W9-AQE-778

An apathy-busting psychology textbook that HOLDS their attention!

Your students' gateway to *ACTIVE* learning

In this captivating and accessible introduction to psychology, Dennis Coon intrigues students with the excitement of discovery as he engages them in ***active***—rather than reactive—studying! The book's nationally praised SQ4R learning system is further enhanced for this edition, so even difficult-to-reach students are engaged in your psychology course. Students are guided through every key topic with an active process of Survey, Question, Read, Reflect, Review, and Recite. This edition's turbo-charged SQ4R is just one in this book's repertoire of apathy-busting features. Including an overall streamlining for even greater accessibility and a thoughtful updating throughout every chapter, Dennis Coon and new contributor John Mitterer also add:

- Intriguing coverage of the field's **LATEST** topics and research—*See page 2 of this PREVIEW.*
- **NEW** *Discovering Psychology* boxes and other tools that strengthen the book's SQ4R learning tool—*See page 3.*
- Many **NEW** *Focus on Research* and *The Clinical File* features that encourage students to think reflectively like psychologists—*See page 4.*
- A wealth of **CURRENT** applications boxes that focus on the real-life value of psychology—*See page 5.*
- Diversity-related topics integrated throughout as well as **NEW** and updated *Human Diversity* boxes—*See page 5.*

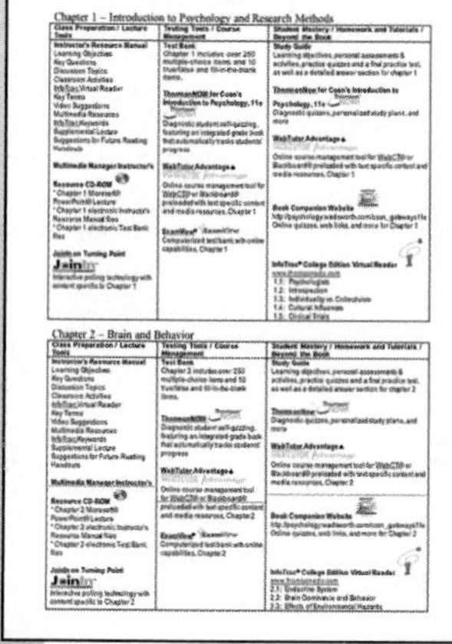
Resource Integration Guide

Chapter 1 – Introduction to Psychology and Research Methods

Chapter 2 – Brain and Behavior

ALSO AVAILABLE!

Many NEW and enhanced online and media resources! For instance, **ThomsonNOW™**, a powerful, assignable online learning companion that assesses each student's study needs through diagnostic tests. And for instructors, the **Resource Integration Guide, JoinIn™ on TurningPoint®**, the **Multimedia Manager**, and many others. *Refer to pages 6–8 of this PREVIEW for details.*

THOMSON
WADSWORTH

Turn the page to begin your tour ▸

Captivating writing incorporates NEW material and interesting research in every chapter

In an accessible, example-laced style that grabs and holds students' attention, Dennis Coon and new contributor John Mitterer present the field's latest research, most vital controversies, and new topics. For example, you'll find new and updated discussion of the following:

- **Gender bias in research,** including the under-representation of women (Chapter 1)
- **Differences between men's and women's brains,** featuring updated material on this fascinating topic (Chapter 2)
- **Life-span development issues,** including cognitive adaptations to abuse, and an easy-to-understand presentation of Kohlberg's theory of moral development (Chapter 4)
- **The failure of subliminal advertising and self-help tapes** (Chapter 5)
- **"Sane hallucinations"** and the Charles Bonnet syndrome (Chapter 6)
- **Hypnopompic (upon awakening) imagery** and how it may be misinterpreted in verifying purported alien sightings (Chapter 7)
- **Recovered/false memory,** including new information in this ongoing debate (Chapter 9)
- **Snap intuitive judgments** and their surprising accuracy (Chapter 10)
- **Emotional intelligence** and the value of positive emotions, authentic happiness, and emotional maturity (Chapter 12)
- **Gender and sexuality topics,** including the latest on HIV and AIDS, sex role socialization, aphrodisiacs, and sexual orientation (Chapter 13)
- **Human personality strengths,** based on new research by Martin Seligman and others doing research in positive psychology (Chapter 14)
- **Health psychology,** behavioral risk factors, and health-promoting behaviors (Chapter 15)
- **Stress disorders,** glutamate levels and schizophrenia, mental illness and violence (Chapter 16)
- **The relationship between culture and therapy** (Chapter 17)

Brain and Behavior 61

side the brain (● Figure 2.11). An electric current is then used to destroy a small amount of brain tissue. Again, changes in behavior give clues about the purpose of the affected area. Using a weaker current, it is also possible to *activate* target areas, rather than remove them. This is called ESB, for **electrical stimulation of the brain.** ESB can call forth behavior with astonishing power. Instantly, it can bring about aggression, alertness, escape, eating, drinking, sleeping, movement, euphoria, memories, speech, tears, and more. Using ESB, researchers are creating a three-dimensional brain "atlas" showing the sensory, motor, and emotional responses that can be elicited from various parts of the brain. It promises to be a valuable guide for medical treatment, as well as for exploring the brain (Clark, Boutros, & Mendez, 2005; Yoshida, 1993).

Could ESB be used to control a person against his or her will? It might seem that you could use ESB to control a person much like a robot. But the details of behaviors and emotions elicited with ESB are modified by personality and circumstances. Sci-fi movies to the contrary, it would be impossible for a ruthless dictator to enslave people by "radio controlling" their brains.

To find out what individual neurons are doing, we need to use micro-electrode recording. A *micro-electrode* is an extremely thin ... salty fluid. The tip of a micro-electrode is ... of a *single* neuron.

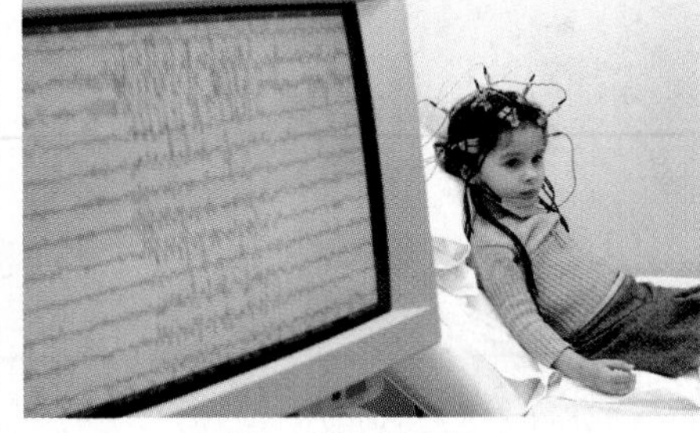

A.J.Photo/Photo Researchers, Inc.

● **Figure 2.12** An EEG recording.

New Images of the Living Brain

Many of the brain's riddles have been solved with the methods just described, plus others based on drugs and brain chemistry. Yet each technique lets us see only a part of the whole picture. What if we could "peek" inside an intact brain while a person is thinking, perceiving, and reacting? Rather than seeing individual musical notes or small musical phrases, what if we could see the ... images

Attitudes and Sexual Behavior—The Changing Sexual Landscape

Has there been a "sexual revolution"? If a woman and a man living 100 years ago could be transported to the present, what would they think about today's sexual values and practices? Undoubtedly, they would be stunned by the changes that have taken place.

ABC-TV/The Kobal Collection/Bratka, Moshe

Twenty years ago, television soap operas were tame, gossipy melodramas. Today they are sexy, gossipy melodramas that frequently feature steamy on-screen lovemaking.

Changing ... intercourse. In a 1959 Roper poll, 88 percent of those interviewed agreed that premarital sex is wrong. In a more recent Gallup Poll, only 40 percent of adults believed that premarital sex is unacceptable (Gallup Poll, 1991). By the 1990s, over 70 percent of young men and women approved of premarital sex (Wells & Twenge, 2005). Similar changes have occurred in attitudes toward extramarital sex, homosexuality, sex education, and related issues.

Behavior

Have changing attitudes been translated into behavior? Changes in attitudes are still larger than changes in actual sexual behavior. Mostly, there is greater *tolerance* for sexual activity, especially that *engaged in by others*. For example, a magazine poll found that 80

Recent Trends

Are there any "hot topics" in psychology today? Yes, biopsychology is an especially fast-growing area. Eventually, biopsychologists expect to explain all behavior in terms of physical mechanisms, such as brain activity and genetics. Cognitive science is another rapidly expanding area. As mentioned earlier, cognitive psychologists study thoughts, expectations, memory, language, perception, problem solving, consciousness, creativity, and other mental processes. With all this renewed interest in thinking, psychology has finally "regained consciousness" (Robins, Gosling, & Craik, 1998). Recently, these two topics have been joined. *Cognitive neuroscience* is an attempt to discover connections between mental events and activity in the brain. For instance, we would like to know what happens in the brain when you think, remember, feel happy, or pay attention (Schall, 2004).

Positive Psychology

Psychology is being used to treat emotional trauma, manage pain, relieve depression, and much more. Because there is a pressing need to solve human problems, psychologists have paid much at-

BRIDGES

Behaviorism, Gestalt psychology, psychoanalytic theory, and humanism have given rise to various forms of psychotherapy. **See Chapter 17 for more information about how psychological disorders are treated.**

> *Almost effortlessly, the student learns about psychological research and theory because the writing style is so fluid and personable.*
>
> **Donna Alexander**
> **John Tyler Community College**

The latest topics and research findings

This edition's enhanced SQ4R method helps students stop to reflect, think critically, and study for success

Dennis Coon is psychology's leader in using the SQ4R method, which to date has given more than a million students a concrete tool for active involvement in their learning and success in the psychology course. With this edition's fully integrated SQ4R method, students focus on every key topic using an active six-step process, which guides them from **Survey**, to **Question**, **Read**, **Reflect**, **Review**, and **Recite.** Not only holding students' attention, SQ4R gives them the satisfaction of interactive discovery and the reward of improved grades.

KNOWLEDGE BUILDER

Psychologists and Their Specialties

REFLECT

You're going to meet four psychologists at a social gathering. How many would you expect to be therapists in private practice? Odds are that only two will be clinical (or counseling) psychologists and only one of these will work in private practice. On the other hand, at least one out of the four (and probably two) will work at a college or university.

LEARNING CHECK

1. Which of the following can prescribe drugs?
   a. a psychologist c. a psychotherapist
   b. a psychiatrist d. a counselor
2. A psychologist who specializes in treating human emotional difficulties is called a ________________ psychologist.
3. Roughly 40 percent of psychologists specialize in counseling psychology. T or F?
4. Who among the following would most likely be involved in the detection of learning disabilities?
   a. a consumer psychologist c. an experimental psychologist
   b. a forensic psychologist d. a school psychologist

CRITICAL THINKING

5. If most psychologists work in applied settings, why is basic research still of great importance?

Answers: 1. b 2. clinical or counseling 3. F 4. d 5. Because practitioners benefit from basic psychological research in the same way that physicians benefit from basic research in biology. Discoveries in basic science form the knowledge base that leads to useful applications.

Knowledge Builder sections throughout—each now includes a series of Reflect and Critical Thinking questions.

◀ SQ4R's new Reflect step—offering an even stronger focus on critical thinking
Using one of cognitive psychology's core principles—the idea that reflective processing of new information is an effective way to foster understanding and form lasting memories—this edition now includes **Reflect**, a cognitively enhanced step in the **SQ4R** process that helps students harness critical thinking to enrich their understanding of, and memory for, psychology's broad concepts and great diversity of topics.

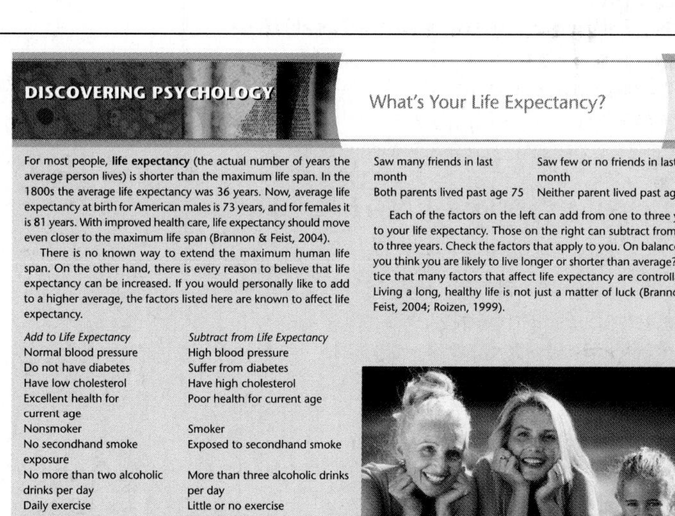

DISCOVERING PSYCHOLOGY What's Your Life Expectancy?

For most people, **life expectancy** (the actual number of years the average person lives) is shorter than the maximum life span. In the 1800s the average life expectancy was 36 years. Now, average life expectancy at birth for American males is 73 years, and for females it is 81 years. With improved health care, life expectancy should move even closer to the maximum life span (Brannon & Feist, 2004).

There is no known way to extend the maximum human life span. On the other hand, there is every reason to believe that life expectancy can be increased. If you would personally like to add to a higher average, the factors listed here are known to affect life expectancy.

Add to Life Expectancy	*Subtract from Life Expectancy*
Normal blood pressure	High blood pressure
Do not have diabetes	Suffer from diabetes
Have low cholesterol	Have high cholesterol
Excellent health for current age	Poor health for current age
Nonsmoker	Smoker
No secondhand smoke exposure	Exposed to secondhand smoke
No more than two alcoholic drinks per day	More than three alcoholic drinks per day
Daily exercise	Little or no exercise
Low-fat diet	High-fat diet
Eat fruits and vegetables daily	No fruits and vegetables
	Divorced or single
	One or more major disruptive events last year
Saw many friends in last month	Saw few or no friends in last month
Both parents lived past age 75	Neither parent lived past age 75

Each of the factors on the left can add from one to three years to your life expectancy. Those on the right can subtract from one to three years. Check the factors that apply to you. On balance, do you think you are likely to live longer or shorter than average? Notice that many factors that affect life expectancy are controllable. Living a long, healthy life is not just a matter of luck (Brannon & Feist, 2004; Roizen, 1999).

Royalty-Free/Corbis

▲ NEW Discovering Psychology boxes—opportunities to "try it" and then, reflect
Enabling students to observe interesting facets of their own behavior or do self-assessments, these new *Discovering Psychology* boxes offer students many great opportunities to reflect on what they are learning—and link chapter information to their own experiences. Topics include: "What's Your Life Expectancy?" "What's Your Attachment Style?" "Are You Color-Blind?" "Can Sex Be Assigned?" "Crazy for a Day," "I'm Not Prejudiced, Right?" and many more.

CRITICAL THINKING Testing Common-Sense Beliefs

It may seem that psychological research confirms what we already know from everyday experience. Why waste time and money confirming the obvious? Actually, common-sense beliefs are often wrong. See if you can tell which of the following common-sense beliefs are true and which are false (Landau & Bavaria, 2003).

- The basis of the baby's love for his mother is the fact that his mother fills his physiological need for food. True or False?
- Most humans use only 10 percent of their potential brain power. True or False?
- Blind people have unusually sensitive organs of touch. True or False?
- The more motivated you are, the better you will do at solving a complex problem. True or False?
- The weight of evidence suggests that the major factor in forgetting is the decay of memory traces with time. True or False?
- Psychotherapy has its greatest success in the treatment of psychotic patients who have lost touch with reality. True or False?
- Personality tests reveal one's basic motives, including those you may not be aware of. True or False?
- To change people's behavior toward members of ethnic minority groups, we must first change their attitudes. True or False?
- "The study of the mind" is the best brief definition of psychology today. True or False?
- Boys and girls exhibit no behavioral differences until environmental influences begin to produce such differences. True or False?

It turns out that research has shown that *all* of these common-sense beliefs are false. Yet in a survey, *all* of the beliefs were accepted as true by a large number of college students (Landau & Bavaria, 2003). How did you do?

We can all benefit from being more reflective in evaluating common-sense beliefs. When you find yourself wondering about the truth of a particular belief, apply your critical thinking skills by asking whether the belief makes logical sense. Can it be explained by any of the concepts in this book? Can you imagine what sort of research might yield empirical evidence to get you closer to the truth? Critical Thinking boxes like this one will appear throughout this book to help you be more reflective and think critically about human behavior.

▲ Many NEW and updated Critical Thinking boxes help students distinguish empirically evaluated research from common-sense beliefs.

> ***. . . Very engaging. As a matter of fact, I haven't seen many texts that measure up to it. . . . The Knowledge Builders are good for students who don't use study guides but could use direction for review of material.***
>
> **Patricia Kemerer**
> **Ivy Tech Community College**

With NEW *Discovering Psychology* boxes, and more!

Students get an inside look at psychological research and its relevance to their lives

▶ NEW and updated Focus on Research boxes

Found throughout this edition, *Focus on Research* boxes help students relate interesting new research to their everyday lives. Many new and updated topics are included:

- "Investigating the Placebo Effect" extends the usual discussion of placebos by exploring how they help people make sense of their experiences.
- "Neural Network Flies F-22 Jet Fighter" discusses hybrots, which are an innovative way of studying neural networks.
- "The Long-Term Potential of a Memory Pill" explores the phenomenon of long-term potentiation as a neurological underpinning to memory.

Brain and Behavior 57

FOCUS ON RESEARCH — Neural Network Flies F-22 Jet Fighter

Neurons cooperate in networks to carry out even the simplest of tasks. To study neural networks, researchers have created hybrid robots ("hybrots") combining living neurons with artificial components (Potter, Wagenaar, & DeMaarse, in press). To build a hybrot, start with a grid of about 60 small metal electrodes in a small glass dish. When you add living neurons and the right nutrients, the neurons interconnect to form a neural network.

You can now input information to the hybrot by delivering different patterns of electrical stimulation to electrodes in the neural network. You can also register the hybrot's output by measuring the resulting pattern of electrical activity in the neural network. One hybrot was connected to an F-22 fighter jet simulator program. Input about a simulated flight was delivered to the neural network through patterns of electrical stimulation. The hybrot's output was measured and translated into instructions to control the F-22. Again and again, the simulator program input flight data and the hybrot output flight instructions. At first, the hybrot couldn't fly the fighter jet, but with practice it learned to control the simulation, keeping the jet level under a wide range of simulated weather conditions!

Further research with hybrots may lead to real-world applications that can fly unmanned aircraft, disable bombs, or help damaged human brains control prosthetic devices. Also, by measuring how hybrots change with training, we may learn a lot more about how natural neural networks grow and change with experience.

chemicals reduce the pain so that it is not too disabling (Drolet et al., 2001).

Ultimately, brain regulators may help explain depression, schizophrenia, drug addiction, and other puzzling topics. For example, women who suffer from severe premenstrual pain and distress have unusually low endorphin levels (Straneva et al., 2002).

The Nervous System—Wired for Action

Jamal and Vicki are playing catch with a Frisbee. This may look fairly simple. However, to merely toss the Frisbee or catch it, a huge amount of information must be sensed, interpreted, and directed to countless muscle fibers. As they play, Jamal and Vicki's neural circuits are ablaze with activity. Let's explore the "wiring diagram" that makes their Frisbee game possible.

Neurons and Nerves

myelin help nerve impulses move faster. Instead of passing down the entire length of the axon, the action potential leaps from gap to gap. Without the added speed this allows, it would probably be impossible to brake in time to avoid many automobile accidents. When the myelin layer is damaged, a person may suffer from numbness, weakness, or paralysis. That, in fact, is what happens in multiple sclerosis, a disease that occurs when the immune system attacks and destroys the myelin in a person's body.

A thin layer of cells called the **neurilemma** (NOOR-rih-LEM-ah) is also wrapped around most axons outside the brain and spinal cord (return to Figure 2.1). The neurilemma forms a "tunnel" that damaged fibers can follow as they repair themselves.

Neural Networks

As you can see in ● Figures 2.7 and 2.8, the **central nervous system (CNS)** consists of the brain and spinal cord. The brain is the central "comp...

THE CLINICAL FILE — The Matrix: Do Phantoms Live Here?

In the popular *Matrix* film trilogy, Neo, as played by Keanu Reeves, discovers that he is imprisoned in a phantom world by machines that are stealing human energy for their own use. What would you say if you found out that the idea of a "matrix" is not totally farfetched, and that your own brain may be creating a *neuromatrix* that is responsible for your perceptions of your own body? Welcome to the world of phantom limbs.

A person who suffers an amputation doesn't need to believe in the *Matrix* to encounter phantoms. Most amputees have **phantom limb** sensations for months or years after losing a limb (Fraser, 2002). For some, the missing limb continues to feel as if it is present, just as it always did. Because the phantom limb feels so "real," a patient with a recently amputated leg may inadvertently try to walk on it, risking further injury. Sometimes phantom limbs feel like they are stuck in awkward positions. For instance, one man can't sleep on his back because his missing arm feels like it is twisted behind him. Worst of all, perhaps, are the amputees who suffer from phantom limb pain, which may be severe, can last for years, and is very difficult to treat (Halbert, Crotty, & Cameron, 2002).

What causes phantom limbs? Phantom limb pain cannot be explained by gate-control theory (Hunter, Katz, & Davis, 2003). Because pain cannot be coming from the missing limb (after all, it's missing), it cannot pass through pain gates to the brain. Instead, according to Ronald Melzack (1993, 1999), the brain creates a body image called the *neuromatrix*, which ultimately creates our sense of bodily self. Although amputation may remove a limb, as far as the neuromatrix in the brain is concerned, the limb still exists. Medical imaging techniques have made it possible to confirm that sensory and motor areas of the brain are more active when a person feels a phantom limb (Rosen et al., 2001). Even though pain signals no longer emanate from the amputated limb, the neuromatrix may continue to interpret other sensory experiences as pain coming from the missing limb.

Sometimes the brain gradually reorganizes to adjust for the sensory loss (Wu & Kaas, 2002). For example, a person who loses an arm may at first have a phantom arm and hand. After many years, the phantom may shrink, until only a hand is felt at the shoulder. Perhaps more vividly than others, people with phantom limbs are reminded that the sensory world as we know it is constructed, moment by moment, not by some futuristic machines but by our very own neuromatrix in our brains.

THE CLINICAL FILE — Staying in Touch with Reality

Just imagine that often, and without warning, you hear a voice shouting, "Buckets of blood!" or see blood spattering across the walls of your bedroom. Chances are people would think you are mentally disturbed. Hallucinations are a major symptom of psychosis, dementia, epilepsy, migraine headaches, alcohol withdrawal, and drug intoxication (Spence & David, 2004) and are one of the clearest signs that a person has "lost touch with reality."

Yet consider the case of mathematician John Nash (the subject of *A Beautiful Mind*, the winner of the 2002 Oscar for best film). Even though Nash suffered from schizophrenia, he eventually learned to use his ability to engage in *reality testing* to sort out which of his experiences were perceptions and which were hallucinations. Unlike John Nash, most people who experience full-blown hallucinations also have a limited ability to reality test (Hohwy & Rosenberg, 2005).

Curiously, "sane hallucinations" also occur. *Charles Bonnet syndrome* is a rare condition that afflicts mainly older people who are partially blind but not mentally disturbed. They may "see" people, animals, buildings, plants, and other objects appear and disappear in front of their eyes. One older man suffering from partial blindness and leukemia complained of seeing animals in his house, including cattle and bears (Jacob et al., 2004). However, people experiencing "sane hallucinations" can more easily tell that their hallucinations aren't real because their capacity to reality test is not impaired.

Such unusual experiences show how powerfully the brain seeks meaningful patterns in sensory input and the role reality testing plays in our normal perceptual experience.

◀ NEW and updated The Clinical File boxes

Focusing on therapies, disorders, mental health, and personal adjustment, *The Clinical File* boxes expose students to clinical topics that illustrate the relevance of chapter concepts. New and updated topics such as these hold students' attention:

- "Staying in Touch with Reality" explores the breakdown of reality testing, the usually effortless distinction we all make between reality and fantasy.
- "Coping with Chemo" discusses the application of classical conditioning to help patients cope with conditioned nausea from chemotherapy.
- "The Matrix: Do Phantoms Live Here?" adds discussion of the neuromatrix theory of phantom limb pain.

. . . In 25 years of teaching, this is one of the best-written texts I have encountered.

H. Mitzi Doane
University of Minnesota–Duluth

An emphasis on applied and positive psychologies, as well as inclusive coverage of "Human Diversity"

▶ Updated Psychology in Action sections

Found at the end of every chapter, high-interest *Psychology in Action* sections discuss ways that students can use their growing knowledge of psychology's concepts to improve their understanding of common life issues and experiences, such as emotional intelligence, motivation and emotion, well-being and happiness, and effective parenting.

PSYCHOLOGY IN ACTION

Emotional Intelligence—The Fine Art of Self-Control

The Greek philosopher Aristotle had a recipe for handling relationships smoothly. You must be able, he said, be angry with the right person, to the t degree, at the right time, for the right ose, and in the right way." Psycholo- Peter Salovey and John Mayer call self-control "emotional intelligence." otional intelligence refers to a combina- of skills, such as empathy, self-control, self-awareness (Salovey & Mayer, 1997). h skills can make us more flexible, adapt- , and emotionally mature (Bonanno et 2004).

eople who excel in life tend to be emo- ally intelligent (Fisher & Ashanasy, 2000; rabian, 2000). Indeed, the costs of poor tional skills can be high. They range n problems in marriage and parenting oor physical health. A lack of emotional lligence can ruin careers and sabotage ievement. Perhaps the greatest toll falls hildren and teenagers. For them, hav- poor emotional skills can contribute to ression, eating disorders, unwanted preg- cy, aggression, violent crime, and poor demic performance (Parker et al., 2004). s, in many life circumstances emotional lligence is as important as IQ (Dulewicz iggs, 2000).

re there specific skills that make up emo- al intelligence? Many elements contribute motional intelligence (Mayer et al., 1). Descriptions of some of the most ortant skills follows.

Self-awareness Emotionally intelligent people are tuned in to their own feelings. For example, they are able to recognize quickly if they are angry, or envious, or feeling guilty, or depressed. This is valuable because many people have disruptive emotions without being able to pinpoint why they are uncomfortable. Those who are more self-aware are keenly sensitive to their own feelings.

Empathy Empathetic people accurately perceive emotions in others and sense what others are feeling. They are good at "reading" facial expressions, tone of voice, and other signs of emotion.

Managing emotions Emotional intelligence involves an ability to manage your own emotions and those of others. For example, you know how to calm down when you are angry and you also know how to calm others. As Aristotle noted so long ago, people who are emotionally intelligent have an ability to amplify or restrain emotions, depending on the situation (Bonanno et al., 2004).

Understanding emotions Emotions contain useful information. For instance, anger is a cue that something is wrong; anxiety indicates uncertainty; embarrassment communicates shame; depression means we feel helpless; enthusiasm tells us we're excited. People who are emotionally intelligent know what causes various emotions, what they mean, and how they affect behavior.

Using emotion People who are emotionally intelligent use their feelings to enhance thinking and decision making. For example, if you can remember how you reacted emotionally in the past, it can help you react better to new situations. Emotional intelligence also involves using emotions to promote personal growth and improve relationships with others. For instance, you may have noticed that helping someone else makes you feel better, too. Likewise, when good fortune comes their way, people who are emotionally smart share the news with others. Almost always, doing so strengthens relationships and increases emotional well-being (Gable et al., 2004).

Emotional Flexibility

In general, being emotionally intelligent means accepting that emotions are an essential part of who we are and how we survive. There is a natural tendency to enjoy positive emotions like joy or love, while treating negative emotions as unwelcome misery. However, negative emotions can also be valuable and constructive. For example, persistent distress may impel a person to seek help, mend a relationship, or find a new direction in life (Plutchik, 2003).

Often, the "right" choices in life can only be defined by taking personal values, needs, and emotions into account. Extremely rational approaches to making choices can produce sensible but emotionally empty decisions. Good decisions often combine emotion with reason. In short, emotional intelligence is the ability to consciously make your emotions work for you.

Positive Psychology and Positive Emotions

It's obvious that joy, interest, contentment, love, and similar emotions are pleasant and rewarding. However, as psychologist Barbara Fredrickson has pointed out, positive emotions have other benefits. Negative emotions are associated with actions that probably helped our ancestors save their skins: escaping, attacking, expelling poison, and the like. As useful as these reactions may be, they tend to narrow our focus of attention and limit our ideas about possible actions. In contrast, positive emotions tend to broaden

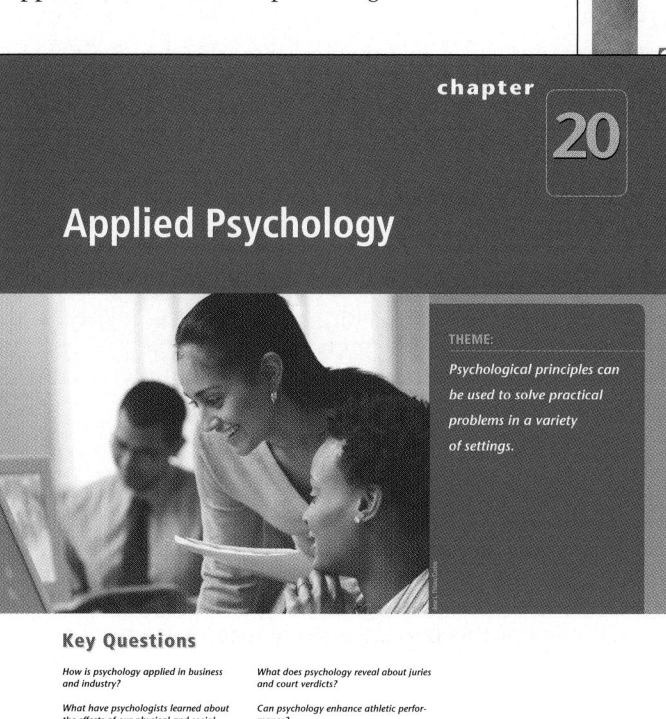

chapter 20

Applied Psychology

THEME: *Psychological principles can be used to solve practical problems in a variety of settings.*

Key Questions

How is psychology applied in business and industry?

What have psychologists learned about the effects of our physical and social environments?

How has psychology improved education?

What does psychology reveal about juries and court verdicts?

Can psychology enhance athletic performance?

What can be done to improve communication at work?

◀ A comprehensive Chapter 20, "Applied Psychology"

This current chapter shows students how psychological principles can be used to solve practical problems in everyday settings, such as in the workplace, the environment, school, and sports. For example, this chapter's exceptional, real-world coverage of industrial-organizational psychology includes discussion of organizational culture, organizational citizenship, workplace anger, and more.

▶ NEW and updated Human Diversity boxes

In addition to a thorough integration of diversity topics throughout the book, *Human Diversity* boxes highlight many current, diversity-related issues, such as the impact of poverty on child development, cultural differences in the types of information we store in memory, and how cultural heritage can aid or impair problem solving.

HUMAN DIVERSITY

Do They See What We See?

According to psychologist Richard Nisbett and his colleagues, people from different cultures do, in fact, perceive the world differently. European Americans are individualistic people who tend to focus on the self and their sense of personal control. In contrast, East Asians are collectivist people who tend to focus on interpersonal relationships and social responsibility. As a consequence, European Americans tend to explain a person's actions in terms of internal factors ("he did it because he chose to do it"), whereas East Asians tend to explain a person's actions in terms of the context ("he did it because it was his responsibility to his family") (Norenzayan & Nisbett, 2000).

Do such cultural differences affect our everyday perception of objects and events? Apparently they do. In one study, American and Japanese participants were shown drawings of everyday scenes, such as a farm. Later, they saw a slightly changed version of the scene. Some of the changes were to the focal point, or figure of the scene. Other changes were to the surrounding context, or ground. The American participants, it turns out, were better at detecting changes in the figure of a scene, whereas the Japanese participants were better at detecting alterations to the ground (Nisbett & Miyamoto, 2005).

To explain this difference, Chua, Boland, and Nisbett (2005) presented American and Chinese participants with pictures of a figure (such as a tiger) placed on a ground (such as a jungle) and monitored their eye-movement patterns. The American participants focused their eye movements on the figure, whereas the Chinese participants made more eye movements around the ground. In other words, Westerners have a relatively narrow focus of attention, whereas Easterners have a broader focus of attention. Apparently, the society we live in can, indeed, influence even our most basic perceptual habits.

Discussions of positive psychology throughout the book

Love, happiness, creativity, well-being, self-confidence, achievement . . . These and many other topics associated with positive psychology are integrated throughout this book to help students gain an appreciation of the many emotional and intellectual tools available within psychology to enhance their lives.

It's so easy to move from this text to online enrichment

NEW! ThomsonNOW™
Just what you need to do NOW!
Available at no additional cost when packaged with each new copy of the textbook, this dynamic, online study system features a series of diagnostic tests (by Britton Mace, Southern Utah University) and *Personalized Study* plans with learning modules, eBook files, and other media that enable students to discover those areas of the text in which they need to focus their efforts. Also includes an instructor grade book. *Turn to the inside front cover of this book for details.*

Book Companion Website
www.thomsonedu.com/psychology/coon
When you adopt this textbook, you and your students receive a rich array of teaching and learning materials, including chapter-by-chapter online tutorial quizzes, a final exam, web links for each text chapter, flash cards, and more.

WebTutor™ Advantage on WebCT® and Blackboard®
On WebCT®: 0-495-09738-1
On Blackboard®: 0-495-09739-X
Log on and go—or customize in any way you choose! This versatile online tool is filled with preloaded content from Coon's text, including video clips, practice quizzes, and more—all organized by text chapter. WebTutor™ Advantage effectively pairs course management capabilities with text-specific learning tools—saving you time! View a demo at **www.thomsonedu.com/webtutor.**

InfoTrac® College Edition with InfoMarks®
Includes millions of current topic-related articles
This fully searchable database contains more than 20 years' worth of full-text articles (not abstracts) from more than 5,000 diverse sources, such as top academic journals, newsletters, and up-to-the minute periodicals. The database also includes access to InfoMarks®—stable URLs that can be linked to articles and searches. Access is available for packaging with each copy of this book. For more information, visit **www.thomsonedu.com/infotrac.**

vMentor™
Live, one-on-one tutoring from a subject expert
vMentor™ gives your students access to virtual office hours with one-on-one, online tutoring help. In vMentor's virtual classroom, students interact with a tutor and other students using two-way audio, an interactive whiteboard for illustrating the problem, and instant messaging. To ask a question, students simply click to "raise a hand." Access is available for packaging with each new copy of this book. *For proprietary, college, and university adopters only.*

Thomson InSite for Writing and Research™
With Turnitin® originality checker
InSite features a full suite of writing, peer review, online grading, and e-portfolio applications. It is an all-in-one tool that helps instructors manage the flow of papers electronically and allows students to submit papers and peer reviews online. Also included in the suite is Turnitin, an "originality checker" that offers a simple solution for instructors who want a strong deterrent against plagiarism, as well as encouragement for students to employ proper research techniques. Access is available for packaging with each new copy of this book. For more information, visit **www.thomsonedu.com/insite.**

These innovative resources are indispensable to course preparation and presentation

Multimedia Manager Instructor's Resource CD-ROM: A Microsoft® PowerPoint® Tool
0-495-09744-6
The Multimedia Manager helps you to enhance your Microsoft® PowerPoint® lecture with art from this textbook, videos, animations, and your own materials! This one-stop lecture and course preparation tool makes it easy for you to assemble, edit, publish, and present custom lectures for your course, using Microsoft PowerPoint. The Multimedia Manager provides text-specific lecture outlines (by Andrew Getzfeld, New Jersey City University), art from the textbook, videos, animations, a full *Instructor's Resource Manual, Test Bank,* and other resources.

JoinIn™ on TurningPoint®
0-495-09745-4
JoinIn on TurningPoint is the easiest way to turn your PowerPoint software into a powerful, audience-response vehicle. With just a click on a hand-held device, your students can respond to multiple-choice questions, short polls, interactive exercises, and peer review questions. You can take attendance, collect student demographics to better assess student needs, and even administer quizzes without collecting paper or grading. Please consult your local Thomson Wadsworth representative for details, or for a demonstration, visit **www.thomsonedu.com/thomsontechnology.**

Instructor's Resource Manual
0-495-09735-7
by Wanda McCarthy, Clermont College, University of Cincinnati. This thoroughly revised manual is organized into an easy-to-use lecture format—and is packaged in a convenient three-ring binder that you can personalize. Included is a large selection of class activity handouts, as well as learning objectives, lecture enhancements, role-playing scenarios, value-clarification statements, journal questions, media suggestions, and Internet resources.

Test Bank
0-495-09736-5
by Jeannette Murphey, Meridian Community College. Featuring approximately 5,600 multiple-choice test items organized by chapter and objective, this *Test Bank* offers nearly twice the number of questions that are included with most other introductory psychology texts. Fill-in-the-blank and true/false, as well as multiple-choice questions, are also available online.

ExamView® Computerized Testing
0-495-09737-3
*Contains all **Test Bank** questions electronically!* You'll create, deliver, and customize tests and study guides (both print and online) in minutes with this easy-to-use assessment and tutorial system.

Psychology Digital Video Library 3.0 CD-ROM
0-495-09063-8
A diversified selection of approximately 100 classic and contemporary clips, this CD-ROM offers a convenient way to access an appropriate clip for every lecture. Included is footage of prominent psychologists, as well as demonstrations and simulations of important experiments.

The Wadsworth Psychology Film and Video Library
Qualified adopters can choose from a great variety of continually updated DVD and video options, including selections from Insight Media, Films for the Humanities and Sciences, Annenberg/CPB Discovering Psychology, The Pennsylvania State University's PCR: Films and Videos in the Behavioral Sciences, and more.

Due to contractual reasons, certain ancillaries are available only in higher education or U.S. domestic markets. Minimum purchase may apply to receive the ancillaries at no charge.

Resources that help students succeed in your course

Gateways to Psychology: Concept Maps and Concept Reviews
0-495-09741-1
This essential study aid offers a handy reference to psychology's "Gateway" concepts—the key transformative ideas every student should know. *Concept Maps* (by Art VanDeventer, Thomas Nelson Community College) help students see how ideas are interconnected. *Concept Reviews* (by Melissa Acevedo, Valencia Community College) contain 30 multiple-choice questions for each text chapter.

Study Guide
0-495-09734-9
Written by Thuy Karafa, Ferris State University, and Dennis Coon, the *Study Guide* offers seamless integration with the text. The guide is structured around the active learning system (Survey, Question, Read, Reflect, Review, Recite) and offers many opportunities for practice, self-testing, and review. Features include a "Chapter Overview," "Recite and Review" (fill-in-the-blank), a "Mastery Test" (multiple-choice) for each chapter in the book, and an updated Language Development Guide.

Available Summer 2006!
Further Readings Booklet
Features articles that enrich textbook topics by taking students into fascinating realms of psychology.

Also available to supplement student learning . . .

Critical Thinking in Psychology: Separating Sense from Nonsense, Second Edition
by John Ruscio, Elizabethtown College
0-534-63459-1

Challenging Your Preconceptions: Thinking Critically About Psychology, Second Edition
by Randolph A. Smith, Kennesaw State University
0-534-26739-4

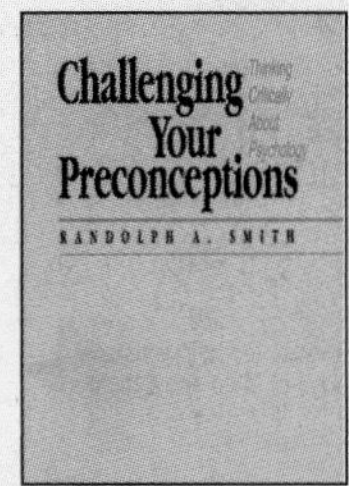

Writing Papers in Psychology: A Student Guide to Research Papers, Essays, Proposals, Posters, and Handouts, Seventh Edition
by Ralph L. Rosnow, Temple University, and Mimi Rosnow
0-534-53331-0

Introduction to Positive Psychology
by William C. Compton, Middle Tennessee University
0-534-64453-8

Writing with Style: APA Style Made Easy, Third Edition
by Lenore T. Szuchman, Barry University
0-534-63432-X

Careers in Psychology: Opportunities in a Changing World
by Tara L. Kuther, Western Connecticut State University, and Robert D. Morgan, Texas Tech University
0-534-61776-X

Please contact your Thomson Wadsworth representative with questions about availability of any of these items.

Introduction to Psychology

Gateways to Mind and Behavior

ELEVENTH EDITION

Dennis Coon

John O. Mitterer
Brock University

Australia • Brazil • Canada • Mexico • Singapore • Spain
United Kingdom • United States

Introduction to Psychology: Gateways to Mind and Behavior,
Eleventh Edition
Dennis Coon / John O. Mitterer

Senior Psychology Editor: Marianne Taflinger
Development Editor: Kristin Makarewycz
Editorial Assistant: Lucy Faridany
Technology Project Manager: Amanda Kaufmann
Marketing Assistant: Natasha Coats
Marketing Communications Manager: Kelley McAllister
Project Manager, Editorial Production: Jerilyn Emori
Creative Director: Rob Hugel
Senior Art Director: Vernon Boes
Print Buyers: Karen Hunt, Barbara Britton
Permissions Editor: Roberta Broyer
Production Service: Lisa Royse, Graphic World Inc.
Text Designer: Liz Harasymczuk
Photo Researcher: Kathleen Olson
Cover Designer: Gopa&Ted2, Inc.
Cover Image: Jeffrey Allen Cable/Botanica/Getty Images
Compositor: Graphic World Inc.
Text and Cover Printer: Courier Corporation/Kendallville

Printed in the United States of America
1 2 3 4 5 6 7 10 09 08 07 06

Library of Congress Control Number: 2006926245

Student Edition: ISBN 0-495-09155-3

Loose-leaf Edition: ISBN 0-495-09747-0

Thomson Higher Education
10 Davis Drive
Belmont, CA 94002-3098
USA

For more information about our products, contact us at:
Thomson Learning Academic Resource Center
1-800-423-0563

For permission to use material from this text or product, submit a request online at **http://www.thomsonrights.com.**
Any additional questions about permissions can be submitted by e-mail to **thomsonrights@thomson.com.**

About the Authors

After earning a doctorate in psychology from the University of Arizona, Dennis Coon taught for 22 years at Santa Barbara City College, California. Throughout his career, Dr. Coon has especially enjoyed the challenge of teaching introductory psychology. He and his wife, Sevren, have returned to Tucson, where he continues to teach, write, edit, and consult.

Dr. Coon is the author of *Introduction to Psychology* and *Psychology: A Journey,* as well as *Essentials of Psychology.* Together, these texts have been used by over 2 million students. Dr. Coon frequently serves as a reviewer and consultant to publishers, and he edited the best-selling trade book, *Choices*. He also helped design modules for PsychNow!, Wadsworth's interactive CD-ROM.

In his leisure hours, Dr. Coon enjoys hiking, photography, painting, woodworking, and music. He also designs, builds, and plays classical and steel string acoustic guitars. He has published articles on guitar design and occasionally offers lectures on this topic, in addition to his more frequent presentations on psychology.

New contributor John Mitterer was awarded his Ph.D. in cognitive psychology from McMaster University. Currently, Dr. Mitterer teaches at Brock University, where he has taught over 20,000 introductory psychology students. He is the recipient of the 2003 Brock University Distinguished Teaching Award, a 2003 Ontario Confederation of University Faculty Associations (OCUFA) Teaching Award, a 2004 3M Teaching Fellowship, and the 2005 Canadian Psychological Association Award for Distinguished Contributions to Education and Training in Psychology.

Dr. Mitterer's primary research focus is on basic cognitive processes in learning and teaching. As a consultant for a variety of companies, such as Bell Northern Research, Unisys Corporation, IBM Canada, and computer-game developer Silicon Knights, he has applied cognitive principles. His professional focus, however, is in applying cognitive principles to the improvement of undergraduate education. In support of his introductory psychology course, he has been involved in the production of textbook materials for both students and instructors and has adapted an introductory psychology textbook for use in Canada. Dr. Mitterer has published and lectured on undergraduate instruction throughout Canada and the United States. He continues to work on his ultimate dream, a fully integrated, instructional learning environment for the teaching and learning of introductory psychology, including textbook, electronic, and web-based components.

In his spare time, Dr. Mitterer strives to become a better golfer and to attain his life goal of seeing all of the bird species in the world. To this end, he recently went to Peru, South Africa, Venezuela, and Australia.

Brief Contents

Introduction: The Psychology of Studying 1

1 Introduction to Psychology and Research Methods 11
Psychology in Action: Psychology in the News—Separating Fact from Fiction 46

2 Brain and Behavior 51
Psychology in Action: Handedness—If Your Brain Is Right, What's Left? 77

3 Child Development 83
Psychology in Action: Effective Parenting—Raising Healthy Children 115

4 From Birth to Death: Life-Span Development 121
Psychology in Action: Well-Being and Happiness—What Makes a Good Life? 150

5 Sensation and Reality 155
Psychology in Action: Controlling Pain—This Won't Hurt a Bit 184

6 Perceiving the World 188
Psychology in Action: Perception and Objectivity—Believing Is Seeing 217

7 States of Conciousness 223
Psychology in Action: Exploring and Using Dreams 256

8 Conditioning and Learning 261
Psychology in Action: Behavioral Self-Management—A Rewarding Project 291

9 Memory 296
Psychology in Action: Mnemonics—Memory Magic 324

10 Cognition, Language, and Creativity 329
Psychology in Action: Enhancing Creativity—Brainstorms 356

Intelligence 362

Psychology in Action: How Intelligent Are Intelligence Tests? 382

Motivation and Emotion 387

Psychology in Action: Emotional Intelligence—The Fine Art of Self-Control 422

Gender and Sexuality 426

Psychology in Action: Sexual Problems—When Pleasure Fades 450

Personality 458

Psychology in Action: Barriers and Bridges—Understanding Shyness 491

Health, Stress, and Coping 496

Psychology in Action: Stress Management 525

16 **Psychological Disorders 531**

Psychology in Action: Suicide—Lives on the Brink 563

Therapies 569

Psychology in Action: Self-Management and Finding Professional Help 596

Social Behavior 604

Psychology in Action: Assertiveness Training—Standing Up for Your Rights 627

Attitudes, Culture, and Human Relations 631

Psychology in Action: Multiculturalism—Living with Diversity 656

Applied Psychology 661

Psychology in Action: Improving Communication at Work 686

Appendix: Behavioral Statistics 690

Glossary G-1
References R-1
Photo Credits C-1
Name Index N-1
Subject Index S-1

Contents

Introduction: The Psychology of Studying 1

The SQ4R Method—How to Tame a Textbook 1
How to Use *Gateways to Mind and Behavior* 2
Effective Note-Taking—Good Students, Take Note! 3
Using and Reviewing Your Notes 3
Study Strategies—Making a Habit of Success 4
Self-Regulated Learning—Academic All-Stars 5
Procrastination—Avoiding the Last-Minute Blues 5
Time Management 5
Goal Setting 6
Make Learning an Adventure 6
Taking Tests—Are You "Test Wise"? 6
General Test-Taking Skills 6
Using Electronic Media—Netting New Knowledge 7
Electronic Journeys 7
The Psychology Resource Center 8
Psych Sites 8
Multimedia CD-ROMs 9
A Final Word 9
Web Resources 10
Interactive Learning 10

1 Introduction to Psychology and Research Methods 11

Preview: Why Study Psychology? 12
Psychology—Spotlight on Behavior 12
What Is Psychology? 12
Seeking Empirical Evidence 12
Psychological Research 13
Science and Critical Thinking 14
Research Specialties 14
Animals and Psychology 15
Psychology's Goals 16
A Brief History of Psychology—Psychology's Family Album 17
Into the Lab 17
Structuralism 17
Functionalism 18
Behaviorism 18
Gestalt Psychology 19
The Role of Women in Psychology's Early Days 19
Psychoanalytic Psychology 20
Humanistic Psychology 21
Psychology Today—Five Views of Behavior 21
Recent Trends 22
Positive Psychology 22
Summary 22
Human Diversity—Appreciating Social and Cultural Differences 22
The Impact of Culture 23
Psychologists—Guaranteed Not to Shrink 24
Psychologists 25
Other Mental Health Professionals 26
The Profession of Psychology 27
Specialties in Psychology 27
Scientific Research—How to Think Like a Psychologist 28
The Scientific Method 29
Research Methods 31
Naturalistic Observation—Psychology Steps Out! 31
Limitations 31
Recording Observations 32
Correlational Studies—In Search of the Perfect Relationship 32
Correlation Coefficients 32
Relationships in Psychology 33
The Psychology Experiment—Where Cause Meets Effect 35
Variables and Groups 35
Evaluating Results 36
Placebo Effects—Sugar Pills and Saltwater 37
Controlling Placebo Effects 37
The Experimenter Effect 38
The Clinical Method—Data by the Case 39
Survey Method—Here, Have a Sample 40
Critical Thinking Revisited—Evaluating Claims and Evidence 42
A Case Study of Critical Thinking 42
Pseudo-Psychologies—Palms, Planets, and Personality 43
Uncritical Acceptance 44
Positive Instances 44
The Barnum Effect 44
Summary: Science and Critical Thinking 45

Psychology in Action:
Psychology in the News—Separating Fact from Fiction 46
Chapter in Review 48
Web Resources 50
Interactive Learning 50
Feature Boxes (Highlights)
- **Critical Thinking:** Testing Common-Sense Beliefs 13
- **The Clinical File:** The Golden Psi 25
- **Discovering Psychology:** Is a Career in Psychology Right for You? 27
- **Focus on Research:** Investigating the Placebo Effect—Can Placebos Heal? 38
- **Human Diversity:** Is There a Gender Bias in Psychological Research? 41

2 Brain and Behavior 51

Preview: Finding Music in Tofu 52

Neurons—Building a "Biocomputer" 52
Parts of a Neuron 52
The Nerve Impulse 52
Synapses and Neurotransmitters 55
The Nervous System—Wired for Action 57
Neurons and Nerves 57
Neural Networks 57
Research Methods—Charting the Brain's Inner Realms 60
New Images of the Living Brain 61
The Cerebral Cortex—My, What a Big Brain You Have! 63
Cerebrum 63
Cerebral Hemispheres 64
Hemispheric Specialization 65
Lobes of the Cerebral Cortex 67
The Subcortex—At the Core of the (Brain) Matter 71
The Hindbrain 71
The Forebrain 72
The Magnificent Brain 73
The Endocrine System—Hormones and Behavior 74
Psychology in Action:
Handedness—If Your Brain Is Right, What's Left? 77
Chapter in Review 81
Web Resources 82
Interactive Learning 82
Feature Boxes (Highlights)
- **Discovering Psychology:** Dollars, Drag Racing, and the Nervous System 56
- **Focus on Research:** Neural Network Flies F-22 Jet Fighter 57
- **The Clinical File:** A Stroke of Bad Luck 66
- **Human Diversity:** His and Her Brains? 70
- **Critical Thinking:** If You Change Your Mind Do You Change Your Brain? 74

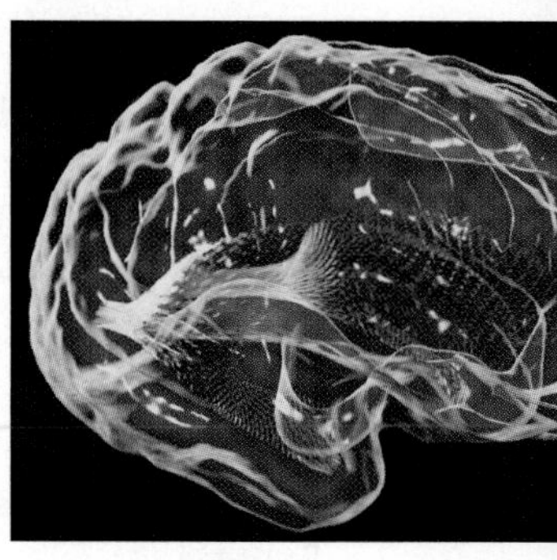

3 Child Development 83

Preview: A Star Is Born—Here's Amy! 84

Heredity and Environment—The Nurture of Nature 84
Heredity 84
Genetic Programming 85
Environment 86
Prenatal Influences 87
Childbirth 88
Deprivation and Enrichment 88
Nature-Nurture Interactions 90
The Newborn Baby—The Basic Model Comes with Options 90
The World of the Neonate 91
Maturation 93
Motor Development 93
Emotional Development 94
Social Development—Baby, I'm Stuck on You 95
Social Referencing 95
Imprinting 96
Attachment 97
Attachment Quality 97
Motherless Monkeys 99
Day Care 100
Play and Social Skills 100
Affectional Needs 100
Maternal and Paternal Influences—Life with Mom and Dad 101
Optimal Caregiving 101
Parenting Styles 102
Ethnic Differences: Four Flavors of Parenting 103
Side Effects of Child Discipline 104
Positive Psychology: Resilience in Childhood 105
Language Development—Fast-Talking Babies 106
Language Acquisition 106
Language and the Terrible Twos 106
The Roots of Language 106

Cognitive Development—How Do Children Learn to Think? 109
Piaget's Theory of Cognitive Development 110
Piaget and Parenting 112
Piaget Today 112
Vygotsky's Sociocultural Theory 114
Psychology in Action:
Effective Parenting—Raising Healthy Children 115
Chapter in Review 119
Web Resources 120
Interactive Learning 120
Feature Boxes (Highlights)
- **Human Diversity:** Children of Poverty 89
- **The Clinical File:** Beyond Homesickness 97
- **Discovering Psychology:** What's Your Attachment Style? 98
- **Critical Thinking:** The Pampered Child 105
- **Focus on Research:** A Child's Theory of Mind—Other People, Other Minds 111

From Birth to Death: Life-Span Development 121

Preview: The Story of a Lifetime 122
The Cycle of Life—Rocky Road or Garden Path? 122
The Life Span in Perspective 124
Problems of Childhood—Why Parents Get Gray Hair 125
Normal Childhood Problems 125
Serious Childhood Problems 127
Feeding Disturbances 127
Toilet-Training Disturbances 127
Speech Disturbances 127
Learning Disorders 128
Attention-Deficit/Hyperactivity Disorder 128
Conduct Disorder 128
Autism 128
Child Abuse—Cycles of Violence 129
Characteristics of Abusive Parents 129
The Abuse Cycle 130
Preventing Child Abuse 130
Adolescence—The Best of Times, the Worst of Times 132
Puberty 132
Early and Late Maturation 132
The Search for Identity 133
The Transition to Adulthood 135
Moral Development—Growing a Conscience 135
Moral Dilemmas 136
Justice or Caring? 136
Challenges of Adulthood—Charting Life's Ups and Downs 138
Adult Development 138
A Midlife Crisis? 139
Middle Age 140
Positive Psychology: Well-Being at Midlife 140
Aging—Will You Still Need Me When I'm 64? 141
The Course of Aging 141
Positive Psychology: Successful Aging 143
Ageism 145
Countering Myths About Aging 145
Death and Dying—The Curtain Falls 146
Reactions to Impending Death 146
Bereavement and Grief 148
Psychology in Action:
Well-Being and Happiness—What Makes a Good Life? 150
Chapter in Review 152
Where to Write for Information 153
Web Resources 153
Interactive Learning 154
Feature Boxes (Highlights)
- **The Clinical File:** Children and Divorce—What Are the Risks? 126
- **Focus on Research:** Trapped by Anger: The "Rage Radar" of Abused Children 130
- **Human Diversity:** The Twixters 135
- **Discovering Psychology:** What's Your Life Expectancy? 143
- **Critical Thinking:** Near-Death Experiences—Back from the Brink 148

Sensation and Reality 155

Preview: Sensation—A Window on the World 156
General Properties of Sensory Systems—What You See Is What You Get 156
Sensory Analysis and Coding 156
Psychophysics—Life at the Limit 158
Difference Thresholds 158
Perceptual Defense and Subliminal Perception 158
Vision—Catching Some Rays 160
Structure of the Eye 160
Rods and Cones 161
Color Vision—There's More to It Than Meets the Eye 165
Color Theories 165
Color Blindness and Color Weakness 166

Dark Adaptation—Let There Be Light! 167
Hearing—Good Vibrations 170
Mechanisms of Hearing 170
Smell and Taste—The Nose Knows When the Tongue Can't Tell 173
The Sense of Smell 174
Taste and Flavors 175
The Somesthetic Senses—Flying by the Seat of Your Pants 177
The Skin Senses 177
The Vestibular System 179
Adaptation, Attention, and Gating—Tuning In and Tuning Out 180
Sensory Adaptation 180
Selective Attention 181
Sensory Gating 181
Psychology in Action:
Controlling Pain—This Won't Hurt a Bit 184
Chapter in Review 186
Web Resources 187
Interactive Learning 187
Feature Boxes (Highlights)
- **Critical Thinking:** Subliminal Seduction or Subliminal Myths? 159
- **Focus on Research:** Blindsight: The "What" and the "Where" of Vision 164
- **Discovering Psychology:** Are You Color-Blind? 168
- **The Clinical File:** Artificial Hearing 172
- **Discovering Psychology:** Are You a Superstar? 176
- **The Clinical File:** The Matrix: Do Phantoms Live Here? 183

6 Perceiving the World 188

Preview: Murder! 189
Perceptual Constancies—Taming an Unruly World 189
Perceptual Organization—Getting It All Together 191
Gestalt Principles 191
Depth Perception—What If the World Were Flat? 195
Muscular Cues 196
Stereoscopic Vision 197
Pictorial Cues for Depth—A Deep Topic 199
Pictorial Depth Cues 199
Perceptual Learning—What If the World Were Upside Down? 202
Perceptual Habits 203
Adaptation Level 205
Illusions 206
Motives and Perception—May I Have Your . . . Attention! 209
Attention and Perception 209
Habituation 210
Motives and Attention 210
Perceptual Expectancies—On Your Mark, Get Set 211
Ready, Set, Perceive 212
Extrasensory Perception—Do You Believe in Magic? 213
An Appraisal of ESP 214
Stage ESP 215
Psychology in Action:
Perception and Objectivity—Believing Is Seeing 217
Chapter in Review 221
Web Resources 222
Interactive Learning 222
Feature Boxes (Highlights)
- **Focus on Research:** Designing for Human Use 193
- **Human Diversity:** Do They See What We See? 205
- **The Clinical File:** Staying in Touch with Reality 206
- **Critical Thinking:** The "Boiled Frog Syndrome" 211

7 States of Consciousness 223

Preview: A Visit to Several States (of Consciousness) 224
States of Consciousness—The Many Faces of Awareness 224
Altered States of Consciousness 224
Sleep—A Nice Place to Visit 224
The Need for Sleep 225
Sleep Patterns 227
Stages of Sleep—The Nightly Roller-Coaster Ride 228
Stages of Sleep 229
Two Basic Kinds of Sleep 230
REM Sleep and Dreaming 230
Sleep Disturbances—Showing Nightly: Sleep Wars! 232
Insomnia 232
Sleepwalking and Sleeptalking 233
Nightmares and Night Terrors 233
Sleep Apnea 234

Dreams—A Separate Reality? 235
REM Sleep Revisited 235
Dream Worlds 235
Dream Theories 236
Hypnosis—Look into My Eyes 237
Hypnotic Susceptibility 237
Stage Hypnosis 239
Sensory Deprivation—Life on a Sensory Diet 240
Disruptive Effects 240
Benefits of Sensory Restriction 240
Drug-Altered Consciousness—The High and Low of It 242
How Drugs Affect the Brain 243
Dependence 244
Patterns of Abuse 244
Uppers—Amphetamines, Cocaine, MDMA, Caffeine, Nicotine 244
Cocaine 245
MDMA ("Ecstasy") 246
Caffeine 246
Nicotine 247
Downers—Sedatives, Tranquilizers, and Alcohol 249
Barbiturates 249
GHB 249
Tranquilizers 249
Alcohol 250
Marijuana—What's in the Pot? 253
Hallucinogens 253
Marijuana 253
Dangers of Marijuana Use 254
Psychology in Action:
Exploring and Using Dreams 256
Chapter in Review 259
Web Resources 260
Interactive Learning 260
Feature Boxes (Highlights)
- **Critical Thinking:** What Is It Like to Be a Bat? 225
- **Human Diversity:** Consciousness and Culture 226
- **The Clinical File:** Teenage Sleep Zombies 227
- **Focus on Research:** Abducted by Space Aliens? 231
- **Discovering Psychology:** Swinging Suggestions 239

8 Conditioning and Learning 261

Preview: What Did You Learn in School Today? 262
What Is Learning—Does Practice Make Perfect? 262
Classical Conditioning 262
Operant Conditioning 263
Classical Conditioning—Does the Name Pavlov Ring a Bell? 263
Pavlov's Experiment 264
Principles of Classical Conditioning—Teach Your Little Brother to Salivate 265
Acquisition 265
Expectancies 266
Extinction and Spontaneous Recovery 266
Generalization 266
Discrimination 266
Classical Conditioning in Humans—An Emotional Topic 267
Conditioned Emotional Responses 267
Vicarious, or Secondhand, Conditioning 268
Operant Conditioning—Can Pigeons Play Ping-Pong? 269
Positive Reinforcement 270
Acquiring an Operant Response 270
The Timing of Reinforcement 271
Shaping 272
Operant Extinction 272
Negative Reinforcement 273
Punishment 273
Operant Reinforcers—What's Your Pleasure? 274
Primary Reinforcers 274
Secondary Reinforcers 274
Feedback 276
Learning Aids 276
Partial Reinforcement—Las Vegas, a Human Skinner Box? 278
Schedules of Partial Reinforcement 279
Stimulus Control—Red Light, Green Light 280
Punishment—Putting the Brakes on Behavior 282
Variables Affecting Punishment 282
Using Punishment Wisely 283
Side Effects of Punishment 284
Cognitive Learning—Beyond Conditioning 286
Cognitive Maps 286
Latent Learning 286
Modeling—Do as I Do, Not as I Say 288
Observational Learning 288
Modeling and Television 289

Psychology in Action:
Behavioral Self-Management—A Rewarding Project 291
Chapter in Review 294
Web Resources 295
Interactive Learning 295
Feature Boxes (Highlights)
- **The Clinical File:** Coping with Chemo 265
- **The Clinical File:** Blink If Your Brain Is Healthy 268
- **Discovering Psychology:** Conditioning and Conservation: Learning to Act Locally 277
- **Critical Thinking:** You Mean Video Games Might Be Bad for Me? 290

9 Memory 296

Preview: "What the Hell's Going on Here?" 297

Stages of Memory—Do You Have a Mind Like a Steel Trap? Or a Sieve? 297
Sensory Memory 297
Short-Term Memory 298
Long-Term Memory 298
Short-Term Memory—Do You Know the Magic Number? 300
Recoding 300
Rehearsing Information 300
Long-Term Memory—Where the Past Lives 301
Constructing Memories 301
Organizing Memories 303
Skill Memory and Fact Memory 304
Measuring Memory—The Answer Is on the Tip of My Tongue 306
Recalling Information 306
Recognizing Information 306
Relearning Information 307
Implicit and Explicit Memories 308
Exceptional Memory—Wizards of Recall 308
Eidetic Imagery 308
Exceptional Memory 309
Memory Champions 310
Forgetting—Why We, Uh, Let's See; Why We, Uh . . . Forget! 311
When Encoding Fails 312
Memory Decay 313
Cue-Dependent Forgetting 313
Interference 314
Transfer of Training 316
Repression and Suppression of Memories 316
Flashbulb Memories 317
Memory Formation—Some "Shocking" Findings 318
Consolidation 318
The Brain and Memory 319
Improving Memory—Keys to the Memory Bank 321
Memory Strategies 321
Psychology in Action:
Mnemonics—Memory Magic 324
Chapter in Review 327
Web Resources 328
Interactive Learning 328
Feature Boxes (Highlights)
- **Human Diversity:** Cows, Memories, and Culture 299
- **Focus on Research:** Telling Wrong from Right in Forensic Memory 303
- **Discovering Psychology:** Card Magic! 312
- **The Clinical File:** The Recovered Memory/False Memory Debate 317
- **Focus on Research:** The Long-Term Potential of a Memory Pill 320

10 Cognition, Language, and Creativity 329

Preview: Gizmos and Doohickeys 330

What Is Thinking?—It's All in Your Head! 330
Some Basic Units of Thought 330
Mental Imagery—Does a Frog Have Lips? 331
The Nature of Mental Images 331
Concepts—I'm Positive, It's a Whatchamacallit 333
Forming Concepts 333
Types of Concepts 334
Language—Don't Leave Home Without It 336
The Structure of Language 337
The Animal Language Debate 338
Problem Solving—Getting an Answer in Sight 341
Mechanical Solutions 341
Solutions by Understanding 341
Heuristics 341
Insightful Solutions 342
Common Barriers to Problem Solving 344
Artificial Intelligence—I Compute, Therefore I Am 345
AI and Cognition 345

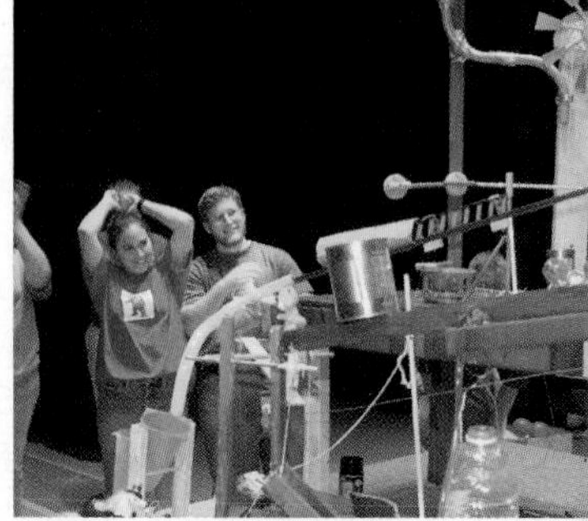

Creative Thinking—Down Roads Less Traveled 347
Tests of Creativity 349
Stages of Creative Thought 350
Positive Psychology: The Creative Personality 351
Logic and Intuition—Mental Shortcut? Or Dangerous Detour? 352
Intuition 353
Psychology in Action:
Enhancing Creativity—Brainstorms 356
Chapter in Review 360
Web Resources 361
Interactive Learning 361
Feature Boxes (Highlights)
- **Human Diversity:** *Si o No, Oui ou Non,* Yes or No? 337
- **Human Diversity:** How to Weigh an Elephant 344
- **Focus on Research:** Daydreams, Fantasy, and Creativity 349
- **The Clinical File:** Madness and Creativity 352
- **Critical Thinking:** Have You Ever Thin Sliced Your Teacher? 353

11 Intelligence 362
Preview: What Day Is It? 363
Defining Intelligence—Intelligence Is . . . You Know, It's . . . 363
Defining Intelligence 364
Reliability and Validity 364
Testing Intelligence—The IQ and You 365
Five Aspects of Intelligence 365
Intelligence Quotients 366
The Wechsler Tests 369
Group Tests 369
Variations in Intelligence—The Numbers Game 370
The Mentally Gifted—Smart, Smarter, Smartest 371
Gifted Children 371
Mental Retardation—A Difference That Makes a Difference 373
Levels of Retardation 373
Causes of Retardation 374
Organic Sources of Retardation 374
Retardation in Perspective 375
Heredity and Environment—Super Rats and Family Trees 376
Hereditary Influences 376
Environmental Influences 377
New Approaches to Intelligence—Intelligent Alternatives 379
The Intelligent Nervous System 379
Intelligent Information Processing 380
Multiple Intelligences 380
Psychology in Action:
How Intelligent Are Intelligence Tests? 382
Chapter in Review 385
Web Resources 386
Feature Boxes (Highlights)
- **Human Diversity:** Intelligence—How Would a Fool Do It? 366
- **The Clinical File:** Autistic Savants—Fragile Genius 373
- **Critical Thinking:** You Mean Video Games Might Be Good for Me? 378
- **Focus on Research:** Inspecting Intelligence 379

12 Motivation and Emotion 387
Preview: The Sun Sets Twice in Utah 388
Motivation—Forces That Push and Pull 388
A Model of Motivation 388
Primary Motives and Homeostasis 390
Hunger—Pardon Me, My Hypothalamus Is Growling 390
Brain Mechanisms 391
Obesity 393
Behavioral Dieting 394
Other Factors in Hunger 395
Eating Disorders 396
Culture, Ethnicity, and Dieting 397
Primary Motives Revisited—Thirst, Sex, and Pain 397
Thirst 398
Pain 398
The Sex Drive 398
Stimulus Drives—Skydiving, Horror Movies, and the Fun Zone 399
Arousal Theory 400
Levels of Arousal 400
Circadian Rhythms 402
Learned Motives—The Pursuit of Excellence 404
Opponent-Process Theory 404
Social Motives 404
The Need for Achievement 405
The Key to Success? 405

Motives in Perspective—A View from the Pyramid 406
- Intrinsic and Extrinsic Motivation 407
- Turning Play into Work 407

Inside an Emotion—How Do You Feel? 409
- Primary Emotions 409
- The Brain and Emotion 410

Physiology and Emotion—Arousal, Sudden Death, and Lying 411
- Fight or Flight 411
- Lie Detectors 412

Expressing Emotions—Making Faces and Talking Bodies 414
- Facial Expressions 414

Theories of Emotion—Several Ways to Fear a Bear 417
- The James-Lange Theory (1884–1885) 417
- The Cannon-Bard Theory (1927) 418
- Schachter's Cognitive Theory of Emotion 418
- The Facial Feedback Hypothesis 419
- A Contemporary Model of Emotion 420

Psychology in Action:
Emotional Intelligence—The Fine Art of Self-Control 422

Chapter in Review 424
Web Resources 425
Interactive Learning 425
Feature Boxes (Highlights)
- **Discovering Psychology:** What's Your BMI? (We've Got Your Number.) 393
- **Human Diversity:** Xtreme! 401
- **Critical Thinking:** To Catch a Terrorist 413
- **Focus on Research:** Crow's-Feet and Smiles Sweet 415
- **The Clinical File:** Suppressing Emotion—Is It Healthy? 420

Gender and Sexuality 426

Preview: That Magic Word 427

Sexual Development—Circle One: *XX* or *XY*? 427
- Female or Male? 427
- Prenatal Sexual Development 429
- Gender Identity 430
- Origins of Male–Female Differences 431
- Gender Roles 431
- Gender Role Socialization 433

Androgyny—Are You Masculine, Feminine, or Androgynous? 434
- Psychological Androgyny 434

Sexual Behavior—Mapping the Erogenous Zone 436
- Sexual Arousal 436

Sexual Orientation—Who Do You Love? 438
- Homosexuality 439

Human Sexual Response—Sexual Interactions 440
- Comparing Male and Female Responses 442

Atypical Sexual Behavior—Trench Coats, Whips, Leathers, and Lace 442
- Paraphilias 443

Attitudes and Sexual Behavior—The Changing Sexual Landscape 444
- Is the Revolution Over? 445
- The Crime of Rape 445

STDs and Safer Sex—Choice, Risk, and Responsibility 447
- AIDS 448
- Behavioral Risk Factors 448
- Risk and Responsibility 449

Psychology in Action:
Sexual Problems—When Pleasure Fades 450

Chapter in Review 456
Web Resources 457
Interactive Learning 457
Feature Boxes (Highlights)
- **Discovering Psychology:** What's Your BMI? (We've Got Your Number.) 393
- **Human Diversity:** Xtreme! 401
- **Critical Thinking:** To Catch a Terrorist 412
- **Focus on Research:** Crow's-Feet and Smiles Sweet 415
- **The Clinical File:** Suppressing Emotion—Is It Healthy? 420

Personality 458

Preview: The Hidden Essence 459

The Psychology of Personality—Do You Have Personality? 459
- Traits 460
- Types 460
- Self-Concept 461
- Personality Theories 462

The Trait Approach—Describe Yourself in 18,000 Words or Less 463
- Predicting Behavior 463
- Describing People 464
- Classifying Traits 464
- The Big Five 465
- Traits, Consistency, and Situations 466
- Do We Inherit Personality? 466

Psychoanalytic Theory—Id Came to Me in a Dream 468
The Structure of Personality 469
The Dynamics of Personality 470
Personality Development 471
Psychodynamic Theories—Freud's Descendants 472
Alfred Adler (1870–1937) 473
Karen Horney (1885–1952) 473
Carl Jung (1875–1961) 473
Learning Theories of Personality—Habit I Seen You Before? 474
How Situations Affect Behavior 475
Personality = Behavior 475
Social Learning Theory 476
Behavioristic View of Development 477
Humanistic Theory—Peak Experiences and Personal Growth 479
Maslow and Self-Actualization 479
Positive Psychology: Positive Personality Traits 480
Carl Rogers's Self Theory 480
Humanistic View of Development 482
Personality Theories—Overview and Comparison 482
Personality Assessment—Psychological Yardsticks 484
The Interview 484
Direct Observation and Rating Scales 485
Personality Questionnaires 486
Projective Tests of Personality—Inkblots and Hidden Plots 487
The Rorschach Inkblot Test 488
The Thematic Apperception Test 488
Sudden Murderers—A Research Example 490
Psychology in Action:
Barriers and Bridges—Understanding Shyness 491
Chapter in Review 493
Web Resources 494
Interactive Learning 495
Feature Boxes (Highlights)
- **Human Diversity:** Self-Esteem and Culture—Hotshot or Team Player 462
- **Discovering Psychology:** What's Your Musical Personality? 463
- **The Clinical File:** Perfectly Miserable 467
- **Critical Thinking:** The Minnesota Twins 468
- **Critical Thinking:** Honesty Tests—Do They Tell the Truth? 488

15 Health, Stress, and Coping 496

Preview: Taylor's (Not So Very) Fine Adventure 497
Health Psychology—Here's to Your Good Health 497
Behavioral Risk Factors 497
Health-Promoting Behaviors 499
Early Prevention 499
Community Health 500
Positive Psychology: Wellness 500
Stress—Thrill or Threat? 501
When Is Stress a Strain? 501
Appraising Stressors 503
Coping with Threat 504
Frustration—Blind Alleys and Lead Balloons 505
Reactions to Frustration 505
Coping with Frustration 507
Conflict—Yes, No, Yes, No, Yes, No, Well, Maybe 507
Managing Conflicts 509
Psychological Defense—Mental Karate? 510
Learned Helplessness—Is There Hope? 512
Depression 512
Depression, a Problem for Everyone 514
Coping with Depression 514
Stress and Health—Unmasking a Hidden Killer 515
Life Events and Stress 515
Psychosomatic Disorders 517
Biofeedback 517
The Cardiac Personality 520
Hardy Personality 521
The Value of Social Support 522
The General Adaptation Syndrome 522
Stress, Illness, and the Immune System 523
Psychology in Action:
Stress Management 525
Chapter in Review 529
Web Resources 530
Interactive Learning 530
Feature Boxes (Highlights)
- **The Clinical File:** Burnout—The High Cost of Caring 502
- **The Clinical File:** Coping with Traumatic Stress 504
- **Human Diversity:** Acculturative Stress—Stranger in a Strange Land 518
- **Critical Thinking:** It's All in Your Mind 519
- **Discovering Psychology:** Feeling Stressed? You've Got a Friend 523

16 Psychological Disorders 531

Preview: Beware the Helicopters 532

Normality—What Is Normal? 532
- Core Features of Disordered Behavior 534

Classifying Mental Disorders—Problems by the Book 535
- An Overview of Psychological Disorders 535
- General Risk Factors 538
- Insanity 540

Personality Disorders—Blueprints for Maladjustment 540
- Maladaptive Personality Patterns 541
- Antisocial Personality 541

Anxiety-Based Disorders—When Anxiety Rules 542
- Adjustment Disorders 542
- Anxiety Disorders 543
- Obsessive-Compulsive Disorder 544
- Stress Disorders 545
- Dissociative Disorders 546
- Somatoform Disorders 546

Anxiety and Disorder—Four Pathways to Trouble 547
- Psychodynamic Approach 548
- Humanistic-Existential Approaches 548
- Behavioral Approach 548
- Cognitive Approach 548

Psychotic Disorders—Life in the Shadow of Madness 549
- The Nature of Psychosis 549

Delusional Disorders—An Enemy Behind Every Tree 551
- Paranoid Psychosis 552

Schizophrenia—Shattered Reality 552
- Disorganized Schizophrenia 552
- Catatonic Schizophrenia 553
- Paranoid Schizophrenia 553
- Undifferentiated Schizophrenia 554
- The Causes of Schizophrenia 555
- The Schizophrenic Brain 556
- Implications 557

Mood Disorders—Peaks and Valleys 558
- Major Mood Disorders 559
- What Causes Mood Disorders? 560

Disorders in Perspective—Psychiatric Labeling 562
- Social Stigma 562
- A Look Ahead 562

Psychology in Action:
Suicide—Lives on the Brink 563

Chapter in Review 566
Web Resources 567
Interactive Learning 568
Feature Boxes (Highlights)
- **Discovering Psychology:** Crazy for a Day 533
- **Critical Thinking:** The Politics of Madness 534
- **Human Diversity:** Running Amok with Cultural Maladies 538
- **Critical Thinking:** Are the Mentally Ill Prone to Violence? 554

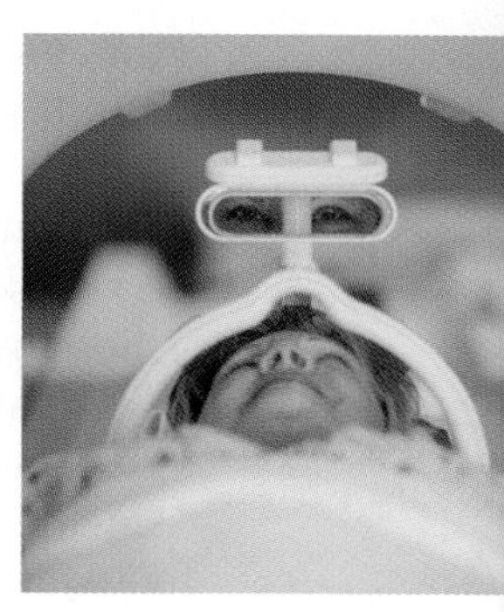

17 Therapies 569

Preview: Cold Terror on a Warm Afternoon 570

Psychotherapy—Getting Better by the Hour 570
- Dimensions of Therapy 570

Origins of Therapy—Bored Skulls and Hysteria on the Couch 571

Psychoanalysis—Expedition into the Unconscious 572
- Psychoanalysis Today 573

Humanistic Therapies—Restoring Human Potential 574
- Client-Centered Therapy 574
- Existential Therapy 575
- Gestalt Therapy 575

Therapy at a Distance—Psych Jockeys and Cybertherapy 576
- Media Psychologists 576
- Telephone Therapists 576
- Cybertherapy 577
- Telehealth 577

Behavior Therapy—Healing by Learning 578
- Aversion Therapy 578
- Desensitization 579

Operant Therapies—All the World Is a Skinner Box? 582
- Nonreinforcement and Extinction 582
- Reinforcement and Token Economies 583

Cognitive Therapy—Think Positive! 584
- Cognitive Therapy for Depression 584
- Rational-Emotive Behavior Therapy 585

Group Therapy—People Who Need People 586
- Psychodrama 586
- Family Therapy 587
- Group Awareness Training 587

Psychotherapy—An Overview 588
- Core Features of Psychotherapy 589
- The Future of Psychotherapy 590
- Basic Counseling Skills 590

Medical Therapies—Psychiatric Care 592
- Drug Therapies 592
- Shock 593
- Psychosurgery 594
- Hospitalization 594
- Community Mental Health Programs 595

Psychology in Action:
Self-Management and Finding Professional Help 596

Chapter in Review 601

Web Resources 603

Interactive Learning 603

Feature Boxes (Highlights)
- **Discovering Psychology:** Feeling a Little Tense? Relax! 580
- **Focus on Research:** Eye Movement Desensitization and Reprocessing—Watching Trauma Fade? 581
- **Discovering Psychology:** Ten Irrational Beliefs—Which Do You Hold? 585
- **Critical Thinking:** How Do We Know Therapy Actually Works? 588
- **Discovering Psychology:** Therapy and Culture—A Bad Case of "Ifufunyane" 590

18 Social Behavior 604

Preview: We Are Social Animals 605

Humans in a Social Context—People, People, Everywhere 605
- Roles 605
- Group Structure and Cohesion 606

Personal Space—Invisible Boundaries 608
- Spatial Norms 608

Social Perception—Behind the Mask 609
- Attribution Theory 609
- Actor and Observer 610

The Need for Affiliation—Come Together 612
- Social Comparison Theory 612

Interpersonal Attraction—Social Magnetism? 613
- Physical Proximity 613
- Physical Attractiveness 614
- Competence 614
- Similarity 614
- Self-Disclosure 614
- Social Exchange Theory 615

Loving and Liking—Dating, Rating, Mating 616
- Love and Attachment 616
- Evolution and Mate Selection 617

Social Influence—Follow the Leader 619
- Conformity 619

Social Power—Who Can Do What to Whom? 621

Obedience—Would You Electrocute a Stranger? 621
- Milgram's Obedience Studies 622

Compliance—A Foot in the Door 624
- Passive Compliance 625

Psychology in Action:
Assertiveness Training—Standing Up for Your Rights 627

Chapter in Review 629

Web Resources 630

Interactive Learning 630

Feature Boxes (Highlights)
- **Focus on Research:** Touch and Status 607
- **The Clinical File:** Self-Handicapping—Smoke Screen for Failure 611
- **Critical Thinking:** Groupthink—Agreement at Any Cost 620
- **Discovering Psychology:** Quack Like a Duck 623
- **Critical Thinking:** How to Drive a Hard Bargain 625

19 Attitudes, Culture, and Human Relations 631

Preview: Doomsday for the Seekers 632

Attitudes—Belief + Emotion + Action 632
- Attitude Formation 632
- Attitudes and Behavior 634
- Attitude Measurement 634

Attitude Change—Why the Seekers Went Public 634
- Persuasion 634
- Cognitive Dissonance Theory 635

Forced Attitude Change—Brainwashing and Cults 636
- Brainwashing 637
- Cults 637

Prejudice—Attitudes That Injure 639
- Becoming Prejudiced 639
- The Prejudiced Personality 641

Intergroup Conflict—The Roots of Prejudice 641
- Experiments in Prejudice 643

Aggression—The World's Most Dangerous Animal 647
Instincts 647
Biology 648
Frustration 648
Social Learning 648
The World According to TV 649
Preventing Aggression 650
Prosocial Behavior—Helping Others 653
Bystander Intervention 653
Who Will Help Whom? 654
Positive Psychology: Everyday Heroes 654
Psychology in Action:
Multiculturalism—Living with Diversity 656
Chapter in Review 658
Web Resources 659
Interactive Learning 660
Feature Boxes (Highlights)
- **Discovering Psychology:** I'm Not Prejudiced, Right? 640
- **Human Diversity:** Choking on Stereotypes 643
- **Critical Thinking:** Terrorists, Enemies, and Infidels 644
- **Focus on Research:** Pornography and Aggression Against Women—Is There a Link? 650
- **The Clinical File:** School Violence—Warning Signs and Remedies 652

20 Applied Psychology 661
Preview: The Towering Inferno 662
Industrial-Organizational Psychology—Psychology at Work 662
Personnel Psychology 662
Job Analysis 663
Selection Procedures 663
Theories of Management—What Works at Work? 666
Theory X and Theory Y 666
Job Satisfaction 667
Job Enrichment 668
Organizational Culture 669
Environmental Psychology—Life in the Big City 670
Environmental Influences 672
Stressful Environments 672
Toxic Environments 675
Sustainable Lifestyles 675
Environmental Problem Solving 677
Conclusion 678
Educational Psychology—An Instructive Topic 679
Elements of a Teaching Strategy 679
Psychology and Law—Judging Juries 680
Jury Behavior 680
Jury Selection 681
Sports Psychology—The Athletic Mind 682
Motor Skills 684
Positive Psychology: Peak Performance 684
Psychology in Action:
Improving Communication at Work 686
Chapter in Review 688
Web Resources 689
Interactive Learning 689
Feature Boxes (Highlights)
- **Focus on Research:** The Sweet Smell of Success? Not Always. 664
- **Focus on Research:** Flextime 668
- **The Clinical File:** Desk Rage and Healthy Organizations 669
- **Focus on Research:** Territoriality 671
- **Discovering Psychology:** Planet in Peril? 675
- **Human Diversity:** Peanut Butter for the Mind: Designing Education for Everyone 680
- **Critical Thinking:** Death-Qualified Juries 682

Appendix: Behavioral Statistics 690
Preview: Statistics from "Heads" to "Tails" 691
Descriptive Statistics—Psychology by the Numbers 691
Graphical Statistics 691
Measures of Central Tendency 692
Measures of Variability 694
Standard Scores 694
The Normal Curve 695
Inferential Statistics—Significant Numbers 696
Samples and Populations 696
Significant Differences 696
Correlation—Rating Relationships 697
Relationships 697
The Correlation Coefficient 698
Appendix in Review 700
Web Resources 700
Interactive Learning 700

Glossary G-1
References R-1
Photo Credits C-1
Name Index N-1
Subject Index S-1

Preface to the Eleventh Edition

An Invitation to the Student

Psychology is an exciting field. It is at once familiar, exotic, surprising, and challenging. What, really, could be more intriguing than our evolving understanding of human behavior?

Psychology is about each of us. It asks us to adopt a reflective attitude as we inquire, "How can we step outside of ourselves to look objectively at how we live, think, feel, and act?" Psychologists believe the answer is through careful thought, observation, and inquiry. As simple as that may seem, thoughtful reflection takes practice to develop. It is the guiding light for all that follows in this text.

Reading *Gateways to Mind and Behavior*

In a separate booklet titled *Gateways to Psychology: Concept Maps and Concept Reviews,* which accompanies this text, you will find a list of "Gateways to Psychology." These concepts are summaries of psychology's "big ideas" and enduring principles. While you don't need to memorize the Gateway concepts, you can use them to review the most important points in each chapter. Ultimately, the Gateway concepts will provide a good summary of what you learned in this course.

Studying *Gateways to Mind and Behavior*

We probably don't have to tell you that learning psychology depends on how you study this book, as well as how you read it. To help you get off to a good start, we strongly encourage you to read our short Introduction, which precedes Chapter 1. The Introduction describes study skills, including the SQ4R method, which you can use to get the most out of this text and your psychology course. It also tells how you can explore psychology through the Internet, electronic databases, and interactive CDs.

Each chapter of this book will take you into a different realm of psychology, such as personality, abnormal behavior, memory, consciousness, and child development. Each realm is complex and fascinating in its own right, with many pathways, landmarks, and interesting detours to discover. *Introduction to Psychology: Gateways to Mind and Behavior* is your passport to an adventure in learning. It is, in a very real sense, written about you, for you, and to you.

An Invitation to the Instructor

Marcel Proust wrote, "The real voyage of discovery consists not in seeing new landscapes but in having new eyes." It is in this spirit that we invite you to make full use of this book to help you change the way your students see human behavior. Accordingly, we have written this book to promote an interest in human behavior, including an appreciation of the practical applications of psychology, the richness of human diversity, and the field of positive psychology. At the same time, we have structured this book to facilitate the application of learning and critical-thinking skills. Without such skills, students cannot easily go, as Jerome Bruner put it, "beyond the information given" (Bruner, 1973).

To help students read more effectively, we continue to open every chapter with a list of "Key Questions" that students can use as powerful advance organizers for digesting new information (e.g., Ausubel, 1978). These questions are addressed throughout the chapter and form the basis for the summaries at the end of every chapter.

In a separate booklet, *Gateways to Psychology: Concept Maps and Concept Reviews,* students will find lists of "Gateways to Psychology." These summarize the "take home" ideas every student should remember 10 years after reading this text. As a whole, they are capable of transforming the way students view human behavior.

Now widely emulated, earlier editions of *Introduction to Psychology* revolutionized textbooks by using psychology to help students learn more effectively. We continue that tradition of innovation in this edition. To help students study more effectively, we have updated the SQ4R method to promote active learning, better long-term retention of ideas, and a reflective attitude that lies at the heart of critical thinking.

Specifically, in this edition we have replaced "Relate" with "Reflect" so that SQ4R now refers to the steps Survey, Question, Read, Recite, Reflect, and Review. This change has allowed us to expand the Reflect step to strengthen the relationship between learning and doing the kinds of elaborative processing and critical thinking that characterize the reflective student (Gadzella, 1995).

Readability and Narrative Emphasis

Selecting a textbook is half the battle in teaching a successful course. A good text does much of the work of imparting information to your students. This frees class time for your discussion, extra topics, or media presentations. It also leaves students asking for more. When a book overwhelms students or cools their interest, teaching and learning suffer.

Many introductory psychology students are reluctant readers. No matter how interesting a text may be, its value is lost if students fail to read it. That's why we've worked hard to make this a clear, readable, and engaging text. We want students to read this book with genuine interest and enthusiasm, not merely as an obligation.

To encourage students to read, we made a special effort to weave narrative threads through every chapter. Everyone loves a good story, and the story of psychology is among the most compelling to be told. Throughout *Introduction to Psychology,* we have used intriguing anecdotes and examples to propel reading and sustain interest. As students explore concepts, they are encouraged to think about ideas and relate them to their own experiences. For example, the tide of human compassion unleashed by the 2004 Asian tsunami and the 2005 hurricane season in the Southern United States are used to illustrate human altruism.

Practical Applications

Introduction to Psychology is designed to give students a clear grasp of major concepts without burying them in details. At the same time, it offers a broad overview that reflects psychology's rich heritage of ideas. We think students will find this book informative and intellectually stimulating. Moreover, we have emphasized the many ways that psychology relates to practical problems in daily life.

A major feature of this book is the *Psychology in Action* section found at the end of each chapter. These high-interest discussions bridge the gap between theory and practical application. We believe it is fair for students to ask, "Does this mean anything to me? Can I use it? Why should I learn it if I can't?" The *Psychology in Action* features show students how to solve problems and manage their own behavior. This allows them to see the benefits of adopting new ideas, and it breathes life into psychology's concepts.

An Integrated Study Guide

The chapters of this text are divided into short segments by special sections called *Knowledge Builders*. Each *Knowledge Builder* challenges students to relate concepts to their own experiences, to quiz themselves, and to think critically about psychology.

If students would like even more feedback and practice, *Chapter Quizzes* are available in the *Gateways to Psychology: Concept Maps and Concept Reviews* booklet, a traditional Study Guide is available, and students can use a web-based course-management tool called *WebTutor™ Advantage* to take online quizzes or practice with electronic flash cards. A free booklet, *Gateways to Psychology: Concept Maps and Concept Reviews,* accompanies every new copy of the text and includes Gateway concepts for every chapter, concept maps of key concepts, and concept reviews (comprised of a 30-item multiple-choice quiz for each chapter). Available to qualified adopters, please consult your local sales representative for details.

Electronic Resources

To encourage further exploration, students will find a section called *Web Resources* at the end of each chapter. The websites described there offer a wealth of information on topics related to psychology. Students are also directed to relevant articles in *InfoTrac® College Edition,* Wadsworth's exclusive online college library. All chapters include a list of relevant modules in *PsychNow! 2.0.* This excellent CD-ROM from Wadsworth provides students with a rich assortment of interactive learning experiences, animations, and simulations.

On the web, students can visit this text's *Book Companion Website,* where they will find quizzes, a final exam, chapter-by-chapter web links, flash cards, an audio glossary, and more (www.thomsonedu.com/psychology/coon).

Students can also make use of *ThomsonNOW for Coon's Introduction to Psychology: Gateways to Mind and Behavior,* eleventh edition, a web-based, personalized study system that provides a pretest and a posttest for each chapter and separate chapter quizzes. *ThomsonNOW for Coon's Introduction to Psychology,* eleventh edition, can also create personalized study plans—which include rich media such as videos, animations, and learning modules—that point students to areas in the text that will help them master course content. An additional set of integrative questions helps students pull all of the material together.

Human Diversity

Today's students reflect the multicultural, multifaceted nature of contemporary society. In *Introduction to Psychology,* students will find numerous discussions of human diversity, including differences in race, ethnicity, culture, gender, abilities, sexual orientation, and age. Too often, such differences needlessly divide people into opposing groups. Our aim throughout this text is to discourage stereotyping, prejudice, discrimination, and intolerance. We've tried to make this book gender neutral and sensitive to diversity issues. All pronouns and examples involving females and males are equally divided by gender. In artwork, photographs, and examples, we have tried to portray the rich diversity of humanity. In addition, a boxed feature, *Human Diversity,* appears throughout the book, providing the student with examples of how to be more reflective about human diversity.

Many topics and examples in this book encourage students to appreciate social, physical, and cultural differences and to accept them as a natural part of being human.

Positive Psychology

In January 2000, Martin Seligman and Mihaly Csikszentmihalyi co-edited a special issue of *American Psychologist* devoted to optimal functioning, happiness, and "positive psychology." Over the past 100 years, psychologists have paid ample attention to the negative side of human behavior. This is easy to understand because we urgently need to find remedies for human problems. However, Seligman and Csikszentmihalyi have urged us to also study positive psychology. What do we know, for instance, about love, happiness, creativity, well-being, self-confidence, and achievement? Throughout this book, we have attempted to answer such questions for students. Our hope is that students who read this book will gain an appreciation for the potential we all have for optimal functioning. Also, of course, we hope that they will leave introductory psychology with emotional and intellectual tools they can use to enhance their lives.

How Chapter Features Support the SQ4R Method

Introduction to Psychology was the first college text with an SQ4R, active-learning format. Through Dennis Coon's pioneering efforts, this book has made learning psychology a rewarding experience for more than 2 million students. With their feedback and

TABLE 1

***Human Diversity and Culture in* Introduction to Psychology**

Chapter 1: Introduction to Psychology and Research Methods

- Cultural psychology
- Human diversity, appreciating social and cultural differences
- The impact of culture
- Cultural relativity
- A broader view of diversity
- Human diversity and representative samples

Chapter 2: Brain and Behavior

- Nerve grafting for people with spinal injuries
- Hypopituitary dwarfism
- Handedness and laterality
- Computer aids for people with total paralysis

Chapter 3: Child Development

- Ethnic differences in child-rearing
- The relationship between culture and babbling
- Parentese in different cultures
- Piagetian stages and cultural influences
- Sociocultural influences on cognitive development (Vygotsky)

Chapter 4: From Birth to Death: Life-Span Development

- Adolescent status and culture
- Diversity and the adolescent search for identity
- Ethnicity and personal identity
- Culture and moral reasoning
- 20-somethings and emerging adulthood
- Ageism and myths about the elderly

Chapter 6: Perceiving the World

- The "other race" effect in facial recognition
- Culture and the recognition of pictorial depth cues
- Culture and the Müller-Lyer illusion
- Cross-racial perceptions (eyewitness accuracy)
- Cultural differences in perception

Chapter 7: States of Consciousness

- States of consciousness and culture
- The cultural context of drug use

Chapter 8: Conditioning and Learning

- Comparing U.S. television content with cultures that limit televised violence

Chapter 9: Memory

- Aging and memory
- Cultural influences on memory
- Eyewitnesses and cross-racial recognition
- Labeling and the ability to remember people from other social groups

Chapter 10: Cognition, Language, and Creativity

- Social stereotypes and cognition
- The effects of unconscious prejudice on word recognition
- Affect of word meanings on thinking (of celebrity names)
- Linguistic misunderstandings between cultures
- The pros and cons of bilingualism
- Cultural differences in the use of phonemes
- The deaf community and gestural languages
- Cultural barriers to problem solving

Chapter 11: Intelligence

- Age and IQ
- The developmentally disabled
- Race, culture, ethnicity, and intelligence
- Cultural differences in intelligence (as taught to children)
- Culture-fair intelligence testing
- A critique of *The Bell Curve*
- Bias in the use of IQ tests for educational placement

Chapter 12: Motivation and Emotion

- Cultural values and food preferences
- Culture, ethnicity, and dieting
- Pain avoidance and cultural conditioning
- The influence of culture on emotional expressions
- Cultural differences in the occurrence of emotion
- Cultural differences in facial expressions
- Cultural learning and body language

Chapter 13: Gender and Sexuality

- Gender-role stereotypes
- Culture and gender roles
- Androgyny
- Sexual orientation
- Sexual activity and teenage pregnancy rates
- Gender-role stereotyping and rape
- Rates of HIV/AIDS infection and death

Chapter 14: Personality

- Self-esteem and culture

Chapter 15: Health, Stress, and Coping

- Scapegoating of ethnic group members
- Culture shock and acculturative stress

Chapter 16: Psychological Disorders

- How culture affects judgments of psychopathology
- Culture-specific psychological "disorders"
- Ethnic group differences in psychopathology

Chapter 17: Therapies

- Cultural issues in counseling and psychotherapy
- Culturally aware therapists

Chapter 18: Social Behavior

- Cultural differences in norms governing personal space
- Gendered friendships
- Male-female differences in mate preferences
- Evolutionary perspectives on male and female mate selection

Chapter 19: Attitudes, Culture, and Human Relations

- Racial prejudice and discrimination
- Ethnocentrism
- Social stereotypes
- Cultural differences in hostility and aggression
- Symbolic prejudice
- Rejection and demonization of out-groups
- Experiments in creating and reducing prejudice
- Multiculturalism
- Breaking the prejudice habit
- Cultural awareness

Chapter 20: Applied Psychology

- How cultural differences affect living in space habitats

TABLE 2

***Gender in* Introduction to Psychology**

Chapter 1: Introduction to Psychology and Research Methods

- The psychology of gender
- Women in psychology
- A broader view of diversity
- Gender bias in research

Chapter 2: Brain and Behavior

- Oversecretion of sex hormones (and virilism and pre-puberty)
- Male-female differences in brain lateralization

Chapter 3: Child Development

- Parenting styles and gender-role development

Chapter 4: From Birth to Death: Life-Span Development

- Comparing male and female moral reasoning
- Comparing male and female midlife transitions
- Menopause versus the climacteric
- Gender and happiness

Chapter 7: States of Consciousness

- Lung-cancer deaths caused by smoking
- Metabolism of alcohol
- Affects of alcohol on sexual performance
- Sexual affects of Ecstasy

Chapter 8: Conditioning and Learning

- Affects of television on children's perceptions of sex roles
- Affects of television on children's level of aggression

Chapter 11: Intelligence

- Sex and IQ
- Gender and genetic mutations

Chapter 12: Motivation and Emotion

- Pain avoidance and cultural conditioning
- Social obstacles to achievement for women
- How hormones affect sex drive
- Gender differences in emotion

Chapter 13: Gender and Sexuality

- Psychosocial differences between men and women
- Intersexuality
- Controversy about gender differences in ability (left brain/right brain)
- Gender roles
- Gender-role stereotypes
- Culture and gender roles
- Gender-role socialization
- Likeability of women successful at "man's work"
- Androgyny
- Sexual arousal (after watching erotic films)
- Sexual activity
- Sexual orientation
- Role of hormones in sex drive
- Gender differences in sexual response
- Sexual double standard
- Gender-role stereotyping and rape
- Rates of HIV/AIDS infection and death

Chapter 14: Personality

- Social learning of male and female traits

Chapter 15: Health, Stress, and Coping

- Sex differences in seeking social support

Chapter 16: Psychological Disorders

- How gender affects judgments of psychopathology
- Gender differences in rates of anxiety disorders
- Sex differences in rates of clinical depression
- Gender differences in suicide (attempt and completion)

Chapter 18: Social Behavior

- Gender differences in touching (as related to status)
- Double standards for male and female performance
- Influence of physical attractiveness
- Male-female differences in mate preferences
- Gendered friendships
- Male-female differences in loving and liking
- Evolutionary perspectives on male and female mate selection

Chapter 19: Attitudes, Culture, and Human Relations

- Levels of testosterone and aggression
- Affects of pornography on sexual violence against women

TABLE 3

***Positive Psychology in* Introduction to Psychology**

Altruism and helping behavior (Ch. 19)
Androgyny and adaptability (Ch. 13)
Appreciating human diversity (Chs. 1, 19)
Characteristics of the gifted (Ch. 11)
Constructive child discipline (Ch. 3)
Dreams and creativity (Ch. 7)
Elements of positive mental health (Ch. 16)
Emotional intelligence (Ch. 12)
Enhancing creativity (Ch. 10)
Enriching early development (Ch. 3)
Ethical research (Ch. 1)
Exceptional memory (Ch. 9)
Facilitating cognitive development (Ch. 3)
Friendship and attraction (Ch. 18)
Fully functioning person (Ch. 14)
Hardiness and happiness (Ch. 15)
Health-promoting behaviors (Ch. 15)
Health-promoting conditions in therapy (Ch. 17)
Healthy organizations (Ch. 20)
Helping behaviors (Ch. 19)
High achievers (Ch. 12)
Hope (Ch. 15)
Humanistic psychology (Chs. 1, 12, 14, 17)
Improving memory (Ch. 9)
Intrinsic motivation and creativity (Ch. 12)
Jigsaw classrooms (Ch. 19)
Loving and liking (Ch. 18)
Meditation (Ch. 15)
Meta-needs (Ch. 12)
Moral behavior (Ch. 4)
Multiculturalism (Ch. 19)
Multiple intelligences (Ch. 11)
Optimal caregiving (Ch. 3)
Peak performance (Chs. 12, 20)
Perceptual awareness (Ch. 6)
Positive states of consciousness (Ch. 7)
Promoting secure attachment (Ch. 3)
Promoting self-esteem in children (Ch. 3)
Prosocial behavior (Ch. 19)
Quality day care (Ch. 3)
Repair of brain damage (Ch. 2)
Self-actualization (Chs. 1, 12, 14)
Self-confidence (Ch. 14)
Self-efficacy (Ch. 14)
Self-esteem (Ch. 14)
Self-regulated learning (Introduction)
Successful aging (Ch. 4)
Superordinate goals (Ch. 19)
Well-being and happiness (Ch. 4)
Wellness (Ch. 15)

generous help from many professors, we have continued to refine the unique features of *Gateways*.

Notice how the steps of the SQ4R method—*survey, question, read, recite, reflect,* and *review*—are incorporated into the chapter design.

Survey Features at the beginnings of chapters help students build cognitive maps of upcoming topics, thus serving as advance organizers. Students begin with a chapter Theme and a list of Key Questions. Key Questions identify the main points students should search for as they read. Next, a short Preview arouses interest, gives an overview of the chapter, and focuses attention on the task at hand. These chapter-opening features invite students to read with a purpose and thus engage in active information processing.

Question Throughout each chapter, frequent italicized Guide Questions also serve as advance organizers. That is, Guide Questions prompt students to look for important ideas as they read and thus promote active learning. They also establish a dialogue in which the questions and reactions of students are anticipated. This clarifies difficult points—in a lively give-and-take between questions and responses.

Read We've made every effort to make this a clear, readable text. To further aid comprehension, we've used a full array of traditional learning aids. These include boldface terms (with phonetic pronunciations), bullet summaries, a robust illustration program, summary tables, a name index, a subject index, and a detailed glossary. As an additional aid, figure and table references in the text are marked with small geometric shapes. These "placeholders" make it easier for students to return to reading after they have paused to view a table or figure.

An integrated Running Glossary aids reading comprehension by providing precise definitions directly in context. When important terms first appear, they are immediately defined. In this way, students get clear definitions when and where they need them—in the general text itself. In addition, a parallel Running Glossary defines key terms. The Running Glossary makes it easier for students to find, study, and review important terms.

Recite Every few pages, a *Knowledge Builder* gives students a chance to test their understanding and recall of preceding topics. The *Knowledge Builders* are small, built-in study guides that include a Learning Check (a short, noncomprehensive quiz), which helps students actively process information and assess their progress. Learning Check questions are not as difficult as in-class tests, and they are just a sample of what students could be asked about various topics. Students who miss any items are asked to backtrack and clarify their understanding before reading more. Completing Learning Checks serves as a form of recitation to enhance learning.

Reflect Cognitive psychology tells us that elaboration, the reflective processing of new information, is one of the best ways to foster understanding and form lasting memories (Gadzella, 1995). The more elaborated that processing, the richer the understanding and the better the resulting memory.

Self-reference, a particularly powerful form of elaboration, makes new information more meaningful by relating it to what is already known (Klein and Kihlstrom, 1986). New in this edition are the *Discovering Psychology* boxes. These "try-it" demonstrations allow students to observe interesting facets of their own behavior or do self-assessment exercises, thus linking new chapter information to the student's concrete experience.

To help students further elaborate their new understanding, each *Knowledge Builder* includes a series of Reflect questions. These questions also encourage students to associate new concepts with personal experiences and prior knowledge.

A course in psychology also naturally contributes to deeper forms of reflection, such as the development of critical-thinking abilities. To further facilitate reflection, each *Knowledge Builder* also includes one or more Critical Thinking questions. These stimulating questions challenge students to think critically and analytically about psychology. Each is followed by a brief answer with which students can compare their own thoughts. Many of these answers are based on research and are informative in their own right.

In addition, several boxed highlights encourage other forms of reflective thought. The *Critical Thinking* and *Focus on Research* boxes model a reflective approach to the theoretical and empirical foundations of critical thinking in psychology. In addition, *Human Diversity* boxes encourage reflection on the variability of the human experience, and *The Clinical File* boxes encourage reflection on the clinical applications of psychology.

Finally, *Bridges* appear throughout the text. Each *Bridge* links a topic under discussion to further discussion elsewhere in the book. This feature invites students to reflect on the rich interconnection of ideas that characterizes contemporary psychology.

Review As noted previously, all important terms appear in a Running Glossary throughout the book, which aids review. As also noted, a *Psychology in Action* section shows students how psychological concepts relate to practical problems, including problems in their own lives. The information found in *Psychology in Action* helps reinforce learning by illustrating psychology's practicality.

Next, a point-by-point summary provides a concise synopsis of all major concepts. The Chapter in Review summary is organized around the same Key Questions found at the beginning of the chapter. This brings the SQ4R process full circle and provides closure with respect to the learning objectives of each chapter.

Critical Thinking

The active, questioning nature of the SQ4R method is, in itself, an inducement to think critically. Many of the Guide Questions that introduce topics in the text act as models of critical thinking. So do the *Critical Thinking, Focus on Research, Human Diversity, Discovering Psychology,* and *The Clinical File* boxes. Furthermore, Chapter 1 contains a discussion of critical-thinking skills and a rational appraisal of pseudo-psychologies. In addition, the research methods portion of Chapter 1 is basically a short course on how to think clearly about behavior. It is augmented by tips about how to critically evaluate claims in the popular media. Chapter

10 (Cognition, Language, and Creativity) includes many topics that focus on thinking skills. Taken together, these features will help students gain thinking skills of lasting value.

Introduction to Psychology: Gateways to Mind and Behavior —What's New?

Thanks to psychology's vitality, this text is improved in many ways. The eleventh edition of *Introduction to Psychology: Gateways to Mind and Behavior* features some of the most recent and interesting information in psychology. The following annotations highlight some of the new topics and features that appear in this edition.

Introduction: The Psychology of Studying

The SQ4R framework has been updated to place more emphasis on critical thinking. Throughout this book, the term *relate* has been replaced by the term *reflect* to show that relating new information to personal experience and thinking critically about new information are both forms of reflective cognition. In addition, the Introduction shows students how to read effectively, study more efficiently, take good notes, prepare for tests, take tests, create study schedules, and avoid procrastination.

Chapter 1: Introduction to Psychology and Research Methods

- A new *Discovering Psychology* box, "Is a Career in Psychology Right for You?" presents students with a questionnaire to evaluate their interest in a career in psychology.
- A revised table gives a better view of the early development of psychology.
- A new *Focus on Research* box, "Investigating the Placebo Effect—Can Placebos Heal?" extends the usual discussion of placebos by exploring how placebo effects help people make sense of their experiences.
- A new *Critical Thinking* box, "Testing Common-Sense Beliefs," helps students draw a sharper distinction between common-sense beliefs and empirical research.
- *The Clinical File* box, "The Golden Psi," offers an updated discussion of media portrayals of psychologists.
- The treatment of gender bias in research has been expanded to reflect the several ways in which women have been underrepresented as subjects and researchers in psychology.

Chapter 2: Brain and Behavior

- A new *Discovering Psychology* box, "Dollars, Drag Racing, and the Nervous System," shows students a way to measure their own neural processing time, thus giving them some direct experience of their own nervous systems at work.
- A new *Focus on Research* box, "Neural Network Flies F-22 Jet Fighter," discusses hybrots, which are an innovative new way of studying neural networks.
- An updated *The Clinical File* box, "A Stroke of Bad Luck," introduces students to the study of brain injuries through the case of a neuroscientist who diagnosed his own stroke and wrote about it.
- A new *Critical Thinking* box, "If You Change Your Mind Do You Change Your Brain?" explores the relationship between the mind and the brain through the topic of neuroplasticity.
- The discussion of differences between men's and women's brains has been updated.

Chapter 3: Child Development

- A new *Discovering Psychology* box, "What's Your Attachment Style?" explores the relationship between infant attachment and adult attachment styles.
- The discussion of children's theory of mind has been updated.
- A new *Critical Thinking* box, "The Pampered Child," discusses the negative effects of excessively high self-esteem.
- A new *Human Diversity* box, "Children of Poverty," explores the impact of poverty on child development.
- Research updates enhance discussions of the Mozart effect, sensitive periods and language, temperament, infant facial preferences, the social smile, and parenting.

Chapter 4: From Birth to Death: Life-Span Development

- A new *Discovering Psychology* box, "What's Your Life Expectancy?" invites students to calculate their life expectancy.
- A new *Human Diversity* box, "The Twixters," explores the phenomenon of emerging adulthood and its cross-cultural variability.
- The discussion of divorce has been updated to better reflect the resilience many children exhibit when faced by the dissolution of their parents' marriage.
- The treatment of children's remarkable cognitive adaptations to child abuse has been expanded.
- The presentation of Kohlberg's theory of moral development has been restructured to make it easier to understand.

Chapter 5: Sensation and Reality

- The Ishihara test of color blindness is featured in a new hands-on *Discovering Psychology* box, "Are You Color-Blind?"
- *The Clinical File* box, "The Matrix: Do Phantoms Live Here?" has been updated with a discussion of the neuromatrix theory of phantom limb pain.
- The section on subliminal perception has been updated to include a discussion of the failure of attempts of advertisers and politicians to influence people with subliminal methods. The failure of subliminal self-help tapes is also discussed.
- Through the phenomenon of visual agnosia, a new *Focus on Research* box explores the dorsal and ventral visual pathways.

Chapter 6: Perceiving the World

- The *Focus on Research* box, "Designing for Human Use," has been updated to include a discussion of feeling present virtually in remote environments (telepresence) and the machines that provide touch feedback in telepresence systems (haptic interfaces).

- A new *The Clinical File* box, "Do They See What We See?" explores perceptual differences between members of individualist and collectivist cultures.
- The discussion of "sane hallucinations" has been updated to include the Charles Bonnet syndrome.

Chapter 7: States of Consciousness

- A new *Critical Thinking* box, "What Is It Like to Be a Bat?" discusses the difficulty of knowing other minds from a subjective rather than an objective point of view.
- A new *Discovering Psychology* box, "Swinging Suggestions," uses the Chevreul pendulum to give students insight into hypnosis and the basic suggestion effect.
- A new *Focus on Research* box, "Abducted by Space Aliens?" explains how purported alien abductions may be based on misinterpretations of hypnopompic (upon awakening) imagery.

Chapter 8: Conditioning and Learning

- A new *The Clinical File* box, "Coping with Chemo," explores the application of classical conditioning principles to help patients cope with conditioned nausea from chemotherapy.
- The discussion of how learning principles can be used to foster environmental recycling has been expanded.
- The discussion of violence in video games has been updated as "You Mean Video Games Might Be Bad for Me?" in the *Critical Thinking* box to counterpoint a new *Critical Thinking* box in Chapter 11, titled "You Mean Video Games Might Be Good for Me?"

Chapter 9: Memory

- A new *Human Diversity* box, "Cows, Memories, and Culture," briefly explores cultural differences in the types of information we store in memory.
- The treatment of both hypnosis and the cognitive interview as techniques for investigating people's memories of crimes has been updated and unified in a new *Focus on Research* box, "Telling Wrong from Right in Forensic Memory."
- An interesting new *Discovering Psychology* box, "Card Magic!" uses a popular "card trick" to show how distraction and encoding failure affect memory.
- The discussion of the recovered memory/false memory debate has been updated.
- A new *Focus on Research* box, "The Long-Term Potential of a Memory Pill," explores the phenomenon of long-term potentiation as a neurological underpinning to memory.

Chapter 10: Cognition, Language, and Creativity

- A new *Human Diversity* box, "How to Weigh an Elephant," explains how one's cultural heritage can aid or impair problem solving.
- A new *Critical Thinking* box, "Have You Ever Thin Sliced Your Teacher?" offers a discussion of the surprising accuracy of snap intuitive judgments.
- The *Human Diversity* box, "*Si o No, Oui ou Non,* Yes or No?" has been updated.

Chapter 11: Intelligence

- A new *Human Diversity* box, "Intelligence—How Would a Fool Do It?" stresses cross-cultural differences in the definition of intelligence.
- *The Clinical File* box on autistic savants now features Kim Peek, who served as the model for Dustin Hoffman's character in the movie *Rain Man.*
- The discussion of the relationship of intelligence to race has been updated to show that race may not even constitute a useful genetic categorization of human beings.
- The presentation of the effects of adoption on IQ has been updated.
- A new *Critical Thinking* box, "You Mean Video Games Might Be Good For Me?" explores why IQ scores have been on a rapid rise throughout the developed world.

Chapter 12: Motivation and Emotion

- An engaging new vignette opens this chapter to promote interest in the modules that follow. The chapter has also been streamlined for greater interest and readability.
- A new *Discovering Psychology* box, "What's Your BMI? (We've Got Your Number.)" shows students how to find out if their current body weight is healthy or potentially risky.
- The discussion of hunger now discusses how large food portions (especially fast-food portions) contribute to overeating and the obesity epidemic.
- New art helps students better understand connections between emotional reactions and activity in the autonomic system.
- A new *Human Diversity* box, "Xtreme!" explores individual differences in degree of sensation-seeking.
- A new *Critical Thinking* box, "To Catch a Terrorist," explores new methods of lie detection (infrared face scans, fMRI).
- A revised discussion of emotional intelligence discusses the value of positive emotions, authentic happiness, and the skills that comprise emotional maturity.

Chapter 13: Gender and Sexuality

- *The Clinical File* box, "Bruce or Brenda—Can Sex Be Assigned?" has been updated and now refers to the case of David Reimer, who was reassigned to be a girl but later challenged the reassignment.
- A new *Discovering Psychology* box, "Man's Work," summarizes a recent study showing that self-assertive, achievement-oriented behaviors are frowned upon in women.
- Information about HIV and AIDS reflects the latest findings.
- Additional updates address male-female intellectual differences, sex role socialization, the hormonal basis of sex drive, aphrodisiacs, sexual orientation, and patterns of sexual behavior in the United States.

Chapter 14: Personality

- A new *Discovering Psychology* box, "What's Your Musical Personality?" describes an interesting study that relates personality traits to musical tastes.

- A brief new section presents research on the human strengths identified by Martin Seligman and other positive psychologists.
- This chapter also benefits from brief research updates on self-esteem, the consistency of traits, trait-situation interactions, the Big Five, and shyness.

Chapter 15: Health, Stress, and Coping

- Suggestions for coping with conflict and frustration have been moved into the chapter. This places the suggestions in context and it shortens the *Psychology in Action* feature.
- The discussion of health psychology and behavioral risk factors has been updated and streamlined.
- A revised discussion presents the latest research on health-promoting behaviors.
- Two brief, new positive psychology sections discuss interesting links among hardiness, optimism, happiness, social support, stress reduction, and health.
- A new *Discovering Psychology* box, "Feeling Stressed? You've Got a Friend," describes research showing that thinking about a friend, or even a pet, can reduce stress when people are in difficult situations.
- *The Clinical File* box, "Coping with Traumatic Stress," has been updated.
- A new *Critical Thinking* box, "It's All in Your Mind," contrasts the medical model of disease with the biopsychosocial model of health.
- This chapter also includes detailed updates on behavioral risk factors, the disease-prone personality, refusal skills training, unpredictability and stress, job burnout, the nature of threat, coping with threat, hostility and the Type A personality, psychoneuroimmunology, and stress management.

Chapter 16: Psychological Disorders

- The section of this chapter that discusses anxiety disorders is more concise, and it includes updated information about stress disorders.
- A new *Discovering Psychology* box, "Crazy for a Day," helps students appreciate how powerfully social norms constrain our actions and how they contribute to judgments of normality.
- The *Human Diversity* box, "Running Amok with Cultural Maladies," now includes an updated discussion of culture-bound syndromes and the introduction of *dhat,* a unique culture-specific syndrome.
- A revised table clarifies differences between various personality disorders.
- A new table presents the anxiety disorders in a way that will help students recognize and remember them.
- *The Critical Thinking* box titled "The Politics of Madness" has been updated and now refers to anarchia, an old diagnostic category referring to a form of insanity that leads one to seek a more democratic society.
- An updated discussion of biochemical explanations of schizophrenia now includes the influence of glutamate levels on dopamine systems.
- The discussion of mental illness and violence has been updated.

Chapter 17: Therapies

- A new *Discovering Psychology* box, "Feeling a Little Tense? Relax!" teaches students the tension-release method of deep muscle relaxation. This exercise provides insight into desensitization and prepares students for a later discussion of self-directed desensitization.
- A new *Critical Thinking* box, "How Do We Know Therapy Actually Works?" addresses the issues involved in assessing the effectiveness of a therapy.
- A new *Human Diversity* box, "Therapy and Culture—A Bad Case of 'Ifufunyane,'" explores the idea relationship between culture and therapy.

Chapter 18: Social Behavior

- The *Critical Thinking* box, "Groupthink—Agreement at Any Cost," has been updated.
- A new *Discovering Psychology* box, "Quack Like a Duck," recasts a classic classroom exercise as an in-text demonstration of obedience.

Chapter 19: Attitudes, Culture, and Human Relations

- A new *Discovering Psychology* box, "I'm Not Prejudiced, Right?" invites students to assess their prejudices with an implicit association test.
- The treatment of stereotype threat has been updated.
- More information is presented about symbolic prejudice and the unconscious origins of discrimination.
- We have updated the section on the causes of human aggression, including the effects of media violence.
- The *Critical Thinking* box, "Terrorists, Enemies, and Infidels," about stereotyping of other cultural groups in times of war has been updated.
- Research on pornography and violence against women has been updated.
- *The Clinical File* box on school violence has been updated.
- A brief new section, "Positive Psychology: Everyday Heroes," discusses various ways in which "we do well by doing good."

Chapter 20: Applied Psychology

- A new *Discovering Psychology* box, "Planet in Peril?" is designed to alert students to a variety of threats to the environment and apprise them of an emerging ecological worldview.
- A new *Human Diversity* box, "Peanut Butter for the Mind," introduces students to universal instructional design, which stresses the need to create educational materials that are effective for a wide range of learners.

A Complete Course—Teaching and Learning Supplements

A rich array of supplements accompanies *Introduction to Psychology: Gateways to Mind and Behavior,* including several that make use of the latest technologies. These supplements are designed to make teaching and learning more effective. Many are available free to professors or students. Others can be packaged with this text at a discount. For more information on any of the listed resources, please call the Thomson Learning™ Academic Resource Center at 1-800-423-0563.

Student Support Materials

Introductory students must learn a multitude of abstract concepts, which can make a first course in psychology difficult. The materials listed here will greatly improve students' chances for success.

Gateways to Psychology: Concept Maps and Concept Reviews Concept maps created by A.D. VanDeventer of Thomas Nelson Community College and quiz items updated by Melissa Acevedo, Valencia Community College. For each chapter of the text, this booklet includes the Gateway concepts, a concept map, and a 30-item multiple-choice practice exam (ISBN: 0-495-09741-1).

Study Guide with Language Development Guide The *Study Guide,* written by Thuy Karafa of Ferris State University and Dennis Coon, is an invaluable student resource. It contains a variety of study tools, including Chapter Overviews, Recite and Review (fill-in-the-blank), Connections (matching), Check Your Memory (true/false), Final Survey and Review (fill-in-the-blank), and Mastery Test. A language development section, updated by Thuy Karafa, clarifies idioms, special phrases, cultural and historical allusions, and difficult vocabulary (ISBN: 0-495-09734-9).

Further Readings to Accompany Introduction to Psychology: Gateways to Mind and Behavior Each selection in this booklet explores a given topic, such as "How do concerns about self-presentation affect behavior?" and then comes to a set of practical conclusions about the issue. Issues range from the effect of culture on counseling and psychotherapy, the role of touching in personal relationships, how biology influences learning, and more (ISBN: 0-495-01691-8).

Careers in Psychology: Opportunities in a Changing World, 2e This informative booklet, written by Tara L. Kuther, is a Wadsworth exclusive. The pamphlet describes the field of psychology as well as how to prepare for a career in psychology. Career options and resources are also discussed. *Careers in Psychology* can be packaged with this text at no additional cost to students (ISBN 0-495-09078-6).

Multimedia CD-ROMs

Interactive CD-ROMs make it possible for students to directly experience some of the phenomena they are studying. The following CDs from Wadsworth provide a wealth of engaging modules and exercises.

PsychNow!™ Interactive Experiences in Psychology 2.0 This exciting CD-ROM was created by Joel Morgovsky, Lonnie Yandell, Elizabeth Lynch, and project consultant Dennis Coon. At the end of each chapter of this text, students will find a list of *PsychNow!* modules they can access for additional, "hands-on" learning. *PsychNow!* provides stunning graphics and animations, interesting video clips, interactive exercises, and web links, bringing psychology to life. With *PsychNow!,* students can do more than just read about a topic—they can read, watch, listen, react, and reflect on the meaning of their own responses. *PsychNow!,* which is available for Macintosh and Windows, contains 39 fully interactive modules that will enhance their understanding, 8 "Interact Now" Collaborative Labs, and "Quiz Game Now" quizzes. Students can also conduct 15 different "Interactive Research Experiments" in areas such as neurocognition, perception, memory, concepts, and imagery. *PsychNow! 2.0* can be packaged with this text for a discount; contact your sales representative for details (ISBN: 0-534-59046-2).

Sniffy™ the Virtual Rat, Lite Version 2.0 There's no better way to master the basic principles of learning than working with a real laboratory rat. However, this is usually impractical in introductory psychology courses. *Sniffy the Virtual Rat* offers a fun, interactive alternative to working with lab animals. This innovative and entertaining software teaches students about operant and classical conditioning by allowing them to condition a virtual rat. Users begin by training Sniffy to press a bar to obtain food. Then they progress to studying the effects of reinforcement schedules and simple classical conditioning. In addition, special "Mind Windows" enable students to visualize how Sniffy's experiences in the Skinner Box produce learning. The Sniffy CD-ROM includes a Lab Manual that shows students how to set up various operant and classical conditioning experiments. *Sniffy™ the Virtual Rat, Lite Version 2.0* may be packaged with this text for a discount (ISBN: 0-534-63357-9).

Online Resources

The Internet is providing new ways to exchange information and enhance education. In psychology, Wadsworth is at the forefront in making use of this exciting technology.

Book Companion Website As users of this text, you and your students will have access to the Book Companion Website for *Introduction to Psychology* at www.thomsonedu.com/psychology/coon. Access is free and no pin is required. This outstanding site features chapter-by-chapter online tutorial quizzes, a final exam, chapter-by-chapter web links, flash cards, and more!

ThomsonNOW™ Available free to students, this web-based study aid, by Britton Mace, Southern Utah University, helps your students discover the areas of text where they need to focus their efforts through a series of diagnostic pretests and posttests, personalized study plans—which include rich media such as videos, animations, and learning modules—that parallel the modules in the book, eBook files, and other integrated media elements. Included with *ThomsonNOW™* is *vMentor™*, which gives students access to free one-on-one, online tutoring help from a subject-area expert with a copy of the text. Students can use *ThomsonNOW™ for Coon's Introduction to Psychology,* eleventh edition, without any instructor setup or involvement, but an Instructor Gradebook is also available for you to monitor student progress (ISBN: 0-495-09748-9).

InfoTrac® College Edition *InfoTrac College Edition* is a powerful online learning resource, consisting of thousands of full-text articles from hundreds of journals and periodicals. Students using *Introduction to Psychology: Gateways to Mind and Behavior* receive 4 months of free access to *InfoTrac College Edition.* This fully searchable database offers over 20 years' worth of full-text articles from thousands of scholarly and popular sources—updated daily and available 24 hours a day from any computer with Internet access. By doing a simple keyword search, students can quickly generate a list of relevant articles from thousands of possibilities. Then they can select full-text articles to read, explore, and print for reference or further study. *InfoTrac College Edition*'s collection of articles can be useful for doing reading and writing assignments that reach beyond the pages of this text. Students also have access to *InfoWrite,* which provides extensive resources for writing papers, including suggested topics, APA guidelines, and more. (For more information, go to www.thomsonedu.com/psychology/coon.)

WebTutor™ Advantage This online supplement helps students succeed by taking them into an environment rich with study and mastery tools, communication aids, and additional course content. For students, *WebTutor* offers real-time access to a full array of study tools, including videos, animations, flash cards (with audio), practice quizzes and tests, online tutorials, exercises, asynchronous discussion, a whiteboard, and an integrated e-mail system. Students will also have integrated access to *InfoTrac College Edition,* the online library, as well as to the *Newbury House Online Dictionary,* an interactive dictionary that gives users instant access to definitions (including audio pronunciations).

Professors can use *WebTutor Advantage* to offer virtual office hours, post syllabi, set up threaded discussions, track student progress on quizzes, and more. You can customize the content of *WebTutor* in any way you choose, including uploading images and other resources, adding web links, and creating course-specific practice materials (*WebTutor Advantage* on *WebCT,* ISBN: 0-495-09738-1; *Advantage* on *Blackboard,* ISBN: 0-495-09739-X).

Essential Teaching Resources

As every professor knows, teaching an introductory psychology course is a tremendous amount of work. The supplements listed here should not only make life easier for you, they should also make it possible for you to concentrate on the more creative and rewarding facets of teaching.

Instructor's Resource Manual The *Instructor's Manual,* by Wanda McCarthy, Clermont College, University of Cincinnati, contains resources designed to streamline and maximize the effectiveness of your course preparation. In a three-ring binder format for the first time, this IRM is a treasure trove—from the introduction section, which includes a Resource Integration Guide, to a full array of chapter resources. Each chapter includes learning objectives, discussion questions, lecture enhancements, role-playing scenarios, "one-minute motivators," broadening-our-cultural-horizons exercises, journal questions, suggestions for further reading, media suggestions, web links, and *InfoTrac College Edition* Virtual Reader exercises (ISBN: 0-495-09735-7).

Test Bank The *Test Bank* was prepared by Jeannette Murphey of Meridian Community College. It includes over 4,500 multiple-choice questions organized by chapter and by learning objectives. All items, which are classified as factual, conceptual, or applied, include correct answers and page references from the text. All questions new to this edition are identified by an asterisk (ISBN: 0-495-09736-5).

***ExamView™* Computerized Testing** This software helps you create, deliver, and customize tests and study guides (both in print and online). In just minutes, this easy-to-use system can generate the assessment and tutorial materials your students need. *ExamView* offers both a Quick Test Wizard and an Online Test Wizard that guide you step-by-step through the process of creating tests. *ExamView* shows the test you are creating on the screen exactly as it will print or display online. Using a database prepared by Sandra Madison, you can build tests of up to 250 questions using up to 12 question types. *ExamView*'s complete word-processing capabilities also allow you to enter an unlimited number of new questions or edit existing questions (ISBN: 0-495-09737-3).

WebTutor™ Advantage With *WebTutor™ Advantage's* text-specific, pre-formatted content and total flexibility, you can easily create and manage your own custom course website. WebTutor Advantage's course management tools give you the ability to provide virtual office hours, post syllabi, set up threaded discussions, track student progress, and access password-protected Instructor Resources for lectures and class preparation. This powerful resource also provides videos, animations, and robust communication tools, such as a course calendar, asynchronous discussion, real-time chat, a whiteboard, and an integrated e-mail system. And both versions now come with a daily news feed from NewsEdge, an authoritative source for late-breaking news (*WebTutor™ Advantage* for *Blackboard,* ISBN: 0-495-09739-X; *WebTutor™ Advantage* for *WebCT,* ISBN: 0-495-09738-1).

Multimedia Manager Instructor's Resource CD-ROM: A Microsoft® PowerPoint® Tool This one-stop lecture and class preparation tool was created by Andrew Getzfeld of New Jersey City University. It contains ready-to-use slides in Microsoft® PowerPoint® and allows you to assemble, edit, publish, and present custom lectures for your course. You can easily create a personalized, media-enhanced presentation by combining text-specific lecture outlines and art from this text along with your own materials. In addition, all videos from Wadsworth's Psychology Digital Video Library 3.0 can be easily integrated into PowerPoint® for more interactive presentations. The CD-ROM also contains a full Instructor's Manual and Test Bank in Microsoft Word (ISBN: 0-495-09744-6).

JoinIn™ on TurningPoint® JoinIn™ content for Response Systems allows you to transform your assessment tools with instant in-class quizzes and polls. Wadsworth's exclusive agreement to offer TurningPoint® software lets you pose book-specific questions and display students' answers seamlessly within the Microsoft PowerPoint slides of your own lecture, in conjunction with the "clicker" hardware of your choice (ISBN: 0-495-09746-2).

Transparency Acetates If you customarily use transparencies in class, a nice set is available to illustrate and enliven your lectures. Approximately 150 text-specific transparencies, selected by Dennis Coon, make it easy to display tables, graphs, charts, and drawings from this text (ISBN: 0-534-61466-3).

Videotapes and Films

Wadsworth offers a variety of videotapes and films to enhance classroom presentations. Many video segments in the Wadsworth collection pertain directly to major topics in this text, making them excellent lecture supplements.

Wadsworth Film and Video Library for Introductory Psychology Adopters can select from a variety of continually updated film and video options. The Wadsworth Film and Video Library includes selections from the *Discovering Psychology* series, the *Annenberg* series, and *Films for Humanities*. Contact your local sales representative or Wadsworth Marketing at 1-877-999-2350 for details.

Psychology Digital Video Library Version 3.0 CD-ROM This CD-ROM contains a diverse selection of more than 100 classic and contemporary clips, including "Little Albert," the "Action Potential of a Neuron," "Parts of the Brain," and many more! The digital library offers a convenient way to access an appropriate clip for every lecture. An accompanying *Digital Video Handbook* offers a detailed description, approximate running time, and references to related media clips. It also offers objective quizzing and critical-thinking questions for each clip, as well as instructions on how to embed clips into your PowerPoint presentations. Available exclusively to instructors who adopt Wadsworth psychology texts (ISBN: 0-534-57671-0).

Wadsworth Media Guide for Introductory Psychology This essential instructor resource, edited by Russell J. Watson, contains hundreds of video and feature film recommendations for all major topics in introductory psychology (ISBN: 0-534-17585-6).

Supplementary Books

No text can cover all of the topics that might be included in an introductory psychology course. If you would like to enrich your course, or make it more challenging, the Wadsworth titles listed here may be of interest.

Challenging Your Preconceptions: Thinking Critically About Psychology, Second Edition This paperbound book, written by Randolph Smith, helps students strengthen their critical-thinking skills. Psychological issues such as hypnosis and repressed memory, statistical seduction, the validity of pop psychology, and other topics arc used to illustrate the principles of critical thinking (ISBN: 0-534-26739-4).

Writing Papers in Psychology: A Student Guide The sixth edition of *Writing Papers in Psychology,* by Ralph L. Rosnow and Mimi Rosnow, is a valuable "how to" manual for writing term papers and research reports. This new edition has been updated to reflect the latest APA guidelines. The book covers each task with examples, hints, and two complete writing samples. Citation ethics, how to locate information, and new research technologies are also covered (ISBN: 0-534-52395-1).

Cross-Cultural Perspectives in Psychology How well do the concepts of psychology apply to various cultures? What can we learn about human behavior from cultures different from our own? These questions lie behind a collection of original articles written by William F. Price and Rich Crapo. The fourth edition of *Cross-Cultural Perspectives in Psychology* contains articles on North American ethnic groups as well as cultures from around the world (ISBN: 0-534-54653-6).

Summary

We sincerely hope that teachers and students will consider this book and its supporting materials a refreshing change from the ordinary. Creating it has been quite an adventure. In the pages that follow, we believe students will find an attractive blend of the theoretical and the practical, plus many of the most exciting ideas in psychology. Most of all, we hope that students using this book will discover that reading a college textbook can be entertaining and enjoyable.

Acknowledgments

Psychology is a cooperative effort requiring the talents and energies of a large community of scholars, teachers, researchers, and students. Like most endeavors in psychology, this book reflects the efforts of many people. We deeply appreciate the contributions of the following professors who have, over the years, supported this text's evolution:

Faren R. Akins
University of Arizona

Avis Donna Alexander
John Tyler Community College

Clark E. Alexander
Arapahoe Community College

Tricia Alexander
Long Beach City College

Dennis Anderson
Butler Community College

Lynn Anderson
Wayne State University

Nancy L. Ashton
R. Stockton College of New Jersey

Scott A. Bailey
Texas Lutheran University

Frank Barbehenn
Bucks County Community College

Michael Bardo
University of Kentucky

Larry W. Barron
Grand Canyon University

Linda M. Bastone
Purchase College, SUNY

Brian R. Bate
Cuyahoga Community College

Hugh E. Bateman
Jones Junior College

Evelyn Blanch-Payne
Oakwood College

Cheryl Bluestone
Queensborough Community College–CUNY

Galen V. Bodenhausen
Michigan State University

Aaron U. Bolin
Arkansas State University

Tom Bond
Thomas Nelson Community College

John Boswell
University of Missouri, St. Louis

Anne Bright
Jackson State Community College

Soheila T. Brouk
Gateway Technical College

Derek Cadman
El Camino Community College

James F. Calhoun
University of Georgia

Dennis Cogan
Texas Tech University

Lorry Cology
Owens College

William N. Colson
Norfolk State College

Chris Cozby
California State University, Fullerton

Corinne Crandell
Broome County Community College

Thomas L. Crandell
Broome County Community College

Charles Croll
Broome Community College

Daniel B. Cruse
University of Miami

Keith E. Davis
University of South Carolina–Columbia

Diane DeArmond
University of Missouri, Kansas City

Patrick T. DeBoll
St. John's University

Dawn Delaney
University of Wisconsin–Whitewater

Jack Demick
Suffolk University

Lorraine P. Dieudonne
Foothill College

H. Mitzi Doane
University of Minnesota–Duluth

Wendy Domjan
University of Texas at Austin

Roger A. Drake
Western State College of Colorado

John Dworetzky
Glendale Community College

Bill Dwyer
Memphis State University

Thomas Eckle
Modesto Community College

David Edwards
Iowa State University

Raymond Elish
Cuyahoga Community College

Diane Feibel
University of Cincinnati–Raymond Walters College

Paul W. Fenton
University of Wisconsin, Stout

Dave Filak
Joliet Junior College

Oney D. Fitzpatrick, Jr.
Lamar University

Linda E. Flickinger
Saint Clair County Community College

William F. Ford
Bucks County Community College

Marie Fox
Metropolitan State College of Denver

Chris Fraser
Gippsland Institute of Advanced Education

Christopher Frost
Southwest Texas State University

Eugenio J. Galindro
El Paso Community College

Irby J. Gaudet
University of Southwestern Louisiana

David Gersh
Houston Community College

David A. Gershaw
Arizona Western College

Andrew R. Getzfeld
New Jersey City University

Carolyn A. Gingrich
South Dakota State University

Perilou Goddard
Northern Kentucky University

Michael E. Gorman
Michigan Technological University

Peter Gram
Pensacola Junior College

David A. Gries
State University of New York, Farmingdale

R.J. Grisham
Indian River Community College

John Grivas
Monash University

Anne Groves
Montgomery College

Michael B. Guyer
John Carroll University

Janice Hartgrove-Freile
North Harris College

Raquel Henry
Kingwood College

Callina Henson
Oakland Community College–Auburn Hills

Anne Hester
Pennsylvania State University–Hazleton Campus

Gregory P. Hickman
The Pennsylvania State University–Fayette

Don Hockenbury
Tulsa Junior College

Sidney Hockman
Nassau Community College

Barbara Honhart
Lansing Community College

John C. Johanson
Winona State University

James A. Johnson
Sam Houston State University

Myles E. Johnson
Normandale Community College

Pat Jones
Brevard Community College

Richard Kandus
Menifee Valley Campus

Bruno M. Kappes
University of Alaska–Anchorage

Charles Karis
Northeastern University

John P. Keating
University of Washington

Patricia Kemerer
Ivy Tech Community College

Cindy Kennedy
Sinclair Community College

Shaila Khan
Tougaloo College

Richard R. Klene
University of Cincinnati

Ronald J. Kopcho
Mercer Community College

Mary Kulish
Thomas Nelson Community College

Billie Laney
Central Texas College

Phil Lau
DeAnza College

Robert Lawyer
Delgado Community College

Walter Leach
College of San Mateo

Christopher Legrow
Marshall University

Lindette I. Lent
Arizona Western College

Elizabeth Levin
Laurentian University

Julie Lewis
Georgian College

Elise B. Lindenmuth
York College of Pennsylvania

Linda Lockwood
Metropolitan State College of Denver

Philip Lom
West Connecticut State University

Cheryl S. Lynch
University of Louisiana–Lafayette

Salvador Macias, III
University of South Carolina, Sumter

Abe Marrero
Rogers State University

Al Mayer
Portland Community College

Michael Jason McCoy
Cape Fear Community College

Edward R. McCrary III
El Camino College

Yancy B. McDougal
University of South Carolina, Spartanburg

Mark McGee
Texas A&M University

Angela McGlynn
Mercer County Community College

Mark McKinley
Lorain County Community College

Chelley Merrill
Tidewater Community College

Beth Moore
Madisonville Community College

Feleccia R. Moore-Davis
Houston Community College System

Edward J. Morris
Owensboro Community College

Edward Mosley
Pasiac County Community College

James Murray
San Jacinto University

Gary Nallan
University of North Carolina–Ashville

Andrew Neher
Cabrillo College

Don Nelson
Indiana State University

Steve Nida
Franklin University

Peggy Norwood
Tidewater Community College

James P. B. O'Brien
Tidewater Community College

Frances O'Keefe
Tidewater Community College

Steve G. Ornelas
Central Arizona College

Laura Overstreet
Tarrant County College

Darlene Pacheco
Moorpark College

Lisa K. Paler
College of New Rochelle

Debra Parish
Tomball College

Cora F. Patterson
University of Southwestern Louisiana

Leon Peek
North Texas State University

John Pennachio
Adirondack Community College

Peter Phipps
Sullivan County Community College

Steven J. Pollock
Moorpark College

Jack Powell
University of Hartford

Ravi Prasad
Texas Tech University

Derrick L. Proctor
Andrews University

Douglas Pruitt
West Kentucky Community College

Robin Raygor
Anoka-Ramsey Community College

Richard Rees
Glendale Community College

Paul A. Rhoads
Williams College

Harvey Richman
Columbus State University

Marcia Rossi
Tuskegee University

Jeffrey Rudski
Mulhenberg College

James J, Ryan
University of Wisconsin, La Crosse

John D. Sanders
Butler County Community College

Nancy Sauerman
Kirkwood Community College

Michael Schuller
Fresno City College

Pamela E. Scott-Johnson
Spelman College

Carol F. Shoptaugh
Southwest Missouri State University

Harold I. Siegel
Rutgers University

Richard Siegel
University of Massachusetts, Lowell

Nancy Simpson
Trident Technical College

Madhu Singh
Tougaloo College

Glenda Smith
North Harris Community College

Steven M. Smith
Texas A&M University

Francine Smolucha
Moraine Valley Community College

Michael C. Sosulski
College of DuPage

Lynn M. Sprott
Jefferson Community College

Donald M. Stanley
North Harris County College

Julie E. Stokes
California State University–Fullerton

Catherine Grady Strathern
University of Cincinnati

Harvey Taub
Staten Island Community College

Christopher Taylor
University of Arizona

Carol Terry
University of Oklahoma

Laura Thompson
New Mexico State University

Richard Townsend
Miami-Dade Community College–Kendall Campus

Bruce Trotter
Santa Barbara City College

Susan Troy
Northeast Iowa Community College

Pat Tuntland
Pima College

Paul E. Turner
David Lipscomb University

A.D. VanDeventer
Thomas Nelson Community College

Mark Vernoy
Palomar College

Charles Verschoor
Miami-Dade Community College–Kendall Campus

Frank Vitro
Texas Women's University

John Vojtisek
Castleton State College

Francis Volking
Saint Leo University

David W. Ward
Arkansas Tech University

Paul J. Wellman
Texas A&M University

Sharon Whelan
University of Kentucky

Robert Wiley
Montgomery College

Thomas Wilke
University of Wisconsin, Parkside

Carl D. Williams
University of Miami

Don Windham
Roane State Community College

Kaye D. Young
North Iowa Area Community College

Michael Zeller
Mankato State University

Margaret C. Zimmerman
Virginia Wesleyan College

Otto Zinser
East Tennessee State College

Producing *Introduction to Psychology: Gateways to Mind and Behavior* and its supplements was a formidable task. We are especially indebted to each of the following individuals for supporting this book: Susan Badger, Sean Wakely, Eve Howard, Vicki Knight.

We are grateful to Marianne Taflinger for her wisdom, creativity, humor, and unflagging support. Marianne has unmistakably made this a better book.

We also wish to thank the individuals at Wadsworth who have so generously shared their knowledge and talents over the past year. These are the people who made it happen: Kristin Makarewycz, Vernon Boes, Jerilyn Emori, Jennifer Alexander, Lucy Faridany, Caroline Croley, and Darin Derstine.

It has been a pleasure to work with such a gifted group of professionals and many others at Wadsworth. We especially want to thank Kristin Makarewycz for her valuable editorial assistance.

introduction

The Psychology of Studying

Eric Audras/PhotoAlto/Jupiterimages

Even if you're an excellent student, you may be able to improve your study skills. Students who get good grades tend to work *smarter*, not just longer or harder (Hofer & Yu, 2003). To help you get a good start, let's look at several ways to improve studying.

The SQ4R Method—How to Tame a Textbook

How much do you typically remember after you've read a textbook chapter? If the answer is "Nada," "Zip minus 1," or simply "Not enough," it may be time to try the **SQ4R method.** SQ4R stands for *survey, question, read, recite, reflect,* and *review.* These six steps can help you learn as you read, remember more, and review effectively:

S = *Survey.* Skim through a chapter before you begin reading it. Start by looking at topic headings, figure captions, and summaries. Try to get an overall picture of what lies ahead. Because this book is organized into short sections, you can survey just one section at a time if you prefer.

Q = *Question.* As you read, turn each topic heading into one or more questions. For example, when you read the heading

SQ4R method An active study-reading technique based on these steps: survey, question, read, recite, reflect, and review.

"Stages of Sleep" you might ask, "Is there more than one stage of sleep?" "What are the stages of sleep?" "How do they differ?" Asking questions helps you read with a purpose.

R1 = *Read.* The first R in SQ4R stands for read. As you read, look for answers to the questions you asked. Read in short "bites," from one topic heading to the next, then stop. For difficult material you may want to read only a paragraph or two at a time.

R2 = *Recite.* After reading a small amount, you should pause and recite or rehearse. That is, try to mentally answer your questions. Better yet, summarize what you just read in brief notes. Making notes will show you what you know and don't know, so you can fill gaps in your knowledge (Peverly et al., 2003).

If you can't summarize the main ideas, skim over each section again. Until you can remember what you just read, there's little point to reading more. After you've studied a short "bite" of text, turn the next topic heading into questions. Then read to the following heading. Remember to look for answers as you read and to recite or take notes before moving on. Ask yourself repeatedly, "What are the main ideas here?"

Repeat the question–read–recite cycle until you've finished an entire chapter (or just from one Knowledge Builder to the next, if you want to read shorter units).

R3 = *Reflect.* As you read, try to relate new facts, terms, and concepts to information you already know well or to your own experiences. You've probably noticed that it is especially easy to remember ideas that are personally meaningful, so try to relate the ideas you read about to your own life. This may be the most important step in the SQ4R method. The more genuine interest you can bring to your reading, the more you will learn (Hartlep & Forsyth, 2000).

R4 = *Review.* When you're done reading, skim back over a section or the entire chapter, or read your notes. Then check your memory by reciting and quizzing yourself again. Try to make frequent, active review a standard part of your study habits. (See ● Figure I.1.)

Does this really work? Yes. Using a reading strategy improves learning and grades (Chastain & Thurber, 1989; Taraban, Rynearson, & Kerr, 2000). Simply reading straight through a chapter can give you "intellectual indigestion." That's why it's better to stop often to think, question, recite, reflect, review, and "digest" information as you read.

How to Use *Gateways to Mind and Behavior*

You can apply the SQ4R method to any text. However, this book is designed to help you actively learn psychology.

Survey

Each chapter opens with a chapter survey that includes a *Preview* as well as lists of *Key Questions* that will be covered. You can use these features to identify important ideas as you begin reading. The *Preview* should help you get interested in the topics you will be reading about. The *Key Questions* are a good guide to the kinds of information to look for as you read. After you've studied the *Key Questions,* take a few minutes to do your own survey of the chapter. As you do, try to build a "mental map" of upcoming topics.

Question

How can I use the SQ4R method to make reading more interesting and effective? One of the key steps is to ask yourself lots of questions while you read. Guide Questions like the one that began this paragraph will help you focus on seeking information as you read. However, be sure to ask your own questions, too. Try to actively interact with your textbooks as you read.

Read

As an aid to reading, important terms are printed in **boldface type** and defined where they first appear. (Some are followed by pronunciations—capital letters show which syllables are accented.) You'll also find a *running glossary* in the lower right-hand corner of pages you are reading, so you never have to guess about the meaning of technical terms. If you want to look up a term from a lecture or another chapter, check the main *Glossary.* This "mini-dictionary" is located near the end of the book. Perhaps you should take a moment to find it now. In addition, many figures and tables help you quickly grasp important concepts.

Recite and Reflect

Every few pages, a learning guide called a *Knowledge Builder* provides chances to think, rehearse, reflect, and test your memory. (Don't forget to also take notes or recite on your own.) If you want to study in smaller "bites," this book is divided into short sections that end with Knowledge Builders, which make good stopping points.

This book also encourages you to reflect more deeply about what you are reading. Boxed *Discovering Psychology* highlights in-

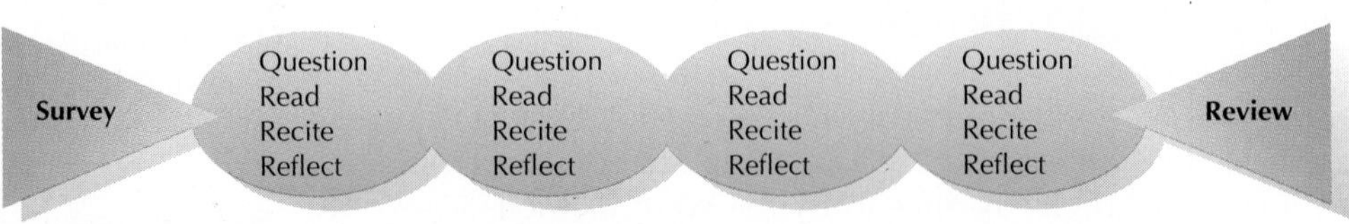

● **Figure I.1** The SQ4R method promotes active learning and information processing. You should begin with a survey of the chapter or a shorter section, depending on how much you plan to read. Then, you should proceed through cycles of questioning, reading, reciting, and reflecting, and conclude with a review of the section or the entire chapter.

vite you to relate psychology to your own life. The *Critical Thinking* and *Focus on Research* highlights invite you to reflect on the theoretical and empirical dimensions of psychology, both core components of critical thinking in psychology. In addition, *Human Diversity* encourages you to reflect on the rich variability of human experience and *The Clinical File* encourages you to reflect on clinical applications of psychology, a topic of intrinsic interest to many of you.

Review

Each chapter concludes with a point-by-point summary called *Chapter in Review* that will help you identify important ideas to remember. You can also use the running glossary in the margin for further review, as well as reviewing boldface terms, figures, and tables.

■ Table I.1 summarizes how this text helps you apply the SQ4R method. Even with all this help, there is still much more you can do on your own.

TABLE I.1

Using the SQ4R Method

Survey
- Preview
- Key Questions
- Topic Headings
- Figure Captions

Question
- Topic Headings
- Guide Questions
- In-Text Dialogue Questions

Read
- Topic Headings
- Boldface Terms
- Running Glossary (in margin)
- Figures and Tables

Recite
- Learning Check Questions (in Knowledge Builders)
- Practice Quizzes (online)
- Notes (make them while reading)

Reflect
- Reflect Questions (in Knowledge Builders)
- Critical Thinking Questions (in Knowledge Builders)
- Boxed Highlights (throughout the text)

Review
- Chapter in Review
- Running Glossary (in margin)
- Boldface Terms
- Figure and Tables
- Practice Quizzes (online)
- Study Guide

Effective Note-Taking—Good Students, Take Note!

Reading strategies may be good for studying, but what about taking notes in class? Sometimes it's hard to know what's important. Like effective reading, good notes come from actively seeking information. People who are **active listeners** avoid distractions and skillfully gather ideas. Here's a listening/note-taking plan that works for many students. The letters LISAN, pronounced like the word *listen,* will help you remember the steps.

L = *Lead. Don't follow.* Try to anticipate what your teacher will say by asking yourself questions. Questions can come from study guides, reading assignments, or your own curiosity.

I = *Ideas.* Every lecture is based on a core of ideas. Usually, an idea is followed by examples or explanations. Ask yourself often, "What is the main idea now? What ideas support it?"

S = *Signal words.* Listen for words that tell you what direction the instructor is taking. For instance, here are some signal words:

There are three reasons why . . .	Here come ideas
Most important is . . .	Main idea
On the contrary . . .	Opposite idea
As an example . . .	Support for main idea
Therefore . . .	Conclusion

A = *Actively listen.* Sit where you can get involved and ask questions. Bring questions you want answered from the last lecture or from your text. Raise your hand at the beginning of class or approach your professor before the lecture. Do anything that helps you stay active, alert, and engaged.

N = *Note taking.* Students who take accurate lecture notes tend to do well on tests (Williams & Eggert, 2002). However, don't try to be a tape recorder. Listen to everything, but be selective and write down only key points. If you are too busy writing, you may not grasp what your professor is saying. When you're taking notes, it might help to think of yourself as a reporter who is trying to get a good story (Ryan, 2001).

Actually, most students take reasonably good notes—and then don't use them! Many students wait until just before exams to review. By then, their notes have lost much of their meaning. If you don't want your notes to seem like hieroglyphics or "chicken scratches," it pays to review them every day (Luckie & Smethurst, 1998).

Using and Reviewing Your Notes

When you review, you will learn more if you take the extra steps listed here (Gadzella, 1995; Kiewra et al., 1991; King, 1992, 1995; Luckie & Smethurst, 1998).

Active listener A person who knows how to maintain attention, avoid distractions, and actively gather information from lectures.

- As soon as you can, improve your notes by filling in gaps, completing thoughts, and looking for connections among ideas.
- Remember to link new ideas to what you already know.
- Summarize your notes. Boil them down and organize them.
- After each class session, write down at least seven major ideas, definitions, or details that are likely to become test questions. Then, make up questions from your notes and be sure you can answer them.

Summary

The letters LISAN are a guide to active listening, but listening and good note taking are not enough. You must also review, organize, reflect, extend, and think about new ideas. Use active listening to get involved in your classes and you will undoubtedly learn more (Luckie & Smethurst, 1998).

Study Strategies—Making a Habit of Success

Grades depend nearly as much on effort as they do on "intelligence." However, don't forget that good students work more *efficiently,* not just harder. Many study practices are notoriously poor, such as recopying lecture notes, studying class notes but not the textbook (or the textbook but not class notes), outlining chapters, answering study questions with the book open, and "group study" (which often becomes a party). The best students emphasize *quality:* They study their books and notes in depth and attend classes regularly. It's a mistake to blame poor grades on events "beyond your control." Students who are motivated to succeed usually get better grades (Perry et al., 2001). Let's consider a few more things you can do to improve your study habits.

Study in a Specific Place

Ideally, you should study in a quiet, well-lighted area free of distractions. If possible, you should also have at least one place where you *only study.* Do nothing else at that spot: Keep magazines, MP3 players, friends, cell phones, pets, posters, video games, puzzles, food, lovers, sports cars, elephants, pianos, televisions, hang gliders, kazoos, and other distractions out of the area. In this way, the habit of studying will become strongly linked with one specific place. Then, rather than trying to force yourself to study, all you have to do is go to your study area. Once there, you'll find it is relatively easy to get started.

Use Spaced Study Sessions

It is reasonable to review intensely before an exam. However, you're taking a big risk if you are only "cramming" (learning new information at the last minute). Spaced practice is much more efficient (Naveh-Benjamin, 1990). **Spaced practice** consists of a large number of relatively short study sessions. Long, uninterrupted study sessions are called **massed practice.** (If you "massed up" your studying, you probably messed it up too.)

Cramming places a big burden on memory. Usually, you shouldn't try to learn anything new about a subject during the last day before a test. It is far better to learn small amounts every day and review frequently (Luckie & Smethurst, 1998).

Try Mnemonics

Learning has to start somewhere, and memorizing is often the first step. Many of the best ways to improve memory are covered in Chapter 9. Let's consider just one technique here.

A **mnemonic** (nee-MON-ik) is a memory aid. Most mnemonics link new information to ideas or images that are easy to remember. For example, what if you want to remember that the Spanish word for duck is *pato* (POT-oh)? To use a mnemonic, you could picture a duck in a pot or a duck wearing a pot for a hat. Likewise, to remember that the cerebellum controls coordination, you might picture someone named "Sarah Bellum" who is very coordinated. For best results, make your mnemonic images exaggerated or bizarre, vivid, and interactive (Campos & Perez, 1997). There are many ways to create mnemonics. If you would like to learn more about memory strategies, see Chapter 9.

Test Yourself

A great way to improve grades is to take several practice tests before the real one in class. In other words, studying should include **self-testing,** in which you pose questions to yourself. You can use flash cards, Learning Check questions, online quizzes, a study guide, or other means. As you study, ask many questions and be sure you can answer them. Studying without self-testing is like practicing for a basketball game without shooting any baskets.

For more convenient self-testing, your professor may make a *Study Guide* or a separate booklet of *Practice Quizzes* available. You can use either to review for tests. Practice quizzes are also available on the Internet, as described later. However, don't use practice quizzes as a substitute for studying your textbook and lecture notes. Trying to learn from quizzes alone will probably *lower* your grades. It is best to use quizzes to find out what topics you need to study more (Brothen & Wambach, 2001).

Overlearn

Many students *underprepare* for exams, and most *overestimate* how well they will do. A solution to both problems is **overlearning,** in which you continue studying beyond your initial mastery of a topic. In other words, plan to do extra study and review *after* you think you are prepared for a test.

Here's another reason for overlearning: Students who expect to take an essay test (usually the hardest kind) do better on essay, multiple-choice, and short-answer tests (Foos & Clark, 1983). Before tests, students ask, "Will it be essay or multiple choice?" But as you can see, *it is best to approach all tests as if they will be essays.* That way, you will learn more completely, so you really "know your stuff."

Mnemonics make new information more familiar and memorable. Forming an image of a duck wearing a pot for a hat might help you remember that *pato* is the Spanish word for duck.

Self-Regulated Learning—Academic All-Stars

Think of a topic you are highly interested in, such as music, sports, fashion, cars, cooking, politics, or movies. Whatever the topic, you have probably learned a lot about it—painlessly. How could you make your college work more like voluntary learning? An approach called self-regulated learning might be a good start. **Self-regulated learning** is active, self-guided study (Zimmerman, 1996a). Here's how you can change passive studying into goal-oriented learning

1. *Set specific, objective learning goals.* Try to begin each learning session with specific goals in mind. What knowledge or skills are you trying to master? What do you hope to accomplish? (Schunk, 1990).
2. *Plan a learning strategy.* How will you accomplish your goals? Make daily, weekly, and monthly plans for learning. Then put them into action.
3. *Be your own teacher.* Effective learners silently give themselves guidance and ask themselves questions. For example, as you are learning, you might ask yourself, "What are the important ideas here? What do I remember? What don't I understand? What do I need to review? What should I do next?"
4. *Monitor your progress.* Self-regulated learning depends on self-monitoring. Exceptional learners keep records of their progress toward learning goals (pages read, hours of studying, assignments completed, and so forth). They quiz themselves, use study guides, and find other ways to check their understanding while learning.
5. *Reward yourself.* When you meet your daily, weekly, or monthly goals, reward your efforts in some way, such as going to a movie or buying a new CD. Be aware that self-praise also rewards learning. Being able to say, "Hey, I did it!" or "Good work!" and knowing that you deserve it can be very rewarding. In the long run, success, self-improvement, and personal satisfaction are the real payoffs for learning.
6. *Evaluate your progress and goals.* It is a good idea to frequently evaluate your performance records and goals. Are there specific areas of your work that need improvement? If you are not making good progress toward long-range goals, do you need to revise your short-term targets?
7. *Take corrective action.* If you fall short of your goals you may need to adjust how you budget your time. You may also need to change your learning environment to deal with distractions such as watching TV, daydreaming, talking to friends, or testing the structural integrity of the walls with your stereo system.

If you discover that you lack necessary knowledge or skills, ask for help, take advantage of tutoring programs, or look for information beyond your courses and textbooks. Knowing how to regulate and control learning can be a key to life-long enrichment and personal empowerment.

Procrastination—Avoiding the Last-Minute Blues

All of these study techniques are fine. But what can I do about procrastination? A tendency to procrastinate is almost universal. (When campus workshops on procrastination are offered, many students never get around to signing up!) Even when procrastination doesn't lead to failure, it can cause much suffering. Procrastinators work only under pressure, skip classes, give false reasons for late work, and feel ashamed of their last-minute efforts (Burka & Yuen, 1990). They also tend to feel stressed and are ill more often (Tice & Baumeister, 1997).

Why do so many students procrastinate? Many students equate grades with their personal worth. That is, they act as if grades tell whether they are good, smart people who will succeed in life. By procrastinating they can blame poor work on a late start, rather than a lack of ability (Beck, Koons, & Milgrim, 2000). After all, it wasn't their best effort, was it?

Perfectionism is a related problem. If you expect the impossible, it's hard to start an assignment. Students with high standards often end up with all-or-nothing work habits (Onwuegbuzie, 2000).

Time Management

Most procrastinators must eventually face the self-worth issue. Nevertheless, most can improve by learning study skills and better time management. We have already discussed general study skills, so let's consider time management in a little more detail.

Spaced practice Practice spread over many relatively short study sessions.

Massed practice Practice done in a long, uninterrupted study session.

Mnemonic A memory aid or strategy.

Self-testing Evaluating learning by posing questions to yourself.

Overlearning Continuing to study and learn after you think you've mastered a topic.

Self-regulated learning Active, self-guided learning.

A **weekly time schedule** is a written plan that allocates time for study, work, and leisure activities. To prepare your schedule, make a chart showing all of the hours in each day of the week. Then fill in times that are already committed: sleep, meals, classes, work, team practices, lessons, appointments, and so forth. Next, fill in times when you will study for various classes. Finally, label the remaining hours as open or free times.

Each day, you can use your schedule as a checklist. That way you'll know at a glance which tasks are done and which still need attention (Luckie & Smethurst, 1998).

You may also find it valuable to make a **term schedule** that lists the dates of all quizzes, tests, reports, papers, and other major assignments for each class.

The beauty of sticking to a schedule is that you know you are making an honest effort. It will also help you avoid feeling bored while you are working or guilty when you play.

Be sure to treat your study times as serious commitments, but respect your free times, too. And remember, students who study hard and practice time management *do* get better grades (Britton & Tesser, 1991; Leeming, 1997).

Goal Setting

As mentioned earlier, students who are active learners set **specific goals** for studying. Such goals should be clear-cut and measurable (Schunk, 1990). If you find it hard to stay motivated, try setting goals for the semester, the week, the day, and even for single study sessions. Also, be aware that more effort early in a course can greatly reduce the "pain" and stress you will experience later (Brown, 1991). If your professors don't give frequent assignments, set your own day-by-day goals. That way, you can turn big assignments into a series of smaller tasks that you can actually complete (Ariely & Wertenbroch, 2002). An example would be reading, studying, and reviewing 8 pages a day to complete a 40-page chapter in 5 days. For this book, reading from one Knowledge Builder to the next each day might be a good pace. Remember, many small steps can add up to an impressive journey.

Study Skills Checklist

Time Management
- Make formal schedule
- Set specific goals

Study Habits
- Study in specific area
- Pace study and review
- Create memory aids
- Test yourself
- Overlearn

Reading
- Use SQ4R method
- Study while reading
- Review frequently

Note Taking
- Listen actively
- Use LISAN method
- Review notes frequently

● **Figure I.2** Study skills checklist.

Make Learning an Adventure

A final point to remember is that you are most likely to procrastinate if you think a task will be unpleasant (Pychyl et al., 2000). Learning can be hard work. Nevertheless, many students find ways to make schoolwork interesting and enjoyable. Try to approach your schoolwork as if it were a game, a sport, an adventure, or simply a way to become a better person. The best educational experiences are challenging, yet fun (Ferrari & Scher, 2000).

Virtually every topic is interesting to someone, somewhere. I'm not particularly interested in the sex life of South American tree frogs. However, a biologist might be fascinated. (Another tree frog might be, too.) If you wait for teachers to "make" their courses interesting, you are missing the point. Interest is a matter of *your attitude*. (See ● Figure I.2 for a summary of study skills.)

Taking Tests—Are You "Test Wise"?

If I read and study effectively, is there anything else I can do to improve my grades? You must also be able to show what you know on tests. Here are some suggestions for improving your test-taking skills.

General Test-Taking Skills

You'll do better on all types of tests if you observe the following guidelines (Wood & Willoughby, 1995).

1. Read all directions and questions carefully. They may give you good advice or clues.
2. Quickly survey the test before you begin.
3. Answer easy questions before spending time on more difficult ones.
4. Be sure to answer all questions.
5. Use your time wisely.
6. Ask for clarification when necessary.

Several additional strategies can help you do better on objective tests.

Objective Tests

Objective tests (multiple-choice and true–false items) require you to recognize a correct answer among wrong ones or a true statement versus a false one. Here are some strategies for taking objective tests.

1. First, relate the question to what you know about the topic. Then, read the alternatives. Does one match the answer you expected to find? If none match, reexamine the choices and look for a *partial* match.
2. Read *all* the choices for each question before you make a decision. Here's why: If you immediately think that *a* is correct

and stop reading, you might miss seeing a better answer like "both *a* and *d*."

3. Read rapidly and skip items you are unsure about. You may find "free information" in later questions that will help you answer difficult items.
4. Eliminate certain alternatives. With a four-choice multiple-choice test, you have one chance in four of guessing right. If you can eliminate two alternatives, your guessing odds improve to 50-50.
5. Unless there is a penalty for guessing, be sure to answer any skipped items. Even if you are not sure of the answer, you may be right. If you leave a question blank, it is automatically wrong. When you are forced to guess, don't choose the longest answer or the letter you've used the least. Both strategies lower scores more than random guessing does.
6. There is a bit of folk wisdom that says, "Don't change your answers on a multiple-choice test. Your first choice is usually right." Careful study of this idea has shown it is *false*. If you change answers you are three times more likely to gain points than to lose them (Geiger, 1991). This is especially true if you feel *very* uncertain of your first answer. ("When in doubt, scratch it out!") When you have doubts, your second answer is more likely to be correct (Harvil & Davis, 1997).
7. Remember, you are searching for the one *best* answer to each question. Some answers may be partly true, yet flawed in some way. If you are uncertain, try rating each multiple-choice alternative on a 1-to-10 scale. The answer with the highest rating is the one you are looking for.
8. Few circumstances are *always* or *never* present. Answers that include superlatives such as *most, least, best, worst, largest,* or *smallest* are often false (Luckie & Smethurst, 1998).

Essay Tests

Essay questions are a weak spot for students who lack organization, don't support their ideas, or don't directly answer the question. When you take an essay exam try the following:

1. Read the question carefully. Be sure to note key words, such as *compare, contrast, discuss, evaluate, analyze,* and *describe*. These words all demand a certain emphasis in your answer.
2. Think about your answer for a few minutes and list the main points you want to make. Just write them as they come to mind. Then rearrange the ideas in a logical order and begin writing. Elaborate plans or outlines are not necessary (Torrance et al., 1991).
3. Don't beat around the bush or pad your answer. Be direct. Make a point and support it. Get your list of ideas into words.
4. Look over your essay for errors in spelling and grammar. Save this for last. Your *ideas* are of first importance. You can work on spelling and grammar separately if they affect your grades.

Short-Answer Tests

Tests that ask you to fill in a blank, define a term, or list specific items can be difficult. Usually, the questions themselves contain little information. If you don't know the answer, you won't get much help from the questions.

The best way to prepare for short-answer tests is to overlearn the details of the course. As you study, pay special attention to lists of related terms.

Again, it is best to start with the questions you're sure you know. Follow that by completing items you think you probably know. Questions you have no idea about can be left blank (Luckie & Smethurst, 1998).

Again, for your convenience, ● Figure I.2 provides a checklist summary of the main study skills we have covered.

Using Electronic Media—Netting New Knowledge

Did you know that "Google" is now officially an English verb, as in the question, "Did you google that?" meaning, "Did you look it up on the web using the Google search engine?" The Internet and electronic media have become incredibly popular ways to explore topics ranging from amnesia to zoophobia. Let's see how you can use these technologies to learn more about psychology.

Electronic Journeys

The **Internet** is a network of computers that communicate through the phone system and other electronic links. An important subpart of the Internet is the **World Wide Web**, or just plain "web," an interlinked system of information "sites" or "pages." A website is just a collection of information stored on a computer. Through the Internet, you can retrieve web pages from other computers and display them on your own screen. Thus, if you know the URL, the electronic "address" of a website, you can view the information it contains. Almost all web pages also have links to other websites. These **links** let you jump from one site to the next to find more information.

Google It

To find psychological information on the Internet you'll need a computer and an Internet connection. If you don't own a computer, you can usually use one on campus to access the Internet.

Weekly time schedule A written plan that allocates time for study, work, and leisure activities during a one-week period.

Term schedule A written plan that lists the dates of all major assignments for each of your classes for an entire semester or quarter.

Specific goal A goal with a clearly defined and measurable outcome.

Internet An electronic network that enables computers to communicate with one another, usually through the telephone system.

World Wide Web A system of information "sites" accessible through the Internet.

Links Connections built into Internet sites that let you "jump" from one site to the next.

Various software browsers make it easier to navigate around the Internet and receive information. A **browser** allows you to see text, images, sounds, and video clips stored on other computers. Browsers also keep lists of your favorite Internet addresses so that you can return to them.

The Psychology Resource Center

How would I find information about psychology on the Internet? Your first stop on the Internet should be the Psychology Resource Center. This site supports students who are using Wadsworth textbooks to learn psychology. Here's what you'll find there:

Online Quizzes. You can use these chapter-by-chapter multiple-choice quizzes to practice for tests and check your understanding.

Interactive Activities. The demonstrations and mini-experiments in this feature allow you to directly experience various psychological principles.

Internet Resources. This area is a "launching pad" that will take you to other psychology-related sites on the Internet. If a site sounds interesting, a click of the mouse will take you to it.

Online Flash Cards. These online flash cards allow you to practice terms and concepts interactively.

Hot Topics. This section features a news item or current event that is explored from a psychological perspective. After you've thought about a topic, you can share your opinions with others in an online discussion.

Discussion Forum. In the Discussion Forum you'll have a chance to share your ideas with psychology students from all over the country.

Research and Teaching Showcase. Here you'll find regularly updated summaries of presentations, articles, or other teaching and research materials.

Archives. Using the Archives, you can quickly search for current and past articles from Hot Topics and the Research and Teaching Showcase.

Meet the Author. Meet the author of your text in an interactive, multimedia presentation.

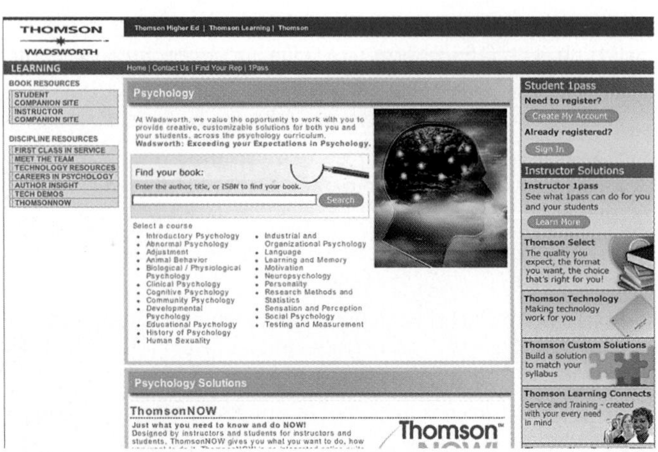

Wadsworth's Psychology Resource Center gives you online access to a variety of valuable learning aids and interesting materials.

The Wadsworth Psychology Study Center is located at www.thomsonedu.com/psychology. Be sure to visit this site for valuable information about how to improve your grades and enhance your appreciation of psychology. You can follow the "Find Companion Sites" link to locate quizzes and other materials related to this text.

Psych Sites

You'll find a list of interesting websites you may want to explore at the end of each chapter in this book. The best way to reach these sites is through the Psychology Resource Center. We have not included web addresses here because they often change or may become inactive. At the Psychology Resource Center you'll find up-to-date links for websites listed in this book. The sites we've listed are generally of high quality. However, be aware that information on the Internet is not always accurate. It is wise to approach all websites with a healthy dose of skepticism.

InfoTrac College Edition

InfoTrac College Edition is an online university library of articles from more than 700 publications. These articles cover a multitude of topics in psychology. You can read them online or print complete articles right from InfoTrac College Edition. InfoTrac College Edition is great for writing reports, doing research, or just reading more about psychology.

InfoTrac College Edition is located at www.thomsonedu.com. You will need a password to use this service. If InfoTrac College Edition was included with this textbook, you already have a password. Otherwise, you can buy a subscription to InfoTrac College Edition at the campus bookstore.

PsycINFO

Psychological knowledge can also be found in specialized online databases. One of the best is PsycINFO, offered by the American Psychological Association. **PsycINFO** provides summaries of the scientific and scholarly literature in psychology. Each record in PsycINFO consists of an abstract (short summary), plus notes about the author, title, source, and other details (● Figure I.3). All entries are indexed using key terms. Thus, you can search for various topics by entering words such as "drug abuse," "postpartum depression," or "creativity."

You can gain access to PsycINFO in several ways. Many colleges and universities subscribe to PsycINFO or to a related CD-ROM version called PsycLIT. If this is the case, you can usually search PsycINFO from a terminal in the college library or computercenter—for free. PsycINFO can also be accessed through the Internet, either directly or through APA's PsycDIRECT service. For more information on how to gain access to PsycINFO, check this website: www.apa.org/psycinfo.

The APA Website

The APA maintains an online library of general-interest articles on aging, anger, children and families, depression, divorce, emotional health, kids and the media, sexuality, stress, testing issues, women and men, and other topics. These articles are available to the pub-

TITLE Combat exposure and adult psychosocial adjustment among U.S. Army veterans serving in Vietnam, 1965-1971.

ABSTRACT (from the journal abstract) This study investigated the relationship between combat exposure and adult antisocial behavior in a sample of 2,490 male Army veterans of the Vietnam War who completed questionnaires about their psychological functioning. After adjustment for history of childhood behavior problems, posttraumatic stress disorder diagnosis, and demographic and military characteristics, it was found that veterans who experienced high and very high levels of combat were twice as likely to report adult antisocial behavior as veterans with no or low levels of combat and were also more likely to meet criteria for antisocial personality disorder. The results indicate that exposure to traumatic events during late adolescence or early adulthood is associated with multiple adult adjustment problems in vocational, interpersonal, and societal functioning. Treatment focusing on the effects of the trauma is likely to be necessary but not sufficient for improving affected veterans' behavior. (PsycINFO Database Record (c) 2002 APA, all rights reserved)

AUTHOR Barrett, Drue H.; Resnick, Heidi S.; Foy, David W.; Dansky, Bonnie S.; Flanders, W. Dana; Stroup, Nancy E.

AFFILIATION Barrett, D. H.: Ctrs for Disease Control & Prevention, National Ctr for Environmental Health, Atlanta, GA, US

SOURCE Journal of Abnormal Psychology. 1996 Nov Vol 105(4) 575-581

● **Figure I.3** This is a sample abstract from the PsycINFO database. If you search for the term "antisocial behavior" you will find this article and many more in PsychINFO. (This record is reprinted with permission of the American Psychological Association, publisher of the PsycINFO Database, all rights reserved. May not be reproduced without prior permission.)

lic for free. They are well worth consulting when you have questions about psychological issues. You'll find them at www.apa.org. For links to recent articles in newspapers and magazines, be sure to check the APA's PsycPORT page at www.psycport.com.

Please do take some of the "electronic journeys" described here. You might be surprised by the fascinating information that awaits you. Investigating psychology on your own is one of the best ways to enrich an already valuable course.

Multimedia CD-ROMs

Multimedia CD-ROMs are an exciting recent development in education. A single CD can store reams of text and thousands of pieces of art. All of the information contained in traditional print

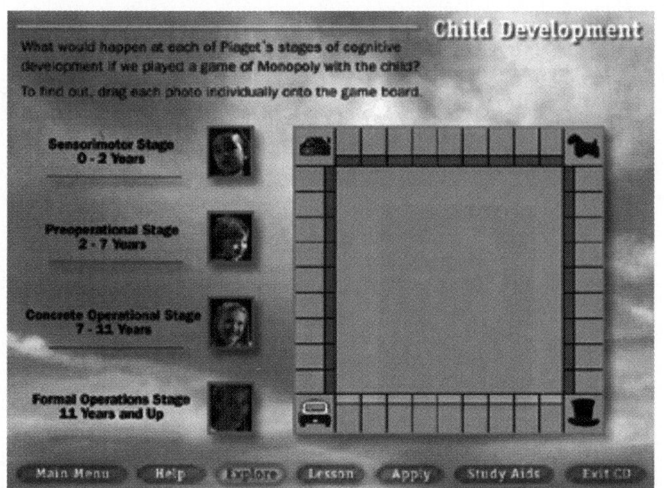

● **Figure I.4** A sample screen from *PsychNow! 2.0.*

textbooks can easily fit on a CD for display on a computer screen. In addition, CDs are capable of presenting animations, audio clips, film clips, and interactive exercises. A CD you may be interested in trying is *PsychNow!*, offered by Wadsworth to complement this textbook.

PsychNow!

Using this dynamic multimedia CD allows you to actively explore the world of psychology. Full audio and video presentations will help you discover interesting principles—often by observing your own behavior (● Figure I.4). *PsychNow!* includes many interactive demonstrations, experiments, games, and activities, all designed to expand your understanding. Rather than just reading about concepts, *PsychNow!* makes it possible to experience them directly. With the click of a mouse you can call up a large variety of helpful materials that make learning psychology more exciting than ever.

Using Multimedia CD-ROMs

PsychNow! and similar CD-ROMs can be used alone or in conjunction with a textbook. At the end of each chapter in this book you'll find a list of *PsychNow!* modules. Using these materials will allow you to see psychology come to life in ways that are not possible in a printed text. If you would like to be part of the electronic revolution in psychology, give *PsychNow!* a try.

A Final Word

There is a distinction in Zen between "live words" and "dead words." Live words come from personal experience; dead words are "about" a subject. This book can only be a collection of dead words unless you accept the challenge of making an intellectual journey. You will find many helpful, useful, and exciting ideas in the pages that follow. To make them yours, you must set out to *actively* learn as much as you can. The ideas presented here should get you off to a good start. Good luck!

For more information, consult any of the following books.

Burka, J. B., & Yuen, L. M. (1990). *Procrastination: Why You Do It; What to Do About It.* Cambridge, MA: Perseus Books.

Campanelli, J. F., & Price, J. L. (1991). *Write in Time: Essay Exam Strategies.* Ft. Worth, TX: Holt, Rinehart & Winston.

Hettich, P. I. (1998). *Learning Skills for College and Career.* Belmont, CA: Wadsworth.

Luckie, W., & Smethurst, W. (1998). *Study Power.* Cambridge, MA: Brookline.

Rosnow, R. L., & M. Rosnow. (2006). *Writing Papers in Psychology: A Student Guide.* Belmont, CA: Wadsworth.

Rowe, B. (1998). *College Survival Guide: Hints and References to Aid College Students.* Belmont, CA: Wadsworth.

Browser Software that facilitates access to text, images, sounds, video, and other information stored in formats used on the Internet.

PsycINFO A searchable, online database that provides brief summaries of the scientific and scholarly literature in psychology.

KNOWLEDGE BUILDER

Study Skills

REFLECT

Which study skills do you think would help you the most? Which techniques do you already use? Which do you think you should try? How else could you improve your performance as a student? To what extent do you already engage in self-regulated learning? What additional steps could you take to become a more active, goal-oriented learner?

LEARNING CHECK

1. The four R's in SQ4R stand for "read, recite, reflect, and review." T or F?
2. When using the LISAN method, students try to write down as much of a lecture as possible so that their notes are complete. T or F?
3. Spaced study sessions are usually superior to massed practice. T or F?
4. According to recent research, you should almost always stick with your first answer on multiple-choice tests. T or F?
5. To use the technique known as overlearning, you should continue to study after you feel you have begun to master a topic. T or F?
6. Setting learning goals and monitoring your progress are important parts of ______________ learning.
7. Procrastination is related to seeking perfection and equating self-worth with grades. T or F?
8. An Internet browser is typically used to search CD-ROM databases for articles on various topics. T or F?

CRITICAL THINKING

9. How are the SQ4R method and the LISAN method related?

Answers: 1. T 2. F 3. T 4. F 5. T 6. self-regulated 7. T 8. F 9. Both encourage people to actively seek information as a way of learning more effectively.

Web Resources

Internet addresses frequently change. To find the sites listed here, visit www.thomsonedu.com/psychology/coon for an updated list of Internet addresses and direct links to relevant sites.

***Psychology: Gateways to Mind and Behavior* Website** Online quizzes, flash cards, and other helpful study aids for this text. www.thomsonedu.com/psychology/coon

How to Succeed as a Student Advice on how to be a college student. Topics from studying to housing to preparation for work are included.

Library Research in Psychology Hints on how to do library research in psychology.

Psychology Glossary You can use this glossary to get additional definitions for common psychological terms.

Study Skills More information on SQ4R, taking tests, note taking, and time management.

ThomsonNOW™ Go to www.thomsonedu.com to link to ThomsonNOW, your online study tool. First take the **Pre-Test** for this chapter to get your **Personalized Study Plan,** which will identify topics you need to review and direct you to online resources. Then take the **Post-Test** to determine what concepts you have mastered and what you still need work on.

InfoTrac College Edition For recent articles on studying, use Subject Guide search for STUDY SKILLS. Go to www.thomsonedu.com/psychology/coon.

Interactive Learning

PsychNow! Version 2.0 Interact with the material with *PsychNow!*'s animations, video clips, experiments, and interactive assessments. For this chapter, go to *1a. Study Skills* for more information on how to improve your study skills.

chapter 1

Introduction to Psychology and Research Methods

Corbis Images/jupiterimages

THEME:

Psychology is science and a profession. Scientific observation is the most powerful way to answer questions about behavior.

Key Questions

What is psychology? What are its goals?

How did psychology emerge as a field of knowledge?

What are the major trends and specialties in psychology?

How do psychologists collect information?

How is an experiment performed?

What other research methods do psychologists use?

How does psychology differ from false explanations of behavior?

How dependable is psychological information in the popular media?

Preview

Why Study Psychology?

You are a universe, a collection of worlds within worlds. Your brain is possibly the most complicated device in existence. Through its action you are capable of art, music, science, war, philosophy, love, hatred, and charity. You are the most challenging riddle ever written, a mystery at times even to yourself. Your thoughts, emotions, and actions—your behavior and conscious experience—are the subject of this book.

Look around you: Newspapers, radio, magazines, television, and the Internet are brimming with psychological topics. Psychology is an ever-changing panorama of people and ideas. You really can't call yourself educated without knowing something about it. And, although we might envy those who have walked on the moon or explored the ocean's depths, the ultimate frontier still lies close to home. Psychology can help you better understand yourself and others. This book is a guided tour of human behavior. We hope you enjoy the adventure. What, really, could be more fascinating than a journey of self-discovery?

Psychology—Spotlight on Behavior

Psychology touches us in many ways. Psychology is about memory, stress, therapy, love, persuasion, hypnosis, perception, death, conformity, creativity, learning, personality, aging, intelligence, sexuality, emotion, happiness, and much more. Psychologists use scientific investigation to study, describe, understand, predict, and control human behavior.

Psychology is both a *science* and a *profession.* Some psychologists are scientists who do research to create new knowledge. Others are teachers who pass knowledge on to students. Still others apply psychology to solve problems in mental health, education, business, sports, law, and medicine (Halpern, 2003). Later we will return to the profession of psychology. For now, let's focus on how knowledge is created. Whether they work in a lab, a classroom, or a clinic, all psychologists rely on information from scientific research.

Jeff Greenberg/PhotoEdit

Psychologists are highly trained professionals. In addition to the psychological knowledge they possess, psychologists learn specialized skills in counseling and therapy, measurement and testing, research and experimentation, statistics, diagnosis, treatment, and many other areas.

What Is Psychology?

The word *psychology* comes from the roots *psyche,* which means "mind," and *logos,* meaning "knowledge or study." However, when did you last see or touch a "mind"? Because the mind can't be studied directly, **psychology** is now defined as the scientific study of behavior and mental processes.

What does behavior refer to in the definition of psychology? Anything you do—eating, sleeping, talking, or sneezing—is a behavior. So are dreaming, gambling, watching television, learning Spanish, basket weaving, and reading this book. Naturally, we are interested in *overt behaviors* (observable actions and responses). But psychologists also study *covert behaviors.* These are hidden, internal events, such as thinking and remembering (Leary, 2004).

Seeking Empirical Evidence

At various times in the last 100 years, experts have stated that "Heavier-than-air flying machines are impossible," "Radio has no future," "X-rays are a hoax," and "Computers will never serve any practical purpose." Obviously, all of these ideas proved to be wrong.

Self-appointed "authorities" are also often wrong about human behavior. Because of this, psychologists have a special respect for *empirical evidence* (information gained from direct observation). We study behavior directly and collect data (observed facts) so that we can draw valid conclusions (Martin, 2004). Would you say it's true, for instance, that "You can't teach an old dog new tricks"? Why argue about it? As psychologists, we would simply get ten "new" dogs, ten "used" dogs, and ten "old" dogs and then try to teach them all a new trick to find out!

CRITICAL THINKING

Testing Common-Sense Beliefs

It may seem that psychological research confirms what we already know from everyday experience. Why waste time and money confirming the obvious? Actually, common-sense beliefs are often wrong. See if you can tell which of the following common-sense beliefs are true and which are false (Landau & Bavaria, 2003).

- The basis of the baby's love for his mother is the fact that his mother fills his physiological need for food. True or False?
- Most humans use only 10 percent of their potential brain power. True or False?
- Blind people have unusually sensitive organs of touch. True or False?
- The more motivated you are, the better you will do at solving a complex problem. True or False?
- The weight of evidence suggests that the major factor in forgetting is the decay of memory traces with time. True or False?
- Psychotherapy has its greatest success in the treatment of psychotic patients who have lost touch with reality. True or False?
- Personality tests reveal one's basic motives, including those you may not be aware of. True or False?
- To change people's behavior toward members of ethnic minority groups, we must first change their attitudes. True or False?
- "The study of the mind" is the best brief definition of psychology today. True or False?
- Boys and girls exhibit no behavioral differences until environmental influences begin to produce such differences. True or False?

It turns out that research has shown that *all* of these common-sense beliefs are false. Yet in a survey, *all* of the beliefs were accepted as true by a large number of college students (Landau & Bavaria, 2003). How did you do?

We can all benefit from being more reflective in evaluating common-sense beliefs. When you find yourself wondering about the truth of a particular belief, apply your critical thinking skills by asking whether the belief makes logical sense. Can it be explained by any of the concepts in this book? Can you imagine what sort of research might yield empirical evidence to get you closer to the truth? Critical Thinking boxes like this one will appear throughout this book to help you be more reflective and think critically about human behavior.

Basically, the empirical approach says, "Let's take a look" (Stanovich, 2004). Have you ever wondered if drivers become more hostile when it's blazing hot outside? Douglas Kenrick and Steven MacFarlane (1986) decided to find out. They parked a car at a green light in a one-lane intersection in Phoenix, Arizona, in temperatures ranging from 88°F to 116°F. Then they recorded the number of times other frazzled drivers (in cars without air-conditioning) honked at the stalled car and how long they honked. The results are shown in ● Figure 1.1. Notice that when it was very hot, drivers spent more time leaning on the horn (which may be why cars have horns instead of cannons).

Isn't the outcome of this study fairly predictable? In this instance, you may have guessed how drivers would react. You might even see this research as doing little more than confirming common-sense beliefs. However, the results of many studies are surprising or unexpected. Take a moment and read "Testing Common-Sense Beliefs" for more information. Even in the case of this research, it's possible that drivers become lethargic in hot weather, not more aggressive. Thus, the study tells us something interesting about frustration, discomfort, and aggression.

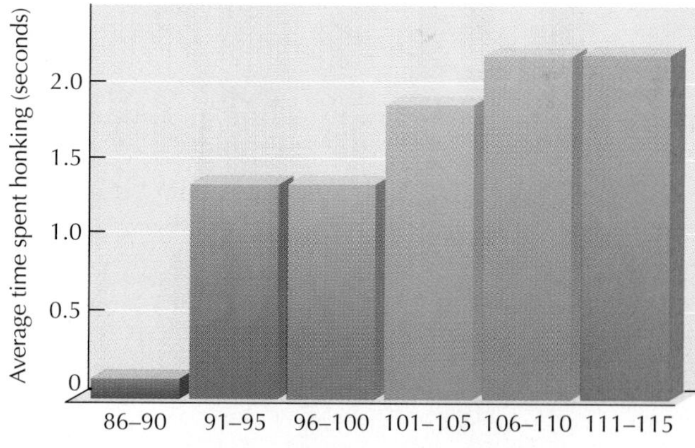

● **Figure 1.1** Results of an empirical study. The graph shows that horn honking by frustrated motorists becomes more likely as air temperature increases. This suggests that physical discomfort is associated with interpersonal hostility. Riots and assaults also increase during hot weather. Here we see a steady rise in aggression as temperatures go higher. However, research done by other psychologists has shown that hostile actions that require physical exertion, such as fist fights, may become *less* likely at very high temperatures. (Data from Kenrick & MacFarlane, 1986.)

Psychological Research

Many fields, such as history, law, art, and business, are interested in human behavior. How is psychology different? Psychology's great strength is that it uses **scientific observation** to answer questions

Psychology The scientific study of behavior and mental processes.

Scientific observation An empirical investigation that is structured so that it answers questions about the world.

about behavior (Stanovich, 2004). For instance, some parents believe that the music of Mozart increases babies' intelligence. Is this true? Many popular magazines and books say yes. Scientific testing says no.

Of course, some topics can't be studied because of ethical or practical concerns. More often, questions go unanswered for lack of a suitable **research method** (a systematic process for answering scientific questions). In the past, for example, we had to take the word of people who say they never dream. Then the EEG (electroencephalograph, or brain-wave machine) was invented. Certain EEG patterns, and the presence of eye movements, can reveal that a person is dreaming. People who "never dream," it turns out, dream frequently. If they are awakened during a dream they vividly remember it. Thus, the EEG helped make the study of dreaming more scientific.

Science and Critical Thinking

Because we all deal with human behavior every day, we tend to think that we already know what is true in psychology. For example, many people believe that punishment (a spanking) is a good way to reinforce learning in children. However, scientific studies have shown that spanking is a poor way to discipline young children. Such studies illustrate why critical thinking is important in psychology. **Critical thinking** is the ability to evaluate, compare, analyze, critique, and synthesize information. Critical thinkers analyze the evidence supporting their beliefs, they question assumptions, and they look for alternate conclusions. For example, with regard to spanking, a critical thinker would ask, "Does punishment work? If so, when? Under what conditions does it not work? What are its drawbacks? Are there better ways to guide learning?" (Halpern, 2000).

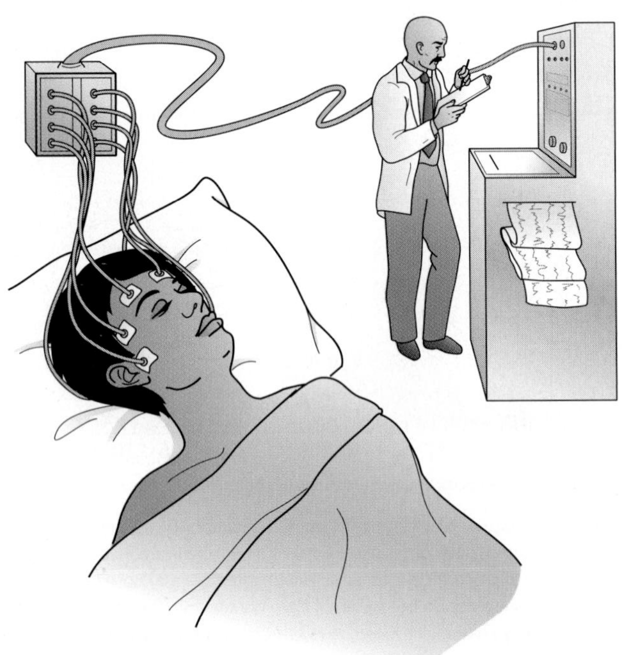

The scientific study of dreaming was made possible by use of the EEG, a device that records the tiny electrical signals generated by the brain as a person sleeps. The EEG converts these electrical signals into a written record of brain activity. Certain shifts in brain activity, coupled with the presence of rapid eye movements, are strongly related to dreaming. (See Chapter 7 for more information.)

Thinking About Behavior

The core of critical thinking is a willingness to actively *evaluate* ideas. True knowledge comes from constantly revising and improving our understanding of the world. As Susan Blackmore (2001) said when her studies caused her to abandon some long-held beliefs, "Admitting you are wrong is always hard—even though it's a skill that every psychologist has to learn."

Critical thinking is built on four basic principles (Gill, 1991; Shore, 1990):

1. *Few "truths" transcend the need for empirical testing.* It is true that religious beliefs and personal values may be held without supporting evidence, but most other ideas can be evaluated by applying the rules of logic and evidence.
2. *Judging the quality of evidence is crucial.* Imagine that you are a juror in a courtroom, judging claims made by two battling lawyers. To decide correctly, you can't just weigh the amount of evidence. You must also critically evaluate the *quality* of the evidence. Then you can give greater weight to the most credible facts.
3. *Authority or claimed expertise does not automatically make an idea true.* Just because a teacher, guru, celebrity, or authority is convinced or sincere doesn't mean you should automatically believe him or her. Always ask, "What evidence convinced her or him? How good is it? Is there a better explanation?"
4. *Critical thinking requires an open mind.* Be prepared to consider daring departures and go wherever the evidence leads. However, don't become so "open-minded" that you are simply gullible. Critical thinkers strike a balance between open-mindedness and healthy skepticism. They are ready to change their views when new evidence arises (Bartz, 2002).

Research Specialties

What kinds of topics do psychologists study? Here's a sample of what various psychologists might say about their work:

"In general, *developmental psychologists* study the course of human growth and development, from conception until death. I'm especially interested in how young children develop the ability to think, speak, perceive, and act."

"I'm also interested in how people get to be the way they are. Like other *learning theorists,* I study how and why learning occurs in humans and animals. Right now I'm investigating how patterns of reward affect learning."

"I'm a *personality theorist.* I study personality traits, motivation, and individual differences. I am especially interested in the personality profiles of highly creative college students."

"As a *sensation and perception psychologist,* I investigate how we discern the world through our senses. I am studying how we recognize familiar faces."

Mireille Vauier/Woodfin Camp/PictureQuest

Eric A. Wessman/Stock, Boston Inc./PictureQuest

Anne-Marie Weber/Getty Images

Greg Johnston/Lonely Planet Images

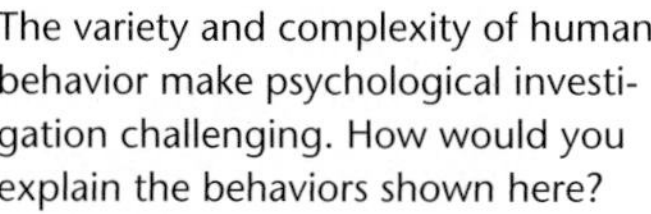

The variety and complexity of human behavior make psychological investigation challenging. How would you explain the behaviors shown here?

"*Comparative psychologists* study and compare the behavior of different species, especially animals. Personally, I'm fascinated by the communication abilities of porpoises."

"*Biopsychologists* are interested in how behavior relates to biological processes, especially activities in the nervous system. I've been doing some exciting research on how the brain controls hunger."

"*Cognitive psychologists* are primarily interested in thinking. I want to know how reasoning, problem solving, memory, and other mental processes relate to human behavior."

"*Gender psychologists* study differences between females and males. I want to understand how gender differences are influenced by biology, child rearing, education, and stereotypes."

"*Social psychologists* explore human social behavior, such as attitudes, persuasion, riots, conformity, leadership, racism, and friendship. My own interest is interpersonal attraction. I analyze how friendships develop."

"*Cultural psychologists* study the ways in which culture affects human behavior. The language you speak, the foods you eat, how your parents disciplined you, what laws you obey, who you regard as 'family,' whether you eat with a spoon or your fingers—these and countless other details of behavior are strongly influenced by culture."

"*Evolutionary psychologists* are interested in how our behavior is guided by patterns that evolved during the long history of humankind. I am studying some interesting trends in male and female mating choices that don't seem to be merely learned or based on culture."

This small sample should give you an idea of the diversity of psychological research. It also hints at some of the kinds of information we will explore in this book.

Animals and Psychology

Research involving animals was mentioned in some of the preceding examples. Why is that? You may be surprised to learn that psychologists are interested in the behavior of *any* living creature—from flatworms to humans. Indeed, some comparative psychologists

Research method A systematic approach to answering scientific questions.

Critical thinking An ability to evaluate, compare, analyze, critique, and synthesize information.

Some of the most interesting research with animals has focused on attempts to teach primates to communicate with sign language. Such research has led to better methods for teaching language to aphasic children (children with serious language impairment). (See Chapter 10 for more information.)

spend their entire careers studying rats, cats, dogs, turtles, or chimpanzees.

Sometimes psychologists use **animal models** to discover principles that apply to humans. For instance, animal studies have helped us understand stress, learning, obesity, aging, sleep, and many other topics. Psychology also benefits animals. For example, caring for endangered species in zoos relies on behavioral studies. Overall, about 8 percent of all psychological research is done with animals (McCarty, 1998).

Psychology's Goals

What do psychologists hope to achieve? In general, the goals of psychology as a science are to *describe, understand, predict,* and *control* behavior. Beyond that, psychology's ultimate goal is to benefit humanity (O'Neill, 2005). What do psychology's goals mean in practice? Imagine that we would like to answer questions such as these: What happens when the right side of the brain is injured? Is there more than one type of memory? How do hyperactive children interact with their parents?

Description

Answering psychological questions requires a careful description of behavior. **Description**, or naming and classifying, is typically based on making a detailed record of behavioral observations.

But a description doesn't explain anything, does it? Right. Useful knowledge begins with accurate description, but descriptions fail to answer the important "why" questions. *Why* do more women attempt suicide, and *why* do more men complete it? *Why* are people more aggressive when they are uncomfortable? *Why* are bystanders often unwilling to help in an emergency?

Understanding

We have met psychology's second goal when we can explain an event. That is, **understanding** usually means we can state the causes of a behavior. Take our last "why" question as an example: Research on "bystander apathy" reveals that people often fail to help when *other* possible helpers are nearby. Why? Because a "diffusion of responsibility" occurs. Basically, no one feels personally obligated to pitch in. As a result, the more potential helpers there are, the less likely it is that anyone will help (Darley & Latané, 1968). Now we can explain a perplexing problem.

Prediction

Psychology's third goal, **prediction**, is the ability to forecast behavior accurately. Notice that our explanation of bystander apathy makes a prediction about the chances of getting help. If you've ever been stranded on a busy freeway with car trouble, you'll recognize the accuracy of this prediction: Having many potential helpers nearby is no guarantee that anyone will stop to help.

Control

Description, explanation, and prediction seem reasonable, but is control a valid goal? Control may seem like a threat to personal freedom. However, to a psychologist, **control** simply refers to altering conditions that affect behavior. If we suggest changes in a classroom that help children learn better, we have exerted control. If a clinical psychologist helps a person overcome a terrible fear of heights, control is involved. Control is also involved in designing airplanes to keep pilots from making fatal errors. Clearly, psychological control must be used wisely and humanely.

In summary, psychology's goals are a natural outgrowth of our desire to understand behavior. Basically, they boil down to asking the following questions:

- What is the nature of this behavior? (description)
- Why does it occur? (understanding and explanation)
- Can we forecast when it will occur? (prediction)
- What conditions affect it? (control)

BRIDGES

Bystander apathy and conditions that influence whether people will help in an emergency are of great interest to social psychologists.

See Chapter 19, pages 653–654, for details.

KNOWLEDGE BUILDER

The Science of Psychology

REFLECT

At first, many students think that psychology is primarily about abnormal behavior and psychotherapy. Did you? How would you describe the field now?

LEARNING CHECK

To check your memory, see if you can answer these questions. If you miss any, skim over the preceding material before continuing to make sure you understand what you just read.

1. Psychology is the ________________ study of ____________ ____________ and ____________ processes.
2. The best psychological information is typically based on
   a. proven theories
   b. opinions of experts and authorities
   c. anthropomorphic measurements
   d. empirical evidence
3. In psychological research, animal ________________ may be used to discover principles that apply to human behavior.
4. Which of the following questions relates most directly to the goal of *understanding* behavior?
   a. Do the scores of men and women differ on tests of thinking abilities?
   b. Why does a blow to the head cause memory loss?
   c. Will productivity in a business office increase if room temperature is raised or lowered?
   d. What percentage of college students suffer from test anxiety?

Match the following research areas with the topics they cover.

_____ **5.** Developmental psychology
_____ **6.** Learning
_____ **7.** Personality
_____ **8.** Sensation and perception
_____ **9.** Biopsychology
_____ **10.** Social psychology
_____ **11.** Comparative psychology

A. Attitudes, groups, leadership
B. Conditioning, memory
C. The psychology of law
D. Brain and nervous system
E. Child psychology
F. Individual differences, motivation
G. Animal behavior
H. Processing sensory information

CRITICAL THINKING

12. All sciences are interested in controlling the phenomena they study. True or false?

Answers: 1. scientific, behavior, mental **2.** d **3.** models **4.** b **5.** E **6.** B **7.** F **8.** H **9.** D **10.** A **11.** G **12.** False. Astronomy and archaeology are examples of sciences that do not share psychology's fourth goal.

A Brief History of Psychology—Psychology's Family Album

Psychology began long ago as a part of philosophy, the study of knowledge, reality, and human nature. In contrast, psychology's brief history as a science dates back only about 120 years. Of course, to some students any history is "not short enough!" Nevertheless, to understand psychology now, we need to explore its past.

Into the Lab

The science of psychology began in 1879 at Leipzig, Germany. There, the "father of psychology," Wilhelm Wundt (VILL-helm Voont), set up a laboratory to study conscious experience. How, he wondered, do we form sensations, images, and feelings? To find out, Wundt observed and measured stimuli of various kinds (lights, sounds, weights). A **stimulus** is any physical energy that evokes a sensory response (stimulus: singular; stimuli [STIM-you-lie]: plural). Wundt then used **introspection**, or "looking inward," to probe his reactions to various stimuli. (If you stop reading right now and carefully examine your thoughts, feelings, and sensations, you will have done some introspecting.)

Archives of the History of American Psychology, University of Akron

Wilhelm Wundt, 1832–1920. Wundt is credited with making psychology an independent science, separate from philosophy. Wundt's original training was in medicine, but he became deeply interested in psychology. In his laboratory, Wundt investigated how sensations, images, and feelings combine to make up personal experience.

Wundt called his approach *experimental self-observation* because he used both trained introspection and objective measurement (Lieberman, 1979). There were many limitations to Wundt's methods. Nevertheless, he got psychology off to a good start by insisting on careful observation and measurement.

Structuralism

Wundt's ideas were carried to the United States by Edward B. Titchener (TICH-in-er). Titchener called Wundt's ideas **structuralism** because they dealt with the structure of mental life. Essentially, the structuralists hoped to analyze experience into basic "elements" or "building blocks."

How could they do that? You can't analyze experience like a chemical compound, can you? Perhaps not, but the structuralists tried, mostly by using introspection. For instance, an observer might heft an apple and decide that she had experienced the elements "hue" (color), "roundness," and "weight." Another question that might have interested a structuralist is, "What basic tastes mix together to create complex flavors as different as liver, lime, bacon, and burnt-almond fudge?"

Animal model In research, an animal whose behavior is used to derive principles that may apply to human behavior.

Description In scientific research, the process of naming and classifying.

Understanding In psychology, understanding is achieved when the causes of a behavior can be stated.

Prediction An ability to accurately forecast behavior.

Control Altering conditions that influence behavior.

Stimulus Any physical energy sensed by an organism.

Introspection To look within; to examine one's own thoughts, feelings, or sensations.

Structuralism The school of thought concerned with analyzing sensations and personal experience into basic elements.

Introspection proved to be a poor way to answer many questions. Why? Because the structuralists frequently *disagreed.* And when they did, there was no way to settle differences. If two people came up with different lists of basic taste sensations, for example, who could say which was right? Despite such limitations, "looking inward" is still used in studies of problem solving, hypnosis, meditation, moods, and many other topics (Mayer & Hanson, 1995).

Functionalism

William James, an American scholar, broadened psychology to include animal behavior, religious experience, abnormal behavior, and other interesting topics. James's brilliant first book, *Principles of Psychology* (1890), helped establish the field as a serious discipline (Benjafield, 2004).

The term **functionalism** comes from an interest in how the mind functions to help us survive and adapt. James regarded consciousness as an ever-changing *stream* or *flow* of images and sensations—not a set of lifeless building blocks, as the structuralists claimed.

The functionalists admired Charles Darwin, who deduced that creatures evolve in ways that favor survival. According to Darwin's principle of **natural selection**, physical features that help animals adapt to their environments are retained in evolution. Similarly, the functionalists wanted to find out how the mind, perception, habits, and emotions help us adapt and survive.

What effect did functionalism have on psychology? Functionalism brought the study of animals into psychology. It also promoted educational psychology (the study of learning, teaching, classroom dynamics, and related topics). Learning makes us more adaptable, so the functionalists tried to find ways to improve education. For similar reasons, functionalism gave rise to industrial psychology, the study of people at work.

Archives of the History of American Psychology, University of Akron

William James, 1842–1910. William James was the son of philosopher Henry James Sr. and the brother of novelist Henry James. During his long academic career, James taught anatomy, physiology, psychology, and philosophy at Harvard University. James believed strongly that ideas should be judged in terms of their practical consequences for human conduct.

BRIDGES

Educational psychology and industrial psychology are two major applied specialties.

See Chapter 20 for more information.

Behaviorism

Functionalism was soon challenged by **behaviorism,** the study of observable behavior. Behaviorist John B. Watson objected strongly to the study of the "mind" or "conscious experience." "Introspection," he said, "is unscientific." Watson realized that he could study the behavior of animals even though he couldn't ask them questions or know what they were thinking (Watson, 1913/1994). He simply observed the relationship between **stimuli** (events in the environment) and an animal's **responses** (any muscular action, glandular activity, or other identifiable behavior). Why not, he asked, apply the same objectivity to human behavior?

Watson soon adopted Russian physiologist Ivan Pavlov's (ee-VAHN PAV-lahv) concept of *conditioning* to explain most behavior. (A *conditioned response* is a learned reaction to a particular stimulus.) Watson enthusiastically proclaimed, "Give me a dozen healthy infants, well-formed, and my own special world to bring them up in and I'll guarantee to take any one at random and train him to become any type of specialist I might select—doctor, lawyer, artist, merchant-chief, and yes, beggarman and thief" (Watson, 1913/1994).

Would most psychologists agree with Watson's claim? Today, most would consider it an overstatement. Just the same, behaviorism helped make psychology a natural science, rather than a branch of philosophy (Richelle, 1995).

Radical Behaviorism

One of the best-known modern behaviorists, B. F. Skinner (1904–1990), said, "In order to understand human behavior we must take into account what the environment does to an organism before and after it responds. Behavior is shaped and maintained by its consequences" (Skinner, 1971). As a "radical behaviorist," Skinner also believed that mental events are not needed to explain behavior (Richelle, 1995).

According to Skinner, our behavior is controlled by rewards, or positive reinforcers. To study learning, Skinner created his famous

Archives of the History of American Psychology, University of Akron

John B. Watson, 1878–1958. Watson's intense interest in observable behavior began with his doctoral studies in biology and neurology. Watson became a psychology professor at Johns Hopkins University in 1908 and advanced his theory of behaviorism. He remained at Johns Hopkins until 1920, when he left for a career in the advertising industry!

conditioning chamber or "Skinner box." With it, he could present stimuli to animals and record specific responses (see Chapter 8, "Operant Conditioning"). Many of Skinner's ideas came from work with rats and pigeons. Nevertheless, he believed that the same laws of behavior apply to all organisms, including humans.

Skinner was convinced that a "designed culture" based on positive reinforcement could encourage desirable behavior. Too often, he believed, misguided rewards lead us into destructive actions that create problems such as overpopulation, pollution, and war.

Cognitive Behaviorism Strict behaviorists can be criticized for ignoring the role that thinking plays in our lives. One critic even charged that Skinnerian psychology had "lost consciousness." However, many criticisms have been answered by **cognitive behaviorism**, a view that combines cognition (thinking) and conditioning to explain behavior (Sperry, 1995). As an example, let's say you frequently visit a particular website because it offers free games. A behaviorist would say that you visit the site because you are rewarded by the pleasure of game playing each time you go there. A cognitive behaviorist would add that, in addition, you *expect* to find free games at the site. This is the cognitive part of your behavior.

Behaviorists deserve credit for much of what we know about learning, conditioning, and the proper use of reward and punishment. Behaviorism is also the source of behavior therapy, which uses learning principles to change problem behaviors such as overeating, unrealistic fears, or temper tantrums. (See Chapter 17 for more information.)

Neena Leen/*Life Magazine*/Timepix/Getty Images

B. F. Skinner, 1904–1990. Skinner studied simple behaviors under carefully controlled conditions. The "Skinner box" you see here has been widely used to study learning in simplified animal experiments. In addition to advancing psychology, Skinner hoped that his radical brand of behaviorism would improve human life.

Gestalt Psychology

Imagine that you just played "Happy Birthday" on a tuba. Next, you play it on a high-pitched violin. None of the tuba's sounds are duplicated by the violin. Yet we notice something interesting: The melody is still completely recognizable—as long as the *relationships* between the notes remains the same.

Now, what would happen if you played the notes of "Happy Birthday" in the correct order, but at a rate of one per hour? What would we have? Nothing! The separate notes would no longer be a melody. Perceptually, the melody is somehow more than the individual notes that define it.

It was observations like these that launched the Gestalt school of thought. The German word *Gestalt* means "form, pattern, or whole." **Gestalt psychologists** studied thinking, learning, and perception in whole units, not by analyzing experiences into parts. Their slogan was, "The whole is greater than the sum of its parts." (See ● Figure 1.2.)

Max Wertheimer (VERT-hi-mer), a German psychologist, was the first person to advance the Gestalt viewpoint. It is a mistake, he said, to analyze psychological events into pieces, or "elements," as the structuralists did. Like a melody, many experiences resist being broken into smaller units. For this reason, studies of perception and personality have been especially influenced by the Gestalt viewpoint. Gestalt psychology also inspired a type of psychotherapy. If you are curious about what Gestalt therapy is like, look ahead to Chapter 17.

The Role of Women in Psychology's Early Days

Were all the early psychologists men? Women were actively discouraged from seeking advanced degrees in the late 1800s. Nevertheless, women have contributed to psychology from the beginning

Functionalism School of psychology concerned with how behavior and mental abilities help people adapt to their environments.

Natural selection Darwin's theory that evolution favors those plants and animals best suited to their living conditions.

Behaviorism School of psychology that emphasizes the study of overt, observable behavior.

Response Any muscular action, glandular activity, or other identifiable aspect of behavior.

Cognitive behaviorism An approach that combines behavioral principles with cognition (perception, thinking, anticipation) to explain behavior.

Gestalt psychology A school of psychology emphasizing the study of thinking, learning, and perception in whole units, not by analysis into parts.

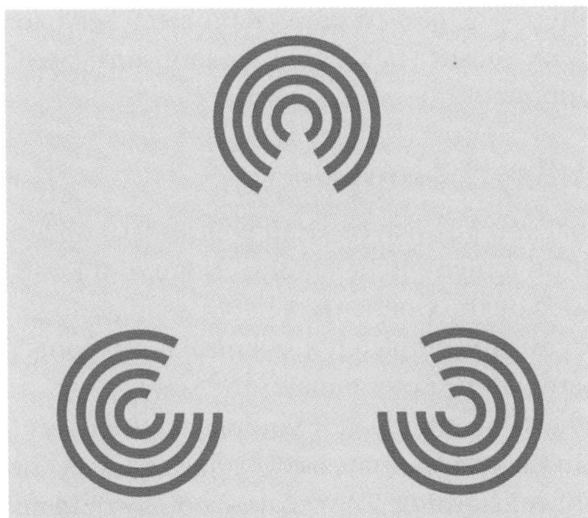

● **Figure 1.2** The design you see here is entirely made up of broken circles. However, as the Gestalt psychologists discovered, our perceptions have a powerful tendency to form meaningful patterns. Because of this tendency, you will probably see a triangle in this design, even though it is only an illusion. Your whole perceptual experience exceeds the sum of its parts.

Archives of the History of American Psychology, University of Akron

Max Wertheimer, 1880–1941. Wertheimer first proposed the Gestalt viewpoint to help explain perceptual illusions. He later promoted Gestalt psychology as a way to understand not only perception, problem solving, thinking, and social behavior, but also art, logic, philosophy, and politics.

(Minton, 2000). By 1906 in America, about 1 psychologist in every 10 was a woman. Who were these "foremothers" of psychology? Three who became well known are Mary Calkins, Christine Ladd-Franklin, and Margaret Washburn.

Mary Calkins did valuable research on memory. She was also the first woman president of the American Psychological Association, in 1905. Christine Ladd-Franklin studied color vision. In 1906 she was ranked among the 50 most important psychologists in America. In 1908 Margaret Washburn published an influential textbook on animal behavior, titled *The Animal Mind.*

The first woman to be awarded a Ph.D. in psychology was Margaret Washburn, in 1894. Over the next 15 years many more women followed her pioneering lead. Today, two out of three graduate students in psychology are women, and in recent years, nearly 75 percent of all college graduates with a major in psychology have been women. Clearly, psychology has become fully open to both men and women (Furumoto & Scarborough, 1986; Howard et al., 1986a; Madigan & O'Hara, 1992; Martin, 1995).

Psychoanalytic Psychology

As American psychology grew more scientific, an Austrian doctor named Sigmund Freud was developing his own theories. Freud believed that mental life is like an iceberg: only a small part is exposed to view. He called the area of the mind that lies outside of personal awareness the **unconscious.** According to Freud, our behavior is deeply influenced by unconscious thoughts, impulses, and desires—especially those concerning sex and aggression. Freud's ideas opened new horizons in art, literature, and history, as well as psychology (Gedo, 2002).

Freud theorized that many unconscious thoughts are threatening; hence, they are **repressed** (held out of awareness). But sometimes, he said, they are revealed by dreams, emotions, or slips of the tongue. ("Freudian slips" are often humorous, as when a student who is tardy for class says, "I'm sorry I couldn't get here any later.")

Freud believed that all thoughts, emotions, and actions are *determined.* In other words, nothing is an accident: If we probe deeply enough we will find the causes of every thought or action. Freud was also among the first to appreciate that childhood affects adult personality ("The child is father to the man"). Most of all, perhaps, Freud is known for creating **psychoanalysis**, the first "talking therapy." Freudian psychotherapy explores unconscious conflicts and emotional problems (see Chapter 17).

It wasn't very long before some of Freud's students began to promote their own theories. Several who modified Freud's ideas became known as neo-Freudians (*neo* means "new" or "recent").

Archives of the History of American Psychology, University of Akron

Mary Calkins, 1863–1930.

Archives of the History of American Psychology, University of Akron

Christine Ladd-Franklin, 1847–1930.

Archives of the History of American Psychology, University of Akron

Margaret Washburn, 1871–1939.

Neo-Freudians accept much of Freud's theory but revise parts of it. Many, for instance, place less emphasis on sex and aggression and more on social motives and relationships. Some well-known neo-Freudians are Alfred Adler, Anna Freud (Freud's daughter), Karen Horney (HORN-eye), Carl Jung (yoong), Otto Rank (rahnk), and Erik Erikson. Today, Freud's legacy is evident in various **psychodynamic theories,** which emphasize internal motives, conflicts, and unconscious forces (Westen, 1998).

Humanistic Psychology

Humanism is a view that focuses on subjective human experience. Humanistic psychologists are interested in human problems, potentials, and ideals.

How is the humanistic approach different from others? Carl Rogers, Abraham Maslow, and other humanists rejected the Freudian idea that we are ruled by unconscious forces. They were also uncomfortable with the behaviorist emphasis on conditioning. Both views have a strong undercurrent of **determinism** (the idea that behavior is determined by forces beyond our control). Instead, the humanists stress our ability to make voluntary choices, or **free will.** Of course, past experiences do affect us. Nevertheless, humanists believe that people can freely *choose* to live more creative, meaningful, and satisfying lives.

Humanists helped stimulate interest in psychological needs for love, self-esteem, belonging, self-expression, creativity, and spirituality. Such needs, they believe, are as important as our biological urges for food and water.

How scientific is the humanistic approach? Initially, humanists were less interested in treating psychology as a science. They stressed subjective factors, such as one's self-image, self-evaluation, and frame of reference. (*Self-image* is your perception of your own body, personality, and capabilities. *Self-evaluation* refers to appraising yourself as good or bad. A *frame of reference* is a mental perspective used to interpret events.) Today, humanists still seek to understand how we perceive ourselves and experience the world. However, most now do research to test their ideas, just as other psychologists do (Schneider, Bugental, & Pierson, 2001).

Maslow's concept of self-actualization is a special feature of humanism. **Self-actualization** refers to fully developing one's potential and becoming the best person possible. According to humanists, everyone has this potential. Humanists seek ways to help it emerge. (See ■ Table 1.1 for a summary of psychology's early development.)

Archives of the History of American Psychology, University of Akron

Sigmund Freud, 1856–1939. For more than 50 years, Freud probed the unconscious mind. In doing so, he altered modern views of human nature. His early experimentation with a "talking cure" for hysteria is regarded as the beginning of psychoanalysis. Through psychoanalysis, Freud added psychological treatment methods to psychiatry.

Psychology Today—Five Views of Behavior

At one time, loyalty to each school of thought was fierce, and clashes were common. Today, viewpoints such as functionalism and Gestalt psychology have blended into newer, broader perspectives. Also, some early systems, such as structuralism, have disappeared entirely. Certainly, specialties still exist. But today, many psychologists are *eclectic* (ek-LEK-tik): they draw from a variety of perspectives. Even so, five major views shape modern psy-

Bettmann/Corbis

Abraham Maslow, 1908–1970. As a founder of humanistic psychology, Maslow was interested in studying people of exceptional mental health. Such self-actualized people, he believed, make full use of their talents and abilities. Maslow offered his positive view of human potential as an alternative to the schools of behaviorism and psychoanalysis.

Unconscious Contents of the mind that are beyond awareness, especially impulses and desires not directly known to a person.

Repression The unconscious process by which memories, thoughts, or impulses are held out of awareness.

Psychoanalysis A Freudian approach to psychotherapy emphasizing the exploration of unconscious conflicts.

Neo-Freudian A psychologist who accepts the broad features of Freud's theory but has revised the theory to fit his or her own concepts.

Psychodynamic theory Any theory of behavior that emphasizes internal conflicts, motives, and unconscious forces.

Humanism An approach to psychology that focuses on human experience, problems, potentials, and ideals.

Determinism The idea that all behavior has prior causes that would completely explain one's choices and actions if all such causes were known.

Free will The idea that human beings are capable of freely making choices or decisions.

Self-actualization The ongoing process of fully developing one's personal potential.

TABLE 1.1

The Early Development of Psychology

PERSPECTIVE	DATE	NOTABLE EVENTS
Experimental psychology	1875	• First psychology course offered by William James
	1878	• First American Ph.D. in psychology awarded
	1879	• Wilhelm Wundt opens first psychology laboratory in Germany
	1883	• First American psychology lab founded at Johns Hopkins University
	1886	• First American psychology textbook written by John Dewey
Structuralism	1898	• Edward Titchener advances psychology based on introspection
Functionalism	1890	• William James publishes *Principles of Psychology*
	1892	• American Psychological Association founded
Psychodynamic psychology	1895	• Sigmund Freud publishes first studies
	1900	• Freud publishes *The Interpretation of Dreams*
Behaviorism	1906	• Ivan Pavlov reports his research on conditioned reflexes
	1913	• John Watson presents behavioristic view
Gestalt psychology	1912	• Max Wertheimer and others advance Gestalt viewpoint
Humanistic psychology	1942	• Carl Rogers publishes *Counseling and Psychotherapy*
	1943	• Abraham Maslow publishes "A Theory of Human Motivation"

chology. These are the *psychodynamic, behavioristic,* and *humanistic* views, plus modern *cognitive* and *biopsychological* perspectives (■ Table 1.2) (Robins, Gosling, & Craik, 1998).

Recent Trends

Are there any "hot topics" in psychology today? Yes, biopsychology is an especially fast-growing area. Eventually, biopsychologists expect to explain all behavior in terms of physical mechanisms, such as brain activity and genetics. Cognitive science is another rapidly expanding area. As mentioned earlier, cognitive psychologists study thoughts, expectations, memory, language, perception, problem solving, consciousness, creativity, and other mental processes. With all this renewed interest in thinking, psychology has finally "regained consciousness" (Robins, Gosling, & Craik, 1998). Recently, these two topics have been joined. *Cognitive neuroscience* is an attempt to discover connections between mental events and activity in the brain. For instance, we would like to know what happens in the brain when you think, remember, feel happy, or pay attention (Schall, 2004).

Positive Psychology

Psychology is being used to treat emotional trauma, manage pain, relieve depression, and much more. Because there is a pressing need to solve human problems, psychologists have paid much attention to the negative side of human behavior. However, psychologists have recently begun to ask, "What do we know about love, happiness, creativity, well-being, self-confidence, and achievement?" Together, such topics make up **positive psychology**, the study of human strengths, virtues, and optimal behavior (Seligman & Csikszentmihalyi, 2000). We know a lot about what's unhealthy and wrong. Positive psychology is an attempt to learn what people are doing right. Recall, for instance, that Abraham Maslow studied people who were leading especially effective lives (Froh, 2004). Now that psychologists are starting to study human strengths more formally, we are beginning to be able to say what makes up a "good life" (Compton, 2005). You will find many topics from positive psychology in this book. Ideally, they will help make your own life more positive and fulfilling (Simonton & Baumeister, 2005).

BRIDGES

Behaviorism, Gestalt psychology, psychoanalytic theory, and humanism have given rise to various forms of psychotherapy.

See Chapter 17 for more information about how psychological disorders are treated.

Summary

As you can see, it is helpful to view human behavior from more than one perspective. This is also true in another sense. We are rapidly becoming a multicultural society, made up of people from many different nations. How has this affected psychology? The next section explains why it is important for all of us to be aware of cultural differences.

Human Diversity—Appreciating Social and Cultural Differences

Jerry, who is Japanese American, is married to an Irish Catholic American. Here is what Jerry, his wife, and their children did on New Year's Day:

> We woke up in the morning and went to Mass at St. Brigid's, which has a black gospel choir. . . . Then we went to the Japanese-American Commu-

TABLE 1.2

Five Ways to Look at Behavior

CONSCIOUS / UNCONSCIOUS	**Psychodynamic View** Key Idea: *Behavior is directed by forces within one's personality that are often hidden or unconscious.* Emphasizes internal impulses, desires, and conflicts—especially those that are unconscious; views behavior as the result of clashing forces within personality; somewhat negative, pessimistic view of human nature.
S > R	**Behavioristic View** Key Idea: *Behavior is shaped and controlled by one's environment.* Emphasizes the study of observable behavior and the effects of learning; stresses the influence of external rewards and punishments; neutral, scientific, somewhat mechanistic view of human nature.
Self / Self-image / Self-evaluation	**Humanistic View** Key Idea: *Behavior is guided by one's self-image, by subjective perceptions of the world, and by needs for personal growth.* Focuses on subjective, conscious experience, human problems, potentials, and ideals; emphasizes self-image and self-actualization to explain behavior; positive, philosophical view of human nature.
	Biopsychological View Key Idea: *Human and animal behavior is the result of internal physical, chemical, and biological processes.* Seeks to explain behavior through activity of the brain and nervous system, physiology, genetics, the endocrine system, biochemistry, and evolution; neutral, reductionistic, mechanistic view of human nature.
INPUT / Processing / OUTPUT	**Cognitive View** Key Idea: *Much human behavior can be understood in terms of the mental processing of information.* Concerned with thinking, knowing, perception, understanding, memory, decision making, and judgment; explains behavior in terms of information processing; neutral, somewhat computer-like view of human nature.

nity Center for the Oshogatsu New Year's program and saw Buddhist archers shoot arrows to ward off evil spirits for the year. Next, we ate traditional rice cakes as part of the New Year's service and listened to a young Japanese-American storyteller. On the way home, we stopped in Chinatown and after that we ate Mexican food at a taco stand (Njeri, 1991).

Jerry and his family reflect a new norm of cultural diversity. About one third of the population in the United States is now African American, Hispanic, Asian American, Native American, or Pacific Islander. In some large cities, "minority" groups are already the majority (Schmitt, 2001).

The Impact of Culture

In the past, psychology was based mostly on the cultures of North America and Europe. Now we must ask, "Do the principles of Western psychology apply to people in all cultures? Are some psychological concepts invalid in other cultures? Are any universal?" Regardless, one thing is clear: Most of what we think, feel, and do is influenced in one way or another by the social and cultural worlds in which we live (Lehman, Chiu, & Schaller, 2004).

Cultural Relativity

Imagine that you are a psychologist. Your client, Linda, who is a Native American, tells you that spirits live in the trees near her home. Is Linda suffering from a delusion? Is she abnormal? Obviously, you will misjudge Linda's mental health if you fail to take her cultural beliefs into account. **Cultural relativity** (the idea that behavior must be judged relative to the values of the culture in which it occurs) can greatly affect the diagnosis of mental disorders (Alarcon, 1995). Cases like Linda's teach us to be wary of using inappropriate standards when judging others or comparing groups.

A Broader View of Diversity

In addition to cultural differences, age, ethnicity, gender, religion, disability, and sexual orientation all affect the **social norms** that guide behavior. Social norms are rules that define acceptable and expected behavior for members of various groups. All too often, the unstated standard for judging what is "average," "normal," or "correct" is the behavior of white, middle-class males (Reid, 2002). To fully understand human behavior, psychologists need to know how people differ, as well as the ways in which we are all alike. To be effective, psychologists must be sensitive to people who are ethnically and culturally different from themselves (APA, 2003). For the same reason, respecting human diversity can enrich your life, as well as your understanding of psychology (Cushner, 2003; Denmark, Rabinowitz, & Sechzer, 2005; Guthrie, 2004).

In a moment we will further explore what psychologists do. First, here are some questions to enhance your learning.

Positive psychology The study of human strengths, virtues, and effective functioning.

Cultural relativity The idea that behavior must be judged relative to the values of the culture in which it occurs.

Social norms Unspoken rules that define acceptable and expected behavior for members of a group.

KNOWLEDGE BUILDER

History and Major Perspectives

REFLECT

Which school of thought most closely matches your own view of behavior? Do you think any of the early schools offers a complete explanation of why we behave as we do? What about the five contemporary perspectives? Can you explain why so many psychologists are eclectic?

A group of psychologists were asked to answer this question: "Why did the chicken cross the road?" Their answers are listed next. Can you identify their theoretical orientations?

The chicken had been rewarded for crossing road in the past.

The chicken had an unconscious wish to become a trivet.

The chicken was trying to solve the problem of how to reach the other side of the road.

The chicken felt a need to explore new possibilities as a way to actualize its potential.

The chicken's motor cortex was activated by messages from its hypothalamus.

LEARNING CHECK

Match:

1. _____ Philosophy
2. _____ Wundt
3. _____ Structuralism
4. _____ Functionalism
5. _____ Behaviorism
6. _____ Gestalt
7. _____ Psychodynamic
8. _____ Humanistic
9. _____ Cognitive
10. _____ Washbur
11. _____ Biopsychology

A. Against analysis; studied whole experiences
B. "Mental chemistry" and introspection
C. Emphasizes self-actualization and personal growth
D. Interested in unconscious causes of behavior
E. Interested in how the mind aids survival
F. First woman Ph.D. in psychology
G. Studied stimuli and responses, conditioning
H. Part of psychology's "long past"
I. Concerned with thinking, language, problem solving
J. Used introspection and careful measurement
K. Relates behavior to the brain, physiology, and genetics
L. Also known as engineering psychology

12. Who among the following was not an historic woman psychologist?
    a. Calkins
    b. Ladd-Franklin
    c. Washburn
    d. Watson
13. A psychotherapist is working with a person from an ethnic group other than her own. She should be aware of how cultural relativity and _______________ affect behavior.
    a. the anthropomorphic error
    b. operational definitions
    c. biased sampling
    d. social norms

CRITICAL THINKING

14. Modern sciences like psychology are built on observations that can be verified by two or more independent observers. Did structuralism meet this standard? Why or why not?

Answers: **1.** H **2.** J **3.** B **4.** E **5.** G **6.** A **7.** D **8.** C **9.** I **10.** F **11.** K **12.** d **13.** d **14.** No, it did not. The downfall of structuralism was that each observer examined the contents of his or her own mind, which is something that no other person can observe.

Joseph Sohm/Stock, Boston

To fully understand human behavior, personal differences based on age, race, culture, ethnicity, gender, and sexual orientation must be taken into account.

BRIDGES

Psychotherapy can be less effective if a therapist and client come from different cultures.

See Chapter 17, page 590, for a discussion of the impact of culture on therapy.

Psychologists—Guaranteed Not to Shrink

Question: What is the difference between a psychologist and a psychiatrist?

Answer: About $30 an hour. (And going up.)

Contrary to common belief, clinical psychology is not the only specialty in the field. Only a little more than half of all psychologists study mental disorders or do therapy. Others apply their expertise to problems in research, education, medicine, health, business, the environment, and other nonclinical areas. Also, clinical psychologists are not the only people who work in the field of mental health. Often, they coordinate their efforts with other specially trained professionals. What are the differences among psychologists, psychiatrists, psychoanalysts, counselors, and other mental health professionals? Certainly, they're not all "shrinks." Each has a specific blend of training and skills.

THE CLINICAL FILE

The Golden Psi

About 75 percent of all psychologists help people directly and nearly all psychologists aid people in one way or another (Peterson, 1995). As you read this book you may find yourself wondering whether a particular concept can be used to solve mental and behavioral problems. In "The Clinical File" boxes like this one, you will find examples to help you reflect on how psychology can be used to help people.

Public impressions of psychologists are often inaccurate. Perhaps this occurs because so many stereotyped images appear in movies and on television. For example, in the 2005 comedy *Prime* a therapist listens to a patient describe intimate details of her relationship with a man without telling the patient that the man is her son. No ethical therapist would ever engage in such behavior, yet it is not unusual in the movies. Other films have featured psychologists who are more disturbed than their patients (such as Jack Nicholson's character in *Anger Management*) or psychologists who are bumbling buffoons (such as Billy Crystal's character in *Analyze This*). Evil, mind-controlling therapists who victimize or seduce patients are another popular Hollywood stereotype. Such characters may be dramatic and entertaining, but they seriously distort public perceptions of responsible and hardworking psychologists (Schultz, 2004; Sleek, 1998).

To combat these stereotypes, the American Psychological Association created the Golden Psi Media Award for the responsible portrayal of mental health professionals. (The Greek letter *psi*, written ψ, symbolizes psychology.) The 2004 Golden Psi went to two episodes of the television program *Law & Order: Special Victims Unit.* In both episodes, a psychiatrist acts professionally, despite intense pressures to act otherwise. In one episode, for example, the psychiatrist refuses to medicate a schizophrenic man (without his permission) to force him to reveal the location of an abducted child. In a second episode, the psychiatrist testifies at the trial of a man who is accused of raping and killing Arabs. The defense attorney argues that these acts are "in the man's genes" and therefore out of his control. The psychiatrist testifies about how much the environment influences behavior and how the killer is, in fact, responsible for his crimes.

Universal Studios/The Kobal Collection

In the film *Prime* Meryl Streep plays a therapist who listens to her patient, played by Uma Thurman, describe intimate details of her relationship with a man. However, the therapist neglects to tell her patient that the man is her son. Such premises are typical of the way psychologists and psychotherapy are misrepresented in the media.

Interestingly, the Golden Psi has never been awarded to a movie, going instead to television programs. Apparently this pattern occurs because most movies try to be dramatic and sensational, whereas some television programs try to be more realistic (Schultz, 2004).

Psychologists

A **psychologist** is highly trained in the methods, knowledge, and theories of psychology. Psychologists usually have a master's degree or a doctorate. These degrees typically require several years of postgraduate training. Psychologists may teach, do research, give psychological tests, or serve as consultants to business, industry, government, or the military. (There are many popular misconceptions about psychologists. See "The Golden Psi.")

Psychologists interested in emotional problems specialize in clinical or counseling psychology (see ■ Table 1.3). **Clinical psychologists** treat psychological problems or do research on therapies and mental disorders. In contrast, **counseling psychologists** tend to treat milder problems, such as troubles at work or school. However, such differences are fading, and many counseling psychologists now work full time as therapists.

To enter the profession of psychology, it is best to have a doctorate (Ph.D., Psy.D., or Ed.D.). Most clinical psychologists have a Ph.D. degree and follow a scientist-practitioner model. That is, they are trained to do either research or therapy. Many do both. Other clinicians earn the Psy.D. (Doctor of Psychology) degree, which emphasizes therapy skills rather than research (Peterson, 2001).

Have you ever wondered what it takes to become a psychologist? See "Is a Career in Psychology Right for You?"

Psychologist A person highly trained in the methods, factual knowledge, and theories of psychology.

Clinical psychologist A psychologist who specializes in the treatment of psychological and behavioral disturbances or who does research on such disturbances.

Counseling psychologist A psychologist who specializes in the treatment of milder emotional and behavioral disturbances.

TABLE 1.3

Kinds of Psychologists and What They Do

SPECIALTY		TYPICAL ACTIVITIES
Biopsychology	B*	Does research on the brain, nervous system, and other physical origins of behavior
Clinical	A	Does psychotherapy; investigates clinical problems; develops methods of treatment
Cognitive	B	Studies human thinking and information processing abilities
Community	A	Promotes community-wide mental health through research, prevention, education, and consultation
Comparative	B	Studies and compares the behavior of different species, especially animals
Consumer	A	Researches packaging, advertising, marketing methods, and characteristics of consumers
Counseling	A	Does psychotherapy and personal counseling; researches emotional disturbances and counseling methods
Cultural	B	Studies the ways in which culture, subculture, and ethnic group membership affect behavior
Developmental	A, B	Conducts research on infant, child, adolescent, and adult development; does clinical work with disturbed children; acts as consultant to parents and schools
Educational	A	Investigates classroom dynamics, teaching styles, and learning; develops educational tests, evaluates educational programs
Engineering	A	Does applied research on the design of machinery, computers, airlines, automobiles, and so on, for business, industry, and the military
Environmental	A, B	Studies the effects of urban noise, crowding, attitudes toward the environment, and human use of space; acts as a consultant on environmental issues
Forensic	A	Studies problems of crime and crime prevention, rehabilitation programs, prisons, courtroom dynamics; selects candidates for police work
Gender	B	Does research on differences between males and females, the acquisition of gender identity, and the role of gender throughout life
Health	A, B	Studies the relationship between behavior and health; uses psychological principles to promote health and prevent illness
Industrial-organizational	A	Selects job applicants, does skills analysis, evaluates on-the-job training, improves work environments and human relations in organizations and work settings
Learning	B	Studies how and why learning occurs; develops theories of learning
Medical	A	Applies psychology to manage medical problems, such as the emotional impact of illness, self-screening for cancer, compliance in taking medicine
Personality	B	Studies personality traits and dynamics; develops theories of personality and tests for assessing personality traits
School	A	Does psychological testing, referrals, emotional and vocational counseling of students; detects and treats learning disabilities; improves classroom learning
Sensation and perception	B	Studies the sense organs and the process of perception; investigates the mechanisms of sensation and develops theories about how perception occurs
Social	B	Investigates human social behavior, including attitudes, conformity, persuasion, prejudice, friendship, aggression, helping, and so forth

*Research in this area is typically applied (A), basic (B), or both (A, B).

Other Mental Health Professionals

A **psychiatrist** is a medical doctor who treats mental disorders, usually by doing psychotherapy. However, psychiatrists can also prescribe drugs, which is something psychologists usually cannot do. This is changing, however. Psychologists in New Mexico and Louisiana can now legally prescribe drugs. It will be interesting to see whether other states grant similar privileges (Daw, 2002).

To be a psychoanalyst, you must have a moustache and goatee, spectacles, a German accent, and a well-padded couch—or so the TV and movie stereotype goes. Actually, to become a **psychoanalyst** you must have an M.D. or Ph.D. degree plus further specialized training in the theory and practice of Freudian psychoanalysis. In other words, either a physician or a psychologist may become an analyst by completing more training in a specific type of psychotherapy.

DISCOVERING PSYCHOLOGY Is a Career in Psychology Right for You?

The more you can reflect on new ideas by relating them to your own life, the better you will understand and remember them. Thus, as you read this book you should ask yourself often if psychological concepts, theories, or research findings are relevant to you. As you do, you might make connections that will be genuinely helpful to you. "Discovering Psychology" boxes like this one will help you be more reflective about how psychology relates to your own life.

In our first Discovering Psychology box, let's explore whether you would enjoy becoming a psychologist. You can find out by answering the following questions:

1. I have a strong interest in human behavior. True or False?
2. I am good at recognizing patterns, evaluating evidence, and drawing conclusions. True or False?
3. I am emotionally stable. True or False?
4. I have good communication skills. True or False?
5. I find theories and ideas challenging and stimulating. True or False?
6. My friends regard me as especially sensitive to the feelings of others. True or False?
7. I enjoy planning and carrying out complex projects and activities. True or False?
8. Programs and popular books about psychology interest me. True or False?
9. I enjoy working with other people. True or False?
10. Clear thinking, objectivity, and keen observation appeal to me. True or False?

If you answered "True" to most of these questions, a career in psychology might be a good choice for you. And remember that many psychology majors also succeed in occupations such as management, public affairs, social services, business, sales, and education.

In many states, counselors also do mental health work. A **counselor** is an adviser who helps solve problems with marriage, career, school, work, or the like. To be a licensed counselor (such as a marriage and family counselor, a child counselor, or a school counselor) typically requires a master's degree plus one or two years of full-time supervised counseling experience. Counselors offer practical helping skills and do not treat serious mental disorders.

Psychiatric social workers play an important role in many mental health programs. They apply social science principles to help patients in clinics and hospitals. Most hold an M.S.W. (Master of Social Work) degree. Often, they assist psychologists and psychiatrists as part of a team. Their typical duties include evaluating patients and families, conducting group psychotherapy, or visiting a patient's home, school, or job to alleviate problems.

The Profession of Psychology

Does a person have to have a license to practice psychology? At one time it was possible in many states for anyone to "hang out a shingle" as a "psychologist." Now psychologists must meet rigorous educational and legal requirements. To work as a clinical or counseling psychologist you must have a license issued by a state examining board. However, the law does not prevent you from calling yourself anything else you choose—therapist, rebirther, primal feeling facilitator, cosmic aura balancer, or Rolfer—or from selling your "services" to anyone willing to pay. Beware of people with self-proclaimed titles. Even if their intentions are honorable, they may have little training. A licensed psychologist who chooses to use a particular type of therapy is not the same as someone "trained" solely in that technique.

Ethics

Most psychologists take pride in following a professional code that stresses (1) high levels of competence, integrity, and responsibility; (2) respect for people's rights to privacy, dignity, confidentiality, and personal freedom; and, above all, (3) protection of the client's welfare. Psychologists are also expected to use their knowledge to contribute to society. Many do volunteer work in the communities in which they live ("Ethical," 2002; Sullivan et al., 1998).

Specialties in Psychology

Do all psychologists do therapy and treat abnormal behavior? No. Only about 58 percent are clinical and counseling psychologists. The rest are found in other specialties. At present, the American Psychological Association (APA) consists of more than 50 divi-

Psychiatrist A medical doctor with additional training in the diagnosis and treatment of mental and emotional disorders.

Psychoanalyst A mental health professional (usually a medical doctor) trained to practice psychoanalysis.

Counselor A mental health professional who specializes in helping people with problems not involving serious mental disorder; for example, marriage counselors, career counselors, or school counselors.

Psychiatric social worker A mental health professional trained to apply social science principles to help patients in clinics and hospitals.

sions, each reflecting special skills or interests. Some of the major specialties are listed in ■ Table 1.3 (also see ● Figure 1.3). Nearly 30 percent of all psychologists are employed full-time at colleges or universities, where they teach and do research, consulting, or therapy. Some do *basic research,* in which they seek knowledge for its own sake. For example, a psychologist might study memory simply to understand how it works. Others do *applied research* to solve immediate practical problems, such as finding ways to improve the memory of eyewitnesses to crimes. Some do both types of research.

In a moment we'll take a closer look at how research is done. Before that, here's a brief review and a chance to do a little research on how much you've learned.

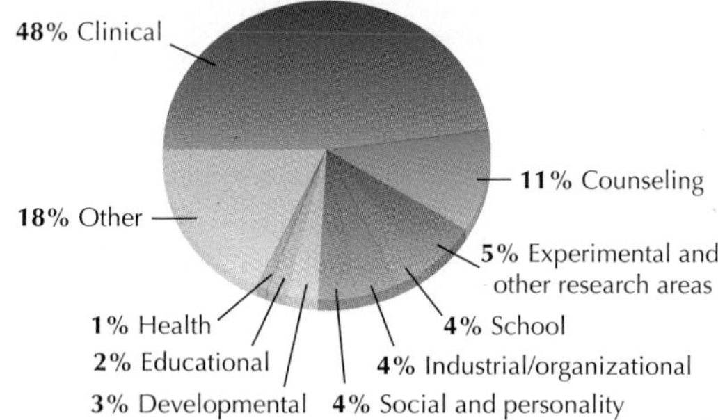

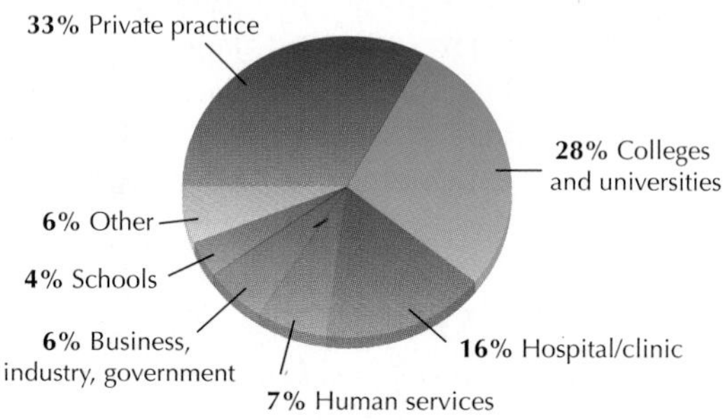

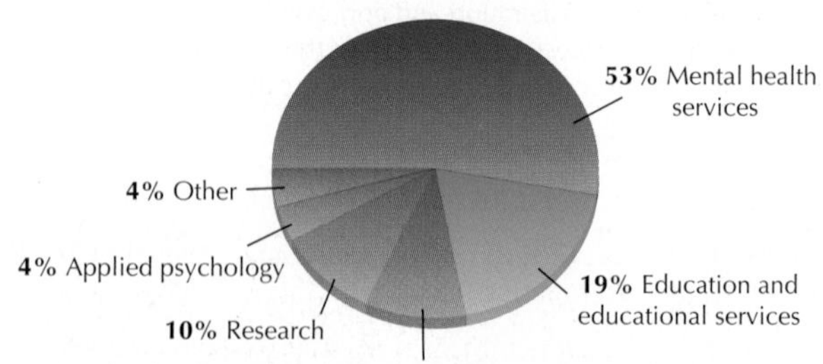

● **Figure 1.3** *(a)* Specialties in psychology. Percentages are approximate. *(b)* Where psychologists work. *(c)* The main activities psychologists do at work. Any particular psychologist might do several of these activities during a work week (APA, 1998). As you can see, most psychologists specialize in applied areas and work in applied settings.

KNOWLEDGE BUILDER

Psychologists and Their Specialties

REFLECT

You're going to meet four psychologists at a social gathering. How many would you expect to be therapists in private practice? Odds are that only two will be clinical (or counseling) psychologists and only one of these will work in private practice. On the other hand, at least one out of the four (and probably two) will work at a college or university.

LEARNING CHECK

1. Which of the following can prescribe drugs?
   a. a psychologist c. a psychotherapist
   b. a psychiatrist d. a counselor
2. A psychologist who specializes in treating human emotional difficulties is called a ________________ psychologist.
3. Roughly 40 percent of psychologists specialize in counseling psychology. T or F?
4. Who among the following would most likely be involved in the detection of learning disabilities?
   a. a consumer psychologist c. an experimental psychologist
   b. a forensic psychologist d. a school psychologist

CRITICAL THINKING

5. If most psychologists work in applied settings, why is basic research still of great importance?

Answers: 1. b **2.** clinical or counseling **3.** F **4.** d **5.** Because practitioners benefit from basic psychological research in the same way that physicians benefit from basic research in biology. Discoveries in basic science form the knowledge base that leads to useful applications.

Scientific Research—How to Think Like a Psychologist

Suppose that your grandfather goes back to college. What do people say? "Ah . . . never too old to learn." And what do they say when he loses interest and quits? "Well, you can't teach an old dog new tricks." Let's examine another *common-sense statement.* It is often said that "absence makes the heart grow fonder." Those of us separated from friends and lovers can take comfort in this knowledge—until we remember, "Out of sight, out of mind"! Much of what passes for common sense is equally vague and inconsistent. Notice also that most of these B.S. statements work best after the fact. (B.S., of course, stands for *Before Science.*)

As we have noted, *scientific* observations must be *systematic* so that they reveal something about behavior (Stanovich, 2004). To use an earlier example, little would be gained if you drove around a city during the summer and made haphazard observations of aggressive horn honking.

Dan McCoy/Rainbow

Applying the scientific method to the study of behavior requires careful observation. Here, a psychologist videotapes a session in which a child's thinking abilities are being tested.

The Scientific Method

The **scientific method** is based on careful collection of evidence, accurate description and measurement, precise definition, controlled observation, and repeatable results (Leary, 2004). In its ideal form the scientific method has six elements:

1. Making observations
2. Defining a problem
3. Proposing a hypothesis
4. Gathering evidence/testing the hypothesis
5. Publishing results
6. Theory building

Let's take a closer look at some elements of the scientific method.

Hypothesis Testing

Yes, what does "proposing a hypothesis" mean? A **hypothesis** (hi-POTH-eh-sis) is a tentative explanation of an event or relationship. In common terms, a hypothesis is a *testable* hunch or educated guess about behavior. For example, you might hypothesize that "frustration encourages aggression." How could you test this hypothesis? First you would have to decide how you are going to frustrate people. (This part might be fun.) Then you will need to find a way to measure whether or not they become more aggressive. (Not so much fun if you plan to be nearby.) Your observations would then provide evidence to confirm or disconfirm the hypothesis.

Operational Definitions

Because we cannot see or touch frustration, it must be defined operationally. An **operational definition** states the exact procedures used to represent a concept. Operational definitions allow abstract ideas to be tested in real-world terms (see ● Figure 1.4). For example, you might define frustration as "interrupting an adult before he or she can finish a puzzle and win a $100 prize." Aggression might be defined as "the number of times a frustrated individual insults the person who prevented work on the puzzle."

Clever Hans

Several steps of the scientific method can be illustrated with the story of Clever Hans, a famous "wonder horse" (Rosenthal, 1965). Clever Hans seemed to solve difficult math problems, which he answered by tapping his hoof. If you asked Hans, "What is 12 times 2, minus 18?" Hans would tap his hoof six times. This was so astonishing that a scientist decided to find out if Hans really could do arithmetic. Assume that you are the scientist and that you are just itching to discover how Hans *really* does his trick.

Can a Horse Add?

Your investigation of Hans's math skills would probably begin with careful *observation* of both the horse and his owner. Assume that these observations fail to reveal any obvious cheating. Then the *problem* becomes more clearly *defined:* What signals Hans to start and stop tapping his hoof? Your first *hypothesis* might be that the owner is giving Hans a signal. Your proposed *test* would be to make the owner leave the room. Then someone else could ask Hans questions. Your test would either confirm or deny the owner's role. This *evidence* would

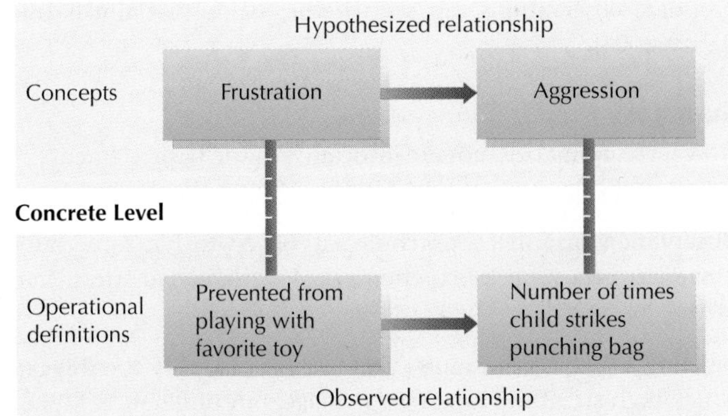

● **Figure 1.4** Operational definitions are used to link concepts with concrete observations. Do you think the examples given are reasonable operational definitions of frustration and aggression? Operational definitions vary in how well they represent concepts. For this reason, many different experiments may be necessary to draw clear conclusions about hypothesized relationships in psychology.

Scientific method Testing the truth of a proposition by careful measurement and controlled observation.

Hypothesis The predicted outcome of an experiment or an educated guess about the relationship between variables.

Operational definition Defining a scientific concept by stating the specific actions or procedures used to measure it. For example, "hunger" might be defined as "the number of hours of food deprivation."

support or eliminate the cheating hypothesis. By changing the conditions under which you observe Hans, you have *controlled* the situation to gain more information from your observations.

Incidentally, Hans could still answer when his owner was out of the room. But a brilliant series of controlled observations revealed Hans's secret. If Hans couldn't see the questioner, he couldn't answer. It seems that questioners always *lowered their heads* (to look at Hans's hoof) after asking a question. This was Hans's cue to start tapping. When Hans had tapped the correct number, a questioner would always *look up* to see if Hans was going to stop. This was Hans's cue to stop tapping!

Theories

What about theory formulation? Because Clever Hans's ability to do math was an isolated problem, no theorizing was involved. However, in actual research, a **theory** acts as a map of knowledge (Halpern, 2003). Good theories summarize observations, explain them, and guide further research (● Figure 1.5). Without theories of forgetting, personality, stress, mental illness, and the like, psychologists would drown in a sea of disconnected facts (Stanovich, 2004).

Publication

Scientific information must always be *publicly available*. The results of psychological studies are usually published in professional journals (see ■ Table 1.4). That way, anyone willing to make appropriate observations can see whether or not a claim is true (Leary, 2004).

Summary

Now let's summarize more realistically. All the basic elements of the scientific method are found in the example that follows.

Observation Suzanne, a psychologist, observes that some business managers seem to experience less work-related stress than others do.

Defining a Problem Suzanne's problem is to identify the ways in which high-stress and low-stress managers are different.

Observation Suzanne carefully questions managers about how much stress they experience. These additional observations suggest that low-stress managers believe they have more control over their work.

Proposing a Hypothesis Suzanne hypothesizes that having control over difficult tasks reduces stress.

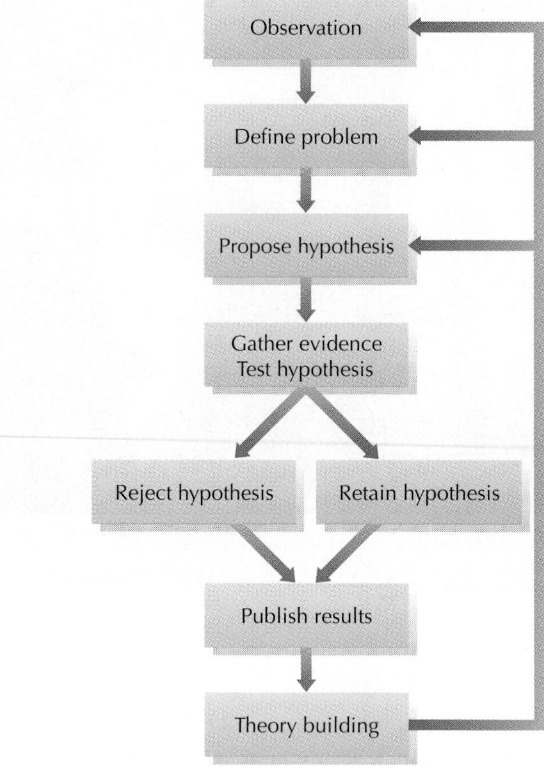

● **Figure 1.5** Psychologists use the logic of science to answer questions about behavior. Specific hypotheses can be tested in a variety of ways, including naturalistic observation, correlational studies, controlled experiments, clinical studies, and the survey method. Psychologists revise their theories to reflect the evidence they gather. New or revised theories then lead to new observations, problems, and hypotheses.

Gathering Evidence/Testing the Hypothesis Suzanne designs an experiment in which people must solve a series of very difficult problems. In one group, people solve the problems at a forced pace, dictated by Suzanne. In another group, they are allowed to set the pace themselves. While working, the second group reports lower stress levels than the first did. This suggests that Suzanne's hypothesis is correct.

Publishing Results In a scholarly article, Suzanne carefully describes the question she investigated, the methods she used, and the results of her experiment. The article is published in the *Journal of Clinical Psychology.*

Theory Building Drawing on the results of similar experiments, Suzanne and other psychologists create a theory to explain why having control over a task helps reduce stress.

BRIDGES

IQ tests serve as operational definitions of intelligence. Without such tests, it would be difficult to study intelligence.

See Chapter 11, pages 366–369.

BRIDGES

One of the major limitations of Freudian personality theory is that many of its concepts are not testable or falsifiable.

See Chapter 14, page 472.

TABLE 1.4

Outline of a Research Report

- **Abstract** Research reports begin with a very brief summary of the study and its findings. The abstract allows you to get an overview without reading the entire article.
- **Introduction** The introduction describes the question to be investigated. It also provides background information by reviewing prior studies on the same or related topics.
- **Method** This section tells how and why observations were made. It also describes the specific procedures used to gather data. That way, other researchers can repeat the study to see if they get the same results.
- **Results** The outcome of the investigation is presented. Data may be graphed, summarized in tables, or statistically analyzed.
- **Discussion** The results of the study are discussed in relation to the original question. Implications of the study are explored and further studies may be proposed.

Baron Hugo van Lawick/National Geographic Society

● **Figure 1.6** A special moment in Jane Goodall's naturalistic study of chimpanzees. A chimp uses a grass stem to extract a meal from a termite nest. Goodall's work also documented the importance of long-term emotional bonds between chimpanzee mothers and their offspring, as well as fascinating differences in the behavior and "personalities" of individual chimps (Goodall, 1990).

Research Methods

Psychologists gather evidence and test hypotheses in many ways: They observe behavior as it unfolds in natural settings (**naturalistic observation**); they make measurements to discover relationships between events (**correlational method**); they use the powerful technique of controlled experimentation (**experimental method**); they study psychological problems and therapies in clinical settings (**clinical method**); and they use questionnaires to poll large groups of people (**survey method**). Let's see how each of these is used to advance psychological knowledge.

Naturalistic Observation—Psychology Steps Out!

Psychologists sometimes actively observe behavior in a *natural setting* (the typical environment in which a person or animal lives). The work of Jane Goodall provides a good example. She and her staff have been observing chimpanzees in Tanzania since 1960. A quote from her book, *In the Shadow of Man,* captures the excitement of a scientific discovery:

> Quickly focusing my binoculars, I saw that it was a single chimpanzee, and just then he turned my direction. . . . He was squatting beside the red earth mound of a termite nest, and as I watched I saw him carefully push a long grass stem into a hole in the mound. After a moment he withdrew it and picked something from the end with his mouth. I was too far away to make out what he was eating, but it was obvious that he was actually using a grass stem as a tool. (● Figure 1.6) (Excerpt from *In the Shadow of Man* by Jane Goodall. Copyright © 1971 by Hugo and Jane Van Lawick-Goodall. Reprinted by permission of Houghton Mifflin Company. All rights reserved.)

Notice that naturalistic observation only provides *descriptions* of behavior. To *explain* observations we may need information from other research methods. Just the same, Goodall's discovery helped us realize that humans are not the only tool-making animals (Lavallee, 1999).

Chimpanzees in zoos use objects as tools. Doesn't that demonstrate the same thing? Not necessarily. Naturalistic observation allows us to study behavior that hasn't been tampered with by outside influences. Only by observing chimps in their natural environment can we tell if they use tools without human interference.

Limitations

Doesn't the presence of human observers affect the animals' behavior? Yes. The observer effect is a major problem. The **observer effect** refers to changes in a subject's behavior caused by an awareness of being observed. Naturalists must be very careful to keep their distance and avoid "making friends" with the animals they are watching. Likewise, if you are interested in schoolyard bullying,

Theory A system of ideas designed to interrelate concepts and facts in a way that summarizes existing data and predicts future observations.

Naturalistic observation Observing behavior as it unfolds in natural settings.

Correlational method Making measurements to discover relationships between events.

Experimental method Investigating behavior through controlled experimentation.

Clinical method Studying psychological problems and therapies in clinical settings.

Survey method Using questionnaires and surveys to poll large groups of people.

Observer effect Changes in a person's behavior brought about by an awareness of being observed.

you can't simply stroll onto a playground and start taking notes. As a stranger, your presence would probably change children's behavior. When possible, this problem can be minimized by concealing the observer. Another solution is to use hidden recorders. For example, a naturalistic study of playground aggression was done with video cameras and remote microphones (Pepler, Craig, & Roberts, 1998).

Observer bias is a related problem in which observers see what they expect to see or record only selected details. For instance, teachers in one study were told to watch normal elementary school children who had been labeled (for the study) as "learning disabled," "mentally retarded," "emotionally disturbed," or "normal." Sadly, teachers gave the children very different ratings, depending on the labels used (Foster & Ysseldyke, 1976). In some situations, observer bias can have serious consequences. For example, psychotherapists tend to get better results with the type of therapy they favor (Lambert, 1999).

The Anthropomorphic Error

A special trap that must be avoided while observing animals is the **anthropomorphic** (AN-thro-po-MORE-fik) **error.** This is the error of attributing human thoughts, feelings, or motives to animals—especially as a way of explaining their behavior (Blumberg & Wasserman, 1995).

Why is it risky to attribute motives or emotions to animals? The temptation to assume that an animal is "angry," "jealous," "bored," or "guilty" can be strong, but it can lead to false conclusions. If you have pets at home, you probably already know how difficult it is to avoid anthropomorphizing.

Recording Observations

Psychologists doing naturalistic studies make a special effort to minimize bias by keeping a formal log of data and observations, called an **observational record.** As suggested in the study of playground aggression, videotaping often provides the best record of all (Pepler & Craig, 1995).

Despite its problems, naturalistic observation can supply a wealth of information and raise many interesting questions. In most scientific research it is an excellent starting point.

Correlational Studies—In Search of the Perfect Relationship

Let's say a psychologist notes an association between the IQs of parents and their children, or between beauty and social popularity, or between anxiety and test performance, or even between crime and the weather. In each instance, two observations or events are **correlated** (linked together in an orderly way).

A **correlational study** finds the degree of relationship, or correlation, between two existing traits, behaviors, or events. First, two factors of interest are measured. Then a statistical technique is used to find their degree of correlation. (See the Statistics Appendix near the end of this book for more information.) For example, we could find the correlation between the number of hours slept at night and afternoon sleepiness. If the correlation is large, knowing how long a person sleeps at night would allow us to predict his or her degree of sleepiness in the afternoon. Likewise, afternoon sleepiness could be used to predict the duration of nighttime sleep.

Correlation Coefficients

How is the degree of correlation expressed? The strength and direction of a relationship can be expressed as a **coefficient of correlation.** This is simply a number falling somewhere between +1.00 and −1.00 (see the Appendix). If the number is zero or close to zero, the association between two measures is weak or nonexistent. For example, the correlation between shoe size and intelligence is zero. (Sorry, size 12 readers.) If the correlation is +1.00, a perfect positive relationship exists; if it is −1.00, a perfect negative relationship has been discovered.

Correlations in psychology are rarely perfect, but the closer the coefficient is to +1.00 or −1.00, the stronger the relationship. For example, identical twins tend to have almost identical IQs. In contrast, the IQs of parents and their children are only generally similar. The correlation between the IQs of parents and children is .35; between identical twins it's .86.

What do the terms "positive" and "negative" correlation mean? A **positive correlation** shows that increases in one measure are matched by increases in the other (or decreases correspond with decreases). For example, there is a positive correlation between high school grades and college grades; students who do better in high school tend to do better in college (and the reverse). In a **negative correlation,** increases in the first measure are associated with decreases in the second (● Figure 1.7). We might observe, for instance, that the higher the air temperature, the lower the activity level of animals in a zoo.

Would that show that air temperature causes changes in activity level? It might seem so, but we cannot be sure without performing an experiment.

Correlation and Causation

Correlational studies help us discover relationships and make predictions. However, correlation *does not demonstrate causation.* Just because two things *appear* to be related does not mean that **causation** (a cause-and-effect connection) exists (Halpern, 2003). The animals' activity might be affected by seasonal changes in weight, hormone levels, or even the feeding schedule at the zoo. Just because one thing to be related to another does not mean that a cause-and-effect connection exists.

BRIDGES

Correlations between the IQs of family members are used to estimate the degree to which intelligence is affected by heredity and environment.

See Chapter 11, pages 376–378.

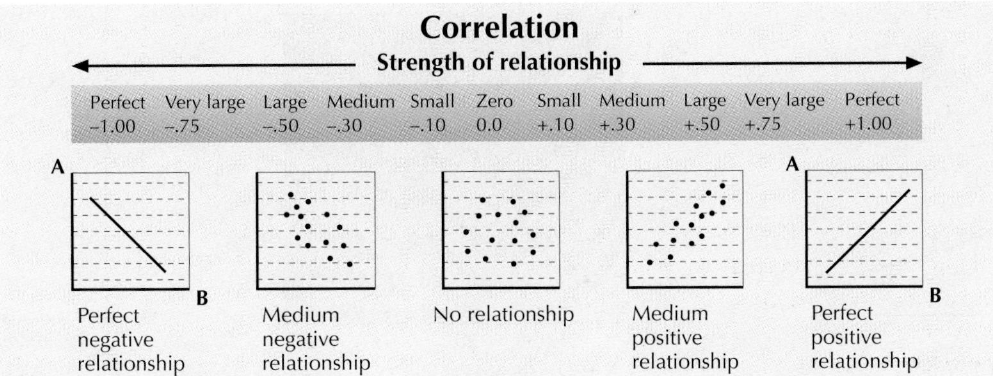

● **Figure 1.7** The correlation coefficient tells how strongly two measures are related. These graphs show a range of relationships between two measures, A and B. If a correlation is negative, increases in one measure are associated with decreases in the other. (As B gets larger, A gets smaller.) In a positive correlation, increases in one measure are associated with increases in the other. (As B gets larger, A gets larger.) The center-left graph ("medium negative relationship") might result from comparing anxiety level (B) with test scores (A): Higher anxiety is associated with lower scores. The center graph ("no relationship") would result from plotting a person's shoe size (B) and his or her IQ (A). The center-right graph ("medium positive relationship") could be a plot of grades in high school (B) and grades in college (A) for a group of students: Higher grades in high school are associated with higher grades in college.

Here is another example of mistaking correlation for causation: What if a psychologist discovers that the blood of patients with schizophrenia contains a certain chemical not found in the general population? Does this show that the chemical *causes* schizophrenia? It may seem so, but schizophrenia could cause the chemical to form. Or both schizophrenia and the chemical might be caused by some unknown third factor, such as the typical diet in mental hospitals.

Just because one thing *appears* to cause another does not *confirm* that it does. This fact can be seen clearly in the case of obviously noncausal relationships. For example, there is a correlation between the number of churches in American cities and the number of bars; the more churches, the more bars. Does this mean that drinking makes you religious? Does it mean that religion makes you thirsty? No one, of course, would leap to such conclusions about cause and effect. But in less obvious situations, it's tempting. (The real connection is that both the number of churches and the number of bars are related to the population size of cities.)

Relationships in Psychology

Do students who study more get better grades? To answer this question we could record how long a number of students study each week. Then we could match hours studied with grades earned. Suppose we find that low study times correspond to low grades. Likewise, high amounts of studying are associated with high grades. If this were the case, there would be a positive relationship between studying and grades. Similarly, we might discover that students who watch many hours of television tend to get lower grades than those who watch few hours. (This is the well-known TV zombie effect.) This time, a negative relationship would exist. That is, low viewing times go with high grades, and high viewing times go with low grades. Obviously, these examples are only hypothetical. However, when real patterns can be identified, they have great value. Relationships summarize large amounts of data and allow us to make accurate predictions.

Graphical Data

Drawing graphs of relationships can help clarify their nature. For instance, ● Figure 1.8 shows the results of a memory experiment. Before being tested, subjects learned from one to twenty word lists. The question was, "How well would they remember the last list?" The graph shows that when participants learned only one list, they remembered 80 percent of it. When they learned four lists, their scores on the last list dropped to 43 percent (blue arrows). When they memorized ten other lists, their recall fell even more, to 22 percent (red arrows). Overall, there was a negative relationship between the number of lists memorized and

Observer bias The tendency of an observer to distort observations or perceptions to match his or her expectations.

Anthropomorphic error The error of attributing human thoughts, feelings, or motives to animals, especially as a way of explaining their behavior.

Observational record A detailed summary of observed events or a videotape of observed behavior.

Correlation The existence of a consistent, systematic relationship between two events, measures, or variables.

Correlational study A nonexperimental study designed to measure the degree of relationship (if any) between two or more events, measures, or variables.

Coefficient of correlation A statistical index ranging from −1.00 to +1.00 that indicates the direction and degree of correlation.

Positive correlation A statistical relationship in which increases in one measure are matched by increases in the other (or decreases correspond with decreases).

Negative correlation A statistical relationship in which increases in one measure are matched by decreases in the other.

Causation The act of causing some effect.

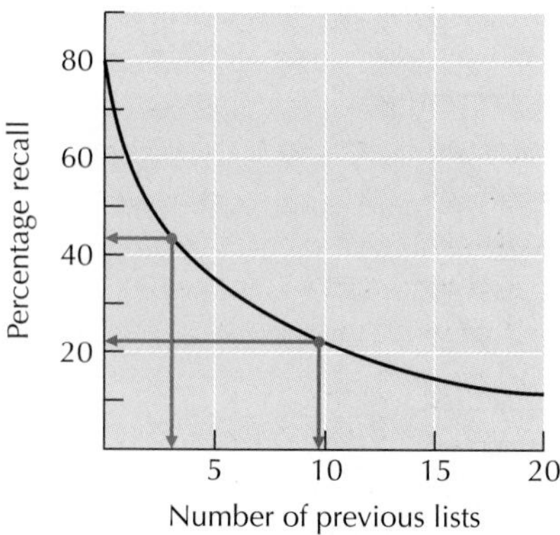

● **Figure 1.8** Effects of interference on memory. A graph of the approximate relationship between percentage recalled and number of different word lists memorized. Adapted from Underwood, 1957

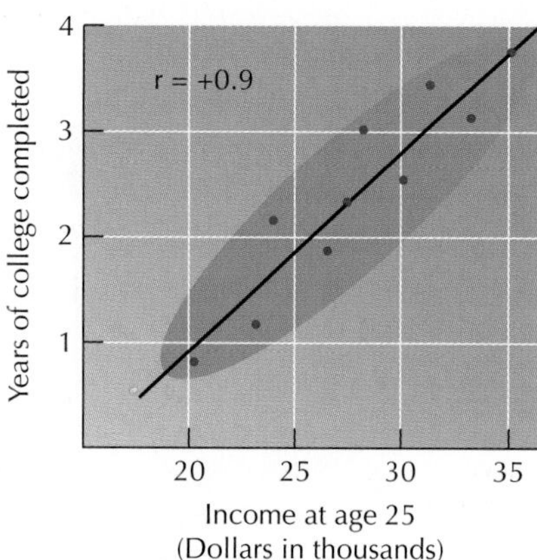

● **Figure 1.9** The relationship between years of college completed and personal income (hypothetical data).

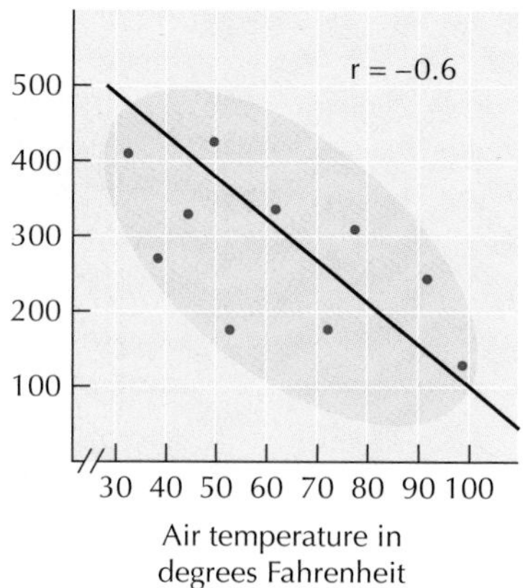

● **Figure 1.10** The relationship between air temperature and amount of coffee consumed (hypothetical data.)

recall of the last list. (The meaning of this finding is discussed in Chapter 9. For now, let's just say that you shouldn't memorize a telephone book before studying for a test.)

Some graphs reveal **linear** (straight-line) **relationships.** Others are **curvilinear** (kur-vih-LIN-ee-er) and consist of a curved line, like Figure 1.8. In either case, relationships need not be perfect to be useful. Suppose, for instance, that we randomly select 10 people. We then compare the years of college completed with each person's income at age 25. Results like those shown in ● Figure 1.9 would make it clear that there is a strong positive relationship between education and earnings. Remember that such correlations do not prove education increases earnings. Nevertheless, a pattern like this might be of great interest to a high school student thinking about whether to attend college.

The shaded area and the colored line in ● Figure 1.9 show that the relationship is approximately linear, but not perfect. (If it were perfect, all the dots would lie on the colored line.) The correlation coefficient (*r*) also shows that the relationship is strong and positive, but not perfect. (How often do you find a perfect relationship?) If the relationship *were* perfect, the coefficient would be 1.00.

For comparison, ● Figure 1.10 plots more hypothetical data. Assume that the manager of a college cafeteria has recorded the amount of coffee sold on 10 different days, as well as the air temperature on each day. Notice again that the relationship appears to be linear. However, this time it is negative. Also note how the shaded area and the correlation coefficient both indicate a weaker relationship. Even so, knowing the correlation between temperature and coffee drinking would help anyone planning how much "mud" to brew each morning.

On a higher plane, psychologists seek to identify relationships concerning memory, perception, stress, aging, therapy, and a host of similar topics. Much of this book is a summary of such relationships.

The best way to be confident that a cause-and-effect relationship exists is to perform a controlled experiment. You'll learn how in the next section.

KNOWLEDGE BUILDER

Research Methods, Naturalistic Observation, and Correlation

REFLECT

You probably hypothesize daily about why people act the way they do. Do you seek to verify your hypotheses? Usually we closely observe others to determine whether our "educated guesses" about them are correct. But casual observation can be misleading. To really test a hypothesis, systematic observation and formal research methods are necessary.

If you were going to do some informal naturalistic observation in your psychology classroom, what behavior would you observe and record?

See if you can identify at least one positive relationship and one negative relationship that involves human behavior.

LEARNING CHECK

1. Most of psychology can rightfully be called common sense because psychologists prefer naturalistic observation to controlled observation. T or F?
2. A psychologist does a study to see if having control over difficult tasks reduces stress. In the study he will be testing an
   a. experimental hypothesis c. empirical definition
   b. operational definition d. anthropomorphic theory
3. Two major problems in naturalistic observation are the effects of the observer and observer bias. T or F?
4. The ______________________ fallacy involves attributing human feelings and motives to animals.
5. Correlation typically does not demonstrate causation. T or F?
6. Which correlation coefficient represents the strongest relationship?
   a. −0.86 b. +0.66 c. +0.10 d. +0.09

CRITICAL THINKING

7. Can you think of some additional "common-sense" statements that contradict each other?

8. Adults who often ate Frosted Flakes cereal as children now have half the cancer rate seen in adults who never ate Frosted Flakes. What do you think explains this strange correlation?

Answers: 1. F **2.** a **3.** T **4.** anthropomorphic **5.** T **6.** a **7.** There are many examples. Here are a few more to add to the ones you thought of: "You can't make a silk purse out of a sow's ear," versus "Clothes make the man (or woman)." "He (or she) who hesitates is lost," versus "Haste makes waste." "Birds of a feather flock together," versus "Opposites attract." **8.** The correlation is related to an age bias in the group of people studied. Older adults have higher cancer rates than younger adults, and Frosted Flakes weren't available during the childhoods of older people. Thus, Frosted Flakes appear to be related to cancer, when age is the real connection (Tierny, 1987).

The Psychology Experiment—Where Cause Meets Effect

Psychologists want to be able explain *why* we act the way we do. Sometimes this can be achieved with naturalistic observation or correlations. However, usually we must do an experiment to discover the *causes* of behavior. Experiments bring cause-and-effect relationships into sharp focus, allowing us to answer the important "why" questions in psychology.

The most powerful research tool is an **experiment** (a formal trial undertaken to confirm or disconfirm a hypothesis). Psychologists carefully control conditions in experiments to identify cause-and-effect relationships. To perform an experiment you would do the following:

1. Directly vary a condition you think might affect behavior.
2. Create two or more groups of subjects. These groups should be alike in all ways *except* the condition you are varying.
3. Record whether varying the condition has any effect on behavior.

Assume that you want to find out if hunger affects memory. First, you would form two groups of people. Then you could give the members of one group a memory test while they are hungry. The second group would take the same test after eating a meal. By comparing average memory scores for the two groups, you could tell if hunger affects memory.

As you can see, the simplest psychological experiment is based on two groups of **subjects** (animals or people whose behavior is investigated). One group is called the *experimental group;* the other becomes the *control group.* The control group and the experimental group are treated exactly alike except for the condition you intentionally vary. This condition is called the *independent variable.*

Variables and Groups

A **variable** is any condition that can change and that might affect the outcome of the experiment. Identifying causes and effects in an experiment involves three types of variables:

1. **Independent variables** are conditions altered or varied by the experimenter, who sets their size, amount, or value. Independent variables are suspected *causes* for differences in behavior.
2. **Dependent variables** measure the results of the experiment. That is, they reveal the *effects* that independent variables have on *behavior.* Such effects are often revealed by measures of performance, such as test scores.
3. **Extraneous variables** are conditions that a researcher wishes to prevent from affecting the outcome of the experiment.

We can apply these terms to our hunger/memory experiment in this way: Hunger is the independent variable—we want to know if hunger affects memory. Memory (defined by scores on the memory test) is the dependent variable—we want to know if the ability to memorize depends on how hungry a person is. All other conditions that could affect memory scores are extraneous. Examples are the number of hours slept the night before the test, intelligence, or difficulty of the questions.

As you can see, an **experimental group** consists of subjects exposed to the independent variable (hunger in the preceding example). Members of the **control group** are exposed to all conditions except the independent variable.

Let's examine another simple experiment. Suppose you notice that you seem to study better while listening to music. This suggests the hypothesis that music improves learning. We could test this idea by forming an experimental group that studies with music. A control group would study without music. Then we could compare their scores on a test.

Is a control group really needed? Can't people just study with music on to see if they do better? Without a control group it would be impossible

Linear relationship A relationship that forms a straight line when graphed.

Curvilinear relationship A relationship that forms a curved line when graphed.

Experiment A formal trial undertaken to confirm or disconfirm a fact or principle.

Experimental subjects Humans or animals whose behavior is investigated in an experiment.

Variable Any condition that changes or can be made to change; a measure, event, or state that may vary.

Independent variable In an experiment, the condition being investigated as a possible cause of some change in behavior. The values that this variable takes are chosen by the experimenter.

Dependent variable In an experiment, the condition (usually a behavior) that is affected by the independent variable.

Extraneous variables Conditions or factors excluded from influencing the outcome of an experiment.

Experimental group In a controlled experiment, the group of subjects exposed to the independent variable or experimental condition.

Control group In a controlled experiment, the group of subjects exposed to all experimental conditions or variables *except* the independent variable.

to tell if music had any effect on learning. The control group provides a *point of reference* for comparison with scores of the experimental group. If the average test score of the experimental group is higher than the average of the control group, we can conclude that music improves learning. If there is no difference, it's obvious that the independent variable had no effect on learning.

In this experiment, the amount learned (indicated by scores on the test) is the *dependent variable*. We are asking, Does the independent variable *affect* the dependent variable? (Does music affect or influence learning?)

Experimental Control

How do we know that the people in one group aren't more intelligent than those in the other group? It's true that personal differences might affect the experiment. However, they can be controlled by randomly assigning people to groups. **Random assignment** means that a subject has an equal chance of being in either the experimental group or the control group. Randomization evenly balances personal differences in the two groups. In our musical experiment, this could be done by simply flipping a coin for each subject: heads, the subject is in the experimental group; tails, it's the control group. This would result in few differences in the number of people in each group who are geniuses or dunces, hungry, hung over, tall, music lovers, or whatever.

Other *extraneous,* or outside, variables—such as the amount of study time, the sex of subjects, the temperature in the room, the time of day, the amount of light, and so forth—must also be prevented from affecting the outcome of an experiment. But how? Usually this is done by making all conditions (except the independent variable) *exactly* alike for both groups. When all conditions are the same for both groups—*except* the presence or absence of music—then a difference in the amount learned *must* be caused by the music (● Figure 1.11).

Cause and Effect

Now let's summarize. In an experiment two or more groups of subjects are treated differently with respect to the independent variable. In all other ways they are treated the same. That is, extraneous variables are equalized for all groups. The effect of the independent variable (or variables) on some behavior (the dependent variable) is then measured. In a carefully controlled experiment, the independent variable is the only possible *cause* for any *effect* noted in the dependent variable. This allows clear cause-and-effect connections to be identified (● Figure 1.12).

Evaluating Results

How can we tell if the independent variable really made a difference? The problem is handled statistically. Reports in psychology journals almost always include the statement, "Results were **statistically significant.**" What this means is that the obtained results would occur very rarely by chance alone. To be statistically significant, a difference must be large enough so that it would occur by chance in less than 5 experiments out of 100. (See the Statistics Appendix for more information.) Of course, findings also become more convincing when they can be *replicated* (repeated) by other researchers.

Meta-Analysis

As you might guess, numerous studies are done on important topics in psychology. Although each study adds to our understanding, the results of various studies don't always agree. Let's say we are interested in whether males or females tend to be greater risk takers. A computer search would reveal that more than 100 studies have investigated various types of risk-taking (for example, smoking, fast driving, or unprotected sex).

Is there a way to combine the results of the studies? Yes, a statistical technique called **meta-analysis** can be used to combine the results of many studies as if they were all part of one big study (Rosenthal & DiMatteo, 2001). In other words, a meta-analysis is a study of the results of other studies. In recent years, meta-analysis has been used

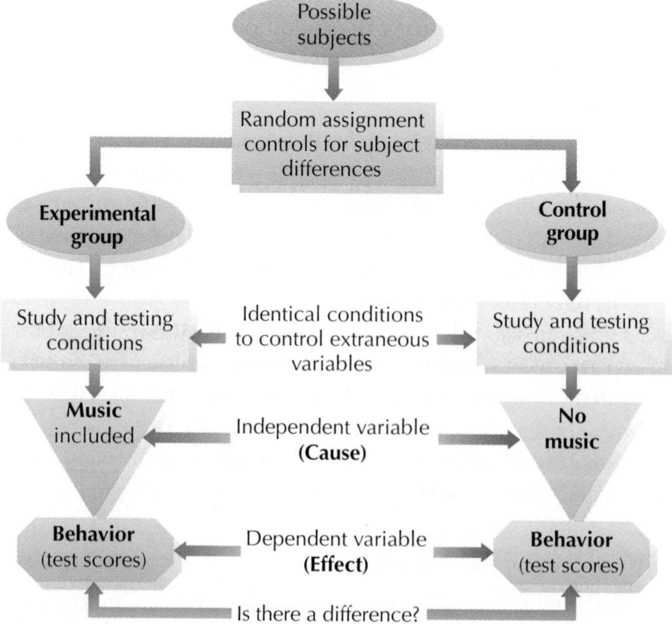

● **Figure 1.11** Elements of a simple psychological experiment to assess the effects of music during study on test scores.

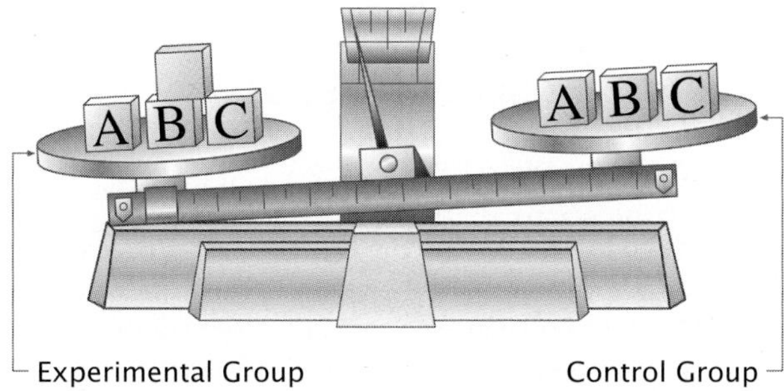

● **Figure 1.12** Experimental control is achieved by balancing extraneous variables for the experimental group and the control group. For example, the average age (A), education (B), and intelligence (C) of group members could be made the same for both groups. Then we could apply the independent variable to the experimental group. If their behavior (the dependent variable) changes (in comparison with the control group), the change must be caused by the independent variable.

to summarize and synthesize mountains of psychological research. This allows us to see the big picture and draw conclusions that might be missed in a single, small-scale study. Oh, and about that risk-taking question: A meta-analysis showed that males do tend to take more risks than females (Byrnes, Miller, & Schafer, 1999). (The most frequent last words uttered by deceased young males is rumored to be, "Hey, watch this!")

Placebo Effects—Sugar Pills and Saltwater

Let's do an experiment to see if the drug amphetamine (a stimulant) affects learning: Before studying, members of our experimental group take an amphetamine pill. Control group members get nothing. Later, we assess how much each subject learned. Does this experiment seem valid? Actually, it is seriously flawed.

Why? The experimental group took the drug and the control group didn't. Differences in the amount they learned must have been caused by the drug, right? No, because the drug wasn't the only difference between the groups. People in the experimental group swallowed a pill, and control subjects did not. Without using a placebo (plah-SEE-bo), it is impossible to tell if the drug affects learning. It could be that those who swallowed a pill *expected* to do better. This alone might have affected their performance, even if the pill didn't.

What is a placebo? Why would it make a difference? A **placebo** is a fake pill or injection. Inert substances such as sugar pills and saline (saltwater) injections are common placebos. Thus, if a placebo has any effect, it must be based on suggestion, rather than chemistry (Moerman, 2002).

The **placebo effect** (changes in behavior caused by belief that one has taken a drug) can be powerful. For instance, a saline injection is 70 percent as effective as morphine in reducing pain. That's why doctors sometimes prescribe placebos. Placebos have been shown to affect pain, anxiety, depression, alertness, tension, sexual arousal, cravings for alcohol, and many other processes (Kirsch & Lynn, 1999).

How could an inert substance have any effect? Placebos alter our expectations about our own emotional and physical reactions. Because we associate taking medicine with feeling better, we expect placebos to make us feel better, too (Stewart-Williams, 2004). After a person takes a placebo, there is a reduction in brain activity linked with pain, so the effect is not imaginary (Wager et al., 2004).

Controlling Placebo Effects

To control for placebo effects, we could use a **single-blind experiment.** In this case, subjects do not know if they are receiving a real drug or a placebo. All subjects get a pill or injection. People in the experimental group get a real drug, and those in the control group get a placebo. Because subjects are *blind* as to whether they received the drug, their expectations are the same. Any difference in their behavior must be caused by the drug.

Keeping subjects "blind" is not necessarily enough, however. In a **double-blind experiment** neither subjects nor experimenters know who received a drug and who took a placebo. This keeps researchers from unconsciously influencing subjects. Typically, someone else prepares the pills or injections so that experimenters don't know until after testing who got what. Double-blind testing has shown that about 50 percent of the effectiveness of antidepressant drugs, such as the "wonder drug"

Random assignment The use of chance (for example, flipping a coin) to assign subjects to experimental and control groups.

Statistical significance Experimental results that would rarely occur by chance alone.

Meta-analysis A statistical technique for combining the results of many studies on the same subject.

Placebo An inactive substance given in the place of a drug in psychological research or by physicians who wish to treat a complaint by suggestion.

Placebo effect Changes in behavior due to expectations that a drug (or other treatment) will have some effect.

Single-blind experiment An arrangement in which subjects remain unaware of whether they are in the experimental group or the control group.

Double-blind experiment An arrangement in which both subjects and experimenters are unaware of whether subjects are in the experimental group or the control group.

FOCUS ON RESEARCH

Abducted by Space Aliens?

In upcoming chapters you will find other "Focus on Research" boxes like this one. These boxes will help you reflect on the role of research methods in psychology.

Because the placebo effect is based, in part, on suggestion, it is tempting to conclude that placebos have no value. You might even think it is wrong for doctors to deliberately use placebos to "fool" their patients (Moerman, 2002). But some research methods suggest otherwise. For example, in one study patients recovering from surgery were given morphine. Some patients knew they were getting the morphine because they watched a doctor give them an injection. Patients in another group received the same dose of morphine, but they didn't know they were getting it. (The drug was given through an infusion machine to which the patients were already connected.) Thus, the experimental group received a visible medical treatment and the control group got a concealed medical treatment (Benedetti, Maggi, & Lopiano, 2003).

What were the results? Patients who knew they were getting morphine experienced more pain relief than patients who didn't know they'd been given a painkiller. One way to interpret this result is that a placebo effect is *always* present when medicines are administered. This suggests that doctors should administer medicine as openly as possible. That way, patients benefit from the medicine *and* the placebo effect. In other words, medicine works best when doctors help people *make sense* of their medical condition, to maximize healing (Moerman, 2002).

Prozac, is due to the placebo effect (Kirsch & Sapirstein, 1998). Much of the popularity of herbal health remedies is also based on the placebo effect (Seidman, 2001). (See "Investigating the Placebo Effect" for more information about how psychologists study placebos.)

Esbin-Anderson/The Image Works

The placebo effect is a major factor in medical treatments. Would you also expect the placebo effect to occur in psychotherapy? (It does, which complicates studies on the effectiveness of new psychotherapies.)

Sometimes researchers themselves affect experiments by influencing the behavior of their subjects. Let's see how this occurs.

The Experimenter Effect

How could a researcher influence subjects? The **experimenter effect** (changes in behavior caused by the unintended influence of an experimenter) is a common problem. In essence, experimenters run the risk of finding what they expect to find. This occurs because humans are very sensitive to hints about what is expected of them (Rosenthal, 1994).

The experimenter effect even applies outside the laboratory. Psychologist Robert Rosenthal (1973) reports an example of how expectations influence people: At the U.S. Air Force Academy Preparatory School, 100 airmen were randomly assigned to five different math classes. Their teachers did not know about this random placement. Instead, each teacher was told that his or her students had unusually high or low ability. Students in the classes labeled "high ability" improved much more in math scores than those in "low-ability" classes. Yet, initially, all of the classes had students of equal ability.

Apparently, the teachers subtly communicated their expectations to students. Most likely, they did this through tone of voice, body language, and by giving encouragement or criticism. Their "hints," in turn, created a self-fulfilling prophecy that affected the students. A *self-fulfilling prophecy* is a prediction that prompts people to act in ways that make the prediction come true. For instance, many teachers underestimate the abilities of ethnic minority children, which hurts the students' chances for success (Weinstein, Gregory, & Strambler, 2004). In short, people sometimes become what we prophesy for them. It is wise to remember that others tend to live *up* or *down* to our expectations for them (Madon, Jussim, & Eccles, 1997; Madon et al., 2001).

KNOWLEDGE BUILDER

The Psychology Experiment

REFLECT

In a sense, we all conduct little experiments to detect cause-and-effect connections. If you are interested in gardening, for example, you might try adding plant food to one bed of flowers but not another. The question then becomes, "Does the use of plant food (the independent variable) affect the size of the flowers (the dependent variable)?" By comparing unfed plants (the control group) with those receiving plant food (the experimental group) you could find out if plant food is worth using. Can you think of at least one informal experiment you've run in the last month? What were the variables? What was the outcome?

LEARNING CHECK

1. To understand cause and effect, a simple psychological experiment is based on creating two groups: the ______________ group and the ______________ group.
2. There are three types of variables to consider in an experiment: ______________ variables (which are manipulated by the experimenter); ______________ variables (which measure the outcome of the experiment); and ______________ variables (factors to be excluded in a particular experiment).
3. A researcher performs an experiment to learn if room temperature affects the amount of aggression displayed by college students under crowded conditions in a simulated prison environment. In this experiment, the independent variable is which of the following?
   a. room temperature
   b. the amount of aggression
   c. crowding
   d. the simulated prison environment
4. A procedure used to control both the placebo effect and the experimenter effect in drug experiments is the
   a. correlation method
   b. extraneous prophecy
   c. double-blind technique
   d. random assignment of subjects

CRITICAL THINKING

5. There is a loophole in the statement, "I've been taking vitamin C tablets, and I haven't had a cold all year. Vitamin C is great!" What is the loophole?
6. How would you determine if sugary breakfasts affect children's activity levels and their ability to learn in school?
7. People who believe strongly in astrology have personality characteristics that actually match, to a degree, those predicted by their astrological signs. Can you explain why this occurs?

Answers: 1. experimental, control **2.** independent, dependent, extraneous **3.** a **4.** c **5.** The statement implies that vitamin C prevented colds. However, not getting a cold could just be a coincidence. A controlled experiment with a group given vitamin C and a control group not taking vitamin C would be needed to learn if vitamin C actually has any effect on susceptibility to colds. **6.** An actual experiment on this question used a double-blind design in which children were given a breakfast drink containing either 50 grams of sucrose (sugar), a placebo (aspartame), or only a very small amount of sucrose. Observed changes in activity levels and in scores on a learning task did not support the view that sugar causes major changes in children's behavior (Rosen et al., 1988). **7.** Belief in astrology can create a self-fulfilling prophecy in which people alter their behaviors and self-concepts to match their astrological signs (van Rooij, 1994).

The Clinical Method—Data by the Case

It can be difficult or impossible to use the experimental method to study mental disorders, such as depression or psychosis. Many experiments are impractical, unethical, or impossible to do. In such instances, a **case study** (an in-depth focus on a single subject) may be the best source of information. Clinical psychologists rely heavily on case studies, especially as a way to investigate rare or unusual problems.

Case studies may sometimes be thought of as **natural clinical tests** (accidents or other natural events that provide psychological data). Gunshot wounds, brain tumors, accidental poisonings, and similar disasters have provided much information about the human brain. One remarkable case from the history of psychology is reported by Dr. J. M. Harlow (1868). Phineas Gage, a young foreman on a work crew, had a 13-pound steel rod blown through the front of his brain by a dynamite explosion (● Figure 1.13). Amazingly, he survived the accident. Within 2 months Gage could walk, talk, and move normally, but the injury forever changed his personality. Instead of the honest and dependable worker he had been before, Gage became a surly, foul-mouthed liar. Dr. Harlow carefully recorded all details of what was perhaps the first in-depth case study of an accidental frontal lobotomy (the destruction of front brain matter).

When a Los Angeles carpenter named Michael Melnick suffered a similar injury, he recovered completely, with no lasting ill effects. Melnick's very different reaction to a similar injury shows why psychologists prefer controlled experiments and often use lab animals for studies of the brain. Case studies lack formal control groups, which limits the conclusions that can be drawn. Nonetheless, case studies are especially valuable for studying rare events, such as unusual mental disorders, childhood "geniuses," or "rampage" school shootings (Harding, Fox, & Mehta, 2002). Also, case studies of psychotherapy have provided many useful ideas about how to treat emotional problems (Hersen, 2002).

Case studies can provide special opportunities to answer interesting questions. For instance, a classic case study in psychology concerns four identical quadruplets, known as the Genain sisters. In addition to having identical genes, all four women became schizophrenic before age 25 (Rosenthal & Quinn, 1977). The Genains, who are now in their late sixties, have been in and out of mental hospitals all their lives. The fact that they share identical genes suggests that mental disorders are influenced by heredity. The fact that some of the sisters are more disturbed than others suggests that environmental conditions also affect mental illness.

Experimenter effect Changes in subjects' behavior caused by the unintended influence of an experimenter's actions.

Case study An in-depth focus on all aspects of a single person.

Natural clinical test An accident or other natural event that allows the gathering of data on a psychological phenomenon of interest.

Indeed, Myra, the least ill of the four, was the only sister who was able to avoid her father, an alcoholic who terrorized, spied on, and sexually molested the girls. (See Chapter 13 for more information about the causes of schizophrenia.)

The Genain sisters have been studied for 40 years. The chances of four identical quads all becoming schizophrenic are about one in 1.5 billion. Thus, cases like theirs provide insights that can't be obtained by any other means (Edwards, 1998; Mirsky et al., 2000).

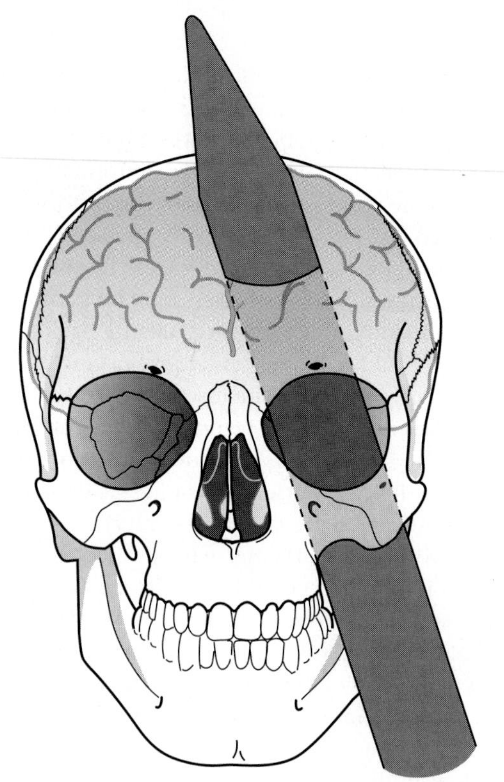

● **Figure 1.13** Some of the earliest information on the effects of damage to frontal areas of the brain came from a case study of the accidental injury of Phineas Gage.

Survey Method—Here, Have a Sample

Sometimes psychologists would like to ask everyone in the world a few well-chosen questions: "Do you drink alcoholic beverages? How often per week?" "What form of discipline did your parents use when you were a child?" "What is the most creative thing you've done?" The answers to such questions can reveal much about people's behavior, but because it is impossible to question everyone, doing a survey is often more practical.

In the **survey method**, public polling techniques are used to answer psychological questions (Tourangeau, 2004). Typically, people in a representative sample are asked a series of carefully worded questions. A **representative sample** is a small group that accurately reflects a larger population. A good sample must include the same proportion of men, women, young, old, professionals, blue-collar workers, Republicans, Democrats, whites, African Americans, Latinos, Asians, and so on as found in the population as a whole. In contrast, a **biased sample** does not accurately reflect characteristics of the whole population.

Pretesting of survey questions can usually remove those that are bad, confusing, or easily misunderstood. Also, new computerized surveys can ask a different series of questions, depending on the answers to the first few items. This helps avoid asking unnecessary questions and it brings a person's responses into sharper focus (Krosnick, 1999).

A **population** is an entire group of animals or people belonging to a particular category (for example, all college students or all married women). Ultimately, we are interested in entire populations, but by selecting a smaller sample we can draw conclusions about the larger group without polling each and every person. Representative samples are often obtained by *randomly* selecting who will be included (● Figure 1.14). (Notice that this is similar to randomly assigning subjects to groups in an experiment.)

In recent years, 93 percent of human subjects in psychology experiments have been recruited from introductory psychology courses (Sieber & Saks, 1989). The majority of these subjects have

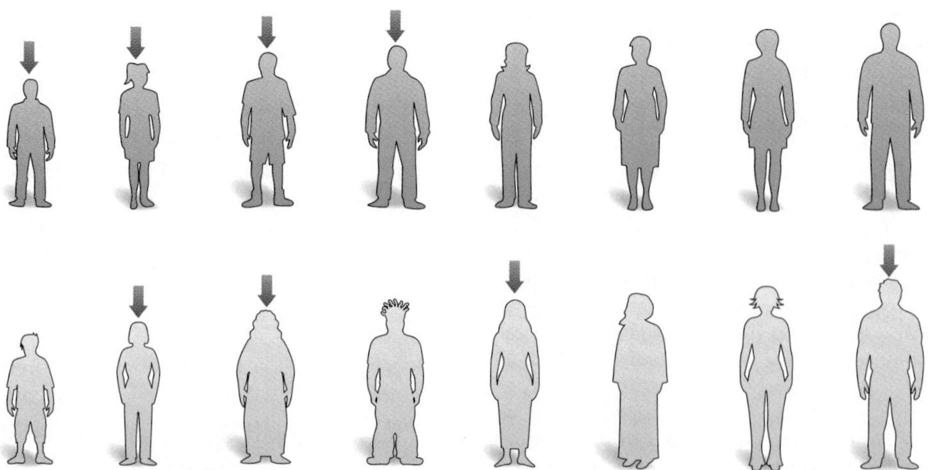

● **Figure 1.14** If you were conducting a survey in which a person's height might be an important variable, the upper, nonrandom sample would be very unrepresentative. The lower sample, selected using a table of random numbers, better represents the group as a whole.

Is There a Gender Bias in Psychological Research?

As you read through this book you may find yourself wondering whether or not a particular concept, theory, or research finding applies equally well to women and men, to members of various races or ethnic groups, or to people of different ages or sexual orientations. "Human Diversity" boxes like this one will help you be more reflective about our multicultural, multifaceted society. Here, let's begin with a basic question: Is there is a gender bias in the research process itself?

Many doctors continue to recommend that adults take an aspirin a day to help prevent a heart attack. Both men and women are given this advice. The problem? Not a single woman was included in the sample on which the advice is based. Although females make up more than half the population, they continue to be neglected in psychological and medical research (Hyde, 2004).

This oversight is just one form of **gender bias in research.** This term refers to the tendency for females to be underrepresented as research subjects and female topics to be ignored by many investigators. Consequently, the investigators assumed that conclusions based on men also apply to women. But without directly studying women it is impossible to know how often this assumption is wrong. A related problem occurs when researchers combine results from men and women. Doing so can hide important male–female differences. An additional problem is that unequal numbers of men and women may volunteer for some kinds of research. For example, in studies of sexuality, more male college students volunteer to participate than females (Wiederman, 1999). What a surprise!

Another form of gender bias in research occurs when women are underrepresented among the researchers themselves. In one example, Laurence Kohlberg (1969) proposed a theory about how we develop moral values. His studies suggested that women were morally "immature" because they were not as concerned with justice as men were. However, few women were involved in doing the studies and the researchers merely *assumed* that theories based on men also apply to women. In response, Carol Gilligan (1982) provided evidence that women were more likely to make moral choices based on caring, rather than justice. From this point of view, it was men who were morally immature. Today, we recognize that both justice and caring perspectives may be essential to adult wisdom (see Chapter 4 for more details).

Similar biases exist concerning the race, ethnicity, age, and sexual orientation of researchers and participants in psychological research (Denmark, Rabinowitz, & Sechzer, 2005; Guthrie, 2004). Far too many conclusions are created by and/or based on small groups of people who do not represent the rich tapestry of humanity. However, the solution to such problems is straightforward: We need to encourage a wider array of people to become researchers and, when possible, researchers need to include a wider array of people in their studies. In recognition of human diversity, many researchers are doing just that (Reid, 2002).

been white members of the middle class and most of the researchers themselves have been white males (Guthrie, 2004). None of this automatically invalidates the results of psychology experiments. However, it may place some limitations on their meanings. (See "Is There a Gender Bias in Psychological Research?") The distinguished psychologist Edward Tolman once noted that much of psychology is based on two sets of subjects: rats and college sophomores. Tolman urged scientists to remember that rats are certainly not people and that college sophomores may not be!

Internet Surveys

Recently, psychologists have started doing surveys and experiments on the Internet. Web-based research has the advantage of low cost and it can reach very large groups of people. Internet studies have provided interesting information about topics such as anger, decision making, racial prejudice, what disgusts people, religion, sexual attitudes, and much more. Biased samples can limit web-based research, but psychologists are finding ways to gather valid information with it (Birnbaum, 2004; Gosling et al., 2004).

Social Desirability

Even well-designed surveys may be limited by another problem. If a psychologist were to ask you detailed questions about your sexual history and current sexual behavior, how accurate would your replies be? Would you exaggerate? Would you be embarrassed? Replies to survey questions are not always accurate or

Survey method The use of public polling techniques to answer psychological questions.

Representative sample A small, randomly selected part of a larger population that accurately reflects characteristics of the whole population.

Biased sample A subpart of a larger population that does not accurately reflect characteristics of the whole population.

Population An entire group of animals or people belonging to a particular category (for example, all college students or all married women).

Gender bias (in research) A tendency for females and female issues to be underrepresented in research, psychological or otherwise.

truthful. Many people show a distinct *courtesy bias* (a tendency to give "polite" or socially desirable answers). For example, answers to questions concerning sex, drinking or drug use, income, and church attendance tend to be less than truthful. Likewise, the week after an election more people will say they voted than actually did (Krosnick, 1999).

Summary

Despite their limitations, surveys frequently produce valuable information. For instance, the survey method was used to find out how often sexual harassment occurs and to raise public awareness about the problem (Janus & Janus, 1993). To sum up, the survey method can be a powerful research tool. Like other methods, it has limitations, but new techniques and strategies are providing valuable information about our behavior (Tourangeau, 2004).

Is so much emphasis on science really necessary in psychology? In a word, yes. As we have seen, science is a powerful way of asking questions about the world and getting trustworthy answers. (■ Table 1.5 summarizes many of the important ideas we have covered.)

Critical Thinking Revisited—Evaluating Claims and Evidence

Even if you never do any research of you own, you can benefit from the efforts of others. Many beliefs about human behavior can be evaluated by applying critical thinking to published evidence. For example, here's a typical scene: An anxious mother watches her son eat a candy bar and says, "Watch, it's like lighting a fuse on a skyrocket. He'll be bouncing off the walls in a few minutes." Is she right? Will a "sugar buzz" make her son "hyper"? How would you evaluate the claim that sugar adversely affects behavior? Here are some basic steps.

1. *State the claim clearly. What are its implications?* It's important to spell out what you would expect to see if the claim is true.
2. *Gather evidence.* Look for evidence both for and against the claim. Evidence may come from many sources, such as casual observations, opinions of authorities, published studies, or direct scientific observation.
3. *Evaluate the evidence.* Is the evidence consistent with the claim? If the information is conflicting, what conclusion does the strongest evidence support? (In general, scientific observations provide the highest-quality evidence.)
4. *Draw a conclusion.* If you have carefully evaluated the arguments and evidence bearing on a claim, you should have little trouble drawing a valid conclusion.

A Case Study of Critical Thinking

To see how the preceding steps apply, let's return to the question about sugar. What we want to know is this: Does eating excessive amounts of sugar adversely affect children's behavior? What are the implications of this claim? If it is true, children who eat sugar should display measurable changes in behavior.

Anecdotal Evidence

What evidence is there to support the claim? It should be easy to find parents who will attest that their children become high-strung after eating sugar. However, parents are not likely to be objective observers. Beliefs about "sugar highs" are common and could easily color parents' views.

Casual Observation

Perhaps it would help to observe children directly. Let's say you decide to watch children at a birthday party, where you know they will eat a lot of sugary foods. As predicted by the claim, children at the party become loud and boisterous after eating cake, ice cream,

TABLE 1.5

Comparison of Psychological Research Methods

	ADVANTAGES	DISADVANTAGES
Naturalistic Observation	Behavior is observed in a natural setting; much information is obtained, and hypotheses and questions for additional research are formed	Little or no control is possible; observed behavior may be altered by the presence of the observer; observations may be biased; causes cannot be conclusively identified
Correlational Method	Demonstrates the existence of relationships; allows prediction; can be used in lab, clinic, or natural setting	Little or no control is possible; relationships may be coincidental; cause-and-effect relationships cannot be confirmed
Experimental Method	Clear cause-and-effect relationships can be identified; powerful controlled observations can be staged; no need to wait for natural event	May be somewhat artificial; some natural behavior not easily studied in laboratory (field experiments may avoid these objections)
Clinical Method	Takes advantage of "natural clinical trials" and allows investigation of rare or unusual problems or events	Little or no control is possible; does not provide a control group for comparison, subjective interpretation is often necessary, a single case may be misleading or unrepresentative
Survey Method	Allows information about large numbers of people to be gathered; can address questions not answered by other approaches	Obtaining a representative sample is critical and can be difficult to do; answers may be inaccurate; people may not do what they say or say what they do

and candy. How persuasive is this evidence? Actually, it is seriously flawed. Birthday parties expose children to bright lights, loud noises, and unfamiliar situations. Any of these conditions, and others as well, could easily explain the children's "hyper" activity.

Authority

For nearly 50 years many doctors, teachers, nutritionists, and other "experts" have emphatically stated that sugar causes childhood misbehavior. Should you believe them? Unfortunately, most of these "expert" opinions are based on anecdotes and casual observations that are little better than those we have already reviewed.

Formal Evidence

The truth is, parents, casual observers, and many authorities have been wrong. Dr. Mark Wolraich and his colleagues reviewed 23 scientific studies on sugar and children. In each study, children consumed known amounts of sugar and were then observed or tested. The clear-cut conclusion in all of the studies was that sugar does not affect aggression, mood, motor skills, or cognitive skills (Wolraich, Wilson, & White, 1995).

Studies like those we just reviewed tend to be convincing because they are based on systematic, controlled observation. To evaluate psychological questions, you will often have to rely on similar published evidence. But don't just accept the study's conclusions. It is important to review the evidence yourself and decide if it is convincing. Our next topic illustrates the pitfalls of failing to scientifically test ideas.

Pseudo-Psychologies—Palms, Planets, and Personality

For an interesting contrast, let's see how some false beliefs compare with real psychology. A **pseudo-psychology** (SUE-doe-psychology) is any unfounded system that resembles psychology. (*Pseudo* means "false.") Pseudo-psychologies change little over time because their followers avoid evidence that contradicts their beliefs (Kelly & Saklofske, 1994). Scientists, in contrast, actively look for contradictions as a way to advance knowledge. They skeptically evaluate and critique their own theories (Woodward & Goodstein, 1996).

Would you hire this man? Here's a sample of your author's handwriting. What do you think it reveals? Your interpretations are likely to be as accurate (or inaccurate) as those of a graphologist.

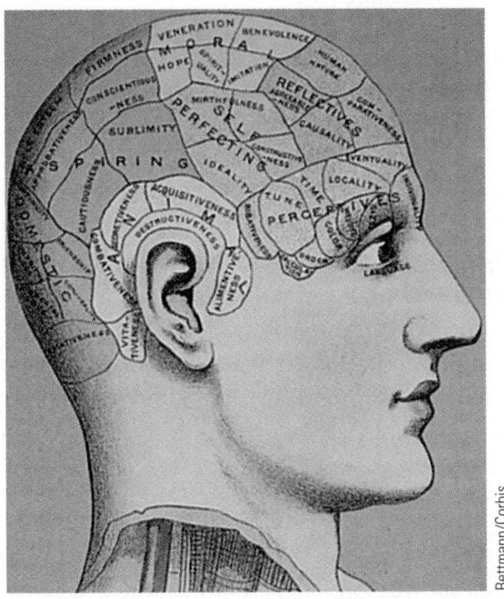

Bettmann/Corbis

Phrenology was an attempt to assess personality characteristics by examining various areas of the skull. Phrenologists used charts such as the one shown here as guides. Like other pseudo-psychologists, phrenologists made no attempt to empirically verify their concepts.

Unlike the real thing, pseudo-psychologies are not based on scientific testing. For instance, *palmistry* is a false system that claims lines on the hand reveal personality and predict the future. Despite the overwhelming evidence against this, palmists can still be found separating the gullible from their money in many cities. A similar false system is *phrenology,* which claims that personality traits are revealed by the shape of the skull. Phrenology was popularized in the nineteenth century by Franz Gall, a German anatomy teacher. Modern research has long since shown that bumps on the head have nothing to do with talents or abilities. In fact, the phrenologists were so far off that they listed the part of the brain that controls hearing as a center for "combativeness"!

At first glance, a pseudo-psychology called *graphology* might seem more reasonable. Graphologists claim that personality traits are revealed by handwriting. Based on such claims, some companies use graphologists to select job candidates. This is troubling because graphologists score close to zero on tests of accuracy in rating personality (Ben-Shakhar et al., 1986). In fact, graphologists do no better than untrained college students in rating personality and job performance (Neter & Ben-Shakhar, 1989; Rafaeli & Klimoski, 1983). Even a graphological society recently concluded that handwriting analysis should not be used to select people for jobs (Simner & Goffin, 2003). (By the way, graphology's failure at revealing personality should be separated from its value for detecting forgeries.)

Pseudo-psychology Any false and unscientific system of beliefs and practices that is offered as an explanation of behavior.

Graphology might seem harmless enough. However, this false system has been used to determine who is hired, given bank credit, or selected for juries. In these and similar situations, pseudo-psychologies do, in fact, harm people (Barker, 1993).

If pseudo-psychologies have no scientific basis, how do they survive and why are they popular? There are several reasons, all of which can be demonstrated by a critique of astrology. Astrology is probably the most popular pseudo-psychology. Astrology holds that the positions of the stars and planets at the time of one's birth determine personality traits and affect behavior. Like other pseudo-psychologies, astrology has repeatedly been shown to have no scientific validity (Kelly, 1998, 1999; Stewart, 1996). The objections to astrology are numerous and devastating:

1. The zodiac has shifted in the sky by one full constellation since astrology was first set up. However, most astrologers simply ignore this shift. (In other words, if astrology calls you a Scorpio you are really a Libra, and so forth.)
2. There is no connection between the "compatibility" of couples' astrological signs and their marriage and divorce rates.
3. Studies have found no connection between astrological signs and leadership, physical characteristics, career choices, or personality traits.
4. Astrologers have failed to explain why the moment of birth should be more important than the moment of conception.
5. A study of more than 3,000 predictions by famous astrologers found that only a small percentage were fulfilled. These "successful" predictions tended to be vague ("There will be a tragedy somewhere in the east in the spring") or easily guessed from current events.
6. If astrologers are asked to match people with their horoscopes, they do no better than would be expected by chance (Kelly, 1999).
7. A few astrologers have tried to test astrology. Their results have been just as negative as those obtained by critics (Kelly, 1998, 1999; Martens & Trachet, 1998; Stewart, 1996).

In short, astrology doesn't work.

Then why does astrology often seem to work? The following discussion tells why.

Uncritical Acceptance

If you have ever had your astrological chart done, you may have been impressed with its apparent accuracy. However, such perceptions are typically based on **uncritical acceptance** (the tendency to believe positive or flattering descriptions of yourself). Many astrological charts are made up of mostly flattering traits. Naturally, when your personality is described in *desirable* terms, it is hard to deny that the description has the "ring of truth." How much acceptance would astrology receive if a birth sign read like this:

> Virgo: You are the logical type and hate disorder. Your nitpicking is unbearable to your friends. You are cold, unemotional, and usually fall asleep while making love. Virgos make good doorstops.

Positive Instances

Even when an astrological description contains a mixture of good and bad traits it may seem accurate. To find out why, read the following personality description.

> **Your Personality Profile**
>
> You have a strong need for other people to like you and for them to admire you. You have a tendency to be critical of yourself. You have a great deal of unused energy which you have not turned to your advantage. While you have some personality weaknesses, you are generally able to compensate for them. Your sexual adjustment has presented some problems for you. Disciplined and controlled on the outside, you tend to be worrisome and insecure inside. At times you have serious doubts as to whether you have made the right decision or done the right thing. You prefer a certain amount of change and variety and become dissatisfied when hemmed in by restrictions and limitations. You pride yourself on being an independent thinker and do not accept other opinions without satisfactory proof. You have found it unwise to be too frank in revealing yourself to others. At times you are extroverted, affable, sociable, while at other times you are introverted, wary, and reserved. Some of your aspirations tend to be pretty unrealistic.*

Does this describe your personality? A psychologist read this summary individually to college students who had taken a personality test. Only 5 students out of 79 thought that the description was inaccurate. Another study found that people rated this "personality profile" as more accurate than their actual horoscopes (French et al., 1991).

Reread the description and you will see that it contains both sides of several personality dimensions ("At times you are extroverted . . . while at other times you are introverted"). Its apparent accuracy is an illusion based on the **fallacy of positive instances**, in which we remember or notice things that confirm our expectations and forget the rest. The pseudo-psychologies thrive on this effect. For example, you can always find "Leo characteristics" in a Leo. If you looked, however, you could also find "Gemini characteristics," "Scorpio characteristics," or whatever.

The fallacy of positive instances is used by various "psychic mediums" who pretend to communicate with the deceased friends and relatives of audience members. An analysis of their performances shows that the number of "hits" (correct statements) made by these fakes tends to be very low. Nevertheless, many viewers are impressed because of the natural tendency to remember apparent hits and ignore misses. Also, embarrassing misses are edited out before the shows appear on television (Nickell, 2001).

The Barnum Effect

Pseudo-psychologies also take advantage of the **Barnum effect**, which is a tendency to consider personal descriptions accurate if they are stated in general terms. P. T. Barnum, the famed circus

*Reprinted with permission of author and publisher from R. E. Ulrich, T. J. Stachnik, and N. R. Stainton, "Student acceptance of generalized personality interpretations," *Psychological Reports,* 13, 1963, 831–834.

Non Sequitur

Non Sequitur, © 1993. Reprinted by permission of Universal Press Syndicate.

showman, had a formula for success: "Always have a little something for everybody." Like the all-purpose personality profile, palm readings, fortunes, horoscopes, and other products of pseudo-psychology are stated in such general terms that they can hardly miss. There is always "a little something for everybody." To observe the Barnum effect, read *all 12* of the daily horoscopes found in newspapers for several days. You will find that predictions for other signs fit events as well as those for your own sign do.

Pseudo-psychologies may seem like no more than a nuisance, but they can do harm. For instance, people seeking treatment for psychological disorders may become the victims of self-appointed "experts" who offer ineffective, pseudo-scientific "therapies" (Kalal, 1999). Valid psychological principles are based on observation and evidence, not fads, opinions, or wishful thinking.

Summary: Science and Critical Thinking

Most of us would be skeptical when buying a used car. But all too often we may be tempted to "buy" outrageous claims about topics such as the occult, the Bermuda Triangle, UFOs, herbal "cures," Tarot cards, healing crystals, "miraculous" therapies, and so forth. To put the principles of science and critical thinking into action, here are some questions to ask over and over again as you evaluate new information (Bartz, 1990):

1. What claims are being made?
2. What test (if any) of these claims has been made?
3. Who did the test? How good is the evidence?
4. What was the nature and quality of the tests? Are they credible? Can they be repeated?
5. How reliable and trustworthy were the investigators? Do they have conflicts of interest? Do their findings appear to be objective? Has any other independent researcher duplicated the findings?
6. Finally, how much credibility can the claim be given? High, medium, low, provisional?

A Look Ahead

To help you get the most out of psychology, each chapter of this text includes a "Psychology in Action" section like the one that follows. There you will find ideas you can actually use, now or in the future. To complete our discussion, let's take a critical look at information reported in the popular press. You should find this an interesting way to conclude our first tour of psychology and its methods.

KNOWLEDGE BUILDER

Cases Studies, the Survey Method, and Critical Thinking

REFLECT

If you were going to do a case study of a celebrity or other public feature, who would you choose? What aspect of the person's behavior would you investigate?

Have you ever known someone who suffered a brain injury or disease? How did his or her behavior change? Was the change clear-cut enough to serve as a natural clinical test?

If you could ask only three questions in a psychological survey, what would they be? What population would you be interested in studying? How would you obtain a valid sample? Is it likely that any of your questions would be affected by a courtesy bias?

It is nearly impossible to get through a day without encountering people who believe in pseudo-psychologies or who make unscientific or unfounded statements. How stringently do you evaluate your own beliefs and the claims made by others?

LEARNING CHECK

1. Case studies can often be thought of as natural tests and are frequently used by clinical psychologists. T or F?
2. For the survey method to be valid, a representative sample of people must be polled. T or F?
3. The phenomenon of multiple personality would most likely be investigated by use of
   a. a representative sample
   b. a correlational experiment
   c. the double-blind procedure
   d. case studies
4. A problem with the survey method is that answers to questions may not always be ________________ or ________________.
5. People who abuse certain "designer drugs" develop neurological symptoms similar to Parkinson's disease. Studying damage to the brains of these people would provide a ________________ test of theories about the causes of Parkinson's.

Uncritical acceptance The tendency to believe generally positive or flattering descriptions of oneself.

Fallacy of positive instances The tendency to remember or notice information that fits one's expectations while forgetting discrepancies.

Barnum effect The tendency to consider a personal description accurate if it is stated in very general terms.

6. The fallacy of positive instances refers to graphology's accepted value for the detection of forgeries. T or F?
7. Personality descriptions provided by pseudo-psychologies are stated in general terms, which provide "a little something for everybody." This fact is the basis of the
   a. palmist's fallacy
   b. uncritical acceptance pattern
   c. fallacy of positive instances
   d. Barnum effect

CRITICAL THINKING

8. A psychologist conducting a survey at a shopping mall (The Gallery of Wretched Excess) flips a coin before stopping passersby. If the coin shows heads, he interviews the person; if it shows tails, he skips that person. Has the psychologist obtained a random sample?
9. Each New Year's Day, phony "psychics" make predictions about events that will occur during the coming year. The vast majority of these predictions are wrong, but the practice continues each year. Can you explain why?

Answers: 1. T **2.** T **3.** d **4.** accurate, truthful **5.** natural clinical **6.** F **7.** d **8.** The psychologist's coin flips *might* produce a reasonably good sample of people *at the mall*. The real problem is that people who go to the mall may be mostly from one part of town, from upper income groups, or from some other nonrepresentative group. The psychologist's sample is likely to be seriously flawed. **9.** Because of the fallacy of positive instances, people only remember predictions that seemed to come true and forget all of the errors. Incidentally, "predictions" that appear to be accurate are usually easily deduced from current events or are stated in very general terms to take advantage of the Barnum effect.

PSYCHOLOGY IN ACTION

Psychology in the News—Separating Fact from Fiction

Psychology is a popular topic in magazines and newspapers. Unfortunately, much of what you will read is based on wishful thinking rather than science. Here are some suggestions for separating high-quality information from misleading fiction.

Suggestion 1: Be skeptical. Reports in the popular press tend to be made uncritically and with a definite bias toward reporting "astonishing" findings. Remember, saying, "That's incredible" means, "That's not believable"—which is often true.

Example 1: Some years ago, news articles described an amazing new "sixth sense" called "dermo-optical perception." A few gifted people, the articles claimed, could use their fingertips to identify colors and read print while blindfolded.

In reality, such "abilities" are based on what stage magicians call a "nose peek." It is impossible to prepare a blindfold (without damaging the eyes) that does not leave a tiny space on each side of the nose. Were the people who claimed to have "X-ray eyes" taking nose peeks? Apparently they were, because "dermo-optical abilities" disappeared as soon as the opportunity to peek was controlled.

Example 2: The *National Enquirer* once reported that "Top University Researchers Reveal . . . 8 million Americans may have been abducted by UFOs." However, one of the researchers cited in the article actually concluded, "The public can rest assured that there is no evidence that millions of Americans are being abducted." In other words, the *Enquirer* story completely *reversed* the real findings. You'll find similar misinformation and sensationalism throughout the popular media. Be on guard.

Example 3: The Internet is awash with rumors, hoaxes, half-truths, and urban legends. One recent classic was a story about the health department in Oregon seeking a Klingon interpreter for mental health patients who only speak in the fictional language used on the *Star Trek* TV series.

This tale started when a newspaper reported that Klingon was on a list of languages that some psychiatric patients claimed they could speak. The article specifically noted that "in reality, no patient has yet tried to communicate in Klingon." Nevertheless, as the story spread around the web, the idea that Oregon was looking for someone fluent in Klingon had become a "fact" (O'Neill, 2003).

Suggestion 2: Consider the source of information. It should come as no surprise that information used to sell a product often reflects a desire for profit rather than the objective truth. Here is a typical advertising claim: "Government tests prove that no pain reliever is stronger or more effective than Brand X aspirin." A statement like this usually means that there was *no difference* between the products tested. No other pain reliever was stronger or more effective—but none was weaker either.

Keep the source in mind when reading the claims of makers of home biofeedback machines, sleep-learning devices, subliminal tapes, and the like. Remember that psychological services may be merchandised as well. Be wary of expensive courses that promise instant mental health and happiness, increased efficiency, memory, ESP or psychic ability, control of the unconscious mind, an end to smoking, and so on. Usually they are promoted with a few testimonials and many unsupported claims (Lilienfeld, 2005).

Psychic claims should be viewed with special caution. Stage mentalists make a living by deceiving the public. Understandably, they are highly interested in promoting belief in their nonexistent powers. Psychic phenomena, when (and if) they do occur, are quite unpredictable. It would be impossible for a mentalist to do three shows a night, six nights a week, without consistently using deception. The same is true of the so-called psychic advisors promoted in TV commercials. These charlatans make use of the Barnum effect to create an illusion that they know private information about the people who call them (Nickell, 2001).

Suggestion 3: Ask yourself if there was a control group. The key importance of a control group in any experiment is often overlooked by the unsophisticated—an error to which you are no longer susceptible. The popular press is full of reports of "experiments" performed without control groups: "Talking to Plants Speeds Growth"; "Special Diet Controls Hyperactivity in Children"; "Food Shows Less Spoilage in Pyramid Chamber"; "Graduates of Firewalking Seminar Risk Their Soles."

Consider the last example for a moment. In recent years, expensive commercial courses have been promoted to teach people to walk barefoot on hot coals. (Why anyone would want to do this is itself an interesting question.) Firewalkers supposedly protect their feet with a technique called "neurolinguistic programming." Many people have paid good money to learn the technique, and most do manage a quick walk on the coals. But is the technique necessary? And is anything remarkable happening? We need a comparison group.

Fortunately, physicist Bernard Leikind has provided one. Leikind showed with volunteers that anyone (with reasonably callused feet) can walk over a bed of coals without being burned. The reason is that the coals, which are light, fluffy carbon, transmit little heat when touched. The principle involved is similar to briefly putting your hand in a hot oven. If you touch a pan, you will be burned because metal transfers heat efficiently. But if your hand stays in the heated air you'll be fine because air transmits little heat (Mitchell, 1987). Mystery solved.

Suggestion 4: Look for errors in distinguishing between correlation and causation. As you now know, it is dangerous to presume that one thing *caused* another just because they are correlated. In spite of this, you will see many claims based on questionable correlations. Here's an example of mistaking correlation for causation: Jeanne Dixon, an astrologer, once answered a group of prominent scientists—who had declared that there is no scientific foundation for astrology—by saying, "They would do well to check the records at their local police stations, where they will learn that the rate of violent crime rises and falls with lunar cycles." Dixon, of course, believes that the moon affects human behavior.

If it is true that violent crime is more frequent at certain times of the month, doesn't that prove her point? Far from it. Increased crime could be due to darker nights, the fact that many people expect others to act crazier, or any number of similar factors. More important, direct studies of the alleged "lunar effect" have shown that it doesn't occur (Simon, 1998; Wilkinson et al., 1997). Moonstruck criminals, along with "moon madness," are a fiction (Raison, Klein, & Steckler, 1999).

Suggestion 5: Be sure to distinguish between observation and inference. If you see a person *crying,* is it correct to assume that she or he is *sad?* Although it seems reasonable to make this assumption, it is actually quite risky. We can observe objectively that the person is crying, but to *infer* sadness may be in error. It could be that the individual has just peeled 5 pounds of onions. Or maybe he or she just won a million-dollar lottery or is trying contact lenses for the first time.

Psychologists, politicians, physicians, scientists, and other experts often go far beyond the available facts in their claims. This does not mean that their inferences, opinions, and interpretations have no value; the opinion of an expert on the causes of mental illness, criminal behavior, learning problems, or whatever can be revealing. But be careful to distinguish between fact and opinion.

Suggestion 6: Beware of oversimplifications, especially those motivated by monetary gain. Courses or programs that offer a "new personality in three sessions," "six steps to love and fulfillment in marriage," or newly discovered "secrets of unlocking the

John Nordell/The Image Works

Firewalking is based on simple physics, not on any form of supernatural psychological control. The temperature of the coals may be as high as 1,200°F. However, coals are like the air in a hot oven: They are very inefficient at transferring heat during brief contact.

powers of the mind" should be immediately suspect.

An excellent example of oversimplification is provided by a brochure entitled, "Dr. Joyce Brothers Asks: How Do You Rate as a 'Superwoman'?" Dr. Brothers, a "media" psychologist who has no private practice and is not known for research, wrote the brochure as a consultant for the Aerosol Packaging Council of the Chemical Specialties Manufacturers Association. A typical suggestion in this brochure tells how to enhance a marriage: "Sweep him off to a weekend hideaway. Tip: When he's not looking spray a touch of your favorite *aerosol* cologne mist on the bed sheets and pillows" (italics added). Sure, Joyce.

Suggestion 7: Remember, "for example" is not proof. After reading this chapter you should be sensitive to the danger of selecting single examples. If you read, "Law student passes state bar exam using sleep-learning device," don't rush out to buy one. Systematic research has shown that these devices are of little or no value (Druckman & Bjork, 1994; Wood et al., 1992). A corollary to this suggestion is to ask, "Are the reported observations important or widely applicable?"

Examples, anecdotes, single cases, and testimonials are all potentially deceptive. Unfortunately, *individual cases* tell nothing about what is true *in general* (Stanovich, 2004). For instance, studies of large groups of people show that smoking increases the likelihood of lung cancer. It doesn't matter if you know a lifelong heavy smoker who is 94 years old. The general finding is the one to remember.

Summary We are all bombarded daily with such a mass of new information that it is difficult to absorb it. The available knowledge, even in a limited area like psychology, biology, medicine, or contemporary rock music, is so vast that no single person can completely know and comprehend it. With this situation in mind, it becomes increasingly important that you become a critical, selective, and informed consumer of information.

KNOWLEDGE BUILDER

Psychology in the Media

REFLECT

Do you tend to assume that a statement must be true if it is in print, on television, or made by an authority? How actively do you evaluate and question claims found in the media? Could you be a more critical consumer of information? *Should* you be a more critical consumer of information?

LEARNING CHECK

1. Newspaper accounts of dermo-optical perception have generally reported only the results of carefully designed psychological experiments. T or F?
2. Stage mentalists and psychics often use deception in their acts. T or F?
3. Blaming the lunar cycle for variations in the rate of violent crime is an example of mistaking correlation for causation. T or F?
4. To investigate possible links between drinking milk and delinquent behavior, it would be desirable to create an experimental group that consumes large amounts of milk and a control group that drinks none. T or F?

CRITICAL THINKING

5. Mystics have shown that fresh eggs can be balanced on their large ends during the vernal equinox when the sun is directly over the equator, day and night are equal in length, and the world is in perfect balance. What is wrong with their observation?

Answers: 1. F **2.** T **3.** T **4.** T **5.** The mystics have neglected to ask if eggs can be balanced at other times. They can. The lack of a control group gives the illusion that something amazing is happening, but the equinox has nothing to do with egg balancing (Halpern, 2003).

Chapter in Review

What is psychology? What are its goals?

- Psychology is the scientific study of behavior and mental processes.
- Psychologists seek empirical evidence based on scientific observation.
- Critical thinking and high-quality evidence are used to judge the truth of propositions about human behavior.
- Some major areas of research in psychology are comparative, learning, sensation, perception, personality, biopsychology, motivation and emotion, social, cognitive, developmental,

the psychology of gender, cultural psychology, and evolutionary psychology.
- Some psychologists are directly interested in animal behavior. Others study animals as models of human behavior.
- As a science, psychology's goals are to describe, understand, predict, and control behavior.

How did psychology emerge as a field of knowledge?
- The first psychological laboratory was established in Germany by Wilhelm Wundt, who tried to study conscious experience.
- The first school of thought in psychology was structuralism, a kind of "mental chemistry" based on introspection and analysis.
- Structuralism was followed by functionalism, behaviorism, and Gestalt psychology.
- Psychodynamic approaches, such as Freud's psychoanalytic theory, emphasize the unconscious origins of behavior.
- Humanistic psychology accentuates subjective experience, human potentials, and personal growth.

What are the major trends and specialties in psychology?
- Five main streams of thought in modern psychology are behaviorism, humanism, the psychodynamic approach, biopsychology, and cognitive psychology.
- Today there is an eclectic blending of many viewpoints within psychology.
- Psychologists have recently begun to formally study positive aspects of human behavior, or positive psychology.
- Although psychologists, psychiatrists, psychoanalysts, and counselors all work in the field of mental health, their training and methods differ considerably.
- Clinical and counseling psychologists, who do psychotherapy, represent only two of dozens of specialties in psychology.
- Other representative areas of specialization are industrial, educational, consumer, school, developmental, engineering, medical, environmental, forensic, community, psychometric, and experimental psychology.
- Psychological research may be basic or applied.

How do psychologists collect information?
- Scientific research provides the highest quality information about behavior.
- In the scientific method, systematic observation is used to test hypotheses about behavior and mental events.
- The results of scientific studies are made public so that others can evaluate them, learn from them, and use them to produce further knowledge.
- Important elements of a scientific investigation include observing, defining a problem, proposing a hypothesis, gathering evidence/testing the hypothesis, publishing results, and forming a theory.
- Concepts must be defined operationally before they can be studied empirically.
- Naturalistic observation is a starting place in many investigations.
- Three problems with naturalistic observation are the effects of the observer on the observed, observer bias, and an inability to explain observed behavior.
- In the correlational method, relationships between two traits, responses, or events are measured.
- A correlation coefficient is computed to gauge the strength of the relationship. Correlations allow prediction, but they do not demonstrate cause-and-effect connections.
- Relationships in psychology may be positive or negative, linear or curvilinear.
- Cause-and-effect relationships are best identified by controlled experiments.

How is an experiment performed?
- Experiments involve two or more groups of subjects that differ only with regard to the independent variable.
- Effects on the dependent variable are then measured. All other conditions (extraneous variables) are held constant.
- Psychological experiments are set up so the independent variable is the only possible cause of a change in the dependent variable. In this way, clear cause-and-effect connections can be identified.
- To be taken seriously, the results of an experiment must be statistically significant (they would occur very rarely by chance alone).
- In experiments that involve drugs, a placebo must be given to control for the effects of expectations. If a double-blind procedure is used, neither subjects nor experimenters know who received a drug.
- A related problem is the experimenter effect (a tendency for experimenters to unconsciously influence the outcome of an experiment). Expectations can create a self-fulfilling prophecy, in which a person changes in the direction of the expectation.

What other research methods do psychologists use?
- Case studies and natural clinical tests provide insights into human behavior that can't be gained by other methods.
- In the survey method, people in a representative sample are asked a series of carefully worded questions.
- Obtaining a representative sample of people is crucial when the survey method is used to study large populations.

How does psychology differ from false explanations of behavior?
- Critical thinking is central to the scientific method, to psychology, and to effective behavior in general.
- Critical thinking is the ability to evaluate, compare, analyze, critique, and synthesize information.

- To judge the validity of a claim, it is important to gather evidence for and against the claim and to evaluate the *quality* of the evidence.
- Numerous pseudo-psychologies exist. These false systems are often confused with valid psychology. Belief in pseudo-psychologies is based in part on uncritical acceptance, the fallacy of positive instances, and the Barnum effect.

How dependable is psychological information found in popular media?

- Information in the mass media varies greatly in quality and accuracy.
- It is wise to approach such information with skepticism and caution. Critical thinking and skepticism about media reports is often necessary to separate facts from fallacies.
- Problems in media reports are often related to biased or unreliable sources of information, uncontrolled observation, misleading correlations, false inferences, oversimplification, use of single examples, and unrepeatable results.

Web Resources

Internet addresses frequently change. To find the sites listed here, visit www.thomsonedu.com/psychology/coon for an updated list of Internet addresses and direct links to relevant sites.

***Psychology: Gateways to Mind and Behavior* Website** Online quizzes, flash cards, and other helpful study aids for this text. www.thomsonedu.com/psychology/coon

American Psychological Association Home page of the APA, with links to PsychNET, student information, member information, and more.

American Psychological Society Home page of the APS, with links to information, services, and Internet resources.

Ethical Principles of Psychologists and Code of Conduct The full text of the ethical principles that guide professional psychologists.

Psychweb This award-winning page provides a multitude of services and links.

Psycoloquy An online journal with short articles on all areas of psychology.

PsycPORT This site is a large database of psychological information, including daily updates on news related to psychology.

The Jane Goodall Institute Information about Goodall's work at Gombe, in Tanzania, where she has studied and protected wild chimpanzees for more than 40 years.

The Wadsworth Psychology Study Center From the publishers of this book, this site offers a study center for this text, with online activities, links to multimedia brochures, catalogues, software demos, and more. Go to www.thomsonedu.com/psychology.

Today in the History of Psychology Events in the history of psychology by the date.

ThomsonNOW™ Go to www.thomsonedu.com to link to ThomsonNow, your online study tool. First take the **Pre-Test** for this chapter to get your **Personalized Study Plan,** which will identify topics you need to review and direct you to online resources. Then take the **Post-Test** to determine what concepts you have mastered and what you still need work on.

InfoTrac College Edition For recent articles related to the pseudo-psychologies discussed in this chapter, use a Key Words search for PHRENOLOGY and ASTROLOGY. You can also use a Key Words search for PSYCHOLOGICAL RESEARCH. Go to www.thomsonedu.com/psychology/coon.

Interactive Learning

***PsychNow! Version 2.0* CD-ROM** Interact with the material with *PsychNow!*'s animations, video clips, experiments, and interactive assessments. For this chapter, go to *1b. Psychology and Its History, 1c. Research Methods,* and *1d. Critical Thinking in Psychology* to better understand psychology's history, its research methods, and the importance of critical thinking.

chapter 2

Brain and Behavior

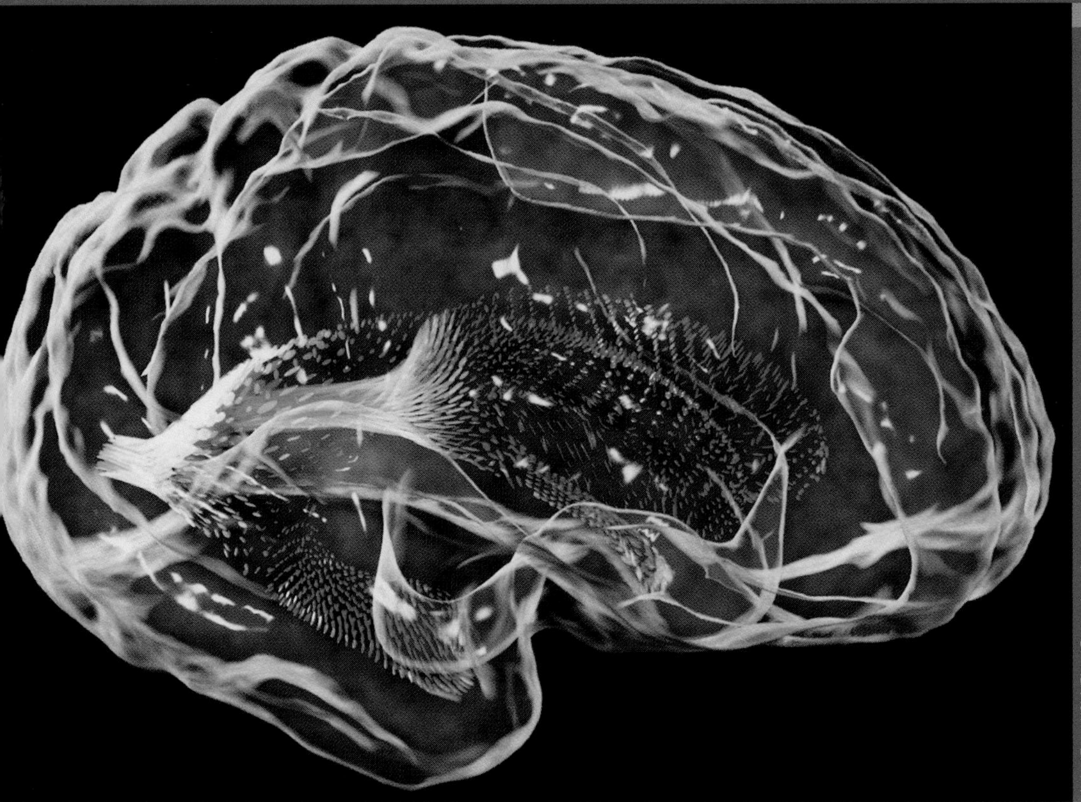

Arthur Toga, UCLA/Photo Researchers, Inc.

THEME:

Brain activity is the source of human consciousness, intelligence, and behavior.

Key Questions

How do nerve cells operate and communicate?

What are the functions of major parts of the nervous system?

How do we know how the brain works?

How is the brain organized, and what do its higher structures do?

Why are the brain's association areas important? What happens when they are injured?

What kinds of behaviors are controlled by the subcortex?

Does the glandular system affect behavior?

How do right- and left-handed individuals differ?

Is brain damage always permanent?

Preview

Finding Music in Tofu

When we watch gifted musicians, we often think about the brain. One of us recently saw Yo-Yo Ma, a master cellist, play a Bach suite with such skill that he was utterly amazed. If Ma had been an athlete, you would say he was "in the zone." His performance was unforgettable. Of course, in everything from rock to rap, musicians regularly make music that no machine could duplicate. A virtual Carlos Santana? A mechanical Tori Amos? We don't think so. That's why music is a good example of the central role the brain plays in all that is human.

Your brain is the size of a grapefruit. It weighs about 3 pounds and looks a lot like tofu. The next time you are in a market that sells beef brains, stop and have a look. What you will see is similar to your own brain, only smaller. How could such a squishy little blob of tissue allow us to make music of exquisite beauty? To seek a cure for cancer? To fall in love? Or read a book like this one?

Each nerve cell in your brain is linked to as many as 15,000 others. This network makes it possible to process immense amounts of information. In fact, there may be more *possible* pathways between the neurons in your brain than there are atoms in the entire universe! Undeniably, the human brain is the most amazing of all computers.

Scientists use the power of the brain to study the brain. Yet even now we must wonder if the brain will ever completely understand itself. Nevertheless, it is clear that answers to many age-old questions about the mind, consciousness, and knowledge lie buried within the brain. Let's visit this fascinating realm.

Neurons—Building a "Biocomputer"

All of your thoughts, feelings, and actions can be traced back to electrical impulses flashing through spidery nerve cells within the brain. Although they may seem far removed from daily life, everything you do begins with these tiny cells. Let's see how nerve cells operate, how the nervous system is "wired," and how scientists study the brain.

The brain consists of some 100 billion **neurons** (NOOR-ons: individual nerve cells). Neurons carry and process information. They also activate muscles and glands. A single neuron is not very smart—it would take at least several just to make you blink. Yet when neurons form vast networks they produce intelligence and consciousness. Neurons are linked to one another in tight clumps and long "chains." Each neuron receives messages from many others and sends its own message on. Millions of neurons must send messages at the same time to produce even the most fleeting thought (Clark, Boutros, & Mendez, 2005). When Carlos Santana plays a guitar riff, literally billions of neurons are involved.

Parts of a Neuron

What does a neuron look like? What are its main parts? Although no two neurons are exactly alike, most have four basic parts (● Figure 2.1). The **dendrites** (DEN-drytes), which look like tree roots, receive messages from other neurons. The **soma** (SOH-mah: cell body) does the same. In addition, the soma sends messages of its own (nerve impulses) down a thin fiber called the **axon** (AK-sahn).

Most axons end in **axon terminals.** These "branches" link up with the dendrites and somas of other neurons, allowing information to pass from neuron to neuron. Some axons are only 0.1 millimeter long (about the width of a pencil line). Others stretch up to a meter through the nervous system (from the base of your spine to your big toe, for instance). Like miniature cables, axons carry messages through the brain and nervous system. Altogether, your brain contains about 3 million miles of axons (Hyman, 1999).

Now let's summarize with a metaphor. Imagine that you are standing in a long line of people who are holding hands. A person on the far right end of the line wants to silently send a message to the person on the left end. She does this by pressing the hand of the person to her left, who presses the hand of the person to his left, and so on. The message arrives at your right hand (your dendrites). You decide whether to pass it on (you are the soma). The message goes out through your left arm (the axon). With your left hand (the axon terminals), you squeeze the hand of the person to your left, and the message moves on.

The Nerve Impulse

Electrically charged molecules called *ions* (EYE-ons) are found inside each neuron (● Figure 2.2). Other ions lie outside the cell. Some ions have a positive electrical charge, and some are negative. Different numbers of these "plus" and "minus" charges exist in-

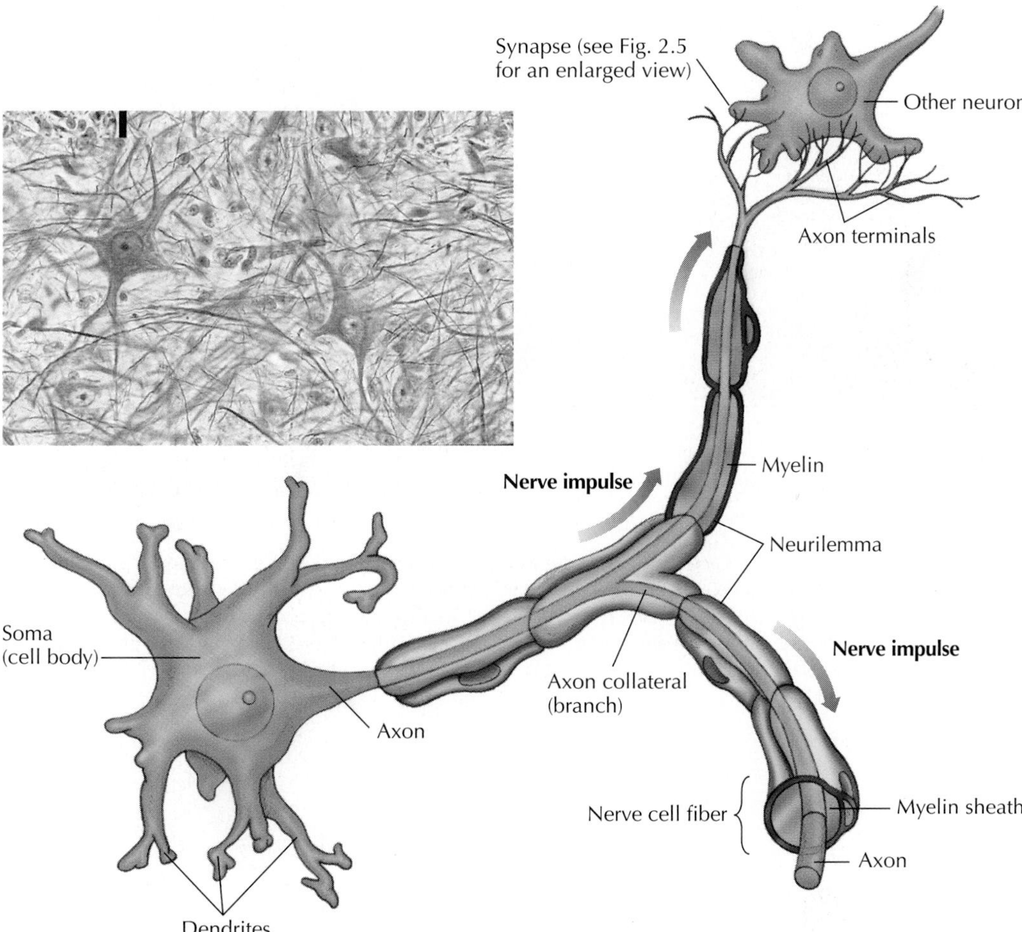

● **Figure 2.1** A neuron, or nerve cell. In the right foreground you can see a nerve cell fiber in cross section. The upper left photo gives a more realistic picture of the shape of neurons. Nerve impulses usually travel from the dendrites and soma to the branching ends of the axon. The nerve cell shown here is a motor neuron. The axons of motor neuron stretch from the brain and spinal cord to muscles or glands of the body.

side and outside of nerve cells. As a result, the inside of each neuron in your brain has an electrical charge of about minus 70 millivolts. (A millivolt is one thousandth of a volt.) This charge allows each neuron in your brain to act like a tiny biological battery.

The electrical charge of an inactive neuron is called its **resting potential.** But neurons seldom get much rest: Messages arriving from other neurons raise and lower the resting potential. If the electrical charge rises to about minus 50 millivolts, the neuron will reach its **threshold,** or trigger point for firing (see ● Figure 2.2). It's as if the neuron says, "Ah ha! It's time to send a message to my neighbors." When a neuron reaches −50 millivolts, an **action potential,** or nerve impulse, sweeps down the axon at up to 200 miles per hour (● Figure 2.3). That may seem fast, but it still takes at least a split second to react. That's one reason why hitting a 95-mile-per-hour major league fastball is so difficult. (See "Dollars, Drag Racing, and the Nervous System.")

What happens during an action potential? The axon membrane is pierced by tiny tunnels or "holes," called **ion channels.** Normally, these tiny openings are blocked by molecules that act like "gates" or "doors." During an action potential, the gates pop open. This allows sodium ions (Na^+) to rush into the axon (Carlson, 2005). The channels first open near the soma. Then gate after gate opens down the length of the axon as the action potential zips along (● Figure 2.4).

Each action potential is an *all-or-nothing event* (a nerve impulse occurs completely or not at all). Picture the axon as a row of dominoes set on end. Tipping over the dominoes is an all-or-nothing act. Once the first domino drops, a wave of falling blocks will zip rapidly to the end of the line. Similarly, when a nerve impulse is triggered near the soma, a wave of activity (the action potential)

Neuron An individual nerve cell.

Dendrites Neuron fibers that receive incoming messages.

Soma The main body of a neuron or other cell.

Axon Fiber that carries information away from the cell body of a neuron.

Axon terminals Branching fibers at the ends of axons.

Resting potential The electrical charge of a neuron at rest.

Threshold The point at which a nerve impulse is triggered.

Action potential The nerve impulse.

Ion channels Tiny openings through the axon membrane.

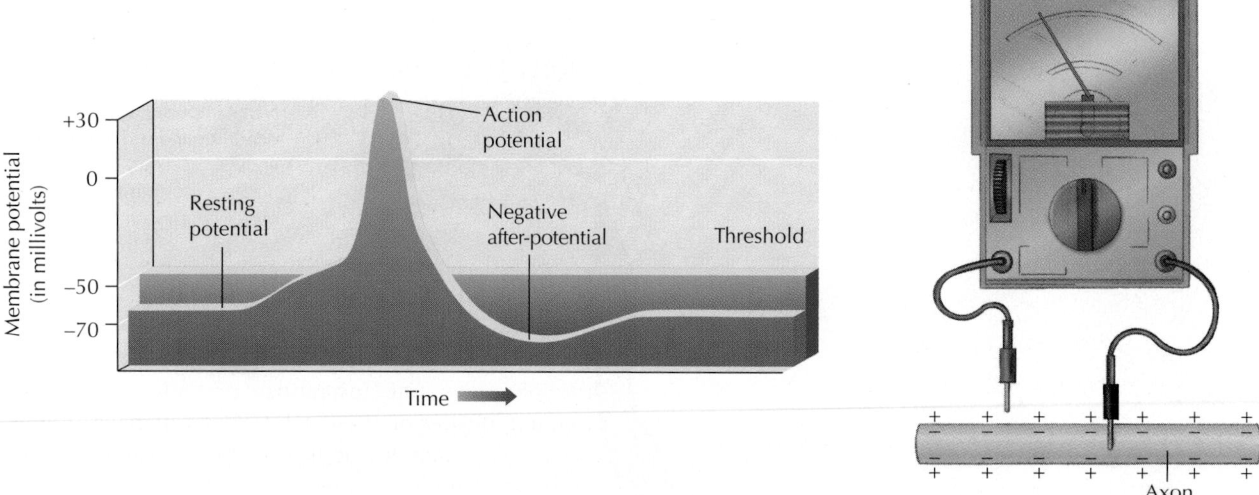

● **Figure 2.2** Electrical probes placed inside and outside an axon measure its activity. (The scale is exaggerated here. Such measurements require ultra-small electrodes, as described later in this chapter.) The inside of an axon at rest is about −60 to −70 millivolts, compared with the outside. Electrochemical changes in a neuron generate an action potential. When sodium ions (Na^+) that have a positive charge rush into the cell, its interior briefly becomes positive. This is the action potential. After the action potential, positive potassium ions (K^+) flow out of the axon and restore its negative charge. (See Figure 2.3 for further explanation.)

● **Figure 2.3** The inside of an axon normally has a negative electrical charge. The fluid surrounding an axon is normally positive. As an action potential passes along the axon, these charges reverse so that the interior of the axon briefly becomes positive.

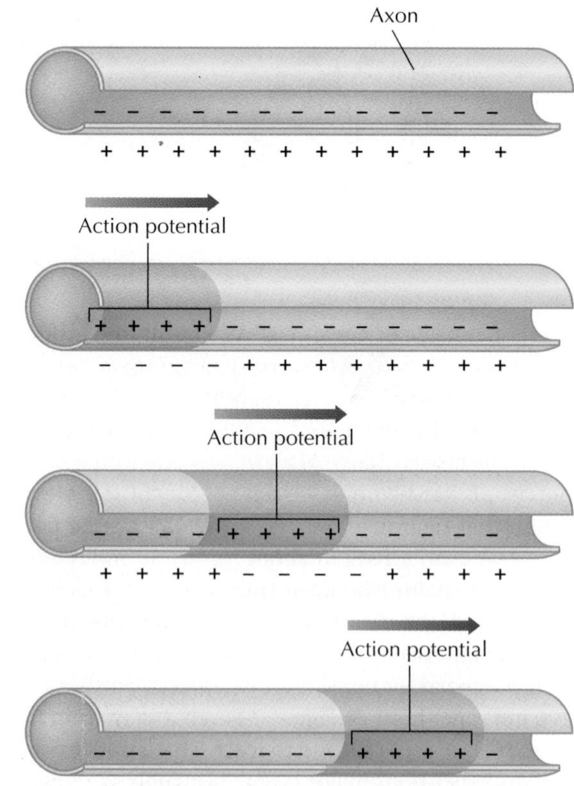

travels down the axon. This is what happens in neuron after neuron as Yo-Yo Ma's brain tells his hands what to do next, note after note.

After each nerve impulse, the cell briefly dips below its resting level and it becomes less willing to fire. This **negative after-potential** occurs because potassium ions (K^+) flow out of the neuron while the membrane gates are open (● Figure 2.4). After a nerve impulse, ions flow both into and out of the axon, recharging it for more action. In our model, the row of dominoes is quickly set up again. Soon, the axon is ready for another wave of activity.

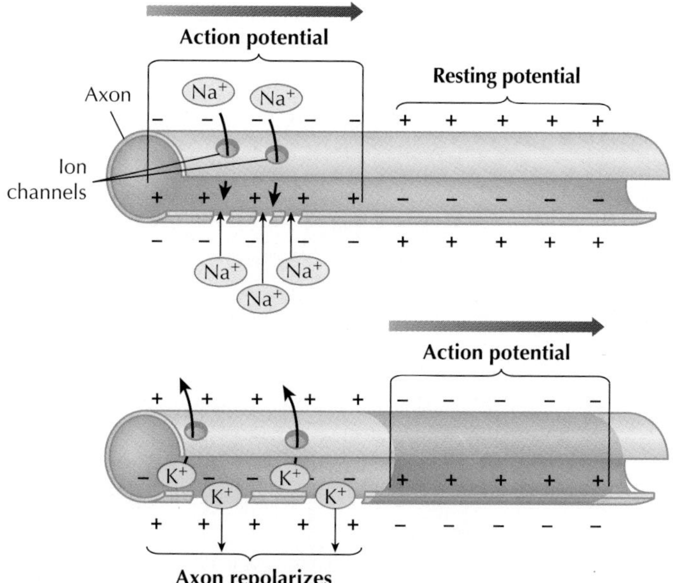

● **Figure 2.4** The interior of an axon. The right end of the top axon is at rest. Thus, it has a negative charge inside. An action potential begins when ion channels open and sodium ions (Na^+) rush into the axon. In this drawing, the action potential would travel from left to right along the axon. In the lower axon, the action potential has moved to the right. After it passes, potassium ions (K^+) flow out of the axon. This quickly renews the negative charge inside the axon so that it can fire again. Sodium ions that enter the axon during an action potential are pumped out more slowly. Removing them restores the original resting potential.

Synapses and Neurotransmitters

How does information move from one neuron to another? The nerve impulse is primarily electrical. That's why electrically stimulating the brain affects behavior. To prove the point, researcher José Delgado once entered a bullring with a cape and a radio transmitter. The bull charged. Delgado retreated. At the last instant the speeding bull stopped short. Why? Because Delgado's radio activated electrodes (metal wires) placed deep within the bull's brain. These, in turn, stimulated "control centers" that brought the bull to a halt.

In contrast to the nerve impulse, communication between neurons is chemical. The microscopic space between two neurons, over which messages pass, is called a **synapse** (SIN-aps) (● Figure 2.6). When an action potential reaches the tips of the axon terminals, **neurotransmitters** (NOOR-oh-TRANS-mit-ers) are released into the sy naptic gap. Neurotransmitters are chemicals that alter activity in neurons.

Let's return to the people standing in a line. To be more accurate, you and the others shouldn't be holding hands. Instead, each person should have a squirt gun in his or her left hand. To pass along a message, you would squirt the right hand of the person to your left. When that person notices this "message," he or she would squirt the right hand of the person to the left, and so on.

When chemical molecules cross over a synapse, they attach to special receiving areas on the next neuron (● Figure 2.6). These tiny **receptor sites** on the cell membrane are sensitive to neurotransmitters. The sites are found in large numbers on nerve cell bodies and dendrites. Muscles and glands have receptor sites, too.

Do neurotransmitters always trigger an action potential in the next neuron? No. Some transmitters *excite* the next neuron (move it closer to firing). Others *inhibit* it (make firing less likely). At any instant, a single neuron may receive hundreds or thousands of messages. If several "exciting" messages arrive close in time, the neuron will fire—but only if it doesn't get too many "inhibiting" messages that push it *away* from its trigger point. In this way, messages are *combined* before a neuron "decides" to fire its all-or-nothing action potential. Multiply these events by 100 billion neurons and 100 trillion synapses and you have an amazing computer—one that could easily fit inside a shoe box.

More than 100 transmitter chemicals are found in the brain. Some examples are acetylcholine, epinephrine, norepinephrine, serotonin, dopamine, histamine, and various amino acids. Disturbances of any of these substances can have serious consequences. For example, too little dopamine can cause the muscle tremors of Parkinson's disease. Too much dopamine may cause schizophrenia.

Many drugs imitate, duplicate, or block neurotransmitters. For example, **acetylcholine** (ah-SEET-ul-KOH-leen) normally activates muscles. Without acetylcholine, our musical friend Yo-Yo Ma couldn't even move, much less play Bach. That's exactly how the drug curare (cue-RAH-ree) causes paralysis. By attaching to receptor sites on muscles, curare competes with acetylcholine. This prevents acetylcholine from activating muscle cells. As a result, a person or animal given curare cannot move—a fact known to South American Indians of the Amazon River Basin, who use curare as an arrow poison for hunting.

Neural Regulators

More subtle brain activities are affected by chemicals called **neuropeptides** (NOOR-oh-PEP-tides). Neuropeptides do not carry messages directly. Instead, they *regulate* the activity of other neurons. By doing so, they affect memory, pain, emotion, pleasure, moods, hunger, sexual behavior, and other basic processes. For example, when you touch something hot, you jerk your hand away. The messages for this action are carried by neurotransmitters. At the same time, pain may cause the brain to release *enkephalins* (en-KEF-ah-lins). These opiate-like neural regulators relieve pain and stress. Related chemicals called *endorphins* (en-DORF-ins) are released by the pituitary gland. Together, these

Negative after-potential A drop in electrical charge below the resting potential.

Synapse The microscopic space between two neurons, over which messages pass.

Neurotransmitter Any chemical released by a neuron that alters activity in other neurons.

Receptor sites Areas on the surface of neurons and other cells that are sensitive to neurotransmitters or hormones.

Acetylcholine The neurotransmitter released by neurons to activate muscles.

Neuropeptides Brain chemicals that regulate the activity of neurons.

DISCOVERING PSYCHOLOGY Dollars, Drag Racing, and the Nervous System

In the sport of drag racing, victory depends on a driver's reaction time. When a light signals the start of a race, the driver must react as quickly as possible, usually in less than a half second. To test your own reaction time, have a friend hold a dollar bill from the top, as shown in ● Figure 2.5. Spread your thumb and fingers about 2 in. apart and place them around the bill, near the middle of Washington's portrait. Watch the bill intently. Without warning, your friend should release the bill. When you see it begin to move, try to catch it by pressing your thumb and fingers together. Most likely, the bill will slip through your fingers. It takes a split second for you to see the bill's movement, process that information in your brain, and send signals to your hand, causing it to move. Because neural processing takes time, our experiences and reactions lag slightly behind events in the world. In fact, your sense of control over your actions is partly an illusion. For instance, if you decide to wiggle your finger, your brain will begin a series of events that leads to finger movement. This activity will start *before* you begin to feel that you are intentionally moving your finger (Obhi & Haggard, 2004)!

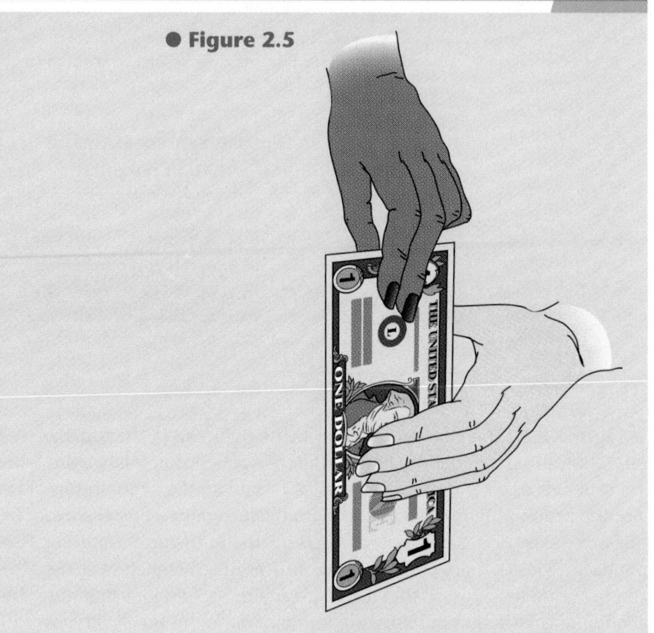

● **Figure 2.5**

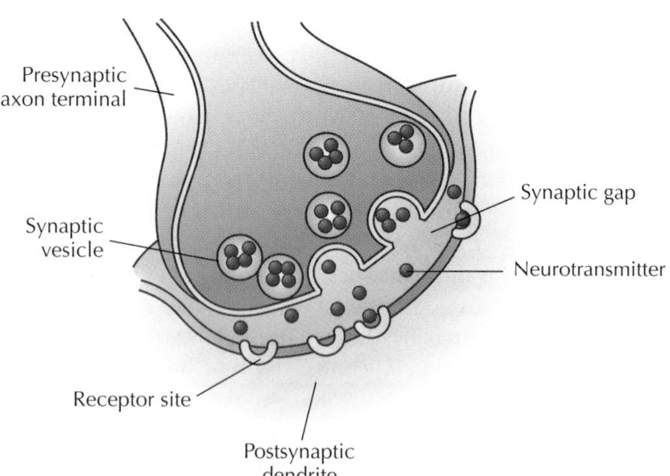

● **Figure 2.6** A highly magnified view of a synapse. Neurotransmitters are stored in tiny sacs called synaptic vesicles (VES-ih-kels). When a nerve impulse reaches the end of an axon, the vesicles move to the surface and release neurotransmitters. These molecules cross the synaptic gap to affect the next neuron. The size of the gap is exaggerated here; it is actually only about one millionth of an inch. Some transmitter molecules excite the next neuron and some inhibit its activity.

Spencer Grant/PhotoEdit

Endophins protect us at times of stress. A "real-life" example of this effect can be found among sport parachutists. Right after novices make their first jump, they have elevated endorphin levels and they are less sensitive to pain (Janssen & Arntz, 2001).

FOCUS ON RESEARCH

Neural Network Flies F-22 Jet Fighter

Neurons cooperate in networks to carry out even the simplest of tasks. To study neural networks, researchers have created hybrid robots ("hybrots") combining living neurons with artificial components (Potter, Wagenaar, & DeMaarse, in press). To build a hybrot, start with a grid of about 60 small metal electrodes in a small glass dish. When you add living neurons and the right nutrients, the neurons interconnect to form a neural network.

You can now input information to the hybrot by delivering different patterns of electrical stimulation to electrodes in the neural network. You can also register the hybrot's output by measuring the resulting pattern of electrical activity in the neural network. One hybrot was connected to an F-22 fighter jet simulator program. Input about a simulated flight was delivered to the neural network through patterns of electrical stimulation. The hybrot's output was measured and translated into instructions to control the F-22. Again and again, the simulator program input flight data and the hybrot output flight instructions. At first, the hybrot couldn't fly the fighter jet, but with practice it learned to control the simulation, keeping the jet level under a wide range of simulated weather conditions!

Further research with hybrots may lead to real-world applications that can fly unmanned aircraft, disable bombs, or help damaged human brains control prosthetic devices. Also, by measuring how hybrots change with training, we may learn a lot more about how natural neural networks grow and change with experience.

chemicals reduce the pain so that it is not too disabling (Drolet et al., 2001).

Ultimately, brain regulators may help explain depression, schizophrenia, drug addiction, and other puzzling topics. For example, women who suffer from severe premenstrual pain and distress have unusually low endorphin levels (Straneva et al., 2002).

The Nervous System—Wired for Action

Jamal and Vicki are playing catch with a Frisbee. This may look fairly simple. However, to merely toss the Frisbee or catch it, a huge amount of information must be sensed, interpreted, and directed to countless muscle fibers. As they play, Jamal and Vicki's neural circuits are ablaze with activity. Let's explore the "wiring diagram" that makes their Frisbee game possible.

Neurons and Nerves

Are neurons the same as nerves? No. Neurons are tiny cells. You would need a microscope to see one. **Nerves** are large bundles of axons. You can easily see nerves without magnification.

Many nerves are white because they contain axons coated with a fatty layer called **myelin** (MY-eh-lin). Small gaps in the myelin help nerve impulses move faster. Instead of passing down the entire length of the axon, the action potential leaps from gap to gap. Without the added speed this allows, it would probably be impossible to brake in time to avoid many automobile accidents. When the myelin layer is damaged, a person may suffer from numbness, weakness, or paralysis. That, in fact, is what happens in multiple sclerosis, a disease that occurs when the immune system attacks and destroys the myelin in a person's body.

A thin layer of cells called the **neurilemma** (NOOR-rih-LEM-ah) is also wrapped around most axons outside the brain and spinal cord (return to Figure 2.1). The neurilemma forms a "tunnel" that damaged fibers can follow as they repair themselves.

Neural Networks

As you can see in ● Figures 2.7 and 2.8, the **central nervous system (CNS)** consists of the brain and spinal cord. The brain is the central "computer" of the nervous system. The power of the brain arises from the cooperation of large numbers of neurons connected together into *neural networks*. Each neural network in the brain is, in turn, connected to other neural networks. Jamal must use this "computer" to anticipate when and where the Frisbee will arrive. To learn more about how to study neural networks, see "Neural Network Flies F-22 Jet Fighter."

BRIDGES

Under some circumstances, pain can produce feelings of relaxation or euphoria.

Endorphins underlie this effect, as explained in Chapter 5, pages 181–183.

Nerve A bundle of neuron axons.

Myelin A fatty layer coating some axons.

Neurilemma A layer of cells that encases many axons.

Central nervous system (CNS) The brain and spinal cord.

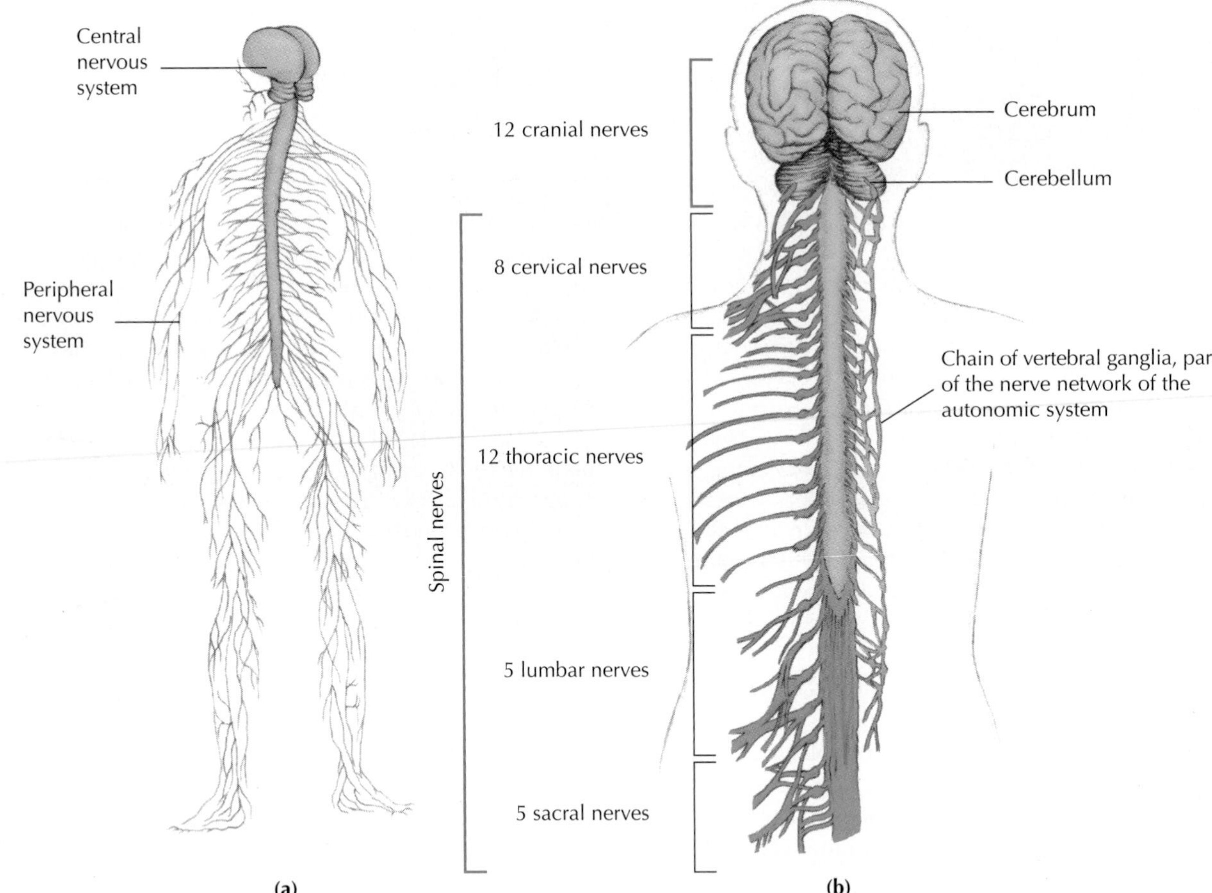

● **Figure 2.7** *(a)* Central and peripheral nervous systems. *(b)* Spinal nerves, cranial nerves, and the autonomic nervous system.

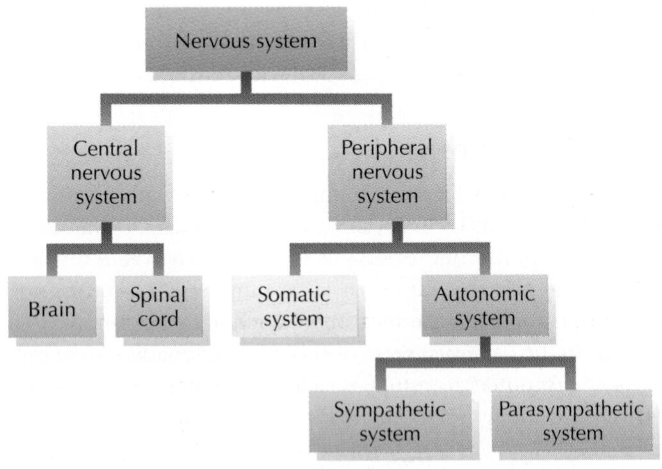

● **Figure 2.8** Subparts of the nervous system.

Jamal's brain communicates with the rest of his body through a large "cable" called the spinal cord. From there, messages flow through the **peripheral nervous system (PNS).** This intricate network of nerves carries information to and from the CNS.

A serious injury to the brain or spinal cord is usually permanent. However, scientists are starting to make progress repairing damaged neurons in the CNS. For instance, they have partially repaired cut spinal cords in rats. First they close the gap with nerve fibers from outside the spinal cord. Then they biochemically coax the severed spinal nerve fibers to grow through the "tunnels" provided by the implanted fibers. Within months, rats treated this way regain some use of their hind legs (Cheng, Cao, & Olson, 1996). Imagine what that could mean to a person confined to a wheelchair. Although it is unwise to raise false hopes, medical researchers have begun the first human trials in which nerve grafts will be used to repair damaged spinal cords (Levesque & Neuman, 1999). Nevertheless, it is wise to take good care of your own CNS. That means using seatbelts when you drive, wearing a helmet if you ride a motorcycle or bicycle, wearing protective gear for sports, and avoiding activities that pose a risk to the head or spinal cord.

The Peripheral Nervous System

The peripheral system can be divided into two major parts (see ● Figure 2.8). The **somatic system** carries messages to and from the sense organs and skeletal muscles. In general, it controls voluntary behavior, such as when Vicki tosses the Frisbee or B. B. King plays the blues. In contrast, the **autonomic system** serves the internal organs and glands. The word *autonomic* means "self-

Each year spinal cord injuries rob many thousands of people of the ability to move. Yet there is growing hope that nerve grafting techniques may someday make it possible for some of these people to walk again.

governing." Activities governed by the autonomic nervous system (ANS) are mostly "vegetative," or automatic, such as heart rate, digestion, and perspiration. Thus, messages carried by the somatic system can make your hand move, but they cannot cause your eyes to dilate. Likewise, messages carried by the ANS can stimulate digestion, but they cannot help you write a letter. If Jamal feels a flash of anger when he misses a catch, a brief burst of activity will spread through his autonomic system.

The ANS can be divided into the sympathetic and parasympathetic branches. Both are related to emotional responses, such as crying, sweating, heart rate, and other involuntary behavior (● Figure 2.9). The ANS and the somatic system work together to coordinate the body's internal reactions to events in the world outside. For example, if a snarling dog lunges at you, the somatic system will control your leg muscles so that you can run. At the same time, the autonomic system will raise your blood pressure, quicken your heart, and so forth.

BRIDGES

The ANS plays a central role in our emotional lives. In fact, without the ANS a person would feel little emotion.

See Chapter 12, pages 411–412 for more information about the ANS and emotion.

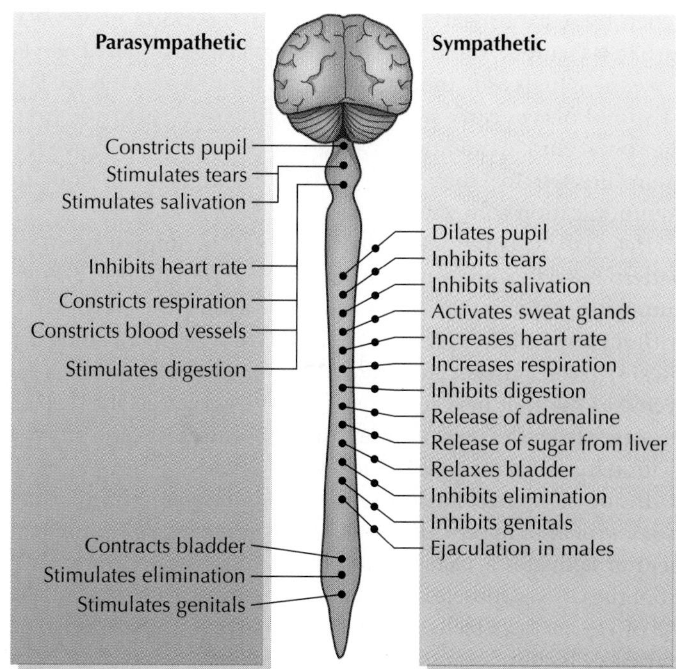

● **Figure 2.9** Sympathetic and parasympathetic branches of the autonomic nervous system.

How do the branches of the autonomic system differ? The **sympathetic branch** is an "emergency" system. It prepares the body for "fight or flight" during times of danger or high emotion. In essence, it arouses the body for action. (Yo-Yo Ma once left his $2 million cello in a taxi. No doubt his sympathetic nervous system was quite active when he first noticed his error.)

The **parasympathetic branch** quiets the body and returns it to a lower level of arousal. It is most active soon after an emotional event. The parasympathetic branch also helps keep vital functions such as heart rate, breathing, and digestion at moderate levels.

Of course, both branches of the ANS are always active. At any given moment, their combined activity determines whether your body is relaxed or aroused.

The Spinal Cord

As mentioned earlier, the spinal cord connects the brain to other parts of the body. If you severed this "cable," you would see columns of *white matter* (bundles of axons covered with myelin).

Peripheral nervous system (PNS) All parts of the nervous system outside the brain and spinal cord.

Somatic system The system of nerves linking the spinal cord with the body and sense organs.

Autonomic system The system of nerves carrying information to and from the internal organs and glands.

Sympathetic branch A part of the ANS that arouses the body.

Parasympathetic branch A part of the ANS that quiets the body.

When these axons leave the spinal cord, they form nerves. Return to ● Figure 2.7*b* and you will see that 30 pairs of spinal nerves leave the spinal cord. Another pair (not shown) leaves the tip. The 31 **spinal nerves** carry sensory and motor messages to and from the spinal cord. In addition, 12 pairs of **cranial nerves** leave the brain directly. Together, these nerves keep your entire body in communication with your brain.

How is the spinal cord related to behavior? The simplest behavior pattern is a **reflex arc**, which occurs when a stimulus provokes an automatic response. Such reflexes occur within the spinal cord, without any help from the brain (see ● Figure 2.10). Imagine that Vicki steps on a thorn. (Yes, they're still playing catch.) Pain is detected in her foot by a **sensory neuron** (a nerve cell that carries messages from the senses toward the CNS). Instantly, the sensory neuron fires off a message to Vicki's spinal cord.

Inside the spinal cord, the sensory neuron synapses with a *connector neuron* (a nerve cell that links two others). The connector neuron activates a *motor neuron* (a cell that carries commands from the CNS to muscles and glands). The muscle fibers are made up of *effector cells* (cells capable of producing a response). The muscle cells contract and cause Vicki's foot to withdraw. Note that no brain activity is required for a reflex arc to occur. Vicki's body will react automatically to protect itself.

In reality, even a simple reflex usually triggers more complex activity. For example, muscles of Vicki's other leg must contract to support her as she shifts her weight. Even this can be done by the spinal cord, but it involves many more cells and several spinal nerves. Also, the spinal cord normally informs the brain of its actions. As her foot pulls away from the thorn, Vicki will feel the pain and think, "Ouch, what was that?"

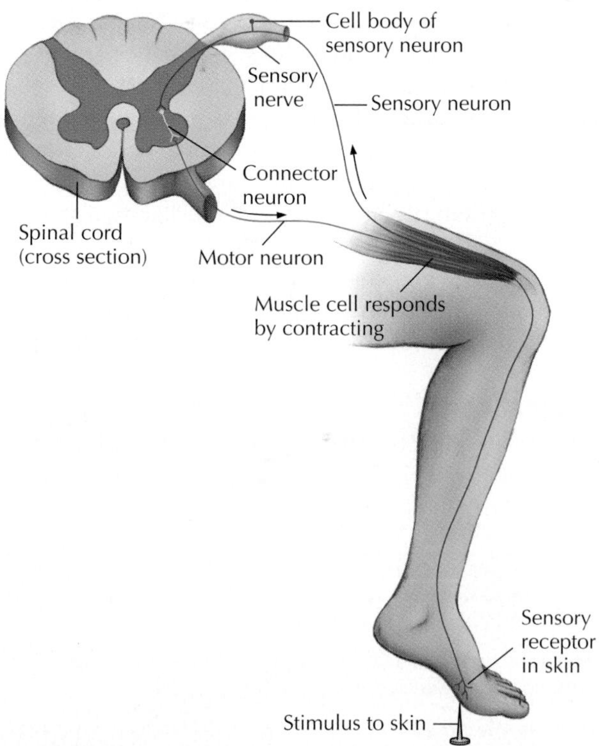

● **Figure 2.10** A simple sensory-motor (reflex) arc. A simple reflex is set in motion by a stimulus to the skin (or other part of the body). The nerve impulse travels to the spinal cord and then back out to a muscle, which contracts. Reflexes provide an "automatic" protective device for the body.

Perhaps you have realized how adaptive it is to have a spinal cord capable of responding on its own. Such automatic responses leave the brains of our Frisbee aces free to deal with more important information—such as the location of trees, lampposts, and attractive onlookers—as they take turns making grandstand catches.

In a few moments, we will probe more deeply into the brain. Before we do, let's explore some of the research tools biopsychologists use.

Research Methods—Charting the Brain's Inner Realms

Biopsychology is the study of how biological processes, the brain, and the nervous system relate to behavior. Many of the functions of the brain have been identified through **clinical studies.** Such studies examine how brain diseases or injuries affect personality, behavior, or sensory capacities. A related experimental technique is based on **ablation** (ab-LAY-shun: surgical removal) of parts of the brain (● Figure 2.11). When ablation causes changes in behavior or sensations, we gain insight into the purpose of the missing "part." An alternative approach is to use electrical stimulation to "turn on" brain structures. For example, you can activate the brain's surface by touching it with a small electrified wire called an **electrode.** When this is done during brain surgery, patients can describe how the stimulation affected them. (The brain has no pain receptors, so surgery can be done while a patient is awake. Only local painkillers are used for the scalp and skull. Any volunteers?)

Even structures below the surface of the brain can be activated or removed. In **deep lesioning** (LEE-zhun-ing), a thin wire electrode, insulated except at the tip, is lowered into a target area in-

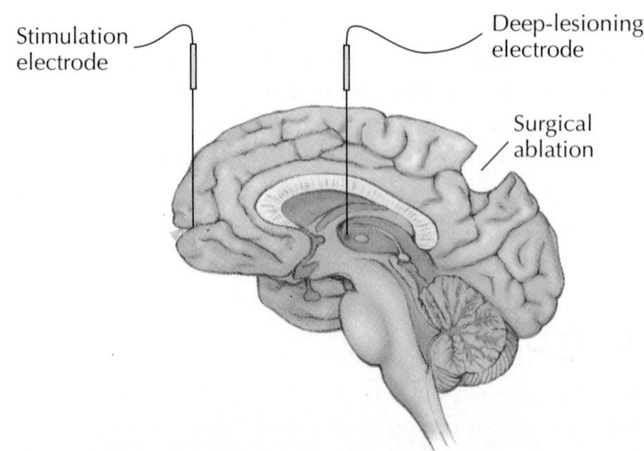

● **Figure 2.11** The functions of brain structures are explored by selectively activating or removing them. Brain research is often based on electrical stimulation, but chemical stimulation is also used at times.

side the brain (● Figure 2.11). An electric current is then used to destroy a small amount of brain tissue. Again, changes in behavior give clues about the purpose of the affected area. Using a weaker current, it is also possible to *activate* target areas, rather than remove them. This is called ESB, for **electrical stimulation of the brain.** ESB can call forth behavior with astonishing power. Instantly, it can bring about aggression, alertness, escape, eating, drinking, sleeping, movement, euphoria, memories, speech, tears, and more. Using ESB, researchers are creating a three-dimensional brain "atlas" showing the sensory, motor, and emotional responses that can be elicited from various parts of the brain. It promises to be a valuable guide for medical treatment, as well as for exploring the brain (Clark, Boutros, & Mendez, 2005; Yoshida, 1993).

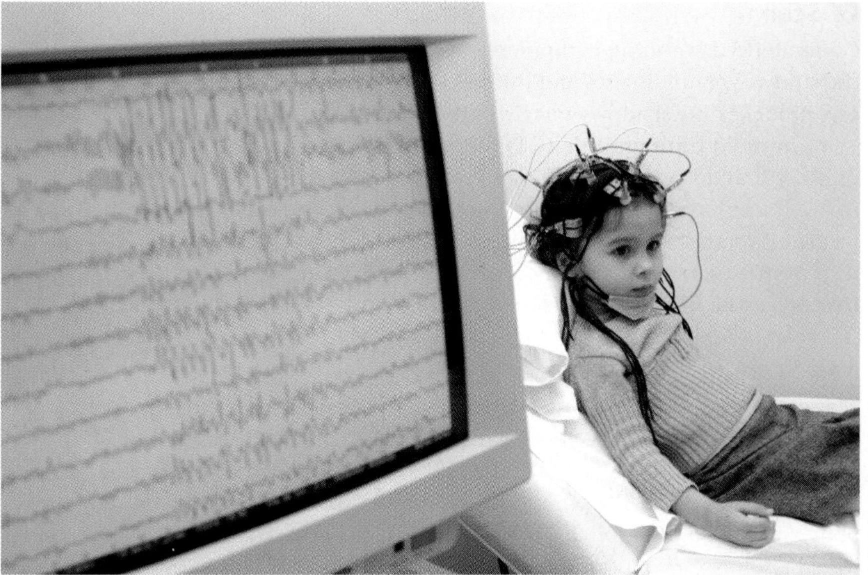

AJPhoto/Photo Researchers, Inc.

● **Figure 2.12** An EEG recording.

Could ESB be used to control a person against his or her will? It might seem that you could use ESB to control a person much like a robot. But the details of behaviors and emotions elicited with ESB are modified by personality and circumstances. Sci-fi movies to the contrary, it would be impossible for a ruthless dictator to enslave people by "radio controlling" their brains.

To find out what individual neurons are doing, we need to use micro-electrode recording. A *micro-electrode* is an extremely thin glass tube filled with a salty fluid. The tip of a micro-electrode is small enough to detect the electrical activity of a *single* neuron. Watching the action potentials of just one neuron provides a fascinating glimpse into the true origins of behavior. (The action potential shown in ● Figure 2.2 was recorded with a micro-electrode.)

What about the bigger picture? Is it possible to record what the brain is doing as a whole? Yes, it is, with electroencephalography (ee-LEK-tro-in-SEF-ah-LOG-ruh-fee). This technique measures the waves of electrical activity produced by the brain. Small disk-shaped metal plates are placed on a person's scalp. Electrical impulses from the brain are detected by these electrodes and sent to an **electroencephalograph (EEG).** The EEG amplifies these weak signals (brain waves) and records them on a moving sheet of paper or a computer screen (● Figure 2.12). Using an EEG, scientists can record activity in the brain without invading the skull. Various brain-wave patterns reveal tumors, epilepsy, and other diseases, as well as how brain activity changes during sleep, daydreaming, hypnosis, coma, and other mental states.

BRIDGES

The EEG has been quite valuable in studies of sleep and dreaming.

Chapter 7, pages 229–230, explains how changes in brain waves help define various stages of sleep.

New Images of the Living Brain

Many of the brain's riddles have been solved with the methods just described, plus others based on drugs and brain chemistry. Yet each technique lets us see only a part of the whole picture. What if we could "peek" inside an intact brain while a person is thinking, perceiving, and reacting? Rather than seeing individual musical notes or small musical phrases, what if we could see the brain's entire ongoing symphony? Computer-enhanced images are now making this age-old dream possible.

Spinal nerves Major nerves that carry sensory and motor messages in and out of the spinal cord.

Cranial nerves Major nerves that leave the brain without passing through the spinal cord.

Reflex arc The simplest behavior, in which a stimulus provokes an automatic response.

Sensory neuron A nerve cell that carries information from the senses toward the CNS.

Clinical study A detailed investigation of a single person, especially one suffering from some injury or disease.

Ablation Surgical removal of tissue.

Electrode Any device (such as a wire, needle, or metal plate) used to electrically stimulate nerve tissue or to record its activity.

Deep lesioning Removal of tissue within the brain by use of an electrode.

Electrical stimulation of the brain (ESB) Direct electrical stimulation and activation of brain tissue.

Electroencephalograph (EEG) A device that detects, amplifies, and records electrical activity in the brain.

CT Scan

Computerized scanning equipment has virtually revolutionized the study of brain diseases and injuries. At best, conventional X-rays produce only shadowy images of the brain.

Computed tomographic (CT) scanning is a specialized type of X-ray that does a much better job of making the brain visible. In a CT scan, X-ray information is collected by a computer and formed into an image of the brain. A CT scan can reveal the effects of strokes, injuries, tumors, and other brain disorders. These, in turn, can be related to a person's behavior.

MRI Scan

Magnetic resonance imaging (MRI) uses a strong magnetic field to produce an image of the body's interior. During an MRI scan, the body is placed inside a magnetic field. Processing by a computer then creates a three-dimensional model of the brain or body. Any two-dimensional plane, or slice, of the body can be selected and displayed as an image on a computer screen. This allows us to peer into the living brain almost as if it were transparent. In ● Figure 2.13, a precise "slice" from the middle of the three-dimensional MRI data reveals a brain tumor (see arrow).

A **functional MRI (fMRI)** goes one step further by making brain *activity* visible. For example, the motor areas on the surface of the brain would be highlighted in an fMRI image if Yo-Yo Ma bowed his cello. Such images allow scientists to pinpoint areas in the brain responsible for thoughts, feelings, and actions.

Is it true that most people use only 10 percent of their brain capacity? No, this is a myth. Brain scans show that all parts of the brain are active during waking hours. Obviously, some people make better use of their innate brain power than others do. Nevertheless, there are no great hidden or untapped reserves of mental capacity in a normally functioning brain.

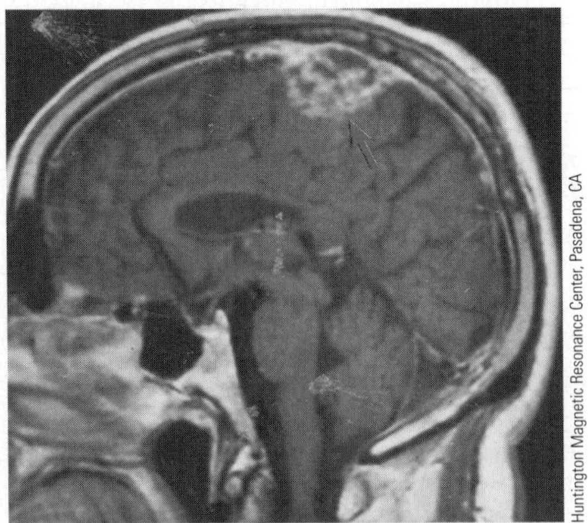

● **Figure 2.13** An MRI scan of the brain.

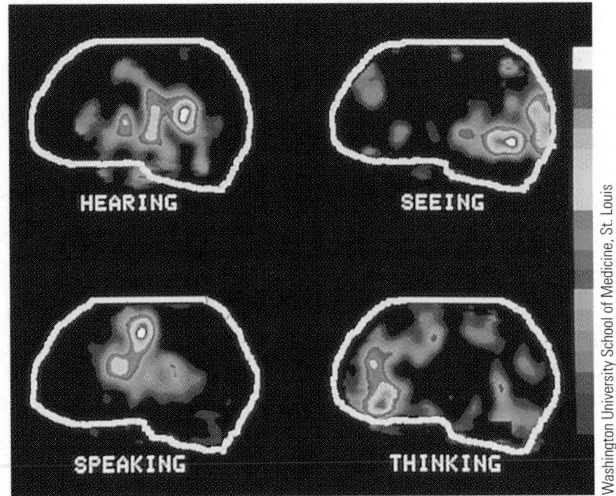

● **Figure 2.14** PET scans.

PET Scan

Positron emission tomography (PET) images are perhaps the most remarkable of all. A **PET scan** detects positrons (subatomic particles) emitted by weakly radioactive glucose (sugar) as it is consumed by the brain. Because the brain runs on glucose, a PET scan shows which areas are using energy. Higher energy use corresponds with higher activity. Thus, by placing positron detectors around the head and sending data to a computer, it is possible to create a moving, color picture of changes in brain activity. As you can see in ● Figure 2.14, PET scans reveal that very specific brain areas are active when you are reading a word, hearing a word, saying a word, or thinking about the meaning of a word (Petersen et al., 1988). It is just a matter of time until even brighter beacons are flashed into the shadowy inner world of thought. (See ● Figure 2.15.)

BRIDGES

PET scans suggest that different patterns of brain activity accompany major psychological disorders, such as depression or schizophrenia.

See Chapter 16, pages 554 and 556–557.

KNOWLEDGE BUILDER

Neurons, the Nervous System, and Brain Research

REFLECT

To cope with all of the technical terms in this chapter, think of neurons as strange little creatures. How do they act? What excites them? How do they communicate? To remember the functions of major branches of the nervous system, think about what you *couldn't* do if each part were missing.

You suspect that a certain part of the brain is related to memory. How could you use clinical studies, ablation, deep lesioning, and ESB to study the structure? You are interested in finding out how single neurons in the optic nerve respond when the eye is exposed to light. What technique will you use? You want to know which areas of the brain's surface are most active when a person sees a face. What methods will you use?

LEARNING CHECK

1. The ____________ and __________ are receiving areas where information from other neurons is accepted.
2. Nerve impulses are carried down the ________________ to the ____________ ________________.
3. The ____________ potential becomes an ____________ potential when a neuron passes the threshold for firing.
4. Neuropeptides are transmitter substances that help regulate the activity of neurons. T or F?
5. The somatic and autonomic systems are part of the ________ ________ nervous system.
6. Sodium and potassium ions flow through ion channels in the synapse to trigger a nerve impulse in the receiving neuron. T or F?
7. The simplest behavior sequence is a ________________ __________.
8. The parasympathetic nervous system is most active during times of high emotion. T or F?
9. Which of the following research techniques has the most in common with clinical studies of the effects of brain injuries?
   a. EEG recording   c. micro-electrode recording
   b. deep lesioning   d. PET scan

CRITICAL THINKING

10. What effect would you expect a drug to have if it blocked passage of neurotransmitters across the synapse?
11. Deep lesioning is used to ablate an area in the hypothalamus of a rat. After the operation, the rat seems to lose interest in food and eating. Why would it be a mistake to conclude that the ablated area is a "hunger center"?

Answers: **1.** dendrites, soma **2.** axon, axon terminals **3.** resting, action **4.** T **5.** peripheral **6.** F **7.** reflex arc **8.** F **9.** b **10.** Such a drug could have wide-ranging effects. If the drug blocked excitatory synapses, it would depress brain activity. If it blocked inhibitory messages, it would act as a powerful stimulant. **11.** Because other factors might explain the apparent loss of appetite. For example, the taste or smell of food might be affected, or the rat might simply have difficulty swallowing. It is also possible that hunger originates elsewhere in the brain and the ablated area merely relays messages that cause the rat to eat.

The Cerebral Cortex—My, What a Big Brain You Have!

Many parts of your brain are surprisingly similar to corresponding brain areas in lower animals, such as lizards. Superior human intelligence is related to the fact that our brains have a large cerebrum. The wrinkled surface of the cerebrum can be divided into smaller areas known as lobes. Parts of various lobes are responsible for the ability to see, hear, move, think, and speak. Thus, a map of the cerebrum is in some ways like a map of human behavior, as we shall see.

Cerebrum

In many ways we are pretty unimpressive creatures. Animals surpass humans in almost every category of strength, speed, and sensory sensitivity. The one area in which we excel is intelligence.

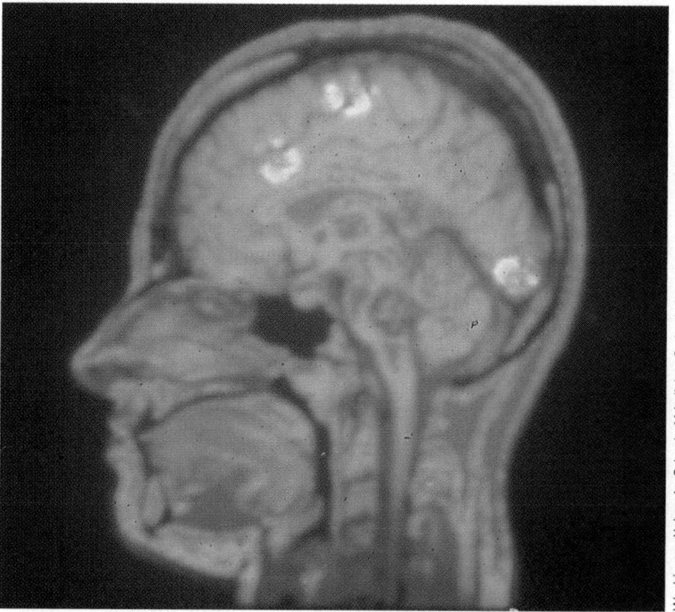

Washington University School of Medicine, St. Louis

● **Figure 2.15** The bright spots you see here were created by a PET scan. They are similar to the spots in Figure 2.14. However, here they have been placed over an MRI scan so that the brain's anatomy is visible. The three bright spots are areas in the left brain related to language. The spot on the right is active during reading. The top-middle area is connected with speech. The area to the left in the frontal lobe is linked with thinking about a word's meaning (Montgomery, 1989).

Do humans have the largest brains? Surprisingly, no. Elephant brains weigh 13 pounds, and whale brains weigh 19 pounds. At 3 pounds, the human brain seems puny—until we compare brain weight to body weight. We then find that an elephant's brain is 1/1,000 of its weight; the ratio for sperm whales is 1 to 10,000. The ratio for humans is 1 to 60. If someone tells you that you have a "whale of a brain" be sure to find out if they mean size or ratio!

As we move from lower to higher animals, more of the brain is devoted to the *cerebrum* (SER-eh-brum or ser-REE-brum: two large hemispheres that cover the upper part of the brain). ● Figure 2.16 shows the increased relative size of the human cerebrum. Its outer layer is known as the **cerebral** (seh-REE-brel or ser-EH-brel) **cortex.** Although the cortex is only 3 millimeters thick (one tenth of an inch), it contains 70 percent of the neurons in the central nervous system. It is largely responsible for our ability to use lan-

Computed tomographic (CT) scan Computed tomography scan; a computer-enhanced X-ray image of the brain or body.

MRI scan Magnetic resonance imaging; a computer-enhanced three-dimensional representation of the brain or body based on the body's response to a magnetic field.

fMRI scan Magnetic resonance imaging that records brain activity.

PET scan Positron emission tomography; a computer-generated image of brain activity based on glucose consumption in the brain.

Cerebral cortex The outer layer of the cerebrum.

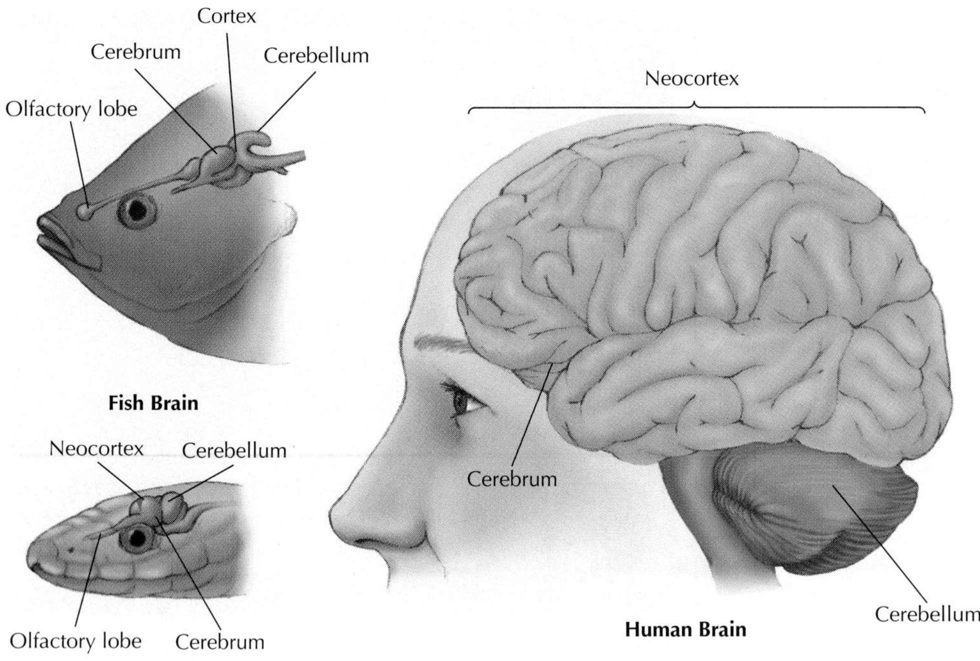

● **Figure 2.16**

guage, make tools, acquire complex skills, and live in complex social groups (Gibson, 2002). Without the cortex, humans wouldn't be much smarter than toads.

Corticalization

The cerebral cortex looks a little like a giant, wrinkled walnut. It covers most of the brain with a mantle of *gray matter* (spongy tissue made up mostly of cell bodies). The cortex in lower animals is small and smooth. In humans it is twisted, folded, and very large. The fact that humans are more intelligent than other animals is particularly related to this **corticalization** (KORE-tih-kal-ih-ZAY-shun), or increase in the size and wrinkling of the cortex.

Does having a larger brain make a person smarter? A small positive correlation exists between intelligence and brain size (Flashman et al., 1997; Wickett, Vernon, & Lee, 2000). However, size *alone* does not determine human intelligence. Brain efficiency has as much to do with intelligence as brain size does (Gazzaniga, 1995).

Psychologist Richard J. Haier and his colleagues found that the brains of people who perform well on mental tests consume less energy than those of poor performers (Haier et al., 1988). Haier measured brain activity with a PET scan. Recall that a PET scan records the amount of glucose (sugar) used by brain cells. The harder neurons work, the more sugar they use (● Figure 2.17).

What did PET scans reveal when subjects took a difficult reasoning test? Surprisingly, the brains of those who scored lowest on the test used the most glucose. Although we might assume that smart brains are hardworking brains, the reverse appears to be true. Brighter subjects actually used less energy than poor performers did. Haier believes this shows that intelligence is related to brain efficiency: Less efficient brains work harder and still accomplish less. We've all had days like that!

Cerebral Hemispheres

The cortex is composed of two sides, or *cerebral hemispheres* (half-globes). The two hemispheres are connected by a thick band of fibers called the *corpus callosum* (KORE-pus kah-LOH-sum) (● Figure 2.18). The left side of the brain mainly controls the right side of the body. Likewise, the right brain mainly controls left body areas. When our friend Marge had a stroke, her right hemisphere suffered damage. (A stroke occurs when an artery carrying blood to the brain becomes blocked, causing some brain tissue to die.) In Marge's case, the stroke caused some paralysis and loss of sensation on the left side of her body.

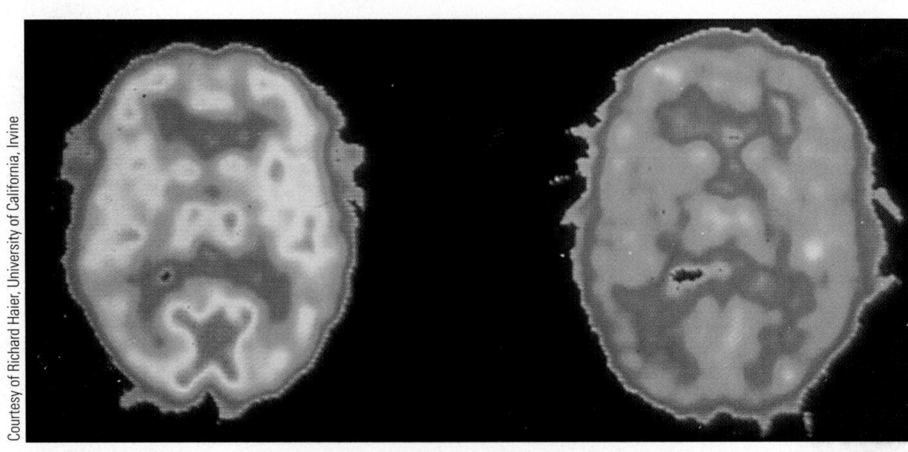

● **Figure 2.17** In the images you see here, red, orange, and yellow indicate high consumption of glucose; green, blue, and pink show areas of low glucose use. The PET scan of the brain on the left shows that a man who solved 11 out of 36 reasoning problems burned more glucose than the man on the right, who solved 33.

Courtesy of Richard Haier, University of California, Irvine

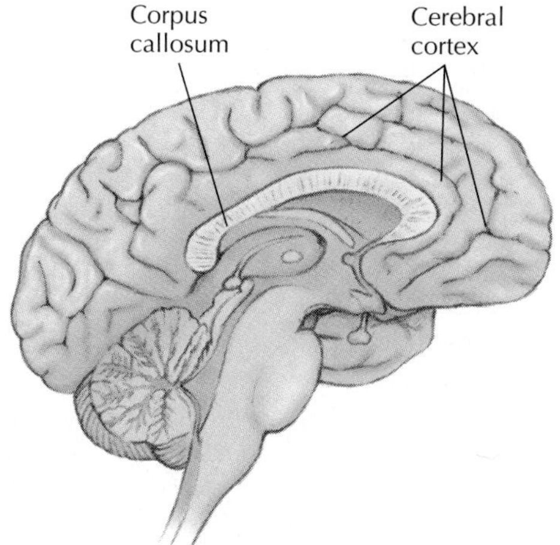

● **Figure 2.18**

Damage to the right hemisphere may also cause a curious problem called *spatial neglect.* Affected patients pay no attention to the left side of visual space (see ● Figure 2.19). Often, the patient will not eat food on the left side of a plate. Some even refuse to acknowledge a paralyzed left arm as their own (Springer & Deutsch, 1998). If you point to the "alien" arm, the patient is likely to say, "Oh, that's not my arm. It must belong to someone else." To learn more about strokes, see "A Stroke of Bad Luck").

● **Figure 2.19** Spatial neglect. A patient with right-hemisphere damage was asked to copy three model drawings. Notice the obvious neglect of the left side in his drawings. Similar instances of neglect occur in many patients with right-hemisphere damage. (From *Left Brain, Right Brain,* Revised Edition, by S. P. Springer and G. Deutsch, copyright 1981, 1985, 1989, 1993, 1998. Reprinted with the permission of W. H. Freeman and Company.)

Hemispheric Specialization

In 1981, Roger Sperry (1914–1994) won a Nobel prize for his remarkable discovery that the right and left brain hemispheres perform differently on tests of language, perception, music, and other capabilities.

How is it possible to test only one side of the brain? One way is to work with people who've had a **"split-brain" operation.** In this rare type of surgery, the corpus callosum is cut to control severe epilepsy. The result is essentially a person with two brains in one body. After the surgery it is a simple matter to send information to one hemisphere or the other (see ● Figure 2.20).

"Split Brains"

After the right and left brain are separated, each hemisphere will have its own separate perceptions, concepts, and impulses to act.

How does a split-brain person act after the operation? Having two "brains" in one body can create some interesting dilemmas.

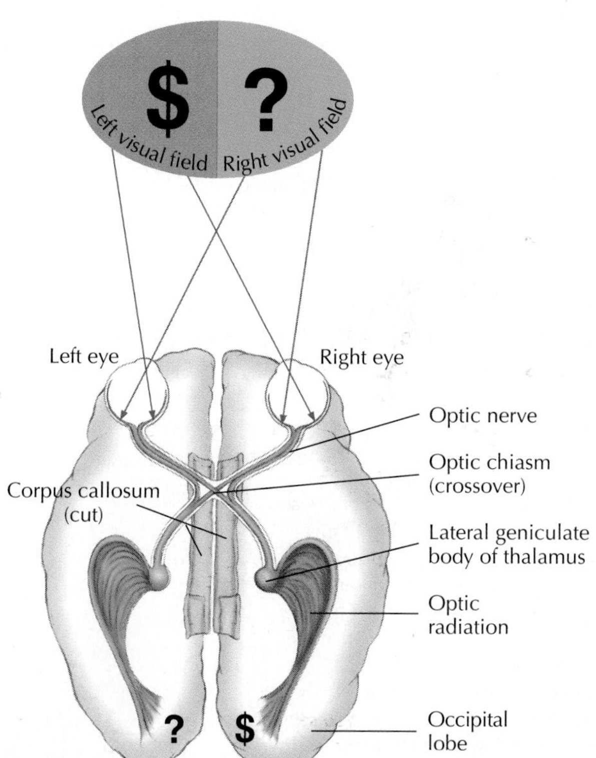

● **Figure 2.20** Basic nerve pathways of vision. Notice that the left portion of each eye connects only to the left half of the brain; likewise, the right portion of each eye connects to the right brain. When the corpus callosum is cut, a "split brain" results. Then visual information can be directed to one hemisphere or the other by flashing it in the right or left visual field as the person stares straight ahead.

Corticalization An increase in the relative size of the cerebral cortex.

"Split-brain" operation Cutting the corpus callosum.

THE CLINICAL FILE

A Stroke of Bad Luck

One morning Bryan Kolb lost his left hand. Up early to feed his cat, he could not see his hand, or anything else to his upper left side. Kolb, a Canadian biopsychologist, instantly realized that he had suffered a right hemisphere stroke. He drove to the hospital where he argued with the doctors about his own diagnosis (he was right, of course!). He eventually resumed his career and even wrote a fascinating account of his case (Kolb, 1990).

Strokes and other brain injuries can hit like a thunderbolt. Almost instantly, victims realize that something is wrong. You would, too, if you suddenly found that you couldn't move, or feel parts of your body, or see, or speak. However, some brain injuries are not so obvious. Many involve less dramatic, but equally disabling, changes in personality, thinking, judgment, or emotions. Although major brain injuries are easy enough to spot, psychologists also look for more subtle signs that the brain is not working properly. **Neurological soft signs,** as they are called, include clumsiness, an awkward gait, poor hand-eye coordination, and other problems with perception or fine muscle control. These telltale signs are "soft" in the sense that they aren't direct tests of the brain, like an EEG or CT scan. Bryan Kolb initially diagnosed himself entirely with soft signs. Soft signs help psychologists diagnose problems ranging from childhood learning disorders to full-blown psychosis (Borod et al., 2002; Chen et al., 2001; Gepner & Mestre, 2002; Karow et al., 2001; Stuss & Levine, 2002).

When one split-brain patient dressed himself, he sometimes pulled his pants down with one hand and up with the other. Once, he grabbed his wife with his left hand and shook her violently. Gallantly, his right hand came to her aid and grabbed the aggressive left hand (Gazzaniga, 1970). However, such conflicts are actually rare. That's because both halves of the brain normally have about the same experience at the same time. Also, if a conflict arises, one hemisphere usually overrides the other.

Split-brain effects are easiest to see in specialized testing. For example, we could flash a dollar sign to the right brain and a question mark to the left brain of a patient named Tom. (● Figure 2.20 shows how this is possible.) Next, Tom is asked to draw what he saw, using his left hand, out of sight. Tom's left hand draws a dollar sign. If Tom is then asked to point with his right hand to a picture of what his hidden left hand drew, he will point to a question mark (Sperry, 1968). In short, for the split-brain person, one hemisphere may not know what is happening in the other. This has to be the ultimate case of the "right hand not knowing what the left hand is doing"! ● Figure 2.21 provides another example of split-brain testing.

Left Brain

- Language
- Speech
- Writing
- Calculation
- Time sense
- Rhythm
- Ordering of complex movements

Right Brain

- Nonverbal
- Perceptual skills
- Visualization
- Recognition of patterns, faces, melodies
- Recognition and expression of emotion
- Spatial skills
- Simple language comprehension

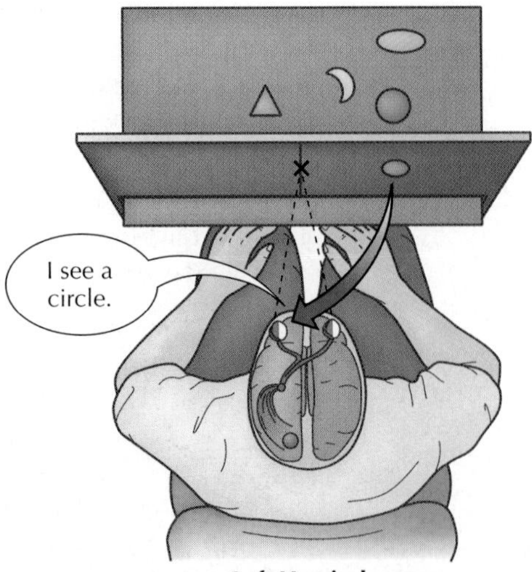

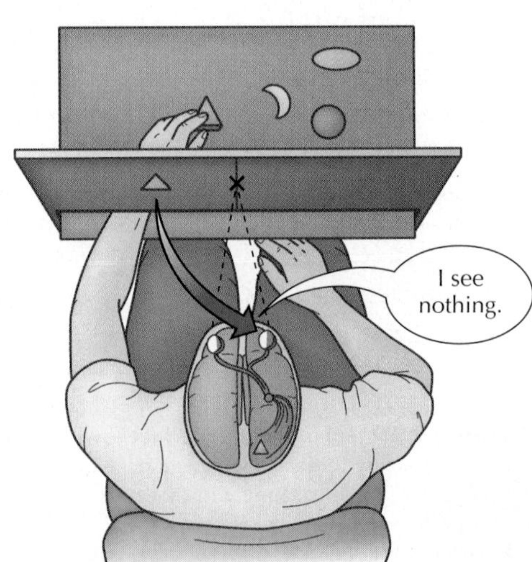

● **Figure 2.21** If a circle is flashed to the left brain and a split-brain patient is asked to say what she or he saw, the circle is easily named. The person can also pick out the circle by touching shapes with the right hand, out of sight on a tabletop. However, the left hand will be unable to identify the shape. If a triangle is flashed to the right brain, the person cannot say what was seen (speech is controlled by the left hemisphere). The person will also be unable to identify the correct shape by touch with the right hand. Now, however, the left hand will have no difficulty picking out the hidden triangle. Separate testing of each hemisphere reveals distinct specializations, as listed earlier.

Right Brain/Left Brain

Earlier it was stated that the hemispheres differ in abilities; in what ways are they different? Roughly 95 percent of us use our left brain for language (speaking, writing, and understanding). In addition, the left hemisphere is superior at math, judging time and rhythm, and coordinating the order of complex movements, such as those needed for speech.

In contrast, the right hemisphere can produce only the simplest language and numbers. Working with the right brain is like talking to a child who can say only a dozen words or so. To answer questions, the right hemisphere must use nonverbal responses, such as pointing at objects (see ● Figure 2.21).

Although it is poor at producing language, the right brain is especially good at perceptual skills, such as recognizing patterns, faces, and melodies; putting together a puzzle; or drawing a picture. It is also helps you express emotions and detect the emotions that other people are feeling (Borod et al., 1998; Stuss & Alexander, 2000).

Even though the right hemisphere is nearly "speechless," it is superior at some aspects of understanding language. If the right side of the brain is damaged, people lose their ability to understand jokes, irony, sarcasm, implications, and other nuances of language. Basically, the right hemisphere helps us see the overall context in which something is said (Beeman & Chiarello, 1998). For instance, let's say you tell a patient with right-brain damage the following joke:

> "Dad," said Jason, "I'm late for soccer practice. Would you do my math homework for me?"
>
> The boy's father answered, "Son, it just wouldn't be right."
>
> "That's okay," replied Jason. "You could at least try, right?"

When asked what this story means, the patient might say, "The father doesn't want to do it, but the son is persistent." Without the right brain's ability to perceive context, the patient doesn't get the joke about the father's math abilities. The left hemisphere understands the words, one at a time, but it can't grasp the bigger picture.

One Brain, Two Styles

In general, the left hemisphere is mainly involved with *analysis* (breaking information into parts). It also processes information *sequentially* (in order, one item after the next). The right hemisphere appears to process information *simultaneously* and *holistically* (all at once) (Springer & Deutsch, 1998).

To summarize further, you could say that the right hemisphere is better at assembling pieces of the world into a coherent picture; it sees overall patterns and general connections. The left brain focuses on small details (see ● Figure 2.22). The right brain sees the wide-angle, global view; the left zooms in on specifics (Heinze et al., 1998; Hellige, 1993; Huebner, 1998).

Do people normally do puzzles or draw pictures with just the right hemisphere? Do they do other things with only the left? Numerous books have been written about how to use the right brain to manage, teach, draw, ride horses, learn, and even make love (Clark, Boutros, & Mendez, 2005). Such books oversimplify right- and left-brain differences. Although it's true that some tasks may make *more* use of one hemisphere or the other, in most "real world" activities the hemispheres share the work. Each does the parts it does best and shares information with the other side.

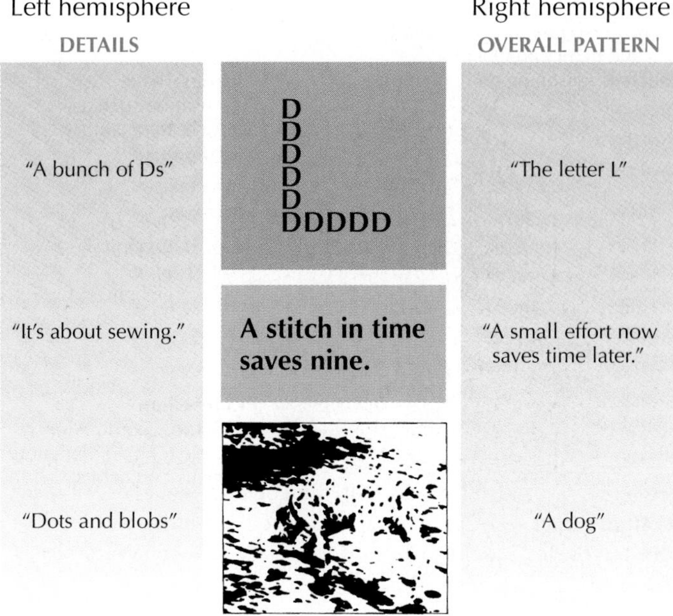

● **Figure 2.22** The left and right brain have different information processing styles. The right brain gets the big pattern; the left focuses on small details.

Popular books and courses that claim to teach "right-brain thinking" also ignore the fact that everyone already uses the right brain for thinking (Gazzaniga, Ivry, & Mangun, 2002). To do anything well requires the talents and processing abilities of both hemispheres. A smart brain is one that grasps both the details and the overall picture at the same time (Ornstein, 1997). For instance, during a concert Yo-Yo Ma will use his left brain to judge time and rhythm and coordinate the order of his hand movements. At the same time, he will use his right brain to recognize and organize melodies.

Lobes of the Cerebral Cortex

Each of the two hemispheres of the cerebral cortex can be divided into several smaller *lobes*. Some of the lobes of the cerebral cortex are defined by larger fissures on the surface of the cerebrum. Others are regarded as separate areas because their functions are quite different. (See ● Figure 2.23.)

The Occipital Lobes

At the back of the brain we find the **occipital** (awk-SIP-ih-tal) **lobes,** the primary visual area of the cortex. Patients with tumors (cell growths that interfere with brain activity) in the occipital lobes experience blind spots in their vision.

Neurological soft signs Subtle behavioral signs of brain dysfunction, including clumsiness, an awkward gait, poor hand-eye coordination, and other perceptual and motor problems.

Occipital lobes Portion of the cerebral cortex where vision registers in the brain.

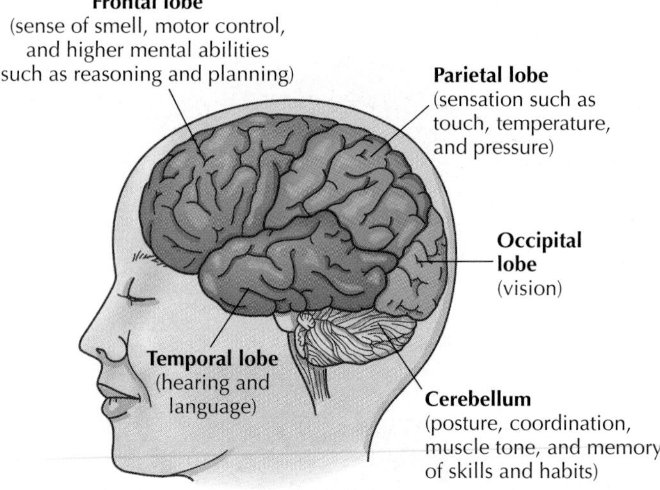

● **Figure 2.23**

Do the visual areas of the cortex correspond directly to what is seen? Images are mapped onto the cortex, but the map is greatly stretched and distorted (Carlson, 2005). It is important to avoid thinking of the visual area as being like a little TV screen in the brain. Visual information creates complex patterns of activity in nerve cells; it does *not* make a TV-like image.

The Parietal Lobes

Bodily sensations register in the **parietal** (puh-RYE-ih-tal) **lobes,** located just above the occipital lobes. Touch, temperature, pressure, and other somatic sensations flow into the **somatosensory** (SO-mat-oh-SEN-so-ree) **area** of the parietal lobes. Again, we find that the map of bodily sensations is distorted. The drawing in ● Figure 2.24 shows that the cortex reflects the *sensitivity* of body areas, not their size. For example, the lips are large in the drawing because of their great sensitivity, whereas the back and trunk, which are less sensitive, are much smaller. Notice that the hands are also large in the map of body sensitivity—which is obviously an aid to musicians, typists, watchmakers, massage therapists, lovers, and brain surgeons.

The Temporal Lobes

The temporal lobes are located on each side of the brain. Auditory information projects directly to the **temporal lobes,** making them the main site where hearing registers. If we did a PET scan of your brain and played your favorite MP3, your temporal lobes would light up. Likewise, if we could stimulate the auditory area of your temporal lobe, you would "hear" a series of sound sensations.

For most people, the left temporal lobe also contains a language "center." (For 5 percent of all people, the area is on the right temporal lobe.) Damage to the temporal lobe can severely limit ability to use language. (More on this later.)

The Frontal Lobes

The **frontal lobes** are associated with higher mental abilities. This area is also responsible for the control of movement. Specifically, an arch of tissue over the top of the brain, called the **motor cortex,** directs the body's muscles. If this area is stimulated with an electrical current, various parts of the body will twitch or move. Like the somatosensory area, the motor cortex corresponds to the importance of bodily areas, not to their size. The hands, for example, get more area than the feet (see ● Figure 2.24). If you've ever wondered why your hands are more dextrous than your feet, it's partly because more motor cortex is devoted to the hands. Incidentally, learning and experience can alter these "motor maps." For instance, violin, viola, and cello players like Yo-Yo Ma have larger "hand maps" in the cortex (Hashimoto et al., 2004).

The frontal lobes are also related to more complex behaviors. If the frontal lobes are damaged, a patient's personality and emotional life may change dramatically. (Remember Phineas Gage, the railroad foreman described in Chapter 1?) Reasoning or planning may also be affected. Patients with damage to the frontal lobes often get "stuck" on mental tasks and repeat the same wrong answers over and over (Goel & Grafman, 1995). PET scans suggest that much of what we call intelligence is related to increased activity in the frontal areas of the cortex (Duncan et al., 2000). Sadly, drug abuse can damage this important area of the brain (Liu et al., 1998).

Association Areas

Only a small part of the cerebral cortex directly controls the body and receives information from the senses. All the surrounding areas, which are called the **association cortex,** combine and process information from the senses. If you see a rose, the association areas help you recognize it and name it. The association cortex also contributes to higher mental abilities. For example, a person with damage to association areas in the left hemisphere may suffer **aphasia** (ah-FAZE-yah: an impaired ability to use language).

One type of aphasia is related to **Broca's** (BRO-cahs) **area,** a "speech center" on the left frontal lobe (Leonard, 1997). Damage to Broca's area causes great difficulty in speaking or writing. Typically, a patient's grammar and pronunciation are poor and speech is slow and labored. For example, the person may say "bife" for bike, "seep" for sleep, or "zokaid" for zodiac. Generally, the person knows what she or he wants to say but can't seem to utter the words (Geschwind, 1979).

A second language site, called **Wernicke's** (VER-nick-ees; see ● Figure 2.23) **area,** lies on the left temporal lobe. If it is damaged, the person has problems with the *meaning* of words, not their pronunciation. Someone with Broca's aphasia might say "tssair" when shown a picture of a chair. In contrast, a Wernicke's patient might say "stool" (Leonard, 1997).

One of the most fascinating results of brain injury is **agnosia** (ag-KNOW-zyah: an inability to identify seen objects). This condition is sometimes referred to as "mindblindness." For example, if we show Alice, an agnosia patient, a candle, she will describe it as "a long narrow object that tapers at the top." Alice can even draw the candle accurately, but she cannot name it. However, if

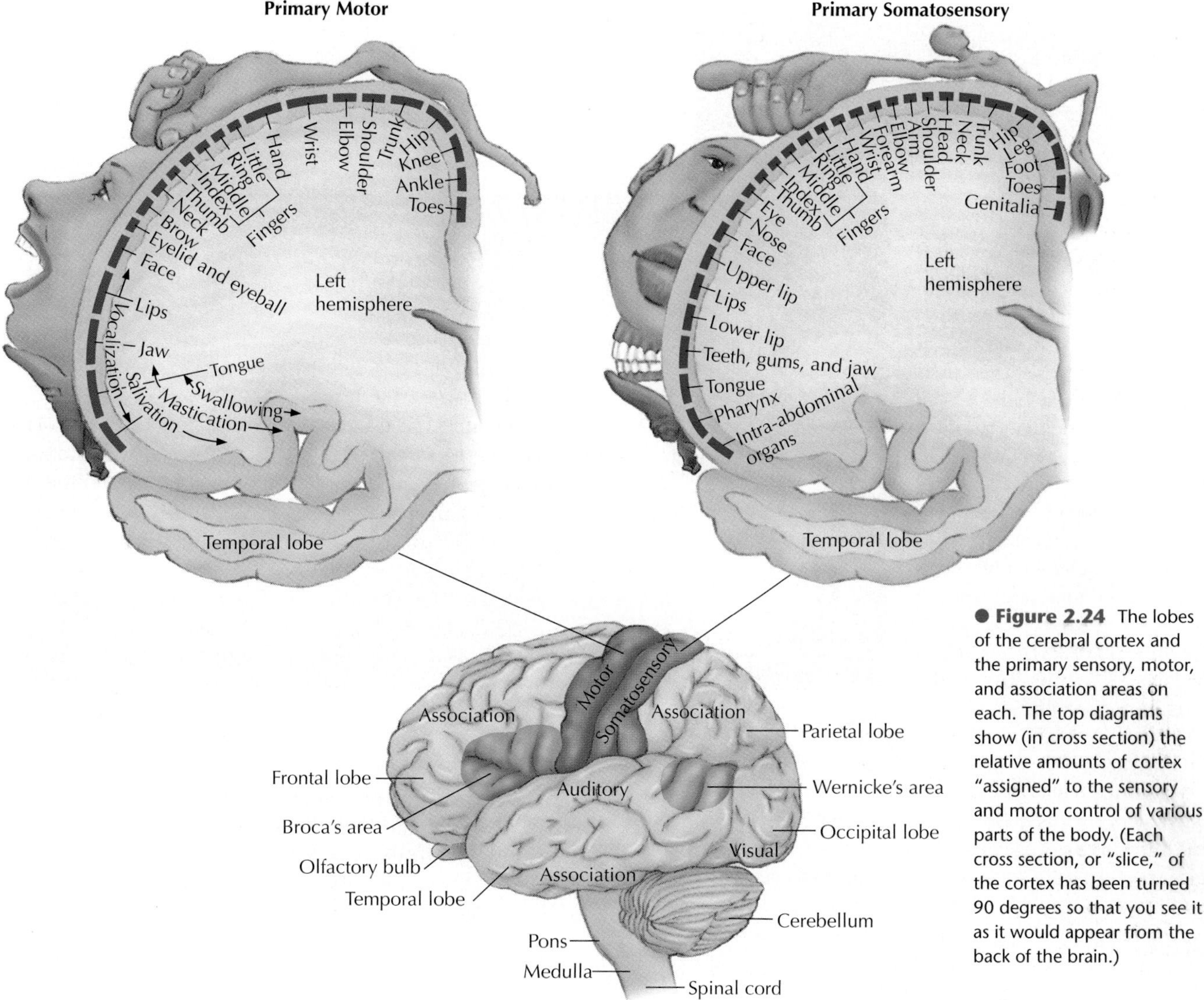

● **Figure 2.24** The lobes of the cerebral cortex and the primary sensory, motor, and association areas on each. The top diagrams show (in cross section) the relative amounts of cortex "assigned" to the sensory and motor control of various parts of the body. (Each cross section, or "slice," of the cortex has been turned 90 degrees so that you see it as it would appear from the back of the brain.)

she is allowed to *feel* the candle, she will name it immediately (Warrington & McCarthy, 1995). In short, Alice can still see color, size, and shape. She just can't perceive the meanings of objects (De Haan et al., 1995).

Are agnosias limited to objects? No. A fascinating form of "mind-blindness" is **facial agnosia**, an inability to perceive familiar faces. One patient with facial agnosia couldn't recognize her husband or mother when they visited her in the hospital, and she was unable to identify pictures of her children. However, as soon as a visitor spoke she knew them immediately by their voices (Benton, 1980).

Areas devoted to recognizing faces lie on the underside of the occipital lobes. These areas appear to have no other function. Why would part of the brain be set aside solely for identifying faces? From an evolutionary standpoint it is not really so surprising. After all, we are social animals, for whom facial recognition is very important. This specialization is just one example of what a marvelous organ of consciousness we possess. But do the brains of different people differ? Could we find specialization from brain to brain? Perhaps. "His and Her Brains?" explains why.

Parietal lobes Area of the brain where bodily sensations register.

Somatosensory area A receiving area for bodily sensations.

Temporal lobes Areas that include the sites where hearing registers in the brain.

Frontal lobes A brain area associated with movement, the sense of smell, and higher mental functions.

Motor cortex A brain area associated with control of movement.

Association cortex All areas of the cerebral cortex that are not primarily sensory or motor in function.

Aphasia A speech disturbance resulting from brain damage.

Broca's area A language area related to grammar and pronunciation.

Wernicke's area An area related to language comprehension.

Agnosia An inability to grasp the meaning of stimuli, such as words, objects, or pictures.

Facial agnosia An inability to recognize familiar faces.

HUMAN DIVERSITY

His and Her Brains?

Are men's and women's brains specialized? Yes, to some extent. Many physical differences between the brains of men and women have been reported, although the interpretation of these differences remains controversial. In one group of studies, researchers used brain imaging to observe brain activity while people did language tasks. As they worked, both men and women showed increased activity in Broca's area, on the left side of the brain, exactly as expected. Surprisingly, however, both the left *and* the right brain were activated in more than half the women tested (Shaywitz & Gore, 1995; see ● Figure 2.25). Despite this difference, in one of the studies, the two sexes performed equally well on the task, which involved sounding out words (Shaywitz et al., 1995). The researchers concluded that nature has given the brain different routes to the same ability.

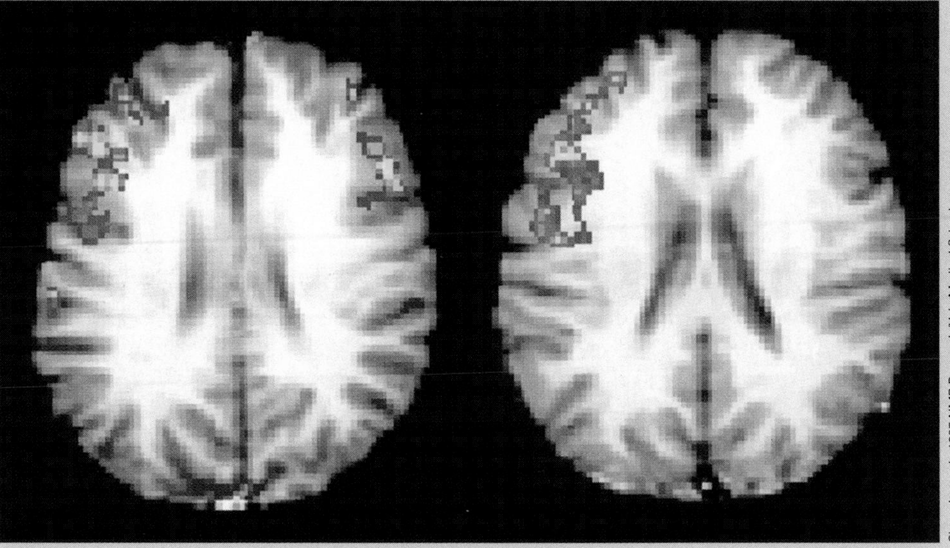

● **Figure 2.25** Language tasks activate the left side of the brain in men and both sides in many women.

In a study of men and women with similar IQs, brain images revealed major differences in the parts of their brains involved in intelligence (Haier et al., 2004). In general, the men had more grey matter (neuron cell bodies), whereas the women had more white matter (neuron axons coated in myelin). Further, both the grey and white matter of the women was more concentrated in their frontal lobes than that of the men. In contrast, the men's grey matter was split between the frontal and parietal lobes, whereas their white matter was concentrated in the temporal lobe. Whatever else these differences mean, they show that the human brain can be specialized in different ways to arrive at the same capabilities.

As you can see, the bulk of our daily experience and all of our understanding of the world can be traced to the sensory, motor, and association areas of the cortex. The human brain is among the most advanced and sophisticated of the brain-bearing species on earth. This, of course, is no guarantee that this marvelous "biocomputer" will be put to full use. Still, we must stand in awe of the potential it represents.

KNOWLEDGE BUILDER

Cerebral Cortex and Lobes of the Brain

REFLECT

Learning the functions of the brain lobes is like learning areas on a map. Try drawing a map of the cortex. Can you label all of the different "countries" (lobes)? Can you name their functions? Where is the motor cortex? The somatosensory area? Broca's area? Keep redrawing the map until it becomes more detailed and you can do it easily.

LEARNING CHECK

See if you can match the following:

1. _____ Corpus callosum
2. _____ Occipital lobes
3. _____ Parietal lobes
4. _____ Temporal lobes
5. _____ Frontal lobes
6. _____ Association cortex
7. _____ Aphasias
8. _____ Corticalization
9. _____ Left hemisphere
10. _____ Right hemisphere
11. _____ "Split brain"
12. _____ Agnosia

A. Visual area
B. Language, speech, writing
C. Motor cortex and abstract thinking
D. Spatial skills, visualization, pattern recognition
E. Speech disturbances
F. Causes sleep
G. Increased ratio of cortex in brain
H. Bodily sensations
I. Treatment for severe epilepsy
J. Inability to identify seen objects
K. Fibers connecting the cerebral hemispheres
L. Cortex that is not sensory or motor in function
M. Hearing

CRITICAL THINKING

13. If you wanted to increase the surface area of the cerebrum so that more cerebral cortex would fit within the skull, how would you do it?
14. What would be some of the possible advantages and disadvantages to having a "split brain"?
15. If your brain were removed, replaced by another, and moved to a new body, which would you consider to be yourself, your old body with the new brain, or your new body with the old brain?

Answers: 1. K **2.** A **3.** H **4.** M **5.** C **6.** L **7.** E **8.** G **9.** B **10.** D **11.** I **12.** J **13.** One solution would be to gather the surface of the cortex into folds, just as you might if you were trying to fit a large piece of cloth into a small box. This, in fact, is probably why the cortex is more convoluted (folded or wrinkled) in higher animals. **14.** If information were properly routed to each brain hemisphere, it would be possible to have both hands working simultaneously on conflicting tasks. However, such possible benefits would apply only under highly controlled conditions. **15.** Although there is no "correct" answer to this question, your personality, knowledge, personal memories, and self-concept all derive from brain activity—which makes a strong case for your old brain in a new body being more nearly the "real you."

The Subcortex—At the Core of the (Brain) Matter

You could lose large portions of your cerebrum and still survive. Not so with the **subcortex**, the brain structures immediately below the cerebral cortex. Serious damage to the subcortex (lower brain) can be fatal. Hunger, thirst, sleep, attention, sex, breathing, and many other vital functions are controlled by parts of the subcortex. Let's take a quick tour of these brain areas.

This area can be divided into the brainstem (or hindbrain), the midbrain, and the forebrain. (The forebrain also includes the cerebral cortex, which we have already discussed because of its size and importance.) For our purposes the midbrain can be viewed as a link between the forebrain and the brainstem. Therefore, let us focus on the rest of the subcortex (see ● Figure 2.26).

The Hindbrain

Why are the lower brain areas so important? As the spinal cord joins the brain, it widens into the brainstem. The **brainstem** consists mainly of the medulla (meh-DUL-ah) and the cerebellum (ser-ah-BEL-uhm). The **medulla** contains centers important for the reflex control of vital life functions, including heart rate, breathing, swallowing, and the like. Various drugs, diseases, and injuries can disrupt the medulla and end or endanger life. That's why a karate chop to the back of the neck can be extremely dangerous.

The **pons**, which looks like a small bump on the brainstem, acts as a bridge between the medulla and other brain areas. In addition to connecting with many other locations, including the cerebellum, the pons influences sleep and arousal.

The cerebellum, which looks like a miniature cerebral cortex, lies at the base of the brain. The **cerebellum** primarily regulates posture, muscle tone, and muscular coordination. The cerebellum also stores memories related to skills and habits. Again we see that experience shapes the brain: Musicians, who practice special motor skills throughout their lives, have larger than average cerebellums (Hutchinson et al., 2003).

What happens if the cerebellum is injured? Without the cerebellum, tasks like walking, running, and playing music become impossible. The first symptoms of a crippling disease called *spinocerebellar degeneration* are tremor, dizziness, and muscular weakness. Eventually, victims have difficulty merely standing, walking, or feeding themselves.

BRIDGES

The cerebellum stores "know how" or "skill memories." "Know what" memories, such as remembering a person's name or knowing what the cerebellum does, are stored elsewhere in the brain.

See Chapter 9, pages 304–305.

Reticular Formation

A network of fibers and cell bodies called the **reticular** (reh-TICK-you-ler) **formation (RF)** lies inside the medulla and brainstem. As messages flow into the brain, the RF gives priority to some while turning others aside. By doing so, the RF influences *attention.* The RF doesn't fully mature until adolescence, which may be why children have such short attention spans. The RF also modifies outgoing commands to the body. In this way the RF affects muscle tone, posture, and movements of the eyes, face, head, body, and limbs. At the same time, the RF controls reflexes involved in breathing, sneezing, coughing, and vomiting.

The RF also keeps us vigilant, alert, and awake. Incoming messages from the sense organs branch into a part of the RF called the **reticular activating system (RAS).** The RAS bombards the cortex with stimulation, keeping it active and alert. For instance, let's say a sleepy driver rounds a bend and sees a deer standing in the road. The driver snaps to attention and applies the brakes. She can thank her RAS for arousing the rest of her brain and averting an

Subcortex All brain structures below the cerebral cortex.

Brainstem The lowest portions of the brain, including the cerebellum, medulla, pons, and reticular formation.

Medulla The structure that connects the brain with the spinal cord and controls vital life functions.

Pons An area on the brainstem that acts as a bridge between the medulla and other structures.

Cerebellum A brain structure that controls posture and coordination.

Reticular formation (RF) A network within the medulla and brainstem; associated with attention, alertness, and some reflexes.

Reticular activating system (RAS) A part of the reticular formation that activates the cerebral cortex.

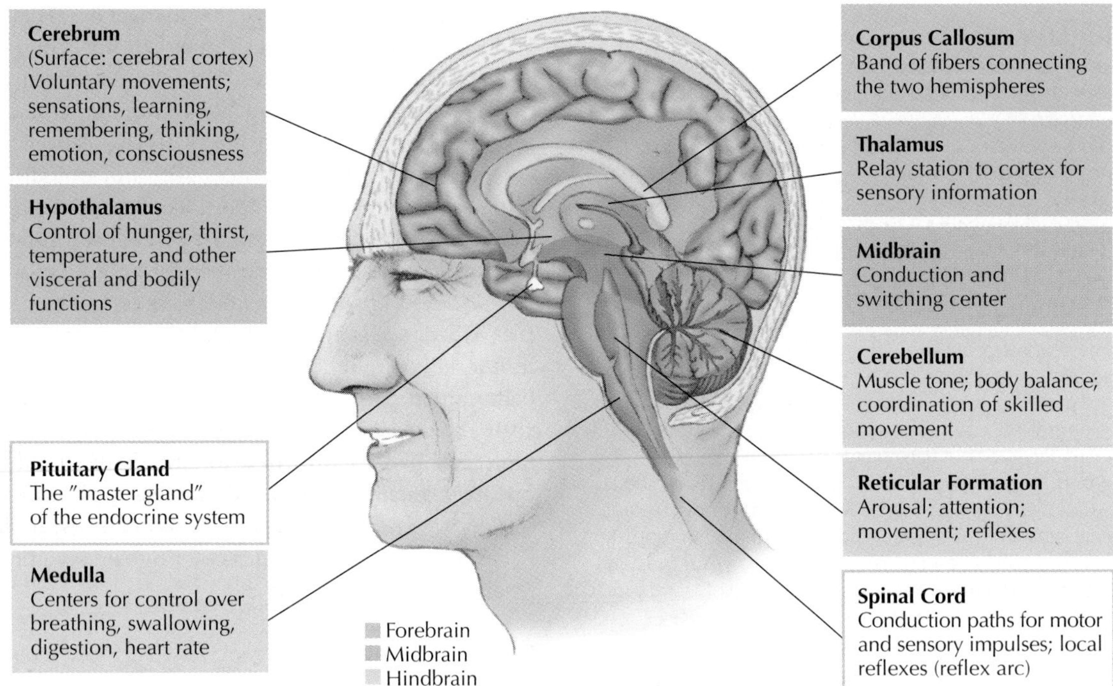

● **Figure 2.26** This simplified drawing shows the main structures of the human brain and describes some of their most important features. (You can use the color code in the foreground to identify which areas are part of the forebrain, midbrain, and hindbrain.)

accident. If you're getting sleepy while reading this chapter, try pinching your ear—a little pain will cause the RAS to momentarily arouse your cortex.

The Forebrain

Like hidden gemstones, two of the most important parts of your body lie buried deep within your brain. The thalamus (THAL-uh-mus) and an area just below it called the hypothalamus (HI-po-THAL-uh-mus) are key parts of the forebrain (see ● Figure 2.26).

How could these be any more important than other areas already described? The **thalamus** acts as a final "switching station" for sensory messages on their way to the cortex. Vision, hearing, taste, and touch all pass through this small, football-shaped structure. Thus, injury to even small areas of the thalamus can cause deafness, blindness, or loss of any other sense, except smell.

The human hypothalamus is about the size of a small grape. Small as it may be, the **hypothalamus** is a kind of master control center for emotion and many basic motives (Carlson, 2005). The hypothalamus affects behaviors as diverse as sex, rage, temperature control, hormone release, eating and drinking, sleep, waking, and emotion. The hypothalamus is basically a "crossroads" that connects many areas of the brain. It is also the final pathway for many kinds of behavior. That is, the hypothalamus is the last place where many behaviors are organized or "decided on" before messages leave the brain, causing the body to react.

BRIDGES

The hypothalamus has a powerful effect on hunger, thirst, sex, and other basic motives.

See Chapter 12, pages 390–391.

The Limbic System

As a group, the hypothalamus, parts of the thalamus, the amygdala, the hippocampus, and other structures make up the limbic system (● Figure 2.27). The **limbic system** has a major role in producing emotion and motivated behavior. Rage, fear, sexual response, and intense arousal can be obtained from various points in the limbic system. Laughter, a delightful part of human social life, also has its origins in the limbic system (Cardoso, 2000).

During evolution, the limbic system was the earliest layer of the forebrain to develop. In lower animals, the limbic system helps organize basic survival responses: feeding, fleeing, fighting, or reproduction. In humans, a clear link to emotion remains. The **amygdala** (ah-MIG-dah-luh), in particular, is strongly related to fear. For example, during medical testing one woman reacted with a sudden outburst of fear and anger when the amygdala was stimulated, saying, "I feel like I want to get up from this chair! Please don't let me do it! I don't want to be mean! I want to get something and just tear it up!" (King, 1961).

The amygdala provides a primitive, "quick pathway" to the cortex. Like lower animals, we are able to react to dangerous stimuli before we fully know what is going on. In situations where

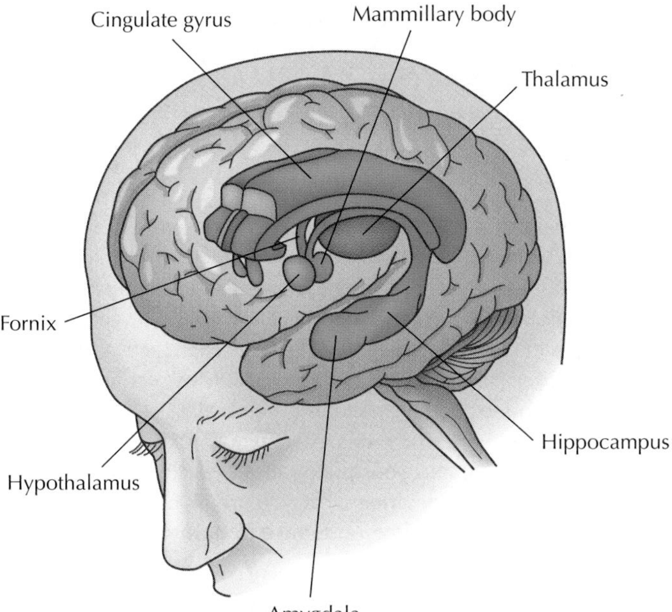

● **Figure 2.27** Parts of the limbic system are shown in this highly simplified drawing. Although only one side is shown, the hippocampus and the amygdala extend out into the temporal lobes at each side of the brain. The limbic system is a sort of "primitive core" of the brain strongly associated with emotion.

true danger exists, such as in military combat, the amygdala's rapid response may aid survival. However, disorders of the brain's fear system can be very disruptive. An example is the war veteran who involuntarily dives into the bushes when he hears a car backfire (Fellous & LeDoux, 2005; LaBar & LeDoux, 2002).

Some parts of the limbic system have taken on extra, higher-level functions. A part called the **hippocampus** (HIP-oh-CAMP-us) is important for forming lasting memories (Bigler et al., 1996). The hippocampus lies inside the temporal lobes, which is why stimulating the temporal lobes can produce memory-like or dream-like experiences. The hippocampus also helps us navigate through space. Your right hippocampus will become more active, for instance, if you mentally plan a drive across town (Maguire et al., 1997).

Psychologists have discovered that animals will learn to press a lever to deliver a dose of electrical stimulation to the limbic system. The animals act like the stimulation is satisfying or pleasurable. Indeed, several areas of the limbic system act as reward, or "pleasure," pathways. Many are found in the hypothalamus, where they overlap with areas that control thirst, sex, and hunger. Commonly abused drugs, such as cocaine, amphetamine, heroin, nicotine, marijuana, and alcohol activate many of the same pleasure pathways. This appears to explain, in part, why these drugs are so powerfully rewarding (Wise & Rompre, 1989). You might also be interested to know that music you would describe as "thrilling" activates pleasure systems in your brain. This may explain some of the appeal of music that can send shivers down the spine (Blood & Zatorre, 2001). (It may also explain why people will pay so much for concert tickets!)

Punishment, or "aversive," areas have also been found in the limbic system. When these locations are activated, animals show discomfort and will work hard to turn off the stimulation. Because much of our behavior is based on seeking pleasure and avoiding pain, these discoveries continue to fascinate psychologists.

The Magnificent Brain

Given the amount of information covered in our journey through the brain, a short review is in order. We have seen that the human brain is an impressive assembly of billions of sensitive cells and nerve fibers. The brain controls vital bodily functions, keeps track of the external world, issues commands to the muscles and glands, responds to current needs, regulates its own behavior, and even creates the "mind" and the magic of consciousness—*all* at the same time. (See "If You Change Your Mind Do You Change Your Brain?")

A final note of caution is now in order. For the sake of simplicity we have assigned functions to each "part" of the brain as if it were a computer. This is only a half-truth. In reality, the brain is a vast information-processing system. Incoming information scatters all over the brain and converges again as it goes out through the spinal cord, to muscles and glands. The overall system is much, much more complicated than our discussion of separate "parts" implies. In addition, the brain constantly revises its circuits in response to changing life experiences (Kolb & Whishaw, 2005).

BRIDGES

Unconscious fear produced by the amygdala seems to explain why people who survive horrible experiences, such as a plane crash, can have debilitating fears years later.

See the discussion of stress disorders in Chapter 16, pages 545–546.

Thalamus A brain structure that relays sensory information to the cerebral cortex.

Hypothalamus A small area of the brain that regulates emotional behaviors and motives.

Limbic system A system in the forebrain that is closely linked with emotional response.

Amygdala A part of the limbic system associated with fear responses.

Hippocampus A part of the limbic system associated with storing memories.

CRITICAL THINKING

If You Change Your Mind Do You Change Your Brain?

You can always change your mind. But does that have anything to do with your brain? The relationship of the mind to the brain (and the rest of the body) has been debated by philosophers for centuries. Biopsychologists argue that every mental event involves a brain event.

In one study, people suffering from spider phobias were treated with cognitive behavior therapy (see Chapter 17). After therapy, they could actually touch spiders (although they might not have been ready to appear on *Fear Factor*). Their fMRI brain images revealed reduced activity in the brain areas involved in the phobia (Paquette et al., 2003). Not only did they change their minds about spiders, they literally changed their brains.

In another study, stroke patients with left hemisphere damage were given language comprehension training to help them overcome aphasia. Not only did the training help improve the patients' language comprehension, but PET scans revealed that their undamaged right hemispheres became more active to compensate for their damaged left hemispheres (Musso et al., 1999). Again, a learning experience changed their brains.

Just think. As you study this psychology textbook you are changing your mind, and your brain, about psychology. There is even a fancy phrase to describe what you are doing: self-directed neuroplasticity. Every time you undertake to learn something, you are reshaping your living brain.

The Endocrine System—Hormones and Behavior

Our behavior is not solely a product of the nervous system. The endocrine (EN-duh-krin) glands form a second communication system in the body. Hormones can affect everything from puberty to personality, giantism to jet lag. The **endocrine system** is made up of glands that secrete chemicals directly into the bloodstream or lymph system (see ● Figure 2.28). These chemicals, called **hormones**, are carried throughout the body, where they affect both internal activities and visible behavior. Hormones are related to neurotransmitters. Like other transmitter chemicals, hormones activate cells in the body. To respond, the cells must have receptor sites for the hormone.

How do hormones affect behavior? Although we are seldom aware of them, hormones affect us in many ways. Here is a brief sample: Hormone output from the adrenal glands rises during stressful situations; androgens ("male" hormones) are related to the sex drive in both males and females; hormones secreted during times of high emotion intensify memory formation; at least some of the emotional turmoil of adolescence is due to elevated hormone levels; different hormones prevail when you are angry, rather than fearful. Something as routine as watching a movie can alter hormone levels. After watching violent scenes from *The Godfather,* men had higher levels of the male hormone testosterone. For both men and women, watching a romantic film boosted a hormone that's linked to relaxation and reproduction (Schultheiss, Wirth, & Stanton, 2004). Because these are just samples, let's consider some additional effects hormones have on the body and behavior.

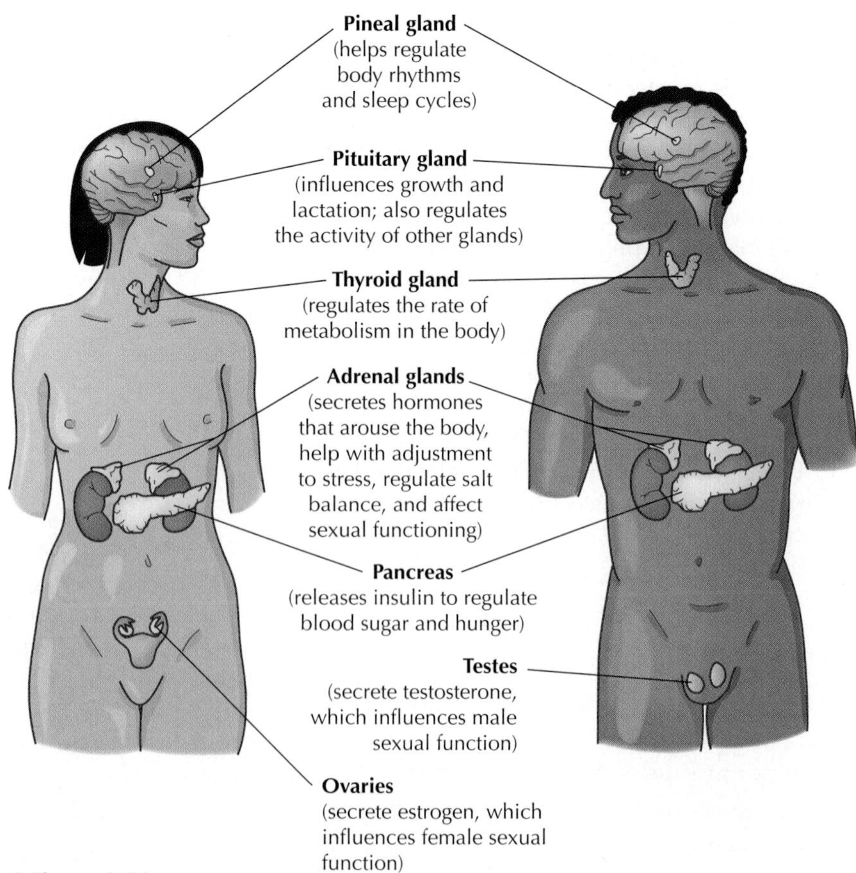

● **Figure 2.28**

Getty Images

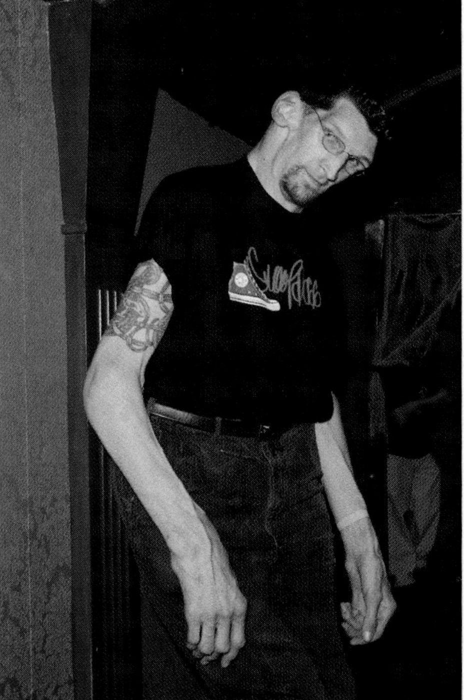
Amanda Edwards/Getty Images

Underactivity of the pituitary gland may produce a dwarf. Verne Troyer, best known for playing Mini-Me in the *Austin Powers* movies, has enjoyed an impressive career as an actor. Overactivity of the pituitary gland may produce a giant. Until his premature death in 2005, actor Mathew McGrory was best know for his role as Karl the Giant in the 2003 movie *Big Fish.*

The pituitary is a pea-size globe hanging from the base of the brain (return to ● Figure 2.27). One of the pituitary's more important roles is to regulate growth. During childhood, the pituitary secretes a hormone that speeds body development. If too little **growth hormone** is released, a person may remain far smaller than average. If this condition is not treated, a child may be 6 to 12 inches shorter than age-mates. As adults, some will have *hypopituitary* (HI-po-pih-TU-ih-ter-ee) *dwarfism.* Such individuals are perfectly proportioned, but tiny. Regular injections of growth hormone can raise a hypopituitary child's height by several inches, usually to the short side of average.

Too much growth hormone produces *giantism* (excessive bodily growth). Secretion of too much growth hormone late in the growth period causes *acromegaly* (AK-row-MEG-uh-lee), a condition in which the arms, hands, feet, and facial bones become enlarged. Acromegaly produces prominent facial features, which some people have used as a basis for careers as character actors, wrestlers, and the like.

The pituitary also governs the functioning of other glands (especially the thyroid, adrenal glands, and ovaries or testes). These glands in turn regulate such bodily processes as metabolism, responses to stress, and reproduction. In women, the pituitary controls milk production during pregnancy.

BRIDGES

Melatonin can be used to reset the body's "clock" and minimize jet lag for long-distance pilots, air crews, and travelers.

See Chapter 12, pages 402–403.

The **pituitary** is often called the "master gland" because its hormones influence other endocrine glands. But the master has a master: The pituitary is directed by the hypothalamus, which lies directly above it. In this way, the hypothalamus affects glands throughout the body. This, then, is the major link between the brain and the glandular system (Carlson, 2005).

The pineal (pin-EE-ul) gland was once considered a useless remnant of evolution. In certain fishes, frogs, and lizards, the gland is associated with a well-developed light-sensitive organ, or so-called third eye. In humans, the function of the **pineal gland** is just now coming to light (so to speak). The pineal gland releases a hormone called **melatonin** (mel-ah-TONE-in) in response to daily variations in light. Melatonin levels in the bloodstream rise at dusk and peak around midnight and fall again as morning approaches. This light-driven cycle helps control body rhythms and sleep cycles (Kennaway & Wright, 2002).

Endocrine system Glands whose secretions pass directly into the bloodstream or lymph system.

Hormone A glandular secretion that affects bodily functions or behavior.

Growth hormone A hormone, secreted by the pituitary gland, that promotes bodily growth.

Pituitary gland The "master gland" whose hormones influence other endocrine glands.

Pineal gland Gland in the brain that helps regulate body rhythms and sleep cycles.

Melatonin Hormone released by the pineal gland in response to daily cycles of light and dark.

The **thyroid gland,** located in the neck, regulates metabolism. As you may remember from a biology course, metabolism is the rate at which energy is produced and expended in the body. By altering metabolism, the thyroid can have a sizable effect on personality. A person suffering from *hyperthyroidism* (an overactive thyroid) tends to be thin, tense, excitable, and nervous. An underactive thyroid (*hypothyroidism*) in an adult can cause inactivity, sleepiness, slowness, and obesity. In infancy, hypothyroidism limits development of the nervous system, leading to severe mental retardation (see Chapter 11).

When you are frightened or angry, some important reactions prepare your body for action: Your heart rate and blood pressure rise, stored sugar is released into the bloodstream for quick energy, your muscles tense and receive more blood, and your blood is prepared to clot more quickly in case of injury. As we discussed earlier, these changes are controlled by the autonomic nervous system. Specifically, the sympathetic branch of the ANS causes the hormones *epinephrine* (ep-eh-NEF-rin) and *norepinephrine* to be released by the adrenal glands. (Epinephrine is also known as adrenaline, which may be more familiar to you.) **Epinephrine,** which is associated with fear, tends to arouse the body. **Norepinephrine** also tends to arouse the body, but it is linked with anger.

The **adrenal glands** are located just under the back of the rib cage, atop the kidneys. The *adrenal medulla,* or inner core of the adrenal glands, is the source of epinephrine and norepinephrine. The *adrenal cortex,* or outer "bark" of the adrenal glands, produces a set of hormones called corticoids (KOR-tih-coids). The corticoids regulate salt balance in the body, help the body adjust to stress, and provide a secondary source of sex hormones.

An oversecretion of the adrenal sex hormones can cause *virilism* (exaggerated male characteristics). For instance, a woman may grow a beard or a man's voice may become so low it is difficult to understand. Oversecretion early in life can cause *premature puberty* (full sexual development during childhood). One of the most remarkable cases on record is that of a 5-year-old Peruvian girl who gave birth to a son (Strange, 1965).

While we are on the topic of sex hormones, there is a related issue worth mentioning. One of the principal androgens, or "male" hormones, is testosterone, which is supplied in small amounts by the adrenal glands. (The testes are the main source of testosterone in males.) Perhaps you have heard about the use of anabolic steroids by athletes who want to "bulk up" or promote muscle growth. Most of these drugs are synthetic versions of testosterone.

Although many athletes believe otherwise, there is no evidence that steroids improve performance, and they may cause serious side effects. Problems include voice deepening or baldness in women and shrinkage of the testicles, sexual impotence, or breast enlargement in men. Younger adolescents who use steroids are at an increased risk of heart attack and stroke, liver damage, or stunted growth (Bahrke, Yesalis, & Brower, 1998). Dangerous increases in hostility and aggression ("roid rage") have also been linked with steroid use (Hartgens & Kuipers, 2004). Understandably, almost all major sports organizations ban the use of anabolic steroids.

Getty Images

During his bid for the major league home run record, baseball star Mark McGwire admitted to using a steroid drug banned by the NFL and the Olympics but not by Major League Baseball. Many athletes have been disqualified, banned from competing, or stripped of medals for steroid use.

In this brief discussion of the endocrine system we have considered only a few of the more important glands. Nevertheless, this should give you an appreciation of how completely behavior and personality are tied to the ebb and flow of hormones in the body.

A Look Ahead

In the upcoming Psychology in Action section, we will return to the brain to see how hand preference relates to brain organization. You'll also find out if being right- or left-handed affects your chances of living to a ripe old age.

KNOWLEDGE BUILDER

Subcortex and Endocrine System

REFLECT

If Mr. Medulla met Ms. Cerebellum at a party, what would they say their roles are in the brain? Would a marching band in a "reticular formation" look like a network? Would it get your attention? If you were standing in the final path for behavior leaving the brain, would you be in the thalamus? Or in the hy-*path*-alamus (please forgive the misspelling)? When you are emotional, do you wave your limbs around (and does your limbic system become more active)?

Name as many of the endocrine glands as you can. Which did you leave out? Can you summarize the functions of each of the glands?

LEARNING CHECK

1. Three major divisions of the brain are the brainstem or ______________, the ______________, and the ______________.
2. Reflex centers for heartbeat and respiration are found in the
   a. cerebellum c. medulla
   b. thalamus d. RF
3. A portion of the reticular formation, known as the RAS, serves as an ______________ system in the brain.
   a. activating c. adjustment
   b. adrenal d. aversive
4. The ______________ is a final relay, or "switching station," for sensory information on its way to the cortex.
5. "Reward" and "punishment" areas are found throughout the ______________ system, which is also related to emotion.
6. Undersecretion from the thyroid can cause
   a. dwarfism c. obesity
   b. giantism d. mental retardation
7. The body's ability to resist stress is related to the action of the adrenal ______________.

CRITICAL THINKING

8. Subcortical structures in humans are quite similar to corresponding lower brain areas in animals. Why would knowing this allow you to predict, in general terms, what functions are controlled by the subcortex?
9. Where in all the brain's "hardware" do you think the mind is found? What is the relationship between mind and brain?

Answers: 1. hindbrain, midbrain, forebrain **2.** c **3.** a **4.** thalamus **5.** limbic **6.** c, d (in infancy) **7.** cortex **8.** Because the subcortex must be related to basic functions common to all higher animals: motives, emotions, sleep, attention, and vegetative functions, such as heart rate, breathing, and temperature regulation. The subcortex also routes and processes incoming information from the senses and outgoing commands to the muscles. **9.** This question, known as the mind–body problem, has challenged thinkers for centuries. One recent view is that mental states are "emergent properties" of brain activity. That is, brain activity forms complex patterns that are, in a sense, more than the sum of their parts. Or, to use a rough analogy, if the brain were a musical instrument, then mental life would be like music played on that instrument.

PSYCHOLOGY IN ACTION

Handedness—If Your Brain Is Right, What's Left?

In the English language, "what's right is right," but what's left may be wrong. We have left-handed compliments, people with "two left feet," those who are left out, and the left-handed. On the other hand (so to speak), we have the right way, the right angle, the "right-hand man" (or woman), righteousness, and the right-handed.

What causes **handedness** (a preference for the right or left hand)? Why are there more right-handed than left-handed people? How do left-handed and right-handed people differ? Does being left-handed create any problems—or benefits? The answers to these questions lead us back to the brain, where handedness begins. Let's see what research has revealed about handedness, the brain, and you.

Hand Dominance

Write your name on a sheet of paper, first using your right hand and then your left. You were probably much more comfortable writing with your dominant hand. This is interesting because there's no real difference in the strength or dexterity of the hands themselves. The agility of your dominant hand is an outward expression of superior motor control on one side of the brain. If you are right-handed, there is literally more area on the left side of your brain devoted to controlling your right hand. If you are left-handed, the reverse applies (Volkmann et al., 1998). To better assess your handedness, which is a matter of degree

Thyroid gland Endocrine gland that helps regulate the rate of metabolism.

Epinephrine An adrenal hormone that tends to arouse the body; epinephrine is associated with fear. (Also known as adrenaline.)

Norepinephrine An adrenal hormone that tends to arouse the body; norepinephrine is associated with anger. (Also known as noradrenaline.)

Adrenal glands Endocrine glands that arouse the body, regulate salt balance, adjust the body to stress, and affect sexual functioning.

Handedness A preference for the right or left hand in most activities.

(Coren, 1992), circle an answer for each of the questions that follow.

Are You Right- or Left-Handed?

1. Which hand do you normally use to write? Right Left Either
2. Which hand would you use to throw a ball at a target? Right Left Either
3. Which hand do you use to hold your toothbrush? Right Left Either
4. Which hand do you use to hold a knife when cutting food? Right Left Either
5. With which hand do you hold a hammer when hitting a nail? Right Left Either
6. When you thread a needle, which hand holds the thread? Right Left Either

To find your score, count the number of "Rights" you circled and multiply by 3. Then multiply the number of "Eithers" by 2. Next count the number of "Lefts" you circled. Now add all three totals and compare the result with the following scale (adapted from Coren, 1992).

17–18 Strongly right-handed
15–16 Moderately right-handed (mixed)
13–14 Mildly right-handed (mixed)
12 Ambidextrous
10–11 Mildly left-handed (mixed)
8–9 Moderately left-handed (mixed)
6–7 Strongly left-handed

A majority of people (about 77 percent) are strongly right- or left-handed. The rest show some inconsistency in hand preference. As ■ Table 2.1 indicates, such differences can affect performance in some sports. (Contrary to popular belief, there is no overall handedness advantage in baseball. However, there are situations that favor one hand or the other. For instance, it is best to have a lefty pitch to a left-handed batter [Goldstein & Young, 1996].) Away from sports, left-handedness has an undeserved bad reputation. The supposed clumsiness of lefties is merely a result of living in a right-handed world: If it can be gripped, turned, or pulled, it's probably designed for the right hand. Even toilet handles are on the right side.

If a person is strongly left-handed, does that mean the right hemisphere is dominant? Not necessarily. It's true that the right hemisphere controls the left hand, but a left-handed person's language-producing, **dominant hemisphere** may be on the opposite side of the brain.

Brain Dominance

About 97 percent of right-handers process speech in the left hemisphere and are left-brain dominant (● Figure 2.29). A good 68 percent of left-handers produce speech from the left hemisphere, just as right-handed people do. About 19 percent of all lefties and 3 percent of righties use their right brain for language. Some left-handers (approximately 12 percent) use both sides of the brain for language processing. All told, 94 percent of the population uses the left brain for language (Coren, 1992).

TABLE 2.1

Sports and Handedness

SPORT	HANDEDNESS ADVANTAGE
Baseball	No overall left or right advantage
Boxing	Left
Fencing	Left
Basketball	Mixed and ambidextrous
Ice hockey	Mixed and ambidextrous
Field hockey	Mixed and ambidextrous
Tennis	Strong left or strong right
Squash	Strong left or strong right
Badminton	Strong left or strong right

Adapted from Coren, 1992.

Left-handers have an advantage in sports such as fencing and boxing. Most likely, their movements are less familiar to opponents, who usually face right-handers (Coren, 1992).

Bob Daemmrich/The Image Works

Is there any way for a person to tell which of his or her hemispheres is dominant? One interesting clue is the way you write. Right-handed individuals who write with a straight hand, and lefties who write with a hooked hand, are usually left-brain dominant for language. Left-handed people who write with their hand below the line, and righties who use a hooked position, are usually right-brain dominant (Levy & Reid, 1976). Another hint is provided by hand gestures. If you gesture mostly with your right hand as you talk, you probably process language in your left hemisphere. Gesturing with your left hand is associated with right-brain language processing (Hellige, 1993).

Are your friends right brained or left brained (see ● Figure 2.30)? Before you leap to any conclusions, be aware that writing position and gestures are not foolproof. The only sure way to check brain dominance is to do a medical test that involves briefly anesthetizing one cerebral hemisphere at a time (Springer & Deutsch, 1998).

Handedness

How common is left-handedness, and what causes it? Ninety percent of all humans are right-handed; 10 percent are left-handed. In the past, many left-handed children were forced to use their right hand for writing, eating, and other skills. But as fetal ultrasound images show, clear hand preferences are apparent even before birth (Hepper, McCartney, & Shannon, 1998) (see ● Figure 2.31). This suggests that handedness cannot be dictated. Parents should never try to force a left-handed child to use the right hand. To do so may create speech or reading problems.

Is handedness inherited from parents? Studies of twins show that hand preferences are not directly inherited like eye color or skin color (Reiss et al., 1999; Ross et al., 1999). Yet two left-handed parents are more likely to have a left-handed child than two right-handed parents are (McKeever, 2000). The best evidence to date shows that handedness is influenced by a single gene on the X (female) chromosome (Jones & Martin, 2001). However, learning, birth traumas, and social pressure to use the right hand can also affect which hand you end up favoring (McKeever et al., 2000; Provins, 1997).

Are there any drawbacks to being left-handed? A minority of lefties owe their hand preference to birth traumas (such as prematurity, low birth weight, and breech birth). These individuals have higher rates of allergies, learning disorders, and other

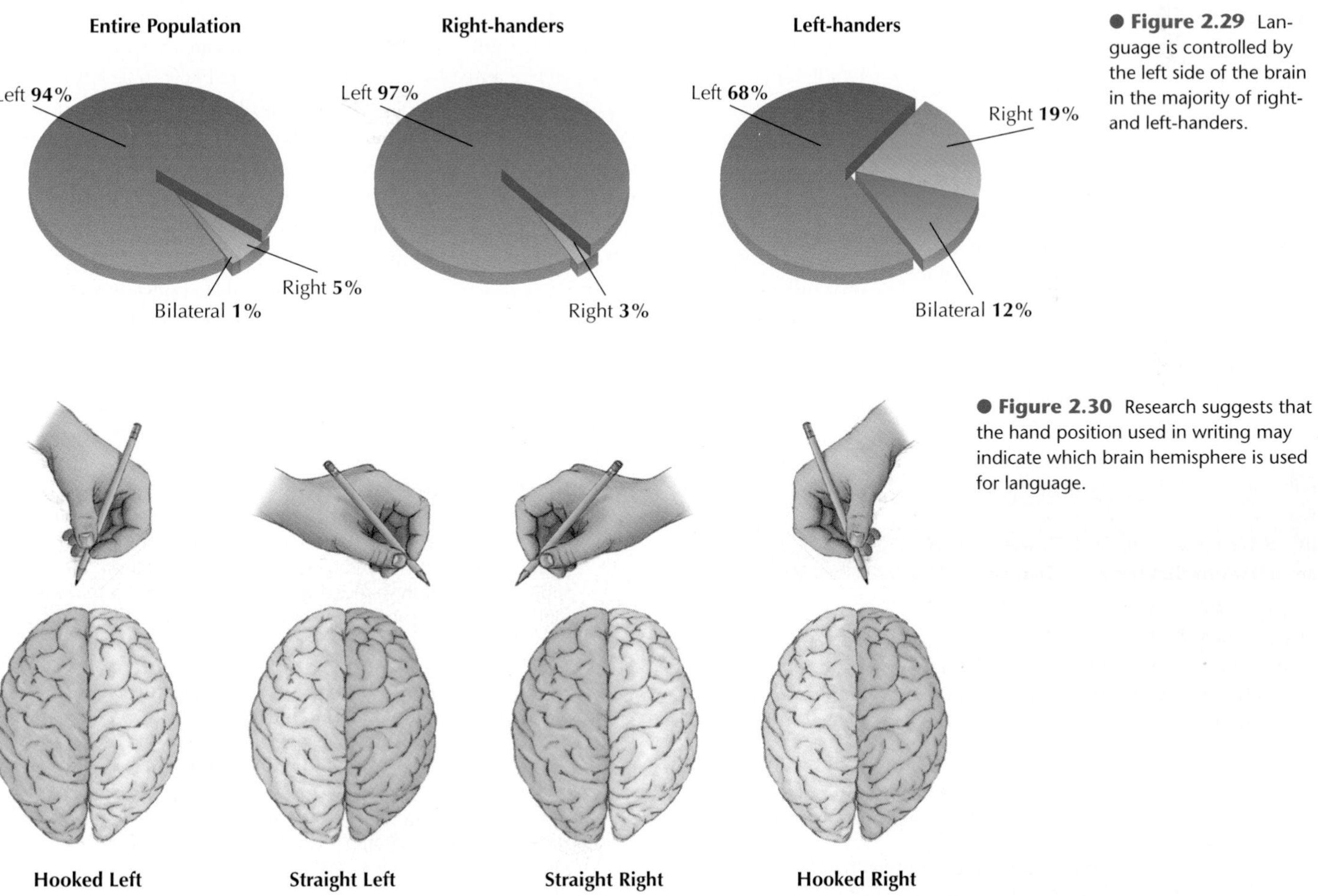

● **Figure 2.29** Language is controlled by the left side of the brain in the majority of right- and left-handers.

● **Figure 2.30** Research suggests that the hand position used in writing may indicate which brain hemisphere is used for language.

Dominant hemisphere A term usually applied to the side of a person's brain that produces language.

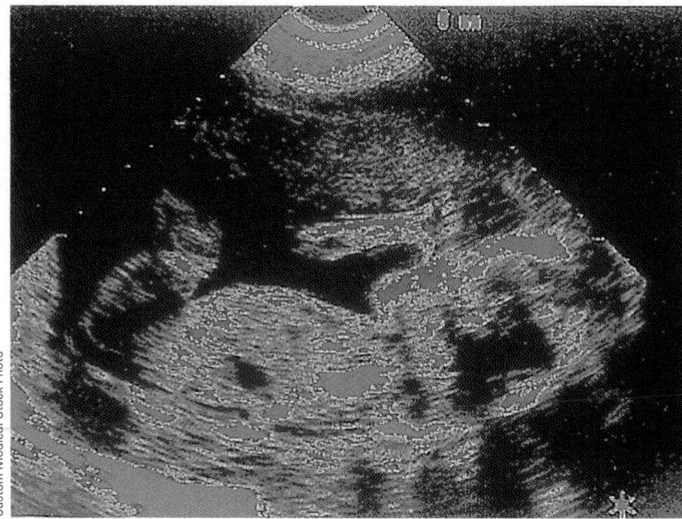

● **Figure 2.31** In this ultrasound image, a 4-month-old fetus sucks her right thumb. A study by psychologist Peter Hepper suggests that she will continue to prefer her right hand after she is born and that she will be right-handed as an adult.

Custom Medical Stock Photo

problems (Betancur et al., 1990). But in most instances left-handedness is unrelated to intelligence or the overall incidence of illness and accidents (McManus et al., 1988; Porac et al., 1998).

Then why do right-handed people seem to live longer than left-handed people? It is true that there is a shortage of very old lefties. However, this does not mean that the left-handed die early. It just reflects the fact that, in the past, more left-handed children were forced to become right-handed. That makes it look like many lefties don't survive to old age. In reality, they do, but many of them are masquerading as righties (Martin & Freitas, 2002)!

Advantage Left

Actually, there are some clear advantages to being left-handed. Throughout history a notable number of artists have been lefties, from Leonardo da Vinci and Michelangelo to Pablo Picasso and M. C. Escher. Conceivably, because the right hemisphere is superior at imagery and visual abilities, there is some advantage to using the left hand for drawing or painting (Springer & Deutsch, 1998). At the least, lefties are definitely better at visualizing three-dimensional objects. This may be why there are more left-handed architects, artists, and chess players than would be expected (Coren, 1992).

Lateralization refers to specialization in the abilities of the brain hemispheres. One striking feature of lefties is that they are generally less lateralized than the right-handed. In fact, even the physical size and shape of their cerebral hemispheres are more alike. If you are a lefty you can take pride in the fact that your brain is less lopsided than most! In general, left-handers are more symmetrical on almost everything, including eye dominance, fingerprints—even foot size (Polemikos & Papaeliou, 2000).

In some situations less lateralization may be a real advantage. For instance, individuals who are moderately left-handed or ambidextrous seem to have better than average pitch memory, which is a basic musical skill. Correspondingly, more musicians are ambidextrous than would normally be expected (Springer & Deutsch, 1998). Math abilities may also benefit from fuller use of the right hemisphere. Students who are extremely gifted in math are much more likely to be left-handed or ambidextrous (Benbow, 1986). Even where ordinary arithmetic skills are concerned, lefties seem to excel (Annett & Manning, 1990).

The clearest advantage of being left-handed shows up when there is a brain injury. Because of their milder lateralization, left-handed individuals typically experience less language loss after damage to either brain hemisphere, and they recover more easily (Geschwind, 1979). Maybe having "two left feet" isn't so bad after all.

KNOWLEDGE BUILDER

Handedness and Brain Lateralization

REFLECT

Think for a moment about what you "knew" about handedness and left-handed people before you read this section. Which of your beliefs were correct? How has your knowledge about handedness changed?

LEARNING CHECK

1. About 97 percent of left-handed people process language on the left side of the brain, the same as right-handed people do. T or F?
2. Left-handed individuals who write with their hand below the line are likely to be right-brain dominant. T or F?
3. People basically learn to be right- or left-handed. T or F?
4. In general, left-handed individuals show less lateralization in the brain and throughout the body. T or F?

CRITICAL THINKING

5. News reports that left-handed people tend to die younger have been flawed in an important way: The average age of people in the left-handed group was younger than that of subjects in the right-handed group. Why would this make a difference in the conclusions drawn?

Answers: 1. F **2.** T **3.** F **4.** T **5.** Because we can't tell if handedness or average age accounts for the difference in death rates. For example, if we start with a group of 20- to 30-year-old people, in which some die, the average age of death has to be between 20 and 30. If we start with a group of 30- to 40-year-old people, in which some die, the average age of death has to be between 30 and 40. Thus, the left-handed group might have an earlier average age at death simply because members of the group were younger to start with.

Chapter in Review

How do nerve cells operate and communicate?

- All behavior can be traced to the activity of neurons, which carry information from one cell to another.
- Axons are the basic conducting fibers of neurons, but dendrites, the soma, and axon terminals are also involved in communication.
- The firing of an action potential (nerve impulse) is basically an electrical event.
- Communication between neurons is chemical: Neurotransmitters cross the synapse, attach to receptor sites, and excite or inhibit the receiving cell.
- Chemicals called neuropeptides regulate activity in the brain.

What are the functions of major parts of the nervous system?

- The nervous system can be divided into the central nervous system and the peripheral nervous system, which includes the somatic (bodily) and autonomic (involuntary) nervous systems.
- The peripheral nervous system carries sensory information to the brain and motor commands to the body.
- "Vegetative" and automatic bodily processes are controlled by the autonomic nervous system, which has a sympathetic branch and a parasympathetic branch.

How do we know how the brain works?

- Brain research relies on clinical studies, electrical stimulation, ablation, deep lesioning, electrical recording, microelectrode recording, and EEG recording.
- To map the brain, researchers activate or disable specific areas and observe changes in behavior.
- Computer-enhanced images are providing three-dimensional pictures of the living human brain and its activity. Examples of such techniques are CT scans, MRI scans, and PET scans.

How is the brain organized, and what do its various areas do?

- The human brain is marked by advanced corticalization, or enlargement of the cerebral cortex.
- The left cerebral hemisphere contains speech or language "centers" in most people. It also specializes in writing, calculating, judging time and rhythm, and ordering complex movements.
- The right hemisphere is largely nonverbal. It excels at spatial and perceptual skills, visualization, and recognition of patterns, faces, and melodies.
- The left hemisphere is good at analysis and it processes small details sequentially. The right hemisphere detects overall patterns; it processes information simultaneously and holistically.
- "Split brains" have been created in animals and humans by cutting the corpus callosum. The split-brain individual shows a remarkable degree of independence between the right and left hemispheres.
- The most basic functions of the lobes of the cerebral cortex are as follows: occipital lobes—vision; parietal lobes—bodily sensation; temporal lobes—hearing and language; frontal lobes—motor control, speech, and abstract thought. Damage to any of these areas will impair the named functions.

Why are the brain's association areas important? What happens when they are injured?

- Association areas on the cortex are neither sensory nor motor in function. They are related to more complex skills, such as language, memory, recognition, and problem solving.
- Damage to either Broca's area or Wernicke's area causes speech and language problems known as aphasias.
- Damage in other areas may cause agnosia, the inability to identify objects by sight.

What kinds of behaviors are controlled by the subcortex?

- The subcortex consists of the hindbrain, midbrain, and lower parts of the forebrain.
- The brain can be subdivided into the forebrain, midbrain, and hindbrain. The subcortex includes several crucial brain structures found at all three levels, below the cortex.
- The medulla contains centers essential for reflex control of heart rate, breathing, and other "vegetative" functions.
- The cerebellum maintains coordination, posture, and muscle tone.
- The reticular formation directs sensory and motor messages, and part of it, known as the RAS, acts as an activating system for the cerebral cortex.
- The thalamus carries sensory information to the cortex. The hypothalamus exerts powerful control over eating, drinking,

---

Lateralization Differences between the two sides of the body, especially differences in the abilities of the brain hemispheres.

sleep cycles, body temperature, and other basic motives and behaviors.
- The limbic system is strongly related to emotion. It also contains distinct reward and punishment areas and an area known as the hippocampus that is important for forming memories.

Is behavior affected by the glandular system?
- Hormones from the endocrine glands enter the bloodstream and affect activities all over the body.
- Endocrine glands serve as a chemical communication system within the body. Behavior, moods, and personality are influenced by the ebb and flow of hormones in the bloodstream.
- Many of the endocrine glands are influenced by the pituitary (the "master gland"), which is in turn influenced by the hypothalamus. Thus, the brain controls the body through the fast nervous system and the slower endocrine system.

In what ways do right- and left-handed individuals differ?
- Brain dominance and brain activity determine whether you are right-handed, left-handed, or ambidextrous.
- Most people are strongly right-handed. A minority are strongly left-handed. A few have moderate or mixed hand preferences or they are ambidextrous. Thus, handedness is not a simple either/or trait.
- The vast majority of people are right-handed and therefore left-brain dominant for motor skills. Ninety-seven percent of right-handed persons and 68 percent of the left-handed also produce speech from the left hemisphere.
- Left-handed people tend to be less strongly lateralized than right-handed people (their brain hemispheres are not as specialized).

> Web Resources

Internet addresses frequently change. To find the sites listed here, visit www.thomsonedu.com/psychology/coon for an updated list of Internet addresses and direct links to relevant sites.

***Psychology: Gateways to Mind and Behavior* Website** Online quizzes, flash cards, and other helpful study aids for this text. www.thomsonedu.com/psychology/coon.

Brain Briefings Articles on a variety of topics in neuroscience.

Brain Connection Explains brain research to the public, including common myths about the brain, the effects of various chemicals, how brain research applies to education, and more.

Lorin's Left-Handedness Site Answers to common questions about left-handedness.

Probe the Brain Explore the motor homunculus of the brain interactively.

The Brain Quiz Answer questions about the brain and get instant feedback.

The Brain: A Work in Progress A set of related articles about the brain.

The Human Brain: Dissections of the Real Brain Detailed photographs and drawings of the human brain.

The Endocrine System Describes the endocrine system and hormones.

ThomsonNOW™ Go to www.thomsonedu.com to link to ThomsonNow, your online study tool. First take the **Pre-Test** for this chapter to get your **Personalized Study Plan,** which will identify topics you need to review and direct you to online resources. Then take the **Post-Test** to determine what concepts you have mastered and what you still need work on.

InfoTrac College Edition For recent articles related to brain mapping, use a Key Words search for MAGNETIC RESONANCE IMAGING and ELECTROENCEPHALOGRAPHY. Go to www.thomsonedu.com/psychology/coon.

Interactive Learning

***PsychNow! Version 2.0* CD-ROM** Interact with the material with *PsychNow!'s* animations, video clips, experiments, and interactive assessments. For this chapter, go to *3a. Neurons and Synaptic Transmission* and *3b. Brain and Behavior* to better understand synaptic transmission and how the brain impacts behavior.

chapter

3

Child Development

FogStock/Index Stock Imagery

THEME:

The principles of development help us better understand not only children, but our own behavior as well.

Key Questions

How do heredity and environment affect development?

What can newborn babies do?

What influence does maturation have on early development?

Of what significance is a child's emotional bond with parents?

How important are parenting styles?

How do children acquire language?

How do children learn to think?

How do effective parents discipline their children?

Preview

A Star Is Born—Here's Amy!

Olivia has just given birth to her first child, Amy. Frankly, at the moment Amy looks something like a pink prune, with pudgy arms, stubby legs, and lots of wrinkles. She also has the face of an angel—at least in her parents' eyes. As Olivia and her husband, Tom, look at Amy, they wonder, "How will her life unfold? What kind of a person will she be?"

What if we could skip ahead through Amy's childhood and observe her at various ages? What could we learn? Seeing the world through her eyes would be fascinating and instructive. For example, younger children are very literal in their use of language. When she was 3, Amy thought her bath was too hot and said to Tom, "Make it warmer, Daddy." At first, Tom was confused. The bath was already fairly hot. But then he realized that what she really meant was, "Bring the water closer to the temperature we call *warm.*" It makes perfect sense if you look at it that way.

Today we can merely guess about Amy's future. However, psychologists have studied many thousands of children. Their findings tell a fascinating story about human growth and development. Let's let Olivia, Tom, and Amy represent parents and children everywhere, as we see what psychology can tell us about the challenges of growing up. Tracing Amy's development might even help you answer the question, "How did I become the person I am today?"

Heredity and Environment—The Nurture of Nature

Children are the heart of **developmental psychology** (the study of progressive changes in behavior and abilities). However, human development involves every stage of life, from conception to death (or "the womb to the tomb"). Some events in life, such as achieving sexual maturity, are mostly governed by heredity. Others, such as learning to swim or use a computer, are primarily a matter of environment. But which is more important, heredity or environment? Let's consider some evidence on both sides of the nature-nurture debate.

Heredity

Heredity ("nature") refers to genetically passing characteristics from parents to children. An incredible number of personal features are set at conception, when a sperm and an ovum (egg) unite.

How does heredity operate? Every human cell contains 46 **chromosomes**, which hold the coded instructions of heredity (● Figure 3.1). A notable exception is sperm cells and ova, which contain only 23 chromosomes. Thus, Amy received 23 chromosomes from Olivia and 23 from Tom. This is her genetic heritage.

Chromosomes are made up of **DNA** (deoxyribonucleic [dee-OX-see-RYE-bo-new-KLEE-ik] acid). DNA is a long, ladder-like chain of chemical molecules (● Figure 3.2). The order of these molecules, or organic bases, acts as a code for genetic information. The DNA in each cell contains a record of all the instructions needed to make a human—with room left over to spare.

Genes are small areas of DNA that affect a particular process or personal characteristic. Sometimes, a single gene is responsible for an inherited feature, such as Amy's eye color. Most characteristics, however, are **polygenic** (pol-ih-JEN-ik), or controlled by many genes working in combination.

Genes may be dominant or recessive. When a gene is **dominant**, the feature it controls will appear every time the gene is present. When a gene is **recessive**, it must be paired with a second recessive gene before its effect will be expressed. For example, if Amy got a blue-eye gene from Tom and a brown-eye gene from Olivia, Amy will be brown-eyed, because brown-eye genes are dominant.

If brown-eye genes are dominant, why do two brown-eyed parents sometimes have a blue-eyed child? If each parent has two brown-eye genes, the couple's children can only be brown-eyed. But what if

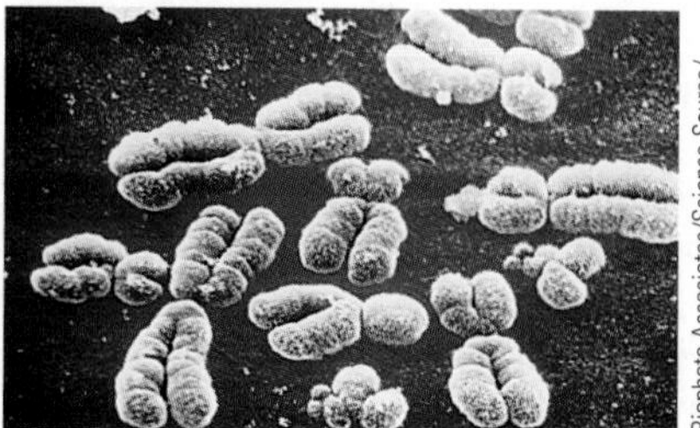

Biophoto Associates/Science-Source/Photo Researchers, Inc.

● **Figure 3.1** This image, made with a scanning electron microscope, shows several pairs of human chromosomes. (Colors are artificial.)

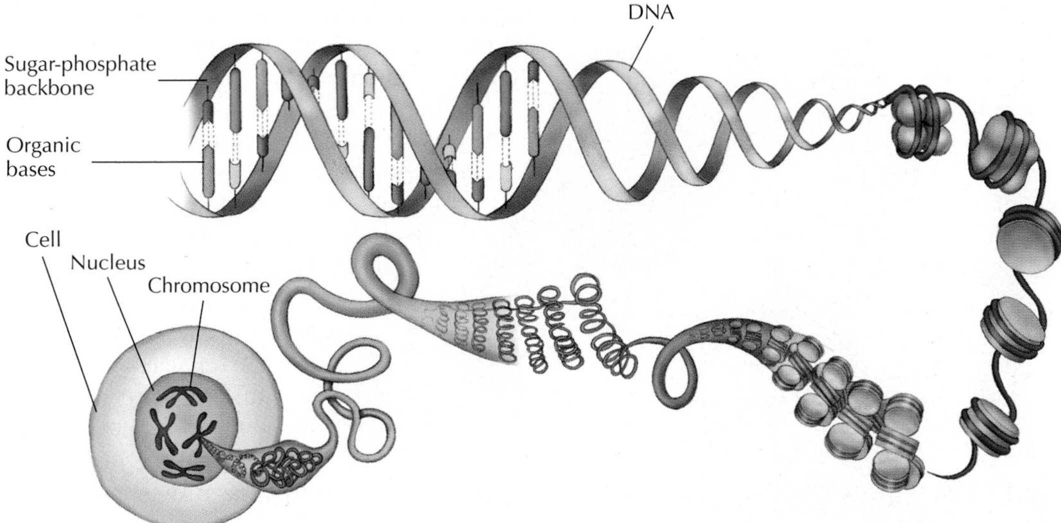

● **Figure 3.2** *(Top left)* Linked molecules (organic bases) make up the "rungs" on DNA's twisted "molecular ladder." The order of these molecules serves as a code for genetic information. The code provides a genetic blueprint that is unique for each individual (except identical twins). The drawing shows only a small section of a DNA strand. An entire strand of DNA is composed of billions of smaller molecules. *(Bottom left)* The nucleus of each cell in the body contains chromosomes made up of tightly wound coils of DNA. (Don't be misled by the drawing: Chromosomes are microscopic in size, and the chemical molecules that make up DNA are even smaller.)

each parent has one brown-eye gene and one blue-eye gene? In that case the parents would both have brown eyes. Yet there is a one in four chance that their children will get two blue-eye genes and have blue eyes (● Figure 3.3).

Genetic Programming

Heredity influences events from conception to senescence (seh-NESS-ens: aging) and death (see ■ Table 3.1). That's why the **human growth sequence**, or overall pattern of physical development, is universal. Heredity also determines eye color, skin color, and susceptibility to some diseases. To a degree, genetic instructions affect body size and shape, height, intelligence, athletic potential, personality traits, sexual orientation, and a host of other details (Klug & Cummings, 2003). Score one for those who favor heredity as the more important factor in development!

Temperament

How soon do hereditary differences appear? Some appear right away. For instance, newborn babies differ noticeably in **temperament.** This is the physical core of personality. It includes sensitivity, irritability, distractibility, and typical mood (Kagan, 2000). About 40 percent of all newborns are *easy children,* who are relaxed and

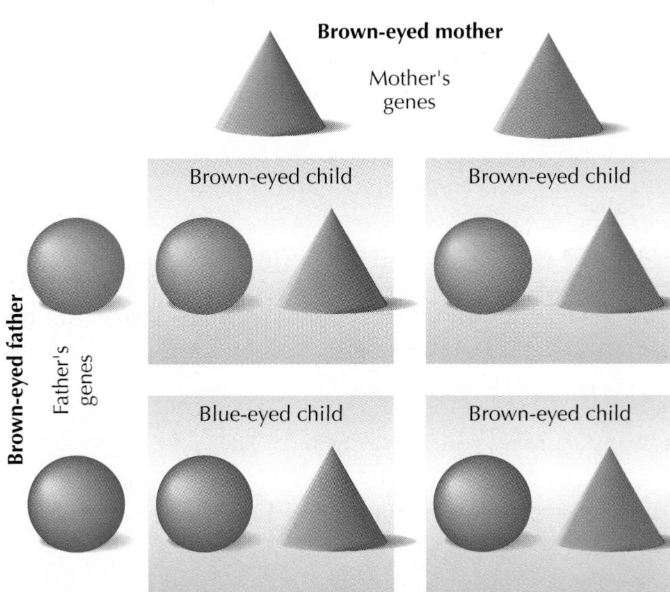

● **Figure 3.3** Gene patterns for children of brown-eyed parents, where each parent has one brown-eye gene and one blue-eye gene. Because the brown-eye gene is dominant, one out of every four children will be blue-eyed. Thus, there is a significant chance that two brown-eyed parents will have a blue-eyed child.

Developmental psychology The study of progressive changes in behavior and abilities from conception to death.

Heredity ("nature") The transmission of physical and psychological characteristics from parents to offspring through genes.

Chromosomes Thread-like "colored bodies" in the nucleus of each cell that are made up of DNA.

DNA Deoxyribonucleic acid, a molecular structure that contains coded genetic information.

Genes Specific areas on a strand of DNA that carry hereditary information.

Polygenic characteristics Personal traits or physical properties that are influenced by many genes working in combination.

Dominant gene A gene whose influence will be expressed each time the gene is present.

Recessive gene A gene whose influence will be expressed only when it is paired with a second recessive gene.

Human growth sequence The pattern of physical development from conception to death.

Temperament The physical core of personality, including emotional and perceptual sensitivity, energy levels, typical mood, and so forth.

agreeable. Ten percent are *difficult children,* who are moody, intense, and easily angered. *Slow-to-warm-up children* (about 15 percent) are restrained, unexpressive, or shy. The remaining children do not fit neatly into a single category (Chess & Thomas, 1986).

Imagine that we start with some infants who are very shy and some who are very bold. By the time they are 4 to 5 years old, most of these children will be only moderately shy or bold. This suggests that inherited temperaments are modified by learning (Kagan, 1999). In other words, nurture immediately enters the picture.

Environment

Environment ("nurture") refers to the sum of all external conditions that affect a person. The environments in which a child grows up can have a powerful impact on development. Humans today are genetically very similar to cave dwellers who lived 30,000 years ago. Nevertheless, a bright baby born today could learn to become almost anything—a ballet dancer, an engineer, a gangsta rapper, or a biochemist who likes to paint in watercolors—but an Upper Paleolithic baby could have only become a hunter or food gatherer. Score one for the environmentalists!

Early experiences can have very lasting effects. For example, children who are abused may suffer life-long emotional problems (Rutter, 1995). At the same time, extra care can sometimes reverse the effects of a poor start in life (Bornstein & Tamis-LeMonda, 2001). In short, environmental forces guide human development, for better or worse, throughout life.

Myrleen Ferguson Cate/PhotoEdit

Identical twins. Twins who share identical genes (identical twins) demonstrate the powerful influence of heredity. Even when they are reared apart, identical twins are strikingly alike in motor skills, physical development, and appearance. At the same time, twins are less alike as adults than they were as children, which shows environmental influences are at work (McCartney, Bernieri, & Harris, 1990).

TABLE 3.1

Human Growth Sequence

PERIOD	DURATION	DESCRIPTIVE NAME
Prenatal period	From conception to birth	Zygote
Germinal period	First 2 weeks after conception	Embryo
Embryonic period	2–8 weeks after conception	Fetus
Fetal period	From 8 weeks after conception to birth	Neonate
Neonatal period	From birth to a few weeks after birth	
Infancy	From a few weeks after birth until child is walking securely; some children walk securely at less than a year, while others may not be able to until age 17–18 months	Infant
Early childhood	From about 15–18 months until about 2–2½ years	Toddler
	From age 2–3 to about age 6	Preschool child
Middle childhood	From about age 6 to age 12	School-age child
Pubescence	Period of about 2 years before puberty	
Puberty	Point of development at which biological changes of pubescence reach a climax marked by sexual maturity	
Adolescence	From the beginning of pubescence until full social maturity is reached (difficult to fix duration of this period)	Adolescent
Adulthood	From adolescence to death; sometimes subdivided into other periods as shown at left	Adult
Young adulthood (19–25)		
Adulthood (26–40)		
Maturity (41 plus)		
Senescence	No defined limit that would apply to all people; extremely variable; characterized by marked physiological and psychological deterioration	Adult (senile), "old age"

*Note: There is no exact beginning or ending point for various growth periods. The ages are approximate, and each period may be thought of as blending into the next. (Table courtesy of Tom Bond.)

Sensitive Periods

Why do some experiences have more lasting effects than others? Part of the answer lies in **sensitive periods.** These are times when children are more susceptible to particular types of environmental influences. Events that occur during a sensitive period can permanently alter the course of development (Bornstein, 1989). For instance, if a woman has German measles during early pregnancy, her child may be born with heart defects, cataracts, or hearing loss. Later in pregnancy, the child would escape without damage.

Often, certain events must occur during a sensitive period for a person to develop normally. For example, forming a loving bond with a caregiver early in life seems to be crucial for optimal development. Likewise, babies who don't hear normal speech during their first year may have impaired language abilities (Thompson & Nelson, 2001).

Prenatal Influences

The impact of nurture actually starts before birth. Although the intrauterine environment (interior of the womb) is highly protected, environmental conditions can affect the developing child. For example, when Olivia was pregnant, Amy's fetal heart rate and movements increased when loud sounds or vibrations penetrated the womb (Kisilevsky et al., 2004).

If Olivia's health or nutrition had been poor, or if she contracted German measles, syphilis, or HIV; used drugs; or was exposed to X-rays or atomic radiation, Amy might have been harmed. In such cases babies can suffer from **congenital problems** or "birth defects." These problems affect the developing fetus and become apparent at birth. In contrast, **genetic disorders** are inherited from parents. Examples are sickle cell anemia, hemophilia, cystic fibrosis, muscular dystrophy, albinism, and some types of mental retardation.

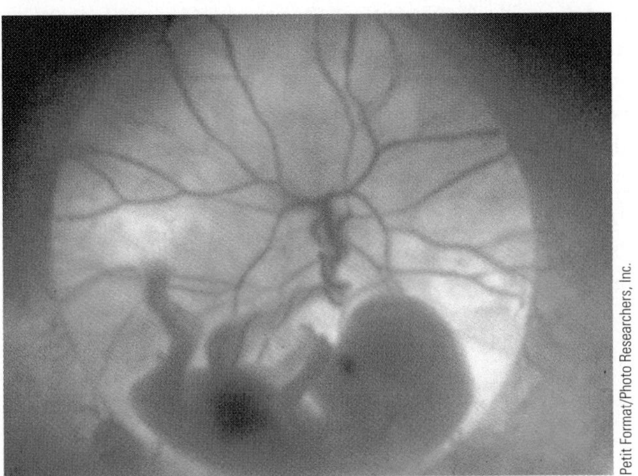

Petit Format/Photo Researchers, Inc.

Because of the rapid growth of basic structures, the developing fetus is sensitive to a variety of diseases, drugs, and sources of radiation. This is especially true during the first trimester (3 months) of gestation (pregnancy).

BRIDGES

Child abuse is a serious problem, but steps can be taken to prevent it.

See Chapter 4, pages 129–131, for more information.

Fetal Vulnerability

How is it possible for the embryo or the fetus to be harmed? No direct intermixing of blood takes place between a mother and her unborn child. Yet some substances—especially drugs—do reach the fetus. If a mother is addicted to morphine, heroin, or methadone, her baby may be born with an addiction. Repeated heavy drinking during pregnancy causes *fetal alcohol syndrome* (FAS). Affected infants have low birth weight, a small head, bodily defects, and facial malformations. Many also suffer from emotional, behavioral, and mental handicaps (Golden, 2005; Mattson et al., 1998).

Tobacco is also harmful. Smoking during pregnancy greatly reduces oxygen to the fetus. Heavy smokers risk miscarrying or having premature, underweight babies who are more likely to die soon after birth (Slotkin, 1998). Children of smoking mothers score lower on tests of language and mental ability (Fried et al., 1992). In other words, an unborn child's future can go "up in smoke."

Teratogens

Anything capable of causing birth defects is called a **teratogen** (teh-RAT-uh-jen). Sometimes women are exposed to powerful teratogens, such as radiation, lead, pesticides, or PCBs without knowing it (Eliot, 1999). But pregnant women do have direct control over many teratogens. For example, a woman who takes cocaine runs a serious risk of injuring her fetus (Espy, Kaufmann, & Glisky, 1999; Swanson et al., 1999). In short, when a pregnant woman takes drugs, her unborn child does too.

Healthy Pregnancies/Healthy Babies

What can parents do to minimize prenatal risks? Several basic practices help promote successful pregnancies and healthy babies (Bradley, 1995). These include the following:

- Maintaining good nutrition during pregnancy
- Learning relaxation and stress-reduction techniques to ease the transition to motherhood
- Avoiding teratogens and other harmful substances

Environment ("nurture") The sum of all external conditions affecting development, including especially the effects of learning.

Sensitive period During development, a period of increased sensitivity to environmental influences. Also, a time during which certain events must take place for normal development to occur.

Congenital problems Problems or defects that originate during prenatal development in the womb.

Genetic disorders Problems caused by defects in the genes or by inherited characteristics.

Teratogen Radiation, a drug, or other substance capable of altering fetal development in ways that cause birth defects.

Ted Wood

Some of the typical features of children suffering from fetal alcohol syndrome include a small nonsymmetrical head, a short nose, a flattened area between the eyes, oddly shaped eyes, and a thin upper lip. Many of these features become less noticeable by adolescence. However, mental retardation and other problems commonly follow the FAS child into adulthood. The child shown here represents a moderate example of FAS.

- Getting adequate exercise during pregnancy
- Obtaining general education about pregnancy and childbirth

Childbirth

Does the way a child is born make a difference in later development? Yes. In a traditional **medicated birth** the mother is given analgesics (painkillers) or general anesthetics, which cause a loss of consciousness. It is wise to use general anesthetics as little as possible, because they usually block a mother's awareness of giving birth, and some infants are born partially anesthetized. In addition, drugs can reduce oxygen flow to the fetus. For such reasons, babies tend to lag in muscular and neural development if their mothers were heavily anesthetized.

Although medicated births are declining, 95 percent of all deliveries in the United States and Canada use some painkillers. Certainly, a mother should not feel guilty if she needs pain relief. Drugs injected near the spinal cord (an epidural block) can greatly reduce pain without affecting the child or decreasing the mother's alertness.

Prepared Childbirth

What can parents do to give babies a good start in life while avoiding overmedicated births? In **prepared childbirth**, parents learn behavioral techniques to manage discomfort and facilitate labor. The most popular approach is the Lamaze (la-MAHZ) method, developed by French physician Ferdinand Lamaze.

Early in pregnancy, Lamaze instructors explain the entire birth process in detail to ease fears and anxieties. Expectant mothers then learn methods of breathing and muscular control that reduce pain. Another important element is training the father, a partner, or a friend to give emotional support to the mother during childbirth. Prepared childbirth typically shortens labor and reduces pain. Prepared parents are more likely to experience birth as a time of great joy (Mackey, 1995). For Olivia and Tom it made birth a celebration of life, rather than a medical problem.

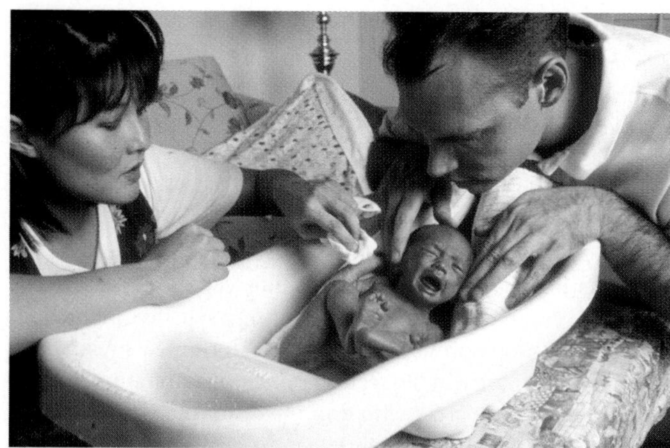

Michael Newman/PhotoEdit

Changing attitudes toward childbirth have encouraged mothers and fathers to actively prepare for birth and to participate more fully in caring for the newborn.

Deprivation and Enrichment

The brain of a newborn baby has fewer **dendrites** (nerve cell branches) and **synapses** (connections between nerve cells) than an adult brain (see ● Figure 3.4). However, during the first 3 years of life millions of new connections form in the brain every day. At the same time, unused connections disappear. As a result, early learning environments literally shape the developing brain, through "blooming and pruning" of synapses (Nelson, 1999). This is especially true of environments that can be described as *enriched* or *deprived*. **Deprivation** refers to a lack of normal stimulation, nutrition, comfort, or love. **Enrichment** exists when envi-

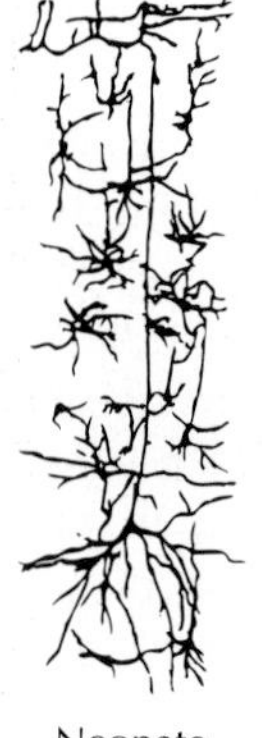

● **Figure 3.4** A rapid increase in brain synapses continues until about age 4. At that point, children actually have more brain synapses than adults do. Then, after age 10, the number slowly declines, reaching adult levels at about age 16. (Reprinted by permission of the publisher from *The Postnatal Development of the Human Cerebral Cortex,* Vols. I–III by Jesse LeRoy Conel, Cambridge, MA: Harvard University Press, Copyright © 1935, 1975 by the President and Fellows of Harvard College.)

HUMAN DIVERSITY

Children of Poverty

We all know that being poor is no fun. But does it actually hurt children? Sadly, the answer is "yes" (Allhusen et al., 2005). Poverty can have dramatic effects on the development of children in at least two ways (Sobolewski & Amato, 2005).

First, poor parents may not be able to give their children needed resources. In the extreme, they may lack nutritious meals, access to health care, and a safe neighborhood to live in. As a result, poor children are more vulnerable to a host of health problems, such as infectious diseases and injuries (Bradley & Corwyn, 2002). Typically, impoverished children also lack educational toys, books, home computers, and other learning resources. As a result, they may lag in cognitive development and educational achievement.

A second problem is that the stress associated with poverty can be hard on parents as well. This can lead to marital discord, less positive parenting, and poorer parent–child relationships. The resulting emotional turmoil can damage a child's socioemotional development. In the extreme, it may lead to an increased risk for mental illness and delinquent behavior (Bradley & Corwyn, 2002).

By the age of 5, children who grow up in poor homes tend to have lower IQs. They are also more fearful, unhappy, and prone to hostile or aggressive behavior (Carnegie Corporation, 1994; McLoyd, 1998). As adults, the children of poverty can remain trapped in a vicious cycle of poverty. Because one in seven American families fall below the poverty line, this grim reality plays itself out in millions of American homes every day (Sobolewski & Amato, 2005).

ronments are intentionally made more complex, intellectually stimulating, and emotionally supportive.

What happens when children suffer severe deprivation? Tragically, a few mistreated children have spent their first years in closets, attics, and other restricted environments. When they are first discovered, these children are usually mute, retarded, and emotionally damaged. Fortunately, such extreme deprivation is unusual. Nevertheless, milder levels of perceptual, intellectual, or emotional deprivation occur in many families, especially those that must cope with poverty (see "Children of Poverty"). Later in childhood, damage may result from a lack of intellectual stimulation or from parents who are cold, neglectful, or rejecting. In light of this, it is wise to view all of childhood as a *relatively sensitive period* (Barnet & Barnet, 1998; Nelson, 1999).

Anna Kaufman Moon/Stock, Boston

Children who grow up in poverty run a high risk of experiencing many forms of deprivation. There is evidence that lasting damage to social, emotional, and cognitive development occurs when children must cope with severe early deprivation (Evans, 2004).

Enriched Environments

Can improved environments enhance development? To answer this question, psychologists have created *enriched environments* that are especially novel, complex, and stimulating. To illustrate, let's consider rats raised in a sort of "rat wonderland." Their cages were filled with platforms, ladders, cubbyholes, and colorful patterns. As adults, these rats were superior at learning mazes. In addition, they had larger, heavier brains, with a thicker cortex (Benloucif, Bennett, & Rosenzweig, 1995). Of course, it's a long leap from rats to people, but an actual increase in brain size is impressive. If extra stimulation can enhance the "intelligence" of a lowly rat, it's

BRIDGES

Adults experience a number of disruptive effects when they are deprived of perceptual stimulation.

See Chapter 7, pages 240–241, for details.

Medicated birth The common practice in Western medicine of giving painkilling drugs during labor and birth.

Prepared childbirth A collection of techniques designed to manage discomfort and facilitate birth so that the use of painkilling drugs can be avoided or minimized.

Dendrites Nerve-cell fibers that receive incoming messages from other nerve cells.

Synapse A connection point between two nerve cells over which messages pass.

Deprivation In development, the loss or withholding of normal stimulation, nutrition, comfort, love, and so forth; a condition of lacking.

Enrichment Deliberately making an environment more novel, complex, and perceptually or intellectually stimulating.

likely that human infants also benefit from enrichment. Many studies have shown that enriched environments do, in fact, improve abilities or enhance development. It would be wise for Tom and Olivia to make a point of nourishing Amy's mind, as well as her body (Dieter & Emory, 1997).

What can parents do to enrich a child's environment? Parents can encourage exploration and stimulating play by noticing what holds their baby's interest. It is better to "childproof" a house than to strictly limit what a child can touch. There is also value in actively enriching sensory experiences. Babies should be surrounded by colors, music, people, and things to see, taste, smell, and touch. Children progress most rapidly when they have responsive parents and stimulating play materials at home (Bradley et al., 1989; Luster & Dubow, 1992).

Most people recognize that babies need lots of "tender loving care" for their physical needs. But as our discussion has shown, tender loving care should include a baby's psychological needs as well. The effects of deprivation and enrichment appear to apply to *all* areas of development. It would be a good idea to place perceptual and intellectual stimulation, affection, and personal warmth high on any list of infant needs.

Nature-Nurture Interactions

As Amy passes through life she will have to learn countless bits of information: how to eat with a fork; the names of animals; proper etiquette at a wedding; how to use a computer. This knowledge reflects billions of connections in the brain. No conceivable amount of genetic programming could make it possible. With this fact in mind, the outcome of the nature-nurture debate is clear: Heredity and environment are both important. Heredity gives us a variety of potentials and limitations. These, in turn, are affected by environmental influences, such as learning, nutrition, disease, and culture. Thus, the person you are today reflects a constant *interaction,* or interplay, between the forces of nature and nurture (Gopnik, Meltzoff, & Kuhl, 1999).

Reciprocal Influences

Because of differences in temperament, some babies are more likely than others to smile, cry, vocalize, reach out, or pay attention. As a result, babies rapidly become active participants in their own development. Growing infants alter their parents' behavior at the same time they are changed by it. For example, Amy is an easy baby who smiles frequently and is easily fed. This encourages Olivia to touch, feed, and sing to Amy. Olivia's affection rewards Amy, causing her to smile more. Soon, a dynamic relationship blossoms between mother and child. The reverse also occurs: Difficult children make parents unhappy and elicit more negative parenting (Parke, 2004).

A person's **developmental level** is his or her current state of physical, emotional, and intellectual development. To summarize, three factors combine to determine your developmental level at any stage of life. These are *heredity, environment,* and your *own behavior,* each tightly interwoven with the others.

KNOWLEDGE BUILDER

Heredity and Environment

REFLECT

Do you think that heredity or environment best explains who you are today? Can you think of clear examples of the ways in which heredity and environmental forces have affected your development?

What kind of temperament did you have as an infant? How did it affect your relationship with your parents or caregivers?

What advice would you give a friend who has just become pregnant? Be sure to consider the prenatal environment, sensitive periods, and birth options.

LEARNING CHECK

1. In the "nature-nurture" debate, the term *nature* primarily refers to
   a. senescence c. prenatal teratogens
   b. the existence of sensitive periods d. heredity
2. Areas of the DNA molecule called genes are made up of dominant and recessive chromosomes. T or F?
3. If a personal trait is controlled by a single dominant gene, the trait cannot be
   a. hereditary c. influenced by chromosomes
   b. related to DNA sequences d. polygenic
4. Which of the following represents a correct sequence?
   a. zygote, fetus, embryo, neonate, infant
   b. zygote, embryo, neonate, fetus, infant
   c. embryo, zygote, fetus, neonate, infant
   d. zygote, embryo, fetus, neonate, infant
5. "Slow-to-warm-up" children can be described as restrained, unexpressive, or shy. T or F?
6. Deprivation has an especially strong impact on development during
   a. the reciprocal stage c. the polygenic stage
   b. sensitive periods d. the social play phase
7. As a child develops there is a continuous ______________________ between the forces of heredity and environment.

CRITICAL THINKING

8. Environmental influences can interact with hereditary programming in an exceedingly direct way. Can you guess what it is?

Answers: 1. d 2. F 3. d 4. d 5. T 6. b 7. interaction 8. Environmental conditions sometimes turn specific genes on or off, thus directly affecting the expression of genetic tendencies (Gottlieb, 1998).

The Newborn Baby—The Basic Model Comes with Options

Infants have mental capacities that continue to surprise researchers and delight parents. The emergence of a baby's mental life, physical abilities, and emotions is closely related to maturation of the brain, nervous system, and body. Let's see how the infant's world unfolds.

At birth the human *neonate* (NEE-oh-nate: newborn infant) will die if not cared for. Newborn babies cannot lift their heads, turn over, or feed themselves. Does this mean they are inert and unfeeling? Definitely not! Neonates like Amy can see, hear, smell, taste, and respond to pain and touch. Although their senses are less acute, babies are very responsive. Amy will follow a moving object with her eyes and will turn in the direction of sounds.

Amy also has a number of adaptive infant reflexes. To elicit the *grasping reflex,* press an object in the neonate's palm and she will grasp it with surprising strength. Many infants, in fact, can hang from a raised bar, like little trapeze artists. The grasping reflex aids survival by helping infants avoid falling. You can observe the *rooting reflex* (reflexive head turning and nursing) by touching Amy's cheek. Immediately, she will turn toward your finger, as if searching for something.

How is such turning adaptive? The rooting reflex helps infants find a bottle or a breast. Then, when a nipple touches the infant's mouth, the *sucking reflex* (rhythmic nursing) helps her obtain needed food. This is a genetically programmed action (Koepke & Bigelow, 1997). At the same time, food rewards nursing. Because of this, babies quickly learn to nurse more actively. Again, we see how the interplay of nature and nurture alters a baby's behavior.

The *Moro reflex* is also interesting. If Amy's position is changed abruptly or if she is startled by a loud noise, she will make a hugging motion. This reaction has been compared to the movements baby monkeys use to cling to their mothers. (We leave it to the reader's imagination to decide if there is any connection.)

Newborn babies display a special interest in the human face. A preference for seeing their mother's face develops rapidly and encourages social interactions between mother and baby.

Margaret Miller/Photo Researchers, Inc.

The World of the Neonate

Thirty years ago, many people thought of newborn babies as mere bundles of reflexes, like those just described. But infants are capable of much more. For example, Andrew Meltzoff and Keith Moore (1983) found that babies are born mimics. ● Figure 3.5 shows Meltzoff as he sticks out his tongue, opens his mouth, and purses his lips at a 20-day-old girl. Will she imitate him? Videotapes of babies confirm that they imitate adult facial gestures. As early as 9 months of age, infants can imitate actions a day after seeing them (Heimann & Meltzoff, 1996). Such mimicry obviously aids rapid learning in infancy.

How intelligent are neonates? Babies are smarter than many people think. From the earliest days of life, babies seem to be trying to learn how the world works. They immediately begin to look, touch, taste, and otherwise explore their surroundings. From an evolutionary perspective, a baby's mind is designed to soak up information, which it does at an amazing pace (Gopnik, Meltzoff, & Kuhl, 1999).

In the first weeks and months of life, babies are increasingly able to think, to learn from what they see, to make predictions, and to search for explanations. For example, Jerome Bruner (1983) observed that 3- to 8-week-old babies seem to understand that a person's voice and body should be connected. If a baby hears his mother's voice coming from where she is standing, the baby will remain calm. If her voice comes from a loudspeaker several feet away, the baby will become agitated and begin to cry.

Another look into the private world of infants can be drawn from testing their vision, which is challenging because infants cannot talk. Robert Fantz invented a device called a *looking chamber* to find out what infants can see and what holds their attention (● Figure 3.6*a*). Imagine that Amy is placed on her back inside the chamber, facing a lighted area above. Next, two objects are placed in the chamber. By observing the movements of Amy's eyes and the images they reflect, we can tell what she is looking at. Such tests show that adult vision is about 30 times sharper, but babies can see large patterns, shapes, and edges.

Fantz found that 3-day-old babies prefer complex patterns, such as checkerboards and bull's-eyes, to simpler colored rectangles. Other researchers have learned that infants are excited by circles, curves, and bright lights (● Figure 3.6*b*) (Brown, 1990a). Immediately after birth, Amy will be aware of changes in the position of objects (Slater et al., 1990). When she is 6 months old she will be able to recognize categories of objects that differ in shape or color. By 9 months of age she will be able to tell the difference between dogs and birds or other groups of animals (Mandler & McDonough, 1998). So there really is a person inside that little body!

Neonates can most clearly see objects about a foot away. It is as if they are best prepared to see the people who love and care for them. Perhaps that's why babies have a special fascination with human faces. Just *hours* after they are born, babies begin to prefer seeing their mother's face, rather than a stranger's (Walton, Bower, & Bower, 1992). When babies are only 2 to 5 days old they will pay more attention to a person who is gazing directly at them,

Developmental level An individual's current state of physical, emotional, and intellectual development.

● **Figure 3.5** Infant imitation. In the top row of photos, Andrew Meltzoff makes facial gestures at an infant. The bottom row records the infant's responses. Videotapes of Meltzoff and of tested infants helped ensure objectivity.

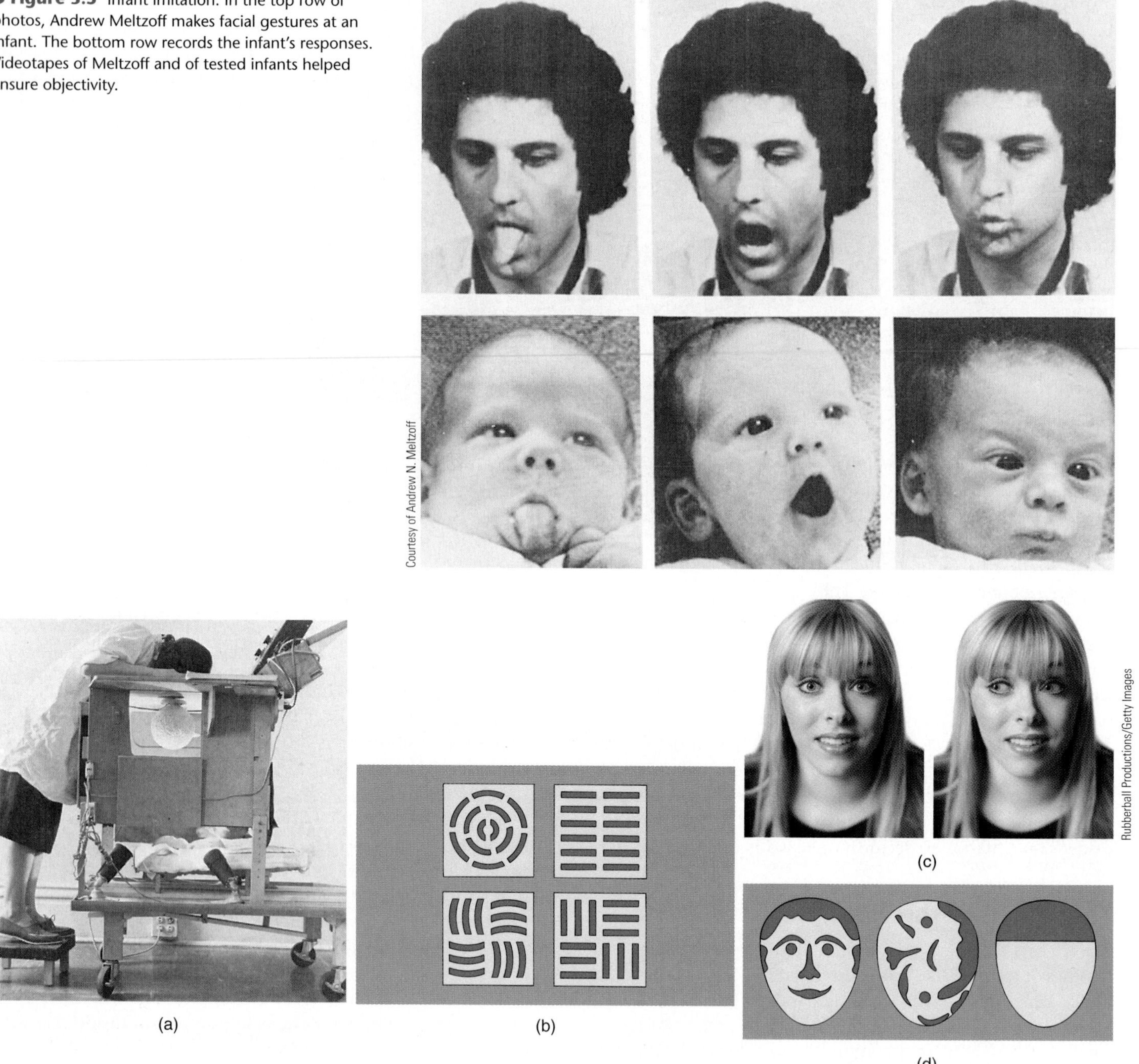

● **Figure 3.6** *(a)* Eye movements and fixation points of infants are observed in Fantz's "looking chamber." *(b)* Thirteen-week-old infants prefer concentric and curved patterns like those on the left to nonconcentric and straight-line patterns like those on the right. *(c)* When they are just days old, infants pay more attention to the faces of people who are gazing directly at them. *(d)* Infants look at normal faces longer than at scrambled faces and at both faces longer than designs, like the one on the right. (Photo [a] courtesy of David Linton. Drawing from "The Origin of Form Perception" by Robert L. Fantz, Copyright © 1961 by Scientific American, Inc. All rights reserved.)

rather than one who is looking away (Farroni et al., 2004) (● Figure 3.6*c*).

In a looking chamber, most infants will spend more time looking at a human face pattern than a scrambled face or a colored oval (● Figure 3.6*d*). When real human faces are used, infants prefer familiar faces to unfamiliar faces. However, this reverses at about age 2. At that time, unusual objects begin to interest the child. For instance, Jerome Kagan (1971) showed face masks to 2-year-olds. Kagan found that the toddlers were fascinated by a face with eyes on the chin and a nose in the middle of the forehead. He believes the babies' interest came from a need to understand why the scrambled face differed from what they had come to expect. Such behavior is further evidence that babies actively try to make sense of their surroundings (Gopnik, Meltzoff, & Kuhl, 1999).

● **Figure 3.7** Motor development. Most infants follow an orderly pattern of motor development. Although the order in which children progress is similar, there are large individual differences in the ages at which each ability appears. The ages listed are averages for American children. It is not unusual for many of the skills to appear 1 or 2 months earlier than average or several months later (Frankenburg & Dodds, 1967; Harris & Liebert, 1991). Parents should not be alarmed if a child's behavior differs some from the average.

Maturation

The emergence of many basic abilities is closely tied to **maturation** (physical growth and development of the body, brain, and nervous system). Maturation will be especially evident as Amy learns motor skills, such as crawling and walking. Of course, the *rate* of maturation varies from child to child. Nevertheless, the *order* of maturation is almost universal. For instance, Amy will be able to sit without support from Tom before she has matured enough to crawl. Indeed, infants around the world typically sit before they crawl, crawl before they stand, and stand before they walk (● Figure 3.7).

What about my weird cousin Emo who never crawled? Like cousin Emo, a few children substitute rolling, creeping, or shuffling for crawling. A very few move directly from sitting to standing and walking (Robson, 1984). Even so, their motor development is orderly. In general, muscular control spreads in a pattern that is *cephalocaudal* (SEF-eh-lo-KOD-ul: from head to toe) and *proximodistal* (PROK-seh-moe-DIS-tul: from the center of the body to the extremities). Even if cousin Emo flunked Elementary Crawling, his motor development followed the standard top-down, center-outward pattern.

Motor Development

Although maturation has a big impact, motor skills don't simply "emerge." Amy must learn to control her actions. When babies are beginning to crawl or walk, they actively try new movements and select those that work. Amy's first efforts may be flawed—a wobbly crawl or some shaky first steps. However, with practice, babies "tune" their movements to be smoother and more effective. Such learning is evident from the very first months of life (Thelen, 2000) (see ● Figure 3.8).

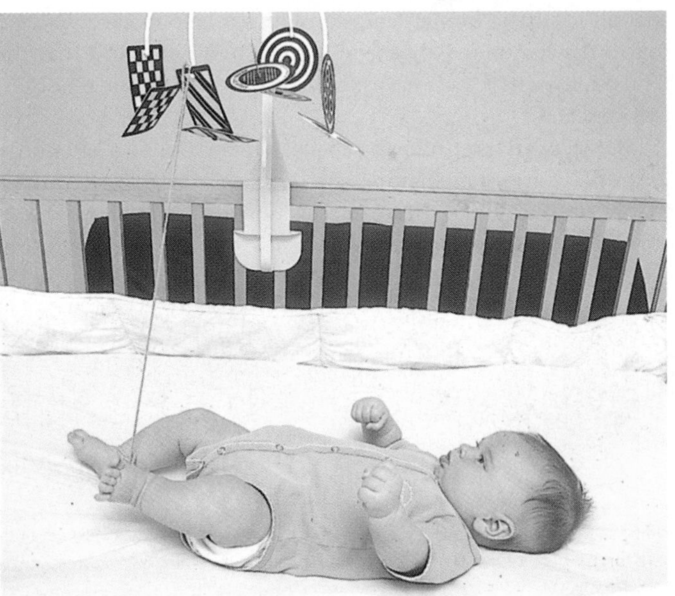

Michael Newman/PhotoEdit

● **Figure 3.8** Psychologist Carolyn Rovee-Collier has shown that babies as young as 3 months old can learn to control their movements. In her experiments, babies lie on their backs under a colorful crib mobile. A ribbon is tied around the baby's ankle and connected to the mobile. Whenever babies spontaneously kick their legs, the mobile jiggles and rattles. Within a few minutes, infants learn to kick faster. Their reward for kicking is a chance to see the mobile move (Hayne & Rovee-Collier, 1995).

Maturation The physical growth and development of the body and nervous system.

Readiness

At what ages will Amy be ready to feed herself, to walk alone, or to say goodbye to diapers? Such milestones tend to be governed by a child's **readiness** for rapid learning. That is, minimum levels of maturation must occur before some skills can be learned. Parents are asking for failure when they try to force a child to learn skills too early (Luxem & Christophersen, 1994). It is impossible, for instance, to teach children to walk or use a toilet before they have matured enough to control their bodies.

Consider the eager parents who toilet trained an 18-month-old child in 10 trying weeks of false alarms and "accidents." If they had waited until the child was 24 months old, they might have succeeded in just 3 weeks. Parents may control when toilet training starts, but maturation tends to dictate when it will be completed (Luxem & Christophersen, 1994). The average age for *completed* toilet training is about 3 years (girls a little earlier, boys a little later) (Schum et al., 2001). So why fight nature? (The wet look is in.)

Emotional Development

Early emotional development also follows a pattern closely tied to maturation. Even the **basic emotions** of *anger, fear,* and *joy*—which appear to be unlearned—take time to develop. General *excitement* is the only emotional state newborn infants clearly express. However, as Tom and Olivia can tell you, a baby's emotional life blossoms rapidly. One researcher (Bridges, 1932) observed that all the basic human emotions appear before age 2. Bridges found that emotions appear in a consistent order and that the first basic split is between pleasant and unpleasant emotions (● Figure 3.9).

Many experts continue to believe that emotions unfold slowly as the nervous system matures (Camras, Sullivan, & Michel, 1993; Matias & Cohn, 1993). However, psychologist Carroll Izard thinks that infants can express several basic emotions as early as 10 weeks of age. When Izard looks carefully at the faces of babies, he sees abundant signs of emotion (see ● Figure 3.10). The most common infant expression, he found, is not excitement, but *interest*—followed by *joy, anger,* and *sadness* (Izard et al., 1995).

If Izard is right, then emotions are "hard-wired" by heredity and related to evolution. Perhaps that's why smiling is one of a baby's most common reactions. Smiling probably helps babies survive by inviting parents to care for them (Izard et al., 1995).

At first, a baby's smiling is haphazard. By the age of 2 to 3 months, however, infants smile more frequently when another person is nearby. This **social smile** is especially rewarding to parents. On the other hand, when new parents see and hear a crying baby, they feel annoyed, irritated, disturbed, or unhappy. Babies the world over, it seems, rapidly become capable of letting others know what they like and dislike. (Prove this to yourself sometime by driving a baby buggy.)

With dazzling speed, human infants are transformed from helpless babies to independent people. Early growth is extremely rapid. By her third year, Amy will have a unique personality and she will be able to stand, walk, talk, and explore. At no other time after birth does development proceed more rapidly. During the same period, Amy's relationships with other people will expand as well. Before we explore that topic, here's a chance to review what you've learned.

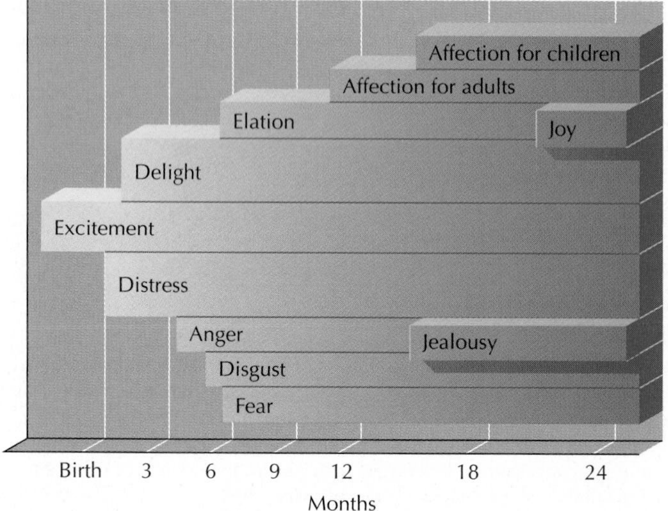

● **Figure 3.9** The traditional view of infancy holds that emotions are rapidly differentiated from an initial capacity for excitement. (After K.M.B. Bridges, 1932. Reprinted by permission of the Society for Research in Child Development, Inc.)

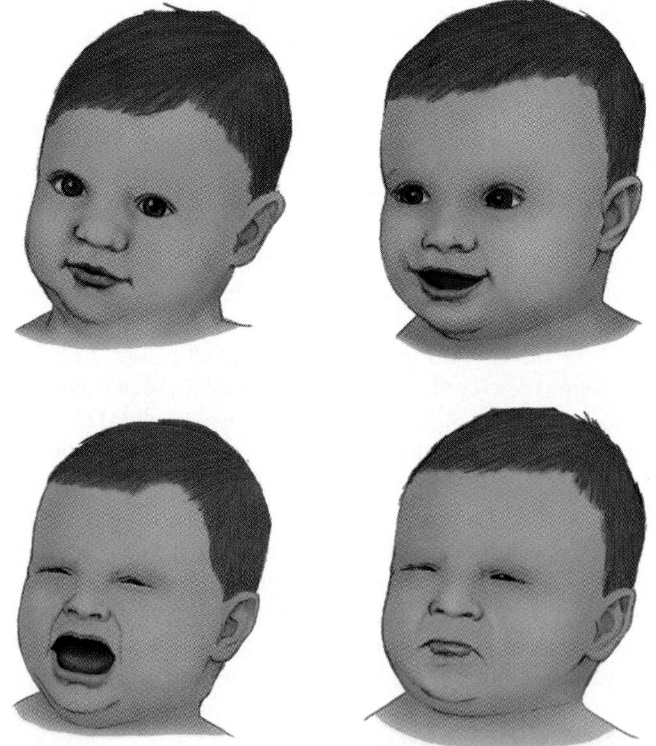

● **Figure 3.10** Infants display many of the same emotional expressions as adults do. Carroll Izard believes such expressions show that distinct emotions appear within the first months of life. Other theorists argue that specific emotions come into focus more gradually, as an infant's nervous system matures. Either way, parents can expect to see a full range of basic emotions by the end of a baby's first year. By the time babies are 18 months old, they begin to gain control over some of their emotional expressions (Izard & Abe, 2004).

KNOWLEDGE BUILDER

The Neonate and Early Maturation

REFLECT

What infant reflexes have you observed? How would maturation affect the chances of teaching an infant to eat with a spoon? Can you give an example of how heredity and environment interact during motor development?

To know what a baby is feeling, would it be more helpful to be able to detect delight and distress (Bridges) or joy, anger, and sadness (Izard)?

LEARNING CHECK

1. If an infant is startled, it will make movements similar to an embrace. This is known as the
   a. grasping reflex c. Moro reflex
   b. rooting reflex d. adaptive reflex
2. After age 2, infants tested in a looking chamber show a marked preference for familiar faces and simpler designs. T or F?
3. Cephalocaudal and proximodistal patterns show the effects of ______________ on motor development.
   a. enriched environments c. scaffolding
   b. maturation d. sensitive periods
4. General excitement or interest is the clearest emotional response present in newborn infants, but meaningful expressions of delight and distress appear soon after. T or F?
5. Early in life, the learning of basic skills is most effective when parents respect the
   a. principle of early maturation
   b. value of reactive maternal involvement
   c. principle of readiness
   d. fact that babies cannot imitate adult actions until they are 18 months old

CRITICAL THINKING

6. If you were going to test newborn infants to see if they prefer their own mothers' faces to those of strangers, what precautions would you take?

Answers: 1. c 2. F 3. b 4. T 5. c 6. In one study of the preferences of newborns, the hair color and complexion of strangers was matched to that of the mothers. Also, only the mother's or stranger's face was visible during testing. Finally, a scent was used to mask olfactory (smell) cues so that an infant's preference could not be based on the mother's familiar odor (Bushnell, Sai, & Mullin, 1989).

Social Development—Baby, I'm Stuck on You

Like all humans, babies are social creatures. Their early **social development** lays a foundation for relationships with parents, siblings, friends, and relatives. A first basic step into the social world involves becoming aware of oneself as a separate person. When you look in a mirror, you recognize the image staring back as your own—except, perhaps, early on Monday mornings. Would Amy recognize herself at age 1? At age 2? Like many such events, initial self-awareness depends on maturation of the nervous system. In a typical test of self-recognition, infants are shown images of themselves on a TV. Most infants have to be 15 months old before they recognize themselves (Lewis & Brooks-Gunn, 1979). Together with an increased interest in others, self-awareness begins to form the core of social development (Asendorpf, 1996; Kagan, 1991). Growing self-awareness also makes it possible to feel *social* emotions, such as embarrassment, shame, guilt, and pride (Lewis, 1992).

Social Referencing

At about the same time that self-awareness appears, infants become more aware of others. Have you noticed how adults sometimes glance at the facial expressions of others to decide how to respond to them? **Social referencing** (observing others to obtain information or guidance) can also be observed in babies.

In one study, babies were placed on a visual cliff. (A visual cliff is pictured in Chapter 6.) The deep side of the cliff was just high enough so that the babies were tempted to cross it, but did not. Most babies placed on the edge of the cliff repeatedly looked at

Chris Lowe/Index Stock Imagery

A sense of self, or self-awareness, develops at about age 18 months. Before children develop self-awareness, they do not recognize their own image in a mirror. Typically, they think they are looking at another child. Some children hug the child in the mirror or go behind it looking for the child they see there (Lewis, 1995).

Readiness A condition that exists when maturation has advanced enough to allow the rapid acquisition of a particular skill.

Basic emotions The first distinct emotions to emerge in infancy.

Social smile Smiling elicited by social stimuli, such as seeing a parent's face.

Social development The development of self-awareness, attachment to parents or caregivers, and relationships with other children and adults.

Social referencing Observing others in social situations to obtain information or guidance.

their mothers. As they did, the mothers made faces at them. (All for science, of course.) When the mothers posed faces of joy or interest, most babies crossed the deep side of the cliff. When mothers displayed fear or anger, few babies crossed (Sorce et al., 1985). Thus, by the end of their first year, infants are aware of the facial expressions of others and seek guidance from them—especially from mother (Hirshberg & Svejda, 1990; Stenberg & Hagekull, 1997). Again, we see the roots of an important social skill.

The real core of social development is found in the emotional attachments that human babies form with their caregivers. Before we consider that topic, let's see what we can learn from some baby animals.

Imprinting

Konrad Lorenz (1903–1989) was an Austrian **ethologist** who studied the natural behavior patterns of animals. Lorenz wondered why baby geese follow their mothers. The obvious explanation seemed to be, "It's instinctive," but Lorenz showed otherwise.

Mother Lorenz

Normally the first large moving object a baby goose sees is its mother. Lorenz hatched geese in an incubator, so the first moving object they saw was Lorenz. From then on, these baby geese followed Lorenz. They even reacted to his call as if he were their mother (Lorenz, 1937).

As you can see, baby geese aren't born knowing that they should follow a mother goose. Instead, they are born with a tendency to follow large moving objects. Normally that would be their mother. But it need not be. Mother-goose following is acquired during a sensitive period when baby geese are exposed to an adult goose (or whatever else happens to be around). The rapid and early learning of permanent behavior patterns of this type is called **imprinting.**

If a newly hatched duck or goose doesn't imprint on its mother (or some other object) within 30 hours, it never will (Hess, 1959). (Ducklings have been imprinted on decoys, rubber balls, wooden blocks, and other unlikely objects.) In many animals, imprinting has lifelong consequences (Lorenz, 1962).

Revenge of the Jackdaw

Imprinting normally serves to attach a young animal to its mother. It also guides the selection of a mate of the same species at sexual maturity. In another of Lorenz's experiments, a jackdaw (European crow) imprinted on him. When the bird reached sexual maturity, Lorenz became the target of its mating ritual. Part of this ritual involves stuffing worms into the mouth of the intended mate—as a surprised Lorenz learned while asleep on the lawn one day. When Lorenz refused its gift, the jackdaw stuffed a worm in Lorenz's ear. (Showing, perhaps, that it's not nice to fool Mother Nature!)

Nina Leen/TimePix

"Mother" Lorenz leads his charges. The goslings have imprinted on Lorenz because he was the first moving object they saw after they hatched.

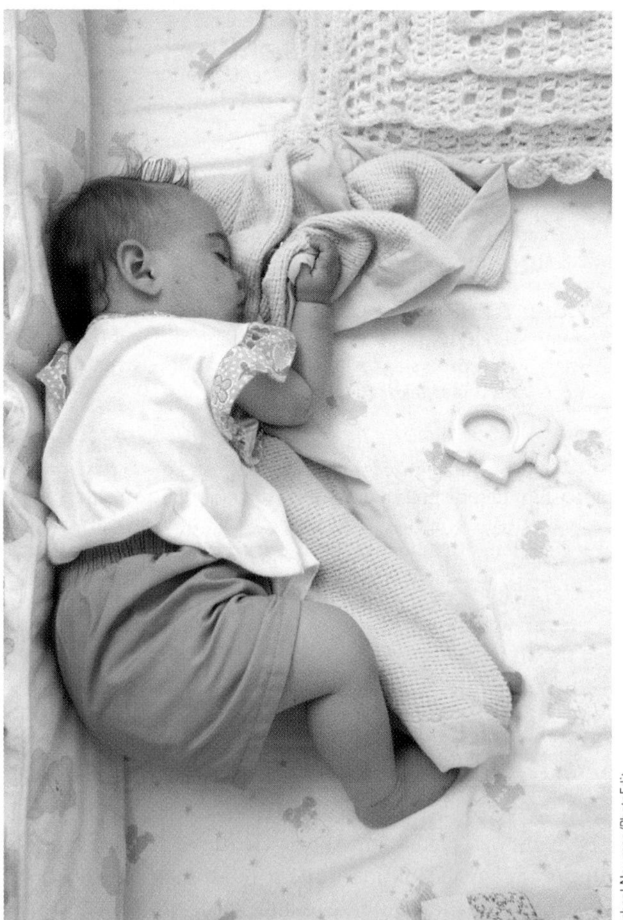

Michael Newman/PhotoEdit

Most parents are familiar with the storm of crying that sometimes occurs when babies are left alone at bedtime. Bedtime distress can be a mild form of separation anxiety. As many parents know, it is often eased by the presence of "security objects," such as a stuffed animal or favorite blanket (Morelli et al., 1992).

THE CLINICAL FILE

Beyond Homesickness

Camp counselors know the look: Doleful eyes, anxious, and forlorn, a homesick child is easy to spot. But such distress can be more serious than the "summer-camp blues." At some point in their lives, about 5 percent of all children (1 in 20) suffer from **separation anxiety disorder.** These children are miserable when they are separated from their parents, whom they cling to or constantly follow. Some fear that they will get lost and never see their parents again. They are reluctant to leave home, go to camp, sleep over at a friend's house, or go on errands. Seventy-five percent refuse to go to school, which can seriously jeopardize their academic future.

What causes separation anxiety disorder? Some children are more vulnerable to the disorder, indicating a genetic component (Cronk et al., 2005). Environmental stressors also play a role. The problem may begin after a child faces stresses such as illness, experiencing the death of a relative or pet, moving to a new neighborhood, or changing schools. Whatever the triggering event, separation anxiety should not be ignored. It can seriously impede a child's emotional development. Although children tend to grow out of the disorder (Kearney et al., 2003), if separation anxiety is intense or lasts for more than a month parents should seek professional help for their child (DSMIV-TR, 2000; Masi, Mucci, & Millepiedi, 2001).

Ryan McVay/Getty Images

Attachment

Does imprinting occur in humans? True imprinting is limited to birds and a few other animals. However, human infants do form an **emotional attachment**, or close emotional bond, to their primary caregivers. There is a sensitive period (roughly the first year of life) during which this must occur for optimal development. Returning to Amy's story, we find that attachment keeps her close to Olivia, who provides safety, stimulation, and a secure "home base" from which Amy can go exploring. Like other mothers, Olivia began to cultivate a bond with Amy just hours after giving birth, by touching her and holding her (Kaitz et al., 1995). For most infants, a clear sign of emotional bonding appears around 8 to 12 months of age. At that time Amy will display **separation anxiety** (crying and signs of fear) when she is left alone or with a stranger. Mild separation anxiety is normal. When it is more intense, it may reveal a problem. See "Beyond Homesickness" for details.

You may have heard that bonding is especially powerful during the first few hours after birth (Klaus et al., 1995). However, careful studies have generally failed to support a "superglue" version of the bonding concept. Although long-term infant attachments are a reality, "instant bonding" appears to be a myth (Eyer, 1994).

Attachment Quality

According to psychologist Mary Ainsworth (1913–1999), the quality of attachment is revealed by how babies act when their mothers return after a brief separation. Infants who are **securely attached** have a stable and positive emotional bond. They are upset by the mother's absence and seek to be near her when she returns. **Insecure-avoidant** infants have an anxious emotional

Ethologist A person who studies the natural behavior patterns of animals.

Imprinting A rapid and relatively permanent type of learning that occurs during a limited period early in life.

Separation anxiety disorder Severe and prolonged distress displayed by children when they are separated from their parents or caregivers.

Emotional attachment An especially close emotional bond that infants form with their parents, caregivers, or others.

Separation anxiety Uneasiness displayed by infants when they are separated from their parents or caregivers.

Secure attachment A stable and positive emotional bond.

Insecure-avoidant attachment An anxious emotional bond marked by a tendency to avoid reunion with a parent or caregiver.

DISCOVERING PSYCHOLOGY

What's Your Attachment Style?

Do our first attachments continue to affect us as adults? Some psychologists believe they do by influencing how we relate to friends and lovers (Bridges, 2003; Sroufe et al., 2005). Read the following statements and see which best describes your adult relationships.

Secure Attachment Style

In general, I think most other people are well intentioned and trustworthy.
I find it relatively easy to get close to others.
I am comfortable relying on others and having others depend on me.
I don't worry much about being abandoned by others.
I am comfortable when other people want to get close to me emotionally.

Avoidant Attachment Style

I tend to pull back when things don't go well in a relationship.
I am somewhat skeptical about the idea of true love.
I have difficulty trusting my partner in a romantic relationship.
Other people tend to be too eager to seek commitment from me.
I get a little nervous if anyone gets too close emotionally.

Ambivalent Attachment Style

I have often felt misunderstood and unappreciated in my romantic relationships.
My friends and lovers have been somewhat unreliable.
I love my romantic partner, but I worry that she or he doesn't really love me.
I would like to be closer to my romantic partner, but I'm not sure I trust her or him.

Do any of the preceding statements sound familiar? If so, they may describe your adult attachment style. Most adults have a secure attachment style that is marked by caring, supportiveness, and understanding. However, it's not unusual to have an avoidant attachment style that reflects a tendency to resist intimacy and commitment to others (Collins et al., 2002). An ambivalent attachment style is marked by mixed feelings about love and friendship (Tidwell, Reis, & Shaver, 1996). Do you see any similarities between your present relationships and your attachment experiences as a child?

bond. They tend to turn away from the mother when she returns. **Insecure-ambivalent attachment** is also an anxious emotional bond. In this case, babies are ambivalent: They both seek to be near the returning mother and angrily resist contact with her. (See ● Figure 3.11.)

Attachment can have lasting effects. Infants who are securely attached at 1 year of age show more resiliency, curiosity, problem-solving ability, and social skill in preschool (Collins & Gunnar, 1990). In contrast, attachment failures can be damaging. Consider, for example, the plight of children raised in overcrowded Romanian orphanages. These children got almost no attention from adults for the first year or two of their lives. Some have now been adopted by American and Canadian families, but many are poorly attached to their new parents. Some, for instance, will wander off with strangers, are anxious and remote, and don't like to be touched or to make eye contact with others. In short, for some children a lack of affectionate care early in life leaves lasting emotional scars (O'Conner et al., 2003).

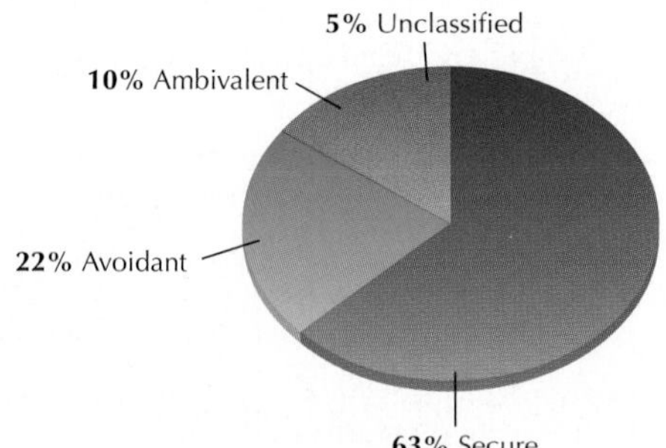

● **Figure 3.11** In the United States, about two thirds of all children from middle-class families are securely attached. About one child in three is insecurely attached. (Percentages are approximate. From Kaplan, 1998.)

Promoting Secure Attachment

The key to secure attachment is a mother who is accepting and sensitive to her baby's signals and rhythms. Poor attachment occurs when a mother's actions are inappropriate, inadequate, intrusive, overstimulating, or rejecting. An example is the mother who tries to play with a drowsy infant or who ignores a baby who is looking at her and vocalizing. The link between sensitive caregiving and secure attachment appears to apply to other cultures as well as our own (Posada et al., 2002).

What about attachment to fathers? Fathers of securely attached infants tend to be outgoing, agreeable, and happy in their marriage. In general, a warm family atmosphere tends to produce secure children (Belsky, 1996).

What effect does the arrival of a second child have on attachment? Attachment security often drops for a firstborn child when a second baby arrives. Aware parents, therefore, make a special effort to involve their firstborn child in the excitement of the "new arrival." They also give the firstborn extra attention and affection

(Teti, 1996). (For another view of attachment, see "What's Your Attachment Style?")

Another dimension of attachment is illustrated by studies of baby monkeys, as described next.

Motherless Monkeys

To investigate mother–infant relationships, Harry Harlow separated baby rhesus monkeys from their mothers at birth. The real mothers were replaced with **surrogate** (substitute) **mothers.** Some were made of cold, unyielding wire. Others were covered with soft terry cloth (● Figure 3.12). When the infants were given a choice between the two mothers, they spent most of their time clinging to the cuddly terry-cloth mother. This was true even when the wire mother held a bottle, making her the source of food. The "love" and attachment displayed toward the cloth replicas was identical to that shown toward natural mothers. For example, when frightened by rubber snakes, wind-up toys, and other "fear stimuli," the infant monkeys ran to their cloth mothers and clung to them for security.

Courtesy of Harry Harlow, University of Wisconsin Primate Laboratory

● **Figure 3.12** An infant monkey clings to a cloth-covered surrogate mother. Baby monkeys become attached to the cloth "contact-comfort" mother but not to a similar wire mother. This is true even when the wire mother provides food. Contact comfort may also underlie the tendency of children to become attached to inanimate objects, such as blankets or stuffed toys. However, a study of 2- to 3-year-old "blanket-attached" children found that they were no more insecure than others (Passman, 1987). (So, maybe Linus is okay after all.) (Courtesy of Harry Harlow, University of Wisconsin Primate Laboratory.)

Contact Comfort

These classic studies suggest that "contact comfort" is an important part of attachment. **Contact comfort** refers to the pleasant, reassuring feeling infants get from touching something soft and warm, especially their mother.

The emotional well-being of human infants is also related to contact comfort (Eliot, 1999). Touching helps shape "body maps" in a baby's brain that affect tactile sensitivity and motor skills. Premature babies, in particular, benefit greatly from tender touching, which can have a big effect on their social and emotional health at age 2 (Weiss et al., 2001).

Breast-feeding

The value of contact comfort is one reason why psychologists advocate breast-feeding infants. Breast-feeding virtually guarantees that a baby will receive touching and handling. In addition, mothers produce *colostrum* (kuh-LOSS-trum: a fluid rich in proteins) for the first few days after giving birth. Colostrum carries antibodies from the mother to the newborn. This helps prevent certain infectious diseases. Colostrum is also easier for the newborn to digest than cow's milk and infant formulas.

Breast-feeding may have other benefits as well. One study found that breast-fed babies grow up to be smarter adults. Danish men and women who were breast-fed for 7 to 9 months as infants

Brownie Harris/Corbis

Extra touching, massage, and human contact is especially beneficial for premature and low-birth-weight infants.

Insecure-ambivalent attachment An anxious emotional bond marked by both a desire to be with a parent or caregiver and some resistance to being reunited.

Surrogate mother A substitute mother (often an inanimate dummy in animal research).

Contact comfort A pleasant and reassuring feeling human and animal infants get from touching or clinging to something soft and warm, usually their mother.

have intelligence test scores that average 6 points higher than people who were breast-fed for 1 month or less. Most likely, these IQ gains reflect better nourishment of the developing brain and the benefits of a close mother–infant relationship (Mortensen et al., 2002).

Unfortunately, the number of women worldwide who breast-feed their babies is declining. This is due, in part, to United Nations efforts to encourage mothers in AIDS-ravaged parts of the world to use infant formula rather than breast milk to feed their babies (because the virus is transmitted through breast milk). In addition, large businesses actively promote sales of infant formulas in developing countries. Many companies give free samples of their products to new mothers, a practice that discourages many mothers from trying breast-feeding (Dermer, 1998).

What about women who can't breast-feed? The observed IQ boost could also have another source: Mothers who take time to breast-feed probably interact more with their youngsters throughout childhood. Thus, mothers who can't breast-feed should make an extra effort to hold, touch, nurture, and interact with their babies (Mortensen et al., 2002).

Day Care

Does commercial child care interfere with the quality of attachment? It depends on the quality of day care. Overall, *high-quality* day care does not adversely affect attachment to parents (National Institute of Child Health and Human Development, 1999). In fact, children in high-quality day care tend to have better relationships with their mothers and fewer behavior problems. They also have better cognitive skills and language abilities (Burchinal et al., 2000; Vandell, 2004). Thus, high-quality day care can actually improve children's social and mental skills (Scarr, 1998).

However, all of the positive effects just noted are *reversed* for low-quality day care (● Figure 3.13). Poor-quality day care can actually create behavior problems that didn't exist beforehand (Pierrehumbert et al., 2002). Parents are wise to carefully evaluate and monitor the quality of day care their children receive.

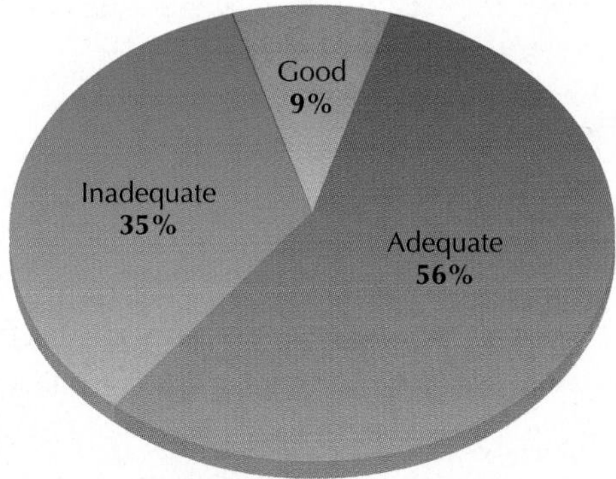

● Figure 3.13 This graph shows the results of a study of child care in homes other than the child's. In most cases, parents paid for this care, although many of the caregivers were unlicensed. As you can see, child care was "good" in only 9 percent of the homes. In 35 percent of the homes it was rated as inadequate (Mehren, 1994).

Quality

What should parents look for when they evaluate the quality of child care? Low-quality day care *is* risky and it *may* weaken attachment. Parents seeking quality should insist on *at least* the following: (1) a small number of children per caregiver, (2) small overall group size (12 to 15), (3) trained caregivers, (4) minimal staff turnover, and (5) a stable day-care experience (Howes, 1997). (Also, avoid any child-care center with the words "zoo," "menagerie," or "stockade" in its name.)

Play and Social Skills

A chance to play with other children is one of the side benefits of day care. For instance, in one corner a 2-year-old stacks colored blocks, pounds on them with a toy truck, and then chews on the truck. On the other side of the room some 5-year-olds have built a "store" out of cardboard boxes. For the next half hour, one child is the "owner" and the others are "customers." With just a 3-year difference in age, we see a dramatic change in how children play.

Naturally, play is fun for children. It's also serious business. Children use play to explore the world and to practice skills—especially social skills. By the time children are 4 or 5 they will have progressed from **solitary play** (playing alone) to **cooperative play** (in which two or more children must coordinate their actions). Children engaged in cooperative play take parts or play roles, follow rules, and lead or follow others. Playing this way helps them learn to handle cooperation and competition, conflicts, power, role taking, and communication.

Cooperative play is a big step toward participating in social life. It's easy for adults to dismiss play as silly or trivial. In fact, play is one of the most important activities of childhood (Kaplan, 1998).

Affectional Needs

A baby's **affectional needs** (needs for love and affection) are every bit as important as more obvious needs for food, water, and physical care. All things considered, creating a bond of trust and affection between the infant and at least one other person is a key event during the first year of life. Parents are sometimes afraid of "spoiling" babies with too much attention, but for the first year or two this is nearly impossible. In fact, a later capacity to experience warm and loving relationships may depend on it.

KNOWLEDGE BUILDER

Social Development

REFLECT

As an adult, how does social referencing affect your behavior?

Think of a child you know who seems to be securely attached and another who seems to be insecurely attached. How do the children differ? Do their parents treat them differently?

Do you think you were securely or insecurely attached as a child? Are there any parallels in your relationships today?

LEARNING CHECK

1. Clear signs of self-awareness or self-recognition are evident in most infants by the time they reach 8 months of age. T or F?
2. Social ____________________ of parents' facial expressions is evident in infants by the time they are 1 year old.
3. A clear sign that infant attachment is beginning to occur is found in the presence of
   a. a social smile c. social scaffolding
   b. separation anxiety d. affectional needs
4. A baby who turns away from his mother when she returns after a brief separation shows signs of having which type of attachment?
   a. insecure-avoidant c. solitary-ambivalent
   b. insecure-ambivalent d. maternal-disaffectional

CRITICAL THINKING

5. Can you think of another way to tell if infants have self-awareness?
6. Attachment quality is usually attributed to the behavior of parents or caregivers. How might infants contribute to the quality of attachment?

Answers: **1.** F **2.** referencing **3.** b **4.** a **5.** Another successful method is to secretly rub a spot of rouge on an infant's nose. The child is then placed in front of a mirror. The question is, "Will the child touch the red spot?" showing recognition of the mirror image as his or her own? The probability that a child will do so jumps dramatically during the second year. **6.** An infant's behavior patterns, temperament, and emotional style may greatly influence parents' behavior. As a result, infants can affect attachment as much as parents do (Oatley & Jenkins, 1992).

Maternal and Paternal Influences—Life with Mom and Dad

What does it mean to be a good parent? Are children affected differently by mothers and fathers? How do parental styles of discipline affect children? Psychologists have investigated each of these questions. Let's investigate their findings.

For the first few years of life, caregivers are the center of a child's world, making the quality of mothering and fathering very important. For example, one classic study focused on **maternal influences** (all the effects a mother has on her child). Researchers began by selecting children who were very competent (A children) or low in competence (C children). As they observed younger and younger children, it soon became apparent that A and C patterns were already set by age 3. To learn how this was possible, psychologists visited homes and observed **caregiving styles** (White & Watts, 1973). What they saw ranged from the "super mother" to the "zoo-keeper mother." Super mothers went out of their way to provide educational experiences and let their children initiate activities. This style produced A children, who were competent in most areas of development. At the other end of the scale, zoo-keeper mothers gave their children good physical care but interacted with them very little. Their child-care routines were rigid and highly structured. The result was C children, who approached problems inflexibly.

Optimal Caregiving

More recent studies mirror the earlier findings: Optimal caregiving involves *proactive educational interactions* with a child (Olson, Bates, & Kaskie, 1992). For example, Olivia is a proactive mother who talks to Amy and helps her explore her surroundings. This speeds Amy's mental growth and minimizes behavior problems.

Optimal caregiving also depends on the *goodness of fit,* or compatibility, of parent and child temperaments (Chess & Thomas, 1986). For instance, Damion is a slow-to-warm-up child who has impatient parents. Damion will probably have more problems than he would with easy-going parents.

A third ingredient of caregiving is *parental responsiveness* to a child's feelings, needs, rhythms, and signals. When Amy is a month old, Olivia should focus on touching, holding, feeding, and stimulating her. When Amy is a year old, give-and-take interactions that promote Amy's social skills will be more important. Thus, effective mothers adjust their behavior to meet their children's changing needs (Heermann, Jones, & Wikoff, 1994). In general, the most effective parents tend to be intelligent, good at managing their own emotions, and focused on family, work, and childrearing (Pulkkinen et al., 2002).

Paternal Influences

Aren't you overlooking the effects of fathering? Yes, fathers make a unique contribution to parenting (Videon, 2005). Studies of **paternal influences** (the sum of all effects a father has on his child) reveal that fathers typically act as playmates for infants (Parke, 1995). In many homes, fathers spend 4 or 5 times more hours playing with infants than they do in caregiving. It's true that fathers are getting more involved, but mothers still spend much more time on child care (de Luccie & Davis, 1991).

It might seem that the father's role as a playmate makes him less important. Not so. From birth onward, fathers pay more visual attention to children than mothers do. Fathers are much more tactile (lifting, tickling, and handling the baby), more physically arousing (engaging in rough-and-tumble play), and more likely to engage in unusual play (imitating the baby, for example) (Crawley & Sherrod, 1984). In comparison, mothers speak to infants more, play more conventional games (such as peekaboo),

Solitary play Playing alone.

Cooperative play Play in which two or more children must coordinate their actions; if children don't cooperate the game ends.

Affectional needs Emotional needs for love and affection.

Maternal influences The aggregate of all psychological effects mothers have on their children.

Caregiving styles Identifiable patterns of parental caretaking and interaction with children.

Paternal influences The aggregate of all psychological effects fathers have on their children.

Fathering typically makes a contribution to early development that differs in emphasis from mothering.

and, as noted, spend much more time in caregiving (● Figure 3.14). Amy's playtime with Tom is actually very valuable. Young children who spend a lot of time playing with their fathers tend to be more competent in many ways (Pettit et al., 1998).

Overall, fathers can be as affectionate, sensitive, and responsive as mothers are. Nevertheless, infants tend to get very different views of males and females. Females, who offer comfort, nurturance, and verbal stimulation, tend to be close at hand. Males come and go, and when they are present, action, exploration, and risk-taking prevail. It's no wonder, then, that the caregiving styles of mothers and fathers have a major impact on children's gender role development (Lindsay, Mize, & Pettit, 1997; Videon, 2005).

As a child matures and becomes more independent, parents must find ways to control the child's behavior. ("No, you may not smear pudding on Daddy's face.") Such attempts can have a variety of effects, as described next.

Parenting Styles

Psychologist Diana Baumrind (1991) has studied the effects of three major styles of parenting. See if you recognize the styles she describes.

Authoritarian parents enforce rigid rules and demand strict obedience to authority. Typically they view children as having few rights but adult-like responsibilities. The child is expected to stay out of trouble and to accept, without question, what parents regard as right or wrong. ("Do it because I say so.") The children of authoritarian parents are usually obedient and self-controlled. But they also tend to be emotionally stiff, withdrawn, apprehensive, and lacking in curiosity.

Overly permissive parents give little guidance, allow too much freedom, or don't hold children accountable for their actions. Typically, the child has rights similar to an adult's but few responsibilities. Rules are not enforced, and the child usually gets his or her way. ("Do whatever you want.") Permissive parents tend to produce dependent, immature children who misbehave frequently. Such children are aimless and likely to "run amok."

Baumrind describes **authoritative parents** as those who supply firm and consistent guidance, combined with love and affection. Such parents balance their own rights with those of their children. They control their children's behavior in a caring, responsive, non-authoritarian way. ("Do it for this reason.") Effective parents are firm and consistent, not harsh or rigid. In general, they encourage the child to act responsibly, to think, and to make good decisions. This style produces children who are competent, self-controlled, independent, assertive, and inquiring (Baumrind, 1991).

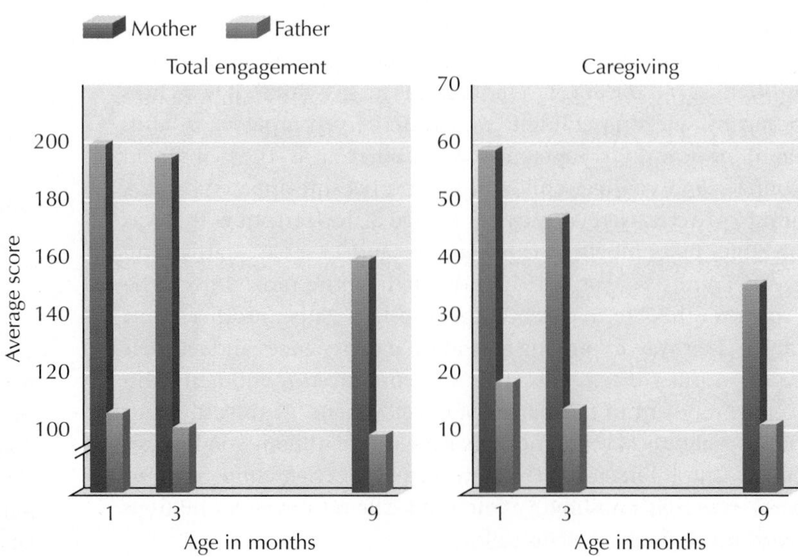

● Figure 3.14 Mother–infant and father–infant interactions. These graphs show what occurred on routine days in a sample of 72 American homes. The graph on the left records the total amount of contact parents had with their babies, including such actions as talking to, touching, hugging, or smiling at the infant. The graph on the right shows the amount of caregiving (diapering, washing, feeding, and so forth) done by each parent. Note that in both cases mother–infant interactions greatly exceed father–infant interactions. (Adapted from Belsky et al., 1984.)

Baby Blues

Close to Home

"All right now, give Mommy the super-glue."

Culture

Do ethnic differences in parenting affect children in distinctive ways? Diana Baumrind's conclusions are probably most valid for families of European descent. Child rearing in other ethnic groups often reflects different customs and beliefs. Cultural differences are especially apparent with respect to the meaning attached to a child's behavior. Is a particular behavior "good" or "bad"? Should it be encouraged or discouraged? The answer will depend greatly on parents' cultural values (Rubin, 1998).

Ethnic Differences: Four Flavors of Parenting

Making generalizations about groups of people is always risky. Nevertheless, some typical differences in child-rearing patterns have been observed in North American ethnic communities (Kaplan, 1998).

African-American Families

Traditional African-American values emphasize loyalty and interdependence among family members, security, developing a positive identity, and not giving up in the face of adversity. African-American parents typically stress obedience and respect for elders. Child discipline tends to be fairly strict, but many African-American parents see this as a necessity, especially if they live in urban areas where safety is a concern. Self-reliance, resourcefulness, and an ability to take care of oneself in difficult situations are also qualities that African-American parents seek to promote in their children (Parke, 2004).

Hispanic Families

Like African-American parents, Hispanic parents tend to have relatively strict standards of discipline. They also place a high value on family values, family pride, and loyalty. Hispanic families are typically affectionate and indulgent toward younger children. However, as children grow older they are expected to learn social skills and to be calm, obedient, courteous, and respectful. In fact, such social skills may be valued more than cognitive skills (Delgado & Ford, 1998). In addition, Hispanic parents tend to stress cooperation more than competition. Such values can put Hispanic children at a disadvantage in highly competitive, Anglo-American culture.

Asian-American Families

Asian cultures tend to be group oriented, and they emphasize interdependence among individuals. In contrast, Western cultures value individual effort and independence. This difference is often reflected in Asian-American child-rearing practices. Asian-American children are taught that their behavior can bring either pride or shame to the family. Therefore, they are obliged to set aside their own desires when the greater good of the family is at

Authoritarian parents Parents who enforce rigid rules and demand strict obedience to authority.

Overly permissive parents Parents who give little guidance, allow too much freedom, or do not require the child to take responsibility.

Authoritative parents Parents who supply firm and consistent guidance combined with love and affection.

Jeff Greenberg/PhotoEdit

In ethnic communities, norms for effective parenting often differ in subtle ways from parenting styles in Euro-American culture.

stake (Parke, 2004). Parents tend to act as teachers who encourage hard work, moral behavior, and achievement. For the first few years, parenting is lenient and permissive. However, after about age 5, Asian-American parents begin to expect respect, obedience, self-control, and self-discipline from their children.

Arab-American Families

In Middle Eastern cultures, children are expected to be polite, obedient, disciplined, and conforming. Punishment generally consists of spankings, teasing, or shaming in front of others. Arab-American fathers tend to be strong authority figures who demand obedience so that the family will not be shamed by a child's bad behavior. Success, generosity, and hospitality are highly valued in Arab-American culture. The pursuit of family honor encourages hard work, thrift, conservatism, and educational achievement. The welfare of the family is emphasized over individual identity. Thus, Arab-American children are raised to respect their parents, members of their extended family, and other adults as well (Erikson & Al-Timimi, 2001).

Implications

Child rearing shows considerable variation around the world. In fact, many of the things we do in North America, such as forcing young children to sleep alone, would be considered odd or wrong in other cultures. In the final analysis, parenting can only be judged if we know what culture or ethnic community a child is being prepared to enter (Bornstein et al., 1998).

Side Effects of Child Discipline

When parents fail to provide *discipline* (guidance regarding acceptable behavior), children become antisocial, aggressive, and insecure. Effective discipline is fair but loving, authoritative yet sensitive. It socializes a child without destroying the bond of love and trust between parent and child.

Types of Discipline

Parents typically discipline children in one of three ways. **Power assertion** refers to physical punishment or a show of force, such as taking away toys or privileges. As an alternative, some parents use **withdrawal of love** (withholding affection) by refusing to speak to a child, threatening to leave, rejecting the child, or otherwise acting as if the child is temporarily unlovable. **Management techniques** combine praise, recognition, approval, rules, reasoning, and the like to encourage desirable behavior. Each of these approaches can control a child's behavior, but their side effects differ considerably.

What are the side effects? Power-oriented techniques—particularly harsh or severe physical punishment—are associated with fear, hatred of parents, and a lack of spontaneity and warmth. Severely punished children also tend to be defiant, rebellious, and aggressive (Patterson, 1982). Despite its drawbacks, power assertion is the most popular mode of discipline (Papps et al., 1995).

Withdrawal of love produces children who tend to be self-disciplined. You could say that such children have developed a good conscience. Often, they are described as "model" children or as unusually "good." But as a side effect, they are also frequently anxious, insecure, and dependent on adults for approval.

Management techniques also have limitations. Most important is the need to carefully adjust to a child's level of understanding. Younger children don't always see the connection between rules, explanations, and their own behavior. Nevertheless, management techniques receive a big plus in another area. Psychologist Stanley Coopersmith (1968) found a direct connection between discipline and a child's self-esteem.

Self-Esteem

If you regard yourself as a worthwhile person, you have **self-esteem.** High self-esteem is essential for emotional health. Individuals with low self-esteem don't think much of themselves as people. In elementary school, children with high self-esteem tend to be more popular, cooperative, and successful in class. Children with low self-esteem are more withdrawn and tend to perform below average (Hay, Ashman, & Van Kraayenoord, 1998).

How does discipline affect self-esteem? Coopersmith (1968) found that low self-esteem is related to physical punishment and the withholding of love. And why not? What messages do children receive if a parent beats them or tells them they are not worthy of love?

BRIDGES

Punishment has important effects on learning.

For more tips on how to use punishment wisely, see Chapter 8, pages 283–285.

CRITICAL THINKING The Pampered Child

Surely high self-esteem is the key to psychological health, whereas low self-esteem is at the root of childhood misbehavior. The child whose authoritarian father belittles him at home is the one who becomes a bully at school and the child whose parents ignore her becomes a loner, vulnerable to falling in with a bad crowd. These are the problem kids, right?

Although low self-esteem can lead to problems, so can excessively high self-esteem, according to clinical psychologist Maggie Mamen. In her book, *Pampered Child Syndrome,* Mamen (2004) suggests that many modern parents are trying to be more humane in their parenting style. To "empower" their children, they impose few limits on behavior, and to make them feel special, they give their children everything they want.

Mamen suggests that such good intentions can backfire, leaving parents with children who have developed an artificially high level of self-esteem and a sense of entitlement. That is, overly permissive parenting produces spoiled, self-indulgent children who have little self-control (Baumrind, 1991). Their sense of entitlement can lead them to bully other children to get their way or even to engage in criminal activity. As adults, such children may become addicted to seeking ways to enhance their self-esteem. For example, they may place excessive importance on being physically attractive, leading to stress, drug and alcohol use, and eating disorders (Crocker & Park, 2004).

High self-esteem is promoted by management techniques. Thus, it is best to minimize physical punishment and avoid unnecessary withdrawal of love. Children who feel that their parents support them emotionally tend to have high self-esteem (Hay, Ashman, & Van Kraayenoord, 1998; Nielsen & Metha, 1994). But can self-esteem ever get too high? See "The Pampered Child."

Positive Psychology: Resilience in Childhood

Children may face daunting hurdles as they are growing up, such as poverty, divorce, violence, or illness. Yet despite such adversity, children prove to be amazingly *resilient* (good at bouncing back after bad experiences) and develop the strengths they need to thrive in difficult circumstances (Masten, 2001).

Psychologists have tried to find ways to encourage resilience in children. Their work suggests again that warm, authoritative parenting is important (Kim-Cohen et al., 2004; Masten, 2001). In addition, effective parents teach their children how to manage emotions and use positive coping skills (Eisenberg et al., 2003; Lynch et al., 2004). Children who have self-esteem and feel connected to caring adults are likely to be resilient, capable, and successful. For this, and many other reasons, competent parenting is well worth the effort.

KNOWLEDGE BUILDER

Parental Influences

REFLECT

Picture a mother you know who seems to be a good caregiver. Which of the optimal caregiving behaviors does she engage in?

Do you know any parents who have young children and who are authoritarian, permissive, or authoritative? What are their children like?

What do you think are the best ways to discipline children? How would your approach be classified? What are its advantages and disadvantages?

LEARNING CHECK

1. Three important elements of effective mothering are _____ _______________ maternal involvement; parental _______________ to a child's feelings; needs, rhythms, and signals, and compatibility between parent and child _______________.
2. Fathers are more likely to act as playmates for their children, rather than caregivers. T or F?
3. According to Diana Baumrind's research, effective parents are authoritarian in their approach to their children's behavior. T or F?
4. Psychologist Diana Baumrind describes parents who enforce rigid rules and demand strict obedience as
   a. authoritative c. proactive-reactive
   b. permissive-repressive d. authoritarian
5. Which form of child discipline tends to make children insecure, anxious, and hungry for approval?
   a. withdrawal of love c. power assertion
   b. management techniques d. authoritative techniques

Power assertion The use of physical punishment or coercion to enforce child discipline.

Withdrawal of love Withholding affection to enforce child discipline.

Management techniques Combining praise, recognition, approval, rules, and reasoning to enforce child discipline.

Self-esteem Regarding oneself as a worthwhile person; a positive evaluation of oneself.

6. Coopersmith found that high self-esteem in childhood is related to discipline based on either management techniques or withdrawal of love. T or F?

CRITICAL THINKING

7. Why is it risky to make generalizations about child-rearing differences for various ethnic groups?
8. If power assertion is a poor way to discipline children, why do so many parents use it?

Answers: 1. proactive, responsiveness, temperaments **2.** T **3.** d **4.** T **5.** a **6.** F **7.** Because there may be as much variation within ethnic groups as there is between them. For example, there are sizable differences in the child-rearing styles of Hispanic parents from Puerto Rico, Argentina, and Guatemala. **8.** Most parents discipline their children in the same ways that they themselves were disciplined. Parenting is a responsibility of tremendous importance, for which most people receive almost no training.

Language Development—Fast-Talking Babies

There's something almost miraculous about a baby's first words. As infants, how did we manage to leap into the world of language? As will soon be apparent, social development provides a foundation for language learning. But before we probe that connection, let's begin with a quick survey of language development.

Language Acquisition

Language development is closely tied to maturation (Gleason, 2005). As every parent knows, babies can cry from birth on. By 1 month of age they use crying to gain attention. Typically, parents can tell if an infant is hungry, angry, or in pain from the tone of the crying (Kaplan, 1998). Around 6 to 8 weeks of age, babies begin **cooing** (the repetition of vowel sounds such as "oo" and "ah").

By 7 months of age, Amy's nervous system will mature enough to allow her to grasp objects, smile, laugh, sit up, and **babble.** In the babbling stage, the consonants *b, d, m,* and *g* are combined with the vowel sounds to produce meaningless language sounds: *dadadadada* or *bababa.* At first, babbling is the same around the world. But soon the language spoken by parents begins to have an influence. That is, Japanese babies start to babble in a way that sounds like Japanese, Mexican babies babble in Spanish-like sounds, and so forth (Gopnik, Meltzoff, & Kuhl, 1999; Kuhl, 2004).

At about 1 year of age, children can stand alone for a short time and respond to real words such as *no* or *hi.* Soon afterward, the first connection between words and objects forms, and children may address their parents as "Mama" or "Dada." By age 18 months to 2 years, Amy will have learned to stand and walk alone. By then, her vocabulary may include from 24 to 200 words. At first there is a *single-word stage,* during which children use one word at a time, such as "go," "juice," or "up." Soon after, words are arranged in simple two-word sentences called *telegraphic speech:* "Want-Teddy," "Mama-gone."

Language and the Terrible Twos

At about the same time that children begin to put two or three words together they become much more independent. Two-year-olds understand some of the commands parents make, but they are not always willing to carry them out. A child like Amy may assert her independence by saying, "No drink," "Me do it," "My cup, my cup," and the like. It can be worse, of course. A 2-year-old may look at you intently, make eye contact, listen as you shout "No, no," and still pour her juice on the cat.

During their second year, children become increasingly capable of mischief and temper tantrums (Kaplan, 1998). Thus, calling this time "the terrible twos" is not entirely inappropriate. One-year-olds can do plenty of things parents don't want them to do. However, it's usually 2-year-olds who do things *because* you don't want them to (Gopnik, Meltzoff, & Kuhl, 1999).

Perhaps parents can take some comfort in knowing that a stubborn, negative 2-year-old is simply becoming more independent. When Amy is 2, Olivia and Tom would be wise to remember, "This, too, shall pass." After age 2, the child's comprehension and use of words takes a dramatic leap forward (Reznick & Goldfield, 1992). From this point on, vocabulary and language skills grow at a phenomenal rate. By first grade, Amy will be able to understand around 8,000 words and use about 4,000. She will have truly entered the world of language.

The Roots of Language

In a classic study, William Condon and Louis Sander (1974) filmed newborn infants listening to various sounds. A frame-by-frame analysis of the films showed something astonishing: Infants move

Baby Blues

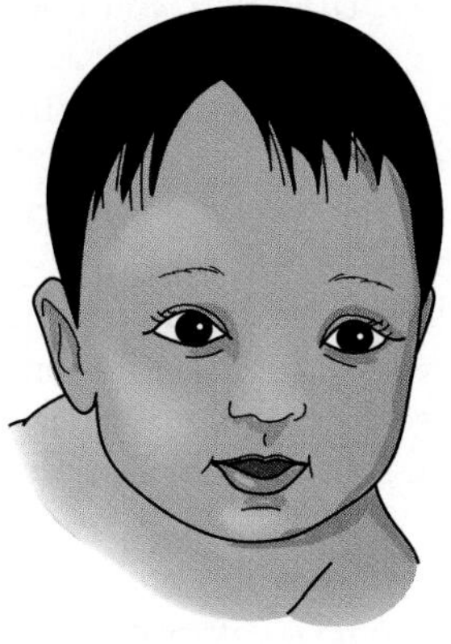
85
Medium high positive

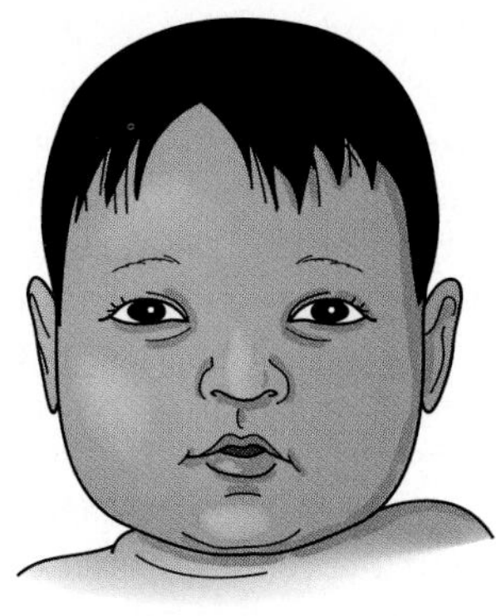
50
Neutral attention

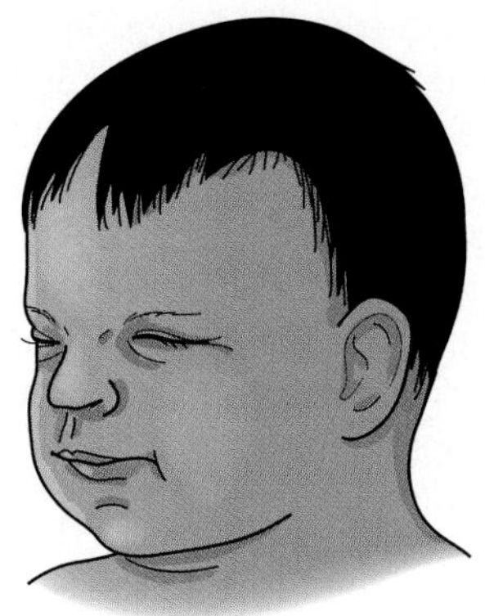
20
Avert

● **Figure 3.15** Infant engagement scale. These samples from a 90-point scale show various levels of infant engagement, or attention. Babies participate in prelanguage "conversations" with parents by giving and withholding attention and by smiling, gazing, or vocalizing. (From Beebe et al., 1982)

their arms and legs to the rhythms of human speech. Random noise, rhythmic tapping, or disconnected vowel sounds will not produce a "language dance." Only natural speech has this effect.

Why do day-old infants "dance" to speech but not other sounds? One possibility is that language recognition is innate. Linguist Noam Chomsky (1975, 1986) has long claimed that humans have a **biological predisposition**, or hereditary readiness, to develop language. According to Chomsky, language patterns are inborn, much like a child's ability to coordinate walking. If such inborn language recognition does exist, it may explain why children around the world use a limited number of patterns in their first sentences. Typical patterns include the following (Mussen et al., 1979):

Identification:	"See kitty."
Nonexistence:	"Allgone milk."
Possession:	"My doll."
Agent-Action:	"Mama give."
Negation:	"Not ball."
Question:	"Where doggie?"

Does Chomsky's theory explain why language develops so rapidly? Perhaps. But many psychologists believe that Chomsky underestimates the impact of learning (Tomasello, 2003). *Psycholinguists* (specialists in the psychology of language) have shown that imitation of adults and rewards for correctly using words (as when a child asks for a cookie) are an important part of language learning. Also, babies actively participate in language learning by asking questions, such as, "What dis?" (Domingo & Goldstein-Alpern, 1999).

When a child makes a language error, parents typically repeat the child's sentence, with needed corrections (Bohannon & Stanowicz, 1988). More important is the fact that parents and children begin to communicate long before the child can speak. Months of shared effort precede a child's first word. From this point of view, an infant's "language dance" reflects a readiness to interact *socially* with parents, not innate language recognition. The next section explains why.

Early Communication

How do parents communicate with infants before they can talk? Parents go to a great deal of trouble to get babies to smile and vocalize (● Figure 3.15). In doing so, they quickly learn to change their actions to keep the infant's attention, arousal, and activity at optimal levels. A familiar example is the "I'm-Going-to-Get-You Game." In it, the adult says, "I'm gonna getcha. . . . I'm gonna getcha. . . . I'm gonna getcha. . . . Gotcha!" Through such games, adults and babies come to share similar rhythms and expectations (Stern, 1982). Soon a system of shared **signals** is created, including touching, vocalizing, gazing, and smiling. These help lay a foundation for later language use. Specifically, signals establish a pattern of "conversational" *turn-taking* (alternate sending and receiving of messages).

Olivia	*Amy*
(smiles)	
"Oh what a nice little smile!"	
"Yes, isn't that nice?"	
"There."	
"There's a nice little smile."	(burps)
"Well, pardon you!"	
"Yes, that's better, isn't it?"	
"Yes."	(vocalizes)
"Yes."	(smiles)
"What's so funny?"	

Cooing Spontaneous repetition of vowel sounds by infants.

Babbling The repetition by infants of meaningless language sounds (including both vowel and consonant sounds).

Biological predisposition The presumed hereditary readiness of humans to learn certain skills, such as how to use language, or a readiness to behave in particular ways.

Signal In early language development, any behavior, such as touching, vocalizing, gazing, or smiling, that allows nonverbal interaction and turn-taking between parent and child.

From the outside, such exchanges may look meaningless. In reality, they represent real communication. Amy's vocalizations and attention provide a way of interacting emotionally with Olivia and Tom. Infants as young as 4 months engage in vocal turn-taking with adults (also, see ● Figure 3.16) (Jaffe et al., 2001). The more children interact with parents, the faster they learn to talk and the faster they learn thinking abilities (Hart & Risley, 1999). A recent study found that 6-week-old babies gaze at an adult's face in rhythm with the adult's speech (Crown et al., 2002). Unmistakably, social relationships contribute to early language learning (Tomasello, 2003).

Parentese

When they talk to infants, parents use an exaggerated pattern of speaking called **parentese.** Typically, they raise their tone of voice, use short, simple sentences, and repeat themselves more. They also slow their rate of speaking and use exaggerated voice inflections: "Did Amy eat it A-L-L UP?"

What is the purpose of such changes? Parents are apparently trying to help their children learn language. When a baby is still babbling, parents tend to use long, adult-style sentences, but as soon as the baby says its first word they switch to parentese. By the time babies are 4 months old they prefer parentese over normal speech (Cooper et al., 1997).

In addition to being simpler, parentese has a distinct "musical" quality (Fernald & Mazzie, 1991). No matter what language mothers speak, the melodies, pauses, and inflections they use to comfort, praise, or give warning are universal. Psychologist Anne Fernald has found that mothers of all nations talk to their babies with similar changes in pitch. For instance, we praise babies with a rising, then falling pitch ("BRA-vo!" "GOOD girl!"). Warnings are delivered in a short, sharp rhythm ("Nein! Nein!" "Basta! Basta!" "Not! Dude!"). To give comfort, parents use low, smooth, drawn-out tones ("Oooh poor baaa-by." "Oooh pobrecito.") A high-pitched, rising melody is used to call attention to objects ("See the pretty BIRDIE?") (Fernald, 1989).

Note that parentese is not literally "baby talk." Many parents can't seem to resist imitating a baby's "cute" mispronunciations of words, like "wa-wa" (water) or "pah-getty" (spaghetti). This is harmless enough for a short time. However, continued use of baby talk may slow language learning. Unless parents help their children pronounce words correctly, a child can easily reach school age still using baby talk. ("Teacher, can I go wee-wee.")

Parentese helps parents get babies' attention, communicate with them, and teach them language (Kaplan et al., 1995). Later, as a child's speaking improves, parents tend to adjust their speech to the child's language ability. Especially from 18 months to 4 years of age, parents seek to clarify what a child says and prompt the child to say more. Two typical strategies are as follows (Newman & Newman, 1987):

Expansion:	*Child:*	Doggie bite.
	Parent:	Yes, the dog bit *the toy.*
Prompting:	*Child:*	Doggie briggle.
	Parent:	What did the doggie do?

In summary, some elements of language are innate. Nevertheless, our inherited tendency to learn language does not determine

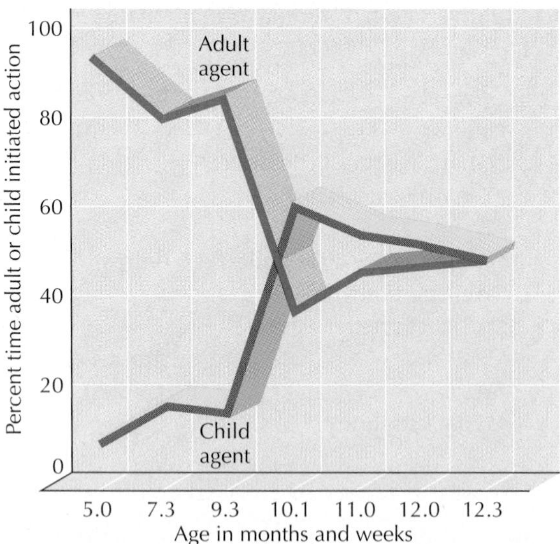

● **Figure 3.16** This graph shows the development of turn-taking in games played by an infant and his mother. For several months Richard responded to games such as peekaboo and "hand-the-toy-back" only when his mother initiated action. At about 9 months, however, he rapidly began to initiate action in the games. Soon, he was the one to take the lead about half of the time. Learning to take turns and to direct actions toward another person underlies basic language skills. (From *Child's Talk: Learning to Use Language* by Jerome Bruner. Copyright © 1983 by Jerome Bruner. Used by permission of W. W. Norton & Company, Inc.)

Just as they do when speaking, parents use a distinctive style when they sing to an infant. Even people who speak another language can tell if a recorded song was sung to an infant or an adult. Likewise, lullabies remain recognizable when electronic filtering removes words (Trehub et al., 1993a, 1993b).

whether we will speak English or Vietnamese, Spanish or Russian. Environmental forces also influence whether a person develops simple or sophisticated language skills. The first 7 years of life are a sensitive period in language learning (Eliot, 1999). Clearly, a full flowering of speech requires careful cultivation.

KNOWLEDGE BUILDER

Language Development

REFLECT

In order, see if you can name and imitate the language abilities you had as you progressed from birth to age 2 years. Now see if you can label and imitate some basic elements of parentese.

In your own words, state at least one argument for and one argument against Chomsky's view of language acquisition.

You are going to spend a day with a person who speaks a different language than you do. Do you think you would be able to communicate with the other person? How does this relate to language acquisition?

LEARNING CHECK

1. The development of speech and language usually occurs in which order?
   a. crying, cooing, babbling, telegraphic speech
   b. cooing, crying, babbling, telegraphic speech
   c. babbling, crying, cooing, telegraphic speech
   d. crying, babbling, cooing, identification
2. Simple two-word sentences are characteristic of ____________ ____________ speech.
3. Noam ____________ has advanced the idea that language acquisition is built on innate patterns.
4. Prelanguage turn-taking and social interactions would be of special interest to a psycholinguist. T or F?
5. Parents talk to young children with a raised tone of voice and an exaggerated pattern of speaking that is called
   a. transformational grammar
   b. telegraphic speech
   c. signal switching
   d. parentese

CRITICAL THINKING

6. The children of professional parents hear more words per hour than the children of welfare parents, and they also tend to score higher on tests of mental abilities. How else could their higher scores be explained?

Answers: 1. a 2. telegraphic 3. Chomsky 4. T 5. d 6. Children in professional homes receive many educational benefits that are less common in welfare homes. Yet even when such differences are taken into account, brighter children tend to come from richer language environments (Hart & Risley, 1999).

Cognitive Development—How Do Children Learn to Think?

Now that we have Amy talking, let's move on to a broader view of intellectual development. Jean Piaget (Jahn pea-ah-ZHAY) provided some of the first great insights into how children develop thinking abilities. Piaget observed that children's cognitive skills progress through a series of stages. Although Piaget's theory has been very valuable, psychologists continue to update his ideas. Also, many psychologists have become interested in how children learn the intellectual skills valued by their culture. Typically, children do this with guidance from skilled "tutors" (parents and others). This section explores children's mental development.

How different is a child's understanding of the world from that of an adult? Generally speaking, their thinking is less abstract. Children use fewer generalizations, categories, and principles. They also tend to base their understanding on particular examples and objects they can see or touch.

Before the age of 6 or 7, thinking is very concrete. Younger children cannot make **transformations** in which they must mentally change the shape or form of a substance (such as clay or water). Let's visit Amy at age 5: If you show her a short, wide glass full of milk and a tall, narrow glass (also full), she will tell you that the taller glass contains more milk. Amy will tell you this even if she watches you pour milk from the short glass into an empty, tall glass. She is not bothered by the fact that the milk appears to be transformed from a smaller to a larger amount. Instead, she responds only to the fact that *taller* seems to mean *more* (see ● Figure 3.17). After about age 7, children are no longer fooled by this situation. Perhaps that's why 7 has been called the "age of reason." From age 7 on, we see a definite trend toward more logical, adult-like thought (Flavell, 1992).

Tony Freeman/PhotoEdit

● **Figure 3.17** Children younger than age 7 intuitively assume that a volume of liquid increases when it is poured from a short, wide container into a taller, thinner one. This boy thinks the tall container holds more than the short one. Actually each holds the same amount of liquid. Children make such judgments based on the height of the liquid, not its volume.

Parentese A pattern of speech used when talking to infants, marked by a higher-pitched voice, short, simple sentences, repetition, slower speech, and exaggerated voice inflections.

Transformation The mental ability to change the shape or form of a substance (such as clay or water) and to perceive that its volume remains the same.

Is there any pattern to the growth of intellect in childhood? According to the Swiss psychologist and philosopher Jean Piaget (1951, 1952), there is.

Piaget's Theory of Cognitive Development

Jean Piaget believed that all children pass through a series of distinct stages in intellectual development. Many of his ideas came from observing his own children as they solved various thought problems. (It is tempting to imagine that Piaget's illustrious career was launched one day when his wife said to him, "Watch the children for a while, will you, Jean?")

Mental Adaptations

Piaget was convinced that intellect grows through processes he called assimilation and accommodation. **Assimilation** refers to using existing mental patterns in new situations. Let's say that a plastic hammer is the favorite toy of a boy named Benjamin, who pounds on blocks with it. For his birthday Benjamin gets an oversize toy wrench. If he uses the wrench for pounding, it has been assimilated to an existing knowledge structure.

In **accommodation,** existing ideas are modified to fit new requirements. For instance, a younger child might think that a dime is worth less than a (larger) nickel. However, as children begin to spend money, they must alter their ideas about what "more" and "less" mean. Thus, new situations are assimilated to existing ideas, and new ideas are created to accommodate new experiences.

Piaget's ideas have deeply affected our view of children (Beilin, 1992). The following is a brief summary of what he found.

Yves De Braine/stockphoto.com

Jean Piaget—philosopher, psychologist, and keen observer of children.

The Sensorimotor Stage (0–2 Years)

In the first 2 years of life, Amy's intellectual development will be largely nonverbal. She will be mainly concerned with learning to coordinate her movements with information from her senses. Also, **object permanence** (an understanding that objects continue to exist when they are out of sight) emerges at this time. Sometime during their first year, babies begin to actively pursue disappearing objects. By age 2, they can anticipate the movement of an object behind a screen. For example, when watching an electric train, Amy will look ahead to the end of a tunnel, rather than staring at the spot where the train disappeared.

In general, developments in this stage indicate that the child's conceptions are becoming more *stable.* Objects cease to appear and disappear magically, and a more orderly and predictable world replaces the confusing and disconnected sensations of infancy.

The Preoperational Stage (2–7 Years)

During this period, children begin to think *symbolically* and use language. But the child's thinking is still very **intuitive** (it makes little use of reasoning and logic). (Do you remember thinking as a child that the sun and the moon followed you when you took a walk?) In addition, the child's use of language is not as sophisticated as it might seem. Children have a tendency to confuse words with the objects they represent. If Benjamin calls a toy block a "car" and you use it to make a "house," he may be upset. To children, the name of an object is as much a part of the object as its size, shape, and color. This seems to underlie a preoccupation with name-calling. To the preoperational child, insulting words may really hurt. Consider one rather protected youngster who was angered by her older brother. Searching for a way to retaliate against her larger and stronger foe, she settled on, "You panty-girdle!" It was the worst thing she could think of saying.

FogStock LLC/Index Stock Imagery

Crossing a busy street can be dangerous for the preoperational child. Because their thinking is still egocentric, younger children cannot understand why the driver of a car can't see them if they can see the car. Children younger than 7 years also cannot consistently judge speeds and distances of oncoming cars. Adults can easily overestimate the "street smarts" of younger children. It is advisable to teach children to cross with a light, in crosswalks, or with assistance.

FOCUS ON RESEARCH

A Child's Theory of Mind—Other People, Other Minds

Why are young children so egocentric? In many instances it's because they have a limited understanding of mental states, such as desires, beliefs, thoughts, intentions, and feelings. In other words, it could be said that they have a very simplified **theory of mind** (Flavell, 1999).

The following example is based on theory-of-mind research. Imagine that you show 5-year-old Kobe a candy box. "What do you think is inside?" you ask. "Candy," Kobe replies. Then you let Kobe look inside, where he finds a surprise: The box contains crayons, not candy. "Kobe," you ask, "what will your friend Max think is inside the box if I show it to him?" Kobe replies, "Candy!" amused at the thought that Max is going to get fooled, too.

Now imagine that we try the procedure again, this time with Shelia, who is only 3 years old. Like Kobe, Shelia thinks she will find candy in the box. She opens the box and sees the crayons. Now we ask Shelia what she thinks Max will expect to find in the box. "Crayons," she replies. Because Shelia knows that there are crayons in the box, she assumes that everyone else does, too. It's as if only one reality exists for Shelia. She doesn't seem to understand that the minds of other people contain different information, beliefs, thoughts, and so forth (Gopnik, Meltzoff, & Kuhl, 1999).

Children around the world normally gain a richer understanding of mental life between the ages of 3 and 5. One study found this to be the case for children in five different cultures, Thailand, India, Peru, Samoa, and Canada (Callaghan et al., 2005). However, according to a Turkish study, children with little opportunity to interact with adults, such as children living in a boarding home, may take longer to develop this understanding (Yagmurlu et al., 2005). Regardless, as young children's "theory of mind" becomes more accurate, they are able to participate more fully in the complex psychological world in which we all live.

During the preoperational stage, the child is also quite **egocentric** (unable to take the viewpoint of other people). The child's ego seems to stand at the center of his or her world. To illustrate, show Amy a two-sided mirror. Then hold it between you and her, so that she can see herself in it. If you ask her what she thinks *you* can see, she imagines that you see *her* face reflected in the mirror, instead of your own. Such egocentrism explains why children can seem exasperatingly selfish or uncooperative at times. If Benjamin blocks your view by standing in front of the TV, he assumes that you can see it if he can. If you ask him to move so that you can see better, he may move so that he can see better! Benjamin is not being selfish in the ordinary sense. He just doesn't realize that your view differs from his (see "A Child's Theory of Mind").

The Concrete Operational Stage (7–11 Years)

An important development during this stage is mastery of **conservation** (the concept that mass, weight, and volume remain unchanged when the shape of objects changes). Children have learned conservation when they understand that rolling a ball of clay into a "snake" does not increase the amount of clay. Likewise, pouring liquid from a tall, narrow glass into a shallow dish does not reduce the amount of liquid. In each case the volume remains the same despite changes in shape or appearance. The original amount is *conserved* (see ● Figure 3.17).

During the concrete operational stage, children begin to use concepts of time, space, and number. The child can think logically about very concrete objects or situations, categories, and principles. Such abilities explain why children stop believing in Santa Claus when they reach this stage. Because they can conserve volume, they realize that Santa's sack couldn't possibly hold enough toys for millions of girls and boys.

Assimilation In Piaget's theory, the application of existing mental patterns to new situations (that is, the new situation is assimilated to existing mental schemes).

Accommodation In Piaget's theory, the modification of existing mental patterns to fit new demands (that is, mental schemes are changed to accommodate new information or experiences).

Sensorimotor stage Stage of intellectual development during which sensory input and motor responses become coordinated.

Object permanence Concept, gained in infancy, that objects continue to exist even when they are hidden from view.

Preoperational stage Period of intellectual development during which children begin to use language and think symbolically, yet remain intuitive and egocentric in their thought.

Intuitive thought Thinking that makes little or no use of reasoning and logic.

Theory of mind A child's current understanding of the mind, including the desires, beliefs, intentions, and feelings of others.

Egocentric thought Thought that is self-centered and fails to consider the viewpoints of others.

Concrete operational stage Period of intellectual development during which children become able to use the concepts of time, space, volume, and number, but in ways that remain simplified and concrete, rather than abstract.

Conservation In Piaget's theory, mastery of the concept that the weight, mass, and volume of matter remains unchanged (is conserved) even when the shape or appearance of objects changes.

Another important development at this time is the ability to *reverse* thoughts or mental operations. A conversation with a 4-year-old boy in the preoperational stage shows what happens when a child's thinking *lacks* reversibility (Phillips, 1969).

"Do you have a brother?"
"Yes."
"What's his name?"
"Jim."
"Does Jim have a brother?"
"No."

Reversibility of thought allows children in the concrete operational stage to recognize that if $4 \times 2 = 8$, then 2×4 does, too. Younger children must memorize each relationship separately. Thus, a preoperational child may know that $4 \times 9 = 36$ without being able to tell you what 9×4 equals.

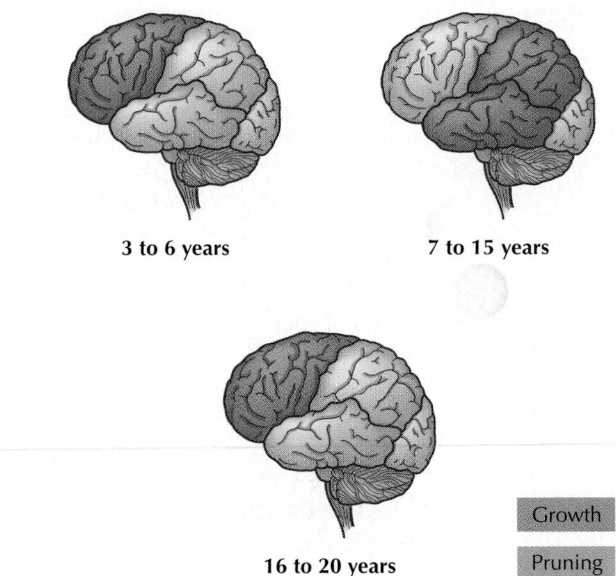

● **Figure 3.18** Between the ages of 3 and 6 a tremendous wave of growth occurs in connections among neurons in the frontal areas of the brain. This corresponds to the time when children make rapid progress in their ability to think symbolically. Between ages 7 and 15, peak synaptic growth shifts to the temporal and parietal lobes. During this period children become increasingly adept at using language, a specialty of the temporal lobes. In the late teens, the brain actively destroys unneeded connections, especially in the frontal lobes. This pruning of synapses sharpens the brain's capacity for abstract thinking (Restak, 2001).

The Formal Operations Stage (11 Years and Up)

After about the age of 11, children begin to break away from concrete objects and specific examples. Thinking is based more on **abstract principles,** such as "democracy," "honor," or "correlation." Children who reach this stage can think about their thoughts, and they become less egocentric. Older children and young adolescents also gradually become able to consider **hypothetical possibilities** (suppositions, guesses, or projections). For example, if you ask a younger child, "What do you think would happen if it suddenly became possible for people to fly?" the child might respond, "People can't fly." Older children are able to consider such possibilities.

Full adult intellectual ability is attained during the stage of formal operations. Older adolescents are capable of inductive and deductive reasoning, and they can comprehend math, physics, philosophy, psychology, and other abstract systems. They can learn to test hypotheses in a scientific manner. Of course, not everyone reaches this level of thinking. Also, many adults can think formally about some topics, but their thinking becomes concrete when the topic is unfamiliar. This implies that formal thinking may be more a result of culture and learning than maturation. In any case, after late adolescence, improvements in intellect are based on gaining knowledge, experience, and wisdom rather than on any leaps in basic thinking capacity.

Piaget and Parenting

How can parents apply Piaget's ideas? Piaget's theory suggests that the ideal way to guide intellectual development is to provide experiences that are only slightly novel, unusual, or challenging. Remember, a child's intellect develops mainly through accommodation. It is usually best to follow a *one-step-ahead strategy,* in which your teaching efforts are aimed just beyond a child's current level of comprehension (Heckhausen, 1987). (This idea is discussed more in a moment.)

Parents should avoid **forced teaching,** or "hothousing," which is like trying to force plants to bloom prematurely (Hyson et al., 1991). Forcing children to learn reading, math, gymnastics, swimming, or music at an accelerated pace can bore or oppress them. True intellectual enrichment respects the child's interests. It does not make the child feel pressured to perform (Alvino et al., 1996).

For example, every morning Mateo's mother drills him with flash cards in hopes that he will learn to read before any of the neighborhood children. In the afternoon, Mateo watches educational videotapes about pre-math skills. Every evening, a Mozart sonata fills Mateo's room, repeating over and over. Mateo is taking dancing lessons and learning sign language. Are his parents facilitating his cognitive development? Perhaps not. Mateo is 2 and a half. Although his parents obviously mean well, intellectual "enrichment" that does not match a child's needs is of little value.

For your convenience, ■ Table 3.2 briefly summarizes each Piagetian stage. To help you remember Piaget's theory, the table describes what would happen at each stage if we played a game of *Monopoly* with the child. You'll also find brief suggestions about how to relate to children in each stage.

Piaget Today

Piaget's theory is a valuable "road map" for understanding how children think. However, many psychologists are convinced that Piaget gave too little credit to the effects of learning. For example, children of pottery-making parents can correctly answer questions about the conservation of clay at an earlier age than Piaget would have predicted (Bransford et al., 1986). According to learn-

TABLE 3.2

Piaget—A Guide for Parents

PIAGET	*MONOPOLY* GAME	GUIDELINES FOR PARENTS
Sensorimotor Stage (0–2 Years)		
The stage during which sensory input and motor responses become coordinated.	The child puts houses, hotels, and dice in her mouth and plays with "Chance" cards.	Active play with a child is most effective at this stage. Encourage explorations in touching, smelling, and manipulating objects. Peekaboo is a good way to establish the permanence of objects.
Preoperational Stage (2–7 Years)		
The period of cognitive development when children begin to use language and think symbolically, yet remain intuitive and egocentric.	The child plays *Monopoly* but makes up her own rules and cannot understand instructions.	Specific examples and touching or seeing things continues to be more useful than verbal explanations. Learning the concept of conservation may be aided by demonstrations with liquids, beads, clay, and other substances.
Concrete Operational Stage (7–11 Years)		
The period of cognitive development during which children begin to use concepts of time, space, volume, and number, but in ways that remain simplified and concrete.	The child understands basic instructions and will play by the rules but is not capable of hypothetical transactions dealing with mortgages, loans, and special pacts with other players.	Children are beginning to use generalizations, but they still require specific examples to grasp many ideas. Expect a degree of inconsistency in the child's ability to apply concepts of time, space, quantity, and volume to new situations.
Formal Operations Stage (11 Years and Up)		
The period of intellectual development marked by a capacity for abstract, theoretical, and hypothetical thinking.	The child no longer plays the game mechanically; complex and hypothetical transactions unique to each game are now possible.	It is now more effective to explain things verbally or symbolically and to help children master general rules and principles. Encourage the child to create hypotheses and to imagine how things could be.

ing theorists, children continuously gain specific knowledge; they do not undergo stage-like leaps in general mental ability (Siegler, 2004). On the other hand, the growth in connections between brain cells occurs in waves that parallel some of Piaget's stages (see ● Figure 3.18). Thus, the truth may lie somewhere between Piaget's stage theory and modern learning theory.

On a broad scale, many of Piaget's *observations* have held up well. However, his *explanations* for the growth of thinking abilities in childhood continue to be debated. Where early infancy is concerned, even Piaget's observations may need revision. It looks like Piaget greatly underestimated the thinking abilities of infants during the sensorimotor stage.

Infant Cognition

What evidence is there that Piaget underestimated infant abilities? Piaget believed that infants younger than 1 year of age cannot think. Babies, he said, have no memory of people and objects that are out of sight. Yet we now know that infants begin forming representations of the world very early in life. For example, babies as young as 3 months of age appear to know that objects are solid and do not disappear when out of view (Baillargeon, 2004; Johnson & Nanez, 1995).

Why did Piaget fail to detect the thinking skills of infants? Most likely, he mistook babies' limited *physical* skills for *mental* incompetence. Piaget's tests required babies to search for objects or reach out and touch them. Newer, more sensitive methods are uncovering abilities Piaget missed. One such method takes advantage of the fact that babies, like adults, act surprised when they see something "impossible" or unexpected occur. To make use of this effect, psychologist Renee Baillargeon (1991) puts on little "magic shows" for infants. In her "theater" babies watch as possible and impossible events occur with toys or other objects. Some 3-month-old infants act surprised and gaze longer at impossible events. An example is seeing two solid objects appear to pass through each other. By the time they are 8 months old, babies can remember where objects are (or should be) for at least 1 minute (● Figure 3.19).

Piaget believed that abilities like those described in ● Figure 3.19 emerge only after a long sensorimotor period of develop-

Reversibility of thought Recognition that relationships involving equality or identity can be reversed (for example, if A × B, then B × A).

Formal operations stage Period of intellectual development characterized by thinking that includes abstract, theoretical, and hypothetical ideas.

Abstract principles Concepts and ideas removed from specific examples and concrete situations.

Hypothetical possibilities Suppositions, guesses, or projections.

Forced teaching Accelerated learning at a pace dictated by an adult.

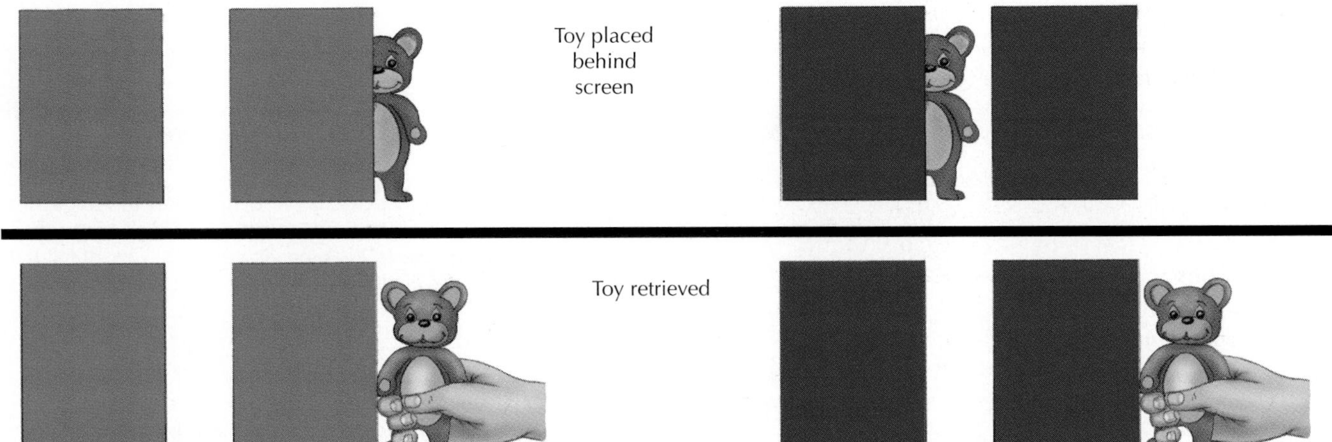

● **Figure 3.19** The panels on the left show a possible event, in which an infant watches as a toy is placed behind the right of two screens. After a delay of 70 seconds, the toy is brought into view from behind the right screen. In the two panels on the right, an impossible event occurs. The toy is placed behind the left screen and retrieved from behind the right. (A duplicate toy was hidden there before testing.) Eight-month-old infants react with surprise when they see the impossible event staged for them. Their reaction implies that they remember where the toy was hidden. Infants appear to have a capacity for memory and thinking that greatly exceeds what Piaget claimed is possible during the sensorimotor period. (Adapted from Baillargeon et al., 1989.)

ment. However, evidence continues to mount that babies are born with the capacity to form concepts about the world or to acquire this ability early in life (Eimas, Quinn, & Cowan, 1994). It looks as if further study is likely to refine and amend the ideas that grew from Piaget's fateful decision to "watch the children for a while."

Another criticism of Piaget is that he underestimated the impact of culture on mental development. The next section tells how Amy will go about mastering the intellectual tools valued by her culture.

Vygotsky's Sociocultural Theory

Psychologists are also interested in the *sociocultural theory* of Russian scholar Lev Vygotsky (1896–1934). Vygotsky's key insight is that children's thinking develops through dialogues with more capable persons (Vygotsky, 1962, 1978).

How does that relate to intellectual growth? So far, no one has ever published *A Child's Guide to Life on Earth.* Instead, children must learn about life from various "tutors," such as parents, teachers, and older siblings. Even if *A Child's Guide to Life on Earth* did exist, we would need a separate version for every culture. It is not enough for children to learn how to think. Each must also learn specific intellectual skills valued by his or her culture.

Like Piaget, Vygotsky believed that children actively seek to discover new principles. However, Vygotsky emphasized that many of a child's most important "discoveries" are guided by skillful tutors. Developmental psychologist David Shaffer (2002) offers the following example:

> Annie, a 4-year-old, has just received her first jigsaw puzzle as a birthday present. She attempts to work the puzzle but gets nowhere until her father comes along, sits down beside her, and gives her some tips. He suggests that it would be a good idea to put together the corners first, points to the pink area at the edge of one corner piece and says, "Let's look for another pink piece." When Annie seems frustrated, he places two interlocking pieces near each other so that she will notice them, and when Annie succeeds, he offers words of encouragement. As Annie gradually gets the hang of it, he steps back and lets her work more and more independently (p. 260).

Interactions like this are most helpful when they take place within a child's **zone of proximal development.**

What did Vygotsky mean by that? The word *proximal* means close or nearby. Vygotsky realized that, at any given time, some tasks are just beyond a child's reach. The child is close to having the mental skills needed to do the task, but it is a little too complex to be mastered alone. However, children working within this zone can make rapid progress if they receive sensitive guidance from a skilled partner (LeBlanc & Bearison, 2004).

Vygotsky also emphasized a process he called **scaffolding.** A scaffold is a framework or temporary support. Vygotsky believed that adults help children learn how to think by "scaffolding," or supporting, their attempts to solve problems or discover principles. To be most effective, scaffolding must be responsive to a child's needs. For example, as Annie's father helped her with the puzzle, he tailored his hints and guidance to match her evolving abilities. The two of them worked together, step by step, so that Annie could better understand how to assemble a puzzle. In a sense, Annie's father set up a series of temporary bridges that helped her move into new mental territory. As predicted by Vygotsky's theory, the cognitive skills of 3- to 6-year-old children are closely related to the amount of scaffolding their mothers provide (Smith, Landry, & Swank, 2000).

During their collaborations with others, children learn important cultural beliefs and values. For example, imagine that a boy wants to know how many hockey cards he has. His mother helps him stack and count the cards, moving each card to a new stack as they count it. She then shows him how to write the number on a slip of paper to help him remember it. This teaches the child not only about counting but also that writing is valued in our culture. In other parts of the world, a child learning to count might be shown how to make notches on a stick or tie knots in a cord.

Implications

Vygotsky saw that grown-ups play a crucial role in what children know. As they try to decipher the world, children rely on adults to help them understand how things work. Vygotsky further noticed that adults unconsciously adjust their behavior to give children the information they need to solve problems that interest the child. In this way, children use adults to learn about their culture and society (Gopnik, Meltzoff, & Kuhl, 1999; LeBlanc & Bearison, 2004).

KNOWLEDGE BUILDER

Cognitive Development

REFLECT

You are going to make cookies with children of various ages. See if you can name each of Piaget's stages and give an example of what a child in that stage might be expected to do.

You have been asked to help a child learn to use a pocket calculator to do simple addition. How would you go about identifying the child's zone of proximal development for this task? How would you scaffold the child's learning?

LEARNING CHECK

Match each item with one of the following stages.

A. Sensorimotor B. Preoperational C. Concrete operational D. Formal operations

1. _____ egocentric thought
2. _____ abstract or hypothetical
3. _____ purposeful movement
4. _____ intuitive thought
5. _____ conservation
6. _____ reversibility thought
7. _____ object permanence
8. _____ nonverbal development
9. Piaget believed that a child's understanding of the world grows through the mental processes of assimilation and
   a. intuition c. egocentricism
   b. accommodation d. reversibility
10. Newer methods for testing infant thinking abilities frequently make note of whether an infant is ____________ by seemingly ____________ events.
11. Vygotsky believed that adults help children learn how to think by using a process he called
   a. reversible thinking c. accommodation
   b. scaffolding d. moral reasoning

CRITICAL THINKING

12. Using Piaget's theory as a guide, at what age would you expect a child to recognize that a Styrofoam cup has weight?
13. Forced teaching ignores what principle of early maturation and development?

Answers: 1. B **2.** D **3.** A **4.** B **5.** C **6.** C **7.** A **8.** A **9.** b **10.** surprised, impossible **11.** b **12.** Seventy-five percent of 4- to 6-year-olds say that a Styrofoam cup has no weight after lifting it! Most children judge weight intuitively (by the way an object feels) until they begin to move into the concrete operational stage (Smith, Carey, & Wiser, 1985). **13.** Readiness.

PSYCHOLOGY IN ACTION

Effective Parenting—Raising Healthy Children

When parents fail to give children a good start in life, everybody suffers—the child, the parents, and society as a whole. Children need to grow up with a capacity for love, joy, fulfillment, responsibility, and self-control. Most people discipline their children in the same way they were disciplined. Unfortunately, this means many parents make the same mistakes their parents did (Covell, Grusec, & King, 1995).

Two key ingredients of effective parenting are communication and discipline. In each area, parents must strike a balance between freedom and guidance.

Zone of proximal development Refers to the range of tasks a child cannot yet master alone but that she or he can accomplish with the guidance of a more capable partner.

Scaffolding The process of adjusting instruction so that it is responsive to a beginner's behavior and supports the beginner's efforts to understand a problem or gain a mental skill.

Consistency

How can parents strike a healthy balance? Children should feel free to express their deepest feelings. However, this does not mean they can act in whatever way they please. Rather, the child is allowed to move freely within well-defined boundaries for acceptable behavior. Of course, individual parents may choose limits that are more "strict" or less "strict." But this choice is less important than **consistency** (maintaining stable rules of conduct). Consistent discipline gives a child a sense of security and stability. Inconsistency makes the child's world seem insecure and unpredictable.

What does consistent discipline mean in practice? To illustrate the errors parents often make, let's consider some examples of *inconsistency* (Fontenelle, 1989).

- Saying one thing and doing something else. You tell the child, "Bart, if you don't eat your Brussels sprouts you can't have any dessert." Then you feel guilty and offer him some dessert.
- Making statements you don't mean. "If you don't quiet down, I'm going to stop the car and make you walk home."
- Overstating consequences. "Look what you did to the flower bed. You can't ever ride your bike again."
- Changing *no* to *yes,* especially to quiet a nagging child. An example is the parent who first refuses to buy the child a toy and later gives in and buys it.
- Not checking to see if the child has actually done something you requested, such as picking up clothes or making a bed.
- Contradicting the rules your spouse has set for the child. Parents need to agree on guidelines for child discipline and not undermine each other's efforts.
- Not meaning what you say the first time. Children quickly learn how many times they can be warned before they are actually about to be punished.
- Responding differently to the same misbehavior. One day a child is sent to his room for fighting with his sister. The next day the fighting is overlooked.

Random discipline makes children feel angry and confused because they cannot control the consequences of their own behavior. Inconsistency also gives children the message, "Don't believe what I say because I usually don't mean it."

Constructive Discipline

At one time or another, most parents use power assertion, withdrawal of love, or management techniques to control their children. Each mode of discipline has its place. However, physical punishment and withdrawal of love should always be used with caution. Here are some guidelines:

1. Parents should separate disapproval of the act from disapproval of the child. Instead of saying, "I'm going to punish you because *you are bad,*" say, "I'm upset about *what you did.*"
2. State specifically what misbehavior you are punishing. Explain why you have set limits on this kind of conduct.
3. Punishment should never be harsh or injurious. Don't physically punish a child while you are angry. Also remember that the message, "I don't love you right now," can be more painful and damaging than any spanking.
4. Punishment, such as a scolding or taking away privileges, is most effective when done immediately. This statement is especially true for younger children.
5. Spanking and other forms of physical punishment are not particularly effective for children younger than age 2. The child will only be confused and frightened. Spankings also become less effective after age 5 because they tend to humiliate the child and breed resentment.
6. Many psychologists believe that children should never be spanked. If you do use physical punishment, reserve it for situations that pose an immediate danger to younger children; for example, when a child runs into the street.
7. Remember, too, that it is usually more effective to reward children when they are being good than it is to punish them for misbehavior.

After age 5, management techniques are the most effective form of discipline, especially techniques that emphasize communication and the relationship between parent and child.

The Parent–Child Relationship

The heart of child management is the relationship between parents and their children. Parenting experts Don Dinkmeyer, Sr. and Gary McKay (1997) believe that there are four basic ingredients of positive parent–child interactions.

- Mutual respect. Effective parents try to avoid nagging, hitting, debating, and talking down to their children. They also avoid doing things for their children that children can do for themselves. Constantly stripping children of opportunities to learn and take responsibility prevents them from becoming independent and developing self-esteem.
- Shared enjoyment. Effective parents spend some time each day with their children, doing something that both the parent and child enjoy.
- Love. This goes almost without saying, but many parents assume their children know that they are loved. It is important to show them you care—in words and by actions such as hugging.
- Encouragement. Children who get frequent encouragement come to believe in themselves. Effective parents don't just

Calvin and Hobbes

praise their children for success, winning, or good behavior. They also recognize a child's *progress and attempts to improve*. Show you have faith in children by letting them try things on their own and by encouraging their efforts.

Effective Communication

Creative communication is another important ingredient of successful child management (Bath, 1996). Child expert Haim Ginott (1965) believed that making a distinction between feelings and behavior is the key to clear communication. Because children (and parents, too) do not choose how they feel, it is important to allow free expression of feelings.

Accepting Feelings

The child who learns to regard some feelings as "bad," or unacceptable, is being asked to deny a very real part of his or her experience. Ginott encouraged parents to teach their children that all feelings are appropriate; it is only actions that are subject to disapproval. Many parents are unaware of just how often they block communication and the expression of feelings in their children. Consider this typical conversation excerpted from Ginott's (1965) classic book:

> *Son:* I am stupid, and I know it. Look at my grades in school.
> *Father:* You just have to work harder.
> *Son:* I already work harder and it doesn't help. I have no brains.
> *Father:* You are smart, I know.
> *Son:* I am stupid, I know.
> *Father:* (loudly) You are not stupid!
> *Son:* Yes, I am!
> *Father:* You are not stupid. Stupid!

By debating with the child, the father misses the point that his son *feels* stupid. It would be far more helpful for the father to encourage the boy to talk about his feelings. For instance, he might say, "You really feel that you are not as smart as others, don't you? Do you feel this way often? Are you feeling bad at school?" In this way, the child is given a chance to express his emotions and to feel understood. The father might conclude by saying, "Look, son, in my eyes you are a fine person. But I understand how you feel. Everyone feels stupid at times."

Encouragement

Again, it is valuable to remember that supportive parents encourage their children. In terms of communication, encouragement sounds like this (Dinkmeyer et al., 1997):

> "It looks like you enjoyed that."
> "I have confidence in you; you'll make it."
> "It was thoughtful of you to ____________."
> "Thanks. That helped a lot."
> "You really worked hard on that."
> "You're improving. Look at the progress you've made."

I-Messages

Communication with a child can also be the basis of effective discipline. Child psychologist Thomas Gordon (1970) offers a useful suggestion. Gordon believes that parents should send *I-messages* to their children, rather than *you-messages*.

What's the difference? **You-messages** take the form of threats, name-calling, accusing, bossing, lecturing, or criticizing. Generally, you-messages tell children what's "wrong" with them. An **I-message** tells children what effect their behavior had on you. For example, after a hard day's work, Maria wants to sit down and rest awhile. She begins to relax with a newspaper when her 5-year-old daughter starts banging loudly on a toy drum. Most parents would respond with a you-message:

> "You go play outside this instant." (bossing)
> "Don't ever make such a racket when someone is reading." (lecturing)
> "You're really pushing it today, aren't you?" (accusing)
> "You're a spoiled brat." (name-calling)
> "You're going to get a spanking!" (threatening)

Gordon suggests sending an I-message such as, "I am very tired, and I would like to read. I feel upset and can't read with so much noise." This forces the child to accept responsibility for the effects of her actions.

To summarize, an I-message states the behavior to which you object. It then clearly tells the child the consequence of his or her behavior and how that makes you feel. Here's a "fill-in-the-blanks" I-message: "When you [state the child's behavior], I feel [state your feelings] because [state the consequences of the child's behavior]." For

Consistency With respect to child discipline, the maintenance of stable rules of conduct.

You-message A message that threatens, accuses, bosses, lectures, or criticizes another person.

I-message A message that states the effect someone else's behavior has on you.

example, "When you go to Jenny's without telling me, I worry that something might have happened to you because I don't know where you are" (Dinkmeyer et al., 1997).

Using Natural and Logical Consequences

Sometimes events automatically discourage misbehavior. For example, a child who refuses to eat dinner will get uncomfortably hungry. A child who throws a temper tantrum may gain nothing but a sore throat and a headache if the tantrum is ignored (Fontenelle, 1989). In such instances, a child's actions have **natural consequences** (intrinsic effects). In situations that don't produce natural consequences, parents can set up **logical consequences** (rational and reasonable effects). For example, a parent might say, "We'll go to the zoo when you've picked up all those toys," or "You can play with your dolls as soon as you've taken your bath," or "You two can stop arguing or leave the table until you're ready to join us."

The concept of logical, parent-defined consequences can be combined with I-messages to handle many day-to-day instances of misbehavior. The key idea is to use an I-message to set up consequences and then give the child a choice to make: "Michelle, we're trying to watch TV. You can settle down and watch with us or go play elsewhere. You decide which you'd rather do" (Dinkmeyer et al., 1997).

How could Maria have dealt with her 5-year-old—the one who was banging on a drum? A response that combines an I-message with logical consequences would be, "I would like for you to stop banging on that drum; otherwise, please take it outside." If the child continues to bang on the drum inside the house, then she has caused the toy to be put away. If she takes it outside, she has made a decision to play with the drum in a way that respects her mother's wishes. In this way, both parent and child have been allowed to maintain a sense of self-respect and a needless clash has been averted.

After you have stated consequences and let the child decide, be sure to respect the child's choice. If the child repeats the misbehavior, you can let the consequences remain in effect longer. But later give the child another chance to cooperate.

With all child-management techniques, remember to be firm, kind, consistent, respectful, and encouraging. Most of all, try every day to live the message you wish to communicate.

KNOWLEDGE BUILDER

Parenting and Child Discipline

REFLECT

What do you think are the best ways to balance freedom and restraint in child discipline?

Parents can probably never be completely consistent. Think of a time when your parents were inconsistent in disciplining you. How did it affect you?

To what extent do the four basic ingredients of positive parent–child interactions apply to any healthy relationship?

Think of a you-message you have recently given a child, family member, roommate, or spouse. Can you change it into an I-message?

LEARNING CHECK

1. Effective discipline gives children freedom within a structure of consistent and well-defined limits. T or F?
2. One good way to maintain consistency in child management is to overstate the consequences for misbehavior. T or F?
3. Spankings and other physical punishments are most effective for children under the age of 2. T or F?
4. Giving recognition for progress and attempts to improve is an example of parental ________________.
5. Which type of child discipline take the form of threats, name-calling, accusing, bossing, lecturing, or criticizing?
   a. I-messages c. logical consequences
   b. you-messages d. natural consequences
6. In situations where natural consequences are unavailable or do not discourage misbehavior, parents should define logical consequences for a child. T or F?

CRITICAL THINKING

7. Several Scandinavian countries have made it illegal for parents to spank their own children. Does this infringe on the rights of parents?

Answers: 1. T **2.** F **3.** F **4.** encouragement **5.** b **6.** T **7.** Such laws are based on the view that it should be illegal to physically assault any person, regardless of their age. Although parents may believe they have a "right" to spank their children, it can be argued that children need special protection because they are small, powerless, and dependent.

Chapter in Review

How do heredity and environment affect development?

- The nature-nurture controversy concerns the relative contributions to development of heredity (nature) and environment (nurture).
- Hereditary instructions are carried by the chromosomes and genes in each cell of the body. Most characteristics are polygenic and reflect the combined effects of dominant and recessive genes.
- Heredity is also involved in differences in temperament. Most infants fall into one of three temperament categories: easy children, difficult children, and slow-to-warm-up children.
- During sensitive periods in development, infants experience an increased sensitivity to specific environmental influences.
- Prenatal development is subject to environmental influences in the form of diseases, drugs, radiation, and the mother's diet, health, and emotions. Various teratogens can cause prenatal damage to the fetus, resulting in congenital problems.
- Early perceptual, intellectual, and emotional deprivation seriously retards development.
- Deliberate enrichment of the environment has a beneficial effect on development in infancy.
- Heredity and environment are inseparable and interacting forces. Therefore, a child's developmental level reflects heredity, environment, and the effects of the child's own behavior.

What can newborn babies do?

- The human neonate has a number of adaptive reflexes, including the grasping, rooting, sucking, and Moro reflexes. Neonates show immediate evidence of learning and of appreciating the consequences of their actions.
- Tests in a looking chamber reveal a number of visual preferences in the newborn. The neonate is drawn to bright lights and circular or curved designs.
- Infants prefer human face patterns, especially familiar faces. In later infancy, interest in the unfamiliar emerges.

What influence does maturation have on early development?

- Maturation of the body and nervous system underlies the orderly sequence of motor, cognitive, emotional, and language development.
- The rate of maturation, however, varies from person to person. Also, learning contributes greatly to the development of basic motor skills.
- Emotions develop in a consistent order from the generalized excitement observed in newborn babies. Three of the basic emotions—fear, anger, and joy—may be unlearned.
- Many early skills are subject to the principle of readiness.

Of what significance is a child's emotional bond with parents?

- Emotional attachment of human infants is a critical early event.
- Infant attachment is reflected by separation anxiety. The quality of attachment can be classified as secure, insecure-avoidant, or insecure-ambivalent.
- High-quality day care does not appear to harm children. Low-quality care can be risky.
- Engaging in cooperative play is an important milestone in social development.
- Meeting a baby's affectional needs is as important as meeting needs for physical care.

How important are parenting styles?

- Studies suggest that caregiving styles have a substantial impact on emotional and intellectual development.
- Whereas mothers typically emphasize caregiving, fathers tend to function as playmates for infants.
- Optimal caregiving includes proactive maternal involvement, responsiveness to a child's needs and signals, and a good fit between the temperaments of parents and their children.
- Three major parental styles are authoritarian, permissive, and authoritative (effective). When judged by its effects on children, authoritative parenting appears to benefit children the most.
- Effective parental discipline tends to emphasize child-management techniques (especially communication), rather than power assertion or withdrawal of love.

How do children acquire language?

- Language development proceeds from control of crying, to cooing, then babbling, then use of single words, and then to telegraphic speech.

Natural consequences The effects that naturally tend to follow a particular behavior.

Logical consequences Reasonable consequences that are defined by parents.

- The underlying patterns of telegraphic speech suggest a biological predisposition to acquire language. This innate predisposition is augmented by learning.
- Prelanguage communication between parent and child involves shared rhythms, nonverbal signals, and turn-taking.
- Motherese or parentese is a simplified, musical style of speaking used by parents to help their children learn language.

How do children learn to think?

- The intellect of a child is less abstract than that of an adult. Jean Piaget theorized that intellectual growth occurs through a combination of assimilation and accommodation.
- Piaget also held that children go through a fixed series of cognitive stages. The stages and their approximate age ranges are sensorimotor (0–2), preoperational (2–7), concrete operational (7–11), and formal operations (11–adulthood).
- Learning principles provide an alternate explanation that assumes cognitive development is continuous; it does not occur in stages.
- Recent studies of infants younger than 1 year suggest that they are capable of thought well beyond that observed by Piaget.
- Lev Vygotsky's sociocultural theory emphasizes that a child's mental abilities are advanced by interactions with more competent partners. Mental growth takes place in a child's zone of proximal development, where a more skillful person may scaffold the child's progress.

How do effective parents discipline their children?

- Responsibility, mutual respect, consistency, love, encouragement, and clear communication are features of effective parenting.
- Much misbehavior can be managed by use of I-messages and the application of natural and logical consequences.

 Web Resources

Internet addresses frequently change. To find the sites listed here, visit www.thomsonedu.com/psychology/coon for an updated list of Internet addresses and direct links to relevant sites.

***Psychology: Gateways to Mind and Behavior* Website** Online quizzes, flash cards, and other helpful study aids for this text. www.thomsonedu.com/psychology/coon.

Choosing Quality Child Care Provides information on issues related to quality child care.

Depression after Delivery A site devoted to providing information about postpartum depression.

Diving into the Gene Pool From the Exploratorium, teaches about modern genetics.

Human Relations Publications Covers over 50 topics spanning the entire range of human development.

I Am Your Child Information for parents of children up to 3 years of age.

Jean Piaget Archives: Biography The life of Jean Piaget, plus five photos from birth to old age.

Parenthood Web A comprehensive site for parents.

Sesame Street Parents An expert description of physical development from birth to 11.

The Parent's Page Comprehensive site full of links for expectant couples and new parents.

ThomsonNOW™ Go to www.thomsonedu.com to link to ThomsonNow, your online study tool. First take the **Pre-Test** for this chapter to get your **Personalized Study Plan,** which will identify topics you need to review and direct you to online resources. Then take the **Post-Test** to determine what concepts you have mastered and what you still need work on.

InfoTrac College Edition For recent articles related to Piaget and Vygotsky, use Key Words search for COGNITION IN INFANTS. Go to www.thomsonedu.com/psychology/coon.

 Interactive Learning

***PsychNow! Version 2.0* CD-ROM** Interact with the material with *PsychNow!'s* animations, video clips, experiments, and interactive assessments. For this chapter, go to *2a. Infant Development, 2b. Child Development, 2c. Adolescent Development,* and *2d. Adult Development, Aging, and Death* to get a better understanding of human development.

chapter 4

From Birth to Death: Life-Span Development

Michael Newman/PhotoEdit

THEME:

Development over a lifetime reflects a delicate balance between stability and change.

Key Questions

What are the typical tasks and dilemmas through the life span?

What are some of the more serious childhood problems?

Why is adolescent development especially challenging?

How do we develop morals and values?

What happens psychologically during adulthood?

What are the psychological challenges of aging?

How do people typically react to death and bereavement?

What factors contribute most to a happy and fulfilling life?

Preview

The Story of a Lifetime

Everyone is born. Everyone will die. This is the short summary of a life. Although it's accurate, the story certainly leaves out a lot, doesn't it? How might we develop a fuller picture of what happens during a lifetime?

Perhaps we could begin by studying interesting lives. For example, what do Jennifer Lopez, Tiger Woods, Hillary Clinton, Bill Gates, Oprah Winfrey, John Glenn, Maya Angelou, and J. K. Rowling have in common? Of course, they've all been uncommonly successful. Yet beyond that, their lives appear to be quite different. However, if we consider many people and look beyond surface differences, all lives follow at least some general patterns. Why should this be so? What do you and I have in common with Jennifer Lopez or Tiger Woods? The answer is that we all face similar challenges in growing up, becoming an adult, and aging. Also, we are all affected by the same universal principles that guide human development.

Each of us will face problems on the path to healthy development. Some obstacles, such as learning to walk or finding a personal identity, are universal. Others are unusual or specialized. In addition to such challenges, psychologists have probed the question, "What makes a good life?" Their findings, which are described in this chapter, may provide a road map you can use to make your own life happier, more meaningful, and more fulfilling.

The challenges of development extend far beyond childhood and into old age. Let's scan some of the milestones, challenges, problems, and potentials you are likely to encounter across the life span.

The Cycle of Life—Rocky Road or Garden Path?

Each of us can take pride in being "one of a kind." There really is no such thing as a "typical person" or a "typical life." Nevertheless, broad similarities can be found in the **life stages** of infancy, childhood, adolescence, young adulthood, middle adulthood, and old age. Each stage confronts us with new **developmental tasks** that must be mastered for optimal development. Examples are learning to read in childhood, adjusting to sexual maturity in adolescence, and establishing a career as an adult. Every life is also marked by a number of **developmental milestones.** These are notable events, markers, or turning points in personal development. Some examples include graduating from school, voting for the first time, getting married, watching a child leave home (or move back!), the death of a parent, becoming a grandparent, retirement, and one's own death. In the following pages we will examine development from a **life-span perspective.** Life-span psychologists study both continuity and change in behavior during a lifetime (Kaplan, 1998).

In an influential book titled *Childhood and Society* (1963), personality theorist Erik Erikson (1903–1994) suggests that we face a specific *psychosocial dilemma,* or "crisis," at each stage of life. A **psychosocial dilemma** is a conflict between personal needs and the social world. Resolving each dilemma creates a new balance between a person and society. A string of "successes" leads to healthy development and a satisfying life. Unfavorable outcomes throw us off balance, making it harder to deal with later crises. Life becomes a "rocky road" and personal growth is stunted. ■ Table 4.1 lists Erikson's dilemmas.

What are the major developmental tasks and life crises? A brief description of each psychosocial dilemma follows.

TABLE 4.1

Erikson's Psychosocial Dilemmas

AGE	CHARACTERISTIC DILEMMA
Birth to 1 year	Trust versus mistrust
1 to 3 years	Autonomy versus shame and doubt
3 to 5 years	Initiative versus guilt
6 to 12 years	Industry versus inferiority
Adolescence	Identity versus role confusion
Young adulthood	Intimacy versus isolation
Middle adulthood	Generativity versus stagnation
Late adulthood	Integrity versus despair

Erik Erikson (1903–1994) is best known for his life-stage theory of human development. His last book, *Vital Involvement in Old Age,* published in 1986, described his ideas about successful aging.

Stage One, First Year of Life: Trust Versus Mistrust

During the first year of life, children are completely dependent on others. Erikson believes that a basic attitude of trust or mistrust is formed at this time. **Trust** is established when babies are given warmth, touching, love, and physical care. **Mistrust** is caused by inadequate or unpredictable care and by parents who are cold, indifferent, or rejecting. Basic mistrust may later cause insecurity, suspiciousness, or an inability to relate to others. Notice that trust comes from the same conditions that help babies become securely attached to their parents (see Chapter 3).

Stage Two, 1 to 3 Years: Autonomy Versus Shame and Doubt

In stage two, children express their growing self-control by climbing, touching, exploring, and trying to do things for themselves. Parents can foster a sense of **autonomy** by encouraging children to try new skills. However, the child's first efforts can be crude. Often, they result in spilling, falling, wetting, and other "accidents." Thus, parents who ridicule or overprotect their children may cause them to **doubt** their abilities and feel **shameful** about their actions.

Stage Three, 3 to 5 Years: Initiative Versus Guilt

In stage three, children move beyond simple self-control and begin to take initiative (drawing on the walls with Crayolas, for instance). Through play, children learn to make plans and carry out tasks. Parents reinforce **initiative** by giving children freedom to play, ask questions, use imagination, and choose activities. Feelings of **guilt** about initiating activities are formed if parents criticize severely, prevent play, or discourage a child's questions.

Stage Four, 6 to 12 Years: Industry Versus Inferiority

The challenges of middle childhood are symbolized by that fateful day when you started school. With dizzying speed your world expanded beyond your family, and you faced a whole series of new developmental tasks.

Erikson describes the elementary school years as the child's "entrance into life." In school, children begin to learn skills valued by society, and success or failure can affect their feelings of adequacy. Children learn a sense of **industry** if they win praise for productive activities, such as building, painting, cooking, reading, and studying. If a child's efforts are regarded as messy, childish, or inadequate, feelings of **inferiority** result. For the first time, teachers, classmates, and adults outside the home can be as important as parents in shaping attitudes toward oneself.

Stage Five, Adolescence: Identity Versus Role Confusion

Adolescence is often a turbulent time. Caught between childhood and adulthood, teens face some unique problems. For Erikson, answering the question, "Who am I?" is the primary task during this stage of life. Mental, physical, and sexual maturation bring new feelings, a new body, and new attitudes (● Figure 4.1). Adolescents must build a consistent **identity** out of their talents, values, life history, relationships, and their culture (Douvan, 1997). Conflicting experiences as a student, friend, athlete, worker, son or daughter, lover, and so forth must be integrated into a unified sense of self (more on this later). Persons who fail to develop a sense of identity suffer from **role confusion.** That is, they are uncertain about who they are and where they are going.

Life stages Widely recognized periods of life corresponding to broad phases of development.

Developmental task Any skill that must be mastered, or personal change that must take place, for optimal development.

Developmental milestone A significant turning point or marker in personal development.

Life-span perspective The study of continuity and change in behavior over a lifetime.

Psychosocial dilemma A conflict between personal impulses and the social world that affects development.

Trust versus mistrust A conflict early in life centered on learning to trust others and the world.

Autonomy versus shame and doubt A conflict created when growing self-control (autonomy) is pitted against feelings of shame or doubt.

Initiative versus guilt A conflict centered around learning to take initiative while overcoming feelings of guilt about doing so.

Industry versus inferiority A conflict in middle childhood centered around lack of support for industrious behavior, which can result in feelings of inferiority.

Identity versus role confusion A major conflict of adolescence, involving the need to establish a consistent personal identity.

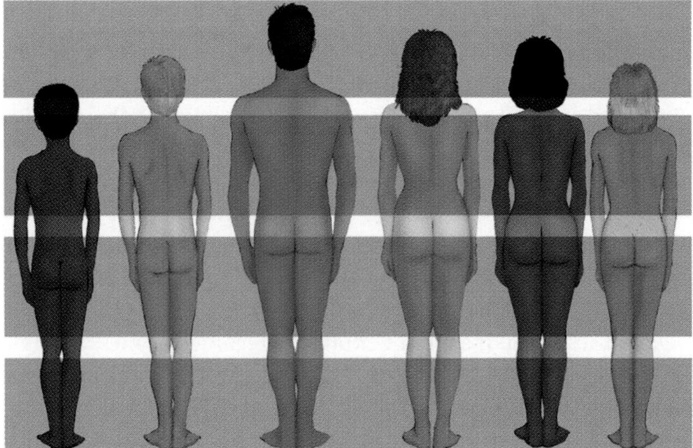

● **Figure 4.1** Dramatic differences in physical size and maturity are found in adolescents of the same age. The girls pictured are all 13, the boys 16. Maturation that occurs earlier or later than average can affect the "search for identity." (Adapted from "Growing Up" by J. M. Tanner. Copyright © September 1973 by Scientific American, Inc. All rights reserved.)

Jeff Greenberg

According to Erikson, an interest in future generations characterizes optimal adult development.

Stage Six, Young Adulthood: Intimacy Versus Isolation

What does Erikson believe is the major conflict in early adulthood? In stage six, the individual feels a need for *intimacy* in his or her life. After establishing a stable identity, a person is prepared to share meaningful love or deep friendship with others. By **intimacy**, Erikson means an ability to care about others and to share experiences with them. In line with Erikson's view, 75 percent of college-age men and women rank a good marriage and family life as important adult goals (Bachman & Johnson, 1979). Yet marriage or sexual involvement is no guarantee of intimacy: Many adult relationships remain superficial and unfulfilling. Failure to establish intimacy with others leads to a deep sense of **isolation** (feeling alone and uncared for in life). This often sets the stage for later difficulties.

Stage Seven, Middle Adulthood: Generativity Versus Stagnation

According to Erikson, an interest in guiding the next generation provides emotional balance in mature adulthood. Erikson called this quality **generativity.** It is expressed by caring about oneself, one's children, and future generations. Generativity may be achieved by guiding one's own children or by helping other children (as a teacher or coach, for example). Productive or creative work can also express generativity. In any case, a person's concerns and energies must turn outward, to include the welfare of others and society as a whole. Failure to do this is marked by a **stagnant** concern with one's own needs and comforts. Life loses meaning, and the person feels bitter, dreary, and trapped (Peterson & Klohnen, 1995).

Stage Eight, Late Adulthood: Integrity Versus Despair

What does Erikson see as the conflicts of old age? Old age is a time of reflection. According to Erikson, a person must be able to look back over life with acceptance and satisfaction. The person who has lived richly and responsibly develops a sense of **integrity** (self-respect). This allows the person to face aging and death with dignity. If previous life events are viewed with regret, the elderly person experiences **despair** (heartache and remorse). In this case, life seems like a series of missed opportunities. The person feels like a failure and knows it's too late to reverse what has been done. Aging and the threat of death then become sources of fear and depression.

The Life Span in Perspective

To squeeze a lifetime into a few pages, we must ignore countless details. Although much is lost, the net effect is a clearer picture of an entire life cycle. Are Erikson's stages an exact map of your future? Probably not. Still, the dilemmas he described are major events in the lives of many people. Knowing about them may allow you to anticipate typical trouble spots in life. You may also be better prepared to understand how friends and relatives are feeling at various stages in life.

Now that we've completed a whirlwind birth-to-death tour, we will revisit several points in life for a closer look at various challenges, tasks, and problems. Before we begin, it might be a good idea to complete the Knowledge Builder that follows.

KNOWLEDGE BUILDER

The Life Cycle

REFLECT

See if you can think of a person you know who is facing one of Erikson's psychosocial dilemmas. Now see if you can think of specific people who seem to be coping with each of the other dilemmas.

LEARNING CHECK

As a way to improve your memory, you might find it helpful to summarize Erikson's eight life stages. Complete this do-it-yourself summary and compare your answers to those given below.

Stage	Crisis	Favorable outcome
First year of life	**1.** ____________ vs. **2.** ____________	Faith in the environment and in others
Ages 1–3	Autonomy vs. **3.** ____________	Feelings of self-control and adequacy
Ages 3–5	**4.** ____________ vs. guilt	Ability to begin one's own activities
Ages 6–12	Industry vs. **5.** ____________	Confidence in productive skills, learning how to work
Adolescence	**6.** ____________ vs. role confusion	An integrated image oneself as a unique person
Young adulthood	Intimacy vs. **7.** ____________	Ability to form bonds of love and friendship with others
Middle adulthood	Generativity vs. **8.** ____________	Concern for family, society, and future generations
Late adulthood	**9.** ____________ vs. **10.** ____________	Sense of dignity and fulfillment, willingness to face death

CRITICAL THINKING

11. Trying to make generalizations about development throughout life is complicated by at least one major factor. What do you think it is?

Answers: 1. trust **2.** mistrust **3.** shame or doubt **4.** initiative **5.** inferiority **6.** identity **7.** isolation **8.** stagnation **9.** integrity **10.** despair **11.** Different *cohorts* (groups of people born in the same year) live in different historical times. People born in various decades may have very different life experiences. This makes it difficult to identify universal patterns (Stewart & Ostrove, 1998).

Problems of Childhood—Why Parents Get Gray Hair

Most children have at least a few minor behavioral problems while growing up. However, some children have more serious difficulties. If left untreated, learning disorders, hyperactivity, and similar disorders can have lifelong consequences. This section explores a variety of problems children may face.

Can you remember a time in childhood when your actions led to a disaster or a near-disaster? It shouldn't be hard. It's a wonder that many of us survive childhood at all. Where one of your authors grew up, digging underground tunnels, wiggling down chimneys, hopping on trains, jumping off houses, crawling through storm drains—and worse—were common childhood adventures.

Stress is a normal part of life—even in childhood. Certainly this doesn't mean that parents should intentionally stress their children. However, it does suggest that children need not be completely sheltered from distress. Overprotection, or "smother love," can be as damaging as overstressing a child. (*Overprotection* refers to excessively shielding a child from ordinary stresses.)

Normal Childhood Problems

Most children do a good job of keeping stress at comfortable levels when *they* initiate an activity. At a public swimming pool, for instance, some children can be observed making death-defying leaps from the high dive, whereas others stick close to the wading area. If there's no immediate danger, it is reasonable to let chil-

Jonathan Nourok/PhotoEdit

Childhood can be a challenging period of life. However, most children do a good job of keeping stress at comfortable levels when they initiate an activity.

Intimacy versus isolation The challenge in early adulthood of establishing intimacy with friends, family, a lover, or a spouse versus experiencing a sense of isolation.

Generativity versus stagnation A conflict of middle adulthood in which stagnant concern for oneself is countered by interest in guiding the next generation.

Integrity versus despair A conflict in old age between feelings of personal integrity and the despair that occurs when previous life events are viewed with regret.

THE CLINICAL FILE

Children and Divorce—What Are the Risks?

Almost half of all marriages in the United States end in divorce. Close to 60 percent of children born in the 1990s will live, at some point, in single-parent families. Stepfamilies make up about 1 of 6 two-parent families. One of every 10 children will experience at least two parental divorces before they are 16 years old! What are the consequences of "serial marriage"?

Studies show that children from divorced families and stepfamilies tend to be more distressed and have more behavior problems than the children of intact families. Children from divorced and remarried families are more likely to have problems in school, to be involved in delinquency and drug use, to be loners, and to have low self-esteem. Often, these problems continue into adolescence and adulthood (Wallerstein, Lewis, & Blakeslee, 2000).

That's a pretty bleak picture. Does it apply to all children from divorced families? Actually, 75 to 80 percent of children from divorced families and stepfamilies do not have serious problems (Hetherington & Kelly, 2002). Besides, it may be troubled marriages, and not divorce, that actually create problems. Kelly and Emery (2003) found that children display similar problems if their parents have a troubled marriage and remain together. This suggests that the problems of the children of divorce often begin years before the actual divorce.

Regardless, divorce is stressful. Although most children possess the resilience to adjust, some children are more vulnerable than others. When a marriage breaks up, distraught parents are often less able to nurture and supervise their children—at a time when children need it the most. Also, conflict is more common in families struggling to reshape themselves. The combination of vulnerability, impaired parenting, and conflict can be hard on a child (Hetherington & Kelly, 2002).

Many children say that their parents' divorce was one of their most painful life experiences. Although behavior problems are not inevitable, single parents and parents in blended families should be aware of the importance of making extra efforts to support and nurture children whose world has been turned upside down.

dren get stuck in trees, make themselves dizzy, squabble with other children, and so forth. Getting into a few scrapes can help prepare a child to cope with later challenges. (If one of your authors hadn't crawled through a few storm pipes, his adult interest in plumbing the depths of the psyche might have gone down the drain.)

Typical Difficulties

How can you tell if a child is being subjected to too much stress? Child specialist Stella Chess identified several difficulties experienced at times by almost every child. They are normal reactions to the unavoidable stresses of growing up.

1. All children occasionally have *sleep disturbances,* including wakefulness, nightmares, or a desire to get into their parents' bed.
2. *Specific fears* of the dark, dogs, school, or a particular room or person are also common.
3. Most children will be *overly timid* at times, allowing themselves to be bullied by other children.
4. Temporary periods of *general dissatisfaction* may occur, when nothing pleases the child.
5. Children also normally display periods of *general negativism.* Repeatedly saying "no" or refusing to do anything requested is typical of such times.
6. Another normal problem is *clinging.* Children who "cling" refuse to leave the sides of their mothers or do anything on their own. (However, see the discussion of attachment disorder in Chapter 3.)
7. Development does not always advance smoothly. *Reversals* or *regressions* to more infantile behavior occur with almost all children (Chess, Thomas, & Birch, 1976).

Rivalry and Rebellion

An added problem in the elementary school years is *sibling rivalry* (competition among brothers and sisters). It is normal for a certain amount of jealousy, rivalry, and even hostility to develop between siblings. In fact, some sibling conflict may be constructive. A limited amount of aggressive give-and-take between siblings provides an opportunity to learn emotional control, self-assertion, and good sportsmanship (Bank & Kahn, 1982). Parents can help keep such conflicts within bounds by not "playing favorites" and by not comparing one child with another. Supportive and affectionate fathering, in particular, seems to minimize conflicts and jealousy among siblings (Rolling & Belsky, 1992).

Parents should also expect to see some *childhood rebellion* (open defiance of adult authority). Most school-age children rebel at times against parental rules. Being with other children offers a chance to "let off steam" by doing some of the things the adult world forbids. It is normal for children to be messy, noisy, hostile, or destructive to a moderate degree.

Keep in mind that "normal problems" that intensify or last for long periods may become serious disturbances. Some examples of more serious problems are identified in the following discussion. (Also, see "Children and Divorce" for information on one common source of childhood behavior problems.)

Serious Childhood Problems

By the time he was 5, Billy had not learned to talk. He threw wild temper tantrums and never seemed to sleep. He got into closets and tore up his mother's dresses and urinated on her clothes. He smashed furniture and spread detergent and cereal all over the floors. Billy attacked his mother, sometimes going for her throat with his teeth. He once tried to stuff his baby brother in a toy box.

Billy refused to eat anything but cold, greasy hamburgers from a local fast-food business. To get through a week, his parents had to buy dozens of hamburgers. Then they hid them around the house, so Billy wouldn't eat them all at once. While driving, they had to detour around fast-food restaurants to prevent Billy from frothing at the mouth and trying to jump out the window (Moser, 1965). Billy, you may note, was not an average 5-year-old.

What was his problem? Billy was an *autistic* child. His problem is rare. Few children get off to as bad a start in life as Billy. However, emotional disturbances affect more children than many people realize. Let's consider some of the more serious problems that parents may face.

Feeding Disturbances

Children with feeding disturbances may vomit, refuse food for no reason, or drastically overeat or undereat. Overeating (eating in excess of daily caloric needs) can be a serious problem. Some parents overfeed simply because they think a fat baby is healthy or "cute." Others, who feel unloved, may compensate by showering their child with "love" in the form of food. Whatever the case, overfed children develop eating habits that become a lifelong handicap.

Serious cases of undereating, or self-starvation, are called **anorexia nervosa** (AN-or-REX-yah ner-VOH-sah: nervous loss of appetite). Although it is becoming more common among adolescent males (Gila et al., 2005), the victims of anorexia nervosa are still predominantly adolescent females. Many have conflicts about maturing sexually and facing adulthood. By starving themselves, girls can limit figure development and stop menstruation. As we will discuss in Chapter 10, unrealistic standards of thinness and beauty also contribute to self-starvation (Simpson, 2002).

Pica (PIE-ka: a craving for unnatural foods) is a disorder in which children eat or chew on all sorts of inedible substances, such as plaster and chalk. Some try to eat things like buttons, rubber bands, mud, or paint flakes. Paint may contain lead, which is highly poisonous. Pica is a serious problem, but it usually can be treated with various behavioral techniques (Woods, Miltenberger, & Lumley, 1996).

BRIDGES

Parents should be aware that a child with language delays or learning problems could be developmentally disabled (mentally retarded).

See Chapter 11, pages 373–375, for more information.

Toilet-Training Disturbances

The two most common toilet-training problems are **enuresis** (EN-you-REE-sis: lack of bladder control) and **encopresis** (EN-coh-PREE-sis: lack of bowel control). Both wetting and soiling can be an expression of frustration or hostility. But parents should not be overly alarmed by some delays in toilet training or by a few "accidents." As mentioned in Chapter 3, 30 months is the average age for completing toilet training. It is not unusual, however, for some children to take 6 months longer (age 3).

Sometimes, the problem is purely physical. For example, some bed wetters simply do not wake up when they need to go to the bathroom. These children can be helped by limiting how much they drink in the evening. They should also use the toilet before going to bed, and they can be rewarded for "dry" nights. For older children, learning self-control strategies can be effective (Ronen & Wozner, 1995). In all cases, understanding, tact, and sympathy help. Where more serious problems exist, parents should seek professional help (Goin, 1998).

Speech Disturbances

Delayed speech (learning to talk after the normal age for language development) is another serious handicap. For example, at age 5 Tommy was still using telegraphic speech: "Me go. Outdoor. Mama in car now. Dink Tommy cup." Delayed speech like Tommy's is sometimes caused by a lack of intellectual stimulation at home. Other possible causes are parents who discourage a child's attempts to grow up, childhood stresses, mental retardation, and emotional disturbances.

Stuttering (chronic stumbling in speech) is a second major language problem. In the past, many parents were blamed for "causing" stuttering. Now, researchers believe the problem involves speech-timing mechanisms in the brain. Stuttering is four times more common in males and it seems to be partially inherited (Felsenfeld, 1996).

Although parents don't cause stuttering, they can certainly make it worse. Children who fear that they are about to stutter are, in fact, more likely to stutter. That's why parents should avoid criticizing speech difficulties. With support from parents and formal speech therapy, many children do overcome stuttering (Venkatagiri, 2005).

Anorexia nervosa Active self-starvation or a sustained loss of appetite that has psychological origins.

Pica Eating or chewing on inedible objects or substances such as chalk, ashes, and the like.

Enuresis An inability to control urination, particularly with regard to bed-wetting.

Encopresis A lack of bowel control; "soiling."

Delayed speech Speech that begins well after the normal age for language development has passed.

Stuttering Chronic hesitation or stumbling in speech.

Learning Disorders

Soon after Gary started school, he became shy and difficult. He couldn't seem to pay attention in class or finish his assignments. Gary's teacher suspected a learning disorder, and a specialist confirmed it. **Learning disorders** include problems with reading, math, or writing. Gary's specific problem was **dyslexia** (dis-LEX-ee-uh), an inability to read with understanding. Because of it, he often felt confused and "stupid" in class, although his intelligence was normal.

From 10 to 15 percent of school-age children have some dyslexia, or "word blindness." When dyslexic children try to read, they often reverse letters (such as seeing *b* for *d*) and words (*was* and *saw*, for example). Dyslexia is caused by a malfunction of language processing areas on the left side of the brain. It is typically treated with exercises in hearing, touch, and vision that improve reading skills.

Attention-Deficit/Hyperactivity Disorder

One of the more serious childhood problems is **attention-deficit/hyperactivity disorder** (**ADHD**). The child with ADHD is constantly in motion and cannot concentrate. She or he talks rapidly, can't pay attention, rarely finishes work, and is impulsive. ADHD afflicts 4 to 6 percent of all children, and five times as many boys as girls. Unless it is carefully managed, ADHD can lead to school drop-outs and antisocial behavior (Hinshaw, 2002).

What causes ADHD? Brain areas for language, motor control, and attention are impaired by chemical imbalances (Sagvolden & Sergeant, 1998). ADHD tends to run in families, which suggests it may be hereditary (Zametkin, 1995). Many parents believe that hyperactive behavior is triggered by eating sugar. However, sugary diets have no effect at all on the behavior of either normal or hyperactive children. "Sugar highs" are a myth (Wolraich, Wilson, & White, 1995).

How is ADHD treated? Treatment for ADHD includes drugs, behavioral management approaches, and family counseling. Physicians typically use the stimulant drug Ritalin (methylphenidate) to control ADHD. It might seem that stimulants would make hyperactivity worse. However, the drugs lengthen the ADHD child's attention span and reduce impulsiveness (Diller, 1998).

Ritalin is a potent, amphetamine-like drug. In view of this, it is remarkable that 5 percent (1 in 20) of all U.S. school-age boys take Ritalin for ADHD. The drug's possible side effects include insomnia, weight loss, irritability, depression, and slowed growth.

Many experts worry that Ritalin is overused. Drugs, they suspect, are sometimes being prescribed for ordinary misbehavior, not because a child actually has ADHD. Ritalin does seem to be effective when the diagnosis of ADHD is accurate. The problem is that doctors, parents, and teachers may be tempted to use drugs to control children who are merely disobedient (Diller, 1998).

For many ADHD children, behavior modification is as effective as drug treatment (Carlson et al., 1992). **Behavior modification** is the application of learning principles to change or eliminate maladaptive or abnormal behavior. (See Chapter 17 for more information.) The basic idea is to reward the child with ADHD for being calm and paying attention (Hoff & DuPaul, 1998).

David Young-Wolff/PhotoEdit

The ADHD child's inability to hold still and pay attention can seriously disrupt learning.

Conduct Disorder

Earlier we noted that minor instances of childhood rebellion can be perfectly normal. See if you think the following qualifies as childhood rebellion: Lucas started smoking, smashing windows, and getting in fights in the third grade. By the time he was in the fifth grade, he had broken another child's arm with a baseball bat. Lucas bullies classmates, is cruel to smaller children, and has tortured animals in his neighborhood. He has been caught shoplifting, and he steals from unlocked cars.

Lucas suffers from a **conduct disorder** (DSM-IV-TR, 2000). Affected children are aggressive, they harm others, they engage in vandalism, they lie or steal, and they persistently violate rules. As a result, children with conduct disorders are usually in trouble at home, at school, and in the community.

Despite their "tough" image, children suffering from conduct disorders tend to have low self-esteem. Much of their antisocial behavior can be traced to the fact that they can't handle frustration. They anger easily, have outbursts of temper, and become reckless. They also tend to be insensitive to the feelings of others. Conduct disorders are more common in males, but females may be affected, too. Females are more likely to engage in truancy, lying, and substance use; to run away; or to be victimized on the streets as prostitutes. Overall, the outlook is bleak for children with conduct disorders—unless parents seek professional help for their children.

Autism

Children who suffer from **autism** (AWE-tiz-um) are lost in their own thoughts, fantasies, and private impulses. Autism is one of the most severe childhood problems. It affects 1 in 2,500 children, boys four times more often than girls. Autistic children are locked into their own private worlds and have no interest in affection or other people (Sigman, 1995). For instance, the autistic child doesn't respond any more to a photo of his mother's face than he does to the face of a stranger (Dawson et al., 2002).

In addition to being extremely isolated, an autistic child may throw gigantic temper tantrums—sometimes including self-destructive behavior such as head banging. Many autistic children are mute. If they speak at all, they may infuriatingly parrot back everything said, a pattern called **echolalia** (EK-oh-LAY-lee-ah). Some autistic children also engage in repetitive actions such as rocking, flapping their arms, or waving their fingers in front of their eyes. In addition, they may show no response to an extremely loud noise (sensory blocking), or they may spend hours watching a water faucet drip (sensory "spin-out"). Finally, autistic children don't seem to understand what other people are thinking—or even that they do think. This makes autistic persons very inept in social situations (Firth, 1993).

Do parents cause autism? No, autism is caused by congenital defects in the brain. The symptoms of autism appear before a child is 1 year old (Baranek, 1999). That's why autistic babies are aloof and do not cuddle or mold to their parents' arms. Medical scans reveal that the brains of autistic adults are larger than normal. This suggests that something goes wrong during development of the autistic brain (Piven, Arndt, & Palmer, 1995).

Can anything be done for an autistic child? Even with help, only about 25 percent of all autistic children approach normalcy and only 2 percent are able to live alone. Nevertheless, almost all autistic children can make progress with proper care. When treatment begins early, behavior modification is particularly successful.

Do you remember Billy, the autistic child described earlier? Billy was one of the first patients in a pioneering program designed by psychologist Ivar Lovaas. Billy was selected because of his unusual appetite for hamburgers. Teaching Billy to talk illustrates one aspect of his treatment. It began with his learning to blow out a match—making a sound like "who." Each time he made the "who" sound, Billy was rewarded with a bite of his beloved hamburgers. Next he was rewarded for babbling meaningless sounds. If he accidentally said a word, he was rewarded. After several weeks, he was able to say words such as *ball, milk, mama,* and *me.* Through this painstaking process, Billy was eventually taught to talk. (This technique, which is called operant shaping, is discussed further in Chapter 8.)

In a behavior modification program, each of an autistic child's maladaptive behaviors is altered using reward and punishment. In addition to food, therapists have found that sensory stimulation, such as tickling or music, is very reinforcing for autistic children. And strangely enough, following actions such as head banging and hand biting with punishment can swiftly end self-destructive behavior. When such efforts are combined with home treatment by parents, considerable progress can be made. A few children, in fact, approach near-normal functioning (McEachin, Smith, & Lovaas, 1993).

BRIDGES

Psychologists suspect that autistic children fail to develop a normal "theory of mind" about the thoughts, feelings, and intentions of other people.

See Chapter 3, page 111, for a brief discussion of the theory of mind concept.

Autism and other severe childhood problems are a monumental challenge to the ingenuity of psychologists, educators, and parents. However, great strides have been made. There is reason to believe that in the future even more help will be available for children who get a bad start in life.

Child Abuse—Cycles of Violence

Sadly, no account of problems in development would be complete without a brief discussion of *child abuse* (physical or emotional harm caused by violence, mistreatment, or neglect). Child abuse is widespread (Barnet & Barnet, 1998). From 3.5 to 14 percent of all children are physically abused by parents. That means more than 2 million children are physically battered each year in the United States and Canada (Finkelhor & Dziuba-Leatherman, 1994).

Characteristics of Abusive Parents

What are abusive parents like? Typically they have a high level of stress and frustration in their lives. Common problems include depression, loneliness, marital discord, unemployment, drug abuse, divorce, family violence, heavy drinking, and work anxieties ("A Nation's," 1995; Famularo et al., 1992).

Some parents know they are mistreating a child but are unable to stop. Other abusive parents literally hate their children or are disgusted by their needs, sloppiness, crying, or dirty diapers. Abusive mothers tend to believe their children are *intentionally* annoying them. In many cases, troubled parents expect the child to love them and make them happy. When the child (who is usually under 3 years old) cannot meet such unrealistic demands, the parent reacts with lethal anger. Parents who are feeling stressed and who believe in physical punishment are especially likely to abuse their children (Crouch & Behl, 2001).

Learning disorder Any problem with thinking, perception, language, attention, or activity levels that tends to impair learning ability.

Dyslexia An inability to read with understanding, often caused by a tendency to misread letters (by seeing their mirror images, for instance).

Attention-deficit/hyperactivity disorder (ADHD) A behavioral problem characterized by short attention span, restless movement, and impaired learning capacity.

Behavior modification Applying principles of learning to change or eliminate maladaptive or abnormal behavior.

Conduct disorder A pattern in which children consistently violate rules and behave aggressively and destructively.

Autism A severe disorder involving mutism, sensory spin-outs, sensory blocking, tantrums, unresponsiveness to others, and other difficulties.

Echolalia A compulsion, sometimes observed in autistic children, to repeat everything that is said.

FOCUS ON RESEARCH

Trapped by Anger: The "Rage Radar" of Abused Children

Although bruises or broken bones may heal, the emotional scars created by the nightmarish emotional world of the abused child can last for many years. Abused children may be withdrawn, depressed, fearful, angry, or aggressive. More subtle changes also occur. For example, according to psychologist Seth Pollak and his colleagues, abused children develop a finely tuned "rage radar."

Abused children are experts at quickly detecting anger in adult faces. Nine-year-old children were asked to judge whether a series of faces were happy, sad, angry, or fearful. Some of the faces were pure examples of each emotion. Others were a blend of emotions. For instance, a face might be 20 percent angry and 80 percent fearful. Both abused and nonabused children were equally good at judging whether a face was happy, sad, or fearful. However, abused kids were much more sensitive to any hints of anger. In a series of faces that progressed from 100 percent sad to 100 percent angry, abused children could detect rage in faces that were only 40 percent angry. Nonabused children didn't start seeing the anger until a face was 70 percent angry (● Figure 4.2) (Pollak & Kistler, 2002).

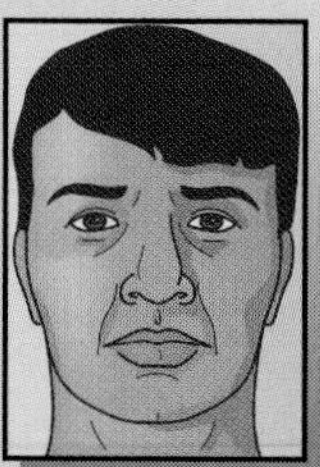

● **Figure 4.2** Abused children could detect signs of rage in faces that were only 40 percent angry. Nonabused children couldn't see the anger until facial expressions were at least 70 percent angry (Pollak & Kistler, 2002).

Once abused children pick up the early warning signs of anger, they also tend to focus on it longer than nonabused children do (Pollak & Tolley-Schell, 2003; Pollak et al., 2005). Being keenly attuned to signs of anger is probably a "survival skill" for abused children. Yet it also leaves them "trapped" by anger, quick to detect its telltale signs and slow to shift attention away from it. As a result, abused children may grow up to be hypersensitive to normal expressions of anger in their adult relationships.

The Abuse Cycle

A cycle of violence that flows from one generation to the next is at the core of much child abuse. In short, many abused children later become abusive adults (Oliver, 1993). Roughly one third of all parents who were abused as children mistreat their own children (Knutson, 1995). A second third are likely to abuse their children when they are feeling stressed. Such parents simply never learned to love, communicate with, or discipline a child.

How do caring parents who were abused as children differ from abusive parents who continue the cycle of violence? Those who break the cycle are more likely to have received emotional support from a caring adult during childhood. They are also more likely to have received therapy or to have an emotionally supportive mate (Egeland, Jacobvitz, & Sroufe, 1988). Without such support, childhood abuse greatly increases the lifetime risk of emotional problems, substance abuse, and violence (Malinosky-Rummell & Hansen, 1993; Mullen et al., 1996). (Also see "Trapped by Anger: The 'Rage Radar' of Abused Children.")

Preventing Child Abuse

What can be done about child abuse? Many public agencies have teams to identify battered or neglected children. However, legal "cures" leave a lot to be desired. The courts can take custody of a child, or the parents may voluntarily agree to place the child in a foster home. Foster care can be an improvement, but it may also further traumatize the child. In some cases the child is allowed to remain with the parents, but under court supervision. Even then, there is a chance of further injury unless the parents get help. Some of the most effective programs teach parents child-care skills, how to manage stress, anger control, and how to avoid using corporal punishment (Fetsch, Schultz, & Wahler, 1999; Reppucci, Woolard, & Fried, 1999). It would be best if such skills were taught in high school, before potential abusers become parents.

Helpful Strategies

Self-help groups of former child abusers and community volunteers are a major aid to parents. One such group is Parents Anonymous, an organization of parents who help each other stop abusing children. Local groups set up networks of members that parents can call in an abuse crisis. Parents also learn how to curb violent impulses and how to cope with their children. Experts recommend that a parent who is tempted to shake or strike a crying infant should try any of the following (Evans, 1993):

- Leave the room and call a friend.
- Put on some soothing music.
- Take 10 deep breaths and calm yourself; then take 10 more.
- Move to another room and do some exercise.
- Take a shower.

- Sit down, close your eyes, and vividly imagine yourself in a pleasant place.
- If none of the preceding strategies work, seek professional help. (Telephone numbers are listed at the end of this chapter.)

It is also important to remember that emotional abuse can be just as damaging as physical abuse. Parents inflict long-lasting emotional scars when they neglect, humiliate, intimidate, or terrorize their children.

Dangerous Attitudes

Another way of preventing child abuse is by changing attitudes. Many parents continue to believe it is their "right" to slap or hit their children. In a *USA Today* poll, 67 percent of adults agreed that "a good, hard spanking" is sometimes necessary to discipline a child. For many parents, "sometimes" occurs quite often: On average, parents report spanking their children 2.5 times a week (Holden, Coleman, & Schmidt, 1995). Roughly 25 percent of all American parents have used an object to spank their children. Thus, one parent in four has at least flirted with serious child abuse (Gershoff, 2002).

Widespread acceptance of physical punishment creates an atmosphere in which angry parents can easily lose control and abuse their children. Even parents who would never strike a child may fall prey to "shaken baby syndrome." In such cases, an angry parent violently shakes an infant (often one that won't stop crying). The result can be brain injuries that cause mental retardation, blindness, or even death.

As a society we seem to say, "Violence is okay if the child isn't injured; if the child is injured, then it's child abuse." Of course, when the child is injured, it's too late to take back the violence. By condoning punishment that borders on abuse, we greatly raise the chances of injury. The best solution to physical abuse may lie in rethinking our attitudes about the rights of children (Gershoff, 2002). If it is against the law to hit other adults, prisoners, and even animals, why is it okay to hit children?

Fortunately, public opinion regarding spanking is starting to shift. Several states have banned spanking in schools, and in 11 countries it is now illegal for parents to physically punish their children. However, child victimization will continue as long as we as a society tolerate it.

KNOWLEDGE BUILDER

Problems of Childhood

REFLECT

What normal problems could first-time parents expect their children to have? Can you also describe some of the more serious problems that occur?

You have been hired as director of a nonprofit agency that is concerned with child abuse. What would you have your staff do to reduce child abuse in your community?

LEARNING CHECK

1. Occasional reversals and regressions to more infantile behavior are sure signs that a significant childhood problem exists. T or F?
2. Sleep disturbances and specific fears can be a sign of significant childhood problems when they are prolonged or exaggerated. T or F?
3. A moderate amount of sibling rivalry is considered normal. T or F?
4. Encopresis is the formal term for lack of bladder control. T or F?
5. The ADHD child is lost in his or her own private world. T or F?
6. Approximately 30 percent of all parents who were abused as children mistreat their own children. T or F?

CRITICAL THINKING

7. Regarding so-called anorexia nervosa, is it really possible to be too thin in today's fashion-conscious society?

Answers: 1. F 2. T 3. T 4. F 5. F 6. T 7. It certainly is! Anorexia nervosa is best described as pathological self-starvation. Often it leads to serious health problems, and sometimes even to death. See Chapter 12 for details.

BRIDGES

Is it better, then, to "spare the rod"? How do we know that won't "spoil the child"?

See Chapter 8, pages 284–285, for further discussion of why it may not be helpful to physically punish children.

Adolescence—The Best of Times, the Worst of Times

Adolescence is a time of change, exploration, exuberance, and youthful searching. It can also be a time of worry and problems, especially in today's world. It might even be fair to describe adolescence as "the best of times, the worst of times." During adolescence, a person's identity and moral values come into sharper focus. Just in case you weren't taking notes in junior high, let's survey the challenges of this colorful chapter of life.

Adolescence is the culturally defined period between childhood and adulthood. Socially, the adolescent is no longer a child, yet not quite an adult. Almost all cultures recognize this transitional status. However, the length of adolescence varies greatly from culture to culture. For example, most 14-year-old girls in North America live at home and go to school. In contrast, many 14-year-old females in rural villages of the Near East are married and have children. In our culture, 14-year-olds are adolescents. In others, they may be adults.

Is marriage the primary criterion for adult status in North America? No, it's not even one of the top three criteria. Today, the most widely accepted standards are (1) taking responsibility for oneself, (2) making independent decisions, and (3) becoming financially independent. In practice, this typically means breaking away from parents by taking a job and setting up a separate residence (Arnett, 2001, 2004).

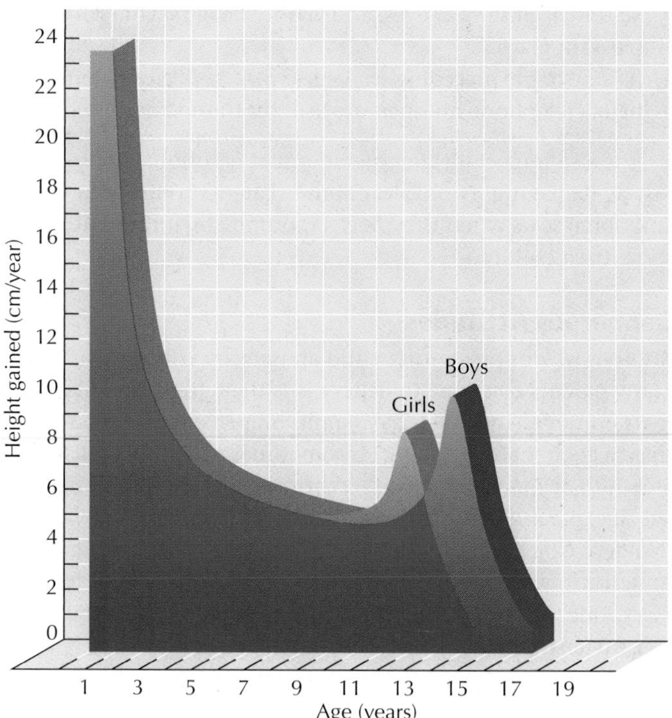

● **Figure 4.3** The typical rate of growth for boys and girls. Notice that growth in early adolescence equals that for ages 1 to 3. Note too the earlier growth spurt for girls.

Puberty

Many people confuse adolescence with **puberty.** However, puberty is a *biological* event, not a social status. During puberty, hormonal changes promote rapid physical growth and sexual maturity. Interestingly, the peak **growth spurt** (accelerated growth rate) during puberty occurs earlier for girls than for boys (● Figure 4.3). This difference explains the 1- to 2-year period when girls tend to be taller than boys. (Remember going to dances where the girls towered over the boys?) For girls the onset of puberty typically occurs between 9 and 12 years of age. For most boys the age range is 11 to 14 years.

Biologically, most people reach reproductive maturity in the early teens. Social and intellectual maturity, however, may lie years ahead. Young adolescents often make fateful decisions that affect their entire lives, even though they are immature in cognitive development, knowledge, and social experience. The tragically high rates of teenage pregnancy and drug abuse in many Western nations are prime examples. The younger an adolescent becomes sexually active, delinquent, or involved with drugs, the greater the resulting damage (White & DeBlassie, 1992). Other major risks during adolescence include alcohol abuse, smoking, eating disorders, suicide, risk-taking, violence, sexually transmitted diseases, and school failure (Johnson & Roberts, 1999). However, this may paint too grim a picture. Despite such risks, most people do manage to weather adolescence without developing any serious psychological problems (Steinberg, 2001).

Early and Late Maturation

When you were going through puberty, did you ever spend *hours* preparing to attend a party, dance, or other social event? If you did, you weren't alone. Puberty tends to dramatically increase body awareness and concerns about physical appearance. In many instances, dissatisfaction is related to the *timing* of puberty. Girls who are temporarily "too tall," boys who are "too small," and both boys and girls who lag in sexual development are likely to be upset about their bodies (Petersen et al., 1991).

How much difference does the timing of puberty make? Because puberty involves so many rapid changes, it can be stressful for just about anyone. When puberty comes unusually early or late, its impact may be magnified—for both good and bad.

Timing

For boys, maturing early is generally beneficial. Typically, it enhances their self-image and gives them an advantage socially and athletically. For such reasons, early maturing boys tend to be more poised, relaxed, dominant, self-assured, and popular. However, early-maturing boys are also more likely to get into trouble with drugs, alcohol, truancy, fighting, and antisocial behavior (Steinberg, 2001). In comparison, late-maturing boys tend to be anxious about being behind in development. However, after they catch up they tend to be more eager, talkative, self-assertive, and tolerant of themselves than average maturers (Dusek, 1996).

For girls, the advantages of early maturation are less clear-cut. In elementary school, physically advanced girls tend to have *less* prestige among peers. They also have poorer self-images (Crawford et al., 2004). This may be because they are larger and heavier than their classmates. By junior high, however, early development includes sexual features. This leads to a more positive body image, *greater* peer prestige, and adult approval (Brooks-Gunn & Warren, 1988). In contrast, late-maturing girls have the possible advantage of usually growing taller and thinner than early-maturing girls. Other relevant findings are that early-maturing girls date sooner and are more independent and more active in school; they are also more often in trouble at school and more likely to engage in early sex (Flannery et al., 1993). For all girls, changes in self-confidence, body image, sexual maturity, and relationships with friends and family tend to be prominent issues during adolescence (Steinberg, 2001).

As you can see, there are costs and benefits associated with both early and late puberty. One added cost of early maturation is that it may force premature identity formation. When a teenager begins to look like an adult, she or he may be treated like an adult. Ideally, this change can encourage greater maturity and independence. But what happens when a person is treated as an adult before he or she is emotionally ready? Then the search for identity may end too soon, leaving the person with a distorted, poorly formed sense of self.

Bettmann/Corbis

David Young-Wolff/PhotoEdit

Typical clothing worn by young adolescents 50 years ago and today.

Hurried into Adulthood?

Psychologist David Elkind (2001) believes that many parents are hurrying their children's development. Elkind is concerned about parents who try to raise their babies' IQs, force them to "read" flash cards, or have them swimming and doing gymnastics before they are 3 months old. Such pushing, he believes, partly explains why more children have recently begun to show serious stress symptoms. Moreover, hurried children are turning into hurried teenagers—urged by parents and the media alike to grow up fast. Elkind believes that too many teenagers are left without the guidance, direction, and support they need to become healthy adults (Elkind, 1984). In part, this occurs because many parents are too busy dealing with demands outside the family and expect their children to "take care of themselves" (Elkind, 1995).

Elkind's main point is that today's teenagers have adulthood thrust on them too soon. Violence, drug abuse, X-rated movies, youth crime, teenage pregnancy, divorce and single-parent families, date rape, aimless schools—all this, and more, strikes Elkind as evidence that there is no place for teenagers in today's society.

According to Elkind, the traditional **social markers** of adolescence have all but disappeared. (Social markers are visible or tangible signs that indicate a person's social status or role—such as a driver's license or a wedding ring.) As an example, Elkind notes that clothing for children and teenagers is increasingly adult-like. Girls especially are urged to wear seductive clothing and revealing swimsuits.

Clearly, Elkind is stating a clinical opinion. It's possible that his view exaggerates the problem somewhat—indeed, much of what he says is debatable. Nevertheless, his portrayal of hurried adolescents as "all grown up with no place to go" is highly thought-provoking.

The Search for Identity

As discussed earlier, identity formation is a key task of adolescence. Of course, problems of identity occur at other times too. But in a very real sense, puberty signals that it's time to begin forming a new, more mature self-image (Douvan, 1997). Many problems stem from unclear standards about the role adolescents should play within society. Are they adults or children? Should they be autonomous or dependent? Should they work or play? Such ambiguities make it difficult for young people to form clear images of themselves and of how they should act (Alsaker, 1995).

Answering the question, "Who am I?" is also spurred by cognitive development. After adolescents have attained the stage of formal operations, they are better able to ask questions about their place in the world and about morals, values, politics, and social relationships. Then, too, being able to think about hypothetical possibilities allows the adolescent to contemplate the future and ask more realistically, "Who will I be?" (Suls, 1989).

Ethnic youths often encounter negative stereotypes that can cause confusion about personal identity and lower self-esteem (de las Fuentes & Vasquez, 1999). Ethnic adolescents are also torn be-

Adolescence The culturally defined period between childhood and adulthood.

Puberty The biologically defined period during which a person matures sexually and becomes capable of reproduction.

Growth spurt An often dramatic acceleration in physical growth that coincides with puberty.

Social markers Visible or tangible signs that indicate a person's social status or role.

tween popular culture and their families and ethnic communities. For them, the question is often not just, "Who am I?" Rather, it is, "Who am I at home? Who am I at school? Who am I with friends from my neighborhood?" As a result, ethnic teens face the question of how they should think of themselves. Is Lori an American or a Chinese American? Is Jaime a Chicano, a Mexicano, or a Mexican American?

Teens who take pride in their ethnic heritage have higher self-esteem, a better self-image, and a stronger sense of personal identity (Roberts et al., 1999; Tse, 1999; Verkuyten & Lay, 1998). Incidentally, the same can be said of anyone who is "different." Sexual orientation and disabilities, for instance, create many of the same conflicts that ethnicity does. Enhanced group pride, positive models, and a more tolerant society could do much to keep a broad range of options open to *all* adolescents (Vasquez & de las Fuentes, 1999).

Parents and Teens

What effects do parents have on identity formation? The adolescent search for identity frequently leads to conflict with parents. This is especially true in early adolescence (Laursen et al., 1998). However, some disagreement with parents is probably necessary for growth of a separate identity. A complete lack of conflict may mean that the adolescent is afraid to seek independence.

Actually, adolescents and parents tend to agree about basic topics such as religion, marriage, and morals. Even though teens disagree with parents more than they did as children, less conflict occurs than might be expected (Fuligni, 1998). (This may be because teens spend so little time at home!) The conflicts that do occur tend to be over superficial differences regarding styles of dress, manners, social behavior, and the like. However, superficial disputes sometimes mask struggles about more basic issues, such as substance use, dangerous driving, and sex. For instance, parents who resist a 13-year-old's request to begin dating may actually be concerned about sex, not dating (Arnett, 1999).

Adolescents naturally desire more freedom, but they do not want their parents to abruptly abandon them. Teenagers do best when they are given gradual increases in personal freedom and opportunities to make decisions. In the majority of cases, adolescents who ask their parents for emotional or practical support actually receive it (Valery, O'Conner, & Jennings, 1997). Problems occur when parents crack down too hard or throw their hands up and surrender control over the adolescent's behavior (Eccles et al., 1993). As was true in childhood, authoritative (warm but firm) parenting continues to be the best approach during the teen years (see Chapter 3) (Steinberg, 2000).

Imaginary Audiences

David Elkind has noted an interesting pattern in adolescent thought. According to Elkind (1984), many teenagers are preoccupied with **imaginary audiences** (people they imagine are watching them). In other words, teenagers may act like others are aware of their thoughts and feelings. Sometimes this leads to painful self-consciousness—as in thinking that *everyone* is staring at a bad haircut you just received. The imaginary audience also seems to underlie attention-seeking "performances" involving outlandish dress or behavior. In any case, adolescents become very concerned with controlling the impressions they make on others. For many, being "on stage" in this way helps define and shape an emerging identity.

Peer Groups

In high school were you a jock, prep, brain, hacker, surfer, criminal, cowboy, punk, mod, rapper, druggy, warthog, dervish, gargoyle, or aardvark? (Well, okay, we made up the last four—the rest are real.) Increased identification with *peer groups* is quite common during adolescence. A **peer group** consists of people who share similar social status. To an extent, membership in such groups gives a measure of security and a sense of identity apart from the family. Beyond this, group membership provides practice in belonging to a social network. Children tend to see themselves more as members of families and small friendship groups, not as members of society as a whole. Therefore, gaining a broader, member-of-society perspective can be a major step toward adulthood (Hill, 1993).

Aren't groups also limiting? Yes, they are. Conformity to peer values peaks in early adolescence, but it remains strong at least through high school. Throughout this period there is always a danger of allowing group pressure to **foreclose** (shut down) personal growth (Newman & Newman, 1987). Cliques, in particular, can be very confining because members typically don't socialize with people outside the clique (Degirmencioglu et al., 1998).

The Twixters

Meet 22-year-old Kirsten:

> When our mothers were our age, they were engaged. . . . They at least had some idea what they were going to do with their lives. . . . I, on the other hand, will have a dual degree in majors that are ambiguous at best and impractical at worst [English and political science], no ring on my finger and no idea who I am, much less what I want to do. . . . Under duress, I will admit that this is a pretty exciting time. Sometimes, when I look out across the wide expanse that is my future, I can see beyond the void. I realize that having nothing ahead to count on means I now have to count on myself; that having no direction means forging one of my own. (Page, 1999)

Are you a twixter like Kirsten? Twentysomething, still living at home, not yet married, no children, no settled career? Are twixters self-indulgent individuals trapped in a "maturity gap" (Galambos, Barker, & Tilton-Weaver, 2003) or part of a cultural phenomenon of "emerging adulthood" (Arnett, 2000)? According to American psychologist Jeffrey Arnett (2000, 2004), emerging adulthood is increasingly characteristic of affluent Westernized cultures that allow young people to take longer to settle into their adult roles.

In England they are called "Kippers" (Kids In Parents' Pockets Eroding Retirement Savings), in Italy they are "Mammone" (won't give up on mother's cooking), and in Germany they are "Nesthocker" (nest squatters). In less affluent countries, as in less affluent parts of America, however, most adolescents continue to "become adults" at much younger ages (Arnett & Galambos, 2003). Thus, words like *childhood* or *adulthood* cannot be defined solely in terms of physical maturation. If we look at various cultures, it's clear that there is simply no definite age when we magically stop being children or become adults (Arnett, 2004).

The Transition to Adulthood

By the end of high school, many adolescents have not yet sufficiently explored various interests, values, vocations, skills, or ideologies on their own. Perhaps that is why many students view moving on to work or college as a chance to break out of earlier roles—to expand or reshape personal identity. For many who choose college, the effect may be more a matter of placing further changes in identity on hold. By doing so, college students keep open the possibility of changing majors, career plans, personal style, and so on. Typically, commitment to an adult identity grows stronger in later college years (Arnett, 2000, 2004).

Michael Siluk/The Image Works

Membership in friendship groups, cliques, "posses," or "crews" helps adolescents build an identity apart from their relationship to parents. However, over-identification with a clannish group that rejects anyone who looks or acts different can limit personal growth.

Careers today are increasingly technological and information based. As a result, the amount of education required for young people to prepare for jobs is stretching ever longer. In addition, young people have more control over their lives than they did in past decades. Many now wait until the late twenties to get married and have children. Because of such changes, a new phase of life has appeared in many countries. A period of *emerging adulthood* now stretches from the late teens to the mid-twenties. During this time, young people tend to actively explore love, work, and worldviews. Changes in residence, lovers, and jobs are common at this time. Thus, young people today prolong identity explorations into their twenties before they commit to long-term choices in love and work (Arnett, 2000, 2002, 2004). (See "The Twixters.")

Moral Development—Growing a Conscience

A person with a terminal illness is in great pain. She is pleading for death. Should extraordinary medical efforts be made to keep her alive? If a friend of yours desperately needed to pass a test and asked you to help him cheat, would you do it? These are *moral* questions, or questions of conscience.

Imaginary audience The group of people a person imagines is watching (or will watch) his or her actions.

Peer group A group of people who share similar social status.

Foreclosed identity A premature end to the search for personal identity.

Moral development starts in childhood and continues into young adulthood. During this period, we acquire values, beliefs, and thinking abilities that guide responsible behavior. Moral values are especially likely to come into sharper focus during adolescence, as capacities for self-control and abstract thinking increase (Fabes et al., 1999). Let's take a brief look at this interesting aspect of personal development.

Moral Dilemmas

How are moral values acquired? Psychologist Lawrence Kohlberg (1981a) held that we learn moral values through thinking and reasoning. To study moral development, Kohlberg posed dilemmas to children of different ages. The following is one of the moral dilemmas he used (adapted from Kohlberg, 1969).

> A woman was near death from cancer, and there was only one drug that might save her. It was discovered by a druggist who was charging 10 times what it cost to make the drug. The sick woman's husband could only pay $1,000, but the druggist wanted $2,000. He asked the druggist to sell it cheaper or to let him pay later. The druggist said no. So the husband became desperate and broke into the store to steal the drug for his wife. Should he have done that? Was it wrong or right? Why?

Each child was asked what action the husband should take. Kohlberg classified the reasons given for each choice and identified three levels of moral development. Each is based not so much on the choices made, but on the reasoning used to arrive at a choice.

At the **preconventional level**, moral thinking is guided by self-interest and the consequences of actions (punishment, reward, or an exchange of favors). For example, a person at this level might say:

> "He shouldn't steal the drug because he could get caught and sent to jail" (avoiding punishment).
>
> "It won't do him any good to steal the drug because he will go to jail and his wife will probably die before he gets out" (self-interest).

In the **conventional level,** reasoning is based on a desire to please others or to follow socially accepted rules and values:

> "He shouldn't steal the drug because others will think he is a thief. His wife would not want to be saved by thievery" (avoiding the disapproval of others).
>
> "Although his wife needs the drug, he should not break the law to get it. His wife's condition does not justify stealing, which is legally wrong" (traditional morality of authority).

The advanced moral reasoning of the **postconventional level** follows higher, self-accepted moral principles, not those supplied by outside authorities. For example, the person might reason as follows:

> "He should not steal the drug. The druggist's decision is reprehensible, but I think it is of great importance to respect the rights of others" (social contract).
>
> "He should steal the drug and then inform the authorities that he has done so. He will have to face a penalty, but he will have saved a human life" (self-chosen ethical principles).

As these examples imply, Kohlberg believed that each level of moral reasoning has two stages (see ■ Table 4.2). In time, Kohlberg found it necessary to combine stages 5 and 6 because it was difficult to separate them (Kohlberg, 1981b). He was firm in his belief, however, that morality develops in preconventional, conventional, and postconventional phases.

Does everyone eventually reach the highest level? People advance through the stages at different rates and many fail to reach the postconventional stage. In fact, many do not even reach the conventional level. For instance, a survey in England revealed that 11 percent of men and 3 percent of women would commit murder for $1 million if they could be sure of getting away with the crime ("They'd Kill," 1991).

The preconventional stages (1 and 2) are most characteristic of young children and delinquents (Nelson, Smith, & Dodd, 1990). The conventional, group-oriented morals of stages 3 and 4 are typical of older children and most adults. Kohlberg estimated that only about 20 percent of the adult population achieves postconventional morality, representing self-direction and higher principles. (It would appear that few of these people enter politics!)

Moral development is a promising topic for further study. As an example, consider the work of psychologist Carol Gilligan.

Justice or Caring?

Gilligan (1982) pointed out that Kohlberg's system is concerned mainly with *justice*. Based on studies of women who faced real-life

TABLE 4.2

Kohlberg's Stages of Moral Development

Preconventional
Stage 1: Punishment orientation. Actions are evaluated in terms of possible punishment, not goodness or badness; obedience to power is emphasized.
Stage 2: Pleasure-seeking orientation. Proper action is determined by one's own needs; concern for the needs of others is largely a matter of "you scratch my back and I'll scratch yours," not of loyalty, gratitude, or justice.
Conventional
Stage 3: Good boy/good girl orientation. Good behavior is that which pleases others in the immediate group or which brings approval; the emphasis is on being "nice."
Stage 4: Authority orientation. In this stage the emphasis is on upholding law, order, and authority, doing one's duty, and following social rules.
Postconventional
Stage 5: Social-contract orientation. Support of laws and rules is based on rational analysis and mutual agreement; rules are recognized as open to question but are upheld for the good of the community and in the name of democratic values.
Stage 6: Morality of individual principles. Behavior is directed by self-chosen ethical principles that tend to be general, comprehensive, or universal; high value is placed on justice, dignity, and equality.

Bananastock/jupiterimages

Each of us faces moral dilemmas, both large and small, every day. Dishonesty on taxes, sexual faithfulness, abortion, speeding, found valuables, temptations to lie, honesty in business—these and many other situations raise moral questions. A moral dilemma familiar to most students involves being unprepared for an exam. Sadly, the majority of American children function at the preconventional level of moral development at school: A 1990 poll found that two thirds would cheat to pass an important exam.

dilemmas, Gilligan argued that there is also an ethic of *caring* about others. As one illustration, Gilligan presented the following story to 11- to 15-year-old American children.

The Porcupine and the Moles

> Seeking refuge from the cold, a porcupine asked to share a cave for the winter with a family of moles. The moles agreed. But because the cave was small, they soon found they were being scratched each time the porcupine moved about. Finally, they asked the porcupine to leave. But the porcupine refused, saying, "If you moles are not satisfied, I suggest that you leave."

Boys who read this story tended to opt for justice in resolving the dilemma: "It's the moles' house. It's a deal. The porcupine leaves." In contrast, girls tended to look for solutions that would keep all parties happy and comfortable, such as, "Cover the porcupine with a blanket."

Gilligan's point is that male psychologists have, for the most part, defined moral maturity in terms of justice and autonomy. From this perspective, a woman's concern with relationships can look like a weakness rather than a strength. (A woman who is concerned about what pleases or helps others would be placed at stage 3 in Kohlberg's system.) But Gilligan believes that caring is also a major element of moral development, and she suggests that males may lag in achieving it (Gilligan & Attanucci, 1988).

Does the evidence support Gilligan's position? Several studies have found little or no difference in men's and women's overall moral reasoning abilities (Glover, 2001; Wilson, 1995). Indeed, both men and women may use caring *and* justice to make moral decisions. The moral yardstick they use appears to depend on the situation they face (Wark & Krebs, 1996). Just the same, Gilligan deserves credit for identifying a second major way in which moral choices are made. It can be argued that our best moral choices combine justice and caring, reason and emotion—which may be what we mean by wisdom (Pasupathi & Staudinger, 2001).

Developing a "moral compass" is only one of the challenges of moving into adulthood. We'll explore others in a moment. Before you read more, here's a summary and a chance to check your progress.

KNOWLEDGE BUILDER

Adolescence and Moral Development

REFLECT

To what extent does the concept of identity formation apply to your own experience during adolescence? Did you mature early, average, or late? How do you think the timing of puberty affected you? In what ways did peer group membership affect your personal identity?

At what stage of moral development was former U.S. President Bill Clinton functioning in his highly-publicized affair with Monica Lewinsky?

LEARNING CHECK

1. In most societies, adolescence begins with the onset of puberty and ends with its completion. T or F?
2. Early maturing boys tend to experience more clear-cut advantages than do early maturing girls. T or F?
3. According to David Elkind, the traditional markers of adolescence and adulthood have been blurred. T or F?
4. The imaginary audience refers to conformity pressures that adolescents believe adults apply to them. T or F?
5. According to Kohlberg, the conventional level of moral development is marked by a reliance on outside authority. T or F?
6. Self-interest and avoiding punishment are elements of postconventional morality. T or F?
7. About 80 percent of all adults function at the postconventional level of moral reasoning. T or F?
8. Gilligan regards gaining a sense of justice as the principal basis of moral development. T or F?

CRITICAL THINKING

9. Elkind suggests that many adolescents are "hurried into adulthood." Yet many young people live at home longer than ever before (often into their early twenties). Does this contradict Elkind's thesis?

Answers: 1. F 2. T 3. T 4. F 5. T 6. F 7. F 8. F 9. Not necessarily. Prolonged dependence on parents appears to be based on economic pressures, not on an extension of adolescent social status.

Moral development The development of values, beliefs, and thinking abilities that act as a guide regarding what is acceptable behavior.

Preconventional moral reasoning Moral thinking based on the consequences of one's choices or actions (punishment, reward, or an exchange of favors).

Conventional moral reasoning Moral thinking based on a desire to please others or to follow accepted rules and values.

Postconventional moral reasoning Moral thinking based on carefully examined and self-chosen moral principles.

Challenges of Adulthood—Charting Life's Ups and Downs

Wherever you may be in life, there is much to be learned from those who have gone before you. What are the typical patterns of adult development? Do people experience a midlife crisis? What factors are related to well-being at midlife? How much of the impact of aging is biological? How much is social or cultural? What are the keys to successful aging? Psychologists have sought empirical answers to these questions and others that map the road ahead.

Adult Development

After a "settling down" period somewhere in the twenties, adult development is uniform and uninteresting, right? Wrong! A fairly predictable series of challenges is associated with development from adolescence to old age.

What personality changes and psychological developments can a person look forward to in adulthood? Further study has added important detail to the events discussed by Erikson. One informative account is based on clinical work by Roger Gould, a psychiatrist interested in adult personality. Gould's (1975) research reveals that common patterns for North American adults are as follows.

Ages 16 to 18: Escape from Dominance

Ages 16 to 18 are marked by a struggle to escape from parental dominance. Efforts to do so cause considerable anxiety about the future and conflicts about continuing dependence on parents.

Ages 18 to 22: Leaving the Family

Most people break away from their families in their early twenties. Leaving home is usually associated with building new friendships with other adults. These friends serve as substitutes for the family and as allies in the process of breaking ties. (This phase and part of the next correspond to the period of emerging adulthood described earlier.)

Ages 22 to 28: Building a Workable Life

The trend in the mid-twenties is to seek mastery of the real world. Two dominant activities are striving for accomplishment (seeking competence) and reaching out to others. Note that the second activity corresponds to Erikson's emphasis on seeking intimacy at this time. Married couples in this age group tend to place a high value on "togetherness."

Ages 29 to 34: Crisis of Questions

Around the age of 30 many people experience a minor life crisis. The heart of this crisis is a serious questioning of what life is all about. People tend to ask themselves, "Is this it?" and confidence in previous choices and values can waver. Unsettled by these developments, the person actively searches for a style of living that will bring more meaning to life. Marriages are particularly vulnerable during this time of dissatisfaction. Extramarital affairs and divorces are common symptoms of the "crisis of questions."

Ages 35 to 43: Crisis of Urgency

People of ages 35 to 43 are typically beginning to become more aware of the reality of death. Having a limited number of years to live begins to exert pressure on the individual. Intensified attempts are made to succeed at a career or to achieve one's life goals. Generativity, in the form of nurturing, teaching, or serving others, helps alleviate many of the anxieties of this stage.

Ages 43 to 50: Attaining Stability

The urgency of the previous stage gives way to a calmer acceptance of one's fate in the late forties. The predominant feeling is that the die is cast and that former decisions can be lived with. Those who have families begin to appreciate their children as individuals and ease up on their tendency to extend their own goals to their children's behavior.

Age 50 and Up: Mellowing

After age 50 a noticeable mellowing occurs. Emphasis is placed on sharing day-to-day joys and sorrows. There is less concern with glamour, wealth, accomplishment, and abstract goals. Many of the tensions of earlier years give way to a desire to savor life and its small pleasures. (A study of typical life goals and concerns at various ages parallels many of the points made by Gould. See ■ Table 4.3.)

Notice in the preceding descriptions that in many ways early adulthood is more emotionally turbulent than midlife or old age. This is borne out by a recent national survey in which younger adults reported feeling more negative emotions than older adults did. Likewise, older adults are more likely than younger adults to say they often feel happy, truly alive, and peaceful (● Figure 4.4). Despite all of the emphasis on youth in our culture, middle age and beyond can be a relatively rich period of life in which people feel secure, happy, and self-confident (Rubenstein, 2002).

Psychologists aim for universal accounts of development. It should be clear, however, that Gould's summary is highly idealized. Each person's path through life is unique. Also, adult development varies greatly in different cultures and at different times in history (Stewart & Ostrove, 1998). Accordingly, Gould's description is merely a starting point for understanding typical pat-

TABLE 4.3

Typical Life Goals and Concerns

	Typical goals are related to:	Typical concerns are related to:
Young adults	Education and family	Relationships and friends
Middle-aged	Children's lives and personal property worries	Occupation
Elderly	Good health, retirement, leisure, community	Health fears

Nurmi, 1992

TABLE 4.4

Three Views of Development Challenges

	ERIKSON	GOULD	LEVINSON
Childhood	Trust/mistrust (1) Autonomy/shame, doubt (1–3) Initiative/guilt (3–5) Industry/inferiority (6–12)		
Adolescence	Identity/confusion (12–18)	Escape from dominance (16–18)	Early adulthood transition (17–22)
Early Adulthood	Intimacy/isolation	Leaving the family (18–22) Building a workable life (22–28) Crisis of questions (29–34)	Early adulthood transition (17–22) Age 30 transition (28–33)
Middle Adulthood	Generativity/self-absorption	Crisis of urgency (35–43) Attaining stability (43–50) Mellowing (50+)	Midlife transition (40–45) Age 50 transition (50–55)
Late Adult			Late adult transition (60–65)
Old Age	Integrity/despair		

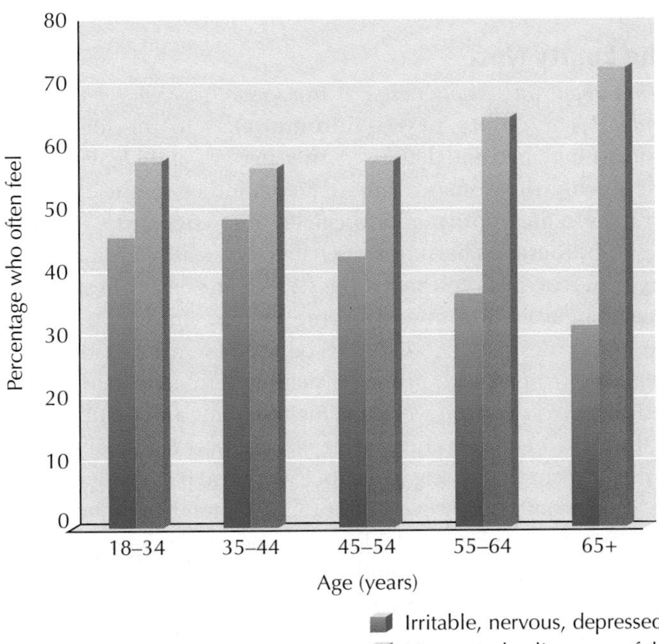

● **Figure 4.4** Negative emotions are more common before age 50 than after. The frequency of positive feelings tends to increase from midlife on into old age.

terns in adult development. Let's see what we can learn from other investigations.

A Midlife Crisis?

Gould describes two "crisis" points in adult development. How common is it to have a "midlife crisis"? Serious difficulties at the midpoint of life are certainly not universal. A study of more than 8,000 Americans found that only 23 percent (about 1 in 4) believed they had experienced a midlife crisis. In other words, most people thrive during middle adulthood and have no special problems (Brim et al., 1999).

If a midlife crisis does occur, what does it look like? Psychologist Daniel Levinson carried out an in-depth study of adulthood and identified five periods when people typically make major transitions (■ Table 4.4). A **transition period** ends one life pattern and opens the door to new possibilities (Levinson, 1986). At such times, people address concerns about their identity, work, and relationships to others.

Levinson's first study focused on the lives of men. As they approached the midlife transition (between the ages of 37 and 41), most men went through a period of instability, anxiety, and change. (Notice that this corresponds closely to Gould's crisis-of-urgency period.) In a later study, Levinson found that most of what he learned about men also applies to women (Levinson & Levinson, 1996).

Of the men Levinson studied, roughly half defined the midlife period as a "last chance" to achieve their goals. Such goals were often stated as a key event, such as reaching a certain income or becoming a supervisor, a full professor, a shop steward, and so forth. For these men the midlife period was stressful but manageable.

A smaller percentage of men experienced a serious midlife decline. Many of these men had to face the fact that they had chosen a dead-end job or lifestyle. Others had achieved financial success but felt that what they were doing was pointless.

In a third pattern, a few hardy individuals appeared to "break out" of a seriously flawed life structure. For them, a decision to "start over" was typically followed by 8 to 10 years of rebuilding.

Transition period Time span during which a person leaves an existing life pattern behind and moves into a new pattern.

In what ways does the midlife transition differ for women? Compared with men, women were less likely to enter adulthood with clearly formulated "goals." As a result, they were less likely to define "success" in terms of some key event. Rather than focusing on external goals, women tended to seek changes in personal identity at midlife. For example, a woman might become more self-reliant and independent—qualities she may have regarded as "masculine" earlier in life (Levinson & Levinson, 1996). But make no mistake, midlife can be challenging for women, too. In a survey of middle-aged women, two thirds said they made major changes in their lives between ages 37 and 43 (Stewart & Vandewater, 1999).

Midcourse Corrections

In summary, people tend to move through cycles of stability and transition in their adult lives (Ornstein & Isabella, 1990). However, it is more common to make a "midcourse correction" at midlife than it is to survive a "crisis" (Stewart & Ostrove, 1998). Ideally, the midlife transition involves reworking old identities, achieving valued goals, finding one's own truths, and preparing for old age. Taking stock may be especially valuable at midlife, but reviewing past choices to prepare for the future is helpful at any age (Lewchanin & Zubrod, 2001). For some people, difficult turning points in life can serve as "wake-up calls" that create opportunities for personal growth (Wethington, 2003).

Middle Age

When individuals reach their forties and fifties, declining vigor, strength, and youthfulness make it clear that more than half their years are gone. At the same time, greater stability often comes from letting go of the "impossible dream." That is, there is an increased attempt to be satisfied with the direction one's life has taken and to accept that hoped-for life goals may no longer be possible (Lachman, 2004).

For most women during this era, menopause represents the first real encounter with growing "old" (Rossi, 2004). At **menopause**, which occurs at an average age of 51, monthly menstruation ends, and a woman is no longer able to bear children. At the same time, the level of the hormone estrogen drops—sometimes altering mood or appearance. Menopause also can cause physical symptoms, such as fatigue and "hot flashes" (a sudden uncomfortable sensation of heat) or night sweats. Many of the small discomforts of menopause appear to be related to disrupted bodily rhythms. They are, in other words, a little like suffering from jet lag (Gannon, 1993).

A few women find menopause as difficult as adolescence, and some experience anxiety, irritability, or depression at this time. Most women, however, are neutral about no longer being able to bear a child. Many, in fact, express relief at being freed from concerns about pregnancy, birth control, and menstruation. All considered, the vast majority of women easily take "the pause" in stride, with no major emotional problems (Stewart & Ostrove, 1998). Some of those who do have problems can benefit from hormone replacement therapy (HRT), in which estrogen is temporarily taken to reduce the symptoms of menopause. However, many women regard menopause as a natural part of aging, rather than a medical problem. Also, HRT can increase other health risks, so it is not a good choice for all women (Marriott & Wenk, 2004).

Do men go through similar changes? Males do not undergo any physical change that is as abrupt as menopause. With aging, production of the male hormone testosterone gradually declines. **Andropause** (reduced testosterone levels) can lead to a decrease in sex drive, alertness, strength, bone density, and height. Fatigue, depression, insomnia, and obesity may occur. However, men remain fertile at this time, and any changes they experience tend to be gradual (Wespes & Schulman, 2002).

For some men the changes that come with andropause can be fairly disturbing. Some appear to pass through a **climacteric** (kly-MAK-ter-ik: "change of life") marked by major changes in appearance and physical vigor (Sternbach, 1998). For most men, such symptoms are probably psychological in origin. Some doctors are trying to treat andropause with hormones. However, the value of such treatment is debated. As is the case with women and menopause, some experts question if it is a good idea to treat normal aging as a medical problem (Wespes & Schulman, 2002).

The Empty Nest

What about the "empty nest"? Is it a special problem for women at midlife? The **empty nest syndrome** refers to the idea that a woman may become depressed after her last child leaves home. Supposedly, the woman's self-esteem plummets as one of her major roles in life (mother and caregiver) is downgraded. The empty nest syndrome has been hotly debated. Is it real? Or is it based on sexist stereotypes? Research suggests that an "empty nest" can be psychologically disruptive for some women. But which women? An empty nest is more likely to be a problem for traditionally feminine women who primarily define themselves as wives and mothers. Women who work outside the home are less likely to be disturbed when their children depart (Stewart & Ostrove, 1998). It might seem that trying to balance work and parenting would be hard on women. However, multiple roles tend to be beneficial. For instance, working outside the home can provide added income, social support, experiences with success, a broader perspective, more equality with men, and more sophistication (Barnett & Hyde, 2001).

Positive Psychology: Well-Being at Midlife

The pitfalls of adulthood are all too familiar: marital discord, divorce, career difficulties, unemployment, health problems, financial pressures, legal conflicts, and personal tragedies—to name but a few. How do people maintain a state of well-being as they run the gauntlet of modern life? Psychologist Carol Ryff (1995) believes that well-being during adulthood has six elements:

- Self-acceptance
- Positive relations with others
- Autonomy (personal freedom)
- Environmental mastery

- A purpose in life
- Continued personal growth

Based on a national survey, Ryff found that personal growth and having a sense of purpose in life tend to decline with increasing age. However, these declines are offset by increases in two other areas (● Figure 4.5). As people age, positive relations with others tend to increase, along with mastery of the complex demands of life (Ryff & Keyes, 1995). Thus, sharing life's joys and sorrows with others, coupled with a better understanding of how the world works, can help carry people through the midlife period and into their later years (Ryff & Singer, 2000). In fact, feeling emotionally close to others is a key ingredient of well-being throughout adulthood (Reis et al., 2000).

Signs of aging may be unmistakable in middle age, but people are also at their peak in many respects. Instead of emphasizing decline, many of today's adults seek active, healthy lifestyles. This can make the middle-age years a positive experience, not something to be dreaded or endured.

After the late fifties, the problems an individual faces in maintaining a healthy and meaningful life are complicated by the inevitable process of aging. How unique are the problems of older people, and how severely do they challenge the need to maintain integrity and personal comfort? We will look at some answers in the next section.

Aging—Will You Still Need Me When I'm 64?

Some years ago, students at Long Beach City College in California elected Pearl Taylor their spring festival queen. Ms. Taylor had everything necessary to win: looks, intelligence, personality, and campus-wide popularity. At about the same time, citizens of Raleigh, North Carolina, elected Isabella Cannon as their mayor.

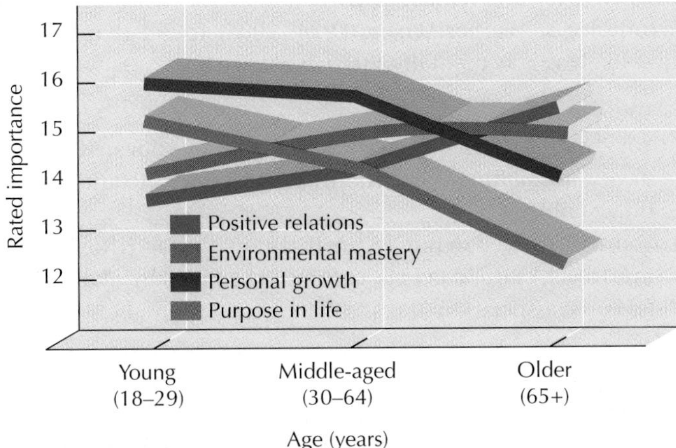

● **Figure 4.5** Feelings of personal growth and that one has a purpose in life tend to decline with increasing age. However, positive relations with other people and mastery of the environment tend to increase. Thus, the basis for a continued sense of well-being makes an interesting shift between young adulthood and old age. (Graph courtesy of Dr. Carol Ryff.)

What's so remarkable about these events? Not too much really, except that Pearl was 90 years old when elected, and Isabella was 73. Both are part of the graying of North America. Currently, some 35 million North Americans are older than 65. By the year 2020, some 60 million persons in the United States and Canada, or one out of every five, will be 65 years of age or older (● Figure 4.6). These figures make the elderly the fastest-growing segment of society. Understandably, psychologists have become increasingly interested in aging. You should be too. If you are now in your twenties, you will be part of the "grandparent boom" in 2020.

What is life like for the aged? There are large variations in aging. Most of us have known elderly persons at both extremes: those who are active, healthy, satisfied, lucid, and alert, and those who are confused, child-like, or dependent. Despite such variations, some generalizations can be made.

The Course of Aging

Biological aging refers to age-related changes in physiological functioning. Aging is a gradual process that begins quite early in life. Peak functioning in most physical capacities reaches a maximum by about 25 to 30 years of age (● Figure 4.7). Thereafter, gradual declines occur in muscular strength, flexibility, circulatory efficiency, speed of response, sensory acuity, and other functions (Birren & Fisher, 1995). Given the natural course of aging, it is extremely unlikely that a 50-year-old, or even a 40-year-old, will ever hold the world record for the 100-meter dash (Schulz & Heckhausen, 1996).

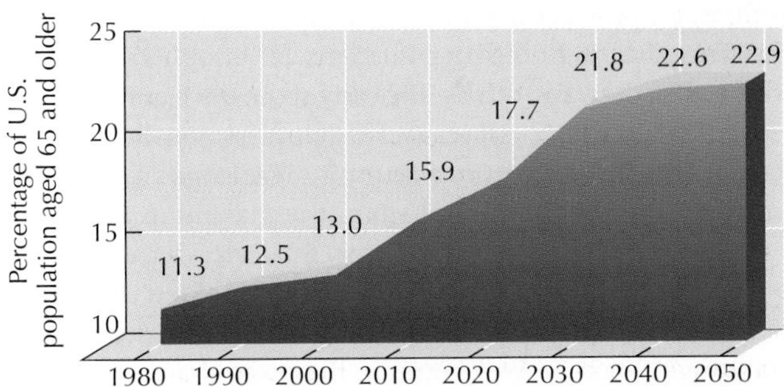

● **Figure 4.6** Longer life expectancy will produce an unprecedented increase in the percentage of the population older than 65. The "boom" is expected to start about now and peak by about 2030 to 2050 (Taeuber, 1993).

Menopause The female "change of life" signaled by the end of regular monthly menstrual periods.

Andropause A gradual decline in testosterone levels in older men.

Climacteric A point during late middle age when males experience a significant change in health, vigor, or appearance.

Empty nest syndrome Psychological disturbance experienced by some women after their last child leaves home.

Biological aging Physiological changes that accompany growing older.

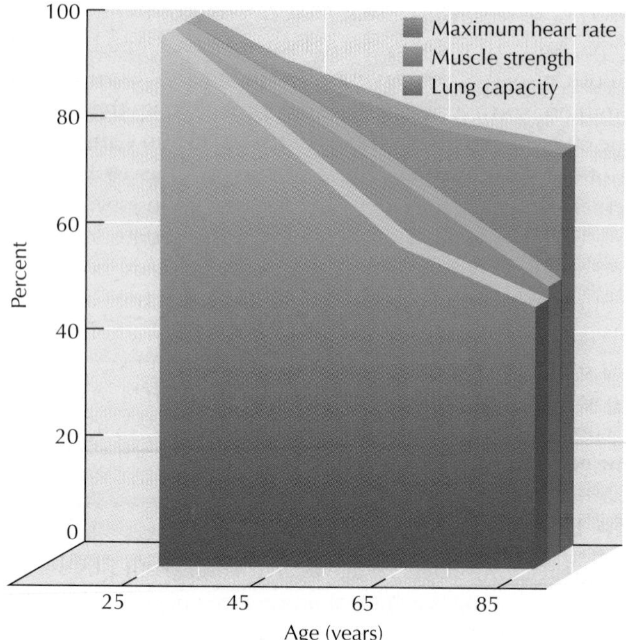

● **Figure 4.7** Physical aging, which is biologically programmed, progresses steadily from early adulthood onward. Regular exercise, good health practices, and a positive attitude can help minimize the impact of physical aging.

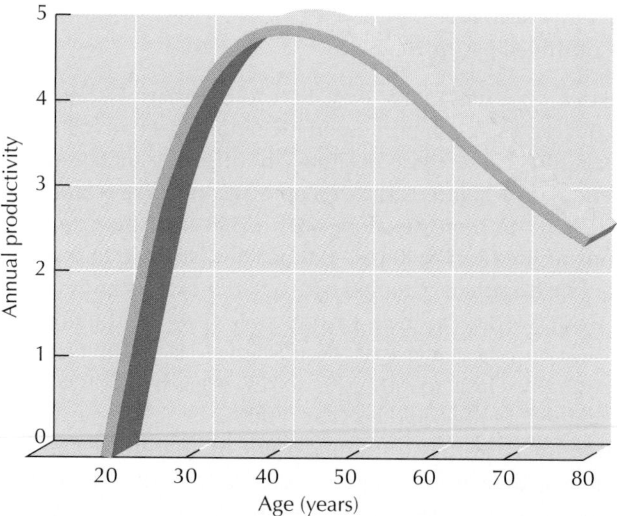

● **Figure 4.8** At what point during life are people most productive? On average, when do people make their greatest contributions to fields such as science, literature, philosophy, music, and the visual arts? No matter how achievement is tallied, productivity tends to rise rapidly to a single peak that is followed by a slow decline. The graph you see here is typical of contributions to the field of psychology. Fields such as poetry, pure math, and theoretical physics have earlier peaks, around the early thirties or even the late twenties. Other fields, such as novel writing, history, philosophy, medicine, and scholarship are marked by peaks in the late forties, fifties, or even sixties. (After Simonton, 1988.)

So people are "over the hill" by 30? Hardly! Prime abilities come at different ages for different activities. Peak performances for professional football and baseball players usually occur in the mid-twenties; for professional bowlers, the mid-thirties; for artists and musicians, the fifties; and for politicians, philosophers, business or industrial leaders, and others, the early sixties (● Figure 4.8).

Whatever the biological causes of aging, humans seem to grow, mature, age, and die within a set time. The length of our lives is limited by the **maximum life span** (the maximum age humans can attain under optimal conditions). Estimates of the maximum human life span place it around 120 years. The oldest documented age ever achieved is 122 years, by Jeanne Calment, a French woman who died in 1997. Among the more than 5 billion persons currently living, only two or three will reach the age of 115. (See "What's Your Life Expectancy?")

The prospect of physical aging may seem threatening. However, it is wrong to believe that most elderly people are sickly, infirm, or senile. Only about 5 percent of those older than 65 are in nursing homes. In fact, the percentage of elderly who are chronically disabled has declined greatly in the last 10 years (Rowe & Kahn, 1998). As for the possibility of a mental slide, the human brain does not shrink, wilt, perish, or deteriorate with age. It normally continues to function well through as many as 9 decades.

Mental Abilities

Gerontologists (jer-ON-TOL-o-jists: those who study aging), estimate that only 25 percent of the disability of old people is medical. The remaining 75 percent is social, political, and cultural. This view is backed up by intelligence test scores, which decline little with aging. Although it is true that **fluid abilities** (those requiring speed or rapid learning) may diminish, many **crystallized abilities** (learned knowledge and skills), such as vocabulary and stored-up facts, actually improve—at least into the sixties (Baltes, Staudinger, & Lindenberger, 1999; Schaie, 2005) (see ● Figure 4.9).

Many elderly persons are at least as mentally able as the average young adult. On intellectual tests, top scorers over the age of 65 match the average for men younger than 35. What sets these silver-haired stars apart? Typically they are people who have continued to work and remain intellectually active (Salthouse, 2004). Gerontologist Warner Schaie (1994, 2005) found that you are most likely to stay mentally sharp in old age if

1. You remain healthy.
2. You live in a favorable environment (you are educated and have a stimulating occupation, above-average income, and an intact family).
3. You are involved in intellectually stimulating activities (reading, travel, cultural events, continuing education, clubs, professional associations).

BRIDGES

The most common cause of dementia in old age is Alzheimer's disease.

See page 551 in Chapter 16 for a discussion of this devastating illness.

DISCOVERING PSYCHOLOGY

What's Your Life Expectancy?

For most people, **life expectancy** (the actual number of years the average person lives) is shorter than the maximum life span. In the 1800s the average life expectancy was 36 years. Now, average life expectancy at birth for American males is 73 years, and for females it is 81 years. With improved health care, life expectancy should move even closer to the maximum life span (Brannon & Feist, 2004).

There is no known way to extend the maximum human life span. On the other hand, there is every reason to believe that life expectancy can be increased. If you would personally like to add to a higher average, the factors listed here are known to affect life expectancy.

Add to Life Expectancy	*Subtract from Life Expectancy*
Normal blood pressure	High blood pressure
Do not have diabetes	Suffer from diabetes
Have low cholesterol	Have high cholesterol
Excellent health for current age	Poor health for current age
Nonsmoker	Smoker
No secondhand smoke exposure	Exposed to secondhand smoke
No more than two alcoholic drinks per day	More than three alcoholic drinks per day
Daily exercise	Little or no exercise
Low-fat diet	High-fat diet
Eat fruits and vegetables daily	No fruits and vegetables
Happily married	Divorced or single
No major disruptive events last year	One or more major disruptive events last year
Saw many friends in last month	Saw few or no friends in last month
Both parents lived past age 75	Neither parent lived past age 75

Each of the factors on the left can add from one to three years to your life expectancy. Those on the right can subtract from one to three years. Check the factors that apply to you. On balance, do you think you are likely to live longer or shorter than average? Notice that many factors that affect life expectancy are controllable. Living a long, healthy life is not just a matter of luck (Brannon & Feist, 2004; Roizen, 1999).

Royalty-Free/Corbis

4. You have a flexible personality.
5. You are married to a smart spouse.
6. You maintain your perceptual processing speed.
7. You were satisfied with your accomplishments in midlife.

A shorter summary of the preceding is, "Those who live by their wit die with their wits."

Positive Psychology: Successful Aging

In general, what kind of person adjusts most successfully to aging? Two theories have been proposed to explain successful adjustment to aging. **Disengagement theory** assumes it is normal and desirable for people to withdraw from society as they age (Cumming & Henry, 1961). According to this view, the elderly welcome disen-

Maximum life span The biologically defined maximum number of years humans can live under optimal conditions.

Gerontologist One who scientifically studies aging and its effects.

Fluid abilities Innate, nonlearned abilities based on perceptual, motor, or intellectual speed and flexibility.

Crystallized abilities Abilities that a person has intentionally learned; accumulated knowledge and skills.

Life expectancy The average number of years a person of a given sex, race, and nationality can expect to live.

Disengagement theory of aging Theory stating that it is normal for older people to withdraw from society and from roles they held earlier.

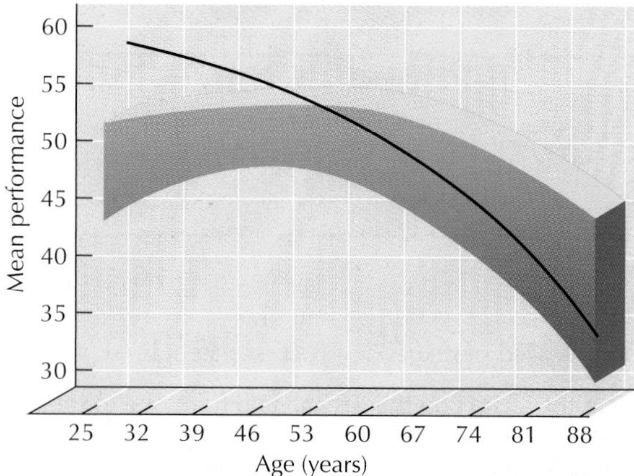

● **Figure 4.9** Average performance at various ages for verbal, numeric, spatial, and reasoning abilities all fall within the blue area of this graph. Notice that, in general, mental abilities show modest gains from young adulthood to early middle age. After that, they begin a slow decline. Notice, too, that most abilities at age 70 return to about the same levels found at age 25. Only after age 80 do declines become large enough to make a practical difference in mental abilities. One exception is perceptual speed (black line). This fluid ability declines steadily after age 25. (Adapted from Schaie, 1994.)

At age 77, John Glenn became the oldest person to fly into space, in October 1998. Glenn was also the first American astronaut to orbit Earth, in 1962. As Glenn's space adventure shows, aging does not inevitably bring an end to engaging in challenging activities. The same is true of productive and creative work. Many artists, writers, composers, poets, and scientists have continued to make contributions to society during the seventh, eighth, and even ninth decades of their lives.

gagement from roles they are less able to fulfill. Likewise, society benefits from disengagement, as younger persons with new energy and skills fill positions vacated by aging individuals.

Certainly we have all known people who disengaged from society as they grew older. Nevertheless, disengagement theory seems to describe successful aging as a retreat. Although disengagement may be common, it is not necessarily ideal (Clair, Karp, & Yoels, 1994).

What does the second theory say? The second theory of optimal aging is a sort of "use-it-or-lose-it" view. **Activity theory** assumes that activity is the essence of life at any age. Activity theory predicts that people who remain active physically, mentally, and socially will adjust better to aging (Havighurst, 1961). Thus, if a person is forced to give up particular roles or activities, they should be replaced with others. That way, the aging person is able to maintain a better self-image, greater satisfaction, and more social support—resulting in more successful aging.

Which theory is correct? The majority of studies support the activity theory (Clair, Karp, & Yoels, 1994). At the same time, some people do seek disengagement, so neither theory is absolutely "correct." Actually, successful aging probably requires a combination of continued activity and selective disengagement. The best mix appears to include being productive, as well as enjoying leisure activities (Herzog et al., 1998).

Compensation and Optimization

Learning to compensate for age-related changes is one of the real keys to remaining active and happy in old age. In fact, the challenge at any age is to make good use of your potentials (Schroots, 1996). Gerontologist Paul Baltes believes this occurs when people use a strategy of "selective optimization with compensation." That is, older people should focus on what they can still do, find ways to perform well, and compensate for any age-related losses. Baltes offers the following as an example:

> When the concert pianist Arthur Rubinstein, as an 80-year-old, was asked in a television interview how he managed to maintain such a high level of expert piano playing, he hinted at the coordination of three strategies. First, he played fewer pieces (selection); he practiced these pieces more often (optimization); and to counteract his loss in mechanical speed he now used a kind of impression management, such as playing more slowly before fast segments to make the latter appear faster (compensation). (Baltes, Staudinger, & Lindenberger, 1999)

Another key to successful aging is spending as much time as possible doing the things one finds meaningful. Activities done just "to pass the time" tend to lower happiness in old age (Everard, 1999). Finally, people age best when they are able to maintain *control* of their lives (Schulz & Heckhausen, 1996).

Seniors with Attitude

People older than 50 who have a positive outlook about aging live an average of 7.5 years longer than those who take a dim view of old age. People with a positive outlook on aging were likely to agree with statements such as, "I have as much pep as I did last year." Pessimists tended to agree with statements such as, "Things keep getting worse as I get older." Longer life expectancy is also partly related to a person's "will to live." People who want to live life fully describe themselves as feeling "worthy," "hopeful," and "full." Those with a weak will to live see themselves as "worthless," "hopeless," or "empty."

How could a person's attitude affect how long they live? It's possible that negative attitudes increase an aging person's levels of stress. More stress, in turn, may accelerate bodily damage and susceptibility to disease. On the other hand, it's nice to know that positive self-perceptions and a good attitude toward aging can add years to your life expectancy (Levy et al., 2002).

Ageism

You have almost certainly encountered ageism in one way or another. **Ageism**, which refers to discrimination or prejudice based on age, can oppress the young as well as the old. For instance, a person applying for a job may just as well be told "You're too young" as "You're too old." In some societies ageism is based on respect for the elderly. In Japan, for instance, aging is seen as positive, and greater age brings more status and respect (Kimmel, 1988). In most Western nations, however, ageism tends to have a negative impact on older individuals. Usually, it is expressed as a rejection of the elderly. The concept of "oldness" is often used to expel people from useful work: Too often, retirement is just another name for dismissal and unemployment.

Stereotyping is a major facet of ageism. Popular stereotypes of the "dirty old man," "meddling old woman," "senile old fool," and the like help perpetuate the myths underlying ageism. Contrast such images to those associated with youthfulness: The young are perceived as fresh, whole, attractive, energetic, active, emerging, and appealing. Yet even positive stereotypes can be a problem. For example, if older people are perceived as financially well-off, wise, or experienced, it can blind others to the real problems of the elderly (Gatz & Pearson, 1988). The important point is that age-based stereotypes are often wrong. A tremendous diversity exists among the elderly—ranging from the infirm and demented to aerobic-dancing grandmothers.

Lori Adamski Peek/Getty Images

Social centers and exercise programs for senior citizens are a direct expression of the benefits predicted by activity theory. Remaining active may also give older persons a feeling of *control* over their lives. As we will discuss further in Chapter 15, feelings of control contribute to mental and physical well-being.

Countering Myths About Aging

What can be done about ageism? One of the best ways to combat ageism is to confront stereotypes with facts. For example, studies show that in many occupations older workers perform better at jobs requiring *both* speed and skill (Giniger et al., 1983). Gradual slowing with age is a reality. But often it can be offset by experience, skill, or expertise (Schaie, 1988, 2005). Overall, very little loss of job performance occurs as workers grow older. In the professions, wisdom and expertise can usually more than compensate for any loss of mental quickness. People who become experts in various fields often reach their peak between the ages of 30 and 50. They then maintain high levels of performance into old age through regular practice of their skills (Ericsson, 2000). Basing retirement solely on a person's age makes little sense (Baltes, Staudinger, & Lindenberger, 1999).

Myth Versus Fact

Taking a broader view, Bernice Neugarten (1916–2001), a pioneer in the study of aging, examined the lives of 200 people between the ages of 70 and 79 (Neugarten, 1971). Neugarten found that 75

Jeff Greenberg/Index Stock Imagery

In the United States, commercial airline pilots are required to retire at age 60. However, in the 35 years since this age was set, many changes have taken place in life expectancy and the nature of flying. There is no reason why a person who is physically healthy cannot continue flying beyond age 60. Actual job performance is probably the best measure of a pilot's ability to continue working (Birren & Fisher, 1995). The same is true of most jobs.

Activity theory Theory stating that the best adjustment to aging occurs when people remain active mentally, socially, and physically.

Ageism Discrimination or prejudice based on a person's age.

percent of these people were satisfied with their lives after retirement. Similarly, another study found that only 30 percent of retirees find retirement stressful (Bosse et al., 1991). Neugarten's findings also refuted other myths about aging.

1. Old persons generally do not become isolated and neglected by their families. Most *prefer* to live apart from their children.
2. Old persons are rarely placed in mental hospitals by uncaring children.
3. Old persons who live alone are not necessarily lonely or desolate.
4. Few elderly persons ever show signs of senility or mental decay, and few ever become mentally ill.

In short, most of the elderly studied by Neugarten were integrated, active, and psychologically healthy. A major study at the Harvard Medical School identified four psychological characteristics shared by the healthiest, happiest older people (Vaillant, 2002):

- Optimism, hope, and an interest in the future
- Gratitude and forgiveness; an ability to focus on what is good in life
- Empathy; an ability to share the feelings of others and see the world through their eyes
- Connection with others; an ability to reach out, to give and receive social support

Enlightened views of aging call for an end to the forced obsolescence of the elderly. As a group, older people represent a valuable source of skill, knowledge, and energy that we can't afford to cast aside. As we face the challenges of this planet's uncertain future, we need all the help we can get!

KNOWLEDGE BUILDER

Adulthood and Aging

REFLECT

Do any of the patterns of adult development described by Gould match your own experience? Using Gould's summary as a guide, what do you expect to be major issues during the next 5, 10, and 15 years of your life?

Do you know anyone who seems to be making a difficult life transition? How well is he or she handling it?

See if you can describe three instances of ageism you have witnessed.

LEARNING CHECK

1. According to Gould, building a workable life tends to be the dominant activity during which age range?
   a. 18–22 c. 29–34
   b. 22–28 d. 35–43
2. Levinson's description of a "midlife crisis" corresponds roughly to Gould's
   a. escape from dominance c. crisis of urgency
   b. crisis of questions d. settling down period
3. Nearly everyone experiences a midlife crisis sometime around age 40. T or F?
4. The average male experiences menopause between the ages of 45 and 50. T or F?
5. Many indications of biological aging start to become evident as early as the mid-twenties. T or F?
6. An expert on the problems of aging is called a ______________ ______________.
7. The activity theory of optimal aging holds that aging individuals should restrict their activities and withdraw from former community activities. T or F?
8. After age 65, a large proportion of older people show significant signs of mental disability and most require special care. T or F?

CRITICAL THINKING

9. Why might you reasonably question Gould's and Levinson's accounts of adult development?
10. In Japan, aging is seen as positive, and growing older brings increased status and respect. Is this an example of ageism?

Answers: 1. b **2.** c **3.** F **4.** F **5.** T **6.** gerontologist **7.** F **8.** F **9.** Both Gould and Levinson may be describing typical patterns of adult development *in Western societies*. It is doubtful that these patterns apply equally well to all cultures. **10.** Yes it is. Even when the elderly are revered, they are being *prejudged* on the basis of age. Also, giving higher status to the elderly relegates the young to lower status—another instance of ageism.

Death and Dying—The Curtain Falls

"I'm not afraid of dying. I just don't want to be there when it happens."
Woody Allen

The statistics on death are very convincing: One out of one dies. It might seem that as people grow older they would fear death more. However, older persons actually have fewer death fears than younger people. Older people more often fear the *circumstances* of dying, such as pain or helplessness, rather than death itself (Thorson & Powell, 1990). These findings seem to show a general lack of death fears, but they may actually reflect a widespread denial of death. Notice how denial is apparent in the language used to talk about death: Often we speak of a dead person as having "passed away," "expired," "gone to God," or "gone to rest" (Morgan, 1995).

Many people have little direct experience with death until they, themselves, are fairly old (Morgan, 1995). The average person's exposure to death consists of the artificial and unrealistic portrayals of death on TV. By the time the average person is 17 years old, she or he will have witnessed roughly 18,000 TV deaths. With few exceptions these are *homicides*, not deaths due to illness or aging.

Reactions to Impending Death

A direct account of emotional responses to death comes from the work of **thanatologist** (than-ah-TOL-oh-jist: one who studies death) Elisabeth Kübler-Ross (1975). After her death in 2004,

Death may be inevitable, but it can be faced with dignity and, sometimes, even humor. Mel Blanc's famous sign-off, "That's all folks," is engraved on a marble headstone over his grave. Blanc was the voice of Bugs Bunny, Porky Pig, and many other cartoon characters.

Kübler-Ross was named one to the 100 greatest minds of the 20th century by *Time* magazine. Over the years she spent hundreds of hours at the bedsides of the terminally ill, where she observed five basic emotional reactions to impending death.

1. **Denial and isolation.** A typical first reaction is to deny death's reality and isolate oneself from information confirming that death is really going to occur. Initially the person may be sure that "it's all a mistake." "Surely," she or he thinks, "the lab reports have been mixed up or the doctor made an error." This sort of denial may proceed to attempts to avoid any reminder of the situation.
2. **Anger.** Many dying individuals feel anger and ask, "Why me?" As they face the ultimate threat of having life torn away, their anger may spill over into rage toward the living. Even good friends may temporarily evoke anger because their health is envied.
3. **Bargaining.** In another common reaction, the terminally ill bargain with themselves or with God. The dying person thinks, "Just let me live a little longer and I'll do anything to earn it." Individuals may bargain for time by trying to be "good" ("I'll never smoke again"), by righting past wrongs, or by praying that if they are granted more time they will dedicate themselves to their religion.
4. **Depression.** As death draws near and the person begins to recognize that it cannot be prevented, feelings of futility, exhaustion, and deep depression may set in. The person realizes she or he will be separated from friends, loved ones, and the familiar routines of life, and this causes a profound sadness.
5. **Acceptance.** If death is not sudden, many people manage to come to terms with dying and accept it calmly. The person who accepts death is neither happy nor sad, but at peace with the inevitable. Acceptance usually signals that the struggle with death has been resolved. The need to talk about death ends, and silent companionship from others is frequently all the person desires.

Not all terminally ill persons display all these reactions, nor do they always occur in this order. Individual styles of dying vary greatly, according to emotional maturity, religious belief, age, education, the attitudes of relatives, and so forth. Generally, there does tend to be a movement from initial shock, denial, and anger toward eventual acceptance. However, some people who seem to have accepted death may die angry and raging against the inevitable. Conversely, the angry fighter may let go of the struggle and die peacefully. In general, your approach to dying will mirror your style of living. Ideally, dying involves successful coping, acceptance, inner strength, and finding meaning in one's final passage (Yedidia & MacGregor, 2001). For many people, to die well is no less an accomplishment than to live well.

It is best not to think of Kübler-Ross's list as a fixed series of stages to go through in order. It is an even bigger mistake to assume that someone who does not show all the listed emotional reactions is somehow deviant or immature. Rather, the list describes typical reactions to impending death. Note, as well, that many of the same reactions accompany any major loss, be it divorce, loss of a home due to fire, death of a pet, or loss of a job.

Implications

How can I make use of this information? First, it can help both the dying and survivors to recognize and cope with periods of depression, anger, denial, and bargaining. Second, it helps to realize that close friends or relatives may feel many of the same emotions before or after a person's death because they, too, are facing a loss.

Perhaps the most important thing to recognize is that the dying person needs to share feelings with others and to discuss death openly. Too often, dying persons feel isolated and separated from others by the wall of silence erected by doctors, nurses, and family members. Adults tend to "freeze up" with someone who is dying. A simple willingness to be with the person and to honestly share his or her feelings can help bring dignity, acceptance, and meaning to death (Holstein, 1997).

Hospices have recently emerged as an alternative to hospitalization for terminally ill patients and their families (Kleespies, 2004). Hospices make it easier to understand what the dying person is going through and make it easier for families to offer support at this important time. The father of one of us died in late 2004 at a hospice in Canada. Hospice staff worked with the family to help the patient die an "appropriate death," as free from physical, emotional, social, and spiritual pain as possible. The result was a positive death in which a resilient human being was able to end his life with dignity (Nakashima & Canda, 2005). Thanatologist Kirsti Dyer (2001) has this advice:

- Be yourself and relate person to person.
- Be ready to listen again and again.
- Be respectful.
- Be aware of feelings and nonverbal cues.

Thanatologist A specialist who studies emotional and behavioral reactions to death and dying.

CRITICAL THINKING

Near-Death Experiences—Back from the Brink

Emergency room doctors work feverishly over a heart attack victim. "I think we've lost him," says one of the doctors. The patient, who appears to have died, hears the doctor's words, then a buzzing sound. From somewhere above, he sees his own lifeless body on the table. Then he enters a dark tunnel and passes into an area of bright light. There, he is met by a "being of light" who shows him a rapid playback of his entire life. At some point he reaches a barrier. He is completely at peace and feels engulfed by love, but he knows he must go back. Suddenly, he is in his body again. One of the doctors exclaims, "Look, his heart's beating!" The patient recovers. For the rest of his life, he is profoundly affected by his journey to the threshold of death and back.

The preceding description contains all the core elements of a **near-death experience (NDE)** (a pattern of experiences that may occur when a person is clinically dead and then resuscitated). During an NDE, people typically experience all or most of the following: feeling separated from their bodies, entering darkness or a tunnel, seeing a light, entering the light, a life review, and feeling at peace (Lester, 2000; Morris & Knafl, 2003). Nevertheless, NDEs can vary greatly from person to person and are affected by cultural beliefs (Knoblauch, Schmied, & Schnettler, 2001; McClenon, 2005).

Many people regard NDEs as spiritual experiences that seem to verify the existence of an afterlife. In contrast, medical explanations attribute NDEs to the physiological reactions of an oxygen-starved brain (● Figure 4.10). Indeed, many elements of NDEs can be produced by other conditions, such as hallucinogenic drugs, migraine headaches, general anesthetics, insulin shock, extreme fatigue, high fever, or just falling asleep (Blackmore, 2005; Wettach, 2000). Likewise, researchers recently found an area in the brain that produces out-of-body experiences when it is stimulated (Blanke et al., 2004).

Regardless of the ultimate meaning of NDEs, near-death experiences can profoundly change personality and life goals (Morris & Knafl, 2003). Many near-death survivors claim that they are no longer motivated by greed, competition, or material success. Instead, they become more concerned about the needs of other people (Kinnier et al., 2001). As many near-death survivors have learned, death can be an excellent yardstick for measuring what is really important in life.

● **Figure 4.10** Visual sensations in the form of a tunnel of light or a spiral can be induced by many conditions other than near-death experiences. Such patterns appear to be related to activity in the visual cortex of the brain—especially activities that occur when the brain is deprived of oxygen (Blackmore, 2005).

- Be comfortable with silence.
- Be genuine.
- Most of all, be there.

Emotional reactions to impending death tell us little about what it is actually like to die. As you will soon discover, however, many people have "died" and then lived to tell about it. See "Near-Death Experiences" for information about some very close encounters with death.

Bereavement and Grief

Typically, a period of grief follows **bereavement** (the loss of a friend or relative to death). **Grief** (intense sorrow and distress) is a natural and normal reaction as survivors adjust to their loss. Bereavement can make a person feel vulnerable or worthless. It typically changes one's views of the world and the future. Understandably, there's a lot to work through emotionally when you lose someone you love (Gluhoski, 1995).

Grief tends to follow a predictable pattern (Parkes, 1979; Schulz, 1978). Grief usually begins with a period of *shock* or emotional numbness. For a brief time the bereaved remain in a dazed state in which they may show little emotion. Most find it extremely difficult to accept the reality of their loss. This phase usually ends by the time of the funeral, which unleashes tears and bottled-up feelings of despair.

Initial shock is followed by sharp *pangs of grief*. These are episodes of painful yearning for the dead person and, sometimes, anguished outbursts of anger. During this period the wish to have the dead person back is intense. Often, mourners continue to think of the dead person as alive. They may hear his or her voice and see the deceased vividly in dreams. For some time, agitated distress alternates with silent despair, and suffering is acute.

The first powerful reactions of grief gradually give way to weeks or months of *apathy* (listlessness), *dejection* (demoralization), and *depression* (deep despondency). The person faces a new emotional landscape with a large gap that cannot be filled. Life seems to lose

Craig Aurness/Corbis

As cultural rituals, funerals and memorial services are rites of separation and leave-taking. Funerals encourage a release of emotion and provide a sense of closure for survivors, who must come to terms with the death of a loved one (Morgan, 1995).

much of its meaning, and a sense of futility dominates. The mourner is usually able to resume work or other activities after 2 or 3 weeks. However, insomnia, loss of energy and appetite, and similar signs of depression may continue.

Little by little, the bereaved person accepts what cannot be changed and makes a new beginning. Pangs of grief may still occur, but they are less severe and less frequent. Memories of the dead person, though still painful, now include positive images and nostalgic pleasure. At this point, the person can be said to be moving toward *resolution* (acceptance and rebuilding). For many people, the pain of grieving will have eased considerably by the end of about 1 year (Lindstrom, 1995). However, it is not unusual for 2 to 3 years to pass before grief is fully resolved. At a lower level of intensity, mourning the loss of someone you love can continue indefinitely (Rando, 1995).

As was true of approaching death, individual reactions to grief vary considerably. The amount of pain a person feels depends on his or her personality, the relationship to the deceased, the nature of the death (was it natural, a homicide, suicide, peaceful, agonized?), and the bereaved person's social situation—especially the amount of support she or he receives from others (Rando, 1995).

Is it true that suppressing grief leads to more problems later? It has long been assumed that suppressing grief may later lead to more severe and lasting depression. However, there is little evidence to support this idea. A lack of intense grief does not usually predict later problems. In fact, some people do better if they restrict their emotions and upsetting thoughts after the death of a loved one (Lindstrom, 2002). Bereaved persons should work through their grief at their own pace and in their own way—without worrying about whether they are grieving too much or too little (Stroebe et al., 2002). Time doesn't heal all wounds, but with the passage of time the pain of loss does lessen. Some additional suggestions for coping with grief follow.

Coping with Grief

- Acknowledge and accept that the person is gone.
- Face the loss directly and do not isolate yourself.
- Discuss your feelings with relatives and friends.
- Do not block out your feelings with drugs or alcohol.
- Allow grief to progress naturally; neither hurry nor suppress it.
- Honor the memory of the deceased, but accept the need to rebuild your life. (Coni et al., 1984; Rando, 1995)

A Look Ahead

The subject of death brings us full circle in the cycle of life. In the upcoming Psychology in Action section, we will probe the question, "What makes a good life?" But first, it's time for a study break.

KNOWLEDGE BUILDER

Death and Dying

REFLECT

Briefly summarize your beliefs about death. Which concepts in the preceding discussion confirm your prior thoughts? Which contradict them? Can you summarize the typical reactions to impending death? What can you learn from the near-death experiences of others?

LEARNING CHECK

1. In the reaction that Kübler-Ross describes as bargaining, the dying individual asks, "Why me?" T or F?
2. A dazed state of shock or numbness is typical of the first phase of grief. T or F?
3. Near-death experiences provide clear evidence for the existence of an afterlife. T or F?
4. Most evidence supports the idea that suppressing grief leads to later problems, such as severe depression. T or F?

CRITICAL THINKING

5. Why do you think it is best not to think of Kübler-Ross's list as a fixed series of stages to go through in order?

Answers: 1. F **2.** T **3.** F **4.** F **5.** When Kübler-Ross's observations were first published, nurses sometimes chastised dying patients for "being in the wrong stage" or "not progressing quickly enough" to the next stage. Also, some dying individuals felt guilty because they hadn't "achieved acceptance." Obviously, these examples represent a serious misunderstanding of the emotional reactions to dying that Kübler-Ross noted.

Near-death experience (NDE) A pattern of subjective experiences that may occur when a person is clinically dead and then resuscitated.

Bereavement Period of emotional adjustment that follows the death of a loved one.

Grief An intense emotional state that follows the death of a lover, friend, or relative.

PSYCHOLOGY IN ACTION

Well-Being and Happiness—What Makes a Good Life?

What makes you happy? Love? Money? Music? Sports? Partying? Religion? Clearly, there is no simple, universal formula for happiness. And what does it mean to have a good life? Is it a matter of health? Achievement? Friendship? Leisure? Personal growth? Again, there are no simple answers. Both happiness and living a "good life" depend greatly on individual needs and cultural values. Nevertheless, psychologists are beginning to understand some aspects of what it means to be happy and live well. Their findings provide valuable hints about how to live a successful life.

Happiness

Most people want to be happy. But what does that mean? To study happiness, psychologist Ed Diener and his associates have focused on what they call **subjective well-being.** According to them, feelings of well-being, or happiness, occur when people are satisfied with their lives, have frequent positive emotions, and have relatively few negative emotions (Diener et al., 1999).

Life Satisfaction

What does life satisfaction refer to? You are high in life satisfaction if you strongly agree with the following statements (from the "Satisfaction with Life Scale," Pavot & Diener, 1993):

- In most ways my life is close to my ideal.
- The conditions of my life are excellent.
- I am satisfied with my life.
- So far I have gotten the important things I want in life.
- If I could live my life over, I would change almost nothing.

These statements seem to cover a lot of what it means to be happy. However, Dienster and his colleagues believe day-to-day emotional experiences are also important.

Emotions

Imagine that several pleasant or rewarding events have occurred today. These events caused you to experience moments of laughter, joy, delight, and satisfaction. As a result, you feel happy and life seems good. In contrast, imagine that your day was marred by a series of unpleasant or punishing events, which left you feeling sad. In reality, of course, we rarely have entirely good or bad days. Life is a mixture of rewarding and punishing events, so everyone feels both positive and negative emotions. It's possible for the same person to have lots of positive feelings *and* lots of negative feelings. That's why happiness is not just a matter of having good feelings. The happiest people are those who have many positive emotional experiences and relatively few negative experiences (Diener et al., 1999).

Life Events

Then do good and bad events in life dictate whether a person is happy? Happiness is related to good and bad life events, but the impact is smaller than you might imagine. The reason for this is that happiness tends to come from within a person. Subjective well-being is affected by our goals, choices, emotions, values, and personality. The way you perceive, interpret, and manage events is as important as the nature of the events themselves. People who are good at dodging life's hard knocks tend to create their own "luck." As a result, they are happier and seem to negotiate life's demands more smoothly (Eronen & Nurmi, 1999).

Esbin/Anderson/The Image Works

Personal Factors

What about factors such as income, age, or marital status? Are they related to happiness? Personal characteristics have only a small connection with overall happiness. Let's see why.

Wealth

It is tempting to think that wealth brings happiness. But does it? To a small degree wealthier people are happier than poorer people. However, the overall association between money and happiness is weak. In fact, people who win lotteries are often *less* happy than they were before. Instant riches usually bring new stresses into a person's life that tend to cancel out any positive effects of wealth. In short, money may make it possible to buy the good things in life, but money can't buy a good life. Happiness usually must come from other sources (King & Napa, 1998).

Education

More-educated people tend to be a little happier than the less educated. However, this is most likely just another way of saying that there is a small connection between wealth and happiness. Higher education generally results in higher income and more social status.

Marriage

Married people report greater happiness than people who are divorced, separated, or single. It could be that happier people are simply more likely to get married. But a better explanation for this association is that happy people are more likely to get married and stay married. Most people get a small boost in happiness immediately after getting married. However, most eventually return to about the same level of happiness they had before they tied the knot (Lucas et al., 2003).

Religion

There is a small but positive association between happiness and holding spiritual beliefs. Religious beliefs may add to feelings of purpose and meaning in life, resulting in greater happiness. Another possibility is that church membership may simply provide social support that softens the impact of life's negative events.

Age

The stereotype of the crotchety old person who is dissatisfied with everything is inaccurate. Life satisfaction and happiness generally *do not* decline with age. People are living longer and staying healthier, which has greatly delayed age-related declines. When declines do occur, older people today seem better able to cope with them.

Sex

Overall, men and women do not differ in happiness. However, women do have a tendency to experience higher emotional highs and lower lows than men do. Thus, more women are found among those rare individuals who are extremely happy or unhappy.

Work

People who are satisfied with their jobs tend to be happier, but the association is weak. If fact, it probably just reflects the fact that job satisfaction is a large part of greater life satisfaction.

Personality

With respect to happiness and personality, it may be fair to paraphrase the movie character Forest Gump and say, "Happy is as happy does." To a degree, some people are more temperamentally disposed to be happy, regardless of life events. In general, happier people also tend to be extraverted (outgoing), optimistic, and worry-free. This combination probably influences the balance of positive and negative emotions a person feels (Diener et al., 1999).

Goals and Happiness

The preceding account gives some insight into who is happy, but we can learn more by examining people's goals. To know if someone is happy, it is helpful to ask, "What is this person trying to do in life? How well is she or he succeeding at it?"

Do you want to be healthy and physically fit? To do well in school? To be liked by friends? To own a shopping mall? A Ferrari? The goals people choose vary widely. Nevertheless, one generalization we can make is that people tend to be happy if they are meeting their personal goals. This is especially true if you feel you are making progress, on a day-to-day basis, on smaller goals that relate to long-term, life goals (King, Richards, & Stemmerich, 1998; McGregor & Little, 1998).

The importance of personal goals helps explain why specific circumstances tell us so little about happiness. It is often difficult to know if an event is good or bad without knowing what a person is trying to achieve in life (Diener et al., 1999).

It seems that people who attain their goals are sometimes no happier than before. If making progress toward one's goals brings happiness, how could that be?

Meaning and Integrity

Canadian psychologists Ian McGregor and Brian Little believe they can explain why achieving one's goals doesn't always lead to happiness. Consider the highly successful person who is absorbed in his or her accomplishments. All it may take is a crisis, like a child's illness or the death of a friend, to make life feel meaningless. But meaning can be restored and the crisis resolved if the person begins to act with integrity. Thus, McGregor and Little believe that optimal human functioning involves integrity as well as an ability to accomplish goals. "Doing well," they say, is associated with happiness. In contrast, "being yourself" is associated with leading a meaningful life. In short, the goals we pursue must express our core interests and values if we are to live with integrity (McGregor & Little, 1998).

McGregor and Little give examples of the kinds of "personal projects" (short-term goals) and long-term goals that occupy us: "finish my calculus assignment," "help the poor," "take a trip to Florida," "lose weight," "earn an M.A. in psychology," "play professional hockey," "become a police officer with investments in property and live comfortably." Among a welter of possibilities such as these, the question becomes, "To what extent does this project feel distinctly like me—like a personal trademark, as opposed to something alien or imposed?" Such goals are crucial because overall well-being is a combination of happiness and meaning. Pursuing goals that are inconsistent with personal interests and values can leave a person feeling uneasy, bothered, and uncomfortable (McGregor & Little, 1998).

Conclusion

In summary, happier persons tend to be married, comfortable with their work, extraverted, religious, optimistic, and generally satisfied with their lives. They also are making progress toward their goals (Diener et al., 1999). However, attaining goals that do not express our deeper interests and values may add little to happiness (Sheldon & Elliot, 1999).

What, then, makes a good life? Earlier in this chapter we noted that purpose and meaning are important sources of well-being at midlife (Ryff, 1995). Actually, this appears to be true at any point in life. As we have seen, a good life is one that is happy *and* meaningful (Emmons, 2003).

We are most likely to experience a meaningful life when we act with integrity. It's interesting that this agrees with Erikson's analysis at the beginning of this chapter. Although achievement and external goals may preoccupy younger persons, integrity becomes increasingly important later in life (McGregor & Little, 1998).

"To thine own self be true" may seem like a cliché, but it's actually not a bad place to begin a search for a happy and satisfying life.

Subjective well-being General life satisfaction combined with frequent positive emotions and relatively few negative emotions.

KNOWLEDGE BUILDER

Well-Being and Happiness

REFLECT

How do you think you would rate on each of the three components of subjective well-being? What other factors discussed in this section are related to your own level of happiness?

It is common for students to pursue goals and personal projects that are imposed on them. Which of your activities do you regard as most meaningful? How do they relate to your personal beliefs and values?

LEARNING CHECK

1. Subjective well-being consists of a mixture of ________________ ________________, positive emotions, and negative emotions.
2. People who experience many positive emotions are, by definition, very happy. T or F?
3. Happiness has only a small positive correlation with wealth. T or F?
4. Single persons are generally happier than those who are married. T or F?
5. Making progress day by day toward important ____________ ____________ is a major source of happiness.

CRITICAL THINKING

6. Under what circumstances would you expect having money to be more strongly associated with happiness?

Answers: **1.** life satisfaction **2.** F **3.** T **4.** F **5.** life goals **6.** In poorer countries, where life can be harsh, the association between material wealth and happiness is stronger than it is in North America.

Chapter in Review

What are the typical tasks and dilemmas through the life span?

- Life-span psychologists study continuity and change in behavior from birth to death.
- According to Erikson, each life stage provokes a specific psychosocial dilemma.
- In addition to the dilemmas identified by Erikson, we recognize that each life stage requires successful mastery of certain developmental tasks.

What are some of the more serious childhood problems?

- Few children grow up without experiencing some of the normal problems of childhood, including negativism, clinging, specific fears, sleep disturbances, general dissatisfaction, regression, sibling rivalry, and rebellion.
- Major areas of difficulty in childhood are toilet training (including enuresis and encopresis); feeding disturbances, such as overeating, anorexia nervosa (self-starvation), and pica (eating nonfood substances); speech disturbances (delayed speech, stuttering); learning disorders, including dyslexia; attention-deficit/hyperactivity disorder; conduct disorder; and other problems.
- Childhood autism is representative of some of the more severe problems that can occur. Some cases of autism are being treated successfully with behavior modification.
- Child abuse is a major problem for which few solutions currently exist. Roughly 30 percent of all abused children become abusive adults. Emotional support and therapy appear to help break the cycle of abuse.

Why is adolescent development especially challenging?

- Adolescence is a culturally defined social status. Puberty is a biological event.
- Early maturation is beneficial mostly for boys; its effects are mixed for girls. One danger of early maturation is premature identity formation.
- Adolescent identity formation is accelerated by cognitive development and influenced by parents and peer groups.

How do we develop morals and values?

- Lawrence Kohlberg theorized that moral development passes through a series of stages revealed by moral reasoning.
- Kohlberg identified preconventional, conventional, and postconventional levels of morality.
- Kohlberg emphasized a morality of justice. Adults appear to base moral choices on either justice or caring, depending on the situation.
- People in some cultures may prefer to use justice as the primary standard for making moral choices; in other cultures a morality of caring is preferred.

What happens psychologically during adulthood?

- Certain relatively consistent events mark adult development in Western societies. These range from escaping parental dominance in the late teens to a noticeable acceptance of one's lot in life during the fifties.
- A midlife crisis affects some people in the 37 to 41 age range, but this is by no means universal. Even if no crisis occurs, people tend to move through repeated cycles of stability and transition throughout adulthood.
- Adjustment to later middle age can be complicated for women by menopause. To a lesser degree, some men may experience a climacteric.
- Well-being during adulthood consists of six elements: self-acceptance, positive relations with others, autonomy, environmental mastery, having a purpose in life, and continued personal growth.

What are the psychological challenges of aging?

- Both the number and the proportion of older people in the population has grown.
- Biological aging begins between 25 and 30, but peak performance in specific pursuits may come at various points throughout life.
- Intellectual declines associated with aging are limited, at least through one's seventies. This is especially true of individuals who remain mentally active.
- With regard to successful aging, disengagement theory holds that withdrawal from society is necessary and desirable in old age. Activity theory counters that optimal adjustment to aging is tied to continuing activity and involvement. There is an element of truth to each, but activity theory applies to more people.
- The best adaptation to aging is based on selection, optimization, and compensation, which together allow people to continue to perform tasks well.
- Ageism refers to prejudice, discrimination, and stereotyping on the basis of age. It affects people of all ages but is especially damaging to older people. Most ageism is based on stereotypes, myths, and misinformation.

How do people typically react to death and bereavement?

- Typical emotional reactions to impending death are denial, anger, bargaining, depression, and acceptance.
- Near-death experiences frequently result in significant changes in personality, values, and life goals.
- Bereavement also brings forth a typical series of grief reactions, ranging from shock to final acceptance.

What factors contribute most to a happy and fulfilling life?

- Subjective well-being (happiness) is a combination of general life satisfaction, plus more positive emotions than negative emotions.
- Life events and various demographic factors have relatively little influence on happiness.
- People with extraverted (outgoing), optimistic, and worry-free personalities tend to be happier.
- Making progress toward one's goals is associated with happiness.
- Overall well-being is a combination of happiness and meaning in life, which comes from pursuing goals that have integrity (they express one's deeper interests and values).

Where to Write for Information

Anorexia Nervosa National Association of Anorexia Nervosa and Associated Disorders, Box 271, Highland Park, IL 60035.

Autism The National Society for Autistic Children, 101 Richmond St., Huntington, WV 25701, or Autism Society of America, Suite C1017, 1234 Massachusetts Ave. NW, Washington, DC 20005.

Child Abuse Parents Anonymous, call toll-free, (800) 421-0353, to find local chapters, or call the National Child Abuse Hot Line, toll-free, (800) 422-4453.

Hospice The National Hospice Organization, 1901 North Ft. Meyer Drive, Arlington, VA 22180.

Hyperactivity Department of Health, Education, and Welfare, Office of the Secretary, Secretary's Committee on Mental Retardation, Washington, DC 20201.

Learning Disorders National Association for Children with Learning Disabilities, 5225 Grace St., Pittsburgh, PA 15236.

Living Will Society for the Right to Die, 250 West 57th St., New York, NY 10107.

Web Resources

Internet addresses frequently change. To find the sites listed here, visit www.thomsonedu.com/psychology/coon for an updated list of Internet addresses and direct links to relevant sites.

***Psychology: Gateways to Mind and Behavior* Website** Online quizzes, flash cards, and other helpful study aids for this text. www.thomsonedu.com/psychology/coon

Alzheimer's Association Has many links to material on Alzheimer's disease.

Mental Health Risk Factors for Adolescents Links to resources concerning eating disorders, drug abuse, suicide, and other topics.

MIDMAC Reports on a major study of middle age.

The AARP Webplace Home page of the American Association of Retired Persons.

Webster's Death, Dying, and Grief Guide An index to sites on death, dying, and grief.

What Works for Girls A summary of research about what contributes positively to healthy development.

ThomsonNOW™ Go to www.thomsonedu.com to link to ThomsonNow, your online study tool. First take the **Pre-Test** for this chapter to get your **Personalized Study Plan,** which will identify topics you need to review and direct you to online resources. Then take the **Post-Test** to determine what concepts you have mastered and what you still need work on.

InfoTrac College Edition For recent articles related to maltreatment of children, use Key Words search for CHILD ABUSE. Go to www.thomsonedu.com/psychology/coon.

Interactive Learning

***PsychNow! Version 2.0* CD-ROM** Interact with the material with *PsychNow!'s* animations, video clips, experiments, and interactive assessments. For this chapter, go to *2c. Adolescent Development* and *2d. Adult Development, Aging, and Death* to get a better understanding of adolescent and adult development.

chapter

5

Sensation and Reality

Douglas Kirkland/Corbis

THEME:

Sensory systems link us to the external world and shape the flow of information to the brain.

Key Questions

In general, how do sensory systems function?

What are the limits of our sensory sensitivity?

How is vision accomplished?

How do we perceive colors?

What are the mechanisms of hearing?

How do the chemical senses operate?

What are the somesthetic senses and why are they important?

Why are we more aware of some sensations than others?

How can pain be reduced in everyday situations?

Preview

Sensation—A Window on the World

At this very moment you are bathed in a swirling kaleidoscope of light, heat, pressure, vibrations, molecules, radiation, and mechanical forces. Without the senses, all of this would seem like nothing more than a void of darkness and silence. The next time you drink in the beauty of a sunset, a flower, or a friend, remember this: Sensation makes it all possible.

What would the world be like if new senses could be added—if we could "see" gamma rays, "hear" changes in barometric pressure, or "taste" light? We can only guess. It is far easier to imagine losing or regaining a sensory system. Consider the words of Bob Edens, who had his sight restored at age 51 after being blind since birth:

> I never would have dreamed that yellow is so . . . so yellow. I don't have the words, I'm amazed by yellow. But red is my favorite color. I just can't believe red. I can't wait to get up each day to see what I can see. I saw some bees the other day, and they were magnificent. I saw a truck drive by in the rain and throw a spray in the air. It was marvelous. And did I mention, I saw a falling leaf just drifting through the air?

If you are ever tempted to take sensory impressions for granted, remember Bob Edens. As his words show, sensation is our window on the world. All our meaningful behavior, our awareness of physical reality, and our ideas about the universe ultimately spring from the senses. It may be no exaggeration then, to claim that this chapter is quite . . . "sensational."

General Properties of Sensory Systems—What You See Is What You Get

Vision gives us amazingly wide access to the world. In one instant you can view a star light-years away, and in the next you can peer into the microscopic universe of a dewdrop. Yet vision also narrows what we observe. Like the other senses, vision acts as a *data reduction system*. It selects, analyzes, and filters information until only the most important data remain (Sekuler & Blake, 2006).

How does data reduction take place? Some selection occurs because sensory receptors are biological transducers. A *transducer* is a device that converts one kind of energy into another. For example, an electric guitar converts string vibrations into electrical signals, which are amplified and fed to a speaker. Pluck a string and the speaker will blast out sound. However, stimuli that don't cause the string to move will have no effect. For instance, if you shine a light on the string, or pour cold water on it, the speaker will remain silent. (The owner of the guitar, however, might get quite loud at this point!) Similarly, each sensory organ is most sensitive to a select type and range of energy that it converts to nerve impulses. For instance, visible light is just a small slice of the *electromagnetic spectrum* (entire spread of electromagnetic wavelengths). The spectrum also includes infrared and ultraviolet light, radio waves, television broadcasts, gamma rays, and other energies (look ahead at ● Figure 5.3). If your eyes weren't limited in sensitivity, you would "see" a disorienting jumble of different energies.

Sensory Analysis and Coding

What we experience is greatly influenced by **sensory analysis.** As they process information, the senses divide the world into important **perceptual features** (basic stimulus patterns). For vision, such features include lines, shapes, edges, spots, colors, and other patterns. Look at ● Figure 5.1 and notice how eye-catching the single vertical line is among a group of slanted lines. This effect, which is called *pop-out,* occurs because your visual system is highly sensitive to perceptual features (Ramachandran, 1992).

In some instances, the senses act as *feature detectors* because they are attuned to very specific stimuli. Frog eyes, for example, are highly sensitive to small, dark, moving spots. In other words, they are basically "tuned" to detect bugs flying nearby (Lettvin, 1961). But the insect (spot) must be moving, or the frog's "bug detectors" won't work. A frog could starve to death surrounded by dead flies.

After they have selected and analyzed information, sensory systems must *code* it. **Sensory coding** refers to changing important features of the world into messages understood by the brain (Hubel & Wiesel, 1979). To see coding at work, try closing your eyes for a moment. Then take your fingertips and press firmly on your eyelids. Apply enough pressure to "squash" your eyes slightly. Do this for about 30 seconds and observe what happens. (Readers with eye problems or contact lenses should not try this.)

Did you "see" stars, checkerboards, and flashes of color? These are called *phosphenes* (FOSS-feens: visual sensations caused by mechanical excitation of the retina). They occur because the eye's

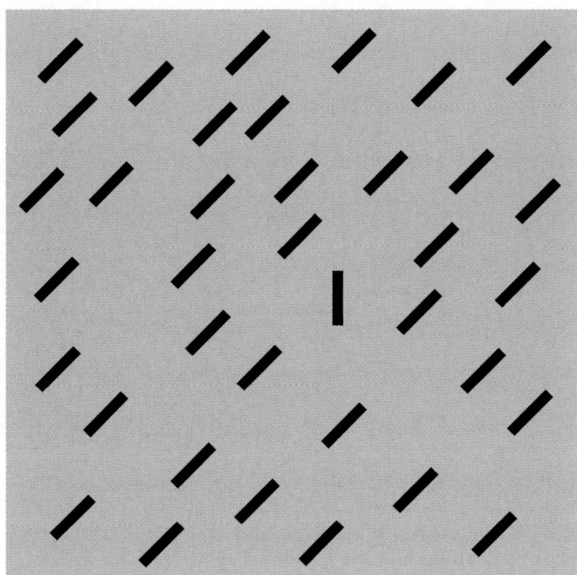

Figure 5.1 Visual pop-out (adapted from Ramachandran, 1992). Pop-out is so basic that babies as young as 3 months respond to it (Quinn & Bhatt, 1998).

sensations you are feeling. Sensory localization may someday make it possible to artificially restore sight, hearing, or other senses. In fact, researchers have already used a miniature television camera to send electrical signals to the brain (Dobelle, 2000; Normann et al., 1999). As you can see in ● Figure 5.2, a grid of tiny electrodes stimulates the visual cortex. One man who has an implant of this type can "see" 100 dots of light. Like a sports scoreboard, these lights can be used to form crude letters (Dobelle, 2000). Eventually, a larger number of dots could make reading, and "seeing" large objects, such as furniture and doorways, possible (Normann et al., 1999).

It is fascinating to realize that "seeing" and "hearing" take place in the brain, not in the eye or ear. Information arriving from the sense organs creates **sensations.** When the brain organizes sensations into meaningful patterns, we speak of **perception**, which will be covered in Chapter 6. In a moment you will learn how each of the senses operates. But first, let's explore a little more. How sensitive are we to our "sensational" world?

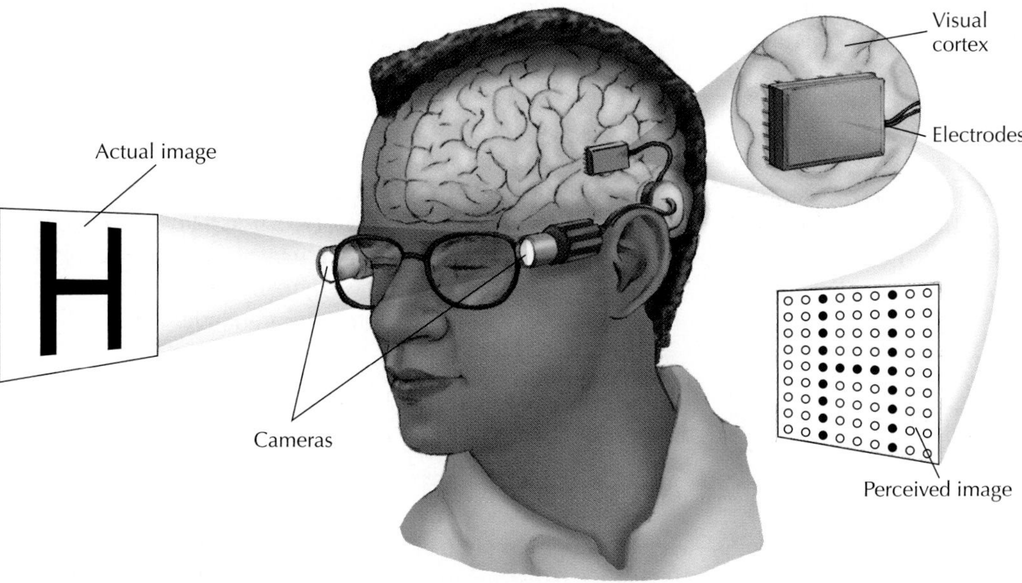

Figure 5.2 An artificial visual system.

receptor cells, which normally respond to light, are also somewhat sensitive to pressure. Notice though, that the eye is only prepared to code stimulation—including pressure—into visual features. As a result, you experience light sensations, not pressure. Also important in producing this effect is *sensory localization* in the brain.

Sensory localization means that the type of sensation you experience depends on which brain area is activated. Some brain areas receive visual information, others receive auditory information, and still others receive taste or touch (see Chapter 2). Knowing which brain areas are active tells us, in general, what kinds of

Sensory analysis Separation of sensory information into important elements.

Perceptual features Basic elements of a stimulus, such as lines, shapes, edges, or colors.

Sensory coding Codes used by the sense organs to transmit information to the brain.

Sensation The immediate response in the brain caused by excitation of a sensory organ.

Perception The mental process of organizing sensations into meaningful patterns.

Psychophysics—Life at the Limit

What is the quietest sound that can be heard? The weakest light that can be seen? The lightest touch that can be felt? The sense organs are our link to reality. What are their limits? In an approach called **psychophysics,** physical stimuli are measured and related to dimensions of the sensations we experience, such as loudness, brightness, or taste. A basic question psychophysics asks is, "What is the minimum amount of energy necessary for a sensation to occur?" The answer defines the **absolute threshold** for a sensory system.

Testing for absolute thresholds shows just how sensitive we are. For example, it only takes three photons of light striking the retina of the eye to produce a sensation. A photon (FOE-tahn: one quantum of energy) is the smallest possible "package" of light. Responding to three photons is like seeing a candle flame 30 miles away! ■ Table 5.1 gives approximate absolute thresholds for the five major senses.

Some sensory systems have upper limits as well as lower ones. For example, if we test for pitch sensitivity (higher and lower tones), we find that humans can hear sounds down to 20 hertz (vibrations per second) and up to about 20,000 hertz. This is an impressive range—from the lowest rumble of a pipe organ to the highest squeak of a stereo "tweeter." On the lower end, the threshold is as low as practical. If your ears could sense tones below 20 hertz, you would hear the movements of your own muscles. Imagine how disturbing it would be to hear your body creak and groan like an old ship as you move.

The 20,000 hertz upper threshold for human hearing, on the other hand, could easily be higher. Dogs, bats, cats, and other animals can hear sounds well above this limit. That's why a "silent" dog whistle (which may make sounds as high as 40,000 to 50,000 hertz) can be heard by dogs but not by humans. For dogs, the sound exists. For humans it is beyond awareness. It's easy to see how thresholds define the limits of the sensory world in which we live. (If you want to buy a stereo system for your dog, you will have a hard time finding one that reproduces sounds above 20,000 hertz!)

TABLE 5.1

Absolute Thresholds

SENSORY MODALITY	ABSOLUTE THRESHOLD
Vision	Candle flame seen at 30 miles on a clear dark night
Hearing	Tick of a watch under quiet conditions at 20 feet
Taste	1 teaspoon of sugar in 2 gallons of water
Smell	1 drop of perfume diffused into a three-room apartment
Touch	A bee's wing falling on your cheek from 1 centimeter above

From Galanter, 1962

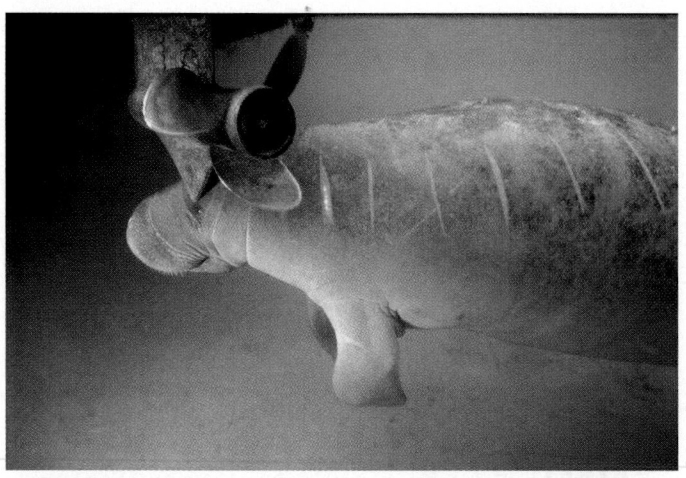

Absolute thresholds define the sensory worlds of humans and animals, sometimes with serious consequences. The endangered Florida manatee ("sea cow") is a peaceful, plant-eating creature that can live for more than 60 years. For the last decade, the number of manatees killed by boats has climbed alarmingly. The problem? Manatees have poor sensitivity to the low-frequency sounds made by slow-moving boats. Current laws require boats to slow down in manatee habitats, which may actually increase the risk to these gentle giants (Gerstein, 2002).

Difference Thresholds

Psychophysics also involves the study of **difference thresholds.** Here we are asking, "How much must a stimulus change (increase or decrease) before it becomes just noticeably different?" The study of **just noticeable differences (JNDs)** led to one of psychology's first natural "laws." **Weber's** (VAY-bears) **law** can be roughly stated as follows: The amount of change needed to produce a JND is a constant proportion of the original stimulus intensity. Here are some Weber's proportions for common judgments:

Pitch	1/333 (1/3 of 1 percent)
Weight	1/50 (2 percent)
Loudness	1/10 (10 percent)
Taste	1/5 (20 percent)

Notice how much more sensitive hearing is than taste. Very small changes in pitch and loudness are easy to detect. If a voice or a musical instrument that is off pitch by 1/3 of 1 percent, you'll probably notice it. For taste, we find that a 20-percent change is necessary to produce a JND. If a cup of coffee has 5 teaspoons of sugar in it, you will have to add 1 more (1/5 of 5) before it will be noticeably sweeter. If you're salting soup, it takes a lot of cooks to spoil the broth!

Perceptual Defense and Subliminal Perception

Wouldn't the absolute threshold be different for different people? Not only do absolute thresholds vary for different people, they also change from time to time for a single person. The type of stimulus, the state of your nervous system, and the costs of false "detections" all make a difference. Emotional factors are also important.

CRITICAL THINKING

Subliminal Seduction or Subliminal Myths?

Could subliminal perception ever be used against us? The sensationalistic book *Subliminal Seduction* (Key, 1973) voiced popular fears of attempts to influence us through subliminal messages embedded in advertising. But could it work?

In a famous early attempt, a New Jersey theater flashed the words *Eat popcorn* and *Drink Coca-Cola* on the screen for 1/3,000 second every 5 seconds during movies. Dramatic claims that popcorn and Coke sales increased as a result later turned out to be falsehoods. The advertising "expert" responsible admitted he faked the whole thing. By lying about his ability to control audiences, he had hoped to gain customers for his marketing business (Pratkanis, 1992).

A more recent attempt at subliminal seduction provided a curious moment in the 2000 U.S. presidential campaign. A TV commercial criticizing Democratic candidate Al Gore's Medicare proposal included the word "RATS" flashed for 1/30 of a second across the phrase "The Gore prescription plan: Bureaucrats decide." Although Republican candidate George W. Bush made light of the situation, someone in the Bush campaign had clearly intended to use subliminal advertising to influence voters.

In an interesting twist, some businesses actually sell subliminal messages to people who want them to work. Each year, consumers spend millions of dollars on so-called subliminal self-help tapes and CDs. "Subliminal messages" embedded in relaxing music or the soothing sounds of ocean waves purportedly influence "subconscious motivation" to help listeners lose weight, relieve pain, find romance, succeed financially, improve grades, and so forth.

In one study, students who listened to subliminal messages meant to improve their study habits, and, hence, their grades, performed no better than students who just listened to relaxing ocean sounds without subliminal messages and students who listened to nothing at all (Russell, Rowe, & Smouse, 1991). Even when people want to be influenced by subliminal messages, they have no impact. People who think they have been helped by subliminal messages have experienced nothing more than a placebo effect (Froufe & Schwartz, 2001).

To summarize, there is evidence that, although subliminal perception can occur, subliminal stimuli are basically weak stimuli. But subliminal seduction turns out to be a subliminal myth. There is little evidence that subliminal messages can persuade us or greatly influence our behavior (Shrum, 2004; Trappey, 1996), even when we want them to. Advertisers are better off using the loudest, clearest, most attention-demanding stimuli available—as most do (Smith & Rogers, 1994).

Unpleasant stimuli, for example, may *raise* the threshold for recognition. This resistance to perceiving threatening or disturbing stimuli is called **perceptual defense.** It was first revealed in experiments on the perception of "dirty" and "clean" words (McGinnies, 1949). So-called dirty words such as "whore," "rape," "bitch," and "penis" were briefly flashed on a screen. Such words took longer to recognize than did "clean" words such as "wharf," "rope," "batch," and "pencil."

Couldn't it be that people wanted to be really sure they had seen a word like "penis" before saying it? Yes, especially in 1949! For years, psychologists worried about this and other flaws in the original experiment. But others have also found that perceptual defense occurs. For example, new mothers who are emotionally depressed take longer than nondepressed women to recognize pictures related to pregnancy, birth, and babies (David et al., 1990). Apparently, we process stimuli on more than one level. This allows us to resist information that causes anxiety, discomfort, or embarrassment (Mogg et al., 1993).

Is that "subliminal" perception? Basically, yes. Anytime information is processed below the normal *limen* (LIE-men: threshold or limit) for awareness, it is *subliminal.* **Subliminal perception** was demonstrated by a study in which college students saw photos of a person flashed on a screen. Each time before the face appeared, it was preceded by a subliminal image. Some were images that made viewers feel good (such as cute kittens). Others made them feel bad (for example, a face on fire). All of the emotional images were flashed too briefly to be recognized. Nevertheless, they altered the impressions students formed of the target person (Krosnick et al., 1992). Apparently, some emotional impact gets through, even when a stimulus is below the level of conscious awareness (Arndt, Allen, & Greenberg, 2001). To find out if such effects could be applied to advertising, read "Subliminal Seduction or Subliminal Myths?"

Psychophysics Study of the relationship between physical stimuli and the sensations they evoke in a human observer.

Absolute threshold The minimum amount of physical energy necessary to produce a sensation.

Difference threshold A change in stimulus intensity that is detectable to an observer.

Just noticeable difference (JND) Any noticeable difference in a stimulus.

Weber's law The just noticeable difference is a constant proportion of the original stimulus intensity.

Perceptual defense Resistance to perceiving threatening or disturbing stimuli.

Subliminal perception Perception of a stimulus below the threshold for conscious recognition.

It's now time to examine each of the senses in more detail. In the next section, we will begin with vision, which is perhaps the most magnificent sensory system of all. Before you read more, it might be a good idea to stop and review some of the ideas we have covered.

KNOWLEDGE BUILDER

Sensation and Psychophysics

REFLECT

How does sensation affect what you are experiencing right now? What if data reduction didn't occur? What if you could transduce other energies? What if your senses were tuned to detect different perceptual features? What if your absolute thresholds were higher or lower for each sense? How would the sensory world you live in change?

LEARNING CHECK

1. Sensory receptors are biological ________________, or devices for converting one type of energy to another.
2. Lettvin found that a frog's eyes are especially sensitive to phosphenes. T or F?
3. Important features of the environment are transmitted to the brain through a process known as
   a. phosphenation c. detection
   b. coding d. programming
4. The minimum amount of stimulation necessary for a sensation to occur defines the ________________________ __________ ________________.
5. A stimulus that causes discomfort or embarrassment may have to be viewed longer before it is perceived because of _______ ______________________ _______________________.
6. Subliminal stimuli have been shown to have a powerful effect on the behavior of viewers, especially when embedded in movies. T or F?

CRITICAL THINKING

7. Is a doorbell a transducer?
8. If the human ear were more sensitive than it is now, our hearing would be impaired. How could this be true?
9. Can you think of another way in which McGinnies's original experiment on perceptual defense was flawed?
10. When promoters of self-help "subliminal tapes" are challenged to provide evidence that their products work, what study do you think they most often cite?

Answers: 1. transducers **2.** F **3.** b **4.** absolute threshold **5.** perceptual defense **6.** F **7.** In a broad sense, it is. The button converts mechanical energy from your finger into an electrical signal that is converted again into mechanical energy in order to strike a bell; the physical vibrations of the bell then produce sound waves that are transduced into nerve impulses by the ears of the person in the house. **8.** Under ideal conditions, vibrations of the eardrum as small as one billionth of a centimeter (one tenth the diameter of a hydrogen atom) can be heard. Therefore, if your ears were more sensitive, they would convert the random movement of air molecules into a constant roaring or hissing noise. **9.** So-called clean words occur more frequently in everyday speech and writing. This alone could make them easier to recognize than "dirty" words. **10.** Good guess! That's right, it's the faked "Eat popcorn/drink Coca-Cola" study (Pratkanis, 1992).

Vision—Catching Some Rays

Because of vision's great importance, we will explore it in more detail than the other senses. Let's begin with the basic dimensions of light and vision. As we have noted, various wavelengths of light make up the **visible spectrum** (electromagnetic energies to which the eyes respond). Visible light starts at "short" wavelengths of 400 *nanometers* (nan-OM-et-er: one billionth of a meter), which we sense as purple or violet. Longer light waves produce blue, green, yellow, orange, and red, which has a wavelength of 700 nanometers (● Figure 5.3).

The term *hue* refers to the basic color categories of red, orange, yellow, green, blue, indigo, and violet. As just noted, various hues (or color sensations) correspond to the wavelength of the light that reaches our eyes. White light, in contrast, is a mixture of many wavelengths. Hues (colors) from a narrow band of wavelengths are very *saturated,* or "pure." (An intense "fire-engine" red is more saturated than a muddy "brick" red.) A third dimension of vision, *brightness,* corresponds roughly to the amplitude, or height, of light waves. Waves of greater amplitude are "taller," carry more energy, and cause the colors we see to appear brighter or more intense. For example, the same "brick" red would look bright under intense, high-energy illumination and drab under dim light.

Structure of the Eye

Is it true that the eye is like a camera? In some ways, it is. Both cameras and eyes have a *lens* to focus images on a light-sensitive layer at the back of a closed space. In a camera, this layer is the film. In the eye, it is a layer of *photoreceptors* (light-sensitive cells) in the **retina,** an area about the size and thickness of a postage stamp (● Figure 5.4).

How does the eye focus? Most focusing is done at the front of the eye by the *cornea,* a clear membrane that bends light inward. The lens makes additional, smaller adjustments. Your eye's focal point changes when muscles attached to the lens alter its shape. This process is called **accommodation.** In cameras, focusing is done more simply—by changing the distance between the lens and the film.

Visual Problems

Focusing is also affected by the shape of the eye. If your eye is too short, you won't be able to focus nearby objects but distant objects will be sharp. This is called **hyperopia** (HI-per-OPE-ee-ah: farsightedness). If your eyeball is too long, images fall short of the retina and you won't be able to focus distant objects. This results in **myopia** (my-OPE-ee-ah: nearsightedness). When the cornea or the lens is misshapen, part of vision will be focused and part will be fuzzy. In this case, the eye has more than one focal point, a problem called **astigmatism** (ah-STIG-mah-tiz-em). All three visual defects can be corrected by placing glasses (or contact lenses) in front of the eye to change the path of light (● Figure 5.5).

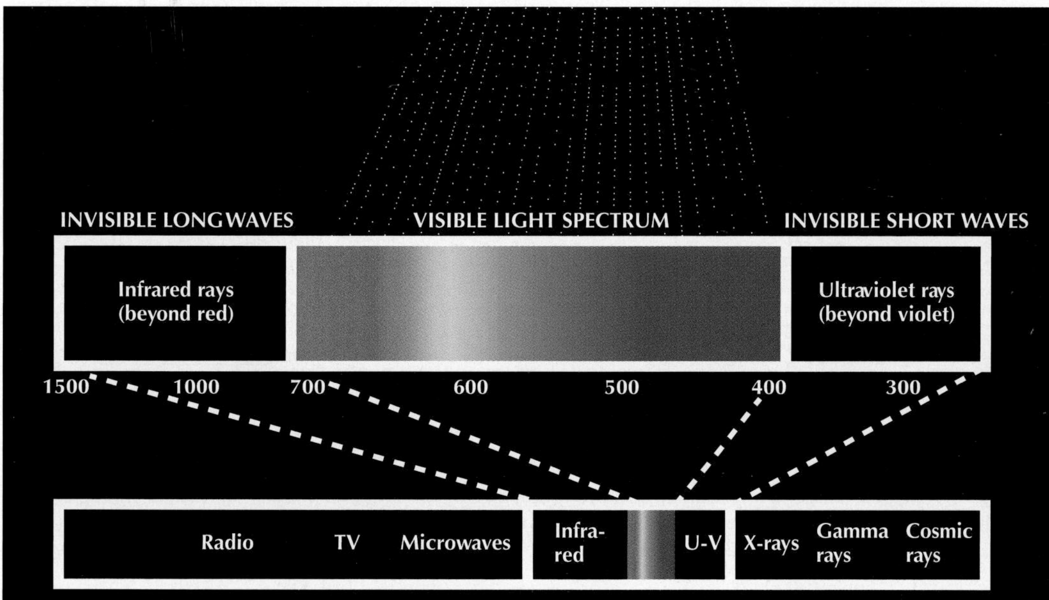

Figure 5.3 The visible spectrum.

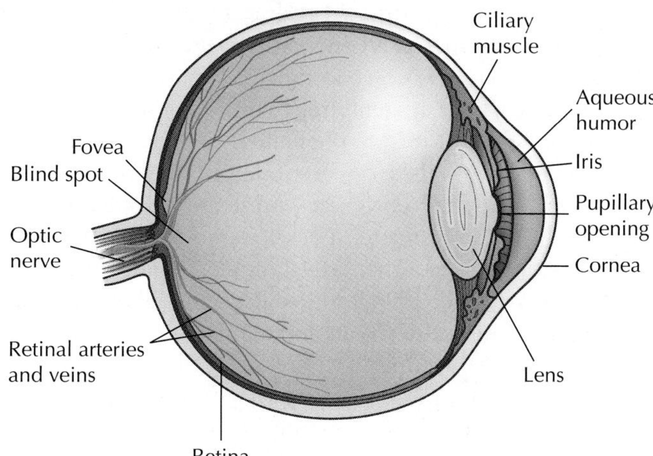

Figure 5.4 The human eye, a simplified view.

As people age, the lens becomes less flexible and less able to accommodate. The result is **presbyopia** (prez-bee-OPE-ee-ah: old vision, or farsightedness due to aging). Perhaps you have seen a grandparent or older friend reading a newspaper at arm's length because of presbyopia. If you now wear glasses for nearsightedness, you may need bifocals as you age. (Unless your arms grow longer in the meantime.) Bifocal lenses correct near vision *and* distance vision.

Light Control

There is one more major similarity between the eye and a camera. In front of the lens in both is a mechanism that controls the amount of light entering. In the eye, this mechanism is the *iris;* in a camera, it is the diaphragm (● Figure 5.6). The **iris** is a colored circular muscle that expands and contracts. As it does, it changes the size of the **pupil** (the opening at the center of the eye).

The retina can adapt to changing light conditions, but only slowly. By making rapid adjustments, the iris allows us to move quickly from darkness to bright sunlight, or the reverse. In dim light the pupils dilate (enlarge), and in bright light they constrict (narrow). When the iris is wide open, the pupil is 17 times larger than at its smallest. Were it not for this, you would be blinded for some time after walking into a darkened room.

Rods and Cones

Unlike a camera, the eye has two types of "film," consisting of receptor cells called *rods* and *cones*. The **cones**, numbering about 6.5 million in each eye, work best in bright light. They also produce color sensations and pick up fine details. In contrast, the **rods,**

Visible spectrum That part of the electromagnetic spectrum to which the eyes are sensitive.

Retina The light-sensitive layer of cells at the back of the eye.

Accommodation Changes in the shape of the lens of the eye.

Hyperopia Difficulty focusing nearby objects (farsightedness).

Myopia Difficulty focusing distant objects (nearsightedness).

Astigmatism Defects in the cornea, lens, or eye that cause some areas of vision to be out of focus.

Presbyopia Farsightedness caused by aging.

Iris Circular muscle that controls the amount of light entering the eye.

Pupil The opening at the front of the eye through which light passes.

Cones Visual receptors for colors and daylight visual acuity.

Rods Visual receptors for dim light that produce only black and white sensations.

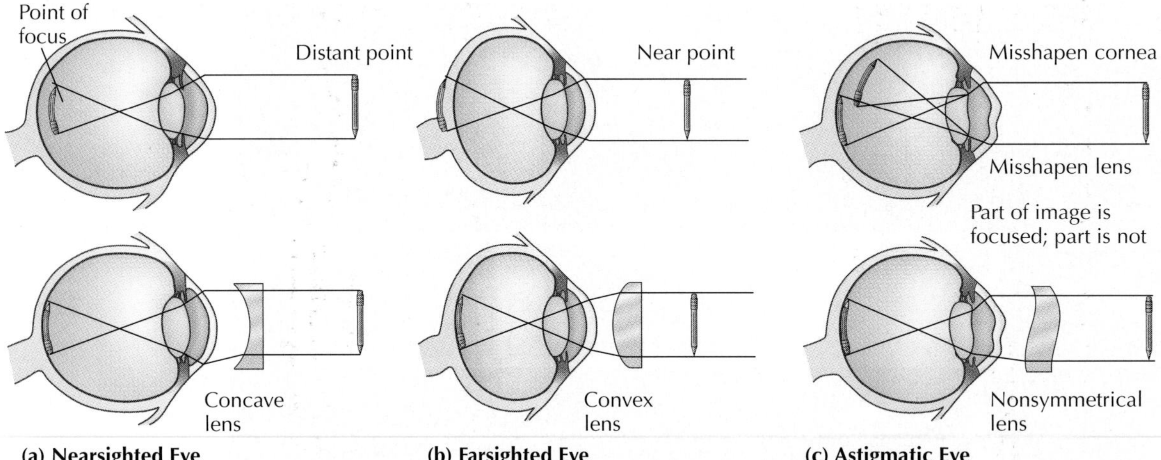

Figure 5.5 Visual defects and corrective lenses: *(a)* A myopic (longer than usual) eye. The concave lens spreads light rays just enough to increase the eye's focal length. *(b)* A hyperopic (shorter than usual) eye. The convex lens increases refraction (bending), returning the point of focus to the retina. *(c)* An astigmatic (lens or cornea not symmetrical) eye. In astigmatism, parts of vision are sharp and parts are unfocused. Lenses to correct astigmatism are unsymmetrical.

Figure 5.6 The iris and diaphragm.

numbering about 100 million, are unable to detect colors (● Figure 5.7). Pure rod vision is black and white. However, the rods are much more sensitive to light than the cones are. The rods therefore allow us to see in very dim light. Notice in ● Figure 5.7 that light does not fall directly on the rods and cones. It must pass through the outer layers of the retina. Note, too, that the rods and cones face the *back* of the eye! Only about one half of the light falling on the front of the eye ever reaches the rods and cones—testimony to the eye's amazing light sensitivity.

Surprisingly, the retina has a "hole" in it: Each eye has a **blind spot** because there are no receptors where the optic nerve leaves the eye (● Figure 5.8*a*). The blind spot shows that vision depends greatly on the brain. If you close one eye, part of what you see will fall on the blind spot of your open eye. Why isn't there a gap in your vision? The answer is that the visual cortex of the brain actively fills in the gap with patterns from surrounding areas (● Figure 5.8*b*). By closing one eye, you can visually "behead" other people by placing their images on your blind spot. (Just a hint for some classroom fun.) The brain can also "erase" distracting information. Roll your eyes all the way to the right and then close your right eye. You should clearly see your nose in your left eye's field of vision. Now, open your right eye again and your nose will nearly disappear as your brain disregards its presence.

From the retina on, vision becomes a complex system for analyzing patterns of light. It's tempting to think of vision as a movie-like projection of "pictures" to the brain. However, this mistaken notion immediately raises the question, "Who's watching the movie?" Thanks to the Nobel prize–winning work of biopsychologists David Hubel and Torsten Wiesel, we now know that vision acts more like a computer than a television or movie camera.

Hubel and Wiesel directly recorded the activities of single cells in the brain's visual cortex in cats and monkeys. As they did, they noted the area of the retina to which each cell responded. Then they aimed lights of various sizes and shapes at the retina and recorded how often the corresponding brain cell fired nerve impulses (● Figure 5.9).

The results were fascinating. Many brain cells responded only to lines of a certain width or orientation. These same cells didn't get the least bit "excited" over a dot of light or overall illumination. Other cells responded only to lines at certain angles, or lines of certain lengths, or lines moving in a particular direction (Hubel, 1979; Hubel & Wiesel, 1979).

The upshot of such findings is that cells in the brain, like the frog's retina described earlier, act as feature detectors. The brain seems to first analyze information into lines, angles, shading, movement, and other basic features. Then, other brain areas combine these features into meaningful visual experiences. (This concept is discussed further in Chapter 6.) Reading this page is a direct result of such feature analysis. Given the size of the task, it's little wonder that as much as 30 percent of the human brain may be involved in vision. (To further follow the pathways visual information takes through the brain, see "Blindsight: The 'What' and the 'Where' of Vision.")

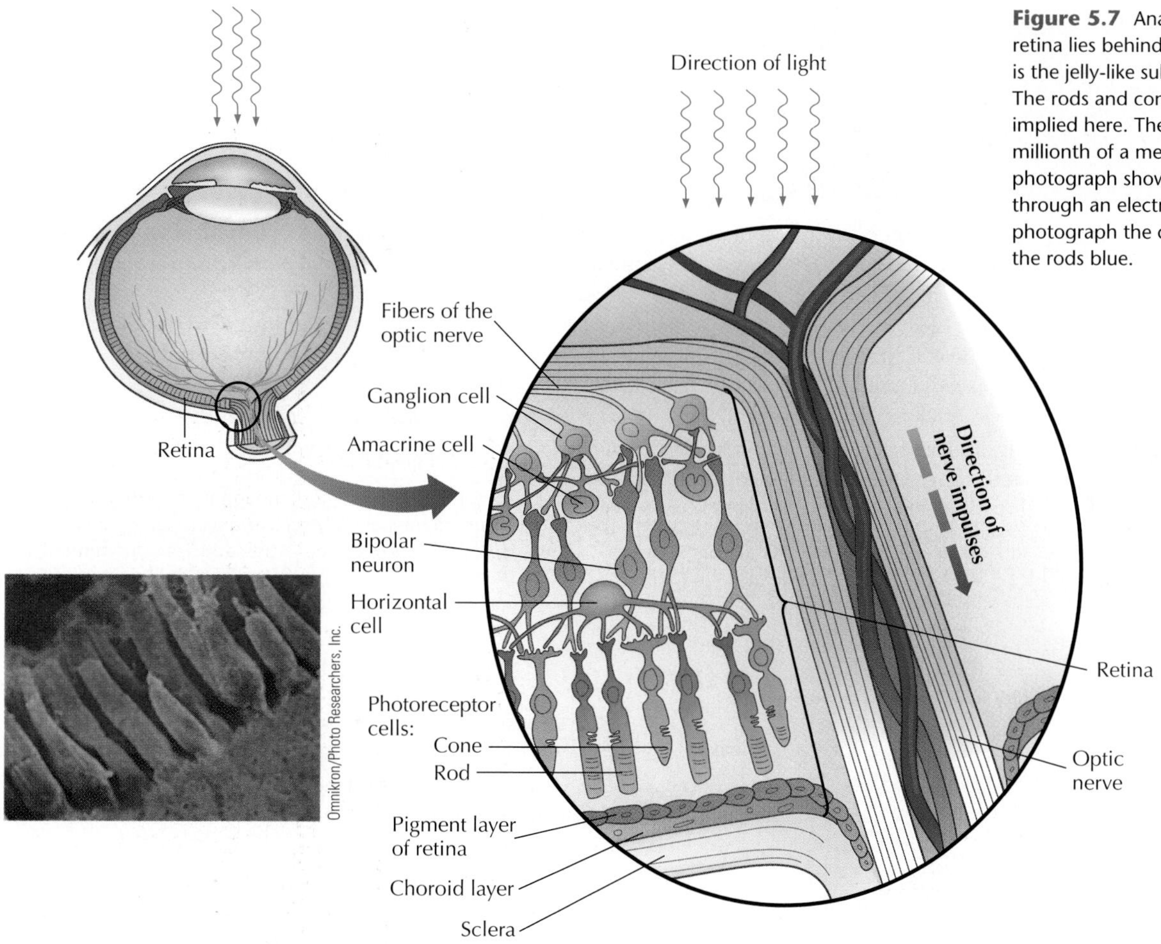

Omnikron/Photo Researchers, Inc.

Figure 5.7 Anatomy of the retina. The retina lies behind the vitreous humor, which is the jelly-like substance that fills the eyeball. The rods and cones are much smaller than implied here. The smallest are 1 micron (one millionth of a meter) wide. The lower-left photograph shows rods and cones as seen through an electron microscope. In the photograph the cones are colored green and the rods blue.

Figure 5.8 Experiencing the blind spot. *(a)* With your right eye closed, stare at the upper-right cross. Hold the book about 1 foot from your eye and slowly move it back and forth. You should be able to locate a position that causes the black spot to disappear. When it does, it has fallen on the blind spot. With a little practice you can learn to make people or objects you dislike disappear too! *(b)* Repeat the procedure described, but stare at the lower cross. When the white space falls on the blind spot, the black lines will appear to be continuous. This may help you understand why you do not usually experience a blind spot in your visual field.

Blind spot An area of the retina lacking visual receptors.

FOCUS ON RESEARCH

Blindsight: The "What" and the "Where" of Vision

Meet D. F., who suffered brain damage that caused severe *visual agnosia* (Goodale et al., 1991; James et al., 2003). If D. F. was shown an object, she could not recognize it. Remarkably, even though she couldn't recognize objects, D. F. could successfully manipulate them. For example, in one test she was given a card and asked to insert it into a slot at a certain angle. Although she could not describe the slot's orientation, she had no difficulty in inserting the card into it. You could say that D. F. displayed *blindsight:* When shown an object, she was *blind* to *what* the object was, but she had enough *sight* to know *where* it was in her visual field.

What patients like D. F. teach us is that the brain has assigned the job of seeing to different brain regions. One series of regions, the *ventral pathway,* is responsible for the "what" of vision, whereas another series of regions, the *dorsal pathway,* is responsible for the "where" of vision (Deco, Rolls, & Horowitz, 2004). D. F. suffered damage in her ventral pathway so she could not process the "what" of vision, but her intact dorsal pathway could still process the "where" of vision.

What happens if someone suffers brain damage to the dorsal pathway? In a rare case, a woman with just such damage had great difficulty crossing the street. Although she had no trouble recognizing cars (the what), she could not tell *where* they were. She could not even distinguish approaching cars from parked cars (Zeki, 1991).

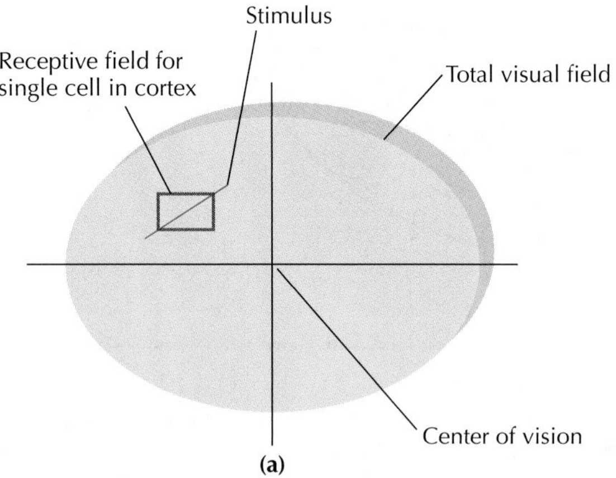

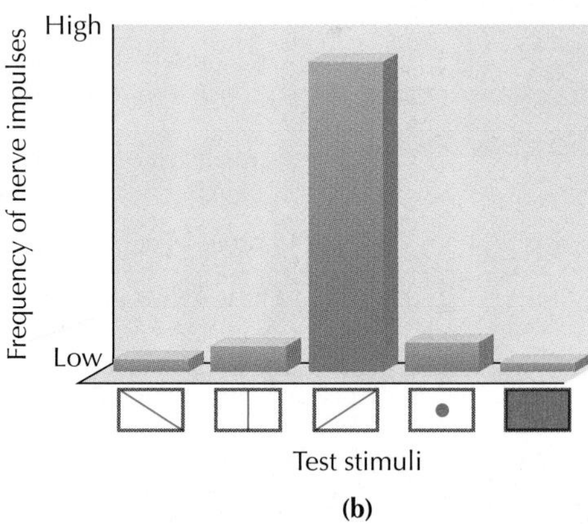

Figure 5.9 *(a)* A "typical" brain cell responds to only a small area of the total field of vision. In this example, the cell responds to stimuli that fall above and left of the center of vision. The bar graph *(b)* illustrates how a brain cell may act as a feature detector. Notice how the cell primarily responds to just one type of stimulus. (Adapted from Hubel, 1979.)

Visual Acuity

The rods and cones also affect **visual acuity**, or sharpness. The cones lie mainly at the center of the eye. In fact, the **fovea** (FOE-vee-ah: a small cup-shaped area in the middle of the retina) contains only cones—about 50,000 of them. Like a newspaper photograph made of many small dots, the tightly packed cones in the fovea produce the sharpest images. Normal acuity is designated as 20/20 vision: At 20 feet in distance, you can distinguish what the average person can see at 20 feet (● Figure 5.10). If your vision is 20/40, you can only see at 20 feet what the average person can see at 40 feet. If your vision is 20/200, everything is a blur and you need glasses! Vision that is 20/12 would mean that you can see at 20 feet what the average person must be 8 feet nearer to see. That's much better than average acuity. American astronaut Gordon Cooper, who claimed to see railroad lines in northern India from 100 miles above, had 20/12 vision.

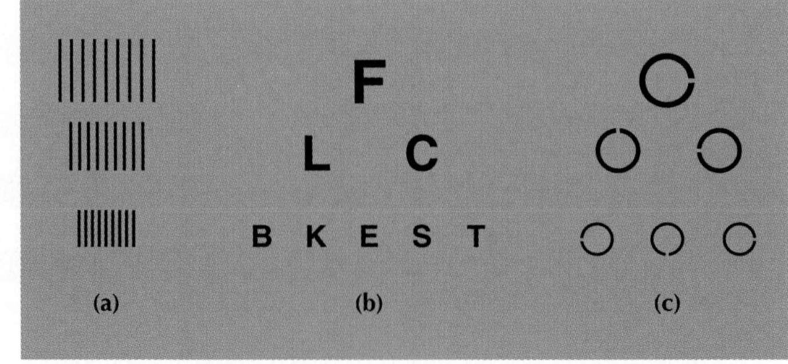

Figure 5.10 Tests of visual acuity. Here are some common tests of visual acuity. In *(a)* sharpness is indicated by the smallest grating still seen as individual lines. The Snellen chart *(b)* requires that you read rows of letters of diminishing size until you can no longer distinguish them. The Landolt rings *(c)* require no familiarity with letters. All that is required is a report of which side has a break in it.

Peripheral Vision

What is the purpose of the rest of the retina? Areas outside the fovea also get light, creating a large region of **peripheral** (side) **vision.** The rods are most numerous about 20 degrees from the center of the retina, so much of our peripheral vision is rod vision. Although rod vision is not very sharp, the rods are quite sensitive to *movement* in peripheral vision. To experience this characteristic of the rods, look straight ahead and hold your hand beside your head, at about 90 degrees. Wiggle your finger and slowly move your hand forward until you can detect motion. You will become aware of the movement before you can actually "see" your finger.

Seeing "out of the corner of the eye" is important for sports, driving, and walking down dark alleys. People who suffer from *tunnel vision* (a loss of peripheral vision) feel as if they are wearing blinders. Tunnel vision can also occur temporarily when we are overloaded by a task. For example, if you were playing a demanding video game you might be excused for not noticing that a friend had walked up beside you (Williams, 1995).

The rods are also highly responsive to dim light. Because most rods are 20 degrees to each side of the fovea, the best night vision is obtained by looking *next to* an object you wish to see. Test this yourself some night by looking at, and next to, a very dim star.

Color Vision—There's More to It Than Meets the Eye

What would you say is the brightest color? Red? Yellow? Blue? Actually, there are two answers to this question, one for the rods and one for the cones. The cones are most sensitive to the *yellowish green* part of the spectrum. In other words, if all colors are tested in daylight (with each reflecting the same amount of light), then yellowish green appears *brightest.* Yellow-green fire trucks and the bright yellow vests worn by roadside work crews are a reflection of this fact.

To what color are the rods most sensitive? Remember that the rods do not produce color sensations. If you were looking at a very dim colored light, you wouldn't see any color. Even so, one light would appear brighter than the others. When tested this way, the rods are most sensitive to *blue-green* lights. Thus, at night or in dim light, when rod vision prevails, the brightest-colored light will be one that is blue or blue-green. For this reason, police and highway patrol cars in many states now have blue emergency lights for night work. Also, you may have wondered why the taxiway lights at airports are blue. It seems like a poor choice, but blue is actually highly visible to pilots.

Tom McCarthy/PhotoEdit

Yellow-green fire trucks are far more visible in daylight because their color matches the cones' sensitivity peak. However, many cities continue to prefer red trucks because of tradition.

Color Theories

How do the cones produce color sensations? The **trichromatic** (TRY-kro-MAT-ik) **theory** of color vision holds that there are three types of cones, each most sensitive to red, green, or blue. Other colors result from combinations of these three. Black and white sensations are produced by the rods.

A basic problem with the trichromatic theory is that four colors of light—red, green, blue, and yellow—seem to be primary (you can't get them by mixing other colors). Also, why is it impossible to have a reddish green or a yellowish blue? These problems led to the development of a second view, known as the **opponent-process theory,** which states that vision analyzes colors into "either-or" messages. That is, the visual system can produce messages for either red or green, yellow or blue, black or white. Coding one color in a pair (red, for instance) seems to block the opposite message (green) from coming through. As a result, a reddish green is impossible, but a yellowish red (orange) can occur.

According to opponent-process theory, fatigue caused by making one response produces an afterimage of the opposite color as the system recovers. *Afterimages* are visual sensations that persist after a stimulus is removed—like seeing a spot after a flashbulb goes off. To see an afterimage of the type predicted by opponent-process theory, look at ● Figure 5.11 and follow the instructions there.

Which color theory is correct? Both! The three-color theory applies to the retina, where three different types of *visual pigments* (light-sensitive chemicals) have been found. As predicted, each pigment is most sensitive to light in roughly the red, green, or

Visual acuity The sharpness of visual perception.

Fovea An area at the center of the retina containing only cones.

Peripheral vision Vision at the edges of the visual field.

Trichromatic theory Theory of color vision based on three cone types: red, green, and blue.

Opponent-process theory Theory of color vision based on three coding systems (red or green, yellow or blue, black or white).

Figure 5.11 Negative afterimages. Stare at the dot near the middle of the flag for at least 30 seconds. Then look immediately at a plain sheet of white paper or a white wall. You will see the American flag in its normal colors. Reduced sensitivity to yellow, green, and black in the visual system, caused by prolonged staring, results in the appearance of complementary colors. Project the afterimage of the flag on other colored surfaces to get additional effects.

blue region. The three types of cones fire nerve impulses at different rates to produce various color sensations (● Figure 5.12).

In contrast, the opponent-process theory seems to explain what happens in optic pathways and the brain *after* information leaves the eye. For example, nerve cells can be found in the brain that are excited by the color red and inhibited by the color green. So both theories are "correct." One explains what happens in the eye itself. The other explains how colors are analyzed after messages leave the eye (Gegenfurtner & Kiper, 2003).

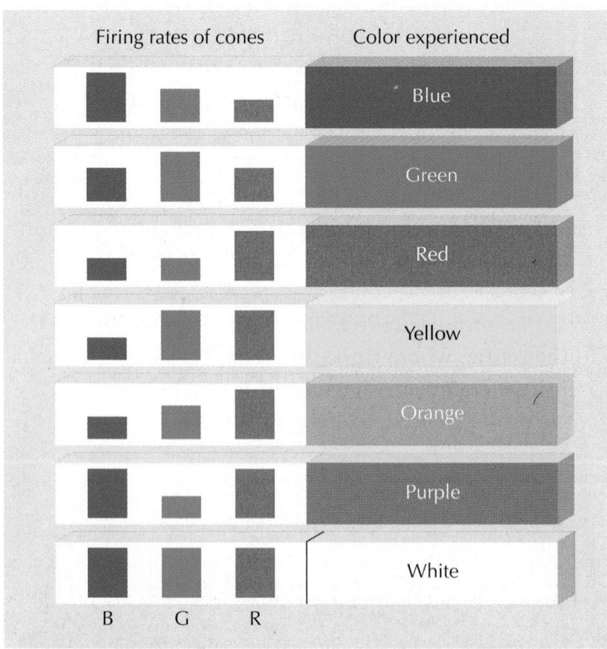

Figure 5.12 Firing rates of blue, green, and red cones in response to different colors. The taller the colored bar, the higher the firing rates for that type of cone. As you can see, colors are coded by differences in the activity of all three types of cones in the normal eye. (Adapted from Goldstein, 2004.)

Constructing Colors

The preceding explanations present a fairly mechanical view of how colors are sensed. In reality, color experiences are more complex. For example, the apparent color of an object is influenced by the colors of other nearby objects. This effect is called **simultaneous color contrast.** It occurs because brain cell activity in one area of the cortex can be altered by activity in nearby areas. Simultaneous contrast can make it difficult to paint a picture or decorate a room. If you add a new color to a canvas or a room, all of the existing colors will suddenly look different. Typically, each time a new color is added, all the other colors must be adjusted (see ● Figure 5.13).

More striking than simultaneous contrast is the fact that color experiences are *actively constructed* in the brain. The brain does not simply receive prepackaged color messages. It must generate color from the data it receives. As a result, it is possible to experience color where none exists (see ● Figure 5.14 for an example). Indeed, all of our experiences are at least partially constructed from the information surrounding us. (We'll explore this idea further in the next chapter.)

Color Blindness and Color Weakness

Do you know anyone who regularly draws hoots of laughter by wearing clothes of wildly clashing colors? Or someone who sheepishly tries to avoid saying what color an object is? If so, you probably know someone who is color-blind.

What is it like to be color-blind? What causes color blindness? A person who is **color-blind** cannot perceive colors. It is as if the world is a black-and-white movie. The color-blind person either lacks cones

Figure 5.13 Notice how different the gray-blue color looks when it is placed on different backgrounds. Unless you are looking at a large, solid block of color, simultaneous contrast is constantly affecting your color experiences.

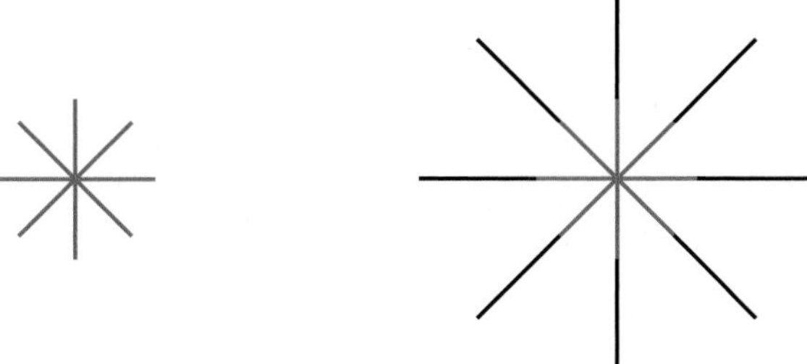

Figure 5.14 On the left is a "star" made of red lines. On the right, the red lines are placed on top of longer black lines. Now, in addition to the red lines, you will see a glowing red disk, with a clear border. Of course, no red disk is printed on this page. No ink can be found between the red lines. The glowing red disk exists only in your mind. (After Hoffman, 1999, p. 111.)

or has cones that do not function normally (Deeb, 2004). Such total color blindness is rare. In *color weakness,* or partial color blindness, a person can't see certain colors. Approximately 8 percent of all males (but less than 1 percent of women) have red-green color weakness. These people see both reds and greens as the same color, usually a yellowish brown (see ● Figure 5.15). Another type of color weakness, involving yellow and blue, is extremely rare (Hsia & Graham, 1997). (See "Are You Color-Blind?")

Color blindness is caused by changes in the genes that control red, green, and blue pigments in the cones. Red-green color weakness is a recessive, sex-linked trait. That means it is carried on the *X,* or female, chromosome. Women have two *X* chromosomes, so if they receive only one defective color gene, they still have normal vision. Color-weak men, however, have only one *X* chromosome, so they can inherit the defect from their mothers (who usually don't display any color weakness).

How can color-blind individuals drive? Don't they have trouble with traffic lights? Red-green color-weak individuals have normal vision for yellow and blue, so their main problem is telling red lights from green. In practice, that's not difficult. The red light is always on top, and the green light is brighter than the red. Also, "red" traffic signals have yellow mixed in with the red and a "green" light is really blue-green.

Figure 5.15 Color blindness and color weakness. *(a)* Photograph illustrates normal color vision. *(b)* Photograph is printed in blue and yellow and gives an impression of what a red-green color-blind person sees. *(c)* Photograph simulates total color blindness. If you are totally color-blind, all three photos will look nearly identical.

Dark Adaptation—Let There Be Light!

What happens when the eyes adjust to a dark room? **Dark adaptation** is the dramatic increase in retinal sensitivity to light that occurs after a person enters the dark. Consider walking into a theater. If you enter from a brightly lighted lobby, you practically need to be led to your seat. After a short time, however, you can see the entire room in detail (including the couple kissing over in the corner). It takes about 30 to 35 minutes of complete darkness to reach maximum visual sensitivity (● Figure 5.17). At that point, your eye will be 100,000 times more sensitive to light (Goldstein, 2004).

What causes dark adaptation? Like the cones, the rods contain a light-sensitive visual pigment. When struck by light, visual pigments *bleach,* or break down chemically. (The afterimages caused by flashbulbs are a direct result of this bleaching.) To restore light

Simultaneous color contrast Changes in perceived hue that occur when a colored stimulus is displayed on backgrounds of various colors.

Color blindness A total inability to perceive colors.

Dark adaptation Increased retinal sensitivity to light.

DISCOVERING PSYCHOLOGY

Are You Color-Blind?

How can I tell if I am color-blind? Surprisingly, it is not as obvious as you might think; some of us reach adulthood without knowing. The *Ishihara test* is commonly used to measure color blindness and weakness. In the test, numbers and other designs made of dots are placed on a background also made of dots (● Figure 5.16). The background and the numbers are of different colors (red and green, for example). A person who is color-blind sees only a jumble of dots. If you have normal color vision you can detect the numbers or designs (Birch & McKeever, 1993; Coren, Ward, & Enns, 2004). The chart below Figure 5.16 lists what people with normal color vision, and color blindness, see. Because ● Figure 5.16 is just a replica, it is not a definitive test of color blindness. Nevertheless, if you can't see all of the embedded designs, you may be color-blind or color-weak.

Figure 5.16 A replica of the Ishihara test for color blindness.

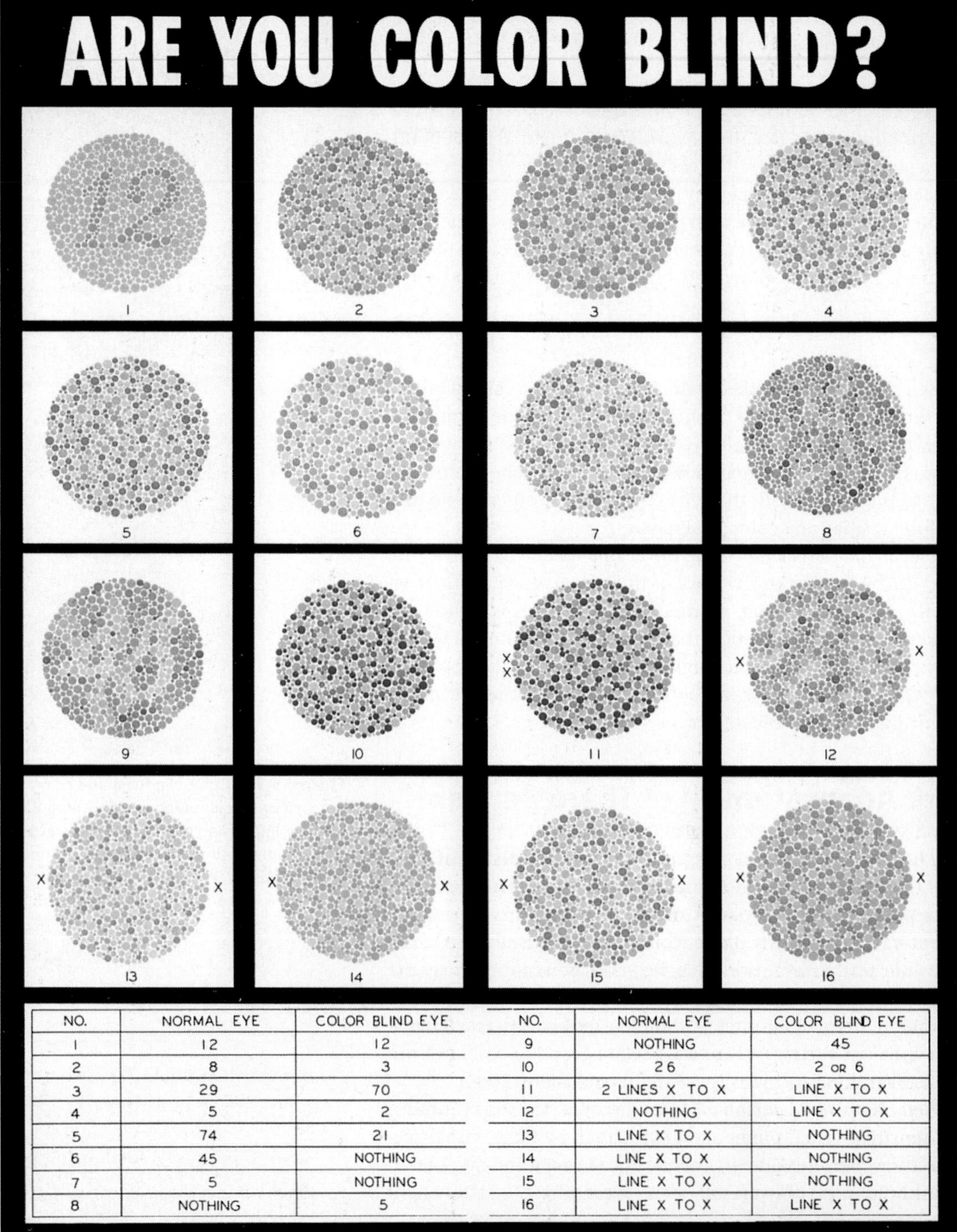

NO.	NORMAL EYE	COLOR BLIND EYE	NO.	NORMAL EYE	COLOR BLIND EYE
1	12	12	9	NOTHING	45
2	8	3	10	26	2 OR 6
3	29	70	11	2 LINES X TO X	LINE X TO X
4	5	2	12	NOTHING	LINE X TO X
5	74	21	13	LINE X TO X	NOTHING
6	45	NOTHING	14	LINE X TO X	NOTHING
7	5	NOTHING	15	LINE X TO X	NOTHING
8	NOTHING	5	16	LINE X TO X	LINE X TO X

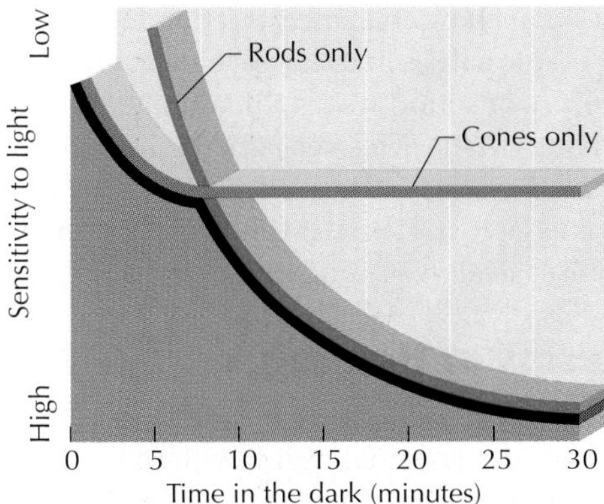

Figure 5.17 Typical course of dark adaptation. The black line shows how the threshold for vision lowers as a person spends time in the dark. (A lower threshold means that less light is needed for vision.) The green line shows that the cones adapt first, but they soon cease adding to light sensitivity. Rods, shown by the red line, adapt more slowly. However, they continue to add to improved night vision long after the cones are fully adapted.

sensitivity, the visual pigments must recombine, which takes time. Night vision is due mainly to an increase in **rhodopsin** (row-DOP-sin), the rod pigment. When completely dark adapted, the human eye is almost as sensitive to light as the eye of an owl.

Before artificial lighting, humans gradually adapted to the dark at sunset. Now, we are often caught in temporary semi-blindness. Usually this isn't dangerous, but it can be. Even though dark adaptation takes a long time, it can be wiped out by just a few seconds of viewing bright light. Try this demonstration:

See (and Don't See) for Yourself

Spend 15 or 20 minutes in a darkened room. At the end of this time, you should be able to see clearly. Now, close your left eye and cover it tightly with your hand. Turn on a bright light for 1 or 2 seconds and look at it with your right eye. With the light off again, compare the vision in your two eyes, first opening one and then the other. You will be completely blinded in your right eye.

As you can see, just a few seconds of exposure to bright white light can completely wipe out dark adaptation. That's why you should be sure to avoid looking at oncoming headlights when you are driving at night—especially the newer bluish-white zenon lights.

Under normal conditions, glare recovery takes about 20 seconds, plenty of time for an accident. After a few drinks, it may take 30 to 50 percent longer because alcohol dilates the pupils, allowing more light to enter. Note, too, that dark adaptation occurs more slowly as we grow older. This is one reason why injuries caused by falling in the dark become more common among the elderly (McMurdo & Gaskell, 1991).

Is there any way to speed up dark adaptation? The rods are *insensitive* to extremely red light. To take advantage of this fact, submarines and airplane cockpits are illuminated with red light. So are the ready rooms for fighter pilots and their ground crews. In each case, people are able to move quickly into the dark without having to adapt. Because the red light doesn't stimulate the rods, it is as if they had already spent time in the dark.

Red light allows dark adaptation to occur because it provides little or no stimulation to the rods.

Can eating carrots really improve vision? One chemical "ingredient" of rhodopsin is *retinal,* which the body makes from vitamin A. (Retinal is also called *retinene.*) When too little vitamin A is available, less rhodopsin is produced. Thus, a person lacking vitamin A may develop night blindness. In **night blindness,** the person can see normally in bright light while using the cones, but becomes blind at night when the rods must function. Carrots are an excellent source of vitamin A, so they could improve night vision for someone suffering a deficiency, but not the vision of anyone with an adequate diet (Carlson, 2005).

KNOWLEDGE BUILDER

Vision

REFLECT

Pretend you are a beam of light. What will happen to you at each step as you pass into the eye and land on the retina? What will happen if the eye is not perfectly shaped? How will the retina know you've arrived? How will it tell what color of light you are? What will it tell the brain about you?

Rhodopsin The light-sensitive pigment in the rods.

Night blindness Blindness under conditions of low illumination.

LEARNING CHECK

1. The ________ ________ is made up of electromagnetic radiation with wavelengths between 400 and 700 nanometers.
2. Hyperopia is related to
   a. farsightedness c. corneal astigmatism
   b. having an elongated eye d. lack of cones in the fovea
3. In dim light, vision depends mainly on the ________. In brighter light, color and fine detail are produced by the ________.
4. The fovea has the greatest visual acuity due to the large concentration of rods found there. T or F?
5. Hubel and Wiesel found that cells in the visual cortex of the brain function as ________ ________.
6. The term "20/20 vision" means that a person can see at 20 feet what can normally be seen from 20 feet. T or F?
7. For the cones, the most visible color is
   a. reddish orange c. yellow-orange
   b. blue-green d. yellowish green
8. The eyes become more sensitive to light at night because of a process known as ________ ________.

CRITICAL THINKING

9. William James once said, "If a master surgeon were to cross the auditory and optic nerves, we would hear lightning and see thunder." Can you explain what James meant?
10. Sensory transduction in the eye takes place first in the cornea, then in the lens, then in the retina. T or F?

Answers: 1. visible spectrum **2.** a **3.** rods, cones **4.** F **5.** feature detectors **6.** T **7.** d **8.** dark adaptation **9.** The explanation is based on localization of function: If a lightning flash caused re-routed messages from the eyes to activate auditory areas of the brain, we would experience a sound sensation. Likewise, if the ears transduced a thunderclap, and sent impulses to the visual area, a sensation of light would occur. **10.** False. The cornea and lens bend and focus light rays, but they do not change light to another form of energy. No change in the *type* of energy takes place until the retina converts light to nerve impulses.

Hearing—Good Vibrations

Rock, classical, jazz, rap, country, hip-hop—whatever your musical taste, you have probably been moved by the riches of sound. Hearing also collects information from all around the body, such as detecting the approach of an unseen car (Yost, 2000). Vision, in all its glory, is limited to stimuli in front of the eyes (unless, of course, your "shades" have rearview mirrors attached).

What is the stimulus for hearing? If you throw a stone into a quiet pond, a circle of waves will spread in all directions. In much the same way, sound travels as a series of invisible waves of *compression* (peaks) and *rarefaction* (RARE-eh-fak-shun: valleys) in the air. Any vibrating object—a tuning fork, the string of a musical instrument, or the vocal cords—will produce sound waves (rhythmic movement of air molecules). Other materials, such as fluids or solids, can also carry sound. But sound does not travel in a vacuum. Movies that show characters reacting to the "roar" of alien starships or titanic battles in deep space are in error.

The *frequency* of sound waves (the number of waves per second) corresponds to the perceived *pitch* (higher or lower tone) of a sound. The *amplitude,* or physical "height," of a sound wave tells how much energy it contains. Psychologically, amplitude corresponds to sensed *loudness* (sound intensity) (● Figure 5.18).

Mechanisms of Hearing

How are sounds converted to nerve impulses? Hearing involves an elaborate chain of events that begins with the *pinna* (PIN-ah: the visible, external part of the ear). In addition to being a good place to hang earrings, the pinna acts like a funnel to concentrate sounds. After they are guided into the ear canal, sound waves collide with the *tympanic membrane* (eardrum), setting it in motion. This, in turn, causes three small bones (the *auditory ossicles*) (OSS-ih-kuls) to vibrate (● Figure 5.19). The ossicles are the malleus (MAL-ee-us), incus, and stapes (STAY-peas). Their common names are the hammer, anvil, and stirrup. The ossicles link the eardrum with the *cochlea* (KOCK-lee-ah: a snail-shaped organ that makes up the inner ear). The stapes is attached to a membrane on the cochlea called the *oval window.* As the oval window moves back and forth, it makes waves in a fluid inside the cochlea.

The cochlea is really the organ of hearing, because it is here that tiny **hair cells** detect waves in the fluid. The hair cells are part of the **organ of Corti** (KOR-tee), which makes up the center part of the cochlea (● Figure 5.20). A set of *stereocilia* (STER-ee-oh-SIL-ih-ah), or "bristles," atop each hair cell brush against the tectorial membrane when waves ripple through the fluid surrounding the organ of Corti. As the stereocilia are bent, nerve impulses are triggered, which then flow to the brain. (Are your ears "bristling" with sound?)

How are higher and lower sounds detected? The **frequency theory** of hearing states that as pitch rises, nerve impulses of a corresponding frequency are fed into the auditory nerve. That is, an 800-hertz tone produces 800 nerve impulses per second. (*Hertz* refers to the number of vibrations per second.) This explains how

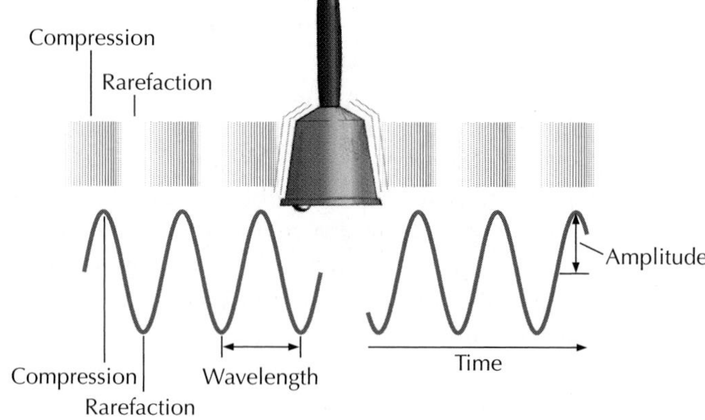

Figure 5.18 Waves of compression in the air, or vibrations, are the stimulus for hearing. The frequency of sound waves determines their pitch. The amplitude determines loudness.

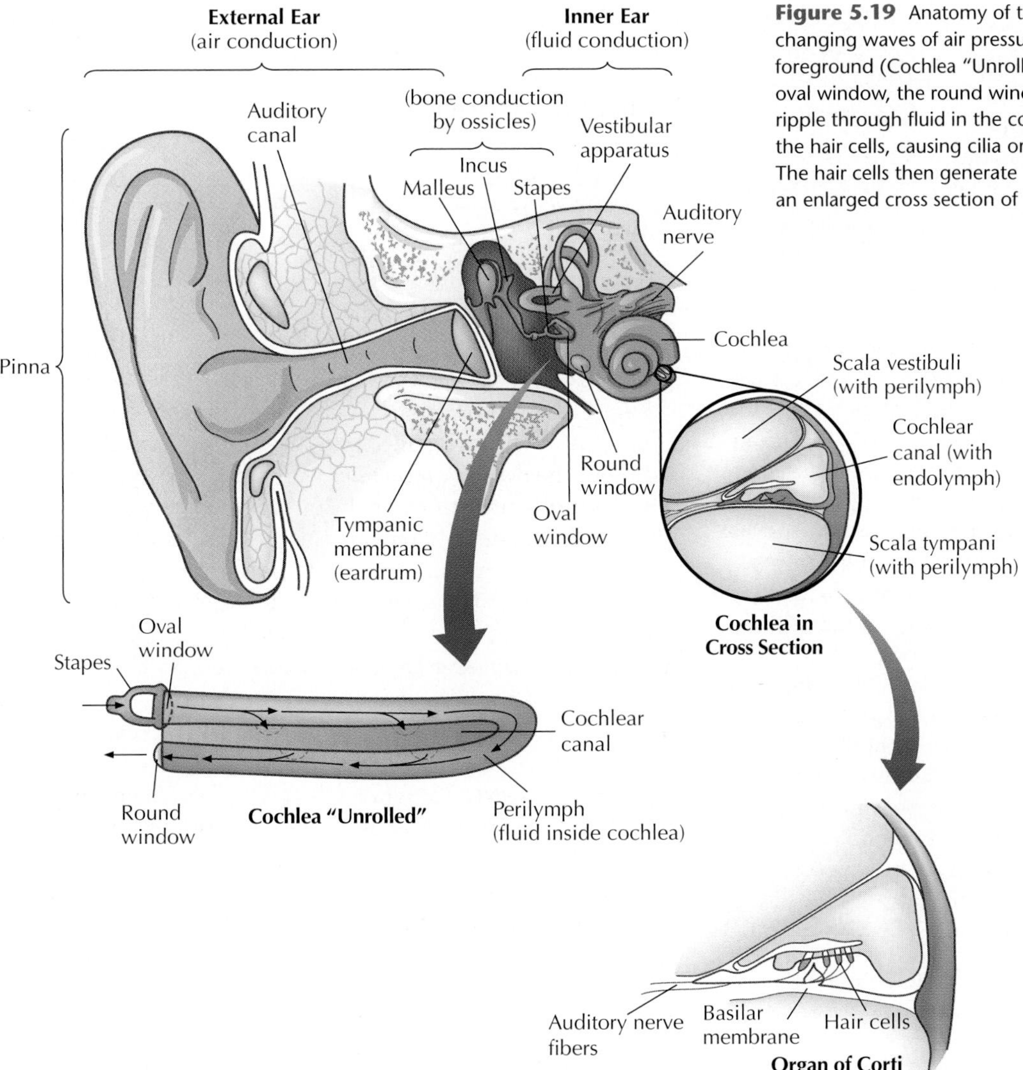

Figure 5.19 Anatomy of the ear. The entire ear is a mechanism for changing waves of air pressure into nerve impulses. The inset in the foreground (Cochlea "Unrolled") shows that as the stapes moves the oval window, the round window bulges outward, allowing waves to ripple through fluid in the cochlea. The waves move membranes near the hair cells, causing cilia or "bristles" on the tips of the cells to bend. The hair cells then generate nerve impulses carried to the brain. (See an enlarged cross section of cochlea in Figure 5.20.)

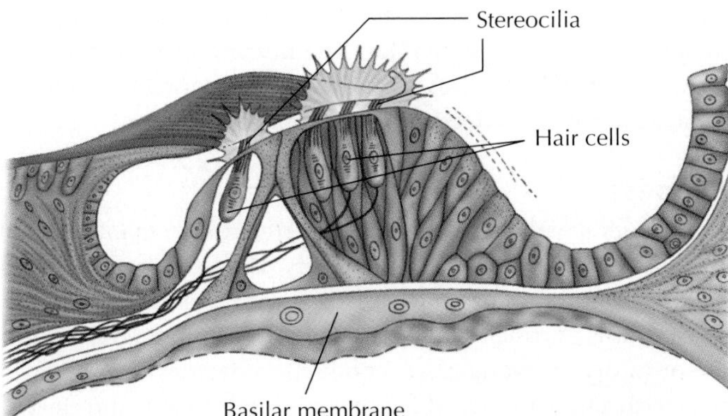

Figure 5.20 A closer view of the hair cells shows how movement of fluid in the cochlea causes the bristling "hairs" or cilia to bend, generating a nerve impulse.

Hair cells Receptor cells within the cochlea that transduce vibrations into nerve impulses.

Organ of Corti Center part of the cochlea, containing hair cells, canals, and membranes.

Frequency theory Holds that tones up to 4,000 hertz are converted to nerve impulses that match the frequency of each tone.

THE CLINICAL FILE

Artificial Hearing

In many cases of "nerve" deafness, the nerve is actually intact. This finding has spurred the development of cochlear implants that bypass hair cells and stimulate the auditory nerves directly (● Figure 5.22).

As you can see in ● Figure 5.22, wires from a microphone carry electrical signals to an external coil. A matching coil under the skin picks up the signals and carries them to one or more areas of the cochlea. The latest implants make use of place theory to separate higher and lower tones. This has allowed some formerly deaf persons to hear human voices, music, and other higher-frequency sounds. About 60 percent of all multichannel implant patients can understand some spoken words and appreciate music (Leal et al., 2003; Tye-Murray et al., 1995). Some deaf children learn to speak. Those who receive a cochlear implant before age 2 learn spoken language at a near normal rate (Dorman & Wilson, 2004).

At present, artificial hearing remains crude. All but the most successful cochlear implant patients describe the sound as "like a radio that isn't quite tuned in." In fact, 30 percent of all adults who have tried implants have given up on them. But cochlear implants are improving. And even now it is hard to argue with enthusiasts like Kristen Cloud. Shortly after Kristen received an implant, she was able to hear a siren and avoid being struck by a speeding car. She says simply, "The implant saved my life."

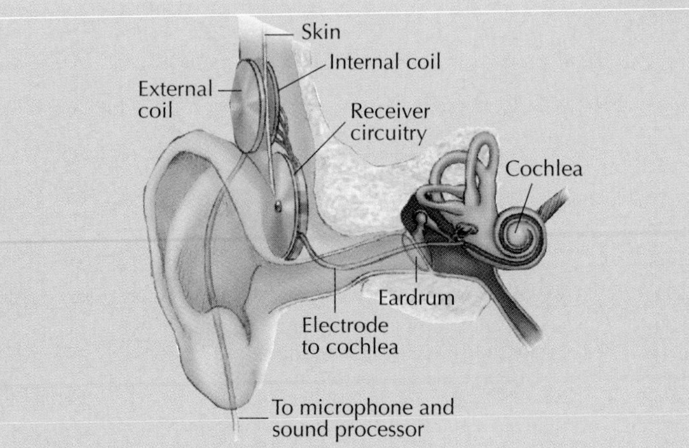

Figure 5.22 A cochlear implant, or "artificial ear."

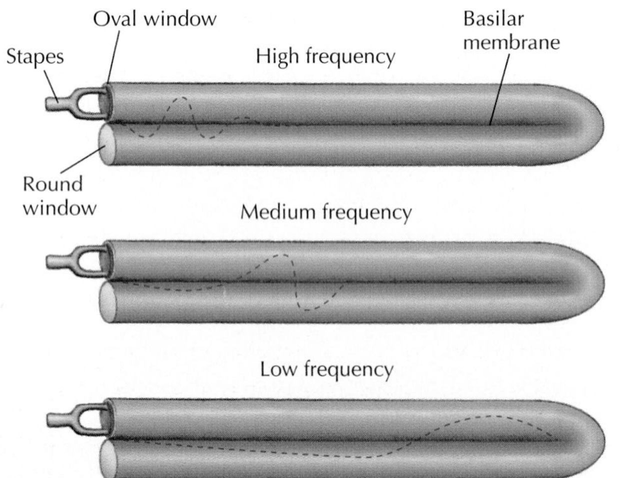

Figure 5.21 Here we see a simplified side view of the cochlea "unrolled." Remember that the basilar membrane is the elastic "roof" of the lower chamber of the cochlea. The organ of Corti, with its sensitive hair cells, rests atop the basilar membrane. The colored line shows where waves in the cochlear fluid cause the greatest deflection of the basilar membrane. (The amount of movement is exaggerated in the drawing.) Hair cells respond most in the area of greatest movement, which helps identify sound frequency.

sounds up to about 4,000 hertz reach the brain. But what about higher tones? **Place theory** states that higher and lower tones excite specific areas of the cochlea. High tones register most strongly at the base of the cochlea (near the oval window). Lower tones, on the other hand, mostly move hair cells near the outer tip of the cochlea (● Figure 5.21). Pitch is signaled by the area of the cochlea most strongly activated. Incidentally, place theory also explains why hunters sometimes lose hearing in a narrow pitch range. "Hunter's notch," as it is called, occurs when hair cells are damaged in the area affected by the pitch of gunfire.

Deafness

What causes other types of deafness? There are two main types of deafness. **Conduction deafness** occurs when the transfer of vibrations from the eardrum to the inner ear is weak. For example, the eardrums or ossicles may be damaged or immobilized by disease or injury. In many cases, conduction deafness can be overcome with a hearing aid, which makes sounds louder and clearer.

Nerve deafness results from damage to the hair cells or auditory nerve. Hearing aids are of no help in this case because auditory messages are blocked from reaching the brain. However, artificial hearing systems are making it possible for some persons with nerve deafness to break through the wall of silence. (See "Artificial Hearing.")

Many jobs, hobbies, and pastimes can cause **stimulation deafness**, which occurs when very loud sounds damage hair cells (as in hunter's notch). The hair cells, which are about as thin as a cobweb, are very fragile (● Figure 5.23). By the time you are 65, more than 40 percent of them will be gone. If you work in a noisy environment or enjoy loud music, motorcycling, snowmobiling, hunting, or similar pursuits, you may be risking stimulation deafness. Dead hair cells are never replaced: When you abuse them you lose them.

How loud must a sound be to be hazardous? The danger of hearing loss depends on both the loudness of sound and how long you are exposed to it. Daily exposure to 85 decibels or more may cause permanent hearing loss (Sekuler & Blake, 2006). Even short periods at 120 decibels (a rock concert) may cause a *temporary threshold shift* (a partial, transitory loss of hearing). Brief exposure to 150 decibels (a jet airplane nearby) can cause permanent deafness.

You might find it interesting to check the decibel ratings of some of your activities in ● Figure 5.24. Don't be fooled by the numbers, though. Decibels are plotted on a logarithmic scale (like earthquake intensity!). Every 20 decibels increases the sound pressure by a factor of 10. In other words, a rock concert at 120 decibels is not just twice as powerful as a normal voice at 60 decibels. It is actually 1,000 times stronger.

Be aware that highly amplified musical concerts, iPod-style stereo headphones, and "boom-box" car stereos can also damage your hearing. If *tinnitus* (tin-NYE-tus: a ringing or buzzing sensation) follows exposure to loud sounds, chances are that hair cells have been damaged. Almost everyone has tinnitus at times, especially with increasing age. But after repeated sounds that produce this warning, you can expect to become permanently hard-of-hearing. A study of people who regularly go to amplified concerts found that 44 percent had tinnitus and most had some hearing loss (Meyer-Bisch, 1996).

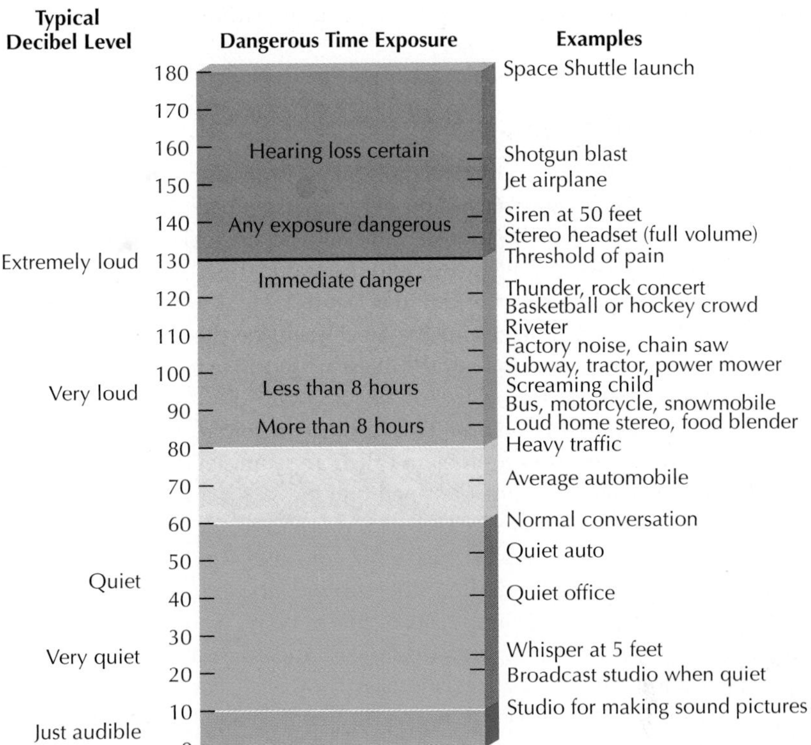

Figure 5.24 Loudness ratings and potential hearing damage.

The next time you are exposed to a very loud sound, remember Figure 5.24 and take precautions against damage. (Remember, too, that for temporary ear protection, fingers are always handy.)

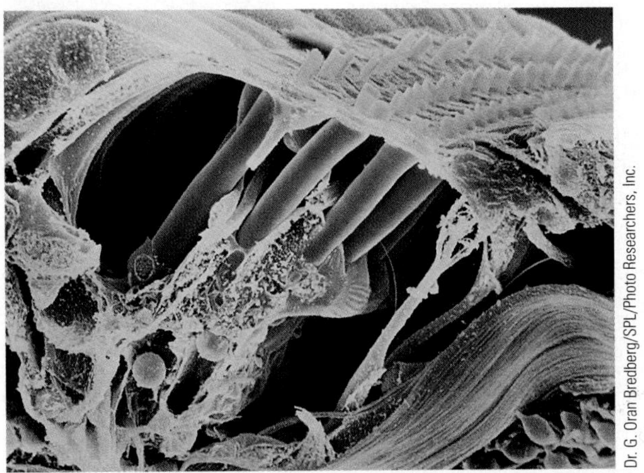

Figure 5.23 A highly magnified electron microscope photo of the cilia (orange bristles) on the top of human hair cells. (Colors are artificial.)

Smell and Taste—The Nose Knows When the Tongue Can't Tell

Unless you are a wine taster, a perfume blender, a chef, or a gourmet, you may think of **olfaction** (smell) and **gustation** (taste) as minor senses. Certainly you could survive without these two *chemical senses* (receptors that respond to chemical molecules). Just the same, smell and taste occasionally prevent poisonings and they add pleasure to our lives. Skilled novelists always include descriptions of odors and tastes in their writings. Perhaps they intuitively realize that a scene is incomplete without smells and

Place theory Theory that higher and lower tones excite specific areas of the cochlea.

Conduction deafness Poor transfer of sounds from the eardrum to the inner ear.

Nerve deafness Deafness caused by damage to the hair cells or auditory nerve.

Stimulation deafness Damage caused by exposing the hair cells to excessively loud sounds.

Olfaction The sense of smell.

Gustation The sense of taste.

tastes. Likewise, this chapter would be incomplete without a description of the chemical senses.

The Sense of Smell

Smell receptors respond to airborne molecules. As air enters the nose, it passes over roughly 5 million nerve fibers embedded in the lining of the upper nasal passages. Molecules passing over the fibers trigger nerve signals that are sent to the brain. The extreme close-up of an olfactory receptor cell in ● Figure 5.25*c* shows the thread-like fibers that project into the air flow inside the nose. Receptor proteins on the surface of the fibers are sensitive to various airborne molecules.

How are different odors produced? This is still an unfolding mystery. One hint comes from a problem called **anosmia** (an-OZE-me-ah: defective smell), a sort of "smell blindness" for a single odor. Anosmia suggests there are receptors for specific odors. Indeed, molecules having a particular odor are quite similar in shape. Specific shapes produce the following types of odors: floral (flower-like), camphoric (camphor-like), musky (have you ever smelled a sweaty musk ox?), minty (mint-like), and etherish (like ether or cleaning fluid). This does not mean, however, that there are just five different olfactory receptors. In humans, 300 to 400 types of smell receptors are believed to exist (Herz, 2001).

Does the existence of 400 different types of receptors mean that we can sense only 400 different odors? No, molecules trigger activity in different *combinations* of odor receptors. Thus, humans can detect at least 10,000 different odors. Just as you can make many thousands of words from the 26 letters of the alphabet, many combinations of receptors are possible, resulting in many different odors. The brain uses the distinctive patterns of messages it gets from the olfactory receptors to recognize particular scents (Laurent et al., 2001; Malnic, Hirono, & Buck, 1999).

It appears that different-shaped "holes," or "pockets," exist on the surface of olfactory receptors. Like a piece fits in a puzzle, chemicals produce odors when part of a molecule matches a hole of the same shape. This is the **lock and key theory.** Scents are also identified, in part, by the *location* of the receptors in the nose that are activated by a particular odor. Finally, the *number of activated receptors* tells the brain how strong an odor is (Freeman, 1991).

One person out of 100 cannot smell at all (Gilbert & Wysocki, 1987). These people typically find that olfaction is not such a minor sense after all. One person, for instance, almost died because he couldn't smell the smoke when his apartment building caught fire. Even in everyday terms, total anosmia can be a real loss. Many anosmics are unable to cook, and they may be poisoned by spoiled food.

What causes anosmia? Risks include infections, allergies, and blows to the head (which may tear the olfactory nerves). Exposure to chemicals such as ammonia, photo-developing chemicals, and hair-dressing potions can also cause anosmia. If you value your sense of smell, be careful what you breathe (Herz, 2001).

It might seem that various odors are inherently good or bad smelling. But newborn infants show no signs to reacting more strongly to "good" versus "bad" odors. Recently, the U.S. military tried to create a stink bomb that could be used for clearing people out of an area. No matter how foul the smell, nothing could be found that was universally repelling. It appears that likes and dislikes for various scents are learned (Herz, 2001). For example, a person who smelled roses for the first time at her mother's funeral might dislike the scent of roses. Or one who smelled a skunk for the first time during a backyard birthday party might like the scent of skunk. If you don't like the fetid, rotten odor of "ripe" cheeses, you just grew up in the wrong culture!

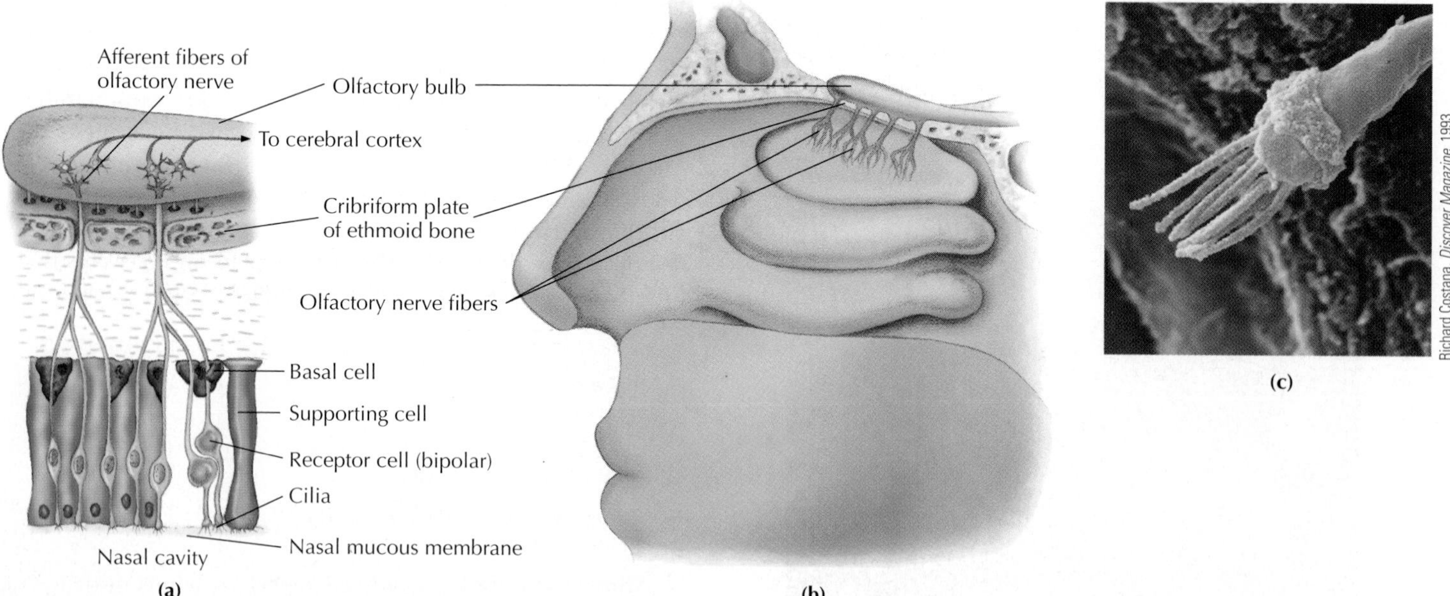

Figure 5.25 Receptors for the sense of smell (olfaction). *(a)* Olfactory nerve fibers respond to gaseous molecules. Receptor cells are shown in cross section. *(b)* Olfactory receptors are located in the upper nasal cavity. *(c)* An extreme close-up of an olfactory receptor shows fibers that sense gaseous molecules of various shapes.

Pheromones: A Sixth Sense?

Among animals, **pheromones** (FAIR-oh-moans: airborne chemical signals) greatly affect mating, sexual behavior, recognizing family members, and territorial marking. For example, when a female pig is exposed to the pheromones in a male pig's breath, she immediately becomes sexually receptive.

The *vomeronasal* (voh-MARE-oh-NAZE-ul) *organ* (VNO) is the sense organ for pheromones. Until recently, humans were assumed to have only a vestigial VNO or none at all. Now, however, scientists believe they have located the VNO in humans (Hays, 2003). The suspected human vomeronasal organ looks like a small pit inside the nose (one on each side of the septum). These pits are lined with nerve cells and respond to chemicals that are suspected pheromones (Benson, 2002).

What would a pheromone smell like? Pheromones are not smelled, felt, seen, tasted, or heard. In humans, pheromones appear to produce vague feelings, such as well-being, attraction, unease, or anxiety. When people say that their relationships are influenced by good or bad "chemistry," there may be some truth to it. Pheromones could add to the intoxicating feelings of romantic attraction or the sourness of instant dislike. In fact, one group of researchers believe that adding a pheromone to aftershave lotion can make men more sexually attractive (McCoy & Pitino, 2002). (However, the most likely human pheromones are found in underarm sweat, which is not exactly an enticing thought.)

Critics doubt that human pheromones directly release sexual behavior. Instead, they probably affect a person's general mood. Even then, social context appears to influence the effect. For instance, the ability of pheromones to induce a positive mood depends on whether a person of the opposite sex is nearby (Jacob, Hayreh, & McClintock, 2001).

Evidence for the existence of human pheromones remains preliminary and controversial. (Men shouldn't expect "Boar's Breath" cologne to be offered anytime soon!) Nevertheless, the possibilities are intriguing (Ebster & Kirk-Smith, 2005). For instance, human pheromones appear to explain why the menstrual cycles of women who live together tend to become synchronized. It's also possible that pheromones may one day be used to decrease anxiety, curb hunger, relieve premenstrual discomforts, or aid sex therapy. Only further study will tell whether searching for a sixth sense makes sense.

Tim Davis/Getty Images

Taste and Flavors

There are at least four basic taste sensations: *sweet, salt, sour,* and *bitter.* We are most sensitive to bitter, less sensitive to sour, even less sensitive to salt, and least sensitive to sweet. This order may have helped prevent poisonings when most humans foraged for food, because bitter and sour foods are more likely to be inedible.

Many experts now believe that a fifth taste quality exists. The Japanese word *umami* (oo-MAH-me) describes a pleasant savory or "brothy" taste associated with certain amino acids in chicken soup, some meat extracts, kelp, tuna, human milk, cheese, and soy beans. The receptors for *umami* are sensitive to glutamate, a substance found in MSG (Lindemann, 2000). Perhaps MSG's reputation as a "flavor enhancer" is based on the pleasant *umami* taste (Bellisle, 1999). At the very least, we may finally know why chicken soup is such a "comfort food."

If there are only four or five tastes, how can there be so many different flavors? Flavors seem more varied because we tend to include sensations of texture, temperature, smell, and even pain ("hot" chili peppers) along with taste. Smell is particularly important in determining flavor. If you plug your nose and eat small bits of apple, potato, and onion, they will "taste" almost exactly alike. So do gourmet jelly beans! It is probably fair to say that subjective flavor is one half smell. That's why food loses its "taste" when you have a cold.

Taste buds (taste-receptor cells) are mainly located on the top side of the tongue, especially around the edges. However, a few are found elsewhere inside the mouth (● Figure 5.26). As food is chewed, it dissolves and enters the taste buds, where it sets off nerve impulses to the brain (Northcutt, 2004). Much like smell, sweet and bitter tastes appear to be based on a lock-and-key match between molecules and intricately shaped receptors. Saltiness and sourness, however, are triggered by a direct flow of charged atoms into the tips of taste cells (Lindemann, 2001).

People seem to have very different tastes. Why is that? Some differences are genetic. The chemical phenylthiocarbamine (FEEN-il-thigh-oh-CAR-bah-meen), or PTC, tastes bitter to about 70 percent of those tested and has no taste for the other 30 percent. More generally, taste sensitivity is related to how many taste buds you have on your tongue. Some people have as few as 500 taste buds, whereas others have as many as 10,000. Those with many taste buds are "supertasters" who need only half as much sugar in their coffee to make it sweet (Pennisi, 1992). (See "Are You a Supertaster?")

Anosmia Loss or impairment of the sense of smell.

Lock and key theory Holds that odors are related to the shapes of chemical molecules.

Pheromone An airborne chemical signal.

Taste bud The receptor organ for taste.

DISCOVERING PSYCHOLOGY

Are You a Superstar?

Spicy foods? Some like it hot. Others breathe fire if a dish contains a tiny bit too much pepper. And what about sweets? One person's sumptuous delight is another's cloying goo. Clearly, all tongues are not created equal (Bartoshuk et al., 2004). To learn a little more about taste sensitivity, try the following tests, devised by Linda Bartoshuk and Laurie Lucchina of Yale University (Bartoshuk, Duffy, & Miller, 1994).

Sweet

Place one-half cup of sugar in a measuring cup and add enough water to make one cup of solution. Rinse your mouth with plain water. Use a cotton swab dipped in the sugar solution to coat the front half of your tongue, including the tip. Wait a few seconds and rate the sensation of sweetness according to the taste scale.

Taste Scale

Barely detectable | Weak | Moderate | Strong | Very strong | Strongest imaginable sensation

0 10 20 30 40 50 60 70 80 90 100

Spicy

Add one teaspoon of Tabasco sauce to one cup of water. Coat one-half inch of your tongue, starting at the tip. Keep your tongue outside of your mouth until the burning sensation peaks. Rate the sensation of "heat" you feel on the scale.

Results

■ Table 5.2 shows typical ratings for nontasters and supertasters. Most people, of course, fall in between these extremes. About one in four is a supertaster.

Sensitivity to tastes has a genetic basis (Bartoshuk, 2000). Supertasters tend to have stronger tastes for sweet, bitter, and irritants such as alcohol and capsaicin (the chemical that makes chilies hot). Women are more often supertasters. Nontasters tend to prefer sweets and fatty foods, which may be why supertasters tend to be slimmer than nontasters.

TABLE 5.2

Average Taste-Test Ratings

	NONTASTER	SUPERTASTER
Sweet	32	56
Spicy	31	64

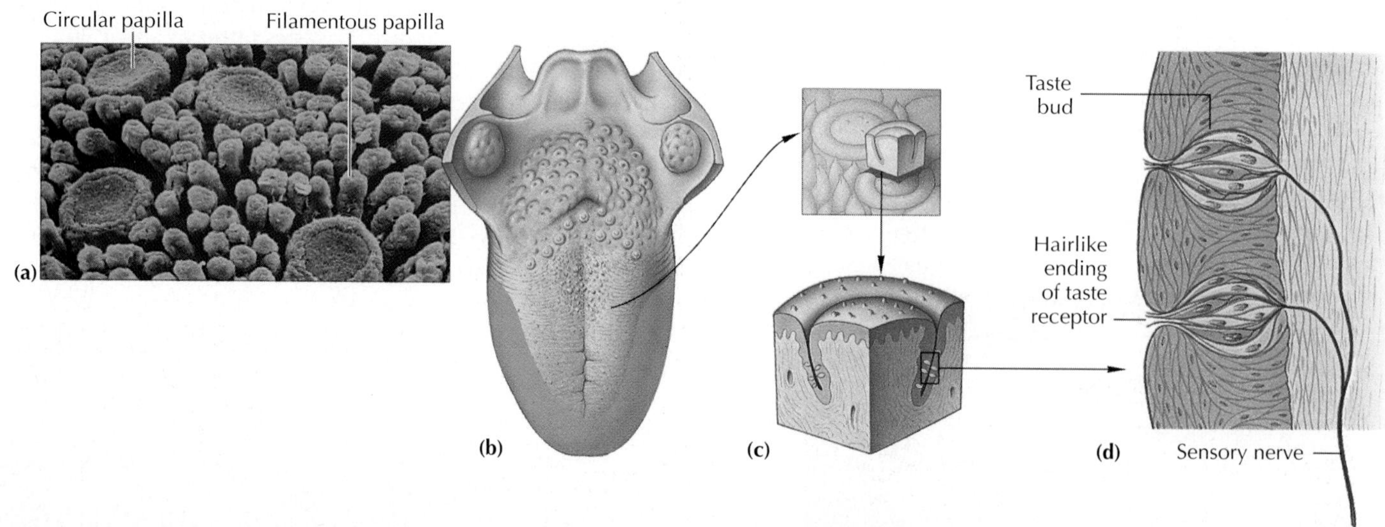

Figure 5.26 Receptors for taste: *(a)* The tongue is covered with small protrusions called *papillae. (b)* Most taste buds are found around the top edges of the tongue (shaded area). However, some are located elsewhere, including under the tongue. Stimulation of the central part of the tongue causes no taste sensations. All four primary taste sensations occur anywhere that taste buds exist. *(c)* An enlarged drawing shows that taste buds are located near the base of papillae. *(d)* Detail of a taste bud. These receptors also occur in other parts of the digestive system, such as the lining of the mouth.

The sense of taste also varies with age. Taste cells only live for several days. With aging, cell replacement slows, so the sense of taste diminishes. That's why many foods you disliked in childhood may seem appetizing now. Children who will not eat broccoli, spinach, liver, and so on may be having a very different taste experience than an adult. Aside from this fact, however, most taste preferences are acquired. Would you eat the coagulated secretion of the modified skin glands of a cow after it had undergone bacterial decomposition? If you would, you are a *cheese* fancier!

KNOWLEDGE BUILDER

Hearing, Smell, and Taste

REFLECT

Close your eyes and listen to the sounds around you. As you do, try to mentally trace the events necessary to convert vibrations in the air into the sounds you are hearing. Review the discussion of hearing if you leave out any steps.

What is your favorite food odor? What is your favorite taste? Can you explain how you are able to sense the aroma and taste of foods?

LEARNING CHECK

1. The frequency of a sound wave corresponds to how loud it is. T or F?
2. Which of the following is *not* a part of the cochlea?
   a. ossicles c. tympanic membrane
   b. pinna d. all of the above
3. Which of the following is *not* important for the transduction of sound?
   a. pinna d. oval window
   b. ossicles e. hair cells
   c. phosphenes
4. According to the place theory of hearing, higher tones register most strongly near the base of the cochlea. T or F?
5. Nerve deafness occurs when the auditory ossicles are damaged. T or F?
6. Daily exposure to sounds with a loudness of ______ decibels may cause permanent hearing loss.
7. Cochlear implants have been used primarily to overcome
   a. conduction deafness c. nerve deafness
   b. stimulation deafness d. tinnitus
8. Olfaction appears to be at least partially explained by the ______ ______ ______ theory of molecule shapes and receptor sites.
9. From the standpoint of survival, we are fortunate that we are least sensitive to bitter tastes. T or F?

CRITICAL THINKING

10. Why do you think your voice sounds so different when you hear a tape recording of your speech?
11. Smell and hearing differ from vision in a way that may aid survival. What is it?

Answers: **1.** F **2.** d **3.** c **4.** T **5.** F **6.** 85 **7.** c **8.** lock and key **9.** F **10.** The answer lies in another question: How else might vibrations from the voice reach the cochlea? Other people hear your voice only as it is carried through the air. You hear not only that sound, but also vibrations conducted by the bones of your skull. **11.** Both smell and hearing can detect stimuli (including signals of approaching danger) around corners, behind objects, and behind the head.

The Somesthetic Senses—Flying by the Seat of Your Pants

A gymnast "flying" through a routine on the uneven bars may rely as much on the **somesthetic senses** as on vision (*soma* means "body"; *esthetic* means "feel"). Even the most routine activities, such as walking, running, or passing a sobriety test, would be impossible without somesthetic information from the body. You would find it very difficult to move, stay upright, or even stay alive without touch, pain, balance, and other bodily senses. They are an essential part of our sensory world.

What are the somesthetic senses? Somesthetic sensitivity includes the **skin senses** (touch), the **kinesthetic senses** (receptors in muscles and joints that detect body position and movement), and the **vestibular senses** (receptors in the inner ear for balance, gravity, and acceleration). Let's begin with the skin senses.

The Skin Senses

It's difficult to imagine what life would be like without the sense of touch, but the plight of Ian Waterman gives a hint. After an illness, Waterman permanently lost all feeling below his neck. Now, in order to know what position his body is in he has to be able to see it. If he moves with his eyes closed, he has no idea where he is moving. If the lights go out in a room, he's in big trouble (Cole, 1995).

Skin receptors produce at least five different sensations: *light touch, pressure, pain, cold,* and *warmth.* Receptors with particular shapes appear to specialize somewhat in various sensations (● Figure 5.27). However, the surface of the eye, which has only free nerve endings, can produce all five sensations (Carlson, 2005). Altogether, the skin has about 200,000 nerve endings for temperature, 500,000 for touch and pressure, and 3 million for pain.

Doe s the number of receptors in an area of skin relate to its sensitivity? Yes. Your skin could be "mapped" by applying heat, cold, touch, pressure, or pain to points all over your body. Such testing would show that the number of skin receptors varies and that sensitivity generally matches the number of receptors in a given area. As a rough-and-ready illustration, try this two-point touch test:

> The density of touch receptors on various body areas can be checked by having a friend apply two pencil points to the skin with varying distances between them. Without looking, you should respond "one" or "two" each time. Record the distance between the pencils each time you feel two points.

Somesthetic sense Sensations produced by the skin, muscles, joints, viscera, and organs of balance.

Skin senses The senses of touch, pressure, pain, heat, and cold.

Kinesthetic senses The senses of body movement and positioning.

Vestibular senses The senses of balance, position in space, and acceleration.

Skin receptors Sensory organs for light touch, pressure, pain, cold, and warmth.

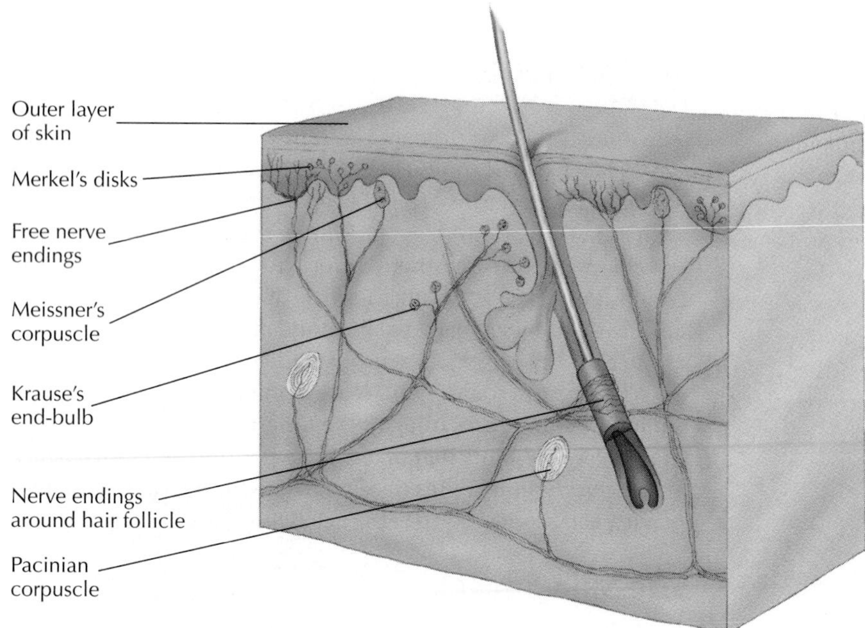

Figure 5.27 The skin senses include touch, pressure, pain, cold, and warmth. This drawing shows different forms the skin receptors can take. The only clearly specialized receptor is the pacinian corpuscle, which is highly sensitive to pressure. Free nerve endings are receptors for pain and any of the other sensations. For reasons that are not clear, cold is sensed near the surface of the skin and warmth is sensed deeper (Carlson, 2005).

You should find that two points are recognizable when they are 1/10 inch apart on the fingertips, 1/4 inch on the nose, and 3 inches at the middle of the back. Generally speaking, important areas such as the lips, tongue, face, hands, and genitals have a higher density of receptors. Of course, the sensation you ultimately feel will depend on brain activity.

Pain

There are many more pain receptors than other kinds. Why is pain so heavily represented, and does the concentration of pain receptors also vary? Like the other skin senses, pain receptors vary in their distribution. An average of about 232 pain points per square centimeter are found behind the knee, 184 per centimeter on the buttocks, 60 on the pad of the thumb, and 44 on the tip of the nose. (Is it better then, to be pinched on the nose than behind the knee? It depends on what you like!)

Pain fibers are also found in the internal organs. Stimulation of these fibers causes **visceral pain.** Curiously, visceral pain is often felt on the surface of the body, at a site some distance from the point of origin. Experiences of this type are called **referred pain** (● Figure 5.28). For example, a person having a heart attack may feel pain in the left shoulder, arm, or even the little finger.

Pain from the skin, muscles, joints, and tendons is known as **somatic** (bodily) **pain.** Somatic pain carried by *large nerve fibers* is sharp, bright, fast, and seems to come from specific body areas. This is the body's **warning system.** Give yourself a small jab with a pin and you will feel this type of pain. As you do this, notice that warning pain quickly disappears. Much as we may dislike warning pain, it is usually a signal that the body has been, or is about to be, damaged. Without warning pain, we would be unable to detect or prevent injury. Children who are born with a rare inherited insensitivity to pain repeatedly burn themselves, break bones, bite their tongues, and become ill without knowing it (Larner et al., 1994).

A second type of somatic pain is carried by *small nerve fibers.* This type is slower, nagging, aching, widespread, and very unpleasant. It gets worse if the pain stimulus is repeated. This is the body's **reminding system.** It reminds the brain that the body has been injured. Sadly, the reminding system can cause agony long after an injury has healed or in terminal illnesses, when the reminder is useless. This chapter's Psychology in Action section describes some ways to control pain. If you got carried away with the earlier pin demonstration, maybe you should read ahead now!

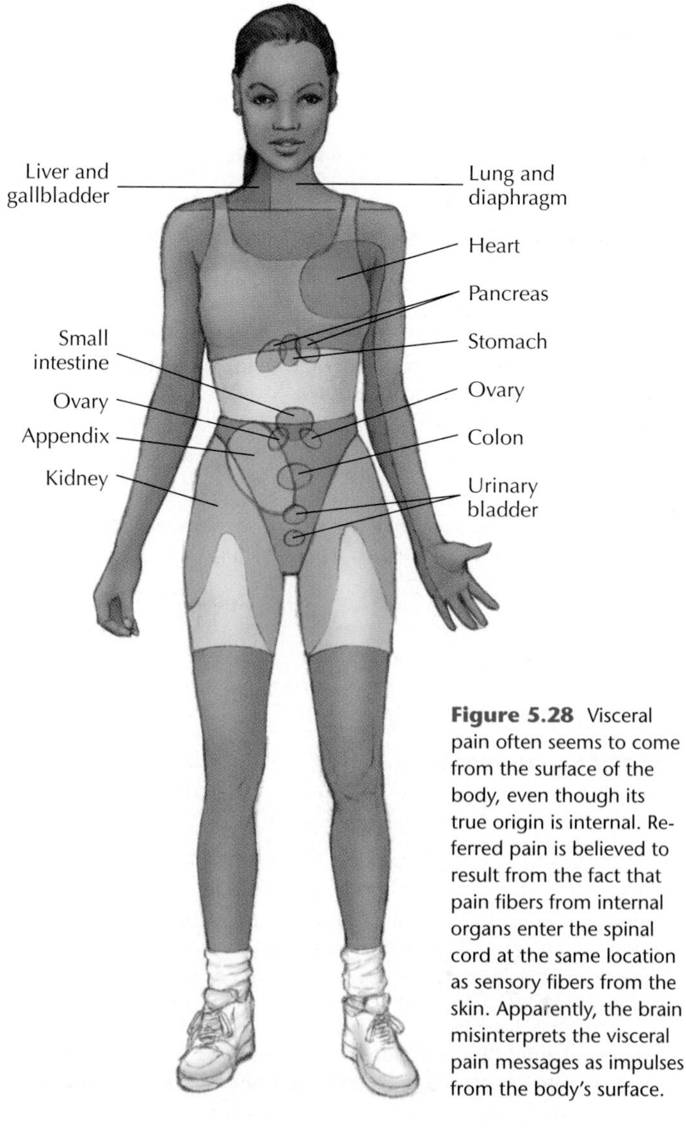

Figure 5.28 Visceral pain often seems to come from the surface of the body, even though its true origin is internal. Referred pain is believed to result from the fact that pain fibers from internal organs enter the spinal cord at the same location as sensory fibers from the skin. Apparently, the brain misinterprets the visceral pain messages as impulses from the body's surface.

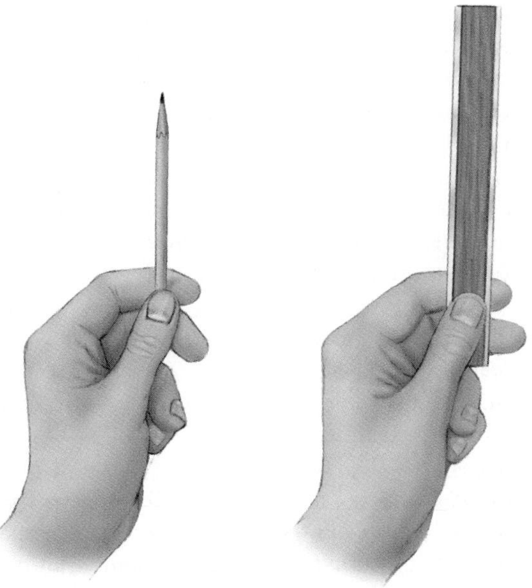

Figure 5.29 Hold a variety of elongated objects upright between your fingertips. Close your eyes and move each object about. Your ability to estimate the size, length, shape, and orientation of each object will be quite accurate. (After Turvey, 1996.)

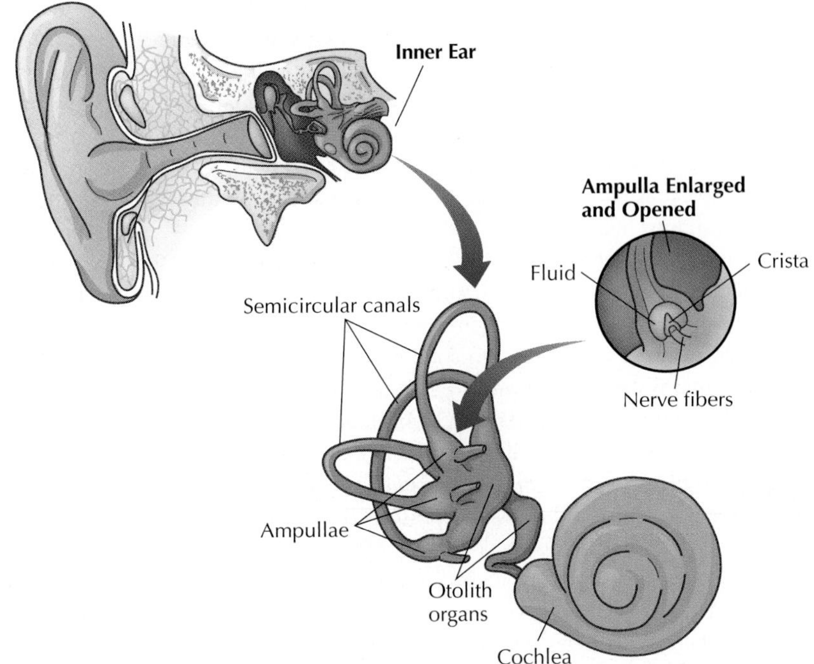

Figure 5.30 The vestibular system. (See text for explanation.)

JSC/NASA

Weightlessness presents astronauts with a real challenge in sensory adaptation.

Dynamic Touch

A carpenter swings a hammer with practiced precision. A juggler fluidly tosses and catches five balls. An ice hockey player embeds his stick in an opposing player's helmet. In sports and everyday life, touch is rarely static. Most skilled performances rely on **dynamic touch**, which combines sensations from skin receptors with kinesthetic information from the muscles and tendons.

Studies have shown that dynamic touch provides surprisingly detailed information about objects, such as their size and shape (see ● Figure 5.29). How are we able to make such judgments? Psychologist M. T. Turvey has found that most bodily motions form an arc or a combination of arcs. Dynamic touch is largely a matter of sensing the *inertia* of objects as they move through these arcs. The fact that dynamic touch is a reliable source of information is what makes it possible for us to use a wide range of tools, utensils, and objects as if they were extensions of our bodies (Turvey, 1996).

The Vestibular System

Space flight might look like fun. But if you ever get a ride into space, it is about 70 percent likely that your first experience in orbit will be throwing up (Davis et al., 1988). Weightlessness and space flight affect the vestibular system, often causing severe motion sickness (● Figure 5.30). Within the vestibular system, fluid-filled sacs called *otolith* (OH-toe-lith) *organs* are sensitive to movement, acceleration, and gravity. The otolith organs contain tiny crystals in a soft, gelatin-like mass. The tug of gravity or rapid head movements can cause the mass to shift. This, in turn, stimulates hair-like receptor cells, allowing us to sense gravity, acceleration, and movement through space (Lackner & DiZio, 2005).

Visceral pain Pain originating in the internal organs.

Referred pain Pain that is felt in one part of the body but comes from another.

Somatic pain Pain from the skin, muscles, joints, and tendons.

Warning system Pain based on large nerve fibers; warns that bodily damage may be occurring.

Reminding system Pain based on small nerve fibers; reminds the brain that the body has been injured.

Dynamic touch Touch experienced when the body is in motion; a combination of sensations from skin receptors, muscles, and joints.

Three fluid-filled tubes called the *semicircular canals* are the sensory organs for balance. If you could climb inside these tubes, you would find that head movements cause the fluid to swirl about. As the fluid moves, it bends a small "flap," or "float," called the *crista,* that detects movement in the semicircular canals. A crista can be found within each *ampulla* (am-PULL-ah), a wider part of the canal. The bending of each crista again stimulates hair cells and signals head rotation.

What causes motion sickness? According to **sensory conflict theory,** we feel dizziness and nausea when sensations from the vestibular system don't match sensations from our eyes and body (Warwick-Evans et al., 1998). On solid ground, information from the vestibular system, vision, and kinesthesis usually matches. However, in a heaving, pitching boat, car, or airplane, a serious mismatch can occur—causing disorientation and heaving of another kind.

Why would sensory conflict cause nausea? You can probably blame (or thank) evolution. Many poisons disturb the vestibular system, vision, and the body. Therefore, we may have evolved so that we react to sensory conflict by vomiting to expel poison. The value of this reaction, however, may be of little comfort to anyone who has ever been "green" and miserable with motion sickness.

In space, sensory conflict can be especially intense. During weightlessness, merely pulling on one's shoes can result in a backward somersault. Under such conditions, the otolith organs send unexpected signals to the brain, and head movements are no longer confirmed by the semicircular canals. Few of the messages the brain receives from the vestibular system and kinesthetic receptors agree with a lifetime of past experience (Yardley, 1992).

What can be done to minimize motion sickness? Whether you are in outer space, playing a particularly intense video game, or just sitting in the backseat of a moving car, motion sickness is a very unpleasant experience. If you face motion sickness, there are a few things you can try that should help (Harm, 2002; Jackson, 1994). If you know beforehand that you might be at risk, consider taking nonprescription motion sickness pills. If you are trapped in the moment, try minimizing sensory conflict by moving your head as little as possible. Either close your eyes, fixate on an unmoving point (such as the horizon), or look above the horizon at the unmoving sky. Also, lie down if you can. The otoliths are less sensitive to vertical movements when you are horizontal, and your head will move less. Finally, anxiety intensifies motion sickness. Try slow, deep breathing (Jokerst et al., 1999) and other relaxation techniques that you can use when needed (Jackson, 1994). (Relaxation methods are described in Chapter 17 of this book.)

How long does it take to adapt to weightlessness? Space sickness usually disappears in 2 or 3 days. Recent research suggests that this adaptation occurs because astronauts shift to using visual cues instead of vestibular information. Later, this same shift can cause "earth sickness." Immediately after returning to Earth (especially after very long missions), some astronauts have experienced dizziness and nausea. All had considerable difficulty in standing with their eyes closed for the first day or two (Von Baumgarten et al., 1984).

Space sickness is only one of the behavioral challenges of space travel. In fact, the long-term effects of space flight are still largely unknown. Although space missions seem relatively routine, astronauts remain true pioneers in a strange and alien sensory environment.

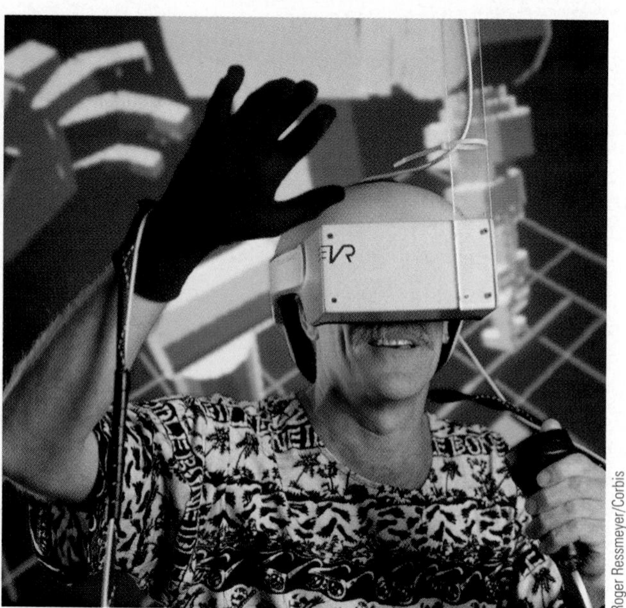

Roger Ressmeyer/Corbis

Many people become nauseated the first time they experience virtual reality. Why? Because virtual reality also creates a sensory conflict: Computer-generated visual images change as if the viewer's body is in motion, but the vestibular system tells viewers that they are standing still (Harm, 2002). The result? The scenery may not be real but the nausea is.

Adaptation, Attention, and Gating—Tuning In and Tuning Out

You are surrounded by sights, sounds, odors, tastes, and touch sensations. Which are you aware of? Each of the senses we have described is continuously active. Even so, many sensory events never reach awareness because of *sensory adaptation, selective attention,* and *sensory gating.* Let's see how information is filtered by these processes.

Sensory Adaptation

Think about walking into a house where fried fish, sauerkraut, broccoli, and head cheese were prepared for dinner. (Some dinner!) You would probably pass out at the door, yet people who had been in the house for some time wouldn't be aware of the food odors. Why? Because sensory receptors respond less to unchanging stimuli, a process called **sensory adaptation.**

Fortunately, the olfactory (smell) receptors adapt quickly. When exposed to a constant odor, they send fewer and fewer nerve impulses to the brain until the odor is no longer noticed. Adaptation to pressure from a wristwatch, waistband, ring, or glasses is based on the same principle. Sensory receptors generally respond best to *changes* in stimulation. No one wants or needs to be reminded 16 hours a day that his shoes are on.

If change is necessary to prevent sensory adaptation, why doesn't vision undergo adaptation like the sense of smell does? If you stare at something, it certainly doesn't go away. The rods and cones, like other receptor cells, would respond less to a constant stimulus. However, the eye normally makes thousands of tiny movements every minute. These movements are caused by *physiological nystagmus* (nis-TAG-mus: involuntary tremors of the eye muscles). Although they are too small to be seen, the movements shift visual images from one receptor cell to another.

Constant eye movement ensures that images always fall on fresh, unfatigued rods and cones. Evidence for this comes from fitting people with a contact lens that has a miniature slide projector attached to it (● Figure 5.31*a*). Because the projector follows the exact movements of the eye, an image can be stabilized on the retina. When this is done, projected geometric designs fade from view within a few seconds (Pritchard, 1961). You can get a similar effect by staring at ● Figure 5.31*b*. Because the lighter circle does not form a distinct edge, the retina adapts to the brightness difference. As it does, the circle gradually disappears.

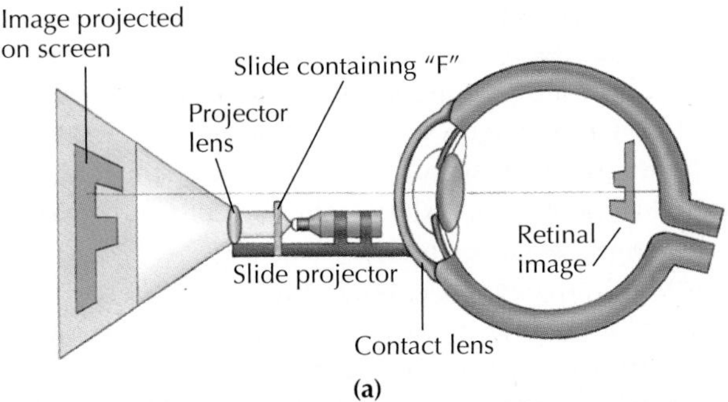

Figure 5.31 Stabilized images. *(a)* A miniature slide projector attached to a contact lens moves each time the eye moves. As a result, the projected image disappears in a few seconds because it does not move on the retina. *(b)* A similar effect occurs when changes in brightness do not define a distinct edge. In this case, eye movements cannot prevent adaptation. Therefore, if you stare at the dot, the lighter area will disappear. (After Cornsweet, 1970.)

Selective Attention

As you sit reading this page, receptors for touch and pressure in the seat of your pants are sending nerve impulses to your brain. Although these sensations have been present all along, you were probably not aware of them until just now. This "seat-of-the-pants phenomenon" is an example of **selective attention** (voluntarily focusing on a specific sensory input). We are able to "tune in on" a single sensory message while excluding others. Another familiar example of this is the "cocktail party effect." When you are in a group of people, surrounded by voices, you can still select and attend to the voice of the person you are facing. Or if that person gets dull, you can eavesdrop on conversations all over the room. (Be sure to smile and nod your head occasionally!) Actually, no matter how interesting your companion may be, your attention will probably shift away if you hear your own name spoken somewhere in the room (Conway, Cowan, & Bunting, 2001). We do find what others say about us to be very interesting, don't we?

Sensory Gating

What makes selective attention possible? Selective attention appears to be based on the ability of brain structures to select and divert incoming sensory messages (Sekuler & Blake, 2006). But what about messages that haven't reached the brain? Is it possible that some are blocked while others are allowed to pass? Evidence suggests there are *sensory gates* that control the flow of incoming nerve impulses in just this way. In particular, **sensory gating** refers to facilitating or blocking sensory messages in the spinal cord (Melzack, 1993; Melzack & Wall, 1996).

Pain Gates

A fascinating example of sensory gating is provided by Ronald Melzack and Patrick Wall (1996), who study "pain gates" in the spinal cord. Melzack and Wall noticed, as you may have, that one type of pain will sometimes cancel another. Their **gate control theory** suggests that pain messages from different nerve fibers pass through the same neural "gate" in the spinal cord. If the gate is "closed" by one pain message, other messages may not be able to pass through (Humphries, Johnson, & Long, 1996).

Sensory conflict theory Explains motion sickness as the result of a mismatch between information from vision, the vestibular system, and kinesthesis.

Sensory adaptation A decrease in sensory response to an unchanging stimulus.

Selective attention Voluntarily focusing on a specific sensory input.

Sensory gating Alteration of sensory messages in the spinal cord.

Gate control theory Proposes that pain messages pass through neural "gates" in the spinal cord.

How is the gate closed? Messages carried by large, fast nerve fibers seem to close the spinal pain gate directly. Doing so can prevent slower, "reminding system" pain from reaching the brain. Pain clinics use this effect by applying a mild electrical current to the skin. Such stimulation, felt only as a mild tingling, can greatly reduce more agonizing pain.

Messages from small, slow fibers seem to take a different route. After going through the pain gate, they pass on to a "central biasing system" in the brain. Under some circumstances, the brain then sends a message back down the spinal cord, closing the pain gates (see ● Figure 5.32). Melzack and Wall believe that gate control theory explains the painkilling effects of *acupuncture.*

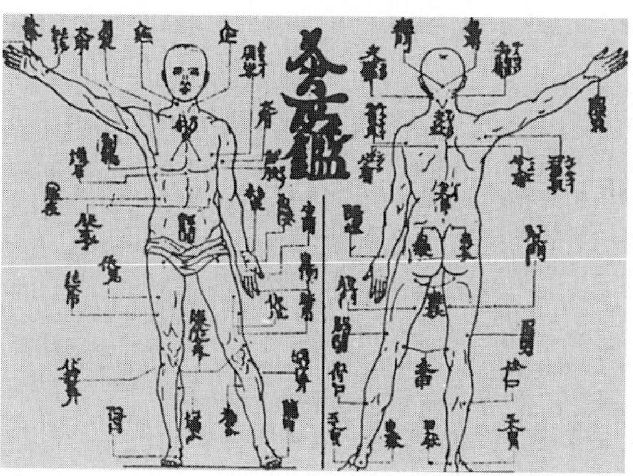

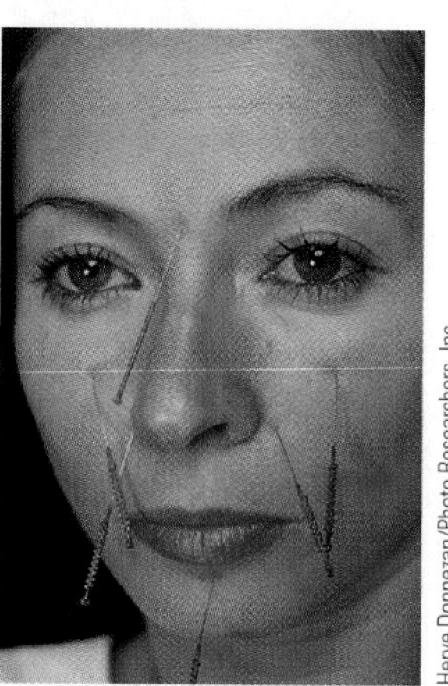

(left) An acupuncturist's chart. *(right)* Thin stainless steel needles are inserted into areas defined by the chart. Modern research has begun to explain the painkilling effects of acupuncture (see text). Acupuncture's claimed ability to cure diseases is more debatable.

Acupuncture is the Chinese medical art of relieving pain and illness by inserting thin needles into the body. As the acupuncturist's needles are twirled, heated, or electrified, they activate small pain fibers. These relay through the biasing system to close the gates to intense or chronic pain (Melzack & Wall, 1996). Studies have shown that acupuncture produces short-term pain relief for 50 to 80 percent of patients tested (Ernst, 1994; Murray, 1995).

Acupuncture has an interesting side effect not predicted by sensory gating. People given acupuncture often report feelings of lightheadedness, relaxation, or euphoria. How are these feelings explained? The answer seems to lie in the body's ability to produce opiate-like chemicals. To combat pain, the brain causes the pituitary gland to release a painkilling chemical called **beta-endorphin** (BAY-tah-en-DOR-fin: from *endo,* "within," and *orphin,* "opiate"). Chemically, beta-endorphin is quite similar to morphine.

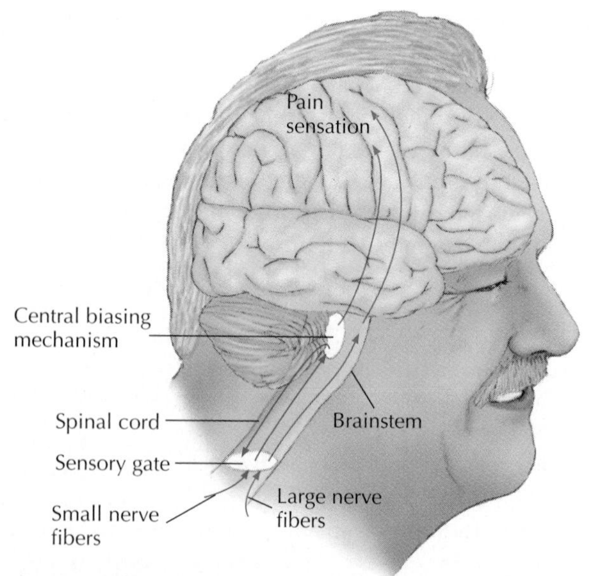

Figure 5.32 A sensory gate for pain. A series of pain impulses going through the gate may prevent other pain messages from passing through. Or pain messages may relay through a "central biasing mechanism" that exerts control over the gate, closing it to other impulses.

Such discoveries help explain the painkilling effect of placebos (fake pills or injections), which raise endorphin levels. A release of endorphins also seems to underlie "runner's high," masochism, acupuncture, and the euphoria sometimes associated with childbirth, painful initiation rites, or eating hot chili peppers (Sternberg et al., 1998). In each case, pain and stress cause the release of endorphins. These in turn induce feelings of pleasure or euphoria similar to being "high" on morphine.

The "high" often felt by long-distance runners serves as a good example of the endorphin effect. In one experiment, subjects were tested for pain tolerance. After running 1 mile, each was tested again. In the second test, all could withstand pain about 70 percent longer than before. The runners were then given naloxone, a drug that blocks the effects of endorphins. Following another 1-mile run the subjects were tested again. This time they had lost their earlier protection from pain (Haier et al., 1988). A similar effect occurs with first-time parachute jumpers. After the jump, their endorphin levels increase dramatically and they are much less sensitive to pain (Janssen & Arntz, 2001). Actually, these observations tie in nicely with the idea of pain gates. The central biasing system, which closes pain gates in the spinal cord, is highly sensitive to morphine and other opiate painkillers (Melzack & Wall, 1996). People who say they are "addicted" to running, or bungee jumping, or eating spicy foods may be closer to the truth than they realize. (But can pain gates and endorphins explain every type of pain? See "The Matrix: Do Phantoms Live Here?")

Conclusion and a Look Ahead

The senses supply raw data to the brain, but the information remains mostly meaningless until it is interpreted. It's as if the senses provide only the jumbled pieces of a complex puzzle. In the next chapter we will explore some perceptual processes that help us put the puzzle together.

A variety of psychological factors affect the severity of pain. Because you may not want to try acupuncture or electrical stimulation to control everyday pain, the following discussion describes several practical ways to reduce pain. Before we turn to that useful topic, here's a chance to rehearse what you've learned.

THE CLINICAL FILE

The Matrix: Do Phantoms Live Here?

In the popular *Matrix* film trilogy, Neo, as played by Keanu Reeves, discovers that he is imprisoned in a phantom world by machines that are stealing human energy for their own use. What would you say if you found out that the idea of a "matrix" is not totally farfetched, and that your own brain may be creating a *neuromatrix* that is responsible for your perceptions of your own body? Welcome to the world of phantom limbs.

A person who suffers an amputation doesn't need to believe in the *Matrix* to encounter phantoms. Most amputees have **phantom limb** sensations for months or years after losing a limb (Fraser, 2002). For some, the missing limb continues to feel as if it is present, just as it always did. Because the phantom limb feels so "real," a patient with a recently amputated leg may inadvertently try to walk on it, risking further injury. Sometimes phantom limbs feel like they are stuck in awkward positions. For instance, one man can't sleep on his back because his missing arm feels like it is twisted behind him. Worst of all, perhaps, are the amputees who suffer from phantom limb pain, which may be severe, can last for years, and is very difficult to treat (Halbert, Crotty, & Cameron, 2002).

What causes phantom limbs? Phantom limb pain cannot be explained by gate-control theory (Hunter, Katz, & Davis, 2003). Because pain cannot be coming from the missing limb (after all, it's missing), it cannot pass through pain gates to the brain. Instead, according to Ronald Melzack (1993, 1999), the brain creates a body image called the *neuromatrix,* which ultimately creates our sense of bodily self. Although amputation may remove a limb, as far as the neuromatrix in the brain is concerned, the limb still exists. Medical imaging techniques have made it possible to confirm that sensory and motor areas of the brain are more active when a person feels a phantom limb (Rosen et al., 2001). Even though pain signals no longer emanate from the amputated limb, the neuromatrix may continue to interpret other sensory experiences as pain coming from the missing limb.

Sometimes the brain gradually reorganizes to adjust for the sensory loss (Wu & Kaas, 2002). For example, a person who loses an arm may at first have a phantom arm and hand. After many years, the phantom may shrink, until only a hand is felt at the shoulder. Perhaps more vividly than others, people with phantom limbs are reminded that the sensory world as we know it is constructed, moment by moment, not by some futuristic machines but by our very own neuromatrix in our brains.

KNOWLEDGE BUILDER

Somesthetic Senses, Adaptation, Attention, and Gating

REFLECT

Stand on one foot with your eyes closed. Now touch the tip of your nose with your index finger. Which of the somesthetic senses did you use to perform this feat?

Imagine you are on a boat ride with a friend who starts to feel queasy. Can you explain to your friend what causes motion sickness and what she or he can do to prevent it?

As you sit reading this book, which sensory inputs have undergone adaptation? What new inputs can you become aware of by shifting your focus of attention?

LEARNING CHECK

1. Which of the following is a somesthetic sense?
   a. gustation c. rarefaction
   b. olfaction d. kinesthesis
2. An ability to sense the inertia of objects as we move them through space is the basis for ______________________ ______________________.
3. Pain that originates in the internal organs is sometimes felt on the surface of the body as "referred pain." T or F?
4. Warning pain is carried by ____________ nerve fibers.
5. Head movements are detected primarily in the semicircular canals, gravity by the otolith organs. T or F?
6. Sensory conflict theory appears to explain space sickness, but it does not seem to apply to other types of motion sickness. T or F?
7. *Sensory adaptation* refers to an increase in sensory response that accompanies a constant or unchanging stimulus. T or F?
8. The brain-centered ability to influence what sensations we will receive is called
   a. sensory gating c. selective attention
   b. central adaptation d. sensory biasing
9. The painkilling effects of acupuncture appear to result from ______________ ______________ and the release of beta-endorphin.

CRITICAL THINKING

10. What special precautions would you have to take to test the ability of acupuncture to reduce pain?
11. In a very real sense, we all live slightly in the past. How could that be true?

Answers: 1. d **2.** dynamic touch **3.** T **4.** large **5.** T **6.** F **7.** F **8.** c **9.** sensory gating **10.** At the very least, you would have to control for the placebo effect by giving fake acupuncture to control group members. However, a true double-blind study would be difficult to do. Acupuncturists would always know if they were giving a placebo treatment or the real thing, which means they might unconsciously influence subjects. **11.** For all of the senses, it takes a split second for sensory receptors to sense a change in external stimuli and for a neural message to arrive at the brain. Therefore, by the time we are aware of an event, such as a very brief flash of light, it is already over.

Beta-endorphin A natural, painkilling brain chemical similar to morphine.

Phantom limb The illusory sensation that a limb still exists after it is lost through accident or amputation.

PSYCHOLOGY IN ACTION

Controlling Pain—This Won't Hurt a Bit

In some cultures, people endure tattooing, stretching, cutting, and burning with little apparent pain. How is such insensitivity achieved? Very likely the answer lies in four factors that anyone can use to reduce pain. These are (1) anxiety, (2) control, (3) attention, and (4) interpretation (McMahon & Koltzenburg, 2005).

Anxiety

The basic sensory message of pain can be separated from emotional reactions to it. Fear or high levels of anxiety almost always increase pain. (**Anxiety** is a feeling of apprehension or uneasiness similar to fear, but based on an unclear threat.) A dramatic reversal of this effect is the surprising lack of pain displayed by soldiers wounded in battle. Being excused from further combat apparently produces a flood of relief. This emotional state leaves many soldiers insensitive to wounds that would agonize a civilian (Melzack & Wall, 1996). In general, unpleasant emotions increase pain and pleasant emotions decrease it (Meagher, Arnau, & Rhudy, 2001).

Pain is a complex experience. In addition to producing a physical sensation, pain messages activate areas of the brain associated with emotion. If you are fearful or anxious, the emotional part of pain will be magnified and you will feel more intense pain. Reducing fear and anxiety is one of several things you can do to diminish pain.

Esbin-Anderson/Photo Network/PictureQuest

Control

If you can regulate a painful stimulus, you have **control** over it. A moment's reflection should convince you that the most upsetting pain is that over which you have no control. Loss of control seems to increase pain by increasing anxiety and emotional distress. People who are allowed to regulate, avoid, or control a painful stimulus suffer less. In general, the more control one *feels* over a painful stimulus, the less pain is experienced (Wells, 1994).

Attention

Distraction can also radically reduce pain. As you'll recall, **attention** refers to voluntarily focusing on a specific sensory input. Pain, even though it is highly persistent, can be selectively "tuned out" (at least partially), just like any other sensation. Subjects in one experiment who were in intense pain experienced the greatest relief when they were distracted by the task of watching for signal lights to come on (Johnson et al., 1998). Another example is provided by burn patients, who must undergo excruciating pain while their bandages are changed. Recently, video games and virtual reality have been used to distract them from their pain, which helps immensely (Hoffman et al., 2001).

Have you ever temporarily forgotten about a toothache or similar pain while absorbed in a movie or book? As this suggests, concentrating on pleasant, soothing images can be especially helpful (Fernandez & Turk, 1989). Instead of listening to the whirr of a dentist's drill, for example, you might imagine that you are lying in the sun on a beach, listening to the roar of the surf. Or, take an iPod along and crank up your favorite MP3. At home, music can be a good distractor from chronic pain (Good, 1995; Michel & Chesky, 1995).

Interpretation

The meaning, or **interpretation**, you give a stimulus also affects pain (Turk & Melzack, 2001). For example, if you give a child a swat on the behind while playing, you'll probably get a burst of laughter. Yet the same swat given as punishment may bring tears. The effects of interpretation are illustrated by an experiment in which thinking of pain as pleasurable (denying the pain) greatly increased pain tolerance (Neufeld, 1970). Another study found that people who believe a painful procedure will improve their health feel less pain during the procedure (Staats et al., 1998).

BRIDGES

In addition to reducing pain, prepared childbirth has other benefits.

See Chapter 3, page 88.

Coping with Pain

How can these facts be applied? In a sense, they already are applied to childbirth. *Prepared childbirth training,* which promotes birth with a minimum of drugs or painkillers, uses all four factors. To prepare for natural childbirth, the expectant mother learns in great detail what to anticipate at each stage of labor. This greatly relieves her fears and anxieties. During labor, she attends to sensations that mark her progress and she adjusts her breathing accordingly. Her attention is shifted to sensations other than pain, resulting in less discomfort (Leventhal et al., 1989). Also, her positive attitude is maintained by use of the term "contractions" rather than "labor pains." Finally, because of her months of preparation and her active participation, she feels *in control* of the situation.

Natural childbirth techniques reduce pain by an average of about 30 percent. Many women find this reduction quite helpful. However, it is important to remember that labor can produce very severe pain. A woman should not feel guilty if she needs painkillers during labor. Many women who have had prepared childbirth training still end up asking for an epidural block.

For moderate pain, it can make quite a difference to reduce anxiety, redirect attention, and increase control. When you anticipate pain (during a trip to the doctor, dentist, and so on), you can lower anxiety by making sure that you are *fully informed.* Be sure that someone explains everything that will happen or could happen to you. Also, be sure to fully discuss any fears you have. If you are physically tense, you can use relaxation exercises to lower your level of arousal. Relaxation methods involve tensing and then releasing muscles in various parts of the body. A typical technique is described in detail in the Psychology in Action section of Chapter 17. (The desensitization procedure described there may also help reduce anxiety.)

Distraction and Reinterpretation

Some dentists are now equipped to help you shift attention away from pain. Patients are actively distracted with video games and headphones playing music. In other situations, focusing on some external object may help you shift attention away from pain. Pick a tree outside a window, a design on the wall, or some other stimulus and examine it in great detail. Prior practice in meditation can be a tremendous aid to such attention shifts. Research suggests that distraction of this type works best for mild or brief pain. For chronic or strong pain, reinterpretation is more effective (McCaul & Malott, 1984).

Counterirritation

Is there any way to increase control over a painful stimulus? Practically speaking, the choices may be limited. You may be able to arrange a signal with a doctor or dentist that will give you control over whether a painful procedure will continue. A second possibility is more unusual. Ronald Melzack's gate control theory of pain suggests that sending *mild* pain messages to the spinal cord and brain may effectively close the neurological gates to more severe or unpredictable pain. Medical texts have long recognized this effect. Physicians have found that intense surface stimulation of the skin can control pain from other parts of the body. Likewise, a brief, mildly painful stimulus can relieve more severe pain. Such procedures, known as **counterirritation**, are evident in some of the oldest techniques used to control pain: applying ice packs, hot-water bottles, mustard packs, vibration, or massage to other parts of the body (Kakigi et al., 1993).

These facts suggest a way to minimize pain that is based on increased control, counterirritation, and the release of endorphins. If you pinch yourself, you can easily *create and endure* pain equal to that produced by many medical procedures (receiving an injection, having a tooth drilled, and so on). The pain doesn't seem too bad because you have control over it, and it is predictable.

This fact can be used to *mask* one pain with a second painful stimulus that is under your control. For instance, if you are having a tooth filled, try pinching yourself or digging a fingernail into a knuckle while the dentist is working. Focus your attention on the pain you are creating, and increase its intensity anytime the dentist's work becomes more painful. This suggestion may not work for you, but casual observation suggests that it can be a useful technique for controlling pain in some circumstances. Generations of children have used it to take the edge off a spanking.

Anxiety Apprehension or uneasiness similar to fear but based on an unclear threat.

Control Where pain is concerned, *control* refers to an ability to regulate the pain stimulus.

Attention Voluntarily focusing on a specific sensory input.

Interpretation Where pain is concerned, the meaning given to a stimulus.

Counterirritation Using mild pain to block more intense or long-lasting pain.

KNOWLEDGE BUILDER

Pain Control

REFLECT

Think about a strategy you have used for reducing pain at the doctor, dentist, or some other painful situation. Did you alter anxiety, control, attention, or interpretation? Can you think of any ways in which you have used counterirritation to lessen pain?

LEARNING CHECK

1. Like heightened anxiety, increased control tends to increase subjective pain. T or F?
2. In one experiment, subjects given the task of watching signal lights experienced less pain than subjects who paid attention to the pain stimulus. T or F?
3. Imagining a pleasant experience can be an effective way of reducing pain in some situations. T or F?
4. The concept of counterirritation holds that relaxation and desensitization are key elements of pain control. T or F?

CRITICAL THINKING

5. What measures would you take to ensure that an experiment involving pain is ethical?

Answers: 1. F **2.** T **3.** T **4.** F **5.** Experiments that cause pain must be handled with care and sensitivity. Participation must be voluntary, the source of pain must be noninjurious, and subjects must be allowed to quit at any time.

Chapter in Review

In general, how do sensory systems function?

- Sensory organs transduce physical energies into nerve impulses.
- Because of selectivity, limited sensitivity, feature detection, and coding patterns, the senses act as data reduction systems.
- Sensory response can be partially understood in terms of localization of function in the brain.

What are the limits of our sensory sensitivity?

- The minimum amount of physical energy necessary to produce a sensation defines the absolute threshold. The amount of change necessary to produce a just noticeable difference in a stimulus defines a difference threshold. The study of thresholds and related topics is called psychophysics.
- Threatening or anxiety-provoking stimuli may raise the threshold for recognition, an effect called perceptual defense.
- Any stimulus below the level of conscious awareness is said to be subliminal. There is evidence that subliminal perception occurs, but subliminal advertising is largely ineffective.

How is vision accomplished?

- The visible spectrum consists of electromagnetic radiation in a narrow range.
- The eye is a visual system, not a photographic one. Individual cells in the visual cortex of the brain act as feature detectors to analyze visual information.
- Four common visual defects are myopia (nearsightedness), hyperopia (farsightedness), presbyopia (loss of accommodation), and astigmatism.
- The rods and cones are photoreceptors making up the retina of the eye.
- The rods specialize in night vision, seeing black and white, and motion detection.
- The cones, found exclusively in the fovea and otherwise toward the middle of the eye, specialize in color vision, acuity, and daylight vision.
- Much peripheral vision is supplied by the rods.

How do we perceive colors?

- The rods and cones differ in color sensitivity. *Yellowish green* is brightest for cones, *blue-green* for the rods (although they will see it as colorless). Color vision is explained by the trichromatic theory in the retina and by the opponent-process theory in the visual system beyond the eyes.
- Total color blindness is rare, but 8 percent of males and 1 percent of females are red-green color-weak. Color weakness is a sex-linked trait carried on the *X* chromosome. The Ishihara test is used to detect color blindness and color weakness.
- Dark adaptation, an increase in sensitivity to light, is caused by increased concentration of visual pigments in both the rods and the cones but mainly by rhodopsin recombining in the rods. Vitamin A deficiencies may cause night blindness.

What are the mechanisms of hearing?

- Sound waves are the stimulus for hearing. They are transduced by the eardrum, auditory ossicles, oval window, cochlea, and ultimately, hair cells.
- The frequency theory and place theory of hearing together explain how pitch is sensed.
- Three basic types of deafness are nerve deafness, conduction deafness, and stimulation deafness.

How do the chemical senses operate?

- Olfaction (smell) and gustation (taste) are chemical senses responsive to airborne or liquefied molecules. It is also suspected that humans are sensitive to pheromones, although the evidence for this sense remains preliminary.
- The lock and key theory partially explains smell. In addition, the location of the olfactory receptors in the nose helps identify various scents.
- Sweet and bitter tastes are based on a lock-and-key coding of molecule shapes. Salty and sour tastes are triggered by a direct flow of ions into taste receptors.

What are the somesthetic senses, and why are they important?

- The somesthetic senses include the skin senses, vestibular senses, and kinesthetic senses (receptors that detect muscle and joint positioning).
- The skin senses include touch, pressure, pain, cold, and warmth. Sensitivity to each is related to the number of receptors found in an area of skin.
- Distinctions can be made among various types of pain, including visceral pain, somatic pain, referred pain, warning system pain, and reminding system pain.
- Various forms of motion sickness are related to messages received from the vestibular system, which senses gravity and movement.
- According to sensory conflict theory, motion sickness is caused by a mismatch of visual, kinesthetic, and vestibular sensations. Motion sickness can be avoided by minimizing sensory conflict.

Why are we more aware of some sensations than others?

- Incoming sensations are affected by sensory adaptation (a reduction in the number of nerve impulses sent), by selective attention (selection and diversion of messages in the brain), and by sensory gating (blocking or alteration of messages flowing toward the brain).
- Selective gating of pain messages apparently takes place in the spinal cord. Gate control theory proposes an explanation for many pain phenomena, except phantom limb pain.

How can pain be reduced in everyday situations?

- Pain is greatly affected by anxiety, attention, control over the stimulus, the interpretation placed on an experience, and counterirritation. Pain can therefore be reduced by controlling these factors.

Web Resources

Internet addresses frequently change. To find the sites listed here, visit www.thomsonedu.com/psychology/coon for an updated list of Internet addresses and direct links to relevant sites.

***Psychology: Gateways to Mind and Behavior* Website** Online quizzes, flash cards, and other helpful study aids for this text. www.thomsonedu.com/psychology/coon

HEARNET A page that promotes ear protection for rock musicians.

How We See A tutorial on the basic processes of vision.

Interactive Illustrations of Color Perception Examples of how colors interact with each other.

Questions and Answers About Pain Control Answers common questions about pain control.

Smell Olfaction and problems with smelling are defined.

Smell and Taste Disorders FAQ Questions and answers about smell and taste disorders.

Vestibular Disorders Association Provides links to sites concerned with vestibular problems.

ThomsonNOW™ Go to www.thomsonedu.com to link to ThomsonNow, your online study tool. First take the **Pre-Test** for this chapter to get your **Personalized Study Plan,** which will identify topics you need to review and direct you to online resources. Then take the **Post-Test** to determine what concepts you have mastered and what you still need work on.

InfoTrac College Edition For recent articles related to pain control, use Key Words search for ANXIETY and COUNTERIRRITATION. Go to www.thomsonedu.com/psychology/coon.

Interactive Learning

***PsychNow! Version 2.0* CD-ROM** Interact with the material with *PsychNow!'s* animations, video clips, experiments, and interactive assessments. For this chapter, go to *4a. Vision and Hearing* and *4b. Chemical and Somesthetic Senses* to learn more about these senses.

chapter

6

Perceiving the World

THEME:

Perception is an active process; perceptual impressions are not always accurate representations of events.

Key Questions

What are perceptual constancies, and what is their role in perception?

What basic principles do we use to group sensations into meaningful patterns?

How is it possible to see depth and judge distance?

What effect does learning have on perception?

How is perception altered by attention, motives, values, and expectations?

Is extrasensory perception possible?

How reliable are eyewitness reports?

Preview

Murder!

One of your authors was in a supermarket when an 8-year-old girl suddenly came running around a corner. She looked back and screamed, "Stop! Stop! You're killing him! You're killing my father!" Here is your author's account of what followed:

> I retraced the girl's path and saw two men on the floor, struggling violently. The guy on top had his victim by the throat. There was blood everywhere. It was a murder in progress! As a witness, I would have told a jury what I just told you, were it not for an important fact: No murder ever took place that day at the supermarket. When the police arrived, they quickly discovered that the "guy on the bottom" had passed out and hit his head. That caused the cut (actually quite minor) that explained the "blood everywhere." The "guy on top" saw the first man fall and was trying to loosen his collar. Obviously, the girl had misunderstood what was happening to her father. As a psychologist, I still find it fascinating that her words so dramatically influenced what I saw.

In the last chapter we discussed sensation, the process of bringing information into the nervous system. This chapter is about **perception,** or how we assemble sensations into meaningful patterns. As we perceive events, the brain actively selects, organizes, and integrates sensory information to construct a "picture" or model of the world. This process is so automatic that it can take a drastic misperception like that of your author to call attention to it.

Perception creates faces, melodies, works of art, illusions, and on occasion, "murders" out of the raw material of sensation. Let's see how this takes place.

Perceptual Constancies—Taming an Unruly World

What would it be like to have your vision restored after a lifetime of blindness? In Chapter 5 we met Bob Edens, who, after 50 years of blindness, was overjoyed by the vividness of colors. But a first look at the world can also be disappointing. Newly sighted persons must *learn* to identify objects; to read clocks, numbers, and letters; and to judge sizes and distances (Senden, 1960). Learning to "see" can be quite frustrating. For instance, a cataract patient named Mr. S. B. had been blind since birth. After an operation restored his sight at age 52, Mr. S. B. struggled to use his vision. At first, he could judge distance only in familiar situations (Gregory, 2000). One day he was found crawling out of a hospital window to get a closer look at traffic on the street. It's easy to understand his curiosity, but he had to be restrained. His room was on the fourth floor!

Why would Mr. S. B. try to crawl out of a fourth-story window? Couldn't he at least tell distance from the size of the cars? No, you must be familiar with objects to use their size to judge distance. Try holding your left hand a few inches in front of your nose and your right hand at arm's length. Your right hand should appear to be about half the size of your left hand. Still, you know your right hand did not suddenly shrink, because you have seen it many times at various distances. We call this **size constancy:** The perceived size of an object remains the same, even though the size of its image on the retina changes.

To perceive your hand accurately, you had to draw on past experience. Some perceptions are so basic they seem to be *native* (inborn). An example is the ability to see a line on a piece of paper. Likewise, even newborn babies show some evidence of size constancy (Slater, Mattock, & Brown, 1990). However, many of our perceptions are *empirical,* or based on prior experience. For instance, cars, houses, and people look like toys when seen from an unfamiliar perspective, such as from the top of a skyscraper. This suggests that although some size constancy is innate, it is also affected by learning.

In **shape constancy** the shape of an object remains stable, even though the shape of its retinal image changes. You can demonstrate shape constancy by looking at this page from directly overhead

Perception The mental process of organizing sensations into meaningful patterns.

Size constancy The perceived size of an object remains constant, despite changes in its retinal image.

Shape constancy The perceived shape of an object is unaffected by changes in its retinal image.

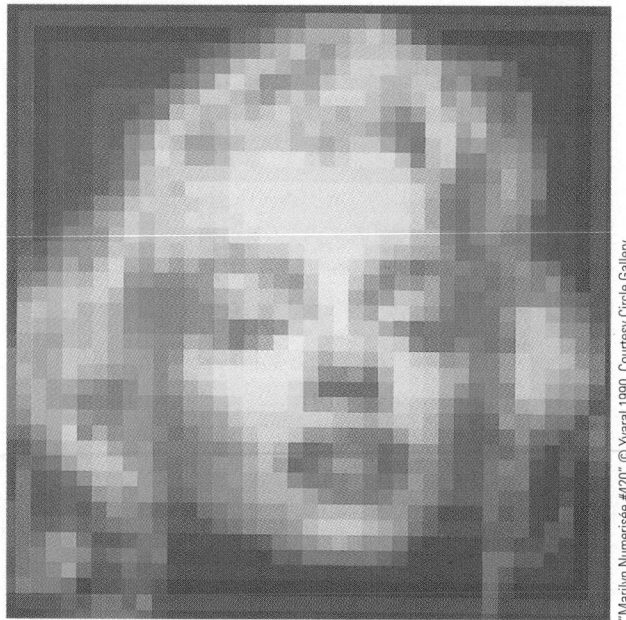

Visual perception involves finding meaningful patterns in complex stimuli. If you look closely at this painting by the artist Yvaral, you will see that it is entirely made up of small, featureless squares. An infant or newly sighted person would see only a jumble of meaningless colors. But because the squares form a familiar pattern, you should easily see Marilyn Monroe's face. (Or is that Madonna?)

Almost everyone's family album has at least one photo like this. Extreme viewing angles can make maintaining size constancy difficult, even for familiar objects.

and then from an angle. Obviously, the page is rectangular, but most of the images that reach your eyes are distorted. Yet although the book's image changes, your perception of its shape remains constant. (For additional examples, see ● Figure 6.1.) On the highway, alcohol intoxication impairs size and shape constancy, adding to the accident rate among drunk drivers (Farrimond, 1990).

Let's say that you are outside in bright sunlight. Beside you, a friend is wearing a gray skirt and a white blouse. Suddenly a cloud shades the sun. It might seem that the blouse would grow dimmer, but it still appears to be bright white. This happens because the blouse continues to reflect a larger *proportion* of light than nearby objects. **Brightness constancy** refers to the fact that the brightness of objects appears to stay the same as lighting conditions change. However, this holds true only if the blouse and other objects are all illuminated by the same amount of light. You could make an area on your friend's gray skirt look whiter than the shaded blouse by shining a bright spotlight on the skirt.

To summarize, the energy patterns reaching our senses are constantly changing, even when they come from the same object. Size, shape, and brightness constancy rescue us from a confusing world in which objects would seem to shrink and grow, change shape as if made of rubber, and light up or fade like neon lamps. Gaining these constancies was only one of the hurdles Mr. S. B. faced in learning to see. In the next section, we will consider some others.

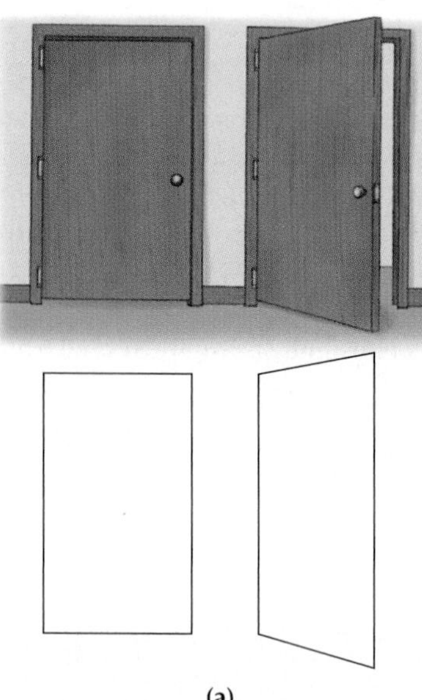

(a)

(b)

● **Figure 6.1** Shape constancy. *(a)* When a door is open, its image actually forms a trapezoid. Shape constancy is indicated by the fact that it is still perceived as a rectangle. *(b)* With great effort you may be able to see this design as a collection of flat shapes. However, if you maintain shape constancy, the distorted squares strongly suggest the surface of a sphere. (From *Spherescapes-1* by Scott Walter and Kevin McMahon, 1983.)

Perceptual Organization—Getting It All Together

We have seen that Mr. S. B. had to *learn* to understand his visual sensations. He was soon able to tell time from a large clock and read block letters he had known only from touch. At a zoo, he recognized an elephant from descriptions he had heard. However, handwriting meant nothing to him for more than a year after he regained sight, and many objects were meaningless until he touched them. Thus, although Mr. S. B. had visual *sensations,* his ability to *perceive* remained limited.

How are sensations organized into meaningful perceptions? The simplest organization involves grouping some sensations into an object, or figure, that stands out on a plainer background. **Figure-ground organization** is probably inborn, because it is the first perceptual ability to appear after cataract patients regain sight. In normal figure-ground perception, only one figure is seen. In *reversible figures,* however, figure and ground can be switched. In ● Figure 6.2 it is equally possible to see either a wineglass figure on a dark background or two face profiles on a light background. As you shift from one pattern to the other, you should get a clear sense of what figure-ground organization means.

Gestalt Principles

How do we separate a figure from its background? The Gestalt psychologists (see Chapter 1) studied this question in detail. They concluded that even if you were seeing for the first time, several factors would bring some order to your perceptions (● Figure 6.3).

● **Figure 6.2** A reversible Figure-ground design. Do you see two faces in profile or a wineglass?

1. **Nearness.** All other things being equal, stimuli that are near one another tend to be grouped together (Kubovy & Holcombe, 1998). Thus, if three people stand near one another and a fourth person stands 10 feet away, the adjacent three will be seen as a group and the distant person as an outsider (see ● Figure 6.3*a*).
2. **Similarity.** "Birds of a feather flock together," and stimuli that are similar in size, shape, color, or form tend to be grouped together (see ● Figure 6.3*b*). Picture two bands marching side by side. If their uniforms are different colors, the bands will be seen as two separate groups, not as one large group.
3. **Continuation, or continuity.** Perceptions tend toward simplicity and continuity. In ● Figure 6.3*c* it is easier to visualize a wavy line on a squared-off line than it is to see a complex row of shapes.
4. **Closure.** Closure refers to the tendency to *complete* a figure so that it has a consistent overall form. Each of the drawings in ● Figure 6.3*d* has one or more gaps, yet each is perceived as a recognizable figure. The "shapes" that appear in the two right drawings in ● Figure 6.3*d* are *illusory figures* (implied shapes that are not actually bounded by an edge or an outline). Even young children see these shapes, despite knowing that they are "not really there." Illusory figures reveal that our tendency to form shapes—even with minimal cues—is powerful.
5. **Contiguity.** A principle that can't be shown in ● Figure 6.3 is contiguity, or nearness in time *and* space. Contiguity is often responsible for the perception that one thing has *caused* another (Michotte, 1963). A psychologist friend of ours demonstrates this principle in class by knocking on his head with one hand while knocking on a wooden table (out of sight) with the other. The knocking sound is perfectly timed with the movements of his visible hand. This leads to the irresistible perception that his head is made of wood.
6. **Common region.** As you can see in ● Figure 6.3*e,* stimuli that are found within a common region or area tend to be seen as a group (Palmer, 1992). On the basis of similarity and nearness, the stars in ● Figure 6.3*e* should be one group and the dots another. However, the colored backgrounds define regions that create three groups of objects (four stars, two stars plus two dots, and four dots). Perhaps the principle of common region explains why we tend to mentally group together people from a particular country, state, province, or geographic region.

To learn about how the principles that guide perceptual organization can be applied to practical problems, see "Designing for Human Use."

Brightness constancy The apparent (or relative) brightness of objects remains the same as long as they are illuminated by the same amount of light.

Figure-ground organization Part of a stimulus appears to stand out as an object (figure) against a less prominent background (ground).

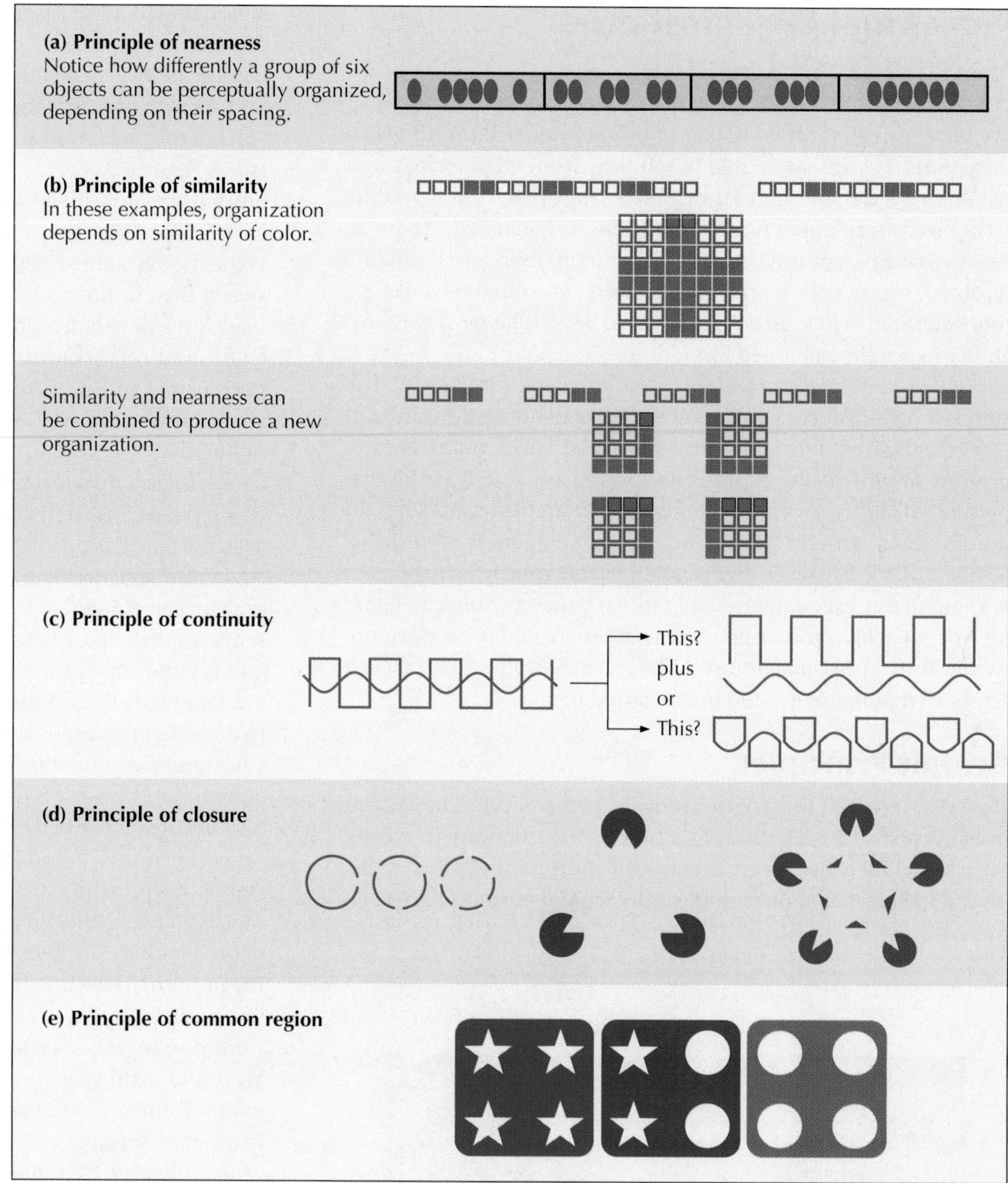

● **Figure 6.3** How we organize perceptions.

Clearly, the Gestalt principles shape our day-to-day perceptions, but so do learning and past experience. Take a moment and look for the camouflaged animal pictured in ● Figure 6.5. (Camouflage patterns break up figure-ground organization). If you had never seen similar animals before, could you have located this one? Mr. S. B. would have been at a total loss to find meaning in such a picture.

In a way, we are all detectives, seeking patterns in what we see. In this sense, a meaningful pattern represents a **perceptual hypothesis,** or initial guess about how to organize sensations. Have you ever seen a "friend" in the distance, only to have the person turn into a stranger as you drew closer? Preexisting ideas and expectations *actively* guide our interpretation of sensations (Most et al., 2005).

The active nature of perception is perhaps most apparent for *ambiguous stimuli* (patterns allowing more than one interpretation). If you look at a cloud, you may discover dozens of ways to organize its contours into fanciful shapes and scenes. Even clearly defined stimuli may permit more than one interpretation. Look at Necker's cube in ● Figure 6.6 if you doubt that perception is an active process. Visualize the top cube as a wire box. If you stare at the cube, its organization will change. Sometimes it will seem to project upward, like the lower left cube; other times it will project downward. The difference lies in how your brain interprets the same information. In short, we actively *construct* meaningful perceptions; we do not passively record the events and stimuli around us (Coren, Ward, & Enns, 2004).

In some instances, a stimulus may offer such conflicting information that perceptual organization becomes impossible. For example, the tendency to make a three-dimensional object out of a drawing is frustrated by the "three-pronged widget" (● Figure 6.7), an *impossible figure.* Such patterns cannot be organized into

FOCUS ON RESEARCH

Designing for Human Use

Machines are of little value unless humans can operate them effectively. An awkward pocket calculator might just as well be a paperweight. An automobile design that blocks large areas of the driver's vision could be deadly. To design machines for human use, an **engineering psychologist (human factors engineer)** must make them *compatible* with our sensory and motor capacities (Gamache, 2004). For example, displays must be easy to perceive, controls must be easy to use, and the tendency to make errors must be minimized (● Figure 6.4). (A *display* is any dial, screen, light, or other device used to provide information about a machine's activity to a human user. A *control* is any knob, handle, button, lever, or other device used to alter the activity of a machine.)

Human factors engineers helped design many of the machines we rely on each day, such as telephones, "user-friendly" computers, home appliances, cameras, personal digital assistants (PDAs), airplane controls, and traffic signals. A recent challenge is the design of machines that allow *telepresence,* a sense of presence in remote environments. For example, in 2001 a surgeon in New York became the first to use *telesurgery* to remove the diseased gallbladder of a patient an ocean away in France. Because a good surgeon relies extensively on the sense of touch, it is important to improve *haptic interfaces,* which are designed to provide touch feedback in telepresence systems (Lederman & Klatsky, 2004; Lederman et al., 2004).

Psychologist Donald Norman (1994) refers to successful human factors engineering as **natural design,** which makes use of perceptual signals that people understand naturally, without needing to learn them. An example is the row of vertical buttons in elevators that mimic the layout of the floors. This is simple, natural, and clear. Effective design also provides *feedback* (information about the effect of making a response). The audible click designed into many computer keyboards is a good example. As Norman points out, the cause of many accidents is not just "human error." The real culprit is poor design.

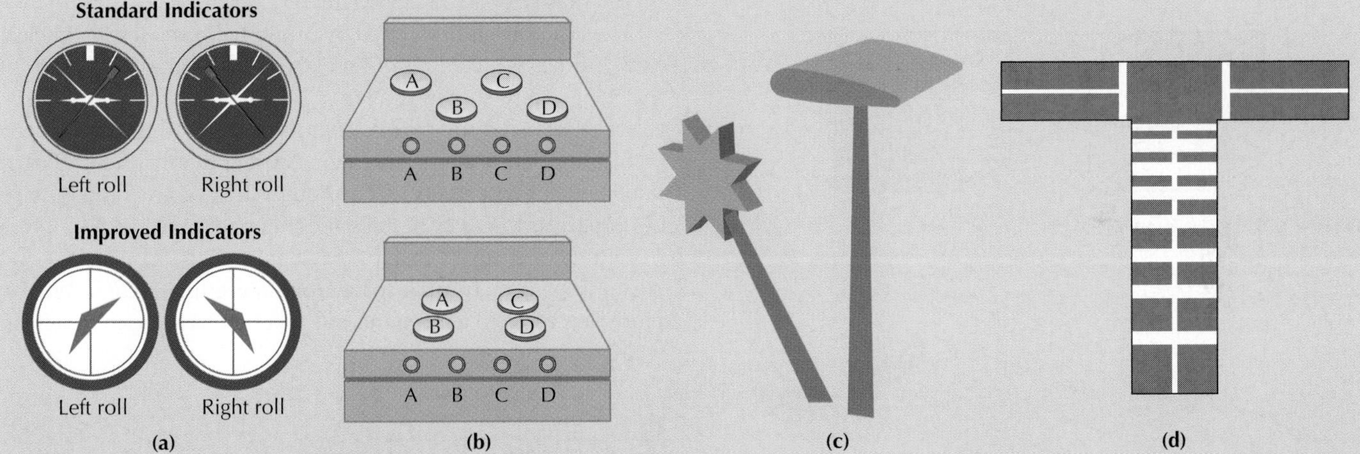

● **Figure 6.4** Human factors engineering. *(a)* Early roll indicators in airplanes were perceptually confusing and difficult to read (top). Improved displays are clear even to nonpilots. Which would you prefer if you were flying an airplane in heavy fog? *(b)* Even on a stove, the placement of controls is important. During simulated emergencies, people made no errors in reaching for the controls on the top stove. In contrast, they erred 38 percent of the time with the bottom arrangement (Chapanis & Lindenbaum, 1959). *(c)* Sometimes the shape of a control is used to indicate its function, to discourage errors. For example, the left control might be used to engage and disengage the gears of an industrial machine, whereas the right control might operate the landing flaps on an airplane. *(d)* This design depicts a street intersection viewed from above. Psychologists have found that painting white lines across the road makes drivers feel like they are traveling faster. This effect is even stronger if the lines get progressively closer together. Placing lines near dangerous intersections or sections of highway has dramatically lowered accident rates.

stable, consistent, or meaningful perceptions. If you cover either end of the drawing in ● Figure 6.7, it makes sense perceptually. However, a problem arises when you try to organize the entire drawing. Then, the conflicting information it contains prevents you from forming a stable perception.

Is the ability to understand drawings learned? Humans almost always appear to understand lines that represent the *edges of*

Perceptual hypothesis An initial guess regarding how to organize (perceive) a stimulus pattern.

Engineering psychology (human factors engineering) A specialty concerned with making machines and work environments compatible with human perceptual and physical capacities.

Natural design Human factors engineering that makes use of naturally understood perceptual signals.

E.R. Degginger/Animals Animals

● **Figure 6.5** A challenging example of perceptual organization. Once the camouflaged insect (known as a giant walking stick) becomes visible, it is almost impossible to view the picture again without seeing the insect.

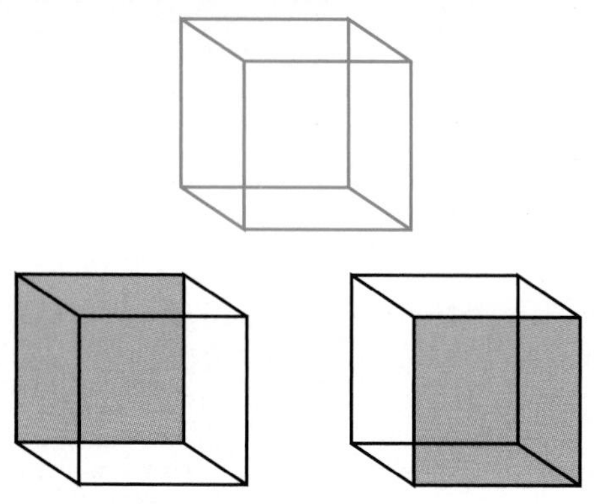

● **Figure 6.6** Necker's cube.

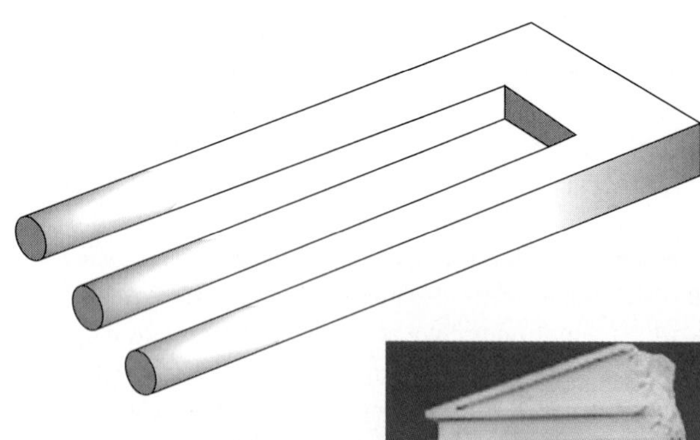

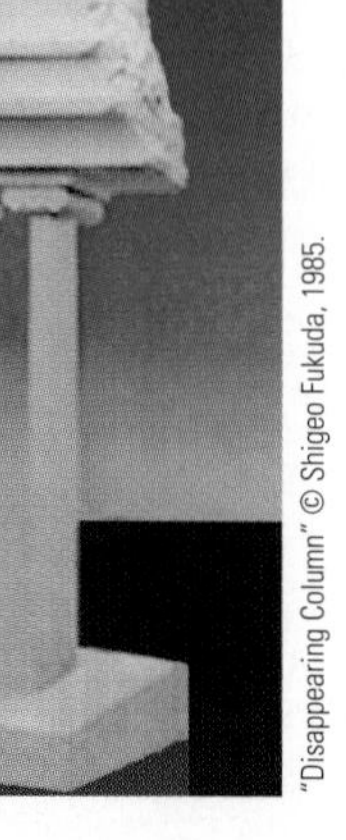

"Disappearing Column" © Shigeo Fukuda, 1985.

● **Figure 6.7** *(Above)* An impossible figure—the "three-pronged widget." *(Below)* It might seem that including more information in a drawing would make perceptual conflicts impossible. However, Japanese artist Shigeo Fukuda has shown otherwise.

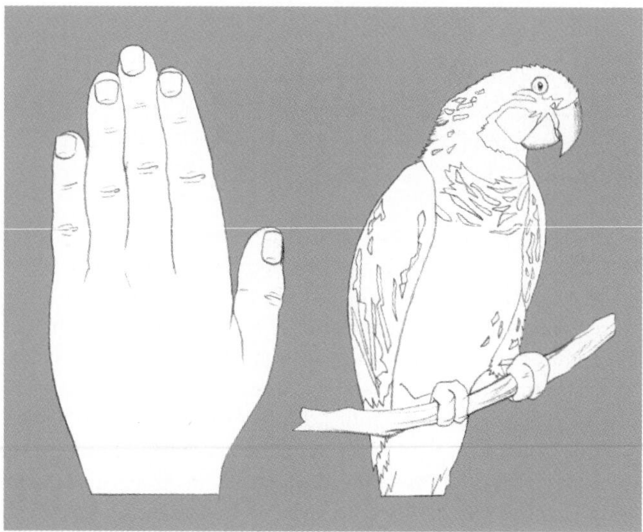

● **Figure 6.8** Stimuli similar to those used by Kennedy (1983) to study the kinds of information universally recognized in drawings. (See text for explanation.)

surfaces. We also have no problem with a single line used to depict the *parallel edges* of a narrow object, such as a rope. Something that we *do not* easily recognize is lines showing color boundaries on the surface of an object (Kennedy, 1983).

The last point is illustrated by the Songe, a small tribe in Papua New Guinea, which does not make or use line drawings. As a test, the Songe were shown drawings like that in ● Figure 6.8. They easily recognized the parrot from its outlines. But lines showing color boundaries confused them. Most thought that the parrot had been cut repeatedly, even though the lines matched the colors of parrots they saw in daily life (Kennedy, 1983).

One of the most amazing perceptual feats is our capacity to create three-dimensional space from flat retinal images. We'll explore that topic in a moment, but first here's a chance to rehearse what you've learned.

KNOWLEDGE BUILDER

Perceptual Constancies and Gestalt Principles

REFLECT

If you needed to explain the perceptual constancies to a friend, what would you say? Why are the constancies important for maintaining a stable perceptual world?

As you look around the area in which you are now, how are the Gestalt principles helping to organize your perceptions? Try to find a specific example for each principle.

LEARNING CHECK

1. Which among the following are subject to basic perceptual constancy?
   a. figure-ground organization
   b. size
   c. ambiguity
   d. brightness
   e. continuity
   f. closure
   g. shape
   h. nearness

2. The first and most basic perceptual organization to emerge when sight is restored to a blind person is:
   a. continuity c. recognition of numbers and letters
   b. nearness constancy d. figure-ground
3. At times, meaningful perceptual organization represents a ________________, or "guess," held until the evidence contradicts it.
4. The design known as Necker's cube is a good example of an impossible figure. T or F?
5. There is evidence that humans universally recognize line drawings depicting the edges of ________________ and narrow parallel lines.
6. An important element of engineering psychology is making ________________ and ________________ compatible with human perceptual capacities. This is often best accomplished through ________________ design.

CRITICAL THINKING

7. People who have taken psychedelic drugs, such as LSD or mescaline, often report that the objects and people they see appear to be changing in size, shape, and brightness. This suggests that such drugs disrupt what perceptual process?

Answers: 1. b, d, g 2. d 3. hypothesis 4. F 5. surfaces 6. displays, controls, natural 7. Perceptual constancies (size, shape, and brightness).

Mark Richards/PhotoEdit

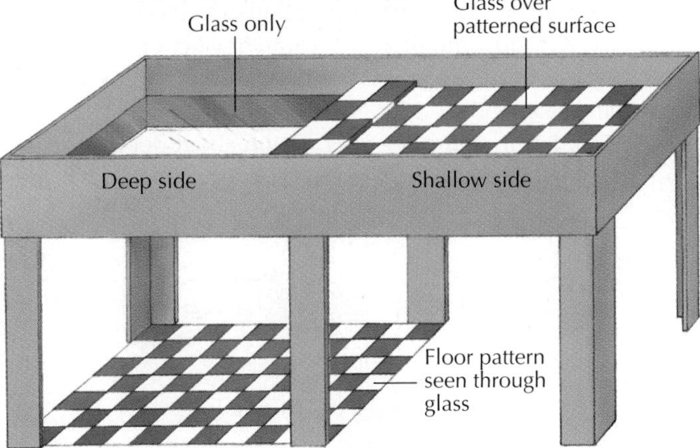

● **Figure 6.9** Human infants and newborn animals refuse to go over the edge of the visual cliff.

Depth Perception—What If the World Were Flat?

Close one of your eyes, hold your head very still, and stare at a single point across the room. If you don't move your head or eyes, your surroundings will appear to be almost flat, like a painting or photograph. But even under these conditions you will still have some sense of depth. Now, open both eyes and move your head and eyes as usual. Suddenly, the "3-D" perceptual world returns. How are we able to perceive depth and space?

Depth perception is the ability to see three-dimensional space and to accurately judge distances. Without depth perception, you would be unable to drive a car or ride a bicycle, play catch, shoot baskets, thread a needle, or simply navigate around a room. The world would look like a flat surface.

Mr. S. B. had trouble with depth perception after his sight was restored. Is depth perception learned? Some psychologists (nativists) hold that depth perception is inborn. Others (the empiricists) view it as learned. Most likely, depth perception is partly learned and partly innate. Some evidence on the issue comes from work with the *visual cliff*. Basically, a visual cliff is a glass-topped table (● Figure 6.9). On one side a checkered surface lies directly beneath the glass. On the other side, the checkered surface is 4 feet below. This makes the glass look like a tabletop on one side and a cliff, or drop-off, on the other.

To test for depth perception, 6- to 14-month-old infants were placed in the middle of the visual cliff. This gave them a choice of crawling to the shallow side or the deep side. (The glass prevented them from doing any "skydiving" if they chose the deep side.) Most infants chose the shallow side. In fact, most refused the deep side even when their mothers tried to call them toward it (Gibson & Walk, 1960).

If the infants were at least 6 months old when they were tested, isn't it possible that they learned to perceive depth? Yes, it is, so let's consider another test. Psychologist Jane Gwiazda fitted infants with goggles that make some designs stand out three-dimensionally while others remain flat. By watching head movements, Gwiazda could tell when babies first became aware of the 3-D designs. As in other tests, this occurred at age 4 months. The nearly universal emergence of depth perception at this time suggests that it depends more on brain maturation than on individual learning (Aslin & Smith, 1988). It is very likely that at least a basic level of depth perception is innate.

Then why do some babies crawl off tables or beds? As soon as infants become active crawlers, they refuse to cross the deep side of the visual cliff (Campos et al., 1978). But even babies who perceive depth may not be able to catch themselves if they slip. A

Depth perception The ability to see three-dimensional space and to accurately judge distances.

lack of coordination—not an inability to see depth—probably explains most "crash landings" after about 4 months of age.

How do adults perceive depth? We also learn to use a variety of *depth cues* as aids to perceiving three-dimensional space. **Depth cues** are features of the environment and messages from the body that supply information about distance and space. Some cues will work with just one eye *(monocular cues),* whereas others require two eyes *(binocular cues).*

Muscular Cues

As their name implies, muscular cues come from the body. One such cue is *accommodation,* the bending of the lens to focus on nearby objects. Sensations from muscles attached to each lens flow back to the brain. Changes in these sensations help us judge distances within about 4 feet of the eyes. This information is available even if you are just using one eye, so accommodation is a monocular cue. Beyond 4 feet, accommodation has limited value. Obviously, it is more important to a watchmaker or a person trying to thread a needle than it is to a basketball player or someone driving an automobile.

A second bodily source of information about depth is *convergence,* a binocular cue. When you look at a distant object, the lines of vision from your eyes are parallel. However, when you look at something 50 feet or less in distance, your eyes must converge (turn in) to focus the object (● Figure 6.10).

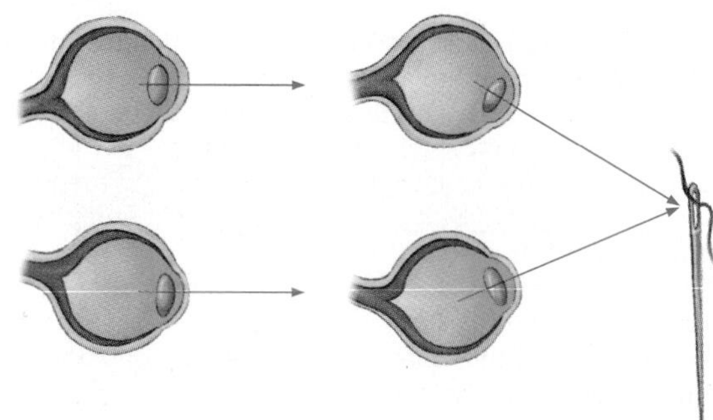

● **Figure 6.10** The eyes must converge, or turn in toward the nose, to focus close objects. The eyes shown are viewed from above the head.

You are probably not aware of it, but whenever you estimate a distance under 50 feet (as when you play catch or zap flies with your personal laser), you are using convergence. How? Muscles attached to the eyeball control convergence. These muscles feed information on eye position to the brain to help it judge distance.

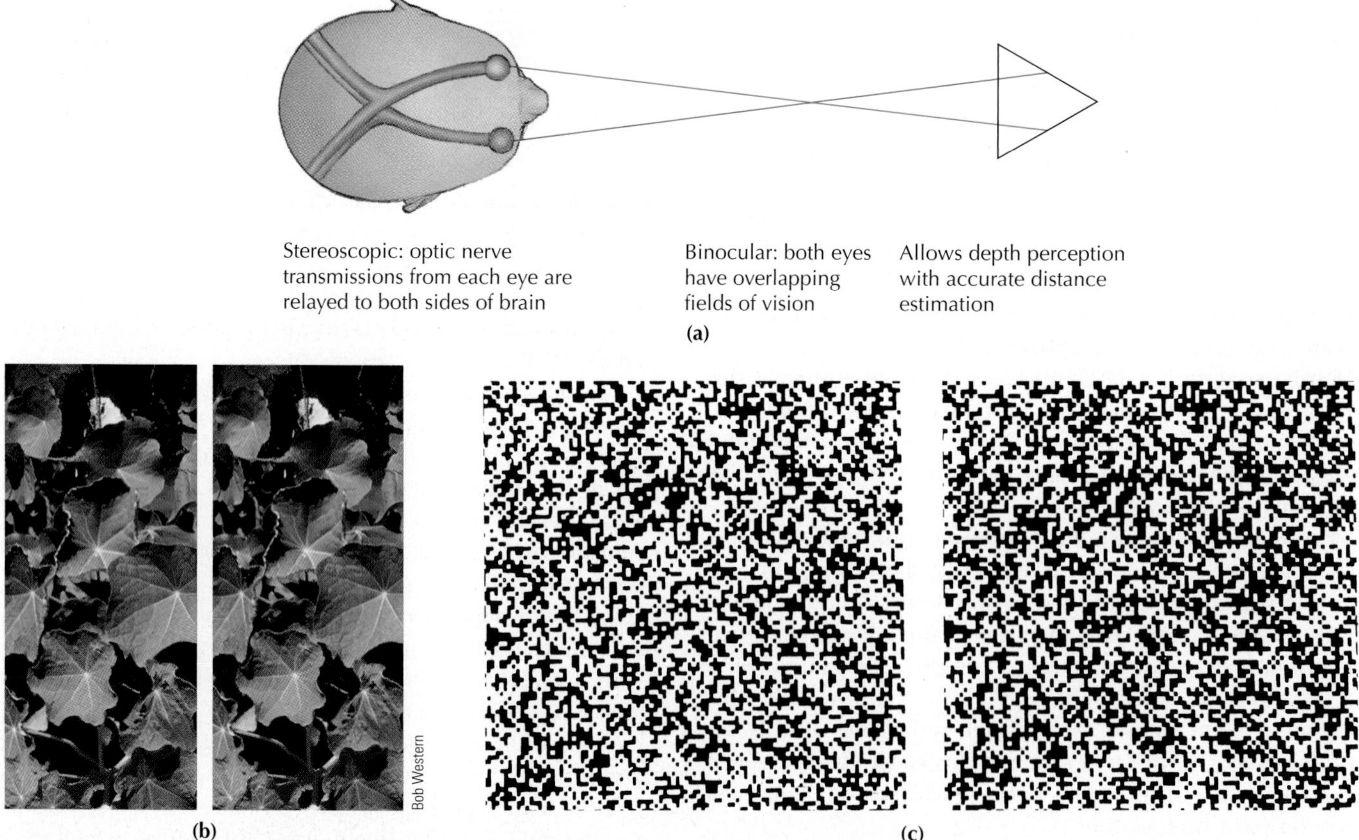

● **Figure 6.11** *(a)* Stereoscopic vision. *(b)* The photographs show what the right and left eyes would see when viewing a plant. Hold the page about 6 to 8 inches from your eyes. Allow your eyes to cross and focus on the overlapping image between the two photos. Then try to fuse the leaves into one image. If you are successful, the third dimension will appear like magic. *(c)* Now do the same with the random dot stereogram, but with your eyes 10 inches from the page. With luck, you will see a diamond shape hovering over the background. (See text for explanation.) (Julez, 1971; reprinted by permission of Bela Julez.)

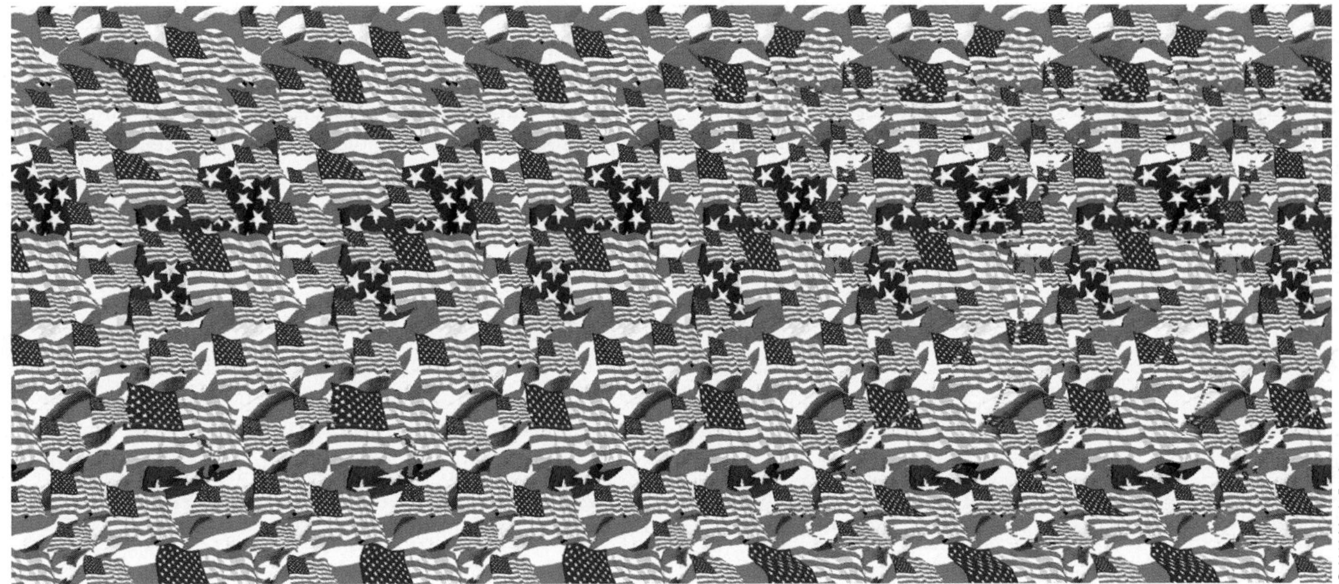

● **Figure 6.12** This popular style of computer-generated art creates a 3-D illusion by superimposing two patterns. There are mismatches between some areas of the two patterns. This simulates retinal disparity and creates a sensation of depth. To get the 3-D effect, hold the stereogram about 8 inches from the end of your nose. Relax your eyes and look *through* the art, as if you were focusing on something in the distance. If you're patient, you may see a 3-D globe.

You can feel convergence by exaggerating it: Focus on your fingertip and bring it toward your eyes until they almost cross. At that point you can feel the sensations from the muscles that control eye movement.

Stereoscopic Vision

The most basic source of depth perception is *retinal disparity* (a discrepancy in the images that reach the right and left eyes). Retinal disparity, which is a binocular cue, is based on the fact that the eyes are about 2.5 inches apart. Because of this, each eye receives a slightly different view of the world. When the two images are fused into one overall image, **stereoscopic vision** (three-dimensional sight) occurs. The result is a powerful sensation of depth (● Figure 6.11).

Retinal disparity can be used to produce 3-D movies by filming with two cameras separated by several inches. Later, both images are simultaneously projected on a screen. Audience members wear glasses that filter out one of the images to each eye. Because each eye gets a separate image, normal stereoscopic vision is duplicated. Try the following demonstration of retinal disparity and fusion.

Totally Tubular

Roll a piece of paper into a tube. Close your left eye. Hold the tube to your right eye like a telescope. Look through the tube at some object in the distance. Place your left hand against the tube halfway down its length and in front of your left eye. Now open your left eye. You should see a "hole" in your hand. You couldn't expect a professional photographer to do a better job of blending the two images than your visual system does automatically.

How does retinal disparity produce depth? Perceiving depth is more than a simple blending of two "pictures" of the world. In ● Figure 6.11*c* you will find two *random dot stereograms* (patterns of dots that produce an illusion of depth). Notice that they contain no objects, lines, or edges. Just the same, when the stereograms are properly viewed (one to each eye), a center area seems to float above the background. Such designs show that the brain is very sensitive to any *mismatch* of information from the eyes. In ● Figure 6.11*c,* depth comes from shifting dots in the center of one square so that they do not match dots in the other square (Howard & Rogers, 2001a, 2000b; Julesz, 1971). (Also see ● Figure 6.12.)

To a large extent, three-dimensional space is woven from countless tiny differences between what the right and left eyes see. Direct studies of the brain have shown that visual areas do, in fact, contain cells that detect disparities (Cumming & DeAngelis, 2001).

If disparity is so important, can a person with one eye perceive depth? A one-eyed person lacks convergence and retinal disparity, and accommodation helps us judge short distances only. That means a person with only one eye will have limited depth perception. Try driving a car or riding a bicycle with one eye closed. You will find yourself braking too soon or too late, and you will have difficulty estimating your speed. ("But officer, my psychology text said

Depth cues Perceptual features that impart information about distance and three-dimensional space.

Stereoscopic vision Perception of space and depth caused chiefly by the fact that the eyes receive different images.

to . . .") Despite this, you will be able to drive, although it will be more difficult than usual. A person with one eye can even successfully land an airplane—a task that depends strongly on depth perception. Overall, stereoscopic vision is ten times better for judging depth than perception based on just one eye (Rosenberg, 1994).

It is tempting to assume that higher animals perceive depth much as we do. Although this is sometimes true, there are many exceptions. Let's explore some examples of how a "bird's-eye" view of the world might differ from our own.

A Bird's-Eye View

It might seem that birds would have acute stereoscopic vision, and some do. But most birds are prey for other animals. When you spend life as a potential meal, it's important to detect approaching predators. That's why many birds have an unusually wide field of view (● Figure 6.13*a* and *b*). An extreme case is the American woodcock, a bird that can survey a 360-degree panorama without moving its eyes or head. The trade-off for this wide-angle view is a very limited area of binocular vision (● Figure 6.13*c*). But to the woodcock, an ability to spot hungry predators is probably more valuable than depth perception.

What does the world look like to a woodcock? Computer scientist Ping-Kang Hsiung (1990) used optical ray-tracing to simulate the woodcock's view (● Figure 6.13*e* and *f*). As you can see in ● Figure 6.13, even a pretty foxy predator would have trouble sneaking up on a woodcock.

Most variations in vision have a purpose. Scientists theorize that human depth perception is an evolutionary holdover—from life in the treetops. The superb depth perception that helped our distant ancestors swing from branch to branch now helps us swing at a softball or avoid erratic drivers in traffic. Perhaps it's too bad that a little of the woodcock's wide-angle vision didn't get thrown in as well (Waldvogel, 1990).

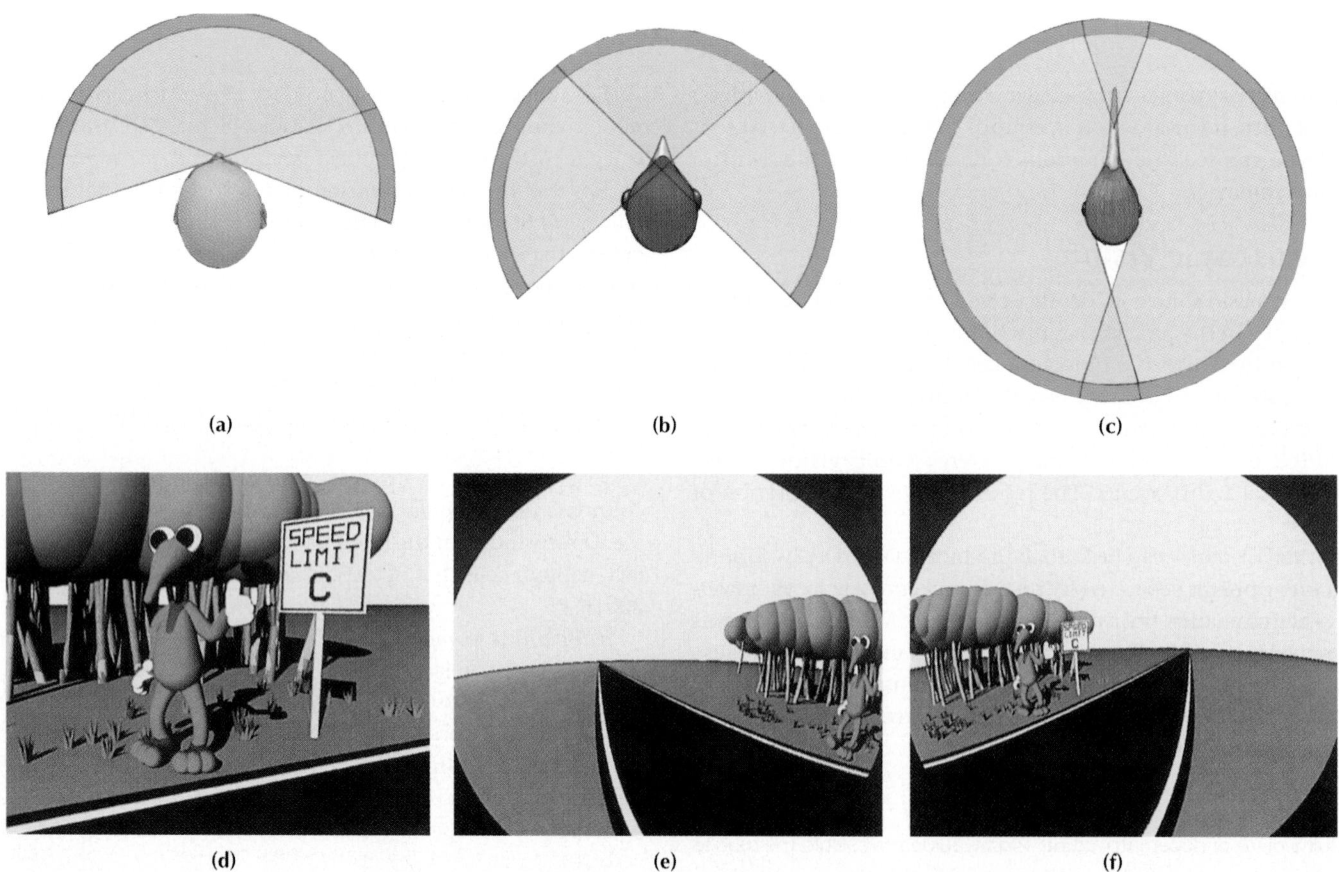

● **Figure 6.13** *(a)* When viewed from above the head, a human's field of view for the right and left eyes contains a large area of overlapping, stereoscopic vision (darker shading). *(b)* The barn swallow's vision, like that of many birds, covers a much wider field of view than ours. Although the swallow's area of binocular vision is smaller than a human's, the swallow has sharper peripheral vision. *(c)* A bird called the American woodcock can see all the way around its head. Binocular vision is limited to a narrow band, but an extremely wide field of view helps the woodcock detect predators. (Adapted from Waldvogel, 1990.) *(d)* This image, created by Ping-Kang Hsiung (1990), shows how an imaginary scene would look to a person standing across the road from a rather strange hitchhiker. *(e, f)* This is what a woodcock's left and right eyes would see if the bird were at the same point as the human in view *d*. (Computer graphics courtesy of Dr. Hsiung.)

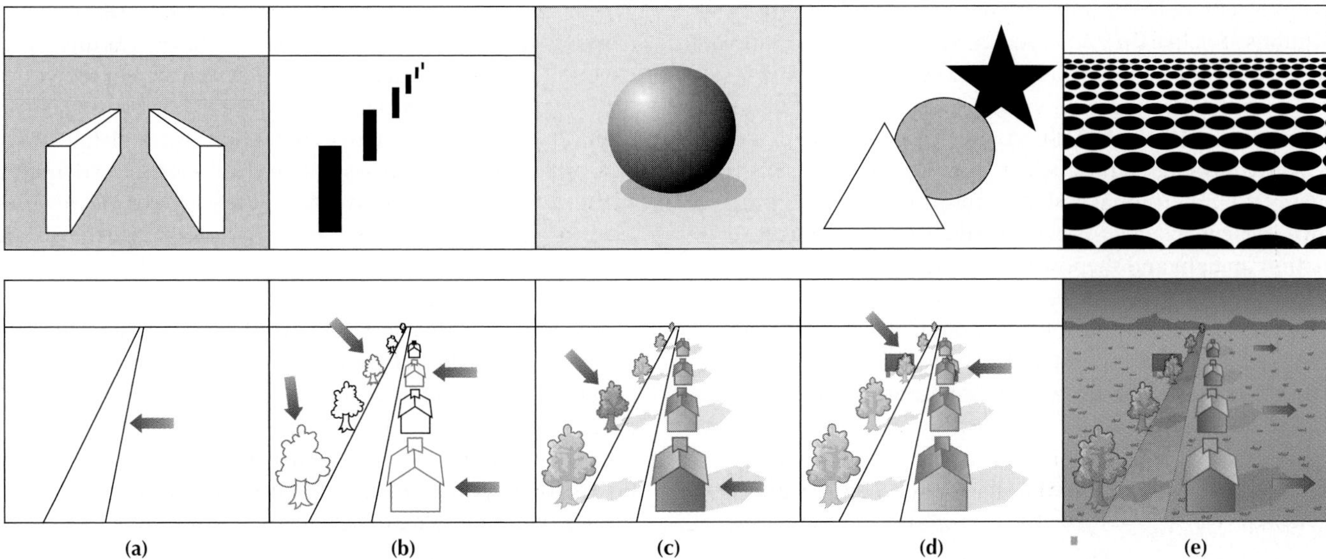

● **Figure 6.14** *(a)* Linear perspective. *(b)* Relative size. *(c)* Light and shadow. *(d)* Overlap. *(e)* Texture gradients. Drawings in the top row show fairly "pure" examples of each of the pictorial depth cues. In the bottom row, the pictorial depth cues are used to assemble a more realistic scene.

Pictorial Cues for Depth—A Deep Topic

A good movie, painting, or photograph can create a convincing sense of depth where none exists. And, as noted, a one-eyed person can learn to gauge depth.

How is the illusion of depth created on a two-dimensional surface, and how is it possible to judge depth with one eye? The answers lie in the pictorial depth cues, all of which are monocular (they will work with just one eye). **Pictorial depth cues** are features found in paintings, drawings, and photographs that impart information about space, depth, and distance. To understand how these cues work, imagine that you are looking outdoors through a window. If you trace everything you see onto the glass, you will have an excellent drawing, with convincing depth. If you then analyze what is on the glass you will find the following features.

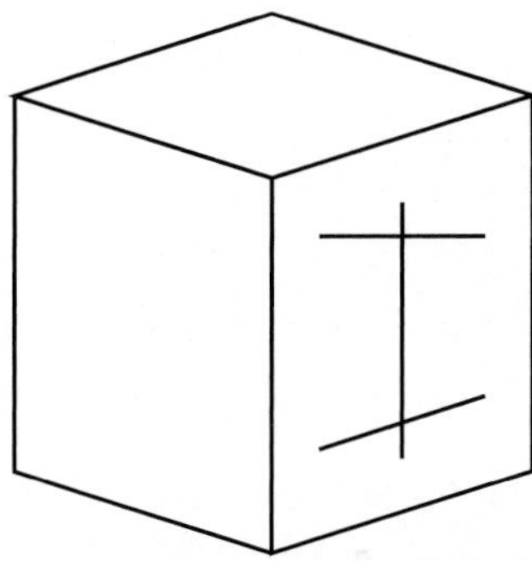

Linear perspective is a very powerful cue for depth. Because of the depth cues implied in this drawing, the upper cross on the vertical line appears to be diagonal. It is actually a right angle. The lower cross, which appears to be a right angle, is actually diagonal to the vertical line. (After Enns & Coren, 1995.)

● **Figure 6.15** On a dry lake bed, relative size is just about the only depth cue available for judging the camera's distance from this vintage aircraft. What do you estimate the distance to be? For the answer, look ahead to Figure 6.20.

Pictorial Depth Cues

1. **Linear perspective.** This cue is based on the apparent convergence of parallel lines in the environment. If you stand between two railroad tracks, they appear to meet near the horizon, even though they actually remain parallel. Their convergence implies great distance. Because you know they are parallel, their convergence implies great distance (● Figure 6.14*a*).
2. **Relative size.** If an artist wishes to depict two objects of the same size at different distances, the artist makes the more distant object smaller (● Figure 6.14*b*). Films in the *Star Wars* series create sensational illusions of depth by rapidly changing the image size of planets, space stations, and starships. (Also see ● Figure 6.15.)
3. **Height in the picture plane.** Objects that are placed higher (closer to the horizon line) in a drawing tend to be perceived

Pictorial depth cues Features found in paintings, drawings, and photographs that impart information about space, depth, and distance.

as more distant. In the upper frame of ● Figure 6.14*b* the black columns look like they are receding into the distance partly because they become smaller but also because they move higher in the drawing.

4. **Light and shadow.** Most objects are lighted in ways that create patterns of light and shadow. Copying such patterns can give a two-dimensional design a three-dimensional appearance (● Figure 6.14*c*). (Also, see ● Figure 6.16 for more information on light and shadow.)
5. **Overlap.** Overlap (or *interposition*) is a depth cue that occurs when one object partially blocks another object. Hold your hands up and have a friend try to tell from across the room which is nearer. Relative size will give the answer if one hand is much nearer to your friend than the other. But if one hand is only slightly closer, your friend may have difficulty—until you slide one hand in front of the other. Overlap then removes any doubt (● Figure 6.14*d*).
6. **Texture gradients.** Changes in texture also contribute to depth perception. If you stand in the middle of a cobblestone street, the street will look coarse near your feet. However, its texture will get smaller and finer if you look into the distance (● Figure 6.14*e*).
7. **Aerial perspective.** Smog, fog, dust, and haze add to the apparent distance of an object. Because of aerial perspective, distant objects tend to be hazy, washed out in color, and lacking in detail. Aerial haze is often most noticeable when it is missing. If you have ever seen a distant mountain range on a crystal-clear day, it might have looked like it was only a few miles away.
8. **Relative motion.** Relative motion, also known as *motion parallax* (PAIR-ah-lax), can be seen by looking out a window and moving your head from side to side. Notice that nearby objects appear to move a sizable distance as your head moves. In comparison, trees, houses, and telephone poles that are farther away appear to move slightly in relation to the background. Distant objects like hills, mountains, or clouds don't seem to move at all.

● **Figure 6.16** *(Above)* We typically make two assumptions when using light and shadow to judge depth in a picture or drawing. First, we usually assume that light comes mainly from one direction. Second, we tend to assume that the source of light is above pictured objects. Squint a little to blur the image you see here. You should perceive a collection of globes projecting outward. If you turn this page upside down, the globes should become cavities. (After Ramachandran, 1995.) *(Below)* The famed Dutch artist M. C. Escher violated both assumptions about light to create the dramatic illusions of depth found in his 1955 lithograph *Convex and Concave.* In this print, light appears to come from all sides of the scene.

When combined, pictorial cues can create a powerful illusion of depth. (See ■ Table 6.1 for a summary of all the depth cues we have discussed.)

Is motion parallax really a pictorial cue? Strictly speaking it is not, except in movies, television, or animated cartoons. However, when parallax is present, we almost always perceive depth. Much of the apparent depth of a good movie comes from relative motion captured by the camera. ● Figure 6.17 illustrates an interesting feature of motion parallax. Imagine that you are in a bus and watching the passing scenery (with your gaze at a right angle to the road). Under these conditions, nearby objects will appear to rush *backward.* Those farther away, such as distant mountains, will seem to move very little or not at all. Objects that are more

TABLE 6.1

Summary of Visual Depth Cues

BINOCULAR CUES
- Convergence
- Retinal disparity

MONOCULAR CUES
- Accommodation
- Pictorial depth cues (listed below)
  - Linear perspective
  - Relative size
  - Height in the picture plane
  - Light and shadow
  - Overlap
  - Texture gradients
  - Aerial perspective
  - Relative motion (motion parallax)

● **Figure 6.17** The apparent motion of objects viewed during travel depends on their distance from the observer. Apparent motion can also be influenced by an observer's point of fixation. At middle distances, objects closer than the point of fixation appear to move backward; those beyond the point of fixation appear to move forward. Objects at great distances, such as the sun or moon, always appear to move forward.

remote, such as the sun or moon, will appear to move in the *same* direction you are traveling. (This is why the moon appears to "follow" you when you take a stroll at night.)

Are pictorial depth cues universal, like the understanding of basic drawings noted earlier? Not entirely. Some cultures use only selected pictorial cues to represent depth. People in these cultures may not easily recognize other cues (Deregowski, 1972). For example, researcher William Hudson tested members of remote tribes who do not use relative size to show depth in drawings. These people perceive simplified drawings as flat designs. As you can see in ● Figure 6.18, they do not assume, as we do, that a larger image means that an object is closer. Of course, members of non-Western cultures can learn to interpret drawings of depth if they are given a chance to practice (Mshelia & Lapidus, 1990).

The Moon Illusion

How do the depth perception cues relate to daily experience? We constantly use both pictorial cues and bodily cues to sense depth and judge distances. Depth cues also produce an intriguing effect called the **moon illusion** (perceiving the moon as larger when it is low in the sky). When the moon is on the horizon, it tends to look like a silver dollar. When it is directly overhead, it looks more like a dime. Contrary to what some people believe, the moon is not magnified by the atmosphere. But the moon *looks* nearly twice as large when it's low in the sky (Ross & Plug, 2002). This occurs, in part, because the moon's *apparent distance* is greater when it is near the horizon than when it is overhead (Kaufman & Kaufman, 2000).

But if it seems farther away, shouldn't it look smaller? No. When the moon is overhead, few depth cues surround it. In contrast, when you see the moon on the horizon, it is behind houses, trees, telephone poles, and mountains. These objects add numerous depth cues, which cause the horizon to seem more distant than the sky overhead. Picture two balloons, one 10 feet away and the second 20 feet away. Suppose the more distant balloon is inflated until its image matches the image of the nearer balloon. How do we know the more distant balloon is larger? Because its image is the same size as a balloon that is closer. Similarly, the moon makes the same-size image on the horizon as it does overhead. However, the horizon seems more distant because more depth cues are present. As a result, the horizon moon must be perceived as larger (Kaufman & Kaufman, 2000) (see ● Figure 6.19).

● **Figure 6.18** A Hudson test picture. Two-dimensional perceivers assume the hunter is trying to spear the distant elephant rather than the nearby antelope. Some acquaintance with conventions for representing depth in pictures and photographs seems necessary. (From "Pictorial Perception and Culture" by J. B. Deregowski. © 1972 Scientific American, Inc. All rights reserved.)

● **Figure 6.19** The Ponzo illusion may help you understand the moon illusion. Picture the two white bars as resting on the railroad tracks. In the drawing, the upper bar is the same length as the lower bar. However, because the upper bar appears to be farther away than the lower bar, we perceive it as longer. The same logic applies to the moon illusion.

Moon illusion The apparent change in size that occurs as the moon moves from the horizon (large moon) to overhead (small moon).

This explanation is known as the **apparent-distance hypothesis** (the horizon seems more distant than the night sky). You can test it by removing depth cues while looking at a horizon moon. Try looking at the moon through a rolled-up paper tube or make your hands into a "telescope" and look at the next large moon you see. It will immediately appear to shrink when viewed without depth cues (Ross & Plug, 2002).

To what extent has the apparent-distance hypothesis been confirmed? The father and son team of Lloyd and James Kaufman projected images of the moon on a mirror. This allowed them to superimpose an artificial moon on the sky. In addition, the mirrors were moveable. Volunteer observers reported that as the moon moved closer, it appeared to get smaller. This effect was most dramatic when the moon was near the horizon, where more depth cues are found. This is the strongest confirmation yet of the apparent-distance theory (Kaufman & Kaufman, 2000).

Dennis Coon

● **Figure 6.20** Before you can use familiar size to judge distance, objects must actually be the size you assume they are. Either these men are giants, or the model airplane was closer than you may have thought when you looked at Figure 6.15.

KNOWLEDGE BUILDER

Depth Perception

REFLECT

Part of the rush of excitement produced by action movies and video games is based on the sense of depth they create. Return to the list of pictorial depth cues. What cues have you seen used to portray depth? Try to think of specific examples in a movie or game you have seen recently.

LEARNING CHECK

1. The visual cliff is used to test for infant sensitivity to linear perspective. T or F?
2. Write an *M* or a *B* after each of the following to indicate if it is a monocular or binocular depth cue.
   accommodation _____ convergence _____ retinal disparity _____ linear perspective _____ motion parallax _____ overlap _____ relative size _____
3. Which of the depth cues listed in question 2 are based on muscular feedback? _____________________.
4. Interpretation of pictorial depth cues requires no prior experience. T or F?
5. The apparent-distance hypothesis provides a good explanation of the
   a. moon illusion
   b. horizontal-vertical illusion
   c. Zulu illusion
   d. effects of inattentional blindness

CRITICAL THINKING

6. Scientists believe that the famous Dutch artist Rembrandt had a visual defect that prevented him from perceiving depth. (He had a wandering eye.) How might this have aided him as an artist?

Answers: 1. F **2.** accommodation (M), convergence (B), retinal disparity (B), linear perspective (M), motion parallax (M), overlap (M), relative size (M) **3.** accommodation or convergence **4.** F **5.** a **6.** An artist must transfer a three-dimensional scene onto a flat canvas. Because Rembrandt could not see depth, it might have been easier for him to put what he saw onto a two-dimensional surface.

Perceptual Learning—What If the World Were Upside Down?

England is one of the few countries in the world where people drive on the left side of the road. Because of this reversal, it is not unusual for visitors to step off curbs in front of cars—after carefully looking for traffic in the *wrong* direction. As this example suggests, learning has a powerful impact on perception.

How does learning affect perception? The term **perceptual learning** refers to changes in the brain that alter how we process sensory information (Ahissar, 1999). For example, to use a computer, you must learn to pay attention to specific stimuli, such as icons, commands, and signals. We also learn to tell the difference between stimuli that seemed identical at first. An example is the novice chef who discovers how to tell the difference between dried basil, oregano, and tarragon. In other situations, we learn to

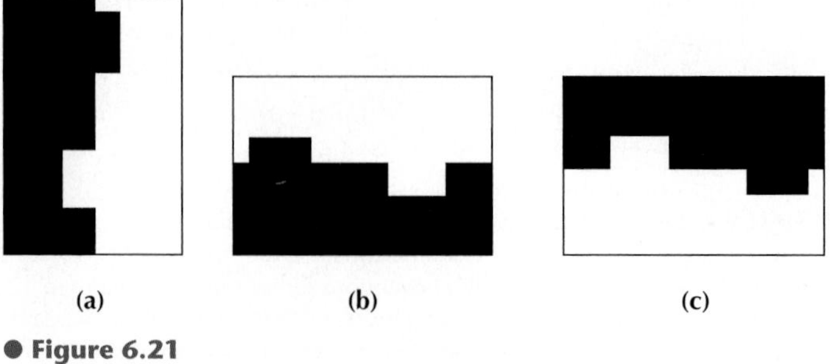

● **Figure 6.21**

Bettmann/Corbis

● **Figure 6.22** The effects of prior experience on perception. The doctored face looks far worse when viewed right side up because it can be related to past experience.

focus on just one part of a group of stimuli. This saves us from having to process all of the stimuli in the group. For instance, a linebacker in football may be able to tell if the next play will be a run or a pass by watching one or two key players, rather than the entire opposing team (Goldstone, 1998).

Even something as simple as figure-ground perception is affected by learning. For example, if you cut a shape out of dark paper and place it on a white background, other people are more likely to see it as a figure if it resembles a familiar object. As another example, in ● Figure 6.21*a* you can probably shift between seeing the white shape or the black shape as an object. Now look at ● Figure 6.21*b*. Does the lower black shape seem more like it's the figure than the upper white shape? Next consider ● Figure 6.21*c*. Notice how the white area in Figure 6.4*c* seems like it has become the figure. In our daily experience, objects below the horizon are usually closer to us. Also, we typically see more objects below the horizon than above it. Because of such experiences, we are more likely to perceive areas below the "horizon" line in a drawing as objects or figures (Vecera, Vogel, & Woodman, 2002). Does this mean you should figure that figures are close to the ground?

Perceptual Habits

In general, learning creates **perceptual habits** (ingrained patterns of organization and attention) that affect our daily experience. Stop for a moment and look at ● Figure 6.22. The left face looks somewhat unusual, to be sure. But the distortion seems mild—until you turn the page upside down. Viewed normally, the face looks quite grotesque. Why is there a difference? Apparently, most people have little experience with upside-down faces. Perceptual learning, therefore, has less impact on our perceptions of an upside-down face. With a face in the normal position, you know what to expect and where to look. Also, you tend to see the entire face as a recognizable pattern. When a face is inverted, we are forced to perceive its individual features separately (Bartlett & Searcy, 1993).

Before we continue, read aloud the short phrase in ● Figure 6.23. Did you read, "Paris in the spring"? If so, look again. The word *the* appears twice in the phrase. Because of past experience with the English language, good readers often overlook the repeated word. Again, the effects of perceptual learning are apparent.

Magicians rely on perceptual habits when they use sleight of hand to distract observers while performing tricks. Another kind of "magic" is related to consistency. It is usually safe to assume that a room is shaped roughly like a box. This need not be true, however. An *Ames room* (named for the man who designed it) is a lopsided space that appears square when viewed from a certain

● **Figure 6.23**

Apparent-distance hypothesis An explanation of the moon illusion stating that the horizon seems more distant than the night sky.

Perceptual learning Changes in perception that can be attributed to prior experience.

Perceptual habits Well-established patterns of perceptual organization and attention.

point (● Figure 6.24). This illusion is achieved by carefully distorting the proportions of the walls, floor, ceiling, and windows. Because the left corner of the Ames room is farther from a viewer than the right, a person standing in that corner looks very small; one standing in the nearer, shorter right corner looks very large. A person who walks from the left to the right corner, will seem to "magically" grow larger.

As mentioned earlier, the brain is especially sensitive to **perceptual features** such as lines, shapes, edges, spots, and colors. At least some of this sensitivity appears to be learned. Colin Blakemore and Graham Cooper raised kittens in a room with only vertical stripes on the walls. Another set of kittens saw only horizontal stripes. When returned to normal environments, the "horizontal" cats could easily jump onto a chair, but when walking on the floor, they bumped into chair legs. "Vertical" cats, on the other hand, easily avoided chair legs, but they missed when trying to jump to horizontal surfaces. The cats raised with vertical stripes were "blind" to horizontal lines, and the "horizontal" cats acted as if vertical lines were invisible. In such cases, there is an actual decrease in brain cells tuned to the missing features.

Perceptual features might seem removed from daily experience. Nevertheless, they can have a profound effect on human behavior. In recognizing faces, for example, a consistent *other-race effect* occurs. This is a sort of "they all look alike to me" bias in perceiving persons from other racial and ethnic groups. In tests of facial recognition, people are much better at recognizing faces of their own race than others. One reason for this difference is that we typically have more experience with people from our own race. As a result, we become very familiar with the features that help us recognize different persons. For other groups, we lack the perceptual expertise needed to accurately separate one face from another (Sporer, 2001). Okay, so maybe people from different races or ethnic groups have developed perceptual habits that lead them to see in-group faces differently, but we all see everything else more or less the same way, right? For an answer, see "Do They See What We See?"

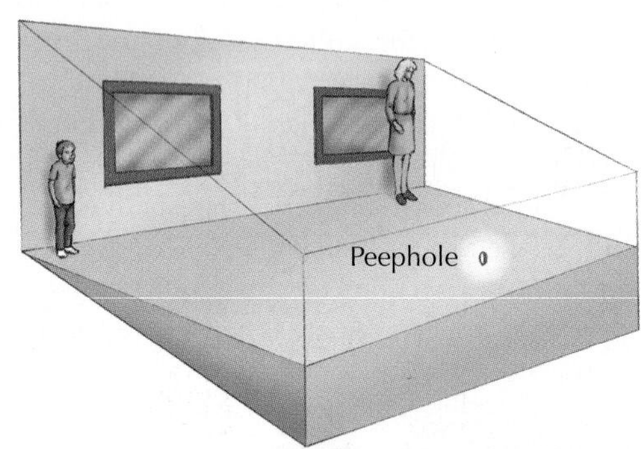

● **Figure 6.24** The Ames room. From the front, the room looks normal; actually, the right-hand corner is very short, and the left-hand corner is very tall. In addition, the left side of the room slants away from viewers. The diagram shows the shape of the room and reveals why people appear to get bigger as they cross the room toward the nearer, shorter right corner.

Inverted Vision

Would it be possible for an adult to adapt to a completely new perceptual world? An answer comes from an experiment in which a person wore goggles that turned the world upside down and reversed objects from right to left. At first, even the simplest tasks—walking, eating, and so forth—were incredibly difficult. Imagine trying to reach for a door handle and watching your hand shoot off in the wrong direction .

Participants in the experiment also reported that head movements made the world swing violently through space, causing severe headaches and nausea. Yet after several days they began to adapt to inverted vision. Their success, although not complete, was impressive.

Did everything turn upright again for the humans? No. While they wore the goggles, their visual images remained upside down. But in time they learned to perform most routine activities, and their inverted world began to seem relatively normal. In later experiments, some people wearing inverting lenses were able to successfully drive cars. One person even flew an airplane (Kohler, 1962). These feats are like driving or flying upside down, with right and left reversed. Some ride!

Interacting with a new visual world through *active movement* (self-generated action) seems to be a key to rapid adaptation. In

Inverted vision. Adaptation to complete inversion of the visual world is possible, but challenging.

HUMAN DIVERSITY

Do They See What We See?

According to psychologist Richard Nisbett and his colleagues, people from different cultures do, in fact, perceive the world differently. European Americans are individualistic people who tend to focus on the self and their sense of personal control. In contrast, East Asians are collectivist people who tend to focus on interpersonal relationships and social responsibility. As a consequence, European Americans tend to explain a person's actions in terms of internal factors ("he did it because he chose to do it"), whereas East Asians tend to explain a person's actions in terms of the context ("he did it because it was his responsibility to his family") (Norenzayan & Nisbett, 2000).

Do such cultural differences affect our everyday perception of objects and events? Apparently they do. In one study, American and Japanese participants were shown drawings of everyday scenes, such as a farm. Later, they saw a slightly changed version of the scene. Some of the changes were to the focal point, or figure of the scene. Other changes were to the surrounding context, or ground. The American participants, it turns out, were better at detecting changes in the figure of a scene, whereas the Japanese participants were better at detecting alterations to the ground (Nisbett & Miyamoto, 2005).

To explain this difference, Chua, Boland, and Nisbett (2005) presented American and Chinese participants with pictures of a figure (such as a tiger) placed on a ground (such as a jungle) and monitored their eye-movement patterns. The American participants focused their eye movements on the figure, whereas the Chinese participants made more eye movements around the ground. In other words, Westerners have a relatively narrow focus of attention, whereas Easterners have a broader focus of attention. Apparently, the society we live in can, indeed, influence even our most basic perceptual habits.

one experiment, people wore glasses that grossly distorted vision. Those who walked on their own adapted more quickly than persons pushed around in a wheeled cart (Held, 1971). Why does movement help? Probably because commands sent to the muscles can be related to sensory feedback. Remaining immobile would be like watching a weird movie over which you have no control. There would be little reason for any perceptual learning to occur.

Andrew G. Wood/Photo Researchers, Inc.

Even small distortions of the visual world may necessitate perceptual learning. For example, the size, distance, and curvature of objects appear distorted underwater. Experiments confirm that professional divers gradually correct for these distortions as they gain experience with them (Vernoy, 1989).

Adaptation Level

The external *context* in which a stimulus is judged is an important factor affecting perception. **Context** refers to information surrounding a stimulus. For example, a man 6 feet in height will look "tall" when surrounded by others of average height, and "short" among a group of professional basketball players. In ● Figure 6.25, the center circle is the same size in both designs. But like the

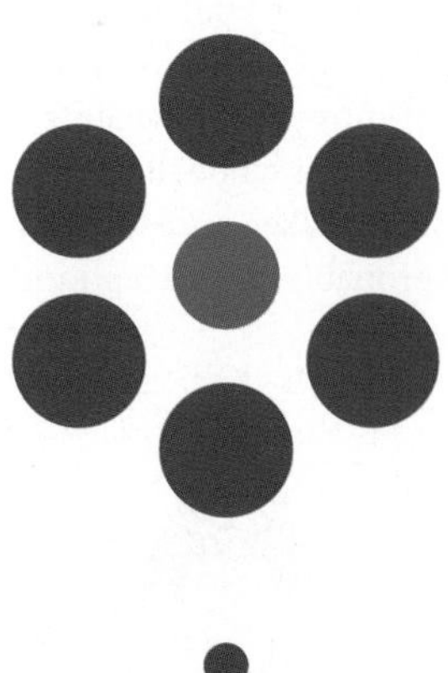

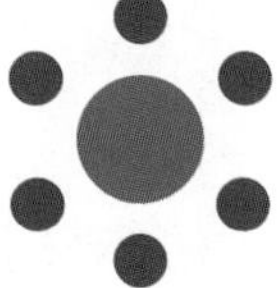

● **Figure 6.25** Are the center dots in both figures the same size?

Perceptual features Important elements of a stimulus pattern, such as lines, shapes, edges, spots, and colors.

Context Information surrounding a stimulus.

THE CLINICAL FILE

Staying in Touch with Reality

Just imagine that often, and without warning, you hear a voice shouting, "Buckets of blood!" or see blood spattering across the walls of your bedroom. Chances are people would think you are mentally disturbed. Hallucinations are a major symptom of psychosis, dementia, epilepsy, migraine headaches, alcohol withdrawal, and drug intoxication (Spence & David, 2004) and are one of the clearest signs that a person has "lost touch with reality."

Yet consider the case of mathematician John Nash (the subject of *A Beautiful Mind,* the winner of the 2002 Oscar for best film). Even though Nash suffered from schizophrenia, he eventually learned to use his ability to engage in *reality testing* to sort out which of his experiences were perceptions and which were hallucinations. Unlike John Nash, most people who experience full-blown hallucinations also have a limited ability to reality test (Hohwy & Rosenberg, 2005).

Curiously, "sane hallucinations" also occur. *Charles Bonnet syndrome* is a rare condition that afflicts mainly older people who are partially blind but not mentally disturbed. They may "see" people, animals, buildings, plants, and other objects appear and disappear in front of their eyes. One older man suffering from partial blindness and leukemia complained of seeing animals in his house, including cattle and bears (Jacob et al., 2004). However, people experiencing "sane hallucinations" can more easily tell that their hallucinations aren't real because their capacity to reality test is not impaired.

Such unusual experiences show how powerfully the brain seeks meaningful patterns in sensory input and the role reality testing plays in our normal perceptual experience.

man in different company, context alters the circle's apparent size. The importance of context is also shown by ● Figure 6.26. What do you see in the middle? If you read across, context causes it to be organized as a 13. Reading down makes it a B.

In addition to external contexts, we all have personal **frames of reference** (internal standards for judging stimuli). If you were asked to lift a 10-pound weight, would you label it light, medium, or heavy? The answer to this question depends on your **adaptation level** (the "medium point" of your personal frame of reference). Each person's adaptation level is constantly modified by experience (Helson, 1964). If most of the weights you lift in day-to-day life *average* around 10 pounds, you will call a 10-pound weight medium. If you are a watchmaker and spend your days lifting tiny watch parts, you will probably call a 10-pound weight heavy. If you work as a furniture mover, your adaptation level will exceed 10 pounds and you will call a 10-pound weight light. (If you are an aging rock star, you will no doubt call everything "heavy," man.)

A

12 13 14

C

● **Figure 6.26** Context alters the meaning of the middle figure.

Illusions

Perceptual learning is responsible for a number of *illusions*. In an **illusion**, length, position, motion, curvature, or direction is consistently misjudged. Note that illusions are distorted perceptions of stimuli that actually exist. In a **hallucination**, people perceive objects or events that have no external reality (Lepore, 2002). For example, they hear voices that are not there (see "Staying in Touch with Reality"). If you think you see a 3-foot-tall butterfly, you can confirm you are hallucinating by trying to touch its wings. To detect an illusion, you may have to measure a drawing or apply a straightedge to it.

Illusions are a fascinating challenge to our understanding of perception. On occasion, they also have practical uses. An illusion called *stroboscopic* (strobe-oh-SKOP-ik) *movement* puts the "motion" in motion pictures. **Stroboscopic movement** refers to the illusory motion perceived when objects are shown in rapidly changing positions. The strobe lights used on dance floors reverse this illusion. Each time the strobe flashes, it "freezes" dancers in particular positions. However, if the light flashes fast enough, normal motion is seen. In a similar way, movies project a rapid series of "snapshots," so the gaps in motion are imperceptible.

Can other illusions be explained? Not in all cases, or to everyone's satisfaction. Generally speaking, size and shape constancy, habitual eye movements, continuity, and perceptual habits combine in various ways to produce the illusions in ● Figure 6.27. Rather than attempt to explain all of the pictured illusions, let's focus on one deceptively simple example.

Dennis Coon

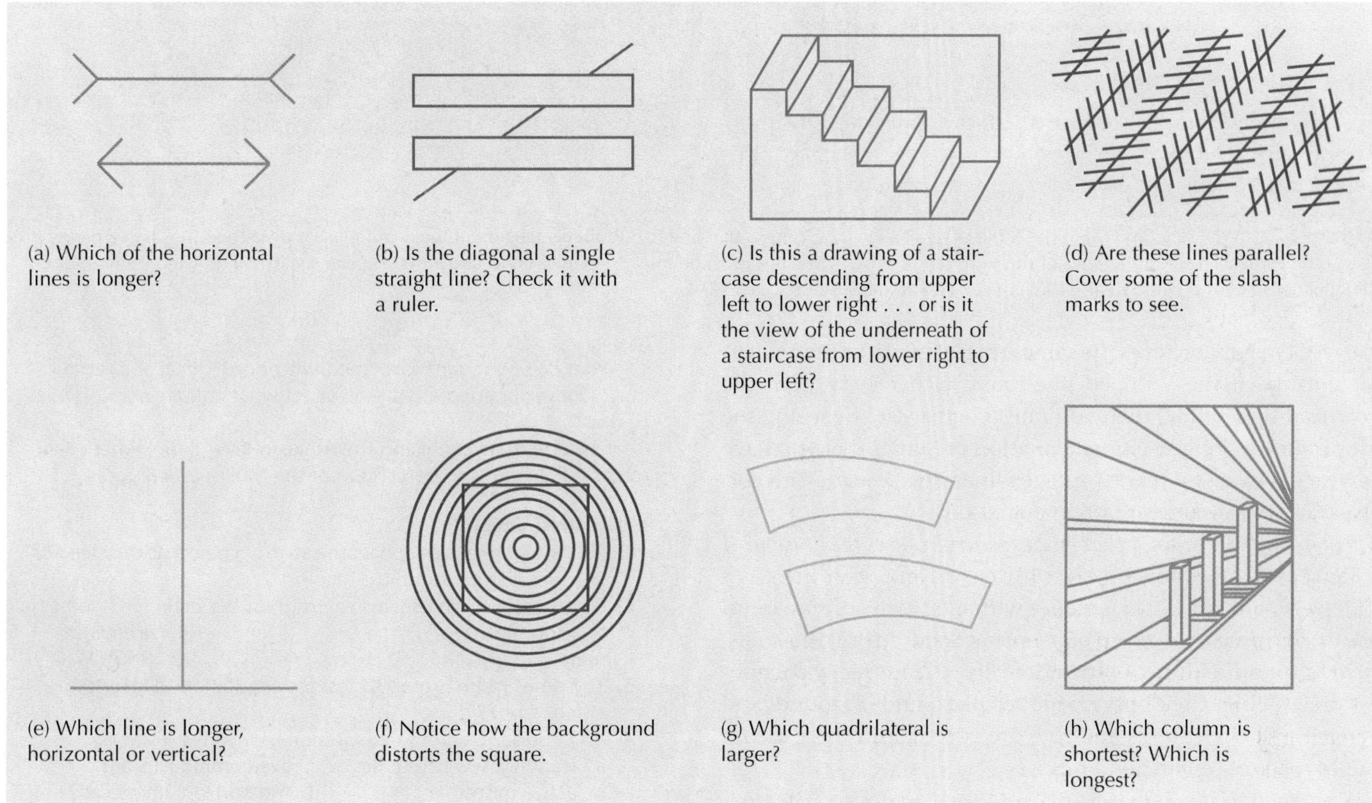

(a) Which of the horizontal lines is longer?

(b) Is the diagonal a single straight line? Check it with a ruler.

(c) Is this a drawing of a staircase descending from upper left to lower right . . . or is it the view of the underneath of a staircase from lower right to upper left?

(d) Are these lines parallel? Cover some of the slash marks to see.

(e) Which line is longer, horizontal or vertical?

(f) Notice how the background distorts the square.

(g) Which quadrilateral is larger?

(h) Which column is shortest? Which is longest?

● **Figure 6.27** Some interesting perceptual illusions. Such illusions are a normal part of visual perception.

Consider the drawing in ● Figure 6.27*a*. This is the familiar **Müller-Lyer** (MEOO-ler-LIE-er) **illusion**, in which the horizontal line with arrowheads appears shorter than the line with V's. A quick measurement will show that they are the same length. How can we explain this illusion? Evidence suggests it is based on a lifetime of experience with the edges and corners of rooms and buildings. Richard Gregory (2000) believes you see the horizontal line with the V's as if it were the corner of a room viewed from inside (● Figure 6.28). The line with arrowheads, on the other hand, suggests the corner of a room or building seen from outside. In other words, cues that suggest a 3-D space alter our perception of a two-dimensional design (Enns & Coren, 1995).

When discussing the moon illusion earlier, we said that if two objects make images of the same size, the more distant object must be larger. This is known formally as **size-distance invariance** (the size of an object's image is precisely related to its distance from

Frame of reference An internal perspective relative to which events are perceived and evaluated.

Adaptation level An internal or mental "average" or "medium" point that is used to judge amounts.

Illusion A misleading or distorted perception.

Hallucination An imaginary sensation, such as seeing, hearing, or smelling something that does not exist in the external world.

Stroboscopic movement Illusion of movement in which an object is shown in a rapidly changing series of positions.

Müller-Lyer illusion Two equal-length lines tipped with inward or outward pointing V's appear to be of different lengths.

Size-distance invariance The strict relationship between the distance an object lies from the eyes and the size of its image.

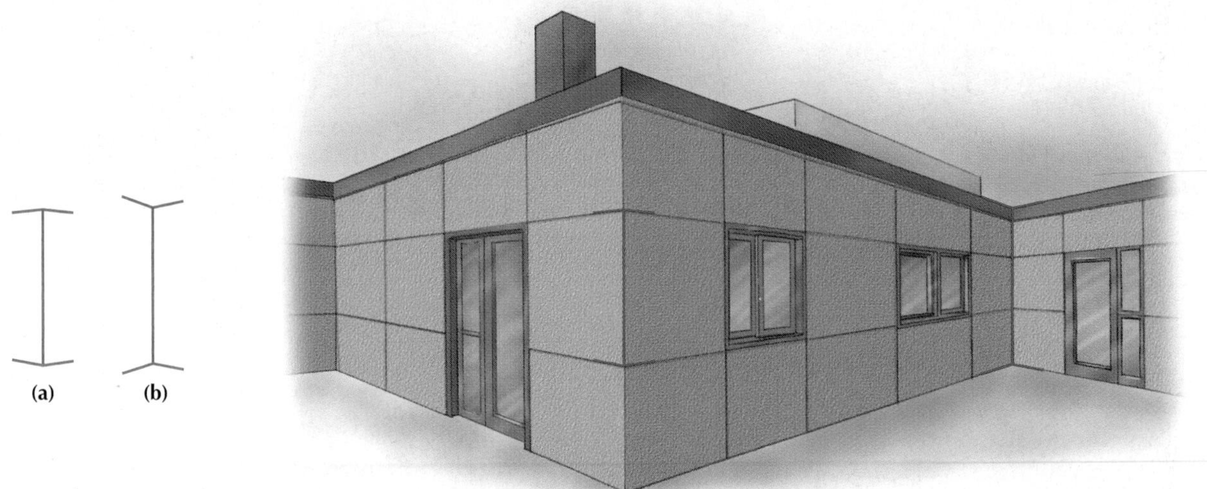

● **Figure 6.28** Why does line *(b)* in the Müller-Lyer illusion look longer than line *(a)*? Probably because it looks more like a distant corner than a nearer one. Because the vertical lines form images of the same length, the more "distant" line must be perceived as larger. As you can see in the drawing on the right, additional depth cues accentuate the Müller-Lyer illusion. (After Enns & Coren, 1995.)

the eyes). Gregory believes the same concept explains the Müller-Lyer illusion. If the V-tipped line looks farther away than the arrowhead-tipped line, then you must compensate by seeing the V-tipped line as longer. This explanation presumes that you have had years of experience with straight lines, sharp edges, and corners—a pretty safe assumption in our culture.

Is there any way to show that past experience causes the illusion? If we could test someone who saw only curves and wavy lines as a child, we would know if experience with a "square" culture is important. Fortunately, a group of people in South Africa, the Zulus, live in a "round" culture. In their daily lives, Zulus rarely encounter a straight line: Their huts are shaped like rounded mounds and arranged in a circle, tools and toys are curved, and there are no straight roads or square buildings.

What happens if a Zulu looks at the Müller-Lyer design? The typical Zulu villager does not experience the illusion. At most, she or he sees the V-tipped line as *slightly* longer than the other (Gregory, 1990). This seems to confirm the importance of past experience and perceptual habits in determining our view of the world. But, like many topics in psychology, room for debate remains. The Müller-Lyer illusion also seems to be partly based on directly misperceiving the location of the ends of the lines (Morgan, Hole, & Glennerster, 1990). Thus, it could be that both apparent size and misperception cause the illusion.

KNOWLEDGE BUILDER

Perceptual Learning

REFLECT

How has perceptual learning affected your ability to safely drive a car? For example, what do you pay attention to at intersections? Where do you habitually look as you are driving?

What do you regard as a "medium-priced" meal at a restaurant? Does your adaptation level affect what you are comfortable paying?

If you spent a year hiking the Amazon River Basin, what effect might it have on your perception of the Müller-Lyer illusion?

LEARNING CHECK

1. Perceptual habits may become so ingrained that they lead us to misperceive a stimulus. T or F?
2. Perceptual learning seems to program the brain for sensitivity to important ______________ of the environment.
3. The Ames room is used to test for adaptation to inverted vision. T or F?
4. An important factor in adaptation to inverted vision is
   a. learning new categories
   b. active movement
   c. overcoming illusions
   d. the horizontal-vertical invariance
5. Size-distance relationships appear to underlie which two illusions? ______________ and ______________
6. An adaptation level represents a personal "medium point," or internal ______________ ___ ______________.

CRITICAL THINKING

7. What size object do you think you would have to hold at arm's length to cover up a full moon?

Answers: 1. T 2. features 3. F 4. b 5. moon illusion, Müller-Lyer illusion 6. frame of reference 7. The most popular answers range from a quarter to a softball. Actually, a pea held in the outstretched hand will cover a full moon (Kunkel, 1993). If you listed an object larger than a pea, be aware that perceptions, no matter how accurate they seem, may distort reality.

Motives and Perception—May I Have Your . . . Attention!

You are surrounded by sights, sounds, odors, tastes, and touch sensations. Which are you aware of? The first stage of perception is attention. As you may recall from Chapter 5, **selective attention** refers to the fact that we give some messages priority and put others on hold (Klein, 2004). You might find it helpful to think of selective attention as a *bottleneck,* or narrowing in the information channel linking the senses to perception. When one message enters the bottleneck, it seems to prevent others from passing through (see ● Figure 6.29). Imagine, for instance, that you are a pilot preparing to land a jumbo jet. You need to be sure the flaps are down. Just as you are about to check them, your copilot says something to you. If you then fail to notice the flaps are still up, an air disaster is just seconds away.

Have you ever felt overloaded when trying to do several things at once? **Divided attention** arises when you must divide your mental effort among tasks, each of which requires more or less attention. Divided attention is related to our limited *capacity* for storing and thinking about information. For example, when people first learn to drive, almost all of their attention is needed to steer, brake, shift, and so forth. However, as a skill becomes more automatic, it requires less attention. In driving, greater skill frees mental capacity for other things, such as tuning the car's radio or carrying on a conversation (Desimone & Duncan, 1995). Yet even as some driving skills become automated, divided attention can be hazardous. Many automobile accidents occur when people are using cell phones, tending to children, looking for dropped objects, reading maps, touching up their makeup, and the like.

Are some stimuli more attention getting than others? Yes. Very *intense* stimuli usually command attention. Stimuli that are brighter, louder, or larger tend to capture attention: A gunshot in a library would be hard to ignore. If a brightly colored hot-air balloon ever lands at your college campus, it will almost certainly draw a crowd.

Repetitious stimuli, repetitious stimuli, repetitious stimuli, repetitious stimuli, repetitious stimuli, repetitious stimuli are also attention getting. A dripping faucet at night makes little noise by normal standards, but because of repetition, it may become as attention getting as a single sound many times louder. This effect is used repeatedly, so to speak, in television and radio commercials.

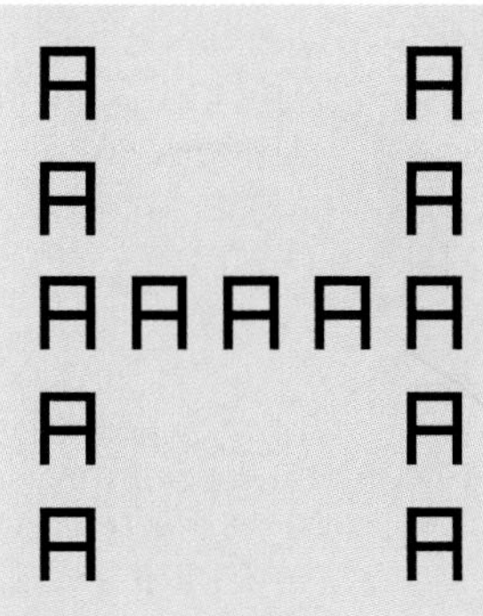

● **Figure 6.29** The attentional "spotlight" can be widened or narrowed. If you focus on local details in this drawing you will see the letter *A* repeated 13 times. If you broaden your field of attention to encompass the overall pattern, you will see the letter *H.* (After Lamb & Yund, 1996.)

Bob Daemmrich/The Image Works

In many sports, experts are much better than beginners at paying attention to key information. Compared with novices, experts scan actions and events more quickly and focus on only the most meaningful information. This allows experts to make decisions and react more quickly (Bard, Fleury, & Goulet, 1994).

ATTENTION IS ALSO **FREQUENTLY** RELATED TO contrast OR *change* IN STIMULATION. The contrasting type styles in the preceding sentence draw attention because they are *unexpected.* Geoffrey Loftus and Norman Mackworth (1978) found that people who look at drawings like ● Figure 6.30 focus first and longest on unexpected objects (the octopus, in this case).

Attention and Perception

As we take in information, attention is the key that unlocks the door to perception. In fact, psychologists Arien Mack and Irvin Rock believe that perception cannot occur without attention. Let's say, for example, that you are staring intently at a computer screen, waiting to see if a black cross will appear. The cross flashes on the screen for a split second and you say, "Yes I saw the cross." At the same time, a small blue square is flashed near the cross, also for a split second. Do you see it, too? Amazingly, when people are tested in this way, many never see the blue square. While their attention is intensely focused on one object, they are blind to another—even though it is right in front of their eyes. The image of the blue square falls on the retina, but it might as well be invisible. Mack

Selective attention Giving priority to a particular incoming sensory message.

Divided attention Allotting mental space or effort to various tasks or parts of a task.

● **Figure 6.30** One of the drawings used by Loftus and Mackworth (1978) to investigate attention. Observers attend to unexpected objects longer than they do to expected objects. In this drawing, observers looked longer at the octopus than they did at a tractor placed in the same spot. What do you think would happen if a tractor were shown upside down or on the roof of the barn? (From "Cognitive Determinants of Fixation Location During Picture Viewing," by G. R. Loftus and N. H. MacWorth, *Journal of Experimental Psychology: Human Perception and Performance,* 4th ed., 1978, pp. 565–572.)

and Rock call this effect **inattentional blindness** (blindness caused by not attending to a stimulus) (Mack & Rock, 1998). Not seeing something that is plainly before your eyes is most likely to occur when your attention is narrowly focused (Mack, 2002).

Inattentional blindness is vividly illustrated by the work of psychologists Daniel Simons and Christopher Chabris. In one study, Simons and Chabris showed participants a film of two basketball teams, one wearing black shirts and the other wearing white. Observers were asked to watch the film closely and count how many times a basketball passed between members of one of the teams, while ignoring the other team. As observers watched and counted, a person wearing a gorilla suit walked into the middle of the basketball game, faced the camera, thumped its chest, and walked out of view. Half the observers failed to notice this rather striking event (Simons & Chabris, 1999). In a similar way, using a cell phone while driving can cause inattentional blindness. Instead of ignoring a gorilla, you might miss seeing another car, a motorcyclist, or a pedestrian while your attention is focused on the phone (Strayer, Drews, & Johnston, 2003).

Habituation

Change, contrast, and incongruity are perhaps the most basic sources of attention. We quickly **habituate** (respond less) to predictable and unchanging stimuli. Notice that repetition without variation leads to habituation. Repetition is attention getting when it is irritating or annoying. A dripping faucet varies in timing just enough to gain attention. In contrast, we quickly habituate to the steady tick of a clock.

How does habituation differ from sensory adaptation? As described in Chapter 5, *adaptation* decreases the actual number of sensory messages sent to the brain. When messages do reach the brain, the body has a sort of "What is it?" reaction, known as an *orientation response*. An **orientation response** (OR) prepares us to receive information from a stimulus: The pupils enlarge, brain-wave patterns shift, breathing stops briefly, blood flow to the head increases, and we turn toward the stimulus. Have you ever seen someone do a double take? If so, you have observed an orientation response.

Now, think about what happens when you buy a new CD. At first the music holds your attention all the way through. But when the CD becomes "old," all the songs may play without your really attending to them. When a stimulus is repeated *without change,* the OR habituates, or decreases. (Also, see "The 'Boiled Frog Syndrome.'")

Interestingly, creative people habituate *more slowly* than average. We might expect that they would rapidly become bored with a repeated stimulus. Instead, it seems that creative people actively attend to stimuli, even those that are repeated (Colin, Moore, & West, 1996).

Motives and Attention

Motives also play a role in shaping our perceptions. For example, if you are hungry, food-related words are more likely to gain your attention than nonfood words (Mogg et al., 1998). Advertisers, of course, know that their pitch will be more effective if it gets your attention. That's why ads are loud, repetitious, and often intentionally irritating. They also take advantage of two motives that are widespread in our society: *anxiety* and *sex*. Everything from mouthwash to automobile tires is merchandised by using sex to gain attention. Other ads combine sex with anxiety. Deodorant, soaps, toothpaste, and countless other articles are pushed in ads that play on desires to be attractive, to have "sex appeal," or to avoid embarrassment.

In addition to directing attention, motives may alter what is perceived. As part of a supposed study of "the dating practices of college students," male volunteers were shown a picture of a female student and asked to give a first impression of how attractive she was. Before making these ratings, each person read one of two

● **Figure 6.31** Emotionally significant stimuli influence attention. (M. H. Erdelyi and A. G. Applebaum, "Cognitive Masking: The Disruptive Effects of an Emotional Stimulus upon the Perception of Contiguous Neural Items," *Bulletin of the Psychonomic Society,* 1973, I, pp. 59–61. Reprinted by permission.)

CRITICAL THINKING — The "Boiled Frog Syndrome"

As we have noted, the perceptual system is impressed most by dramatic changes. Humans evolved to detect sharp changes and distinctive events, such as the sudden appearance of a lion, a potential mate, or sources of food. We are far less able to detect gradual changes.

Perceptual capacities that aided survival when humans were hunters and gatherers can now be a handicap. Many of the threats facing civilization develop very slowly. Examples include the stockpiling of nuclear warheads, degradation of the environment, global deforestation, global warming, erosion of the ozone layer, and runaway human population growth.

Randy Ury/Corbis

Robert Ornstein, a psychologist, and Paul Ehrlich, a biologist, believe that many of the large-scale threats we face are similar to the "boiled frog syndrome." Frogs placed in a pan of water that is slowly heated cannot detect the gradual rise in temperature. They will sit still until they die. Like the doomed frogs, many people seem unable to detect gradual but deadly trends in modern civilization (Ornstein & Ehrlich, 1989).

To avoid disasters, it may take a conscious effort by large numbers of people to see the "big picture" and reverse lethal but easily overlooked patterns (O'Neill, 2005). The relatively new field of *community psychology* is dedicated to helping overcome our own narrow perspectives to perceive important larger patterns (Nelson & Prilleltensky, 2005). Understanding how perception shapes "reality" may ultimately prove to be a matter of life or death. Are you paying attention?

short written passages: One was sexually arousing and the other was not. The important finding was that men who read the more arousing passage rated the female as more attractive (Stephan et al., 1971). This result may come as no surprise if you have ever been infatuated with someone and then fallen out of love. A person who once seemed highly attractive may look quite different when your feelings change.

An emotional stimulus can shift attention away from other information. In an experiment, members of a Jewish organization watched as pictures like ● Figure 6.31 were flashed on a screen for a split second. In another instance of inattentional blindness, people were less likely to recognize symbols around the drawing's edge when the center item was an emotional symbol like the swastika (Erdelyi & Appelbaum, 1973). This effect probably explains why fans of opposing sports teams often act as if they had seen two completely different games.

Perceptual Expectancies—On Your Mark, Get Set

On a piece of paper, draw a circle about 3 inches in diameter. Inside the circle, above and to the left of center, make a large black dot, about one-half inch in diameter. Make another dot inside the circle above and to the right of center. Now, still inside the circle, draw an arc, curved upward and about 2 inches long just below the center of the circle. If you followed these instructions, your reaction might now be, "Oh! Why didn't you just say to draw a happy face?"

Like the happy face drawing, perception seems to proceed in two major ways. In **bottom-up processing**, we analyze information starting at the "bottom" with small sensory units (features) and build upward to a complete perception. The reverse also seems to occur. In **top-down processing** preexisting knowledge is used to rapidly organize features into a meaningful whole. Bottom-up processing is like putting together a picture puzzle you've never seen before: You must assemble small pieces until a recognizable pattern appears. Top-down processing is like putting together a puzzle you have solved many times: After only a few pieces are in place, you begin to see outlines of the final picture.

Both types of processing are illustrated by ● Figure 6.32. Also, return to Figure 6.5, the giant walking stick. The first time you saw the photo you probably processed it bottom-up, picking out features until the insect was recognizable. This time, because of top-down processing, you should see the insect instantly. Another

Inattentional blindness Failure to perceive a stimulus that is in plain view, but not the focus of attention.

Habituation A decrease in perceptual response to a repeated stimulus.

Orientation response Bodily changes that prepare an organism to receive information from a particular stimulus.

Bottom-up processing Organizing perceptions by beginning with low-level features.

Top-down processing Applying higher-level knowledge to rapidly organize sensory information into a meaningful perception.

● **Figure 6.32** This painting by abstract artist Al Held is 9 feet by 9 feet. If you process the painting "bottom-up," all you will see is two small dark geometric shapes. Would you like to try some top-down processing? Knowing the painting's title will allow you to apply your knowledge and see the painting in an entirely different way. The title? It's *The Big N.* Can you see it now?

good example of top-down processing is found in perceptual expectancies.

Ready, Set, Perceive

What is a perceptual expectancy? A runner in the starting blocks at a track meet is *set* to respond in a certain way. Likewise, past experience, motives, context, or suggestions may create a **perceptual expectancy (or set)** that prepares you to perceive in a certain way. If a car backfires, runners at a track meet may jump the gun. When drawing a face, a beginning artist tends to think "nose, mouth, eyes, ears" and tries to draw what he or she *thinks* each of these features looks like instead of what they *actually* look like (Cohen & Bennett, 1997). As a matter of fact, we all frequently jump the gun when perceiving. In essence, an expectancy is a perceptual hypothesis we are *very likely* to apply to a stimulus—even if applying it is inappropriate.

Perceptual sets often lead us to see what we *expect* to see. For example, let's say you are driving across the desert. You are very low on gas. Finally, you see a sign approaching. On it are the words FUEL AHEAD. You relax, knowing you will not be stranded. But as you draw nearer, the words on the sign become FOOD AHEAD. Most people have had similar experiences in which expectations altered their perceptions. To observe perceptual expectancies firsthand, perform the demonstration described in ● Figure 6.33.

Perceptual expectancies are frequently created by *suggestion.* This is especially true of perceiving other people. In one classic experiment, a psychology professor arranged for a guest lecturer to teach his class. Half the students in the class were given a page of notes that described the lecturer as a "rather *cold* person, industrious, critical, practical, and determined." The other students got notes describing him as a "rather *warm* person, industrious, critical, practical, and determined" (Kelley, 1950; italics added). Students who received the "cold" description perceived the lecturer as unhappy and irritable and didn't volunteer in class discussion. Those who got the "warm" description saw the lecturer as happy and good-natured, and they actively took part in discussion with him. In the same way, labels such as "punk," "mental patient," "queer," "illegal immigrant," "bitch," and so on, are very likely to distort perceptions.

Those are extremes. Does it really make that much difference what you call someone or something? Perceptual categories, especially those defined by labels, do make a difference. This is especially true in perceiving people, where even trained observers may be influenced. For example, in one study, psychotherapists were shown a videotaped interview. Half of the therapists were told that the man being interviewed was applying for a job. The rest were told that the man was a mental patient. Therapists who

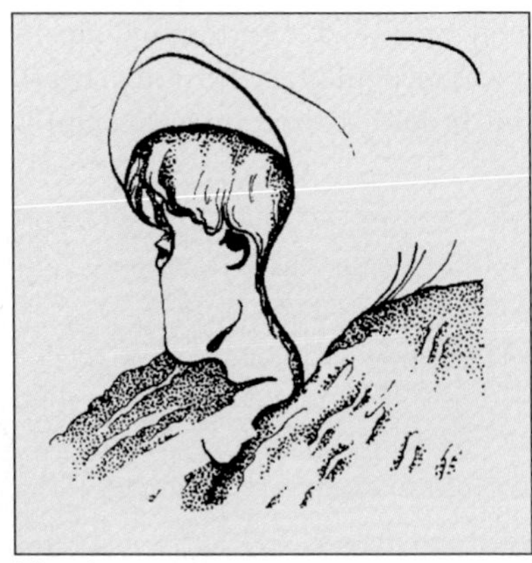
View I

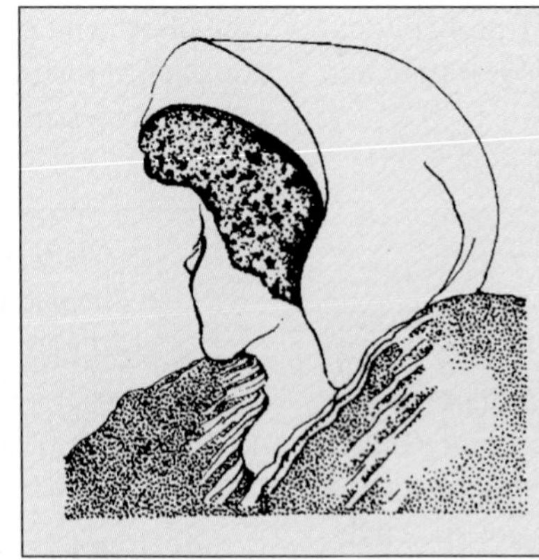
View II

View III

● **Figure 6.33** "Young woman/old woman" illustrations. As an interesting demonstration of perceptual expectancy, show some of your friends view I and some view II (cover all other views). Next show your friends view III and ask them what they see. Those who saw view I should see the old woman in view III; those who saw view II should see the young woman in view III. Can you see both? (After Leeper, 1935.)

thought the man was a job applicant perceived him as "realistic," "sincere," and "pleasant." Those who thought he was a patient perceived him as "defensive," "dependent," and "impulsive" (Langer & Abelson, 1974).

In the next section, we will go beyond normal perception to ask, "Is extrasensory perception possible?" Before we do that, here's a chance to answer the question, "Is remembering the preceding discussion possible?"

KNOWLEDGE BUILDER

Attention and Perceptual Expectancies

REFLECT

Have you ever tried to listen to two people who were talking to you at the same time? What happens to your ability to process information when there's a conflict in selective attention?

You have almost certainly misperceived a situation at some time because of a perceptual expectancy or the influence of motives. How were your perceptions influenced?

LEARNING CHECK

1. Selective attention is promoted by all but one of the following. Which does not fit?
   a. habituation c. change
   b. contrast d. intensity
2. The occurrence of an orientation response shows that habituation is complete. T or F?
3. Changes in brain waves and increased blood flow to the head are part of an OR. T or F?
4. Research shows that heightened sexual arousal can cause a person to perceive members of the opposite sex as more physically attractive. T or F?
5. In top-down processing of information, individual features are analyzed and assembled into a meaningful whole. T or F?
6. When a person is prepared to perceive events in a particular way, it is said that a perceptual expectancy or ______________ exists.
7. Perceptual expectancies are greatly influenced by the existence of mental categories and labels. T or F?

CRITICAL THINKING

8. Cigarette advertisements in the United States are required to carry a warning label about the health risks of smoking. How have tobacco companies made these labels less visible?

Answers: 1. a 2. F 3. T 4. T 5. F 6. set 7. T 8. Advertisers place health warnings in the corners of ads, where they attract the least possible attention. Also, the labels are often placed on "busy" backgrounds so that they are partially camouflaged. Finally, the main images in ads are designed to strongly attract attention. This further distracts readers from seeing the warnings.

Extrasensory Perception—Do You Believe in Magic?

About half of the general public believes in the existence of extrasensory perception. Very few psychologists share this belief. Actually, it's surprising that even more people aren't believers. ESP and other paranormal events are treated as accepted facts in many movies and television programs. What is the evidence for and against extrasensory perception?

Uri Geller, a self-proclaimed "psychic," once agreed to demonstrate his claimed paranormal abilities. During testing, it seemed that Geller could sense which of ten film canisters contained a hidden object, he correctly guessed the number that would come up on a die shaken in a closed box, and he reproduced drawings sealed in envelopes.

Was Geller cheating, or was he using some ability beyond normal perception? There is little doubt that Geller was cheating (Randi, 1997). But how? The answer lies in a discussion of **extrasensory perception** (ESP)—the purported ability to perceive events in ways that cannot be explained by known sensory capacities.

Parapsychology is the study of ESP and other **psi** (pronounced "sigh") **phenomena** (events that seem to defy accepted scientific laws). Parapsychologists seek answers to the questions raised by three basic forms that ESP could take:

1. **Clairvoyance.** The purported ability to perceive events or gain information in ways that appear unaffected by distance or normal physical barriers.
2. **Telepathy.** Extrasensory perception of another person's thoughts, or more simply, the purported ability to read someone else's mind.
3. **Precognition.** The purported ability to perceive or accurately predict future events. Precognition may take the form of prophetic dreams that foretell the future.

While we are at it, we might as well toss in another purported psi ability:

4. **Psychokinesis.** The purported ability to exert influence over inanimate objects by willpower ("mind over matter"). (Psychokinesis cannot be classed as a type of ESP, but it is frequently studied by parapsychologists.)

Perceptual expectancy (or set) A readiness to perceive in a particular manner, induced by strong expectations.

Extrasensory perception The purported ability to perceive events in ways that cannot be explained by known capacities of the sensory organs.

Parapsychology The study of extranormal psychological events, such as extrasensory perception.

Psi phenomena Events that seem to lie outside the realm of accepted scientific laws.

Clairvoyance The purported ability to perceive events at a distance or through physical barriers.

Telepathy The purported ability to directly know another person's thoughts.

Precognition The purported ability to accurately predict future events.

Psychokinesis The purported ability to mentally alter or influence objects or events.

An Appraisal of ESP

Psychologists as a group are highly skeptical about psi abilities. If you've ever had an apparent clairvoyant or telepathic experience you might be convinced that ESP exists. However, the difficulty of excluding *coincidence* makes such experiences less conclusive than they might seem. Consider a typical "psychic" experience: During the middle of the night, a woman away for a weekend visit suddenly had a strong impulse to return home. When she arrived she found the house on fire with her husband asleep inside (Rhine, 1953). An experience like this is striking, but it does not confirm the reality of ESP. If, by coincidence, a hunch turns out to be correct, it may be *reinterpreted* as precognition or clairvoyance (Marks, 2000). If it is not confirmed, it will simply be forgotten. Most people don't realize it, but such coincidences occur quite often.

Formal investigation of psi events owes much to the late J. B. Rhine, who tried to study ESP objectively. Many of Rhine's experiments made use of the **Zener cards** (a deck of 25 cards, each bearing one of five symbols) (● Figure 6.34). In a typical clairvoyance test, people tried to guess the symbols on the cards as they were turned up from a shuffled deck. Pure guessing in this test will produce an average score of 5 "hits" out of 25 cards.

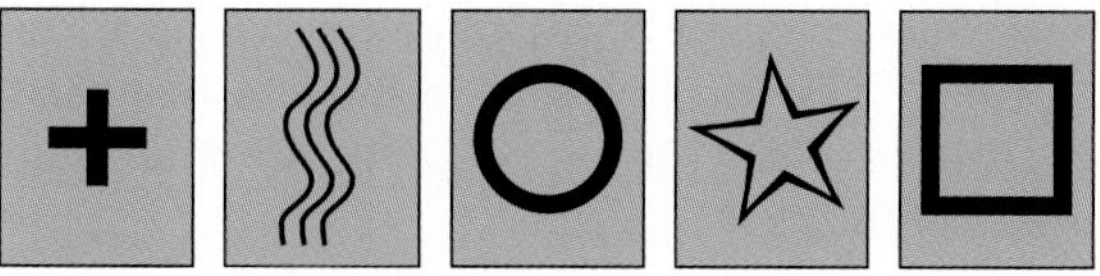

● **Figure 6.34** ESP cards used by J. B. Rhine, an early experimenter in parapsychology.

Susan Van Etten/PhotoEdit

Most so-called psychics are simply keen observers. The "psychic" begins a "reading" by making general statements about a person. The "psychic" then plays "hot and cold" by attending to the person's facial expressions, body language, or tone of voice. When the "psychic" is "hot" (on the right track), the "psychic" continues to make similar statements about the person. If the person's reactions signal that the "psychic" is "cold," the psychic drops that topic or line of thought and tries another (Schouten, 1994).

Fraud and Skepticism

Unfortunately, some of Rhine's most dramatic early experiments used badly printed Zener cards that allowed the symbols to show faintly on the back. It is also very easy to cheat, by marking cards with a fingernail or by noting marks on the cards caused by normal use. Even if this were not the case, there is evidence that early experimenters sometimes unconsciously gave people cues about cards with their eyes, facial gestures, or lip movements. In short, none of the early studies in parapsychology were done in a way that eliminated the possibility of fraud or "leakage" of helpful information (Alcock, Burns, & Freeman, 2003).

Modern parapsychologists are now well aware of the need for double-blind experiments, security and accuracy in record keeping, meticulous control, and repeatability of experiments (Milton & Wiseman, 1997). In the last 10 years, hundreds of experiments have been reported in parapsychological journals. Many of them seem to support the existence of psi abilities.

Then why do most psychologists remain skeptical about psi abilities? For one thing, fraud continues to plague the field. It is remarkable, for instance, that many parapsychologists chose to ignore a famous "psychic's" habit of peeking at ESP cards during testing (Cox, 1994). As one critic put it, positive ESP results usually mean "Error Some Place" (Marks, 1990). The more closely psi experiments are examined, the more likely it is that claimed successes will evaporate (Alcock, 2003; Stokes, 2001).

The need for skepticism is especially great anytime there's money to be made from purported psychic abilities. For example, the owners of the "Miss Cleo" TV-psychic operation were convicted of felony fraud in 2002. "Miss Cleo," supposedly a Jamaican psychic, was really just an actress from Los Angeles. People who paid $4.99 a minute for a "reading" from "Miss Cleo" actually reached one of several hundred operators. These people were hired through ads that read, "No experience necessary." Despite being entirely faked, the "Miss Cleo" scam brought in more than $1 billion before it was shut down.

Statistics and Chance

Inconsistency is a major problem in psi research. For every study with positive results, there are others that fail (Alcock, 2003; Hansel, 1980). It is rare—in fact, almost unheard of—for a person to maintain psi ability over any sustained period of time (Jahn, 1982). ESP researchers believe this "decline effect" shows that parapsychological skills are very fragile. But critics argue that a person who only temporarily scores above chance has just received credit for a **run of luck** (a statistically unusual outcome that could occur by chance alone). When the run is over, it is not

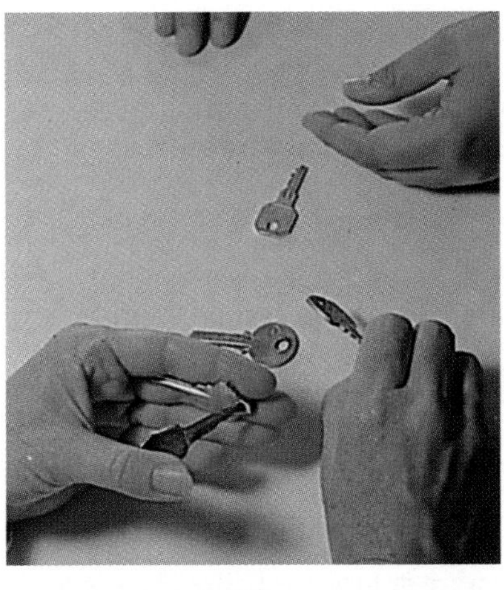
(a)

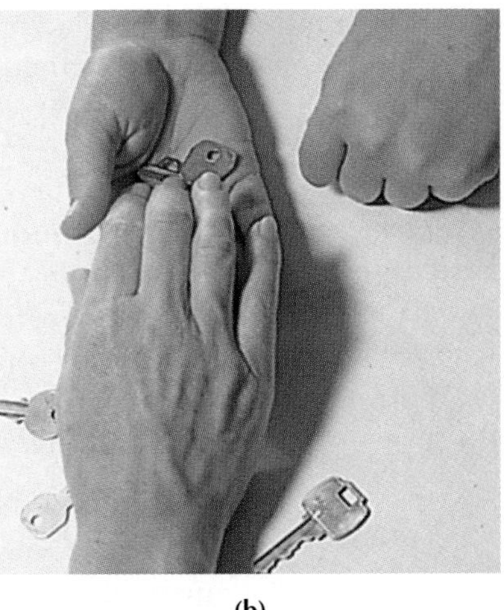
(b)

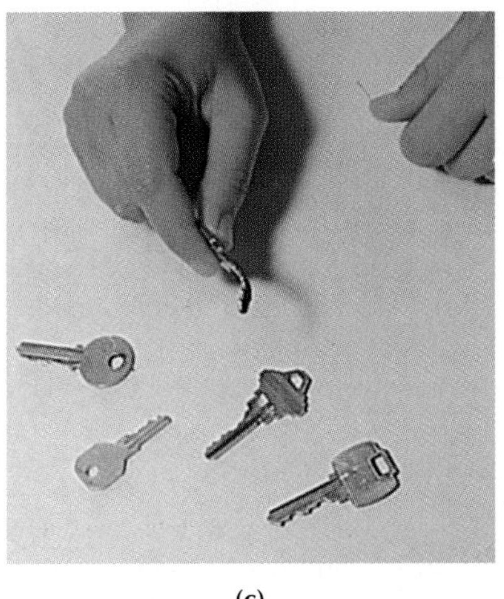
(c)

Dennis Coon

● **Figure 6.35** Fake psychokinesis. *(a)* The performer shows an observer several straight keys. While doing so, he bends one of the keys by placing its tip in the slot of another key. Normally, this is done out of sight, behind the "psychic's" hand. It is clearly shown here so that you can see how the deception occurs. *(b)* Next, the "psychic" places the two keys in the observer's hand and closes it. By skillful manipulation, the observer has been kept from seeing the bent key. The performer then "concentrates" on the keys to "bend them with psychic energy." *(c)* The bent key is revealed to the observer. "Miracle" accomplished! (Adapted from Randi, 1983.)

fair to assume that ESP is temporarily gone. We must count *all* attempts.

To understand the run-of-luck criticism, imagine that you flip a coin 100 times and record the results. You then flip another coin 100 times, again recording the results. The two lists are compared. For any 10 pairs of flips, we would expect heads or tails to match 5 times. Let's say that you go through the list and find a set of 10 pairs where 9 out of 10 matched. This is far above chance expectation. But does it mean that the first coin "knew" what was going to come up on the second coin? The idea is obviously silly.

Now, what if a person guesses 100 times what will come up on a coin. Again, we might find a set of 10 guesses that matches the results of flipping the coin. Does this mean that the person, for a time, had precognition—then lost it? Parapsychologists tend to believe the answer is yes. Skeptics assume that nothing more than random matching occurred, as in the two-coin example.

Inconclusive Research

Unfortunately, many of the most spectacular findings in parapsychology simply cannot be **replicated** (Hyman, 1996a). Even the same researchers using the same experimental subjects typically can't get similar results every time (Schick & Vaughn, 2001). More important, improved research methods usually result in fewer positive results (Hyman, 1996b).

Reinterpretation is also a problem in psi experiments. For example, ex-astronaut Edgar Mitchell claimed he did a successful telepathy experiment from space. Yet news accounts never mentioned that on some trials Mitchell's "receivers" scored above chance, whereas on others they scored *below* chance. Although you might assume that below-chance trials were failures to find telepathy, Mitchell reinterpreted them as "successes," claiming that they represented intentional "psi missing." But, as skeptics have noted, if both high scores and low scores count as successes, how can you lose?

Of course, in many ESP tests the outcome is beyond debate. A good example is provided by recent ESP experiments done through newspapers, radio, and television. In these mass media studies, people attempted to identify ESP targets from a distance. Such studies allow large numbers of people to be tested. The results of more than 1.5 million ESP trials recently done through the mass media are easy to summarize: There was no significant ESP effect (Milton & Wiseman, 1999). Zero. Zip. Nada. Clearly, state lottery organizers have nothing to fear!

Stage ESP

If psychic phenomena do occur, they certainly can't be controlled well enough to be used by entertainers. **Stage ESP** simulates ESP for the purpose of entertainment. Like stage magic, it is based on sleight of hand, deception, and patented gadgets (● Figure 6.35). A case in point is Uri Geller, a former nightclub magician who "astounded" audiences—and some scientists—with apparent telepathy, psychokinesis, and precognition.

It's now clear that tests of Geller's performance were incredibly sloppy. For instance, Geller reproduced sealed drawings in a room next to the one where the drawings were made. Original reports

Zener cards A deck of 25 cards bearing various symbols and used in early parapsychological research.

Run of luck A statistically unusual outcome (as in getting five heads in a row when flipping a coin) that could still occur by chance alone.

Replicate To reproduce or repeat.

Stage ESP The simulation of ESP for the purpose of entertainment.

failed to mention that there was a hole in the wall between the rooms, through which Geller could have heard descriptions of the pictures as they were being drawn. Likewise, in the "die in the box" tests Geller was allowed to hold the box, shake it, and have the honor of opening it (Randi, 1997; Wilhelm, 1976).

Why weren't such details reported? Sensational and uncritical reporting of apparent paranormal events is widespread. Hundreds of books, articles, and television programs are produced each year by people who are getting rich by promoting unsupported claims. If a person did have psychic powers, he or she would not have to make a living by entertaining others. A quick trip to a casino would allow the person to retire for life.

Implications

After close to 130 years of investigation, it is still impossible to say conclusively whether psi events occur. As we have seen, a close look at psi experiments often reveals serious problems of evidence, procedure, and scientific rigor (Alcock, Burns, & Freeman, 2003; Hyman, 1996b; Marks, 2000; Stokes, 2001). It is also interesting to note that a survey of leading parapsychologists and skeptics found that almost all in both camps said their belief in psi had decreased (Blackmore, 1989). Yet being a skeptic does not mean a person is against something. It means that you are unconvinced. The purpose of this discussion, then, has been to counter the *uncritical* acceptance of psi events that is rampant in the media.

What would it take to scientifically demonstrate the existence of ESP? Quite simply, a set of instructions that would allow any competent, unbiased observer to produce a psi event under standardized conditions that rule out any possibility of fraud (Schick & Vaughn, 2001). In fact, professional magician and skeptic James Randi even offers a $1,000,000 prize to anyone who can demonstrate evidence of psi events under standardized conditions (no one has claimed the prize yet; you can read all about it at www.randi.org). Undoubtedly, some intrepid researchers will continue their attempts to supply just that. Others remain skeptics and consider 130 years of inconclusive efforts reason enough to abandon the concept of ESP (Marks, 2000). At the least, it seems essential to be carefully skeptical of evidence reported in the popular press or by researchers who are uncritical "true believers." (But then, you already knew we were going to say that, didn't you!)

Ziggy

A Look Ahead

In this chapter we have moved from basic sensations to the complexities of perceiving people and events. We have also probed some of the controversies concerning ESP. In the Psychology in Action section, we will return to "everyday" perception for a look at perceptual awareness.

KNOWLEDGE BUILDER

Extrasensory Perception

REFLECT

Let's say that a friend of yours is an avid fan of TV shows that feature paranormal themes. See if you can summarize for her or him what is known about ESP. Be sure to include evidence for and against the existence of ESP and some of the thinking errors associated with nonskeptical belief in the paranormal.

LEARNING CHECK

1. Four purported psi events investigated by parapsychologists are clairvoyance, telepathy, precognition, and ______________ ______________.
2. The Zener cards were used in early studies of
   a. psi phenomena c. the Müller-Lyer illusion
   b. inattentional blindness d. top-down processing
3. Natural, or "real-life," occurrences are regarded as the best evidence for the existence of ESP. T or F?
4. Skeptics attribute positive results in psi experiments to statistical runs of luck. T or F?
5. Replication rates are very high for ESP experiments. T or F?

CRITICAL THINKING

6. What would you estimate is the chance that two people will have the same birthday (day and month, but not year) in a group of 30 people?
7. A "psychic" on television offers to fix broken watches for viewers. Moments later, dozens of viewers call the station to say that their watches miraculously started running again. What have they overlooked?

Answers: 1. psychokinesis 2. a 3. F 4. T 5. F 6. Most people assume that this would be a relatively rare event. Actually there is a 71 percent chance that two people will share a birthday in a group of 30. Most people probably underestimate the natural rate of occurrence of many seemingly mysterious coincidences (Alcock, Burns, & Freeman, 2003). 7. When psychologists handled watches awaiting repair at a store, 57 percent began running again, with no help from a "psychic." Believing the "psychic's" claim also overlooks the impact of big numbers: If the show reached a large audience, at least a few "broken" watches would start working merely by chance.

PSYCHOLOGY IN ACTION

Perception and Objectivity—Believing Is Seeing

Have you ever seen the sun set? You may think you have. Yet, in reality, we know the sun does not "set." Instead, our viewing angle changes as the earth turns, until the sun is obscured by the horizon. Want to try the alternative? This evening, stand facing the west. With practice, you can learn to feel yourself being swept backward on the rotating surface of the earth as you watch an unmoving sun recede in the distance.

This radical shift in perspective illustrates the limitations of "objective" observation. Like most experiences, seeing a "sunset" is a **perceptual reconstruction** (mental model) of an external event. Another way of appreciating this is to realize that it takes about 50 milliseconds for a visual signal to move from the retina to the brain. Therefore, the images we see are always slightly in the past. An event that happens quickly, like the pop of a flashbulb, may be over by the time we perceive it.

As we have seen, perception reflects the needs, expectations, attitudes, values, and beliefs of the perceiver. In this light, the phrase "seeing is believing" must be modified. Clearly, we see what we believe, as well as believe what we see (● Figure 6.36).

In some cases, subjective perception nurtures the personal vision valued in art, music, poetry, and scientific innovation. Often, however, it is a real liability.

Eyewitness

In the courtroom, eyewitness testimony can be a key to proving guilt or innocence. The claim "I saw it with my own eyes" carries a lot of weight with a jury. Most jurors (unless they have taken a psychology course) tend to assume that eyewitness testimony is nearly infallible (Durham & Dane, 1999). Even police officers, who are presumably more familiar with witnesses, generally believe that eyewitnesses are rarely incorrect (Kebbell & Milne, 1998). But to put it bluntly, eyewitness testimony is frequently wrong.

What about witnesses who are certain that their perceptions were accurate? Should juries believe them? Actually, having confidence in your testimony has almost no bearing on its accuracy (Wells, 1993)! Psychologists are gradually convincing lawyers, judges, and police that eyewitness errors are common

● Figure 6.36 It is difficult to look at this simple drawing without perceiving depth. Yet the drawing is nothing more than a collection of flat shapes. Turn this page counterclockwise 90 degrees and you will see 3 C's, one within another. When the drawing is turned sideways, it seems nearly flat. However, if you turn the page upright again, a sense of depth will reappear. Clearly, you have used your knowledge and expectations to *construct* an illusion of depth. The drawing itself would only be a flat design if you didn't invest it with meaning.

AP/Wide World Photo

Even in broad daylight, eyewitness testimony is untrustworthy. In 2001 an American Airlines airliner crashed near Kennedy International Airport in New York. Hundreds of people saw the plane go down. Half of them said the plane was on fire. Flight recorders showed there was no fire. One witness in five saw the plane make a right turn. An equal number saw it make a left turn! As one investigator commented, the best witness may be a "kid under 12 years old who doesn't have his parents around." Adults, it seems, are easily swayed by their expectations.

Perceptual reconstruction A mental model of external events.

(Yarmey, 2003). Even so, thousands of people have been wrongfully convicted (Scheck, Neufeld, & Dwyer, 2000). Unfortunately, perception rarely provides an "instant replay" of events. As stated earlier, impressions formed when a person is surprised, threatened, or under stress are especially prone to distortion (Yuille & Daylen, 1998). In addition, being questioned tends to make witnesses more confident about what they saw, even if they are wrong. Thus, police questioning can actually degrade the value of the testimony witnesses give later, in court (Shaw, 1996).

Because impressions formed when a person is surprised, threatened, or under stress are especially prone to distortion, witnesses to crimes often disagree. As a dramatic demonstration of this problem, a college professor was attacked by an actor in a staged assault. Immediately after the event, 141 witnesses were questioned in detail. Their descriptions were then compared with a videotape made of the staged "crime." The total accuracy score for the group (on features such as appearance, age, weight, and height of the assailant) was only *25 percent* of the maximum possible (Buckhout, 1974). Similarly, a study of real eyewitness cases found that the *wrong person* was chosen from police lineups 25 percent of the time (Levi, 1998).

Wouldn't the victim of a crime remember more than a mere witness? Not necessarily. A revealing study found that eyewitness accuracy is virtually the same for witnessing a crime (seeing a pocket calculator stolen) as it is for being a victim (seeing one's own watch stolen) (Hosch & Cooper, 1982). Placing more weight on the testimony of victims may be a serious mistake. In many crimes, victims fall prey to *weapon focus*. Understandably, they fix their entire attention on the knife, gun, or other weapon used by an attacker. In doing so, they fail to notice details of appearance, dress, or other clues to identity (Steblay, 1992). Additional factors that consistently lower eyewitness accuracy are summarized in ■ Table 6.2 (Kassin et al., 2001).

Implications

Now that DNA testing is available, more than 100 people who were convicted of murder, rape, and other crimes in the United States have been exonerated. Each of these innocent people was convicted mainly on the basis of eyewitness testimony. Each also spent *years* in prison before being cleared (Foxhall, 2000). How often are everyday perceptions as inaccurate or distorted as those of an emotional eyewitness? The answer we have been moving toward is very frequently. Bearing this in mind may help you be more tolerant of the views of others and more cautious about your own objectivity. It may also encourage more frequent *reality testing* on your part.

What do you mean by reality testing? In any situation having an element of doubt or uncertainty, **reality testing** involves obtaining additional information to check your

TABLE 6.2

Factors Affecting the Accuracy of Eyewitness Perceptions

SOURCES OF ERROR	SUMMARY OF FINDINGS
1. Wording of questions	An eyewitness's testimony about an event can be affected by how the questions put to that witness are worded.
2. Postevent information	Eyewitness testimony about an event often reflects not only what was actually seen but also information obtained later on.
3. Attitudes, expectations	An eyewitness's perception and memory of an event may be affected by his or her attitudes and expectations.
4. Alcohol intoxication	Alcohol intoxication impairs later ability to recall events.
5. Cross-racial perceptions	Eyewitnesses are better at identifying members of their own race than they are at identifying people of other races.
6. Weapon focus	The presence of a weapon impairs an eyewitness's ability to accurately identify the culprit's face.
7. Accuracy confidence	An eyewitness's confidence is not a good predictor of his or her accuracy.
8. Exposure time	The less time an eyewitness has to observe an event, the less well she or he will perceive and remember it.
9. Unconscious transference	Eyewitnesses sometimes identify as a culprit someone they have seen in another situation or context.
10. Color perception	Judgments of color made under monochromatic light (such as an orange street light) are highly unreliable.
11. Stress	Very high levels of stress impair the accuracy of eyewitness perceptions.

Adapted from Kassin et al., 2001.

BRIDGES

Distortions in memory also affect the accuracy of eyewitness testimony.

See Chapter 9, pages 303–307.

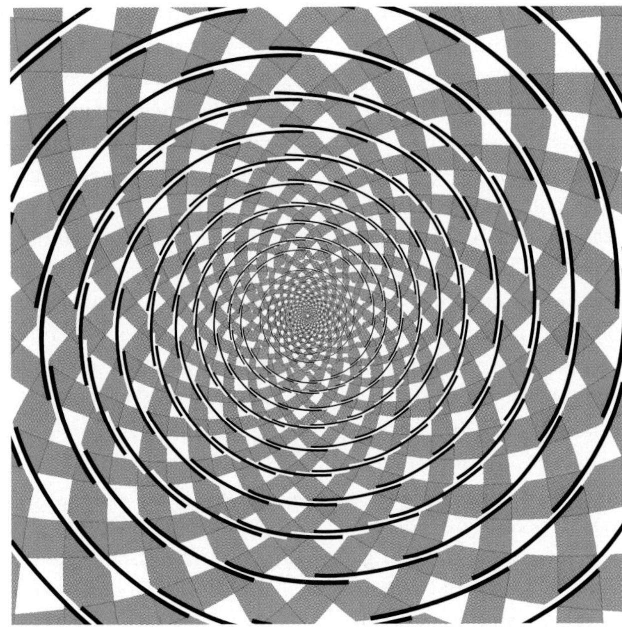

● **Figure 6.37** The limits of pure perception. Even simple designs are easily misperceived. Fraser's spiral is actually a series of concentric circles. The illusion is so powerful that people who try to trace one of the circles sometimes follow the illusory spiral and jump from one circle to the next. (After Seckel, 2000.)

perceptions. ● Figure 6.37 shows a powerful illusion called Fraser's spiral. What appears to be a spiral is actually made up of a series of closed circles. Most people cannot spontaneously see this reality. Instead, they must carefully trace one of the circles to confirm what is "real" in the design.

Psychologist Sidney Jourard once offered a more pertinent example of reality testing. One of Jourard's students believed her roommate was stealing from her. The student gradually became convinced of her roommate's guilt but said nothing. As her distrust and anger grew, their relationship turned cold and distant. Finally, at Jourard's urging, she confronted her roommate. The roommate cleared herself immediately and expressed relief when the puzzling change in their relationship was explained (Jourard, 1974). With their friendship reestablished, the true culprit was soon caught. (The cleaning woman did it!)

If you have ever concluded that someone was angry, upset, or unfriendly without checking the accuracy of your perceptions, you have fallen into a subtle trap. Personal objectivity is an elusive quality, requiring frequent reality testing to maintain. At the very least, it pays to ask a person what she or he is feeling when you are in doubt. Clearly, most of us could learn to be better "eyewitnesses" to daily events.

Positive Psychology: Perceptual Awareness

Do some people perceive things more accurately than others? Humanistic psychologist Abraham Maslow (1969) believed that some people perceive themselves and others with unusual accuracy. Maslow characterized these people as especially alive, open, aware, and mentally healthy. He found that their perceptual styles were marked by immersion in the present; a lack of self-consciousness; freedom from selecting, criticizing, or evaluating; and a general "surrender" to experience. The kind of perception Maslow described is like that of a mother with her newborn infant, a child at Christmas, or two people in love.

In daily life, we quickly habituate (respond less) to predictable and unchanging stimuli. Habituation is a type of learning—basically, we learn to cease paying attention to familiar stimuli. As we discussed previously, when you buy a new CD, the music initially holds your attention all the way through. But when the CD becomes "old," all the songs may play without your really attending to them. When a stimulus is repeated *without change,* our response to it habituates, or decreases. Remember, creative people habituate *more slowly* than average. We might expect that they would rapidly become bored with a repeated stimulus. Instead, it seems that creative people actively attend to stimuli, even those that are repeated (Colin, Moore, & West, 1996).

The Value of Paying Attention

Whereas the average person has not reached perceptual restriction of the "if you've seen one tree, you've seen them all" variety, the fact remains that most of us tend to look at a tree and classify it into the perceptual category of "trees in general" without really appreciating the miracle standing before us. How, then, can we bring about **dishabituation** (a reversal of habituation) on a day-to-day basis? Does perceptual clarity require years of effort? Fortunately, a more immediate avenue is available. The deceptively simple key to dishabituation is this: Pay attention. The following quote summarizes the importance of attention:

> One day a man of the people said to Zen Master Ikkyu: "Master, will you please write for me some maxims of the highest wisdom?"
>
> Ikkyu immediately took his brush and wrote the word "Attention."
>
> "Is that all?" asked the man. "Will you not add something more?"
>
> Ikkyu then wrote twice running: "Attention. Attention."
>
> "Well," remarked the man rather irritably, "I really don't see much depth or subtlety in what you have just written."
>
> Then Ikkyu wrote the same word three times running: "Attention. Attention. Attention." Half angered, the man

Reality testing Obtaining additional information to check on the accuracy of perceptions.

Dishabituation A reversal of habituation.

demanded, "What does that word 'Attention' mean anyway?"

And Ikkyu answered gently: "Attention means attention." (Kapleau, 1966)

To this we can add only one thought, provided by the words of poet William Blake: "If the doors of perception were cleansed, man would see everything as it is, infinite."

How to Become a Better "Eyewitness" to Life

Here's a summary of ideas from this chapter to help you maintain and enhance perceptual awareness and accuracy.

1. *Remember that perceptions are reconstructions of reality.* Learn to regularly question your own perceptions. Are they accurate? Could another interpretation fit the facts? What assumptions are you making? Could they be false? How might your assumptions be distorting your perceptions?
2. *Break perceptual habits and interrupt habituation.* Each day, try to do some activities in new ways. For example, take different routes when you travel to work or school. Do routines, such as brushing your teeth or combing your hair, with your nonpreferred hand. Try to look at friends and family members as if they are persons you just met for the first time.
3. *Shift adaptation levels and broaden frames of reference by seeking out-of-the-ordinary experiences.* The possibilities here range from trying foods you don't normally eat to reading opinions very different from your own. Experiences ranging from a quiet walk in the woods to a trip to an amusement park may be perceptually refreshing.
4. *Beware of perceptual sets.* Anytime you pigeonhole people, objects, or events, there is a danger that your perceptions will be distorted by expectations or preexisting categories. Be especially wary of labels and stereotypes. Try to see people as individuals and events as unique, one-time occurrences.
5. *Be aware of the ways in which motives and emotions influence perceptions.* It is difficult to avoid being swayed by your own interests, needs, desires, and emotions. But be aware of this trap and actively try to see the world through the eyes of others. Taking the other person's perspective is especially valuable in disputes or arguments. Ask yourself, "How does this look to her or him?"
6. *Make a habit of engaging in reality testing.* Actively look for additional evidence to check the accuracy of your perceptions. Ask questions, seek clarifications, and find alternative channels of information. Remember that perception is not automatically accurate. You could be wrong—we all are frequently.
7. *Pay attention.* Make a conscious effort to pay attention to other people and your surroundings. Don't drift through life in a haze. Listen to others with full concentration. Watch their facial expressions. Make eye contact. Try to get in the habit of approaching perception as if you are going to have to testify later about what you saw and heard.

KNOWLEDGE BUILDER

Perceptual Awareness and Accuracy

REFLECT

Because perceptions are reconstructions or models of external events, we should all engage in more frequent reality testing. Can you think of a recent event when a little reality testing would have saved you from misjudging a situation?

To improve your own perceptual awareness and accuracy, which strategies would you emphasize first?

LEARNING CHECK

1. Most perceptions can be described as active reconstructions of external reality. T or F?
2. Inaccuracies in eyewitness perceptions obviously occur in "real life," but they cannot be reproduced in psychology experiments. T or F?
3. Accuracy scores for facts provided by witnesses to staged crimes may be as low as 25 percent correct. T or F?
4. Victims of crimes are more accurate eyewitnesses than are impartial observers. T or F?
5. *Reality testing* is another term for dishabituation. T or F?
6. A good antidote to perceptual habituation can be found in conscious efforts to
   a. reverse sensory gating
   b. pay attention
   c. achieve visual accommodation
   d. counteract shape constancy

CRITICAL THINKING

7. Return for a moment to the incident described at the beginning of this chapter. What perceptual factors were involved in the first version of the "murder"? How did the girl affect what was seen?

Answers: 1. T **2.** F **3.** T **4.** F **5.** F **6.** b **7.** The girl's misperception, communicated so forcefully to one of your authors, created a powerful expectancy that influenced what he perceived. Also, the event happened quickly (the exposure time was brief), and the stressful or emotional nature of the incident encouraged his own misperception.

Chapter in Review

What are perceptual constancies, and what is their role in perception?

- Perception is the process of assembling sensations into a usable mental representation of the world.
- In vision, the image projected on the retina is constantly changing, but the external world appears stable and undistorted because of size, shape, and brightness constancy.

What basic principles do we use to group sensations into meaningful patterns?

- The most basic organization of sensations is a division into figure and ground (object and background).
- A number of factors contribute to the organization of sensations. These are nearness, similarity, continuity, closure, contiguity, common region, and combinations of the preceding. Basic elements of line drawings appear to be universally recognized.
- A perceptual organization may be thought of as a hypothesis held until evidence contradicts it. Perceptual organization shifts for ambiguous stimuli. Impossible figures resist stable organization altogether.

How is it possible to see depth and judge distance?

- Depth perception (the ability to perceive three-dimensional space and judge distances) is present in basic form soon after birth (as shown by testing with the visual cliff and other methods).
- Depth perception depends on the muscular cues of accommodation (bending of the lens) and convergence (inward movement of the eyes). Stereoscopic vision is created mainly by retinal disparity and the resulting overlap and mismatch of visual sensations.
- Various pictorial cues also underlie depth perception. They are linear perspective, relative size, height in the picture plane, light and shadow, overlap, texture gradients, aerial haze, and relative motion (motion parallax). All are monocular depth cues (only one eye is needed to make use of them).
- The moon illusion appears to be best explained by the apparent distance hypothesis, which emphasizes the greater number of depth cues present when the moon is on the horizon.

What effect does learning have on perception?

- Perceptual habits influence the ways in which we organize and interpret sensations. Studies of inverted vision show that even the most basic organization is subject to a degree of change. Active movement speeds adaptation to a new perceptual environment.
- Perceptual judgments are not made in a vacuum. They are almost always related to context or to an internal frame of reference called the adaptation level.
- One of the most familiar of all illusions, the Müller-Lyer illusion, seems to be related to perceptual learning, linear perspective, size-distance invariance relationships, and mislocating the end points of the figure.

How is perception altered by attention, motives, values, and expectations?

- Attention is selective, and it may be divided among various activities. Attention is closely related to stimulus intensity, repetition, contrast, change, and incongruity.
- The phenomenon called inattentional blindness suggests that there can be no perception without attention.
- Attention is accompanied by an orientation response. When a stimulus is repeated without change, the orientation response undergoes habituation.
- Personal motives and values often alter perceptions by changing the evaluation of what is seen or by altering attention to specific details.
- Perceptions may be based on top-down or bottom-up processing of information.
- Attention, prior experience, suggestion, and motives combine in various ways to create perceptual sets, or expectancies. These prepare a person to perceive or misperceive in a particular way.

Is extrasensory perception possible?

- Parapsychology is the study of purported psi phenomena, including clairvoyance, telepathy, precognition, and psychokinesis.
- Research in parapsychology remains controversial owing to a variety of problems and shortcomings. The bulk of the evidence to date is against the existence of ESP. Stage ESP is based on deception and tricks.

How reliable are eyewitness reports?

- Perception is an active reconstruction of events. This is one reason why eyewitness testimony is surprisingly unreliable. Eyewitness accuracy is further damaged by weapon focus and a number of similar factors.

- Perceptual accuracy is enhanced by reality testing, dishabituation, and conscious efforts to pay attention. It is also valuable to break perceptual habits, to broaden frames of reference, to beware of perceptual sets, and to be aware of the ways in which motives and emotions influence perceptions.

 Web Resources

Internet addresses frequently change. To find the sites listed here, visit www.thomsonedu.com/psychology/coon for an updated list of Internet addresses and direct links to relevant sites.

***Psychology: Gateways to Mind and Behavior* Website** Online quizzes, flash cards, and other helpful study aids for this text. www.thomsonedu.com/psychology/coon.

IllusionWorks A large collection of visual illusions.

Perceptual Processes A wide-ranging tutorial on perception.

Stereogram Links Provides links to stereograms and information about stereograms, including how to create your own.

The Joy of Visual Perception An online book about visual perception.

Vision Test An on-screen vision test.

Visual Illusions Gallery Presents 21 visual illusions.

ThomsonNOW™ Go to www.thomsonedu.com to link to ThomsonNow, your online study tool. First take the **Pre-Test** for this chapter to get your **Personalized Study Plan**, which will identify topics you need to review and direct you to online resources. Then take the **Post-Test** to determine what concepts you have mastered and what you still need work on.

InfoTrac College Edition For recent articles related to ESP, use Key Words search for EXTRASENSORY PERCEPTION. Go to www.thomsonedu.com/psychology/coon.

 Interactive Learning

***PsychNow!* Version 2.0 CD-ROM** Interact with the material with *PsychNow!'s* animations, video clips, experiments, and interactive assessments. For this chapter, go to *4c. Perception* to learn more about perceptual processes.

chapter 7

States of Consciousness

Image Source/SuperStock

THEME:

Understanding states of consciousness can promote self-awareness and enhance personal effectiveness.

Key Questions

What is an altered state of consciousness?

What are the effects of sleep loss or changes in sleep patterns?

Are there different stages of sleep?

How does dream sleep differ from dreamless sleep?

What are the causes of sleep disorders and unusual sleep events?

Do dreams have meaning?

How is hypnosis done, and what are its limitations?

How does sensory deprivation affect consciousness?

What are the effects of the more commonly used psychoactive drugs?

How are dreams used to promote personal understanding?

Preview

A Visit to Several States (of Consciousness)

In New Zealand, a Maori tohunga (priest) performs a night-long ritual to talk to the spirits who created the world in the mythical period the Aborigines call Dreamtime.

In Toronto, Canada, three businesspeople head for a popular tavern after a stressful day.

In the American Southwest, a Navajo elder gives his congregation peyote tea, a sacrament in the Native American Church, as a drumbeat resounds in the darkness.

In Northern Ireland, a nun living in a convent spends an entire week in silent prayer and contemplation.

In Los Angeles, California, an aspiring actor consults a hypnotist for help in reducing her stage fright.

In Berkeley, California, an artist spends 2 hours in a flotation chamber to clear her head before resuming work on a large painting.

At a park in Amsterdam, a group of street musicians smoke a joint and sing for spare change.

In Tucson, Arizona, one of your authors pours himself another cup of coffee.

What do all these people have in common? Each person seeks to alter consciousness—in different ways, to different degrees, and for different reasons. As these examples suggest, consciousness can take many forms. In the discussion that follows, we will begin with the familiar realms of sleep and dreaming and then move to more exotic states of consciousness.

States of Consciousness—The Many Faces of Awareness

To be conscious means to be aware. **Consciousness** consists of all the sensations, perceptions, memories, and feelings you are aware of at any instant (Hobson, 2001; Koch, 2004). (See "What Is It Like to Be a Bat?"). We spend most of our lives in **waking consciousness**, a state of clear, organized alertness. In waking consciousness we perceive times, places, and events as real, meaningful, and familiar. But states of consciousness related to fatigue, delirium, hypnosis, drugs, and euphoria may differ markedly from "normal" awareness. Everyone experiences at least some altered states, such as sleep, dreaming, and daydreaming. In everyday life, changes in consciousness may also accompany long-distance running, music, lovemaking, or other circumstances.

Altered States of Consciousness

How are altered states distinguished from normal awareness? During an **altered state of consciousness** (ASC), changes occur in the quality and pattern of mental activity. Typically there are distinct shifts in our perceptions, emotions, memories, time sense, thoughts, feelings of self-control, and suggestibility (Tart, 1986). Definitions aside, most people know when they have experienced an ASC.

Are there other causes of ASCs? In addition to the ones mentioned, we could add the following: sensory overload (for example, a rave, Mardi Gras crowd, or mosh pit), monotonous stimulation (such as "highway hypnotism" on long drives), unusual physical conditions (for example, high fever, hyperventilation, dehydration, sleep loss, near-death experiences), restricted sensory input, and many other possibilities. In some instances, altered states have important cultural meanings. (See "Consciousness and Culture" for more information.)

An unconscious person will die without constant care. Yet as crucial as consciousness is, we can't really explain how it occurs. Nevertheless, it is possible to identify various states of consciousness and to explore the role they play in our lives. Let's begin with a guided tour of sleep and dreaming.

Sleep—A Nice Place to Visit

Each of us will spend some 25 years of life asleep. Contrary to common belief, you are not totally unresponsive during sleep. For instance, you are more likely to awaken if you hear your own name spoken, instead of another's. Likewise, a sleeping mother may ignore a jet thundering overhead but wake at the slightest whimper of her child. It's even possible to do simple tasks while asleep. In one experiment, people learned to avoid an electric shock by touching a switch each time a tone sounded. Eventually, they could do it without waking. (This is much like the basic survival skill of turning off your alarm clock without waking.) Of course, sleep does impose limitations. Don't expect to learn math, a foreign language, or other complex skills while asleep (Druckman & Bjork, 1994; Wood et al., 1992).

CRITICAL THINKING

What Is It Like to Be a Bat?

Imagine hurtling through the air on leather wings while shrieking noisily. Suddenly, the echo of your own voice draws your attention to a moth that is frantically trying to evade you. You careen after it, twisting through the pitch-black jungle. Dodging trees and other bats, you catch the moth and savor your first meal of the still-young night.

In his famous essay, "What Is It Like to Be a Bat?" Thomas Nagel (1974) points out that we can learn a lot about bats from an objective, *third-person* point of view. Scientifically, we know that bats use echolocation to hunt insects at night. But what does that *feel* like from a subjective, *first-person* point of view? Have you ever been curious about what it is like to be a bat, or a dog, or a cat? What runs through Rover's mind when he sniffs other dogs? Does Rover have dreams? Are they as strange as ours? Do cats ever worry about the future? Do they like music? Do animals feel joy?

According to Nagel, we cannot directly know the first-person experience of animals (or even other people, for that matter). However, it is reasonable to assume that bats must experience *something,* whereas inanimate objects, such as rocks, experience *nothing.*

The difficulty of knowing other minds is why behaviorism replaced introspectionism early in psychology's history. (Remember Chapter 1?) A basic challenge for psychology is to use objective studies of the brain and behavior to help us understand the mind and consciousness, which are fundamentally first-person phenomena (Grossenbacher, 2001; Hobson, 2001; Koch, 2004).

Because sleep is familiar, many people think they know all about it. Before reading more, test your knowledge with the following Sleep Quiz. Were you surprised by any of the answers? Let's see what we know about our "daily retreat from the world."

Sleep Quiz

1. People can learn to sleep for just a few hours a night and still function well. T or F?
2. Everyone dreams every night. T or F?
3. The brain rests during sleep. T or F?
4. Resting during the day can replace lost sleep. T or F?
5. As people get older, they sleep more. T or F?
6. Alcohol may help a person get to sleep, but it disturbs sleep later during the night. T or F?
7. If a person goes without sleep long enough, death will occur. T or F?
8. Dreams mostly occur during deep sleep. T or F?
9. A person prevented from dreaming would soon go crazy. T or F?
10. Sleepwalking occurs when a person acts out a dream. T or F?

Answers: 1. F 2. T 3. F 4. F 5. F 6. T 7. T 8. F 9. F 10. F

Timothy Ross/The Image Works

● **Figure 7.1** Not all animals sleep, but like humans, those that do have powerful sleep needs. For example, dolphins must voluntarily breathe air, which means they face the choice of staying awake or drowning. The dolphin solves this problem by sleeping on just one side of its brain at a time! The other half of the brain, which remains awake, controls breathing (Jouvet, 1999).

The Need for Sleep

How strong is the need for sleep? Sleep is an innate **biological rhythm** that can never be entirely ignored (Lavie, 2001). Of course, sleep will give way temporarily, especially at times of great danger. As comedian and filmmaker Woody Allen once put it, "The lion and the lamb shall lie down together, but the lamb will not be very sleepy." However, there are limits to how long humans can go without sleep. A rare disease that prevents sleep always ends with stupor, coma, and death (Oliwenstein, 1993). (● See Figure 7.1.)

Imagine placing an animal on a moving treadmill over a pool of water. Even under these conditions, animals soon drift into repeated microsleeps. A **microsleep** is a brief shift in brain activity to the pat-

Consciousness Mental awareness of sensations, perceptions, memories, and feelings.

Waking consciousness A state of normal, alert awareness.

Altered state of consciousness A condition of awareness distinctly different in quality or pattern from waking consciousness.

Biological rhythm Any repeating cycle of biological activity, such as sleep and waking cycles or changes in body temperature.

Microsleep A brief shift in brain-wave patterns to those of sleep.

HUMAN DIVERSITY

Consciousness and Culture

In many cultures, rituals of healing, prayer, purification, or personal transformation are accompanied by altered states of consciousness.

Throughout history, people have found ways to alter consciousness. A dramatic example is the sweat lodge ceremony of the Sioux Indians. During the ritual, several men sit in total darkness inside a small chamber heated by coals. Cedar smoke, bursts of steam, and sage fill the air. The men chant rhythmically. The heat builds. At last they can stand it no more. The door is thrown open. Cooling night breezes rush in. And then? The cycle begins again—often to be repeated four or five times more.

Like the Yoga practices of Hindu mystics or the dances of the Whirling Dervishes of Turkey, the ritual "sweats" of the Sioux are meant to cleanse the mind and body. When they are especially intense, they bring altered awareness and personal revelation.

People seek some altered states for pleasure, as is often true of drug intoxication. Yet as the Sioux illustrate, many cultures regard altered consciousness as a pathway to personal enlightenment. Indeed, all cultures and most religions recognize and accept some alterations of consciousness. However, the meaning given to these states varies greatly—from signs of "madness" and "possession" by spirits, to life-enhancing breakthroughs. Thus, cultural conditioning greatly affects what altered states we recognize, seek, consider normal, and attain (de Rios & Grob, 2005; Heath, 2001).

tern normally recorded during sleep. When you drive, remember that microsleeps can lead to macro-accidents. Even if your eyes are open, you can fall asleep for a few seconds. Roughly 2 out of every 100 highway crashes are caused by sleepiness (Lyznicki et al., 1998). By the way, if you are struggling to stay awake while driving, you should stop, quit fighting it, and take a short nap. Coffee helps too, but briefly giving in to sleep helps more (Horne & Reyner, 1996).

Sleep Deprivation

How long could a person go without sleep? With few exceptions, 4 days or more without sleep becomes hell for everyone. For example, a disc jockey named Peter Tripp once stayed awake for 200 hours to raise money for charity. After 100 hours, Tripp began to hallucinate: He saw cobwebs in his shoes and watched in terror as a tweed coat became a suit of "furry worms." By the end of 200 hours, Tripp was unable to distinguish between his hallucinations and reality (Luce, 1965). Despite Tripp's breakdown, longer sleepless periods are possible. The world record is held by Randy Gardner, who at age 17 went 268 hours (11 days) without sleep. Surprisingly, Randy needed only 14 hours of sleep to recover. As Randy found, most symptoms of **sleep deprivation** (sleep loss) are reversed by a single night's rest.

What are the costs of sleep loss? Age and personality make a big difference. Although Peter Tripp's behavior became quite bizarre, Randy Gardner was less impaired. However, make no mistake: Sleep is a necessity. At various times, Randy's speech was slurred, and he couldn't concentrate, remember clearly, or name common objects (Coren, 1996). Sleep loss also typically causes trembling hands, drooping eyelids, inattention, irritability, staring, increased pain sensitivity, and general discomfort (Doran, Van Dongen, & Dinges, 2001; Naitoh et al., 1989).

Most people who have not slept for 2 or 3 days can still do interesting or complex mental tasks (Binks, Waters, & Hurry, 1999), but they have trouble paying attention, staying alert, and doing simple or boring routines. For a driver, pilot, or machine operator, this can spell disaster (Fairclough & Graham, 1999). If a task is monotonous (such as factory work or air traffic control), no amount of sleep loss is safe (Gillberg & Akerstedt, 1998). In fact, if you lose just 1 hour of sleep a night, it can affect your mood, memory, ability to pay attention, and even your health (Everson, 1998; Maas, 1999). (See "Teenage Sleep Zombies.")

How can I tell how much sleep I really need? Pick a day when you feel well rested. Then sleep that night until you wake without an alarm clock. If you feel rested when you wake up, that's your natural sleep need. If you're sleeping fewer hours than you need, you're building up a sleep debt (Maas, 1999).

Severe sleep loss can cause a temporary **sleep-deprivation psychosis** (loss of contact with reality) like Peter Tripp suffered. Confusion, disorientation, delusions, and hallucinations are typical of this reaction. Fortunately, such "crazy" behavior is uncom-

THE CLINICAL FILE

Teenage Sleep Zombies

Did you ever have to fight to stay awake in a high school class? *Hypersomnia* (hi-per-SOM-nee-ah: excessive daytime sleepiness) is a common problem during adolescence (Carskadon, Acebo, & Jenni, 2004). The reason? Rapid physical changes during puberty increase the need for sleep. However, sleep time tends to decease during the teen years (Fukuda & Ishihara, 2001). At a time when they need more sleep, many adolescents get less.

If teenagers are sleep deprived, why don't they just sleep more? As children enter puberty, they begin to stay up later at night. However, they must get up early to attend school, regardless of when they went to bed. As a result, many teens are seriously sleep deprived during the week. Then, on the weekend, they sleep longer and get up late in the morning (LaBerge et al., 2001). After sleeping extra amounts for 2 days, many teens have difficulty falling asleep Sunday night. On Monday, they have to get up early for school, and the sleep loss cycle begins again.

What can be done about teenage sleep deprivation? Psychologists have persuaded some school districts to start classes later so that high school students can sleep longer. Studies suggest that this schedule improves learning and reduces behavior problems. In fact, it looks like some of the "storm and stress" of adolescence may be ordinary grouchiness caused by sleep loss (Mitru, Millrood, & Mateika, 2002).

Calvin and Hobbes

mon. Hallucinations and delusions rarely appear before 60 hours of wakefulness (Naitoh et al., 1989).

Sleep Patterns

Sleep was described as an innate biological rhythm. What does that mean? Daily sleep and waking periods create a variety of **sleep patterns.** Rhythms of sleep and waking are so steady that they continue for many days, even when clocks and light-dark cycles are removed. However, under such conditions, humans eventually shift to a sleep-waking cycle that averages slightly more than 24 hours (24 hours and 10 minutes, to be exact) (Czeisler et al., 1999). This suggests that external time markers, especially light and dark, help tie our sleep rhythms to days that are exactly 24 hours long (● Figure 7.2). Otherwise, many of us would drift into our own unusual sleep cycles (Lavie, 2001).

What is the normal range of sleep? A few individuals can get by on only an hour or two of sleep a night—and feel perfectly fine. However, this is rare. Only 8 percent of the population are **short sleepers,** averaging 5 hours of sleep or less per night. On the other end of the scale we find **long sleepers,** who doze 9 hours or more (and tend to be daytime worriers) (McCann & Stewin, 1988). Most of us sleep on a familiar 7- to 8-hour-per-night schedule. For a few people, however, it is quite normal to sleep as little as 5 hours per night or as much as 11 hours. Urging everyone to sleep 8 hours would be like advising everyone to wear medium-size shoes.

Do elderly people need more sleep? Sleep needs actually remain fairly constant as people age. However, older people rarely get the sleep they need. Total sleep time declines throughout life. Those older than 50 average only 6 hours of sleep a night. In contrast,

BRIDGES

Daily sleep cycles can be disrupted by rapid travel across time zones (jet lag) and by shift work.

See Chapter 12, pages 402–403, for more information.

Sleep deprivation Being prevented from getting desired or needed amounts of sleep.

Sleep-deprivation psychosis A major disruption of mental and emotional functioning brought about by sleep loss.

Sleep patterns The order and timing of daily sleep and waking periods.

Short sleeper A person who averages 5 hours of sleep or less per night.

Long sleeper A person who averages 9 hours of sleep or more per night.

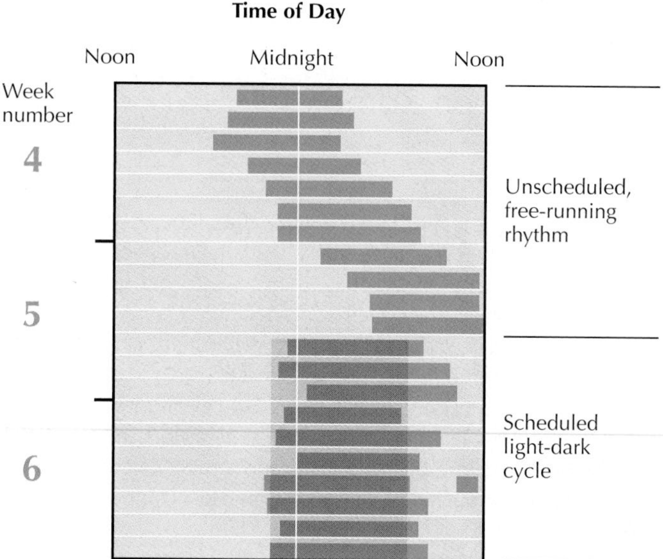

● **Figure 7.2** Sleep rhythms. Bars show periods of sleep during the fourth, fifth, and sixth weeks of an experiment with a human subject. During unscheduled periods, the subject was allowed to select times of sleep and lighting. The result was a sleep rhythm of about 25 hours. Notice how this free-running rhythm began to advance around the clock. When periods of darkness were scheduled (colored area), the rhythm quickly resynchronized with 24-hour days. (Adapted from Czeisler et al., 1981.)

infants spend up to 20 hours a day sleeping, usually in 2- to 4-hour cycles.

As they mature, most children go through a "nap" stage and eventually settle into a steady cycle of sleeping once a day (● Figure 7.3). Perhaps we should all continue to take an afternoon "siesta." Midafternoon sleepiness is a natural part of the sleep cycle. That's why brief, well-timed naps can help people like truck drivers and hospital interns, who often must fight to stay alert (Batejat & Lagarde, 1999).

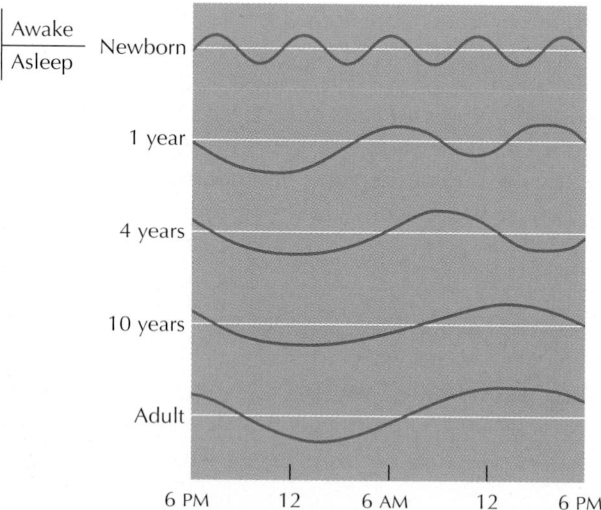

● **Figure 7.3** Development of sleep patterns. Short cycles of sleep and waking gradually become the night-day cycle of an adult. Although most adults don't take naps, midafternoon sleepiness is a natural part of the sleep cycle. (After Williams et al., 1964.)

Busy people may be tempted to sleep less. However, people on *shortened* cycles—for example, 3 hours of sleep to 6 hours awake—often can't get to sleep when the cycle calls for it. This is why astronauts continue to sleep on their normal earth schedule while in space. Adapting to *longer*-than-normal days is more promising. Such days can be tailored to match natural sleep patterns, which have a ratio of 2 to 1 between time awake and time asleep (16 hours awake and 8 hours asleep). For instance, one study showed that 28-hour "days" work for some people. Overall, however, sleep is a "gentle tyrant." Sleep patterns may be bent and stretched, but they rarely yield entirely to human whims (Akerstedt et al., 1993).

Stages of Sleep—The Nightly Roller-Coaster Ride

What causes sleep? Early sleep experts thought that something in the bloodstream must cause sleep. But conjoined twins, whose bodies are joined at birth, show that this is false. It's not unusual for one twin to be asleep while the second is awake (● Figure 7.4). During waking hours, a **sleep hormone** (sleep-promoting chemical) collects in the brain and spinal cord, *not* in the blood. If this substance is extracted from one animal and injected into another, the second animal will sleep deeply for many hours (Cravatt et al., 1995). Notice, however, that this explanation is incomplete. For example, why would a well-rested person have to fight to stay awake during a boring midday meeting?

Whether you are awake or asleep right now depends on the *balance* between separate sleep and waking systems. Brain circuits and chemicals in one of the systems promote sleep. A network of brain cells in the other system responds to chemicals that inhibit sleep. The two systems seesaw back and forth, switching the brain between sleep and wakefulness (Lavie, 2001). Note that the brain does not "shut down" during sleep. Rather, the *pattern* of activity changes. The total amount of activity remains fairly constant (Steriade & McCarley, 1990).

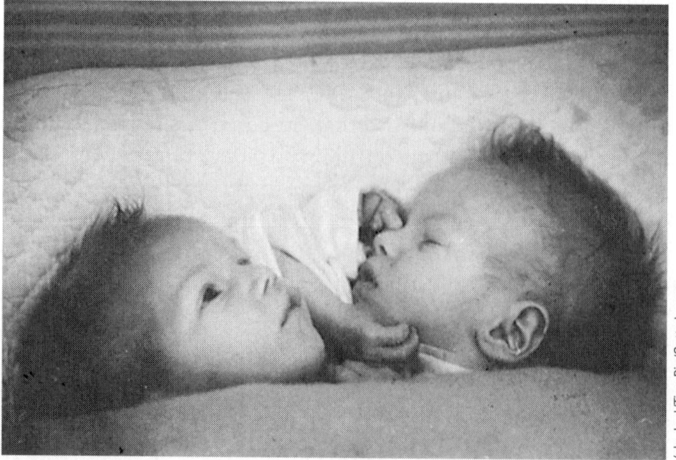

● **Figure 7.4** These conjoined twins share the same blood supply, yet one sleeps while the other is awake.

Stages of Sleep

How does brain activity change when you fall asleep? Sleep activity can be measured with an **electroencephalograph** (eh-LEK-tro-en-SEF-uh-lo-graf), or **EEG.** The brain generates tiny electrical signals (brain waves) that can be amplified and recorded. When you are awake and alert, the EEG reveals a pattern of small fast waves called **beta waves** (● Figure 7.5). Immediately before sleep, the pattern shifts to larger and slower waves called **alpha waves.** (Alpha waves also occur when you are relaxed and allow your thoughts to drift.) As the eyes close, breathing becomes slow and regular, the pulse rate slows, and body temperature drops. Soon after, four separate **sleep stages** occur.

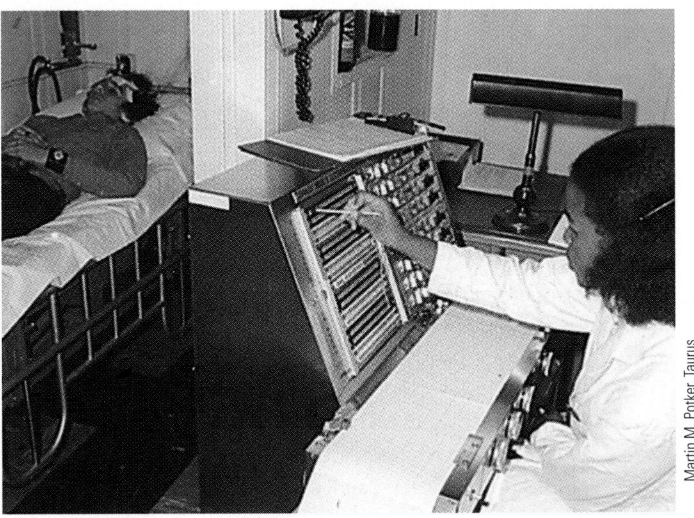

Martin M. Potker, Taurus

(a)

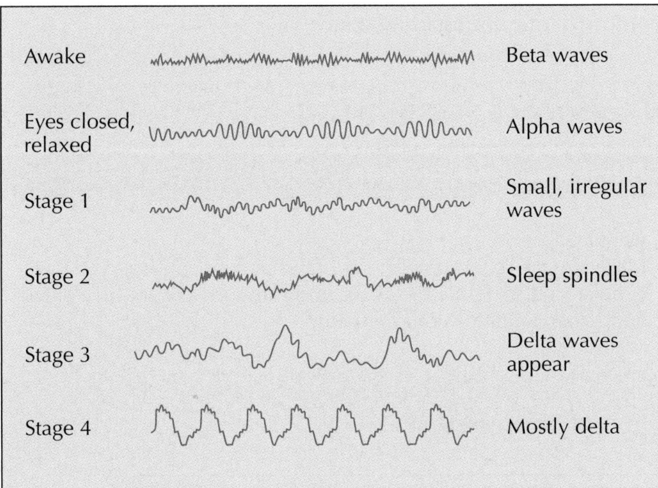

(b)

● **Figure 7.5** *(a)* Photograph of an EEG recording session. The man in the background is asleep. *(b)* Changes in brain-wave patterns associated with various stages of sleep. Actually, most wave types are present at all times, but they occur more or less frequently in various sleep stages.

BRIDGES

The EEG is also used to study brain activity and to detect abnormal conditions caused by diseases.

See Chapter 2, page 61, for more information.

Stage 1

As you enter **light sleep** (stage 1 sleep), your heart rate slows even more. Breathing becomes more irregular. The muscles of your body relax. This may trigger a reflex muscle twitch called a *hypnic* (HIP-nik: sleep) *jerk.* (This is quite normal, so have no fear about admitting to your friends that you fell asleep with a hypnic jerk.) In stage 1 sleep the EEG is made up mainly of small, irregular waves with some alpha waves. Persons awakened at this time may or may not say they were asleep.

Stage 2

As sleep deepens, body temperature drops further. Also, the EEG begins to include **sleep spindles,** which are short bursts of distinctive brain-wave activity (Gottselig, Bassetti, & Achermann, 2002). Spindles seem to mark the true boundary of sleep. Within 4 minutes after spindles appear, most people will say they were asleep.

Stage 3

In stage 3, a new brain wave, the delta wave, begins to appear. **Delta waves** are very large and slow. They signal a move to deeper sleep and a further loss of consciousness.

Stage 4

Most people reach **deep sleep** (the deepest level of normal sleep) in about 1 hour. Stage 4 brain waves are almost pure delta, and the sleeper is in a state of oblivion. If you make a loud noise during stage 4, the sleeper will wake up in a state of confusion and may

Sleep hormone A sleep-promoting substance found in the brain and spinal cord.

Electroencephalograph (EEG) A device designed to detect, amplify, and record electrical activity in the brain.

Beta waves Small, fast brain waves associated with being awake and alert.

Alpha waves Large, slow brain waves associated with relaxation and falling asleep.

Sleep stages Levels of sleep identified by brain-wave patterns and behavioral changes.

Light sleep Stage 1 sleep, marked by small irregular brain waves and some alpha waves.

Sleep spindles Distinctive bursts of brain-wave activity that indicate a person is asleep.

Delta waves Large, slow brain waves that occur in deeper sleep (stages 3 and 4).

Deep sleep Stage 4 sleep; the deepest form of normal sleep.

not remember the noise. After spending some time in stage 4, the sleeper returns (through stages 3 and 2) to stage 1. Further shifts between deeper and lighter sleep occur throughout the night (● Figure 7.6).

Two Basic Kinds of Sleep

If you watch a person sleep, you will soon notice that the sleeper's eyes occasionally move under the eyelids. These **rapid eye movements (REMs)** are associated with dreaming (● Figure 7.6). Roughly 85 percent of the time, people awakened during REMs report vivid dreams. In addition to rapid eye movements, **REM sleep** is marked by a return of fast, irregular EEG patterns similar to stage 1 sleep. In fact, the brain is so active during REM sleep that it looks as if the person is awake (Hobson et al., 1998). Some eye movements correspond to dream activities: Dream that you are watching a tennis match, and you will probably move your eyes from side to side. However, people who were born blind still have REMs, so eye movements are not just a result of "watching" dream images (Shafton, 1995). REM sleep is easy to observe in pets, such as dogs and cats. Watch for eye movements and irregular breathing. (You can forget about your pet iguana, though. Reptiles show no signs of REM sleep.)

REM and NREM Sleep

The two most basic states of sleep are REM sleep with its associated dreaming and **non-REM (NREM) sleep,** which occurs during stages 1, 2, 3, and 4 (Jouvet, 1999). NREM sleep is dream free about 90 percent of the time. Your first period of stage 1 sleep usually lacks REMs and dreams. Each later return to stage 1 is usually accompanied by REMs. Dreams during REM sleep tend to be longer, clearer, more detailed, more bizarre, and more "dream-like" than thoughts and images that occur in NREM sleep (Hobson, Pace-Schott, & Stickgold, 2000). Also, brain areas associated with imagery and emotion become more active during REM sleep. This may explain why REM dreams tend to be more vivid than NREM dreams (Braun, Balkin, & Herscovitch, 1998).

What is the function of NREM sleep? NREM sleep increases after physical exertion and may help us recover from bodily fatigue. In comparison, daytime stress tends to increase REM sleep. REM sleep totals only about 90 minutes per night (about the same as a feature-length movie). Yet its link with dreaming makes it as important as NREM sleep. REM sleep may rise dramatically when there is a death in the family, trouble at work, a marital conflict, or other emotionally charged events.

REM Sleep and Dreaming

What happens to the body when a person dreams? REM sleep is a time of high emotion. The heart beats irregularly. Blood pressure and breathing waver. Both males and females appear to be sexually aroused: Males usually have an erection, and genital blood flow increases in women. This occurs for all REM sleep, so it is not strictly related to erotic dreams (Jouvet, 1999).

During REM sleep, your body becomes quite still, as if you were paralyzed. Imagine for a moment the results of acting out some of your recent dreams. Very likely, REM-sleep paralysis prevents some hilarious—and dangerous—nighttime escapades. When it fails, some people thrash violently, leap out of bed, and may attack their bed partners. A lack of muscle paralysis during REM sleep is called *REM behavior disorder.* One patient suffering from the disorder tied himself to his bed every night. That way, he couldn't jump up and crash into furniture or walls (Shafton, 1995). Yet sometimes sleep paralysis can go a little too far (see "Abducted by Space Aliens?")

In a moment we will survey some additional sleep problems—if you are still awake. First, here are a few questions to check your memory of our discussion so far.

KNOWLEDGE BUILDER

Altered States and Sleep

REFLECT

Make a quick list of some altered states of consciousness you have experienced. What do they have in common? How are they different? What conditions caused them?

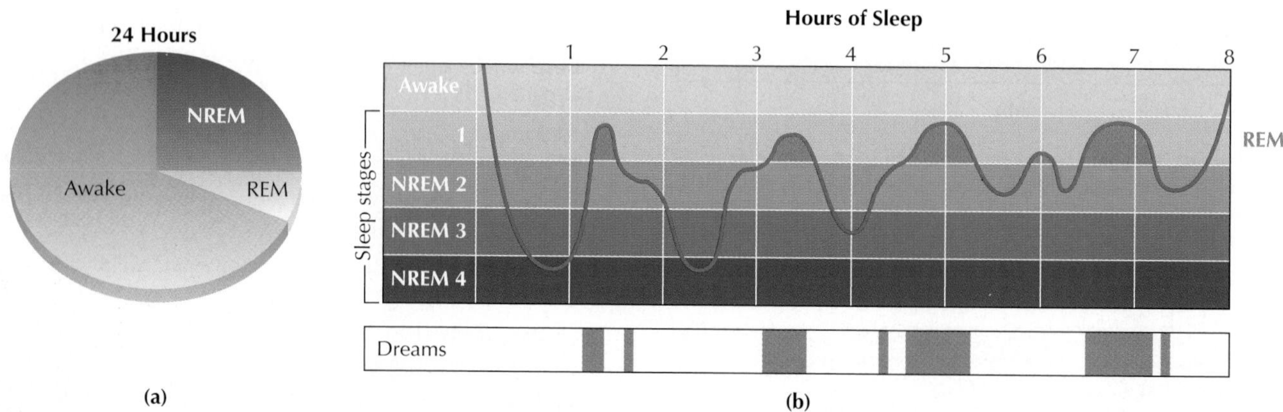

● **Figure 7.6** *(a)* Average proportion of time adults spend daily in REM sleep and NREM sleep. REM periods add up to about 20 percent of total sleep time. *(b)* Typical changes in stages of sleep during the night. Notice that dreams mostly coincide with REM periods.

FOCUS ON RESEARCH

Abducted by Space Aliens?

Imagine opening your eyes shortly before dawn, attempting to roll over in your bed, and suddenly realizing that you are entirely paralyzed. While lying helplessly on your back and unable to cry out for help, you become aware of sinister figures lurking in your bedroom. As they move closer to your bed, your heart begins to pound violently and you feel as if you are suffocating. You hear buzzing sounds and feel electrical sensations shooting throughout your body. Within moments, the visions vanish and you can move once again. Terrified, you wonder what has just happened. (McNally & Clancy, 2005, p. 114)

Researchers Richard McNally and Susan Clancy have given us a better understanding of experiences like that just described. Although sleep paralysis normally prevents us from moving during REM sleep, up to 30 percent of us have experienced sleep paralysis after beginning to wake up. During such episodes, people often have *hypnopompic* ("upon awakening") hallucinations, which may include vague images of alien beings. Although most of us shrug off these benign but definitely unusual experiences, some people try to make sense of them. Earlier in history, people interpreted these hallucinated intruders as angels, demons, or witches. As our culture changes, so too do the interpretations. More recently, some people have interpreted these experiences as evidence of alien abductions and even sexual abuse (McNally & Clancy, 2005).

Detroit Institute of the Arts/SuperStock

Swiss artist Henry Fuseli drew on hypnopompic imagery as an inspiration for his famous painting, *The Nightmare.*

Imagine that you are a counselor at a sleep clinic. You must explain the basics of sleep and dreaming to a new client who knows little about these topics. Can you do it?

LEARNING CHECK

1. Changes in the quality and pattern of mental activity define
   a. an EEG c. SIDS
   b. an REM d. an ASC
2. Alyssa experiences a microsleep while driving. Most likely, this indicates that she
   a. was producing mostly beta waves
   b. had high levels of sleep hormones in her bloodstream
   c. switched from delta waves to alpha waves
   d. was sleep deprived
3. Delusions and hallucinations typically continue for several days after a sleep-deprived individual returns to normal sleep. T or F?
4. Older adults, and particularly the elderly, sleep more than children do because the elderly are more easily fatigued. T or F?
5. Which of the following would normally be most incompatible with moving your arms and legs while asleep?
   a. REM sleep c. delta waves
   b. sleep spindles d. NREM sleep
6. Rapid eye movements indicate that a person is in deep sleep. T or F?
7. Alpha waves are to presleep drowsiness as ______________ ______________ are to stage 4 sleep.

CRITICAL THINKING

8. Why might it be better for the unscheduled human sleep–waking cycle to average more than 24 hours, instead of less?
9. Biologically, what advantages might sleeping provide?

Answers: 1. d **2.** d **3.** F **4.** F **5.** a **6.** F **7.** delta waves **8.** Sleep experts theorize that the 25-hour average leaves a little "slack" in the cycle. External time markers can then retard the bodily cycle slightly to synchronize it with light-dark cycles. If the bodily cycle were shorter than 24 hours, we all might have to "stretch" every day to adjust. **9.** Lowering bodily activity and metabolism during sleep may help conserve energy and lengthen life. Also, natural selection may have favored sleep because animals that remained active at night probably had a higher chance of being killed. (I'll bet they had more fun, though.)

Rapid eye movements (REMs) Swift eye movements during sleep.

REM sleep Sleep marked by rapid eye movements and a return to stage 1 EEG patterns.

Non-REM (NREM) sleep Non–rapid eye movement sleep characteristic of stages 2, 3, and 4.

Sleep Disturbances—Showing Nightly: Sleep Wars!

Sleep quality has taken a beating in North America. Artificial lighting, frenetic schedules, exciting pastimes, smoking, drinking, overstimulation, and many other factors have contributed to a near epidemic of sleep problems. Sleep disturbances are a serious risk to health and happiness. Sleep clinics treat thousands of people each year who suffer from sleep disorders or complaints (see ■ Table 7.1). Let's explore some of the more interesting problems these people face.

TABLE 7.1

Sleep Disturbances—Things That Go Wrong in the Night

Hypersomnia	Excessive daytime sleepiness. This can result from depression, insomnia, narcolepsy, sleep apnea, sleep drunkenness, periodic limb movements, drug abuse, and other problems.
Insomnia	Difficulty in getting to sleep or staying asleep; also, not feeling rested after sleeping.
Narcolepsy	Sudden, irresistible, daytime sleep attacks that may last anywhere from a few minutes to a half hour. Victims may fall asleep while standing, talking, or even driving.
Nightmare disorder	Vivid, recurrent nightmares that significantly disturb sleep.
Periodic limb movement syndrome	Muscle twitches (primarily affecting the legs) that occur every 20 to 40 seconds and severely disturb sleep.
REM behavior disorder	A failure of normal muscle paralysis, leading to violent actions during REM sleep.
Restless legs syndrome	An irresistible urge to move the legs to relieve sensations of creeping, tingling, prickling, aching, or tension.
Sleep apnea	During sleep, breathing stops for 20 seconds or more until the person wakes a little, gulps in air, and settles back to sleep; this cycle may be repeated hundreds of times per night.
Sleep drunkenness	A slow transition to clear consciousness after awakening; sometimes associated with irritable or aggressive behavior.
Sleep terror disorder	The repeated occurrence of night terrors that significantly disturb sleep.
Sleep-wake schedule disorder	A mismatch between the sleep-wake schedule demanded by a person's bodily rhythm and that demanded by the environment.
Sleepwalking disorder	Repeated incidents of leaving bed and walking about while asleep.

Bond & Wooten, 1996; DSM-IV-TR, 2000; Hauri & Linde, 1990

Insomnia

Staring at the ceiling at 2 AM is pretty low on most people's list of favorite pastimes. Yet about 30 percent of all adults have had insomnia. Roughly 9 percent have a serious or chronic problem. **Insomnia** includes difficulty in going to sleep, frequent nighttime awakenings, waking too early, or a combination of these problems. Insomnia can harm people's work, health, and relationships (Sateia & Nowell, 2004).

Types and Causes of Insomnia

Worry, stress, and excitement can cause *temporary insomnia* and a self-defeating cycle. First, excess mental activity ("I can't stop turning things over in my mind") and heightened arousal block sleep. Then, frustration and anger over not being able to sleep cause more worry and arousal. This further delays sleep, which causes more frustration, and so on (Espie, 2002). A good way to beat this cycle is to avoid fighting it. It is usually best to get up and do something useful or satisfying when you can't sleep. (Reading a textbook might be a good choice of useful activities.) Return to bed only when you begin to feel that you are struggling to stay awake. If sleeping problems last for more than 3 weeks, then a diagnosis of *chronic insomnia* can be made.

Drug-dependency insomnia (sleep loss caused by withdrawal from sleeping pills) can also occur. North Americans spend well over one-half billion dollars a year on sleeping pills. There is real irony in this expense. Nonprescription sleeping pills such as Sominex, Nytol, and Sleep-Eze have little sleep-inducing effect. Even worse are barbiturates. These prescription sedatives decrease both stage 4 sleep and REM sleep, drastically lowering sleep quality. In addition, many users become "sleeping-pill junkies" who need an ever-greater number of pills to get to sleep. Victims must be painstakingly weaned from their sleep medicines. Otherwise, terrible nightmares and "rebound insomnia" may drive them back to drug use. It's worth remembering that although alcohol and other depressant drugs may help a person get to sleep, they greatly reduce sleep quality (Lobo & Tufik, 1997).

Behavioral Remedies for Insomnia

If sleeping pills are a poor way to treat insomnia, what can be done? Sleep specialists now prefer to treat insomnia with lifestyle changes and behavioral techniques (Walsh & Scweitzer, 1999). Treatment for chronic insomnia usually begins with a careful analysis of a patient's sleep habits, lifestyle, stress levels, and medical problems. All of the approaches discussed here are helpful for treating insomnia (Swanson, 1999). Of the methods listed, stimulus control and sleep restriction are the most effective (Chesson et al., 1999):

1. **Stimulus control.** One of the best ways to combat insomnia is also the simplest. Insisting on a regular schedule helps establish a firm body rhythm, greatly improving sleep. This is best achieved by exercising **stimulus control**, which refers to linking a response with specific stimuli. It is important to get up and go to sleep at the same time each day, including weekends (Bootzin & Epstein, 2000). (As noted earlier regarding ad-

olescent sleep loss, many people upset their sleep rhythms by staying up late on weekends.). In addition, insomniacs are told to avoid doing anything but sleeping when they are in bed. They are not to study, eat, watch TV, read, pay the bills, worry, or even think in bed. (Lovemaking is okay, however.) In this way, only sleeping and relaxation become associated with going to bed at specific times (Bootzin & Epstein, 2000).

2. **Sleep restriction.** Even if an entire night's sleep is missed, it is important not sleep late in the morning, nap more than 1 hour, sleep during the evening, or go to bed early the following night. Instead, restricting sleep to normal bedtime hours avoids fragmenting sleep rhythms (Lacks & Morin, 1992).
3. **Paradoxical intention.** Another helpful approach is to remove the pressures of *trying* to go to sleep. Instead, the goal becomes trying to keep the eyes open (in the dark) and stay awake as long as possible (Horvath & Goheen, 1990). This allows sleep to come unexpectedly and lowers performance anxiety (Espie, 2002).
4. **Relaxation.** Some insomniacs lower their arousal before sleep by using a physical or mental strategy for relaxing, such as progressive muscle relaxation (see Chapter 17), meditation, or blotting out worries with calming images. It is also helpful to schedule time in the early evening to write down worries or concerns and plan what to do about them the next day; in this way, they are set aside before you go to bed.
5. **Exercise.** Strenuous exercise during the day promotes sleep. It is best if done about 6 hours before bedtime (Maas, 1999). However, exercise in the evening is helpful only if it is very light.
6. **Food intake.** What you eat can affect how easily you get to sleep. Eating starchy foods increases the amount of *tryptophan* (TRIP-tuh-fan: an amino acid) reaching the brain. More tryptophan, in turn, increases the amount of serotonin in the brain. Serotonin is associated with relaxation, a positive mood, and sleepiness. Thus, to promote sleep, try eating a snack that is nearly all starch. Good sleep-inducing snacks are cookies, bread, pasta, oatmeal, pretzels, bagels, and dry cereal. If you really want to drop the bomb on insomnia, try eating a baked potato (which may be the world's largest sleeping pill!) (Sahelian, 1998).
7. **Stimulants.** Stimulants, such as coffee and cigarettes, should be avoided. It is also worth remembering that alcohol, although not a stimulant, impairs sleep quality.

Sleepwalking and Sleeptalking

Sleepwalking is eerie and fascinating. **Somnambulists** (som-NAM-bue-lists: those who sleepwalk) avoid obstacles, descend stairways, and on rare occasions may step out of windows or in front of automobiles. The sleepwalker's eyes are usually open, but a blank face and shuffling feet reveal that the person is asleep. If you find someone sleepwalking, you should gently guide the person back to bed. Awakening a sleepwalker does no harm, but it is not necessary.

Does sleepwalking occur during dreaming? No. Remember that people are normally immobilized during REM sleep. EEG studies have shown that somnambulism occurs during NREM stages 3 and 4 (Stein & Ferber, 2001). **Sleeptalking** also occurs mostly in NREM stages of sleep. The link with deep sleep explains why sleeptalking makes little sense and why sleepwalkers are confused and remember little when awakened (DSM-IV-TR, 2000).

BRIDGES

Learning how to achieve deep relaxation is a highly useful skill.

See Chapter 17, pages 579–580, for more information.

Nightmares and Night Terrors

Stage 4 sleep is also the realm of night terrors. These frightening episodes are quite different from ordinary nightmares (■ Table 7.2). A **nightmare** is simply a bad dream that takes place during REM sleep. Nightmares, which occur about twice a month, are usually brief and easily remembered (Wood & Bootzin, 1990). During stage 4 **night terrors,** a person suffers total panic and may hallucinate frightening dream images into the bedroom. An attack may last 15 to 20 minutes. When it is over, the person awakens drenched in sweat but only vaguely remembers the terror. Because night terrors occur during NREM sleep (when the body is not immobilized), victims may sit up, scream, get out of bed, or run around the room. Victims remember little afterward. (Other family members, however, may have a story to tell.) Night terrors are most common in childhood, but they continue to plague about 2 out of every 100 adults (Kataria, 2004; Ohayon et al., 1999).

How to Eliminate a Nightmare

Is there any way to stop a recurring nightmare? A bad nightmare can be worse than any horror movie. It's easy to leave a theater, but we often remain trapped in terrifying dreams. Nevertheless, most nightmares can be banished by following three simple steps. First, write down your nightmare, describing it in detail. Next, change the dream any way you wish, being sure to spell out the details of the new dream. The third step is **imagery rehearsal,** in which you mentally rehearse the changed dream before you fall asleep again (Krakow & Neidhardt, 1992). Imagery rehearsal may work because it makes upsetting dreams familiar while a person is

Insomnia Difficulty in getting to sleep or staying asleep.

Stimulus control Linking a particular response with specific stimuli.

Somnambulists People who sleepwalk; occurs during NREM sleep.

Sleeptalking Speaking that occurs during NREM sleep.

Nightmare A bad dream that occurs during REM sleep.

Night terror A state of panic during NREM sleep.

Imagery rehearsal Mentally rehearsing and changing a nightmare in an attempt to prevent it from reoccurring.

TABLE 7.2

Was It a Nightmare or a Night Terror?

	NIGHTMARE	NIGHT TERROR
Stage of sleep	REM	NREM
Activity	Slight or no movement	Violent body movement, sits up, cries out, may run
Emotion	Fear or anxiety	Terror and disorganizing panic
Mental state when awakened	Coherent, can be calmed	Incoherent, disoriented, cannot be calmed, may be hallucinating
Physiological changes	No perspiration	Perspires heavily
Recall	Dream activity usually remembered	Amnesia for episode

awake and feeling safe. Or perhaps it mentally "reprograms" future dream content. In any case, the technique has helped many people (Krakow et al., 1996).

Narcolepsy

One of the most dramatic sleep problems is **narcolepsy** (NAR-koe-lep-see), or sudden, irresistible sleep attacks. These last anywhere from a few minutes to a half hour. Victims may fall asleep while standing, talking, or even driving. Emotional excitement, especially laughter, commonly triggers narcolepsy. (Tell an especially good joke and a narcoleptic may fall asleep.) More than half of all victims also suffer from **cataplexy** (CAT-uh-plex-see), a sudden temporary paralysis of the muscles, leading to complete body collapse. It's easy to understand why narcolepsy can devastate careers and relationships (Broughton & Broughton, 1994).

Because sudden paralysis happens during dreaming, is there a connection between narcolepsy and REM sleep? Yes, narcoleptics tend to fall directly into REM sleep. Thus, the narcoleptic's sleep attacks and paralysis appear to occur when REM sleep intrudes into the waking state (Mignot, 2001).

Fortunately, narcolepsy is rare. It runs in families, which suggests that it is hereditary (Chabas et al., 2003). In fact, this has been confirmed by breeding several generations of narcoleptic dogs. (These dogs, by the way, are simply outstanding at learning the trick "Roll over and play dead.") There is no known cure for narcolepsy, but stimulant drugs may cut down the frequency of attacks. Scheduling a long nap each day also helps narcoleptics manage their sleep attacks (Mullington & Broughton, 1993).

Sleep Apnea

Some sage once said, "Laugh and the whole world laughs with you; snore and you sleep alone." Nightly "wood sawing" is often harmless, but it can signal a serious problem. A person who snores loudly, with short silences and loud gasps or snorts, may suffer from apnea (AP-nee-ah: interrupted breathing). In **sleep apnea,** breathing stops for periods of 20 seconds to 2 minutes. As the need for oxygen becomes intense, the person wakes a little and gulps in air. She or he then settles back to sleep. But soon, breathing stops again. This cycle is repeated hundreds of times a night. As you might guess, apnea victims are extremely sleepy during the day (DSM-IV-TR, 2000).

What causes sleep apnea? Some cases occur because the brain stops sending the signals that maintain breathing. Another cause is blockage of the upper air passages. In addition to the misery it causes, apnea seriously endangers health. Anyone who snores loudly should seek treatment. The most effective treatments are weight loss, surgery for breathing obstructions, and use of a CPAP (continuous positive airway pressure) mask to aid breathing during sleep (Koenig, 1996).

SIDS

Sleep apnea is suspected as one cause of **sudden infant death syndrome (SIDS),** or "crib death." Each year 1 out of every 500 babies is a victim of SIDS. In the "typical" crib death, a slightly premature or small baby with some signs of a cold or cough is bundled up and put to bed. A short time later, parents find the child has died. A baby deprived of air will normally struggle to begin breathing again. However, SIDS babies seem to have a weak arousal reflex. This prevents them from changing positions and resuming breathing after an episode of apnea (Horne et al., 2001).

Babies at risk for SIDS must be carefully watched for the first 6 months of life. To aid parents in this task, a special monitor may be used that sounds an alarm when breathing or pulse becomes weak (● Figure 7.7). The list that follows gives some danger signals for SIDS.

- The mother is a teenager.
- The baby is premature.
- The baby has a shrill, high-pitched cry.
- The baby engages in "snoring," breath-holding, or frequent awakening at night.
- The baby breathes mainly through an open mouth.
- The baby remains passive when its face rolls into a pillow or blanket.
- The baby's bed contains soft objects such as pillows, quilts, comforters, or sheepskins.
- Parents or other adults in the home are smokers.

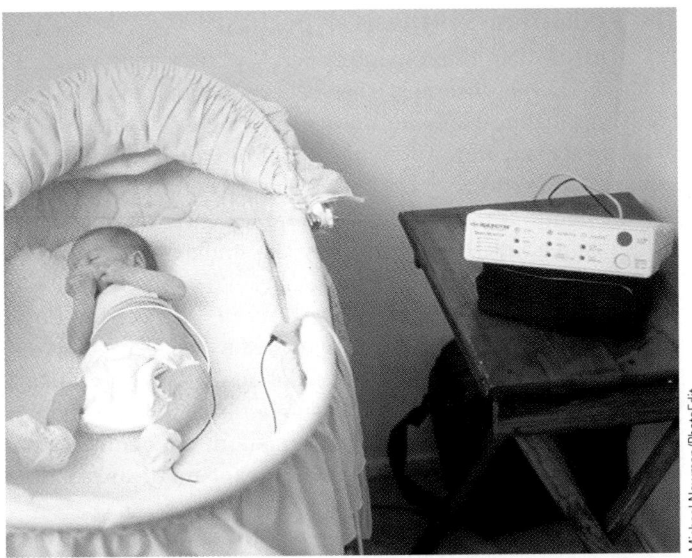
Michael Newman/PhotoEdit

● **Figure 7.7** Infants at risk for SIDS are often attached to devices that monitor breathing and heart rate during sleep. An alarm sounds to alert parents if either pulse or respiration falters. SIDS rarely occurs after an infant is 1 year old. Babies at risk for SIDS should be placed on their sides or on their backs.

"Back to Sleep"

Pop quiz: Should babies be placed face down or face up in bed? Sleeping position is another major risk factor for SIDS. Healthy infants are better off sleeping on their backs or sides. (Premature babies, those with respiratory problems, and those who often vomit may need to sleep face down. Ask a pediatrician for guidance.) At least one third of all SIDS cases involve babies who were placed face down. Remember, "*back* to sleep" is the safest position for most infants (Hauck et al., 2002).

Dreams—A Separate Reality?

When REM sleep was discovered in 1952, it ushered in a "Golden Era" of dream inquiry. To conclude our discussion of sleep, let's consider some age-old questions about dreaming.

Does everyone dream? Do dreams occur in an instant? Most people dream four or five times a night, but not all people remember their dreams. "Nondreamers" are often surprised by their dreams when first awakened during REM sleep. Dreams are usually spaced about 90 minutes apart. The first dream lasts only about 10 minutes; the last averages 30 minutes and may run as long as 50. Dreams, therefore, occur in real time, not as a "flash" (Shafton, 1995).

REM Sleep Revisited

How important is REM sleep? Is it essential for normal functioning? To answer these questions, sleep expert William Dement awakened volunteers each time they entered REM sleep. Soon, their need for "dream time" grew more urgent. By the fifth night, many had to be awakened 20 or 30 times to prevent REM sleep. When the volunteers were finally allowed to sleep undisturbed, they dreamed extra amounts. This effect, called an **REM rebound**, explains why alcoholics have horrible nightmares after they quit drinking. Alcohol suppresses REM sleep and sets up a powerful rebound when it is withdrawn. It's worth remembering that alcohol, like other depressant drugs, greatly reduces sleep quality (Lobo & Tufik, 1997).

Dement's volunteers complained of memory lapses, poor concentration, and anxiety. For a while, it was thought that people deprived of REM sleep might go crazy. But later experiments showed that missing *any* sleep stage can cause a rebound for that stage. In general, daytime disturbances are related to the *total amount* of sleep lost, not to the *type* of sleep lost (Devoto et al., 1999).

The Value of REM Sleep

What then, is the purpose of REM sleep? Early in life, REM sleep may stimulate the developing brain. Newborn babies spend a hearty 8 or 9 hours a day in REM sleep. That's about 50 percent of their total sleep time. In adulthood, REM sleep may prevent sensory deprivation during sleep, and it may help us process emotional events. REM sleep also seems to help us sort and integrate memories, especially memories about strategies that help us solve problems (Stickgold et al., 2001). Speaking very loosely, it's as if the dreaming brain were reviewing messages left on a telephone answering machine, deciding which are worth keeping. During the day, when information is streaming in, the brain may be too busy to efficiently select useful memories. When the conscious brain is "off-line," we are better able to build new memories. Although we have much to learn, it's clear that REM sleep and dreaming are valuable for keeping the brain in good working order (Stickgold et al., 2001).

Dream Worlds

Calvin Hall, a noted dream expert, collected and analyzed more than 10,000 dream reports (Hall, 1966a; Hall et al., 1982). Hall found that most dreams reflect everyday events. The favorite dream setting is a familiar room in a house. Action usually takes place between the dreamer and two or three other emotionally important people—friends, enemies, parents, or employers. Dream actions are also mostly familiar: running, jumping, riding, sitting, talking, and watching. About half of all dreams have sexual elements. Dreams of flying, floating, and falling occur less frequently.

Narcolepsy A sudden, irresistible sleep attack.

Cataplexy A sudden temporary paralysis of the muscles.

Sleep apnea Repeated interruption of breathing during sleep.

Sudden infant death syndrome (SIDS) The sudden, unexplained death of an apparently healthy infant.

REM rebound The occurrence of extra rapid eye movement sleep following REM sleep deprivation.

Are most dreams happy or sad? If you ask people in the morning what they dreamed about, they mention more unpleasant emotions than pleasant emotions (Merritt et al., 1994). However, it may be that dreams of fear, anger, or sadness are easier to remember. When people are awakened during REM sleep, they report equal numbers of positive and negative emotions (Fosse, Stickgold, & Hobson, 2001).

Dream Theories

How meaningful are dreams? Most theorists agree that dreams reflect our waking thoughts, fantasies, and emotions (Beck, 2004; Cartwright & Lamberg, 1992). Thus, the real question might be, "How deep should we dig in interpreting dreams?" Some theorists believe that dreams have deeply hidden meanings. Others regard dreams as nearly meaningless. Let's examine both views.

Psychodynamic Dream Theory

Sigmund Freud's landmark book, *The Interpretation of Dreams* (1900), first advanced the idea that many dreams are based on **wish fulfillment** (an expression of unconscious desires). Thus, a student who is angry with a teacher might dream of embarrassing the teacher in class, a lonely person may dream of romance, or a hungry child may dream of food.

Freud's **psychodynamic theory** of dreaming emphasizes internal conflicts and unconscious forces. Although many of his ideas are attractive, there is evidence against them. For example, volunteers in a study of starvation showed no particular increase in dreams about food and eating. In general, dreams show few signs of directly expressing hidden wishes (Fisher & Greenberg, 1996).

Freud's response to critics, no doubt, would have been that dreams rarely express needs so directly. One of Freud's key insights is that ideas in dreams are expressed as *images* or pictures, rather than in words. Freud believed that dreams express unconscious desires and conflicts as disguised **dream symbols** (images that have deeper symbolic meaning). For instance, death might be symbolized by a journey; children, by small animals; or sexual intercourse, by horseback riding or dancing. Similarly, a woman sexually attracted to her best friend's husband might dream of stealing her friend's wedding ring and placing it on her own hand, an indirect symbol of her true desires.

Do all dreams have hidden meanings? Probably not. Even Freud realized that some dreams are trivial "day residues" or carryovers from ordinary waking events. On the other hand, dreams do tend to reflect a person's current concerns, so Freud wasn't entirely wrong (Nikles et al., 1998).

BRIDGES

Interpreting dreams is an important part of Freudian psychoanalysis, a psychodynamic therapy.

See Chapter 17, pages 572–573.

The Activation-Synthesis Hypothesis

Psychiatrists Allan Hobson and Robert McCarley have a radically different view of dreaming. They believe that during REM sleep, brain cells that normally control eye movements, balance, and actions are activated. However, messages from the cells are blocked from reaching the body, so no movement occurs. Nevertheless, the cells continue to tell higher brain areas of their activities. Struggling to interpret this information, the brain searches through stored memories and manufactures a dream (Hobson, 2000).

How does that help explain dream content? Let's use the classic chase dream as an example. In such dreams we feel we are running but not going anywhere. This occurs because the brain is told the body is running, but it gets no feedback from the motionless legs. To make sense of this information, the brain creates a chase drama. A similar process probably explains dreams of floating or flying.

Hobson and McCarley call their view the **activation-synthesis hypothesis.** Hobson explains that several parts of the brain are "turned on" (activated) during REM sleep. This triggers sensations, motor commands, and memories. The cortex of the brain, which also becomes more active during REM sleep, synthesizes this activity into stories and visual images. However, frontal areas of the cortex, which control higher mental abilities, are mostly shut down during REM sleep. This explains why dreams are more primitive and more bizarre than daytime thoughts (Hobson, 2000). Viewed this way, dreams are merely a different type of thinking that occurs during sleep (McCarley, 1998).

Note that the activation-synthesis hypothesis doesn't rule out the idea that dreams have meaning. Because dreams are created from memories and past experiences, they can tell us quite a lot about a person's mental life, emotions, and concerns (Hobson, 2000). However, many psychologists continue to believe that dreams have deeper meaning (Shafton, 1995; White & Taytroe, 2003). There seems to be little doubt that dreams can make a difference in our lives: Veteran sleep researcher William Dement once dreamed that he had lung cancer. In the dream a doctor told Dement he would die soon. At the time, Dement was smoking two packs of cigarettes a day. He says, "I will never forget the surprise, joy, and exquisite relief of waking up. I felt reborn." Dement quit smoking the following day. (For more information about dreaming, see this chapter's Psychology in Action.)

KNOWLEDGE BUILDER

Sleep Disturbances and Dreaming

REFLECT

Almost everyone suffers from insomnia at least occasionally. Are any of the techniques for combating insomnia similar to strategies you have discovered on your own?

How many sleep disturbances can you name (including those listed in Table 7.1)? Are there any that you have experienced? Which do you think would be most disruptive?

Do you think the activation-synthesis hypothesis provides an adequate explanation of your own dreams? Have you had dreams that seem to reflect Freudian wish fulfillment? Do you think your dreams have symbolic meaning?

LEARNING CHECK

1. People who suffer from sudden daytime sleep attacks have which sleep disorder?
   a. narcolepsy c. somnambulism
   b. REM behavior disorder d. sleep spindling
2. Eating a snack that is nearly all starch can promote sleep because it increases __________ in the brain.
   a. beta waves c. EEG activity
   b. tryptophan d. hypnic cycling
3. Night terrors, sleepwalking, and sleeptalking all occur during stage 1, NREM sleep. T or F?
4. Sleep ________________ is suspected as one cause of SIDS.
5. Which of the following is *not* a behavioral remedy for insomnia?
   a. daily hypersomnia c. progressive relaxation
   b. stimulus control d. paradoxical intention
6. The favored setting for dreams is
   a. work c. outdoors or unfamiliar places
   b. school d. familiar rooms
7. Sorting and integrating memories is one function of
   a. activation-synthesis cycles c. deep sleep
   b. REM sleep d. NREM sleep
8. According to the activation-synthesis model of dreaming, dreams are constructed from ______________________________ to explain messages received from nerve cells controlling eye movement, balance, and bodily activity.

CRITICAL THINKING

9. Even without being told that somnambulism is an NREM event, you could have predicted that sleepwalking doesn't occur during dreaming. Why?

Answers: 1. a 2. b 3. F 4. apnea 5. a 6. d 7. b 8. memories 9. Because people are immobilized during REM sleep and REM sleep is strongly associated with dreaming. This makes it unlikely that sleepwalkers are acting out dreams.

Hypnosis—Look into My Eyes

"Your body is becoming heavy. You can barely keep your eyes open. You are so tired you can't move. Relax. Let go. Relax. Close your eyes and relax." These are the last words a textbook should ever say to you, and the first a hypnotist might say.

Hypnosis is an altered state of consciousness, characterized by narrowed attention and openness to suggestion (Kallio & Revonsuo, 2003; Kosslyn et al., 2000). Not all psychologists accept this definition. To some, hypnosis is merely a blend of conformity, relaxation, imagination, obedience, and role-playing (Braffman & Kirsch, 1999). Either way, hypnosis can be explained by normal principles. It is not mysterious or "magical."

Interest in hypnosis began in the 1700s with Austrian doctor Franz Mesmer, whose name gave us the term *mesmerize* (to hypnotize). Mesmer believed he could cure disease with magnets. Mesmer's strange "treatments" are related to hypnosis because they actually relied on the power of suggestion, not magnetism. For a time, Mesmer enjoyed quite a following. In the end, however, his theories of "animal magnetism" were rejected and he was branded a fraud.

The term *hypnosis* was coined by English surgeon James Braid. The Greek word *hypnos* means "sleep," and Braid used it to describe the hypnotic state. Today we know that hypnosis is *not* sleep. Confusion about this point remains because some hypnotists give the suggestion, "Sleep, sleep." However, EEG patterns recorded during hypnosis are different from those observed when a person is asleep or pretending to be hypnotized (Barabasz, 2000).

Hypnotic Susceptibility

Can everyone be hypnotized? About 8 people out of 10 can be hypnotized, but only 4 out of 10 will be good hypnotic subjects. People who are imaginative and prone to fantasy are often highly responsive to hypnosis (Silva & Kirsch, 1992). But people who lack these traits may also be hypnotized. If you are willing to be hypnotized, chances are good that you could be. Hypnosis depends more on the efforts and abilities of the hypnotized person than the skills of the hypnotist (Kirsch & Lynn, 1995). But make no mistake, people who are hypnotized are not merely faking their responses (Perugini et al., 1998).

Hypnotic susceptibility refers to how easily a person can become hypnotized. It is measured by giving a series of suggestions and counting the number of times a person responds. A typical hypnotic test is the *Stanford Hypnotic Susceptibility Scale* shown in ■ Table 7.3. In the test, various suggestions are made, and the person's response is noted. For instance, you might be told that your left arm is becoming more and more rigid and that it will not bend. If you can't bend your arm during the next 10 seconds, you have shown a susceptibility to hypnotic suggestions. (Also see ● Figure 7.8.)

Inducing Hypnosis

How is hypnosis done? Could I be hypnotized against my will? Hypnotists use many different methods. Still, all techniques encourage a person (1) to focus attention on what is being said, (2) to relax and feel tired, (3) to "let go" and accept suggestions easily, and (4)

Wish fulfillment Freudian belief that many dreams express unconscious desires.

Psychodynamic theory Any theory of behavior that emphasizes internal conflicts, motives, and unconscious forces.

Dream symbols Images in dreams that serve as visible signs of hidden ideas, desires, impulses, emotions, relationships, and so forth.

Activation-synthesis hypothesis An attempt to explain how dream content is affected by motor commands in the brain that occur during sleep but are not carried out.

Hypnosis An altered state of consciousness characterized by narrowed attention and increased suggestibility.

Hypnotic susceptibility One's capacity for becoming hypnotized.

TABLE 7.3

Stanford Hypnotic Susceptibility Scale

SUGGESTED BEHAVIOR	CRITERION OF PASSING
1. Postural sway	Falls without forcing
2. Eye closure	Closes eyes without forcing
3. Hand lowering (left)	Lowers at least 6 inches by end of 10 seconds
4. Immobilization (right arm)	Arm rises less than 1 inch in 10 seconds
5. Finger lock	Incomplete separation of fingers at end of 10 seconds
6. Arm rigidity (left arm)	Less than 2 inches of arm bending in 10 seconds
7. Hands moving together	Hands at least as close as 6 inches after 10 seconds
8. Verbal inhibition (name)	Name unspoken in 10 seconds
9. Hallucination (fly)	Any movement, grimacing, acknowledgment of effect
10. Eye catalepsy	Eyes remain closed at end of 10 seconds
11. Posthypnotic (changes chairs)	Any partial movement response
12. Amnesia test	Three or fewer items recalled

Adapted from Weitzenhoffer & Hilgard, 1959.

● **Figure 7.8** In one test of hypnotizability, subjects attempt to pull their hands apart after hearing suggestions that their fingers are "locked" together.

to use vivid imagination (Druckman & Bjork, 1994). Basically, you must cooperate to become hypnotized. Many theorists believe that all hypnosis is really self-hypnosis *(autosuggestion)*. From this perspective, a hypnotist merely helps another person follow a series of suggestions. These suggestions, in turn, alter sensations, perceptions, thoughts, feelings, and behaviors (Druckman & Bjork, 1994; Kirsch & Lynn, 1995). (See "Swinging Suggestions.")

What does it feel like to be hypnotized? You might be surprised at some of your actions during hypnosis. You also might have mild feelings of floating, sinking, anesthesia, or separation from your body. Personal experiences vary widely. A key element in hypnosis is the **basic suggestion effect** (a tendency of hypnotized persons to carry out suggested actions as if they were involuntary). Hypnotized persons feel like their actions and experiences are *automatic*—they seem to happen without effort. However, hypnotized people generally remain in control of their behavior and aware of what is going on. For instance, most people will not act out hypnotic suggestions that they consider immoral or repulsive (such as undressing in public or harming someone) (Kirsch & Lynn, 1995). Here is how one person described his hypnotic session:

> I felt lethargic, my eyes going out of focus and wanting to close. My hands felt real light. . . . I felt I was sinking deeper into the chair. . . . I felt like I wanted to relax more and more. . . . My responses were more automatic. I didn't have to *wish* to do things so much or *want* to do them. . . . I just did them. . . . I felt floating . . . very close to sleep. (Hilgard, 1968)

Hypnosis may also cause a *dissociation,* or "split," in awareness. To illustrate, researcher Ernest Hilgard (1904–2001) asked hypnotized subjects to plunge one hand into a painful bath of ice water. Subjects told to feel no pain said they felt none. The same subjects were then asked if there was any part of their mind that did feel pain. With their free hand, many wrote, "It hurts," or "Stop it, you're hurting me," while they continued to act pain free (Hilgard 1977, 1978). Thus, one part of the hypnotized person says there is no pain and acts as if there is none. Another part, which Hilgard calls the *hidden observer,* is aware of the pain but remains in the background. The **hidden observer** is a detached part of the hypnotized person's awareness that silently observes events.

Effects of Hypnosis

What can (and cannot) be achieved with hypnosis? Many abilities have been tested during hypnosis, leading to the following conclusions (Burgess & Kirsch, 1999; Chaves, 2000; Kirsch & Lynn, 1995):

1. **Superhuman acts of strength.** Hypnosis has no more effect on physical strength than instructions that encourage a person to make his or her best effort.
2. **Memory.** There is some evidence that hypnosis can enhance memory (Wagstaff, et al., 2004). However, it frequently increases the number of false memories as well. For this reason, many states now bar persons from testifying in court if they were hypnotized to improve their memory of a crime they witnessed.
3. **Amnesia.** A person told not to remember something heard during hypnosis may claim not to remember. In some instances

DISCOVERING PSYCHOLOGY Swinging Suggestions

Here's a demonstration you can use to gain insight into hypnosis. Tie a short length of string (about 6 inches) to a small, heavy object, such as a ring or a small metal nut. Hold the ring at eye level, about a foot from your face. Concentrate on the ring and notice that it will begin to move, ever so slightly. As it does, focus all your attention on the ring. Narrow your attention to a beam of energy and mentally push the ring away from you. Each time the ring swings away, push on it, using only mental force. Then release it and let it swing back toward you. Continue to mentally push and release the ring until it is swinging freely. For the best results, try this now, before reading more.

Did the ring move? If it did, you used autosuggestion to influence your own behavior in a subtle way. Suggestions that the ring would swing caused your hand to make tiny micro-muscular movements. These, in turn, caused the ring to move—no special mental powers or supernatural forces are involved.

As is true of hypnotic suggestion, the ring's movement probably seemed to be automatic. Obviously, you could just intentionally swing the ring. However, if you responded to suggestion, the movement seemed to happen without any effort on your part. In the same way, when people are hypnotized, their actions seem to occur without any voluntary intent. Incidentally, autosuggestion likely underlies other phenomena, such as how Ouija boards spell out answers to questions despite no apparent conscious interference. Autosuggestion also plays a role in many forms of self-therapy.

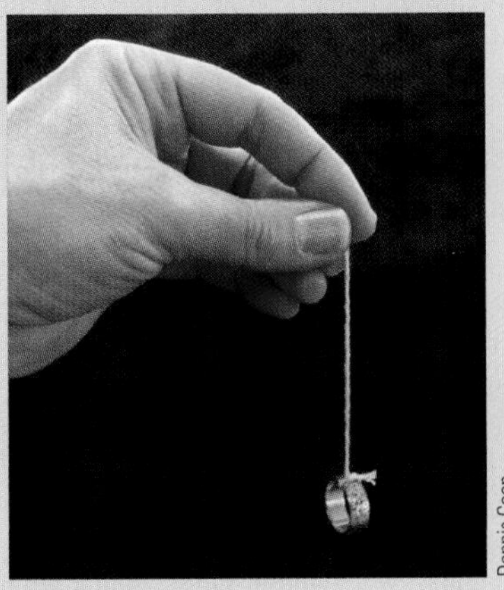
Dennis Coon

this may be nothing more than a deliberate attempt to avoid thinking about specific ideas. However, brief memory loss of this type actually does seem to occur (Bowers & Woody, 1996).

4. **Pain relief.** Hypnosis can relieve pain (Eimer, 2000; Keefe, Abernethy, & Campbell, 2005). It can be especially useful when chemical painkillers are ineffective. For instance, hypnosis can reduce phantom limb pain (Oakley, Whitman, & Halligan, 2002). (As discussed in Chapter 5, amputees sometimes feel phantom pain that seems to come from a missing limb.)
5. **Age regression.** Given the proper suggestions, some hypnotized people appear to "regress" to childhood. However, most theorists now believe that "age-regressed" subjects are only acting out a suggested role.
6. **Sensory changes.** Hypnotic suggestions concerning sensations are among the most effective. Given the proper instructions, a person can be made to smell a small bottle of ammonia and respond as if it were a wonderful perfume. It is also possible to alter color vision, hearing sensitivity, time sense, perception of illusions, and many other sensory responses.

BRIDGES

Should the police use hypnosis to enhance the memories of witnesses? The evidence generally says no.

See Chapter 9, page 303.

Hypnosis is a valuable tool. It can help people relax, feel less pain, and make better progress in therapy (Kirsch, Montgomery, & Sapirstein, 1995). Generally, hypnosis is more successful at changing subjective experiences than it is at modifying behaviors such as smoking or overeating. In short, hypnotic effects are useful, but seldom amazing (Chaves, 2000; Druckman & Bjork, 1994).

Stage Hypnosis

On stage the hypnotist intones, "When I count to three, you will imagine that you are on a train to Disneyland and growing younger and younger as the train approaches." Responding to these suggestions, grown men and women begin to giggle and squirm like children on their way to a circus.

How do stage entertainers use hypnosis to get people to do strange things? They don't. Little or no hypnosis is needed to do a good hypnosis act. **Stage hypnosis** is often merely a simulation of hypnotic effects. T. X. Barber, an authority on hypnosis, says that stage hypnotists make use of several features of the stage setting to perform their act (Barber, 1970).

Basic suggestion effect The tendency of hypnotized persons to carry out suggested actions as if they were involuntary.

Hidden observer A detached part of the hypnotized person's awareness that silently observes events.

Stage hypnosis Use of hypnosis to entertain; often, merely a simulation of hypnosis for that purpose.

1. **Waking suggestibility.** We are all more or less open to suggestion, but on stage people are unusually cooperative because they don't want to "spoil the act." As a result, they will readily follow almost any instruction given by the entertainer.
2. **Selection of responsive subjects.** Participants in stage hypnotism (all *volunteers*) are first "hypnotized" as a group. Then, anyone who doesn't yield to instructions is eliminated.
3. **The hypnosis label disinhibits.** Once a person has been labeled "hypnotized," she or he can sing, dance, act silly, or whatever, without fear or embarrassment. On stage, being "hypnotized" takes away personal responsibility for one's actions.
4. **The hypnotist as a "director."** After volunteers loosen up and respond to a few suggestions, they find that they are suddenly the stars of the show. Audience response to the antics on stage brings out the "ham" in many people. All the "hypnotist" needs to do is direct the action.
5. **The stage hypnotist uses tricks.** Stage hypnosis is about 50 percent taking advantage of the situation and 50 percent deception. One of the more impressive stage tricks is to rigidly suspend a person between two chairs. This is astounding only because the audience does not question it. Anyone can do it, as is shown in the photographs and instructions in ● Figure 7.9. Try it!

To summarize, hypnosis is real, and it can significantly alter private experience. Hypnosis is a useful tool in a variety of settings. Nightclubs, however, are not one of these settings. Stage "hypnotists" entertain; they rarely hypnotize.

Sensory Deprivation—Life on a Sensory Diet

Throughout history, sensory deprivation has been one of the most widely used means of altering consciousness. **Sensory deprivation** (SD) refers to any major reduction in the amount or variety of sensory stimulation.

What happens when stimulation is greatly reduced? A hint comes from reports by prisoners in solitary confinement, arctic explorers, high-altitude pilots, long-distance truck drivers, and radar operators. When faced with limited or monotonous stimulation, people sometimes have bizarre sensations, dangerous lapses in attention, and wildly distorted perceptions. To find out why, D. O. Hebb paid volunteers to undergo sensory deprivation under controlled conditions.

In Hebb's classic experiments, subjects spent several days lying on their backs in a small cubicle. To prevent vision, they wore darkened goggles. Gloves and cardboard cuffs restricted touch. In the background, a constant hissing noise masked all other sounds. Do these conditions sound interesting? If you were placed in similar circumstances, you might be in for a surprise. Few subjects could take more than 2 or 3 days of sensory deprivation without "pushing the panic button."

Disruptive Effects

What sort of changes take place during sensory deprivation? A person may misjudge time and have trouble concentrating. After emerging from sensory deprivation, some people experience color distortions, heightened visual illusions, slower reactions, and a brief warping of visual lines and spaces. Volunteers in some early studies also reported strange and vivid images.

Spurred by such reports, researchers soon created an ingenious array of sensory deprivation environments, and volunteers seeking a drugless high flocked to experiments. Most were disappointed, however. We now know that true hallucinations are rare during sensory deprivation. The fanciful, dream-like visions that sometimes occur are more likely to be **hypnagogic** (hip-nuh-GAH-jik) **images** (images like those that occur just before sleep). These images may be vivid and surprising, but they are rarely mistaken for real objects. Hypnagogic images are linked to an increase in the number of *theta waves* produced by the brain. These brain waves, in the 4- to 7-cycle-per-second range, are usually recorded just before sleep. Sensory deprivation also increases their occurrence (Taylor, 1983).

Benefits of Sensory Restriction

In recent years, psychologists have begun to explore the possible benefits of sensory deprivation. Much of this work has involved sensory restriction in small isolation tanks like the one pictured in ● Figure 7.10.

Sensory Enhancement

How could sensory deprivation be beneficial? One of the most consistent aftereffects of sensory deprivation is increased sensory acuity. That is, vision, hearing, touch, and taste are temporarily more

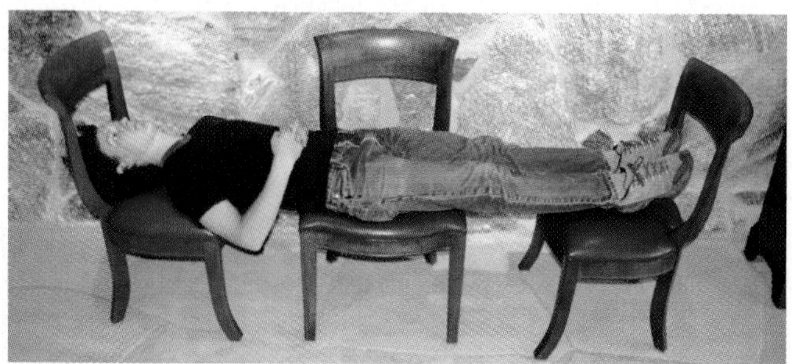

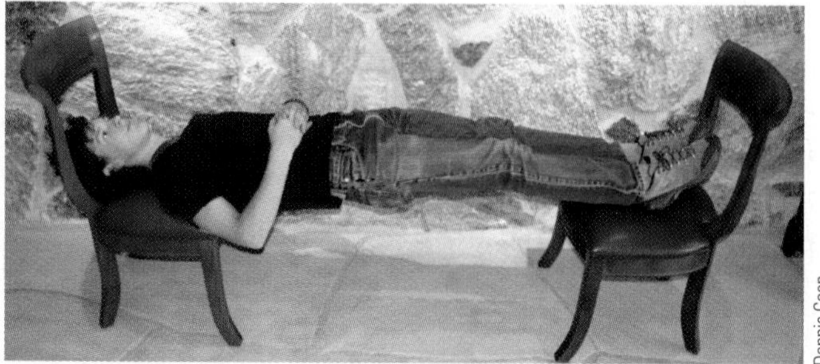

Dennis Coon

● **Figure 7.9** Arrange three chairs as shown. Have someone recline as shown. Ask him to lift slightly while you remove the middle chair. Accept the applause gracefully! (Concerning hypnosis and similar phenomena, the moral, of course, is, "Suspend judgment until you have something solid to stand on.")

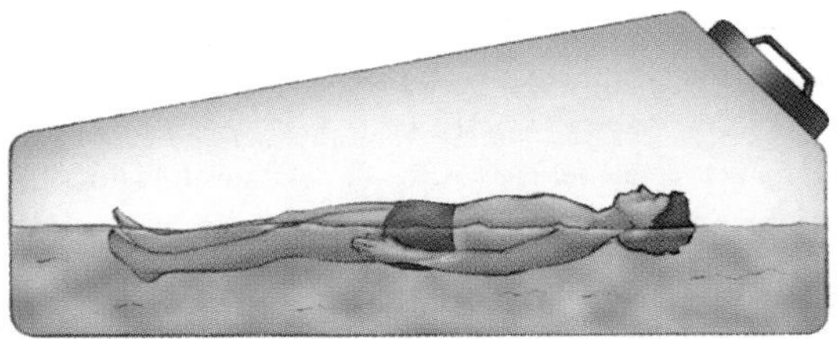

● **Figure 7.10** A sensory isolation chamber. Small flotation tanks like the one pictured have been used by psychologists to study the effects of mild sensory deprivation. Subjects float in darkness and silence. The shallow body-temperature water contains hundreds of pounds of Epsom salts so that subjects float near the surface. Mild sensory deprivation produces deep relaxation.

sensitive. This effect could be used to reawaken the dulled senses of someone who is listless or overworked. At the very least, wearing earplugs for a day might be an interesting prelude to hearing a musical concert!

Relaxation

As we already noted, prolonged sensory deprivation is stressful and uncomfortable. Yet, oddly, brief periods of restricted sensation can be very relaxing. An hour or two spent in a flotation tank, for instance, causes a large drop in blood pressure, muscle tension, and other signs of stress (van Dierendonck & Te Nijenhuis, 2005). Of course, it could be argued that a warm bath has the same effect. But evidence suggests that brief sensory deprivation is one of the surest ways to induce deep relaxation (Suedfeld & Borrie, 1999)

Changing Habits

Psychologists have also found that mild sensory deprivation can help people quit smoking, lose weight, and reduce their use of alcohol and drugs (Borrie, 1990–1991; Cooper, Adams, & Scott, 1988; Suedfeld, 1990). Canadian researcher Peter Suedfeld calls such benefits restricted environmental stimulation therapy, or **REST.** In one study, Suedfeld tested the effects of standard antismoking messages. These were then compared with the effects of the same messages combined with sensory deprivation. He found that roughly equal numbers of people succeeded in stopping smoking with either treatment. But 3 months later, members of the REST group were smoking 40 percent less than the others (Suedfeld, 1990). Another study found similar benefits for people in a weight-loss program based on sensory deprivation (Borrie & Suedfeld, 1980).

How does sensory deprivation help? Tape-recorded suggestions to eat less or stop smoking are played for clients in a flotation tank. It may be that deep relaxation makes a person less likely to argue against or otherwise resist suggestions. In addition, REST temporarily increases mental and behavioral flexibility. Perhaps this is because spending time in a restricted environment completely interrupts a person's routines and behavior patterns. In any case, REST can "loosen" belief systems and behavior patterns in ways that make it easier to change bad habits (Suedfeld & Borrie, 1999).

Prospects

After years of being viewed only as a disruptive state, sensory deprivation may yet prove to have additional benefits. For example, REST shows promise as a way to stimulate creative thinking (Norlander et al., 1998). REST sessions also enhance performance in skilled sports, such as gymnastics, tennis, basketball, darts, archery, and marksmanship (Druckman & Bjork, 1994; Norlander et al., 1999). There is also evidence that REST can relieve chronic pain and reduce stress (Kjellgren et al., 2001). Clearly, there is much yet to be learned from studying "nothingness."

KNOWLEDGE BUILDER

Hypnosis and Sensory Deprivation

REFLECT

How have your beliefs about hypnosis changed after reading the preceding section? Can you think of specific examples in which hypnosis was misrepresented? For example, in high school assemblies, stage acts, movies, or TV dramas?

Have you experienced any form of sensory restriction or sensory deprivation? How did you react? Would you be willing to try REST to break a bad habit?

LEARNING CHECK

1. The term *hypnotism* was coined by a British surgeon named
   a. Franz Mesmer c. T. A. Kreskin
   b. James Stanford d. James Braid
2. Only 4 out of 10 people can be hypnotized. T or F?
3. Which of the following can most definitely be achieved with hypnosis?
   a. unusual strength c. improved memory
   b. pain relief d. sleep-like brain waves
4. Which of the following is not a disruptive effect observed during or immediately after sensory deprivation?
   a. impaired time sense c. elevated blood pressure
   b. difficulty concentrating d. heightened visual illusions
5. Vivid images during sensory deprivation usually can be best described as
   a. daydreams c. hallucinations
   b. hypnagogic d. hypodynamic
6. Prolonged periods of sensory deprivation lower anxiety and induce deep relaxation. T or F?

CRITICAL THINKING

7. What kind of control group would you need to identify the true effects of hypnosis?

Answers: 1. d 2. F 3. b 4. c 5. b 6. F 7. Most experiments on hypnosis include a control group in which people are asked to simulate being hypnotized. Without such controls, the tendency of subjects to cooperate with experimenters makes it difficult to identify true hypnotic effects.

Sensory deprivation Any major reduction in the amount or variety of sensory stimulation.

Hypnagogic images Vivid mental images that may occur just as one enters stage 1 sleep.

REST Restricted environmental stimulation therapy.

TABLE 7.4

Comparison of Psychoactive Drugs

NAME	CLASSIFICATION	MEDICAL USE	USUAL DOSE	DURATION OF EFFECT
Alcohol	Sedative-hypnotic	Solvent, antiseptic	Varies	1–4 hours
Amphetamines	Stimulant	Relief of mild depression, control of narcolepsy and hyperactivity	2.5–5 milligrams	4 hours
Barbiturates	Sedative-hypnotic	Sedation, relief of high blood pressure, anticonvulsant	50–100 milligrams	4 hours
Benzodiazepines	Anxiolytic (antianxiety drug)	Tranquilizer	2–100 milligrams	10 minutes–8 hours
Caffeine	Stimulant	Counteract depressant drugs, treatment of migraine headaches	Varies	Varies
Cocaine	Stimulant, local anesthetic	Local anesthesia	Varies	Varied, brief periods
Codeine	Narcotic	Ease pain and coughing	30 milligrams	4 hours
GHB	Sedative-hypnotic	Experimental treatment of narcolepsy, alcoholism	1–3 grams (powder)	1–3 hours
Heroin	Narcotic	Pain relief	Varies	4 hours
LSD	Hallucinogen	Experimental study of mental function, alcoholism	100–500 milligrams	10 hours
Marijuana (THC)	Relaxant, euphoriant; in high doses, hallucinogen	Treatment of glaucoma and side effects of chemotherapy	1–2 cigarettes	4 hours
MDMA	Stimulant/hallucinogen	None	125 milligrams	4–6 hours
Mescaline	Hallucinogen	None	350 micrograms	12 hours
Methadone	Narcotic	Pain relief	10 milligrams	4–6 hours
Morphine	Narcotic	Pain relief	15 milligrams	6 hours
PCP	Anesthetic	None	2–10 milligrams	4–6 hours, plus 12-hour recovery
Psilocybin	Hallucinogen	None	25 milligrams	6–8 hours
Tobacco (nicotine)	Stimulant	Emetic (nicotine)	Varies	Varies

Question marks indicate conflict of opinion. It should be noted that illicit drugs are frequently adulterated and thus pose unknown hazards to the user.

Drug-Altered Consciousness—The High and Low of It

Drug abuse has been one of the most persistent of all social problems in Western nations. The problem is that drugs that can ease pain, induce sleep, or end depression have a high potential for abuse (Goldberg, 2003). Add alcohol and illicit drugs to the menu and it's little wonder that so many lives are damaged by drug use.

The surest way to alter human consciousness is to administer a **psychoactive drug** (a substance capable of altering attention, judgment, memory, time sense, self-control, emotion, or perception) (Julien, 2004). Most psychoactive drugs can be placed on a scale ranging from stimulation to depression. A **stimulant** is a substance that increases activity in the body and nervous system. A **depressant** does the reverse. ● Figure 7.11 shows various drugs and their approximate effects. A more complete summary of frequently abused psychoactive drugs is given in ■ Table 7.4.

TABLE 7.4

Comparison of Psychoactive Drugs

EFFECTS SOUGHT	LONG-TERM SYMPTOMS	PHYSICAL DEPENDENCE POTENTIAL	PSYCHOLOGICAL DEPENDENCE POTENTIAL	ORGANIC DAMAGE POTENTIAL
Sense alteration, anxiety reduction, sociability	Cirrhosis, toxic psychosis, neurologic damage, addiction	Yes	Yes	Yes
Alertness, activeness	Loss of appetite, delusions, hallucinations, toxic psychosis	Yes	Yes	Yes
Anxiety reduction, euphoria	Addiction with severe withdrawal symptoms, possible convulsions, toxic psychosis	Yes	Yes	Yes
Anxiety relief	Irritability, confusion, depression, sleep disorders	Yes	Yes	No, but can affect fetus
Wakefulness, alertness	Insomnia, heart arrhythmias, high blood pressure	No?	Yes	Yes
Excitation, talkativeness	Depression, convulsions	Yes	Yes	Yes
Euphoria, prevent withdrawal discomfort	Addiction, constipation, loss of appetite	Yes	Yes	No
Intoxication, euphoria, relaxation	Anxiety, confusion, insomnia, hallucinations, seizures	Yes	Yes	No?
Euphoria, prevent withdrawal discomfort	Addiction, constipation, loss of appetite	Yes	Yes	No*
Insightful experiences, exhilaration, distortion of senses	May intensify existing psychosis, panic reactions	No	No?	No?
Relaxation; increased euphoria, perceptions, sociability	Possible lung cancer, other health risks	No	Yes	Yes?
Excitation, euphoria	Personality change, hyperthermia, liver damage	No	Yes	Yes
Insightful experiences, exhilaration, distortion of senses	May intensify existing psychosis, panic reactions	No	No?	No?
Prevent withdrawal discomfort	Addiction, constipation, loss of appetite	Yes	Yes	No
Euphoria, prevent withdrawal discomfort	Addiction, constipation, loss of appetite	Yes	Yes	No*
Euphoria	Unpredictable behavior, suspicion, hostility, psychosis	Debated	Yes	Yes
Insightful experiences, exhilaration, distortion of senses	May intensify existing psychosis, panic reactions	No	No?	No?
Alertness, calmness, sociability	Emphysema, lung cancer, mouth and throat cancer, cardiovascular damage, loss of appetite	Yes	Yes	Yes

*Persons who inject drugs under nonsterile conditions run a high risk of contracting AIDS, hepatitis, abscesses, or circulatory disorders.

How Drugs Affect the Brain

How do drugs alter consciousness? Psychoactive drugs influence the activity of brain cells. Typically, drugs imitate or alter neurotransmitters, the chemicals that carry messages between brain cells. Some drugs, such as ecstasy, amphetamine, and some antidepressants, cause more neurotransmitters to be released, increasing the activity of brain cells. Other drugs slow the removal of neurotransmitters after they are released. This prolongs the action of transmit-

Psychoactive drug A substance capable of altering attention, memory, judgment, time sense, self-control, mood, or perception.

Stimulant A substance that increases activity in the body and nervous system.

Depressant A substance that decreases activity in the body and nervous system.

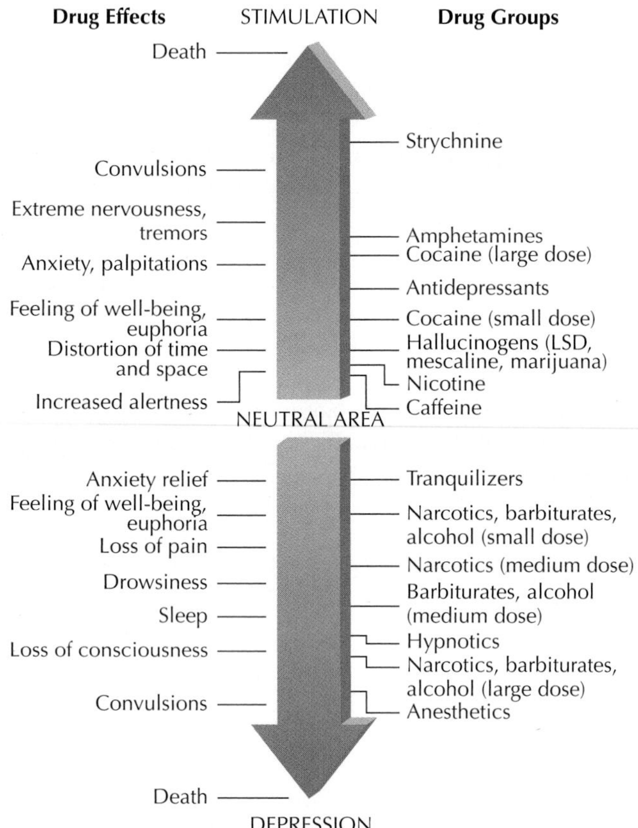

● **Figure 7.11** Spectrum and continuum of drug action. Many drugs can be rated on a stimulation-depression scale according to their effects on the central nervous system. Although LSD, mescaline, and marijuana are listed here, the stimulation-depression scale is less relevant to these drugs. The principal characteristic of such hallucinogens is their mind-altering quality.

ter chemicals and typically has a stimulating effect (cocaine works in this way). Other drugs, such as nicotine and opiates, directly stimulate brain cells by mimicking neurotransmitters. Another possibility is illustrated by alcohol and tranquilizers. These drugs affect certain types of brain cells that cause relaxation and relieve anxiety. Some drugs fill receptor sites on brain cells and block incoming messages. Other possibilities also exist, which is why drugs can have such a wide variety of effects on the brain (Julien, 2004).

All addictive drugs stimulate the brain's reward circuitry, producing feelings of pleasure. As one expert put it, addictive drugs fool brain-reward pathways: "As a result, the reward pathway signals, 'That felt good. Let's do it again. Let's remember exactly how we did it.'" This creates a compulsion to repeat the drug experience. It's the hook that eventually snares the addict (Restak, 2001). Adolescents are especially susceptible to addiction because brain systems that restrain risk-taking are not as mature as those that reward pleasure-seeking (Chambers, Taylor, & Potenza, 2003).

Dependence

Drug dependence falls into two broad categories. When a person compulsively uses a drug to maintain bodily comfort, a **physical dependence** (addiction) exists. Addiction occurs most often with drugs that cause **withdrawal symptoms** (physical illness that follows removal of a drug) (Julien, 2004). Withdrawal from drugs such as alcohol, barbiturates, and opiates can cause violent flu-like symptoms of nausea, vomiting, diarrhea, chills, sweating, and cramps. Addiction is often accompanied by a **drug tolerance** (reduced response to a drug). This leads users to take larger and larger doses to get the desired effect.

Persons who develop a **psychological dependence** believe that a drug is necessary to maintain feelings of comfort or well-being. Usually, they intensely crave the drug and its rewarding qualities (Feldman & Meyer, 1996). Psychological dependence can be just as powerful as physical addiction. That's why some psychologists define addiction as any compulsive habit pattern. By this definition, a person who has lost control over drug use, for whatever reason, is addicted. In fact, most people who answer yes to both of the following questions have an alcohol or drug problem and should seek professional help (Brown et al., 1997):

- In the last year, did you ever drink or use drugs more than you meant to?
- Have you felt you wanted or needed to cut down on your drinking or drug use in the last year?

Patterns of Abuse

Some drugs, of course, have a higher potential for abuse than others. Heroin is certainly more dangerous than caffeine. However, this is only one side of the picture. It can be as useful to classify drug-taking *behavior* as it is to rate drugs. For example, some people remain social drinkers for life, whereas others become alcoholics within weeks of taking their first drink. In this sense, drug use can be classified as *experimental* (short-term use based on curiosity), *social-recreational* (occasional social use for pleasure or relaxation), *situational* (use to cope with a specific problem, such as needing to stay awake), *intensive* (daily use with elements of dependence), or *compulsive* (intense use and extreme dependence). The last three categories of drug taking tend to be damaging no matter what drug is used.

Drugs of Abuse

Note in ■ Table 7.4 that the drugs most likely to lead to physical dependence are alcohol, amphetamines, barbiturates, cocaine, codeine, heroin, methadone, morphine, and tobacco (nicotine). Using *any* of the drugs listed in ■ Table 7.4 can result in psychological dependence. Note too that people who take drugs intravenously are at high risk for developing hepatitis and acquired immunodeficiency syndrome (AIDS) (see Chapter 13). The discussion that follows focuses on the drugs most often abused by students.

Uppers—Amphetamines, Cocaine, MDMA, Caffeine, Nicotine

Amphetamines are synthetic stimulants. Common street names for amphetamine are "speed," "bennies," "dex," "go," and "uppers." These drugs were once widely prescribed for weight loss or depression. Today, the only fully legitimate medical use of amphetamines is to treat narcolepsy, childhood hyperactivity, and overdoses of depressant drugs. Illicit use of amphetamines is widespread, however, especially by people seeking to stay awake and by those who think drugs can improve mental or physical performance.

Methamphetamine is a more potent variation of amphetamine. It can be snorted, injected, or eaten. Of the various types of amphetamine, methamphetamine has created the largest drug problem. "Crank," "speed," "meth," or "crystal," as it is known on the street, can be made cheaply in backyard labs and sold for massive profits. In addition to ruining lives through addiction, it has fueled a violent criminal subculture.

Amphetamines rapidly produce a drug tolerance. Most abusers end up taking ever larger doses to get the desired effect. Eventually, some users switch to injecting methamphetamine ("speed") directly into the bloodstream. True speed freaks typically go on binges lasting several days, after which they "crash" from lack of sleep and food.

Abuse

How dangerous are amphetamines? Amphetamines pose many dangers. Large doses can cause nausea, vomiting, extremely high blood pressure, fatal heart attacks, and disabling strokes. It is important to realize that amphetamines speed up the use of bodily resources; they do not magically supply energy. After an amphetamine binge, people suffer from crippling fatigue, depression, confusion, uncontrolled irritability, and aggression. Repeated amphetamine use damages the brain. Amphetamines can also cause amphetamine psychosis, a loss of contact with reality. Affected users have paranoid delusions that someone is out to get them. Acting on these delusions, they may become violent, resulting in suicide, self-injury, or injury to others (Kratofil, Baberg, & Dimsdale, 1996).

A potent smokable form of crystal methamphetamine has added to the risks of stimulant abuse. This drug, known as "ice" on the street, is highly addictive. Like "crack," the smokable form of cocaine, it produces an intense high. But also like crack (discussed in a moment), crystal methamphetamine leads very rapidly to compulsive abuse and severe drug dependence.

BRIDGES

The symptoms of amphetamine psychosis and paranoid schizophrenia are nearly identical.

This suggests that both are based on similar changes in brain chemistry. See Chapter 16, page 556.

Cocaine

Cocaine ("coke," "snow," "blow") is a powerful central nervous system stimulant extracted from the leaves of the coca plant. Cocaine produces feelings of alertness, euphoria, well-being, power, boundless energy, and pleasure (Julien, 2004). At the turn of the twentieth century, dozens of nonprescription potions and cure-alls contained cocaine. It was during this time that Coca-Cola was indeed the "real thing." From 1886 until 1906, when the U.S. Pure Food and Drug Act was passed, Coca-Cola contained cocaine (which has since been replaced with caffeine).

How does cocaine differ from amphetamines? The two are very much alike in their effects on the central nervous system. The main difference is that amphetamine lasts several hours; cocaine is snorted and quickly metabolized, so its effects last only about 15 to 30 minutes.

Abuse

How dangerous is cocaine? Cocaine is one of the most dangerous drugs of abuse. Even casual or first-time users risk having convulsions, a heart attack, or a stroke (Cregler & Mark, 1985; Lacayo, 1995). When rats and monkeys are given free access to cocaine, they find it irresistible. Many, in fact, end up dying of convulsions from self-administered overdoses of the drug. Cocaine increases the chemical messengers dopamine (DOPE-ah-meen) and nor-

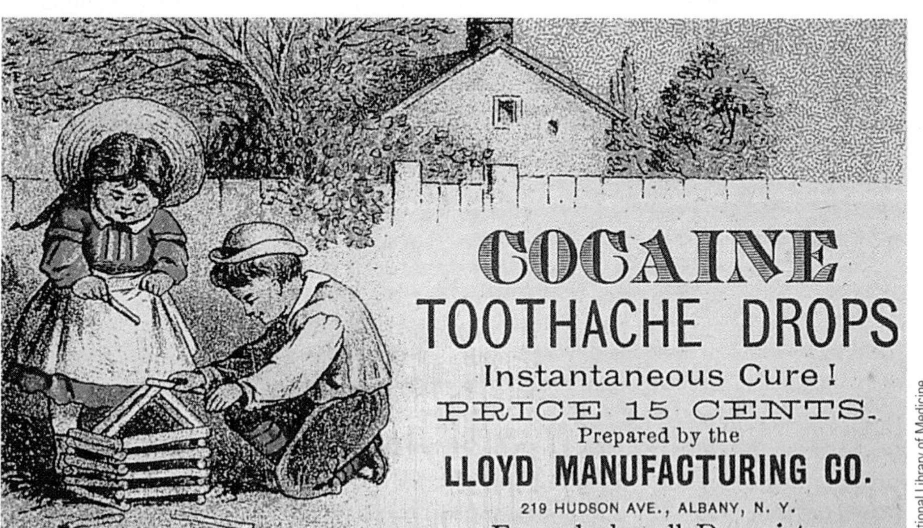

Cocaine was the main ingredient in many nonprescription elixirs before the turn of the twentieth century. Today cocaine is recognized as a powerful and dangerous drug. Its high potential for abuse has damaged the lives of countless users.

Physical dependence Physical addiction, as indicated by the presence of drug tolerance and withdrawal symptoms.

Withdrawal symptoms Physical illness and discomfort following the withdrawal of a drug.

Drug tolerance A reduction in the body's response to a drug.

Psychological dependence Drug dependence that is based primarily on emotional or psychological needs.

adrenaline (nor-ah-DREN-ah-lin). Noradrenaline arouses the brain, and dopamine produces a "rush" of pleasure. This combination is so powerfully rewarding that cocaine users run a high risk of becoming compulsive abusers (Aston-Jones & Druhan, 1999). A person who stops using cocaine does not experience heroin-like withdrawal symptoms. But cocaine can be highly addictive. The brain adapts to cocaine abuse in ways that upset its chemical balance, causing depression when cocaine is withdrawn. First, there is a jarring "crash" of mood and energy. Within a few days, the person enters a long period of fatigue, anxiety, paranoia, boredom, and **anhedonia** (an-he-DAWN-ee-ah: an inability to feel pleasure). Before long, the urge to use cocaine becomes intense. So, although cocaine does not fit the classic pattern of addiction, it is ripe for compulsive abuse. Even a person who gets through withdrawal may crave cocaine months or years later (Withers et al., 1995). If cocaine were cheaper, 9 out of 10 users would progress to compulsive abuse. In fact, rock cocaine ("crack," "rock," or "*roca*"), which is cheaper, produces very high abuse rates. Here are some signs of cocaine abuse (Pursch, 1983):

- *Compulsive use.* If cocaine is available—say, at a party—you can't say no to it.
- *Loss of control.* Once you have had some cocaine, you will keep using it until you are exhausted or the cocaine is gone.
- *Disregarding consequences.* You don't care if the rent gets paid, your job is endangered, your lover disapproves, or your health is affected, you'll use cocaine anyway.

Cocaine's capacity for abuse and social damage rivals that of heroin. Anyone who thinks she or he has a cocaine problem should seek advice at a drug clinic or a Cocaine Anonymous meeting. Quitting cocaine is extremely difficult. Nevertheless, three out of four cocaine abusers who remain in treatment do succeed in breaking their coke dependence (Simpson et al., 1999).

MDMA ("Ecstasy")

The drug MDMA (methylenedioxymethamphetamine, or "Ecstasy") is also chemically similar to amphetamine. In addition to producing a rush of energy, users say it makes them feel closer to others and heightens sensory experiences. Ecstasy causes brain cells to release extra amounts of serotonin. The physical effects of MDMA include dilated pupils, elevated blood pressure, jaw clenching, loss of appetite, and elevated body temperature (Braun, 2001). Although some users believe that Ecstasy increases sexual pleasure, it *diminishes* sexual performance, impairing erection in 40 percent of men and retarding orgasm in both men and women. (Zemishlany, Aizenberg, & Weizman, 2001).

Abuse

The use of Ecstasy in North America has dramatically increased in the last 5 years. At least 1 in 20 college students has tried Ecstasy. What are the consequences of such widespread use? Serious problems are beginning to surface. Every year, emergency room doctors see more MDMA cases, including a steady increase in MDMA-related deaths. Some of these incidents are caused by elevated body temperature (hyperthermia) or heart arrhythmias, which can lead to collapse. Ecstasy users at "rave" parties try to prevent overheating by drinking water to cool themselves. This may help to a small degree, but the risk of fatal heat exhaustion is real. MDMA can also cause severe liver damage, which can be fatal (Braun, 2001). In addition, Ecstasy users are more likely to abuse alcohol and other drugs, to neglect studying, to party excessively, and to engage in risky sex (Strote, Lee, & Wechsler, 2002).

It may take another decade before Ecstasy's full impact on health emerges. For now, we know that repeated use of MDMA damages serotonergic brain cells. This damage lasts for years. It leads to feelings of anxiety or depression that can persist for months after a person stops taking Ecstasy. In addition, heavy users typically do not score well on tests of mental functioning or memory (Morgan, 2000; Zakzanis & Young, 2001). Many of the drugs sold as "Ecstasy" are impure or adulterated with other substances. Despite its street name, Ecstasy may be a ticket to agony for many users (Kuhn & Wilson, 2001).

Caffeine

Caffeine is the most frequently used psychoactive drug in North America. (And that's not counting Seattle!) Caffeine stimulates the brain by blocking chemicals that normally inhibit or slow nerve activity (Julien, 2004). Its effects become apparent with doses as small as 50 milligrams, the amount found in about one-half cup of brewed coffee. Physically, caffeine causes sweating, talkativeness, tinnitus (ringing in the ears), and hand tremors (Nehlig, 2004). Psychologically, caffeine suppresses fatigue or drowsiness and increases feelings of alertness (Smith, Sturgess, & Gallagher, 1999). Some people have a hard time starting a day (or writing another paragraph) without it.

How much caffeine did you consume today? It is common to think of coffee as the major source of caffeine, but there are many others. Caffeine is found in tea, many soft drinks (especially colas), chocolate, and cocoa (■ Table 7.5). More than 2,000 nonprescription drugs also contain caffeine, including stay-awake pills, cold remedies, and many name-brand aspirin products.

Abuse

Are there any serious drawbacks to using caffeine? Frequent abuse of caffeine may result in an unhealthy dependence known as **caffeinism.** Insomnia, irritability, loss of appetite, chills, racing heart, and elevated body temperature are all signs of caffeinism. Many people with these symptoms drink 15 or 20 cups of coffee a day. However, even at lower dosages, caffeine can intensify anxiety and other psychological problems (Hogan, Hornick, & Bouchoux, 2002).

Caffeine has a variety of health risks. Caffeine encourages the growth of breast cysts in women, and it may contribute to bladder cancer, heart problems, and high blood pressure. Pregnant women should consider giving up caffeine entirely because of a suspected link between caffeine and birth defects. Pregnant women who consume six cups or more of coffee a day double the risk of having a miscarriage (Klebanoff et al., 1999).

It is customary to think of caffeine as a nondrug. But as few as 2.5 cups of coffee a day (or the equivalent) can be a problem. People who consume even such modest amounts may experience anxiety, depression, fatigue, headaches, and flu-like symptoms during withdrawal (Silverman et al., 1992). About half of all caffeine users show some signs of dependence (Hughes et al., 1998). It is wise to remember that caffeine *is* a drug and use it in moderation.

Nicotine

Nicotine is a natural stimulant found mainly in tobacco. Next to caffeine, it is the most widely used psychoactive drug (Julien, 2004).

How does nicotine compare with other stimulants? Nicotine is a potent drug. It is so toxic that it is sometimes used to kill insects! In large doses it causes stomach pain, vomiting and diarrhea, cold sweats, dizziness, confusion, and muscle tremors. In very large doses, nicotine may cause convulsions, respiratory failure, and death. For a nonsmoker, 50 to 75 milligrams of nicotine taken in a single dose could be lethal. (Chain-smoking about 17 to 25 cigarettes will produce this dosage.) Most first-time smokers get sick on one or two cigarettes. In contrast, a heavy smoker may inhale 40 cigarettes a day without feeling ill. This indicates that regular smokers build a tolerance for nicotine (Stolerman & Jarvis, 1995).

THE FAR SIDE® By GARY LARSON

The real reason dinosaurs became extinct

Abuse

How addictive is nicotine? A vast array of evidence confirms that nicotine is very addictive (Spinella, 2005). Among regular smokers who are 15 to 24 years old, 60 percent are addicted (Breslau et al., 2001). For many smokers, withdrawal from nicotine causes headaches, sweating, cramps, insomnia, digestive upset, irritability, and a sharp craving for cigarettes (Killen & Fortmann, 1997). These symptoms may last from 2 to 6 weeks and may be worse than heroin withdrawal. Indeed, relapse patterns are nearly identical for alcoholics, heroin addicts, cocaine abusers, and smokers who try to quit (Stolerman & Jarvis, 1995). A staggering 8 out of 10 people who quit smoking relapse within 1 year (Jarvik, 1995).

TABLE 7.5

Average Caffeine Content of Various Foods

Average Caffeine Content of Various Foods
Instant coffee (5 ounces), 64 milligrams
Percolated coffee (5 ounces), 108 milligrams
Drip coffee (5 ounces), 145 milligrams
Decaf. coffee (5 ounces), 3 milligrams
Black tea (5 ounces), 42 milligrams
Canned ice tea (17 ounces), 30 milligrams
Cocoa drink (6 ounces), 8 milligrams
Chocolate drink (8 ounces), 14 milligrams
Sweet chocolate (1 ounce), 20 milligrams
Colas (12 ounces), 50 milligrams
Soft drinks (12 ounces), 0–52 milligrams

Impact on Health

How serious are the health risks of smoking? A burning cigarette releases a large variety of potent *carcinogens* (car-SIN-oh-jins: cancer-causing substances). Lung cancer and other cancers caused by smoking are now considered the single most preventable cause of death in the United States and Canada. Among men, 97 percent of lung cancer deaths are caused by smoking. For women, 74

Anhedonia An inability to feel pleasure.

Caffeinism Excessive consumption of caffeine, leading to dependence and a variety of physical and psychological complaints.

The Everett Collection

Actress and comedienne Lily Tomlin, here shown portraying one of her comedic characters, Ernestine, once took up smoking for a role in a movie *(Shadows and Fog)* and developed a four-pack-a-day habit. As Tomlin's experience shows, the best way to avoid developing a nicotine addiction is to not begin smoking in the first place.

percent of all lung cancers are due to smoking. Here are some sobering facts about smoking:

Smoking Facts

- Every cigarette reduces a smoker's life expectancy by 7 minutes.
- Smoking is the number-one cause of deaths in the United States and Canada—more than the number of deaths from alcohol, drugs, car accidents, and AIDS combined.
- Worldwide, smoking kills 5 million people every year.
- In the United States alone, smoking-related medical costs total $50 billion a year. Taxpayers pick up the bill for 43 percent of this total.
- Forty percent of all smokers who develop throat cancer try smoking again.
- Each year, only one out of five smokers who tries to quit smoking succeeds.
- Some tobacco companies manipulate nicotine levels in their cigarettes to keep smokers addicted.
- Daily exposure to secondhand smoke at home or work causes a 24 to 39 percent increase in cancer risk to nonsmokers.

If you think smoking is harmless or that there's no connection between smoking and cancer, you're kidding yourself. The scientific link between tobacco smoking and cancer is undeniable. Skeptics please note: Wayne McLaren, who portrayed the rugged "Marlboro Man" in cigarette ads, died of lung cancer at age 51. By the way, urban cowboys and Skol bandits, the same applies to chewing tobacco and snuff. Users of smokeless tobacco run a four to six times higher risk of developing oral cancer. Smokeless tobacco also causes shrinkage of the gums, contributes to heart disease, and is as addicting as cigarettes (Christian & McDonald, 1987; Foreyt, 1987).

Smokers don't just risk their own health, they also endanger those who live and work nearby. Secondary smoke causes 20 percent of all lung cancers. Nonsmoking women who are married to smokers are 30 percent more likely to get lung cancer. It is particularly irresponsible of smokers to expose young children to secondhand smoke (Abramson, 1993).

Quitting Smoking

Is it better for a person to quit smoking abruptly or taper down gradually? For many years, smokers were advised to quit cold turkey. The current view is that quitting all at once isn't as effective as tapering off. Going cold turkey makes quitting an all-or-nothing proposition. Smokers who smoke even one cigarette after "quitting forever" tend to feel they've failed. Many figure they might just as well resume smoking. Those who quit gradually accept that success may take many attempts, spread over several months.

There are many ways in which smoking can be gradually reduced. For example, the smoker can (1) delay having a first cigarette in the morning and then try to delay a little longer each day, (2) gradually reduce the total number of cigarettes smoked each day, or (3) quit completely, but for just 1 week, then quit again, a week at a time, for as many times as necessary to make it stick

Mark C. Burnett/Stock, Boston

A study of fifth to twelfth graders found that those who smoke are less likely than nonsmokers to believe the health warning labels on cigarette packs (Cecil, Evans, & Stanley, 1996). Smokers in general are less likely to believe that smoking poses a serious risk to health.

BRIDGES

Behavioral self-management techniques can be very useful for breaking habits such as smoking.

See Chapter 8, pages 291–293, and Chapter 17, pages 596–601.

(Pierce, 1991). Gradually stretching the time periods between cigarettes is a key part of this program. Scheduled smoking apparently helps people learn to cope with the urge to smoke. As a result, people using this method are more likely to succeed. Also, they more often remain permanent nonsmokers than people using other approaches (Cinciripini et al., 1997).

Whatever approach is taken, quitting smoking is not easy (Abrams et al., 2003). Many people find that using nicotine patches or gum helps them get through the withdrawal period. Also, as we have noted, anyone trying to quit should be prepared to make several attempts before succeeding. But the good news is tens of millions of people have quit.

Downers—Sedatives, Tranquilizers, and Alcohol

How do downers differ from the stimulant drugs? The most widely used downers, or depressant drugs, are alcohol, barbiturates, gamma hydroxybutyrate (GHB), and benzodiazepine (ben-zoe-die-AZ-eh-peen) tranquilizers. These drugs are much alike in their effects. In fact, barbiturates and tranquilizers are sometimes referred to as "solid alcohol." Let's examine the properties of each.

Barbiturates

Barbiturates are sedative drugs that depress brain activity. Common barbiturates include amobarbital, pentobarbital, secobarbital, and Tuinal. On the street they are known as "downers," "blue heavens," "yellow jackets," "purple hearts," "goof balls," "reds," "pink ladies," "rainbows," or "tooies." Medically, barbiturates are used to calm patients or to induce sleep. At mild dosages, barbiturates have an effect similar to alcohol intoxication. Higher dosages can cause severe mental confusion or even hallucinations. Overdoses can easily cause coma or death. Barbiturates are often taken in excess amounts because a first dose may be followed by others, as the user becomes uninhibited or forgetful. Overdoses first cause a loss of consciousness. Then they severely depress brain centers that control heartbeat and breathing. The result is death (McKim, 1997).

GHB

Would you swallow a mixture of degreasing solvent and drain cleaner to get high? Apparently, a lot of people would. A mini-epidemic of GHB use has taken place in recent years, especially at nightclubs and raves. GHB ("goop," "scoop," "max," "Georgia Home Boy") is a central nervous system depressant that relaxes and sedates the body. Users describe its effects as being similar those of to alcohol. Mild GHB intoxication tends to produce euphoria, a desire to socialize, and a mild loss of inhibitions. GHB's intoxicating effects typically last 3 to 4 hours, depending on the dosage.

Abuse

At lower dosages, GHB can relieve anxiety and produce relaxation. However, as the dose increases, its sedative effects may result in nausea, a loss of muscle control, and either sleep or a loss of consciousness. Higher dosages can cause coma, breathing failure, and death. GHB inhibits the gag reflex, so some users choke to death on their own vomit. Potentially fatal doses of GHB are only three times the amount typically taken by users. This narrow margin of safety has led to numerous overdoses, especially when GHB is combined with alcohol. An overdose causes sleep or deep sedation from which the person cannot be awakened.

In March 2000, the U.S. government classified GHB as a controlled substance, making its possession a felony crime. Clinical evidence increasingly suggests that GHB is addictive and a serious danger to users. Two out of three frequent users have lost consciousness after taking GHB. Heavy users who stop taking GHB have withdrawal symptoms that include anxiety, agitation, tremor, delirium, and hallucinations (Miotto et al., 2001).

As if the preceding weren't enough reason to be leery of GHB, here's one more to consider: GHB is often manufactured in homes with recipes and ingredients purchased on the Internet. As mentioned earlier, it can be produced by combining degreasing solvent with drain cleaner (Falkowski, 2000). If you want to degrease your brain, GHB will do the trick.

Tranquilizers

A *tranquilizer* is a drug that lowers anxiety and reduces tension. Doctors prescribe benzodiazepine tranquilizers to alleviate nervousness and stress. Valium is the best-known drug in this family; others are Xanax, Halcion, and Librium. Even at normal dosages these drugs can cause drowsiness, shakiness, and confusion. When used at too high a dosage or for too long a time, benzodiazepines have strong addictive potential (McKim, 1997).

A drug sold under the trade name Rohypnol (ro-HIP-nol) has added to the problem of tranquilizer abuse. This drug, which is related to Valium, is cheap and ten times more potent. It lowers inhibitions and produces relaxation or intoxication. Large doses induce short-term amnesia and sleep. "Roofies," as they are known on the street, are odorless and tasteless. They have been used to spike drinks, which are given to the unwary. Drugged victims are then sexually assaulted or raped while they are unconscious (Navarro, 1995). (Be aware, however, that drinking too much alcohol is by far the most common prelude to rape.)

Abuse

Repeated use of barbiturates can cause physical dependence. Some abusers suffer severe emotional depression that may end in suicide. Similarly, when tranquilizers are used at too high a dosage or for too long a time, addiction can occur. Many people have learned the hard way that their legally prescribed tranquilizers are as dangerous as many illicit drugs (McKim, 1997).

Combining barbiturates or tranquilizers with alcohol is extremely risky. When mixed, the effects of both drugs are multiplied by a **drug interaction** (one drug enhances the effect of another).

Drug interaction A combined effect of two drugs that exceeds the addition of one drug's effects to the other.

Drug interactions are responsible for many hundreds of fatal drug overdoses every year. All too often, depressants are gulped down with alcohol or added to a spiked punch bowl. This is the lethal brew that left a young woman named Karen Ann Quinlan in a coma that lasted 10 years, ending with her death. It is no exaggeration to restate that mixing depressants with alcohol can be deadly.

Alcohol

Alcohol is the common name for ethyl alcohol, the intoxicating element in fermented and distilled liquors. Contrary to popular belief, alcohol is not a stimulant. The noisy animation at drinking parties is due to alcohol's effect as a *depressant.* As ● Figure 7.12 shows, small amounts of alcohol reduce inhibitions and produce feelings of relaxation and euphoria. Larger amounts cause ever-greater impairment of the brain until the drinker loses consciousness. Alcohol is also not an aphrodisiac. Rather than enhancing sexual arousal, it usually impairs performance, especially in males. As William Shakespeare observed long ago, drink "provokes the desire, but it takes away the performance."

Some people become aggressive and want to argue or fight when they are drunk. Others become relaxed and friendly. How can the same drug have such different effects? When a person is drunk, thinking and perception become dulled or shortsighted, a condition that has been called **alcohol myopia** (my-OH-pea-ah). Only the most obvious and immediate stimuli catch a drinker's attention. Worries and "second thoughts" that would normally restrain behavior are banished from the drinker's mind. That's why many behaviors become more extreme when a person is drunk. On college campuses, drunken students tend to have accidents, get into fights,

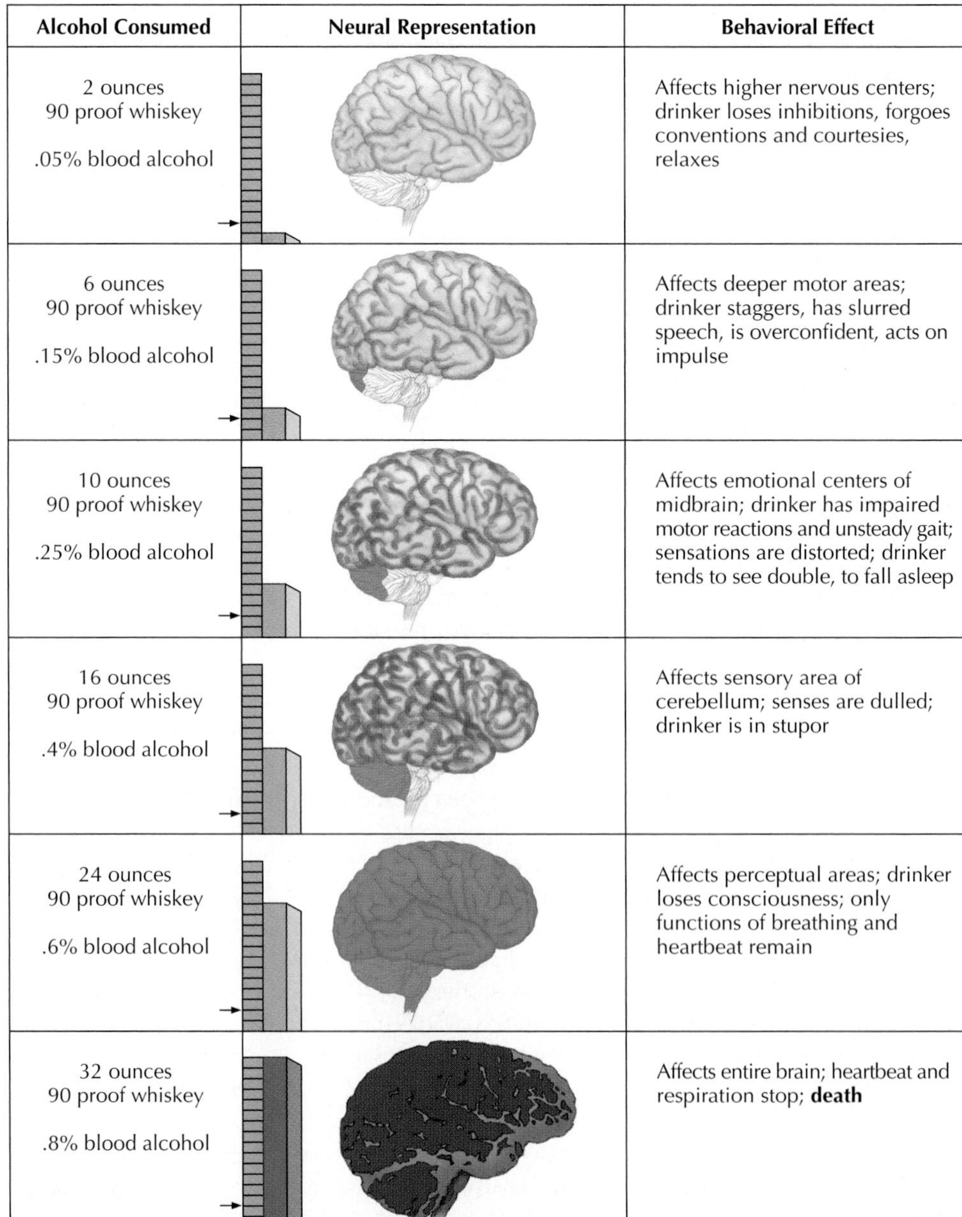

● **Figure 7.12** The behavioral effects of alcohol are related to blood alcohol content and the resulting suppression of higher mental function. Arrows indicate the typical threshold for legal intoxication in the United States. (From Jozef Cohen, *Eyewitness Series in Psychology,* p. 44. Copyright © Rand McNally and Company. Reprinted by permission.)

sexually assault others, or engage in risky sex. They also destroy property and disrupt the lives of students who are trying to sleep or study (Brower, 2002).

Abuse

Alcohol, the world's favorite depressant, breeds our biggest drug problem. An estimated 25 million people in the United States and Canada have serious drinking problems. In the United States alone, 75,000 people die every year from alcohol-related diseases and car crashes. The level of alcohol abuse among adolescents and young adults is alarming. Seventy percent of college students have engaged in binge drinking. For fraternity and sorority members, the figure jumps to 84 percent. **Binge drinking** is defined as downing five drinks or more in a short time (four drinks for women). Apparently, many students think it's entertaining to get completely wasted and throw up on their friends. However, binge drinking is a serious sign of alcohol abuse. It is responsible for 1,400 college student deaths each year and thousands of trips to the emergency room (Wechsler et al., 2002).

Binge drinking is of special concern because the brain continues to develop into the early twenties. Research has shown that teenagers and young adults who drink too much may lose as much as 10 percent of their brain power—especially their memory capacity (Brown et al., 2000). Such losses can have a long-term impact on a person's chances for success in life. In short, getting drunk is a slow but sure way to get stupid (Obernier et al., 2002; Wechsler & Wuethrich, 2002).

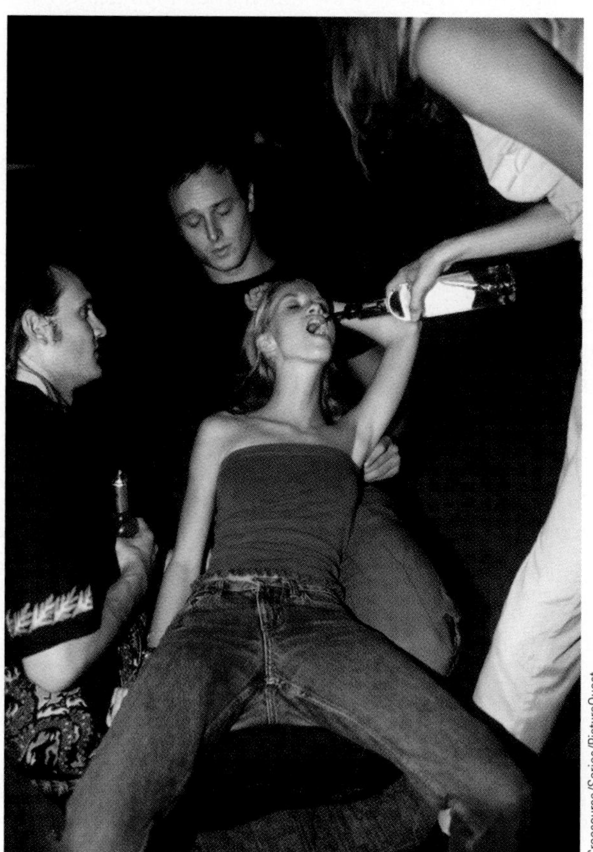

Creasource/Series/PictureQuest

Binge drinking and alcohol abuse have become serious problems among college students. Many alcohol abusers regard themselves as "moderate" drinkers, which suggests that they are in denial about how much they actually drink (Grant & Dawson, 1997).

At Risk

Children of alcoholics and those who have other relatives who abuse alcohol are at greater risk for becoming alcohol abusers themselves. The increased risk appears to be partly genetic. It is based on the fact that some people have stronger cravings for alcohol after they drink (Hutchison et al., 2002). Women also face some special risks. For one thing, alcohol is absorbed faster and metabolized more slowly by women's bodies. As a result, women get intoxicated from less alcohol than men do. Women who drink are also more prone to liver disease, osteoporosis, and depression. As few as three drinks a week may increase a woman's risk of breast cancer by 50 percent.

Positive reinforcement—drinking for pleasure—motivates most people who consume alcohol. What sets alcohol abusers apart is that they also drink to cope with negative emotions, such as anxiety and depression. That's why alcohol abuse increases with the level of stress in people's lives. People who drink to relieve bad feelings are at great risk of becoming alcoholics (Kenneth, Carpenter, & Hasin, 1998).

Recognizing Problem Drinking

What are the signs of alcohol abuse? Because alcohol abuse is such a common problem, it is important to recognize the danger signals of growing dependency. The path from a social drinker to an alcohol abuser to an alcoholic is often subtle. Jellinek (1960) gives these typical steps in the development of a drinking problem:

1. **Initial phase.** At first, the social drinker begins to turn more often to alcohol to relieve tension or to feel good. Four danger signals in this period that signal excessive dependence on alcohol are:

   Increasing consumption. The individual drinks more and more and may begin to worry about his or her drinking.

   Morning drinking. Morning drinking is a dangerous sign, particularly when it is used to combat a hangover or to "get through the day."

   Regretted behavior. The person engages in extreme behavior while drunk that leaves her or him feeling guilty or embarrassed.

   Blackouts. Abusive drinking may be revealed by an inability to remember what happened during intoxication.

2. **Crucial phase.** A crucial turning point comes as the person begins to lose control over drinking. At this stage, there is still some control over when and where a first drink is taken. But one drink starts a chain reaction, leading to a second and a third, and so on.

Alcohol myopia Shortsighted thinking and perception that occurs during alcohol intoxication.

Binge drinking Consuming five drinks or more in a short time (four drinks for women).

3. **Chronic phase.** At this point, the person is alcohol dependent. Victims drink compulsively and continuously. They rarely eat, they become intoxicated from far less alcohol than before, and they crave alcohol when deprived of it. Work, family ties, and social life all deteriorate. The person's self-drugging is usually so compulsive that when given a choice, the bottle comes before friends, relatives, employment, and self-esteem. The person is an addict.

The Development of a Drinking Problem

To add to this summary, the following lists will help you form a more detailed picture of how alcohol abuse develops.

Early Warnings

- You are beginning to feel guilty about your drinking.
- You drink more than you used to and tend to gulp your drinks.
- You try to have a few extra drinks before or after drinking with others.
- You have begun to drink at certain times or to get through certain situations.
- You drink to relieve feelings of boredom, depression, anxiety, or inadequacy.
- You are sensitive when others mention your drinking.
- You have had memory blackouts or have passed out while drinking.

Signals Not to Be Ignored

- There are times when you need a drink.
- You drink in the morning to overcome a hangover.
- You promise to drink less and are lying about your drinking.
- You often regret what you have said or done while drinking.
- You have begun to drink alone.
- You have weekend drinking bouts and Monday hangovers.
- You have lost time at work or school because of drinking.
- You are noticeably drunk on important occasions.
- Your relationship to family and friends has changed because of your drinking.

Perhaps the simplest way to identify problem drinkers is to ask a single question: "When was the last time you had more than five drinks (four for women) in a day?" Eighty-six percent of the people who answer "less than 3 months ago" are alcohol abusers (Williams & Vinson, 2001).

Moderated Drinking

Many social-recreational drinkers could do a far better job of managing their use of alcohol. Almost everyone has been to a party spoiled by someone who drank too much too fast. Those who avoid overdrinking have a better time, and so do their friends. But how do you avoid drinking too much? After all, as one wit once observed, "The conscience dissolves in alcohol." Psychologists Roger Vogler and Wayne Bartz (1982, 1992) provide a partial answer.

Vogler and Bartz observe that drinking makes you feel good while blood alcohol is rising and remains below a level of about 0.05. In this range, people feel relaxed, euphoric, and sociable. At higher levels they go from moderately intoxicated to thoroughly drunk. Later, as blood alcohol begins to fall, those who overdrink become sick and miserable. ■ Table 7.6 shows the approximate amount per hour that can be consumed without exceeding the 0.05 blood alcohol level. (Even at this level, driving may be impaired.) By pacing themselves, those who choose to drink can remain comfortable, pleasant, and coherent during a long social event. In short, if you drink, it might be wise to learn your "magic" number from Table 7.6.

It takes skill to regulate drinking in social situations, where the temptation to drink can be strong. If you choose to drink, here are some guidelines that may be helpful.

Paced Drinking

1. Think about your drinking beforehand and plan how you will manage it.
2. Drink slowly, eat while drinking, and make every other drink (or more) a nonalcoholic beverage.
3. Limit drinking primarily to the first hour of a social event or party. Pace your drinking using the information from Table 7.6.
4. Practice how you will politely but firmly refuse drinks.
5. Learn how to relax, meet people, and socialize without relying on alcohol.

Adapted from Vogler & Bartz, 1992.

Limiting your own drinking may help others as well. When people are tempted to drink too much, their main reason for stopping is that "other people were quitting and deciding they'd had enough" (Johnson, 2002).

Treatment

Treatment for alcohol dependence begins with sobering up the person and cutting off the supply. This phase is referred to as **detoxification** (literally, "to remove poison"). It frequently produces all the symptoms of drug withdrawal and can be extremely

TABLE 7.6

Drinking in Moderation

APPROXIMATE NUMBER OF DRINKS PER HOUR TO STAY BELOW 0.05 BLOOD ALCOHOL*

YOUR WEIGHT (POUNDS)	MALE	FEMALE
100	0.75	0.60
120	1.00	0.75
140	1.25	0.90
160	1.30	1.00
180	1.50	1.10
200	1.60	1.20
220	1.80	1.35

One drink = 12 ounces beer, 4 ounces wine, 2.5 ounces brandy, or 1.25 ounces 80 proof liquor.
*Table entries are approximate, owing to individual differences in metabolism, recency of meals, and other factors. Estimates are from tables prepared by Vogler and Bartz (1982, 1992).

unpleasant. The next step is to try to restore the person's health. Heavy abuse of alcohol usually causes severe damage to body organs and the nervous system. After alcoholics have "dried out" and some degree of health has been restored, they may be treated with tranquilizers, antidepressants, or psychotherapy. Unfortunately, the success of these procedures has been limited.

One mutual-help approach that has been fairly successful is Alcoholics Anonymous (AA). AA acts on the premise that it takes a former alcoholic to understand and help a current alcoholic. Participants at AA meetings admit that they have a problem, share feelings, and resolve to stay "dry" one day at a time. Other group members provide support for those struggling to end dependency. (Cocaine Anonymous and Narcotics Anonymous use the same approach.)

Eighty-one percent of those who remain in AA for more than 1 year get through the following year without a drink. However, AA's success rate may simply reflect the fact that members join voluntarily, meaning they have admitted they have a serious problem (Morgenstern et al., 1997). Sadly, it seems that alcohol abusers will often not face their problems until they have "hit rock bottom." If they are willing, though, AA presents a practical approach to the problem.

Two newer groups offer a rational, nonspiritual approach to alcohol abuse that better fits the needs of some people. These are Rational Recovery and Secular Organizations for Sobriety (SOS). Other alternatives to AA include medical treatment, group therapy, and individual psychotherapy (Institute of Medicine, 1990). There is a strong tendency for abusive drinkers to deny they have a problem. The sooner they seek help, the better.

Marijuana—What's in the Pot?

Marijuana and hashish are derived from the hemp plant *Cannabis sativa.* Marijuana ("pot," "herb," "weed") consists of the leaves and flowers of the hemp plant. Hashish is a resinous material scraped from *Cannabis* leaves. The main active chemical in marijuana is tetrahydrocannabinol (tet-rah-hydro-cah-NAB-ih-nol), or THC for short. THC is a mild **hallucinogen** (hal-LU-sin-oh-jin: a substance that alters sensory impressions).

Hallucinogens

The drug LSD (lysergic acid diethylamide or "acid") is perhaps the best-known hallucinogen. Even when taken in tiny amounts, LSD can produce hallucinations and psychotic-like disturbances in thinking and perception. Two other common hallucinogens are mescaline (peyote) and psilocybin ("magic mushrooms"). Incidentally, the drug PCP (phencyclidine or "angel dust") can have hallucinogenic effects. However, PCP, which is an anesthetic, also has stimulant and depressant effects. This potent combination can cause extreme agitation, disorientation, violence—and too often, tragedy. All of the hallucinogens, including marijuana, typically affect neurotransmitter systems that carry messages between brain cells (Julien, 2004).

Artists have tried at times to capture the effects of hallucinogens. Here, the artist depicts visual experiences he had while under the influence of LSD.

Marijuana

Marijuana's psychological effects include a sense of euphoria or well-being, relaxation, altered time sense, and perceptual distortions. At high dosages, however, paranoia, hallucinations, and delusions can occur (Palfai & Jankiewicz, 1991). All considered, marijuana intoxication is relatively subtle by comparison to drugs such as LSD or alcohol (Kelly et al., 1990). Despite this, driving a car while high on marijuana can be extremely hazardous. As a matter of fact, driving under the influence of any intoxicating drug is dangerous.

No overdose deaths from marijuana have been reported. However, marijuana cannot be considered harmless. Particularly worrisome is the fact that THC accumulates in the body's fatty tissues, especially in the brain and reproductive organs. Even if a person smokes marijuana just once a week, the body is never entirely free of THC. Scientists have located a specific receptor site on the surface of brain cells where THC binds to produce its effects (● Figure 7.13). These receptor sites are found in large numbers in the cerebral cortex, which is the seat of human consciousness (Matsuda et al., 1990). In addition, THC receptors are found in areas involved in the control of skilled movement. Naturally occurring chemicals similar to THC may help the brain cope with pain and stress. However, when THC is used as a drug, high dosages can cause paranoia, hallucinations, and dizziness (Julien, 2004).

Detoxification In the treatment of alcoholism, the withdrawal of the patient from alcohol.

Hallucinogen A substance that alters or distorts sensory impressions.

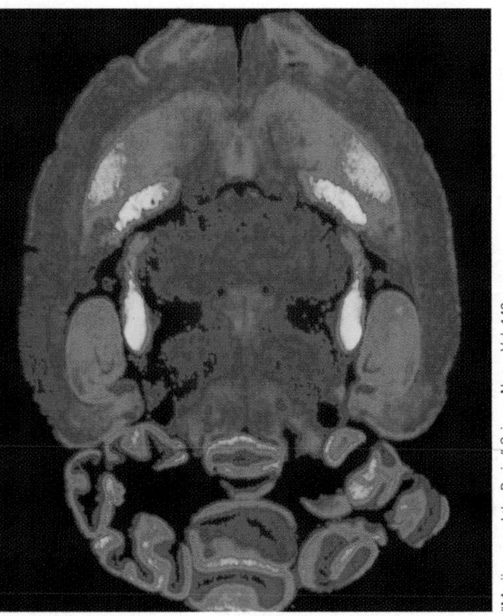

"Marijuana and the Brain," Science News, Vol. 143

● **Figure 7.13** This thin slice of a rat's brain has been washed with a radioactive THC-like drug. Yellowish areas show where the brain is rich in THC receptors. In addition to the cortex, or outer layer of the brain, THC receptors are found in abundance in areas involved in the control of coordinated movement. Naturally occurring chemicals similar to THC may help the brain cope with pain and stress. However, when THC is used as a drug, large doses can cause paranoia, hallucinations, and dizziness (Julien, 2004).

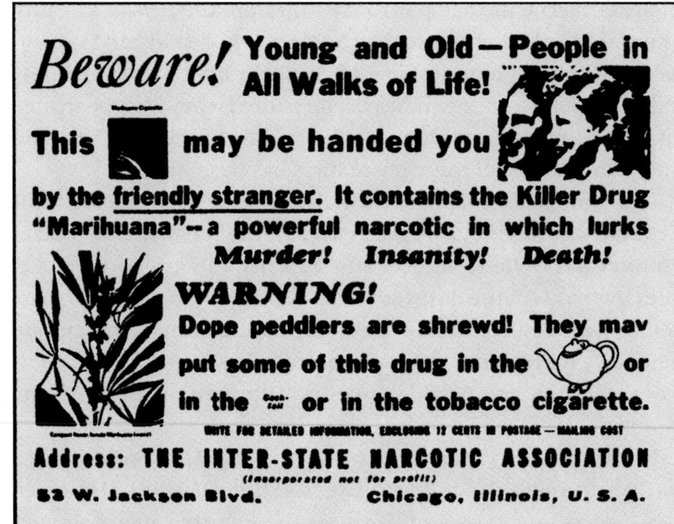

Courtesy of Dr. Lester Grinspoon/Harvard Medical School

An outdated antimarijuana poster demonstrates the kind of misinformation that has long been attached to this drug. Research has finally begun to sort out what risks are associated with use of marijuana.

Does marijuana produce physical dependence? Studies of long-term heavy users of marijuana in Jamaica, Greece, and Costa Rica failed to find any physical dependence (Carter, 1980; Rubin & Comitas, 1975; Stefanis et al., 1977). Marijuana's potential for abuse lies primarily in the realm of psychological dependence, not physical addiction. Nevertheless, frequent users of marijuana find it very difficult to quit, so dependence is a risk (Budney et al., 1999; Haney et al., 1999).

Dangers of Marijuana Use

There have been very alarming reports in the press about the dangers of marijuana. Are they accurate? In the past it was widely reported that marijuana causes brain damage, genetic damage, and a loss of motivation. Each of these charges can be criticized for being based on poorly done or inconclusive research. But that doesn't mean that marijuana gets a clean bill of health. For about a day after a person smokes marijuana, his or her attention, coordination, and short-term memory are impaired (Pope, Gruber, & Yurgelun-Todd, 1995). Frequent marijuana users show small declines in learning, memory, attention, and thinking abilities (Solowij et al., 2002). When surveyed at age 29, nonusers are healthier, earn more, and are more satisfied with their lives than people who smoke marijuana regularly (Ellickson, Martino, & Collins, 2004).

People who smoke five or more joints a week score 4 points lower on IQ tests. This is enough to dull their learning capacity. In fact, many people who have stopped using marijuana say they quit because they were bothered by short-term memory loss and concentration problems. Fortunately, IQ scores and other cognitive measures rebound in about a month after a person quits using marijuana (Fried et al., 2002; Grant et al., 2001). In other words, people who smoke dope may act like dopes, but if they quit, there's a good chance they will regain their mental abilities.

Health Risks

After many years of conflicting information, some of marijuana's health hazards are also being clarified. Marijuana's long-term effects include the following health risks:

1. In regular users, marijuana causes precancerous changes in lung cells. At present, no direct link between marijuana and lung cancer has been proved, but it is suspected. Marijuana smoke contains 50 percent more cancer-causing hydrocarbons and 16 times more tar than tobacco smoke does. Thus, smoking several "joints" a week may be the equivalent of smoking a dozen cigarettes a day (Barsky et al., 1998).
2. Marijuana temporarily lowers sperm production in males, and users produce more abnormal sperm. This could be a problem for a man who is marginally fertile and wants to have a family (Schuel et al., 1999).
3. In experiments with female monkeys, THC causes abnormal menstrual cycles and disrupts ovulation. Other animal studies show that THC causes a higher rate of miscarriages and that it can reach the developing fetus. As is true for so many other drugs, it appears that marijuana should be avoided during pregnancy.
4. THC can suppress the body's immune system, increasing the risk of disease.
5. In animals, marijuana causes genetic damage within cells of the body. It is not known to what extent this happens in humans, but it does suggest that marijuana can be detrimental to health.

6. Activity levels in the cerebellum are lower than normal in marijuana abusers. This may explain why chronic marijuana users tend to show some loss of coordination (Volkow et al., 1996).
7. There is some evidence that THC damages parts of the brain important for memory (Chan et al., 1998).
8. Children whose mothers smoked marijuana during pregnancy show lowered ability to succeed in challenging, goal-oriented activities (Fried & Smith, 2001).

When the preceding findings are compared with the studies of veteran marijuana users, it is clear that no one can say with certainty that marijuana is extremely harmful or completely safe. Although much is still unknown, marijuana appears to be in a class with two other potent drugs—tobacco and alcohol. Only future research will tell for sure "what's in the pot."

A Look Ahead

Of the many states of consciousness we have discussed, dreaming remains one of the most familiar—and the most surprising. Are there lessons to be learned from dreams? What personal insights lie hidden in the ebb and flow of dream images? The Psychology in Action section probes such questions.

KNOWLEDGE BUILDER

Psychoactive Drugs

REFLECT

What legal drugs did you use in the last year? Did any have psychoactive properties? How do psychoactive drugs differ from other substances in their potential for abuse?

LEARNING CHECK

1. Which of the drugs listed below are known to cause a physical dependence?
   a. heroin
   b. morphine
   c. codeine
   d. methadone
   e. barbiturates
   f. alcohol
   g. caffeine
   h. amphetamines
   i. nicotine
   j. cocaine
   k. GHB
2. Hyperthermia, heart arrhythmias, and severe liver damage are major risks in the use of
   a. marijuana
   b. benzodiazepine
   c. MDMA
   d. GHB
3. Cocaine is very similar to which of the following in its effects on the central nervous system?
   a. Seconal
   b. codeine
   c. cannabis
   d. amphetamine
4. Drug interaction is a special danger when a person combines
   a. marijuana and amphetamine
   b. barbiturates and alcohol
   c. alcohol and cocaine
   d. marijuana and THC
5. One drink starts a chain reaction leading to a second and a third in the crucial phase of problem drinking. T or F?
6. Treatment for alcohol dependence begins with sobering up the person and cutting off the supply. This is referred to as
   a. "hitting bottom"
   b. the crucial phase
   c. detoxification
   d. clinical anhedonia
7. Addictive drugs stimulate the brain's reward circuitry by affecting
   a. neurotransmitters
   b. alpha waves
   c. tryptophan levels
   d. delta spindles

CRITICAL THINKING

8. The U.S. government, which helps fund antismoking campaigns and smoking-related health research, also continues to subsidize tobacco growers. Can you explain this contradiction?
9. Why do you think there is such a contrast between the laws regulating marijuana and those regulating alcohol and tobacco?

Answers: **1.** All but g **2.** c **3.** d **4.** b **5.** T **6.** c **7.** a **8.** Neither can we. **9.** Drug laws in Western societies reflect cultural values and historical patterns of use. Inconsistencies in the law often cannot be justified on the basis of pharmacology, health risks, or abuse potential.

PSYCHOLOGY IN ACTION

Exploring and Using Dreams

At one time or another, almost everyone has had a dream that seemed to have deep meaning. What strategies do psychologists use to interpret dreams? Let's start with Sigmund Freud's approach.

To unlock dreams, Freud identified four **dream processes**, or mental filters, that disguise the meanings of dreams. The first is **condensation**, in which several people, objects, or events are combined into a single dream image. A dream character that looks like a teacher, acts like your father, talks like your mother, and is dressed like your employer might be a condensation of authority figures in your life.

Displacement is a second way of disguising dream content. Displacement may cause important emotions or actions of a dream to be redirected toward safe or seemingly unimportant images. Thus, a student angry at his parents might dream of accidentally wrecking their car instead of directly attacking them.

A third dream process is **symbolization**. As mentioned earlier, Freud believed that dreams are often expressed in images that are symbolic rather than literal. That's why it helps to ask what feelings or ideas a dream image might symbolize. Let's say, for example, that a student dreams of coming to class naked. A literal interpretation would be that the student is an exhibitionist. A more likely symbolic meaning is that the student feels vulnerable or unprepared in the class.

Secondary elaboration is the fourth method by which dream meanings are disguised. **Secondary elaboration** is the tendency to make a dream more logical and to add details when remembering it. The fresher a dream memory is, the more useful it is likely to be.

Courtesy of Maryanne Mott

Dream images may contain symbolic messages, as well as literal meanings. If you find yourself wearing a mask in a dream, for instance, it could relate to important roles that you play at school, work, or home. It could also mean that you want to hide or that you are looking forward to a costume party. To accurately interpret a dream, it is important to learn your own "vocabulary" of dream images and meanings. Keeping a dream diary is the first step toward gaining valuable insights.

Looking for condensation, displacement, symbolization, and secondary elaboration may help you unlock your dreams. But there are other techniques that may be more effective. Dream theorist Calvin Hall (1974a) preferred to think of dreams as plays and the dreamer as a playwright. Hall admitted that dream images and ideas tend to be more primitive than waking thoughts. Nevertheless, much can be learned by simply considering the *setting, cast of characters, plot,* and *emotions* portrayed in a dream.

Another dream theorist, Rosalind Cartwright, suggests that dreams are primarily "feeling statements." According to her, the overall *emotional tone* (underlying mood) of a dream is a major clue to its meaning. Is the dream comical, threatening, joyous, or depressing? Were you lonely, jealous, frightened, in love, or angry? Cartwright believes that exploring everyday dream life can be a source of personal enrichment and personal growth (Cartwright & Lamberg, 1992).

In many ways, dreams can be thought of as messages *from* yourself *to* yourself. Thus, the way to understand dreams is to remember them, write them down, look for the messages they contain, and become deeply acquainted with *your own* symbol system. Here's how.

How to Catch a Dream

1. Before retiring, plan to remember your dreams. Keep a pen and paper or a tape recorder beside your bed.
2. If possible, arrange to awaken gradually without an alarm. Natural awakening almost always follows soon after a REM period.
3. If you rarely remember your dreams, you may want to set an alarm clock to go off an hour before you usually awaken. Although less desirable than awakening naturally, this may let you catch a dream.
4. Upon awakening, lie still and review the dream images with your eyes closed. Try to recall as many details as possible.

5. If you can, make your first dream record (whether by writing or by tape) with your eyes closed. Opening your eyes will disrupt dream recall.
6. Review the dream again and record as many additional details as you can remember. Dream memories disappear quickly. Be sure to describe feelings as well as the plot, characters, and actions of the dream.
7. Put your dreams into a permanent dream diary. Keep dreams in chronological order and review them periodically. This procedure will reveal recurrent themes, conflicts, and emotions. It almost always produces valuable insights.
8. Remember, a number of drugs suppress dreaming (see ■ Table 7.7).

Dream Work

Because each dream has several possible meanings or levels of meaning, there is no fixed way to work with it. Telling the dream to others and discussing its meaning can be a good start. Describing it may help you relive some of the feelings in the dream. Also, family members or friends may be able to offer interpretations to which you would be blind. Watch for verbal or visual puns and other playful elements in dreams. For example, if you dream that you are in a wrestling match and your arm is pinned behind your back, it may mean that you feel someone is "twisting your arm" in real life.

The meaning of most dreams will yield to a little detective work. Rosalind Cartwright suggests asking a series of questions about dreams you would like to understand (Cartwright & Lamberg, 1992).

Probing Dreams

1. Who was in the dream? Do you recognize any of the characters?
2. What was happening? Were you active in the dream or watching it transpire? Did someone else do something to you?
3. Where did the action of the dream take place? Have you seen the setting or any part of it in real life, or was it a fantasy scene?
4. What was the time frame? What was your age in the dream?
5. Who is responsible for what happened in the dream?
6. Who are you in your dreams? Are you someone you would like to be or someone you'd rather not be?

If you still have trouble seeing the meaning of a dream, you may find it helpful to use a technique developed by Fritz Perls. Perls, the originator of Gestalt therapy, considered most dreams special messages about what's missing in our lives, what we avoid doing, or feelings that need to be "re-owned." Perls believed that dreams are a way of filling in gaps in personal experience (Perls, 1969).

An approach that Perls found helpful is to "take the part of" or "speak for" each of the characters and objects in the dream. In other words, if you dream about a strange man standing behind a doorway, you would speak aloud to the man, then answer for him. To use Perls's method, you would even speak for the door, perhaps saying something like, "I am a barrier. I keep you safe, but I also keep you locked inside. The stranger has something to tell you. You must risk opening me to learn it."

TABLE 1.1

Effects of Selected Drugs on Dreaming

DRUG	EFFECT ON REM SLEEP
Alcohol	Decrease
Amphetamines	Decrease
Barbiturates	Decrease
Caffeine	None
Cocaine	Decrease
Ecstasy	Decrease (by interrupting sleep)
LSD	Slight increase
Marijuana	Slight decrease or no effect
Opiates	Decrease
Valium	Decrease

A particularly interesting dream exercise is to continue a dream as waking fantasy so that it may be concluded or carried on to a more meaningful ending. As the world of dreams and your personal dream language become more familiar, you will doubtless find many answers, paradoxes, intuitions, and insights into your own behavior.

Using Your Dreams

Creative people tend to remember more dreams (Schredl, 1995). It could be that such people just pay more attention to their dreams. But dream theorist Gordon Globus (1987) believes that dreams make a major contribution to creativity. Globus points out that some of our most creative moments take place during dreaming. Even unimaginative people may create amazing worlds each night in their dreams. For many of us, this rich ability to create is lost in the daily rush of sensory input. How might we tap the creative power of dreams that is so easily lost during waking?

Dreams and Creativity

History is full of cases where dreams have been a pathway to creativity and discovery. A striking example is provided by Dr. Otto Loewi, a pharmacologist and winner of a Nobel prize. Loewi had spent years studying the chemical transmission of nerve impulses. A tremendous breakthrough in his research came when he dreamed of an experiment 3 nights in a row. The first 2 nights he woke up and scribbled the experiment on a pad. But the next morning, he couldn't tell what the notes meant. On the third night, he got up after having the dream. This time, instead of making notes he went straight to his laboratory and performed the crucial experiment. Loewi later said that if the experiment had occurred to him while awake he would have rejected it.

Dream processes Mental filters that hide the true meanings of dreams.

Condensation Combining several people, objects, or events into a single dream image.

Displacement Directing emotions or actions toward safe or unimportant dream images.

Symbolization The nonliteral expression of dream content.

Secondary elaboration Making a dream more logical and complete while remembering it.

Loewi's experience gives some insight into using dreams to produce creative solutions. Inhibitions are reduced during dreaming, which may be especially useful in solving problems that require a fresh point of view.

Being able to take advantage of dreams for problem solving is improved if you "set" yourself before retiring. Before you go to bed, try to think intently about a problem you wish to solve. Steep yourself in the problem by stating it clearly and reviewing all relevant information. Then use the suggestions listed in the previous section to catch your dreams. Although this method is not guaranteed to produce a novel solution or a new insight, it is certain to be an adventure. About half of a group of college students using the method for 1 week recalled a dream that helped them solve a personal problem (Barrett, 1993).

Lucid Dreaming

If you would like to press further into the territory of dreams, you may want to learn lucid dreaming, a relatively rare, but fascinating experience. During a **lucid dream** a person feels as if she or he is fully awake within the dream world and capable of normal thought and action. If you ask yourself, "Could this be a dream?" and answer "Yes," you are having a lucid dream (Blackmore, 1991).

Stephen LaBerge and his colleagues at the Stanford University Sleep Research Center have used a unique approach to show that lucid dreams are real and that they occur during REM sleep. In the sleep lab, lucid dreamers agree to make prearranged signals when they become aware they are dreaming. One such signal is to look up abruptly in a dream, causing a distinct upward eye movement. Another signal is to clench the right and left fists (in the dream) in a prearranged pattern. In other words, lucid dreamers can partially overcome REM sleep paralysis. Such signals show very clearly that lucid dreaming and voluntary action in dreams is possible (LaBerge, 1981, 1985; Moss, 1989).

How would a person go about learning to have lucid dreams? Dream researcher Stephen LaBerge found he could greatly increase lucid dreaming by following this simple routine: When you awaken spontaneously from a dream, take a few minutes to try to memorize it. Next, engage in 10 to 15 minutes of reading or any other activity requiring full wakefulness. Then while lying in bed and returning to sleep, say to yourself, "Next time I'm dreaming, I want to remember I'm dreaming." Finally, visualize yourself lying in bed asleep while in the dream you just rehearsed. At the same time, picture yourself realizing that you are dreaming. Follow this routine each time you awaken (substitute a dream memory from another occasion if you don't awaken from a dream). Researchers have also found that stimulation from the vestibular system tends to increase lucidity. Thus, sleeping in a hammock, a boat, or on a waterbed might increase the number of lucid dreams you have (Leslie & Ogilvie, 1996).

Why would anyone want to have more lucid dreams? Researchers are interested in lucid dreams because they provide a tool for understanding dreaming. Using subjects who can signal while they are dreaming makes it possible to explore dreams with firsthand data from the dreamer's world itself.

On a more personal level, lucid dreaming can convert dreams into a nightly "workshop" for emotional growth. Consider, for example, a recently divorced woman who kept dreaming that she was being swallowed by a giant wave. Rosalind Cartwright asked the woman to try swimming the next time the wave engulfed her. She did, with great determination, and the nightmare lost its terror. More important, her revised dream made her feel that she could cope with life again. For reasons such as this, people who have lucid dreams tend to feel a sense of emotional well-being (Wolpin et al., 1992). Dream expert Allan Hobson believes that learning to voluntarily enter altered states of consciousness (through lucid dreaming or self-hypnosis, for example) has allowed him to have enlightening experiences without the risks of taking mind-altering drugs (Hobson, 2001). So, day or night, don't be afraid to dream a little.

KNOWLEDGE BUILDER

Exploring and Using Dreams

REFLECT

Some people are very interested in remembering and interpreting their dreams. Others pay little attention to dreaming. What importance do you place on dreams? Do you think dreams and dream interpretation can increase self-awareness?

LEARNING CHECK

1. Which is *not* one of the four dream processes identified by Freud?
   a. condensation b. lucidity c. displacement d. symbolization
2. In secondary elaboration, one dream character stands for several others. T or F?
3. Calvin Hall's approach to dream interpretation emphasizes the setting, cast, plot, and emotions portrayed in a dream. T or F?
4. Rosalind Cartwright stresses that dreaming is a relatively mechanical process having little personal meaning. T or F?
5. Both alcohol and LSD cause a slight increase in dreaming. T or F?
6. "Taking the part of" or "speaking for" dream elements is a dream interpretation technique originated by Fritz Perls. T or F?
7. Recent research shows that lucid dreaming occurs primarily during NREM sleep or micro-awakenings. T or F?

CRITICAL THINKING

8. The possibility of having a lucid dream raises an interesting question: If you were dreaming right now, how could you prove it?

Answers: 1. b **2.** F **3.** T **4.** F **5.** F **6.** T **7.** F **8.** In waking consciousness, our actions have consequences that produce immediate sensory feedback. Dreams lack such external feedback. Thus, trying to walk through a wall or doing similar tests would reveal if you were dreaming.

Chapter in Review

What is an altered state of consciousness?

- States of awareness that differ from normal, alert, waking consciousness are called altered states of consciousness (ASCs). Altered states are especially associated with sleep and dreaming, hypnosis, sensory deprivation, and psychoactive drugs.
- Cultural conditioning greatly affects what altered states a person recognizes, seeks, considers normal, and attains.

What are the effects of sleep loss and changes in sleep patterns?

- Sleep is an innate biological rhythm essential for survival. Higher animals and people deprived of sleep experience involuntary microsleeps.
- Moderate sleep loss mainly affects vigilance and performance on routine or boring tasks. Extended sleep loss can (somewhat rarely) produce a temporary sleep-deprivation psychosis.
- Sleep patterns show some flexibility, but 7 to 8 hours remains average. The amount of daily sleep decreases steadily from birth to old age. Once-a-day sleep patterns, with a 2:1 ratio of waking to sleep, are most efficient for most people.

Are there different stages of sleep?

- Sleep occurs in four stages. Stage 1 is light sleep, and stage 4 is deep sleep. The sleeper alternates between stages 1 and 4 (passing through stages 2 and 3) several times each night.

How does dream sleep differ from dreamless sleep?

- There are two basic sleep states: rapid eye movement (REM) sleep and non-REM (NREM) sleep. REM sleep is much more strongly associated with dreaming than non-REM sleep is.
- Dreaming and REMs occur mainly during light sleep, similar to stage 1. Dreaming is accompanied by emotional arousal but relaxation of the skeletal muscles.
- People deprived of dream sleep show a REM rebound when allowed to sleep without interruption. However, total sleep loss seems to be more important than loss of a single stage.
- In addition to several other possible functions, REM sleep appears to aid the processing of memories.

What are the causes of sleep disorders and unusual sleep events?

- Sleepwalking and sleeptalking occur during NREM sleep. Night terrors occur in NREM sleep, whereas nightmares occur in REM sleep. Narcolepsy (sleep attacks) and cataplexy are caused by a sudden shift to stage 1 REM patterns during normal waking hours.
- Sleep apnea (interrupted breathing) is one source of insomnia and daytime hypersomnia (sleepiness).
- Apnea is suspected as one cause of sudden infant death syndrome (SIDS). Exposure to secondhand smoke is a major risk factor for SIDS. With only a few exceptions, healthy infants should sleep face up or on their sides.
- Insomnia may be temporary or chronic. When it is treated through the use of drugs, sleep quality is often lowered and drug-dependency insomnia may develop.
- Behavioral approaches to managing insomnia, such as sleep restriction and stimulus control, are quite effective.

Do dreams have meaning?

- Most dream content is about familiar settings, people, and actions. Dreams more often involve negative emotions than positive emotions.
- The Freudian, or psychodynamic, view is that dreams express unconscious wishes, frequently hidden by dream symbols.
- Many theorists have questioned Freud's view of dreams. For example, the activation-synthesis model portrays dreaming as a physiological process.

How is hypnosis done, and what are its limitations?

- Hypnosis is an altered state characterized by narrowed attention and increased suggestibility. (Not all psychologists agree that hypnotic effects require an alteration of consciousness.)
- Hypnosis appears capable of producing relaxation, controlling pain, and altering perceptions. Stage hypnotism takes advantage of typical stage behavior and uses deception to simulate hypnosis.

How does sensory deprivation affect consciousness?

- Extreme or unusual stimulus conditions often induce altered states of consciousness. A prime example is sensory deprivation.

Lucid dream A dream in which the dreamer feels awake and capable of normal thought and action.

- Prolonged sensory deprivation is stressful and disruptive. However, brief sensory deprivation can enhance sensitivity and promote relaxation. Sensory deprivation also appears to aid the breaking of long-standing habits and it facilitates creative thinking.

What are the effects of the more commonly used psychoactive drugs?

- A psychoactive drug is a substance that affects the brain in ways that alter consciousness. Most psychoactive drugs can be placed on a scale ranging from stimulation to depression.
- Drugs may cause a physical dependence (addiction), a psychological dependence, or both. The physically addicting drugs are alcohol, amphetamines, barbiturates, cocaine, codeine, GHB, heroin, methadone, morphine, nicotine, and tranquilizers. All psychoactive drugs can lead to psychological dependence.
- Drug use can be classified as experimental, recreational, situational, intensive, and compulsive. Drug abuse is most often associated with the last three.
- Stimulant drugs are readily abused because of the period of depression that often follows stimulation. The greatest risks are associated with amphetamines (especially methamphetamine), cocaine, MDMA, and nicotine, but even caffeine can be a problem. Nicotine includes the added risk of lung cancer, heart disease, and other health problems.
- Barbiturates and tranquilizers are depressant drugs whose action is similar to that of alcohol. The overdose level for barbiturates and GHB is close to the intoxication dosage, making them dangerous drugs. Mixing barbiturates, tranquilizers, or GHB and alcohol may result in a fatal drug interaction.
- Alcohol is the most heavily abused drug in common use today. The development of a drinking problem is usually marked by an initial phase of increasing consumption, a crucial phase, in which a single drink can set off a chain reaction, and a chronic phase, in which a person lives to drink and drinks to live.
- Marijuana is subject to an abuse pattern similar to alcohol. Studies have linked chronic marijuana use with lung cancer, various mental impairments, and other health problems.

How can dreams be used to promote personal understanding?

- Dreams may be used to promote self-understanding. Freud held that the meaning of dreams is hidden by condensation, displacement, symbolization, and secondary elaboration.
- Hall emphasizes the setting, cast, plot, and emotions of a dream. Cartwright's view of dreams as feeling statements and Perls's technique of speaking for dream elements are also helpful. Dreams may be used for creative problem solving, especially when dream control is achieved through lucid dreaming.

 Web Resources

Internet addresses frequently change. To find the sites listed here, visit www.thomsonedu.com/psychology/coon for an updated list of Internet addresses and direct links to relevant sites.

***Psychology: Gateways to Mind and Behavior* Website** Online quizzes, flash cards, and other helpful study aids for this text. www.thomsonedu.com/psychology/coon.

Alcoholics Anonymous (AA) Home page of Alcoholics Anonymous.

Circadian Rhythms Basic information about circadian rhythms and jet lag.

Cocaine Anonymous Offers advice and information on how to quit cocaine addiction.

Drugs and Behavior Links Comprehensive links to topics in drugs and behavior.

Marijuana Anonymous Offers advice and information on how to quit smoking marijuana.

Self-Scoring Alcohol Check Up A short quiz for identifying drinking problems.

SleepNet Information about sleep and sleep disorders, with many links to other sites.

Sudden Infant Death and Other Infant Death Information about SIDS, with links to related topics.

Antidrug.com Advice to parents and other adults about how to help children resist drug use.

The Reality of Hypnosis An extended discussion of hypnosis.

ThomsonNOW™ Go to www.thomsonedu.com to link to ThomsonNow, your online study tool. First take the **Pre-Test** for this chapter to get your **Personalized Study Plan,** which will identify topics you need to review and direct you to online resources. Then take the **Post-Test** to determine what concepts you have mastered and what you still need work on.

InfoTrac College Edition For recent articles related to the Psychology in Action feature, use Key Words search for DREAMS. Go to www.thomsonedu.com/psychology/coon.

 Interactive Learning 

***PsychNow!* Version 2.0 CD-ROM** Interact with the material with *PsychNow!'s* animations, video clips, experiments, and interactive assessments. For this chapter, go to *3c. Sleep and Dreaming* and *3d. Psychoactive Drugs* for more explanation on sleep, dreams, and drugs.

chapter

8

Conditioning and Learning

Jeff Greenberg/PhotoEdit

THEME:

The principles of learning can be used to understand and manage behavior.

Key Questions

What is learning?

How does classical conditioning occur?

Does conditioning affect emotions?

How does operant conditioning occur?

Are there different kinds of operant reinforcement?

How are we influenced by patterns of reward?

What does punishment do to behavior?

What is cognitive learning?

Does learning occur by imitation?

How does conditioning apply to practical problems?

Preview

What Did You Learn in School Today?

When one of your authors was in college, he discovered an intriguing flaw in the dorm plumbing: Flush a toilet while someone was taking a shower and the cold water pressure would suddenly drop. This caused the shower to become scalding hot. Naturally, the shower victim screamed in terror as his reflexes caused him to leap backward in pain. Soon he discovered that if *all* the toilets were flushed at once, the effects were multiplied many times over!

A toilet has to be one of the world's most uninspiring stimuli. But for a time, a whole flock of college students twitched involuntarily whenever they heard a toilet flush. Their reactions were the result of classical conditioning, a basic type of learning. Classical conditioning is one of the topics of this chapter.

Now, let's say that you are at school and you feel like you are "starving to death." You locate a vending machine and deposit your last two quarters to buy a candy bar. Then you press the button, and . . . nothing happens. Being civilized and in complete control, you press the other buttons, try the coin return, and look for an attendant. Still nothing. Your stomach growls. Impulsively, you give the machine a little kick (just to let it know how you feel). Then, as you turn away, out pops a candy bar plus 25 cents change. Once this happens, chances are good that you will repeat the "kicking response" in the future. If it pays off several times more, kicking vending machines may become a regular feature of your behavior. In this case, learning is based on operant conditioning (also called instrumental learning).

Classical and operant conditioning reach into every corner of our lives. Are you ready to learn more about learning? If so, read on!

What Is Learning—Does Practice Make Perfect?

Most behavior is learned. Imagine if you suddenly lost all you had ever learned. What could you do? You would be unable to read, write, or speak. You couldn't feed yourself, find your way home, drive a car, play the bassoon, or "party." Needless to say, you would be totally incapacitated. (Dull, too!) **Learning** is a relatively permanent change in behavior due to experience. Notice that this definition excludes temporary changes caused by motivation, fatigue, maturation, disease, injury, or drugs. Each of these can alter behavior, but none qualifies as learning.

Isn't learning the result of practice? It depends on what you mean by practice. Merely repeating a response will not necessarily produce learning. You could close your eyes and swing a tennis racket hundreds of times without learning anything about tennis. Reinforcement is the key to learning. **Reinforcement** refers to any event that increases the probability that a response will occur again. A response is any identifiable behavior. Responses may be observable actions, such as blinking, eating a piece of candy, or turning a doorknob. They can also be internal, such as having a faster heartbeat.

To teach a dog a trick, we could reinforce correct responses by giving the dog some food each time it sits up. Similarly, you could teach a child to be neat by praising him for picking up his toys. Learning can also occur in other ways. For instance, if a girl gets stung by a bee, she may learn to associate pain with bees and to fear them. In this case, the girl's fear is reinforced by the discomfort she feels immediately after seeing the bee. Later, you'll discover how such varied experiences lead to learning.

Antecedents and Consequences

Unlocking the secrets of learning begins with noting what happens before and after a response. Events that precede a response are called **antecedents.** For example, Ashleigh, age 3, has learned that when she hears a truck pull into the driveway, it means that Daddy is home. Ashleigh runs to the front door, where she gets a hug from her father. Effects that follow a response are **consequences.** The hug is what reinforces Ashleigh's tendency to run to the door. As this suggests, paying careful attention to the "before and after" of learning is a key to understanding it.

Classical Conditioning

Classical conditioning is based on what happens before we respond. It begins with a stimulus that reliably triggers a response. Imagine, for example, that a puff of air (the stimulus) is aimed at your eye. The air puff will make you blink (a response) every time. The eyeblink is a **reflex** (automatic, nonlearned response).

Now, assume that we sound a horn (another stimulus) just before each puff of air hits your eye. If the horn and the air puff occur together many times, what happens? Soon, the horn alone will make you blink. Clearly, you've learned something. Before, the horn didn't make you blink. Now it does. Similarly, if your mouth waters each time you eat a cookie, you may learn to salivate when you merely *see* a cookie, a picture of cookies, a cookie jar, or other stimuli that preceded salivation.

In **classical conditioning**, an antecedent stimulus that doesn't produce a response is linked with one that does (a horn is associated with a puff of air to the eye, for example). We can say that learning has occurred when the new stimulus will also elicit (bring forth) responses (● Figure 8.1).

Operant Conditioning

In **operant conditioning**, learning is based on the consequences of responding. A response may be followed by a reinforcer (such as food). Or by punishment. Or by nothing. These results determine whether a response is likely to be made again (see ● Figure 8.1). For example, if you wear a particular hat and get lots of compliments (reinforcement), you are likely to wear it more often. If people snicker, insult you, call the police, or scream (punishment), you will probably wear it less often.

Now that you have an idea of what happens in the two basic kinds of learning, let's look at classical conditioning in more detail.

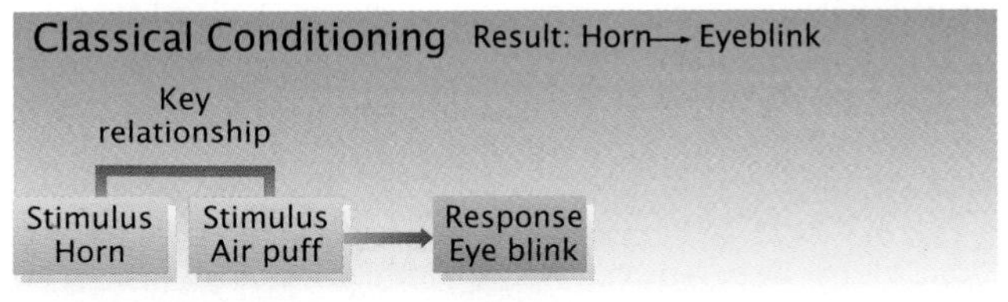

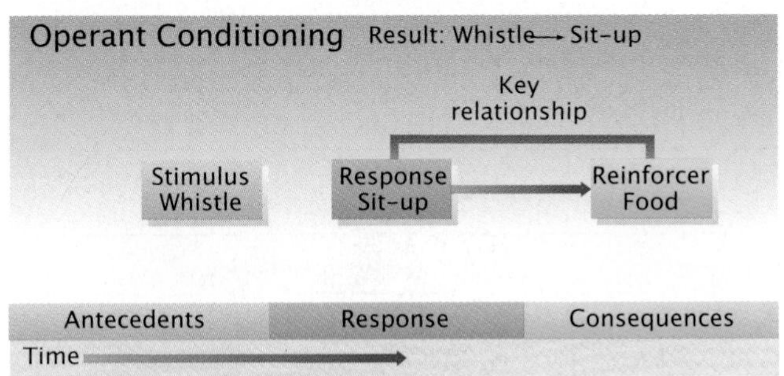

● **Figure 8.1** In classical conditioning, a stimulus that does not produce a response is paired with a stimulus that does elicit a response. After many such pairings, the stimulus that previously had no effect begins to produce a response. In the example shown, a horn precedes a puff of air to the eye. Eventually the horn alone will produce an eyeblink. In operant conditioning, a response that is followed by a reinforcing consequence becomes more likely to occur on future occasions. In the example shown, a dog learns to sit up when it hears a whistle.

Classical Conditioning—Does the Name Pavlov Ring a Bell?

How was classical conditioning discovered? At the beginning of the twentieth century, something happened in the lab of Russian physiologist Ivan Pavlov that brought him lasting fame: Pavlov's subjects drooled at him.

Actually, Pavlov was studying digestion. To observe salivation, he placed meat powder or some tidbit on a dog's tongue. After doing this many times, Pavlov noticed that his dogs were salivating *before* the food reached their mouths. Later, the dogs even began to salivate when they saw Pavlov enter the room. Was this misplaced affection? Pavlov knew better. Salivation is normally a reflex. For the animals to salivate at the mere sight of food, some type of learning must have occurred. Pavlov called it *conditioning* (● Figure 8.2). Because of its importance in psychology's history, it is now called *classical conditioning* (also known as *Pavlovian conditioning* or *respondent conditioning*).

● **Figure 8.2** An apparatus for Pavlovian conditioning. A tube carries saliva from the dog's mouth to a lever that activates a recording device (far left). During conditioning, various stimuli can be paired with a dish of food placed in front of the dog. The device pictured here is more elaborate than the one Pavlov used in his early experiments.

Learning Any relatively permanent change in behavior that can be attributed to experience.

Reinforcement Any event that increases the probability that a particular response will occur.

Antecedents Events that precede a response.

Consequences Effects that follow a response.

Reflex An innate, automatic response to a stimulus; for example, an eyeblink.

Classical conditioning A form of learning in which reflex responses are associated with new stimuli.

Operant conditioning Learning based on the consequences of responding.

Pavlov's Experiment

How did Pavlov study conditioning? After Pavlov observed that food made his dogs salivate, he began his classic experiments (see ● Figure 8.2). To begin, he rang a bell. At first, the bell was a neutral stimulus (the dogs did not respond to it by salivating). Immediately after Pavlov rang the bell, he placed meat powder on the dog's tongue, which caused reflex salivation. This sequence was repeated many times: bell, meat powder, salivation; bell, meat powder, salivation. Eventually (as conditioning took place), the dogs began to salivate when they heard the bell (● Figure 8.3). By association, the bell, which before had no effect, began to evoke the same response that food did. This was shown by sometimes ringing the bell alone. Then the dog salivated, even though no food had been placed in its mouth.

Psychologists use several terms to describe these events. The bell starts out as a **neutral stimulus** (NS). In time, the bell becomes a **conditioned stimulus** (CS) (a stimulus that, because of learning, will elicit a response). The meat powder is an **unconditioned stimulus** (US) (a stimulus innately capable of producing a response). Notice that the dog did not have to learn to respond to the US. Such stimuli naturally trigger reflexes or emotional reactions.

Because a reflex is innate, or "built in," it is called an **unconditioned** (nonlearned) **response** (UR). Reflex salivation was the UR in Pavlov's experiment. When Pavlov's bell also produced salivation, the dog was making a new response. Thus, salivation had become a **conditioned** (learned) **response** (CR) (see ● Figure 8.3). ■ Table 8.1 summarizes the important elements of classical conditioning.

Are all these terms really necessary? Yes, because they help us recognize similarities in various instances of learning. Let's summarize the terms using an earlier example:

Before Conditioning	**Example**
US → UR	Puff of air → eye blink
NS → no effect	Horn → no effect
After Conditioning	**Example**
CS → CR	Horn → eye blink

Now let's see if we can explain the shower and flushing toilet example described earlier. The unconditioned, or nonlearned, response was a reflex jump from the hot water. The unconditioned stimulus was the hot water. The conditioned stimulus was the sound of a flushing toilet. That is, the flushing sound was at first neutral and had no effect. But as a result of conditioning, it became capable of triggering a reflex. See "Coping with Chemo" for an example of how classical conditioning is being used to solve a clinical problem.

TABLE 8.1

Elements of Classical Conditioning

ELEMENT	SYMBOL	DESCRIPTION	EXAMPLE
Neutral stimulus	NS	A stimulus that does not evoke a response	Bell
Unconditioned stimulus	US	A stimulus innately capable of eliciting a response	Meat powder
Conditioned stimulus	CS	A stimulus that evokes a response because it has been repeatedly paired with an unconditioned stimulus	Bell
Unconditioned response	UR	An innate reflex response elicited by an unconditioned stimulus	Reflex salivation
Conditioned response	CR	A learned response elicited by a conditioned stimulus	Salivation

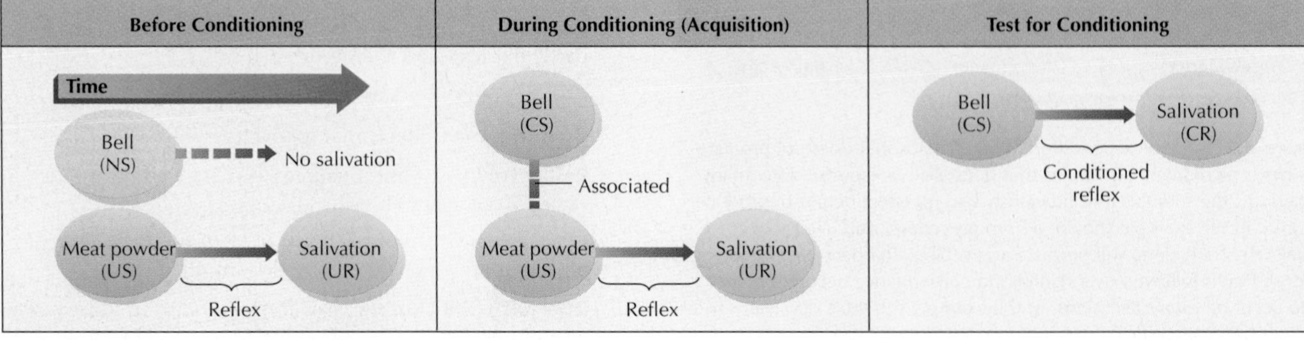

● **Figure 8.3** The classical conditioning procedure.

THE CLINICAL FILE

Coping with Chemo

Our hearts go out to children with cancer. Even the treatment, chemotherapy, makes them miserable because it causes nausea and vomiting. In a cruel twist, nausea can occur *before* a chemotherapy session begins. Typically, it is triggered by certain sights or tastes, like the sight of the treatment center or the taste of a food the child ate before an earlier chemotherapy session.

In classical conditioning terms, chemotherapy is a US that leads to nausea, which is a UR. The sight of the treatment center or the taste of food eaten before treatment is a neutral stimulus that is associated with nausea and vomiting, making it a CS. These sights or tastes can now elicit anticipatory nausea (a CR) even at times when the child doesn't receive chemotherapy (Chance, 2006).

In nature, many species are *biologically prepared* to associate specific locations and tastes with nausea. For example, animals that eat contaminated food get sick and vomit. Later, the same locations or tastes trigger anticipatory nausea and vomiting. These reactions discourage animals from eating potentially dangerous food.

Unfortunately, conditioned nausea can also affect young cancer patients. Imagine that Gita's parents lovingly give her pizza, her favorite meal, before she has her first chemotherapy session. The chemotherapy makes her nauseous and she vomits. From that time on, the taste of pizza makes her feel sick.

Is there any way to prevent conditioned nausea? No, but classical conditioning can provide some relief (Taylor, 2002). For instance, meals eaten before chemotherapy can be flavored with an unusual taste, such as peppermint. The unique flavor "attracts" the conditioning, so that other tastes don't become linked with nausea. In this way, Gita can continue to enjoy her favorite meal, pizza, during the course of her treatments (Bovbjerg et al., 1992).

Principles of Classical Conditioning—Teach Your Little Brother to Salivate

To observe conditioning, you could ring a bell and squirt lemon juice into a child's mouth. By repeating this procedure several times, you could condition the child to salivate to the bell. The child might then be used to explore other aspects of classical conditioning. Let's see how conditioning occurs.

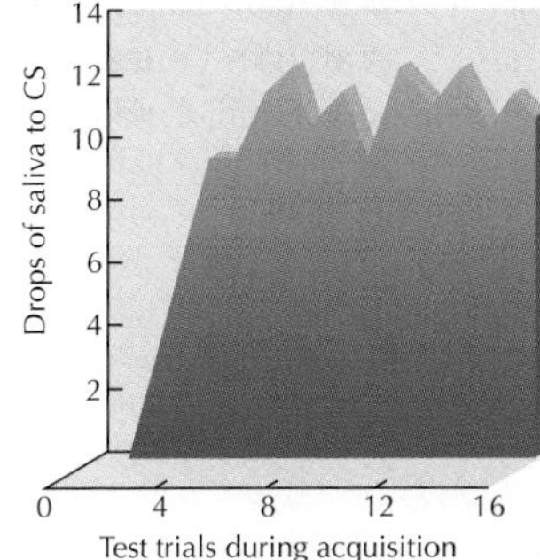

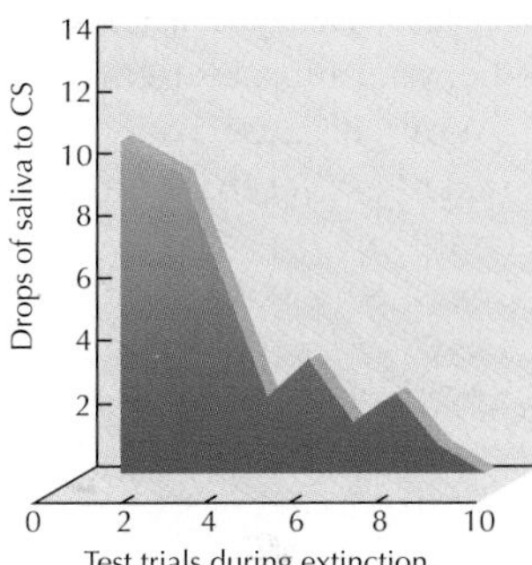

● **Figure 8.4** Acquisition and extinction of a conditioned response. (After Pavlov, 1927.)

Acquisition

During **acquisition**, or training, a conditioned response must be reinforced (strengthened) (● Figure 8.4). Classical conditioning is *reinforced* when the CS is followed by, or paired with, an unconditioned stimulus. For our child, the bell is the CS, salivating is the UR, and the sour lemon juice is a US. To reinforce salivating to the bell, we must link the bell with the lemon juice. Conditioning will be most rapid if the US (lemon juice) follows *immediately* after the CS (the bell). With most reflexes, the optimal delay between CS and US is from one-half second to about 5 seconds (Chance, 2006).

Higher Order Conditioning

Once a response is learned, it can bring about **higher order conditioning.** In this case, a well-learned CS is used to reinforce further learning. That is, the CS has become strong enough to be used like an unconditioned stimulus. Let's illustrate again with our salivating child.

As a result of earlier learning, the bell now makes the boy salivate. (No lemon juice is needed.) To go a step further, you could clap your hands and then ring the bell. (Again, no lemon juice

Neutral stimulus A stimulus that does not evoke a response.

Conditioned stimulus A stimulus that evokes a response because it has been repeatedly paired with an unconditioned stimulus.

Unconditioned stimulus A stimulus innately capable of eliciting a response.

Unconditioned response An innate reflex response elicited by an unconditioned stimulus.

Conditioned response A learned response elicited by a conditioned stimulus.

Acquisition The period in conditioning during which a response is reinforced.

Higher order conditioning Classical conditioning in which a conditioned stimulus is used to reinforce further learning; that is, a CS is used as if it were a US.

would be used.) Through higher order conditioning, the child would soon learn to salivate when you clapped your hands (● Figure 8.5). (This little trick could be a real hit with friends and neighbors.)

Higher order conditioning extends learning one or more steps beyond the original conditioned stimulus. Many advertisers use this effect by pairing images that evoke good feelings (such as people smiling and having fun) with pictures of their products. Obviously, they hope that you will learn, by association, to feel good when you see their products (Johnsrude et al., 1999; Priluck & Till, 2004).

Expectancies

Many psychologists believe that classical conditioning is related to information that might aid survival. According to this *informational view,* we look for associations among events. Doing so creates new mental **expectancies,** or expectations about how events are interconnected.

How does classical conditioning alter expectancies? Notice that the conditioned stimulus reliably predicts that the unconditioned stimulus is about to appear (Rescorla, 1987). During conditioning, the brain learns to *expect* that the US will follow the CS. As a result, the brain prepares the body to respond to the US. Here's an example: When you are about to get a shot with a hypodermic needle, your muscles tighten and there is a catch in your breathing. Why? Because your body is preparing for pain. You have learned to expect that getting poked with a needle will hurt. This

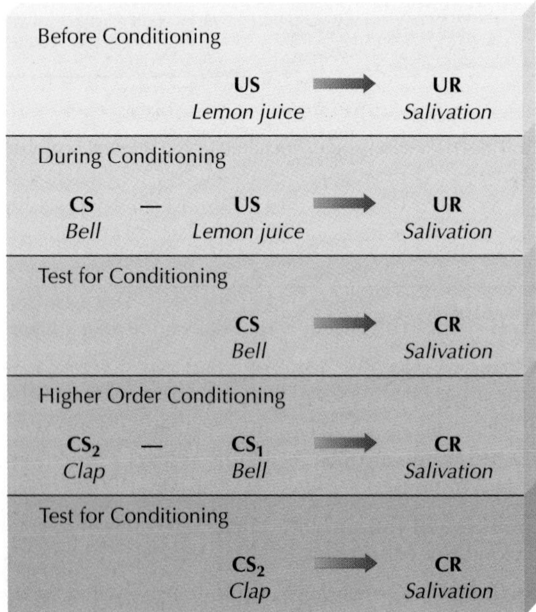

● **Figure 8.5** Higher order conditioning takes place when a well-learned conditioned stimulus is used as if it were an unconditioned stimulus. In this example, a child is first conditioned to salivate to the sound of a bell. In time, the bell will elicit salivation. At that point, you could clap your hands and then ring the bell. Soon, after repeating the procedure, the child would learn to salivate when you clapped your hands.

expectancy, which was acquired during classical conditioning, changes your behavior.

Extinction and Spontaneous Recovery

After conditioning has occurred, what would happen if the US no longer followed the CS? If the US never again follows the CS, conditioning will extinguish, or fade away. Let's return to the boy and the bell. If you ring the bell many times and do not follow it with lemon juice, the boy's expectancy that "bell precedes lemon juice" will weaken. As it does, he will lose his tendency to salivate when he hears the bell. Thus, we see that classical conditioning can be weakened by removing the contingency between the conditioned and unconditioned stimulus (see ● Figure 8.4). This process is called **extinction.**

If conditioning takes a while to build up, shouldn't it take time to reverse? Yes. In fact, it may take several extinction sessions to completely reverse conditioning. Let's say that we ring the bell until the child quits responding. It might seem that extinction is complete. However, the boy will probably respond to the bell again on the following day, at least at first. The return of a learned response after apparent extinction is called **spontaneous recovery.** It explains why people who have had car accidents may need many slow, calm rides before their fear of driving extinguishes.

Generalization

After conditioning, other stimuli similar to the CS may also trigger a response. This is called **stimulus generalization.** For example, we might find that our child salivates to the sound of a ringing telephone or doorbell, even though they were never used as conditioning stimuli.

It is easy to see the value of stimulus generalization. Consider the child who burns her finger while playing with matches. Most likely, lighted matches will become conditioned fear stimuli for her. But will she fear only matches? Because of stimulus generalization, she should also have a healthy fear of flames from lighters, fireplaces, stoves, and so forth. It's fortunate that generalization extends learning to related situations. Otherwise, we would all be far less adaptable.

As you may have guessed, stimulus generalization has limits. As stimuli become less like the original CS, responding decreases. If you condition a person to blink each time you play a particular note on a piano, blinking will decline as you play higher or lower notes. If the notes are *much* higher or lower, the person will not respond at all (● Figure 8.6). Stimulus generalization explains why many stores carry imitations of nationally known products. For many customers, positive attitudes conditioned to the real products tend to generalize to the cheaper knockoffs (Till & Priluck, 2000).

Discrimination

Let's consider one more idea with our salivating child (who by now must be ready to hide in the closet). Suppose we again condition the child, with a bell as the CS. As an experiment, we occasionally sound a buzzer instead of ringing the bell. However, the buzzer is never followed by the US (lemon juice). At first, the child

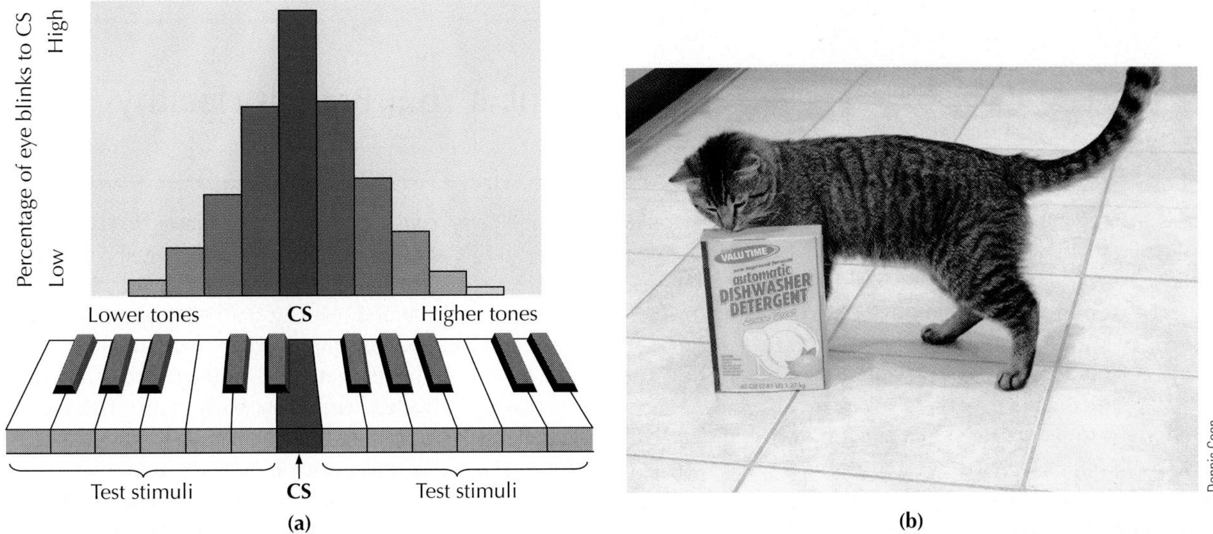

● **Figure 8.6** (a) Stimulus generalization. Stimuli similar to the CS also elicit a response. *(b)* This cat has learned to salivate when it sees a cat food box. Because of stimulus generalization, it also salivates when shown a similar-looking detergent box.

salivates when he hears the buzzer (because of generalization). But after we sound the buzzer several times more, the child will stop responding to it. Why? In essence, the child's generalized response to the buzzer has extinguished. As a result, he has learned to *discriminate,* or respond differently, to the bell and the buzzer.

Stimulus discrimination is the ability to respond differently to various stimuli. As an example, you might remember the feelings of anxiety or fear you had as a child when your mother's or father's voice changed to its you're-in-a-heap-of-trouble tone. (Or the dreaded give-me-that-PlayStation-Portable tone.) Most children quickly learn to discriminate voice tones associated with punishment from those associated with praise or affection.

Classical Conditioning in Humans—An Emotional Topic

How much human learning is based on classical conditioning? At its simplest, classical conditioning depends on reflex responses. As mentioned earlier, a reflex is a dependable, inborn stimulus-and-response connection. For example, your hand reflexively draws back from pain. Bright light causes the pupil of the eye to narrow. A puff of air directed at your eye will make you blink. (See "Blink If Your Brain Is Healthy.") Various foods elicit salivation. Any of these reflexes, and others as well, can be associated with a new stimulus. At the very least, you have probably noticed how your mouth waters when you see or smell a bakery. Even pictures of food may make you salivate (a photo of a sliced lemon is great for this).

Conditioned Emotional Responses

In addition to simple reflexes, more complex *emotional,* or "gut," responses may be linked to new stimuli. For instance, if your face reddened when you were punished as a child, you may blush now when you are embarrassed or ashamed. Or think about the effects of associating pain with a dentist's office during your first visit. On later visits, did your heart pound and your palms sweat *before* the dentist began?

Many *involuntary,* autonomic nervous system, responses ("fight-or-flight" reflexes) are linked with new stimuli and situations by classical conditioning. For example, learned reactions worsen many cases of hypertension (high blood pressure). Traffic jams, arguments with a spouse, and similar situations can become conditioned stimuli that trigger a dangerous rise in blood pressure (Reiff, Katkin, & Friedman, 1999).

Of course, emotional conditioning also applies to animals. One of the most common mistakes people make with pets (especially dogs) is hitting them if they do not come when called. Calling the animal then becomes a conditioned stimulus for fear and withdrawal. No wonder the pet disobeys when called on future occasions. Parents who belittle, scream at, or physically abuse their children make the same mistake.

Expectancy An anticipation concerning future events or relationships.

Extinction The weakening of a conditioned response through removal of reinforcement.

Spontaneous recovery The reappearance of a learned response after its apparent extinction.

Stimulus generalization The tendency to respond to stimuli similar to, but not identical to, a conditioned stimulus.

Stimulus discrimination The learned ability to respond differently to similar stimuli.

THE CLINICAL FILE

Blink If Your Brain Is Healthy

Dementia is a terrifying mental disorder. Imagine how it would feel to lose your ability to read, think, recognize family members, or do ordinary tasks. Dementia (duh-MEN-sha) is caused by various brain diseases, including many associated with aging (see Chapter 16). Eventually, people with dementia suffer major declines in memory, judgment, language, and thinking abilities. Yet in its early stages dementia may be nearly invisible.

It is important to detect dementia as soon as possible so that treatment can begin early. However, most tests for dementia are based on higher mental abilities, such as memory or reasoning. By the time a person has problems in these areas, dementia is already fairly advanced.

How else could dementia be detected? Psychologist Diana Woodruff-Pak has proposed a new way to tell if a person is in the early stages of dementia. While exploring the effects of aging on eyeblink conditioning (see, e.g., Bellebaum & Daum, 2004), Woodruff-Pak noticed that eyeblink conditioning was especially slowed in a dementia patient 6 years before other tests showed any signs of trouble. As a very basic form of learning, classical conditioning appears to be quite sensitive to changes in the hippocampus of the brain, one of the brain areas dementia attacks.

Eyeblink conditioning is simple to do and nonthreatening to patients. In the future, it may be a valuable addition to standard mental tests. In fact, it may eventually be possible to detect dementia "in the blink of an eye" (Woodruff-Pak, 2001).

Learned Fears

Some phobias (FOE-bee-ahs) are also based on emotional conditioning. A *phobia* is a fear that persists even when no realistic danger exists. Fears of animals, water, heights, thunder, fire, bugs, elevators, and the like, are common. Psychologists believe that many phobias begin as **conditioned emotional responses** (CERs). (A CER is a learned emotional reaction to a previously neutral stimulus.) People who have phobias can often trace their fears to a time when they were frightened, injured, or upset by a particular stimulus. Many spider phobias, for example, start in childhood. Just one bad experience in which you were frightened or disgusted by a spider may condition fears that last for years (de Jong & Muris, 2002; Merckelbach & Muris, 1997).

Stimulus generalization and higher order conditioning can spread CERs to other stimuli (Gewirtz & Davis, 1998). As a result, what began as a limited fear may become a disabling phobia (● Figure 8.7). However, a therapy called **desensitization** is now widely used to extinguish fears, anxieties, and phobias. This is done by gradually exposing the phobic person to feared stimuli while she or he remains calm and relaxed. Incidentally, desensitization works on animals, too. For example, dogs have been desensitized for fears of fireworks, thunder, airplanes, bees, hot-air balloons, and other frightening stimuli (Rogerson, 1997).

Undoubtedly, we acquire many of our likes, dislikes, and fears as conditioned emotional responses. As noted before, advertisers try to achieve the same effect by pairing products with pleasant images and music. So do many students on a first date.

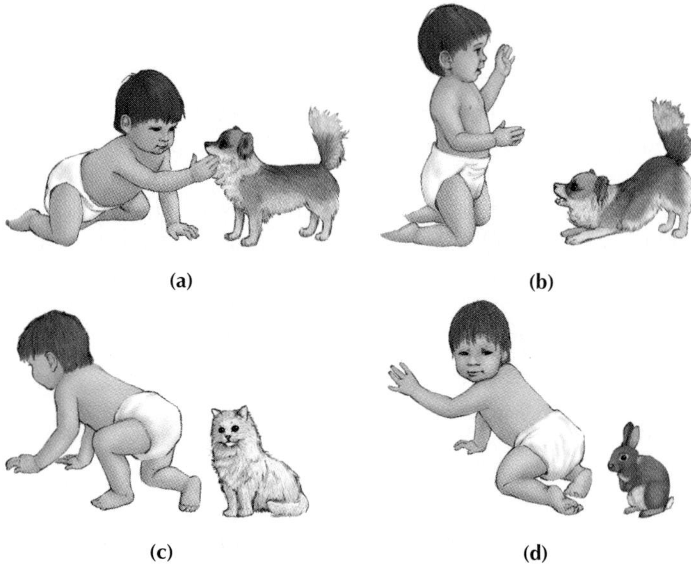

● **Figure 8.7** Hypothetical example of a CER becoming a phobia. Child approaches dog *(a)* and is frightened by it *(b)*. Fear generalizes to other household pets *(c)* and later to virtually all furry animals *(d)*.

BRIDGES

Desensitization is a type of behavior therapy. (Behavior therapists apply the principles of learning to change human behavior patterns.)

See Chapter 17, pages 579–580, for details.

Vicarious, or Secondhand, Conditioning

Conditioning also occurs indirectly, which adds to its impact on us. Let's say, for example, that you watch another person get an electric shock. Each time, a signal light comes on before the shock is delivered. Even if you don't receive a shock yourself, you will soon develop a CER to the light (Bandura & Rosenthal, 1966). Children who learn to fear thunder by watching their parents react to it have undergone similar conditioning.

Vicarious classical conditioning occurs when we learn to respond emotionally to a stimulus by observing another person's emotional reactions. Such "secondhand" learning affects feelings in many situations. For example, "horror" movies filled with screaming actors probably add to fears of snakes, caves, spiders, heights, and other terrors. If movies can affect us, we might expect the emotions of parents, friends, and relatives to have even more impact. How, for instance, does a city child learn to fear snakes and respond emotionally to mere pictures of them? Being told that "snakes are dangerous" may not explain the child's *emotional* response. More likely, the child has observed others reacting fearfully to the word *snake* or to snake images on television (Ollendick & King, 1991).

The emotional attitudes we develop toward foods, political parties, ethnic groups, escalators—whatever—are probably conditioned not only by direct experiences but vicariously as well. No one is born prejudiced—all attitudes are learned. Parents may do well to look in a mirror if they wonder how or where a child "picked up" a particular fear or emotional attitude (Mineka & Hamida, 1998).

KNOWLEDGE BUILDER

Classical Conditioning

REFLECT

US, CS, UR, CR—How will you remember these terms? First, you should note that we are interested in either a stimulus (S) or a response (R). What else do we need to know? Each S or R can be either conditioned (C) or unconditioned (U).

Can a stimulus provoke a response before any learning has occurred? If it can, then it's a US. Do you have to learn to respond to the stimulus? Then it's a CS.

Does a response occur without being learned? Then it's a UR. If it has to be learned, then it's a CR.

LEARNING CHECK

1. The concept of reinforcement applies to both
   a. antecedents and consequences
   b. neutral stimuli and rewards
   c. classical and operant conditioning
   d. acquisition and spontaneous recovery
2. Classical conditioning, studied by the Russian physiologist ____________________, is also referred to as ____________________ conditioning.
3. You smell the odor of cookies being baked and your mouth waters. Apparently, the odor of cookies is a __________ and your salivation is a __________.
   a. CR, CS c. consequence, neutral stimulus
   b. CS, CR d. reflex, CS
4. The informational view says that classical conditioning is based on changes in mental ____________________ about the CS and US.
5. After you have acquired a conditioned response, it may be weakened by
   a. spontaneous recovery c. removing reinforcement
   b. stimulus generalization d. following the CS with a US
6. When a conditioned stimulus is used to reinforce the learning of a second conditioned stimulus, higher order conditioning has occurred. T or F?
7. Psychologists theorize that many phobias begin when a CER generalizes to other, similar situations. T or F?
8. Three-year-old Josh sees his five-year-old sister get chased by a neighbor's dog. Now Josh is as afraid of the dog as his sister is. Josh's fear is a result of
   a. stimulus discrimination c. spontaneous recovery
   b. vicarious conditioning d. higher order conditioning

CRITICAL THINKING

9. Lately you have been getting a shock of static electricity every time you touch a door handle. Now there is a hesitation in your door-opening movements. Can you analyze this situation in terms of classical conditioning?

Answers: 1. c **2.** Pavlov, respondent **3.** b **4.** expectancies **5.** c **6.** T **7.** T **8.** b **9.** Door handles have become conditioned stimuli that elicit the reflex withdrawal and muscle tensing that normally follows getting a shock. This conditioned response has also generalized to other handles.

Operant Conditioning—Can Pigeons Play Ping-Pong?

Operant conditioning applies to all living creatures and explains much day-to-day behavior. The principles of operant learning are among the most powerful tools in psychology. You won't regret learning how to use them. Operant conditioning can be used to alter the behavior of pets, children, and other adults, and your own behavior, too.

As stated earlier, in **operant conditioning** (or instrumental learning) we associate responses with their consequences. The basic principle is simple: Acts that are reinforced tend to be repeated. Pioneer learning theorist Edward L. Thorndike called this the **law of effect** (the probability of a response is altered by the effect it has). Learning is strengthened each time a response is followed by a satisfying state of affairs. Think of the earlier example of the vending machine. Because kicking the machine had the effect of producing food and money, the odds of repeating the "kicking

Conditioned emotional response An emotional response that has been linked to a previously nonemotional stimulus by classical conditioning.

Desensitization Reducing fear or anxiety by repeatedly exposing a person to emotional stimuli while the person is deeply relaxed.

Vicarious classical conditioning Classical conditioning brought about by observing another person react to a particular stimulus.

Operant conditioning Learning based on the consequences of responding.

Law of effect Responses that lead to desirable effects are repeated; those that produce undesirable results are not.

response" increased. Likewise, if you like jokes, you are much more likely to tell a joke to several different friends if each of them laughs at it. If the first three people frown when they hear the joke, you may not tell it again.

Classical conditioning is passive. It simply "happens to" the learner when a US follows a CS. In operant conditioning, the learner actively "operates on" the environment. Thus, operant conditioning refers mainly to learning *voluntary* responses. For example, pushing buttons on a TV remote control is a learned operant response. Pushing a particular button is reinforced by gaining the result you desire, such as changing channels or muting an obnoxious commercial. (See ■ Table 8.2 for a further comparison of classical and operant conditioning.)

Positive Reinforcement

The idea that reward affects learning is certainly nothing new to parents (and other trainers of small animals). However, parents, as well as teachers, politicians, supervisors, and even you, may use reward in ways that are inexact or misguided. A case in point is the term *reward*. To be correct, it is better to say *reinforcer*. Why? Because rewards do not always increase responding. If you try to give licorice candy to a child as a "reward" for good behavior, it will work only if the child likes licorice. What is reinforcing for one person may not be for another. As a practical rule of thumb, psychologists define an **operant reinforcer** as any event that follows a response and increases its probability of occurring again (● Figure 8.8).

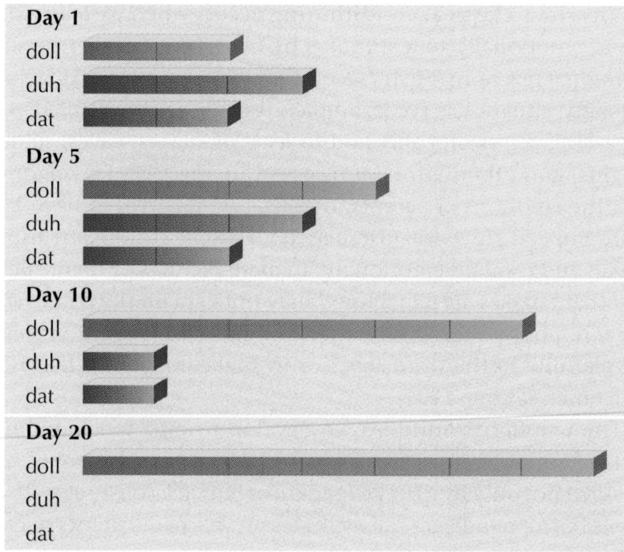

● **Figure 8.8** Assume that a child who is learning to talk points to her favorite doll and says either "doll," "duh," or "dat" when she wants it. Day 1 shows the number of times the child uses each word to ask for the doll (each block represents one request). At first, she uses all three words interchangeably. To hasten learning, her parents decide to give her the doll only when she names it correctly. Notice how the child's behavior shifts as operant reinforcement is applied. By day 20, saying "doll" has become the most probable response.

Acquiring an Operant Response

Many studies of instrumental learning have been done in a **conditioning chamber**, an apparatus designed to study operant conditioning in animals. This device is also called a Skinner box, after B. F. Skinner, who invented it (● Figure 8.9). A look into a typical Skinner box will clarify the process of operant conditioning.

The Adventures of Mickey Rat

A hungry rat is placed in a small cage-like chamber. The walls are bare except for a metal lever and a tray into which food pellets can be dispensed (see ● Figure 8.9).

Frankly, there's not much to do in a Skinner box. This increases the chances that our subject will make the response we want to reinforce, which is pressing the bar. Also, hunger keeps the animal motivated to seek food and actively *emit*, or freely give off, a variety of responses. Now let's take another look at our subject.

Further Adventures of Mickey Rat

For a while our subject walks around, grooms, sniffs at the corners, or stands on his hind legs—all typical rat behaviors. Then it happens. He places his paw on the lever to get a better view of the top of the cage. *Click!* The lever depresses, and a food pellet drops into the tray. The rat walks to the tray, eats the pellet, then grooms himself. Up and exploring the cage again, he leans on the lever. *Click!* After a trip to the food tray, he returns to the bar and sniffs it, then puts his foot on it. *Click!* Soon the rat settles into a smooth pattern of frequent bar pressing.

TABLE 8.2

Comparison of Classical and Operant Conditioning

	CLASSICAL CONDITIONING	OPERANT CONDITIONING
Nature of response	Involuntary, reflex	Spontaneous, voluntary
Reinforcement	Occurs *before* response (CS paired with US)	Occurs *after* response (response is followed by reinforcing stimulus or event)
Role of learner	Passive (response is *elicited* by US)	Active (response is emitted)
Nature of learning	Neutral stimulus becomes a CS through association with a US	Probability of making a response is altered by consequences that follow it
Learned expectancy	US will follow CS	Response will have a specific effect

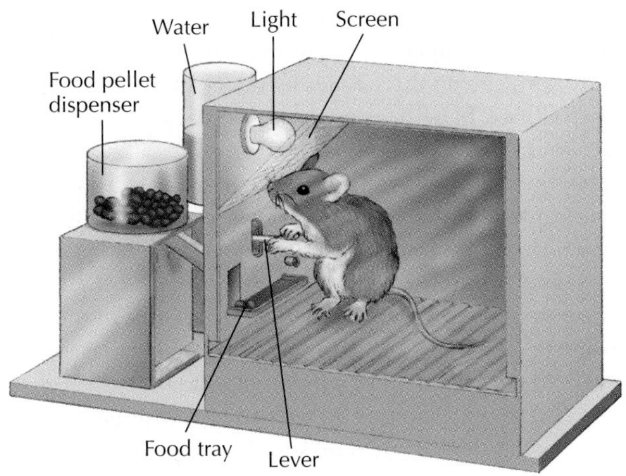

● **Figure 8.9** The Skinner box. This simple device, invented by B. F. Skinner, allows careful study of operant conditioning. When the rat presses the bar, a pellet of food or a drop of water is automatically released. (A photograph of a Skinner box appears in Chapter 1.)

Notice that the rat did not acquire a new skill in this situation. He was already able to press the bar. Reinforcement only alters how *frequently* he presses the bar. In operant conditioning, new behavior patterns are molded by increasing the probability that various responses will be made.

Information

Like classical conditioning, operant learning is based on information and expectancies. In operant conditioning, *we learn to expect that a certain response will have a certain effect at certain times* (Pierce & Cheney, 2004). That is, we learn that a particular stimulus is associated with a particular response that is associated with reinforcement (Dragoi & Staddon, 1999). From this point of view, a reinforcer tells a person or an animal that a response was "right" and worth repeating.

● Figure 8.10 shows how operant reinforcement can change behavior. The results are from an effort to teach a severely disturbed 9-year-old child to say "Please," "Thank you," and "You're welcome." As you can see, during the initial, baseline period, the child rarely used the word *please.* Typically, he just grabbed objects and became angry if he couldn't have them. However, when he was reinforced for saying "Please," he soon learned to use the word nearly every time he wanted something. When the child said "Please" he was reinforced in three ways: He received the object he asked for (a crayon, for example); he was given a small food treat, such as a piece of candy, popcorn, or a grape; and he was praised for his good behavior (Matson et al., 1990).

Contingent Reinforcement

Operant reinforcement works best when it is *response contingent* (kon-TIN-jent). That is, it must be given only after a desired response has occurred. If the disturbed child received reinforcers haphazardly, his behavior wouldn't have changed at all. In situations ranging from studying to working hard on the job, contingent reinforcement also affects the *performance* of responses. For example, ● Figure 8.11 shows the performance of 38 major league pitchers who signed multiyear contracts for large salaries. When salary was no longer contingent on good performance, there was a rapid decline in innings pitched and in the number of wins. During the same 6-year period, the performance of pitchers on 1-year contracts remained fairly steady. In similar ways, operant principles greatly affect behavior in homes, schools, and businesses. It is always worthwhile to arrange reinforcers so that they encourage productive and responsible behavior.

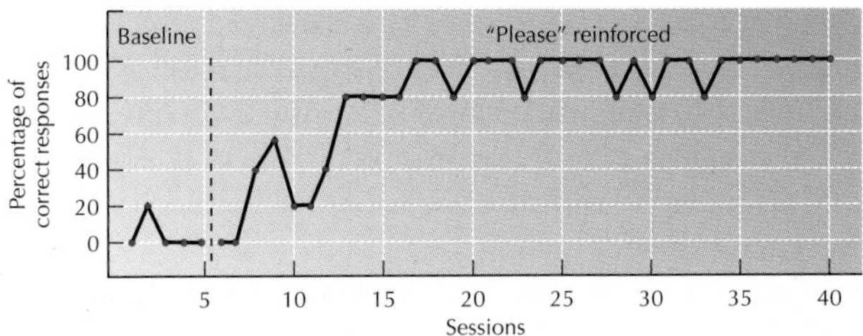

● **Figure 8.10** Reinforcement and human behavior. The percentage of times that a severely disturbed child said "Please" when he wanted an object was increased dramatically by reinforcing him for making a polite request. Reinforcement produced similar improvements in saying "Thank you" and "You're welcome," and the boy applied these terms in new situations as well. (Adapted from Matson et al., 1990.)

The Timing of Reinforcement

Operant reinforcement is most effective when it rapidly follows a correct response. For rats in a Skinner box, very little learning occurs when the delay between bar pressing and receiving food

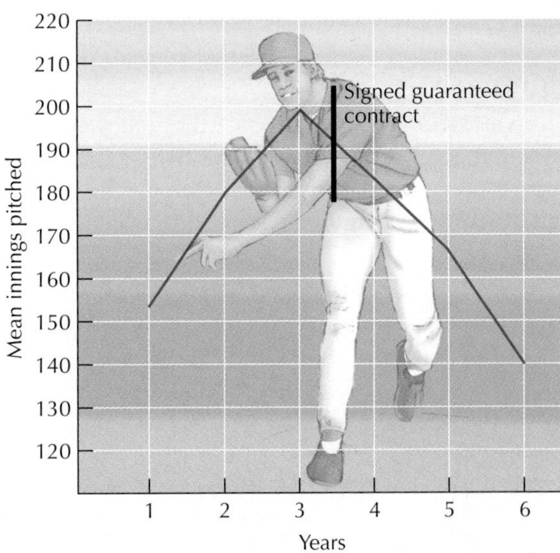

● **Figure 8.11** Average number of innings pitched by major league baseball players before and after signing long-term guaranteed contracts. (Data from O'Brien et al., 1981.)

Operant reinforcer Any event that reliably increases the probability or frequency of responses it follows.

Conditioning chamber An apparatus designed to study operant conditioning in animals; a Skinner box.

reaches 50 seconds. If the food reward is delayed more than about a minute and a half, no learning occurs (Perin, 1943) (● Figure 8.12). In general, you will be most successful if you present a reinforcer *immediately* after a response you wish to change. Thus, a child who is helpful or courteous should be immediately praised for her good behavior.

Let's say I work hard all semester in a class to get an A grade. Wouldn't the delay in reinforcement keep me from learning anything? No, for several reasons. First, as a mature human you can anticipate future reward. Second, you get reinforced by quiz and test grades all through the semester. Third, a single reinforcer can often maintain a long response chain (a linked series of actions that lead to reinforcement). A simplified example of **response chaining** is provided by Barnabus, a rat trained by psychologists at Brown University.

The Great Barnabus

By carefully working from the last response to the first, Barnabus was trained to make an ever-longer chain of responses to obtain a single food pellet. When in top form, Barnabus was able to climb a spiral staircase, cross a narrow bridge, climb a ladder, pull a toy car with a chain, get into the car, pedal it to a second staircase, climb the staircase, wriggle through a tube, climb onto an elevator and descend to a platform, press a lever to receive a food pellet, and . . . start over! (Pierrel & Sherman, 1963)

Many of the things we do every day involve similar response chains. The long series of events necessary to prepare a meal is rewarded by the final eating. A violinmaker may carry out thousands of steps for the final reward of hearing a first musical note. Tying a shoe is a short but familiar response chain.

Are You Superstitious?

Reinforcers affect not only the response they follow but also other responses that occur shortly before. This helps explain many human superstitions. If a golfer taps her club on the ground three times and then hits an unusually fine shot, what happens? The successful shot reinforces not only the correct swing but also the three taps. If this happens a few times more, the golfer may superstitiously tap her club three times before every shot.

Superstitious behaviors are repeated because they appear to produce reinforcement, even though they are actually unnecessary (Pisacreta, 1998). If you get the large half of a wishbone and have good fortune soon after, you may credit your luck to the wishbone. If you walk under a ladder and then break a leg, you may avoid ladders in the future. Each time you avoid a ladder and nothing bad happens, your superstitious action is reinforced. Belief in magic can also be explained along such lines. Rituals to bring rain, ward off illness, or produce abundant crops very likely earn the faith of participants because they occasionally appear to succeed. Besides, better safe than sorry!

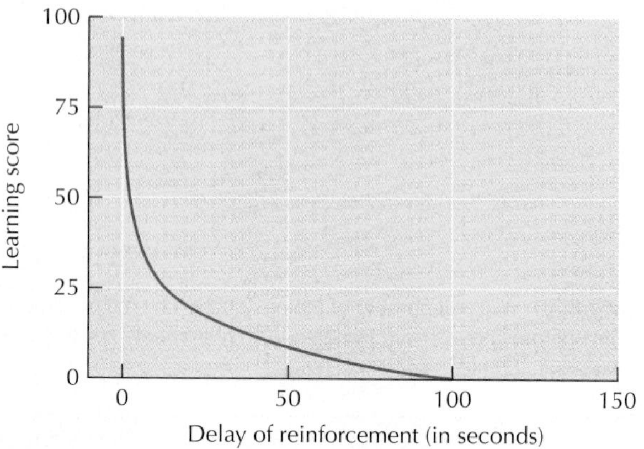

● **Figure 8.12** The effect of delay of reinforcement. Notice how rapidly the learning score drops when reward is delayed. Animals learning to press a bar in a Skinner box showed no signs of learning if food reward followed a bar press by more than 100 seconds (Perin, 1943).

Shaping

How is it possible to reinforce responses that rarely occur? Even in a barren Skinner box, it could take a long time for a rat to accidentally press the bar and get a food pellet. We might wait forever for more complicated responses to occur. For example, you would have to wait a long time for a duck to accidentally walk out of its cage, turn on a light, play a toy piano, turn off the light, and walk back to its cage. If this is what you wanted to reward, you would never get the chance.

Then how are the animals on TV and at amusement parks taught to perform complicated tricks? The answer lies in **shaping,** which is the gradual molding of responses to a desired pattern. Let's look again at our subject, Mickey Rat.

Mickey Rat Shapes Up

Assume that the rat has not yet learned to press the bar. He also shows no signs of interest in the bar. Instead of waiting for the first accidental bar press, we can shape his behavior. At first, we settle for just getting him to face the bar. Any time he turns toward the bar, he is reinforced with a bit of food. Soon Mickey spends much of his time facing the bar. Next, we reinforce him every time he takes a step toward the bar. If he turns toward the bar and walks away, nothing happens. But when he faces the bar and takes a step forward, *click!* His responses are being shaped.

By changing the rules about what makes a successful response, we can gradually train the rat to approach the bar and press it. In other words, *successive approximations* (ever-closer matches) to a desired response are reinforced during shaping. B. F. Skinner once taught two pigeons to play Ping-Pong in this way (● Figure 8.13). Shaping applies to humans, too. Let's say you want to study more, clean the house more often, or exercise more. In each case, it would be best to set a series of gradual, daily goals. Then you can reward yourself for small steps in the right direction (Watson & Tharp, 2002).

Operant Extinction

Would a rat stop bar pressing if no more food arrived? Yes, but not immediately. Learned responses that are not reinforced gradually fade away. This process is called **operant extinction.** Just as ac-

Yale Joel/Life Magazine/TimePix/Getty Images

● **Figure 8.13** Operant conditioning principles were used to train these pigeons to play Ping-Pong.

quiring an operant response takes time, so does extinction. For example, if a TV program repeatedly bores you, watching the program will probably extinguish over time.

Even after extinction seems complete, the previously reinforced response may return. If a rat is removed from a Skinner box after extinction and given a short rest, the rat will press the bar again when returned to the box. Similarly, a few weeks after they give up on buying state lottery tickets, many people are tempted to try again.

Does extinction take as long the second time? If reinforcement is still withheld, a rat's bar pressing will extinguish again, usually more quickly. The brief return of an operant response after extinction is another example of spontaneous recovery (mentioned earlier regarding classical conditioning). Spontaneous recovery is very adaptive. After a rest period, the rat responds again in a situation that produced food in the past: "Just checking to see if the rules have changed!"

Marked changes in behavior occur when reinforcement and extinction are combined. For example, parents often unknowingly reinforce children for *negative attention seeking* (using misbehavior to gain attention). Children are generally ignored when they are playing quietly. They get attention when they become louder and louder, yell "Hey, Mom!" at the top of their lungs, throw tantrums, show off, or break something. Granted, the attention they get is often a scolding, but attention is a powerful reinforcer, nevertheless. Parents report dramatic improvements when they *ignore* their children's disruptive behavior and praise or attend to a child who is quiet or playing constructively.

Negative Reinforcement

Until now, we have stressed **positive reinforcement**, which occurs when a pleasant or desirable event follows a response. How else could operant learning be reinforced? The time has come to consider negative reinforcement, which occurs when making a response removes an unpleasant event. Don't be fooled by the word negative. Negative reinforcement also increases responding. However, it does so by ending discomfort.

Let's say that you have a headache and take an aspirin. Your aspirin taking will be negatively reinforced if the headache stops. Likewise, a rat could be taught to press a bar to get food (positive reinforcement), or the rat could be given a continuous mild shock (through the floor of its cage) that is turned off by a bar press (negative reinforcement). Either way, the rat will learn to press the bar more often. Why? Because it leads to a desired state of affairs (food or an end to pain). Here are two additional examples of negative reinforcement:

> While walking outside, your hands get so cold they hurt. You take a pair of gloves out of your backpack and put them on, ending the pain. (Putting on the gloves is negatively reinforced.)
>
> A politician who irritates you is being interviewed on the evening news. You change channels so you won't have to listen to him. (Channel changing is negatively reinforced.)

Punishment

Many people mistake negative reinforcement for punishment. However, **punishment** refers to following a response with an **aversive** (unpleasant) consequence. Punishment *decreases* the likelihood that the response will occur again. As noted, negative reinforcement *increases* responding. The difference can be seen in a hypothetical example. Let's say you live in an apartment and your neighbor's stereo is blasting so loudly that your ears hurt. If you pound on the wall and the volume suddenly drops (negative reinforcement), future wall pounding will be more likely. But if you pound on the wall and the volume increases (punishment) or if the neighbor comes over and pounds on you (more punishment), wall pounding becomes less likely. Here are two examples of punishment, in which an unpleasant result follows a response:

> You're a passenger in a friend's car on a long trip. You try to read a book to pass the time, but you get carsick. Henceforth, you won't read while riding in a car. (Reading was punished by nausea.)
>
> Every time you give advice to a friend she suddenly turns cold and distant. Lately, you've stopped offering her advice. (Giving advice was punished by rejection.)

Response chaining The assembly of separate responses into a series of actions that lead to reinforcement.

Superstitious behavior A behavior repeated because it seems to produce reinforcement, even though it is actually unnecessary.

Shaping Gradually molding responses to a final desired pattern.

Operant extinction The weakening or disappearance of a nonreinforced operant response.

Negative reinforcement Occurs when a response is followed by an end to discomfort or by the removal of an unpleasant event.

Positive reinforcement Occurs when a response is followed by a reward or other positive event.

Punishment Any event that follows a response and *decreases* its likelihood of occurring again.

Aversive stimulus A stimulus that is painful or uncomfortable.

TABLE 8.3

Behavioral Effects of Various Consequences

	CONSEQUENCE OF MAKING A RESPONSE	EXAMPLE	EFFECT ON RESPONSE PROBABILITY
Positive reinforcement	Positive event begins	Food given	Increase
Negative reinforcement	Negative event ends	Pain stops	Increase
Punishment	Negative event begins	Pain begins	Decrease
Punishment (response cost)	Positive event ends	Food removed	Decrease
Nonreinforcement	Nothing	—	Decrease

Isn't it also punishing to have privileges, money, or other positive things taken away for making a particular response? Yes. Punishment also occurs when a reinforcer or positive state of affairs is removed, such as losing privileges. This second type of punishment is called **response cost.** Parents who "ground" their teenage children for misbehavior are applying response cost. Parking tickets and other fines are also based on response cost. For your convenience, Table 8.3 summarizes four basic consequences of making a response.

Operant Reinforcers—What's Your Pleasure?

For humans, learning may be reinforced by anything from an M&M candy to a pat on the back. In categorizing reinforcers, useful distinctions can be made between *primary reinforcers, secondary reinforcers,* and *feedback.* Operant reinforcers of all types have a large impact on our lives. Let's examine them in more detail.

Primary Reinforcers

Primary reinforcers are natural, nonlearned, and rooted in biology: They produce comfort, end discomfort, or fill an immediate physical need. Food, water, and sex are obvious examples. Every time you open the refrigerator, walk to a drinking fountain, turn up the heat, or order a double latte, your actions reflect primary reinforcement.

In addition to obvious examples, there are other less natural primary reinforcers. One of the most powerful is *intracranial stimulation* (ICS). ICS involves direct activation of "pleasure centers" in the brain (Olds & Fobes, 1981) (● Figure 8.14).

Wiring a Rat for Pleasure

Use of brain stimulation for reward requires the permanent implantation of tiny electrodes in specific areas of the brain. A rat "wired for pleasure" can be trained to press the bar in a Skinner box to deliver electrical stimulation to its own brain. Some rats will press the bar thousands of times per hour to obtain brain stimulation. After 15 or 20 hours of constant pressing, animals sometimes collapse from exhaustion. When they revive, they begin pressing again. If the reward circuit is not turned off, an animal will ignore food, water, and sex in favor of bar pressing.

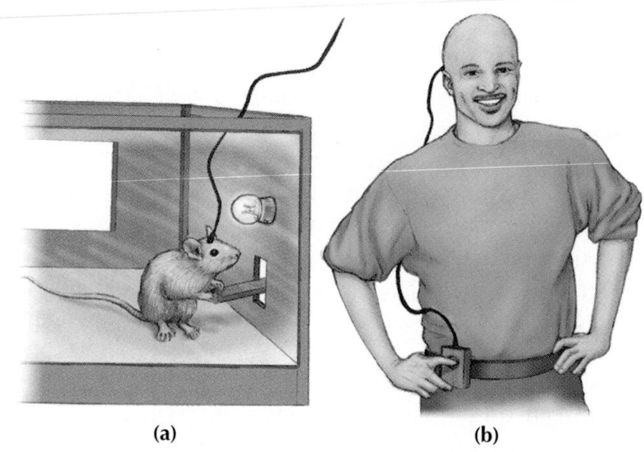

● **Figure 8.14** In the apparatus shown in *(a),* the rat can press a bar to deliver mild electric stimulation to a "pleasure center" in the brain. Humans also have been "wired" for brain stimulation, as shown in *(b).* However, in humans, this has been done only as an experimental way to restrain uncontrollable outbursts of violence. Implants have not been done merely to produce pleasure.

Many natural primary reinforcers activate the same pleasure pathways in the brain that make ICS so powerful (McBride, Murphy, & Ikemoto, 1999).

One shudders to think what might happen if brain implants were easy and practical to do. (They are not.) Every company from Playboy to Microsoft would have a device on the market, and we would have to keep a closer watch on politicians than usual!

Secondary Reinforcers

In some traditional societies, learning is still strongly tied to food, water, and other primary reinforcers. Most of us, however, respond to a much broader range of rewards and reinforcers. Money, praise, attention, approval, success, affection, grades, and the like, all serve as learned or **secondary reinforcers.**

BRIDGES

Electrical stimulation is a valuable tool for studying the functions of various brain structures.

See Chapter 2, page 61.

How does a secondary reinforcer gain its ability to promote learning? Some secondary reinforcers are simply associated with a primary reinforcer. For example, if you would like to train a dog to follow you ("heel") when you take a walk, you could reward the dog with small food treats for staying near you. If you praise the dog each time you give it a treat, praise will become a secondary reinforcer. In time, you will be able to skip giving treats and simply praise your pup for doing the right thing. The same principle applies to children. One reason that parents' praise becomes a secondary reinforcer is because it is frequently associated with food, candy, hugs, and other primary reinforcers.

Tokens

Secondary reinforcers that can be *exchanged* for primary reinforcers gain their value more directly. Printed money obviously has little or no value of its own. You can't eat it, drink it, or sleep with it. However, it can be exchanged for food, water, lodging, and other necessities.

A **token reinforcer** is a tangible secondary reinforcer, such as money, gold stars, poker chips, and the like. In a series of classic experiments, chimpanzees were taught to work for tokens. The chimps were first trained to put poker chips into a "Chimp-O-Mat" vending machine. Each chip dispensed a few grapes or raisins. Once the animals had learned to exchange tokens for food, they would learn new tasks to earn the chips. To maintain the value of the tokens, the chimps were occasionally allowed to use the "Chimp-O-Mat" (● Figure 8.15) (Cowles, 1937; Wolfe, 1936).

A major advantage of tokens is that they don't lose reinforcing value as quickly as primary reinforcers do. For instance, if you use candy to reinforce a retarded child for correctly naming things, the child might lose interest once he is satiated (fully satisfied) or no longer hungry. It would be better to use tokens as immediate rewards for learning. Later, the child could exchange his tokens for candy, toys, or other treats.

Chimp-O-Mat, Yukes Regional Primate Research Center, Emory University

● **Figure 8.15** Poker chips normally have little or no value for chimpanzees, but this chimp will work hard to earn them once he learns that the "Chimp-O-Mat" will dispense food in exchange for them.

Tokens have been used in similar ways with troubled children and adults in special programs, and even in ordinary elementary school classrooms (Spiegler & Guevremont, 2003) (● Figure 8.16). In each case the goal is to provide an immediate reward for learning. Typically, tokens may be exchanged for food, desired goods, special privileges, or trips to movies, amusement parks, and so forth. Many parents find that tokens greatly reduce discipline problems with younger children. For example, children can earn points or gold stars during the week for good behavior. If they earn enough tokens, they are allowed on Sunday to choose one item out of a "grab bag" of small prizes.

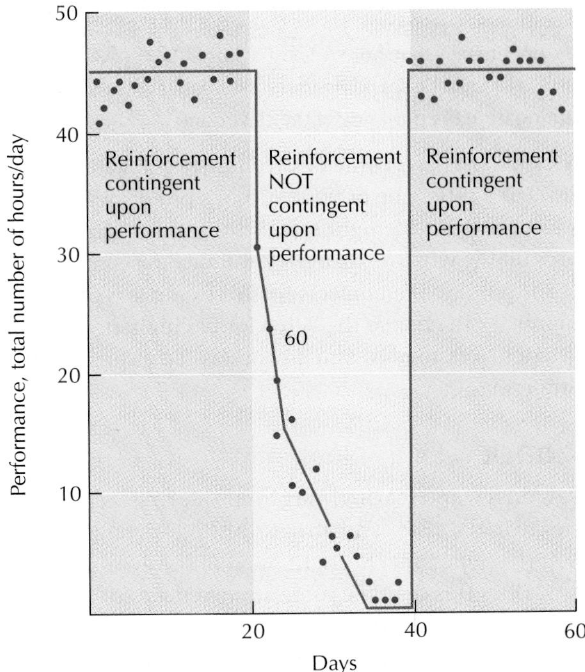

● **Figure 8.16** Reinforcement in a token economy. This graph shows the effects of using tokens to reward socially desirable behavior in a mental hospital ward. Desirable behavior was defined as cleaning, making the bed, attending therapy sessions, and so forth. Tokens earned could be exchanged for basic amenities such as meals, snacks, coffee, game-room privileges, or weekend passes. The graph shows more than 24 hours per day because it represents the total number of hours of desirable behavior performed by all patients in the ward. (Adapted from Ayllon & Azrin, 1965.)

Response cost Removal of a positive reinforcer after a response is made.

Primary reinforcers Nonlearned reinforcers; usually those that satisfy physiological needs.

Secondary reinforcer A learned reinforcer; often one that gains reinforcing properties by association with a primary reinforcer.

Token reinforcer A tangible secondary reinforcer such as money, gold stars, poker chips, and the like.

Social Reinforcers

As we have noted, learned desires for attention and approval, which are called **social reinforcers**, often influence human behavior. This fact can be used in a classic, if somewhat mischievous, demonstration.

Shaping a Teacher

For this activity, about one half (or more) of the students in a classroom must participate. First, select a target behavior. This should be something like "lecturing from the right side of the room." (Keep it simple, in case your teacher is a slow learner.) Begin training in this way: Each time the instructor turns toward the right or takes a step in that direction, participating students should look *really* interested. Also, smile, ask questions, lean forward, and make eye contact. If the teacher turns to the left or takes a step in that direction, participating students should lean back, yawn, check out their split ends, close their eyes, or generally look bored. Soon, without being aware of why, the instructor should be spending most of his or her time each class period lecturing from the right side of the classroom.

This trick has been a favorite of psychology graduate students for decades. For a time, one of your author's professors delivered all of her lectures from the right side of the room while toying with the cords on the window shades. (We added the cords the second week!) The point to remember from this example is that attention and approval can change the behavior of children, family members, friends, roommates, and coworkers. Be aware of what you are reinforcing.

Feedback

His eyes, driven and blazing, dart from side to side. His left hand twitches, dances, rises, and strikes, hitting its target again and again. At the same time, his right hand furiously spins in circular motions. Does this describe some strange neurological disorder? Actually, it depicts 10-year-old Vikram as he plays his favorite video game, an animated skateboarding adventure!

How did Vikram learn the complex movements needed to excel at virtual skateboarding? After all, he was not rewarded with food or money. The answer lies in the fact that Vikram's favorite video game provides two key elements that underlie learning: *a responsive environment* and *information.*

Every time a player moves, a video game responds instantly with sounds, animated actions, and a higher or lower score. The machine's responsiveness and the information flow it provides can be very motivating if you want to win. The same principle applies to many other learning situations: If you are trying to learn to use a computer, to play a musical instrument, to cook, or to solve math problems, reinforcement comes from knowing that you achieved a desired result.

The adaptive value of information helps explain why much human learning occurs in the absence of obvious reinforcers, such as food or water. Humans readily learn responses that merely have a desired effect or that bring a goal closer. Let's explore this idea further.

Knowledge of Results

Imagine that you are asked to throw darts at a target. Each dart must pass over a screen that prevents you from telling if you hit the target. If you threw 1,000 darts, we would expect little improvement in your performance because no *feedback* is provided. **Feedback** (information about the effect a response had) is particularly important in human learning. Vikram's video game did not explicitly reward him for correct responses. Yet because it provided feedback, rapid learning took place.

How can feedback be applied? Increased feedback (also called **knowledge of results**, or **KR**) almost always improves learning and performance (Lee & Carnahan, 1990). If you want to learn to play a musical instrument, to sing, to speak a second language, or to deliver a speech, tape-recorded feedback can be very helpful. In sports, videotapes are used to improve everything from tennis serves to pick-off moves in baseball. (Taped replays of this kind are most helpful when a skilled coach directs attention to key details.) Whenever you are trying to learn a complex skill, it pays to get more feedback (Wulf, Shea, & Matschiner, 1998). (Also, see "Conditioning and Conservation: Learning to Act Locally.")

Learning Aids

How do these techniques make use of feedback? Feedback is most effective when it is *frequent, immediate,* and *detailed.* **Programmed instruction** teaches students in a format that presents information in small amounts, gives immediate practice, and provides continuous feedback to learners. Frequent feedback keeps learners from practicing errors. It also lets students work at their own pace. (A small sample of programmed instruction is shown in ● Figure 8.17 so that you can see what the format looks like.) Programmed learning can be done in book form or presented by a computer (Mabry, 1998).

In *computer-assisted instruction* (CAI), learning is aided by computer-presented information and exercises. In addition to giving learners immediate feedback, the computer can give hints about why an answer was wrong and what is needed to correct it (Light, 1997). Although the final level of skill or knowledge gained is not necessarily higher, CAI can save much time and effort. In addition, people often do better with feedback from a computer because they can freely make mistakes and learn from them (Schneider & Shugar, 1990). For example, CAI can give medical students unlimited practice at diagnosing diseases from symptoms, such as "acute chest pain" (Papa et al., 1999).

BRIDGES

A token economy is a system for managing and altering behavior through reinforcement of selected responses.

See Chapter 17, pages 583–584.

DISCOVERING PSYCHOLOGY

Conditioning and Conservation: Learning to Act Locally

We psychologists enjoy seeing behavioral principles used to solve practical problems. One area of behavior very much in need of attention is our "throw-away" society. We burn fossil fuels, destroy forests, use chemical products, and strip, clear, and farm the land. In doing so, we alter the very face of the earth. What can be done? One approach involves changing the *consequences* of wasteful energy use, polluting, and the like.

At the level of governments, for example, energy taxes can be used to increase the cost of using fossil fuels (response cost). On the reinforcement side of the equation, rebates can be offered for installing insulation, or buying energy-efficient appliances or cars, and tax breaks can be given to companies that take steps to preserve the environment.

According to the famous dictum *think globally, act locally,* the most effective actions take place at the local level. But too many of us feel powerless to influence the health of our earth. But imagine just how much could be achieved if, on a day-to-day basis, we ordinary people recycled materials such as paper, steel, glass, aluminum, and plastic. One approach is through *civic environmentalism,* giving state and local authorities more power over their local environment (Abel & Stephan, 2000). This creates conditions in which we ordinary citizens have more control over, and responsibility for, our local environments.

Again, behavioral principles come into play. For instance, people who set their own goals for recycling tend to meet them. Likewise, when families, work groups, factories, and dorms receive weekly feedback about how much they recycled, they typically recycle more. Recycling is also more effective when entire families participate, with some family members (usually mom, of course) reinforcing the recycling behavior of other family members (Meneses & Asunción, 2005). We also know that people are most likely to continue recycling if they feel a sense of satisfaction from helping protect the environment (Werner & Makela, 1998). Is such satisfaction sufficiently reinforcing to encourage more people to reduce, reuse, and recycle? We certainly hope so.

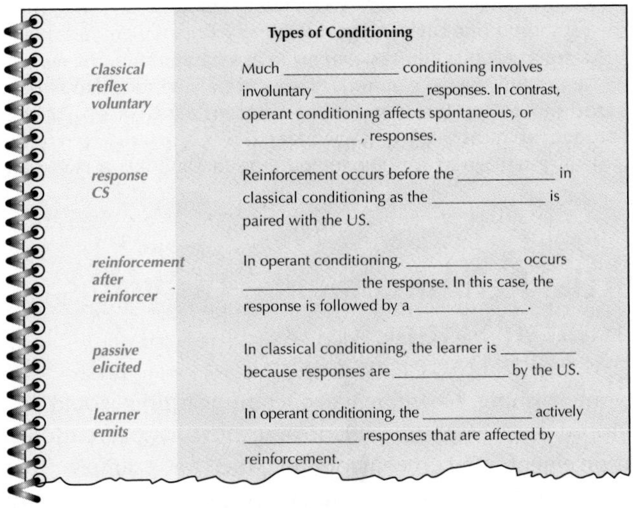

Types of Conditioning

classical *reflex* *voluntary*	Much ______ conditioning involves involuntary ______ responses. In contrast, operant conditioning affects spontaneous, or ______, responses.
response *CS*	Reinforcement occurs before the ______ in classical conditioning as the ______ is paired with the US.
reinforcement *after* *reinforcer*	In operant conditioning, ______ occurs ______ the response. In this case, the response is followed by a ______.
passive *elicited*	In classical conditioning, the learner is ______ because responses are ______ by the US.
learner *emits*	In operant conditioning, the ______ actively ______ responses that are affected by reinforcement.

● **Figure 8.17** To sample a programmed instruction format, try covering the terms on the left with a piece of paper. As you fill in the blanks, uncover one new term for each response. In this way, your correct (or incorrect) responses will be followed by immediate feedback. (Actually, this is a somewhat simplified example. In true programmed instruction, new ideas are presented along with opportunities to practice them.)

Some CAI programs, called *serious games,* make use of instructional games in which stories, competition with a partner, sound effects, and game-like graphics increase interest and motivation (● Figure 8.18) (Stoney & Wild, 1998). Educational simulations go a step further by allowing students to explore an imaginary situation or "micro-world" that simulates real-world problems. By seeing the effects of their choices, students discover basic principles of physics, biology, psychology, or other subjects (Cordova & Lepper, 1996).

Psychologists are only now beginning to fully explore the value and limits of CAI. Nevertheless, it seems likely that their efforts will improve not only education but our understanding of human learning as well.

Let's pause now for some learning exercises so that you can get some feedback about your mastery of the preceding ideas.

Social reinforcer Reinforcement based on receiving attention, approval, or affection from another person.

Feedback Information returned to a person about the effects a response has had; also known as knowledge of results.

Knowledge of results (KR) Informational feedback.

Programmed instruction Any learning format that presents information in small amounts, gives immediate practice, and provides continuous feedback to learners.

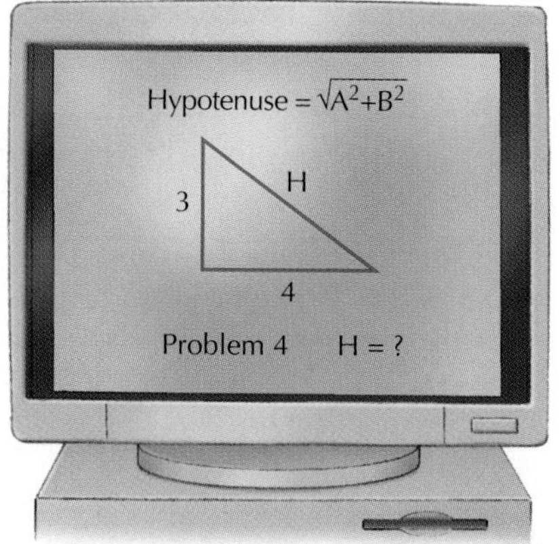

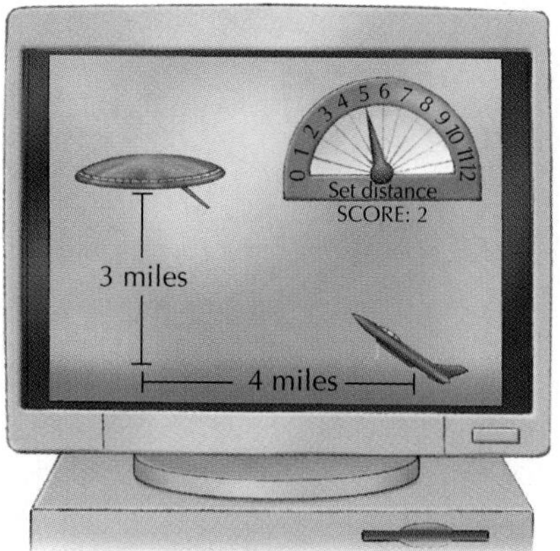

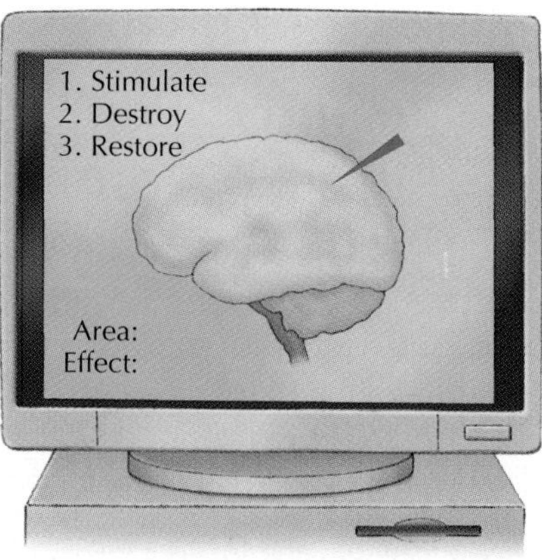

● **Figure 8.18** Computer-assisted instruction. The screen on the left shows a typical drill-and-practice math problem, in which students must find the hypotenuse of a triangle. The center screen presents the same problem as an instructional game to increase interest and motivation. In the game, a child is asked to set the proper distance on a ray gun in the hovering space ship to "vaporize" an attacker. The screen on the right depicts an educational simulation. Here, students place a "probe" at various spots in a human brain. They then "stimulate," "destroy," or "restore" areas. As each area is altered, it is named on the screen and the effects on behavior are described. This allows students to explore basic brain functions on their own.

KNOWLEDGE BUILDER

Operant Conditioning

REFLECT

How have your thoughts about the effects of "rewards" changed now that you've read about operant conditioning? Can you explain the difference between positive reinforcement, negative reinforcement, and punishment? Can you give an example of each concept from your own experience?

A friend of yours punishes his dog all the time. What advice would you give him about how to use reinforcement, extinction, and shaping, instead of punishment?

LEARNING CHECK

1. Responses in operant conditioning are ________________, whereas those in classical conditioning are passive, ________ ________ responses.
2. Changing the rules in small steps so that an animal (or person) is gradually trained to respond as desired is called ________ ________________.
3. Extinction in operant conditioning is also subject to ________ of a response.
   a. successive approximations c. automation
   b. shaping d. spontaneous recovery
4. Positive reinforcers increase the rate of responding and negative reinforcers decrease it. T or F?
5. Primary reinforcers are those learned through classical conditioning. T or F?
6. Which is a correct match?
   a. social reinforcer–primary reinforcement
   b. token reinforcer–secondary reinforcement
   c. ICS–secondary reinforcement
   d. negative reinforcer–punishment
7. Superstitious responses are those that are
   a. shaped by secondary reinforcement
   b. extinguished
   c. prepotent
   d. unnecessary to obtain reinforcement
8. Knowledge of results, or KR, is also known as ______________ __________.
9. CAI is based on the same principles as
   a. negative reinforcement c. higher order conditioning
   b. programmed instruction d. stimulus generalization

CRITICAL THINKING

10. How might operant conditioning principles be used to encourage people to pick up litter? (What rewards could be offered, and how might the cost of rewards be kept low?)

Answers: **1.** voluntary or emitted, involuntary or elicited **2.** shaping **3.** d **4.** F **5.** F **6.** b **7.** d **8.** feedback **9.** b **10.** A strategy that has been used with some success is to hold drawings for various prizes, such as movie or concert passes. Each time a person turns in a specific amount of litter, she or he receives one chance (a token) to enter in the drawing. Giving refunds for cans and bottles is another way to reinforce recycling of litter.

Partial Reinforcement—Las Vegas, a Human Skinner Box?

Anyone wishing to influence operant learning would be ill equipped to do so without knowing how various patterns of reinforcement affect behavior. Imagine, for example, that a mother wants to reward her child for turning off the lights when he leaves a room. Contrary to what you might think, she would be well advised to reinforce only some of her son's correct responses. Why should this be so? You'll find the answer in the following discussion.

B. F. Skinner, so the story goes, was studying operant conditioning when he ran short of food pellets. In order to continue, he arranged for a pellet to reward every other response. Thus began the formal study of **schedules of reinforcement** (plans for determining which responses will be reinforced). Until now, we have treated operant reinforcement as if it were continuous. **Continuous reinforcement** means that a reinforcer follows every correct response. This is fine for the lab, but it has little to do with the real world. Most of our responses are more inconsistently rewarded. In daily life, learning is usually based on **partial reinforcement,** in which reinforcers do not follow every response.

Partial reinforcement can be given in several patterns. Each has a distinct effect on behavior. In addition to these (which will be explored in a moment), there is a general effect: Responses acquired by partial reinforcement are highly resistant to extinction. For some obscure reason, lost in the lore of psychology, this is called the **partial reinforcement effect.**

How does getting reinforced part of the time make a habit stronger? If you have ever visited Las Vegas or a similar gambling mecca, you have probably seen row after row of people playing slot machines. To gain insight into partial reinforcement, imagine that you are making your first visit to Las Vegas. You put a dollar in a slot machine and pull the handle. Ten dollars spills into the tray. Using one of your newly won dollars, you pull the handle again. Another payoff! Let's say this continues for 15 minutes. Every pull is followed by a payoff. Suddenly each pull is followed by nothing. Obviously, you would respond several times more before giving up. However, when continuous reinforcement is followed by extinction, the message soon becomes clear: No more payoffs.

Contrast this with partial reinforcement. Again, imagine that this is your first encounter with a slot machine. You put a dollar in the machine five times without a payoff. You are just about to quit, but decide to play once more. Bingo! The machine returns $20. After this, payoffs continue on a partial schedule; some are large, and some are small. All are unpredictable. Sometimes you hit 2 in a row, and sometimes 20 or 30 pulls go unrewarded.

Now let's say the payoff mechanism is turned off again. How many times do you think you would respond this time before your handle-pulling behavior extinguished? Because you have developed the expectation that any play may be "the one," it will be hard to resist just one more play . . . and one more . . . and one more. Also, because partial reinforcement includes long periods of nonreward, it will be harder to discriminate between periods of reinforcement and extinction. It is no exaggeration to say that the partial reinforcement effect has left many people penniless. Even psychologists visiting Las Vegas may get "cleaned out"—and they should know better!

Christoph Wilhelm/Getty Images

The one-armed bandit (slot machine) is a dispenser of partial reinforcement.

Schedules of Partial Reinforcement

Partial reinforcement can be given in many different patterns. Let's consider the four most basic, which have some interesting effects on us. Typical responses to each pattern are shown in ● Figure 8.19. Results such as these are obtained when a cumulative recorder is connected to a Skinner box. The device consists of a moving strip of paper and a mechanical pen that jumps upward each time a response is made. Rapid responding causes the pen to draw a steep line; a horizontal line indicates no response. Small tick marks on the lines show when a reinforcer was given.

Fixed Ratio (FR)

What would happen if a reinforcer followed only every other response? Or what if we followed every third, fourth, fifth, or other number of responses with reinforcement? Each of these patterns

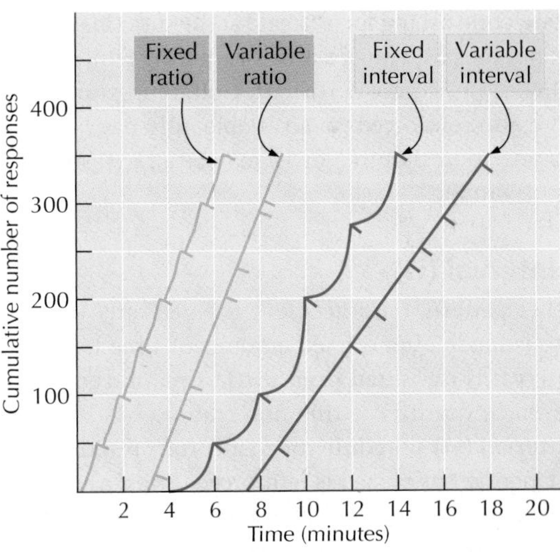

● **Figure 8.19** Typical response patterns for reinforcement schedules.

Schedule of reinforcement A rule or plan for determining which responses will be reinforced.

Continuous reinforcement A schedule in which every correct response is followed by a reinforcer.

Partial reinforcement A pattern in which only a portion of all responses are reinforced.

Partial reinforcement effect Responses acquired with partial reinforcement are more resistant to extinction.

is a **fixed ratio (FR) schedule** (a set number of correct responses must be made to obtain a reinforcer). Notice that in an FR schedule the ratio of reinforcers to responses is fixed: FR-2 means that every other response is rewarded; FR-3 means that every third response is reinforced; in an FR-10 schedule, exactly 10 responses must be made to obtain a reinforcer.

Fixed ratio schedules produce very high response rates (● Figure 8.19). A hungry rat on an FR-10 schedule will quickly run off 10 responses, pause to eat, and will then run off 10 more. A similar situation occurs when factory or farm workers are paid on a piecework basis. When a fixed number of items must be produced for a set amount of pay, work output is high.

Variable Ratio (VR)

In a **variable ratio (VR) schedule** a varied number of correct responses must be made to get a reinforcer. Instead of reinforcing every fourth response (FR-4), for example, a person or animal on a VR-4 schedule gets rewarded *on the average* every fourth response. Sometimes 2 responses must be made to obtain a reinforcer; sometimes it's 5; sometimes, 4; and so on. The actual number varies, but it averages out to 4 (in this example). Variable ratio schedules also produce high response rates.

VR schedules seem less predictable than FR. Does that have any effect on extinction? Yes. Because reinforcement is less predictable, VR schedules tend to produce greater resistance to extinction than fixed ratio schedules. Playing a slot machine is an example of behavior maintained by a variable ratio schedule. Another would be a child asking for a "treat" at the supermarket. The number of times the child must ask before getting reinforced varies, so the child becomes quite persistent. Golf, tennis, and many other sports are also reinforced on a variable ratio basis: An average of perhaps one good shot in 5 or 10 may be all that's needed to create a sports fanatic.

Fixed Interval (FI)

In another pattern, reinforcement is given only when a correct response is made after a fixed amount of time has passed. This time interval is measured from the last reinforced response. Responses made during the time interval are not reinforced. In a **fixed interval (FI) schedule** the first correct response made after the time period has passed is reinforced. Thus, a rat on an FI-30-second schedule has to wait 30 seconds after the last reinforced response before a bar press will pay off again. The rat can press the bar as often as it wants during the interval, but it will not be rewarded.

Fixed interval schedules produce *moderate response rates*. These are marked by spurts of activity mixed with periods of inactivity. Animals working on an FI schedule seem to develop a keen sense of the passage of time (Eckerman, 1999). For example:

Mickey Rat Takes a Break

Mickey Rat, trained on an FI-60-second schedule, has just been reinforced for a bar press. What does he do? He saunters around the cage, grooms himself, hums, whistles, reads magazines, and polishes his nails. After 50 seconds, he walks to the bar and gives it a press—just testing. After 55 seconds, he gives it two or three presses, but there's still no payoff. Fifty-eight seconds, and he settles down to rapid pressing, 59 seconds, 60 seconds, and he hits the reinforced press. After one or two more presses (unrewarded), he wanders off again for the next interval.

Is getting paid weekly an FI schedule? Pure examples of fixed interval schedules are rare, but getting paid each week at work does come close. Notice, however, that most people do not work faster just before payday, as an FI schedule predicts. A closer parallel would be having a report due every 2 weeks for a class. Right after turning in a paper, your work would probably drop to zero for a week or more. Then, as the next due date draws near, a work frenzy occurs. Another fixed interval example is checking a Thanksgiving turkey in the oven. Typically, the frequency of checking increases as the time for the turkey to be done draws near (Chance, 2006).

Variable Interval (VI)

Variable interval (VI) schedules are a variation on fixed intervals. Here, reinforcement is given for the first correct response made after a varied amount of time. On a VI-30-second schedule, reinforcement is available after an interval that averages *30 seconds*.

VI schedules produce *slow, steady response rates* and tremendous resistance to extinction (Lattal et al., 1998). When you dial a phone number and get a busy signal, reward (getting through) is on a VI schedule. You may have to wait 30 seconds or 30 minutes. If you are like most people, you will doggedly dial over and over again until you get a connection. Success in fishing is also on a VI schedule—which may explain the bulldog tenacity of many anglers (Chance, 2006).

Stimulus Control—Red Light, Green Light

When you are driving, your behavior at intersections is controlled by the red or green light. In similar fashion, many of the stimuli we encounter each day act like stop or go signals that guide our behavior. To state the idea more formally, stimuli that consistently precede a rewarded response tend to influence when and where the response will occur. This effect is called **stimulus control.** Notice how it works with our friend Mickey Rat.

Lights Out for Mickey Rat

While learning the bar-pressing response, Mickey has been in a Skinner box illuminated by a bright light. During several training sessions, the light is alternately turned on and off. When the light is on, a bar press will produce food. When the light is off, bar pressing goes unrewarded. We soon observe that the rat presses vigorously when the light is on and ignores the bar when the light is off.

In this example, the light signals what consequences will follow if a response is made. Evidence for stimulus control could be shown by turning the food delivery *on* when the light is *off*. A well-trained animal might never discover that the rules had changed. A similar example of stimulus control would be a child learning to ask for candy when her mother is in a good mood, but not asking at other times. Likewise, we pick up phones that are ringing, but rarely answer phones that are silent. Thus, a simplified summary of stimulus control is this: Notice something, do something, get something (Powell, Symbaluk, & Macdonald, 2005).

Generalization

Two important aspects of stimulus control are generalization and discrimination. Let's return to the example of the vending machine (from the chapter Preview) to illustrate these concepts. First, generalization.

Is generalization the same in operant conditioning as it is in classical conditioning? Basically, yes. **Operant stimulus generalization** is the tendency to respond to stimuli similar to those that preceded operant reinforcement. That is, a reinforced response tends to be made again when similar antecedents are present. Assume, for instance, that you have been reliably rewarded for kicking one particular vending machine. Your kicking response tends to occur in the presence of that machine. It has come under stimulus control. Now let's say that there are three other machines on campus identical to the one that pays off. Because they are similar, your kicking response will very likely transfer to them. If each of these machines also pays off when kicked, your kicking response may *generalize* to other machines only mildly similar to the original. Similar generalization explains why children may temporarily call all men *daddy*—much to the embarrassment of their parents.

Discrimination

Meanwhile, back at the vending machine. . . . As stated earlier, to discriminate means to respond differently to varied stimuli. Because one vending machine reinforced your kicking response, you began kicking other identical machines (generalization). Because these also paid off, you began kicking similar machines (more generalization). If kicking these new machines has no effect, the kicking response that generalized to them will extinguish because of nonreinforcement. Thus, your response to machines of a particular size and color is consistently rewarded, whereas the same response to different machines is extinguished. Through **operant stimulus discrimination** you have learned to differentiate between antecedent stimuli that signal reward and nonreward. As a result, your response pattern will shift to match these **discriminative stimuli** (stimuli that precede reinforced and nonreinforced responses).

A discriminative stimulus that most drivers are familiar with is a police car on the freeway. This stimulus is a clear signal that a specific set of reinforcement contingencies applies. As you have probably observed, the presence of a police car brings about rapid reductions in driving speed, lane changes, tailgating, and in Los Angeles, gun battles.

The role of discriminative stimuli may be clarified by an interesting feat achieved by Jack, a psychologist friend of one of your authors. Here is his account of what Jack did:

Carleton Ray/Photo Researchers, Inc.

Stimulus control. Operant shaping was used to teach this whale to "bow" to an audience. Fish were used as reinforcers. Notice the trainer's hand signal, which serves as a discriminative stimulus to control the performance.

> Jack decided to teach his cat to say its name. To begin, he gave the cat a pat on the back. If the cat meowed in a way that sounded anything like its name, Jack immediately gave the cat a small amount of food. If the cat made this unusual meow at other times, it received nothing. This process was repeated many times each day.

Fixed ratio (FR) schedule A set number of correct responses must be made to get a reinforcer. For example, a reinforcer is given for every four correct responses.

Variable ratio (VR) schedule A varied number of correct responses must be made to get a reinforcer. For example, a reinforcer is given after three to seven correct responses; the actual number changes randomly.

Fixed interval (FI) schedule A reinforcer is given only when a correct response is made after a set amount of time has passed since the last reinforced response. Responses made during the time interval are not reinforced.

Variable interval (VI) schedule A reinforcer is given for the first correct response made after a varied amount of time has passed since the last reinforced response. Responses made during the time interval are not reinforced.

Stimulus control Stimuli present when an operant response is acquired tend to control when and where the response is made.

Operant stimulus generalization The tendency to respond to stimuli similar to those that preceded operant reinforcement.

Operant stimulus discrimination The tendency to make an operant response when stimuli previously associated with reward are present and to withhold the response when stimuli associated with nonreward are present.

Discriminative stimuli Stimuli that precede rewarded and nonrewarded responses in operant conditioning.

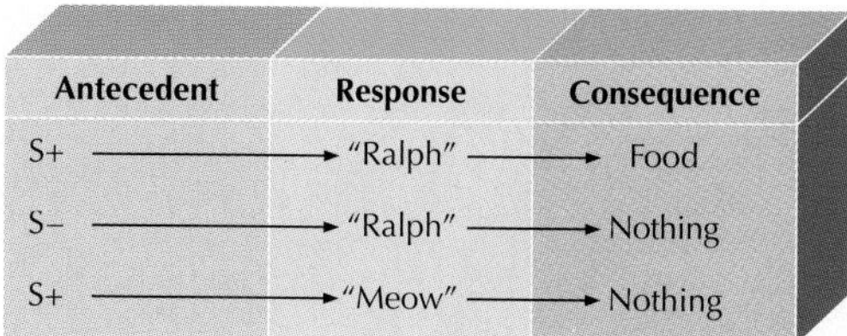

● **Figure 8.20** A diagram of Ralph the cat's discrimination training.

By gradual shaping, the cat's meow was made to sound very much like its name. Also, this peculiar meow came under stimulus control: When it received a pat on the back, the cat said its name; without the pat, it remained silent or meowed normally.

I should add at this point that I was unaware that Jack had a new cat or that he had trained it. I went to visit him one night and met the cat on the front steps. I gave the cat a pat on the back and said, "Hi kitty, what's your name?" Imagine my surprise when the cat immediately replied, "Ralph"!

Psychologists symbolize a stimulus that precedes reinforced responses as an S+. Discriminative stimuli that precede unrewarded responses are symbolized as S− (Chance, 2006). Thus, ● Figure 8.20 summarizes Ralph's training.

Stimulus discrimination is also aptly illustrated by the "sniffer" dogs that locate drugs and explosives at airports and border crossings. Operant discrimination is used to teach these dogs to recognize contraband. During training, they are reinforced only for approaching containers baited with drugs or explosives.

Stimulus discrimination clearly has a tremendous impact on human behavior. Learning to recognize different automobile brands, birds, animals, wines, types of music, and even the answers on psychology tests all depends, in part, on operant discrimination learning.

KNOWLEDGE BUILDER

Partial Reinforcement and Stimulus Control

REFLECT

Think of something you do that is reinforced only part of the time. Do you pursue this activity persistently? How have you been affected by partial reinforcement?

See if you can think of at least one everyday example of the four basic schedules of reinforcement.

Doors that are meant to be pushed outward have metal plates on them. Those that are meant to be pulled inward have handles. Do these discriminative stimuli affect your behavior? (If they don't, how's your nose doing?)

LEARNING CHECK

1. Two aspects of stimulus control are ________________ and ________________.
2. Responding tends to occur in the presence of discriminative stimuli associated with reinforcement and tends not to occur in the presence of discriminative stimuli associated with nonreinforcement. T or F?
3. Stimulus generalization refers to making an operant response in the presence of stimuli similar to those that preceded reinforcement. T or F?
4. Moderate response rates that are marked by spurts of activity and periods of inactivity are characteristic of
   a. FR schedules c. FI schedules
   b. VR schedules d. VI schedules
5. Partial reinforcement tends to produce slower responding and reduced resistance to extinction. T or F?
6. The schedule of reinforcement associated with playing slot machines and other types of gambling is
   a. fixed ratio c. fixed interval
   b. variable ratio d. variable interval

CRITICAL THINKING

7. A business owner who pays employees an hourly wage wants to increase productivity. How could the owner make more effective use of reinforcement?
8. How could you use conditioning principles to teach a dog or a cat to come when called?

Answers: 1. generalization, discrimination **2.** T **3.** T **4.** c **5.** F **6.** b **7.** Continuing to use fixed interval rewards (hourly wage or salary) would guarantee a basic level of income for employees. To reward extra effort, the owner could add some fixed ratio reinforcement (such as incentives, bonuses, commissions, or profit sharing) to employees' pay. **8.** An excellent way to train a pet to come when you call is to give a distinctive call or whistle each time you feed the animal. This makes the signal a secondary reinforcer and a discriminative stimulus for reward (food). Of course, it also helps to directly reinforce an animal with praise, petting, or food for coming when called.

Punishment—Putting the Brakes on Behavior

Spankings, reprimands, fines, jail sentences, firings, failing grades, and the like, are commonly used to control behavior. Clearly, the story of learning is unfinished without a return to the topic of punishment. Recall that **punishment** lowers the probability that a response will occur again. To be most effective, punishment must be given contingently (only after an undesired response occurs).

Punishers, like reinforcers, are defined by observing their effects on behavior. A **punisher** is any consequence that reduces the frequency of a target behavior. It is not always possible to know ahead of time what will act as a punisher for a particular person. For example, when Jason's mother reprimanded him for throwing toys, he stopped doing it. In this instance, the reprimand was a punisher. However, Chris is starved for attention of any kind from his parents, who both work full-time. For Chris, a reprimand, or even a spanking, might actually reinforce toy throwing. Remember, too, that a punisher can be either the onset of an unpleasant event or the removal of a positive state of affairs (response cost).

Variables Affecting Punishment

How effective is punishment? Many people assume that punishment stops unacceptable behavior. Is this always true? Actually the effectiveness of punishers depends greatly on their *timing,*

Tony Freeman/PhotoEdit

Punishers are consequences that lower the probability that a response will be made again. Receiving a traffic citation is directly punishing because the driver is delayed and reprimanded. Paying a fine and higher insurance rates add to the punishment in the form of response cost.

consistency, and *intensity*. Punishment works best when it occurs as the response is being made, or *immediately* afterward (timing), and when it is given *each time* a response occurs (consistency). Thus, you could effectively (and humanely) punish a dog that barks incessantly by spraying water on its nose each time it barks. About 10 to 15 such treatments are usually enough to greatly reduce barking. This would not be the case if you applied punishment haphazardly or long after the barking stopped. If you discover that your dog dug up a tree and ate it while you were gone, punishing the dog hours later will do little good. Likewise, the commonly heard childhood threat, "Wait till your father comes home, then you'll be sorry," just makes the father a feared brute; it doesn't effectively punish an undesirable response.

Severe punishment (following a response with an intensely aversive or unpleasant stimulus) can be extremely effective in stopping behavior. If 3-year-old Beavis sticks his finger in a light socket and gets a shock, that may be the last time he *ever* tries it. More often, however, punishment only temporarily *suppresses* a response. If the response is still reinforced, punishment may be particularly ineffective. Responses suppressed by mild punishment usually reappear later. If 7-year-old Alissa sneaks a snack from the refrigerator before dinner and is punished for it, she may pass up snacks for a short time. But because snack sneaking was also rewarded by the sneaked snack, she will probably try sneaky snacking again, sometime later (the sneaky little devil).

This fact was demonstrated by slapping rats on the paw as they were bar pressing in a Skinner box. Two groups of well-trained rats were placed on extinction. One group was punished with a slap for each bar press, whereas the other group was not. It might seem that the slap would cause bar pressing to extinguish more quickly. Yet this was not the case, as you can see in ● Figure 8.21. Punishment temporarily slowed responding, but it did not cause more rapid extinction. Slapping the paws of rats or children has little permanent effect on a reinforced response. It is worth stating again, however, that intense punishment may permanently suppress responding, even for actions as basic as eating. Animals severely punished while eating may never eat again (Bertsch, 1976).

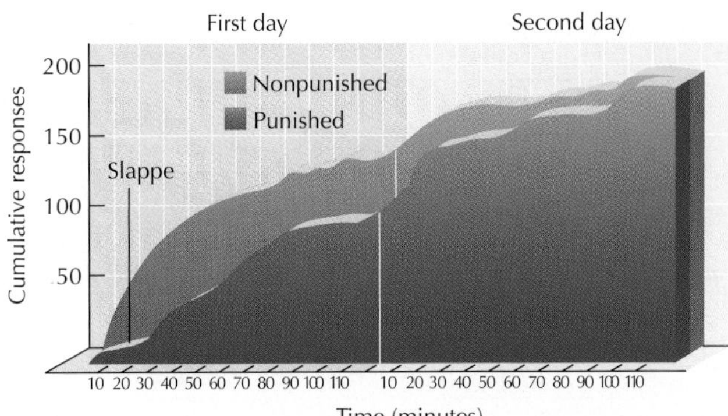

● **Figure 8.21** The effect of punishment on extinction. Immediately after punishment, the rate of bar pressing is suppressed, but by the end of the second day, the effects of punishment have disappeared. (After Skinner, *The Behavior of Organisms* © 1938 D. Appleton-Century Co., Inc. Reprinted by permission of Prentice Hall, Inc.)

BRIDGES

Learning principles are only one element of effective child management.

See Chapter 3, pages 115–118, for additional techniques.

Using Punishment Wisely

In light of its drawbacks, should punishment be used to control behavior? Parents, teachers, animal trainers, and the like, have three basic tools to control simple learning: (1) Reinforcement strengthens responses, (2) nonreinforcement causes responses to extinguish, and (3) punishment suppresses responses. (Consult ● Figure 8.22 to refresh your memory about the different types of reinforcement and punishment.) These tools work best in combination.

There are times when punishment may be necessary to manage the behavior of an animal, child, or even another adult. If you feel that you must punish, here are some tips to keep in mind.

1. *Use the minimum punishment necessary to suppress misbehavior.* If punishment is used at all, it should always be mild. In a situation that poses immediate danger, such as when a child reaches for something hot or a dog runs into the street, mild punishment may prevent disaster. Punishment in such cases works best when it produces actions *incompatible* with the response you want to suppress. Let's say a child reaches toward a stove burner. Would a swat on the bottom serve as an effective punisher? Probably so. It would be better, however, to slap the

Punishment The process of suppressing a response.

Punisher Any event that decreases the probability or frequency of responses it follows.

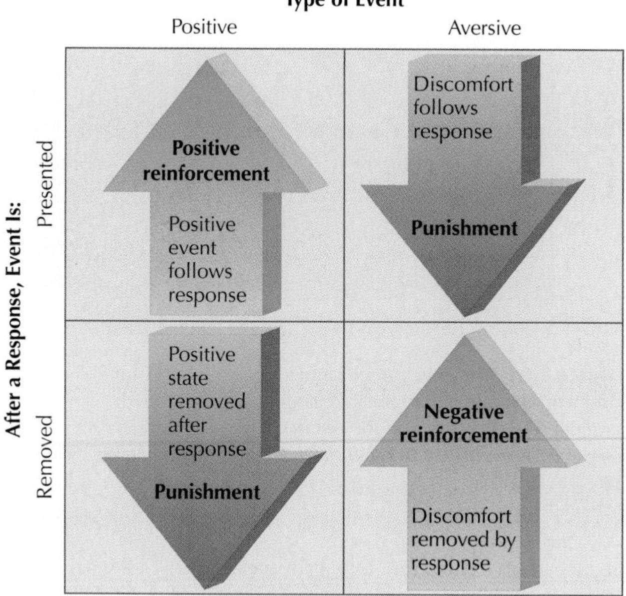

● **Figure 8.22** Types of reinforcement and punishment. The impact of an event depends on whether it is presented or removed after a response is made. Each square defines one possibility: Arrows pointing upward indicate that responding is increased; downward-pointing arrows indicate that responding is decreased. (Adapted from Kazdin, 1975.)

child's outstretched hand so that it will be *withdrawn* from the source of danger. Taking away privileges or other positive reinforcers (response cost) is usually best for older children and adults. Often, a verbal rebuke or a scolding is enough.

2. *Avoid harsh punishment such as spanking.* Harsh or excessive punishment has serious negative side effects. (Never slap a child's face, for instance.) Parents should minimize spanking or avoid it entirely (Gershoff, 2002). Although most children show no signs of long-term damage from spanking as long as spanking is backed up by supportive parenting, emotional damage does occur if spankings are severe, frequent, or coupled with harsh parenting (Baumrind, Larzelere, & Cowan, 2002). In addition, frequent spanking tends to increase aggression, and it leads to more problem behaviors, not fewer (McLoyd & Smith, 2002; Saadeh, Rizzo, & Roberts, 2002). In fact, antispanking laws have been passed in a number of countries around the world.
3. *Don't use punishment at all if you can discourage misbehavior in other ways.* Even mild punishment will be ineffective if reinforcers are still available in the situation. That's why it is best to also reward an alternate, desired response. For example, a child who has a habit of taking toys from her sister should not just be reprimanded for it. She should also be praised for cooperative play and sharing her toys with others. Punishment tells a person or an animal that a response was "wrong." However, it does not say what the "right" response is, so it *does not teach new behaviors.* If reinforcement is missing, punishment becomes less effective (Gershoff, 2002). Make liberal use of positive reinforcement, especially praise, to encourage good behavior. Also, try extinction first: See what happens if you ignore a problem behavior; or shift attention to a desirable activity and then reinforce it with praise. Remember, it is much more effective to strengthen and encourage desirable behaviors than it is to punish unwanted behaviors (Gershoff, 2002).
4. *Apply punishment during, or immediately after, misbehavior.* Of course, immediate punishment is not always possible. With older children and adults, you can bridge the delay by clearly stating what act you are punishing. If you cannot punish an animal immediately, wait for the next instance of misbehavior.
5. *Be consistent.* Be very clear about what you regard as misbehavior. Punish every time the misbehavior occurs. Don't punish for something one day and ignore it the next. If you are usually willing to give a child three chances, don't change the rule and explode without warning after a first offense. Both parents should try to punish their children for the same things and in the same way.
6. *Expect anger from a punished person.* Briefly acknowledge this anger, but be careful not to reinforce it. Be willing to admit your mistake if you wrongfully punish someone or if you punished too severely.
7. *Punish with kindness and respect.* Allow the punished person to retain self-respect. For instance, do not punish a person in front of others, if possible. A strong, trusting relationship tends to minimize behavior problems. Ideally, others should want to behave well to get your praise, not because they fear punishment.

Side Effects of Punishment

What are the drawbacks of using punishment? The basic problem with punishment is that it is aversive (painful or uncomfortable). As a result, people and situations associated with punishment tend, through classical conditioning, to become feared, resented, or disliked. The aversive nature of punishment makes it especially poor to use when teaching children to eat politely or in toilet training.

Escape and Avoidance

A second major problem is that aversive stimuli encourage escape and avoidance learning. In **escape learning** we learn to make a response in order to end an aversive stimulus. Escape learning simply reflects the operation of negative reinforcement, as the following example shows.

> A dog is placed in a two-compartment cage called a shuttle box. If the dog is shocked while in one of the compartments, it will quickly learn to jump to the other compartment to *escape* the shock. If a buzzer is sounded 10 seconds before each shock begins, the dog will soon learn to associate the buzzer with shock. It will then *avoid* pain by jumping *before* the shock begins (Solomon & Wynne, 1953).

Avoidance learning appears to involve *both* classical and operant conditioning (Levis, 1989). In a shuttle box a dog first learns, through classical conditioning, to fear the buzzer. (The buzzer is a CS, which is followed by shock, a US for pain and fear.) Each time the buzzer sounds, the dog becomes fearful. But by jumping to the "safe" compartment the dog can end the unpleasant fear it feels. Therefore, learning to jump *before* the onset of the shock is negatively reinforced by fear reduction. This is the operant part of avoidance learning.

Once avoidance is learned it is very persistent. The electric shock in a shuttle box can be turned off, yet the dog will continue to leap from the compartment each time the buzzer sounds. This fact is rather puzzling: If the buzzer is never followed by shock, why doesn't fear of the buzzer extinguish? The dog, it seems, has learned to *expect* that the buzzer will be followed by shock. If the dog leaves before the shock would normally occur, it gets no new information to change the expectancy (Chance, 2006).

Escape and avoidance learning are a regular part of daily experience. For example, if you work with a loud and obnoxious person, you may at first escape from conversations with him to obtain relief. Later you may dodge him altogether. This is an example of **avoidance learning** (making a response to postpone or prevent discomfort). Each time you sidestep him, your avoidance is again reinforced by a sense of relief. In many situations involving frequent punishment, similar desires to escape and avoid are activated. For example, children who run away from punishing parents (escape) may soon learn to lie about their behavior (avoidance) or to spend as much time away from home as possible (also an avoidance response).

Aggression

A third problem with punishment is that it can greatly increase *aggression*. Animals react to pain by attacking whomever or whatever else is around (Azrin et al., 1965). A common example is the faithful dog that nips its owner during a painful procedure at the veterinarian's office. Likewise, humans who are in pain have a tendency to lash out at others.

We also know that one of the most common responses to frustration is aggression. Generally speaking, punishment is painful, frustrating, or both. Punishment, therefore, sets up a powerful environment for learning aggression. When a child is spanked, the child may feel angry, frustrated, and hostile. What if the child then goes outside and hits a brother, a sister, or a neighbor? The danger is that aggressive acts may feel good because they release anger and frustration. If so, aggression has been rewarded and will tend to occur again in other frustrating situations.

A study of children found that those who are physically punished are more likely to engage in aggressive, impulsive, antisocial behavior (Straus & Mouradian, 1998). Another study of angry adolescent boys found that they were severely punished at home. This suppressed their misbehavior at home but made them more aggressive elsewhere. Parents were often surprised to learn that their "good boys" were in trouble for fighting at school (Bandura & Walters, 1959). Yet another study of classroom discipline problems found that physical punishment, yelling, and humiliation are generally ineffective. Positive reinforcement, in the form of praise, approval, and reward, is much more likely to quell classroom disruptions, defiance, and inattention (Tulley & Chiu, 1995).

Should You Punish or Not?

To summarize, the most common error in using punishment is to rely on it alone for training or discipline. The overall emotional adjustment of a child or pet disciplined mainly by reward is usually superior to one disciplined mainly by punishment. Frequent punishment makes a person or an animal unhappy, confused, anxious, aggressive, and fearful (Gershoff, 2002).

Parents and teachers should be aware that using punishment can be "habit forming." When children are being noisy, messy, disrespectful, or otherwise misbehaving, the temptation to punish them can be strong. The danger is that punishment often works. When it does, a sudden end to the adult's irritation acts as a negative reinforcer. This encourages the adult to use punishment more often in the future (Alberto & Troutman, 1998). Immediate silence may be "golden," but its cost can be very high in terms of a child's emotional health. "Sparing the rod" will not spoil a child. In fact, the reverse is true: Two recent studies found that young children with behavior problems were harshly punished at home (Brenner & Fox, 1998; DeKlyen et al., 1998).

KNOWLEDGE BUILDER

Punishment

REFLECT

Think of how you were punished as a child. Was the punishment immediate? Was it consistent? What effect did these factors have on your behavior? Was the punishment effective? Which of the side effects of punishment have you witnessed or experienced?

LEARNING CHECK

1. Negative reinforcement increases responding; punishment suppresses responding. T or F?
2. Three factors that greatly influence the effects of punishment are timing, consistency, and ______________.
3. Mild punishment tends to only temporarily __________ a response that is also reinforced.
   a. enhance c. replace
   b. aggravate d. suppress

BRIDGES

The connection between frustration and aggression is strong. But does frustration always produce aggression?

For more information, see Chapter 15, pages 505–506, and Chapter 19, pages 648–649.

Escape learning Learning to make a response in order to end an aversive stimulus.

Avoidance learning Learning to make a response in order to postpone or prevent discomfort.

4. Three undesired side effects of punishment are (1) conditioning of fear and resentment, (2) encouragement of aggression, and (3) the learning of escape or ______________ responses.
5. Using punishment can be "habit forming" because putting a stop to someone else's irritating behavior can ______________ ______________ the person who applies the punishment.

CRITICAL THINKING

6. Using the concept of partial reinforcement, can you explain why inconsistent punishment is especially ineffective?
7. Escape and avoidance learning have been applied to encourage automobile seat belt use. Can you explain how?

Answers: 1. T **2.** intensity **3.** d **4.** avoidance **5.** negatively reinforce **6.** An inconsistently punished response will continue to be reinforced on a partial schedule, which makes it even more resistant to extinction. **7.** Many automobiles have an unpleasant buzzer that sounds if the ignition key is turned before the driver's seat belt is fastened. Most drivers quickly learn to fasten the belt to stop the annoying sound. This is an example of escape conditioning. Avoidance conditioning is evident when a driver learns to buckle up before the buzzer sounds.

Cognitive Learning—Beyond Conditioning

Is all learning just a connection between stimuli and responses? Much learning can be explained by classical and operant conditioning. But, as we have seen, even basic conditioning has "mental" elements. As a human, you can anticipate future reward or punishment and react accordingly. (You may wonder why this doesn't seem to work when a doctor or dentist says, "This won't hurt a bit." Here's why: They lie!) There is no doubt that human learning includes a large *cognitive,* or mental, dimension. As humans, we are greatly affected by information, expectations, perceptions, mental images, and the like.

Loosely speaking, **cognitive learning** refers to understanding, knowing, anticipating, or otherwise making use of information-rich higher mental processes. Cognitive learning extends beyond basic conditioning into the realms of memory, thinking, problem solving, and language. Because these topics are covered in later chapters, our discussion here is limited to a first look at learning beyond conditioning.

Cognitive Maps

How do you navigate around the town you live in? Is it fair to assume that you have simply learned to make a series of right and left turns to get from one point to another? It is far more likely that you have an overall mental picture of how the town is laid out. This *cognitive map* acts as a guide even when you must detour or take a new route. A **cognitive map** is an internal representation of an area, such as a maze, city, or campus. Even the lowly rat—not exactly a mental giant—learns *where* food is found in a maze, not just which turns to make to reach the food (Tolman et al., 1946). If you have ever learned your way through some of the levels found in many video games, you will have a good idea of what a cognitive map is. In a sense, cognitive maps also apply to other kinds of knowledge. For instance, it could be said that you have been developing a "map" of psychology while reading this book. That's why students sometimes find it helpful to draw pictures or diagrams of how they envision concepts fitting together.

Latent Learning

Cognitive learning is also revealed by latent (hidden) learning. **Latent learning** occurs without obvious reinforcement and remains hidden until reinforcement is provided. Here's an example from a classic animal study: Two groups of rats were allowed to explore a maze. The animals in one group found food at the far end of the maze. Soon, they learned to rapidly make their way through the maze when released. Rats in the second group were unrewarded and showed no signs of learning. But later, when the "uneducated" rats were given food, they ran the maze as quickly as the rewarded group (Tolman & Honzik, 1930). Although there was no outward sign of it, the unrewarded animals had learned their way around the maze. Their learning, therefore, remained latent at first (● Figure 8.23).

How did they learn if there was no reinforcement? Just satisfying curiosity can be enough to reward learning (Harlow & Harlow, 1962). In humans, latent learning is related to higher-level abilities, such as anticipating future reward. For example, if you give an attractive classmate a ride home, you may make mental notes about how to get to his or her house, even if a date is only a remote future possibility.

Discovery Learning

Much of what is meant by cognitive learning is summarized by the word *understanding.* Each of us has, at times, learned ideas by *rote* (repetition and memorization). Although rote learning is efficient, many psychologists believe that learning is more lasting and flexible when people *discover* facts and principles on

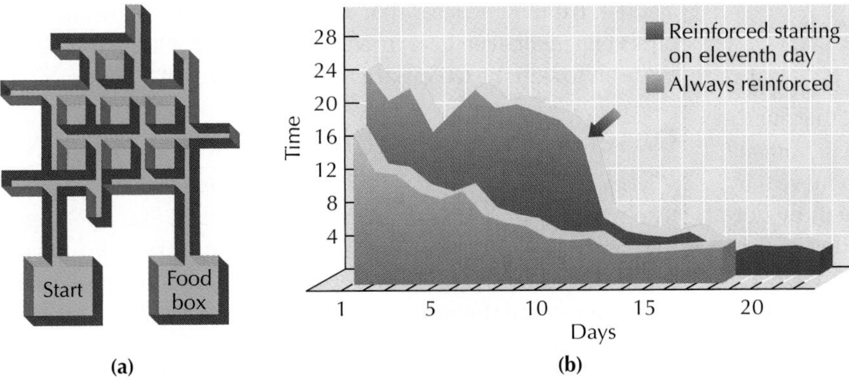

● **Figure 8.23** Latent learning. *(a)* The maze used by Tolman and Honzik to demonstrate latent learning by rats. *(b)* Results of the experiment. Notice the rapid improvement in performance that occurred when food was made available to the previously unreinforced animals. This indicates that learning had occurred but that it remained hidden or unexpressed. (Adapted from Tolman & Honzik, 1930.)

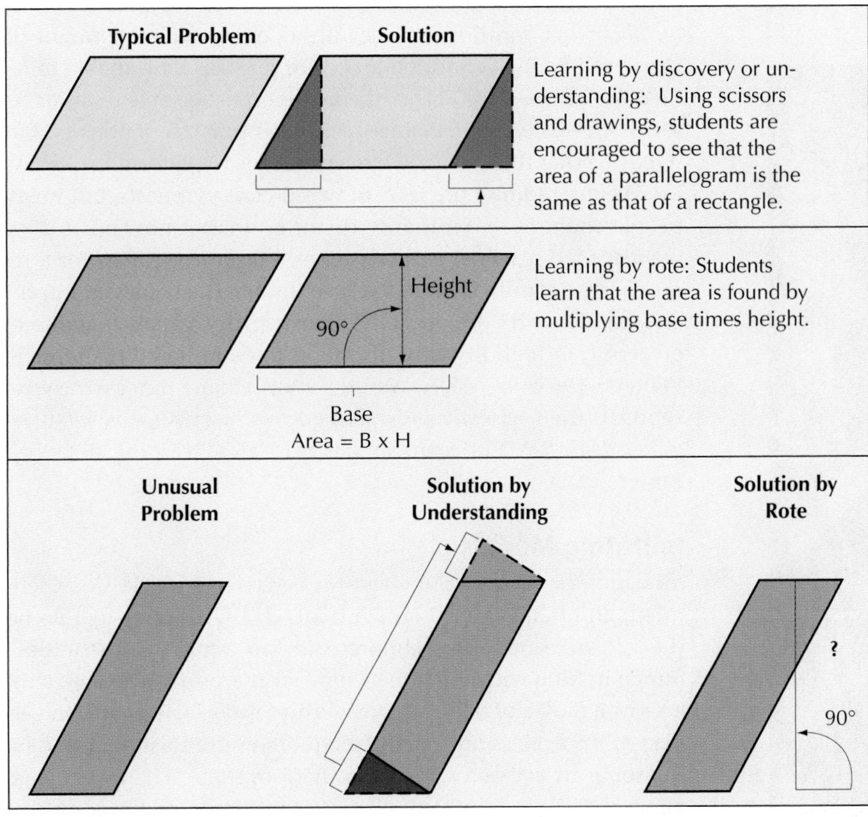

● **Figure 8.24** Learning by understanding and by rote. For some types of learning, understanding may be superior, although both types of learning are useful. (After Wertheimer, 1959.)

their own. In **discovery learning**, skills are gained by insight and understanding instead of by rote (de Jong & van Joolingen, 1998).

As long as learning occurs, what difference does it make if it is by discovery or by rote? ● Figure 8.24 illustrates the difference. Two groups of students were taught to calculate the area of a parallelogram by multiplying the height by the length of the base. Some were encouraged to see that a "piece" of a parallelogram could be "moved" to create a rectangle. Later, they were better able to solve unusual problems in which the height times base formula didn't seem to work. Students who simply memorized a rule were confused by the same problems (Wertheimer, 1959). As this implies, discovery leads to a better understanding of new or unusual problems. When possible, people should try new strategies and discover new solutions during learning (McDaniel & Schlager, 1990). However, this doesn't mean that students are supposed to stumble around and rediscover the principles of math, physics, biology, or chemistry. The best teaching strategies are based on *guided discovery,* in which students are given enough freedom to actively think about problems and enough guidance so that they gain useful knowledge (Mayer, 2004).

Cognitive learning Higher-level learning involving thinking, knowing, understanding, and anticipation.

Cognitive map Internal images or other mental representations of an area (maze, city, campus, and so forth) that underlie an ability to choose alternative paths to the same goal.

Latent learning Learning that occurs without obvious reinforcement and that remains unexpressed until reinforcement is provided.

Discovery learning Learning based on insight and understanding.

Modeling—Do as I Do, Not as I Say

The class watches intently as a skilled potter pulls a spinning ball of clay into the form of a vase. There is little doubt that many skills are learned by what Albert Bandura (1971) calls *observational learning,* or *modeling.* **Observational learning** is achieved by watching and imitating the actions of another person or by noting the consequences of the person's actions. In other words, modeling is any process in which information is imparted by example, before direct practice is allowed (Rosenthal & Steffek, 1991).

The value of learning by observation is obvious: Imagine trying to *tell* someone how to tie a shoe, do a dance step, crochet, or play a guitar. Bandura believes that anything that can be learned from direct experience can be learned by observation. Often, this allows a person to skip the tedious trial-and-error stage of learning.

Mark Andersen/Rubberball/Jupiterimages

Observational learning often imparts large amounts of information that would be difficult to obtain by reading instructions or memorizing rules.

Observational Learning

It seems obvious that we learn by observation, but how does it occur? By observing a **model** (someone who serves as an example), a person may (1) learn new responses, (2) learn to carry out or avoid previously learned responses (depending on what happens to the model for doing the same thing), or (3) learn a general rule that can be applied to various situations.

For observational learning to occur, several things must take place. First, the learner must pay *attention* to the model and *remember* what was done. (A beginning auto mechanic might be interested enough to watch an entire tune-up, but unable to remember all the steps.) Next, the learner must be able to *reproduce* the modeled behavior. (Sometimes this is a matter of practice, but it may be that the learner will never be able to perform the behavior. We may admire the feats of world-class gymnasts, but many people could never reproduce them, no matter how much they practiced.) If a model is *successful* at a task or *rewarded* for a response, the learner is more likely to imitate the behavior. In general, models who are attractive, trustworthy, capable, admired, powerful, or high in status also tend to be imitated (Bandura & Walters, 1963; Brewer & Wann, 1998). Finally, once a new response is tried, *normal reinforcement determines whether it will be repeated thereafter.* (Notice the similarity to latent learning, described earlier.)

Imitating Models

Modeling has a powerful effect on behavior. In a classic experiment, children watched an adult attack a large blow-up "Bo-Bo the Clown" doll. Some children saw an adult sit on the doll, punch it, hit it with a hammer, and kick it around the room. Others saw a movie of these actions. A third group saw a cartoon version of the aggression. Later, the children were frustrated by having some attractive toys taken away from them. Then, they were allowed to play with the Bo-Bo doll. Most imitated the adult's attack (● Figure 8.25). Some even added new aggressive acts of their own! Interestingly, the cartoon was only slightly less effective in encouraging aggression than the live adult model and the filmed model (Bandura et al., 1963).

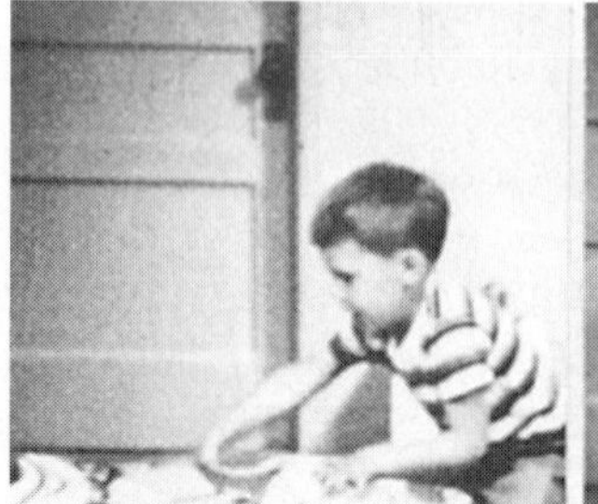

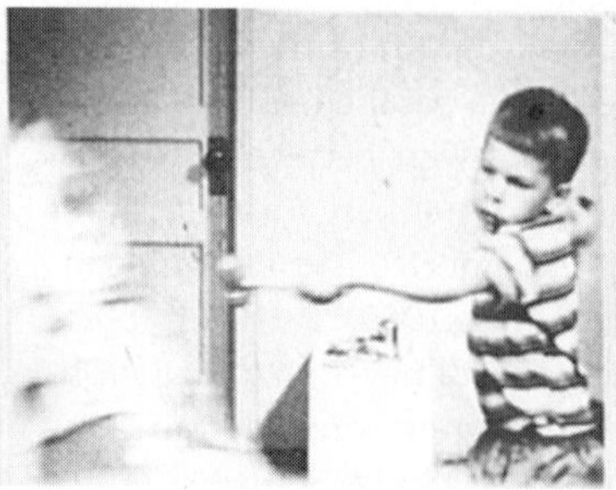
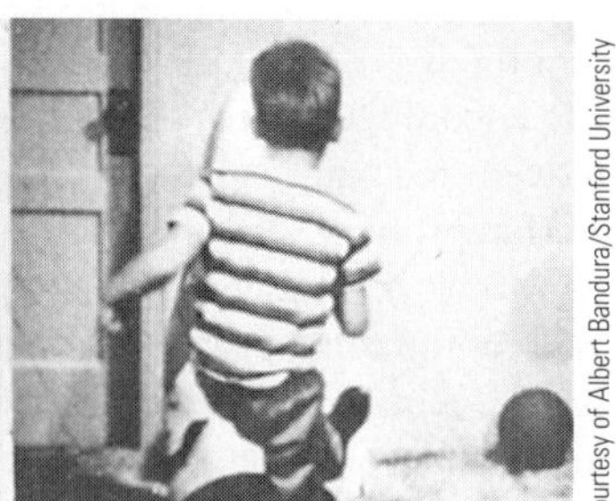

Courtesy of Albert Bandura/Stanford University

● **Figure 8.25** A nursery school child imitates the aggressive behavior of an adult model he has just seen in a movie.

Then do children blindly imitate adults? No. Remember that observational learning only prepares a person to duplicate a response. Whether it is actually imitated depends on whether the model was rewarded or punished for what was done. Nevertheless, when parents tell a child to do one thing but model a completely different response, children tend to imitate what the parents *do*, and *not* what they *say* (Bryan & Walbek, 1970). Thus, through modeling, children learn not only attitudes, gestures, emotions, and personality traits, but fears, anxieties, and bad habits as well. A good example is the children of smokers, who are much more likely to try smoking than children from smoke-free homes (Rowe et al., 1996).

Now, consider a typical situation: Little Raymond has just been interrupted at play by his older brother, Robert. Angry and frustrated, he screams at Robert. This behavior interrupts his father Frank's TV watching. Father promptly spanks little Raymond, saying, "This will teach you to hit your big brother." And it will. Because of modeling effects, it is unrealistic to expect a child to "Do as I say, not as I do." The message Frank has given the child is clear: "You have frustrated me; therefore, I will hit you." The next time little Raymond is frustrated, it won't be surprising if he imitates his father and hits his brother.

Modeling and Television

Does television promote observational learning? The impact of TV can be found in these figures: By the time the average person has graduated from high school, she or he will have viewed some 15,000 hours of TV, compared with only 11,000 hours spent in the classroom. In that time, viewers will have seen some 18,000 murders and countless acts of robbery, arson, bombing, torture, and beatings. Children watching Saturday morning cartoons see a chilling 26 or more violent acts each hour (Pogatchnik, 1990). Even G-rated cartoons average 10 minutes of violence per hour (Yokota & Thompson, 2000). In short, typical TV viewers are exposed to a massive dose of media violence, which tends to promote observational learning of aggression (Bushman & Anderson, 2001).

Life Before and After TV

What effect does the North American penchant for TV watching have on behavior? To answer this question, a team of researchers found a town in northwestern Canada that did not receive TV broadcasts. Discovering that the town was about to get TV, the team seized a rare opportunity. Tannis Williams and her colleagues carefully tested residents of the town just before TV arrived and again 2 years later. This natural experiment revealed that after the tube came to town:

- Reading development among children declined (Corteen & Williams, 1986).
- Children's scores on tests of creativity dropped (Harrison & Williams, 1986).
- Children's perceptions of sex roles became more stereotyped (Kimball, 1986).
- There was a significant increase in both verbal and physical aggression (● Figure 8.26). This occurred for both boys and girls, and it applied equally to children who were high or low in aggression before they began watching TV (Joy et al., 1986).

Tony Freeman/PhotoEdit

Televised violence may promote observational learning of aggression. In addition to providing poor behavioral models, constant exposure to aggressive imagery can lower viewers' emotional sensitivity to violence.

Televised Aggression

The last finding comes as no surprise. Studies show conclusively that if large groups of children watch a great deal of televised violence, they will be more prone to behave aggressively (Bushman & Anderson, 2001; Hughes & Hasbrouck, 1996). In other words, not all children will become more aggressive, but many will. Especially during adolescence, viewing lots of violence on television is associated with actual increases in aggression against others (Johnson et al., 2002). It's little wonder that a large panel of medical and psychological experts recently concluded that media violence is a serious threat to public health (Bushman & Anderson, 2001).

Does the same conclusion apply to video games? See "You Mean Video Games Might Be Bad for Me?" for some recent evidence.

Is it fair to say, then, that televised violence causes aggression in viewers, especially children? Fortunately, that would be an ex-

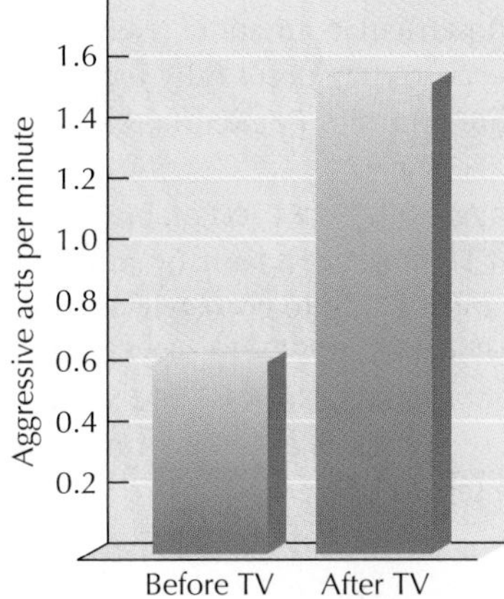

● Figure 8.26 This graph shows the average number of aggressive acts per minute before and after television broadcasts were introduced into a Canadian town. The increase in aggression after television watching began was significant. Two other towns that already had television were used for comparison. Neither showed significant increases in aggression during the same time period. (Data compiled from Joy et al., 1986.)

Observational learning Learning achieved by watching and imitating the actions of another or noting the consequences of those actions.

Model A person who serves as an example in observational learning.

CRITICAL THINKING

You Mean Video Games Might Be Bad for Me?

Today's kids can experience more gore in a day than most people used to experience in a lifetime, even during military combat. For example, in one popular video game you can kill an entire marching band with a flame-thrower. Some of your victims won't die right away. They will just writhe in pain, begging you to finish them off.

What effects do such experiences have on people who play violent video games? Recent reviews of a large number of studies lead to the unmistakable conclusion that violent video games increase aggressive behavior in children and young adults (Anderson & Bushman, 2002; Anderson, 2004). As with TV, young children are especially susceptible to fantasy violence in video games (Anderson et al., 2003; Bensley & Van Eenwyk, 2001).

One study illustrates the impact of video game violence. First, college students played a very violent video game (Mortal Kombat) or a nonviolent one (PGA Tournament Golf). Next, they competed with another student (actually an actor) in a task that allowed aggression and retaliation to take place. Students who played Mortal Kombat were much more likely to aggress, by punishing their competitor (Bartholow & Anderson, 2002). (Don't mess with someone who just played Mortal Kombat!)

How does video game violence increase aggressive behavior? One possibility is that repeated exposure to violence desensitizes players, making them less likely to react negatively to violence and, hence, more prone to engage in it (Bartholow, Sestir, & Davis, 2005; Funk, 2005). Another possibility is that by practicing violence against other people, players may learn to be aggressive in real life (Unsworth & Ward, 2001). The new generation of virtual reality and Internet-based games allow players to learn the skills of stalking and attacking each other. (Before you write off video games altogether, read "You Mean Video Games Might Be Good for Me?" in Chapter 11.)

aggeration. Televised violence can make aggression more *likely,* but it does not invariably "cause" it to occur for any given child. Many other factors affect the chances that hostile thoughts will be turned into actions. Among children, one such factor is the extent to which a child *identifies* with aggressive characters (Huesmann et al., 1983). That's why it is so sad to find TV *heroes* behaving aggressively, as well as villains (Boyatzis, Matillo, & Nesbitt, 1995). Younger children, in particular, are more likely to be influenced by such programs because they don't fully recognize that the characters and stories are fantasies (McKenna & Ossoff, 1998).

Youngsters who believe that aggression is an acceptable way to solve problems, who believe that TV violence is realistic, and who identify with TV characters are most likely to copy televised aggression (Huesmann, Moise, & Podolski, 1997). In view of such findings, it is understandable that Canada, Norway, and Switzerland have restricted the amount of permissible violence on television. Should all countries do the same?

A Look Ahead

Conditioning principles are often derived from animal experiments. However, it should be apparent that the same principles apply to human behavior. Perhaps the best way to appreciate this fact is to observe how reinforcement affects your own behavior. With this in mind, the upcoming Psychology in Action section proposes a personal experiment in operant conditioning. Don't miss this coming attraction!

KNOWLEDGE BUILDER

Cognitive Learning and Imitation

REFLECT

Try to think of at least one personal example of each of these concepts: cognitive map, latent learning, discovery learning.

Describe a skill you have learned primarily through observational learning. How did modeling help you learn?

What entertainment or sports personalities did you identify with when you were a child? How did it affect your behavior?

LEARNING CHECK

1. An internal representation of relationships is referred to as a ____________ ____________.
2. Learning that suddenly appears when a reward or incentive for performance is given is called
   a. discovery learning c. rote learning
   b. latent learning d. reminiscence
3. Psychologists use the term ____________ to describe observational learning.
4. If a model is successful, rewarded, attractive, or high in status, his or her behavior is
   a. difficult to reproduce c. more likely to be imitated
   b. less likely to be attended to d. subject to positive transfer
5. Children who observed a live adult behave aggressively became more aggressive; those who observed movie and cartoon aggression did not. T or F?

6. Children are most likely to imitate TV characters with whom they identify. T or F?
7. Children who watch a great deal of televised violence are more prone to be aggressive, an effect that is best explained by
   a. negative reinforcement
   b. shaping and successive approximations
   c. observational learning
   d. vicarious classical conditioning

CRITICAL THINKING

8. Draw a map of your school's campus as you picture it now. Draw a map of the campus as you pictured it after your first visit. Why do the maps differ?
9. Children who watch many aggressive programs on television tend to be more aggressive than average. Why doesn't this observation prove that televised aggression causes aggressive behavior?

Answers: 1. cognitive map **2.** b **3.** modeling **4.** c **5.** F **6.** T **7.** c **8.** Your cognitive map of the campus has undoubtedly become more accurate and intricate over time as you have added details to it. Your drawings should reflect this change. **9.** Because the observation is based on a correlation. Children who are already aggressive may choose to watch more aggressive programs, rather than being made aggressive by them. It took experimental studies to verify that televised aggression promotes aggression by viewers.

PSYCHOLOGY IN ACTION

Behavioral Self-Management—A Rewarding Project

This discussion could be the start of one of the most personal applications of psychology in this book. Many people have learned to use reinforcement to alter or manage their own behavior (Watson & Tharp, 2002). This, then, is an invitation to carry out a self-management project of your own. Would you like to increase the number of hours you spend studying each week? Would you like to exercise more, attend more classes, concentrate longer, or read more books? All these activities and many others can be improved by following the rules described here.

Self-Managed Behavior

The principles of operant conditioning can be adapted to manage your own behavior (Martin & Pear, 2003). Here's how:

1. **Choose a target behavior.** Identify the activity you want to change.
2. **Record a baseline.** Record how much time you currently spend performing the target activity or count the number of desired or undesired responses you make each day.
3. **Establish goals.** Remember the principle of shaping and set realistic goals for gradual improvement on each successive week. Also, set daily goals that add up to the weekly goal.
4. **Choose reinforcers.** If you meet your daily goal, what reward will you allow yourself? Daily rewards might be watching television, eating a candy bar, socializing with friends, playing a musical instrument, or whatever you enjoy. Also establish a weekly reward. If you reach your weekly goal, what reward will you allow yourself? A movie? A dinner out? A weekend hike?
5. **Record your progress.** Keep accurate records of the amount of time spent each

Rubberball/SuperStock

day on the desired activity or the number of times you make the desired response.

6. **Reward successes.** If you meet your daily goal, collect your reward. If you fall short, be honest with yourself and skip the reward. Do the same for your weekly goal.
7. **Adjust your plan as you learn more about your behavior.** Overall progress will reinforce your attempts at self-management.

If you have trouble finding rewards, or if you don't want to use the entire system, remember that anything done often can serve as reinforcement. This is known as the **Premack principle.** It is named after David Premack, a psychologist who popularized its use. For example, if you watch television every night and want to study more, make it a rule not to turn on the set until you have studied for an hour (or whatever length of time you choose). Then lengthen the requirement each week. Here is a sample of one student's plan:

1. *Target behavior:* number of hours spent studying for school.
2. *Recorded baseline:* an average of 25 minutes per day for a weekly total of 3 hours.
3. *Goal for the first week:* an increase in study time to 40 minutes per day; weekly goal of 5 hours total study time. *Goal for second week:* 50 minutes per day and 6 hours per week. *Goal for third week:* 1 hour per day and 7 hours per week. *Ultimate goal:* to reach and maintain 14 hours per week study time.
4. *Daily reward for reaching goal:* 1 hour of guitar playing in the evening; no playing if the goal is not met. *Weekly reward for reaching goal:* going to a movie or buying a DVD.

Self-Recording

Even if you find it difficult to give and withhold rewards, you are likely to succeed. Simply knowing that you are reaching a desired goal can be reward enough. The key to any self-management program, therefore, is **self-recording** (keeping records of response frequencies). The concept is demonstrated by students in a psychology course. Some of the students recorded their study time and graphed their daily and weekly study behavior. Even though no extra rewards were offered, these students earned better grades than others who were not required to keep records (Johnson & White, 1971).

As discussed earlier, feedback is also valuable for changing personal behavior. Feedback can help you decrease bad habits as well as increase desirable responses. Keep track of the number of times daily that you arrive late to class, smoke a cigarette, watch an hour of TV, drink a cup of coffee, bite your fingernails, swear, or whatever you are interested in changing. A simple tally on a piece of paper will do, or you can get a small mechanical counter like those used to keep golf scores or count calories. Record keeping helps break patterns, and the feedback can be motivating as you begin to make progress.

Good Ways to Break Bad Habits

How can I use learning principles to break a bad habit? By using the methods we have discussed, you can reinforce yourself for *decreasing* unwanted behaviors, such as swearing, biting your nails, criticizing others, smoking, drinking coffee, watching TV too much, or engaging in any other behavior you choose to target. However, breaking bad habits may require some additional techniques. Here are four strategies to help you change bad habits.

Alternative Responses

A good strategy for change is to try to get the same reinforcement with a new response.

Example: Marta often tells jokes at the expense of others. Her friends sometimes feel hurt by her sharp-edged humor. Marta senses this and wants to change. What can she do? Usually, Marta's joke telling is reinforced by attention and approval. She could just as easily get the same reinforcement by giving other people praise or compliments. Making a change in her behavior should be easy because she will continue to receive the reinforcement she seeks.

Extinction

Try to discover what is reinforcing an unwanted response and remove, avoid, or delay the reinforcement (Ferster et al., 1962).

Example: Fatima has developed a habit of taking longer and longer "breaks" to watch TV when she should be studying. Obviously, TV watching is reinforcing her break taking. To improve her study habits, Fatima could delay reinforcement by studying at the library or some other location a good distance from her TV.

Response Chains

Break up response chains that precede an undesired behavior. The key idea is to scramble the chain of events that leads to an undesired response (Watson & Tharp, 2002).

Example: Almost every night Ignacio comes home from work, turns on the TV, and eats a whole bag of cookies or chips. He then takes a shower and changes clothes. By dinnertime he has lost his appetite. Ignacio realizes he is substituting junk food for dinner. Ignacio could solve the problem by breaking the response chain that precedes dinner. For instance, he could shower immediately when he gets home, or he could avoid turning on the television until after dinner.

Cues and Antecedents

Try to avoid, narrow down, or remove stimuli that elicit the bad habit.

Example: Raul wants to cut down on smoking. He has taken many smoking cues out of his surroundings by removing ashtrays, matches, and extra cigarettes from his house, car, and office. This is a good first step. Drug cravings are strongly related to cues conditioned to the drug, such as the odor of cigarettes (Lazev et al., 1999). Raul should try narrowing antecedent stimuli even more. He could begin by smoking only in the lounge at work, never in his office or in his car. He could then limit his smoking to home. Then to only one room at home. Then to one chair at home. If he succeeds in getting this far, he may want to limit his smoking to only one unpleasant place, such as a bathroom, basement, or garage (Goldiamond, 1971).

Contracting

If you try the techniques described here and have difficulty sticking with them, you may want to try behavioral contracting. In a **behavioral contract,** you state a specific problem behavior you want to control or a goal you want to achieve. Also state the rewards you will receive, privileges you will forfeit, or punishments you must accept. The contract should be typed and signed by you and a person you trust.

A behavioral contract can be quite motivating, especially when mild punishment is part of the agreement. Here's an example reported by Nurnberger and Zimmerman (1970): A student working on his Ph.D. had completed all requirements but his dissertation, yet for 2 years had not written a single page. A contract was drawn up for him in which he agreed to meet weekly deadlines on the number of pages he would complete. To make sure he would meet the deadlines, he wrote postdated checks. These were to be forfeited if he failed to reach his goal for the week. The checks were made out to organizations he despised (the Ku Klux Klan and American Nazi Party). From the time he signed the contract until he finished his degree, the student's work output was greatly improved.

Getting Help

Attempting to manage or alter your own behavior may be more difficult than it sounds. If you feel you need more information, consult either of the books listed here. You will also find helpful advice in the Psychology in Action section of Chapter 17. If you do try a self-modification project but find it impossible to reach your goals, be aware that professional advice is available.

Where to Obtain More Information

Watson, D. L., & Tharp, R. G. (2002). *Self-directed behavior.* Belmont, CA: Wadsworth.

Williams, R. L., & Long, J. D. (1991). *Toward a self-managed life style.* Boston: Houghton Mifflin.

KNOWLEDGE BUILDER

Behavioral Self-Management

REFLECT

Even if you don't expect to carry out a self-management project right now, outline a plan for changing your own behavior. Be sure to describe the behavior you want to change, set goals, and identify reinforcers.

LEARNING CHECK

1. After a target behavior has been selected for reinforcement, it's a good idea to record a baseline so that you can set realistic goals for change. T or F?
2. Self-recording, even without the use of extra rewards, can bring about desired changes in target behaviors. T or F?
3. The Premack principle states that behavioral contracting can be used to reinforce changes in behavior. T or F?
4. A self-management plan should make use of the principle of shaping by setting a graduated series of goals. T or F?
5. Eleni ends up playing dozens of solitaire games on her computer each time she tries to work on a term paper for her history class. Eventually she does get to work on the paper, but only after a long delay. To break this bad habit Eleni removes the solitaire icon from her computer screen so that she won't see it when she begins work. Eleni has used which strategy for breaking bad habits?
   a. alternative responses c. avoid cues
   b. extinction d. contracting

CRITICAL THINKING

6. How does setting daily goals in a behavioral self-management program help maximize the effects of reinforcement?

Answers: 1. T **2.** T **3.** F **4.** T **5.** c **6.** Daily performance goals and rewards reduce the delay of reinforcement, which maximizes its impact.

Premack principle Any high-frequency response can be used to reinforce a low-frequency response.

Self-recording Self-management based on keeping records of response frequencies.

Behavioral contract A formal agreement stating behaviors to be changed and consequences that apply.

Chapter in Review

What is learning?

- Learning is a relatively permanent change in behavior due to experience. Learning resulting from conditioning depends on reinforcement. Reinforcement increases the probability that a particular response will occur.
- Classical, or respondent, conditioning and instrumental, or operant, conditioning are two basic types of learning.
- In classical conditioning, a previously neutral stimulus begins to elicit a response through association with another stimulus.
- In operant conditioning, the frequency and pattern of voluntary responses are altered by their consequences.

How does classical conditioning occur?

- Classical conditioning, studied by Pavlov, occurs when a neutral stimulus (NS) is associated with an unconditioned stimulus (US).
- The US causes a reflex called the unconditioned response (UR). If the NS is consistently paired with the US, it becomes a conditioned stimulus (CS) capable of producing a response by itself. This response is a conditioned (learned) response (CR).
- When the conditioned stimulus is followed by the unconditioned stimulus, conditioning is reinforced (strengthened).
- From an informational view, conditioning creates expectancies, which alter response patterns. In classical conditioning, the CS creates an expectancy that the US will follow.
- Higher order conditioning occurs when a well-learned conditioned stimulus is used as if it were an unconditioned stimulus, bringing about further learning.
- When the CS is repeatedly presented alone, conditioning is extinguished (weakened or inhibited). After extinction seems to be complete, a rest period may lead to the temporary reappearance of a conditioned response. This is called spontaneous recovery.
- Through stimulus generalization, stimuli similar to the conditioned stimulus will also produce a response. Generalization gives way to stimulus discrimination when an organism learns to respond to one stimulus, but not to similar stimuli.

Does conditioning affect emotions?

- Conditioning applies to visceral or emotional responses as well as simple reflexes. As a result, conditioned emotional responses (CERs) also occur.
- Irrational fears called phobias may be CERs. Conditioning of emotional responses can occur vicariously (secondhand) as well as directly.

How does operant conditioning occur?

- Operant conditioning occurs when a voluntary action is followed by a reinforcer. Reinforcement in operant conditioning increases the frequency or probability of a response. This result is based on the law of effect.
- Complex operant responses can be taught by reinforcing successive approximations to a final desired response. This is called shaping. It is particularly useful in training animals.
- If an operant response is not reinforced, it may extinguish (disappear). But after extinction seems complete, it may temporarily reappear (spontaneous recovery).

Are there different kinds of operant reinforcement?

- In positive reinforcement, reward or a pleasant event follows a response. In negative reinforcement, responses that end discomfort tend to be repeated.
- Primary reinforcers are "natural," physiologically based rewards. Intracranial stimulation of "pleasure centers" in the brain can also serve as a primary reinforcer.
- Secondary reinforcers are learned. They typically gain their reinforcing value by direct association with primary reinforcers or because they can be exchanged for primary reinforcers. Tokens and money gain their reinforcing value in this way.
- Feedback, or knowledge of results, aids learning and improves performance. It is most effective when it is immediate, detailed, and frequent.
- Programmed instruction breaks learning into a series of small steps and provides immediate feedback. Computer-assisted instruction (CAI) does the same but has the added advantage of providing alternative exercises and information when needed. Four variations of CAI are drill and practice, instructional games, educational simulations, and interactive multimedia instruction.

How are we influenced by patterns of reward?

- Delay of reinforcement greatly reduces its effectiveness, but long chains of responses may be built up so that a single reinforcer maintains many responses.
- Superstitious behaviors often become part of response chains because they *appear* to be associated with reinforcement.
- Reward or reinforcement may be given continuously (after every response) or on a schedule of partial reinforcement. Partial reinforcement produces greater resistance to extinction.
- The four most basic schedules of reinforcement are fixed ratio, variable ratio, fixed interval, and variable interval. Each produces a distinct pattern of responding.

- Stimuli that precede a reinforced response tend to control the response on future occasions (stimulus control). Two aspects of stimulus control are generalization and discrimination.
- In generalization, an operant response tends to occur when stimuli similar to those preceding reinforcement are present.
- In discrimination, responses are given in the presence of discriminative stimuli associated with reinforcement (S+) and withheld in the presence of stimuli associated with nonreinforcement (S−).

What does punishment do to behavior?

- Punishment decreases responding. Punishment occurs when a response is followed by the onset of an aversive event or by the removal of a positive event (response cost).
- Punishment is most effective when it is immediate, consistent, and intense. Mild punishment tends to only temporarily suppress responses that are also reinforced or were acquired by reinforcement.
- The undesirable side effects of punishment include the conditioning of fear to punishing agents and situations associated with punishment, the learning of escape and avoidance responses, and the encouragement of aggression.

What is cognitive learning?

- Cognitive learning involves higher mental processes, such as understanding, knowing, or anticipating. Even in relatively simple learning situations, animals and people seem to form cognitive maps (internal representations of relationships).
- In latent learning, learning remains hidden or unseen until a reward or incentive for performance is offered.
- Discovery learning emphasizes insight and understanding, in contrast to rote learning.

Does learning occur by imitation?

- Much human learning is achieved through observation, or modeling. Observational learning is influenced by the personal characteristics of the model and the success or failure of the model's behavior. Studies have shown that aggression is readily learned and released by modeling.
- Television characters can act as powerful models for observational learning. Televised violence increases the likelihood of aggression by viewers.

How does conditioning apply to practical problems?

- Operant principles can be readily applied to manage behavior in everyday settings. When managing one's own behavior, self-reinforcement, self-recording, feedback, and behavioral contracting are all helpful.
- Four strategies that can help change bad habits are reinforcing alternative responses, promoting extinction, breaking response chains, and avoiding antecedent cues.

Web Resources

Internet addresses frequently change. To find the sites listed here, visit www.thomsonedu.com/psychology/coon for an updated list of Internet addresses and direct links to relevant sites.

***Psychology: Gateways to Mind and Behavior* Website** Online quizzes, flash cards, and other helpful study aids for this text. www.thomsonedu.com/psychology/coon.

Animal Training at Sea World Explains how marine mammals are trained at Sea World.

Memory A short tutorial on classical conditioning, operant conditioning, and cognitive learning.

Methods for Changing Behavior Teaches you how to modify your own behavior.

Observational Learning Presents Bandura's original work on modeling, with graphs.

Oppatoons Cartoons of rats undergoing conditioning.

Studying Television Violence An article on television violence.

ThomsonNOW™ Go to www.thomsonedu.com to link to ThomsonNow, your online study tool. First take the **Pre-Test** for this chapter to get your **Personalized Study Plan,** which will identify topics you need to review and direct you to online resources. Then take the **Post-Test** to determine what concepts you have mastered and what you still need work on.

InfoTrac College Edition For recent articles related to the impact of television, use Key Words search for VIOLENCE ON TELEVISION. Go to www.thomsonedu.com/psychology/coon.

Interactive Learning

***PsychNow!* Version 2.0 CD-ROM** Interact with the material with *PsychNow!*'s animations, video clips, experiments, and interactive assessments. For this chapter, go to *5a. Classical Conditioning, 5b. Operant Conditioning,* and *5c. Observational Learning* to get more information on conditioning and learning.

chapter

9

Memory

THEME:

Memory is not like a tape recorder or a video camera: Memories change as they are stored and retrieved.

Richard Heinzen/SuperStock

Key Questions

Is there more than one type of memory?

What are the features of each type of memory?

Is there more than one type of long-term memory?

How is memory measured?

What are "photographic" memories?

What causes forgetting?

How accurate are everyday memories?

What happens in the brain when memories are formed?

How can memory be improved?

Preview

"What the Hell's Going on Here?"

It's February and Steven is cross-country skiing on the ice of Lake Michigan. He realizes he is very cold and decides to turn back. In a few minutes comes a new realization: He is lost. Wandering on the ice, he grows numb and very, very tired.

Put yourself in Steven's shoes, and you will appreciate the shock of what happened next. Steven clearly recalls wandering lost and alone on the ice. Immediately after that, he remembers waking up in a field. But as he looked around, Steven knew something was wrong. It was a warm spring day! In his backpack he found running shoes, swimming goggles, and a pair of glasses—all unfamiliar. As he looked at his clothing—also unfamiliar—Steven thought to himself, "What the hell's going on here?" Fourteen months had passed since he left to go skiing (Loftus, 1980). How did he get to the field? Steven couldn't say. He had lost over a year of his life to total amnesia.

As Steven's amnesia vividly shows, life without memory would be meaningless. Imagine the terror of having all your memories wiped out. You would have no identity, no knowledge, and no life history (Behrend, Beike, & Lampinen, 2004). You wouldn't recognize friends or family members. When you looked in a mirror, a stranger would stare back at you. In a very real sense, we are our memories.

This chapter discusses memory and forgetting. By reading it you'll almost certainly discover ways to improve your memory.

Stages of Memory—Do You Have a Mind Like a Steel Trap? Or a Sieve?

Do you remember what you had for breakfast this morning? Or what happened on September 11, 2001? Of course you do. But how is it possible for us to so easily travel back in time? Let's begin with a look at basic memory systems. An interesting series of events must occur before we can say, "I remember."

Many people think of memory as "a dusty storehouse of facts." In reality, **memory** is an active system that receives, stores, organizes, alters, and recovers information (Lieberman, 2004). In some ways memory acts like a computer (● Figure 9.1). Incoming information is first **encoded**, or changed into a usable form. This step is like typing data into a computer. Next, information is **stored**, or held in the system. (As we will see in a moment, human memory can be pictured as three separate storage systems.) Finally, memories must be **retrieved**, or taken out of storage, to be useful. If you're going to remember all of the 9,856 new terms on your next psychology exam, you must successfully encode, store, and retrieve them.

What are the three separate memory systems just mentioned? Psychologists have identified three stages of memory. To be stored for a long time, information must pass through all three (● Figure 9.2).

● **Figure 9.1** In some ways, a computer acts like a mechanical memory system. Both systems process information, and both allow encoding, storage, and retrieval of data.

Sensory Memory

Let's say a friend asks you to pick up several things at a market. How will you remember them? Information first enters **sensory memory**, which can hold an exact copy of what you see or hear, for a few seconds or less. For instance, look at a flower and then

Memory The mental system for receiving, encoding, storing, organizing, altering, and retrieving information.

Encoding Converting information into a form in which it will be retained in memory.

Storage Holding information in memory for later use.

Retrieval Recovering information from storage in memory.

Sensory memory The first stage of memory, which holds an exact record of incoming information for a few seconds or less.

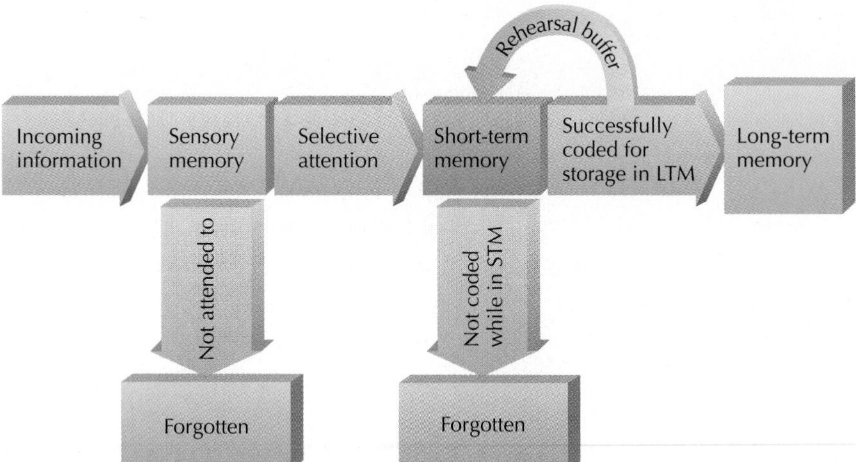

● **Figure 9.2** Remembering is thought to involve at least three steps. Incoming information is first held for a second or two by sensory memory. Information selected by attention is then transferred to temporary storage in short-term memory. If new information is not rapidly encoded or rehearsed, it is forgotten. If it is transferred to long-term memory, it becomes relatively permanent, although retrieving it may be a problem. The preceding is a useful, but highly simplified, *model* of memory; it may not be literally true of what happens in the brain (Eysenck & Keane, 1995).

close your eyes. An **icon** (EYE-kon), or fleeting mental image, of the flower will persist for about one half second. Similarly, when you hear information, sensory memory stores it as an *echo* for up to 2 seconds (Schweickert, 1993). An **echo** is a brief flurry of activity in the auditory system. In general, sensory memory holds information just long enough to move it to the second memory system (Neath, 2002).

Short-Term Memory

Not everything we see or hear stays in memory. Imagine that a radio is playing in the background as your friend reads her shopping list. Will you remember what the announcer says, too? Probably not, because *selective attention* (focusing on a selected portion of sensory input) controls what information moves on to short-term memory. **Short-term memory (STM)** holds small amounts of information for brief periods. By paying attention to your friend, you will place her shopping list in short-term memory (while you ignore the voice on the radio saying, "Buy Burpo Butter").

How are short-term memories encoded? Short-term memories can be stored as images. But more often they are stored *phonetically* (by sound), especially in recalling words and letters (Neath, 2002). If you are introduced to Tim at a party and you forget his name, you are more likely to call him by a name that sounds like Tim (Jim, Kim, or Slim, for instance), rather than a name that sounds different, such as Bob or Mike. Your friend with the shopping list may be lucky if you don't bring home jam instead of ham and soap instead of soup!

Short-term memory briefly stores small amounts of information. When you dial a phone number or briefly remember a shopping list, you are using STM. Notice that information is quickly "dumped" from STM and forever lost. Short-term memory prevents our minds from storing useless names, dates, telephone numbers, and other trivia.

As you may have noticed when dialing a telephone, STM is very sensitive to *interruption,* or *interference.* You've probably had something like this happen: Someone leaves a phone number on your answering machine. You repeat the number to yourself as you start to dial. Then the doorbell rings and you rush to see who is there. When you return to the phone, you have completely forgotten the number. You listen to the message again and memorize the number. This time as you begin to dial, someone asks you a question. You answer, turn to the phone, and find that you have forgotten the number. Notice again that STM can handle only small amounts of information. It is very difficult to do more than one task at a time in STM (Miyake, 2001).

Working Memory

Short-term memory is often used for more than just storing information. When STM is combined with other mental processes, it provides an area of **working memory** where we do much of our thinking. Working memory acts as a sort of "mental scratchpad." It briefly holds the information we need when we are thinking and solving problems (Tuholski, Engle, & Baylis, 2001). Whenever you do mental arithmetic, put together a puzzle, plan a meal, follow directions, or read a book, you are using working memory (Baddeley, 2003).

Long-Term Memory

If STM is so limited, how do we remember for longer periods of time? Information that is important or meaningful is transferred to **long-term memory (LTM)**, which acts as a lasting storehouse for knowledge. LTM contains everything you know about the world—from aardvark to zucchini, math to MTV, facts to fantasy. Yet there appears to be no danger of running out of room. LTM can hold nearly limitless amounts of information. In fact, the more you know, the easier it becomes to add new information to memory. This is the reverse of what we would expect if LTM could be "filled up" (Eysenck & Keane, 1995). It is also one of many reasons for getting an education.

HUMAN DIVERSITY

Cows, Memories, and Culture

As noted, we are most likely to remember information that is personally meaningful. If you were on a farm and saw twenty cows walk by, do you think you could remember the age, color, sex, and condition of all of them? Unless you are a dairy farmer, doing so would be quite a feat of memory. However, for a Maasai person from East Africa, it would be easy. Livestock are very important in Maasai culture; wealth among the Maasai is measured by the number of cattle owned. Thus, the Maasai are prepared to code and store information about cattle that would be difficult for many people in the United States to remember.

Culture affects our memories in other interesting ways. For example, American culture emphasizes individuals, whereas Chinese culture emphasizes membership in groups. In a recent study, European-American and Chinese adults were asked to recall twenty memories from any time in their lives. As expected, American memories tended to be self-centered: Most people remembered surprising events and what they did during the events. Chinese adults, in contrast, remembered important social or historical events and their own interactions with family members, friends, and others (Wang & Conway, 2004). Thus, in the United States, personal memories tend to be about "me"; in China they tend to be about "us."

Malcolm Linton/Liaison/Getty Images

Are long-term memories also encoded as sounds? They can be. But typically, long-term memories are stored on the basis of *meaning,* not sound. If you make an error in LTM, it will probably be related to meaning. For example, if you are trying to recall the word *barn* from a memorized list, you are more likely to mistakenly say *shed* or *farm* than *yarn* or *darn.* If you can link information in STM to knowledge already stored in LTM, it gains meaning. This makes it easier to remember. As an example, try to memorize this story:

> With hocked gems financing him, our hero bravely defied all scornful laughter. "Your eyes deceive," he had said, "An egg, not a table, correctly typifies this unexplored planet." Now three sturdy sisters sought proof. Forging along, days became weeks as many doubters spread fearful rumors about the edge. At last from nowhere welcome winged creatures appeared, signifying momentous success. (Adapted from Dooling & Lachman, 1971)

This odd story emphasizes the impact that meaning has on memory. People given the title of the story were able to remember it far better than those not given a title. See if the title helps you as much as it did them: "Columbus Discovers America."

Dual Memory

Most of our daily memory chores are handled by STM and LTM. To summarize their connection, picture short-term memory as a small desk at the front of a huge warehouse full of filing cabinets (LTM). As information enters the warehouse, it is first placed on the desk. Because the desk is small, it must be quickly cleared off to make room for new information. Unimportant items are simply tossed away. Meaningful or important information is placed in the files (LTM). (See "Cows, Memories, and Culture.") When we want to use knowledge from LTM to answer a question, the information is returned to STM. Or, in our analogy, a folder is taken out of the files (LTM) and moved to the desk (STM), where it can be used.

Now that you have a general picture of memory it is time to explore STM and LTM in more detail. But first, here's a chance to rehearse what you've learned.

Icon A mental image or visual representation.

Echo A brief continuation of sensory activity in the auditory system after a sound is heard.

Short-term memory (STM) The memory system used to hold small amounts of information for relatively brief time periods.

Working memory Another name for short-term memory, especially when it is used for thinking and problem solving.

Long-term memory (LTM) The memory system used for relatively permanent storage of meaningful information.

KNOWLEDGE BUILDER

Memory Systems

REFLECT

Wave a pencil back and forth in front of your eyes while focusing on something in the distance. The pencil's image looks transparent. Why? (Because sensory memory briefly holds an image of the pencil. This image persists after the pencil passes by.)

Think of a time today when you used short-term memory (such as briefly remembering a phone number, an Internet address, or someone's name). How long did you retain the information? How did you encode it? How much do you remember now?

How is long-term memory helping you read this sentence? If the words weren't already stored in LTM, could you read at all? How else have you used LTM today?

LEARNING CHECK

Match: **A.** Sensory memory **B.** STM **C.** LTM

1. _____ Working memory
2. _____ Holds information for a few seconds or less
3. _____ Stores an icon or echo
4. _____ Permanent, unlimited capacity
5. _____ Temporarily holds small amounts of information
6. _____ Selective attention determines its contents
7. STM is improved by interruption, or interference, because attention is more focused at such times. T or F?

CRITICAL THINKING

8. Why is sensory memory important to filmmakers?

Answers: **1.** B **2.** A **3.** A **4.** C **5.** B **6.** B **7.** F **8.** Without sensory memory, a movie would look like a flickering series of still pictures. The brief persistence of icons in sensory memory is what blends one movie frame into the next.

Short-Term Memory—Do You Know the Magic Number?

To make good use of your memory, it is valuable to know more about the characteristics of STM and LTM. It's time to dig deeper into the inner workings of our primary memory systems.

How much information can be held in short-term memory? For an answer, read the following numbers once. Then close the book and write as many as you can in the correct order.

8 5 1 7 4 9 3

This is called a digit-span test. It is a measure of attention and short-term memory. If you were able to correctly repeat 7 digits, you have an average short-term memory. Now try to memorize the following list, reading it only once.

7 1 8 3 5 4 2 9 1 6 3 4

This series was probably beyond your short-term memory capacity. Psychologist George Miller found that short-term memory is limited to the "magic number" 7 (plus or minus 2) **information bits** (Miller, 1956). A bit is a single meaningful "piece" of information, such as a digit. It is as if short-term memory has 7 "slots" or "bins" into which separate items can be placed. Actually, a few people can remember up to 9 bits, and for some types of information 5 bits is the limit. Thus, an *average* of 7 information bits can be held in short-term memory (Neath, 2002).

When all of the "slots" in STM are filled, there is no room for new information. Picture how this works at a party: Let's say your hostess begins introducing everyone who is there, "Chun, Dasia, Marco, Roseanna, Cholik, Shawn, Kyrene . . ." "Stop," you think to yourself. But she continues, "Nelia, Jay, Efren, Frank, Marietta, Jorge, Patty, Amit, Ricky." The hostess leaves, satisfied that you have met everyone. And you spend the evening talking with Chun, Dasia, and Ricky, the only people whose names you remember!

Recoding

Before we continue, test your short-term memory again, this time on letters. Read the following letters once, then look away and try to write them in the proper order.

T V I B M U S N Y M C A

Notice that there are 12 letters, or "bits" of information. This should be beyond the 7-item limit of STM. However, because the letters are in four groups, or *chunks* of information, many students are able to memorize them. **Information chunks** are made up of bits of information grouped into larger units.

How does chunking help? Chunking **recodes** (reorganizes) information into units that are already in LTM. For example, you may have noticed that NY is the abbreviation for New York. If so, the two bits N and Y became one chunk. In an experiment that used lists like this one, people remembered best when the letters were read as familiar meaningful chunks: TV, IBM, USN, YMCA (Bower & Springston, 1970). If you recoded the letters this way, you probably remembered the entire list.

Chunking suggests that STM holds about 5 to 7 of whatever units we are using. A single chunk could be made up of numbers, letters, words, phrases, or familiar sentences (Barsalou, 1992). Picture STM as a small desk again. Through chunking, we combine several items into one "stack" of information. This allows us to place 7 stacks on the desk, where before there was only room for 7 separate items. While you are studying, try to find ways to link 2, 3, or more separate facts or ideas into larger chunks, and your memory will improve. Psychologist Nelson Cowan (2001) believes that STM may actually hold only 4 items, unless some chunking has occurred. The clear message is that creating information chunks is the key to making good use of your short-term memory.

Rehearsing Information

How long do short-term memories last? They disappear very rapidly. However, you can prolong a memory by silently repeating it, a process called **maintenance rehearsal.** You have probably briefly remembered an address or telephone number this way. In a sense, rehearsing information allows you to "hear" it many times, not just once (Nairne, 2002). The more times a short-term memory is rehearsed, the greater its chances of being stored in LTM (Barsalou, 1992).

What if rehearsal is prevented, so a memory cannot be recycled or moved to LTM? Without maintenance rehearsal, STM is incredibly brief. In one experiment, subjects heard meaningless syllables like XAR followed by a number like 67. As soon as subjects heard the number, they began counting backward by threes (to prevent them from repeating the syllable). After a delay of only 18 seconds, their memory scores fell to zero (Peterson & Peterson, 1959).

After *18 seconds* without rehearsal, the short-term memories were gone forever! Part of this rapid loss can be explained by the testing procedures used (Goldstein, 2005). In daily life, short-term memories usually last longer. Just the same, if you are introduced to someone, and the name slips out of STM, it is gone forever. To escape this awkward situation you might try saying something like, "I'm curious, how do you spell your name?" Unfortunately, the response is often an icy reply like, "B-O-B S-M-I-T-H, it's really not too difficult." To avoid embarrassment, pay careful attention to the name, repeat it to yourself several times, and try to use it in the next sentence or two—before you lose it (Neath, 2002).

Elaborative rehearsal, which makes information more meaningful, is a far better way to form lasting memories. Elaborative rehearsal links new information to memories that are already in LTM. When you are studying, you will remember more if you elaborate, extend, and reflect about the meaning of information. As you read, try to frequently ask yourself "why" questions, such as, "Why would that be true?" (Willoughby et al., 1997). Also, try to relate new ideas to your own experiences and knowledge (Hartlep & Forsyth, 2000).

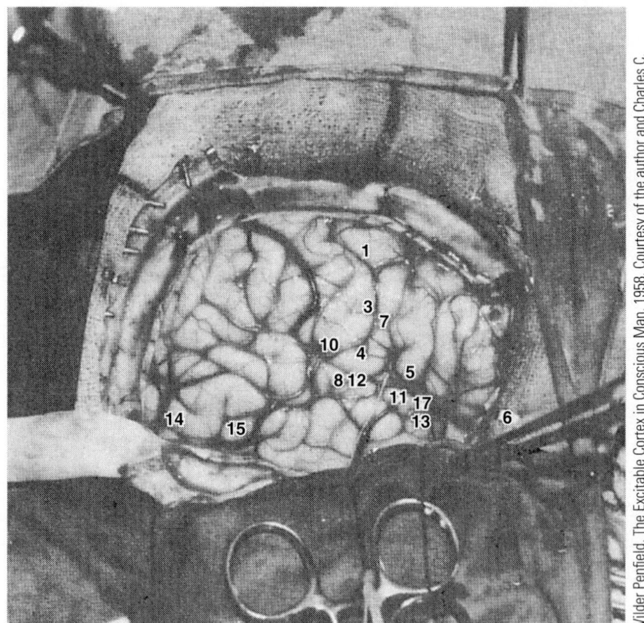

● **Figure 9.3** Exposed cerebral cortex of a patient undergoing brain surgery. Numbers represent points that reportedly produced "memories" when electrically stimulated. A critical evaluation of such reports suggests that they are more like dreams than memories. This fact raises questions about claims that long-term memories are permanent.

Try It Yourself: How's Your Memory?

To better appreciate the next topic, pause for a moment and read the words you see here. Read through the list once. Then continue reading the next section of this chapter.

bed dream blanket doze pillow nap snore mattress alarm clock rest slumber nod sheet bunk cot cradle groggy

Long-Term Memory—Where the Past Lives

An electrode touched the patient's brain. Immediately she said, "Yes, sir, I think I heard a mother calling her little boy somewhere. It seemed to be something happening years ago. It was somebody in the neighborhood where I live." A short time later the electrode was applied to the same spot. Again the patient said, "Yes, I hear the same familiar sounds, it seems to be a woman calling, the same lady" (Penfield, 1958). A woman undergoing brain surgery made these statements. There are no pain receptors in the brain, so the patient was awake as her brain was electrically stimulated (● Figure 9.3). When activated, some brain areas seemed to produce vivid memories of long-forgotten events.

Permanence

Are all of our experiences permanently recorded in memory? Results like those described led neurosurgeon Wilder Penfield to claim that the brain records the past like a "strip of movie film, complete with sound track" (Penfield, 1957). But as you know, this is an exaggeration. Many events never get past short-term memory. Also, brain stimulation produces memory-like experiences in only about 3 percent of cases. Most reports resemble dreams more than memories, and many are clearly imaginary. Memory experts now believe that long-term memories are only *relatively* permanent (Barsalou, 1992). Perfect, eternal memories are a myth.

Constructing Memories

There's another reason for doubting that all of our experiences are permanently recorded. As new long-term memories are stored, older memories are often updated, changed, lost, or *revised* (Lieberman, 2004). To illustrate this point, in a classic study Elizabeth Loftus and John Palmer (1974) showed people a filmed automobile accident. Afterward, some participants were asked to estimate how fast the cars were going when they "smashed" into each

Information bits Meaningful units of information, such as numbers, letters, words, or phrases.

Information chunks Information bits grouped into larger units.

Recoding Reorganizing or modifying information to assist storage in memory.

Maintenance rehearsal Silently repeating or mentally reviewing information to hold it in short-term memory.

Elaborative rehearsal Rehearsal that links new information with existing memories and knowledge.

other. For others the words "bumped," "contacted," or "hit" replaced "smashed." One week later, each person was asked, "Did you see any broken glass?" Those asked earlier about the cars that "smashed" into each other were more likely to say yes. (No broken glass was shown in the film.) The new information ("smashed") was included in memories and altered them.

Try It Yourself: Old or New?

Now, without looking back to the list of words you read a few minutes ago, see if you can tell which of the following are "old" words (items from the list you read) and which are "new" words (items that weren't on the list). Mark each of the following words as old or new:

sofa sleep lamp kitchen

Updating memories is called **constructive processing.** Gaps in memory, which are common, may be filled in by logic, guessing, or new information (Schacter, Norman, & Koutstaal, 1998). Indeed, it is possible to have "memories" for things that never happened (such as remembering broken glass at an accident when there was none) (Loftus, 2003). In a study by Sharon Hannigan and Mark Reinitz, college students saw photographs that depicted common activities, such as shopping for groceries or eating at a restaurant. In some cases, the photos showed an unusual event. For example, in one sequence a woman at a grocery store passes a pile of oranges on the floor. Two days later, the students saw the photos again. This time, however, new photos were included that *explained* how the unusual event occurred (● Figure 9.4). For instance, the woman at the market is shown pulling an orange from the bottom of a stack of oranges. Sixty-eight percent of the students were sure they remembered seeing this image (Hannigan & Reinitz, 2001).

As the preceding examples show, thoughts, inferences, and mental associations may be mistaken for true memories (Loftus, 2003). People in Elizabeth Loftus's experiments who had these *pseudo-memories* (false memories) were often quite upset to learn they had given false "testimony" (Loftus & Ketcham, 1994).

Tom Carter/Index Stock Imagery

Eyewitness memories are notoriously inaccurate. By the time witnesses are asked to testify in court, information they learned after an incident may blend into their original memories.

Dennis Coon

● **Figure 9.4** Suppose you are shown a series of photographs that depict various scenes related to having lunch at the campus commons. One of the photos shows an unexpected event (the spilled soda). If you were to see all of the photos again a few days later, it's likely that you would remember seeing the image on the right, even though it wasn't in the original group of photos. When we see an unexplained event, we are very likely to think about its cause. Later, it is easy to mistake these thoughts for an actual memory (Hannigan & Reinitz, 2001).

Try It Yourself: And Now, the Results

Return now and look at the labels you wrote on the "old or new" word list. If you answered as most people do, this exercise may help you appreciate how often we have false memories. All of the listed words are "new." None was on the original list!

If you thought you "remembered" that "sleep" was on the original list, you had a false memory. The word *sleep* is associated with most of the words on the original list, which creates a strong impression that you saw it before (Roediger & McDermott, 1995).

False long-term memories are a common problem in police work. For example, a witness may select a photo of a suspect from police files or see a photo in the news. Later, the witness identifies the suspect in a lineup or in court. Did the witness really remember the suspect from the scene of the crime? Or was it from the more recently seen photograph? Under some circumstances, innocent people have been "remembered" and named as criminals (Schacter, 2001).

Does new information "overwrite" existing memories? No, the real problem is that we often can't remember the *source* of a memory. This can lead witnesses to "remember" a face that they actually saw somewhere other than the crime scene (Schacter, Norman, & Koutstaal, 1998). Many tragic cases of mistaken identity occur this way.

Is there any way to avoid such problems? Forensic psychologists have tried a variety of techniques to help improve the memory of witnesses. "Telling Wrong from Right in Forensic Memory" examines research on this intriguing question.

To summarize, forming and using memories is an active, creative, highly personal process. Our memories are colored by emotions, judgments, and quirks of personality. If you and a friend were joined at the hip and you went through life side-by-side, you would still have different memories. What we remember depends

FOCUS ON RESEARCH

Telling Wrong from Right in Forensic Memory

Imagine that you are a forensic psychologist, investigating a crime. Unfortunately, your witness can't remember much of what happened. What can you, as a "memory detective," do to help?

Could hypnosis improve the witness's memory? It might seem so. In one case in California, 26 children were abducted from a school bus and held captive for ransom. Under hypnosis, the bus driver recalled the license plate number of the kidnappers' van. This memory helped break the case. Such successes seem to imply that hypnosis can improve memory. But does it?

Research has shown that hypnosis increases false memories more than it does true ones. Eighty percent of the new memories produced by hypnotized subjects in one classic experiment were *incorrect* (Dywan & Bowers, 1983). This is in part because a hypnotized person is more likely than normal to use imagination to fill in gaps in memory. Also, if a questioner asks misleading or suggestive questions, hypnotized persons tend to weave the information into their memories (Scoboria et al., 2002). To make matters worse, even when a memory is completely false, the hypnotized person's confidence in it can be unshakable (Burgess & Kirsch, 1999). Thus, hypnosis sometimes uncovers more information, as it did with the bus driver (Schreiber & Schreiber, 1999). However, when it does, there is no sure way to tell which memories are false and which are true (Newman & Thompson, 2001).

Is there a better way to improve eyewitness memory? To help police detectives, R. Edward Geiselman and Ron Fisher created the **cognitive interview,** a technique for jogging the memory of eyewitnesses (Fisher & Geiselman, 1987). The key to this approach is recreating the crime scene. Witnesses revisit the scene in their imaginations or in person. That way, aspects of the crime scene, such as sounds, smells, and objects, provide helpful retrieval cues. Back in the context of the crime, the witness is encouraged to recall events in different orders and from different viewpoints. Every new memory, no matter how trivial it may seem, can serve as a cue to trigger the retrieval of yet more memories.

When used properly, the cognitive interview produces 35 percent more correct information than standard questioning (Davis, McMahon, & Greenwood, 2005; Geiselman et al., 1986). This improvement comes without adding to the number of false memories elicited, as occurs with hypnosis, and it is more effective in actual police work (Ginet & Py, 2001; Kebbell & Wagstaff, 1998).

A. Ramey/PhotoEdit

Some police detectives, following the advice of psychologists, recreate crime scenes to help witnesses remember what they saw. Typically, people return to the scene at the time of day the crime occurred. They are also asked to wear the same clothing they wore and go through the same motions as they did before the crime. With so many memory cues available, witnesses sometimes remember key items of information they hadn't recalled before.

on what we pay attention to, what we regarded as meaningful or important, and what we feel strongly about (Schacter, 2000).

Organizing Memories

Long-term memory stores huge amounts of information in a lifetime. How are we able to find specific memories? The answer is that each person's "memory index" is highly organized.

Do you mean that information is arranged alphabetically, as in a dictionary? Not a chance! If we ask you to name a black and white animal that lives on ice, is related to a chicken, and cannot fly, you don't have to go from aardvark to zebra to find the answer. You will probably only think of black and white birds living in the Antarctic. Which of these cannot fly? *Voila,* the answer is a penguin.

Information in LTM may be arranged according to rules, images, categories, symbols, similarity, formal meaning, or personal meaning (Lieberman, 2004). In recent years, psychologists have begun to develop a picture of the *structure,* or organization, of memories. *Memory structure* refers to the pattern of associations among items of information. For example, assume that you are given two statements, to which you must answer yes or no: (1) *A*

Constructive processing Reorganizing or updating memories on the basis of logic, reasoning, or the addition of new information.

Cognitive interview Use of various cues and strategies to improve the memory of eyewitnesses.

canary is an animal. (2) *A canary is a bird.* Which do you answer more quickly? Most people can say that *A canary is a bird* faster than they can recognize that *A canary is an animal* (Collins & Quillian, 1969). Why should this be so? Psychologists believe that a **network model** of memory explains why. According to this view, LTM is organized as a network of linked ideas (● Figure 9.5). When ideas are "farther" apart, it takes a longer chain of associations to connect them. The more two items are separated, the longer it takes to answer. In terms of information links, *canary* is probably "close" to *bird* in your "memory files." *Animal* and *canary* are farther apart. Remember though, this has nothing to do with alphabetical order. We are talking about a system of linked meanings.

Redintegrative Memories

Networks of associated memories may help explain a common experience: Imagine finding a picture taken on your sixth birthday or tenth Christmas. As you look at the photo, one memory leads to another, which leads to another, and another. Soon you have unleashed a flood of seemingly forgotten details. This process is called redintegration (ruh-DIN-tuh-GRAY-shun).

Redintegrative memories seem to spread through the "branches" of memory networks. Many people find that such memories are also touched off by distinctive odors out of the past—from a farm visited in childhood, Grandma's kitchen, the seashore, a doctor's office, the perfume or aftershave of a former lover, and so on. The key idea in redintegration is that one memory serves as a cue to trigger another. As a result, an entire past experience may be reconstructed from one small recollection.

How many types of long-term memory are there? It is becoming clear that more than one type of long-term memory exists. Let's probe a little farther into the mysteries of memory.

Skill Memory and Fact Memory

A curious thing happens to many people who develop amnesia. Amnesic patients may be unable to learn a telephone number, an address, or a person's name. Yet the same patients can learn to solve complex puzzles in a normal amount of time (Squire & Zola-Morgan, 1988) (● Figure 9.6). These and other observations have led many psychologists to conclude that long-term memories fall into at least two categories. One is called *procedural memory* (or skill memory). The other is *declarative memory* (also sometimes called fact memory).

Skills

Procedural memory includes basic conditioned responses and learned actions, such as those involved in typing, driving, or swinging a golf club. Memories such as these can be fully expressed only as actions (or "know-how"). It is likely that skill memories register in "lower" brain areas, especially the cerebellum. They represent the more basic "automatic" elements of conditioning, learning, and memory (Gabrieli, 1998).

Facts

Declarative memory stores specific factual information, such as names, faces, words, dates, and ideas. Declarative memories are expressed as words or symbols. For example, knowing that Peter Jackson directed both the *Lord of the Rings* trilogy and the latest remake of *King Kong* is a declarative memory. This is the type of memory that a person with amnesia lacks and that most of us take for granted. Declarative memory can be further divided into *semantic memory* and *episodic memory* (Tulving, 2000).

Semantic Memory

Most of our basic factual knowledge about the world is almost totally immune to forgetting. The names of objects, the days of the week or months of the year, simple math skills, the seasons, words and language, and other general facts are all quite lasting. Such impersonal facts make up a part of LTM called **semantic memory.** Semantic memory serves as a mental dictionary or encyclopedia of basic knowledge.

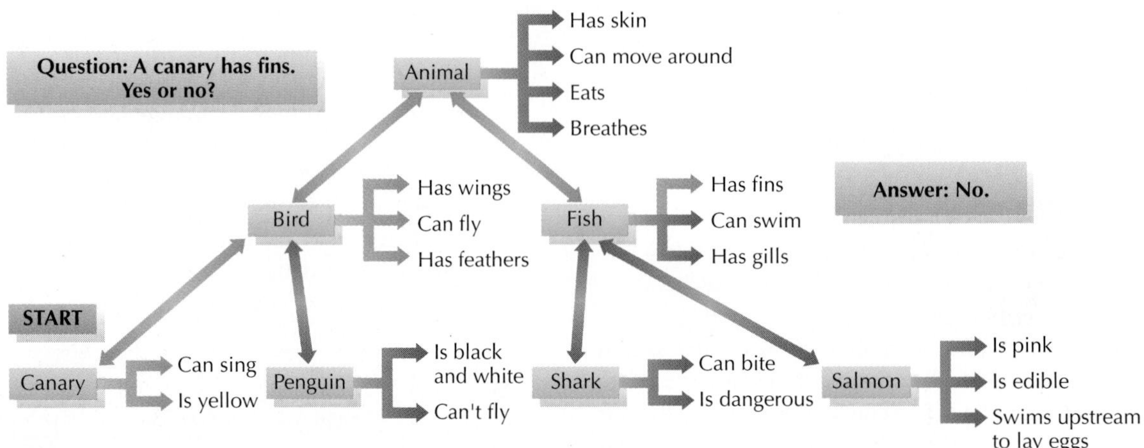

● **Figure 9.5** A hypothetical network of facts about animals shows what is meant by the structure of memory. Small networks of ideas such as this are probably organized into larger and larger units and higher levels of meaning. (Adapted from Collins & Quillian, 1969.)

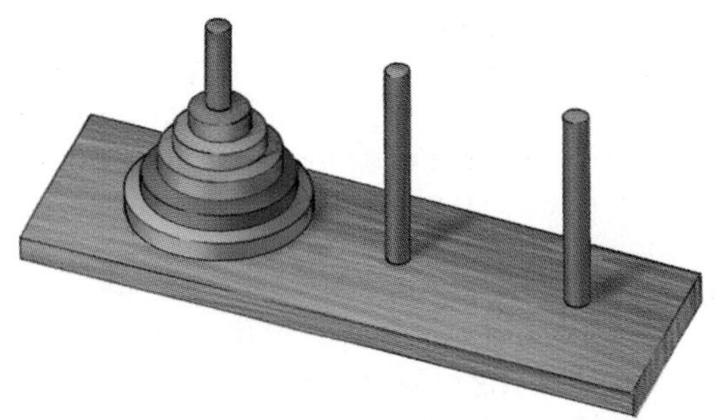

● **Figure 9.6** The tower puzzle. In this puzzle, all the colored disks must be moved to another post, without ever placing a larger disk on a smaller one. Only one disk may be moved at a time, and a disk must always be moved from one post to another (it cannot be held aside). An amnesic patient learned to solve the puzzle in 31 moves, the minimum possible. Even so, each time he began, he protested that he did not remember ever solving the puzzle before and that he did not know how to begin. Evidence like this suggests that memories for skills are distinct from memories for facts.

Episodic Memory

Semantic memory has no connection to times or places. It would be rare, for instance, to remember when and where you first learned the names of the seasons. In contrast, **episodic** (ep-ih-SOD-ik) **memory** is an "autobiographical" record of personal experiences. It stores life events (or "episodes") day after day, year after year. Can you remember your seventh birthday? Your first date? An accident you witnessed? What you did yesterday? All are episodic memories. Note that episodic memories are about the "what," "where," and "when" of our lives. More than a simple ability to store information, they make it possible for us to mentally travel back in time and *re-experience* events (Tulving, 2002).

Are episodic memories as lasting as semantic memories? In general, episodic memories are more easily forgotten than semantic memories. This is because new information constantly pours into episodic memory. Stop for a moment and remember where and when you first met your best friend. That was an episodic memory. Notice that you now remember that you just remembered something. You have a new episodic memory in which you remember that you remembered while reading this text! It's easy to see how much we ask of our memory.

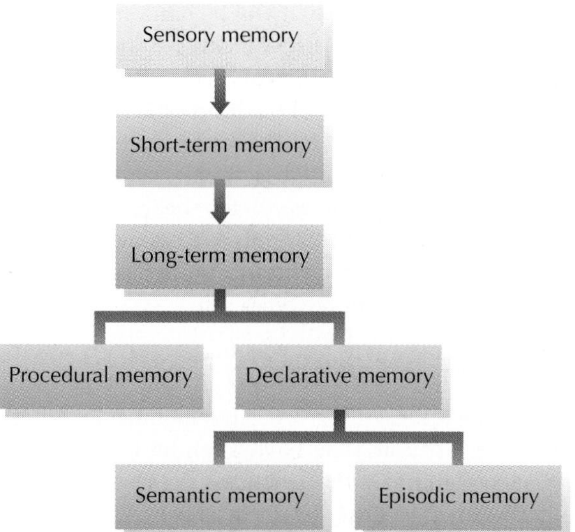

● **Figure 9.7** In the model shown here, long-term memory is divided into procedural memory (learned actions and skills) and declarative memory (stored facts). Declarative memories can be either semantic (impersonal knowledge) or episodic (personal experiences associated with specific times and places).

How Many Types of Memory?

In answer to the question posed at the beginning of this section, it is very likely that three kinds of long-term memories exist: procedural memory and two types of declarative memory, semantic and episodic (Mitchell, 1989; Squire, Knowlton, & Musen, 1993) (● Figure 9.7). Although other types of memory may be discovered, it appears that some pieces of the puzzle are falling into place.

KNOWLEDGE BUILDER

STM and LTM

REFLECT

Telephone numbers are divided into an area code (3 digits) and a 7-digit number that is divided into 3 digits, plus 4 more. Can you relate this practice to STM? How about to chunking and recoding?

Think about how you've used your memory in the last hour. See if you can identify an example of each of the following: a procedural memory, a declarative memory, a semantic memory, and an episodic memory.

LEARNING CHECK

1. Information is best transferred from STM to LTM when a person engages in
   a. maintenance chunking c. elaborative networking
   b. maintenance recoding d. elaborative rehearsal
2. Constructive processing is often responsible for creating pseudo-memories. T or F?
3. Electrical stimulation of the brain has shown conclusively that all memories are stored permanently, but not all memories can be retrieved. T or F?

Network model A model of memory that views it as an organized system of linked information.

Redintegrative memories Memories that are reconstructed or expanded by starting with one memory and then following chains of association to other, related memories.

Procedural memory Long-term memories of conditioned responses and learned skills.

Declarative memory That part of long-term memory containing specific factual information.

Semantic memory A subpart of declarative memory that records impersonal knowledge about the world.

Episodic memory A subpart of declarative memory that records personal experiences that are linked with specific times and places.

4. Memories elicited under hypnosis are more vivid, complete, and reliable than normal. T or F?
5. The existence of redintegrative memories is best explained by ____________ models of memory.
   a. network c. implicit
   b. TOT d. eidetic
6. Which of the following is a type of skill memory?
   a. semantic memory c. episodic memory
   b. declarative memory d. procedural memory

CRITICAL THINKING

7. Parents sometimes warn children not to read comic books, fearing that they will learn less in school if they "fill their heads up with junk." Why is this warning unnecessary?

Answers: 1. d 2. T 3. F 4. F 5. a 6. d 7. Because the more information you have in long-term memory, the greater the possibilities for linking new information to it. Generally, the more you know, the more you can learn—even if some of what you know is "junk."

Measuring Memory—The Answer Is on the Tip of My Tongue

You either remember something or you don't, right? Wrong. Partial memories are common. For instance, imagine that a clerk helps you at a clothing store. Will you remember her 6 months later? Probably not—unless you happen to see her again at the mall. If you remember her then, you will have used a type of partial memory called *recognition*.

Partial memory is also demonstrated by the **tip-of-the-tongue** (TOT) **state.** This is the feeling that a memory is available, but not quite retrievable. It is as if an answer or a memory is just out of reach—on the "tip of your tongue." For instance, in one study, people listened to theme music from popular TV shows. Then they tried to name the program the tune came from. This produced TOT experiences for about one out of five tunes (Riefer, Keveri, & Kramer, 1995).

The items listed next may induce the TOT state. See if you can name the defined words. (*Answers are at the bottom of this page.)

What's on the Tip of Your Tongue?

1. A person who collects and studies postage stamps
2. To officially renounce a throne
3. A nylon strip surfaced with tiny hooks that fasten to another strip surfaced with uncut pile
4. Produced by humans rather than natural
5. The pictorial system of writing used in ancient Egypt
6. A small fish that attaches itself to a shark

In a classic TOT study, university students read the definitions of words such as *sextant, sampan,* and *ambergris.* Students who "drew a blank" and couldn't name a defined word were asked to give any other information they could. Often, they could guess the first and last letter and the number of syllables of the word they were seeking. They also gave words that sounded like or meant the same thing as the defined word (Brown & McNeill, 1966). Did any of these signs of the TOT state occur as you read the definitions above?

Closely related to the TOT state is the fact that people can often tell beforehand if they are likely to remember something. This is called the **feeling of knowing** (Nelson, 1987). Feeling-of-knowing reactions are easy to observe on TV game shows, where they occur just before contestants are allowed to answer.

Because memory is not an all-or-nothing event, there are several ways of measuring it. Notice that whether you have "remembered" depends on how you are tested. Three commonly used **memory tasks** (tests of memory) are recall, recognition, and relearning. Let's see how they differ.

Recalling Information

What is the name of the first song on your favorite CD? Who won the World Series last year? Who wrote *Hamlet?* If you can answer these questions you are using **recall**, a direct retrieval of facts or information. Tests of recall often require *verbatim* (word-for-word) memory. If you study a poem until you can recite it without looking at it, you are recalling it. If you complete a fill-in-the-blank question, you are using recall. When you answer an essay question by providing facts and ideas, you are also using recall, even though you didn't learn your essay verbatim.

The order in which information is memorized has an interesting effect on recall. To experience it, try to memorize the following list, reading it only once:

bread, apples, soda, ham, cookies, rice, lettuce, beets, mustard, cheese, oranges, ice cream, crackers, flour, eggs

If you are like most people, it will be hardest for you to recall items from the middle of the list. ● Figure 9.8 shows the results of a similar test. Notice that most errors occur with middle items of an ordered list. This is the **serial position effect.** You can remember the last items on a list because they are still in STM. The first items are also remembered well because they entered an "empty" short-term memory. This allows you to rehearse the items so they move into long-term memory (Addis & Kahana, 2004). The middle items are neither held in short-term memory nor moved to long-term memory, so they are often lost.

Recognizing Information

Try to write down everything you can remember learning from a class you took last year. (You have 3 minutes, which should be more than enough time!) If you actually did this, you might conclude that you had learned very little. However, a more sensitive test based on recognition could be used. In **recognition memory**, previously learned material is correctly identified. For instance, you could take a multiple-choice test on facts and ideas from the course. Because you would only have to recognize correct answers, we would probably find that you had learned a lot.

* 1. philatelist 2. abdicate 3. Velcro 4. artificial 5. hieroglyphics 6. remora

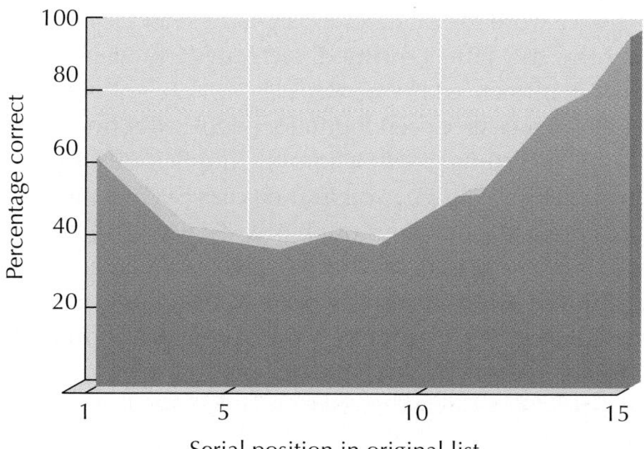

● **Figure 9.8** The serial position effect. The graph shows the percentage of subjects correctly recalling each item in a 15-item list. Recall is best for the first and last items. (Data from Craik, 1970.)

Police lineups make use of the sensitivity of recognition memory. However, unless great care is taken, false identifications are still possible (Wells, 2001).

SW Production/Index Stock Imagery

Recognition memory can be amazingly accurate for pictures and photographs. One investigator showed people 2,560 photographs at a rate of one every 10 seconds. Each person was then shown 280 pairs of photographs. Each pair included an "old" picture (from the first set of photos) and a similar "new" image. Subjects could tell 85 to 95 percent of the time which photograph they had seen before (Haber, 1970). This finding may explain why people so often say, "I may forget a name, but I never forget a face." (It's also why we rarely need to see our friends' vacation photos more than once.)

Recognition is usually superior to recall. That's why police departments use photographs or a lineup to identify criminal suspects. Witnesses who disagree when they try to recall a suspect's height, weight, age, or eye color often agree completely when they merely need to recognize the person.

Is recognition always superior? It depends greatly on the kind of *distractors* used. These are false items included with an item to be recognized. If distractors are very similar to the correct item, memory may be poor. A reverse problem occurs when only one choice looks like it could be correct. This can produce a *false positive,* or false sense of recognition, like the false memory you had earlier when you thought you remembered seeing the word *sleep.*

There have been instances in which witnesses described a criminal as black, tall, or young. Then a lineup was held in which a suspect was the only African American among whites, the only tall suspect, or the only young person. In such cases a false identification is very likely. A better method is to have *all* the distractors look like the person witnesses described. Also, to reduce false positives, witnesses should be warned that the culprit *may not be present* (Wells et al., 1999). Many hundreds of people have been put in jail on the basis of mistaken eyewitness memories. To avoid tragic mistakes, it's far better to show witnesses one photo at a time (a sequential lineup). For each photo, the witness must decide whether the person is the culprit before another photo is shown (Wells, 2001; Wells & Olsen, 2003).

Relearning Information

In another classic experiment, a psychologist read a short passage in Greek to his son every day when the boy was between 15 months and 3 years of age. At age 8, the boy was asked if he remembered the Greek passage. He showed no evidence of recall. He was then shown selections from the passage he heard and selections from other Greek passages. Could he recognize the one he heard as an infant? "It's all Greek to me!" he said, indicating a lack of recognition (and drawing a frown from everyone in the room).

Had the psychologist stopped, he might have concluded that no memory of the Greek remained. However, the child was then asked to memorize the original quotation and others of equal difficulty. This time his earlier learning became evident. The boy memorized the passage he had heard in childhood 25 percent faster than the others (Burtt, 1941). As this experiment suggests, **relearning** is typically the most sensitive measure of memory.

When a person is tested by relearning, how do we know a memory still exists? As with the boy described, relearning is measured by a *savings score* (the amount of time saved when relearning information). Let's say it takes you 1 hour to memorize all the names in a telephone book. (It's a small town.) Two years later you relearn

Tip-of-the-tongue state The feeling that a memory is available but not quite retrievable.

Feeling of knowing A feeling that allows people to predict beforehand whether they will be able to remember something.

Memory task Any task designed to test or assess memory.

Recall To supply or reproduce memorized information with a minimum of external cues.

Serial position effect The tendency to make the most errors in remembering the middle items of an ordered list.

Recognition memory An ability to correctly identify previously learned information.

Relearning Learning again something that was previously learned. Used to measure memory of prior learning.

them in 45 minutes. Because you "saved" 15 minutes, your savings score would be 25 percent (15 divided by 60 times 100). Savings of this type are a good reason for studying a wide range of subjects. It may seem that learning algebra, history, or a foreign language is wasted if you don't use the knowledge immediately. But when you do need such information, you will be able to relearn it quickly.

Implicit and Explicit Memories

Many memories remain outside of conscious awareness. For example, if you know how to type, it is apparent that you know where the letters are on the keyboard. But how many typists could correctly label blank keys in a drawing of a keyboard? Many people find that they cannot directly remember such information, even though they "know" it.

Who were the last three presidents of the United States? What did you have for breakfast today? What is the title of the Black Eyed Peas latest album? Explicit memory is used in answering each of these questions. **Explicit memories** are past experiences that are consciously brought to mind. Recall, recognition, and the tests you take in school rely on explicit memories. In contrast, **implicit memories** lie outside of awareness (Roediger, 1990). That is, we are not aware that a memory exists. Nevertheless, implicit memories—such as unconsciously knowing where the letters are on a keyboard—greatly influence our behavior (Neath, 2002).

Priming

How is it possible to show that a memory exists if it lies outside of awareness? Psychologists first noticed implicit memory while studying memory loss caused by brain injuries. Let's say, for example, that a patient is shown a list of common words, such as *chair, tree, lamp, table,* and so on. A few minutes later, the patient is asked to recall words from the list. Sadly, he has no memory of the words.

Now, instead of asking the patient to explicitly recall the list, we could "prime" his memory by giving him the first two letters of each word. "We'd like you to say a word that begins with these letters," we tell him. "Just say whatever comes to mind." Of course, many words could be made from each pair of letters. For example, the first item (from chair) would be the letters CH. The patient could say "child," "chalk," "chain," "check," or many other words. Instead, he says "chair," a word from the original list. The patient is not aware that he is remembering the list, but as he gives a word for each letter pair, almost all are from the list. Apparently, the letters **primed** (activated) hidden memories, which then influenced his answers.

Can you label the letter keys on this blank keyboard? If you can, you probably used implicit memory to do it.

Similar effects have been found for people with normal memories. As the preceding example implies, implicit memories are often revealed by giving a person limited cues, such as the first letter of words or partial drawings of objects. Typically, the person believes that he or she is just saying whatever comes to mind. Nevertheless, information previously seen or heard affects his or her answers (Rueckl & Galantucci, 2005). Some nutritionists like to say, "You are what you eat." In the realm of memory it appears that we are what we experience—to a far greater degree than once realized.

Exceptional Memory—Wizards of Recall

Can you remember how many doors there are in your house or apartment? To answer a question like this, many people form **internal images** (mental pictures) of each room and count the doorways they visualize. As this example implies, many memories are stored as mental images (Roeckelein, 2004).

Stephen Kosslyn, Thomas Ball, and Brian Reiser (1978) found an interesting way to show that memories do exist as images. Participants first memorized a sort of treasure map similar to the one shown in ● Figure 9.9*a*. They were then asked to picture a black dot moving from one object, such as one of the trees, to another, such as the hut at the top of the island. Did people really form an image to do this task? It seems they did. As shown in ● Figure 9.9*b*, the time it took to "move" the dot was directly related to actual distances on the map.

Is the "treasure map" task an example of photographic memory? In some ways, internal memory images do have "photographic" qualities. However, the term *photographic memory* is more often used to describe a type of memory called eidetic imagery.

Eidetic Imagery

Eidetic (eye-DET-ik) **imagery** occurs when a person has visual images clear enough to be "scanned" or retained for at least 30 seconds. Internal memory images can be "viewed" mentally with the eyes closed. In contrast, eidetic images are "projected" out in front of a person. That is, they are best "seen" on a plain surface, such as a blank piece of paper. In this respect, eidetic images are somewhat like the afterimages you might have after looking at a flashbulb or a brightly lit neon sign (Kunzendorf, 1989).

Eidetic memory is most common in childhood, with about 8 children in 100 having eidetic images. In one series of tests, children were shown a picture from *Alice's Adventures in Wonderland* (● Figure 9.10). To test your eidetic imagery, look at the picture and read the instructions there.

Now, let's see how much you remember. Can you say (without looking again) which of Alice's apron strings is longer? Are the cat's front paws crossed? How many stripes are on the cat's tail?

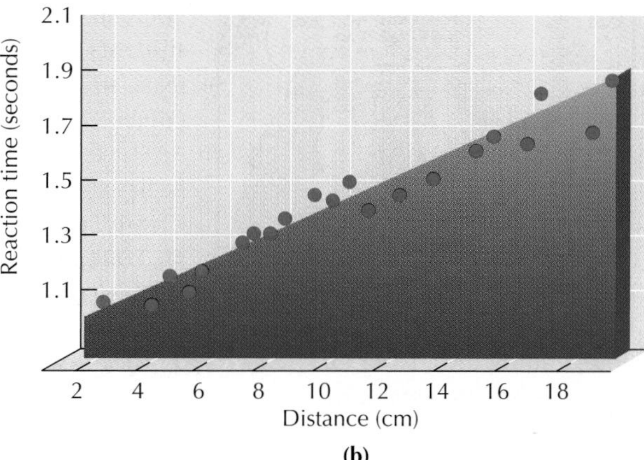

(a) (b)

● **Figure 9.9** (a) "Treasure map" similar to the one used by Kosslyn, Ball, and Reiser (1978) to study images in memory. *(b)* This graph shows how long it took subjects to move a visualized spot various distances on their mental images of the map. (See text for explanation.)

● **Figure 9.10** A test picture like that used to identify children with eidetic imagery. To test your eidetic imagery, look at the picture for 30 seconds. Then look at a blank surface and try to "project" the picture onto it. If you have good eidetic imagery, you will be able to see the picture in detail. Return now to the text and try to answer the questions there. (Redrawn from an illustration in Lewis Carroll's *Alice's Adventures in Wonderland.*)

After the picture was removed from view, one 10-year-old boy was asked what he saw. He replied, "I see the tree, gray tree with three limbs. I see the cat with stripes around its tail." Asked to count the stripes, the boy replied, "There are about 16" (a correct count!). The boy then went on to describe the remainder of the picture in striking detail (Haber, 1969).

Don't be disappointed if you didn't do too well when you tried your eidetic skills. Most eidetic imagery disappears during adolescence and becomes rare by adulthood (Kunzendorf, 1989). Actually, this may not be too much of a loss. The majority of eidetic memorizers have no better long-term memory than average.

Exceptional Memory

Let's return now to the concept of internal memory images. In rare instances, such images may be so vivid that it is reasonable to say that a person has "photographic memory." A notable example was reported by Aleksandr Luria (1968) in his book, *The Mind of a Mnemonist.* Luria studied a man he called Mr. S who had practically unlimited memory for visual images. Mr. S could remember almost everything that ever happened to him with incredible accuracy. Luria tried to test Mr. S's memory by using longer and longer lists of words or numbers. However, he soon discovered that no matter how long the list, Mr. S was able to recall it without error. Mr. S could memorize, with equal ease, strings of digits, meaningless consonants, mathematical formulas, and poems in foreign languages. His memory was so powerful that he had to devise ways to *forget*—such as writing information on a piece of paper and then burning it.

Mr. S's abilities might seem fantastic to any college student. However, Mr. S remembered so much that he couldn't separate important facts from trivia or facts from fantasy (Neath, 2002). For instance, if you asked him to read this chapter he might remember every word. Yet he might also recall all the images each

Explicit memory A memory that a person is aware of having; a memory that is consciously retrieved.

Implicit memory A memory that a person does not know exists; a memory that is retrieved unconsciously.

Priming Facilitating the retrieval of an implicit memory by using cues to activate hidden memories.

Internal images Mental images or visual depictions used in memory and thinking.

Eidetic imagery The ability to retain a "projected" mental image long enough to use it as a source of information.

word made him think of and all the sights, sounds, and feelings that occurred as he was reading. Therefore, finding the answer for a specific question, writing a logical essay, or even understanding a single sentence was very difficult for him. If you didn't have selective memory you would recall all the ingredients on your cereal box, every street number you've seen, and countless other scraps of information.

Few people in history have possessed memory abilities like Mr. S's. Nonetheless, you probably know at least one person who has an especially good memory. Is superior memory a biological gift? Or do excellent memorizers merely make better-than-average use of normal memory capacities? Let's investigate further.

Strategies for Remembering

At first, a student volunteer named Steve could remember 7 digits—a typical score for a college student. Could he improve with practice? For 20 months Steve practiced memorizing ever-longer lists of digits. Ultimately, he was able to memorize around 80 digits, like this sample:

92842048050842268953990190252912807999706606574717310601080585269726026357332135

How did Steve do it? Basically, he worked by chunking digits into meaningful groups containing 3 or 4 digits each. Steve's avid interest in long-distance running helped greatly. For instance, to him the first three digits above represented 9 minutes and 28 seconds, a good time for a 2-mile run. When running times wouldn't work, Steve used other associations, such as ages or dates, to chunk digits (Ericsson & Chase, 1982). It seems apparent that Steve's success was based on learned strategies. By using similar memory systems, other people have trained themselves to equal Steve's feat (Bellezza, Six, & Phillips, 1992).

Psychologist Anders Ericsson (2000) believes that exceptional memory is merely a learned extension of normal memory. As evidence, he notes that Steve's short-term memory did not improve during months of practice. For example, Steve could still memorize only 7 consonants. Steve's phenomenal memory for numbers grew as he figured out new ways to encode digits and store them in LTM.

Researchers studying Rajan Mahadevan have drawn similar conclusions about his spectacular memory for long strings of digits. In 1981 Rajan earned a place in the *Guinness Book of World Records* by reciting the first 31,811 digits of *pi!* Yet, like Steve, Rajan's memory for most other types of information is average. His exceptional memory seems to be based on highly practiced strategies for encoding and storing digits (Thompson, Cowan, & Frieman, 1993). By using similar memory systems, college students have even managed to duplicate some of Mr. S's feats, such as memorizing a 50-digit matrix in 3 minutes (Higbee, 1997).

Steve and Rajan began with normal memory for digits. Both extended their memory abilities by diligent practice. Clearly, exceptional memory can be learned (Ericsson et al., 2004). However, we still have to wonder, do some people have naturally superior memories?

Memory Champions

Each year the World Memory Championship is held in England. There, a variety of mental athletes compete to see who had the best memory. To remain in the running, each contestant has to rapidly memorize daunting amounts of information, such as long lists of unrelated words and numbers. Psychologists John Wilding and Elizabeth Valentine saw this event as an opportunity to study exceptional memory and persuaded the contestants to take some additional memory tests. These ranged from ordinary (recall a story), to challenging (recall the telephone numbers of 6 different people), to diabolical (recall 48 numerals arranged in rows and columns; recognize 14 previously seen pictures of snowflakes among 70 new photos) (Wilding & Valentine, 1994a).

Wilding and Valentine found that exceptional memorizers

- Use memory strategies and techniques
- Have specialized interests and knowledge that make certain types of information easier to encode and recall
- Have naturally superior memory abilities, often including vivid mental images

The first two points confirm what we learned from Steve's acquired memory ability. Many of the contestants, for example, actively used memory strategies called *mnemonics* (nee-MON-iks). Specialized interests and knowledge also helped for some tasks. For example, one contestant, who is a mathematician, was exceedingly good at memorizing numbers (Wilding & Valentine, 1994a).

Several of the memory contestants were able to excel on tasks that prevented the use of learned strategies and techniques. This observation implies that superior memory ability can be a "gift"

8 7 3 7 9 2 6 8
2 0 1 1 7 4 9 5
0 1 7 5 8 7 8 3
1 9 4 7 6 0 6 9
3 6 1 6 8 1 5 4
4 5 2 4 0 2 9 7

This number matrix is similar to the ones contestants in the World Memory Championship had to memorize. To be scored as correct, digits had to be recalled in their proper positions (Wilding & Valentine, 1994a).

as well as a learned skill. Wilding and Valentine conclude that exceptional memory may be based on either natural ability or learned strategies. Usually it requires both. In fact, most super memorizers use strategies to augment whatever natural talents they have. Some of their strategies are described in this chapter's Psychology in Action section. Please do remember to read it.

KNOWLEDGE BUILDER

Memory Tasks and Exceptional Memory

REFLECT

Have you experienced the TOT state recently? Were you able to retrieve the word you were seeking? If not, what could you remember about it?

Do you prefer tests based primarily on recall or recognition? Have you observed a savings effect while relearning information you studied in the past (such as in high school)?

Can you think of things you do that are based on implicit memories? For instance, how do you know which way to turn various handles in your house, apartment, or dorm? Do you have to explicitly think, "Turn it to the right," before you act?

What kinds of information are you good at remembering? Why do you think your memory is better for those topics?

LEARNING CHECK

1. Four techniques for measuring or demonstrating memory are ______ ______ ______ ______
2. Essay tests require ______ of facts or ideas.
3. As a measure of memory, a savings score is associated with
   a. recognition c. relearning
   b. eidetic images d. reconstruction
4. The two most sensitive tests of memory are
   a. recall and redintegration c. recognition and relearning
   b. recall and relearning d. recognition and digit-span
5. Priming is used to reveal which type of memories?
   a. explicit c. skill
   b. sensory d. implicit
6. Children with eidetic imagery typically have no better than average long-term memory. T or F?
7. For most people, having an especially good memory is based on
   a. maintenance rehearsal c. phonetic imagery
   b. constructive processing d. learned strategies

CRITICAL THINKING

8. Mr. S had great difficulty remembering faces. Can you guess why?

Answers: 1. recall, recognition, relearning, priming 2. recall 3. c 4. c 5. d 6. T 7. d 8. Mr. S's memory was so specific that faces seemed different and unfamiliar if he saw them from a new angle or if a face had a different expression on it than when Mr. S last saw it.

Forgetting—Why We, Uh, Let's See; Why We, Uh . . . Forget!

Forgetting is one of the more vexing aspects of memory. For example, why is it hard to remember facts you learned for a test just a week or two later? Again, the more you know about how we "lose" memories, the better you will be able to hang on to them.

Most forgetting tends to occur immediately after memorization. Herman Ebbinghaus (1885) famously tested his own memory at various time intervals after learning. Ebbinghaus wanted to be sure he would not be swayed by prior learning, so he memorized *nonsense syllables*. These are meaningless three-letter words such as CEF, WOL, and GEX. The importance of using meaningless words is shown by the fact that VEL, FAB, and DUZ are no longer used on memory tests. People who recognize these words as detergent names find them very easy to remember. This is another reminder that relating new information to what you already know can improve memory.

By waiting various lengths of time before testing himself, Ebbinghaus plotted a **curve of forgetting.** This graph shows the amount of information remembered after varying lengths of time (● Figure 9.11). Notice that forgetting is rapid at first and is then followed by a slow decline. The same applies to meaningful information, but the forgetting curve is stretched over a longer time. As you might expect, recent events are recalled more accurately than those from the remote past (O'Connor et al., 2000). Thus, you are more likely to remember that *Crash* won the "Best Picture" Academy Award in 2006 than you are to remember that *American Beauty* won it in 1999.

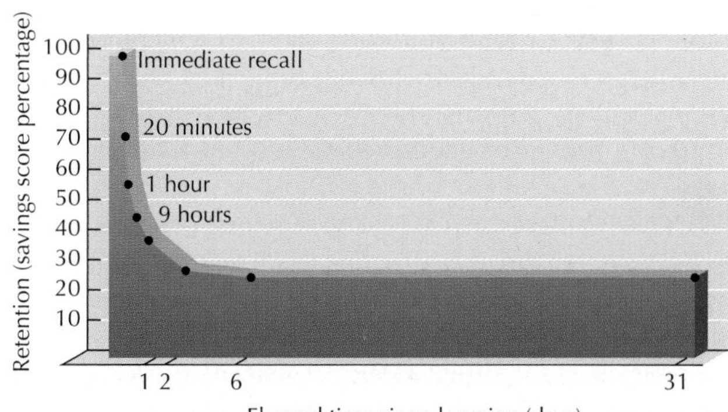

● **Figure 9.11** The curve of forgetting. This graph shows the amount remembered (measured by relearning) after varying lengths of time. Notice how rapidly forgetting occurs. The material learned was nonsense syllables. Forgetting curves for meaningful information also show early losses followed by a long, gradual decline, but overall, forgetting occurs much more slowly. (After Ebbinghaus, 1885.)

Curve of forgetting A graph that shows the amount of memorized information remembered after varying lengths of time.

DISCOVERING PSYCHOLOGY

Card Magic!

● Figure 9.12

Pick a card from the six shown in ● Figure 9.12. Look at it closely and be sure you can remember which card is yours. Now, snap your fingers and look at the cards in ● Figure 9.13.

Poof! Only five cards remain, and the card you chose has disappeared. Obviously, you could have selected any one of the six cards in ● Figure 9.12. How did we know which one to remove?

This trick is based entirely on an illusion of memory. Recall that you were asked to concentrate on one card among the six cards in ● Figure 9.12. That prevented you from paying attention to the other cards, so they weren't stored in your memory (Mangels, Picton, & Craik, 2001). The five cards you see below are all new (none is shown in ● Figure 9.12). Because you couldn't find your card in the "remaining five," it looked like your card disappeared. What looked like "card magic" is actually memory magic. Now return to "When Encoding Fails" and continue reading to learn more about forgetting.

● Figure 9.13

As a student, you should note that a short delay between reviewing and taking a test minimizes forgetting. However, this is no reason for cramming. Most students make the error of *only* cramming. If you cram, you don't have to remember for very long, but you may not learn enough in the first place. If you use short, daily study sessions *and* review intensely before a test, you will get the benefit of good preparation and a minimum time lapse.

The Ebbinghaus curve shows less than 30 percent remembered after only 2 days have passed. Is forgetting really that rapid? No, not always. Meaningful information is not lost nearly as quickly as nonsense syllables. After 3 years, students who took a university psychology had forgotten about 30 percent of the facts they learned. After that, little more forgetting occurred (Conway et al., 1992). Actually, as learning grows stronger, some knowledge may become nearly permanent (Bahrick, 1984). Semantic memories and implicit memories (both mentioned earlier) appear to be very lasting (Bower, 1990).

"I'll never forget old, old . . . oh, what's his name?" Forgetting is both frustrating and embarrassing. Why *do* we forget? The Ebbinghaus curve gives a general picture of forgetting, but it doesn't explain it. For explanations we must search further. Before we do, look at "Card Magic!" where you will find an interesting demonstration.

When Encoding Fails

Whose head is on a U.S. penny? Which way is it facing? What is written at the top of a penny? Can you accurately draw and label a penny? In an interesting experiment, Ray Nickerson and Marilyn Adams (1979) asked a large group of students to draw a penny. Few could. Well then, could the students at least recognize a drawing of a real penny among fakes? (see ● Figure 9.14). Again, few could.

The most obvious reason for forgetting is also the most commonly overlooked. Obviously, few of us ever encode the details of a penny. In many cases, we "forget" because of **encoding failure.** That is, a memory was never formed in the first place (the card trick you just saw is another example). If you are bothered by frequent forgetting or absent-mindedness it is wise to ask yourself, "Have I been storing the information in the first place?" (Schacter, 2001). When 140 college professors were asked what they do to improve their memories, the favorite technique was to *write things down* (Park et al., 1990). Making notes prevents information from slipping out of short-term memory before you can review it and store it more **permanently.**

College Students, They're All Alike!

Encoding failures also affect our memories of people. Imagine yourself in this situation: As you are walking on campus, a young man, who looks like a college student, approaches you and asks

● **Figure 9.14** Some of the distractor items used in a study of recognition memory and encoding failure. Penny A is correct but was seldom recognized. Pennies G and J were popular wrong answers. (Adapted from Nickerson & Adams, 1979.)

for directions. While you are talking, two workers carrying a door pass between you and the young man. While your view is blocked by the door, another man takes the place of the first. Now you are facing a different person than the one who was there just seconds earlier. If this happened to you, do you think you would notice the change? Remarkably, only half of the people tested in this way noticed the switch (Simons & Levin, 1998)!

How could anyone fail to notice that one stranger had been replaced by another? The people who didn't remember the first man were all older adults. College students weren't fooled by the switch. Apparently, older adults encoded the first man in very general terms as a "college student." As a result, that's all they remembered about him. Because his replacement also looked like a college student, they thought he was the same person (Simons & Levin, 1998).

Actually, we all tend to categorize strangers in general terms: Is the person young or old, male or female, a member of my ethnic group or another? This tendency is one reason why eyewitnesses are better at identifying members of their own ethnic group than persons from other groups (Kassin et al., 2001). It may seem harsh to say so, but during brief social contacts, people really do act as if members of other ethnic groups "all look alike." Of course, this bias disappears when people get acquainted and learn more about one another as individuals.

Memory Decay

One view of forgetting holds that **memory traces** (changes in nerve cells or brain activity) decay (fade or weaken) over time. **Memory decay** appears to be a factor in the loss of sensory memories. Such fading also applies to short-term memory. Information stored in STM seems to initiate a brief flurry of activity in the brain that quickly dies out. Short-term memory therefore operates like a "leaky bucket": New information constantly pours in, but it rapidly fades away and is replaced by still newer information. Let's say that you are trying to remember a short list of letters, numbers, or words after seeing or hearing them once. If it takes you more than 4 to 6 seconds to repeat the list, you will forget some of the items (Dosher & Ma, 1998).

Disuse

Is it possible that the decay of memory traces also explains long-term forgetting? That is, could long-term memory traces fade from **disuse** (infrequent retrieval) and eventually become too weak to retrieve? There is evidence that memories not retrieved and "used" or rehearsed become weaker over time (Schacter, 2001). However, disuse alone cannot fully explain forgetting.

Disuse doesn't seem to account for our ability to recover seemingly forgotten memories through redintegration, relearning, and priming. It also fails to explain why some unused memories fade, whereas others are carried for life. A third contradiction will be recognized by anyone who has spent time with the elderly. People growing senile may become so forgetful that they can't remember what happened a week ago. Yet at the same time your Uncle Oscar's recent memories are fading, he may have vivid memories of trivial and long-forgotten events from the past. "Why, I remember it as clearly as if it were yesterday," he will say, forgetting that the story he is about to tell is one he told earlier the same day. In short, disuse offers no more than a partial explanation of long-term forgetting.

If decay and disuse don't fully explain forgetting, what does? Let's briefly consider some additional possibilities.

Cue-Dependent Forgetting

Often, memories appear to be *available* but not *accessible.* An example is having an answer on the "tip of your tongue." You know the answer is there, but it remains just "out of reach." This suggests that many memories are "forgotten" because **memory cues** (stimuli associated with a memory) are missing when the time comes to retrieve information. For example, if you were asked, "What were you doing on Monday afternoon of the third week in September 2 years ago?" your reply might be, "Come on, how should I know?" However, if you were reminded, "That was the day the courthouse burned," or "That was the day Stacy had her automobile accident," you might remember immediately.

Encoding failure Failure to store sufficient information to form a useful memory.

Memory traces Physical changes in nerve cells or brain activity that take place when memories are stored.

Memory decay The fading or weakening of memories assumed to occur when memory traces become weaker.

Disuse Theory that memory traces weaken when memories are not periodically used or retrieved.

Memory cue Any stimulus associated with a particular memory. Memory cues usually enhance retrieval.

The presence of appropriate cues almost always enhances memory (Nairne, 2002). In theory, for instance, memory will be best if you study in the same room where you will be tested. Because this is often impossible, when you study, try to visualize the room where you will be tested. Doing so can enhance memory later (Jerabek & Standing, 1992). Similarly, people remember better if the same odor (such as lemon or lavender) is present when they study and are tested (Parker, Ngu, & Cassaday, 2001). If you wear a particular perfume or cologne while you prepare for a test, it might be wise to wear it when you take the test.

State-Dependent Learning

Have you heard the story about the drunk who misplaced his wallet and had to get drunk again to find it? Although this tale is often told as a joke, it is not too farfetched. The bodily state that exists during learning can be a strong cue for later memory, an effect known as **state-dependent learning** (Neath, 2002). Being very thirsty, for instance, might prompt you to remember events that took place on another occasion when you were thirsty. Because of such effects, information learned under the influence of a drug is best remembered when the drugged state occurs again (Slot & Colpaert, 1999).

A similar effect applies to emotional states (Wessel & Wright, 2004). For instance, Gordon Bower (1981) found that people who learned a list of words while in a happy mood recalled them better when they were again happy. People who learned while they felt sad remembered best when they were sad (● Figure 9.15). Similarly, if you are in a happy mood, you are more likely to remember recent happy events (Salovey & Singer, 1989). If you are in a bad mood, you will tend to have unpleasant memories (Eich et al., 1990). Such links between emotional cues and memory could explain why couples who quarrel often end up remembering—and rehashing—old arguments.

External cues like those found in a photograph, in a scrapbook, or during a walk through an old neighborhood often aid recall of seemingly lost memories. For many veterans, finding a familiar name engraved in the Vietnam Veterans Memorial unleashes a flood of memories.

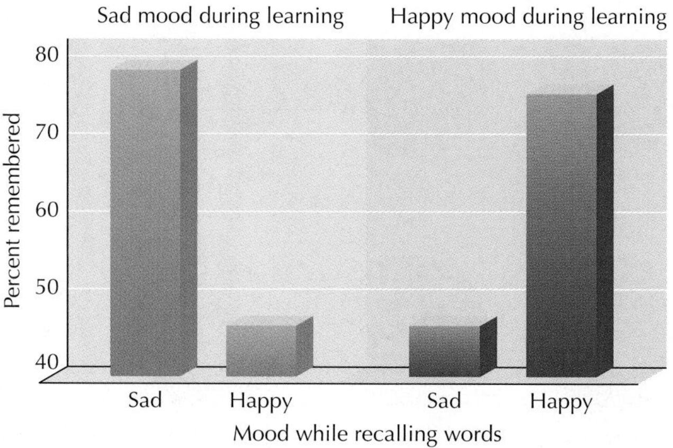

● **Figure 9.15** The effect of mood on memory. Subjects best remembered a list of words when their mood during testing was the same as their mood was when they learned the list. (Adapted from Bower, 1981.)

Interference

Further insight into forgetting comes from a classic experiment in which college students learned lists of nonsense syllables. After studying, students in one group slept for 8 hours and were then tested for memory of the lists. A second group stayed awake for 8 hours and went about business as usual. When members of the second group were tested, they remembered *less* than the group that slept (● Figure 9.16.) This difference is based on the fact that new learning can interfere with previous learning. **Interference** refers to the tendency for new memories to impair retrieval of older memories (and the reverse). It seems to apply to both short-term and long-term memory (Lustig et al., 2001; Nairne, 2002).

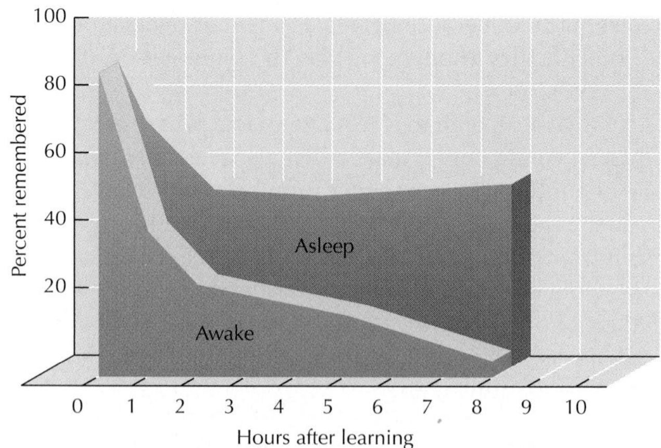

● **Figure 9.16** The amount of forgetting after a period of sleep or of being awake. Notice that sleep causes less memory loss than activity that occurs while one is awake. (After Jenkins & Dallenbach, 1924.)

BRIDGES

Sleep can improve memory in another way: REM sleep and dreaming appear to help us form certain types of memories. **See Chapter 7, pages 230–231.**

How could anyone lose something as large as a car? If you park your car in a different place every day you may have experienced forgetting caused by interference. Today's memory about your car's location is easily confused with memories from yesterday, and the day before, and the day before that.

Andy Reynolds/Getty Images

It is not completely clear if new memories alter existing memory traces or if they make it harder to "locate" (retrieve) earlier memories. In any case, there is no doubt that interference is a major cause of forgetting (Neath, 2002). College students who memorized 20 lists of words (one list each day) were able to recall only 15 percent of the last list. Students who learned only one list remembered 80 percent (Underwood, 1957) (● Figure 9.17).

Order Effects

The sleeping college students remembered more because retroactive (RET-ro-AK-tiv) interference was held to a minimum. **Retroactive interference** refers to the tendency for new learning to inhibit retrieval of old learning. Avoiding new learning prevents retroactive interference. This doesn't exactly mean you should hide in a closet after you study for an exam. However, you should avoid studying other subjects until the exam. Sleeping after study can help you retain memories, and reading, writing, or even watching TV may cause interference.

Retroactive interference is easily demonstrated in the laboratory by this arrangement:

Experimental group:	**Learn A**	**Learn B**	**Test A**
Control group:	**Learn A**	**Rest**	**Test A**

Imagine yourself as a member of the experimental group. In task A, you learn a list of telephone numbers. In task B, you learn a list of Social Security numbers. How do you score on a test of task A (the telephone numbers)? If you do not remember as much as the control group that learns *only* task A, then retroactive interference has occurred. The second thing learned interfered with memory of the first thing learned; the interference went "backward," or was "retroactive" (● Figure 9.18).

Proactive (pro-AK-tiv) interference is a second basic source of forgetting. **Proactive interference** occurs when prior learning

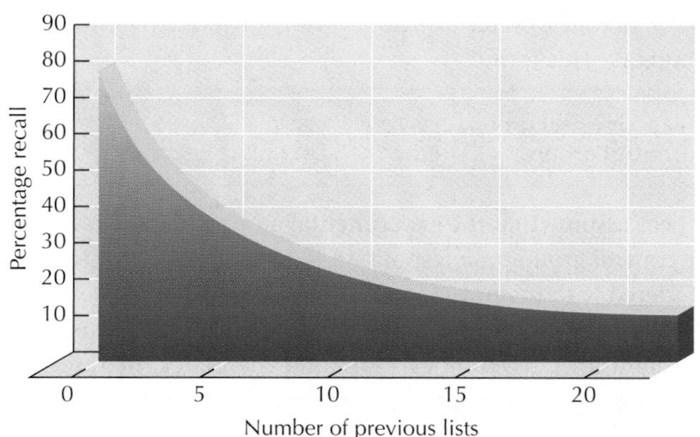

● Figure 9.17 Effects of interference on memory. A graph of the approximate relationship between percentage recalled and number of different word lists memorized. (Adapted from Underwood, 1957.)

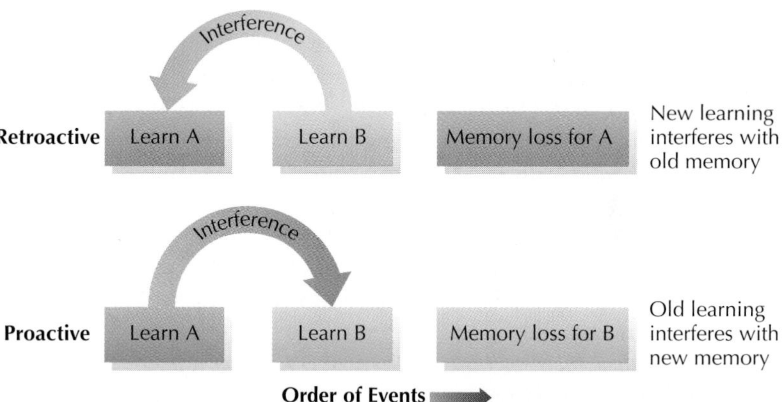

● Figure 9.18 Retroactive and proactive interference. The order of learning and testing shows whether interference is retroactive (backward) or proactive (forward).

State-dependent learning Memory influenced by one's bodily state at the time of learning and at the time of retrieval. Improved memory occurs when the bodily states match.

Interference The tendency for new memories to impair retrieval of older memories, and the reverse.

Retroactive interference The tendency for new memories to interfere with the retrieval of old memories.

Proactive interference The tendency for old memories to interfere with the retrieval of newer memories.

inhibits recall of later learning. A test for proactive interference would take this form:

Experimental group:	**Learn A**	**Learn B**	**Test B**
Control group:	**Rest**	**Learn B**	**Test B**

Let's assume that the experimental group remembers less than the control group on a test of task B. In that case, learning task A interfered with memory for task B.

Then proactive interference goes "forward"? Yes. For instance, if you cram for a psychology exam and then later the same night cram for a history exam, your memory for the second subject studied (history) will be less accurate than if you had studied only history. (Because of retroactive interference, your memory for psychology would probably also suffer.) The greater the similarity in the two subjects studied, the more interference takes place. The moral, of course, is don't procrastinate in preparing for exams. The more you can avoid competing information, the more likely you are to recall what you want to remember (Anderson & Bell, 2001).

The interference effects we have described apply primarily to memories of verbal information, such as the contents of this chapter. When you are learning a skill, similarity can sometimes be beneficial, rather than disruptive. The next section explains how this occurs.

Transfer of Training

Two people begin mandolin lessons. One already plays the violin. The other is a trumpet player. All other things being equal, which person will initially do better in learning the mandolin? If you chose the violin player you have an intuitive grasp of what positive transfer is. (The strings on a mandolin are tuned the same as a violin.) **Positive transfer** takes place when mastery of one task aids mastery of a second task. Another example would be learning to balance and turn on a bicycle before learning to ride a motorcycle or motor scooter. Likewise, surfing and skateboarding skills transfer to snowboarding.

Is there such a thing as negative transfer? There is indeed. In **negative transfer,** skills developed in one situation conflict with those required to master a new task. Learning to back a car with a trailer attached to it is a good example. Normally, when you are backing a car, the steering wheel is turned in the direction you want to go, the same as when moving forward. However, when backing a trailer, you must turn the steering wheel *away* from the direction you want the trailer to go. This situation results in negative transfer, and often creates comical scenes at campgrounds and boat launching ramps.

On a more serious note, many tragic crashes caused by negative transfer finally led to greater standardization of airplane cockpits. Fortunately, negative transfer is usually brief, and it occurs less often than positive transfer. Negative transfer is most likely to occur when a new response must be made to an old stimulus. If you have ever encountered a pull-type handle on a door that must be pushed open, you will appreciate this point.

Repression and Suppression of Memories

Take a moment and scan over the events of the last few years of your life. What kinds of things most easily come to mind? Many people remember happy, positive events better than disappointments and irritations (Linton, 1979). A clinical psychologist would call this tendency **repression,** or motivated forgetting. Through repression, painful, threatening, or embarrassing memories are held out of consciousness (Anderson et al., 2004). An example is provided by soldiers who have repressed some of the horrors they saw during combat (Karon & Widener, 1997, 1998).

The forgetting of past failures, upsetting childhood events, the names of people you dislike, or appointments you don't want to keep may reveal repression. People prone to repression tend to be extremely sensitive to emotional events. As a result, they use repression to protect themselves from threatening thoughts (Mendolia et al., 1996).

It's possible that some adults who were sexually abused as children have repressed memories of their mistreatment. It's also possible that such memories may surface during psychotherapy or other circumstances. However, caution is required any time accusations are made on the basis of seemingly "recovered" memories. In what appeared to be an extreme case of repression, Eileen Franklin testified in court in 1990 that her father, George Franklin, abducted, raped, and killed 8-year-old Susan Nason in 1969. Eileen testified that the memory surfaced one day as she looked into the eyes of her own young daughter. Her father was convicted solely on the basis of her "repressed" memory. However, the conviction was overturned when DNA tests cleared her father of a second murder she also accused him of committing. As the Franklin case illustrates, trying to separate true memories from fantasies is a major headache for psychologists and the courts. See "The Recovered Memory/False Memory Debate" for further cautions.

Rick Martin/San Jose Mercury News

Eileen Franklin's father was convicted on the basis of her "repressed" memories. He was later cleared by DNA testing.

THE CLINICAL FILE

The Recovered Memory/False Memory Debate

Many sexually abused children develop problems that persist into adulthood. In some instances, they repress all memory of the abuse. According to some psychologists, uncovering these hidden memories can be an important step toward regaining emotional health (Palm & Gibson, 1998).

Although the preceding may be true, the search for repressed memories of sexual abuse has itself been a problem. Cases have surfaced in which families were torn apart by accusations of sexual abuse that later turned out to be completely false (Porter et al., 2003). For example, Gary Ramona lost his marriage and his $400,000-a-year job when his daughter Holly alleged that he molested her throughout her childhood. To prove to Holly that her memories were true, the therapists gave her the drug Amytal, and told her that it was a "truth drug." (Amytal is a hypnotic drug that induces a twilight state of consciousness. People do not automatically tell the truth while under its influence.) Ramona sued Holly's therapists, claiming that they had been irresponsible. After reviewing the evidence, a jury awarded Gary Ramona $500,000 in damages. In a way, Gary Ramona was lucky. Most people who are falsely accused have no way to prove their innocence (Loftus & Ketcham, 1994).

Why would anyone have false memories about such disturbing events? Several popular books and a few misguided therapists have actively encouraged people to find repressed memories of abuse. Hypnosis, guided visualization, suggestion, age regression, and similar techniques can elicit fantasies that are mistaken for real memories. As we saw earlier in this chapter, it is easy to create false memories, especially by using hypnosis (Loftus, 2003; Loftus & Bernstein, 2005).

In an effort to illustrate how easy it is to implant false memories and to publicize *false memory syndrome,* memory expert Elizabeth Loftus once even deliberately implanted a false memory in actor Alan Alda. As the host of the television series *Scientific American Frontiers,* he was scheduled to interview Loftus. Before the interview, Alda was asked to fill out a questionnaire about his tastes in food. When he arrived, Loftus told Alda that his answers revealed that he must once have gotten sick after eating hard-boiled eggs (which was false). Later that day, at a picnic, Alda would not eat hard-boiled eggs (Loftus, 2003).

Certainly, some memories of abuse that return to awareness are genuine and must be dealt with. However, there is little doubt that some "recovered" memories are pure fantasy. No matter how real a recovered memory may seem, it could be false, unless it can be verified by others, or by court or medical records (Olio, 2004).

A few years ago, an "epidemic" of recovered memories took place. Today, psychologists have developed new guidelines for therapists to minimize the risk of influencing clients' memories. Nevertheless, false claims about childhood abuse still occasionally make the news. The saddest thing about such claims is that they deaden public sensitivity to actual abuse. Childhood sexual abuse is widespread. Awareness of its existence must not be repressed.

If I try to forget a test I failed, am I repressing it? No. Repression can be distinguished from **suppression**, an active, conscious attempt to put something out of mind. By not thinking about the test, you have merely suppressed a memory. If you choose to, you can remember the test. Clinicians consider true repression an *unconscious* event. When a memory is repressed we may be unaware that forgetting has even occurred.

Recently, some psychologists have questioned whether repression exists (Court & Court, 2001). However, there is evidence that we can choose to actively avoid remembering upsetting information (Anderson, 2001). If you have experienced a painful emotional event, you will probably avoid all thoughts associated with it. This tends to keep cues out of mind that could trigger a painful memory. In time, your active suppression of the memory may become true repression (Anderson & Green, 2001; Bowers & Farvolden, 1996).

BRIDGES

Clinical psychologists regard repression as one of the major psychological defenses we use against emotional threats.

See Chapter 15, pages 510–511, for details.

Flashbulb Memories

Why are some traumatic events vividly remembered, whereas others are repressed? Psychologists use the term **flashbulb memories** to describe images that seem to be frozen in memory at times of personal tragedy, accident, or other emotionally significant events (Finkenauer et al., 1998).

Positive transfer Mastery of one task aids learning or performing another.

Negative transfer Mastery of one task conflicts with learning or performing another.

Repression Unconsciously pushing unwanted memories out of awareness.

Suppression A conscious effort to put something out of mind or to keep it from awareness.

Flashbulb memories Memories created at times of high emotion that seem especially vivid.

Depending on your age, you may have a "flashbulb" memory for the Pearl Harbor attack, the assassinations of John F. Kennedy and Martin Luther King, the *Challenger* or *Columbia* space shuttle disasters, or the terrorist attack on the World Trade Center in New York (Paradis et al., 2004). Flashbulb memories are most often formed when an event is surprising, important, or emotional (Rubin, 1985). They are frequently associated with public tragedies, but memories of positive events may also have "flashbulb" clarity.

Flashbulb memories seem to be very detailed. Often, they focus primarily on how you reacted to the event. ■ Table 9.1 lists some memories that had "flashbulb" clarity for at least 50 percent of a group of college students. How vivid are the memories they trigger for you? (Note again that both positive and negative events are listed.)

The term *flashbulb memories* was first used to describe recollections that seemed to be unusually vivid and permanent. It has become clear, however, that flashbulb memories are not always accurate (Harsch & Neisser, 1989). More than anything else, what sets flashbulb memories apart is that we tend to place great *confidence* in them—even when they are wrong (Niedzwienska, 2004). Perhaps that's because we review emotionally charged events over and over and tell others about them. Also, public events such as wars, earthquakes, and assassinations reappear many times in the news, which highlights them in memory (Wright, 1993). Over time, flashbulb memories tend to crystallize into consistent, if not entirely accurate, landmarks in our lives (Schmolck, Buffalo, & Squire, 2000; Winningham, Hyman, & Dinnel, 2000).

TABLE 9.1

Bright Flashes of Memory

MEMORY CUE	PERCENTAGE OF STUDENTS WITH FLASHBULB MEMORIES
A car accident you were in or witnessed	85
When you first met your college roommate	82
The night of your high school graduation	81
The night of your senior prom (if you went or not)	78
An early romantic experience	77
A time you had to speak in front of an audience	72
When you first got your college admissions letter	65
Your first date—the moment you met him/her	57

From Rubin, 1985

AP/Wide World Photo

It is highly likely that you have a flashbulb memory about where you were when you first learned about the terrorist attack on the World Trade Center in New York. If someone alerted you about the news, you will remember that person's call and you will have clear memories about how you reacted to seeing the collapse of the towers.

Memory Formation—Some "Shocking" Findings

One possibility overlooked in our discussion of forgetting is that memories may be lost as they are being formed. For example, a head injury may cause a "gap" in memories preceding the accident. *Retrograde amnesia,* as this is called, involves forgetting events that occurred before an injury or trauma. In contrast, *anterograde amnesia* involves forgetting events that follow an injury or trauma. (An example of this type of amnesia is discussed in a moment.)

Consolidation

Retrograde amnesia can be understood if we assume that it takes a certain amount of time to move information from short-term memory to long-term memory. The forming of a long-term memory is called **consolidation** (Squire, Knowlton, & Musen, 1993). You can think of consolidation as being somewhat like writing your name in wet concrete. Once the concrete is set, the information (your name) is fairly lasting, but while it is setting, it can be wiped out (amnesia) or scribbled over (interference).

Consider a classic experiment on consolidation, in which a rat is placed on a small platform. The rat steps down to the floor and receives a painful electric shock. After one shock, the rat can be returned to the platform repeatedly, but it will not step down. Obviously, the rat remembers the shock. Would it remember if consolidation were disturbed?

Interestingly, one way to prevent consolidation is to give a different kind of shock called **electroconvulsive shock (ECS).** ECS is a mild electric shock to the brain. It does not harm the animal, but it does destroy any memory that is being formed. If each painful shock (the one the animal remembers) is followed by ECS (which wipes out memories during consolidation), the rat will step down over and over. Each time, ECS will erase the memory of the painful shock.

What would happen if ECS were given several hours after the learning? Recent memories are more easily disrupted than older memories (Gold, 1987). If enough time is allowed to pass between learning and ECS, the memory will be unaffected because consolidation is already complete. That's why people with mild head injuries lose only memories from just before the accident, whereas older memories remain intact (Lieberman, 2004). Likewise, you would forget more if you studied, stayed awake 8 hours, and then slept 8 hours than you would if you studied, slept 8 hours, and were awake for 8 hours. Either way, 16 hours would pass. However, less forgetting would occur in the second instance because more consolidation would occur before interference begins (Nesca & Koulack, 1994).

Where does consolidation take place in the brain? Actually, many parts of the brain are responsible for memory, but the **hippocampus** is particularly important. The hippocampus acts as a sort of "switching station" between short-term and long-term memory (Gabrieli, 1998). The hippocampus does this, in part, by growing new neurons. New neurons probably store information by making new connections within the brain (Macklis, 2001).

Humans who have hippocampal damage usually show a striking inability to store new memories (Bigler et al., 1996). A patient described by Brenda Milner provides a vivid example. Two years after an operation damaged his hippocampus, a 29-year-old patient continued to give his age as 27. He also reported that it seemed as if the operation had just taken place (Milner, 1965). His memory of events before the operation remained clear, but he found forming new long-term memories almost impossible. When his parents moved to a new house a few blocks away on the same street, he could not remember the new address. Month after month, he read the same magazines over and over without finding them familiar. If you were to meet this man, he would seem fairly normal because he still has short-term memory. But if you were to leave the room and return 15 minutes later, he would act as if he had never seen you before. Years ago his favorite uncle died, but he suffers the same grief anew each time he is told of the death. Lacking the ability to form new lasting memories, he lives eternally in the present (Corkin, 2002).

BRIDGES

ECS has been used as a psychiatric treatment for severe depression. Used in this way, electroshock therapy also causes memory loss.

See Chapter 17, pages 594–595.

The Brain and Memory

Somewhere within the 3-pound mass of the human brain lies all we know: ZIP codes, faces of loved ones, history, favorite melodies, the taste of an apple, and much, much more. Where is this information? Karl Lashley, a pioneering brain researcher, set out in the 1920s to find an **engram**, or memory trace. Lashley taught animals to run mazes and then removed parts of their brains to see how memory of the maze changed. After 30 years he had to concede defeat: Engrams are not located in any one area of the brain. It mattered little which part of the brain's cortex he removed. Only the *amount* removed was related to memory loss.

Lashley's conclusion remains true for specific memories (Squire, 2004). However, some areas of the cerebral cortex *are* more important to memory than others. Patterns of blood flow in the cerebral cortex (the wrinkled outer layer of the brain) can be used to map brain activity. ● Figure 9.19 shows the results of measuring blood flow while people were thinking about a semantic memory *(a)* or an episodic memory *(b)*. In the map, green indicates areas that are more active during semantic thinking. Reds show areas of greater activity during episodic thinking. The brain in view *c* shows the difference in activity between views *a* and *b*. The resulting pattern indicates that the front of the cortex is re-

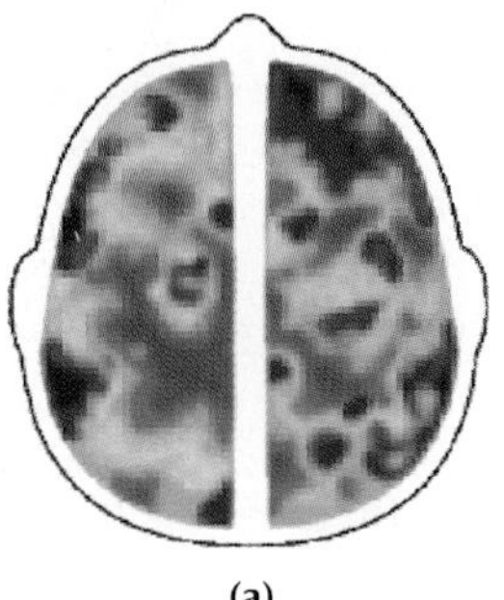
(a)

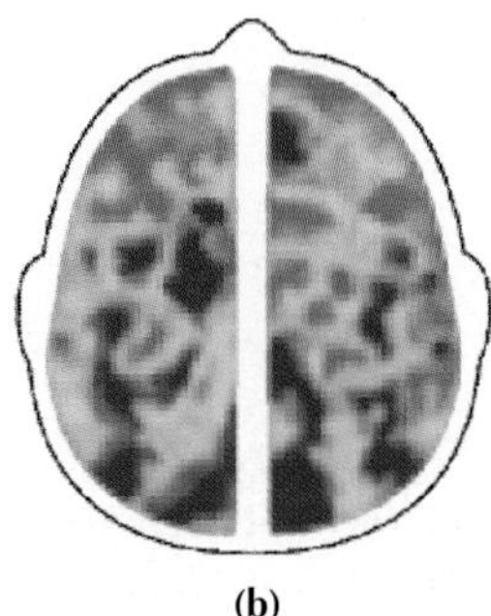
(b)

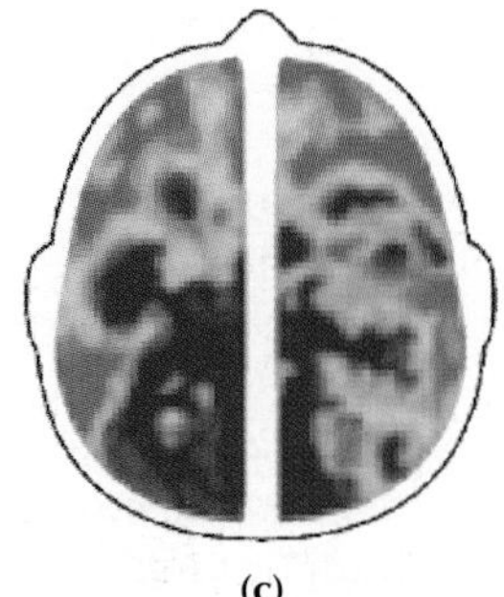
(c)

● **Figure 9.19** Patterns of blood flow in the cerebral cortex (wrinkled outer layer of the brain) change as areas become more or less active. Thus, blood flow can be used to draw "maps" of brain activity. This drawing, which views the brain from the top, shows the results of measuring cerebral blood flow while people were thinking about a semantic memory *(a)* or an episodic memory *(b)*. In the map, green indicates areas that are more active during semantic thinking. Reds show areas of greater activity during episodic thinking. The brain in view *c* shows the difference in activity between views *a* and *b*. The resulting pattern suggests that the front of the cortex is related to episodic memory. Areas toward the back and sides of the brain, especially the temporal lobes, are more associated with semantic memory (Gabrieli, 1998; Tulving, 1989, 2002).

Consolidation Process by which relatively permanent memories are formed in the brain.

Electroconvulsive shock (ECS) An electric current passed directly through the brain, producing a convulsion.

Hippocampus A brain structure associated with emotion and the transfer of information from short-term memory to long-term memory.

Engram A "memory trace" in the brain.

FOCUS ON RESEARCH

The Long-Term Potential of a Memory Pill

At long last, scientists may have found the chemical "signature" that records memories in everything from snails to rats to humans. If two brain cells become more active at the same time, the connections between them grow stronger (Squire & Kandel, 2000). This process is called *long-term potentiation.* After it occurs, an affected brain cell will respond more strongly to messages from other cells. The brain appears to use this mechanism to form lasting memories (García-Junco-Clemente, Linares-Clemente, & Fernández-Chacón, 2005).

How has that been demonstrated? Electrically stimulating parts of the brain involved in memory, such as the hippocampus, can decrease long-term potentiation (Ivanco & Racine, 2000). For example, using electroconvulsive shock to overstimulate memory areas in the brains of rats interferes with long-term potentiation (Trepel & Racine, 1998). It also causes memory loss—just as it does when humans are given ECS for depression.

Will researchers ever produce a "memory pill" for people with normal memory? It's a growing possibility. Drugs that *increase* long-term potentiation also tend to improve memory (Shakesby, Anwyl, & Rowan, 2002). For example, rats administered such drugs could remember the correct path through a maze better than rats not given the drug (Service, 1994). Such findings suggest that memory can be and will be artificially enhanced (Schacter, 2000). However, the possibility of something like a "physics pill" or a "math pill" still seems remote.

lated to episodic memory. Back areas are more associated with semantic memory (Tulving, 1989, 2002).

To summarize (and simplify greatly), the hippocampus handles memory consolidation (Zola & Squire, 2001). Once long-term memories are formed, they appear to be stored in the cortex of the brain (Gabrieli, 1998; Teng & Squire, 1999).

How are memories recorded in the cortex? Scientists are beginning to identify the exact ways in which nerve cells record information. For example, Eric Kandel and his colleagues have studied learning in the marine snail *aplysia* (ah-PLEEZ-yah). Kandel found that learning in *aplysia* occurs when certain nerve cells in a circuit alter the amount of transmitter chemicals they release (Kandel, 1999). Learning also alters the activity, structure, and chemistry of brain cells. Such changes determine which connections get stronger and which become weaker. This "reprograms" the brain and records information (Abel & Lattal, 2001; Klintsova & Greenough, 1999).

Scientists continue to study various chemicals, especially neurotransmitters, that affect memory. If their research succeeds, it may be possible to help the millions of persons who suffer from memory impairment (Elli & Nathan, 2001). (See "The Long-Term Potential of a Memory Pill.")

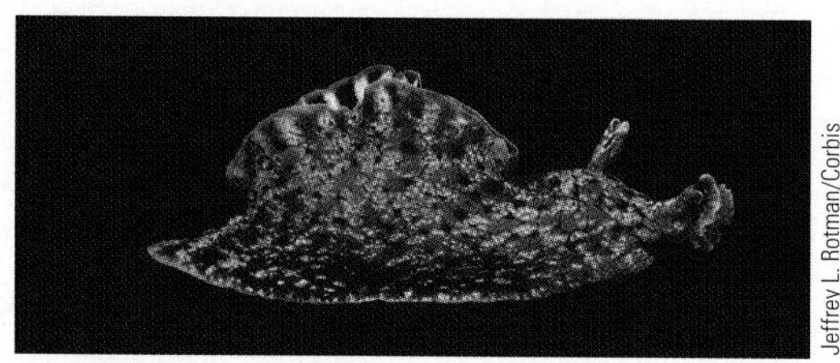

Jeffrey L. Rotman/Corbis

An *aplysia.* The relatively simple nervous system of this sea animal allows scientists to study memory as it occurs in single nerve cells.

KNOWLEDGE BUILDER

Forgetting

REFLECT

Which of the following concepts best explain why you have missed some answers on psychology tests: encoding failure, decay, disuse, memory cues, interference?

Do you know someone whose name you have a hard time remembering? Do you like or dislike that person? Do you think your difficulty is an instance of repression? Suppression? Interference? Encoding failure?

Have you had a flashbulb memory? How vivid is the memory today? How accurate do you think it is?

Here's a mnemonic tip: Elephants are supposed to have good memories, but a *hippo campus* is the place to go if you want to learn to consolidate memories.

LEARNING CHECK

1. According to the Ebbinghaus curve of forgetting, we forget slowly at first and then a rapid decline occurs. T or F?
2. Which explanation seems to account for the loss of short-term memories?
   a. decay c. repression
   b. disuse d. interference
3. When memories are available but not accessible, forgetting may be cue dependent. T or F?
4. When learning one thing makes it more difficult to recall another, forgetting may be caused by ____________________.
5. You are asked to memorize long lists of telephone numbers. You learn a new list each day for 10 days. When tested on list 3, you remember less than a person who only learned the first three lists. Your larger memory loss is probably caused by
   a. disuse c. regression
   b. retroactive interference d. proactive interference

6. If you consciously succeed at putting a painful memory out of mind, you have used
   a. redintegration c. negative rehearsal
   b. suppression d. repression
7. Flashbulb memories could be thought of as the reverse of
   a. repressed memories c. retroactive memories
   b. proactive memories d. episodic memories
8. Retrograde amnesia results when consolidation is speeded up. T or F?

CRITICAL THINKING

9. Based on state-dependent learning, why do you think that music often strongly evokes memories?
10. You must study French, Spanish, psychology, and biology in one evening. What do you think would be the best order in which to study these subjects so as to minimize interference?
11. There may be another way to explain why flashbulb memories are so long lasting. Can you think of one?

Answers: 1. F **2.** a and d **3.** T **4.** interference **5.** b **6.** b **7.** a **8.** F **9.** Music tends to affect the mood that a person is in, and moods tend to affect memory (Balch & Lewis, 1996). **10.** Any order that separates French from Spanish and psychology from biology would work (for instance: French, psychology, Spanish, biology). **11.** Memories of emotionally significant events may be unusually strong because such memories are rehearsed more frequently. People usually mentally review emotionally charged events many times.

Improving Memory—Keys to the Memory Bank

No matter how good your memory may be, there are probably times when you wish it were better. While we're waiting around for the arrival of a memory pill, this section describes some ways to immediately improve your memory skills.

Tatiana Cooley won a national memory contest held in New York. To win, she had to memorize long lists of words and numbers, the order of the cards in a shuffled deck, a 54-line poem, and 100 names and faces. Tatiana thinks that memorization is fun. You might expect that she would also be good at everyday memory chores. On the contrary, Tatiana describes herself as "incredibly absent-minded." When asked how many brothers and sisters she has, she replies, "Six, er seven, er six." The year she graduated from high school? She pauses for a several seconds, "1990." The elementary school grade she was in when she won a regional spelling bee? She can't remember. Ever fearful of forgetting, Tatiana keeps a daily to-do list and surrounds herself with a thicket of Post-It notes (Levinson, 1999).

Memory Strategies

What can we learn about memory from Tatiana? First, we should all be more tolerant of occasional memory lapses. Even memory champions have less than perfect memories! As we have seen in this chapter, memory is not like a tape recorder or a video camera. Information is frequently lost, and memories change as they are stored and retrieved. This can be frustrating at times, but it's also a good thing. The flexibility of human memory allows us to focus on what's important and meaningful, even though it also contributes to some inaccuracies. Tatiana's success as a "memory athlete" also suggests that making full use of memory requires effort and practice. Let's see how you can improve your memory.

Knowledge of Results

Learning proceeds best when feedback, or *knowledge of results,* allows you to check your progress. Feedback can help you identify ideas that need extra practice. In addition, knowing that you have remembered or answered correctly is rewarding. A prime way to provide feedback for yourself while studying is *recitation.*

Recitation

If you are going to remember something, eventually you will have to retrieve it. *Recitation* refers to summarizing aloud while you are learning. Recitation forces you to practice retrieving information. When you are reading a text, you should stop frequently and try to remember what you have just read by restating it in your own words. In one experiment, the best memory score was earned by a group of students who spent 80 percent of their time reciting and only 20 percent reading (Gates, 1958). Maybe students who talk to themselves aren't crazy after all.

Rehearsal

The more you *rehearse* (mentally review) information as you read, the better you will remember it. But remember that maintenance rehearsal alone is not very effective. Elaborative rehearsal, in which you look for connections to existing knowledge, is far better. Thinking about facts helps link them together in memory. To learn college-level information, you must make active use of rehearsal strategies (Nist, Sharman, & Holschuh, 1996).

Selection

The Dutch scholar Erasmus said that a good memory should be like a fish net: It should keep all the big fish and let the little ones escape. If you boil down the paragraphs in most textbooks to one or two important terms or ideas, your memory chores will be more manageable. Practice very selective marking in your texts and use marginal notes to further summarize ideas. Most students mark their texts too much instead of too little. If everything is underlined, you haven't been selective. And, very likely, you didn't pay much attention in the first place (Peterson, 1992).

Organization

Assume that you must memorize the following list of words: north, man, red, spring, woman, east, autumn, yellow, summer, boy, blue, west, winter, girl, green, south. This rather difficult list could be reorganized into *chunks* as follows: north-east-south-west, spring-summer-autumn-winter, red-yellow-green-blue, man-woman-boy-girl. This simple reordering made the second list much easier to learn when college students were tested on both lists (Deese & Hulse, 1967). Organizing class notes and summarizing chapters can be quite helpful (Dickinson & O'Connell, 1990). You may even want to summarize your summaries so that the overall network of ideas becomes clearer and simpler. Summaries improve memory by encouraging better encoding of information (Hadwin, Kirby, & Woodhouse, 1999).

Whole Versus Part Learning

If you have to memorize a speech, is it better to try to learn it from beginning to end? Or in smaller parts like paragraphs? Generally it is better to practice whole packages of information rather than smaller parts (*whole learning*). This is especially true for fairly short, organized information. An exception is that learning parts may be better for extremely long, complicated information. In *part learning,* subparts of a larger body of information are studied (such as sections of a textbook chapter). To decide which approach to use, remember to study the *largest meaningful amount of information* you can at one time.

For very long or complex material, try the *progressive-part method,* by breaking a learning task into a series of short sections. At first, you study part A until it is mastered. Next, you study parts A and B; then A, B, and C; and so forth. This is a good way to learn the lines of a play, a long piece of music, or a poem (Ash & Holding, 1990). After the material is learned, you should also practice by starting at points other than A (at C, D, or B, for example). This helps prevent getting "lost" or going blank in the middle of a performance.

Serial Position

Whenever you must learn something in order, be aware of the serial position effect. As you will recall, this is the tendency to make the most errors in remembering the middle of a list. If you are introduced to a long line of people, the names you are likely to forget will be those in the middle, so you should make an extra effort to attend to them. You should also give extra practice to the middle of a list, poem, or speech. Try to break long lists of information into short sub-lists, and make the middle sub-lists the shortest of all.

Cues

The best *memory cues* (stimuli that aid retrieval) are those that were present during encoding (Reed, 1996). For example, students in one study had the daunting task of trying to recall a list of 600 words. As they read the list (which they did not know they would be tested on), the students gave three other words closely related in meaning to each listed word. In a test given later, the words each student supplied were used as cues to jog his or her memory. The students recalled an astounding 90 percent of the original word list (Mantyla, 1986).

Now read the following sentence:

The fish bit the swimmer.

If you were tested a week from now, you would be more likely to recall the sentence if you were given a memory cue. And, surprisingly, the word *shark* would work better as a reminder than *fish* would. The reason for this is that most people think of a shark when they read the sentence. As a result, *shark* becomes a potent memory cue (Schacter, 2000).

The preceding examples show, once again, that it often helps to *elaborate* information as you learn. When you study, try to use new names, ideas, or terms in several sentences. Also, form images that include the new information and relate it to knowledge you already have (Pressley et al., 1988). Your goal should be to knit meaningful cues into your memory code to help you retrieve information when you need it (● Figure 9.20).

Robbie Jack/Corbis

● **Figure 9.20** Actors can remember large amounts of complex information for many months, even when learning new roles in between. During testing, they remember their lines best when they are allowed to move and gesture as they would when performing. Apparently their movements supply cues that aid recall (Noice & Noice, 1999).

Overlearning

Numerous studies have shown that memory is greatly improved when you **overlearn.** That is, when study is continued beyond bare mastery. After you have learned material well enough to remember it once without error, you should continue studying. Overlearning is your best insurance against going blank on a test because of being nervous.

Spaced Practice

To keep boredom and fatigue to a minimum, try alternating short study sessions with brief rest periods. This pattern, called **spaced practice,** is generally superior to **massed practice,** in which little or no rest is given between learning sessions. By improving attention and consolidation, three 20-minute study sessions can produce more learning than 1 hour of continuous study. There's an old joke that goes, "How do you get to Carnegie Hall?" The answer is, "Practice, practice, practice." A better answer would be "Practice, wait awhile, practice, wait awhile, practice" (Neath, 2002).

Perhaps the best way to make use of spaced practice is to *schedule* your time. To make an effective schedule, designate times during the week before, after, and between classes when you will study particular subjects. Then treat these times just as if they were classes you had to attend.

Sleep and Memory

Remember that sleeping after study reduces interference. However, unless you are a "night person," late evening may not be a very efficient time for you to study. Also, you obviously can't sleep after every study session or study everything just before you sleep. That's why your study schedule should include ample breaks between subjects, as described earlier. Using your breaks and free time in a schedule is as important as living up to your study periods.

Hunger and Memory

People who are hungry almost always score lower on memory tests. So mother was right, it's a good idea to make sure you've had a good breakfast or lunch before you take tests at school (Martin & Benton, 1999; Smith, Clark, & Gallagher, 1999).

Extend How Long You Remember

When you are learning new information, test yourself repeatedly. As you do, gradually lengthen the amount of time that passes before you test yourself again. For example, if you are studying German words on flash cards, look at the first card and then move it a few cards back in the stack. Do the same with the next few cards. When you get to the first "old" card, test yourself on it and check the answer. Then, move it farther back in the stack. Do the same with other "old" cards as they come up. When "old" cards come up for the third time, put them clear to the back of the stack (Cull, Shaughnessy, & Zechmeister, 1996).

Review

If you have spaced your practice and overlearned, review will be like icing on your study cake. Reviewing shortly before an exam cuts down the time during which you must remember details that may be important for the test. When reviewing, hold the amount of new information you try to memorize to a minimum. It may be realistic to take what you have actually learned and add a little more to it at the last minute by cramming. But remember that more than a little new learning may interfere with what you already know.

Using a Strategy to Aid Recall

Successful recall is usually the result of a planned *search* of memory (Reed, 1996). For example, one study found that students were most likely to recall names that eluded them if they made use of partial information (Reed & Bruce, 1982). The students were trying to answer questions such as, "He is best remembered as the scarecrow in the Judy Garland movie *The Wizard of Oz.*" (The answer is Ray Bolger.) Partial information that helped students remember included impressions about the length of the name, letter sounds within the name, similar names, and related information (such as the names of other characters in the movie). A similar helpful strategy is to go through the alphabet, trying each letter as the first sound of a name or word you are seeking.

The *cognitive interview* described earlier in this chapter (see "Telling Wrong from Right in Forensic Memory") offers some further hints for recapturing context and jogging memories:

1. Say or write down *everything* you can remember that relates to the information you are seeking. Don't worry about how trivial any of it seems; each bit of information you remember can serve as a cue to bring back others.
2. Try to recall events or information in different orders. Let your memories flow out backward or out of order, or start with whatever impressed you the most.
3. Recall from different viewpoints. Review events by mentally standing in a different place. Or try to view information as another person would remember it. When taking a test, for instance, ask yourself what other students or your professor would remember about the topic.
4. Mentally put yourself back in the situation where you learned the information. Try to mentally recreate the learning environment or relive the event. As you do, include sounds, smells, details of weather, nearby objects, other people present, what you said or thought, and how you felt as you learned the information (Fisher & Geiselman, 1987).

A Look Ahead

Psychologists still have much to learn about the nature of memory and how to improve it. For now, one thing stands out clearly: People who have good memories excel at organizing information and making it meaningful. With this in mind, the Psychology in Action discussion for this chapter tells how you can combine organization and meaning into a powerful method for improving memory.

KNOWLEDGE BUILDER

Improving Memory

REFLECT

Return to the topic headings in the preceding pages that list techniques for improving memory. Place a check mark next to those that you have used recently. Review any you didn't mark and think of a specific example of how you could use each technique at school, at home, or at work.

LEARNING CHECK

1. To improve memory, it is reasonable to spend as much or more time reciting as reading. T or F?
2. Organizing information while studying has little effect on memory because long-term memory is already highly organized. T or F?
3. The progressive-part method of study is best suited to long and complex learning tasks. T or F?
4. Sleeping immediately after studying is highly disruptive to the consolidation of memories. T or F?
5. As new information is encoded and rehearsed it is helpful to elaborate on its meaning and connect it to other information. T or F?
6. The cognitive interview helps people remember more by providing
   a. memory cues
   b. a serial position effect
   c. phonetic priming
   d. massed practice

CRITICAL THINKING

7. What advantages would there be to taking notes as you read a textbook, as opposed to underlining words in the text?

Answers: 1. T **2.** F **3.** T **4.** F **5.** T **6.** a **7.** Note-taking is a form of recitation, it encourages elaborative rehearsal and facilitates the organization and selection of important ideas, and your notes can be used for review.

Spaced practice A practice schedule that alternates study periods with brief rests.

Massed practice A practice schedule in which studying continues for long periods, without interruption.

PSYCHOLOGY IN ACTION

Mnemonics—Memory Magic

Some stage performers use memory as part of their acts. Do they have eidetic imagery? Various "memory experts" entertain by memorizing the names of everyone at a banquet, the order of all the cards in a deck, long lists of words, or other seemingly impossible amounts of information. Such feats may seem like magic, but if they are, you can have a magic memory too. These tricks are performed through the use of *mnemonics* (nee-MON-iks) (Lieberman, 2004; Wilding & Valentine, 1994b). A **mnemonic** is any kind of memory system or aid. In some cases, mnemonic strategies increase recall ten-fold (Patten, 1990).

Some mnemonic systems are so common that almost everyone knows them. If you are trying to remember how many days there are in a month, you may find the answer by reciting, "Thirty days hath September . . ." Physics teachers often help students remember the colors of the spectrum by giving them the mnemonic "Roy G. Biv": **R**ed, **O**range, **Y**ellow, **G**reen, **B**lue, **I**ndigo, **V**iolet. The budding sailor who has trouble telling port from starboard may remember that port and left both have four letters or may remind herself, "I *left* port." And what beginning musician hasn't remembered the notes represented by the lines and spaces of the musical staff by learning "F-A-C-E" and "**E**very **G**ood **B**oy **D**oes **F**ine."

Mnemonic techniques are ways to avoid *rote* learning (learning by simple repetition). The superiority of mnemonic learning as opposed to rote learning has been demonstrated many times. For example, Gordon Bower (1973) asked college students to study 5 different lists of 20 unrelated words. At the end of a short study session, subjects tried to recall all 100 items. People using mnemonics remembered an average of 72 items, whereas members of a control group using rote learning remembered an average of 28.

Stage performers rarely have naturally superior memories. Instead, they make extensive use of memory systems to perform their feats (Wilding & Valentine, 1994b). Few of these systems are of practical value to you as a student, but the principles underlying mnemonics are. By practicing mnemonics you should be able to greatly improve your memory with little effort (Dretzke & Levin, 1996).

Here, then, are the basic principles of mnemonics.

1. **Use mental pictures.** Visual pictures, or images, are generally easier to remember than words. Turning information into mental pictures is therefore very helpful. Make these images as vivid as possible (Campos & Perez, 1997).
2. **Make things meaningful.** Transferring information from short-term memory to long-term memory is aided by making it meaningful. If you encounter technical terms that have little or no immediate meaning for you, *give* them meaning, even if you have to stretch the term to do so. (This point is clarified by the examples following this list.)
3. **Make information familiar.** Connect it to what you already know. Another way to get information into long-term memory is to connect it to information already stored there. If some facts or ideas in a chapter seem to stay in your memory easily, associate other more difficult facts with them.
4. **Form bizarre, unusual, or exaggerated mental associations.** Forming images that make sense is better in most situations. However, when associating two ideas, terms, or especially mental images, you may find that the more outrageous and exaggerated the association, the more likely you are to remember. Bizarre images make stored information more *distinctive* and therefore easier to retrieve

Ulrike Welsch

Mnemonics can be an aid in preparing for tests. However, because mnemonics help most in the initial stages of storing information, it is important to follow through with other elaborative learning strategies.

(Worthen & Marshall, 1996). Imagine, for example, that you have just been introduced to Mr. Rehkop. To remember his name, you could picture him wearing a police uniform. Then replace his nose with a ray gun. This bizarre image will provide two hints when you want to remember Mr. Rehkop's name: *ray* and *cop* (Carney, Levin, & Stackhouse, 1997). This technique works for other kinds of information, too. College students who used exaggerated mental associations to remember the names of unfamiliar animals outperformed students who just used rote memory (Carney & Levin, 2001). Bizarre images mainly help improve immediate memory, and they work best for fairly simple information (Robinson-Riegler & McDaniel, 1994). Nevertheless, they can be a first step toward learning.

A sampling of typical applications of mnemonics should make these four points clearer to you.

Example 1

Let's say you have 30 new vocabulary words to memorize in Spanish. You can proceed by rote memorization (repeat them over and over until you begin to get them), or you can learn them with little effort by using the keyword method (Pressley, 1987). In the **keyword method** a familiar word or image is used to link two other words or items. To remember that the word *pajaro* (pronounced PAH-hah-ro) means bird, you can link it to a "key" word in English: *Pajaro* (to me) sounds like "parked car-o." Therefore, to remember that *pajaro* means bird, you might visualize a parked car jam-packed full of birds. You should try to make this image as vivid and exaggerated as possible, with birds flapping and chirping and feathers flying everywhere. Similarly, for the word *carta* (which means "letter"), you might imagine a shopping *cart* filled with postal letters.

Exaggerated mental images can link two words or ideas in ways that aid memory. Here, the keyword method is used to link the English word *letter* with the Spanish word *carta.*

If you link similar keywords and images for the rest of the list, you may not remember them all, but you will get most without any more practice. As a matter of fact, if you have formed the *pajaro* and *carta* images just now, it is going to be almost impossible for you to ever see these words again without remembering what they mean. The keyword method is also superior when you want to work "backward" from an English word to a foreign vocabulary word (Hogben & Lawson, 1992).

What about a year from now? How long do keyword memories last? Mnemonic memories work best in the short run. Later, they may be more fragile than conventional memories. That's why it's usually best to use mnemonics during the initial stages of learning (Carney & Levin, 1998). To create more lasting memories, you'll need to use the techniques discussed earlier in this chapter.

Example 2

Let's say you have to learn the names of all the bones and muscles in the human body for biology. You are trying to remember that the jawbone is the *mandible.* This one is easy because you can associate it to a *man nibbling,* or maybe you can picture a *man dribbling* a basketball with his jaw (make this image as ridiculous as possible). If the muscle name *latissimus dorsi* gives you trouble, familiarize it by turning it into *"the ladder misses the door, sigh."* Then picture a ladder glued to your back where the muscle is found. Picture the ladder leading up to a small door at your shoulder. Picture the ladder missing the door. Picture the ladder sighing like an animated character in a cartoon.

This seems like more to remember, not less; and it seems like it would cause you to misspell things. Mnemonics are not a complete substitute for normal memory; they are an aid to normal memory. Mnemonics are not likely to be helpful unless you make extensive use of *images* (Willoughby et al., 1997). Your mental pictures will come back to you easily. As for misspellings, mnemonics can be thought of as a built-in hint in your memory. Often, when taking a test, you will find that the slightest hint is all you need to remember correctly. A mnemonic image is like having someone leaning over your shoulder who says, "Psst, the name of that muscle sounds like 'ladder misses the door, sigh.'" If misspelling continues to be a problem, try to create memory aids for spelling, too.

Here are two more examples to help you appreciate the flexibility of a mnemonic approach to studying.

Example 3

Your art history teacher expects you to be able to name the artist when you are shown slides as part of exams. You have seen many of the slides only once before in class. How will you remember them? As the slides are shown in class, make each artist's name into an object or image. Then picture the object *in* the paintings done by the artist. For example, you can picture Van Gogh as a *van* (automobile) *going* through the middle of each Van Gogh painting. Picture the van running over things and knocking things over. Or, if you remember that Van Gogh cut off his ear, picture a giant bloody ear in each of his paintings.

Example 4

If you have trouble remembering history, try to avoid thinking of it as something from the dim past. Picture each historical personality as a person you know right now (a friend, teacher, parent, and so on). Then picture these people doing whatever the historical figures did. Also, try visualizing battles or other events as if they were happening in your town or make parks and schools into countries. Use your imagination.

How can mnemonics be used to remember things in order? Here are three techniques that are helpful.

Mnemonic Any kind of memory system or aid.

Keyword method As an aid to memory, using a familiar word or image to link two items.

1. **Form a story or a chain.** To remember lists of ideas, objects, or words in order, try forming an exaggerated association (mental image) connecting the first item to the second, then the second to the third, and so on. To remember the following short list in order—elephant, doorknob, string, watch, rifle, oranges—picture a full-size *elephant* balanced on a *doorknob* playing with a *string* tied to him. Picture a *watch* tied to the string, and a *rifle* shooting *oranges* at the watch. This technique can be used quite successfully for lists of 20 or more items. In one test, people who used a linking mnemonic did much better at remembering lists of 15 and 22 errands (Higbee et al., 1990). Try it next time you go shopping and leave your list at home. Another helpful strategy is to make up a short story that links all of the items on a list you want to remember (McNamara & Scott, 2001).
2. **Take a mental walk.** Ancient Greek orators had an interesting way to remember ideas in order when giving a speech. Their method was to take a mental walk along a familiar path. As they did, they associated topics with the images of statues found along the walk. You can do the same thing by "placing" objects or ideas along the way as you mentally take a familiar walk (Neath, 2002).
3. **Use a system.** Many times, the first letters or syllables of words or ideas can be formed into another word that will serve as a reminder of order. "Roy G. Biv" is an example. As an alternative, learn the following: 1 is a bun, 2 is a shoe, 3 is a tree, 4 is a door, 5 is a hive, 6 is sticks, 7 is heaven, 8 is a gate, 9 is a line, 10 is a hen. To remember a list in order, form an image associating bun with the first item on your list. For example, if the first item is *frog,* picture a "frog-burger" on a bun to remember it. Then, associate shoe with the second item, and so on.

If you have never used mnemonics, you may still be skeptical, but give this approach a fair trial. Most people find they can greatly extend their memory through the use of mnemonics. But remember, like most things worthwhile, remembering takes effort.

KNOWLEDGE BUILDER

Mnemonics

REFLECT

As an exercise, see if you can create mnemonics for the words *icon, implicit memory,* and *mnemonic.* The best mnemonics are your own, but here are some examples to help you get started. An icon is a visual image: Picture an *eye* in a *can* to remember that icons store visual information. Implicit memories are "hidden": Picture an *imp* hiding in memory. A mnemonic is a memory aid: Imagine writing a phone number on your knee to remember it. Imagine your *knee moaning, "Ick,* you shouldn't write on me."

Now, go through the glossary items in this chapter and make up mnemonics for any terms you have difficulty remembering.

LEARNING CHECK

1. Memory systems and aids are referred to as ______________.
2. Which of the following is least likely to improve memory?
   a. using exaggerated mental images
   b. forming a chain of associations
   c. turning visual information into verbal information
   d. associating new information to information that is already known or familiar
3. Bizarre images make stored information more distinctive and therefore easier to retrieve. T or F?
4. Bower's 1973 study showed that, in general, mnemonics only improve memory for related words or ideas. T or F?
5. The keyword method is a commonly used
   a. cognitive interviewing technique
   b. massed practice strategy
   c. mnemonic technique
   d. first step in the progressive-part method

CRITICAL THINKING

6. How are elaborative rehearsal and mnemonics alike?

Answers: 1. mnemonics **2.** c **3.** T **4.** F **5.** c **6.** Both attempt to relate new information to information stored in LTM that is familiar or already easy to retrieve.

Chapter in Review

Is there more than one type of memory?

- Memory is an active, computer-like system that encodes, stores, and retrieves information.
- Humans appear to have three interrelated memory systems. These are sensory memory, short-term memory (STM, also called working memory), and long-term memory (LTM).

What are the features of each type of memory?

- Sensory memory is exact but very brief. Through selective attention, some information is transferred to STM.
- STM has a capacity of about 5 to 7 bits of information, but this can be extended by chunking, or recoding. Short-term memories are brief and very sensitive to interruption, or interference; however, they can be prolonged by maintenance rehearsal.
- LTM functions as a general storehouse of information, especially meaningful information. Elaborative rehearsal helps transfer information from STM to LTM. Long-term memories are relatively permanent, or lasting. LTM seems to have an almost unlimited storage capacity.
- LTM is subject to constructive processing, or ongoing revision and updating. LTM is highly organized to allow retrieval of needed information. The pattern, or structure, of memory networks is the subject of current memory research.
- Redintegrative memories are reconstructed as each memory provides a cue for the next memory.

Is there more than one type of long-term memory?

- Within long-term memory, declarative memories for facts seem to differ from procedural memories for skills.
- Declarative memories may be further categorized as semantic memories or episodic memories.

How is memory measured?

- The tip-of-the-tongue state shows that memory is not an all-or-nothing event. Memories may therefore be revealed by recall, recognition, relearning, or priming.
- In recall, memory proceeds without explicit cues, as in an essay exam. Recall of listed information often reveals a serial position effect (middle items on the list are most subject to errors).
- A common test of recognition is the multiple-choice question.
- In relearning, "forgotten" material is learned again, and memory is indicated by a savings score.
- Recall, recognition, and relearning mainly measure explicit memories. Other techniques, such as priming, are necessary to reveal implicit memories.

What are "photographic" memories?

- Eidetic imagery (photographic memory) occurs when a person is able to project an image onto a blank surface.
- Eidetic imagery is rarely found in adults. However, many adults have internal memory images, which can be very vivid.
- Exceptional memory can be learned by finding ways to directly store information in LTM.
- Learning has no effect on the limits of STM. Some people may have exceptional memories that exceed what can be achieved through learning.

What causes forgetting?

- Forgetting and memory were extensively studied by Herman Ebbinghaus. His work shows that forgetting is most rapid immediately after learning (the curve of forgetting).
- Failure to encode information is a common cause of "forgetting."
- Forgetting in sensory memory and STM probably reflects decay of memory traces in the nervous system. Decay or disuse of memories may also account for some LTM loss.
- Often, forgetting is cue dependent. The power of cues to trigger memories is revealed by state-dependent learning and the link between moods and memory.
- Much forgetting in both STM and LTM can be attributed to interference.
- When recent learning interferes with retrieval of prior learning, retroactive interference has occurred.
- If old learning interferes with new learning, proactive interference has occurred.

How accurate are everyday memories?

- Repression is the forgetting of painful, embarrassing, or traumatic memories.
- Repression is thought to be unconscious, in contrast to suppression, which is a conscious attempt to avoid thinking about something.
- Independent evidence has verified that some recovered memories of childhood sexual abuse are true. However, others have been shown to be false.
- In the absence of confirming or disconfirming evidence, there is currently no way to separate true memories from

fantasies. Caution is advised for all concerned with attempts to retrieve supposedly hidden memories.

What happens in the brain when memories are formed?

- Retrograde amnesia and the effects of electroconvulsive shock (ECS) may be explained by the concept of consolidation.
- Consolidation theory holds that engrams (permanent memory traces) are formed during a critical period after learning. Until they are consolidated, long-term memories are easily destroyed.
- The hippocampus is a brain area that has been linked with consolidation of memories. Once memories are consolidated, they appear to be stored in the cortex of the brain.
- The search within the brain for engrams has now settled on changes in nerve cells and how they interconnect.

How can memory be improved?

- Memory can be improved by using feedback, recitation, and rehearsal; by selecting and organizing information; and by using the progressive-part method, spaced practice, overlearning, and active search strategies. Effects of serial position, sleep, review, cues, and elaboration should also be kept in mind when studying or memorizing.
- Mnemonic systems use mental images and unusual associations to link new information with familiar memories already stored in LTM. Such strategies give information personal meaning and make it easier to recall.

Web Resources

Internet addresses frequently change. To find the sites listed here, visit www.thomsonedu.com/psychology/coon for an updated list of Internet ad dresses and direct links to relevant sites.

***Psychology: Gateways to Mind and Behavior* Website** Online quizzes, flash cards, and other helpful study aids for this text. www.thomsonedu.com/psychology/coon.

Active Brain Areas in Working Memory A three-dimensional MRI reconstruction of a person's brain while holding letters in working memory.

Exploratorium: Memory Demonstrations and articles related to memory from an exceptional science museum.

False-Memory Test Use the materials in this site to induce false memories in others (for demonstration purposes).

Memories Are Made of . . . Article from *Scientific American* discusses memory-enhancing drugs for Alzheimer's patients.

Memory Techniques and Mnemonics Links to information on mnemonics.

Questions and Answers About Memories of Childhood Abuse From APA, a summary of the repressed memory issue.

Repressed and Recovered Memories Site devoted to the recovered memory controversy; has links to both sides of the controversy.

The Machinery of Thought *Scientific American* article describes research on the physiology of memory.

The Magical Number Seven, Plus or Minus Two Full text of George Miller's original article.

ThomsonNOW™ Go to www.thomsonedu.com to link to ThomsonNow, your online study tool. First take the **Pre-Test** for this chapter to get your **Personalized Study Plan,** which will identify topics you need to review and direct you to online resources. Then take the **Post-Test** to determine what concepts you have mastered and what you still need work on.

InfoTrac College Edition For recent articles on the Psychology in Action feature, use Key Words search for MNEMONICS. Go to www.thomsonedu.com/psychology/coon.

Interactive Learning

***PsychNow!* Version 2.0 CD-ROM** Interact with the material with *PsychNow!*'s animations, video clips, experiments, and interactive assessments. For this chapter, go to *5d. Memory Systems* and *5e. Forgetting* to learn more about how our memory works.

chapter 10

Cognition, Language, and Creativity

Dave Umberger/AP Wide World Photos

THEME:

The origins of intelligent behavior lie in thinking, language, problem solving, and creativity.

Key Questions

What is the nature of thought?

In what ways are images related to thinking?

How are concepts learned? Are there different kinds of concepts?

What is the role of language in thinking?

Can animals be taught to use language?

What do we know about problem solving?

What is artificial intelligence?

What is the nature of creative thinking?

How accurate is intuition?

What can be done to promote creativity?

Preview

Gizmos and Doohickeys

Cartoonist Rube Goldberg was famous for drawing wacky machines that did simple tasks in hilarious ways. A typical Rube Goldberg device consisted of pulleys, switches, levers, mousetraps, balloons, fans, dancing cows, and other strange items.

Today, thanks to the Theta Tau engineering fraternity, students can honor Goldberg's zany inspiration while testing their own creativity. In a contest held at Purdue University, students invent machines to do tasks such as sticking a stamp on a letter, teeing up a golf ball, or screwing a lightbulb into a socket. Of course, any engineering student worth his or her calculator could easily create a machine to do such things. The real challenge in the National Rube Goldberg Machine Contest is to build a gadget that does something simple in the most complicated way imaginable. For instance, Doug Shoenenberger and Paul Calhoun won with a contraption that loads a disc into a CD player in 35 mind-boggling steps.

Students like Doug and Paul obviously enjoy complexity, novelty, and problem solving. At higher levels, these are the same qualities that define many of history's geniuses, such as Einstein, Darwin, Mozart, Newton, Michelangelo, Galileo, Madame Curie, Edison, Martha Graham, and others (Michalko, 1998).

Like all creative activities, the Rube Goldberg contest raises questions about human cognition. How do we think? How are we able to solve problems? How do people create works of art, science, and literature? How many engineering students does it take to screw in a lightbulb? For some preliminary answers, we will investigate thinking, problem solving, and creativity in the pages that follow.

What Is Thinking?—It's All in Your Head!

Humans are highly adaptable creatures. We live in deserts, jungles, mountains, frenzied cities, placid retreats, and, recently, in space stations. Unlike other species, our success owes more to intelligence and thinking abilities than it does to physical strength or speed (Solso, MacLin, & MacLin, 2005). Let's see how concepts, language, and mental images make thinking possible.

Cognition refers to mentally processing information. Our thoughts take many forms, including daydreaming, problem solving, and reasoning (to name but a few). Although thinking is not limited to humans, imagine trying to teach an animal to match the feats of Shakuntala Devi, who holds the "world record" for mental calculation. Devi once multiplied two 13-digit numbers (7,686,369,774,870 times 2,465,099,745,779) in her head, giving the answer in 28 seconds. (That's 18,947,668,104,042,434, 089,403,730 if you haven't already figured it out.)

AP/Wide World Photos

The power of thought is beautifully expressed by Stephen W. Hawking, a theoretical physicist and one of the best-known scientific minds of modern times. Now in his early sixties, Hawking has suffered since age 13 from amyotrophic lateral sclerosis, a disabling condition also known as Lou Gehrig's disease. Today, he can control only his left hand, and he cannot speak. Nevertheless, his brain remains fiercely active. With courage and determination, he has used his intellect to advance our understanding of the universe.

Some Basic Units of Thought

At its most basic, thinking is an *internal representation* (mental expression) of a problem or situation. (Picture a chess player who mentally tries out several moves before actually touching a chess piece.) The power of being able to mentally represent problems is dramatically illustrated by chess grand master Miguel Najdorf, who once simultaneously played 45 chess games, while blindfolded. How did Najdorf do it? Like most people, he used the basic units of thought: images, concepts, and language (or symbols). **Images** are picture-like mental representations. **Concepts** are ideas that represent categories of objects or events. **Language** consists of words or symbols, and rules for combining them. Thinking often involves all three units. For example, blindfolded chess players rely on visual images, concepts ("Game 2 begins with a strategy called an English opening"), and the notational system, or "language," of chess.

In a moment we will delve further into imagery, concepts, and language. Be aware, however, that thinking involves attention, pattern recognition, memory, decision making, intuition, knowledge, and more. This chapter is only a sample of what cognitive psychology is about.

B.Busco/Getty Images

An ability to mentally rotate objects is very valuable for people who work in industrial design and drafting.

Mental Imagery—Does a Frog Have Lips?

Ninety-seven percent of us have visual images and 92 percent have auditory images. More than 50 percent have imagery for movement, touch, taste, smell, and pain. Thus, mental images are sometimes more than just "pictures." For example, your image of a bakery may also include its delicious odor. Some people have a rare form of imagery called **synesthesia** (sin-es-THEE-zyah). For these individuals, images cross normal sensory barriers (Martino & Marks, 2001). For instance, listening to music may produce a burst of colors or tastes, as well as sound sensations (Robertson & Sagiv, 2005). Despite such variations, most of us use images to think, remember, and solve problems. For instance, we may use mental images to do the following:

- Make a decision or solve a problem (choosing what clothes to wear; figuring out how to arrange furniture in a room).
- Change feelings (thinking of pleasant images to get out of a bad mood; imagining yourself as thin to stay on a diet).
- Improve a skill or prepare for some action (using images to improve a swimming stroke; mentally rehearsing how you will ask for a raise).
- Aid memory (picturing Mr. Cook wearing a chef's hat, so you can remember his name).

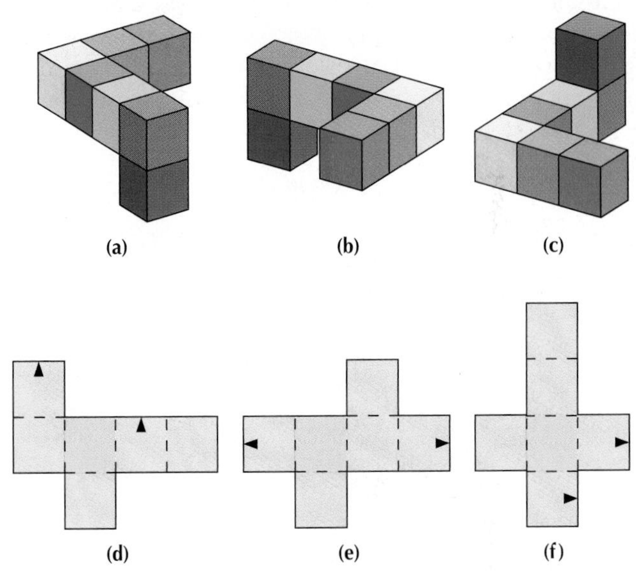

● **Figure 10.1** Imagery in thinking. *(Top)* Subjects were shown a drawing similar to *(a)* and drawings of how *(a)* would look in other positions, such as *(b)* and *(c)*. Subjects could recognize *(a)* after it had been "rotated" from its original position. However, the more *(a)* was rotated in space, the longer it took to recognize it. This result suggests that subjects actually formed a three-dimensional image of *(a)* and rotated the image to see if it matched (Shepard, 1975). *(Bottom)* Try your ability to manipulate mental images: Each of these shapes can be folded to make a cube; in which do the arrows meet? (After Kosslyn, 1985.)

The Nature of Mental Images

Mental images are not flat, like photographs. Researcher Stephen Kosslyn showed this by asking people, "Does a frog have lips and a stubby tail?" Unless you often kiss frogs, you will probably tackle this question by using mental images. Most people picture a frog, "look" at its mouth, and then mentally "rotate" the frog in mental space to check its tail (Kosslyn, 1983). Mental rotation is partly based on imagined movements (● Figure 10.1). That is, we mentally "pick up" an object and turn it around (Richter et al., 2000; Wexler, Kosslyn, & Berthoz, 1998).

Cognition The process of thinking or mentally processing information (images, concepts, words, rules, and symbols).

Image Most often, a mental representation that has picture-like qualities; an icon.

Concept A generalized idea representing a class of related objects or events.

Language Words or symbols, and rules for combining them, that are used for thinking and communication.

Synesthesia Experiencing one sense in terms normally associated with another sense; for example, "seeing" colors when a sound is heard.

"Reverse Vision"

What happens in the brain when a person has visual images? Seeing something in your "mind's eye" is similar to seeing real objects. Information from the eyes normally activates the brain's primary visual area, creating an image (● Figure 10.2). Other brain areas then help us recognize the image by relating it to stored knowledge. When you form a mental image, the system works in reverse. Brain areas where memories are stored send signals back to the visual cortex, where once again, an image is created (Ganis, Thompson, & Kosslyn, 2004; Kosslyn, Thompson, & Alpert, 1995). For example, if you visualize a friend's face right now, the area of your brain that specializes in perceiving faces will become more active (O'Craven & Kanwisher, 2000).

Using Mental Images

How are images used to solve problems? We use *stored images* (information from memory) to apply past experiences to problem solving. Let's say you are asked, "How many ways can you use an empty egg carton?" You might begin by picturing uses you have already seen, such as sorting buttons into a carton. To give more original answers, you will probably need to use *created images,* which are assembled or invented, rather than simply remembered. Thus, an artist may completely picture a proposed sculpture before beginning work. People with good imaging abilities tend to score higher on tests of creativity (Morrison & Wallace, 2001). In fact, Albert Einstein, Thomas Edison, Lewis Carroll, and many other of history's most original intellects relied heavily on imagery (West, 1991).

Does the "size" of a mental image affect thinking? To find out, first picture a cat sitting beside a housefly. Now try to "zoom in" on the cat's ears so you see them clearly. Next, picture a rabbit sitting beside an elephant. How quickly can you "see" the rabbit's front feet? Did it take longer than picturing the cat's ears?

When a rabbit is pictured with an elephant, the rabbit's image must be small because the elephant is large. Using such tasks, Stephen Kosslyn found that the smaller an image is, the harder it is to "see" its details. To put this finding to use, try forming oversize images of things you want to think about. For example, to understand electricity, picture the wires as large pipes with electrons the

Vision

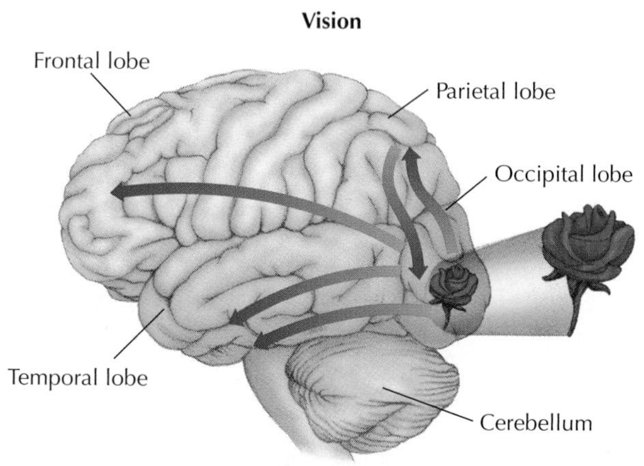

Visual Image

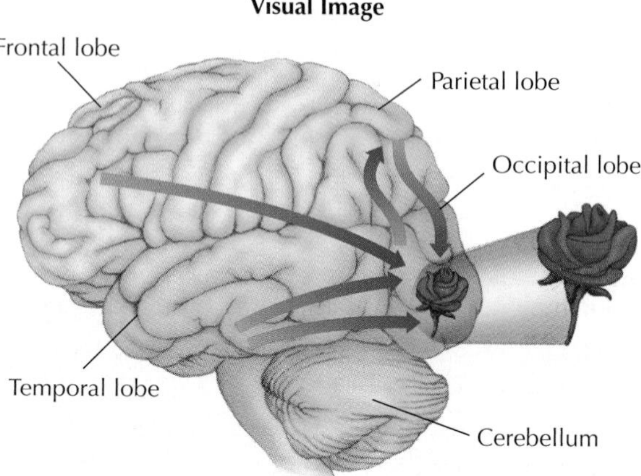

● **Figure 10.2** When you see a flower, its image is represented by activity in the primary visual area of the cortex, at the back of the brain. Information about the flower is also relayed to other brain areas. If you form a mental image of a flower, information follows a reverse path. The result, once again, is activation of the primary visual area.

Dennis Coon

The Church of the Sacred Family in Barcelona, Spain, was designed by Antonio Gaudi. Could a person lacking mental imagery design such a masterpiece? Three people out of 100 find it impossible to produce mental images and 3 out of 100 have very strong imagery. Most artists, architects, designers, sculptors, and film makers have excellent visual imagery.

size of golf balls moving through them; to understand the human ear, explore it (in your mind's eye) like a large cave; and so forth.

Kinesthetic Imagery

How do muscular responses relate to thinking? In a sense, we think with our bodies as well as our heads. *Kinesthetic images* are created from muscular sensations (Oyama & Ichikawa, 1990). Such images help us think about movements and actions. As you think and talk, kinesthetic sensations tend to guide the flow of ideas. For example, if you try to tell a friend how to make bread, you may move your hands as if kneading the dough. Or try answering this question: Which direction do you turn the hot-water handle in your kitchen to shut off the water? Most people haven't simply memorized the words, "Turn it clockwise," or "Turn it counterclockwise." Instead you will probably "turn" the faucet in your imagination before answering. You may even make a turning motion with your hand before answering.

Kinesthetic images are especially important in music, sports, dance, skateboarding, martial arts, and other movement-oriented skills. People with good kinesthetic imagery learn such skills faster than those with poor imagery (Glisky, Williams, & Kihlstrom, 1996).

Thinking is often accompanied by tiny, nearly imperceptible *micromovements* in our muscles. For example, if you imagine lifting a weight, a burst of activity will occur in the muscles of your motionless arm (Bakker, Boschker, & Chung, 1996). Such micromovements are an outward expression of the brain activity that accompanies kinesthetic images (Parsons et al., 1995). If you would like to demonstrate the link between muscular activity and thinking, ask a friend who was in a sports event to describe what happened. Along with a description, you will probably get an "instant replay" of the high points!

Brian Bailey/Getty Images

Rock climbers use kinesthetic imagery to learn climbing routes and to plan their next few moves (Smyth & Waller, 1998).

Concepts—I'm Positive, It's a Whatchamacallit

A **concept** is an idea that represents a category of objects or events. Concepts help us identify important features of the world. That's why experts in various areas of knowledge are good at classifying objects. Bird watchers, tropical fish fanciers, 5-year-old dinosaur enthusiasts, and other experts all learn to look for identifying details that beginners tend to miss. If you are knowledgeable about a topic, such as horses, flowers, or football, you literally see things differently than less well-informed people do (Johnson & Mervis, 1997).

Forming Concepts

How are concepts learned? **Concept formation** is the process of classifying information into meaningful categories (Ashby & Maddox, 2005). At its most basic, concept formation is based on experience with **positive** and **negative instances** (examples that belong, or do not belong, to the concept class). Concept formation is not as simple as it might seem. Imagine a child learning the concept of *dog*.

Dog Daze

A child and her father go for a walk. At a neighbor's house, they see a medium-size dog. The father says, "See the dog." As they pass the next yard, the child sees a cat and says, "Dog!" Her father corrects her, "No, that's a *cat*." The child now thinks, "Aha, dogs are large and cats are small." In the next yard, she sees a Pekingese and says, "Cat!" "No, that's a dog," replies her father.

The child's confusion is understandable. At first she might even mistake a Pekingese for a dust mop. However, with more positive and negative instances, the child will eventually recognize everything from Great Danes to Chihuahuas as members of the same category—dogs.

Concept A generalized idea representing a class of related objects or events.

Concept formation The process of classifying information into meaningful categories.

Positive instance In concept learning, an object or event that belongs to the concept class.

Negative instance In concept learning, an object or event that does not belong to the concept class.

As adults, we often acquire concepts by learning or forming *rules*. A **conceptual rule** is a guideline for deciding whether objects or events belong to a concept class. For example, a triangle must be a closed shape with three sides made of straight lines. Rules are an efficient way to learn concepts, but examples remain important. It's unlikely that memorizing rules would allow a new listener to accurately categorize *punk, hip-hop, fusion, salsa, heavy metal, grunge rock,* and *rap* music.

Types of Concepts

Are there different kinds of concepts? Yes, **conjunctive concepts**, or "and concepts," are defined by the presence of two or more features. In other words, an item must have "this feature *and* this feature *and* this feature." For example, a *motorcycle* must have two wheels *and* an engine *and* handlebars.

Relational concepts are based on how an object relates to something else, or how its features relate to one another. All of the following are relational concepts: *larger, above, left, north,* and *upside down*. Another example is *sister,* which is defined as "a female considered in her relation to another person having the same parents."

Disjunctive concepts have at *least one* of several possible features. These are "either/or" concepts. To belong to the category, an item must have "this feature *or* that feature *or* another feature." For example, in baseball, a *strike* is *either* a swing and a miss *or* a pitch over the plate *or* a foul ball. The either/or quality of disjunctive concepts makes them hard to learn.

Prototypes

When you think of the concept *bird,* do you mentally list the features that birds have? Probably not. In addition to rules and features, we use **prototypes**, or ideal models, to identify concepts (Burnett et al., 2005; Rosch, 1977). A robin, for example, is a model bird; an ostrich is not. In other words, some items are better examples of a concept than others are. Which of the drawings in ● Figure 10.3 best represents a cup? At some point, as a cup grows taller or wider it becomes a vase or a bowl. How do we know when the line is crossed? Probably, we mentally compare objects to an "ideal" cup, like number 5. That's why it's hard to identify concepts when we can't come up with relevant prototypes. What, for example, are the objects shown in ● Figure 10.4? As you can see, prototypes are especially helpful when we are asked to categorize complex stimuli (Minda & Smith, 2001).

Connotative Meaning

Generally speaking, concepts have two types of meaning. The **denotative meaning** of a word or concept is its exact definition. The **connotative meaning** is its emotional or personal meaning. The denotative meaning of the word *naked* (having no clothes) is the same for a nudist as it is for a movie censor, but we could expect their connotations to differ. Connotative differences can influence how we think about important issues. For example, the term *enhanced radiation device* has a more positive connotation than *neutron bomb* does (Gruner & Tighe, 1995).

Can you clarify what a connotative meaning is? Yes, connotative meaning can be measured with a technique called the *semantic differential,* as shown in ● Figure 10.5. When we rate words or concepts, most of their connotative meaning boils down to the dimensions *good/bad, strong/weak,* and *active/passive*. (Sounds like

● **Figure 10.3** When does a cup become a bowl or a vase? Deciding whether an object belongs to a conceptual class is aided by relating it to a prototype, or ideal example. Subjects in one experiment chose number 5 as the "best" cup. (After Labov, 1973.)

If you had never seen a cherimoya before, how would you decide if it is a vegetable or a fruit (or something from another planet)? A definition such as, "the edible part of a plant developed from a flower" might not help much. Instead, you could focus on specific features, such as flavor, odor, and texture. You might also compare a cherimoya with familiar fruits. Can a fruit be green? Yes, apples are. Do other fruits have inedible skins? Yes, bananas do. Are other fruits sweet? Yes, most are. And so forth. To gain further confidence, you might relate a cherimoya to a "model" fruit such as an apple or a peach (Storms, De Boeck, & Ruts, 2001).

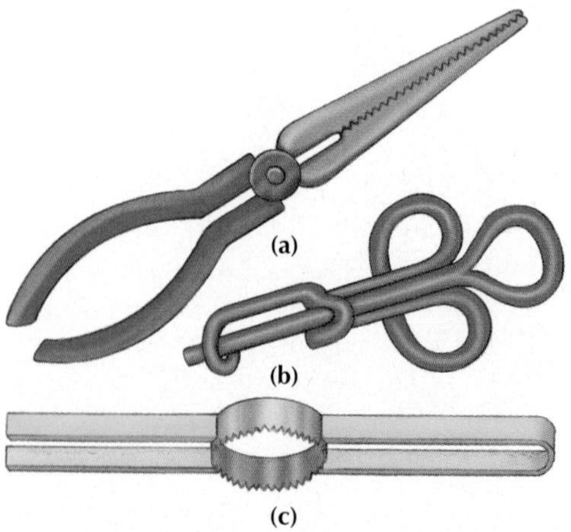

● **Figure 10.4** Use of prototypes in concept identification. Even though its shape is unusual, item *(a)* can be related to a model (an ordinary set of pliers) and thus recognized. But what are items *(b)* and *(c)*? If you don't recognize them, look ahead to ● Figure 10.6. (After Bransford & McCarrell, 1977.)

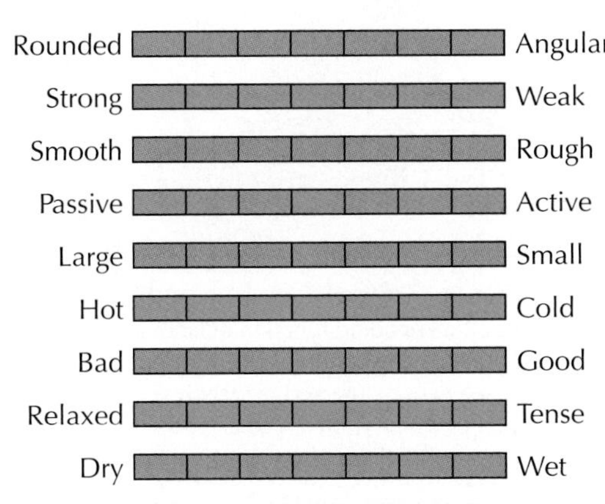

● **Figure 10.5** This is an example of Osgood's semantic differential. The connotative meaning of the word *jazz* can be established by rating it on the scales. Mark your own rating by placing dots or X's in the spaces. Connect the marks with a line; then have a friend rate the word and compare your responses. It might be interesting to do the same for *rock and roll, classical,* and *rap.* You also might want to try the word *psychology.* (From Osgood. Copyright © 1952 American Psychological Association. Reprinted by permission.)

a good movie title, doesn't it: *The Good, the Bad, the Strong, the Weak, the Active, the Passive, Spongebob Squarepants Movie.*) These dimensions give words very different connotations, even when their denotative meanings are similar. For example, I am *conscientious;* you are *careful;* he is *nitpicky!*

Faulty Concepts

Using inaccurate concepts often leads to thinking errors. For example, *social stereotypes* are oversimplified concepts of groups of people. Stereotypes about men, African Americans, women, conservatives, liberals, police officers, or other groups often muddle thinking about members of the group. A related problem is *all-or-nothing thinking* (one-dimensional thought). In this case, we classify things as absolutely right or wrong, good or bad, fair or unfair, black or white, honest or dishonest. Thinking this way prevents us from appreciating the subtleties of most life problems.

KNOWLEDGE BUILDER

Images and Concepts

REFLECT

Name some ways in which you have used imagery in the thinking you have done today. Were the images you used created or stored? Were any synesthetic or kinesthetic?

Write a conceptual rule for the following idea: *unicycle.* Were you able to define the concept with a rule? Would positive and negative instances help make the concept clearer for others?

A true sports car has two seats, a powerful engine, good brakes, and excellent handling. What kind of a concept is the term *sports car?* What do you think of as a prototypical sports car?

LEARNING CHECK

1. List three basic units of thought: ____________, ____________, ____________
2. Synesthesia is the use of kinesthetic sensations as a vehicle for thought. T or F?
3. Humans appear capable of forming three-dimensional images that can be moved or rotated in mental space. T or F?
4. Our reliance on imagery in thinking means that problem solving is impaired by micromovements. T or F?
5. A *mup* is defined as anything that is small, blue, and hairy. *Mup* is a ____________ concept.
6. The connotative meaning of the word *naked* is "having no clothes." T or F?
7. Stereotyping is an example of oversimplification in thinking. T or F?

CRITICAL THINKING

8. It takes longer to answer the question, "Does a frog have lips and a stubby tail?" than the question, "Does a frog have lips?" Can you think of an explanation other than mental rotation to explain this difference?
9. A Democrat and a Republican are asked to rate the word *democratic* on the semantic differential. Under what conditions would their ratings be most alike?

Answers: 1. images, concepts, and language or symbols (others could be listed) **2.** F **3.** T **4.** F **5.** conjunctive **6.** F **7.** T **8.** The first question could simply be more difficult. The difficulty of questions must be carefully matched in studies of mental imagery. **9.** If they both assume the word refers to a form of government, not a political party or a candidate.

BRIDGES

Stereotypes have a major impact on social behavior and frequently contribute to prejudice and discrimination.

See Chapter 19, pages 641–644, for more information.

Conceptual rule A formal rule for deciding whether an object or event is an example of a particular concept.

Conjunctive concept A class of objects that have two or more features in common. (For example, to qualify as an example of the concept an object must be both red *and* triangular.)

Relational concept A concept defined by the relationship between features of an object or between an object and its surroundings (for example, "greater than," "lopsided").

Disjunctive concept A concept defined by the presence of at least one of several possible features. (For example, to qualify an object must be either blue *or* circular.)

Prototype An ideal model used as a prime example of a particular concept.

Denotative meaning The exact, dictionary definition of a word or concept; its objective meaning.

Connotative meaning The subjective, personal, or emotional meaning of a word or concept.

Language—Don't Leave Home Without It

As we have seen, thinking may occur without language. Everyone has searched for a word to express an idea that exists as a vague image or feeling. Nevertheless, most thinking relies heavily on language, because words *encode* (translate) the world into symbols that are easy to manipulate (● Figure 10.6).

The study of meaning in words and language is known as **semantics.** It is here that the link between language and thought becomes most evident. Suppose, on an intelligence test, you were asked to circle the word that does not belong in this series:

SKYSCRAPER CATHEDRAL TEMPLE PRAYER

Wine tasting illustrates the encoding function of language. To communicate their experiences to others, wine connoisseurs must put taste sensations into words. The wine you see here is "marked by deeply concentrated nuances of plum, blackberry, and currant, with a nice balance of tannins and acid, building to a spicy oak finish." (Don't try this with a Pop-tart!)

If you circled *prayer,* you answered as most people do. Now try another problem, again circling the odd item:

CATHEDRAL PRAYER TEMPLE SKYSCRAPER

Did you circle *skyscraper* this time? The new order subtly alters the meaning of the last word (Mayer, 1995). This occurs because words get much of their meaning from *context.* For example, the word *shot* means different things when we are thinking of marksmanship, bartending, medicine, photography, or golf (Miller, 1999).

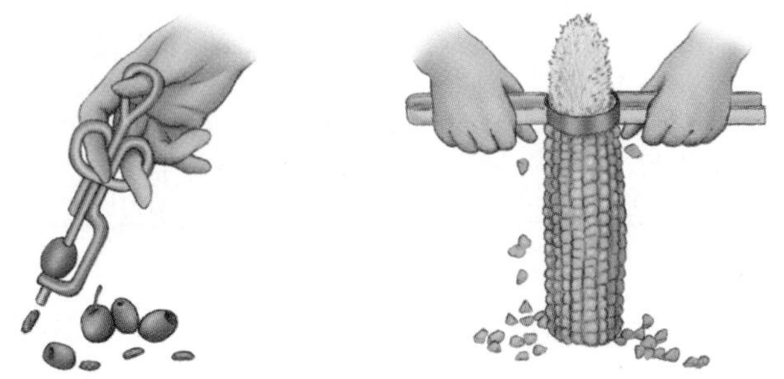

● **Figure 10.6** Context can substitute for a lack of appropriate prototypes in concept identification.

Semantics affect thinking when the words we use alter meaning: Has one country's army "invaded" another? Or "effected a protective incursion"? Is the city reservoir "half full" or "half empty"? Would you rather eat "prime beef" or "dead cow"?! More subtle effects also occur. For example, most people have difficulty quickly naming the color of the ink used to print the words in the middle two rows of ● Figure 10.7. The word meanings are just too strong to ignore. A related effect occurred in a study of celebrity names. Some of the celebrities were European American and some were African American. Their names, in turn, were sometimes printed in black letters and sometimes in white letters. When black letters were used for a name such as Bill Cosby, people quickly identified the color. When white letters were used, color recognition was slower. The reverse pattern occurred when white celebrity names were printed in white letters (faster recognition) or black letters (slower recognition) (Karylowski et al., 2002). Unmistakably, word meanings "color" our thoughts.

Translating languages can cause a rash of semantic problems. Perhaps the San Jose, California, public library can be excused for displaying a large banner that was supposed to say "You are welcome" in a native Philippine language. The banner actually said "You are circumcised." Likewise, we may forgive Pepsi for translating "Come alive, you Pepsi generation," into Thai as "Pepsi

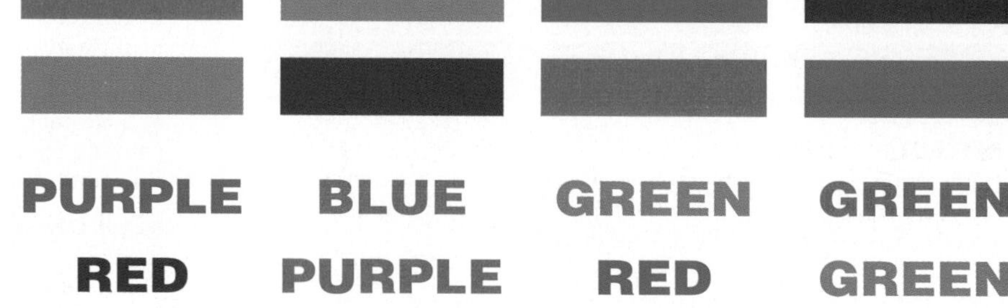

● **Figure 10.7** The Stroop interference task. Test yourself by naming the colors in the top two rows as quickly as you can. Then name the colors of the *ink* used to print the words in the middle two rows (do not read the words themselves). Was it harder to name the ink color in the middle two rows? Now, name the ink color used in the bottom two rows of words. Was it harder to name the ink color in the last row than it was in the next-to-last row? Return to the text for an explanation of these effects.

HUMAN DIVERSITY

Si o No, Oui ou Non, Yes or No?

Bilingualism is the ability to speak two languages. Some people learn both a first and a second language together. Others learn one language and then another. In either case, age can make a big difference: To gain fluency in a second language and speak it with a native accent, learning must usually begin before age 6 (Genesee, 1994), although even adults learners can become fluent with enough effort (Hakuta, Bialystok, & Wiley, 2003).

Millions of American children do not speak English at home. At school, many of these children are "immersed" in English, where they are expected to "sink or swim." When minority children are plunged into English-only classrooms, they are likely to experience *subtractive bilingualism.* That is, they usually end up losing some proficiency in their native language. Such children are at risk for being less than fully competent in *both* their first and second languages. In addition, they tend to fall behind educationally. As they struggle with English, their grasp of arithmetic, social studies, science, and other subjects may suffer. In short, English-only instruction can leave them poorly prepared to succeed in the majority culture (Genesee, 1994; Matthews & Matthews, 2004).

For majority children, the picture can be quite different, because learning a second language is almost always beneficial. It poses no threat to the child's home language, and it improves a variety of general cognitive skills. This has been called *additive bilingualism* because learning a second language adds to a child's overall competence (Hinkel, 2005).

An approach called **two-way bilingual education** offers a way to retain the benefits of bilingualism and avoid its drawbacks. In such programs native speakers and children with limited English skills are taught part of the day in English and part in a second language. This approach has proved to be very successful (Lessow-Hurley, 2005). Both native and minority language speakers become fluent in two languages and they perform as well or better than single-language students in English and general academic abilities.

Then why isn't two-way bilingual education more widely used? For one thing, all types of bilingual education tend to be politically unpopular among majority language speakers. Language is a major sign of group membership. Even where the majority culture is highly dominant, some of its members may feel that recent immigrants and "foreign languages" are eroding their culture. Yet an ability to think and communicate in a second language is a wonderful gift. Although minority children are certainly at a disadvantage if they do not become proficient in English, native English speakers may be shortchanged by English-only schools as well.

Studies of bilingual students in Canada and the United States have found that those who achieve a high level of ability in two languages have better mental flexibility, general language skills, control of attention, and problem-solving abilities (Bialystok, 2001; Craik & Bialystok, 2005; Cromdal, 1999). Fostering bilingualism may turn out to be one of the best ways to improve competitiveness in our rapidly globalizing information economy.

brings your ancestors back from the dead." However, in more important situations, such as in international diplomacy, avoiding semantic confusion may be vital.

Language plays a major role in defining ethnic communities and other social groups. Thus, language can be a bridge or a barrier between cultures. See "*Si o No, Oui ou Non,* Yes or No?" for a brief discussion of the pros and cons of bilingual education.

The Structure of Language

What does it take to make a language? First, a language must provide symbols that can stand for objects and ideas (Jay, 2003). The symbols we call words are built out of **phonemes** (FOE-neems: basic speech sounds) and **morphemes** (MOR-feems: speech sounds collected into meaningful units, such as syllables or words). For instance, in English the sounds *m, b, w,* and *a* cannot form a syllable *mbwa.* In Swahili, they can. (Also, see ● Figure 10.8.)

Next, a language must have a **grammar,** or set of rules for making sounds into words and words into sentences. One part of grammar, known as **syntax,** concerns rules for word order. Syntax is important because rearranging words almost always changes the meaning of a sentence: "Dog bites man" versus "Man bites dog."

Traditional grammar is concerned with "surface" language—the sentences we actually speak. Linguist Noam Chomsky has focused instead on the unspoken rules we use to change core ideas into various sentences. Chomsky (1986) believes that we do not

Semantics The study of meanings in language.

Bilingualism An ability to speak two languages.

Two-way bilingual program A program in which English-speaking children and children with limited English proficiency are taught half the day in English and half in a second language.

Phonemes The basic speech sounds of a language.

Morphemes The smallest meaningful units in a language, such as syllables or words.

Grammar A set of rules for combining language units into meaningful speech or writing.

Syntax Rules for ordering words when forming sentences.

● **Figure 10.8** Animals around the world make pretty much the same sounds. Notice, however, how various languages use slightly different phonemes to express the sound a duck makes.

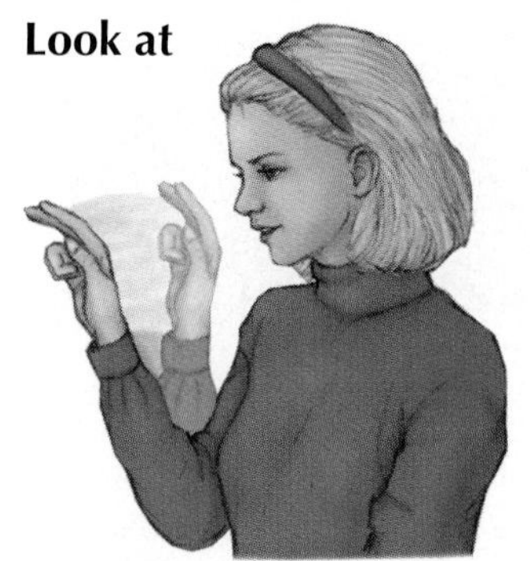

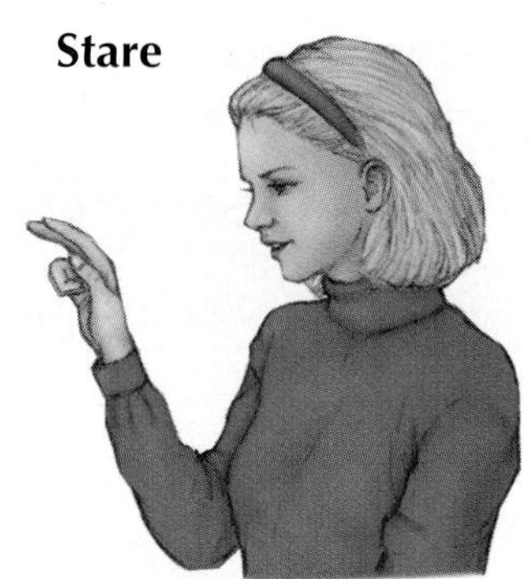

● **Figure 10.9** ASL has only 3,000 root signs, compared with roughly 600,000 words in English. However, variations in signs make ASL a highly expressive language. For example, the sign LOOK-AT can be varied in ways to make it mean look at me, look at her, look at each, stare at, gaze, watch, look for a long time, look at again and again, reminisce, sightsee, look forward to, predict, anticipate, browse, and many more variations.

learn all the sentences we might ever say. Rather, we actively *create* them by applying **transformation rules** to universal, core patterns. We use these rules to change a simple declarative sentence to other voices or forms (past tense, passive voice, and so forth). For example, the core sentence "Dog bites man" can be transformed to these patterns (and others as well):

Past: The dog bit the man.
Passive: The man was bitten by the dog.
Negative: The dog did not bite the man.
Question: Did the dog bite the man?

Children seem to be using transformation rules when they say things such as, "I runned home." That is, the child applied the normal past tense rule to the irregular verb *to run.*

A true language is also *productive*—it can generate new thoughts or ideas. In fact, words can be rearranged to produce a nearly infinite number of sentences. Some are silly: "Please don't feed me to the goldfish." Some are profound: "We hold these truths to be self-evident, that all men are created equal." In either case, the productive quality of language makes it a powerful tool for thinking.

Gestural Languages

Contrary to common belief, language is not limited to speech. Consider the case of Ildefonso, a young man who was born deaf. At age 24, Ildefonso had never communicated with another human, except by mime. Then, at last, Ildefonso had a breakthrough: After much hard work with a sign language teacher, he understood the link between a cat and the gesture for it. At that magic moment, he grasped the idea that "cat" could be communicated to another person, just by signing the word.

American Sign Language (ASL), a gestural language, made Ildefonso's long-awaited breakthrough possible. ASL is not pantomime or a code. It is a true language, like German, Spanish, or Japanese. In fact, those who use other gestural languages, such as French Sign, Chinese Sign, Yiddish Sign, or Old Kentish Sign, do not understand ASL.

Both speech and signing follow similar universal language patterns. Of course, ASL has a *spatial* grammar, syntax, and semantics all its own (● Figure 10.9). Just the same, signing children pass through the stages of language development at about the same age as speaking children do. Some psychologists now believe that speech evolved from gestures, far back in human history (Corballis, 2002). Do you ever make hand gestures when you are speaking on the phone? If so, you may be displaying a remnant of the gestural origins of language. Gestures help us string words together as we speak (Morsella & Krauss, 2004). Some people would have difficulty speaking with their hands tied to their sides.

Sign languages naturally arise out of a need to communicate visually. But they also embody a personal identity and define a distinct community. Sign is the true voice of the deaf and hearing impaired. Those who "speak" sign share not just a language, but a rich culture as well (Liddell, 2003; Meier, 1991; Schaller, 1991; Singleton & Newport, 2004;).

The Animal Language Debate

Do animals use language? Animals do communicate. The cries, gestures, and mating calls of animals have broad meanings immediately understood by other animals of the same species (Premack,

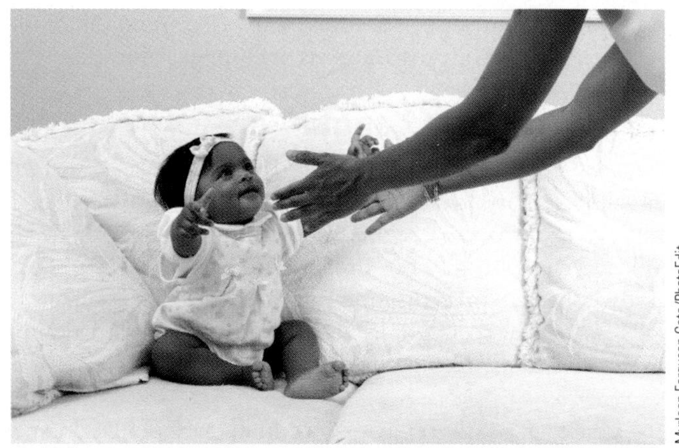

Infants can express the idea "pick me up" in gestures before they can make the same request in words. Their progression from gestures to speech may mirror the evolution of human language abilities (Stokoe, 2001).

1983). For the most part, however, natural animal communication is quite limited. Even apes and monkeys make only a few dozen distinct cries, which carry messages such as "attack," "flee," or "food here." More important, animal communication lacks the productive quality of human language. For example, when a monkey gives an "eagle distress call," it means something like, "I see an eagle." The monkey has no way of saying, "I don't see an eagle," or "Thank heavens that wasn't an eagle," or "That sucker I saw yesterday was some huge eagle" (Pinker & Jackendoff, 2005). Let's consider some of psychology's successes and failures in trying to teach animals to use language.

Talking Chimps

Early attempts to teach chimps to talk were a dismal failure. The world record was held by Viki, a chimp who could say only four words (*mama, papa, cup,* and *up*) after 6 years of intensive training (Fleming, 1974; Hayes, 1951). (Actually, all four words sounded something like a belch.) Then there was a breakthrough. Beatrix and Allen Gardner used operant conditioning and imitation to teach a female chimp named Washoe to use American Sign Language. Washoe was soon able to put together primitive sentence strings like "Come-gimme sweet," "Out please," "Gimme tickle," and "Open food drink." At her peak, Washoe could construct six-word sentences and use about 240 signs (Gardner & Gardner, 1989).

A chimp named Sarah was another well-known pupil of human language. David Premack taught Sarah to use 130 "words" consisting of plastic chips arranged on a magnetized board (● Figure 10.10). From the beginning of her training, Sarah was required to use proper word order. She learned to answer questions; to label things "same" or "different"; to classify objects by color, shape, and size; and to form compound sentences (Premack & Premack, 1983). One of Sarah's top achievements was her use of conditional sentences. A *conditional statement* contains a qualification, often in the if/then form: "If Sarah take apple, then Mary give Sarah chocolate." "If Sarah take banana, then Mary no give Sarah chocolate" (● Figure 10.11).

Can it be said with certainty that the chimps understand such interchanges? Most researchers working with chimps believe that they have indeed communicated with them. Especially striking are the chimps' spontaneous responses. Washoe once "wet" on psychologist Roger Fouts's back while riding on his shoulders. When Fouts asked, with some annoyance, why she had done it, Washoe signed, "It's funny!"

Criticisms

Such interchanges are impressive. But communication and real language usage are different things. Even untrained chimps use simple gestures to communicate with humans. For example, a chimp will point at a banana that is out of reach, while glancing back and forth between the banana and a person standing nearby (Leavens & Hopkins, 1998). (The meaning of the gesture is clear. The meaning of the exasperated look on the chimp's face is less certain, but it probably means, "Yes, give me the banana, you idiot.")

Some psychologists doubt that apes can really use language. For one thing, chimps rarely "speak" without prompting from humans. Also, the apes may be simply performing operant responses to get food or other "goodies" (Hixon, 1998). By making certain signs, the apes then manipulate their trainers to get what they want.

You might say the critics believe the apes have made monkeys out of their trainers. However, studies show that chimps hold real

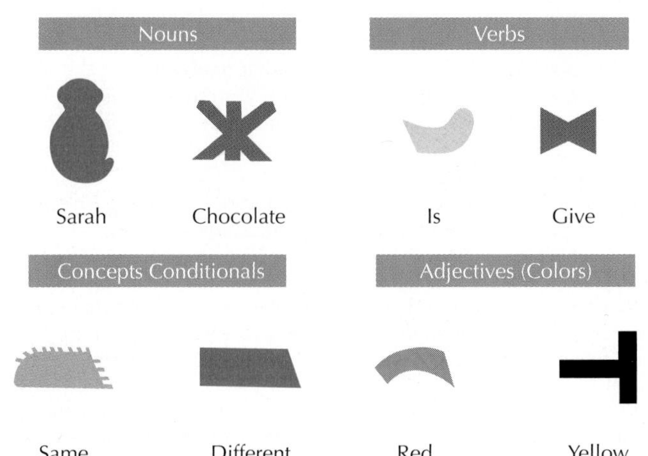

● **Figure 10.10** Here is a sample of some of the word-symbols that Sarah chimpanzee used to communicate with humans. (After Premack & Premack, 1972.)

● **Figure 10.11** After reading the message "Sarah insert apple pail banana dish" on the magnetic board, Sarah performed the actions as directed. (From "Teaching Language to an Ape" by Ann J. Premack and David Premack. Copyright © 1972 by Scientific American, Inc. All rights reserved.)

Transformation rules Rules by which a simple declarative sentence may be changed to other voices or forms (past tense, passive voice, and so forth).

conversations, even when people are not around to cue them. Only 5 percent of these conversations concern food (Fouts, Fouts, & Schoenfield, 1984; Greenfield & Savage-Rumbaugh, 1993). When "conversing" with humans, chimps reply in patterns that are similar to young children (Jensvold & Gardner, 2000), So, maybe the chimps will make monkeys out of the critics.

Problems with Syntax

At this point, numerous chimps, a gorilla named Koko, and an assortment of dolphins and sea lions have learned to communicate with word symbols of various kinds. Yet even if some criticisms can be answered, linguists remain unconvinced that animals can truly use language. The core issue is that problems with syntax (word order) have plagued almost all animal language studies. For example, when a chimp named Nim Chimpsky (no relation to Noam Chomsky) wanted an orange, he would typically signal a grammarless string of words: "Give orange me give eat orange me eat orange give me eat orange give me you." This might be communication, but it is not language.

Lexigrams

More recently, Kanzi, a pygmy chimpanzee studied by Duane Rumbaugh and Sue Savage-Rumbaugh, has learned to communicate by pushing buttons on a computer keyboard. Each of the 250 buttons is marked with a **lexigram**, or geometric word-symbol (● Figure 10.12). Using the lexigrams, Kanzi can create primitive sentences several words long. He can also understand about 650 spoken sentences. During testing, Kanzi hears spoken words over headphones, so his caretakers cannot visually prompt him (Savage-Rumbaugh, Shanker, & Taylor, 1998; Savage-Rumbaugh & Lewin, 1996).

Kanzi's sentences consistently follow correct word order. Like a child learning language, Kanzi picked up some rules from his caregivers (Savage-Rumbaugh & Lewin, 1996). However, he has developed other patterns on his own. For example, Kanzi usually places action symbols in the order he wants to carry them out, such as "chase tickle" or "chase hide." In this respect, Kanzi's grammar is on a par with that of a 2-year-old child (Savage-Rumbaugh et al., 1993).

Robin Nelson/PhotoEdit

● **Figure 10.12** Kanzi's language learning has been impressive. He can comprehend spoken English words. He can identify lexigram symbols when he hears corresponding words. He can use lexigrams when the objects they refer to are absent and he can, if asked, lead someone to the object. All these skills were acquired through observation, not conditioning (Savage-Rumbaugh & Lewin, 1996; Savage-Rumbaugh et al., 1990).

Kanzi's ability to invent a simple grammar may help us better understand the roots of human language. It is certainly the strongest answer yet to critics (Benson et al., 2002). On the other hand, Chomsky insists that if chimps were biologically capable of language they would use it on their own. Although the issue is far from resolved, such research may unravel the mysteries of language learning. In fact, it has already been helpful for teaching language to children with serious language impairments.

KNOWLEDGE BUILDER

Language

REFLECT

Here's some mnemonic help: You use a *phone* to send *phonemes.* To *morph* them into words you have to hit them with a *grammar.* What wrong is with sentence this? (The answer is not a *sin tax,* but it still may tax you.)

Just for fun, see if you can illustrate the productive quality of language by creating a sentence that no one has ever spoken before.

You must learn to communicate with an alien life-form (from the planet Encodon) whose language cannot be reproduced by the human voice. Do you think it would it be better to use a gestural language or lexigrams? Why?

LEARNING CHECK

1. True languages are ______________ because they can be used to generate new possibilities.
2. The basic speech sounds are called ______________; the smallest meaningful units of speech are called ______________.
3. Two-way bilingual education almost always has a subtractive effect on general academic abilities. T or F?
4. Noam Chomsky believes that we create an infinite variety of sentences by applying ______________ to universal language patterns.
5. ASL can be used to communicate, but it is not a true language. T or F?
6. One of the chimpanzee Sarah's most outstanding achievements was the construction of sentences involving
   a. negation c. adult grammar
   b. conditional relationships d. unprompted questions
7. Critics consider "sentences" constructed by apes to be simple ______________ responses having little meaning to the animal.
8. Kanzi's use of lexigrams has suffered from the same problems with syntax as other animal-language studies. T or F?

CRITICAL THINKING

9. Chimpanzees and other apes are intelligent and entertaining animals. If you were doing language research with a chimp, what major problem would you have to guard against?

Answers: 1. productive 2. phonemes, morphemes 3. F 4. transformation rules 5. F 6. b 7. operant 8. F 9. The problem of anthropomorphizing (ascribing human characteristics to animals) is especially difficult to avoid when researchers spend many hours "conversing" with chimps.

Problem Solving—Getting an Answer in Sight

We all solve many problems every day. Problem solving can be as commonplace as figuring out how to make a nonpoisonous meal out of leftovers or as significant as developing a cure for cancer. How do we solve such problems? In addition to exploring this question directly, we will also see what has been learned by trying to create machines that solve problems "intelligently."

A good way to start a discussion of problem solving is to solve a problem. Give this one a try.

> A famous ocean liner (the *Queen Ralph*) is steaming toward port at 20 miles per hour. It is 50 miles from shore when a seagull takes off from its deck and flies toward port. At the same instant, a speedboat leaves port at 30 miles per hour. The bird flies back and forth between the speedboat and the *Queen Ralph* at a speed of 40 miles per hour. How far will the bird have flown when the two boats pass?

If you don't immediately see the answer to this problem, read it again. (The answer is revealed in "Insightful Solutions.")

Mechanical Solutions

For routine problems, a **mechanical solution** may be adequate. Mechanical solutions are achieved by trial and error or by rote. If you forget the combination to your bike lock, you may be able to discover it by trial and error. In an era of high-speed computers, many trial-and-error solutions are best left to machines. A computer could generate all possible combinations of the five numbers on the lock in a split second. (Of course, it would take a long time to try them all.) When a problem is solved by *rote,* thinking is guided by an **algorithm,** or learned set of rules that always leads to a correct solution. A simple example of an algorithm is the steps needed to divide one number into another (by doing arithmetic, not by using a calculator).

If you have a good background in math, you may have solved the problem of the bird and the boats by rote. (We hope you didn't. There is an easier solution.)

Solutions by Understanding

Many problems cannot be solved mechanically. In that case, **understanding** (deeper comprehension of a problem) is necessary. Try this problem:

> A person has an inoperable stomach tumor. A device is available that produces rays that at high intensity will destroy tissue (both healthy and diseased). How can the tumor be destroyed without damaging surrounding tissue? (Students were also shown the sketch in ● Figure 10.13.)

What does this problem show about problem solving? German psychologist Karl Duncker did a classic series of studies in which he gave college students this problem. Duncker asked them to think aloud as they worked. He found that successful students first had to discover the *general properties* of a correct solution. A **general solution** defines the requirements for success, but not in enough detail to guide further action. This phase was complete when students realized that the intensity of the rays had to be lowered on their way to the tumor. Then, in the second phase, they proposed a number of **functional** (workable) **solutions** and selected the best one (Duncker, 1945). (One solution is to focus weak rays on the tumor from several angles. Another is to rotate the person's body, to minimize exposure of healthy tissue.)

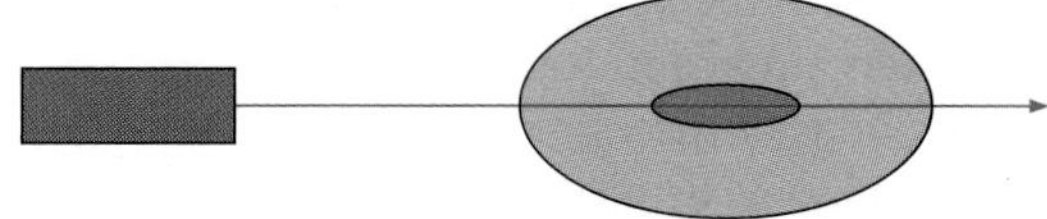

● **Figure 10.13** A schematic representation of Duncker's tumor problem. The dark spot represents a tumor surrounded by healthy tissue. How can the tumor be destroyed without injuring surrounding tissue? (After Duncker, 1945.)

It might help to summarize with a more familiar example. Almost everyone who has tried the Rubik's cube puzzle begins at the mechanical, *trial-and-error level.* If you want to take the easy route, printed instructions are available that give the steps for a *rote* solution. In time, those who persist begin to *understand* the *general properties* of the puzzle. After that, they can solve it consistently.

Heuristics

"You can't get there from here," or so it often seems when facing a problem. Solving problems often requires a strategy. If the number of alternatives is small, a **random search strategy** may work. This is another example of trial-and-error thinking in which all possibilities are tried, more or less randomly. Imagine that you are traveling and you decide to look up an old friend, J. Smith, in a city you are visiting. You open the phone book and find 47 J. Smiths listed. Of course, you could dial each number until you find the right one. "Forget it," you say to yourself. "Is there any way I can narrow the search?" "Oh, yeah! I remember hearing that Janet lives by the beach." Then you take out a map and call only the numbers with addresses near the waterfront (Ellis & Hunt, 1992).

The approach used in this example is a **heuristic** (hew-RIS-tik: a strategy for identifying and evaluating problem solutions). Typi-

Lexigram A geometric shape used as a symbol for a word.

Mechanical solution A problem solution achieved by trial and error or by a fixed procedure based on learned rules.

Algorithm A learned set of rules that always leads to the correct solution of a problem.

Understanding In problem solving, a deeper comprehension of the nature of the problem.

General solution A solution that correctly states the requirements for success but not in enough detail for further action.

Functional solution A detailed, practical, and workable solution.

Random search strategy Trying possible solutions to a problem in a more or less random sequence.

Heuristic Any strategy or technique that aids problem solving, especially by limiting the number of possible solutions to be tried.

cally, a heuristic is a "rule of thumb" that *reduces the number of alternatives* thinkers must consider (Solso, MacLin, & MacLin, 2005). This raises the odds of success, although it does not guarantee a solution. Here are some heuristic strategies that often work:

- Try to identify how the current state of affairs differs from the desired goal. Then find steps that will reduce the difference.
- Try working backward from the desired goal to the starting point or current state.
- If you can't reach the goal directly, try to identify an intermediate goal or subproblem that at least gets you closer.
- Represent the problem in other ways, with graphs, diagrams, or analogies, for instance.
- Generate a possible solution and test it. Doing so may eliminate many alternatives, or it may clarify what is needed for a solution.

Ideal Problem Solving

Perhaps the most valuable heuristic of all is having a *general* thinking strategy. In a classic formulation, psychologist John Bransford and his colleagues list five steps that they believe lead to effective problem solving: **i**dentify, **d**efine, **e**xplore, **a**ct, and **l**ook and learn (Bransford & Stein, 1984; Bransford et al., 1986). Notice that the first letters of the steps spell *ideal.*

To apply the ideal thinking strategy you should *identify* the problem, *define* it clearly, and then *explore* possible solutions and relevant knowledge. Next, you must *act* by trying a possible solution or hypothesis. Finally, you should *look* at the results and *learn* from them. Of course, each attempted solution may identify further subproblems. These can again be tackled with the "ideal" steps until a final satisfactory solution is found.

Insightful Solutions

A thinker who suddenly solves a problem has experienced **insight.** Insight is so rapid and clear that we may wonder why we didn't see the solution sooner (Schilling, 2005). Insights are usually based on reorganizing a problem. This allows us to see problems in new ways and makes their solutions seem obvious (Durso, Rea, & Dayton, 1994).

Let's return now to the problem of the boats and the bird. The best way to solve it is by insight. Because the boats will cover the 50-mile distance in exactly 1 hour, and the bird flies 40 miles per hour, the bird will have flown 40 miles when the boats meet. No math is necessary if you have insight into this problem. ● Figure 10.14 lists some additional insight problems you may want to try.

In an interesting experiment, college students rated how "warm" (close to an answer) they felt while solving insight problems. Those who had insights usually jumped directly from "cold" to the correct answer. Students who only got "warmer" usually produced wrong answers (Metcalfe, 1986). Thus, you may be headed for a mistake if an insight is *not* rapid. Real insight tends to be an all-or-nothing event (Smith & Kounios, 1996).

The Nature of Insight

Psychologists Robert Sternberg and Janet Davidson (1982) believe that insight involves three abilities. The first is *selective encoding,* which refers to selecting information that is relevant to a prob-

Water lilies

Problem: Water lilies growing in a pond double in area every 24 hours. On the first day of spring, only one lily pad is on the surface of the pond. Sixty days later, the pond is entirely covered. On what day is the pond half-covered?

Twenty dollars

Problem: Jessica and Blair both have the same amount of money. How much must Jessica give Blair so that Blair has $20 more than Jessica?

How many pets?

Problem: How many pets do you have if all of them are birds except two, all of them are cats except two, and all of them are dogs except two?

Between 2 and 3

Problem: What one mathematical symbol can you place between 2 and 3 that results in a number greater than 2 and less than 3?

One word

Problem: Rearrange the letters NEWDOOR to make one word.

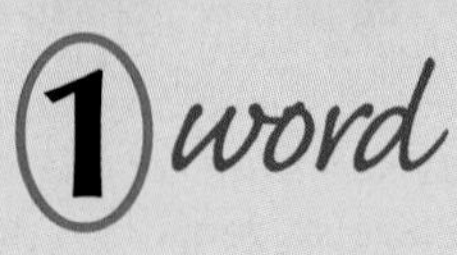

2 ? 3

1 word

● **Figure 10.14** Insight problems (see ■ Table 10.1 for solutions).

lem, while ignoring distractions. For example, consider the following problem:

> If you have white socks and black socks in your drawer, mixed in the ratio of 4 to 5, how many socks will you have to take out to make sure of having a pair of the same color?

A person who fails to recognize that "mixed in a ratio of 4 to 5" is irrelevant will be less likely to come up with the correct answer of 3 socks.

Insight also relies on *selective combination,* or bringing together seemingly unrelated bits of useful information. Try this sample problem:

> With a 7-minute hourglass and an 11-minute hourglass, what is the simplest way to time the boiling of an egg for 15 minutes?

The answer requires using both hourglasses in combination. First, the 7-minute and the 11-minute hourglasses are started running. When the 7-minute hourglass runs out, it's time to begin boiling the egg. At this point, 4 minutes remain on the 11-minute hourglass. Thus, when it runs out it is simply turned over. When it runs out again, 15 minutes will have passed.

A third source of insights is *selective comparison.* This is the ability to compare new problems with old information or with problems already solved. A good example is the hat rack problem, in which subjects must build a structure that can support an overcoat in the middle of a room. Each person is given only two long sticks and a C-clamp to work with. The solution, shown in ● Figure 10.15, is to clamp the two sticks together so that they are wedged between the floor and ceiling. If you were given this problem, you would be more likely to solve it if you first thought of how pole lamps are wedged between floor and ceiling. (See "How to Weigh an Elephant.")

Fixations

One of the most important barriers to problem solving is **fixation,** the tendency to get "hung up" on wrong solutions or to become blind to alternatives. Usually this occurs when we place unnecessary restrictions on our thinking (Isaak & Just, 1995). How, for example, could you plant four small trees so that each is an equal distance from all the others? (The answer is shown in ● Figure 10.16.)

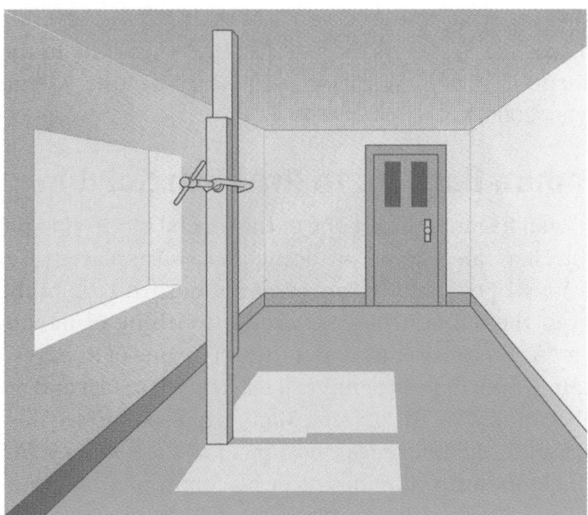

● **Figure 10.15** Solution to the hat rack problem.

A prime example of restricted thinking is **functional fixedness.** This is an inability to see new uses (functions) for familiar objects or for things that were used in a particular way (German & Barrett, 2005). If you have ever used a dime as a screwdriver, you've overcome functional fixedness.

How does functional fixedness affect problem solving? Karl Duncker illustrated the effects of functional fixedness by asking students to mount a candle on a vertical board so the candle could burn normally. Duncker gave each student three candles, some matches, some cardboard boxes, some thumbtacks, and other items. Half of Duncker's subjects received these items *inside* the cardboard boxes. The others were given all the items, including the boxes, spread out on a tabletop.

Duncker found that when the items were in the boxes, solving the problem was very difficult. Why? If students saw the boxes as *containers,* they didn't realize the boxes might be part of the solution. (If you haven't guessed the solution, check ● Figure 10.17.) Undoubtedly, we could avoid many fixations by being more flexible in categorizing the world (Langer, 2000). For instance, creative thinking could be facilitated in the container problem by saying, "This *could be* a box," instead of "This *is* a box." When tested with the candle problem, 5-year-old children show no signs of functional fixedness. Apparently, this is because they have had

● **Figure 10.16** Four trees can be placed equidistant from one another by piling dirt into a mound. Three of the trees are planted equal distances apart around the base of the mound. The fourth tree is planted on the top of the mound. If you were fixated on arrangements that involve level ground, you may have been blind to this three-dimensional solution.

Insight A sudden mental reorganization of a problem that makes the solution obvious.

Fixation The tendency to repeat wrong solutions or faulty responses, especially as a result of becoming blind to alternatives.

Functional fixedness A rigidity in problem solving caused by an inability to see new uses for familiar objects.

HUMAN DIVERSITY

How to Weigh an Elephant

Does the culture we grow up in affect our ability to use selective comparison to solve problems? See if you can solve this problem:

> A treasure hunter wanted to explore a cave, but he was afraid that he might get lost. Obviously, he did not have a map of the cave; all that he had with him were some common items such as a flashlight and a bag. What could he do to make sure he did not get lost trying to get back out of the cave later? (Adapted from Chen, Mo, & Honomichl, 2004.)

To solve his problem, the man could leave a trail of small objects, such as pebbles or sand, while traveling through the cave, and then follow this trail out to exit.

Seventy-five percent of American college students, but only 25 percent of Chinese students, were able to solve the cave problem. Why was there such a difference in the two groups? It seems that American students benefited from having heard the story of Hansel and Gretel when they were growing up. As you may recall, Hansel and Gretel were able to find their way out of the woods because Hansel made a trail of bread crumbs that led back home (Chen, Mo, & Honomichl, 2004).

Now try this problem:

> In a village by a river, the chief of a tribe guards a sacred stone statue. Every year, the chief goes downriver to the next village to collect taxes. There, he places the statue in a tub at one end of a hanging balance. To pay their taxes, the villagers have to fill a tub at the other end of the scale with gold coins until the scale balances. This year, the chief forgot to bring his balance scale. How can he figure out how much gold to collect to match the statue's weight? (Adapted from Chen, Mo, & Honomichl, 2004.)

To solve this problem, the chief could put a tub in the river and place the statue in the tub. Then he could mark the water level on the outside of the tub. To pay their taxes, the villagers would have to put gold coins in the tub until it sank to the same level as it did when the statue was in it.

Sixty-nine percent of Chinese students, but only 8 percent of American students were able to solve this problem. Again, it seems that being exposed to a similar problem in the past was helpful. Most Chinese are familiar with a traditional tale about weighing an elephant that is too big to put on a scale. In the story, the elephant is placed in a boat and the water level is marked. After the elephant is removed, the boat is filled with small stones until the water again reaches the mark. Then, each of the stones is weighed on a small scale and the total weight of the elephant is calculated (Chen, Mo, & Honomichl, 2004).

Every culture prepares its members to solve some types of problems more easily than others. As a result, learning about other cultures can make us more flexible and resourceful thinkers—and that's no fairytale.

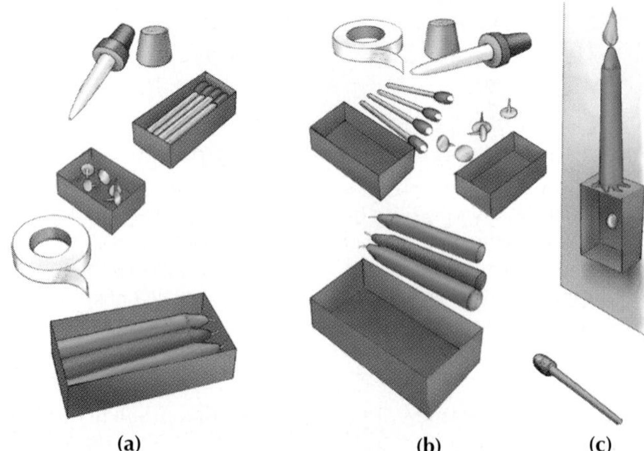

● **Figure 10.17** Materials for solving the candle problem were given to subjects in boxes *(a)* or separately *(b)*. Functional fixedness caused by condition *(a)* interfered with solving the problem. The solution to the problem is shown in *(c)*.

less experience with the use of various objects. It is sometimes said that to be more creative, you should try to see the world without preconceptions, as if through the eyes of a child. In the case of functional fixedness that may actually be true (German & Defeyter, 2000).

Common Barriers to Problem Solving

Functional fixedness is just one of the mental blocks that prevent insight. Here's an example of another: A $5 bill is placed on a table and a stack of objects is balanced precariously on top of the bill. How can the bill be removed without touching or moving the objects? A good answer is to split the bill on one of its edges. Gently pulling from opposite ends will tear the bill in half and remove it without toppling the objects. Many people fail to see this solution because they have learned not to destroy money (Adams, 1988). Notice again the impact of placing something in a category, in this case, "things of value" (which should not be destroyed). Other common mental blocks can hinder problem solving, too, as listed here.

1. **Emotional barriers:** inhibition and fear of making a fool of oneself, fear of making a mistake, inability to tolerate ambiguity, excessive self-criticism
   Example: An architect is afraid to try an unconventional design because she fears that other architects will think it is frivolous.
2. **Cultural barriers:** values that hold that fantasy is a waste of time; that playfulness is for children only; that reason, logic, and numbers are good; that feelings, intuitions, pleasure, and humor are bad or have no value in the serious business of problem solving
   Example: A corporate manager wants to solve a business problem, but becomes stern and angry when members of his marketing team joke playfully about possible solutions.
3. **Learned barriers:** conventions about uses (functional fixedness), meanings, possibilities, taboos
   Example: A cook doesn't have any clean mixing bowls and fails to see that he could use a frying pan as a bowl.
4. **Perceptual barriers:** habits leading to a failure to identify important elements of a problem
   Example: A beginning artist concentrates on drawing a vase of flowers without seeing that the "empty" spaces around the vase are part of the composition, too.

Much of what we know about thinking comes from direct studies of how people solve problems. Yet, surprisingly, much can also be learned from machines. As the next section explains, computerized problem solving provides a fascinating "laboratory" for testing ideas about how we think.

Artificial Intelligence—I Compute, Therefore I Am

It's been a long time since Johann Sebastian Bach, the eighteenth-century German composer, last wrote any music. But listeners sometimes mistake music created by Kemal Ebcioglu for Bach's work. Ebcioglu wrote a computer program that creates harmonies

TABLE 10.1

Solutions to Insight Problems

Water lilies:	Day 59
Twenty dollars:	$10
How many pets?:	Three (one bird, one cat, and one dog)
Between 2 and 3:	A decimal point
One word:	ONE WORD (You may object that the answer is two words, but the problem called for the answer to be "one word," and it is.)

Archiv/Photo Researchers, Inc.

Courtesy of Cray Computer

Two composers. The one on the left was a genius who wrote sublime, multivoiced harmonies. The one on the right has created reasonably good, if uninspired, music. Computer models of thought can approximate intelligent human behavior. However, rule-based computer "thinking" still lacks the flexibility, creativity, and common sense of human intelligence.

remarkably similar to Bach's. By analyzing Bach's music, Ebcioglu came up with 350 rules that govern harmonization. The result is a program that displays *artificial intelligence.*

Artificial intelligence (AI) refers to computer programs capable of doing things that require intelligence when done by people (Russell & Norvig, 2003). Artificial intelligence is based on the fact that many tasks—from harmonizing music to medical diagnosis—can be reduced to a set of rules applied to a body of information. AI is valuable in situations where speed, vast memory, and persistence are required. In fact, AI programs are better at some tasks than humans are. An example is world chess champion Garry Kasparov's loss, in 1997, to a computer called Deep Blue.

AI and Cognition

Artificial intelligence provides a way to probe how we comprehend language, make decisions, and solve problems. Increasingly, AI is being used as a research tool in *computer simulations* and *expert systems.*

Computer simulations are programs that attempt to duplicate human behavior, especially thinking, decision making, or problem solving. Here, the computer acts as a "laboratory" for testing models of cognition. If a computer program behaves as humans do (including making the same errors), then the program may be a good model of how we think.

Artificial intelligence Any artificial system (often a computer program) that is capable of human-like problem solving or intelligent responding.

Computer simulations Computer programs that mimic some aspect of human thinking, decision making, or problem solving.

Most computer models of problem solving are based on a **means-ends analysis.** Typically, the program compares the current state of affairs to the desired end state or goal and attempts to reduce the difference. After each step, the program tests to see if the difference is greater or less than before. This cycle is repeated until the problem is solved. Models such as this may seem removed from real life, but much human thinking and problem solving has a means-ends quality to it (Anderson, 2005). The following quotation provides an everyday example:

> I want to take my son to nursery school. What's the difference between what I have and what I want? Distance. What changes distance? My car. My car won't start. What is needed to make it start? A new battery. What has new batteries? An auto repair shop. I need to have the shop come to my house and put in a new battery. But the shop doesn't know I need a battery. What is the problem? Communication. What allows communication? A telephone. (And so on.) (Adapted from Newell & Simon, 1972)

Expert systems are a second major form of AI. **Expert systems** are computer programs that respond as a human expert would. They have demystified some human abilities by converting complex skills into clearly stated rules a computer can follow. Expert systems can predict the weather, analyze geological formations, diagnose disease, play chess, read, tell when to buy or sell stocks, and perform many other tasks.

Experts and Novices

Working with artificial intelligence has helped especially to clarify how novices differ from experts. Research on chess masters, for example, shows that their skills are based on specific *organized knowledge* (systematic information) and *acquired strategies* (learned tactics). In other words, becoming a star performer does not come from some general strengthening of the mind. Master chess players don't necessarily have better memories than beginners (except for realistic chess positions) (Gobet & Simon, 1996) (see ● Figure 10.18). And, typically, they don't explore more moves ahead than lesser players.

What does set master players apart is their ability to recognize *patterns* that suggest what lines of play should be explored next (Anderson, 2005). This helps eliminate a large number of possible moves. The chess master, therefore, does not waste time exploring unproductive pathways. Experts are better able to see the true nature of problems and to define them in terms of general principles (Anderson, 2005).

Expertise also allows more *automatic processing,* or fast, fairly effortless thinking based on experience with similar problems. Automatic processing frees "space" in short-term memory, making it easier to work on the problem. At the highest skill levels, expert performers tend to rise above rules and plans. Their decisions, thinking, and actions become rapid and fluid. Thus, when a chess master recognizes a pattern on the chessboard, the most desirable tactic comes to mind almost immediately (Klein et al., 1995).

The Future of AI

AI may lead to robots that recognize voices and that speak and act "intelligently." But cognitive scientists are becoming aware that machine "intelligence" is ultimately "blind" outside its underlying set of rules. In contrast, human cognition is much more flexible. For example, u cann understnd wrds thet ar mizpeld. Computers are very literal and easily stymied by such errors. Let's say you are exchanging instant messages with a computer in another room and can ask it questions. If the machine can "fool" you into thinking it is a human, it could be argued that it is intelligent. To date, no machine has come close to passing this test (Moor, 2001).

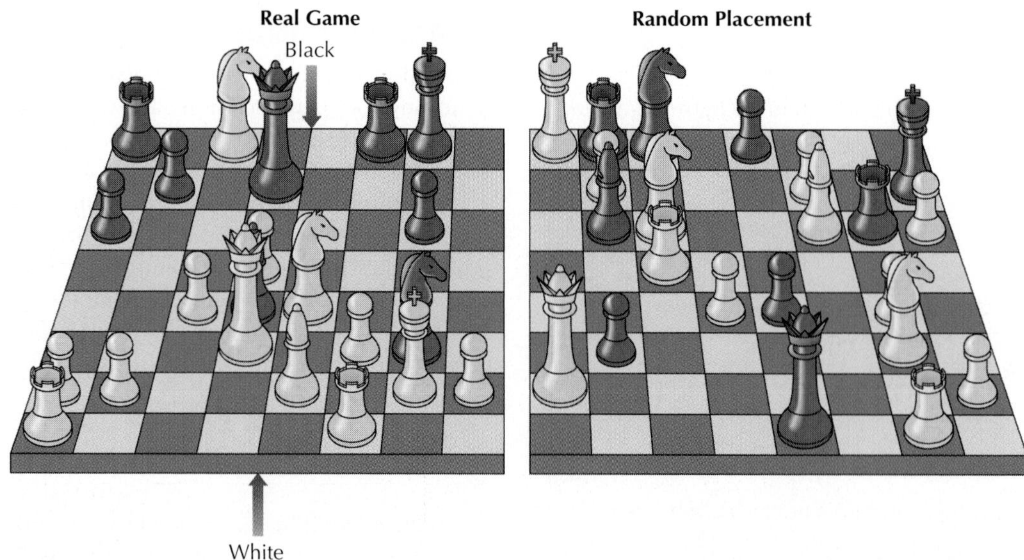

● **Figure 10.18** The left chessboard shows a realistic game. The right chessboard is a random arrangement of pieces. Expert chess players can memorize the left board at a glance, yet they are no better than beginners at memorizing the random board (Saariluoma, 1994). Their superior recall of realistic positions is based on a learned ability to see meaningful patterns among pieces. Such patterns change groups of pieces into large chunks that match knowledge stored in long-term memory (Gobet & Simon, 1996).

Humans are able to take into account exceptions, context, and interpretations as they think. We also make commitments and take responsibility for our actions. A rule-driven expert system processes information without regard for the meaning of actions. Expert systems may never be able to anticipate the infinite number of possible events that could occur. As a result, their actions might be disastrous in unanticipated situations. Clearly, artificial intelligence is not likely to soon replace the human touch in many areas. Although Bach might have been fascinated by AI, it is doubtful that his musical magic will be eclipsed by a machine.

KNOWLEDGE BUILDER

Problem Solving and Artificial Intelligence

REFLECT

Identify at least one problem you have solved mechanically or by rote. Now identify a problem you solved by understanding. Did the second problem involve finding a general solution or a functional solution? Or both? What heuristics did you use to solve the problem?

What is the best insightful solution you've ever come up with? Did it involve selective encoding, combination, or comparison?

Can you think of time when you overcame functional fixedness to solve a problem?

LEARNING CHECK

1. Insight refers to rote, or trial-and-error, problem solving. T or F?
2. The first phase in problem solving by understanding is to discover the general properties of a correct solution. T or F?
3. Problem-solving strategies that guide the search for solutions are called ____________________.
4. A common element underlying insight is that information is encoded, combined, and compared ____________________.
   a. mechanically c. functionally
   b. by rote d. selectively
5. The term *fixation* refers to the point at which a helpful insight becomes fixed in one's thinking. T or F?
6. Two aspects of artificial intelligence are computer simulations and automatic processing. T or F?
7. Computer simulations are often used to test models of human cognition. T or F?
8. Organized knowledge, acquired strategies, and automatic processing are all characteristics of human expertise. T or F?
9. Expert systems can be described as broadly intelligent because their rules and heuristics apply to almost any problem-solving situation. T or F?

CRITICAL THINKING

10. Do you think that it is true that "a problem clearly defined is a problem half solved"?
11. Is it ever accurate to describe a machine as "intelligent"?

Answers: 1. F **2.** T **3.** heuristics **4.** d **5.** F **6.** F **7.** T **8.** T **9.** F **10.** Although that might be an overstatement, it is true that clearly defining a starting point and the desired goal can serve as a heuristic in problem solving. **11.** As stated, rule-driven expert systems may appear "intelligent" within a narrow range of problem solving. However, they are idiots at everything else. This is usually not what we have in mind when discussing human intelligence.

Creative Thinking—Down Roads Less Traveled

Original ideas have changed the course of human history. Much of what we now take for granted in art, medicine, music, technology, and science was once regarded as radical or impossible. How do creative thinkers achieve the breakthroughs that advance us into new realms? Creativity is elusive. Nevertheless, psychologists have learned a great deal about how creativity occurs and how to promote it, as you will soon learn.

We have seen that problem solving may be mechanical, insightful, or based on understanding. To this we can add that thinking may be **inductive** (going from specific facts or observations to general principles) or **deductive** (going from general principles to specific situations). Thinking may also be **logical** (proceeding from given information to new conclusions on the basis of explicit rules) or **illogical** (intuitive, associative, or personal).

What distinguishes creative thinking from more routine problem solving? Creative thinking involves all of these thinking styles, plus *fluency, flexibility,* and *originality.* Let's say that you would like to find creative uses for the millions of automobile tires discarded each year. The creativity of your suggestions could be rated in this way: **Fluency** is defined as the total number of suggestions you are able to make. **Flexibility** is the number of times you shift from one class of possible uses to another. **Originality** refers to how novel or unusual your ideas are. By counting the number of times you showed fluency, flexibility, and originality, we could rate your creativity, or capacity for *divergent thinking* (Baer, 1993; Runco, 2004).

Means-ends analysis An analysis of how to reduce the difference between the present state of affairs and a desired goal.

Expert systems Computer programs designed to respond as a human expert would; programs based on the knowledge and rules that underlie human expertise in specific topics.

Inductive thought Thinking in which a general rule or principle is inferred from a series of specific examples; for instance, inferring the laws of gravity by observing many falling objects.

Deductive thought Thought that applies a general set of rules to specific situations; for example, using the laws of gravity to predict the behavior of a single falling object.

Logical thought Drawing conclusions on the basis of formal principles of reasoning.

Illogical thought Thought that is intuitive, haphazard, or irrational.

Fluency In tests of creativity, fluency refers to the total number of solutions produced.

Flexibility In tests of creativity, flexibility is indicated by the number of different types of solutions produced.

Originality In tests of creativity, originality refers to how novel or unusual solutions are.

The first paper clip was patented in 1899. Competition for sales, combined with divergent thinking, has resulted in a remarkable array of alternative designs. These are drawings of just a few of the variations that have appeared over the years. (After Kim, 2000.)

Fluency is an important part of creative thinking. Mozart produced more than 600 pieces of music. Picasso (shown here) created more than 20,000 artworks. Shakespeare wrote 154 sonnets. Not all of these works were masterpieces. However, a fluent outpouring of ideas fed the creative efforts of each of these geniuses.

In routine problem solving or thinking, there is one correct answer, and the problem is to find it. This leads to **convergent thinking** (lines of thought converge on the answer). **Divergent thinking** is the reverse, in which many possibilities are developed from one starting point (Baer, 1993). (See ■ Table 10.2 for some examples.) Rather than repeating learned solutions, creative thinking produces new answers, ideas, or patterns (Michalko, 1998).

Divergent thinking is also a characteristic of daydreaming. Before we discuss divergent thinking further, let's take a brief detour into the realm of fantasy (if you're not there already; see "Daydreams, Fantasy, and Creativity").

TABLE 10.2

Convergent and Divergent Problems

Convergent Problems

- What is the area of a triangle that is 3 feet wide at the base and 2 feet tall?
- Erica is shorter than Zoey but taller than Carlo, and Carlo is taller than Jared. Who is the second tallest?
- If you simultaneously drop a baseball and a bowling ball from a tall building, which will hit the ground first?

Divergent Problems

- What objects can you think of that begin with the letters BR?
- How could discarded aluminum cans be put to use?
- Write a poem about fire and ice.

Isn't creativity more than divergent thinking? What if a person comes up with a large number of useless answers to a problem? A good question. Divergent thinking is an important part of creativity, but there is more to it. To be creative, the solution to a problem must be more than novel, unusual, or original. It must also be *practical* if it is an invention and *sensible* if it is an idea. This is the dividing line between a "harebrained scheme" and a "stroke of genius." In other words, the creative person uses reasoning and critical thinking to *evaluate* new ideas once they are produced (Runco, 2003).

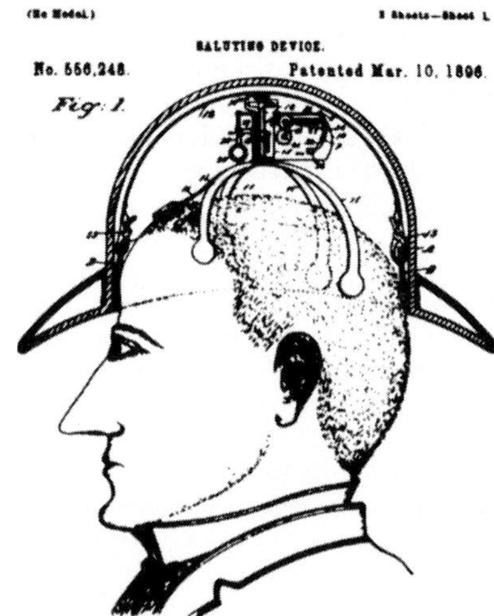

Hat-tipping device. According to the patent, it is for "automatically effecting polite salutations by the elevation and rotation of the hat on the head of the saluting party when said person bows to the person or persons saluted." In addition to being original or novel, a creative solution must fit the demands of the problem. Is this a creative solution to the "problem" of hat tipping?

BRIDGES

Like fantasy, dreams can contribute to creative problem solving.

See Chapter 7, pages 257–258.

FOCUS ON RESEARCH

Daydreams, Fantasy, and Creativity

Has your reading of this chapter been interrupted by a **daydream** (vivid waking fantasy)? Psychologist Eric Klinger (1990) fitted volunteers with pagers and asked them to record what they were doing or thinking whenever he "beeped" them. Surprisingly, Klinger found that about half of our waking thoughts are occupied by daydreams. What do we know about this unique mental state?

Content

In general, daydreams mirror our desires, fears, and anxieties in a fairly direct way. Klinger says, "When you're happy you have happy daydreams, when you're sad you have sad daydreams, and when you're angry you have angry daydreams." Because daydreams are fairly straightforward in meaning, they can be a good source of personal insights. Sleeping dreams, in contrast, tend to be more complex and difficult to analyze (Klinger, 1990, 2000).

Two of the most common daydream plots are the *conquering hero* and the *suffering martyr* themes. In a *conquering hero* fantasy, the daydreamer gets the starring role as a famous, rich, or powerful person: a celebrity, athlete, musician, famous surgeon, brilliant lawyer, or magnificent lover. Themes such as these seem to reflect needs for mastery and escape from the frustrations of everyday life. *Suffering martyr* daydreams center on feelings of being neglected, hurt, rejected, or unappreciated by others. In such fantasies, others end up regretting their past actions and realizing what a wonderful person the daydreamer was all along.

Benefits

Daydreams often fill a need for stimulation during routine or boring tasks. They also improve our ability to delay immediate pleasures so that future goals can be achieved. In everyday terms, fantasy can be an outlet for frustrated impulses. If you have a momentary urge to bash the fool in front of you on the highway, substituting fantasy for action may avert disaster.

Perhaps the greatest value of fantasy is its contribution to creativity. In the imaginative realm of fantasy, anything is possible—a quality allowing for tremendous fluency and flexibility of thought. For most people, fantasy and daydreaming are associated with positive emotional adjustment, lower levels of aggression, and greater mental flexibility or creativity (Klinger, 1990, 2000; Langens & Schmalt, 2002). Perhaps that's why Albert Einstein was, in his own words, "disorderly and a dreamer."

Problem finding is another characteristic of creative thinking. Many of the problems we solve are "presented" to us—by employers, teachers, circumstances, or life in general. **Problem finding** involves actively seeking problems to solve. When you are thinking creatively, a spirit of discovery prevails: You are more likely to find unsolved problems and *choose* to tackle them. Thus, problem finding may be a more creative act than the convergent problem solving that typically follows it (Runco, 2004).

Tests of Creativity

There are several ways to measure divergent thinking. In the *Unusual Uses Test,* you would be asked to think of as many uses as possible for some object, such as the tires mentioned earlier. In the *Consequences Test,* you would list the consequences that would follow a basic change in the world. For example, you might be asked, "What would happen if everyone suddenly lost the sense of balance and could no longer stay upright?" People try to list as many reactions as possible. If you were to take the *Anagrams Test,* you would be given a word such as *creativity* and asked to make as many new words as possible by rearranging the letters. Each of these tests can be scored for fluency, flexibility, and originality. (For an example of other tests of divergent thinking, see ● Figure 10.19.) Tests of divergent thinking seem to tap something quite different from intelligence. Generally, there is little correlation between creativity tests and IQ test scores (Wallach, 1985).

Creativity tests have been useful, but they are not the whole story. If you want to predict whether a person will be creative in the future, it helps to look at two more kinds of information (Feldhusen & Goh, 1995):

- The *products* of creative thinking (such as essays, poems, drawings, or constructed objects) are often more informative than test results. When creative people are asked to actually produce something, others tend to judge their work as creative. (The Rube Goldberg machines described earlier are a good example.)
- A simple listing of a person's *past creative activities and achievements* is an excellent guide to the likelihood that she or he will be creative in the future.

Convergent thought Thinking directed toward discovery of a single established correct answer; conventional thinking.

Divergent thought Thinking that produces many ideas or alternatives; a major element in original or creative thought.

Daydream A vivid waking fantasy.

Problem finding The active discovery of problems to be solved.

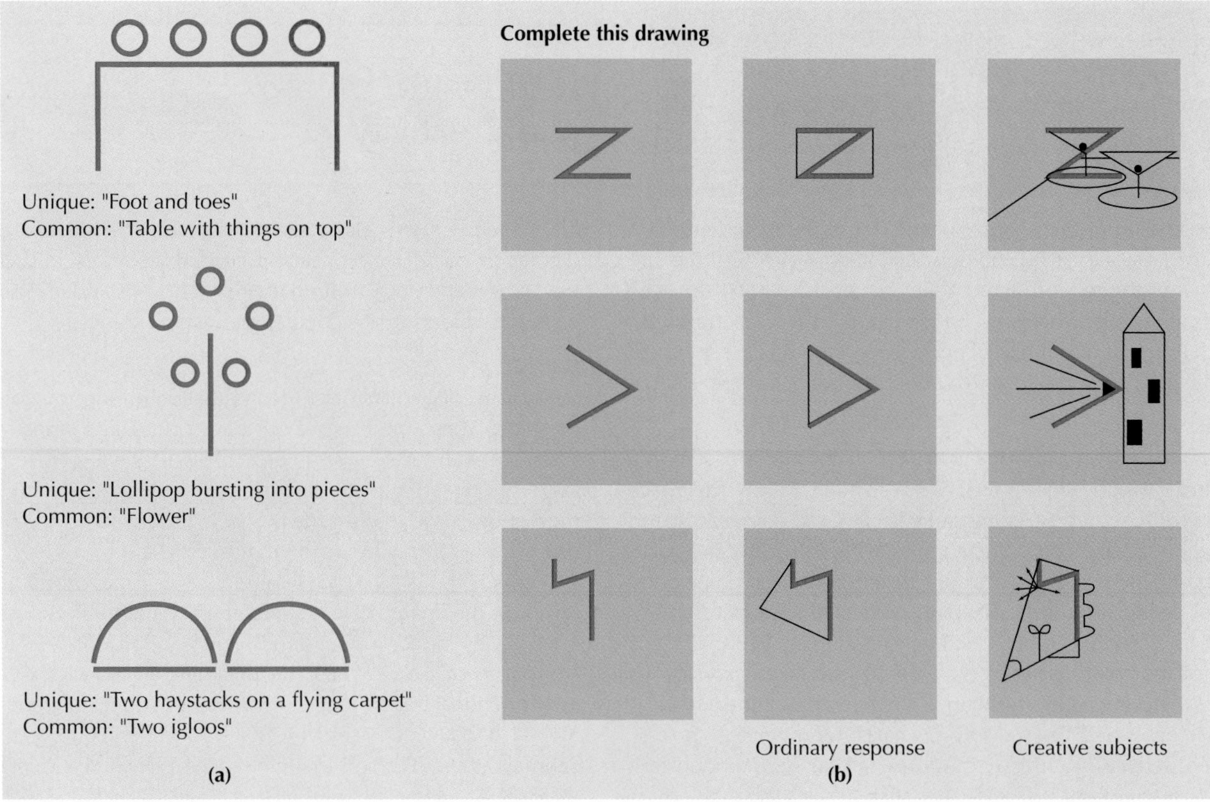

Figure 10.19 Some tests of divergent thinking. Creative responses are more original and more complex ([*a*] after Wallach & Kogan, 1965; [*b*] after Barron, 1958).

Stages of Creative Thought

Is there any pattern to creative thinking? Typically, five stages occur during creative problem solving:

1. **Orientation.** As a first step, the person defines the problem and identifies its most important dimensions.
2. **Preparation.** In the second stage, creative thinkers saturate themselves with as much information about the problem as possible.
3. **Incubation.** Most major problems produce a period during which all attempted solutions will be futile. At this point, problem solving may proceed on a subconscious level: Although the problem seems to have been set aside, it is still "cooking" in the background.
4. **Illumination.** The stage of incubation is often ended by a rapid insight or series of insights. These produce the "Aha!" experience, often depicted in cartoons as a light bulb appearing over the thinker's head.
5. **Verification.** The final step is to test and critically evaluate the solution obtained during the stage of illumination. If the solution proves faulty, the thinker reverts to the stage of incubation.

Of course, creative thought is not always so neat. Nevertheless, the stages listed are a good summary of the most typical sequence of events.

You may find it helpful to relate the stages to the following more or less true story. Legend has it that the king of Syracuse (a city in ancient Greece) once suspected that his goldsmith had substituted cheaper metals for some of the gold in a crown and kept the extra gold. Archimedes, a famous mathematician and thinker, was given the problem of discovering whether the king had been cheated.

Archimedes began by defining the problem *(orientation):* "How can I tell what metals have been used in the crown without damaging it?" He then checked all known methods of analyzing metals *(preparation).* All involved cutting or melting the crown, so he was forced to temporarily set the problem aside *(incubation).* Then one day as he stepped into his bath, Archimedes suddenly knew he had the solution *(illumination).* He was so excited he is said to have run naked through the streets shouting, "Eureka, eureka!" (I have found it, I have found it!).

On observing his own body floating in the bath, Archimedes realized that different metals of equal weight would displace different amounts of water. A pound of brass, for example, occupies more space than a pound of gold, which is denser. All that remained was to test the solution *(verification).* Archimedes placed an amount of gold (equal in weight to that given the goldsmith) in a tub of water. He marked the water level and removed the gold. He then placed the crown in the water. Was the crown pure gold? If it was, it would raise the water to exactly the same level. Unfortunately, the purity of the crown and the fate of the goldsmith are to this day unknown! (Too bad Archimedes didn't grow up in China. If he had heard the "weighing-the-elephant" tale, he might have quickly solved the crown problem.)

The preceding account is a good general description of creative thinking. However, creative thinking can be highly complex. Rather than springing from sudden insights, much creative problem solving is **incremental** (Weisenberg, 1986). That is, it is the end result of many small steps. This is certainly true of many inventions, which build on earlier ideas.

Some authors believe that truly exceptional creativity requires a rare combination of thinking skills, personality, and a supportive social environment. This mix, they believe, accounts for creative giants such as Edison, Freud, Mozart, Picasso, Tolstoy, and others (Tardif & Sternberg, 1988).

Roger Viollet/Getty Images

T. J. Florian/Rainbow

John Barr/Getty Images

The development of modern aircraft has been highly creative and quite rapid. Even so, it has been marked more by incremental progress than by dramatic breakthroughs.

Positive Psychology: The Creative Personality

What makes a person creative? According to the popular stereotype, highly creative people are eccentric, introverted, neurotic, socially inept, unbalanced in their interests, and on the edge of madness. Although some artists and musicians cultivate this public image, there is little truth in it. Direct studies of creative individuals paint a very different picture (Winner, 2003). (However, read "Madness and Creativity" to learn about an important exception.)

1. For people of normal intelligence, there is a small positive correlation between creativity and IQ. In other words, smarter people have a slight tendency to be more creative. But, for the most part, at any given level of IQ, some people are creative and some are not. An average IQ is 100. The average college graduate has an IQ of 120. This is more than high enough to allow a person to write novels, do scientific research, or pursue other creative work (Finke, 1990). IQs above 120 do not seem to add anything more to creative ability (Sternberg & Lubart, 1995).
2. Creative people usually have a greater-than-average range of knowledge and interests, and they are more fluent in combining ideas from various sources. They are also good at using mental images and metaphors in thinking (Riquelme, 2002).
3. Creative people are open to a wide variety of experiences. They accept irrational thoughts and are uninhibited about their feelings and fantasies (McCrae, 1987). They tend to use broad categories, to question assumptions, to break mental sets, and they find order in chaos. They also experience more unusual states of consciousness, such as vivid dreams and mystical experiences (Ayers, Beaton, & Hunt, 1999).
4. Creative people enjoy symbolic thought, ideas, concepts, and possibilities. They tend to be interested in truth, form, and beauty, rather than in fame or success. Their creative work is an end in itself (Sternberg & Lubart, 1995).
5. Highly creative people value their independence and prefer complexity. However, they are unconventional and nonconforming primarily in their work; otherwise they do not have unusual, outlandish, or bizarre personalities.

Could Bill Gates manage the Boston Red Sox? Probably not. It is widely accepted that people tend to be creative in particular skills or pursuits. For example, a person who is a creative writer might be an uncreative artist or businessperson. Perhaps this is because creativity favors a prepared mind. Those who are creative in a particular field often build on a large store of existing knowledge (Kaufman & Baer, 2002). Yoshiro NakaMats, a Japanese inventor who holds more than 2,000 patents, sees such preparation as a way to gain the freedom to think creatively.

Incremental problem solving Thinking marked by a series of small steps that lead to an original solution.

THE CLINICAL FILE

Madness and Creativity

You've probably heard that "genius is next to insanity." Is there really any link between madness and creativity? Generally, the answer is no. The vast majority of creative people do not suffer from mental disorders. (The jury is out on Ozzy Osbourne, however.) And most people who are mentally ill are not especially creative (Ghadirian, Gregoire, & Kosmidis, 2001).

A notable exception to the preceding conclusion concerns mood disorders. A person with a mood disorder may be manic (agitated, elated, and hyperactive), depressed, or both. (See Chapter 16 for more information.) One study found that parents with a history of mood swings, as well as their children, scored higher in creativity than did normal parents and their children (Simeonova et al., 2005). Further, many of history's renowned artists, writers, poets, and composers apparently suffered from mood disorders (Jamison, 1999). For example, the composer Robert Schumann wrote most of his music during several "high" periods when he was mildly manic. When he was depressed, his output plunged. Similar patterns marked the work of Vincent Van Gogh, Edgar Allan Poe, Emily Dickinson, Ernest Hemmingway, and many others (Jamison, 1999; McDermott, 2001).

The connection between mood swings and creativity may be mainly a matter of productivity. It's easy to understand why creative persons would more actively paint, write, or compose when they are manic and have boundless energy. Also, people who are manic tend to have illogical thoughts. Such thinking can enhance creativity by promoting unusual connections among ideas (Anderegg & Gartner, 2001).

Again, it is important to emphasize that most creative people are not mentally disturbed and most mentally disturbed people are not creative. Nevertheless, a few talented (and often miserable) individuals do appear to ride an emotional roller coaster to highs and lows of creativity (Kaufman, 2001).

Can creativity be learned? It is beginning to look as if some creative thinking skills can be taught. In particular, you can become more creative by practicing divergent thinking, and by taking risks, analyzing ideas, and seeking unusual connections between ideas (Baer, 1993; Sternberg, 2001).

Logic and Intuition—Mental Shortcut? Or Dangerous Detour?

At the same time that irrational, intuitive thought may contribute to creative problem solving, it can also lead to thinking errors. Before we discuss intuitive thinking, try the following problems.

Many thinking errors begin with flawed reasoning. Simple sequences of logic can be arranged as a set of *premises* (assumptions) and a *conclusion.* This format is called a **syllogism.** A syllogism can be evaluated for the *validity* of its reasoning and for the *truth* of its *conclusion.* It is entirely possible to draw true conclusions using faulty logic or to draw false conclusions using valid logic. The following examples show how this is possible.

BRIDGES

Humanistic psychologist Abraham Maslow believed that we must live honestly and creatively to make full use our potentials.

See Chapter 14, pages 479–480, for a discussion of self-actualization.

Syllogism 1
All humans are mortal. (Major premise)
All women are humans. (Minor premise)
Therefore, all women are mortal. (Conclusion)

As you can see from ● Figure 10.20, the logic in this example is valid. Because our premises are true, the conclusion is true. The diagram shows all women included within the boundaries of mortals.

Syllogism 2
All women are humans.
All humans are mortal.
Therefore, all mortals are women.

In this example, the conclusion is false because the reasoning is invalid. The diagram for Syllogism 1 shows that all mortals are not women. Notice how little the information has to be changed to produce a false conclusion. Now consider these statements:

Syllogism 3
All psychologists are weird.
Mary is a psychologist.
Therefore, Mary is weird.

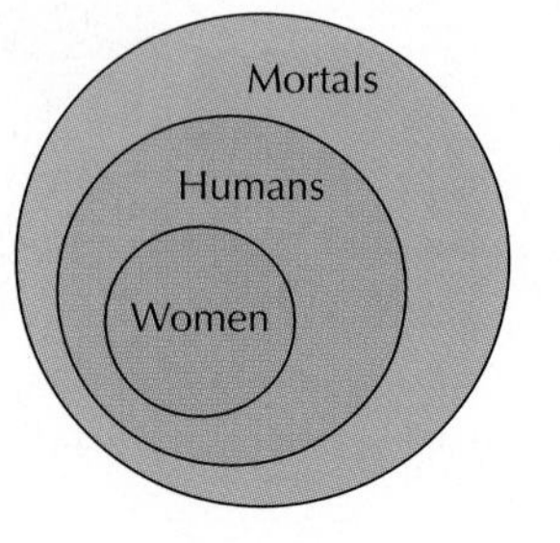

● **Figure 10.20**

CRITICAL THINKING

Have You Ever Thin Sliced Your Teacher?

Think back to your least favorite teacher (not your current one, of course!). How long did it take you to figure out that he or she wasn't going to make your list of star teachers?

In an intriguing study, psychologist Nalini Ambady asked people to watch video clips of teachers they did not know. After watching three ten-second segments, participants were asked to rate the teachers. Amazingly, their ratings correlated highly with year-end course evaluations made by actual students (Ambady & Rosenthal, 1993). Ambady obtained the same result when she presented an even thinner "slice" of teaching behavior, just three two-second clips. A mere 6 seconds is all that participants needed to form intuitive judgments of the instructors' teaching!

In his recent book, *Blink,* Malcolm Gladwell (2005) argues that this was not a case of hurried irrationality. Instead, it was "thin-slicing," or quickly making sense of thin slivers of experience. According to Gladwell, these immediate, intuitive reactions can sometimes form the basis of more carefully reasoned judgments. They are a testament to the power of the *cognitive unconscious,* which is a part of the brain that does automatic, unconscious processing (Wilson, 2002). Far from being irrational, intuition may be an important part of how we think.

The trick, of course, is figuring out when thin slicing can be trusted and when it can't. After all, first impressions aren't always right. For example, have you ever had a teacher you came to appreciate only after classes were well under way or only after the course was over? In many circumstances, quick impressions are most valuable when you take the time to verify them through further observation.

In this case the reasoning is valid, but the conclusion is false because the first premise is false. All psychologists are *not* weird. (Honest!) Now let's analyze one more example.

Syllogism 4
All ducks have wings.
All birds have wings.
Therefore, all ducks are birds.

This sequence shows the importance of paying close attention to logic. The reasoning appears to be valid because the conclusion is true. However, substitute *bats* or *airplanes* for *ducks* and see how the conclusion reads. It is a good idea to get in the habit of questioning the logic used by politicians, advertisers, and psychologists, too, for that matter.

Intuition

If you are formally trained in logic, you may actually think in logical sequences like the preceding examples. However, most people take a more intuitive approach to reasoning. For instance, we tend to abandon logical reasoning if a conclusion contradicts our personal beliefs (Markovits & Nantel, 1989). The following problems capture the flavor of much of the reasoning we do.

Problem 1 An epidemic breaks out, and 600 people are about to die. Doctors have two choices. If they give drug A, 200 lives will be saved. If they give drug B, there is a one-third chance that 600 people will be saved, and a two-thirds chance that none will be saved. Which drug should they choose?

Problem 2 Again, 600 people are about to die, and doctors must make a choice. If they give drug A, 400 people will die. If they give drug B, there is a one-third chance that no one will die, and a two-thirds chance that 600 will die. Which drug should they choose?

Most people choose drug A for the first problem and drug B for the second. This is fascinating because the two problems are identical. The only difference is that the first is stated in terms of lives saved, the second in terms of lives lost. Yet even people who realize that their answers are contradictory find it difficult to change them (Kahneman & Tversky, 1972, 1973).

As the example shows, we often make decisions intuitively, rather than logically or rationally. **Intuition** is quick, impulsive thought. It may provide fast answers, but it can also be misleading and sometimes disastrous. (see "Have You Ever Thin Sliced Your Teacher?")

Two noted psychologists, Daniel Kahneman (KON-eh-man) and Amos Tversky (tuh-VER-ski) (1937–1996), have studied how we make decisions in the face of uncertainty. They have found that human judgment is often seriously flawed (Kahneman, 2003). Let's explore some common intuitive thinking errors, so you will be better prepared to avoid them.

Representativeness

One very common pitfall in judgment is illustrated by this question: Which is more probable?

A. Venus Williams will lose the first set of a tennis match but win the match.
B. Venus Williams will lose the first set.

Tversky and Kahneman (1982) found that most people regard statements like A as more probable than B. However, this intuitive

Syllogism A format for analyzing logical arguments.

Intuition Quick, impulsive thought that does not make use of formal logic or clear reasoning.

answer overlooks an important fact: The likelihood of two events occurring together is lower than the probability of either one alone. (For example, the probability of getting one head when flipping a coin is one half, or .5. The probability of getting two heads when flipping two coins is one fourth, or .25.) Therefore, A is less likely to be true than B.

According to Tversky and Kahneman, such faulty conclusions are based on the **representativeness heuristic.** That is, we tend to give a choice greater weight if it seems to be representative of what we already know. Thus, you probably compared the information about Venus Williams with your mental model of what a tennis pro's behavior should be like. Answer A seems to better represent the model. Therefore, it seems more likely than answer B, even though it isn't. In courtrooms, jurors are more likely to think a defendant is guilty if the person appears to fit the profile of a person likely to commit a crime (Davis & Follette, 2002). For example, a young single male from a poor neighborhood would be more likely to be judged guilty of theft than a middle-aged married father from an affluent suburb.

Emotion

Feelings also tend to affect good judgment. When we must make a choice, our emotional reactions to various alternatives can determine what intuitively seems to be the right answer. Emotions such as fear, hope, anxiety, liking, or disgust can eliminate possibilities from consideration or promote them to the top of the list (Kahneman, 2003). For many people, choosing which political candidate to vote for is a good example of how emotions can cloud clear thinking. Rather than comparing candidates' records and policies, it is tempting to vote for the person we like, rather than the person who is most qualified for the job.

Underlying Odds

A second common error in judgment involves ignoring the **base rate,** or underlying probability, of an event. People in one experiment were told that they would be given descriptions of 100 people—70 lawyers and 30 engineers. Subjects were then asked to guess, without knowing anything about a person, whether she or he was an engineer or a lawyer. All correctly stated the probabilities as 70 percent for lawyer and 30 percent for engineer. Participants were then given this description:

> Dick is a 30-year-old man. He is married with no children. A man of high ability and high motivation, he promises to be quite successful in his field. He is well liked by his colleagues.

Notice that the description gives no new information about Dick's occupation. He could still be either an engineer or a lawyer. Therefore, the odds should again be estimated as 70–30. However, most people changed the odds to 50–50. Intuitively it seems that Dick has an equal chance of being either an engineer or a lawyer. But this guess completely ignores the underlying odds.

Perhaps it is fortunate that we do at times ignore underlying odds. Were this not the case, how many people would get married in the face of a 50-percent divorce rate? Or how many would start high-risk businesses? On the other hand, people who smoke, drink and then drive, or skip wearing auto seat belts ignore rather high odds of injury or illness. In many high-risk situations, ignoring base rates is the same as thinking you are an exception to the rule.

Framing

The most general conclusion about intuition is that the way a problem is stated, or **framed,** affects decisions (Tversky & Kahneman, 1981). As the first example in this discussion revealed, people often give different answers to the same problem if it is stated in slightly different ways. To gain some added insight into framing, try another thinking problem:

> A couple are divorcing. Both parents seek custody of their only child, but custody can be granted to just one parent. If you had to make a decision based on the following information, to which parent would you award custody of the child?
>
> **Parent A:** average income, average health, average working hours, reasonable rapport with the child, relatively stable social life.
>
> **Parent B:** above-average income, minor health problems, lots of work-related travel, very close relationship with the child, extremely active social life.

Most people choose to award custody to Parent B, the parent who has some drawbacks but also several advantages (such as above-average income). That's because people tend to look for *positive qualities* that can be *awarded* to the child. However, how would you choose if you were asked this question: Which parent should be denied custody? In this case, most people choose to deny custody to Parent B. Why is Parent B a good choice one moment and a poor choice the next? It's because the second question asked who should be *denied* custody. To answer this question, people tend to look for *negative qualities* that would *disqualify* a parent. As you can see, the way a question is framed can channel us down a narrow path so we attend to only part of the information provided, rather than weighing all the pros and cons (Shafir, 1993).

Usually, the *broadest* way of framing or stating a problem produces the best decisions. However, people often state problems in increasingly narrow terms until a single, seemingly "obvious" answer emerges. For example, to select a career, it would be wise to consider pay, working conditions, job satisfaction, needed skills, future employment outlook, and many other factors. Instead, such decisions are often narrowed to thoughts such as, "I like to write, so I'll be a journalist," "I want to make good money and law pays well," or "I can be creative in photography." Framing decisions so narrowly greatly increases the risk of making a poor choice. If you would like to think more critically and analytically, it is important to pay attention to how you are defining problems before you try to solve them. Remember, shortcuts to answers often short-circuit clear thinking.

Wisdom

People can be intelligent without being wise. For example, a person who does well in school and on IQ tests may make a total mess of her life. Likewise, people can be intelligent without being creative, and clear, rational thinking can lead to correct, but uninspired, answers (Sternberg, 2001). In many areas of human life, wisdom represents a mixture of convergent thinking, intelligence, and reason, spiced with creativity and originality. People who are wise approach life with openness and tolerance (Helson & Srivastava, 2002).

A Look Ahead

We have discussed only some of the intuitive errors made in the face of uncertainty. In the upcoming Psychology in Action section we will return to the topic of creative thinking for a look at ways to promote creativity.

KNOWLEDGE BUILDER

Creativity and Intuition

REFLECT

Make up a question that would require convergent thinking to answer. Now do the same for divergent thinking.

Which of the tests of creativity described in the text do you think you would do best on? (Look back if you can't remember them all.)

To better remember the stages of creative thinking, make up a short story that includes these words: *orient, prepare, in Cuba, illuminate, verify.*

How many of the characteristics of creative individuals apply to you?

Explain in your own words how representativeness and base rates contribute to thinking errors.

LEARNING CHECK

1. Fluency, flexibility, and originality are characteristics of
   a. convergent thought
   b. deductive thinking
   c. creative thought
   d. trial-and-error solutions
2. List the typical stages of creative thinking in the correct order.
   ______ ______ ______ ______ ______ ______
3. Reasoning and critical thinking tend to block creativity; these are noncreative qualities. T or F?
4. To be creative an original idea must also be practical or feasible. T or F?
5. Intelligence and creativity are highly correlated; the higher a person's IQ is, the more likely he or she is to be creative. T or F?
6. In evaluating a syllogism, it is possible to draw a true conclusion with faulty logic or a false conclusion with valid logic. T or F?
7. Kate is single, outspoken, and very bright. As a college student, she was deeply concerned with discrimination and other social issues and participated in several protests. Which statement is more likely to be true?
   a. Kate is a bank teller.
   b. Kate is a bank teller and a feminist.

CRITICAL THINKING

8. A coin is flipped four times with one of the following results: *(a)* H T T H, *(b)* T T T T, *(c)* H H H H, *(d)* H H T H. Which sequence would most likely precede getting a head on the fifth coin flip?

Answers: 1. c **2.** orientation, preparation, incubation, illumination, verification **3.** F **4.** T **5.** F **6.** T **7.** a **8.** The chance of getting a head on the fifth flip is the same in each case. Each time you flip a coin, the chance of getting a head is 50 percent, no matter what happened before. However, many people intuitively think that *b* is the answer because a head is "overdue," or that *c* is correct because the coin is "on a roll" for heads.

Representativeness heuristic A tendency to select wrong answers because they seem to match preexisting mental categories.

Base rate The basic rate at which an event occurs over time; the basic probability of an event.

Framing In thought, the terms in which a problem is stated or the way that it is structured.

PSYCHOLOGY IN ACTION

Enhancing Creativity—Brainstorms

Thomas Edison once explained his creativity by saying, "Genius is 1 percent inspiration and 99 percent perspiration." Many studies of creativity show that "genius" and "eminence" owe as much to persistence and dedication as they do to inspiration (Ericsson & Charness, 1994; Winner, 2003). A study of creative artists revealed that many regard creativity as "hard work" (Glueck, Ernst, & Unger, 2002).

Once it is recognized that creativity can be hard work, then something can be done to enhance it. Here are some suggestions on how to begin.

1. Break mental sets and challenge assumptions. A **mental set** is the tendency to perceive a problem in a way that blinds us to possible solutions. Mental sets are a major barrier to creative thinking. Usually they lead us to see a problem in preconceived terms that impede our problem-solving attempts. (Fixations and functional fixedness, which were described earlier, are specific types of mental sets.)

Try the problems pictured in ● Figure 10.21. If you have difficulty, try asking yourself what assumptions you are making. The problems are designed to demonstrate the limiting effects of a mental set. (The answers to these problems, along with an explanation of the sets that prevent their solution, are found in ● Figure 10.22.)

Sometimes, problems themselves produce a disruptive set. For example, see if you can unscramble each group of letters on the following list to make words that use all of the letters:

MEST __________________
LFAE __________________
DUB __________________
STKAL __________________
OTOR __________________
LTEPA __________________

Now try a new list:

FINEK __________________
OPONS __________________
KROF __________________
PUC __________________
SDIH __________________
LTEPA __________________

Did you notice that the last problem was the same in each case? Many people don't and end up solving the problem twice. To complete the first list *(stem, leaf, bud, stalk, root),* the item LTEPA is usually unscrambled as *petal.* In the second list *(knife, spoon, fork, cup, dish),* LTEPA becomes *plate* for many people.

Now that you have been forewarned about the danger of faulty assumptions, see if you can correctly answer the following questions.

1. A farmer had 19 sheep. All but 9 died. How many sheep did the farmer have left?
2. It is not unlawful for a man living in Winston-Salem, North Carolina, to be buried west of the Mississippi River. T or F?
3. Some months have 30 days, some have 31. How many months have 28 days?
4. I have two coins that together total 30 cents. One of the coins is not a nickel. What are the two coins?
5. If there are 12 one-cent candies in a dozen, how many two-cent candies are there in a dozen?

These questions are designed to cause thinking errors. Here are the answers:

> 1. Nineteen—9 alive and 10 dead. 2. F. It is against the law to bury a living person anywhere. 3. All of them. 4. A quarter and a nickel. One of the coins is not a nickel, but the other one is! 5. 12.

If you got caught on any of the questions, consider it an additional reminder of the value of actively challenging the assumptions you are making in any instance of problem solving.

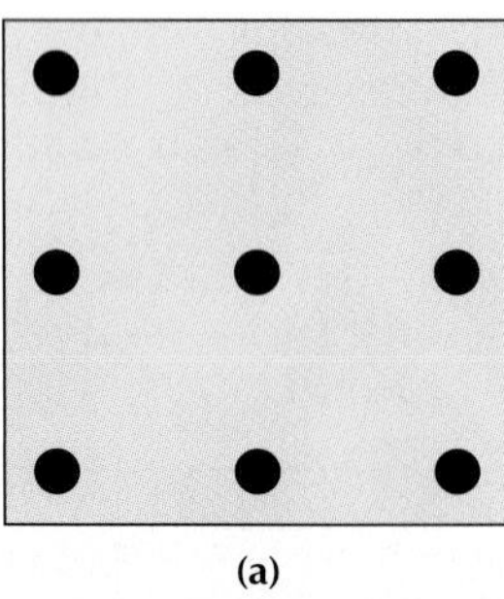

(a)

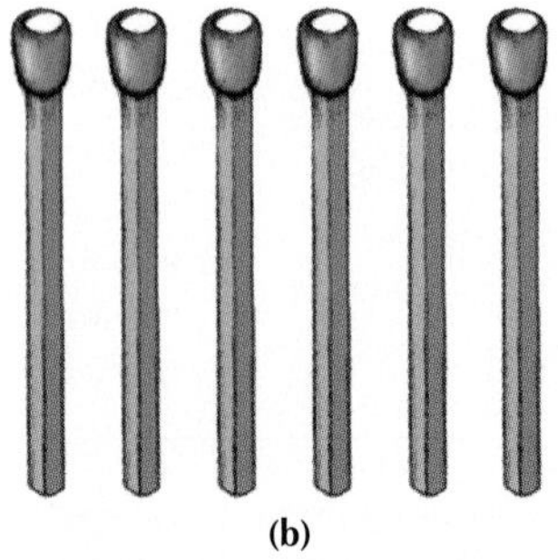

(b)

● **Figure 10.21** (a) Nine dots are arranged in a square. Can you connect them by drawing four continuous straight lines without lifting your pencil from the paper? *(b)* Six matches must be arranged to make four triangles. The triangles must be the same size, with each side equal to the length of one match. (The solutions to these problems appear in Figure 10.23.)

Define problems broadly. An effective way to break mental sets is to enlarge the definition of a problem. For instance, assume your problem is to design a better doorway. This is likely to lead to ordinary solutions. Why not change the problem to design a better way to get through a wall? Now your solutions will be more original. Best of all might be to state the problem as follows: Find a better way to define separate areas for living and working. This could lead to truly creative solutions (Adams, 1988).

Let's say you are leading a group that's designing a new can opener. Wisely, you ask the group to think about *opening* in general, rather than about can openers. This was just the approach that led to the pop-top can. As the design group discussed the concept of opening, one member suggested that nature has its own openers, like the soft seam on a pea pod. Instead of a new can-opening tool, the group invented the self-opening can (Stein, 1974).

Restate the problem in different ways. Stating problems in novel ways also tends to produce more creative solutions. See if you can cross out six letters to make a single word out of the following:

CSRIEXLEATTTERES

If you're having difficulty, it may be that you need to restate the problem. Were you trying to cross out six letters? The real solution is to cross out the letters in the words "six letters," which yields the word CREATE.

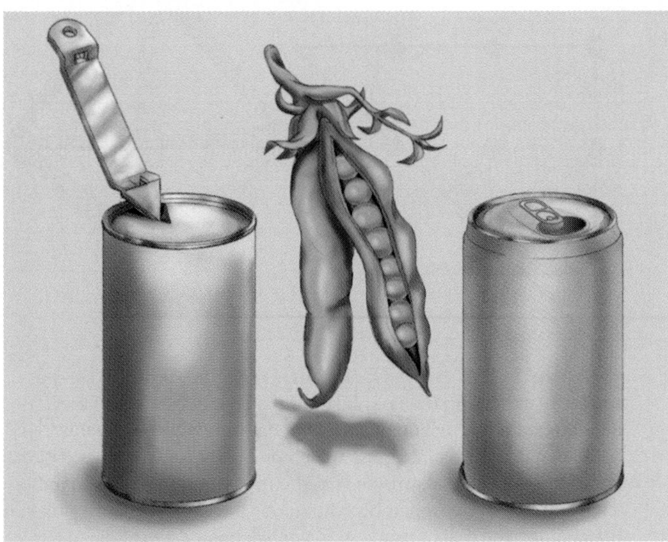

One way to restate a problem is to imagine how another person would view it. What would a child, engineer, professor, mechanic, artist, psychologist, judge, or minister ask about the problem? Also, don't be afraid to ask "silly" or playful questions. Here are some examples:

If the problem were alive, what would it look like?
If the problem were edible, how would it taste?
How would the problem look from an airplane? How does it look from underneath?
Is any part of the problem pretty? Ugly? Stupid? Friendly?
If the problem could speak, what would it say?

At the very least, you should almost always ask the following questions:

What information do I have?
What don't I know?
What can I extract from the known information?
Have I used all of the information?
What additional information do I need?
What are the parts of the problem?
How are the parts related?
How could the parts be related?
Is this in any way like a problem I've solved before?

Remember, to think more creatively you must find ways to jog yourself out of mental sets and habitual modes of thought (Michalko, 1998).

4. Create the right atmosphere. Various experiments show that people make more original, spontaneous, and imaginative responses when exposed to others (role models) doing the same. If you want to become more creative, spend more time around creative people. This is the premise underlying much education in art, theater, dance, and music (Sternberg & Lubart, 1995).

5. Allow time for incubation. Trying to hurry or to force a solution may simply encourage fixation on a dead end. Creativity takes time. You need to be able to revise or embellish initial solutions, even those based on rapid insight. If you are feeling hurried by a sense of time pressure, you are much less likely to think creatively almost always (Amabile, Hadley, & Kramer, 2002).

Incubation is especially fruitful when you are exposed to external cues that relate to the problem (remember Archimedes' bath?). For example, Johannes Gutenberg, creator of the printing press, realized while at a wine harvest that the mechanical pressure used to crush grapes could also be used to imprint letters on paper (Dorfman, Shames, & Kihlstrom, 1996).

6. Seek varied input. Remember, creativity requires divergent thinking. Rather than digging deeper with logic, you are attempting to shift your mental "prospecting" to new areas. As an example of this strategy, Edward de Bono (1992) recommends that you randomly look up words in the dictionary and relate them to the problem. Often the words will trigger a fresh perspective or open a new avenue. For instance, let's say you are asked to come up with new ways to clean oil off a beach. Following de Bono's suggestion, you would read the following randomly selected words, relate each to the problem, and see what thoughts are triggered: *weed, rust, poor, magnify, foam, gold, frame, hole, diagonal, vacuum, tribe, puppet, nose, link, drift, portrait, cheese, coal.* You may get similar benefits from relating various objects to a problem. Or take a walk, skim through a newspaper, or look through a stack of photographs to see what thoughts they trigger (Michalko, 1998). Exposing yourself to a wide variety of information is a good way to encourage divergent thinking (Clapham, 2001).

7. Look for analogies. Many "new" problems are really old problems in new clothing

Mental set A predisposition to perceive or respond in a particular way.

(Siegler, 1989). Representing a problem in a variety of ways is often the key to solution. Most problems become easier to solve when they are effectively represented. For example, consider this problem:

> Two backpackers start up a steep trail at 6 AM. They hike all day, resting occasionally, and arrive at the top at 6 PM. The next day they start back down the trail at 6 AM. On the way down they stop several times and vary their pace. They arrive back at 6 PM. On the way down, one of the hikers, who is a mathematician, tells the other that she has realized that they will pass a point on the trail at exactly the same time as they did the day before. Her nonmathematical friend finds this hard to believe, because on both days they have stopped and started many times and changed their pace. The problem: Is the mathematician right?

Perhaps you will see the answer to this problem immediately. If not, think of it this way: What if there were two pairs of backpackers, one going up the trail, the second coming down, and both hiking *on the same day*? As one pair of hikers goes up the trail and the other goes down, they *must* pass each other at some point on the trail, right? Therefore, at that point they will be at the same place at the same time. Now, would your conclusion change if one of the pairs was going up the trail one day and the other was coming down the trail the next? If you mentally draw their path up the mountain and then visualize them coming back down it the next day, do you see that at some point the two paths will meet at the same point at the same time on both days? Well, what if it were the same pair of hikers going up one day and coming back down the next? See, the mathematician was right.

8. Take sensible risks. A willingness to go against the crowd is a key element in doing creative work. Unusual and original ideas may be rejected at first by conventional thinkers. Often, creative individuals must persevere and take some risks before their ideas are widely accepted. For example, Post-It notes were invented by an engineer who accidentally created a weak adhesive. Rather than throw the mixture out, the engineer put it to a highly creative new use. However, it took him some time to convince others that a "bad" adhesive could be a useful product. Today, stick-on notepapers are one of the 3-M Company's most successful products (Sternberg & Lubart, 1995).

9. Delay evaluation. Various studies suggest that people are most likely to be creative when they are given the freedom to play with ideas and solutions without having to worry about whether they will be evaluated. In the first stages of creative thinking, it is important to avoid criticizing your efforts. Worrying about the correctness of solutions tends to inhibit creativity (Basadur, Runco, & Vega, 2000). This idea is expanded in the discussion that follows.

An alternative approach to enhancing creativity is called *brainstorming*. Although brainstorming is a group technique, it can be applied to individual problem solving as well.

Brainstorming

The essence of **brainstorming** is that producing and evaluating ideas are kept separate. In group problem solving, each person is encouraged to produce as many ideas as possible without fear of criticism (Buyer, 1988). This encourages divergent thinking. Some of the most successful brainstorming takes place on computer networks, where each person's fears of being evaluated are minimized (Siau, 1996).

Only at the end of a brainstorming session are ideas reconsidered and evaluated. As ideas are freely generated, an interesting **cross-stimulation effect** takes place in which one participant's ideas trigger ideas from others (Brown, Dane, & Durham, 1998).

The basic rules for successful brainstorming are as follows (Michalko, 1998):

1. Criticism of ideas is absolutely barred. Defer evaluation until later in the session.
2. Modification or combination with other ideas is encouraged. Don't worry about giving credit for ideas or keeping them neat. Mix them up!
3. Quantity of ideas is sought. In the early stages of brainstorming, quantity is more important than quality. Try to generate lots of ideas.
4. Unusual, remote, or wild ideas are sought. Let your imagination run amok!
5. Record ideas as they occur.
6. Elaborate or improve on the most promising ideas.

It is important to be persistent when you are brainstorming. Most groups give up too soon, usually when the flow of new ideas begins to slow (Nijstad, Stroebe, & Lodewijkx, 1999).

How is brainstorming applied to individual problem solving? The essential point to remember is to *suspend judgment.* Ideas should first be produced without regard for logic, organization, accuracy, practicality, or any other evaluation. In writing an essay, for instance, you would begin by writing ideas in any order, the more the better, just as they occur to you. Later you would go back and reorganize, rewrite, and criticize your efforts.

As an aid to following rules 2, 3, and 4 of the brainstorming method, you might find this checklist helpful for encouraging original thought. It can be used to see if you have overlooked a possible solution.

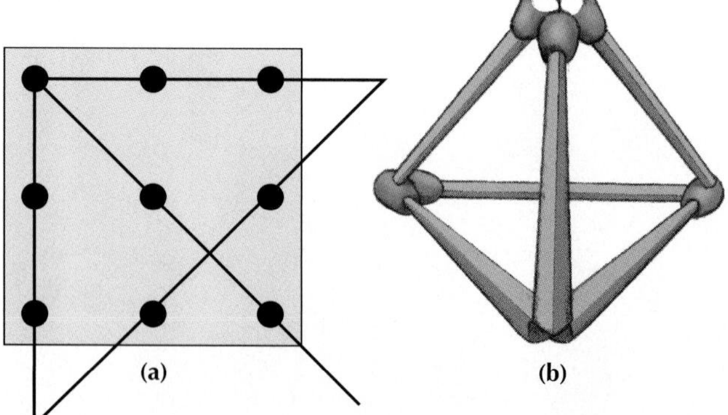

● **Figure 10.22** Problem solutions. *(a)* The dot problem can be solved by extending the lines beyond the square formed by the dots. Most people assume incorrectly that they may not do this. *(b)* The match problem can be solved by building a three-dimensional pyramid. Most people assume that the matches must be arranged on a flat surface. If you remembered the four-tree problem from earlier in the chapter, the match problem may have been easy to solve.

Creativity Checklist

1. **Redefine.** Consider other uses for all elements of the problem. (This is designed to alert you to fixations that may be blocking creativity.)
2. **Adapt.** How could other objects, ideas, procedures, or solutions be adapted to this particular problem?
3. **Modify.** Imagine changing anything and everything that could be changed.
4. **Magnify.** Exaggerate everything you can think of. Think on a grand scale.
5. **Minify.** What if everything were scaled down? What if all differences were reduced to zero? "Shrink" the problem down to size.
6. **Substitute.** How could one object, idea, or procedure be substituted for another?
7. **Rearrange.** Break the problem into pieces and shuffle them.
8. **Reverse.** Consider reverse orders and opposites and turn things inside out.
9. **Combine.** This one speaks for itself.

By making a habit of subjecting a problem to each of these procedures, you should be able to greatly reduce the chances that you will overlook a useful, original, or creative solution.

Living More Creatively

Many people who think in conventional ways live intelligent, successful, and fulfilling lives. Just the same, creative thinking can add spice to life and lead to exciting personal insights. Psychologist Mihalyi Csikszentmihalyi (sik-sent-me-HALE-yee) (1997) makes these recommendations about how to become more creative:

- Find something that surprises you every day.
- Try to surprise at least one person every day.
- If something sparks your interest, follow it.
- Make a commitment to doing things well.
- Seek challenges.
- Take time for thinking and relaxing.
- Start doing more of what you really enjoy, less of what you dislike.
- Try to look at problems from as many viewpoints as you can.

Even if you don't become more creative by following these suggestions, they are still good advice. Life is not a standardized test with a single set of correct answers. It is much more like a blank canvas on which you can create designs that uniquely express your talents and interests. To live more creatively, you must be ready to seek new ways of doing things. Try to surprise at least one person today—yourself, if no one else.

KNOWLEDGE BUILDER

Enhancing Creativity

REFLECT

Review the preceding pages and note which methods you could use more often to improve the quality of your thinking. Now mentally summarize the points you especially want to remember.

LEARNING CHECK

1. Fixations and functional fixedness are specific types of mental sets. T or F?
2. The incubation period in creative problem solving usually lasts just a matter of minutes. T or F?
3. Exposure to creative models has been shown to enhance creativity. T or F?
4. In brainstorming, each idea is critically evaluated as it is generated. T or F?
5. Defining a problem broadly produces a cross-stimulation effect that can inhibit creative thinking. T or F?

CRITICAL THINKING

6. What mode of thinking does the "Creativity Checklist" (redefine, adapt, modify, magnify, and so forth) encourage?

Answers: 1. T 2. F 3. T 4. F 5. F 6. Divergent thinking.

Brainstorming Method of creative thinking that separates the production and evaluation of ideas.

Cross-stimulation effect In group problem solving, the tendency of one person's ideas to trigger ideas from others.

Chapter in Review

What is the nature of thought?

- Thinking is the manipulation of internal representations of external stimuli or situations.
- Three basic units of thought are images, concepts, and language or symbols.

In what ways are images related to thinking?

- Most people have internal images of one kind or another. Images may be stored or created. Sometimes they cross normal sense boundaries in a type of imagery called synesthesia.
- Images used in problem solving may be three-dimensional, they may be rotated in space, and their size may change.
- Kinesthetic images are created by produced, remembered, or imagined actions. Kinesthetic sensations and micromovements seem to help structure the flow of thought for many people.

How are concepts learned? Are there different kinds of concepts?

- A concept is a generalized idea of a class of objects or events.
- Concept formation may be based on positive and negative instances or, more commonly, on rule learning. In practice, concept identification frequently makes use of prototypes, or general models of the concept class.
- Concepts may be classified as conjunctive ("and" concepts), disjunctive ("either/or" concepts), or relational.
- The denotative meaning of a word or concept is its dictionary definition. Connotative meaning is personal or emotional. Connotative meaning can be measured with the semantic differential.
- Oversimplification and stereotyping contribute to thinking errors.

What is the role of language in thinking?

- Language allows events to be encoded into symbols for easy mental manipulation. Thinking in language is influenced by meaning. The study of meaning is called *semantics*.
- Language carries meaning by combining a set of symbols or signs according to a set of rules (grammar), which includes rules about word order (syntax). A true language is productive and can be used to generate new ideas or possibilities.
- Complex gestural systems, such as American Sign Language, are true languages.

Can animals be taught to use language?

- Animal communication is relatively limited because it lacks symbols that can be rearranged easily.
- Attempts to teach chimpanzees systems such as American Sign Language suggest to some that primates are capable of language use. Others question this conclusion. Studies that make use of lexigrams provide the best evidence yet of animal language use.

What do we know about problem solving?

- The solution to a problem may be arrived at mechanically (by trial and error or by rote application of rules), but mechanical solutions are often inefficient or ineffective, except where aided by computer.
- Solutions by understanding usually begin with discovery of the general properties of an answer. Next comes the proposal of a number of functional solutions.
- Problem solving is frequently aided by heuristics. These are strategies that typically narrow the search for solutions. The ideal strategy is a general heuristic.
- When understanding leads to a rapid solution, it is said that insight has occurred. Three elements of insight are selective encoding, selective combination, and selective comparison. Insight and other problem solving can be blocked by fixation. Functional fixedness is a common fixation, but emotional blocks, cultural values, learned conventions, and perceptual habits are also problems.

What is artificial intelligence?

- Artificial intelligence refers to any artificial system that can perform tasks that require intelligence when done by people.
- Two principal areas of artificial intelligence research are computer simulations and expert systems.
- Computer simulations of human problem solving are usually based on a means-ends analysis.
- Expert human problem solving is based on organized knowledge and acquired strategies, rather than some general improvement in thinking ability.
- Artificial intelligence is helping scientists explore the nature of human thought, knowledge, and expertise.

What is the nature of creative thinking?

- To be creative, a solution must be practical and sensible as well as original. Creative thinking requires divergent thought, characterized by fluency, flexibility, and originality. Tests of creativity measure these qualities.
- Daydreaming and fantasy are a source of much divergent thinking.

- Five stages often seen in creative problem solving are orientation, preparation, incubation, illumination, and verification. Not all creative thinking fits this pattern. Much creative activity is based on incremental problem solving.
- Studies suggest that creative persons share a number of identifiable characteristics, most of which contradict popular stereotypes. There appears to be only a slight correlation between IQ and creativity.

How accurate is intuition?

- Intuitive thinking often leads to errors. Wrong conclusions may be drawn when an answer seems highly representative of what we already believe to be true.
- A second problem is ignoring the base rate (or underlying probability) of an event.
- Clear thinking is usually aided by stating or framing a problem in broad terms.

What can be done to improve thinking and to promote creativity?

- Various strategies that promote divergent thinking tend to enhance creative problem solving.
- In group situations, brainstorming may lead to creative solutions. The principles of brainstorming can also be applied to individual problem solving.

Web Resources

Internet addresses frequently change. To find the sites listed here, visit www.thomsonedu.com/psychology/coon for an updated list of Internet addresses and direct links to relevant sites.

***Psychology: Gateways to Mind and Behavior* Website** Online quizzes, flash cards, and other helpful study aids for this text. www.thomsonedu.com/psychology/coon.

Creativity Web Multiple links to resources on creativity.

The Psychology of Invention An exploration of how invention and discovery happen.

The Question of Primate Language This article from the National Zoo discusses primate communication and intelligence.

ThomsonNOW™ Go to www.thomsonedu.com to link to ThomsonNow, your online study tool. First take the **Pre-Test** for this chapter to get your **Personalized Study Plan,** which will identify topics you need to review and direct you to online resources. Then take the **Post-Test** to determine what concepts you have mastered and what you still need work on.

InfoTrac College Edition For recent articles on the controversies surrounding bilingual education, use Key Words search for BILINGUALISM. Go to www.thomsonedu.com/psychology/coon.

Interactive Learning

***PsychNow!* Version 2.0 CD-ROM** Interact with the material with *PsychNow!*'s animations, video clips, experiments, and interactive assessments. For this chapter, go to *5f. Cognition and Language* and *5g. Problem Solving and Creativity* to learn more about how we process information and solve problems.

chapter

11

Intelligence

THEME:

Measuring intelligence is worthwhile, but tests provide limited definitions of intelligent behavior.

Key Questions

How do psychologists define intelligence?

What are the qualities of a good psychological test?

What are typical IQ tests like?

How do IQ scores relate to gender, age, and occupation?

What does IQ tell us about genius?

What causes mental retardation?

How do heredity and environment affect intelligence?

How have views of intelligence changed in recent years?

Preview

What Day Is It?

Ask George, "In which recent years did April 21 fall on a Sunday?" With little hesitation he will answer, "2002, 1996, 1991, 1985, 1974, 1968, 1963, 1957, 1946." Surprisingly, this gives only a hint of his ability. If encouraged, George will go back as far as 1700—with complete accuracy! His calendar calculations cover at least 6,000 years: With equal ease he can identify February 15, 2002, as a Friday or August 28, 1591, as a Wednesday.

Is he a genius? George's abilities are even more amazing because he is mentally retarded. George cannot add, subtract, multiply, or divide even simple numbers (Horwitz et al., 1965). His strange talent is an example of the *savant syndrome,* in which an island of brilliance is found in a sea of retardation. In the savant syndrome, a person of limited intelligence shows exceptional mental ability in a narrow area, such as mental arithmetic, calendar calculations, art, or music (Miller, 1999; Treffert, 2000).

The striking contrast between George's general retardation and his unusual ability is a fitting introduction to the challenge of trying to define and measure intelligence. Quite frankly, we are still searching for answers to questions like these: Is intelligence a general trait or a collection of specific skills? Is intelligence affected by the genetic "wheel of fortune"? How much is it nurtured by environment? Is it possible to create an intelligence test that is fair to all people? How important is intelligence for "success"? Because our understanding of intelligence is rapidly changing, we cannot hope to give final answers to all these questions.

For the sake of clarity, let's first assume that intelligence *can* be measured. That way, we can use IQ scores to answer some important questions about intelligence. Later, we will consider questions that have been raised about intelligence tests and the meaning of their results.

Defining Intelligence—Intelligence Is . . . You Know, It's . . .

Intelligence cannot be seen, it has no mass, and it occupies no space. Nevertheless, we feel certain it exists. Let's compare two children:

> When she was 14 months old, Anne H. wrote her own name. She taught herself to read at age 2. At age 5, she astounded her kindergarten teacher by bringing a notebook computer to class—on which she was reading an encyclopedia. At 10 she breezed through an entire high school algebra course in 12 hours.
>
> Billy A., who is 10 years old, can write his name and can count, but he has trouble with simple addition and subtraction problems and finds multiplication impossible. He has been held back in school twice and is still incapable of doing the work his 8-year-old classmates find easy.

Anne is considered a genius; Billy, a slow learner. There seems little doubt that they differ in intelligence.

Wait! Anne's ability is obvious, but how do we know that Billy isn't just lazy? This is the same question that Alfred Binet faced in 1904 (Jarvin & Sternberg, 2003). The minister of education in Paris had asked Binet to find a way to distinguish slower students from the more capable (or the capable but lazy). In a flash of brilliance, Binet and an associate created a test made up of "intellectual" questions and problems. Next, they learned which questions an average child could answer at each age. By giving children the test, they could tell if a child was performing up to his or her potential (Kaufman, 2000).

Binet's approach gave rise to modern intelligence tests. At the same time, it launched nearly 100 years of heated debate. Part of the debate is related to the basic difficulty of defining intelligence (Sternberg, Grigorenko, & Kidd, 2005).

Modern intelligence tests are widely used to measure cognitive abilities. When properly administered, such tests provide an operational definition of intelligence.

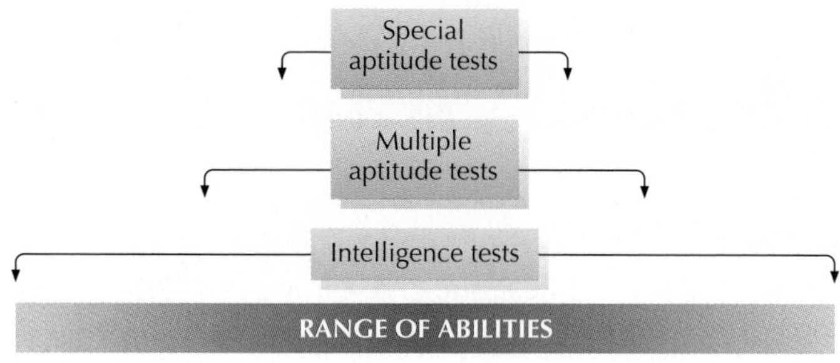

● **Figure 11.1** Special aptitude tests measure a person's potential for achievement in a limited area of ability, such as manual dexterity. Multiple aptitude tests measure potentials in broader areas, such as college work, law, or medicine. Intelligence tests measure a very wide array of aptitudes and mental abilities.

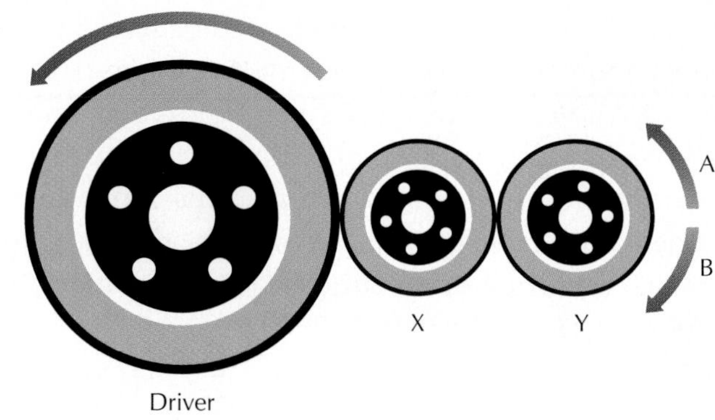

1. If the driver turns in the direction shown, which direction will wheel Y turn? A B

2. Which wheel will turn the slowest? Driver X Y

● **Figure 11.2** Sample questions like those found on tests of mechanical aptitude. (The answers are A and the Driver.)

Defining Intelligence

Is there an accepted definition of intelligence? In general, **intelligence** is the global capacity to act purposefully, to think rationally, and to deal effectively with the environment. Intelligence also involves reasoning, problem-solving ability, knowledge, memory, and successful adaptation to one's surroundings (Sternberg, 2004). Beyond this there is much disagreement. In fact, many psychologists simply accept an **operational definition** of intelligence, by spelling out the procedures they use to measure it. Thus, by selecting test items, a psychologist is saying in a very direct way, "This is what I mean by intelligence." A test that measures memory, reasoning, and verbal fluency offers a very different definition of intelligence than one that measures strength of grip, shoe size, length of the nose, or the person's best *Super Mario Brothers* video game score.

Aptitudes

As a child, Hedda displayed an aptitude for art. Today, Hedda is a successful graphic artist. How does an aptitude like Hedda's differ from general intelligence? An **aptitude** is a capacity for learning certain abilities. Persons with mechanical, artistic, or musical aptitudes are likely to do well in careers involving mechanics, art, or music, respectively (● Figure 11.1).

Are there tests for aptitudes? How are they different from intelligence tests? Aptitude tests measure a narrower range of abilities than intelligence tests do. For example, **special aptitude tests** predict whether you will succeed in a single area, such as clerical work or computer programming (● Figure 11.2). **Multiple aptitude tests** measure two or more types of ability. These tests tend to be more like intelligence tests. The well-known *Scholastic Assessment Test* (SAT), which measures aptitudes for language, math, and reasoning, is a multiple aptitude test. So are the tests required to enter graduate schools of law, medicine, business, and dentistry. The broadest aptitude measures are **general intelligence tests**, which assess a wide variety of mental abilities (Cohen & Swerdlik, 2005).

Reliability and Validity

Suppose that a deranged psychologist, Professor Ike Q. Tester, decides to write an intelligence test (the *I. Q. Tester IQ Test*). As a concerned citizen, there are two questions you should ask about Tester's test: "Is it *reliable*?" and "Is it *valid*?"

BRIDGES

Psychologists use a variety of aptitude tests to select people for employment and to advise people about choosing careers. **See Chapter 20, pages 664–665.**

What does reliability refer to? If you weigh yourself several times in a row, a reliable bathroom scale gives the same weight each time. Likewise, a **reliable** test must give approximately the same score each time a person takes it. In other words, the scores should be *consistent* and highly correlated. It is easy to see why unreliable tests have little value. Imagine a medical test for pregnancy or breast cancer, for instance, which gives positive and negative responses for the same woman on the same day.

To check the reliability of the *I. Q. Tester IQ Test,* we could give it to a large group of people. Then each person could be tested again a week later to establish *test-retest reliability.* We also might want to know if scores on one half of the test items match scores on the other half *(split-half reliability).* If Professor Tester decides to offer two versions of his test, we could compare scores on one version to scores on the other *(equivalent-forms reliability).*

By comparing such scores we find that the *Tester Test* is quite reliable. In fact, the scores are identical each time the test is given: Everyone scores zero (except Professor Tester, who scores 100 percent and thereby proclaims himself the only human with any intelligence).

Let's concede to Tester that his test is reliable (but for the wrong reasons). A more important question then becomes, "Is the test valid?" Now Tester becomes testy. He knows his test is invalid and that it will have to be withdrawn.

Obviously we have been playing with a silly example. A test has **validity** when it measures what it claims to measure. By no stretch of imagination could a test of intelligence be valid if the person who wrote it is the only one who can pass it.

How is validity established? Validity is usually demonstrated by comparing test scores to actual performance. This is called *criterion validity.* Scores on a test of legal aptitude, for example, might be compared to grades in law school. If high scores correlate with high grades, or some other standard (criterion) of success, the test might be valid. Unfortunately, many "free" tests you will encounter, such as those found in magazines and on the Internet, have little or no validity.

Tester's Last Stand

Let's return to Professor Tester for a final point. Although he admits that his test has problems, Professor Tester claims that at least it is *objective.* Is he right? Actually, he might be. If the *I. Q. Tester IQ Test* gives the same score when corrected by different people it is an **objective test.** However, objectivity is not enough to guarantee a fair test. Useful tests must also be *standardized.*

Test standardization refers to two things. First, it means that standard procedures are used in giving the test. The instructions, answer forms, amount of time to work, and so forth, are the same for everyone. Second, it means finding the **norm,** or average score, made by a large group of people like those for whom the test was designed. Without standardization, we couldn't fairly compare the scores of people taking the test at different times. And without norms, there would be no way to tell if a score is high, low, or average.

Later in this chapter we will address the question of whether intelligence tests are valid. For now, let's take a practical approach and learn about some popular standardized tests.

Testing Intelligence—The IQ and You

American psychologists quickly saw the value of Alfred Binet's test. In 1916, Lewis Terman and others at Stanford University revised it for use in North America. After more revisions, the *Stanford-Binet Intelligence Scales, Fifth Edition* continues to be widely used. The original Stanford-Binet assumed that a child's intellectual abilities improve with each passing year. Today, the Stanford-Binet (SB5) is still primarily made up of age-ranked questions. Naturally, these questions get a little harder at each age level. The SB5 is appropriate for people from age 2 to 90 years and scores on the test are very reliable (Roid, 2003).

Five Aspects of Intelligence

The SB5 measures five cognitive factors (types of mental abilities) that make up general intelligence. These are *fluid reasoning, knowledge, quantitative reasoning, visual-spatial processing,* and *working memory.* Each factor is measured with verbal questions (those involving words and numbers) and nonverbal questions (items that use pictures and objects). Let's see what each factor looks like.

Fluid Reasoning

This factor tests reasoning ability with questions like the following:

How are an apple, a plum, and a banana different from a beet?
An apprentice is to a master as a novice is to an ________.

Intelligence An overall capacity to think rationally, act purposefully, and deal effectively with the environment.

Operational definition The operations (actions or procedures) used to measure a concept.

Aptitude A capacity for learning certain abilities.

Special aptitude test Test to predict a person's likelihood of succeeding in a particular area of work or skill.

Multiple aptitude test Test that measures two or more aptitudes.

General intelligence test A test that measures a wide variety of mental abilities.

Reliability The ability of a test to yield the same score, or nearly the same score, each time it is given to the same person.

Validity The ability of a test to measure what it purports to measure.

Objective test A test that gives the same score when different people correct it.

Test standardization Establishing standards for administering a test and interpreting scores.

Norm An average score for a designated group of people.

Intelligence—How Would a Fool Do It?

Imagine being asked to sort some objects into categories. Wouldn't it be smart to separate the clothes, containers, implements, and foods into separate piles? Not necessarily. When members of the Kpelle culture in Liberia were asked to sort objects, they grouped them together by function. For example, a potato (food) would be placed together with a knife (implement). When the Kpelle were asked why they grouped the objects this way, they often said that's how a wise man would do it. The researchers finally asked the Kpelle, "How would a fool do it?" Only then did the Kpelle sort the objects into the nice, neat categories we Westerners prefer.

This anecdote, related by cultural psychologist Patricia Greenfield (1997), raises serious questions about the limits of intelligence testing. For example, the Cree people of Northern Canada value visual skills needed to find food on the frozen tundra (Darou, 1992). The Puluwat people in the South Pacific prize oceangoing navigation skills necessary to get from island to island (Sternberg, 2004). And so it goes, from culture to culture. Each culture teaches its children the kinds of "intelligence" valued in that culture—how the wise man would do it, not a fool (Correa-Chávez, Rogoff, & Arauz, 2005). In view of such differences, psychologists have tried to create "culture-fair" intelligence tests. Some have even stressed the need to rethink the concept of intelligence itself. We'll discuss both of these ideas in this chapter's Psychology in Action section.

> "I knew my bag was going to be in the last place I looked, so I looked there first." What is silly or impossible about that?

Other items ask people to fill in the missing shape in a group of shapes, and to tell a story that explains what's going on in a series of pictures.

Knowledge

This factor assesses the person's knowledge about a wide range of topics.

> Why is yeast added to bread dough?
> What does cryptic mean?
> What is silly or impossible about this picture? (For example, a bicycle has square wheels.)

Quantitative Reasoning

Test items for this factor measure a person's ability to solve problems involving numbers. Here are some samples:

> If I have six marbles and you give me another one, how many marbles will I have?
> Given the numbers 3, 6, 9, 12, what number would come next?
> If a shirt is being sold for 50 percent of the normal price, and the price tag is $60, what is the cost of the shirt?

Visual-Spatial Processing

People who have visual-spatial skills are good at putting picture puzzles together and copying geometric shapes (such as triangles, rectangles, and circles). Other questions ask test takers to reproduce patterns of blocks and choose pictures that show how a piece of paper would look if it were folded or cut. Verbal questions can also require visual-spatial abilities:

> Suppose that you are going east, then turn right, then turn right again, then turn left. In what direction are you facing now?

Working Memory

This part of the SB5 measures the ability to use short-term memory. Some typical memory tasks include:

> Correctly remember the order of colored beads on a stick.
> After hearing several sentences, name the last word from each sentence.
> Repeat a series of digits (forward or backward) after hearing them once.
> After seeing several objects, point to them in the same order as they were presented.

If you were to take the SB5, it would yield a score for general intelligence, verbal intelligence, nonverbal intelligence, and each of the five cognitive factors (Bain & Allin, 2005; Roid, 2003). For another perspective on the kinds of tasks used in the SB5, see "Intelligence—How Would a Fool Do It?"

Intelligence Quotients

Imagine that a child named Yuan can answer questions that an average 7-year-old can answer. How smart is she? Actually, we can't say yet, because we don't know how old Yuan is. If she is 10, she's not very smart. If she's 5, she is very bright. Thus, to estimate a child's intelligence we need to know both her **chronological age** (age in years) and her **mental age** (average intellectual performance).

Mental age is based on the level of age-ranked questions a person can answer. For example, at ages 8 or 9, very few children can define the word *connection*. At age 10, 10 percent can. At age 13, 60 percent can. Thus, a 13-year-old of average ability can define *connection.* If we had only this one item to test children with, those who answered correctly would be given a mental age of 13. When scores from many such items are combined, a child's overall mental age can be found. ■ Table 11.1 is a sample of items that persons of average intelligence can answer at various ages.

Mental age is a good measure of actual ability. But mental age says nothing about whether overall intelligence is high or low, compared with other people of the same age. To find out what a particular mental age means, we must also consider a person's chronological age. Then we can relate mental age to actual age. This yields an **IQ**, or **intelligence quotient.** A quotient results from dividing one number into another. When the Stanford-Binet was first used, IQ was defined as mental age (MA) divided by chronological age (CA) and multiplied by 100. (Multiplying by 100 changes the IQ into a whole number, rather than a decimal.)

$$\frac{\text{MA}}{\text{CA}} \times 100 = \text{IQ}$$

An advantage of the original IQ was that intelligence could be compared among children with different chronological and mental ages. For instance, 10-year-old Justin has a mental age of 12. Thus, his IQ is 120:

$$\frac{\text{(MA) } 12}{\text{(CA) } 10} \times 100 = 120 \text{ (IQ)}$$

Justin's friend Suke also has a mental age of 12. However, Suke's chronological age is 12, so his IQ is 100:

$$\frac{\text{(MA) } 12}{\text{(CA) } 12} \times 100 = 100 \text{ (IQ)}$$

The IQ shows that 10-year-old Justin is brighter than his 12-year-old friend Suke, even though their intellectual skills are about the same. Notice that a person's IQ will be 100 when mental age equals chronological age. An IQ score of 100 is therefore defined as average intelligence.

Then does a person with an IQ score below 100 have below average intelligence? Not unless the IQ is well below 100. An IQ of 100 is the *mathematical* average (or mean) for such scores. However, average intelligence is usually defined as any score from 90 to 109. The important point is that IQ scores will be over 100 when mental age is higher than age in years (● Figure 11.3). IQ scores below 100 occur when a person's age in years exceeds his or her mental age. An example of the second situation would be a 15-year-old with an MA of 12:

$$\frac{12}{15} \times 100 = 80 \text{ (IQ)}$$

TABLE 11.1

Sample Items from the Stanford-Binet Intelligence Scale

2 years old	On a large paper doll, points out the hair, mouth, feet, ears, nose, hands, and eyes. When shown a tower built of four blocks, builds one like it.
3 years old	When shown a bridge built of three blocks, builds one like it. When shown a drawing of a circle, copies it with a pencil.
4 years old	Fills in the missing word when asked, "Brother is a boy; sister is a ____________." "In daytime it is light; at night it is ____________." Answers correctly when asked, "Why do we have houses?" "Why do we have books?"
5 years old	Defines ball, hat, and stove. When shown a drawing of a square, copies it with a pencil.
9 years old	Answers correctly when examiner says, "In an old graveyard in Spain they have discovered a small skull which they believe to be that of Christopher Columbus when he was about 10 years old. What is foolish about that?" Answers correctly when asked, "Tell me the name of a color that rhymes with head." "Tell me a number that rhymes with tree."
Adult	Can describe the difference between laziness and idleness, poverty and misery, character and reputation. Answers correctly when asked, "Which direction would you have to face so your right hand would be toward the north?"

Source: L. Terman & M. Merrill, Stanford-Binet Intelligence Scale, 1937. Revised edition, 1960b. Houghton Mifflin Co.

AP/Wide World Photo

● **Figure 11.3** With a score of 230, Marilyn vos Savant has the highest IQ ever officially recorded. When she was only 7 years and 9 months old, vos Savant could answer questions that the average 13-year-old can answer. At ages 8, 9, and 10, she got perfect scores on the Stanford-Binet scale. Now in her 50s, she is a well-published author and recently became the host of an *Ask Marilyn* segment for CBS TV News.

Chronological age A person's age in years.

Mental age The average mental ability displayed by people of a given age.

Intelligence quotient (IQ) An index of intelligence defined as mental age divided by chronological age and multiplied by 100.

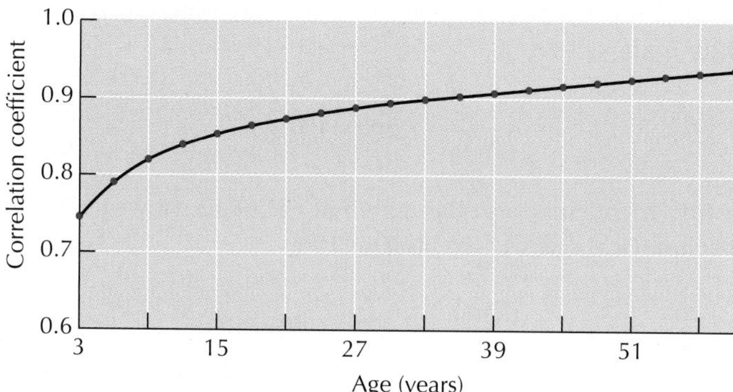

● **Figure 11.4** The stability or reliability of IQ scores increases rapidly in early childhood. Scores are very consistent from early adulthood to late middle age (Schuerger & Witt, 1989).

Deviation IQs

The preceding examples may give you insight into IQ scores. However, it's no longer necessary to directly calculate IQs. Instead, modern tests use **deviation IQs.** These scores are based on a person's relative standing in his or her age group. That is, they tell how far above or below average the person's score falls. (For more information, see the "Behavioral Statistics" appendix near the end of this book.) Tables supplied with the test are then used to convert a person's relative standing in the group to an IQ score (Neisser et al., 1996). For example, if you score at the 50th percentile, half the people your age who take the test score higher than you and half score lower. In this case, your IQ score is 100. If you score at the 84th percentile, your IQ score is 115. If you score at the 97th percentile, your IQ score is 130.

The Stability of IQ

How old do children have to be before their IQ scores become stable? IQ scores are not very dependable until about age 6 (Schuerger & Witt, 1989). IQ scores measured at age 2 correlate only .31 with those measured at age 18. In other words, knowing a child's IQ at age 2 tells us very little about what his or her IQ will be 16 years later. (Recall that a perfect correlation is 1.00 and a correlation of 0.00 occurs when scores are unrelated.) However, IQs do become more reliable as children grow older. After middle childhood, IQ scores usually change very little (Canivez & Watkins, 1998). The average change during retesting is only about 5 points in either direction (● Figure 11.4).

How much are IQs affected by age? IQs reflect a person's education, maturity, and experience, as well as innate intelligence. As a result, test scores show a small, gradual increase until about age 40 (Eichorn, Hunt, & Honzik, 1981). This trend, of course, is an average. Some

TABLE 11.2

Sample Items Similar to Those Used on the WAIS-III

VERBAL SUBTESTS	SAMPLE ITEMS
Information	How many wings does a bird have? Who wrote *Paradise Lost?*
Digit span	Repeat from memory a series of digits, such as 3 1 0 6 7 4 2 5, after hearing it once.
General	What is the advantage of keeping money in the bank?
Comprehension	Why is copper often used in electrical wires?
Arithmetic	Three men divided 18 golf balls equally among themselves. How many golf balls did each man receive? If 2 apples cost 15¢ what will be the cost of a dozen apples?
Similarities	In what way are a lion and a tiger alike? In what way are a saw and a hammer alike?
Vocabulary	The test consists simply of asking, "What is a ________?" or "What does ________ mean?" The words cover a wide range of difficulty or familiarity.
PERFORMANCE SUBTESTS	**DESCRIPTION OF ITEM**
Picture arrangement	Arrange a series of cartoon panels to make a meaningful story.
Picture completion	What is missing from these pictures?
Block design	Copy designs with blocks (as shown at right).
Object assembly	Put together a jigsaw puzzle.
Digit symbol	Fill in the symbols:

1	2	3	4
X	III	I	0

3	4	1	3	4	2	1	2

Courtesy of The Psychological Corporation.

TABLE 11.3

Items from the* Army Alpha *Subtest on "Common Sense"

The *Army Alpha* was given to World War I army recruits in the United States as a way to identify potential officers. In these sample questions, note the curious mixture of folk wisdom, scientific information, and moralism (Kessen & Cahan, 1986). Other parts of the test were more like modern intelligence tests.

Hulton-Deusch Collection/Corbis

1. If plants are dying for lack of rain, you should
   - water them
   - ask a florist's advice
   - put fertilizer around them
2. If the grocer should give you too much money in making change, what is the right thing to do?
   - buy some candy for him with it
   - give it to the first poor man you meet
   - tell him of his mistake
3. If you saw a train approaching a broken track you should
   - telephone for an ambulance
   - signal the engineer to stop the train
   - look for a piece of rail to fit in
4. Some men lose their breath on high mountains because
   - the wind blows their breath away
   - the air is too rare
   - it is always cold there
5. We see no stars at noon because
   - they have moved to the other side of the earth
   - they are much fainter than the sun
   - they are hidden behind the sky

people make fairly large gains in IQ, whereas others have sizable losses. How do the two groups differ? In general, those who gain in IQ are exposed to intellectual stimulation during early adulthood. Those who decline typically suffer from chronic illnesses, drinking problems, or unstimulating lifestyles (Honzik, 1984).

Some studies have found slow declines in IQ after middle age, whereas others indicate little or no change due to aging. As you may recall from Chapter 4, these contradictory results can be explained in this way: When we emphasize comprehension or general knowledge, IQs decline very little until advanced age. However, test items requiring perceptual speed or rapid insight decline rapidly after middle age (Brody, 1992; Lawrence, Myerson, & Hale, 1998). Overall, age-related losses are small for most healthy, well-educated individuals (Weintraub, 2003).

The most striking link between intelligence and aging occurs in the last years of life. Apparently, death is foreshadowed by changes in the brain. An abrupt **terminal decline** in IQ can be measured about 5 years before death, even when a person appears to be in good health (Suedfeld & Piedrahita, 1984).

The Wechsler Tests

Is the Stanford-Binet the only intelligence test? A widely used alternative is the *Wechsler Adult Intelligence Scale—Third Edition* (WAIS-III). A version for children is called the *Wechsler Intelligence Scale for Children—Third Edition* (WISC-III).

The Wechsler tests are similar to the Stanford-Binet, but different in important ways. For one thing, the WAIS-III was specifically designed to test adult intelligence. The original Stanford-Binet was better suited for children and adolescents. The latest Stanford-Binet (the SB5) can now be used for all ages, but the WAIS was the first "adult" IQ test. Like the Stanford-Binet, the Wechsler tests yield a single overall IQ. In addition, the WAIS and WISC give separate scores for **performance** (nonverbal) **intelligence** and **verbal** (language- or symbol-oriented) **intelligence.** (Note that this feature was also recently added to the SB5.) The abilities measured by the Wechsler tests and some sample test items are listed in ■ Table 11.2.

Group Tests

The SB5 and the Wechsler tests are **individual intelligence tests,** which are given to a single person by a trained specialist. In contrast, **group intelligence tests** can be given to a large group of people with minimal supervision. Group tests usually require people to read, to follow instructions, and to solve problems of logic, reasoning, mathematics, or spatial skills. The first group intelligence test was the *Army Alpha,* developed for World War I military inductees. As you can see in ■ Table 11.3, intelligence testing has come a long way since then.

Deviation IQ An IQ obtained statistically from a person's relative standing in his or her age group; that is, how far above or below average the person's score was relative to other scores.

Terminal decline An abrupt decline in measured intelligence about five years before death.

Performance intelligence Intelligence measured by solving puzzles, assembling objects, completing pictures, and other nonverbal tasks.

Verbal intelligence Intelligence measured by answering questions involving vocabulary, general information, arithmetic, and other language- or symbol-oriented tasks.

Individual intelligence test A test of intelligence designed to be given to a single individual by a trained specialist.

Group intelligence test Any intelligence test that can be administered to a group of people with minimal supervision.

Scholastic Aptitude Tests

If you're wondering if you have ever taken an intelligence test, the answer is probably yes. As mentioned earlier, the *Scholastic Assessment Test* is a multiple aptitude test. So are the *American College Test* (ACT) and the *College Qualification Test* (CQT). Each of these group tests is designed to predict your chances for success in college. Because the tests measure general knowledge and a variety of mental aptitudes, each can also be used to estimate intelligence.

KNOWLEDGE BUILDER

Intelligence Tests

REFLECT

If you were going to write an intelligence test, what kinds of questions would you ask? How much would your questions resemble those on standard intelligence tests? Would you want to measure any mental skills not covered by established tests?

LEARNING CHECK

1. The first successful intelligence test was developed by ______________________.
2. If we define intelligence by writing a test, we are using
   a. a circular definition c. an operational definition
   b. an abstract definition d. a chronological definition
3. Place an R or a V after each operation to indicate if it would be used to establish the reliability or the validity of a test.
   a. Compare score on one half of test items to score on the other half. ( )
   b. Compare scores on test to grades, performance ratings, or other measures. ( )
   c. Compare scores from the test after administering it on two separate occasions. ( )
   d. Compare scores on alternate forms of the test. ( )
4. IQ was originally defined as ______________ times 100.
5. The ability to answer general information and comprehension questions shows the most rapid decline during aging. T or F?
6. The WAIS-III is a group intelligence test. T or F?
7. Establishing norms and uniform procedures for administering a test are elements of standardization. T or F?
8. Scores on modern intelligence tests are based on one's deviation IQ (relative standing among test takers) rather than on the ratio between mental age and chronological age. T or F?

CRITICAL THINKING

9. A person who displays the savant syndrome might score well on a special ______________________ test, while scoring very low on an ______________________ test.

Answers: 1. Alfred Binet 2. c 3. a. (R), b. (V), c. (R), d. (R) 4. MA/CA 5. F 6. F 7. T 8. T 9. aptitude, intelligence

Variations in Intelligence—The Numbers Game

IQ scores are classified as shown in ■ Table 11.4. A look at the percentages reveals a definite pattern. The distribution (or scattering) of IQ scores approximates a **normal** (bell-shaped) **curve.** That is, most scores fall close to the average and very few are found at the extremes. ● Figure 11.5 shows this characteristic of measured intelligence.

TABLE 11.4

Distribution of Adult IQ Scores on the WAIS-III

IQ	DESCRIPTION	PERCENTAGE
Above 130	Very superior	2.2
120–129	Superior	6.7
110–119	Bright normal	16.1
90–109	Average	50.0
80–89	Dull normal	16.1
70–79	Borderline	6.7
Below 70	Mentally retarded	2.2

Sex

On the average, do males and females differ in intelligence? IQ scores cannot answer this question because test items were selected to be equally difficult for both sexes. However, men and women do not appear to differ in overall intelligence (Hyde, 2004). On the other hand, tests like the WAIS-III allow us to compare the intellectual strengths and weaknesses of men and women. For decades, women, as a group, performed best on items that require verbal ability, vocabulary, and rote learning. Men, in contrast, were best at items that require spatial visualization and math. Today, such male–female differences have almost disappeared among children and young adults. The small differences that remain appear to be based on a tendency for parents and educators to encourage males, more than females, to learn math and spatial skills.

IQ and Achievement

How do IQ scores relate to success in school, jobs, and other endeavors? IQ differences of a few points tell us little about a person. But if we look at a broader ranges of scores the differences do become

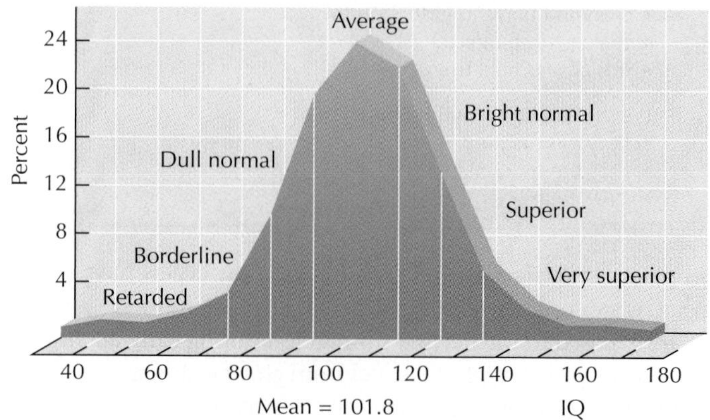

● **Figure 11.5** Distribution of Stanford-Binet Intelligence Test scores for 3,184 children. (After Terman & Merrill, 1960.)

meaningful. For example, a person with an IQ of 100 would probably struggle with college, whereas one with an IQ of 120 would do just fine.

The correlation between IQ and school grades is .50—a sizable association. If grades depended solely on IQ, the connection would be even stronger. However, motivation, special talents, off-campus educational opportunities, and many other factors influence grades and school success. The same is true of "real world" success beyond school. IQ is also not a good predictor of success in art, music, writing, dramatics, science, and leadership. Tests of creativity are much more strongly related to achievement in these areas (Neisser et al., 1996; Runco, 2004).

As you might expect, IQ is also related to job status. Persons holding white-collar, professional positions average higher IQs than those in blue-collar settings. For example, accountants, lawyers, and engineers average about 125 in IQ. In contrast, miners and farm workers average about 90 (Brody, 1992). It is important to note, however, that a range of IQ scores can be found in all occupations. Many people of high intelligence, because of choice or circumstance, have "low-ranking" jobs.

Does the link between IQ and occupation show that professional jobs require more intelligence? Not as clearly as you might think. Higher-status jobs often require an academic degree. As a result, hiring for professional jobs is biased in favor of a particular type of intelligence, namely, the kind measured by intelligence tests (McClelland, 1994; Neisser et al., 1996). This bias probably inflates the apparent association between professional jobs and IQ. The more IQ-like tests are used to select people for jobs, the stronger the association between IQ and job status. In fact, it can be argued that high-status groups use such tests to protect their "territory" (Tittle & Rotolo, 2000).

When IQs are extreme—below 70 or above 140—their link to an individual's potential for success becomes unmistakable. Only about 3 percent of the population falls in these ranges. Nevertheless, millions of people have exceptionally high or low IQs. Discussions of the mentally gifted and mentally retarded follow.

The Mentally Gifted—Smart, Smarter, Smartest

How high is the IQ of a genius? Only 2 people out of 100 score above 130 on IQ tests. These bright individuals are usually described as "gifted." Less than one half of one percent of the population scores above 140. These people are certainly gifted or perhaps even "geniuses." However, some psychologists reserve the term *genius* for people with even higher IQs or those who are exceptionally creative (Hallahan & Kauffman, 2006).

Gifted Children

Do high IQ scores in childhood predict later ability? To directly answer this question, Lewis Terman selected 1,500 children with IQs of 140 or more. Terman followed this gifted group (the "Termites," as he called them) into adulthood. By doing so, Terman corrected several popular misconceptions about high intelligence (Shurkin, 1992).

Misconception: The gifted tend to be peculiar, socially backward people.
Fact: On the contrary, Terman's gifted subjects, and gifted people in general, are socially skilled and above average in leadership (Feldhusen & Westby, 2003).
Misconception: Early ripe means later rot; the gifted tend to fizzle out as adults.
Fact: This is false. When they were retested as adults, Terman's subjects again scored in the upper IQ ranges.
Misconception: The very bright are physically inferior "eggheads," "nerds," or weaklings.
Fact: As a group, the gifted were above average in height, weight, and physical appearance.
Misconception: Highly intelligent persons are more susceptible to mental illness ("Genius is next to insanity").
Fact: Terman demonstrated conclusively that the gifted enjoy better than average mental health and a greater *resistance* to mental illness. In general, the highly gifted tend to be very well adjusted psychologically (Garland & Zigler, 1999; Norman et al., 1999).
Misconception: Intelligence has little to do with success, especially in practical matters.
Fact: The success of Terman's subjects was striking. Far more of them than average completed college, earned advanced degrees, and held professional positions. As a group, the gifted produced dozens of books, thousands of scientific articles, and hundreds of short stories and other publications (Shurkin, 1992; Terman & Oden, 1959). As noted earlier, IQ scores are not generally good predictors of real-world success. However, when scores are in the gifted range, the likelihood of outstanding achievement does seem to be higher.

Giftedness and Achievement

Were all of the gifted children superior as adults? No. Remember that high IQ reveals *potential*. It does not guarantee success. Marilyn vos Savant, with an IQ of 230, has contributed little to science, literature, or art. Nobel-prize-winning physicist Richard Feynman, whom many regard as a genius, had an IQ of 122 (Michalko, 1998). As adults, some of the Terman's gifted subjects committed crimes, were unemployable, or were unhappy misfits.

BRIDGES

One exception exists in which genius does seem to be linked with mental illness. Some of history's outstanding writers and composers appear to have suffered from bipolar disorder.
See Chapter 10, page 352.

Normal curve A bell-shaped curve characterized by a large number of scores in a middle area, tapering to very few extremely high and low scores.

How did the more successful gifted persons differ from the less successful? Most of the successful Termites had educated parents who valued learning and encouraged them to do the same. In general, successful gifted persons tend to have strong *intellectual determination*—a desire to know, to excel, and persevere (Winner, 2003). Gifted or not, most successful persons tend to be *persistent* and *motivated* to learn. No one is paid to sit around being *capable* of achievement. What you do is always more important than what you should be able to do. That's why a child's talents are most likely to blossom when they are nurtured with support, encouragement, education, and effort (Freeman, 1995).

Identifying Gifted Children

How might a parent spot an unusually bright child? Early signs of giftedness are not always purely "intellectual." **Giftedness** can be either the possession of a high IQ or special talents or aptitudes. The following signs may reveal that a child is gifted: A tendency to seek out older children and adults; an early fascination with explanations and problem solving; talking in complete sentences as early as 2 or 3 years of age; an unusually good memory; precocious talent in art, music, or number skills; an early interest in books, along with early reading (often by age 3); showing of kindness, understanding, and cooperation toward others (Alvino et al., 1996).

Notice that this list goes beyond straight "academic" intelligence. Children may be gifted in ways other than having a high IQ. In fact, if artistic talent, mechanical aptitude, musical aptitude, athletic potential, and so on, are considered, 19 out of 20 children have a special "gift" of one kind or another. Limiting giftedness to high IQ can shortchange children with special talents or potentials. This is especially true of ethnic minority children, who may be the victims of subtle biases in standardized intelligence tests. These children, as well as children with physical disabilities, are less likely to be recognized as gifted (Robinson & Clinkenbeard, 1998).

Dan McCoy/Rainbow

Christiana Dittmann/Rainbow

It is wise to remember that there are many ways in which a child may be gifted. Many schools now offer Gifted and Talented Education programs for students with a variety of special abilities—not just for those who score well on IQ tests.

Mobile Press Register/Getty Images

Michael Kearney is the youngest college graduate in the world. He attended high school at 5, earned an A.S. degree in geology at 8, and a B.A. degree in anthropology at age 10. Although it is clear that Michael is gifted, his rapid progress in school required motivation and effort. Also, his experience is atypical. Skipping grades can be risky because even bright children may feel out of place with older students.

GATE Programs

Being exceptionally bright is not without its problems. Usually, parents and teachers must make adjustments to help gifted children make the most of their talents (Silverman, 1998). The gifted child may become bored in classes designed for average children. This can lead to misbehavior or clashes with teachers who think the gifted child is a show-off or smart aleck. Extremely bright children may also find classmates less stimulating than older children or adults. In recognition of these problems, many schools now provide special Gifted and Talented Education (GATE) classes for gifted children. Such programs combine classroom enrichment with fast-paced instruction to satisfy the gifted child's appetite for intellectual stimulation (Gottfried & Gottfried, 1994). Since 1988, the federally funded Jacob K. Javits Gifted and Talented Children and Youth Education Act has provided funds for research into gifted and talented education programs.

In the next section, we will discuss mental retardation. Before you begin, take a few moments to read "Autistic Savants—Fragile Genius," where you will find information about a strange mixture of brilliance and mental disability.

BRIDGES

All children benefit from enriched environments.

For a discussion of enrichment and some guidelines for parents, see Chapter 3, pages 89–90.

THE CLINICAL FILE: Autistic Savants—Fragile Genius

Meet Kim Peek, who is an autistic savant like George, the calendar calculator mentioned earlier. Kim, who served as the model for Dustin Hoffman's character in the movie *Rain Man,* began to memorize books at 18 months of age. To date, Kim has completely memorized 9,000 books. He also knows all of the zip codes and area codes in the United States, and can provide accurate travel directions between any two major U.S. cities. Upon hearing any of hundreds of pieces of classical music, he can instantly discuss the music in detail, name the composer, and tell when and where the piece was composed and first performed. In middle age, Kim is even learning to play all of that music (Treffert & Christensen, 2005).

Once, four months after reading a Tom Clancy novel, *The Hunt for Red October,* Kim was asked about a character, a Russian radio operator. He immediately named the character, gave the page number on which a description appeared, and accurately recited several paragraphs about the character (Treffert & Christensen, 2005).

Other savants have exceptional abilities in music, mechanics, math, and remembering names or numbers. At the same time, each of these people is of very low general intelligence or suffers from autism (Detterman & Ruthsatz, 1999; Miller, 1999). In most respects they are "slow." Kim Peek, for example, has poor coordination and cannot even button his own clothes. He also has difficulty with abstract thought (Treffert & Christensen, 2005).

Do savants have special mental powers not shared by most people? One theory holds that the performances of many savants result from intense practice (Miller, 1999). Take George's amazing knowledge of dates, for instance. Perpetual calendars have only 14 different yearly "templates." Many calendar calculators memorize the 14 templates and learn how to tell which one applies to a particular year. This allows persons of below normal intelligence to perform an impressive mental feat. But intense practice can't explain a talent such as Kim's prodigious memory.

Another possibility is that some mental disabilities free savants from the "distractions" of language, concepts, and higher-level thought. This allows them to focus with crystal clarity on music, drawing, prime numbers, license plates, TV commercials, and other specific information. Although the savant syndrome hasn't been fully explained, it shows that extraordinary abilities can exist apart from general intelligence. Perhaps each of us harbors embers of mental brilliance that intense practice could fan into full flame.

Mental Retardation—A Difference That Makes a Difference

A person with mental abilities far below average is termed **mentally retarded** or **developmentally disabled.** Retardation begins at an IQ of approximately 70 or below. However, a person's ability to perform *adaptive behaviors* (basic skills such as dressing, eating, communicating, shopping, and working) also figures into evaluating retardation (*DSM-IV-TR,* 2000; Hallahan & Kauffman, 2006).

Levels of Retardation

Below an IQ of 70, retardation is classified as shown in ■ Table 11.5. The listed IQ ranges are approximate because IQ scores normally vary a few points. The terms in the right-hand column are

Giftedness Either the possession of a high IQ or special talents or aptitudes.

Mental retardation The presence of a developmental disability, an IQ score below 70, or a significant impairment of adaptive behavior.

TABLE 11.5

Levels of Mental Retardation

IQ RANGE	DEGREE OF RETARDATION	EDUCATIONAL CLASSIFICATION	REQUIRED LEVEL OF SUPPORT
50–55 to 70	Mild	Educable	Intermittent
35–40 to 50–55	Moderate	Trainable	Limited
20–25 to 35–40	Severe	Dependent	Extensive
Below 20–25	Profound	Life support	Pervasive

DSM-IV-TR, 2000

listed only to give you a general impression of each IQ range. Unless they are used cautiously, such terms can needlessly limit the educational goals of retarded persons (*DSM-IV-TR,* 2000).

Are the retarded usually placed in institutions? No. Total care is only necessary for the *profoundly* retarded (IQ below 25). Many of these individuals live in group homes or with their families. The *severely* retarded (IQ of 25–40) and *moderately* retarded (IQ of 40–55) are capable of mastering basic language and self-help skills. Many become self-supporting by working in sheltered workshops (special simplified work environments). The *mildly* retarded (IQ of 55–70) make up about 85 percent of all those affected. This group can benefit from carefully structured education. As adults, these persons, as well as the *borderline retarded* (IQ 70–85), are capable of living alone and they may marry. However, they tend to have difficulties with many of the demands of adult life (Zetlin & Murtaugh, 1990).

Causes of Retardation

What causes mental retardation? In 30 to 40 percent of cases, no known biological problem can be identified. In many such instances the degree of retardation is mild, in the 50–70 IQ range.

Stan Godlweski/Getty Images

These youngsters are participants in the Special Olympics—an athletic event for the mentally retarded. It is often said of the Special Olympics that "everyone is a winner—participants, coaches, and spectators."

Often, other family members are also mildly retarded. **Familial retardation**, as this is called, occurs mostly in very poor households, where nutrition, intellectual stimulation, medical care, and emotional support may be inadequate. This suggests that familial retardation is based largely on an impoverished environment. Thus, better nutrition, education, and early childhood enrichment programs could prevent many cases of retardation (Hunt, 1995).

Organic Sources of Retardation

About half of all cases of mental retardation are *organic,* or related to physical disorders (Das, 2000). These include *birth injuries* (such as lack of oxygen during delivery), and *fetal damage* (prenatal damage from disease, infection, or drugs). *Metabolic disorders,* which affect energy production and use in the body, also cause retardation. Some forms of retardation are linked to *genetic abnormalities,* such as missing genes, extra genes, or defective genes. Malnutrition and exposure to lead, PCBs, and other toxins early in childhood can also cause organic retardation (Bryant & Maxwell, 1999). Let's briefly look at several distinctive problems.

Phenylketonuria (PKU)

The problem called **phenylketonuria** (FEN-ul-KEET-uh-NURE-ee-ah) is a genetic disease. Children who have PKU lack an important enzyme. This causes phenylpyruvic (FEN-ul-pye-ROO-vik) acid (a destructive chemical) to collect within their bodies. PKU is also linked to very low levels of dopamine, an important chemical messenger in the brain. If PKU goes untreated, severe retardation typically occurs by age 3.

PKU can be detected in newborn babies by routine medical testing. Affected children are usually placed on a diet low in phenylalinine, the substance the child's body can't handle. Carefully following this diet will usually prevent retardation. (Phenylalinine is present in many foods. You might be interested to know that it is also found in Aspartame, the artificial sweetener in diet colas.)

Microcephaly

The word **microcephaly** (MY-kro-SEF-ah-lee) means small-headedness. The microcephalic person suffers a rare abnormality in which the skull is extremely small or fails to grow. This forces the brain to develop in a limited space, causing severe retardation. Although they are typically institutionalized, microcephalic persons are usually affectionate, well-behaved, and cooperative.

Hydrocephaly

Hydrocephaly (HI-dro-SEF-ah-lee: "water on the brain") is caused by a buildup of cerebrospinal fluid within brain cavities. Pressure from this fluid can damage the brain and enlarge the head. Hydrocephaly is not uncommon—about 10,000 hydocephalic babies are born each year in the United States and Canada. However, thanks to new medical procedures, most of these infants will lead nearly normal lives. A surgically implanted tube drains fluid from the brain into the abdomen and minimizes brain damage. Although affected children score below average on mental tests, severe retardation usually can be prevented (Rourke et al., 2002).

Cretinism

Cretinism (KREET-un-iz-um) is another type of retardation that appears in infancy. It results from an insufficient supply of thyroid hormone. In some parts of the world, cretinism is caused by a lack of iodine in the diet (the thyroid glands require iodine to function normally). Iodized salt has made this source of retardation rare in developed nations. Cretinism causes stunted physical and intellectual growth that cannot be reversed. Fortunately, cretinism is easily detected in infancy. Once detected, it can be treated with thyroid hormone replacement, before permanent damage occurs.

Down Syndrome

In 1 out of 800 babies, the disorder known as **Down syndrome** causes moderate to severe retardation and a shortened life expectancy of around 49 years. Distinctive features of this problem are almond-shaped eyes, a slightly protruding tongue, a stocky build, and stubby hands with deeply creased palms.

It is now known that Down syndrome children have an extra 21st chromosome. This condition, which is called trisomy-21, results from flaws in the parents' egg or sperm cells. Thus, while Down syndrome is *genetic,* it is not usually *hereditary* (it doesn't "run in the family").

The age of parents is a major factor in Down syndrome. As people age, their reproductive cells are more prone to errors during cell division. This raises the odds that an extra chromosome will be present. As you can see in the following figures, the older a women is, the greater the risk:

Mother's age	Incidence of Down syndrome
Early 20s	1/2000
Early 40s	1/105
Late 40s	1/12

Fathers, and possibly especially older fathers, also add to the risk; in a small percentage of cases the father is the source of the extra chromosome (Savage et al., 1998). Older adults who plan to have children should carefully consider the odds shown here.

There is no "cure" for Down syndrome. However, these children are usually loving and responsive, and they make progress in a caring environment. At a basic level, Down syndrome children can do most of the things that other children can, only slower. The best hope for Down syndrome children, therefore, lies in specially tailored educational programs that enable them to lead fuller lives.

Fragile-X Syndrome

The second most common form of genetic mental retardation (after Down syndrome) is **fragile-X syndrome** (Hallahan & Kauffman, 2006). Unlike Down syndrome, fragile-X syndrome is hereditary—it *does* run in families. The problem is related to a thin, frail-looking area on the *X* (female) chromosome. Because fragile-X is sex linked (like color blindness), boys are most often affected, at a rate of about 1 out of every 1,200 (Rose, 1995).

Fragile-X males generally have long, thin faces and big ears. Physically, they are usually larger than average during childhood, but smaller than average after adolescence. Up to three fourths of all fragile-X males suffer from hyperactivity and attention disorders. Many also have a peculiar tendency to avoid eye contact with others.

Fragile-X males are only mildly retarded during early childhood, but they are often severely or profoundly retarded as adults. When learning adaptive behaviors, they tend to do better with daily living skills than with language and social skills (Hallahan & Kauffman, 2006).

Retardation in Perspective

It is important to remember that developmentally disabled persons are not handicapped where their feelings are concerned. They are sensitive to rejection and easily hurt by teasing or ridicule. Likewise, they respond warmly to love and acceptance. Everyone has a right to self-respect and a place in the community. This is especially important during childhood, when the support of others adds greatly to the retarded person's chances of becoming a well-adjusted member of society.

KNOWLEDGE BUILDER

Variations in Intelligence

REFLECT

If you measure the heights of all the people in your psychology class, most people will be clustered around an average height. Very few will be extremely tall or extremely short. Does this ring a bell? Do you think it's normal? (It is, of course; most measured human characteristics form a normal curve, just as IQs do.)

Do you think that giftedness should be defined by high IQ or having special talents (or both)? To increase your chances of succeeding in today's society, would you prefer to be smart or

Familial retardation Mild mental retardation associated with homes that are intellectually, nutritionally, and emotionally impoverished.

Phenylketonuria A genetic disease that allows phenylpyruvic acid to accumulate in the body.

Microcephaly A disorder in which the head and brain are abnormally small.

Hydrocephaly A buildup of cerebrospinal fluid within brain cavities.

Cretinism Stunted growth and mental retardation caused by an insufficient supply of thyroid hormone.

Down syndrome A genetic disorder caused by the presence of an extra chromosome; results in mental retardation.

Fragile-X syndrome A genetic form of mental retardation caused by a defect in the *X* chromosome.

talented (or both)? How about smart, talented, motivated, and lucky!?

As a psychologist you are asked to assess a child's degree of retardation. Will you rely more on IQ or the child's level of adaptive behavior? Would you be more confident in your judgment if you took both factors into account?

LEARNING CHECK

1. The distribution of IQs approximates a ________________ ______ (bell-shaped) curve.
2. The association between IQ and high-status professional jobs proves that such jobs require more intelligence. T or F?
3. Differences in the intellectual strengths of men and women have grown larger in recent years. T or F?
4. Only about 6 percent of the population scores above 140 on IQ tests. T or F?
5. An IQ score below 90 indicates mental retardation. T or F?
6. Many cases of mental retardation without known organic causes appear to be ________________.

Match:

7. ____ PKU
8. ____ Microcephaly
9. ____ Hydrocephaly
10. ____ Cretinism
11. ____ Down syndrome
12. ____ Fragile-X

A. Too little thyroid hormone
B. Very small brain
C. 47 chromosomes
D. Lack of an important enzyme
E. Excess of cerebrospinal fluid
F. Abnormal female chromosome
G. Caused by a lack of oxygen at birth

CRITICAL THINKING

13. Lewis Terman took great interest in the lives of many of the "Termites." He even went so far as to advise them about what kinds of careers they should pursue. What error of observation did Terman make?

Answers: **1.** normal **2.** F **3.** F **4.** F **5.** F **6.** familial **7.** D **8.** B **9.** E **10.** A **11.** C **12.** F **13.** Terman may have unintentionally altered the behavior of the people he was studying. Although Terman's observations are generally regarded as valid, he did break a basic rule of scientific observation.

Heredity and Environment—Super Rats and Family Trees

Is intelligence inherited? This seemingly simple question is loaded with controversy. Some psychologists believe that intelligence is strongly affected by heredity. Others feel that environment is dominant. Let's examine some evidence for each view.

In a classic study of genetic factors in learning, Tryon (1929) managed to breed separate strains of "maze-bright" and "maze-dull" rats (animals that were extremely "bright" or "stupid" at learning mazes). After several generations of breeding, the slowest "super rat" outperformed the best "dull" rat. This and other studies of **eugenics** (selective breeding for desirable characteristics) suggest that some traits are highly influenced by heredity.

That may be true, but is maze-learning really a measure of intelligence? No, it isn't. Tryon's study seemed to show that intelligence is inherited, but later researchers found that the "bright" rats were simply more motivated by food and less easily distracted during testing. When they weren't chasing after rat chow, the "bright" rats were no more intelligent than the supposedly dull rats. Thus, Tryon's study did demonstrate that behavioral characteristics can be influenced by heredity. However, it was inconclusive concerning intelligence. Because of such problems, animal studies cannot tell us with certainty how heredity and environment affect intelligence. Let's see what human studies reveal.

Hereditary Influences

Most people are aware of a moderate similarity in the intelligence between parents and their children, or between brothers and sisters. As ● Figure 11.6 shows, the closer two people are on a family tree, the more alike their IQs are likely to be.

Does that indicate that intelligence is hereditary? Not necessarily. Brothers, sisters, and parents share similar environments as well as similar genes (Grigorenko, 2005). To separate heredity and environment, we need to make some selected comparisons.

Twin Studies

Notice in ● Figure 11.6 that the IQ scores of fraternal twins are more alike than those of ordinary brothers and sisters. **Fraternal twins** come from two separate eggs fertilized at the same time. They are no more genetically alike than ordinary siblings. Why then, should the twins' IQ scores be more similar? The reason is environmental: Parents treat twins more alike than ordinary siblings, resulting in a closer match in IQs.

More striking similarities are observed with **identical twins**, who develop from a single egg and have identical genes. At the top of ● Figure 11.6 you can see that identical twins who grow up in the same family have highly correlated IQs. This is what we would expect with identical heredity and very similar environments. Now, let's consider what happens when identical twins are reared apart. As you can see, the correlation drops, but only from .86 to .72. Psychologists who emphasize genetics believe figures like these show that differences in adult intelligence are roughly 50 percent hereditary (Casto, DeFries, & Fulker, 1995; Neisser et al., 1996).

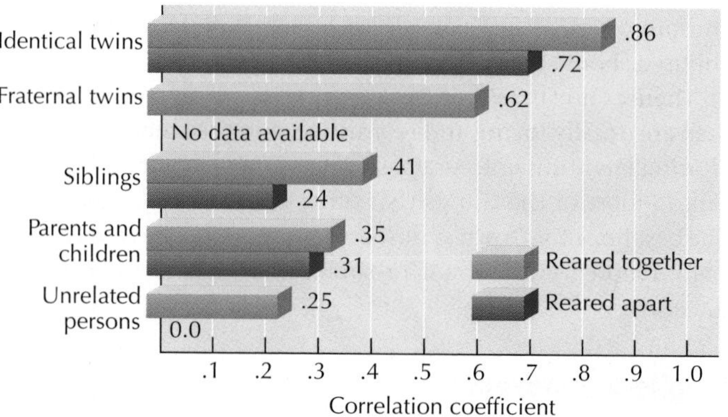

● **Figure 11.6** Approximate correlations between IQ scores for persons with varying degrees of genetic and environmental similarity. Notice that the correlations grow smaller as the degree of genetic similarity declines. Also note that a shared environment increases the correlation in all cases. (Estimates from Bouchard, Jr., 1983; Henderson, 1982.)

How do environmentalists interpret the figures? They point out that some separated identical twins differ by as much as 20 IQ points. In every case where this occurs there are large educational and environmental differences between the twins. Also, separated twins are almost always placed in homes socially and educationally similar to those of their birth parents. This would tend to inflate apparent genetic effects by making the separated twins' IQs more alike. Another frequently overlooked fact is that twins grow up in the same environment *before birth* (in the womb). If this environmental similarity is taken into account, intelligence would seem to be less than 50 percent hereditary (Devlin, Daniels, & Roeder, 1997).

Environmental Influences

Strong evidence for an environmental view of intelligence comes from families having one adopted child and one biological child. As ● Figure 11.7 shows, parents contribute genes *and* environment to their biological child. With an adopted child they contribute only environment. If intelligence is highly genetic, the IQs of biological children should be more like their parents' IQs than the IQs of adopted children are. However, studies show that children reared by the same mother resemble her in IQ to the same degree. It doesn't matter whether they share her genes (Kamin, 1981; Weinberg, 1989).

Another way to see environmental effects is to compare children adopted by parents of high or low socio-economic status. As you might predict, children who grow up in high-status homes develop higher IQs than those reared by lower-status parents. Presumably, the higher socio-economic homes provide an enriched environment, with better nutrition, greater educational opportunities, and other advantages (Capron & Duyme, 1992).

IQ and Environment

How much can environment alter intelligence? In one study, striking increases in IQ occurred in 25 children who were moved from an orphanage and were eventually adopted by parents who gave them love, a family, and a stimulating home environment. Once considered mentally retarded and unadoptable, the children gained an average of 29 IQ points. A second group of initially less "retarded" children, who stayed in the orphanage, *lost* an average of 26 IQ points (Skeels, 1966)! In another study, placing normal black children into adoptive families increased the children's IQs by an average of 13 points (Nisbett, 2005), bringing them into line with those of white children.

A particularly dramatic environmental effect is the Flynn effect, the fact that 14 nations have shown average IQ gains of from

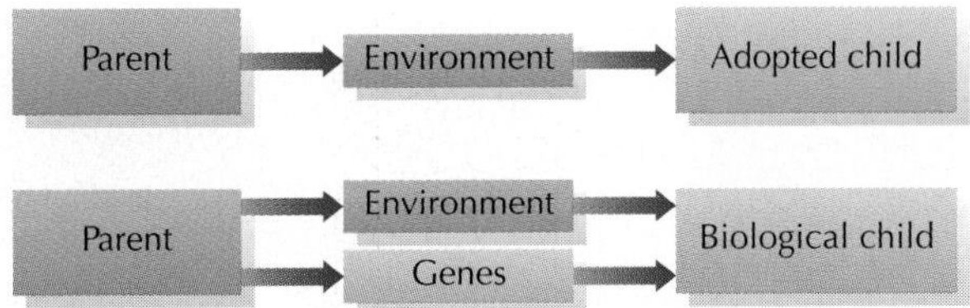

● **Figure 11.7** Comparison of an adopted child and a biological child reared in the same family. (After Kamin, 1981.)

5 to 25 points during the last 30 years (Dickens & Flynn, 2001; Flynn, 1990). These IQ boosts, averaging 15 points, occurred in far too short a time for genetics to explain them. It is more likely that the gains reflect environmental forces, such as improved education, nutrition, and living in a technologically complex society (Johnson, 2005). If you've ever tried to play a computer game or set up a wireless network in your home, you'll understand why people may be getting better at answering IQ test questions (Neisser, 1997). The highlight "You Mean Video Games Might Be Good for Me?" explores this idea further.

If environment makes a difference, can intelligence be taught? The traditional answer is "no." Brief coaching, for instance, has little positive effect on aptitude and intelligence test scores (Brody, 1992). More encouraging results can be found in **early childhood education programs,** which provide longer-term stimulating intellectual experiences for disadvantaged children. In one study, children from low-income families were given enriched environments from early infancy through preschool. By age 2 their IQ scores were already higher than those in a control group. More important, they were still 5 points higher 7 years later (Campbell & Ramey, 1994). High-quality enrichment programs such as Head Start can prevent children from falling behind in school (Barnet & Barnet, 1998; Ramey, Ramey, & Lanzi, 2001).

Later schooling can also have an impact on IQ. Stephen Ceci found that people who leave school lose up to 6 points in IQ per year. Dropping out of school in the eighth grade can reduce a person's adult IQ by up to 24 points. Conversely, IQ rises as people spend more time in school (Ceci, 1991). Israeli psychologist Reuven Feuerstein (FOY-er-shtine) and his colleagues have developed a program they call Instrumental Enrichment. Through hundreds of hours of guided problem solving, students learn to avoid the thinking flaws that lower IQ scores (Feuerstein et al., 1986). Feuerstein and others have shown that such training can improve thinking abilities and even raise IQs (Feuerstein et al., 2004; Skuy et al., 2002; Tzuriel & Shamir, 2002).

BRIDGES

Identical twins also tend to have similar personality traits. This suggests that heredity contributes to personality, as well as intelligence.

See Chapter 14, pages 466–468.

Eugenics Selective breeding for desirable characteristics.

Fraternal twins Twins conceived from two separate eggs.

Identical twins Twins who develop from a single egg and have identical genes.

Early childhood education program Programs that provide stimulating intellectual experiences, typically for disadvantaged preschoolers.

CRITICAL THINKING

You Mean Video Games Might Be Good for Me?

The *Flynn effect* suggests that environmental factors influence intelligence (Schooler, 1998). However, we are left with the question, "Which factors?" Psychologist Steven Johnson (2005) believes that contemporary culture is responsible. Although he agrees that much popular media content is too violent or sexual in nature (see Chapter 8, "You Mean Video Games Might Be Bad for Me?"), he points out that video games, the Internet, and even television are becoming more complex. As a result, they demand ever greater cognitive effort from us. In other words, it is as important to understand *how* we experience the environment as it is to understand *what* we experience.

For example, early video games, such as Pong or PacMan, offered simple, repetitive visual experiences. In contrast, today's best-selling games, such as *Halo 2* or *The Sims,* offer rich, complicated experiences that can take forty or more hours of intense problem solving to complete. Furthermore, players must usually figure out the rules by themselves. Instructions for completing popular games, which have been created by fans, are typically much longer than chapters in this textbook. Only a complex and engaging game would prompt players to use such instructions, much less write them for others to use (Johnson, 2005).

According to Johnson, other forms of popular culture have also become more complex, including the Internet and computer software. Even popular television has become more cognitively demanding. For example, compared with television dramas of the past, modern dramas weave plot lines and characters through an entire season of programs. In the end, popular culture may well be inviting us to read, reflect, and problem solve more than ever before.

With our growing understanding of how people think, and with the tireless aid of computers, it may become common in schools to "teach intelligence." Most important, improved education and training in thinking skills can improve the intellectual abilities of all children, regardless of what their IQ scores are (Hunt, 1995; Perkins, 1995). Even if "teaching intelligence" doesn't raise IQ scores, it can give children the abilities they need to think better and succeed in life (Perkins & Grotzer, 1997).

Summary

To sum up, few psychologists seriously believe that heredity is not a major factor in intelligence, and all acknowledge that environment affects it. Estimates of the impact of heredity and environment continue to vary. But ultimately both camps agree that improving social conditions and education can raise intelligence.

There is probably no limit to how far *down* intelligence can go in an extremely poor environment. On the other hand, heredity does seem to impose upper limits on IQ, even under ideal conditions. It is telling, nevertheless, that gifted children tend to come from homes where parents spend time with their children, an-

● **Figure 11.8** Attempts to measure the speed of mental processing have taken several forms. In this example, the person must make a rapid choice based on the position of a colored stimulus flashed on a computer screen. A faster reaction time is assumed to reflect faster processing of information. In some experiments brain responses are measured directly, through electrodes attached to the scalp.

BRIDGES

Impoverished and unstimulating environments can severely restrict mental development during early childhood.

See Chapter 3, pages 89–90, for more information.

FOCUS ON RESEARCH

Inspecting Intelligence

Look quickly at ● Figure 11.9*a*. Which "leg" of the drawing is longer, the right or the left? It's a pretty easy question, isn't it? However, if similar drawings are flashed on a screen for only a split second, the task becomes much harder. And, strange as it may seem, it may reveal something about intelligence (Petrill et al., 2001).

Stimuli like those in ● Figure 11.9 are used to measure **inspection time**—the amount of time a person must inspect (look at) a stimulus to make a correct judgment about it. In a real inspection time task, a stimulus like the one on the left appears for a few milliseconds. It is then followed immediately by a second stimulus, like 11.9*b*. (The second stimulus keeps people from using afterimages or sensory memory to make decisions about the first stimulus.)

In inspection time studies, we want to know how quickly a person's nervous system can take in enough information to make a correct decision. As simple as this measure may seem, it correlates about −.45 with IQ scores. (The correlation is negative because shorter inspection times are associated with higher IQs.) Similar findings have also been obtained in studies of auditory inspection times (Bates, 2005; McCrory & Cooper, 2005).

In addition, brain areas that control higher mental abilities become more active during inspection time testing (Deary et al., 2001). Such observations suggest that having a quick nervous system is part of what it means to be quick, smart, swift, or brainy (Grudnik & Kranzler, 2001; Osmon & Jackson, 2002).

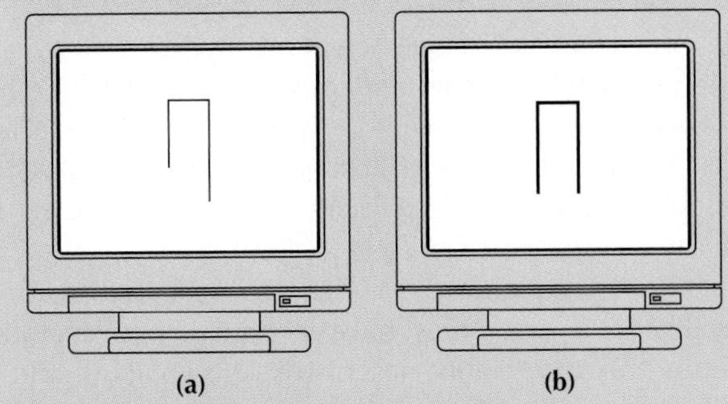

● **Figure 11.9** Stimuli like those used in inspection time tasks.

swer their questions, and encourage intellectual exploration (Snowden & Christian, 1999).

The fact that intelligence is partly determined by heredity tells us little of any real value. Genes are fixed at birth. Improving the environments in which children learn and grow is the main way in which we can assure that they reach their full potential (Turkheimer, 1998).

As a final summary, it might help to think of inherited intellectual potential as a rubber band that is stretched by outside forces. A long rubber band may be stretched more easily, but a shorter one can be stretched to the same length if enough force is applied. Of course, a superior genetic gift may allow for a higher maximum IQ. In the final analysis, intelligence reflects development as well as potential, nurture as well as nature (Grigorenko, 2005; Rose, 1995).

New Approaches to Intelligence—Intelligent Alternatives

Until now, we have treated intelligence as a quality that can be measured, like height or weight. Recently, three new ways of looking at intelligence have emerged:

- Some psychologists are investigating the neural basis for intelligence. How, they ask, does the nervous system contribute to differences in IQ?
- A second new approach views intelligent behavior as an expression of thinking skills. Cognitive psychologists believe that the nervous system is like a fast computer—it's of little value unless you know how to use it.
- A third trend involves newer, broader definitions of intelligence. Many psychologists have begun to question the narrow focus on analytic thinking found in traditional IQ tests (Perkins, 1995).

The Intelligent Nervous System

Do intelligent people have faster nervous systems? In an attempt to answer this question, researchers are measuring how fast people process various kinds of information (Bates, 2005). For example, psychologists have looked at how long it takes people to react when making a choice (● Figure 11.8). The flurry of brain activity that follows exposure to a stimulus has also been recorded. Such studies attempt to measure a person's **speed of processing**, which is assumed to reflect the brain's speed and efficiency (Budak et al., 2005; Deary & Stough, 1996; Reed, Vernon, & Johnson, 2004).

Inspection time The amount of time a person must look at a stimulus to make a correct judgment about it.

Speed of processing The speed with which a person can mentally process information.

Does rapid information processing really have anything to do with intelligence? See "Inspecting Intelligence" for an answer.

Intelligent Information Processing

Much intelligent behavior is an expression of good thinking skills. Cognitive psychologist David Perkins believes that how smart you are depends on three factors:

- Relatively fixed **neural intelligence** (the speed and efficiency of the nervous system)
- **Experiential intelligence** (specialized knowledge and skills acquired over time)
- **Reflective intelligence** (an ability to become aware of one's own thinking habits)

Little can be done to change neural intelligence. However, by adding to personal knowledge and learning to think better, people can become more intelligent (Perkins, 1995). The effects of Feuerstein's Instrumental Enrichment program (described earlier) are a good example of how reflective intelligence can be improved.

Many psychologists now believe that to make full use of innate intelligence a person must have good **metacognitive skills.** *Meta* means "beyond," so metacognitive skills go above and beyond ordinary thinking. Such skills involve an ability to manage your own thinking and problem solving. Typically this means breaking problems into parts, establishing goals and subgoals, monitoring your progress, and making corrections. Learning metacognitive skills is the surest avenue to becoming more intelligent (Hunt, 1995).

Multiple Intelligences

At an elementary school, a student who is two grades behind in reading shows his teacher how to solve a difficult computer programming problem. In a nearby room, one of his classmates, who is poor in math, plays an intricate piece of music on a piano. Both of these children show clear signs of intelligence. Yet each might score below average on a traditional IQ test. Such observations have convinced many psychologists that it is time to forge new, broader definitions of intelligence. Their basic goal is to better predict "real-world" success—not just the likelihood of success in school (Sternberg, 1996).

Frames of Mind

One such psychologist is Howard Gardner of Harvard University. Gardner (1993, 1999, 2003) theorizes that there are actually eight different kinds of intelligence. These are different mental "languages" that people use for thinking. Each is listed below, with examples of pursuits that make use of them.

1. *language* (linguistic abilities)—writer, lawyer, comedian
2. *logic and math* (numeric abilities)—scientist, accountant, programmer
3. *visual and spatial thinking* (pictorial abilities)—engineer, inventor, artist
4. *music* (musical abilities)—composer, musician, music critic
5. *bodily-kinesthetic skills* (physical abilities)—dancer, athlete, surgeon
6. *intrapersonal skills* (self-knowledge)—poet, actor, minister
7. *interpersonal skills* (social abilities)—psychologist, teacher, politician
8. *naturalist skills* (an ability to understand the natural environment)—biologist, medicine man, organic farmer

To simplify a great deal, people can be "word smart," "number smart," "picture smart," "musically smart," "body smart," "self smart," "people smart," and "nature smart." In addition, Gardner (1999, 2003) has recently explored the idea that a ninth type of intelligence exists. People who have *existential intelligence* think about ultimate concerns, such as the meaning of life, love, death, and the human condition. Great thinkers such as Aristotle, Confucius, Plato, and Socrates had high levels of existential intelligence.

Most of us are probably strong in only a few types of intelligence. In contrast, geniuses like Albert Einstein seem to be able to use nearly all of the intelligences, as needed, to solve problems.

BRIDGES

Metacognitive skills are a large part of what it means to be an expert in a particular topic or field.

See Chapter 10, page 346, for a discussion of expertise.

Getty Images

According to Howard Gardner's theory, bodily-kinesthetic skills reflect one of eight distinct types of intelligence.

If Gardner's theory of **multiple intelligences** is correct, traditional IQ tests measure only a part of real-world intelligence—namely, linguistic, logical-mathematical, and spatial abilities. A further implication is that our schools may be wasting a lot of human potential (Campbell, Campbell, & Dickinson, 2003). For example, some children might find it easier to learn math or reading if these topics were tied into art, music, dance, drama, and so on.

Not all psychologists agree with Gardner's broader definition of intelligence. His view, in fact, is at odds with studies that suggest that scores on IQ tests mainly reflect an underlying "general intelligence" or general ability factor (often referred to as *g*) (Brody, 2000; Neisser et al., 1996). This **g-factor** is said to explain the high correlations found among scores on various tests of intellectual ability and achievement (Robinson, 1999). Gardner's reply would probably be that such correlations only show how narrowly traditional tests define intelligence. In any case, it seems likely that in the future intelligence will not be so strongly equated with IQ. Already, many schools are using Gardner's theory to cultivate a wider range of skills and talents (Campbell, Campbell, & Dickinson, 2003; Gardner, 2002).

A Look Ahead

As promised earlier, the Psychology in Action section of this chapter addresses questions concerning the validity of intelligence tests and their fairness to various groups. The issues raised go to the heart of the question, "What is intelligence?" In addition to being highly interesting and culturally relevant, this topic should round out your understanding of intelligence.

KNOWLEDGE BUILDER

Heredity, Environment, and New Views of Intelligence

REFLECT

Why do you think studies of hereditary and environmental influences on intelligence have provoked such emotional debate? Which side of the debate would you expect each of the following people to favor: teacher, parent, school administrator, politician, medical doctor, liberal, conservative, bigot?

Would you rather have your own intelligence measured with a speed of processing test or a traditional IQ test? Why?

Here's a mnemonic: *New experiences reflect* three kinds of intelligence. Can you define *neural, experiential,* and *reflective* intelligence in your own words?

Make your own list of specialized intelligences. How many items on your list correspond to the eight intelligences identified by Gardner?

LEARNING CHECK

1. Selective breeding for desirable characteristics is called ______________________.
2. The closest similarity in IQs would be observed for
   a. parents and their children
   b. identical twins reared apart
   c. fraternal twins reared together
   d. siblings reared together
3. Most psychologists believe that intelligence is 90 percent hereditary. T or F?
4. Except for slight variations during testing, IQ cannot be changed. T or F?
5. Environmental effects are probably more capable of lowering IQ than of raising it. T or F?
6. Inspection time has been used as a measure of ____________ ______ intelligence.
   a. experiential c. reflective
   b. neural d. analytical
7. According to Howard Gardner's theory, which of the following is not measured by traditional IQ tests?
   a. intrapersonal skills c. logical skills
   b. spatial skills d. linguistic skills

CRITICAL THINKING

8. Dropping out of school can lower tested IQ and attending school can raise it. What do these observations reveal about intelligence *tests?*

Answers: 1. eugenics **2.** b **3.** F **4.** F **5.** T **6.** b **7.** a **8.** Such observations remind us that intelligence tests are affected by learning and that they measure knowledge, as well as innate cognitive abilities.

Neural intelligence The innate speed and efficiency of a person's brain and nervous system.

Experiential intelligence Specialized knowledge and skills acquired through learning and experience.

Reflective intelligence An ability to become aware of one's own thinking habits.

Metacognitive skills An ability to manage one's own thinking and problem-solving efforts.

Multiple intelligences Howard Gardner's theory that there are several specialized types of intellectual ability.

g-factor A core of general intellectual ability that is assumed to explain the high correlations among various measures of intelligence.

PSYCHOLOGY IN ACTION

How Intelligent Are Intelligence Tests?

During their lifetimes, most people take an intelligence test, or one of the closely related scholastic aptitude tests. If you have ever taken an individually administered IQ test, you may actually know what your IQ is. If not, the following self-administered test will provide a rough estimate of your IQ. Most people are curious about how they would score on an intelligence test. Why not give the Dove test a try?

If you scored 14 on this exam, your IQ is approximately 100, indicating average intelligence. If you scored 10 or less, you are mentally retarded. With luck and the help of a special educational program, we may be able to teach you a few simple skills!

Isn't the Dove Test a little unfair? No, it is *very* unfair. It was written in 1971 by African-American sociologist Adrian Dove as "a half serious attempt to show that we're just not talking the same language." Dove tried to slant his test as much in favor of urban African-American culture as he believes the typical intelligence test is biased toward a white middle-class background (Jones, 2003). (Because of its age, the test is probably now also unfair even for African-Americans under 35.)

Dove's test is a thought-provoking reply to the fact that African-American children score an average of about 15 points lower on standardized IQ tests than European American children. By reversing the bias, Dove has shown that intelligence tests are not equally valid for all groups. As Jerome Kagan says, "If the Wechsler and Binet scales were translated into Spanish, Swahili, and Chinese and given to every 10-year-old in Latin America, East Africa, or China, the majority would obtain IQ scores in the mentally retarded range." The problem is that people in other cultures do not share the same values, knowledge, and language patterns that underlie IQ tests written for use in North America (Greenfield, 1997).

Culture-Fair Testing

Certainly we cannot believe that children of different cultures are all retarded. The fault must lie in the test. Cultural values,

Dove Counterbalance Intelligence Test

Time limit: 5 minutes.
Circle the correct answer.

1. T-bone Walker got famous for playing what?
a. trombone b. piano c. T-flute d. guitar e. "hambone"
2. A "gas head" is a person who has a
a. fast-moving car. b. stable of "lace." c. "process." d. habit of stealing cars. e. long jail record for arson.
3. If you throw the dice and 7 is showing on the top, what is facing down?
a. 7 b. snake eyes c. boxcars d. little joes e. 11
4. Cheap chitlings (not the kind you purchase at a frozen-food counter) will taste rubbery unless they are cooked long enough. How soon can you quit cooking them to eat and enjoy them?
a. 45 minutes b. two hours c. 24 hours d. one week (on a low flame) e. one hour
5. Bird or Yardbird was the jacket jazz lovers from coast to coast hung on
a. Lester Young b. Peggy Lee c. Benny Goodman d. Charlie Parker e. Birdman of Alcatraz
6. A "handkerchief head" is
a. a cool cat b. a porter c. an Uncle Tom d. a hoddi e. a preacher
7. Jet is
a. an East Oakland motorcycle club b. one of the gangs in West Side Story c. a news and gossip magazine d. a way of life for the very rich
8. "Bo Diddly" is a
a. game for children b. down-home cheap wine c. down-home singer d. new dance e. Moejoe call
9. Which word is most out of place here?
a. splib b. blood c. gray d. spook e. black
10. If a pimp is uptight with a woman who gets state aid, what does he mean when he talks about "Mother's Day"?
a. second Sunday in May b. third Sunday in June c. first of every month d. none of these e. first and fifteenth of every month
11. Many people say that "Juneteenth" (June 10th) should be made a legal holiday because this was the day when
a. the slaves were freed in the United States b. the slaves were freed in Texas c. the slaves were freed in Jamaica d. the slaves were freed in California e. Martin Luther King was born f. Booker T. Washington died
12. If a man is called a "blood," then he is a
a. fighter b. Mexican-American c. Black d. hungry hemophile e. red man or Indian
13. What are the Dixie Hummingbirds?
a. a part of the KKK b. a swamp disease c. a modern gospel group d. a Mississippi Negro paramilitary strike force e. deacons
14. The opposite of square is
a. round b. up c. down d. hip e. lame

ANSWERS

1. d 2. c 3. a 4. c 5. d 6. c 7. c 8. c 9. c
10. c 11. b 12. c 13. c 14. d

traditions, and experiences can greatly affect performance on tests designed for Western cultures (Neisser et al., 1996; Sternberg & Grigorenko, 2005). To avoid this problem, some psychologists have tried to develop culture-fair tests that do not disadvantage certain groups. A **culture-fair test** is designed to minimize the importance of skills and knowledge that may be more common in some cultures than in others. (For a sample of culture-fair test items, see ● Figure 11.10.) For example, our culture places a high value on logic and formal reasoning. Other cultures regard intuition as an important part of what it means to be smart (Norenzayan et al., 2002).

Culture-fair tests attempt to measure intelligence without, as much as possible, being influenced by a person's verbal skills, cultural background, and educational level (see "Intelligence—How Would a Fool Do It?"). Their value lies not just in testing people from other cultures. They are also useful for testing children in the United States who come from poor communities, rural areas, or ethnic minority families (Stephens et al., 1999). However, no intelligence test can be entirely free of cultural influences. For instance, our culture is very "visual," because children are constantly exposed to television, movies, video games, and the like. Thus, compared with children in developing countries, a child who grows up in the United States may be better prepared to take *both* nonverbal tests and traditional IQ tests.

Because the concept of intelligence exhibits such diversity across cultures, many psychologists have begun to stress the need to rethink the concept of intelligence itself (Greenfield, 1997; Sternberg & Grigorenko, 2005). If we are to find a truly culture-fair way to measure intelligence, we first need to identify those core cognitive skills that lie at the heart of human intelligence the world around (Sternberg, 2004).

The Bell Curve—Race, Culture, and IQ

Biased tests are not the only IQ issue African Americans have confronted. In 1994, Richard Herrnstein and Charles Murray proclaimed, in a book titled *The Bell Curve,* that African-Americans score below average in IQ because of their "genetic heritage." Herrnstein and Murray's most inflammatory claim is that the poor, whatever ethnic group they may belong to, are genetically incapable of climbing out of poverty (Herrnstein & Murray, 1994).

Psychologists have responded to such claims with a number of counterarguments. First, it is no secret that as a group African Americans are more likely than European Americans to live in environments that are physically, educationally, and intellectually impoverished. When unequal education is part of the equation, IQs tell us little about how heredity affects intelligence (Neisser et al., 1996; Sternberg, Grigorenko, & Kidd, 2005).

A second argument against Herrnstein and Murray is that they overlook the point made by the Dove test. The assumptions, biases, and content of standard IQ tests do not always allow meaningful comparisons between ethnic, cultural, or racial groups (Helms, 1992; Miller-Jones, 1989). As Leon Kamin (1981) says, "The important fact is that we cannot say which sex (or race) might be more intelligent, because we have no way of measuring 'intelligence.' We have only IQ tests."

Kamin's point is that the makers of IQ tests decided in advance to use test items that would give men and women equal IQ scores. It would be just as easy to put together an IQ test that would give African Americans and European Americans equal scores. Differences in IQ scores are not a fact of nature, but a decision by the test makers. That's why European Americans do better on IQ tests written by European Americans, and African Americans do better on IQ tests devised by African Americans. Another example of this fact is an intelligence test made up of 100 words selected from the *Dictionary of Afro-American Slang.* Williams (1975) gave the test to 100 black and 100 white high school students in St. Louis and found that the black group averaged 36 points higher than the white group.

Many psychologists have evaluated the claims made in *The Bell Curve.* Most have concluded there is no scientific evidence that group differences in average IQ are based on genetics. In fact, studies that used actual blood group testing found no significant correlations between ethnic ancestry and IQ scores. According to Bonham, Warshauer-Baker, & Collins (2005), this is because it does not even make genetic sense to talk about "races" at all, because obvious external markers, like skin color, have little to do with underlying genetic differences. The conclusions that Herrnstein and Murray drew in *The Bell Curve* reflect their political beliefs and biases, not scientific facts. Group differences in IQ scores are based on cultural

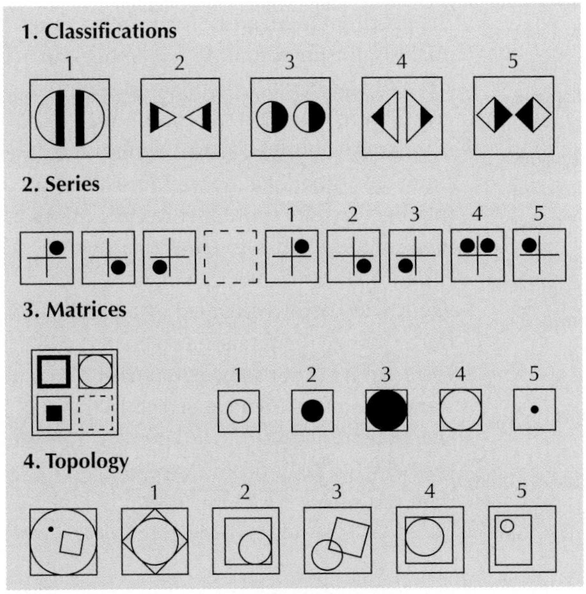

1. Classifications

2. Series

3. Matrices

4. Topology

● **Figure 11.10** No intelligence test can be entirely free of cultural bias. However, culture-fair intelligence tests try to minimize the effects of growing up in various cultures. The following sample items are from a culture-fair test. 1. Which pattern is different from the remaining four? (Number 3.) 2. Which of the five figures on the right would properly continue the three on the left—that is, fill the blank? (Number 5.) 3. Which of the figures on the right should go in the square on the left to make it look right? (Number 2.) 4. At left, the dot is outside the square and inside the circle. In which of the figures on the right could you put a dot outside the square and inside the circle? (Number 3.) (Courtesy of Cattell.)

Culture-fair test A test designed to minimize the importance of skills and knowledge that may be more common in some cultures than in others.

and environmental differences, not on heredity (Neisser et al., 1996; Nisbett, 2005; Williams & Ceci, 1997).

Questioning IQ—Beyond the Numbers Game

African Americans are not the only segment of the population with reason to question the validity of intelligence testing and the role of heredity in determining intelligence. The clarifications they have won extend to others as well.

Consider the 9-year-old child confronted with this question on an intelligence test: "Which of the following does not belong with the others? Roller skates, airplane, train, bicycle." If the child fails to answer "airplane," does it reveal a lack of intelligence? It can be argued that an intelligent choice could be based on any of these alternatives: Roller skates are not typically used for transportation; an airplane is the only nonland item; a train can't be steered; a bicycle is the only item with just two wheels. The parents of a child who misses this question may have reason to be angry, because educational systems tend to classify children and then make the label stick.

Court decisions have led some states to outlaw the use of intelligence tests in public schools. Criticism of intelligence testing has also come from the academic community. Harvard University psychologist David McClelland believes that IQ is of little value in predicting real competence to deal effectively with the world. McClelland concedes that IQ predicts school performance, but when he compared a group of college students with straight A's to another group with poor grades, he found no differences in later career success (McClelland, 1994).

Standardized Testing

In addition to IQ tests, 400 to 500 million standardized multiple-choice tests are given in schools and workplaces around the nation each year. Many, like the *Scholastic Assessment Test,* may determine whether a person is admitted to college. Other tests—for employment, licensing, and certification—directly affect the lives of thousands by qualifying or disqualifying them for jobs.

Widespread reliance on standardized intelligence tests and aptitude tests raises questions about the relative good and harm they do. On the positive side, tests can open opportunities as well as close them. A high test score may allow a disadvantaged youth to enter college, or it may identify a child who is bright but emotionally disturbed. Test scores may also be fairer and more objective than arbitrary judgments made by admissions officers or employment interviewers. Also, tests *do* accurately predict academic performance. The fact that academic performance *does not* predict later success may call for an overhaul of college course work, not an end to testing.

High-Stakes Testing On the negative side, mass testing can occasionally exclude people of obvious ability. In one case, a student who was seventh in his class at Columbia University, and a member of Phi Beta Kappa, was denied entrance to law school because he had low scores on the *Law School Admissions Test.* Other complaints relate to the frequent appearance of bad or ambiguous questions on standardized tests, overuse of class time to prepare students for the tests (instead of teaching general skills), and in the case of intelligence tests, the charge that tests are often biased. Also, most standardized tests demand passive recognition of facts, assessed with a multiple-choice format. They do not, for the most part, test a person's ability to think critically or creatively or to apply knowledge to solve problems. Various "high-stakes tests," which can make or break a person's career, could be improved by (1) removing all questions that favor one group over another; (2) using video-based testing, when possible, to reduce the importance of verbal skills; and (3) providing a pre-test orientation for all test takers, so that people who can afford coaching won't have an unfair advantage (Sackett et al., 2001).

What should we make of the positive and negative aspects of standardized testing? Robert Glaser (1986) says we should remember that tests are "limited tools for limited purposes." Glaser also says that tests are now used primarily to *select* people. In schools they could instead be used to *adapt* instruction to the strengths, weaknesses, and needs of each student—thereby increasing the chances of success.

Conclusion

An application of the preceding discussion to your personal understanding of intelligence can be summarized in this way: Intelligence tests are a two-edged sword; we have learned much from their use, yet they have the potential to do great harm. In the final analysis, it is important to remember—as Howard Gardner has pointed out—that creativity, motivation, physical health, mechanical aptitude, artistic ability, and numerous other qualities not measured by intelligence tests contribute to the achievement of life goals. Also remember that IQ is not intelligence. IQ is an *index* of intelligence (as narrowly defined by a particular test). Change the test and you change the score. An IQ is not some permanent number stamped on the forehead of a child that forever determines his or her potential. The real issue is what skills people have, not what their test scores are (Hunt, 1995).

KNOWLEDGE BUILDER

Intelligence Testing in Perspective

REFLECT

Do you think it would be possible to create an intelligence test that is universally culture-fair? What would its questions look like? Can you think of any type of question that wouldn't favor the mental skills emphasized by some culture, somewhere in the world?

Funding for schools in some states varies greatly in rich and poor neighborhoods. Imagine that a politician opposes spending more money on disadvantaged students because she believes it would "just be a waste." Using the controversy surrounding *The Bell Curve* as a guide, what arguments can you offer against her assertion?

In your own opinion, what are the advantages of using standardized tests to select applicants for college, graduate school, and professional schools? What are the disadvantages?

LEARNING CHECK

1. The WAIS-III, Binet-4, and Dove Test are all culture-fair intelligence scales. T or F?
2. Herrnstein and Murray's claim that heredity accounts for racial differences in average IQ ignores environmental differences and the cultural bias inherent in standard IQ tests. T or F?
3. IQ scores predict school performance. T or F?
4. IQ is not intelligence; it is one index of intelligence. T or F?

CRITICAL THINKING

5. Assume that a test of memory for words is translated from English to Spanish. Would the Spanish version of the test be equal in difficulty to the English version?

Answers: **1.** F **2.** T **3.** T **4.** T **5.** Probably not, because the Spanish words might be longer or shorter than the same words in English. The Spanish words might also sound more or less alike than words on the original test. Translating an intelligence test into another language can subtly change the meaning and difficulty of test items.

Chapter in Review

How do psychologists define intelligence?

- Intelligence refers to one's general capacity to act purposefully, think rationally, and deal effectively with the environment.
- In practice, intelligence is operationally defined by the creation of intelligence tests.
- General intelligence is distinguished from specific aptitudes. Special aptitude tests and multiple aptitude tests are used to assess a person's capacities for learning various abilities. Aptitude tests measure a narrower range of abilities than general intelligence tests do.

What are the qualities of a good psychological test?

- To be of any value, a psychological test must be reliable (give consistent results). A worthwhile test must also have validity, meaning that it measures what it claims to measure.
- Widely used intelligence tests are objective (they give the same result when scored by different people) and standardized (the same procedures are always used in giving the test, and norms have been established so that scores can be interpreted).

What are typical IQ tests like?

- The first practical intelligence test was assembled by Alfred Binet. A modern version of Binet's test is the *Stanford-Binet Intelligence Scales, Fifth Edition.* A second major intelligence test is the *Wechsler Adult Intelligence Scale—Third Edition* (WAIS-III). The WAIS-III measures both verbal and performance intelligence.
- In addition to individual tests, intelligence tests have also been produced for use with groups. A group test of historical interest is the *Army Alpha.* The SAT, the ACT, and the CQT are group scholastic aptitude tests. Although narrower in scope than IQ tests, they bear some similarities to them.

How do IQ scores relate to gender, age, and occupation?

- Intelligence is expressed in terms of an intelligence quotient (IQ). IQ is defined as mental age (MA) divided by chronological age (CA) and then multiplied by 100. An "average" IQ of 100 occurs when mental age equals chronological age.
- Modern IQ tests no longer calculate IQs directly. Instead the final score reported by the test is a deviation IQ.
- IQ scores become fairly stable at about age 6, and they become increasingly reliable thereafter. On the average, IQ scores continue to gradually increase until middle age. Later intellectual declines are moderate for most people until their seventies. Shortly before death, a more significant terminal decline in intelligence is often observed.
- The distribution of IQ scores approximates a normal curve. There are no overall differences between males and females in tested intelligence. However, very small gender differences may result from the intellectual skills our culture encourages males and females to develop.

- IQ is related to school grades and job status. The second association may be somewhat artificial because educational credentials are required for entry into many occupations.

What does IQ tell us about genius?

- People with IQs in the gifted or "genius" range of above 140 tend to be superior in many respects.
- By criteria other than IQ, a large proportion of children might be considered gifted or talented in one way or another. Intellectually gifted children often have difficulties in average classrooms and benefit from special accelerated programs.
- People with the savant syndrome combine retardation or mental disability with exceptional ability in a very limited skill.

What causes mental retardation?

- The terms mentally retarded and developmentally disabled are applied to those whose IQ falls below 70 or who lack various adaptive behaviors.
- Further classifications of retardation are mild (50–55 to 70), moderate (35–40 to 50–55), severe (20–25 to 35–40), and profound (below 20–25). Chances for educational success are related to the degree of retardation.
- About 50 percent of the cases of mental retardation are organic, being caused by birth injuries, fetal damage, metabolic disorders, or genetic abnormalities. The remaining cases are of undetermined cause.
- Many cases of subnormal intelligence are thought to be the result of familial retardation, a generally low level of educational and intellectual stimulation in the home, coupled with poverty and poor nutrition.
- Six distinct forms of organic retardation are phenylketonuria (PKU), microcephaly, hydrocephaly, cretinism, Down syndrome, and fragile-X syndrome.

How do heredity and environment affect intelligence?

- Studies of eugenics in animals and familial relationships in humans demonstrate that intelligence is partially determined by heredity. However, environment is also important, as revealed by changes in tested intelligence induced by schooling and stimulating environments.
- There is evidence that some elements of intelligence can be taught. Intelligence therefore reflects the combined effects of both heredity and environment in the development of intellectual abilities.

How have views of intelligence changed in recent years?

- Some psychologists are investigating the *neural basis* for intelligence, especially the speed of processing various kinds of information.
- Cognitive psychologists believe that successful intelligence depends on thinking and problem-solving skills. Metacognitive skills, in particular, contribute greatly to intelligent behavior.
- Many psychologists have begun to forge new, broader definitions of intelligence. Howard Gardner's theory of multiple intelligences is a good example of this trend.

Are IQ tests fair to all racial and cultural groups?

- Traditional IQ tests often suffer from a degree of cultural bias. For this and other reasons, it is wise to remember that IQ is merely an index of intelligence and that intelligence is narrowly defined by most tests.
- The use of standard IQ tests for educational placement of students (especially into special education classes) has been prohibited by law in some states. Whether this is desirable and beneficial to students is currently being debated.

Web Resources

Internet addresses frequently change. To find the sites listed here, visit www.thomsonedu.com/psychology/coon for an updated list of Internet addresses and direct links to relevant sites.

***Psychology: Gateways to Mind and Behavior* Website** Online quizzes, flash cards, and other helpful study aids for this text. www.thomsonedu.com/psychology/coon.

Be Careful of How You Define Intelligence An article about cross-cultural differences in intelligence.

Helping Your Highly Gifted Child Advice for parents of gifted children.

Introduction to Mental Retardation Answers to basic question about mental retardation.

IQ Tests Provides links to a number of IQ tests.

The Bell Curve Flattened An article that summarizes objections to *The Bell Curve.*

The Knowns and Unknowns of Intelligence From the APA, what is known about intelligence and intelligence tests.

ThomsonNOW™ Go to www.thomsonedu.com to link to ThomsonNow, your online study tool. First take the **Pre-Test** for this chapter to get your **Personalized Study Plan,** which will identify topics you need to review and direct you to online resources. Then take the **Post-Test** to determine what concepts you have mastered and what you still need work on.

InfoTrac College Edition For more information on the controversy concerning the book *The Bell Curve,* use Key Words search for BELL CURVE. Go to www.thomsonedu.com/psychology/coon.

chapter

12

Motivation and Emotion

Mike Brinson/Getty Images

THEME:

Our behavior is energized and directed by motives and emotions.

Key Questions

What is motivation? Are there different types of motives?

What causes hunger? Overeating? Eating disorders?

Is there more than one type of thirst?

In what ways are pain avoidance and the sex drive unusual?

How does arousal relate to motivation?

What are social motives? Why are they important?

Are some motives more basic than others?

What happens during emotion?

Can "lie detectors" really detect lies?

How accurately do "body language" and the face express emotions?

How do psychologists explain emotions?

What does it mean to have "emotional intelligence"?

Preview

The Sun Sets Twice in Utah

Sevren and Dennis had been backpacking for a week in the Unitas Mountains of Utah. Every day they enjoyed new trails, inspiring vistas, fresh air, and lots of wildlife. Best of all, neither of them wore a watch.

After a long hike one day, they reached a lake, just as darkness fell. The light was fading quickly, so they set up a tent, cooked dinner, and prepared to eat. Neither of them had an appetite, but they didn't want to wake up hungry in the middle of the night, so they ate anyway. Then they washed dishes and climbed into their tent, where they tried to get to sleep. That's when the sun came up.

Pulling back the tent flap, they looked around in amazement to discover bright sunshine outside. It was late afternoon. They had *hours* of daylight left before nightfall!

Heavy, dark clouds had covered most of the western sky when our wayward hikers first arrived at the lake. Apparently, an approaching storm blocked the sun, reducing the forest to twilight. When the storm retreated, the sun came out again. No wonder they weren't hungry or sleepy! Fortunately, no one else was there to laugh at them—although they did have a good laugh themselves.

This chapter is about the motives and emotions that underlie human behavior. As our hikers' experience suggests, even "simple" motivated activities, such as eating, are not solely under the control of the body. In many instances, external cues, expectations, learning, cultural values, and other factors influence our motives, actions, and goals (R. C. Beck, 2004).

Let's begin with basic motives, such as hunger and thirst, and then explore how emotions affect us. Although emotions can be the spice of life, they are sometimes the spice of death as well. Read on to find out why.

Motivation—Forces That Push and Pull

What do you plan to do today? What are your goals? Why do you pursue them? How vigorously do you try to reach them? When are you satisfied? When do you give up? These are all questions about motivation, or why we act as we do. Let's begin with a basic model of motivation and an overview of types of motives.

Motivation refers to the dynamics of behavior—the ways in which our actions are *initiated, sustained, directed,* and *terminated* (Petri, 2003). Imagine that a student named Omar is studying psychology in the library. He begins to feel hungry and can't concentrate. His stomach growls and he decides to buy an apple from a vending machine. The machine is empty, so he goes to the cafeteria. Closed. Omar drives home, where he cooks a meal and eats it. At last his hunger is satisfied, and he resumes studying. Notice how Omar's food seeking was *initiated* by a bodily need. His search was *sustained* because the need was not immediately met, and his actions were *directed* by possible sources of food. Finally, achieving his goal *terminated* his food seeking.

A Model of Motivation

Many motivated activities begin with a **need**, or internal deficiency. The need that initiated Omar's search was a depletion of key substances in his body. Needs cause a **drive** (an energized motivational state) to develop. The drive was hunger, in Omar's case. Drives activate a **response** (an action or series of actions) designed to attain a **goal** (the "target" of motivated behavior). Reaching a goal that satisfies the need will end the chain of events. Thus, a simple model of motivation can be shown in this way:

NEED → DRIVE → RESPONSE → GOAL
(NEED REDUCTION) ←

Aren't needs and drives the same thing? No, because the strength of needs and drives can differ. If you begin fasting today, your bodily need for food will increase every day. However, you would probably feel less "hungry" on the seventh day of fasting than you did on the first. Although your need for food steadily increases, the hunger drive comes and goes.

Now let's observe Omar again. It's Saturday night: For dinner, Omar has soup, salad, a large steak, a baked potato, four pieces of bread, two pieces of cheesecake, and three cups of coffee. After dinner, he complains that he is "too full to move." Soon after, Omar's roommate arrives with a strawberry pie. Omar exclaims that strawberry pie is his favorite dessert and eats three large pieces! Is this hunger? Certainly, Omar's dinner satisfied his biological needs for food.

● **Figure 12.1** Needs and incentives interact to determine drive strength *(top). (a)* Moderate need combined with a high-incentive goal produces a strong drive. *(b)* Even when a strong need exists, drive strength may be moderate if a goal's incentive value is low. It is important to remember, however, that incentive value lies "in the eye of the beholder" *(photo).* No matter how hungry, few people would be able to eat the pictured grubworms.

How does that change the model of motivation? Omar's "pie lust" illustrates that motivated behavior can be energized by the "pull" of external stimuli, as well as by the "push" of internal needs.

Incentives

The "pull" of a goal is called its **incentive value** (the goal's appeal beyond its ability to fill a need). Some goals are so desirable (strawberry pie, for example) that they can motivate behavior in the absence of an internal need. Other goals are so low in incentive value that they may be rejected even if they meet the internal need. Fresh, live grubworms, for instance, are highly nutritious. However, it is doubtful that you would eat one no matter how hungry you might be.

Usually, our actions are energized by a mixture of internal needs *and* external incentives. That's why a strong need may change an unpleasant incentive into a desired goal. Perhaps you've never eaten a grubworm, but we'll bet you've eaten some pretty horrible leftovers when the refrigerator was bare. The incentive value of goals also helps explain motives that don't seem to come from internal needs, such as drives for success, status, or approval (● Figure 12.1).

Types of Motives

For our purposes, motives can be divided into three major categories:

1. **Primary motives** are based on biological needs that must be met for survival. The most important primary motives are hunger, thirst, pain avoidance, and needs for air, sleep, elimination of wastes, and regulation of body temperature. Primary motives are innate.
2. **Stimulus motives** express our needs for stimulation and information. Examples include activity, curiosity, exploration, manipulation, and physical contact. Although such motives also appear to be innate, they are not strictly necessary for survival.
3. **Secondary motives** are based on learned needs, drives, and goals. Learned motives help explain many human activities, such as making music, creating a web page, or trying to win the skateboarding finals in the X Games. Many secondary motives are related to learned needs for power, affiliation (the need to be

Motivation Internal processes that initiate, sustain, and direct activities.

Need An internal deficiency that may energize behavior.

Drive The psychological expression of internal needs or valued goals. For example, hunger, thirst, or a drive for success.

Response Any action, glandular activity, or other identifiable behavior.

Goal The target or objective of motivated behavior.

Incentive value The value of a goal above and beyond its ability to fill a need.

Primary motives Innate motives based on biological needs.

Stimulus motives Innate needs for stimulation and information.

Secondary motives Motives based on learned needs, drives, and goals.

with others), approval, status, security, and achievement. Fear and aggression also appear to be greatly affected by learning.

Primary Motives and Homeostasis

How important is food in your life? Water? Sleep? Air? Temperature regulation? Finding a public rest room? For most of us, satisfying biological needs is so routine that we tend to overlook how much of our behavior they direct. But exaggerate any of these needs through famine, shipwreck, poverty, near drowning, bitter cold, or drinking 10 cups of coffee, and their powerful grip on behavior becomes evident. We are, after all, still animals in many ways.

Biological drives are essential because they maintain *homeostasis* (HOE-me-oh-STAY-sis), or bodily equilibrium (Cannon, 1932).

What is homeostasis? The term **homeostasis** means "standing steady," or "steady state." Optimal levels exist for body temperature, for chemicals in the blood, for blood pressure, and so forth. When the body deviates from these "ideal" levels, automatic reactions begin to restore equilibrium (Deckers, 2005). Thus, it might help to think of homeostasis as being similar to a thermostat set at a particular temperature.

A (Very) Short Course on Thermostats

When room temperature falls below the level set on a thermostat, the heat is automatically turned on to warm the room. When the heat equals or slightly exceeds the ideal temperature, it is automatically turned off. In this way room temperature is kept in a state of equilibrium hovering around the ideal level.

The first reactions to disequilibrium in the human body are also automatic. For example, if you become too hot, more blood will flow through your skin and you will begin to perspire, thus lowering body temperature. Usually, we are not aware of such changes, unless continued disequilibrium drives us to seek shade, warmth, food, or water.

KNOWLEDGE BUILDER

Overview of Motivation

REFLECT

Motives help explain why we do what we do. See if you can think of something you do that illustrates the concepts of need, drive, response, and goal. Does the goal in your example vary in incentive value? What effects do high- and low-incentive-value goals have on your behavior?

Mentally list some primary motives you have satisfied today. Some stimulus motives. Some secondary motives. How did each influence your behavior?

LEARNING CHECK

Classify the following needs or motives by placing the correct letter in the blank.

A. Primary motive B. Stimulus motive C. Secondary motive

1. _____ curiosity
2. _____ status
3. _____ sleep
4. _____ thirst
5. _____ achievement
6. _____ physical contact
7. Motives ______________, sustain, and ______________ activities.
8. The maintenance of bodily equilibrium is called thermostasis. T or F?
9. Desirable goals are motivating because they are high in
   a. secondary value
   b. stimulus value
   c. homeostatic value
   d. incentive value

CRITICAL THINKING

10. Many people mistakenly believe that they suffer from "hypoglycemia" (low blood sugar), which is often blamed for fatigue, difficulty concentrating, irritability, and other symptoms. Why is it unlikely that many people actually have hypoglycemia?

Answers: 1. B **2.** C **3.** A **4.** A **5.** C **6.** B **7.** initiate, direct **8.** F **9.** d **10.** Because of homeostasis: Blood sugar is normally maintained within narrow bounds. Although blood sugar levels fluctuate enough to affect hunger, true hypoglycemia is an infrequent medical problem.

Hunger—Pardon Me, My Hypothalamus Is Growling

You get hungry, you find food, and you eat: Hunger might seem like a "simple" motive, but only recently have we begun to understand it. Hunger provides a good model of how internal and external factors direct our behavior. And, as we will see later, many of the principles that explain hunger also apply to thirst.

What causes hunger? When you feel hungry, you probably think of your stomach. That's why Walter Cannon and A. L. Washburn decided to see if stomach contractions cause hunger. In an early study, Washburn trained himself to swallow a balloon, which could be inflated through an attached tube. This allowed Cannon to record the movements of Washburn's stomach (● Figure 12.2). When Washburn's stomach contracted, he reported that he felt "hunger pangs." In view of this, the two scientists concluded that hunger is nothing more than the contractions of an empty stomach (Cannon & Washburn, 1912). (Unfortunately, this proved to be an inflated conclusion.)

For many people, hunger produces an overall feeling of weakness or shakiness, rather than a "growling" stomach. Of course, eating *does* slow when the stomach is stretched or distended (full). (Remember last Thanksgiving?) However, we now know that the stomach is not essential for feeling hunger. Even people who have had their stomachs removed for medical reasons continue to feel hungry and eat regularly (Woods et al., 2000).

Then what does cause hunger? One important signal for hunger is lowered levels of glucose (sugar) in the blood (Campfield et al., 1996). Strange as it may seem, the liver also affects hunger.

The liver? Yes, the liver responds to a lack of bodily "fuel" by sending nerve impulses to the brain. These "messages" contribute to a desire to eat (Woods et al., 2000).

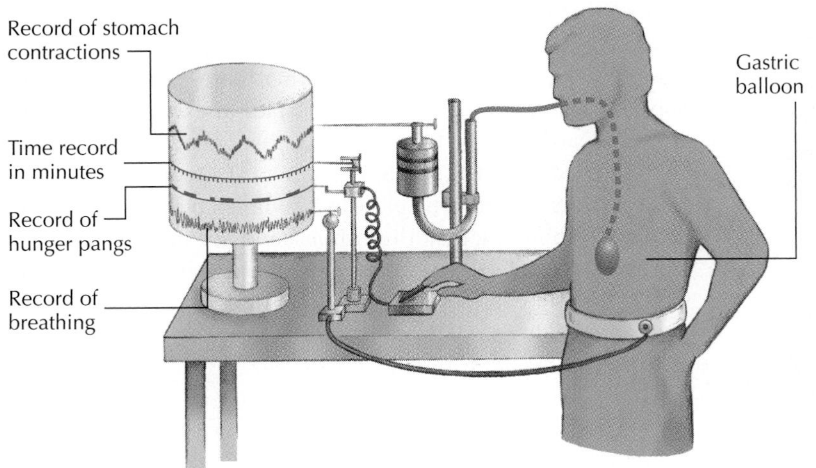

● **Figure 12.2** In Cannon's early study of hunger, a simple apparatus was used to simultaneously record hunger pangs and stomach contractions. (After Cannon, 1934.)

Brain Mechanisms

What part of the brain controls hunger? When you are hungry, many parts of the brain are affected, so no single "hunger center" exists. However, a small area called the **hypothalamus** (HI-po-THAL-ah-mus) regulates many motives, including hunger, thirst, and the sex drive (● Figure 12.3).

The hypothalamus is sensitive to levels of sugar in the blood (and other substances described in a moment). It also receives neural messages from the liver and the stomach. When combined, these signals determine if you are hungry or not (Woods et al., 2000).

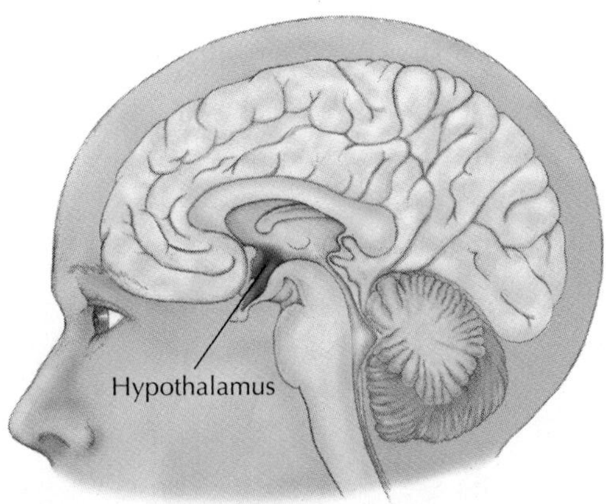

● **Figure 12.3** Location of the hypothalamus in the human brain.

BRIDGES

The hypothalamus directly affects many basic motives.

For more information about its role in controlling behavior, see Chapter 2, page 72.

One part of the hypothalamus acts as a *feeding system* that initiates eating. If the *lateral hypothalamus* is "turned on" with an electrified probe, even a well-fed animal will immediately begin eating. (The term *lateral* simply refers to the sides of the hypothalamus. See ● Figure 12.4.) If the same area is destroyed, the animal will never eat again.

A second area in the hypothalamus is part of a *satiety system,* or "stop mechanism" for eating. If the *ventromedial hypothalamus* (VENT-ro-MEE-dee-al) is destroyed, dramatic overeating results. (*Ventromedial* refers to the bottom middle of the hypothalamus.) Rats with such damage will eat until they balloon up to weights of 1,000 grams or more (● Figure 12.5). A normal rat weighs about 180 grams. To put this weight gain in human terms, picture someone you know who weighs 180 pounds growing to a weight of 1,000 pounds.

The *paraventricular nucleus* (PAIR-uh-ven-TRICK-you-ler) of the hypothalamus also affects hunger (● Figure 12.4). This area helps keep blood sugar levels steady by both starting and stopping eating. The paraventricular nucleus is very sensitive to a substance called *neuropeptide Y* (NPY). If NPY is present in large amounts, an

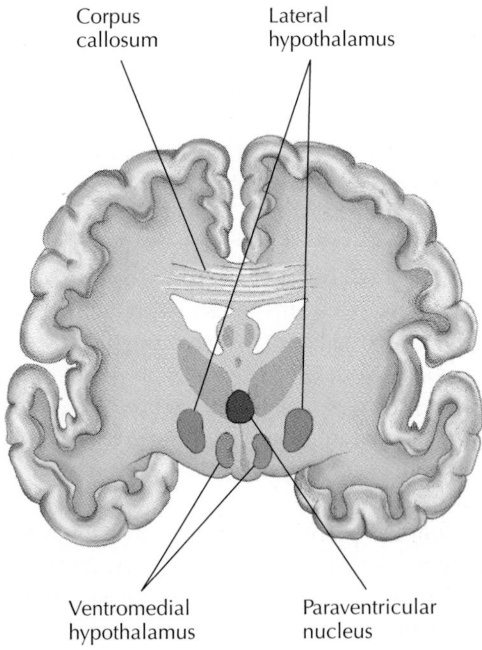

● **Figure 12.4** This is a cross section through the middle of the brain (viewed from the front of the brain). Indicated areas of the hypothalamus are associated with hunger and the regulation of body weight.

Homeostasis A steady state of bodily equilibrium.

Hypothalamus A small area at the base of the brain that regulates many aspects of motivation and emotion, especially hunger, thirst, and sexual behavior.

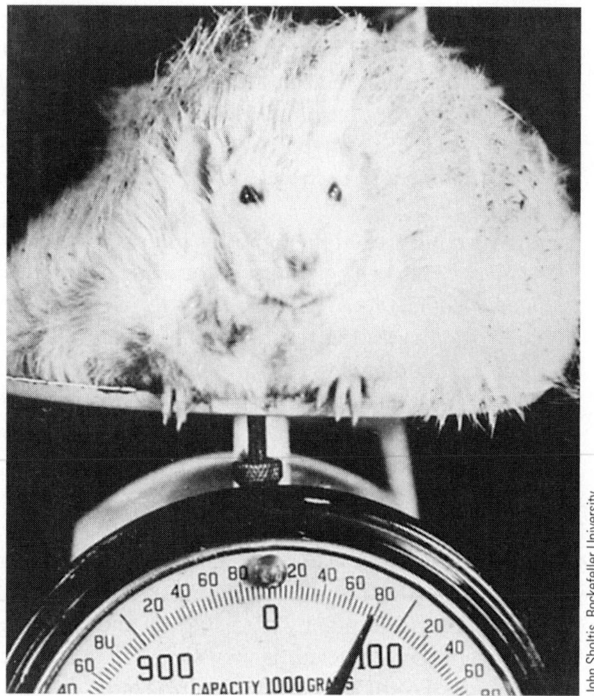

John Sholtis, Rockefeller University

● **Figure 12.5** Damage to the hunger satiety system in the hypothalamus can produce a very fat rat, a condition called hypothalamic *hyperphagia* (Hi-per-FAGE-yah: overeating). This rat weighs 1,080 grams. (The pointer has gone completely around the dial and beyond.)

animal will eat until it cannot hold another bite (Woods et al., 2000). Incidentally, the hypothalamus also responds to a chemical in marijuana, which can produce intense hunger (the "munchies") (Di Marzo et al., 2001).

How do we know when to stop eating? A chemical called glucagon-like peptide 1 (GLP-1) causes eating to cease. After you eat a meal, GLP-1 is released by the intestines. From there, it travels in the bloodstream to the brain. When enough GLP-1 arrives, your desire to eat ends (Nori, 1998; Turton et al., 1996). It takes at least 10 minutes for the hypothalamus to respond after you begin eating. That's why you are less likely to overeat if you eat slowly, which gives your brain time to get the message that you've had enough (Liu et al., 2000).

The substances we have reviewed are only some of the chemical signals that start and stop eating (Geary, 2004). Others continue to be discovered. In time, they may make it possible to artificially control hunger. If so, better treatments for extreme obesity and self-starvation could follow (Batterham et al., 2003; Woods et al., 2000).

Set Point

In addition to knowing when to start eating, and when a meal is over, your body needs to regulate weight over longer periods of time. This is done by monitoring the amount of fat stored in the body (Woods, Seeley, & Porte, 1998). Basically, your body has a **set point** for the proportion of fat it maintains. The set point acts like a "thermostat" for fat levels. Your own set point is the weight you maintain when you are making no effort to gain or lose weight. When your body goes below its set point, you will feel hungry most of the time. On the other hand, fat cells release a substance called *leptin* when your "spare tire" is well inflated. Leptin is carried in the bloodstream to the brain, where it tells us to eat less (Mercer et al., 1998; Williams et al., 2004).

Set points are only one piece in a complex puzzle that's worth solving. Obesity is a major health risk and, for many, a source of social stigma and low self-esteem. Roughly 65 percent of adults in the United States are overweight (● Figure 12.6). As a result, obesity is overtaking smoking as a cause of needless deaths (Murray, 2001b). (See "What's Your BMI?")

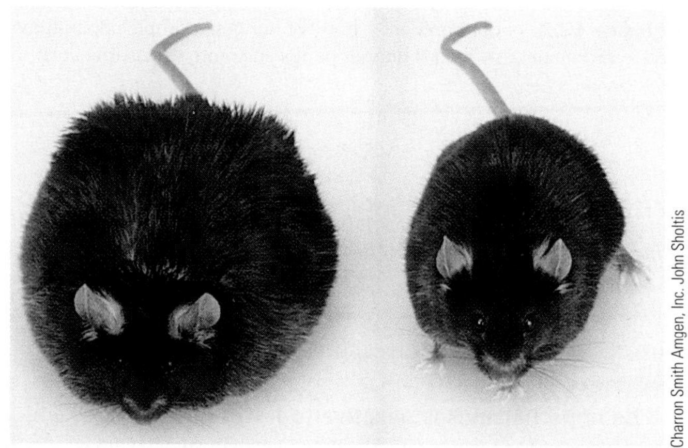
Charron Smith Amgen, Inc. John Sholtis

The mouse on the left has a genetic defect that prevents its fat cells from producing normal amounts of leptin. Without this chemical signal, the mouse's body acts as if its set point for fat storage is, shall we say, rather high.

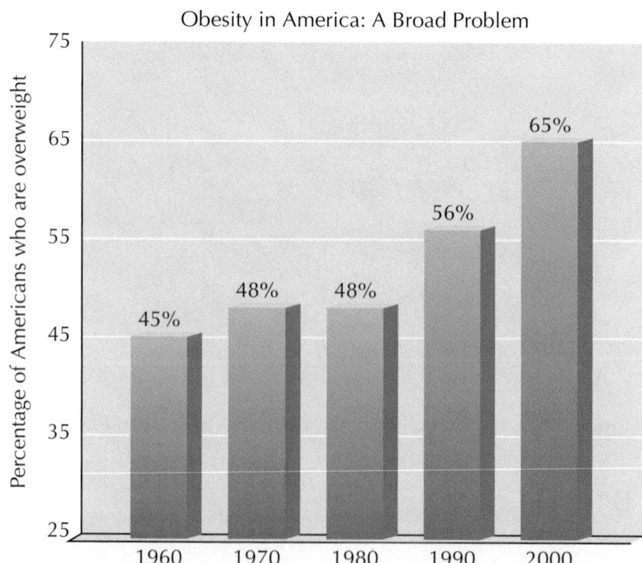

● **Figure 12.6** A near epidemic of obesity and has occurred in the United States during the last 20 years, with 65 percent of all Americans now classified as overweight (CDC, 2003).

DISCOVERING PSYCHOLOGY What's Your BMI? (We've Got Your Number.)

From the standpoint of fashion, you may already have an opinion about whether you are overweight. But how do you rate from a medical perspective? Obesity is directly linked to heart disease, high blood pressure, stroke, diabetes, and premature death. But how heavy do you have to be to endanger your health? A measure called the *body mass index* (BMI) can be used to assess where you stand on the weight scale (so to speak). You can calculate your BMI by using the following formula:

$$\text{BMI} = \frac{\text{(your weight in pounds)}}{\text{(height in inches) (height in inches)}} \times 703$$

To use the formula, take your height in inches and multiply that number by itself (square the number). Then divide the result into your weight in pounds. Multiply the resulting number by 703 to obtain your BMI. For example, a person who weighs 220 pounds and is 6 feet 3 inches tall has a BMI of 27.5.

$$\frac{\text{(220 pounds)}}{\text{(75 inches) (75 inches)}} \times 703 = 27.5$$

Now, compare your BMI to the following scale:

Underweight	less than 18.5
Normal weight	18.5 to 24.9
Overweight	25 to 29.9
Obesity	30 or greater

If your BMI is greater than 25 you should be concerned. If it is greater than 30, your weight may be a serious health risk. (There are two exceptions: The BMI may overestimate body fat if you have a muscular build, and it may underestimate body fat in older persons who have lost muscle mass.) Losing weight and keeping it off can be very challenging. However, if you're overweight, lowering your BMI is well worth the effort. In the long run, it could save your life.

Obesity

Why do people overeat? If internal needs alone controlled eating, fewer people would overeat. However, most of us are also sensitive to *external eating cues.* These are signs and signals linked with food. Do you tend to eat more when food is attractive, highly visible, and easy to get? If so, then external cues affect your food intake. In cultures like ours, where food is plentiful, external cues often lead to overeating (Woods et al., 2000). For example, many college freshmen gain weight rapidly during their first three months on campus (the famous "Frosh 15"). All-you-can-eat dining halls in the dorms and nighttime snacking appear to be the culprits (Levitsky et al., 2003).

Large food portions contribute to overeating. A fast food meal consisting of a hamburger, medium fries, and a medium soda averages 1,200 calories, which is over half the daily caloric need for an adult. Make that a double burger, add cheese, super-size the fries and the drink and you will consume two thirds of the food you need in a day, in just one meal. Notice, too, that people tend to eat all the food they have paid for, even if it is more than they need.

Royalty-Free/Corbis

Is it true that people also overeat when they are emotionally upset? Yes. People with weight problems are just as likely to eat when they are anxious, angry, or sad as when hungry (Schotte, Cools, & McNally, 1990). Furthermore, obese individuals are often unhappy in our fat-conscious culture. The result is overeating, which leads to emotional distress and still more overeating (Rutledge & Linden, 1998).

Diet

A diet is not just a way to lose weight. Your current diet is defined by the types and amounts of food you regularly eat. Some diets actually encourage overeating. For instance, placing animals on a "supermarket" diet leads to gross obesity. In one classic experiment, rats were given meals of chocolate chip cookies, salami, cheese, bananas, marshmallows, milk chocolate, peanut butter, and fat. These pampered rodents gained almost three times as much weight as rats that ate only laboratory chow (Sclafani & Springer, 1976). (Rat chow is a dry mixture of several bland grains. If you were a rat, you'd probably eat more cookies than rat chow, too.)

People are also sensitive to dietary content. In general, *sweetness,* high *fat content,* and *variety* tend to encourage overeating (Lucas & Sclafani, 1990). Sadly, our culture provides the worst kinds of foods for people who suffer from obesity. For instance, restaurant food tends to be higher in fat and calories than meals made at home. The convenience-food industry also tends to pro-

Set point The proportion of body fat that tends to be maintained by changes in hunger and eating.

mote cheap, tasty products that are loaded with fat and sugar (Brownell, 2003).

Large meals are another problem. For example, food portions at restaurants in the United States are 25 percent larger, or more, than they are in France. Far fewer people are obese in France, most likely, because they simply eat less. The French also take longer to eat a meal, which discourages overeating (Rozin et al., 2003).

An added problem faced by people who want to control their weight concerns the way evolution prepared us to store fat when food is plentiful.

Evolution and Yo-Yo Dieting

If dieting works, why are hundreds of "new" diets published each year? The answer is that although dieters do lose weight, most regain it soon after they stop dieting. In fact, many people end up weighing even more than before. Why should this be so? Dieting (starving) slows the body's rate of metabolism (the rate at which energy is used up). In effect, a dieter's body becomes highly efficient at *conserving* calories and storing them as fat (Pinel, Assanand, & Lehman, 2000).

Apparently, evolution prepared us to save energy when food is scarce and to stock up on fat when food is plentiful. Briefly starving yourself, therefore, may have little lasting effect on weight. "Yo-yo dieting," or repeatedly losing and gaining weight, is especially dangerous. Frequent changes in weight can dramatically slow the body's metabolic rate. This makes it harder to lose weight each time a person diets and easier to regain weight when the diet ends. Frequent weight changes also increase the risk of heart disease and premature death (Wang & Brownell, 2005). To avoid bouncing between feast and famine requires a permanent change in eating habits and exercise—a topic we will return to soon.

To summarize, overeating is related to internal and external influences, diet, emotions, genetics, exercise, and many other factors. We live in a culture that provides inexpensive, good-tasting food everywhere, and a brain that evolved to say, "Eat whenever food is available." We eat more when we are given more, and big portions combined with rapid eating can override a natural sense of fullness. For such reasons, scientists are still a long way from winning the "battle of the bulge." Nevertheless, many people have learned to take control of eating by applying the principles of behavioral dieting.

Behavioral Dieting

As we have noted, dieting is usually followed by rapid weight gains. If you really want to lose weight you must overhaul your eating habits, an approach called **behavioral dieting.** Here are some helpful behavioral techniques.

1. **Get yourself committed to weight loss.** Involve other people in your efforts. Programs such as Overeaters Anonymous or Take Off Pounds Sensibly can be a good source of social support.
2. **Exercise.** No diet can succeed for long without an increase in exercise, because exercise lowers the body's set point. Stop saving steps and riding elevators. Add activity to your routine in every way you can think of. To lose weight, you must use more calories than you take in. Burning just 200 extra calories a day can help prevent rebound weight gains. That's just 30 minutes a day of walking or light exercise. The more frequently and vigorously you exercise, the more weight you will lose (Jeffery & Wing, 2001).
3. **Learn your eating habits by observing yourself and keeping a "diet diary."** Begin by making a complete, 2-week record of when and where you eat, what you eat, and the feelings and events that occur just before and after eating. Is a roommate, relative, or spouse encouraging you to overeat? What are your most "dangerous" times and places for overeating?
4. **Learn to weaken your personal eating cues.** When you have learned when and where you do most of your eating, avoid these situations. Try to restrict your eating to one room, and do not read, watch TV, study, or talk on the phone while eating. Require yourself to interrupt what you are doing in order to eat.
5. **Count calories, but don't starve yourself.** To lose, you must eat less, and calories allow you to keep a record of your food intake. If you have trouble eating less every day, try dieting 4 days a week. People who diet intensely every other day lose as much as those who diet moderately every day (Viegener et al., 1990).
6. **Develop techniques to control the act of eating.** Begin by taking smaller portions. Carry to the table only what you plan to eat. Put all other food away before leaving the kitchen. Eat slowly, sip water between bites of food, leave food on your plate, and stop eating before you are completely full. As mentioned earlier, you should be especially wary of the extra-large servings at fast-food restaurants. Saying "super-size me" too often can, indeed, leave you super sized (Murray, 2001b).
7. **Avoid snacks.** It is generally better to eat several small meals a day than three large ones (Assanand, Pinel, & Lehman, 1998). However, high-calorie snacks tend to be eaten *in addition to* meals. If you have an impulse to snack, set a timer for 20 minutes and see if you are still hungry then. Delay the impulse to snack several times if possible. Dull your appetite by filling up on raw carrots, bouillon, water, coffee, or tea.
8. **Chart your progress daily.** Record your weight, the number of calories eaten, and whether you met your daily goal. Set realistic goals by cutting down calories gradually. Losing about a pound per week is realistic, but remember, you are changing habits, not just dieting. Diets don't work!

9. **Set a "threshold" for weight control.** Maintaining weight loss can be even more challenging than losing weight. A study found that people who successfully maintained weight losses had a regain limit of 3 pounds or less. In other words, if they gained more than 2 or 3 pounds, they immediately began to make corrections in their eating habits and amount of exercise (Brownell et al., 1986).

Be patient with this program. It takes years to develop eating habits. You can expect it to take at least several months to change them. If you are unsuccessful at losing weight with these techniques, you might find it helpful to seek the aid of a psychologist familiar with behavioral weight-loss techniques.

Other Factors in Hunger

As research on overeating suggests, "hunger" is affected by more than bodily needs for food. Let's consider some additional factors.

Cultural Factors

Learning to think of some foods as desirable and others as revolting has a large impact on what we eat. In North America we would never consider eating the eyes out of the steamed head of a monkey, but in some parts of the world they are considered a delicacy. By the same token, vegans and vegetarians think it is barbaric to eat any kind of meat. In short, cultural values (widely held beliefs about the desirability of various objects and activities) greatly affect the *incentive value* of foods.

Taste

Even tastes for "normal" foods vary considerably. For example, if you are well fed, leptin dulls the tongue's sensitivity to sweet tastes (Kawai et al., 2000). That's why you may lose your "sweet tooth" when you are full. Actually, if you eat too much of any particular food, it will become less appealing. This probably helps us maintain variety in our diets. However, it also encourages obesity in societies where tasty foods are plentiful. If you overdose on fried chicken or French fries, moving on to some cookies or chocolate cheesecake certainly won't do your body much good (Pinel, Assanand, & Lehman, 2000).

It is easy to acquire a **taste aversion,** or active dislike, for a particular food. This can happen if a food causes sickness or if it is merely associated with nausea (Jacobsen et al., 1993). Not only do we learn to avoid such foods, but they too can become nauseating. A friend of ours, who once became ill after eating a cheese Danish (well, actually, *several*), has never again been able to come face to face with this delightful pastry.

If getting sick occurs long after eating, how does it become associated with a particular food? A good question. Taste aversions are a type of classical conditioning. As stated in Chapter 8, a long delay between the CS and US usually prevents conditioning. However, psychologists theorize that we have a biological tendency to associate an upset stomach with foods eaten earlier. Such learning is usually protective. Yet, sadly, many cancer patients suffer taste aversions long after the nausea of their drug treatments has passed (Stockhorst, Klosterhalfen, & Steingrueber, 1998).

If you like animals, you will be interested in an imaginative approach to an age-old problem. In many rural areas, predators are poisoned, trapped, or shot by ranchers. These practices have nearly wiped out the timber wolf, and in some areas the coyote faces a similar end. How might the coyote be saved without a costly loss of livestock?

In a classic experiment, coyotes were given lamb tainted with lithium chloride. Coyotes who took the bait became nauseated and vomited. After one or two such treatments, they developed **bait shyness**—a lasting distaste for the tainted food (Gustavson & Garcia, 1974). If applied consistently, taste aversion conditioning might solve many predator–livestock problems. (Perhaps this technique could even be used to protect roadrunners from the Wiley Coyote!)

BRIDGES

Bait shyness is similar to human aversion conditioning, which is used to help people control bad habits, such as smoking, drinking, or nail biting.

See Chapter 17, pages 578–579, to explore this connection.

Behavioral dieting Weight reduction based on changing exercise and eating habits, rather than temporary self-starvation.

Taste aversion An active dislike for a particular food.

Bait shyness An unwillingness or hesitation on the part of animals to eat a particular food.

Like humans and other animals, coyotes develop taste aversions when food is associated with nausea.

Taste aversions may also help people avoid severe nutritional imbalances. For example, if you go on a fad diet and eat only grapefruit, you will eventually begin to feel ill. In time, associating your discomfort with grapefruit may create an aversion to it and restore some balance to your diet.

Eating Disorders

Under the sheets of her hospital bed Krystal looks like a skeleton. If her **anorexia nervosa** (AN-uh-REK-see-yah ner-VOH-sah: self-starvation) cannot be stopped, Krystal may die of malnutrition. Victims of anorexia, who are mostly adolescent females (5 to 10 percent are male), suffer devastating weight losses from severe, self-inflicted dieting (Cooper, 2005; Polivy & Herman, 2002).

Do anorexics lose their appetite? No, many continue to feel hungry, yet struggle to starve themselves to excessive thinness. A compulsive desire to lose weight causes them to actively avoid food. However, this does not prevent them from feeling physical hunger. Often, anorexia starts with "normal" dieting that slowly begins to dominate the person's life. In time, anorexics suffer debilitating health problems. From 5 to 8 percent (more than 1 in 20) die of malnutrition (Polivy & Herman, 2002). ■ Table 12.1 lists the symptoms of anorexia nervosa.

Bulimia nervosa (bue-LIHM-ee-yah) is a second major eating disorder. Bulimic persons gorge on food, then vomit or take laxatives to avoid gaining weight (see ■ Table 12.1). Like anorexia, most victims of bulimia are girls or women. Approximately 5 percent of college women are bulimic, and as many as 61 percent have milder eating problems. Bingeing and purging can seriously damage health. Typical risks include sore throat, hair loss, muscle spasms, kidney damage, dehydration, tooth erosion, swollen salivary glands, menstrual irregularities, loss of sex drive, and even heart attack.

Causes

What causes anorexia and bulimia? Women who suffer from eating disorders are extremely dissatisfied with their bodies. Usually, they have distorted views of themselves and exaggerated fears of becoming fat. Many overestimate their body size by 25 percent or more. As a result, they think they are disgustingly "fat" when they are actually wasting away (● Figure 12.7) (Gardner & Bokenkamp, 1996; Polivy & Herman, 2002). Many of these problems are related to harmful messages in the media. Girls who spend a lot of time reading teen magazines are more likely to have distorted body images and unrealistic ideas about how they compare with others (Martinez-Gonzalez et al., 2003).

TABLE 12.1

Recognizing Eating Disorders

Anorexia nervosa

- Body weight below 85 percent of normal for one's height and age.
- Refusal to maintain body weight in normal range.
- Intense fear of becoming fat or gaining weight, even though underweight.
- Disturbance in one's body image or perceived weight.
- Self-evaluation is unduly influenced by body weight.
- Denial of seriousness of abnormally low body weight.
- Absence of menstrual periods.
- Purging behavior (vomiting or misuse of laxatives or diuretics).

Bulimia nervosa

- Normal or above-normal weight.
- Recurring binge eating.
- Eating within an hour or two an amount of food that is much larger than most people would consume.
- Feeling a lack of control over eating.
- Purging behavior (vomiting or misuse of laxatives or diuretics).
- Excessive exercise to prevent weight gain.
- Fasting to prevent weight gain.
- Self-evaluation is unduly influenced by body weight.

DSM-IV-TR, 2000.

Anorexia nervosa is far more dangerous than many people realize. This haunting photo shows popular singer Karen Carpenter shortly before she died of starvation-induced heart failure. Many other celebrities have struggled with eating disorders, including Paula Abdul, Kirstie Alley, Fiona Apple, Victoria Beckham (Posh Spice), Princess Diana, Tracey Gold, Janet Jackson, and Mary-Kate Olsen.

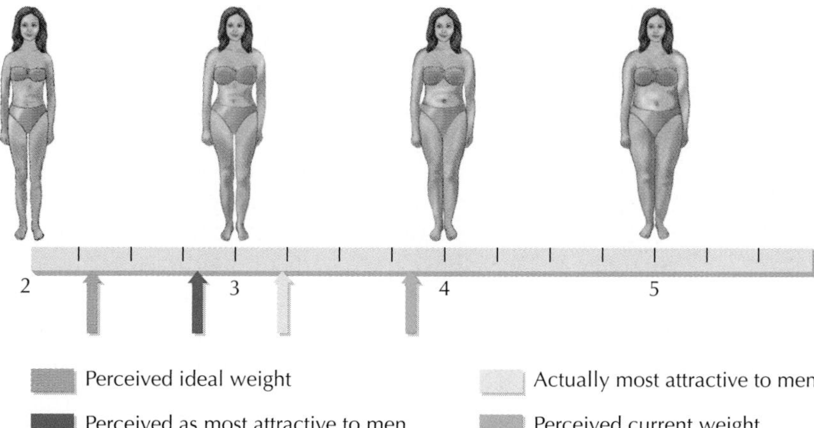

● **Figure 12.7** Women with abnormal eating habits were asked to rate their body shape on a scale similar to the one you see here. As a group, they chose ideal figures much thinner than what they thought their current weights were. (Most women say they want to be thinner than they currently are, but to a lesser degree than women with eating problems.) Notice that the women with eating problems chose an ideal weight that was even thinner than what they thought men prefer. This is not typical of most women. In this study, only women with eating problems wanted to be thinner than what they thought men find attractive (Zellner, Harner, & Adler, 1989).

Evan Agostini/Getty Images

The relentless parade of atypically thin models in the media contributes to eating disorders. People with eating disorders are much more likely to report being influenced by unrealistic body ideals in the media (Murray, Touyz, & Beumont, 1996).

Anorexic teens are usually described as "perfect" daughters—helpful, considerate, conforming, and obedient. Many seem to be seeking perfect control in their lives by being perfectly slim (Pliner & Haddock, 1996). People suffering from bulimia are also concerned with control. Typically they are obsessed with thoughts of weight, food, eating, and ridding themselves of food. As a result, they feel guilt, shame, self-contempt, and anxiety after a binge. Vomiting reduces their anxiety, which makes purging highly reinforcing (Powell & Thelen, 1996).

Treatment

People suffering from eating disorders need professional help. Treatment for anorexia usually begins with giving drugs to relieve obsessive fears of gaining weight. Then a medical diet is used to restore weight and health. Next, a counselor may help patients work on the emotional conflicts that led to weight loss. For bulimia, behavioral counseling may include self-monitoring of food intake. The urge to vomit can be treated with extinction training. A related cognitive-behavioral approach focuses on changing the thinking patterns and beliefs about weight and body shape that perpetuate eating disorders (Byrne & McLean, 2002; Cooper, 2005).

Most people suffering from eating disorders will not seek help on their own. Typically, it takes strong urging by family or friends to get victims into treatment.

Culture, Ethnicity, and Dieting

Women with eating disorders are not alone in having body image problems. In Western cultures, many women learn to see themselves as "objects" that are evaluated by others. As a result, they try to shape their bodies to the cultural ideal of slimness through dieting (Fredrickson et al., 1998).

Just looking at a fashion magazine tends to leave women less satisfied with their weight and anxious to be thinner (Simpson, 2002). However, women from some cultural backgrounds appear to be less susceptible to the glorification of slimness. For example, Asian-American college students are only half as likely to diet as other college women are (Tsai, Hoerr, & Song, 1998). Within the African-American and Pacific-Islander communities there is a general preference for a fuller and shapelier figure. In these groups a larger body size is associated with high social status, health, and beauty (Flynn & Fitzgibbon, 1998; Ofosu, Lafreniere, & Senn, 1998). Clearly, what constitutes an attractive body style is a matter of opinion.

Primary Motives Revisited—Thirst, Sex, and Pain

Most biological motives work in ways that are similar to hunger. For example, thirst is only partially controlled by dryness of the mouth. If you were to take a drug that made your mouth constantly wet, or dry, your water intake would remain normal. Like hunger, thirst is regulated by separate *thirst* and *thirst satiety* systems in the hypothalamus. Also like hunger, thirst is strongly affected by learning and cultural values.

Anorexia nervosa Active self-starvation or a sustained loss of appetite that has psychological origins.

Bulimia nervosa Excessive eating (gorging) usually followed by self-induced vomiting and/or taking laxatives.

Thirst

You may not have noticed, but there are actually two kinds of thirst. **Extracellular thirst** occurs when water is lost from the fluids surrounding the cells of your body. Bleeding, vomiting, diarrhea, sweating, and drinking alcohol cause this type of thirst (Petri, 2003). When a person loses both water and minerals in any of these ways—especially by perspiration—a slightly salty liquid may be more satisfying than plain water.

Why would a thirsty person want to drink salty water? The reason is that before the body can retain water, minerals lost through perspiration (mainly salt) must be replaced. In lab tests, animals greatly prefer saltwater after salt levels in their bodies are lowered (Strickler & Verbalis, 1988). Similarly, some nomadic peoples of the Sahara Desert prize blood as a beverage, probably because of its saltiness. (Maybe they should try Gatorade?)

A second type of thirst occurs when you eat a salty meal. In this instance your body does not lose fluid. Instead, excess salt causes fluid to be drawn out of cells. As the cells "shrink," **intracellular thirst** is triggered. Thirst of this type is best quenched by plain water.

The drives for food, water, air, sleep, and elimination are all similar in that they are generated by a combination of activities in the body and the brain, and they are influenced by various external factors. However, the sex drive and the drive to avoid pain are more unusual.

Pain

How is the drive to avoid pain different? Hunger, thirst, and sleepiness come and go in a fairly regular cycle each day. Pain avoidance, by contrast, is an **episodic drive** (ep-ih-SOD-ik). That is, it occurs in distinct episodes when bodily damage takes place or is about to occur. Most drives prompt us to actively seek a desired goal (food, drink, warmth, and so forth). Pain prompts us to *avoid* or *eliminate* sources of discomfort.

Alain Evrard/Photo Researchers, Inc.

Tolerance for pain and the strength of a person's motivation to avoid discomfort are greatly affected by cultural practices and beliefs.

Some people feel they must be "tough" and not show any distress. Others complain loudly at the smallest ache or pain. The first attitude raises pain tolerance, and the second lowers it. As this suggests, the drive to avoid pain is partly learned. That's why members of some societies endure cutting, burning, whipping, tattooing, and piercing of the skin that would agonize most people (but apparently not devotees of piercing and "body art"). In general, we learn how to react to pain by observing family members, friends, and other role models (McMahon & Koltzenburg, 2005).

The Sex Drive

Many psychologists do not think of sex as a primary motive, because sex (contrary to anything your personal experience might suggest) is not necessary for *individual* survival. It is necessary, of course, for *group* survival.

The term sex drive refers to the strength of one's motivation to engage in sexual behavior. In lower animals the sex drive is directly related to hormones. Female mammals (other than humans) are interested in mating only when their fertility cycles are in the stage of **estrus**, or "heat." Estrus is caused by a release of **estrogen** (a female sex hormone) into the bloodstream. Hormones are important in males as well. In most animals, castration will abolish the sex drive. But in contrast to females, the normal male animal is almost always ready to mate. His sex drive is primarily aroused by the behavior and scent of a receptive female. Therefore, in many species mating is closely tied to female fertility cycles.

How much do hormones affect human sex drives? Hormones affect the human sex drive, but not as directly as in animals (Crooks & Baur, 2005). The sex drive in men is related to the amount of androgens (male hormones) provided by the testes. When the supply of androgens dramatically increases at puberty, so does the male sex drive. Likewise, the sex drive in women is related to their estrogen levels (Graziottin, 1998). However, "male" hormones also affect the female sex drive. In addition to estrogen, a woman's body produces small amounts of androgens. When their androgen levels increase, many women experience a corresponding increase in sex drive (Van Goozen et al., 1995).

The link between hormones and the sex drive grows weaker as we ascend the biological scale. For example, there is no connection between female sexual activity and women's monthly menstrual cycles. In humans, mental, cultural, and emotional factors determine sexual expression. However, our liberation from hormones is not total. Human males lose their sex drive after castration, and some women lose sexual desire when taking birth control pills.

Human sexual behavior and attitudes are discussed in detail in Chapter 13. For now it is enough to note that the sex drive is largely **non-homeostatic** (relatively independent of bodily need states). In humans, the sex drive can be aroused at virtually any time by almost anything. It therefore shows no clear relationship to deprivation (the amount of time since the drive was last satisfied). Certainly, an increase in desire may occur as time passes. But recent sexual activity does not prevent sexual desire from occurring again. Notice, too, that people may seek to arouse the sex drive as well as to reduce it. This unusual quality makes the sex drive capable of motivating a wide range of behaviors. It also explains why sex is used to sell almost everything imaginable.

The non-homeostatic quality of the sex drive can be shown in this way: A male animal is allowed to copulate until it seems to have no further interest in sexual behavior. Then a new sexual partner is provided. Immediately the animal resumes sexual activity. This pattern is called the *Coolidge effect* after former U.S. president Calvin Coolidge. What, you might ask, does Calvin Coolidge have to do with the sex drive? The answer is found in the following story.

While touring an experimental farm, Coolidge's wife reportedly asked if a rooster mated just once a day. "No ma'am," she was told, "he mates dozens of times each day." "Tell that to the president," she said, with a faraway look in her eyes. When President Coolidge reached the same part of the tour, his wife's message was given to him. His reaction was to ask if the dozens of matings were with the same hen. No, he was told, different hens were involved. "Tell *that* to Mrs. Coolidge," the president is said to have replied.

KNOWLEDGE BUILDER

Hunger, Thirst, Pain, and Sex

REFLECT

Think of the last meal you ate. What caused you to feel hungry? What internal signals told your body to stop eating? How sensitive are you to external eating cues? Have you developed any taste aversions?

A friend of yours seems to be engaging in yo-yo dieting. Can you explain to her or him why such dieting is ineffective?

If you wanted to provoke extracellular thirst in yourself, what would you do? How could you make intracellular thirst occur?

LEARNING CHECK

1. The hunger satiety system in the hypothalamus signals the body to start eating when it receives signals from the liver or detects changes in blood sugar. T or F?
2. Maintaining your body's set point for fat is closely linked with the amount of __________ in the bloodstream.
   a. hypothalamic factor-1
   b. ventromedial peptide-1
   c. NPY
   d. leptin
3. People who diet frequently tend to benefit from practice: They lose weight more quickly each time they diet. T or F?
4. Bingeing and purging are most characteristic of people who have
   a. taste aversions
   b. anorexia
   c. bulimia
   d. strong sensitivity to external eating cues
5. In addition to changing eating habits, a key element of behavioral dieting is
   a. exercise
   b. well-timed snacking
   c. better eating cues
   d. commitment to "starving" every day
6. A cancer patient has little appetite for food several weeks after the nausea caused by chemotherapy has ended. Her loss of appetite is probably best explained by
   a. increased NPY in the brain
   b. a conditioned taste aversion
   c. the after effects of yo-yo dieting
   d. a loss of extracellular hunger
7. Thirst may be either intracellular or __________________.
8. Pain avoidance is an __________________ drive.
9. Sexual behavior in animals is largely controlled by estrogen levels in the female and the occurrence of estrus in the male. T or F?

CRITICAL THINKING

10. Kim, who is overweight, is highly sensitive to external eating cues. How might her wristwatch contribute to her overeating?

Answers: 1. F **2.** d **3.** F **4.** c **5.** a **6.** b **7.** extracellular **8.** episodic **9.** F **10.** The time of day can influence eating, especially for externally cued eaters, who tend to get hungry at mealtimes, irrespective of their internal needs for food.

Stimulus Drives—Skydiving, Horror Movies, and the Fun Zone

Are you full of energy right now? Are you feeling tired? Clearly, the level of arousal you are experiencing is closely linked with your motivation. Are there ideal levels of arousal for different people and different activities? Let's find out.

Most people enjoy a steady "diet" of new movies, novels, tunes, fashions, games, news, websites, and adventures. Yet **stimulus drives,** which reflect needs for information, exploration, manipulation, and sensory input, go beyond mere entertainment. Stimulus drives also help us survive. As we scan our surroundings, we constantly identify sources of food, danger, shelter, and other key details. Stimulus drives are readily apparent in animals as well as humans. For example, monkeys will quickly learn to solve a mechanical puzzle made up of interlocking metal pins, hooks, and latches (Butler, 1954) (● Figure 12.8). No food treats or other external rewards are needed to get them to explore and manipulate their surround-

Extracellular thirst Thirst caused by a reduction in the volume of fluids found between body cells.

Intracellular thirst Thirst triggered when fluid is drawn out of cells due to an increased concentration of salts and minerals outside the cell.

Episodic drive A drive that occurs in distinct episodes.

Estrus Changes in the sexual drives of animals that create a desire for mating; particularly used to refer to females in heat.

Estrogen Any of a number of female sex hormones.

Non-homeostatic drive A drive that is relatively independent of physical deprivation cycles or bodily need states.

Stimulus drives Drives based on needs for exploration, manipulation, curiosity, and stimulation.

● **Figure 12.8** Monkeys happily open locks that are placed in their cage. Because no reward is given for this activity, it provides evidence for the existence of stimulus needs.

ings. The monkeys seem to work for the sheer fun of it. The drive for stimulation can even be observed in infants. By the time a child can walk, there are few things in the home that have not been tasted, touched, viewed, handled, or, in the case of toys, destroyed!

Arousal Theory

Are stimulus drives homeostatic? Yes. According to **arousal theory** we try to keep arousal at an optimal level (Hancock & Ganey, 2003; Hebb, 1966). In other words, when your level of arousal is too low or too high, you will seek ways to raise or lower it.

What do you mean by arousal? Arousal refers to activation of the body and the nervous system. Arousal is zero at death; it is low during sleep; it is moderate during normal daily activities; and it is high at times of excitement, emotion, or panic. Arousal theory assumes that we become uncomfortable when arousal is too low ("I'm bored") or when it is too high, as in fear, anxiety, or panic ("The dentist will see you now"). Most adults vary their activities to maintain a comfortable level of activation. Music, parties, sports, conversation, sleep, surfing the web, and the like are combined to keep arousal at moderate levels. The right mix of activities prevents boredom *and* overstimulation.

Sensation Seekers

Do people vary in their needs for stimulation? Picture a city dweller who is visiting the country. Before long, she begins to complain that it is "too quiet," and seeks some "action." Now imagine a country dweller who is visiting the city. Very soon, she finds the city "overwhelming" and seeks peace and quiet. These examples are extremes, but arousal theory also suggests that people learn to seek particular levels of arousal.

Sensation seeking is a trait of people who prefer high levels of stimulation. Whether you are high or low in sensation seeking is probably based on how your body responds to new, unusual, or intense stimulation (Zuckerman, 1990, 2002). People high in sensation seeking tend to be bold and independent, and they value change. They also report more sexual partners than low scorers, they are more likely to smoke, and they prefer spicy, sour, and crunchy foods over bland foods. Low sensation seekers are orderly, nurturant, and giving, and they enjoy the company of others. Which are you? (Most people fall somewhere between the extremes. See "Xtreme!")

Levels of Arousal

Is there an ideal level of arousal for peak performance? If we set aside individual differences, most people perform best when their arousal level is *moderate*. Let's say that you have to take an essay exam. If you are sleepy or feeling lazy (arousal level too low), your performance will suffer. If you are in a state of anxiety or panic about the test (arousal level too high), you will also perform below par. Thus, the relationship between arousal and performance forms an *inverted U function* (a curve in the shape of an upside-down U) (● Figure 12.9) (Hancock & Ganey, 2003).

The inverted U tells us that at very low levels of arousal you're not sufficiently energized to perform well. Performance will improve as your arousal level increases, up to the middle of the curve. Then it begins to drop off, as you become emotional, frenzied, or disorganized. For example, imagine trying to start a car

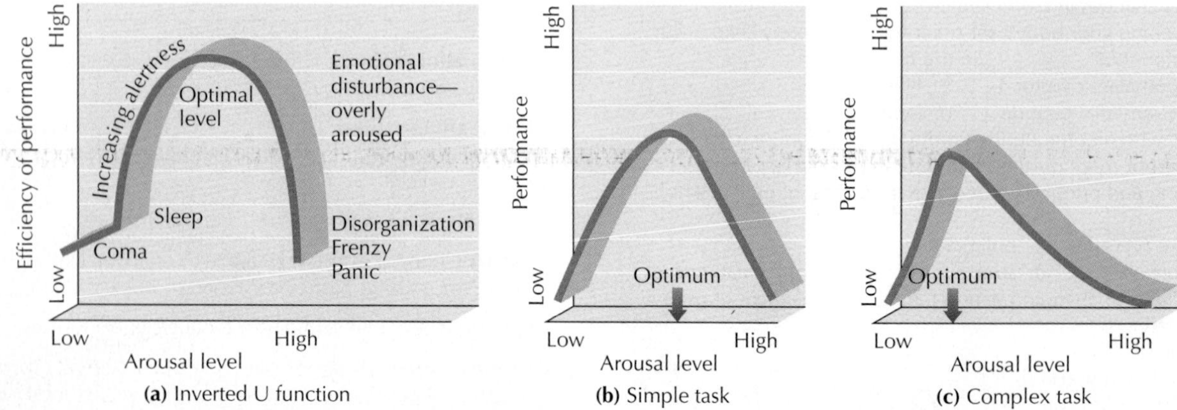

● **Figure 12.9** *(a)* The general relationship between arousal and efficiency can be described by an inverted U curve. The optimal level of arousal or motivation is higher for a simple task *(b)* than for a complex task *(c)*.

HUMAN DIVERSITY

Xtreme!

Where would you prefer to go on your next summer vacation? How about a week with your best friends at a cottage on a nearby lake? Or a shopping and museum trip to New York City? Better yet, how about cage diving with great white sharks in South Africa? If the shark adventure attracts you, you are probably high in sensation seeking and would be interested in a vacation that includes activities like bungee-jumping, scuba diving, skiing, surfing, sky diving, or white water rafting (Pizam et al., 2004).

Marvin Zuckerman (1990, 2000) has devised a test to measure differences in sensation seeking. His *Sensation-Seeking Scale* (SSS) includes statements like the samples shown here (from Zuckerman, 1996):

Thrill and adventure seeking
- I would like to try parachute jumping.
- I think I would enjoy the sensations of skiing very fast down a high mountain slope.

Experience seeking
- I like to explore a strange city or section of town myself, even if it means getting lost.
- I like to try new foods that I have never tasted before.

Disinhibition
- I like wild, "uninhibited" parties.
- I often like to get high (drinking liquor or smoking marijuana).

Boredom susceptibility
- I can't stand watching a movie that I've seen before.
- I like people who are sharp and witty, even if they do sometimes insult others.

So who are the potential cage divers? Perhaps it's not surprising that SSS scores tend to be higher among men and younger people (Butkovic & Bratko, 2003; Roberti, 2004). SSS scores also vary across cultures. In one study of eleven different cultures, people from America, Israel, and Ireland scored higher on the SSS than people from South Africa, Slovakia, Sicily, or Gabon (Pizam et al., 2004).

Exciting lives aside, there is a dark side to sensation seeking as well. High sensation seekers are also more likely to engage in high-risk behaviors such as substance abuse (Horvath et al., 2004) and casual unprotected sex (Gullette & Lyons, 2005).

Jeffrey L. Rotman

Thrill seeking is an element of the sensation-seeking personality.

stalled on a railroad track, with a speeding train bearing down on you. That's what the high-arousal end of the curve feels like.

Is performance always best at moderate levels of arousal? No, the ideal level of arousal depends on the complexity of a task. If a task is relatively simple, it is best for arousal to be high. When a task is more complex, your best performance will occur at lower levels of arousal. This relationship is called the **Yerkes-Dodson law** (see ● Figure 12.9). It applies to a wide variety of tasks and to measures of motivation other than arousal.

Some examples of the Yerkes-Dodson law might be helpful. At a track meet, it is almost impossible for sprinters to get too aroused for a race. The task is direct and uncomplicated: Run as fast as you can for a short distance. On the other hand, a basketball player making a game-deciding free throw faces a more sensitive and complex task. Excessive arousal is almost certain to hurt his or her performance. In school, most students have had experience with "test anxiety," a familiar example of how too much arousal can lower performance.

BRIDGES

One of the best ways to avoid test anxiety is to improve your study skills. If test anxiety is a problem for you, it would be wise to return to the Introduction in this text and review the learning and test-taking skills described there.

See the Introduction.

Arousal theory Assumes that people prefer to maintain ideal, or comfortable, levels of arousal.

Yerkes-Dodson law A summary of the relationships among arousal, task complexity, and performance.

Coping with Test Anxiety

Then is it true that by learning to calm down, a person would do better on tests? Usually, but not always. **Test anxiety** is a mixture of *heightened physiological arousal* (nervousness, sweating, pounding heart) and *excessive worry*. This combination—arousal plus worry—tends to distract students with a rush of upsetting thoughts and feelings (Gierl & Rogers, 1996). Studies show that students are typically most anxious when they don't know the material. If this is the case, calming down simply means you will remain calm while failing. Here are some suggestions for coping with test anxiety:

1. **Preparation.** *Hard work* is the most direct antidote for test anxiety. Many anxious students simply study too little, too late. That's why improving your study skills is a good way to reduce test anxiety (Jones & Petruzzi, 1995). The best solution is to *overprepare* by studying long before the "big day." Well-prepared students score higher, worry less, and are less likely to panic (Zohar, 1998).
2. **Relaxation.** Learning to relax is another way to lower test anxiety (Ricketts & Galloway, 1984). You can learn self-relaxation skills by looking at Chapter 14, where a relaxation technique is described. Emotional support also helps (Stöber, 2004). If you are test anxious, discuss the problem with your professors or study for tests with a supportive classmate.
3. **Rehearsal.** To reduce your nervousness, rehearse how you will cope with upsetting events. Before taking a test, imagine yourself going blank, running out of time, or feeling panicked. Then calmly plan how you will handle each situation—by keeping your attention on the task, by focusing on one question at a time, and so forth (Watson & Tharp, 2001).
4. **Restructuring Thoughts.** Another helpful strategy involves listing the upsetting thoughts you have during exams. Then you can learn to combat worries with calming, rational replies (Jones & Petruzzi, 1995). (These are called *coping statements;* see Chapter 12 for more information.) Let's say you think, "I'm going to fail this test and everybody will think I'm stupid." A good reply to this upsetting thought would be to say, "If I prepare well and control my worries, I will probably pass the test. Even if I don't, it won't be the end of the world. My friends will still like me, and I can try to improve on the next test."

Students who cope well with exams usually try to do the best they can, even under trying circumstances. Becoming a more confident test taker can actually increase your scores, because it helps you remain calm. With practice, most people can learn to be less testy at test-taking time (Smith, 2002; Zeidner, 1995).

Circadian Rhythms

We have seen that moment-to-moment changes in activation can have a major impact on performance. What about larger cycles of arousal? Do they also affect energy levels, motivation, and performance? Scientists have long known that bodily activity is guided by internal "biological clocks." Every 24 hours, your body undergoes a cycle of changes called **circadian** (SUR-kay-dee-AN) **rhythms** (*circa:* about; *diem:* a day) (Antle & Mistlberger, 2005).

Throughout the day, large changes take place in body temperature, blood pressure, and amino acid levels (● Figure 12.10). Also affected are the activities of the liver, kidneys, and endocrine glands. These activities, and many others, peak sometime each day. Output of the hormone adrenaline, which arouses the body, is often three to five times greater during the day. Most people are more energetic and alert at the high point of their circadian rhythms (Natale & Cicogna, 1996).

People with shorter circadian rhythms are "day people," who wake up alert, peak early in the day, and fall asleep early in the evening. People with longer rhythms are "night people," who wake up groggy, peak in the afternoon or early evening, and stay up late (Duffy, Rimmer, & Czeisler, 2001). Such differences are so basic that when a day person rooms with a night person, both are more likely to give their relationship a negative rating (Carey, Stanley, & Biggers, 1988). This is easy to understand: What could be worse than having someone bounding around cheerily when you're half asleep, or the reverse?

Shift Work and Jet Lag

Circadian rhythms are most noticeable whenever there is a major shift in time schedules. Businesspersons, diplomats, athletes, and other time zone travelers tend to make errors or perform poorly when their body rhythms are disturbed (Rader & Hicks, 1987). If you travel great distances east or west, the peaks and valleys of your circadian rhythms will be out of phase with the sun and clocks. For example, you might find that you are wide awake and alert at midnight. Your low point, in contrast, occurs during the middle of the day (return to ● Figure 12.10). Shift work has the

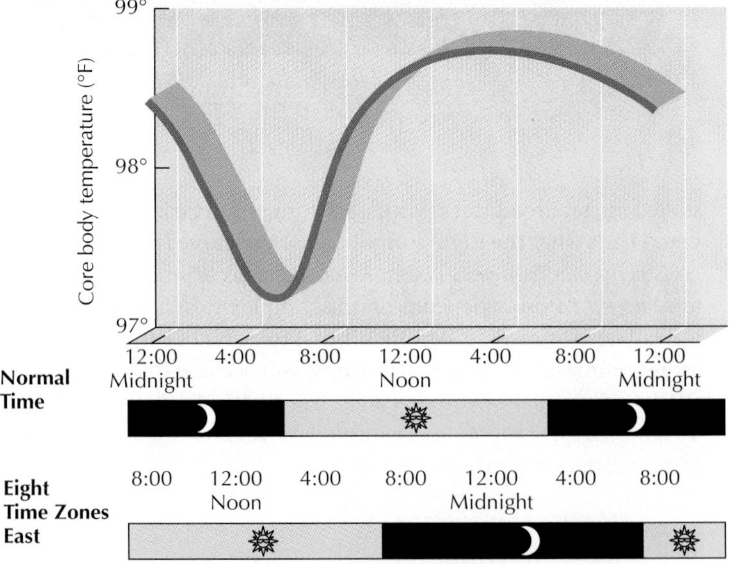

● **Figure 12.10** Core body temperature is a good indicator of a person's circadian rhythm. Most people reach a low point 2–3 hours before their normal waking time. It's no wonder that both the Chernobyl and Three-Mile Island nuclear power plant accidents occurred around 4 AM. Rapid travel to a different time zone, shift work, depression, and illness can throw sleep and waking patterns out of synchronization with the body's core rhythm. Mismatches of this kind are very disruptive (Hauri & Linde, 1990).

same effect, causing fatigue, inefficiency, irritability, upset stomach, and depression (Akerstedt, 1990).

How fast do people adapt to time shifts? For major time zone shifts (5 hours or more) it can take from several days to 2 weeks to resynchronize. Adaptation to jet lag is slowest when you stay indoors, where you can sleep and eat on "home time." Getting outdoors, where you must sleep, eat, and socialize on the new schedule, speeds adaptation. A 5-hour dose of bright sunlight early each day is particularly helpful for resetting your circadian rhythm in a new time zone (Czeisler et al., 1989). The same principle can be applied to shift work by bathing workers in bright light during their first few night shifts (Eastman et al., 1994).

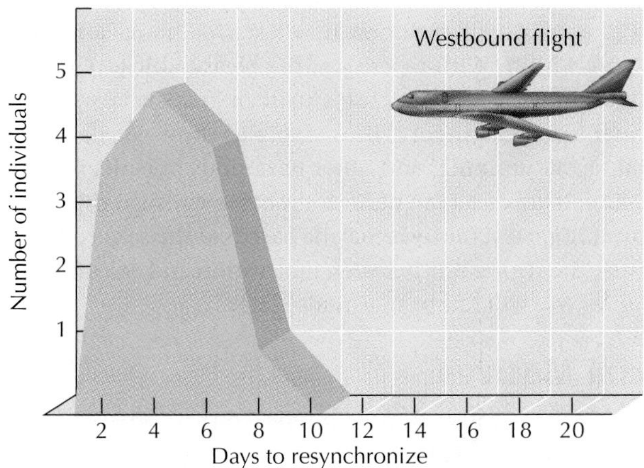

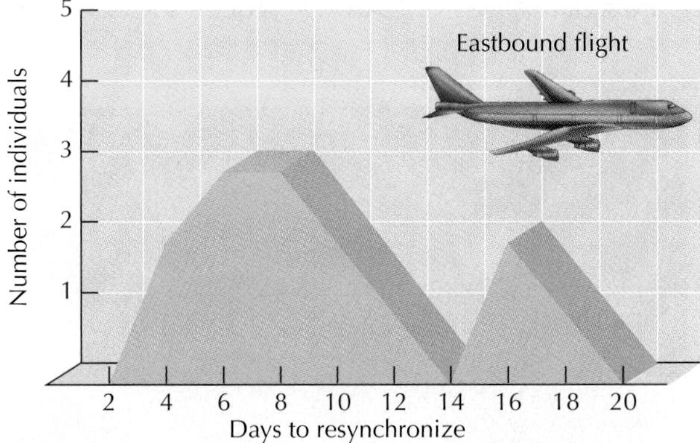

● **Figure 12.11** Time required to adjust to air travel across six time zones. The average time to resynchronize was shorter for westbound travel than for eastbound flights. (Data from Beljan et al., 1972; cited by Moore-Ede, Sulzman, & Fuller, 1982.)

The *direction* of travel also affects adaptation (Herxheimer, & Waterhouse, 2003). If you fly west, adapting is relatively easy, taking an average of 4 to 5 days. If you fly east, adapting takes 50 percent longer, or more (● Figure 12.11). Why is there a difference? The answer is that when you fly east the sun comes up *earlier* (relative to your "home" time). Let's say that you live in Los Angeles and fly to New York. Getting up at 7 AM in New York will be like getting up at 4 AM in Los Angeles. If you fly west, the sun comes up later, and it is easier for most people to "advance" (stay up later and sleep in) than it is to shift backward. Likewise, work shifts that "rotate" backward (night, evening, day) are more disruptive than those that advance (day, evening, night). Best of all are work shifts that do not change: Even continuous night work is less upsetting than rotating shifts (Lac & Chamoux, 2004).

What does all of this have to do with those of us who are not shift workers or world travelers? There are few college students who have not at one time or another "burned the midnight oil," especially for final exams. During any strenuous period, it is wise to remember that departing from your regular schedule is likely to cost more than it's worth. Often, you can do as much during 1 hour in the morning as you could have in 3 hours of work after midnight. The 2-hour difference in efficiency might as well be spent sleeping. If you feel you must deviate from your normal schedule, do it gradually over a period of days.

In general, if you can anticipate an upcoming body rhythm change (when traveling, before finals week, or when doing shift work), it is best to *preadapt* to your new schedule. Preadaptation is the gradual matching of sleep–waking cycles to a new time schedule. Before traveling, for instance, you should go to sleep one hour later (or earlier) each day until your sleep cycle matches the time at your destination. If you are unable to do that, it at least helps to fly early in the day when you fly east. When you fly west, it is better to fly late. (Remember, the *E* in *east* matches the *E* in *early*.)

Studies of flight crews show that jet lag can also be minimized by a hormone called melatonin (mel-ah-TONE-in). Melatonin is normally produced at night by the pineal gland and suppressed during daylight (Sharkey & Eastman, 2002). Melatonin has a strong impact on the timing of body rhythms and sleep cycles. As far as the brain is concerned, it's bedtime when melatonin levels rise (Shanahan et al., 1999).

To reset the body's clock in a new time zone, a small amount of melatonin can be taken about an hour before bedtime. This dose is continued for as many days as necessary to ease jet lag. The same treatment can be used for rotating work shifts (Comperatore et al, 1996; Sharkey & Eastman, 2002).

BRIDGES

Changes in melatonin levels are thought to partly explain winter depressions that occur when people endure several months of long dark days.

See Chapter 16, pages 561–562.

Test anxiety High levels of arousal and worry that seriously impair test performance.

Circadian rhythms Cyclical changes in bodily functions and arousal levels that vary on a schedule approximating a 24-hour day.

Flight crews often suffer severe disruptions in their sleep cycles. For example, a crew that leaves Los Angeles at 4 PM, bound for London, will arrive in 8 hours. Crew members' bodies, which are on California time, will act as if it is 12 AM. Yet in London, it will be 8 AM. Recent studies confirm that melatonin can help people adjust more rapidly to such time-zone changes.

Learned Motives—The Pursuit of Excellence

Many motives are acquired directly. It is easy enough to see that praise, money, success, pleasure, and similar reinforcers affect our goals and desires. But how do people learn to enjoy activities that are at first painful or frightening? Why do people climb rocks, jump out of airplanes, run marathons, take sauna baths, or swim in frozen lakes? For an answer, let's examine a related situation.

When a person first tries a drug such as heroin, he or she feels a "rush" of pleasure. However, as the drug wears off, discomfort and craving occurs. The easiest way to end the discomfort is to take another dose—as most drug users quickly learn. But in time, habituation takes place; the drug stops producing pleasure, although it will end discomfort. At the same time, the after effects of the drug grow more painful. At this point, the drug user has acquired a powerful new motive. In a vicious cycle, heroin relieves discomfort, but it guarantees that withdrawal will occur again in a few hours.

Opponent-Process Theory

Psychologist Richard L. Solomon (1980) offers an intriguing explanation for drug addiction and other learned motives. According to his **opponent-process theory**, if a stimulus causes a strong emotion, such as fear or pleasure, an opposite emotion tends to occur when the stimulus ends. For example, if you are in pain, and the pain ends, you will feel a pleasant sense of relief. If a person feels pleasure, as in the case of drug use, and the pleasure ends, it will be followed by craving or discomfort. If you are in love and feel good when you are with your lover, you will be uncomfortable when she or he is absent.

What happens if the stimulus is repeated? Solomon assumes that when a stimulus is repeated, our response to it habituates, or gets weaker. First-time skydivers, for instance, are almost always terrified. But with repeated jumps, fear decreases, until finally the skydiver feels a "thrill" instead of terror (Roth et al., 1996). In contrast, emotional aftereffects get stronger with repetition. After a first jump, beginning parachutists feel a brief but exhilarating sense of relief. After many such experiences, seasoned skydivers can get a "rush" of euphoria that lasts for hours after a jump (● Figure 12.12). With repetition, the pleasurable aftereffect gets stronger and the initial "cost" (pain or fear) gets weaker. The opponent-process theory thus explains how skydiving, rock climbing, ski jumping, and other hazardous pursuits become reinforcing. If you are a fan of horror movies, carnival rides, or bungee jumping, your motives may be based on the same effect. (Notice, too, the strong link between motivation and emotion in such examples. We will return to this idea later.)

Social Motives

Some of your friends are more interested than others in success, achievement, competition, money, possessions, status, love, approval, grades, dominance, power, or belonging to groups—all of which are *social motives* or goals. We acquire **social motives** in

● **Figure 12.12** A sport parachutist takes the plunge. The typical emotional sequence for a first jump is anxiety before, terror during, and relief after the jump. After many jumps the emotional sequence becomes eagerness before, a thrill during, and exhilaration after a jump. The new sequence strongly reinforces skydiving.

complex ways, through socialization and cultural conditioning. The behavior of outstanding artists, scientists, athletes, educators, and leaders is best understood in terms of such learned needs, particularly the need for achievement.

The Need for Achievement

To many people, being "motivated" means being interested in achievement. In a later chapter we will investigate aggression, helping, affiliation, seeking approval, and other social motives. For now, let us focus on the **need for achievement** (nAch), which is a desire to meet an internal standard of excellence (McClelland, 1961). People with high needs for achievement strive to do well any time they are evaluated.

Is that like the aggressive businessperson who strives for success? Not necessarily. Needs for achievement may lead to wealth and prestige, but people who are high achievers in art, music, science, or amateur sports may excel without seeking riches. Such people typically enjoy challenges and they relish a chance to test their abilities (Puca & Schmalt, 1999).

Power

The need for achievement differs from a **need for power,** which is a desire to have impact or control over others (McClelland, 1975). People with strong needs for power want their importance to be visible: They buy expensive possessions, wear prestigious clothes, and exploit relationships. In some ways the pursuit of power and financial success is the dark side of the American dream. People whose main goal in life is to make lots of money tend to be poorly adjusted and unhappy (Kasser & Ryan, 1993).

Characteristics of Achievers

David McClelland (1917–1998) and others have probed the need for achievement. Using a simple measure, McClelland found that he could predict the behavior of high and low achievers. For instance, McClelland compared people's occupations with scores on an achievement test they took as college sophomores. Fourteen years later, those who scored high in nAch tended to have jobs that involved risk and responsibility (McClelland, 1965).

Here's a test: In front of you are five targets. Each is placed at an increasing distance from where you are standing. You are given a beanbag to toss at the target of your choice. Target A, anyone can hit; target B, most people can hit; target C, some people can hit; target D, very few people can hit; target E is rarely if ever hit. If you hit A, you will receive $2; B, $4; C, $8; D, $16; and E, $32. You get only one toss. Which one would you choose? McClelland's research suggests that if you have a high need for achievement, you will select C or perhaps D. Those high in nAch are *moderate* risk takers. When faced with a problem or a challenge, persons high in nAch avoid goals that are too easy.

Why do they pass up sure success? They do it because easy goals offer no sense of satisfaction. They also avoid long shots because there is either no hope of success, or "winning" will be due to luck rather than skill. Persons low in nAch select sure things or impossible goals. Either way, they don't have to take any responsibility for failure.

Desires for achievement and calculated risk taking lead to success in many situations. People high in nAch complete difficult tasks, they earn better grades, and they tend to excel in their occupations. College students high in nAch attribute success to their own ability, and failure to insufficient effort. Thus, high nAch students are more likely to renew their efforts when they perform poorly. When the going gets tough, high achievers get going.

The Key to Success?

What does it take to achieve extraordinary success? Psychologist Benjamin Bloom did an interesting study of America's top concert pianists, Olympic swimmers, sculptors, tennis players, mathematicians, and research neurologists. Bloom (1985) found that drive and determination, not great natural talent, led to exceptional success.

The first steps toward high achievement began when parents exposed their children to music, swimming, scientific ideas, and so forth, "just for fun." At first, many of the children had very ordinary skills. One Olympic swimmer, for instance, remembers repeatedly losing races as a 10-year-old. At some point, however, the children began to actively cultivate their abilities. Before long, parents noticed the child's rapid progress and found an expert in-

AP/Wide World Photo

The person with high needs for achievement strives to do well in any situation in which evaluation takes place.

Opponent-process theory States that strong emotions tend to be followed by an opposite emotional state; also the strength of both emotional states changes over time.

Social motives Learned motives acquired as part of growing up in a particular society or culture.

Need for achievement The desire to excel or meet some internalized standard of excellence.

Need for power The desire to have social impact and control over others.

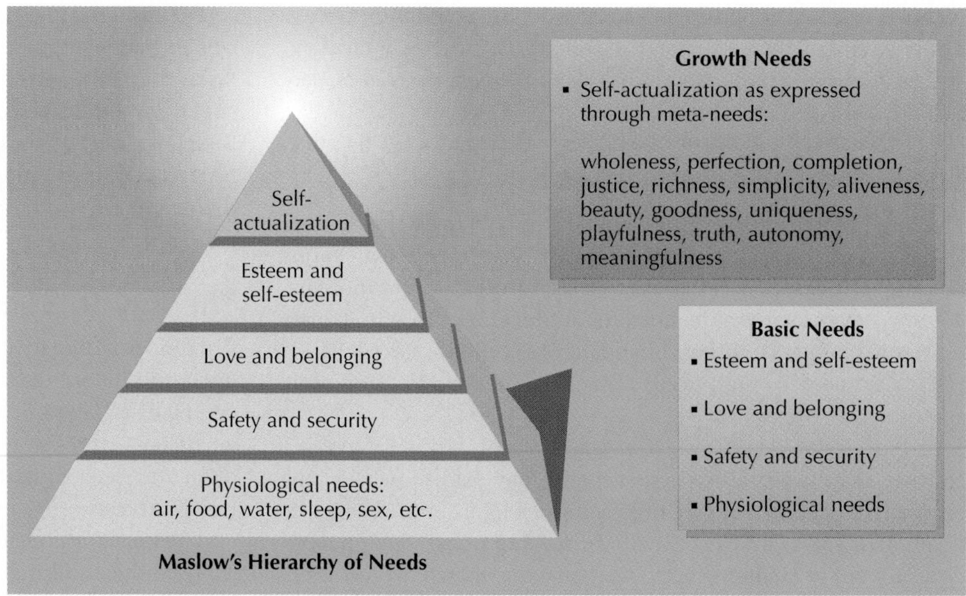

● **Figure 12.13** Maslow believed that lower needs in the hierarchy are dominant. Basic needs must be satisfied before growth motives are fully expressed. Desires for self-actualization are reflected in various meta-needs (see text).

structor or coach. After more successes, the youngsters began "living" for their talent and practiced many hours daily. This continued for many years before they reached truly outstanding heights of achievement.

The upshot of Bloom's work is that talent is nurtured by dedication and hard work (R. C. Beck, 2004). It is most likely to blossom when parents actively support a child's special interest and emphasize doing one's best at all times. Studies of child prodigies and eminent adults also show that intensive practice and expert coaching are common ingredients of high achievement. Elite performance in music, sports, chess, the arts, and many other pursuits requires at least 10 years of dedicated practice (Ericsson & Charness, 1994). The old belief that "talent will surface" on its own is largely a myth. This is especially true for talented women, who face a wide variety of social obstacles to exceptional achievement (Noble, Subotnik, & Arnold, 1996).

Self-Confidence

Achieving elite performance may be reserved for the dedicated few. Nevertheless, you may be able to improve everyday motivation by increasing your self-confidence. People with self-confidence believe they can successfully carry out an activity or reach a goal. To enhance self-confidence, it is wise to do the following (Druckman & Bjork, 1994):

- Set goals that are specific and challenging, but attainable.
- Visualize the steps you need to take to reach your goal.
- Advance in small steps.
- When you first acquire a skill, your goal should be to make progress in learning. Later, you can concentrate on improving your performance, compared with other people.
- Get expert instruction that helps you master the skill.
- Find a skilled model (someone good at the skill) to emulate.
- Get support and encouragement from an observer.
- If you fail, regard it as a sign that you need to try harder, not that you lack ability.

Self-confidence affects motivation by influencing the challenges you will undertake, the effort you will make, and how long you will persist when things don't go well. You can be confident that self-confidence is worth cultivating.

Motives in Perspective—A View from the Pyramid

What motivates people who live fully and richly? As you may recall from Chapter 1, Abraham Maslow called the full use of personal potential *self-actualization.* Maslow also described a **hierarchy of human needs**, in which some needs are more basic or powerful than others. Think about the needs that influence your own behavior. Which seem strongest? Which do you spend the most time and energy satisfying? Now look at Maslow's hierarchy (● Figure 12.13). Note that physiological needs are at the base of the pyramid. Because these needs must be met if we are to survive, they tend to be *prepotent,* or dominant over the higher needs. It could be said, for example, that "to a starving person, food is god."

Maslow believed that higher, more fragile needs are expressed only after we satisfy our physiological needs. This is also true of needs for safety and security. Until they are met, we may have little interest in higher pursuits. For instance, a person who is extremely thirsty might have little interest in writing poetry or even talking with friends. For this reason, Maslow described the first four levels of the hierarchy as **basic needs.** Other basic needs include love and belonging (family, friendship, caring), and needs for esteem and self-esteem (recognition and self-respect).

All of the basic needs are *deficiency* motives. That is, they are activated by a *lack* of food, water, security, love, esteem, or other basic needs. At the top of the hierarchy we find **growth needs,** which are expressed as a need for self-actualization. The need for self-actualization is not based on deficiencies. Rather, it is a positive, life-enhancing force for personal growth (Reiss & Havercamp, 2005). Like other humanistic psychologists, Maslow believed that people are basically good. If our basic needs are met, he said, we will tend to move on to actualizing our potentials.

Wheelchair athletes engage in vigorous competition. Maslow considered such behavior an expression of the need for self-actualization.

How are needs for self-actualization expressed? Maslow called the less powerful but humanly important actualization motives **meta-needs** (Maslow, 1970). Meta-needs are an expression of tendencies to fully development your personal potentials. The meta-needs are

1. Wholeness (unity)
2. Perfection (balance and harmony)
3. Completion (ending)
4. Justice (fairness)
5. Richness (complexity)
6. Simplicity (essence)
7. Aliveness (spontaneity)
8. Beauty (rightness of form)
9. Goodness (benevolence)
10. Uniqueness (individuality)
11. Playfulness (ease)
12. Truth (reality)
13. Autonomy (self-sufficiency)
14. Meaningfulness (values)

According to Maslow, we tend to move up through the hierarchy of needs, toward the meta-needs. When the meta-needs are unfulfilled, people fall into a "syndrome of decay" marked by despair, apathy, and alienation.

Maslow's point is that mere survival or comfort is usually not enough to make a full and satisfying life. It's interesting to note, in this regard, that college students who are primarily concerned with money, personal appearance, and social recognition score lower than average in vitality, self-actualization, and general well-being (Kasser & Ryan, 1996).

BRIDGES

Maslow provided few guidelines for promoting self-actualization. However, some suggestions can be gleaned from his writings.

See Chapter 14, pages 480–481, for more about self-actualization.

Maslow's hierarchy is not well documented by research, and many questions can be raised about it. How, for instance, do we explain the actions of people who fast as a means of social protest? How can the meta-need for justice overcome the more basic need for food? (Perhaps the answer is that fasting is temporary and self-imposed.) Despite such objections, Maslow's views are a good way to understand and appreciate the rich interplay of human motives.

Are many people motivated by meta-needs? Maslow estimated that few people are primarily motivated by needs for self-actualization. Most of us are more concerned with esteem, love, or security. Perhaps this is because rewards in our society tend to encourage conformity, uniformity, and security in schools, jobs, and relationships. When was the last time you met a meta-need?

Intrinsic and Extrinsic Motivation

Some people cook for a living and consider it hard work. Others cook for pleasure and dream of opening a restaurant. For some people, carpentry, gardening, writing, photography, or jewelry making is fun. For others the same activities are drudgery they must be paid to do. How can the same activity be "work" for one person and "play" for another?

When you do something for enjoyment or to improve your abilities, your motivation is usually *intrinsic*. **Intrinsic motivation** occurs when we act without any obvious external rewards. We simply enjoy an activity or see it as an opportunity to explore, learn, and actualize our potentials. In contrast, **extrinsic motivation** stems from external factors, such as pay, grades, rewards, obligations, and approval. Most of the activities we think of as "work" are extrinsically rewarded (Baard, Deci, & Ryan, 2004; Ryan & Deci, 2000).

Turning Play into Work

Don't extrinsic incentives strengthen motivation? Yes they can, but not always. In fact, *excessive* rewards can decrease intrinsic motivation and spontaneous interest (Lepper, Keavney, & Drake, 1996; Tang & Hall, 1995). For instance, children who were lavishly rewarded for drawing with felt-tip pens later showed little interest

Hierarchy of human needs Abraham Maslow's ordering of needs, based on their presumed strength or potency.

Basic needs The first four levels of needs in Maslow's hierarchy; lower needs tend to be more potent than higher needs.

Growth needs In Maslow's hierarchy, the higher-level needs associated with self-actualization.

Meta-needs In Maslow's hierarchy, needs associated with impulses for self-actualization.

Intrinsic motivation Motivation that comes from within, rather than from external rewards; motivation based on personal enjoyment of a task or activity.

Extrinsic motivation Motivation based on obvious external rewards, obligations, or similar factors.

in playing with the pens again (Greene & Lepper, 1974). Apparently, "play" can be turned into "work" by *requiring* people to do something they would otherwise enjoy. When we are coerced or "bribed" to act, we tend to feel as if we are "faking it." Employees who lack initiative and teenagers who reject school and learning are good examples of such reactions (Ryan & Deci, 2000).

Creativity

People are more likely to be creative when they are intrinsically motivated. On the job, for instance, salaries and bonuses may increase the amount of work done. However, work *quality* is affected more by intrinsic factors, such as personal interest and freedom of choice (Nakamura & Csikszentmihalyi, 2003). People who are intrinsically motivated usually get personally involved in tasks, which leads to greater creativity (Ruscio, Whitney, & Amabile, 1998).

Psychologist Teresa Amabile lists the following as "creativity killers" on the job:

- Working under surveillance
- Having your choices restricted by rules
- Working primarily to get a good evaluation (or avoid a bad one)
- Working mainly to get more money

Time pressure also kills creativity. Employees are less likely to solve tricky problems and come up with innovative ideas when they work "under the gun" (Amabile, Hadley, & Kramer, 2002). When a person is intrinsically motivated, a certain amount of challenge, surprise, and complexity makes a task rewarding. A person who is extrinsically motivated wants to take the fastest, most direct route to a goal, not the most creative (Sternberg and Lubart, 1995).

How can the concept of intrinsic motivation be applied? Both types of motivation are necessary. But extrinsic motivation shouldn't be overused, especially with children. To summarize, (1) if there's no intrinsic interest in an activity to begin with, you have nothing to lose by using extrinsic rewards; (2) if basic skills are lacking, extrinsic rewards may be necessary at first; (3) extrinsic rewards can focus attention on an activity so real interest will develop; and (4) if extrinsic rewards are used, they should be small and phased out as soon as possible (Greene & Lepper, 1974). It also helps to tell children they seem to be *really interested* in drawing, playing the piano, learning a language, or whatever activity you are rewarding (Cialdini et al., 1998).

At work, it is valuable for managers to find out what each employee's interests and career goals are. People are not solely motivated by money. A chance to do challenging, interesting, and intrinsically rewarding work is often just as important (Campion & McClelland, 1993). In many situations it is important to encourage intrinsic motivation, especially when children are learning new skills.

KNOWLEDGE BUILDER

Stimulus Motives, Learned Motives, Maslow, and Intrinsic Motivation

REFLECT

Does arousal theory seem to explain any of your own behavior? Think of at least one time when your performance was impaired by arousal that was too low or too high. Now think of some personal examples that illustrate the Yerkes-Dodson law.

In situations involving risk and skill, do you like to "go for broke"? Or do you prefer sure things? Do you think you are high, medium, or low in nAch?

Which levels of Maslow's hierarchy of needs occupy most of your time and energy?

Name an activity you do that is intrinsically motivated and one that is extrinsically motivated. How do they differ?

LEARNING CHECK

1. Exploration, manipulation, and curiosity provide evidence for the existence of ____________________ drives.

Rick Friedman/Corbis

Gregory A. Beaumont/® The Great Arcata to Ferndale World Championship Cross Country Kinetic Sculpture Race

People who are intrinsically motivated feel free to explore creative solutions to problems. (*Left.* Dean Kaman, inventor of the Segway personal transportation device. *Right.* "Caffiends at the Beach," an entrant in the Great Arcata to Ferndale World Championship Cross Country Kinetic Sculpture Race.)

2. People who score high on the SSS tend to be extroverted, independent, and individuals who value change. T or F?
3. Complex tasks, such as taking a classroom test, tend to be disrupted by high levels of arousal, an effect predicted by
   a. the Sensation-Seeking Scale
   b. the Yerkes-Dodson law
   c. studies of circadian arousal patterns
   d. studies of the need for achievement
4. Two key elements of test anxiety that must be controlled are ____________ and excessive ____________.
5. People high in nAch
   a. prefer long shots
   b. prefer sure things
   c. are moderate risk takers
   d. prefer change and high levels of stimulation
6. The highest level of Maslow's hierarchy of motives involves
   a. meta-needs
   b. needs for safety and security
   c. needs for love and belonging
   d. extrinsic needs
7. Intrinsic motivation is often undermined in situations in which obvious external rewards are applied to a naturally enjoyable activity. T or F?
8. Which of the following is *not* a characteristic of people who score high on the Sensation-Seeking Scale?
   a. boredom susceptibility c. inhibition
   b. experience seeking d. thrill seeking

CRITICAL THINKING

9. Over 75 percent of all U.S. college freshmen say that "being well-off financially" is an essential life goal. Seventy-three percent indicate that "making more money" was a very important factor in their decision to attend college (Green, 1989). Which meta-needs are fulfilled by "making more money"?

Answers: 1. stimulus 2. T 3. b 4. arousal, worry 5. c 6. a 7. T 8. c
9. None of them.

Inside an Emotion—How Do You Feel?

Picture the faces of terrified people fleeing the collapse of the World Trade Center towers in New York and it's easy to see that motivation and emotion are closely related. Emotions shape our relationships and color our daily activities. What are the basic parts of an emotion? How does the body respond during emotion?

If a mad scientist replaced your best friend's brain with a computer, how would you know that something was wrong? An absence of emotion might be one of the first telltale signs. **Emotion** is characterized by physiological arousal, and changes in facial expressions, gestures, posture, and subjective feelings.

The word *emotion* means "to move," and emotions do indeed move us. First, the body is physically aroused during emotion. Such bodily stirrings are what cause us to say we were "moved" by a play, a funeral, or an act of kindness. Second, we are often motivated, or moved to take action, by emotions such as fear, anger, or joy. Many of the goals we seek make us feel good. Many of the activities we avoid make us feel bad. We feel happy when we succeed and sad when we fail (Oatley & Jenkins, 1992).

Emotions are linked to many basic **adaptive behaviors,** such as attacking, fleeing, seeking comfort, helping others, and reproducing. Such behaviors help us survive and adjust to changing conditions (Plutchik, 2003). However, it is also apparent that emotions can have negative effects. Stage fright or "choking up" in sports can spoil performances. Hate, anger, contempt, disgust, and fear disrupt behavior and relationships. But more often, emotions aid survival. As social animals, it would be impossible for humans to live in groups, cooperate in raising children, and defend one another without positive emotional bonds of love, caring, and friendship (Buss, 2000).

A pounding heart, sweating palms, "butterflies" in the stomach, and other bodily reactions are a major element of fear, anger, joy, and other emotions. Typical **physiological changes** include changes in heart rate, blood pressure, perspiration, and other bodily stirrings. Most are caused by activity in the sympathetic nervous system and by the hormone **adrenaline,** which the adrenal glands release into the bloodstream.

Emotional expressions, or outward signs of what a person is feeling, are another ingredient of emotion. For example, when you are intensely afraid, your hands tremble, your face contorts, your posture becomes tense and defensive, and your voice changes. In general, these expressions serve to tell others what emotions we are experiencing (Hortman, 2003).

Emotional feelings (a person's private emotional experience) are a final major element of emotion. This is the part of emotion with which we are usually most familiar.

Primary Emotions

Are some emotions more basic than others? Yes. Robert Plutchik (2003) has identified eight **primary emotions.** These are fear, surprise, sadness, disgust, anger, anticipation, joy, and trust (acceptance). If the list seems too short, it's because each emotion can vary in *intensity.* When you're angry, for instance, you may feel anything from rage to simple annoyance, as shown in ● Figure 12.14.

Emotion A state characterized by physiological arousal, changes in facial expression, gestures, posture, and subjective feelings.

Adaptive behaviors Actions that aid attempts to survive and adapt to changing conditions.

Physiological changes (in emotion) Alterations in heart rate, blood pressure, perspiration, and other involuntary responses.

Adrenaline A hormone produced by the adrenal glands that tends to arouse the body.

Emotional expression Outward signs that an emotion is occurring.

Emotional feelings The private, subjective experience of having an emotion.

Primary emotions According to Robert Plutchik, the most basic emotions are fear, surprise, sadness, disgust, anger, anticipation, joy, and acceptance.

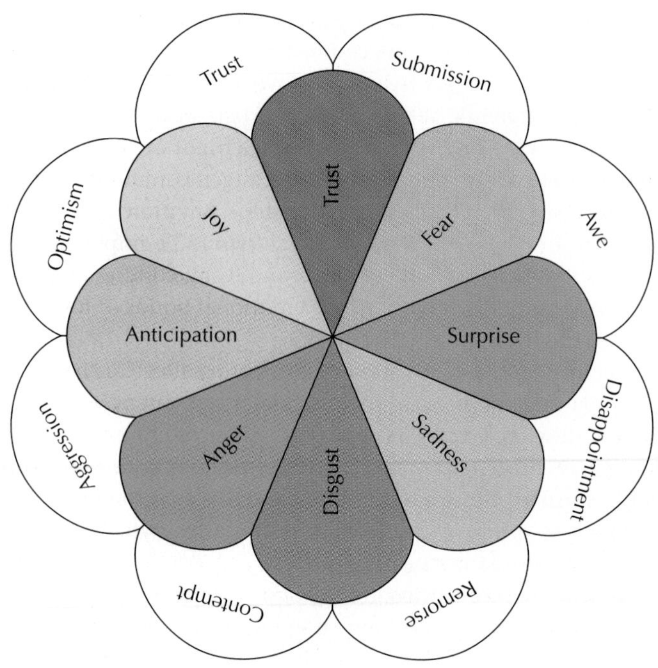

Less intense	Primary emotion	More intense
Interest	Anticipation	Vigilance
Serenity	Joy	Ecstasy
Acceptance	Trust	Admiration
Apprehension	Fear	Terror
Distraction	Surprise	Amazement
Pensiveness	Sadness	Grief
Boredom	Disgust	Loathing
Annoyance	Anger	Rage

● **Figure 12.14** Primary and mixed emotions. In Robert Plutchik's model there are eight primary emotions, as listed in the inner areas. Adjacent emotions may combine to give the emotions listed around the perimeter. Mixtures involving more widely separated emotions are also possible. For example, fear plus anticipation produces anxiety. (Adapted from Plutchik, 2003.)

As shown in ● Figure 12.14, each pair of adjacent emotions can be mixed to yield a third, more complex emotion. Other mixtures are also possible. For example, 5-year-old Tupac feels both joy and fear as he eats a stolen cookie. The result? Guilt—as you may recall from your own childhood. Likewise, jealousy could be a mixture of love, anger, and fear.

A *mood* is the mildest form of emotion (● Figure 12.15). **Moods** are low-intensity emotional states that can last for many hours, or even days. Moods often affect day-to-day behavior by preparing us to act in certain ways. For example, when your neighbor Roseanne is in an irritable mood she may react angrily to almost anything you say. When she is in a happy mood, she can easily laugh off an insult. Happy, positive moods tend to make us more adaptable in several ways. For example, when you are in a good mood, you are likely to make better decisions and you will be more helpful, efficient, creative, and peaceful (Compton, 2005).

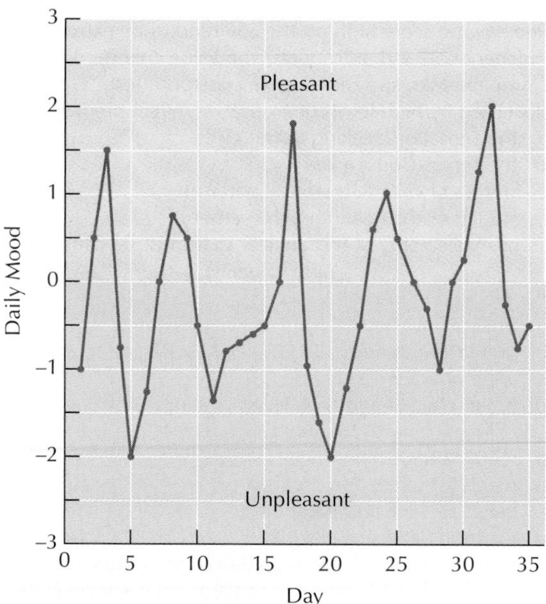

● **Figure 12.15** Folklore holds that people who work or attend school on a weekly schedule experience their lowest moods on "Blue Monday." Actually, moods tend to be generally lower for *most* weekdays than they are on weekends. The graph shown here plots the average daily mood ratings made by a group of college students over a 5-week period. As you can see, many people find that their moods rise and fall on a 7-day cycle. For most students, a low point tends to occur around Monday or Tuesday and a peak on Friday or Saturday. (Adapted from Larsen & Kasimatis, 1990.) In other words, moods are often entrained (pulled along) by weekly schedules.

The Brain and Emotion

Emotions can be either positive or negative. Ordinarily, we might think that positive and negative emotions are opposites. But this is not the case. As Tupac's "cookie guilt" implies, it is possible to have positive and negative emotions at the same time. How is that possible? In the brain, positive emotions are processed mainly in the left hemisphere. In contrast, negative emotions are processed in the right hemisphere. The fact that positive and negative emotions are based on different brain areas helps explain why we can feel happy and sad at the same time (Canli et al., 1998). It also explains why your right foot is more ticklish than your left foot! The left hemisphere controls the right side of the body and processes positive emotions (Smith & Cahusac, 2001). Thus, most people are more ticklish on their right side. If you really want to tickle someone, be sure to "do it right."

Scientists used to think that all emotions are processed by the cerebral cortex. However, this is not always the case. Imagine this test of willpower: Go to a zoo and place your face close to the glass in front of a rattlesnake display. Suddenly, the rattlesnake strikes at your face. Do you flinch? Even though you know you are safe, Joseph LeDoux predicts that you will recoil from the snake's attack (LeDoux, 2000).

LeDoux and other researchers have found that an area of the brain called the **amygdala** (ah-MIG-duh-la) specializes in producing fear (● Figure 12.16). (See Chapter 2 for more information.)

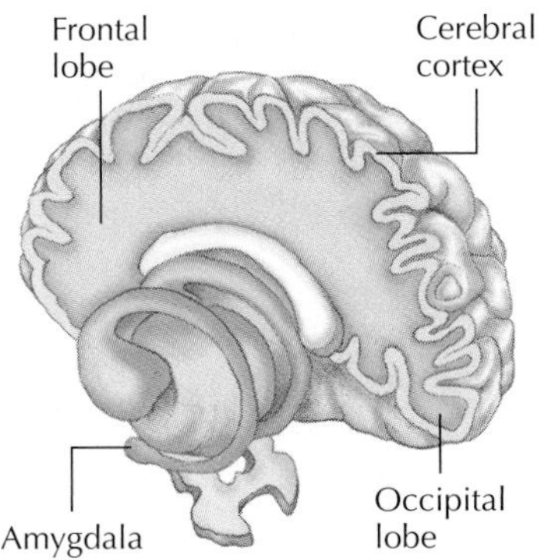

● **Figure 12.16** An amygdala can be found buried within the temporal lobes on each side of the brain (see Chapter 2). The amygdala appears to provide "quick and dirty" processing of emotional stimuli that allows us to react involuntarily to danger.

The amygdala receives sensory information very directly and quickly, bypassing the cortex. As a result, it allows us to respond to potential danger before we really know what's happening. This primitive fear response is not under the control of higher brain centers. The role of the amygdala in emotion may explain why people who suffer from phobias and disabling anxiety often feel afraid without knowing why (Fellous & Ledoux, 2005).

People who suffer damage to the amygdala become "blind" to emotion. An armed robber could hold a gun to the person's head and the person wouldn't feel fear. Such people are also unable to "read" or understand other people's emotions. Many lose their ability to relate normally to friends, family, and coworkers (Goleman, 1995).

Later we will attempt to put all the elements of emotion together into a single picture. But first, we need to look more closely at bodily arousal and emotional expressions.

Physiology and Emotion—Arousal, Sudden Death, and Lying

An African Bushman frightened by a lion and a city dweller frightened by a prowler will react in much the same way (Mesquita & Frijda, 1992). Such encounters usually produce muscle tension, a pounding heart, irritability, dryness of the throat and mouth, sweating, butterflies in the stomach, frequent urination, trembling, restlessness, sensitivity to loud noises, and numerous other bodily changes. These reactions are nearly universal because they are innate. Specifically, they are caused by the **autonomic nervous system (ANS)** (the neural system that connects the brain with internal organs and glands). As you may recall from Chapter 2, activity of the ANS is *automatic,* rather than voluntary.

Fight or Flight

The ANS has two divisions, the sympathetic branch and the parasympathetic branch. The two branches are active at all times. Whether you are relaxed or aroused at any moment depends on the combined activity of both branches (Kalat, 2004).

What does the ANS do during emotion? In general, the **sympathetic branch** activates the body for emergency action—for "fighting or fleeing." It does this by arousing some bodily systems and inhibiting others (● Figure 12.17). These changes have a purpose. Sugar is released into the bloodstream for quick energy, the heart beats faster to supply blood to the muscles, digestion is temporarily slowed, blood flow in the skin is restricted to reduce bleeding, and so forth. Such reactions improve the chances of surviving an emergency.

The **parasympathetic branch** reverses emotional arousal. This calms and relaxes the body. After a period of high emotion, the heart is slowed, the pupils return to normal size, blood pressure drops, and so forth. In addition to restoring balance, the parasympathetic system helps build up and conserve bodily energy.

The parasympathetic system responds much more slowly than the sympathetic system does. That's why a pounding heart, muscle tension, and other signs of arousal don't fade for 20 or 30 minutes after you feel an intense emotion, such as fear. Moreover, after a strong emotional shock, the parasympathetic system may overreact and lower blood pressure too much. This can cause you to become dizzy or to faint after seeing something shocking, such as a horrifying accident.

Sudden Death

An overreaction to intense emotion is called a **parasympathetic rebound.** If the rebound is severe, it can sometimes cause death. In times of war, for instance, combat can be so savage that some soldiers literally die of fear (Moritz & Zamchech, 1946). Apparently, such deaths occur because the parasympathetic nervous system slows the heart to a stop. Even in civilian life this is possible. In one case, a terrified young woman was admitted to a hospital because she felt she was going to die. A backwoods midwife had predicted that the woman's two sisters would die before their 16th and 21st birthdays. Both died as predicted. The midwife also predicted that this woman would die before her 23rd birthday. She was found dead in her hospital bed the day after she was admitted. It was 2 days before her 23rd birthday (Seligman, 1989). The woman was an apparent victim of her own terror.

Mood A low-intensity, long-lasting emotional state.

Amygdala A part of the limbic system (within the brain) that produces fear responses.

Autonomic nervous system (ANS) The system of nerves that connects the brain with the internal organs and glands.

Sympathetic branch A part of the ANS that activates the body at times of stress.

Parasympathetic branch A part of the autonomic system that quiets the body and conserves energy.

Parasympathetic rebound Excess activity in the parasympathetic nervous system following a period of intense emotion.

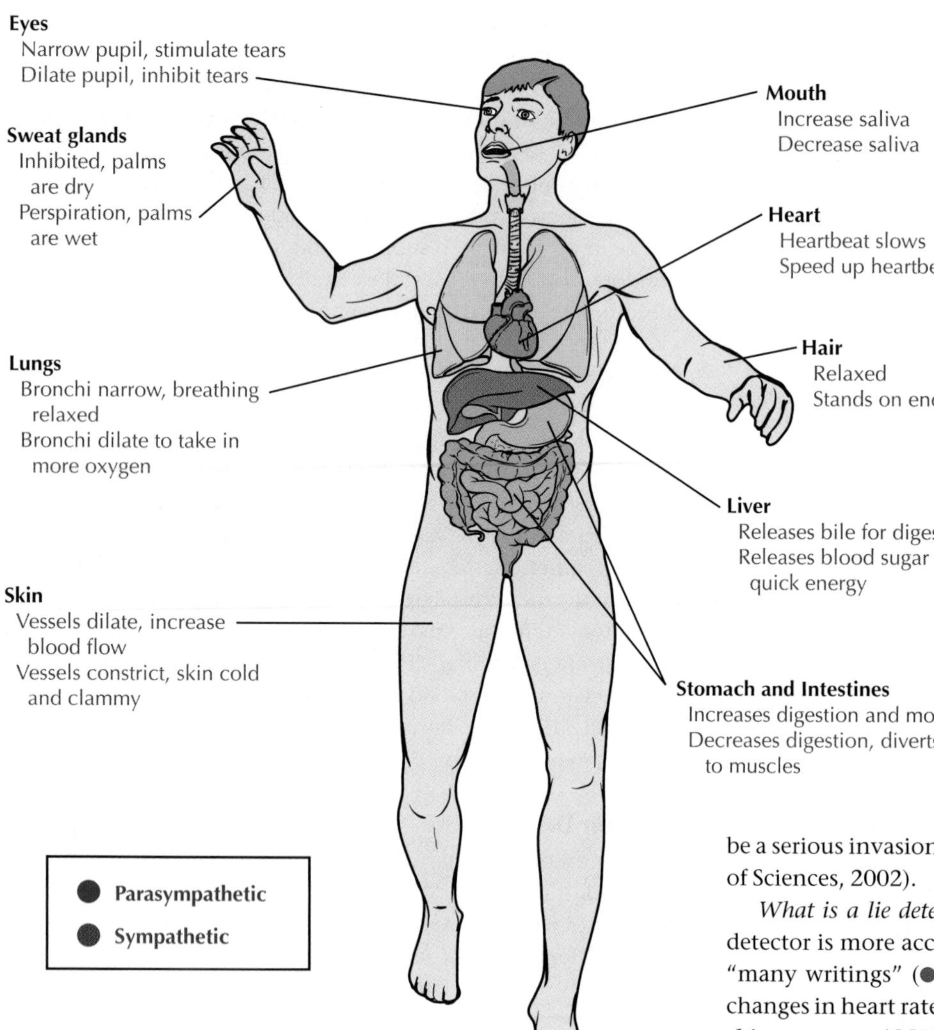

● **Figure 12.17** The parasympathetic branch of the ANS calms and quiets the body. The sympathetic branch arouses the body and prepares it for emergency action.

Is the parasympathetic nervous system always responsible for such deaths? Probably not. For older persons or those with heart problems, sympathetic effects may be enough to bring about heart attack and collapse. For example, five times more people than usual died of heart attacks on the day of a major 1994 earthquake in Los Angeles (Leor, Poole, & Kloner, 1996). In Asia, the number 4 is considered unlucky, and more heart patients die on the fourth day of the month than any other day. Because they fear they will die on an "unlucky day," their chance of dying actually increases (Phillips et al., 2001).

Lie Detectors

Was Michael Jackson guilty? Has Scott Peterson ever told the whole truth about Laci? Has a trusted employee been stealing from the business? The most popular method for detecting lies measures the bodily changes that accompany emotion. However, the accuracy of "lie detector" tests is doubtful, and they can be a serious invasion of privacy (Lykken, 2001; National Academy of Sciences, 2002).

What is a lie detector? Do lie detectors really detect lies? The lie detector is more accurately called a *polygraph,* a word that means "many writings" (● Figure 12.18). A typical **polygraph** records changes in heart rate, blood pressure, breathing, and the **galvanic skin response (GSR).** The GSR is recorded from the hand by electrodes that measure skin conductance or, more simply, sweating. Popularly known as a lie detector because it is used for that purpose by the police, the polygraph was invented in 1915 by psychologist William Marston. He also created the comic book character *Wonder Woman,* a superhero whose "magic lasso" could

Bob Daemmrich/The Image Works

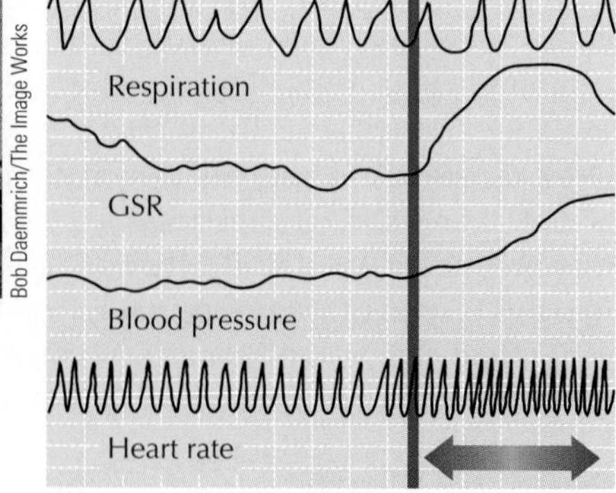

● **Figure 12.18** *(left)* A typical polygraph includes devices for measuring heart rate, blood pressure, respiration, and galvanic skin response. Pens mounted on the top of the machine make a record of bodily responses on a moving strip of paper. *(right)* Changes in the area marked by the arrow indicate emotional arousal. If such responses appear when a person answers a question, he or she may be lying, but other causes of arousal are also possible.

CRITICAL THINKING

To Catch a Terrorist

An airport check-in agent asks a passenger if he packed his own luggage. He says he did. But he is sitting in a booth that creates high-resolution infrared images of the heat patterns on his face. The patterns reveal stress, suggesting that he is lying. His luggage is searched and an otherwise undetectable explosive device is confiscated, averting a potential disaster.

Although this scenario is not yet a reality, it is not as far-fetched as you might think. The growing realization that polygraph tests are not very accurate could not have come at a worse time for national security (Knight, 2004). The infrared scanner is just one alternative technology currently under development. Preliminary research indicates that infrared face scans are at least as accurate as polygraphs at detecting lying (Pavlidis, Eberhardt, & Levine, 2002).

Other new techniques look directly at brain activity, thus bypassing the traditional approach of looking for indirect signs of general emotional arousal. For example, psychologist Daniel Langleben theorizes that a liar must inhibit telling the truth in order to lie (Langleben et al., 2002). Thus, extra brain areas must be activated to tell a lie, which can be seen in fMRI brain images (see Chapter 2) when people are lying.

Even if new techniques are used, a problem remains: How can we avoid falsely classifying liars as truth tellers and truth tellers as liars? Until that can be done with acceptable accuracy, the new technologies may have no more value than the polygraph does.

force people to tell the truth (Grubin & Madsen, 2005). In reality, the polygraph is not a lie detector at all. The device only records *general emotional arousal*—it can't tell the difference between lying and fear, anxiety, or excitement (Lykken, 2001).

When trying to detect a lie, the polygraph operator begins by asking irrelevant (neutral, non-emotional) questions, such as, "Is your name (person's name)?" "Did you eat lunch today?" and so forth. This establishes a "baseline" for normal emotional responses. Then the examiner asks relevant questions: "Did you murder Hensley?" Presumably, only a guilty person will become anxious or emotional if they lie when answering relevant questions.

Wouldn't a person be nervous just from being questioned? Yes, but to minimize this problem, skilled polygraph examiners ask a *series* of questions with critical items mixed among them. An innocent person may respond emotionally to the whole procedure, but only a guilty person is supposed to respond more to key questions. For example, a suspected bank robber might be shown several pictures and asked, "Was the teller who was robbed this person? Was it this person?"

As an alternative, subjects may be asked **control questions,** which are designed to make almost anyone anxious: "Have you ever stolen anything from your place of work?" Typically, such questions are very difficult to answer truthfully with an unqualified no. In theory they show how a person reacts to doubt or misgivings. The person's reaction to critical questions can then be compared with responses to control questions.

Even when questioning is done properly, lie detection may be inaccurate (Grubin & Madsen, 2005). For example, a man named Floyd Fay was convicted of murdering his friend Fred Ery. To prove his innocence, Fay volunteered to take a lie detector test, which he failed. Fay spent 2 years in prison before the real killer confessed to the crime. Psychologist David Lykken (1998, 2001) has documented many cases in which innocent people were jailed after being convicted on the basis of polygraph evidence.

If Floyd Fay was innocent, why did he fail the test? Put yourself in his place, and it's easy to see why. Imagine the examiner asking, "Did you kill Fred?" Because you knew Fred, and you are a suspect, it's no secret that this is a critical question. What would happen to *your* heart rate, blood pressure, breathing, and perspiration under such circumstances?

Proponents of lie detection claim it is 95-percent accurate. But in one study, accuracy was dramatically lowered when people thought about past emotional experiences as they answered irrelevant questions (Ben-Shakhar & Dolev, 1996). Similarly, the polygraph may be thrown off by self-inflicted pain, by tranquilizing drugs, or by people who can lie without anxiety (Waid & Orne, 1982). Worst of all, the test is much more likely to label an innocent person guilty, rather than a guilty person innocent. In studies involving real crimes, an average of one innocent person in five was rated as guilty by the lie detector (Lykken, 2001; Patrick & Iacono, 1989; Saxe, Dougherty, & Cross, 1985). In some instances, these false positives have caused three out of four innocent persons to be labeled guilty. Individuals who believe the polygraph is highly accurate may actually change their statements to be con-

Polygraph A device for recording heart rate, blood pressure, respiration, and galvanic skin response; commonly called a "lie detector."

Galvanic skin response (GSR) A change in the electrical resistance (or inversely, the conductance) of the skin, due to sweating.

Control questions In a polygraph exam, questions that almost always provoke anxiety.

sistent with the test. This, too, can leave an innocent person open to false accusations (Meyer & Youngjohn, 1991). For such reasons, the National Academy of Sciences (2002) recently concluded that polygraph tests should not be used to screen employees. (See "To Catch a Terrorist.")

Despite the lie detector's unreliability, you may be tested for employment or other reasons. Should this occur, the best advice is to remain calm; then actively challenge the outcome if the machine wrongly questions your honesty.

KNOWLEDGE BUILDER

Emotion and Physiological Arousal

REFLECT

How did your most emotional moment of the past week affect your behavior, expressions, feelings, and bodily state? Could you detect both sympathetic and parasympathetic effects?

Make a list of the emotions you consider to be most basic. To what extent do they agree with Plutchik's list?

What did you think about the lie detector test before reading this chapter? What do you think now?

LEARNING CHECK

1. Many of the physiological changes associated with emotion are caused by secretion of the hormone
   a. atropine c. attributine
   b. adrenaline d. amoduline
2. Emotional _______________ often serve to communicate a person's emotional state to others.
3. Awe, remorse, and disappointment are among the primary emotions listed by Robert Plutchik. T or F?
4. Emotional arousal is closely related to activity of the _______ _______________ nervous system.
5. Preparing the body for "fighting or fleeing" is largely the job of the
   a. paraventricular nucleus c. GSR
   b. sympathetic branch d. left hemisphere
6. The parasympathetic system inhibits digestion and raises blood pressure and heart rate. T or F?
7. What bodily changes are measured by a polygraph? _______ _______________

CRITICAL THINKING

8. Can you explain why people "cursed" by shamans or "witch doctors" sometimes actually die?

Answers: 1. b 2. expressions 3. F 4. autonomic 5. b 6. F 7. heart rate, blood pressure, breathing rate, GSR 8. In cultures where there is deep belief in magic or voodoo, a person who thinks that she or he has been cursed may become uncontrollably emotional. After several days of intense terror, a parasympathetic rebound is likely. If the rebound is severe enough, it can lead to physical collapse and death.

Expressing Emotions—Making Faces and Talking Bodies

Next to our own feelings, the expressions of others are the most familiar part of emotion. Are emotional expressions a carryover from human evolution? Charles Darwin thought so. Darwin (1872) observed that angry tigers, monkeys, dogs, and humans all bare their teeth in the same way. Psychologists believe that emotional expressions evolved to communicate our feelings to others, which aids survival. Such messages give valuable hints about what other people are likely to do next (Ekman & Rosenberg, 1997). For instance, in a recent study, people were able to detect angry and scheming faces faster than happy, sad, or neutral faces (● Figure 12.19). Presumably, we are especially sensitive to threatening faces because they warn us of possible harm (Oehman, 2002; Tipples, Atkinson, & Young, 2002.)

Facial Expressions

Are emotional expressions the same for all people? Basic expressions appear to be fairly universal (● Figure 12.20). Children who are born blind have little opportunity to learn emotional expressions from others. Even so, they display joy, sadness, fear, anger, and disgust in the same way as sighted people do (Galati, Scherer, & Ricci-Bitti, 1997).

Some facial expressions are shaped by learning and may be found only in specific cultures. Among the Chinese, for example, sticking out the tongue is a gesture of surprise, not of disrespect or teasing. If a person comes from another culture, it is wise to remember that you may easily misunderstand his or her expressions. At such times, knowing the social *context* in which an expression occurs helps clarify its meaning (Carroll & Russell, 1996; Ekman, 1993). (Also, see "Cultural Differences in Emotion.")

Cultural Differences in Emotion

How many times have you been angry this week? Once? Twice? Several times? If it was more than once, you're not unusual. Anger is a very common emotion in Western cultures. Very likely this is because our culture emphasizes personal independence and a free expression of individual rights and needs. In North America, anger is widely viewed as a "natural" reaction to feeling that you have been treated unfairly.

On the opposite side of the globe, many Asian cultures place a high value on group harmony. In Asia, expressing anger in public is less common and anger is regarded as less "natural." The reason for this is that anger tends to separate people. Thus, being angry is at odds with a culture that values cooperation (Markus, Kitayama, & VandenBos, 1996).

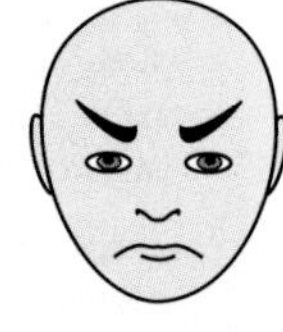

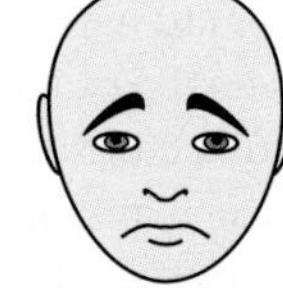

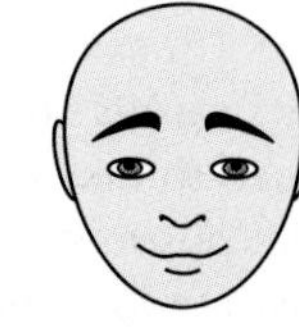

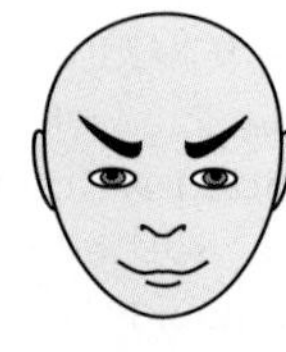

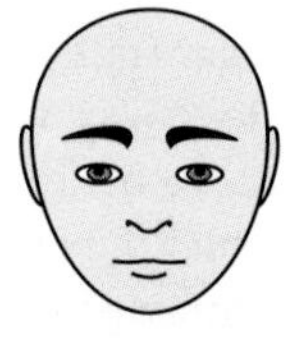

● Figure 12.19 When shown groups of simplified faces (without labels), the angry and scheming faces "jumped out" at people faster than sad, happy, or neutral faces. An ability to rapidly detect threatening expressions probably helped our ancestors survive. (Adapted from Tipples, Atkinson, & Young, 2002.)

FOCUS ON RESEARCH

Crow's-Feet and Smiles Sweet

The next time you see an athletic contest or a beauty pageant on television, look closely at the winner's smile and the smile of the runner-up. Although both people will be smiling, it is likely that the winner's smile will be authentic and the loser's smile will be forced.

We smile for many reasons: to be polite or because of embarrassment, or sometimes to deceive (Frank, 2002; Frank & Ekman, 2004). These "social smiles" are often intentional or forced, and they only involve lifting the corners of the mouth. What does a genuine smile look like? A real smile involves not only the mouth, but also the small muscles around the eyes. These muscles lift the cheeks and make crow's-feet or crinkles in the outside corners of the eyes.

Authentic smiles are called *Duchenne smiles* (after Guilluame Duchenne, a French scientist who studied facial muscles). The muscles around the eyes are very difficult to tighten on command. Hence, to tell if a smile in authentic, or merely posed, look at the corners of a person's eyes, not the mouth (Williams et al., 2001). To put it another way, crow's-feet mean a smile is sweet.

Duchenne smiles signal genuine happiness and enjoyment (Soussignan, 2002). In a recent study, women who had authentic smiles in their college yearbook photos were contacted 6, 22, and 31 years later. At each interval, real smiles in college were associated with more positive emotions and a greater sense of competence. We can only speculate about why this is the case. However, it is likely that smiling signals that a person is helpful or nurturing. This leads to more supportive social relationships and, in a self-fulfilling manner, to greater happiness (Gladstone & Parker, 2002).

Dennis Coon

The face on the left shows a social smile; the one on the right is an authentic, or Duchenne, smile.

Culture also influences positive emotions. In America, we tend to have positive feelings such as pride, happiness, and superiority, which emphasize our role as *individuals*. In Japan, positive feelings are more often linked with membership in groups (friendly feelings, closeness to others, and respect) (Kitayama, Markus, & Kurokawa, 2000). It is common to think of emotion as an individual event. However, as you can see, emotion is shaped by cultural ideas, values, and practices.

Gender and Emotion

Women have a reputation for being "more emotional" than men. Are they? There is little reason to think that men and women differ in their private experiences of emotion. However, in Western cultures women do tend to more openly express sadness, fear, shame, and guilt. Men more often express anger and hostility (Fischer et al., 2004). Why should this be so? The answer again lies in learning: As they are growing up, boys learn to express emotions related to power; girls learn to express emotions related to nurturing others (Wood & Eagly, 2002). For many men, an inability to express feelings is a major barrier to having close, satisfying relationships with others (Bruch, Berko, & Haase, 1998). It may even contribute to tragedies like the murders at Columbine High School in Littleton, Colorado. For many young males, anger is the only emotion they can freely express.

Universal Expressions

Despite cultural differences, facial expressions of *fear, anger, disgust, sadness,* and *happiness* (enjoyment) are recognized around

Gary Conner/PhotoEdit

● **Figure 12.20** Is anger expressed the same way in different cultures? A study of masks from 18 cultures found that those meant to be frightening or threatening were strikingly similar. Shared features included angular, diagonal, or triangular eyes, eyebrows, nose, cheeks, and chin, together with an open, downward-curved mouth. (Keep this list in mind next Halloween.) Obviously, the pictured mask is not meant to be warm and cuddly. Your ability to "read" its emotional message suggests that basic emotional expressions have universal biological roots (Aronoff, Barclay, & Stevenson, 1988).

Sergei Karpukhgin/Reuters/Corbis

The expression of emotion is strongly influenced by learning. As you have no doubt observed, women cry more often, longer, and more intensely than men do. Men begin learning early in childhood to suppress crying—possibly to the detriment of their emotional health (Williams & Morris, 1996). Many men are especially unwilling to engage in public displays of emotion, in contrast to these women, who are grieving for the victims of a 2005 school siege in Breslan, Russia, which left hundreds of children dead.

the world. *Contempt, surprise,* and *interest* may also be universal, but researchers are less certain of these expressions (Ekman, 1993). Notice that this list covers most of the primary emotions described earlier. It's also nice to note that a genuine smile is the most universal and easily recognized facial expression of emotion.

Body Language

If a friend walked up to you and said, "Hey, ugly, what are you doing?" would you be offended? Probably not, because such remarks are usually delivered with a big grin. The facial and bodily gestures of emotion speak a language all their own and add to what a person says.

Kinesics (kih-NEEZ-iks) is the study of communication through body movement, posture, gestures, and facial expressions. Informally, we call it body language. To see a masterful use of body language, turn off the sound on a television and watch a popular entertainer or politician at work.

What kinds of messages are sent with body language? Popular books on body language tend to list particular meanings for gestures. For instance, a woman who stands rigidly, crosses her arms over her chest, or sits with her legs tightly crossed is supposedly sending a "hands off" message. But experts in kinesics emphasize that gestures are rarely this fixed in meaning. The message might simply be, "This room is cold."

It is important to realize cultural learning also affects the meaning of gestures. What, for instance, does it mean if you touch your thumb and first finger together to form a circle? In North America it means "Everything is fine" or "A-okay." In France and Belgium it means "You're worth zero." In southern Italy it means "You're an ass!" (Ekman, Friesen, & Bear, 1984). Thus, when the layer of culturally defined meanings is removed, it is more realistic to say that body language reveals an overall emotional tone (underlying emotional state).

Your face can produce some 20,000 different expressions, which makes it the most expressive part of your body. Most of these are *facial blends* (a mixture of two or more basic expressions). Imagine, for example, that you just received an F on an unfair test. Quite likely, your eyes, eyebrows, and forehead would reveal anger, while your mouth would be turned downward in a sad frown.

Most of us believe we can fairly accurately tell what others are feeling by observing their facial expressions. If thousands of facial blends occur, how do we make such judgments? The answer is that facial expressions can be boiled down to three basic dimensions: *pleasantness–unpleasantness, attention–rejection,* and *activation* (or arousal) (Schlosberg, 1954). By smiling when you give a friend a hard time, you add an emotional message of acceptance to the verbal insult, which changes its meaning. As they say in movie Westerns, it makes a big difference to "Smile when you say that, partner."

Amy Etra/PhotoEdit, Inc.

Emotions are often unconsciously revealed by gestures and body positioning.

The body telegraphs other feelings. The most general "messages" involve *relaxation* or *tension,* and *liking* or *disliking.* Relaxation is expressed by casually positioning the arms and legs, leaning back (if sitting), and spreading the arms and legs. Liking is expressed mainly by leaning toward a person or object. Thus, body positioning can reveal feelings that would normally be concealed. Who do you "lean toward"?

Psychologists John Bargh and Tanya Chartrand have identified an aspect of body language they call the "chameleon effect." This refers to the fact that we often unconsciously mimic the postures, mannerisms, and facial expressions of other people as we interact with them. (We change our gestures to match our surroundings, like a chameleon changes color.) Bargh and Chartrand also found that if another person copies your gestures and physical postures, you are more inclined to like them (Chartrand & Bargh, 1999). This implies that to make a stronger connection with others, it helps to subtly mimic their gestures.

Imagine that you are standing 30 yards from a classroom in which test grades are being announced. As students file out, do you think you could tell—without the aid of facial expressions—who got an A and who got an F? Actually, your task might not be too difficult. Overall *posture* can also indicate one's emotional state. Specifically, when a person is successful, his or her posture is likely to be more erect (Weisfeld & Beresford, 1982) (● Figure 12.21). Psychologists debate whether this tendency is a product of evolution or is simply learned. In any case, standing tall with pride and slumping with dejection do seem to be consistent patterns.

Does body positioning or movement ever reveal lying or deception? Just as a less than genuine smile may betray a liar, so too might body language (Ekman & O'Sullivan, 1991). But the signs are subtle; seemingly obvious clues like shifty eyes, squirming, and nervous movements that involve touching one's own body (rubbing, grooming, scratching, twisting hair, rubbing hands, biting lips, stroking the chin, and so on) are not consistently related to lying (Ekman, 2001).

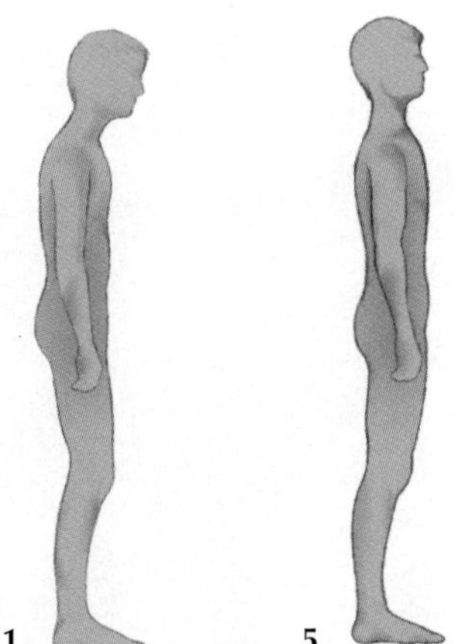

● **Figure 12.21** Posture and success. These drawings show the end points of a five-point scale used to measure erectness of posture. Success by people in various situations was found to be reflected by a more upright posture. (Adapted from Weisfeld & Beresford, 1982.)

On the other hand, the gestures people use to illustrate what they are saying may reveal lying. These gestures, called **illustrators**, tend to *decrease* when a person is telling a lie. In other words, persons who usually "talk with their hands" may be much less animated when they are lying.

Other movements, called *emblems,* can also reveal lying. **Emblems** are gestures that have widely understood meanings within a particular culture. Some examples are the thumbs-up sign, the A-okay sign, the middle-finger insult, a head nod for yes, and a head shake for no. Emblems tend to *increase* when a person is lying. More important, they often reveal true feelings contrary to what the liar is saying. For example, a person might smile and say, "Yes, I'd love to try some of your homemade candied pig's feet," while slowly shaking her head from side to side.

Theories of Emotion—Several Ways to Fear a Bear

Is it possible to explain what takes place during emotion? How are arousal, behavior, cognition, expression, and feelings interrelated? Theories of emotion offer different answers to these questions. Let's investigate some prominent views. Each appears to have a part of the truth, so we will try to put them all together in the end.

The James-Lange Theory (1884–1885)

Common sense tells us that we see a bear, feel fear, become aroused, and run (and sweat and yell). But is this the true order of events? In the 1880s, American psychologist William James (the functionalist) and Danish psychologist Carl Lange proposed that common sense had it backward. According to James and Lange, bodily arousal (such as increased heart rate) does not follow a feeling such as fear. Instead, they argued, *emotional feelings follow bodily arousal.* Thus, we see a bear, run, are aroused, and *then* feel fear as we become aware of our bodily reactions (● Figure 12.22).

To support his ideas, James pointed out that we often do not experience an emotion until after reacting. For example, imagine that you are driving. Suddenly a car pulls out in front of you. You swerve and skid to an abrupt halt at the side of the road. Only after you have come to a stop do you notice your pounding heart, rapid breathing, and tense muscles—and recognize your fear.

Kinesics Study of the meaning of body movements, posture, hand gestures, and facial expressions; commonly called body language.

Illustrators Gestures people use to illustrate what they are saying.

Emblems Gestures that have widely understood meanings within a particular culture.

James-Lange theory States that emotional feelings follow bodily arousal and come from awareness of such arousal.

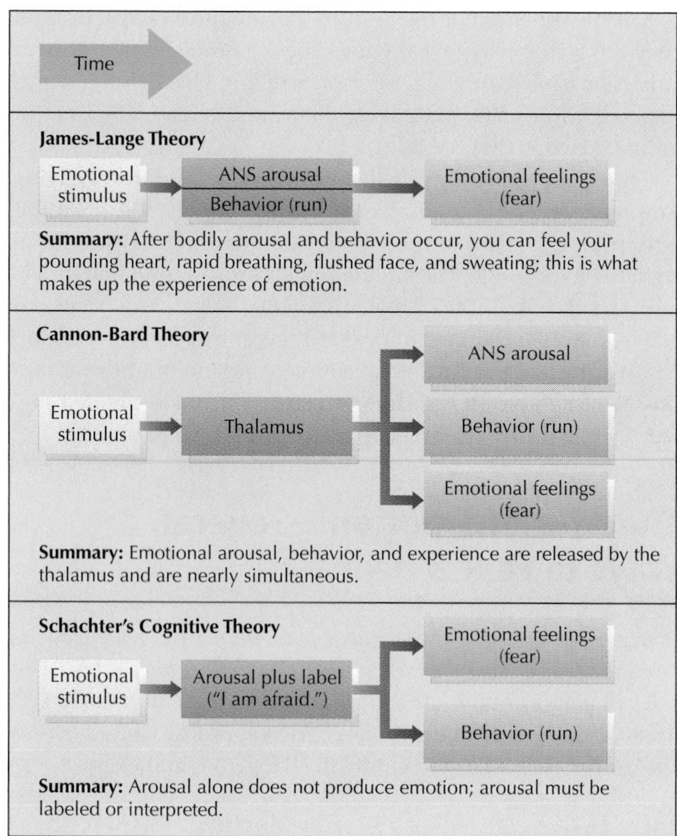

● **Figure 12.22** Theories of emotion.

The Cannon-Bard Theory (1927)

Walter Cannon (1932) and Phillip Bard disagreed with the James-Lange theory. According to them, emotional feelings and bodily arousal *occur at the same time*. Cannon and Bard believed that seeing a bear activates the thalamus in the brain. The thalamus, in turn, alerts the cortex and the hypothalamus for action. The cortex produces our emotional feelings and emotional behavior. The hypothalamus triggers a chain of events that arouses the body. Thus, if you see a dangerous-looking bear, brain activity will simultaneously produce bodily arousal, running, and feeling fear (● Figure 12.22).

Schachter's Cognitive Theory of Emotion

The previous theories are mostly concerned with our physical responses. Stanley Schachter realized that cognitive (mental) factors also enter into emotion. According to Schachter, emotion occurs when we apply a particular *label* to general physical *arousal*. Schachter believed that when we are aroused, we have a need to interpret our feelings. Assume, for instance, that someone sneaks up behind you on a dark street and says, "Boo!" No matter who the person is, your body will be aroused (pounding heart, sweating palms, and so on). If the person is a total stranger, you might interpret this arousal as fear; if the person is a close friend, the arousal may be labeled as surprise or delight. The label (such as anger, fear, or happiness) you apply to bodily arousal is influenced by your past experiences, the situation, and the reactions of others (● Figure 12.22).

Support for the cognitive theory of emotion comes from an experiment in which people watched a slapstick movie (Schachter & Wheeler, 1962). Before viewing the movie, one third of the people received an arousing injection of adrenaline, one third got a placebo (salt water) injection, and one third was given a tranquilizer. People who received the adrenaline rated the movie funniest and laughed the most while watching it. In contrast, those given the tranquilizer were least amused. The placebo group fell in between.

According to the cognitive theory of emotion, individuals who received adrenaline had a stirred-up body, but no explanation for what they were feeling. Consequently, they became happy when the movie implied that their arousal was due to amusement. This and similar experiments make it clear that emotion is much more than just an agitated body. Perception, experience, attitudes, judgment, and many other mental factors also affect the emotions we feel. Schachter's theory would predict, then, that if you met a bear, you would be aroused. If the bear seemed unfriendly, you would interpret your arousal as fear, and if the bear offered to shake your "paw," you would be happy, amazed, and relieved!

Attribution

We now move from slapstick movies and fear of bear bodies to appreciation of bare bodies. Researcher Stuart Valins (1967) added an interesting wrinkle to Schachter's theory of emotion. According to Valins, arousal can be attributed to various sources—a process that alters perceptions of emotion. To demonstrate **attribution**, Valins (1966) showed male college students a series of slides of nude females. While watching the slides, each subject heard an amplified heartbeat that he believed was his own. In reality, subjects were listening to a recorded heartbeat carefully designed to beat *louder* and *stronger* when some (but not all) of the slides were shown.

After watching the slides, each student was asked to say which was most attractive. Students who heard the false heartbeat consistently rated slides paired with a "pounding heart" as the most attractive. In other words, when a student saw a slide and heard his heart beat louder, he attributed his "emotion" to the slide. His interpretation seems to have been, "Now that one I like!" His next

Michael Grecco/Stock, Boston/PictureQuest

Which theory of emotion best describes the reactions of these people? Given the complexity of emotion, each theory appears to possess an element of truth.

reaction, perhaps, was "But why?" Later research suggests that subjects persuaded themselves that the slide really was more attractive in order to explain their apparent arousal (Truax, 1983).

That seems somewhat artificial. Does it really make any difference what arousal is attributed to? Yes. To illustrate attribution in the "real world," consider what happens when parents interfere with the budding romance of a son or daughter. Often, trying to separate a young couple *intensifies* their feelings. Meddling parents add frustration, anger, and fear or excitement (as in seeing each other "on the sly") to the couple's feelings. Because they already care for each other, they are likely to attribute all this added emotion to "true love" (Walster, 1971).

Attribution theory predicts that you are most likely to "love" someone who gets you stirred up emotionally (Foster et al., 1998). This is true even when fear, anger, frustration, or rejection is part of the formula. Thus, if you want to successfully propose marriage, take your intended to the middle of a narrow, windswept suspension bridge over a deep chasm and look deeply into his or her eyes. As your beloved's heart pounds wildly (from being on the bridge, not from your irresistible charms), say, "I love you." Attribution theory predicts that your companion will conclude, "Oh wow, I must love you too."

The preceding is not as farfetched as it may seem. In an ingenious study, a female psychologist interviewed men in a park. Some were on a swaying suspension bridge 230 feet above a river. The rest were on a solid wooden bridge just 10 feet above the ground. After the interview, the psychologist gave each man her telephone number, so he could "find out about the results" of the study. Men interviewed on the suspension bridge were much more likely to give the "lady from the park" a call (Dutton & Aron, 1974). Apparently, these men experienced heightened arousal, which they interpreted as attraction to the experimenter—a clear case of love at first fright!

The Facial Feedback Hypothesis

Schachter added thinking and interpretation (cognition) to our view of emotion, but the picture still seems incomplete. What about expressions? How do they influence emotion? As Charles Darwin observed, the face is very central to emotion—certainly it must be more than just an "emotional billboard."

Psychologist Carrol Izard (1977, 1990) was among the first to suggest that the face does, indeed, affect emotion. According to Izard and others, emotional activity causes innately programmed changes in facial expression. Sensations from the face then provide cues to the brain that help us determine what emotion we are feeling. This idea is known as the **facial feedback hypothesis** (Adelmann & Zajonc, 1989). Stated another way, it says that having facial expressions and becoming aware of them is what leads to emotional experience. Exercise, for instance, arouses the body, but we don't experience this arousal as emotion because it does not trigger emotional expressions.

Psychologist Paul Ekman takes the idea one step further. Ekman believes that "making faces" can actually cause emotion (Ekman, 1993). In one study, participants were guided as they arranged their faces, muscle by muscle, into expressions of surprise, disgust, sadness, anger, fear, and happiness (● Figure 12.23). At the same time, each person's bodily reactions were monitored.

Contrary to what you might expect, "making faces" can affect the autonomic nervous system, as shown by changes in heart rate and skin temperature. In addition, each facial expression produces a different pattern of activity. An angry face, for instance, raises heart rate and skin temperature, whereas disgust lowers both (Ekman et al., 1983). Other studies have confirmed that posed expressions alter emotions and bodily activity (Duclos & Laird, 2001; Soussignan, 2002).

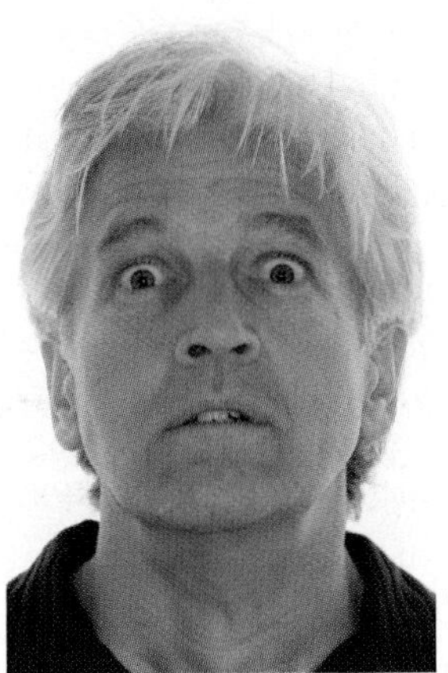

Dennis Coon

● **Figure 12.23** Facial feedback and emotion. Participants in Ekman's study formed facial expressions like those normally observed during emotion. When they did this, emotion-like changes took place in their bodily activity. (After Ekman, Levenson, & Friesen, 1983.)

BRIDGES

Love is one basis for interpersonal attraction, but there are others, such as similarity and proximity.

To learn more about what brings people together, see Chapter 18, pages 616–618.

Cannon-Bard theory States that activity in the thalamus causes emotional feelings and bodily arousal to occur simultaneously.

Schachter's cognitive theory States that emotions occur when physical arousal is labeled or interpreted on the basis of experience and situational cues.

Attribution The mental process of assigning causes to events. In emotion, the process of attributing arousal to a particular source.

Facial feedback hypothesis States that sensations from facial expressions help define what emotion a person feels.

THE CLINICAL FILE

Suppressing Emotion—Is It Healthy?

Emotional life has its ups and downs. While sharing a beautiful day with friends, you can freely express your happiness. But often, we try to appear less emotional than we really are, especially when we are feeling negative emotions. Have you ever been angry with a friend in public? Embarrassed by someone's behavior at a party? Disgusted by someone's table manners or a bad joke? In such circumstances, people are quite good at suppressing outward signs of emotion. However, restraining emotion can actually increase activity in the sympathetic nervous system. In other words, hiding emotion requires a lot of effort.

Suppressing emotions can impair thinking and memory, as you devote energy to self-control. Thus, although suppressing emotion allows us to appear calm and collected on the outside, this cool appearance comes at a high cost (Richards & Gross, 2000). People who suppress emotions cope poorly with life and are prone to depression and other problems (Lynch et al., 2001). Conversely, people who express their emotions generally experience better emotional and physical health (Lumley, 2004; Pennebaker, 2004). Usually, it's better to manage emotions than it is to suppress them. You will find some suggestions for managing emotions in the upcoming Psychology in Action feature.

In a fascinating experiment on facial feedback, people rated how funny they thought cartoons were while holding a pen crosswise in their mouths. Those who held the pen in their teeth thought the cartoons were funnier than did people who held the pen in their lips. Can you guess why? The answer is that if you hold a pen with your teeth, you are forced to form a smile. Holding it with the lips makes a frown. As predicted by the facial feedback hypothesis, emotional experiences were influenced by the facial expressions that people made (Strack, Martin, & Stepper, 1988). Next time you're feeling sad, bite a pen!

It appears, then, that not only do emotions influence expressions, but expressions influence emotions, as shown here (Adelmann & Zajonc, 1989; Duclos & Laird, 2001):

Contracted Facial Muscles	Felt Emotion
Forehead	Surprise
Brow	Anger
Mouth (down)	Sadness
Mouth (smile)	Joy

This could explain an interesting effect you have probably observed. When you are feeling "down," forcing yourself to smile will sometimes be followed by an actual improvement in your mood (Kleinke, Peterson, & Rutledge, 1998).

If smiling can improve a person's mood, is it a good idea to inhibit negative emotions? For an answer, see "Suppressing Emotion—Is It Healthy."

A Contemporary Model of Emotion

To summarize, James and Lange were right that feedback from arousal and behavior adds to our emotional experiences. Cannon and Bard were right about the timing of events. Schachter showed us that cognition is important. In fact, psychologists are increasingly aware that how you *appraise* a situation greatly affects your emotions (Strongman, 1996). **Emotional appraisal** refers to evaluating the personal meaning of a stimulus: Is it good/bad, threatening/supportive, relevant/irrelevant, and so on.

In recent years many new theories of emotion have appeared. Rather than pick one "best" theory, let's put the main points of several theories together in a single contemporary model of emotion (● Figure 12.24).

Imagine that a large snarling dog lunges at you with its teeth bared. A modern view of your emotional reactions goes something like this: An *emotional stimulus* (the dog) is *appraised* (judged) as a threat or other cause for emotion (■ Table 12.2). (You think to yourself, "Uh oh, big trouble!") Your appraisal gives rise to *ANS arousal* (your heart pounds and your body becomes stirred up). The appraisal also releases *innate emotional expressions* (your face twists into a mask of fear and your posture becomes tense). At the same time, your appraisal leads to *adaptive behavior* (you run from the dog). It also causes a change in consciousness that you recognize as the subjective experience of fear. (The intensity of this *emotional feeling* is directly related to the amount of ANS arousal taking place in your body.)

Each element of emotion—ANS arousal, adaptive behavior, subjective experience, and your emotional expressions—may further alter your appraisal of the situation, as well as your thoughts, judgments, and perceptions. Such changes affect each of the other reactions, which again alters your appraisal and interpretation of events. Thus, emotion may blossom, change course, or diminish as it proceeds. Note too that the original emotional stimulus can be external, like the attacking dog, or internal, such as a memory of being chased by a dog, rejected by a lover, or praised by a friend.

BRIDGES

Emotional appraisals have a major impact on the ability to cope with threats and stress, which may ultimately affect your health.

See Chapter 15, pages 503–504.

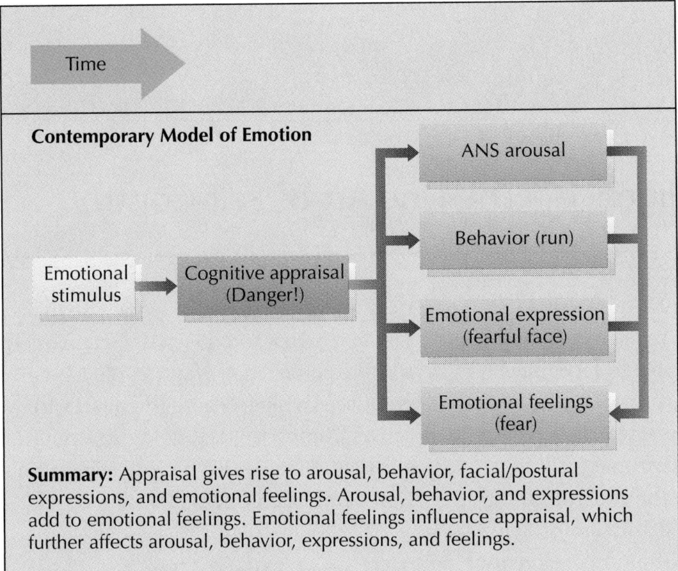

● **Figure 12.24** A contemporary model of emotion.

TABLE 12.2

Appraisals and Corresponding Emotions

APPRAISAL	EMOTION
You have been slighted or demeaned	Anger
You feel threatened	Anxiety
You have experienced a loss	Sadness
You have broken a moral rule	Guilt
You have not lived up to your ideals	Shame
You desire something another has	Envy
You are near something repulsive	Disgust
You fear the worst but yearn for better	Hope
You are moving toward a desired goal	Happiness
You are linked with a valued object or accomplishment	Pride
You have been treated well by another	Gratitude
You desire affection from another person	Love
You are moved by someone's suffering	Compassion

Paraphrased from Lazarus, 1991b.

That's why mere thoughts and memories can make us fearful, sad, or happy (Strongman, 1996).

Our discussion suggests that emotion is greatly influenced by how you think about an event. For example, if another driver "cuts you off" on the highway, you could become very angry. But if you do, you will add 15 minutes of emotional upset to your day. By changing your appraisal, you could just as easily choose to laugh at the other driver's childish behavior—and minimize the emotional wear-and-tear (Gross, 2001).

A Look Ahead

In the Psychology in Action section of this chapter we will look further at the impact of emotional appraisals through an examination of *emotional intelligence*. Before we continue, you might want to appraise your learning with the exercises that follow.

KNOWLEDGE BUILDER

Emotional Expression and Theories of Emotion

REFLECT

Write a list of emotions that you think you can accurately detect from facial expressions. Does your list match Paul Ekman's? Would you be more confident in rating pleasantness–unpleasantness, attention–rejection, and activation? Why?

Which theory seems to best explain your own emotional experiences? Try frowning or smiling for five minutes. Did facial feedback have any effect on your mood? Cover the left column of ■ Table 12.2. Read each emotional label in the right column. What appraisal do you think would lead to the listed emotion? Do the appraisals in the table match your predictions?

LEARNING CHECK

1. Charles Darwin held that emotional expressions aid survival for animals. T or F?
2. A formal term for "body language" is ________________.
3. Which three dimensions of emotion are communicated by facial expressions?
   a. pleasantness–unpleasantness d. anger
   b. complexity e. curiosity–disinterest
   c. attention–rejection f. activation
4. According to the James-Lange theory, emotional experience precedes physical arousal and emotional behavior. (We see a bear, are frightened, and run.) T or F?
5. The Cannon-Bard theory of emotion says that bodily arousal and emotional experience occur ________________.
6. The idea that labeling arousal helps define what emotions we experience is associated with
   a. the James-Lange theory c. the Cannon-Bard theory
   b. Schachter's cognitive theory d. Darwin's theory of innate emotional expressions
7. Subjects in Valin's false heart rate study attributed increases in their heart rate to the action of a placebo. T or F?
8. As you try to wiggle your ears, you keep pulling the corners of your mouth back into a smile. Each time you do, you find yourself giggling. Which of the following provides the best explanation for this reaction?
   a. attribution c. appraisal
   b. the Cannon-Bard theory d. facial feedback

CRITICAL THINKING

9. People with high spinal injuries may feel almost no signs of physiological arousal from their bodies. Nevertheless they still feel emotion, which can be intense at times. What theory of emotion does this observation contradict?

Answers: 1. T **2.** kinesics **3.** a, c, f **4.** F **5.** simultaneously **6.** b **7.** F **8.** d **9.** The James-Lange theory and Schachter's cognitive theory. The facial feedback hypothesis also helps explain the observation.

Emotional appraisal Evaluating the personal meaning of a stimulus or situation.

PSYCHOLOGY IN ACTION

Emotional Intelligence—The Fine Art of Self-Control

The Greek philosopher Aristotle had a recipe for handling relationships smoothly. You must be able, he said, "to be angry with the right person, to the right degree, at the right time, for the right purpose, and in the right way." Psychologists Peter Salovey and John Mayer call such self-control "emotional intelligence." **Emotional intelligence** refers to a combination of skills, such as empathy, self-control, and self-awareness (Salovey & Mayer, 1997). Such skills can make us more flexible, adaptable, and emotionally mature (Bonanno et al., 2004).

People who excel in life tend to be emotionally intelligent (Fisher & Ashanasy, 2000; Mehrabian, 2000). Indeed, the costs of poor emotional skills can be high. They range from problems in marriage and parenting to poor physical health. A lack of emotional intelligence can ruin careers and sabotage achievement. Perhaps the greatest toll falls on children and teenagers. For them, having poor emotional skills can contribute to depression, eating disorders, unwanted pregnancy, aggression, violent crime, and poor academic performance (Parker et al., 2004). Thus, in many life circumstances emotional intelligence is as important as IQ (Dulewicz & Higgs, 2000).

Are there specific skills that make up emotional intelligence? Many elements contribute to emotional intelligence (Mayer et al., 2001). Descriptions of some of the most important skills follows.

Self-awareness Emotionally intelligent people are tuned in to their own feelings. For example, they are able to recognize quickly if they are angry, or envious, or feeling guilty, or depressed. This is valuable because many people have disruptive emotions without being able to pinpoint why they are uncomfortable. Those who are more self-aware are keenly sensitive to their own feelings.

Empathy Empathetic people accurately perceive emotions in others and sense what others are feeling. They are good at "reading" facial expressions, tone of voice, and other signs of emotion.

Managing emotions Emotional intelligence involves an ability to manage your own emotions and those of others. For example, you know how to calm down when you are angry and you also know how to calm others. As Aristotle noted so long ago, people who are emotionally intelligent have an ability to amplify or restrain emotions, depending on the situation (Bonanno et al., 2004).

Understanding emotions Emotions contain useful information. For instance, anger is a cue that something is wrong; anxiety indicates uncertainty; embarrassment communicates shame; depression means we feel helpless; enthusiasm tells us we're excited. People who are emotionally intelligent know what causes various emotions, what they mean, and how they affect behavior.

Using emotion People who are emotionally intelligent use their feelings to enhance thinking and decision making. For example, if you can remember how you reacted emotionally in the past, it can help you react better to new situations. Emotional intelligence also involves using emotions to promote personal growth and improve relationships with others. For instance, you may have noticed that helping someone else makes you feel better, too. Likewise, when good fortune comes their way, people who are emotionally smart share the news with others. Almost always, doing so strengthens relationships and increases emotional well-being (Gable et al., 2004).

Emotional Flexibility

In general, being emotionally intelligent means accepting that emotions are an essential part of who we are and how we survive. There is a natural tendency to enjoy positive emotions like joy or love, while treating negative emotions as unwelcome misery. However, negative emotions can also be valuable and constructive. For example, persistent distress may impel a person to seek help, mend a relationship, or find a new direction in life (Plutchik, 2003).

Often, the "right" choices in life can only be defined by taking personal values, needs, and emotions into account. Extremely rational approaches to making choices can produce sensible but emotionally empty decisions. Good decisions often combine emotion with reason. In short, emotional intelligence is the ability to consciously make your emotions work for you.

Positive Psychology and Positive Emotions

It's obvious that joy, interest, contentment, love, and similar emotions are pleasant and rewarding. However, as psychologist Barbara Fredrickson has pointed out, positive emotions have other benefits. Negative emotions are associated with actions that probably helped our ancestors save their skins: escaping, attacking, expelling poison, and the like. As useful as these reactions may be, they tend to narrow our focus of attention and limit our ideas about possible actions. In contrast, positive emotions tend to broaden our focus. This opens up new possibilities and builds up our personal resources. For instance, emotions such as joy, interest, and contentment create an urge to play, to be creative, to explore, to savor life, to seek new experiences, to integrate, and to grow. In short, positive emotions are not just a pleasant side effect of happy circumstances. They also encourage personal growth and social connection. A capacity for having positive emotions is a basic human strength, and cultivating good feelings is a part of emotional intelligence (Fredrickson, 2001).

Authentic Happiness Psychologists have worked hard to find ways to relieve the negative emotions that make us miserable. Recently, psychologist Martin Seligman has proposed an alternate approach. Rather than trying to fix weaknesses, he believes we are more likely to find genuine happiness by emphasizing our natural strengths. Seligman teaches that happiness can be cultivated by using the strengths we already possess—including kindness, originality, humor, optimism, and generosity. Such strengths are natural buffers against misfortune, and they can help people live more positive, genuinely happy lives (Seligman, 2002).

Becoming Emotionally Smart

Understandably, many psychologists believe that schools should promote emotional competence as well as intellectual skills. The result, they think, would be greater self-control, altruism, and compassion—all basic capacities needed if our society is to thrive.

How would a person learn the skills that make up emotional intelligence? Psychologists are still unsure how to teach emotional intelligence. Nevertheless, it's clear that emotional skills can be learned. Accepting that emotions are valuable is an important first step. There are many valuable lessons to learn from paying close attention to your emotions and the emotions of others. It's a good bet that many of the people you admire the most are not just smart, but also emotionally smart. They are people who know how to offer a toast at a wedding, tell a joke at a roast, comfort the bereaved at a funeral, add to the fun at a party, or calm a frightened child. These are skills worth cultivating.

KNOWLEDGE BUILDER

Emotional Intelligence

REFLECT

Think of a person you know who is smart, but low in emotional intelligence. Think of another person who is smart cognitively and emotionally. How does the second person differ from the first? Which person do you think would make a better parent, friend, supervisor, roommate, or teacher?

LEARNING CHECK

1. People who rate high in emotional intelligence tend to be highly aware of their own feelings and unaware of emotions experienced by others. T or F?
2. Using the information imparted by emotional reactions can enhance thinking and decision making. T or F?
3. Positive emotions may be pleasant, but they tend to narrow our focus of attention and limit the range of possible actions we are likely to consider. T or F?
4. Which of the following is *not* an element of emotional intelligence?
   a. empathy
   b. self-control
   c. misattribution
   d. self-awareness

CRITICAL THINKING

5. You are angry because a friend borrowed money from you and hasn't repaid it. What would be an emotionally intelligent response to this situation?

Answers: 1. F **2.** T **3.** F **4.** c **5.** There's no single right answer to this question. However, rather than being angry it might be better to reflect on whether friendship or money is more important in life. If you appreciate your friend's virtues, accept that no one is perfect, and reappraise the loan as a gift, you could save a valued relationship and reduce your anger at the same time.

Emotional intelligence Emotional competence, including empathy, self-control, self-awareness, and other skills.

Chapter in Review

What is motivation? Are there different types of motives?

- Motives initiate, sustain, and direct activities. Motivation typically involves this sequence: need, drive, goal, and goal attainment (need reduction).
- Behavior can be activated either by needs (push) or by goals (pull). The attractiveness of a goal and its ability to initiate action are related to its incentive value.
- Three principal types of motives are primary motives, stimulus motives, and secondary motives. Most primary motives operate to maintain homeostasis.

What causes hunger? Overeating? Eating disorders?

- Hunger is influenced by a complex interplay between fullness of the stomach, blood sugar levels, metabolism in the liver, and fat stores in the body.
- The most direct control of eating is effected by the hypothalamus, which has areas that act like feeding and satiety systems. The hypothalamus is sensitive to both neural and chemical messages, which affect eating.
- Other factors influencing hunger are the body's set point, external eating cues, the attractiveness and variety of diet, emotions, learned taste preferences and taste aversions, and cultural values.
- Obesity is the result of a complex interplay of internal and external influences, diet, emotions, genetics, and exercise.
- Behavioral dieting is based on techniques that change eating patterns and exercise habits.
- Anorexia nervosa and bulimia nervosa are two prominent eating disorders. Both tend to involve conflicts about self-image, self-control, and anxiety.

Is there more than one type of thirst?

- Like hunger, thirst and other basic motives are affected by a number of bodily factors, but are primarily under the central control of the hypothalamus. Thirst may be either intracellular or extracellular.

In what ways are pain avoidance and the sex drive unusual?

- Pain avoidance is unusual because it is episodic as opposed to cyclic. Pain avoidance and pain tolerance are partially learned.
- The sex drive is also unusual in that it is non-homeostatic.

How does arousal relate to motivation?

- The stimulus motives include drives for exploration, manipulation, change, and sensory stimulation.
- Drives for stimulation are partially explained by arousal theory, which states that an ideal level of bodily arousal will be maintained if possible. The desired level of arousal or stimulation varies from person to person, as measured by the *Sensation-Seeking Scale*.
- Optimal performance on a task usually occurs at *moderate* levels of arousal. This relationship is described by an inverted U function. The Yerkes-Dodson law further states that for simple tasks the ideal arousal level is higher, and for complex tasks it is lower.
- Circadian rhythms of bodily activity are closely tied to sleep, activity, and energy cycles. Time zone travel and shift work can seriously disrupt sleep and bodily rhythms.

What are social motives? Why are they important?

- Social motives are learned through socialization and cultural conditioning. Such motives account for much of the diversity of human motivation. Opponent-process theory explains the operation of some acquired motives.
- One of the most prominent social motives is the need for achievement (nAch). High nAch is correlated with success in many situations, with occupational choice, and with *moderate* risk taking.
- Self-confidence greatly affects motivation in everyday life.

Are some motives more basic than others?

- Maslow's hierarchy of motives categorizes needs as basic and growth oriented. Lower needs in the hierarchy are assumed to be prepotent (dominant) over higher needs. Self-actualization, the highest and most fragile need, is reflected in meta-needs.
- Higher needs in Maslow's hierarchy are closely related to the concept of intrinsic motivation. In many situations, extrinsic motivation can reduce intrinsic motivation, enjoyment, and creativity.

What happens during emotion?

- Emotions are linked to many basic adaptive behaviors. Other major elements of emotion are physiological changes in the body, emotional expressions, and emotional feelings.
- The following are considered to be primary emotions: *fear, surprise, sadness, disgust, anger, anticipation, joy,* and *acceptance*. Other emotions seem to represent mixtures of the primaries.
- The left hemisphere of the brain primarily processes positive emotions. Negative emotions are processed in the right hemisphere.

- The amygdala provides a "quick and dirty" pathway for the arousal of fear that bypasses the cerebral cortex.
- Physical changes associated with emotion are caused by the action of adrenaline, a hormone released into the bloodstream, and by activity in the autonomic nervous system (ANS).
- The sympathetic branch of the ANS is primarily responsible for arousing the body, the parasympathetic branch for quieting it.

Can "lie detectors" really detect lies?

- The polygraph, or "lie detector," measures emotional arousal by monitoring heart rate, blood pressure, breathing rate, and the GSR.
- Under some circumstances, the accuracy of the lie detector can be quite low.

How accurately are emotions expressed by "body language" and the face?

- Basic emotional expressions, such as smiling or baring one's teeth when angry, appear to be unlearned. Facial expressions appear to be central to emotion.
- Body gestures and movements (body language) also express feelings, mainly by communicating emotional tone. Three dimensions of facial expressions are pleasantness–unpleasantness, attention–rejection, and activation. The study of body language is known as kinesics.
- Lying can sometimes be detected from changes in illustrators or emblems and from signs of general arousal.

How do psychologists explain emotions?

- The James-Lange theory says that emotional experience follows the bodily reactions. In contrast, the Cannon-Bard theory says that bodily reactions and emotional experiences are organized in the brain and occur simultaneously.
- Schachter's cognitive theory of emotion emphasizes the importance of the labels we apply to feelings of bodily arousal. In addition, emotions are affected by attribution (ascribing bodily arousal to a particular source).
- The facial feedback hypothesis holds that emotional expressions help define what emotion a person is feeling.
- Contemporary views of emotion place greater emphasis on the effects of cognitive appraisals. Also, all of the elements of emotion are seen as interrelated and interacting.

What does it mean to have "emotional intelligence"?

- Emotional intelligence is the ability to consciously make your emotions work for you in a wide variety of life circumstances.
- Important elements of emotional intelligence include self-awareness, empathy, an ability to manage emotions, understanding emotion, and knowing how to use emotions to enhance thinking, decision making, and relationships.
- Positive emotions are valuable because they tend to broaden our focus and they encourage personal growth and social connection.

Web Resources

Internet addresses frequently change. To find the sites listed here, visit www.thomsonedu.com/psychology/coon for an updated list of Internet addresses and direct links to relevant sites.

***Psychology: Gateways to Mind and Behavior* Website** Online quizzes, flash cards, and other helpful study aids for this text. www.thomsonedu.com/psychology/coon.

Controlling Anger Discusses anger and some strategies for its control.

Eating Disorders Website Home page of a self-help group for those afflicted with eating disorders.

Emotions and Emotional Intelligence Discusses emotional intelligence.

Research on Human Emotions Links to a variety of sources on emotion.

The Validity of Polygraph Examinations Information about the doubtful validity of polygraph examinations.

What's Your Emotional Intelligence Quotient? Visitors may take an online quiz about their E-IQ.

Authentic Happiness This site offers a variety of tests related to happiness and personal strengths.

ThomsonNOW™ Go to www.thomsonedu.com to link to ThomsonNow, your online study tool. First take the **Pre-Test** for this chapter to get your **Personalized Study Plan**, which will identify topics you need to review and direct you to online resources. Then take the **Post-Test** to determine what concepts you have mastered and what you still need work on.

InfoTrac College Edition For recent articles on lie detection, use Key Words search for POLYGRAPH. Go to www.thomsonedu.com/psychology/coon.

Interactive Learning

***PsychNow!* Version 2.0 CD-ROM** Interact with the material with *PsychNow!*'s animations, video clips, experiments, and interactive assessments. For this chapter, go to *6a. Motivation* and *6b. Emotion* to get a better understanding of these processes.

chapter

13

Gender and Sexuality

THEME:

The sexes are more alike than different. Sexuality is a normal and healthy part of human behavior.

David Lo Tai Wai/Getty Images

Key Questions

What are the basic dimensions of sex?

How does one's sense of maleness or femaleness develop?

What is psychological androgyny (and is it contagious)?

What are the most typical patterns of human sexual behavior?

To what extent do females and males differ in sexual response?

What are the most common sexual disorders?

Have recent changes in attitudes affected sexual behavior?

What impacts have sexually transmitted diseases had on sexual behavior?

What are the most common sexual adjustment problems? How are they treated?

Preview

That Magic Word

Sex\seks n 1. One of the two divisions of organisms formed on the distinction of male and female.

"Sex" has many meanings: reproduction, lovemaking, sexual identity, and much more. Of the various meanings, the simplest would seem to be biological sex. What, really, could be simpler? Females are females and males are males, right? Wrong. Even something as basic as biological sex is many sided.

The complexity of sexual identity is illustrated by Dr. Renée Richards's attempt to enter a women's tennis tournament. Dr. Richards is a transsexual. Formerly she was Dr. Richard Raskin, an ophthalmologist. As a man, Richard Raskin was a modestly successful tennis player. After a sex-change operation, Dr. Richards tried to launch a new tennis career as a woman. Other women players protested. Officials finally decided to use a genetic sex test to decide if Dr. Richards could compete. She, in turn, protested the test. Genetically she is still male, but psychologically she is female—she has female genitals, and she functions socially as a female (Hyde & DeLamater, 2000). Is Dr. Richards, then, female or male?

You might view Renée Richards as an unfair example because transsexuals seek to alter their natural sex. For most people, the indicators of maleness or femaleness are in agreement. Nevertheless, it is not unusual to find ambiguities among various aspects of a person's sex.

Sex is probably a topic you already know a lot about. It should be interesting, then, for you to compare your knowledge with the information that follows. Sex and gender have a tremendous impact on relationships, personal identity, and health.

Sexual Development—Circle One: *XX* or *XY*?

One thing we never forget about a person is his or her sex. Considering the number of activities, relationships, conflicts, and choices influenced by sex, it is no wonder that we pay such close attention to it. Contrary to common belief, classifying a person as male or female is not a simple either/or proposition.

Being male or female is partly a matter of biology and partly psychological. The term **sex** refers to whether you are biologically female or male. In contrast, **gender** refers to all the psychological and social traits associated with being male or female (Crooks & Baur, 2005). In other words, after we establish that you are male or female, gender tells us if you are masculine or feminine (as defined by the culture in which you live). Two important aspects of gender are *gender roles* and *gender identity,* which we will discuss soon. For the moment, let's begin with two basic questions: Biologically, what does it mean to be female or male? How do male and female differences develop?

Female or Male?

Males and females differ in both *primary* and *secondary* sexual characteristics. **Primary sexual characteristics** refer to the sexual and reproductive organs themselves: the vagina, ovaries, and uterus in females and the penis, testes, and scrotum in males (see ● Figure 13.1 and ● Figure 13.2; also see ■ Table 13.1). **Secondary sexual characteristics** are more superficial physical features that appear at puberty. These features develop in response to hormonal signals from the pituitary gland. In females, secondary sexual characteristics include breast development, broadening of the hips, and other changes in body shape. Males grow facial and body hair, and the voice deepens. These changes signal that a person is biologically ready to reproduce. Reproductive maturity is especially evident in the female *menarche* (MEN-are-kee: the onset of menstruation). Soon after menarche, monthly ovulation begins. *Ovulation* refers to the release of ova (eggs) from the ovaries. From the first ovulation until *menopause* (the end of regular

Sex One's biological classification as female or male.

Gender Psychological and social characteristics associated with being male or female; defined especially by one's gender identity and learned gender roles.

Primary sexual characteristics Sex as defined by the genitals and internal reproductive organs.

Secondary sexual characteristics Sexual features other than the genitals and reproductive organs—breasts, body shape, facial hair, and so forth.

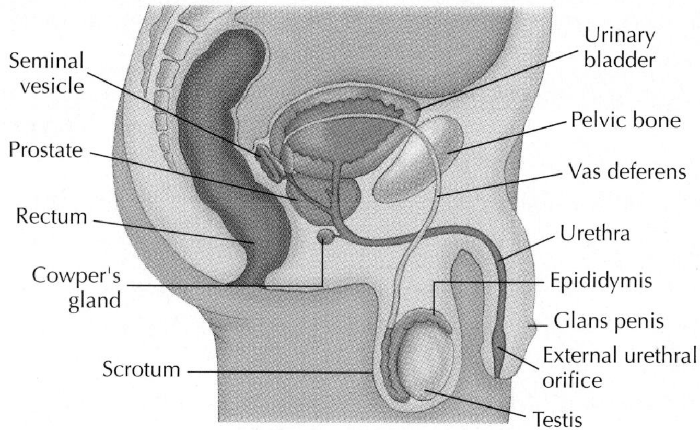

● **Figure 13.1** Cutaway view of internal and external male reproductive structures.

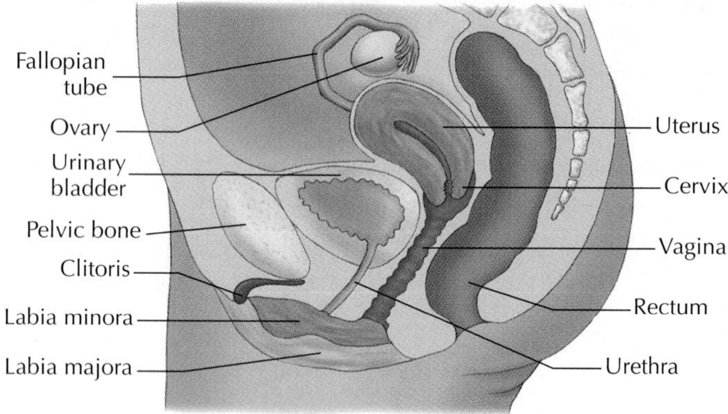

● **Figure 13.2** Cutaway view of internal and external female reproductive structures.

monthly fertility cycles in the late forties or early fifties), women can bear children.

Sex Hormones

What causes the development of sex differences? In general, sexual characteristics are related to the effects of sex hormones. (Hormones are chemical substances secreted by endocrine glands.) The **gonads** (or sex glands) affect sexual development and behavior by secreting **estrogens** (female hormones) and **androgens** (male hormones). The gonads in the male are the testes; female gonads are the ovaries. The adrenal glands (located above the kidneys) also supply sex hormones. At puberty, adrenal hormones add to the development of secondary sexual characteristics.

Interestingly, everyone normally produces both estrogens and androgens. Sex differences are related to the *proportion* of these

BRIDGES

Signs of developing sexual maturity mark the beginning of puberty and a gradual transition to adult status. Menopause is an unmistakable sign of aging.

See Chapter 4, page 140.

TABLE 13.1

Female and Male Sexual Anatomy

Female Reproductive Structures

Cervix (SER-vix) The lower end of the uterus that projects into the vagina.

Clitoris (KLIT-er-iss) Small, sensitive organ made up of erectile tissue; located above the vaginal opening.

Fallopian tube (feh-LOPE-ee-en) One of two tubes that carry eggs from the ovaries to the uterus.

Labia majora (LAY-bee-ah mah-JOR-ah) The larger outer lips of the vulva.

Labia minora (LAY-bee-ah mih-NOR-ah) Inner lips of the vulva, surrounding the vaginal opening.

Ovary (OH-vah-ree) One of the two female reproductive glands; ovaries are the source of hormones and eggs.

Uterus (YOO-ter-us) The pear-shaped muscular organ in which the fetus develops during pregnancy; also known as the womb.

Vagina (vah-JINE-ah) Tube-like structure connecting the external female genitalia with the uterus.

Male Reproductive Structures

Cowper's glands Two small glands that secrete a clear fluid into the urethra during sexual excitement.

Epididymis (ep-ih-DID-ih-mus) A coiled structure at the top of the testes in which sperm are stored.

External urethral orifice (yoo-REE-thral OR-ih-fis) The opening at the tip of the penis through which urine and semen pass.

Glans penis (glanz PEA-nis) The tip of the penis.

Prostate (PROSS-tate) A gland located at the base of the urinary bladder that supplies most of the fluid that makes up semen.

Scrotum (SKROE-tehm) The sac-like pouch that holds the testes.

Seminal vesicles (SEM-in-uhl VES-ih-kuhlz) These two small organs (one on each side of the prostate) supply fluid that becomes part of semen.

Testis (TES-tis, singular; testes, plural) One of the two male reproductive glands; the testes are a source of hormones and sperm.

Vas deferens (vaz DEH-fur-enz) The duct that carries sperm from the testes to the urethra.

Related Structures

Pelvic bone One of the bones at the front of the pelvis (the pelvis connects the spine with the legs).

Rectum The lowest section of the large intestine.

Urethra (yoo-REE-thra) The tube through which urine drains as it leaves the body. In males, semen also passes through the urethra.

Urinary bladder The sac that collects urine before it is eliminated from the body.

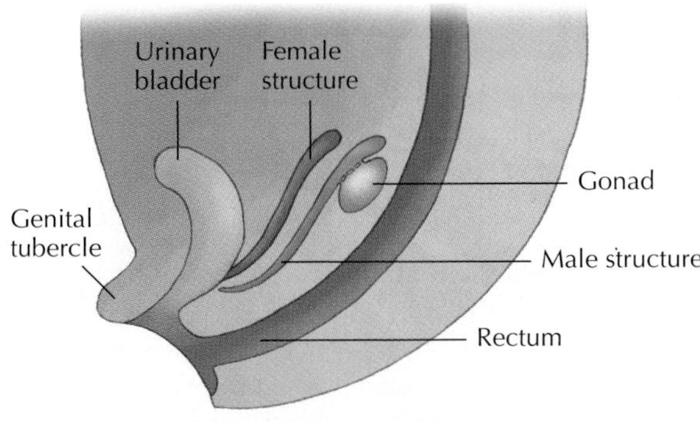

(a) Undifferentiated

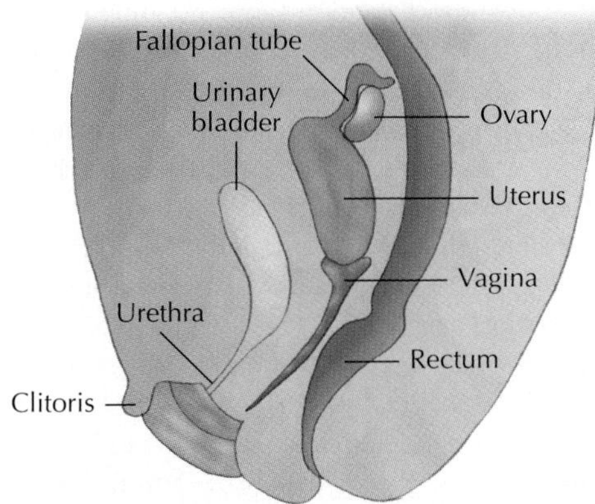

(b) Female *XX* Chromosomes

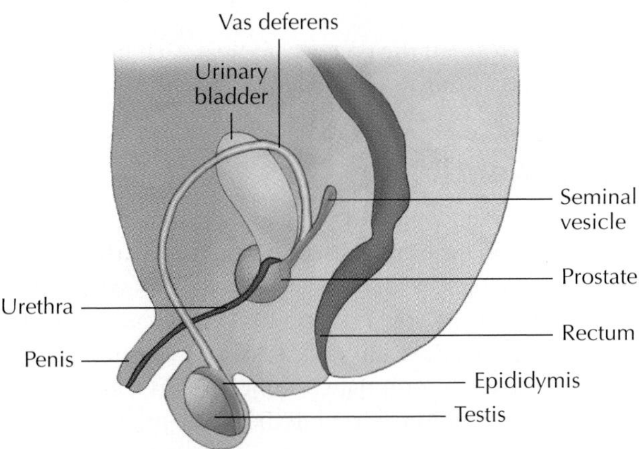

(c) Male *XY* Chromosomes

● **Figure 13.3** Prenatal development of the reproductive organs. Early development of ovaries or testes affects hormonal balance and alters sexual anatomy. *(a)* At first the sex organs are the same in the human female and male. *(b)* When androgens are absent, female structures develop. *(c)* Male sex organs are produced when androgens are present.

hormones found in the body. In fact, prenatal development of male or female anatomy is largely due to the presence or absence of **testosterone** (tes-TOSS-teh-rone: one of the androgens, secreted mainly by the testes) (LeVay & Valente, 2005).

Then is biological sex determined by the sex hormones? Not entirely. As suggested by the chapter preview, sex cannot be reduced to a single dimension.

Dimensions of Sex

At the very least, classifying a person as female or male must take into account the following biological factors: (1) **genetic sex** (*XX* or *XY* chromosomes), (2) **gonadal sex** (ovaries or testes), (3) **hormonal sex** (predominance of androgens or estrogens), (4) **genital sex** (clitoris and vagina in females, penis and scrotum in males). An important nonbiological part of a person's sexual makeup is (5) **gender identity** (one's subjective sense of being male or female). To see why sex must be defined along these five dimensions, let's trace the events involved in becoming female or male.

Prenatal Sexual Development

Becoming male or female starts simply enough. Genetic sex is determined at the instant of conception: Two **X chromosomes** initiate female development; an *X* chromosome plus a **Y chromosome** produces a male. A woman's ovum always provides an *X* chromosome, because she has two *X*s in her own genetic makeup. In contrast, one half of the male's sperm carry *X* chromosomes and the other half *Y*s.

Genetic sex stays the same throughout life. But it alone does not determine biological sex. We must also consider hormonal effects before birth. For the first 6 weeks of prenatal growth, genetically female and male embryos look identical. However, if a *Y* chromosome is present, testes develop in the embryo and supply testosterone. This stimulates growth of the penis and other male structures (● Figure 13.3). In the absence of testosterone, the em-

Gonads The primary sex glands—the testes in males and ovaries in females.

Estrogen Any of a number of female sex hormones.

Androgen Any of a number of male sex hormones, especially testosterone.

Testosterone A male sex hormone, secreted mainly by the testes and responsible for the development of many male sexual characteristics.

Genetic sex Sex as indicated by the presence of *XX* (female) or *XY* (male) chromosomes.

Gonadal sex Sex as indicated by the presence of ovaries (female) or testes (male).

Hormonal sex Sex as indicated by a preponderance of estrogens (female) or androgens (male) in the body.

Genital sex Sex as indicated by the presence of male or female genitals.

Gender identity One's personal, private sense of maleness or femaleness.

X chromosome The female chromosome contributed by the mother; produces a female when paired with another *X* chromosome, and a male when paired with a *Y* chromosome.

Y chromosome The male chromosome contributed by the father; produces a male when paired with an *X* chromosome. Fathers may give either an *X* or a *Y* chromosome to their offspring.

THE CLINICAL FILE

Bruce or Brenda—Can Sex Be Assigned?

After Bruce was born, disaster struck. A normally routine circumcision destroyed his penis. Doctors suggested to his parents that Bruce should be sexually reassigned to become Brenda, a girl. With multiple surgeries and hormone treatments, the doctors said, Brenda would turn out just fine. Following their advice, Brenda wasn't told about the "accident," and she was raised as a girl. For many years, her case was considered a prime example of successful gender reassignment.

However, by puberty Brenda was miserable and suicidal, never quite fitting in with the other girls. In desperation, her parents told her the truth. Initially, Brenda was relieved. She opted for surgical reconstruction as a boy and took the name David. In 2000, he helped author John Colapinto tell his story in *As Nature Made Him* (Colapinto, 2000). After some initial successes as a man, David's marriage and finances failed. Tragically, he committed suicide in 2004.

Although many cases of sexual reassignment are successful, David's case is not unique. Some intersexual children whose sex has been reassigned have had similar experiences. Like David, an intersexual child who is biologically male, but raised as a girl, may continue to feel that she is a boy, especially at puberty when "she" may begin growing a beard. If their "secret" is revealed, intersexual people may feel damaged—that their bodies were surgically altered without their permission (Cull, 2002).

As this discussion implies, a heated controversy exists about the treatment of sex and gender issues in young children (Williams, 2002). Supporters of early sex assignment argue that the benefits usually outweigh the long-term psychological costs (Slijper et al., 2000). Critics of early sex assignment believe that it is better for individuals to accept who they are and to realize that some bodies do not neatly fit into the categories of male and female (Holmes, 2002). Recently, critics have argued, with some success, that rather than impose the choice on them as children, it is better to wait until adulthood, when intersex individuals can then choose for themselves whether or not to have surgery and whether to live as a man or a woman (Thyen, et al., 2005).

Only time will tell which approach is more successful, and for which particular intersex condition. Because sex and gender are complex, the best course of treatment may prove to be different for different people (Rathus, Nevid, & Fichner-Rathus, 2005).

bryo will develop female reproductive organs and genitals, regardless of genetic sex (LeVay & Valente, 2005). It might be said, then, that nature's primary impulse is to make a female. Without testosterone, we would all be women.

Prenatal growth usually matches genetic sex, but not always. A genetic male won't develop male genitals if too little testosterone is available. Even if testosterone is present, an inherited *androgen insensitivity* (unresponsiveness to testosterone) may exist. Again, the result is female development (LeVay & Valente, 2005).

Similarly, androgens must be at low levels or absent for an *XX* embryo to develop as a female. Thus, for both genetic females and males, hormonal problems before birth may produce an **intersexual person** (one who has ambiguous sexual anatomy). For instance, a developing female may be masculinized by the antimiscarriage drug progestin, or by a problem known as the *androgenital syndrome* (an-dro-JEN-ih-tal). In the androgenital syndrome, the child's body produces estrogen, but a genetic abnormality causes the adrenal glands to release too much androgen. In such cases, a female child may be born with genitals that are more male than female.

Can sex be assigned? For a variety of reasons, including transsexuality and intersexuality, it may make sense to reassign the sex of an individual. Surgery can reconfigure the external appearance of the genitals, hormone treatments can shift the chemical balance in the body, and a deliberate effort can be made to transform the person's sense of gender identity. But can it be successful? Experts are divided about the best way to treat such individuals. See "Bruce or Brenda—Can Sex Be Assigned?"

Gender Identity

As stated earlier, gender identity is your personal, private sense of being female or male. Gender identity is at least partly learned.

How is gender identity acquired? Obviously, it begins with *labeling* ("It's a girl," "It's a boy") (Eagly, 2001). Thereafter it is shaped by **gender role socialization** (the process of learning gender behaviors regarded as appropriate for one's sex in a given culture). Gender role socialization reflects all the subtle pressures from parents, peers, and cultural forces that urge boys to "act like boys" and girls to "act like girls." By the time they are just 2 years of age, children are aware of gender role differences (Witt, 1997). At 3 or 4 years of age, gender identity is usually well formed.

Don't intersexual children imply that biology also plays a role in gender identity? Yes, they do. The fact that trying to assign gender is not always successful suggests that hormones may "sex-type" the brain before birth (LeVay & Valente, 2005). Changes in the brain are then thought to alter the chances of developing feminine or masculine traits (Witelson, 1991). Direct evidence for this idea is provided by females exposed to androgens before birth. After birth, their hormones shift to female, and they are raised as girls. Nevertheless, the prenatal exposure to male hormones has a masculinizing effect. During childhood, such girls are typically "tomboys" who prefer the company of boys to girls. However, their masculinization usually does not persist. After adolescence, the girls' tomboyism usually gives way to female interests and gender characteristics (Money, 1987; Money & Mathews, 1982). Cases like these make it clear that both prenatal hormones and later social factors contribute to adult sexual identity (Breedlove, Cooke, & Jordan, 1999).

Origins of Male–Female Differences

In animals, clear links exist between prenatal hormones and male or female behaviors. In humans, biology plays a similar role. That is, prenatal androgens and estrogens subtly influence development of the body, nervous system, and later behavior patterns. Although it would be a mistake to ignore this **biological biasing effect,** most human sex-linked behaviors are influenced much more by learning than is the case for animals (Hare-Mustin & Marecek, 1988; Helgeson, 2005).

At the risk of getting mired in the "battle of the sexes," let's consider one more idea. Some researchers believe that the biological biasing effect imparts different thinking abilities in women and men. Women, they say, are more often "left brained," and men, "right brained." The left brain, you may recall, is largely responsible for language and rote learning. The right brain is superior at spatial reasoning. Thus, some psychologists think that biological differences explain why men (as a group) do slightly better on spatial tasks and math and why women are slightly better at language skills (Hiscock, Perachio, & Inch, 2001). Others, however, strongly reject this theory. To them, such claims are based on shaky evidence and sexist thinking. The most telling evidence on this point may be that female and male scores on the Scholastic Assessment Test are rapidly becoming more alike. The same applies to tests of math ability (Halpern, 2001). The narrowing gap is probably explained by a growing similarity in male and female interests, experiences, and educational goals.

Note also that the differences that do exist between women and men are based on *averages* (● Figure 13.4). Many women are better at math than most men are. Likewise, many men are better at verbal skills than most women are. Scores for women and men overlap so much that it is impossible to predict if any one person will be good or bad at math or language skills simply from knowing his or her sex. There is no biological basis for the unequal treatment women have faced at work, school, and elsewhere. Most male–female performance gaps can be traced to *social* differences in the power and opportunities given to men and women. Unequal power tends to exaggerate differences between men and women, and then makes these artificial differences appear to be real (Goodwin & Fiske, 2001).

BRIDGES

Differences in male and female brains may affect the chances of retaining language abilities after a person suffers a stroke or brain injury.

See "His and Her Brains?" in Chapter 2, page 70.

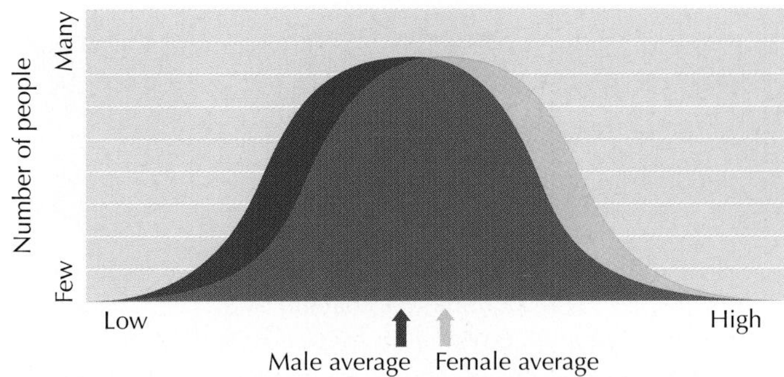

● **Figure 13.4** Recorded differences in various abilities that exist between women and men are based on *averages.* For example, if we were to record the number of men and women who have low, medium, or high scores on tests of language ability, we might obtain graphs like those shown. For other abilities, men would have a higher average. However, such average differences are typically small. As a result, the overlap in female abilities and male abilities is very large (LeVay & Valente, 2005).

Gender Roles

Gender roles probably have as big an influence on sexual behavior as chromosomal, genital, or hormonal factors do. A **gender role** is the favored pattern of behavior expected of each sex. In our culture, boys are encouraged to be strong, fast, aggressive, dominant, and achieving. Traditional females are expected to be sensitive, intuitive, passive, emotional, and "naturally" interested in child rearing. All cultures define gender roles. This often leads to stereotyped thinking, as illustrated by the following riddle:

Question: How many men does it take to change a light bulb?
Answer: None. Real men aren't afraid of the dark.

This joke pokes fun at the North American stereotype of manhood. Despite much progress in the last 20 years, gender role stereotypes continue to have a major impact on women and men.

Gender role stereotypes are oversimplified beliefs about what men and women are actually like. Gender roles influence how we act. Gender role stereotypes, in contrast, treat gender roles as if they were real biological differences. That is, culturally defined ways of acting are turned into false beliefs about what men and women can and can't do.

Intersexual person An individual who has genitals suggestive of both sexes.

Gender role socialization The process of learning gender behaviors considered appropriate for one's sex in a given culture.

Biological biasing effect Hypothesized effect that prenatal exposure to sex hormones has on development of the body, nervous system, and later behavior patterns.

Gender role The pattern of behaviors that is regarded as "male" or "female" by one's culture; sometimes also referred to as a sex role.

Gender role stereotypes Oversimplified and widely held beliefs about the basic characteristics of men and women.

DISCOVERING PSYCHOLOGY

Man's Work

Andrea is the assistant vice president for sales at a large aircraft company. She is responsible for training and supervising junior executives, keeping up with industry trends, and finding new clients. Her work focuses on engine assemblies, hydraulic controls, fuel tanks, servos, and other mechanical parts. In a recent performance review, Andrea received high evaluations. She is regarded as a rising star, based on sales, the number of new client accounts she has produced, and actual dollars earned. Her performance is in the top 5 percent of all employees at her level.

Now that you know a little about Andrea, use the following scale to answer this question: How much do you think you would like this person? (Circle your rating.)

Not at All | Slightly | Somewhat | Moderately | More than Average | Quite a Lot | Very Much

Do you think your rating would be higher if the name *James* replaced *Andrea* in the job summary? In a recent study, college students rated a woman and a man who were equally successful in a traditionally "male" job. The students consistently liked high-performing women *less* than they did men with identical jobs and achievements.

Why are women who are successful at "man's work" considered less likeable? The answer is that women tend to be punished for violating gender norms. Being successful in a "male" job implies that a woman has the "wrong" traits, which are better suited to males. That is, the self-assertive, achievement-oriented behaviors that are valued in men are frowned on in women. Despite the fact that many women have shown that they can excel, many pay a social price for their success (Heilman et al., 2004).

Are women suited to be fighter pilots, corporate presidents, military commanders, or racecar drivers? A person with strong gender role stereotypes might say, "No, because women are not sufficiently aggressive, dominant, or mechanically inclined for such roles." Yet today's women have performed successfully in virtually all realms. Nevertheless, gender role stereotypes persist. The United States has never had a woman president, although the possibility may be nearer: As of 2006, both Hillary Clinton and Condolezza Rice have been mentioned as serious candidates for the 2008 election. Only time will tell.

Gender role stereotypes can be a major career obstacle. For many jobs, your chances of being hired could be reduced by your sex, be it male or female. Unequal pay for comparable work and experience is also a major problem for women. In the professions, women earn only about 75 cents for every dollar earned by men. The rate for women of color is worse—67 cents for black women and a measly 54 cents for Latinas. The male–female pay difference is even found in colleges, where greater awareness of gender fairness should prevail (Kite et al., 2001).

"The committee on women's rights will now come to order."

Like all stereotypes, those based on gender roles ignore the wonderful diversity of humanity. Fortunately, extreme gender stereotyping has declined somewhat in the last 20 years (Helwig, 1998; Kite, 2001). Just the same, in business, academia, medicine, law, sports, and politics, women continue to earn less money and achieve lower status than men do. In other words, many women are still "running in place," hobbled by gender stereotyping (Valian, 1998). (See "Man's Work.")

Culture

A look at other cultures shows that our gender roles are by no means "natural" or universal. For example, in many cultures women do the heavy work because men are considered too weak for it (Best, 2002). In Russia, roughly 75 percent of all medical doctors are women, and women make up a large portion of the workforce. Many more examples could be cited, but one of the most interesting is anthropologist Margaret Mead's (1935) classic observations of the Tchambuli people of New Guinea.

Gender roles for the Tchambuli are a nearly perfect reversal of North American stereotypes. Tchambuli women do the fishing and manufacturing, and they control the power and economic life of the community. Women also take the initiative in courting and sexual relations. Tchambuli men, on the other hand, are expected to be dependent, flirtatious, and concerned with their appearance. Art, games, and theatrics occupy most of the Tchambuli males' time, and men are particularly fond of adorning themselves with flowers and jewelry.

As the Tchambuli show, men and women are expected to act in quite different ways in various cultures. The arbitrary nature of gender roles is also apparent. A man is no less a man if he cooks, sews, or cares for children. A woman is no less a woman if she excels in sports, succeeds in business, or works as an auto mechanic.

Still, adult personality and gender identity are closely tied to cultural definitions of "masculinity" and "femininity."

An interesting side effect of gender role socialization is the imprint it leaves on activities that have nothing to do with sex. For example, it has long been thought that boys are more aggressive than girls and girls have more emotional empathy than boys (Block, 1979; Maccoby & Jacklin, 1974).

Gender Role Socialization

How are gender differences created? Learning gender roles begins immediately. Infant girls are held more gently and treated more tenderly than boys. Both parents play more roughly with sons than with daughters (who are presumed to be more "delicate"). Later, boys are allowed to roam over a wider area without special permission. They are also expected to run errands earlier than girls. Daughters are told that they are pretty and that "nice girls don't fight." Boys are told to be strong and that "tough guys don't cry." Sons are more often urged to control their emotions, except for anger and aggression, which parents tolerate more in boys than in girls.

Toys are strongly sex typed: Parents buy dolls for girls; trucks, tools, and sports equipment for boys. Fathers, especially, tend to encourage their children to play with "appropriate" sex-typed toys (Raag & Rackliff, 1998) (● Figure 13.5). By the time children reach kindergarten they have learned to think that doctors, fire fighters, and pilots are men and that nurses, secretaries, and hairdressers are women (Eagly, 2000; Stroeher, 1994). And why not? The workforce is still highly segregated by sex, and children learn from what they observe. Stereotyped gender roles are even the norm in TV commercials, children's picture books, and video games (Browne, 1998; Dietz, 1998)!

Steve Dunwell Photography, Inc./Index Stock Imagery/PictureQuest

● **Figure 13.5** One study found that even the parents of 2-year-olds strongly encourage their toddlers to play with "sex-appropriate" toys. Parents' nonverbal responses to toys were consistently more positive when a toy matched stereotypes for the child's gender (Caldera, Huston, & O'Brien, 1989).

"Female" and "Male" Behavior

Overall, parents tend to encourage their sons to engage in **instrumental** (goal-directed) **behaviors**, to control their emotions, and to prepare for the world of work. Daughters, on the other hand, are encouraged in **expressive** (emotion-oriented) **behaviors** and, to a lesser degree, are socialized for motherhood.

When parents are told they treat girls and boys differently, many explain that the sexes are just "naturally" different. But what comes first, "natural differences" or the gender-based expectations that create them? In our culture, "male" seems—for many—to be defined as "not female." That is, parents often have a vague fear of expressive and emotional behavior in male children. To them, such behavior implies that a boy is effeminate or a sissy. Many parents who would not be troubled if their daughters engaged in "masculine" play might be upset if their sons played with dolls or imitated "female" mannerisms.

Differences between boys and girls are magnified by sex-segregated play. Beginning around age 3, boys start to play mostly with boys and girls play with girls. And how do they play? Girls tend to play indoors and near adults. They like to cooperate by playing house and other games that require lots of verbal give-and-take. Boys prefer super-hero games and rough-and-tumble play outdoors. They tend to be concerned with dominance or who's the boss. Thus, from an early age males and females tend to grow up in different, gender-defined cultures (Martin & Fabes, 2001).

To summarize, gender role socialization in our society prepares children for a world in which men are expected to be instrumental, conquering, controlling, and unemotional. Women, in contrast, are expected to be expressive, emotional, passive, and dependent. Thus, gender role socialization teaches us to be highly competent in some respects and handicapped in others (Levant, 1996).

Robert Caputo/Stock, Boston

Behaviors that are considered typical and appropriate for each sex (gender roles) vary a great deal from culture to culture. Undoubtedly some cultures magnify sex differences more than others (LeVay & Valente, 2005).

Instrumental behaviors Behaviors directed toward the achievement of some goal; behaviors that are instrumental in producing some effect.

Expressive behaviors Behaviors that express or communicate emotion or personal feelings.

Of course, many people find traditional gender roles acceptable and comfortable. It seems evident, however, that just about everyone will benefit when the more stereotyped and burdensome aspects of gender roles are set aside. The next section explains why.

Androgyny—Are You Masculine, Feminine, or Androgynous?

Are you aggressive, ambitious, analytical, assertive, athletic, competitive, decisive, dominant, forceful, independent, individualistic, self-reliant, and willing to take risks? If so, you are quite "masculine." Are you affectionate, cheerful, childlike, compassionate, flatterable, gentle, gullible, loyal, sensitive, shy, soft-spoken, sympathetic, tender, understanding, warm, and yielding? If so, then you are quite "feminine." What if you have traits from both lists? In that case, you may be *androgynous* (an-DROJ-ih-nus).

The two lists you just read are from the seminal work of psychologist Sandra Bem. By combining 20 "masculine" traits (self-reliant, assertive, and so forth), 20 "feminine" traits (affectionate, gentle), and 20 neutral traits (truthful, friendly) Bem created the *Bem Sex Role Inventory* (BSRI). (Some psychologists prefer to use the term *sex role* instead of gender role.) Next, she and her associates gave the BSRI to thousands of people, asking them to say whether each trait applied to them. Of those surveyed, 50 percent fell into traditional feminine or masculine categories, 15 percent scored higher on traits of the opposite sex, and 35 percent were androgynous, getting high scores on both feminine and masculine items.

BRIDGES

In males, a restricted ability to express emotion is one of the costs of adopting a masculine gender role, at least as it is defined in North America.

See Chapter 12, page 416.

Psychological Androgyny

The word **androgyny** (an-DROJ-ih-nee) literally means "man-woman." Androgyny sounds as if it might have something to do with androids, asexuality, or sex-change operations, but it actually refers to having both feminine and masculine traits (Helgeson, 2005).

Bem is convinced that our complex society requires flexibility with respect to gender roles. She believes that it is necessary for men to be gentle, compassionate, sensitive, and yielding and for women to be forceful, self-reliant, independent, and ambitious—*as the situation requires*. In short, Bem feels that more people should be androgynous.

Adaptability

Bem has shown that androgynous individuals are more adaptable. They seem especially to be less hindered by images of "feminine" or "masculine" behavior. For example, in one study people were given the choice of doing either a "masculine" activity (oil a hinge, nail boards together, and so forth) or a "feminine" activity (prepare a baby bottle, wind yarn into a ball, and so on). Masculine men and feminine women consistently chose to do gender-appropriate activities, even when the opposite choice paid more!

Bem has concluded that rigid gender stereotypes and gender roles can seriously restrict behavior, especially for men (Bem, 1975, 1981). She believes that masculine males have great difficulty expressing warmth, playfulness, and concern—even when they are appropriate. Masculine men, it seems, tend to view such feelings as unacceptably "feminine." Masculine men (let's call them "manly men") also find it hard to accept emotional support from others, particularly from women (Levant, 2001). They tend to be interested in sports, have mostly male friends, dislike feminists, and sit with their knees wide apart (really!) (Twenge, 1999). Problems faced by highly feminine women are the reverse of those faced by masculine men. Such women have trouble being independent and assertive, even when these qualities are desirable.

Over the years androgyny has been variously supported, attacked, and debated. Now, as the dust begins to settle, the picture looks like this:

Androgynous individuals adapt easily to both traditionally "feminine" and "masculine" situations.

Kevin Fitzgerald/Getty Images

Viario Press/Imapress/The Image Works

- Having "masculine" traits primarily means that a person is independent and assertive. Scoring high in "masculinity," therefore, is related to high self-esteem and to success in many situations (Long, 1989).
- Having "feminine" traits primarily means that a person is nurturant and interpersonally oriented. People who score high in "femininity," therefore, are more likely to seek and receive social support. They tend to experience greater social closeness with others and more happiness in marriage (Reevy & Maslach, 2001).

In sum, there are advantages to possessing both "feminine" and "masculine" traits (Guastello & Guastello, 2003; Ickes, 1993). In general, androgynous persons are more flexible when it comes to coping with difficult situations (Jurma & Powell, 1994; Spangenberg & Lategan, 1993) (see ● Figure 13.6). Androgynous persons also tend to be more satisfied with their lives. Apparently, they can use both instrumental and emotionally expressive capacities to enhance their lives and relationships (Dean-Church & Gilroy, 1993; Ramanaiah, Detwiler, & Byravan, 1995).

Interestingly, some men appear to be moving toward more balanced definitions of manhood. For instance, more Mexican-American men than European-American men are androgynous (Sugihara & Warner, 1999). Along the same lines, some Asian-American men, especially those who were born in the United States, appear to be creating a more flexible masculinity free from male dominance. These men link their masculinity with a capacity for caring and they are not afraid of doing "feminine tasks," such as cooking or housework (Chua & Fujino, 1999).

It is worth saying again that many people remain comfortable with traditional views of gender. Nevertheless, "feminine" traits and "masculine" traits can exist in the same person, and androgyny can be a highly adaptive balance.

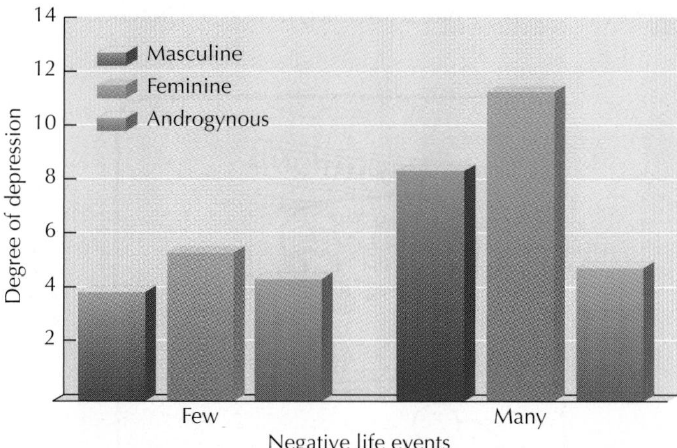

● **Figure 13.6** Another indication of the possible benefits of androgyny is found in a study of reactions to stress. When confronted with an onslaught of negative events, strongly masculine or feminine persons become more depressed than androgynous individuals do. (Adapted from Roos & Cohen, 1987)

KNOWLEDGE BUILDER

Sexual Development, Gender, and Androgyny

REFLECT

You are a pediatrician who has been asked to evaluate a child whose sex seems to be ambiguous. What indicators of sex would you want to check?

Can you remember an example of gender role socialization you experienced as a child? Do you think you were encouraged to engage more in instrumental behaviors or expressive behaviors?

Mentally change your male friends to females and your female friends to males. Can you separate the "human being" or "core person" from your friends' normal gender identities and gender roles?

Think of three people you know, one who is androgynous, one who is traditionally feminine, and one who is traditionally masculine. What advantages and disadvantages do you see in each collection of traits. How do you think you would be classified if you took the BSRI?

LEARNING CHECK

1. ____________ sexual characteristics refer to the sexual and reproductive organs; ____________ sexual characteristics refer to other bodily changes that take place at puberty.
2. All individuals normally produce both androgens and estrogens, although the proportions differ in females and males. T or F?
3. The four basic dimensions of biological sex are: ____________, ____________, ____________, ____________
4. In females, intersexual anatomy may result from
   a. an androgen insensitivity c. excessive estrogen
   b. the androgenital syndrome d. all of these
5. For humans, the biological biasing effect of prenatal hormones tends to override all other influences. T or F?
6. One's private sense of maleness or femaleness is referred to as ____________ ____________.
7. Traditional gender role socialization encourages ____________ behavior in males.
   a. instrumental c. expressive
   b. emotional d. dependent
8. A person who is androgynous is one who scores high on ratings of traits usually possessed by the opposite sex. T or F?
9. For both women and men, having masculine traits is associated with greater happiness in marriage. T or F?

CRITICAL THINKING

10. A problem known as transsexualism exists when a person feels that she or he is trapped in a body of the wrong sex. This problem is therefore defined almost entirely on the basis of which dimension of gender?
11. As children are growing up, the male emphasis on instrumental behavior comes into conflict with the female emphasis on expressive behavior. At what age do you think such conflicts become prominent?

Androgyny The presence of both "masculine" and "feminine" traits in a single person (as masculinity and femininity are defined within one's culture).

12. Could a person be androgynous in a culture where "masculine" and "feminine" traits differ greatly from those on Bem's list?

Answers: **1.** Primary, secondary **2.** T **3.** genetic sex, gonadal sex, hormonal sex, genital sex **4.** b **5.** F **6.** gender identity **7.** a **8.** F **9.** F **10.** Gender identity. **11.** Children segregate themselves into same-sex groups during much of childhood, which limits conflicts between male and female patterns of behavior. However, as children move into adolescence they begin to spend more time with members of the opposite sex. This brings the dominant, competitive style of boys into conflict with the nurturant, expressive style of girls, often placing girls at a disadvantage (Maccoby, 1990). **12.** Yes. Being androgynous means having both masculine and feminine traits *as they are defined within one's culture.*

Sexual Behavior—Mapping the Erogenous Zone

Sexuality is a natural part of being human. A capacity for sexual arousal is apparent at birth or soon after. Researcher Alfred Kinsey verified instances of orgasm in boys as young as 5 months old and girls as young as 4 months (Kinsey, Pomeroy, & Martin, 1948, 1953). Kinsey also found that 2- to 5-year-old children spontaneously touch and exhibit their genitals.

Various types of sexual behavior continue throughout childhood. But as a child matures, cultural norms place greater restrictions on sexual activities. Still, 25 percent of females and 50 percent of males engage in preadolescent sex play. In adulthood, norms continue to shape sexual activity along socially approved lines. In our culture, sex between children, incest (sex between close relatives), prostitution, and extramarital sex are all discouraged.

As was true of gender roles, it's apparent that such restrictions are somewhat arbitrary. Sexual activities of all kinds are more common in cultures that place fewer restrictions on sexual behavior. Apart from cultural norms, it can be said that any sexual act engaged in by consenting adults is "normal" if it does not hurt anyone. (Atypical sexual behavior is discussed later in this chapter.)

Sexual Arousal

Human sexual arousal is complex. It may, of course, be produced by direct stimulation of the body's **erogenous zones** (eh-ROJ-eh-nus: productive of pleasure or erotic desire). Human erogenous zones include the genitals, mouth, breasts, ears, anus, and to a lesser degree, the surface of the entire body. It is clear, however, that more than physical contact is involved: A urological or gynecological exam rarely results in any sexual arousal. Likewise, an unwanted sexual advance may produce only revulsion. Human sexual arousal obviously includes a large cognitive element. Indeed, arousal may be triggered by mere thoughts or images. As one expert put it, the most important sex organ is between your ears. For humans, the mind (or brain) is the ultimate erogenous zone.

Sexual Scripts

In a restaurant we commonly expect certain things to occur. It could even be said that each of us has a restaurant "script" that defines a plot, dialogue, and actions that should take place. Researcher John Gagnon (1977) has pointed out that, similarly, we learn a variety of **sexual scripts,** or unspoken mental plans that guide our sexual behavior. Such scripts determine when and where we are likely to express sexual feelings, and with whom. They provide a "plot" for the order of events in lovemaking and they outline "approved" actions, motives, and outcomes.

When two people follow markedly different scripts, misunderstandings are common. Consider, for instance, what happens when a woman acting out a "friendly-first-date" script is paired with a man following a "seduction" script: The result is often anger, hurt feelings, or worse (Schleicher & Gilbert, 2005). Even newlyweds may find that their sexual "agendas" differ. In such cases, considerable "rewriting" of scripts is often needed for sexual compatibility.

Are men more easily sexually aroused than women? Yes and no. No, because women are just as *physically* responsive as men (Laan et al., 1995). Yes, because women are more sensitive to *emotional* factors than men (Basson et al., 2005). In one study women watched excerpts from two erotic films. One was made by a man for male viewers. The other was directed by a woman and presented from a female point of view. Although women's physical arousal was nearly identical for both films, as measured by a medical recording device, their subjective experiences differed greatly. Many women reported being repulsed, disgusted, and decidedly not aroused by the male-oriented film. When they watched the film made for women, subjects reported more subjective feelings of sexual arousal, more positive emotions, and more interest in the film (Laan et al., 1994).

Why did the women respond so differently? Basically, the male-centered film was a macho fantasy in which the woman was little more than a sexual prop—her pleasure and fulfillment were portrayed as largely unimportant. In the woman-made film, the female character took the initiative in lovemaking and obviously enjoyed it. Clearly, women and men have equal potential for sex-

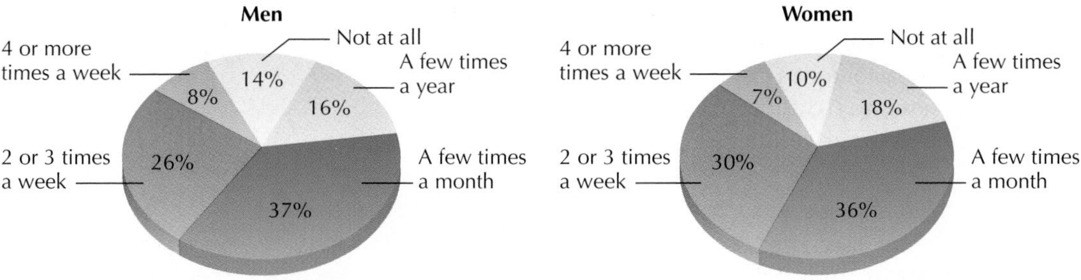

● **Figure 13.7** These graphs show the frequency of sexual intercourse for American adults. To generalize, about one third of the people surveyed have sex twice a week or more, one third a few times a month, and one third a few times a year or not at all. The overall average is about once a week (Laumann et al., 1994).

ual arousal. However, a woman's subjective feelings of arousal tend to be more closely tied to her emotional response to erotic cues. It would appear that many women want to be active partners in lovemaking and they want their needs and preferences to be acknowledged.

Based on the frequency of orgasm (from masturbation or intercourse), the peak of male sexual activity is at age 18. The peak rate of female sexual activity appears to occur a little later (Janus & Janus, 1993). However, male and female sexual patterns are rapidly becoming more alike (Oliver & Hyde, 1993). ● Figure 13.7 shows the results of a major survey of sexual behavior among American adults. As you can see, the frequency of sexual intercourse is very similar for men and women (Laumann et al., 1994). Exaggerating the differences between male and female sexuality is not only inaccurate, it can also create artificial barriers to sexual satisfaction (Wiederman, 2001).

Sex Drive

What causes differences in sex drive? The term **sex drive** refers to the strength of one's motivation to engage in sexual behavior. Attitudes toward sex, sexual experience, and recency of sexual activity are all important, but physical factors also play a role. As discussed in Chapter 12, a man's sex drive is related to the amount of androgens (especially testosterone) supplied by the testes. The connection can be very direct: When a man chats with a woman he finds attractive, his testosterone levels actually increase (Roney, 2003). Likewise, the sex drive in women is related to estrogen levels (Graziottin, 1998). As you may also recall, testosterone also plays a role in female sexuality. A woman's sex drive is closely related to the testosterone level in her bloodstream. Of course, women produce much smaller amounts of testosterone than men do. But that doesn't mean their sex drive is weaker. Women's bodies are more sensitive to testosterone and their sex drive is comparable to males. Testosterone levels decline with age, which can lower sexual desire. However, in some instances, testosterone supplements can restore the sex drive in both men and women (Crooks & Baur, 2005).

BRIDGES

Sexual arousal normally occurs during rapid-eye-movement (REM) sleep, when most dreaming takes place.

See Chapter 7, pages 230–231.

Does alcohol stimulate the sex drive? In general, no. Alcohol is a *depressant*. As such, it may, in small doses, stimulate erotic desire by lowering inhibitions. This effect no doubt accounts for alcohol's reputation as an aid to seduction. (Humorist Ogden Nash once summarized this bit of folklore by saying, "Candy is dandy, but liquor is quicker.") However, in larger doses alcohol suppresses orgasm in women and erections in men. Getting drunk *decreases* sexual desire, arousal, pleasure, and performance (Crowe & George, 1989).

Numerous other drugs are reputed to be aphrodisiacs (af-ruh-DEEZ-ee-aks: substances that increase sexual desire or pleasure). However, like alcohol, a long list of other drugs actually impair sexual response, rather than enhance it. Some examples are ampehtamines, amyl nitrite, barbiturates, cocaine, Ecstasy, LSD, and marijuana. As one expert observed, "Love, however you define it, seems to be the best aphrodisiac of all" (Crooks & Bauer, 2005).

Does removal of the testes or ovaries abolish the sex drive? In lower animals, **castration** (surgical removal of the testicles or ovaries) tends to abolish sexual activity in *inexperienced* animals. In humans, the effects of male and female castration vary. At first, some people experience a loss of sex drive; in others there is no change. (That's why castration of sex offenders is not likely to curb their behavior.) However, after several years almost all subjects report a decrease in sex drive unless they take hormone supplements.

The preceding observations have nothing to do with **sterilization** (surgery to make a man or woman infertile). The vast majority of women and men who choose surgically based birth control (such as a tubal ligation or a vasectomy) do not lose interest in sex. If anything, they may become more sexually active when pregnancy is no longer a concern.

What happens to the sex drive in old age? A natural decline in sex drive typically accompanies aging. As noted earlier, this is related to a reduced output of sex hormones, especially testosterone (Segraves

Erogenous zones Areas of the body that produce pleasure and/or provoke erotic desire.

Sexual script An unspoken mental plan that defines a "plot," dialogue, and actions expected to take place in a sexual encounter.

Sex drive The strength of one's motivation to engage in sexual behavior.

Castration Surgical removal of the testicles or ovaries.

Sterilization Medical procedures such as vasectomy or tubal ligation that make a man or a woman infertile.

& Segraves, 1995) (● Figure 13.8). However, sexual activity need not come to an end. Some people in their eighties and nineties continue to have active sex lives (Skoog, 1996). The crucial factor for an extended sex life appears to be regularity and opportunity. ("Use it or lose it.") People who fairly regularly engage in intercourse have little difficulty in later years (Janus & Janus, 1993).

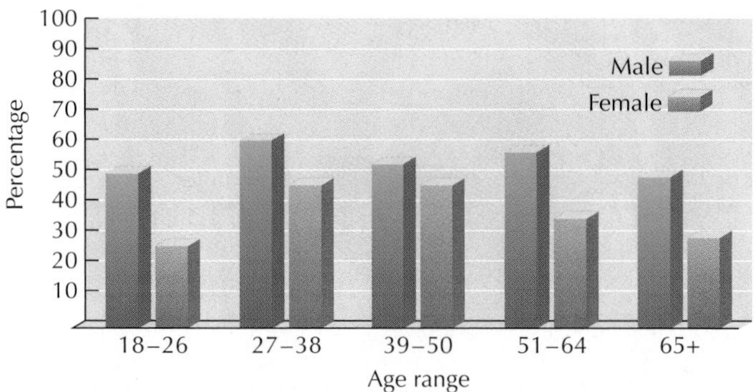

● **Figure 13.9** Percentage of women and men who masturbate. (Data from Janus & Janus, 1993.)

Masturbation

One of the most basic sexual behaviors is **masturbation** (self-stimulation that causes sexual pleasure or orgasm). Self-stimulation has been observed in infants under 1 year of age. In adulthood, female masturbation most often involves rubbing the clitoris or areas near it. Male masturbation usually takes the form of rubbing or stroking the penis.

Do more men masturbate than women? Yes. Of the women who took part in a national survey, 89 percent reported that they had masturbated at some time. Of the males, 95 percent reported that they had masturbated. (Some cynics add, "And the other 5 percent lied!") As ● Figure 13.9 shows, masturbation is a regular feature of the sex lives of many people (Janus & Janus, 1993).

What purpose does masturbation serve? Through masturbation, people discover what pleases them sexually. Masturbation is an important part of the psychosexual development of most adolescents. Among other things, it provides a healthy substitute for sexual involvement at a time when young people are maturing emotionally.

Is it immature for masturbation to continue after marriage? If it is, there are many "immature" people around! Approximately 70 percent of married women and men masturbate at least occasionally. Generally speaking, masturbation is valid at any age and usually has no effect on marital relationships. Contrary to popular myths, people are not compelled to masturbate because they lack a sexual partner. Masturbation is just "one more item on the menu" for people with active sex lives (Laumann et al., 1994).

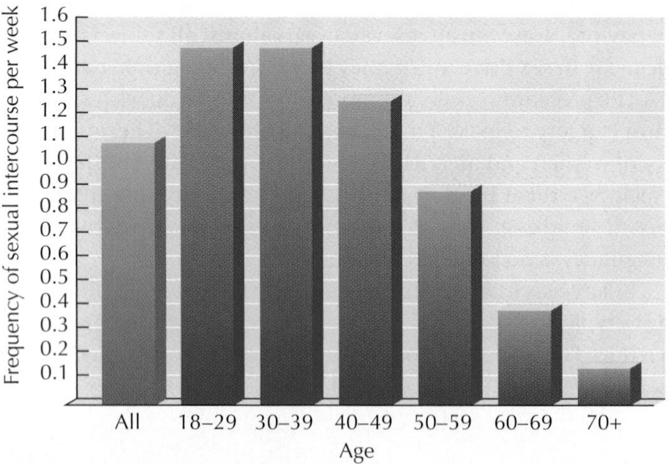

● **Figure 13.8** Average frequency of sexual intercourse per week for adults in the United States. Average intervals for intercourse decline from once every 4 to 5 days in young adulthood, to once every 16 days in the sixties. Remember that averages such as these are lowered by the inclusion of people who are abstinent or who do not have sexual partners (such as many widowed persons). However, the age declines noted here also show up for people who are married, ranging from an average rate of intercourse of twice a week for couples under 30 to once every 3 weeks for those over 70. This suggests that the average frequency of intercourse does decline with advancing age (Smith, 1990).

Is there any way in which masturbation can cause harm? Fifty years ago, a child might have been told that masturbation would cause insanity, acne, sterility, or other such nonsense. "Self-abuse," as it was often called, has enjoyed a long and unfortunate history of religious and medical disapproval. The modern view is that masturbation is a normal sexual behavior (Bockting & Coleman, 2003). Enlightened parents are well aware of this fact. Still, many children are punished or made to feel guilty for touching their genitals. This is unfortunate because masturbation itself is harmless. Typically, its only negative effects are feelings of fear, guilt, or anxiety that arise from learning to think of masturbation as "bad" or "wrong." In an age when people are urged to practice "safer sex," masturbation remains the safest sex of all.

Sexual Orientation—Who Do You Love?

Sexual behavior and romantic relationships are strongly influenced by a person's sexual orientation. **Sexual orientation** refers to your degree of emotional and erotic attraction to members of the same sex, opposite sex, or both sexes. **Heterosexual** people are romantically and erotically attracted to members of the opposite sex. Those who are **homosexual** are attracted to people whose sex matches their own. A person who is **bisexual** is attracted to both men and women. In short, sexual orientation answers these questions: Who are you attracted to? Who do you have erotic fantasies about? Do you love men, or women, or both (Garnets, 2002)?

Sexual orientation is a deep part of personal identity. Starting with their earliest erotic feelings, most people remember being attracted to either the opposite sex or the same sex. The chances are practically nil of an exclusively heterosexual or homosexual person being "converted" from one orientation to the other. If

FOCUS ON RESEARCH

Genes, the Brain, and Sexual Orientation

Why are some people attracted to the opposite sex whereas others prefer members of the same sex? New evidence suggests that sexual orientation is at least partly hereditary. One study found that if one identical twin is homosexual or bisexual, there is a 50-percent chance that the other twin is too. Similar findings lead some researchers to estimate that sexual orientation is from 30 to 70 percent genetic (Mustanski, Chivers, & Bailey, 2002).

How could genes affect sexual orientation? Possibly, heredity shapes areas of the brain that orchestrate sexual behavior. Support for this idea comes from the work of neuroscientists who have shown that various brain structures (LeVay, 1993) and brain chemicals (Kinnunen et al., 2004) do indeed differ in heterosexuals and homosexuals. Other research suggests that sexual orientation is influenced by a gene or genes found on the *X* chromosome. Thus, genetic tendencies for homosexuality may be passed from mothers to their children (Hamer et al., 1993; Hu et al., 1995; Rahman & Wilson, 2003). During human evolution, homosexuality may have developed to reduce competition between males for a limited number of potential female mates (Schuiling, 2004).

Many people mistakenly believe that homosexuality is caused by a hormone imbalance. However, it is *highly unlikely* that adult hormone levels affect sexual orientation. Hormone levels of most gay men and lesbians are within the normal range (Banks & Gartrell, 1995). If hormones do affect sexual orientation, their impact occurs before birth (Mustanski, Chivers, & Bailey, 2002).

It is also a mistake to think that parenting makes children homosexual. There is little difference between the development of children with gay or lesbian parents and those who have heterosexual parents (Patterson, 2002; Wainright, Russell, & Patterson, 2004). Most lesbians and gay men were raised by heterosexual parents, and most children raised by gay or lesbian parents become heterosexual (Garnets, 2002).

All of these findings tend to discredit myths about parents making children homosexual or claims that homosexuality is merely a choice. Although learning contributes to one's sexual orientation, it appears that nature strongly prepares people to be either homosexual or heterosexual (LeVay, 1993). In view of this, discriminating against homosexuals is much like rejecting a person for being blue-eyed or left-handed (Rathus, Nevid, & Fichner-Rathus, 2005).

you are heterosexual, you are probably certain that nothing could ever make you have homoerotic feelings. If so, then you know how homosexual persons feel about the prospects for changing *their* sexual orientation (Seligman, 1994).

But what about people who have had both heterosexual and homosexual relationships? The fact that sexual orientation is usually quite stable doesn't rule out the possibility that for some people erotic feelings may change during the course of a lifetime. However, many such instances involve homosexual people who date or marry members of the opposite sex because of pressures to fit into heterosexual society. When these people realize they are being untrue to themselves, their identity and relationships may shift. Other apparent shifts in orientation probably involve people who are basically bisexual.

What determines a person's sexual orientation? Research suggests that hereditary, biological, social, cultural, and psychological influences combine to produce one's sexual orientation (Garnets, 2002; Van Wyk & Geist, 1995). As one author summarized, "Like much of human behavior, a combination of biological and social factors are most likely involved in the development of sexuality" (Rathus, Nevid, & Fichner-Rathus, 2005). "Genes, the Brain, and Sexual Orientation" summarizes some interesting findings about the origins of sexual orientation.

Homosexuality

As the preceding discussion implies, homosexuality is part of the normal range of variations in sexual orientation (Garnets, 2002). Gay men, lesbians, and bisexuals encounter hostility because they are members of minority groups, not because there is anything inherently wrong with them (Meyer, 1995).

Masturbation Self-stimulation that causes sexual pleasure or orgasm.

Sexual orientation One's degree of emotional and erotic attraction to members of the same sex, opposite sex, or both sexes.

Heterosexual A person romantically and erotically attracted to members of the opposite sex.

Homosexual A person romantically and erotically attracted to same-sex persons.

Bisexual A person romantically and erotically attracted to both men and women.

Based on a national survey, it is estimated that about 7 percent of all adults regard themselves as homosexual or bisexual (Janus & Janus, 1993). Here are the figures:

	Men	**Women**
Heterosexual	91%	95%
Homosexual	4%	2%
Bisexual	5%	3%

A more recent survey of young men found that 6 percent identified themselves as homosexual, so the preceding figures may be low estimates (Bagley & Tremblay, 1998). Nevertheless, among men, *at least* 1 in 25 is homosexual. Among women, *at least* 1 in 50 is a lesbian. About 1 person in 25 is bisexual. Together, these percentages indicate that at least 7 persons out of every 100 are bisexual or homosexual (Janus & Janus, 1993). That means about 60 million people in the United States alone are gay, lesbian, or have a family member who is homosexual (Patterson, 1995).

In contrast to heterosexuals, homosexual persons tend to discover their sexual orientation at a fairly late date—often not until early adolescence. Very likely, this is because they are surrounded by powerful cultural images that contradict their natural feelings. However, most homosexual persons begin to sense that they are different in childhood. By early adolescence, gay men and lesbians begin to feel an attraction to members of the same sex. Gradually, this leads them to question their sexual identity and accept their same-sex orientation (Diamond, 1998).

The problems faced by lesbians and gay men tend to be related to rejection by family and discrimination in hiring and housing. Such unfair treatment is based on homophobia and heterosexism in our society (Meyer, 1995). *Homophobia* refers to prejudice, fear, and dislike directed at homosexuals. *Heterosexism* is the belief that heterosexuality is better or more natural than homosexuality. Understandably, social rejection tends to produce higher rates of anxiety and depression among gay and lesbian people (Cochran, 2001; Gilman et al., 2001). However, anyone facing discrimination and stigma would react in much the same way (Jorm et al., 2002). When such stresses are factored out, homosexual persons are no more likely to have emotional problems than heterosexual people are (Goldfried, 2001). Homosexuality itself is not a problem (Mays & Cochran, 2001).

Most homosexual people have at one time or another suffered verbal abuse—or worse—because of their sexual orientation (Cochran, 2001). Much of this rejection is based on false stereotypes about gay and lesbian people. The following points are a partial reply to such stereotypes. Gay and lesbian people

- Do not try to convert others to homosexuality.
- Do not molest children.
- Are not mentally ill.
- Do not hate persons of the opposite sex.
- Do not, as parents, make their own children gay.
- Do have long-term, caring, monogamous relationships.
- Are no less able to contribute to society than heterosexuals.

Homosexual people are found in all walks of life, at all social and economic levels, and in all cultural groups. They are as diverse in terms of race, ethnicity, age, parenthood, relationships, careers, health, education, politics, and sexual behavior as the heterosexual community (Garnets, 2002). Perhaps as more people come to see gay and lesbian people in terms of their humanity, rather than their sexuality, the prejudices they have faced will wane.

KNOWLEDGE BUILDER

Sexual Behavior and Sexual Orientation

REFLECT

How would you explain the following statement to students in a high school biology class: "Human sexual arousal obviously includes a large cognitive element"?

To what extent does the discussion of sexual arousal and sex drive agree with your own experiences and beliefs? What do you want to remember that you didn't know before?

Which of your prior beliefs about sexual orientation are true? Which are false?

LEARNING CHECK

1. A capacity for sexual arousal is apparent at birth or soon after. T or F?
2. Areas of the body that produce erotic pleasure are called ______________ zones.
3. When exposed to erotic stimuli, men and women vary in their most common emotional reactions, but there appears to be no difference in their levels of physical arousal. T or F?
4. There is some evidence to suggest that sexual activity and sex drives peak later for males than they do for females. T or F?
5. It is possible (and normal) for sexual activity to continue to ages of 80 or 90. T or F?
6. More males than females report that they masturbate. T or F?
7. Masturbation can cause physical harm, according to the latest research reports. T or F?
8. Research suggests that homosexuality is closely related to hormonal imbalances found in roughly 7 percent of all adults. T or F?
9. Whether a person has erotic fantasies about women or men is a strong indicator of his or her sexual orientation. T or F?

CRITICAL THINKING

10. Why do you think that fidelity in marriage is strongly encouraged by law and custom?

Answers: 1. T **2.** erogenous **3.** T **4.** F **5.** T **6.** T **7.** F **8.** F **9.** T **10.** Through marriage laws and customs, human societies tend to foster enduring bonds between sexual partners to help ensure that children are cared for and not just produced (Ainsworth, 1989).

Human Sexual Response—Sexual Interactions

The pioneering work of gynecologist William Masters and psychologist Virginia Johnson greatly expanded our understanding of sexual response (Masters & Johnson, 1966, 1970). In a series of experiments, interviews, and controlled observations, Masters and Johnson directly studied sexual intercourse and masturbation in nearly 700 males and females. This objective information has given us a much clearer picture of human sexuality.

According to Masters and Johnson, sexual response can be divided into four phases: (1) *excitement,* (2) *plateau,* (3) *orgasm,* and (4) *resolution* (● Figure 13.10 and ● Figure 13.11). These four phases can be described as follows:

Excitement phase The first level of sexual response, indicated by initial signs of sexual arousal.

Plateau phase The second level of sexual response, during which physical arousal intensifies.

Orgasm A climax and release of sexual excitement.

Resolution The final phase of sexual response, involving a return to lower levels of sexual tension and arousal.

The four phases are the same for people of all sexual orientations (Garnets & Kimmel, 1991).

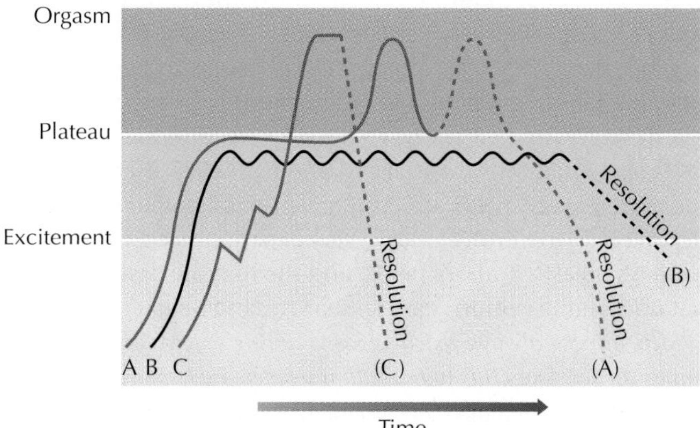

●Figure 13.10 Female sexual response cycle. The green line shows that sexual arousal rises through the excitement phase and levels off for a time during the plateau phase. Arousal peaks during orgasm and then returns to pre-excitement levels. In pattern A, arousal rises from excitement, through the plateau phase, and peaks in orgasm. Resolution may be immediate, or it may first include a return to the plateau phase and a second orgasm (dotted line). In pattern B, arousal is sustained at the plateau phase and slowly resolved without sexual climax. Pattern C shows a fairly rapid rise in arousal to orgasm. Little time is spent in the plateau phase and resolution is fairly rapid. (Reproduced by permission from Frank A. Beach, ed., *Sex and Behavior* [New York: Wiley, 1965]).

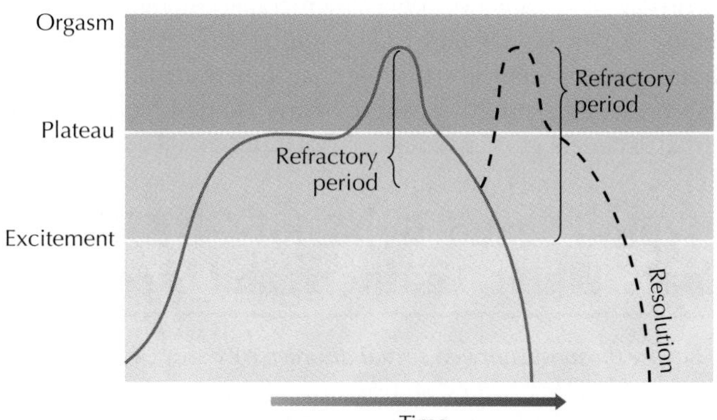

● Figure 13.11 Male sexual response cycle. The green line shows that sexual arousal rises through the excitement phase and levels off for a time during the plateau phase. Arousal peaks during orgasm and then returns to pre-excitement levels. During the refractory period, immediately after orgasm, a second sexual climax is typically impossible. However, after the refractory period has passed, there may be a return to the plateau phase, followed by a second orgasm (dotted line). (Reproduced by permission from Frank A. Beach, ed., *Sex and Behavior* [New York: Wiley, 1965]).

Female Response

In women, the excitement phase is marked by a complex pattern of changes that prepare the vagina for intercourse. At the same time, the nipples become erect, pulse rate rises, and the skin may become flushed. If sexual stimulation ends, the excitement phase will gradually subside. If the person moves into the plateau phase, physical changes and subjective feelings of arousal become more intense. Sexual arousal that ends during this phase tends to ebb more slowly, which may produce considerable frustration. Occasionally, women skip the plateau phase (see ● Figure 13.10). For some women, this is almost always the case.

During orgasm, from 3 to 10 muscular contractions of the vagina, uterus, and related structures discharge sexual tension. Somewhat rarely, a small amount of fluid is released from the urethra during orgasm (Whipple, 2000). Orgasm is usually followed by resolution, a return to lower levels of sexual tension and arousal. After orgasm, about 15 percent of all women return to the plateau phase and may have one or more additional orgasms.

Before the work of Masters and Johnson, theorists debated whether "vaginal orgasms" are different from those derived from stimulation of the clitoris. Sigmund Freud claimed that a "clitoral orgasm" is an "immature" form of female response. Because the clitoris is the female structure comparable to the penis, Freud believed that women whose orgasms centered on the clitoris had not fully accepted their femininity.

Masters and Johnson exploded the Freudian myth by showing that physical responses are the same no matter how an orgasm is produced (Mah & Binik, 2001). As a matter of fact, the inner two thirds of the vagina is relatively insensitive to touch. Most sensations during intercourse come from stimulation of the clitoris and other external areas.

Apparently, sensations from many sources are fused together into the total experience of orgasm. For most women, the clitoris is an important source of pleasurable sensations. Women in one

Excitement phase The first phase of sexual response, indicated by initial signs of sexual arousal.

Plateau phase The second phase of sexual response during which physical arousal is further heightened.

Orgasm A climax and release of sexual excitement.

Resolution The fourth phase of sexual response, involving a return to lower levels of sexual tension and arousal.

study said that they enjoyed vaginal and clitoral stimulation equally. But if they were forced to choose, two thirds said they would prefer clitoral sensations (Fisher, 1973). Similarly, researcher Shere Hite reported that only 26 percent of women regularly reach orgasm during intercourse without separate massaging of the clitoris (Hite, 1976). Thus, to downgrade the "clitoral orgasm" ignores basic female biology.

Male Response

Sexual arousal in the male is signaled by erection of the penis during the excitement phase. There is also a rise in heart rate, increased blood flow to the genitals, enlargement of the testicles, erection of the nipples, and numerous other bodily changes. As is true of female sexual response, continued stimulation moves the male into the plateau phase. Again, physical changes and subjective feelings of arousal become more intense. Further stimulation during the plateau phase brings about a reflex release of sexual tension, resulting in orgasm.

In the mature male, orgasm is usually accompanied by **ejaculation** (release of sperm and seminal fluid). Afterward, it is followed by a short **refractory period** during which a second orgasm is impossible. (Many men cannot even have an erection until the refractory phase has passed.) Only rarely is the male refractory period immediately followed by a second orgasm. Both orgasm and resolution in the male usually do not last as long as they do for females.

Comparing Male and Female Responses

Male and female sexual responses are generally quite similar. However, the differences that do exist can affect sexual adjustment. For example, women typically go through the sexual phases more slowly than men do. During lovemaking, from 10 to 20 minutes is often required for a woman to go from excitement to orgasm. Males may experience all four stages in as little as 4 minutes. However, there is much variation, especially in women. A study of married women found that 50 percent of them reached orgasm if intercourse lasted 1 to 11 minutes; when intercourse lasted 15 minutes or more, the rate increased to 66 percent. Twenty-five percent of the wives said that orgasm occurred within 1 minute of the start of intercourse (Brewer, 1981). (Note that these times refer only to intercourse, not to an entire arousal sequence.) Such differences should be kept in mind by couples seeking sexual compatibility.

Does that mean that a couple should try to time lovemaking to promote simultaneous orgasm? At one time simultaneous orgasm (both partners reaching sexual climax at the same time) was considered the "goal" of lovemaking. Now, it is regarded as an artificial concern that may reduce sexual enjoyment. It is more advisable for couples to seek mutual satisfaction through a combination of intercourse and erotic touching than it is to inhibit spontaneity, communication, and pleasure. A national survey found that the vast majority of American adults no longer feel that simultaneous orgasm is necessary for satisfying lovemaking (Janus & Janus, 1993).

Does the slower response just described mean that women are less sexual than men? Definitely not. During masturbation, 70 percent of females reach orgasm in 4 minutes or less. This casts serious doubts on the idea that women respond more slowly. Slower female response during intercourse probably occurs because stimulation to the clitoris is less direct. It might be said that men simply provide too little stimulation for more rapid female response, not that women are in any way inferior.

Does penis size affect female response? Masters and Johnson found that the vagina adjusts to the size of the penis and that subjective feelings of pleasure and intensity of orgasm are not related to penis size. They also found that although individual differences exist in flaccid penis size, there tends to be much less variation in size during erection. That's why erection has been called the "great equalizer." Contrary to popular belief, there is no relationship between penis size and male sexual potency. Lovemaking involves the entire body. Preoccupation with the size of a woman's breasts, a man's penis, and the like, are based on myths that undermine genuine caring, sharing, and sexual satisfaction.

Men almost always reach orgasm during intercourse, but many women do not. Does this indicate that women are less sexually responsive? Again, the evidence argues against any lack of female sexual responsiveness. It is true that about one woman in three does not experience orgasm during the first year of marriage, and only about 30 percent regularly reach orgasm through intercourse alone. However, this does not imply lack of physical responsiveness, because 90 percent of all women reach orgasm when masturbating.

In another regard, women are clearly more responsive. Only about 5 percent of males are capable of multiple orgasms (and then only after an unavoidable refractory period). Most men are limited to a second orgasm at best. In contrast, Masters and Johnson's findings suggest that most women who regularly experience orgasm are capable of multiple orgasms. According to one survey, 48 percent of all women have had multiple orgasms (Darling, Davidson, & Passarello, 1992). Remember though, that only about 15 percent regularly have multiple orgasms. A woman should not automatically assume that something is wrong if she isn't orgasmic or multi-orgasmic. Many women have satisfying sexual experiences even when orgasm is not involved.

Atypical Sexual Behavior—Trench Coats, Whips, Leathers, and Lace

What are the most common sexual disorders? By strict standards (including the law in some states), any sexual activity other than face-to-face heterosexual intercourse between married adults is atypical or "deviant." But public standards are often at odds with private behavior. Just as the hunger drive is expressed and satisfied in many ways, the sex drive also leads to an immense range of behaviors.

When do variations in sexual behavior become sufficiently atypical to be a problem? Psychologically, the mark of true sexual deviations is that they are compulsive and destructive.

Paraphilias

Sexual deviations, or **paraphilias** (PAIR-eh-FIL-ih-ahs) typically cause guilt, anxiety, or discomfort for one or both participants. The paraphilias cover a wide variety of behaviors, including the following:

Pedophilia—sex with children, or child molesting
Fetishism—sexual arousal associated with inanimate objects
Exhibitionism—"flashing," or displaying the genitals to unwilling viewers
Voyeurism—"peeping," or viewing the genitals of others without their permission
Transvestic fetishism—achieving sexual arousal by wearing clothing of the opposite sex
Sexual sadism—deriving sexual pleasure from inflicting pain
Sexual masochism—desiring pain as part of the sex act
Frotteurism—sexually touching or rubbing against a nonconsenting person, usually in a public place such as a subway

Sexual deviance is a highly emotional subject and many people have misconceptions about it. Two of the most misunderstood problems are exhibitionism and pedophilia. Check your understanding against the information that follows.

Exhibitionism

Exhibitionism is a common problem. Roughly 35 percent of all sexual arrests are for "flashing." Exhibitionists are typically male and married, and most come from strict and repressive backgrounds. Exhibitionists have the highest repeat rate among sexual offenders. Most of them feel a deep sense of inadequacy, which produces a compulsive need to prove their "manhood" by frightening women. Although exhibitionists are usually harmless, those who approach closer than arm's reach may be dangerous. In general, a woman confronted by an exhibitionist can assume that his goal is to shock and alarm her. By becoming visibly upset she actually encourages him (Hyde & DeLamater, 2000).

Child Molestation

Child molesters, who also are usually males, are often pictured as despicable perverts lurking in dark alleys. In fact, most are married and two thirds are fathers. Many are rigid, passive, puritanical, or religious. In one half to two thirds of all cases of pedophilia, the offender is a friend, acquaintance, or relative of the child. Molesters are also often thought of as child rapists, but most molestations rarely exceed fondling (Sue, Sue, & Sue, 1996).

How serious are the effects of a molestation? The impact varies widely. It is affected by how long the abuse lasts and whether genital sexual acts are involved (Freize, 1987). Many authorities believe that a single incident of fondling is unlikely to cause severe emotional harm to a child. For most children the event is frightening, but not a lasting trauma. That's why parents are urged not to overreact to such incidents or to become hysterical. Doing so only further frightens the child. This does not mean, however, that parents should ignore hints from a child that a molestation may have occurred. Here are some hints of trouble that parents should watch for.

Recognizing Signs of Child Molestation

1. The child fears being seen nude (for instance, during bathing), when such fears were absent before.
2. The child develops physical complaints, such as headaches, stomachaches, and other stress symptoms.
3. The child displays anxiety, fidgeting, shame, or discomfort when any reference to sexual behavior occurs.
4. The child becomes markedly emotional and irritable.
5. The child engages in hazardous risk taking, such as jumping from high places or riding a bicycle dangerously in traffic.
6. The child reveals self-destructive or suicidal thoughts, self-blame.
7. The child shows a loss of self-esteem or self-worth.

(Adapted from Frederick, 1987)

How can children protect themselves? Children should be taught to shout "No" if an adult tries to engage them in sexual activity. If children are asked to keep a secret, they should reply that they don't keep secrets. Parents and children also need to be aware that some pedophiles now try to make contact with children on the Internet. If an adult suggests to a child online that they could meet in person, the child should immediately tell his or her parents.

It also helps if children know the tactics typically used by molesters. Interviews with convicted sex offenders revealed the following (Elliott, Browne, & Kilcoyne, 1995):

Tactics of Child Molesters

1. Most molesters act alone.
2. Most assaults take place in the abuser's home.
3. Many abusers gain access to the child through caretaking.
4. Children are targeted at first through bribes, gifts, and games.
5. The abuser tries to lull the child into participation through touch, talking about sex, and persuasion. (This can take place through e-mail or chat rooms on the Internet.)
6. The abuser then uses force, anger, threats, and bribes to gain continued compliance.

Repeated molestations, those that involve force or threats, and incidents that exceed fondling can leave lasting emotional scars. As adults, many victims of incest or molestation develop sexual phobias. For them, lovemaking may evoke vivid and terrifying memories of the childhood victimization. Serious harm is especially likely to occur if the molester is someone the child deeply trusts. Molestations by parents, close relatives, teachers, priests, youth leaders, and similar persons can be quite damaging. In such cases professional counseling is often needed (Saywitz et al., 2000).

Ejaculation The release of sperm and seminal fluid by the male at the time of orgasm.

Refractory period A short time period after orgasm during which males are unable to again reach orgasm.

Paraphilias Compulsive or destructive deviations in sexual preferences or behavior.

As the preceding discussion suggests, the picture of sexual deviance that most often emerges is one of sexual inhibition and immaturity. Typically, some relatively infantile sexual expression (like exhibitionism or pedophilia) is selected because it is less threatening than more mature sexuality.

Many sadists, masochists, fetishists, and transvestites voluntarily associate with people who share their sexual interests. Thus, their behavior may not harm anyone, except when it is extreme. In contrast, pedophilia, exhibitionism, voyeurism, and frotteurism do victimize unwilling participants (Crooks & Bauer, 2005).

All of the paraphilias, unless they are very mild, involve compulsive behavior. As a result, they tend to emotionally handicap people. There is room in contemporary society for a large array of sexual behaviors. Nevertheless, any behavior that becomes compulsive (be it eating, gambling, drug abuse, or sex) is psychologically unhealthy.

Attitudes and Sexual Behavior—The Changing Sexual Landscape

Has there been a "sexual revolution"? If a woman and a man living 100 years ago could be transported to the present, what would they think about today's sexual values and practices? Undoubtedly, they would be stunned by the changes that have taken place. Unmarried couples falling into bed on television; advertisements for bras, skimpy men's underwear, tampons, and cures for "jock itch"; near nudity at the beaches; sexually explicit movies—these and many other elements of contemporary culture would shock a person from the Victorian era.

The word *revolution,* however, suggests rapid change. Has there been a sexual revolution? A look at social changes in the 1960s and 1970s makes it clear that some fundamental alterations have occurred. Liberalized sexual attitudes and access to effective birth control significantly changed sexual behavior. Compared with earlier times, the gap between sexual values and actual behavior has narrowed. For example, traditional morality called for female virginity before marriage. Yet by the 1940s and 1950s, as many as 75 percent of married women had engaged in premarital sex (Strong & DeVault, 1994).

ABC-TV/The Kobal Collection/Brakha, Moshe

Twenty years ago, television soap operas were tame, gossipy melodramas. Today they are sexy, gossipy melodramas that frequently feature steamy on-screen lovemaking.

Attitudes

Changing attitudes can be seen in national polls about premarital intercourse. In a 1959 Roper poll, 88 percent of those interviewed agreed that premarital sex is wrong. In a more recent Gallup Poll, only 40 percent of adults believed that premarital sex is unacceptable (Gallup Poll, 1991). By the 1990s, over 70 percent of young men and women approved of premarital sex (Wells & Twenge, 2005). Similar changes have occurred in attitudes toward extramarital sex, homosexuality, sex education, and related issues.

Behavior

Have changing attitudes been translated into behavior? Changes in attitudes are still larger than changes in actual sexual behavior. Mostly, there is greater *tolerance* for sexual activity, especially that *engaged in by others.* For example, a magazine poll found that 80 percent of all readers considered extramarital sex acceptable under some circumstances (Athenasiou, Shaver, & Tavris, 1970). But two other polls found that, in practice, only about 30 percent of married persons actually had extramarital sexual experience (Rubenstein, 1983; Rubenstein & Tavris, 1987). These are older studies, but the percentage has not changed greatly in the last 50 years. More important, faithfulness in marriage is a widely shared norm. Over a year, only 1.5 percent of married people have sex partners other than their spouse. Americans actually seem to live up to the norm of marital fidelity fairly well (Laumann et al., 1994; T. W. Smith, 1990).

Premarital intercourse rates are a good indication of overall sexual activity. The social upheaval that began in the 1960s led to an especially sharp rise in sexual activity among teenagers. This increase continued into the 1980s, although it slowed in the 1990s. In the 1950s, Kinsey found that 70 percent of males and 33 percent of females had premarital intercourse by age 25. In the 1970s, Morton Hunt obtained premarital intercourse rates of 97 percent for males and about 70 percent for females. Now, 83 percent of all women and 91 percent of all men have premarital sexual experience (Janus & Janus, 1993). To some extent these changes are related to a tendency to postpone marriage. In the

United States alone, over 2 million unmarried couples are living together.

Another major change is that both sexes engage in sexual behavior at earlier ages. For example, a recent study found that 73 percent of all 17-year-old girls were sexually experienced. Nearly half (45 percent) had intercourse for the first time when they were 15 or 16. Sixteen percent had intercourse before they were 15. Pressures to engage in adult behaviors, early physical maturity, and the use of drugs all contribute to early sexual activity (Rosenthal et al., 2001).

The increase in sexual behavior during early adolescence is troubling. The United States has one of the highest teenage pregnancy rates among all industrialized nations. A partial solution to this problem may be to give youths a better understanding of their sexuality. Research confirms that sex education *delays* the age at which young people first engage in sexual intercourse (Sawyer & Smith, 1996). Parents can encourage sexual responsibility in their children by providing close supervision and by stressing the value of delayed sexual involvement (Rosenthal et al., 2001).

Is the Revolution Over?

Talk of a sexual revolution has quieted in recent years, and a conservative countermovement has been visible. Some of the reaction may reflect concern about sexually transmitted diseases. However, a gradual liberalization continues, albeit at a much slower pace (Janus & Janus, 1993). An interesting trend is the fact that people today spend as much of their adult lives (on average) alone, as they do in marriage. As a result, many people are involved in nonmarried sexual relationships (Mahay & Laumann, 2004).

In all, there is ample evidence that sexual behavior has increased in the last 40 years. Although this trend has brought problems, it does not seem to represent a wholesale move toward sexual promiscuity. Even premarital intercourse does not appear to represent a major rejection of traditional values and responsible behavior. The connection between sexuality and love or affection remains strong for most people. Both premarital sex and cohabitation are still widely viewed as preludes to marriage or as temporary substitutes for it. Likewise, other changes in attitudes and behavior appear to reflect a greater acceptance of sexuality rather than a total rejection of earlier values (Crooks & Bauer, 2005).

Slow Death of the Double Standard

A good summary of one major change that has occurred in sexual behavior is found in the phrase "the slow death of the double standard."

The **double standard** refers to using different rules to judge the appropriateness of male and female sexual behavior. In past decades, for example, males were largely forgiven for engaging in premarital sex. Young males who "sowed some wild oats" were widely tolerated. In fact, many were tacitly encouraged to seek casual sex as a step toward manhood. On the other hand, women who were sexually active before marriage ran the risk of being labeled "easy," "bad," or "promiscuous." Clearly, women are more aware of the double standard than men are: 79 percent of men believe it exists, whereas 91 percent of women do (Janus & Janus, 1993).

Similar differences pervade sexual mores and frequently place women in a "separate but not equal" position with regard to sexual behavior (Sprecher & Hatfield, 1996). However, as the gap between female and male sexual patterns continues to close, it is increasingly likely that an end to the double standard is in sight (Schleicher & Gilbert, 2005).

Choices

A more comfortable acceptance of human sexuality is the positive side of changing sexual attitudes and values. The negative side is revealed by the plight of people who are not ready for, or interested in, greater sexual freedom. Apparently, some individuals feel pressured into sexual behavior because it is "expected." Six percent of first sexual intercourse experiences are against the person's will (Bajracharya, Sarvela, & Isberner, 1995).

Pressures to engage in sex probably come as much from the individual as from others. For a greater acceptance of sexuality to be constructive, people must feel that they have the right to say no, as well as the right to choose when, where, how, and with whom they will express their sexuality. As is true elsewhere, freedom must be combined with responsibility, commitment, and caring if it is to have meaning.

The Crime of Rape

The importance of respecting the right to say no is underscored by a recent dramatic increase in **acquaintance (date) rape** (forced intercourse that occurs in the context of a date or other voluntary encounter). From *5 to 15 percent* of all female college students report having been raped. Roughly one half of these rapes were by first dates, casual dates, or romantic acquaintances (Fisher, Cullen, & Daigle, 2005; Koss, 2000).

Men who commit date rape often believe they have done nothing wrong. A typical explanation is, "Her words were saying no, but her body was saying yes" (see "Gender Role Stereotyping and Rape"). But forced sex is rape, even if the rapist doesn't use a knife or become violent. The effects of acquaintance rape are no less devastating than rape committed by a stranger.

Double standard Applying different standards for judging the appropriateness of male and female sexual behavior.

Acquaintance (date) rape Forced intercourse that occurs in the context of a date or other voluntary encounter.

CRITICAL THINKING

Gender Role Stereotyping and Rape

Rape is related to traditional gender role socialization. Traditional feminine stereotypes include the idea that women should not show direct interest in sex. Traditional masculine stereotypes, on the other hand, include the ideas that a man should take the initiative and persist in attempts at sexual intimacy—even when the woman says no (Locke & Mahalik, 2005).

Psychologists James Check and Neil Malamuth believe that such attitudes create a "rape-supportive culture." In their view, rape is only an extreme expression of a system that condones coercive (forced) sexual intimacy. They point out, for instance, that the single most used cry of rapists to their victims is, "You know you want it." And afterward, "There now, you really enjoyed it, didn't you."

In general, research has confirmed a link between acceptance of rape myths and sexual violence toward women (Forbes, Adams-Curtis, & White, 2004). In a classic experimental confirmation of the hypothesis that stereotyped images contribute to rape, male college students were classified as either high or low in gender role stereotyping. Each student then read one of three stories: The first described voluntary intercourse; the second depicted stranger rape; and the third described date rape.

As predicted, college males high in gender role stereotyping were more aroused by the rape stories. Their arousal patterns, in fact, were similar to those found among actual rapists. Moreover, a chilling 44 percent of those tested indicated they would consider rape—especially if they could be sure of not being caught (Check & Malamuth, 1983).

In view of such findings—and the continuing widespread belief that when a woman says no she means yes—it is little wonder that rape occurs every 6 minutes in the United States. Perhaps the time has come for our culture to make it clear that no means no. Educating men about rape myths has been one of the most successful ways of preventing sexual assault (King, 2005; Reppucci, Woolard, & Fried, 1999).

Rape Myths

A study of college men found that many tend to blame *women* for date rape. According to them, women who are raped by an acquaintance actually wanted to have sex (Proite, Dannells, & Benton, 1993). This is just one of several widely held beliefs that qualify as **rape myths** (Jones, Russell, & Bryant, 1998). All of these statements are myths:

- A woman who appears alone in public and dresses attractively is "asking for it."
- When a woman says no she really means yes.
- Many women who are raped actually enjoy it.
- If a woman goes home with a man on a first date she is interested in sex.
- If a woman is sexually active, she is probably lying if she says she was raped.

Men who believe rape myths are more likely to misread a woman's resistance to unwanted sexual advances, assuming that she really means yes when she says no (Forbes, Adams-Curtis, & White, 2004). Add some alcohol to the situation and the risk of sexual assault is even greater: Men who believe rape myths and who have been drinking are especially likely to ignore signals that a woman wants sexual advances to stop (Bernat, Calhoun, & Stolp, 1998; Marx, Gross, & Adams, 1999).

Forcible Rape

Date rape is coercive, but not necessarily violent. **Forcible rape**, which is distressingly common, is carried out under the threat of bodily injury. Rapists often inflict more violence on their victims than is necessary to achieve their goal. Many women feel confident that their chances of being raped are low. But the facts tell a different story (Koss, 1993):

- At least one woman in seven will be raped in her lifetime. Because many rapes go unreported, the true figure is probably one in four.
- In 65 to 80 percent of all cases the rapist is a friend or acquaintance of the victim.
- Five percent of rapes result in pregnancy.
- From 4 to 30 percent of rape victims contract sexually transmitted diseases.

Most authorities no longer think of forcible rape as a primarily sexual act. Rather, it is an act of brutality or aggression based on the need to debase others. Many rapists impulsively take what they want without concern for the feelings of the victim or guilt about their deed. Others harbor deep-seated resentment or outright hatred of women.

Quite often, the rapist's goal is not strictly sexual intercourse; it is to attack, subordinate, humiliate, and degrade the victim. Typical after-effects for the victim include rage, guilt, depression, loss of self-esteem, shame, sexual adjustment problems, and, in many cases, a lasting mistrust of male–female relationships. The impact is so great that most women continue to report fear, anxiety, and sexual dysfunction a year or two after being raped. Even years later, rape survivors are more likely to suffer from depression, alcohol or drug abuse, and other emotional problems.

It is also important to be aware that men can also be the victims of rape, especially homosexual rape (Davies & McCartney,

TABLE 13.2

Common Sexually Transmitted Diseases

STD	MALE SYMPTOMS	FEMALE SYMPTOMS	PREVENTION	TREATMENT
Gonorrhea	Milky discharge from urethra; painful, frequent urination	Vaginal discharge and inflammation, painful urination	Condom/safer sex practices	Antibiotics
Chlamydia	Painful urination, discharge from urethra	Painful urination, discharge from vagina, abdominal pain	Condom/safer sex practices	Antibiotics
Syphilis	Painless sores on genitals, rectum, tongue, or lips; skin rash, fever, headache, aching bones and joints	Same	Condom/safer sex practices	Antibiotics
Genital herpes	Pain or itching on the penis; water blisters or open sores	Pain or itching in the genital area; water blisters or open sores	Condom/safer sex practices	Symptoms can be treated but not cured
Genital warts	Warty growths on genitals	Same	Condom/safer sex practices	Removal by surgery or laser
HIV/AIDS	Prolonged fatigue, swollen lymph nodes, fever lasting more than 10 days, night sweats, unexplained weight loss, purplish lesions on skin, persistent cough or sore throat, persistent colds, persistent diarrhea, easy bruising or unexplained bleeding	Same	Condom/safer sex practices	Can be treated with various drugs but cannot be cured
Hepatitis B	Mild cases may have no symptoms, but infection can cause chronic liver disease, cirrhosis of the liver, or liver cancer	Same	Vaccination	None available
Pelvic inflammatory disease	Does not apply	Intense pain in lower back and/or abdomen, fever	Condom/safer sex practices	Antibiotics

2003). Any man who doubts the seriousness of rape should imagine himself mistakenly placed in jail, where he is violently raped (sodomized) by other inmates. There is no pleasure in rape for victims of either sex. It is truly a despicable crime.

STDs and Safer Sex—Choice, Risk, and Responsibility

In general, most adults favor greater freedom of choice for themselves, including choice about sexual behavior. Yet, as noted, there is some ambivalence toward greater sexual freedom. As the upcoming discussion of AIDS suggests, there are new and compelling reasons for caution in sexual behavior.

A **sexually transmitted disease (STD)** is an infection passed from one person to another by intimate physical contact. Sexually active people run a high risk of getting chlamydia (klah-MID-ee-ah), gonorrhea, hepatitis B, herpes, genital warts, syphilis, and other STDs (see ■ Table 13.2). Many people who carry STDs remain *asymptomatic* (a-SIMP-teh-mat-ik: lacking obvious symptoms). It is easy to have an infection without knowing it. Likewise, it is often impossible to tell if a sexual partner is infectious. Thus, risky sex is a serious hazard. A recent study of sexually active teenage girls engaging in risky sex is a case in point. Nearly 90 percent of the girls thought that they had virtually no chance of getting an STD. In reality, over the next 18 months one in four got chlamydia or gonorrhea (Ethier et al., 2003).

A major problem is the fact that people who are sexually active may have indirect contact with many other people. A recent study of sexual relationships at a high school in a Midwestern city found long chains of sexual contact between students. Thus, a student at the end of the chain might have had sex with only one person, but in reality she or he had indirect contact with dozens or even hundreds of others (Bearman, Moody, & Stovel, 2004).

Rape myths False beliefs about rape that tend to blame the victim and increase the likelihood that some men will think that rape is justified.

Forcible rape Sexual intercourse carried out against the victim's will, under the threat of violence or bodily injury.

Sexually transmitted disease (STD) A disease that is typically passed from one person to the next by intimate physical contact; a venereal disease.

For many sexually active people, the human immunodeficiency virus (HIV) has added a new threat. HIV is a sexually transmitted disease that disables the immune system. Whereas most STDs are treatable, HIV infections can be lethal. Check your knowledge about HIV against the following summary.

AIDS

Acquired immune deficiency syndrome (AIDS) is caused by an HIV infection. As the immune system weakens, other "opportunistic" diseases invade the body. Most AIDS victims eventually die of multiple infections (although newer multidrug therapies have greatly improved the odds of survival). The first symptoms of AIDS may show up as little as 2 months after infection, but they typically don't appear for 10 years. Because of this long incubation period, infected persons often pass the AIDS virus on to others without knowing it. Medical tests can detect an HIV infection. However, for at least the first 6 months after becoming infected, a person can test negative while carrying the virus. A negative test result, therefore, is no guarantee that someone is a "safe" sex partner.

HIV infections are spread by direct contact with body fluids—especially blood, semen, and vaginal secretions. The AIDS virus cannot be transmitted by casual contact. People do not get AIDS from shaking hands, touching or using objects touched by an AIDS patient, eating food prepared by an infected person, social kissing, sweat or tears, sharing drinking glasses, sharing towels, and so forth.

Leonard Lessin/Photo Researchers, Inc.

The AIDS Memorial Quilt was begun in 1985 to commemorate those who have died from AIDS. Today, the quilt has grown to immense size, symbolizing the extent of the AIDS epidemic. Originally the quilt memorialized only homosexual victims. It now includes heterosexual men, women, and children, signifying that AIDS respects no boundaries (Zucker, 1995).

HIV can be spread by all forms of sexual intercourse, and it has affected persons of all sexual orientations. Recently, the AIDS epidemic has spread more quickly among heterosexuals, women, African Americans, Hispanics, and children (Taylor-Seehafer & Rew, 2000). Among 13- to 19-year-olds, two thirds of new HIV cases are female ("HIV/AIDS," 2004). HIV infection is the leading cause of death among women and men between the ages of 25 and 44 (Gayle, 2000). Worldwide, 3 million people die each year from HIV/AIDS and 5 million new infections occur.

Populations at Risk

In North America, those who are at greatest risk for HIV infection remain men who have had sex with other men (homosexual and bisexual men), people who have shared needles (for tattoos or for intravenous drug use), blood transfusion recipients (between 1977 and spring 1985), hemophiliacs (who require frequent blood transfusions), sexual partners of people in the preceding groups, and heterosexuals with a history of multiple partners. Thus, the vast majority of people are not at high risk of HIV infection. Still, 1 in 75 men and 1 in 700 women in North America are now infected with HIV. Each year, 40,000 more people in the United States become infected (Gayle, 2000). In short, people who engage in unsafe sex are gambling with their lives—at very poor odds.

Behavioral Risk Factors

Sexually active people can do much to protect their own health. The behaviors listed here are risky when performed with an infected person.

Risky Behaviors

- Sharing drug needles and syringes
- Anal sex, with or without a condom
- Vaginal or oral sex with someone who injects drugs or engages in anal sex
- Sex with someone you don't know well, or with someone you know has several partners
- Unprotected sex (without a condom) with an infected partner
- Having two or more sex partners (additional partners further increase the risk)

In the United States, between 2 and 4 of every 100 adults put themselves at high risk by engaging in the behaviors just listed (Gayle, 2000).

It's important to remember that you can't tell from appearance if a person is infected. Many people would be surprised to learn that their partners have engaged in behavior that places them both at risk (Seal & Palmer-Seal, 1996).

The preceding high-risk behaviors can be contrasted with the following list of safer sexual practices. Note, however, that unless a person completely abstains, sex can be made safer, but not risk-free.

Safer Sex Practices

- Not having sex
- Sex with one mutually faithful, uninfected partner
- Not injecting drugs
- Discussing contraception with partner
- Being selective regarding sexual partners
- Reducing the number of sexual partners
- Discussing partner's sexual health prior to engaging in sex
- Not engaging in sex while intoxicated
- Using a condom

Sexually active persons should practice safer sex until their partner's sexual history and/or health has been clearly established. And remember, a condom offers little or no protection if it is misused. Sadly, one of three sexually active teens don't know how to use a condom correctly (and virgins of both sexes are even more clueless) (Crosby & Yarber, 2001).

HIV and AIDS initially had a strong impact on sexual behavior in some groups. Among gay men there was a sharp decrease in risky sex and an increase in monogamous relationships. Unfortunately, this trend has recently reversed. Once again, STD rates are rising dramatically among gay men. In part, this may be due to the fact that new medical treatments are helping people with HIV live longer. Many victims simply do not look or act sick. This gives a false impression about the dangers of HIV infection and encourages foolish risk taking (Handsfield, 2001).

Other groups are also not getting the message. The AIDS epidemic has thus far had little impact on the willingness of high school and college age students to engage in risky behavior (casual sex) or to use condoms (Ramirez-Valles, Zimmerman, & Newcomb, 1998). A study of heterosexual adults found that 62 percent did not practice safer sex with their last partner. Most of these "gamblers" knew too little about their partners to be sure they were not taking a big risk. ■ Table 13.3 lists the excuses they gave for engaging in risky sex (Kusseling et al., 1996). For many people, drinking alcohol greatly increases the likelihood of taking sexual risks (Corbin & Fromme, 2002).

Apparently, heterosexual people still don't feel that they are truly at risk. However, *75 percent* of people with the AIDS virus were infected through heterosexual sex. Over the next 20 to 30 years, heterosexual transmission is expected to become the primary means of spreading HIV. Over the next 15 years 65 million more people will die of AIDS unless prevention efforts are greatly expanded (Altman, 2002).

TABLE 13.3

Common Excuses for Not Practicing Safer Sex

REASONS FOR NOT HAVING SAFER SEX	PERCENTAGE GIVING EXCUSE
Condom not available	20
Didn't want to use a condom	19
"Couldn't stop ourselves"	15
Partner didn't want to use a condom	14
Alcohol or drug use	11

Kusseling et al., 1996.

Risk and Responsibility

The threat of HIV/AIDS has forced many people to face new issues of risk and responsibility. Those who do not ensure their own safety are playing Russian roulette with their health. One chilling study of HIV patients—who knew they were infectious—found that 41 percent of those who were sexually active did not always use condoms (Sobel et al., 1996)! Thus, responsibility for "safer sex" rests with each sexually active individual. It is unwise to count on a sexual partner for protection against HIV infection.

A special risk that befalls people in committed relationships is that they often interpret practicing safer sex as a sign of mistrust. Taking precautions could, instead, be defined as a way of showing that you really care about the welfare of your partner (Hammer et al., 1996). Likewise, dating couples who have high levels of emotional, social, and intellectual intimacy are more likely to use contraceptives (Davis & Bibace, 1999).

The sexual revolution was fueled, in part, by "the pill" and other birth control methods. Will the threat of AIDS reverse the tide of changes that occurred in previous decades? Will STD come to mean Sudden Total Disinterest in sex? Will the "germs of endearment" change the terms of endearment? The answers may depend on how quickly people learn to respect the AIDS virus and whether its prevention or cure can be achieved.

A Look Ahead

Even without STDs to worry about, sexual problems are quite common. In the Psychology in Action section we will consider the most frequent complaints and how they are remedied.

KNOWLEDGE BUILDER

Sexual Response, Attitudes, and Behavior

REFLECT

In what ways are sexual responses of members of the opposite sex similar to your own? In what ways are they different?

Based on your own observations of attitudes toward sex and patterns of sexual behavior, do you think there has been a sexual revolution?

You work in a program that provides counseling to AIDS patients. Should you be worried about contracting the disease? Why or why not?

To what extent do movies, music videos, and video games contribute directly to the perpetuation of rape myths? What about indirectly, by portraying gender role stereotypes?

As a counselor, you are working with a young person who seems to be sexually active. What can you tell this person about STDs and safer sex practices?

LEARNING CHECK

1. List the four phases of sexual response identified by Masters and Johnson: ____________, ____________, ____________, ____________
2. Males typically experience ____________ after ejaculation.
   a. an increased potential for orgasm
   b. a short refractory period
   c. the excitement phase
   d. muscular contractions of the uterus
3. The research of Masters and Johnson suggests that the similarities between female and male sexual responses outweigh the differences. T or F?
4. During lovemaking, from 10 to 20 minutes is often required for a woman to go from excitement to orgasm, whereas a male may experience all four stages of sexual response in as little as 4 minutes. T or F?
5. Simultaneous orgasm of the female and male should be the ultimate goal in lovemaking. T or F?
6. Recent research shows that more liberal views regarding sexual behavior have erased the traditional values that link sexual involvement with committed relationships. T or F?
7. Contrary to long-standing belief, it now appears that much female sexual pleasure is focused on
   a. the uterus c. the urethra
   b. the clitoris d. the cervix
8. One woman in 70 will be raped in her lifetime and chances are greater than 50 percent that the rapist will be a friend or acquaintance. T or F?
9. The term ____________ ____________ describes the tendency for the sexual behavior of women and men to be judged differently.
10. Because AIDS is spread by direct contact with body fluids, it can be transmitted by social kissing or contact with food or dishes handled by an AIDS patient. T or F?

CRITICAL THINKING

11. Of the following reasons that teenage boys and girls give for engaging in sex—love, curiosity, sexual gratification, peer pressure, and "everyone's doing it"—which do you think they rank first, and which last?

Answers: 1. excitement, plateau, orgasm, resolution **2.** b **3.** T **4.** T **5.** F **6.** F **7.** b **8.** F **9.** double standard **10.** F **11.** Peer pressure ranks first (cited by 30 percent of those surveyed) and love ranked last (cited by 8 percent) ("Teen sex," 1989).

PSYCHOLOGY IN ACTION

Sexual Problems—When Pleasure Fades

Sexual dysfunctions are far more common than many people realize. Most people who seek sexual counseling have one or more of the following types of problems (*DSM-IV-TR,* 2000; Heiman, 2002):

1. **Desire Disorders:** The person has little or no sexual motivation or desire.
2. **Arousal Disorders:** The person desires sexual activity but does not become sexually aroused.
3. **Orgasm Disorders:** The person does not have orgasms or experiences orgasm too soon or too late.
4. **Sexual Pain Disorders:** The person experiences pain that makes lovemaking uncomfortable or impossible.

There was a time when people suffered such problems in silence. However, in recent years effective treatments have been found for many of the major complaints. Let's briefly investigate the nature, causes, and treatments of sexual dysfunctions.

Desire Disorders

Desire disorders, like most sexual problems, must be defined in relation to a person's age, sex, partner, expectations, and sexual history. It is not at all unusual for a person to briefly lose sexual desire. Typically, erotic feelings return when anger toward a partner fades, or fatigue, illness, and similar temporary problems end. Under what circumstances, then, is loss of desire a dysfunction? First, the loss of desire must be *persistent.* Second, the person must be *troubled by it.* When these two conditions are met, **hypoactive sexual desire** is said to exist. Diminished desire can apply to both sexes. However, it is somewhat more common in women (Heiman, 2002; Read, 1995).

Some people don't merely lack sexual desire; they are *repelled* by sex and seek to avoid it. A person who suffers from **sexual aversion** feels fear, anxiety, or disgust about engaging in sex. Often, the afflicted person still has some erotic feelings. For example, he or she may still masturbate or have sexual fantasies. Nevertheless, the prospect of having sex with another person causes panic or revulsion (*DSM-IV-TR,* 2000).

Sexual desire disorders are common. Possible physical causes include illness, fatigue, hormonal difficulties, and the side effects of medicines. Desire disorders are also associated with psychological factors such as depression, fearing loss of control over sexual urges, strict religious beliefs, fear of pregnancy, marital conflict, fear of closeness, and simple loss of attraction to one's partner (King, 2005; Read, 1995). It is also not uncommon to find that people with desire disorders were sexually mistreated as children (Bakich, 1995).

Treatment

Desire disorders are complex problems. Unless they have a straightforward physical cause, they are difficult to treat. Desire disorders are often deeply rooted in a person's childhood, sexual history, personality, and relationships. In such instances, counseling or psychotherapy is recommended (King, 2005).

Arousal Disorders

A person suffering from an arousal disorder wants to make love but experiences little or no physical arousal. For women, this means vaginal dryness. For men, it means an inability to maintain an erection. Basically, in arousal disorders the body does not cooperate with the person's desire to make love.

Male Erectile Disorder

An inability to maintain an erection for lovemaking is called male **erectile disorder.** This problem, which is also known as erectile dysfunction, was once referred to as *impotence.* However, psychologists now discourage use of the term *impotence* because of its many negative connotations.

Erectile disorders can be primary or secondary. Men suffering from primary erectile dysfunction have never had an erection. Those who previously performed successfully, but then developed a problem, suffer from secondary erectile dysfunction. Either way, persistent erectile difficulties tend to be very disturbing to the man and his sexual partner (Baldo & Eardley, 2005).

How often must a man experience failure for a problem to exist? Ultimately, only the man and his partner can make this judgment. Nevertheless, sex therapists Masters and Johnson (1970) believe that a problem exists when failure occurs on 25 percent or more of a man's lovemaking attempts. Repeated erectile dysfunction should therefore be distinguished from *occasional* erectile problems. Fatigue, anger, anxiety, and drinking too much alcohol can cause temporary erectile difficulties in healthy males. True erectile disorders typically persist for months or years.

It is important to recognize that occasional erectile problems are normal. In fact, "performance demands" or overreaction to the temporary loss of an erection may generate fears and doubts that contribute to a further inhibition of arousal (Abrahamson, Barlow, & Abrahamson, 1989). At such times, it is particularly important for the man's partner to avoid expressing anger, disappointment, or embarrassment. Patient reassurance helps prevent the establishment of a vicious cycle.

What causes erectile disorders? For years, experts held that erectile disorders are rarely caused by physical illness, disease, or damage. Now it is recognized that roughly 40 percent of all cases are *organic,* or physically caused. The origin of the remaining cases is **psychogenic** (a result of emotional factors). Even when erectile dysfunction is organic, however, it is almost always made worse by anxiety, anger, and dejection. If a man can have an erection at times other than lovemaking (during sleep, for instance), the problem probably is not physical (Baldo & Eardley, 2005).

Organic erectile problems have many causes. Typical sources of trouble include alcohol or drug abuse, diabetes, vascular disease, prostate and urological disorders, neurological problems, and reactions to medication for high blood pressure, heart disease, or stomach ulcers. Erectile problems are also a normal part of aging. As men grow older they typically experience a decline in sexual desire and arousal and an increase in sexual dysfunction (Segraves & Segraves, 1995).

According to Masters and Johnson (1970), primary erectile disorders are often related to harsh religious training, early sexual experiences with a seductive mother, sexual molestation in childhood, or other experiences leading to guilt, fear, and sexual inhibition.

Secondary erectile disorders may be related to anxiety about sex in general, guilt because of an extramarital affair, resentment or hostility toward a sexual partner, fear of inability to perform, concerns about STDs, and similar emotions and conflicts (Shires & Miller, 1998). Often the problem starts with repeated sexual failures caused by drinking too much alcohol or by premature ejaculation. In any event, initial doubts soon become severe fears of failure—which further inhibit sexual response.

Treatment

Drugs or surgery may be used in medical treatment of organic erectile disorders. The drug Viagra is successful for about 70 to 80 percent of men with erectile disorders. However, effective treatment should also include counseling to remove fears and psychological blocks (Althof & Seftel, 1995; Heiman, 2002). Fixing the "hydraulics" of erectile problems may not be enough to end the problem. It is important for the man to also regain confidence, improve his relationship with his partner, and learn better lovemaking skills. To free him of conflicts, the man and his partner may be assigned a series of exercises to perform. This technique, called **sensate focus,** directs attention to natural

Hypoactive sexual desire A persistent, upsetting loss of sexual desire.

Sexual aversion Persistent feelings of fear, anxiety, or disgust about engaging in sex.

Erectile disorder An inability to maintain an erection for lovemaking.

Psychogenic Having psychological origins, rather than physical causes.

Sensate focus Form of therapy that directs a couple's attention to natural sensations of sexual pleasure.

sensations of pleasure and builds communication skills (McCabe, 1992).

In sensate focus, the couple is told to take turns caressing various parts of each other's bodies. They are further instructed to carefully avoid any genital contact. Instead, they are to concentrate on giving pleasure and on signaling what feels good to them. This takes the pressure to perform off the man and allows him to learn to give pleasure as a means of receiving it. For many men, sensate focus is a better solution than depending on an expensive drug to perform sexually.

Over a period of days or weeks, the couple proceeds to more intense physical contact involving the breasts and genitals. As inhibitions are reduced and natural arousal begins to replace fear, the successful couple moves on to mutually satisfying lovemaking.

Female Sexual Arousal Disorder

Women who suffer from **female sexual arousal disorder** respond with little or no physical arousal to sexual stimulation. The problem thus appears to correspond directly to male erectile difficulties. As in the male, female sexual arousal disorder may be primary or secondary. Also, it is again important to remember that all women occasionally experience inhibited arousal. In some instances the problem may reflect nothing more than a lack of sufficient sexual stimulation before attempting lovemaking (King, 2005; Read, 1995).

The causes of inhibited arousal in women are similar to those seen in men. Sometimes the problem is medical, being related to illness or the side effects of medicines or contraceptives. Psychological factors include anxiety, anger or hostility toward one's partner, depression, stress, or distracting worries. Some women can trace their arousal difficulties to frightening childhood experiences, such as molestations (often by older relatives), incestuous relations that produced lasting guilt, a harsh religious background in which sex was considered evil, or cold, unloving childhood relationships. Also common is a need to maintain control over emotions, deep-seated conflicts over being female, and extreme distrust of others, especially males (Read, 1995).

Treatment

How does treatment proceed? Treatment typically includes sensate focus, genital stimulation by the woman's partner, and "nondemanding" intercourse controlled by the woman (Segraves & Althof, 2002). With success in these initial stages, full intercourse is gradually introduced. As sexual training proceeds, psychological conflicts and dynamics typically appear, and as they do, they are treated in separate counseling sessions.

Orgasm Disorders

A person suffering from an orgasm disorder either fails to reach orgasm during sexual activity or reaches orgasm too soon or too late. Notice that such disorders are very much based on expectations. For instance, if a man experiences delayed orgasm, one couple might define it as a problem, whereas another might welcome it. It is also worth noting again that some women rarely or never have orgasm and still find sex pleasurable (King, 2005; Read, 1995).

Female Orgasmic Disorder

The most prevalent sexual complaint among women is a persistent inability to reach orgasm during lovemaking. It is often clear in **female orgasmic disorder** that the woman is not completely unresponsive. Rather, she is unresponsive in the context of a relationship—she may easily reach orgasm by masturbation, but not in lovemaking with her partner.

Then couldn't the woman's partner be at fault? Sex therapists try to avoid finding fault or placing blame. However, it is true that the woman's partner must be committed to ensuring her gratification. Roughly two thirds of all women need direct stimulation of the clitoris to reach orgasm. Therefore, some apparent instances of female orgasmic disorder can be traced to inadequate stimulation or faulty technique on the part of the woman's partner. Even when this is true, sexual adjustment difficulties are best viewed as a problem the couple shares, not just as the "woman's problem," the "man's problem," or her "partner's problem."

Treatment

If we focus only on the woman, the most common source of orgasmic difficulties is overcontrol of sexual response. Orgasm requires a degree of abandonment to erotic feelings. It is inhibited by ambivalence or hostility toward the relationship, by guilt, by fears of expressing sexual needs, and by tendencies to control and intellectualize erotic feelings. The woman is unable to let go and enjoy the flow of pleasurable sensations (Segraves & Althof, 2002).

In Helen Kaplan's treatment program at Cornell University, anorgasmic women (those who do not have orgasms) are first trained to focus on their sexual responsiveness through masturbation or vigorous stimulation by a partner. As the woman becomes consistently orgasmic in these circumstances, her responsiveness is gradually transferred to lovemaking with her partner. Couples also typically learn alternative positions and techniques of lovemaking designed to increase clitoral stimulation (Hurlbert & Apt, 1995). At the same time, communication between partners is stressed, especially with reference to the woman's sexual value system (expectations, motivations, and preferences).

Male Orgasmic Disorder

Among males, an inability to reach orgasm was once considered a rare problem. But milder forms of **male orgasmic disorder** account for increasing numbers of clients seeking therapy. Typical background factors are strict religious training, fear of impregnating, lack of interest in the sexual partner, symbolic inability to give of oneself, unacknowledged homosexuality, or the recent occurrence of traumatic life events. Power and commitment struggles within relationships may be important added factors.

Treatment

Treatment for male orgasmic disorder (also known as retarded ejaculation) consists of sensate focus, manual stimulation by the man's partner (which is designed to orient the male to his partner as a source of pleasure), and stimulation to the point of orgasm followed by immediate intercourse and ejaculation. Work also focuses on resolving personal conflicts and marital difficulties underlying the problem.

Premature Ejaculation

Defining premature ejaculation is tricky because of large variations in the time different women take to reach orgasm. Helen Kaplan says that **premature ejaculation** exists when it occurs reflexively or the man cannot tolerate high levels of excitement at the plateau stage of arousal. Basically, ejaculation is premature if it consistently occurs before the man and his partner want it to occur.

Do many men have difficulties with premature ejaculation? Approximately 50 percent of young adult men have problems with premature ejaculation. Theories advanced to explain it have ranged from the idea that it may represent hostility toward the man's sexual partner (because it deprives the partner of satisfaction) to the suggestion that most early male sexual experiences tend to encourage rapid climax (such as those taking place in the back seat of a car and masturbation). H. S. Kaplan (1974) adds that excessive arousal and anxiety over performance are usually present. Also, some men simply engage in techniques that maximize sensation and make rapid orgasm inevitable.

Ejaculation is a reflex. To control it, a man must learn to recognize the physical signals that it is about to occur. Some men have simply never learned to be aware of these signals. Whatever the causes, premature ejaculation can be a serious difficulty, especially in the context of long-term relationships (King, 2005).

Treatment

Treatment for premature ejaculation is highly successful and relatively simple. The most common treatment is a "stop-start" procedure called the **squeeze technique** (Grenier & Byers, 1995). The man's sexual partner stimulates him manually until he signals that ejaculation is about to occur. The man's partner then firmly squeezes the tip of his penis to inhibit orgasm. When the man feels he has control, stimulation is repeated. Later the squeeze technique is used during lovemaking. Gradually, the man acquires the ability to delay orgasm sufficiently for mutually satisfactory lovemaking. During treatment, skills that improve communication between partners are developed, along with a better understanding of the male's sexual response cues (McCarthy & Fucito, 2005).

Sexual Pain Disorders

Pain in the genitals before, during, or after sexual intercourse is called **dyspareunia** (DIS-pah-ROO-nee-ah). Both females and males can experience dyspareunia. However, this problem is actually rare in males. In women, dyspareunia is often related to **vaginismus** (VAJ-ih-NIS-mus), a condition in which muscle spasms of the vagina prevent intercourse (*DSM-IV-TR,* 2000).

Vaginismus is often accompanied by obvious fears of intercourse, and where fear is absent, high levels of anxiety are present. Vaginismus therefore appears to be a phobic response to intercourse. Predictably, its causes include experiences of painful intercourse, rape and/or brutal and frightening sexual encounters, fear of men and of penetration, misinformation about sex (belief that it is injurious), fear of pregnancy, and fear of the specific male partner (Read, 1995; Ward & Ogden, 1994).

Treatment

Treatment of vaginismus is similar to what might be done for a nonsexual phobia. It includes extinction of conditioned muscle spasms by progressive relaxation of the vagina, desensitization of fears of intercourse, and masturbation or manual stimulation to associate pleasure with sexual approach by the woman's partner. Hypnosis has also been used successfully in some cases.

Summary

Solving sexual problems can be difficult. The problems described here are rarely solved without professional help (a possible exception is premature ejaculation). If a serious sexual difficulty is not resolved in a reasonable amount of time, the aid of an appropriately trained psychologist, physician, or counselor should be sought. The longer the problem is ignored, the more difficult it is to solve. But professional help is available.

Relationships and Sexual Adjustment

What can be done to improve sexual adjustment? Often, it is best to view sexual adjustment within the broader context of a relationship (Crooks & Bauer, 2005). Conflict and unresolved anger in other areas frequently take their toll in sexual adjustment, and mutually satisfying relationships tend to carry over into sexual relations. Sex is not a performance or a skill to be mastered like playing tennis. It is a form of communication within a relationship. Couples with strong and caring relationships can probably survive most sexual problems. A couple with a satisfactory sex life but a poor relationship rarely lasts. Marriage expert John Gottman believes that a couple must have at least five times as many positive as negative moments in their marriage if it is to survive (Gottman, 1994).

Disagreements About Sex

When disagreements arise over issues such as frequency of lovemaking, who initiates lovemaking, or what behavior is appropriate, Masters and Johnson believe that the rule should be, "Each partner must accept the other as the final authority on his or her own feelings." Partners are urged to give feedback about their feelings by following what therapists call the "touch and ask" rule: Touching and caressing should often be followed by questions such as, "Does that

Female sexual arousal disorder A lack of physical arousal to sexual stimulation.

Female orgasmic disorder A persistent inability to reach orgasm during lovemaking.

Male orgasmic disorder A persistent inability to reach orgasm during lovemaking.

Premature ejaculation Ejaculation that consistently occurs before the man and his partner want it to occur.

Squeeze technique Method for inhibiting ejaculation by compressing the tip of the penis.

Dyspareunia Genital pain before, during, or after sexual intercourse.

Vaginismus Muscle spasms of the vagina.

feel good?" "Do you like that?" and so forth (Knox, 1984). Satisfying erotic relationships focus on enhancing sexual pleasure for both partners, not on selfish interest in one's own gratification (Kleinplatz, 1996).

When problems do arise, partners are urged to be *responsive* to each other's needs at an *emotional* level and to recognize that all sexual problems are *mutual*. "Failures" should always be shared without placing blame. Masters and Johnson believe that it is particularly important to avoid the "numbers game." That is, couples should avoid being influenced by statistics on the average frequency of lovemaking, by stereotypes about sexual potency, and by the superhuman sexual exploits portrayed in movies and magazines.

Bridges to Sexual Satisfaction

According to sex therapist Barry McCarthy, four elements are necessary for a continuing healthy sexual relationship:

1. **Sexual anticipation**. Looking forward to lovemaking is inhibited by routine and poor communication between partners. It is wise for busy couples to set aside time to spend together. Unexpected, spontaneous lovemaking should also be encouraged.
2. **Valuing one's sexuality.** This is most likely to occur when you develop a respectful, trusting, and intimate relationship with your partner. Such relationships allow both partners to deal with negative sexual experiences when they occur.
3. **Feeling that you deserve sexual pleasure.** As previously noted, the essence of satisfying lovemaking is the giving and receiving of pleasure.
4. **Valuing intimacy.** A sense of closeness and intimacy with one's partner helps maintain sexual desire, especially in long-term relationships (McCarthy, 1995; McCarthy & Fucito, 2005).

Intimacy and Communication

Are there any other guidelines for maintaining a healthy relationship? A study that compared happily married couples with unhappily married couples found that, in almost every regard, the happily married couples showed superior *communication* skills. Three patterns that are almost always related to serious long-term problems in relationships are defensiveness (including whining), stubbornness, and refusal to talk with your partner (the "big freeze") (Gottman & Krokoff, 1989). Many couples find that communication is facilitated by observing the following guidelines.

Avoid "Gunnysacking"

Persistent feelings, whether positive or negative, need to be expressed. Gunnysacking refers to saving up feelings and complaints. These are then "dumped" during an argument or are used as ammunition in a fight. Gunnysacking is very destructive to a relationship.

Be Open About Feelings

Happy couples not only talk more, they convey more personal feelings and show greater sensitivity to their partners' feelings. As one expert put it, "In a healthy relationship, each partner feels free to express his likes, dislikes, wants, wishes, feelings, impulses, and the other person feels free to react with like honesty to these. In such a relationship, there will be tears, laughter, sensuality, irritation, anger, fear, baby-like behavior, and so on."

Don't Attack the Other Person's Character

Whenever possible, expressions of negative feelings should be given as statements of one's own feelings, not as statements of blame. It is far more constructive to say, "It makes me angry when you leave things around the house," than it is to say, "You're a slob!" Remember too, that if you use the words "always" or "never," you are probably mounting a character attack.

Don't Try to "Win" a Fight

Constructive fights are aimed at resolving shared differences, not at establishing who is right or wrong, superior or inferior.

Recognize That Anger Is Appropriate

Constructive and destructive fights are not distinguished by whether or not anger is expressed. A fight is a fight, and anger is appropriate. As is the case with any other emotion in a relationship, anger should be expressed. However, constructive expression of anger requires that couples fight fair by sticking to the real issues and not "hitting below the belt." Resorting to threats, such as announcing, "This relationship is over," is especially damaging.

Try to See Things Through Your Partner's Eyes

Marital harmony is closely related to the ability to put yourself in another person's place (Long & Andrews, 1990). When a conflict arises, always pause and try to take your partner's perspective. Seeing things through your partner's eyes can be a good reminder that no one is ever totally right or wrong in a personal dispute.

Don't Be a "Mind-Reader"

The preceding suggestion should not be taken as an invitation to engage in "mind-reading." Assuming that you know what your partner is thinking or feeling can

"Well, if it doesn't matter who's right and who's wrong, why don't I be right and you be wrong?"

muddle or block communication. Hostile or accusatory mind-reading, like the following examples, can be very disruptive: "You're just looking for an excuse to criticize me, aren't you?" "You don't really want my mother to visit, or you wouldn't say that." Rather than *telling* your partner what she or he thinks, *ask* her or him.

To add to these guidelines, Bryan Strong and Christine DeVault (1994) suggest that if you really want to mess up a relationship, you can almost totally avoid intimacy and communication by doing the following.

Ten Ways to Avoid Intimacy

1. Don't talk about anything meaningful, especially about feelings.
2. Never show your feelings; remain as expressionless as possible.
3. Always be pleasant and pretend everything is okay, even if you are upset or dissatisfied.
4. Always win, never compromise.
5. Always keep busy; that way you can avoid intimacy and make your partner feel unimportant in your life.
6. Always be right; don't let on that you are human.
7. Never argue or you may have to reveal differences and make changes.
8. Make your partner guess what you want. That way, you can tell your partner that she or he doesn't really understand or love you.
9. Always take care of your own needs first.
10. Keep the television set on. Wouldn't you rather be watching TV than talking with your partner?

Remember, to encourage intimacy, wise couples *avoid* the practices in the preceding list.

As a last point, it is worth restating that sexual adjustment and loving relationships are interdependent. When sex goes well, it's 15 percent of a relationship, and when it goes badly it's 85 percent. As a shared pleasure, a form of intimacy, a means of communication, and a haven from everyday tensions, a positive sexual relationship can do much to enhance a couple's mutual understanding and caring. Likewise, an honest, equitable, and affectionate out-of-bed relationship contributes greatly to sexual satisfaction (Rathus, Nevid, & Fichner-Rathus, 2005).

KNOWLEDGE BUILDER

Sexual Problems

REFLECT

In plain language, sexual disorders can be summarized this way: The person doesn't want to do it. The person wants to do it but can't get aroused. The person wants to do it, gets aroused, but has problems with orgasm. The person wants to do it and gets aroused, but lovemaking is uncomfortable. What are the formal terms for each of these possibilities?

We all make mistakes in relationships. Using the discussion in the Psychology in Action as a guide, which mistakes have you avoided? Which would you like to avoid or correct?

LEARNING CHECK

1. Males suffering from primary erectile dysfunction have never been able to have or maintain an erection. T or F?
2. According to the latest figures, most erectile disorders are caused by castration fears. T or F?
3. Sensate focus is the most common treatment for premature ejaculation. T or F?
4. Premature ejaculation is considered the rarest of the male sexual adjustment problems. T or F?
5. As it is for female sexual arousal disorder, the sensate focus technique is a primary treatment mode for male sexual arousal disorder. T or F?
6. Vaginismus, which appears to be a phobic response to sexual intercourse, can also cause dyspareunia. T or F?
7. Masters and Johnson urge sexual partners to recognize that all sexual problems are mutual and not just one partner's problem. T or F?
8. The term *gunnysacking* refers to the constructive practice of hiding anger until it is appropriate to express it. T or F?

CRITICAL THINKING

9. Who would you expect to have the most frequent sex and the most satisfying sex, married couples or single persons?

Answers: **1.** T **2.** F **3.** F **4.** F **5.** T **6.** T **7.** T **8.** F **9.** Contrary to mass media portrayals of sexy singles, married couples have the most sex and are most likely to have orgasms when they do. Greater opportunity, plus familiarity with a partner's needs and preferences probably account for these findings (Laumann et al., 1994).

Chapter in Review

What are the basic dimensions of sex?

- Physically, males and females differ in primary and secondary sexual characteristics.
- Estrogens (female sex hormones) and androgens (male sex hormones) influence the development of primary and secondary sexual characteristics.
- Biological sex consists of genetic sex, gonadal sex, hormonal sex, and genital sex. Sexual character is also affected by gender identity.
- Sexual development begins with genetic sex (*XX* or *XY* chromosomes) and is then influenced by prenatal hormone levels.
- Androgen insensitivity, exposure to progestin, the androgenital syndrome, and similar problems can cause a person to be born with an intersexual condition.
- Many researchers believe that prenatal hormones exert a biological biasing effect that combines with social factors to influence psychosexual development.
- On most psychological dimensions, women and men are more alike than they are different.

How does one's sense of maleness or femaleness develop?

- Male and female behavior patterns are related to learned gender identity and gender role socialization.
- Gender role stereotypes often distort perceptions about the kinds activities for which men and women are suited.
- Gender identity usually becomes stable by age 3 or 4 years.
- Gender role socialization seems to account for most observed female–male gender differences. Parents tend to encourage boys in instrumental behaviors and girls in expressive behaviors.

What is psychological androgyny (and is it contagious)?

- Roughly one third of all persons are androgynous. Approximately 50 percent are traditionally feminine or masculine.
- Psychological androgyny is related to greater behavioral adaptability and flexibility.

What are the most typical patterns of human sexual behavior?

- "Normal" sexual behavior is defined differently by various cultures. There appears to be little difference in sexual responsiveness between females and males.
- Sexual arousal is related to the body's erogenous zones, but mental and emotional reactions are the ultimate source of sexual responsiveness.
- There is evidence that the sex drive peaks at a later age for females than it does for males, although this difference is diminishing.
- Castration may or may not influence sex drive in humans. Sterilization does not alter the sex drive.
- There is a gradual decline in the frequency of sexual intercourse with increasing age. However, many elderly persons remain sexually active and large variations exist at all ages.
- Masturbation is a normal and completely acceptable behavior.
- Sexual orientation refers to one's degree of emotional and erotic attraction to members of the same sex, opposite sex, or both sexes. A person may be heterosexual, homosexual, or bisexual.
- A combination of hereditary, biological, social, and psychological influences combine to produce one's sexual orientation.
- As a group, homosexual men and women do not differ psychologically from heterosexuals.

To what extent do females and males differ in sexual response?

- Human sexual response can be divided into four phases: (1) excitement, (2) plateau, (3) orgasm, and (4) resolution.
- There do not appear to be any differences between "vaginal orgasms" and "clitoral orgasms." Fifteen percent of women are consistently multi-orgasmic, and at least 50 percent are capable of multiple orgasm.
- Males experience a refractory period after orgasm, and only 5 percent of men are multi-orgasmic.
- Mutual orgasm has been abandoned by most sex counselors as the ideal in lovemaking.

What are the most common sexual disorders?

- Atypical sexual behaviors that often cause difficulty are called paraphilias. The paraphilias include pedophilia, fetishism, voyeurism, exhibitionism, transvestic fetishism, sexual sadism, sexual masochism, and frotteurism.
- Exhibitionists are rarely dangerous and can best be characterized as sexually inhibited and immature.
- The effects of child molestation vary greatly, depending on the severity of the molestation and the child's relationship to the molester.

Have recent changes in attitudes affected sexual behavior?

- Attitudes toward sexual behavior have become more liberal, but actual changes in sexual behavior have been more gradual.

- Adolescents and young adults engage in more frequent sexual activity than they did 40 years ago.
- In recent years there has been a greater acceptance of female sexuality and a narrowing of differences in female and male patterns of sexual behavior.
- Forcible rape, acquaintance rape, and rape-supportive attitudes and beliefs are major problems in North America.

What impact have sexually transmitted diseases had on sexual behavior?

- During the last 20 years the incidence of sexually transmitted diseases has steadily increased.
- STDs and the spread of AIDS have had a sizable impact on patterns of sexual behavior, including some curtailment of risk taking.
- Many sexually active people continue to take unnecessary risks with their health by failing to follow safer sex practices.

What are the most common sexual adjustment problems? How are they treated?

- The principal sexual problems are desire disorders, arousal disorders, orgasm disorders, and sexual pain disorders.
- Behavioral methods and counseling techniques have been developed to alleviate many sexual problems.
- Most sexual adjustment problems are closely linked to the general health of a couple's relationship.
- Communication skills that foster and maintain intimacy are the key to successful relationships.

Web Resources

Internet addresses frequently change. To find the sites listed here, visit www.thomsonedu.com/psychology/coon for an updated list of Internet addresses and direct links to relevant sites.

***Psychology: Gateways to Mind and Behavior* Website** Online quizzes, flash cards, and other helpful study aids for this text. www.thomsonedu.com/psychology/coon.

"Friends" Raping Friends Information about date rape.

Go Ask Alice The Sexual Health section of this question-and-answer site offers valuable information and links about sexuality.

Online Sexual Disorders Screening Test for Men A self-scoring test for sexual problems.

Online Sexual Disorders Screening Test for Women A self-scoring test for sexual problems.

Preventing HIV Infection Advice on how to prevent HIV.

Sexual Orientation and Homosexuality—FAQ Answers basic questions about sexual orientation and homosexuality.

ThomsonNOW™ Go to www.thomsonedu.com to link to ThomsonNow, your online study tool. First take the **Pre-Test** for this chapter to get your **Personalized Study Plan,** which will identify topics you need to review and direct you to online resources. Then take the **Post-Test** to determine what concepts you have mastered and what you still need work on.

InfoTrac College Edition For more information on sexually transmitted diseases, use Key Words search for SEXUALLY TRANSMITTED DISEASE. Go to www.thomsonedu.com/psychology/coon.

Interactive Learning

***PsychNow!* Version 2.0 CD-ROM** Interact with the material with *PsychNow!*'s animations, video clips, experiments, and interactive assessments. For this chapter, go to *6e. Human Sexuality* and *8g. Gender and Stereotyping* for a better understanding of sexuality and gender issues.

chapter

14

Personality

THEME:

Personality refers to the consistency we see in personal behavior patterns. Measures of personality reveal individual differences and help predict future behavior.

Andre Forget/AP/Wide World Photo

Key Questions

How do psychologists use the term personality?

What core concepts make up the psychology of personality?

Are some personality traits more basic or important than others?

How do psychodynamic theories explain personality?

What do behaviorists emphasize in their approach to personality?

How do humanistic theories differ from other perspectives?

How do psychologists measure personality?

What causes shyness? What can be done about it?

Preview

The Hidden Essence

Rural Colorado. Our car banged over one last, brain-jarring rut and lurched toward the dilapidated farmhouse. Annette was on the porch, hooting and whooping and obviously happy to see old friends arrive.

If anyone was suited for a move to the "wilds" of Colorado, it was Annette, a strong and resourceful woman. Still, it was hard to imagine a more radical change. After separating from her husband, she had traded a comfortable life in the city for hard times in the high country. Annette was working as a ranch hand and a lumberjack (lumberjill?), trying to make it through some hard winters.

So radical were the changes in Annette's life, we worried that she might be entirely different. She was, on the contrary, more her "old self" than ever.

Perhaps you have had a similar experience. After several years of separation, it is always intriguing to see an old friend. At first you may be struck by how the person has changed. ("Where did you get that haircut!?") Soon, however, you will probably be delighted to discover that the semi-stranger before you is still the person you once knew. It is exactly this core of consistency that psychologists have in mind when they use the term *personality.*

Without doubt, personality touches our daily lives. Falling in love, choosing friends, getting along with coworkers, voting for a president, or coping with your zaniest relatives all raise questions about personality.

What is personality? How does it differ from temperament, character, or attitudes? Is it possible to measure personality? We'll address these questions and more in this chapter.

The Psychology of Personality—Do You Have Personality?

Part of the pleasure of getting to know someone is the fascination of learning who he or she is and how he or she thinks. Each person has a unique pattern of thinking, behaving, and expressing their feelings. In short, everyone has a unique personality. As psychologists, we would like to better understand Annette's personality. What models and concepts can we use?

"Annette has a very optimistic personality." "Ramiro's not handsome, but he has a great personality." "My father's business friends think he's a nice guy. They should see him at home where his real personality comes out." "It's hard to believe Tanya and Nikki are sisters. They have such opposite personalities."

It's obvious that we all frequently use the term *personality.* But if you think that personality means "charm," "charisma," or "style," you have misused the term. Psychologists regard **personality** as a person's unique pattern of thinking, emotions, and behavior (Funder, 2004; Mischel, 2004). In other words, personality refers to the consistency in who you are, have been, and will become. It also refers to the special blend of talents, values, hopes, loves, hates, and habits that makes each of us a unique person.

How is that different from the way most people use the term? Many people confuse personality with *character.* The term **character** implies that a person has been evaluated, not just described (Skipton, 1997). If, by saying someone has "personality," you mean the person is friendly, outgoing, and attractive, you are describing what we regard as good character in our culture. But in some cultures it is deemed good for people to be fierce, warlike, and cruel. So, although everyone in a particular culture has personality, not everyone has character—or at least not good character. (Do you know any good characters?)

Personality is also distinct from *temperament,* the "raw material" from which personalities are formed. **Temperament** refers to the hereditary aspects of your personality, such as your sensitivity, irritability, distractibility, and typical mood (Kagan, 2004). Judging from Annette's adult personality, we would guess that she was an active, happy baby.

Psychologists use a large number of terms to explain personality. It might be wise, therefore, to start with a few key concepts. These ideas should help you keep your bearings as you read this chapter.

Personality A person's unique and relatively stable behavior patterns.

Character Personal characteristics that have been judged or evaluated; a person's desirable or undesirable qualities.

Temperament The hereditary aspects of personality, including sensitivity, activity levels, prevailing mood, irritability, and adaptability.

Does this man have personality? Do you?

Traits

We use the idea of traits every day to talk about personality. For instance, our friend Dan is *sociable, orderly,* and *intelligent.* His sister Kayla is *shy, sensitive,* and *creative.* In general, **personality traits** like these are stable qualities that a person shows in most situations. Typically, traits are inferred from behavior. If you see Dan talking to strangers—first at a supermarket and later at a party—you might deduce that he is "sociable." Once personality traits are identified, they can be used to predict future behavior. For example, noting that Dan is outgoing might lead you to predict that he will be sociable at school or at work. In fact, such consistencies can span many years. A study of women who appeared to be happy in their college yearbook photos (they had genuine smiles) found that most were still happy people 30 years later (Harker & Keltner, 2001).

When Is the Plaster Set?

As we observed in our reunion with Annette, personality traits are usually quite stable (Gustavsson et al., 1997). Think about how little the traits of your best friends have changed in the last 5 years. It would be strange indeed to feel like you were talking with a different person every time you met a friend or an acquaintance.

At what age are personality traits firmly established? During the twenties, personality slowly begins to harden. By age 30, personality has usually stabilized. The person you are at age 30 is, for the most part, the person you will be at age 60 (Costa & McCrae, 1992; Roberts, Caspi, & Moffitt, 2001). However, there is an exception: Most people continue to become more conscientious and agreeable as they mature. In view of these changes, it appears that stereotypes of the "grumpy old man" and "cranky old woman" are largely unfounded (Srivastava, et al., 2003).

BRIDGES

Even newborn babies differ in temperament, which implies that it is hereditary. Temperament has a large impact on how infants interact with their parents.

See Chapter 3, pages 85–86.

Psychologists and employers are especially interested in the personality traits of individuals who hold high-risk, high-stress positions involving public safety, such as police, air traffic controllers, and nuclear power plant employees.

Types

Have you ever asked the question, "What type of person is she (or he)?" A **personality type** refers to people who have *several traits in common* (Larsen & Buss, 2005). Informally, your own thinking might include categories such as the executive type, the athletic type, the motherly type, the hip-hop type, the techno geek, and so forth. If we asked you to define these informal types, you would probably list a different collection of traits for each one.

How valid is it to speak of personality "types"? Over the years, psychologists have proposed many ways to categorize personalities into types. For example, Swiss psychiatrist Carl Jung (yoong) proposed that people are either *introverts* or *extroverts.* An **introvert** is a shy, egocentric person whose attention is focused inward. An **extrovert** is a bold, outgoing person whose attention is directed outward. These terms are so widely used that you may think of yourself and your friends as being one type or the other. However, the wildest, wittiest, most party-loving "extrovert" you know is introverted at times. Likewise, extremely introverted persons are assertive and sociable in some situations. In short, two categories (or even several) are often inadequate to fully capture differences in personality. That's why rating people on a list of traits tends to be more informative than classifying them into two or three types.

Even though types tend to oversimplify personality, they do have value. Most often, types are a shorthand way of labeling people who have several key traits in common. For example, in the next chapter we will discuss Type A personalities. These are people who have personality traits that increase their chance of suffering a heart attack (see ● Figure 14.1). Similarly, you will read in

The four basic personality types

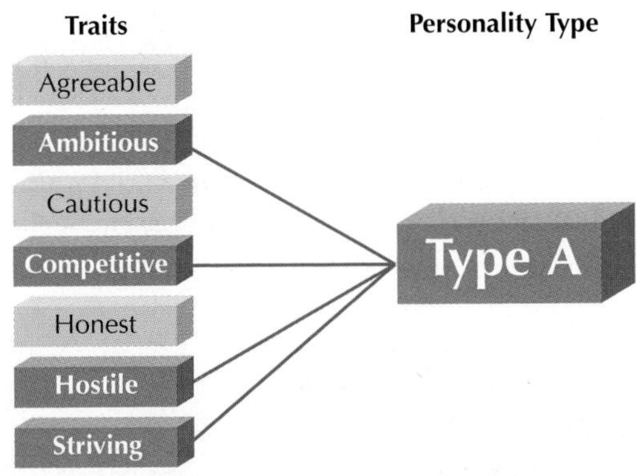

● **Figure 14.1** Personality types are defined by the presence of several specific traits. For example, several possible personality traits are shown in the left column. A person who has a Type A personality typically possesses all or most of the highlighted traits. Type A persons are especially prone to heart disease (see Chapter 15).

Chapter 16 about unhealthy personality types such as the paranoid personality, the dependent personality, and the antisocial personality. Each problem is defined by a specific collection of maladaptive traits.

Self-Concept

Self-concepts provide another way of understanding personality. The rough outlines of your self-concept could be revealed by this request: "Please tell us about yourself." In other words, your **self-concept** consists of all your ideas, perceptions, and feelings about who you are. It is the mental "picture" you have of your own personality.

We creatively build our self-concepts out of daily experiences. Then we slowly revise them as we have new experiences. Once a stable self-concept exists, it tends to guide what we pay attention to, remember, and think about. Because of this, self-concepts can greatly affect our behavior and personal adjustment—especially when they are inaccurate (Larsen & Buss, 2005). For instance, Alesha is a student who thinks she is stupid, worthless, and a failure, despite getting good grades. With such an inaccurate self-concept, she tends to be depressed regardless of how well she does.

Self-Esteem

Note that in addition to having a faulty self-concept, Alesha has low **self-esteem** (a negative self-evaluation). A person with high self-esteem is confident, proud, and self-respecting. One who has low self-esteem is insecure, lacking in confidence, and self-critical. Like Alesha, people with low self-esteem are usually anxious and unhappy.

Self-concepts can be remarkably consistent. In a study, very old people were asked how they had changed over the years. Almost all thought they were essentially the same person they were when they were young (Troll & Skaff, 1997).

Personality trait A stable, enduring quality that a person shows in most situations.

Personality type A style of personality defined by a group of related traits.

Introvert A person whose attention is focused inward; a shy, reserved, self-centered person.

Extrovert A person whose attention is directed outward; a bold, outgoing person.

Self-concept A person's perception of his or her own personality traits.

Self-esteem Regarding oneself as a worthwhile person; a positive evaluation of oneself.

Self-Esteem and Culture—Hotshot or Team Player?

You and some friends are playing soccer. Your team wins, in part because you make some good plays. After the game, you bask in the glow of having performed well. You don't want to brag about being a hotshot, but your self-esteem gets a boost from your personal success.

In Japan, Shinobu and some of his friends are playing soccer. His team wins, in part because he makes some good plays. After the game Shinobu is happy because his team did well. However, Shinobu also dwells on the ways in which he let his team down. He thinks about how he could improve, and he resolves to be a better team player.

These sketches illustrate a basic difference in Eastern and Western psychology. In individualistic cultures such as the United States, self-esteem is based on personal success and outstanding performance (Lay & Verkuyten, 1999). For us, the path to higher self-esteem lies in self-enhancement. We are pumped up by our successes and tend to downplay our faults and failures (Ross et al., 2005).

Asian cultures, such as the Japanese and Chinese cultures, place a greater emphasis on collectivism, or interdependence among people. For them, self-esteem is based on a secure sense of belonging to social groups. As a result, people in Asian cultures are more apt to engage in self-criticism (Ross et al., 2005). By correcting personal faults, they add to the well-being of the group (Kitayama et al., 1997; Kitayama, Markus, & Kurokawa, 2000). And, when the *group* succeeds, individual members feel better about themselves, which raises their self-esteem.

Perhaps self-esteem is still based on success in both Eastern and Western cultures. However, it is fascinating that cultures define success in such different ways (Schmitt & Allik, 2005). The North American emphasis on winning is not the only way to feel good about yourself (Heine & Lehman, 1999).

Self-esteem tends to rise when we experience success or praise. A person who is competent and effective and who is loved, admired, and respected by others will almost always have high self-esteem (Baumeister et al., 2003). (The reasons for having high self-esteem can vary in different cultures. See "Self-Esteem and Culture" for more information.)

People who have low self-esteem typically also suffer from poor self-knowledge. Like Alesha, their self-concepts are inconsistent, inaccurate, and confused. Problems of this type are explored later in this chapter.

What if you "think you're hot," but you're not? Genuine self-esteem is based on an accurate appraisal of your strengths and weaknesses. A positive self-evaluation that is bestowed too easily may not be healthy (Twenge & Campbell, 2001). People who think very highly of themselves (and let others know it) may at first seem confident, but their arrogance quickly turns off other people (Paulhus, 1998).

A related problem plagues people who are incompetent. Such people grossly overestimate their own abilities. For instance, a study found that people who score very low on tests of logic, grammar, and humor think that they are well above average in these areas. Basically, they seem to be too incompetent to recognize their own incompetence. This finding may explain why humor-impaired people (we all know at least one) insist on telling jokes that are not funny (Kruger & Dunning, 1999).

Personality Theories

It would be easy to get lost without a framework for understanding personality. How do our thoughts, actions, and feelings relate to one another? How does personality develop? Why do some

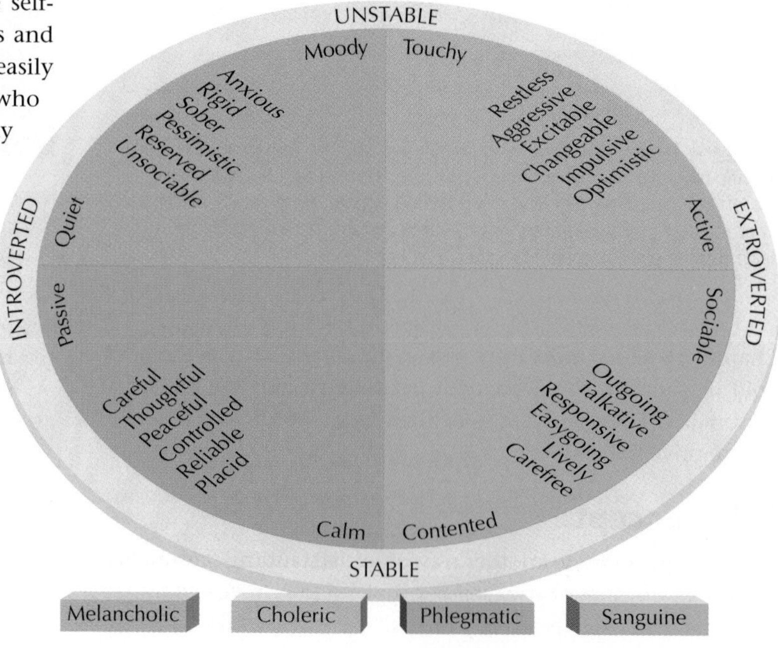

● **Figure 14.2** English psychologist Hans Eysenck (1916–1997) believed that many personality traits are related to whether you are mainly introverted or extroverted and whether you tend to be emotionally stable or unstable (highly emotional). These characteristics, in turn, are related to four basic types of temperament first recognized by the early Greeks. The types are: *melancholic* (sad, gloomy), *choleric* (hot-tempered, irritable), *phlegmatic* (sluggish, calm), and *sanguine* (cheerful, hopeful). (Adapted from Eysenck, 1981.)

DISCOVERING PSYCHOLOGY What's Your Musical Personality?

Even if you like all kinds of music, you probably prefer some styles to others. Of the styles listed here, which three do you enjoy the most? (Circle your choices.)

blues jazz classical folk rock alternative heavy metal country soundtrack religious pop rap/hip-hop soul/funk electronic/dance

In a recent study, Peter Rentfrow and Samuel Gosling found that the types of music people prefer tend to be associated with their personality characteristics. See if your musical tastes match their findings (Rentfrow & Gosling, 2003).

- People who value aesthetic experiences, have good verbal abilities, are liberal, and tolerant of others tend to like music that is reflective and complex (blues, jazz, classical, and folk music).
- People who are curious about new experiences, enjoy taking risks, and are physically active prefer intense, rebellious music (rock, alternative, and heavy metal music).
- People who are cheerful, conventional, extroverted, reliable, helpful, and conservative tend to enjoy upbeat conventional music (country, soundtrack, religious, and pop music).
- People who are talkative, full of energy, forgiving, physically attractive, and who reject conservative ideals tend to prefer energetic, rhythmic music (rap/hip-hop, soul/funk, and electronic/dance music).

Unmistakably, personality traits affect our everyday behavior.

people suffer from psychological problems? How can they be helped? To answer such questions, psychologists have created a dazzling array of theories. A **personality theory** is a system of concepts, assumptions, ideas, and principles proposed to explain personality (● Figure 14.2). In this chapter, we can only explore a few of the many personality theories. The five major perspectives we will consider are the following:

1. **Trait theories** attempt to learn what traits make up personality and how they relate to actual behavior.
2. **Psychodynamic theories** focus on the inner workings of personality, especially internal conflicts and struggles.
3. **Behavioristic theories** place importance on the external environment and on the effects of conditioning and learning.
4. **Social learning theories** attribute differences in personality to socialization, expectations, and mental processes.
5. **Humanistic theories** stress private, subjective experience and personal growth.

With these broad perspectives in mind, let's take a deeper look at personality.

The Trait Approach—Describe Yourself in 18,000 Words or Less

How many words can you think of to describe the personality of a close friend? Your list might be long: Over 18,000 English words refer to personal characteristics. As we have noted, traits are stable qualities that a person shows in most situations. For example, if you are usually friendly, optimistic, and cautious, these qualities are traits of your personality.

What if I am sometimes shy, pessimistic, or uninhibited? The original three qualities are still traits as long as they are most *typical* of your behavior. Let's say our friend Annette approaches most situations with optimism, but tends to expect the worst each time she applies for a job. If her pessimism is limited to this situation or a few others, it is still accurate and useful to describe her as an optimistic person.

Predicting Behavior

As we have noted, separating people into broad types, such as "introvert" or "extrovert," may oversimplify personality. However, introversion/extroversion can also be thought of as a trait. Knowing how you rate on this single dimension would allow us to predict how you will behave in a variety of settings. Where, for example, do you prefer to study in the library? Researchers have found that students high in the trait of extroversion study in noisy locations where there's a good chance of talking with others (Campbell & Hawley, 1982). In the library at Colgate University (where the study was done), you can find extroverted students in the second floor lounge. Or, if you prefer, more introverted students are in the cubicles on the first and third floors! (Other interesting links exist between traits and behavior. See "What's Your Musical Personality?")

Personality theory A system of concepts, assumptions, ideas, and principles used to understand and explain personality.

Describing People

In general, psychologists try to identify traits that best describe a person. Take a moment to check the traits in ■ Table 14.1 that describe your personality. Are the traits you checked of equal importance? Are some stronger or more basic than others? Do any overlap? For example, if you checked "dominant," did you also check "confident" and "bold"? Answers to these questions would interest a trait theorist. To better understand personality, **trait theorists** attempt to analyze, classify, and interrelate traits.

Classifying Traits

Are there different types of traits? Yes, psychologist Gordon Allport (1961) identified several kinds. **Common traits** are characteristics shared by most members of a culture. Common traits tell us how people from a particular nation or culture are similar, or which traits a culture emphasizes. In America, for example, competitiveness is a fairly common trait. Among the Hopi of Northern Arizona, it is relatively rare.

Of course, common traits don't tell us much about individuals. Although many people are competitive in American culture, various people you know may rate high, medium, or low in this trait. Usually we are also interested in these **individual traits**, which describe a person's unique qualities.

Here's an analogy to help you separate common traits from individual traits: If you decide to buy a pet dog, you will want to know the general characteristics of the dog's breed (its common traits). In addition, you will want to know about the "personality" of a specific dog (its individual traits) before you decide to take it home.

TABLE 14.1

Adjective Checklist

Check the traits you feel are characteristic of your personality. Are some more basic than others?

aggressive	organized	ambitious	clever
confident	loyal	generous	calm
warm	bold	cautious	reliable
sensitive	mature	talented	jealous
sociable	honest	funny	religious
dominant	dull	accurate	nervous
humble	uninhibited	visionary	cheerful
thoughtful	serious	helpful	emotional
orderly	anxious	conforming	good-natured
liberal	curious	optimistic	kind
meek	neighborly	passionate	compulsive

Allport also made distinctions between *cardinal traits, central traits,* and *secondary traits.* **Cardinal traits** are so basic that all of a person's activities can be traced to the trait. For instance, compassion was an overriding trait of Mother Teresa's personality. Likewise, Abraham Lincoln's personality was dominated by the cardinal trait of honesty. According to Allport, few people have cardinal traits.

Central Traits

How do central and secondary traits differ from cardinal traits? **Central traits** are the basic building blocks of personality. A surprisingly small number of central traits can capture the essence of a person. For instance, just six traits would provide a good description of Annette's personality: dominant, sociable, honest, cheerful, intelligent, and optimistic. When college students were asked to describe someone they knew well, they mentioned an average of seven central traits (Allport, 1961).

Secondary traits are more superficial personal qualities, such as food preferences, attitudes, political opinions, musical tastes, and so forth. In Allport's terms, a personality description might therefore include the following items.

Name: Jane Doe
Age: 22
Cardinal traits: None
Central traits: Possessive, autonomous, artistic, dramatic, self-centered, trusting
Secondary traits: Prefers colorful clothes, likes to work alone, politically liberal, always late

Source Traits

How can you tell if a personality trait is central or secondary? Raymond B. Cattell (1906–1998) tried to answer this question by directly studying the traits of a large number of people. Cattell began by measuring visible features of personality, which he called **surface traits.** Soon, Cattell noticed that these surface traits often appeared together in groups. In fact, some traits appeared together so often that they seemed to represent a single more basic trait. Cattell called these deeper characteristics **source traits** (Cattell, 1965). They are the core of each individual's personality.

How do source traits differ from Allport's central traits? Allport classified traits subjectively, and it's possible that he was wrong at times. Cattell used a statistical technique called *factor analysis* to look for connections among traits. For example, he found that imaginative people are almost always *inventive, original, curious, creative, innovative,* and *ingenious.* Thus, *imaginative* is a source trait. If you are an imaginative person, we automatically know that you have several other traits, too.

Cattell identified 16 source traits. According to him, all 16 are needed to fully describe a personality. Source traits are measured by a test called the *Sixteen Personality Factor Questionnaire* (often referred to as the 16 PF). Like many personality tests, the 16 PF can be used to produce a **trait profile,** or graph of a person's score on each trait. Trait profiles draw a "picture" of individual personalities, which makes it easier to compare them (● Figure 14.3).

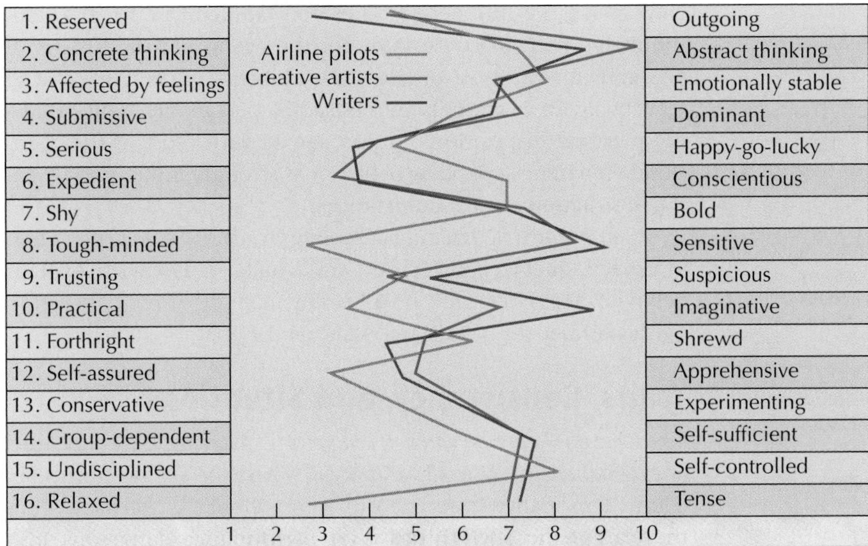

● **Figure 14.3** The 16 source traits measured by Cattell's 16 PF are listed beside the graph. Scores can be plotted as a profile for an individual or a group. The profiles shown here are group averages for airline pilots, creative artists, and writers. Notice the similarity between artists and writers and the difference between these two groups and pilots. (R. B. Cattell, "Personality Pinned Down," 1973. Reprinted by permission of Dr. R. B. Cattell.)

The Big Five

Noel is outgoing and friendly, conscientious, emotionally stable, and smart. His brother Joel is introverted, hostile, irresponsible, emotionally unpredictable, and disinterested in ideas (stupid). You will be spending a week in a space capsule with either Noel or Joel. Who would you choose? If the answer seems obvious, it's because Noel and Joel were described with the **five-factor model**, a system that identifies the five most basic dimensions of personality.

The "Big Five" factors listed in ● Figure 14.4 attempt to further reduce Cattell's 16 factors to just five universal dimensions (McCrae & Costa, 2001; McCrae & Terracciano, 2005). The Big Five may be the best answer of all to the question, "What is the essence of human personality?" (De Raad, 1998; McCrae & Costa, 1997).

Five Key Dimensions

If you would like to compare the personalities of two people, try rating them informally on the five dimensions shown in ● Figure 14.4. For factor 1, *extroversion,* rate how introverted or extroverted each person is. Factor 2, *agreeableness,* refers to how friendly, nurturant, and caring a person is, as opposed to cold, indifferent, self-centered, or spiteful. A person who is *conscientious* (factor 3) is self-disciplined, responsible, and achieving. People low on this factor are irresponsible, careless, and undependable. Factor 4, *neuroticism,* refers to negative, upsetting emotions. People who are high in neuroticism tend to be anxious, emotionally "sour," irritable, and unhappy. Finally, people who rate high on factor 5, *openness to experience,* are intelligent and open to new ideas (McCrae & Costa, 2001).

The beauty of the Big-Five model is that almost any trait you can name will be related to one of the five factors. If you were selecting a college roommate, hiring an employee, or answering a singles ad, you would probably like to know all of the personal dimensions covered by the Big Five. Such traits predict how people will act in various circumstances. For example, people who score high in conscientiousness tend to perform well at work, do well in school, and they rarely have automobile accidents (Arthur & Doverspike, 2001; Barrick, Moun, & Judge, 2001; Chamorro-Premuzic & Furnham, 2003). (Is it possible to be too conscientious? See "Perfectly Miserable" for an answer.)

Before you read the next section, take a moment to answer the questions that follow. Doing so will add to your understanding of a long-running controversy in the psychology of personality.

Rate Yourself: How Do You View Personality?

1. My friends' actions are fairly consistent from day to day and in different situations. T or F?
2. Whether a person is honest or dishonest, kind or cruel, a hero or a coward depends mainly on circumstances. T or F?
3. Most people that I have known for several years have pretty much the same personalities now as they did when I first met them. T or F?
4. The reason that people in some professions (such as teachers, lawyers, or doctors) seem so much alike is because their work requires that they act in particular ways. T or F?
5. One of the first things I would want to know about a potential roommate is what the person's personality is like. T or F?

Trait theorist A psychologist interested in classifying, analyzing, and interrelating traits to understand personality.

Common traits Personality traits that are shared by most members of a particular culture.

Individual traits Personality traits that define a person's unique individual qualities.

Cardinal trait A personality trait so basic that all of a person's activities relate to it.

Central traits The core traits that characterize an individual personality.

Secondary traits Traits that are inconsistent or relatively superficial.

Surface traits The visible or observable traits of one's personality.

Source traits Basic underlying traits of personality; each source trait is reflected in a number of surface traits.

Trait profile A graph of the scores obtained on several personality traits.

Five-factor model Proposes that there are five universal dimensions of personality.

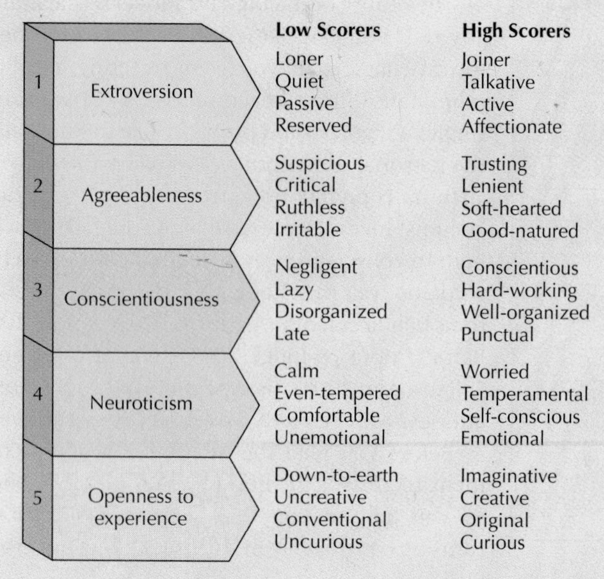

● **Figure 14.4** The Big Five. According to the five-factor model, basic differences in personality can be "boiled down" to the dimensions shown here. The five-factor model answers these essential questions about a person: Is she/he extroverted or introverted? Agreeable or difficult? Conscientious or irresponsible? Emotionally stable or unstable? Smart or unintelligent? These questions cover a large measure of what we might want to know about someone's personality. (Trait descriptions adapted from McCrae & Costa, 1990.)

Eleanor Bentall/Corbis

Knowing where a person stands on the "Big Five" personality factors helps predict his or her behavior. For example, people who score high on conscientiousness tend to be safe drivers who are unlikely to have automobile accidents (Arthur & Doverspike, 2001).

6. I believe that immediate circumstances usually determine how people act at any given time. T or F?
7. To be comfortable in a particular job, a person's personality must match the nature of the work. T or F?
8. Almost anyone would be polite at a wedding reception; it doesn't matter what kind of personality the person has. T or F?

Now count the number of times you marked true for the odd-numbered items. Do the same for the even-numbered items. If you agreed with most of the odd-numbered items, you tend to view behavior as strongly influenced by personality traits or lasting personal dispositions. If you agreed with most of the even-numbered items, you view behavior as strongly influenced by external situations and circumstances.

What if I answered true about equally for odd and even items? Then you place equal weight on traits and situations as ways to explain behavior. This is the view now held by many personality psychologists (Funder, 2004; Mischel & Shoda, 1998).

Traits, Consistency, and Situations

To predict how a person will act, is it better to focus on personality traits or external circumstances? Actually, it's best to take both into account. Personality traits are quite consistent. As we have seen, they can predict such things as job performance, dangerous driving, or successful marriage (Funder, 2004). Yet *situations* also greatly influence our behavior. For instance, it would be unusual for you to dance at a movie or read a book at a football game. Likewise, few people sleep in roller coasters or tell off-color jokes at funerals. However, your personality traits may predict whether you choose to read a book, go to a movie, or attend a football game in the first place. Typically, traits *interact* with situations to determine how we will act (Mischel, 2004).

Trait-situation interactions occur when external circumstances influence the expression of personality traits. For instance, imagine what would happen if you moved from a church to a classroom to a party to a football game. As the setting changed, you would probably become louder and more boisterous. This change would demonstrate situational effects on behavior. At the same time, your personality traits would also be apparent: If you were quieter than average in class, you would probably be quieter than average in the other settings, too. Where do such differences come from? The next section explores one source of personality traits.

Do We Inherit Personality?

How much does heredity affect personality traits? Some breeds of dogs have reputations for being friendly, aggressive, intelligent, calm, or emotional. Such differences fall in the realm of **behavioral genetics**, the study of inherited behavioral traits. We know that facial features, eye color, body type, and many other physical

BRIDGES

Behavioral genetic research has helped us better understand the hereditary origins of intelligence and psychological disorders.

See Chapter 11, pages 377–378, and Chapter 16, page 555.

THE CLINICAL FILE

Perfectly Miserable

Up to a point, wanting to be "perfect" is associated with high achievement. However, having impossibly high standards, a trait called perfectionism, can be a problem. As you might expect, college students who are perfectionists tend to get good grades. Yet some students cross the line into maladaptive perfectionism, which typically *lowers* performance at school and elsewhere (Accordino, Accordino, & Slaney, 2000).

People who suffer from unhealthy perfectionism set unattainably high standards for themselves. This causes them to feel as if they are always failing. Perfectionistic students are self-critical, terrified of making mistakes, and often seriously depressed (Sumi & Kanda, 2002).

For many students, maladaptive perfectionism begins with harsh, perfectionistic parenting. There's nothing wrong with having parents who expect a lot of you—if they are also emotionally supportive. However, parents who are demanding and highly critical may leave a student feeling that nothing she or he does is ever quite good enough. As already noted, this is a recipe for self-doubt and depression.

Authentic Navajo rugs always have a flaw in their intricate designs. Navajo weavers intentionally make a "mistake" in each rug as a reminder that humans are not perfect. There is a lesson in this: It is not always necessary, or even desirable, to be "perfect." To learn from your experiences you must feel free to make mistakes (Castro & Rice, 2003). Success, in the long run, is more often based on seeking "excellence," rather than "perfection" (Enns, Cox, & Clara, 2005).

characteristics are inherited. So are many of our behavioral tendencies (Bouchard, 2004; Rose, 1995). Genetic studies have shown that intelligence, some mental disorders, temperament, and other complex qualities are influenced by heredity. In view of such findings, we also might wonder, "Do genes affect personality?"

Wouldn't comparing the personalities of identical twins help answer the question? It would indeed—especially if the twins were separated at birth or soon after.

Twins and Traits

For two decades, psychologists at the University of Minnesota have been studying identical twins who grew up in different homes. Medical and psychological tests reveal that reunited twins are very much alike, even when they are reared apart (● Figure 14.5) (Bouchard, 2004; Bouchard et al., 1990). Typically, they are astonishingly similar in appearance, voice quality, facial gestures, hand movements, and nervous tics, such as nail biting. Separated twins also tend to have similar talents. If one twin excels at art, music, dance, drama, or athletics, the other is likely to as well—despite wide differences in childhood environment. However, as "The Minnesota Twins" explains, it's wise to be cautious about some reports of extraordinary similarities in reunited twins.

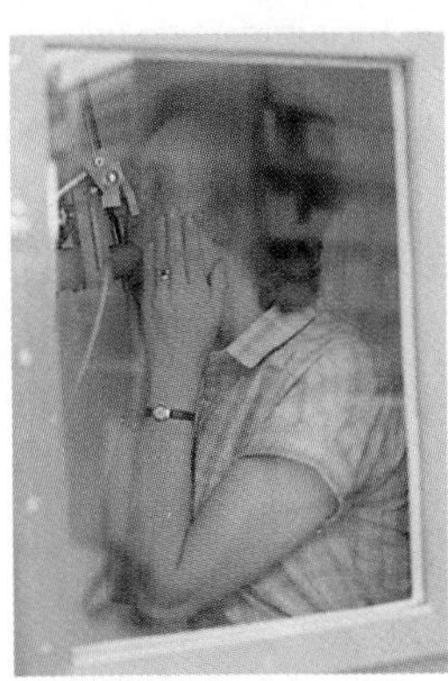

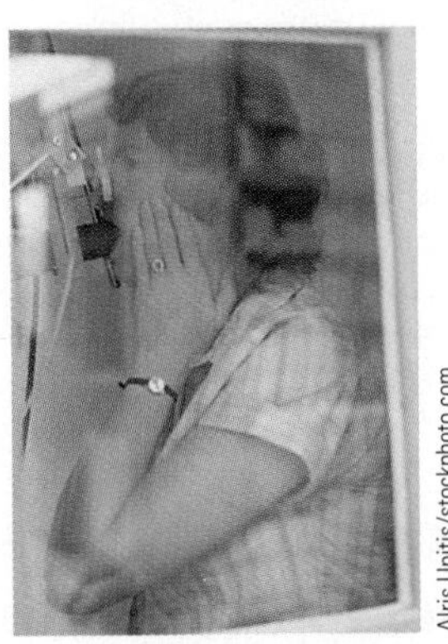

Alris Upitis/stockphoto.com

● Figure 14.5 Reunited identical twins Terry and Margaret undergo lung function tests at the University of Minnesota. Researchers collected a wide range of medical and psychological data for each set of twins.

Summary

Studies of twins make it clear that heredity has a sizable effect on each of us. All told, it seems reasonable to conclude that heredity is responsible for about 25 to 50 percent of the variation in many personality traits (Jang & Livesley, 1998; Loehlin et al., 1998). Notice, however, that the same figures imply personality is shaped as much, or more, by environment as it is by heredity.

Each personality is a unique blend of heredity and environment, biology and culture. We are not—thank goodness—genetically programmed robots whose behavior and personality traits are "wired in" for life. Where you go in life is the result of the choices you make. To a degree, these choices are influenced by inherited tendencies (Saudino et al., 1997). However, they are not merely a product of your genes (Funder, 2004; Rose, 1995).

Trait-situation interaction The influence that external settings or circumstances have on the expression of personality traits.

Behavioral genetics The study of inherited behavioral traits and tendencies.

CRITICAL THINKING

The Minnesota Twins

Many reunited twins in the Minnesota study have displayed similarities far beyond what would be expected on the basis of heredity. The "Jim twins," James Lewis and James Springer, provide a good example. Both Jims had married and divorced women named Linda. Both had undergone police training. One named his first-born son James Allan, the other named *his* first-born son James Alan. Both drove Chevrolets and vacationed at the same beach each summer. Both listed carpentry and mechanical drawing among their hobbies. Both had built benches around trees in their yards. And so forth (Holden, 1980).

Does heredity actually control such details of our lives? Are there child-naming genes and bench-building genes? Of course, the idea is preposterous. How, then, do we explain the eerie similarities in separated twins' lives? Separating hereditary from environmental influences on personality is just not that easy.

The astute reader will realize that completely unrelated persons can also share "amazing" similarities. One study, for instance, compared twins to unrelated pairs of students. The unrelated pairs, who were the same age and sex, were almost as alike as the twins. They had highly similar political beliefs, musical interests, religious preferences, job histories, hobbies, favorite foods, and so on (Wyatt et al., 1984). Why were the unrelated students so similar? Basically, it's because people of the same age and sex live in the same historical times and select from similar societal options.

Imagine that you were separated at birth from a twin brother or sister. If you were reunited with your twin today, what would you do? Quite likely, you would spend the next several days comparing every imaginable detail of your lives. Under such circumstances it is virtually certain that you and your twin would notice and compile a long list of similarities. ("Wow! I use the same brand of toothpaste you do!") Yet two unrelated persons of the same age, sex, and race could probably rival your list—*if* they were as motivated to find similarities.

To summarize, many of the seemingly "astounding" coincidences shared by reunited twins may be a special case of the fallacy of positive instances, described in Chapter 1. Similarities blaze brightly in the memories of reunited twins, whereas differences are ignored.

KNOWLEDGE BUILDER

Personality and Trait Theories

REFLECT

See if you can define or describe the following terms in your own words: personality, character, temperament, trait, type, self-concept, self-esteem.

List six or seven traits that best describe your personality. Which system of traits seems to best match your list, Allport's, Cattell's, or the Big Five?

Choose a prominent trait from your list. Does its expression seem to be influenced by specific situations? Do you think that heredity contributed to the trait?

LEARNING CHECK

1. When someone's personality has been evaluated, we are making a judgment about his or her
   a. temperament c. extroversion
   b. character d. self-esteem
2. A personality type is usually defined by the presence of
   a. all five personality dimensions c. several specific traits
   b. a stable self concept d. a source trait
3. The research methods of ______________ have been used to study the extent to which we inherit personality characteristics.
   a. behavioral genetics c. factor analysis
   b. social learning theory d. trait profiling
4. Central traits are those shared by most members of a culture. T or F?
5. Cattell believes that clusters of ______________ traits reveal the presence of underlying ______________ traits.
6. Which of the following is *not* one of the Big Five personality factors?
   a. submissiveness c. extroversion
   b. agreeableness d. neuroticism
7. To understand personality, it is wise to remember that traits and situations ______________________________ to determine our behavior.

CRITICAL THINKING

8. In what way would memory contribute to the formation of an accurate or inaccurate self-image?
9. Are situations equally powerful in their impact on behavior?

Answers: 1. b 2. c 3. a 4. F 5. surface, source 6. a 7. interact 8. As discussed in Chapter 8, memory is highly selective, and long-term memories are often distorted by recent information. Such properties add to the moldability of self-concept. 9. No. Circumstances can have a strong or weak influence. In some situations, almost everyone will act the same, no matter what their personality traits may be. In other situations, traits may be of greater importance.

Psychoanalytic Theory—Id Came to Me in a Dream

Psychodynamic theorists are not content with studying traits. Instead, they try to probe under the surface of personality—to learn what drives, conflicts, and energies animate us. Psychodynamic

TABLE 14.2

Key Freudian Concepts

Anal stage The psychosexual stage corresponding roughly to the period of toilet training (ages 1 to 3).

Anal-expulsive personality A disorderly, destructive, cruel, or messy person.

Anal-retentive personality A person who is obstinate, stingy, or compulsive, and who generally has difficulty "letting go."

Conscience The part of the superego that causes guilt when its standards are not met.

Conscious Region of the mind that includes all mental contents a person is aware of at any given moment.

Ego The executive part of personality that directs rational behavior.

Ego ideal The part of the superego representing ideal behavior; a source of pride when its standards are met.

Electra conflict A girl's sexual attraction to her father and feelings of rivalry with her mother.

Erogenous zone Any body area that produces pleasurable sensations.

Eros Freud's name for the "life instincts."

Fixation A lasting conflict developed as a result of frustration or overindulgence.

Genital stage Period of full psychosexual development, marked by the attainment of mature adult sexuality.

Id The primitive part of personality that remains unconscious, supplies energy, and demands pleasure.

Latency According to Freud, a period in childhood when psychosexual development is more or less interrupted.

Libido In Freudian theory, the force, primarily pleasure oriented, that energizes the personality.

Moral anxiety Apprehension felt when thoughts, impulses, or actions conflict with the superego's standards.

Neurotic anxiety Apprehension felt when the ego struggles to control id impulses.

Oedipus conflict A boy's sexual attraction to his mother, and feelings of rivalry with his father.

Oral stage The period when infants are preoccupied with the mouth as a source of pleasure and means of expression.

Oral-aggressive personality A person who uses the mouth to express hostility by shouting, cursing, biting, and so forth. Also, one who actively exploits others.

Oral-dependent personality A person who wants to passively receive attention, gifts, love, and so forth.

Phallic personality A person who is vain, exhibitionistic, sensitive, and narcissistic.

Phallic stage The psychosexual stage (roughly ages 3 to 6) when a child is preoccupied with the genitals.

Pleasure principle A desire for immediate satisfaction of wishes, desires, or needs.

Preconscious An area of the mind containing information that can be voluntarily brought to awareness.

Psyche The mind, mental life, and personality as a whole.

Psychosexual stages The oral, anal, phallic, and genital stages, during which various personality traits are formed.

Reality principle Delaying action (or pleasure) until it is appropriate.

Superego A judge or censor for thoughts and actions.

Thanatos The death instinct postulated by Freud.

Unconscious The region of the mind that is beyond awareness, especially impulses and desires not directly known to a person.

theorists believe that many of our actions are based on hidden, or unconscious, thoughts, needs, and emotions.

Psychoanalytic theory, the best-known psychodynamic approach, grew out of the work of Sigmund Freud, a Viennese physician. As a doctor, Freud was fascinated by patients whose problems seemed to be more emotional than physical. From about 1890 until he died in 1939, Freud evolved a theory of personality that deeply influenced modern thought. Let's consider some of its main features (Jacobs, 2003).

The Structure of Personality

How did Freud view personality? Freud's model portrays personality as a dynamic system directed by three mental structures, the **id**, the **ego**, and the **superego.** According to Freud, most behavior involves activity of all three systems. (Freud's theory includes a large number of concepts. For your convenience, they are defined in ■ Table 14.2 rather than in page margins.)

The Id

The id is made up of innate biological instincts and urges. It is self-serving, irrational, impulsive, and totally unconscious. The id operates on the **pleasure principle.** That is, it seeks to freely express pleasure-seeking urges of all kinds. If we were solely under control of the id, the world would be chaotic beyond belief.

The id acts as a well of energy for the entire **psyche** (SIGH-key), or personality. This energy, called **libido** (lih-BEE-doe), flows from the **life instincts** (or **Eros**). According to Freud, libido underlies our efforts to survive, as well as our sexual desires and pleasure seeking. Freud also described a **death instinct. Thanatos,** as he called it, produces aggressive and destructive urges. Freud offered humanity's long history of wars and violence as evidence of such

Psychoanalytic theory Freudian theory of personality that emphasizes unconscious forces and conflicts.

Freud considered personality an expression of two conflicting forces, life instincts and the death instinct. Both are symbolized in this drawing by Allen Gilbert. (If you don't immediately see the death symbolism, stand farther from the drawing.)

urges. Most id energies, then, are aimed at discharging tensions related to sex and aggression.

The Ego

The ego is sometimes described as the "executive," because it directs energies supplied by the id. The id is like a blind king or queen whose power is awesome but who must rely on others to carry out orders. The id can only form mental images of things it desires. The ego wins power to direct behavior by relating the desires of the id to external reality.

Are there other differences between the ego and the id? Yes. Recall that the id operates on the pleasure principle. The ego, in contrast, is guided by the **reality principle.** That is, the ego delays action until it is practical or appropriate. The ego is the system of thinking, planning, problem solving, and deciding. It is in conscious control of the personality.

The Superego

What is the role of the superego? The superego acts as a judge or censor for the thoughts and actions of the ego. One part of the superego, called the **conscience,** reflects actions for which a person has been punished. When standards of the conscience are not met, you are punished internally by guilt *feelings.*

A second part of the superego is the **ego ideal.** The ego ideal reflects all behavior one's parents approved of or rewarded. The ego ideal is a source of goals and aspirations. When its standards are met, we feel *pride.*

The superego acts as an "internalized parent" to bring behavior under control. In Freudian terms, a person with a weak superego will be a delinquent, criminal, or antisocial personality. In contrast, an overly strict or harsh superego may cause inhibition, rigidity, or unbearable guilt.

The Dynamics of Personality

How do the id, ego, and superego interact? Freud didn't picture the id, ego, and superego as parts of the brain or as "little people" running the human psyche. Instead, they are conflicting mental processes. Freud theorized a delicate balance of power among the three. For example, the id's demands for immediate pleasure often clash with the superego's moral restrictions. Perhaps an example will help clarify the role of each part of the personality.

Freud in a Nutshell

Let's say you are sexually attracted to an acquaintance. The id clamors for immediate satisfaction of its sexual desires, but is opposed by the superego (which finds the very thought of sex shocking). The id says, "Go for it!" The superego icily replies, "Never even think that again!" And what does the ego say? The ego says, "I have a plan!"

Of course, this is a drastic simplification, but it does capture the core of Freudian thinking. To reduce tension, the ego could begin actions leading to friendship, romance, courtship, and marriage. If the id is unusually powerful, the ego may give in and attempt a seduction. If the superego prevails, the ego may be forced to *displace* or *sublimate* sexual energies to other activities (sports, music, dancing, push-ups, cold showers). According to Freud, internal struggles and rechanneled energies typify most personality functioning.

Is the ego always caught in the middle? Basically yes, and the pressures on it can be intense. In addition to meeting the conflicting demands of the id and superego, the overworked ego must deal with external reality.

According to Freud, you feel anxiety when your ego is threatened or overwhelmed. Impulses from the id cause **neurotic anxiety** when the ego can barely keep them under control. Threats of punishment from the superego cause **moral anxiety.** Each person develops habitual ways of calming these anxieties, and many resort to using *ego-defense mechanisms* to lessen internal conflicts. Defense mechanisms are mental processes that deny, distort, or otherwise block out sources of threat and anxiety.

Levels of Awareness

Like other psychodynamic theorists, Freud believed that our behavior often expresses unconscious (or hidden) forces. The **unconscious** holds repressed memories and emotions, plus the

BRIDGES

The ego-defense mechanisms that Freud identified are used as a form of protection against stress, anxiety, and threatening events.

See Chapter 15, pages 510–512.

instinctual drives of the id. Interestingly, modern scientists have found that the brain's limbic system does, in fact, seem to trigger unconscious emotions and memories (LeDoux, 2000).

Even though they are beyond awareness, unconscious thoughts, feelings, or urges may slip into behavior in disguised or symbolic form. For example, if you meet someone you would like to know better, you may unconsciously leave a book or a jacket at that person's house to ensure another meeting.

Earlier you said that the id is completely unconscious. Are the actions of the ego and superego unconscious? At times, yes, but they also operate on two other levels of awareness (● Figure 14.6). The **conscious** level includes everything you are aware of at a given moment, including thoughts, perceptions, feelings, and memories. The **preconscious** contains material that can be easily brought to awareness. If you stop to think about a time when you felt angry or rejected, you will be moving this memory from the preconscious to the conscious level of awareness.

The superego's activities also reveal differing levels of awareness. At times we consciously try to live up to moral codes or standards. Yet at other times a person may feel guilty without knowing why. Psychoanalytic theory credits such guilt to unconscious workings of the superego. Indeed, Freud believed that the unconscious origins of many feelings cannot be easily brought to awareness.

Personality Development

How does psychoanalytic theory explain personality development? Freud theorized that the core of personality is formed before age 6 in a series of **psychosexual stages.** Freud believed that erotic childhood urges have lasting effects on development. As you might expect, this is a controversial idea. However, Freud used the terms *sex* and *erotic* very broadly to refer to many physical sources of pleasure.

A Freudian Fable?

Freud identified four psychosexual stages, the **oral, anal, phallic,** and **genital.** (He also described a period of "latency" between the phallic and genital stages. Latency is explained in a moment.) At each stage, a different part of the body becomes a child's primary **erogenous zone** (an area capable of producing pleasure). Each area then serves as the main source of pleasure, frustration, and self-expression. Freud believed that many adult personality traits can be traced to **fixations** in one or more of the stages.

What is a fixation? A fixation is an unresolved conflict or emotional hang-up caused by overindulgence or by frustration. As we describe the psychosexual stages you'll see why Freud considered fixations important.

The Oral Stage

During the first year of life, most of an infant's pleasure comes from stimulation of the mouth. If a child is overfed or frustrated, oral traits may be created. Adult expressions of oral needs include gum chewing, nail biting, smoking, kissing, overeating, and alcoholism.

What if there is an oral fixation? Fixation early in the oral stage produces an **oral-dependent personality.** Oral-dependent persons are gullible (they swallow things easily!) and passive and need lots of attention (they want to be mothered and showered with gifts). Frustrations later in the oral stage may cause aggression, often in the form of biting. Fixations here create cynical, **oral-aggressive** adults who exploit others. They also like to argue ("biting sarcasm" is their forte!).

The Anal Stage

Between the ages of 1 and 3, the child's attention shifts to the process of elimination. When parents attempt toilet training, the child can gain approval or express rebellion or aggression by "holding on" or by "letting go." Therefore, harsh or lenient toilet training can cause an anal fixation that may lock such responses into personality. Freud described the **anal-retentive** (holding-on) **personality** as obstinate, stingy, orderly, and compulsively clean.

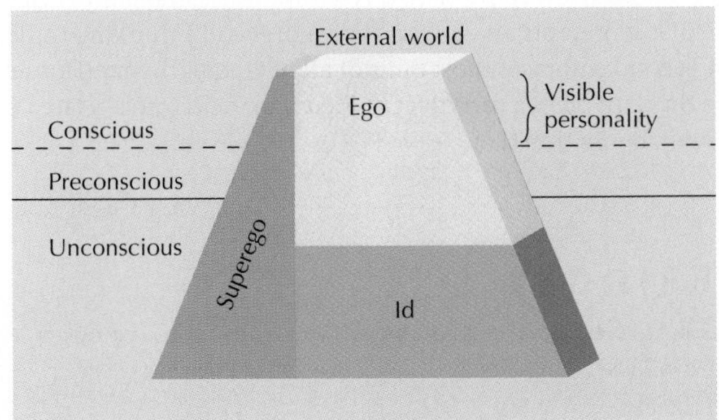

● **Figure 14.6** The approximate relationship between the id, ego, and superego, and the levels of awareness.

Was Freud's ever-present cigar a sign of an oral fixation? Was it a phallic symbol? Was it both? Or was it neither? An inability to say for sure is one of the shortcomings of psychoanalytic theory.

The **anal-expulsive** (letting-go) **personality** is disorderly, destructive, cruel, or messy.

The Phallic Stage

Adult traits of the **phallic personality** are vanity, exhibitionism, sensitive pride, and narcissism (self-love). Freud theorized that phallic fixations develop between the ages of 3 and 6. At this time, increased sexual interest causes the child to be physically attracted to the parent of the opposite sex. In males this attraction leads to an **Oedipus conflict.** In it, the boy feels a rivalry with his father for the affection of his mother. Freud believed that the male child feels threatened by the father (specifically, the boy fears castration). To ease his anxieties, the boy must **identify** with the father. Their rivalry ends when the boy seeks to become more like his father. As he does, he begins to accept the father's values and forms a conscience.

What about the female child? Girls experience an **Electra conflict.** In this case, the girl loves her father and competes with her mother. However, according to Freud, the girl identifies with the mother more gradually.

Freud believed that females already feel castrated. Because of this, they are less driven to identify with their mothers than boys are with their fathers. This, he said, is less effective in creating a conscience. This particular part of Freudian thought has been thoroughly (and rightfully) rejected by modern feminists. It is probably best understood as a reflection of the male-dominated times in which Freud lived.

Latency

According to Freud there is a period of *latency* from age 6 to puberty. Latency is not actually a stage. Rather, it is a quiet time during which psychosexual development is dormant. Freud's belief that psychosexual development is "on hold" at this time is hard to accept. Nevertheless, Freud saw latency as a relatively quiet time compared to the stormy first 6 years of life.

The Genital Stage

At puberty an upswing in sexual energies activates all the unresolved conflicts of earlier years. This upsurge, according to Freud, is the reason why adolescence can be filled with emotion and turmoil. The genital stage begins at puberty. It is marked, during adolescence, by a growing capacity for responsible social–sexual relationships. The genital stage ends with a mature capacity for love and the realization of full adult sexuality.

Critical Comments

As bizarre as Freud's theory might seem, it has been influential for several reasons. First, it pioneered the idea that the first years of life help shape adult personality. Second, it identified feeding, toilet training, and early sexual experiences as critical events in personality formation. Third, Freud was among the first to propose that development proceeds through a series of stages.

Is the Freudian view of development widely accepted? Few psychologists wholeheartedly embrace Freud's theory today. In some cases Freud was clearly wrong. His portrayal of the elementary school years (latency) as free from sexuality and unimportant for personality development is hard to believe. His idea of the role of a stern or threatening father in the development of a strong conscience in males has also been challenged. Studies show that a son is more likely to develop a strong conscience if his father is affectionate and accepting, rather than stern and punishing. Freud also overemphasized sexuality in personality development. Other motives and cognitive factors are of equal importance.

Freud has been criticized for his views of patients who believed they were sexually molested as children. Freud assumed that such events were merely childhood fantasies. This view led to a long-standing tendency to disbelieve children who have been molested and women who have been raped (Brannon, 1996).

Another important criticism is that Freud's concepts are almost impossible to verify scientifically. The theory provides numerous ways to explain almost any thought, action, or feeling *after* it has occurred. However, it leads to few predictions, which makes its claims difficult to test. Although more criticisms of Freud could be listed, the fact remains that there is an element of truth to much of what he said (Jacobs, 2003). Because of this, some clinical psychologists continue to regard Freudian theory as a useful way to think about human problems.

Psychodynamic Theories—Freud's Descendants

Freud's ideas quickly attracted a brilliant following. Just as rapidly, the importance Freud placed on instinctual drives and sexuality caused many to disagree with him. Those who stayed close to the core of Freud's thinking are called *neo-Freudians* (*neo* means "new"). **Neo-Freudians** accepted the broad features of Freud's theory but revised parts of it. Some of the better-known neo-Freudians are Karen Horney, Anna Freud (Freud's daughter), Otto Rank, and Erich Fromm. Other early followers broke away more completely from Freud and created their own opposing theories. This group includes people such as Alfred Adler, Harry Sullivan, and Carl Jung.

The full story of other psychodynamic theories must await your first course in personality. For now, let's sample three views. The first represents an early rejection of Freud's thinking (Adler). The second embraces most but not all of Freud's theory (Horney). The third involves a carryover of Freudian ideas into a related but unique theory (Jung).

BRIDGES

Erik Erikson's psycho*social* stages, which cover development from birth to old age, are a modern offshoot of Freudian thinking.

See Chapter 4, pages 122–124.

Alfred Adler (1870–1937)

Adler broke away from Freud because he disagreed with Freud's emphasis on the unconscious, on instinctual drives, and on the importance of sexuality. Adler believed that we are social creatures governed by social urges, not by biological instincts (Shulman, 2004). In Adler's view, the main driving force in personality is a **striving for superiority.** This striving, he said, is a struggle to overcome imperfections, an upward drive for competence, completion, and mastery of shortcomings.

What motivates "striving for superiority"? Adler believed that everyone experiences feelings of inferiority. This occurs mainly because we begin life as small, weak, and relatively powerless children surrounded by larger and more powerful adults. Feelings of inferiority may also come from our personal limitations. The struggle for superiority arises from such feelings.

Although everyone strives for superiority, each person tries to **compensate** for different limitations, and each chooses a different pathway to superiority. Adler believed that this situation creates a unique **style of life** (or personality pattern) for each individual. According to Adler the core of each person's style of life is formed by age 5. (Adler also believed that valuable clues to a person's style of life are revealed by the earliest memory that can be recalled. You might find it interesting to search back to your earliest memory and contemplate what it tells you.) However, later in his life Adler began to emphasize the existence of a **creative self.** By this he meant that humans create their personalities through choices and experiences.

Karen Horney (1885–1952)

Karen Horney (HORN-eye) remained faithful to most of Freud's theory, but she resisted his more mechanistic, biological, and instinctive ideas. For example, as a woman, Horney rejected Freud's claim that "anatomy is destiny." This view, woven into Freudian psychology, held that males are dominant or superior to females. Horney was among the first to challenge the obvious male bias in Freud's thinking (Eckardt, 2005).

Horney also disagreed with Freud about the causes of neurosis. Freud held that neurotic (anxiety-ridden) individuals are struggling with forbidden id drives that they fear they cannot control. Horney's view was that a core of **basic anxiety** occurs when people feel isolated and helpless in a hostile world. These feelings, she believed, are rooted in childhood. Trouble occurs when an individual tries to control basic anxiety by exaggerating a single mode of interacting with others.

What do you mean by "mode of interacting"? According to Horney, each of us can move *toward* others (by depending on them for love, support, or friendship), we can move *away* from others (by withdrawing, acting like a "loner," or being "strong" and independent), or we can move *against* others (by attacking, competing with, or seeking power over them). Horney believed that emotional health reflects a balance in moving toward, away from, and against others. In her view, emotional problems tend to lock people into overuse of one of the three modes—an insight that remains valuable today.

Carl Jung (1875–1961)

Carl Jung was a student of Freud's, but the two parted ways as Jung began to develop his own ideas. Like Freud, Jung called the conscious part of the personality the ego. However, he further noted that a *persona,* or "mask" exists between the ego and the outside world. The **persona** is the "public self" presented to others. It is most apparent when we adopt particular roles or hide our deeper feelings. As mentioned earlier, Jung believed that actions of the ego may reflect attitudes of *introversion* (in which energy is mainly directed inward), or of *extroversion* (in which energy is mainly directed outward).

Was Jung's view of the unconscious the same as Freud's? Jung used the term *personal unconscious* to refer to what Freud simply called the unconscious (Mayer, 2002). The **personal unconscious** is a mental storehouse for a single individual's experiences, feelings, and memories. But Jung also described a deeper **collective unconscious,** or mental storehouse for unconscious ideas and images shared by all humans. Jung believed that, from the beginning of time, all humans have had experiences with birth, death, power, god figures, mother and father figures, animals, the earth, energy, evil, rebirth, and so on. According to Jung, such universals create **archetypes** (ARE-keh-types: original ideas, images, or patterns).

Archetypes, found in the collective unconscious, are unconscious images that cause us to respond emotionally to symbols of birth, death, energy, animals, evil, and the like (Maloney, 1999). Jung believed that he detected symbols of such archetypes in the art, religion, myths, and dreams of every culture and age. Let us say, for instance, that a man dreams of dancing with his sister. To Freud this would probably be a sign of hidden incestuous feelings. To Jung the image of the sister might represent an unexpressed feminine side of the man's personality and the dream might rep-

Neo-Freudian A theorist who has revised Freud's theory, while still accepting some of its basic concepts.

Striving for superiority According to Adler, this basic drive propels us toward perfection.

Compensation Any attempt to overcome feelings of inadequacy or inferiority.

Style of life The pattern of personality and behavior that defines the pathway each person takes through life.

Creative self The "artist" in each of us that creates a unique identity and style of life.

Basic anxiety A primary form of anxiety that arises from living in a hostile world.

Persona The "mask" or public self presented to others.

Personal unconscious A mental storehouse for a single individual's unconscious thoughts.

Collective unconscious A mental storehouse for unconscious ideas and images shared by all humans.

Archetype A universal idea, image, or pattern, found in the collective unconscious.

resent the cosmic dance that intertwines "maleness" and "femaleness" in all lives.

Are some archetypes more important than others? Two particularly important archetypes are the **anima** (female principle) and the **animus** (male principle). In men, the anima is an unconscious, idealized image of women. This image is based, in part, on real experiences with women (the man's mother, sister, friends). However, the experiences men have had with women throughout history form the true core of the anima. The reverse is true of women, who possess an animus or idealized image of men. The anima in males and the animus in females enable us to relate to members of the opposite sex. The anima and animus also make it possible for people to learn to express both "masculine" and "feminine" sides of their personalities.

Jung regarded the *self archetype* as the most important of all. The **self archetype** represents unity. Its existence causes a gradual movement toward balance, wholeness, and harmony within the personality. Jung felt that we become richer and more completely human when a balance is achieved between the conscious and unconscious, the anima and animus, thinking and feeling, sensing and intuiting, the persona and the ego, introversion and extroversion.

Was Jung talking about self-actualization? Essentially he was. Jung was the first to use the term *self-actualization* to describe a striving for completion and unity. He believed that the self archetype is symbolized in every culture by **mandalas** (magic circles) of one kind or another.

Jung's theory may not be scientific, but clearly he was a man of genius and vision. If you would like to know more about Jung and his ideas, a good starting place is his autobiography, *Memories, Dreams, Reflections* (Jung, 1961).

Alison Wright/Stock, Boston

Jung regarded circular designs as symbols of the self-archetype and representations of unity, balance, and completion within the personality.

KNOWLEDGE BUILDER

Psychodynamic Theories

REFLECT

Try to think of at least one time when your thoughts, feelings, or actions seemed to reflect the workings of each of the following: the id, the ego, and the superego.

Do you know anyone who seems to have oral, anal, or phallic personality traits? Do you think Freud's concept of fixation explains their characteristics?

Do any of your personal experiences support the existence of an Oedipus conflict or an Electra conflict? If not, is it possible that you have repressed feelings related to these conflicts?

If you had to summarize your style of life in one sentence, what would it be?

Which of Horney's three modes of interacting do you think you rely on the most? Do you overuse one of the modes?

Think of the images you have seen in art, mythology, movies, and popular culture. Do any seem to represent Jungian archetypes—especially the self archetype?

LEARNING CHECK

1. List the three divisions of personality postulated by Freud. ________, ________, ________
2. Which division is totally unconscious? ________
3. Which division is responsible for moral anxiety? ________
4. Freud proposed the existence of a life instinct known as Thanatos. T or F?
5. Freud's view of personality development is based on the concept of ________ stages.
6. Arrange these stages in the proper order: phallic, anal, genital, oral. ________
7. Freud considered the anal-retentive personality to be obstinate and stingy. T or F?
8. Karen Horney theorized that people control basic anxiety by moving toward, away from, and ________ others.
9. Carl Jung's theory states that archetypes, which are found in the personal unconscious, exert an influence on behavior. T or F?

CRITICAL THINKING

10. Many adults would find it embarrassing or humiliating to drink from a baby bottle. Can you explain why?

Answers: **1.** id, ego, superego **2.** id **3.** superego **4.** F **5.** psychosexual **6.** oral, anal, phallic, genital **7.** T **8.** against **9.** F **10.** A psychoanalytic theorist would say that it is because the bottle rekindles oral conflicts and feelings of vulnerability and dependence.

Learning Theories of Personality—Habit I Seen You Before?

After exploring psychodynamic theories, you might be relieved to know that behavioral theorists explain personality through straightforward concepts, such as learning, reinforcement, and imitation. Behavioral and social learning theories are based on scientific research, which makes them powerful ways of looking at personality.

How do behaviorists approach personality? According to some critics, as if people are robots like Data of *Star Trek* fame. Actually, the behaviorist position is not nearly that mechanistic, and its value is well established. Behaviorists have shown repeatedly that children can *learn* things like kindness, hostility, generosity, or destructiveness. What does this have to do with personality? Everything, according to the behavioral viewpoint.

Behavioral personality theories emphasize that personality is no more (or less) than a collection of learned behavior patterns. Personality, like other learned behavior, is acquired through classical and operant conditioning, observational learning, reinforcement, extinction, generalization, and discrimination. When Mother says, "It's not nice to make mud pies with Mommy's blender. If we want to grow up to be a big girl, we won't do it again, will we?" she serves as a model and in other ways shapes her daughter's personality.

Strict **learning theorists** reject the idea that personality is made up of traits. They would assert, for instance, that there is no such thing as a trait of "honesty" (Mischel, 2004).

Certainly some people are honest while others are not. How can honesty not be a trait? Learning theorists recognize that some people are honest *more often* than others. But knowing this does not allow us to predict whether a person will be honest in a specific situation. It would not be unusual, for example, to find that a person honored for returning a lost wallet had cheated on a test, bought a term paper, or broken the speed limit. If you were to ask a learning theorist, "Are you an honest person?" the reply might be, "In what situation?"

As you can see, learning theorists are interested in the **situational determinants** (external causes) of our actions. A good example of how situations can influence behavior is a study in which people were intentionally overpaid for doing an assigned task. Under normal circumstances, 80 percent kept the extra money without mentioning it. But as few as 17 percent were dishonest if the situation was altered. For instance, if people thought the money was coming out of the pocket of the person doing the study, far fewer were dishonest (Bersoff, 1999). Thus, situations always interact with our prior learning history to activate behavior.

fotostock/SuperStock

Freud believed that aggressive urges are "instinctual." In contrast, behavioral theories assume that personal characteristics such as aggressiveness are learned. Is this boy's aggression the result of observational learning, harsh punishment, or prior reinforcement?

How Situations Affect Behavior

Situations vary greatly in their impact. Some are powerful. Others are trivial and have little effect on behavior. The more powerful the situation, the easier it is to see what is meant by situational determinants. For example, each of the following situations would undoubtedly have a strong influence on behavior: an armed terrorist walks into a supermarket; you accidentally sit on a lighted cigarette; you find your lover in bed with your best friend. Yet even these situations could provoke very different reactions from different personalities. That's why behavior is always a product of both prior learning and the situations in which we find ourselves (Mischel & Shoda, 1998).

Ultimately, what is predictable about personality is that we respond in consistent ways to certain *types of situations*. Consider, for example, two people who are easily angered: One person might get angry when she is delayed (for example, in traffic or a checkout line), but not when she misplaces something at home; the other person might get angry whenever she misplaces things, but not when she is delayed. Overall, the two women are equally prone to anger, but their anger tends to occur in different patterns and different types of situations (Mischel, 2004).

Personality = Behavior

How do learning theorists view the structure of personality? The behavioral view of personality can be illustrated with an early theory proposed by John Dollard and Neal Miller (1950). In their view, **habits** (learned behavior patterns) make up the structure of personality. As for the dynamics of personality, habits are governed by four elements of learning: *drive, cue, response,* and *reward.*

Anima An archetype representing the female principle.

Animus An archetype representing the male principle.

Self archetype An unconscious image representing, unity, wholeness, completion, and balance.

Mandala A circular design representing balance, unity, and completion.

Behavioral personality theory Any model of personality that emphasizes learning and observable behavior.

Learning theorist A psychologist interested in the ways that learning shapes behavior and explains personality.

Situational determinants External conditions that strongly influence behavior.

Habit A deeply ingrained, learned pattern of behavior.

A **drive** is any stimulus strong enough to goad a person to action (such as hunger, pain, lust, frustration, or fear). **Cues** are signals from the environment. These signals guide **responses** (actions) so that they are most likely to bring about **reward** (positive reinforcement).

How does that relate to personality? Let's say a child named Kindra is frustrated by her older brother Kelvin, who takes a toy from her. Kindra could respond in several ways: She could throw a temper tantrum, hit Kelvin, tell Mother, and so forth. The response she chooses is guided by available cues and the previous effects of each response. If telling Mother has paid off in the past, and the mother is present, telling again may be her immediate response. If a different set of cues exists (if Mother is absent or if Kelvin looks particularly menacing), Kindra may select some other response. To an outside observer, Kindra's actions seem to reflect her personality. To a learning theorist, they simply express the combined effects of drive, cue, response, and reward.

Doesn't this analysis leave out a lot? Yes. Learning theorists first set out to provide a simple, clear model of personality. But in recent years they have had to face a fact that they originally tended to overlook. The fact is this: People think. The new breed of behavioral psychologists—who include perception, thinking, expectations, and other mental events in their views—are called social learning theorists. Learning principles, modeling, thought patterns, perceptions, expectations, beliefs, goals, emotions, and social relationships are combined in **social learning theory** to explain personality (Mischel & Shoda, 1998).

Social Learning Theory

Someone trips you. How do you respond? Your reaction probably depends on whether you think it was planned or an accident. It is not enough to know the setting in which a person responds. We also need to know the person's **psychological situation** (how the person interprets or defines the situation). As another example, let's say you score low on an exam. Do you consider it a challenge to work harder, a sign that you should drop the class, or an excuse to get drunk? Again, your interpretation is important.

Our actions are affected by an **expectancy,** or anticipation, that making a response will lead to reinforcement. To continue the example, if working harder has paid off in the past, it is a likely reaction to a low test score. But to predict your response, we would also have to know if you *expect* your efforts to pay off in the present situation. In fact, expected reinforcement may be more important than actual past reinforcement. And what about the *value* you attach to grades, school success, or personal ability? The concept of **reinforcement value** states that we attach different subjective values to various activities or rewards. This, too, must be taken into account to understand personality.

BRIDGES

Behavioral theories have contributed greatly to the creation of therapies for various psychological problems and disorders.

See the discussion of behavior therapy in Chapter 17, pages 578–581.

Self-Efficacy

An ability to control your own life is the essence of what it means to be human. Because of this, Albert Bandura believes that one of the most important expectancies we develop concerns **self-efficacy** (EF-uh-keh-see: a capacity for producing a desired result). You're attracted to someone in your anthropology class. Will you ask him or her out? You're thinking about learning to snowboard. Will you try it this winter? You're beginning to consider a career in psychology. Will you take the courses you need to get into graduate school? You'd like to exercise more on the weekends. Will you join a hiking club? In these and countless other situations, efficacy beliefs play a key role in shaping our lives by influencing the activities and environments we choose to get into (Bandura, 2001).

Self-Reinforcement

One more idea deserves mention. At times, we all evaluate our actions and may reward ourselves with special privileges or treats for "good behavior." With this in mind, social learning theory adds the concept of self-reinforcement to the behavioristic view. **Self-reinforcement** refers to praising or rewarding yourself for having made a particular response (such as completing a school assignment). Thus, habits of self-praise and self-blame become an important part of personality. In fact, self-reinforcement can be thought of as the social learning theorist's counterpart to the superego.

Rate Yourself: Self-Reinforcement

Check the statements in the list that apply to you.

__ I often think positive thoughts about myself.
__ I frequently meet standards that I set for myself.
__ I try not to blame myself when things go wrong.
__ I usually don't get upset when I make mistakes because I learn from them.
__ I can get satisfaction out of what I do even if it's not perfect.

David Young-Wolff/PhotoEdit

Through self-reinforcement we reward ourselves for personal achievements and other "good" behavior.

__ When I make mistakes I take time to reassure myself.
__ I don't think talking about what you've done right is too boastful.
__ Praising yourself is healthy and normal.
__ I don't think I have to be upset every time I make a mistake.
__ My feelings of self-confidence and self-esteem stay pretty steady.

People who agree with most of these statements tend to have high rates of self-reinforcement (Heiby, 1983).

Self-reinforcement is closely related to high self-esteem. The reverse is also true: Mildly depressed college students tend to have low rates of self-reinforcement. It is not known if low self-reinforcement leads to depression, or the reverse. In either case, self-reinforcement is associated with less depression and greater life satisfaction (Seybolt & Wagner, 1997; Wilkinson, 1997). From a behavioral viewpoint, there is value in learning to be "good to yourself."

Behavioristic View of Development

How do learning theorists account for personality development? Many of Freud's ideas can be restated in terms of learning theory. Dollard and Miller (1950) agree with Freud that the first 6 years are crucial for personality development, but for different reasons. Rather than thinking in terms of psychosexual urges and fixations, they ask, "What makes early learning experiences so lasting in their effects?" Their answer is that childhood is a time of urgent drives, powerful rewards and punishments, and crushing frustrations. Also important is **social reinforcement,** which is based on praise, attention, or approval from others. These forces combine to shape the core of personality.

Critical Situations

Dollard and Miller believe that during childhood four **critical situations** are capable of leaving a lasting imprint on personality. These are (1) feeding, (2) toilet or cleanliness training, (3) sex training, and (4) learning to express anger or aggression.

Why are these of special importance? Feeding serves as an illustration. If children are fed when they cry, it encourages them to actively manipulate their parents. The child allowed to cry without being fed learns to be passive. Thus, a basic active or passive orientation toward the world may be created by early feeding experiences. Feeding can also affect later social relationships because the child learns to associate people with pleasure or with frustration and discomfort.

Toilet and cleanliness training can be a particularly strong source of emotion for both parents and children. Rashad's parents were aghast the day they found him smearing feces about with joyful abandon. They reacted with sharp punishment, which frustrated and confused Rashad. Many attitudes toward cleanliness, conformity, and bodily functions are formed at such times. Studies have also long shown that severe, punishing, or frustrating toilet training can have undesirable effects on personality development (Sears, Maccoby, & Levin, 1957). Because of this, toilet and cleanliness training demand patience and a sense of humor.

What about sex and anger? When, where, and how a child learns to express anger and sexual feelings can leave an imprint on personality. Specifically, permissiveness for sexual and aggressive behavior in childhood is linked to adult needs for power (McClelland & Pilon, 1983). This link probably occurs because permitting such behaviors allows children to get pleasure from asserting themselves. Sex training also involves learning socially defined "male" and "female" gender roles—which also affect personality (Pervin, Cervone, & John, 2005).

Drive Any stimulus (especially an internal stimulus such as hunger) strong enough to goad a person to action.

Cue External stimuli that guide responses, especially by signaling the presence or absence of reinforcement.

Response Any behavior, either observable or internal.

Reward Anything that produces pleasure or satisfaction; a positive reinforcer.

Social learning theory An explanation of personality that combines learning principles, cognition, and the effects of social relationships.

Psychological situation A situation as it is perceived and interpreted by an individual, not as it exists objectively.

Expectancy Anticipation about the effect a response will have, especially regarding reinforcement.

Reinforcement value The subjective value a person attaches to a particular activity or reinforcer.

Self-efficacy Belief in your capacity to produce a desired result.

Self-reinforcement Praising or rewarding oneself for having made a particular response (such as completing a school assignment).

Social reinforcement Praise, attention, approval, and/or affection from others.

Critical situations Situations during childhood that are capable of leaving a lasting imprint on personality.

Becoming Male or Female

From birth onward, children are labeled as boys or girls and encouraged to learn sex-appropriate behavior. According to social learning theory, identification and imitation contribute greatly to personality development and to sex training. **Identification** refers to the child's emotional attachment to admired adults, especially those who provide love and care. Identification typically encourages **imitation**, a desire to act like the admired person. Many "male" or "female" traits come from children's attempts to imitate a same-sex parent with whom they identify.

If children are around parents of both sexes, why don't they imitate behavior typical of the opposite sex as well as of the same sex? You may recall from Chapter 8 that Albert Bandura and others have shown that learning takes place vicariously as well as directly. This means that we can learn without direct reward by observing and remembering the actions of others. But the actions we choose to imitate depend on their outcomes. For example, boys and girls have equal chances to observe adults and other children acting aggressively. However, girls are less likely than boys to imitate aggressive behavior because they rarely see female aggression rewarded or approved. Thus, many arbitrary "male" and "female" qualities are passed on at the same time sexual identity is learned.

A study of preschool teachers found that they are three times more likely to pay attention to aggressive or disruptive boys than to girls acting the same way. Boys who hit other students or broke things typically got loud scoldings. This made them the center of attention for the whole class. In contrast, disruptive girls were given brief, soft rebukes that others couldn't hear (Serbin & O'Leary, 1975). We know that attention of almost any kind reinforces children's behavior. Therefore, it is clear that boys were encouraged to be active and aggressive. Girls got the most attention when they were within arm's reach, more or less clinging to the teacher.

The pattern just described grows stronger throughout elementary school. In all grades, boys are louder, faster, and more boisterous than girls. Day after day, boys receive a disproportionate amount of the teacher's attention (Sadker & Sadker, 1994). It's easy to see that teachers unwittingly encourage girls to be submissive, dependent, and passive. Similar differences in reinforcement probably explain why males are responsible for more aggression than females are. Among adults, rates of murder and assault are consistently higher for men. The roots of this difference appear to lie in childhood.

We have considered only a few examples of the links between social learning and personality. Nevertheless, the connection is unmistakable. When parents accept their children and give them affection, the children become sociable, positive, and emotionally stable, and they have high self-esteem. When parents are rejecting, punishing, sarcastic, humiliating, or neglectful, their children become hostile, unresponsive, unstable, and dependent, and have impaired self-esteem (Triandis & Suh, 2002).

Laura Dwight/PhotoEdit

Adult personality is influenced by identification with parents.

KNOWLEDGE BUILDER

Behavioral and Social Learning Theories

REFLECT

What is your favorite style of food? Can you relate Dollard and Miller's concepts of habit, drive, cue, response, and reward to explain your preference?

Some people love to shop. Others hate it. How have the psychological situation, expectancy, and reinforcement value affected your willingness to "shop till you drop"?

Who did you identify with as a child? What aspects of that person's behavior did you imitate?

LEARNING CHECK

1. Learning theorists believe that personality "traits" really are ____________ acquired through prior learning. They also emphasize ____________ determinants of behavior.
2. Dollard and Miller consider cues the basic structure of personality. T or F?
3. To explain behavior, social learning theorists include mental elements, such as ____________ (the anticipation that a response will lead to reinforcement).
4. Self-reinforcement is to behavioristic theory as superego is to psychoanalytic theory. T or F?
5. Which of the following is *not* a "critical situation" in the behaviorist theory of personality development?
   a. feeding c. language training
   b. sex training d. anger training
6. In addition to basic rewards and punishments, a child's personality is also shaped by ____________ reinforcement.

7. Social learning theories of development emphasize the impact of identification and ______________________.

CRITICAL THINKING

8. The concept of *reinforcement value* is closely related to a motivational principle discussed in Chapter 10. Can you name it?

Answers: **1.** habits, situational **2.** F **3.** expectancies **4.** T **5.** c **6.** social **7.** imitation **8.** Incentive value.

Humanistic Theory—Peak Experiences and Personal Growth

At the beginning of this chapter you met Annette, an interesting personality. A few years ago, Annette and her husband spent a year riding mules across the country as a unique way to see America and get to know themselves better. Where do such desires for personal growth come from? Humanistic theories pay special attention to the fuller use of human potentials and they help bring balance to our overall views of personality.

Humanism focuses on human experience, problems, potentials, and ideals. It is a reaction to the rigidity of traits, the pessimism of psychoanalytic theory, and the mechanical nature of learning theory. At its core is a positive image of what it means to be human. Humanists reject the Freudian view of personality as a battleground for instincts and unconscious forces. Instead, they view human nature as inherently good. (Human nature consists of the traits, qualities, potentials, and behavior patterns most characteristic of the human species.) Humanists also oppose the machine-like overtones of behaviorism. We are not, they say, merely a bundle of moldable responses. Rather, we are creative beings capable of *free choice* (an ability to choose that is not controlled by genetics, learning, or unconscious forces). In short, humanists seek ways to encourage our potentials to blossom.

To a humanist the person you are today is largely the product of all the choices you have made. Humanists also emphasize immediate *subjective experience* (private perceptions of reality), rather than prior learning. They believe that there are as many "real worlds" as there are people. To understand behavior, we must learn how a person subjectively views the world—what is "real" for her or him.

Who are the major humanistic theorists? Many psychologists have added to the humanistic tradition. Of these, the best known are Carl Rogers (1902–1987) and Abraham Maslow (1908–1970). Because Maslow's idea of self-actualization was introduced in Chapter 1, let's begin with a more detailed look at this facet of his thinking.

Maslow and Self-Actualization

Abraham Maslow became interested in people who were living unusually effective lives. How were they different? To find an answer, Maslow began by studying the lives of great men and women, such as Albert Einstein, William James, Jane Addams, Eleanor Roosevelt, Abraham Lincoln, John Muir, and Walt Whitman. From there he moved on to directly study living artists, writers, poets, and other creative individuals.

Along the way, Maslow's thinking changed radically. At first he studied only people of obvious creativity or high achievement. However, it eventually became clear that a housewife, clerk, student, or someone like our friend Annette could live a rich, creative, and satisfying life. Maslow referred to the process of fully developing personal potentials as **self-actualization** (Maslow, 1954). The heart of self-actualization is a continuous search for personal fulfillment (Reiss & Havercamp, 2005; Sumerlin, 1997).

Characteristics of Self-Actualizers

A **self-actualizer** is a person who is living creatively and fully using his or her potentials. In his studies, Maslow found that self-actualizers share many similarities. Whether famous or unknown, well-schooled or uneducated, rich or poor, self-actualizers tend to fit the following profile.

1. **Efficient perceptions of reality.** Self-actualizers are able to judge situations correctly and honestly. They are very sensitive to the fake and dishonest.
2. **Comfortable acceptance of self, others, nature.** Self-actualizers accept their own human nature with all its flaws. The shortcomings of others and the contradictions of the human condition are accepted with humor and tolerance.
3. **Spontaneity.** Maslow's subjects extended their creativity into everyday activities. Actualizers tend to be unusually alive, engaged, and spontaneous.
4. **Task centering.** Most of Maslow's subjects had a mission to fulfill in life or some task or problem outside of themselves to pursue. Humanitarians such as Albert Schweitzer and Mother Teresa represent this quality.
5. **Autonomy.** Self-actualizers are free from reliance on external authorities or other people. They tend to be resourceful and independent.
6. **Continued freshness of appreciation.** The self-actualizer seems to constantly renew appreciation of life's basic goods. A sunset or a flower will be experienced as intensely time after time as it was at first. There is an "innocence of vision," like that of an artist or child.
7. **Fellowship with humanity.** Maslow's subjects felt a deep identification with others and the human situation in general.
8. **Profound interpersonal relationships.** The interpersonal relationships of self-actualizers are marked by deep, loving bonds.

Humanism An approach that focuses on human experience, problems, potentials, and ideals.

Self-actualization The process of fully developing personal potentials.

Self-actualizer One who is living creatively and making full use of his or her potentials.

9. **Comfort with solitude.** Despite their satisfying relationships with others, self-actualizing persons value solitude and are comfortable being alone (Sumerlin & Bundrick, 1996).
10. **Nonhostile sense of humor.** This refers to the wonderful capacity to laugh at oneself. It also describes the kind of humor a man like Abraham Lincoln had. Lincoln probably never made a joke that hurt anybody. His wry comments were a gentle prodding of human shortcomings.
11. **Peak experiences.** All of Maslow's subjects reported the frequent occurrence of *peak experiences* (temporary moments of self-actualization). These occasions were marked by feelings of ecstasy, harmony, and deep meaning. Self-actualizers reported feeling at one with the universe, stronger and calmer than ever before, filled with light, beautiful and good, and so forth.

In summary, self-actualizers feel safe, nonanxious, accepted, loved, loving, and alive.

Maslow's choice of self-actualizing people for study seems pretty subjective. Is it really a fair representation of self-actualization? Although Maslow tried to investigate self-actualization empirically, his choice of people for study was subjective. Undoubtedly there are many ways to make full use of personal potential. Maslow's primary contribution was to draw our attention to the possibility of lifelong personal growth.

What steps can be taken to promote self-actualization? Maslow made few specific recommendations about how to proceed. There is no magic formula for leading a more creative life. Self-actualization is primarily a *process,* not a goal or an end point. As such, it requires hard work, patience, and commitment. Nevertheless, some helpful suggestions can be gleaned from his writings (Maslow, 1954, 1967, 1971). Here are some ways to begin.

1. **Be willing to change.** Begin by asking yourself, "Am I living in a way that is deeply satisfying to me and that truly expresses me?" If not, be prepared to make changes in your life. Indeed, ask yourself this question often and accept the need for continual change.
2. **Take responsibility.** You can become an architect of self by acting as if you are personally responsible for every aspect of your life. Shouldering responsibility in this way helps end the habit of blaming others for your own shortcomings.
3. **Examine your motives.** Self-discovery involves an element of risk. If your behavior is restricted by a desire for safety or security, it may be time to test some limits. Try to make each life decision a choice for growth, not a response to fear or anxiety.
4. **Experience honestly and directly.** Wishful thinking is another barrier to personal growth. Self-actualizers trust themselves enough to accept all kinds of information without distorting it to fit their fears and desires. Try to see yourself as others do. Be willing to admit, "I was wrong," or, "I failed because I was irresponsible."
5. **Make use of positive experiences.** Maslow considered peak experiences temporary moments of self-actualization. Therefore, you might actively repeat activities that have caused feelings of awe, amazement, exaltation, renewal, reverence, humility, fulfillment, or joy.
6. **Be prepared to be different.** Maslow felt that everyone has a potential for "greatness," but most fear becoming what they might. As part of personal growth, be prepared to trust your own impulses and feelings; don't automatically judge yourself by the standards of others. Accept your uniqueness.
7. **Get involved.** With few exceptions, self-actualizers tend to have a mission or "calling" in life. For these people, "work" is not done just to fill deficiency needs, but to satisfy higher yearnings for truth, beauty, community, and meaning. Get personally involved and committed. Turn your attention to problems outside yourself.
8. **Assess your progress.** There is no final point at which one becomes self-actualized. It's important to gauge your progress frequently and to renew your efforts. If you feel bored at school, at a job, or in a relationship, consider it a challenge. Have you been taking responsibility for your own personal growth? Almost any activity can be used as a chance for self-enhancement if it is approached creatively.

Positive Psychology: Positive Personality Traits

It could be said that self-actualizing people are thriving, not just surviving. In recent years, proponents of positive psychology have tried to scientifically study positive personality traits that contribute to happiness and well-being (Keyes & Haidt, 2003; Seligman, 2003). Although their work does not fall within the humanistic tradition, their findings are relevant here.

Martin Seligman, Christopher Peterson, and others have identified six human strengths that contribute to well-being and life satisfaction. Each strength is expressed by the positive personality traits listed here (Peterson & Seligman, 2004).

- **Wisdom and knowledge:** Creativity, curiosity, open-mindedness, love of learning, perspective
- **Courage:** Bravery, persistence, integrity, vitality
- **Humanity:** Love, kindness, social intelligence
- **Justice:** Citizenship, fairness, leadership
- **Temperance:** Forgiveness, humility, prudence, self-control
- **Transcendence:** Appreciation of beauty and excellence, gratitude, hope, humor, spirituality

Which of the positive personality traits are most closely related to happiness? A recent study found that traits of hope, vitality, gratitude, love, and curiosity are strongly associated with life satisfaction (Park, Peterson, & Seligman, 2004). These characteristics, in combination with Maslow's descriptions of self-actualizers, provide a good guide to the characteristics that help people live happy, meaningful lives.

Carl Rogers's Self Theory

Carl Rogers, another well-known humanist, also emphasized the human capacity for inner peace and happiness. The *fully functioning person,* he said, lives in harmony with his or her deepest feelings and impulses. Such people are open to their experiences and they trust their inner urges and intuitions (Rogers, 1961). Rogers believed that this attitude is most likely to occur when a person receives ample amounts of love and acceptance from others.

Personality Structure and Dynamics

Rogers's theory emphasizes the **self**, a flexible and changing perception of personal identity. Much behavior can be understood as an attempt to maintain consistency between our *self-image* and our actions. (Your **self-image** is a total subjective perception of your body and personality.) For example, people who think of themselves as kind tend to be considerate in most situations.

Let's say I know a person who thinks she is kind, but she really isn't. How does that fit Rogers's theory? According to Rogers, we allow experiences that match our self-image into awareness, where they gradually change the self. Information or feelings inconsistent with the self-image are said to be *incongruent.* Thus, a person who thinks she is kind, but really isn't, is in a state of **incongruence.** In other words, there is a discrepancy between her experiences and her self-image. As another example, it would be incongruent to believe that you are a person who "never gets angry," if you spend much of each day seething inside.

Experiences seriously incongruent with the self-image can be threatening, and they are often distorted or denied conscious recognition. Blocking, denying, or distorting experiences prevents the self from changing. This creates a gulf between the self-image and reality. As the self-image grows more unrealistic, the **incongruent person** becomes confused, vulnerable, dissatisfied, or seriously maladjusted (● Figure 14.7). In line with Rogers's observations, a study of college students confirmed that being *authentic* is vital for healthy functioning. That is, we need to feel that our behavior accurately expresses who we are (Sheldon et al., 1997). Please note, however, that being authentic doesn't mean you can do whatever you want. Being true to yourself is no excuse for acting irresponsibly or ignoring the feelings of others.

Humanists consider self-image a central determinant of behavior and personal adjustment.

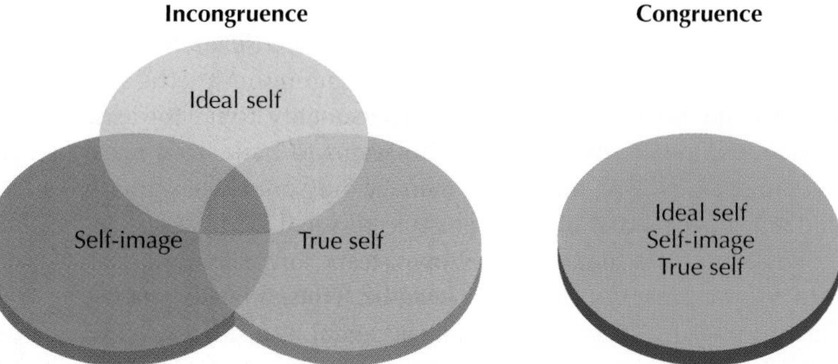

● Figure 14.7 Incongruence occurs when there is a mismatch between any of these three entities: the ideal self (the person you would like to be), your self-image (the person you think you are), and the true self (the person you actually are). Self-esteem suffers when there is a large difference between one's ideal self and self-image. Anxiety and defensiveness are common when the self-image does not match the true self.

When your self-image is consistent with what you really think, feel, do, and experience, you are best able to actualize your potentials. Rogers also considered it essential to have congruence between the self-image and the **ideal self.** The ideal self is similar to Freud's ego ideal. It is an image of the person you would most like to be.

Is it really incongruent not to live up to one's ideal self? Rogers was aware that we never fully attain our ideals. Nevertheless, the greater the gap between the way you see yourself and the way you would like to be, the more tension and anxiety you will experience.

Rogers emphasized that to maximize our potentials, we must accept information about ourselves as honestly as possible. In accord with his thinking, researchers have found that people with a close match between their self-image and ideal self tend to be socially poised, confident, and resourceful. Those with a poor match tend to be depressed, anxious, and insecure (Alfeld-Liro & Sigelman, 1998; Scott & O'Hara, 1993).

BRIDGES

Rogers and other humanistic theorists believe that some psychological disorders are caused a faulty or incongruent self-image.

See Chapter 16, page 548.

Self A continuously evolving conception of one's personal identity.

Self-image Total subjective perception of one's body and personality (another term for self-concept).

Incongruence State that exists when there is a discrepancy between one's experiences and self-image or between one's self-image and ideal self.

Incongruent person A person who has an inaccurate self-image or whose self-image differs greatly from the ideal self.

Ideal self An idealized image of oneself (the person one would like to be).

According to psychologists Hazel Markus and Paula Nurius (1986), our ideal self is only one of a number of *possible selves* (persons we could become or are afraid of becoming). Annette, who was described earlier, is an interesting personality, to say the least. Annette is one of those people who seems to have lived many lives in the time that most of us manage only one. Like Annette, you may have pondered many possible personal identities.

Possible selves translate our hopes, fears, fantasies, and goals into specific images of who we *could* be. Thus, a beginning law student might picture herself as a successful attorney, an enterprising college student might imagine himself as a dot.com entrepreneur, and a person on a diet might imagine both slim and grossly obese possible selves. Such images tend to direct our future behavior (Oyserman et al., 2004).

Of course, almost everyone over age 30 has probably felt the anguish of realizing that some cherished possible selves will never be realized. Nevertheless, there is value in asking yourself not just "Who am I?" but also "Who would I like to become?" As you do, remember Maslow's advice that everyone has a potential for "greatness," but most fear becoming what they might.

Humanistic View of Development

Why do mirrors, photographs, video cameras, and the reactions of others hold such fascination and threat for many people? Carl Rogers's theory suggests it is because they provide information about one's self. The development of a self-image depends greatly on information from the environment. It begins with a sorting of perceptions and feelings: my body, my toes, my nose, I want, I like, I am, and so on. Soon, it expands to include self-evaluation: I am a good person, I did something bad just now, and so forth.

How does development of the self contribute to later personality functioning? Rogers believed that positive and negative evaluations by others cause children to develop internal standards of evaluation called **conditions of worth.** In other words, we learn that some actions win our parents' love and approval whereas others are rejected. More important, parents may label some *feelings* as bad or wrong. For example, a child might be told that it is wrong to feel angry toward a brother or sister—even when anger is justified. Likewise, a little boy might be told that he must not cry or show fear, two very normal emotions.

Learning to evaluate some experiences or feelings as "good" and others as "bad" is directly related to a later capacity for self-esteem, positive self-evaluation, or **positive self-regard,** to use Rogers's term. To think of yourself as a good, lovable, worthwhile person, your behavior and experiences must match your internal conditions of worth. The problem is that this can cause incongruence by leading to the denial of many true feelings and experiences.

To put it simply, Rogers blamed many adult emotional problems on attempts to live by the standards of others. He believed that congruence and self-actualization are encouraged by replacing conditions of worth with **organismic valuing** (a natural, undistorted, full-body reaction to an experience). Organismic valuing is a direct, gut-level response to life that avoids the filtering and distortion of incongruence. It involves trusting one's own feelings and perceptions. Organismic valuing is most likely to develop, Rogers felt, when children (or adults) receive **unconditional positive regard** (unshakable love and approval) from others. That is, when they are "prized" as worthwhile human beings, just for being themselves, without any conditions or strings attached. Although this may be a luxury few people enjoy, we are more likely to move toward our ideal selves if we receive affirmation and support from a close partner (Drigotas et al., 1999).

KNOWLEDGE BUILDER

Humanistic Theory

REFLECT

How do your views of human nature and free choice compare with those of the humanists?

Do you know anyone who seems to be making especially good use of their personal potentials? Does that person fit Maslow's profile of a self-actualizer?

How much difference do you think there is between your self-image, your ideal self, and your true self? Do you think Rogers is right about the effects of applying conditions of worth to your perceptions and feelings?

LEARNING CHECK

1. Humanists view human nature as basically good and they emphasize the effects of subjective learning and unconscious choice. T or F?
2. Maslow used the term ______________________ to describe the tendency of certain individuals to fully use their talents and potentials.
3. According to Rogers, a close match between the self-image and the ideal self creates a condition called incongruence. T or F?
4. Markus and Nurius describe alternative self-concepts that a person may have as "possible selves." T or F?
5. Rogers's theory considers acceptance of conditions of ______ ______________ a troublesome aspect of development of the self.
6. According to Maslow, a preoccupation with one's own thoughts, feelings, and needs is characteristic of self-actualizing individuals. T or F?
7. Maslow regarded ______________ experiences as times of temporary self-actualization.

CRITICAL THINKING

8. What role would "possible selves" have in the choice of a college major?

Answers: 1. F **2.** self-actualization **3.** F **4.** T **5.** worth **6.** F **7.** peak **8.** Career decisions almost always involve, in part, picturing oneself occupying various occupational roles.

Personality Theories—Overview and Comparison

Which personality theory is right? Each theory has added to our understanding by organizing observations of human behavior. Nevertheless, theories can't be fully proved or disproved. We can only

TABLE 14.3

Comparison of Personality Theories

	TRAIT THEORIES	PSYCHOANALYTIC THEORY	BEHAVIORISTIC AND SOCIAL LEARNING THEORIES	HUMANISTIC THEORY
View of human nature	Neutral	Negative	Neutral	Positive
Is behavior free or determined?	Determined	Determined	Determined	Free choice
Principal motives	Depends on one's traits	Sex and aggression	Drives of all kinds	Self-actualization
Personality structure	Traits	Id, ego, superego	Habits, expectancies	Self
Role of unconscious	Minimized	Maximized	Practically nonexistent	Minimized
Conception of conscience	Traits of honesty, etc.	Superego	Self-reinforcement, punishment history	Ideal self, valuing process
Developmental emphasis	Combined effects of heredity and environment	Psychosexual stages	Critical learning situations, identification, and imitation	Development of self-image
Barriers to personal growth	Unhealthy traits	Unconscious conflicts, fixations	Maladaptive habits, unhealthy environment	Conditions of worth, incongruence

ask, "Does the evidence tend to support this theory or disconfirm it?" Yet although theories are neither true nor false, their implications or predictions may be. The best way to judge a theory, then, is in terms of its *usefulness*. Does the theory adequately explain behavior? Does it stimulate new research? Does it suggest how to treat psychological disorders? Each theory has fared differently in these areas (Pervin, Cervone, & John, 2005).

Trait Theories

Traits are very useful for describing and comparing personalities. Many of the personality tests used by clinical psychologists are based on trait theories. However, trait theories tend to have a circular quality. For example, how do we know that a young woman named Carrie has the trait of shyness? Because we frequently observe Carrie avoiding conversations with others. And why doesn't Carrie socialize with others? Because shyness is a trait of her personality. And how do we know she has the trait of shyness? Because we observe that she avoids socializing with others. And so on.

Psychoanalytic Theory

By present standards, psychoanalytic theory seems to exaggerate the impact of sexuality and biological instincts. These distortions were corrected somewhat by the neo-Freudians, but problems remain. One of the most telling criticisms of Freudian theory is that it can explain any psychological event *after* it has occurred. But beforehand it offers little help in predicting future behavior. For this reason, many psychoanalytic concepts are difficult or impossible to test scientifically (Schick & Vaughn, 1995).

Behavioristic and Social Learning Theories

Learning theories have provided a good framework for personality research. Of the major perspectives, the behaviorists have made the best effort to rigorously test and verify their ideas. They have, however, been criticized for understating the impact that temperament, emotion, thinking, and subjective experience have on personality. Social learning theory answers some of these criticisms, but it may still understate the importance of private experience.

Humanistic Theory

A great strength of the humanists is the attention they have given to positive dimensions of personality. As Maslow (1968) put it, "Human nature is not nearly as bad as it has been thought to be. It is as if Freud supplied us with the sick half of psychology and we must now fill it out with the healthy half." Despite their contributions, humanists can be criticized for using "fuzzy" concepts that are difficult to measure and study objectively. Even so, humanistic thought has encouraged many people to seek greater self-awareness and personal growth. Also, humanistic concepts have been very useful in counseling and psychotherapy.

In the final analysis, we need all five major perspectives to explain personality. Each provides a sort of lens through which human behavior can be viewed. In many instances, a balanced picture emerges only when each theory is considered. ■ Table 14.3 provides a final overview of the principal approaches to personality.

Conditions of worth Internal standards used to judge the value of one's thoughts, actions, feelings, or experiences.

Positive self-regard Thinking of oneself as a good, lovable, worthwhile person.

Organismic valuing A natural, undistorted, full-body reaction to an experience.

Unconditional positive regard Unshakable love and approval given without qualification.

Personality Assessment—Psychological Yardsticks

Measuring personality can help predict how people will behave at work, at school, and in therapy. However, painting a detailed picture can be a challenge. In many instances, it requires several of the techniques described in this unit. To capture a personality as unique as Annette's, it might take all of them!

How is personality "measured"? Psychologists use interviews, observation, questionnaires, and projective tests to assess personality (Derlega, Winstead, & Jones, 2005). Each method has strengths and limitations. For this reason, they are often used in combination.

Formal personality measures are refinements of more casual ways of judging a person. At one time or another, you have probably "sized up" a potential date, friend, or roommate by engaging in conversation (interview). Perhaps you have asked a friend, "When I am delayed I get angry. Do you?" (questionnaire). Maybe you watch your professors when they are angry or embarrassed to learn what they are "really" like when they're caught off-guard (observation). Or possibly you have noticed that when you say, "I think people feel . . . ," you may be expressing your own feelings (projection). Let's see how psychologists apply each of these methods to probe personality.

The Interview

In an **interview**, direct questioning is used to learn about a person's life history, personality traits, or current mental state. In an *unstructured interview,* conversation is informal and topics are taken up freely as they arise. In a *structured interview,* information is gathered by asking a planned series of questions.

How are interviews used? Interviews are used to identify personality disturbances; to select people for jobs, college, or special programs; and to study the dynamics of personality. Interviews also provide information for counseling or therapy. For instance, a counselor might ask a depressed person, "Have you ever contemplated suicide? What were the circumstances?" The counselor might then follow by asking, "How did you feel about it?" or, "How is what you are now feeling different from what you felt then?"

In addition to providing information, interviews make it possible to observe a person's tone of voice, hand gestures, posture, and facial expressions. Such "body language" cues are important because they may radically alter the message sent, as when a person claims to be "completely calm" but trembles uncontrollably.

Computerized Interviews

If you were distressed and went to a psychologist or psychiatrist, what is the first thing she or he might do? Typically, a **diagnostic interview** is used to find out how a person is feeling and what complaints or symptoms he or she has. In many cases, such interviews are based on a specific series of questions. Because the questions are always the same, some researchers have begun to wonder, "Why not let a computer ask them?"

The results of computerized interviews have been promising. In one study, people were interviewed by both a computer and a psychiatrist. Eighty-five percent of these people thought the computer did an acceptable interview (Dignon, 1996). Another study found that a computerized interview was highly accurate at identifying psychiatric disorders and symptoms. It also closely agreed with diagnoses made by psychiatrists (Marion, Shayka, & Marcus, 1996). Thus, it may soon become common for people to "Tell it to the computer," at least in the first stages of seeking help (Peters, Clark, & Carroll, 1998).

Limitations

Interviews give rapid insight into personality, but they have limitations. For one thing, interviewers can be swayed by preconceptions. A person identified as a "housewife," "college student," "high school athlete," "punk," "computer nerd," or "ski bum" may be misjudged because of an interviewer's personal biases. Second, an interviewer's own personality, or even gender, may influence a client's behavior. When this occurs, it can accentuate or distort the person's apparent traits (Pollner, 1998). A third problem is that people sometimes try to deceive interviewers. For example, a person accused of a crime might try to avoid punishment by pretending to be mentally disabled.

A fourth problem is the **halo effect**, which is the tendency to generalize a favorable or unfavorable first impression to an entire personality. Because of the halo effect, a person who is likable or physically attractive may be rated more mature, intelligent, or

Zia Soleil/Getty Images

What is your initial impression of the person wearing the gray jacket? If you think that she looks friendly, attractive, or neat, your subsequent perceptions might be altered by a positive first impression. Interviewers are often influenced by the halo effect (see text).

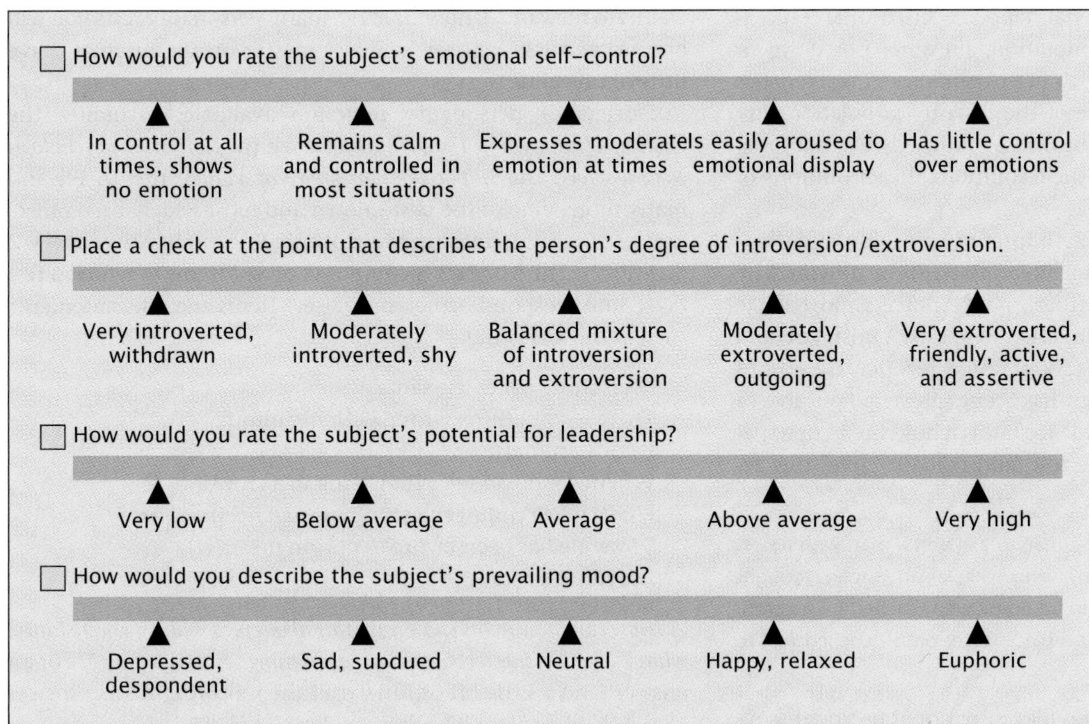

● **Figure 14.8** Sample rating scale items. To understand how the scale works, imagine someone you know well. Where would you place check marks on each of the scales to rate that person's characteristics?

mentally healthy than she or he actually is. The halo effect is something to keep in mind at job interviews. First impressions do make a difference (Lance, LaPointe, & Stewart, 1994).

Even with their limitations, interviews are a respected method of assessment. In many cases, interviews are the first step in evaluating personality and an essential prelude to therapy. Nevertheless, interviews may not be enough. Usually, they must be supplemented by other measures and tests (Meyer et al., 2001).

Direct Observation and Rating Scales

Are you fascinated by airports, bus depots, parks, taverns, subway stations, or other public places? Many people relish a chance to observe the actions of others. When used for assessment, **direct observation** (looking at behavior) is a simple extension of this natural interest in "people watching." For instance, a psychologist might arrange to observe a disturbed child as she plays with other children. Is the child withdrawn? Does she become hostile or aggressive without warning? By careful observation, the psychologist can identify the girl's personality traits and clarify the nature of her problems.

Wouldn't observation be subject to the same problems of misperception as an interview? Yes. Misperceptions can be a difficulty, which is why rating scales are sometimes used (● Figure 14.8). A **rating scale** is a list of personality traits or aspects of behavior that can be used to evaluate a person. Rating scales limit the chance that some traits will be overlooked while others are exaggerated (Merenda, 1996). Perhaps they should be a standard procedure for choosing a roommate, spouse, or lover!

An alternative approach is to do a **behavioral assessment** by counting the frequency of specific behaviors. In this case, observers record *actions,* not what traits they think a person has. For example, a psychologist working with hospitalized mental patients might note the frequency of a patient's aggression, self-care, speech, and unusual behaviors. Behavioral assessments can also be used to probe thought processes. In one study, for example, students high in math anxiety were asked to think aloud while doing math problems. Later, their thoughts were analyzed to pinpoint why they had math fears (Blackwell et al., 1985).

Situational Testing

In **situational testing,** real-life conditions are simulated so that a person's spontaneous reactions can be observed. Such tests assume that the best way to learn how people react is to put them in

Interview (personality) A face-to-face meeting held for the purpose of gaining information about an individual's personal history, personality traits, current psychological state, and so forth.

Diagnostic interview An interview used to find out how a person is feeling and what complaints or symptoms he or she has.

Halo effect The tendency to generalize a favorable or unfavorable first impression to unrelated details of personality.

Direct observation Assessing behavior through direct surveillance.

Rating scale A list of personality traits or aspects of behavior on which a person is rated.

Behavioral assessment Recording the frequency of various behaviors.

Situational test Simulating real-life conditions so that a person's reactions may be directly observed.

realistic situations and watch what happens. Situational tests expose people to frustration, temptation, pressure, boredom, or other conditions capable of revealing personality characteristics (Weekley & Jones, 1997). Some of the recently popular "reality TV" programs, such as *Survivor,* bear some similarity to situational tests—which may account for their ability to attract millions of viewers.

How are situational tests done? An interesting example of situational testing is the judgmental firearms training provided by many police departments. At times, police officers must make split-second decisions about using their weapons. A mistake could be fatal. In a typical shoot–don't shoot test, actors play the part of armed criminals. As various high-risk scenes are acted out live or on videotape, officers must decide to shoot or hold fire. A newspaper reporter who once took the test (and failed it) gives this account (Gersh, 1982):

> I judged wrong. I was killed by a man in a closet, a man with a hostage, a woman interrupted when kissing her lover, and a man I thought was cleaning a shotgun. . . . I shot a drunk who reached for a comb, and a teenager who pulled out a black water pistol. Looked real to me.

In addition to the training it provides, situational testing uncovers police cadets who lack the good judgment needed to carry a gun out on the street.

Personality Questionnaires

Personality questionnaires are paper-and-pencil tests that reveal personality characteristics. Questionnaires are more objective than interviews or observation. (An **objective test** gives the same score when different people correct it.) Questions, administration, and scoring are all standardized so that scores are unaffected by any biases an examiner may have. However, this is not enough to ensure accuracy. A good test must also be reliable and valid. A test is **reliable** if it yields close to the same score each time it is given to the same person. A test has **validity** if it measures what it claims to measure. Unfortunately, many personality tests you will encounter, such as those in magazines or on the Internet, have little or no validity.

David McNew Newsmakers/Getty Images

A police officer undergoes judgmental firearms training. Variations on this situational test are used by a growing number of police departments. All officers must score a passing grade.

Dozens of personality tests are available, including the *Guilford-Zimmerman Temperament Survey,* the *California Psychological Inventory,* the *Allport-Vernon Study of Values,* the 16 PF, and many more. One of the best-known and most widely used objective tests is the **Minnesota Multiphasic Personality Inventory-2 (MMPI-2).** The MMPI-2 is composed of 567 items to which a test taker must respond "true" or "false." Items include statements such as the following:

Everything tastes the same.
There is something wrong with my mind.
I enjoy animals.
Whenever possible I avoid being in a crowd.
I have never indulged in any unusual sex practices.
Someone has been trying to poison me.
I daydream often.*

How can these items show anything about personality? For instance, what if a person has a cold so that "everything tastes the same"? For an answer (and a little bit of fun), read the following items. Answer "Yes," "No," or "Don't bother me, I can't cope!"

I would enjoy the work of a chicken flicker.
My eyes are always cold.
Frantic screaming makes me nervous.
I believe I smell as good as most people.
I use shoe polish to excess.
The sight of blood no longer excites me.
As an infant I had very few hobbies.
Dirty stories make me think about sex.
I stay in the bathtub until I look like a raisin.
I salivate at the sight of mittens.
I never finish what I

These items were written by humorist Art Buchwald (1965) and psychologist Carol Sommer to satirize personality questionnaires. Such questions may seem ridiculous, but they are not very different from the real thing. How, then, do the items on tests such as the MMPI-2 reveal anything about personality? The answer is that a single item tells little about personality. For example, a person who agrees that "Everything tastes the same" might simply have a cold. It is only through *patterns* of response that personality dimensions are revealed.

*Reproduced by permission. Copyright 1989, University of Minnesota Press.

BRIDGES

Reliability and validity are important characteristics of all psychological tests, especially intelligence and aptitude tests.

See Chapter 11, pages 364–365.

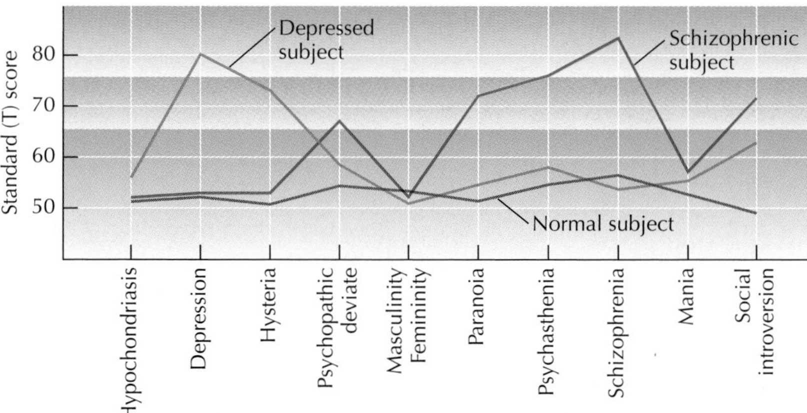

● **Figure 14.9** An MMPI-2 profile showing hypothetical scores indicating normality, depression, and psychosis. High scores begin at 66 and very high scores at 76. An unusually low score (40 and below) may also reveal personality characteristics or problems.

Items on the MMPI-2 were selected for their ability to correctly identify persons with particular psychological problems (Butcher, 2005). For instance, if depressed persons consistently answer a series of items in a particular way, it is assumed that others who answer the same way are also prone to depression. As silly as the gag items in the preceding lists may seem, it is possible that some could actually work in a legitimate test. But before an item could be part of a test, it would have to be shown to correlate highly with some trait or dimension of personality.

The MMPI-2 measures 10 major aspects of personality (listed in ■ Table 14.4). After the MMPI-2 is scored, results are charted graphically as an **MMPI-2 profile** (● Figure 14.9). By comparing a person's profile to scores produced by typical, normal adults, a psychologist can identify various personality disorders (Butcher, 2005). Additional scales can identify substance abuse, eating disorders, Type A (heart-attack prone) behavior, repression, anger, cynicism, low self-esteem, family problems, inability to function in a job, and other problems (Hathaway & McKinley, 1989).

How accurate is the MMPI-2? Personality questionnaires are only accurate if people tell the truth about themselves. Because of this, the MMPI-2 has additional **validity scales** that reveal whether a person's scores should be discarded. The validity scales detect attempts by test takers to "fake good" (make themselves look good) or "fake bad" (make it look like they have problems). Other scales uncover defensiveness or tendencies to exaggerate shortcomings and troubles. When taking the MMPI-2, it is best to answer honestly, without trying to second-guess the test.

A clinical psychologist trying to decide if a person has emotional problems would be wise to take more than the MMPI-2 into account. Test scores are informative, but they can incorrectly label some people (Cronbach, 1990). ("Honesty Tests" discusses a related problem.) Fortunately, clinical judgments usually rely on information from interviews, tests, and other sources. Also, despite their limitations, it is reassuring to note that psychological assessments are at least as accurate as commonly used medical tests (Meyer et al., 2001).

Projective Tests of Personality—Inkblots and Hidden Plots

Projective tests take a different approach to personality. Interviews, observation, rating scales, and inventories try to directly identify overt, observable traits (Vane & Guarnaccia, 1989). By contrast, projective tests seek to uncover deeply hidden or *unconscious* wishes, thoughts, and needs.

As a child you may have delighted in finding faces and objects in cloud formations. Or perhaps you have learned something about your friends' personalities

TABLE 14.4

MMPI-2 Basic Clinical Subscales

1. **Hypochondriasis** (HI-po-kon-DRY-uh-sis). Exaggerated concern about one's physical health.
2. **Depression.** Feelings of worthlessness, hopelessness, and pessimism.
3. **Hysteria.** The presence of physical complaints for which no physical basis can be established.
4. **Psychopathic deviate.** Emotional shallowness in relationships and a disregard for social and moral standards.
5. **Masculinity/femininity.** One's degree of traditional "masculine" aggressiveness or "feminine" sensitivity.
6. **Paranoia.** Extreme suspiciousness and feelings of persecution.
7. **Psychasthenia** (sike-as-THEE-nee-ah). The presence of obsessive worries, irrational fears (phobias), and compulsive (ritualistic) actions.
8. **Schizophrenia.** Emotional withdrawal and unusual or bizarre thinking and actions.
9. **Mania.** Emotional excitability, manic moods or behavior, and excessive activity.
10. **Social introversion.** One's tendency to be socially withdrawn.

Personality questionnaire A paper-and-pencil test consisting of questions that reveal aspects of personality.

Objective test A test that gives the same score when different people correct it.

Reliability The ability of a test to yield nearly the same score each time it is given to the same person.

Validity The ability of a test to measure what it purports to measure.

Minnesota Multiphasic Personality Inventory-2 (MMPI-2) One of the best-known and most widely used objective personality questionnaires.

MMPI-2 profile A graphic representation of an individual's scores on each of the primary scales of the MMPI-2.

Validity scales Scales that tell whether test scores should be invalidated for lying, inconsistency, or "faking good."

CRITICAL THINKING

Honesty Tests—Do They Tell the Truth?

Each year, millions of anxious job seekers take paper-and-pencil honesty tests given by companies that hope to avoid hiring dishonest workers (Spector, 2005). **Honesty tests** (also known as integrity tests) assume that poor attitudes toward dishonest acts predispose a person to dishonest behavior. Examples include attitudes toward taking office supplies home or leaving work early. Most of the tests also ask people how honest they think the average person is and how honest they are in comparison. Surprisingly, many job applicants willingly rate their own honesty as below average (Neuman & Baydoun, 1998). (You have to admire them for being honest about it!) Honesty tests also ask about prior brushes with the law, past acts of theft or deceit, and attitudes toward alcohol and drug use.

Is honesty testing valid? This question is still very much in dispute. Some psychologists believe that the best honesty tests are sufficiently valid to be used for making hiring decisions (Ones & Viswesvaran, 2001). Others, however, remain unconvinced. Most studies have failed to demonstrate that honesty tests can accurately *predict* if a person will be a poor risk on the job (Horn, Nelson & Brannick, 2004; Ones, Viswesvaran, & Schmidt, 2003). Psychologists are also concerned because honesty tests are often administered by untrained people. Yet another cause for concern is the fact that 96 percent of test takers who fail are *falsely labeled* as dishonest (Camara & Schneider, 1994). In North America alone, that means well over a million workers a year are wrongly accused of being dishonest (Rieke & Guastello, 1995).

Some states have banned the use of honesty tests as the sole basis for deciding whether to hire a person. Yet it's easy to understand why employers want to do whatever they can to reduce theft and dishonesty in the workplace. The pressures to use honesty tests are intense. No doubt, the debate about honesty testing will continue. Honest.

from their reactions to movies or paintings. If so, you will have some insight into the rationale for projective tests. In a **projective test**, a person is asked to describe ambiguous stimuli or make up stories about them. Describing an unambiguous stimulus (a picture of an automobile, for example) tells little about your personality. But when you are faced with an unstructured stimulus, you must organize what you see in terms of your own life experiences. Everyone sees something different in a projective test, and what is perceived can reveal the inner workings of personality.

Projective tests have no right or wrong answers, which makes them difficult to fake (Vane & Guarnaccia, 1989). Moreover, projective tests can be a rich source of information, because responses are not restricted to simple true/false or yes/no answers.

The Rorschach Inkblot Test

Is the inkblot test a projective technique? The inkblot test, or **Rorschach** (ROAR-shock) **Technique**, is one of the oldest and most widely used projective tests. Developed by Swiss psychologist Hermann Rorschach in the 1920s, it consists of 10 standardized inkblots. These vary in color, shading, form, and complexity.

How does the test work? First, a person is shown each blot and asked to describe what she or he sees in it (● Figure 14.10). Later the psychologist may return to a blot, asking the person to identify specific sections of it, to expand previous descriptions, or to give new impressions about what it contains. Obvious differences in content—such as "blood dripping from a dagger" versus "flowers blooming in a field"—are important for identifying personal conflicts and fantasies. But surprisingly, content is less important than what parts of the inkblot are used to organize images. These factors allow psychologists to detect emotional disturbances by observing how a person perceives the world (Hilsenroth, 2000). The Rorschach is especially good at detecting psychosis, one of the most serious of all mental disorders (Ganellen, 1996).

The Thematic Apperception Test

Another popular projective test is the **Thematic Apperception Test (TAT)** developed by personality theorist Henry Murray (1893–1988).

How does the TAT differ from the Rorschach? The TAT consists of 20 sketches depicting various scenes and life situations (● Figure 14.11). During testing, a person is shown each sketch and asked to make up a story about the people in it. Later, the person looks at each sketch a second or a third time and elaborates on previous stories or creates new stories.

BRIDGES

Schizophrenia and other psychotic disorders are associated with severe disturbances in thinking and perception. Such disturbances are usually readily apparent during projective testing.

See Chapter 16, pages 549–550.

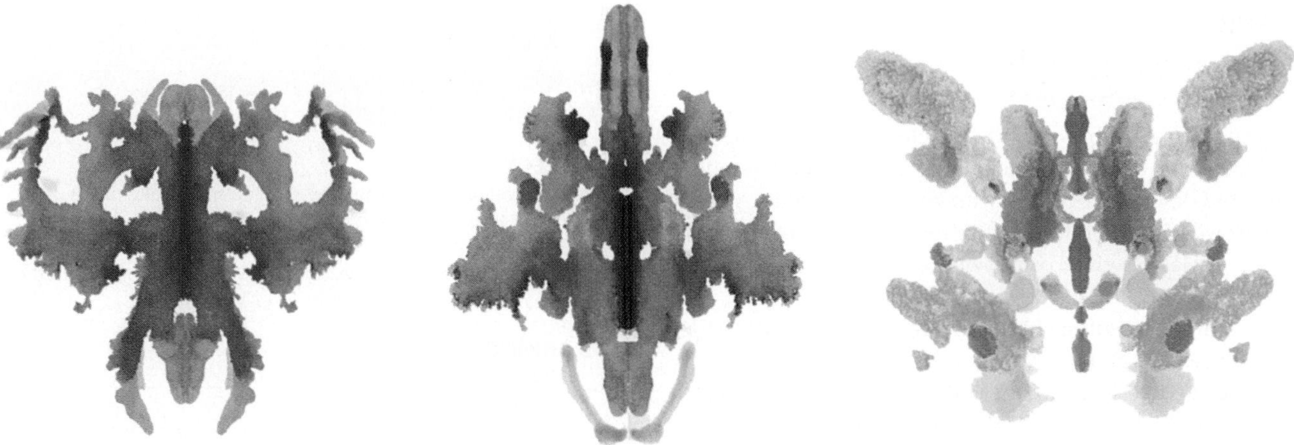

●**Figure 14.10** Inkblots similar to those used on the Rorschach. What do you see?

●**Figure 14.11** This is a picture like those used for the Thematic Apperception Test. If you wish to simulate the test, tell a story that explains what led up to the pictured situation, what is happening now, and how the action will end.

To score the TAT, a psychologist analyzes the content of the stories. Interpretations focus on how people feel, how they interact, what events led up to the incidents depicted in the sketch, and how the story will end. For example, TAT stories told by bereaved college students typically include themes of death, grief, and coping with loss (Balk et al., 1998).

A psychologist might also count the number of times the central figure in a TAT story is angry, overlooked, apathetic, jealous, or threatened. Here is a story written by a student to describe ● Figure 14.11:

> The girl has been seeing this guy her mother doesn't like. The mother is telling her that she better not see him again. The mother says, "He's just like your father." The mother and father are divorced. The mother is smiling because she thinks she is right. But she doesn't really know what the girl wants. The girl is going to see the guy again, anyway.

As this example implies, the TAT is especially good at revealing feelings about a person's social relationships (Alvarado, 1994).

Limitations of Projective Testing

Although projective tests have been popular, their validity is considered lowest among tests of personality (Lilienfeld, 1999). Objectivity and reliability (consistency) are also low for different users of the TAT and Rorschach. Note that after a person interprets an ambiguous stimulus, the scorer must interpret the person's (sometimes) ambiguous responses. In a sense, the interpretation of a projective test may be a projective test for the scorer!

Despite their drawbacks, projective tests still have value (Weiner, 1997). This is especially true when they are used as part of a *test battery* (collection of assessment devices and interviews). In the hands of a skilled clinician, projective tests can be a good way to detect major conflicts, to get clients to talk about upsetting topics, and to set goals for therapy (O'Roark, 2001).

Honesty test A paper-and-pencil test designed to detect attitudes, beliefs, and behavior patterns that predispose a person to dishonest behavior.

Projective tests Psychological tests making use of ambiguous or unstructured stimuli.

Rorschach Technique A projective test comprised of 10 standardized inkblots.

Thematic Apperception Test (TAT) A projective test consisting of 20 different scenes and life situations about which respondents make up stories.

Sudden Murderers—A Research Example

Personality assessments provide us with clues to some of the most perplexing human events. Consider Fred Cowan, a model student in school and described by those who knew him as quiet, gentle, and a man who loved children. Despite his size (6 feet tall, 250 pounds), Fred was described by a coworker as "someone you could easily push around."

Fred Cowan represents a puzzling phenomenon: We occasionally read in the news about sudden murderers—gentle, quiet, shy, good-natured people who explode without warning into violence (Lee, Zimbardo, & Bertholf, 1977). Two weeks after he was suspended from his job, Fred returned to work determined to get even with his supervisor. Unable to find the man, he killed four coworkers and a policeman before taking his own life.

Isn't such behavior contrary to the idea of personality traits? It might seem that sudden murderers are newsworthy simply because they are unlikely candidates for violence. On the contrary, research conducted by Melvin Lee, Philip Zimbardo, and Minerva Bertholf suggests that sudden murderers explode into violence *because* they are shy, restrained, and inexpressive, not in spite of it. These researchers studied prisoners at a California prison. Ten were inmates whose homicide was an unexpected first offense. Nine were criminals with a record of habitual violence prior to murder. Sixteen were inmates convicted of nonviolent crimes.

Did the inmates differ in personality makeup? Each of the inmates took a battery of tests, including the MMPI, a measure of shyness, and an adjective checklist. Personal interviews were also done with each inmate. As expected, the sudden murderers were passive, shy, and overcontrolled (restrained) individuals. The habitually violent inmates were "masculine" (aggressive), undercontrolled (impulsive), and less likely to view themselves as shy than the inmates convicted of nonviolent crimes (Lee, Zimbardo, & Bertholf, 1977).

Psychologists have learned that quiet, overcontrolled individuals are likely to be especially violent if they ever lose control. Their attacks are usually triggered by a minor irritation or frustration, but the attack reflects years of unexpressed feelings of anger and belittlement. When sudden murderers finally release the strict controls they have maintained on their behavior, a furious and frenzied attack ensues. Usually it is totally out of proportion to the offense against them and many have amnesia for their violent actions.

In comparison, the previously violent murderers showed very different reactions. Although they killed, their violence was moderate—usually only enough to do the necessary damage. Typically, they felt they had been cheated or betrayed and that they were doing what was necessary to remedy the situation or maintain their manhood (Lee, Zimbardo, & Bertholf, 1977).

A Look Ahead

The preceding example illustrates how some of the concepts and techniques discussed in this chapter can be applied to further our understanding. The Psychology in Action section that follows should add balance to your view of personality. Don't be shy. Read on!

KNOWLEDGE BUILDER

Personality Assessment

REFLECT

How do *you* assess personality? Do you informally make use of any of the methods described in this chapter?

You are a candidate for a desirable job. Your personality is going to be assessed by a psychologist. What method (or methods) would you prefer that she or he use? Why?

LEARNING CHECK

1. Planned questions are used in a ________________ interview.
2. The halo effect is the tendency of an interviewer to influence what is said by the interviewee. T or F?
3. Which of the following is considered the most objective measure of personality?
   a. rating scales
   b. personality questionnaires
   c. projective tests
   d. TAT
4. Situational testing allows direct ________________ of personality characteristics.
5. A psychotic person would probably score highest on which MMPI-2 scale?
   a. depression
   b. hysteria
   c. schizophrenia
   d. mania
6. The use of ambiguous stimuli is most characteristic of
   a. interviews
   b. projective tests
   c. personality inventories
   d. direct observation
7. The content of one's responses to the MMPI-2 is considered an indication of unconscious wishes, thoughts, and needs. T or F?
8. Doing a behavioral assessment requires direct observation of the person's actions or a direct report of the person's thoughts. T or F?
9. A surprising finding is that sudden murderers are usually undercontrolled, very masculine, and more impulsive than average. T or F?
10. A test is considered valid if it consistently yields the same score when the same person takes it on different occasions. T or F?

CRITICAL THINKING

11. Can you think of one more reason why personality traits may not be accurately revealed by interviews?
12. Projective testing would be of greatest interest to which type of personality theorist?

Answers: 1. structured **2.** F **3.** b **4.** observation **5.** c **6.** b **7.** F **8.** T **9.** F **10.** F **11.** Because of trait-situation interactions, a person may not behave in a normal fashion while being evaluated in an interview. **12.** Psychodynamic: Because projective testing is designed to uncover unconscious thoughts, feelings, and conflicts.

PSYCHOLOGY IN ACTION

Barriers and Bridges—Understanding Shyness

As a personality trait, **shyness** refers to a tendency to avoid others, as well as feelings of anxiety, preoccupation, and social inhibition (uneasiness and strain when socializing) (Bruch, 2001). Shy persons fail to make eye contact, retreat when spoken to, speak too quietly, and display little interest or animation in conversations. Do you

- Find it hard to talk to strangers?
- Lack confidence with people?
- Feel uncomfortable in social situations?
- Feel nervous with people who are not close friends?

If so, you may be part of the *50 percent* of college students who consider themselves shy (Carducci & Stein, 1988). Mild shyness may be no more than a nuisance. However, extreme shyness is often associated with depression, loneliness, fearfulness, social anxiety, inhibition, and low self-esteem (Henderson, 1997; Jackson et al., 2002).

Elements of Shyness

What causes shyness? To begin with, shy persons often lack *social skills* (proficiency at interacting with others). Many simply have not learned how to meet people or how to start a conversation and keep it going. **Social anxiety** (a feeling of apprehension in the presence of others) is also a factor in shyness. Almost everyone feels nervous in some social situations (such as meeting an attractive stranger). Typically, this is a reaction to evaluation fears (fears of being inadequate, embarrassed, ridiculed, or rejected). Although fears of rejection are common, they are much more frequent or intense for shy persons (Jackson, Towson, & Narduzzi, 1997). A third problem for shy persons is a *self-defeating bias* (distortion) in their thinking. Specifically, shy persons almost always blame themselves when a social encounter doesn't go well. They are unnecessarily self-critical in social situations (Lundh et al., 2002).

Situational Causes of Shyness

Shyness is most often triggered by *novel* or *unfamiliar* social situations. A person who does fine with family or close friends may become shy and awkward when meeting a stranger. Shyness is also magnified by formality, by meeting someone of higher status, by being noticeably different from others, or by being the focus of attention (as in giving a speech) (Buss, 1980).

Don't most people become cautious and inhibited in such circumstances? Yes. That's why we need to see how the personalities of shy and non-shy persons differ.

Dynamics of the Shy Personality

There is a tendency to think that shy persons are wrapped up in their own feelings and thoughts. But surprisingly, researchers Jonathan Cheek and Arnold Buss (1979) found no connection between shyness and **private self-consciousness** (attention to inner feelings, thoughts, and fantasies). Instead, they discovered that shyness is linked to **public self-consciousness** (acute awareness of oneself as a social object).

Digital Vision/Getty Images

BRIDGES

From 3 to 5 percent of North Americans are so shy that they suffer from "social anxiety disorder" and need treatment.

See Chapter 16, page 544, for more information.

Shyness A tendency to avoid others plus uneasiness and strain when socializing.

Social anxiety A feeling of apprehension in the presence of others.

Private self-consciousness Preoccupation with inner feelings, thoughts, and fantasies.

Public self-consciousness Intense awareness of oneself as a social object.

Persons who rate high in public self-consciousness are intensely concerned about what others think of them (Buss, 1980). They worry about saying the wrong thing or appearing foolish. In public, they may feel "naked" or as if others can "see through them." Such feelings trigger anxiety or outright fear during social encounters, leading to awkwardness and inhibition (Buss, 1986). The shy person's anxiety, in turn, often causes her or him to misperceive others in social situations (Schroeder, 1995).

As mentioned, almost everyone feels anxious in at least some social situations. But there is a key difference in the way shy and not-shy persons *label* this anxiety. Shy persons tend to consider their social anxiety a *lasting personality trait*. Shyness, in other words, becomes part of their self-concept. In contrast, not-shy persons believe that *external situations* cause their occasional feelings of shyness. When not-shy persons feel anxiety or "stage fright," they assume that almost anyone would feel as they do under the same circumstances (Zimbardo, Pilkonis, & Norwood, 1978).

Labeling is important because it affects *self-esteem*. In general, not-shy persons tend to have higher self-esteem than shy persons. This is because not-shy persons give themselves credit for their social successes and they recognize that failures are often due to circumstances. In contrast, shy people blame themselves for social failures, never give themselves credit for successes, and expect to be rejected (Buss, 1980; Jackson et al., 2002).

Shy Beliefs

What can be done to reduce shyness? While directing a shyness clinic, psychologist Michel Girodo (1978) observed that shyness is often maintained by unrealistic or self-defeating beliefs. Here's a sample of such beliefs.

1. *If you wait around long enough at a social gathering, something will happen.*
   Comment: This is really a cover-up for fear of starting a conversation. For two people to meet, at least one has to make an effort, and it might as well be you.
2. *Other people who are popular are just lucky when it comes to being invited to social events or asked out.*
   Comment: Except for times when a person is formally introduced to someone new, this is false. People who are more active socially typically make an effort to meet and spend time with others. They join clubs, invite others to do things, strike up conversations, and generally leave little to luck.
3. *The odds of meeting someone interested in socializing are always the same, no matter where I am.*
   Comment: This is another excuse for inaction. It pays to seek out situations that have a higher probability of leading to social contact, such as clubs, teams, and school events.
4. *If someone doesn't seem to like you right away, they really don't like you and never will.*
   Comment: This belief leads to much needless shyness. Even when a person doesn't show immediate interest, it doesn't mean the person dislikes you. Liking takes time and opportunity to develop.

Unproductive beliefs like the preceding can be replaced with statements such as the following.

1. I've got to be active in social situations.
2. I can't wait until I'm completely relaxed or comfortable before taking a social risk.
3. I don't need to pretend to be someone I'm not; it just makes me more anxious.
4. I may think other people are harshly evaluating me, but actually I'm being too hard on myself.
5. I can set reasonable goals for expanding my social experience and skills.
6. Even people who are very socially skillful are never successful 100 percent of the time. I shouldn't get so upset when an encounter goes badly. (Adapted from Girodo, 1978.)

Social Skills

Learning social skills takes practice. There is nothing "innate" about knowing how to meet people or start a conversation. Social skills can be directly practiced in a variety of ways. It can be helpful, for instance, to get a tape recorder and listen to several of your conversations. You may be surprised by the way you pause, interrupt, miss cues, or seem disinterested. Similarly, it can be useful to look at yourself in a mirror and exaggerate facial expressions of surprise, interest, dislike, pleasure, and so forth. By such methods, most people can learn to put more animation and skill into their self-presentation. (For a discussion of related skills, see the section on self-assertion in Chapter 18.)

Conversation

One of the simplest ways to make better conversation is by learning to ask questions. A good series of questions shifts attention to the other person and shows you are interested. Nothing fancy is needed. You can do fine with questions such as, "Where do you (work, study, live)? Do you like (dancing, travel, music)? How long have you (been at this school, worked here, lived here)?" After you've broken the ice, the best questions are often those that are *open ended* (they can't be answered yes or no):

> "What parts of the country have you seen?" (as opposed to, "Have you ever been to Florida?")
> "What's it like living on the West Side?" (as opposed to, "Do you like living on the West Side?")
> "What kinds of food do you like?" (as opposed to, "Do you like Chinese cooking?")

It's easy to see why open-ended questions are helpful. In replying to open-ended questions, people often give "free information" about themselves. This extra information can be used to ask other questions or to lead into other topics of conversation.

This brief sampling of ideas is no substitute for actual practice. Overcoming shyness requires a real effort to learn new skills and test old beliefs and attitudes. It may even require the help of a counselor or therapist. At the very least, a shy person must be willing to take social risks. Breaking down the barriers of shyness will always include some awkward or unsuccessful encounters. Nevertheless, the rewards are powerful: human companionship and personal freedom.

KNOWLEDGE BUILDER

Understanding Shyness

REFLECT

If you are shy, see if you can summarize how social skills, social anxiety, evaluation fears, self-defeating thoughts, and public self-consciousness contribute to your social inhibition. If you're not shy, imagine how you would explain these concepts to a shy friend.

LEARNING CHECK

1. Surveys show that 14 percent of American college students consider themselves shy. T or F?
2. Social anxiety and evaluation fears are seen almost exclusively in shy individuals; the non-shy rarely have such experiences. T or F?
3. Unfamiliar people and situations most often trigger shyness. T or F?
4. Contrary to what many people think, shyness is *not* related to
   a. private self-consciousness
   b. social anxiety
   c. self-esteem
   d. blaming oneself for social failures
5. Shy persons tend to consider their social anxiety to be a
   a. situational reaction c. public efficacy
   b. personality trait d. habit
6. Changing personal beliefs and practicing social skills can be helpful in overcoming shyness. T or F?

CRITICAL THINKING

7. Shyness is a trait of Vonda's personality. Like most shy people, Vonda is most likely to feel shy in unfamiliar social settings. Vonda's shy behavior demonstrates that the expression of traits is governed by what concept?

Answers: 1. F **2.** F **3.** T **4.** T **5.** b **6.** a **7.** trait-situation interactions (again)

Chapter in Review

How do psychologists use the term *personality?*

- Personality is made up of one's unique and enduring behavior patterns.
- Character is personality evaluated, or the possession of desirable qualities.
- Temperament refers to the hereditary and physiological aspects of one's emotional nature.

What core concepts make up the psychology of personality?

- Personality traits are lasting personal qualities that are inferred from behavior.
- Personality types group people into categories on the basis of shared traits or similar characteristics.
- Behavior is influenced by self-concept, which is a perception of one's own personality traits.
- A positive self-evaluation leads to high self-esteem. Low self-esteem is associated with stress, unhappiness, and depression.
- Personality theories combine interrelated assumptions, ideas, and principles to explain personality.

Are some personality traits more basic or important than others?

- Trait theories identify qualities that are most lasting or characteristic of a person.
- Allport made useful distinctions between common traits and individual traits and among cardinal, central, and secondary traits.
- Cattell's trait theory attributes visible surface traits to the existence of underlying source traits. Cattell used factor analysis to identify 16 source traits.
- Source traits are measured by the *Sixteen Personality Factor Questionnaire* (16 PF). Like other trait measures, the outcome of the 16 PF may be graphed as a trait profile.
- The five-factor model identifies five universal dimensions of personality: extroversion, agreeableness, conscientiousness, neuroticism, and openness to experience.
- Traits interact with situations to determine behavior. Neither factor alone fully explains our actions.
- Behavioral genetics and studies of separated identical twins suggest that heredity contributes significantly to adult personality traits.

How do psychodynamic theories explain personality?

- Like other psychodynamic approaches, Sigmund Freud's psychoanalytic theory emphasizes unconscious forces and conflicts within the personality.
- In Freud's theory, personality is made up of the id, ego, and superego.
- Libido, derived from the life instincts, is the primary energy running the personality. Conflicts within the personality may cause neurotic anxiety or moral anxiety and motivate use of ego-defense mechanisms.

- The personality operates on three levels, the conscious, preconscious, and unconscious.
- The Freudian view of personality development is based on a series of psychosexual stages: the oral, anal, phallic, and genital stages. Fixation at any stage can leave a lasting imprint on personality.
- Neo-Freudian theorists accepted the broad features of Freudian psychology, but developed their own views. Three representative neo-Freudians are Alfred Adler, Karen Horney, and Carl Jung.

What do behaviorists emphasize in their approach to personality?

- Behavioral theories of personality emphasize learning, conditioning, and immediate effects of the environment.
- Learning theorists generally stress the effects of prior learning and situational determinants of behavior.
- Learning theorists John Dollard and Neal Miller consider habits the basic core of personality. Habits express the combined effects of drive, cue, response, and reward.
- Social learning theory adds cognitive elements, such as perception, thinking, and understanding to the behavioral view of personality. Examples of such concepts include the psychological situation, expectancies, and reinforcement value. Some social learning theorists treat "conscience" as a case of self-reinforcement.
- The behavioristic view of personality development holds that social reinforcement in four situations is critical. The critical situations are feeding, toilet or cleanliness training, sex training, and anger or aggression training. Identification and imitation are of particular importance in sex training.

How do humanistic theories differ from other perspectives?

- Humanistic theory emphasizes subjective experience and needs for self-actualization.
- Abraham Maslow's study of self-actualizers identified characteristics they share, ranging from efficient perceptions of reality to frequent peak experiences.
- Carl Rogers's theory views the self as an entity that emerges from personal experience. Experiences that match the self-image are symbolized (admitted to consciousness), whereas those that are incongruent are excluded.
- The incongruent person has a highly unrealistic self-image and/or a mismatch between the self-image and the ideal self. The congruent or fully functioning person is flexible and open to experiences and feelings.
- In the development of personality, humanists are primarily interested in the emergence of a self-image and in self-evaluations.
- As parents apply conditions of worth to children's behavior, thoughts, and feelings, children begin to do the same. Internalized conditions of worth then contribute to incongruence and disrupt the organismic valuing process.

How do psychologists measure personality?

- Techniques typically used for personality assessment are interviews, observation, questionnaires, and projective tests.
- Structured and unstructured interviews provide much information, but they are subject to interviewer bias and misperceptions. The halo effect may also lower the accuracy of an interview.
- Direct observation, sometimes involving situational tests, behavioral assessment, or the use of rating scales, allows evaluation of a person's actual behavior.
- Personality questionnaires, such as the *Minnesota Multiphasic Personality Inventory-2* (MMPI-2), are objective and reliable, but their validity is open to question.
- Honesty tests, which are essentially personality questionnaires, are widely used by businesses to make hiring decisions. Their validity is hotly debated.
- Projective tests ask a subject to project thoughts or feelings to an ambiguous stimulus or unstructured situation.
- The *Rorschach Technique,* or inkblot test, is a well-known projective technique. A second is the *Thematic Apperception Test* (TAT).
- The validity and objectivity of projective tests are quite low. Nevertheless, projective techniques are considered useful by many clinicians, particularly as part of a test battery.

What causes shyness? What can be done about it?

- Shyness is a mixture of social inhibition and social anxiety. It is marked by heightened public self-consciousness and a tendency to regard one's shyness as a lasting trait.
- Shyness can be lessened by changing self-defeating beliefs and by improving social skills.

Web Resources

Internet addresses frequently change. To find the sites listed here, visit www.thomsonedu.com/psychology/coon for an updated list of Internet addresses and direct links to relevant sites.

***Psychology: Gateways to Mind and Behavior* Website** Online quizzes, flash cards, and other helpful study aids for this text. www.thomsonedu.com/psychology/coon.

About Humanistic Psychology Discusses the history and future of humanistic psychology.

FAQ About Psychological Tests Answers to commonly asked questions about tests and testing.

Freud Net Offers links to information on Freud and psychoanalysis.

Personality and IQ Tests Multiple links to personality tests and IQ tests that are scored online.

ThomsonNOW™ Go to www.thomsonedu.com to link to ThomsonNow, your online study tool. First take the **Pre-Test** for this chapter to get your **Personalized Study Plan**, which will identify topics you need to review and direct you to online resources. Then take the **Post-Test** to determine what concepts you have mastered and what you still need work on.

InfoTrac College Edition For recent articles related to heritability of personality traits, use Key Words search for TWIN STUDIES. Go to www.thomsonedu.com/psychology/coon.

Interactive Learning

***PsychNow!* Version 2.0 CD-ROM** Interact with the material with *PsychNow!*'s animations, video clips, experiments, and interactive assessments. For this chapter, go to *7a. Theories of Personality* and *7e. Assessment* to learn more about personality theory and assessment.

chapter 15

Health, Stress, and Coping

THEME:

Health is affected greatly by lifestyle and behavior patterns, especially those related to stress.

Royalty-Free/Corbis

Key Questions

What is health psychology? How does behavior affect health?

What is stress? What factors determine its severity?

What causes frustration and what are typical reactions to it?

Are there different types of conflict? How do people react to conflict?

What are defense mechanisms?

What do we know about coping with feelings of helplessness and depression?

How is stress related to health and disease?

What are the best strategies for managing stress?

Preview

Taylor's (Not So Very) Fine Adventure

Somehow, Taylor had managed to survive the rush of make-or-break term papers, projects, and classroom speeches. Then it was on to finals, where his tests seemed perfectly timed to inflict as much suffering as possible. His two hardest exams fell on the same day! Great. What luck!

On the last day of finals, Taylor got caught in a traffic jam on his way to school. Two drivers cut him off, and another gave him a one-finger salute. When Taylor finally got to campus the parking lot was swarming with frantic students. Most of them, like him, were within minutes of missing a final exam. At last, Taylor spied an empty space. As he started toward it, a Volkswagen darted around the corner and into "his" place. The driver of the car behind him began to honk impatiently. For a moment, Taylor was seized by a colossal desire to run over anything in sight.

Finally, after a week and a half of stress, pressure, and frustration, Taylor's finals were over. Sleep deprivation, gallons of coffee, junk food, and equal portions of cramming and complaining had carried him through. He was off for the summer. At last, he could kick back, relax, and have some fun. Or could he? Just four days after the end of school, Taylor got a bad cold, followed by bronchitis that lasted for nearly a month.

Taylor's experience illustrates what happens when stress, emotion, personal habits, and health collide. Although the timing of his cold might have been a coincidence, odds are it wasn't. Periods of stress are frequently followed by illness (Biondi & Zannino, 1997).

In the first part of this chapter we will explore a variety of behavioral health risks. Then we will look more closely at what stress is and how it affects us. After that, we will stress ways of coping with stress, so you can do a better job of staying healthy than Taylor did.

Health Psychology—Here's to Your Good Health

Health is priceless. It's also free. Despite the high cost of health-care, one of the most important sources of health is free for the taking. Health psychologists have shown that many of the diseases that bedevil us are caused by unhealthy behavior. Let's see which personal habits contribute the most to leading a long, healthy, and happy life.

Most people agree that health is important—especially their own. Yet half of all deaths in North America are primarily due to unhealthy behavior (Mokdad et al., 2004). **Health psychology** aims to do something about such deaths by using behavioral principles to promote health and prevent illness. Psychologists working in the allied field of **behavioral medicine** apply psychology to manage medical problems, such as diabetes or asthma. Their interests include pain control, helping people cope with chronic illness, stress-related diseases, self-screening for diseases (such as breast cancer), and similar topics (Brannon & Feist, 2004).

Behavioral Risk Factors

Around the turn of the twentieth century, people primarily died from infectious diseases and accidents. Today, people generally die from **lifestyle diseases**, which are related to health-damaging personal habits. Examples include heart disease, stroke, and lung cancer (McGinnis & Foege, 1993) (● Figure 15.1). Clearly, some lifestyles promote health, whereas others lead to illness and death. As one observer put it, "We have met the enemy and he is us."

What kinds of behavior are you referring to as unhealthy? Some causes of illness are beyond our control, but many behavioral risks can be reduced. **Behavioral risk factors** are actions that increase the chances of disease, injury, or early death. For example, approximately 435,000 people die every year from smoking-related diseases. Similarly, being overweight *doubles* the chance of dying from cancer or heart disease. Roughly 60 percent of all American adults are overweight. As a result, obesity may soon overtake smoking as the main cause of preventable deaths. Being fat is not just a matter of fashion—in the long run it could kill

Health psychology Study of the ways in which behavioral principles can be used to prevent illness and promote health.

Behavioral medicine The study of behavioral factors in medicine, physical illness, and medical treatment.

Lifestyle disease A disease related to health-damaging personal habits.

Behavioral risk factors Behaviors that increase the chances of disease, injury, or premature death.

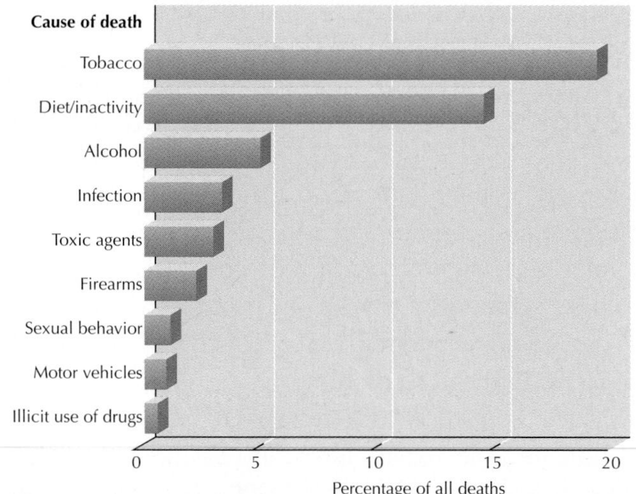

● **Figure 15.1** The nine leading causes of death in the United States are shown in this graph. As you can see, eight of the top nine causes are directly related to behavioral risk factors (infection is the exception). At least half of all deaths can be traced to unhealthful behavior. The percentage of day-to-day health problems related to unhealthful behavior is even higher (Mokdad et al., 2004). (Data from McGinnis & Foege, 2002.)

TABLE 15.1

Percentage of U.S. High School Students Who Engaged in Health-Endangering Behaviors

RISKY BEHAVIOR	PERCENTAGE
Rode with drinking driver (previous month)	35
Were in a physical fight (previous year)	42
Carried a weapon (previous month)	22
Had five or more drinks on one occasion (previous month)	30
Have used marijuana	33
Have engaged in sexual intercourse	53
Did not use condom during last sexual intercourse	47
Smoked cigarettes (previous month)	31
Ate high-fat food (previous day)	34
No vigorous exercise (previous week)	34

Kolbe, Collins, & Cortese, 1997.

you. A person who is overweight at age 20 can expect to lose 5 to 20 years of life expectancy (Fontaine et al., 2003).

Each of the following factors is a major behavioral risk (Baum & Posluszny, 1999): high levels of stress, untreated high blood pressure, cigarette smoking, abuse of alcohol or other drugs, overeating, inadequate exercise, unsafe sexual behavior, exposure to toxic substances, violence, excess sun exposure, reckless driving, and disregarding personal safety (accidents). Seventy percent of all medical costs are related to just six of the listed factors—smoking, alcohol and drug abuse, poor diet, insufficient exercise, and risky sexual practices (Orleans, Gruman, & Hollendonner, 1999).

■ Table 15.1 shows how many high school students in the United States engage in risky behaviors of the kind listed here. The health habits you have by the time you are 18 or 19 greatly affect your health, happiness, and life expectancy years later (Vaillant & Mukamal, 2001).

Specific risk factors are not the only concern. Some people have a general **disease-prone personality** that leaves them depressed, anxious, hostile, and . . . frequently ill. In contrast, people who are intellectually resourceful, compassionate, optimistic, and non-hostile tend to enjoy good health (Taylor et al., 2000). Depression, in particular, is likely to damage health. People who are depressed eat poorly, sleep poorly, rarely exercise, fail to use seat belts in cars, smoke more, and so on (Allgower, Wardle, Steptoe, 2001).

Lifestyle

In your mind's eye, fast-forward an imaginary film of your life all the way to old age. Do it twice—once with a lifestyle including a large number of behavioral risk factors, and again without them. It should be obvious that many small risks can add up, dramatically raising the chance of illness. If stress is a frequent part of your life, visualize your body seething with emotion, day after day. If you smoke, picture a lifetime's worth of cigarette smoke blown through your lungs in a week. If you drink, take a lifetime of alcohol's assaults on the brain, stomach, and liver and squeeze them into a month: Your body would be poisoned, ravaged, and soon dead. If you eat a high-fat, high-cholesterol diet, fast-forward a lifetime of heart-killing plaque clogging your arteries.

This discussion is not meant to be a sermon. It is merely a reminder that risk factors do make a difference. To make matters

Darren Robb/Getty Images

Jeffrey Allan Salter/Corbis

In the long run, behavioral risk factors and lifestyles do make a difference in health and life expectancy.

TABLE 15.2

Major Health-Promoting Behaviors

SOURCE	DESIRABLE BEHAVIORS
Nutrition	Eating a balanced, low-fat diet; appropriate caloric intake; maintenance of healthy body weight
Exercise	At least 30 minutes of aerobic exercise, 5 days per week
Blood pressure	Lower blood pressure with diet and exercise, or medicine if necessary
Alcohol and drugs	No more than two drinks per day; abstain from using drugs
Tobacco	Do not smoke; do not use smokeless tobacco
Sleep and relaxation	Avoid sleep deprivation; provide for periods of relaxation every day
Sex	Practice safer sex; avoid unplanned pregnancy
Injury	Curb dangerous driving habits, use seat belts; minimize sun exposure; forgo dangerous activities
Stress	Learn stress management; lower hostility

worse, unhealthy lifestyles almost always create multiple risks. That is, people who smoke are also likely to drink excessively. Those who overeat usually do not get enough exercise, and so on (Emmons et al., 1998). Even infectious diseases are often linked to behavioral risks. For example, pneumonia and other infections occur at high rates in people who have cancer, heart disease, lung disease, or liver disease. Thus, many deaths attributed to infections can actually be traced to smoking, poor diet, or alcohol abuse (Mokdad et al., 2004).

Health-Promoting Behaviors

To prevent disease, health psychologists first try to remove behavioral risk factors. All the medicine in the world may not be enough to restore health without changes in behavior. We all know someone who has had a heart attack or lung disease who couldn't change the habits that led to their illness.

In some cases, diseases can be treated or prevented by making relatively minor, but very specific changes in behavior. For example, hypertension (high blood pressure) can be deadly. Yet for some people simple lifestyle changes will fend off this "silent killer." Here's the recipe for lower blood pressure: lose weight, consume less sodium (salt), use alcohol sparingly, and get more exercise (Georgiades et al., 2000).

In addition to removing risk factors, psychologists are interested in getting people to increase behaviors that promote health. Health-promoting behaviors include such obvious practices as getting regular exercise, controlling smoking and alcohol use, maintaining a balanced diet, getting good medical care, and managing stress (Glik, Kronenfeld, & Jackson, 1996). In fact, a recent medical study revealed that just four of these factors can greatly increase life expectancy. The risk of dying was cut by 65 percent during a 10-year period for adults who were careful about diet, alcohol, exercise, and smoking (Knoops et al., 2004).

Do health-promoting behaviors seem restrictive or burdensome? They don't have to be. For instance, maintaining a healthy diet doesn't mean surviving on tofu and wheat grass. The healthiest people in the study just described ate a tasty "Mediterranean diet," high in fruit, vegetables, and fish and low in red meat and dairy products. Likewise, you don't need to exercise like an Olympic athlete to benefit from physical activity. All you need is 30 minutes of exercise (the equivalent of a brisk walk) three or four times a week. Almost everyone can fit such "lifestyle physical activity" into his or her schedule (Pescatello, 2001).

What about alcohol? Moderation in drinking doesn't mean that you must be a teetotaler. Consuming one or two alcoholic drinks per day is generally safe for most people, especially if you remain alcohol free two or three days a week. However, having three or more drinks a day greatly increases the risk of stroke, cirrhosis of the liver, cancer, high blood pressure, heart disorders, and other diseases (Knoops et al., 2004).

To summarize, a small number of behavioral patterns accounts for many common health problems (Kolbe, Collins, & Cortese, 1997). ■ Table 15.2 lists several major ways to promote good health.

Early Prevention

Of the behavioral risks we have discussed, smoking is the largest preventable cause of death and the single most lethal factor (Mokdad et al., 2004). As such, it illustrates the prospect for preventing illness.

Disease-prone personality A personality type associated with poor health; marked by persistent negative emotions, including anxiety, depression, and hostility.

What have health psychologists done to lessen the risks? Attempts to "immunize" youths against pressures to start smoking are a good example. The smoker who says, "Quitting is easy, I've done it dozens of times," states a basic truth—only one smoker in ten has long-term success at quitting. Thus, the best way to deal with smoking is to prevent it before it becomes a lifelong habit. For example, school-based prevention programs have used quizzes about smoking, antismoking art contests, poster and T-shirt giveaways, antismoking pamphlets for parents, and questions for students to ask their parents (Biglan et al., 1996). Such efforts are designed to persuade kids that smoking is dangerous and "uncool." Apparently, many teens are getting the message, as attitudes toward smoking are now more negative than they were twenty years ago (Chassin et al., 2003).

Some of the best antismoking programs include **refusal skills training.** In this case, youths learn to resist pressures to begin smoking (or using other drugs). For example, junior high students can role-play ways to resist smoking pressures from peers, adults, and cigarette ads. Similar methods can be applied to other health risks, such as sexually transmitted diseases and teen pregnancy (Wandersman & Florin, 2003).

The latest health programs also teach students general life skills. The idea is to give kids skills that will help them cope with day-to-day stresses. That way, they will be less tempted to escape problems through drug use or other destructive behaviors. **Life skills training** includes practice in stress reduction, self-protection, decision making, goal setting, self-control, and social skills (Tobler et al., 2000).

Community Health

In addition to early prevention, health psychologists have had some success with **community health campaigns.** These are community-wide education projects designed to lessen major risk factors. Health campaigns inform people of risks such as stress, alcohol abuse, high blood pressure, high cholesterol, smoking, STDs, or excessive sun exposure. This is followed by efforts to motivate people to change their behavior. Campaigns sometimes provide *role models* (positive examples) who show people how to improve their own health. They also direct people to services for health screening, advice, and treatment. Health campaigns may reach people through the mass media, public schools, health fairs, their work, or self-help programs. Such programs are increasingly successful in helping people make healthful changes in their behavior (Orleans, 2000).

Positive Psychology: Wellness

Health is not just an absence of disease. People who are truly healthy enjoy a positive state of **wellness** or well-being. Maintaining wellness is a life-long pursuit and, hopefully, a labor of love. People who attain optimal wellness are both physically and psychologically healthy. They are happy, optimistic, self-confident individuals who can bounce back emotionally from adversity (Tugade, Fredrickson, & Barrett, 2004).

People who enjoy a sense of well-being also have supportive relationships with others, they do meaningful work, and they live in a clean environment. Many of these aspects of wellness are addressed elsewhere in this book. In this chapter we will give special attention to the effect that stress has on health and sickness. Understanding stress and learning to control it can improve not only your health, but the quality of your life as well (Suinn, 2001). For these reasons, a discussion of stress and stress management follows.

KNOWLEDGE BUILDER

Health Psychology

REFLECT

If you were to work as a health psychologist would you be more interested in preventing disease or managing it?

Make a list of the major behavioral risk factors that apply to you. Are you laying the foundation for a lifestyle disease?

Which of the health-promoting behaviors listed in Table 15.2 would you like to increase?

If you were designing a community health campaign, who would you use as role models of healthful behavior?

LEARNING CHECK

1. Adjustment to chronic illness and the control of pain are topics that would more likely be of interest to a specialist in ________________ ________________ rather than to a health psychologist.
2. With respect to health, which of the following is *not* a major behavioral risk factor?
   a. overexercise c. stress
   b. cigarette smoking d. high blood pressure
3. Lifestyle diseases related to just six behaviors account for 70 percent of all medical costs. The behaviors are smoking, alcohol and drug abuse, poor diet, insufficient exercise, and
   a. driving too fast c. unsafe sex
   b. excessive sun exposure d. exposure to toxins
4. Health promoting behaviors that combat hypertension include the following: lose weight, consume less sodium, use alcohol sparingly, and get more
   a. sleep c. carbohydrates
   b. exercise d. cholesterol
5. Health psychologists tend to prefer ________________ rather than modifying habits (like smoking) that become difficult to break once they are established.
6. The disease-prone personality is marked by ________________ ________, anxiety, and hostility.

CRITICAL THINKING

7. The general public is increasingly well informed about health risks and healthful behavior. Can you apply the concept of reinforcement to explain why so many people fail to act on this information?

Answers: 1. behavioral medicine **2.** a **3.** c **4.** b **5.** prevention **6.** depression **7.** Many of the health payoffs are delayed by months or years, greatly lessening the immediate rewards for healthful behavior.

Stress—Thrill or Threat?

Although stress is a natural part of life, it can be a major behavioral risk factor if it is prolonged or severe. It might seem that stressful events "happen to" people. Although this is sometimes the case, more often stress is a matter of how we perceive events and react to them. Because of this, stress can often be managed or controlled. This unit explains how stress occurs and typical reactions to it.

Stress can be dangerous if it is prolonged or severe, but it isn't always bad. As stress researcher Hans Selye (SEL-yay) (1976) observed, "To be totally without stress is to be dead." That's because **stress** is the mental and physical condition that occurs when we adjust or adapt to the environment. Unpleasant events such as work pressures, marital problems, or financial woes naturally produce stress. But so do travel, sports, a new job, mountain climbing, dating, and other positive activities. Even if you aren't a thrill seeker, a healthy lifestyle may include a fair amount of *eustress* (good stress). Activities that provoke "good stress" are usually challenging, rewarding, and energizing.

A **stress reaction** begins with the same autonomic nervous system arousal that occurs during emotion. Imagine you are standing at the top of a wind-whipped ski jump for the first time. Internally, there would be a rapid surge in your heart rate, blood pressure, respiration, muscle tension, and other ANS responses. *Short-term* stresses of this kind can be uncomfortable, but they rarely do any damage. (Your landing might be another matter, however.) Later we will describe the *long-term* physical impact of prolonged stress—which can do harm (Sternberg, 2000). For now, here's a list of some of the typical signs or symptoms of ongoing stress (Doctor & Doctor, 1994).

Emotional signs: Anxiety, apathy, irritability, mental fatigue
Behavioral signs: Avoidance of responsibilities and relationships, extreme or self-destructive behavior, self-neglect, poor judgment
Physical signs: Excessive worry about illness, frequent illness, exhaustion, overuse of medicines, physical aliments and complaints

Other than when it is long lasting, why is stress sometimes damaging and sometimes not? Stress reactions are complex. Let's examine some of the chief factors that determine whether or not stress is harmful.

When Is Stress a Strain?

It goes almost without saying that some events are more likely to cause stress than others. A **stressor** is a condition or event that challenges or threatens a person. Police officers, for instance, suffer from a high rate of stress-related diseases. The threat of injury or death, plus occasional confrontations with angry, drunk, or hostile citizens, takes a toll. A major factor is the *unpredictable* nature of police work. An officer who stops a car to issue a traffic ticket never knows if a cooperative citizen or an armed gang member is waiting inside.

A revealing study shows how unpredictability adds to stress. In a series of one-minute trials, college students breathed air through a mask. On some trials, the air contained 20 percent more carbon dioxide (CO_2) than normal. If you were to inhale this air, you would feel anxious, stressed, and a little like you were suffocating. Students tested this way hated the "surprise" doses of CO_2. They found it much less stressful to be told in advance which trials would include a choking whiff of CO_2 (Lejuez, et al. 2000).

Pressure is another element of stress, especially job stress. **Pressure** occurs when a person must meet *urgent* external demands or expectations (Weiten, 1998). For example, we feel pressured when activities must be speeded up, when deadlines must be met, when extra work is added, or when we must work near maximum capacity for long periods. Most students who have survived final exams are familiar with the effects of pressure.

What if I set deadlines for myself? Does it make a difference where the pressure comes from? Yes. People generally feel more stress in situations over which they have little or no control (Taylor et al., 2000). Consider, for example, a study in which college students tried to avoid electric shocks. During testing, some students were allowed to select their own rest periods; others were told when they could rest. Students allowed to control their own rest periods had lower stress levels (as measured by blood pressure) than those who were given no choice (DeGood, 1975).

To summarize, when emotional "shocks" are *intense* or *repeated, unpredictable, uncontrollable,* and linked to *pressure,* stress will be magnified and damage is likely to result. (See ■ Table 15.3 for a rating of jobs that contain these elements.) At work, people face many of these sources of stress every day. In fact, chronic job stress sometimes results in *burnout,* a pattern of emotional exhaustion (see "Burnout—The High Cost of Caring").

Refusal skills training Program that teaches youths how to resist pressures to begin smoking. (Can also be applied to other drugs, and health risks.)

Life skills training A program that teaches stress reduction, self-protection, decision making, self-control, and social skills.

Community health campaign A community-wide education program that provides information about how to lessen risk factors and promote health.

Wellness A positive state of good health; more than the absence of disease.

Stress The mental and physical condition that occurs when a person must adjust or adapt to the environment.

Stress reaction The physical response to stress, consisting mainly of bodily changes related to autonomic nervous system arousal.

Stressor A specific condition or event in the environment that challenges or threatens a person.

Pressure A stressful condition that occurs when a person must meet urgent external demands or expectations.

THE CLINICAL FILE

Burnout—The High Cost of Caring

Margo, a young nurse, realizes with dismay that she has "lost all patience with her patients" and wishes they would "go somewhere else to be sick." Margo's feelings are a clear sign of job **burnout,** a condition in which workers are physically, mentally, and emotionally drained (Greenglass, Burke, & Moore, 2003). Burnout has three aspects (Maslach, Schaufeli, & Leiter, 2001).

- Emotional exhaustion: Affected persons are fatigued, tense, apathetic, and suffer from physical ailments. They feel "used up" and "empty."
- Cynicism or detachment: Burned-out workers have an "I don't give a damn anymore" attitude and they treat clients coldly, as if they were objects.
- Feelings of reduced personal accomplishment: Burned-out workers do poor work and feel helpless, hopeless, or angry.

Burnout may occur in any job, but it is a special problem in emotionally demanding helping professions, such as nursing, teaching, social work, childcare, counseling, or police work. Often, the most idealistic and caring workers are the ones who burn out. As some say, "You have to be on fire to burn out" (Maslach, Schaufeli, & Leiter, 2001).

If we wish to keep caring people in the helping professions, it may be necessary to adjust workloads, rewards, and the amount of control people have in their jobs (Maslach, Schaufeli, & Leiter, 2001). In general, social support helps people from many cultures resist burnout (Pines et al., 2002). For example, support groups at work help caregivers deal with stress by allowing them to talk about their feelings and problems at work (Greenglass, Burke, & Konarski, 1998).

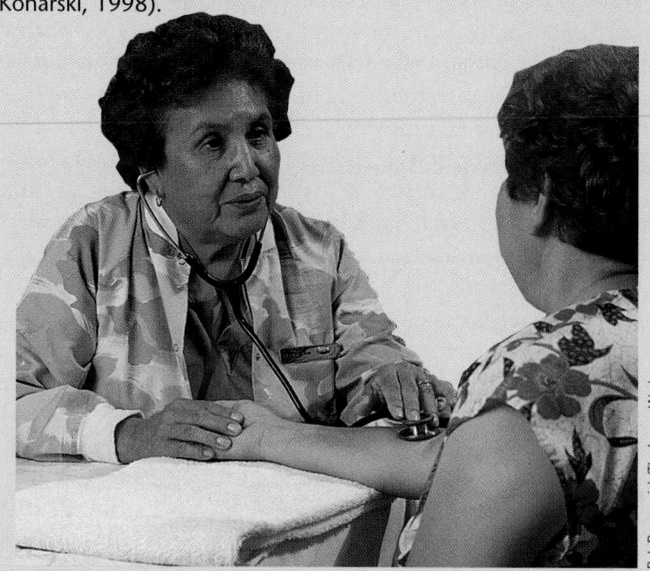
Bob Daemmrich/The Image Works

The helping professions require empathy, caring, and emotional involvement. As a result, caregivers risk depleting their emotional resources and ability to cope. Over time, this can lead to burnout.

Daniel G. Lavoie/Corbis

Air traffic control is stressful work. Employees must pay intense attention for long periods of time, they have little control over the pace of work, and the consequences of making a mistake can be dire.

TABLE 15.3

The Ten Most Stressful Jobs

JOB	RANK
U.S. president	1
firefighter	2
senior corporate executive	3
Indy-class race car driver	4
taxi driver	5
surgeon	6
astronaut	7
police officer	8
NFL football player	9
air-traffic controller	10

L. Krantz, 1995.

Appraising Stressors

It might seem that stressful events "happen to" us. Sometimes this is true, but as noted in Chapter 10, our emotions are greatly affected by how we appraise situations. That's why some people are distressed by events that others view as a thrill or a challenge (eustress). Ultimately, stress depends on how you perceive a situation. Our friend Akihito would find it stressful to listen to five of his son's rap CDs in a row. His son Takashi would find it stressful to listen to *one* of his father's opera CDs. To know if you are stressed, we must know what meaning you place on events. As we will see in a moment, whenever a stressor is appraised as a *threat* (potentially harmful), a powerful stress reaction follows (Folkman & Moskowitz, 2004; Lazarus, 1991b).

"Am I Okay or in Trouble?"

Situation: You have been selected to give a speech to 300 people. Or a doctor tells you that you must undergo a dangerous and painful operation. Or the one true love of your life walks out the door. What would your emotional response to these events be? How do you cope with an emotional threat?

According to Richard Lazarus (1991b), there are two important steps in managing a threat. The first is a **primary appraisal,** in which you decide if a situation is relevant or irrelevant, positive or threatening. In essence, this step answers the question, "Am I okay or in trouble?" Then you make a **secondary appraisal,** in which you assess your resources and choose a way to meet the threat or challenge. ("What can I do about this situation?") Thus, the way a situation is "sized up" greatly affects our ability to cope with it (● Figure 15.2). Public speaking, for instance, can be appraised as an intense threat or as a chance to perform. Emphasizing the threat—by imagining failure, rejection, or embarrassment—obviously invites disaster (Lazarus, 1993).

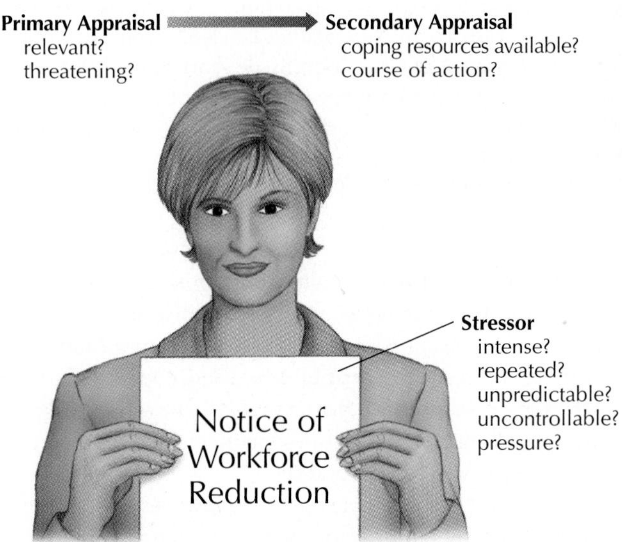

● **Figure 15.2** Stress is the product of an interchange between a person and the environment.

THE FAR SIDE® By GARY LARSON

"The fuel light's on, Frank! We're all going to die! ... Wait, wait. ... Oh, my mistake—that's the intercom light."

The Nature of Threat

What does it mean to feel threatened by a stressor? Certainly in most day-to-day situations it doesn't mean you think your life is in danger. (Unless, of course, you owe money to "Eddie The Enforcer.") Threat has more to do with the idea of control. We are particularly prone to feel stressed when we can't—or think we can't—control our immediate environment. In short, a *perceived* lack of control is just as threatening as an actual lack of control (DasGupta, 1992). If your answer to the question, "What can I do about this situation?" is "nothing," you will feel emotionally stressed.

A sense of control also comes from believing you can reach desired goals. It is threatening to feel that we lack *competence* to cope with life's demands (Bandura, 2001). Because of this, the in-

Burnout A job-related condition of mental, physical, and emotional exhaustion.

Primary appraisal Deciding if a situation is relevant to oneself and if it is a threat.

Secondary appraisal Deciding how to cope with a threat or challenge.

THE CLINICAL FILE

Coping with Traumatic Stress

Traumatic experiences produce psychological injury or intense emotional pain. Victims of **traumatic stresses,** such as war, torture, rape, assassination, plane crashes, natural disasters, or street violence, may suffer from nightmares, flashbacks, insomnia, irritability, nervousness, grief, emotional numbing, and depression. There is little doubt that the 2005 hurricane season caused these effects in the Gulf Coast states. Like most traumatic stresses, the impact, especially of hurricanes Katrina and Rita, was overwhelming.

People who personally witness or survive a disaster are most affected by traumatic stress. Twenty percent of the people who lived close to Ground Zero in New York suffered serious stress disorders (Galea et al., 2002). Yet even those who experience horror at a distance may be traumatized (Galea & Resnick, 2005). Among U.S. adults who only saw the September 11th terrorist attacks on television, 44 percent had at least some stress symptoms (Schuster et al., 2001).

Traumatic stress produces feelings of helplessness and vulnerability (Fields & Margolin, 2001). Victims realize that disaster could strike again without warning. In addition to feeling threatened, many victims sense that they are losing control of their lives (Scurfield, 2002).

What can people do about such reactions? Psychologists recommend the following:

- Identify what you are feeling and talk to others about your fears and concerns.
- Think about the skills that have helped you overcome adversity in the past and apply them to the present situation.
- Continue to do the things that you enjoy and that make life meaningful (LeDoux & Gorman, 2001).
- Get support from others. This is a major element in recovery from all traumatic events.
- Give yourself time to heal. Fortunately, most people are more resilient than they think.

When traumatic stresses are severe or repeated, some people have even more serious symptoms. They suffer from crippling anxiety or become emotionally numb. Typically, they can't stop thinking about the disturbing event, they anxiously avoid anything associated with the event, and they are constantly fearful or nervous. (These are the symptoms of *stress disorders,* which are discussed in Chapter 16.) Such reactions can leave victims emotionally handicapped for months or years after a disaster. If you feel that you are having trouble coping with a severe emotional shock, consider seeking help from a psychologist or other professional.

Ken Cedeno/Corbis

There can be little doubt that hurricane Katrina's assault on New Orleans was a traumatically stressful event. Even people who merely witnessed the disaster on television suffered from stress symptoms.

tensity of your body's stress reaction often depends on what you think and tell yourself about a stressor. That's why it's valuable to learn to think in ways that ward off the body's stress response. (Some strategies for controlling upsetting thoughts are described in the Psychology in Action section of this chapter.)

Coping with Threat

You have appraised a situation as threatening. What will you do next? There are two major choices. Both involve thinking and acting in ways that help us handle stressors. In **emotion-focused coping**, we try to control our emotional reactions to the situation. For example, a distressed person may distract herself by listening to music, take a walk to relax, or seek emotional support from others. In contrast, **problem-focused coping** is aimed at managing or correcting the distressing situation itself. Some examples are making a plan of action or concentrating on your next step (Folkman & Moskowitz, 2004).

Couldn't both types of coping occur together? Yes. Sometimes the two types of coping aid one another. For instance, quieting your emotions may make it easier for you find a way to solve a problem. Say, for example, that a woman feels anxious as she steps to the podium to give a speech. If she does some deep breathing to reduce her anxiety (emotion-focused coping) she will be better able to glance over her notes to improve her delivery (problem-focused coping).

It is also possible for coping efforts to clash. For instance, if you have to make a difficult decision, you may suffer intense emotional distress. In such circumstances there is a temptation to make a quick, ill-advised choice, just to end the suffering. Doing so may allow you to cope with your emotions, but it shortchanges problem-focused coping.

In general, problem-focused coping tends to be especially useful when you are facing a controllable stressor—that is, a situation you can actually do something about. Emotion-focused efforts are best suited to managing stressors you cannot control (Folkman & Moskowitz, 2004). To improve your chances of coping effectively, the stress-fighting strategies described in this chapter include a mixture of both techniques.

So far, our discussion has focused on everyday stresses. How do people react to the extreme stresses imposed by war, violence, or disaster? "Coping with Traumatic Stress" discusses this important topic.

Frustration—Blind Alleys and Lead Balloons

Do you remember how frustrated Taylor was when he couldn't find a parking place? **Frustration** is a negative emotional state that occurs when people are prevented from reaching desired goals. In Taylor's case, the goal of finding a parking space was blocked by another car.

Obstacles of many kinds cause frustration. A useful distinction can be made between external and personal sources of frustration. *External frustration* is based on conditions outside a person that impede progress toward a goal. All of the following are external frustrations: getting stuck with a flat tire; having a marriage proposal rejected; finding the cupboard bare when you go to get your poor dog a bone; finding the refrigerator bare when you go to get your poor tummy a T-bone; finding the refrigerator gone when you return home; being chased out of the house by your starving dog. In other words, external frustrations are based on *delays, failure, rejection, loss,* and other direct blocking of motivated behavior.

Notice that external obstacles can be either *social* (slow drivers, tall people in theaters, people who cut into lines) or *nonsocial* (stuck doors, a dead battery, rain on the day of the game). If you ask ten of your friends what has frustrated them recently, most will probably mention someone's behavior ("My sister wore one of my dresses when I wanted to wear it," "My supervisor is unfair," "My history teacher grades too hard"). As social animals, we humans are highly sensitive to social sources of frustration (Peeters, Buunk, & Schaufeli, 1995; Taylor, 2006). That's probably why unfair treatment associated with racial or ethnic prejudice is a major source of frustration and stress in the lives of many African Americans and other minority group members (Clark, et al. 1999).

Frustration usually increases as the *strength, urgency,* or *importance* of a blocked motive increases. Taylor was especially frustrated in the parking lot because he was late for an exam. Likewise, an escape artist submerged in a tank of water and bound with 200 pounds of chain would become *quite* frustrated if a trick lock jammed. Remember, too, that motivation becomes stronger as we near a goal. As a result, frustration is more intense when a person runs into an obstacle very close to a goal. If you've ever missed an A grade by 5 points, you were probably very frustrated. If you've missed an A by 1 point—well, frustration builds character, right?

A final factor affecting frustration is summarized by the old phrase "the straw that broke the camel's back." The effects of *repeated* frustrations can accumulate until a small irritation sets off an unexpectedly violent response. A case in point is the fact that people with long daily commutes are more likely to display "road rage" (angry, aggressive driving) (Harding et al., 1998).

Personal frustrations are based on personal characteristics. If you are 4 feet tall and aspire to be a professional basketball player, you very likely will be frustrated. If you want to go to medical school but can earn only D grades, you will likewise be frustrated. In both examples, frustration is actually based on personal limitations. Yet failure may be *perceived* as externally caused. We will return to this point in a discussion of stress management. In the meantime, let's look at some typical reactions to frustration.

Reactions to Frustration

Aggression is any response made with the intent of harming a person or an object. It is one of the most persistent and frequent responses to frustration (Anderson & Bushman, 2002). The frustration–aggression link is so common, in fact, that experiments are hardly necessary to show it. A glance at almost any newspaper will provide examples like the one that follows.

Justifiable Autocide

Burien, Washington (AP)—Barbara Smith committed the assault, but police aren't likely to press charges. Her victim was an old Oldsmobile, which failed once too often to start.

When Officer Jim Fuda arrived at the scene, he found one beat-up car, a broken baseball bat and a satisfied 23-year-old Seattle woman.

"I feel good," Ms. Smith reportedly told the officer. "That car's been giving me misery for years and I killed it."

Traumatic stresses Extreme events that cause psychological injury or intense emotional pain.

Emotion-focused coping Managing or controlling one's emotional reaction to a stressful or threatening situation.

Problem-focused coping Directly managing or remedying a stressful or threatening situation.

Frustration A negative emotional state that occurs when one is prevented from reaching a goal.

Aggression Any response made with the intent of harming some person or object.

Does frustration always cause aggression? Aren't there other reactions? Although the connection is strong, frustration does not always incite aggression. More often, frustration is met first with *persistence,* often in the form of more vigorous efforts and varied responses (● Figure 15.3). For example, if you put your last quarter in a vending machine and pressing the button has no effect, you will probably press harder and faster (vigorous effort). Then you will press all the other buttons (varied response). Persistence may help you reach your goal by getting *around* a barrier. However, if the machine *still* refuses to deliver, or return your quarter, you may become aggressive and kick the machine (or at least tell it what you think of it).

Persistence can be very adaptive. Overcoming a barrier ends the frustration and allows the need or motive to be satisfied. The same is true of aggression that removes or destroys a barrier. Picture a small band of nomadic humans, parched by thirst but separated from a water hole by a menacing animal. It is easy to see that attacking the animal may ensure their survival. In modern society such direct aggression is seldom acceptable. If you find a long line at the drinking fountain, aggression is hardly appropriate. Because direct aggression is discouraged, it is frequently *displaced.*

How is aggression displaced? Directing aggression toward a source of frustration may be impossible, or it may be too dangerous. If you are frustrated by your boss at work or by a teacher at school, the cost of direct aggression may be too high (losing your job or failing a class). Instead, the aggression may be displaced, or redirected, toward whomever or whatever is available. Targets of **displaced aggression** tend to be safer, or less likely to retaliate, than the original source of frustration. At one time or another, you have probably lashed out at a friend or relative who was not the real cause of your annoyance. As this suggests, excessive anger over a minor irritation is a common form of displaced aggression (Miller et al., 2003).

Sometimes long *chains* of displacement occur, in which one person displaces aggression to the next. For instance, a businesswoman who is frustrated by high taxes reprimands an employee, who swallows his anger until he returns home and then yells at his wife, who in turn yells at the children, who then tease the dog. The dog chases the cat, which later knocks over the canary cage.

Psychologists attribute much hostility to displaced aggression. A disturbing example is the finding that when unemployment increases, so does child abuse (Steinberg, Catalano, & Dooley, 1981). In a pattern known as **scapegoating,** a person or a group is blamed for conditions not of their making. A *scapegoat* is a person who has become a habitual target of displaced aggression. Despite recent progress, many minority groups continue to face hostility based on scapegoating. Think, for example, about the hostility expressed toward recent immigrants during times of economic hardship. In many communities, layoffs and job losses are closely linked to increased violence (Catalano, Novaco, & McConnell, 1997). Or think about the hostility expressed toward anyone in the United States who looked even vaguely "foreign" after the September 11th terrorist attacks.

I have a friend who dropped out of school to hitchhike around the country. He seemed very frustrated before he quit. What type of response to frustration is that? Another major reaction to frustration is escape, or withdrawal. It is stressful and unpleasant to be frustrated. If other reactions do not reduce frustration, a person may try to escape. **Escape** may mean actually leaving a source of frustration (dropping out of school, quitting a job, leaving an unhappy marriage), or it may mean psychologically escaping. Two common forms of psychological escape are apathy (pretending not to care) and the use of drugs such as cocaine, alcohol, marijuana, or narcotics. (Notice that these are examples of *ineffective* emotion-focused coping.) (See ● Figure 15.3 for a summary of common reactions to frustration.)

Person
Goal
Barrier
Frustration

Goal
Persistence, vigorous effort

Goal
Variability, circumvention

Goal
Direct aggression

Goal
Displaced aggression

Goal
Withdrawal, escape

● **Figure 15.3** Frustration and common reactions to it.

Tony Anderson/Getty Images

Bumper cars seem to bring out aggressive impulses in many drivers. Wild smash-ups are part of the fun, but are some drivers displacing aggressive urges related to frustration in other areas of their lives?

Coping with Frustration

In a classic experiment, a psychologist studying frustration placed rats on a small platform at the top of a tall pole. Then he forced them to jump off the platform toward two elevated doors, one locked and the other unlocked. If the rat chose the correct door, it swung open and the rat landed safely on another platform. Rats who chose the locked door bounced off it and fell into a net far below.

The problem of choosing the open door was made unsolvable and very frustrating by randomly alternating which door was locked. After a time, most rats adopted a stereotyped response. That is, they chose the same door every time. This door was then permanently locked. All the rat had to do was to jump to the other door to avoid a fall, but time after time the rat bounced off the locked door (Maier, 1949).

Isn't that an example of persistence? No. Persistence that is *inflexible* can turn into "stupid," stereotyped behavior like that of a rat on a jumping stand. When dealing with frustration, you must know when to quit and establish a new direction. Here are some suggestions to help you avoid needless frustration.

1. Try to identify the source of your frustration. Is it external or personal?
2. Is the source of frustration something that can be changed? How hard would you have to work to change it? Is it under your control at all?
3. If the source of your frustration can be changed or removed, are the necessary efforts worth it?

The answers to these questions help determine if persistence will be futile. There is value in learning to accept gracefully those things that cannot be changed.

It is also important to distinguish between *real* barriers and *imagined* barriers. All too often we create our own imaginary barriers. For example, Corazon wants a part-time job to earn extra money. At the first place she applied, she was told that she didn't have enough "experience." Now she complains of being frustrated because she wants to work but cannot. She needs "experience" to work, but can't get experience without working. She has quit looking for a job.

Is Corazon's need for experience a real barrier? Unless she applies for *many* jobs it is impossible to tell if she has overestimated its importance. For her the barrier is real enough to prevent further efforts, but with persistence she might locate an "unlocked door." If a reasonable amount of effort does show that experience is essential, it might be obtained in other ways—through temporary volunteer work, for instance.

Conflict—Yes, No, Yes, No, Yes, No, Well, Maybe

Conflict occurs whenever a person must choose between contradictory needs, desires, motives, or demands. Choosing between college and work, marriage and single life, or study and failure are common conflicts. There are four basic forms of conflict. As we will see, each has its own properties (● Figure 15.4 and ● Figure 15.5).

Approach-Approach Conflicts

A simple **approach-approach conflict** comes from having to choose between two positive, or desirable, alternatives. Choosing between tutti-frutti-coconut-mocha-champagne ice and orange-marmalade-peanut butter-coffee swirl at the ice cream parlor may throw you into a temporary conflict. However, if you really like both choices, your decision will be quickly made. Even when more important decisions are at stake, approach-approach conflicts tend to be the easiest to resolve. The old fable about the mule that died of thirst and starvation while standing between a bucket of water and a bucket of oats is obviously unrealistic. When both options are positive, the scales of decision are easily tipped one direction or the other.

Avoidance-Avoidance Conflicts

Being forced to choose between two negative, or undesirable, alternatives creates an **avoidance-avoidance conflict.** A person in an avoidance conflict is caught between "the devil and the deep

● **Figure 15.4** Three basic forms of conflict. For this woman, choosing between pie and ice cream is a minor approach-approach conflict; deciding whether to take a job that will require weekend work is an approach-avoidance conflict; and choosing between paying higher rent and moving is an avoidance-avoidance conflict.

Displaced aggression Redirecting aggression to a target other than the actual source of one's frustration.

Scapegoating Blaming a person or a group of people for conditions not of their making.

Escape Reducing discomfort by leaving frustrating situations or by psychologically withdrawing from them.

Conflict A stressful condition that occurs when a person must choose between incompatible or contradictory alternatives.

Approach-approach conflict Choosing between two positive, or desirable, alternatives.

Avoidance-avoidance conflict Choosing between two negative, or mutually undesirable, alternatives.

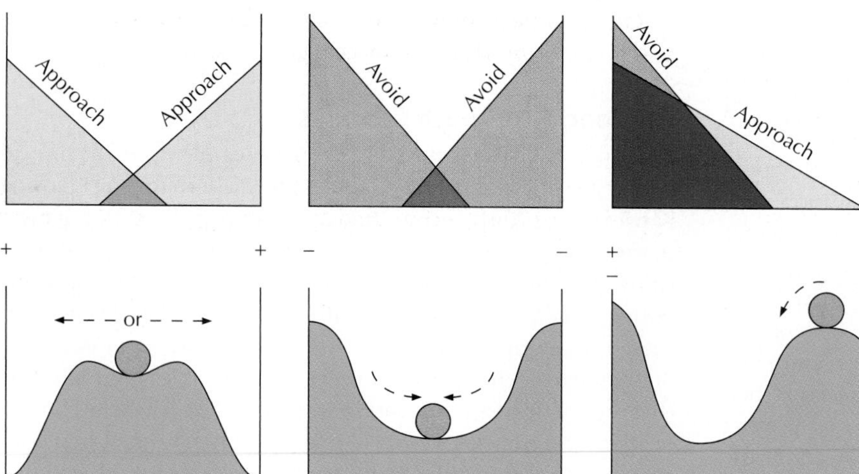

● **Figure 15.5** Conflict diagrams. As shown by the colored areas in the graphs, desires to approach and to avoid increase near a goal. The effects of these tendencies are depicted below each graph. The "behavior" of the ball in each example illustrates the nature of the conflict above it. An approach conflict *(left)* is easily decided. Moving toward one goal will increase its attraction *(graph)* and will lead to a rapid resolution. (If the ball moves in either direction, it will go all the way to one of the goals.) In an avoidance conflict *(center),* tendencies to avoid are deadlocked, resulting in inaction. In an approach-avoidance conflict *(right),* approach proceeds to the point where desires to approach and avoid cancel each other. Again, these tendencies are depicted *(below)* by the action of the ball. (Graphs after Miller, 1944.)

blue sea," between "the frying pan and the fire," or between "a rock and a hard place." In real life, double-avoidance conflicts involve dilemmas such as choosing between unwanted pregnancy and abortion, the dentist and tooth decay, a monotonous job and poverty, or dorm food and starvation.

Suppose I don't object to abortion. Or suppose that I consider any pregnancy sacred and not to be tampered with? Like many other stressful situations, these examples can be defined as conflicts only on the basis of personal needs and values. If a woman wants to end a pregnancy and does not object to abortion, she experiences no conflict. If she would not consider abortion under any circumstances, there is also no conflict.

Avoidance conflicts often have a "damned if you do, damned if you don't" quality. In other words, both choices are negative, but *not choosing* may be impossible or equally undesirable. To illustrate, imagine the plight of a person trapped in a hotel fire 20 stories from the ground. Should she jump from the window and almost surely die on the pavement? Or should she try to dash through the flames and almost surely die of smoke inhalation and burns? When faced with a choice such as this, it is easy to see why people often *freeze,* finding it impossible to decide or take action. A trapped individual may first think about the window, approach it, and then back away after looking down 20 stories. Next, she may try the door and again back away as heat and smoke billow in. In actual disasters of this sort, people are often found dead in their rooms, victims of an inability to take action.

Indecision, inaction, and freezing are not the only reactions to double-avoidance conflicts. Because avoidance conflicts are stressful and rarely solved, people sometimes pull out of them entirely. This reaction, called *leaving the field,* is another form of escape. It may explain the behavior of a student who could not attend school unless he worked. However, if he worked he could not earn passing grades. His solution after much conflict and indecision? He joined the navy.

Approach-Avoidance Conflicts

Approach-avoidance conflicts are also difficult to resolve. In some ways they are more troublesome than avoidance conflicts because people seldom escape them. A person in an **approach-avoidance conflict** is "caught" by being attracted to, and repelled by, the same goal or activity. Attraction keeps the person in the situation, but its negative aspects cause turmoil and distress. For example, a high school student arrives to pick up his date for the first time. He is met at the door by her father, who is a professional wrestler—7 feet tall, 300 pounds, and entirely covered with hair. The father gives the boy a crushing handshake and growls that he will break him in half if the girl is not home on time. The student considers the girl attractive and has a good time. But does he ask her out again? It depends on the relative strength of his attraction and his fear. Almost certainly he will feel *ambivalent* about asking her out again, knowing that another encounter with her father awaits him.

Ambivalence (mixed positive and negative feelings) is a central characteristic of approach-avoidance conflicts. Ambivalence is usually translated into *partial approach* (Miller, 1944). Because our student is still attracted to the girl, he may spend time with her at school and elsewhere. But he may not actually date her again. Some more realistic examples of approach-avoidance conflicts are planning to marry someone your parents strongly disapprove of, wanting to be in a play but suffering stage fright, wanting to buy a car but not wanting to make monthly payments, and wanting to eat when you're already overweight. Many of life's important decisions have approach-avoidance dimensions.

Multiple Conflicts

Aren't real-life conflicts more complex than the ones described here? Yes. Conflicts are rarely as clear-cut as those described. People in conflict are usually faced with several dilemmas at once, so several types of conflict may be intermingled. The fourth type of conflict moves us closer to reality. In a **double approach-avoidance conflict** each alternative has both positive and negative qualities. For example, you are offered two jobs: One has good pay but poor hours and dull work; the second has interesting work and excellent hours, but low pay. Which do you select? This situation is more typical of the choices we must usually make. It offers neither completely positive nor completely negative options.

As with single approach-avoidance conflicts, people faced with double approach-avoidance conflicts feel ambivalent about each choice. This causes them to *vacillate,* or waver between the alternatives. Just as you are about to choose one such alternative, its undesirable aspects tend to loom large. So, what do you do? You swing back toward the other choice. If you have ever been romantically attracted to two people at once—each having qualities you like and dislike—then you have probably experienced vacillation. Another example that may be familiar is trying to decide between two college majors, each with advantages and disadvantages.

In real life it is common to face **multiple approach-avoidance conflicts** in which several alternatives each have positive and negative features. An example would be trying to choose which automobile to buy among several brands. On a day-to-day basis, most multiple approach-avoidance conflicts are little more than an annoyance. When they involve major life decisions, such as choosing a career, a school, a mate, or a job, they can add greatly to the amount of stress we experience.

Managing Conflicts

How can I handle conflicts more effectively? Most of the suggestions made earlier concerning frustration also apply to conflicts. However, here are some additional things to remember when you are in conflict or must make a difficult decision.

1. Don't be hasty when making important decisions. Take time to collect information and to weigh pros and cons. Hasty decisions are often regretted. Even if you do make a faulty decision, it will trouble you less if you know that you did everything possible to avoid a mistake.
2. Try out important decisions *partially* when possible. If you are thinking about moving to a new town, try to spend a few days there first. If you are choosing between colleges, do the same. If classes are in progress, sit in on some. If you want to learn to scuba dive, rent equipment for a reasonable length of time before buying.
3. Look for workable compromises. Again, it is important to get all available information. If you think that you have only one or two alternatives and they are undesirable or unbearable, seek the aid of a teacher, counselor, minister, or social service agency. You may be overlooking possible alternatives these people will know about.
4. When all else fails, make a decision and live with it. Indecision and conflict exact a high cost. Sometimes it is best to select a course of action and stick with it unless it is very obviously wrong after you have taken it.

Conflicts are a normal part of life. With practice you can learn to manage many of the conflicts you will face.

KNOWLEDGE BUILDER

Stress, Frustration, and Conflict

REFLECT

What impact did pressure, control, predictability, repetition, and intensity have on your last stress reaction?

What type of coping do you tend to use when you face a stressor such as public speaking or taking an important exam?

Think of a time when you were frustrated. What was your goal? What prevented you from reaching it? Was your frustration external or personal?

Have you ever displaced aggression? Why did you choose another target for your hostility?

Review the major types of conflict and think of a conflict you have faced that illustrates each type. Did your reactions match those described in the text?

LEARNING CHECK

1. Emotional exhaustion, cynicism, and reduced accomplishment are characteristics of job ____________.
2. Stress tends to be greatest when a situation is appraised as a ____________ and a person does not feel ____________ to cope with the situation.
3. According to Richard Lazarus, choosing a way to meet a threat or challenge takes place during the
   a. primary stress reaction c. primary appraisal
   b. secondary stress reaction d. secondary appraisal
4. Which of the following is *not* a common reaction to frustration?
   a. ambivalence c. displaced aggression
   b. aggression d. persistence
5. Sampson Goliath is 7 feet tall and weighs 300 pounds. He has failed miserably in his aspirations to become a jockey. The source of his frustration is mainly ____________.
6. Aggression is an especially common reaction to
   a. frustration c. approach conflicts
   b. the primary appraisal d. ambivalence
7. Displaced aggression is closely related to the pattern of behavior known as
   a. scapegoating c. stereotyped responding
   b. leaving the field d. burnout
8. Inaction and freezing are most characteristic of avoidance-avoidance conflicts. T or F?
9. You would be most likely to experience vacillation if you found yourself in

Approach-avoidance conflict Being attracted to and repelled by the same goal or activity.

Ambivalence Mixed positive and negative feelings or simultaneous attraction and repulsion.

Double approach-avoidance conflict Being simultaneously attracted to and repelled by each of two alternatives.

Multiple approach-avoidance conflict Being simultaneously attracted to and repelled by each of several alternatives.

a. an approach-approach conflict
b. an avoidance-avoidance conflict
c. a double approach-avoidance conflict
d. the condition called emotion-focused coping

CRITICAL THINKING

10. Which do you think would produce more stress: (a) Appraising a situation as mildly threatening but feeling like you are totally incompetent to cope with it? Or (b) appraising a situation as very threatening but feeling that you have the resources and skills to cope with it?

11. Being frustrated is unpleasant. If some action, including aggression, ends frustration, why might we expect the action to be repeated on other occasions?

Answers: 1. burnout **2.** threat, competent **3.** d **4.** a **5.** personal **6.** a **7.** a **8.** T **9.** c **10.** There is no correct answer here because individual stress reactions vary greatly. However, the secondary appraisal of a situation often determines just how stressful it is. Feeling incapable of coping is very threatening. **11.** If a response ends discomfort, the response has been negatively reinforced. This makes it more likely to occur in the future (see Chapter 8).

Psychological Defense—Mental Karate?

Threatening situations are often accompanied by an unpleasant emotion called **anxiety.** When you are anxious you feel tense, uneasy, apprehensive, worried, and vulnerable. This unpleasant state can lead to emotion-focused coping that is *defensive* in nature (Lazarus, 1991a). Psychodynamic psychologists have identified various defenses that shield us from anxiety. Defense mechanisms allow us to reduce anxiety caused by stressful situations or our own shortcomings.

What are psychological defense mechanisms and how do they reduce anxiety? A **defense mechanism** is any mental process used to avoid, deny, or distort sources of threat or anxiety, including threats to one's self-image. Many of the defenses were first identified by Sigmund Freud, who assumed they operate *unconsciously.* Often, defense mechanisms create large blind spots in awareness. For instance, you might know an extremely stingy person who is completely unaware that he is a tightwad.

Everyone has at one time or another used defense mechanisms. Let's consider some of the most common. (A more complete listing is given in ■ Table 15.4.)

Denial

One of the most basic defenses is **denial** (protecting oneself from an unpleasant reality by refusing to accept it or believe it). Denial is closely linked with death, illness, and similar painful and threatening events. For instance, if you were told that you had only 3 months to live, how would you react? Your first thoughts might be, "Aw, come on, someone must have mixed up the X-rays," or, "The doctor must be mistaken," or simply, "It can't be true!" Similar denial and disbelief are common reactions to the unexpected death of a friend or relative: "It's just not real. I don't believe it. I just don't believe it!"

BRIDGES

Severe anxiety can be extremely disruptive. It is the basis for some of the most common psychological disorders.

See Chapter 16, page 542.

TABLE 15.4

Psychological Defense Mechanisms

Compensation Counteracting a real or imagined weakness by emphasizing desirable traits or seeking to excel in the area of weakness or in other areas.

Denial Protecting oneself from an unpleasant reality by refusing to perceive it.

Fantasy Fulfilling unmet desires in imagined achievements or activities.

Identification Taking on some of the characteristics of an admired person, usually as a way of compensating for perceived personal weaknesses or faults.

Intellectualization Separating emotion from a threatening or anxiety-provoking situation by talking or thinking about it in impersonal "intellectual" terms.

Isolation Separating contradictory thoughts or feelings into "logic-tight" mental compartments so that they do not come into conflict.

Projection Attributing one's own feelings, shortcomings, or unacceptable impulses to others.

Rationalization Justifying your behavior by giving reasonable and "rational," but false, reasons for it.

Reaction formation Preventing dangerous impulses from being expressed in behavior by exaggerating opposite behavior.

Regression Retreating to an earlier level of development or to earlier, less demanding habits or situations.

Repression Unconsciously preventing painful or dangerous thoughts from entering awareness.

Sublimation Working off unmet desires, or unacceptable impulses, in activities that are constructive.

Repression

Freud noticed that his patients had tremendous difficulty recalling shocking or traumatic events from childhood. It seemed that powerful forces were holding these painful memories from awareness. Freud called this **repression.** He believed that we protect ourselves by repressing threatening thoughts and impulses. Feelings of hostility toward a family member, the names of people we dislike, and past failures are common targets of repression. Recent research suggests that you are most likely to repress information that threatens your self-image (Mendolia, 2002).

JUMP START reprinted by permission of United Feature Syndicate, Inc.

Reaction Formation

In a **reaction formation**, impulses are not just repressed; they are also held in check by exaggerating opposite behavior. For example, a mother who unconsciously resents her children may, through reaction formation, become absurdly overprotective and overindulgent. Her real thoughts of "I hate them" and "I wish they were gone" are replaced by "I love them" and "I don't know what I would do without them." The mother's hostile impulses are traded for "smother" love, so that she won't have to admit she hates her children. Thus, the basic idea in a reaction formation is that the individual acts out an opposite behavior to block threatening impulses or feelings.

Regression

In its broadest meaning, **regression** refers to any return to earlier, less demanding situations or habits. Most parents who have a second child have to put up with at least some regression by the older child. Threatened by a new rival for affection, an older child may regress to childish speech, bed-wetting, or infantile play after the new baby arrives. If you've ever seen a child get homesick at summer camp or on a vacation, you've observed regression. The child wants to go home, where it's "safe." An adult who throws a temper tantrum or a married adult who "goes home to mother" is also regressing.

Projection

Projection is an unconscious process that protects us from the anxiety we would feel if we were to discern our faults. A person who is projecting tends to see his or her own feelings, shortcomings, or unacceptable impulses in others. **Projection** lowers anxiety by exaggerating negative traits in others. This justifies one's own actions and directs attention away from personal failings.

One of your authors once worked for a greedy shop owner who cheated many of his customers. This same man considered himself a pillar of the community and a good Christian. How did he justify to himself his greed and dishonesty? He believed that everyone who entered his store was bent on cheating *him* any way they could. In reality, few, if any, of his customers shared his motives, but he projected his own greed and dishonesty onto them.

Rationalization

Every teacher is familiar with this strange phenomenon: On the day of an exam, an incredible wave of disasters sweeps through the city. Mothers, fathers, sisters, brothers, aunts, uncles, grandparents, friends, relatives, and pets become ill or die. Motors suddenly fall out of cars. Books are lost or stolen. Alarm clocks go belly-up and ring no more.

The making of excuses comes from a natural tendency to explain our behavior. **Rationalization** refers to justifying personal actions by giving "rational" but false reasons for them. When the explanation you give for your behavior is reasonable and convincing—but not the real reason—you are *rationalizing*. For example, Taylor failed to turn in an assignment made at the beginning of the semester in one of his classes. Here's the explanation he gave his professor:

> My car broke down 2 days ago, and I couldn't get to the library until yesterday. Then I couldn't get all the books I needed because some were checked out, but I wrote what I could. Then last night, as the last straw, the cartridge in my printer ran out, and since all the stores were closed, I couldn't finish the paper on time.

When asked why he left the assignment until the last minute (the real reason it was late), Taylor offered another set of rationalizations. Like many people, Taylor had difficulty seeing himself without the protection of his rationalizations.

All of the defense mechanisms described seem pretty undesirable. Do they have a positive side? People who overuse defense mechanisms become less adaptable, because they consume great amounts of emotional energy to control anxiety and maintain an unrealistic self-image. Defense mechanisms do have value, though. Often, they help keep us from being overwhelmed by immediate threats. This can provide time for a person to learn to cope in a more effective, problem-focused manner. If you recognize some of your own behavior in the descriptions here, it is hardly a sign that you are hopelessly defensive. As noted earlier, most people occasionally use defense mechanisms.

Two defense mechanisms that have a decidedly more positive quality are compensation and sublimation.

Compensation

Compensatory reactions are defenses against feelings of inferiority. A person who has a defect or weakness (real or imagined) may go to unusual lengths to overcome the weakness or to *compensate* for it by excelling in other areas. One of the pioneers of "pumping iron" in America is Jack LaLanne. LaLanne made a successful career out of bodybuilding in spite of the fact that he was thin and sickly as a young man. Or perhaps it would be more accurate to say *because* he was thin and sickly. There are dozens of examples of **compensation** at work. A childhood stutterer may excel in debate at college. As a child, Helen Keller was unable to see or hear,

Anxiety Apprehension, dread, or uneasiness similar to fear but based on an unclear threat.

Defense mechanism A habitual and often unconscious psychological process used to reduce anxiety.

but she became an outstanding thinker and writer. Perhaps Doc Watson, Ray Charles, Stevie Wonder, and other blind entertainers were drawn to music because of their handicap.

Sublimation

The defense called **sublimation** (sub-lih-MAY-shun) is defined as working off frustrated desires (especially sexual desires) through socially acceptable activities. Freud believed that art, music, dance, poetry, scientific investigation, and other creative activities could serve to rechannel sexual energies into productive behavior. Freud also felt that almost any strong desire could be sublimated. For example, a very aggressive person may find social acceptance as a professional soldier, boxer, or football player. Greed may be refined into a successful business career. Lying may be sublimated into storytelling, creative writing, or politics.

Sexual motives appear to be the most easily and widely sublimated. Freud would have had a field day with such modern pastimes as surfing, motorcycle riding, drag racing, and dancing to or playing rock music, to name but a few. People enjoy each of these activities for a multitude of reasons, but it is hard to overlook the rich sexual symbolism apparent in each.

Learned Helplessness—Is There Hope?

What would happen if a person's defenses failed or if the person appraised a threatening situation as hopeless? Martin Seligman studied the case of a young marine who seemed to have adapted to the stresses of being held prisoner during the Vietnam War. The marine's health was related to a promise made by his captors: If he cooperated, they said, he would be released on a certain date. As the date approached, his spirits soared. Then came a devastating blow. He had been deceived. His captors had no intention of ever releasing him. He immediately lapsed into a deep depression, refused to eat or drink, and died shortly thereafter.

Scott Cunningham/Getty Images

For some players—and fans—football probably allows sublimation of aggressive urges. *Quake 4* and similar computer games may serve the same purpose.

That seems like an extreme example. Does anything similar occur outside of concentration camps? Apparently so. For example, researchers in Finland found that even in everyday life, people who feel a sense of hopelessness die at elevated rates (Everson, Goldberg, & Salonen, 1996).

To explain such patterns psychologists have focused on the concept of learned helplessness (Seligman, 1989). **Learned helplessness** is an acquired inability to overcome obstacles and avoid aversive stimuli. To observe learned helplessness, let's see what happens when animals are tested in a shuttle box (● Figure 15.6). If placed in one side of a divided box, dogs will quickly learn to leap to the other side to escape an electric shock. If they are given a warning before the shock occurs (for example, a light that dims), most dogs learn to avoid the shock by leaping the barrier before the shock arrives. This is true of most dogs, but not those who have learned to feel helpless (Overmier & LoLordo, 1998).

How is a dog made to feel helpless? Before being tested in the shuttle box, a dog can be placed in a harness (from which the dog cannot escape). The dog is then given several painful shocks. The animal is helpless to prevent these shocks. When placed in the shuttle box, dogs prepared this way react to the first shock by crouching, howling, and whining. None of them try to escape. They helplessly resign themselves to their fate. After all, they have already learned that there is nothing they can do about shock.

As the shuttle box experiments suggest, helplessness is a psychological state that occurs when events *appear to be uncontrollable* (Seligman, 1989). Helplessness also afflicts humans. It is a common reaction to repeated failure and to unpredictable or unavoidable punishment. A prime example is college students who feel helpless about their schoolwork. Such students tend to procrastinate, give up easily, and drop out of school (McKean, 1994; Perry, 2003).

Where humans are concerned, attributions (discussed in Chapter 12) have a large effect on helplessness. Persons who are made to feel helpless in one situation are more likely to act helpless in other situations if they attribute their failure to *lasting, general* factors. An example would be concluding, "I must be stupid," after doing poorly on a test in a biology class. In contrast, attributing a low score to specific factors in the situation ("I'm not too good at the type of test my biology professor uses" or "I'm not very interested in biology") tends to prevent learned helplessness from spreading (Alloy et al., 1984).

Depression

Seligman and others have pointed out the similarities between learned helplessness and **depression.** Both are marked by feelings of despondency, powerlessness, and hopelessness. "Helpless" ani-

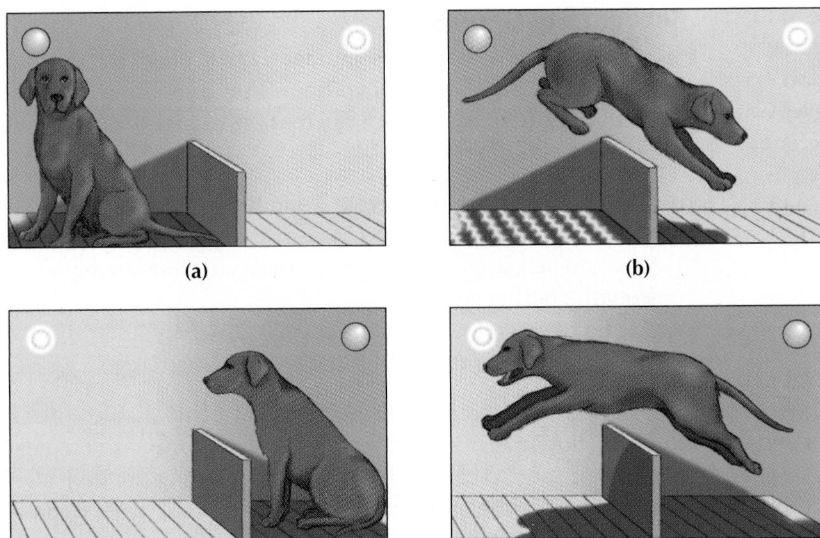

● **Figure 15.6** In the normal course of escape and avoidance learning, a light dims shortly before the floor is electrified *(a)*. Because the light does not yet have meaning for the dog, the dog receives a shock (noninjurious, by the way) and leaps the barrier *(b)*. Dogs soon learn to watch for the dimming of the light *(c)* and to jump before receiving a shock *(d)*. Dogs made to feel "helpless" rarely even learn to escape shock, much less to avoid it.

mals display decreased activity, lowered aggression, blunted appetite, and a loss of sex drive. Humans suffer from similar effects and also tend to see themselves as failing, even when they're not (Seligman, 1989).

Depression is one of the most widespread emotional problems, and it undoubtedly has many causes. However, learned helplessness seems to explain many cases of depression and hopelessness. For example, Seligman (1972) describes the fate of Archie, a 15-year-old boy. For Archie, school is an unending series of shocks and failures. Other students treat him as if he's stupid; in class he rarely answers questions because he doesn't know some of the words. He feels knocked down everywhere he turns. These may not be electric shocks, but they are certainly emotional "shocks," and Archie has learned to feel helpless to prevent them. When he leaves school his chances of success will be poor. He has learned to passively endure whatever shocks life has in store for him. Archie is not alone in this regard. Hopelessness is almost always a major element of depression (Ciarrochi, Dean, & Anderson, 2002).

Hope

Does Seligman's research give any clues about how to "unlearn" helplessness? With dogs, an effective technique is to forcibly drag them away from shock into the "safe" compartment. After this is done several times, the animals regain "hope" and feelings of control over the environment. Just how this can be done with humans is a question psychologists are exploring. It seems obvious, for instance, that someone like Archie would benefit from an educational program that would allow him to "succeed" repeatedly.

In **mastery training**, responses are reinforced that lead to mastery of a threat or control over one's environment. Animals who undergo such training become more resistant to learned helplessness (Volpicelli et al., 1983). For example, animals that first learn to escape shock become more persistent in trying to flee inescapable shock. In effect, they won't give up, even when the situation really is "hopeless."

Such findings suggest that we might be able to "immunize" people against helplessness and depression by allowing them to master difficult challenges. The Outward Bound schools, in which people pit themselves against the rigors of mountaineering, whitewater canoeing, and wilderness survival, might serve as a model for such a program.

BRIDGES

Depression is a complex problem that takes many forms and has many causes.

See Chapter 16, pages 558–562.

Mastery training can occur informally when people learn to cope with challenges. For example, 18- to 21-year-old trainees on a transatlantic sailing voyage showed marked improvements in their ability to cope with stress (Norris & Weinman, 1996).

Learned helplessness A learned inability to overcome obstacles or to avoid punishment; learned passivity and inaction to aversive stimuli.

Depression A state of despondency marked by feelings of powerlessness and hopelessness.

Mastery training Reinforcement of responses that lead to mastery of a threat or control over one's environment.

The value of hope should not be overlooked. As fragile as this emotion seems to be, it is a powerful antidote to depression and helplessness. As an individual, you may find hope in religion, nature, human companionship, or even technology. Wherever you find it, remember its value: Hope is among the most important of all human emotions. Having positive beliefs, such as optimism, hope, and a sense of meaning and control is closely related to overall well-being (Taylor et al., 2000, 2003).

Depression, a Problem for Everyone

During the school year, nearly 80 percent of all college students suffer some symptoms of depression. At any given time, from 16 to 30 percent of the student population is depressed (McLennan, 1992; Wong & Whitaker, 1993). Why should so many students be "blue"? Various problems contribute to depressive feelings. Here are some of the most common:

1. Stresses from college work and pressures to choose a career can leave students feeling that they are missing out on fun or that all their hard work is meaningless.
2. Isolation and loneliness are common when students leave their support groups behind. In the past, family, a circle of high school friends, and often a boyfriend or girlfriend could be counted on for support and encouragement.
3. Problems with studying and grades frequently trigger depression. Many students start college with high aspirations and little prior experience with failure. At the same time, many lack basic skills necessary for academic success and are afraid of failure (Martin & Marsh, 2003).
4. Depression can be triggered by the breakup of an intimate relationship, either with a former boyfriend or girlfriend or with a newly formed college romance.
5. Students who find it difficult to live up to their idealized images of themselves are especially prone to depression (Scott & O'Hara, 1993).
6. An added danger is that depressed students are more likely to abuse alcohol, which is a depressant (Camatta & Nagoshi, 1995).

Barbara Stitzer/PhotoEdit

In a survey, college students reported that they were depressed from one to two times a month. These episodes lasted from a few hours to several days.

Recognizing Depression

Most people know, obviously enough, when they are "down." Aaron Beck, an authority on depression, suggests you should assume that more than a minor fluctuation in mood is involved when five conditions exist:

1. You have a consistently negative opinion of yourself.
2. You engage in frequent self-criticism and self-blame.
3. You place negative interpretations on events that usually wouldn't bother you.
4. The future looks bleak and negative.
5. You feel that your responsibilities are overwhelming.

What can be done to combat depression? Bouts of the college blues are closely related to stressful events. Learning to manage college work and to challenge self-critical thinking can help alleviate mild school-related depression. See "Coping with Depression" for some helpful suggestions.

Attacks of the college blues are common and should be distinguished from more serious cases of depression. Severe depression is a serious problem that can lead to suicide or a major impairment of emotional functioning. In such cases it would be wise to seek professional help.

Coping with Depression

If you don't do well on a test or a class assignment, how do you react? If you see it as a small, isolated setback, you probably won't feel too bad. However, if you feel like you have "blown it" in a big way, depression may follow. Students who strongly link everyday events to long-term goals (such as a successful career or high income) tend to overreact to day-to-day disappointments (McIntosh, Harlow, & Martin, 1995).

What does the preceding tell us about the college blues? The implication is that it's important to take daily tasks one step at a time and chip away at them. That way, you are less likely to feel overwhelmed, helpless, or hopeless. Beck and Greenberg (1974) suggest that when you feel "blue" you should make a *daily schedule* for yourself. Try to schedule activities to fill up every hour during the day. It is best to start with easy activities and progress to more difficult tasks. Check off each item as it is completed. That way, you will begin to break the self-defeating cycle of feeling helpless and falling further behind. (Depressed students spend much of their time sleeping.) A series of small accomplishments, successes, or pleasures may be all that you need to get going again. However, if you are lacking skills needed for success in college, ask for help in getting them. Don't remain "helpless."

Feelings of worthlessness and hopelessness are usually supported by self-critical or negative thoughts. Beck and Greenberg recommend writing down such thoughts as they occur, especially those that immediately precede feelings of sadness. After you have collected these thoughts, write a rational answer to each. For example, the thought "No one loves me" should be answered with a list of those who do care. (See Chapter 17 for more information.) One more point to keep in mind is this: When events begin to improve, try to accept it as a sign that better times lie ahead. Positive events are most likely to end depression if you view them as stable and continuing, rather than temporary and fragile (Needles & Abramson, 1990).

KNOWLEDGE BUILDER

Defense Mechanisms, Helplessness, and Depression

REFLECT

We tend to be blind to our own reliance on defense mechanisms. Return to the definitions in Table 15.4 and see if you can think of one example of each defense that you have observed someone else using.

Have you ever felt helpless in a particular situation? What caused you to feel that way? Does any part of Seligman's description of learned helplessness match your own experience?

Imagine that a friend of yours is suffering from the college blues. What advice would you give your friend?

LEARNING CHECK

1. The psychological defense known as denial refers to the natural tendency to explain or justify one's actions. T or F?
2. Fulfilling frustrated desires in imaginary achievements or activities defines the defense mechanism of
   a. compensation c. fantasy
   b. isolation d. sublimation
3. In compensation, one's own undesirable characteristics or motives are attributed to others. T or F?
4. Of the defense mechanisms, two that are considered relatively constructive are
   a. compensation e. regression
   b. denial f. rationalization
   c. isolation g. sublimation
   d. projection
5. Depression in humans is similar to ________________ ________________ observed in animal experiments.
6. Learned helplessness tends to occur when events appear to be
   a. frustrating c. uncontrollable
   b. in conflict d. problem-focused
7. At any given time, over one half of the college student population suffers symptoms of depression. T or F?
8. Frequent self-criticism and self-blame are a natural consequence of doing college work. T or F?

CRITICAL THINKING

9. Learned helplessness is most closely related to which of the factors that determine the severity of stress?

Answers: 1. F 2. c 3. F 4. a, g 5. learned helplessness 6. c 7. F 8. F 9. Feelings of incompetence and lack of control.

Stress and Health—Unmasking a Hidden Killer

At the beginning of this chapter you read about Taylor, a student who became ill after a stressful final exam period. Was Taylor's illness a coincidence? Psychologists have now firmly established that stress affects our health. Let's see how this occurs. We will also explore some factors that limit the health risks we face. Because we live in a fast-paced and often stressful society, these are topics worth stressing.

Disaster, depression, and sorrow often precede illness. As Taylor (our intrepid student) learned after finals week, stressful events reduce the body's natural defenses against disease. More surprising is the finding that *life changes*—both good and bad—can increase susceptibility to accidents or illness. Major changes in our surroundings or routines require us to be vigilant, on guard, and ready to react. Over long time periods, this can be quite stressful (Sternberg, 2000).

Life Events and Stress

How can I tell if I am subjecting myself to too much stress? Dr. Thomas Holmes and his associates developed the first rating scale to estimate the health hazards we face when stresses add up (Holmes & Masuda, 1972). More recently, Mark Miller and Richard Rahe updated the scale for use today. The **Social Readjustment Rating Scale (SRRS)** is reprinted in ■ Table 15.5. Notice that the impact of life events is expressed in **life change units (LCUs)** (numerical values assigned to each life event).

As you read the scale, note again that positive life events may be as costly as disasters. Marriage rates 50 life change units, even though it is usually a happy event. You'll also see many items that read "Change in . . ." This means that an improvement in life conditions can be as costly as a decline. A stressful adjustment may be required in either case.

To use the scale, add up the LCUs for all life events you have experienced during the last year and compare the total to the following standards.

0–150: No significant problems
150–199: Mild life crisis (33 percent chance of illness)
200–299: Moderate life crisis (50 percent chance of illness)
300 or more: Major life crisis (80 percent chance of illness)

According to Holmes, there is a high chance of illness or accident when your LCU total exceeds 300 points. A more conservative rating of stress can be obtained by totaling LCU points for only the previous 6 months.

Many of the listed life changes don't seem relevant to young adults or college students. Does the SRRS apply to them? The SRRS tends to be more appropriate for older, more established adults. However, the health of college students is also affected by stressful events, such as entering college, changing majors, or the breakup of a steady relationship (Crandall, Preisler, & Ausspprung, 1992). (For a student-oriented rating of stress, see ■ Table 15.8 in the Psychology in Action section of this chapter.)

Social Readjustment Rating Scale (SRRS) A scale that rates the impact of various life events on the likelihood of illness.

Life change units (LCUs) Numerical values assigned to each life event on the SRRS.

TABLE 15.5

Social Readjustment Rating Scale

RANK	LIFE EVENT	LIFE CHANGE UNITS	RANK	LIFE EVENT	LIFE CHANGE UNITS
1	Death of spouse or child	119	23	Mortgage or loan greater than $10,000	44
2	Divorce	98	24	Change in responsibilities at work	43
3	Death of close family member	92	25	Change in living conditions	42
4	Marital separation	79	26	Change in residence	41
5	Fired from work	79	27	Begin or end school	38
6	Major personal injury or illness	77	28	Trouble with in-laws	38
7	Jail term	75	29	Outstanding personal achievement	37
8	Death of close friend	70	30	Change in work hours or conditions	36
9	Pregnancy	66	31	Change in schools	35
10	Major business readjustment	62	32	Christmas	30
11	Foreclosure on a mortgage or loan	61	33	Trouble with boss	29
12	Gain of new family member	57	34	Change in recreation	29
13	Marital reconciliation	57	35	Mortgage or loan less than $10,000	28
14	Change in health or behavior of family member	56	36	Change in personal habits	27
15	Change in financial state	56	37	Change in eating habits	27
16	Retirement	54	38	Change in social activities	27
17	Change to different line of work	51	39	Change in number of family get-togethers	26
18	Change in number of arguments with spouse	51	40	Change in sleeping habits	26
19	Marriage	50	41	Vacation	25
20	Spouse begins or ends work	46	42	Change in church activities	22
21	Sexual difficulties	45	43	Minor violations of the law	22
22	Child leaving home	44			

Miller & Rahe, 1997; reproduced by permission.

Evaluation

People differ greatly in their reactions to the same event. For such reasons, the SRRS is at best a rough index of stress. Nevertheless, it's hard to ignore a study in which people were deliberately exposed to the virus that causes common colds. The results were nothing to sneeze at: If a person had a high stress score, she or he was much more likely to actually get a cold (Cohen, Waltzman, & Fisher, 1993). In view of such findings, a high LCU score should be taken seriously. If your score goes much over 300, an adjustment in your activities or lifestyle may be needed. Remember, "To be forewarned is to be forearmed."

The Hazards of Hassles

There must be more to stress than major life changes. Isn't there a link between ongoing stresses and health? In addition to having a direct impact, major life events spawn countless daily frustrations and irritations (Pillow, Zautra, & Sandler, 1996). Also, many of us face ongoing stresses at work or at home that do not involve major life changes. In view of these facts, psychologist Richard Lazarus and his associates studied the impact of minor but frequent stresses. Lazarus (1981) calls such distressing daily annoyances **hassles,** or **microstressors** (see ■ Table 15.6).

In a year-long study, 100 men and women recorded the hassles they endured. Participants also reported on their physical and mental health. As Lazarus suspected, frequent and severe hassles turned out to be better predictors of day-to-day health than major life events were. However, major life events did predict changes in health 1 or 2 years after the events took place. It appears that daily hassles are closely linked to immediate health and psychological well-being (Crowther et al., 2001; Treharne, Lyons, & Tupling, 2001). Major life changes have more of a long-term impact.

Marriage is usually a positive life event. Nevertheless, the many changes it brings can be stressful.

TABLE 15.6

Examples of Daily Hassles

Examples of Daily Hassles
Too many responsibilities or commitments
Problems with work, boss, or coworkers
Unexpected house guests
Inconsiderate neighbors
Noisy, messy, or quarreling children
Regrets over past decisions
Having trouble making decisions
Money worries or concerns
Not enough time for family, relaxation, entertainment
Loneliness, social isolation, separated from family
Physical illness, symptoms, complaints
Concerns about weight, appearance
Frustrations with daily chores
Delays, transportation problems
Paperwork, filling out forms
Misplacing or losing things
Noise, pollution, deteriorating neighborhoods
Bad weather
Crime, disturbing news events

What can be done about a high LCU score or feeling excessively hassled? A good response is to use stress management skills. For serious problems, stress management should be learned directly from a therapist or a stress clinic. When ordinary stresses are involved, there is much you can do on your own. An upcoming discussion of stress management will give you a start. In the meantime, take it easy!

One way to guarantee that you will experience a large number of life changes and hassles is to live in a foreign culture. "Acculturative Stress" offers a brief glimpse into some of the consequences of culture shock.

Psychosomatic Disorders

As we have seen, chronic or repeated stress can damage physical health, as well as upset emotional well-being. Prolonged stress reactions are closely related to a large number of psychosomatic (SIKE-oh-so-MAT-ik) illnesses. In **psychosomatic disorders** (*psyche:* mind; *soma:* body), psychological factors contribute to actual bodily damage or to damaging changes in bodily functioning. Psychosomatic problems, therefore, are *not* the same as hypochondria. **Hypochondriacs** (HI-po-KON-dree-aks) imagine that they have diseases. There is nothing imaginary about asthma, a migraine headache, or high blood pressure. Severe psychosomatic disorders can be fatal. The person who says, "Oh it's *just* psychosomatic," doesn't understand how serious stress-related diseases really are (see "It's All in Your Mind").

The most common psychosomatic problems are gastrointestinal and respiratory (stomach pain and asthma, for example), but many others exist. Typical problems include eczema (skin rash), hives, migraine headaches, rheumatoid arthritis, hypertension (high blood pressure), colitis (ulceration of the colon), and heart disease. Actually, these are only the major problems. Many lesser health complaints are also stress related. Typical examples include sore muscles, headaches, neckaches, backaches, indigestion, constipation, chronic diarrhea, fatigue, insomnia, premenstrual problems, and sexual dysfunctions (Taylor, 2006). For some of these problems biofeedback may be helpful. The next section explains how.

Biofeedback

Psychologists have discovered that people can learn to control bodily activities once thought to be involuntary. This is done by applying informational feedback to bodily control, a process called

Hassle Any distressing, day-to-day annoyance; also called a *microstressor.*

Psychosomatic disorders Illnesses in which psychological factors contribute to bodily damage or to damaging changes in bodily functioning.

Hypochondriac A person who complains about illnesses that appear to be imaginary.

Acculturative Stress—Stranger in a Strange Land

Around the world, an increasing number of emigrants and refugees must adapt to dramatic changes in language, dress, values, and social customs. For many, the result is a period of culture shock or **acculturative stress** (stress caused by adapting to a foreign culture). Typical reactions to acculturative stress are anxiety, hostility, depression, alienation, physical illness, or identity confusion (Rummens, Beiser, & Noh, 2003). For many young immigrants, acculturative stress is a major source of mental health problems (Yeh, 2003).

The severity of acculturative stress is related, in part, to how a person adapts to a new culture. Four main patterns are the following (Berry, 1990; Berry et al., 2005):

Morton Beebe/Corbis

One of the best antidotes for acculturative stress is a society that tolerates or even celebrates ethnic diversity. Although some people find it hard to accept new immigrants, the fact is, nearly everyone's family tree includes people who were once strangers in a strange land.

Integration—maintain your old cultural identity but participate in the new culture

Separation—maintain your old cultural identity and avoid contact with the new culture

Assimilation—adopt the new culture as your own and have contact with its members

Marginalization—reject your old culture but suffer rejection by members of the new culture

To illustrate each pattern, let's consider a family that has immigrated to the United States from the imaginary country of Farlandia.

> The father favors integration. He is learning English and wants to get involved in American life. At the same time, he is a leader in the Farlandian-American community and spends much of his leisure time with other Farlandian-Americans. His level of acculturative stress is low.
>
> The mother only speaks Farlandish and only interacts with other Farlandian-Americans. She remains almost completely separate from American society. Her stress level is high.
>
> The teenage daughter is annoyed by hearing Farlandish spoken at home, by her mother's serving only Farlandian food, and by having to spend her leisure time with her extended Farlandian family. She would prefer to speak English and to be with her American friends. Her desire to assimilate creates moderate stress.
>
> The son doesn't particularly value his Farlandian heritage, yet his schoolmates reject him because he speaks with a Farlandian accent. He feels trapped between two cultures. His position is marginal and his stress level is high.

To summarize, those who feel marginalized tend to be highly stressed; those who seek to remain separate are also highly stressed; those who pursue integration into their new culture are minimally stressed; and those who assimilate are moderately stressed.

As you can see, integration and assimilation are the best options. However, a big benefit of assimilating is that people who embrace their new culture experience fewer social difficulties. For many, this justifies the stress of adopting new customs and cultural values (Ward & Rana-Deuba, 1999).

biofeedback. If we were to say to you, "Raise the temperature of your right hand," you probably couldn't, because you wouldn't know if you were succeeding. To make your task easier, we could attach a sensitive thermometer to your hand. The thermometer could be wired so that an increase in temperature would activate a signal light. Then, all you would have to do is try to keep the light on as much as possible. With practice and the help of biofeedback, you could learn to raise your hand temperature at will.

Biofeedback holds promise as a way to treat some psychosomatic problems (● Figure 15.7). For instance, people have been trained to prevent migraine headaches with biofeedback. Sensors are taped to patients' hands and foreheads. Patients then learn to redirect blood flow away from the head to their extremities. Because migraine headaches involve excessive blood flow to the head, biofeedback helps patients reduce the frequency of their headaches (Gauthier, Cote, & French, 1994; Kropp et al., 1997).

Early successes led many to predict that biofeedback would offer a cure for psychosomatic illnesses, anxiety, phobias, drug abuse, and a long list of other problems. In reality, biofeedback has proved helpful, but not an instant cure (Schwartz & Andrasik,

CRITICAL THINKING

It's All in Your Mind

Have you ever had someone dismiss a health concern by saying, "It's all in your mind," as if your problem might be imaginary? For centuries the *medical model* has dominated Western thinking. From this perspective, health is an absence of illness and your body is a complex biological machine that can break down and become ill. Sometimes, you inflict the damage yourself through poor lifestyle choices, such as smoking or overeating. Sometimes, an external cause, such as a virus, is the culprit. In either event, the problem is physical and your mind has little to do with it. Moreover, physical problems call for physical treatments ("Take your medicine"), so your mind has little to do with your recovery.

Over the last fifty years, the medical model has slowly given way to the *biopsychosocial model.* This view states that diseases are caused by a combination of biological, psychological, and social factors. Most important, the biopsychosocial model defines health as a state of well-being that we can *actively* attain and maintain (Oakley, 2004). Instead of passively getting treatments from a doctor, this model says that you play a role in fostering your own health. Thus, it may no longer be inaccurate to say, "It's all in your mind," *if* you mean that a person's beliefs—which affect behavior—can have a dramatic impact on health. So, as you take responsibility for your own well-being, remember that in some ways health is all in your mind!

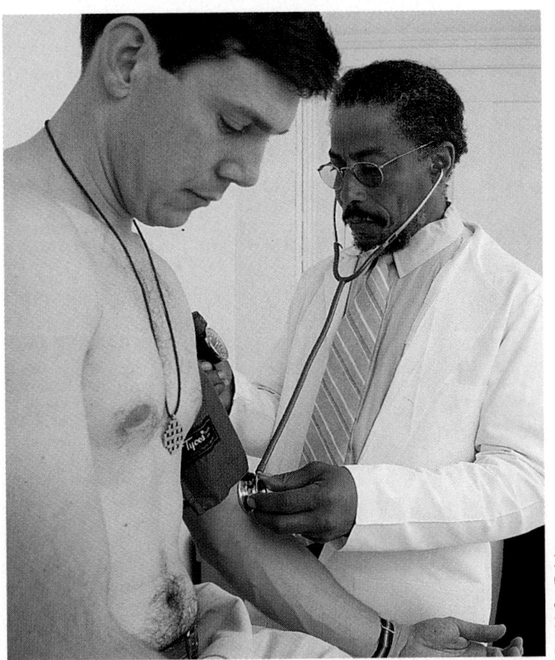

It is estimated that at least half of all patients who see a doctor have a psychosomatic disorder or an illness that is complicated by psychosomatic symptoms.

2003). Biofeedback can help relieve muscle-tension headaches, migraine headaches, and chronic pain (Buckelew et al., 1998; Middaugh & Pawlick, 2002). It shows promise for lowering blood pressure and controlling heart rhythms (Lal et al., 1998; Rau, Bührer, & Weitkunat, 2003). The technique has been used with some success to control epileptic seizures and hyperactivity in children (Sterman, 1996). Insomnia also responds to biofeedback therapy (Barowsky, Moskowitz, & Zweig, 1990).

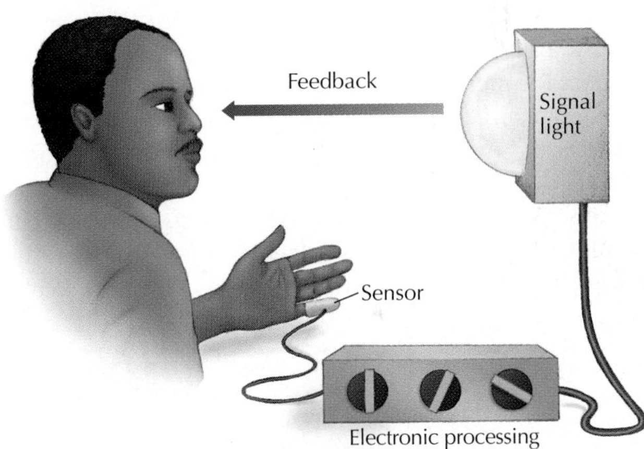

● **Figure 15.7** In biofeedback training bodily processes are monitored and processed electronically. A signal is then routed back to the patient through headphones, signal lights, or other means. This information helps the patient alter bodily activities not normally under voluntary control.

How does biofeedback help? Some researchers believe that many of its benefits arise from *general relaxation.* Others stress that there is no magic in biofeedback itself. The method simply acts as a "mirror" to help a person perform tasks involving *self-regulation.* Just as a mirror does not comb your hair, biofeedback does not do anything by itself. It can, however, help people make desired changes in their behavior (Weems, 1998).

Acculturative stress Stress caused by the many changes and adaptations required when a person moves to a foreign culture.

Biofeedback Information given to a person about his or her ongoing bodily activities; aids voluntary regulation of bodily states.

The Cardiac Personality

It would be a mistake to assume that stress is the sole cause of psychosomatic diseases. Genetic differences, organ weaknesses, and learned reactions to stress combine to do damage. Personality also enters the picture. As mentioned earlier, a general disease-prone personality type exists. To a degree, there are also "headache personalities," "asthma personalities," and so on. The best documented of such patterns is the "cardiac personality"—a person at high risk for heart disease.

Two cardiologists, Meyer Friedman and Ray Rosenman, offer a glimpse at how some people create stress for themselves. In a landmark study of heart problems, Friedman and Rosenman (1983) classified people as either **Type A personalities** (those who run a high risk of heart attack) or **Type B personalities** (those who are unlikely to have a heart attack). Then they did an 8-year follow-up, finding more than twice the rate of heart disease in Type A's than in Type B's (Rosenman et al., 1975).

Type A

What is the Type A personality like? Type A people are hard driving, ambitious, highly competitive, achievement oriented, and striving. Type A people believe that with enough effort they can overcome any obstacle, and they "push" themselves accordingly.

Perhaps the most telltale signs of a Type A personality are *time urgency* and chronic *anger* or *hostility*. Type A's seem to chafe at the normal pace of events. They hurry from one activity to another, racing the clock in self-imposed urgency. As they do, they feel a constant sense of frustration and anger. Feelings of anger and hostility, in particular, are strongly related to increased risk of heart attack (Niaura et al., 2002). One study found that 15 percent of a group of 25-year-old doctors and lawyers who scored high on a hostility test were dead by age 50. The most damaging pattern may occur in hostile persons who keep their anger "bottled up." Such people seethe with anger, but don't express it outwardly. This increases their pulse rate and blood pressure and puts a tremendous strain on the heart (Bongard, al'Absi, & Lovallo, 1998).

To summarize, there is growing evidence that anger or hostility may be the core lethal factor of Type A behavior (Krantz & McCeney, 2002; Niaura et al., 2002). To date, hundreds of studies have supported the validity of the Type A concept. In view of this, Type A's would be wise to take their increased health risks seriously.

How are Type A people identified? Characteristics of Type A people are summarized in the short self-identification test presented in ■ Table 15.7. If most of the list applies to you, you might be a Type A. However, confirmation of your type would require more

Hisham Ibrahim/Getty Images

Individuals with Type A personalities feel a continuous sense of anger, irritation, and hostility.

TABLE 15.7

Characteristics of the Type A Person

Check the items that apply to you. Do you

______	Have a habit of explosively accentuating various key words in ordinary speech even when there is no need for such accentuation?
______	Finish other persons' sentences for them?
______	*Always* move, walk, and eat rapidly?
______	Quickly skim reading material and prefer summaries or condensations of books?
______	Become easily angered by slow-moving lines or traffic?
______	Feel an impatience with the rate at which most events take place?
______	Tend to be unaware of the details or beauty of your surroundings?
______	Frequently strive to think of or do two or more things simultaneously?
______	Almost always feel vaguely guilty when you relax, vacation, or do absolutely nothing for several days?
______	Tend to evaluate your worth in quantitative terms (number of A's earned, amount of income, number of games won, and so forth)?
______	Have nervous gestures or muscle twitches, such as grinding your teeth, clenching your fists, or drumming your fingers?
______	Attempt to schedule more and more activities into less time and in so doing make fewer allowances for unforeseen problems?
______	Frequently think about other things while talking to someone?
______	Repeatedly take on more responsibilities than you can comfortably handle?

Shortened and adapted from Meyer Friedman and Ray H. Rosenman, *Type A Behavior and Your Heart* (New York: Knopf, 1983).

powerful testing methods. Also, remember that the original definition of Type A behavior was probably too broad. The key psychological factors that increase heart disease risk appear to be anger, hostility, and mistrust (Krantz & McCeney, 2002; Smith et al., 2004). Also, although Type A behavior appears to promote heart disease, depression or distress may be what finally triggers a heart attack (Denollet & Van Heck, 2001; Dinan, 2001).

Because our society places a premium on achievement, competition, and mastery, it is not surprising that many people develop Type A personalities. The best way to avoid the self-made stress this causes is to adopt behavior that is the opposite of that listed in ■ Table 15.7 (Karlberg, Krakau, & Unden, 1998). It is entirely possible to succeed in life without sacrificing your health or happiness in the process. People who frequently feel angry and hostile toward others may benefit from the advice of Redford Williams, a physician interested in Type A behavior.

Strategies for Reducing Hostility

According to Redford Williams, reducing hostility involves three goals. First, you must stop mistrusting the motives of others. Second, you must find ways to reduce how often you feel anger, indignation, irritation, and rage. Third, you must learn to be kinder and more considerate. Based on his clinical experience, Williams (1989) recommends 12 strategies for reducing hostility and increasing trust.

1. Become aware of your angry, hostile, and cynical thoughts by logging them in a notebook. Record what happened, what you thought and felt, and what actions you took. Review your hostility log at the end of each week.
2. Admit to yourself and to someone you trust that you have a problem with excessive anger and hostility.
3. Interrupt hostile, cynical thoughts whenever they occur. (The Psychology in Action section of Chapter 17 explains a thought-stopping method you can use for this step.)
4. When you have an angry, hostile, or cynical thought about someone, silently look for the ways in which it is irrational or unreasonable.
5. When you are angry, try to mentally put yourself in the other person's shoes.
6. Learn to laugh at yourself and use humor to defuse your anger.
7. Learn reliable ways to relax. Two methods are described in this chapter's Psychology in Action section. Another can be found in the Psychology in Action discussion of Chapter 17.
8. Practice trusting others more. Begin with situations where no great harm will be done if the person lets you down.
9. Make an effort to listen more to others and to really understand what they are saying.
10. Learn to be assertive, rather than aggressive, in upsetting situations. (See Chapter 18 for information about self-assertion skills.)
11. Rise above small irritations by pretending that today is the last day of your life.
12. Rather than blaming people for mistreating you, and becoming angry over it, try to forgive them. We all have shortcomings.

Hardy Personality

How do Type A people who do not develop heart disease differ from those who do? Psychologists Salvatore Maddi and others have studied people who have a **hardy personality.** Such people seem to be unusually resistant to stress. The first study of hardiness began with two groups of managers at a large utility company. All of the managers held high-stress positions. Yet some tended to get sick after stressful events, whereas others were rarely ill. How did the people who were thriving differ from their "stressed-out" colleagues? Both groups seemed to have traits typical of the Type A personality, so that wasn't the explanation. They were also quite similar in most other respects. The main difference was that the hardy group seemed to hold a worldview that consisted of three traits (Maddi, Kahn, & Maddi, 1998):

1. They had a sense of personal *commitment* to self, work, family, and other stabilizing values.
2. They felt that they had *control* over their lives and their work.
3. They had a tendency to see life as a series of *challenges,* rather than as a series of threats or problems.

How do such traits protect people from the effects of stress? Persons strong in *commitment* find ways of turning whatever they are doing into something that seems interesting and important. They tend to get involved rather than feeling alienated.

Persons strong in *control* believe that they can more often than not influence the course of events around them. This prevents them from passively seeing themselves as victims of circumstance.

Finally, people strong in *challenge* find fulfillment in continual growth. They seek to learn from their experiences, rather than accepting easy comfort, security, and routine (Maddi, Kahn, & Maddi, 1998). Indeed, many "negative" experiences can actually enhance personal growth—if you have support from others and the skills needed to cope with challenge (Armeli, Gunthert, & Cohen, 2001).

Positive Psychology: Hardiness, Optimism, and Happiness

Good and bad events occur in all lives. What separates happy people from those who are unhappy is largely a matter of attitude. Happy people tend to see their lives in more positive terms, even when trouble comes their way. For example, happier people tend to

Type A personality A personality type with an elevated risk of heart disease; characterized by time urgency, anger, and hostility.

Type B personality All personality types other than Type A; a low cardiac-risk personality.

Hardy personality A personality style associated with superior stress resistance.

find humor in disappointments. They look at setbacks as challenges. They are strengthened by losses (Lyubomirsky & Tucker, 1998). In short, happiness tends to be related to hardiness (Brebner, 1998). Why is there a connection? As psychologist Barbara Fredrickson has pointed out, positive emotions tend to broaden our mental focus. Emotions such as joy, interest, and contentment create an urge to play, to be creative, to explore, to savor life, to seek new experiences, to integrate, and to grow. When you are stressed, experiencing positive emotions can make it more likely that you will find creative solutions to your problems. Positive emotions also tend to reduce the bodily arousal that occurs when we are stressed, possibly limiting stress-related damage (Fredrickson, 2003).

Elsewhere in this chapter, we have noted the value of optimism, which goes hand in hand with hardiness and happiness. Optimists tend to expect that things will turn out well. This motivates them to actively cope with adversity. They are less likely to be stopped by temporary setbacks, and more likely to deal with problems head-on. Pessimists are more likely to ignore or deny problems. The result of such differences is that optimists are less stressed and anxious than pessimists. They are also in better health than pessimists. In general, optimists tend to take better care of themselves because they believe that their efforts to stay healthy will succeed (Peterson & Chang, 2003).

The Value of Social Support

Social support (close, positive relationships with others) provides one more important antidote to stress. People with close, supportive relationships tend to be happy, hardy, optimistic, and healthy (Kiecolt-Glaser et al., 2002). Apparently, support from family and friends serves as a buffer to cushion the impact of stressful events. (See "Feeling Stressed? You've Got a Friend.")

Women tend to make better use of social support than men do. Women who are stressed seek support and they nurture others. Men are more likely to become aggressive or to withdraw emotionally (Taylor et al., 2000). This may be why "manly men" won't ask for help, whereas women in trouble call their friends!

Tim Pannell/Corbis

Support from family and friends acts as a major buffer against stress.

Where stress is concerned, many men could benefit from adopting women's tendency to tend to and befriend others.

How else might social support help? Most people share positive events, such as marriages, births, graduations, and birthdays, with others. When things go well, we like to tell others about them. Sharing such events tends to amplify positive emotions and to further increase social support. In many ways, the sharing of good news is an important means by which positive events contribute to individual well-being (Gable et al., 2004).

The General Adaptation Syndrome

At this point we have left a very basic issue unexplained: How does stress, and our response to it, translate into disease? The answer seems to lie in the body's defenses against stress, a pattern known as the general adaptation syndrome.

The **general adaptation syndrome (G.A.S.)** is a series of bodily reactions to prolonged stress. Canadian physiologist Hans Selye (1976) noticed that the first symptoms of almost any disease or trauma (poisoning, infection, injury, or stress) are almost identical. Selye's studies showed that the body responds in the same way to any stress, be it infection, failure, embarrassment, a new job, trouble at school, or a stormy romance.

What pattern does the body's response to stress take? The G.A.S. consists of three stages: an alarm reaction, a stage of resistance, and a stage of exhaustion (Selye, 1976).

In the **alarm reaction**, your body mobilizes its resources to cope with added stress. The pituitary gland signals the adrenal glands to produce more adrenaline, noradrenaline, and cortisol. As these stress hormones are dumped into the bloodstream, some bodily processes are speeded up and others are slowed. This allows bodily resources to be applied where they are needed (Haddy & Clover, 2001).

We should all be thankful that our bodies automatically respond to emergencies. But brilliant as this emergency system is, it can also cause problems. In the first phase of the alarm reaction, people have such symptoms as headache, fever, fatigue, sore muscles, shortness of breath, diarrhea, upset stomach, loss of appetite, and a lack of energy. Notice that these are also the symptoms of being sick, of stressful travel, of high-altitude sickness, of final exams week, and (possibly) of falling in love!

During the **stage of resistance**, bodily adjustments to stress stabilize. As the body's defenses come into balance, symptoms of the alarm reaction disappear. Outwardly, everything seems normal. However, this appearance of normality comes at a high cost. The body is better able to cope with the original stressor, but its resistance to other stresses is lowered (● Figure 15.8). For example, animals placed in extreme cold become more resistant to the cold, but more susceptible to infection. It is during the stage of resistance that the first signs of psychosomatic disorders begin to appear.

Continued stress leads to the **stage of exhaustion** in which the body's resources are drained and stress hormones are depleted. Unless a way of relieving stress is found, the result will be a psychosomatic disease, a serious loss of health, or complete collapse.

The G.A.S. may sound melodramatic if you are young and healthy or if you've never endured prolonged stress. However, stress

DISCOVERING PSYCHOLOGY

Feeling Stressed? You've Got a Friend

Here's an interesting exercise to try: Briefly answer the following four questions about a specific person you are currently close to—someone you can turn to when you need help, advice, or encouragement.

1. What do you value or appreciate most about this person?
2. What does this person value or appreciate most about you?
3. What does this person do for you that is supportive or helpful?
4. How do you feel about this person after being away from her or him for a few hours or a few days?
(Adapted from Smith, Ruiz, & Uchino, 2004.)

Do you feel more relaxed and at ease after answering these questions? In a recent study, the questions were used to get people to think about a close, supportive person for a few minutes. After that, subjects had to give a stressful speech. For some participants, thinking about a supportive person helped lower their stress levels (Smith, Ruiz, & Uchino, 2004).

The preceding study suggests that you may be able to reduce the stress you feel in difficult situations by thinking about a person who supports and encourages you. If that doesn't help, and you own a pet, there may be a good alternative strategy. Many people view their pets as loving, supportive companions who are better, in some ways, than humans. In another study, some people were asked to do stressful tasks alone, whereas others had a friend, a spouse, or a pet present. Under these conditions, the greatest amount of stress relief occurred when a pet (dog or cat) was present (Allen, Blascovich, & Mendes, 2002). Thus, if you have a pet, you might find it helpful to imagine the animal by your side when you face a stressful situation. Silently talking to your furry friend can be quite calming. In any case, whether your comfort comes from a human or an animal companion, it's valuable to remind yourself that "you've got a friend."

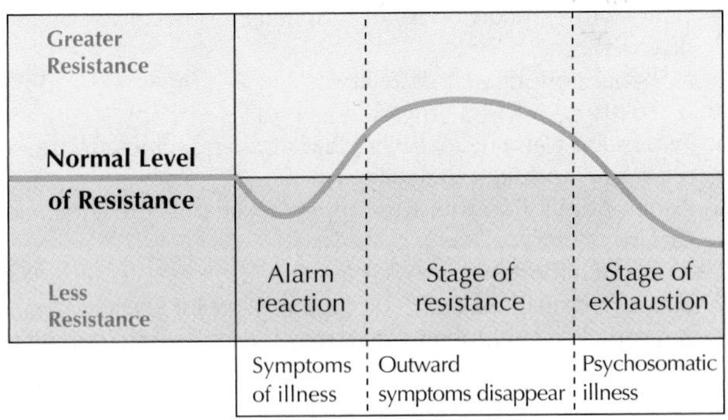

● **Figure 15.8** The general adaptation syndrome. During the initial alarm reaction to stress, resistance falls below normal. It rises again as bodily resources are mobilized, and it remains high during the stage of resistance. Eventually, resistance falls again as the stage of exhaustion is reached. (From *The Stress of Life* by Hans Selye. Copyright © 1978 by Hans Selye. Used by permission of McGraw-Hill Book Company.)

should not be taken lightly. When Selye examined animals in the later stages of the G.A.S., he found that their adrenal glands were enlarged and discolored. There was intense shrinkage of internal organs, such as the thymus, spleen, and lymph nodes, and many animals had stomach ulcers. In addition to such direct effects, stress can disrupt the body's immune system, as described next.

Stress, Illness, and the Immune System

How else might stress affect health? An answer can be found in your body's **immune system**, which mobilizes defenses (such as white blood cells) against invading microbes and other disease agents. The immune system is regulated, in part, by the brain. Because of this link, stress and upsetting emotions can affect the immune system in ways that increase susceptibility to disease (Miller, Cohen, & Ritchey, 2002). (By the way, the study of links among behavior, stress, disease, and the immune system is called **psychoneuroimmunology** [Kiecolt-Glaser et al., 2002]. Try dropping that into a conversation sometime if you want to see a stress reaction!)

Studies show that the immune system is weakened in students during major exam times. Immunity is also lowered by divorce,

Social support Close, positive relationships with other people.

General adaptation syndrome (G.A.S.) A series of bodily reactions to prolonged stress; occurs in three stages: alarm, resistance, and exhaustion.

Alarm reaction First stage of the G.A.S., during which bodily resources are mobilized to cope with a stressor.

Stage of resistance Second stage of the G.A.S., during which bodily adjustments to stress stabilize, but at a high physical cost.

Stage of exhaustion Third stage of the G.A.S., at which time the body's resources are exhausted and serious health consequences occur.

Immune system System that mobilizes bodily defenses (such as white blood cells) against invading microbes and other disease agents.

Psychoneuroimmunology Study of the links among behavior, stress, disease, and the immune system.

Tom Stewart/Corbis

Stress and negative emotions lower immune system activity and increase inflammation. This, in turn, raises our vulnerability to infection, worsens illness, and delays recovery.

bereavement, a troubled marriage, job loss, depression, and similar stresses (Gilbert et al., 1996; Herbert & Cohen, 1993). Lowered immunity explains why the "double whammy" of getting sick when you are trying to cope with prolonged or severe stress is so common (Biondi & Zannino, 1997). Stress causes the body to release substances that increase inflammation. This is part of the body's self-protective response to threats, but it can prolong infections and delay healing (Kiecolt-Glaser et al., 2002). It's also worth noting again the value of positive emotions. Happiness, laughter, and delight tend to strengthen immune system response. Doing things that make you happy can protect your health (Rosenkranz et al., 2003).

Could reducing stress help prevent illness? Yes. Various psychological approaches, such as support groups, relaxation exercises, guided imagery, and stress management training can actually boost immune system functioning (Kiecolt-Glaser & Glaser, 1992). By doing so, they help promote and restore health. For example, stress management reduced the severity of cold and flu symptoms in a group of university students (Reid, Mackinnon, & Drummond, 2001).

There is even evidence that stress management can improve the chances of survival following life-threatening diseases, such as cancer, heart disease, and HIV/AIDS (Schneiderman et al., 2001). With some successes to encourage them, psychologists are now searching for the best combination of treatments to help people resist disease (Miller & Cohen, 2001).

A Look Ahead

The work we have reviewed here has drawn new attention to the fact that each of us has a personal responsibility for maintaining and promoting health. In the Psychology in Action section that follows, we will look at what you can do to better cope with stress and the health risks that it entails. But first, the following questions may help you maintain a healthy grade on your next psychology test.

KNOWLEDGE BUILDER

Stress and Health

REFLECT

Pick a year from your life that was unusually stressful. Use the SRRS to find your LCU score for that year. Do you think there was a connection between your LCU score and your health? Or have you observed more of a connection between microstressors and your health?

Mindy complains about her health all the time, but she actually seems to be just fine. An acquaintance of Mindy's dismisses her problems by saying, "Oh, she's not really sick. It's just psychosomatic." What's wrong with this use of the term *psychosomatic*?

Do you think you are basically a Type A or a Type B personality? To what extent do you possess traits of the hardy personality?

Can you say psychoneuroimmunology? Have you impressed anyone with the word yet?

LEARNING CHECK

1. Ratings on the SRRS are based on the total number of _______ a person has for the preceding year.
   a. hassles c. STDs
   b. LCUs d. psychosomatic illnesses
2. Holmes's SRRS appears to predict long-range changes in health, whereas the frequency and severity of daily microstressors is closely related to immediate ratings of health. T or F?
3. Ulcers, migraine headaches, and hypochondria are all frequently psychosomatic disorders. T or F?
4. Which of the following is *not* classified as a psychosomatic disorder?
   a. hypertension c. eczema
   b. colitis d. thymus
5. Two major elements of biofeedback training appear to be relaxation and self-regulation. T or F?
6. Anger, hostility, and mistrust appear to be the core lethal factors in
   a. hypochondria c. the G.A.S.
   b. learned helplessness d. Type A behavior
7. A sense of commitment, challenge, and control characterizes the hardy personality. T or F?
8. The first signs of psychosomatic disorders begin to appear during the stage of
   a. alarm c. resistance
   b. exhaustion d. appraisal
9. Research shows that social support from family and friends has little effect on the health consequences of stress. T or F?
10. Students taking stressful final exams are more susceptible to the cold virus, a pattern best explained by the concept of
    a. the disease-prone personality c. emotion-focused coping
    b. psychoneuroimmunology d. reaction formation
11. Whereas stressful incidents suppress the immune system, stress management techniques have almost no effect on immune system functioning. T or F?

CRITICAL THINKING

12. People with a hardy personality type appear to be especially resistant to which of the problems discussed earlier in this chapter?

Answers: 1. b 2. T 3. F 4. d 5. T 6. d 7. T 8. a 9. F 10. b 11. F 12. Learned helplessness.

PSYCHOLOGY IN ACTION

Stress Management

Stress management is the use of behavioral strategies to reduce stress and improve coping skills. As promised, this section describes strategies for managing stress. Before you continue reading, you may want to assess your level of stress again, this time using a scale developed for undergraduate students (see ■ Table 15.8). Like the SRRS, high scores on the *College Life Stress Inventory* suggest that you have been exposed to health-threatening levels of stress (Renner & Mackin, 1998).

The *College Life Stress Inventory* is scored by adding the ratings for all of the items that have happened to you in the last year. The scale below is an approximate guide to the meaning of your score. But remember, stress is an internal state. If you are good at coping with stressors, a high score may not be a problem for you.

2351+	Extremely high
1911–2350	Very high
1471–1910	High
1031–1470	Average
591–1030	Below average
151–590	Low
0–150	Very low

Now that you have a picture of your current level of stress, what can you do about it? The simplest way of coping with stress is to modify or remove its source—by leaving a stressful job, for example. Obviously this is often impossible, which is why learning to manage stress is so important.

As shown in ● Figure 15.9, stress triggers *bodily effects, upsetting thoughts,* and *ineffective behavior.* Also shown is the fact that

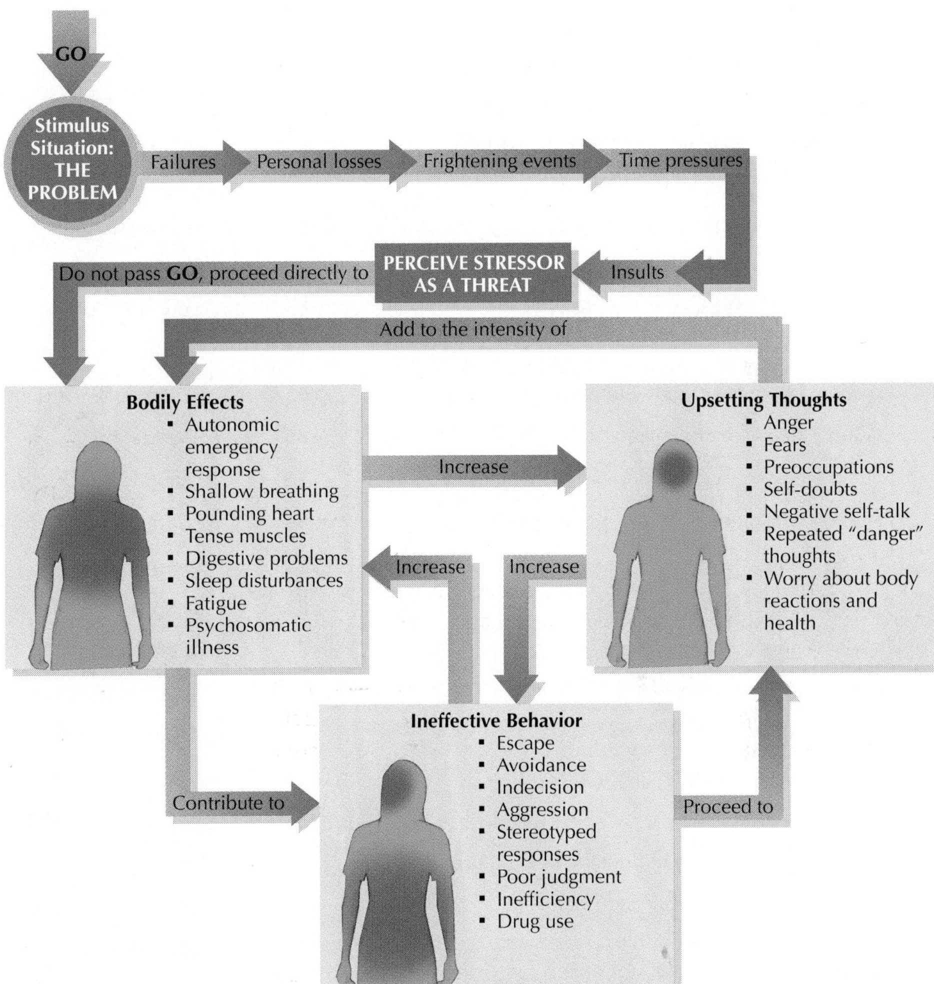

● **Figure 15.9** The stress game. (Adapted from Rosenthal and Rosenthal, 1980.)

Stress management The application of behavioral strategies to reduce stress and improve coping skills.

TABLE 15.8

College Life Stress Inventory

Circle the "stress rating" number for any item that has happened to you in the last year, then add them.

EVENT	STRESS RATING	EVENT	STRESS RATING
Being raped	100	Lack of sleep	69
Finding out that you are HIV-positive	100	Change in housing situation (hassles, moves)	69
Being accused of rape	98	Competing or performing in public	69
Death of a close friend	97	Getting in a physical fight	66
Death of a close family member	96	Difficulties with a roommate	66
Contracting a sexually transmitted disease (other than AIDS)	94	Job changes (applying, new job, work hassles)	65
Concerns about being pregnant	91	Declaring a major or concerns about future plans	65
Finals week	90	A class you hate	62
Concerns about your partner being pregnant	90	Drinking or use of drugs	61
Oversleeping for an exam	89	Confrontations with professors	60
Flunking a class	89	Starting a new semester	58
Having a boyfriend or girlfriend cheat on you	85	Going on a first date	57
Ending a steady dating relationship	85	Registration	55
Serious illness in a close friend or family member	85	Maintaining a steady dating relationship	55
Financial difficulties	84	Commuting to campus or work, or both	54
Writing a major term paper	83	Peer pressures	53
Being caught cheating on a test	83	Being away from home for the first time	53
Drunk driving	82	Getting sick	52
Sense of overload in school or work	82	Concerns about your appearance	52
Two exams in one day	80	Getting straight A's	51
Cheating on your boyfriend or girlfriend	77	A difficult class that you love	48
Getting married	76	Making new friends; getting along with friends	47
Negative consequences of drinking or drug use	75	Fraternity or sorority rush	47
Depression or crisis in your best friend	73	Falling asleep in class	40
Difficulties with parents	73	Attending an athletic event (e.g., football game)	20
Talking in front of a class	72		

Renner & Mackin, 1998.

each element worsens the others in a vicious cycle. Indeed, the basic idea of the "Stress Game" is that once it begins, *you lose*—unless you take action to break the cycle. The information that follows tells how.

Managing Bodily Reactions

Much of the immediate discomfort of stress is caused by fight-or-flight emotional responses. The body is ready to act, with tight muscles and a pounding heart. If action is prevented, we merely remain "uptight." A sensible remedy is to learn a reliable, drug-free way of relaxing.

Exercise

Stress-based arousal can be dissipated by using the body. Any full-body exercise can be effective. Swimming, dancing, jumping rope, yoga, most sports, and especially walking are valuable outlets. Regular exercise alters hormones, circulation, muscle tone, and a number of other aspects of physical functioning. Together, such changes can reduce anxiety and lower the risks for disease (Linden, 2005; Salmon, 2001).

Be sure to choose activities that are vigorous enough to relieve tension, yet enjoyable enough to be done repeatedly. Exercising for stress management is most effective when it is done daily. As little as 30 minutes of total exercise per day, even if it occurs in short 10- to 20-minute sessions, can improve mood and energy (Hansen, Stevens, & Coast, 2001).

Meditation

Many stress counselors recommend *meditation* for quieting the body and promoting relaxation. To learn more about meditation and its effects, read the article "Meditation—The 20-Minute Vacation" in the booklet that came with this text. For now, it is enough to state that meditation is easy to learn—taking an expensive commercial course is unnecessary.

Meditation is one of the most effective ways to relax (Deckro et al., 2002). But be aware that listening to or playing music, taking nature walks, enjoying hobbies, and the like can be meditations of sorts. Anything that reliably interrupts upsetting thoughts and promotes relaxation can be helpful.

Progressive Relaxation

It is possible to relax systematically, completely, and by choice. To learn the details of how this is done, consult Chapter 17 of this book. The basic idea of **progressive relaxation** is to tighten all the muscles in a given area of your body (the arms, for instance) and then voluntarily relax them. By first tensing and relaxing each area of the body, you can learn what muscle tension feels like. Then when each area is relaxed, the change is more noticeable and more controllable. In this way it is possible, with practice, to greatly reduce tension.

Guided Imagery

In a technique called **guided imagery**, people visualize images that are calming, relaxing, or beneficial in other ways. Relaxation, for instance, can be promoted by visualizing peaceful scenes. Pick several places where you feel safe, calm, and at ease. Typical locations might be a beach or lake, the woods, floating on an air mattress in a warm pool, or lying in the sun at a quiet park. To relax, vividly imagine yourself in one of these locations. In the visualized scene, you should be alone and in a comfortable position. It is important to visualize the scene as realistically as possible. Try to feel, taste, smell, hear, and see what you would actually experience in the calming scene. Practice forming such images several times a day for about 5 minutes each time. When your scenes become familiar and detailed they can be used to reduce anxiety and encourage relaxation (Rosenthal, 1993). Remember, too, that imagining that a supportive friend or a loving pet is nearby can reduce tension and anxiety (Allen, Blascovich, & Mendes, 2002; Smith, Ruiz, & Uchino, 2004).

Modifying Ineffective Behavior

Stress is often made worse by our misguided responses to it. The following suggestions may help you deal with stress more effectively.

Slow Down

Remember that stress can be self-generated. Try to deliberately do things at a slower pace—especially if your pace has speeded up over the years. Tell yourself, "What counts most is not if I get there first, but if I get there at all," or "My goal is distance, not speed."

Organize

Disorganization creates stress. Try to take a fresh look at your situation and get organized. Setting priorities can be a real stress fighter. Ask yourself what's really important and concentrate on the things that count. Learn to let go of trivial but upsetting irritations. And above all, when you are feeling stressed, remember to K.I.S.: Keep It Simple. (Some people prefer K.I.S.S.: Keep It Simple, Stupid.)

Strike a Balance

Work, school, family, friends, interests, hobbies, recreation, community, church—there are many important elements in a satisfying life. Damaging stress often comes from letting one element—especially work or school—get blown out of proportion. Your goal should be quality in life, not quantity. Try to strike a balance between challenging "good stress" and relaxation. Remember, when you are "doing nothing" you are actually doing something very important: Set aside time for "me acts" such as loafing, browsing, puttering, playing, and napping.

Recognize and Accept Your Limits

Many of us set unrealistic and perfectionist goals. Given that no one can ever be perfect, this attitude leaves many people feeling inadequate, no matter how well they have performed. Set gradual, achievable goals for yourself. Also, set realistic limits on what you try to do on any given day. Learn to say no to added demands or responsibilities.

Write About Your Feelings

If you don't have someone you can talk to about stressful events, you might try expressing your thoughts and feelings in writing. Several studies have found that students who write about their upsetting experiences, thoughts, and feelings are better able to cope with stress. They also experience fewer illnesses, and they get better grades (Pennebaker & Francis, 1996). Writing about your feelings tends to leave your mind clearer. This makes it easier to pay attention to life's challenges and come up with effective coping strategies (Klein & Boals, 2001a, 2001b).

After you write about your feelings, it helps to make specific plans for coping with upsetting experiences (Cameron & Nicholls, 1998). As an alternative, you might want to try writing about positive experiences. In a recent study, college students who wrote about intensely positive experiences had fewer illnesses over the next 3 months. Writing for just 20 minutes a day for 3 days improved the students' moods and had a surprisingly long-lasting effect on their health (Burton & King, 2004).

Avoiding Upsetting Thoughts

Assume you are taking a test. Suddenly you realize that you are running short of time. If you say to yourself, "Oh no, this is terrible,

Progressive relaxation A method for producing deep relaxation of all parts of the body.

Guided imagery Intentional visualization of images that are calming, relaxing, or beneficial in other ways.

I've blown it now," your body's response will probably be sweating, tenseness, and a knot in your stomach. On the other hand, if you say, "I should have watched the time, but getting upset won't help, I'll just take one question at a time," your stress level will be much lower.

As stated earlier, stress is greatly affected by the views we take of events. Physical symptoms and a tendency to make poor decisions are increased by negative thoughts or "self-talk." In many cases what you say to yourself can be the difference between coping and collapsing (Matheny et al., 1996).

Coping Statements

Psychologist Donald Meichenbaum has popularized a technique called **stress inoculation.** In it, clients learn to fight fear and anxiety with an internal monologue of positive coping statements. First, clients learn to identify and monitor **negative self-statements** (self-critical thoughts that increase anxiety). Negative thoughts are a problem because they tend to directly elevate physical arousal. To counter this effect, clients learn to replace negative statements with coping statements from a supplied list. Eventually they are encouraged to make their own lists (Saunders et al., 1996).

How are coping statements applied? **Coping statements** are reassuring and self-enhancing. They are used to block out, or counteract, negative self-talk in stressful situations. Before giving a short speech, for instance, you would replace "I'm scared," "I can't do this," "My mind will go blank and I'll panic," or "I'll sound stupid and boring" with "I'll give my speech on something I like," or "I'll breathe deeply before I start my speech," or "My pounding heart just means I'm psyched up to do my best." Additional examples of coping statements follow.

Preparing for Stressful Situation

I'll just take things one step at a time.
If I get nervous I'll just pause a moment.
Tomorrow I'll be through it.
I've managed to do this before.
What exactly do I have to do?

Confronting the Stressful Situation

Relax now, this can't really hurt me.
Stay organized, focus on the task.
There's no hurry, take it step by step.
Nobody's perfect, I'll just do my best.
It will be over soon, just be calm.

Meichenbaum cautions that saying the "right" things to yourself may not be enough to improve stress tolerance. You must practice this approach in actual stress situations. Also, it is important to develop your own personal list of coping statements by finding what works for you. Ultimately, the value of learning this and other stress management skills ties back into the idea that much stress is self-generated. Knowing that you can manage a demanding situation is in itself a major antidote for stress. In a recent study, college students who learned stress inoculation not only had less anxiety and depression, but better self-esteem as well (Schiraldi & Brown, 2001).

Lighten Up

Humor is worth cultivating as a way to reduce stress. A good sense of humor can lower your distress/stress reaction to difficult events (Lefcourt & Thomas, 1998). In addition, an ability to laugh at life's ups and downs is associated with better immunity to disease (McClelland & Cheriff, 1997). Don't be afraid to laugh at yourself and at the many ways in which we humans make things difficult for ourselves. You've probably heard the following advice about everyday stresses: "Don't sweat the small stuff, and it's all small stuff." Humor is one of the best antidotes for anxiety and emotional distress because it helps put things into perspective (Cann, Holt, & Calhoun, 1999; Henman, 2001). The vast majority of events are only as stressful as you allow them to be. Have some fun. It's perfectly healthy.

KNOWLEDGE BUILDER

Coping with Stress

REFLECT

If you were going to put together a "tool kit" for stress management, what items would you include?

LEARNING CHECK

1. Exercise, meditation, and progressive relaxation are considered effective ways of countering negative self-statements. T or F?
2. A person using progressive relaxation for stress management is most likely trying to control which component of stress?
   a. bodily reactions c. ineffective behavior
   b. upsetting thoughts d. the primary appraisal
3. Exercise, meditation, progressive relaxation, and guided imagery would be least likely to help a person who is in the G.A.S. stage of
   a. alarm c. exhaustion
   b. resistance d. adaptation
4. While taking a stressful classroom test you say to yourself, "Stay organized, focus on the task." It's obvious that you are using
   a. guided imagery c. LCUs
   b. coping statements d. guided relaxation

CRITICAL THINKING

5. Steve always feels extremely pressured when the due date arrives for his major term papers. How could he reduce stress in such instances?

Answers: 1. F **2.** a **3.** c **4.** b **5.** The stress associated with doing term papers can be almost completely eliminated by making a long-term assignment into many small daily or weekly assignments. Students who habitually procrastinate are often amazed at how pleasant college work can be once they renounce "brinkmanship."

Chapter in Review

What is health psychology? How does behavior affect health?

- Health psychologists are interested in behavior that helps maintain and promote health.
- Studies of health and illness have identified a number of behavioral risk factors and health-promoting behaviors.
- Health psychologists have pioneered efforts to prevent the development of unhealthy habits and to improve well-being through community health campaigns.

What is stress? What factors determine its severity?

- Stress occurs when demands are placed on an organism to adjust or adapt.
- Stress is more damaging in situations involving pressure, a lack of control, unpredictability of the stressor, and intense or repeated emotional shocks.
- Stress is intensified when a situation is perceived as a threat and when a person does not feel competent to cope with it.
- In work settings, prolonged stress can lead to burnout.
- The primary appraisal of a situation greatly affects our emotional response to it. Stress reactions, in particular, are related to an appraisal of threat.
- During a secondary appraisal some means of coping with a situation is selected. Coping may be either problem focused or emotion focused or both.

What causes frustration and what are typical reactions to it?

- Frustration is the negative emotional state that occurs when progress toward a goal is blocked. Sources of frustration may be usefully classified as external or personal.
- External frustrations are based on delay, failure, rejection, loss, and other direct blocking of motives. Personal frustration is related to personal characteristics over which one has little control.
- Frustrations of all types become more intense as the strength, urgency, or importance of the blocked motive increases.
- Major behavioral reactions to frustration include persistence, more vigorous responding, circumvention, direct aggression, displaced aggression (including scapegoating), and escape or withdrawal.

Are there different types of conflict? How do people react to conflict?

- Conflict occurs when one must choose between contradictory alternatives.
- Five major types of conflict are approach-approach, avoidance-avoidance, approach-avoidance, double approach-avoidance, and multiple approach-avoidance.
- Approach-approach conflicts are usually the easiest to resolve.
- Avoidance conflicts are difficult to resolve and are characterized by inaction, indecision, freezing, and a desire to escape (called leaving the field).
- People usually remain in approach-avoidance conflicts, but fail to fully resolve them. Approach-avoidance conflicts are associated with ambivalence and partial approach.
- Vacillation is a common reaction to double approach-avoidance conflicts.

What are defense mechanisms?

- Anxiety, threat, or feelings of inadequacy frequently lead to the use of defense mechanisms. These are habitual psychological strategies used to avoid or reduce anxiety.
- A large number of defense mechanisms have been identified, including compensation, denial, fantasy, intellectualization, isolation, projection, rationalization, reaction formation, regression, repression, and sublimation.

What do we know about coping with feelings of helplessness and depression?

- Learned helplessness has been used as a model for understanding depression. Mastery training acts as one major antidote to helplessness.
- Depression is a major, and surprisingly common, emotional problem. Actions and thoughts that counter feelings of helplessness tend to reduce depression.
- The college blues are a relatively mild form of depression. Learning to manage college work and to challenge self-critical thinking can help alleviate the college blues.

How is stress related to health and disease?

- Work with the *Social Readjustment Rating Scale* indicates that multiple life changes can increase long-range susceptibility to accident or illness.

Stress inoculation Use of positive coping statements to control fear and anxiety.

Negative self-statements Self-critical thoughts that increase anxiety and lower performance.

Coping statements Reassuring, self-enhancing statements that are used to stop self-critical thinking.

- Immediate psychological and mental health is more closely related to the intensity and severity of daily hassles or microstressors.
- Intense or prolonged stress may cause damage in the form of psychosomatic problems.
- Psychosomatic (mind-body) disorders have no connection to hypochondria, the tendency to imagine that one has some terrible disease.
- During biofeedback training, bodily processes are monitored and converted to a signal that tells what the body is doing. With practice, biofeedback allows alteration of many bodily activities. It shows promise for the alleviation of some psychosomatic illnesses.
- People with Type A personalities are competitive, striving, hostile, and impatient. These characteristics—especially hostility—double the risk of heart attack.
- People who have traits of the hardy personality seem to be resistant to stress, even if they also have Type A traits.
- The body reacts to stress in a series of stages called the general adaptation syndrome (G.A.S.).
- The stages of the G.A.S. are alarm, resistance, and exhaustion. The pattern of bodily reactions and changes in resistance observed in the G.A.S. follows closely the pattern observed in the development of psychosomatic disorders.
- Studies of psychoneuroimmunology show that stress also lowers the body's immunity to disease.

What are the best strategies for managing stress?

- The damaging effects of stress can be reduced with stress management techniques.
- All of the following are good ways to manage bodily reactions to stress: exercise, meditation, progressive relaxation, and guided imagery.
- To minimize ineffective behavior when you are stressed you can slow down, get organized, balance work and relaxation, accept your limits, and write about your feelings.
- Learning to use coping statements is a good way to combat upsetting thoughts.

> Web Resources

Internet addresses frequently change. To find the sites listed here, visit www.thomsonedu.com/psychology/coon for an updated list of Internet addresses and direct links to relevant sites.

***Psychology: Gateways to Mind and Behavior* Website** Online quizzes, flash cards, and other helpful study aids for this text. www.thomsonedu.com/psychology/coon.

Burnout Test A short questionnaire on job burnout.

Coping with Terrorism Information about emotional reactions to terrorism; provided by the American Psychological Association.

Focus on Stress A series of articles about stress.

HealthyWay A set of pages on health, nutrition, addictions, disabilities, sexuality, fitness. and much more.

Preventive Health Center A general source of information on how to maintain health and prevent disease.

Stress Management: Review of Principles Links to articles on stress management.

Stress, Anxiety, Fears, and Psychosomatic Disorders A comprehensive source on stress, anxiety, and related disorders.

Type A Behavior Describes Type A behavior, with links to an online test and related sites.

ThomsonNOW™ Go to www.thomsonedu.com to link to ThomsonNow, your online study tool. First take the **Pre-Test** for this chapter to get your **Personalized Study Plan**, which will identify topics you need to review and direct you to online resources. Then take the **Post-Test** to determine what concepts you have mastered and what you still need work on.

InfoTrac College Edition For recent articles related to the college blues and more serious forms of depression, use Key Words search for MENTAL DEPRESSION. Go to www.thomsonedu.com/psychology/coon.

Interactive Learning

***PsychNow!* Version 2.0 CD-ROM** Interact with the material with *PsychNow!*'s animations, video clips, experiments, and interactive assessments. For this chapter, go to *6c. Coping with Emotion* and *6d. Stress and Health* to learn more about how emotion and stress affect our health.

chapter 16

Psychological Disorders

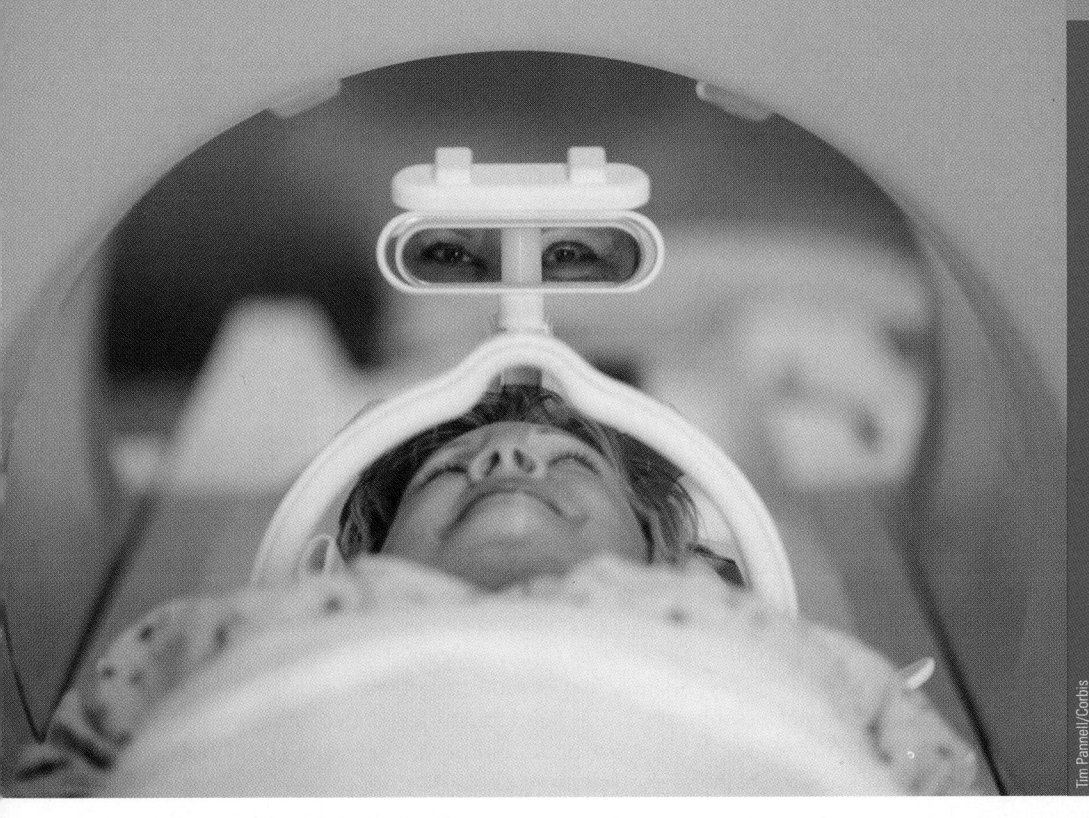

Tim Pannell/Corbis

THEME:

Judgments of normality are relative, but psychological disorders clearly exist and need to be classified, explained, and treated.

Key Questions

How is normality defined, and what are the major psychological disorders?

What is a personality disorder?

What problems result when a person suffers high levels of anxiety?

How do psychologists explain anxiety-based disorders?

What are the general characteristics of psychotic disorders?

How do delusional disorders differ from other psychotic disorders?

What forms does schizophrenia take? What causes it?

What are mood disorders? What causes depression?

Why do people commit suicide? Can suicide be prevented?

Preview

Beware the Helicopters

"The helicopters. Oh no, not the helicopters. Have come to tear the feathers out of my frontal lobes. Help me, nurse, help me, can't you hear them? Gotta get back into my body to save it. . . . The doctor is thinking I would make good glue."

These are the words of Carol North, a psychiatrist who survived schizophrenia. In addition to being plagued by hallucinated helicopters, Carol heard voices that said, "Be good," "Do bad," "Stand up," "Sit down," "Collide with the other world," "Do you want a cigar?" (North, 1987).

Carol North's painful journey into the shadows of madness left her incapacitated for nearly 20 years. Her case is but one hint of the magnitude of mental health problems. Here are the facts on psychological disorders:

- Of every 100 persons, one will become so severely disturbed as to require hospitalization at some point in his or her lifetime.
- Some 3 to 6 percent of the aged suffer from organic psychoses.
- Some 7 percent of the population has an anxiety-related disorder.
- One of every eight school-age children is seriously maladjusted.
- From 10 to 20 percent or more of all adults suffer a major depression in their lifetime.
- Each year in North America, more than 2 million people are admitted to hospitals for psychiatric treatment.

What does it mean to be "crazy"? A hundred years ago, doctors and nonprofessionals alike used terms such as "crazy," "insane," "cracked," and "lunatic" quite freely. The "insane" were thought of as bizarre and definitely different from the rest of us. Today, our understanding of psychological disorders is more sophisticated. To draw the line between normal and abnormal, we must weigh some complex issues. We'll explore some of them in this chapter, as well as an array of psychological problems.

Normality—What Is Normal?

Deciding if a person's behavior is abnormal is harder than it might seem. The conservative, church-going housewife down the street might be flagrantly psychotic and a lethal danger to her children. The reclusive eccentric who hangs out at the park could be the sanest person in town. Let's begin our discussion with some basic factors that affect judgments of normality. "That guy is really wacko. His porch lights are dimming." "Yeah, the butter's sliding off his waffle. I think he's ready to go postal." Informally, it's tempting to make snap judgments about mental health. However, to seriously classify people as psychologically unhealthy raises complex and age-old issues. The scientific study of mental, emotional, and behavioral disorders is known as **psychopathology.** The term also refers to mental disorders themselves, such as schizophrenia or depression, and to behavior patterns that make people unhappy and impair their personal growth (Butcher, Mineka, & Hooley, 2004).

Defining abnormality can be tricky. We might begin by saying that psychopathology is characterized by *subjective discomfort* (private feelings of pain, unhappiness, or emotional distress) like Carol North endured.

But couldn't a person be seriously disturbed without feeling discomfort? Yes. Psychopathology doesn't always cause personal anguish. A person suffering from mania might feel elated and "on top of the world." Also, a *lack* of discomfort may reveal a problem. For example, if you showed no signs of grief after the death of a close friend, we might suspect psychopathology. In practice, subjective discomfort explains most instances in which people voluntarily seek professional help.

Some psychologists use statistics to define normality more objectively. **Statistical abnormality** refers to scoring very high or low on some dimension, such as intelligence, anxiety, or depression. Anxiety, for example, is a feature of several psychological disorders. To measure it, we could create a test to learn how many people show low, medium, or high levels of anxiety. Usually, the results of such tests will form a *normal* (bell-shaped) *curve.* (*Normal* in this case refers only to the *shape* of the curve.) Notice that most people score near the middle of a normal curve; very few have extremely high and low scores (● Figure 16.1). A person who deviates from the average by being anxious all the time (high anxiety) might be abnormal. So, too, might a person who never feels anxiety.

DISCOVERING PSYCHOLOGY

Crazy for a Day

Performing a mildly abnormal behavior is a good way to get a sense of how social norms define "normality" in daily life. Here's your assignment: Do something strange in public and observe how people react to you. (Please don't do anything dangerous, harmful, or offensive—and don't get arrested!) Here are some deviant behaviors that other students have staged:

- Sit in the dining area of a fast-food restaurant and loudly carry on a conversation with an imaginary companion.
- Stand in a busy hallway on campus and adopt a Kung Fu stance. Remain in that position for 10 minutes.
- Walk around campus on a sunny day while wearing a raincoat and carrying an open umbrella. Keep the umbrella over your head when you are inside buildings.
- Stick one finger in your nose and another in your ear. Walk through a busy shopping mall.
- Cover your head with aluminum foil for a day.

Does the idea of performing any of these actions make you uncomfortable? If so, you may not need to do anything more to appreciate how powerfully social norms constrain our actions. As we have noted, social nonconformity is just one facet of abnormal behavior. Nevertheless, actions that are regarded as "strange" within a particular culture are often the first sign to others that a person has a problem.

Then statistical abnormality tells us nothing about the meaning of deviations from the norm? Right. It is as statistically "abnormal" (unusual) for a person to score above 145 on an IQ test as it is to score below 55. However, only the lower score is regarded as "abnormal" or undesirable (Wakefield, 1992). In the same sense, it is unusual for a person to speak four languages or to win an event at the Olympics, but these are desirable, if rare, accomplishments.

Statistical definitions also can't tell us *where to draw the line* between normality and abnormality. To take a new example, we could obtain the average frequency of sexual intercourse for persons of a particular age, sex, sexual orientation, and marital status. Clearly, a person who feels driven to have sex dozens of times a day has a problem. But as we move back toward the norm we face the problem of drawing lines. How often does a normal behavior have to occur before it becomes abnormal? As you can see, statistical boundary lines tend to be somewhat arbitrary (Comer, 2005).

Atypical behavior or nonconformity may underlie some disorders. **Social nonconformity** refers to disobeying public standards for acceptable conduct. Extreme nonconformity can lead to destructive or self-destructive behavior. (Think, for instance, of a drug abuser or a prostitute.) However, we must be careful to separate unhealthy nonconformity from creative lifestyles. Many eccentric "characters" are charming and emotionally stable. Note, too, that strictly following social norms is no guarantee of mental health. In some cases, psychopathology involves rigid conformity. (See "Crazy for a Day.")

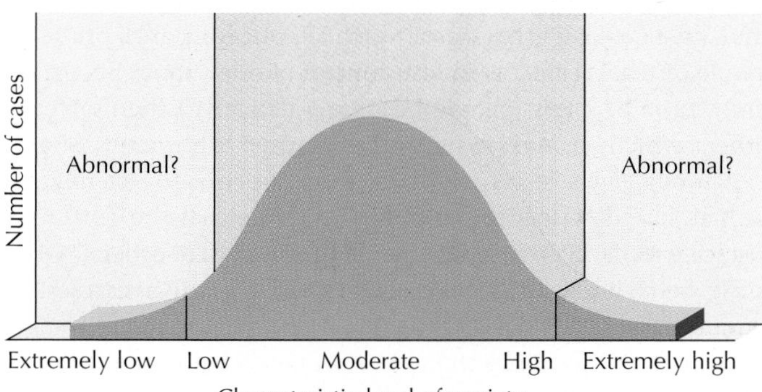

● **Figure 16.1** The number of people displaying a personal characteristic may help define what is statistically abnormal.

Rick Friedman/Corbis

Social nonconformity does not automatically indicate psychopathology.

Psychopathology The scientific study of mental, emotional, and behavioral disorders; also, abnormal or maladaptive behavior.

Statistical abnormality Abnormality defined on the basis of an extreme score on some dimension, such as IQ or anxiety.

Social nonconformity Failure to conform to societal norms or the usual minimum standards for social conduct.

CRITICAL THINKING

The Politics of Madness

The year is 1840. You are a slave who has tried repeatedly to escape from a cruel and abusive master. An expert is consulted about your "abnormal" behavior. His conclusion? You are suffering from "drapetomania," a mental "disorder" that causes slaves to run away (Wakefield, 1992). Your "cure"? The expert will cut off your toes.

As this example suggests, psychiatric terms are easily abused. Historically, some have been applied to culturally disapproved behaviors that are not really disorders. One of our personal favorites is the diagnosis of "anarchia," a form of insanity that leads one to seek a more democratic society (Brown, 1990b). All of the following were also once considered disorders: childhood masturbation, lack of vaginal orgasm, self-defeating personality (applied mainly to women), homosexuality, and nymphomania (a woman with a healthy sexual appetite) (Wakefield, 1992). Even today, race, gender, and social class continue to affect the diagnosis of various disorders (Nathan & Langenbucher, 1999; Poland & Caplan, 2004).

Gender is probably the most common source of bias in judging normality because standards tend to be based on males (Nolen-Hoeksema, 2004; Widiger, 2005). According to psychologist Paula Caplan (1995) and others, women are penalized both for conforming to female stereotypes and for ignoring them. If a woman is independent, aggressive, and unemotional, she may be considered "unhealthy." Yet at the same time, a woman who is vain, emotional, irrational, and dependent on others (all "feminine" traits in our culture) may be classified as a histrionic or dependent personality (Bornstein, 1996). Indeed, a majority of persons classified as having dependent personality disorder are women. In view of this, Paula Caplan asks, why isn't there a category called "delusional dominating personality disorder" for obnoxious men (Caplan, 1995)?

The differences we have reviewed illustrate the subtle influence that culture can have on perceptions of disorder and normality. Be cautious before you leap to conclusions about the mental health of others (*DSM-IV-TR,* 2000). (They might be doing an assignment for their psychology class!)

A young woman ties a thick rubber cord around her ankles, screams hysterically, and jumps headfirst off a bridge. Thirty years ago, the woman's behavior might have seemed completely crazy. Today, it is a routine form of entertainment. Before any behavior can be defined as abnormal, we must consider the *situational context* (social situation, behavioral setting, or general circumstances) in which it occurs. Is it normal to stand outside and water a lawn with a hose? It depends on whether it is raining. Is it abnormal for a grown man to remove his pants and expose himself to another man or woman in a place of business? It depends on whether the other person is a bank clerk or a doctor!

Almost any imaginable behavior can be considered normal in some contexts. In mid-October 1972, an airplane carrying a rugby team crashed in the snow-capped Andes of South America. Incredibly, 16 of the 45 people onboard survived 73 days in deep snow and subfreezing temperatures. They were forced to use extremely grim measures to do so—they ate the bodies of those who died in the crash.

As implied by our earlier discussion of social norms, culture is one of the most influential contexts in which any behavior is judged. In some cultures it is considered normal to defecate or urinate in public or to appear naked in public. In our culture such behaviors would be considered unusual or abnormal. In Muslim cultures, women who remain completely housebound are considered normal or even virtuous. In Western cultures they might be diagnosed as suffering from a disorder called agoraphobia (Fabrega, 2004). (Agoraphobia is described later in this chapter.)

Thus, *cultural relativity* (the idea that judgments are made relative to the values of one's culture) can affect the diagnosis of psychological disorders. (See "The Politics of Madness.") Still, *all* cultures classify people as abnormal if they fail to communicate with others or are consistently unpredictable in their actions.

Core Features of Disordered Behavior

If abnormality is so hard to define, how are judgments of psychopathology made? It's clear that all of the standards we have discussed are *relative*. However, abnormal behavior does have two core features. First, it is **maladaptive.** Rather than helping people cope successfully, abnormal behavior makes it more difficult for them to meet the demands of day-to-day life. Second, people suffering from psychological disorders *lose the ability to control* their thoughts, behaviors, or feelings adequately. For example, gambling is not a problem if people bet for entertainment and can maintain self-control. However, compulsive gambling is a sign of psychopathology. The voices that Carol North kept hearing are a prime example of what it means to lose control of one's thoughts. In the most extreme cases, people become a danger to themselves or others, which is clearly maladaptive (Hansell & Damour, 2004).

Various levels of functioning—from superior to severely disturbed—are described in ■ Table 16.1. Note that the bottom of the scale reads, "Persistent danger of hurting self or others." Obviously, behavior at that level is maladaptive and involves a serious loss of control.

In practice, deciding that a person needs help usually occurs when the person *does something* (hits a person, hallucinates, stares into space, collects rolls of toilet paper, and so forth) that *annoys* or *gains the attention* of a person in a *position of power* in the per-

TABLE 16.1

Levels of Functioning

SCALE	LEVEL OF FUNCTIONING	EXAMPLES
100	Superior functioning in a wide range of activities. No symptoms.	Life's problems never seem to get out of hand. Person is sought by others because of his or her many positive qualities.
90	Absent or minimal symptoms, functioning well in all areas, no more than everyday problems.	Has mild anxiety before exams, occasional arguments with family members.
80	If symptoms are present, they are brief and common reactions to stressors. No more than slight impairment in relationships, work, or school.	Has difficulty concentrating after family arguments, is falling behind in schoolwork.
70	Some mild symptoms, or some difficulty with relationships, work, or school.	Mood is depressed and has mild insomnia. Has been truant at school and has stolen things at home.
60	Moderate symptoms or moderate problems with relationships, work, or school.	Emotions are blunted, speech evasive, occasional panic attacks, no friends, unable to keep a job.
50	Serious symptoms or any serious impairments in relationships, work, or school.	Person has suicidal thoughts, engages in obsessional rituals, shoplifts, has no friends, is unable to keep a job.
40	Some impairment in grasp of reality or in communication, plus major impairments in work or school relationships, judgment, thinking or mood	Speech is illogical, obscure, or irrelevant. Person is depressed and avoids friends, neglects family, and is unable to work
30	Behavior is considerably affected by delusions or hallucinations; or, person is seriously impaired in communication or judgment; or, is unable to function in almost all areas.	Person is sometimes incoherent; acts grossly inappropriately; is preoccupied with suicide; stays in bed all day; has no job, home, or friends.
20	Some danger of hurting self or others; or, occasionally fails to maintain minimal personal hygiene; or, communication is grossly impaired.	Person makes tentative suicide attempts, is frequently violent and manically excited, smears own feces, is either incoherent or mute.
10	Persistent danger of severely hurting self or others; or, persistent inability to maintain minimal personal hygiene; or, serious suicidal acts.	Repeatedly violent, maintains almost no personal hygiene, has made potentially lethal suicide attempts.

Adapted from *Global Assessment of Functioning Scale,* DSM-IV, 1994.

son's life (an employer, teacher, parent, spouse, or the person himself or herself). That person then *does something* about it. (A police officer may be called, the person may be urged to see a psychologist, a relative may start commitment proceedings, or the person may voluntarily seek help.)

Classifying Mental Disorders—Problems by the Book

Psychological problems are classified by using the *Diagnostic and Statistical Manual of Mental Disorders* (*DSM-IV-TR,* 2000). The DSM helps psychologists correctly identify mental disorders and select the best therapies to treat them (First & Pincus, 2002).

A **mental disorder** is a significant impairment in psychological functioning. If you were to glance through *DSM-IV-TR,* you would see many disorders described, including those in ■ Table 16.3 (on page 539). It's impossible here to discuss all of these problems. Major disorders are listed in the table so you can see the types of problems found in the DSM. (You don't need to memorize all of them.) The descriptions that follow will give you an overview of some selected problems.

An Overview of Psychological Disorders

People suffering from **psychotic disorders** have "retreated from reality." That is, they suffer from hallucinations and delusions and they are socially withdrawn. Psychotic disorders are severely disabling and often lead to hospitalization. Typically, psychotic patients cannot control their thoughts and actions. For example, a college student who became psychotic told his father, "It's the strangest thing. I hear voices, hundreds of them, telling me that everyone wants me dead. It's like all the radios of the world blaring all the stations at once, and it doesn't stop. It jams my brain." (Weisburd, 1990). Psychotic symptoms occur in schizophrenia, delusional disorders, and some mood disorders. Also, psychosis

Maladaptive behavior Behavior that makes it difficult to adapt to the environment and meet the demands of day-to-day life.

Mental disorder A significant impairment in psychological functioning.

Psychotic disorder A severe mental disorder characterized by a retreat from reality, by hallucinations and delusions, and by social withdrawal.

TABLE 16.2

Some Selected Categories of Psychopathology

PROBLEM	PRIMARY SYMPTOM	TYPICAL SIGNS OF TROUBLE
Psychotic disorders	Loss of contact with reality	You hear or see things that others don't; your mind has been playing tricks on you
Mood disorders	Mania or depression	You feel sad and hopeless; or you talk too loud and too fast and have a rush of ideas and feelings that others think are unreasonable
Anxiety disorders	High anxiety or anxiety-based distortions of behavior	You have anxiety attacks and feel like you are going to die; or you are afraid to do things that most people can do; or you spend unusual amounts of time doing things like washing your hands or counting your heartbeats
Somatoform disorders	Bodily complaints without an organic (physical) basis	You feel physically sick, but your doctor says nothing is wrong with you; or you suffer from pain that has no physical basis; or you are preoccupied with thoughts about being sick
Dissociative disorders	Amnesia, feelings of unreality, multiple identities	There are major gaps in your memory of events; you feel like you are a robot or a stranger to yourself; others tell you that you have done things that you don't remember doing
Personality disorders	Unhealthy personality patterns	Your behavior patterns repeatedly cause problems at work, at school, and in your relationships with others
Sexual and gender identity disorders	Disturbed gender identity, deviant sexual behavior, problems in sexual adjustment	You feel that you are a man trapped in a woman's body (or the reverse); or you can only gain sexual satisfaction by engaging in highly atypical sexual behavior; or you have problems with sexual desire, arousal, or performance
Substance-related disorders	Disturbances related to drug abuse or dependence	You have been drinking too much, using illegal drugs, or taking prescription drugs more often than you should

American Psychiatric Association

DSM-IV-TR is not the only system for classifying mental disorders. Nevertheless, most activities in mental health settings—from diagnosis to therapy to billing of insurance companies—are influenced by the DSM. *DSM-IV-TR* is both a scientific document and a social one. Major disorders are well-documented problems. Some problems, however, have little to do with "mental illness." Instead, they are primarily socially disapproved behaviors.

may be related to medical problems, drug abuse, and other conditions. (■ Table 16.2 provides a simplified list of major disorders.)

Organic mental disorders are problems caused by brain pathology; that is, by drug damage, diseases of the brain, injuries, poisons, and so on (● Figure 16.2). A person with organic disorders may have severe emotional disturbances, impaired thinking, memory loss, personality changes, delirium, or psychotic symptoms (Nolen-Hoeksema, 2004).

In reality, almost all mental disorders are partly biological (Hansell & Damour, 2004). That's why *DSM-IV-TR* does not list "organic mental disorders" as a separate category. Nevertheless, all of the following problems are closely associated with organic damage: delirium, dementia, amnesia, and other cognitive disorders; mental disorders due to a general medical condition; and substance-related disorders (drug abuse).

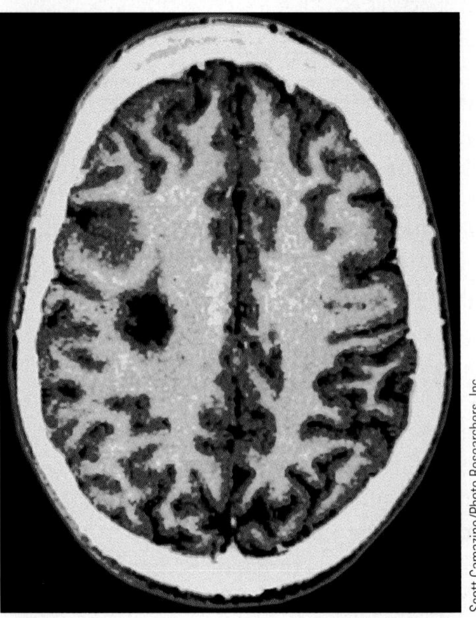

Scott Camazine/Photo Researchers, Inc.

● **Figure 16.2** This MRI scan of a human brain (viewed from the top) reveals a tumor (dark spot). Mental disorders sometimes have organic causes of this sort. However, in many instances no organic damage can be found.

Mood disorders are primarily defined by the presence of extreme, intense, and long-lasting emotions. Afflicted persons may be *manic,* meaning agitated, elated, and hyperactive, or they may be *depressed*. Some people with mood disorders alternate between mania and depression and they may have psychotic symptoms as well.

Anxiety disorders are marked by fear or anxiety and by distorted behavior. Some anxiety disorders involve feelings of panic. Others take the form of phobias (irrational fears) or just overwhelming anxiety and nervousness. Two additional anxiety disorders are post-traumatic stress disorder and acute stress disorder. Obsessive-compulsive behavior patterns are also associated with high anxiety. (These problems are described later in this chapter.)

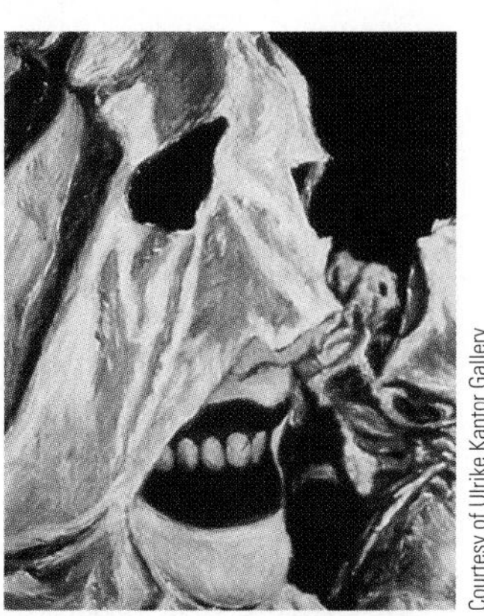

Courtesy of Ulrike Kantor Gallery

The self-portraits shown here were painted by Andy Wilf during a four year period. At that time, Wilf is said to have increasingly abused drugs and alcohol. This dramatic series of images is a record of his self-destructive descent into a private hell. The third painting shows a shrouded skull—and foretells the artist's fate. Wilf died of a drug overdose. Drug abuse is but one of the many psychopathologies, or "problems in living," psychologists seek to alleviate.

Somatoform (so-MAT-oh-form) **disorders** occur when a person has physical symptoms that mimic disease or injury (paralysis, blindness, illness, or chronic pain, for example), for which there is no identifiable physical cause. In such cases, psychological factors appear to explain the symptoms.

A person with a **dissociative disorder** may have temporary amnesia or multiple personalities. Also included in this category are frightening episodes of depersonalization, in which people feel like they are outside of their bodies, are behaving like robots, or are lost in a dream world.

Personality disorders are deeply ingrained, unhealthy personality patterns. Such patterns usually appear in adolescence and continue through much of adult life. They include paranoid (overly suspicious), narcissistic (self-loving), dependent, borderline, and antisocial personality types, as well as others.

Sexual and gender identity disorders include any of a wide range of difficulties with sexual identity, deviant sexual behavior, or sexual adjustment. In gender identity disorders, sexual identity does not match a person's physical sex and the person may seek a sex-change operation. Deviations in sexual behavior known as *paraphilias* include exhibitionism, fetishism, voyeurism, and so on. Also found in this category are a variety of *sexual dysfunctions* (problems in sexual desire, arousal, or response). (Sexual dysfunctions are discussed in Chapter 13.)

Substance-related disorders involve abuse of, or dependence on, psychoactive drugs. Typical culprits include alcohol, barbiturates, opiates, cocaine, amphetamines, hallucinogens, marijuana, and nicotine. A person with a substance disorder cannot stop using the drug and may also suffer from withdrawal symptoms, delirium, dementia, amnesia, psychosis, emotional outbursts, sexual problems, and sleep disturbances.

BRIDGES

Problems with drug abuse and dependence are discussed in the article "Drug Abuse—Many Questions, Few Answers" in the booklet that came with this text and in Chapter 7.

See pages 242–244.

Shouldn't neurosis be listed here? Neurosis was once a recognized mental disorder. However, it is no longer included in the DSM because the term *neurosis* is too imprecise. Behavior that psychologists used to refer to as "neurotic" is now part of anxiety, somatoform, or dissociative disorders. Even though **neurosis** is an outdated term, you may hear it used to loosely refer to problems involving excessive anxiety.

In addition to the formal mental disorders we have reviewed, many cultures have names for "unofficial" psychological "disorders." See "Running Amok with Cultural Maladies" for some samples.

Mood disorder A major disturbance in mood or emotion, such as depression or mania.

Anxiety disorder Disruptive feelings of fear, apprehension, or anxiety, or distortions in behavior that are anxiety related.

Somatoform disorder Physical symptoms that mimic disease or injury for which there is no identifiable physical cause.

Dissociative disorder Temporary amnesia, multiple personality, or depersonalization.

Personality disorder A maladaptive personality pattern.

Sexual and gender identity disorders Any of a wide range of difficulties with sexual identity, deviant sexual behavior, or sexual adjustment.

Substance-related disorder Abuse of or dependence on a mood- or behavior-altering drug.

Neurosis An outdated term once used to refer, as a group, to anxiety disorders, somatoform disorders, dissociative disorders, and some forms of depression.

Running Amok with Cultural Maladies

Every culture recognizes the existence of psychopathology, and most have at least a few folk names for afflictions you won't find in *DSM-IV-TR*. Called *culture-bound syndromes,* here are some examples from around the world (López & Guarnaccia, 2000; "Outline for Cultural," 2000; Sumathipala, Siribaddana, & Bhugra, 2004):

- **Amok** Men in Malaysia, Laos, the Philippines, and Polynesia who believe they have been insulted are sometimes known to go amok. After a period of brooding they erupt into an outburst of violent, aggressive, or homicidal behavior randomly directed at people and objects.
- **Ataque de nervios** Among Latinos from the Caribbean, the symptoms of an *ataque de nervios* (attack of nerves) include shouting, crying, trembling, aggression, threats of suicide, and seizures or fainting. *Ataques de nervios* frequently occur after a stressful event, such as the death of a close relative, divorce, or an accident involving a family member.
- **Ghost sickness** Among many American Indian tribes, people who become preoccupied with death and the deceased are said to suffer from ghost sickness. The symptoms of ghost sickness include bad dreams, weakness, loss of appetite, fainting, dizziness, fear, anxiety, hallucinations, loss of consciousness, confusion, feelings of futility, and a sense of suffocation.
- **Koro** In south and east Asia, a man may experience sudden and intense anxiety that his penis (or, in females, the vulva and nipples) will recede into the body. In addition to the terror this incites, victims also believe that advanced cases of *koro* can cause death. A similar fear of shrinking genitals has also been reported from West Africa (Dzokoto, & Adams, 2005).
- **Locura** Latinos in the United States and Latin America use the term *locura* to refer to people who suffer from chronic psychotic symptoms such as incoherence, agitation, auditory and visual hallucinations, inability to follow social rules, unpredictability, and violence.
- **Zar** In North African and Middle Eastern societies, *zar* is said to occur when spirits possess an individual. *Zar* is marked by shouting, laughing, hitting the head against a wall, singing, or weeping. Victims may become apathetic or withdrawn and they may refuse to eat or carry out daily tasks.
- **Dhat** In Indian society, *dhat* is the fear of the loss of semen during nocturnal emissions. A man suffering from *dhat* will feel anxious and perhaps also guilty. He may also experience fatigue, loss of appetite, weakness, anxiety, and sexual dysfunction.

It's clear that people have a need to label and categorize disturbed behavior. As you can see, however, folk terminology tends to be vague. The terms listed here provide little guidance about the true nature of a person's problems or the best ways to treat them. That's why the DSM is based on empirical data and clinical observations. Otherwise, psychologists and psychiatrists would be no better than folk healers when making diagnoses (Ancis, Chen, & Schultz, 2004).

By the way, culture-bound disorders occur in all societies. For example, American psychologists Pamela Keel and Kelly Klump believe that bulimia is primarily a syndrome of Western cultures, including the United States (Keel & Klump, 2003).

General Risk Factors

What causes mental and psychological disorders like those listed in ■ Table 16.2? We will soon explore the causes of some specific problems. For now, it is worth noting that a variety of risk factors contribute to psychopathology.

- **Social conditions:** poverty, stressful living conditions, homelessness, social disorganization, overcrowding
- **Family factors:** parents who are immature, mentally disturbed, criminal, or abusive; severe marital strife; extremely poor child discipline; disordered family communication patterns
- **Psychological factors:** stress, low intelligence, learning disorders, lack of control or mastery
- **Biological factors:** genetic defects or inherited vulnerabilities, poor prenatal care, very low birth weight, chronic physical illness or disability, exposure to toxic chemicals or drugs, head injuries

Ethnic Group Membership

Culture also influences our susceptibility to various psychological disorders. For example, a recent study found that some disorders are less common in three ethnic groups than they are among European-Americans (Zhang & Snowden, 1999).

- Compared with European-Americans, African Americans are less likely to suffer from depression, obsessive-compulsive disorder, substance abuse, antisocial personality disorder, and anorexia nervosa.
- Compared with European-Americans, Asian Americans are less like to suffer from schizophrenia, mania or bipolar disorders, panic, somatization, substance abuse, and antisocial personality.
- Hispanic Americans have lower rates of schizophrenia, obsessive-compulsive disorder, panic, and substance abuse than European-Americans do.

TABLE 16.3

Major* DSM-IV-TR *Categories

Disorders usually first diagnosed in infancy, childhood, or adolescence

Mental retardation
Example: Mild mental retardation
Learning disorders
Example: Reading disorder
Motor skills disorder
Example: Developmental coordination disorder
Communication disorders
Example: Stuttering
Pervasive developmental disorders
Example: Autistic disorder
Attention-deficit and disruptive behavior disorders
Example: Attention-deficit/hyperactivity disorder
Feeding and eating disorders of infancy or early childhood
Example: Pica (eating inedible substances)
Tic disorders
Example: Tourette's disorder
Elimination disorders
Example: Enuresis (bedwetting)
Other disorders of infancy, childhood, or adolescence
Example: Separation anxiety disorder

Delirium, dementia, amnestic, and other cognitive disorders

Delirium
Example: Delirium due to a general medical condition
Dementia
Example: Dementia of the Alzheimer's type
Amnestic disorders (memory loss)
Example: Amnestic disorder due to a general medical condition
Cognitive disorder not otherwise specified

Mental disorders due to a general medical condition not elsewhere classified

Catatonic disorder due to a general medical condition
Personality change due to a general medical condition
Mental disorder not otherwise specified due to a general medical condition

Substance-related disorders

Example: Cocaine use disorders

Schizophrenia and other psychotic disorders

Schizophrenia
Example: Schizophrenia, paranoid type
Schizophreniform disorder
Schizoaffective disorder
Delusional disorder
Example: Delusional disorder, grandiose type
Brief psychotic disorder
Shared psychotic disorder (folie a deux)
Psychotic disorder due to a general medical condition
Substance-induced psychotic disorder
Psychotic disorder not otherwise specified

Mood disorders

Depressive disorders
Example: Major depressive disorder
Bipolar disorders
Example: Bipolar I disorder
Mood disorder due to a general medical condition
Substance-induced mood disorder
Mood disorder not otherwise specified

Anxiety disorders

Example: Panic disorder

Somatoform disorders

Example: Conversion disorder

Factitious disorders (faked disability or illness)

Example: Factitious disorder

Dissociative disorders

Example: Dissociative identity disorder

Sexual and gender identity disorders

Sexual dysfunctions
Example: Sexual arousal disorders
Paraphilias
Example: Voyeurism
Sexual disorder not otherwise specified
Gender identity disorders
Example: Gender identity disorder

Eating disorders

Example: Anorexia nervosa

Sleep disorders

Primary sleep disorders
Dyssomnias
Example: Primary insomnia
Parasomnias
Example: Sleep terror disorder
Sleep disorders related to another mental disorder
Example: Insomnia related to posttraumatic stress disorder
Other sleep disorders
Example: Substance-induced sleep disorder

Impulse control disorders not elsewhere classified

Example: Kleptomania

Adjustment disorders

Example: Adjustment disorder

Personality disorders

Example: Antisocial personality disorder

It is probably fair to say that the social world and the psychological world interact on an equal footing to produce human behavior. For this reason, cultural factors can influence the expression of psychological disorders. Different values, support networks, stress levels, behavior patterns, family ties, and cultural beliefs can have a big impact on overall mental health (López & Guarnaccia, 2000).

Insanity

Which of the mental disorders causes insanity? None. **Insanity** is a legal term. It refers to an inability to manage one's affairs or foresee the consequences of one's actions. People who are declared insane are not legally responsible for their actions. If necessary, they can be involuntarily committed to a mental hospital.

Legally, insanity is established by testimony from expert witnesses (psychologists and psychiatrists). An *expert witness* is a person recognized by a court of law as being qualified to give opinions on a specific topic. People who are involuntarily committed are usually judged to be a danger to themselves or to others, or they are severely mentally disabled. Involuntary commitments happen most often when people are brought to emergency rooms. Then, if two doctors agree that the person will either commit suicide or hurt someone else, she or he is put into the hospital (Gorman, 1996).

KNOWLEDGE BUILDER

Normality and Psychopathology

REFLECT

Think of an instance of abnormal behavior you have witnessed. By what formal standards would the behavior be regarded as abnormal? In what way was the behavior maladaptive?

What disorders would the following sentences help you remember? An anxious psychotic in a bad mood asked for an organic substance. "First you have to fill out a somato form and tell us what sex or gender you are," he was told. "Don't diss my personality," he replied.

LEARNING CHECK

1. The core feature of abnormal behavior is that it is
   a. statistically unusual c. socially nonconforming
   b. maladaptive d. a source of subjective discomfort
2. One of the most powerful contexts in which judgments of normality and abnormality are made is
   a. the family c. religious systems
   b. occupational settings d. culture
3. Amnesia, multiple identities, and depersonalization are possible problems in
   a. mood disorders c. psychosis
   b. somatoform disorders d. dissociative disorders
4. Which among the following is *not* a major psychological problem listed in *DSM-IV-TR*?
   a. mood disorders c. insanity
   b. personality disorders d. anxiety disorders
5. People are said to have "retreated from reality" when they suffer from
   a. psychotic disorders c. somatoform disorders
   b. mood disorders d. personality disorders
6. Koro and locura are
   a. somatoform disorders c. folk terminology
   b. forms of psychosis d. organic mental disorders
7. Someone who engages in one of the paraphilias has what type of disorder?
   a. dissociative c. substance
   b. somatoform d. sexual
8. Which of the following is a *legal* concept?
   a. neurosis c. drapetomania
   b. psychosis d. insanity

CRITICAL THINKING

9. Brian, a fan of grunge rock, occasionally wears a skirt in public. Does Brian's cross-dressing indicate that he has a mental disorder?
10. Many states began to restrict use of the insanity defense after John Hinkley Jr., who tried to murder former U.S. President Ronald Reagan, was acquitted by reason of insanity. What does this trend reveal about insanity?

Answers: 1. b **2.** d **3.** d **4.** c **5.** a **6.** c **7.** d **8.** d **9.** Probably not. Undoubtedly, Brian's cross-dressing is socially disapproved by many people. Nevertheless, to be classified as a mental disorder it must cause him to feel disabling shame, guilt, depression, or anxiety. The cultural relativity of behavior like Brian's is revealed by the fact that it is fashionable and acceptable for women to wear men's clothing. **10.** It emphasizes that insanity is a legal concept, not a psychiatric diagnosis. Laws reflect community standards. When those standards change, lawmakers may seek to alter definitions of legal responsibility.

Personality Disorders—Blueprints for Maladjustment

"Get out of here and leave me alone so I can die in peace," Judy screamed at her nurses in the seclusion room of the psychiatric hospital. On one of her arms, long dark red marks mingled with the scars of previous suicide attempts. Judy once bragged that her record was 67 stitches. Today, the nurses had to strap her into restraints to keep her from gouging her own eyes. She was given a sedative and slept for 12 hours. She woke calmly and asked for her therapist—even though her latest outburst began when he canceled a morning appointment and changed it to afternoon.

Judy has a condition called *borderline personality disorder.* Although she is capable of working, Judy has repeatedly lost jobs because of her turbulent relationships with other people. At times she can be friendly and a real charmer. At other times she is extremely unpredictable, moody, and even suicidal. Being a friend to Judy can be a fearsome challenge. Canceling an appointment, forgetting a special date, a wrong turn of phrase—these and similar small incidents may trigger Judy's rage or a suicide attempt. Like other people with borderline personality disorder, Judy is extremely sensitive to ordinary criticism, which leaves her feeling rejected and abandoned. Typically, she reacts with anger, self-hatred, and impulsive behavior. These "emotional storms" damage her personal relationships and leave her confused about who she is (Siever & Koenigsberg, 2000).

Maladaptive Personality Patterns

As stated earlier, a person with a personality disorder has maladaptive personality traits. For example, people with a paranoid personality disorder are suspicious, hypersensitive, and wary of others. Narcissistic persons need constant admiration, and they are lost in fantasies of power, wealth, brilliance, beauty, or love. The dependent personality suffers from extremely low self-confidence. Dependent persons allow others to run their lives and they place everyone else's needs ahead of their own. People with a histrionic personality disorder constantly seek attention by dramatizing their emotions and actions.

Typically, patterns such as the ones just described begin during adolescence or even childhood. Thus, personality disorders are deeply rooted and usually span many years. The list of personality disorders is long (■ Table 16.4), so let us focus on a single frequently misunderstood problem, the antisocial personality.

TABLE 16.4

Personality Disorders and Typical Degree of Impairment

Moderate Impairment	
Dependent	You lack confidence and you are extremely submissive and dependent on others (clinging)
Histrionic	You are dramatic and flamboyant; you exaggerate your emotions to get attention from others
Narcissistic	You think you are wonderful, brilliant, important, and worthy of constant admiration
Antisocial	You are irresponsible, lack guilt or remorse, and engage in antisocial behavior, such as aggression, deceit, or recklessness
High Impairment	
Obsessive-compulsive	You demand order, perfection, control, and rigid routine at all times
Schizoid	You feel very little emotion and can't form close personal relationships with others
Avoidant	You are timid, uncomfortable in social situations, and fear evaluation
Severe Impairment	
Borderline	Your self-image, moods, and impulses are erratic, and you are extremely sensitive to any hint of criticism, rejection, or abandonment by others
Paranoid	You deeply distrust others and are suspiciousness of their motives, which you perceive as insulting or threatening
Schizotypal	You are a loner, you engage in extremely odd behavior, and your thought patterns are bizarre, but you are not actively psychotic

DSM-IV-TR, 2000; Millon, 1981.

Antisocial Personality

What are the characteristics of an antisocial personality? A person with an **antisocial personality** lacks a conscience. Such people are impulsive, selfish, dishonest, emotionally shallow, and manipulative. Antisocial persons, who are sometimes called *sociopaths* or *psychopaths,* are poorly socialized and seem to be incapable of feeling guilt, shame, fear, loyalty, or love (*DSM-IV-TR,* 2000).

Are sociopaths dangerous? Sociopaths tend to have a long history of conflict with society. Many are delinquents or criminals who may be a threat to the general public (Rice, 1997). However, sociopaths are rarely the crazed murderers you may have seen

Cary Wolinsky/Stock, Boston

More than 65 percent of all persons with antisocial personalities have been arrested, usually for crimes such as robbery, vandalism, or rape.

BRIDGES

Personality patterns usually become stable by age 30. This makes personality disorders difficult to treat.

See Chapter 14, page 460.

Insanity A legal term that refers to a mental inability to manage one's affairs or to be aware of the consequences of one's actions.

Antisocial personality A person who lacks a conscience, is emotionally shallow, impulsive, and selfish, and tends to manipulate others.

portrayed on TV and in movies. In fact, many sociopaths are "charming" at first. Their "friends" only gradually become aware of the sociopath's lying and self-serving manipulation. Many successful businesspersons, entertainers, politicians, and other seemingly normal people have psychopathic leanings. Basically, antisocial persons coldly use others and cheat their way through life (Rice, 1997). A recent study found that psychopaths are "blind" to signs of disgust in others. This may add to their capacity for cruelty and their ability to use others (Kosson et al., 2002).

Causes

What causes sociopathy? Typically, people with antisocial personalities were emotionally deprived, neglected, and physically abused as children (Pollock et al., 1990). Adult sociopaths also display subtle neurological problems (● Figure 16.3). For example, they have unusual brain-wave patterns that suggest underarousal of the brain. This may explain why sociopaths tend to be thrill seekers. Quite likely, they are searching for stimulation strong enough to overcome their chronic underarousal and feelings of "boredom" (Hare, 1996, 2002).

In a revealing study, psychopaths were shown extremely grisly and unpleasant photographs of mutilations. The photos were so upsetting that they visibly startle normal people. The psychopaths, however, showed no startle response to the photos (Levenston et al., 2000). (They didn't "bat an eyelash.") Those with antisocial personalities might therefore be described as *emotionally cold*. They simply do not feel normal pangs of conscience, guilt, or anxiety (Hare, 1996). Again, this coldness seems to account for an unusual ability to calmly lie, cheat, steal, or take advantage of others.

Can sociopathy be treated? Antisocial personality disorders are rarely treated with success (Hare, 2002). All too often, sociopaths manipulate therapy, just like any other situation. If it is to their advantage to act "cured," they will do so. However, they return to their former behavior patterns as soon as possible. On a more positive note, antisocial behavior does tend to decline somewhat after age 40, even without treatment.

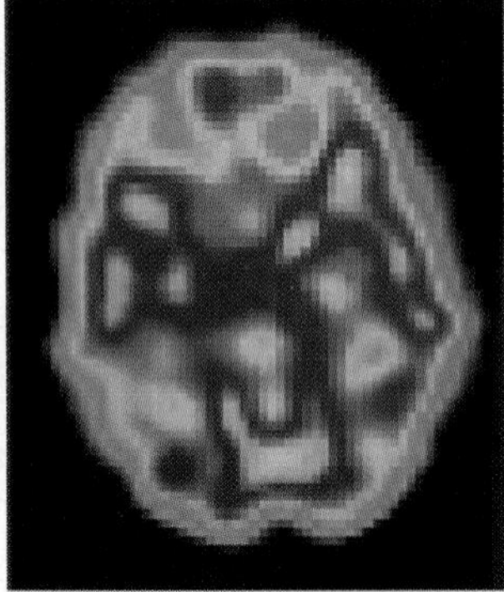

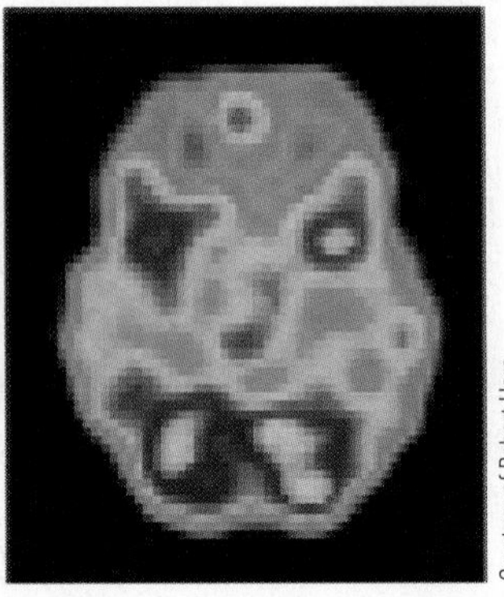

Courtesy of Robert Hare

● **Figure 16.3** Using PET scans, Canadian psychologist Robert Hare found that the normally functioning brain *(left)* lights up with activity when a person sees emotion-laden words such as "maggot" or "cancer." But the brain of a psychopath *(right)* remains inactive, especially in areas associated with feelings and self-control. When Dr. Hare showed the right image to several neurologists, one asked, "Is this person from Mars?"

An individual with an antisocial personality feels very little anxiety. At the other end of the scale, people who have lots of anxiety also suffer from debilitating problems, as described next.

Anxiety-Based Disorders—When Anxiety Rules

Anxiety refers to feelings of apprehension, dread, or uneasiness. We all feel anxiety, but anxiety that is out of proportion to a situation may reveal a problem. An example is a college student named Jian, who became unbearably anxious when he took exams. By the time Jian went to see a counselor, he had skipped several tests and was in danger of dropping out of school. In general, anxiety-related problems like Jian's involve the following:

- High levels of anxiety and/or restrictive, self-defeating behavior patterns
- A tendency to use elaborate defense mechanisms or avoidance responses to get through the day
- Pervasive feelings of stress, insecurity, inferiority, and dissatisfaction with life

People with anxiety-related problems feel threatened, but they don't do anything constructive about it. They struggle to control themselves, but they remain ineffective and unhappy (Rachman, 2004). On any given day, roughly 7 percent of the adult population is suffering from an anxiety disorder.

If anxiety is a normal emotion, when does it signify a problem? A problem exists when intense anxiety prevents people from doing what they want or need to do. Also, their anxieties are out of control—they simply cannot stop worrying.

Adjustment Disorders

Do such problems cause a "nervous breakdown"? People suffering from anxiety-based problems may be miserable, but they rarely experience a "breakdown." Actually, the term *nervous breakdown* has no formal meaning. Nevertheless, a problem known as an *adjustment disorder* does come close to being something of a "breakdown."

Adjustment disorders occur when ordinary stresses push people beyond their ability to cope with life. Examples of such stresses are losing a job, intense marital strife, and chronic physical illness. People suffering from an adjustment disorder may be extremely irritable, anxious, apathetic, or depressed. They also have trouble sleeping, lose their appetite, and suffer from various physical complaints. Often, their problems can be relieved by rest, sedation, supportive counseling, and a chance to "talk through" their fears and anxieties (*DSM-IV-TR,* 2000).

BRIDGES

Excessive use of psychological defense mechanisms is a feature of many anxiety disorders.

See Chapter 15, pages 510–512.

How is an adjustment disorder different from an anxiety disorder? The outward symptoms are similar. However, adjustment disorders disappear when a person's life circumstances improve. People suffering from anxiety disorders seem to generate their own misery, regardless of what's happening around them. They feel that they must be on guard against *future* threats that *could happen* at any time (Barlow, 2000).

Anxiety Disorders

In most anxiety disorders, distress seems greatly out of proportion to a person's circumstances. For example, consider the following description of Ethel B:

> She was never completely relaxed, and complained of vague feelings of restlessness, and a fear that something was "just around the corner." Although she felt that she had to go to work to help pay the family bills, she could not bring herself to start anything new for fear that something terrible would happen on the job. She had experienced a few extreme anxiety attacks during which she felt "like I couldn't breathe, like I was sealed up in a transparent envelope. I thought I was going to have a heart attack. I couldn't stop shaking." (From *Fundamentals of Behavior Pathology* by Suinn. Copyright © 1975. Reprinted by permission of John Wiley & Sons, Inc.*)

Distress like Ethel B's is a key ingredient in anxiety disorders. It also may underlie dissociative and somatoform disorders, where maladaptive behavior serves to reduce anxiety and discomfort. To deepen your understanding, let's first examine the anxiety disorders themselves (■ Table 16.5). Then we will see how anxiety contributes to other problems.

TABLE 16.5

Anxiety Disorders

TYPE OF DISORDER	TYPICAL SIGNS OF TROUBLE
Generalized anxiety disorder	You have been extremely anxious or worried for 6 months
Panic disorder (without agoraphobia)	You are anxious much of the time and have sudden panic attacks
Panic disorder (with agoraphobia)	You have panic attacks and are afraid that they might occur in public places, so you rarely leave home
Agoraphobia (without a history of panic disorder)	You fear that something extremely embarrassing will happen if you leave home (but you don't have panic attacks)
Specific phobia	You have an intense fear of specific objects, activities, or locations
Social phobia	You fear social situations where people can watch, criticize, embarrass, or humiliate you
Obsessive-compulsive disorder	Your thoughts make you extremely nervous and compel you to rigidly repeat certain actions or routines
Acute stress disorder	You are tormented for less than a month by the emotional aftereffects of horrible events you have experienced
Posttraumatic stress disorder	You are tormented for more than a month by the emotional aftereffects of horrible events you have experienced

DSM-IV-TR, 2000.

Generalized Anxiety Disorder

A person with a **generalized anxiety disorder** has been extremely anxious and worried for at least 6 months. Sufferers typically complain of sweating, a racing heart, clammy hands, dizziness, upset stomach, rapid breathing, irritability, and poor concentration. Overall, more women than men have these symptoms (Brawman-Mintzer & Lydiard, 1996).

Was Ethel B's problem a generalized anxiety disorder? No, her *anxiety attacks* reveal that she suffered from panic disorder.

Panic Disorder (without Agoraphobia)

In a **panic disorder (without agoraphobia)** people are highly anxious and also feel sudden, intense, unexpected panic. During a panic attack, victims experience chest pain, a racing heart, dizziness, choking, feelings of unreality, trembling, or fears of losing control. Many believe that they are having a heart attack, are going insane, or are about to die. Needless to say, this pattern leaves victims unhappy and uncomfortable much of the time. Again, the majority of people who suffer from panic disorder are women (Sansone, Sansone, & Righter, 1998).

To get an idea of how a panic attack feels, imagine that you are trapped in your stateroom on a sinking ocean liner (the *Titanic*?). The room fills with water. When only a small air space remains near the ceiling and you are gasping for air, you'll know what a panic attack feels like.

Panic Disorder (with Agoraphobia)

In a **panic disorder (with agoraphobia)** people suffer from chronic anxiety and sudden panic. In addition, they have **agoraphobia** (ah-go-rah-FOBE-ee-ah), which is an intense, irrational *fear that a panic attack will occur* in a public place or unfamiliar situation. That is, agoraphobics intensely fear leaving their home

*Additional Suinn quotes in this chapter are from the same source.

Adjustment disorder An emotional disturbance caused by ongoing stressors within the range of common experience.

Generalized anxiety disorder The person is in a chronic state of tension and worries about work, relationships, ability, or impending disaster.

Panic disorder (without agoraphobia) The person is in a chronic state of anxiety and also has brief moments of sudden, intense, unexpected panic.

Panic disorder (with agoraphobia) A chronic state of anxiety and brief moments of sudden panic. The person fears that these panic attacks will occur in public places or unfamiliar situations.

and familiar surroundings. Typically, they find ways of avoiding places that frighten them—such as crowds, open roads, supermarkets, automobiles, and so on. As a result, some agoraphobics are prisoners in their own homes (*DSM-IV-TR,* 2000).

Agoraphobia

The problem known as **agoraphobia** can also occur without panic. In this case, people *fear that something extremely embarrassing will happen* if they leave home or enter an unfamiliar situation. For example, an agoraphobic person may refuse to go outside because he or she fears having a sudden attack of dizziness, or diarrhea, or shortness of breath. Going outside the home alone, being in a crowd, standing in line, crossing a bridge, or riding in a car can be impossible for an agoraphobic person (*DSM-IV-TR,* 2000). About 7 percent of all adults suffer from agoraphobia (with or without panic) during their lifetime (Magee, Eaton, & Wittchen, 1996).

Brent Stirton/The Image Bank/Getty Images

For a person with a strong fear of snakes (ophidiophobia), merely looking at this picture may be unsettling.

Specific Phobia

As we noted earlier, phobias are intense, irrational fears that a person cannot shake off, even when there is no real danger. In a **specific phobia,** the person's fear, anxiety, and avoidance are focused on particular objects, activities, or situations. People affected by phobias recognize that their fears are unreasonable, but they cannot control them. For example, a person with a spider phobia would find it impossible to ignore a *picture* of a spider, even though a photograph can't bite anyone (Miltner et al., 2004). Specific phobias can be linked to nearly any object or situation. Many have been given names, such as these:

Acrophobia—fear of heights
Astraphobia—fear of storms, thunder, lightning
Arachnophobia—fear of spiders
Aviophobia—fear of airplanes
Claustrophobia—fear of closed spaces
Hematophobia—fear of blood
Microphobia—fear of germs
Nyctophobia—fear of darkness
Pathophobia—fear of disease
Pyrophobia—fear of fire
Xenophobia—fear of strangers
Zoophobia—fear of animals

By combining the appropriate root word with the word *phobia,* any number of unlikely fears can be named. Some are *acarophobia,* a fear of itching; *zemmiphobia,* fear of the great mole rat; *phobosophobia,* fear of fear; *arachibutyrophobia,* fear of peanut butter sticking to the roof of the mouth, and *hippopotomonstrosesquipedaliophobia,* fear of long words!

Almost everyone has a few mild phobias, such as fearing heights, closed spaces, or bugs and crawly things. A phobic disorder differs from such garden-variety fears in that it produces overwhelming fear. True phobias may lead to vomiting, wild climbing and running, or fainting. For a phobic disorder to exist, the person's fear must disrupt his or her daily life. Phobic persons are so threatened that they will go to almost any length to avoid the feared object or situation, such as driving 50 miles out of the way to avoid crossing a bridge. About 11 percent of all adults have phobic disorders during their lifetime (Magee, Eaton, & Wittchen, 1996).

Social Phobia

In a **social phobia,** people fear situations in which they can be observed, evaluated, embarrassed, or humiliated by others. This leads them to avoid certain social situations, such as eating, writing, using the rest room, or speaking in public. When such situations cannot be avoided, people endure them with intense anxiety or distress. It is common for them to have uncomfortable physical symptoms, such as a pounding heart, shaking hands, sweating, diarrhea, mental confusion, and blushing. Social phobias greatly impair a person's ability to work, attend school, and form personal relationships (*DSM-IV-TR,* 2000). About 13 percent of all adults are affected by social phobias at one time or another (Fones, Manfro, & Pollack, 1998).

Obsessive-Compulsive Disorder

People who suffer from **obsessive-compulsive disorder** are preoccupied with certain distressing thoughts and they feel compelled to perform certain behaviors. You have probably experienced a mild obsessional thought, such as a song or stupid commercial jingle that repeats over and over in your mind. This may be irritating, but it's usually not terribly disturbing. True obsessions are images or thoughts that force their way into awareness against a person's will. They are so disturbing that they cause intense anxiety. The most common obsessions are about violence or harm (such as poisoning one's spouse or being hit by a car), about being "dirty" or "unclean," about whether one has performed some action (such as turning off the stove), and about committing immoral acts (Barlow, 2001).

Obsessions usually give rise to compulsions. These are irrational acts that a person feels driven to repeat. Often, compulsive acts help control or block out anxiety caused by an obsession. For example, a minister who finds profanities popping into her mind might start compulsively counting her heartbeat. Doing this would prevent her from thinking "dirty" words.

Many compulsive people are *checkers* or *cleaners*. For instance, a young mother who repeatedly pictures a knife plunging into her baby might check once an hour to make sure all the knives in her house are locked away. Doing so may reduce her anxieties, but it will probably also take over her life. Likewise, a person who feels "contaminated" from touching ordinary objects because "germs are everywhere" may be driven to wash his hands hundreds of times a day. Typically, such compulsive behavior will continue even after the person's hands become raw and painful (Tallis, 1996).

Of course, not all obsessive-compulsive disorders are so dramatic. Many simply involve extreme orderliness and rigid routine. Compulsive attention to detail and rigidly following rules helps keep activities totally under control and makes the highly anxious person feel more secure. (Notice that if such patterns are long-standing, but less intense, they are classified as a personality disorder.)

Stress Disorders

What happens when people endure sudden disasters, such as floods, tornadoes, earthquakes, or horrible accidents? Often, psychological damage follows such events. **Stress disorders** occur when people experience stresses outside the range of normal human experience. They affect many political hostages, combat veterans, prisoners of war, and victims of terrorism, torture, violent crime, child molestation, rape, or domestic violence, or people who have witnessed a death or serious injury (Creamer, Burgess, & McFarlane, 2001; Jones, Hughes, & Unterstaller, 2001).

Symptoms of stress disorders include repeatedly reliving the traumatic event, avoiding reminders of the event, and blunted emotions. Also common are insomnia, nightmares, wariness, poor concentration, irritability, and explosive anger or aggression. If such reactions last *less* than a month after a traumatic event, the problem is called an **acute stress disorder.** If they last *more* than a month, the person is suffering from **posttraumatic stress disorder** (PTSD) (Shalev, 2001).

If a situation causes distress, anxiety, or fear, we tend to avoid it in the future. This is a normal survival instinct. However, vic-

Paula Bronstein/Getty Images

In December 2004, a tsunami killed more than 250,000 people in southern Asia. In the aftermath of such disasters, many survivors suffer from acute stress reactions. For some, the flare-up of anxiety and distress lasts for months or years after the stressful event, an example of a posttraumatic stress reaction.

Bettmann/Corbis

Dennis Coon

The severe obsessions and compulsions of billionaire Howard Hughes led him to live as a recluse for over 20 years. Hughes had an intense fear of contamination. To avoid infection, he constructed sterile, isolated environments in which his contact with people and objects was strictly limited by complicated rituals. Before handling a spoon, for instance, Hughes had his attendants wrap the handle in tissue paper and seal it with tape. A second piece of tissue was then wrapped around the first before he would touch it (Hodgson & Miller, 1982). A spoon prepared as Hughes required is shown at right.

Agoraphobia (without panic) The person fears that something extremely embarrassing will happen to them if they leave the house or enter unfamiliar situations.

Specific phobia An intense, irrational fear of specific objects, activities, or situations.

Social phobia An intense, irrational fear of being observed, evaluated, embarrassed, or humiliated by others in social situations.

Obsessive-compulsive disorder An extreme preoccupation with certain thoughts and compulsive performance of certain behaviors.

Stress disorder A significant emotional disturbance caused by stresses outside the range of normal human experience.

Acute stress disorder A psychological disturbance lasting up to 1 month following stresses that would produce anxiety in anyone who experienced them.

Posttraumatic stress disorder A psychological disturbance lasting more than 1 month following stresses that would produce anxiety in anyone who experienced them.

tims of PTSD fail to recover from these reactions (Breslau, 2001; Yehuda, 2002). Military combat is especially likely to cause PTSD. The constant threat of death and the gruesome sights and sounds of war take a terrible toll. For instance, psychologists are already seeing high rates of PTSD among soldiers involved in combat in Iraq (Hoge et al., 2004). Sadly, 8 percent of military veterans still suffer from PTSD decades after they were in combat (Dirkzwager, Bramsen, & Van Der Ploeg, 2001). Even among the general population, nearly 1 adult out of 12 has suffered from posttraumatic stress at some time (Kessler, Sonnega, & Nelson, 1995).

Dissociative Disorders

In dissociative reactions we see striking episodes of *amnesia, fugue,* or *multiple identity.* **Dissociative amnesia** is an inability to recall one's name, address, or past. **Dissociative fugue** (fewg) involves sudden, unplanned travel away from home and confusion about personal identity. Dissociations are often triggered by highly traumatic events, as the following case illustrates (Lipschitz et al., 1996).

> An American soldier in the Vietnam War wandered into the countryside and ambushed Vietcong soldiers without any memory of his actions. His fugue and amnesia were triggered when he discovered the dead body of a Vietnamese child he had adopted. Later, in therapy, he was able to remember the incident: "After 15 years in the Army, he was all I had. It's all my fault! It's all my fault! If I had just taken you over to the hooch, you wouldn't be there, man! It's not fair. They ain't gotta kill kids." (Spiegel, 1986)

As you can see, forgetting personal identity and fleeing unpleasant situations can serve as defenses against intolerable anxiety.

A person suffering from a **dissociative identity disorder** has two or more separate identities or personality states. (Note that identity disorders are not the same as schizophrenia. Schizophrenia, which is a psychotic disorder, is discussed later in this chapter.) A dramatic example of multiple identity is described in the book *Sybil* (Schreiber, 1973). Sybil reportedly had 16 different personality states. Each identity had a distinct voice, vocabulary, and posture. One personality could play the piano (not Sybil), but the others could not.

When an identity other than Sybil was in control, Sybil experienced a "time lapse," or memory blackout. Sybil's amnesia and alternate identities first appeared during childhood. As a girl she was beaten, locked in closets, perversely tortured, sexually abused, and almost killed. Sybil's first dissociations allowed her to escape by creating another person who would suffer torture in her place. Identity disorders often begin with unbearable childhood experiences, like Sybil endured. A history of childhood trauma, especially sexual abuse, is found in more than 95 percent of persons whose personalities split into multiple identities (Scroppo et al. 1998; Simeon et al., 2002).

Flamboyant cases like Sybil's have led some experts to question the existence of multiple personalities (Casey, 2001). However, a majority of psychologists continue to believe that multiple identity is a real, if rare, problem (Cormier & Thelen, 1998).

Therapy for dissociative identity disorders may make use of hypnosis, which allows contact with the various personality states. The goal of therapy is *integration* and *fusion* of the identities into a single, balanced personality. Fortunately, multiple identity disorders are far rarer in real life than they are in TV dramas!

Somatoform Disorders

Have you ever known someone who appeared to be healthy but seemed to constantly worry about disease? These people are preoccupied with bodily functions, such as their heartbeat or breathing or digestion. Minor physical problems—even a small sore or an occasional cough—may convince them that they have cancer or some other dreaded disease. Typically, they can't give up their fears of illness, even if doctors can find no medical basis for their complaints (Korol, Craig, & Firestone, 2003).

Are you describing hypochondria? Yes. In **hypochondriasis** (HI-po-kon-DRY-uh-sis), people interpret normal bodily sensations as proof that they have a terrible disease. In a related problem called **somatization disorder** (som-ah-tuh-ZAY-shun), people express their anxieties through various bodily complaints. That is, they suffer from problems such as vomiting or nausea, shortness of breath, difficulty swallowing, or painful menstrual periods. Typically, the person feels ill much of the time and visits doctors repeatedly. Most sufferers take medicines or other treatments, but

Bruce Ayres/Getty Images

Uncontrollable sneezing, which may continue for days or weeks, is often a conversion disorder. In such cases, sneezing is atypical in rate and rhythm. In addition, the person's eyes do not close during a sneeze and sneezing does not occur during sleep. (A normal sneeze is shown here.) All of these signs suggest that the cause of the sneezing is psychological, not physical (Fochtmann, 1995).

BRIDGES

Don't confuse somatoform disorders with psychosomatic illnesses, which occur when stress causes real physical damage to the body.

See Chapter 15, pages 522–524.

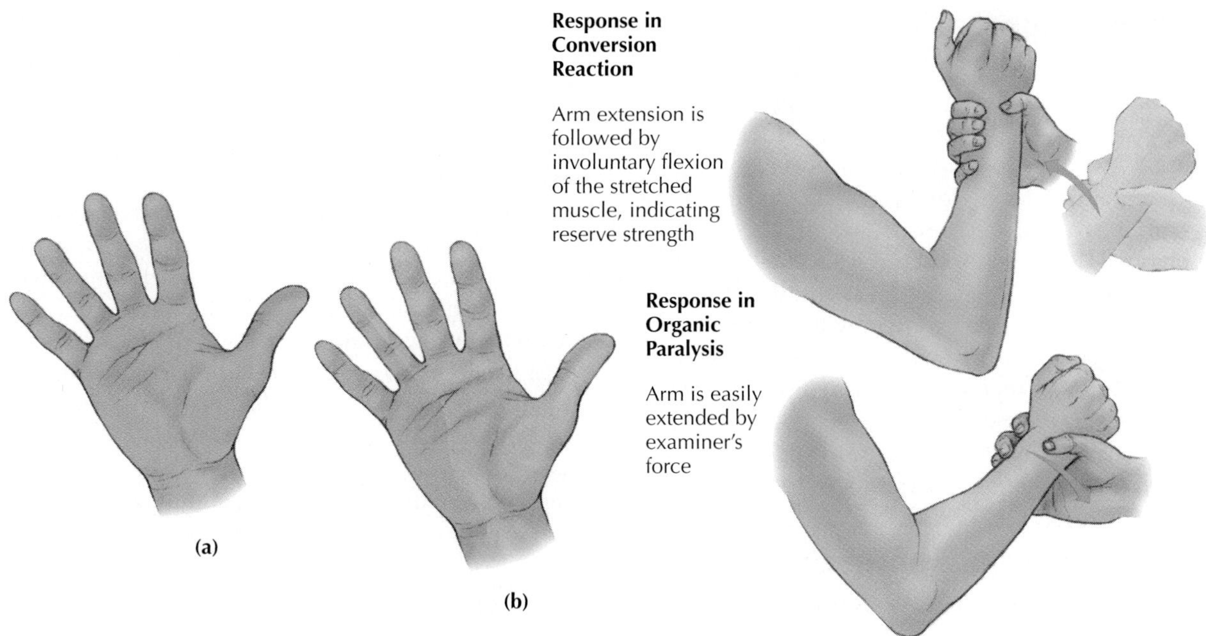

● **Figure 16.4** *(left)* "Glove" anesthesia is a conversion reaction involving loss of feeling in areas of the hand that would be covered by a glove *(a)*. If the anesthesia were physically caused, it would follow the pattern shown in *(b)*. *(right)* To test for organic paralysis of the arm, an examiner can suddenly extend the arm, stretching the muscles. A conversion reaction is indicated if the arm pulls back involuntarily. (Adapted from Weintraub, 1983.)

no physical cause can be found for their distress. Similarly, a person with **pain disorder** is disabled by pain that has no identifiable physical basis.

A rarer somatoform disorder ("body-form" disorder) is called a *conversion reaction.* In a **conversion disorder,** severe emotional conflicts are "converted" into symptoms that actually disturb physical functioning or closely resemble a physical disability. For instance, a soldier might become deaf or lame or develop "glove anesthesia" just before a battle.

What is "glove anesthesia"? "Glove anesthesia" is a loss of sensitivity in the areas of the skin that would normally be covered by a glove. Glove anesthesia shows that conversion symptoms often contradict known medical facts. The system of nerves in the hands does not form a glove-like pattern and could not cause such symptoms (● Figure 16.4).

If symptoms disappear when a victim is asleep, hypnotized, or anesthetized, a conversion reaction must be suspected (Russo et al., 1998). Another sign to watch for is that victims of conversion reactions are strangely unconcerned about suddenly being disabled.

Anxiety and Disorder—Four Pathways to Trouble

What causes the problems described in the preceding discussion? Because we are both biological and social creatures, it is not surprising that susceptibility to anxiety-based disorders appears to be partly inherited (Rachman, 2004). Studies show that being high strung, nervous, or emotional runs in families. For example, 60 percent of children born to parents suffering from panic disorder have a fearful, inhibited temperament. Such children are irritable and wary as infants, shy and fearful as toddlers, and quiet and cautious introverts in elementary school. By the time they reach adulthood, they are at high risk for anxiety problems, such as panic attacks, in adulthood (Barlow, 2000).

At least four major psychological perspectives on the causes of anxiety-based disorders exist. These are (1) the *psychodynamic* approach, (2) the *humanistic-existential* approach, (3) the *behavioral* approach, and (4) the *cognitive* approach.

Dissociative amnesia Loss of memory (partial or complete) for important information related to personal identity.

Dissociative fugue Sudden travel away from home, plus confusion abut one's personal identity.

Dissociative identity disorder The presence of two or more distinct personalities (multiple personality).

Hypochondriasis A preoccupation with fears of having a serious disease. Ordinary physical signs are interpreted as proof that the person has a disease, but no physical disorder can be found.

Somatization disorder Afflicted persons have numerous physical complaints. Typically, they have consulted many doctors, but no organic cause for their distress can be identified.

Pain disorder Pain that has no identifiable physical cause and appears to be of psychological origin.

Conversion disorder A bodily symptom that mimics a physical disability but is actually caused by anxiety or emotional distress.

Psychodynamic Approach

The term *psychodynamic* refers to internal motives, conflicts, unconscious forces, and other dynamics of mental life. Freud was the first to propose a psychodynamic explanation for what he called "neurosis." According to Freud, disturbances like those we have described represent a raging conflict among subparts of the personality—the id, ego, and superego.

Freud emphasized that intense anxiety can be caused by forbidden id impulses for sex or aggression that threaten to break through into behavior. The person constantly fears doing something "crazy" or forbidden. She or he may also be tortured by guilt, which the superego uses to suppress forbidden impulses. Caught in the middle, the ego is eventually overwhelmed. This forces the person to use rigid defense mechanisms and misguided, inflexible behavior to prevent a disastrous loss of control (see Chapter 14).

Humanistic-Existential Approaches

Humanistic theories emphasize subjective experience, human problems, and personal potentials. Humanistic psychologist Carl Rogers regarded emotional disorders as the end product of a faulty self-image or self-concept (Rogers, 1959). Rogers believed that anxious individuals have built up unrealistic mental images of themselves. This leaves them vulnerable to contradictory information. Let's say, for example, that an essential part of Cheyenne's self-image is the idea that she is highly intelligent. If Cheyenne does poorly in school, she may deny or distort her perceptions of herself and the situation. Should Cheyenne's anxiety become severe, she may resort to using defense mechanisms. A conversion reaction, anxiety attacks, or similar symptoms could also result from threats to her self-image. These symptoms, in turn, would become new threats that provoke further distortions. Soon, she would fall into a vicious cycle of maladjustment and anxiety that feeds on itself once started.

Existentialism focuses on the elemental problems of existence, such as death, meaning, choice, and responsibility. Psychologists who take a more existential view stress that unhealthy anxiety reflects a loss of *meaning* in one's life. According to them, we must show *courage* and *responsibility* in our choices if life is to have meaning. Too often, they say, we give in to "existential anxiety" and back away from life-enhancing choices. Existential anxiety is the unavoidable anguish that comes from knowing we are personally responsible for our lives. Hence, we have a crushing need to choose wisely and courageously as we face life's empty and impersonal void.

From the existential view, people who are unhappy and anxious are living in "bad faith." That is, they have collapsed in the face of the awesome responsibility to choose a meaningful existence. In short, they have lost their way in life. From this point of view, making choices that don't truly reflect what you value, feel, and believe can make you sick.

Behavioral Approach

Behaviorist approaches emphasize overt, observable behavior and the effects of learning and conditioning. Behaviorists assume that the "symptoms" we have discussed are learned, just as other behaviors are. You might recall from Chapter 7, for instance, that phobias can be acquired through classical conditioning. Similarly, anxiety attacks may reflect conditioned emotional responses that generalize to new situations. As another example, the hypochondriac's "sickness behavior" may be reinforced by the sympathy and attention he or she gets.

One point that all theorists agree on is that disordered behavior is ultimately self-defeating and paradoxical. A paradox is a contradiction. The contradiction in self-defeating behavior is that it makes the person more miserable in the long run, even though it temporarily lowers anxiety.

But if the person becomes more miserable in the long run, how does the pattern get started? The behavioral explanation is that self-defeating behavior begins with avoidance learning (described in Chapter 8). Avoidance learning occurs when making a response delays or prevents the onset of a painful or unpleasant stimulus. Here's a quick review to refresh your memory:

> An animal is placed in a special cage. After a few minutes a light comes on, followed a moment later by a painful shock. Quickly, the animal escapes into a second chamber. After a few minutes, a light comes on in this chamber, and the shock is repeated. Soon the animal learns to avoid pain by moving before the shock occurs. Once an animal learns to avoid the shock, it can be turned off altogether. A well-trained animal may avoid the nonexistent shock indefinitely.

The same analysis can be applied to human behavior. A behaviorist would say that the powerful reward of immediate relief from anxiety keeps self-defeating avoidance behaviors alive. This view, known as the **anxiety reduction hypothesis,** seems to explain why the behavior patterns we have discussed often look very "stupid" to outside observers.

Cognitive Approach

The cognitive view is that distorted thinking causes people to magnify ordinary threats and failures, which leads to distress (Provencher, Dugas, & Ladouceur, 2004). For example, Terrie, who is socially phobic, constantly has upsetting thoughts about being evaluated. One reason for this is that people with social phobias tend to be perfectionists. Like other social phobics, Terrie is excessively concerned about mistakes. She also perceives criticism where none exists (Juster et al., 1996). Terrie tends to focus too much attention on herself, which intensifies her anxiety in social situations (Woody, 1996). Even when socially phobic persons are successful, distorted thinking leads them to think they have failed (Barlow, 2001). In short, changing the thinking patterns of anxious individuals like Terrie can greatly lessen their fears (Poulton & Andrews, 1996).

Implications

There is probably a core of truth to all four psychological explanations. For this reason, understanding anxiety-based disorders may be aided by combining parts of each perspective. Each viewpoint also suggests a different approach to treatment. Because there are many possibilities, therapy is discussed later, in Chapter 17.

KNOWLEDGE BUILDER

Personality Disorders and Anxiety-Based Disorders

REFLECT

Many of the qualities that define personality disorders exist to a minor degree in normal personalities. Try to think of a person you know who has some of the characteristics described for each type of personality disorder.

Which of the anxiety disorders would you *least* want to suffer from? Why?

What minor obsessions or compulsions have you experienced?

What is the key difference between a stress disorder and an adjustment disorder? (Review both discussions if you don't immediately know the answer.)

Which of the four psychological explanations of anxiety-based disorders do you find most convincing?

LEARNING CHECK

1. Which of the following personality disorders is associated with an inflated sense of self-importance and a constant need for attention and admiration?
   a. narcissistic c. paranoid
   b. antisocial d. manipulative
2. Antisocial personality disorders are difficult to treat, but there is typically a decline in antisocial behavior a year or two after adolescence. T or F?
3. When prolonged unemployment, a bad marriage, or physical illness pushes a person beyond his or her ability to cope, it is most likely that which of the following problems will occur?
   a. a dissociative disorder c. an adjustment disorder
   b. agoraphobia d. a conversion disorder
4. Panic disorder can occur with or without agoraphobia, but agoraphobia cannot occur alone, without the presence of a panic disorder. T or F?
5. Alice has a phobic fear of blood. What is the formal term for her fear?
   a. nyctophobia c. pathophobia
   b. hematophobia d. pyrophobia
6. A person who intensely fears eating, writing, or speaking in public suffers from ______________________ ____________________.
7. "Checkers" and "cleaners" suffer from which disorder?
   a. acarophobia
   b. panic disorder with agoraphobia
   c. generalized anxiety disorder
   d. obsessive-compulsive disorder
8. The symptoms of acute stress disorders last less than 1 month; posttraumatic stress disorders last more than 1 month. T or F?
9. Which of the following is *not* a dissociative disorder?
   a. fugue c. conversion reaction
   b. amnesia d. multiple identity
10. According to the __________ view, anxiety disorders are the end result of a faulty self-image.
    a. psychodynamic c. behaviorist
    b. humanistic d. cognitive

CRITICAL THINKING

11. Many of the physical complaints associated with anxiety disorders are closely related to activity of what part of the nervous system?

Answers: 1. a 2. F 3. c 4. F 5. b 6. social phobia 7. d 8. T 9. c 10. b 11. The autonomic nervous system (ANS), especially the sympathetic branch of the ANS.

Psychotic Disorders—Life in the Shadow of Madness

Imagine that a member of your family has been hearing voices, is talking strangely, has covered her head with aluminum foil, and believes that houseflies are speaking to her in code. If you observed such symptoms, would you concerned? Of course you would, and rightly so. Psychotic disorders are among the most serious of all mental problems.

A person who is psychotic undergoes a number of striking changes in thinking, behavior, and emotion. Basic to all of these changes is the fact that **psychosis** reflects a loss of contact with shared views of reality (psycho*sis*, singular; psycho*ses*, plural). The following comments, made by two psychotic patients, illustrate what is meant by a "split" from reality (Torrey, 1988).

> Everything is in bits. You put the picture up bit by bit into your head. It's like a photograph that's torn in bits and put together again. If you move it's frightening.
>
> Last week I was with a girl and suddenly she seemed to get bigger and bigger, like a monster coming nearer and nearer.

The Nature of Psychosis

What are the major features of psychotic disorders? Delusions and hallucinations are core features, but there are others as well.

People who suffer from **delusions** hold false beliefs that they insist are true, regardless of how much the facts contradict them. An example is a 43-year-old schizophrenic man who was convinced he was pregnant (Mansouri & Adityanjee, 1995).

Are there different types of delusions? Yes, some common types of delusions are (1) *depressive* delusions, in which people feel that they have committed horrible crimes or sinful deeds; (2) *somatic* delusions, such as believing your body is "rotting away" or that it is emitting foul odors; (3) delusions of *grandeur,* in which people think they are extremely important; (4) delusions of *influence,* in which people feel they are being controlled or influenced by others or by unseen forces; (5) delusions of *persecution,* in which people believe that others are "out to get them"; and (6) delusions of *reference,* in which people assign great personal meaning to unrelated events. For instance, delusional people sometimes think that television programs are giving them a special personal message (*DSM-IV-TR,* 2000).

Anxiety reduction hypothesis Explains the self-defeating nature of avoidance responses as a result of the reinforcing effects of relief from anxiety.

Psychosis A withdrawal from reality marked by hallucinations and delusions, disturbed thought and emotions, and personality disorganization.

Delusion A false belief held against all contrary evidence.

Hallucinations are imaginary sensations, such as seeing, hearing, or smelling things that don't exist in the real world. The most common psychotic hallucination is hearing voices, like the voice that told Carol North to "Collide with the world." Sometimes these voices command patients to hurt themselves. Unfortunately, many people obey (Kasper, Rogers, & Adams, 1996). More rarely, psychotic people may feel "insects crawling under their skin," taste "poisons" in their food, or smell "gas" their "enemies" are using to "get" them. Sensory changes, such as anesthesia (numbness, or a loss of sensation) or extreme sensitivity to heat, cold, pain, or touch, can also occur.

During a psychotic episode, emotions are often severely disturbed. For instance, the psychotic person may be wildly elated, depressed, hyperemotional, or apathetic. Sometimes psychotic patients display *flat affect,* a condition in which the face is frozen in a blank expression. However, behind their "frozen masks," psychotic people continue to feel emotions just as strongly as ever (Sison et al., 1996).

Some psychotic symptoms can be thought of as a primitive type of communication. That is, many patients can only use their actions to say, "I need help," or "I can't handle it any more." Disturbed verbal communication is a nearly universal symptom of psychosis. In fact, psychotic speech tends to be so garbled and chaotic that it sometimes sounds like a "word salad."

Major disturbances such as those just described—as well as added problems with thinking, memory, and attention—bring about personality disintegration and a break with reality. *Personality disintegration* occurs when a person's thoughts, actions, and emotions are no longer coordinated. When psychotic disturbances and a fragmented personality are evident for weeks or months, the person has suffered a psychosis (*DSM-IV-TR,* 2000) (see ■ Table 16.6).

Benelux Press/Getty Images

A scene in a state mental hospital.

Organic Psychosis

As we will see later, psychotic disorders appear to involve physical changes in the brain. In a sense, then, all psychoses are partly organic. However, the general term *organic psychosis* is usually reserved for problems involving clear-cut brain injuries or diseases. For example, poisoning by lead or mercury can damage the brain and cause hallucinations, delusions, and a loss of emotional control (● Figure 16.5). A particularly dangerous situation is found in old buildings that contain leaded paints. Lead tastes sweet. Thus, young children may be tempted to eat leaded paint flakes as if they were candy. Children who eat leaded paint can become psychotic or retarded (Mielke, 1999).

TABLE 16.6

Warning Signs of Psychotic Disorders and Major Mood Disorders

- You express bizarre thoughts or beliefs that defy reality
- You have withdrawn from family members and other relationships
- You hear unreal voices or sees things others don't
- You are extremely sad, persistently despondent, or suicidal
- You are excessively energetic and have little need for sleep
- You lose your appetite, sleep excessively, and have no energy
- You exhibit extreme mood swings
- You believe someone is trying to get you
- You have engaged in antisocial, destructive, or self-destructive behavior

Harvey et al., 1996; Sheehy & Cournos, 1992.

Bettmann/Corbis

● **Figure 16.5** The Mad Hatter, from Lewis Carroll's *Alice's Adventures in Wonderland.* History provides numerous examples of psychosis caused by toxic chemicals. Carroll's Mad Hatter character is modeled after an occupational disease of the eighteenth and nineteenth centuries. In that era, hat makers were heavily exposed to mercury used in the preparation of felt. Consequently, many suffered brain damage and became psychotic, or "mad" (Kety, 1979).

Leaded paints also release powdered lead into the air. Children may breathe the powder or eat it after handling contaminated toys. Other sources of lead are soldered water pipes, old lead-lined drinking fountains, lead-glazed pottery, and lead deposited years ago from automobile exhaust. On a much larger scale, "poisoning" of another type, in the form of drug abuse, can also produce psychotic symptoms (*DSM-IV-TR*, 2000).

The most common organic problem is **dementia** (duh-MEN-sha), a serious mental impairment in old age caused by deterioration of the brain. In dementia, we see major disturbances in memory, reasoning, judgment, impulse control, and personality. This combination usually leaves people confused, suspicious, apathetic, or withdrawn. Some common causes of dementia are circulatory problems, repeated strokes, or general shrinkage and atrophy of the brain. The majority of people who suffer from dementia slowly lose their mental abilities without becoming psychotic. However, some do develop delusions and lose contact with reality. The most common cause of dementia is *Alzheimer's disease*.

Alzheimer's disease (ALLS-hi-merz) is one of the most fearsome problems of aging. Alzheimer's victims slowly lose the ability to work, cook, drive, read, write, or do arithmetic. Eventually they are mute and bedridden. Alzheimer's disease appears to be caused by unusual webs and tangles in the brain that damage areas important for memory and learning (Ingram, 2003). Understandably, efforts to find a cure for Alzheimer's disease are expanding. For some of us, such efforts may be a race against time.

Joe Sohm/The Image Works

The soil and dust in cities and near busy streets is often heavily contaminated with lead. This lead came from automobile exhaust before leaded gasoline was banned. Young children frequently put objects and their hands in their mouths. This, then, is a major source of lead poisoning for many children. Paving play areas or covering them with clean soil can greatly reduce lead exposure (Mielke, 1999).

Alan Oddie/PhotoEdit, Inc.

Former U.S. President Ronald Reagan was diagnosed with Alzheimer's disease in 1995. Like many Alzheimer's victims, Reagan slipped into a slow mental decline. He died in 2004.

Delusional Disorders—An Enemy Behind Every Tree

People with delusional disorders usually do not suffer from hallucinations, emotional excesses, or personality disintegration. Even so, their break with reality is unmistakable. The main feature of **delusional disorders** is the presence of deeply held false beliefs, which may take the following forms (*DSM-IV-TR*, 2000):

- **Erotomanic type:** In this disorder, people have erotic delusions that they are loved by another person, especially by someone famous or of higher status.
- **Grandiose type:** In this case, people suffer from the delusion that they have some great, unrecognized talent, knowledge, or insight. They may also believe that they have a special relationship with an important person or with God or that they are a famous person. (If the famous person is alive, the deluded person regards her or him as an imposter.)
- **Jealous type:** An example of this type of delusion would be having an all-consuming, but unfounded, belief that your spouse or lover is unfaithful.
- **Persecutory type:** Delusions of persecution involve belief that you are being conspired against, cheated, spied on, followed, poisoned, maligned, or harassed.
- **Somatic type:** People suffering from somatic delusions typically believe that their bodies are diseased or rotting, or infested with insects or parasites, or that parts of their bodies are defective.

Although they are false, and sometimes far-fetched, all of these delusions are about experiences that could occur in real life (Manschreck, 1996). In other types of psychosis, delusions tend

Hallucination An imaginary sensation, such as seeing, hearing, or smelling things that don't exist in the real world.

Dementia Serious mental impairment in old age caused by physical deterioration of the brain.

Alzheimer's disease An age-related disease characterized by memory loss, mental confusion, and, in its later stages, a nearly total loss of mental abilities.

Delusional disorder A psychosis marked by severe delusions of grandeur, jealousy, persecution, or similar preoccupations.

to be more bizarre. For example, a person with schizophrenia might believe that space aliens have replaced all of his internal organs with electronic monitoring devices. In contrast, people with ordinary delusions merely believe that someone is trying to steal their money, that they are being deceived by a lover, that the FBI is watching them, and the like (*DSM-IV-TR,* 2000).

Paranoid Psychosis

The most common delusional disorder, often called **paranoid psychosis**, centers on delusions of persecution. Many self-styled reformers, crank letter writers, conspiracy theorists, "UFO abductees," and the like suffer paranoid delusions. Paranoid individuals often believe that they are being cheated, spied on, followed, poisoned, harassed, or plotted against. Usually they are intensely suspicious, believing they must be on guard at all times.

The evidence such people find to support their beliefs usually fails to persuade others. Every detail of the paranoid person's existence is woven into a private version of "what's really going on." Buzzing during a telephone conversation may be interpreted as "someone listening"; a stranger who comes to the door asking for directions may be seen as "really trying to get information"; and so forth.

People suffering paranoid delusions are rarely treated. It is almost impossible for them to accept that they need help. Anyone who suggests that they have a problem simply becomes part of the "conspiracy" to "persecute" them.

Paranoid people frequently lead lonely, isolated, and humorless lives dominated by constant suspicion and hostility. Although they are not necessarily dangerous to others, they can be. People who believe that the Mafia, "government agents," terrorists, or a street gang is slowly closing in on them may be moved to violence by their irrational fears. Imagine that a stranger comes to the door to ask a paranoid person for directions. If the stranger has his hand in his coat pocket, he could become the target of a paranoid attempt at "self-defense."

Delusional disorders are rare. By far, the most common form of psychosis is schizophrenia. Let's explore schizophrenia in more detail and see how it differs from a delusional disorder.

Schizophrenia—Shattered Reality

Schizophrenia (SKIT-soh-FREN-nee-uh) is marked by delusions, hallucinations, apathy, thinking abnormalities, and a "split" between thought and emotion. In schizophrenia, emotions may become blunted or very inappropriate. For example, if a person with schizophrenia is told his mother just died, he might smile, or giggle, or show no emotion at all. Schizophrenic delusions may include the idea that the person's thoughts and actions are being controlled, that thoughts are being broadcast (so others can hear them), that thoughts have been "inserted" into the person's mind, or that thoughts have been removed. In addition, schizophrenia involves withdrawal from contact with others, a loss of interest in external activities, a breakdown of personal habits, and an inability to deal with daily events (Neufeld et al., 2003). Of every 100 people, 1 person will become schizophrenic, and roughly half of all the people admitted to mental hospitals are schizophrenic (*DSM-IV-TR,* 2000).

Remember the person with psychosis who said, "Everything is in bits. . . . It's like a photograph that's torn in bits and put together again"? Many schizophrenic symptoms appear to be related to problems with *selective attention*. In other words, it is hard for people with schizophrenia to focus on one item of information at a time. Having an impaired "sensory filter" in their brains may be why they are overwhelmed by a jumble of thoughts, sensations, images, and feelings (Heinrichs, 2001).

Do people with schizophrenia have two personalities? No. How many times have you heard people say something like, "David was so warm and friendly yesterday, but today he's as cold as ice. He's so schizophrenic that I don't know how to react." Such statements show how often the term *schizophrenic* is misused. As you know, a person who displays two or more personalities has a dissociative disorder and is not "schizophrenic." Neither, of course, is a person like David, whose behavior is merely inconsistent.

Is there more than one type of schizophrenia? Schizophrenia appears to be a group of related disturbances. It has four major subtypes (*DSM-IV-TR,* 2000):

- **Disorganized type:** Schizophrenia marked by incoherence, grossly disorganized behavior, bizarre thinking, and flat or grossly inappropriate emotions.
- **Catatonic type:** Schizophrenia marked by stupor, rigidity, unresponsiveness, posturing, mutism, and, sometimes, agitated, purposeless behavior.
- **Paranoid type:** Schizophrenia marked by a preoccupation with delusions or by frequent auditory hallucinations related to a single theme, especially grandeur or persecution.
- **Undifferentiated type:** Schizophrenia in which there are prominent psychotic symptoms, but none of the specific features of catatonic, disorganized, or paranoid types.

Disorganized Schizophrenia

The disorder known as disorganized schizophrenia (sometimes called hebephrenic schizophrenia) comes close to matching the stereotyped images of "madness" seen in movies. In **disorganized schizophrenia**, personality disintegration is almost complete: Emotions, speech, and behavior are all highly disorganized. The result is silliness, laughter, and bizarre or obscene behavior, as shown by this intake interview of a patient named Edna:

> *Dr.* I am Dr. _____. I would like to know something more about you.
> *Patient* You have a nasty mind. Lord! Lord! Cats in a cradle.
> *Dr.* Tell me, how do you feel?
> *Patient* London's bell is a long, long dock. Hee! Hee! (Giggles uncontrollably.)
> *Dr.* Do you know where you are now?
> *Patient* D_____n! S_____t on you all who rip into my internals! The grudgerometer will take care of you all! (Shouting) I am the Queen, see my magic, I shall turn you all into smidgelings forever!
> *Dr.* Your husband is concerned about you. Do you know his name?

> *Patient* (Stands, walks to and faces the wall) Who am I, who are we, who are you, who are they, (turns)
> I . . . I . . . I . . . I! (Makes grotesque faces.)
>
> Edna was placed in the women's ward where she proceeded to masturbate. Occasionally, she would scream or shout obscenities. At other times she giggled to herself. She was known to attack other patients. She began to complain that her uterus was attached to a "pipeline to the Kremlin" and that she was being "infernally invaded" by Communism. (Suinn, 1975)

Disorganized schizophrenia typically develops in adolescence or young adulthood. Chances of improvement are limited, and social impairment is usually extreme (*DSM-IV-TR,* 2000).

Catatonic Schizophrenia

The catatonic person seems to be in a state of total panic (Fink & Taylor, 2003). **Catatonic schizophrenia** brings about a stuporous condition in which odd positions may be held for hours or even days. These periods of rigidity may be similar to the tendency to "freeze" at times of great emergency or panic. Catatonic individuals appear to be struggling desperately to control their inner turmoil. One sign of this is the fact that stupor may occasionally give way to agitated outbursts or violent behavior. The following excerpt describes a catatonic episode.

> Manuel appeared to be physically healthy upon examination. Yet he did not regain his awareness of his surroundings. He remained motionless, speechless, and seemingly unconscious. One evening an aide turned him on his side to straighten out the sheet, was called away to tend another patient, and forgot to return. Manuel was found the next morning, still on his side, his arm tucked under his body, as he had been left the night before. His arm was turning blue from lack of circulation, but he seemed to be experiencing no discomfort. (Suinn, 1975)

Peter Granser/Laif/Aurora Photos

In disorganized schizophrenia, behavior is marked by silliness, laughter, and bizarre or obscene behavior.

Notice that Manuel did not speak. *Mutism,* along with a marked decrease in responsiveness to the environment, makes patients with catatonic schizophrenia difficult to "reach." Fortunately, this bizarre disorder has become rare in Europe and North America (*DSM-IV-TR,* 2000).

Paranoid Schizophrenia

Paranoid schizophrenia is the most common schizophrenic disorder. As in paranoid delusional disorders, **paranoid schizophrenia** centers on delusions of grandeur and persecution. However, paranoid schizophrenics also hallucinate, and their delusions are more bizarre and unconvincing than those in a delusional disorder (Freeman & Garety, 2004).

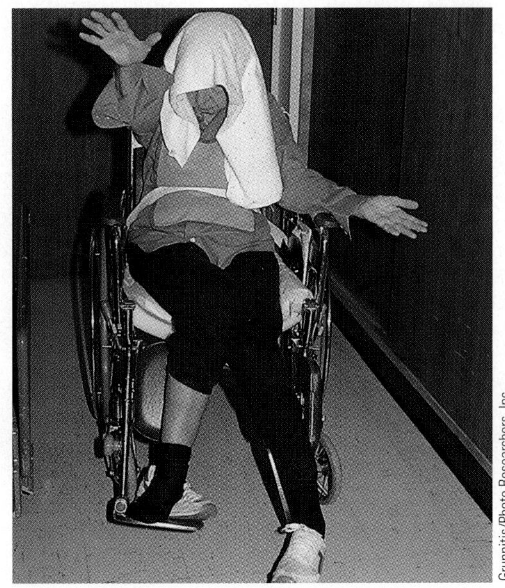

Grunnitis/Photo Researchers, Inc.

Can the rigid postures and stupor of a person with catatonic schizophrenia be understood in terms of abnormal body chemistry? Environment? Heredity?

Paranoid psychosis A delusional disorder centered especially on delusions of persecution.

Schizophrenia A psychosis characterized by delusions, hallucinations, apathy, and a "split" between thought and emotion.

Disorganized schizophrenia Schizophrenia marked by incoherence, grossly disorganized behavior, bizarre thinking, and flat or grossly inappropriate emotions.

Catatonic schizophrenia Schizophrenia marked by stupor, rigidity, unresponsiveness, posturing, mutism, and, sometimes, agitated, purposeless behavior.

Paranoid schizophrenia Schizophrenia marked by a preoccupation with delusions or by frequent auditory hallucinations related to a single theme, especially grandeur or persecution.

CRITICAL THINKING

Are the Mentally Ill Prone to Violence?

News reports and television programs tend to exaggerate the connection between mental illness and violence (Corrigan et al., 2005). Such media reports both create and reflect deeply held beliefs about mental disorders in our society. Such beliefs are important because they affect laws and personal attitudes toward the mentally ill. For example, people who strongly believe that the mentally ill are prone to violence are typically afraid to have former mental patients as neighbors, coworkers, or friends (Corrigan & Watson, 2005).

The reality is just the opposite. According to the MacArthur Study of Mental Disorder and Violence, the largest study ever conducted on this question, mentally ill individuals who are not also substance abusers are no more prone to violence than are normal individuals (Monahan et al., 2001). There are only a few exceptions, and in those cases the risk is not very large (Noble, 1997; Rice, 1997):

- Only persons who are *actively psychotic* are more violence prone than nonpatients. That is, if a person is experiencing delusions and hallucinations, the risk of violence is elevated. Other mental problems are unrelated to violence.
- Only persons *currently* experiencing psychotic symptoms are at increased risk for violence. Violent behavior is not related to having been a mental patient in the past or having had psychotic symptoms in the past.

Although Jeffrey Dahmer's case is extreme, he is typical of the mentally disordered persons who make the evening news. Most have committed murder or some other heinous crime. This gives the impression that the mentally ill are violent and dangerous. In reality, only a tiny percentage of all mentally disordered persons are more violent than average. (Dahmer was killed in prison by another inmate in 1994.)

Curt Borgwardt/Corbis Sygma

Thus, most news stories give a false impression. Only a small minority of the actively mentally ill poses an increased risk. Even when we consider people who are actively psychotic, we find that the vast majority are not violent. Former mental patients, in particular, are no more likely to be violent than people in general. No matter how disturbed a person may have been, she or he merits respect and compassion.

The risk of violence from mental patients is actually many times lower than that from persons who have the following attributes: young, male, poor, and intoxicated (Corrigan & Watson, 2005). Remember, people who are not mentally ill commit the overwhelming majority of violent crimes.

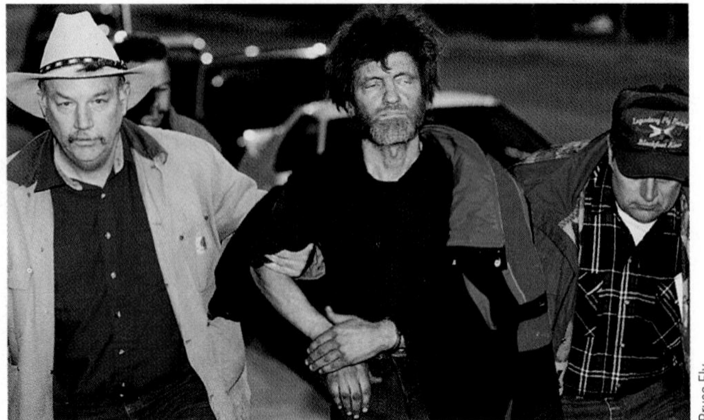

Bruce Ely

● **Figure 16.6** Over a period of years, Theodore Kaczynski mailed bombs to unsuspecting victims, many of whom were maimed or killed. As a young adult, Kaczynski was a brilliant mathematician. At the time of his arrest, he had become the Unabomber—a reclusive "loner" who deeply mistrusted other people and modern technology. After his arrest, Kaczynski was judged to be suffering from paranoid schizophrenia.

Thinking that their minds are being controlled by God, the government, or "cosmic rays from space," or that someone is trying to poison them, people suffering from paranoid schizophrenia may feel forced into violence to "protect" themselves. An example is James Huberty, who brutally murdered 21 people at a McDonald's restaurant in San Ysidro, California. Huberty, who had paranoid schizophrenia, felt persecuted and cheated by life. Shortly before he announced to his wife that he was "going hunting humans," Huberty had been hearing hallucinated voices (● Figure 16.6).

How dangerous are the mentally ill? Many people believe that the mentally ill are dangerous. Are they right? You might be surprised by the answer, found in "Are the Mentally Ill Prone to Violence?"

Undifferentiated Schizophrenia

The three types of schizophrenia just described occur most often in textbooks. In reality, patients may shift from one pattern to another at different times. Many patients, therefore, are simply

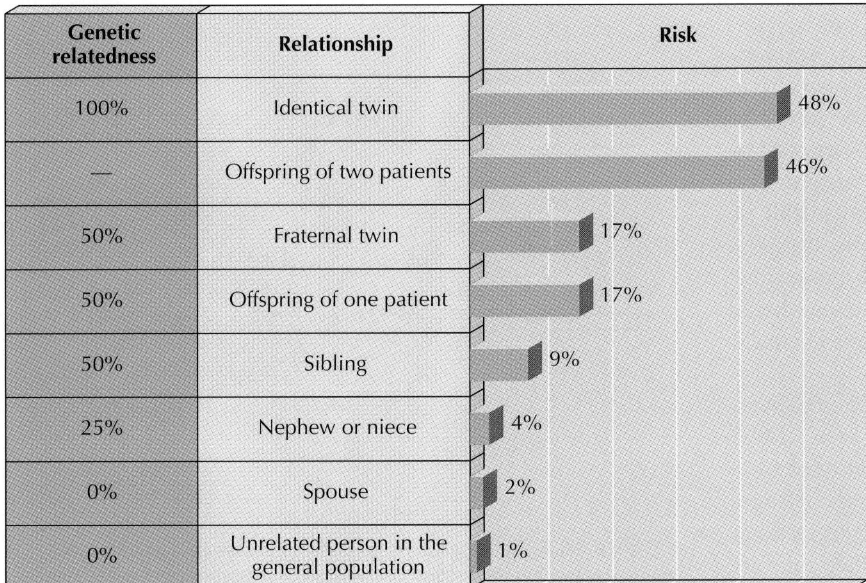

● **Figure 16.7** Lifetime risk of developing schizophrenia is associated with how closely a person is genetically related to a schizophrenic person. A shared environment also increases the risk. (Estimates from Lenzenweger & Gottesman, 1994.)

classified as suffering from **undifferentiated schizophrenia**, in which the specific features of catatonic, disorganized, or paranoid types are missing. Diagnosing schizophrenia is fairly subjective. All things considered, however, there is no doubt that schizophrenia is real or that its treatment is a major challenge.

The Causes of Schizophrenia

Former British Prime Minister Winston Churchill once described a question that perplexed him as "a riddle wrapped in a mystery inside an enigma." The same words might describe the causes of schizophrenia.

Environment

What causes schizophrenia? An increased risk of developing schizophrenia may begin at birth or even before. Women who are exposed to the influenza (flu) virus or to rubella (German measles) during the middle of pregnancy have children who are more likely to become schizophrenic (Brown et al., 2001). Malnutrition during pregnancy and complications at the time of birth can have a similar impact. Possibly, such events disturb brain development, leaving people more vulnerable to a psychotic break with reality (Walker et al., 2004).

Early **psychological trauma** (a psychological injury or shock) may also add to the risk. Often, the victims of schizophrenia were exposed to violence, sexual abuse, death, divorce, separation, or other stresses in childhood (Walker et al., 2004). Living in a troubled family is a related risk factor. In a disturbed family environment, stressful relationships, communication patterns, and negative emotions prevail. For example, a 15-year study found that the chance of developing schizophrenia is related to deviant communication within families (Goldstein, 1985). Deviant communication patterns cause anxiety, confusion, anger, conflict, and turmoil. Typically, disturbed families interact in ways that are laden with guilt, prying, criticism, negativity, and emotional attacks (Bressi, Albonetti, & Razzoli, 1998; Davison & Neale, 2006).

Although they are attractive, environmental explanations alone are not enough to account for schizophrenia. For example, when the children of schizophrenic parents are raised away from their chaotic home environment, they are still more likely to become psychotic (Walker et al., 2004).

Heredity

Does that mean that heredity affects the risk of developing schizophrenia? There is now little doubt that heredity is a factor in schizophrenia. It appears that some individuals inherit a *potential* for developing schizophrenia. They are, in other words, more *vulnerable* to the disorder than others are (Fowles, 1992; Walker et al., 2004).

How has that been shown? If one identical twin becomes schizophrenic (remember, identical twins have identical genes), then the other twin has a *48 percent* chance of also becoming schizophrenic (Lenzenweger & Gottesman, 1994). The figure for twins can be compared to the risk of schizophrenia for the population in general, which is 1 percent. (See ● Figure 16.7 for other relationships.) In general, schizophrenia is clearly more common among close relatives and it tends to run in families (Plomin & Rende, 1991). There's even a case on record of *four* identical quadruplets *all* developing schizophrenia (Mirsky et al., 2000). In light of such evidence, researchers are now beginning to search for specific genes related to schizophrenia.

A problem exists with current genetic explanations of schizophrenia: Very few people with schizophrenia have children. How could a genetic defect be passed from one generation to the next if afflicted people don't reproduce? One possible answer is suggested by the fact that the older a man is when he fathers a child, the more likely it is that the child will develop schizophrenia. Apparently, genetic mutations occur in aging male reproductive cells and increase the risk of schizophrenia (as well as other medical problems) (Malaspina et al., 2001; Malaspina et al., 2005; Sipos et al., 2004).

Undifferentiated schizophrenia Schizophrenia lacking the specific features of catatonic, disorganized, or paranoid types.

Psychological trauma A psychological injury or shock, such as that caused by violence, abuse, neglect, separation, and so forth.

Brain Chemistry

How could someone inherit a susceptibility to schizophrenia? Amphetamine, LSD, PCP ("angel dust"), and similar drugs produce effects that partially mimic the symptoms of schizophrenia. Also, the same drugs (phenothiazines) used to treat LSD overdoses tend to alleviate psychotic symptoms. Facts such as these suggest that biochemical abnormalities (disturbances in brain chemicals or neurotransmitters) may occur in schizophrenic people. It is possible that the schizophrenic brain produces some substance similar to a *psychedelic* (mind-altering) drug. At present, one likely candidate is dopamine (DOPE-ah-meen), an important chemical messenger found in the brain.

Many researchers believe that schizophrenia is related to overactivity in brain dopamine systems (Abi-Dargham et al., 1998; Kapur & Lecrubier, 2003). Another possibility is that dopamine receptors become super-responsive to normal amounts of dopamine (Port & Seybold, 1995). Dopamine appears to trigger a flood of unrelated thoughts, feelings, and perceptions, which may account for the voices, hallucinations, and delusions of schizophrenia. The implication is that schizophrenic people may be on a sort of drug trip caused by their own bodies (● Figure 16.8). In short, most evidence suggests that schizophrenia is a brain disease.

Dopamine is not the only brain chemical that has caught scientists' attention. For instance, the neurotransmitter glutamate also appears to be related to schizophrenia (Belsham, 2001). People who take the hallucinogenic drug PCP, which affects glutamate, have symptoms that closely mimic schizophrenia (Murray, 2002). This occurs because glutamate influences brain activity in areas that control emotions and sensory information (Tsai & Coyle, 2002). Another tantalizing connection is the fact that stress alters glutamate levels, which in turn alter dopamine systems (Moghaddam, 2002). The story is far from complete, but it appears that dopamine, glutamate, and other brain chemicals partly explain the devastating symptoms of schizophrenia (Sawa & Snyder, 2002; Walker et al., 2004).

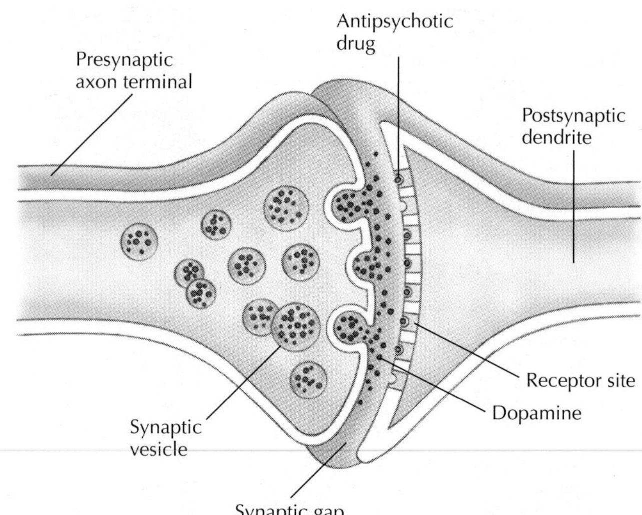

● **Figure 16.8** Dopamine normally crosses the synapse between two neurons, activating the second cell. Antipsychotic drugs bind to the same receptor sites as dopamine does, blocking its action. In people suffering from schizophrenia, a reduction in dopamine activity can quiet a person's agitation and psychotic symptoms.

The Schizophrenic Brain

Medical researchers have long hoped for a way to directly observe the schizophrenic brain. Three medical techniques are now making it possible. One, called a *CT scan,* provides an X-ray picture of the brain. (CT stands for computed tomography, or computer-enhanced X-ray images.) ● Figure 16.9 shows a CT scan of the brain of John Hinkley Jr., who shot former U.S. President Ronald Reagan and three other men in 1981. In the ensuing trial, Hinkley was declared insane. As you can see, his brain differed from the norm. Specifically, it had wider surface fissuring.

Derik Bayes/Courtesy Guttman-Maclay *Life* Picture Service

This series of paintings by Louis Wain reflects a troubled personality. Wain was a British illustrator who became schizophrenic in middle age. As Wain's psychosis progressed, his cat paintings became highly abstract and fragmented. In many ways, Wain's paintings resemble the perceptual changes caused by psychedelic drugs such as mescaline and LSD. Recent research suggests that psychosis may, in fact, be the result of mind-altering changes in brain chemistry.

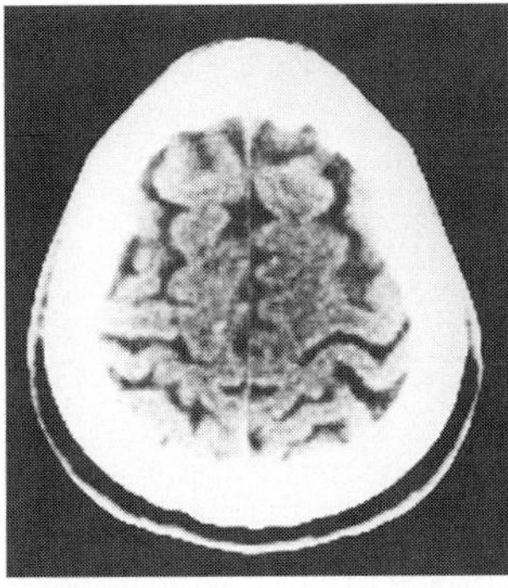

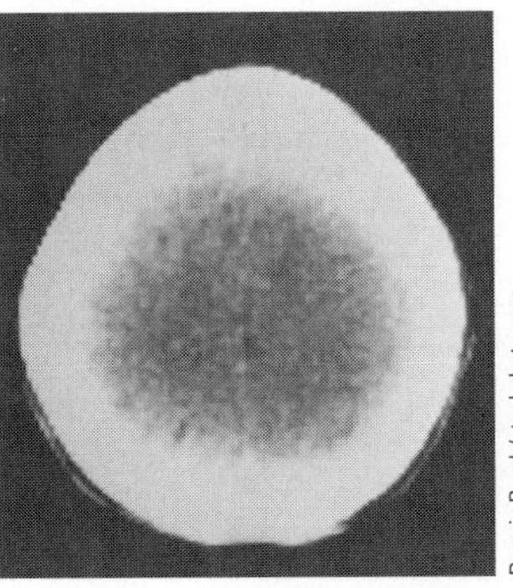

Dennis Brack/stockphoto.com

● **Figure 16.9** *(left)* CT scan of would-be presidential assassin John Hinkley Jr., taken when he was 25. The X-ray image shows widened fissures in the wrinkled surface of Hinkley's brain. *(right)* CT scan of a normal 25-year-old's brain. In most young adults the surface folds of the brain are pressed together too tightly to be seen. As a person ages, surface folds of the brain normally become more visible. Pronounced brain fissuring in young adults may be a sign of schizophrenia, chronic alcoholism, or other problems.

MRI scans (magnetic resonance imaging) are allowing researchers to peer inside the schizophrenic brain. What they find is that schizophrenic people tend to have enlarged ventricles (fluid-filled spaces within the brain) (Sharma et al., 1998). Other brain regions also appear to be abnormal. It is telling that the affected areas are crucial for regulating motivation, emotion, perception, actions, and attention (Gur et al., 1998; Walker et al., 2004).

A third technique, called a *PET scan* (positron emission tomography), provides an image of brain activity. To make a PET scan, a radioactive sugar solution is injected into a vein. When the sugar reaches the brain, an electronic device measures how much is used in each area. These data are then translated into a color map, or scan, of brain activity (● Figure 16.10). Researchers are finding patterns in such scans that are consistently linked with schizophrenia, affective disorders, and other problems. For instance, activity tends to be abnormally low in the frontal lobes of the schizophrenic brain (Velakoulis & Pantelis, 1996). In the future, PET scans may be used to accurately diagnose schizophrenia. For now, PET scans show that there is a clear difference in schizophrenic brain activity.

Implications

In summary, the emerging picture of psychotic disorders such as schizophrenia takes this form: Anyone subjected to enough stress may be pushed to a psychotic break. (Battlefield psychosis is an example.) However, some people inherit a difference in brain chemistry or brain structure that makes them more susceptible—even to normal life stresses.

BRIDGES

Brain scans have provided valuable new insights into brain structures and activities.

See Chapter 2, pages 61–63.

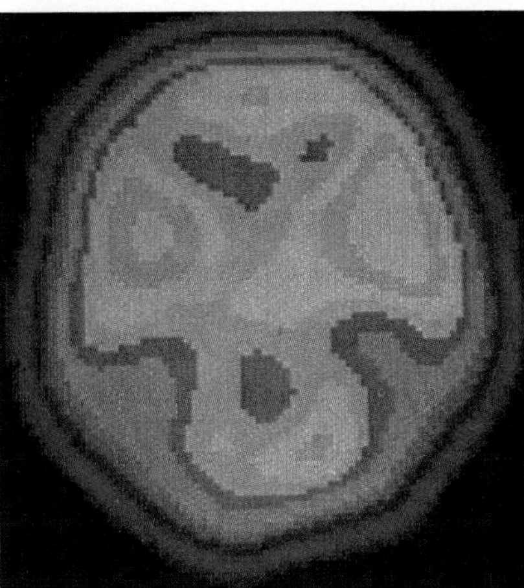

NORMAL

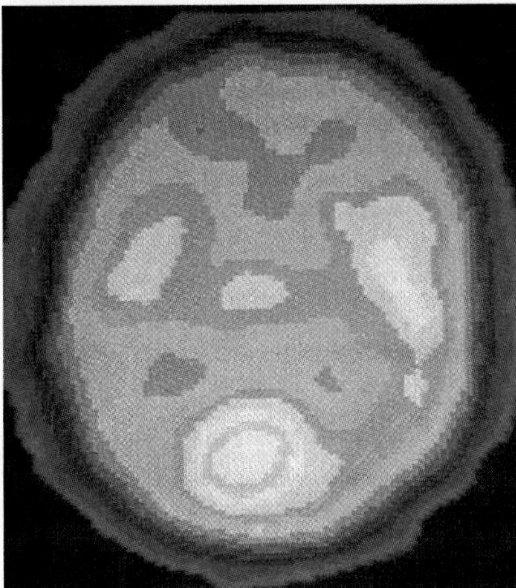

SCHIZOPHRENIC

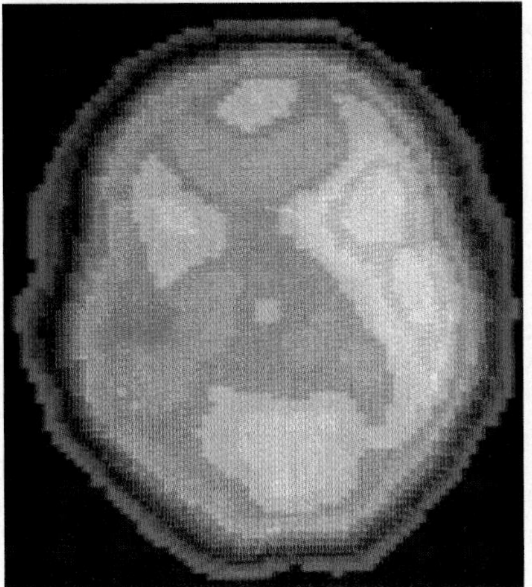

MANIC-DEPRESSIVE

The Brookhaven National Laboratory

● **Figure 16.10** Positron emission tomography produces PET scans of the human brain. In the scans shown here, red, pink, and orange indicate lower levels of brain activity; white and blue indicate higher activity levels. Notice that activity in the schizophrenic brain is quite low in the frontal lobes (top area of each scan) (Velakoulis & Pantelis, 1996). Activity in the manic-depressive brain is low in the left brain hemisphere and high in the right brain hemisphere. The reverse is more often true of the schizophrenic brain. Researchers are trying to identify consistent patterns like these to aid diagnosis of mental disorders.

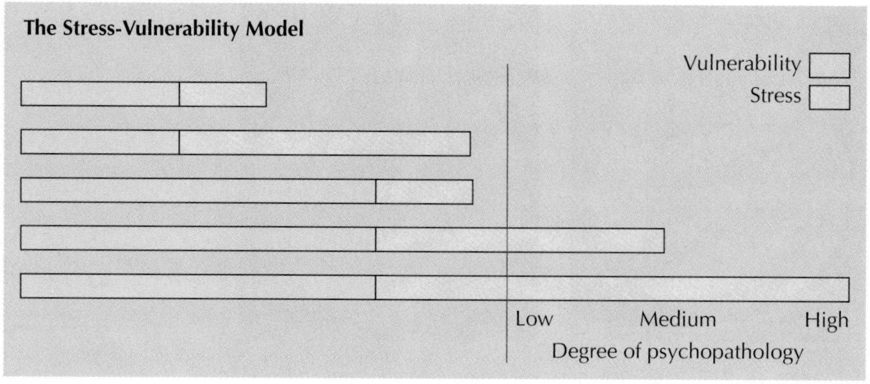

● **Figure 16.11** Various combinations of vulnerability and stress may produce psychological problems. The top bar shows low vulnerability and low stress. The result? No problem. The same is true of the next bar down, where low vulnerability is combined with moderate stress. Even high vulnerability (third bar) may not lead to problems if stress levels remain low. However, when high vulnerability combines with moderate or high stress (bottom two bars) the person "crosses the line" and suffers from psychopathology.

The Stress-Vulnerability Model

Vulnerability
Stress
Low Medium High
Degree of psychopathology

Thus, the right mix of inherited potential and environmental stress brings about mind-altering changes in brain chemicals and brain structure. This explanation is called a **stress-vulnerability model.** It attributes psychotic disorders to a blend of environmental stress and inherited susceptibility (Walker et al., 2004). The model seems to apply to other forms of psychopathology as well, such as depression (● Figure 16.11).

Despite advances in our understanding, psychosis remains "a riddle wrapped in a mystery inside an enigma." Let us hope that recent progress toward a cure for schizophrenia will continue.

KNOWLEDGE BUILDER

Psychosis, Delusional Disorders, and Schizophrenia

REFLECT

What did you think psychosis was like before you read about it? How has your understanding changed? If you were writing a "recipe" for psychosis, what would the main "ingredients" be?

If you were asked to play the role of a paranoid person for a theater production, what symptoms would you emphasize?

You have been asked to explain the causes of schizophrenia to the parents of a schizophrenic teenager. What would you tell them?

LEARNING CHECK

1. Carol wrongly believes that her body is "rotting away." She is suffering from
   a. depressive hallucinations c. flat affect
   b. a delusion d. Alzheimer's disease
2. Colin, who has suffered a psychotic break, is hearing voices. This symptom is referred to as
   a. flat affect c. a word salad
   b. hallucination d. organic delusions
3. A psychosis caused by lead poisoning would be regarded as an organic disorder. T or F?
4. Hallucinations and personality disintegration are the principal features of paranoid psychosis. T or F?
5. Which of the following is *not* one of the subtypes of schizophrenia?
   a. erotomanic type c. paranoid type
   b. catatonic type d. disorganized type
6. Environmental explanations of schizophrenia emphasize emotional trauma and
   a. manic parents c. psychedelic interactions
   b. schizoaffective interactions d. disturbed family relationships
7. The ______ ______ of a schizophrenic person runs a 48 percent chance of also becoming psychotic.
8. Biochemical explanations of schizophrenia have focused on excessive amounts of ______ in the brain.
   a. radioactive sugar c. PCP
   b. webs and tangles d. dopamine and glutamate
9. The stress-vulnerability model of psychosis explains mental disorders as a product of environmental stresses and
   a. psychological trauma
   b. deviant communication
   c. exposure to the flu virus during pregnancy
   d. heredity

CRITICAL THINKING

10. Researchers have found nearly double the normal number of dopamine receptor sites in the brains of schizophrenics. Why might that be important?
11. Enlarged surface fissures and ventricles are frequently found in the brains of chronic schizophrenics. Why is it a mistake to conclude that such features cause schizophrenia?

Answers: 1. b **2.** b **3.** T **4.** F **5.** a **6.** d **7.** identical twin **8.** d **9.** d **10.** Because of the extra receptors, schizophrenics may get psychedelic effects from normal levels of dopamine in the brain. **11.** Because correlation does not confirm causation. Structural brain abnormalities are merely *correlated* with schizophrenia. They could be additional symptoms, rather than causes, of the disorder.

Mood Disorders—Peaks and Valleys

For some people, minor bouts of depression are as common as colds. But extreme swings of mood can be as disabling as a serious physical illness. In fact, depression can be deadly, because depressed persons may be suicidal. It is difficult to imagine how bleak and hopeless the world looks to a person who is deeply depressed, or how "crazy" it can be to ride a wave of mania. Let's explore mood disorders and their causes.

Nobody loves you when you're down and out—or so it seems. Psychologists have come to realize that **mood disorders** (major disturbances in emotion) are among the most serious of all. Two general types of mood disorder are depressive disorders and bipolar disorders (Nevid & Greene, 2005) (see ■ Table 16.7). In **depressive disorders,** sadness and despondency are exaggerated, prolonged, or unreasonable. Signs of a depressive disorder are de-

TABLE 16.7

DSM-IV-TR Classification of Mood Disorders

PROBLEM	PRIMARY SYMPTOM	TYPICAL SIGNS OF TROUBLE
Depressive Disorders		
Major depressive disorder	Extreme emotional depression for at least 2 weeks	You feel extremely sad, worthless, fatigued, and empty; you are unable to feel pleasure; you are having thoughts of suicide.
Dysthymic disorder	Moderately depressed mood on most days during the last 2 years	You feel down and depressed more days than not; your self-esteem and energy levels have been low for many months.
Bipolar Disorders		
Bipolar I disorder	Extreme mania and depression	At times you have little need for sleep, can't stop talking, your mind races, and everything you do is of immense importance; at other times you feel extremely sad, worthless, and empty.
Bipolar II disorder	Emotional depression and at least one episode of mild mania	Most of the time you feel extremely sad, worthless, fatigued, and empty; however, at times you feel unusually good, cheerful, energetic, or "high."
Cyclothymic disorder	Periods of moderate depression and moderate mania for at least 2 years	You have been experiencing upsetting emotional ups and downs for many months.

jection, hopelessness, and an inability to feel pleasure or to take interest in anything. Other common symptoms are fatigue, disturbed sleep and eating patterns, feelings of worthlessness, a very negative self-image, and thoughts of suicide. In **bipolar disorders**, people go both "up" and "down" emotionally (*DSM-IV-TR,* 2000).

In North America, between 10 and 20 percent of the adult population has had a major depressive episode at some time (*DSM-IV-TR,* 2000). On any given day, roughly 5 percent of the population is suffering from a mood disorder.

Some mood disorders are long lasting but relatively moderate problems. If a person is mildly depressed for at least 2 years, the problem is called a **dysthymic disorder** (dis-THY-mik). If depression alternates with periods when the person's mood is cheerful, expansive, or irritable, the problem is a **cyclothymic disorder** (SIKE-lo-THY-mik). Even at this level, mood disorders can be debilitating. However, major mood disorders are much more damaging.

Major Mood Disorders

Major mood disorders are characterized by emotional extremes. The person who only goes "down" emotionally suffers from a **major depressive disorder.** During major depressive episodes everything looks bleak and hopeless. The person has feelings of failure, sinfulness, worthlessness, and total despair. Suffering is intense and the person may become extremely subdued, withdrawn, or intensely suicidal. Severe depression is a serious threat. Suicide attempted during a major depression is rarely a "plea for help." Usually, the person intends to succeed and may give no prior warning.

In a **bipolar I disorder,** people experience both extreme mania and deep depression. During manic episodes, the person is loud, elated, hyperactive, grandiose, and energetic. Manic patients may go bankrupt in a matter of days, get arrested, or go on a binge of promiscuous sex. During periods of depression, the person is deeply despondent and possibly suicidal.

In a **bipolar II disorder** the person is mostly sad and guilt ridden, but has had one or more mildly manic episodes (called *hypomania*). That is, in a bipolar II disorder both elation and depression occur, but the person's mania is not as extreme as in a bipolar I disorder. Bipolar II patients who are hypomanic usually just manage to irritate everyone around them. They are excessively cheerful, aggressive, or irritable, and they may brag, talk too fast, interrupt conversations, or spend too much money (Gorman, 1996).

Stress-vulnerability model Attributes psychosis to a combination of environmental stress and inherited susceptibility.

Mood disorder Major disturbances in mood or emotion, such as depression or mania.

Depressive disorders Emotional disorders primarily involving sadness, despondency, and depression.

Bipolar disorders Emotional disorders involving both depression and mania or hypomania.

Dysthymic disorder Moderate depression that persists for 2 years or more.

Cyclothymic disorder Moderate manic and depressive behavior that persists for 2 years or more.

Major mood disorders Disorders marked by lasting extremes of mood or emotion and sometimes accompanied by psychotic symptoms.

Major depressive disorder A mood disorder in which the person has suffered one or more intense episodes of depression.

Bipolar I disorder A mood disorder in which a person has episodes of mania (excited, hyperactive, energetic, grandiose behavior) and also periods of deep depression.

Bipolar II disorder A mood disorder in which a person is mostly depressed (sad, despondent, guilt ridden) but has also had one or more episodes of mild mania (hypomania).

In serious cases of depression it is impossible for a person to function at work or at school. Sometimes, depressed individuals cannot even feed or dress themselves. In cases of depression and/or mania that are even more severe, the person may also lose touch with reality and display psychotic symptoms. About 14 percent of patients in mental hospitals have major mood disorders.

How do major mood disorders differ from dysthymic and cyclothymic disorders? As mentioned, the major mood disorders involve more severe emotional changes. Also, major mood disorders more often appear to be **endogenous** (en-DODGE-eh-nus: produced from within) rather than a reaction to external events.

What Causes Mood Disorders?

Depression and other mood disorders have resisted adequate explanation and treatment. Some scientists are focusing on the biology of mood changes. They are interested in brain chemicals and transmitter substances, especially serotonin, noradrenaline, and dopamine levels. Their findings are incomplete, but progress has been made. For example, the chemical *lithium carbonate* can be effective for treating some cases of bipolar depression.

Other researchers seek psychological explanations. Psychoanalytic theory, for instance, holds that depression is caused by repressed anger. This rage is displaced and turned inward as self-blame and self-hate. As discussed in Chapter 15, behavioral theories of depression emphasize learned helplessness (LoLordo, 2001; Seligman, 1989). Cognitive psychologists believe that self-criticism and negative, distorted, or self-defeating thoughts underlie many cases of depression. (This view is discussed in Chapter 17.) Clearly, life stresses trigger many mood disorders (Kessler, 1997). This is especially true for people who have personality traits and thinking patterns that make them vulnerable to depression (Franche & Dobson, 1992; Miranda, 1992).

Darren Robb/Getty Images

In major depressive disorders, suicidal impulses can be intense and despair total.

Gender and Depression

Overall, women are twice as likely as men to experience depression (Kuehner, 2003). Researchers believe that social and environmental conditions are the main reason for this difference (Stoppard & McMullen, 2003). Factors that contribute to women's greater risk of depression include conflicts about birth control and pregnancy, work and parenting, and the strain of providing emotional support for others. Marital strife, sexual and physical abuse, and poverty are also factors. Nationwide, women and children are most likely to live in poverty. As a result, poor women frequently suffer the stresses associated with single parenthood, loss of control over their lives, poor housing, and dangerous neighborhoods (Russo, 1990). One study found that women in the United States were most likely to be depressed if they had these characteristics: low education, unmarried, Latina, high stress levels, and feelings of hopelessness (Myers et al., 2002).

Postpartum Depression

One source of women's depression is fairly easy to identify. After pregnancy and childbirth, many women face a high risk of becoming depressed.

Two weeks after her child was born, Makemba realized something was wrong. She could no longer ignore that she was extremely irritable, fatigued, tearful, and depressed. "Shouldn't I be happy?" she wondered. "What's wrong with me?"

Many women are surprised to learn that they face a risk of depression after giving birth. The two most common forms of the problem are maternity blues and postpartum depression. (The term *postpartum* refers to the time period following childbirth.)

An estimated 25 to 50 percent of all women experience **maternity blues,** a mild depression that usually lasts from 1 to 2 days after childbirth. These "third-day blues" are marked by crying, fitful sleep, tension, anger, and irritability. For most women, such reactions are a normal part of adjusting to childbirth. The depression is usually brief and not too severe.

For some women, maternity blues can be the beginning of a serious depression. Roughly 13 percent of all women who give birth develop **postpartum depression,** a moderately severe depression that begins within 3 months following childbirth. Typical signs of postpartum depression are mood swings, despondency, feelings of inadequacy, and an inability to cope with the new baby. Depression of this kind may last anywhere from 2 months to about a year. Women are not the only ones to suffer when postpartum depression strikes. A depressed mother can seriously affect her child's rate of development (Cooper & Murray, 2001).

Stress and anxiety before birth and negative attitudes toward child rearing increase the risk of postpartum depression. A poor marital relationship and lack of support from the father are also danger signs. Part of the problem may be hormonal: After a woman gives birth, her estrogen levels can drop, altering her mood (Harris, 1996).

Women who become depressed tend to see their husbands as unsupportive. Therefore, educating new parents about the importance of supporting one another may reduce the risk of depression. Groups where new mothers can discuss their feelings are also helpful. If depression is severe or long lasting, new mothers should seek professional help.

Biology and Depression

As you might guess, the fact that major mood disorders appear to be endogenous implies that genetics may be involved, especially in bipolar disorders (Gershon et al., 1998). As a case in point, if one identical twin is depressed, the other has an 80 percent chance of suffering depression, too. For nontwin siblings the probability is 35 percent. As we have noted, psychological causes are important in many cases of depression. But for major mood disorders, biological factors seem to play a larger role. Surprisingly, one additional source of depression is related to the seasons.

Seasonal Affective Disorder

Unless you have experienced a winter of "cabin fever" in the far north, you may be surprised to learn that the rhythms of the seasons underlie some depressions. Researcher Norman Rosenthal has found that some people suffer from **seasonal affective disorder** (SAD), or depression that only occurs during the fall and winter months. Almost anyone can get a little depressed when days are short, dark, and cold. But when a person's symptoms are lasting and disabling, the problem may be SAD. Here are some of the major symptoms of SAD (Rosenthal, 1993):

- **Oversleeping and difficulty staying awake:** Your sleep patterns may be disturbed and waking very early in the morning is common.
- **Fatigue:** You feel too tired to maintain a normal routine.
- **Craving:** You hunger for carbohydrates and sweets, leading to overeating and weight gain.
- **Inability to cope:** You feel irritable and stressed.
- **Social withdrawal:** You become unsocial in the winter but are socially active during other seasons.

Starting in the fall, people with SAD sleep longer but more poorly. During the day they feel tired and drowsy, and they tend to overeat. With each passing day they become more sad, anxious, irritable, and socially withdrawn.

Although their depressions are not severe, many victims of SAD face each winter with a sense of foreboding. SAD is especially prevalent in northern latitudes, where days are very short during the winter (Booker & Hellekson, 1992) (● Figure 16.12). For instance, one study found that 13 percent of college students living in northern New England showed signs of suffering from SAD (Low & Feissner, 1998). The students most likely to be affected were those who had moved from the south to attend college!

Seasonal depressions are related to the release of more melatonin during the winter. This hormone, which is secreted by the pineal gland in the brain, regulates the body's response to changing light conditions (Wehr et al., 2001). That's why 80 percent of SAD patients can be helped by extra doses of bright light, a remedy called phototherapy (● Figure 16.13). **Phototherapy** involves ex-

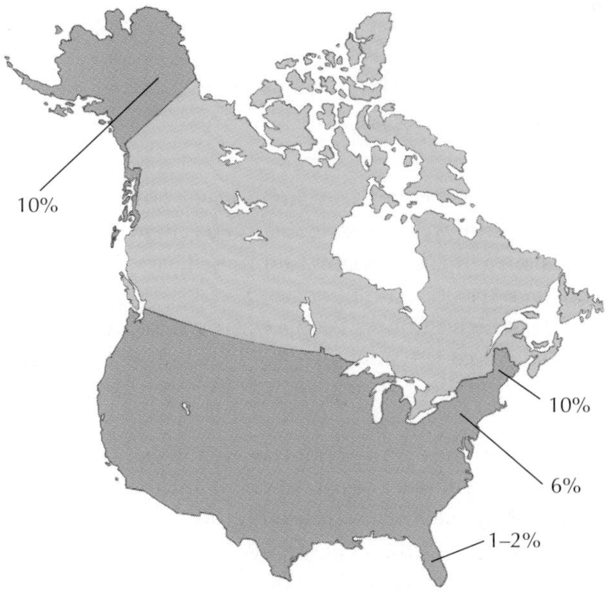

● Figure 16.12 Seasonal affective disorder appears to be related to reduced exposure to daylight during the winter. SAD affects 1 to 2 percent of Florida's population, about 6 percent of the people living in Maryland and New York City, and nearly 10 percent of the residents of New Hampshire and Alaska (Booker & Hellekson, 1992).

Dan McCoy/Rainbow

● Figure 16.13 An hour or more of bright light a day can dramatically reduce the symptoms of seasonal affective disorder. Treatment is usually necessary from fall through spring. Light therapy typically works best when it is used early in the morning (Lewy et al., 1998).

Endogenous depression Depression that appears to be produced from within (perhaps by chemical imbalances in the brain), rather than as a reaction to life events.

Maternity blues A brief and relatively mild state of depression often experienced by mothers 2 or 3 days after giving birth.

Postpartum depression A mild to moderately severe depression that begins within 3 months following childbirth.

Seasonal affective disorder Depression that occurs only during fall and winter; presumably related to decreased exposure to sunlight.

Phototherapy A treatment for seasonal affective disorder that involves exposure to bright, full-spectrum light.

posing SAD patients to one or more hours of very bright fluorescent light each day (Neumeister, 2004). This is best done early in the morning, where it simulates dawn in the summer (Avery et al., 2001). For many SAD sufferers a hearty dose of morning "sunshine" appears to be the next best thing to vacationing in the tropics.

Disorders in Perspective—Psychiatric Labeling

As we conclude our survey of psychological disorders, a caution is in order. The terms we have reviewed in this chapter aid communication about human problems. But if used carelessly, they can hurt people. Everyone has felt or acted "crazy" during brief periods of stress or high emotion. People with psychological disorders have problems that are more severe or long lasting than most of us experience. Otherwise, they may not be that different from you or me.

A fascinating study carried out by psychologist David Rosenhan illustrates the impact of psychiatric labeling. Rosenhan and several colleagues had themselves committed to mental hospitals with a diagnosis of "schizophrenia" (Rosenhan, 1973). After being admitted, each of these "pseudo-patients" dropped all pretense of mental illness. Yet even though they acted completely normal, none of the researchers was ever recognized by hospital *staff* as a phony patient. Real patients were not so easily fooled. It was not unusual for a patient to say to one of the researchers, "You're not crazy, you're checking up on the hospital!" or, "You're a journalist."

To record his observations, Rosenhan took notes by carefully jotting things on a small piece of paper hidden in his hand. However, he soon learned that stealth was totally unnecessary. Rosenhan simply walked around with a clipboard, recording observations. No one questioned this behavior. Rosenhan's note taking was just regarded as a symptom of his "illness." This observation clarifies why staff members failed to detect the fake patients. Because they were in a mental ward, and because they had been *labeled* schizophrenic, anything the pseudo-patients did was seen as a symptom of psychopathology.

As Rosenhan's study shows, it is far better to label *problems* than to label people. Think of the difference in impact between saying, "You are experiencing a serious psychological disorder," and saying, "You're a schizophrenic." Which statement would you prefer to have said about yourself?

Social Stigma

An added problem with psychiatric labeling is that it frequently leads to prejudice and discrimination. That is, the mentally ill in our culture are often *stigmatized* (rejected and disgraced). People who have been labeled mentally ill (at any time in their lives) are less likely to be hired. They also tend to be denied housing and they are more likely to be falsely accused of crimes. Thus, people who are grappling with mental illness may be harmed as much by social stigma as they are by their immediate psychological problems (Corrigan & Penn, 1999).

A Look Ahead

Treatments for psychological problems range from counseling and psychotherapy to mental hospitalization and drug therapy. Because they vary greatly, a complete discussion of therapies is found in the next chapter. For now, it's worth noting that many milder mental disorders can treated successfully. Even major disorders may respond well to drugs and other techniques (see ● Figure 16.14). It is wrong to fear "former mental patients" or to exclude them from work, friendships, and other social situations. A struggle with major depression or a psychotic episode does not inevitably lead to lifelong dysfunction. Too often, however, they lead to unnecessary rejection based on groundless fears (Sarason & Sarason, 2005).

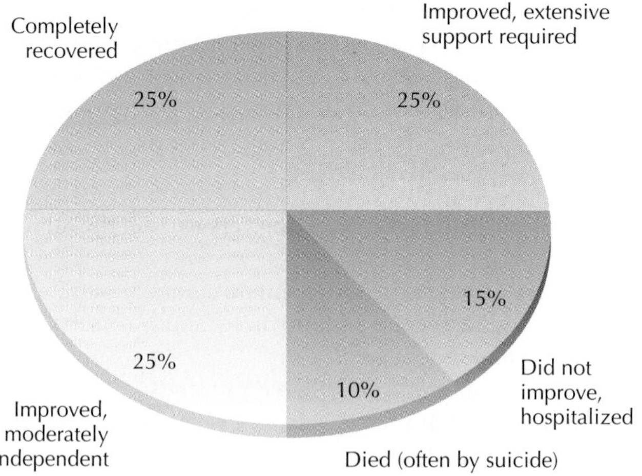

● Figure 16.14 At least one schizophrenic patient in four had completely recovered 10 years after being diagnosed. Three out of four had improved. New treatments for schizophrenia and other major mental disorders may improve these odds. (Source: *FDA Consumer,* 1993.)

BRIDGES

In addition to its role in producing SAD, melatonin regulates normal circadian rhythms.

See Chapter 12, pages 402–403.

BRIDGES

Labels and categories greatly influence our perceptions in many circumstances.

See Chapter 6, pages 211–213.

Let's conclude with a look at a widely misunderstood problem: By the time you finish reading this page, someone in the United States will have attempted suicide. What can be done about suicide? The upcoming Psychology in Action provides some answers.

KNOWLEDGE BUILDER

Mood Disorders

REFLECT

On a piece of paper write "Bipolar Disorders" and "Depressive Disorders." How much of Table 16.7 can you fill in under these headings? Keep reviewing until you can recreate the table (in your own words).

LEARNING CHECK

1. Dysthymic disorder is to depression as cyclothymic disorder is to manic-depression. T or F?
2. Major mood disorders, especially bipolar disorders, often appear to be endogenous. T or F?
3. Learned helplessness is emphasized by ____________ theories of depression.
   a. humanistic c. behaviorist
   b. biological d. psychoanalytic
4. The fact that lithium carbonate is effective in treating some cases of bipolar depression suggests that the causes of bipolar disorders are at least partly ____________.
   a. biological c. environmental
   b. existential d. exogenous
5. Roughly 13 percent of all new mothers experience the maternity blues, which are the first stage of postpartum depression. T or F?
6. Depression that occurs only in the winter is likely to be classified as
   a. SAD c. bipolar
   b. PTSD d. endogenous

CRITICAL THINKING

7. How might relationships contribute to the higher rates of depression experienced by women?

Answers: **1.** T **2.** T **3.** c **4.** a **5.** F **6.** a **7.** Women tend to be more focused on relationships than men are. When listing the stresses in their lives, depressed women consistently report higher rates of relationship problems, such as loss of a friend, spouse, or lover, problems getting along with others, and illnesses suffered by people they care about. Depressed men tend to mention issues such as job loss, legal problems, or work problems (Kendler, Thornton, & Prescott, 2001).

PSYCHOLOGY IN ACTION

Suicide—Lives on the Brink

"Suicide: A permanent solution to a temporary problem."

Suicide ranks as the seventh most common cause of death in North America. Roughly 1 person out of 100 attempts suicide during his or her life. We tend to be very concerned about the high rates of murder in North America. However, for every two people who die by homicide, three will kill themselves. Sooner or later you are likely to be affected by the suicide attempt of someone you know. Check your knowledge of suicide against the following information.

What factors affect suicide rates? Suicide rates vary greatly, but some general patterns do emerge.

Season

Contrary to popular belief, suicide rates are lower than average between Thanksgiving and Christmas (Phillips & Wills, 1987). On the other hand, more suicides take place at New Year's than on any other day. A "Monday effect" also exists, with higher suicide rates occurring on the first day of the week (McCleary et al., 1991).

Sex

Men have the questionable honor of being better at suicide than women. Four times as many men as women *complete* suicide, but women make more attempts. Male suicide attempts are more lethal because men typically use a gun or an equally fatal method

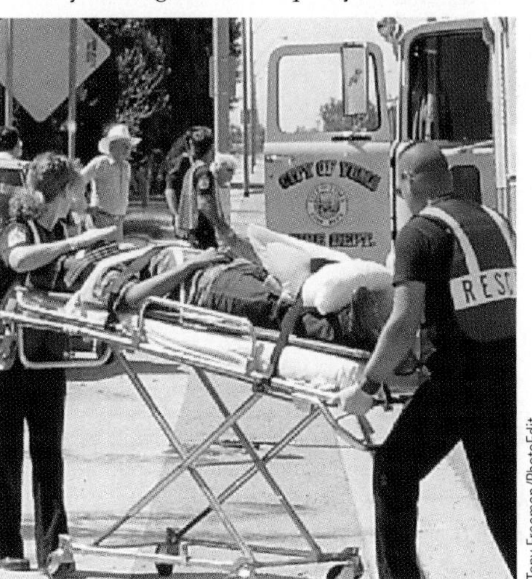

Tony Freeman/PhotoEdit

(Garland & Zigler, 1993). Women most often attempt a drug overdose, so there's a better chance of help arriving before death occurs. Sadly, women are beginning to use more deadly methods and may soon equal men in their likelihood of death by suicide.

Age

Age is also a factor in suicide. Suicide rates gradually rise during adolescence. They then sharply increase during young adulthood (ages 20–24). From then until age 84 the rate continues to gradually rise with advancing age. As a result, more than half of all suicide victims are over 45 years old. White males 65 years and older are particularly at risk.

In recent years there has been a steady increase in the suicide rates for adolescents and young adults (Diekstra & Garnefski, 1995) (● Figure 16.15). Among college students, suicide is the second leading cause of death (Jamison, 2001). School is a factor in some suicides, but only in the sense that suicidal students were not living up to their own extremely high standards. Many were good students. Other important factors in student suicide are chronic health problems (real or imagined) and interpersonal difficulties (some suicides are rejected lovers, but others are simply withdrawn and friendless people).

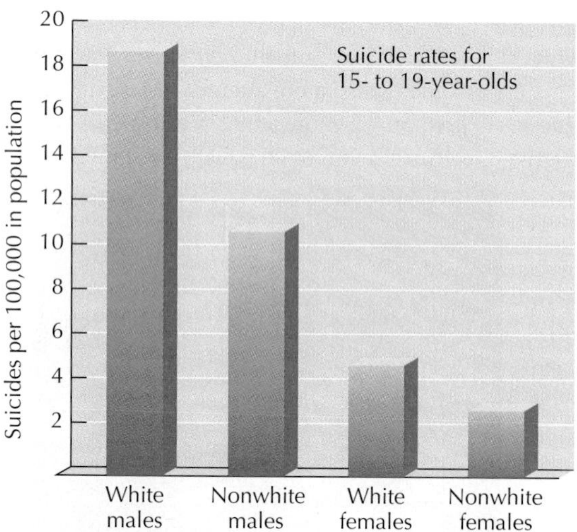

● Figure 16.15 Adolescent suicide rates vary for different racial and ethnic groups. Higher rates occur among whites than among nonwhites. White male adolescents run the highest risk of suicide. Considering gender alone, it is apparent that more male than female adolescents commit suicide. This is the same as the pattern observed for adults.

Income

Some professions, such as medicine and psychiatry, have higher than average suicide rates. Overall, however, suicide is equally a problem for the rich and the poor.

Marital Status

Marriage (when successful) may be the best natural guard against suicidal impulses. The highest suicide rates are found among the divorced, the next-highest rates occur among the widowed, lower rates are recorded for single persons, and married individuals have the lowest rates of all.

Immediate Causes of Suicide

Why do people try to kill themselves? The best explanation for suicide may simply come from a look at the conditions that precede it. The following are all major *risk factors* for suicide (Hall, Platt, & Hall, 1999; Rudd, Joiner, & Rajab, 2001):

- Drug or alcohol abuse
- A prior suicide attempt
- Depression or other mood disorder
- Feelings of hopelessness, worthlessness
- Antisocial, impulsive, or aggressive behavior
- Severe anxiety, panic attacks
- Family history of suicidal behavior
- Shame, humiliation, failure, or rejection
- Availability of a firearm

Suicidal people usually have a history of trouble with family, a lover, or a spouse. Often they have drinking or drug abuse problems, sexual adjustment problems, or job difficulties. Depression is a factor in 70 percent of all suicides (Lecomte & Fornes, 1998). Factors such as these lead to a preoccupation with death as a way to end the person's suffering.

Typically, suicidal people isolate themselves from others, feel worthless, helpless, and misunderstood, and want to die. An extremely negative self-image and severe feelings of *hopelessness* are warnings that the risk of suicide is very high (Beck et al., 1990; Boergers, Spirito, & Donaldson, 1998). A long history of such conditions is not always necessary to produce a desire for suicide. Anyone may temporarily reach a state of depression severe enough to attempt suicide. Most dangerous for the average person are times of divorce, separation, rejection, failure, and bereavement. Each situation can seem intolerable and motivate an intense desire to die, to escape, or to obtain relief (Boergers, Spirito, & Donaldson, 1998). For young people, feelings of anger and hostility add to the danger. When the impulse to harm others is turned inward, the risk of suicide increases dramatically (Jamison, 2001).

Preventing Suicide

Is it true that people who talk about or threaten suicide are rarely the ones who try it? No, this is a major fallacy. Of every ten potential suicides, eight give warning beforehand. A person who threatens suicide should be taken seriously (see ● Figure 16.16). A suicidal person may say nothing more than, "I feel sometimes like I'd be better off dead." Warnings may also come indirectly. If a friend gives you a favorite ring and says, "Here, I won't be needing this anymore," or comments, "I guess I won't get my watch fixed—it doesn't matter anyway," it may be a plea for help. The warning signs in the list that follows—especially if they are observed in combination—can signal an impending suicide attempt (Leenaars, Lester, & Wenckstern, 2005; Slaby, Garfinkel, & Garfinkel, 1994).

- Withdrawal from contact with others
- Sudden swings in mood
- Recent occurrence of life crisis or emotional shock
- Personality change

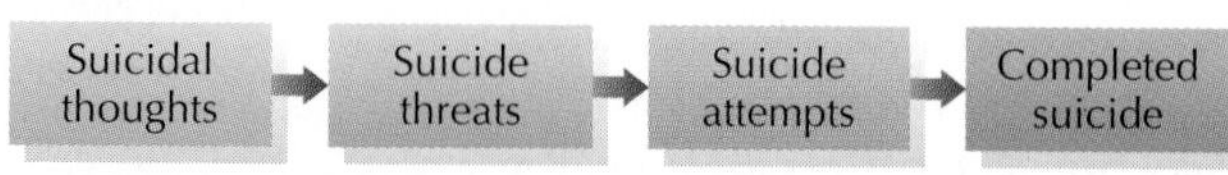

● Figure 16.16 Suicidal behavior usually progresses from suicidal thoughts, to threats, to attempts. A person is unlikely to make an attempt without first making threats. Thus, suicide threats should be taken seriously (Garland & Zigler, 1993).

- Gift giving of prized possessions
- Depression/hopelessness
- Aggression and/or risk taking
- Single-car accident
- Preoccupation with death
- Drug use
- Death imagery in art
- Direct threats to commit suicide

Is it true that suicide can't be prevented, that the person will find a way to do it anyway? No. Suicide attempts usually come when a person is alone, depressed, and unable to view matters objectively. You *should* intervene if someone seems to be threatening suicide.

It is estimated that about two thirds of all suicide attempts are made by people who do not really want to die. Almost a third more are characterized by a "to be or not to be" attitude. These people are *ambivalent* or undecided about dying.

Only 3 to 5 percent of suicide cases involve people who really want to die. Most people, therefore, are relieved when someone comes to their aid. Remember that suicide is almost always a cry for help and that you *can* help. As suicide expert Edwin Shneidman (1987a) puts it, "Suicidal behavior is often a form of communication, a cry for help born out of pain, with clues and messages of suffering and anguish and pleas for response."

How to Help

What is the best thing to do if someone hints they are thinking about suicide? It helps to know some of the common characteristics of suicidal thoughts and feelings (Shneidman, 1987b; Leenaars, Lester, & Wenckstern, 2005):

1. **Escape.** Everyone at times feels like running away from an upsetting situation. Running away from home, quitting school, abandoning a marriage—these are all departures. Suicide, of course, is the ultimate escape. It helps when suicidal persons see that the natural wish for escape doesn't have to be expressed by ending it all.
2. **Unbearable psychological pain.** Emotional pain is what the suicidal person is seeking to escape. A goal of anyone hoping to prevent suicide should be to reduce the pain in any way possible. Ask the person, "Where does it hurt?" Suicide occurs when pain exceeds a person's resources for coping with pain.
3. **Frustrated psychological needs.** Often, suicide can be prevented if a distressed person's frustrated needs can be identified and eased. Is the person deeply frustrated in his or her search for love, achievement, trust, security, or friendship?
4. **Constriction of options.** The suicidal person feels helpless and decides that death is the *only* solution. The person has narrowed all his or her options solely to death. The rescuer's goal, then, is to help broaden the person's perspective. Even when all the choices are unpleasant, suicidal persons can usually be made to see that their *least unpleasant option* is better than death.

Knowing these patterns will give some guidance in talking to a suicidal person. In addition, your most important task may be to establish *rapport* (a harmonious connection) with the person. You should offer support, acceptance, and legitimate caring.

Remember that a suicidal person feels misunderstood. Try to accept and understand the feelings the person is expressing. Acceptance should also extend to the idea of suicide itself. It is completely acceptable to ask, "Are you thinking of suicide?"

Establishing communication with suicidal persons may be enough to carry them through a difficult time. You may also find it helpful to get day-by-day commitments from them to meet for lunch, share a ride, and the like. Let the person know you *expect* her or him to be there. Such commitments, even though small, can be enough to tip the scales when a person is alone and thinking about suicide.

Don't end your efforts too soon. A dangerous time for suicide is when a person suddenly seems to get better after a severe depression. This often means the person has finally decided to end it all. The improvement in mood is deceptive because it comes from an anticipation that suffering is about to end.

Crisis Intervention

Most cities have mental health crisis intervention teams or centers for suicide prevention. Both have staff members trained to talk with suicidal persons over the phone. Give a person who seems to be suicidal the number of one of these services. Urge the person to call you or the other number if she or he becomes frightened or impulsive. Or better yet, help the person make an appointment to get psychological treatment (Garland & Zigler, 1993).

The preceding applies mainly to persons who are having mild suicidal thoughts. If a person actually threatens suicide, you must act more quickly. Ask how the person plans to carry out the suicide. A person who has a *specific, workable plan,* and the means to carry it out, should be asked to accompany you to the emergency ward of a hospital.

If a person seems on the verge of attempting suicide, don't worry about overreacting. Call the police, crisis intervention, or a rescue unit. Needless to say, you should call immediately if a person is in the act of attempting suicide or if a drug has already been taken. The majority of suicide attempts come at temporary low points in a person's life and may never be repeated. Get involved—you may save a life! But remember, if a suicide attempt seems to be imminent, don't hesitate to immediately seek professional assistance.

KNOWLEDGE BUILDER

Suicide and Suicide Prevention

REFLECT

You're working a suicide hotline and you take a call from a very distressed young man. What risk factors will you look for as he tells you about his anguish?

What are the common characteristics of suicidal thoughts and feelings identified by Edwin Shneidman? If a friend of yours were to express any of these thoughts or feelings, how would you respond?

LEARNING CHECK

1. More women than men use guns in their suicide attempts. T or F?
2. Although the overall suicide rate has remained about the same, there has been a decrease in adolescent suicides. T or F?
3. Suicide is equally a problem of the rich and the poor. T or F?
4. The highest suicide rates are found among the divorced. T or F?
5. The majority (two thirds) of suicide attempts fall in the "to be or not to be" category. T or F?
6. The risk that a person may attempt suicide is greatest if the person has
   a. a concrete, workable plan
   b. had a recent life crisis
   c. withdrawn from contact with others
   d. frustrated psychological needs

CRITICAL THINKING

7. If you follow the history of popular music, see if you can answer this question: What two major risk factors contributed to the 1994 suicide of Kurt Cobain, lead singer for the rock group Nirvana?

Answers: 1. F **2.** F **3.** T **4.** T **5.** T **6.** a **7.** Drug or alcohol abuse and availability of a firearm.

Chapter in Review

How is normality defined, and what are the major psychological disorders?

- Psychopathology refers to maladaptive behavior and to the scientific study of mental disorders.
- Definitions of normality usually take into account the following: subjective discomfort, statistical abnormality, social nonconformity, and the cultural or situational context of behavior.
- Two key elements in judgments of disorder are that a person's behavior must be maladaptive and it must involve a loss of control.
- Major mental disorders include psychotic disorders, dementia, substance-related disorders, mood disorders, anxiety disorders, somatoform disorders, dissociative disorders, personality disorders, and sexual or gender identity disorders.
- Insanity is a legal term defining whether a person may be held responsible for his or her actions. Sanity is determined in court on the basis of testimony by expert witnesses.

What is a personality disorder?

- Personality disorders are deeply ingrained maladaptive personality patterns.
- Sociopathy is a common personality disorder. Antisocial persons seem to lack a conscience. They are emotionally unresponsive, manipulative, shallow, and dishonest.

What problems result when a person suffers high levels of anxiety?

- Anxiety disorders, dissociative disorders, and somatoform disorders are characterized by high levels of anxiety, rigid defense mechanisms, and self-defeating behavior patterns.
- The term *nervous breakdown* has no formal meaning. However, "emotional breakdowns" do correspond somewhat to the occurrence of an adjustment disorder.
- Anxiety disorders include generalized anxiety disorder, panic disorder with or without agoraphobia, agoraphobia (without panic), specific phobias, social phobia, obsessive-compulsive disorders, posttraumatic stress disorder, and acute stress disorder.
- Dissociative disorders may take the form of dissociative amnesia, dissociative fugue, or dissociative identity disorder.
- Somatoform disorders center on physical complaints that mimic disease or disability. Four examples of somatoform disorders are hypochondriasis, somatization disorder, somatoform pain disorder, and conversion disorders.

How do psychologists explain anxiety-based disorders?

- The psychodynamic approach emphasizes unconscious conflicts as the cause of disabling anxiety.
- The humanistic approach emphasizes the effects of a faulty self-image.

- The behaviorists emphasize the effects of previous learning, particularly avoidance learning.
- Cognitive theories of anxiety focus on distorted thinking, judgment, and attention.

What are the general characteristics of psychosis?

- Psychosis is a break in contact with reality that is marked by delusions, hallucinations, sensory changes, disturbed emotions, disturbed communication, and personality disintegration.
- An organic psychosis is based on known injuries or diseases of the brain.
- Some common causes of organic psychosis are poisoning, drug abuse, and dementia (especially Alzheimer's disease).

How do delusional disorders differ from other forms of psychosis?

- Delusional disorders are almost totally based on the presence of delusions of grandeur, persecution, infidelity, romantic attraction, or physical disease.
- The most common delusional disorder is paranoid psychosis. Paranoid persons may be violent if they believe they are threatened.

What forms does schizophrenia take? What causes it?

- Schizophrenia involves a split between thought and emotion, delusions, hallucinations, and communication difficulties.
- Disorganized schizophrenia is marked by extreme personality disintegration and silly, bizarre, or obscene behavior. Social impairment is usually extreme.
- Catatonic schizophrenia is associated with stupor, mutism, and odd postures. Sometimes violent and agitated behavior also occurs.
- In paranoid schizophrenia (the most common type), outlandish delusions of grandeur and persecution are coupled with psychotic symptoms and personality breakdown.
- Current explanations of schizophrenia emphasize a combination of early trauma, environmental stress, inherited susceptibility, and abnormalities in the brain.
- Environmental factors that increase the risk of schizophrenia include viral infection or malnutrition during the mother's pregnancy, birth complications, early psychological trauma, and a disturbed family environment.
- Heredity is a major factor in schizophrenia.
- Recent biochemical studies have focused on the brain transmitter dopamine and its receptor sites.
- The dominant explanation of schizophrenia, and other problems as well, is the stress-vulnerability model.

What are mood disorders? What causes depression?

- Mood disorders primarily involve disturbances of mood or emotion, producing manic or depressive states. Severe mood disorders may include psychotic features.
- In a dysthymic disorder, depression is long lasting, though moderate. In a cyclothymic disorder, people suffer from long-lasting, though moderate, swings between depression and elation.
- Bipolar disorders combine mania and depression. In a bipolar I disorder the person swings between severe mania and severe depression. In a bipolar II disorder the person is mostly depressed, but has had periods of mild mania.
- A major depressive disorder involves extreme sadness and despondency but no signs of mania.
- Major mood disorders are partially explained by genetic vulnerability and changes in brain chemistry. Other important factors are loss, anger, learned helplessness, stress, and self-defeating thinking patterns.
- Many women experience a brief period of depression, called the maternity blues, shortly after giving birth. Some women suffer from a more serious and lasting condition called postpartum depression.
- Seasonal affective disorder (SAD), which occurs during the winter months, is another common form of depression. SAD is typically treated with phototherapy.

Why do people commit suicide? Can suicide be prevented?

- Suicide is statistically related to such factors as age, sex, and marital status.
- In individual cases, the potential for suicide is best identified by a desire to escape, unbearable psychological pain, frustrated psychological needs, and a constriction of options.
- Suicide can often be prevented by the efforts of family, friends, and mental health professionals.

Web Resources

Internet addresses frequently change. To find the sites listed here, visit www.thomsonedu.com/psychology/coon for an updated list of Internet addresses and direct links to relevant sites.

***Psychology: Gateways to Mind and Behavior* Website** Online quizzes, flash cards, and other helpful study aids for this text. www.thomsonedu.com/psychology/coon.

A Guide to Depressive and Manic Depressive Illness A complete overview of mood disorders.

Anxiety Disorders Information and links to sites about anxiety disorders.

Depression After Delivery A site devoted to providing information about postpartum depression.

DSM-IV Questions and Answers Answers to common questions about the DSM-IV.

Internet Mental Health Comprehensive page on mental health, with links to many other sites.

National Alliance for the Mentally Ill Home page of the group, with links.

National Institute of Mental Health Links to public information, news and events, and research activities.

Personality Disorders Multiple links to information on personality disorders and their treatment.

Understanding Schizophrenia An extensive look at schizophrenia.

ThomsonNOW™ Go to www.thomsonedu.com to link to ThomsonNow, your online study tool. First take the **Pre-Test** for this chapter to get your **Personalized Study Plan**, which will identify topics you need to review and direct you to online resources. Then take the **Post-Test** to determine what concepts you have mastered and what you still need work on.

InfoTrac College Edition For recent articles related to the Psychology in Action feature, use Key Words search for SUICIDE PREVENTION. Go to www.thomsonedu.com/psychology/coon.

Interactive Learning

***PsychNow!* Version 2.0 CD-ROM** Interact with the material with *PsychNow!*'s animations, video clips, experiments, and interactive assessments. For this chapter, go to *7c. Abnormality and Psychopathology* and *7d. Nonpsychotic, Psychotic, and Affective Disorders* for more information on psychological disorders.

chapter 17

Therapies

Zigy Kalnuv/Getty Images

THEME:

Psychotherapies are based on a common core of therapeutic principles. Medical therapies treat the physical causes of psychological disorders. In many cases, these approaches are complementary.

Key Questions

How do psychotherapies differ? How did psychotherapy originate?

Is Freudian psychoanalysis still used?

What are the major humanistic therapies?

What is behavior therapy?

How is behavior therapy used to treat phobias, fears, and anxieties?

What role does reinforcement play in behavior therapy?

Can therapy change thoughts and emotions?

Can psychotherapy be done with groups of people?

What do various therapies have in common?

How do psychiatrists treat psychological disorders?

How are behavioral principles applied to everyday problems?

How could a person find professional help?

Preview

Cold Terror on a Warm Afternoon

The warm Arizona sun was shining brightly. Outside, an assortment of small birds sang sweetly. Susan's psychology professor could hear them between her frightened sobs.

As psychologists, we meet many students with personal problems. Still, Susan's teacher was surprised to see her at his office door. Her excellent work in class and her healthy, casual appearance left him unprepared for her first words. "I feel like I'm losing my mind," she said. "Can I talk to you?"

In the next hour, Susan described her own personal hell. Her calm appearance hid a world of crippling fear, anxiety, and depression. At work, she was deathly afraid of talking to coworkers and customers. Her social phobia led to frequent absenteeism and embarrassing behavior. At each job she held, it was only a matter of time until she got fired.

At school Susan felt "different" and was sure that other students could tell she was "weird." Several disastrous romances had left her terrified of men. Lately she had been so depressed that she thought of suicide. Often, she became terrified for no apparent reason. Each time, her heart pounded wildly and she felt that she was about to completely lose control.

Susan's request for help was an important turning point. Emotional conflicts had made her existence a nightmare. At a time when she was becoming her own worst enemy, Susan realized she needed help from another person. In Susan's case, that person was a talented psychologist to whom her teacher referred her. With psychotherapy, the psychologist was able to help Susan come to grips with her emotions and regain her balance.

This chapter discusses methods used to alleviate problems like Susan's. First, we will describe therapies that emphasize the value of gaining *insight* into personal problems. Then, we will focus on *behavior therapies* and *cognitive therapies,* which directly change troublesome actions and thoughts. Later, we will conclude with *medical therapies,* which are based on psychiatric drugs and other physical treatments.

Psychotherapy—Getting Better by the Hour

Psychotherapy refers to any psychological technique that can bring about positive changes in personality, behavior, or personal adjustment. In most cases, psychotherapy is based on a dialogue between therapists and their clients. Some therapists also use learning principles to directly alter troublesome behaviors.

Therapists have many approaches to choose from: psychoanalysis, desensitization, Gestalt therapy, client-centered therapy, cognitive therapy, and behavior therapy—to name but a few. As we will see, each therapy emphasizes different concepts and methods. For this reason, the best approach for a particular person or problem may vary.

Dimensions of Therapy

The terms listed here describe basic aspects of various therapies. Notice that more than one term may apply to a particular therapy. For example, it is possible to have a directive, action-oriented group therapy or a nondirective, individual, insight-oriented therapy.

- **Individual therapy:** A therapy involving only one client and one therapist.
- **Group therapy:** A therapy session in which several clients participate at the same time.
- **Insight therapy:** Any psychotherapy whose goal is to lead clients to a deeper understanding of their thoughts, emotions, and behavior.
- **Action therapy:** Any therapy designed to bring about direct changes in troublesome thoughts, habits, feelings, or behavior, without seeking insight into their origins or meanings.
- **Directive therapy:** Any approach in which the therapist provides strong guidance.
- **Nondirective therapy:** A style of therapy in which clients assume responsibility for solving their own problems; the therapist assists, but does not guide or give advice.
- **Time-limited therapy:** Any therapy begun with the expectation that it will last only a limited number of sessions.

- **Supportive therapy:** An approach in which the therapist's goal is to offer support, rather than to promote personal change. A person trying to get through an emotional crisis or one who wants to solve day-to-day problems may benefit from supportive therapy.
- **Positive therapy:** Techniques designed to enhance personal strengths, rather than "fix" weaknesses.

Myths

Psychotherapy has been depicted as a complete personal transformation—a sort of "major overhaul" of the psyche. But therapy is *not* equally effective for all problems. Chances of improvement are fairly good for phobias, low self-esteem, some sexual problems, and marital conflicts. More complex problems can be difficult to solve. For many people, the major benefit of therapy is that it provides comfort, support, and a way to make constructive changes (Hellerstein et al., 1998).

In short, it is often unrealistic to expect psychotherapy to undo a person's entire past history. Yet even when problems are severe, therapy may help a person gain a new perspective or learn behaviors to better cope with life. Psychotherapy can be hard work for both clients and therapists. But when it succeeds, few activities are more worthwhile. ■ Table 17.1 lists some of the elements of positive mental health that therapists seek to restore or promote.

It's also a mistake to think that psychotherapy is only used to solve problems or end a crisis. Even if a person is already doing well, therapy can be a way to promote personal growth (Buck, 1990). Therapists in the positive psychology movement are developing ways to help people make use of their personal strengths. Rather than trying to fix what is "wrong" with a person, they seek to nurture positive traits and actively solve problems (Compton, 2005).

TABLE 17.1

Elements of Positive Mental Health

Elements of Positive Mental Health
• Personal autonomy and independence
• A sense of identity
• Feelings of personal worth
• Skilled interpersonal communication
• Sensitivity, nurturance, and trust
• Genuine and honest with self and others
• Self-control and personal responsibility
• Committed and loving personal relationships
• Capacity to forgive others and oneself
• Personal values and a purpose in life
• Self-awareness and motivation for personal growth
• Adaptive coping strategies for managing stresses and crises
• Fulfillment and satisfaction in work
• Good habits of physical health

Adapted from Bergin, 1991.

Origins of Therapy—Bored Skulls and Hysteria on the Couch

Early treatments for mental problems give good reasons to appreciate modern therapies. Archaeological findings dating to the Stone Age suggest that most primitive approaches were marked by fear and superstitious belief in demons, witchcraft, and magic. One of the more dramatic "cures" practiced by primitive "therapists" was a process called *trepanning* (treh-PAN-ing; also sometimes spelled *trephining*). In modern usage, trepanning is any surgical procedure in which a hole is bored in the skull. In the hands of primitive therapists it meant boring, chipping, or bashing holes into a patient's head. Presumably this was done to relieve pressure or release evil spirits (● Figure 17.1). Actually, many "patients" didn't survive the "treatment," which suggests that trepanning may have simply been an excuse to kill people who were unusual.

During the Middle Ages, treatments for mental illness in Europe focused on **demonology**, the study of demons and persons plagued by spirits. Medieval "therapists" commonly blamed abnormal behavior on supernatural forces, such as possession by the devil, or on curses from witches and wizards. As a cure, they

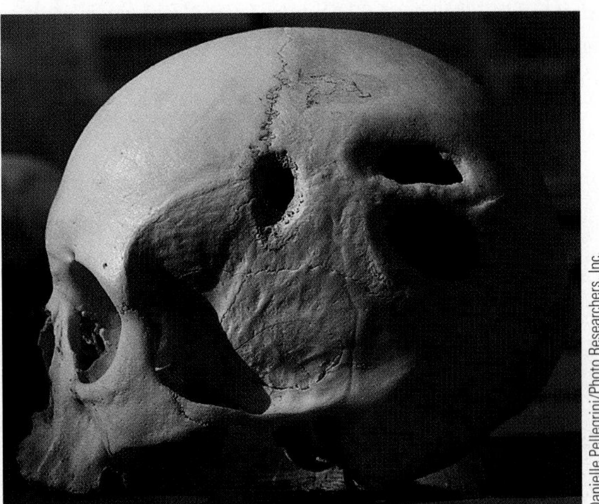

Danielle Pellegrini/Photo Researchers, Inc.

● **Figure 17.1** Primitive "treatment" for mental disorders sometimes took the form of boring a hole in the skull. This example shows signs of healing, which means the patient survived the treatment. Many didn't.

Psychotherapy Any psychological technique used to facilitate positive changes in a person's personality, behavior, or adjustment.

Demonology In medieval Europe, the study of demons and the treatment of persons "possessed" by demons.

used exorcism to "cast out evil spirits." For the fortunate, exorcism was a religious ritual. More often, physical torture was used to make the body an inhospitable place for the devil to reside. A modern analysis of "demonic possession" suggests that some victims were suffering from dissociative disorders (van der Hart, Lierens, & Goodwin, 1996).

One reason for the rise of demonology may lie in *ergotism* (AIR-got-ism), a psychotic-like condition caused by ergot poisoning. In the Middle Ages, rye (grain) fields were often infested with ergot fungus. Ergot, we now know, is a natural source of LSD and other mind-altering chemicals. Eating tainted bread could have caused symptoms that were easily mistaken for bewitchment or madness. Pinching sensations, muscle twitches, facial spasms, delirium, and hallucinations are all signs of ergot poisoning (Matossian, 1982). Thus, many people "treated" by demonologists may have been doubly victimized.

It wasn't until 1793 that the emotionally disturbed were regarded as "mentally ill" and given compassionate treatment. That was the year a French doctor named Philippe Pinel changed the Bicêtre Asylum in Paris from a squalid "madhouse" into a mental hospital by unchaining the inmates. Although it has been over 200 years since Pinel began humane treatment, the process of improving care continues today.

When was psychotherapy developed? The first true psychotherapy was created by Sigmund Freud about 100 years ago (Jacobs, 2003). As a physician in Vienna, Freud was intrigued by cases of *hysteria*. People suffering from hysteria have physical symptoms (such as paralysis or numbness) for which no physical causes can be found. (Such problems are now called somatoform disorders, as discussed in Chapter 16.) Slowly, Freud became convinced that hysteria was related to deeply hidden unconscious conflicts. Based on this insight, Freud developed a therapy called *psychoanalysis*. Because it is the "granddaddy" of more modern therapies, let us examine psychoanalysis in some detail.

Mary Evans Picture Library/Photo Researchers, Inc.

Bettmann/Corbis

(left) Many early asylums were no more than prisons with inmates held in chains. *(right)* One late-nineteenth-century "treatment" was based on swinging the patient in a harness—presumably to calm the patient's nerves.

Psychoanalysis—Expedition into the Unconscious

Isn't psychoanalysis the therapy where the patient lies on a couch? Freud's patients usually reclined on a couch during therapy, while Freud sat out of sight taking notes and offering interpretations. This procedure was supposed to encourage a free flow of thoughts and images from the unconscious. However, it is the least important element of psychoanalysis and many modern analysts have abandoned it.

How did Freud treat emotional problems? Freud's theory stressed that "neurosis" and "hysteria" are caused by repressed memories, motives, and conflicts—particularly those stemming from instinctual drives for sex and aggression. Although they are hidden, these forces remain active in the personality and they cause some people to develop rigid ego-defenses and compulsive, self-defeating behavior. Thus, the main goal of **psychoanalysis** is to reduce internal conflicts that lead to emotional suffering (Marcus, 2002).

Freud relied on four basic techniques to uncover the unconscious roots of neurosis (Freud, 1949). These are *free association, dream analysis, analysis of resistance,* and *analysis of transference.*

Free Association

Saying whatever comes to mind is the basis for **free association.** Patients must speak without worrying whether ideas are painful, embarrassing, or illogical. Thoughts are simply allowed to move freely from one idea to the next, without self-censorship. The purpose of free association is to lower defenses so that unconscious thoughts and feelings can emerge (Hoffer & Youngren, 2004).

Dream Analysis

Freud believed that dreams provide a "royal road to the unconscious" because they freely express forbidden desires and unconscious feelings. Such feelings are found in the **latent content**

Archive/Photo Researchers, Inc.

Pioneering psychotherapist Sigmund Freud in his office.

(hidden, symbolic meaning) of dreams. Normally, we only remember a dream's **manifest content** (obvious, visible meaning), which tends to disguise information from the unconscious.

Freud was especially interested in unconscious messages revealed by **dream symbols** (images that have personal or emotional meanings). Let's say a young man reports a dream in which he pulls a pistol from his waistband and aims at a target while his wife watches. The pistol repeatedly fails to discharge, and the man's wife laughs at him. Freud might have seen this as an indication of repressed feelings of sexual impotence, with the gun serving as a disguised image of the penis.

Analysis of Resistance

When free associating or describing dreams, patients may *resist* talking about or thinking about certain topics. Such **resistances** (blockages in the flow of ideas) reveal particularly important unconscious conflicts. As analysts become aware of resistances, they bring them to the patient's awareness so the patient can deal with them realistically. Rather than being roadblocks in therapy, resistances can be challenges and guides (May, 1996).

Analysis of Transference

Transference is the tendency to "transfer" feelings to a therapist that match those the patient had for important persons in his or her past. At times, the patient may act as if the analyst is a rejecting father, an unloving or overprotective mother, or a former lover, for example. As the patient re-experiences repressed emotions, the therapist can help the patient recognize and understand them. Troubled persons often provoke anger, rejection, boredom, criticism, and other negative reactions from others. Effective therapists learn to avoid reacting as others do and playing the patient's habitual "games." This, too, contributes to therapeutic change (Marcus, 2002).

Psychoanalysis Today

What is the status of psychoanalysis today? Traditional psychoanalysis called for three to five therapy sessions a week, often for many years. Today, most patients are only seen once or twice per week, but treatment may still go on for years (Friedman et al., 1998). Because of the huge amounts of time and money this requires, psychoanalysts have become relatively rare. Nevertheless, psychoanalysis made a major contribution to modern therapies by highlighting the importance of unconscious conflicts (Rangell, 2002).

Many therapists have switched to doing **brief psychodynamic therapy**, which uses direct questioning to reveal unconscious conflicts (Book & Luborsky, 1998). Modern therapists also actively provoke emotional reactions that will lower defenses and provide insights (Davanloo, 1995). Interestingly, brief therapy seems to accelerate recovery. Patients seem to realize that they need to get to the heart of their problems quickly (Messer & Kaplan, 2004).

The development of newer, more streamlined dynamic therapies is in part due to questions about whether traditional psychoanalysis "works." One critic, Hans J. Eysenck (1994), suggested that psychoanalysis simply takes so long that patients experience a *spontaneous remission* of symptoms (improvement due to the mere passage of time). How could we tell if a particular therapy, or the passage of time is responsible for a person's improvement? Typically, some patients are randomly assigned for treatment, whereas others are placed on a waiting list. If members of this *waiting-list control group,* who receive no treatment, improve at the same rate as those in therapy, the therapy may be of little value.

How seriously should the possibility of spontaneous remission be taken? It's true that problems ranging from hyperactivity to anxiety improve with the passage of time. However, researchers have confirmed psychoanalysis does, in fact, produce improvement in a majority of patients (Doidge, 1997).

The real value of Eysenck's critique is that it encouraged psychologists to try new ideas and techniques. Researchers began to ask, "When psychoanalysis works, why does it work? What parts of it are essential and which are unnecessary?" Modern therapists have given surprisingly varied answers to these questions. Upcoming sections will acquaint you with some of the therapies currently in use.

BRIDGES

Some theorists dispute the psychodynamic claim that dreams have symbolic meaning.

See Chapter 7, page 236.

Psychoanalysis A Freudian therapy that emphasizes the use of free association, dream interpretation, resistances, and transference to uncover unconscious conflicts.

Free association In psychoanalysis, the technique of having a client say anything that comes to mind, regardless of how embarrassing or unimportant it may seem.

Latent dream content The hidden or symbolic meaning of a dream, as revealed by dream interpretation and analysis.

Manifest dream content The surface, "visible" content of a dream; dream images as they are remembered by the dreamer.

Dream symbols Images in dreams whose personal or emotional meanings differ from their literal meanings.

Resistance A blockage in the flow of free association; topics the client resists thinking or talking about.

Transference The tendency of patients to transfer feelings to a therapist that correspond to those the patient had for important persons in his or her past.

Brief psychodynamic therapy A modern therapy based on psychoanalytic theory but designed to produce insights more quickly.

KNOWLEDGE BUILDER

Psychotherapy and Psychoanalysis

REFLECT

How has your understanding of psychotherapy changed? How many types of therapy can you name?

Make a list describing what you think it means to be mentally healthy. How well does your list match the items in Table 17.1?

The use of trepanning, demonology, and exorcism all implied that the mentally ill are "cursed." To what extent are the mentally ill rejected and stigmatized today?

Try to free associate (aloud) for 10 minutes. How difficult was it? Did anything interesting surface?

Can you explain, in your own words, the role of dream analysis, resistances, and transference in psychoanalysis?

LEARNING CHECK

Match:

_____ **1.** Directive therapies	**A.** Change behavior
_____ **2.** Action therapies	**B.** Place responsibility on the client
_____ **3.** Insight therapies	**C.** The client is guided strongly
_____ **4.** Nondirective therapies	**D.** Seek understanding

5. An approach that is incompatible with insight therapy is
a. individual therapy c. nondirective therapy
b. action therapy d. group therapy

6. A scientific explanation of Medieval "possessions" by "demons" is related to the effects of
a. ergot poisoning c. exorcism
b. trepanning d. unconscious transference

7. Pinel is famous for his use of exorcism. T or F?

8. In psychoanalysis, an emotional attachment to the therapist is called
a. free association c. resistance
b. manifest association d. transference

CRITICAL THINKING

9. Waiting-list control groups help separate the effects of therapy from improvement related to the mere passage of time. What other type of control group might be needed to learn if therapy is truly beneficial?

Answers: 1. C **2.** A **3.** D **4.** B **5.** b **6.** a **7.** F **8.** d **9.** Placebo therapy is sometimes used to assess the benefits of real therapy. Placebo therapy superficially resembles the real thing, but lacks key elements that are thought to be therapeutic.

Humanistic Therapies—Restoring Human Potential

When most people picture clinical psychologists at work, they probably imagine them doing insight therapy. As stated earlier, insight therapists help clients gain a deeper understanding of their thoughts, emotions, and behavior. Let's sample a variety of insight-oriented approaches, including therapies done at a distance, by telephone or over the Internet.

Better self-knowledge was the goal of traditional psychoanalysis. However, Freud claimed that his patients could expect only to change their "hysterical misery into common unhappiness"! Humanistic therapies are more optimistic. Most assume that it is possible for people to use their potentials fully and live rich, rewarding lives. Psychotherapy is seen as a way to give mental health a chance to emerge.

Client-Centered Therapy

What is client-centered therapy? How is it different from psychoanalysis? Psychoanalysts delve into the unconscious. Psychologist Carl Rogers (1902–1987) found it more beneficial to explore *conscious* thoughts and feelings. The psychoanalyst tends to take a position of authority, stating what dreams, thoughts, or memories "mean." In contrast, Rogers believed that what is right or valuable for the therapist may be wrong for the client. (Rogers preferred the term *client* to *patient* because "patient" implies a person is "sick" and needs to be "cured.") Consequently, the client determines what will be discussed during each session. Thus, **client-centered therapy** (also called **person-centered therapy**) is nondirective and based on insights from conscious thoughts and feelings (Schneider, 2002).

If the client runs things, what does the therapist do? The therapist's job is to create a safe "atmosphere of growth." The therapist provides opportunities for change, but the client must actively seek to solve his or her problems. The therapist cannot "fix" the client (Bohart & Tallman, 1996).

Health-Promoting Conditions

Rogers believed that effective therapists maintain four basic conditions. First, the therapist offers the client **unconditional positive regard** (unshakable personal acceptance). The therapist refuses to react with shock, dismay, or disapproval to anything the client says or feels. Total acceptance by the therapist is the first step to self-acceptance by the client.

Second, the therapist attempts to achieve genuine **empathy** by trying to see the world through the client's eyes and feeling some part of what the client is feeling.

As a third essential condition, the therapist strives to be **authentic** (genuine and honest). The therapist must not hide behind a professional role. Rogers believed that phony fronts destroy the growth atmosphere sought in client-centered therapy.

Fourth, the therapist does not make interpretations, propose solutions, or offer advice. Instead, the therapist **reflects** (rephrases, summarizes, or repeats) the cli-

Courtesy of Dr. Natalie Rogers

Psychotherapist Carl Rogers, who originated client-centered therapy.

ent's thoughts and feelings. This allows the therapist to act as a psychological "mirror" so clients can see themselves more clearly. Rogers theorized that a person armed with a realistic self-image and greater self-acceptance will gradually discover solutions to life's problems.

Personal Growth

Like other humanistic psychologists, Carl Rogers (1980) believed deeply that humans have a natural urge to seek health and self-growth. Rogers's belief is movingly expressed by the following words:

> I remember that in my boyhood the bin in which we stored our winter's supply of potatoes was in the basement, several feet below a small window. The conditions were unfavorable, but pale white sprouts . . . would grow two or three feet in length as they reached toward the light of the distant window. The sprouts were, in their bizarre, futile growth, a sort of desperate expression of the directional tendency I have been describing. . . . In dealing with clients whose lives have been terribly warped, in working with men and women on the back wards of state hospitals, I often think of those potato sprouts. . . . The clue to understanding their behavior is that they are striving, in the only ways that they perceive as available to them, to move toward growth, toward becoming. To healthy persons, the results may seem bizarre and futile but they are life's desperate attempt to become itself. This potent constructive tendency is an underlying basis of the person-centered approach.

Existential Therapy

According to the existentialists, "being in the world" (existence) creates deep conflicts. Each of us must deal with the realities of death. We must face the fact that we create our private world by making choices. We must overcome isolation on a vast and indifferent planet. Most of all, we must confront feelings of meaninglessness.

What do these concerns have to do with psychotherapy? **Existential therapy** focuses on the problems of existence, such as meaning, choice, and responsibility. Like client-centered therapy, it promotes self-knowledge and self-actualization. However, there are important differences. Client-centered therapy seeks to uncover a "true self" hidden behind a screen of defenses. In contrast, existential therapy emphasizes free will, the human ability to make choices. Accordingly, existential therapists believe you can *choose to become* the person you want to be.

Existential therapists try to give clients the *courage* to make rewarding and socially constructive choices. Typically, therapy focuses on *death, freedom, isolation,* and *meaninglessness,* the "ultimate concerns" of existence (Yalom, 1980). These universal human challenges include an awareness of one's mortality, the responsibility that comes with freedom to choose, being alone in your own private world, and the need to create meaning in your life.

One example of existential therapy is Victor Frankl's **logotherapy**, which emphasizes the need to find and maintain meaning in life. Frankl (1904–1997) based his approach on experiences he had as a prisoner in a Nazi concentration camp. In the camp, Frankl saw countless prisoners break down as they were stripped of all hope and human dignity (Frankl, 1955). Those who survived with their sanity did so because they managed to hang on to a sense of meaning *(logos)*. Even in less dire circumstances, a sense of purpose in life adds greatly to psychological well-being (Lantz, 1998).

What does the existential therapist do? The therapist helps clients discover self-imposed limitations in personal identity. To be successful, the client must fully accept the challenge of changing his or her life (Bugental & Sterling, 1995). A key aspect of existential therapy is *confrontation,* in which clients are challenged to examine their values and choices and to take responsibility for the quality of their existence (Gerwood, 1998).

An important part of confrontation is the unique, intense, here-and-now *encounter* between two human beings. When existential therapy is successful, it brings about a renewed sense of purpose and a reappraisal of what's important in life. Some clients even experience an emotional rebirth, as if they had survived a close brush with death. As Marcel Proust wrote, "The real voyage of discovery consists not in seeing new landscapes but in having new eyes."

Gestalt Therapy

Gestalt therapy is based on the idea that perception, or *awareness,* is disjointed and incomplete in maladjusted persons. The German word *Gestalt* means "whole," or "complete." **Gestalt therapy** helps people rebuild thinking, feeling, and acting into connected wholes. This is achieved by expanding personal awareness; by accepting responsibility for one's thoughts, feelings, and actions; and by filling in gaps in experience (Yontef, 1995).

What do you mean by gaps in experience? Gestalt therapists believe that we often shy away from expressing or "owning" upsetting feel-

---

Client-centered (or person-centered) therapy A nondirective therapy based on insights gained from conscious thoughts and feelings; emphasizes accepting one's true self.

Unconditional positive regard An unqualified, unshakable acceptance of another person.

Empathy A capacity for taking another's point of view; the ability to feel what another is feeling.

Authenticity In Carl Rogers's terms, the ability of a therapist to be genuine and honest about his or her own feelings.

Reflection In client-centered therapy, the process of rephrasing or repeating thoughts and feelings expressed by clients so they can become aware of what they are saying.

Existential therapy An insight therapy that focuses on the elemental problems of existence, such as death, meaning, choice, and responsibility; emphasizes making courageous life choices.

Logotherapy A form of existential therapy that emphasizes the need to find and maintain meaning in one's life.

Gestalt therapy An approach that focuses on immediate experience and awareness to help clients rebuild thinking, feeling, and acting into connected wholes; emphasizes the integration of fragmented experiences.

ings. This creates a gap in self-awareness that may become a barrier to personal growth. For example, a person who feels anger after the death of a parent might go for years without fully expressing it. This and similar threatening gaps may impair emotional health.

The Gestalt approach is more directive than client-centered or existential therapy and it emphasizes immediate experience. Working either one-to-one or in a group setting, the Gestalt therapist encourages clients to become more aware of their moment-to-moment thoughts, perceptions, and emotions (Cole, 1998). Rather than discussing *why* clients feel guilt, anger, fear, or boredom, they are encouraged to have these feelings in the "here and now" and become fully aware of them. The therapist promotes awareness by drawing attention to a client's posture, voice, eye movements, and hand gestures. Clients may also be asked to exaggerate vague feelings until they become clear. Gestalt therapists believe that expressing such feelings allows people to "take care of unfinished business" and break through emotional impasses.

Gestalt therapy is often associated with the work of Frederick (Fritz) Perls (1969). In all his writings, Perls's basic message comes through clearly: Emotional health comes from knowing what you *want* to do, not dwelling on what you *should* do, *ought* to do, or *should want* to do (Rosenberg & Lynch, 2002). Another way of stating this idea is that emotional health comes from taking full responsibility for one's feelings and actions. For example, it means changing "I can't" to "I won't," or "I must" to "I choose to."

How does Gestalt therapy help people discover their real wants? Above all else, Gestalt therapy emphasizes *present* experience. Clients are urged to stop intellectualizing and talking *about* feelings. Instead, they learn to live now; live here; stop imagining; experience the real; stop unnecessary thinking; taste and see; express rather than explain, justify, or judge; give in to unpleasantness and pain just as to pleasure; and surrender to being as you are (Naranjo, 1970). Gestalt therapists believe that, paradoxically, the best way to change is to become who you really are (Yontef, 1995).

Because of their emphasis on verbal interaction, humanistic therapies may be conducted at a distance, by telephone or e-mail. Let's investigate this possibility.

Therapy at a Distance—Psych Jockeys and Cybertherapy

How valid are psychological services offered over the phone and on the Internet? For better or worse, psychotherapy and counseling are rapidly becoming high-tech. Today, psychological services are available through radio, telephone, videoconferencing, e-mail, and Internet chat rooms (Maheu et al., 2004). What are the advantages and disadvantages of getting help "online"? What are the risks and possible benefits?

Media Psychologists

By now, you have probably heard a phone-in radio psychologist. On a typical program, callers describe problems arising from child abuse, loneliness, love affairs, phobias, sexual adjustment, or depression. The radio psychologist then offers reassurance, advice, or suggestions for getting help. Talk-radio psychology and similar TV programs may seem harmless, but they raise some important questions. For instance, is it reasonable to give advice without knowing anything about a person's background? Could the advice do harm? What good can a psychologist do in 3 minutes or even an hour?

In defense of themselves, media psychologists point out that listeners and viewers may learn solutions to their problems by hearing others talk. Many also stress that their work is educational, not therapeutic. Nevertheless, the question arises: When does advice become therapy? The American Psychological Association urges media psychologists to discuss problems only of a general nature, instead of actually counseling anyone. For example, if a caller complains about insomnia, the radio psychologist should talk about insomnia in general, not probe the caller's personal life.

By giving information, advice, and social support, media psychologists probably do help some people. Even so, a good guide for anyone tempted to call a radio psychologist or get advice from a TV psychologist might be "let the consumer beware."

Telephone Therapists

The same caution applies to telephone therapists. These "counselors" can be reached through 900-number services for $3 to $4 per minute. To date, there is no evidence that commercial telephone counseling is effective. Successful face-to-face therapy is based on a continuing *relationship* between two people. Telephone therapy is also seriously limited by a lack of visual cues, such as facial expressions and body language (Haas, Benedict, & Kobos, 1996).

It's important to note that legitimate therapists may use the phone to calm, console, or advise clients between therapy sessions. Others are experimenting with actually doing therapy by telephone. For example, after the attack on the World Trade Center towers, many rescue personnel needed counseling. To fill the need,

Getty Images

Media psychologists have been urged to educate without actually doing therapy on the air. Some overstep this boundary, however. Do you think popular TV psychologist Dr. Phil sometimes goes too far?

a phone network was created to link emergency workers with psychologists all over the country (Murray, 2001a; Shore, 2003).

Under the right circumstances, telephone therapy can be as successful as face-to-face therapy (Day & Schneider, 2002). For example, in one recent effort, telephone counseling helped improve success rates for smokers who wanted to quit (Rabius et al., 2004). Another study showed that depressed people benefited from telephone therapy (Simon et al., 2004). Nevertheless, it's worth saying again that the value of commercial telephone therapists is questionable. Consumers might well ask themselves, "How much confidence would I place in a physician who would make a diagnosis over the phone?" Many telephone "therapists" actually may be just untrained operators (Newman, 1994).

Cybertherapy

You can find almost anything on the Internet. Recently, "cybertherapy," psychological advice, support groups, and self-help magazines have been added to the list. Some services, such as support groups, are free. Online counseling or advice, in contrast, is typically offered for a fee. Some online therapists will "discuss" problems with you through e-mail messages. Others merely answer questions or give advice concerning specific problems.

Online counseling and advice services do have some advantages. For one thing, clients can remain anonymous. Thus, a person who might hesitate to see a psychologist can seek help privately, online. Likewise, the Internet can link people who live in rural areas with psychologists living in large cities. And, compared with traditional office visits, cybertherapy is less expensive.

As with radio talk shows and telephone counselors, many objections can be raised about online psychological services. Clearly, brief e-mail messages are no way to make a diagnosis. And forget about facial expressions or body language—not even tone of voice reaches the cybertherapist. Typing emoticons like little smiley faces or frowns is a poor substitute for real human interaction. Another problem is that e-mail counseling may not be completely confidential. In some cases, highly personal messages could be intercepted and misused. Of special concern is the fact that "cybershrinks" may or may not be trained professionals (Bloom, 1998). And even if they are, questions exist about whether a psychologist licensed in one state can legally do therapy in another state, via the Internet. Despite such objections, psychologists are actively exploring the possibility of providing therapy over the Internet, at least for certain types of problems (Lange et al., 2001).

Telehealth

Many of the drawbacks we have discussed can be solved with videoconferencing. In this approach, therapists provide services to people who live too far away to be seen in person. A two-way audio–video link allows the client and therapist to see one another on TV screens and to talk via speakerphones. Doing therapy this way still lacks the close personal contact of face-to-face interaction. However, it does remove many of the objections to doing therapy at a distance. It's very likely that "telehealth" services will become a major source of mental health care in coming years (Jerome et al., 2000).

Implications

As you can see, psychological services that rely on electronic communication may serve some useful purposes. However, the value of therapy offered by commercial telephone "counselors" and Internet "therapists" remains questionable. The very best advice given by media psychologists, telephone counselors, or cybertherapists may be, "You should consider discussing this problem with a psychologist or counselor in your own community."

KNOWLEDGE BUILDER

Insight Therapies

REFLECT

Here's a mnemonic for the elements of client-centered therapy: Picture a therapist saying "I ear u" to a client. The E stands for empathy, A for authenticity, R for reflection, and U for unconditional positive regard.

What would an existential therapist say about the choices you have made so far in your life? Should you be choosing more "courageously"?

You are going to play the role of a therapist for a classroom demonstration. How would you act if you were a client-centered therapist? An existential therapist? A Gestalt therapist?

A neighbor of yours is thinking about getting counseling on the Internet. What would you tell her about the pros and cons of distance therapy?

LEARNING CHECK

Match:

_____ **1.** Client-centered therapy	**A.** Electronic advice
_____ **2.** Gestalt therapy	**B.** Unconditional positive regard
_____ **3.** Existential therapy	**C.** Gaps in awareness
_____ **4.** Cybertherapy	**D.** Choice and becoming

5. The Gestalt therapist tries to *reflect* a client's thoughts and feelings. T or F?

6. Filling in gaps in immediate self-awareness is one of the principal goals of

a. supportive therapy c. person-centered therapy
b. existential therapy d. Gestalt therapy

7. Confrontation and encounter are concepts of existential therapy. T or F?

8. To date, the most acceptable type of "distance therapy" is

a. media psychology
b. commercial telephone counseling
c. Internet-based cybertherapy
d. telehealth

CRITICAL THINKING

9. How might using the term *patient* affect the relationship between an individual and a therapist?

Answers: 1. B **2.** C **3.** D **4.** A **5.** F **6.** d **7.** T **8.** d **9.** The terms *doctor* and *patient* imply a large gap in status and authority between the individual and his or her therapist. Client-centered therapy attempts to narrow this gap by making the person the final authority concerning solutions to his or her problems. Also, the word *patient* implies that a person is "sick" and needs to be "cured." Many regard this as an inappropriate way to think about human problems.

Behavior Therapy—Healing by Learning

Five times a day, for several days, Brooks Workman stopped what she was doing and vividly imagined opening a soft-drink can. She then pictured herself bringing the can to her mouth and placing her lips on it. Just as she was about to drink, hordes of roaches poured out of the can and scurried into her mouth—writhing, twitching, and wiggling their feelers (Williams & Long, 1991).

Why would anyone imagine such a thing? Brooks Workman's behavior is not as strange as it may seem. Her goal was self-control: Brooks was drinking too many soft drinks and she wanted to cut down. The method she chose (called *covert sensitization*) is a form of behavior therapy (Cautela & Kearney, 1986). **Behavior therapy** is the use of learning principles to make constructive changes in behavior. Behavioral approaches include behavior modification, aversion therapy, desensitization, token economies, and other techniques (Forsyth & Savsevitz, 2002).

Behavior therapists believe that deep insight into one's problems is often unnecessary for improvement. Instead, they try to directly alter troublesome thoughts and actions. Brooks Workman didn't need to probe into her past or her emotions and conflicts; she simply wanted to break her habit of drinking too many soft drinks. Even when more serious problems are at stake, techniques like the one she used are valuable.

In general, how does behavior therapy work? Behavior therapists assume that people have *learned* to be the way they are. If they have learned responses that cause problems, then they can change them by *relearning* more appropriate behaviors. Broadly speaking, **behavior modification** refers to any use of classical or operant conditioning to directly alter human behavior (Miltenberger, 2004; Spiegler & Guevremont, 2003). (Some therapists prefer to call this approach *applied behavior analysis*.)

How does classical conditioning work? I'm not sure I remember. Classical conditioning is a form of learning in which simple responses (especially reflexes) are associated with new stimuli. Perhaps a brief review would be helpful. In classical conditioning, a neutral stimulus is followed by an *unconditioned stimulus* (US) that consistently produces an unlearned reaction, called the *unconditioned response* (UR). Eventually, the previously neutral stimulus begins to produce this response directly. The response is then called a *conditioned response* (CR), and the stimulus becomes a *conditioned stimulus* (CS). Thus, for a child the sight of a hypodermic needle (CS) is followed by an injection (US), which causes anxiety or fear (UR). Eventually the sight of a hypodermic (the conditioned stimulus) may produce anxiety or fear (a conditioned response) *before* the child gets an injection. (For a more thorough review of classical conditioning, return to Chapter 8.)

What does classical conditioning have to do with behavior modification? Classical conditioning can be used to associate discomfort with a bad habit, as Brooks Workman did. More powerful versions of this approach are called aversion therapy.

Aversion Therapy

Imagine that you are eating an apple. Suddenly you discover that you just bit a large green worm in half. You vomit. Months pass before you can eat an apple again without feeling ill. It's apparent that you have developed a conditioned aversion to apples. (A *conditioned aversion* is a learned dislike or negative emotional response to some stimulus.)

How are conditioned aversions used in therapy? In **aversion therapy**, an individual learns to associate a strong aversion to an undesirable habit such as smoking, drinking, or gambling. Aversion therapy has been used to cure hiccups, sneezing, stuttering, vomiting, nail-biting, bed-wetting, compulsive hair-pulling, alcoholism, and the smoking of tobacco, marijuana, or crack cocaine. Actually, aversive conditioning happens every day. For example, not many physicians who treat lung cancer are smokers, nor do many emergency room doctors drive without using their seat belts (Eifert & Lejuez, 2000).

Puffing Up an Aversion

The fact that nicotine is toxic makes it easy to create an aversion that helps people give up smoking. Behavior therapists have found that electric shock, nauseating drugs, and similar aversive stimuli are not required to make smokers uncomfortable. All that is needed is for the smoker to smoke—rapidly, for a long time, at a forced pace. During rapid smoking, clients are told to smoke continuously, taking a puff every 6 to 8 seconds. Rapid smoking continues until the smoker is miserable and can stand it no more. By then, most people are thinking, "I never want to see another cigarette for the rest of my life."

Rapid smoking has long been known as an effective behavior therapy for smoking (Tiffany, Martin, & Baker, 1986). Nevertheless, anyone tempted to try rapid smoking should realize that it is very unpleasant. Without the help of a therapist, most people quit too soon for the procedure to succeed. In addition, rapid smoking can be dangerous. It should only be done with professional supervision. (An alternative method that is more practical is described in the Psychology in Action section of this chapter.)

Aversive Therapy for Drinking

Another excellent example of aversion therapy was pioneered by the work of Roger Vogler and his associates (1977). Vogler worked with alcoholics who were unable to stop drinking. For many clients, aversion therapy is a last chance. While drinking an alcoholic beverage, clients receive a painful (although not injurious) electric shock to the hand. Most of the time, these shocks occur as the client is beginning to take a drink of alcohol.

These *response-contingent shocks* (shocks that are linked to a response) obviously take the pleasure out of drinking. Shocks also cause the alcohol abuser to develop a conditioned aversion to drinking. Normally, the misery caused by alcohol abuse comes long after the act of drinking—too late to have much effect. But if alcohol can be linked with *immediate* discomfort, then drinking will begin to make the individual very uncomfortable.

Is it really acceptable to treat clients this way? People are often disturbed (shocked?) by such methods. However, clients usually *volunteer* for aversion therapy because it helps them overcome a destructive habit. Indeed, commercial aversion programs for overeating, smoking, and alcohol abuse have attracted many willing customers. More important, aversion therapy can be justified by its long-term benefits. As behaviorist Donald Baer put it, "A small number of brief, painful experiences is a reasonable exchange for the interminable pain of a lifelong maladjustment."

Desensitization

Assume that you are a swimming instructor who wants to help a child named Jamie overcome fear of the high diving board. How might you proceed? Directly forcing Jamie off the high board could be a psychological disaster. Obviously, a better approach would be to begin by teaching her to dive off the edge of the pool. Then she could be taught to dive off the low board, followed by a platform 6 feet above the water and then an 8-foot platform. As a last step, Jamie could try the high board.

Who's Afraid of a Hierarchy?

This rank-ordered series of steps is called a **hierarchy.** The hierarchy allows Jamie to undergo *adaptation.* Gradually, she adapts to the high dive and overcomes her fear. When Jamie has conquered her fear, we can say that *desensitization* (dee-SEN-sih-tih-ZAY-shun) has occurred (Spiegler & Guevremont, 2003).

Desensitization is also based on **reciprocal inhibition** (using one emotional state to block another) (Wolpe & Plaud, 1997). For instance, it is impossible to be anxious and relaxed at the same time. If we can get Jamie onto the high board in a relaxed state, her anxiety and fear will be inhibited. Repeated visits to the high board should cause fear in this situation to disappear. Again we would say that Jamie has been desensitized. Typically, **systematic desensitization** (a guided reduction in fear, anxiety, or aversion) is attained by gradually approaching a feared stimulus while maintaining relaxation.

What is desensitization used for? Desensitization is primarily used to help people unlearn phobias (intense, unrealistic fears) or strong anxieties. For example, each of these people might be a candidate for desensitization: a teacher with stage fright, a student with test anxiety, a salesperson who fears people, or a newlywed with an aversion to sexual intimacy.

Performing Desensitization

How is desensitization done? First, the client and the therapist *construct a hierarchy.* This is a list of fear-provoking situations, arranged from least disturbing to most frightening. Second, the client is taught *exercises that produce deep relaxation.* (See "Feeling a Little Tense? Relax!") Once the client is relaxed, she or he proceeds to the third step by trying to *perform the least disturbing item* on the list. For a fear of heights (acrophobia), this might be "(1) Stand on a chair." The first item is repeated until no anxiety is felt. Any change from complete relaxation is a signal that clients must relax again before continuing. Slowly, clients move up the hierarchy: "(2) Climb to the top of a small stepladder," "(3) Look down a flight of stairs," and so on, until the last item is performed without fear: "(20) Fly in an airplane."

For many phobias, desensitization works best when people are directly exposed to the stimuli and situations they fear (Oest et al., 2001). For something like a simple spider phobia, this exposure can even be done in groups (Oest, 1996). Also, for some fears (such as fear of riding an elevator) desensitization may be completed in a single session (Sturges & Sturges, 1998).

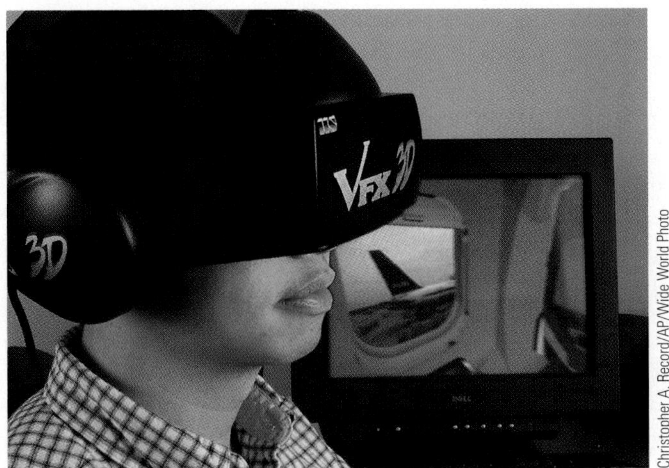

Christopher A. Record/AP/Wide World Photo

Programs for treating fears of flying combine relaxation, systematic desensitization, group support, and lots of direct exposure to airliners. Many such programs conclude with a brief flight, so that participants can "test their wings."

Behavior therapy Any therapy designed to actively change behavior.

Behavior modification The application of learning principles to change human behavior, especially maladaptive behavior.

Aversion therapy Suppressing an undesirable response by associating it with aversive (painful or uncomfortable) stimuli.

Hierarchy A rank-ordered series of higher and lower amounts, levels, degrees, or steps.

Reciprocal inhibition The presence of one emotional state can inhibit the occurrence of another, such as joy preventing fear or anxiety inhibiting pleasure.

Systematic desensitization A reduction in fear, anxiety, or aversion brought about by planned exposure to aversive stimuli.

DISCOVERING PSYCHOLOGY Feeling a Little Tense? Relax!

The key to desensitization is relaxation. To inhibit fear, you must *learn* to relax. One way to voluntarily relax is by using the **tension-release method.** To achieve deep muscle relaxation, try the following exercise.

> Tense the muscles in your right arm until they tremble. Hold them tight as you slowly count to 10 and then let go. Allow your hand and arm to go limp and to relax completely. Repeat the procedure. Releasing tension two or three times will allow you to feel whether or not your arm muscles have relaxed. Repeat the tension-release procedure with your left arm. Compare it with your right arm. Repeat until the left arm is equally relaxed. Apply the tension-release technique to your right leg; to your left leg; to your abdomen; to your chest and shoulders. Clench and release your chin, neck, and throat. Wrinkle and release your forehead and scalp. Tighten and release your mouth and face muscles. As a last step, curl your toes and tense your feet. Then release.

If you carried out these instructions, you should be noticeably more relaxed than you were before you began.

Practice the tension-release method until you can achieve complete relaxation quickly (5 to 10 minutes). After you have practiced relaxation once a day for a week or two, you will begin to be able to tell when your body (or a group of muscles) is tense. Also, you will begin to be able to relax on command. This is a valuable skill that you can apply in any situation that makes you feel tense or anxious.

Vicarious Desensitization

I understand how some fears could be desensitized by gradual approach—as in the case of the child on the high dive. But what if it's not practical to directly act out the steps of a hierarchy? For a fear of heights, the steps of the hierarchy might be acted out. However, if this is impractical the problem can be handled by having clients observe *models* who are performing the feared behavior (● Figure 17.2) (Eifert & Lejuez, 2000). A model is a person (either live or filmed) who serves as an example for observational learning. If such **vicarious desensitization** (secondhand learning) can't be used, there is yet another option. Fortunately, desensitization works almost as well when a person *vividly imagines* each step in the hierarchy (Deffenbacher & Suinn, 1988). If the steps can be visualized without anxiety, fear in the actual situation is reduced. Because imagining feared stimuli can be done at a therapist's office, it is the most common way of doing desensitization.

Virtual Reality Exposure

Desensitization is an *exposure therapy.* Like other such therapies, it involves exposing people to feared stimuli until their fears extinguish. In an important new development, psychologists are using virtual reality to treat phobias. Virtual reality is a computer-generated, three-dimensional "world" that viewers enter by wearing a head-mounted video display. **Virtual reality exposure** presents computerized fear stimuli to patients in a realistic, yet carefully controlled fashion (Wiederhold & Weiderhold, 2004). It has already been used to treat acrophobia (fear of heights), fears of flying and driving and public speaking, spider phobias, and claustrophobia (Arbona et al., 2004; Giuseppe, 2005; Hoffman et al., 2003; Lee et al., 2002; Wald and Taylor, 2000) (see ● Figure 17.3).

Desensitization has been one of the most successful behavior therapies. A second new technique may provide yet another way to lower fears, anxieties, and psychological pain. See "Eye Movement Desensitization and Reprocessing" for the details.

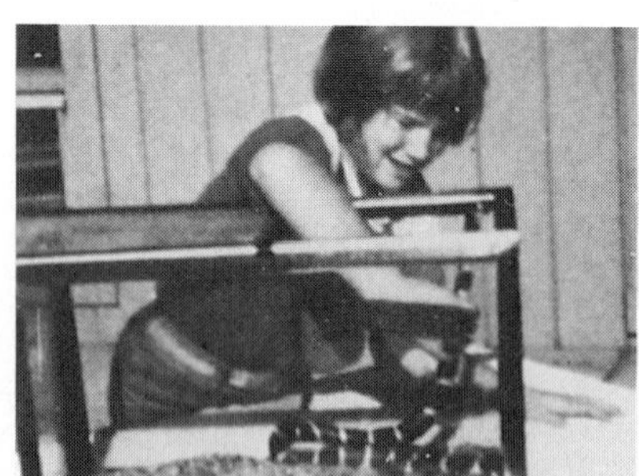

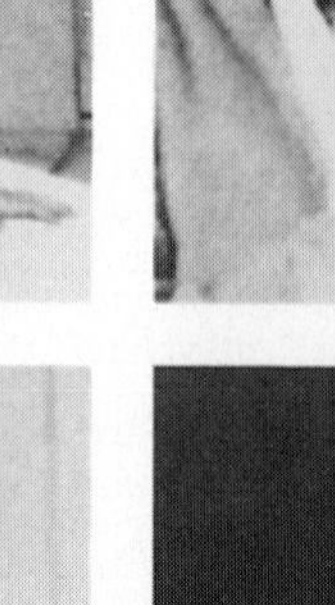

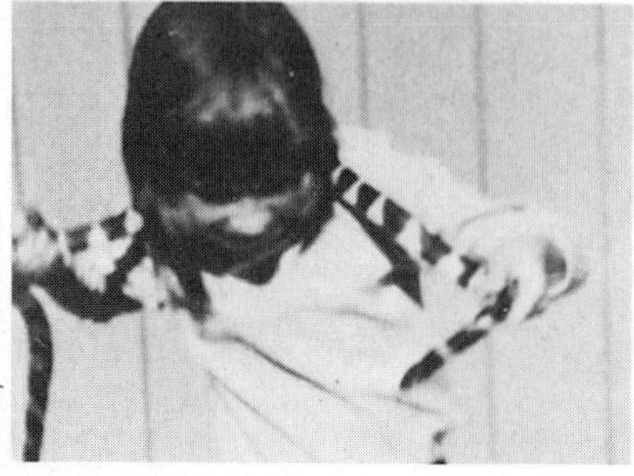

Courtesy of Albert Bandura

● **Figure 17.2** Treatment of a snake phobia by vicarious desensitization. The photographs show models interacting with snakes. To overcome their own fears, phobic subjects observed the models. (Bandura, Blanchard, & Ritter, 1969. Photos courtesy of Albert Bandura.)

FOCUS ON RESEARCH

Eye Movement Desensitization and Reprocessing—Watching Trauma Fade?

Traumatic events produce painful memories. Disturbing flashbacks often haunt victims of accidents, disasters, molestations, muggings, rapes, or emotional abuse. Recently, Dr. Francine Shapiro developed **eye movement desensitization and reprocessing (EMDR)** to help ease traumatic memories and posttraumatic stress.

In a typical EMDR session, the client is asked to visualize the images that most upset her or him. At the same time, a pencil (or other object) is moved rapidly from side to side in front of the person's eyes. Watching the moving object causes the person's eyes to dart swiftly back and forth. After about 30 seconds, patients describe any memories, feelings, and thoughts that emerged and discuss them with the therapist. These steps are repeated until troubling thoughts and emotions no longer surface (Shapiro, 2001; Shapiro & Forrest, 2004).

A number of studies suggest that EMDR lowers anxieties and takes the pain out of traumatic memories (Carlson et al., 1998; Scheck, Schaeffer, & Gillette, 1998; Silver et al., 2005). However, EMDR is highly controversial. Some studies, for example, have found that eye movements add nothing to the treatment. The apparent success of EMDR may simply be based on gradual exposure to upsetting stimuli, like in other forms of desensitization (Cahill, Carrigan, & Frueh, 1999; Davidson & Parker, 2001). On the other hand, some researchers continue to find that EMDR is superior to traditional therapies (Ironson et al., 2002; Rogers & Silver, 2002).

Is EMDR a breakthrough? Or will it prove to be a case of wishful thinking? Given the frequency of traumas in modern society, it shouldn't be long before we find out.

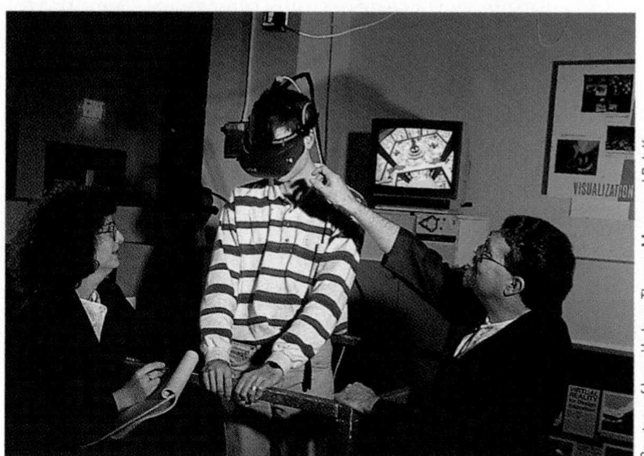

Courtesy of Larry Hodges, Thomas Meyer, and Rob Kooper

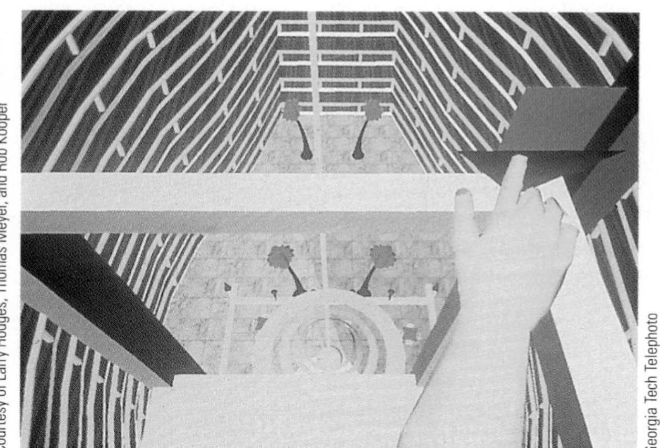

Georgia Tech Telephoto

● **Figure 17.3** *(left)* Dr. Barbara Rothbaum and Dr. Larry Hodges show how a virtual reality system is used to expose people to feared stimuli. Many patients would rather face feared stimuli in a virtual environment than in a real physical environment. *(right)* A computer image from a virtual elevator. Over an 8-week period, patients who suffered from acrophobia "rode" in the elevator. Each session took them to greater heights.

KNOWLEDGE BUILDER

Behavior Therapy

REFLECT

Can you describe three problems for which you think behavior therapy would be an appropriate treatment?

A friend of yours has a dog that goes berserk during thunderstorms. You own a CD of a thunderstorm. How could you use the CD to desensitize the dog? (Hint: The CD-player has a volume control.)

Tension-release method A procedure for systematically achieving deep relaxation of the body.

Vicarious desensitization A reduction in fear or anxiety that takes place vicariously ("secondhand") when a client watches models perform the feared behavior.

Virtual reality exposure Use of computer-generated images to present fear stimuli. The virtual environment responds to a viewer's head movements and other inputs.

Eye movement desensitization and reprocessing (EMDR) A technique for reducing fear or anxiety; based on holding upsetting thoughts in mind while rapidly moving the eyes from side to side.

Have you ever become naturally desensitized to a stimulus or situation that at first made you anxious (for instance, heights, public speaking, or driving on freeways)? How would you explain your reduced fear?

LEARNING CHECK

1. What two types of conditioning are used in behavior modification? ______________ and ______________
2. Shock, pain, and discomfort play what role in conditioning an aversion?
   a. conditioned stimulus   c. unconditioned stimulus
   b. unconditioned response   d. conditioned response
3. If shock is used to control drinking, it must be ______________ contingent.
4. What two principles underlie systematic desensitization? ______________ and ______________
5. When desensitization is carried out through the use of live or filmed models, it is called
   a. cognitive therapy   c. covert desensitization
   b. flooding   d. vicarious desensitization
6. The three basic steps in systematic desensitization are as follows: construct a hierarchy, flood the person with anxiety, and imagine relaxation. T or F?
7. In EMDR therapy, computer-generated virtual reality images are used to expose patients to fear-provoking stimuli. T or F?

CRITICAL THINKING

8. Alcoholics who take a drug called Antabuse become ill after drinking alcohol. Why, then, don't they develop an aversion to drinking?
9. A natural form of desensitization often takes place in hospitals. Can you guess what it is?

Answers: 1. classical (or respondent), operant **2.** c **3.** response **4.** adaptation, reciprocal inhibition **5.** d **6.** F **7.** F **8.** Their discomfort is delayed enough to prevent it from being closely associated with drinking. Fortunately, there are safer, better ways to do aversion therapy (Wilson, 1987). **9.** Doctors and nurses learn to relax and remain calm at the sight of blood because of their frequent exposure to it.

Operant Therapies—All the World Is a Skinner Box?

Aversion therapy and desensitization are based on classical conditioning. Where does operant conditioning fit in? As you may recall, operant conditioning refers to learning based on the consequences of making a response. The operant principles most often used by behavior therapists to deal with human behavior are as follows:

1. **Positive reinforcement.** Responses that are followed by reward tend to occur more frequently. If children whine and get attention, they will whine more frequently. If you get A's in your psychology class, you may become a psychology major.
2. **Nonreinforcement.** A response that is not followed by reward will occur less frequently.
3. **Extinction.** If a response is not followed by reward after it has been repeated many times, it will go away. After winning three times, you pull the handle on a slot machine thirty times more without a payoff. What do you do? You go away. So does the response of handle pulling (for that particular machine, at any rate).
4. **Punishment.** If a response is followed by discomfort or an undesirable effect, the response will be suppressed (but not necessarily extinguished).
5. **Shaping.** Shaping means rewarding actions that are closer and closer approximations to a desired response. For example, to reward a retarded child for saying "ball," you might begin by rewarding the child for saying anything that starts with a *b* sound.
6. **Stimulus control.** Responses tend to come under the control of the situation in which they occur. If you set your clock 10 minutes fast, it may be easier to leave the house on time in the morning. Your departure is under the stimulus control of the clock, even though you know it is fast.
7. **Time out.** A time-out procedure usually involves removing the individual from a situation in which reinforcement occurs. Time out is a variation of nonreinforcement: It prevents reward from following an undesirable response. For example, children who fight with each other can be sent to separate rooms and allowed out only when they are able to behave more calmly (Olson & Roberts, 1987). (For a more thorough review of operant learning, return to Chapter 8.)

As simple as these principles may seem, they have been used very effectively to overcome difficulties in work, home, school, and industrial settings. Let's see how.

Nonreinforcement and Extinction

An extremely overweight mental patient had a persistent and disturbing habit: She stole food from other patients. No one could persuade her to stop stealing or to diet. For the sake of her health, a behavior therapist assigned her a special table in the ward dining room. If she approached any other table, she was immediately removed from the dining room. Because her attempts to steal food went unrewarded, they rapidly disappeared. In addition, any attempt to steal from others caused the patient to miss her own meal (Ayllon, 1963).

What operant principles did the therapist in this example use? The therapist used *nonreward* to produce *extinction.* The most frequently occurring human behaviors lead to some form of reward. An undesirable response can be eliminated by *identifying* and *removing* the rewards that maintain it. But people don't always do things for food, money, or other obvious rewards. Most of the rewards maintaining human behavior are subtler. *Attention, approval,* and *concern* are common yet powerful reinforcers for humans (● Figure 17.4).

Nonreward and extinction can eliminate many problem behaviors, especially in schools, hospitals, and institutions. Often, difficulties center around a limited number of particularly disturbing responses. Time out is a good way to remove such responses, usually by refusing to pay attention to a person who is misbehaving. For example, 14-year-old Terrel periodically appeared in the nude in the activity room of a training center for disturbed adolescents. This behavior always generated a great deal

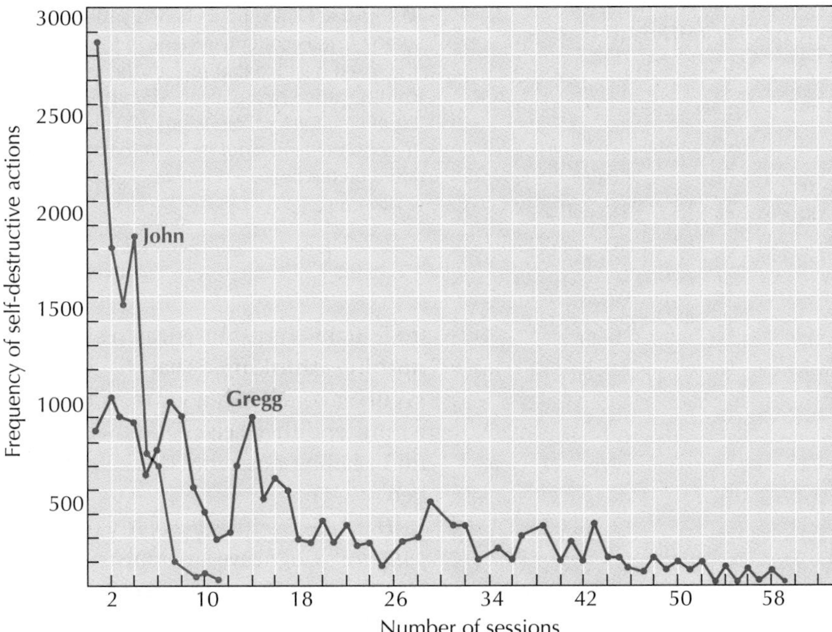

● **Figure 17.4** This graph shows extinction of self-destructive behavior in two autistic boys. Before extinction began, the boys received attention and concern from adults for injuring themselves. During extinction, the adults were taught to ignore the boys' self-damaging behavior. As you can see, the number of times that the boys tried to injure themselves declined rapidly. (Adapted from Lovaas & Simmons, 1969.)

of attention from staff and other patients. Usually Terrel was returned to his room and confined there. During this "confinement," he often missed doing his usual chores. As an experiment he was placed on time out. The next time he appeared nude, counselors and other staff members greeted him normally and then ignored him. Attention from other patients rapidly subsided. Sheepishly he returned to his room and dressed.

Reinforcement and Token Economies

A distressing problem therapists sometimes face is how to break through to severely disturbed patients who won't talk. Conventional psychotherapy offers little hope of improvement for such patients.

What can be done for them? One widely used approach is based on *tokens* (symbolic rewards, such as plastic chips, that can be exchanged for real rewards). Tokens may be printed slips of paper, check marks, points, or gold stars. Whatever form they take, tokens serve as rewards because they may be exchanged for candy, food, cigarettes, recreation, or privileges, such as private time with a therapist, outings, or watching TV. Tokens are used in mental hospitals, halfway houses, schools for the retarded, programs for delinquents, and ordinary classrooms. They usually produce dramatic improvements in behavior (Dickerson, Tenhula, & Green-Paden, 2005; Mohanty, Pati, & Kumar, 1998; Reitman et al., 2004).

BRIDGES

Tokens provide an effective way to change behavior because they are secondary reinforcers.

See Chapter 8, page 275–276.

By using tokens, a therapist can *immediately reward* positive responses. For maximum impact, therapists select specific *target behaviors* (actions or other behaviors the therapist seeks to modify). Target behaviors are then reinforced with tokens. For example, a mute mental patient might first be given a token each time he or she says a word. Next, tokens may be given for speaking a complete sentence. Later, the patient could gradually be required to speak more often, then to answer questions, and eventually to carry on a short conversation in order to receive tokens. In this way, deeply withdrawn patients have been returned to the world of normal communication.

Full-scale use of tokens in an institutional setting produces a *token economy*. In a **token economy,** patients are rewarded with tokens for a wide range of socially desirable or productive activities (Spiegler & Guevremont, 2003). They must *pay* tokens for privileges and for engaging in problem behaviors (● Figure 17.5). For example, tokens are given to patients who get out of bed, dress themselves, take required medication, arrive for meals on time, and so on. Constructive activities, such as gardening, cooking, or cleaning, may also earn tokens. Patients must *exchange* tokens for meals and private rooms, movies, passes, off-ward activities, and other privileges. They are *charged* tokens for staying in bed, disrobing in public, talking to themselves, fighting, crying, and similar target behaviors (Morisse et al., 1996).

Token economies can radically change a patient's overall adjustment and morale. Patients are given an incentive to change, and they are held responsible for their actions. The use of tokens may seem manipulative, but it actually empowers patients. Many "hopelessly" retarded, mentally ill, and delinquent people have been returned to productive lives by means of token economies (Corrigan, 1997). By the time they are ready to leave, patients may be earning tokens on a weekly basis for maintaining sane, responsible, and productive behavior (Miltenberger, 2004). Typically, the most effective token economies are those that gradually switch from tokens to *social rewards* such as praise, recognition, and approval. Such rewards are what patients will receive when they return to family, friends, and community.

Token economy A therapeutic program in which desirable behaviors are reinforced with tokens that can be exchanged for goods, services, activities, and privileges.

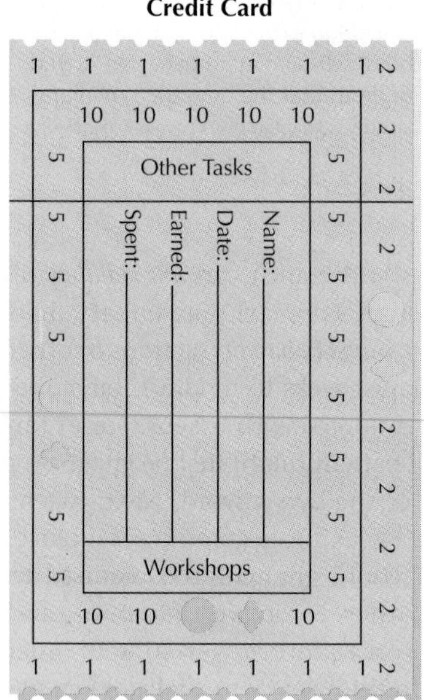

OXNARD DAY TREATMENT CENTER
CREDIT INCENTIVE SYSTEM

EARN CREDITS BY		SPEND CREDITS FOR	
MONITOR DAILY	15	COFFEE	5
MENU PLANNING CHAIRMAN	50	LUNCH	10
PARTICIPATE	5	EXCEPT THURSDAY	15
BUY FOOD AT STORE	10	BUS TRIP	5
COOK FOR/PREPARE LUNCH	5	BOWLING	8
WIPE OFF KITCHEN TABLE	3	GROUP THERAPY	5
WASH DISHES	5-10	PRIVATE STAFF TIME	5
DRY AND PUT AWAY DISHES	5	DAY OFF	5-20
MAKE COFFEE AND CLEAN URN	15	WINDOW SHOPPING	5
CLEAN REFRIGERATOR	20	REVIEW WITH DR.	10
ATTEND PLANNING CONFERENCE	1	DOING OWN THING	1
OT PREPARATION	1-5	LATE 1 PER EVERY 10 MIN	
COMPLETE OT PROJECT	5	PRESCRIPTION FROM DR.	10
RETURN OT PROJECT	2		
DUST AND POLISH TABLES	5		
PUT AWAY GROCERIES	3		
CLEAN TABLE	5		
CLEAN 6 ASH TRAYS	2		
CLEAN SINK	5		
CARRY OUT CUPS & BOTTLES	5		
CLEAN CHAIRS	5		
CLEAN KITCHEN CUPBOARDS	5		
ASSIST STAFF	5		
ARRANGE MAGAZINES NEATLY	3		
BEING ON TIME	5		
MONITOR-ANN			

● **Figure 17.5** Shown here is a token used in one token economy system. In this instance the token is a card that records the number of credits earned by a patient. Also pictured is a list of credit values for various activities. Tokens may be exchanged for items or for privileges listed on the board. (After photographs by Robert P. Liberman.)

Cognitive Therapy—Think Positive!

How would a behavior therapist treat a problem like depression? None of the techniques described seem to apply. As we have discussed, behavior therapists usually try to change troublesome actions. However, in recent years cognitive therapists have become interested in what people think, believe, and feel, as well as how they act. In general, **cognitive therapy** helps clients change thinking patterns that lead to troublesome emotions or behaviors (Dobson, Backs-Dermott, & Dozois, 2000). For example, compulsive handwashing can be greatly reduced just by changing a client's thoughts and beliefs about dirt and contamination (Jones & Menzies, 1998). Cognitive therapy is used as a remedy for many problems, but it has been especially successful in treating depression (Chambless & Ollendick, 2001).

Cognitive Therapy for Depression

As you may recall from Chapter 15, Aaron Beck (1991) believes that negative, self-defeating thoughts underlie depression. According to Beck, depressed persons see themselves, the world, and the future in negative terms. Beck believes this occurs because of major distortions in thinking. The first is **selective perception**, which refers to perceiving only certain stimuli in a larger array. If five good things happen during the day and three bad things, depressed people focus only on the bad. A second thinking error in depression is **overgeneralization**, the tendency to think that an upsetting event applies to other, unrelated situations. An example would be considering yourself a total failure, or completely worthless, if you were to lose a part-time job or fail a test. To complete the picture, depressed persons tend to magnify the importance of undesirable events by engaging in **all-or-nothing thinking.** That is, they see events as completely good or bad, right or wrong, and themselves as either successful or failing miserably (Beck, 2002; Gilbert, 2001).

How do cognitive therapists alter such patterns? Cognitive therapists make a step-by-step effort to correct negative thoughts that lead to depression or similar problems. At first, clients are taught to recognize and keep track of their own thoughts. The client and therapist then look for ideas and beliefs that cause depression, anger, and avoidance. For example, here's how a therapist might challenge all-or-nothing thinking (Burns & Persons, 1982):

> *Patient:* I'm feeling even more depressed. No one wants to hire me, and I can't even clean up my apartment. I feel completely incompetent!
>
> *Therapist:* I see. The fact that you are unemployed and have a messy apartment proves that you are completely incompetent?
>
> *Patient:* Well . . . I can see that doesn't add up.

Next, clients are asked to gather information to test their beliefs. For instance, a depressed person might list his or her activities for a week. The list is then used to challenge all-or-nothing thoughts, such as "I had a terrible week" or "I'm a complete failure." With more coaching, clients learn to alter their thoughts in ways that improve their moods, actions, and relationships.

Cognitive therapy is as effective as drugs for treating many cases of depression. More important, people who have adopted new thinking patterns are less likely to become depressed again—a benefit that drugs can't impart (Dozois & Dobson, 2004; Gloaguen et al., 1998).

In an alternate approach, cognitive therapists look for an *absence* of effective coping skills and thinking patterns, not for the *presence* of self-defeating thoughts (Dobson, Backs-Dermott, & Dozois, 2000). The aim is to teach clients how to cope with anger, depression, shyness, stress, and similar problems. Stress inoculation, which was described in Chapter 15, is a good example of this approach.

Cognitive therapy is a rapidly expanding specialty. Before we leave the topic, let's explore another widely used cognitive therapy.

DISCOVERING PSYCHOLOGY

Ten Irrational Beliefs—Which Do You Hold?

Rational-emotive behavior therapists have identified numerous beliefs that commonly lead to emotional upsets and conflicts. See if you recognize any of the following irrational beliefs:

1. I must be loved and approved by almost every significant person in my life or it's awful and I'm worthless.
   Example: "One of my roommates doesn't seem to like me. I must be a total zero."
2. I should be completely competent and achieving in all ways to be a worthwhile person.
   Example: "I don't understand my chemistry class. I guess I really am a stupid person."
3. Certain people I must deal with are thoroughly bad and should be severely blamed and punished for it.
   Example: "The old man next door is such a pain. I'm going to play my stereo even louder the next time he complains."
4. It is awful and upsetting when things are not the way I would very much like them to be.
   Example: "I should have gotten a B in that class. The teacher is unfair."
5. My unhappiness is always caused by external events; I cannot control my emotional reactions.
   Example: "You make me feel awful. I would be happy if it weren't for you."
6. If something unpleasant might happen, I should keep dwelling on it.
   Example: "I'll never forget the time my boss insulted me. I think about it every day at work."
7. It is easier to avoid difficulties and responsibilities than to face them.
   Example: "I don't know why my wife seems angry. Maybe it will just pass by if I ignore it."
8. I should depend on others who are stronger than I am.
   Example: "I couldn't survive if he left me."
9. Because something once strongly affected my life, it will do so indefinitely.
   Example: "My girlfriend dumped me during my junior year in college. I don't know if I can ever trust a woman again."
10. There is always a perfect solution to human problems and it is awful if this solution is not found.
    Example: "I'm so depressed about politics in this country. It all seems hopeless."
    (Adapted from Beck, 2002; Ellis, 2004; Rohsenow & Smith, 1982)

If any of the listed beliefs sound familiar, you may be creating unnecessary emotional distress for yourself by holding on to unrealistic expectations.

Rational-Emotive Behavior Therapy

Rational-emotive behavior therapy (REBT) attempts to change irrational beliefs that cause emotional problems. According to Albert Ellis (1995, 2004), the basic idea of rational-emotive behavior therapy is as easy as A-B-C. Ellis assumes that people become unhappy and develop self-defeating habits because they have unrealistic or faulty *beliefs*.

How are beliefs important? Ellis analyzes problems in this way: The letter A stands for an *activating experience,* which the person assumes to be the cause of C, an *emotional consequence*. For instance, a person who is rejected (the activating experience) feels depressed, threatened, or hurt (the consequence). Rational-emotive behavior therapy shows the client that the real problem is what comes between A and C: In between is B, the client's irrational and unrealistic *beliefs*. In this example, an unrealistic belief leading to unnecessary suffering is, "I must be loved and approved by everyone at all times." REBT holds that events do not *cause* us to have feelings. We feel as we do because of our beliefs (Kottler, 2004). (For some examples, see "Ten Irrational Beliefs—Which Do You Hold?")

Ellis (1979, 2004) says that most irrational beliefs come from three core ideas, each of which is unrealistic:

1. I *must* perform well and be approved of by significant others. If I don't, then it is awful, I cannot stand it, and I am a rotten person.

BRIDGES

The REBT explanation of emotional distress is related to the effects of emotional appraisals.

See Chapter 12, pages 420–421.

Cognitive therapy A therapy directed at changing the maladaptive thoughts, beliefs, and feelings that underlie emotional and behavioral problems.

Selective perception Perceiving only certain stimuli among a larger array of possibilities.

Overgeneralization Blowing a single event out of proportion by extending it to a large number of unrelated situations.

All-or-nothing thinking Classifying objects or events as absolutely right or wrong, good or bad, acceptable or unacceptable, and so forth.

Rational-emotive behavior therapy (REBT) An approach that states that irrational beliefs cause many emotional problems and that such beliefs must be changed or abandoned.

2. You *must* treat me fairly. When you don't, it is horrible, and I cannot bear it.
3. Conditions *must* be the way I want them to be. It is terrible when they are not, and I cannot stand living in such an awful world.

It's easy to see that such beliefs can lead to much grief and needless suffering in a less than perfect world. Rational-emotive behavior therapists are very directive in their attempts to change a client's irrational beliefs and "self-talk." The therapist may directly attack clients' logic, challenge their thinking, confront them with evidence contrary to their beliefs, and even assign "homework." Here, for instance, are some examples of statements that dispute irrational beliefs (after Kottler, 2004):

- "Where is the evidence that you are a loser just because you didn't do well this one time?"
- "Who said the world should be fair? That's your rule."
- "What are you telling yourself to make yourself feel so upset?"
- "Is it really terrible that things aren't working out as you would like? Or is it just inconvenient?"

Many of us would probably do well to give up our irrational beliefs. Improved self-acceptance and a better tolerance of daily annoyances are the benefits of doing so.

The value of cognitive approaches is further illustrated by three techniques (*covert sensitization, thought stopping,* and *covert reinforcement*) described in this chapter's Psychology in Action section. A little later you can see what you think of them.

KNOWLEDGE BUILDER

Operant Therapies and Cognitive Therapies

REFLECT

See if you can give a personal example of how the following principles have affected your behavior: positive reinforcement, extinction, punishment, shaping, stimulus control, and time out.

You are setting up a token economy for troubled elementary school children. What target behaviors will you attempt to reinforce? For what behaviors will you charge tokens?

We all occasionally engage in negative thinking. Can you remember a time recently when you engaged in selective perception? Overgeneralization? All-or-nothing thinking?

Which of REBT's irrational beliefs have affected your feelings? Which beliefs would you like to change?

LEARNING CHECK

1. Behavior modification programs aimed at extinction of an undesirable behavior typically make use of what operant principles?
   a. punishment and stimulus control
   b. punishment and shaping
   c. nonreinforcement and time out
   d. stimulus control and time out
2. Attention can be a powerful ________________ for humans.
3. Token economies depend on the time-out procedure. T or F?
4. Tokens basically allow the operant shaping of desired responses or "target behaviors." T or F?
5. According to Beck, selective perception, overgeneralization, and ________________ thinking are cognitive habits that underlie depression.
6. The B in the A-B-C of REBT stands for
   a. behavior c. being
   b. belief d. Beck
7. REBT teaches people to change the antecedents of irrational behavior. T or F?

CRITICAL THINKING

8. In Aaron Beck's terms, a belief such as, "I must perform well or I am a rotten person," involves what two thinking errors?

Answers: **1.** c **2.** reinforcer **3.** F **4.** T **5.** all-or-nothing **6.** b **7.** F **8.** Overgeneralization and all-or-nothing thinking.

Group Therapy—People Who Need People

To complete our discussion of psychotherapies, we will begin with a brief look at group therapy. Group therapy has certain advantages, not the least of which is reduced cost. After that, we will try to identify the core features and helping skills that make psychotherapy "work." To conclude, we will explore medical approaches to treating mental disorders.

Group therapy is psychotherapy done with more than one person. Most of the therapies we have discussed can be adapted for use in groups. Psychologists first tried working with groups because there was a shortage of therapists. Surprisingly, group therapy has turned out to be just as effective as individual therapy and it has some special advantages (Burlingame, Fuhriman, & Mosier, 2003).

What are the advantages? In group therapy, a person can *act out* or directly experience problems. Doing so often produces insights that might not occur from merely talking about an issue. In addition, other group members with similar problems can offer support and useful input. Group therapy is especially good for helping people understand their personal relationships (McCluskey, 2002). For reasons such as these, a number of specialized groups have emerged. Because they range from Alcoholics Anonymous to Marriage Encounter, we will sample only a few examples.

Psychodrama

One of the first groups was developed by Jacob L. Moreno (1953), who called his technique psychodrama. In **psychodrama,** clients act out personal conflicts with others who play supporting roles. Through role-playing, the client re-enacts incidents that cause problems in real life. For example, Don, a disturbed teenager, might act out a typical family fight, with the therapist playing his father and with other clients playing his mother, brothers, and sisters. Moreno believed that insights gained in this way transfer to real-life situations.

Therapists using psychodrama often find that role reversals are helpful. A **role reversal** involves taking the part of another person to learn how he or she feels. For instance, Don might role-play his father or mother, to better understand their feelings. A related method is the **mirror technique**, in which clients observe another person re-enact their behavior. Thus, Don might briefly join the audience and watch as another group member plays his role. This would allow him to see himself as others do. Later, the group may summarize what happened and reflect on its meaning (Turner, 1997).

Family Therapy

Family relationships are the source of great pleasure, and all too often, of great pain. In **family therapy**, husband, wife, and children work as a group to resolve the problems of each family member. Family therapy tends to be brief and focused on specific problems, such as frequent fights or a depressed teenager. For some types of problems, family therapy may be superior to other approaches (Capuzzi, 2003; Pinsof, Wynne, & Hambright, 1996).

Family therapists believe that a problem experienced by one family member is really the whole family's problem. If the entire pattern of behavior in a family doesn't change, improvements in any single family member may not last. Thus, family members work together to improve communication, to change destructive patterns, and to see themselves and each other in new ways. This helps them reshape distorted perceptions and interactions directly, with the very persons with whom they have troubled relationships (Goldfried, Greenberg, & Marmar, 1990).

Does the therapist work with the whole family at once? Family therapists treat the family as a unit, but they may not meet with the entire family at each session. If a family crisis is at hand, the therapist may first try to identify the most resourceful family members, who can help solve the immediate problem. The therapist and family members may then work on resolving more basic conflicts and on improving family relationships (Griffin, 2002).

Jon Bradley/Getty Images

A group therapy session. Group members offer mutual support while sharing problems and insights.

Group Awareness Training

During the 1960s and 1970s, the human potential movement led many people to seek personal growth experiences. Often, their interest was expressed by participation in sensitivity training or encounter groups.

What is the difference between sensitivity and encounter groups? Sensitivity groups tend to be less confrontational than encounter groups. Participants in **sensitivity groups** take part in exercises that gently enlarge self-awareness and sensitivity to others. For example, in a "trust walk," participants expand their confidence in others by allowing themselves to be led around while blindfolded.

Encounter groups are based on an honest expression of feelings, and intensely personal communication may take place. Typically, the emphasis is on tearing down defenses and false fronts. Because there is a danger of hostile confrontation, participation is safest when members are carefully screened and a trained leader guides the group. Encounter group "casualties" are rare, but they do occur (Shaffer & Galinsky, 1989).

In business settings, psychologists still use the basic principles of sensitivity and encounter groups—truth, self-awareness, and self-determination—to improve employee relationships. Specially designed encounter groups for married couples are also widely held (Harway, 2004).

There has also been much public interest in various forms of large-group awareness training. **Large-group awareness training** refers to programs that claim to increase self-awareness and facilitate constructive personal change. Lifespring, Actualizations, the Forum, and similar commercial programs are examples. Like the smaller groups that preceded them, large-group trainings combine psychological exercises, confrontation, new viewpoints, and group dynamics to promote personal change.

Group therapy Psychotherapy conducted in a group setting to make therapeutic use of group dynamics.

Psychodrama A therapy in which clients act out personal conflicts and feelings in the presence of others who play supporting roles.

Role reversal Taking the role of another person to learn how one's own behavior appears from the other person's perspective.

Mirror technique Observing another person re-enact one's own behavior, like a character in a play; designed to help persons see themselves more clearly.

Family therapy Technique in which all family members participate, both individually and as a group, to change destructive relationships and communication patterns.

Sensitivity group A group experience consisting of exercises designed to increase self-awareness and sensitivity to others.

Encounter group A group experience that emphasizes intensely honest interchanges among participants regarding feelings and reactions to one another.

Large-group awareness training Any of a number of programs (many of them commercialized) that claim to increase self-awareness and facilitate constructive personal change.

CRITICAL THINKING

How Do We Know Therapy Actually Works?

Why is it risky to believe people who say their therapy was effective? An old joke among doctors is that a cold lasts a week without treatment and seven days with it. Perhaps the same is true of therapy. Someone who feels better after 6 months of therapy may have experienced a spontaneous remission—they just feel better because so much time has passed. Or perhaps the crisis which triggered the therapy is now nearly forgotten. Or maybe some sort of therapy placebo effect has occurred. Also, it's possible that the person has received help from other people, such as family, friends, or clergy.

In order to rule out similar explanations, we need to use some of the research methods described in Chapter 1. Ideally, we would randomly divide a group of clients into an experimental group who receive therapy and a control group who do not. When this is done, it is not unusual for the control group to show some improvement, even without receiving therapy (Lambert & Ogles, 2002). We can conclude that the therapy itself was effective only if the experimental group shows *more* improvement than the control group.

But isn't it unethical to withhold treatment from someone who really needs therapy? That's right. One way to deal with this is to use a *waiting-list control group* consisting of individuals who are waiting to see a therapist and who will, eventually, also receive therapy.

When the results of many experiments are combined (using the statistical technique of *meta-analysis* described in Chapter 1), the effectiveness of therapy becomes clear (see, e.g., Lipsey & Wilson, 1993). Recently, studies have shown that some therapies are most effective for specific disorders (Bradley et al., 2005; Eddy et al., 2004). For example, behavioral, cognitive-behavioral, and drug therapies are particularly helpful in treating obsessive-compulsive disorder.

Are sensitivity, encounter, and awareness groups really psychotherapies? These experiences tend to be positive, but they produce only moderate benefits (Faith, Wong, & Carpenter, 1995). Moreover, many of the claimed benefits may simply result from a kind of **therapy placebo effect**, in which improvement is based on a client's belief that therapy will help. Positive expectations, a break in daily routine, and an excuse to act differently can have quite an impact. Also, less ambitious goals may be easier to attain. For example, one program succeeded in teaching stress-management techniques in a large group setting (Timmerman, Emmelkamp, & Sanderman, 1998). Because of their versatility, groups undoubtedly will continue to be a major tool for solving problems and improving lives.

Psychotherapy—An Overview

How effective is psychotherapy? Judging the outcome of therapy is tricky. In a national survey, nearly nine out of ten people who had sought mental health care said their lives improved as a result of the treatment (Kotkin, Daviet, & Gurin, 1996; "Mental health," 1995). Unfortunately you can't just take people's word for it (see "How Do We Know Therapy Actually Works?") Fortunately, there is more direct evidence that therapy is beneficial. Hundreds of studies show a strong pattern of positive effects for psychotherapy, counseling, and other psychological treatments (Barlow, 2004; Lambert & Cattani-Thompson, 1996).

In general, then, psychotherapy works (Moras, 2002). Of course, results vary in individual cases. For some people therapy is immensely helpful; for others it is unsuccessful; overall it is effective for more people than not. Speaking more subjectively, a real success, in which a person's life is changed for the better, can be worth the frustration of several cases in which little progress is made.

It is common to think of therapy as a long, slow process. But this is not always the case. Research shows that about 50 percent of all patients feel better after only eight therapy sessions. After 26 sessions, roughly 75 percent have improved (Howard et al., 1986) (● Figure 17.6). The typical "dose" of therapy is one hourly session per week. This means that the majority of patients improve

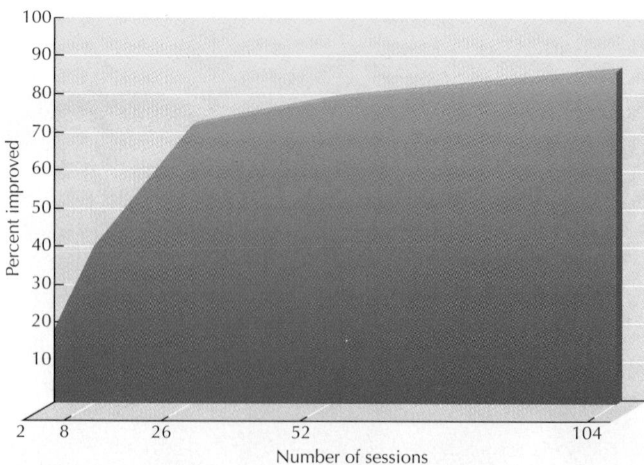

● **Figure 17.6** The dose-improvement relationship in psychotherapy. This graph shows the percentage of patients who improved after varying numbers of therapy sessions. Notice that the most rapid improvement took place during the first 6 months of once-a-week sessions. (From Howard et al., 1986.)

TABLE 17.2

Comparison of Psychotherapies

	INSIGHT OR ACTION?	DIRECTIVE OR NONDIRECTIVE?	INDIVIDUAL OR GROUP?	THERAPY'S STRENGTH*
Psychoanalysis	Insight	Directive	Individual	Searching honesty
Brief psychodynamic therapy	Insight	Directive	Individual	Productive use of conflict
Client-centered therapy	Insight	Nondirective	Both	Acceptance, empathy
Existential therapy	Insight	Both	Individual	Personal empowerment
Gesalt therapy	Insight	Directive	Both	Focus on immediate awareness
Behavior therapy	Action	Directive	Both	Observable changes in behavior
Cognitive therapy	Action	Directive	Individual	Constructive guidance
Rational-emotive behavior therapy	Action	Directive	Individual	Clarity of thinking and goals
Psychodrama	Insight	Directive	Group	Constructive re-enactments
Family therapy	Both	Directive	Group	Shared responsibility for problems

*This column based in part on Andrews (1989).

after 6 months of therapy and half feel better in just 2 months. Keep in mind that people often suffer for several years before seeking help. In view of this, such rapid improvement is impressive.

Core Features of Psychotherapy

What do psychotherapies have in common? We have sampled only a few of the many therapies in use today. For a summary of major differences among psychotherapies, see ■ Table 17.2. To add to your understanding, let us briefly summarize what all techniques have in common.

Psychotherapies of various types share all or most of these goals: restoring hope, courage, and optimism; gaining insight; resolving conflicts; improving one's sense of self; changing unacceptable patterns of behavior; finding purpose; mending interpersonal relations; and learning to approach problems rationally (Frank & Frank, 2004; Seligman, 1998). To accomplish these goals, psychotherapies offer the following:

1. Therapy provides a *caring relationship* between the client and therapist, called a **therapeutic alliance.** Emotional rapport, warmth, friendship, understanding, acceptance, and empathy are the basis for this relationship. The therapeutic alliance unites the client and therapist as they work together to solve the client's problems. The strength of this alliance has a major impact on whether therapy succeeds (Kozart, 2002; Martin, Garske, & Davis, 2000; Stiles et al., 1998).
2. Therapy offers a *protected setting* in which emotional *catharsis* (release) can take place. Therapy is a sanctuary in which the client is free to express fears, anxieties, and personal secrets without fearing rejection or loss of confidentiality (Weiss, 1990).
3. All therapies to some extent offer an *explanation* or *rationale* for the client's suffering. In addition, they propose a line of action that will end this suffering.
4. Therapy provides clients with a *new perspective* about themselves and their situations and a chance to practice *new behaviors* (Crencavage & Norcross, 1990). Insights gained during therapy can bring about lasting changes in clients' lives (Grande et al., 2003).

If you recall that our discussion began with trepanning and demonology, it is clear that psychotherapy has come a long way. Still, the search for ways to improve psychotherapy remains an urgent challenge for those who devote their lives to helping others. For example, as our appreciation of ethnic diversity grows, both within the United States and internationally, the cross-cultural applicability of psychotherapy becomes a pressing concern (Draguns, Gielen, & Fish, 2004). (See "Therapy and Culture—A Bad Case of 'Ifufunyane.'")

Therapy placebo effect Improvement caused not by the actual process of therapy but by a client's expectation that therapy will help.

Therapeutic alliance A caring relationship that unites a therapist and a client in working to solve the client's problems.

DISCOVERING PSYCHOLOGY

Therapy and Culture—A Bad Case of "Ifufunyane"

At the age of 23, the patient was clearly suffering from "ifufunyane," a form of bewitchment common in the Xhosa culture of South Africa. However, he was treated at a local hospital by psychiatrists, who said he had schizophrenia and gave him antipsychotic drugs. The drugs helped, but his family shunned his fancy medical treatment and took him to a traditional healer who gave him herbs for his ifufunyane. Unfortunately, he got worse and was readmitted to the hospital. This time, the psychiatrists included the patient's family in his treatment. Together, they agreed to treat him with a combination of antipsychotic drugs *and* traditional herbs. This time, the patient got much better and his ifufunyane was alleviated, too (Niehaus, et al. 2005).

As this example illustrates, therapists need to take the culture of their clients into account when treating them. It is valuable for a therapist to understand the client's culture, speak the language, and even be from the same culture. Also, it is often particularly helpful to be able to blend traditional healing methods with contemporary Western therapies (Draguns, Gielen, & Fish, 2004). (For more information, see "Cultural Issues in Counseling and Psychotherapy" in the booklet that accompanies this text.)

In some instances, an appreciation of one's cultural heritage may be the best therapy. For example, suicide rates are tragically high among many North American aboriginal peoples. According to one survey, suicide rates among aboriginal groups are often hundreds of times above average. However, for some groups they are rather rare. Intriguingly, aboriginal groups that are actively preserving their own culture have the lowest suicide rates (Chandler & Lalonde, 1998; Chandler et al., 2003). In fact, suicide was historically rare among native peoples living exclusively within their own cultures (Leenaars et al., 1999). Thus, in some cases, the healing force of maintaining one's cultural heritage may be more helpful than a modern psychotherapist.

Master Therapists

Because therapies have much in common, a majority of psychologists have become *eclectic* in their work (Kopta et al., 1999). *Eclectic* therapists use whatever methods best fit a particular problem (Norcross, 2005). In addition, some seek to combine the best elements of various therapies into more general systems.

What do the most capable therapists have in common? One study of master therapists found that they share several characteristics (Jennings & Skovholt, 1999). The most effective therapists

- Are enthusiastic learners
- Draw on their experience with similar problems
- Value complexity and ambiguity
- Are emotionally open
- Are mentally healthy and mature
- Nurture their own emotional well-being
- Realize that their emotional health affects their work
- Have strong social skills
- Cultivate a working alliance
- Expertly use their social skills in therapy

Notice that this list also could describe the kind of person most of us would want to talk to when facing a life crisis.

The Future of Psychotherapy

What will psychotherapy look like in the future? A group of experts predicted the following (Norcross, Hedges, & Prochaska, 2002):

- There will be an increase in the use of short-term therapy and solution-focused, problem-solving approaches.
- More therapy will be provided by master's-level practitioners (counselors, social workers, and psychiatric nurses).
- The use of lower-cost Internet services, telephone counseling, paraprofessionals, and self-help groups will grow.
- The use of psychiatrists and psychoanalysis will decrease.

As you might guess, many of these predicted changes are based on pressures to reduce the cost of mental health services. Another interesting cost-saving measure is the idea that computers may be able to treat some relatively minor problems. In a recent study, clients worked through ten computer-guided sessions that helped them identify a problem, form a plan of action, and work through carrying out the plan. Most were satisfied with the help they received (Jacobs et al., 2001).

In another major development, attempts are being made to make a list of "empirically supported therapies." These are techniques that have been shown to "work" for specific types of problems. In other words, they are therapies that have been validated through lab studies and work in clinics (Miller & Binder, 2002; Nathan, Stuart, & Dolan, 2000).

Basic Counseling Skills

A number of general helping skills can be distilled from the various approaches to therapy. These are points to keep in mind if you would like to comfort a person in distress, such as a troubled friend or relative (■ Table 17.3).

TABLE 17.3

Helping Behaviors

To help another person gain insight into a personal problem it is valuable to keep the following comparison in mind.

BEHAVIORS THAT HELP	BEHAVIORS THAT HINDER
Active listening	Probing painful topics
Acceptance	Judging/moralizing
Reflecting feelings	Criticism
Open-ended questioning	Threats
Supportive statements	Rejection
Respect	Ridicule/sarcasm
Patience	Impatience
Genuineness	Placing blame
Paraphrasing	Opinionated statements

Adapted from Kottler, 2004.

Gilles Mingasson/Getty Images

Teams of psychologists and counselors are often assembled to provide support to victims of major accidents and natural disasters. Because their work is stressful and often heart wrenching, relief workers also benefit from on-site counseling. Expressing emotions and talking about feelings are major elements of disaster counseling.

Active Listening

People frequently talk "at" each other without really listening. A person with problems needs to be heard. Make a sincere effort to listen to and understand the person. Try to accept the person's message without judging it or leaping to conclusions. Let the person know you are listening, through eye contact, posture, your tone of voice, and your replies (Kottler, 2004).

Clarify the Problem

People who have a clear idea of what is wrong in their lives are more likely to discover solutions. Try to understand the problem from the person's point of view. As you do, check your understanding often. For example, you might ask, "Are you saying that you feel depressed just at school? Or in general?" Remember, a problem well defined is often half solved.

Focus on Feelings

Feelings are neither right nor wrong. By focusing on feelings you can encourage the outpouring of emotion that is the basis for catharsis. Passing judgment on what is said just makes people defensive. For example, a friend confides that he has failed a test. Perhaps you know that he studies very little. If you say, "Just study more and you would do better," he will probably become defensive or hostile. Much more can be accomplished by saying, "You must feel very frustrated," or simply, "How do you feel about it?"

Avoid Giving Advice

Many people mistakenly think that they must solve problems for others. Remember that your goal is to provide understanding and support, not solutions. Of course, it is reasonable to give advice when you are asked for it, but beware of the trap of the "Why don't you . . . ? Yes, but . . ." game. According to psychotherapist Eric Berne (1964), this "game" follows a pattern: Someone says, "I have this problem." You say, "Why don't you do thus and so?" The person replies, "Yes, but . . ." and then tells you why your suggestion won't work. If you make a new suggestion the reply will once again be, "Yes, but . . ." Obviously, the person either knows more about his or her personal situation than you do or he or she has reasons for avoiding your advice. The student described earlier knows he needs to study. His problem is to understand why he doesn't *want* to study.

Accept the Person's Frame of Reference

W. I. Thomas said, "Things perceived as real are real in their effects." Try to resist imposing your views on the problems of others. Because we all live in different psychological worlds, there is no "correct" view of a life situation. A person who feels that his or her viewpoint has been understood feels freer to examine it objectively and to question it. (Accepting and understanding the perspective of another person can be especially difficult when cultural differences exist. See "Cultural Issues in Counseling and Psychotherapy" in the booklet that accompanies this text.)

Reflect Thoughts and Feelings

One of the best things you can do when offering support to another person is to give feedback by simply restating what is said. This is also a good way to encourage a person to talk. If your friend seems to be at a loss for words, *restate* or *paraphrase* his or her last sentence. Here's an example.

Friend: I'm really down about school. I can't get interested in any of my classes. I flunked my Spanish test, and somebody stole my notebook for psychology.

You: You're really upset about school, aren't you?

Friend: Yeah, and my parents are hassling me about my grades again.

You: You're feeling pressured by your parents?
Friend: Yeah, damn.
You: It must make you angry to be pressured by them.

As simple as this sounds, it is very helpful to someone trying to sort out feelings. Try it. If nothing else, you'll develop a reputation as a fantastic conversationalist!

Silence

Studies show that counselors tend to wait longer before responding than do people in everyday conversations. Pauses of 5 seconds or more are not unusual, and interrupting is rare. Listening patiently lets the person feel unhurried and encourages her or him to speak freely (Goodman, 1984).

Questions

Because your goal is to encourage free expression, *open questions* tend to be the most helpful. A *closed question* is one that can be answered yes or no. Open questions call for an open-ended reply. Say, for example, that a friend tells you, "I feel like my boss has it in for me at work." A closed question would be, "Oh yeah? So, are you going to quit?" Open questions, such as, "Do you want to talk about it?" or "How do you feel about it?" are more likely to be helpful.

Maintain Confidentiality

Your efforts to help will be wasted if you fail to respect the privacy of someone who has confided in you. Put yourself in the person's place. Don't gossip.

These guidelines are not an invitation to play "junior therapist." Professional therapists are trained to approach serious problems with skills far exceeding those described here. However, the points made help define the qualities of a therapeutic relationship. They also emphasize that each of us can supply two of the greatest mental health resources available at any cost: friendship and honest communication.

BRIDGES

Open questions are an effective way to begin and sustain a conversation.

See Chapter 14, page 492.

Medical Therapies—Psychiatric Care

Psychotherapy may be applied to anything from a brief crisis to a full-scale psychosis. However, most psychotherapists *do not* treat patients with major depressive disorders, schizophrenia, or other severe conditions. Major mental disorders are more often treated medically (Julien, 2004).

Three main types of **somatic** (bodily) **therapy** are *pharmacotherapy, electroconvulsive therapy,* and *psychosurgery.* Somatic therapy is often done in the context of psychiatric hospitalization. All the somatic approaches have a strong medical slant and they are typically administered by psychiatrists.

Drug Therapies

The atmosphere in psychiatric wards and mental hospitals changed radically in the mid-1950s with the widespread adoption of pharmacotherapy (FAR-meh-koe-THER-eh-pea). **Pharmacotherapy** refers to the use of drugs to treat emotional disturbances. Drugs may relieve the anxiety attacks and other discomforts of milder psychological disorders. More often, however, they are used to combat schizophrenia and major mood disorders.

What sorts of drugs are used in pharmacotherapy? Three major types of drugs are used. **Anxiolytics** (such as Valium) produce relaxation or reduce anxiety. **Antidepressants** are mood-elevating drugs that combat depression. **Antipsychotics** (also called **major tranquilizers**) have tranquilizing effects and, in addition, reduce hallucinations and delusions. (See ■ Table 17.4 for examples of each class of drugs.)

Are drugs a valid approach to treatment? Drugs have shortened hospital stays and they have greatly improved the chances that people will recover from major psychological disorders. Drug therapy has also made it possible for many people to return to the community, where they can be treated on an outpatient basis.

Limitations of Drug Therapy

Few experts would argue for a return to the conditions that existed before pharmacotherapy became available. However, drugs do have drawbacks. For example, 15 percent of patients taking major tranquilizers for long periods develop a neurological disorder that causes rhythmic facial and mouth movements (Chakos et al., 1996). Newer drugs are often hailed as medical "miracles."

TABLE 17.4

Commonly Prescribed Psychiatric Drugs

CLASS	EXAMPLES (TRADE NAMES)	EFFECTS
Minor tranquilizers (antianxiety drugs)	Ativan, Halcion, Librium, Restoril, Valium, Xanax	Reduce anxiety, tension, fear
Antidepressants	Anafranil, Elavil, Nardil, Norpramin, Parnate, Paxil, Prozac, Tofranil, Zoloft	Counteract depression
Antipsychotics (major tranquilizers)	Clozaril, Haldol, Mellaril, Navane, Risperdal, Thorazine	Reduce agitation, delusions, hallucinations, thought disorders

Courtesy of Rodger Casier

The work of artist Rodger Casier illustrates the value of psychiatric care. Despite having a form of schizophrenia, Casier produces artwork that has received public acclaim and has been featured in professional journals.

However, all drugs involve a trade-off between benefits and risks. For example, the drug Clozaril (clozapine) can relieve the symptoms of schizophrenia in some previously "hopeless" cases (Buchanan et al., 1998). But Clozaril is nearly as dangerous as it is helpful: Of every 100 patients taking the drug, 2 suffer from a potentially fatal blood disease.

Is the risk worth it? Many experts think it is, because chronic schizophrenia robs people of almost everything that makes life worth living. It's possible, of course, that newer drugs will improve the risk–benefit ratio in the treatment of severe problems like schizophrenia. For example, the drug Risperdal (risperidone) appears to be as effective as Clozaril, without the lethal risk. But even the best new drugs are not cure-alls. They help some people and relieve some problems, but not all. It is noteworthy that for serious mental disorders a combination of medication and psychotherapy almost always works better than drugs alone. Nevertheless, where schizophrenia and major mood disorders are concerned, drugs will undoubtedly remain the primary mode of treatment (Thase & Kupfer, 1996; Walker et al., 2004).

Shock

In **electroconvulsive therapy (ECT)** a 150-volt electrical current is passed through the brain for slightly less than a second. This rather drastic medical treatment for depression triggers a convulsion and causes the patient to lose consciousness for a short time. Muscle relaxants and sedative drugs are given before ECT to soften its impact. Treatments are given in a series of six to eight sessions spread over 3 to 4 weeks.

How does shock help? Actually, it is the seizure activity that is believed to be helpful. Proponents of ECT claim that shock-induced seizures alter the biochemical and hormonal balance in the brain and body, bringing an end to severe depression and suicidal behavior (Fink, 2000). Others have charged that ECT works only by confusing patients so they can't remember why they were depressed.

The ECT Debate

Not all professionals support the use of ECT. However, most experts seem to agree on the following: (1) At best, ECT produces only temporary improvement—it gets the patient out of a bad spot, but it must be combined with other treatments; (2) ECT can cause memory losses in some patients; (3) ECT should be used only after other treatments have failed; and (4) to lower the chance of a relapse, ECT should be followed by antidepressant drugs (Sackeim et al., 2001). All told, ECT is considered by many

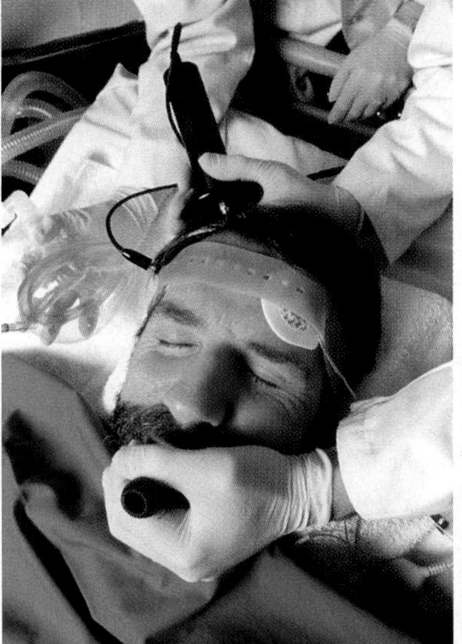

Will & Deni McIntyre/Photo Researchers, Inc.

In electroconvulsive therapy, electrodes are attached to the head and a brief electrical current is passed through the brain. ECT is used in the treatment of severe depression.

Somatic therapy Any bodily therapy, such as drug therapy, electroconvulsive therapy, or psychosurgery.

Pharmacotherapy The use of drugs to alleviate the symptoms of emotional disturbance.

Anxiolytics Drugs (such as Valium) that produce relaxation or reduce anxiety.

Antidepressants Mood-elevating drugs.

Antipsychotics Drugs that, in addition to having tranquilizing effects, also tend to reduce hallucinations and delusional thinking. (Also called major tranquilizers.)

Electroconvulsive therapy (ECT) A treatment for severe depression, consisting of an electric shock passed directly through the brain, which induces a convulsion.

to be a valid treatment for selected cases of depression—especially when it rapidly ends wildly self-destructive or suicidal behavior (Pagnin et al., 2004). It's interesting to note that most ECT patients feel that the treatment helped them. Most, in fact, would have it done again (Bernstein et al., 1998).

Psychosurgery

The most extreme medical treatment is **psychosurgery** (any surgical alteration of the brain). The best-known psychosurgery is the lobotomy. In the *prefrontal lobotomy* the frontal lobes were surgically disconnected from other brain areas. This procedure was supposed to calm persons who didn't respond to any other type of treatment.

When the lobotomy was first introduced in the 1940s, there were enthusiastic claims for its success. But later studies suggested that some patients were calmed, some showed no change, and some became mental "vegetables." Lobotomies also produced a high rate of undesirable side effects, such as seizures, blunted emotions, major personality changes, and stupor. At about the same time that such problems became apparent, the first antipsychotic drugs became available. Soon after, the lobotomy was abandoned (Mashour, Walker, & Martuza, 2005; Pressman, 1998).

To what extent is psychosurgery used now? Psychosurgery is still considered valid by many neurosurgeons. However, most now use *deep lesioning,* in which small target areas are destroyed in the brain's interior. The appeal of deep lesioning is that it can have fairly specific effects. For instance, patients suffering from a severe type of obsessive-compulsive disorder may be helped by psychosurgery (Cumming et al., 1995).

It is worth remembering that psychosurgery cannot be reversed. Whereas a drug can be given or taken away, you can't take back psychosurgery. Many critics argue that psychosurgery should be banned altogether, whereas others continue to report success with brain surgery. All things considered, it is perhaps most accurate, even after decades of use, to describe psychosurgery as an experimental technique. Nevertheless, it may have value as a remedy for some very specific disorders (Fenton, 1998; Mashour, Walker, & Martuza, 2005).

Hospitalization

Mental hospitalization for major mental disorders involves placing a person in a protected setting where medical therapy is provided. Hospitalization, by itself, can be a form of treatment. Staying in a hospital takes patients out of situations that may be sustaining their problems. For example, people with drug addictions may find it nearly impossible to resist the temptations for drug abuse in their daily lives. Hospitalization can help them make a clean break from their self-destructive behavior patterns (Gorman, 1996).

At their best, hospitals are sanctuaries that provide diagnosis, support, refuge, and therapy. This is generally true of psychiatric units in general hospitals and private psychiatric hospitals. At worst, confinement to an institution can be a brutal experience that leaves people less prepared to face the world than when they arrived. This is more often the case in large state mental hospitals (Gorman, 1996).

In most instances, hospitals are best used as a last resort, after other forms of treatment within the community have been exhausted. Actually, most psychiatric patients do as well with short-term hospitalization as they do with longer periods. For this reason, the average stay in psychiatric hospitals is now just 20 days, rather than 3 to 4 months, as it was 20 years ago.

A new trend in treatment is **partial hospitalization.** In this approach, some patients spend their days in the hospital, but go home at night. Others attend therapy sessions during the evening. A major advantage of partial hospitalization is that patients can go home and practice what they've been learning. Eventually, most return to normal life. Overall, partial hospitalization is as effective as full hospitalization (Sledge et al., 1996).

Deinstitutionalization

In the last 30 years the population in large mental hospitals has dropped by two thirds. This is largely a result of **deinstitutionalization**, or reduced use of full-time commitment to mental institutions. Long-term "institutionalization" can lead to dependency, isolation, and continued emotional disturbance (Chamberlin & Rogers, 1990). Deinstitutionalization was meant to remedy this problem.

BRIDGES

Deep lesioning is one of several methods used to investigate the brain's inner workings.

For more information, see Chapter 2, pages 60–61.

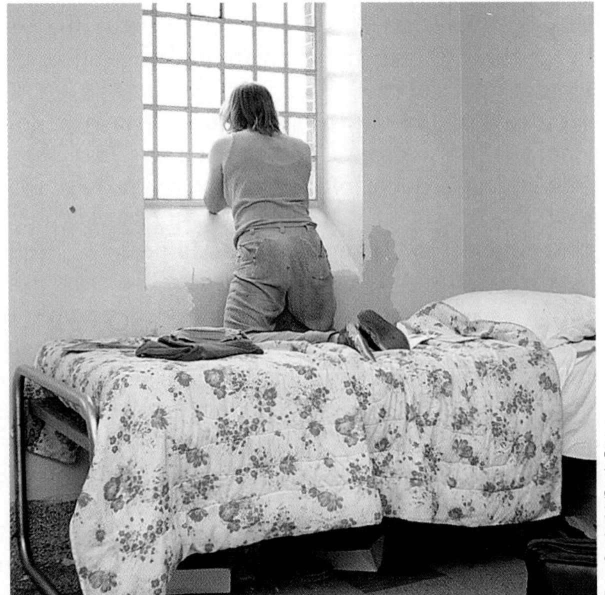

Peter Southwick/Stock, Boston

Depending on the quality of the institution, hospitalization may be a refuge or a brutalizing experience. Many state "asylums" or mental hospitals are antiquated and in need of drastic improvement.

How successful has deinstitutionalization been? In truth, its success has been limited (Talbott, 2004). Many states reduced mental hospital populations primarily as a way to save money. The upsetting result is that many chronic patients have been discharged to hostile communities without adequate care. Many former patients have joined the ranks of the homeless. Others are repeatedly jailed for minor crimes. Sadly, patients who trade hospitalization for unemployment, homelessness, and social isolation all too often end up rehospitalized or in jail (Goldman, 1998).

Large mental hospitals may no longer be warehouses for society's unwanted, but many former patients are no better off in bleak nursing homes, single-room hotels, board-and-care homes, shelters, or jails. One in five of the 2 million Americans who are in jail or prison are mentally ill—three times the number who are in mental hospitals (Human Rights Watch, 2003). These figures suggest that jails are replacing mental hospitals as our society's "solution" for mental illness. Yet, ironically, high-quality care is available in almost every community. As much as anything, a simple lack of money prevents large numbers of people from getting the help they need (Torrey, 1996).

Halfway houses may be a better way to ease patients' return to the community (Anthony, Cohen, & Kennard, 1990). **Halfway houses** are short-term group living facilities for people making the transition from an institution (mental hospital, prison, and so forth) to independent living. Typically, they offer supervision and support, without being as restricted and medically oriented as hospitals. They also keep people near their families. Most important, halfway houses can reduce a person's chances of being readmitted to a hospital (Courtesy, Ward-Alexander, & Katz, 1990).

Community Mental Health Programs

Community mental health centers are a bright spot in the area of mental health care. **Community mental health centers** offer a wide range of mental health services and psychiatric care. Such centers try to help people avoid hospitalization and find answers to mental health problems (Burns, 2004). Typically, they do this by providing short-term treatment, counseling, outpatient care, emergency services, and suicide prevention.

Ed Kashi/Corbis

A well-run half-way house can be a humane and cost-effective way to ease former mental patients back into the community (Courtesy, Ward-Alexander, & Katz, 1990).

If it is like most, the primary aim of the mental health center in your community is to directly aid troubled citizens. Its second goal is likely to be *prevention*. Consultation, education, and **crisis intervention** (skilled management of a psychological emergency) are used to prevent problems before they become serious. Also, some centers attempt to raise the general level of mental health in a community by combating unemployment, delinquency, and drug abuse (Levine, Toro, & Perkins, 1993).

How have community mental health centers done in meeting their goals? In practice, they have concentrated much more on providing clinical services than they have on preventing problems. This appears to be primarily the result of wavering government support (translation: money). Overall, community mental health centers have succeeded in making psychological services more accessible than ever before. Many of their programs rely on **paraprofessionals** (individuals who work in a near-professional capacity under the supervision of more highly trained staff). Some paraprofessionals are ex-addicts, ex-alcoholics, or ex-patients who have "been there." Many more are persons (paid or volunteer) who have skills in tutoring, crafts, or counseling or who are simply warm, understanding, and skilled at communication. Often, paraprofessionals are more approachable than "doctors." This encourages people to seek mental health services that they might otherwise be reluctant to use (Everly, 2002).

A Look Ahead

In the Psychology in Action section that follows we will return briefly to behavioral approaches. There you will find a number of useful techniques that you may be able to apply to your own behavior. You'll also find a discussion of when to seek professional help and how to find it. Here's your authors' professional advice: This is information you won't want to skip.

Psychosurgery Any surgical alteration of the brain designed to bring about desirable behavioral or emotional changes.

Mental hospitalization Placing a person in a protected, therapeutic environment staffed by mental health professionals.

Partial hospitalization An approach in which patients receive treatment at a hospital during the day, but return home at night.

Deinstitutionalization Reduced use of full-time commitment to mental institutions to treat mental disorders.

Halfway house A community-based facility for individuals making the transition from an institution (mental hospital, prison, and so forth) to independent living.

Community mental health center A facility offering a wide range of mental health services, such as prevention, counseling, consultation, and crisis intervention.

Crisis intervention Skilled management of a psychological emergency.

Paraprofessional An individual who works in a near-professional capacity under the supervision of a more highly trained person.

KNOWLEDGE BUILDER

Group Therapy, Helping Skills, and Medical Therapies

REFLECT

Would you rather participate in individual therapy or group therapy? What advantages and disadvantages do you think each has?

Based on your own experience, how valid do you think it is to say that within families "a problem for one is a problem for all"?

What lies at the "heart" of psychotherapy? How would you describe it to a friend?

Which of the basic counseling skills do you already use? Which would improve your ability to help a person in distress?

If a family member of yours became severely depressed, what therapies would be available to him or her? What are the pros and cons of each choice?

LEARNING CHECK

1. In psychodrama, people attempt to form meaningful wholes out of disjointed thoughts, feelings, and actions. T or F?
2. Most large-group awareness trainings make use of Gestalt therapy. T or F?
3. The mirror technique is frequently used in
   a. exposure therapy c. family therapy
   b. psychodrama d. ECT
4. Research shows that about half of all patients feel better after their first ____ therapy sessions.
   a. 8 c. 24
   b. 16 d. 26
5. Emotional rapport, warmth, understanding, acceptance, and empathy are the core of
   a. the therapeutic alliance c. role reversals
   b. large-group awareness training d. action therapy
6. Culturally skilled therapists do all but one of the following; which does *not* apply?
   a. Are aware of the client's degree of acculturation.
   b. Use helping resources within the client's cultural group.
   c. Adapt standard techniques to match cultural stereotypes.
   d. Are aware of their own cultural values.
7. ECT is a modern form of pharmacotherapy. T or F?
8. Currently, the frontal lobotomy is the most widely used form of psychosurgery. T or F?
9. Major tranquilizers are also known as
   a. anxiolytics c. antidepressants
   b. antipsychotics d. prefrontal sedatives
10. Deinstitutionalization is an advanced form of partial hospitalization. T or F?

CRITICAL THINKING

11. In your opinion, do psychologists have a duty to protect others who may be harmed by their clients? For example, if a patient has homicidal fantasies about his ex-wife, should she be informed?
12. Residents of Berkeley, California, voted on a referendum to ban the use of ECT within city limits. Do you think that the use of certain psychiatric treatments should be controlled by law?

Answers: 1. F **2.** F **3.** b **4.** a **5.** a **6.** c **7.** F **8.** F **9.** b **10.** F **11.** According to the law, there is a duty to protect others where a therapist could, with little effort, prevent serious harm. However, this duty can conflict with a client's rights to confidentiality and with client-therapist trust. Therapists often must make difficult choices in such situations. **12.** The question of who can prescribe drugs, do surgery, and administer ECT *is* controlled by law. However, psychiatrists strongly object to residents, city councils, or government agencies making *medical* decisions.

PSYCHOLOGY IN ACTION

Self-Management and Finding Professional Help

"Throw out the snake oil, ladies and gentlemen, and throw away your troubles. Doctor B. Havior Modification is here to put an end to all human suffering."

True? Well, not quite. Behavior therapy is not a cure-all. Its use is often quite complicated and requires a great deal of expertise. Still, behavior therapy offers a straightforward solution to many problems.

Covert Reward and Punishment—Boosting Your "Willpower"

As mentioned elsewhere in this book, you should seek professional help when a significant problem exists. For lesser difficulties you may want to try applying behavioral principles yourself. Let us see how this might be done.

"Have you ever decided to quit smoking cigarettes, watching television too much, eating too much, drinking too much, or driving too fast?"

"Well, one of those applies. I have decided several times to quit smoking."

"When have you decided?"

"Usually after I am reminded of how dangerous smoking is—like when I heard that my uncle had died of lung cancer. He smoked constantly."

"If you have decided to quit 'several times' I assume you haven't succeeded."

"No, the usual pattern is for me to become upset about smoking and then to cut down for a day or two."

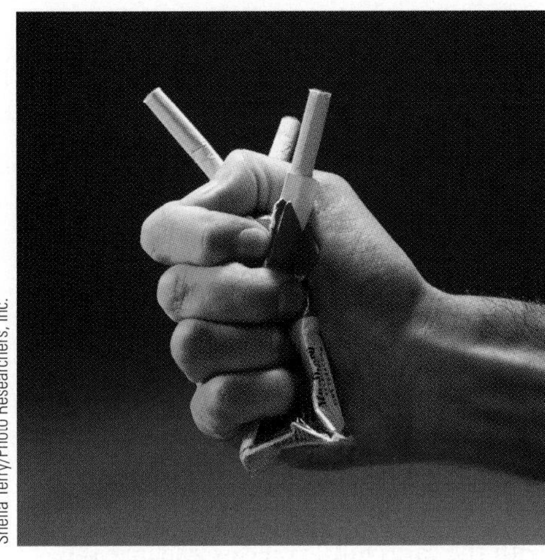
Sheila Terry/Photo Researchers, Inc.

"You forget the disturbing image of your uncle's death, or whatever, and start smoking again."
"Yes, I suppose if I had an uncle die every day or so, I might actually quit!"

The use of intensive behavioral principles, such as electric shock, to condition an aversion seems remote from everyday problems. Even naturally aversive actions are difficult to apply to personal behavior. As mentioned earlier, for instance, rapid smoking is difficult for most smokers to carry out on their own. And what about a problem like overeating? It would be difficult indeed to eat enough to create a lasting aversion to overeating. (Although it's sometimes tempting to try.)

In view of such limitations, psychologists have developed an alternative procedure that can be used to curb smoking, overeating, and other habits (Cautela & Bennett, 1981; Cautela & Kearney, 1986).

Covert Sensitization

In **covert sensitization,** aversive imagery is used to reduce the occurrence of an undesired response. Here's how it's done: Obtain six 3×5 cards and on each write a brief description of a scene related to the habit you wish to control. The scene should be so *disturbing* or *disgusting* that thinking about it would temporarily make you very uncomfortable about indulging in the habit. For smoking, the cards might read as follows:

- I am in a doctor's office. The doctor looks at some reports and tells me I have lung cancer. She says a lung will have to be removed and sets a date for the operation.
- I am in bed under an oxygen tent. My chest feels caved in. There is a tube in my throat. I can barely breathe.
- I wake up in the morning and smoke a cigarette. I begin coughing up blood.
- My lover won't kiss me because my breath smells bad.
- Other cards would continue along the same line.

For overeating the cards might read like this:

- I am at the beach. I get up to go for a swim and I overhear people whispering to each other, "Isn't that fat disgusting?"
- I am at a store buying clothes. I try on several things that are too small. The only things that fit look like rumpled sacks. Salespeople are staring at me.
- Other cards would continue along the same line.

The trick, of course, is to get yourself to imagine or picture vividly each of these disturbing scenes *several times* a day. Imagining the scenes can be accomplished by placing them under *stimulus control.* Simply choose something you do *frequently* each day (such as getting a cup of coffee or getting up from your chair). Next make a rule: Before you can get a cup of coffee or get up from your chair, or whatever you have selected as a cue, you must take out your cards and *vividly picture* yourself engaging in the action you wish to curb (eating or smoking, for example). Then *vividly picture* the scene described on the top card. Imagine the scene for 30 seconds.

After visualizing the top card, move it to the bottom so the cards are rotated. Make up new cards each week. The scenes can be made much more upsetting than the samples given here. The samples are toned down to keep you from being "grossed out."

Covert sensitization can also be used directly in situations that test your self-control. If you are trying to lose weight, for instance, you might be able to turn down a tempting dessert in this way: As you look at the dessert, visualize maggots crawling all over it. If you make this image as vivid and nauseating as possible, losing your appetite is almost a certainty. If you want to apply this technique to other situations, be aware that vomiting scenes are especially effective. Covert sensitization may sound as if you are "playing games with yourself," but it can be a great help if you want to cut down on a bad habit (Cautela & Kearney, 1986). Try it!

Thought Stopping

As discussed earlier, behavior therapists accept that thoughts, like visible responses, can also cause trouble. Think of times when you have repeatedly "put yourself down" mentally or when you have been preoccupied by needless worries, fears, or other negative and upsetting thoughts. If you would like to gain control over such thoughts, thought stopping may help you do it.

In **thought stopping**, aversive stimuli are used to interrupt or prevent upsetting thoughts. The simplest thought-stopping technique makes use of mild punishment to suppress upsetting mental images and internal "talk." Simply place a large, flat rubber band around your wrist. As you go through the day apply this rule: Each time you catch yourself thinking the upsetting image or thought, pull the rubber band away from your wrist and snap it. You need not make this terribly painful. Its value lies in drawing your attention to how often you form negative thoughts and in interrupting the flow of thoughts. Strong punishment is not required.

It seems like this procedure might be abandoned rapidly. Is there an alternative? A second thought-stopping procedure requires only that you interrupt upsetting thoughts each time they occur. Begin by setting aside time each day during which you will deliberately think the unwanted thought. As you begin to form the thought, shout "Stop!" aloud, with

Covert sensitization Use of aversive imagery to reduce the occurrence of an undesired response.

Thought stopping Use of aversive stimuli to interrupt or prevent upsetting thoughts.

conviction. (Obviously, you should choose a private spot for this part of the procedure!)

Repeat the thought-stopping procedure 10 to 20 times for the first 2 or 3 days. Then switch to shouting "Stop!" covertly (to yourself) rather than aloud. Thereafter, thought stopping can be carried out throughout the day, whenever upsetting thoughts occur (Williams & Long, 1991). After several days of practice, you should be able to stop unwanted thoughts whenever they occur.

Covert Reinforcement

Earlier we discussed how punishing images can be used to decrease undesirable responses, such as smoking or overeating. Many people also find it helpful to covertly *reinforce* desired actions. **Covert reinforcement** is the use of positive imagery to reinforce desired behavior. For example, suppose your target behavior is, once again, not eating dessert. If this were the case, you could do the following (Cautela & Bennett, 1981; Cautela & Kearney, 1986):

> Imagine that you are standing at the dessert table with your friends. As dessert is passed, you politely refuse and feel good about staying on your diet.

These images would then be followed by imagining a pleasant, reinforcing scene:

> Imagine that you are your ideal weight. You look really slim in your favorite color and style. Someone you like says to you, "Gee, you've lost weight. I've never seen you look so good."

For many people, of course, actual direct reinforcement (as described in the Psychology in Action section of Chapter 8) is the best way to alter behavior. Nevertheless, covert or "visualized" reinforcement can have similar effects. To make use of covert reinforcement, choose one or more target behaviors and rehearse them mentally. Then follow each rehearsal with a vivid, rewarding image.

Self-Directed Desensitization—Overcoming Common Fears

You have prepared for 2 weeks to give a speech in a large class. As your turn approaches, your hands begin to tremble. Your heart pounds and you find it difficult to breathe. You say to your body, "Relax!" What happens? Nothing! That's why the first step in desensitization is learning to relax voluntarily, by using the tension-release method described earlier in this chapter. As an alternative, you might want to try imagining a very safe, pleasant, and relaxing scene. Some people find such images as relaxing as the tension-release method (Rosenthal, 1993). Another helpful technique is to do some deep breathing. Typically, a person who is breathing deeply is relaxed. Shallow breathing involves little movement of the diaphragm. If you place your hand on your abdomen, it will move up and down if you are breathing deeply.

Once you have learned to relax, the next step is to identify the fear you would like to control and construct a hierarchy.

Procedure for Constructing a Hierarchy

Make a list of situations (related to the fear) that make you anxious. Try to list at least ten situations. Some should be very frightening and others only mildly frightening. Write a short description of each situation on a separate 3 × 5 card. Place the cards in order from the least disturbing situation to the most disturbing. Here is a sample hierarchy for a student afraid of public speaking:

1. Being given an assignment to speak in class
2. Thinking about the topic and the date the speech must be given
3. Writing the speech; thinking about delivering the speech
4. Watching other students speak in class the week before the speech date
5. Rehearsing the speech alone; pretending to give it to the class
6. Delivering the speech to my roommate; pretending my roommate is the teacher
7. Reviewing the speech on the day it is to be presented
8. Entering the classroom; waiting and thinking about the speech
9. Being called; standing up; facing the audience
10. Delivering the speech

Using the Hierarchy

When you have mastered the relaxation exercises and have the hierarchy constructed, set aside time each day to work on reducing your fear. Begin by performing the relaxation exercises. When you are completely relaxed, visualize the scene on the first card (the least frightening scene). If you can *vividly* picture and imagine yourself in the first situation twice *without a noticeable increase in muscle tension,* proceed to the next card. Also, as you progress, relax yourself between cards.

Each day, stop when you reach a card that you cannot visualize without becoming tense in three attempts. Each day, begin one or two cards before the one on which you stopped the previous day. Continue to work with the cards until you can visualize the last situation without experiencing tension (techniques are based on Wolpe, 1974).

By using this approach you should be able to reduce the fear or anxiety associated with things such as public speaking, entering darkened rooms, asking questions in large classes, heights, talking to members of the opposite sex, and taking tests. Even if you are not always able to reduce a fear, you will have learned to place relaxation under voluntary control. This alone is valuable because controlling unnecessary tension can increase energy and efficiency.

Seeking Professional Help—When, Where, and How?

Chance are good that at some point you or someone in your family will benefit from mental health services of one kind or another. In a recent survey, half of all American households had someone who received mental health treatment during the preceding year (Chamberlin, 2004).

How would I know if I should seek professional help at some point in my life? Although there is no simple answer to this question, the following guidelines may be helpful.

1. If your level of psychological discomfort (unhappiness, anxiety, or depression, for example) is comparable to a level of physical discomfort that would cause you to see a doctor or dentist, you should consider seeing a psychologist or a psychiatrist.
2. Another signal to watch for is significant changes in behavior, such as the quality of your work (or schoolwork), your rate of

absenteeism, your use of drugs (including alcohol), or your relationships with others.

3. Perhaps you have urged a friend or relative to seek professional help and were dismayed because he or she refused to do so. If *you* find friends or relatives making a similar suggestion, recognize that they may be seeing things more clearly than you are.
4. If you have persistent or disturbing suicidal thoughts or impulses, you should seek help immediately.

Locating a Therapist

If I wanted to talk to a therapist, how would I find one? Here are some suggestions that could help you get started.

1. **The yellow pages.** Psychologists are listed in the telephone book under "Psychologist," or in some cases under "Counseling Services." Psychiatrists are generally listed as a subheading under "Physicians." Counselors are usually found under the heading "Marriage and Family Counselors." These listings will usually put you in touch with individuals in private practice.
2. **Community or county mental health centers.** Most counties and many cities offer public mental health services. (These are listed in the phone book.) Public mental health centers usually provide counseling and therapy services directly, and they can refer you to private therapists.
3. **Mental health associations.** Many cities have mental health associations organized by concerned citizens. Groups such as these usually keep listings of qualified therapists and other services and programs in the community.
4. **Colleges and universities.** If you are a student, don't overlook counseling services offered by a student health center or special student counseling facilities.
5. **Newspaper advertisements.** Some psychologists advertise their services in newspapers. Also, low-cost "outreach" clinics occasionally try to make their presence known to the public by advertising. In either case, you should carefully inquire into a therapist's training and qualifications. Without the benefit of a referral from a trusted person, it is wise to be cautious.
6. **Crisis hotlines.** The typical crisis hotline is a telephone service staffed by community volunteers. These people are trained to provide information concerning a wide range of mental health problems. They also have lists of organizations, services, and other resources in the community where you can go for help.

■ Table 17.5 summarizes all of the sources for psychotherapy, counseling, and referrals we have discussed, as well as some additional possibilities.

Options *How would I know what kind of a therapist to see? How would I pick one?* The choice between a psychiatrist and a psychologist is somewhat arbitrary. Both are trained to do psychotherapy. Although a psychiatrist can administer somatic therapy and prescribe drugs, a psychologist can work in conjunction with a physician if such services are needed. Psychologists and psychiatrists are equally effective as therapists (Seligman, 1995).

Fees for psychiatrists are usually higher, averaging about $160 to $200 an hour. Psychologists average about $100 an hour. Counselors and social workers typically charge about $80 per hour. Group therapy averages only about $40 an hour because the therapist's fee is divided among several people.

Be aware that most health insurance plans will pay for psychological services. If fees are a problem, keep in mind that many therapists charge on a sliding scale, or ability-to-pay basis, and that community mental health centers almost always charge on a sliding scale. In one way or another, help is almost always available for anyone who needs it.

Some communities and college campuses have counseling services staffed by sympathetic paraprofessionals or peer counselors. These services are free or very low cost. As mentioned earlier, paraprofessionals are people who work in a near-professional capacity under professional supervision. **Peer counselors** are nonprofessional persons who have learned basic counseling skills. There

TABLE 17.5

Mental Health Resources

- Family doctors (for referrals to mental health professionals)
- Mental health specialists, such as psychiatrists, psychologists, social workers, or mental health counselors
- Health maintenance organizations (HMOs)
- Community mental health centers
- Hospital psychiatry departments and outpatient clinics
- University- or medical school–affiliated programs
- State hospital outpatient clinics
- Family service/social agencies
- Private clinics and facilities
- Employee assistance programs
- Local medical, psychiatric, or psychological societies

National Institute of Mental Health.

Covert reinforcement Using positive imagery to reinforce desired behavior.

Peer counselor A nonprofessional person who has learned basic counseling skills.

is a natural tendency, perhaps, to doubt the abilities of paraprofessionals. However, many studies have shown that paraprofessional counselors are often as effective as professionals (Christensen & Jacobson, 1994).

Also, don't overlook self-help groups, which can add valuable support to professional treatment. Members of a self-help group typically share a particular type of problem, such as eating disorders or coping with an alcoholic parent. **Self-help groups** offer members mutual support and a chance to discuss problems. In many instances helping others also serves as therapy for those who give help (Burlingame & Davies, 2002). For some problems, self-help groups may be the best choice of all (Fobair, 1997).

Qualifications You can usually find out about a therapist's qualifications simply by asking. A reputable therapist will be glad to reveal his or her background. If you have any doubts, credentials may be checked and other helpful information can be obtained from local branches of any of the following organizations. You can also write to the addresses listed here.

American Family Therapy Association
2020 Pennsylvania Ave. N.W., Suite 273
Washington, DC 20006

American Psychiatric Association
1400 K Street N.W.
Washington, DC 20005

American Psychological Association
750 1st Street N.E.
Washington, DC 20002

American Association of Humanistic Psychology
7 Hartwood Dr.
Amherst, NY 14226

Canadian Psychiatric Association
200–237 Argyle
Ottawa, ONT K2P1B8

National Mental Health Association
1021 Prince St.
Alexandria, VA 22314

The question of how to pick a particular therapist remains. The best way is to start with a short consultation with a respected psychiatrist, psychologist, or counselor. This will allow the person you consult to evaluate your difficulty and recommend a type of therapy or a therapist who is likely to be helpful. As an alternative you might ask the person teaching this course for a referral.

Evaluating a Therapist *How would I know whether or not to quit or ignore a therapist?* A balanced look at psychotherapies suggests that all *techniques* are about equally successful (Wampold et al., 1997). However, all *therapists* are not equally successful. Far more important than the approach used are the therapist's personal qualities (Norcross, 2002). The most consistently successful therapists are those who are willing to use whatever method seems most helpful for a client. They are also marked by personal characteristics of warmth, integrity, sincerity, and empathy (Jennings & Skovholt, 1999). Former clients consistently rate the person doing the therapy as more important than the type of therapy used (Elliott & Williams, 2003)

It is perhaps most accurate to say that at this stage of development, psychotherapy is an art, not a science. The *relationship* between a client and therapist is the therapist's most basic tool (Hubble, Duncan, & Miller, 1999; Norcross, 2002). This is why you must trust and easily relate to a therapist for therapy to be effective. Here are some danger signals to watch for in psychotherapy:

- Sexual advances by therapist
- Therapist makes repeated verbal threats or is physically aggressive
- Therapist is excessively blaming, belittling, hostile, or controlling
- Therapist makes excessive small talk; talks repeatedly about his or her own problems
- Therapist encourages prolonged dependence on him or her
- Therapist demands absolute trust or tells client not to discuss therapy with anyone else

Clients who like their therapist are generally more successful in therapy (Talley, Strupp, & Morey, 1990). An especially important part of the therapeutic alliance is agreement about the goals of therapy. It is therefore a good idea to think about what you would like to accomplish by entering therapy. Write down your goals and discuss them with your therapist during the first session. Your first meeting with a therapist should also answer all of the following questions (Somberg, Stone, & Claiborn, 1993):

- Will the information I reveal in therapy remain completely confidential?
- What risks do I face if I begin therapy?
- How long do you expect treatment to last?
- What form of treatment do you expect to use?
- Are there alternatives to therapy that might help me as much or more?

It's always tempting to avoid facing up to personal problems. With this in mind, you should give a therapist a fair chance and not give up too easily. But don't hesitate to change therapists or to terminate therapy if you lose confidence in the therapist or if you don't relate well to the therapist as a person.

KNOWLEDGE BUILDER

Self-Management and Finding Professional Help

REFLECT

How could you use covert sensitization, thought stopping, and covert reinforcement to change your behavior? Try to apply each technique to a specific example.

Just for practice, make a fear hierarchy for a situation you find frightening. Does vividly picturing items in the hierarchy make you tense or anxious? If so, can you intentionally relax using the tension-release method?

Assume that you want to seek help from a psychologist or other mental health professional. How would you proceed? Take some time to actually find out what mental health services are available to you.

LEARNING CHECK

1. Covert sensitization and thought stopping combine aversion therapy and cognitive therapy. T or F?
2. Like covert aversion conditioning, covert reinforcement of desired responses is also possible. T or F?
3. The tension-release method is an important part of
   a. covert reinforcement c. desensitization
   b. thought stopping d. REBT
4. Items in a desensitization hierarchy should be placed in order from the least disturbing to the most disturbing. T or F?
5. The first step in desensitization is to place the visualization of disturbing images under stimulus control. T or F?
6. Persistent emotional discomfort is a clear sign that professional psychological counseling should be sought. T or F?
7. Community mental health centers rarely offer counseling or therapy themselves; they only do referrals. T or F?
8. In many instances, a therapist's personal qualities have more of an effect on the outcome of therapy than does the type of therapy used. T or F?

CRITICAL THINKING

9. Would it be acceptable for a therapist to urge a client to break all ties with a troublesome family member?

Answers: 1. T **2.** T **3.** c **4.** T **5.** F **6.** T **7.** F **8.** T **9.** Such decisions must be made by clients themselves. Therapists can help clients evaluate important decisions and feelings about significant persons in their lives. However, actively urging a client to sever a relationship borders on unethical behavior.

Chapter in Review

How do psychotherapies differ? How did psychotherapy originate?

- Psychotherapies may be classified as insight, action, directive, nondirective, or supportive therapies, and combinations of these.
- Therapies may be conducted either individually or in groups, and they may be time limited.
- Primitive approaches to mental illness were often based on belief in supernatural forces.
- Demonology attributed mental disturbance to demonic possession and prescribed exorcism as the cure.
- In some instances, the actual cause of bizarre behavior may have been ergot poisoning.
- More humane treatment began in 1793 with the work of Philippe Pinel in Paris.

Is Freudian psychoanalysis still used?

- Freud's psychoanalysis was the first formal psychotherapy. Psychoanalysis seeks to release repressed thoughts and emotions from the unconscious.
- The psychoanalyst uses free association, dream analysis, and analysis of resistance and transference to reveal health-producing insights.
- Some critics argue that traditional psychoanalysis receives credit for spontaneous remissions of symptoms. However, psychoanalysis is successful for many patients.
- Brief psychodynamic therapy (which relies on psychoanalytic theory but is brief and focused) is as effective as other major therapies.

What are the major humanistic therapies?

- Client-centered (or person-centered) therapy is nondirective and is dedicated to creating an atmosphere of growth.
- Unconditional positive regard, empathy, authenticity, and reflection are combined to give the client a chance to solve his or her own problems.
- Existential therapies, such as Frankl's logotherapy, focus on the end result of the choices one makes in life. Clients are encouraged through confrontation and encounter to exercise free will and to take responsibility for their choices.

Self-help group A group of people who share a particular type of problem and provide mutual support to one another.

- Gestalt therapy emphasizes immediate awareness of thoughts and feelings. Its goal is to rebuild thinking, feeling, and acting into connected wholes and to help clients break through emotional blockages.
- Media psychologists, telephone counselors, and cybertherapists may, on occasion, do some good. However, each has serious drawbacks, and the effectiveness of telephone counseling and cybertherapy has not been established.
- Therapy by videoconferencing shows more promise as a way to provide mental health services at a distance.

What is behavior therapy?

- Behavior therapists use various behavior modification techniques that apply learning principles to change human behavior.
- In aversion therapy, classical conditioning is used to associate maladaptive behavior (such as smoking or drinking) with pain or other aversive events in order to inhibit undesirable responses.

How is behavior therapy used to treat phobias, fears, and anxieties?

- Classical conditioning also underlies systematic desensitization, a technique used to overcome fears and anxieties. In desensitization, gradual adaptation and reciprocal inhibition break the link between fear and particular situations.
- Typical steps in desensitization are as follows: Construct a fear hierarchy, learn to produce total relaxation, and perform items on the hierarchy (from least to most disturbing).
- Desensitization may be carried out with real settings or it may be done by vividly imagining the fear hierarchy or by watching models perform the feared responses.
- In some cases, virtual reality exposure can be used to present fear stimuli in a controlled manner.
- A new technique called eye movement desensitization and reprocessing (EMDR) shows promise as a treatment for traumatic memories and stress disorders. At present, however, EMDR is highly controversial.

What role does reinforcement play in behavior therapy?

- Behavior modification also makes use of operant principles, such as positive reinforcement, nonreinforcement, extinction, punishment, shaping, stimulus control, and time-out. These principles are used to extinguish undesirable responses and to promote constructive behavior.
- Nonreward can extinguish troublesome behaviors. Often this is done by simply identifying and eliminating reinforcers, particularly attention and social approval.
- To apply positive reinforcement and operant shaping, tokens are often used to reinforce selected target behaviors.
- Full-scale use of tokens in an institutional setting produces a token economy. Toward the end of a token economy program, patients are shifted to social rewards such as recognition and approval.

Can therapy change thoughts and emotions?

- Cognitive therapy emphasizes changing thought patterns that underlie emotional or behavioral problems. Its goals are to correct distorted thinking and/or teach improved coping skills.
- In a variation of cognitive therapy called rational-emotive behavior therapy (REBT), clients learn to recognize and challenge their own irrational beliefs.

Can psychotherapy be done with groups of people?

- Group therapy may be a simple extension of individual methods or it may be based on techniques developed specifically for groups.
- In psychodrama, individuals enact roles and incidents resembling their real-life problems. In family therapy, the family group is treated as a unit.
- Although they are not literally psychotherapies, sensitivity and encounter groups attempt to encourage positive personality change. In recent years, commercially offered large-group awareness trainings have become popular. However, the therapeutic benefits of such programs are questionable.

What do various therapies have in common?

- To alleviate personal problems, all psychotherapies offer a caring relationship, emotional rapport, a protected setting, catharsis, explanations for the client's problems, a new perspective, and a chance to practice new behaviors.
- Many basic counseling skills underlie a variety of therapies. These include listening actively, helping to clarify the problem, focusing on feelings, avoiding the giving of unwanted advice, accepting the person's perspective, reflecting thoughts and feelings, being patient during silences, using open questions when possible, and maintaining confidentiality.

How do psychiatrists treat psychological disorders?

- Three medical, or somatic, approaches to treatment are pharmacotherapy, electroconvulsive therapy (ECT), and psychosurgery. All three techniques are controversial to a degree because of questions about effectiveness and side effects.
- Community mental health centers seek to avoid or minimize mental hospitalization. They also seek to prevent mental health problems through education, consultation, and crisis intervention.

How are behavioral principles applied to everyday problems?

- Cognitive techniques can be an aid to managing personal behavior.
- In covert sensitization, aversive images are used to discourage unwanted behavior.
- Thought stopping uses mild punishment to prevent upsetting thoughts.
- Covert reinforcement is a way to encourage desired responses by mental rehearsal.

- Desensitization pairs relaxation with a hierarchy of upsetting images in order to lessen fears.

How could a person find professional help?

- In most communities, a competent and reputable therapist can be located with public sources of information or through a referral.
- Practical considerations such as cost and qualifications enter into choosing a therapist. However, the therapist's personal characteristics are of equal importance.

 Web Resources

Internet addresses frequently change. To find the sites listed here, visit www.thomsonedu.com/psychology/coon for an updated list of Internet addresses and direct links to relevant sites.

***Psychology: Gateways to Mind and Behavior* Website** Online quizzes, flash cards, and other helpful study aids for this text. www.thomsonedu.com/psychology/coon.

Basics of Cognitive Therapy An overview of cognitive therapy, with suggested readings.

How to Find Help for Life's Problems Provides information on psychotherapy and advice on how to choose a psychotherapist.

NetPsychology Explores the delivery of psychological services on the Internet.

Psychological Self-Help An online book about self-improvement.

Science & Pseudoscience Review in Mental Health A review of therapies that are considered to be scientifically dubious.

The Effectiveness of Psychotherapy A summary of the Consumer Reports survey on the effectiveness of psychotherapy.

Types of Therapies Describes four different approaches to therapy. Also has information about choosing a therapist.

Web Counselor Typical personal problems are presented along with examples of advice.

ThomsonNOW™ Go to www.thomsonedu.com to link to ThomsonNow, your online study tool. First take the **Pre-Test** for this chapter to get your **Personalized Study Plan**, which will identify topics you need to review and direct you to online resources. Then take the **Post-Test** to determine what concepts you have mastered and what you still need work on.

InfoTrac College Edition For more information about topics in the Psychology in Action feature, use Key Words search for PSYCHOTHERAPY. Go to www.thomsonedu.com/psychology/coon.

 Interactive Learning

***PsychNow!* Version 2.0 CD-ROM** Interact with the material with *PsychNow!*'s animations, video clips, experiments, and interactive assessments. For this chapter, go to *7b. Major Psychological Therapies* to learn more about different types of psychotherapies.

chapter 18

Social Behavior

THEME:

Humans are social animals. We live in a social world in which our behavior is frequently influenced by the presence of others.

Paul Chesley/Getty Images

Key Questions

How does group membership affect individual behavior?

What unspoken rules govern the use of personal space?

How do we perceive the motives of others, and the causes of our own behavior?

Why do people affiliate?

What factors influence interpersonal attraction?

What have social psychologists learned about conformity, social power, obedience, and compliance?

How does self-assertion differ from aggression?

Preview

We Are Social Animals

To live alone, one must be either an animal or a god.
Aristotle
No man is an island, entire of itself.
John Donne

Here's your assignment: You have been given a written message and the name, address, and occupation of the person who should receive it. The "target person" lives over 1,500 miles away, in a city you have never visited. You can move the message by mail, but you may send it only to a first-name acquaintance. That person, in turn, must mail the message to a first-name acquaintance. The message is to be moved in this fashion until it reaches the target person, whom the previous person must know by name.

Sound impossible? Social psychologist Stanley Milgram once asked people to try moving messages in this way. Amazingly, about one in five made it. Many were *handed* to the target person by a friend or an acquaintance. Even more amazing is the fact that, on average, only seven people were needed to link two strangers separated by half a continent (Korte & Milgram, 1970; Milgram, 1967)!

How is that possible? Each of us is part of a rich tapestry of social relationships. You probably know at least dozens of people by name. Each of them knows dozens more people, who each know still more people, and so on. Thus, each social relationship connects with many others. By following all the social links, you could reach millions of people, just seven "layers" out.

Undeniably, humans are social animals. Although you may like being alone at times, the fact is, humans are social animals. Imagine if you were deprived of all contact with your family and friends. You would probably find it painfully lonely and disorienting.

Social behavior has been the target of an immense amount of study—too much, in fact, for us to cover in detail. Therefore, this chapter and the next are social psychology "samplers." We hope that you will find the topics interesting and thought provoking.

Humans in a Social Context—People, People, Everywhere

Families, teams, crowds, tribes, companies, parties, troops, bands, sects, gangs, crews, clans, communities, nations. Participation in various groups is a basic fact of social life. How do groups influence our behavior? Because you are a member of a group called "psychology class," it would be wise to find out.

Social psychology is the scientific study of how individuals behave, think, and feel in social situations (that is, in the presence, actual or implied, of others) (Baron & Byrne, 2006). Every day, there is a fascinating interplay between our own behavior and that of people around us. We are born into an organized society. Established values, expectations, and behavior patterns are present when we arrive. So too is **culture**, an ongoing pattern of life that is passed from one generation to the next. To appreciate the impact of culture, think about how you have been affected by language, marriage customs, concepts of ownership, and sex roles.

Roles

We all belong to many overlapping social groups: families, teams, church groups, work groups, and so on. In each group we occupy a *position* in the *structure* of the group. **Social roles** are patterns of behavior expected of persons in various social positions. For instance, playing the role of mother, boss, or student involves different sets of behaviors and expectations. Some roles are *ascribed* (they are assigned to a person or are not under personal control): male or female, son, adolescent, inmate. *Achieved roles* are voluntarily attained by special effort: spouse, teacher, scientist, band leader.

Social psychology The scientific study of how individuals behave, think, and feel in social situations.

Culture An ongoing pattern of life, characterizing a society at a given point in history.

Social role Expected behavior patterns associated with particular social positions (such as daughter, worker, student).

Bonnie Kamin/PhotoEdit

Roles have a powerful impact on social behavior. What kinds of behavior do you expect from your teachers? What behaviors do they expect from you? What happens if either of you fails to match the other's expectations?

What effect does role-playing have on behavior? Roles streamline daily interactions by allowing us to anticipate what others will do. When a person is acting as a doctor, mother, clerk, or police officer, we expect certain behaviors. However, roles have a negative side too. Many people experience **role conflicts,** in which two or more roles make conflicting demands on them. Consider, for example, a teacher who must flunk a close friend's daughter, a mother who has a full-time job, and a soccer coach whose son is on the team, but isn't a very good athlete. Likewise, the clashing demands of work, family, and school create role conflicts for many students (Hammer, Grigsby, & Woods, 1998; Senécal, Julien, & Guay, 2003).

Survivor and other "reality" programs on television have offered an interesting, if voyeuristic, look at some of the best and worst aspects of human behavior. However, such programs have nothing over the most revealing experiments in social psychology. For example, a classic study done by Phil Zimbardo and his students at Stanford University showed dramatically how social settings influence our behavior.

In the study, normal healthy male college students were paid to serve as "inmates" and "guards" in a simulated prison (Zimbardo, Haney, & Banks, 1973). After just 2 days in "jail," the inmates grew restless and defiant. When they staged a disturbance, the guards unmercifully suppressed the rebellion. Over the next few days, the guards clamped down with increasing brutality. In a surprisingly short time, the fake convicts looked like real prisoners: They were dejected, traumatized, passive, and dehumanized. Four of them had to be released because they were crying, confused, or severely depressed. Each day, the guards tormented the prisoners with more commands, insults, and demeaning tasks. After 6 days the experiment was halted.

What had happened? Apparently, the assigned social roles—prisoner and guard—were so powerful that in just a few days the experiment became "reality" for those involved. Afterward, it was difficult for many of the guards to believe their own behavior. As one recalls, "I was surprised at myself. I made them call each other names and clean toilets out with their bare hands. I practically considered the prisoners cattle" (Zimbardo, Haney, & Banks, 1973). We tend to think of people as inherently good or bad. But students in the Stanford prison study were randomly assigned to be prisoners or guards. Clearly, the origins of many destructive human relationships can be found in destructive roles.

Group Structure and Cohesion

Are there other dimensions of group membership? Two important dimensions of any group are its structure and cohesiveness. **Group structure** consists of the network of roles, communication pathways, and power in a group. Organized groups such as an army or an athletic team have a high degree of structure. Informal friendship groups may or may not be very structured.

Group cohesiveness refers to the degree of attraction among group members or the strength of their desire to remain in the group. Members of cohesive groups literally stick together: They tend to stand or sit close together, they pay more attention to one another, and they show more signs of mutual affection. Also, their behavior tends to be closely coordinated (Chansler, Swamidass, & Cammann, 2003). Cohesiveness is the basis for much of the power that groups exert over us. Therapy groups, businesses, sports teams, and the like seek to increase cohesion because it helps people work together (Craig & Kelly, 1999).

In-Groups

Cohesiveness is particularly strong for **in-groups** (groups with which a person mainly identifies). Very likely, your own in-group is defined by a combination of social dimensions, such as nationality, ethnicity, age, education, religion, income, political values, gender, sexual orientation, and so forth. In-group membership helps define who we are socially. Predictably, we tend to attribute positive traits to our in-group and negative qualities to **out-groups** (groups with which we do not identify). We also tend to exaggerate differences between members of out-groups and our own group. This sort of "us-and-them" thinking seems to be a basic fact of social life. It also sets the stage for conflict between groups and for racial and ethnic prejudice—topics we will explore in the next chapter.

Status

In addition to defining roles, a person's social position within groups determines his or her **status,** or level of social power and importance. Higher status bestows special privileges and respect. For example, in a classic experiment, researchers left dimes in phone booths. When people entered the booths, a researcher approached and said, "Excuse me, I think I left a dime here a few minutes ago. Did you find it?" Seventy-seven percent of the people returned the money when the researcher was well dressed. Only 38 percent returned it to poorly dressed researchers (Bickman, 1974). You don't have to be in a phone booth for this to work. In

FOCUS ON RESEARCH

Touch and Status

Pause for a moment and think about who you touch during a typical day. Do you think that social status affects your patterns of touching and being touched by others?

It would be surprising if touching weren't affected by status. Touch is one of the most basic forms of communication. Its message can be one of warmth, friendship, caring, nurturance, or sexual interest (see Chapter 13). In addition, touching is a "privilege" of power and high status (Guéguen, 2002). Older persons, for instance, are more likely to touch younger persons than the reverse. Likewise, people of high socioeconomic status are more likely to touch those of lower status.

Even in situations where persons touch each other equal amounts, there is an important difference. When a person of higher status touches one of lower status, the contact is more likely to be "personal" or familiar. When lower-status persons touch those of higher status, it is more likely to be formal or impersonal, such as a handshake (Hall, 1996; Hall, Coats, & LeBeau, 2005).

There is one more difference worth noting. Men, by virtue of their higher status and greater power in society, are more likely to touch women than women are to touch men (Major, Schmidlin, & Williams, 1990). This difference is highly visible in most work settings: Picture a male boss touching his female secretary on the shoulder or arm to get her attention; she, in turn, never touches him. Although women have moved toward equal status with men, patterns of social touching suggest that subtle inequalities in power and dominance persist.

most situations, we are more likely to comply with a request made by a high-status (well-dressed) person (Guéguen, 2002). Perhaps the better treatment given "higher status" persons explains some of our society's preoccupation with expensive clothes, cars, and other status symbols. (For another perspective on the effects of status differences, see "Touch and Status.")

Norms

We are also greatly affected by group norms. A **norm** is a widely accepted (but often unspoken) standard for appropriate behavior. If you have the slightest doubt about the power of norms, try this test: Walk into a crowded supermarket, get in a checkout line, and begin singing loudly in your fullest voice. Probably only 1 person in 100 could actually carry out these instructions.

The impact of norms is shown by an interesting study of littering. The question was, "Does the amount of trash in an area affect littering?" To find out, people were given flyers as they walked into a public parking garage. As you can see in ● Figure 18.1, the more litter there was on the floor, the more likely people were to add to it by dropping their flyer. Apparently, seeing that others had already littered implied a lax norm about whether littering is acceptable. The moral? The cleaner a public area is kept, the less likely people are to "trash" it (Cialdini, Reno, & Kallgren, 1990).

How are norms formed? One early study of group norms made use of a striking illusion called the **autokinetic effect.** In a completely darkened room, a stationary pinpoint of light will appear

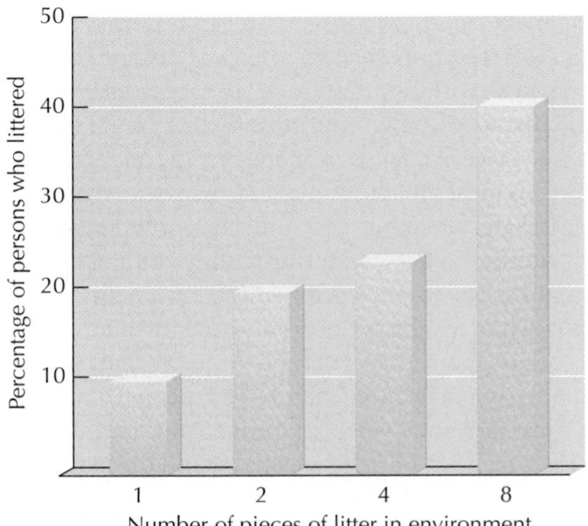

● **Figure 18.1** Results of an experiment on norms concerning littering. The prior existence of litter in a public setting implies that littering is acceptable. This encourages others to "trash" the area. (From Cialdini, Reno, & Kallgren, 1990.)

Role conflict Trying to occupy two or more roles that make conflicting demands on behavior.

Group structure The network of roles, communication pathways, and power in a group.

Group cohesiveness The degree of attraction among group members or their commitment to remaining in the group.

In-group A group with which a person identifies.

Out-group A group with which a person does not identify.

Status An individual's position in a social structure, especially with respect to power, privilege, or importance.

Norm An accepted (but often unspoken) standard of conduct for appropriate behavior.

Autokinetic effect The apparent movement of a stationary pinpoint of light displayed in a darkened room.

to drift or move about. (The light is therefore *autokinetic,* or "self-moving.") Muzafer Sherif (1906–1988) found that people give very different estimates of how far the light moves. However, when two or more people announce their estimates at the same time, their judgments rapidly converge. This is an example of *social influence,* in which one person's behavior is changed by the actions of others (Brehm, & Kassin, & Fein, 2005). We will return to social influence later. For now, it is enough to note that a convergence of attitudes, beliefs, and behaviors tends to take place in many groups (Crano, 2000).

Norms are often based on our *perceptions* of what others think and do. For example, a majority of college students believe that they are more troubled about excessive drinking on campus than other students are. Apparently, many students are fooled by this false norm. Ironically, they help create this false impression by not speaking up. If disapproving students actually outnumber "party animals," then campus norms for acceptable drinking should be fairly conservative, which is usually not the case (Prentice & Miller, 1993).

A vivid example of how norms influence behavior is found in unspoken rules that govern the use of *personal space.* Because personal space is an intriguing topic in its own right, let's take a moment to examine it.

Personal Space—Invisible Boundaries

Each person has an invisible "spatial envelope" that defines his or her **personal space.** This is an area surrounding the body that is regarded as private and subject to personal control. Basically, personal space extends "I" or "me" boundaries past the skin to the immediate environment.

What effect does personal space have on behavior? Regulating personal space affects many social interactions. Powerful norms define the interpersonal distance we regard as appropriate for formal business, casual conversation, waiting in line with strangers, and other situations or settings.

The use of space in public places is governed by unspoken norms, or "rules," about what is appropriate.

The systematic study of rules for the use of personal space is called **proxemics** (prok-SEE-miks) (Hall, 1974). You can demonstrate personal space and the nature of proxemics by "invading" the space of another person. The next time you are talking with an acquaintance, move closer and watch the reaction. Most people show signs of discomfort and step back to re-establish their original distance. Those who hold their ground will turn to the side, look away, or position an arm in front of themselves as a barrier. If you persistently edge toward your subjects, it should be easy to move them back several feet. Such norms may explain why people who feel offended by another person sometimes say, "Get out of my face."

Would this technique work with a good friend? Possibly not. Norms governing comfortable or acceptable distances vary according to relationships as well as activities. Hall (1966) identified four basic zones: *intimate, personal, social,* and *public* distance (● Figure 18.2).

Spatial Norms

Cultural differences also affect spatial norms. In many Middle Eastern countries people hold their faces only inches apart while talking. In Western Europe, the English sit closer together when conversing than the French do. The Dutch, on the other hand, sit farther apart than the French (Remland, Jones, & Brinkman, 1991). In many parts of the world, merely crossing a border can dramatically change spatial behavior (Beaulieu, 2004). The distances listed below apply to face-to-face interactions in North America.

1. **Intimate distance.** For the majority of people, the most private and exclusive space extends about 18 inches out from the skin. Entry within this space (face to face) is reserved for special people or special circumstances. Lovemaking, comforting others, and cuddling children all take place within this space.
2. **Personal distance.** This is the distance maintained in comfortable interaction with friends. It extends from about 18 inches to 4 feet from the body. Personal distance basically keeps people within "arm's reach" of each other.
3. **Social distance.** Impersonal business and casual social gatherings take place in a range of about 4 to 12 feet. This distance eliminates most touching, and it formalizes conversation by requiring greater voice projection. "Important people" in many business offices use the imposing width of their desks to maintain social distance. A big smelly cigar helps, too.
4. **Public distance.** This is the distance at which formal interactions occur (about 12 feet or more from the body). When people are separated by more than 12 feet, people look "flat" and they must raise their voices to speak to one another. Formal speeches, lectures, business meetings, and the like are conducted at public distance.

Because spatial behavior is very consistent, you can learn about your relationship to others by observing the distance you comfortably hold between yourselves. Watch for this dimension in your daily activities. But be aware of cultural differences. Other-

● **Figure 18.2** Typical spatial zones (in feet) for face-to-face interactions in North America. Often, we must stand within intimate distance of others in crowds, buses, subways, elevators, and other public places. At such times, privacy is maintained by avoiding eye contact, by standing shoulder to shoulder or back to back, and by positioning a purse, bag, package, or coat as a barrier to spatial intrusions.

wise, you might misread another person's spatial behavior. People of different nationalities often have different norms for personal space (Beaulieu, 2004). When they do, both are likely to be uncomfortable when talking, as one tries to move closer and the other keeps moving back. This can lead to misunderstandings in which one person feels that the other is being too familiar, while that person feels rejected.

We have now explored some basic facts of social life and a striking example of group norms. In the next section we will consider a kind of impromptu detective work that we engage in as we try to guess the motives of others and the causes of their actions. Let's see how this is done.

AFP/Getty Images

In 2005, in the aftermath of hurricane Katrina, many celebrities, including actor Sean Penn, went to New Orleans to help hurricane victims. As you watched these events, did you attribute the celebrities' actions to selfless concern for the suffering in New Orleans? Or were the celebrities motivated by a selfish desire to hog the limelight? Such attributions greatly affect how we perceive and respond to the social behavior of others.

Social Perception—Behind the Mask

Every day we must guess how people will act, often from small shreds of evidence. We do this through a process called **attribution.** As we observe others, we make inferences about them. Why did Vonda insult Sutchai? Why did Nick change his college major? Why does Kirti talk so fast when she's around men? In answering such questions we *attribute* people's behavior to various causes. Whether we are right or wrong about the causes of their behavior, our conclusions affect how *we* act. To learn how we fill in the "person behind the mask," let's explore the making of attributions.

Attribution Theory

Two people enter a restaurant and order different meals. Nell tastes her food, then salts it. Bert salts his food before he tastes it. How would you explain their behavior? In Nell's case, you might assume that the *food* needed salt. If so, you have attributed her actions to an **external cause** (one that lies outside a person). With Bert, you might be more inclined to conclude that he must really *like* salt. If so, the cause of his behavior is internal. **Internal causes,** such as needs, personality traits, and Bert's taste for salt, lie within the person.

BRIDGES

Attributing bodily arousal to various sources can also have a large impact on emotions.

See Chapter 12, pages 418–419.

Personal space An area surrounding the body that is regarded as private and subject to personal control.

Proxemics Systematic study of the human use of space, particularly in social settings.

Intimate distance The most private space immediately surrounding the body (up to about 18 inches from the skin).

Personal distance The distance maintained when interacting with close friends (about 18 inches to 4 feet from the body).

Social distance Distance at which impersonal interaction takes place (about 4 to 12 feet from the body).

Public distance Distance at which formal interactions, such as giving a speech, occur (about 12 feet or more from the body).

Attribution The process of making inferences about the causes of one's own behavior, and that of others.

External cause A cause of behavior that is assumed to lie outside a person.

Internal cause A cause of behavior assumed to lie within a person—for instance, a need, preference, or personality trait.

What effects do such interpretations have? It is difficult to fully understand social behavior without considering the attributions that we make. For instance, let's say that Tam, who is in one of your classes, seems to avoid you. You see Tam at a market. Do you say hello to him? It could depend on how you have explained Tam's actions to yourself. Have you assumed his avoidance is caused by shyness? Coincidence? Dislike? Many factors affect such judgments. Let's examine a few.

Making Attributions

According to Harold Kelley (1921–2003), one of the originators of attribution theory, when we make attributions we are sensitive to how *consistent* and *distinctive* a person's behavior is (Kelley, 1967). A person's behavior is *consistent* if it changes very little when we observe it on many different occasions. The first time that Tam avoided you he might have just been in a bad mood. However, if Tam has consistently avoided you, it's not likely that he was in a bad mood every time. That rules out coincidence. Still, Tam's avoidance could mean he is shy, not that he dislikes you. That's why distinctiveness is also important. When we watch other people, *distinctiveness* refers to noting that their behavior occurs only under specific circumstances. If you notice that Tam seems to avoid other people too, you may conclude that he is shy or unfriendly. If his avoidance is consistently and distinctively linked only with you, you will probably assume he dislikes you. You could be wrong, of course, but your behavior toward him will change just the same.

To deduce causes, we typically take into account the behavior of the *actor* (the person of interest), the *object* the person's action is directed toward, and the *setting* (social or physical environment) in which the action occurs (Kelley, 1967). Imagine for example, that someone compliments you on your taste in clothes. If you are at a picnic, you may attribute this compliment to what you are wearing (the "object"), unless, of course, you're wearing your worst "grubbies." If you are, you may simply assume that the person (or "actor") is friendly or tactful. However, if you are in a clothing store and a salesperson compliments you, you will probably attribute the compliment to the setting. It's still possible that the salesperson actually likes what you are wearing. Nevertheless, when we make attributions we are very sensitive to the *situational demands* affecting other people's behavior. **Situational demands** are pressures to behave in certain ways in particular settings and social situations. If you see Tam at a funeral, and he is quiet and polite, it will tell you little about his motives and personality traits. The situation demands such behavior.

When situational demands are strong, we tend to *discount* (downgrade) internal causes as a way of explaining a person's behavior. Actually, this is true anytime strong external causes for behavior are present. For example, you have probably discounted the motives of professional athletes who praise shaving creams, hair tonics, deodorants, and the like. Obviously, the large sums of money they receive fully explain their endorsements. It's not necessary to assume they actually *like* the potions they sell. ("Self-Handicapping—Smoke Screen for Failure" discusses a related phenomenon.)

Yet another factor affecting attribution is *consensus* (or agreement). When many people act alike (there is a consensus in their behavior), it implies that their behavior is externally caused. For example, if millions of people go to see the latest Hollywood blockbuster, we tend to say *the movie* is good. If someone you know goes to see a movie six times, when others are staying away in droves, the tendency is to assume that *the person* likes "that type of movie."

Actor and Observer

Let's say that at the last five parties you have attended, you've seen a woman named Macy. Based on this, you assume that Macy is very outgoing and likes to socialize. You see Macy at yet another gathering and mention that she seems to like parties. She says, "Actually, I hate these parties, but I get invited to play my tuba at them. My music teacher says I need to practice in front of an audience, so I keep attending these dumb events. Want to hear a Sousa march?"

We seldom know the real reasons for others' actions. That is why we tend to infer causes from *circumstances*. However, in doing so, we often make mistakes like the one with Macy. The most common error is to attribute the actions of others to internal causes (Follett & Hess, 2002; Jones & Nisbett, 1971). This mistake is called the **fundamental attributional error.** We tend to think the actions of others have internal causes even if they are actually caused by external forces or circumstances.

Where our own behavior is concerned, we are more likely to think that external causes explain most of our actions. In other words, there is an **actor–observer bias** in how we explain behavior. As *observers,* we consistently attribute the behavior of others to their wants, motives, and personality traits (this is the fundamental attributional error). As *actors,* we tend to find external explanations for our own behavior (Krueger, Ham, & Linford, 1996). No doubt you chose your major in school because of what it has to offer. Other students choose *their* majors because of the kind of people they are. Other people who don't leave tips in restaurants

Distressed couples tend to attribute their partners' actions to the worst possible motives, such as bad intentions or selfishness. Thus, attributional styles may lead to serious conflicts in marriage and other relationships (Holtzworth-Munroe & Hutchinson, 1993; Noller & Ruzzene, 1991).

THE CLINICAL FILE

Self-Handicapping—Smoke Screen for Failure

Have you ever known someone who got drunk before taking an exam or making a speech? Why would a person risk failure in this way? Often, the reason lies in **self-handicapping** (arranging to perform under conditions that impair performance). By providing an excuse for poor performance, self-handicapping makes people feel better in situations where they might fail (Kimble & Hirt, 2005).

What if a person succeeds while "handicapped"? Well, then, so much the better. The person's self-image then gets a boost because she or he succeeded under conditions that normally lower performance (Murray & Warden, 1992).

Do you believe that "you either have it or you don't" where ability is concerned? If so, you may be particularly prone to self-handicapping. By working with a handicap, people can avoid any chance of discovering that they "don't have it" (Rhodewalt, 1994)! For instance, college athletes often protect their self-esteem by practicing *less* before important games or events (Bailis, 2001; Kuczka & Treasure, 2005). That way, if they don't do well, they have an excuse for their poor performance.

Drinking alcohol is one of the most popular—and dangerous—self-handicapping strategies. A person who is drunk can attribute failure to being "loaded," while accepting success if it occurs. Examples of using alcohol for self-handicapping include being drunk for school exams, job interviews, or an important first date. A person who gets drunk at such times should be aware that coping with anxiety in this way can lead to serious alcohol abuse (Zuckerman & Tsai, 2005).

Any time you set up excuses for a poor performance, you are self-handicapping. Other examples of self-handicapping include making a half-hearted effort, claiming to be ill, and procrastinating (Urdan & Midgley, 2001). Incidentally, men are more likely than women to self-handicap (Kimble & Hirt, 2005).

Most of us have used self-handicapping at times. Indeed, life would be harsh if we didn't sometimes give ourselves a break from accepting full responsibility for success or failure. Self-handicapping is mainly a problem when it becomes habitual. When it does, it typically leads to lower self-esteem, poor adjustment, and poor health (Zuckerman, Kieffer, & Knee, 1998; Zuckerman & Tsai, 2005). So, watch out for self-handicapping, but try not to be too hard on yourself.

are cheapskates. If you don't leave a tip it's because the service was bad. And, of course, other people are always late because they are irresponsible. You are late because you were held up by events beyond your control.

As you can see, attribution theory summarizes how we think about ourselves and others, including the errors we tend to make. In addition, attribution theory has highlighted some practical problems. Let's conclude with a brief example.

Ye Old Double Standard

Research on attribution has revealed an interesting double standard regarding the abilities of men and women. In a classic study by Kay Deaux and Tim Emswiller (1974), men and women overheard a male or female perform extremely well on a perception task. Each person was then asked to rate whether the test taker's success was due to ability, luck, or some combination of the two. Both men and women attributed male success mainly to skill and women's performances mainly to luck! This was true even though male and female performances were identical.

As early as *kindergarten,* boys tend to take credit for successes. Girls, in contrast, tend to discount their own performances ("put themselves down") (Burgner & Hewstone, 1993). In general, there is a strong tendency to assume, "He's skilled, she's lucky," when assessing the performances of men and women (Swim & Sanna, 1996). Throughout life, such attributions no doubt dog the heels of many talented and successful women.

KNOWLEDGE BUILDER

Social Behavior, Personal Space, and Attribution

REFLECT

What are the most prominent roles you play? Which are achieved and which are ascribed? How do they affect your behavior? What conflicts do they create?

Stand in front of a large object. Using a tape measure, place yourself at distances corresponding to each of the personal space zones. Who do you usually interact with in each zone?

Situational demands Unstated expectations that define desirable or appropriate behavior in various settings and social situations.

Fundamental attributional error The tendency to attribute the behavior of others to internal causes (personality, likes, and so forth)

Actor–observer bias When making attributions, the tendency to attribute the behavior of others to internal causes while attributing one's own behavior to external causes (situations and circumstances).

Self-handicapping Arranging to perform under conditions that usually impair performance, so as to have an excuse for a poor showing.

Think of a time when your attributions were affected by consistency and distinctiveness. Did situational demands also affect your judgments?

Have you ever engaged in self-handicapping? Try to relate the concept to a specific example.

How often do you commit the fundamental attributional error? Again, try to think of a specific example that illustrates the concept.

LEARNING CHECK

1. Male, female, and adolescent are examples of ____________ roles.
2. Status refers to a set of expected behaviors associated with a social position. T or F?
3. Research has shown that the number of first-name acquaintances needed to interconnect two widely separated strangers averages about seven people. T or F?
4. The Stanford prison experiment demonstrated the powerful influence of the autokinetic effect on behavior. T or F?
5. Social psychology is the study of how people behave in ____________________________.
6. If two people position themselves 5 feet apart while conversing, they are separated by a gap referred to as ____________ _______ distance.
7. When situational demands are strong, we tend to attribute a person's actions to internal causes. T or F?
8. The fundamental attributional error is to attribute the actions of others to internal causes. T or F?

CRITICAL THINKING

9. The Stanford prison experiment also illustrates a major concept of personality theory (Chapter 14), especially social learning theory. Can you name it?
10. How could the autokinetic effect contribute to UFO sightings?

Answers: 1. ascribed 2. F 3. T 4. F 5. social situations or the presence of others 6. social 7. F 8. T 9. It is the idea that behavior is often strongly influenced by situations rather than by personal traits. 10. Any point of light in the night sky may appear to move because of the autokinetic effect. This could cause a stationary light to look like it is flying or changing direction rapidly.

The Need for Affiliation—Come Together

Why do people choose to congregate with others? We have already observed that the **need to affiliate** (a desire to associate with other people) appears to be a basic human trait. But why? Probably because affiliation helps meet needs for approval, support, friendship, and information. We also seek the company of others to alleviate fear or anxiety. An experiment in which college women were threatened with electric shock serves as an illustration.

Zilstein's Shock Shop

A man introduced as Dr. Gregor Zilstein ominously explained to arriving subjects, "We would like to give each of you a series of electric shocks . . . these shocks will hurt, they will be painful." In the room was a frightening electrical device that seemed to verify Zilstein's plans. While waiting to be shocked, each subject was given a choice of waiting alone or with other subjects. Women frightened in this way more often chose to wait with others; those who expected the shock to be "a mild tickle or tingle" were more willing to wait alone (Schachter, 1959).

Apparently, the frightened women found it comforting to be with others. Should we conclude that "misery loves company"? Actually, that's not entirely correct. In a later experiment, women expecting to be shocked were given the option of waiting with other shock recipients, with women waiting to see their college advisors, or alone. Most women chose to wait with other future "victims." In short, misery loves miserable company! In general, we prefer to be with people in circumstances similar to our own (Gump & Kulik, 1997).

Is there a reason for that? Yes. Other people provide information for evaluating our own reactions. When a situation is threatening or unfamiliar, or when a person is in doubt, *social comparisons* act as a guide for behavior (Banaji & Prentice, 1994).

Social Comparison Theory

If you want to know how tall you are, you simply get out a tape measure. But how do you know if you are a good athlete, worker, parent, or friend? How do you know if your views on politics, religion, or grunge rock are unusual or widely shared? When there are no objective standards, the only available yardstick is provided by comparing yourself to others (Miller, 2006).

Social psychologist Leon Festinger (1919–1989) theorized that group membership fills needs for **social comparison** (comparing your own actions, feelings, opinions, or abilities to those of others). Have you ever "compared notes" with other students after taking

Mark Richards/PhotoEdit

High school class reunions are notorious for the rampant social comparison they often encourage. Apparently it's hard to resist comparing yourself to former classmates to see how you are doing in life.

an exam? ("How did you do?" "Wasn't that last question hard?") If you have, you were satisfying needs for social comparison.

Typically, we don't make social comparisons randomly or on some ultimate scale. Meaningful evaluations are based on comparing yourself with people of similar backgrounds, abilities, and circumstances (Miller, Turnbull, & McFarland, 1988). To illustrate, let's ask a student named Wendy if she is a good tennis player. If Wendy compares herself to a professional, the answer will be no. But this tells us little about her *relative* ability. Within her tennis group, Wendy is regarded as an excellent player. On a fair scale of comparison, Wendy knows she is good and she takes pride in her tennis skills. In the same way, thinking of yourself as successful, talented, responsible, or fairly paid depends entirely on whom you choose for comparison. Thus, a desire for social comparison influences which groups we join.

In addition to providing information, social comparisons may, at times, be made in ways that reflect desires for self-protection or self-enhancement (Schwinghammer, Stapel, & Blanton, 2006). If you feel threatened, you may make a **downward comparison** by contrasting yourself with a person who ranks lower on some dimension (Banaji & Prentice, 1994). For example, if you have a part-time job and your employer cuts your hours, you may comfort yourself by thinking about a friend who just lost a job.

What about upward comparisons? Do they occur, too? As Wendy's tennis playing suggests, comparing yourself with people of much higher ability will probably just make you feel bad (Tyler & Feldman, 2006). However, **upward comparisons**, in which we compare ourselves to a person who ranks higher on some dimension, are sometimes used for self-improvement. One way that Wendy can learn to improve her tennis skills is to compare herself with players who are only a little better than she is (Collins, 1996).

In general, social comparison theory holds that desires for self-evaluation, self-protection, and self-enhancement provide motives for associating with others. In doing so, they influence which groups we join.

Don't people also affiliate out of attraction for one another? They do, of course. The next section tells why.

Interpersonal Attraction—Social Magnetism?

"Birds of a feather flock together." "Familiarity breeds contempt." "Opposites attract." "Absence makes the heart grow fonder." Are these statements true? Actually, the folklore about friendship is, at best, a mixture of fact and fiction.

What does attract people to each other? **Interpersonal attraction** (affinity to another person) is the basis for most voluntary social relationships (Berscheid & Regan, 2005). As you might expect, we look for friends and lovers who are kind and understanding, who have attractive personalities, and who like us in return (Sprecher, 1998). Deciding whether you would like to know another person can happen very quickly, sometimes within just minutes of meeting (Sunnafrank, Ramirez, & Metts, 2004). In daily life, several factors influence attraction, as described next.

Physical Proximity

Our choice of friends (and even lovers) is based more on *physical proximity* (nearness) than we might care to admit. For example, the closer people live to each other, the more likely they are to become friends. Likewise, lovers may think they have found the "one and only" person in the universe for them. In reality, they have probably found the best match in a 5-mile radius (Buss, 1985)! Marriages are not made in heaven—they are made in schools, businesses, churches, bars, clubs, and neighborhoods.

A main reason for proximity's effect is that it increases the *frequency of contact* between people. A variety of experiments show that we are generally attracted to people with whom we have frequent contact (Saegert, Swap, & Zajonc, 1973). (If you have a reluctant sweetheart, be careful not to send too many love letters—she or he might run off with the letter carrier!) In short, there does seem to be a "boy-next-door" or "girl-next-door" effect in romantic attraction, and a "folks-next-door" effect in friendship. But notice that frequent contact has also become common through Internet chat rooms and e-mail, which can lead to romance at a distance.

Jeff Greenberg/Rainbow

What attracts people to each other? Proximity and frequency of contact have a surprisingly large impact.

Need to affiliate The desire to associate with other people.

Social comparison Making judgments about ourselves through comparison with others.

Downward comparison Comparing yourself with a person who ranks lower than you on some dimension.

Upward comparison Comparing yourself with a person who ranks higher than you on some dimension.

Interpersonal attraction Social attraction to another person.

Physical Attractiveness

People who are *physically attractive* are regarded as good-looking by others. Beautiful people are generally rated as more appealing than average. This is due, in part, to the *halo effect,* a tendency to generalize a favorable impression to unrelated personal characteristics. Because of it, we assume that attractive people are also likable, intelligent, warm, witty, mentally healthy, and socially skilled (Feingold, 1992). Basically, we act as if "what is beautiful is good." Even characters in Hollywood movies tend to be portrayed more favorably if they are beautiful (Smith, McIntosh, & Bazzini, 1999).

There are limits to the traits we associate with beauty. For instance, we do not expect beautiful people to be more honest or concerned about others (Johnson, 1991)! And in reality, physical attractiveness has almost *no* connection to intelligence, talents, or abilities (Feingold, 1992).

Being physically attractive can be an advantage for both males and females (Mehrabian & Blum, 2003). Good-looking people are less lonely, less socially anxious, more popular, more socially skilled, and more sexually experienced than unattractive people (Feingold, 1992). Where romance is concerned, physical attractiveness has more influence on a woman's fate than on a man's (Feingold, 1990). For instance, there is a strong relationship between a woman's physical beauty and her frequency of dating. For men, looks are unrelated to dating frequency. When men and women first meet beauty affects attractiveness more for women and personality more for men (Berry & Miller, 2001).

Do these findings seem shallow and sexist? If so, it may be reassuring to know that beauty is a factor mainly in initial acquaintance (Keller & Young, 1996). Later, more substantial personal qualities become important (Berscheid, 1994, 2000). It takes more than appearance to make a lasting relationship.

Competence

People who are *competent* have knowledge or ability. All other things being equal, we are more attracted to people who are talented or competent. However, there's an interesting twist to this.

John W. Gertz/zefa/Corbis

Physical beauty can be socially advantageous because of the widespread belief that "what is beautiful is good." However, physical beauty is generally unrelated to actual personal traits and talents.

In a revealing classic study, college students listened to audio tapes of candidates for a "College Quiz Bowl." Two of the candidates seemed to be highly intelligent. The other two were of average ability. In addition, one "intelligent" candidate and one "average" candidate clumsily spilled coffee on himself. Later, students rated the intelligent candidate who spilled his coffee as *most* attractive. The *least* attractive person was the candidate who was average and clumsy (Aronson, 1969). Thus, the superior but clumsy person was more attractive than the person who was only superior. Apparently, we like people who are competent but imperfect—which makes them more "human."

Similarity

Take a moment to make a list of your closest friends. What do they have in common (other than the joy of knowing you)? It is likely that their ages are similar to yours and you are of the same sex and ethnicity. There will be exceptions, of course. But similarity on these three dimensions is the general rule for friendships.

Similarity refers to how alike you are to another person in background, age, interests, attitudes, beliefs, and so forth. In everything from marriage to casual acquaintance, similar people are attracted to each other (Brehm, 2002). And why not? It's reinforcing to see our beliefs and attitudes shared by others. It shows we are "right" and reveals that they are clever people as well (Alicke, Yurak, & Vredenburg, 1996)!

Does similarity also influence mate selection? Yes, in choosing a mate, we tend to marry someone who is like us in almost every way, a pattern called **homogamy** (huh-MOG-ah-me) (Blackwell & Lichter, 2004). Studies show that married couples are highly similar in age, education, ethnicity, and religion. To a lesser degree, they are also similar in attitudes and opinions, mental abilities, status, height, weight, and eye color. In case you're wondering, homogamy also applies to unmarried couples who are living together (Blackwell & Lichter, 2000, 2004). Homogamy is probably a good thing. The risk of divorce is highest among couples with sizable differences in age and education (Tzeng, 1992).

Self-Disclosure

How do people who are not yet friends learn if they are similar? To get acquainted you must be willing to talk about more than just the weather, sports, or nuclear physics. At some point you must begin to share private thoughts and feelings and reveal yourself to others. This process, which is called **self-disclosure,** is essential for developing close relationships. In general, as friends talk, they gradually deepen the level of liking, trust, and self-disclosure (Levesque, Steciuk, & Ledley, 2002).

We more often reveal ourselves to persons we like than to those we find unattractive. Disclosure also requires a degree of trust. Many people play it safe, or "close to the vest," with people they do not know well. Indeed, self-disclosure is governed by unspoken rules about what's acceptable. Moderate self-disclosure leads to *reciprocity* (a return in kind). *Overdisclosure,* however, causes suspicion and reduces attraction. Overdisclosure exceeds what is appropriate for a relationship or social situation. For example, imag-

Excessive self-disclosure is a staple of many television talk shows. Guests frequently reveal intimate details about their personal lives, including private family matters, sex and dating, physical or sexual abuse, major embarrassments, and criminal activities. Viewers probably find such intimate disclosures entertaining, rather than threatening, because they don't have to reciprocate.

ine standing in line at a market and having the stranger in front of you say, "Lately I've been thinking about how I really feel about myself. I think I'm pretty well adjusted, but I occasionally have some questions about my sexual adequacy."

When self-disclosure proceeds at a moderate pace, it builds trust, intimacy, reciprocity, and positive feelings. When it is too rapid or inappropriate, we are likely to "back off" and wonder about the person's motives. However, it's interesting to note that in Internet chat rooms, people often feel freer to express their true feelings, which can lead to genuine, face-to-face friendships (Bargh, McKenna, & Fitzsimons, 2002).

Is self-disclosure similar for men and women? Women and men display an interesting difference in patterns of self-disclosure, as described next.

Gendered Friendships

Two male friends share lunch at a restaurant. In the next hour they talk about sports, cars, sports cars, the *Sports Illustrated* swimsuit edition, sports, cars, and golf. (Did we mention sports and cars?) Janis, who was at a nearby table, overheard the entire conversation. Here's her summary of what the men said to each other: "Absolutely nothing!"

In North American culture most male friendships are *activity based.* That is, men tend to do things together—a pattern that provides companionship without closeness.

The friendships of women are more often based on *shared feelings and confidences.* If two female friends spent an afternoon together and did not reveal problems, private thoughts, and feelings to one another, they would assume that something was wrong. For women, friendship is a matter of talking about shared concerns and intimate matters.

Actually, the differences between male and female friendships are smaller than implied here. Men do know *something* about the private thoughts and feelings of their friends. Nevertheless, most contemporary men do not form close friendships with other men. Many could probably learn something from female friendships: Men live their friendships side by side; women live them face-to-face (Bank & Hansford, 2000).

Social Exchange Theory

Self-disclosure involves an exchange of personal information, but other exchanges also occur. In fact, many relationships can be understood as an ongoing series of **social exchanges** (transfers of attention, information, affection, favors, and the like between two people). In many social exchanges, people try to maximize their rewards while minimizing their "costs." When a friendship or love relationship ceases to be attractive, people often say, "I'm not getting anything out of it any more." Actually, they probably are, but their costs—in terms of effort, irritation, or lowered self-esteem—have exceeded their rewards.

According to **social exchange theory,** we unconsciously weigh social rewards and costs. For a relationship to last, it must be *profitable* (its rewards must exceed its costs) for both parties. For instance, Troy and Helen have been dating for 2 years. Although they still have fun at times, they also frequently argue and bicker. If the friction in their relationship gets much stronger, it will exceed the rewards of staying together. When that happens they will probably split up (Gottman, 1994).

Actually, just being profitable is not the whole story. It is more accurate to say that a relationship needs to be *profitable enough.* Generally, the balance between rewards and costs is judged in comparison with what we have come to expect from past experience. The personal standard a person uses to evaluate rewards and costs is called the **comparison level.** The comparison level is high for people with histories of satisfying and rewarding relationships. It is lower for someone whose relationships have been unsatisfying. Thus, the decision to continue a relationship is affected by your personal comparison level. A lonely person, or one whose friendships have been marginal, might stay in a relationship that you would consider unacceptable.

Homogamy Marriage of two people who are similar to one another.

Self-disclosure The process of revealing private thoughts, feelings, and one's personal history to others.

Social exchange Any exchange between two people of attention, information, affection, favors, or the like.

Social exchange theory Theory stating that rewards must exceed costs for relationships to endure.

Comparison level A personal standard used to evaluate rewards and costs in a social exchange.

Loving and Liking—Dating, Rating, Mating

Does romantic attraction differ from interpersonal attraction? In "Love—Stalking an Elusive Emotion" in the booklet accompanying this textbook we noted that **romantic love** is marked by high levels of interpersonal attraction and emotional arousal. We also discussed various types of love that result from combinations of intimacy, passion, and commitment. In Western cultures, sexual desire is also regarded as an important part of romantic attraction (Berscheid & Regan, 2005).

To get another angle on love, psychologist Zick Rubin (1973) chose to think of it as an attitude held by one person toward another. This allowed him to develop "liking" and "love" scales to measure each "attitude" (see ● Figure 18.3). Next, he asked dating couples to complete each scale twice, once with their date in mind and once for a close friend of the same sex.

What were the results? Love for partners and friends differed more than liking did (■ Table 18.1). (**Liking** is affection without passion or deep commitment.) Basically, dating couples like *and* love their partners, but mostly just like their friends. Women, however, were a little more "loving" of their friends than were men. Does this reflect real differences in the strength of male friendships and female friendships? Maybe not, because it is more acceptable in our culture for women to express love for one another than it is for men. Nevertheless, another study confirmed that dating couples feel a mixture of love and friendship for their partners. In fact, 44 percent of a group of dating persons named their romantic partner as their closest friend (Hendrick & Hendrick, 1993).

TABLE 18.1

Average Love and Liking Scores for Date and Same-Sex Close Friend

Attitude toward dating partner	LOVE SCORE	LIKING SCORE
Women	89.5	88.5
Men	89.4	84.7
Attitude toward close friend	**LOVE SCORE**	**LIKING SCORE**
Women	65.3	80.5
Men	55.0	79.1

Rubin, 1970.

Love Scale

1. If ________ were feeling bad, my first duty would be to cheer him (her) up.
2. I feel that I can confide in ________ about virtually everything.
3. I find it easy to ignore ________'s faults.

Liking Scale

1. When I am with ________, we are almost always in the same mood.
2. I think that ________ is unusually well adjusted.
3. I would highly recommend ________ for a responsible job.

● **Figure 18.3** Sample love-scale and liking-scale items. Each scale consists of 13 items similar to those shown. Scores on these scales correspond to other indications of love and liking. (Reprinted by permission of Zick Rubin.)

Love and friendship differ in another interesting way. Romantic love, in contrast to simple liking, usually involves deep **mutual absorption** of the lovers. In other words, lovers (unlike friends) attend almost exclusively to one another. It's not surprising, then, that couples who score high on Rubin's love scale spend more time gazing into each other's eyes than do couples who score low on the scale.

What do romantic partners see when they gaze into each other's eyes? A final interesting characteristic of romantic love is lovers' ability to see their partners in idealized ways. Nobody's perfect, of course. That's why it's no surprise that relationships are most likely to persist when lovers idealize one another. Doing so doesn't just blind them to their partner's faults, it actually helps them create the relationship they wish for (Murray, Holmes, & Griffin, 1996).

Love and Attachment

Sheela has been dating Paul for over a year. Although they have had some rough spots, Sheela is comfortable, secure, and trusting in her love for Paul. Charlene, in contrast, has had a long series of unhappy romances with men. She is basically a loner who has difficulty trusting others. Like Sheela, Eduardo has been dating the same person for a year. However, his relationship with Tanya has been stormy and troubled. Eduardo is strongly attracted to Tanya. Yet he is also in a constant state of anxiety over whether she really loves him.

Sheela, Charlene, and Eduardo might be surprised to learn that the roots of their romantic relationships may lie in childhood. There is growing evidence that early attachments to caregivers (see Chapter 3) can have a lasting impact on how we relate to others (Fraley, 2002; Fraley & Shaver, 2000). For example, studies of dating couples have identified secure, avoidant, and ambivalent attachment patterns similar to those seen in early child development (Mikulincer & Nachshon, 1991). Nationally, about 59 percent of all adults have a secure attachment style, 25 percent are avoidant, and 11 percent have anxious attachment styles (Mickelson, Kessler, & Shaver, 1997).

Secure attachment is a stable and positive emotional bond. A secure attachment style like Sheela's is marked by caring, intimacy, supportiveness, and understanding in love relationships. Secure persons regard themselves as friendly, good natured, and likable. They think of others as generally well intentioned, reliable, and trustworthy. People with a secure attachment style find it relatively easy to get close to others. They are comfortable depending on others and having others depend on them. In general, they don't worry too much about being abandoned or about having someone become too emotionally close to them. Most people prefer to have a secure partner, whatever their own style might be (Latty-Mann, & Davis, 1996).

Charlene's **avoidant attachment** style reflects a fear of intimacy and a tendency to resist commitment to others. Avoidant persons tend to pull back when things don't go well in a relationship. The avoidant person is suspicious, aloof, and skeptical about love. She or he tends to see others as either unreliable or overly eager to commit to a relationship. As a result, avoidant persons find it hard to completely trust and depend on others. Avoidant persons get nervous when anyone gets too close emotionally. Basically, they avoid intimacy (Tidwell, Reis, & Shaver, 1996).

Persons like Eduardo have an **ambivalent attachment** style, marked by mixed emotions about relationships. Conflicting feelings of affection, anger, emotional turmoil, physical attraction, and doubt leave them in an unsettled, ambivalent state. Often, ambivalent persons regard themselves as misunderstood and unappreciated. They tend to see their friends and lovers as unreliable and unable or unwilling to commit themselves to lasting relationships. Ambivalent persons worry that their romantic partners don't really love them or may leave them. Although they want to be extremely close to their partners, they are also preoccupied with doubts about the partner's dependability and trustworthiness.

How could emotional attachments early in life affect adult relationships? It appears that we use early attachment experiences to build mental models about affectionate relationships. Later, we use these models as a sort of blueprint for forming, maintaining, and breaking bonds of love and affection (Simpson, 1990). Thus, the quality of childhood bonds to parents or other caregivers may hold a key to understanding how we approach romantic relationships (Fraley & Shaver, 2000). Maybe it's no accident that persons who are romantically available are often described as "unattached."

BRIDGES

Forming a secure attachment to a caregiver is a major event in early child development.

See Chapter 3, pages 97–99.

It is fascinating to think that our relationships may be influenced by events early in childhood. Could the source of adult mating patterns reach even farther back? The next section explores that possibility.

Evolution and Mate Selection

Evolutionary psychology is the study of the evolutionary origins of human behavior patterns. Many psychologists have come to believe that evolution left an imprint on men and women that influences everything from sexual attraction and infidelity to jealousy and divorce. According to David Buss, the key to understanding human mating patterns is not found just in learning, socialization, attachment, or culture. Rather, we must also understand how evolved behavior patterns guide our choices (Buss, 2004).

In a study of 37 cultures on six continents, Buss found the following patterns: Compared with women, men are more interested in casual sex; they prefer younger, more physically attractive partners; and they get more jealous over real or imagined sexual infidelities than they do over a loss of emotional commitment. Compared with men, women prefer slightly older partners who appear to be industrious, higher in status, or economically successful; women are more upset by a partner who becomes emotionally involved with someone else, rather than one who is sexually unfaithful (Buss et al., 1990) (● Figure 18.4).

Why do such differences exist? Buss and others believe that mating preferences evolved in response to the differing reproductive challenges faced by men and women. As a rule, women must invest more time and energy in reproduction and nurturing the young than men do. Consequently, women evolved an interest in whether their partners will stay with them and whether their mates have the resources to provide for their children (Regan et al., 2000).

In contrast, the reproductive success of men depends on their mates' fertility. Men, therefore, tend to look for health, youth, and beauty in a prospective mate, as signs of suitability for reproduction (Regan et al., 2000). This preference, perhaps, is why some older men abandon their first wives in favor of young, beau-

Romantic love Love that is associated with high levels of interpersonal attraction, heightened arousal, mutual absorption, and sexual desire.

Liking A relationship based on intimacy, but lacking passion and commitment.

Mutual absorption With regard to romantic love, the nearly exclusive attention lovers give to one another.

Secure attachment A stable and positive emotional bond.

Avoidant attachment An emotional bond marked by a tendency to resist commitment to others.

Ambivalent attachment An emotional bond marked by conflicting feelings of affection, anger, and emotional turmoil.

Evolutionary psychology Study of the evolutionary origins of human behavior patterns.

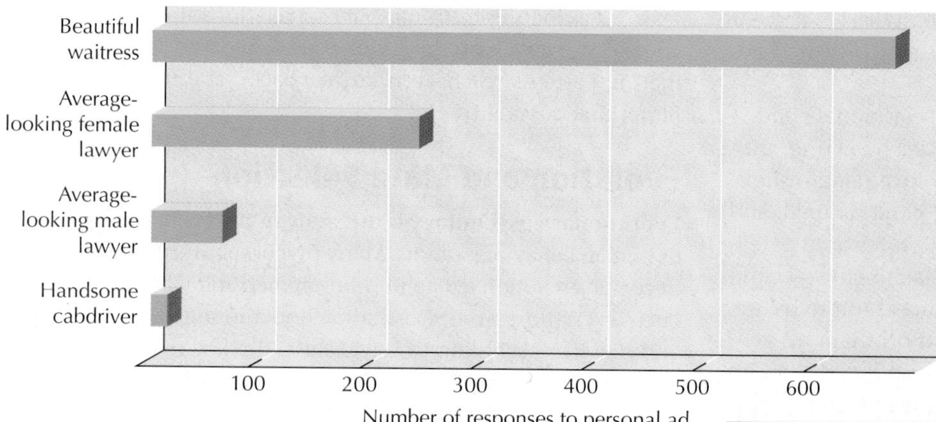

● **Figure 18.4** What do people look for when considering potential dating partners? Here are the results of a study in which personal ads were placed in newspapers. As you can see, men were more influenced by looks, and women by success (Goode, 1996).

According to evolutionary psychologists, women tend to be concerned with whether mates will devote time and resources to a relationship. Men place more emphasis on physical attractiveness and sexual fidelity.

tiful "trophy wives." Evolutionary theory further explains that the male emphasis on mates' sexual fidelity is based on concerns about the paternity of offspring. From a biological perspective, men do not benefit from investing resources in children they did not sire (Schmitt & Buss, 1996).

A sizable body of evidence supports the evolutionary view of mating. However, it is important to remember that evolved mating tendencies are subtle at best and easily overruled by other factors. Some mating patterns may simply reflect the fact that men still tend to control the power and resources in most societies (Feingold, 1992). Also, early research may be misleading because women tend to give "polite" answers to questions about jealousy. Privately, they may be just as furious about a mate's sexual infidelity as any man would be (Harris, 2004).

Whatever the outcome of the debate about evolution and mate selection, it is important to remember this: Potential mates are rated as most attractive if they are kind, secure, intelligent, and supportive (Klohnen & Luo, 2003; Regan et al., 2000). These qualities are love's greatest allies.

KNOWLEDGE BUILDER

Affiliation, Love, Friendship, and Attachment

REFLECT

How has social comparison affected your behavior? Has it influenced who you associate with?

Think of three close friends. Which of the attraction factors described earlier apply to your friendships?

To what extent do Rubin's findings about love and liking match your own experiences?

Can you think of people you know whose adult relationships seem to illustrate each of the three attachments styles described in the preceding section?

LEARNING CHECK

1. Women threatened with electric shock in an experiment generally chose to wait alone or with other women not taking part in the experiment. T or F?
2. The need to affiliate is related to interest in social comparison. T or F?
3. Social comparisons are made pretty much at random. T or F?
4. Interpersonal attraction is increased by all but one of the following. (Which does not fit?)
   a. physical proximity c. similarity
   b. competence d. social costs
5. High levels of self-disclosure are reciprocated in most social encounters. T or F?
6. Women rate their friends higher on the love scale than do men. T or F?
7. The most striking finding about marriage patterns is that most people choose mates whose personalities are quite unlike their own. T or F?
8. Both ambivalent and avoidant attachment patterns are associated with difficulties in trusting a romantic partner. T or F?
9. Compared with men, women tend to be more upset by sexual infidelity than by a loss of emotional commitment on the part of their mates. T or F?

CRITICAL THINKING

10. How have contemporary communications networks altered the effects of proximity on interpersonal attraction?

Answers: 1. F **2.** T **3.** F **4.** d **5.** F **6.** F **7.** F **8.** T **9.** F **10.** As mentioned earlier, it is now possible to interact with another person by telephone, fax, short-wave radio, modem, or similar means. This makes actual physical proximity less crucial in interpersonal attraction, because frequent contact is possible even at great distances.

Social Influence—Follow the Leader

No topic lies nearer the heart of social psychology than **social influence** (changes in behavior induced by the actions of others). When people interact, they almost always affect one another's behavior (Brehm, Kassin, & Fein, 2005; Crano, 2000). For example, in a sidewalk experiment, small groups of people stood on a busy New York City street. On cue they all looked at a sixth-floor window across the street. A camera recorded how many passersby also stopped to stare. The larger the influencing group, the more people were swayed to join in staring at the window (Milgram, Bickman, & Berkowitz, 1969).

Are there different kinds of social influence? Social influence ranges from simple suggestion to intensive indoctrination (brainwashing). Our daily behavior is probably most influenced by group pressures for **conformity** (bringing one's own behavior into agreement with norms or the behavior of others.) Groups of all kinds exert considerable pressures toward uniformity on their members. Conformity typically occurs when people become aware of differences between themselves and the actions, norms, or values of other group members (Baron & Byrne, 2006).

Conformity

When Harry first started working at the Fleegle Flange Factory, he found it easy to process 300 flanges an hour. Others around him averaged only 200. Harry's coworkers told him to slow down and take it easy. "I get bored," he said and continued to do 300 flanges an hour. At first Harry was welcomed, but now conversations broke up when he approached. Other workers laughed at him or ignored him when he spoke. Although he never made a conscious decision to conform, in another week Harry's output had slowed to 200 flanges an hour.

As mentioned earlier, all groups have unspoken rules of conduct called *norms*. The broadest norms, defined by society as a whole, establish "normal" or acceptable behavior in most situations. Comparing hairstyles, habits of speech, dress, eating habits, and social customs in two or more cultures makes it clear that we all conform to social norms. In fact, a degree of uniformity is necessary if we are to interact comfortably. Imagine being totally unable to anticipate the actions of others. In stores, schools, and homes this would be frustrating and disturbing. On the highways it would be lethal.

The Asch Experiment

How strong are group pressures for conformity? One of the first experiments on conformity was staged by Solomon Asch (1907–1996). To fully appreciate it, imagine yourself as a subject. Assume that you are seated at a table with six other students. Your task is actually quite simple: You are shown three lines on a card and you must select the line that matches a "standard" line (● Figure 18.5).

Roy Morsch/Corbis

Conformity is a subtle dimension of daily life. Notice the similarities in the clothing worn by this group of friends.

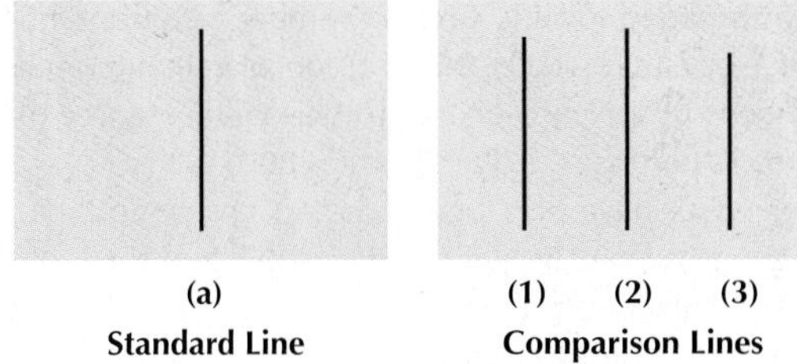

● **Figure 18.5** Stimuli used in Solomon Asch's conformity experiments.

As the testing begins, each person announces an answer for the first card. When your turn comes, you agree with the others. "This isn't hard at all," you say to yourself. For several more trials your answers agree with those of the group. Then comes a shock. All six people announce that line 1 matches the standard, and you were about to say line 2 matches. Suddenly you feel alone and upset. You nervously look at the lines again. The room falls silent. Everyone seems to be staring at you. The experimenter awaits your answer. Do you yield to the group?

In this study the other "students" were all actors who gave the wrong answer on about a third of the trials to create group pressure (Asch, 1956). Real students conformed to the group on about one third of the critical trials. Of those tested, 75 percent yielded at least once. People who were tested alone erred in less than 1 percent of their judgments. Clearly, those who yielded to group pressures were denying what their eyes told them.

Are some people more susceptible to group pressures than others? People with high needs for structure or certainty are more likely

Social influence Changes in a person's behavior induced by the presence or actions of others.

Conformity Bringing one's behavior into agreement or harmony with norms or with the behavior of others in a group.

CRITICAL THINKING

Groupthink—Agreement at Any Cost

As we write this, debate rages about the Iraq war. Why, for example, were no weapons of mass destruction found in Iraq, even though their existence was the major justification for the war in the first place? Was the decision to invade Iraq in 2003 made by a small group of policy makers with little tolerance for dissenting views? Already, it has been suggested that this war may have been a result of **groupthink**—an urge by decision makers to maintain each other's approval, even at the cost of critical thinking (Singer, 2005).

Yale psychologist Irving Janis (1918–1990) first proposed the concept of groupthink in an attempt to understand a series of disastrous decisions made by government officials, in order to understand what happens when people in positions of power fall prey to pressures for conformity (Janis, 1989). The core of groupthink is misguided loyalty. Group members are hesitant to "rock the boat," question sloppy thinking, or tolerate alternative views. This self-censorship leads people to believe they agree more than they actually do (Esser, 1998; Whyte, 2000).

Other crises have also been blamed on groupthink, such as the *Columbia* space shuttle disaster in 2003, and the loss, in 1999, of the $165 million *Mars Climate Orbiter.* In both cases, groupthink contributed to the overlooking of crucial technical flaws that were later found to have caused the disasters. One analysis of 19 international crises found that groupthink contributed to most (Schafer & Crichlow, 1996).

To prevent groupthink, group leaders should take the following steps:

- Define each group member's role as a "critical evaluator."
- Avoid revealing any personal preferences in the beginning.
- State the problem factually, without bias.
- Invite a group member or outside person to play devil's advocate.
- Make it clear that group members will be held accountable for decisions.
- Encourage open inquiry and a search for alternate solutions (Baron, 2005; Chen et al., 1996).

In addition, Janis suggested that there should be a "second-chance" meeting to re-evaluate important decisions. That is, each decision should be reached twice.

In fairness to our decision makers, it is worth noting that the presence of too many alternatives can lead to *deadlock,* which can delay taking necessary action (Kowert, 2002). Regardless, in an age clouded by the threat of war, meltdowns, and similar disasters, even stronger solutions to the problem of groupthink would be welcome. Perhaps we should form a group to think about it?!

to conform. So are people who are anxious, low in self-confidence, or concerned with the approval of others. People who live in cultures that emphasize group cooperation (such as many Asian cultures) are also more likely to conform (Bond & Smith, 1996).

In addition to personal characteristics, certain situations tend to encourage conformity—sometimes with disastrous results. "Groupthink—Agreement at Any Cost" offers a prime example.

Group Factors in Conformity

How do groups enforce norms? In most groups, we have been rewarded with acceptance and approval for conformity and threatened with rejection or ridicule for nonconformity. These reactions are called **group sanctions.** Negative sanctions range from laughter, staring, or social disapproval to complete rejection or formal exclusion. If you've ever felt the sudden chill of disapproval by others, you will understand the power of group sanctions.

Wouldn't the effectiveness of group sanctions depend on the importance of the group? Yes. The more important group membership is to a person, the more he or she will be influenced by other group members. The risk of being rejected can be a threat to our sense of personal identity (Crano, 2000). That's why the Asch experiments are impressive. Because these were only temporary groups, sanctions were informal and rejection had no lasting importance. Just the same, the power of the group was evident.

What other factors, besides importance of the group, affect the degree of conformity? In the sidewalk experiment described earlier, we noted that large groups had more influence. In Asch's face-to-face groups the size of the majority also made a difference, but a surprisingly small one. In other studies, conformity increased dramatically as the majority grew from two to three people. However, a majority of three produced about as much yielding as a majority of eight. The next time you want to talk someone into (or out of) something, take two friends along and see what a difference it makes! (Sometimes it helps if the two are large and mean looking.)

Even more important than the size of the majority is its *unanimity* (total agreement). Having at least one person in your corner can greatly reduce pressures to conform. When Asch gave subjects an ally (who also opposed the majority by giving the correct answer), conformity was lessened. In terms of numbers, a unanimous majority of three is more powerful than a majority of eight with one dissenting. Perhaps this accounts for the rich diversity of human attitudes, beliefs, opinions, and lifestyles. If you can find at least one other person who sees things as you do (no matter how weird), you can be relatively secure in your opposition to other viewpoints. Incidentally, the Internet makes it easier to find that other like-minded person (McKenna & Bargh, 1998)!

KNOWLEDGE BUILDER

Social Influence and Conformity

REFLECT

Identify a recent time when you conformed in some way. How did norms, group pressure, sanctions, and unanimity contribute to your tendency to conform?

What group sanctions have you experienced? What sanctions have you applied to others?

Have you ever been part of a group that seemed to make a bad decision because of groupthink? How could the group have avoided its mistake?

LEARNING CHECK

1. The effect one person's behavior has on another is called ________ ________.
2. Conformity is a normal aspect of social life. T or F?
3. Subjects in Solomon Asch's conformity study yielded on about 75 percent of the critical trials. T or F?
4. Nonconformity is punished by negative group ________ ________.
5. Janis used the term ________ to describe a compulsion among decision-making groups to maintain an illusion of unanimity.

CRITICAL THINKING

6. Would it be possible to be completely nonconforming (that is, to not conform to some group norm)?

Answers: 1. social influence **2.** T **3.** F **4.** sanctions **5.** groupthink **6.** A person who did not follow at least some norms concerning normal social behavior would very likely be perceived as extremely bizarre, disturbed, or psychotic.

Social Power—Who Can Do What to Whom?

Here's something to think about: Strength is a quality possessed by individuals; power is always social—it arises when people come together and disappears when they disperse. In trying to understand the ways in which people are able to influence each other, it is helpful to distinguish among five types of **social power** (the capacity to control, alter, or influence the behavior of another person) (Raven, 1974).

Reward power lies in the ability to reward a person for complying with desired behavior. Teachers try to exert reward power over students with grades. Employers command reward power by their control of wages and bonuses.

Coercive power is based on an ability to punish a person for failure to comply. Coercive power is the basis for most laws, in that fines or imprisonment are used to control behavior.

Legitimate power comes from accepting a person as an agent of an established social order. For example, elected leaders and supervisors have legitimate power. So does a teacher in the classroom. Outside the classroom that power would have to come from another source.

Referent power is based on respect for or identification with a person or a group. The person "refers to" the source of referent power for direction. Referent power is responsible for much of the conformity we see in groups.

Expert power is based on recognition that another person has knowledge necessary for achieving a goal. We allow teachers, lawyers, and other experts to guide behavior because of their ability to produce desired results. Physicians, psychologists, programmers, and plumbers have expert power.

A person who has power in one situation may have very little in another. In those situations where a person has power, she or he is described as an *authority*. In the next section we will investigate **obedience**, a special type of conformity to the demands of an authority. You've probably seen a bumper sticker that says "Question authority." Actually, that's not bad advice if it means "Think critically." However, obedience to authority is a normal part of social life. But what are the limits of obedience? When is it appropriate to resist authority? These are essential questions about how we are affected by social influence based on authority.

Obedience—Would You Electrocute a Stranger?

The question is this: If ordered to do so, would you shock a man with a heart condition who is screaming and asking to be released? Certainly, few people would obey. Or would they? In Nazi Germany, obedient soldiers (once average citizens) helped slaughter over 6 million people in concentration camps. Do such inhumane acts reflect deep character flaws? Are they the acts of heartless psychopaths or crazed killers? Or are they simply the result of obedience to authority? What are the limits of obedience? These are

Groupthink A compulsion by members of decision-making groups to maintain agreement, even at the cost of critical thinking.

Group sanctions Rewards and punishments (such as approval or disapproval) administered by groups to enforce conformity among members.

Social power The capacity to control, alter, or influence the behavior of another person.

Reward power Social power based on the capacity to reward a person for acting as desired.

Coercive power Social power based on the ability to punish others.

Legitimate power Social power based on a person's position as an agent of an accepted social order.

Referent power Social power gained when one is used as a point of reference by others.

Expert power Social power derived from possession of knowledge or expertise.

Obedience Conformity to the demands of an authority.

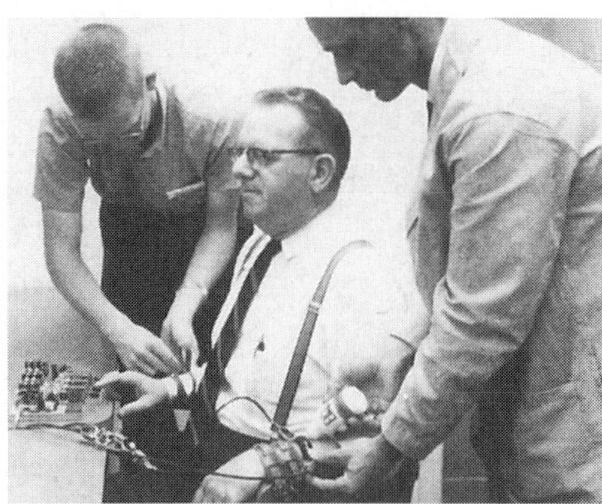
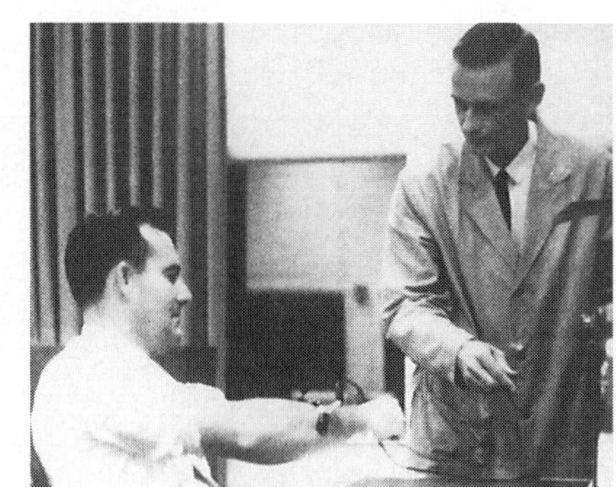

Scenes from the film "Obedience," by Stanley Milgram, The Pennsylvania State University, Audio Visual Services. Used by permission.

● **Figure 18.6** Scenes from Stanley Milgram's study of obedience: the "shock generator," strapping a "learner" into his chair, and a "teacher" being told to administer a severe shock to the learner.

questions that puzzled social psychologist Stanley Milgram (1965) when he began a provocative series of studies on obedience.

How did Milgram study obedience? As was true of the Asch experiments, Milgram's research is best appreciated by imagining yourself as a subject. Place yourself in the following situation.

Milgram's Obedience Studies

Imagine answering a newspaper ad to take part in a "learning" experiment at Yale University. When you arrive, a coin is flipped and a second subject, a pleasant-looking man in his fifties, is designated the "learner." By chance you have become the "teacher."

Your task is to read a list of word pairs. The learner's task is to memorize them. You are to punish him with an electric shock each time he makes a mistake. The learner is taken to an adjacent room and you watch as he is seated in an "electric chair" apparatus. Electrodes are attached to his wrists. You are then escorted to your position in front of a "shock generator." On this device is a row of 30 switches marked from 15 to 450 volts. Corresponding labels range from "Slight Shock" to "Extreme Intensity Shock" and finally "Danger: Severe Shock." Your instructions are to shock the learner each time he makes a mistake. You are to begin with 15 volts and then move one switch (15 volts) higher for each additional mistake (● Figure 18.6).

The experiment begins, and the learner soon makes his first error. You flip a switch. More mistakes. Rapidly you reach the 75-volt level. The learner moans after each shock. At 100 volts he complains that he has a heart condition. At 150 volts he says he no longer wants to continue and demands to be released. At 300 volts he screams and says he can no longer give answers.

At some point, you begin to protest to the experimenter. "That man has a heart condition," you say; "I'm not going to kill that man." The experimenter says, "Please continue." Another shock and another scream from the learner and you say, "You mean I've got to keep going up the scale? No, sir. I'm not going to give him 450 volts!" The experimenter says, "The experiment requires that you continue." For a time the learner refuses to answer any more questions and screams with each shock (Milgram, 1965). Then he falls chillingly silent for the rest of the experiment.

It's hard to believe many people would do this. What happened? Milgram also doubted that many people would obey his orders. When he polled a group of psychiatrists before the experiment, they predicted that less than 1 percent of those tested would obey. The astounding fact is that 65 percent obeyed completely by going all the way to the 450-volt level. Virtually no one stopped short of 300 volts ("Severe Shock") (● Figure 18.7).

Was the learner injured? The time has come to reveal that the "learner" was actually an actor who turned a tape recorder on and off in the shock room. No shocks were ever administered, but the dilemma for the "teacher" was quite real. Subjects protested, sweated, trembled, stuttered, bit their lips, and laughed nervously. Clearly they were disturbed by what they were doing. Nevertheless, most obeyed the experimenter's orders.

Milgram's Follow-Up

Why did so many people obey? Some have suggested that the prestige of Yale University added to subjects' willingness to obey. Could it be that they assumed the professor running the experiment would not really allow anyone to be hurt? To test this possibility, the study was rerun in a shabby office building in nearby Bridgeport, Connecticut. Under these conditions fewer people obeyed (48 percent), but the reduction was minor.

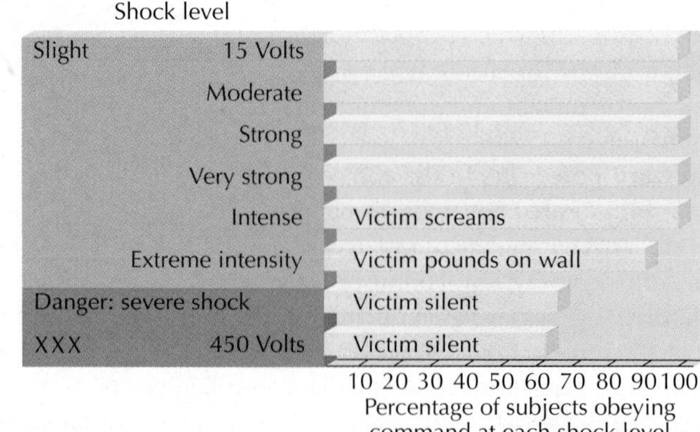

● **Figure 18.7** Results of Milgram's obedience experiment. Only a minority of subjects refused to provide shocks, even at the most extreme intensities. The first substantial drop in obedience occurred at the 300-volt level (Milgram, 1963).

DISCOVERING PSYCHOLOGY

Quack Like a Duck

Imagine your response to the following events. On the first day of class, your psychology professor begins to establish the basic rules of behavior for the course. Draw a line under the first instruction you think you would refuse to carry out.

1. Seats are assigned and you are told to move to a new location.
2. You are told not to talk during class.
3. Your professor tells you that you must have permission to leave early.
4. You are told to bring your textbook to class at all times.
5. Your professor tells you to use only a pencil for taking notes.
6. You are directed to take off your watch.
7. The professor tells you to keep both hands on your desktop at all times.
8. You are instructed to keep both of your feet flat on the floor.
9. You are told to stand up and clap your hands three times.
10. Your professor says, "Stick two fingers up your nose and quack like a duck."

At what point would you stop obeying such orders? In reality, you might find yourself obeying a legitimate authority long after that person's demands had become unreasonable (Aronson, Wilson, & Akert, 2005). What would happen, though, if a few students resisted orders early in the sequence? Would that help free others to disobey? For an answer, return to the discussion of Milgram's experiment for some final remarks.

Milgram was disturbed by the willingness of people to knuckle under to authority and senselessly shock someone. In later experiments, he tried to reduce obedience. He found that the distance between the teacher and the learner was important. When subjects were in the *same room* as the learner, only 40 percent fully obeyed. When they were *face-to-face* with the learner and required to force his hand down on a simulated "shock plate," only 30 percent obeyed (● Figure 18.8). Distance from the authority also had an effect. When the experimenter gave his orders over the phone, only 22 percent obeyed. You may doubt that Milgram's study of obedience applies to you. If so, take a moment to read "Quack Like a Duck."

Percentage complying: 100, 65, 60, 55, 50, 45, 40, 35, 30, 25, 20, 15, 10, 5

"Learner" heard | "Learner" seen | "Learner" touched

● **Figure 18.8** Physical distance from the "learner" had a significant effect on the percentage of subjects obeying orders.

Implications

Milgram's research raises nagging questions about our willingness to commit antisocial or inhumane acts commanded by a "legitimate authority." The excuse so often given by war criminals—"I was only following orders"—takes on new meaning in this light. Milgram suggested that when directions come from an authority, people rationalize that they are not personally responsible for their actions. In locales as diverse as Vietnam, Laos, Rwanda, Bosnia, South Africa, Nicaragua, and Sri Lanka, the tragic result has been "sanctioned massacres" of chilling proportions. Even in everyday life, crimes of obedience are common. In order to keep their jobs, many people obey orders to do things that they know are dishonest, unethical, or harmful (Hamilton & Sanders, 1995).

Rubberball/Jupiterimages

Obedience to authority is often necessary and reasonable; however, it can also be destructive.

Isn't that an overly negative view of obedience? Obedience to authority is obviously necessary and desirable in many circumstances. Just the same, it is probably true, as C. P. Snow (1961) observed, "When you think of the long and gloomy history of man, you will find more hideous crimes have been committed in the name of obedience than in the name of rebellion." With this in mind, let us end on a more positive note. In one of his experiments, Milgram found that group support can greatly reduce destructive obedience. When real subjects saw two other "teachers" (both actors) resist orders and walk out of the experiment, only 10 percent continued to obey. Thus, a personal act of courage or moral fortitude by one or two members of a group may free others to disobey misguided or unjust authority.

Compliance—A Foot in the Door

Pressures to "fit in" and conform are usually indirect. When an authority commands obedience the pressure is direct and difficult to resist. There is a third possibility. The term **compliance** refers to situations in which one person bends to the requests of another person who has little or no authority. Pressures to comply are quite common. For example, a stranger might ask you to yield a phone booth so he can make a call, a saleswoman might suggest that you buy a more expensive watch than you had planned on, or a coworker might ask you for a dollar to buy a cup of coffee.

What determines whether a person will comply with a request? Many factors could be listed, but three stand out as especially interesting.

The Foot-in-the-Door Effect

People who sell door-to-door have long recognized that once they get a foot in the door, a sale is almost a sure thing. To state the **foot-in-the-door principle** more formally, a person who first agrees to a small request is later more likely to comply with a larger demand (Cialdini, 2001). For instance, if someone asked you to put a large, ugly sign in your front yard to promote safe driving, you would probably refuse. If, however, you had first agreed to put a small sign in your window, you would later be much more likely to allow the big sign in your yard (Freedman & Fraser, 1966).

Apparently, the foot-in-the-door effect is based on observing one's own behavior. Seeing yourself agree to a small request helps convince you that you didn't mind doing what was asked. After that, you are more likely to comply with a larger request (Cialdini, 2001).

The Door-in-the-Face Effect

Let's say that a neighbor comes to your door and asks you to feed his dogs, water his plants, and mow his yard while he is out of town for a month. This is quite a major request—one that most people would probably turn down. Feeling only slightly guilty, you tell your neighbor that you're sorry but you can't help him. Now, what if the same neighbor returns the next day and asks if you would at least pick up his mail while he is gone. Chances are very good that you would honor this request, even if you might have originally turned it down, too.

Psychologist Robert Cialdini coined the term **door-in-the-face effect** to describe the tendency for a person who has refused a major request to agree to a smaller request. In other words, after a person has turned down a major request ("slammed the door in your face"), he or she may be more willing to comply with a lesser demand. This strategy works because a person who abandons a large request appears to have given up something. In response, many people feel that they must repay her or him by giving in to the smaller request (Cialdini & Goldstein, 2004). In fact, a good way to get another person to comply with a request is to first do a small favor for the person (Whatley et al., 1999).

The Low-Ball Technique

Anyone who has purchased an automobile will recognize a third way of inducing compliance. Automobile dealers are notorious for convincing customers to buy cars by offering "low-ball" prices that undercut the competition. The dealer first gets the customer to agree to buy at an attractively low price. Then, once the customer is committed, various techniques are used to bump the price up before the sale is concluded.

The **low-ball technique** consists of getting a person committed to act and then making the terms of acting less desirable. Here's another example: A fellow student asks to borrow $25 for a day. This seems reasonable and you agree. However, once you have given your classmate the money, he explains that it would be easier to repay you after payday, in 2 weeks. If you agree, you've succumbed to the low-ball technique. Here's another example: Let's say you ask someone to give you a ride to school in the morning. Only after the person has agreed do you tell her that you have to be there at 6 AM.

Gaining Compliance

To summarize, there are three basic ways to get people to voluntarily comply with a request.

- You can start with a small request that is easy for the person to agree to, and then make a bigger request. (This is the foot-in-the-door strategy.)
- You can make a major request that you know the person will turn down, and then make a smaller request (the one you ac-

CRITICAL THINKING

How to Drive a Hard Bargain

Your local car lot is a good place to see compliance take place. Automobile salespersons play the compliance game daily and get very good at it. If you understand what they are up to, and you are able to critically evaluate their tactics, you will have a far better chance of resisting their sales pressure (Cialdini, 2001; Cialdini & Goldstein, 2004).

A Foot in the Door

The salesperson offers you a test drive. If you accept, you will have made a small commitment of time to a particular car and to the salesperson. The salesperson will then ask you to go to an office and fill out some papers, "just to see what kind of a price" she or he can offer. If you go along, you will be further committed.

The Low-Ball Technique

To get things underway the salesperson will offer you a very good price for your trade-in or will ask you to make an offer on the new car, "any offer, no matter how low." The salesperson will then ask if you will buy the car if she or he can sell it for the price you state. If you say yes, you have virtually bought the car. Most people find it very difficult to walk away once bargaining has reached this stage.

The Hook Is Set

Once buyers are "hooked" by a low-ball offer, the salesperson goes to the manager to have the sale "approved." On returning, the salesperson will tell you with great disappointment that the dealership would lose money on the deal. "Couldn't you just take a little less for the trade-in or pay a little more for the car?" the salesperson will ask. At this point many people hesitate and grumble, but most give in and accept some "compromise" price or trade-in amount.

Evening the Odds

To combat all of the preceding, you must arm yourself with accurate information. In the past, salespeople had a great advantage in negotiating because they knew exactly how much the dealership paid for each car. Now, you can obtain detailed automobile pricing information on the Internet. With such information in hand, you will find it easier to challenge a salesperson's manipulative tactics.

After you've negotiated a final "best offer," get it in writing. Then walk out. Go to another dealer and see if the salesperson will better the price, in writing. When he or she does, return to the first dealership and negotiate for an even better price. Then decide where to buy. Now that you know some of the rules of the "Car Game," you might even enjoy playing it.

tually wanted the person to comply with in the first place). (This is the door-in-the-face strategy.)

- You can make a request and get the person to agree to it. Then change the requirements for fulfilling the request to something the person probably wouldn't have otherwise agreed to do. (This is the low-ball technique.)

One of the main benefits of knowing these strategies is that you can protect yourself from being manipulated by people using them. For example, "How to Drive a Hard Bargain" explains how car salespersons use compliance techniques on customers.

Passive Compliance

Complying with requests is a normal part of daily social life. At times, however, a willingness to comply can exceed what is reasonable. Researcher Thomas Moriarty (1975) has demonstrated excessive, passive compliance under realistic conditions. **Passive compliance** refers to quietly bending to unreasonable demands or unacceptable conditions. Moriarty became interested in the "little murders" of daily life—the personal insults, rebuffs, and sacrifices of dignity that have become so common. Moriarty observed that many people will put up with almost anything to avoid a confrontation. He decided to put this passive, "no-hassle" attitude to experimental test.

BRIDGES

For some people, passive compliance may be an expression of learned helplessness.

See Chapter 15, pages 512–513.

Compliance Bending to the requests of a person who has little or no authority or other form of social power.

Foot-in-the-door effect The tendency for a person who has first complied with a small request to be more likely later to fulfill a larger request.

Door-in-the-face effect The tendency for a person who has refused a major request to subsequently be more likely to comply with a minor request.

Low-ball technique A strategy in which commitment is gained first to reasonable or desirable terms, which are then made less reasonable or desirable.

Passive compliance Passively bending to unreasonable demands or circumstances.

In one experiment, two people (one actually an accomplice) were given a difficult test in a very small room. The subjects were seated back-to-back and left alone to work. As soon as the experimenter left, the phony subject turned on a portable cassette player at full volume. Real subjects who failed to complain were treated to a 17-minute blast of nerve-wracking rock music. The accomplice was instructed to turn the music off only after a third request. In this particular experiment, 80 percent of the subjects said nothing, although they glared, covered their ears, stopped work, and so forth. An interview later showed that most were angry or annoyed, but were afraid to tell the other person to be quiet.

Could it be that people failed to complain because they didn't want to disrupt the testing? Yes, it is possible that the passivity observed in this study is unique to the experimental setting. However, when Moriarty and his students staged loud conversations behind theater patrons or people studying in a library, very few protested. In other naturalistic experiments, people were accosted in phone booths. The experimenter explained that he had left a ring in the booth and asked if the person had found it. When subjects said no, the experimenter demanded that they empty their pockets. Most did.

In these and similar situations, people passively accepted having their personal rights trampled, even when objecting presented no threat to their safety (● Figure 18.9). Overly passive women, in particular, tend to be ripe targets for exploitation, especially by men (Richards, Rollerson, & Phillips, 1991). Have we become "a nation of willing victims"? Certainly, we hope not. Nevertheless, researchers such as Milgram and Moriarty have identified a significant social problem.

A Look Ahead

In the upcoming discussion of Psychology in Action, we will return to the problem of passive behavior to learn how you can better handle difficult social situations. Be assertive, and read on.

● Figure 18.9 In an experiment done at an airport, a smoker intentionally sat or stood near nonsmokers. Only 9 percent of the nonsmokers asked the smoker to stop smoking, even when no-smoking signs were clearly visible nearby (Gibson & Werner, 1994).

Michael Newman/PhotoEdit

KNOWLEDGE BUILDER

Social Power, Obedience, and Compliance

REFLECT

Return to the description of various types of social power. Can you think of a setting in which you have (to a greater or lesser degree) each type of power?

Are you surprised that so many people obeyed orders in Milgram's experiments? Do you think you would have obeyed? How actively do you question authority?

You would like to persuade people to donate to a deserving charity. How, specifically, could you use compliance techniques to get people to donate?

LEARNING CHECK

1. An ability to punish others for failure to obey is the basis for
   a. referent power c. expert power
   b. legitimate power d. coercive power
2. The term *compliance* refers to situations in which a person complies with commands made by a person who has authority. T or F?
3. Obedience in Milgram's experiments was related to
   a. distance between learner and teacher
   b. distance between experimenter and teacher
   c. obedience of other teachers
   d. all of these
4. Obedience is conformity to the commands of an ________________________.
5. By repeating his obedience experiment in a downtown office building, Milgram demonstrated that the prestige of Yale University was the main reason for subjects' willingness to obey in the original experiment. T or F?
6. The research of Thomas Moriarty and others has highlighted the problem of ______________ ______________, rather than obedience to authority.

CRITICAL THINKING

7. Modern warfare allows killing to take place impersonally and at a distance. How does this relate to Milgram's experiments?

Answers: 1. d **2.** F **3.** d **4.** authority **5.** F **6.** passive compliance **7.** There is a big difference between killing someone in hand-to-hand combat and killing someone by lining up images on a video screen. Milgram's research suggests that it is easier for a person to follow orders to kill another human when the victim is at a distance and removed from personal contact.

PSYCHOLOGY IN ACTION

Assertiveness Training—Standing Up for Your Rights

Most of us have been rewarded, first as children and later as adults, for compliant, obedient, or "good" behavior. Perhaps this is why so many people find it difficult to assert themselves. Or perhaps not asserting yourself is related to anxiety about "making a scene" or feeling disliked by others. Whatever the causes, some people suffer tremendous anguish in any situation requiring poise, self-confidence, or self-assertion. Have you ever done any of the following?

- Hesitated to question an error on a restaurant bill because you were afraid of making a scene?
- Backed out of asking for a raise or a change in working conditions?
- Said yes when you wanted to say no?
- Been afraid to question a grade that seemed unfair?

If you have ever had difficulty asserting yourself in similar situations, behavior therapist Joseph Wolpe has a solution for you: a technique called **assertiveness training** (instruction in how to be self-assertive).

What is done in assertiveness training? Assertiveness training is a very direct procedure. By using group exercises, videotapes, mirrors, and staged conflicts, the instructor teaches assertive behavior. People learn to practice honesty, disagreeing, questioning authority, and assertive postures and gestures. As their self-confidence improves, nonassertive clients are taken on "field trips" to shops and restaurants where they practice what they have learned.

Nonassertion requiring therapy is unusual. Nevertheless, many people become tense or upset in at least some situations in which they must stand up for their rights. For this reason, many people have found the techniques and exercises of assertiveness training helpful. If you have ever eaten a carbonized steak when you ordered it rare, or stood in silent rage as a clerk ignored you, the following discussion will be of interest.

Self-Assertion

The first step in assertiveness training is to convince yourself of three basic rights: You have the right to refuse, to request, and to right a wrong. **Self-assertion** involves standing up for these rights by speaking out in your own behalf.

Is self-assertion just getting things your own way? Not at all. A basic distinction can be made between *self-assertion* and *aggressive* behavior. Self-assertion is a direct, honest expression of feelings and desires. It is not exclusively self-serving. People who are nonassertive are usually patient to a fault. Sometimes their pent-up anger explodes with unexpected fury, which can be very destructive to relationships. In contrast to assertive behavior, **aggression** involves hurting another person or achieving one's goals at the expense of another. Aggression does not take into account the feelings or rights of others. It is an attempt to get one's own way no matter what. Assertion techniques emphasize firmness, not attack (■ Table 18.2).

Assertiveness Training

The basic idea in assertiveness training is that each assertive action is practiced until it can be repeated even under stress. For example, let's say it really angers you when a store clerk waits on several people who arrived after you did. To improve your assertiveness in this situation, you would begin by *rehearsing* the dialogue, posture, and gestures you would use to confront the clerk or the other customer. Working in front of a mirror can be very helpful. If possible, you should *role-play* the scene with a friend. Be sure to have your friend take the part of a really aggressive or irresponsible clerk, as well as a cooperative one. Rehearsal and role-playing should also be used when you expect a possible confrontation with someone—for example, if you are going to ask for a raise, challenge a grade, or confront a landlord.

Is that all there is to it? No. Another important principle is **overlearning** (practice that continues after initial mastery of a skill). When you rehearse or role-play assertive behavior, it is essential to continue to practice until your responses become almost automatic. This helps prevent you from getting flustered in the actual situation.

One more technique you may find useful is the **broken record.** This is a self-assertion technique involving repeating a request until it is acknowledged. (In ancient times, when people played phonograph records,

Assertiveness training Instruction in how to be self-assertive.

Self-assertion A direct, honest expression of feelings and desires.

Aggression Hurting another person or achieving one's goals at the expense of another person.

Overlearning Learning or practice that continues after initial mastery of a skill.

Broken record A self-assertion technique involving repeating a request until it is acknowledged.

TABLE 18.2

Comparison of Assertive, Aggressive, and Nonassertive Behavior

	ACTOR	RECEIVER OF BEHAVIOR
Nonassertive behavior	Self-denying, inhibited, hurt, and anxious; lets others make choices; goals not achieved	Feels sympathy, guilt, or contempt for actor; achieves goals at actor's expense
Aggressive behavior	Achieves goals at others' expense; expresses feelings, but hurts others; chooses for others or puts them down	Feels hurt, defensive, humiliated, or taken advantage of; does not meet own needs
Assertive behavior	Self-enhancing; acts in own best interests; expresses feelings; respects rights of others; goals usually achieved; self-respect maintained	Needs respected and feelings expressed; may achieve goal; self-worth maintained

the needle sometimes got "stuck in a groove." When this happened, part of a song might repeat over and over. Hence, the term *broken record* refers to repeating yourself.)

A good way to prevent assertion from becoming aggression is to simply restate your request as many times and in as many ways as necessary. As an illustration, let's say you are returning a pair of shoes to a store. After two wearings the shoes fell apart, but you bought them 2 months ago and no longer have a receipt. The broken record could sound something like this:

Customer: I would like to have these shoes replaced.
Clerk: Do you have a receipt?
Customer: No, but I bought them here, and since they are defective, I would like to have you replace them.
Clerk: I can't do that without a receipt.
Customer: I understand that, but I want them replaced.
Clerk: Well, if you'll come back this afternoon and talk to the manager.
Customer: I've brought these shoes in because they are defective.
Clerk: Well, I'm not authorized to replace them.
Customer: Yes, well, if you'll replace these, I'll be on my way.

Notice that the customer did not attack the clerk or create an angry confrontation. Simple persistence is often all that is necessary for successful self-assertion.

How would I respond assertively to a put-down? Responding assertively to verbal aggression (a "put-down") is a real challenge. The tendency is to respond aggressively, which usually makes things worse. A good way to respond to a put-down uses the following steps: (1) If you are wrong, admit it; (2) acknowledge the person's feelings; (3) assert yourself about the other person's aggression; (4) briskly end the interchange.

Psychologists Robert Alberti and Michael Emmons (1995) offer an example of how to use the four steps. Let's say you accidentally bump into someone. The person responds angrily, "Damn it! Why don't you watch where you're going! You fool, you could have hurt me!" A good response would be to say, "I'm sorry I bumped you. I didn't do it intentionally. It's obvious you're upset, but I don't like your calling me names, or yelling. I can get your point without that."

Now, what if someone insults you indirectly ("I love your taste in clothes, it's so 'folksy.'")? Alberti and Emmons suggest you ask for a clarification ("What are you trying to say?"). This will force the person to take responsibility for the aggression. It can also provide an opportunity to change the way the person interacts with you: "If you really don't like what I'm wearing, I'd like to know it. I'm not always sure I like the things I buy, and I value your opinion."

To summarize, self-assertion does not supply instant poise, confidence, or self-assurance. However, it is a way of combating anxieties associated with life in an impersonal and sometimes intimidating society. If you are interested in more information, you can consult a book entitled *Your Perfect Right* by Alberti and Emmons (1995).

KNOWLEDGE BUILDER

Assertiveness Training

REFLECT

Pick a specific instance when you could have been more assertive. How would you handle the situation if it occurs again?

Think of a specific instance when you were angry and acted aggressively. How could you have handled the situation through self-assertion, instead of aggression?

LEARNING CHECK

1. In assertiveness training, people learn techniques for getting their way in social situations and angry interchanges. T or F?
2. Nonassertive behavior causes hurt, anxiety, and self-denial in the actor, and sympathy, guilt, or contempt in the receiver. T or F?
3. Overlearning should be avoided when rehearsing assertive behaviors. T or F?
4. The "broken record" must be avoided, because it is a basic nonassertive behavior. T or F?

CRITICAL THINKING

5. When practicing self-assertion, do you think it would be better to improvise your own responses or imitate those of a person skilled in self-assertion?

Answers: 1. F **2.** T **3.** F **4.** F **5.** A recent study found that imitating an assertive model is more effective than improvising your own responses (Kipper, 1992). If you know an assertive and self-assured person, you can learn a lot by watching how they handle difficult situations.

Chapter in Review

How does group membership affect individual behavior?

- Humans are social animals enmeshed in a complex network of social relationships. Social psychology studies how individuals behave, think, and feel in social situations.
- Culture provides a broad social context for our behavior. One's position in groups defines a variety of roles to be played.
- Social roles, which may be achieved or ascribed, are particular behavior patterns associated with social positions. When two or more contradictory roles are held, role conflict may occur. The Stanford prison experiment showed that destructive roles may override individual motives for behavior.
- Positions within groups typically carry higher or lower levels of status. High status is associated with special privileges and respect.
- Group structure refers to the organization of roles, communication pathways, and power within a group. Group cohesiveness is basically the degree of attraction among group members.
- Norms are standards of conduct enforced (formally or informally) by groups. The autokinetic effect has been used to demonstrate that norms rapidly form even in temporary groups.

What unspoken rules govern the use of personal space?

- The study of personal space is called proxemics. Four basic spatial zones around each person's body are intimate distance (0–18 inches), personal distance (1½–4 feet), social distance (4–12 feet), and public distance (12 feet or more).

How do we perceive the motives of others, and the causes of our own behavior?

- Attribution theory is concerned with how we make inferences about behavior. A variety of factors affect attribution, including consistency, distinctiveness, situational demands, and consensus.
- The fundamental attributional error is to ascribe the actions of others to internal causes. Because of actor–observer differences, we tend to attribute our own behavior to external causes.
- Self-handicapping involves arranging excuses for poor performance as a way to protect one's self-image or self-esteem.

Why do people affiliate?

- The need to affiliate is tied to additional needs for approval, support, friendship, and information. In addition, research indicates that affiliation is related to reducing anxiety and uncertainty.
- Social comparison theory holds that we affiliate to evaluate our actions, feelings, and abilities. Social comparisons are also made for purposes of self-protection and self-enhancement.

What factors influence interpersonal attraction?

- Interpersonal attraction is increased by physical proximity (nearness), frequent contact, physical attractiveness, competence, and similarity. A large degree of similarity on many dimensions is characteristic of mate selection.
- Self-disclosure occurs more when two people like one another. Self-disclosure follows a reciprocity norm: Low levels of self-disclosure are met with low levels in return, whereas moderate self-disclosure elicits more personal replies. However, overdisclosure tends to inhibit self-disclosure by others.
- According to social exchange theory, we tend to maintain relationships that are profitable; that is, those for which perceived rewards exceed perceived costs.
- Romantic love has been studied as a special kind of attitude. Love can be distinguished from liking by the use of attitude scales. Dating couples like and love their partners but only like their friends. Love is also associated with greater mutual absorption between people.
- Adult love relationships tend to mirror patterns of emotional attachment observed in infancy and early childhood. Secure, avoidant, and ambivalent patterns can be defined on the basis of how a person approaches romantic and affectionate relationships with others.
- Evolutionary psychology attributes human mating patterns to the differing reproductive challenges faced by men and women since the dawn of time.

What have social psychologists learned about conformity, social power, obedience, and compliance?

- In general, social influence refers to alterations in behavior brought about by the behavior of others. Conformity to group pressure is a familiar example of social influence.

- Virtually everyone conforms to a variety of broad social and cultural norms. Conformity pressures also exist within smaller groups. The famous Asch experiments demonstrated that various group sanctions encourage conformity.
- Groupthink refers to compulsive conformity in group decision making. Victims of groupthink seek to maintain each other's approval, even at the cost of critical thinking.
- Social influence is also related to five types of social power: reward power, coercive power, legitimate power, referent power, and expert power.
- Obedience to authority has been investigated in a variety of experiments, particularly those by Milgram. Obedience in Milgram's studies decreased when the victim was in the same room, when the victim and subject were face to face, when the authority figure was absent, and when others refused to obey.
- Compliance with direct requests is another means by which behavior is influenced. Three strategies for inducing compliance are the foot-in-the-door technique, the door-in-the-face approach, and the low-ball technique.
- Recent research suggests that in addition to excessive obedience to authority, many people show a surprising passive compliance to unreasonable requests.

How does self-assertion differ from aggression?

- Self-assertion, as opposed to aggression, involves clearly stating one's wants and needs to others. Learning to be assertive is accomplished by role-playing, rehearsing assertive actions, overlearning, and use of specific techniques, such as the "broken record."

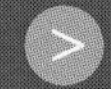

Web Resources

Internet addresses frequently change. To find the sites listed here, visit www.thomsonedu.com/psychology/coon for an updated list of Internet addresses and direct links to relevant sites.

***Psychology: Gateways to Mind and Behavior* Website** Online quizzes, flash cards, and other helpful study aids for this text. www.thomsonedu.com/psychology/coon.

Social Psychology Network A comprehensive site with many links to information about social psychology.

In Your Face Discusses research on facial attractiveness.

Center for Evolutionary Psychology A primer on evolutionary psychology, a reading list, and links.

Evolutionary Psychology for the Common Person Introduces evolutionary psychology; with links to other information on EP.

Preventing Groupthink Offers five ways to prevent groupthink.

Social Psychology Humor Links to cartoons that relate to principles of social psychology.

ThomsonNOW™ Go to www.thomsonedu.com to link to ThomsonNow, your online study tool. First take the **Pre-Test** for this chapter to get your **Personalized Study Plan**, which will identify topics you need to review and direct you to online resources. Then take the **Post-Test** to determine what concepts you have mastered and what you still need work on.

InfoTrac College Edition For recent articles on the Psychology in Action feature, use Key Words search for ASSERTIVENESS. Go to www.thomsonedu.com/psychology/coon.

Interactive Learning

***PsychNow!* Version 2.0 CD-ROM** Interact with the material with *PsychNow!*'s animations, video clips, experiments, and interactive assessments. For this chapter, go to *8a. Helping Others, 8b. Attribution,* and *8c. Social Influence* to get more information on why we help others, how we infer the causes of our own behavior and that of others, and how other people affect our behavior.

chapter 19

Attitudes, Culture, and Human Relations

Nick Clements/Getty Images

THEME:

Social life is complex, but consistent patterns can be found in our attitudes, as well as our positive and negative interactions with others.

Key Questions

What are attitudes? How are they acquired?

How are attitudes measured and changed?

Under what conditions is persuasion most effective?

What is cognitive dissonance? What does it have to do with attitudes and behavior?

Is brainwashing actually possible?

How are people converted to cult membership?

What causes prejudice and intergroup conflict?

What can be done about these problems?

How do psychologists explain human aggression?

Why are bystanders so often unwilling to help in an emergency?

What can be done to lower prejudice and promote social harmony?

Preview

Doomsday for the Seekers

Hardly a year passes without a doomsday group of one kind or another making the news. In a classic example of such groups, a woman named Mrs. Keech claimed she was receiving messages from beings on a planet called Clarion. The aliens told Mrs. Keech they had detected a fault in the Earth that would plunge North America into the sea on December 21. However, Mrs. Keech and her followers, who called themselves the Seekers, had no fear: On December 20, they expected to be met at midnight by a flying saucer and taken to safety in outer space.

December 20 arrived and the Seekers gathered at Mrs. Keech's house. Many had given up jobs and possessions to prepare for departure. Expectations were high and their commitment was total. The news media somehow found out and turned out to report on the proceedings. But as the night wore on, midnight passed and the world continued to exist. It was a bitter and embarrassing disappointment for the Seekers.

Did the group break up then? Our story now takes an amazing twist—one that intrigued social psychologists. Instead of breaking up, the Seekers became *more* convinced than ever before that they were right. At about 5 AM Mrs. Keech said she had received a new message explaining that the Seekers had saved the world.

Before December 20, the Seekers were uninterested in persuading other people that the world was coming to an end. Now they called newspapers and radio stations to convince others of their accomplishment.

How do we explain this strange turn in the behavior of Mrs. Keech's doomsday group? An answer may lie in the concept of *cognitive dissonance.* Cognitive dissonance also helps explain how attitudes change. Watch for Mrs. Keech and a discussion of cognitive dissonance later in this chapter.

Attitudes—Belief + Emotion + Action

What is your attitude toward affirmative action, euthanasia, environmental groups, the death penalty, legalized abortion, junk food, psychology? The answers can have far-reaching effects on your behavior. Attitudes are intimately woven into our actions and views of the world. Our tastes, friendships, votes, preferences, and goals are all touched by attitudes. Let's see how attitudes are formed and changed.

What specifically is an attitude? An **attitude** is a mixture of belief and emotion that predisposes a person to respond to other people, objects, or institutions in a positive or negative way. Attitudes summarize your *evaluation* of objects (Oskamp & Schultz, 2005). As a result, they predict or direct future actions. For example, an approach known as the *misdirected letter technique* shows how actions are closely linked to attitudes.

The Luck of the Irish

During a period of violence in Northern Ireland, attitudes toward the Irish were measured in a sample of English households. Later, wrongly addressed letters were sent to the same households. Each letter had either an English name or an Irish name on it. The question was: Would the "Irish" letters be returned to the Post Office or thrown away? As predicted, letters were more often thrown away by people living in households where anti-Irish attitudes had been measured earlier. (Howitt et al., 1977)

"Your attitude is showing," is sometimes said. Actually, attitudes are expressed through beliefs, emotions, and actions. The **belief component** of an attitude is what you believe about a particular object or issue. The **emotional component** consists of your feelings toward the attitudinal object. The **action component** refers to your actions toward various people, objects, or institutions. Consider, for example, your attitude toward gun control. You will have beliefs about whether gun control would affect rates of crime or violence. You will respond emotionally to guns, finding them either attractive and desirable or threatening and destructive. And you will have a tendency to seek out or avoid gun ownership. The action component of your attitude will probably also include support of organizations that urge or oppose gun control. As you can see, attitudes orient us to the social world. In doing so, they prepare us to act in certain ways (Ajzen, 2001). (For another example, see ● Figure 19.1.)

Attitude Formation

How do people acquire attitudes? Attitudes are acquired in several basic ways. Sometimes, attitudes come from *direct contact* (personal experience) with the object of the attitude—such as oppos-

Issue: Affirmative Action

+	−
Belief component Restores justice Provides equal opportunity	**Belief component** Unfair to majority Reverse discrimination
Emotional component Optimism	**Emotional component** Anger
Action component Vote for affirmative action Donate to groups that support affirmative action	**Action component** Vote against affirmative action Donate to groups that oppose affirmative action

● **Figure 19.1** Elements of positive and negative attitudes toward affirmative action.

ing pollution when a nearby factory ruins your favorite river. Attitudes are also learned through *interaction with others;* that is, through discussion with people holding a particular attitude. For instance, if three of your friends are volunteers at a local recycling center, and you talk with them about their beliefs, you will probably come to favor recycling, too. More generally, there is little doubt that many of our attitudes are influenced by *group membership*. In most groups, pressures to conform shape our attitudes, just as they do our behavior. *Child rearing* (the effects of parental values, beliefs, and practices) also affects attitudes. For example, if both parents belong to the same political party, chances are 2 out of 3 that their children will belong to that party as adults.

There can be no doubt that attitudes are influenced by the *mass media* (all media, such as magazines and television, that reach large audiences). Every day we are coaxed, persuaded, and skillfully manipulated by messages in the mass media. Ninety-nine percent of North American homes have a television set, which is on an average of over 7 hours a day (Steuer & Hustedt, 2002). The information thus channeled into homes has a powerful impact. For instance, frequent viewers mistrust others and overestimate their own chances of being harmed. This suggests that a steady diet of TV violence leads some people to develop a *mean worldview,* in which they regard the world as a dangerous and threatening place (Heath & Gilbert, 1996).

Some attitudes are simply formed through *chance conditioning* (learning that takes place by chance or coincidence) (Olson & Zanna, 1993). Let's say, for instance, that you have had three encounters in your lifetime with psychologists. If all three were neg-

Prakash Singh/AFP/Getty Images

Attitudes are an important dimension of social behavior. They are often greatly influenced by the groups to which we belong.

Attitude A learned tendency to respond to people, objects, or institutions in a positive or negative way.

Belief component What a person thinks or believes about the object of an attitude.

Emotional component One's feelings toward the object of an attitude.

Action component How one tends to act toward the object of an attitude.

ative, you might take an unduly dim view of psychology. In the same way, people often develop strong attitudes toward cities, foods, or parts of the country on the basis of one or two unusually good or bad experiences.

Attitudes and Behavior

Why are some attitudes acted on, whereas others are not? To answer this question, let's consider an example. Assume that a woman named Lorraine knows that automobiles add to air pollution, and she hates smog. Why would Lorraine continue to drive to work every day? Probably it is because the *immediate consequences* of our actions weigh heavily on the choices we make. No matter what Lorraine's attitude may be, it is difficult for her to resist the immediate convenience of driving. Our expectations of how *others will evaluate* our actions are also important. By taking this factor into account, researchers have been able to predict family planning choices, alcohol use by teenagers, re-enlistment in the National Guard, voting on a nuclear power plant initiative, and so forth (Cialdini, 2001). Finally, we must not overlook the effects of long-standing *habits* (Oskamp & Schultz, 2005). Let's say that a "male chauvinist" boss vows to change his sexist attitudes toward female employees. Two months later it would not be unusual for his behavior to show the effects of habit rather than his good intentions.

In short, there are often large differences between attitudes and behavior—particularly between privately held attitudes and public behavior. However, barriers to action typically fall when a person holds an attitude with *conviction.* If you have **conviction** about an issue it evokes strong feelings, you think about it and discuss it often, and you are knowledgeable about it. Attitudes held with passionate conviction often lead to major changes in personal behavior (Oskamp & Schultz, 2005).

Attitude Measurement

How are attitudes measured? Attitudes can be measured several ways. In an **open-ended interview,** people are asked to freely express their attitudes toward a particular issue. For example, a person might be asked, "What do you think about freedom of speech on college campuses?" Attitudes toward social groups can be measured with a **social distance scale.** On such scales people say how willing they are to admit members of a group to various levels of social closeness. These levels range from "would exclude from my country" to "would admit to marriage in my family." If a person is prejudiced toward a group, she or he will prefer to remain socially distant from members of the group (Cover, 1995).

Attitude scales are a widely used measure. **Attitude scales** consist of statements expressing various possible views on an issue (for example, "Socialized medicine would destroy health care in this country," or "This country needs a national health care program"). People typically respond to such statements on a 5-point scale, ranking it from "strongly agree" to "strongly disagree." By combining scores on all items, we can learn if a person accepts or rejects a particular issue. When used in public polls, attitude scales provide useful information about the feelings of large segments of the population.

Attitude Change—Why the Seekers Went Public

Although attitudes are fairly stable, they do change. Some attitude change can be understood in terms of **reference groups** (any group a person uses as a standard for social comparison). It is not necessary to have face-to-face contact with other people for them to be a reference group. It depends instead on whom you identify with or whose attitudes and values you care about (Ajzen, 2001).

In the 1930s Theodore Newcomb studied real-life attitude change among students at Bennington College. Most students came from conservative homes, but Bennington was a very liberal school. Newcomb found that most students shifted significantly toward more liberal attitudes during their 4 years at Bennington. Those who didn't change kept their parents and hometown friends as primary reference groups. This is typified by a student who said, "I decided I'd rather stick to my father's ideas." Those who did change identified primarily with the campus community. Notice that all students could count the college and their families as *membership* groups. However, one group or the other tended to become their point of reference.

Persuasion

What about advertising and other direct attempts to change attitudes? Are they effective? **Persuasion** is any deliberate attempt to change attitudes or beliefs through information and arguments (Brock & Green, 2005). Businesses, politicians, and others who seek to persuade us obviously believe that attitudes can be changed. Billions of dollars are spent yearly on television advertising in the United States and Canada alone. Persuasion can range from the daily blitz of media commercials to personal discussion among friends. In most cases, the success or failure of persuasion can be understood if we consider the *communicator,* the *message,* and the *audience.*

At a community meeting, let's say you have a chance to promote an issue important to you (for or against building a nuclear power plant nearby, for instance). Whom should you choose to

Bob Llewellen/Pictor International Ltd./PictureQuest

Do you exercise regularly? Like students in the Bennington study, your intentions to exercise are probably influenced by the exercise habits of your reference groups (Terry & Hogg, 1996).

Joel Gordon

Persuasion. Would you be likely to be swayed by this group's message? Successful persuasion is related to characteristics of the communicator, the message, and the audience.

make the presentation, and how should that person present it? Research suggests that attitude change is encouraged when the following conditions are met.

1. The communicator is likable, expressive, trustworthy, an expert on the topic, and similar to the audience in some respect.
2. The message appeals to emotions, particularly to fear or anxiety.
3. The message also provides a clear course of action that will, if followed, reduce fear or produce personally desirable results.
4. The message states clear-cut conclusions.
5. The message is backed up by facts and statistics.
6. Both sides of the argument are presented in the case of a well-informed audience.
7. Only one side of the argument is presented in the case of a poorly informed audience.
8. The persuader appears to have nothing to gain if the audience accepts the message.
9. The message is repeated as frequently as possible (Aronson, 1992; Oskamp & Schultz, 2005).

You should have little trouble seeing how these principles are applied to sell everything from underarm deodorants to presidents.

Role-Playing

We all know from personal observation that emotional experiences can dramatically alter attitudes. A good example is the person who gives up drinking after nearly dying in an automobile accident caused by drunkenness. To actively bring about such attitude change, psychologists sometimes create similar experiences through role-playing. For instance, Janis and Mann (1965) asked women who were known smokers to play the role of cancer patients. A doctor told each of the women that he had some bad news: She had lung cancer and would have to undergo immediate surgery. The women played out the part by asking questions about the surgery, if it might fail, and so on. Women in the role-playing group drastically reduced their smoking. Those who listened to a tape recording of similar information showed little change.

Cognitive Dissonance Theory

Why does role-playing have more effect than hearing the same information? Certainly emotional impact and realism have some effect, but part of the explanation also lies in *cognitive dissonance.* Cognitions are thoughts. Dissonance means clashing. The influential theory of **cognitive dissonance** states that contradicting or clashing thoughts cause discomfort. That is, we have a need for *consistency* in our thoughts, perceptions, and images of ourselves (Cooper, Mirabile, & Scher, 2005; Festinger, 1957).

What happens if people act in ways that are inconsistent with their attitudes or self-images? Typically, the contradiction makes them uncomfortable. Such discomfort can motivate people to make their thoughts or attitudes agree with their actions (Oskamp & Schultz, 2005). For example, smokers are told on every pack that cigarettes endanger their lives. They light up and smoke anyway. How do they resolve the tension between this information and their actions? They could quit smoking, but it may be easier to convince themselves that smoking is not really so dangerous. To do this, many smokers seek examples of heavy smokers who have lived long lives, they spend their time with other smokers, and they avoid information about the link between smoking and cancer. According to cognitive dissonance theory, we also tend to reject new information that contradicts ideas we already hold. We're all guilty of this "don't bother me with the facts, my mind is made up" strategy at times.

Conviction Beliefs that are important to a person and that evoke strong emotion.

Open-ended interview An interview in which persons are allowed to freely state their views.

Social distance scale A rating of the degree to which a person would be willing to have contact with a member of another group.

Attitude scale A collection of attitudinal statements with which respondents indicate agreement or disagreement.

Reference group Any group that an individual identifies with and uses as a standard for social comparison.

Persuasion A deliberate attempt to change attitudes or beliefs with information and arguments.

Cognitive dissonance An uncomfortable clash between self-image, thoughts, beliefs, attitudes, or perceptions and one's behavior.

Now recall Mrs. Keech and her doomsday group. Why did their belief in Mrs. Keech's messages *increase* after the world failed to end? Why did the group suddenly become interested in convincing others that they were right? Cognitive dissonance theory explains that after publicly committing themselves to their beliefs, they had a strong need to maintain consistency. In effect, convincing others was a way of adding proof that they were correct (see ■ Table 19.1).

Cognitive dissonance also underlies attempts to convince *ourselves* that we've done the right thing. Here's an example you may recognize: As romantic partners become better acquainted, they sooner or later begin to notice things they don't like about each other. How do they reduce the cognitive dissonance and doubts caused by their partners' shortcomings? Basically, they create stories that change their partners' faults into virtues: He seems cheap, but he's really frugal; she seems egotistical, but she's really self-confident; he's not stubborn, he just has integrity; she's not undependable, she's a free spirit; and so on (Murray & Holmes, 1993).

Making choices often causes dissonance. This is especially true if a rejected alternative seems better than the one selected. To minimize such dissonance, we tend to emphasize positive aspects of what we choose, while downgrading other alternatives. Thus, college students are more likely to think their courses will be good *after* they have registered than they did before making a commitment (Rosenfeld, Giacalone, & Tedeschi, 1983).

TABLE 19.1

Strategies for Reducing Cognitive Dissonance

LeShawn, who is a college student, has always thought of himself as an environmental activist. Recently, LeShawn "inherited" a car from his parents, who were replacing the family "barge." In the past, LeShawn biked or used public transportation to get around. His parents' old car is an antiquated gas-guzzler, but he has begun to drive it every day. How might LeShawn reduce the cognitive dissonance created by the clash between his environmentalism and his use of an inefficient automobile?

STRATEGY	EXAMPLE
Change your attitude	"Cars are not really a major environmental problem."
Add consonant thoughts	"This is an old car, so keeping it on the road makes good use of the resources consumed when it was manufactured."
Change the importance of the dissonant thoughts	"It's more important for me to support the environmental movement politically than it is to worry about how I get to school and work."
Reduce the amount of perceived choice	"My schedule has become too hectic, I really can't afford to bike or take the bus anymore."
Change your behavior	"I'm only going to use the car when it's impossible to bike or take the bus."

After Franzoi, 2002.

Acting contrary to one's attitudes doesn't always bring about change. How does cognitive dissonance explain that? The amount of justification for acting contrary to your attitudes and beliefs affects how much dissonance you feel. (*Justification* is the degree to which a person's actions are explained by rewards or other circumstances.) In a classic study, college students did an extremely boring task (turning wooden pegs on a board), for a *long* time. Afterward, they were asked to help lure others into the experiment by pretending that the task was interesting and enjoyable. Students paid $20 for lying to others did not change their own negative opinion of the task: "That was *really* boring!" Those who were paid only $1 later rated the task as "pleasant" and "interesting." How can we explain these results? Apparently, students paid $20 experienced no dissonance. These students could reassure themselves that anybody would tell a little white lie for $20. Those paid $1 were faced with the conflicting thoughts: "I lied," and " I had no good reason to do it." Rather than admit to themselves that they had lied, these students changed their attitude toward what they had done (Festinger & Carlsmith, 1959) (● Figure 19.2).

We are especially likely to experience dissonance after we cause an event to occur that we wish hadn't taken place (Cooper & Fazio, 1984). Let's say that you agree to help a friend move to a new apartment. The big day arrives and you feel like staying in bed. Actually, you wish you had never promised to help. To reduce dissonance, you may convince yourself that the work will actually be "good exercise," "sort of fun," or that your friend really deserves the help. We often make such adjustments in attitudes to minimize cognitive dissonance.

Forced Attitude Change—Brainwashing and Cults

If you're a history enthusiast, you may associate *brainwashing* with techniques used by the Communist Chinese on prisoners during the Korean War. Through various types of "thought re-

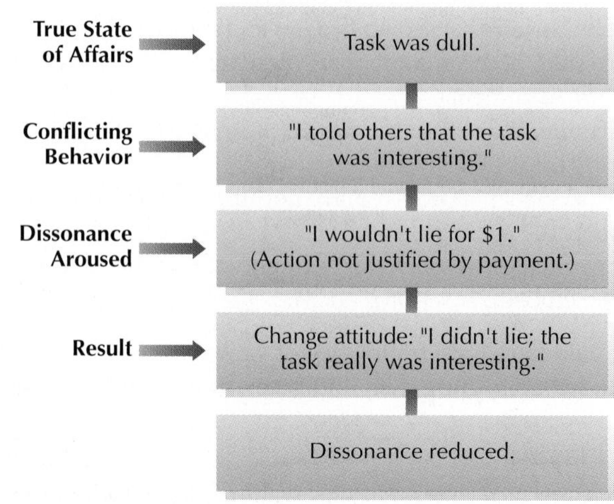

● **Figure 19.2** Summary of the Festinger and Carlsmith (1959) study from the viewpoint of a person experiencing cognitive dissonance.

form," the Chinese were able to coerce 16 percent of these prisoners to sign false confessions. More recently, the mass murder/suicide at Jonestown, the Branch Davidian tragedy at Waco, the Heaven's Gate group suicide in San Diego, and Osama bin Laden's al-Qaeda movement have heightened public interest in forced attitude change.

How does brainwashing differ from other persuasive techniques? As we have noted, advertisers, politicians, educators, religious organizations, and others actively seek to alter attitudes and opinions. To an extent, their persuasive efforts resemble brainwashing, but there is an important difference: **Brainwashing**, or forced attitude change, requires a captive audience. If you are offended by a television commercial, you can tune it out. Prisoners in the POW camps are completely at the mercy of their captors. Complete control over the environment allows a degree of psychological manipulation that would be impossible in a normal setting.

Brainwashing

How does captivity facilitate persuasion? Brainwashing typically begins by making the target person feel completely helpless. Physical and psychological abuse, lack of sleep, humiliation, and isolation serve to *unfreeze,* or loosen, former values and beliefs. When exhaustion, pressure, and fear become unbearable, *change* occurs as the person begins to abandon former beliefs. Prisoners who reach the breaking point may sign a false confession or cooperate to gain relief. When they do, they are suddenly rewarded with praise, privileges, food, or rest. From that point on, a mixture of hope and fear, plus pressures to conform, serves to *refreeze* (solidify) new attitudes (Taylor, 2004).

How permanent are changes caused by brainwashing? In most cases, the dramatic shift in attitudes brought about by brainwashing is temporary. Most "converted" prisoners who returned to the United States after the Korean War eventually reverted to their original beliefs. Nevertheless, brainwashing can be powerful, as shown by the success of cults in recruiting new members.

Cults

Exhorted by their leader, some 900 members of the Reverend Jim Jones's People's Temple picked up paper cups and drank purple Kool-Aid laced with the deadly poison cyanide. Psychologically, the mass suicide at Jonestown in 1978 is not as incredible as it might seem. The inhabitants of Jonestown were isolated in the jungles of Guyana, intimidated by guards, and lulled with sedatives. They were also cut off from friends and relatives and totally accustomed to obeying rigid rules of conduct, which primed them for Jones's final "loyalty test." Of greater psychological interest is the question of how people reach such a state of commitment and dependency.

Why do people join groups such as the People's Temple? The People's Temple was a classic example of a *cult.* A **cult** is an authoritarian group in which the leader's personality is more important than the beliefs she or he preaches. Cult members give their allegiance to this person, who is regarded as infallible, and they follow his or her dictates without question. Almost always, cult members are victimized by their leaders in one way or another. For example, in April 1993, David Koresh and members of his Branch Davidian group perished in a fire at their Waco, Texas, compound. Like Jim Jones had done years before in Jonestown, Koresh took nearly total control of his followers' lives. He told them what to eat, dictated sexual mores, and had errant followers paddled. Followers were persuaded to surrender money, property, and even their children and wives. Like Jones, Koresh also took mistresses and had children out of wedlock. And like other cult leaders, Jones and Koresh demanded absolute loyalty and obedience, with tragic results (Reiterman, 1993).

Psychologist and pioneering brainwashing expert Margaret Singer (1921–2003) studied and aided hundreds of former cult members. Her interviews reveal that in recruiting new members, cults use a powerful blend of guilt, manipulation, isolation, deception, fear, and escalating commitment. In this respect, cults employ high-pressure indoctrination techniques not unlike those used in brainwashing (Singer, 2003; Singer & Addis, 1992). In the United States alone, an estimated 2 to 5 million people have succumbed to the lure of cults (Robinson, Frye, & Bradley, 1997).

Recruitment

Some people studied by Singer were seriously distressed when they joined a cult. Most, however, were simply undergoing a period of mild depression, indecision, or alienation from family and friends (Hunter, 1998). Cult members try to catch potential converts at a time of need—especially when a sense of belonging will be attractive to converts. For instance, many people were ap-

Greg Smith/Corbis

In April 1993, David Koresh and members of his Branch Davidian group perished in an inferno at their Waco, Texas, compound. Authorities believe the fire was set by a cult member, under the direction of Koresh. Like Jim Jones had done years before in Jonestown, Koresh took nearly total control of his followers' lives.

Brainwashing Engineered or forced attitude change involving a captive audience.

Cult A group that professes great devotion to some person and follows that person almost without question; cult members are typically victimized by their leaders in various ways.

proached just after a romance had broken up, or when they were struggling with exams or were trying to become independent from their families (Sirkin, 1990). At such times, people are easily persuaded that joining the group is all they need to do to be happy again (Hunter, 1998).

Conversion

How is conversion achieved? Often it begins with intense displays of affection and understanding ("love bombing"). Next comes isolation from people who are not cult members, and drills, discipline, and rituals (all-night meditation or continuous chanting, for instance). These rituals wear down physical and emotional resistance, discourage critical thinking, and generate feelings of commitment (Langone, 2002).

Many cults make clever use of the foot-in-the-door technique (described in Chapter 18). At first, recruits make small commitments (to stay after a meeting, for example). Then, larger commitments are encouraged (to stay an extra day, to call in sick at work, and so forth). Making a major commitment is usually the final step. The new devotee signs over a bank account or property to the group, moves in with the group, and so forth. Making such major public commitments creates a powerful cognitive dissonance effect. Before long, it becomes virtually impossible for converts to admit they have made a mistake.

Aftermath of the mass suicide at Jonestown. How do cult-like groups recruit new devotees?

Once in the group, members are cut off from family and friends (former reference groups), and the cult can control the flow and interpretation of information to them. Members are isolated from their former value systems and social structures. Conversion is complete when they come to think of themselves more as group members than as individuals. At this point obedience is nearly total (Wexler, 1995).

Why do people stay in cults? Most former members mention guilt and fear as the main reasons for not leaving when they wished they could. Most had been reduced to childlike dependency on the group for meeting all their daily needs (Singer, 2003). After they leave, many former cult members suffer from anxiety, panic attacks, and emotional disturbances much like posttraumatic stress disorder (West, 1993).

Implications

Behind the "throne" from which Jim Jones ruled Jonestown was a sign bearing these words: "Those who do not remember the past are condemned to repeat it." Sadly, another cult-related tragedy occurred in 2001. The terrorist attacks on the United States were carried out by followers of cult leader Osama bin Laden. At his direction, they learned hatred and contempt for everyone outside their band of true believers. If there is a lesson to be learned from such destructive cults, it is this: All true spiritual leaders have taught love and compassion. They also encourage followers to question their beliefs and to reach their own conclusions about how to live. In contrast, destructive cults show how dangerous it is to trade personal independence and critical thinking for security (Goldberg, 2001).

BRIDGES

People suffering from identity confusion, which is common during adolescence, are more susceptible to recruitment by coercive groups.

See Chapter 4, pages 138–139.

KNOWLEDGE BUILDER

Attitudes and Persuasion

REFLECT

Describe an attitude that is important to you. What are its three components?

Which of the various sources of attitudes best explain your own attitudes?

Who belongs to your most important reference group?

Imagine that you would like to persuade voters to support an initiative to preserve a small wilderness area by converting it to a park. Using research on persuasion as a guide, what could you do to be more effective?

How would you explain cognitive dissonance theory to a person who knows nothing about it?

LEARNING CHECK

1. Attitudes have three parts, a __________ component, an __________ component, and an __________ component.
2. Which of the following is associated with attitude formation?
   a. group membership
   b. mass media
   c. chance conditioning
   d. child rearing
   e. all of the preceding
   f. a and d only
3. Because of the immediate consequences of actions, behavior contrary to one's stated attitudes is often enacted. T or F?
4. Items such as "would exclude from my country" or "would admit to marriage in my family" are found in which attitude measure?
   a. a reference group scale
   b. a social distance scale
   c. an attitude scale
   d. an open-ended interview
5. In presenting a persuasive message, it is best to give both sides of the argument if the audience is already well informed on the topic. T or F?
6. Much attitude change is related to a desire to avoid clashing or contradictory thoughts, an idea summarized by __________ __________ theory.
7. Brainwashing differs from other persuasive attempts in that brainwashing requires a __________ __________.
8. Which statement about brainwashing is *false*?
   a. The target person is isolated from others.
   b. Attitude changes brought about by brainwashing are usually permanent.
   c. The first step is unfreezing former values and beliefs.
   d. Cooperation with the indoctrinating agent is rewarded.
9. Margaret Singer found that most former cult members had experienced a major psychological disturbance just prior to joining the cult. T or F?

CRITICAL THINKING

10. Students entering a college gym are asked to sign a banner promoting water conservation. Later, the students shower at the gym. What effect would you expect signing the banner to have on how long students stay in the showers?
11. Cognitive dissonance theory predicts that false confessions obtained during brainwashing are not likely to bring about lasting changes in attitudes. Why?

Answers: 1. belief, emotional, action **2.** e **3.** T **4.** b **5.** T **6.** cognitive dissonance **7.** captive audience **8.** b **9.** F **10.** Cognitive dissonance theory predicts that students who sign the banner will take shorter showers, to be consistent with their publicly expressed support of water conservation. This is exactly the result observed in a study done by social psychologist Elliot Aronson. **11.** Because there is strong justification for such actions. As a result, little cognitive dissonance is created when a prisoner makes statements that contradict his or her beliefs.

Prejudice—Attitudes That Injure

Love and friendship bring people together. Prejudice, which is marked by suspicion, fear, or hatred, has the opposite effect. Prejudice is an all too common part of daily life. What are the origins of prejudice? How can prejudice and hurtful attitudes be reduced? Psychologists have provided valuable insights into these questions (see "I'm Not Prejudiced, Right?").

Prejudice is a negative emotional attitude held toward members of a specific social group. Prejudices may be reflected in the policies of police departments, schools, or government institutions (Dovidio, Glick, & Rudman, 2005). In such cases, prejudice is referred to as **racism, sexism, ageism,** or **heterosexism,** depending on the group affected. Because sexism, ageism, and heterosexism were discussed in earlier chapters, let's focus on racism.

Both racial prejudice and racism lead to **discrimination,** or unequal treatment of people who should have the same rights as others. Discrimination prevents people from doing things they should be able to do, such as buying a house, getting a job, voting, or attending a high-quality school. For example, in many cities, African Americans have been the targets of "racial profiling" in which they are stopped by police without reason. Sometimes, they are merely questioned, but many are cited for minor infractions, such as a cracked taillight or an illegal lane change. For many law-abiding citizens, being detained in this manner is a rude awakening (Harris, 1999). It's also one reason why many African Americans and other persons of color in America distrust police and the legal system (Dovidio et al., 2002).

Becoming Prejudiced

How do prejudices develop? One major theory suggests that prejudice is a form of **scapegoating** (blaming a person or a group for the actions of others or for conditions not of their making). Scapegoating, you may recall, is a type of **displaced aggression** in which hostilities triggered by frustration are redirected at "safer" targets (Nelson, 2002). One interesting classic test of this hypothesis was conducted at a summer camp for young men. The men were given a difficult test they were sure to fail. In addition, completing the test caused them to miss a trip to the movies, which was normally the high point of their weekly entertainment. Attitudes toward Mexicans and Japanese were measured before the test and after the

Prejudice A negative emotional attitude held against members of a particular group of people.

Racism Racial prejudice that has become institutionalized (that is, it is reflected in government policy, schools, and so forth) and that is enforced by the existing social power structure.

Sexism Institutionalized prejudice against members of either sex, based solely on their gender.

Ageism An institutionalized tendency to discriminate on the basis of age; prejudice based on age.

Heterosexism The belief that heterosexuality is better or more natural than homosexuality.

Discrimination Treating members of various social groups differently in circumstances where their rights or treatment should be identical.

Scapegoating Blaming a person or a group for the actions of others or for conditions not of their making.

Displaced aggression Redirecting aggression to a target other than the actual source of one's frustration.

DISCOVERING PSYCHOLOGY

I'm Not Prejudiced, Right?

Are you prejudiced against women working outside the family home? Keep in mind your answer to this explicit question as you read on.

Below you will find a list of 12 words. Your job is to categorize the words. Suppose, for example, that one of the words is *factory.* If you feel that *factory* belongs in the category "Male or Career," then you would touch (or mark) the O to the left of the word. Otherwise, you would mark the O to the right of *factory.*

Now, take 20 seconds to classify each of the words in the list. Place them into the correct categories as quickly and accurately as you can. Got the idea? Ready, set, go!

MALE OR CAREER		**FEMALE OR FAMILY**
O	Daniel	O
O	Sally	O
O	House	O
O	Kitchen	O
O	Merchant	O
O	Company	O
O	Emily	O
O	Relatives	O
O	Employment	O
O	Baby	O
O	Steven	O
O	Executive	O

Now try it again with 12 new words. The only difference is that the categories have changed. Ready, set, go!

MALE OR FAMILY		**FEMALE OR CAREER**
O	Home	O
O	Manager	O
O	Domestic	O
O	Andrew	O
O	In-laws	O
O	Jane	O
O	Workplace	O
O	Sarah	O
O	Office	O
O	Corporation	O
O	Siblings	O
O	John	O

Many people notice that it takes longer to do the second list and that they make more mistakes. Even people who claim they are not prejudiced against women working outside the home will nevertheless be slower and less accurate in classifying words into the categories *Male or Family* as opposed to *Female or Career.* Why is there a difference? For many people, *Female* and *Family* seem to go together better than *Female* and *Career* do.

You just completed a pencil-and-paper version of an *implicit association test* (adapted from Nosek, Greenwald, & Banaji, 2005). If you Google the web you will find that similar tests have been constructed for race, age, religion, ethnicity, disability, sexual orientation, weight, and many other stereotyped categories of people (Blair, 2001; Hofmann et al., 2005; Kite et al., 2005). Apparently, we can harbor implicit (hidden) prejudices even when we do not explicitly own up to them.

men had failed the test and missed the movie. Subjects in this study, all European Americans, consistently rated members of the two ethnic groups lower after being frustrated (Miller & Bugelski, 1970). This effect was easy to observe after the September 11, 2001, terrorist attack in the United States, when people who looked "foreign" became targets for displaced anger and hostility.

At times, the development of prejudice (like other attitudes) can be traced to direct experiences with members of the rejected group. A child who is repeatedly bullied by members of a particular ethnic group might develop a lifelong dislike for all members of the group. Yet even subtle influences, such as parents' attitudes, the depiction of people in books and on TV, and exposure to children of other races can have an impact. By the time they are 3 years of age, many children show signs of race bias (Katz, 2003). Sadly, once prejudices are established, they prevent us from accepting more positive experiences that could reverse the damage (Wilder, Simon, & Faith, 1996).

Distinguished psychologist Gordon Allport (1958) concluded that there are two important sources of prejudice. **Personal prejudice** occurs when members of another social group are perceived as a threat to one's own interests. For example, members of another group may be viewed as competitors for jobs. **Group prejudice** occurs when a person conforms to group norms. Let's say, for instance, that you have no personal reason for disliking out-group members. Nevertheless, your friends, acquaintances, or coworkers expect it of you.

The Prejudiced Personality

Other research suggests that prejudice can be a general personality characteristic. Theodore Adorno and his associates (1950) carefully probed what they called the *authoritarian personality.* These researchers started out by studying anti-Semitism. In the process, they found that people who are prejudiced against one group tend to be prejudiced against *all* out-groups (Perreault & Bourhis, 1999).

What are the characteristics of the prejudice-prone personality? The **authoritarian personality** is marked by rigidity, inhibition, prejudice, and oversimplification. Authoritarians also tend to be very *ethnocentric.* **Ethnocentrism** refers to placing one's own group "at the center," usually by rejecting all other groups. Put more simply, authoritarians consider their own ethnic group superior to others. In fact, authoritarians think they are superior to everyone who is different, not just other ethnic groups (Altemeyer, 2004; Whitley, 1999).

In addition to rejecting out-groups, authoritarians are overwhelmingly concerned with power, authority, and obedience. To measure these qualities, the *F scale* was created (the *F* stands for "fascism"). This attitude scale is made up of statements such as the ones that follow—to which authoritarians readily agree (Adorno et al., 1950).

Authoritarian Beliefs

- Obedience and respect for authority are the most important virtues children should learn.
- People can be divided into two distinct classes: the weak and the strong.
- If people would talk less and work more, everybody would be better off.
- What this country needs most, more than laws and political programs, is a few courageous, tireless, devoted leaders, in whom the people can put their faith.
- Nobody ever learns anything really important except through suffering.
- Every person should have complete faith in some supernatural power whose decisions are obeyed without question.
- Certain religious sects that refuse to salute the flag should be forced to conform to such patriotic action or else be abolished.

As you can see, authoritarians are rather close-minded (Butler, 2000). As children, most were severely punished. As a result, they learned to fear authority (and to covet it) at an early age. In general, people are more likely to express authoritarian beliefs when they feel threatened (Doty, Peterson, & Winter, 1991). An example would be calling for more severe punishment in schools when the economy is bad and job insecurities are high. Authoritarians are not happy people.

It should be readily apparent from the list of authoritarian beliefs that the F scale is slanted toward politically conservative authoritarians. To be fair, psychologist Milton Rokeach (1918–1988) noted that rigid and authoritarian personalities can be found at both ends of the political scale. Rokeach, therefore, preferred to describe rigid and intolerant thinking as *dogmatism.* (**Dogmatism** is an unwarranted certainty in matters of belief or opinion.) Dogmatic persons find it difficult to change their beliefs, even when the evidence contradicts them (Davies, 1993).

Even if we discount the obvious bigotry of the authoritarian personality, racial prejudice runs deep in many nations. Let's probe deeper into the roots of such prejudiced behavior.

Intergroup Conflict—The Roots of Prejudice

An unfortunate by-product of group membership is that it often limits contact with people in other groups. In addition, groups themselves may come into conflict. Both events tend to foster hatred and prejudice toward the out-group. The bloody clash of opposing forces in Israel, Ireland, Africa, and Hometown, U.S.A., are reminders that intergroup conflict is widespread. Daily, we read of jarring strife between political, religious, or ethnic groups.

Shared beliefs concerning *superiority, injustice, vulnerability,* and *distrust* are common triggers for hostility between groups. Pick almost any group in conflict with others and you will find people thinking along these lines: "We are special people who are superior to other groups, but we have been unjustly exploited, wronged, or humiliated [superiority and injustice]. Other groups are a threat to us [vulnerability]. They are dishonest and have repeatedly betrayed us [distrust]. Naturally, we are hostile toward them. They don't deserve our respect or cooperation" (Eidelson & Eidelson, 2003). In addition to hostile beliefs about other groups, conflicts are almost always amplified by stereotyped images of out-group members (Bar-Tal & Labin, 2001).

What exactly is a stereotype? **Social stereotypes** are oversimplified images of people in various groups. There is a good chance that you have stereotyped images of some of the following: African-Americans, European-Americans, Hispanics, Jews, women, Christians, old people, men, Asian-Americans, blue-collar workers, rednecks, politicians, business executives, teenagers, and billionaires. In general, the top three categories on which most stereotypes are based are sex, age, and race (Fiske, 1993; Fiske et al., 2002).

Personal prejudice Prejudicial attitudes held toward persons who are perceived as a direct threat to one's own interests.

Group prejudice Prejudice held out of conformity to group views.

Authoritarian personality A personality pattern characterized by rigidity, inhibition, prejudice, and an excessive concern with power, authority, and obedience.

Ethnocentrism Placing one's own group or race at the center—that is, tending to reject all other groups but one's own.

Dogmatism An unwarranted positiveness or certainty in matters of belief or opinion.

Social stereotypes Oversimplified images of the traits of individuals who belong to a particular social group.

Stereotypes tend to simplify people into "us" and "them" categories. Actually, aside from the fact that they always oversimplify, stereotypes often include a mixture of *positive* and *negative* qualities (Fiske et al., 2002) (● Figure 19.3). ■ Table 19.2 shows stereotyped images of various national and ethnic groups and their changes over a 34-year period. Notice that many of the qualities listed are desirable. Note too, that although the overall trend was a decrease in negative stereotypes, belief in the existence of some negative traits increased.

Even though stereotypes sometimes include positive traits, they are mainly used to maintain control over other people. When a person is stereotyped, the easiest thing for her or him to do is to abide by others' expectations—even if those expectations are demeaning. That's why no one likes to be stereotyped. Being forced into a small, distorted social "box" by stereotyping is limiting and insulting. Stereotypes rob people of their individuality (Maddox, 2004). (See "Choking on Stereotypes.") Without stereotypes there would be far less hate, prejudice, exclusion, and conflict.

In the years since 1967, there have been further declines in negative stereotypes, but also some recent reversals. Some observers believe that racial and ethnic prejudice is on the upswing. But often, today's racism takes the form of **symbolic prejudice**, which is expressed in a disguised fashion. That is, many people realize that crude and obvious racism is socially unacceptable. However, this may not stop them from expressing prejudice in thinly veiled forms when they state their opinions about affirmative action, busing, immigration, crime, and so on. In effect, modern racists find ways to rationalize their prejudice so that it seems to be based on issues other than raw racism. For instance, an African-American candidate and a European-American candidate apply for a job. Both are only moderately qualified for the position. If

NBAE/Getty Images

● **Figure 19.3** Racial stereotypes are common in sports. For example, a recent study confirmed that many people actually do believe that "white men can't jump." This stereotype implies that African-American basketball players are naturally superior in athletic ability. European-American players, in contrast, are falsely perceived as smarter and harder working than African Americans. Such stereotypes set up expectations that distort the perceptions of fans, coaches, and sportswriters. The resulting misperceptions, in turn, help perpetuate the stereotypes (Stone, Perry, & Darley, 1997).

TABLE 19.2

University Students' Characterization of Ethnic Groups, 1933 and 1967

TRAIT	PERCENT CHECKING TRAIT 1933	1967	TRAIT	PERCENT CHECKING TRAIT 1933	1967	TRAIT	PERCENT CHECKING TRAIT 1933	1967
	Americans			Italians			Jews	
Industrious	48	23	Artistic	53	30	Shrewd	79	30
Intelligent	47	20	Impulsive	44	28	Mercenary	49	15
Materialistic	33	67	Musical	32	9	Grasping	34	17
Progressive	27	17	Imaginative	30	7	Intelligent	29	37
	Germans			Irish			Blacks	
Scientific	78	47	Pugnacious	45	13	Superstitious	84	13
Stolid	44	9	Witty	38	7	Lazy	75	26
Methodical	31	21	Honest	32	17	Ignorant	38	11
Efficient	16	46	Nationalistic	21	41	Religious	24	8

Source: M. Karlins, T. L. Coffman, and G. Walters, "On the fading of social stereotypes. Studies in three generations of college students," *Journal of Personality and Social Psychology* 13 (1969):116. Reprinted with permission of the American Psychological Association.

HUMAN DIVERSITY

Choking on Stereotypes

Bill, a retired aircraft mechanic, has agreed to talk to a group of high school students about the early days of commercial aviation. During his talk, Bill is concerned that any slip in his memory will confirm stereotypes about older people being forgetful. Because he is anxious and preoccupied about possible memory lapses, Bill actually does have problems with his memory (Chasteen et al., 2005).

As Bill's example suggests, negative stereotypes can have a self-fulfilling quality. This is especially true in situations in which a person's abilities are evaluated. For example, African-Americans must often cope with negative stereotypes about their academic abilities (Steele & Aronson, 1995). Could such stereotypes actually impair school performance?

Psychologist Claude Steele has amassed evidence that victims of stereotyping tend to feel *stereotype threat.* They can feel threatened when they think they are being judged in terms of a stereotype. The anxiety that this causes can then lower performance, seemingly confirming the stereotype. An experiment Steele did demonstrates this effect. In the study, African-American and European-American college students took a very difficult verbal test. Some students were told the test measured *academic ability.* Others were told that the test was a laboratory *problem-solving task* unrelated to ability. In the ability condition, African-American students performed worse than European Americans. In the problem-solving condition they performed the same as European Americans (Steele, 1997; Steele & Aronson, 1995). A similar effect occurred with women, who scored lower on a math test after being reminded of the stereotype that "women aren't good at math" (Cadinu et al., 2005; Keller, 2002).

In light of such findings, Steele and others are currently working on ways to remove stereotype threat, so that all students can use their potentials more fully (Steele, 1997).

the person making the hiring decision is European American, who gets the job? As you might guess, the European-American candidate is much more likely to be hired. In other words, the European-American candidate will be given "the benefit of the doubt" about his or her abilities, whereas the African-American candidate won't. People making such decisions often believe that they aren't being prejudiced, but they unconsciously discriminate against minorities (Dovidio et al., 2002).

Stereotypes held by the prejudiced tend to be unusually irrational. When given a list of negative statements about other groups, prejudiced individuals agree with most of them. It's particularly revealing that they often agree with conflicting statements. Thus, a prejudiced person may say that Jews are both "pushy" and "standoffish" or that African Americans are both "ignorant" and "sly." In one study, prejudiced persons even expressed negative attitudes toward two nonexistent groups, the "Piraneans" and the "Danirians." (See "Terrorists, Enemies, and Infidels" for further information.) Note, too, that when a prejudiced person meets a pleasant or likable member of a rejected group, the out-group member tends to be perceived as "an exception to the rule," not as evidence against the stereotype. Even when such "exceptional" experiences begin to stack up, a prejudiced person may not change his or her stereotyped belief (Fiske, 1993; Wilder, Simon, & Faith, 1996). Because some elements of prejudice are unconscious, they are very difficult to change (Dovidio et al., 2002).

David Young-Wolff/PhotoEdit

Ethnic pride is gradually replacing stereotypes and discrimination. For example, the African-American festival of Kwanzaa, a holiday celebrated in late December, emphasizes commitment to family, community, and African culture. However, despite affirmations of ethnic heritage, the problem of prejudice is far from solved.

How do stereotypes and intergroup tensions develop? Two experiments, both in unlikely settings and both using children as subjects, offer some insight into these problems.

Experiments in Prejudice

What is it like to be discriminated against? In a unique experiment, elementary school teacher Jane Elliot sought to give her pupils direct experience with prejudice. On the first day of the experiment, Elliot announced that brown-eyed children were to sit in the back of the room and that they could not use the drinking fountain. Blue-eyed children were given extra recess time and got to leave first for lunch. At lunch, brown-eyed children were

Symbolic prejudice Prejudice that is expressed in disguised fashion.

CRITICAL THINKING

Terrorists, Enemies, and Infidels

Sometimes, such as during times of war, normal people are called upon to kill other humans. How do they turn off their emotions and moral standards? Actually they don't. Instead, they convince themselves that their actions are just (Osofsky, Bandura, & Zimbardo, 2005). For example, violence may be seen as necessary to eradicate evil, serve God, or to protect honor, virtue, justice, or freedom.

Whether it's Catholics and Protestants in Northern Ireland, Serbs and Muslims in Bosnia, Hutus and Tutsis in Rwanda, Israelis and Palestinians, or al-Qaeda and the United States, each side believes that attack or counterattack is morally justified. And, whether they are right or wrong, both sides use the same psychological mechanisms to justify violence. In violent conflicts between groups, "the enemy" is always portrayed as evil, monstrous, or less than human. Dehumanizing others makes it seem that they *deserve* hatred and even death. Undoubtedly, this provides a degree of emotional insulation that makes it easier for soldiers to harm other humans. However, it also makes terrorism, torture, murder, and genocide possible (Anderson & Bushman, 2002). Recent examples are the bloody executions of foreigners and indiscriminate suicide attacks by al-Qaeda and Iraqi insurgents in Iraq and the torture of prisoners under American control in facilities like Abu Ghraib prison (Hooks & Mosher, 2005).

A danger in demonizing "the enemy" is that it can lead to misperceptions of the motives and actions of other nations or groups (Silverstein, 1989). Many of the bloodiest conflicts in history have been fueled, in part, by treating "the enemy" as evil and subhuman. Those who actually do hold the moral high ground must be careful not to succumb to the same kind of blind hatred that leads to wanton violence and terrorism. It is also wise to remember that ethnic jokes, racial stereotypes, degrading names, and out-group slurs are small-scale examples of the damage that "enemy" images can do.

AP/Wide World Photo

During the recent civil war in parts of the former Yugoslavia, Bosnian Serbs described mass killing of Muslim civilians as "ethnic cleansing." In reality, the Serb attacks were genocide, in which mothers, fathers, daughters, and sons were slaughtered.

prevented from taking second helpings because they would "just waste it." Brown-eyed and blue-eyed children were kept from mingling, and the blue-eyed children were told they were "cleaner" and "smarter" (Peters, 1971). Eye color might seem like a trivial basis for creating prejudices. However, people primarily use skin color to make decisions about the race of another person (Brown, Dane, & Durham, 1998). Surely, this is just as superficial a way of judging people as eye color is, especially given recent genetic evidence that it does not even make genetic sense to talk about "races" (Bonham, Warshauer-Baker, & Collins, 2005). (See this chapter's Psychology in Action section for further information about the concept of race.)

At first, Elliot made an effort to constantly criticize and belittle the brown-eyed children. To her surprise, the blue-eyed children rapidly joined in and were soon outdoing her in the viciousness of their attacks. The blue-eyed children began to feel superior, and the brown-eyed children felt just plain awful. Fights broke out. Test scores of the brown-eyed children fell.

How lasting were the effects of this experiment? The effects were short lived, because two days later the roles of the children were reversed. Before long, the same destructive effects occurred again, but this time in reverse. The implications of this experiment are unmistakable. In less than one day it was possible to get children to hate each other because of eye color and **status inequalities** (differences in power, prestige, or privileges). Certainly the effects of a lifetime of real racial or ethnic prejudice are infinitely more powerful and destructive. Racism is a major source of stress in the lives of many people of color. Over time, prejudice can have a negative impact on a person's physical and emotional health (Clark et al., 1999).

Equal-Status Contact

What can be done to combat prejudice? Progress has been made through attempts to educate the general public about the lack of justification for prejudice. Changing the belief component of an attitude is one of the most direct means of changing the entire attitude. Thus, when people are made aware that members of various racial and ethnic groups share the same goals, ambitions, feelings, and frustrations as they do, intergroup relations may be improved.

However, this is not the whole answer. As we noted earlier, there is often a wide difference between attitudes and actual behavior. Until nonprejudiced behavior is engineered, changes can be quite superficial. Several lines of thought (including cognitive dissonance theory) suggest that more frequent *equal-status contact* between groups in conflict should reduce prejudice and stereotyping (Olson & Zanna, 1993).

Equal-status contact refers to interacting on an equal footing, without obvious differences in power or status. Much evidence suggests that equal-status contact does, in fact, lessen prejudice. In one early study, European-American women who lived in integrated and segregated housing projects were compared for changes in attitude toward their African-American neighbors. Women in the integrated project showed a favorable shift in attitudes toward members of the other racial group. Those in the segregated project showed no change or actually became more prejudiced than before (Deutsch & Collins, 1951). In other studies, mixed-race groups have been formed at work, in the laboratory, and at schools. The conclusion from such research is that personal contact with a disliked group will induce friendly behavior, respect, and liking. However, these benefits occur only when personal contact is cooperative and on an equal footing (Grack & Richman, 1996).

To test the importance of equal-status contact directly, Gerald Clore and his associates set up a unique summer camp for children. The camp was directed by one European-American male, one European-American female, one African-American male, and one African-American female. Each campsite had three African-American and three European-American campers and one African-American and one European-American counselor. Thus, African-Americans and European-Americans were equally divided in number, power, privileges, and duties. Did the experience make a difference? Apparently it did: Testing showed that the children had significantly more positive attitudes toward opposite-race children after the camp than they did before (Clore, 1976).

Superordinate Goals

Let us now consider a revealing study done with 11-year-old boys. When the boys arrived at a summer camp, they were split into two groups and housed in separate cabins. At first the groups were kept apart to build up separate group identities and friendships. Soon each group had a flag and a name (the "Rattlers" and the "Eagles") and each had staked out its territory. At this point the two groups were placed in competition with each other. After a number of clashes, disliking between the groups bordered on hatred: The boys baited each other, started fights, and raided each other's cabins (Sherif et al., 1961).

Were they allowed to go home hating each other? As an experiment in reducing intergroup conflict, and to prevent the boys from remaining enemies, various strategies to reduce tensions were tried. Holding meetings between group leaders did nothing. When the groups were invited to eat together, the event turned into a free-for-all. Finally, emergencies that required *cooperation* among members of both groups were staged at the camp. For example, the water supply was damaged so that all the boys had to work together to repair it. Creating this and other *superordinate goals* helped restore peace between the two groups. (A **superordinate goal** exceeds or overrides other lesser goals.)

Mary Kate Denny/PhotoEdit

Many school districts in the United States have begun requiring students to wear uniforms. Appearance (including gang colors) is one of the major reasons why kids treat each other differently. Uniforms help minimize status inequalities and in-group/out-group distinctions. In Long Beach, California, a switch to uniforms was followed by a 91 percent drop in student assaults, thefts, vandalism, and weapons and drug violations (Ritter, 1998).

Cooperation and shared goals seem to help reduce conflict by encouraging people in opposing groups to see themselves as members of a single, larger group (Gaertner et al., 2000). Superordinate goals, in other words, have a "we're all in the same boat" effect on perceptions of group membership (Olson & Zanna, 1993). The power of superordinate goals can be seen in the unity that prevailed in the United States for months after the September 11 terrorist attacks. Can such goals exist on a global scale? One example might be a desire to avoid nuclear holocaust. Another that comes to mind is the need to preserve the natural environment on a global scale. Still another is the continuing threat posed by terrorism and religious extremism. Politically, such goals

Status inequalities Differences in the power, prestige, or privileges of two or more persons or groups.

Equal-status contact Social interaction that occurs on an equal footing, without obvious differences in power or status.

Superordinate goal A goal that exceeds or overrides all others; a goal that renders other goals relatively less important.

may be far from universal. But their superordinate quality is clearly evident.

"Jigsaw" Classrooms

Contrary to the hopes of many, integrating public schools often has little positive effect on racial prejudice. In fact, prejudice may be made worse, and the self-esteem of minority students frequently decreases (Aronson, 1992).

If integrated schools provide equal-status contact, shouldn't prejudice be reduced? Theoretically, yes. But in practice, minority-group children often enter schools unprepared to compete on an equal footing. The competitive nature of schools almost guarantees that children will *not* learn to like and understand each other.

With the preceding in mind, social psychologist Elliot Aronson pioneered a way to apply superordinate goals to ordinary classrooms. According to Aronson, such goals are effective because they create **mutual interdependence.** That is, people must depend on one another to meet each person's goals. When individual needs are linked, cooperation is encouraged (Deutsch, 1993).

How has that idea been applied? Aronson has successfully created "jigsaw" classrooms that emphasize cooperation rather than competition. The term *jigsaw* refers to the pieces of a jigsaw puzzle. In a **jigsaw classroom,** each child is given a "piece" of the information needed to complete a project or prepare for a test.

In a typical session, children are divided into groups of five or six and given a topic to study for a later exam. Each child is given his or her "piece" of information and asked to learn it. For example, one child might have information on Thomas Edison's invention of the light bulb; another, facts about his invention of the long-playing phonograph record; and a third, information about Edison's childhood. After the children have learned their parts, they teach them to others in the group. Even the most competitive children quickly realize that they cannot do well without the aid of everyone in the group. Each child makes a unique and essential contribution, so the children learn to listen to and respect each other.

Jonathan Nourok/PhotoEdit

In a "jigsaw" classroom, children help each other prepare for tests. As they teach each other what they know, the children learn to cooperate and to respect the unique strengths of each individual.

Does the jigsaw method work? Compared to children in traditional classrooms, children in jigsaw groups are less prejudiced, they like their classmates more, they have more positive attitudes toward school, their grades improve, and their self-esteem increases (Aronson, 2004; Walker & Crogan, 1998). Such results are quite encouraging. As Kenneth Clark (1965) has said, "Racial prejudice . . . debases all human beings—those who are its victims, those who victimize, and in quite subtle ways, those who are merely accessories."

To summarize, prejudice is reduced when the following are true (Pettigrew, 1998):

- Members of different groups have equal status *within the situation* that brings them together.
- Members of all groups seek a common goal.
- Group members must cooperate to reach the goal.
- Group members spend enough time together for cross-group friendships to develop.

Sports teams are an excellent example of a situation in which all of these conditions apply. The close contact and interdependent effort required in team sports often creates lifelong friendships and breaks down the walls of prejudice.

KNOWLEDGE BUILDER

Prejudice and Intergroup Conflict

REFLECT

Mentally scan over the events of the last week. How would they have changed if prejudices of all types ceased to exist?

Think of the most rigid or dogmatic person you know. Does he or she match the profile of the authoritarian personality?

Stereotypes exist for many social categories, even ordinary ones such as "college student" or "unmarried young adult." What stereotypes do you think you face in daily life?

The director of a youth recreation center is concerned about the amount of conflict she is seeing between boys and girls from different racial and ethnic groups. What advice can you give the director?

LEARNING CHECK

1. As a basis for prejudice, ____________ is frequently related to frustration and displaced ____________.
2. The authoritarian personality tends to be prejudiced against all out-groups, a quality referred to as ____________.
3. Social stereotypes may be both positive and negative. T or F?
4. The stereotypes underlying racial and ethnic prejudice tend to evolve from the superordinate goals that often separate groups. T or F?
5. The term *symbolic prejudice* refers to racism or prejudice that is expressed in disguised or hidden form. T or F?
6. Jane Elliot's classroom experiment in prejudice showed that children could be made to dislike one another
   a. by setting up group competition
   b. by imposing status inequalities
   c. by role-playing
   d. by frustrating all the students

7. Research suggests that prejudice and intergroup conflict may be reduced by ____________ interaction and ____________ goals.

CRITICAL THINKING

8. In court trials, defense lawyers sometimes try to identify and eliminate prospective jurors who have authoritarian personality traits. Can you guess why?

Answers: **1.** scapegoating, aggression **2.** ethnocentrism **3.** T **4.** F **5.** T **6.** b **7.** equal-status, superordinate **8.** Because authoritarians tend to believe that punishment is effective, they are more likely to vote for conviction.

Aggression—The World's Most Dangerous Animal

"I know not with what weapons World War III will be fought, but World War IV will be fought with sticks and stones."

Albert Einstein

Aggression is a human tragedy. Helping others is a source of hope. It might seem that the horrors of war would lead to a worldwide revulsion for killing. In reality, homicide rates have increased in many countries in recent years. What causes aggression? Can violence be reduced? Can we promote prosocial behavior? More than ever, these are pressing questions.

For a time, the City Zoo of Los Angeles, California, had on display two examples of the world's most dangerous animal—the only animal capable of destroying the earth and all other animal species. Perhaps you have already guessed which animal it was. In the cage were two college students, representing the species *Homo sapiens!*

The human capacity for aggression is staggering. It has been estimated that 58 million humans were killed by other humans (an average of nearly one person per minute) during the 125-year period ending with World War II. Murder now ranks as a major cause of death in the United States. One American kills another every 23 minutes—making the United States one of the world's most violent nations. War, homicide, riots, family violence, assassination, rape, assault, forcible robbery, and other violent acts offer sad testimony to the realities of human aggression.

What causes aggression? **Aggression** refers to any action carried out with the intention of harming another person. Aggression has many potential causes. Brief descriptions of some of the major possibilities follow.

Instincts

Some theorists argue we are naturally aggressive creatures, having inherited a "killer instinct" from our animal ancestors. Ethologists theorize that aggression is a biologically rooted behavior observed in all animals, including humans (Blanchard & Blanchard, 2003). (An **ethologist** is a person who studies the natural behavior patterns of animals.) Noted ethologist Konrad Lorenz (1966, 1974) also believed that humans lack certain innate patterns that inhibit aggression in animals. For example, in a dispute over territory, two wolves may growl, lunge, bare their teeth, and fiercely threaten each other. In most instances, though, neither is killed or even wounded. One wolf, recognizing the dominance of the other, will typically bare its throat in a gesture of submission. The dominant wolf could kill in an instant, but it is inhibited by the other wolf's submissive gesture. In contrast, human confrontations of equal intensity almost always end in injury or death.

Getty Images

Ritualized human aggression. Violent and aggressive behavior is so commonplace it may be viewed as entertainment. How "natural" is aggressive behavior?

The idea that humans are "naturally" aggressive has an intuitive appeal, but many psychologists question it. Many of Lorenz's "explanations" of aggression are little more than loose comparisons between human and animal behavior. Just labeling a behavior as "instinctive" does little to explain it. More important, we are left with the question of why some individuals or human cultures (the Arapesh, the Senoi, the Navajo, the Eskimo, and others) show little hostility or aggression. Thankfully, the vast majority of humans *do not* kill or harm others.

Mutual interdependence A condition in which two or more persons must depend on one another to meet each person's needs or goals.

Jigsaw classroom A method of reducing prejudice; each student receives only part of the information needed to complete a project or prepare for a test.

Aggression Any action carried out with the intention of harming another person.

Ethologist A person who studies the natural behavior patterns of animals.

Biology

Despite problems with the instinctive view, aggression may have a biological basis. Physiological studies have shown that some brain areas are capable of triggering or ending aggressive behavior. Also, researchers have found a relationship between aggression and such physical factors as hypoglycemia (low blood sugar), allergy, and specific brain injuries and diseases. For both men and women, higher levels of the hormone testosterone are associated with more aggressive behavior (Banks & Dabbs, 1996; Dabbs, Hargrove, & Heusel, 1996; Harris et al., 1996). Perhaps because of their higher testosterone levels, men are ten times more likely to commit murder than women are (Anderson & Bushman, 2002). However, none of these biological factors can be considered a direct *cause* of aggression (Moore, 2001). Instead, they probably lower the threshold for aggression, making hostile behavior more likely to occur.

The effects of alcohol and other drugs provide another indication of the role of the brain and biology in violence and aggression. A variety of studies show that alcohol is involved in large percentages of murders and violent crimes. Like the conditions already noted, intoxicating drugs seem to lower inhibitions to act aggressively—often with tragic results (Anderson & Bushman, 2002; Ito, Giacalone, & Tedeschi, 1996).

To summarize, the fact that we are biologically *capable* of aggression does not mean that aggression is inevitable or "part of human nature." Twenty eminent scientists who studied the question concluded, "Biology does not condemn humanity to war. . . . Violence is neither in our evolutionary legacy nor in our genes. The same species that invented war is capable of inventing peace" (Scott & Ginsburg, 1994; UNESCO, 1990). Humans are fully capable of learning to inhibit their use of violence. For example, American Quakers, who live in this country's increasingly violent culture, adopt nonviolence as a way of life (Bandura, 2001).

Frustration

Step on a dog's tail and you may get nipped. Frustrate a human and you may get insulted. The **frustration-aggression hypothesis** states that frustration tends to lead to aggression.

Does frustration always produce aggression? Although the connection is strong, a moment's thought will show that frustration does not *always* lead to aggression. Frustration, for instance, may lead to stereotyped responding or perhaps to a state of "learned helplessness" (see Chapter 15). Also, aggression can occur in the absence of frustration. This possibility is illustrated by sports spectators who start fights, throw bottles, tear down goal posts, and so forth, after their team has *won.*

BRIDGES

Various parts of the limbic system in the brain are closely linked with anger and aggression.

See Chapter 2, pages 72–73.

Jon Love/Getty Images

Road rage and some freeway shootings may be a reaction to the frustration of traffic congestion. The fact that automobiles provide anonymity, or a loss of personal identity, may also encourage aggressive actions that would not otherwise occur.

Aversive Stimuli

Frustration probably encourages aggression because it is uncomfortable. Various *aversive stimuli,* which produce discomfort or displeasure, can heighten hostility and aggression (Anderson, Anderson, & Deuser, 1996; Morgan, 2005) (● Figure 19.4). Examples include insults, high temperatures, pain, and even disgusting scenes or odors. Such stimuli probably raise overall arousal levels so that we become more sensitive to **aggression cues** (signals that are associated with aggression) (Carlson, Marcus-Newhall, & Miller, 1990). Aversive stimuli also tend to activate ideas, memories, and expressions associated with anger and aggression (Morgan, 2005).

Some cues for aggression are internal (angry thoughts, for instance). Many are external: Certain words, actions, and gestures made by others are strongly associated with aggressive responses. A raised middle finger, for instance, is an almost universal invitation to aggression in North America. Weapons serve as particularly strong cues for aggressive behavior (Morgan, 2005). The implication of this **weapons effect** seems to be that the symbols and trappings of aggression encourage aggression. A prime example is the fact that murders are almost three times more likely to occur in homes where guns are kept. Nearly 80 percent of the victims in such homes are killed by a family member or acquaintance. Only 4 percent are murdered by strangers (Kellermann et al., 1993).

Social Learning

One of the most widely accepted explanations of aggression is also the simplest. Social learning theory holds that we learn to be aggressive by observing aggression in others (Bandura, 2001).

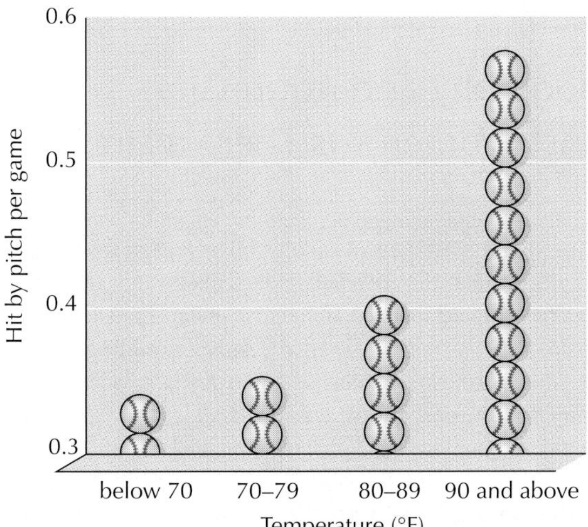

● **Figure 19.4** Personal discomfort caused by aversive (unpleasant) stimuli can make aggressive behavior more likely. For example, studies of crime rates show that the incidence of highly aggressive behavior, such as murder, rape, and assault, rises as the air temperature goes from warm to hot to sweltering (Anderson, 1989). The results you see here further confirm the heat-aggression link. The graph shows that there is a strong association between the temperatures at major league baseball games and the number of batters hit by a pitch during those games. When the temperature exceeds 90°, watch out for that fastball (Reifman, Larrick, & Fein, 1991)!

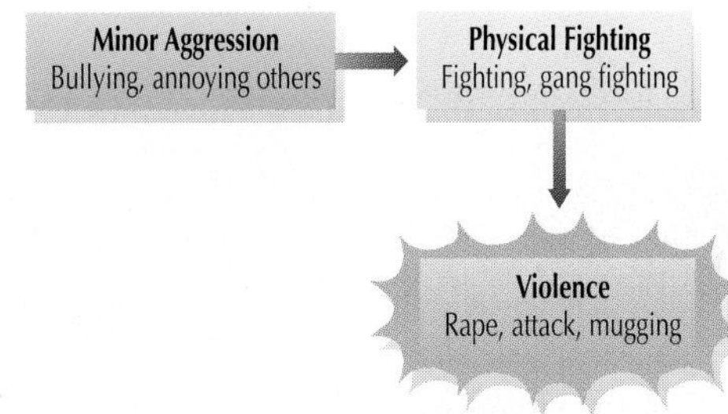

● **Figure 19.5** Violent behavior among delinquent boys doesn't appear overnight. Usually, their capacity for violence develops slowly, as they move from minor aggression to increasingly brutal acts. Overall aggression increases dramatically in early adolescence as boys gain physical strength and more access to weapons (Loeber & Hay, 1997).

To explain behavior, **social learning theory** combines learning principles with cognitive processes, socialization, and modeling. According to this view, there is no instinctive human programming for fistfighting, pipe-bombing, knife wielding, gun loading, 95-mile-an-hour "beanballs," or other violent or aggressive actions. Hence, aggression must be learned (● Figure 19.5). Is it any wonder that people who were the victims of violence during childhood are likely to become violent themselves (Macmillan, 2001)?

Aggressive Models

Social learning theorists predict that people growing up in nonaggressive cultures will themselves be nonaggressive. Those raised in a culture with aggressive models and heroes will learn aggressive responses (Bandura, 2001). Considered in such terms, it is no wonder that America has become one of the most violent of all countries. It is estimated that a violent crime occurs every 54 seconds in the United States. Approximately 40 percent of the population owns firearms. Nationally, 70 percent agree that "when a boy is growing up, it is very important for him to have a few fist-fights." Children and adults are treated to an almost nonstop parade of aggressive models, in the media as well as in actual behavior. We are, without a doubt, an aggressive culture. (See "Pornography and Aggression Against Women—Is There a Link?")

The World According to TV

Did you know that the world is populated primarily by males, professionals, European Americans, and members of the middle class? Did you know that women make up only 28 percent of the population; that one half of all women are teenagers or in their early twenties; that more than one third are unemployed or have no purpose beyond offering emotional support to men or serving as objects of sexual desire? That minorities are generally service workers, criminals, victims, or students? That over one half of all villains have accents? That most victims are single women, young boys, or people of color? If you watch much TV, these are the impressions you get daily on the tube.

Televised Violence

It is clear that TV reality does not match the real world. Every day, TV provides an endless stream of bad models, especially concerning violence. In the United States there are about 188 hours of violent programs per week. Eighty-one percent of all programs contain violence. Murder, robbery, kidnapping, and assault make up 85 percent of TV crimes. In real life, they total about 5 percent. Television is particularly unrealistic about the effects of violence. An astounding 73 percent of violent characters go unpunished and 58 percent of violent acts don't have painful results. Only 16 percent of all programs show any realistic long-term consequences for violence. For children's programs the rate falls to just 5 percent (*National Television Violence Study*, 1995–1996).

How much does TV violence affect children? As Albert Bandura showed in his studies of imitation (Chapter 8), children may learn new aggressive actions by watching violent or aggressive behavior, or they may learn that violence is "okay." Either way, they are more likely to act aggressively. Heroes on TV are as violent as the villains, and they usually receive praise for their violence. There is

Frustration-aggression hypothesis States that frustration tends to lead to aggression.

Aggression cues Stimuli or signals that are associated with aggression and that tend to elicit it.

Weapons effect The observation that weapons serve as strong cues for aggressive behavior.

Social learning theory Combines learning principles with cognitive processes, socialization, and modeling, to explain behavior.

FOCUS ON RESEARCH

Pornography and Aggression Against Women—Is There a Link?

A heated debate has raged for years about the effects of pornography. Early studies suggested that viewing pornography has no major adverse effects. This conclusion appears to remain valid for stimuli that can be described as merely erotic or sexual in content (Malamuth, Addison, & Koss, 2000). However, in recent years there has been a dramatic increase in aggressive-pornographic images in the mass media. **Aggressive pornography** refers to depictions in which violence, threats, or obvious power differences are used to force someone (usually a woman) to engage in sex.

The main finding of studies on aggressive-pornographic stimuli is that they do increase aggression against females in men who are prone to sexual violence (Malamuth, Addison, & Koss, 2000). As researchers Neil Malamuth and Ed Donnerstein (1982) concluded, "Exposure to mass media stimuli that have violent *and* sexual content increases the audience's aggressive-sexual fantasies, beliefs in rape myths, and aggressive behavior." Donnerstein and Daniel Linz (1986) add that media *violence* is most damaging. As they put it, "Violent images, rather than sexual ones, are most responsible for people's attitudes about women and rape." The problem, then, extends far beyond X-rated films and books. Mainstream movies, magazines, music videos, and television programs are equally to blame for reinforcing the myth that women find force or aggression pleasurable (Donnerstein, 2001). It is telling that rapists are sexually aroused by both sexual and nonsexual violence. Clearly, violence is a major dimension of rape and sexual aggression (Forbes & Adams-Curtis, 2001).

now little doubt that widespread exposure to media violence, including video games, contributes to aggression (Anderson et al., 2003; DeGaetano, 2005). Boys and girls who watch a lot of violence on television are much more likely to be aggressive as adults (Huesmann et al., 2003).

In addition to teaching new antisocial actions, television and video games may disinhibit dangerous impulses that viewers already have. **Disinhibition** (the removal of inhibition) results in acting out behavior that normally would be restrained. For example, many TV programs give the message that violence is acceptable behavior that leads to success and popularity. For some people, this message can lower inhibitions against acting out hostile feelings (Anderson et al., 2003).

Another effect of TV violence is that it tends to lower sensitivity to violent acts. As anyone who has seen a street fight or a mugging can tell you, TV violence is sanitized and unrealistic. The real thing is gross, ugly, and gut wrenching. Even when it is graphic, TV violence is viewed in the relaxed and familiar setting of the home. For at least some viewers, this combination diminishes emotional reactions to violent scenes. When Victor Cline and his associates showed a bloody fight film to a group of boys, they found that heavy TV viewers (averaging 42 hours a week) showed much less emotion than those who watched little or no TV (Cline, Croft, & Courrier, 1972). Television, it seems, can cause a **desensitization** (reduced emotional sensitivity) to violence (Huesmann et al., 2003).

Preventing Aggression

What can be done about aggression? Social learning theory implies that "aggression begets aggression." For example, children who are physically abused at home, those who suffer severe physical punishment, and those who merely witness violence in the community are more likely to be involved in fighting, aggressive play, and antisocial behavior at school (Macmillan, 2001; Margolin & Gordis, 2000).

According to social learning theorists, watching a prizefight, sporting event, or violent television program may increase aggression, rather than drain off aggressive urges. A case in point is provided by psychologist Leonard Eron, who spent 22 years following over 600 children into adulthood. Eron (1987) observes, "Among the most influential models for children were those observed on television. One of the best predictors of how aggressive a young man would be at age 19 was the violence of the television programs he preferred when he was 8 years old" (● Figure 19.6). According to Eron, children learn aggressive strategies and actions from TV violence. Because of this, they are more prone to aggress when they face frustrating situations or cues. Others have found that viewers who watch violent videotapes have more aggressive thoughts. As we have noted, violent thoughts often precede violent actions (Bushman & Geen, 1990). Thus, the spiral of aggression might be broken if we did not so often portray it, reward it, and glorify it (Hughes & Hasbrouck, 1996).

BRIDGES

Modeling and observational learning explain much of television's impact on our behavior.

See Chapter 8, pages 288–290.

BRIDGES

Abused children frequently become abusive adults, which is another indication that "aggression begets aggression."

See Chapter 4, pages 129–131.

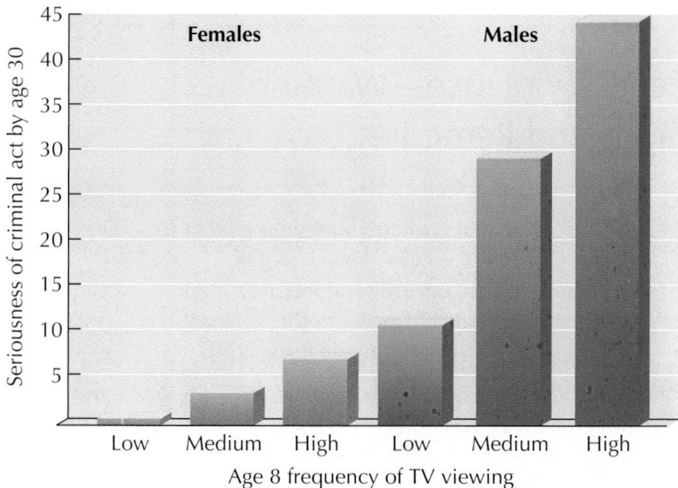

● **Figure 19.6** Although TV violence does not cause aggression, it can encourage it. The likelihood of committing criminal acts by age 30 is related to the amount of TV watching a person did when she or he was a child (Eron, 1987). (Copyright © 1987 by the American Psychological Association, Inc. Reprinted by permission of the author.)

Parents as TV Guides

As the preceding studies show, reduced TV watching is one way to lower aggression. However, other than pulling the plug, what can parents do about television's negative effects on children? Actually, quite a lot. Children typically model parents' TV viewing habits, and they are guided by parents' reactions to programs. Parents can make a big difference if they do the following (Eron, 1986; Frydman, 1999):

1. Limit total viewing time so that television does not dominate your child's view of the world. If necessary, set schedules for when watching TV is allowed. Don't use television as a babysitter.
2. Closely monitor what your child does watch. Change channels or turn off the TV if you object to a program. Be prepared to offer games and activities that stimulate your child's imagination and creativity.
3. Actively seek programs your child will enjoy, especially those that model positive behavior and social attitudes.
4. Watch television with your child so that you can counter what is shown. Help your child distinguish between reality and TV fantasies. Address distortions and stereotypes as they appear on screen.
5. Discuss the social conflicts and violent solutions shown on television. Ask your child in what ways the situations are unrealistic and why the violence shown would not work in the real world. Encourage the child to propose more mature, realistic, and positive responses to situations.
6. Show by your own disapproval that violent TV heroes are not the ones to emulate. Remember, children who identify with TV characters are more likely to be influenced by televised aggression.

By following these guidelines you can help children learn to enjoy television without being overly influenced by programs and advertisers. A recent study found that elementary school children become less aggressive when they decrease the amount of time they spend watching TV and playing video games (Robinson et al., 2001).

TV as a Positive Model

Couldn't TV's impact also be used constructively? There is no denying TV's tremendous power to inform and to entertain. When these features are combined, the effect can be quite constructive. Perhaps the best examples of TV as a positive social force are educational programs such as *Barney and Friends, Sesame Street,* and *Mr. Rogers' Neighborhood.* Numerous research reports have found that the impact of these programs is positive. Clearly, television can teach children while holding their interest and attention.

Prosocial behavior consists of actions toward others that are helpful, constructive, or altruistic (Penner et al., 2005). As a model

The Photo Works/Photo Researchers, Inc.

A study by Jerome and Dorothy Singer found that preschoolers who watch *Barney and Friends* show improved cognitive skills and knowledge—such as knowing colors and shapes, numbers, vocabulary, good manners, and facts about nature and health (deGroot, 1994).

Aggressive pornography Media depictions of sexual violence or of forced participation in sexual activity.

Disinhibition The removal of inhibition; results in acting out behavior that normally would be restrained.

Desensitization A reduction in emotional sensitivity to a stimulus.

Prosocial behavior Behavior toward others that is helpful, constructive, or altruistic.

THE CLINICAL FILE

School Violence—Warning Signs and Remedies

Columbine. Today, years later, most of us still associate this name with the American high school where two students killed twelve fellow students and a teacher, wounded many others, and then killed themselves. Seared into our cultural awareness, the Columbine massacre and other high-profile school shootings never fail to elicit sensationalistic media coverage. They also incite authorities to institute harsh countermeasures like metal detectors in schools, zero-tolerance policies, and student profiling (Cornell, 2005).

Fortunately, school shootings are relatively rare. Nevertheless, they represent the tip of a growing problem of school violence that is better dealt with through careful attention to warning signs and less dramatic remedies (Conoley & Goldstein, 2004).

What are the warning signs for school violence? The following points can help friends, family members, and teachers identify children at risk ("Warning Signs," 2000). A student who is prone to violence

- Consistently does not listen to adults and rejects authority.
- Has trouble paying attention and concentrating.
- Does poorly in school, is disruptive, and skips class.
- Frequently gets in fights, may join a gang, or is involved in stealing or destroying property.
- Is easily frustrated.
- Reacts with extreme anger to criticism or disappointments.
- Feels that life is unfair and blames others or seeks revenge.
- Watches many violent television shows and movies or plays a lot of violent video games.
- Has few friends, and is often publicly rejected or teased by others.
- Has friends who are unruly or aggressive.
- Is cruel or violent toward pets or other animals.
- Drinks alcohol and/or uses inhalants or drugs.

One of the best antidotes to youth violence is a warm and loving family (Pollack, 2001). Depression, pain, hate, and violence often originate in dysfunctional families. To minimize anger, aggression, and violence, parents should do the following:

- Make sure their children are supervised.
- Show by example how children should act.
- Teach children nonaggressive ways to solve problems.
- Avoid hitting their children.
- Be consistent about rules and discipline.
- Make sure children do not have access to guns.
- Try to keep children from seeing violence at home, in the media, or in the community.

Healthy communities also discourage violence (Mateu-Gelabert & Lune, 2003). Parents should get involved in the community and get to know their neighbors. Children benefit from participating in groups that build pride in the community, such as those that organize cleanups of litter or graffiti. Such groups provide a great opportunity for parents, children, and neighbors to spend time together in rewarding activities.

for positive attitudes and responses, TV could be used to promote helping, cooperation, charity, and brotherhood in the same way that it has tended to stereotype and encourage aggression. Over 200 studies have shown that prosocial behavior on TV increases prosocial behavior by viewers (Hearold, 1987). To illustrate, a program called "Youth Against Violence: Choose to De-Fuse" was developed in New York City to help inner-city youths resist violence. The program focused on creating positive peer pressure for choosing nonviolent solutions to conflict. The use of real-life situations, speech, and body language added to the effectiveness of the program (Zimmerman, 1996). (Also see "School Violence—Warning Signs and Remedies" for more information on what individuals can do to prevent violence.)

Anger Control

On a personal level, psychologists have succeeded in teaching some people to control their anger and aggressive impulses. **Anger control** refers to personal strategies for reducing or curbing anger. The key to remaining calm is to define upsetting situations as *problems to be solved.* Therefore, to limit anger, people are taught to do the following:

1. Define the problem as precisely as possible.
2. Make a list of possible solutions.
3. Rank the likely success of each solution.
4. Choose a solution and try it.
5. Assess how successful the solution was, and make adjustments if necessary.

Taking these steps has helped many people to lessen tendencies toward child abuse, family violence, and other destructive outbursts (Meichenbaum, Henshaw, & Himel, 1982).

Beyond this, the question remains: How shall we tame the world's most dangerous animal? There is no easy answer, only a challenge of pressing importance (Lench, 2004). The solution will undoubtedly involve the best efforts of thinkers and researchers from many disciplines.

For the immediate future, it is clear that we need more people who are willing to engage in helpful, altruistic, prosocial behavior. In the next section we will examine some of the forces that operate to prevent people from helping others. Also discussed are a few glimmerings about how to encourage prosocial behavior.

Prosocial Behavior—Helping Others

Late one night, tenants of a Queens, New York, apartment building watched and listened in horror as a young woman named Kitty Genovese was murdered on the sidewalk outside. From the safety of their rooms, no fewer than 38 people heard the agonized screams as her assailant stabbed her, was frightened off, and returned to stab her again.

Kitty Genovese's murder took over 30 minutes, but none of her neighbors tried to help. None even called the police until after the attack had ended. Perhaps it is understandable that no one wanted to get involved. After all, it could have been a violent lovers' quarrel. Or helping might have meant risking personal injury. But what prevented these people from at least calling the police?

Isn't this an example of the alienation of city life? News reports treated this incident as evidence of a breakdown in social ties caused by the impersonality of the city. Although it is true that urban living can be dehumanizing, this does not fully explain such **bystander apathy** (unwillingness of bystanders to offer help during emergencies). According to psychologists John Darley and Bibb Latané (1968), failure to help is related to the number of people present. Over the years many studies have shown that the *more* potential helpers present, the *less* likely people are to help (Latané, Nida, & Wilson, 1981; Miller, 2006).

Why would people be less willing to help when others are present? In Kitty Genovese's case, the answer is that everyone thought *someone else* would help. The dynamics of this effect are easily illustrated: Suppose that two motorists have stalled at the roadside, one on a sparsely traveled country road and the other on a busy freeway. Who gets help first?

On the freeway, where hundreds of cars pass every minute, each driver can assume that someone else will help. Personal responsibility for helping is spread so thin that no one takes action. On the country road, one of the first few people to arrive will probably stop, because the responsibility is clearly theirs. In general, Latané and Darley assume that bystanders are not apathetic or uncaring; they are inhibited by the presence of others.

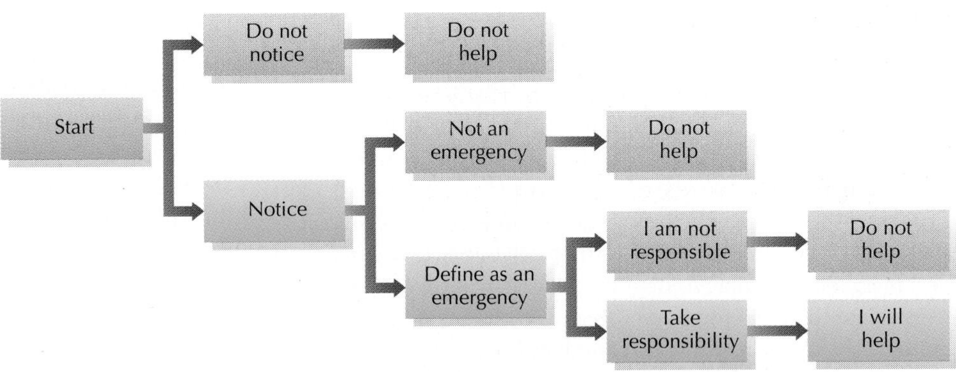

● **Figure 19.7** This decision tree summarizes the steps a person must take before making a commitment to offer help, according to Latané and Darley's model.

Does the person lying on the ground need help? What factors determine whether a person in trouble will receive help in an emergency? Surprisingly, more potential helpers tend to lower the chances that help will be given.

Bystander Intervention

People must pass through four decision points before giving help. First they must notice that something is happening. Next they must define the event as an emergency. Then they must take responsibility. Finally, they must select a course of action (● Figure 19.7). Laboratory experiments have shown that each step can be influenced by the presence of other people.

Noticing

What would happen if you fainted and collapsed on the sidewalk? Would someone stop to help? Would people think you were drunk? Would they even notice you? Latané and Darley suggest that if the sidewalk is crowded, few people will even see you. This has nothing to do with people blocking each other's vision. Instead, it is related to widely accepted norms against staring at others in public. People in crowds typically "keep their eyes to themselves."

Is there any way to show that this is a factor in bystander apathy? To test this idea, students were asked to fill out a questionnaire either alone or in a room full of people. While the students worked, a thick cloud of smoke was blown into the room through a vent.

Most students left alone in the room noticed the smoke immediately. Few of the people in groups noticed the smoke until it actually became difficult to see through it. Subjects working in groups politely kept their eyes on their papers and avoided looking at others (or the smoke). In contrast, those who were alone scanned the room from time to time.

Bystander apathy Unwillingness of bystanders to offer help during emergencies or to become involved in others' problems.

Defining an Emergency

The smoke-filled room also shows the influence others have on defining a situation as an emergency. When subjects in groups finally noticed the smoke, they cast sidelong glances at others in the room. Apparently, they were searching for clues to help interpret what was happening. No one wanted to overreact or act like a fool if there was no emergency. However, as subjects coolly surveyed the reactions of others, they were themselves being watched. In real emergencies, people sometimes "fake each other out" and underestimate the need for action because each person attempts to appear calm. In short, until someone acts, no one acts.

Taking Responsibility

Perhaps the most crucial step in helping is assuming responsibility. In this case, groups limit helping by causing a **diffusion of responsibility** (spreading responsibility among several people).

Is that like the unwillingness of drivers to offer help on a crowded freeway? Exactly. It is the feeling that no one is personally responsible for helping. This problem was demonstrated in an experiment in which students took part in a group discussion over an intercom system. Actually, there was only one real subject in each group; the others were tape-recorded actors. Each subject was placed in a separate room (supposedly to maintain confidentiality), and discussions of college life were begun. During the discussion, one of the "students" simulated an epileptic-like seizure and called out for help. In some cases, subjects thought they were alone with the seizure victim. Others believed they were members of three- or six-person groups.

People who thought they were alone with the "victim" of this staged emergency reported it immediately or tried to help. Some subjects in the three-person groups failed to respond, and those who did were slower. In the six-person groups, over a third of the subjects took no action at all. People in this experiment were obviously faced with a conflict like that in many real emergencies: Should they be helpful and responsible, or should they mind their own business? Many were influenced toward inaction by the presence of others.

People do help in some emergencies. How are these different? It is not always clear what makes the difference. Helping behavior is complex and influenced by many variables. One naturalistic experiment staged in a New York City subway gives a hint of the kinds of things that may be important. When a "victim" (actor) "passed out" in a subway car, he received more help when carrying a cane than when carrying a liquor bottle. More important, however, was the fact that most people were willing to help in either case (Piliavin, Rodin, & Piliavin, 1969).

To better answer the question we need to consider some factors not included in Latané and Darley's account of helping.

Who Will Help Whom?

Many studies suggest that when we see a person in trouble, it tends to cause *heightened arousal* (Dovidio & Penner, 2001). This aroused, keyed-up feeling can motivate us to give aid, but only if the rewards of helping outweigh the costs. Higher costs (such as great effort, personal risk, or possible embarrassment) almost always decrease helping (Foss, 1986). In addition to general arousal, potential helpers may also feel **empathic arousal.** This means they empathize with the person in need or feel some of the person's pain, fear, or anguish. Helping is much more likely when we are able to take the perspective of others and feel sympathy for their plight (Batson & Powell, 2003).

If people feel sad or distressed when another person is in trouble, couldn't it be that they help just to make themselves feel better? It is certainly possible that some helping is actually "selfish." But research has shown that empathy (empathic arousal) really does unleash altruistic motivation based on sympathy and compassion. Most helping, including such altruistic acts as making donations or being kind, is motivated by a true desire to relieve the distress of others (Dovidio, Allen, & Schroeder, 1990).

Empathic arousal is especially likely to motivate helping when the person in need seems to be similar to ourselves (Batson & Powell, 2003). In fact, a feeling of connection to the victim may be one of the most important factors in helping. This, perhaps, is why being in a good mood also increases helping. When we are feeling successful, happy, or fortunate, we may also feel more connected to others (Dovidio & Penner, 2001). In summary, there is a strong **empathy-helping relationship:** We are most likely to help someone in need when we "feel for" that person and experience emotions such as empathy, sympathy, and compassion (Batson, 1990).

Is there anything that can be done to encourage prosocial behavior? People who see others helping are more likely to offer help themselves. Also, persons who give help in one situation tend to perceive themselves as helpful people. This change in self-image encourages them to help in other situations. One more point is that norms of fairness encourage us to help others who have helped us (Dovidio & Penner, 2001). For all these reasons, helping others not only assists them directly, it encourages others to help too.

"De-victimize" Yourself

If you should find yourself in need of help during an emergency, what can you do to avoid being a victim of bystander apathy? The work we have reviewed here suggests that you should make sure that you are noticed, that people realize there's an emergency, and that they need to take action. Being noticed can be promoted in some situations by shouting "Fire!" Bystanders who might run away from a robbery or an assault may rush to see where the fire is. At the very least, remember to not just scream. Instead, you should call out, "Help," or, "I need help right now." Whenever possible, define your situation for bystanders. Say, for instance, "I'm being attacked, call the police." Or, "Stop that man, he has my purse." You can also directly assign responsibility to a bystander by pointing to someone and saying, "You, call the police," or, "I'm injured, I need you to call an ambulance" (Cummins, 1995).

Positive Psychology: Everyday Heroes

Every year awards are given to people who risk their lives while saving the lives of others. These heroes are typically honored for saving people from fires, drowning, animal attacks, electrocution, and suffocation. The majority of people who perform such heroic acts are men, perhaps because of the physical dangers involved. However, there are other heroic, prosocial acts that save lives and involve personal risk. Examples are kidney donors, Peace Corp volunteers, and Doctors of the World volunteers. In such endeavors, we find as many women as men, and often more. It is important to remember, perhaps, that sensational and highly visible acts of heroism are only one of many ways in which people engage in selfless, altruistic behavior (Becker & Eagly, 2004). People who serve as community volunteers, tutors, coaches, blood donors, and the like don't just help others. Often, their efforts contribute to personal growth and make them healthier and happier. Thus, it can be said, "We do well by doing good" (Piliavin, 2003).

A Look Ahead

The Psychology in Action section of this chapter returns to the topic of prejudice for some further thoughts about how to promote tolerance. Don't miss this interesting conclusion to our discussion of social psychology.

KNOWLEDGE BUILDER

Aggression and Prosocial Behavior

REFLECT

Most people have been angry enough at some time to behave aggressively. Which concepts or theories do you think best explain your own aggressive actions?

An elderly woman is at the side of the road, trying to change a flat tire. She obviously needs help. You are approaching her in your car. What must happen before you are likely to stop and help her?

LEARNING CHECK

1. The position of ethologists is that there is no biological basis for aggression. T or F?
2. Higher levels of testosterone are associated with more aggressive behavior. T or F?
3. Frustration and aversive stimuli are more likely to produce aggression when cues for aggressive behavior are present. T or F?
4. Social learning theorists view aggression as primarily related to biological instincts. T or F?
5. Social learning theory holds that exposure to aggressive models helps drain off aggressive energies. T or F?
6. Heavy exposure to television results in lowered emotional sensitivity to violence. T or F?
7. ______________________ behavior refers to actions that are constructive, altruistic, or helpful to others.
8. Defining an event as an emergency is the first step toward bystander intervention. T or F?
9. Seeing that a person in need is similar to ourselves tends to increase empathic arousal and the likelihood that help will be given. T or F?

CRITICAL THINKING

10. If televised violence contributes to aggressive behavior in our society, do you think it is possible that television could also promote prosocial behavior?

Answers: 1. F **2.** T **3.** T **4.** F **5.** F **6.** T **7.** Prosocial **8.** F **9.** T **10.** Yes. TV could be used to promote helping, cooperation, charity, and brotherhood in the same way that it has encouraged aggression. Numerous studies show that prosocial behavior on TV increases prosocial behavior by viewers.

Diffusion of responsibility Spreading the responsibility to act among several people; reduces the likelihood that help will be given to a person in need.

Empathic arousal Emotional arousal that occurs when you feel some of another person's pain, fear, or anguish.

Empathy-helping relationship Observation that we are most likely to help someone else when we feel emotions such as empathy and compassion.

PSYCHOLOGY IN ACTION

Multiculturalism—Living with Diversity

Today's society is more like a "tossed salad" than a cultural "melting pot." Rather than expecting everyone to be alike, psychologists believe that we must learn to respect and appreciate our differences. **Multiculturalism**, as this is called, gives equal status to different ethnic, racial, and cultural groups. It is a recognition and acceptance of human diversity (Fowers & Richardson, 1996).

Breaking the Prejudice Habit

Most people publicly support policies of equality and fairness. Yet many still have lingering biases and negative images of African Americans, Latinos, Asian Americans, and other ethnic minorities. How can we make sense of such conflicting attitudes? Patricia Devine, a social psychologist, has shown that a decision to forsake prejudice does not immediately eliminate prejudiced thoughts and feelings. People who are not prejudiced may continue to respond emotionally to members of other ethnic groups. Quite likely this reflects lingering stereotypes and prejudices learned in childhood (Devine et al., 1991; Dion, 2003).

For many people, becoming less prejudiced begins with sincerely accepting values of tolerance and equality. People who value tolerance feel pangs of guilt or self-criticism when they have intolerant thoughts or feelings (Zuwerink et al., 1996). This motivates them to try to alter their own biased reactions (Dovidio & Gaertner, 1999). But doing so is not easy. Typically, it requires repeated efforts to learn to think, feel, and act differently. Nevertheless, many people have succeeded in overcoming the "prejudice habit" (Devine et al., 1991). If you would like to be more tolerant, the following points may be helpful to you.

Beware of Stereotyping

Stereotypes make the social world more manageable. But placing people in categories almost always causes them to appear more similar than they really are. As a result, we tend to see out-group members as very much alike, even when they are as varied as our friends and family. People who are not prejudiced work hard to actively inhibit stereotyped thoughts and to emphasize fairness and equality (Devine, 1990). A good way to tear down stereotypes is to get to know individuals from various ethnic and cultural groups (Giliovich, Keltner, & Nisbett, 2005).

Seek Individuating Information

When are we most tempted to apply stereotypes? Typically it is when we only have minimal information about a person. Stereotypes help us guess what a person is like and how she or he will act. Unfortunately, these inferences are usually wrong.

One of the best antidotes for stereotypes is **individuating information** (information that helps us see a person as an individual, rather than as a member of a group) (Click, Zion, & Nelson, 1988). Anything that keeps us from placing a person in a particular social category tends to negate stereotyped thinking. When you meet individuals from various backgrounds, focus on the *person,* not the *label* attached to her or him.

A good example of the effects of individuating information comes from a study in Canada of English-speaking students in a French language program. Students who were "immersed" (spent most of their waking hours with French Canadians) became more positive toward them. Immersed students were more likely to say they had come to appreciate and like French Canadians, they were more willing to meet and interact with them, and they saw themselves as less different from French Canadians (Lambert, 1987). In fact, with more subtle kinds of symbolic prejudice, such contact may be the best way to reduce intergroup conflict (Dovidio & Gaertner, 1999)

Don't Fall Prey to Just-World Beliefs

Do you believe that the world is basically fair? Even if you don't, you may believe that the world is sufficiently just so that people generally get what they deserve. It may not be obvious, but such beliefs can directly increase prejudiced thinking (Hafer & Bègue, 2005).

As a result of discrimination, social conditions, and circumstances (such as recent immigration), minorities may occupy lower socioeconomic positions. **Just-world beliefs** (belief that people generally get what they deserve) can lead us to assume that minority group members wouldn't be in such positions if they weren't inferior in some way. This bit of faulty thinking amounts to blaming people who are *victims* of prejudice and discrimination for their plight.

Be Aware of Self-Fulfilling Prophecies

You may recall from Chapter 1 that people tend to act in accordance with the behavior expected by others. If you hold strong stereotypes about members of various groups, a vicious cycle can occur. When you meet someone who is different from yourself, you may treat her or him in a way that is consistent with your stereotypes. If the other person is influenced by your behavior, she or he may act in ways that seem to match your stereotype. This creates a self-fulfilling prophecy and reinforces your belief in the stereotype. (A **self-fulfilling prophecy** is an expectation that prompts people to act in ways that make the expectation come true.)

Remember, Different Does Not Mean Inferior

Some conflicts between groups cannot be avoided. What *can* be avoided is unnecessary **social competition** (rivalry among groups, each of which regards itself as superior to others). The concept of social competition refers to the fact that some individuals seek to enhance their self-esteem by identifying with a group. However, this works only if the group can be seen as superior to others. Because of social competition, groups tend to view themselves as better than their rivals (Baron & Byrne, 2006). In a survey, every major ethnic group in the United States rated itself as better than any other group (Njeri, 1991). This is a little like the fabled town of Lake Woebegone, where all the children are above average.

A person who has high self-esteem does not need to treat others as inferior in order to feel good about himself or herself. Similarly, it is not necessary to degrade other groups in order to feel positive about one's own group identity (Messick & Mackie, 1989). In fact, each ethnic group has strengths that members of other groups could benefit from emulating. For instance, African Americans, Asian Americans, and Latinos emphasize family networks that help buffer them from some of the stresses of daily life (Suinn, 1999).

Understand That Race Is a Social Construction

From the viewpoint of modern genetics, the concept of race has absolutely no meaning (Bonham, Warshauer-Baker, & Collins, 2005; Sternberg, Grigorenko, & Kidd, 2005). Members of various groups are so varied genetically and human groups have intermixed for so many centuries that it is impossible to tell, biologically, to what "race" any given individual belongs. Thus, race is an illusion based on superficial physical differences and learned ethnic identities. Certainly people *act as if* different races exist. But this is a matter of social labeling, not biological reality. To assume that any human group is biologically superior or inferior is simply wrong. In fact, the best available evidence suggests that all people are descended from the same ancient ancestors. The origins of our species lie in Africa, about 100,000 years ago. Among early human populations, darker skin is a protective adaptation to sun exposure near the equator (Jablonski & Chaplin, 2000). Biologically, we are all brothers and sisters under the skin (Graves, 2001; Smedley & Smedley, 2005).

Look for Commonalities

We live in a society that puts a premium on competition and individual effort. One problem with this is that competing with others fosters desires to demean, defeat, and vanquish them. When we cooperate with others we tend to share their joys and suffer when they are in distress (Lanzetta & Englis, 1989). If we don't find ways to cooperate and live in greater harmony, everyone will suffer. That, if nothing else, is one thing that we all have in common. Everyone knows what it feels like to be different. Greater tolerance comes from remembering those times.

Set an Example for Others

People who act in a tolerant fashion can serve as models of tolerance for others. An example is the use of newsletters to promote understanding at an ethnically diverse high school in Houston, Texas. Students wrote stories for the newsletter about situations in which cooperation led to better understanding. For instance, a story about a friendship between Latino and European-American members of a sports team had this headline: "Don't judge somebody until you know them. The color of the skin doesn't matter." Other stories emphasized the willingness of students to get acquainted with people from other ethnic groups and the new perceptions they had of their abilities. After just 5 months of modeling tolerance, hostility between campus ethnic groups was significantly reduced (McAlister et al., 2000).

Tolerance and Cultural Awareness

Living comfortably in a multicultural society means getting to know a little about other groups. Getting acquainted with a person whose cultural background is different from your own can be a wonderful learning experience. No one culture has all the answers or the best ways of doing things. Multicultural populations enrich a community's food, music, arts, and philosophy. Likewise, learning about different racial, cultural, and ethnic groups can be personally rewarding.

The importance of cultural awareness often lies in subtleties and details. For example, in large American cities, many small stores are owned by Korean immigrants. Some of these Korean-American merchants have been criticized for being cold and hostile to their customers. Refusing to place change directly in customers' hands, for instance, helped trigger an African-American boycott of Korean grocers in New York City. The core of the problem was a lack of cultural awareness on both sides.

In America, if you walk into a store, you expect the clerk to be courteous to you. One way of showing politeness is by smiling. But in the Confucian-steeped Korean culture, a smile is reserved for family members and close friends. If a Korean or Korean Ameri-

Multiculturalism Giving equal status, recognition, and acceptance to different ethnic and cultural groups.

Individuating information Information that helps define a person as an individual, rather than as a member of a group or social category.

Just-world beliefs Belief that people generally get what they deserve.

Self-fulfilling prophecy An expectation that prompts people to act in ways that make the expectation come true.

Social competition Rivalry among groups, each of which regards itself as superior to others.

can has no reason to smile, he or she just doesn't smile. There's a Korean saying: "If you smile a lot, you're silly." Expressions such as "thank you" and "excuse me" are also used sparingly and strangers rarely touch each other—not even to return change.

Here's another example of how ignorance of cultural practices can lead to needless friction and misunderstanding: An African-American woman who wanted to ease racial tensions took a freshly baked pie to her neighbors across the way, who were Orthodox Jews. At the front door the woman extended her hand, not knowing that Orthodox Jews don't shake women's hands, unless the woman is a close family member. Once she was inside, she picked up a kitchen knife to cut the pie, not knowing the couple kept a kosher household and used different knives for different foods. The woman's well-intentioned attempt at neighborliness ended in an argument! Knowing a little more about each other's cultures could have prevented both of the conflicts just described.

If the Earth's population could be condensed to just 100 people, with all of the current human ratios maintained, it would look like this:

- There would be 57 Asians, 21 Europeans, 14 from the Western Hemisphere, including North and South America, and 8 from Africa.
- Seventy would be non–European American, and thirty would be European American.
- Sixty-six would be non-Christian and thirty-three Christian.
- Half of the entire village's wealth would be in the hands of only six people, all of them U.S. citizens.
- Half the people in the village would suffer from malnutrition.
- Within the village would be enough nuclear weapons to blow everyone to smithereens many times over.

When you consider the world from such a compressed perspective, the need for tolerance and understanding becomes readily apparent.

KNOWLEDGE BUILDER

Multiculturalism

REFLECT

Which strategies for breaking the prejudice habit do you already use? How could you apply the remaining strategies to become more tolerant?

LEARNING CHECK

1. Multiculturalism refers to the belief that various subcultures and ethnic groups should be blended into a single emergent culture. T or F?
2. Patricia Devine found that many people who don't have prejudiced beliefs still have prejudiced thoughts and feelings in the presence of minority group individuals. T or F?
3. Individuating information tends to be a good antidote for stereotypes. T or F?
4. Just-world beliefs are the primary cause of social competition. T or F?

CRITICAL THINKING

5. Why is it valuable to learn the terms by which members of various groups prefer to be addressed (for example, Mexican American, Latino [or Latina], Hispanic, or Chicano [Chicana])?

Answers: 1. F **2.** T **3.** T **4.** F **5.** Because labels might have negative meanings that are not apparent to persons outside the group. People who are culturally aware allow others to define their own identities, rather than imposing labels on them.

Chapter in Review

What are attitudes? How are they acquired?

- Attitudes are learned dispositions made up of a belief component, an emotional component, and an action component.
- Attitudes may be formed by direct contact, interaction with others, child-rearing practices, and group pressures. Peer-group influences, the mass media, and chance conditioning also appear to be important in attitude formation.

How are attitudes measured and changed?

- Attitudes are typically measured by use of techniques such as open-ended interviews, social distance scales, and attitude scales. Attitudes expressed in these ways do not always correspond to actual behavior.
- Attitude change is related to reference group membership, to deliberate persuasion, and to significant personal experiences (which may be engineered through role-playing).

Under what conditions is persuasion most effective?

- Effective persuasion occurs when characteristics of the communicator, the message, and the audience are well matched. In general, a likable and believable communicator who repeats a credible message that arouses emotion in the audience and states clear-cut conclusions will be persuasive.

What is cognitive dissonance? What does it have to do with attitudes and behavior?

- The maintenance and change of attitudes is closely related to needs for consistency in thoughts and actions. Cognitive dissonance theory explains the dynamics of such needs.
- Cognitive dissonance occurs when there is a clash between thoughts or between thoughts and actions. The amount of reward or justification for one's actions influences whether dissonance occurs. We are motivated to reduce dissonance when it occurs, often by changing beliefs or attitudes.

Is brainwashing actually possible? How are people converted to cult membership?

- Brainwashing is a form of forced attitude change. It depends on control of the target person's total environment. Three steps in brainwashing are unfreezing, changing, and refreezing attitudes and beliefs.
- Many cults recruit new members with high-pressure indoctrination techniques resembling brainwashing. Such groups attempt to catch people when they are vulnerable. Then they combine isolation, displays of affection, discipline and rituals, intimidation, and escalating commitment to bring about conversion.

What causes prejudice and intergroup conflict? What can be done about these problems?

- Prejudice is a negative attitude held toward members of various out-groups. One theory attributes prejudice to scapegoating. A second account says that prejudices may be held for personal reasons (personal prejudice) or simply through adherence to group norms (group prejudice).
- Prejudiced individuals tend to have an authoritarian or dogmatic personality, characterized by rigidity, inhibition, intolerance, oversimplification, and ethnocentrism.
- Intergroup conflict gives rise to hostility and the formation of social stereotypes. Status inequalities tend to build prejudice. Equal-status contact tends to reduce it.
- Psychologists have emphasized the concept of superordinate goals as a key to reducing intergroup conflict, be it racial, religious, ethnic, or national. On a smaller scale, jigsaw classrooms (which encourage cooperation through mutual interdependence) have been shown to be an effective way of combating prejudice.

How do psychologists explain human aggression?

- Aggression and violence are serious social problems and the subject of much current research. Ethological explanations of aggression attribute it to inherited instincts. Biological explanations emphasize brain mechanisms and physical factors related to thresholds for aggression.
- According to the frustration-aggression hypothesis, frustration and aggression are closely linked. Frustration is only one of many aversive stimuli that can arouse a person and make aggression more likely. Aggression is especially likely to occur when aggression cues are present.
- Social learning theory has focused attention on the role of aggressive models in the development of aggressive behavior.

Why are bystanders so often unwilling to help in an emergency?

- Four decision points that must be passed before a person gives help are noticing, defining an emergency, taking responsibility, and selecting a course of action. Helping is less likely at each point when other potential helpers are present.
- Helping is encouraged by general arousal, empathic arousal, being in a good mood, low effort or risk, and perceived similarity between the victim and the helper. For several reasons, giving help tends to encourage others to help too.

What can be done to lower prejudice and promote social harmony?

- Multiculturalism is an attempt to give equal status to different ethnic, racial, and cultural groups.
- Greater tolerance can be encouraged by neutralizing stereotypes with individuating information; by looking for commonalities with others; and by avoiding the effects of just-world beliefs, self-fulfilling prophecies, and social competition.
- Cultural awareness is a key element in promoting greater social harmony.

 Web Resources

Internet addresses frequently change. To find the sites listed here, visit www.thomsonedu.com/psychology/coon for an updated list of Internet addresses and direct links to relevant sites.

***Psychology: Gateways to Mind and Behavior* Website** Online quizzes, flash cards, and other helpful study aids for this text. www.thomsonedu.com/psychology/coon.

Information about Cults and Psychological Manipulation

Ethnic Images in the Comics Articles on the history of ethnic stereotyping in the comics.

Implicit Association Test Online tests that purportedly reveal the unconscious roots of prejudice.

Social Psychology Network A comprehensive site with many links to information about social psychology.

Violence on Television Discusses research and implications of watching violence on television.

ThomsonNOW™ Go to www.thomsonedu.com to link to ThomsonNow, your online study tool. First take the **Pre-Test** for this chapter to get your **Personalized Study Plan**, which will identify topics you need to review and direct you to online resources. Then take the **Post-Test** to determine what concepts you have mastered and what you still need work on.

InfoTrac College Edition For recent articles on coercive attitude change, use Key Words search for CULTS and BRAINWASHING. Go to www.thomsonedu.com/psychology/coon.

Interactive Learning

***PsychNow!* Version 2.0 CD-ROM** Interact with the material with *PsychNow!*'s animations, video clips, experiments, and interactive assessments. For this chapter, go to *8a. Helping Others, 8b. Attribution, 8d. Attitudes and Prejudice,* and *8e. Aggression* to explore both these positive and negative aspects of human relations.

chapter

20

Applied Psychology

Jose L. Pelaez/Corbis

THEME:

Psychological principles can be used to solve practical problems in a variety of settings.

Key Questions

How is psychology applied in business and industry?

What have psychologists learned about the effects of our physical and social environments?

How has psychology improved education?

What does psychology reveal about juries and court verdicts?

Can psychology enhance athletic performance?

What can be done to improve communication at work?

Preview

The Towering Inferno

Alarmed, you sniff the air. "Is that smoke?" you say to yourself. "Yes, something's definitely burning!" You throw open your hotel room door. Outside, a thick black cloud fills the hallway. Somewhere in the choking haze you hear someone shout, "Fire!" "Oh no," you think, "I'm on the 22nd floor. I'd better find the elevator—fast." At that instant you hear the following:

> *Female voice:* "May I have your attention, please. May I have your attention, please."
> *Male voice:* "There has been a fire reported on the 20th floor. While this report is being verified, the building manager would like you to proceed to the stairways and walk down to the 18th floor. Please do not use the elevators, as they may be needed. Please do not use the elevators, but proceed to the stairways." (Loftus, 1979)

All too often, fires in high-rise buildings lead to needless deaths. Using the elevators, for instance, can be fatal. During a fire, they act as chimneys for smoke and poisonous fumes.

In the confusion following a fire alarm, many people ignore posted instructions for safe escape. To remedy the situation, psychologists Jack Keating and Elizabeth Loftus created an unusual, life-saving "fire alarm." The best alarm, they found, is a *voice* that tells people exactly what to do, like the message reproduced above.

As simple as the message seems, it contains certain key elements: (1) Research has shown that switching from a female to a male voice (or the reverse) is very *attention getting;* (2) during emergencies, people like to feel that some *authority* is in control (the "building manager" in this case); (3) the crucial reminder to avoid the elevators is *repeated,* so it will be remembered.

Applied psychology refers to the use of psychological principles and research methods to solve practical problems. Escaping from fires may be a dramatic example of applying psychology, but it is far from unusual. The largest applied areas are clinical and counseling psychology, but there are many others. In fields as diverse as business, education, sports, law, and the environment, psychology is being applied to our lives. Let's see how.

Industrial-Organizational Psychology—Psychology at Work

Do you consider work a blessing? Or a curse? Or do you simply agree that it is "better to wear out than to rust out"? Whatever your attitude, the simple fact is that most adults work for a living. Whether you are employed now or plan to begin a career after college, it helps to know something about the psychology of work and organizations.

Industrial-organizational (I-O) **psychologists** study the behavior of people at work and in organizations (Landy & Conte, 2003). Very likely, their efforts will affect how you are selected for a job and tested, trained, or evaluated for promotion. Most I-O psychologists are employed by the government, industry, and businesses. Typically, they work in two major areas: (1) testing and placement (personnel psychology) and (2) human relations at work. To get a fuller flavor of what I-O psychologists do, look at ■ Table 20.1. As you can see, their interests are quite varied.

The mark of maturity, Sigmund Freud said, is a capacity for love and work. Although most people gladly embrace love, many would just as soon forget work. Yet the fact is, employed adults spend an average of more than 2,000 hours a year at their jobs. With so much time at stake, understanding the world of work is clearly a "survival skill." Let's begin with personnel psychology.

Personnel Psychology

At present, the odds are 9 out of 10 that you are, or will be, employed in business or industry. Thus, nearly everyone who holds a job is sooner or later placed under the "psychological microscope" of personnel selection. **Personnel psychology** is concerned with testing, selection, placement, and promotion of employees (Muchinsky, 2006). Clearly, there is value in knowing how selection for hiring and promotion is done.

TABLE 20.1

Topics of Special Interest to Industrial-Organizational Psychologists

Absenteeism	Pay schedules
Decision making	Personnel selection
Design of organizations	Personnel training
Employee stress	Productivity
Employee turnover	Promotion
Interviewing	Task analysis
Job enrichment	Task design
Job satisfaction	Work behavior
Labor relations	Work environment
Machine design	Work motivation
Management styles	Worker evaluation
Minority workers	

Courtesy of the General Electric Company

● **Figure 20.1** Analyzing complex skills has also been valuable to the U.S. Air Force. When million-dollar aircraft and the lives of pilots are at stake, it makes good sense to do as much training and research as possible on the ground. Air Force psychologists use flight simulators like the one pictured here to analyze the complex skills needed to fly jet fighters. Skills can then be taught without risk on the ground. The General Electric simulator shown here uses a computer to generate full-color images that respond realistically to a pilot's use of the controls.

Job Analysis

How do personnel psychologists make employee selections? Personnel selection begins with **job analysis**, a detailed description of the skills, knowledge, and activities required by a particular job (Borman, Hanson, & Hedge, 1997; Dierdorff & Wilson, 2003). A job analysis may be done by interviewing expert workers or supervisors, by giving them questionnaires, by directly observing work, or by identifying *critical incidents*. **Critical incidents** are situations with which competent employees must be able to cope. The ability to deal calmly with a mechanical emergency, for example, is a critical incident for airline pilots. Once job requirements are known, psychologists can state what skills, aptitudes, and interests are needed (● Figure 20.1). In addition, some psychologists are now doing a broader "work analysis." In this case, they try to identify general characteristics that a person must have to succeed in a variety of work roles, rather than in just a specific job (Hough & Oswald, 2000).

Selection Procedures

After desirable skills and traits are identified, the next step is to learn who has them. Today, the methods most often used for evaluating job candidates include collecting *biodata,* conducting *interviews,* giving *standardized psychological tests,* and the *assessment center* approach. Let's see what each entails.

Biodata

As simple as it may seem, one good way to predict job success is to collect **biodata** (detailed biographical information) from applicants (Borman, Hanson, & Hedge, 1997). The idea behind biodata is that looking at past behavior is a good way to predict future behavior. By learning in detail about a person's life, it is often possible to say whether the person is suited for a particular type of work (Hough & Oswald, 2000).

Some of the most useful items of biodata include past athletic interests, academic achievements, scientific interests, extracurricular activities, religious activities, social popularity, conflict with brothers and sisters, attitudes toward school, and parents' socioeconomic status (Muchinsky, 2006). Such facts tell quite a lot about personality, interests, and abilities. In addition to past experiences, a person's recent life activities also help predict job success (Schmidt, Ones, & Hunter, 1992). For instance, you might think that college grades are unimportant, but college GPA predicts success in many types of work (Hough & Oswald, 2000).

Applied psychology The use of psychological principles and research methods to solve practical problems.

Industrial-organizational psychology A field that focuses on the psychology of work and on behavior within organizations.

Personnel psychology Branch of industrial-organizational psychology concerned with testing, selection, placement, and promotion of employees.

Job analysis A detailed description of the skills, knowledge, and activities required by a particular job.

Critical incidents Situations that arise in a job, with which a competent worker must be able to cope.

Biodata Detailed biographical information about a job applicant.

FOCUS ON RESEARCH

The Sweet Smell of Success? Not Always.

Each year, clothing and cosmetics manufacturers spend huge sums to convince us that their products make us more attractive. Actually, such claims are somewhat justified. You might recall from Chapter 14, for instance, that physically attractive people are often given more positive evaluations in interviews—even on traits that have no connection with appearance. Presumably, this might also apply to the effects of wearing a pleasant perfume or cologne. But does it? In an interesting study, *female* interviewers did, in fact, give higher ratings to job applicants who wore pleasant scents. But *males,* in contrast, gave *lower* ratings to persons who wore perfume or cologne (Baron, 1983).

Psychologist Robert Baron, who carried out this experiment, speculates that the male interviewers were more aware of the scents and resented the implied attempt to influence their ratings. Whatever the case, one thing is clear: If possible, you should learn an interviewer's sex beforehand—if you want to avoid making a flagrant, fragrant error, that is.

In general, indirect efforts to make a good impression, like wearing cologne, dressing well, and flattering the interviewer, are less effective in interviews than direct efforts such as emphasizing your positive traits and past successes (Kristof-Brown, Barrick, & Franke, 2002). However, beware of blatant self-promotion. Excessively "blowing your own horn" tends to lower interviewers' perceptions of competence and suitability for a job (Howard & Ferris, 1996).

Interviews

The traditional personal interview is still one of the most popular ways to select people for jobs or promotions. In a **personal interview,** job applicants are questioned about their qualifications. At the same time, interviewers gain an impression of the applicant's personality (Borman, Hanson, & Hedge, 1997). (Or personalities—but that's another story!)

As discussed in Chapter 14, interviews are subject to the halo effect and similar problems. (Recall that the *halo effect* is the tendency of interviewers to extend favorable or unfavorable impressions to unrelated aspects of an individual's personality.) In addition, interviewees actively engage in *impression management,* seeking to portray a positive image to interviewers (Ellis et al., 2002). It is for reasons like these that psychologists continue to look for ways to improve the accuracy of interviews (see "The Sweet Smell of Success? Not Always"). For instance, recent studies suggest that interviews can be improved by giving them more structure (Hough & Oswald, 2000; Tsai, Chen, & Chiu, 2005). For example, each job candidate should be asked the same questions (Campion, Palmer, & Campion, 1998). However, even with their limitations, interviews are a valid and effective way of predicting how people will perform on the job (Landy, Shankster, & Kohler, 1994).

Psychological Testing

What kinds of tests do personnel psychologists use? General mental ability tests (intelligence tests) tell a great deal about a person's chances of succeeding in various jobs (Schmidt, & Hunter, 1998). So do general personality tests and honesty tests (described in Chapter 14) (Hough & Oswald, 2000). In addition, personnel psychologists often use **vocational interest tests.** These paper-and-pencil tests assess people's interests and match them to interests found among successful workers in various occupations. Tests such as the *Kuder Occupational Interest Survey* and the *Strong-Campbell Interest Inventory* probe interests with items like the following:

I would prefer to
a. visit a museum
b. read a good book
c. take a walk outdoors

Interest inventories typically measure six major themes identified by John Holland (see ■ Table 20.2). If you take an interest test and your choices match those of people in a given occupation, it is assumed that you, too, would be comfortable doing the work they do (Holland, 1997).

Aptitude tests are another mainstay of personnel psychology. Such tests rate a person's potential to learn tasks or skills used in various occupations. Tests exist for clerical, verbal, mechanical, artistic, legal, and medical aptitudes, plus many others. For example, tests of clerical aptitude emphasize the capacity to do rapid, precise, and accurate office work. One section of a clerical aptitude test might therefore ask a person to mark all identical numbers and names in a long list of pairs like those shown here.

49837266	49832766
Global Widgets, Inc.	Global Wigets, Inc.
874583725	874583725
Sevanden Corp.	Sevanden Corp.
Wadsworth Publishing	Wadsworth Publishing

BRIDGES

Aptitude tests are related to intelligence tests.

See Chapter 11, page 364, to learn how they differ.

TABLE 20.2

Vocational Interest Themes

THEMES	SAMPLE COLLEGE MAJORS	SAMPLE OCCUPATIONS
Realistic	Agriculture	Mechanic
Investigative	Physics	Chemist
Artistic	Music	Writer
Social	Education	Counselor
Enterprising	Business	Sales
Conventional	Economics	Clerk

Holland, 1997.

Paper-and-pencil tests sometimes seem far removed from the day-to-day challenges of work. In recent years, psychologists have tried to make employment testing more interesting and relevant. For example, personnel psychologists are developing **multimedia computerized tests.** These tests use computers to present realistic work situations—in living color and stereo sound. As potential employees watch typical work scenes unfold, the action freezes on various problems. The applicant is then asked what she or he would do in that situation. In addition to screening job applicants, multimedia presentations can be used to improve the job skills of current employees. It won't be long before multimedia tests are widely used (Landy, Shankster, & Kohler, 1994; Muchinsky, 2006).

Bill Aron/PhotoEdit, Inc.

Aptitude tests are used to select job candidates and to advise people about what types of work they are likely to be good at.

After college, chances are good that you will encounter an *assessment center.* Many large organizations use **assessment centers** to do in-depth evaluations of job candidates. This approach has become so popular that the list of businesses using it—Ford, IBM, Kodak, Exxon, Sears, and thousands of others—reads like a corporate *Who's Who.*

How do assessment centers differ from the selection methods already described? Assessment centers are primarily used to fill management and executive positions. First, applicants are tested and interviewed. Then they are observed and evaluated in simulated work situations. Specifically, **situational judgment tests** are used to present difficult but realistic work situations to applicants (Borman, Hanson, & Hedge, 1997). For example, in one exercise applicants are given an **in-basket test** that simulates the decision-making challenges executives face. The test consists of a basket full of memos, requests, and typical business problems. Each applicant is asked to quickly read all of the materials and to take appropriate action. In another, more stressful test, applicants take part in a **leaderless group discussion.** This is a test of leadership that simulates group decision making and problem solving. While the group grapples with a realistic business problem, "clerks" bring in price changes, notices about delayed supplies, and so forth. By observing applicants, it is possible to evaluate leadership skills and to see how job candidates cope with stress.

BRIDGES

Situational tests are also used to investigate personality differences.

See Chapter 14, pages 485–486.

Personal interview Formal or informal questioning of job applicants to learn their qualifications and to gain an impression of their personalities.

Vocational interest test A paper-and-pencil test that assesses a person's interests and matches them to interests found among successful workers in various occupations.

Aptitude test A test that rates a person's potential to learn skills required by various occupations.

Multimedia computerized test A test that uses a computer to present life-like situations; test takers react to problems posed by the situations.

Assessment center A program set up within an organization to conduct in-depth evaluations of job candidates.

Situational judgment test Presenting realistic work situations to applicants in order to observe their skills and reactions.

In-basket test A testing procedure that simulates the individual decision-making challenges that executives face.

Leaderless group discussion A test of leadership that simulates group decision making and problem solving.

How well does this approach work? Assessment centers have had considerable success in predicting performance in a variety of jobs, careers, and advanced positions (Landy, Shankster, & Kohler, 1994). One study of women, for instance, found that assessment center predictions of management potential were closely related to career progress 7 years later (Ritchie & Moses, 1983). On the basis of long-range studies, it appears that future success is most clearly predicted by oral communication skills, leadership, energy, resistance to stress, tolerance for uncertainty, need for advancement, and planning skills (Ritchie & Moses, 1983).

As you will soon learn, psychologists working in business do far more than match people with jobs. Let's see how they contribute to management and the quality of work.

Theories of Management—What Works at Work?

At 7 AM each morning at a major manufacturing plant, more than 400 assembly line workers, supervisors, and top executives begin their day talking, joking, and exercising together, all to the beat of amplified music. To say the least, these are unusual working conditions. To understand the rationale behind them, let's consider two basic theories of employee management.

Theory X and Theory Y

One of the earliest attempts to improve worker efficiency was made in 1923 by Frederick Taylor, an engineer. To speed up production, Taylor standardized work routines and stressed careful planning, control, and orderliness. Today, recent versions of Taylor's approach are called *scientific management* (also known as **Theory X**, for reasons explained shortly). **Scientific management** uses time-and-motion studies, task analysis, job specialization, assembly lines, pay schedules, and the like to increase productivity.

It sounds like scientific management treats people as if they were machines. Is that true? To some extent it is. Managers who follow Theory X tend to assume that workers must be goaded or guided into being productive. Many psychologists working in business, of course, are concerned with improving **work efficiency** (defined as maximum output at lowest cost). As a result, they alter conditions they believe will affect workers (such as time schedules, work quotas, bonuses, and so on). Some might even occasionally wish that people would act like well-oiled machines. However, most recognize that psychological efficiency is just as important as work efficiency. **Psychological efficiency** refers to maintaining good morale, labor relations, employee satisfaction, and similar aspects of work behavior. Management styles that ignore or mishandle the human element can be devastatingly costly. Studies have consistently found that happy workers are productive workers (Cote, 1999; Wright & Cropanzano, 2000).

The term *Theory X* was coined by psychologist Douglas McGregor (1960) as a way to distinguish scientific management from a newer management style. McGregor dubbed this newer approach, which emphasizes human relations at work, *Theory Y.*

How is this approach different? **Theory Y** managers assume that workers enjoy autonomy and are willing to accept responsibility. They also assume that worker needs and goals can be meshed with the company's goals, and that people are not naturally passive or lazy. In short, Theory Y assumes that people are industrious, creative, and rewarded by challenging work. It appears that given the proper conditions of freedom and responsibility, many people *will* work hard to gain competence and use their talents.

Many features of Theory Y are illustrated by the Honda plant at Marysville, Ohio. As you may already know, the automobile industry has a long history of labor–management clashes and worker discontent. In fact, outright sabotage by assembly line workers is not uncommon. To avoid such problems, Honda initiated a series of simple, seemingly successful measures. They include the following practices.

- Regardless of their position, all employees wear identical white uniforms. This allows workers and supervisors to interact on a more equal footing and builds feelings of teamwork.
- To further minimize status differences, all employees hold the title *associate.*
- Private offices, separate dining halls, and reserved parking spaces for executives were abolished.
- Employees work alongside company executives, to whom they have easy access.
- Every employee has a say in, and responsibility for, quality control and safety.
- Departmental meetings are held daily. At this time, announcements are discussed, decisions are made, and thoughts are freely shared.

Management Strategies

Two elements that make Theory Y methods effective are *participative management* and *management by objectives.* In **participative management**, employees at all levels are directly involved in decision making. By taking part in decisions that affect them, employees like those at the Honda factory come to see work as a cooperative effort—not as something imposed on them by an egotistical boss. The benefits include greater productivity, more involvement in work, greater job satisfaction, and less job-related stress (Coye & Belohlav, 1995; Kim, 2002).

What does "management by objectives" refer to? In **management by objectives**, workers are given specific goals to meet, so they can tell if they are doing a good job. Typical objectives include reaching a certain sales total, making a certain number of items, or reducing waste by a specific percentage. In any case, workers are free to choose (within limits) how they will achieve their goals. As a result, they feel more independent and take personal responsibility for their work. Workers are especially productive when they receive feedback about their progress toward goals. Clearly, people like to know what the target is, and whether they are succeeding (Neubert, 1998).

Recently, many companies have begun to give *groups* of workers greater freedom and responsibility as well. This is typically done by creating self-managed teams. A **self-managed team** is a

Yellow Dog Productions/Getty Images

Participative management techniques encourage employees at all levels to become involved in decision making. Quite often this arrangement leads to greater job satisfaction.

group of employees who work together toward shared goals. Self-managed teams can typically choose their own methods of achieving results, as long as they are effective. Self-managed teams tend to make good use of the strengths and talents of individual employees. They also promote new ideas and improve motivation. Most of all, they encourage cooperation and teamwork within organizations (Lewis, Goodman, & Fandt, 1995). Workers in self-managed teams are much more likely to feel that they are being treated fairly at work (Chansler, Swamidass, & Cammann, 2003).

How can workers below the management level be involved more in their work? One popular answer is the use of **quality circles.** These are voluntary discussion groups that seek ways to solve business problems and improve efficiency (Jewell, 1998). In contrast to self-managed teams, quality circles usually do not have the power to put their suggestions into practice directly. But good ideas speak for themselves and many are adopted by management. Quality circles have many limitations. Nevertheless, studies verify that greater personal involvement can lead to better performance and job satisfaction (Geehr, Burke, & Sulzer, 1995).

Job Satisfaction

It often makes perfect sense to apply Theory X methods to work. However, doing so without taking worker needs into account can be a case of winning the battle while losing the war. That is, immediate productivity may be enhanced while job satisfaction is lowered. And when job satisfaction is low, absenteeism skyrockets, morale falls, and there is a high rate of employee turnover (leading to higher training costs and inefficiency). Understandably, many of the methods used by enlightened Theory Y managers ultimately improve **job satisfaction,** or the degree to which a person is pleased with his or her work. Job satisfaction is well worth cultivating because positive moods are associated with more cooperation, better performance, a greater willingness to help others, more creative problem solving, and less absenteeism (Brief & Weiss, 2002).

Under what conditions is job satisfaction highest? Basically, job satisfaction comes from a good fit between work and a person's interests, abilities, needs, and expectations (Landy & Conte, 2003; Lubinski, 2000). What, then, do workers consider important? Already in the early 1970s, when American workers were asked to rate the importance of 25 aspects of work, their first 8 choices were as follows (*Work in America,* 1973):

1. Interesting work
2. Enough help and equipment to get the job done
3. Enough information to get the job done
4. Enough authority to get the job done
5. Good pay
6. Opportunity to develop special abilities
7. Job security
8. Seeing the results of one's work

A second survey in the 1980s again found that satisfying, rewarding work ranked first in worker preference. However, high income rose to second place (Weaver & Matthews, 1987). Some observers worry that a swing toward greater materialism has occurred in the last quarter century. Even if this is true, intrinsically interesting work still tops the list. To summarize much research, we can say that job satisfaction is highest when workers are (1) allowed ordinary social contacts with others; (2) given opportunities to use their own judgment and intelligence; (3) recognized for doing well; (4) given a chance to apply their skills; (5) given relative freedom from close supervision; and (6) given opportunities for promotion and advancement. Understandably, the most pro-

Scientific management (Theory X) An approach to managing employees that emphasizes work efficiency.

Work efficiency Maximum output (productivity) at lowest cost.

Psychological efficiency Maintenance of good morale, labor relations, employee satisfaction, and similar aspects of work behavior.

Theory Y A management style that emphasizes human relations at work and that views people as industrious, responsible, and interested in challenging work.

Participative management An approach to management that allows employees at all levels to participate in decision making.

Management by objectives A management technique in which employees are given specific goals to meet in their work.

Self-managed team A work group that has a high degree of freedom with respect to how it achieves its goals.

Quality circle An employee discussion group that makes suggestions for improving quality and solving business problems.

Job satisfaction The degree to which a person is comfortable with or satisfied with his or her work.

FOCUS ON RESEARCH

Flextime

If you've ever worked "9 to 5" you know that traditional time schedules can be confining. They also doom many workers to a daily battle with rush-hour traffic. To improve worker morale, I-O psychologists recommend the use of **flextime,** or flexible working hours. The basic idea of flextime is that starting and quitting times are flexible, as long as employees are present during a core work period (Owen, 1976). For example, employees might be allowed to arrive between 7:30 AM and 10:30 AM and depart between 3:30 PM and 6:30 PM.

Is flextime really an improvement? One analysis of over 30 studies found that flextime has a positive effect on workers' productivity, job satisfaction, absenteeism, and comfort with their work schedules (Baltes et al., 1999).

How does flextime help? Psychologists theorize that it lowers stress and increases feelings of independence, both of which increase productivity and job satisfaction. Another benefit is that flextime is "family friendly." Parents working on a flexible schedule find it much easier to coordinate their work and child-care responsibilities (Frone & Yardley, 1996). When conflicts between work and private life decline, absenteeism usually does too (Baltes et al., 1999). In addition, flextime makes commuting to and from work easier, because flextime commuters do not have to fight peak rush-hour traffic (Lucas & Heady, 2002).

In view of such benefits, two of three large organizations now use flextime. Perhaps we can conclude that it is better, when possible, to bend hours instead of people.

ductive employees are those who are happy at work (Elovainio et al., 2000; Staw, Sutton, & Pelled, 1994). This connection can be seen clearly in the research reported in "Flextime."

Job satisfaction is not entirely a matter of work conditions. Anyone who has ever been employed has probably encountered at least one perpetually grumpy coworker. In other words, workers don't leave their personalities at home. Happy people are more often happy at work and they are more likely to focus on what's good about their job, rather than what's bad (Brief & Weiss, 2002).

Making Career Decisions

When people become seriously dissatisfied with their work, it may be time to seek a new job. This can be a difficult step to take. One way to improve career decisions is to examine how you approach them. Psychologist Irving Janis and writer Dan Wheeler (1978) have described how people typically deal with work dilemmas, especially those that lead to a major change in jobs or careers. Their analysis suggests that there are four basic coping styles. See if you recognize yourself in any of the following descriptions.

- **The Vigilant Style.** This style is the most effective of the four. It describes individuals who evaluate information objectively and make decisions with a clear understanding of the alternatives. Persons using this style make mental "balance sheets" to weigh possible gains and losses before taking action.
- **The Complacent Style.** Persons of this type drift along with a nonchalant attitude toward job decisions. They tend to let chance direct their careers and to take whatever comes along without really making plans.
- **The Defensive-Avoidant Style.** These people are fully aware of the risks and opportunities presented by career choices and dilemmas. However, they are uncomfortable making decisions. This leads them to procrastinate, rationalize, and make excuses for their inaction and indecision.
- **The Hypervigilant Style.** People with this style more or less panic when forced to make career decisions. They may collect hundreds of job announcements and brochures, but they become so frantic that making logical decisions is nearly impossible.

These coping styles may seem exaggerated, but they are easy to observe when people are forced to change jobs or make major alterations in career plans. To relate them to yourself, think about how you have handled vocational decisions to date, or decisions about your college career. Of the four, Janis and Wheeler consider only the vigilant style to be constructive. With this insight, you may be able to improve the quality of your career decisions.

Job Enrichment

For years, the trend in business and industry was to make work more streamlined and efficient and to tie better pay to better work. There is now ample evidence that incentives such as bonuses, earned time off, and profit sharing can increase productivity. However, in recent years far too many jobs have become routine, repetitive, boring, and unfulfilling. To combat the discontent this can breed, many psychologists recommend a strategy called *job enrichment.*

Job enrichment involves making a job more personally rewarding, interesting, or intrinsically motivating. Job enrichment

THE CLINICAL FILE: Desk Rage and Healthy Organizations

"He was really stressed out, and a lot of times it resulted in anger."

"I was upset enough after the meeting with management that I went home. I just said, 'To hell with it. I'm going home. I'm too aggravated to stay here.'"

"The rest of the day I was useless."

"Now I don't talk to him at all unless I have to."

"I got emotional and went outside. Came in about an hour and a half later. I was still very upset, I was mad as hell."

Like road rage on the highways, "desk rage," or workplace anger, is becoming all too common. The preceding statements were made by people who had been involved in angry incidents at work. It's not difficult to understand two common triggers for desk rage: job-related stresses and feeling that one has been treated unfairly can produce intense anger (Spector, 2005). Two other causes that emerged in a recent study are perceived threats to one's self-esteem and work-related conflicts with others (Glomb, 2002).

What can be done about anger and aggression at work? As stated before, healthy organizations display a concern for the well-being of people. The best way to achieve this is through trust, open confrontation of problems, employee empowerment and participation, cooperation, and full use of human potential. Healthy organizations also promote well-being in the following ways (Fuqua & Newman, 2002):

- Rather than always complaining and blaming, group members express sincere gratitude for the efforts of others.
- Everyone makes mistakes. The culture in caring organizations includes a capacity to forgive.
- Everyone needs encouragement at times. Encouragement can inspire workers and give them hope, confidence, and courage.
- Showing sensitivity to other can dramatically change the work environment. Sensitivity can take the form of expressing interest in others and in how they are doing. It also includes respecting the privacy of others.
- Compassion for others is a good antidote for destructive competitiveness and petty game playing.
- People are very different in their needs, values, and experiences. Tolerance and respect for the dignity of others goes a long way toward maintaining individual well-being.

The economic pressures that organizations face can lead to hostile and competitive work environments. However, productivity and quality-of-life at work are closely intertwined. Effective organizations seek to optimize both (Fuqua & Newman, 2002).

has been used with great success by large corporations such as IBM, Maytag, Western Electric, Chrysler, and Polaroid. It usually leads to lower production costs, increased job satisfaction, reduced boredom, and less absenteeism (Lewis, Goodman, & Fandt, 1995; Niehoff et al., 2001).

How is job enrichment done? Merely assigning a person more tasks is usually not enriching. Overloaded workers just feel stressed and they tend to make more errors. Instead, job enrichment applies many of the principles we have discussed. Usually it involves removing some of the controls and restrictions on employees, giving them greater freedom, choice, and authority. In some cases, employees also switch to doing a complete cycle of work. That is, they complete an entire item or project, instead of doing an isolated part of a larger process. Whenever possible, workers are given direct feedback about their work or progress.

BRIDGES

Job enrichment can be thought of as a way of increasing intrinsic motivation.

See Chapter 12, page 669.

True job enrichment increases workers' *knowledge*. That is, workers are encouraged to continuously learn a broad range of skills and information related to their occupations (Campion & McClelland, 1993; Sessa & London, 2006). In short, most people seem to enjoy being good at what they do.

Organizational Culture

Businesses and other organizations, whether they are large or small, develop distinct cultures. Within organizations, **culture** refers to a blend of customs, beliefs, values, attitudes, and rituals. These characteristics give each organization its unique "flavor." Organizational culture includes such things as how people are hired and trained, disciplined, and dismissed. It encompasses

Flextime A work schedule that allows flexible starting and quitting times.

Job enrichment Making a job more personally rewarding, interesting, or intrinsically motivating; typically involves increasing worker knowledge.

Organizational culture The social climate within an organization.

how employees dress, communicate, resolve conflicts, share power, identify with organizational goals and values, negotiate contracts, and celebrate special occasions.

People who fit well into a particular organization tend to contribute to its success in ways that are not specifically part of their job description. For example, they are helpful, conscientious, and courteous. They also display good sportsmanship by avoiding pettiness, gossiping, complaining, and making small problems into big ones. (See "Desk Rage and Healthy Organizations.") Like good citizens, the best workers keep themselves informed about organizational issues by attending meetings and taking part in discussions. Workers with these characteristics display what could be called **organizational citizenship.** Understandably, managers and employers highly value workers who are good organizational citizens (Muchinsky, 2006).

Although we have only scratched the surface of industrial-organizational psychology, it is time to move on for a look at another applied area of great personal relevance. Before we begin, here's a chance to enhance your learning.

KNOWLEDGE BUILDER

Industrial-Organizational Psychology

REFLECT

Which of the various ways of evaluating job applicants do you regard as most valid? Which would you prefer to have applied to yourself?

If you were managing people in a business setting, which of the management concepts discussed in the text do you think you would be most likely to use?

Think of a job you know well (something you have done yourself, or something a person you know does). Could job enrichment be applied to the work? What would you do to increase job satisfaction for people doing similar work?

LEARNING CHECK

1. To gain attention for an emergency announcement, it is better to switch from a male voice to a female voice than it is to do the reverse. T or F?
2. Identifying critical work incidents is sometimes included in a thorough ________ ________.
3. Detailed biographical information about a job applicant is referred to as ________.
4. The Strong-Campbell Inventory is a typical aptitude test. T or F?
5. A leaderless group discussion is most closely associated with which approach to employee selection?
   a. aptitude testing c. job analysis
   b. personal interviews d. assessment center
6. Theory X, or scientific management, is concerned primarily with improving ________ ________.
7. Participative management is often a feature of businesses that adhere to Theory Y. T or F?
8. For the majority of workers, job satisfaction is almost exclusively related to the amount of pay received. T or F?
9. Job enrichment is a direct expression of scientific management principles. T or F?

CRITICAL THINKING

10. In what area of human behavior other than work would a careful task analysis be helpful?

Answers: 1. F **2.** job analysis **3.** biodata **4.** F **5.** d **6.** work efficiency **7.** T **8.** F **9.** F **10.** One such area is sports psychology. As described later in this chapter, sports skills can be broken into subparts, so key elements can be identified and taught. Such methods are an extension of techniques first used for job analyses. To a large extent, attempts to identify the characteristics of effective teaching also rely on task analysis.

Environmental Psychology—Life in the Big City

If cities were drivers, some would get lots of speeding tickets. Others would spend most of their time in the slow lane, watching the scenery go by. Informally, you may have noticed that the pace of life varies from city to city. Psychologist Robert Levine and his students decided to measure the overall tempo of 36 American cities to see how they compare (Levine, 1998).

To rate a city's pace, Levine looked at four indicators: walking speed, working speed, talking speed, and the percentage of men and women wearing watches. The results? The three fastest American cities were Boston, Buffalo, and New York—all in the Northeast. The three slowest cities were in the South and West: Shreveport, Sacramento, and Los Angeles. No surprises here. But Levine's other findings are surprising. Levine and his team also found that there is a correlation between the pace of life and heart disease. Just as there are Type A personalities (heart attack–prone personalities; see Chapter 15), there also seem to be Type A cities. Very likely, Type A people are attracted to fast-paced Type A cities—where they then do their best to keep the pace (Levine, 1998).

F. Pedrick/The Image Works

Various behavioral settings place strong demands on people to act in expected ways.

FOCUS ON RESEARCH

Territoriality

In Chapter 18 we noted that powerful norms govern the use of the space immediately surrounding each person's body. As we move farther from the body, it becomes apparent that personal space also extends to adjacent areas that we claim as our "territory." **Territorial behavior** refers to actions that define a space as one's own or that protect it from intruders. For example, in the library, you might protect your space with a coat, handbag, book, or other personal belonging. "Saving a place" at a theater or a beach also demonstrates the tendency to identify a space as "ours." Even sports teams are territorial, usually showing a home team advantage by playing better on their own home territory than while away and in another team's territory (Neave & Wolfson, 2003).

Respect for the temporary ownership of space is also widespread. It is not unusual for a person to "take over" an entire table or study room by looking annoyed when others intrude. Your own personal territory may include your room, specific seats in many of your classes, or a particular table in the cafeteria or library that "belongs" to you and your friends.

Researchers have found that the more attached you are to an area, the more likely you are to adorn it with obvious **territorial markers** that signal your "ownership." Typical markers include decorations, plants, photographs, or posters. College dorms and business offices are prime places to observe this type of territorial marking. Interestingly, burglars are less likely to break into houses that have lots of obvious territorial cues, such as fences (even if small), parked cars, lawn furniture, exterior lights, and security signs (Brown & Bentley, 1993). "Gated communities" have sprung up in many cities because they mark out a "defensible space" that discourages intrusions (Tijerino, 1998). (A highly territorial bulldog may help, too.)

Joel Gordon

Graffiti, one of the blights of urban life, is an obvious form of territorial marking.

The work of Robert Levine, and psychologists like him, falls into an area known as **environmental psychology**, a specialty concerned with the relationship between environments and human behavior (Gifford, 2002). Environmental psychologists are interested in both **physical environments** (natural or constructed) and **social environments** (defined by groups of people, such as a dance, business meeting, or party). They also give special attention to **behavioral settings** (smaller areas within an environment whose use is well defined, such as an office, locker room, church, casino, or classroom). As you have no doubt noticed, various environments and behavioral settings tend to "demand" certain actions. Consider, for example, the difference between a library and a campus center lounge. In which would a conversation be more likely to occur?

Other major interests of environmental psychologists are personal space, territorial behavior (discussed in "Territoriality"), stressful environments, architectural design, environmental protection, and many related topics (■ Table 20.3).

Organizational citizenship Making positive contributions to the success of an organization in ways that go beyond one's job description.

Territorial behavior Any behavior that tends to define a space as one's own or that protects it from intruders.

Territorial markers Objects and other signals whose placement indicates to others the "ownership" or control of a particular area.

Environmental psychology The formal study of how environments affect behavior.

Physical environments Natural settings, such as forests and beaches, as well as environments built by humans, such as buildings, ships, and cities.

Social environment An environment defined by a group of people and their activities or interrelationships (such as a parade, revival meeting, or sports event).

Behavioral setting A smaller area within an environment whose use is well defined, such as a bus depot, waiting room, or lounge.

TABLE 20.3

Topics of Special Interest to Environmental Psychologists

Architectural design	Noise
Behavioral settings	Personal space
Cognitive maps	Personality and environment
Constructed environments	Pollution
Crowding	Privacy
Energy conservation	Proxemics
Environmental stressors	Resource management
Heat	Territoriality
Human ecology	Urban planning
Littering	Vandalism
Natural environment	

Environmental Influences

Much of our behavior is controlled, in part, by specific types of environments. For example, many shopping malls and department stores are designed like mazes. Their twisting pathways encourage shoppers to linger and wander while looking at merchandise. Likewise, many college classrooms clearly define a speaker–audience relationship. Discussion among students tends to be discouraged by seats that are bolted to the floor, facing an authority at the front of the room (Wong, Somer, & Cook, 1992). Even public bathrooms influence behavior. Because the seating is limited, few people hold meetings there!

Psychologists have found that a variety of environmental factors influence the amount of vandalism that occurs in public places. On the basis of psychological research, many architects now "harden" and "de-opportunize" public settings to discourage vandalism and graffiti (Wise, 1982). Some such efforts limit opportunities for vandalism (doorless toilet stalls, tiled walls). Others weaken the lure of likely targets. (Strangely enough, a raised flowerbed around a sign helps protect it because people resist trampling the flowers to get to the sign.)

Given the personal impact that environments have, it is important to know how we are affected by stressful or unhealthy environments—a topic we will consider next.

Stressful Environments

Everyone has his or her own list of complaints about large cities. Traffic congestion, pollution, crime, and impersonality are urban problems that immediately come to mind. To this list psychologists have added crowding, noise, and overstimulation as major sources of urban stress. Psychological research has begun to clarify the impact of each of these conditions on human functioning (Marsella, 1998).

Crowding

Overpopulation ranks as one of the most serious problems facing the world today. The world's population is now over 6 billion people. World population doubled in the period from 1950 to 1987. It will double again by about 2040 (● Figure 20.2). Each year, the world population grows by roughly 85 million people (Oskamp, 2000).

Experts estimate that the maximum sustainable population of the Earth is between 5 billion and 20 billion persons. This means the Earth has already entered the lower range of its carrying capacity (Cohen, 1995). Further population increases at the present rate could be disastrous. How many more people can the forests, oceans, croplands, and atmosphere support? The most pessimistic experts believe we have *already* exceeded the number of people the Earth can sustain indefinitely (Oskamp, 2000).

Nowhere are the effects of overpopulation more evident than in the teeming cities of many underdeveloped nations. Closer to home, the jammed buses, subways, and living quarters of our own large cities are ample testimony to the stresses of crowding.

Is there any way to assess the effect crowding has on people? One approach is to study the effects of overcrowding among animals. Although the results of animal experiments cannot be considered conclusive for humans, they point to some disturbing effects.

For example? In an interesting classic experiment, John Calhoun (1962) let a group of laboratory rats breed without limit in a confined space. Calhoun provided plenty of food, water, and nesting material for the rats. All that the rats lacked was space. At its peak, the colony numbered 80 rats. Yet it was housed in a cage designed to comfortably hold about 50. Overcrowding in the cage was heightened by the actions of the two most dominant males. These rascals staked out private territory at opposite ends of the cage, gathered harems of 8 to 10 females, and prospered. Their actions

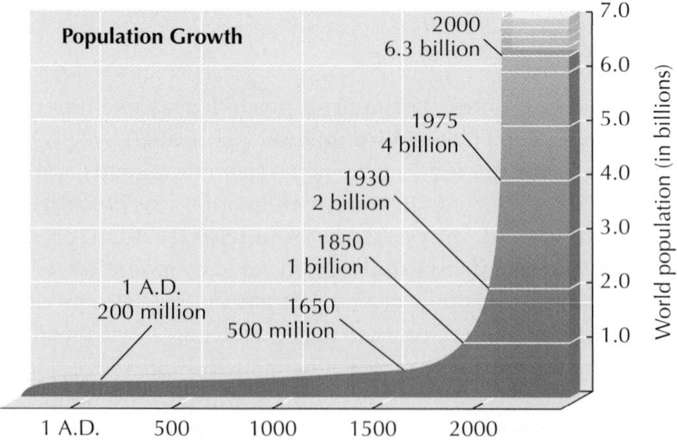

● **Figure 20.2** Population growth has slowed slightly in recent years, but world population still threatens to double again in less than 40 years. Overpopulation and rapid population growth are closely connected with environmental damage, international tensions, and rapid depletion of nonrenewable resources. Some demographers predict that if population growth is not limited voluntarily before it reaches 10 billion, it will be limited by widespread food shortages, disease, infant mortality, and early death (Erlich & Erlich, 1990). (Population Institute)

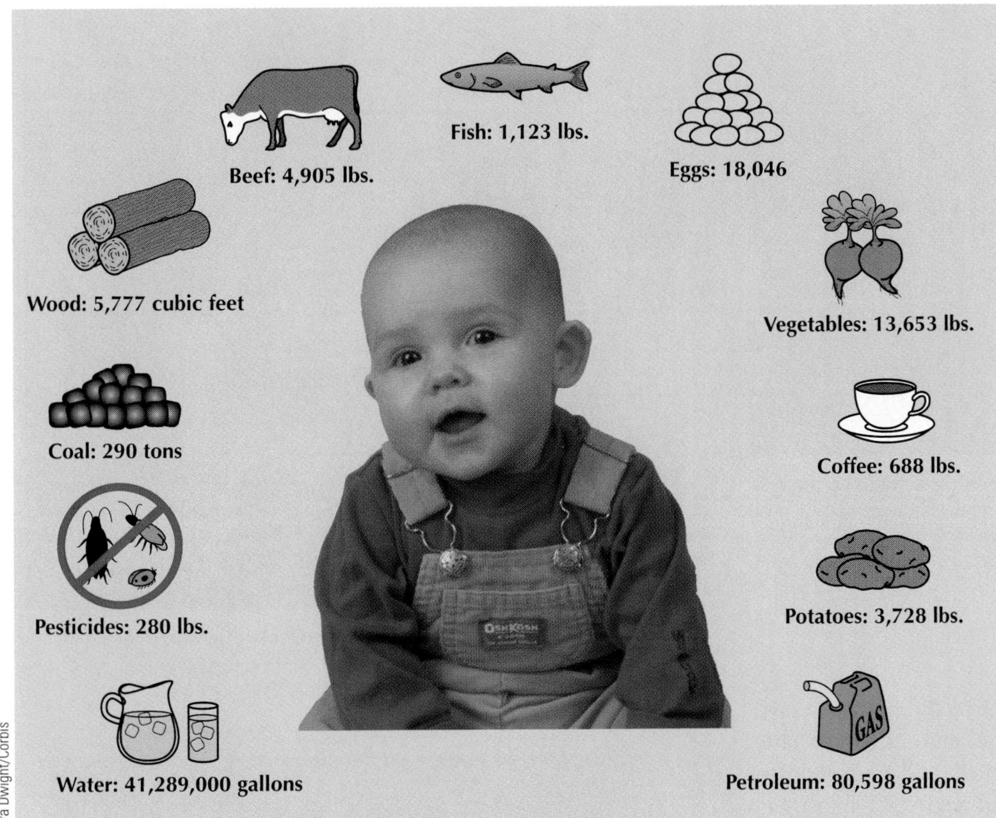

Laura Dwight/Corbis

What will it cost the world to provide for a baby born in the year 2000? Over a lifetime, a person born in North America will consume, on average, the resources shown here ("Bringing Up Baby," 1999).

forced the remaining rats into a small, severely crowded middle area.

What effect did crowding have on the animals? A high rate of pathological behavior developed in both males and females. Females gave up nest building and caring for their young. Pregnancies decreased, and infant mortality ran extremely high. Many of the animals became indiscriminately aggressive and went on rampaging attacks against others. Abnormal sexual behavior was rampant, with some animals displaying hypersexuality and others total sexual passivity. Many of the animals died, apparently from stress-caused diseases. The link between these problems and overcrowding is unmistakable.

But does that apply to humans? Many of the same pathological behaviors can be observed in crowded inner-city ghettos. It is therefore tempting to assume that violence, social disorganization, and declining birthrates as seen in these areas are directly related to crowding. However, the connection has not been so clearly demonstrated with humans. People living in the inner city suffer disadvantages in nutrition, education, income, and health care. These, more than crowding, may deserve the blame. In fact, most laboratory studies using human subjects have failed to produce any serious ill effects by crowding people into small places. Most likely, this is because *crowding* is a psychological condition that is separate from **density** (the number of people in a given space).

How does crowding differ from density? **Crowding** refers to subjective feelings of being overstimulated by social inputs or a loss of privacy. Whether high density is experienced as crowding may depend on relationships among those involved. In an elevator, subway, or prison, high densities may be uncomfortable. In contrast, a musical concert, party, or reunion may be most pleasant at high density levels. Thus, physical crowding may interact with situations to intensify existing stresses or pleasures. However, when crowding causes a *loss of control* over one's immediate social environment, stress is likely to result (Fuller et al., 1996; Pandey, 1999).

Stress probably explains why death rates increase among prison inmates and mental hospital patients who live in crowded conditions. Even milder instances of crowding can have a negative impact. People who live in crowded conditions often become guarded and withdrawn from others (Evans & Lepore, 1993).

Overload

One unmistakable result of high densities and crowding is a state that psychologist Stanley Milgram called **attentional overload.** This is a stressful condition that occurs when sensory stimulation, information, and social contacts make excessive demands on attention. Large cities, in particular, tend to bombard residents with continuous input. The resulting sensory and cognitive overload can be quite stressful.

Milgram (1970) believed that city dwellers learn to prevent attentional overload by engaging only in brief, superficial social contacts, by ignoring nonessential events, and by fending off others with cold and unfriendly expressions. In short, many city dwellers find that a degree of callousness is essential for survival.

Density The number of people in a given space or, inversely, the amount of space available to each person.

Crowding A subjective feeling of being overstimulated by a loss of privacy or by the nearness of others (especially when social contact with them is unavoidable).

Attentional overload A stressful condition caused when sensory stimulation, information, and social contacts make excessive demands on attention.

Daniel Barry/Getty Images

Times Square in New York, New Year's Eve, 2002. High densities do not automatically produce feelings of crowding. The nature of the situation and the relationship between crowd members are also important.

Kind or Callous?

Is there any evidence that such strategies are actually adopted? A fascinating study suggests they are. In several large American cities and smaller nearby towns, a young child stood on a busy street corner and asked passing strangers for help, saying, "I'm lost. Can you call my house?" About 72 percent of those approached in small towns offered to help. Only about 46 percent of those who were asked for help in the cities gave aid. In some cities (Boston and Philadelphia) only about one third were willing to help (Takooshian, Haber, & Lucido, 1977). An analysis of 65 studies confirmed that country people are more likely to help than city people (Steblay, 1987). The least helpful city tested was New York, where the crime rate is high and people are densely packed together (Levine, 2003). Thus, a blunting of sensitivity to the needs of others may be one of the more serious costs of urban stresses and crowding. As described next, noise also contributes to the sensory assault many people endure in urban environments.

The High Cost of Noise

How serious are the effects of daily exposure to noise? A study of children attending schools near Los Angeles International Airport suggests that constant noise can be quite damaging. Children from the noisy schools were compared with similar students attending schools farther from the airport (Cohen et al., 1981). The comparison students were from families of comparable social and economic makeup. Testing showed that children attending the noisy schools had higher blood pressure than those from the quieter schools. They were more likely to give up attempts to solve a difficult puzzle. And they were poorer at proofreading a printed paragraph—a task that requires close attention and concentration. More recent studies of children living near other airports or in noisy neighborhoods have found similar signs of stress, poor reading skills, and other damaging effects (Evans et al., 2001; Haines et al., 2001).

Jeff Greenberg/PhotoEdit

As the late Carl Sagan once said, "When you look closely, you find so many things going wrong with the environment, you are forced to reassess the hypothesis of intelligent life on Earth."

UNEP/Photog/The Image Works

People tend to have prolonged emotional responses to technological disasters. Long after an accidental release of radioactivity by the Three Mile Island nuclear power plant, nearby residents continued to feel stressed and apprehensive (Baum & Fleming, 1993).

The tendency of the noise-battered children to give up or become distracted is a serious handicap. It may even reveal a state of "learned helplessness" (described in Chapter 15) caused by daily, uncontrollable blasts of sound. Even if such damage proves to be temporary, it is clear that **noise pollution** (annoying and intrusive noise) is a major source of environmental stress (Staples, 1996).

DISCOVERING PSYCHOLOGY Planet in Peril?

How seriously do human activities impact the environment? See if you can tell which of the following statements are true and which are false.

1. Worldwide, one in six people suffer from hunger and malnutrition. True or False?
2. By 2025, two thirds of the world's people are likely to be affected by water shortages. True or False?
3. Supplies of oil will begin to decline by 2010. True or False?
4. Continued global warming will lead to increased storms, floods, droughts, and loss of plant and animal species. True or False?
5. Hazardous chemicals are now found in the bodies of all newborn babies. True or False?
6. One in four people worldwide are exposed to unhealthy concentrations of air pollutants. True or False?
7. The world is consuming 20 percent more natural resources a year than the planet can produce. True or False?
8. In the last 30 years, the number of plant and animal species fell 30 percent. True or False?
9. Worldwide energy use has risen by 700 percent in the last 40 years. True or False?
10. Fuel economy in American vehicles hit a 22-year low in 2002. True or False?
11. Polar ice and glaciers around the world are melting at a rate not previously seen in human history. True or False?
12. If fully implemented, the Kyoto Treaty will slow global warming, not prevent it. True or False?

As you may have guessed, all of the preceding statements are true. Given the scope of threats to the natural environment, only a fundamental change in beliefs may be capable of slowing the damage (Bell et al., 2001). The traditional Western view is that humans are superior to other living things, that natural resources are virtually unlimited, and that we can solve any problem through advances in technology. In contrast, an emerging ecological worldview holds that

1. Humans are interdependent with all other living creatures. We benefit from their survival.
2. Many of the things we do have unanticipated negative effects on the environment.
3. Natural resources are limited.
4. Humans must respect the Earth's carrying capacity.

Many problems that will become irreversible in 20 or 30 years depend on what we do now. Increasingly, we ignore what Mother Nature is telling us at our own peril.

Toxic Environments

Human activities drastically change the natural environment. We burn fossil fuels, destroy forests, use chemical products, and strip, clear, and farm the land. In doing so, we alter natural cycles, animal populations, and the very face of the Earth. The long-range impact of such activities is already becoming evident through global warming, the extinction of plants and animals, a hole in the ozone layer, and polluted land, air, water, and oceans (Oskamp, 2002). (See "Planet in Peril?" for more information.)

On a smaller scale there is plenty of evidence that unchecked environmental damage will be costly to our children and descendants. For example, exposure to toxic hazards, such as radiation, pesticides, and industrial chemicals, leads to an elevated risk of physical and mental disease (Baum & Fleming, 1993).

Sustainable Lifestyles

A worldwide ecological crisis is brewing and humans must change course to avoid vast human misery and permanent damage. Of course, corporations and governments do much environmental damage. Thus, many of the solutions will require changes in politics and policies. Ultimately, it will also require changes in individual behavior. Most of the environmental problems we face can be traced back to the human tendency to overuse natural resources (Oskamp, 2000).

Wasted Resources

The rapid worldwide consumption of natural resources is a devastating social problem. Industrialized nations, in particular, are consuming world resources at an alarming rate. North America, for instance, has a little over 5 percent of the world's population. Yet we consume 25 to 30 percent of all the fossil fuels and raw materials used annually. The typical resident of Vancouver, Chicago, or Miami consumes 10 to 1,000 times more resources each day than the average resident of Chile, Ghana, or Zaire (Cohen, 1995). In the face of projected shortages and squandered resources, what can be done to encourage conservation on a personal level?

Noise pollution Stressful and intrusive noise; usually artificially generated by machinery, but also including noises made by animals and humans.

Peter Ginter/Material World

Peter Ginter/Material World

Shown here are the Skeen family of Pearland, Texas, and the Yadev family of Ahraura, India. Each was photographed by the Material World Project, which documented typical families and their possessions around the world. Developed countries presently consume the largest share of world resources. However, population growth is fastest in developing countries and their hunger for material possessions is rapidly expanding. Achieving sustainable levels of population and consumption are two of the greatest challenges of the coming century. (From Menzel et al., 1994.)

Conservation

Try as you might to reduce your use of energy (electricity, for instance), you would probably find it difficult to do. A major problem is that *feedback* about energy use (the monthly bill) arrives long after the temptation to turn up the heat or to leave lights on (see Chapter 8). Psychologists aware of this problem have shown that lower energy bills result from simply giving families daily feedback about their use of gas or electricity.

Programs that give monetary rewards for energy conservation are even more effective. This is especially true for "master-metered" apartment complexes. In such apartments, families do not receive individual bills for their utilities. Consequently, they have no reason to save gas and electricity. Often, they consume about 25 percent more energy than they would in an individually metered apartment (McClelland & Cook, 1980). At this rate of waste, apartment owners can split any savings (from reduced consumption) with their tenants—and still be ahead. Similar factors can greatly increase recycling, as described next.

Reduce, Reuse, Recycle

What can be done to lighten the environmental impact of our "throw-away" society? As we have discussed, reducing consumption is a start. Personally reusing products and materials that would normally be thrown away is also important. In addition, we can recycle materials such as paper, steel, glass, aluminum, and plastic that can be used to make new products.

What can be done to encourage people to recycle? Psychological research has shown that all of the following strategies promote recycling (Oskamp, 1995).

- **Educate.** Learning about environmental problems and pro-environment values at school has been one of the most effective ways to encourage pro-environmental behavior (Zelezny, 1999).
- **Provide monetary rewards.** As mentioned before, monetary rewards encourage conservation. Requiring refundable deposits on glass bottles is a good example of using incentives to increase recycling.
- **Remove barriers.** Anything that makes recycling more convenient helps. A good example is cities that offer curbside pickup of household recyclables. Some cities even accept unsorted recycling materials, which greatly increases participation in recycling programs. On campus, simply putting marked containers in classrooms is a good way to encourage recycling (Ludwig, Gray, & Rowell, 1998).
- **Use persuasion.** Many recycling programs benefit from media campaigns to persuade people to participate.
- **Obtain public commitment.** People who feel they have committed themselves to recycling are more likely to follow through and actually recycle. Sometimes, people are asked to sign "pledge cards" on which they promise to recycle. Another technique involves having people sign a list committing themselves to recycling. Such lists may or may not be pub-

Cleo/PhotoEdit

People are much more likely to recycle if proper attention is given to psychological factors that promote recycling behavior.

lished in a local newspaper. They are just as effective either way.

- **Encourage goal setting.** People who set their own goals for recycling tend to meet them. Goal setting has been used successfully with families, dorms, neighborhoods, offices, factories, and so forth.
- **Give feedback.** Again, feedback proves to be very valuable. Recycling typically increases when families, work groups, dorms, and the like are simply told, on a weekly basis, how much they recycled (Schultz, 1999). Even impersonal feedback can be effective. In one study, signs were placed on recycling containers on a college campus. The signs showed how many aluminum cans had been deposited in the previous week. This simple procedure increased recycling by 65 percent (Larson, Houlihan, & Goernert, 1995).
- **Revise attitudes.** Even people who believe that recycling is worthwhile are likely to regard it as a boring task. Thus, people are most likely to continue recycling if they emphasize the sense of satisfaction they get from contributing to the environment (Werner & Makela, 1998).

Environmental Problem Solving

Although overcrowding, pollution, and overuse of resources rank high on the list of environmental stresses, they are only a few of the many challenges that press for attention. To conclude, let's sample some solutions that psychologists have provided for two more environmental problems.

Problem: Urban Fears

The way people think about the environment greatly affects their behavior. Mental "maps" of various areas, for instance, often guide actions and alter decisions. A case in point is a study done in Philadelphia. There, researchers found that an existing school bus route contributed to truancy. The problem was that many of its stops were at corners where children were afraid of being attacked and beaten (Conyne & Clack, 1981).

Solution

By doing an **environmental assessment**, psychologists develop a picture of environments as they are perceived by the people using them. An assessment often includes such things as charting areas of highest use in buildings, using attitude scales to measure reactions to various settings (such as schools, businesses, and parks), and even having people draw a version of their cognitive map of a building, campus, or city (Coulton, Korbin, & Su, 1996).

In the case of the school children, residents of the neighborhood were asked to rate how much stress they felt when walking in various areas. The result was a contour map (somewhat like a high- and low-pressure weather map) that showed the areas of highest perceived stress. This "stress map" was then used to reroute school buses to "low-pressure" areas.

Problem: Residential Crowding

Anyone who has ever lived in a college dorm knows that at times a dorm hall can be quite a "zoo." Most architects aim to create buildings in which people will be comfortable, happy, and healthy. But sometimes they miss the mark with human behavior. In one well-known experiment, Baum and Valins (1977) found that students housed in long, narrow, corridor-design dormitories often feel crowded and stressed. The crowded students tended to withdraw from others and even made more trips to the campus health center than students living in less-crowded buildings.

Solution

Architectural psychology is the study of the effects buildings have on behavior. By analyzing buildings, psychologists are often able to suggest design changes that solve or avoid problems. For example, Baum and Valins (1979) studied two basic dorm arrangements. One dorm had a long corridor with one central bathroom. As a result, residents were constantly forced into contact

BRIDGES

Learned cognitive maps guide our behavior in a variety of situations.

See Chapter 8, pages 286–287.

Environmental assessment Measurement and analysis of the effects an environment has on the behavior of people within that environment.

Architectural psychology Study of the effects buildings have on behavior and the design of buildings using behavioral principles.

with one another. The other dorm had rooms clustered in threes. Each of these suites shared a small bathroom. Even though the amount of space available to each student was the same in both dorms, students in the long-corridor dorm reported feeling more crowded. They also made fewer friends in their dorm and showed greater signs of withdrawing from social contact.

What sort of solution does this suggest? A later study showed that small architectural changes can greatly reduce stress in high-density living conditions. Baum and Davis (1980) compared students living in a long-corridor dorm housing 40 students to those living in an altered long-corridor dorm. In the altered dorm, Baum and Davis divided the hallway in half with unlocked doors and made three center bedrooms into a lounge area (● Figure 20.3). At the end of the term, students living in the divided dorm reported less stress from crowding. They also formed more friendships and were more open to social contacts. In comparison, students in the long-corridor dorm felt more crowded, stressed, and unfriendly, and they kept their doors shut much more frequently—presumably because they "wanted to be alone."

Similar improvements have been made by altering the interior design of businesses, schools, apartment buildings, mental hospitals, and prisons. In general, the more spaces one must pass through to get from one part of a building to another, the less stressed and crowded people feel (Evans, Lepore, & Schroeder, 1996).

Conclusion

We have had room here only to hint at the creative and highly useful work being done in environmental psychology. Although many environmental problems remain, it is encouraging to see that behavioral solutions exist for at least some of them. Surely, creating and maintaining healthy environments is one of the major challenges facing coming generations (Gifford, 2002; Oskamp, 2000).

We have discussed work and the environment at some length because both have major effects on our lives. To provide a fuller account of the diversity of applied psychology, let's conclude by briefly sampling three additional topics of interest: educational psychology, psychology and law, and sports psychology.

KNOWLEDGE BUILDER

Environmental Psychology

REFLECT

What is the nature of the natural environment, constructed environment, social environment, and behavioral setting you are in right now?

What forms of territorial behavior are you aware of in your own actions?

Have you ever experienced a stressful level of crowding? Was density or control the key factor?

If you were setting up a program to promote recycling on campus, what techniques would you apply?

LEARNING CHECK

1. Although male rats in Calhoun's crowded animal colony became quite pathological, female rats continued to behave in a relatively normal fashion. T or F?
2. To clearly understand behavior, it is necessary to make a distinction between crowding and ____________ (the number of people in a given space).
3. Milgram believed that many city dwellers prevent attentional overload by limiting themselves to superficial social contacts. T or F?
4. Performing an environmental ____________ might be a good prelude to redesigning college classrooms to make them more comfortable and conducive to learning.
5. So far, the most successful approach for bringing about energy conservation is to add monetary penalties to monthly bills for excessive consumption. T or F?

CRITICAL THINKING

6. Many of the most damaging changes to the environment being caused by humans will not be felt until sometime in the future. How does this complicate the problem of preserving environmental quality?

Answers: 1. F **2.** density **3.** T **4.** assessment **5.** F **6.** A delay of consequences (rewards, benefits, costs, and punishers) tends to reduce their impact on immediate behavior.

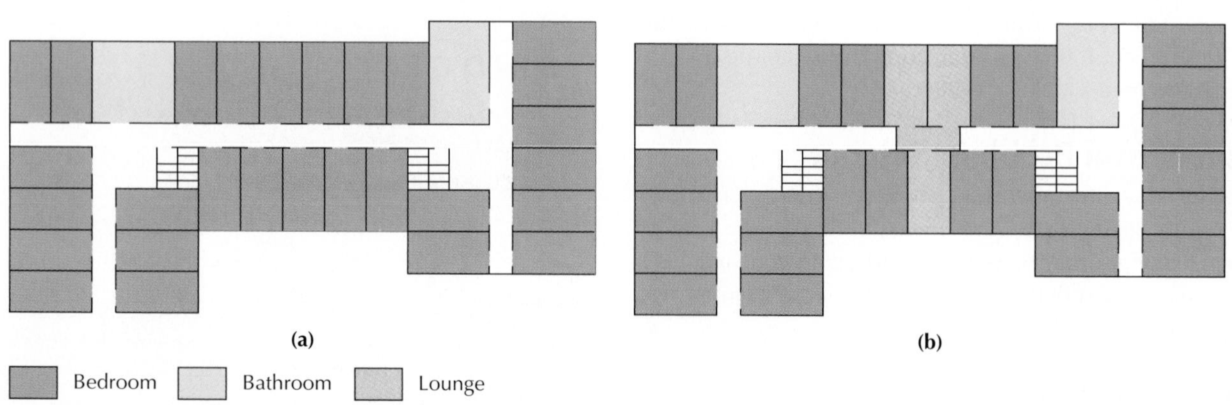

● **Figure 20.3** An architectural solution for crowding. Psychologists divided a dorm hall like that shown in the left diagram *(a)* into two shorter halls separated by unlocked doors and a lounge area *(b)*. This simple change minimized unwanted social contacts and greatly reduced feelings of crowding among dorm residents. (Adapted from Baum & Davis, 1980.)

Educational Psychology—An Instructive Topic

You have just been asked to teach a class of fourth-graders for a day. What will you do? (Assume that bribery, showing them movies, and a field trip to a video arcade are out.) If you ever do try teaching, you might be surprised at how challenging it is. Effective teachers must understand learning, instruction, classroom dynamics, and testing.

What are the best ways to teach? Is there an optimal teaching style for different age groups, topics, or individuals? These and related questions lie at the heart of educational psychology (■ Table 20.4). Specifically, **educational psychology** seeks to understand how people learn and how teachers instruct.

Bill Aron/PhotoEdit, Inc.

Educational psychologists are interested in enhancing learning and improving teaching.

Elements of a Teaching Strategy

Whether it's "breaking in" a new coworker, instructing a friend in a hobby, or helping a child learn to read, the fact is, we all teach at times. The next time you are asked to share your knowledge, how will you do it? One good way to become more effective is to use a specific **teaching strategy**, or planned method of instruction. The example that follows was designed for classroom use, but it applies to many other situations as well (Thornburg, 1984).

Step 1: Learner preparation. Begin by gaining the learner's attention, and focus interest on the topic at hand.
Step 2: Stimulus presentation. Present instructional stimuli (information, examples, and illustrations) deliberately and clearly.
Step 3: Learner response. Allow time for the learner to respond to the information presented (by repeating correct responses or asking questions, for example).
Step 4: Reinforcement. Give positive reinforcement (praise, encouragement) and feedback ("Yes, that's right," "No, this way," and so on) to strengthen correct responses.
Step 5: Evaluation. Test or assess the learner's progress so that both you and the learner can make adjustments when needed.
Step 6: Spaced review. Periodic review is an important step in teaching because it helps strengthen responses to key stimuli.

Effects of Teaching Styles

As a student, I've encountered many different teaching styles. Do different styles affect classroom learning? There is little doubt that teachers can greatly affect student interest, motivation, and creativity. But what styles have what effects? To answer this question, psychologists have compared a number of teaching styles. Two of the most basic are *direct instruction* and *open teaching.*

In **direct instruction,** factual information is presented by lecture, demonstration, and rote practice. In **open teaching,** active teacher–student discussion is emphasized (Peterson, 1979). And

TABLE 20.4

Topics of Special Interest to Educational Psychologists

Aptitude testing	Language learning
Classroom management	Learning theory
Classroom motivation	Moral development
Classroom organization	Student adjustment
Concept learning	Student attitudes
Curriculum development	Student needs
Disabled students	Teacher attitudes
Exceptional students	Teaching strategies
Gifted students	Teaching styles
Individualized instruction	Test writing
Intellectual development	Transfer of learning
Intelligence testing	

BRIDGES

Many effective teaching strategies apply the basic principles of operant conditioning.

See Chapter 8, pages 269–279.

Educational psychology The field that seeks to understand how people learn and how teachers instruct.

Teaching strategy A plan for effective teaching.

Direct instruction Presentation of factual information by lecture, demonstration, and rote practice.

Open teaching Instruction based on active teacher–student discussion.

Peanut Butter for the Mind: Designing Education for Everyone

"Education is the key to unlock the golden door of freedom," said George Washington Carver. Born in 1860, a son of slaves, he invented that universally popular food, peanut butter. In today's ever more complicated world, Carver's words ring truer than ever. Yet educators face an increasingly diverse mix of students: "regular" students, adult learners, students with disabilities, students who speak English as a second language, and students at risk for dropping out (Bowe, 2000). In response, educators have begun to apply *Universal Design for Instruction* (Scott, McGuire, & Shaw, 2003; Udvari-Solner, Villa, & Thousand, 2002). The basic idea is that a good education for one type of student will be a good education for other students as well.

One principle of Universal Design for Instruction is to make use of different instructional methods, such as a lecture, a podcast of the lecture, a group activity, an Internet discussion list, and perhaps student blogs. That way, for example, hearing or visually impaired students can find at least one approach suitable to them, as can adult learners whose work and family responsibilities can make it difficult for them to attend class. At the same time, everyone benefits because we all learn better if we can choose between different ways of experiencing knowledge.

Another principle is to design instructional materials to be simple and intuitive by eliminating unnecessary complexity. Marking schemes for projects can be clearly laid out, course syllabi can be accurate and comprehensive, and handbooks can be created to guide students through difficult homework assignments. Again, such materials are not only easier on special groups of students. They also make learning easier for all of us.

Are these principles being applied to learning in colleges and universities? In short, yes they are (McGuire, & Scott, 2002). Now this is instruction that won't stick to the roof of your mind!

now, the winner: As it turns out, both approaches have certain advantages. Students of direct instruction do slightly better on achievement tests than students in open classrooms (Thornburg, 1984). However, students of open teaching do somewhat better on tests of abstract thinking, creativity, and problem solving. They also tend to be more independent, curious, and positive in their attitudes toward school (Peterson, 1979). At present, it looks as if a balance of teaching styles goes hand in hand with a balanced education.

Although we have viewed only a small sample of educational research, its value for improving teaching and learning should be apparent. Before we leave the topic of education, "Peanut Butter for the Mind: Designing Education for Everyone" offers a peek at where education is going in the new millennium.

Psychology and Law—Judging Juries

One of the best places to see psychology in action is the local courthouse. Jury trials are often fascinating studies in human behavior. Does the defendant's appearance affect the jury's decision? Do the personality characteristics or attitudes of jurors influence how they vote? These and many more questions have been investigated by psychologists interested in law (Bartol & Bartol, 2005). Specifically, the **psychology of law** is the study of the behavioral dimensions of the legal system (see ■ Table 20.5).

Jury Behavior

When a case goes to trial, jurors must listen to days or weeks of testimony and then decide guilt or innocence. How do they reach their decision? Psychologists use **mock juries** (simulated juries) to probe such questions (Spackman et al., 2002). In some mock juries volunteers are simply given written evidence and arguments to read before making a decision. Others watch videotaped trials staged by actors. Either way, studying the behavior of mock juries helps us understand what determines how real jurors vote.

Some of the findings of jury research are unsettling. Studies show that jurors are rarely able to put aside their biases, attitudes, and values while making a decision (Watson, deBortali-Tregerthan, & Frank, 1984). For example, jurors are generally less likely to find

TABLE 20.5

Topics of Special Interest in the Psychology of Law

Arbitration	Juror attitudes
Attitudes toward law	Jury decisions
Bail setting	Jury selection
Capital punishment	Mediation
Conflict resolution	Memory
Criminal personality	Parole board decisions
Diversion programs	Police selection
Effects of parole	Police stress
Expert testimony	Police training
Eyewitness testimony	Polygraph accuracy
Forensic hypnosis	Sentencing decisions
Insanity plea	White-collar crime

attractive defendants guilty (on the basis of the same evidence) than unattractive defendants (Perlman & Cozby, 1983). There is an interesting twist, however. If good looks *helped* a person commit a crime, it can work against her or him in court (Tedeschi, Lindskold, & Rosenfeld, 1985). An example would be a handsome man accused of swindling money from an unmarried middle-aged woman.

A second major problem is that jurors are not very good at separating evidence from other information, such as their perceptions of the defendant, attorneys, witnesses, and what they think the judge wants. For example, if complex scientific evidence is presented, jurors tend to be swayed more by the expertise of the witness than by the evidence itself (Cooper, Bennett, & Sukel, 1996).

Often, jurors' final verdict is influenced by inadmissible evidence, such as mention of a defendant's prior conviction. When jurors are told to ignore information that slips out in court, they find it very hard to do so. A related problem occurs when jurors take into account the severity of the punishment a defendant faces (Sales & Hafemeister, 1985). Jurors are not supposed to let this affect their verdict, but many do.

A fourth area of difficulty arises because jurors usually cannot suspend judgment until all the evidence is in. Typically, they form an opinion early in the trial. It then becomes hard for them to fairly judge evidence that contradicts their opinion.

Problems like these are troubling in a legal system that prides itself on fairness. However, all is not lost. The more severe the crime and the more clear-cut the evidence, the less a jury's quirks affect the verdict (Tedeschi, Lindskold, & Rosenfeld, 1985). Although it is far from perfect, the jury system works reasonably well in most cases.

Jury Selection

Before a trial begins, opposing attorneys are allowed to disqualify potential jurors who may be biased. For example, a person who knows anyone connected with the trial can be excluded. Beyond this, attorneys try to use jury selection to remove people who may cause trouble for them. For instance, jurors who believe rape myths (that some women "ask for it" by their actions or style of dress, for example) are less likely to convict an accused rapist (Watson, deBortali-Tregerthan, & Frank, 1984). In many cases, the composition of a jury has a major effect on the verdict of a trial (Devine et al., 2001).

Only a limited number of potential jurors can be excused. As a result, many attorneys ask psychologists for help in identifying people who will favor or harm their efforts. In **scientific jury selection**, social science principles are applied to the process of choosing a jury. Several techniques are typically used. As a first step, *demographic information* may be collected for each juror. Much can be guessed by knowing a juror's age, sex, race, occupation, education, political affiliation, religion, and socioeconomic status. Most of this information is available from public records.

To supplement demographic information, a *community survey* may be done to find out how local citizens feel about the case.

Getty Images

The behavior of juries and jurors has been extensively studied. The findings of such studies are applied by psychologists who act as advisors to attorneys during the jury selection process. Jury selection in the O. J. Simpson murder trial took 2 months, as defense and prosecution lawyers struggled for the advantage in jury makeup.

The assumption is that jurors probably have attitudes similar to people with backgrounds like their own. Although talking with potential jurors outside the courtroom is not permitted, other information networks are available. For instance, a psychologist may interview relatives, acquaintances, neighbors, and coworkers of potential jurors.

Back in court, psychologists also often watch for *authoritarian personality* traits in potential jurors. Authoritarians tend to believe that punishment is effective, and they are more likely to vote for conviction (Devine et al., 2001). At the same time, the psychologist typically observes potential jurors' *nonverbal behavior.* The idea is to try to learn from body language which side the person favors (Sales & Hafemeister, 1985).

In the United States, murder trials require a special jury—one made up of people who are not opposed to the death penalty. "Death-Qualified Juries" examines the implications of this practice.

BRIDGES

Authoritarian personality traits are also related to ethnocentrism and racial prejudice.

See Chapter 19, pages 641–642.

Psychology of law Study of the psychological and behavioral dimensions of the legal system.

Mock jury A group that realistically simulates a courtroom jury.

Scientific jury selection Using social science principles to choose members of a jury.

CRITICAL THINKING

Death-Qualified Juries

Tony Savion/The Image Works

People in a **death-qualified jury** must favor the death penalty or at least be indifferent to it. That way, jurors are capable of voting for the death penalty if they think it is justified.

In order for the death penalty to have meaning, death-qualified juries may be a necessity. However, psychologists have discovered that the makeup of such juries tends to be biased. Specifically, death-qualified juries are likely to contain a disproportionate number of people who are male, white, high income, conservative, and authoritarian. Such juries are much more likely than average to convict a defendant (Haney, Hurtado, & Vega, 1994; Ogloff, & Chopra, 2004). Given the same facts, jurors who favor the death penalty are more likely to read criminal intent into a defendant's actions (Goodman-Delahunty, Greene, & Hsiao, 1998) and to believe that the death penalty is a deterrent (O'Neil, Patry, & Penrod, 2004). Overall, pro-death jurors are a whopping 44 percent more likely to favor conviction (Allen, Mabry, & McKelton, 1998).

Could death-qualified juries be too willing to convict? It is nearly impossible to say how often the bias inherent in death-qualified juries results in bad verdicts. However, the possibility that some innocent persons have been executed may be one of the inevitable costs of using death as the ultimate punishment.

In the well-publicized case of O. J. Simpson, the ex-football player accused of murdering his wife, a majority of African Americans thought Simpson was innocent during the early stages of the trial. In contrast, the majority of European Americans thought he was guilty. The opinions of both groups changed little over the course of the yearlong trial. (Simpson was eventually acquitted.) The fact that emerging evidence and arguments had little effect on what people believed shows why jury makeup can sometimes decide the outcome of a trial (Brigham & Wasserman, 1999).

Cases like O. J. Simpson's, Michael Jackson's, and Kobe Bryant's raise troubling ethical questions. In each case, wealthy clients had the advantage of psychological jury selection—something most people cannot afford. Attorneys, of course, can't be blamed for trying to improve their odds of winning a case, and because both sides help select jurors, the net effect in most instances is probably a more balanced jury (Sales & Hafemeister, 1985). At its worst, jury analysis leads to unjust verdicts. At its best, it helps to identify and remove only people who would be highly biased (Strier, 1999).

Jury research is perhaps the most direct link between psychology and law, but there are others. Psychologists evaluate people for sanity hearings, do counseling in prisons, advise lawmakers on public policy, help select and train police cadets, and more (Sales & Hafemeister, 1985). In the future, it is quite likely that psychology will have a growing impact on law and the courts.

Sports Psychology—The Athletic Mind

What does psychology have to do with sports? **Sports psychology** is the study of the behavioral dimensions of sports performance (Williams, 2006). As almost all serious athletes soon learn, peak performance requires more than physical training. Mental and emotional "conditioning" are also important. Recognizing this fact, many teams, both professional and amateur, now include psychologists on their staffs. On any given day, a sports psychologist might teach an athlete how to relax, how to ignore distractions, or how to cope with emotions. The sports psychologist might also provide personal counseling for performance-lowering stresses and conflicts (Neff, 1990). Other psychologists are interested in studying factors that affect athletic achievement, such as skill learning, the personality profiles of champion athletes, the effects of spectators, and related topics (■ Table 20.6). In short,

TABLE 20.6

Topics of Special Interest to Sports Psychologists

Achievement motivation	Hypnosis
Athletic personality	Mental practice
Athletic task analysis	Motor learning
Coaching styles	Peak performance
Competition	Positive visualization
Control of attention	Self-regulation
Coping strategies	Skill acquisition
Emotions and performance	Social facilitation
Exercise and mental health	Stress reduction
Goal setting	Team cooperation
Group (team) dynamics	Training procedures

Oliver Maire/Corbis

Sports psychologists have played a significant role in helping prepare athletes for peak performance in the Olympic Games. Stress management, attention regulation, mental imagery, motivation, self-confidence, and many other psychological factors greatly affect athletic performance.

sports psychologists seek to understand and improve sports performance and to enhance the benefits of participating in sports (Williams, 1995).

Sports often provide valuable information on human behavior in general. For example, a study of Little League baseball found that children's self-esteem improved significantly after a season of play (Hawkins & Gruber, 1982). In other work, psychologists have learned that such benefits are most likely to occur when competition, rejection, criticism, and the "one-winner mentality" are minimized. When working with children in sports, it is also important to emphasize fair play, intrinsic rewards, self-control of emotions, independence, and self-reliance (Orlick, 1975). A recent study provides another example of using sports to test ideas about human behavior. Researchers found that when sports teams travel eastward over one or more time zones, they perform more poorly than they do when they travel westward. This is exactly what we would expect from people whose circadian rhythms are disrupted. It provides "real-world" support for other observations about bodily rhythms (Worthen & Wade, 1999).

Adults, of course, may also benefit from sports. For many, the payoffs are stress reduction, a better self-image, and improved general health (Williams, 2006). Researchers have reported, for instance, that running is associated with lower levels of tension, anxiety, fatigue, and depression than is found in the nonrunning population (Gondola & Tuckman, 1982).

Before the advent of sports psychology, it was debatable whether athletes improved because of "homegrown" coaching methods, or in spite of them. For example, in early studies of volleyball and gymnastics, it became clear that people teaching these sports had very little knowledge of crucial, underlying skills (Salmela, 1974, 1975).

How has psychology helped? An ability to do detailed studies of complex skills has been one of the major contributions. In a **task analysis**, sports skills are broken into subparts, so that key elements can be identified and taught. Such methods are an extension of techniques first used for job analyses, as described earlier. For example, it doesn't take much to be off target in the Olympic sport of marksmanship. The object is to hit a bull's-eye the size of a dime at the end of a 165-foot-long shooting range. Nevertheless, an average of 50 bull's-eyes out of 60 shots is not unusual in international competition (prone position).

What does it take—beyond keen eyes and steady hands—to achieve such accuracy? The answer is surprising. Sports psychologists have found that top marksmen consistently squeeze the trigger *between* heartbeats (● Figure 20.4). Apparently the tiny tremor induced by a heartbeat is enough to send the shot astray (Pelton, 1983). Without careful psychological study, it is doubtful that this element of marksmanship would have been identified. Now that its importance is known, competitors have begun to use various techniques—from relaxation training to biofeedback—to steady and control their heartbeat. In the future, the best marksmen may be those who set their sights on mastering their hearts.

Richard Pasley/Stock, Boston

Testing by psychologists has shown that umpires can call balls and strikes more accurately if they stand behind the outside corner of home plate. This position supplies better height and distance information because umpires are able to see pitches pass in front of the batter (Ford et al., 1999).

Death-qualified jury A jury composed of people who favor the death penalty or at least are indifferent to it.

Sports psychology Study of the psychological and behavioral dimensions of sports performance.

Task analysis Breaking complex skills into their subparts.

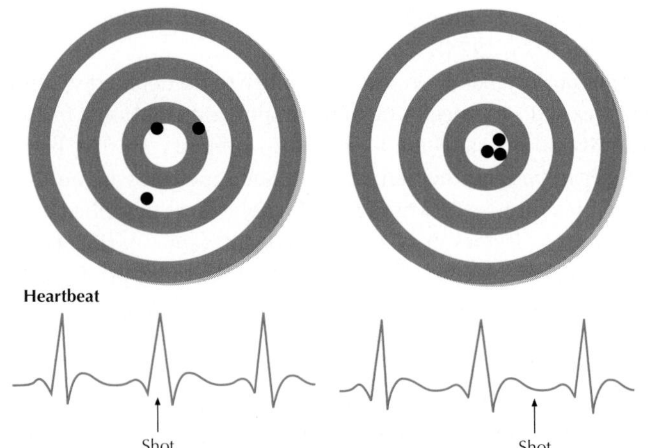

● **Figure 20.4** The target on the left shows what happens when a marksman fires during the heart's contraction. Higher scores, as shown by the three shots on the right, are more likely when shots are made between heartbeats. (Adapted from Pelton, 1983.)

Motor Skills

Sports psychologists are very interested in how we learn motor skills. A **motor skill** is a series of actions molded into a smooth and efficient performance. Typing, walking, pole-vaulting, shooting baskets, playing golf, driving a car, writing, and skiing are all motor skills.

A basketball player may never make exactly the same shot twice in a game. This makes it almost impossible to practice every shot that might occur. How, then, do athletes become skillful? Typically, athletic performances involve learning *motor programs*. A **motor program** is a mental plan or model of what a skilled movement should be like. Motor programs allow an athlete—or a person simply walking across a room—to perform complex movements that fit changing conditions. If, for example, you have learned a "bike-riding" motor program, you can easily ride bicycles of different sizes and types on a large variety of surfaces.

Throughout life you will face the challenge of learning new motor skills. How can psychology make your learning more effective? Studies of sports skills suggest that you should keep the following points in mind for optimal skill learning:

1. Begin by observing and imitating a *skilled model*. Modeling provides a good mental picture of the skill. At this point, try simply to grasp a visual image of the skilled movement.
2. Learn *verbal rules* to back up motor learning. Such rules are usually most helpful in the early phases of skill learning. When first learning cross-country skiing, for example, it is helpful to say, "left arm, right foot, right arm, left foot." Later, as a skill becomes more automated, internal speech may actually get in the way.
3. Practice should be as *lifelike* as possible so that artificial cues and responses do not become a part of the skill. A competitive diver should practice on the board, not on a trampoline. If you want to learn to ski, try to practice on snow, not straw.
4. Get *feedback* from a mirror, videotape, coach, or observer. Whenever possible, get someone experienced in the skill to direct attention to *correct responses* when they occur.
5. When possible, it is better to practice *natural units* rather than breaking the task into artificial parts. When learning to type, it is better to start with real words rather than nonsense syllables.
6. Learn to *evaluate* and *analyze* your own performance. Remember, you are trying to learn a motor program, not just train your muscles. Motor skills are actually very mental.

The last point leads to one more suggestion. Research has shown that **mental practice**, or merely imagining a skilled performance, can aid learning (Martin, Moritz, & Hall, 1999). This technique seems to help by refining motor programs. Of course, mental practice is not superior to actual practice. Mental practice tends to be most valuable after you have mastered a task at a basic level (Tenenbaum, Bar-Eli, & Eyal, 1996; Williams, 2006). When you begin to get really good at a skill, give mental practice a try. You may be surprised at how effective it can be.

Positive Psychology: Peak Performance

One of the most interesting topics in sports psychology is the phenomenon of *peak performance*. During **peak performance,** physical, mental, and emotional states are harmonious and optimal. Many athletes report episodes during which they felt almost as if they were in a trance. The experience has also been called *flow* because the athlete becomes one with his or her performance and flows with it. At such times, athletes experience intense concentration, detachment, a lack of fatigue and pain, a subjective slowing of time, and feelings of unusual power and control (Csikszmentmihalyi, Abuhamdeh, & Nakamura, 2005). It is at just such times that "personal bests" tend to occur.

A curious aspect of flow is that it cannot be forced to happen. In fact, if a person stops to think about it, the flow state goes away. Psychologists are now seeking to identify conditions that facilitate peak performance and the unusual mental state that usually accompanies it (Csikszmentmihalyi, Abuhamdeh, & Nakamura, 2005).

Even though flow may be an elusive state, there is much that athletes can do mentally to improve performance. A starting point is to make sure that their *arousal level is appropriate for the task* at hand. For a sprinter at a track meet that may mean elevating arousal to a very high level. The sprinter could, for example, try to become angry by picturing a rival cheating. For a golfer or a gymnast, lowering arousal may be crucial, in order to avoid "choking" during a big event. One way of controlling arousal is to go through a *fixed routine* before each game or event. Athletes also

BRIDGES

Many of the mental strategies developed by sports psychologists are an extension of stress inoculation techniques.

See Chapter 15, page 528.

learn to use *imagery and relaxation techniques* to adjust their degree of arousal (Gould & Udry, 1994).

Imaging techniques can be used to *focus attention* on the athlete's task and to *mentally rehearse* it beforehand. For example, golf great Jack Nicklaus "watches a movie" in his head before each shot. During events, athletes learn to *use cognitive-behavioral strategies to guide their efforts* in a supportive, positive way (Beauchamp et al., 1996). For instance, instead of berating herself for being behind in a match, a tennis player could use the time between points to savor a good shot or put an error out of mind. In general, athletes benefit from avoiding negative, self-critical thoughts that distract them and undermine their confidence. Finally, top athletes tend to use more *self-regulation strategies,* in which they evaluate their performance and make adjustments to keep it at optimum levels (Anshel, 1995; Kim, Singer, & Radlo, 1996).

The psychological dimension of sport is illustrated by the existence of a small but well documented "home court advantage" in most sports. That is, sports teams are more likely to win at home than they are when they compete "on the road." To some extent, this is based on familiarity with the home court, support from the home crowd, and a lack of travel demands. But most of the advantage occurs because athletes approach home games with greater confidence and optimal arousal levels (Bray & Widmeyer, 2001). When athletes are well matched in skill, small psychological advantages can make a difference between winning and losing.

At present, sports psychology is a very young field, and still much more an art than a science. Nevertheless, interest in the field is rapidly expanding (Petrie & Diehl, 1995).

A Look Ahead

Although we have sampled several major areas of applied psychology, they are by no means the only applied specialties. Others that immediately come to mind are community psychology, military psychology, and health psychology. To conclude, the upcoming Psychology in Action section returns to the world of work, with some advice on how to be an effective communicator.

KNOWLEDGE BUILDER

Psychology Applied to Education, the Law, and Sports

REFLECT

You are going to tutor a young child in arithmetic. How could you use a teaching strategy to improve your effectiveness?

As a student, do you prefer direct instruction or open teaching?

What advice would you give a person who is about to serve on a jury, if she or he wants to make an impartial judgment?

How could you apply the concepts of task analysis, mental practice, and peak performance to a sport you are interested in?

LEARNING CHECK

1. Evaluation of learning is typically the first step in a systematic teaching strategy. T or F?
2. Compared to direct instruction, open teaching produces better scores on achievement tests. T or F?
3. Universal Design for Instruction aims to create educational materials that are useful to ____________ students.
4. Despite their many limitations, one thing that jurors are good at is setting aside inadmissible evidence. T or F?
5. Which of the following is *not* commonly used by psychologists to aid jury selection?
   a. mock testimony c. community surveys
   b. information networks d. demographic data
6. Mental models, called ____________ ____________, appear to underlie well-learned motor skills.
7. Learning verbal rules to back up motor learning is usually most helpful in the early stages of acquiring a skill. T or F?
8. The flow experience is closely linked with instances of ______ ____________ performance.

CRITICAL THINKING

9. When an athlete follows a set routine before an event, what source of stress has she or he eliminated?

Answers: **1.** F **2.** F **3.** all **4.** F **5.** a **6.** motor programs **7.** T **8.** peak **9.** As discussed in Chapter 15, stress is reduced when a person feels in control of a situation. Following a routine helps athletes maintain a sense of order and control so that they are not over-aroused when the time comes to perform.

Motor skill A series of actions molded into a smooth and efficient performance.

Motor program A mental plan or model that guides skilled movement.

Mental practice Imagining a skilled performance to aid learning.

Peak performance A performance during which physical, mental, and emotional states are harmonious and optimal.

PSYCHOLOGY IN ACTION

Improving Communication at Work

"Just a minute, I want to expand on the confusion. This is where I'm assuming we're just going to throw it up for air. I mean, let's tie all this up in loose ends."

"The bottom line is we've got to round-file this puppy ASAP before it goes belly-up. Stan says we're talking mouth-breather here. Copy Monica, Steve, and the bean counters with your input and let's circle the wagons in the AM."

"I was just, like, totally embarrassed, I mean, like abso-double-lutely, totally incinerated, you know? I mean, to the max. I'm all, 'I'm just totally sorry, Mr. Thompson.' And he's all, 'If this is the way you do business, I'm not interested.'"

Each of the people just quoted probably intended to express his or her ideas clearly. As you can see, however, their efforts are less than a model of clarity.

Getting the Message Across

Effective communication is crucial in many work settings. When communication is muddled, important messages may get lost. Feelings can be crushed. Trust may be damaged. Poor decisions are made. Almost always, group effectiveness is impaired.

Clearly, people who work together depend on good communication. Service-oriented work with customers, and ethnocultural diversity in the workforce also put a premium on communication skills. For such reasons, getting a job, keeping it, and excelling in your work all depend on knowing how to communicate clearly with others (Goldstein & Gilliam, 1990).

Effective Communication

To improve your communication skills, or to keep them sharp, remember the following points.

1. **State your ideas clearly and decisively.** News reporters learn to be precise about the "who, what, when, where, how, and why" of events. At work, the same list is a good guide when you are making a request, giving instructions, or answering a question. Rather than saying, "I need someone to give me a hand sometime with some stuff," it would be better to say, "Blake, would you please meet me in the storeroom in 5 minutes? I need help lifting a box." Notice that the second request answers all of these questions: Who? Blake. What? Could you help me? How? By lifting a box. When? In 5 minutes. Where? In the storeroom. Why? It takes two people.

   As you speak, avoid overuse of ambiguous words and phrases ("wiggle words") such as *I guess, I think, kinda, sort of, around, some, about, you know,* and *like.* Here's an example: "Basically, I sort of feel like we should kinda pause. I mean, and, let's see, maybe reconsider, you know, rethink some of this stuff." It would be better to say: "I believe we should revise our plans immediately." Ambiguous messages leave others in doubt as to your true thoughts and wishes and make you sound tentative and less confident in your opinion.

   Also try not to overuse intensifiers (*very, really, absolutely, extra, super, awesome, ultimate, completely,* and so on). Super extra frequent use of such awesome words really causes them to completely lose their ultimate effectiveness.

2. **Eschew the meretricious utilization of polysyllabic locutions. (Don't overuse big words.)** Overuse of obscure vocabulary is often a sign of insecurity. Big words may make you sound important, but they can also blur your message. Which of the following two statements is clearer? "Pulchritude possesses solely cutaneous profundity." Or, "Beauty is only skin deep"?

   Trendy, overused "buzz words" or phrases should also be avoided. Often they are just a way of *sounding like* you are saying something: "Personally, I feel we've got to be more synergistically proactive and start networking in a programmatic fashion if we want to avoid being negatively impacted by future megatrends in the client–purveyor interface." Translation: "I don't have any worthwhile thoughts on the topic."

3. **Avoid excessive use of jargon or slang.** Most professions have their own specialized terminology. Here's an example of some printers' jargon: "TR the last two lines but STET the leading." (Reverse the order of the last two lines but don't change the spacing between them.) Jargon can provide a quick, shorthand way of expressing ideas. However, jargon and technical lingo should be avoided unless you are sure that others are familiar with it. Otherwise, people may misunderstand you or feel left out. Using slang can have the same effect as jargon. Slang that excludes people from a conversation makes them feel belittled. (The second quotation at the beginning of this section is full of slang.)

4. **Avoid loaded words.** Words that have strong emotional meanings (loaded words) can have unintended effects on listeners. For example, the observation "What a stupid-looking tie," implies that anyone who likes the tie is stupid.

In the same way, saying, "I think the supervisor's new schedule is a *dumb* idea," brands anyone who agrees with the schedule as foolish. Good decision making and problem solving require an atmosphere in which people feel that their ideas are respected, even when they disagree.

5. **Use people's names.** Work relationships go more smoothly when you learn names and use them. An impersonal request such as, "Hey you, could you make five copies of this for me?" is not likely to promote future cooperation. Of course, whether you use a first or last name will depend on how formal your relationship to a person is. In any case, learning names is well worth the effort. (The Psychology in Action section of Chapter 9 tells how to improve your memory for names.)
6. **Be polite and respectful.** Being polite is important, but don't be artificially servile or stilted. Overuse of expressions such as *sir, madame, with your permission, if you would be ever so kind,* and so on, can actually be insulting. True politeness puts others at ease. Phony politeness makes people feel that they are being made fun of, or manipulated, or that you are faking it to win approval. Being polite can be difficult when tempers flare. If you have a dispute with someone at work, remember to use the techniques of self-assertion described in Chapter 18.

   In addition to *what* you say, *how* you say it can be important. Psychologist Chris Kleinke (1986) has noted several speech cues that communicate self-confidence and add credibility to your message.
7. **Use an expressive tone of voice.** People who know a subject well or who believe in their point of view usually speak with an expressive, animated tone of voice. Speaking energetically, with good voice inflection, typically adds to one's credibility. Don't, however, use a higher-pitched voice, as this suggests nervousness.
8. **Speak fluently.** Before you speak, try to collect your thoughts so that you can get right to the point. Stammering, repeating yourself, frequent pauses, and overuse of "ahs," "uhms," and "you knows" implies incompetence or nervousness.
9. **Speak quickly.** A brisk rate of speech tends to be persuasive because it implies knowledge, competence, enthusiasm, and confidence. It also helps hold your listener's attention.
10. **Make use of nonverbal cues.** Remember that nonverbal cues, such as facial expressions and hand gestures, can help accentuate your message and structure it for listeners. In Western cultures, making eye contact while speaking is a particularly important nonverbal cue. In a group, don't talk to the ceiling, or to just one person. Try to make eye contact with each person in the group. That way, each feels included and knows that your message is meant for her or him. Another advantage of eye contact is that it lets you watch for feedback from listeners, whose reactions can guide your communication efforts.

Be aware that your behavior sends messages, too. Actions can parallel, amplify, contradict, or undermine what you are saying. For example, being late for a meeting tells others that they are not very important to you. Likewise, your manner of dress, personal grooming—even the way you decorate your personal workspace—all send messages. Think about the message you want to send and be sensitive to nonverbal channels of information.

Being a Good Listener

Effective communication is a two-way street. In addition to expressing yourself clearly you must also be a good listener. We have already discussed good classroom listening habits (Introduction) and listening in counseling situations (Chapter 17). Here are some additional pointers that apply to work settings.

1. **Make an honest effort to pay attention.** Stop what you are doing, actively give the speaker your attention, and resist distractions. Communicate your interest by posture and body position. Make eye contact with the speaker to show your interest.
2. **Try to identify the speaker's purpose.** Is he or she informing, requesting, discussing, persuading, correcting, digressing, or entertaining? Listen for main themes rather than isolated facts. A good listener will be able to answer this question: What is this person's central message? Thus, as you listen, pretend that you will have to summarize the speaker's message for someone else.
3. **Suspend evaluation.** As you listen, try to keep an open mind. Avoid hasty judging, disagreeing, rejecting, or criticizing. There will be time later to think about what was said. After you have heard an entire message, evaluate the information it contains and decide how to use it. Then reply or take action.
4. **Check your understanding.** Let the other person talk, but occasionally acknowledge and confirm what she or he is saying. Restate important parts of the message in your own words to make sure you understand it. Ask questions and clarify points you don't understand. Don't let doubts or ambiguities go unresolved.
5. **Pay attention to nonverbal messages.** Listeners must also be aware of the information provided by gestures, facial expressions, eye contact, touching, body positioning, and voice qualities such as volume, rate, pitch, emphasis, hesitations, and silences. Good listeners are also good observers.
6. **Accept responsibility for effective communication.** As a listener, it is up to you to actively search for meaning and value in what is said. You can facilitate communication as much by being a good listener as you can by being an effective speaker.

The art of effective communication is well worth cultivating. The points made here are basic, but they can go a long way toward ensuring your success at work—like, totally, abso-double-lutely, you know what I mean?

KNOWLEDGE BUILDER

Effective Communication at Work

REFLECT

Effective communication is important in many settings, not just at work. What changes could you make to improve your effectiveness as a listener and a speaker? Use the preceding discussion as a checklist to identify ways in which you could improve.

LEARNING CHECK

1. The sentence, "Copy Monica, Steve, and the bean counters with your input and let's circle the wagons in the AM," shows the danger of using loaded words. T or F?
2. "You've got to REM out some of the TSRs in your AUTOEXEC. BAT file and reboot if you want that software to run." For a beginning computer user, the problem with this message is its overuse of ____________________.
3. An expressive, higher-pitched tone of voice tends to be more persuasive and credible. T or F?
4. Paying attention to nonverbal messages is an element of effective communication for both speakers and listeners. T or F?

CRITICAL THINKING

5. From the perspective of social psychology, effective communication is likely to increase what dimension of group membership?

Answers: 1. F 2. jargon 3. F 4. T 5. Group cohesion.

Chapter in Review

How is psychology applied in business and industry?

- Applied psychology refers to the use of psychological principles and research methods to solve practical problems.
- Industrial-organizational psychologists are interested in the problems people face at work and in organizations. Typically they specialize in personnel psychology and human relations at work.
- Personnel psychologists try to match people with jobs by combining job analysis with a variety of selection procedures. These include gathering biodata, interviewing, giving standardized psychological tests (interest inventories, aptitude tests, and computerized tests), and using assessment centers.
- Two basic approaches to business and industrial management are scientific management (Theory X) and human relations approaches (Theory Y). Theory X is most concerned with work efficiency, whereas Theory Y emphasizes psychological efficiency.
- Theory Y methods include participative management, management by objectives, self-managed teams, and quality circles.
- Job satisfaction is related to productivity, absenteeism, morale, employee turnover, and other factors that affect overall business efficiency.
- Job satisfaction comes from a good fit between work and a person's interests, abilities, needs, and expectations. Job enrichment tends to increase job satisfaction.
- An active, vigilant coping style is most likely to produce good career decisions.
- Workers who fit comfortably within the culture of a business typically show good organizational citizenship.

What have psychologists learned about the effects of our physical and social environments?

- Environmental psychologists are interested in the effects of behavioral settings, physical or social environments, and human territoriality, among many other topics.
- Overpopulation is a major world problem, often reflected at an individual level in crowding.
- Animal experiments indicate that excessive crowding can be unhealthy. However, human research shows that psychological feelings of crowding do not always correspond to density (the number of people in a given space).
- One major consequence of crowding is attentional overload.
- A large number of practical problems—from noise pollution to architectural design—have come under the scrutiny of environmental psychologists. In many cases, effective behavioral solutions to such problems have been found, often as a result of first doing a careful environmental assessment.
- Research has shown that various psychological strategies can promote recycling.

How has psychology improved education?

- Educational psychologists seek to understand how people learn and teachers instruct. They are particularly interested in teaching strategies, and teaching styles, such as direct instruction and open teaching.

What does psychology reveal about juries and court verdicts?

- The psychology of law includes studies of courtroom behavior and other topics that pertain to the legal system. Psychologists also serve various consulting and counseling roles in legal, law enforcement, and criminal justice settings.
- Studies of mock juries show that jury decisions are often far from objective.
- Scientific jury selection is used in attempts to choose jurors who have particular characteristics. In some instances, this may result in juries that have a particular bias or that do not represent the community as a whole.
- A bias toward convicting defendants is characteristic of many death-qualified juries.

Can psychology enhance athletic performance?

- Sports psychologists seek to enhance sports performance and the benefits of sports participation. A careful task analysis of sports skills is one of the major tools for improving coaching and performance.
- A motor skill is a nonverbal response chain assembled into a smooth performance. Motor skills are guided by internal mental models called motor programs.
- Motor skills are refined through direct practice, but mental practice can also contribute to improvement.
- During moments of peak performance, physical, mental, and emotional states are optimal.

What can be done to improve communication at work?

- State your message clearly and precisely. Try to avoid overuse of obscure vocabulary, jargon, slang, and loaded words. Learn and use people's names. Be polite, but not servile. Be expressive when you speak. Pay attention to nonverbal cues and the messages they send.
- To be a good listener, actively pay attention, identify the speaker's purpose and core message, suspend evaluation while listening, check your understanding, and make note of nonverbal information.

Web Resources

Internet addresses frequently change. To find the sites listed here, visit www.thomsonedu.com/psychology/coon for an updated list of Internet addresses and direct links to relevant sites.

***Psychology: Gateways to Mind and Behavior* Website** Online quizzes, flash cards, and other helpful study aids for this text. www.thomsonedu.com/psychology/coon.

Living in Space Articles about the challenges of living in space.

Mars Academy A discussion of crew selection issues for possible trips to Mars.

Newsletter for Educational Psychologists Information and articles about the activities of educational psychologists.

Environmental Psychology From the Canadian Psychological Association; features articles on environmental psychology, with links to other sites.

Sport Psychology Articles, information, and links related to sports psychology.

The Industrial-Organizational Psychologist Online journal concerning I-O psychology.

ThomsonNOW™ Go to www.thomsonedu.com to link to ThomsonNow, your online study tool. First take the **Pre-Test** for this chapter to get your **Personalized Study Plan,** which will identify topics you need to review and direct you to online resources. Then take the **Post-Test** to determine what concepts you have mastered and what you still need work on.

InfoTrac College Edition For recent articles related to the application of psychology to athletics, use Key Words search for SPORTS PSYCHOLOGY. Go to www.thomsonedu.com/psychology/coon.

Interactive Learning

***PsychNow!* Version 2.0 CD-ROM** Interact with the material with *PsychNow!*'s animations, video clips, experiments, and interactive assessments. For this chapter, go to *8f. Environmental Psychology* to learn more about how environments affect our behavior.

appendix

Behavioral Statistics

THEME:

Statistics allow us to summarize the results of psychological studies and draw valid conclusions about behavior.

Dennis Coon

Key Questions

What are descriptive statistics?

How are statistics used to identify an average score?

What statistics do psychologists use to measure how much scores differ from one another?

What are inferential statistics?

How are correlations used in psychology?

Preview

Statistics from "Heads" to "Tails"

Let's say a friend of yours invites you to try your hand at a "game of chance." He offers to flip a coin and pay you a dollar if the coin comes up heads. If the coin shows tails, you must pay him a dollar. He flips the coin: tails—you pay him a dollar. He flips it again: tails. Again: tails. And again: tails. And again: tails.

At this point you are faced with a choice. Should you continue the game in an attempt to recoup your losses? Or should you assume that the coin is biased and quit before you really get "skinned"? Taking out a pocket calculator (and the statistics book you carry with you at all times), you compute the odds of obtaining five tails in a row from an unbiased coin. The probability is 0.031 (roughly 3 times out of 100).

If the coin really is honest, five consecutive tails is a rare event. Wisely, you decide that the coin is probably biased and refuse to play again. (Unless, of course, your "friend" is willing to take "tails" for the next five tosses!)

Perhaps a decision could have been made in this hypothetical example without using statistics. But notice how much clearer the situation becomes when it is expressed statistically.

Psychologists try to extract and summarize useful information from the observations they make. To do so, they use two major types of statistics. **Descriptive statistics** summarize or "boil down" numbers so they become more meaningful and easier to communicate to others. In comparison, **inferential statistics** are used for decision making, for generalizing from small samples, and for drawing conclusions. As was the case in the coin-flipping example, psychologists must often base decisions on limited data. Such decisions are much easier to make with the help of inferential statistics. Let's see how statistics are used in psychology.

Descriptive Statistics—Psychology by the Numbers

Let's say you have completed a study on human behavior. The results seem interesting, but can you really tell what your data reveal just by looking at a jumble of numbers? To get a clear picture of how people behaved, you will probably turn to descriptive statistics. By summarizing the results of your study, statistics will help you draw valid conclusions about what you observed.

Statistics bring greater clarity and precision to psychological thought and research. To see how, let's begin by considering three basic types of descriptive statistics: *graphical statistics,* measures of *central tendency,* and measures of *variability.* Let's start with **graphical statistics**, which present numbers pictorially, so they are easier to visualize.

Graphical Statistics

■ Table A.1 shows simulated scores on a test of hypnotic susceptibility given to 100 college students. With such disorganized data, it is hard to form an overall "picture" of the differences in hypnotic susceptibility. But by using a *frequency distribution,* large amounts of information can be neatly organized and summa-

Descriptive statistics Mathematical tools used to describe and summarize numeric data.

Inferential statistics Mathematical tools used for decision making, for generalizing from small samples, and for drawing conclusions.

Graphical statistics Techniques for presenting numbers pictorially, often by plotting them on a graph.

TABLE A.1

Raw Scores of Hypnotic Susceptibility

55	86	52	17	61	57	84	51	16	64
22	56	25	38	35	24	54	26	37	38
52	42	59	26	21	55	40	59	25	57
91	27	38	53	19	93	25	39	52	56
66	14	18	63	59	68	12	19	62	45
47	98	88	72	50	49	96	89	71	66
50	44	71	57	90	53	41	72	56	93
57	38	55	49	87	59	36	56	48	70
33	69	50	50	60	35	67	51	50	52
11	73	46	16	67	13	71	47	25	77

rized. A **frequency distribution** is made by breaking down the entire range of possible scores into classes of equal size. Next, the number of scores falling into each class is recorded. In ■ Table A.2, the raw data from ■ Table A.1 have been condensed into a frequency distribution. Notice how much clearer the pattern of scores for the entire group becomes.

Frequency distributions are often shown *graphically* to make them more "visual." A **histogram,** or graph of a frequency distribution, is made by labeling class intervals on the *abscissa* (horizontal line) and frequencies (the number of scores in each class) on the *ordinate* (vertical line). Next, bars are drawn for each class interval; the height of each bar is determined by the number of scores in each class (● Figure A.1). An alternate way of graphing scores is the more familiar **frequency polygon** (● Figure A.2). Here, points are placed at the center of each class interval to indicate the number of scores. Then the dots are connected by straight lines.

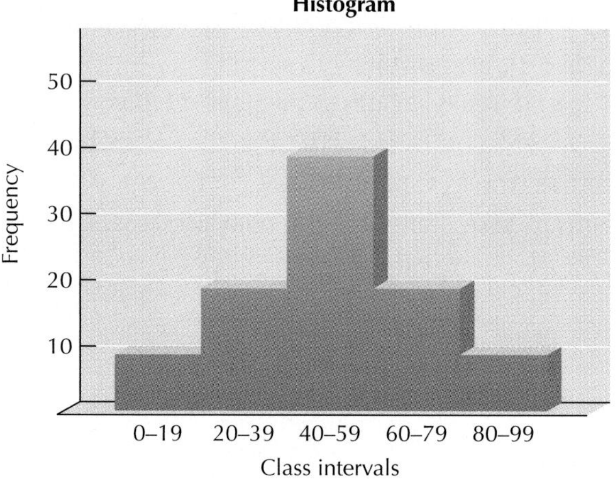

● **Figure A.1** Frequency histogram of hypnotic susceptibility scores contained in Table A.2.

Measures of Central Tendency

Notice in ■ Table A.2 that more scores fall in the range 40–59 than elsewhere. How can we show this fact? A measure of **central tendency** is simply a number describing a "typical score" around

TABLE A.2

Frequency Distribution of Hypnotic Susceptibility Scores

CLASS INTERVAL	NUMBER OF PERSONS IN CLASS
0–19	10
20–39	20
40–59	40
60–79	20
80–99	10

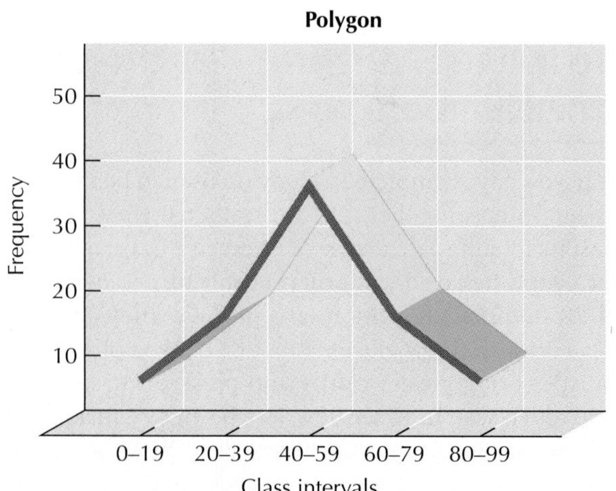

● **Figure A.2** Frequency polygon of hypnotic susceptibility scores contained in Table A.2.

which other scores fall. A familiar measure of central tendency is the mean, or "average." But as we shall see in a moment, there are other types of "averages" that can be used. To illustrate each we need an example: ■ Table A.3 shows the raw data for an imaginary experiment in which two groups of subjects were given a test of memory. Assume that one group was given a drug that might improve memory (let's call the drug Rememberine). The second group received a placebo. Is there a difference in memory scores between the two groups? It's difficult to tell without computing an average.

TABLE A.3

Raw Scores on a Memory Test for Subjects Taking Rememberine or a Placebo

SUBJECT	GROUP 1 REMEMBERINE	GROUP 2 PLACEBO
1	65	54
2	67	60
3	73	63
4	65	33
5	58	56
6	55	60
7	70	60
8	69	31
9	60	62
10	68	61
Sum	650	540
Mean	65	54
Median	66	60

$$\text{Mean} = \frac{\sum X}{N} \text{ or } \frac{\text{Sum of all scores, X}}{\text{number of scores}}$$

$$\text{Mean Group 1} = \frac{65 + 67 + 73 + 65 + 58 + 55 + 70 + 69 + 60 + 68}{10} = \frac{650}{10} = 65$$

$$\text{Mean Group 2} = \frac{54 + 60 + 63 + 33 + 56 + 60 + 60 + 31 + 62 + 61}{10} = \frac{540}{10} = 54$$

Median = the middle score or the mean of the two middle scores*

Median Group 1 = 55 58 60 65 [65 67] 68 69 70 73

$$= \frac{65 + 67}{2} = 66$$

Median Group 2 = 31 33 54 56 [60 60] 60 61 62 63

$$= \frac{60 + 60}{2} = 60$$

* [ ] indicates middle score(s).

The Mean

As one type of "average," the **mean** is calculated by adding all the scores for each group and then dividing by the total number of scores. Notice in ■ Table A.3 that the means reveal a difference between the two groups.

The mean is sensitive to extremely high or low scores in a distribution. For this reason it is not always the best measure of central tendency. (Imagine how distorted it would be to calculate average yearly incomes from a small sample of people that happened to include a multimillionaire.) In such cases the middle score in a group of scores—called the *median*—is used instead.

The Median

The **median** is found by arranging scores from the highest to the lowest and selecting the score that falls in the middle. In other words, half the values in a group of scores fall below the median and half fall above. Consider, for example, the following weights obtained from a small class of college students: 105, 111, 123, 126, 148, 151, 154, 162, 182. The median for the group is 148, the middle score. Of course, if there is an even number of scores, there will be no "middle score." This problem is handled by averaging the two scores that "share" the middle spot. This procedure yields a single number to serve as the median (see bottom panel of ■ Table A.3).

The Mode

A final measure of central tendency is the *mode*. The **mode** is simply the most frequently occurring score in a group of scores. If you were to take the time to count the scores in ■ Table A.3, you would find that the mode of Group 1 is 65, and the mode of Group

Frequency distribution A table that divides an entire range of scores into a series of classes and then records the number of scores that fall into each class.

Histogram A graph of a frequency distribution in which the number of scores falling in each class is represented by vertical bars.

Frequency polygon A graph of a frequency distribution in which the number of scores falling in each class is represented by points on a line.

Central tendency The tendency for a majority of scores to fall in the midrange of possible values.

Mean A measure of central tendency calculated by adding a group of scores and then dividing by the total number of scores.

Median A measure of central tendency found by arranging scores from the highest to the lowest and selecting the score that falls in the middle. That is, half the values in a group of scores fall above the median and half fall below.

Mode A measure of central tendency found by identifying the most frequently occurring score in a group of scores.

2 is 60. The mode is usually easy to obtain. However, the mode can be an unreliable measure, especially in a small group of scores. The mode's advantage is that it gives the score actually obtained by the greatest number of people.

Measures of Variability

Let's say a researcher discovers two drugs that lower anxiety in agitated patients. However, let's also assume that one drug consistently lowers anxiety by moderate amounts, whereas the second sometimes lowers it by large amounts, sometimes has no effect, or may even increase anxiety in some patients. Overall, there is no difference in the *average* (mean) amount of anxiety reduction. Even so, an important difference exists between the two drugs. As this example shows, it is not enough to simply know the average score in a distribution. Usually, we would also like to know if scores are grouped closely together or scattered widely.

Measures of **variability** provide a single number that tells how "spread out" scores are. When the scores are widely spread, this number gets larger. When they are close together it gets smaller. If you look again at the example in ■ Table A.3, you will notice that the scores within each group vary widely. How can we show this fact?

The Range

The simplest way would be to use the **range,** which is the difference between the highest and lowest scores. In Group 1 of our experiment, the highest score is 73 and the lowest is 55; thus, the range is 18 (73 − 55 = 18). In Group 2, the highest score is 63 and the lowest is 31; this makes the range 32. Scores in Group 2 are more spread out than those in Group 1.

The Standard Deviation

A better measure of variability is the **standard deviation** (an index of how much a typical score differs from the mean of a group of scores). To obtain the standard deviation, we find the deviation (or difference) of each score from the mean and then square it (multiply it by itself). These squared deviations are then added and averaged (the total is divided by the number of deviations). Taking the square root of this average yields the standard deviation (■ Table A.4). Notice again that the variability for Group 1 (5.4) is smaller than that for Group 2 (where the standard deviation is 11.3).

TABLE A.4

Computation of the Standard Deviation

GROUP 1 MEAN = 65		
SCORE MEAN	DEVIATION (d)	DEVIATION SQUARED (d^2)
65 − 65 =	0	0
67 − 65 =	2	4
73 − 65 =	8	64
65 − 65 =	0	0
58 − 65 =	−7	49
55 − 65 =	−10	100
70 − 65 =	5	25
69 − 65 =	4	16
60 − 65 =	−5	25
68 − 65 =	3	9
		292

$$SD = \sqrt{\frac{\text{sum of } d^2}{n}} = \sqrt{\frac{292}{10}} = \sqrt{29.2} = 5.4$$

GROUP 2 MEAN = 54		
SCORE MEAN	DEVIATION (d)	DEVIATION SQUARED (d^2)
54 − 54 =	0	0
60 − 54 =	6	36
63 − 54 =	9	81
33 − 54 =	−21	441
56 − 54 =	2	4
60 − 54 =	6	36
60 − 54 =	6	36
31 − 54 =	−23	529
62 − 54 =	8	64
61 − 54 =	7	49
		1276

$$SD = \sqrt{\frac{\text{sum of } d^2}{n}} = \sqrt{\frac{1276}{10}} = \sqrt{127.6} = 11.3$$

Standard Scores

A particular advantage of the standard deviation is that it can be used to "standardize" scores in a way that gives them greater meaning. For example, John and Heather both took psychology midterms, but in different classes. John earned a score of 118, and Heather scored 110. Who did better? It is impossible to tell without knowing what the average score was on each test, and whether John and Heather scored at the top, middle, or bottom of their classes. We would like to have one number that gives all this information. A number that does this is the *z-score.*

To convert an original score to a **z-score,** we subtract the mean from the score. The resulting number is then divided by the standard deviation for that group of scores. To illustrate, Heather had a score of 110 in a class with a mean of 100 and a standard deviation of 10. Therefore, her z-score is +1.0 (■ Table A.5). John's score of 118 came from a class having a mean of 100 and a standard deviation of 18; thus his z-score is also +1.0 (see ■ Table A.5). Originally it looked as if John did better on his midterm than Heather did. But we now see that relatively speaking, their scores were equivalent. Compared to other students, each was an equal distance above average.

TABLE A.5

Computation of a z-score

$$z = \frac{X - \overline{X}}{SD} = \text{or } \frac{\text{score} - \text{mean}}{\text{standard deviation}}$$

$$\text{Susan: } z = \frac{110 - 100}{10} = \frac{+10}{10} = +1.0$$

$$\text{John: } z = \frac{118 - 100}{18} = \frac{+18}{18} = +1.0$$

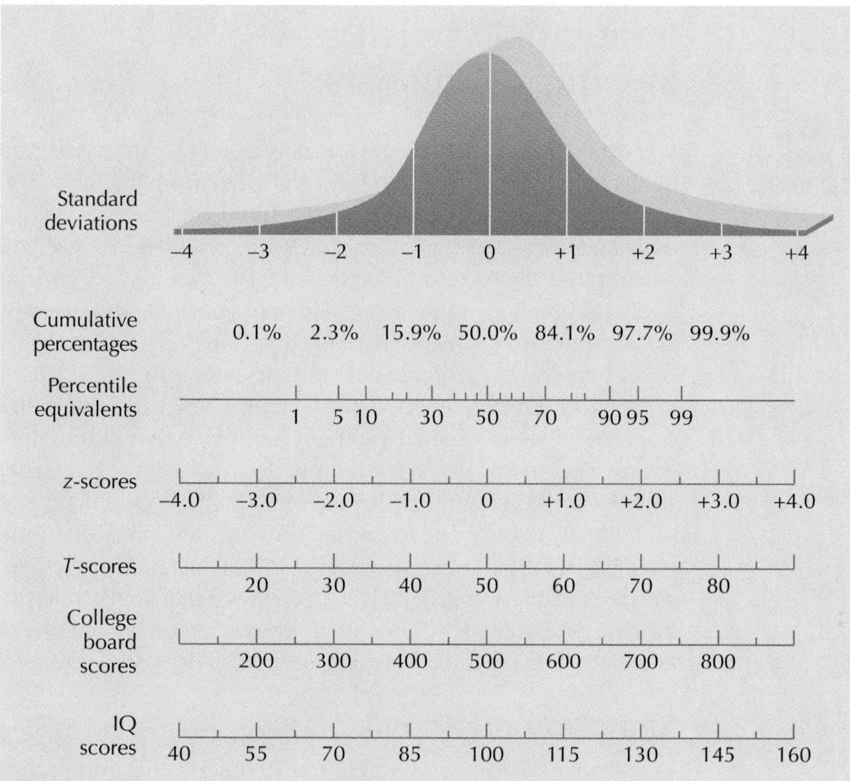

● **Figure A.3** The normal curve. The normal curve is an idealized mathematical model. However, many measurements in psychology closely approximate a normal curve. The scales you see here show the relationship of standard deviations, z-scores, and other measures to the curve.

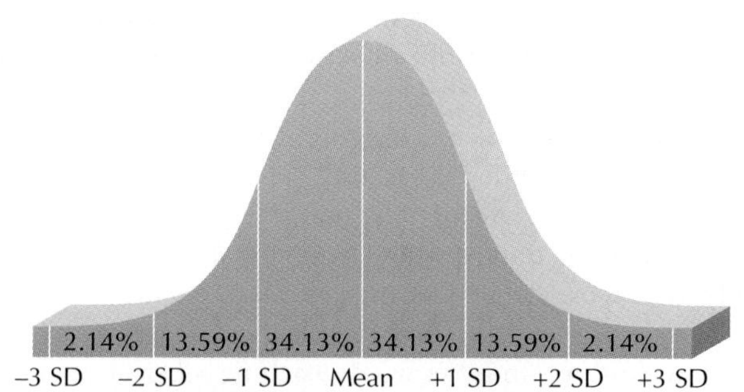

● **Figure A.4** Relationship between the standard deviation and the normal curve.

The Normal Curve

When chance events are recorded, we find that some outcomes have a high probability and occur very often, others have a lower probability and occur infrequently, and still others have little probability and occur rarely. As a result, the distribution (or tally) of chance events typically resembles a *normal curve* (● Figure A.3). A **normal curve** is bell-shaped, with a large number of scores in the middle, tapering to very few extremely high and low scores. Most psychological traits or events are determined by the action of a large number of factors. Therefore, like chance events, measures of psychological variables tend to roughly match a normal curve. For example, direct measurement has shown such characteristics as height, memory span, and intelligence to be distributed approximately along a normal curve. In other words, many people have average height, memory ability, and intelligence. However, as we move above or below average, fewer and fewer people are found.

It is very fortunate that so many psychological variables tend to form a normal curve, because much is known about the curve. One valuable property concerns the relationship between the standard deviation and the normal curve. Specifically, the standard deviation measures off set proportions of the curve above and below the mean. For example, in ● Figure A.4, notice that roughly 68 percent of all cases (IQ scores, memory scores, heights, or whatever) fall between one standard deviation above and below the mean (±1 SD), 95 percent of all cases fall between ±2 SD, and 99 percent of the cases can be found between ±3 SD from the mean.

■ Table A.6 gives a more complete account of the relationship between z-scores and the percentage of cases found in a particular area of the normal curve. Notice, for example, that 93.3 percent of all cases fall below a z-score of 11.5. A z-score of 1.5 on a test (no matter what the original, or "raw," score was) would be a good performance, because roughly 93 percent of all scores fall below this mark. Relationships between the standard deviation (or z-scores) and the normal curve do not change. This makes it possible to compare various tests or groups of scores if they come from distributions that are approximately normal.

KNOWLEDGE BUILDER

Descriptive Statistics

REFLECT

Let's say you ask 100 people how long they sleep each night and record their answers. How could you show these scores graphically?

Variability The tendency for a group of scores to differ in value. Measures of variability indicate the degree to which a group of scores differ from one another.

Range The difference between the highest and lowest scores in a group of scores.

Standard deviation An index of how much a typical score differs from the mean of a group of scores.

z-score A number that tells how many standard deviations above or below the mean a score is.

Normal curve A bell-shaped distribution, with a large number of scores in the middle, tapering to very few extremely high and low scores.

TABLE A.6

Computation of a z-score

Z-SCORE	PERCENTAGE OF AREA TO THE LEFT OF THIS VALUE	PERCENTAGE OF AREA TO THE RIGHT OF THIS VALUE
−3.0 SD	00.1	99.9
−2.5 SD	00.6	99.4
−2.0 SD	02.3	97.7
−1.5 SD	06.7	93.3
−1.0 SD	15.9	84.1
−0.5 SD	30.9	69.1
0.0 SD	50.0	50.0
+0.5 SD	69.1	30.9
+1.0 SD	84.1	15.9
+1.5 SD	93.3	06.7
+2.0 SD	97.7	02.3
+2.5 SD	99.4	00.6
+3.0 SD	99.9	00.1

To find the average amount of sleep for your subjects, would you prefer to know the most frequent score (the mode), the middle score (the median), or the arithmetic average (the mean)?

How could you determine how much sleep times vary? That is, would you prefer to know the highest and lowest scores (the range), or the average amount of variation (the standard deviation)?

How would you feel about receiving your scores on classroom tests in the form of z-scores?

Do you think the distribution of scores in your study of sleep would form a normal curve? Why or why not?

LEARNING CHECK

1. ______________ statistics summarize numbers so they become more meaningful or easier to communicate; ______________ statistics are used for decision making, generalizing, or drawing conclusions.
2. Histograms and frequency polygons are graphs of frequency distributions. T or F?
3. Three measures of central tendency are the mean, the median, and the ______________.
4. If scores are placed in order, from the smallest to the largest, the median is defined as the middle score. T or F?
5. As a measure of variability, the standard deviation is defined as the difference between the highest and lowest scores. T or F?
6. A z-score of −1 tells us that a score fell one standard deviation below the mean in a group of scores. T or F?
7. In a normal curve, 99 percent of all scores can be found between +1 and −1 standard deviations from the mean. T or F?

Answers: 1. Descriptive, inferential 2. T 3. mode 4. T 5. F 6. T 7. F

Inferential Statistics—Significant Numbers

You would like to know if boys are more aggressive than girls. You observe a group of 5-year-old boys and girls on a playground. After collecting data for a week you find that the boys committed more aggressive acts than the girls. Could this difference just be a meaningless fluctuation in aggression? Or does it show conclusively that boys are more aggressive than girls? Inferential statistics were created to answer just such questions.

As stated earlier, **inferential statistics** are techniques that allow us to make inferences. That is, they allow us to generalize from the behavior of small groups of subjects to that of the larger groups they represent. For example, let's say that a researcher studies the effects of a new therapy on a small group of depressed individuals. Is she or he interested only in these particular individuals? Usually not, because except in rare instances, psychologists seek to discover general laws of behavior that apply widely to humans and animals. Undoubtedly the researcher would like to know if the therapy holds any promise for all depressed people.

Samples and Populations

In any scientific study, we would like to observe the entire set, or **population,** of subjects, objects, or events of interest. However, this is usually impossible or impractical. Observing all Catholics, all cancer patients, or all mothers-in-law could be both impractical (because all are large populations) and impossible (because people change denominations, may be unaware of having cancer, and change their status as relatives). In such cases, **samples** (smaller cross sections of a population) are selected, and observations of the samples are used to draw conclusions about the entire population.

For any sample to be meaningful, it must be **representative.** That is, the sample group must truly reflect the membership and characteristics of the larger population. In our earlier hypothetical study of a memory drug, it would be essential for the sample of 20 people to be representative of the general population. A very important aspect of representative samples is that their members are chosen at **random.** In other words, each member of the population must have an equal chance of being included in the sample.

Significant Differences

In our imaginary drug experiment, we found that the average memory score was higher for the group given the drug than it was for persons who didn't take the drug (the placebo group). Certainly this result is interesting, but could it have occurred by chance? If two groups were repeatedly tested (with neither receiving any drug), their average memory scores would sometimes differ. How much must two means differ before we can consider the difference "real" (not due to chance)?

Notice that the question is similar to one discussed earlier: How many tails in a row must we obtain when flipping a coin before we can conclude that the coin is biased? In the case of the coin, we noted that obtaining five tails in a row is a rare event.

Thus, it became reasonable to assume that the coin was biased. Of course, it is possible to get five tails in a row when flipping an honest coin. But because this outcome is unlikely, we have good reason to suspect that something other than chance (a loaded coin, for instance) caused the results. Similar reasoning is used in tests of statistical significance.

Tests of **statistical significance** provide an estimate of how often experimental results could have occurred by chance alone. The results of a significance test are stated as a probability. This probability gives the odds that the observed difference was due to chance. In psychology, any experimental result that could have occurred by chance 5 times (or less) out of 100 (in other words, a probability of .05 or less) is considered *significant*. In our memory experiment, the probability is .025 ($p = .025$) that the group means would differ as they do by chance alone. This allows us to conclude with reasonable certainty that the drug actually did improve memory scores.

Correlation—Rating Relationships

Psychologists are very interested in detecting relationships between events: Are children from single-parent families more likely to misbehave at school? Is wealth related to happiness? Is there a relationship between childhood exposure to lead and IQ at age 10? Is the chance of having a heart attack related to having a hostile personality? All of these are questions about correlation.

Many of the statements that psychologists make about behavior do not result from the use of experimental methods. Rather, they come from keen observations and measures of existing phenomena. A psychologist might note, for example, that the higher a couple's socioeconomic and educational status, the smaller the number of children they are likely to have. Or that grades in high school are related to how well a person is likely to do in college. Or even that as rainfall levels increase within a given metropolitan area, crime rates decline. In these instances, we are dealing with the fact that two variables are **correlating** (varying together in some orderly fashion).

The simplest way of visualizing a correlation is to construct a **scatter diagram.** In a scatter diagram, two measures (grades in high school and grades in college, for instance) are obtained. One measure is indicated by the X axis and the second by the Y axis. The scatter diagram plots the intersection (crossing) of each pair of measurements as a single point. Many such measurement pairs give pictures like those shown in ● Figure A.5.

Relationships

● Figure A.5 also shows scatter diagrams of three basic kinds of relationships between variables (or measures). Graphs *a, b,* and *c* show *positive relationships* of varying strength. As you can see, in a **positive relationship,** increases in the X measure (or score) are matched by increases on the Y measure (or score). An example would be finding that higher IQ scores (X) are associated with higher

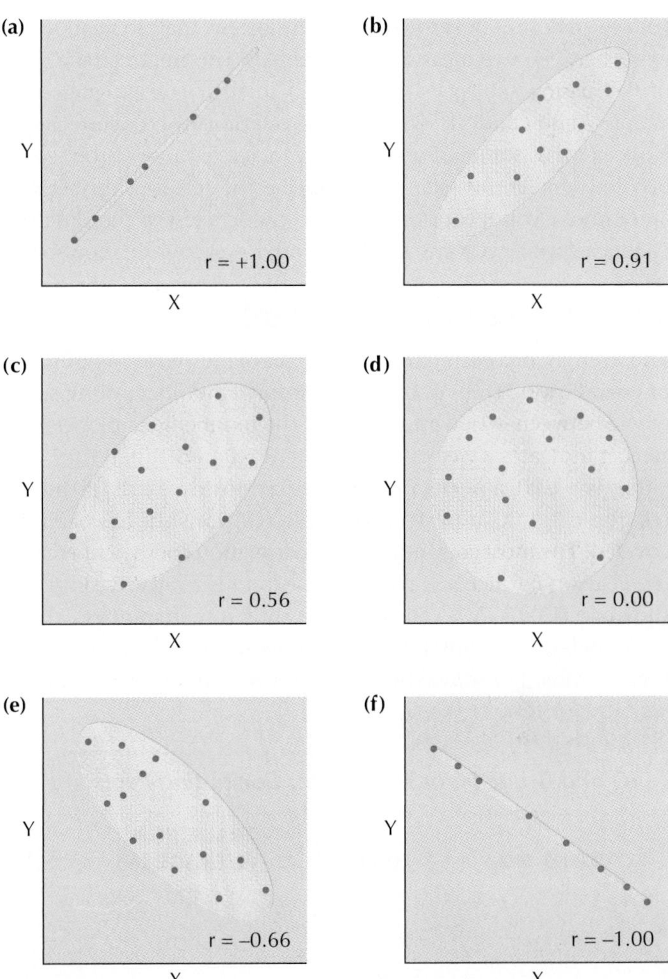

● **Figure A.5** Scatter diagrams showing various degrees of relationship for a positive, zero, and negative correlation.

Population An entire group of animals, people, or objects belonging to a particular category (for example, all college students or all married women).

Sample A smaller subpart of a population.

Representative sample A small, randomly selected part of a larger population that accurately reflects characteristics of the whole population.

Random selection Choosing a sample so that each member of the population has an equal chance of being included in the sample.

Statistical significance The degree to which an event (such as the results of an experiment) is unlikely to have occurred by chance alone.

Correlation The existence of a consistent, systematic relationship between two events, measures, or variables.

Scatter diagram A graph that plots the intersection of paired measures; that is, the points at which paired X and Y measures cross.

Positive relationship A mathematical relationship in which increases in one measure are matched by increases in the other (or decreases correspond with decreases).

college grades (Y). A **zero correlation** suggests that no relationship exists between two measures (see graph *d*). This might be the result of comparing subjects' hat sizes (X) to their college grades (Y). Graphs *e* and *f* both show a **negative relationship** (or correlation). Notice that as values of one measure increase, those of the second become smaller. An example might be the relationship between amount of alcohol consumed and scores on a test of coordination: Higher alcohol levels are correlated with lower coordination scores.

The Correlation Coefficient

The strength of a correlation can also be expressed as a **coefficient of correlation.** This coefficient is simply a number falling somewhere between +1.00 and −1.00. If the number is zero or close to zero, it indicates a weak or nonexistent relationship. If the correlation is +1.00, a **perfect positive relationship** exists; if the correlation is −1.00, a **perfect negative relationship** has been discovered. The most commonly used correlation coefficient is called the Pearson *r*. Calculation of the Pearson *r* is relatively simple, as shown in ■ Table A.7. (The numbers shown are hypothetical.)

As stated in Chapter 1, correlations in psychology are rarely perfect. Most fall somewhere between zero and plus or minus 1. The closer the correlation coefficient is to +1.00 or −1.00, the stronger the relationship. An interesting example of some typical correlations is provided by a study that compared the IQs of adopted children with the IQs of their biological mothers. At age 4, the children's IQs correlated .28 with their biological mothers' IQs. By age 7 the correlation was .35. By age 13 it had grown to .38.

Prediction

Correlations often provide highly useful information. For instance, it is valuable to know that there is a correlation between cigarette smoking and lung cancer rates. Another example is the fact that higher consumption of alcohol during pregnancy is correlated with lower birth weight and a higher rate of birth defects. There is a correlation between the number of recent life stresses experienced and the likelihood of emotional disturbance. Many more examples could be cited, but the point is, correlations help us to identify relationships that are worth knowing.

Correlations are particularly valuable for making *predictions.* If we know that two measures are correlated, and we know a person's score on one measure, we can predict his or her score on the

TABLE A.7

IQ and Grade Point Average for Computing Pearson r

STUDENT NO.	IQ (X)	GRADE POINT AVERAGE (Y)	X SCORE SQUARED (X^2)	Y SCORE SQUARED (Y^2)	X TIMES Y (XY)
1	110	1.0	12,100	1.00	110.0
2	112	1.6	12,544	2.56	179.2
3	118	1.2	13,924	1.44	141.6
4	119	2.1	14,161	4.41	249.9
5	122	2.6	14,884	6.76	317.2
6	125	1.8	15,625	3.24	225.0
7	127	2.6	16,124	6.76	330.2
8	130	2.0	16,900	4.00	260.0
9	132	3.2	17,424	10.24	422.4
10	134	2.6	17,956	6.76	348.4
11	136	3.0	18,496	9.00	408.0
12	138	3.6	19,044	12.96	496.8
Total	1503	27.3	189,187	69.13	3488.7

$$r = \frac{\Sigma XY - \frac{(\Sigma X)(\Sigma Y)}{N}}{\sqrt{\left[\Sigma X^2 - \frac{(\Sigma X)^2}{N}\right]\left[\Sigma Y^2 - \frac{(\Sigma Y)^2}{N}\right]}}$$

$$= \frac{3488.7 - \frac{1503(27.3)}{12}}{\sqrt{\left[189{,}187 - \frac{(1503)^2}{2}\right]\left[69.13\ 2\ \frac{(27.3)^2}{12}\right]}}$$

$$= \frac{69.375}{81.088} = 0.856 = 0.86$$

other. For example, most colleges have formulas that use multiple correlations to decide which applicants have the best chances for success. Usually the formula includes such predictors as high school GPA, teacher ratings, extracurricular activities, and scores on the *Scholastic Assessment Test* (SAT) or some similar test. Although no single predictor is perfectly correlated with success in college, together the various predictors correlate highly and provide a useful technique for screening applicants.

There is an interesting "trick" you can do with correlations that you may find useful. It works like this: If you *square* the correlation coefficient (multiply *r* by itself), you will get a number telling the **percent of variance** (amount of variation in scores) accounted for by the correlation. For example, the correlation between IQ scores and college grade point average is .5. Multiplying .5 times .5 gives .25, or 25 percent. This means that 25 percent of the variation in college grades is accounted for by knowing IQ scores. In other words, with a correlation of .5, college grades are "squeezed" into an oval like the one shown in ● Figure A.5*c*. IQ scores take away some of the possible variation in corresponding grade point averages. If there were no correlation between IQ and grades, grades would be completely free to vary, as shown in ● Figure A.5*d*.

Along the same line, a correlation of +1.00 or −1.00 means that 100 percent of the variation in the Y measure is accounted for by knowing the X measure: If you know a person's X score, you can tell exactly what the Y score is. An example that comes close to this state of affairs is the high correlation (.86) between the IQs of identical twins. In any group of identical twins, 74 percent of the variation in the "Y" twins' IQs is accounted for by knowing the IQs of their siblings (the "X's").

Correlation and Causation

It is very important to recognize that finding a correlation between two measures does not automatically mean that one causes the other: Correlation does not demonstrate causation. When a correlation exists, the best we can say is that two variables are related. Of course, this does not mean that it is impossible for two correlated variables to have a cause-and-effect relationship. Rather, it means that we cannot *conclude,* solely on the basis of correlation, that a causal link exists. To gain greater confidence that a cause-and-effect relationship exists, an experiment must be performed (see Chapter 1).

Often, two correlated measures are related as a result of the influence of a third variable. For example, we might observe that the more hours students devote to studying, the better their grades. Although it is tempting to conclude that more studying produces (causes) better grades, it is possible (indeed, it is probable) that grades and the amount of study time are both related to the amount of motivation or interest a student has.

The difference between cause-and-effect data and data that reveal a relationship of unknown origin is one that should not be forgotten. Because we rarely run experiments in daily life, the information on which we act is largely correlational. This should make us more humble and more tentative in the confidence with which we make pronouncements about human behavior.

KNOWLEDGE BUILDER

Inferential Statistics

REFLECT

Informally, you have probably inferred something about a population of people based on the small sample you have observed directly. How could statistics improve the accuracy of your inferences?

If you were trying to test whether a drug causes birth defects, what level of statistical significance would you use? If you were doing a psychology experiment, what level would you be comfortable with?

See if you can identify at least one positive relationship and one negative relationship involving human behavior that you have observed. How strong to you think the correlation would be in each case? What correlation coefficient would you expect to see?

A woman you know drinks more coffee in the winter than she does in the summer. She also has more colds in the winter. She decides to reduce the amount of coffee she drinks to help prevent colds. What can you tell her about correlation and causation?

LEARNING CHECK

1. In inferential statistics, observations of a ________________ are used to make inferences and draw conclusions about an entire ________________.
2. A representative sample can be obtained by selecting members of the sample at ________________.
3. If the results of an experiment could have occurred by chance alone less than 25 times out of 100, the result is considered statistically significant. T or F
4. A scatter diagram can be used to plot and visualize a ________________ between two groups of scores.
5. In a negative relationship, increases in X scores correspond to decreases in Y scores. T or F?
6. A perfect positive correlation exists when the correlation coefficient is 0.00. T or F?
7. It is important to remember that correlation does not demonstrate ________________.

Answers: 1. sample, population 2. random 3. F 4. correlation 5. T 6. F 7. causation

Zero correlation The absence of a (linear) mathematical relationship between two measures.

Negative relationship A mathematical relationship in which increases in one measure are matched by decreases in the other.

Coefficient of correlation A statistical index ranging from −1.00 to +1.00 that indicates the direction and degree of correlation.

Perfect positive relationship A mathematical relationship in which the correlation between two measures is +1.00.

Perfect negative relationship A mathematical relationship in which the correlation between two measures is −1.00.

Percent of variance A portion of the total amount of variation in a group of scores.

Causation The act of causing some effect.

Appendix in Review

What are descriptive statistics?
- Descriptive statistics organize and summarize numbers.
- Graphical statistics, such as histograms and frequency polygons, are used to represent numbers pictorially.

How are statistics used to identify an average score?
- Measures of central tendency define the "typical score" in a group of scores.
- The mean is found by adding all the scores in a group and then dividing by the total number of scores.
- The median is found by arranging a group of scores from the highest to the lowest and selecting the middle score.
- The mode is the score that occurs most frequently in a group of scores.

What statistics do psychologists use to measure how much scores differ from one another?
- Measures of variability provide a number that shows how much scores vary.
- The range is the difference between the highest score and the lowest score in a group of scores.
- The standard deviation shows how much, on average, all the scores in a group differ from the mean.
- To change an original score into a standard score (or z-score), you must subtract the mean from the score and then divide the result by the standard deviation.
- Standard scores (z-scores) tell, in standard deviation units, how far above or below the mean a score is. This allows meaningful comparisons between scores from different groups.
- Scores that form a normal curve are easy to interpret because the properties of the normal curve are well known.

What are inferential statistics?
- Inferential statistics are used to make decisions, to generalize from samples, and to draw conclusions.
- Most studies in psychology are based on samples. Findings from representative samples are assumed to also apply to entire populations.
- In psychology experiments, differences in the average performance of groups could occur purely by chance. Tests of statistical significance tell us if the observed differences between groups are common or rare. If a difference is large enough to be improbable, it suggests that the results did not occur by chance alone.

How are correlations used in psychology?
- Pairs of scores that vary together in an orderly fashion are said to be correlated.
- The relationship between two variables or measures can be positive or negative.
- Correlation coefficients tell how strongly two groups of scores are related.
- Correlation alone does not demonstrate cause-and-effect links between variables or measures.

Web Resources

Internet addresses frequently change. To find the sites listed here, visit www.thomsonedu.com/psychology/coon for an updated list of Internet addresses and direct links to relevant sites.

***Psychology: Gateways to Mind and Behavior* Website** Online quizzes, flash cards, and other helpful study aids for this text. www.thomsonedu.com/psychology/coon.

Statistics to Use If you enter a series of numbers, this site will calculate basic descriptive statistics and more advanced inferential statistics. www.physics.csbsju.edu/stats.

ThomsonNOW™ Go to www.thomsonedu.com to link to ThomsonNow, your online study tool. First take the **Pre-Test** for this chapter to get your **Personalized Study Plan**, which will identify topics you need to review and direct you to online resources. Then take the **Post-Test** to determine what concepts you have mastered and what you still need work on.

InfoTrac College Edition For recent articles related to inferential statistics, use Key Words search for NORMAL CURVE. Go to www.thomsonedu.com/psychology/coon.

Interactive Learning

***PsychNow!* Version 2.0 CD-ROM** Interact with the material with *PsychNow!*'s animations, video clips, experiments, and interactive assessments. For this chapter, go to *1c. Research Methods* to learn more about how statistics are used in psychological research.

Glossary

Ablation Surgical removal of tissue.

Absolute threshold The minimum amount of physical energy necessary to produce a sensation.

Abstract principles Concepts and ideas removed from specific examples and concrete situations.

Accommodation (perceptual) Changes in the shape of the lens of the eye.

Accommodation (Piaget) In Piaget's theory, the modification of existing mental patterns to fit new demands (that is, mental schemes are changed to accommodate new information or experiences).

Acculturative stress Stress caused by the many changes and adaptations required when a person moves to a foreign culture.

Acetylcholine The neurotransmitter released by neurons to activate muscles.

Acquaintance (date) rape Forced intercourse that occurs in the context of a date or other voluntary encounter.

Acquisition The period in conditioning during which a response is reinforced.

Action component How one tends to act toward the object of an attitude.

Action potential The nerve impulse.

Activation-synthesis hypothesis An attempt to explain how dream content is affected by motor commands in the brain that occur during sleep, but are not carried out.

Active listener A person who knows how to maintain attention, avoid distractions, and actively gather information from lectures.

Activity theory Theory stating that the best adjustment to aging occurs when people remain active mentally, socially, and physically.

Actor–observer bias When making attributions, the tendency to the behavior of others to internal causes while attributing one's own behavior to external causes (situations and circumstances).

Acute stress disorder A psychological disturbance lasting up to 1 month following stresses that would produce anxiety in anyone who experienced them.

Adaptation level An internal or mental "average" or "medium" point that is used to judge amounts.

Adaptive behaviors Actions that aid attempts to survive and adapt to changing conditions.

Adjustment disorder An emotional disturbance caused by ongoing stressors within the range of common experience.

Adolescence The culturally defined period between childhood and adulthood.

Adrenal glands Endocrine glands that arouse the body, regulate salt balance, adjust the body to stress, and affect sexual functioning.

Affectional needs Emotional needs for love and affection.

Ageism An institutionalized tendency to discriminate on the basis of age; discrimination or prejudice based on age.

Aggression Any action carried out with the intention of harming another person or object.

Aggression cues Stimuli or signals that are associated with aggression and that tend to elicit it.

Aggressive pornography Media depictions of sexual violence or of forced participation in sexual activity.

Agnosia An inability to grasp the meaning of stimuli, such as words, objects, or pictures.

Agoraphobia (without panic) The person fears that something extremely embarrassing will happen to them if they leave the house or enter unfamiliar situations.

Alarm reaction First stage of the G.A.S., during which bodily resources are mobilized to cope with a stressor.

Alcohol myopia Shortsighted thinking and perception that occurs during alcohol intoxication.

Algorithm A learned set of rules that always leads to the correct solution of a problem.

All-or-nothing thinking Classifying objects or events as absolutely right or wrong, good or bad, acceptable or unacceptable, and so forth.

Alpha waves Large, slow brain waves associated with relaxation and falling asleep.

Altered state of consciousness (ASC) A condition of awareness distinctly different in quality or pattern from waking consciousness.

Alzheimer's disease An age-related disease characterized by memory loss, mental confusion, and, in its later stages, by a nearly total loss of mental abilities.

Ambivalence Mixed positive and negative feelings or simultaneous attraction and repulsion.

Ambivalent attachment An emotional bond marked by conflicting feelings of affection, anger, and emotional turmoil.

Amphetamine psychosis A loss of contact with reality due to repeated amphetamine use.

Amygdala A part of the limbic system (within the brain) that produces fear responses.

Anal stage The psychosexual stage corresponding roughly to the period of toilet training (ages 1 to 3).

Anal-expulsive personality A disorderly, destructive, cruel, or messy person.

Anal-retentive personality A person who is obstinate, stingy, or compulsive, and who generally has difficulty "letting go."

Androgen Any of a number of male sex hormones, especially testosterone.

Androgyny The presence of both "masculine" and "feminine" traits in a single person (as masculinity and femininity are defined within one's culture).

Andropause A gradual decline in testosterone levels in older men.

Anger control Personal strategies for reducing or curbing anger.

Anhedonia An inability to feel pleasure.

Anima An archetype representing the female principle.

Animal model In research, an animal whose behavior is used to derive principles that may apply to human behavior.

Animus An archetype representing the male principle.

Anorexia nervosa Active self-starvation or a sustained loss of appetite that has psychological origins.

Anosmia Loss or impairment of the sense of smell.

Antecedents Events that precede a response.

Anthropomorphic error The error of attributing human thoughts, feelings, or motives to animals, especially as a way of explaining their behavior.

Antidepressants Mood-elevating drugs.

Antipsychotics Drugs that, in addition to having tranquilizing effects, also tend to reduce hallucinations and delusional thinking. (Also called **major tranquilizers.**)

Antisocial personality A person who lacks a conscience, is emotionally shallow, is impulsive, is selfish, and tends to manipulate others.

Anxiety Apprehension, dread, or uneasiness similar to fear but based on an unclear threat.

Anxiety disorder Disruptive feelings of fear, apprehension, or anxiety, or distortions in behavior that are anxiety related.

Anxiety reduction hypothesis Explains the self-defeating nature of avoidance responses as a result of the reinforcing effects of relief from anxiety.

Anxiolytics Drugs (such as Valium) that produce relaxation or reduce anxiety.

Aphasia A speech disturbance resulting from brain damage.

Apparent-distance hypothesis An explanation of the moon illusion stating that the horizon seems more distant than the night sky.

Applied psychology The use of psychological principles and research methods to solve practical problems.

Approach–approach conflict Choosing between two positive, or desirable, alternatives.

Approach–avoidance conflict Being attracted to and repelled by the same goal or activity.

Aptitude A capacity for learning certain abilities.

Aptitude test A test that rates a person's potential to learn skills required by various occupations.

Archetype A universal idea, image, or pattern, found in the collective unconscious.

Architectural psychology Study of the effects buildings have on behavior and the design of buildings using behavioral principles.

Arousal theory Assumes that people prefer to maintain ideal, or comfortable, levels of arousal.

Artificial intelligence (AI) Any artificial system (often a computer program) that is capable of human-like problem solving or intelligent responding.

Assertiveness training Instruction in how to be self-assertive.

Assessment center A program set up within an organization to conduct in-depth evaluations of job candidates.

Assimilation In Piaget's theory, the application of existing mental patterns to new situations (that is, the new situation is assimilated to existing mental schemes).

Association cortex All areas of the cerebral cortex that are not primarily sensory or motor in function.

Astigmatism Defects in the cornea, lens, or eye that cause some areas of vision to be out of focus.

Attention Voluntarily focusing on a specific sensory input.

Attentional overload A stressful condition caused when sensory stimulation, information, and social contacts make excessive demands on attention.

Attention-deficit/hyperactivity disorder (ADHD) A behavioral problem characterized by short attention span, restless movement, and impaired learning capacity.

Attitude A learned tendency to respond to people, objects, or institutions in a positive or negative way.

Attitude scale A collection of attitudinal statements with which respondents indicate agreement or disagreement.

Attribution The process of making inferences about the causes of one's own behavior, and that of others. In emotion, the process of attributing arousal to a particular source.

Authenticity In Carl Rogers's terms, the ability of a therapist to be genuine and honest about his or her own feelings.

Authoritarian parents Parents who enforce rigid rules and demand strict obedience to authority.

Authoritarian personality A personality pattern characterized by rigidity, inhibition, prejudice, and an excessive concern with power, authority, and obedience.

Authoritative parents Parents who supply firm and consistent guidance combined with love and affection.

Autism A severe disorder involving mutism, sensory spin-outs, sensory blocking, tantrums, unresponsiveness to others, and other difficulties.

Autokinetic effect The apparent movement of a stationary pinpoint of light displayed in a darkened room.

Autonomic nervous system (ANS) The system of nerves that connects the brain with the internal organs and glands.

Autonomy versus shame and doubt A conflict created when growing self-control (autonomy) is pitted against feelings of shame or doubt.

Aversion therapy Suppressing an undesirable response by associating it with aversive (painful or uncomfortable) stimuli.

Aversive stimulus A stimulus that is painful or uncomfortable.

Avoidance learning Learning to make a response in order to postpone or prevent discomfort.

Avoidance–avoidance conflict Choosing between two negative, or mutually undesirable, alternatives.

Avoidant attachment An emotional bond marked by a tendency to resist commitment to others.

Axon Nerve cell fiber that carries information away from the cell body of a neuron.

Axon terminals Branching fibers at the ends of axons.

Babbling The repetition by infants of meaningless language sounds (including both vowel and consonant sounds).

Bait shyness An unwillingness or hesitation on the part of animals to eat a particular food.

Barnum effect The tendency to consider a personal description accurate if it is stated in very general terms.

Base rate The basic rate at which an event occurs over time; the basic probability of an event.

Basic anxiety A primary form of anxiety that arises from living in a hostile world.

Basic emotions The first distinct emotions to emerge in infancy.

Basic needs The first four levels of needs in Maslow's hierarchy; lower needs tend to be more potent than higher needs.

Basic suggestion effect The tendency of hypnotized persons to carry out suggested actions as if they were involuntary.

Behavior modification The application of learning principles to change human behavior, especially maladaptive behavior.

Behavior therapy Any therapy designed to actively change behavior.

Behavioral assessment Recording the frequency of various behaviors.

Behavioral contract A formal agreement stating behaviors to be changed and consequences that apply.

Behavioral dieting Weight reduction based on changing exercise and eating habits, rather than temporary self-starvation.

Behavioral genetics The study of inherited behavioral traits and tendencies.

Behavioral medicine The study of behavioral factors in medicine, physical illness, and medical treatment.

Behavioral personality theory Any model of personality that emphasizes learning and observable behavior.

Behavioral risk factors Behaviors that increase the chances of disease, injury, or premature death.

Behavioral setting A smaller area within an environment whose use is well defined, such as a bus depot, waiting room, or lounge.

Behaviorism School of psychology that emphasizes the study of overt, observable behavior.

Belief component What a person thinks or believes about the object of an attitude.

Bereavement Period of emotional adjustment that follows the death of a loved one.

Beta waves Small, fast brain waves associated with being awake and alert.

Beta-endorphin A natural, painkilling brain chemical similar to morphine.

Biased sample A subpart of a larger population that does not accurately reflect characteristics of the whole population.

Bilingualism An ability to speak two languages.

Binge drinking Consuming five or more drinks in a short time (four drinks for women).

Biodata Detailed biographical information about a job applicant.

Biofeedback Information given to a person about his or her ongoing bodily activities; aids voluntary regulation of bodily states.

Biological aging Physiological changes that accompany growing older.

Biological biasing effect Hypothesized effect that prenatal exposure to sex hormones has on development of the body, nervous system, and later behavior patterns.

Biological predisposition The presumed hereditary readiness of humans to learn certain skills, such as how to use language, or a readiness to behave in particular ways.

Biological rhythm Any repeating cycle of biological activity, such as sleep and waking cycles or changes in body temperature.

Bipolar disorders Emotional disorders involving both depression and mania or hypomania.

Bipolar I disorder A mood disorder in which a person has episodes of mania (excited, hyperactive, energetic, grandiose behavior) and also periods of deep depression.

Bipolar II disorder A mood disorder in which a person is mostly depressed (sad, despondent, guilt ridden) but has also had one or more episodes of mild mania (hypomania).

Bisexual A person romantically and erotically attracted to both men and women.

Blind spot An area of the retina lacking visual receptors.

Bottom-up processing Organizing perceptions by beginning with low-level features.

Brainstem The lowest portions of the brain, including the cerebellum, medulla, pons, and reticular formation.

Brainstorming Method of creative thinking that separates the production and evaluation of ideas.

Brainwashing Engineered or forced attitude change involving a captive audience.

Brief psychodynamic therapy A modern therapy based on psychoanalytic theory but designed to produce insights more quickly.

Brightness constancy The apparent (or relative) brightness of objects remains the same as long as they are illuminated by the same amount of light.

Broca's area A language area related to grammar and pronunciation.

Broken record A self-assertion technique involving repeating a request until it is acknowledged.

Browser Software that facilitates access to text, images, sounds, video, and other information stored in formats used on the Internet.

Bulimia nervosa Excessive eating (gorging) usually followed by self-induced vomiting and/or taking laxatives.

Burnout A job-related condition of mental, physical, and emotional exhaustion.

Bystander apathy Unwillingness of bystanders to offer help during emergencies or to become involved in others' problems.

Caffeinism Excessive consumption of caffeine, leading to dependence and a variety of physical and psychological complaints.

Cannon-Bard theory States that activity in the thalamus causes emotional feelings and bodily arousal to occur simultaneously.

Cardinal trait A personality trait so basic that all of a person's activities relate to it.

Caregiving styles Identifiable patterns of parental caretaking and interaction with children.

Case study An in-depth focus on all aspects of a single person.

Castration Surgical removal of the testicles or ovaries.

Cataplexy A sudden temporary paralysis of the muscles.

Catatonic schizophrenia Schizophrenia marked by stupor, rigidity, unresponsiveness, posturing, mutism, and, sometimes, agitated, purposeless behavior.

Causation The act of causing some effect.

Central nervous system (CNS) The brain and spinal cord.

Central tendency The tendency for a majority of scores to fall in the midrange of possible values.

Central traits The core traits that characterize an individual personality.

Cerebellum A brain structure that controls posture and coordination.

Cerebral cortex The outer layer of the cerebrum.

Character Personal characteristics that have been judged or evaluated; a person's desirable or undesirable qualities.

Chromosomes Thread-like "colored bodies" in the nucleus of each cell that are made up of DNA.

Chronological age A person's age in years.

Circadian rhythms Cyclical changes in bodily functions and arousal levels that vary on a schedule approximating a 24-hour day.

Clairvoyance The purported ability to perceive events at a distance or through physical barriers.

Classical conditioning A form of learning in which reflex responses are associated with new stimuli.

Client-centered (or person-centered) therapy A nondirective therapy based on insights gained from conscious thoughts and feelings; emphasizes accepting one's true self.

Climacteric A point during late middle age when males experience a significant change in health, vigor, or appearance.

Clinical method Studying psychological problems and therapies in clinical settings.

Clinical psychologist A psychologist who specializes in the treatment of psychological and behavioral disturbances or who does research on such disturbances.

Clinical study A detailed investigation of a single person, especially one suffering from some injury or disease.

Coefficient of correlation A statistical index ranging from −1.00 to +1.00 that indicates the direction and degree of correlation.

Coercive power Social power based on the ability to punish others.

Cognition The process of thinking or mentally processing information (images, concepts, words, rules, and symbols).

Cognitive behaviorism An approach that combines behavioral principles with cognition (perception, thinking, anticipation) to explain behavior.

Cognitive dissonance An uncomfortable clash between self-image, thoughts, beliefs, attitudes, or perceptions and one's behavior.

Cognitive interview Use of various cues and strategies to improve the memory of eyewitnesses.

Cognitive learning Higher-level learning involving thinking, knowing, understanding, and anticipation.

Cognitive map Internal images or other mental representations of an area (maze, city, campus, and so forth) that underlie an ability to choose alternative paths to the same goal.

Cognitive therapy A therapy directed at changing the maladaptive thoughts, beliefs, and feelings that underlie emotional and behavioral problems.

Collective unconscious A mental storehouse for unconscious ideas and images shared by all humans.

Color blindness A total inability to perceive colors.

Common traits Personality traits that are shared by most members of a particular culture.

Community health campaign A community-wide education program that provides information about how to lessen risk factors and promote health.

Community mental health center A facility offering a wide range of mental health services, such as prevention, counseling, consultation, and crisis intervention.

Comparison level A personal standard used to evaluate rewards and costs in a social exchange.

Compensation Counteracting a real or imagined weakness, such as feelings of inadequacy or inferiority, by emphasizing desirable traits or seeking to excel in the area of weakness or in other areas.

Compliance Bending to the requests of a person who has little or no authority or other form of social power.

Computer simulations Computer programs that mimic some aspect of human thinking, decision making, or problem solving.

Concept A generalized idea representing a class of related objects or events.

Concept formation The process of classifying information into meaningful categories.

Conceptual rule A formal rule for deciding whether an object or event is an example of a particular concept.

Concrete operational stage Period of intellectual development during which children become able to use the concepts of time, space, volume, and number, but in ways that remain simplified and concrete, rather than abstract.

Condensation Combining several people, objects, or events into a single dream image.

Conditioned emotional response (CER) An emotional response that has been linked to a previously nonemotional stimulus by classical conditioning.

Conditioned response (CR) A learned response elicited by a conditioned stimulus.

Conditioned stimulus (CS) A stimulus that evokes a response because it has been repeatedly paired with an unconditioned stimulus.

Conditioning chamber An apparatus designed to study operant conditioning in animals; a Skinner box.

Conditions of worth Internal standards used to judge the value of one's thoughts, actions, feelings, or experiences.

Conduct disorder A pattern in which children consistently violate rules and behave aggressively and destructively.

Conduction deafness Poor transfer of sounds from the eardrum to the inner ear.

Cones Visual receptors for colors and daylight visual acuity.

Conflict A stressful condition that occurs when a person must choose between incompatible or contradictory alternatives.

Conformity Bringing one's behavior into agreement or harmony with norms or with the behavior of others in a group.

Congenital problems Problems or defects that originate during prenatal development in the womb.

Conjunctive concept A class of objects that have two or more features in common. (For example, to qualify as an example of the concept an object must be both red *and* triangular.)

Connotative meaning The subjective, personal, or emotional meaning of a word or concept.

Conscience The part of the superego that causes guilt when its standards are not met.

Conscious Region of the mind that includes all mental contents a person is aware of at any given moment.

Consciousness Mental awareness of sensations, perceptions, memories, and feelings.

Consequences Effects that follow a response.

Conservation In Piaget's theory, mastery of the concept that the weight, mass, and volume of matter remains unchanged (is conserved) even when the shape or appearance of objects changes.

Consistency With respect to child discipline, the maintenance of stable rules of conduct.

Consolidation Process by which relatively permanent memories are formed in the brain.

Constructive processing Reorganizing or updating memories on the basis of logic, reasoning, or the addition of new information.

Contact comfort A pleasant and reassuring feeling human and animal infants get from touching or clinging to something soft and warm, usually their mother.

Context Information surrounding a stimulus.

Continuous reinforcement A schedule in which every correct response is followed by a reinforcer.

Control Altering conditions that influence behavior. Where pain is concerned, *control* refers to an ability to regulate the pain stimulus.

Control group In a controlled experiment, the group of subjects exposed to all experimental conditions or variables *except* the independent variable.

Control questions In a polygraph exam, questions that almost always provoke anxiety.

Conventional moral reasoning Moral thinking based on a desire to please others or to follow accepted rules and values.

Convergent thought Thinking directed toward discovery of a single established correct answer; conventional thinking.

Conversion disorder A bodily symptom that mimics a physical disability but is actually caused by anxiety or emotional distress.

Conviction Beliefs that are important to a person and that evoke strong emotion.

Cooing Spontaneous repetition of vowel sounds by infants.

Cooperative play Play in which two or more children must coordinate their actions; if children don't cooperate the game ends.

Coping statements Reassuring, self-enhancing statements that are used to stop self-critical thinking.

Correlation The existence of a consistent, systematic relationship between two events, measures, or variables.

Correlational method Making measurements to discover relationships between events.

Correlational study A nonexperimental study designed to measure the degree of relationship (if any) between two or more events, measures, or variables.

Corticalization An increase in the relative size of the cerebral cortex.

Counseling psychologist A psychologist who specializes in the treatment of milder emotional and behavioral disturbances.

Counselor A mental health professional who specializes in helping people with problems not involving serious mental disorder; for example, marriage counselors, career counselors, or school counselors.

Counterirritation Using mild pain to block more intense or long-lasting pain.

Covert reinforcement Using positive imagery to reinforce desired behavior.

Covert sensitization Use of aversive imagery to reduce the occurrence of an undesired response.

Cranial nerves Major nerves that leave the brain without passing through the spinal cord.

Creative self The "artist" in each of us that creates a unique identity and style of life.

Cretinism Stunted growth and mental retardation caused by an insufficient supply of thyroid hormone.

Crisis intervention Skilled management of a psychological emergency.

Critical incidents Situations that arise in a job, with which a competent worker must be able to cope.

Critical situations Situations during childhood that are capable of leaving a lasting imprint on personality.

Critical thinking An ability to evaluate, compare, analyze, critique, and synthesize information.

Cross-stimulation effect In group problem solving, the tendency of one person's ideas to trigger ideas from others.

Crowding A subjective feeling of being overstimulated by a loss of privacy or by the nearness of others (especially when social contact with them is unavoidable).

Crystallized abilities Abilities that a person has intentionally learned; accumulated knowledge and skills.

CT scan Computed tomography scan; a computer-enhanced X-ray image of the brain or body.

Cue An external stimuli that guides responses, especially by signaling the presence or absence of reinforcement.

Cult A group that professes great devotion to some person and follows that person almost without question; cult members are typically victimized by their leaders in various ways.

Cultural relativity The idea that behavior must be judged relative to the values of the culture in which it occurs.

Culture An ongoing pattern of life, characterizing a society at a given point in history.

Culture-fair test A test designed to minimize the importance of skills and knowledge that may be more common in some cultures than in others.

Curve of forgetting A graph that shows the amount of memorized information remembered after varying lengths of time.

Curvilinear relationship A relationship that forms a curved line when graphed.

Cyclothymic disorder Moderate manic and depressive behavior that persists for 2 years or more.

Dark adaptation Increased retinal sensitivity to light.

Daydream A vivid waking fantasy.

Death-qualified jury A jury composed of people who favor the death penalty or at least are indifferent to it.

Decay When referring to memory, the fading or weakening of memories assumed to occur when memory traces become weaker.

Declarative memory That part of long-term memory containing specific factual information.

Deductive thought Thought that applies a general set of rules to specific situations; for example, using the laws of gravity to predict the behavior of a single falling object.

Deep lesioning Removal of tissue within the brain by use of an electrode.

Deep sleep Stage 4 sleep; the deepest form of normal sleep.

Defense mechanism A habitual and often unconscious psychological process used to reduce anxiety.

Deinstitutionalization Reduced use of full-time commitment to mental institutions to treat mental disorders.

Delayed speech Speech that begins well after the normal age for language development has passed.

Delta waves Large, slow brain waves that occur in deeper sleep (stages 3 and 4).

Delusion A false belief held against all contrary evidence.

Delusional disorder A psychosis marked by severe delusions of grandeur, jealousy, persecution, or similar preoccupations.

Dementia Serious mental impairment in old age caused by physical deterioration of the brain.

Demonology In medieval Europe, the study of demons and the treatment of persons "possessed" by demons.

Dendrites Nerve cell fibers that receive incoming messages from other nerve cells.

Denial Protecting oneself from an unpleasant reality by refusing to perceive it or believe it.

Denotative meaning The exact, dictionary definition of a word or concept; its objective meaning.

Density The number of people in a given space or, inversely, the amount of space available to each person.

Dependent variable In an experiment, the condition (usually a behavior) that is affected by the independent variable.

Depressant A substance that decreases activity in the body and nervous system.

Depression A state of despondency marked by feelings of powerlessness and hopelessness.

Depressive disorders Emotional disorders primarily involving sadness, despondency, and depression.

Deprivation In development, the loss or withholding of normal stimulation, nutrition, comfort, love, and so forth; a condition of lacking.

Depth cues Perceptual features that impart information about distance and three-dimensional space.

Depth perception The ability to see three-dimensional space and to accurately judge distances.

Description In scientific research, the process of naming and classifying.

Descriptive statistics Mathematical tools used to describe and summarize numeric data.

Desensitization A reduction in emotional sensitivity to a stimulus. Can be used to deliberately reduce fear or anxiety by repeatedly exposing a person to emotional stimuli while the person is deeply relaxed.

Determinism The idea that all behavior has prior causes that would completely explain one's choices and actions if all such causes were known.

Detoxification In the treatment of alcoholism, the withdrawal of the patient from alcohol.

Developmental level An individual's current state of physical, emotional, and intellectual development.

Developmental milestone A significant turning point or marker in personal development.

Developmental psychology The study of progressive changes in behavior and abilities from conception to death.

Developmental task Any skill that must be mastered, or personal change that must take place, for optimal development.

Deviation IQ An IQ obtained statistically from a person's relative standing in his or her age group; that is, how far above or below average the person's score was relative to other scores.

Diagnostic interview An interview used to find out how a person is feeling and what complaints or symptoms he or she has.

Difference threshold A change in stimulus intensity that is detectable to an observer.

Diffusion of responsibility Spreading the responsibility to act among several people; reduces the likelihood that help will be given to a person in need.

Direct instruction Presentation of factual information by lecture, demonstration, and rote practice.

Direct observation Assessing behavior through direct surveillance.

Discovery learning Learning based on insight and understanding.

Discrimination Treating members of various social groups differently in circumstances where their rights or treatment should be identical.

Discriminative stimuli Stimuli that precede rewarded and nonrewarded responses in operant conditioning.

Disease-prone personality A personality type associated with poor health; marked by persistent negative emotions, including anxiety, depression, and hostility.

Disengagement theory of aging Theory stating that it is normal for older people to withdraw from society and from roles they held earlier.

Dishabituation A reversal of habituation.

Disinhibition The removal of inhibition; results in acting out behavior that normally would be restrained.

Disjunctive concept A concept defined by the presence of at least one of several possible features. (For example, to qualify an object must be either blue *or* circular.)

Disorganized schizophrenia Schizophrenia marked by incoherence, grossly disorganized behavior, bizarre thinking, and flat or grossly inappropriate emotions.

Displaced aggression Redirecting aggression to a target other than the actual source of one's frustration.

Displacement Directing emotions or actions toward safe or unimportant dream images.

Dissociative amnesia Loss of memory (partial or complete) for important information related to personal identity.

Dissociative disorder Temporary amnesia, multiple personality, or depersonalization.

Dissociative fugue Sudden travel away from home, plus confusion about one's personal identity.

Dissociative identity disorder The presence of two or more distinct personalities (multiple personality).

Disuse Theory that memory traces weaken when memories are not periodically used or retrieved.

Divergent thought Thinking that produces many ideas or alternatives; a major element in original or creative thought.

Divided attention Allotting mental space or effort to various tasks or parts of a task.

DNA Deoxyribonucleic acid, a molecular structure that contains coded genetic information.

Dogmatism An unwarranted positiveness or certainty in matters of belief or opinion.

Dominant gene A gene whose influence will be expressed each time the gene is present.

Dominant hemisphere A term usually applied to the side of a person's brain that produces language.

Door-in-the-face effect The tendency for a person who has refused a major request to subsequently be more likely to comply with a minor request.

Double approach–avoidance conflict Being simultaneously attracted to and repelled by each of two alternatives.

Double standard Applying different standards for judging the appropriateness of male and female sexual behavior.

Double-blind experiment An arrangement in which both subjects and experimenters are unaware of whether subjects are in the experimental group or the control group.

Down syndrome A genetic disorder caused by the presence of an extra chromosome; results in mental retardation.

Downward comparison Comparing yourself with a person who ranks lower than you on some dimension.

Dream processes Mental filters that hide the true meanings of dreams.

Dream symbols Images in dreams whose personal or emotional meanings differ from their literal meanings; serve as visible signs of hidden ideas, desires, impulses, emotions, relationships, and so forth.

Drive Any stimulus (especially an internal stimulus such as hunger, thirst, or a drive for success) strong enough to goad a person to action.

Drug interaction A combined effect of two drugs that exceeds the addition of one drug's effects to the other.

Drug tolerance A reduction in the body's response to a drug.

Dynamic touch Touch experienced when the body is in motion; a combination of sensations from skin receptors, muscles, and joints.

Dyslexia An inability to read with understanding, often caused by a tendency to misread letters (by seeing their mirror images, for instance).

Dyspareunia Genital pain before, during, or after sexual intercourse.

Dysthymic disorder Moderate depression that persists for 2 years or more.

Early childhood education program Programs that provide stimulating intellectual experiences, typically for disadvantaged preschoolers.

Echo A brief continuation of sensory activity in the auditory system after a sound is heard.

Echolalia A compulsion, sometimes observed in autistic children, to repeat everything that is said.

Educational psychology The field that seeks to understand how people learn and how teachers instruct.

Ego The executive part of personality that directs rational behavior.

Ego ideal The part of the superego representing ideal behavior; a source of pride when its standards are met.

Egocentric thought Thought that is self-centered and fails to consider the viewpoints of others.

Eidetic imagery The ability to retain a "projected" mental image long enough to use it as a source of information.

Ejaculation The release of sperm and seminal fluid by the male at the time of orgasm.

Elaborative rehearsal Rehearsal that links new information with existing memories and knowledge.

Electra conflict A girl's sexual attraction to her father and feelings of rivalry with her mother.

Electrical stimulation of the brain (ESB) Direct electrical stimulation and activation of brain tissue.

Electroconvulsive shock (ECS) An electric current passed directly through the brain, producing a convulsion.

Electroconvulsive therapy (ECT) A treatment for severe depression, consisting of an electric shock passed directly through the brain, which induces a convulsion.

Electrode Any device (such as a wire, needle, or metal plate) used to electrically stimulate nerve tissue or to record its activity.

Electroencephalograph (EEG) A device that detects, amplifies, and records electrical activity in the brain.

Emblems Gestures that have widely understood meanings within a particular culture.

Emotion A state characterized by physiological arousal, changes in facial expression, gestures, posture, and subjective feelings.

Emotional appraisal Evaluating the personal meaning of a stimulus or situation.

Emotional attachment An especially close emotional bond that infants form with their parents, caregivers, or others.

Emotional component One's feelings toward the object of an attitude.

Emotional expression Outward signs that an emotion is occurring.

Emotional feelings The private, subjective experience of having an emotion.

Emotional intelligence Emotional competence, including empathy, self-control, self-awareness, and other skills.

Emotion-focused coping Managing or controlling one's emotional reaction to a stressful or threatening situation.

Empathic arousal Emotional arousal that occurs when you feel some of another person's pain, fear, or anguish.

Empathy A capacity for taking another's point of view; the ability to feel what another is feeling.

Empathy-helping relationship Observation that we are most likely to help someone else when we feel emotions such as empathy and compassion.

Empty nest syndrome Psychological disturbance experienced by some women after their last child leaves home.

Encoding Converting information into a form in which it will be retained in memory.

Encoding failure Failure to store sufficient information to form a useful memory.

Encopresis A lack of bowel control; "soiling."

Encounter group A group experience that emphasizes intensely honest interchanges among participants regarding feelings and reactions to one another.

Endocrine system Glands whose secretions pass directly into the bloodstream or lymph system.

Endogenous depression Depression that appears to be produced from within (perhaps by chemical imbalances in the brain), rather than as a reaction to life events.

Engineering psychology (human factors engineering) A specialty concerned with making machines and work environments compatible with human perceptual and physical capacities.

Engram A "memory trace" in the brain.

Enrichment Deliberately making an environment more novel, complex, and perceptually or intellectually stimulating.

Enuresis An inability to control urination, particularly with regard to bed-wetting.

Environment ("nurture") The sum of all external conditions affecting development, including especially the effects of learning.

Environmental assessment Measurement and analysis of the effects an environment has on the behavior of people within that environment.

Environmental psychology The formal study of how environments affect behavior.

Epinephrine (adrenaline) An adrenal hormone that tends to arouse the body; epinephrine is associated with fear.

Episodic drive A drive that occurs in distinct episodes.

Episodic memory A subpart of declarative memory that records personal experiences that are linked with specific times and places.

Equal-status contact Social interaction that occurs on an equal footing, without obvious differences in power or status.

Erectile disorder An inability to maintain an erection for lovemaking.

Erogenous zones Areas of the body that produce pleasure and/or provoke erotic desire.

Eros Freud's name for the "life instincts."

Escape Reducing discomfort by leaving frustrating situations or by psychologically withdrawing from them.

Escape learning Learning to make a response in order to end an aversive stimulus.

Estrogen Any of a number of female sex hormones.

Estrus Changes in the sexual drives of animals that create a desire for mating; particularly used to refer to females in heat.

Ethnocentrism Placing one's own group or race at the center that is, tending to reject all other groups but one's own.

Ethologist A person who studies the natural behavior patterns of animals.

Eugenics Selective breeding for desirable characteristics.

Evolutionary psychology Study of the evolutionary origins of human behavior patterns.

Excitement phase The first phase of sexual response, indicated by initial signs of sexual arousal.

Existential therapy An insight therapy that focuses on the elemental problems of existence, such as death, meaning, choice, and responsibility; emphasizes making courageous life choices.

Expectancy An anticipation concerning future events or relationships, including anticipation about the effect a response will have, especially regarding reinforcement.

Experiential intelligence Specialized knowledge and skills acquired through learning and experience.

Experiment A formal trial undertaken to confirm or disconfirm a fact or principle.

Experimental group In a controlled experiment, the group of subjects exposed to the independent variable or experimental condition.

Experimental method Investigating behavior through controlled experimentation.

Experimenter effect Changes in subjects' behavior caused by the unintended influence of an experimenter's actions.

Expert power Social power derived from possession of knowledge or expertise.

Expert systems Computer programs designed to respond as a human expert would; programs based on the knowledge and rules that underlie human expertise in specific topics.

Explicit memory A memory that a person is aware of having; a memory that is consciously retrieved.

Expressive behaviors Behaviors that express or communicate emotion or personal feelings.

External cause A cause of behavior that is assumed to lie outside a person.

Extinction The weakening of a conditioned response through removal of reinforcement.

Extracellular thirst Thirst caused by a reduction in the volume of fluids found between body cells.

Extraneous variables Conditions or factors excluded from influencing the outcome of an experiment.

Extrasensory perception (ESP) The purported ability to perceive events in ways that cannot be explained by known capacities of the sensory organs.

Extrinsic motivation Motivation based on obvious external rewards, obligations, or similar factors.

Extrovert A person whose attention is directed outward; a bold, outgoing person.

Eye movement desensitization and reprocessing (EMDR) A technique for reducing fear or anxiety; based on holding upsetting thoughts in mind while rapidly moving the eyes from side to side.

Facial agnosia An inability to recognize familiar faces.

Facial feedback hypothesis States that sensations from facial expressions help define what emotion a person feels.

Fallacy of positive instances The tendency to remember or notice information that fits one's expectations while forgetting discrepancies.

Familial retardation Mild mental retardation associated with homes that are intellectually, nutritionally, and emotionally impoverished.

Family therapy Technique in which all family members participate, both individually and as a group, to change destructive relationships and communication patterns.

Feedback Information returned to a person about the effects a response has had; also known as knowledge of results.

Feeling of knowing A feeling that allows people to predict beforehand whether they will be able to remember something.

Female orgasmic disorder A persistent inability to reach orgasm during lovemaking.

Female sexual arousal disorder A lack of physical arousal to sexual stimulation.

Figure-ground organization Part of a stimulus appears to stand out as an object (figure) against a less prominent background (ground).

Five-factor model Proposes that there are five universal dimensions of personality.

Fixation (cognition) In problem solving, a tendency to repeat wrong solutions or faulty responses, especially as a result of becoming blind to alternatives.

Fixation (Freudian) A lasting conflict developed as a result of frustration or overindulgence.

Fixed interval (FI) schedule A reinforcer is given only when a correct response is made after a set amount of time has passed since the last reinforced response. Responses made during the time interval are not reinforced.

Fixed ratio (FR) schedule A set number of correct responses must be made to get a reinforcer. For example, a reinforcer is given for every four correct responses.

Flashbulb memories Memories created at times of high emotion that seem especially vivid.

Flexibility In tests of creativity, flexibility is indicated by the number of different types of solutions produced.

Flextime A work schedule that allows flexible starting and quitting times.

Fluency In tests of creativity, fluency refers to the total number of solutions produced.

Fluid abilities Innate, nonlearned abilities based on perceptual, motor, or intellectual speed and flexibility.

fMRI scan Magnetic resonance imaging that records brain activity.

Foot-in-the-door effect The tendency for a person who has first complied with a small request to be more likely later to fulfill a larger request.

Forced teaching Accelerated learning at a pace dictated by an adult.

Forcible rape Sexual intercourse carried out against the victim's will, under the threat of violence or bodily injury.

Foreclosed identity The result of shutting down personal growth.

Formal operational stage Period of intellectual development characterized by thinking that includes abstract, theoretical, and hypothetical ideas.

Fovea An area at the center of the retina containing only cones.

Frame of reference An internal perspective relative to which events are perceived and evaluated.

Fragile-X syndrome A genetic form of mental retardation caused by a defect in the *X* chromosome.

Framing In thought, the terms in which a problem is stated or the way that it is structured.

Fraternal twins Twins conceived from two separate eggs.

Free association In psychoanalysis, the technique of having a client say anything that comes to mind, regardless of how embarrassing or unimportant it may seem.

Free will The idea that human beings are capable of freely making choices or decisions.

Frequency distribution A table that divides an entire range of scores into a series of classes and then records the number of scores that fall into each class.

Frequency polygon A graph of a frequency distribution in which the number of scores falling in each class is represented by points on a line.

Frequency theory Holds that tones up to 4,000 hertz are converted to nerve impulses that match the frequency of each tone.

Frontal lobes A brain area associated with movement, the sense of smell, and higher mental functions.

Frustration A negative emotional state that occurs when one is prevented from reaching a goal.

Frustration–aggression hypothesis States that frustration tends to lead to aggression.

Functional fixedness A rigidity in problem solving caused by an inability to see new uses for familiar objects.

Functional solution A detailed, practical, and workable solution.

Functionalism School of psychology concerned with how behavior and mental abilities help people adapt to their environments.

Fundamental attributional error The tendency to attribute the behavior of others to internal causes (personality, likes, and so forth).

g-factor A core of general intellectual ability that is assumed to explain the high correlations among various measures of intelligence.

Galvanic skin response (GSR) A change in the electrical resistance (or inversely, the conductance) of the skin, due to sweating.

Gate control theory Proposes that pain messages pass through neural "gates" in the spinal cord.

Gender Psychological and social characteristics associated with being male or female; defined especially by one's gender identity and learned gender roles.

Gender bias (in research) A tendency for females and female issues to be underrepresented in research, psychological or otherwise.

Gender identity One's personal, private sense of maleness or femaleness.

Gender role The pattern of behaviors that are regarded as "male" or "female" by one's culture; sometimes also referred to as a sex role.

Gender role socialization The process of learning gender behaviors considered appropriate for one's sex in a given culture.

Gender role stereotypes Oversimplified and widely held beliefs about the basic characteristics of men and women.

General adaptation syndrome (G.A.S.) A series of bodily reactions to prolonged stress; occurs in three stages: alarm, resistance, and exhaustion.

General intelligence test A test that measures a wide variety of mental abilities.

General solution A solution that correctly states the requirements for success but not in enough detail for further action.

Generalized anxiety disorder The person is in a chronic state of tension and worries about work, relationships, ability, or impending disaster.

Generativity versus stagnation A conflict of middle adulthood in which stagnant concern for oneself is countered by interest in guiding the next generation.

Genes Specific areas on a strand of DNA that carry hereditary information.

Genetic disorders Problems caused by defects in the genes or by inherited characteristics.

Genetic sex Sex as indicated by the presence of *XX* (female) or *XY* (male) chromosomes.

Genital sex Sex as indicated by the presence of male or female genitals.

Genital stage Period of full psychosexual development, marked by the attainment of mature adult sexuality.

Gerontologist One who scientifically studies aging and its effects.

Gestalt psychology A school of psychology emphasizing the study of thinking, learning, and perception in whole units, not by analysis into parts.

Gestalt therapy An approach that focuses on immediate experience and awareness to help clients rebuild thinking, feeling, and acting into connected wholes; emphasizes the integration of fragmented experiences.

Giftedness Either the possession of a high IQ or special talents or aptitudes.

Goal The target or objective of motivated behavior.

Gonadal sex Sex as indicated by the presence of ovaries (female) or testes (male).

Gonads The primary sex glands; the testes in males and ovaries in females.

Grammar A set of rules for combining language units into meaningful speech or writing.

Graphical statistics Techniques for presenting numbers pictorially, often by plotting them on a graph.

Grief An intense emotional state that follows the death of a lover, friend, or relative.

Group cohesiveness The degree of attraction among group members or their commitment to remaining in the group.

Group intelligence test Any intelligence test that can be administered to a group of people with minimal supervision.

Group prejudice Prejudice held out of conformity to group views.

Group sanctions Rewards and punishments (such as approval or disapproval) administered by groups to enforce conformity among members.

Group structure The network of roles, communication pathways, and power in a group.

Group therapy Psychotherapy conducted in a group setting to make therapeutic use of group dynamics.

Groupthink A compulsion by members of decision-making groups to maintain agreement, even at the cost of critical thinking.

Growth hormone A hormone, secreted by the pituitary gland, that promotes bodily growth.

Growth needs In Maslow's hierarchy, the higher-level needs associated with self-actualization.

Growth spurt An often dramatic acceleration in physical growth that coincides with puberty.

Guided imagery Intentional visualization of images that are calming, relaxing, or beneficial in other ways.

Gustation The sense of taste.

Habit A deeply ingrained, learned pattern of behavior.

Habituation A decrease in perceptual response to a repeated stimulus.

Hair cells Receptor cells within the cochlea that transduce vibrations into nerve impulses.

Halfway house A community-based facility for individuals making the transition from an institution (mental hospital, prison, and so forth) to independent living.

Hallucination An imaginary sensation, such as seeing, hearing, or smelling things that don't exist in the real world.

Hallucinogen A substance that alters or distorts sensory impressions.

Halo effect The tendency to generalize a favorable or unfavorable first impression to unrelated details of personality.

Handedness A preference for the right or left hand in most activities.

Hardy personality A personality style associated with superior stress resistance.

Hassle Any distressing, day-to-day annoyance; also called a *microstressor*.

Health psychology Study of the ways in which behavioral principles can be used to prevent illness and promote health.

Heredity ("nature") The transmission of physical and psychological characteristics from parents to offspring through genes.

Heterosexism The belief that heterosexuality is better or more natural than homosexuality.

Heterosexual A person romantically and erotically attracted to members of the opposite sex.

Heuristic Any strategy or technique that aids problem solving, especially by limiting the number of possible solutions to be tried.

Hidden observer A detached part of the hypnotized person's awareness that silently observes events.

Hierarchy A rank-ordered series of higher and lower amounts, levels, degrees, or steps.

Hierarchy of human needs Abraham Maslow's ordering of needs, based on their presumed strength or potency.

Higher order conditioning Classical conditioning in which a conditioned stimulus is used to reinforce further learning; that is, a CS is used as if it were a US.

Hippocampus A brain structure in the limbic system associated with emotion and the transfer of information from short-term memory to long-term memory.

Histogram A graph of a frequency distribution in which the number of scores falling in each class is represented by vertical bars.

Homeostasis A steady state of bodily equilibrium.

Homogamy Marriage of two people who are similar to one another.

Homosexual A person romantically and erotically attracted to same-sex persons.

Honesty test A paper-and-pencil test designed to detect attitudes, beliefs, and behavior patterns that predispose a person to dishonest behavior.

Hormonal sex Sex as indicated by a preponderance of estrogens (female) or androgens (male) in the body.

Hormone A glandular secretion that affects bodily functions or behavior.

Human growth sequence The pattern of physical development from conception to death.

Humanism An approach to psychology that focuses on human experience, problems, potentials, and ideals.

Hydrocephaly A buildup of cerebrospinal fluid within brain cavities.

Hyperopia Difficulty focusing nearby objects (farsightedness).

Hypersomnia Excessive daytime sleepiness.

Hypnagogic images Vivid mental images that may occur just as one enters stage 1 sleep.

Hypnosis An altered state of consciousness characterized by narrowed attention and increased suggestibility.

Hypnotic susceptibility One's capacity for becoming hypnotized.

Hypoactive sexual desire A persistent, upsetting loss of sexual desire.

Hypochondriac A person who complains about illnesses that appear to be imaginary.

Hypochondriasis A preoccupation with fears of having a serious disease. Ordinary physical signs are interpreted as proof that the person has a disease, but no physical disorder can be found.

Hypothalamus A small area of the brain that regulates many aspects of motivation and emotion, especially hunger, thirst, and sexual behavior.

Hypothesis The predicted outcome of an experiment or an educated guess about the relationship between variables.

Hypothetical possibilities Suppositions, guesses, or projections.

Icon A mental image or visual representation.

Id The primitive part of personality that remains unconscious, supplies energy, and demands pleasure.

Ideal self An idealized image of oneself (the person one would like to be).

Identical twins Twins who develop from a single egg and have identical genes.

Identification Feeling emotionally connected to a person and seeing oneself as like him or her.

Identity versus role confusion A major conflict of adolescence, involving the need to establish a consistent personal identity.

Illogical thought Thought that is intuitive, haphazard, or irrational.

Illusion A misleading or distorted perception.

Illustrators Gestures people use to illustrate what they are saying.

Image Most often, a mental representation that has picture-like qualities; an icon.

Imagery rehearsal Mentally rehearsing and changing a nightmare in an attempt to prevent it from reoccurring.

Imaginary audience The group of people a person imagines is watching (or will watch) his or her actions.

I-message A message that states the effect someone else's behavior has on you.

Imitation An attempt to match one's own behavior to another person's behavior.

Immune system System that mobilizes bodily defenses (such as white blood cells) against invading microbes and other disease agents.

Implicit memory A memory that a person does not know exists; a memory that is retrieved unconsciously.

Imprinting A rapid and relatively permanent type of learning that occurs during a limited period early in life.

Inattentional blindness Failure to perceive a stimulus that is in plain view, but not the focus of attention.

In-basket test A testing procedure that simulates the individual decision-making challenges that executives face.

Incentive value The value of a goal above and beyond its ability to fill a need.

Incongruence State that exists when there is a discrepancy between one's experiences and self-image or between one's self-image and ideal self.

Incongruent person A person who has an inaccurate self-image or whose self-image differs greatly from the ideal self.

Incremental problem solving Thinking marked by a series of small steps that lead to an original solution.

Independent variable In an experiment, the condition being investigated as a possible cause of some change in behavior. The values that this variable takes are chosen by the experimenter.

Individual intelligence test A test of intelligence designed to be given to a single individual by a trained specialist.

Individual traits Personality traits that define a person's unique individual qualities.

Individuating information Information that helps define a person as an individual, rather than as a member of a group or social category.

Inductive thought Thinking in which a general rule or principle is inferred from a series of specific examples; for instance, inferring the laws of gravity by observing many falling objects.

Industrial-organizational psychology A field that focuses on the psychology of work and on behavior within organizations.

Industry versus inferiority A conflict in middle childhood centered around lack of support for industrious behavior, which can result in feelings of inferiority.

Inferential statistics Mathematical tools used for decision making, for generalizing from small samples, and for drawing conclusions.

Information bits Meaningful units of information, such as numbers, letters, words, or phrases.

Information chunks Information bits grouped into larger units.

In-group A group with which a person identifies.

Initiative versus guilt A conflict centered around learning to take initiative while overcoming feelings of guilt about doing so.

Insanity A legal term that refers to a mental inability to manage one's affairs or to be aware of the consequences of one's actions.

Insecure-ambivalent attachment An anxious emotional bond marked by both a desire to be with a parent or caregiver and some resistance to being reunited.

Insecure-avoidant attachment An anxious emotional bond marked by a tendency to avoid reunion with a parent or caregiver.

Insight A sudden mental reorganization of a problem that makes the solution obvious.

Insomnia Difficulty in getting to sleep or staying asleep.

Inspection time The amount of time a person must look at a stimulus to make a correct judgment about it.

Instrumental behaviors Behaviors directed toward the achievement of some goal; behaviors that are instrumental in producing some effect.

Integrity versus despair A conflict in old age between feelings of personal integrity and the despair that occurs when previous life events are viewed with regret.

Intellectualization Separating emotion from a threatening or anxiety-provoking situation by talking or thinking about it in impersonal "intellectual" terms.

Intelligence An overall capacity to think rationally, act purposefully, and deal effectively with the environment.

Intelligence quotient (IQ) An index of intelligence defined as mental age divided by chronological age and multiplied by 100.

Interference The tendency for new memories to impair retrieval of older memories, and the reverse.

Internal cause A cause of behavior assumed to lie within a person for instance, a need, preference, or personality trait.

Internal images Mental images or visual depictions used in memory and thinking.

Internet An electronic network that enables computers to communicate with one another, usually through the telephone system.

Interpersonal attraction Social attraction to another person.

Interpretation Where pain is concerned, the meaning given to a stimulus.

Intersexual person An individual who has genitals suggestive of both sexes.

Interview (personality) A face-to-face meeting held for the purpose of gaining information about an individual's personal history, personality traits, current psychological state, and so forth.

Intimacy versus isolation The challenge in early adulthood of establishing intimacy with friends, family, a lover, or a spouse, versus experiencing a sense of isolation.

Intimate distance The most private space immediately surrounding the body (up to about 18 inches from the skin).

Intracellular thirst Thirst triggered when fluid is drawn out of cells due to an increased concentration of salts and minerals outside the cell.

Intrinsic motivation Motivation that comes from within, rather than from external rewards; motivation based on personal enjoyment of a task or activity.

Introspection To look within; to examine one's own thoughts, feelings, or sensations.

Introvert A person whose attention is focused inward; a shy, reserved, self-centered person.

Intuition Quick, impulsive thought that does not make use of formal logic or clear reasoning.

Intuitive thought Thinking that makes little or no use of reasoning and logic.

Ion channels Tiny openings through the axon membrane.

Iris Circular muscle that controls the amount of light entering the eye.

Isolation Separating contradictory thoughts or feelings into "logic-tight" mental compartments so that they do not come into conflict.

James-Lange theory States that emotional feelings follow bodily arousal and come from awareness of such arousal.

Jigsaw classroom A method of reducing prejudice; each student receives only part of the information needed to complete a project or prepare for a test.

Job analysis A detailed description of the skills, knowledge, and activities required by a particular job.

Job enrichment Making a job more personally rewarding, interesting, or intrinsically motivating; typically involves increasing worker knowledge.

Job satisfaction The degree to which a person is comfortable with or satisfied with his or her work.

Just noticeable difference (JND) Any noticeable difference in a stimulus.

Just-world beliefs Belief that people generally get what they deserve.

Keyword method As an aid to memory, using a familiar word or image to link two items.

Kinesics Study of the meaning of body movements, posture, hand gestures, and facial expressions; commonly called body language.

Kinesthetic senses The senses of body movement and positioning.

Knowledge of results (KR) Informational feedback.

Language Words or symbols, and rules for combining them, that are used for thinking and communication.

Large-group awareness training Any of a number of programs (many of them commercialized) that claim to increase self-awareness and facilitate constructive personal change.

Latency According to Freud, a period in childhood when psychosexual development is more or less interrupted.

Latent dream content The hidden or symbolic meaning of a dream, as revealed by dream interpretation and analysis.

Latent learning Learning that occurs without obvious reinforcement and that remains unexpressed until reinforcement is provided.

Lateralization Differences between the two sides of the body, especially differences in the abilities of the brain hemispheres.

Law of effect Responses that lead to desirable effects are repeated; those that produce undesirable results are not.

Leaderless group discussion A test of leadership that simulates group decision making and problem solving.

Learned helplessness A learned inability to overcome obstacles or to avoid punishment; learned passivity and inaction to aversive stimuli.

Learning Any relatively permanent change in behavior that can be attributed to experience.

Learning disorder Any problem with thinking, perception, language, attention, or activity levels that tends to impair learning ability.

Learning theorist A psychologist interested in the ways that learning shapes behavior and explains personality.

Legitimate power Social power based on a person's position as an agent of an accepted social order.

Lexigram A geometric shape used as a symbol for a word.

Libido In Freudian theory, the force, primarily pleasure oriented, that energizes the personality.

Life change units (LCUs) Numerical values assigned to each life event on the SRRS.

Life expectancy The average number of years a person of a given sex, race, and nationality can expect to live.

Life skills training A program that teaches stress reduction, self-protection, decision making, self-control, and social skills.

Life stages Widely recognized periods of life corresponding to broad phases of development.

Life-span perspective The study of continuity and change in behavior over a lifetime.

Lifestyle disease A disease related to health-damaging personal habits.

Light sleep Stage 1 sleep, marked by small irregular brain waves and some alpha waves.

Liking A relationship based on intimacy, but lacking passion and commitment.

Limbic system A system in the forebrain that is closely linked with emotional response.

Linear relationship A relationship that forms a straight line when graphed.

Links Connections built into Internet sites that let you "jump" from one site to the next.

Lock and key theory Holds that odors are related to the shapes of chemical molecules.

Logical consequences Reasonable consequences that are defined by parents.

Logical thought Drawing conclusions on the basis of formal principles of reasoning.

Logotherapy A form of existential therapy that emphasizes the need to find and maintain meaning in one's life.

Long sleeper A person who averages 9 hours of sleep or more per night.

Long-term memory (LTM) The memory system used for relatively permanent storage of meaningful information.

Low-ball technique A strategy in which commitment is gained first to reasonable or desirable terms, which are then made less reasonable or desirable.

Lucid dream A dream in which the dreamer feels awake and capable of normal thought and action.

Maintenance rehearsal Silently repeating or mentally reviewing information to hold it in short-term memory.

Major depressive disorder A mood disorder in which the person has suffered one or more intense episodes of depression.

Major mood disorders Disorders marked by lasting extremes of mood or emotion and sometimes accompanied by psychotic symptoms.

Maladaptive behavior Behavior that makes it difficult to adapt to the environment and meet the demands of day-to-day life.

Male orgasmic disorder A persistent inability to reach orgasm during lovemaking.

Management by objectives A management technique in which employees are given specific goals to meet in their work.

Management techniques Combining praise, recognition, approval, rules, and reasoning to enforce child discipline.

Mandala A circular design representing balance, unity, and completion.

Manifest dream content The surface, "visible" content of a dream; dream images as they are remembered by the dreamer.

Massed practice A practice schedule in which studying continues for long periods, without interruption.

Mastery training Reinforcement of responses that lead to mastery of a threat or control over one's environment.

Masturbation Self-stimulation that causes sexual pleasure or orgasm.

Maternal influences The aggregate of all psychological effects mothers have on their children.

Maternity blues A brief and relatively mild state of depression often experienced by mothers 2 or 3 days after giving birth.

Maturation The physical growth and development of the body and nervous system.

Maximum life span The biologically defined maximum number of years humans can live under optimal conditions.

Mean A measure of central tendency calculated by adding a group of scores and then dividing by the total number of scores.

Means–ends analysis An analysis of how to reduce the difference between the present state of affairs and a desired goal.

Mechanical solution A problem solution achieved by trial and error or by a fixed procedure based on learned rules.

Median A central tendency found by arranging scores from the highest to the lowest and selecting the score that falls in the middle. That is, half the values in a group of scores fall above the median and half fall below.

Medicated birth The common practice in Western medicine of giving painkilling drugs during labor and birth.

Medulla The structure that connects the brain with the spinal cord and controls vital life functions.

Melatonin Hormone released by the pineal gland in response to daily cycles of light and dark.

Memory The mental system for receiving, encoding, storing, organizing, altering, and retrieving information.

Memory cue Any stimulus associated with a particular memory. Memory cues usually enhance retrieval.

Memory task Any task designed to test or assess memory.

Memory traces Physical changes in nerve cells or brain activity that take place when memories are stored.

Menopause The female "change of life" signaled by the end of regular monthly menstrual periods.

Mental age The average mental ability displayed by people of a given age.

Mental disorder A significant impairment in psychological functioning.

Mental hospitalization Placing a person in a protected, therapeutic environment staffed by mental health professionals.

Mental practice Imagining a skilled performance to aid learning.

Mental retardation (developmentally disabled) The presence of a developmental disability, an IQ score below 70, or a significant impairment of adaptive behavior.

Mental set A predisposition to perceive or respond in a particular way.

Meta-analysis A statistical technique for combining the results of many studies on the same subject.

Meta-needs In Maslow's hierarchy, needs associated with impulses for self-actualization.

Metacognitive skills An ability to manage one's own thinking and problem-solving efforts.

Microcephaly A disorder in which the head and brain are abnormally small.

Microsleep A brief shift in brain-wave patterns to those of sleep.

Minnesota Multiphasic Personality Inventory-2 (MMPI-2) One of the best-known and most widely used objective personality questionnaires.

Mirror technique Observing another person re-enact one's own behavior, like a character in a play; designed to help persons see themselves more clearly.

MMPI-2 profile A graphic representation of an individual's scores on each of the primary scales of the MMPI-2.

Mnemonic A memory aid or strategy.

Mock jury A group that realistically simulates a courtroom jury.

Mode A measure of central tendency found by identifying the most frequently occurring score in a group of scores.

Model A person who serves as an example in observational learning.

Mood A low-intensity, long-lasting emotional state.

Mood disorder A major disturbance in mood or emotion, such as depression or mania.

Moon illusion The apparent change in size that occurs as the moon moves from the horizon (large moon) to overhead (small moon).

Moral anxiety Apprehension felt when thoughts, impulses, or actions conflict with the superego's standards.

Moral development The development of values, beliefs, and thinking abilities that act as a guide regarding what is acceptable behavior.

Morphemes The smallest meaningful units in a language, such as syllables or words.

Motivation Internal processes that initiate, sustain, and direct activities.

Motor cortex A brain area associated with control of movement.

Motor program A mental plan or model that guides skilled movement.

Motor skill A series of actions molded into a smooth and efficient performance.

MRI scan Magnetic resonance imaging; a computer-enhanced three-dimensional representation of the brain or body based on the body's response to a magnetic field.

Müller-Lyer illusion Two equal-length lines tipped with inward- or outward-pointing V's appear to be of different lengths.

Multiculturalism Giving equal status, recognition, and acceptance to different ethnic and cultural groups.

Multimedia computerized test A test that uses a computer to present lifelike situations; test takers react to problems posed by the situations.

Multiple approach–avoidance conflict Being simultaneously attracted to and repelled by each of several alternatives.

Multiple aptitude test Test that measures two or more aptitudes.

Multiple intelligences Howard Gardner's theory that there are several specialized types of intellectual ability.

Mutual absorption With regard to romantic love, the nearly exclusive attention lovers give to one another.

Mutual interdependence A condition in which two or more persons must depend on one another to meet each person's needs or goals.

Myelin A fatty layer coating some axons.

Myopia Difficulty focusing distant objects (nearsightedness).

Narcolepsy A serious sleep disturbance in which an individual suffers sudden, irresistible sleep attacks.

Natural clinical test An accident or other natural event that allows the gathering of data on a psychological phenomenon of interest.

Natural consequences The effects that naturally tend to follow a particular behavior.

Natural design Human factors engineering that makes use of naturally understood perceptual signals.

Natural selection Darwin's theory that evolution favors those plants and animals best suited to their living conditions.

Naturalistic observation Observing behavior as it unfolds in natural settings.

Near-death experience (NDE) A pattern of subjective experiences that may occur when a person is clinically dead and then resuscitated.

Need An internal deficiency that may energize behavior.

Need for achievement (nAch) The desire to excel or meet some internalized standard of excellence.

Need for power The desire to have social impact and control over others.

Need to affiliate The desire to associate with other people.

Negative after-potential A drop in electrical charge below the resting potential.

Negative correlation A statistical relationship in which increases in one measure are matched by decreases in the other.

Negative instance In concept learning, an object or event that does not belong to the concept class.

Negative reinforcement Occurs when a response is followed by an end to discomfort or by the removal of an unpleasant event.

Negative relationship A mathematical relationship in which increases in one measure are matched by decreases in the other.

Negative self-statements Self-critical thoughts that increase anxiety and lower performance.

Negative transfer Mastery of one task conflicts with learning or performing another.

Neo-Freudian A psychologist who accepts the broad features of Freud's theory but has revised the theory to fit his or her own concepts.

Nerve A bundle of neuron axons.

Nerve deafness Deafness caused by damage to the hair cells or auditory nerve.

Network model A model of memory that views it as an organized system of linked information.

Neural intelligence The innate speed and efficiency of a person's brain and nervous system.

Neurilemma A layer of cells that encases many axons.

Neurological soft signs Subtle behavioral signs of brain dysfunction, including clumsiness, an awkward gait, poor hand–eye coordination, and other perceptual and motor problems.

Neuron An individual nerve cell.

Neuropeptides Brain chemicals that regulate the activity of neurons.

Neurosis An outdated term once used to refer, as a group, to anxiety disorders, somatoform disorders, dissociative disorders, and some forms of depression.

Neurotic anxiety Apprehension felt when the ego struggles to control id impulses.

Neurotransmitter Any chemical released by a neuron that alters activity in other neurons.

Neutral stimulus (NS) A stimulus that does not evoke a response.

Night blindness Blindness under conditions of low illumination.

Night terror A state of panic during NREM sleep.

Nightmare A bad dream that occurs during REM sleep.

Noise pollution Stressful and intrusive noise; usually artificially generated by machinery, but also including noises made by animals and humans.

Nonhomeostatic drive A drive that is relatively independent of physical deprivation cycles or bodily need states.

non-REM (NREM) sleep Non–rapid eye movement sleep characteristic of stages 2, 3, and 4.

Norepinephrine An adrenal hormone that tends to arouse the body; norepinephrine is associated with anger. (Also known as noradrenaline.)

Norm (social) An accepted (but often unspoken) standard of conduct for appropriate behavior.

Norm (testing) An average score for a designated group of people.

Normal curve A bell-shaped distribution, with a large number of scores in the middle, tapering to very few extremely high and low scores.

Obedience Conformity to the demands of an authority.

Object permanence Concept, gained in infancy, that objects continue to exist even when they are hidden from view.

Objective test A test that gives the same score when different people correct it.

Observational learning Learning achieved by watching and imitating the actions of another or noting the consequences of those actions.

Observational record A detailed summary of observed events or a videotape of observed behavior.

Observer bias The tendency of an observer to distort observations or perceptions to match his or her expectations.

Observer effect Changes in a person's behavior brought about by an awareness of being observed.

Obsessive-compulsive disorder An extreme preoccupation with certain thoughts and compulsive performance of certain behaviors.

Occipital lobes Portion of the cerebral cortex where vision registers in the brain.

Oedipus conflict A boy's sexual attraction to his mother, and feelings of rivalry with his father.

Olfaction The sense of smell.

Open teaching Instruction based on active teacher–student discussion.

Open-ended interview An interview in which persons are allowed to freely state their views.

Operant conditioning Learning based on the consequences of responding. Also called instrumental learning.

Operant extinction The weakening or disappearance of a nonreinforced operant response.

Operant reinforcer Any event that reliably increases the probability or frequency of responses it follows.

Operant stimulus discrimination The tendency to make an operant response when stimuli previously associated with reward are present and to withhold the response when stimuli associated with nonreward are present.

Operant stimulus generalization The tendency to respond to stimuli similar to those that preceded operant reinforcement.

Operational definition Defining a scientific concept by stating the specific actions or procedures used to measure it. For example, "hunger" might be defined as "the number of hours of food deprivation."

Opponent-process theory (emotional) States that a strong emotional state tends to be followed by an opposite emotional state; also, the strength of both emotional states changes over time.

Opponent-process theory (sensation) Theory of color vision based on three coding systems (red or green, yellow or blue, black or white).

Oral stage The period when infants are preoccupied with the mouth as a source of pleasure and means of expression.

Oral-aggressive personality A person who uses the mouth to express hostility by shouting, cursing, biting, and so forth. Also, one who actively exploits others.

Oral-dependent personality A person who wants to passively receive attention, gifts, love, and so forth.

Organ of Corti Center part of the cochlea, containing hair cells, canals, and membranes.

Organic mental disorder A mental or emotional problem caused by brain diseases or injuries.

Organismic valuing A natural, undistorted, full-body reaction to an experience.

Organizational citizenship Making positive contributions to the success of an organization in ways that go beyond one's job description.

Organizational culture The social climate within an organization.

Orgasm A climax and release of sexual excitement.

Orientation response Bodily changes that prepare an organism to receive information from a particular stimulus.

Originality In tests of creativity, originality refers to how novel or unusual solutions are.

Out-group A group with which a person does not identify.

Overgeneralization Blowing a single event out of proportion by extending it to a large number of unrelated situations.

Overlearning Continuing to study and learn after you first think you've mastered a topic.

Overly permissive parents Parents who give little guidance, allow too much freedom, or do not require the child to take responsibility.

Pain disorder Pain that has no identifiable physical cause and appears to be of psychological origin.

Panic disorder (with agoraphobia) A chronic state of anxiety and brief moments of sudden panic. The person fears that these panic attacks will occur in public places or unfamiliar situations.

Panic disorder (without agoraphobia) The person is in a chronic state of anxiety and also has brief moments of sudden, intense, unexpected panic.

Paranoid psychosis A delusional disorder centered especially on delusions of persecution.

Paranoid schizophrenia Schizophrenia marked by a preoccupation with delusions or by frequent auditory hallucinations related to a single theme, especially grandeur or persecution.

Paraphilias Compulsive or destructive deviations in sexual preferences or behavior.

Paraprofessional An individual who works in a near-professional capacity under the supervision of a more highly trained person.

Parapsychology The study of extranormal psychological events, such as extrasensory perception.

Parasympathetic branch A part of the autonomic system that quiets the body and conserves energy.

Parasympathetic rebound Excess activity in the parasympathetic nervous system following a period of intense emotion.

Parentese A pattern of speech used when talking to infants, marked by a higher-pitched voice; short, simple sentences; repetition, slower speech; and exaggerated voice inflections.

Parietal lobes Area of the brain where bodily sensations register.

Partial hospitalization An approach in which patients receive treatment at a hospital during the day, but return home at night.

Partial reinforcement A pattern in which only a portion of all responses are reinforced.

Partial reinforcement effect Responses acquired with partial reinforcement are more resistant to extinction.

Participative management An approach to management that allows employees at all levels to participate in decision making.

Passive compliance Passively bending to unreasonable demands or circumstances.

Paternal influences The aggregate of all psychological effects fathers have on their children.

Peak performance A performance during which physical, mental, and emotional states are harmonious and optimal.

Peer counselor A nonprofessional person who has learned basic counseling skills.

Peer group A group of people who share similar social status.

Percent of variance A portion of the total amount of variation in a group of scores.

Perception The mental process of organizing sensations into meaningful patterns.

Perceptual defense Resistance to perceiving threatening or disturbing stimuli.

Perceptual expectancy (or set) A readiness to perceive in a particular manner, induced by strong expectations.

Perceptual features Important elements of a stimulus pattern, such as lines, shapes, edges, spots, and colors.

Perceptual habits Well-established patterns of perceptual organization and attention.

Perceptual hypothesis An initial guess regarding how to organize (perceive) a stimulus pattern.

Perceptual learning Changes in perception that can be attributed to prior experience.

Perceptual reconstruction A mental model of external events.

Perfect negative relationship A mathematical relationship in which the correlation between two measures is −1.00.

Perfect positive relationship A mathematical relationship in which the correlation between two measures is +1.00.

Performance intelligence Intelligence measured by solving puzzles, assembling objects, completing pictures, and other nonverbal tasks.

Peripheral nervous system (PNS) All parts of the nervous system outside the brain and spinal cord.

Peripheral vision Vision at the edges of the visual field.

Persona The "mask" or public self presented to others.

Personal distance The distance maintained when interacting with close friends (about 18 inches to 4 feet from the body).

Personal interview Formal or informal questioning of job applicants to learn their qualifications and to gain an impression of their personalities.

Personal prejudice Prejudicial attitudes held toward persons who are perceived as a direct threat to one's own interests.

Personal space An area surrounding the body that is regarded as private and subject to personal control.

Personal unconscious A mental storehouse for a single individual's unconscious thoughts.

Personality A person's unique and relatively stable behavior patterns.

Personality disorder A maladaptive personality pattern.

Personality questionnaire A paper-and-pencil test consisting of questions that reveal aspects of personality.

Personality theory A system of concepts, assumptions, ideas, and principles used to understand and explain personality.

Personality trait A stable, enduring quality that a person shows in most situations.

Personality type A style of personality defined by a group of related traits.

Personnel psychology Branch of industrial-organizational psychology concerned with testing, selection, placement, and promotion of employees.

Persuasion A deliberate attempt to change attitudes or beliefs with information and arguments.

PET scan Positron emission tomography; a computer-generated image of brain activity based on glucose consumption in the brain.

Phallic personality A person who is vain, exhibitionistic, sensitive, and narcissistic.

Phallic stage The psychosexual stage (roughly ages 3 to 6) when a child is preoccupied with the genitals.

Phantom limb The illusory sensation that a limb still exists after it is lost through accident or amputation.

Pharmacotherapy The use of drugs to alleviate the symptoms of emotional disturbance.

Phenylketonuria A genetic disease that allows phenylpyruvic acid to accumulate in the body.

Pheromone An airborne chemical signal.

Phonemes The basic speech sounds of a language.

Phototherapy A treatment for seasonal affective disorder that involves exposure to bright, full-spectrum light.

Physical dependence Physical addiction, as indicated by the presence of drug tolerance and withdrawal symptoms.

Physical environments Natural settings, such as forests and beaches, as well as environments built by humans, such as buildings, ships, and cities.

Physiological changes (in emotion) Alterations in heart rate, blood pressure, perspiration, and other involuntary responses.

Pica Eating or chewing on inedible objects or substances such as chalk, ashes, and the like.

Pictorial depth cues Features found in paintings, drawings, and photographs that impart information about space, depth, and distance.

Pineal gland Gland in the brain that helps regulate body rhythms and sleep cycles.

Pituitary gland The "master gland" whose hormones influence other endocrine glands.

Place theory Theory that higher and lower tones excite specific areas of the cochlea.

Placebo An inactive substance given in the place of a drug in psychological research or by physicians who wish to treat a complaint by suggestion.

Placebo effect Changes in behavior due to expectations that a drug (or other treatment) will have some effect.

Plateau phase The second phase of sexual response, during which physical arousal is further heightened.

Pleasure principle A desire for immediate satisfaction of wishes, desires, or needs.

Polygenic characteristics Personal traits or physical properties that are influenced by many genes working in combination.

Polygraph A device for recording heart rate, blood pressure, respiration, and galvanic skin response; commonly called a "lie detector."

Pons An area on the brainstem that acts as a bridge between the medulla and other structures.

Population An entire group of animals, people, or objects belonging to a particular category (for example, all college students or all married women).

Positive correlation A statistical relationship in which increases in one measure are matched by increases in the other (or decreases correspond with decreases).

Positive instance In concept learning, an object or event that belongs to the concept class.

Positive psychology The study of human strengths, virtues, and effective functioning.

Positive reinforcement Occurs when a response is followed by a reward or other positive event.

Positive relationship A mathematical relationship in which increases in one measure are matched by increases in the other (or decreases correspond with decreases).

Positive self-regard Thinking of oneself as a good, lovable, worthwhile person.

Positive transfer Mastery of one task aids learning or performing another.

Postconventional moral reasoning Moral thinking based on carefully examined and self-chosen moral principles.

Postpartum depression A mild to moderately severe depression that begins within 3 months following childbirth.

Posttraumatic stress disorder (PTSD) A psychological disturbance lasting more than 1 month following stresses that would produce anxiety in anyone who experienced them.

Power assertion The use of physical punishment or coercion to enforce child discipline.

Precognition The purported ability to accurately predict future events.

Preconscious An area of the mind containing information that can be voluntarily brought to awareness.

Preconventional moral reasoning Moral thinking based on the consequences of one's choices or actions (punishment, reward, or an exchange of favors).

Prediction An ability to accurately forecast behavior.

Prejudice A negative emotional attitude held against members of a particular group of people.

Premack principle Any high-frequency response can be used to reinforce a low-frequency response.

Premature ejaculation Ejaculation that consistently occurs before the man and his partner want it to occur.

Preoperational stage Period of intellectual development during which children begin to use language and think symbolically, yet remain intuitive and egocentric in their thought.

Prepared childbirth A collection of techniques designed to manage discomfort and facilitate birth so that the use of painkilling drugs can be avoided or minimized.

Presbyopia Farsightedness caused by aging.

Pressure A stressful condition that occurs when a person must meet urgent external demands or expectations.

Primary appraisal Deciding if a situation is relevant to oneself and if it is a threat.

Primary emotions According to Robert Plutchik, the most basic emotions are fear, surprise, sadness, disgust, anger, anticipation, joy, and acceptance.

Primary motives Innate motives based on biological needs.

Primary reinforcers Nonlearned reinforcers; usually those that satisfy physiological needs.

Primary sexual characteristics Sex as defined by the genitals and internal reproductive organs.

Priming Facilitating the retrieval of an implicit memory by using cues to activate hidden memories.

Private self-consciousness Preoccupation with inner feelings, thoughts, and fantasies.

Proactive interference The tendency for old memories to interfere with the retrieval of newer memories.

Problem finding The active discovery of problems to be solved.

Problem-focused coping Directly managing or remedying a stressful or threatening situation.

Procedural memory Long-term memories of conditioned responses and learned skills.

Programmed instruction Any learning format that presents information in small amounts, gives immediate practice, and provides continuous feedback to learners.

Progressive relaxation A method for producing deep relaxation of all parts of the body.

Projection Attributing one's own feelings, shortcomings, or unacceptable impulses to others.

Projective tests Psychological tests making use of ambiguous or unstructured stimuli.

Prosocial behavior Behavior toward others that is helpful, constructive, or altruistic.

Prototype An ideal model used as a prime example of a particular concept.

Proxemics Systematic study of the human use of space, particularly in social settings.

Pseudo-psychology Any false and unscientific system of beliefs and practices that is offered as an explanation of behavior.

Psi phenomena Events that seem to lie outside the realm of accepted scientific laws.

Psyche The mind, mental life, and personality as a whole.

Psychiatric social worker A mental health professional trained to apply social science principles to help patients in clinics and hospitals.

Psychiatrist A medical doctor with additional training in the diagnosis and treatment of mental and emotional disorders.

Psychoactive drug A substance capable of altering attention, memory, judgment, time sense, self-control, mood, or perception.

Psychoanalysis A Freudian therapy that emphasizes the use of free association, dream interpretation, resistances, and transference to uncover and reduce unconscious conflicts that lead to emotional suffering.

Psychoanalyst A mental health professional (usually a medical doctor) trained to practice psychoanalysis.

Psychoanalytic theory Freudian theory of personality that emphasizes unconscious forces and conflicts.

Psychodrama A therapy in which clients act out personal conflicts and feelings in the presence of others who play supporting roles.

Psychodynamic theory Any theory of behavior that emphasizes internal conflicts, motives, and unconscious forces.

Psychogenic Having psychological origins, rather than physical causes.

Psychokinesis The purported ability to mentally alter or influence objects or events.

Psychological dependence Drug dependence that is based primarily on emotional or psychological needs.

Psychological efficiency Maintenance of good morale, labor relations, employee satisfaction, and similar aspects of work behavior.

Psychological situation A situation as it is perceived and interpreted by an individual, not as it exists objectively.

Psychological trauma A psychological injury or shock, such as that caused by violence, abuse, neglect, separation, and so forth.

Psychologist A person highly trained in the methods, factual knowledge, and theories of psychology.

Psychology The scientific study of behavior and mental processes.

Psychology of law Study of the psychological and behavioral dimensions of the legal system.

Psychoneuroimmunology Study of the links among behavior, stress, disease, and the immune system.

Psychopathology The scientific study of mental, emotional, and behavioral disorders; also, abnormal or maladaptive behavior.

Psychophysics Study of the relationship between physical stimuli and the sensations they evoke in a human observer.

Psychosexual stages The oral, anal, phallic, and genital stages, during which various personality traits are formed.

Psychosis A withdrawal from reality marked by hallucinations and delusions, disturbed thought and emotions, and personality disorganization.

Psychosocial dilemma A conflict between personal impulses and the social world that affects development.

Psychosomatic disorders Illnesses in which psychological factors contribute to bodily damage or to damaging changes in bodily functioning.

Psychosurgery Any surgical alteration of the brain designed to bring about desirable behavioral or emotional changes.

Psychotherapy Any psychological technique used to facilitate positive changes in a person's personality, behavior, or adjustment.

Psychotic disorder A severe mental disorder characterized by a retreat from reality, by hallucinations and delusions, and by social withdrawal.

PsycINFO A searchable online database that provides brief summaries of the scientific and scholarly literature in psychology

Puberty The biologically defined period during which a person matures sexually and becomes capable of reproduction.

Public distance Distance at which formal interactions, such as giving a speech, occur (about 12 feet or more from the body).

Public self-consciousness Intense awareness of oneself as a social object.

Punisher Any consequence that reduces the frequency of a target behavior.

Punishment Any event that follows a response and *decreases* its likelihood of occurring again. Such events are also known as punishers

Pupil The opening at the front of the eye through which light passes.

Quality circle An employee discussion group that makes suggestions for improving quality and solving business problems.

Racism Racial prejudice that has become institutionalized (that is, it is reflected in government policy, schools, and so forth) and that is enforced by the existing social power structure.

Random assignment The use of chance (for example, flipping a coin) to assign subjects to experimental and control groups.

Random search strategy Trying possible solutions to a problem in a more or less random sequence.

Random selection Choosing a sample so that each member of the population has an equal chance of being included in the sample.

Range The difference between the highest and lowest scores in a group of scores.

Rape myths False beliefs about rape that tend to blame the victim and increase the likelihood that some men will think that rape is justified.

Rapid eye movements (REMs) Swift eye movements during sleep.

Rating scale A list of personality traits or aspects of behavior on which a person is rated.

Rational-emotive behavior therapy (REBT) An approach that states that irrational beliefs cause many emotional problems and that such beliefs must be changed or abandoned.

Rationalization Justifying your behavior by giving reasonable and "rational," but false, reasons for it.

Reaction formation Preventing dangerous impulses from being expressed in behavior by exaggerating opposite behavior.

Readiness A condition that exists when maturation has advanced enough to allow the rapid acquisition of a particular skill.

Reality principle Delaying action (or pleasure) until it is appropriate.

Reality testing Obtaining additional information to check on the accuracy of perceptions.

Recall To supply or reproduce memorized information with a minimum of external cues.

Receptor sites Areas on the surface of neurons and other cells that are sensitive to neurotransmitters or hormones.

Recessive gene A gene whose influence will be expressed only when it is paired with a second recessive gene.

Reciprocal inhibition The presence of one emotional state can inhibit the occurrence of another, such as joy preventing fear or anxiety inhibiting pleasure.

Recoding Reorganizing or modifying information to assist storage in memory.

Recognition memory An ability to correctly identify previously learned information.

Redintegrative memories Memories that are reconstructed or expanded by starting with one memory and then following chains of association to other, related memories.

Reference group Any group that an individual identifies with and uses as a standard for social comparison.

Referent power Social power gained when one is used as a point of reference by others.

Referred pain Pain that is felt in one part of the body but comes from another.

Reflection In client-centered therapy, the process of rephrasing, summarizing, or repeating thoughts and feelings expressed by clients so they can become aware of what they are saying.

Reflective intelligence An ability to become aware of one's own thinking habits.

Reflex An innate, automatic response to a stimulus; for example, an eye blink.

Reflex arc The simplest behavior, in which a stimulus provokes an automatic response.

Refractory period A short time period after orgasm during which males are unable to again reach orgasm.

Refusal skills training Program that teaches youths how to resist pressures to begin smoking. (Can also be applied to other drugs and health risks.)

Regression Retreating to an earlier level of development or to earlier, less demanding habits or situations.

Reinforcement Any event that increases the probability that a particular response will occur.

Reinforcement value The subjective value a person attaches to a particular activity or reinforcer.

Relational concept A concept defined by the relationship between features of an object or between an object and its surroundings (for example, "greater than," "lopsided").

Relearning Learning again something that was previously learned. Used to measure memory of prior learning.

Reliability The ability of a test to yield the same score, or nearly the same score, each time it is given to the same person.

REM rebound The occurrence of extra rapid eye movement sleep following REM sleep deprivation.

REM sleep Sleep marked by rapid eye movements and a return to stage 1 EEG patterns.

Reminding system Pain based on small nerve fibers; reminds the brain that the body has been injured.

Replicate To reproduce or repeat.

Representative sample A small, randomly selected part of a larger population that accurately reflects characteristics of the whole population.

Representativeness heuristic A tendency to select wrong answers because they seem to match preexisting mental categories.

Repression The unconscious process by which memories, thoughts, or impulses are held out of awareness. Also referred to as motivated forgetting.

Research method A systematic approach to answering scientific questions.

Resistance A blockage in the flow of free association; topics the client resists thinking or talking about.

Resolution The fourth phase of sexual response, involving a return to lower levels of sexual tension and arousal.

Response Any muscular action, glandular activity, or other identifiable aspect of behavior.

Response chaining The assembly of separate responses into a series of actions that lead to reinforcement.

Response cost Removal of a positive reinforcer after a response is made.

REST Restricted environmental stimulation therapy.

Resting potential The electrical charge of a neuron at rest.

Reticular activating system (RAS) A part of the reticular formation that activates the cerebral cortex.

Reticular formation (RF) A network within the medulla and brainstem; associated with attention, alertness, and some reflexes.

Retina The light-sensitive layer of cells at the back of the eye.

Retrieval Recovering information from storage in memory.

Retroactive interference The tendency for new memories to interfere with the retrieval of old memories.

Reversibility of thought Recognition that relationships involving equality or identity can be reversed (for example, if A = B, then B = A).

Reward Anything that produces pleasure or satisfaction; a positive reinforcer.

Reward power Social power based on the capacity to reward a person for acting as desired.

Rhodopsin The light-sensitive pigment in the rods.

Rods Visual receptors for dim light that produce only black and white sensations.

Role conflict Trying to occupy two or more roles that make conflicting demands on behavior.

Role reversal Taking the role of another person to learn how one's own behavior appears from the other person's perspective.

Romantic love Love that is associated with high levels of interpersonal attraction, heightened arousal, mutual absorption, and sexual desire.

Rorschach Technique A projective test comprised of ten standardized inkblots.

Run of luck A statistically unusual outcome (as in getting five heads in a row when flipping a coin) that could still occur by chance alone.

Sample A smaller subpart of a population.

Scaffolding The process of adjusting instruction so that it is responsive to a beginner's behavior and supports the beginner's efforts to understand a problem or gain a mental skill.

Scapegoating Blaming a person or a group for the actions of others or for conditions not of their making.

Scatter diagram A graph that plots the intersection of paired measures; that is, the points at which paired X and Y measures cross.

Schachter's cognitive theory States that emotions occur when physical arousal is labeled or interpreted on the basis of experience and situational cues.

Schedule of reinforcement A rule or plan for determining which responses will be reinforced.

Schizophrenia A psychosis characterized by delusions, hallucinations, apathy, and a "split" between thought and emotion.

Scientific jury selection Using social science principles to choose members of a jury.

Scientific management (Theory X) An approach to managing employees that emphasizes work efficiency.

Scientific method Testing the truth of a proposition by careful measurement and controlled observation.

Scientific observation An empirical investigation that is structured so that it answers questions about the world.

Seasonal affective disorder (SAD) Depression that occurs only during fall and winter; presumably related to decreased exposure to sunlight.

Secondary appraisal Deciding how to cope with a threat or challenge.

Secondary elaboration Making a dream more logical and complete while remembering it.

Secondary motives Motives based on learned needs, drives, and goals.

Secondary reinforcer A learned reinforcer; often one that gains reinforcing properties by association with a primary reinforcer.

Secondary sexual characteristics Sexual features other than the genitals and reproductive organs—breasts, body shape, facial hair, and so forth.

Secondary traits Traits that are inconsistent or relatively superficial.

Secure attachment A stable and positive emotional bond.

Selective attention Giving priority, usually voluntarily, to a particular incoming sensory message.

Selective perception Perceiving only certain stimuli among a larger array of possibilities.

Self A continuously evolving conception of one's personal identity.

Self archetype An unconscious image representing, unity, wholeness, completion, and balance.

Self-actualization The ongoing process of fully developing one's personal potential.

Self-actualizer One who is living creatively and making full use of his or her potentials.

Self-assertion A direct, honest expression of feelings and desires.

Self-concept A person's perception of his or her own personality traits.

Self-disclosure The process of revealing private thoughts, feelings, and one's personal history to others.

Self-efficacy Belief in your capacity to produce a desired result.

Self-esteem Regarding oneself as a worthwhile person; a positive evaluation of oneself.

Self-fulfilling prophecy An expectation that prompts people to act in ways that make the expectation come true.

Self-handicapping Arranging to perform under conditions that usually impair performance, so as to have an excuse for a poor showing.

Self-help group A group of people who share a particular type of problem and provide mutual support to one another.

Self-image Total subjective perception of one's body and personality (another term for self-concept).

Self-managed team A work group that has a high degree of freedom with respect to how it achieves its goals.

Self-recording Self-management based on keeping records of response frequencies.

Self-regulated learning Active, self-guided learning.

Self-reinforcement Praising or rewarding oneself for having made a particular response (such as completing a school assignment).

Self-testing Evaluating learning by posing questions to yourself.

Semantic memory A subpart of declarative memory that records impersonal knowledge about the world.

Semantics The study of meanings in language.

Sensate focus Form of therapy that directs a couple's attention to natural sensations of sexual pleasure.

Sensation The immediate response in the brain caused by excitation of a sensory organ.

Sensitive period During development, a period of increased sensitivity to environmental influences. Also, a time during which certain events must take place for normal development to occur.

Sensitivity group A group experience consisting of exercises designed to increase self-awareness and sensitivity to others.

Sensorimotor stage Stage of intellectual development during which sensory input and motor responses become coordinated.

Sensory adaptation A decrease in sensory response to an unchanging stimulus.

Sensory analysis Separation of sensory information into important elements.

Sensory coding Codes used by the sense organs to transmit information to the brain.

Sensory conflict theory Explains motion sickness as the result of a mismatch between information from vision, the vestibular system, and kinesthesis.

Sensory deprivation (SD) Any major reduction in the amount or variety of sensory stimulation.

Sensory gating Alteration of sensory messages in the spinal cord.

Sensory memory The first stage of memory, which holds an exact record of incoming information for a few seconds or less.

Sensory neuron A nerve cell that carries information from the senses toward the CNS.

Separation anxiety Uneasiness displayed by infants when they are separated from their parents or caregivers.

Separation anxiety disorder Severe and prolonged distress displayed by children when they are separated from their parents or caregivers.

Serial position effect The tendency to make the most errors in remembering the middle items of an ordered list.

Set point The proportion of body fat that tends to be maintained by changes in hunger and eating.

Sex One's biological classification as female or male.

Sex drive The strength of one's motivation to engage in sexual behavior.

Sex-linked trait Traits other than sex that are influenced by genes carried on an *X* chromosome (or, rarely, on a *Y* chromosome).

Sexism Institutionalized prejudice against members of either sex, based solely on their gender.

Sexual and gender identity disorders Any of a wide range of difficulties with sexual identity, deviant sexual behavior, or sexual adjustment.

Sexual aversion Persistent feelings of fear, anxiety, or disgust about engaging in sex.

Sexual orientation One's degree of emotional and erotic attraction to members of the same sex, opposite sex, or both sexes.

Sexual script An unspoken mental plan that defines a "plot," dialogue, and actions expected to take place in a sexual encounter.

Sexually transmitted disease (STD) A disease that is typically passed from one person to the next by intimate physical contact; a venereal disease.

Shape constancy The perceived shape of an object is unaffected by changes in its retinal image.

Shaping Gradually molding responses to a final desired pattern.

Short sleeper A person averaging 5 hours of sleep or less per night.

Short-term memory (STM) The memory system used to hold small amounts of information for relatively brief time periods.

Shyness A tendency to avoid others plus uneasiness and strain when socializing.

Signal In early language development, any behavior, such as touching, vocalizing, gazing, or smiling, that allows nonverbal interaction and turn-taking between parent and child.

Simultaneous color contrast Changes in perceived hue that occur when a colored stimulus is displayed on backgrounds of various colors.

Single-blind experiment An arrangement in which subjects remain unaware of whether they are in the experimental group or the control group.

Situational demands Unstated expectations that define desirable or appropriate behavior in various settings and social situations.

Situational determinants External conditions that strongly influence behavior.

Situational judgment test Presenting realistic work situations to applicants in order to observe their skills and reactions.

Situational test Simulating real-life conditions so that a person's reactions may be directly observed.

Size constancy The perceived size of an object remains constant, despite changes in its retinal image.

Size–distance invariance The strict relationship between the distance an object lies from the eyes and the size of its image.

Skin receptors Sensory organs for touch, pressure, pain, cold, and warmth.

Skin senses The senses of touch, pressure, pain, heat, and cold.

Sleep apnea Repeated interruption of breathing during sleep.

Sleep deprivation Being prevented from getting desired or needed amounts of sleep.

Sleep hormone A sleep-promoting substance found in the brain and spinal cord.

Sleep patterns The order and timing of daily sleep and waking periods.

Sleep spindles Distinctive bursts of brain-wave activity that indicate a person is asleep.

Sleep stages Levels of sleep identified by brain-wave patterns and behavioral changes.

Sleep-deprivation psychosis A major disruption of mental and emotional functioning brought about by sleep loss.

Sleeptalking Speaking that occurs during NREM sleep.

Social anxiety A feeling of apprehension in the presence of others.

Social comparison Making judgments about ourselves through comparison with others.

Social competition Rivalry among groups, each of which regards itself as superior to others.

Social development The development of self-awareness, attachment to parents or caregivers, and relationships with other children and adults.

Social distance Distance at which impersonal interaction takes place (about 4 to 12 feet from the body).

Social distance scale A rating of the degree to which a person would be willing to have contact with a member of another group.

Social environment An environment defined by a group of people and their activities or interrelationships (such as a parade, revival meeting, or sports event).

Social exchange Any exchange between two people of attention, information, affection, favors, or the like.

Social exchange theory Theory stating that rewards must exceed costs for relationships to endure.

Social influence Changes in a person's behavior induced by the presence or actions of others.

Social learning theory An explanation of personality that combines learning principles, cognition, and the effects of social relationships.

Social markers Visible or tangible signs that indicate a person's social status or role.

Social motives Learned motives acquired as part of growing up in a particular society or culture.

Social nonconformity Failure to conform to societal norms or the usual minimum standards for social conduct.

Social norms Unspoken rules that define acceptable and expected behavior for members of a group.

Social phobia An intense, irrational fear of being observed, evaluated, embarrassed, or humiliated by others in social situations.

Social power The capacity to control, alter, or influence the behavior of another person.

Social psychology The scientific study of how individuals behave, think, and feel in social situations.

Social Readjustment Rating Scale (SRRS) A scale that rates the impact of various life events on the likelihood of illness.

Social referencing Observing others in social situations to obtain information or guidance.

Social reinforcers Reinforcers, such as attention, approval, and/or affection, provided by other people.

Social role Expected behavior patterns associated with particular social positions (such as daughter, worker, student).

Social smile Smiling elicited by social stimuli, such as seeing a parent's face.

Social stereotypes Oversimplified images of the traits of individuals who belong to a particular social group.

Social support Close, positive relationships with other people.

Solitary play Playing alone.

Soma The main body of a neuron or other cell.

Somatic pain Pain from the skin, muscles, joints, and tendons.

Somatic system The system of nerves linking the spinal cord with the body and sense organs.

Somatic therapy Any bodily therapy, such as drug therapy, electroconvulsive therapy, or psychosurgery.

Somatization disorder Afflicted persons have numerous physical complaints. Typically, they have consulted many doctors, but no organic cause for their distress can be identified.

Somatoform disorder Physical symptoms that mimic disease or injury for which there is no identifiable physical cause.

Somatosensory area A receiving area for bodily sensations.

Somesthetic sense Sensations produced by the skin, muscles, joints, viscera, and organs of balance.

Somnambulism Sleepwalking; occurs during NREM sleep.

Source traits Basic underlying traits of personality; each source trait is reflected in a number of surface traits.

Spaced practice A practice schedule that alternates study periods with brief rests. (Massed practice, in comparison, continues for long periods without interruption.)

Special aptitude test Test to predict a person's likelihood of succeeding in a particular area of work or skill.

Specific goal A goal with a clearly defined and measurable outcome.

Specific phobia An intense, irrational fear of specific objects, activities, or situations.

Speed of processing The speed with which a person can mentally process information.

Spinal nerves Major nerves that carry sensory and motor messages in and out of the spinal cord.

Split-brain operation Cutting the corpus callosum.

Spontaneous recovery The reappearance of a learned response after its apparent extinction.

Sports psychology Study of the psychological and behavioral dimensions of sports performance.

SQ4R method An active study and reading technique based on these steps: survey, question, read, recite, reflect, and review.

Squeeze technique Method for inhibiting ejaculation by compressing the tip of the penis.

Stage ESP The simulation of ESP for the purpose of entertainment.

Stage hypnosis Use of hypnosis to entertain; often, merely a simulation of hypnosis for that purpose.

Stage of exhaustion Third stage of the G.A.S., at which time the body's resources are exhausted and serious health consequences occur.

Stage of resistance Second stage of the G.A.S., during which bodily adjustments to stress stabilize, but at a high physical cost.

Standard deviation An index of how much a typical score differs from the mean of a group of scores.

State-dependent learning Memory influenced by one's bodily state at the time of learning and at the time of retrieval. Improved memory occurs when the bodily states match.

Statistical abnormality Abnormality defined on the basis of an extreme score on some dimension, such as IQ or anxiety.

Statistical significance The degree to which an event (such as the results of an experiment) is unlikely to have occurred by chance alone.

Status An individual's position in a social structure, especially with respect to power, privilege, or importance.

Status inequalities Differences in the power, prestige, or privileges of two or more persons or groups.

Stereoscopic vision Perception of space and depth caused chiefly by the fact that the eyes receive different images.

Sterilization Medical procedures such as vasectomy or tubal ligation that make a man or a woman infertile.

Stimulant A substance that increases activity in the body and nervous system.

Stimulation deafness Damage caused by exposing the hair cells to excessively loud sounds.

Stimulus Any physical energy sensed by an organism.

Stimulus control Linking a particular response with specific stimuli; stimuli present when an operant response is acquired tend to control when and where the response is made.

Stimulus discrimination The learned ability to respond differently to similar stimuli.

Stimulus drives Drives based on needs for exploration, manipulation, curiosity, and stimulation.

Stimulus generalization The tendency to respond to stimuli similar to, but not identical to, a conditioned stimulus.

Stimulus motives Innate needs for stimulation and information.

Storage Holding information in memory for later use.

Stress The mental and physical condition that occurs when a person must adjust or adapt to the environment.

Stress disorder A significant emotional disturbance caused by stresses outside the range of normal human experience.

Stress inoculation Use of positive coping statements to control fear and anxiety.

Stress management The application of behavioral strategies to reduce stress and improve coping skills.

Stress reaction The physical response to stress, consisting mainly of bodily changes related to autonomic nervous system arousal.

Stress-vulnerability model Attributes psychosis to a combination of environmental stress and inherited susceptibility.

Stressor A specific condition or event in the environment that challenges or threatens a person.

Striving for superiority According to Adler, this basic drive propels us toward perfection.

Stroboscopic movement Illusion of movement in which an object is shown in rapidly changing series of positions.

Structuralism The school of thought concerned with analyzing sensations and personal experience into basic elements.

Stuttering Chronic hesitation or stumbling in speech.

Style of life The pattern of personality and behavior that defines the pathway each person takes through life.

Subcortex All brain structures below the cerebral cortex.

Subjective well-being General life satisfaction combined with frequent positive emotions and relatively few negative emotions.

Subjects Animals or people whose behavior is under scientific investigation.

Sublimation Working off unmet desires, or unacceptable impulses, in activities that are constructive.

Subliminal perception Perception of a stimulus below the threshold for conscious recognition.

Substance-related disorder Abuse of, or dependence on, a mood- or behavior-altering drug.

Sudden infant death syndrome (SIDS) The sudden, unexplained death of an apparently healthy infant.

Superego A judge or censor for thoughts and actions.

Superordinate goal A goal that exceeds or overrides all others; a goal that renders other goals relatively less important.

Superstitious behavior A behavior repeated because it seems to produce reinforcement, even though it is actually unnecessary.

Suppression A conscious effort to put something out of mind or to keep it from awareness.

Surface traits The visible or observable traits of one's personality.

Surrogate mother A substitute mother (often an inanimate dummy in animal research).

Survey method Using questionnaires and surveys to poll large groups of people.

Syllogism A format for analyzing logical arguments.

Symbolic prejudice Prejudice that is expressed in disguised fashion.

Symbolization The nonliteral expression of dream content.

Sympathetic branch A part of the ANS that activates the body at times of stress.

Synapse The microscopic space between two neurons, over which messages pass.

Synesthesia Experiencing one sense in terms normally associated with another sense; for example, "seeing" colors when a sound is heard.

Syntax Rules for ordering words when forming sentences.

Systematic desensitization A reduction in fear, anxiety, or aversion brought about by planned exposure to aversive stimuli.

Task analysis Breaking complex skills into their subparts.

Taste aversion An active dislike for a particular food.

Taste bud The receptor organ for taste.

Teaching strategy A plan for effective teaching.

Telepathy The purported ability to directly know another person's thoughts.

Temperament The hereditary aspects of personality, including sensitivity, activity levels, prevailing mood, irritability, and adaptability.

Temperament The physical core of personality, including emotional and perceptual sensitivity, energy levels, typical mood, and so forth.

Temporal lobes Areas that include the sites where hearing registers in the brain.

Tension-release method A procedure for systematically achieving deep relaxation of the body.

Teratogen Radiation, a drug, or other substance capable of altering fetal development in ways that cause birth defects.

Term schedule A written plan that lists the dates of all major assignments for each of your classes for an entire semester or quarter.

Terminal decline An abrupt decline in measured intelligence about 5 years before death.

Territorial behavior Any behavior that tends to define a space as one's own or that protects it from intruders.

Territorial markers Objects and other signals whose placement indicates to others the "ownership" or control of a particular area.

Test anxiety High levels of arousal and worry that seriously impair test performance.

Test standardization Establishing standards for administering a test and interpreting scores.

Testosterone A male sex hormone, secreted mainly by the testes and responsible for the development of many male sexual characteristics.

Thalamus A brain structure that relays sensory information to the cerebral cortex.

Thanatologist A specialist who studies emotional and behavioral reactions to death and dying.

Thanatos The death instinct postulated by Freud.

Thematic Apperception Test (TAT) A projective test consisting of 20 different scenes and life situations about which respondents make up stories.

Theory A system of ideas designed to interrelate concepts and facts in a way that summarizes existing data and predicts future observations.

Theory of mind A child's current understanding of the mind, including the desires, beliefs, intentions, and feelings of others.

Theory Y A management style that emphasizes human relations at work and that views people as industrious, responsible, and interested in challenging work.

Therapeutic alliance A caring relationship that unites a therapist and a client in working to solve the client's problems.

Therapy placebo effect Improvement caused not by the actual process of therapy but by a client's expectation that therapy will help.

Thought stopping Use of aversive stimuli to interrupt or prevent upsetting thoughts.

Threshold The point at which a nerve impulse is triggered.

Thyroid gland Endocrine gland that helps regulate the rate of metabolism.

Tip-of-the-tongue (TOT) state The feeling that a memory is available but not quite retrievable.

Token economy A therapeutic program in which desirable behaviors are reinforced with tokens that can be exchanged for goods, services, activities, and privileges.

Token reinforcer A tangible secondary reinforcer such as money, gold stars, poker chips, and the like.

Top-down processing Applying higher-level knowledge to rapidly organize sensory information into a meaningful perception.

Trait profile A graph of the scores obtained on several personality traits.

Trait theorist A psychologist interested in classifying, analyzing, and interrelating traits to understand personality.

Trait–situation interaction The influence that external settings or circumstances have on the expression of personality traits.

Transference The tendency of patients to transfer feelings to a therapist that correspond to those the patient had for important persons in his or her past.

Transformation The mental ability to change the shape or form of a substance (such as clay or water) and to perceive that its volume remains the same.

Transformation rules Rules by which a simple declarative sentence may be changed to other voices or forms (past tense, passive voice, and so forth).

Transition period Time span during which a person leaves an existing life pattern behind and moves into a new pattern.

Traumatic stresses Extreme events that cause psychological injury or intense emotional pain.

Trichromatic theory Theory of color vision based on three cone types: red, green, and blue.

Trust versus mistrust A conflict early in life centered on learning to trust others and the world.

Two-way bilingual education A program in which English-speaking children and children with limited English proficiency are taught half the day in English and half in a second language.

Type A personality A personality type with an elevated risk of heart disease; characterized by time urgency, anger, and hostility.

Type B personality All personality types other than Type A; a low-cardiac-risk personality.

Unconditional positive regard An unqualified, unshakable acceptance of another person.

Unconditioned response (UR) An innate, unlearned, reflex response elicited by an unconditioned stimulus.

Unconditioned stimulus (US) A stimulus innately capable of eliciting a response.

Unconscious The region of the mind that is beyond awareness, especially impulses and desires not directly known to a person.

Uncritical acceptance The tendency to believe generally positive or flattering descriptions of oneself.

Understanding (problem solving) A deeper comprehension of the nature of a problem.

Understanding (psychology) Understanding is achieved when the causes of a behavior can be stated.

Undifferentiated schizophrenia Schizophrenia lacking the specific features of catatonic, disorganized, or paranoid types.

Upward comparison Comparing yourself with a person who ranks higher than you on some dimension.

Vaginismus Muscle spasms of the vagina.

Validity The ability of a test to measure what it purports to measure.

Validity scales Scales that tell whether test scores should be invalidated for lying, inconsistency, or "faking good."

Variability The tendency for a group of scores to differ in value. Measures of variability indicate the degree to which a group of scores differ from one another.

Variable Any condition that changes or can be made to change; a measure, event, or state that may vary.

Variable interval (VI) schedule A reinforcer is given for the first correct response made after a varied amount of time has passed since the last reinforced response. Responses made during the time interval are not reinforced.

Variable ratio (VR) schedule A varied number of correct responses must be made to get a reinforcer. For example, a reinforcer is given after three to seven correct responses; the actual number changes randomly.

Verbal intelligence Intelligence measured by answering questions involving vocabulary, general information, arithmetic, and other language- or symbol-oriented tasks.

Vestibular senses The senses of balance, position in space, and acceleration.

Vicarious classical conditioning Classical conditioning brought about by observing another person react to a particular stimulus.

Vicarious desensitization A reduction in fear or anxiety that takes place vicariously ("second hand") when a client watches models perform the feared behavior.

Virtual reality exposure Use of computer-generated images to present fear stimuli. The virtual environment responds to a viewer's head movements and other inputs.

Visceral pain Pain originating in the internal organs.

Visible spectrum That part of the electromagnetic spectrum to which the eyes are sensitive.

Visual acuity The sharpness of visual perception.

Vocational interest test A paper-and-pencil test that assesses a person's interests and matches them to interests found among successful workers in various occupations.

Waking consciousness A state of normal, alert awareness.

Warning system Pain based on large nerve fibers; warns that bodily damage may be occurring.

Weapons effect The observation that weapons serve as strong cues for aggressive behavior.

Weber's law The just noticeable difference is a constant proportion of the original stimulus intensity.

Weekly time schedule A written plan that allocates time for study, work, and leisure activities during a 1-week period.

Wellness A positive state of good health; more than the absence of disease.

Wernicke's area An area related to language comprehension.

Wish fulfillment Freudian belief that many dreams express unconscious desires.

Withdrawal of love Withholding affection to enforce child discipline.

Withdrawal symptoms Physical illness and discomfort following the withdrawal of a drug.

Work efficiency Maximum output (productivity) at lowest cost.

Working memory Another name for short-term memory, especially when it is used for thinking and problem solving.

World Wide Web A system of information "sites" accessible through the Internet.

X chromosome The female chromosome contributed by the mother; produces a female when paired with another *X* chromosome, and a male when paired with a *Y* chromosome.

Y chromosome The male chromosome contributed by the father; produces a male when paired with an *X* chromosome. Fathers may give either an *X* or a *Y* chromosome to their offspring.

Yerkes-Dodson law A summary of the relationships among arousal, task complexity, and performance.

You-message A message that threatens, accuses, bosses, lectures, or criticizes another person.

Zener cards A deck of 25 cards bearing various symbols and used in early parapsychological research.

Zero correlation The absence of a (linear) mathematical relationship between two measures.

Zone of proximal development Refers to the range of tasks a child cannot yet master alone but that she or he can accomplish with the guidance of a more capable partner.

z-score A number that tells how many standard deviations above or below the mean a score is.

References

A nation's shame: Fatal child abuse and neglect in the United States. (1995). United States Advisory Board on Child Abuse and Neglect, United States Department of Health and Human Services.

Abel, T., & Lattal, K. M. (2001). Molecular mechanisms of memory acquisition, consolidation and retrieval. *Current Opinion in Neurobiology, 11*(2), 180–187.

Abel, T. D., & Stephan, M. (2000). The limits of civic environmentalism. *American Behavioral Scientist, 44*(4), 614–628.

Abi-Dargham, A., Gil, R., Krystal, J., Baldwin, R., et al. (1998). Increased striatal dopamine transmission in schizophrenia. *American Journal of Psychiatry, 155*(6), 761–767.

Abrahamson, D. J., Barlow, D. H., & Abrahamson, L. S. (1989). Differential effects of performance demand and distraction on sexually functional and dysfunctional males. *Journal of Abnormal Psychology, 98*(3), 241–247.

Abrams, D. B., Brown, R., Niaura, R. S., Emmons, K., et al. (2003). *The tobacco dependence treatment handbook: A guide to best practices*. New York, Guilford.

Abramson, R. (1993). EPA officially links passive smoke, cancer. *Los Angeles Times,* Jan. 8, A27.

Accordino, D. B., Accordino, M. P., & Slaney, R. B. (2000). An investigation of perfectionism, mental health, achievement, and achievement motivation in adolescents. *Psychology in the Schools, 37*(6), 535–545.

Adams, J. (1988). *Conceptual blockbusting*. New York: Norton.

Addis, K. M., & Kahana, M. J. (2004). Decomposing serial learning: What is missing from the learning curve? *Psychonomic Bulletin & Review, 11*(1), 118–174.

Adelmann, P. K., & Zajonc, R. B. (1989). Facial efference and the experience of emotion. *Annual Review of Psychology, 40,* 249–280.

Adorno, T. W., Frenkel-Brunswik, E., Levinson, D. J., & Sanford, R. N. (1950). *The authoritarian personality.* New York: Harper.

Ahissar, M. (1999). Perceptual learning. *Current Directions in Psychological Science, 8*(4), 124–128.

Ainsworth, M. D. (1989). Attachments beyond infancy. *American Psychologist, 44*(4), 709–716.

Ajzen, I. (2001). Nature and operation of attitudes. *Annual Review of Psychology, 52,* 27–58.

Akerstedt, T. (1990). Psychological and psychophysiological effects of shift work. *Scandinavian Journal of Work, Environment & Health, 16*(Suppl. 1), 67–73.

Akerstedt, T., Hume, K., Minors, D., & Waterhouse, J. (1993). Regulation of sleep and naps on an irregular schedule. *Sleep, 16*(8), 736–743.

Alarcon, R. D. (1995). Culture and psychiatric diagnosis: Impact on DSM-IV and ICD-10. *Psychiatric Clinics of North America, 18*(3), 449–465.

Alberti, R., & Emmons, M. (1995). *Your perfect right.* San Luis Obispo, CA: Impact.

Alberto, P. A., & Troutman, A. C. (1998). *Applied behavior analysis for teachers.* Englewood Cliffs, NJ: Prentice Hall

Alcock, J. E. (2003). Give the null hypothesis a chance: Reasons to remain doubtful about the existence of psi. *Journal of Consciousness Studies, 10*(6–7), 29–50.

Alcock, J. E., Burns, J., & Freeman, A. (2003). *Psi wars: Getting to grips with the paranormal*. Exeter, UK: Imprint Academic Press.

Alfeld-Liro, C., & Sigelman, C. K. (1998). Sex differences in self-concept and symptoms of depression during the transition to college. *Journal of Youth & Adolescence, 27*(2), 219–244.

Alicke, M. D., Yurak, T. J., & Vredenburg, D. S. (1996). Using personal attitudes to judge others. *Journal of Research in Personality, 30*(1), 103–119.

Allen, K., Blascovich, J., & Mendes, W. B. (2002). Cardiovascular reactivity in the presence of pets, friends, and spouses: The truth about cats and dogs. *Psychosomatic Medicine, 64*(5), 727–739.

Allen, M., Mabry, E., & McKelton, D. (1998). Impact of juror attitudes about the death penalty on juror evaluations of guilt and punishment: A meta-analysis. *Law & Human Behavior, 22*(6), 715–731.

Allgower, A., Wardle, J., & Steptoe, A. (2001). Depressive symptoms, social support, and personal health behaviors in young men and women. *Health Psychology, 20*(3), 223–227.

Allhusen, V., Belsky, J., Booth-LaForce, C., Bradley, R. H., et al. (2005). Duration and developmental timing of poverty and children's cognitive and social development from birth through third grade. *Child Development, 76*(4), 795–810.

Alloy, L. B., Peterson, C., Abramson, L. Y., & Seligman, M. E. (1984). Attributional style and the generality of learned helplessness. *Journal of Personality & Social Psychology, 46,* 681–687.

Allport, G. W. (1958). *The nature of prejudice.* Garden City, NY: Anchor Books, Doubleday.

Allport, G. W. (1961). *Pattern and growth in personality.* New York: Holt, Rinehart, and Winston.

Alsaker, F. D. (1995). Is puberty a critical period for socialization? *Journal of Adolescence, 18*(4), 427–444.

Altemeyer, B. (2004). Highly dominating, highly authoritarian personalities. *Journal of Social Psychology, 144*(4), 421–447.

Althof, S. E., & Seftel, A. D. (1995). The evaluation and management of erectile dysfunction. *Psychiatric Clinics of North America, 18*(1), 171–192.

Altman, L. K. (2002). AIDS threatens to claim 65M more lives by '20. *Arizona Daily Star,* July 3, A7.

Alvarado, N. (1994). Empirical validity of the Thematic Apperception Test. *Journal of Personality Assessment, 63*(1), 59–79.

Alvino, J., & the Editors of *Gifted Children Monthly*. (1996). *Parents' guide to raising a gifted child.* New York: Ballantine.

Amabile, T., Hadley, C. N., & Kramer, S. J. (2002). Creativity under the gun. *Harvard Business Review, 80*(8), 52–61.

Ambady, N., & Rosenthal, R. (1993). Half a minute: Predicting teacher evaluations from thin slices of nonverbal behavior and physical attractiveness. *Journal of Personality & Social Psychology, 64,* 431–441.

Ancis, J. R., Chen, Y., & Schultz, D. (2004). Diagnostic challenges and the so-called culture-bound syndromes. In J. R. Ancis (Ed.), *Culturally responsive interventions: Innovative approaches to working with diverse populations.* New York: Brunner-Routledge.

Anderegg, D., & Gartner, G. (2001). Manic dedifferentiation and the creative process. *Psychoanalytic Psychology, 18*(2), 365–379.

Anderson, C. A. (1989). Temperature and aggression. *Psychological Bulletin, 106,* 74–96.

Anderson, C. A. (2004). An update on the effects of violent video games. *Journal of Adolescence, 27,* 113–122.

Anderson, C. A., Anderson, K. B., & Deuser, W. E. (1996). Examining an affective aggression framework. *Personality & Social Psychology Bulletin, 22*(4), 366–376.

Anderson, C. A., Berkowitz, L., Donnerstein, E., Huesmann, L. R., et al. (2003). The influence of media violence on youth. *Psychological Science in the Public Interest, 4,* 1–30.

Anderson, C. A., & Bushman, B. J. (2002). Human aggression. *Annual Review of Psychology, 53,* 27–51.

Anderson, J. R. (2005). *Cognitive psychology and its implications* (6th ed.). New York: Worth.

Anderson, M. C., & Bell, T. (2001). Forgetting our facts: The role of inhibitory processes in the loss of propositional knowledge. *Journal of Experimental Psychology: General, 130*(3), 544–570.

Anderson, M. C. (2001). Active forgetting: Evidence for functional inhibition as a source of memory failure. *Journal of Aggression, Maltreatment & Trauma, 4*(2), 185–210.

Anderson, M. C., & Green, C. (2001). Suppressing unwanted memories by executive control. *Nature, 410*(6826), 366–369.

Anderson, M. C., Ochsner, K. N., Kuhl, B., Cooper, J., et al. (2004). Neural systems underlying the suppression of unwanted memories. *Science, 303,* 232–235.

Annett, M., & Manning, M. (1990). Arithmetic and laterality. *Neuropsychologia, 28*(1), 61–69.

Anshel, M. H. (1995). An examination of self-regulatory cognitive-behavioural strategies of Australian elite and non-elite competitive male swimmers. *Australian Psychologist, 30*(2), 78–83.

Anthony, W. A., Cohen, M., & Kennard, W. (1990). Understanding the current facts and principles of mental health systems planning. *American Psychologist, 45*(11), 1249–1252.

Antle, M. C., & Mistlberger, R. E. (2005). Circadian rhythms. In I. Q. Whishaw & B. Kolb (Eds.), *The behavior of the laboratory rat: A handbook with tests*. London: Oxford.

APA. (1998). *APA directory (draft).* American Psychological Association Research Office. Washington, DC: American Psychological Association.

APA. (2003). Guidelines on multicultural education, training, research, practice, and organizational change for psychologists. *American Psychologist, 58*(5), 377–402.

Arbona, C. B., Osma, J., Garcia-Palacios, A., Quero, S., et al. (2004). Treatment of flying phobia using virtual reality: Data from a 1-year follow-up using a multiple baseline design. *Clinical Psychology & Psychotherapy, 11*(5), 311–323.

Ariely, D., & Wertenbroch, K. (2002). Procrastination, deadlines, and performance: Self-control by precommitment. *Psychological Science, 13*(3), 219–224.

Armeli, S., Gunthert, K. C., & Cohen, L. H. (2001). Stressor appraisals, coping, and post-event outcomes: The dimensionality and antecedents of stress-related growth. *Journal of Social & Clinical Psychology, 20*(3), 366–395.

Arndt, J., Allen, J.J.B., & Greenberg, J. (2001). Traces of terror. *Motivation & Emotion, 25*(3), 253–277.

Arnett, J. J. (1999). Adolescent storm and stress, reconsidered. *American Psychologist, 54*(3), 317–326.

Arnett, J. J. (2000). Emerging adulthood. *American Psychologist, 55*(5), 469–480.

Arnett, J. J. (2001). Conceptions of the transition to adulthood. *Journal of Adult Development, 8*(2), 133–143.

Arnett, J. J. (2002). The psychology of globalization. *American Psychologist, 57*(10), 774–783.

Arnett, J. J. (2004). *Emerging adulthood: The winding road from late teens through the twenties*. New York: Oxford University Press.

Arnett, J. J., & Galambos, N. L. (Eds.). (2003). *New directions for*

child and adolescent development: Exploring cultural conceptions of the transition to adulthood. San Francisco: Jossey-Bass.

Aronoff, J., Barclay, A. M., & Stevenson, L. A. (1988). The recognition of threatening facial stimuli. *Journal of Personality & Social Psychology, 54*(4), 647–655.

Aronson, E. (1969). Some antecedents of interpersonal attraction. In W. J. Arnold, & D. Levine (Eds.), *Nebraska Symposium on Motivation.* Lincoln: University of Nebraska Press.

Aronson, E. (1992). *The social animal.* San Francisco: W. H. Freeman.

Aronson, E. (2004). Reducing hostility and building compassion: Lessons from the jigsaw classroom. In A. G. Miller (Ed.), *The social psychology of good and evil.* New York: Guilford.

Aronson, E., Wilson, T. D., & Akert, R. M. (2005). *Social psychology* (5th ed.). Englewood Cliffs, NJ: Prentice Hall.

Arthur, W., & Doverspike, D. (2001). Predicting motor vehicle crash involvement from a personality measure and a driving knowledge test. *Journal of Prevention & Intervention in the Community, 22*(1), 35–42.

Asch, S. E. (1956). Studies of independence and conformity: A minority of one against a unanimous majority. *Psychological Monographs, 70*(416).

Asendorpf, J. B. (1996). Self-awareness and other-awareness. II: Mirror self-recognition, social contingency awareness, and synchronic imitation. *Developmental Psychology, 32*(2), 313–321.

Ash, D. W., & Holding, D. H. (1990). Backward versus forward chaining in the acquisition of a keyboard skill. *Human Factors, 32*(2), 139–146.

Ashby, F. G., & Maddox, W. T. (2005). Human category learning. *Annual Review of Psychology, 56,* 149–178.

Aslin, R. N., & Smith, L. B. (1988). Perceptual development. *Annual Review of Psychology, 39,* 435–473.

Assanand, S., Pinel, J.P.J., & Lehman, D. R. (1998). Personal theories of hunger and eating. *Journal of Applied Social Psychology, 28*(11), 998–1015.

Aston-Jones, G., & Druhan, J. (1999). Breaking the chain of addiction. *Nature, 400*(6742), 317, 319.

Athenasiou, R., Shaver, P., & Tavris, C. (1970). Sex. *Psychology Today, 4*(2), 37–52.

Ausubel, D. P. (1978). In defense of advance organizers: A reply to the critics. *Review of Educational Research, 48,* 251–257.

Avery, D. H., Eder, D. N., Bolte, M. A., Hellekson, C. J., et al. (2001). Dawn simulation and bright light in the treatment of SAD. *Biological Psychiatry, 50*(3), 205–216.

Ayers, L., Beaton, S., & Hunt, H. (1999). The significance of transpersonal experiences, emotional conflict, and cognitive abilities in creativity. *Empirical Studies of the Arts, 17*(1), 73–82.

Ayllon, T. (1963). Intensive treatment of psychotic behavior by stimulus satiation and food reinforcement. *Behavior Research and Therapy, 1,* 53–61.

Ayllon, T., & Azrin, N. H. (1965). The measurement and reinforcement of behavior of psychotics. *Journal of the Experimental Analysis of Behavior, 8,* 357–383.

Azrin, N. H., Hutchinson, R. R., & McLaughlin, R. (1965). The opportunity for aggression as an operant reinforcer during aversive stimulation. *Journal of Experimental Analysis of Behavior, 8,* 171–180.

Baard, P. P., Deci, E. L., & Ryan, R. M. (2004). Intrinsic need satisfaction: A motivational basis of performance and well-being in two work settings. *Journal of Applied Social Psychology, 34*(10), 2045–2068.

Bachman, J. G., & Johnson, L. D. (1979). The freshmen. *Psychology Today, 13,* 78–87.

Baddeley, A. D. (2003). Working memory: Looking back and looking forward. *Nature Reviews Neuroscience, 4*(10), 829–839.

Baer, J. M. (1993). *Creativity and divergent thinking.* Hillsdale, NJ: Erlbaum.

Bagley, C., & Tremblay, P. (1998). On the prevalence of homosexuality and bisexuality, in a random community survey of 750 men aged 18 to 27. *Journal of Homosexuality, 36*(2), 1–18.

Bahrick, H. P. (1984). Semantic memory content in permastore: Fifty years of memory for Spanish learned in school. *Journal of Experimental Psychology: General, 113*(1), 1–37.

Bahrke, M. S., Yesalis, C. E., & Brower, K. J. (1998). Anabolic-androgenic steroid abuse and performance-enhancing drugs among adolescents. *Child & Adolescent Psychiatric Clinics of North America, 7*(4), 821–838.

Bailis, D. S. (2001). Benefits of self-handicapping in sport. *Canadian Journal of Behavioural Science, 33*(4), 213–223.

Baillargeon, R. (1991). Reasoning about the height and location of a hidden object in 4.5- and 6.5-month-old infants. *Cognition, 38*(1), 13–42.

Baillargeon, R. (2004). Infants' reasoning about hidden objects: Evidence for event-general and event-specific expectations. *Developmental Science, 7*(4), 391–424.

Baillargeon, R., De Vos, J., & Graber, M. (1989). Location memory in 8-month-old infants in a non-search AB task. *Cognitive Development, 4,* 345–367.

Bain, S. K., & Allin, J. D. (2005). Stanford-Binet Intelligence Scales, Fifth Edition. *Journal of Psychoeducational Assessment, 23*(1), 87–95.

Bajracharya, S. M., Sarvela, P. D., & Isberner, F. R. (1995). A retrospective study of first sexual intercourse experiences among undergraduates. *Journal of American College Health, 43*(4), 169–177.

Bakich, I. (1995). Hypnosis in the treatment of sexual desire disorders. *Australian Journal of Clinical & Experimental Hypnosis, 23*(1), 70–77.

Bakker, F. C., Boschker, M.S.J., & Chung, T. (1996). Changes in muscular activity while imagining weight lifting using stimulus or response propositions. *Journal of Sport & Exercise Psychology, 18*(3), 313–324.

Balch, W. R., & Lewis, B. S. (1996). Music-dependent memory. *Journal of Experimental Psychology: Learning, Memory, & Cognition, 22*(6), 1354–1363.

Baldo, O., & Eardley, I. (2005). Diagnosis and investigation of men with erectile dysfunction. *Journal of Men's Health & Gender, 2*(1), 79–86.

Balk, D. E., Lampe, S., Sharpe, B., Schwinn, S., et al. (1998). TAT results in a longitudinal study of bereaved college students. *Death Studies, 22*(1), 3–21.

Baltes, B. B., Briggs, T. E., Huff, J. W., Wright, J. A., et al. (1999). Flexible and compressed workweek schedules. *Journal of Applied Psychology, 84*(4), 496–513.

Baltes, P. B., Staudinger, U. M., & Lindenberger, U. (1999). Lifespan psychology. *Annual Review of Psychology, 50,* 471–507.

Banaji, M. R., & Prentice, D. A. (1994). The self in social contexts. *Annual Review of Psychology, 45,* 297–332.

Bandura, A. (1971). *Social learning theory.* New York: General Learning Press.

Bandura, A. (2001). Social cognitive theory. *Annual Review of Psychology, 52,* 1–26.

Bandura, A., Blanchard, E. B., & Ritter, B. (1969). Relative efficacy of desensitization and modeling approaches for inducing behavioral, affective, and attitudinal changes. *Journal of Personality & Social Psychology, 13*(3), 173–199.

Bandura, A., & Rosenthal, T. L. (1966). Vicarious classical conditioning as a function of arousal level. *Journal of Personality & Social Psychology, 3,* 54–62.

Bandura, A., Ross, D., & Ross, S. A. (1963). Vicarious reinforcement and imitative learning. *Journal of Abnormal and Social Psychology, 67,* 601–607.

Bandura, A., & Walters, R. (1959). *Adolescent aggression.* New York: Ronald.

Bandura, A., & Walters, R. (1963). *Social learning and personality development.* New York: Holt.

Bank, B. J., & Hansford, S. L. (2000). Gender and friendship: Why are men's best same-sex friendships less intimate and supportive? *Personal Relationships, 7*(1), 63–78.

Bank, S. P., & Kahn, M. D. (1982). *The sibling bond.* New York: Basic Books.

Banks, A., & Gartrell, N. K. (1995). Hormones and sexual orientation: A questionable link. *Journal of Homosexuality, 28*(3–4), 247–268.

Banks, T., & Dabbs, J. M., Jr. (1996). Salivary testosterone and cortisol in delinquent and violent urban subculture. *Journal of Social Psychology, 136*(1), 49–56.

Barabasz, A. (2000). EEG markers of alert hypnosis. *Sleep & Hypnosis, 2*(4), 164–169.

Baranek, G. T. (1999). Autism during infancy. *Journal of Autism & Developmental Disorders, 29*(3), 213–224.

Barber, T. X. (1970). *Suggested ("hypnotic") behavior: The trance paradigm versus an alternative paradigm.* Harding, MA., Medfield Foundation, Report No. 103.

Bard, C., Fleury, M., & Goulet, C. (1994). Relationship between perceptual strategies and response adequacy in sport situations. *International Journal of Sport Psychology, 25*(3), 266–281.

Barker, E. A. (1993). Evaluating graphology. *Skeptical Inquirer, 17*(Spring), 312–315.

Bargh, J. A., McKenna, K.Y.A., & Fitzsimons, G. M. (2002). Can you see the real me? Activation and expression of the "true self" on the Internet. *Journal of Social Issues, 58*(1), 33–48.

Barlow, D. H. (2000). Unraveling the mysteries of anxiety and its disorders from the perspective of emotion theory. *American Psychologist, 55,* 1247–1263.

Barlow, D. H. (2001). *Anxiety and its disorders* (2nd ed.). New York: Guilford.

Barlow, D. H. (2004). Psychological treatments. *American Psychologist, 59*(9), 869–878.

Barnet, A. B., & Barnet, R. J. (1998). *The youngest minds.* New York: Touchstone.

Barnett, R. C., & Hyde, J. S. (2001). Women, men, work, and family. *American Psychologist, 56*(10), 781–796.

Baron, R.A. (1983) The "sweet smell of success"? The impact of pleasant artificial scents on evaluation of job applicants. *Journal of Applied Psychology, 68,* 709–713.

Baron, R. A., & Byrne, D. E. (2006). *Social psychology* (11th ed.). Boston: Allyn & Bacon.

Baron, R. S. (2005). So right it's wrong: Groupthink and the ubiquitous nature of polarized group decision making. In M. P. Zanna, (Ed.), *Advances in experimental social psychology* (Vol. 37). San Diego: Elsevier.

Barowsky, E. I., Moskowitz, J., & Zweig, J. B. (1990). Biofeedback for disorders of initiating and maintaining sleep. *Annals of the New York Academy of Sciences, 602,* 97–103.

Barrett, D. (1993). The "committee of sleep": A study of dream incubation for problem solving. *Dreaming, 3*(2), 115–122.

Barrick, M. R., Moun, M. K., & Judge, T. A. (2001). Personality and performance at the beginning of the new millennium. *International Journal of Selection & Assessment, 9*(1–2), 9–30.

Barron, F. (1958). The psychology of imagination. *Scientific American, 199*(3), 150–170.

Barsalou, L. W. (1992). *Cognitive psychology.* Hillsdale, NJ: Lawrence Erlbaum.

Barsky, S. H., Roth, M. D., Kleerup, E. C., Simmons, M., et al. (1998). Histopathologic and molecular alterations in bronchial epithelium in habitual smokers of marijuana, cocaine, and/or tobacco. *Journal of the National Cancer Institute, 90*(16), 1198–1205.

Bar-Tal, D., & Labin, D. (2001). The effect of a major event on stereo typing: Terrorist attacks in Israel and Israeli adolescents' perceptions of Palestinians, Jordanians and Arabs. *European Journal of Social Psychology, 31*(3), 265–280.

Bartholow, B. D., & Anderson, C. A. (2002). Effects of violent video games on aggressive behavior. *Journal of Experimental Social Psychology, 38*(3), 283–290.

Bartholow, B. D., Sestir, M. A., & Davis, E. B. (2005). Correlates and consequences of exposure to video game violence: Hostile personality, empathy, and aggressive behavior. *Personality and Social Psychology Bulletin, 31*(11), 1573–1586.

Bartlett, J. C., & Searcy, J. (1993). Inversion and configuration of faces. *Cognitive Psychology, 25*(3), 281–316.

Bartol, C. R., & Bartol, A. M. (Eds.). (2005). *Current perspectives in forensic psychology and criminal justice.* Newbury Park, CA: Sage.

Bartoshuk, L. M. (2000). Psychophysical advances aid the study of genetic variation in taste. *Appetite, 34*(1), 105.

Bartoshuk, L. M., Duffy, V. B., Green, B. G., Hoffman, H. J., et al. (2004). Valid across-group comparisons with labeled scales: The gLMS versus magnitude matching. *Physiology & Behavior, 82*(1), 109–114.

Bartoshuk, L. M., Duffy, V. B., & Miller, I. J. (1994). PTC/PROP taste: Anatomy, psychophysics, and sex effects. *Physiology & Behavior, 56*(6), 1165–1171.

Bartz, W. R. (1990). The basics of critical thought. Personal communication.

Bartz, W. R. (2002). Teaching skepticism via the CRITIC acronym. *Skeptical Inquirer,* Sept.–Oct., 42–44.

Basadur, M., Runco, M. A., & Vega, L. A. (2000). Understanding how creative thinking skills, attitudes and behaviors work together. *Journal of Creative Behavior, 34*(2), 77–100.

Basson, R., Brotto, L. A., Laan, E., Redmond, G., et al. (2005). Assessment and management of women's sexual dysfunctions: Problematic desire and arousal. *Journal of Sexual Medicine, 2*(3), 291–300.

Batejat, D. M., & Lagarde, D. P. (1999). Naps and modafinil as countermeasures for the effects of sleep deprivation on cognitive performance. *Aviation, Space, & Environmental Medicine, 70*(5), 493–498.

Bates, T. C. (2005). Auditory inspection time and intelligence. *Personality & Individual Differences, 38*(1), 115–127.

Bath, H. (1996). Everyday discipline or control with care. *Journal of Child & Youth Care, 10*(2), 23–32.

Batson, C. D. (1990). How social an animal? The human capacity for caring. *American Psychologist, 45*(3), 336–346.

Batson, C. D., & Powell, A. A. (2003). Altruism and prosocial behavior. In T. Millon & M. J. Lerner (Eds.), *Handbook of psychology: Personality and social psychology* (Vol. 5). New York: Wiley.

Batterham, R. L., Cohen, M. A., Ellis, S. M., Le Roux, C. E., et al. (2003). Inhibition of food intake in obese subjects by peptide YY3–36. *New England Journal of Medicine, 349*(Sept. 4), 941–948.

Baum, A., & Davis, G. E. (1980). Reducing the stress of high-density living: An architectural intervention. *Journal of Personality & Social Psychology, 38,* 471–481.

Baum, A., & Fleming, I. (1993). Implications of psychological research on stress and technological accidents. *American Psychologist, 48*(6), 665–672.

Baum, A., & Posluszny, D. M. (1999). Health psychology. *Annual Review of Psychology, 50,* 137–163.

Baum, A., & Valins, S. (Eds.). (1977). *Human response to crowding: Studies of the effects of residential group size.* Hillsdale, NJ: Erlbaum.

Baum, A., & Valins, S. (1979). Architectural mediation of residential density and control: Crowding and the regulation of social contact. *Advances in Experimental and Social Psychology, 12,* 131–175.

Baumeister, R. F., Campbell, J. D., Krueger, J. I., & Vohs, K. D. (2003). Does high self-esteem cause better performance, interpersonal success, happiness, or healthier lifestyles? *Psychological Science in the Public Interest, 4*(1), 1–44.

Baumrind, D. (1991). The influence of parenting style on adolescent competence and substance use. *Journal of Early Adolescence, 11*(1), 56–95.

Baumrind, D., Larzelere, R. E., & Cowan, P. A. (2002). Ordinary physical punishment: Is it harmful? *Psychological Bulletin, 128*(4), 580–589.

Beach, F. A. (Ed.). (1965). *Sex and behavior,* New York: Wiley.

Bearman, P. S., Moody, J., & Stovel, K. (2004). Chains of affection: The structure of adolescent romantic and sexual networks. *American Journal of Sociology, 110*(1), 44–91.

Beauchamp, P. H., Halliwell, W. R., Fournier, J. F., & Koestner, R. (1996). Effects of cognitive-behavioral psychological skills training on the motivation, preparation, and putting performance of novice golfers. *Sport Psychologist, 10*(2), 157–170.

Beaulieu, C.M.J. (2004). Intercultural study of personal space: A case study. *Journal of Applied Social Psychology, 34*(4), 794–805.

Beck, A. T. (1991). Cognitive therapy. *American Psychologist, 46*(4), 368–375.

Beck, A. T. (2004). Cognitive patterns in dreams and daydreams. In R. I. Rosner & W. J. Lyddon (Eds.), *Cognitive therapy and dreams.* New York: Springer.

Beck, A. T., Brown, C., Berchick, R. J., Stewart, B. L., et al. (1990). Relationship between hopelessness and ultimate suicide. *American Journal of Psychiatry, 147*(2), 190–195.

Beck, A. T., & Greenberg, R. L. (1974). *Coping with depression.* New York Institute for Rational Living.

Beck, B. L., Koons, S. R., & Milgrim, D. L. (2000). Correlates and consequences of behavioral procrastination. *Journal of Social Behavior & Personality, 15*(5), 3–13.

Beck, J. S. (2002). Beck therapy approach. In M. Hersen & W. H. Sledge (Eds.), *Encyclopedia of psychotherapy.* San Diego: Academic Press.

Beck, R. C. (2004). *Motivation: Theories and principles* (5th ed.). Englewood Cliffs, NJ: Prentice Hall.

Becker, S. W., & Eagly, A. H. (2004). The heroism of women and men. *American Psychologist, 59*(3), 163–178.

Beebe, B., Gerstman, L., Carson, B., Dolins, M., et al. (1982). Rhythmic communication in the mother–infant dyad. In M. Davis (Ed.), *Interaction rhythms, periodicity in communicative behavior.* New York: Human Sciences Press.

Beeman, M. J., & Chiarello, C. (1998). Complementary right- and left-hemisphere language comprehension. *Current Directions in Psychological Science, 7*(1), 2–8.

Behrend, D. A., Beike, D. R., & Lampinen, J. M. (2004). *The self and memory.* Hove, UK: Psychology Press.

Beilin, H. (1992). Piaget's enduring contribution to developmental psychology. *Developmental Psychology, 28*(2), 191–204.

Beljan, J. R., Rosenblatt, L. S., Hetherington, N. W., Layman, J., et al. (1972). *Human performance in the aviation environment.* NASA Contract no. 2-6657, Pt. Ia, 253–259.

Bell, P. A., Greene, T. C., Fisher, J. D., & Baum, A. (2001). *Environmental Psychology.* Belmont, CA: Wadsworth.

Bellebaum, C., & Daum, I. (2004). Effects of age and awareness on eyeblink conditional discrimination learning. *Behavioral Neuroscience, 118*(6), 1157–1165.

Bellezza, F. S., Six, L. S., & Phillips, D. S. (1992). A mnemonic for remembering long strings of digits. *Bulletin of the Psychonomic Society, 30*(4), 271–274.

Bellisle, F. (1999). Glutamate and the UMAMI taste. *Neuroscience & Biobehavioral Reviews, 23*(3), 423–438.

Belsham, B. (2001). Glutamate and its role in psychiatric illness. *Human Psychopharmacology Clinical & Experimental, 16*(2), 139–146.

Belsky, J. (1996). Parent, infant, and social-contextual antecedents of father–son attachment security. *Developmental Psychology, 32*(5), 905–913.

Belsky, J., Gilstrap, B., & Rovine, M. (1984). The Pennsylvania infant and family development project, I: Stability and change in mother–infant and father–infant interactions in a family setting at one, three, and nine months. *Child Development, 55,* 692–705.

Bem, S. L. (1975). Androgyny vs. the tight little lives of fluffy women and chesty men. *Psychology Today,* Sept., 58–62.

Bem, S. L. (1981). Gender schema theory. A cognitive account of sex typing. *Psychological Review, 88,* 354–364.

Benbow, C. P. (1986). Physiological correlates of extreme intellectual precocity. *Neuropsychologia, 24*(5), 719–725.

Benedetti, F., Maggi, G., & Lopiano, L. (2003). Open versus hidden medical treatments: The patient's knowledge about a therapy affects the therapy outcome. *Prevention & Treatment, 6,* Article 1. Retrieved October 26, 2005, from http://journals.apa.org/prevention/volume6/pre0060001a.html

Benjafield, J. G. (2004). *A history of psychology,* (2nd ed.). Boston: Allyn & Bacon.

Benloucif, S., Bennett, E. L., & Rosenzweig, M. R. (1995). Norepinephrine and neural plasticity: The effects of xylamine on experience-induced changes in brain weight, memory, and behavior. *Neurobiology of Learning & Memory, 63*(1), 33–42.

Ben-Shakhar, G., Bar-Hillel, M., Bilu, Y., Ben-Abba, E., et al. (1986). Can graphology predict occupational success? Two empirical studies and some methodological ruminations. *Journal of Applied Psychology, 71*(4), 645–653.

Ben-Shakhar, G., & Dolev, K. (1996). Psychophysiological detection through the guilty knowledge technique: Effect of mental countermeasures. *Journal of Applied Psychology, 81*(3), 273–281.

Bensley, L., & Van Eenwyk, J. (2001). Video games and real-life aggression. *Journal of Adolescent Health, 29*(4), 244–257.

Benson, E. (2002). Pheromones, in context. *Monitor on Psychology,* Oct., 46–48.

Benson, J., Greaves, W., O'Donnell, M., & Taglialatela, J. (2002). Evidence for symbolic language processing in a Bonobo (Pan paniscus). *Journal of Consciousness Studies, 9*(12), 33–56.

Benton, A. L. (1980). The neuropsychology of facial recognition. *American Psychologist, 35*(Feb.), 176–186.

Bergin, A. E. (1991). Values and religious issues in psychotherapy and mental health. *American Psychologist, 46*(4), 394–403.

Bernat, J. A., Calhoun, K. S., & Stolp, S. (1998). Sexually aggressive men's responses to a date rape analogue. *Journal of Sex Research, 35*(4), 341–348.

Berne, E. (1964). *Games people play.* New York: Grove.

Bernstein H. J., Beale M. D., Burns C., & Kellner C. H. (1998). Patient attitudes about ECT after treatment. *Psychiatric Annals, 28*(9), 524–527.

Berry, D. S., & Miller, K. M. (2001). When boy meets girl: Attractiveness and the five-factor model in opposite-sex interactions. *Journal of Research in Personality, 35*(1), 62–77.

Berry, J. W. (1990). The psychology of acculturation. In R. A. Dienstbier, & J. J. Berman (Eds.), *Nebraska Symposium on Motivation 1989: Cross-cultural perspectives, 37.* Lincoln: University of Nebraska Press.

Berry, J. W., Phinney, J. S, Sam, D. L., & Vedder, P. (2005). *Immigrant youth in cultural transition.* Mahwah, NJ: Erlbaum.

Berscheid, E. (1994). Interpersonal relations. *Annual Review of Psychology, 45,* 79–129.

Berscheid, E. (2000). Attraction. In A. Kazdin (Ed.), *Encyclopedia of psychology.* Washington, DC: American Psychological Association.

Berscheid, E., & Regan, P. (2005). *The psychology of interpersonal relationships.* Englewood Cliffs, NJ: Prentice Hall.

Bersoff, D. M. (1999). Why good people sometimes do bad things: Motivated reasoning and unethical behavior. *Personality & Social Psychology Bulletin, 25*(1), 28–39.

Bertsch, G. J. (1976). Punishment of consummatory and instrumental behavior: A review. *Psychological Record, 26,* 13–31.

Best, D. (2002). Cross-cultural gender roles. In J. Worell (Ed.), *Encyclopedia of women and gender.* New York: Oxford.

Betancur, C., Velez, A., Cabanieu, G., le Moal, M., et al. (1990). Association between left-handedness and allergy: A reappraisal. *Neuropsychologia, 28*(2), 223–227.

Bialystok, E. (2001). *Bilingualism in development: Language, literacy, and cognition.* New York: Cambridge.

Bickman, L. (1974). Clothes make the person. *Psychology Today,* April, 48–51.

Biglan, A., Ary, D., Yudelson, H., & Duncan, T. E. (1996). Experimental evaluation of a modular approach to mobilizing antitobacco influences of peers and parents. *American Journal of Community Psychology, 24*(3), 311–339.

Bigler, E. D., Johnson, S. C., Anderson, C. V., & Blatter, D. D. (1996). Traumatic brain injury and memory: The role of hippocampal atrophy. *Neuropsychology, 10*(3), 333–342.

Binks, P. G., Waters, W. F., & Hurry, M. (1999). Short-term total sleep deprivations does not selectively impair higher cortical functioning. *Sleep, 22*(3), 328–334.

Biondi, M., & Zannino, L. (1997). Psychological stress, neuroimmunomodulation, and susceptibility to infectious diseases in animals and man. *Psychotherapy & Psychosomatics, 66*(1), 3–26.

Birch, J., & McKeever, L. M. (1993). Survey of the accuracy of new pseudoisochromatic plates. *Ophthalmic & Physiological Optics, 13*(1), 35–40.

Birnbaum, M. H. (2004). Human research and data collection via the Internet. *Annual Review of Psychology, 55,* 803–832.

Birren, J. E., & Fisher, L. M. (1995). Rules and reason in the forced retirement of commercial airline pilots at age 60. *Ergonomics, 38*(3), 518–525.

Blackmore, S. (1989). What do we really think? A survey of parapsychologists and sceptics. *Journal of the Society for Psychical Research, 55*(814), 251–262.

Blackmore, S. (1991). Lucid dreaming. *Skeptical Inquirer, 15,* 362–370.

Blackmore, S. (2001). What can the paranormal teach us about consciousness? *Skeptical Inquirer, 25,* 22–27.

Blackmore, S. (2005). *Conversations on consciousness.* Oxford: Oxford University Press.

Blackwell, D. L., & Lichter, D. T. (2000). Mate selection among married and cohabiting couples. *Journal of Family Issues, 21*(3), 275–302.

Blackwell, D. L., & Lichter, D. T. (2004). Homogamy among dating, cohabiting, and married couples. *Sociological Quarterly, 45*(4), 719–737.

Blackwell, R. T., Galassi, J. P., Galassi, M. D., & Watson, T. E. (1985). Are cognitive assessments equal? A comparison of think aloud and thought listing. *Cognitive Therapy and Research, 9,* 399–413.

Blair, I. V. (2001). Implicit stereotypes and prejudice. In G. B. Moscowitz (Ed.), *Cognitive social psychology.* Mahwah, NJ: Erlbaum.

Blanchard, D. C., & Blanchard, R. J. (2003). What can animal aggression research tell us about human aggression? *Hormones & Behavior, 44*(3), 171–177.

Blanke, O., Landis, T., Spinelli, L., & Seeck, M. (2004). Out-of-body experience and autoscopy of neurological origin. *Brain, 127*(2), 243–258.

Block, J. (1979). *Socialization influence of personality development in males and females.* American Psychological Association Master Lecture, Convention of the American Psychological Association, New York City, Sept.

Blood, A. J., & Zatorre, R. J. (2001). Intensely pleasurable responses to music correlate with activity in brain regions implicated in reward and emotion. *Proceedings National Academy of Sciences, 98*(20) 11818–11823.

Bloom, B. (1985). *Developing talent in young people.* New York: Ballantine.

Bloom, J. W. (1998). The ethical practice of WebCounseling. *British Journal of Guidance & Counselling, 26*(1), 53–59.

Blumberg, M. S., & Wasserman, E. A. (1995). Animal mind and the argument from design. *American Psychologist, 50*(3), 133–144.

Bockting, W. O., & Coleman, E. (Eds.), (2003). *Masturbation as a means of achieving sexual health.* New York: Haworth Press.

Boergers, J., Spirito, A., & Donaldson, D. (1998). Reasons for adolescent suicide attempts. *Journal of the American Academy of Child & Adolescent Psychiatry, 37*(12), 1287–1293.

Bohannon, J. N., & Stanowicz, L. B. (1988). The issue of negative evidence: Adult responses to children's language errors. *Developmental Psychology, 24*(5), 684–689.

Bohart, A. C., & Tallman, K. (1996). The active client: Therapy as self-help. *Journal of Humanistic Psychology, 36*(3), 7–30.

Bonanno, G. A., Papa, A., Lalande, K., Westphal, M., et al. (2004). The importance of being flexible. *Psychological Science, 15*(7), 482–487.

Bond, R., & Smith, P. B. (1996). Culture and conformity: A meta-analysis of studies using Asch's (1952, 1956) line judgment task. *Psychological Bulletin, 119*(1), 111–137.

Bond, T., & Wooten, V. (1996). The etiology and management of insomnia. *Virginia Medical Quarterly, 123*(4), 254–255.

Bongard, S., al'Absi, M., & Lovallo, W. R. (1998). Interactive effects of trait hostility and anger expression on cardiovascular reactivity in young men. *International Journal of Psychophysiology, 28*(2), 181–191.

Bonham, V., Warshauer-Baker, E., & Collins, F. S. (2005). Race and ethnicity in the genome era: The complexity of the constructs. *American Psychologist, 60*(1), 9–15.

Book, H. E., & Luborsky, L. (1998). *Brief psychodynamic psychotherapy.* Washington, DC: American Psychological Association.

Booker, J. M., & Hellekson, C. J. (1992). Prevalence of seasonal affective disorder in Alaska. *American Journal of Psychiatry, 149*(9), 1176–1182.

Bootzin, R. R., & Epstein, D. R. (2000). Stimulus control. In K. L. Lichstein & C. M. Morin. *Treatment of late life insomnia.* Thousand Oaks, CA: Sage.

Borman, W. C., Hanson, M. A., & Hedge, J. W. (1997). Personnel psychology. *Annual Review of Psychology, 48,* 299–337.

Bornstein, M. H. (1989). Sensitive periods in development: Structural characteristics and causal interpretations. *Psychological Bulletin, 105*(2), 179–197.

Bornstein, M. H., & Tamis-LeMonda, C. S. (2001). Mother–infant interaction. In A. Fogel & G. Bremmer (Eds.), *Blackwell handbook of infant development.* London: Blackwell.

Bornstein, M. H., Haynes, O. M., Azuma, H., Galperín, C., et al. (1998). A cross-national study of self-evaluations and attributions in parenting. *Developmental Psychology, 34,* 662–676.

Bornstein, R. F. (1996). Sex differences in dependent personality disorder prevalence rates. *Clinical Psychology: Science & Practice, 3*(1), 1–12.

Borod, J. C., Bloom, R. L., Brickman, A. M., Nakhutina, L., et al. (2002). Emotional processing deficits in individuals with unilateral brain damage. *Applied Neuropsychology, 9*(1), 23–36.

Borod, J. C., Cicero, B. A., Obler, L. K., Welkowitz, H. M., et al. (1998). Right hemisphere emotional perception. *Neuropsychology, 12*(3), 446–458.

Borrie, R. A. (1990–1991). The use of restricted environmental stimulation therapy in treating addictive behaviors. *International Journal of the Addictions, 25*(7A–8A), 995–1015.

Borrie, R. A., & Suedfeld, P. (1980). Restricted environmental stimulation therapy in a weight reduction program. *Journal of Behavioral Medicine, 3,* 147–161.

Bosse, R., Aldwin, C. M., Levenson, M. R., & Workman-Daniels, K. (1991). How stressful is retirement? *Journal of Gerontology, 46*(1), 9–14.

Bouchard, T. J., Jr. (1983). Twins—Nature's twice-told tale. In *Yearbook of science and the future.* Chicago: Encyclopedia Britannica.

Bouchard, T. J., Jr. (2004). Genetic influence on human psychological traits: A survey. *Current Directions in Psychological Science, 13*(4), 148–151.

Bouchard, T. J., Jr., Lykken, D. T., McGue, M., Segal, N. L., et al. (1990). Sources of human psychological differences: The Minnesota study of twins reared apart. *Science, 250,* 223–228.

Bovbjerg, D. H., Redd, W. H., Jacobsen, P. B., Manne, S. L., et al. (1992). An experimental analysis of classically conditioned nausea during cancer chemotherapy. *Psychosomatic Medicine,* 54(6), 623–637.

Bowe, F. (2000). *Universal Design in education: Teaching nontraditional students.* Westport, CT: Bergin & Garvey.

Bower, B. (1990). Gone but not forgotten. *Science News, 138*(Nov. 17), 312–314.

Bower, G. H. (1973). How to . . . uh . . . remember. *Psychology Today,* Oct., 63–70.

Bower, G. H. (1981). Mood and memory. *American Psychologist, 36,* 129–148.

Bower, G. H., & Springston, F. (1970). Pauses as recoding points in letter series. *Journal of Experimental Psychology, 83,* 421–430.

Bowers, K. S., & Farvolden, P. (1996). Revisiting a century-old Freudian slip—From suggestion disavowed to the truth repressed. *Psychological Bulletin, 119*(3), 355–380.

Bowers, K. S., & Woody, E. Z. (1996). Hypnotic amnesia and the paradox of intentional forgetting. *Journal of Abnormal Psychology, 105*(3), 381–390.

Boyatzis, C. J., Matillo, G. M., & Nesbitt, K. M. (1995). Effects of "The Mighty Morphin Power Rangers" on children's aggression with peers. *Child Study Journal,* 25(1), 45–55.

Bradley, L. P. (1995). Changing American birth through childbirth education. *Patient Education & Counseling, 25*(1), 75–82.

Bradley, R., Greene, J., Russ, E., Dutra, L., et al. (2005). A multidimensional meta-analysis of psychotherapy for PTSD. *American Journal of Psychiatry, 162*(2), 214–227.

Bradley, R. H., Caldwell, B. M., Rock, S. L., Ramey, C. T., et al. (1989). Home environment and cognitive development in the first 3 years of life: A collaborative study involving six sites and three ethnic groups in North America. *Developmental Psychology, 25*(2), 217–235.

Bradley, R. H., & Corwyn, R. F. (2002). Socioeconomic status and child development. *Annual Review of Psychology, 53,* 377–399.

Braffman, W., & Kirsch, I. (1999). Imaginative suggestibility and hypnotizability. *Journal of Personality & Social Psychology, 77*(3), 578–587.

Brannon, L. (1996). *Gender.* Boston: Allyn & Bacon.

Brannon, L., & Feist, J. (2004). *Health psychology: An introduction to behavior and health* (5th ed.). Belmont, CA: Wadsworth.

Bransford, J. D., & McCarrell, N. S. (1977). A sketch of cognitive approach to comprehension: Some thoughts about understanding what it means to comprehend. In P. N. Johnson-Laird & P. C. Wason (Eds.), *Thinking: Readings in cognitive science.* Cambridge: Cambridge University Press.

Bransford, J. D., Sherwood, R., Vye, N., & Rieser, J. (1986). Teaching thinking and problem solving. *American Psychologist, 41*(10), 1078–1089.

Bransford, J. D., & Stein, B. S. (1984). *The IDEAL problem solver.* New York: Freeman.

Braun, A. R., Balkin, T. J., & Herscovitch, P. (1998). Dissociated pattern of activity in visual cortices and their projections during human rapid eye movement sleep. *Science, 279*(5347), 91–95.

Braun, S. (2001). Seeking insight by prescription. *Cerebrum, 3*(2), 10–21.

Brawman-Mintzer, O., & Lydiard, R. B. (1996). Generalized anxiety disorder: Issues in epidemiology. *Journal of Clinical Psychiatry, 57*(Suppl. 7), 3–8.

Bray, S. R., & Widmeyer, W. N. (2000). Athletes' perceptions of the home advantage. *Journal of Sport Behavior, 23*(1), 1–10.

Brebner, J. (1998). Happiness and personality. *Personality & Individual Differences, 25*(2), 279–296.

Breedlove, S. M., Cooke, B. M., & Jordan, C. L. (1999). The orthodox view of brain sexual differentiation. *Brain, Behavior & Evolution, 54*(1), 8–14.

Brehm, S. S. (2002). *Intimate relationships* (3rd ed.). New York: McGraw-Hill.

Brehm, S. S., Kassin, S. M., & Fein, S. (2005). *Social psychology* (6th ed.). Boston: Houghton Mifflin.

Brenner, V., & Fox, R. A. (1998). Parental discipline and behavior problems in young children. *Journal of Genetic Psychology, 159*(2), 251–256.

Breslau, N. (2001). Outcomes of posttraumatic stress disorder. *Journal of Clinical Psychiatry, 62*(Suppl. 17), 55–59.

Breslau, N., Johnson, E. O., Hiripi, E., & Kessler, R. (2001). Nicotine dependence in the United States. *Archives of General Psychiatry, 58*(9), 810–816.

Bressi, C., Albonetti, S., & Razzoli, E. (1998). "Communication deviance" and schizophrenia. *New Trends in Experimental & Clinical Psychiatry, 14*(1), 33–39.

Brewer, J. S. (1981). Duration of intromission and female orgasm rates. *Medical Aspects of Human Sexuality, 15*(4), 70–71.

Brewer, K. R., & Wann, D. L. (1998). Observational learning effectiveness as a function of model characteristics. *Social Behavior & Personality, 26*(1), 1–10.

Bridges, K.M.B. (1932). Emotional development in early infancy. *Child Development, 3,* 324–334.

Bridges, L. J. (2003). Trust, attachment, and relatedness. In M. H. Bornstein, L. Davidson, et al. (Eds.), *Well-being: Positive development across the life course.* Mahwah, NJ: Erlbaum.

Brief, A. P., & Weiss, H. M. (2002). Organizational behavior. *Annual Review of Psychology, 53,* 279–307.

Brigham, J. C., & Wasserman, A. W. (1999). The impact of race, racial attitude, and gender on reactions to the criminal trial of O. J. Simpson. *Journal of Applied Social Psychology, 29*(7), 1333–1370.

Brim, O. G., Baltes, P. B., Bumpass, L. L., Cleary, P. D., et al. (1999). National survey of midlife development in the United States (MIDUS), 1995–1996. Ann Arbor, MI: DataStat, Inc./Boston, MA: Harvard Medical School, Dept. of Health Care Policy.

"Bringing Up Baby." (1999). *Sierra,* Jan.–Feb., 17.

Britton, B. K., & Tesser, A. (1991). Effects of time-management practices on college grades. *Journal of Educational Psychology, 83(3),* 405–410.

Brock, T. C., & Green, M. C. (Eds.). (2005). *Persuasion: Psychological insights and perspectives* (2nd ed.). Thousand Oaks, CA: Sage.

Brody, N. (1992). *Intelligence.* San Diego, CA: Academic Press.

Brody, N. (2000). Intelligence. In A. Kazdin (Ed.), *Encyclopedia of psychology.* Washington, DC: American Psychological Association.

Brooks-Gunn, J., & Warren, M. P. (1988). The psychological significance of secondary sexual characteristics in nine- to eleven-year-old girls. *Child Development, 59*(4), 1061–1069.

Brothen, T., & Wambach, C. (2001). Effective student use of computerized quizzes. *Teaching of Psychology, 28*(4), 292–294.

Broughton, W. A., & Broughton, R. J. (1994). Psychosocial impact of narcolepsy. *Sleep, 17*(8, Suppl.), S45–S49.

Brower, A. M. (2002). Are college students alcoholics? *Journal of American College Health, 50*(5), 253–255.

Brown, A. M. (1990a). Development of visual sensitivity to light and color vision in human infants: A critical review. *Vision Research, 30*(8), 1159–1188.

Brown, A. S., Cohen, P., Harkavy-Friedman, J., Babulas, V., et al. (2001). Prenatal rubella, premorbid abnormalities, and adult schizophrenia. *Biological Psychiatry, 49*(6), 473–486.

Brown, B. B., & Bentley, D. L. (1993). Residential burglars judge risk. *Journal of Environmental Psychology, 13*(1), 51–61.

Brown, P. (1990b). The name game. *Journal of Mind and Behavior, 11,* 385–406.

Brown, R., & McNeill, D. (1966). The "tip of the tongue" phenomenon. *Journal of Verbal Learning and Verbal Behavior, 5,* 325–337.

Brown, R. L., Leonard, T., Saunders, L. A., & Papasouiotis, O. (1997). A two-item screening test for alcohol and other drug problems. *Journal of Family Practice, 44*(2), 151–160.

Brown, R. T. (1991). Helping students confront and deal with stress and procrastination. *Journal of College Student Psychotherapy, 6*(2), 87–102.

Brown, S. A., Tapert, S. F., Granholm, E., & Delis, D. C. (2000). Neurocognitive functioning of adolescents: Effects of protracted alcohol use. *Alcoholism: Clinical & Experimental Research, 24*(2), 164–171.

Brown, T. D., Dane, F. C., & Durham, M. D. (1998). Perception of race and ethnicity. *Journal of Social Behavior & Personality, 13*(2), 295–306.

Browne, B. A. (1998). Gender stereotypes in advertising on children's television in the 1990s. *Journal of Advertising, 27*(1), 83–96.

Brownell, K. D. (2003). *Food fight.* New York: McGraw-Hill.

Brownell, K. D., Greenwood, M.R.C., Stellar, E., & Shrager, E. E. (1986). The effects of repeated cycles of weight loss and regain in rats. *Physiology and Behavior, 38,* 459–464.

Bruch, M. A. (2001). Shyness and social interaction. In R. Crozier & L. Alden (Eds.), *International handbook of social anxiety.* Sussex, U.K.: Wiley.

Bruch, M. A., Berko, E. H., & Haase, R. F. (1998). Shyness, masculine ideology, physical attractiveness, and emotional inexpressiveness. *Journal of Counseling Psychology, 45*(1), 84–97.

Bruner, J. (1973). *Going beyond the information given.* New York: Norton.

Bruner, J. (1983). *Child's talk.* New York: Norton.

Bryan, J. H., & Walbek, N. H. (1970). Preaching and practicing generosity: Children's actions and reactions. *Child Development, 41,* 329–353.

Bryant, D. M., & Maxwell, K. L. (1999). The environment and mental retardation. *International Review of Psychiatry, 11*(1) 56–67.

Buchanan, R. W., Breier A., Kirkpatrick B., Ball, B., et al. (1998). Positive and negative symptom response to clozapine in schizophrenic patients. *American Journal of Psychiatry, 155*(6), 751–760.

Buchwald, A. (1965). Psyching out. *Washington Post,* June 20.

Buck, L. A. (1990). Abnormality, normality and health. *Psychotherapy, 27*(2), 187–194.

Buckelew, S. P., Conway, R., Parker, J., & Deuser, W. E., et al. (1998). Biofeedback/relaxation training and exercise interventions for fibromyalgia. *Arthritis Care & Research, 11*(3), 196–209.

Buckhout, R. (1974). Eyewitness testimony. *Scientific American, 231,* 23–31.

Budak, F., Filiz, T. M., Topsever, P., & Tan, Ü. (2005). Correlations between nonverbal intelligence and nerve conduction velocities in right-handed male and female subjects. *International Journal of Neuroscience, 115*(5), 613–623.

Budney, A. J., Novy, P. L., & Hughes, J. R. (1999). Marijuana withdrawal among adults seeking treatment for marijuana dependence. *Addiction, 94*(9), 1311–1322.

Bugental, J.F.T., & Sterling, M. M. (1995). Existential-humanistic psychotherapy: New perspectives. In A. S. Gurman & S. B. Messer (Eds.), *Essential psychotherapies.* New York: Guilford.

Burchinal, M. R., Roberts, J. E., Riggins, R., Zeisel, S. A., et al. (2000). Relating quality of center-based child care to early cognitive and language development longitudinally. *Child Development, 71*(2), 339–357.

Burgess, C. A., & Kirsch, I. (1999). Expectancy information as a moderator of the effects of hypnosis on memory. *Contemporary Hypnosis, 16*(1), 22–31.

Burgner, D., & Hewstone, M. (1993). Young children's causal attributions for success and failure. *British Journal of Developmental Psychology, 11*(2), 125–129.

Burka, J. B., & Yuen, L. M. (1990). *Procrastination: Why you do it; What to do about it.* Cambridge, MA: Perseus Books.

Burlingame, G. M., & Davies, R. (2002). Self-help groups. In M. Hersen & W. H. Sledge (Eds.), *Encyclopedia of psychotherapy.* San Diego: Academic Press.

Burlingame, G. M., Fuhriman, A., & Mosier, J. (2003). The differential effectiveness of group psychotherapy: A meta-analytic perspective. *Group Dynamics: Theory, Research, and Practice, 7*(1), 3–12.

Burnett, R. C., Medin, D. L., Ross, N. O., & Blok, S. V. (2005). Ideal is typical. *Canadian Journal of Experimental Psychology. Special Issue on 2003 Festschrift for Lee R. Brooks, 59*(1), 3–10.

Burns, D. D., & Persons, J. (1982). Hope and hopelessness: A cognitive approach. In L. E. Abt & I. R. Stuart (Eds.), *The newer therapies: A sourcebook.* New York: Van Nostrand Reinhold.

Burns, T. (2004). *Community mental health teams: A guide to current practices.* New York: Oxford.

Burton, C. M., & King, L. A. (2004). The health benefits of writing about intensely positive experiences. *Journal of Research in Personality, 38*(2), 150–163.

Burtt, H. E. (1941). An experimental study of early childhood memory: Final report. *Journal of General Psychology, 58,* 435–439.

Bushman, B. J., & Anderson, C. A. (2001). Media violence and the American public. *American Psychologist, 56*(6/7), 477–489.

Bushman, B. J., & Geen, R. G. (1990). Role of cognitive-emotional mediators and individual differences in the effects of media violence on aggression. *Journal of Personality & Social Psychology, 58*(1), 156–163.

Bushnell, L. W., Sai, F., & Mullin, L. T. (1989). Neonatal recognition of the mother's face. *British Journal of Developmental Psychology, 7*(1), 3–15.

Buss, A. H. (1980). *Self-consciousness and social anxiety.* San Francisco: Freeman.

Buss, A. H. (1986). A theory of shyness. In W. H. Jones, J. M. Cheek, et al. (Eds.), *Shyness: Perspectives on research and treatment.* New York: Plenum.

Buss, D. M. (1985). Human mate selection. *American Scientist, 73,* 47–51.

Buss, D. M. (2000). *The dangerous passion.* New York: Free Press.

Buss, D. M. (2004). *Evolutionary psychology: The new science of the mind* (2nd ed.). Boston: Allyn & Bacon.

Buss, D. M., Abbott, M., Angleitner, A., Asherian, A., et al. (1990). International preferences in selecting mates: A study of 37 cultures. *Journal of Cross-Cultural Psychology, 21*(1), 5–47.

Butcher, J. N. (2005). *A beginner's guide to the MMPI-2* (2nd ed.). Washington, DC: American Psychological Association.

Butcher, J. N., Mineka, S., & Hooley, J. (2004). *Abnormal psychology.* Boston: Allyn & Bacon.

Butkovic, A., & Bratko, D. (2003). Generation and sex differences in sensation seeking: Results of the family study. *Perceptual and Motor Skills, 97*(3, Pt. 1), 965–970.

Butler, J. C. (2000). Personality and emotional correlates of right-wing authoritarianism. *Social Behavior & Personality, 28*(1), 1–14.

Butler, R. (1954). Curiosity in monkeys. *Scientific American, 190*(18), 70–75.

Buyer, L. S. (1988). Creative problem solving: A comparison of performance under different instructions. *Journal of Creative Behavior, 22*(1), 55–61.

Byrne, S. M., & McLean, N. J. (2002). The cognitive-behavioral model of bulimia nervosa: A direct evaluation. *International Journal of Eating Disorders, 31,* 17–31.

Byrnes, J. P., Miller, D. C., & Schafer, W. D. (1999). Gender differences in risk taking: A meta-analysis. *Psychological Bulletin, 125*(3), 367–383.

Cadinu, M., Maass, A., Rosabianca, A., & Kiesner, J. (2005). Why do women underperform under stereotype threat? Evidence for the role of negative thinking. *Psychological Science, 16*(7), 572–578.

Cahill, S. P., Carrigan, M. H., & Frueh, B. C. (1999). Does EMDR work? and if so, why? *Journal of Anxiety Disorders, 13*(1–2), 5–33.

Caldera, Y. M., Huston, A. C., & O'Brien, M. (1989). Social interactions and play patterns of parents and toddlers with feminine, masculine, and neutral toys. *Child Development, 60*(1), 70–76.

Calhoun, J. B. (1962). A "behavioral sink." In E. L. Bliss (Ed.), *Roots of behavior.* New York: Harper & Row.

Callaghan, T., Rochat, P., Lillard, A., Claux, M. L., et al. (2005). Synchrony in the onset of mental-state reasoning: Evidence from five cultures. *Psychological Science, 16*(5), 378–384.

Camara, W. J., & Schneider, D. L. (1994). Integrity tests. *American Psychologist, 49*(2), 112–119.

Camatta, C. D., & Nagoshi, C. T. (1995). Stress, depression, irrational beliefs, and alcohol use and problems in a college student sample. *Alcoholism: Clinical & Experimental Research, 19*(1), 142–146.

Cameron, L. D., & Nicholls, G. (1998). Expression of stressful experiences through writing. *Health Psychology, 17*(1), 84–92.

Campanelli, J. F., & Price, J. L. (1991). *Write in time: Essay exam strategies.* Ft. Worth, TX: Holt, Rinehart & Winston.

Campbell, F. A., & Ramey, C. T. (1994). Effect of early intervention on intellectual and academic achievement. *Child Development, 65,* 684–698.

Campbell, J. B., & Hawley, C. W. (1982). Study habits and Eysenck's theory of extraversion–introversion. *Journal of Research in Personality, 16,* 139–146.

Campbell, L., Campbell, B., & Dickinson, D. (2003). *Teaching and learning through multiple intelligences* (3rd ed.). Boston: Allyn & Bacon.

Campfield, L. A., Smith, F. J., Rosenbaum, M., & Hirsch, J. (1996). Human eating: Evidence for a physiological basis using a modified paradigm. *Neuroscience & Biobehavioral Reviews, 20*(1), 133–137.

Campion, M. A., & McClelland, C. L. (1993). Follow-up and extension of interdisciplinary costs and benefits of enlarged jobs. *Journal of Applied Psychology, 78*(3), 339–351.

Campion, M. A., Palmer, D. K., & Campion, J. E. (1998). Structuring employment interviews to improve reliability, validity and users' reactions. *Current Directions in Psychological Science, 7*(3), 77–82.

Campos, A., & Perez, M. J. (1997). Mnemonic images and associated pair recall. *Journal of Mental Imagery, 21*(3–4), 73–82.

Campos, J. J., Hiatt, S., Ramsay, D., Henderson, C., et al. (1978). The emergence of fear on the visual cliff. In M. Lewis & L. A. Rosenblum (Eds.), *The development of affect.* New York: Plenum Press.

Camras, L. A., Sullivan, J., & Michel, G. (1993). Do infants express discrete emotions? *Journal of Nonverbal Behavior, 17*(3), 171–186.

Canivez, G. L., & Watkins, M. W. (1998). Long-term stability of the Wechsler Intelligence Scale for Children—Third Edition. *Psychological Assessment, 10*(3), 285–291.

Canli, T., Desmond, J. E., Zhao, Z., Glover, G., et al. (1998). Hemispheric asymmetry for emotional stimuli detected with fMRI. *Neuroreport, 9*(14) 3233–3239.

Cann, A., Holt, K., & Calhoun, L. G. (1999). The roles of humor and sense of humor in responses to stressors. *Humor: International Journal of Humor Research, 12*(2), 177–193.

Cannon, W. B., & Washburn, A. L. (1912). An exploration of hunger. *American Journal of Physiology, 29,* 441–454.

Cannon, W. B. (1932). *The wisdom of the body.* New York: Norton.

Cannon, W. B. (1934). Hunger and thirst. In C. Murchinson (Ed.), *Handbook of general experimental psychology.* Worcester, MA: Clark University Press.

Caplan, P. J. (1995). *They say you're crazy.* Reading, MA: Addison-Wesley.

Capron, C., & Duyme, M. (1992). Assessment of effects of socio-economic status on IQ in a full cross-fostering study. *Nature, 340,* 552–554.

Capuzzi, D. (2003). *Approaches to group counseling.* Englewood Cliffs, NJ: Prentice Hall.

Cardoso, S. H. (2000). Our ancient laughing brain. *Cerebrum, 2*(4), 15–30.

Carducci, B. J., & Stein, N. D. (1988). *The personal and situational pervasiveness of shyness in college students: A nine-year comparison.* Paper presented at the meeting of the Southeastern Psychological Association, New Orleans, April.

Carey, J. C., Stanley, D. A., & Biggers, J. (1988). Peak alert time and rapport between residence hall roommates. *Journal of College Student Development, 29*(3), 239–243.

Carlson, C. L., Pelhan, W. E., Milich, R., & Dixon, J. (1992). Single and combined effects of methylphenidate and behavior therapy on the classroom performance of children with attention-deficit hyperactivity disorder. *Journal of Abnormal Child Psychology, 20*(2), 213–232.

Carlson, J. G., Chemtob, C. M., Rusnak, K., Hedlund, N. L., et al. (1998). Eye movement desensitization and reprocessing (EDMR) treatment for combat-related post-traumatic stress disorder. *Journal of Traumatic Stress, 11*(1), 3–24.

Carlson, M., Marcus-Hewhall, A., & Miller, N. (1990). Effects of situational aggression cues: A quantitative review. *Journal of Personality & Social Psychology, 58*(4), 622–633.

Carlson, N. R. (2005). *Physiology of behavior* (8th ed.). Boston: Allyn & Bacon.

Carnegie Corporation of New York. (1994). *Starting points: Meeting the needs of our youngest children.* New York: Carnegie Corporation.

Carney, R. N., & Levin, J. R. (1998). Do mnemonic memories fade as time goes by? *Contemporary Educational Psychology, 23*(3), 276–297.

Carney, R. N., & Levin, J. R. (2001). Remembering the names of unfamiliar animals: Keywords as keys to their kingdom. *Applied Cognitive Psychology, 15*(2), 133–143.

Carney, R. N., Levin, J. R., & Stackhouse, T. L. (1997). The face–name mnemonic strategy from a different perspective. *Contemporary Educational Psychology, 22*(3), 399–412.

Carroll, J. M., & Russell, J. A. (1996). Do facial expressions signal specific emotions? Judging emotion from the face in context. *Journal of Personality & Social Psychology, 70*(2), 205–218.

Carskadon, M. A., Acebo, C., & Jenni, O. C. (2004). Regulation of adolescent sleep: Implications for behavior. *Annals of the New York Academy of Science, 1021,* 276–291.

Carter, W. E. (Ed.). (1980). *Cannabis in Costa Rica: A study of chronic marihuana use.* Philadelphia: Institute for the Study of Human Issues.

Cartwright, R., & Lamberg, L. (1992). *Crisis dreaming.* New York: HarperCollins.

Casey, P. (2001). Multiple personality disorder. *Primary Care Psychiatry, 7*(1), 7–11.

Casto, S. D., DeFries, J. C., & Fulker, D. W. (1995). Multivariate genetic analysis of Wechsler Intelligence Scale for Children—Revised (WISC–R) factors. *Behavior Genetics, 25*(1), 25–32.

Castro, J. R., & Rice, K. G. (2003). Perfectionism and ethnicity: Implications for depressive symptoms and self-reported academic achievement. *Cultural Diversity and Ethnic Minority Psychology, 9*(1), 64–78.

Catalano, R., Novaco, R., & McConnell, W. (1997). A model of the net effect of job loss on violence. *Journal of Personality & Social Psychology, 72*(6), 1440–1447.

Cattell, R. B. (1965). *The scientific analysis of personality.* Baltimore: Penguin.

Cattell, R. B. (1973). Personality pinned down. *Psychology Today,* July, 40–46.

Cautela, J. R., & Bennett, A. K. (1981). Covert conditioning. In R. J. Corsini (Ed.), *Handbook of innovative psychotherapies.* New York: Wiley.

Cautela, J. R., & Kearney, A. J. (1986). *The covert conditioning handbook.* New York: Springer.

CDC. (2003). *Overweight, obesity, and healthy weight among persons 20 years of age and over, according to sex, age, race, and Hispanic origin: United States, 1960–62, 1971–74, 1976–80, 1988–94, and 1999–2000.* Atlanta, GA: Centers for Disease Control and Prevention.

Ceci, S. J. (1991). How much does schooling influence general intelligence and its cognitive components? *Developmental Psychology, 27*(5), 703–722.

Cecil, H., Evans, R. J., & Stanley, M. A. (1996). Perceived believability among adolescents of health warning labels on cigarette packs. *Journal of Applied Social Psychology, 26*(6), 502–519.

Chabas, D., Taheri, S., Renier, C., & Mignot, E. (2003). The genetics of narcolepsy. *Annual Review of Genomics and Human Genetics, 4,* 459–483.

Chakos, M. H., Alvir, J. M. J., Woerner, M., & Koreen, A. (1996). Incidence and correlates of tardive dyskinesia in first episode of schizophrenia. *Archives of General Psychiatry, 53*(4), 313–319.

Chamberlin, J. (2004). Survey says: More Americans are seeking mental health treatment. *Monitor on Psychology,* July/Aug., 17.

Chamberlin, J., & Rogers, J. A. (1990). Planning a community-based mental health system. *American Psychologist, 45*(11), 1241–1244.

Chambers, R. A., Taylor, J. R., & Potenza, M. N. (2003). Developmental neurocircuitry of motivation in adolescence: A critical period of addiction vulnerability. *American Journal of Psychiatry, 160*(6), 1041–1052.

Chambless, D. L., & Ollendick, T. H. (2001). Empirically supported psychological interventions. *Annual Review of Psychology, 52,* 685–716.

Chamorro-Premuzic, T., & Furnham, A. (2003). Personality predicts academic performance. *Journal of Research in Personality, 37*(4), 319–338.

Chan, G. C.-K., Hinds, T. R., Impey, S., & Storm, D. R. (1998). Hippocampal neurotoxicity of Δ-sup-9-tetrahydrocannabinol. *Journal of Neuroscience, 18*(14), 5322–5332.

Chance, P. (2006). *Learning and behavior* (5th ed.). Belmont, CA: Wadsworth.

Chandler, M. J., & Lalonde, C. E. (1998). Cultural continuity as a hedge against suicide in Canada's First Nations. *Transcultural Psychiatry, 35*(2), 193–211.

Chandler, M. J., Lalonde, C. E., Sokol, B. W., & Hallett, D. (2003). Personal persistence, identity development, and suicide: A study of Native and non-Native North American adolescents. *Monographs of the Society for Research in Child Development, 68*(2), vii–130.

Chansler, P. A., Swamidass, P. M., & Cammann, C. (2003). Self-managing work teams: An empirical study of group cohesiveness in "natural work groups" at a Harley-Davidson Motor Company plant. *Small Group Research, 34*(1), 101–120.

Chapanis, A., & Lindenbaum, L. E. (1959). A reaction time study of four control-display linkages. *Human Factors, 1,* 1–7.

Chartrand, T. L., & Bargh, J. A. (1999). The chameleon effect: The perception-behavior link and social interaction. *Journal of Personality & Social Psychology, 76*(6), 893–910.

Chassin, L., Presson, C. C., Sherman, S. J., & Kim, K. (2003). Historical changes in cigarette smoking and smoking-related beliefs after 2 decades in a midwestern community. *Health Psychology, 22*(4), 347–353.

Chastain, G., & Thurber, S. (1989). The SQ3R study technique enhances comprehension of an introductory psychology textbook. *Reading Improvement, 26*(1), 94.

Chasteen, A. L., Bhattacharyya, S., Horhota, M., Tam, R., et al. (2005). How feelings of stereotype threat influence older adults' memory performance. *Experimental Aging Research, 31*(3), 235–260.

Chaves, J. F. (2000). Hypnosis. In A. Kazdin (Ed.), *Encyclopedia of psychology*. Washington, DC: American Psychological Association.

Check, J. V. P., & Malamuth, N. M. (1983). Sex role stereotyping and reactions to depictions of stranger versus acquaintance rape. *Journal of Personality & Social Psychology, 45,* 344–356.

Cheek, J., & Buss, A. H. (1979). *Scales of shyness, sociability and self-esteem and correlations among them.* Unpublished research, University of Texas. (Cited by Buss, 1980.)

Chen, E. Y. H., Lam, L. C. W., Chen, R. Y. L., Nguyen, D. G. H., et al. (2001). Neurological signs and sustained attention impairment in schizophrenia. *European Archives of Psychiatry & Clinical Neuroscience, 251*(1), 1–5.

Chen, Z., Lawson, R. B., Gordon, L. R., & McIntosh, B. (1996). Groupthink: Deciding with the leader and the devil. *Psychological Record, 46*(4), 581–590.

Chen, Z., Mo, L., & Honomichl, R. (2004). Having the memory of an elephant. *Journal of Experimental Psychology: General, 133*(3), 415–433.

Cheng, H., Cao, Y., & Olson, L. (1996). Spinal cord repair in adult paraplegic rats: Partial restoration of hind limb function. *Science, 273*(5274), 510.

Chess, S., & Thomas, A. (1986). *Know your child.* New York: Basic.

Chess, S., Thomas, A., & Birch, H. G. (1976). *Your child is a person: A psychological approach to parenthood without guilt.* New York: Penguin.

Chesson, A. L., Anderson, W. M., Littner, M., Davila. D, et al. (1999). Practice parameters for the nonpharmacologic treatment of chronic insomnia. *Sleep, 22,* 1128–1133.

Chomsky, N. (1975). *Reflections on language.* New York: Pantheon.

Chomsky, N. (1986). *Knowledge of language.* New York: Praeger.

Christensen, A., & Jacobson, N. S. (1994). Who (or what) can do psychotherapy. *Psychological Science, 5*(1), 8–14.

Christian, A. G., & McDonald, J. L. (1987). Smokeless tobacco country: From nicotine dependency to oral problems and cancer. *Aviation, Space, & Environmental Medicine, 58*(2), 97–104.

Chua, H. F., Boland, J. E., & Nisbett, R. E. (2005). Cultural variation in eye movements during scene perception. *Proceedings of the National Academy of Sciences of the United States of America, 102*(35), 12629–12633.

Chua, P., & Fujino, D. C. (1999). Negotiating new Asian-American masculinities: Attitudes and gender expectations. *Journal of Men's Studies, 7*(3), 391–413.

Cialdini, R. B. (2001). *Influence: Science and practice* (4th ed.). Boston: Allyn & Bacon.

Cialdini, R. B., Eisenberg, N., & Green, B. L., Rhoads, K., et al. (1998). Undermining the undermining effect of reward on sustained interest. *Journal of Applied Social Psychology, 28*(3), 249–263.

Cialdini, R. B., & Goldstein, N. J. (2004). Social influence: Compliance and conformity. *Annual Review of Psychology, 55,* 591–621.

Cialdini, R. B., Reno, R. R., & Kallgren, C. A. (1990). A focus theory of normative conduct: Recycling the concept of norms to reduce littering in public places. *Journal of Personality & Social Psychology, 58*(6), 1015–1026.

Ciarrochi, J., Dean, F. P., & Anderson, S. (2002). Emotional intelligence moderates the relationship between stress and mental health. *Personality & Individual Differences, 32*(2), 197–209.

Cinciripini, P. M., Wetter, D. W., & McClure, J. B. (1997). Scheduled reduced smoking. *Addictive Behaviors, 22*(6), 759–767.

Clair, J. M., Karp, D. A., & Yoels, W. C. (1994). *Experiencing the life cycle.* Springfield, IL: Charles C Thomas.

Clapham, M. M. (2001). The effects of affect manipulation and information exposure on divergent thinking. *Creativity Research Journal, 13*(3–4), 335–350.

Clark, D., Boutros, N., & Mendez, M. (2005). *The brain and behavior* (2nd ed.). Cambridge: Cambridge University Press.

Clark, K. B. (1965). *Dark ghetto.* New York: Harper & Row.

Clark, R., Anderson, N. B., Clark, V. R., & Williams, D. R. (1999). Racism as a stressor for African Americans. *American Psychologist, 54*(10), 805–816.

Click, P., Zion, C., & Nelson, C. (1988). What mediates sex discrimination in hiring decisions? *Journal of Personality & Social Psychology, 55*(2), 178–186.

Cline, V. B., Croft, R. G., & Courrier, S. (1972). Desensitization of children to television violence. *Journal of Personality & Social Psychology, 27,* 360–365.

Clore, G. L. (1976). Interpersonal attraction: An overview. In *Contemporary topics in social psychology.* Morristown, NJ: General Learning Press.

Cochran, S. D. (2001). Emerging issues in research on lesbians' and gay men's mental health. *American Psychologist,* Nov., 931–947.

Cohen, D. J., & Bennett, S. (1997). Why can't most people draw what they see? *Journal of Experimental Psychology: Human Perception and Performance, 23*(3), 609–621.

Cohen, J. E. (1995). *How many people can the earth support?* New York: Norton.

Cohen, N. L., Waltzman, S. B., & Fisher, S. G. (1993). A prospective, randomized study of cochlear implants. *New England Journal of Medicine, 328*(4), 233–237.

Cohen, R. J., & Swerdlik, M. E. (2005). *Psychological testing and assessment* (6th ed.). New York: McGraw-Hill.

Cohen, S., Evans, G. W., Krantz, D. S., & Stokols, D. (1981). Cardiovascular and behavioral effects of community noise. *American Scientist, 69,* 528–535.

Colapinto, J. (2000). *As nature made him: The boy who was raised as a girl.* New York: HarperCollins.

Cole, J. (1995). *Pride and a daily marathon.* Cambridge, MA: MIT Press.

Cole, P. H. (1998). Affective process in psychotherapy: A Gestalt therapist's view. *Gestalt Journal, 21*(1), 49–72.

Colin, A. K., Moore, K., & West, A. N. (1996). Creativity, oversensitivity, and rate of habituation. *EDRA: Environmental Design Research Association, 20*(4), 423–427.

Collins, A. M., & Quillian, M. R. (1969). Retrieval time from semantic memory. *Journal of Verbal Learning and Verbal Behavior, 8,* 240–247.

Collins, N. L., Cooper, M. L., Albino, A., & Allard, L. (2002). Psychosocial vulnerability from adolescence to adulthood: A prospective study of attachment style differences in relationship functioning and partner choice. *Journal of Personality, 70*(6), 965–1008.

Collins, R. L. (1996). For better or worse: The impact of upward social comparison on self-evaluations. *Psychological Bulletin, 119*(1), 51–69.

Collins, W. A., & Gunnar, M. R. (1990). Social and personality development. *Annual Review of Psychology, 41,* 387–416.

Comer, R. J. (2005). *Fundamentals of abnormal psychology* (4th ed.). New York: Worth.

Comperatore, C. A., Lieberman, H. R., Kirby, A. W., & Adams, B. (1996). Melatonin efficacy in aviation missions requiring rapid deployment and night operations. *Aviation, Space, & Environmental Medicine, 67*(6), 520–524.

Compton, W. C. (2005). *An introduction to positive psychology.* Belmont, CA: Wadsworth.

Condon, W. S., & Sander, L. W. (1974) Synchrony demonstrated between movements of the neonate and adult speech. *Child Development, 45*(2), 456–462.

Coni, N., Davison, W., & Webster, S. (1984). *Ageing.* Oxford: Oxford University Press.

Conoley, J. C., & Goldstein, A. P. (Eds.). (2004). *School violence intervention: A practical handbook* (2nd ed.). New York: Guilford.

Conway, A. R. A., Cowan, N., & Bunting, M. F. (2001). The cocktail party phenomenon revisited. *Psychonomic Bulletin & Review, 8*(2), 331–335.

Conway, M. A., Cohen, G., & Stanhope, N. (1992). Very long-term memory for knowledge acquired at school and university. *Applied Cognitive Psychology, 6*(6), 467–482.

Conyne, R. K., & Clack, R. J. (1981). *Environmental assessment and design.* New York: Praeger.

Cooper, G. D., Adams, H. B., & Scott, J. C. (1988). Studies in REST: I. Reduced Environmental Stimulation Therapy (REST) and reduced alcohol consumption. *Journal of Substance Abuse Treatment, 5*(2), 61–68.

Cooper, J., & Fazio, R. H. (1984). A new look at dissonance theory. *Advances in Experimental Social Psychology, 17,* 226–229.

Cooper, J., Bennett, E. A., & Sukel, H. L. (1996). Complex scientific testimony: How do jurors make decisions? *Law & Human Behavior, 20*(4), 379–394.

Cooper, J., Mirabile, R., & Scher, S. J. (2005). Actions and attitudes: The theory of cognitive dissonance. In T. C. Brock & M. C. Green (Eds.), *Persuasion: Psychological insights and perspectives* (2nd ed). Thousand Oaks, CA: Sage.

Cooper, M. J. (2005). Cognitive theory in anorexia nervosa and bulimia nervosa: Progress, development and future directions. *Clinical Psychology Review, 25*(4), 511–531.

Cooper, P. J., & Murray, L. (2001). The treatment and prevention of postpartum depression and associated disturbances in child development. *Archives of Women's Mental Health, 3*(suppl. 2), 5.

Cooper, R. P., Abraham, J., Berman, S., & Staska, M. (1997). The development of infants' preference for motherese. *Infant Behavior and Development, 20*(4), 477–488.

Coopersmith, S. (1968). Studies in self-esteem. *Scientific American, 218,* 96–106.

Corballis, M. C. (2002). *From hand to mouth: The origins of language.* Princeton, NJ: Princeton University Press.

Corbin, W. R., & Fromme, K. (2002). Alcohol use and serial monogamy as risks for sexually transmitted diseases in young adults. *Health Psychology, 21*(3), 229–236.

Cordova, D. I., & Lepper, M. R. (1996). Intrinsic motivation and the process of learning. *Journal of Educational Psychology, 88*(4), 715–730.

Coren, S. (1992). *The left-hander syndrome.* New York: Free Press.

Coren, S. (1996). *Sleep thieves.* New York: Free Press.

Coren, S., Ward, L. M., & Enns, J. T. (2004). *Sensation and perception* (6th ed.). New York: Wiley.

Corkin, S. (2002). What's new with the amnesic patient H.M.? *Nature Reviews Neuroscience, 3,* 153–160.

Cormier, J. F., & Thelen, M. H. (1998). Professional skepticism of multiple personality disorder. *Professional Psychology: Research and Practice, 29*(2), 163–167.

Cornell, D. G. (2005). School violence: Fears versus facts. In K. Heilbrun, N. E. S. Goldstein, et al. (Eds.), *Juvenile delinquency: Prevention, assessment, and intervention.* New York: Oxford University Press.

Cornsweet, T. N. (1970). *Visual perception.* New York: Academic.

Correa-Chávez, M., Rogoff, B., & Arauz, R. M. (2005). Cultural patterns in attending to two events at once. *Child Development, 76*(3), 664–678.

Corrigan, P. W. (1997). Behavior therapy empowers persons with severe mental illness. *Behavior Modification, 21*(1), 45–61.

Corrigan, P. W., & Penn, D. L. (1999). Lessons from social psychology on discrediting psychiatric stigma. *American Psychologist, 54*(9), 765–776.

Corrigan, P. W., & Watson, A. C. (2005). Findings from the National Comorbidity Survey on the frequency of violent behavior in individuals with psychiatric disorders. *Psychiatry Research, 136*(2–3), 153–162.

Corrigan, P. W., Watson, A. C., Gracia, G., Slopen, N., et al. (2005). Newspaper stories as measures of structural stigma. *Psychiatric Services, 56*(5), 551–556.

Corteen, R. S., & Williams, T. M. (1986). Television and reading skills. In T. M. Williams (Ed.), *The impact of television: A natural experiment in three communities.* Orlando, FL: Academic.

Costa, P. T., & McCrae, R. R. (1992). Multiple uses for longitudinal personality data. *European Journal of Personality, 6(2),* 85–102.

Cote, S. (1999). Affect and performance in organizational settings. *Current Directions in Psychological Science, 8*(2), 65–68.

Coulton, C. J., Korbin, J. E., & Su, M. (1996). Measuring neighborhood context for young children in an urban area. *American Journal of Community Psychology, 24*(1), 5–32.

Coursey, R. D., Ward-Alexander, L., & Katz, B. (1990). Cost-effectiveness of providing insurance benefits for posthospital psychiatric halfway house stays. *American Psychologist, 45*(10), 1118–1126.

Court, J. H., & Court, P. C. (2001). Repression: R. I. P. *Australian Journal of Clinical & Experimental Hypnosis, 29*(1), 8–16.

Covell, K., Grusec, J. E., & King, G. (1995). The intergenerational transmission of maternal discipline and standards for behavior. *Social Development, 4*(1), 32–43.

Cover, J. D. (1995). The effects of social contact on prejudice. *Journal of Social Psychology, 135*(3), 403–405.

Cowan, N. (2001). The magical number 4 in short-term memory. *Behavioral & Brain Sciences, 24*(1), 87–185.

Cowles, J. T. (1937). Food tokens as incentives for learning by chimpanzees. *Comparative Psychology,* Monograph, *14*(5, Whole no. 71).

Cox, W. E. (1994). Exceptional evidence of ESP by a reputed sensitive. *Journal of the Society for Psychical Research, 60*(836), 16–28.

Coye, R. W., & Belohlav, J. A. (1995). An exploratory analysis of employee participation. *Group & Organization Management, 20*(1), 4–17.

Craig, T. Y., & Kelly, J. R. (1999). Group cohesiveness and creative performance. *Group Dynamics, 3*(4), 243–256.

Craik, F. I. M. (1970). The fate of primary items in free recall. *Journal of Verbal Learning and Verbal Behavior, 9,* 143–148.

Craik, F. I. M., & Bialystok, E. (2005). Intelligence and executive control: Evidence from aging and bilingualism. *Cortex, 41*(2), 222–224.

Crandall, C. S., Preisler, J. J., & Aussprung, J. (1992). Measuring life event stress in the lives of college students: The Undergraduate Stress Questionnaire (USQ). *Journal of Behavioral Medicine, 15*(6), 627–662.

Crano, W. D. (2000). Milestones in the psychological analysis of social influence. *Group Dynamics: Theory, Research, and Practice, 4*(1), 68–80.

Cravatt, B. F., Prospero-Garcia O., Siuzdak G., Gilula, N. B., et al. (1995). Chemical characterization of a family of brain lipids that induce sleep. *Science, 268*(5216), 1506–1509.

Crawford, T. N., Cohen, P., Johnson, J. G., Sneed, J. R., et al. (2004). The course and psychosocial correlates of personality disorder symptoms in adolescence: Erikson's developmental theory revisited. *Journal of Youth & Adolescence, 33*(5), 373–387.

Crawley, S. B., & Sherrod, K. B. (1984). Parent–infant play during the first year of life. *Infant Behavior & Development, 7,* 65–75.

Creamer, M., Burgess, P., & McFarlane, A. C. (2001). Post-traumatic stress disorder: Findings from the Australian National Survey of Mental Health and Well-Being. *Psychological Medicine, 31*(7), 1237–1247.

Cregler, L. L., & Mark, H. (1985). Medical complications of cocaine abuse. *New England Journal of Medicine, 315*(23), 1495–1500.

Crencavage, L. M., & Norcross, J. C. (1990). Where are the commonalities among the therapeutic common factors? *Professional Psychology: Research & Practice, 21*(5), 372–378.

Crocker, J., & Park, L. E. (2004). The costly pursuit of self-esteem. *Psychological Bulletin, 130*(3), 392–414.

Cromdal, J. (1999). Childhood bilingualism and metalinguistic skills. *Applied Psycholinguistics, 20*(1), 1–20.

Cronbach, L. (1990). *Essentials of psychological testing.* Reading, PA: Addison-Wesley.

Cronk, N. J., Slutske, W. S., Madden, P. A. F., Bucholz, K. K., et al. (2005). Risk for separation anxiety disorder among girls: Paternal absence, socioeconomic disadvantage, and genetic vulnerability. *Journal of Abnormal Psychology, 113*(2), 237–247.

Crooks, R., & Bauer, K. (2005). *Our sexuality* (9th ed.). Belmont, CA: Wadsworth.

Crosby, R. A., & Yarber, W. L. (2001). Perceived versus actual knowledge about correct condom use among U.S. adolescents: results from a national study. *Journal of Adolescent Health, 28*(5), 415–420.

Crouch, J. L., & Behl, L. E. (2001). Relationships among parental beliefs in corporal punishment, reported stress, and physical child abuse potential. *Child Abuse & Neglect, 25*(3), 413–419.

Crowe, L. C., & George, W. H. (1989). Alcohol and human sexuality: Review and integration. *Psychological Bulletin, 105*(3), 374–386.

Crown, C. L., Feldstein, S., Jasnow, M. D., Beebe, B., et al. (2002). The cross-modal coordination of interpersonal timing. *Journal of Psycholinguistic Research, 31*(1), 1–23.

Crowther, J. H., Sanftner, J., Bonifazi, D. Z., & Shepherd, K. L. (2001). The role of daily hassles in binge eating. *International Journal of Eating Disorders, 29,* 449–454.

Csikszentmihalyi, M. (1997). *Creativity.* New York: HarperCollins.

Csikszentmihalyi, M., Abuhamdeh, S., Nakamura, J. (2005). Flow. In A. J. Elliot & C. S. Dweck, (Eds.), *Handbook of competence and motivation.* New York: Guilford.

Cull, M. (2002). Treatment of intersex needs open discussion. *British Medical Journal, 324*(7342), 919

Cull, W. L., Shaughnessy, J. J., & Zechmeister, E. B. (1996). Expanding understanding of the expanding-pattern-of-retrieval mnemonic. *Journal of Experimental Psychology: Applied, 2*(4) 365–378.

Cumming, B. G., & DeAngelis, G. C. (2001). The physiology of stereopsis. *Annual Review of Neuroscience, 24,* 203–238.

Cumming, E., & Henry, W. E. (1961). *Growing old: The process of disengagement.* New York: Basic.

Cumming, S., Hay, P., Lee, T., & Sachdev, P. (1995). Neuropsychological outcome from psychosurgery for obsessive-compulsive disorder. *Australian & New Zealand Journal of Psychiatry, 29*(2), 293–298.

Cummins, D. D. (1995). *The other side of psychology.* New York: St. Martins.

Cushner, K. (2003). *Human diversity in action: Developing multicultural competencies for the classroom* (2nd ed.). Boston: McGraw-Hill.

Czeisler, C. A., Duffy, J. F., Shanahan, T. L., Brown, E. N., et al. (1999). Stability, precision, and near-24-hour period of the human circadian pacemaker. *Science, 284*(5423), 2177–2181.

Czeisler, C. A., Kronauer, R. E., Allan, J. S., Duffy, J. F., et al. (1989). Bright light induction of strong (Type O) resetting of the human circadian pacemaker. *Science, 244*(June), 1328–1333.

Czeisler, C. A., Richardson, G. S., Zimmerman, J. C., Moore-Ede, M. C., et al. (1981). Entrainment of human circadian rhythms by light-dark cycles: A reassessment. *Photochemistry, Photobiology, 34,* 239–247.

Dabbs, J. M., Jr., Hargrove, M. F., & Heusel, C. (1996). Testosterone differences among college fraternities. *Personality & Individual Differences, 20*(2), 157–161.

Darley, J. M., & Latané, B. (1968). Bystander intervention in emergencies: Diffusion of responsibility. *Journal of Personality & Social Psychology, 8,* 377–383.

Darling, C. A., Davidson, J. K., & Passarello, L. C. (1992). The mystique of first intercourse among college youth: The role of partners, contraceptive practices, and psychological reactions. *Journal of Youth & Adolescence, 21*(1), 97–117.

Darou, W. S. (1992). Native Canadians and intelligence testing. *Canadian Journal of Counselling, 26*(2), 96–99.

Darwin, C. (1872). *The expression of emotion in man and animals.* Chicago: University of Chicago Press.

Das, J. P. (2000). Mental retardation. In A. Kazdin (Ed.), *Encyclopedia of psychology.* Washington, DC: American Psychological Association.

DasGupta, B. (1992). Perceived control and examination stress. *Psychology: A Journal of Human Behavior, 29*(1), 31–34.

Davanloo, H. (1995). Intensive short-term dynamic psychotherapy. *International Journal of Short-Term Psychotherapy, 10*(3–4), 121–155.

David, H., Borgeat, F., & Saucier, J. (1990). The relation between tachystoscopic pictures and neurotic postpartum depression. *Pre- & Peri-Natal Psychology Journal, 4*(3), 219–227.

Davidson, P. R., & Parker, K. C. H. (2001). Eye movement desensitization and reprocessing (EMDR): A meta-analysis. *Journal of Consulting & Clinical Psychology, 69*(2), 305–316.

Davies, M., & McCartney, S. (2003). Effects of gender and sexuality on judgements of victim blame and rape myth acceptance in a depicted male rape. *Journal of Community & Applied Social Psychology, 13*(5), 391–398.

Davies, M. F. (1993). Dogmatism and the persistence of discredited beliefs. *Personality & Social Psychology Bulletin, 19*(6), 692–699.

Davis, D., & Follette, W. C. (2002). Rethinking the probative value of evidence. *Law & Human Behavior, 26*(2), 133–158.

Davis, J. R., Vanderploeg, J. M., Santy, P. A., Jennings, R. T., et al. (1988). Space motion sickness during 24 flights of the Space Shuttle. *Aviation, Space, & Environmental Medicine, 59*(12), 1185–1189.

Davis, M. J., & Bibace, R. (1999). Dating couples and their relationships: Intimacy and contraceptive use. *Adolescence, 34*(133), 1–7.

Davis, M. R., McMahon, M., & Greenwood, K. M. (2005). The efficacy of mnemonic components of the cognitive interview: Towards a shortened variant for time-critical investigations. *Applied Cognitive Psychology, 19*(1), 75–93.

Davison, G. C., & Neale, J. M. (2006). *Abnormal psychology* (10th ed.). San Francisco: Jossey-Bass.

Daw, J. (2002). New Mexico becomes first state to gain Rx privileges. *Monitor on Psychology,* April, 24–25.

Dawson, G., Carver, L., Meltzoff, A. N., Panagiotides, H., et al. (2002). Neural correlates of face and object recognition in young children with autism spectrum disorder, developmental delay and typical development. *Child Development, 73*(3), 700–717.

Day, S. X., & Schneider, P. L. (2002). Psychotherapy using distance technology. *Journal of Counseling Psychology, 49*(4), 499–503.

Dean-Church, L., & Gilroy, F. D. (1993). Relation of sex-role orientation to life satisfaction in a healthy elderly sample. *Journal of Social Behavior & Personality, 8*(1), 133–140.

Deary, I. J., Simonotto, E., Marshall, A., Marshall, I., et al. (2001). The functional anatomy of inspection time. *Intelligence, 29*(6), 497–510.

Deary, I. J., & Stough, C. (1996). Intelligence and inspection time. *American Psychologist, 51*(6), 599–608.

Deaux, K., & Emswiller, T. (1974). Explanation of successful performance on sex-linked tasks: What is skill for the male is luck for the female. *Journal of Personality & Social Psychology, 29,* 80–85.

de Bono, E. (1992). *Serious creativity.* New York: HarperCollins.

Deckers, L. (2005). *Motivation: Biological, psychological, and environmental* (2nd ed.). Boston: Allyn & Bacon.

Deckro, G. R., Ballinger, K. M., Hoyt, M., Wilcher, M., et al. (2002). The evaluation of a mind/body intervention to reduce psychological distress and perceived stress in college students. *Journal of American College Health, 50*(6), 281–287.

Deco, G., Rolls, E. T., & Horwitz, B. (2004). "What" and "Where" in visual working memory: A computational neurodynamical perspective for integrating fMRI and single-neuron data. *Journal of Cognitive Neuroscience, 16*(4), 683–701.

Deeb, S. S. (2004). Molecular genetics of color-vision deficiencies. *Visual Neuroscience, 21*(3), 191–196.

Deese, J., & Hulse, S. J. (1967). *The psychology of learning* (3rd. ed.). New York: McGraw-Hill.

Deffenbacher, J. L., & Suinn, R. M. (1988). Systematic desensitization and the reduction of anxiety. *Counseling Psychologist, 16*(1), 9–30.

DeGaetano, G. (2005). The impact of media violence on developing minds and hearts. In S. Olfman (Ed.), *Childhood lost: How American culture is failing our kids.* Westport, CT: Praeger.

Degirmencioglu, S. M., Urberg, K. A., Tolson, J. M., & Richard, P. (1998). Adolescent friendship networks. *Merrill-Palmer Quarterly, 44*(3), 313–337.

DeGood, D. E. (1975). Cognitive factors in vascular stress responses. *Psychophysiology, 12,* 399–401.

deGroot, G. (1994). Psychologists explain Barney's power. *APA Monitor,* June, 4.

De Haan, E. H. F., Heywood, C. A., Young, A. W., Edelstyn, N., et al. (1995). Ettlinger revisited: The relation between agnosia and sensory impairment. *Journal of Neurology, Neurosurgery & Psychiatry, 58*(3), 350–356.

de Jong, P. J., & Muris, P. (2002). Spider phobia. *Journal of Anxiety Disorders, 16*(1), 51–65.

de Jong, T., & van Joolingen, W. R. (1998). Scientific discovery learning with computer simulations of conceptual domains. *Review of Educational Research, 68*(2), 179–201.

DeKlyen, M., Biernbaum, M. A., Spelz, M. L., & Greenberg, M. T. (1998). Fathers and preschool behavior problems, *Developmental Psychology, 34*(2), 264–275.

de las Fuentes, C., & Vasquez, M. J. T. (1999). Immigrant adolescent girls of color. In N. G. Johnson, M. C. Roberts, et al. (Eds.), *Beyond appearance.* Washington, DC: American Psychological Association.

Delgado, B. M., & Ford, L. (1998). Parental perceptions of child development among low-income Mexican American families. *Journal of Child & Family Studies, 7*(4), 469–481.

de Luccie, M. F., & Davis, A. J. (1991). Father–child relationships from the preschool years through mid-adolescence. *Journal of Genetic Psychology, 152*(2), 225–238.

Denmark, F. L., Rabinowitz, V. C., & Sechzer, J. A. (2005). *Engendering psychology: Women and gender revisited* (2nd ed.). Boston: Allyn & Bacon.

Denollet, J., & Van Heck, G. L. (2001). Psychological risk factors in heart disease. *Journal of Psychosomatic Research, 51*(3), 465–468.

De Raad, B. (1998). Five big, Big Five issues. *European Psychologist, 3*(2), 113–124.

Deregowski, J. B. (1972). Pictorial perception and culture. *Scientific American,* Nov., 82–88.

de Rios, M. D., & Grob, C. S. (2005). Editors' introduction: Ayahuasca use in cross-cultural perspective. *Journal of Psychoactive Drugs, 37*(2), 119–121.

Derlega, V. J., Winstead, B. A., & Jones, W. H. (2005). *Personality: Contemporary theory and research* (3rd ed.). Belmont, CA: Wadsworth.

Dermer, A. (1998). Breastfeeding and women's health. *Journal of Women's Health, 7*(4), 427–433.

Desimone, R., & Duncan, J. (1995). Neural mechanisms of selective visual attention. *Annual Review of Neuroscience, 18,* 193–222.

Detterman, D., & Ruthsatz, J. (1999). Toward a more comprehensive theory of exceptional abilities. *Journal for the Education of the Gifted, 22*(2), 148–158.

Deutsch, M. (1993). Educating for a peaceful world. *American Psychologist, 48*(5), 510–517.

Deutsch, M., & Collins, M. E. (1951). *Interracial housing.* Minneapolis: University of Minnesota Press.

Devine, D. J., Clayton, L. D., Dunford, B. B., Seying, R., et al. (2001). Jury decision making: 45 years of empirical research on deliberating groups. *Psychology, Public Policy, & Law, 7*(3), 622–727.

Devine, P. G. (1990). Stereotypes and prejudice: Their automatic and controlled components. *Journal of Personality & Social Psychology, 56*(1), 5–18.

Devine, P. G., Monteith, M. J., Zuerink, J. R., & Elliot, A. J. (1991). Prejudice with and without compunction. *Journal of Personality & Social Psychology, 60*(6), 817–830.

Devlin, B., Daniels, M., & Roeder, K. (1997). The heritability of IQ. *Nature, 388*(6641), 468–471.

Devoto, A., Lucidi, F., Violani, C., & Bertini, M. (1999). Effects of different sleep reductions on daytime sleepiness. *Sleep, 22*(3), 336–343.

Diamond, L. M. (1998). Development of sexual orientation among adolescent and young adult women. *Developmental Psychology, 34*(5), 1085–1095.

Dickens, W. T., & Flynn, J. R. (2001). Heritability estimates versus large environmental effects: The IQ paradox resolved. *Psychological Review, 108,* 346–369.

Dickerson, F. B., Tenhula, W. N., & Green-Paden, L. D. (2005). The token economy for schizophrenia: Review of the literature and recommendations for future research. *Schizophrenia Research, 75*(2–3), 405–416.

Dickinson, D. J., & O'Connell, D. Q. (1990). Effect of quality and quantity of study on student grades. *Journal of Educational Research, 83*(4), 227–231.

Diekstra, R. F., & Garnefski, N. (1995). On the nature, magnitude, and causality of suicidal behaviors: An international perspective. *Suicide & Life-Threatening Behavior, 25*(1), 36–57.

Diener, E., Suh, E. M., Lucas, R. E.., & Smith, H. L. (1999). Subjective well-being: Three decades of progress. *Psychological Bulletin, 125*(2), 276–302.

Dierdorff, E. C., & Wilson, M. A. (2003). A meta-analysis of job analysis reliability. *Journal of Applied Psychology, 88*(4), 635–646.

Dieter, J. N. I., & Emory, E. K. (1997). Supplemental stimulation of premature infants. *Journal of Pediatric Psychology, 22*(3), 281–295.

Dietz, T. L. (1998). An examination of violence and gender role portrayals in video games. *Sex Roles, 38*(5–6), 425–442.

Dignon, A. M. (1996). Acceptability of a computer-administered psychiatric interview. *Computers in Human Behavior, 12*(2), 177–191.

Diller, L. H. (1998). *Running on ritalin.* New York: Bantam.

Di Marzo, V., Goparaju, S. K., Wang, L., Liu, J., et al. (2001). Leptin-regulated endocannabinoids are involved in maintaining food intake. *Nature, 410*(6830), 822–825.

Dinan, T. G. (2001). Stress, depression and cardiovascular disease. *Stress & Health: Journal of the International Society for the Investigation of Stress, 17*(2), 65–66.

Dinkmeyer, D., Sr., McKay, G. D., & Dinkmeyer, D., Jr. (1997). *The parent's handbook.* Circle Pines, MN: American Guidance Service.

Dion, K. L. (2003). Prejudice, racism, and discrimination. In T. Millon & M. J. Lerner (Eds.), *Personality and social psychology. The comprehensive handbook of psychology* (Vol. 5). New York: Wiley.

Dirkzwager, A. J. E., Bramsen, I., & Van Der Ploeg, H. M. (2001). The longitudinal course of posttraumatic stress disorder symptoms among aging military veterans. *Journal of Nervous & Mental Disease, 189*(12), 846–853.

Dobelle, W. H. (2000). Artificial vision for the blind by connecting a television camera to the visual cortex. *American Society of Artificial Internal Organs, 46,* 3–9.

Dobson, K. S., Backs-Dermott, G. J., & Dozois, D. J. A. (2000). Cognitive and cognitive-behavioral therapies. In C. R. Snyder & R. E. Ingram (Eds.), *Handbook of psychological change: Psychotherapy processes and practices for the 21st century.* New York: Wiley.

Doctor, R. M., & Doctor, J. N. (1994). Stress. *Encyclopedia of human behavior* (Vol. 4). San Diego: Academic Press.

Doidge, N. (1997). Empirical evidence for the efficacy of psychoanalytic psychotherapies and psychoanalysis. *Psychoanalytic Inquiry,* Suppl., 102–150.

Dollard, J., & Miller, N. E. (1950). *Personality and psychotherapy: An analysis in terms of learning, thinking and culture.* New York: McGraw-Hill.

Domingo, R. A., & Goldstein-Alpern, N. (1999). "What dis?" and other toddler-initiated, expressive language-learning strategies. *Infant-Toddler Intervention, 9*(1), 39–60.

Donnerstein, E. (2001). Media violence. In J. Worell (Ed.), *Encyclopedia of gender and women.* San Diego: Academic Press.

Donnerstein, E. I., & Linz, D. G. (1986). The question of pornography. *Psychology Today,* Dec., 56–59.

Dooling, D. J., & Lachman, R. (1971). Effects of comprehension on retention of prose. *Journal of Experimental Psychology, 88,* 216–222.

Doran, S. M., Van Dongen, H. P., & Dinges, D. F. (2001). Sustained attention performance during sleep deprivation. *Archives of Italian Biology, 139,* 253–267.

Dorfman, J., Shames, J., & Kihlstrom, J. F. (1996). Intuition, incubation, & insight. In G. Underwood (Ed.), *Implicit cognition.* New York: Oxford University Press.

Dorman, M. F., & Wilson, B. S. (2004). The design and function of cochlear implants. *American Scientist, 92*(Sept.–Oct.), 436–445.

Dosher, B. A., & Ma, J. (1998). Output loss or rehearsal loop? *Journal of Experimental Psychology: Learning, Memory, & Cognition, 24*(2), 316–335.

Doty, R. M., Peterson, B. E., & Winter, D. G. (1991). *Journal of Personality & Social Psychology, 61*(4), 629–640.

Douvan, E. (1997). Erik Erikson: Critical times, critical theory. *Child Psychiatry & Human Development, 28*(1), 15–21.

Dovidio, J. F., Allen, J. L., & Schroeder, D. A. (1990). Specificity of empathy-induced helping: Evidence for altruistic motivation. *Journal of Personality & Social Psychology, 59*(2), 249–260.

Dovidio, J. F., & Gaertner, S. L. (1999). Reducing prejudice: Combating intergroup biases. *Current Directions in Psychological Science, 8*(4), 101–105.

Dovidio, J. F., Gaertner, S. L., Kawakami, K., & Hodson, G. (2002). Why can't we just get along? *Cultural Diversity and Ethnic Minority Psychology, 8*(2), 88–102.

Dovidio, J. F., Glick, P., & Rudman, L. A. (Eds.). (2005). *On the nature of prejudice: Fifty years after Allport.* Malden, MA: Blackwell.

Dovidio, J. F., & Penner, L. A. (2001). Helping and altruism. In M. Hewstone & M. Brewer (Eds.), *Handbook* *of social psychology*. London: Blackwell.

Dozois, D. J. A., & Dobson, K. S. (Eds.). (2004). *The prevention of anxiety and depression: Theory, research, and practice*. Washington, DC: American Psychological Association.

Dragoi, V., & Staddon, J. E. R. (1999). The dynamics of operant conditioning. *Psychological Review, 106*(1), 20–61.

Draguns, J. G., Gielen, U. P., & Fish, J. M. (2004). Approaches to culture, healing, and psychotherapy. In U. P. Gielen, J. M. Fish, et al. (Eds.), *Handbook of culture, therapy, and healing*. Mahwah, NJ: Lawrence Erlbaum.

Dretzke, B. J., & Levin, J. R. (1996). Assessing students' application and transfer of a mnemonic strategy. *Contemporary Educational Psychology, 21*(1), 83–93.

Drigotas, S. M., Rusbult, C. E., Wieselquist, J., & Whitton, S. W. (1999). Close partner as sculptor of the ideal self: Behavioral affirmation and the Michelangelo phenomenon. *Journal of Personality & Social Psychology, 77*(2), 293–323.

Drolet, G., Dumont, E. C., Gosselin, I., Kinkead, R., et al. (2001). Role of endogenous opioid system in the regulation of the stress response. *Progress in Neuro-Psychopharmacology & Biological Psychiatry, 25*(4), 729–741.

Druckman, D., & Bjork, R. A. (1994). *Learning, remembering, believing: Enhancing human performance*. Washington, DC: National Academy Press.

DSM-IV-TR: Diagnostic and statistical manual of mental disorders (5th ed.). (2000). Washington, DC: American Psychiatric Association.

Duclos, S. E., & Laird, J. D. (2001). The deliberate control of emotional experience through control of expressions. *Cognition and Emotion, 15*, 27–56.

Duffy, J. F., Rimmer, D. W., & Czeisler, C. A. (2001). Association of intrinsic circadian period with morningness-eveningness, usual wake time, and circadian phase. *Behavioral Neuroscience, 115*(4), 895–899.

Dulewicz, V., & Higgs, M. (2000). Emotional intelligence. *Journal of Managerial Psychology, 15*(4), 341–372.

Duncan, J., Seitz, R. J., Kolodny, J., Bor, D., et al. (2000). A neural basis for general intelligence. *Science, 289*, 457–460.

Duncker, K. (1945). On problem solving. *Psychological Monographs, 58*(270).

Durham, M. D., & Dane, F. C. (1999). Juror knowledge of eyewitness behavior. *Journal of Social Behavior & Personality, 14*(2), 299–308.

Durso, F. T., Rea, C. B., & Dayton, T. (1994). Graph-theoretic confirmation of restructuring during insight. *Psychological Science, 5*(2), 94–98.

Dusek, J. B. (1996). *Adolescent development and behavior.* Englewood Cliffs, NJ: Prentice Hall.

Dutton, D. G., & Aron, A. P. (1974). Some evidence for heightened sexual attraction under conditions of high anxiety. *Journal of Personality & Social Psychology, 30*, 510–517.

Dyer, K. A. (2001). Dealing with death and dying in medical education and practice. *Journey of Hearts*. http://www.journeyofhearts.org/jofh/kirstimd/AMSA/outline.htm.

Dywan, J., & Bowers, K. S. (1983). The use of hypnosis to enhance recall. *Science, 222*, 184–185.

Dzokoto, V. A., & Adams, G. (2005). Understanding genital-shrinking epidemics in West Africa: Koro, juju, or mass psychogenic illness? *Culture, Medicine and Psychiatry, 29*(1), 53–78.

Eagly, A. H. (2000). Gender roles. In A. Kazdin (Ed.), *Encyclopedia of psychology*. Washington, DC: American Psychological Association.

Eagly, A. H. (2001). Social role theory of sex differences and similarities. In J. Worell (Ed.), *Encyclopedia of women and gender*. San Diego: Academic Press.

Eastman, C. I., Stewart, K. T., Mahoney, M. P., Liu, L., et al. (1994). Dark goggles and bright light improve circadian rhythm adaptation to night-shift work. *Sleep, 17*(6), 535–543.

Ebbinghaus, H. (1885). *Memory: A contribution to experimental psychology.* Translated by H. A. Ruger & C. E. Bussenius, 1913. New York: New York Teacher's College, Columbia University.

Ebster, C., & Kirk-Smith, M. (2005). The effect of the human pheromone androstenol on product evaluation. *Psychology & Marketing, 22*(9), 739–749.

Eccles, J. S., Midgley, C., Wigfield, A., Buchanan, C. M., et al. (1993). Development during adolescence. *American Psychologist, 48*, 90–101.

Eckardt, M. H. (2005). Karen Horney: A portrait: The 120th anniversary, Karen Horney, September 16, 1885. *American Journal of Psychoanalysis, 65*(2), 95–101.

Eckerman, D. A. (1999). Scheduling reinforcement about once a day. *Behavioural Processes, 45*(1–3), 101–114.

Eddy, K. T., Dutra, L., Bradley, R., & Westen, D. (2004). A multidimensional meta-analysis of psychotherapy and pharmacotherapy for obsessive-compulsive disorder. *Clinical Psychology Review, 24*(8), 1011–1030.

Edwards, D. J. A. (1998). Types of case study work. *Journal of Humanistic Psychology, 38*(3), 36–70.

Egeland, B., Jacobvitz, D., & Sroufe, L. A. (1988). Breaking the cycle of abuse. *Child Development, 59*(4), 1080–1088.

Eich, E., Rachman, S., & Lopatka, C. (1990). Affect, pain, and autobiographical memory. *Journal of Abnormal Psychology, 99*(2) 174–178.

Eichorn, D. H., Hunt, J. V., & Honzik, M. P. (1981). Experience, personality, and IQ: Adolescence to middle age. In D. H. Eichorn, J. A. Clausen, et al. (Eds.), *Present and past in middle life*. New York: Academic Press.

Eidelson, R. J., & Eidelson, J. I. (2003). Dangerous ideas. *American Psychologist, 58*(3), 182–192.

Eifert, G. H., & Lejuez, C. W. (2000). Aversion therapy. In A. E. Kazdin (Ed.), *Encyclopedia of psychology*. Washington, DC: American Psychological Association.

Eimas, P. D., Quinn, P. C., & Cowan, P. (1994). Development of exclusivity in perceptually based categories of young infants. *Journal of Experimental Child Psychology, 58*(3), 418–431.

Eimer, B. N. (2000). Clinical applications of hypnosis for brief and efficient pain management psychotherapy. *American Journal of Clinical Hypnosis, 43*, 17–40.

Eisenberg, N., Valiente, C., Fabes, R. A., Smith, C. L., et al. (2003). The relations of effortful control and ego control to children's resiliency and social functioning. *Developmental Psychology, 39*(4), 761–776.

Ekman, P. (1993). Facial expression and emotion. *American Psychologist, 48*(4), 384–392.

Ekman, P. (2001). *Telling lies: Clues to deceit in the marketplace, politics, and marriage*. New York: Norton.

Ekman, P., Friesen, W. V., & Bear, J. (1984). The international language of gestures. *Psychology Today*, May, 64–69.

Ekman, P., Levenson, R. W., & Friesen, W. V. (1983). Autonomic nervous system activity distinguishes among emotions. *Science, 221*, 1208–1210.

Ekman, P., & O'Sullivan, M. (1991). Who can catch a liar? *American Psychologist, 46*(9), 913–920.

Ekman, P., & Rosenberg, E. (1997). *What the face reveals*. New York: Oxford University Press.

Eliot, L. (1999). *What's going on in there?* New York: Bantam

Elkind, D. (1984). *All grown up & no place to go*. Reading, MA: Addison-Wesley.

Elkind, D. (1995). *Ties that stress*. Cambridge, MA: Harvard University Press.

Elkind, D. (2001). *The hurried child: Growing up too fast too soon* (3rd ed.). Cambridge, MA: Perseus.

Elli, K. A., & Nathan, P. J. (2001). The pharmacology of human working memory. *International Journal of Neuropsychopharmacology, 4*(3), 299–313.

Ellickson, P. L., Martino, S. C., & Collins, R. L. (2004). Marijuana use from adolescence to young adulthood. *Health Psychology, 23*(3), 299–307.

Elliott, M., Browne, K., & Kilcoyne, J. (1995). Child sexual abuse prevention: What offenders tell us. *Child Abuse & Neglect, 19*(5), 579–594.

Elliott, M., & Williams, D. (2003). The client experience of counselling and psychotherapy. *Counselling Psychology Review, 18*(1), 34–38.

Ellis, A. (1979). The practice of rational-emotive therapy. In A. Ellis & J. Whiteley (Eds.), *Theoretical and empirical foundations of rational-emotive therapy.* Monterey, CA: Brooks/Cole.

Ellis, A. (1995). Changing rational-emotive therapy (RET) to rational emotive behavior therapy (REBT). *Journal of Rational-Emotive & Cognitive Behavior Therapy, 13*(2), 85–89.

Ellis, A. (2004). Why rational emotive behavior therapy is the most comprehensive and effective form of behavior therapy. *Journal of Rational-Emotive & Cognitive Behavior Therapy, 22*(2), 85–92.

Ellis, H. C., & Hunt, R. R. (1992). *Fundamentals of cognitive psychology.* Madison, WI: Brown & Benchmark.

Ellis, P. J., West, B. J., Ryan, A. M., & Deshon, R. P. (2002). The use of impression management tactics in structured interviews: A function of question type. *Journal of Applied Psychology, 87*, 1200–1208.

Elovainio, M., Kivimaeki, M., Steen, N., & Kalliomaeki-Levanto, T. (2000). Organizational and individual factors affecting mental health and job satisfaction. *Journal of Occupational Health Psychology, 5*(2), 269–277.

Emmons, K. M., Wechsler, H., Dowdall, G., & Abraham, M. (1998). Predictors of smoking among US college students. *American Journal of Public Health, 88*(1), 104–107.

Emmons, R. A. (2003). Personal goals, life meaning, and virtue. In C. L. M. Keyes & J. Haidt (Eds.), *Flourishing*. Washington, DC: American Psychological Association.

Enns, J. T., & Coren, S. (1995). The box alignment illusion. *Perception & Psychophysics, 57*(8), 1163–1174.

Enns, M. W., Cox, B. J., & Clara, I. P. (2005). Perfectionism and neuroticism: A longitudinal study of specific vulnerability and diathesis-stress models. *Cognitive Therapy and Research, 29*(4), 463–478.

Erdelyi, M. H., & Appelbaum, A. G. (1973). Cognitive masking: The disruptive effect of an emotional stimulus upon the perception of contiguous neutral items. *Bulletin of the Psychonomic Society, 1*, 59–61.

Erickson, C. D., & Al-Timimi, N. R. (2001). Providing mental health services to Arab Americans. *Cultural Diversity and Ethnic Minority Psychology, 7*(4), 308–327.

Ericsson, K. A. (2000). How experts attain and maintain superior performance. *Journal of Aging & Physical Activity, 8*(4), 366–372.

Ericsson, K. A., & Charness, N. (1994). Expert performance. *American Psychologist, 49*(8), 725–747.

Ericsson, K. A., & Chase, W. G. (1982). Exceptional memory. *American Scientist, 70*, 607–615.

Ericsson, K. A., Delaney, P. F., Weaver, G., & Mahadevan, R. (2004). Uncovering the structure of a memorist's superior "basic" memory capacity. *Cognitive Psychology, 49*(3), 191–237.

Erikson, E. H. (1963). *Childhood and society.* New York: Norton.

Erikson, E. H. (1986). *Vital involvement in old age*. New York: Norton.

Erlich, P. R., & Erlich, A. H. (1990). The population explosion. *The Amicus Journal*, Winter, 18–29.

Ernst, E. (1994). Is acupuncture effective for pain control? *Journal of Pain & Symptom Management, 9*(2), 72–74.

Eron, L. D. (1986). Interventions to mitigate the psychological effects of media violence on aggressive behavior. *Journal of Social Issues, 42*(3), 155–169.

Eron, L. D. (1987). The development of aggressive behavior from the perspective of a developing behaviorism. *American Psychologist, 42,* 435–442.

Eronen, S., & Nurmi, J. (1999). Life events, predisposing cognitive strategies and well-being. *European Journal of Personality, 13*(2), 129–148.

Espie, C. A. (2002). Insomnia. *Annual Review of Psychology, 53,* 215–243.

Espy, K. A., Kaufmann, P. M., & Glisky, M. L. (1999). Neuropsychological function in toddlers exposed to cocaine in utero: A preliminary study. *Developmental Neuropsychology, 15*(3), 447–460.

Esser, J. K. (1998). Alive and well after 25 years: A review of groupthink research. *Organizational Behavior & Human Decision Processes, 73*(2–3), 116–141.

Ethical principles of psychologists and code of conduct. (2002). *American Psychologist, 57*(12), 1060–1073.

Ethier, K. A., Kershaw, T., Niccolai, L., Lewis, J. B., et al. (2003). Adolescent women underestimate their susceptibility to sexually transmitted infections. *Sexually Transmitted Infections, 79,* 408–411.

Evans, G. W. (2004). The environment of childhood poverty. *American Psychologist, 59*(2), 77–92.

Evans, G. W., & Lepore, S. J. (1993). Household crowding and social support. *Journal of Personality & Social Psychology, 65*(2), 308–316.

Evans, G. W., Lepore, S. J., & Schroeder, A. (1996). The role of interior design elements in human responses to crowding. *Journal of Personality & Social Psychology, 70*(1), 41–46.

Evans, G. W., Lercher, P., Meis, M., Ising, H., & Kofler, W. W. (2001). Community noise exposure and stress in children. *Journal of the Acoustical Society of America, 109*(3), 1023–1027.

Evans, S. (1993). Keeping cool when the baby won't stop crying. *Los Angeles Times,* Jan. 25, E-2.

Everard, K. M. (1999). The relationship between reasons for activity and older adult well-being. *Journal of Applied Gerontology, 18*(3), 325–340.

Everly, G. S. (2002). Thoughts on peer (paraprofessional) support in the provision of mental health services. *International Journal of Emergency Mental Health, 4*(2), 89–92.

Everson, C. A. (1998). Physiological consequences of sleep deprivation. *Journal of Musculoskeletal Pain, 6*(3), 93–101.

Everson, S. A., Goldberg, D. E., & Salonen, J. T. (1996). Hopelessness and risk of mortality and incidence of myocardial infarction and cancer. *Psychosomatic Medicine, 58*(2), 113.

Eyer, D. E. (1994). Mother–infant bonding: A scientific fiction. *Human Nature, 5*(1), 69–94.

Eysenck, H. J. (Ed.). (1981). *A model for personality.* New York: Springer-Verlag.

Eysenck, H. J. (1994). The outcome problem in psychotherapy: What have we learned? *Behaviour Research & Therapy, 32*(5), 477–495.

Eysenck, M. W., & Keane, M. T. (1995). *Cognitive psychology.* Hove, East Sussex, UK: Erlbaum.

Fabes, R. A., Carlo, G. Kupanoff, K., & Laible, D. (1999). Early adolescence and prosocial/moral behavior. *Journal of Early Adolescence, 19*(1), 5–16.

Fabrega, H., Jr. (2004). Culture and the origins of psychopathology. In U. P. Gielen, J. M., Fish, et al. (Eds.), *Handbook of culture, therapy, and healing.* Mahwah, NJ: Erlbaum.

Fairclough, S. H., & Graham, R. (1999). Impairment of driving performance caused by sleep deprivation or alcohol. *Human Factors, 41*(1), 118–128.

Faith, M. S., Wong, F. Y., & Carpenter, K. M. (1995). Group sensitivity training: Update, meta-analysis, and recommendations. *Journal of Counseling Psychology, 42*(3), 390–399.

Falkowski, C. (2000). *Dangerous drugs.* Center City, MN: Hazelden Information Education.

Famularo, R., Kinscherff, R., & Fenton, T. (1992). Psychiatric diagnoses of abusive mothers. *Journal of Nervous & Mental Disease, 180*(10), 658–661.

Fantz, R. L. (1961). The origin of form perception. *Scientific American,* May, 71.

Farrimond, T. (1990). Effect of alcohol on visual constancy values and possible relation to driving performance. *Perceptual & Motor Skills, 70*(1), 291–295.

Farroni, T., Massaccesi, S., Pividori, D., & Johnson, M. H. (2004). Gaze following in newborns. *Infancy, 5*(1), 39–60.

Feingold, A. (1990). Gender differences in effects of physical attractiveness on romantic attraction. *Journal of Personality & Social Psychology, 59*(5), 981–993.

Feingold, A. (1992). Gender differences in mate selection preferences. *Psychological Bulletin, 111,* 304–341.

Feldhusen, J. F., & Goh, B. E. (1995). Assessing and accessing creativity: An integrative review of theory, research, and development. *Creativity Research Journal, 8*(3), 231–247.

Feldhusen, J. F., & Westby, E. L. (2003). Creative and affective behavior: Cognition, personality, and motivation. In J. Houtz (Ed.), *The educational psychology of creativity. Perspectives on creativity.* Cresskill, NJ: Hampton Press.

Feldman, R. S., & Meyer, J. (1996). *Fundamentals of neuropsychopharmacology.* Sunderland, MA: Sinauer Associates.

Fellous, J.-M., & Ledoux, J. E. (2005). Toward basic principles for emotional processing: What the fearful brain tells the robot. In J.-M. Fellous & M. A. Arbib, (Eds.), *Who needs emotions? The brain meets the robot.* New York: Oxford University Press.

Felsenfeld, S. (1996). Progress and needs in the genetics of stuttering. *Journal of Fluency Disorders, 21*(2), 77–103.

Fenton, G. W. (1998). Neurosurgery for mental disorder. *Irish Journal of Psychological Medicine, 15*(2), 45–48.

Fernald, A. (1989). Intonation and communicative intent in mothers' speech to infants: Is the melody the message? *Child Development, 60*(6), 1497–1510.

Fernald, A., & Mazzie, C. (1991). Prosody and focus in speech to infants and adults. *Developmental Psychology, 27*(2), 209–221.

Fernandez, E., & Turk, D. C. (1989). The utility of cognitive coping strategies for altering pain perception. *Pain, 38*(2), 123–135.

Ferrari, J. R., & Scher, S. J. (2000). Toward an understanding of academic and nonacademic tasks procrastinated by students: The use of daily logs. *Psychology in the Schools, 37*(4), 359–366.

Ferster, C. B., Nurnberger, J. I., & Levitt, E. B. (1962). The control of eating. *Journal of Mathematics, 1,* 87–109.

Festinger, L. (1957). *A theory of cognitive dissonance.* Stanford, CA: Stanford University Press.

Festinger, L., & Carlsmith, J. M. (1959). Cognitive consequences of forced compliance. *Journal of Abnormal and Social Psychology, 58,* 203–210.

Fetsch, R. J., Schultz, C. J., & Wahler, J. J. (1999). A preliminary evaluation of the Colorado rethink parenting and anger management program. *Child Abuse & Neglect, 23*(4), 353–360.

Feuerstein, R., Hoffman, M. B., Rand, Y., & Jensen, M. R. (1986). Learning to learn: Mediated learning experiences and instrumental enrichment. *Special Services in the Schools, 3*(1–2), 49–82.

Feuerstein, R., Rand, Y., Hoffman, M., Hoffman, M., et al. (2004). Cognitive modifiability in retarded adolescents: Effects of Instrumental Enrichment. *Pediatric Rehabilitation, 7*(1), 20–29.

Fields, R. M., & Margolin, J. (2001). *Coping with trauma.* Washington, DC: American Psychological Association.

Fink, M. (2000). Electroshock revisited. *American Scientist, 88*(March–April), 162–167.

Fink, M., & Taylor, M. A. (2003). *Catatonia: A clinician's guide to diagnosis and treatment.* London: Cambridge University Press.

Finke, R. (1990). *Creative imagery.* Hillsdale, NJ: Erlbaum.

Finkelhor, D., & Dziuba-Leatherman, J. (1994). Victimization of children. *American Psychologist, 49*(3), 173–183.

Finkenauer, C., Luminet, O., Gisle, L., El-Ahmadi, A. et al. (1998). Flashbulb memories and the underlying mechanisms of their formation. *Memory & Cognition, 26*(3), 516–531.

First, M. B., & Pincus, H. A. (2002). The DSM-IV text revision: Rationale and potential impact on clinical practice. *Psychiatric Services, 53,* 288–292.

Firth, U. (1993). Autism. *Scientific American,* June, 108–114.

Fischer, A. H., Manstead, A. S. R., Rodriquez Mosquera, P. M., & van Vianen, A. E. M. (2004). Gender and culture differences in emotion. *Emotion, 4*(1), 87–94.

Fisher, B. S., Cullen, F. T., & Daigle, L. E. (2005). The discovery of acquaintance rape: The salience of methodological innovation and rigor. *Journal of Interpersonal Violence, 20*(4), 493–500.

Fisher, C. D., & Ashanasy, N. M. (2000). The emerging role of emotions in work life. *Journal of Organizational Behavior, 21,* 123–129.

Fisher, R. P., & Geiselman, R. E. (1987). Enhancing eyewitness memory with the cognitive interview. In M. M. Grunegerg, P. E. Morris, et al. (Eds.), *Practical aspects of memory: Current research and issues.* Chinchester, U.K.: Wiley.

Fisher, S. (1973). *The female orgasm.* New York: Basic.

Fisher, S., & Greenberg, R. P. (1996). *Freud scientifically reappraised.* New York: Wiley.

Fiske, S. T. (1993). Social cognition and social perception. *Annual Review of Psychology, 44,* 155–194.

Fiske, S. T., Cuddy, A. J. C., Glick, P., & Xu, J. (2002). A model of (often mixed) stereotype content. *Journal of Personality & Social Psychology, 82*(6), 878–902.

Flannery, D. J., Rowe, D. C., & Gulley, B. L. (1993). Impact of pubertal status, timing, and age on adolescent sexual experience and delinquency. *Journal of Adolescent Research, 8*(1), 21–40.

Flashman, L. A., Andreasen, N. C., Flaum, M., & Swayze, V. W., II. (1997). Intelligence and regional brain volumes in normal controls. *Intelligence, 25*(3), 149–160.

Flavell, J. H. (1992). Cognitive development: Past, present, and future. *Developmental Psychology, 28*(6), 998–1005.

Flavell, J. H. (1999). Cognitive development: Children's knowledge about the mind. *Annual Review of Psychology, 50,* 21–45.

Fleming, J. (1974). Field report: The state of the apes. *Psychology Today,* Jan., 46.

Flynn, J. R. (1990). Massive IQ gains on the Scottish WISC: Evidence against Brand et al.'s hypothesis. *Irish Journal of Psychology, 11*(1), 41–51.

Flynn, K. J., & Fitzgibbon, M. (1998). Body images and obesity risk among black females: A review of the literature. *Annals of Behavioral Medicine, 20*(1), 13–24.

Fobair, P. (1997). Cancer support groups and group therapies. *Journal of Psychosocial Oncology, 15*(3–4), 123–147.

Fochtmann, L. J. (1995). Intractable sneezing as a conversion symptom. *Psychosomatics, 36*(2), 103–112.

Folkman, S., & Moskowitz, J. T. (2004). Coping. *Annual Review of Psychology, 55,* 745–774.

Follett, K., & Hess, T. M. (2002). Aging, cognitive complexity, and the fundamental attribution error. *Journals of Gerontology: Series B: Psychological Sciences and Social Sciences, 57B*(4), 312–323.

Fones, C. S. L., Manfro, G. G., & Pollack, M. H. (1998). Social phobia: An update. *Harvard Review of Psychiatry, 5*(5), 247–259.

Fontaine, K. R., Redden, D. T., Wang, C., Westfall, A. O., et al. (2003). Years of life lost due to obesity. *Journal of the American Medical Association, 289,* 187–193.

Fontenelle, D. H. (1989). *How to live with your children.* Tucson, AZ: Fisher Books.

Foos, P. W., & Clark, M. C. (1983). Learning from text: Effects of input order and expected test. *Human Learning, 2,* 177–185.

Forbes, G. B., & Adams-Curtis, L. E. (2001). Experiences with sexual coercion in college males and females. *Journal of Interpersonal Violence, 16*(9), 865–889.

Forbes, G. B., Adams-Curtis, L. E., & White, K. B. (2004). First- and second-generation measures of sexism, rape myths and related beliefs, and hostility toward women: Their interrelationships and association with college students' experiences with dating aggression and sexual coercion. *Violence Against Women, 10*(3), 236–261.

Ford, G. G., Gallagher, S. H., Lacy, B. A., Bridwell, A. M., et al. (1999). Repositioning the home plate umpire to provide enhanced perceptual cues and more accurate ball–strike judgments. *Journal of Sport Behavior, 22*(1), 28–44.

Foreyt, J. P. (1987). The addictive disorders. In G. T. Wilson, C. M. Franks, et al. (Eds.), *Review of behavior therapy: Theory and practice* (Vol. 2). New York: Guilford.

Forsyth, J. P., & Savsevitz, J. (2002). Behavior therapy: Historical perspective and overview. In M. Hersen & W. H. Sledge (Eds.), *Encyclopedia of psychotherapy.* San Diego: Academic Press.

Foss, R. D. (1986). Using social psychology to increase altruistic behavior: Will it help? In M. J. Saks & L. Saxe. (Eds.), *Advances in applied social psychology* (Vol. 3). Hillsdale, NJ: Erlbaum.

Fosse, R., Stickgold, R., & Hobson, J. A. (2001). The mind in REM sleep: Reports of emotional experience. *Sleep: Journal of Sleep & Sleep Disorders Research, 24*(8), 947–955.

Foster, C. A., Witcher, B. S., Campbell, W. K., & Green, J. D. (1998). Arousal and attraction. *Journal of Personality & Social Psychology, 74*(1), 86–101.

Foster, G., & Ysseldyke, J. (1976). Expectancy and halo effects as a result of artificially induced teacher bias. *Contemporary Educational Psychology, 1,* 37–45.

Fouts, R., Fouts, D., & Schoenfield, D. (1984). Sign language conversational interaction between chimpanzees. *Sign Language Studies, 42,* 1–12.

Fowers, B. J., & Richardson, F. C. (1996). Why is multiculturalism good? *American Psychologist, 51*(6), 609–621.

Fowles, D. C. (1992). Schizophrenia: Diathesis-stress revisited. *Annual Review of Psychology, 43,* 303–336.

Foxhall, K. (2000). Suddenly, a big impact on criminal justice. *APA Monitor,* Jan., 36–37.

Fraley, R. C. (2002). Attachment stability from infancy to adulthood: Meta-analysis and dynamic modeling of developmental mechanisms. *Personality and Social Psychology Review, 6*(2), 123–151.

Fraley, R. C., & Shaver, P. R. (2000). Adult romantic attachment: Theoretical developments, emerging controversies, and unanswered questions. *Review of General Psychology. Special Issue: Adult Attachment, 4*(2), 132–154.

Franche, R., & Dobson, K. S. (1992). Self-criticism and interpersonal dependency as vulnerability factors to depression. *Cognitive Therapy & Research, 16*(4), 419–435.

Frank, J. D., & Frank, J. (2004). Therapeutic components shared by all psychotherapies. In A. Freeman, M. J. Mahoney, et al. (Eds.), *Cognition and psychotherapy* (2nd ed.). New York: Springer.

Frank, M. G. (2002). Smiles, lies, and emotion. In M. H. Abel (Ed.), *An empirical reflection on the smile. Mellen studies in psychology* (Vol. 4). Lewiston, NY: Edwin Mellen Press.

Frank, M. G., & Ekman, P. (2004). Appearing truthful generalizes across different deception situations. *Journal of Personality and Social Psychology, 86*(3), 486–495.

Frankenburg, W. K., & Dodds, J. B. (1967). The Denver Developmental Screening Test. *The Journal of Pediatrics, 1,* 181–191.

Frankl, V. (1955). *The doctor and the soul.* New York: Knopf.

Franzoi, S. L. (2002). *Social psychology.* New York: McGraw-Hill.

Fraser, C. (2002). Fact and fiction: A clarification of phantom limb phenomena. *British Journal of Occupational Therapy, 65*(6), 256–260.

Frederick, C. J. (1987) Psychic trauma in victims of crime and terrorism. In G. R. VandenBos & B. K. Bryant (Eds.), *Cataclysms, crises, and catastrophes: Psychology in action.* Washington, DC: American Psychological Association.

Fredrickson, B. L. (2001). The role of positive emotions in positive psychology. *American Psychologist, 56*(3), 218–226.

Fredrickson, B. L. (2003). The value of positive emotions. *American Scientist, 91,* 330–335.

Fredrickson, B. L., Roberts, T., Noll, S. M., Quinn, D. M., et al. (1998). That swimsuit becomes you. *Journal of Personality & Social Psychology, 75*(1), 269–284.

Freedman, J. L., & Fraser, S. C. (1966). Compliance without pressure: The foot-in-the-door technique. *Journal of Personality & Social Psychology, 4,* 195–202.

Freeman, D., & Garety, P. A. (2004). *Paranoia: The psychology of persecutory delusions.* New York: Routledge.

Freeman, J. (1995). Recent studies of giftedness in children. *Journal of Child Psychology & Psychiatry & Allied Disciplines, 36*(4), 531–547.

Freeman, W. J. (1991). The physiology of perception. *Scientific American,* Feb., 78–85.

Freize, I. H. (1987). The female victim. In VandenBos, G. R. & Bryant, B. K. (Eds.), *Cataclysms, crises, and catastrophes: Psychology in action.* Washington, DC: American Psychological Association.

French, C. C., Fowler, M., McCarthy, K., & Peers, D. (1991). A test of the Barnum effect. *Skeptical Inquirer, 15*(4), 66–72.

Freud, S. (1900). *The interpretation of dreams.* London: Hogarth.

Freud, S. (1949). *An outline of psychoanalysis.* New York: Norton.

Fried, P. A., O'Connell, C. M., & Walkinson, B. (1992). 60- and 72-month follow-up of children prenatally exposed to marijuana, cigarettes, and alcohol. *Journal of Developmental & Behavioral Pediatrics, 13*(6), 383–391.

Fried, P. A., & Smith, A. M. (2001). A literature review of the consequences of prenatal marihuana exposure. *Neurotoxicology and Teratology, 23*(1), 1–11.

Fried, P. A., Watkinson, B., James, D., & Gray, R. (2002). Current and former marijuana use: Preliminary findings of a longitudinal study of effects on IQ in young adults. *Canadian Medical Association Journal, 166,* 887–891.

Friedman, M., & Rosenman, R. (1983). *Type A behavior and your heart.* New York: Knopf.

Friedman, R. C., Bucci, W., Christian, C., Drucker, P., et al. (1998). Private psychotherapy patients of psychiatrist psychoanalysts. *American Journal of Psychiatry, 155,* 1772–1774.

Froh, J. J. (2004). The history of positive psychology: Truth be told. *NYS Psychologist, 16*(3), 18–20.

Frone, M. R., & Yardley, J. K. (1996). Workplace family-supportive programmes. *Journal of Occupational & Organizational Psychology, 69*(4), 351–366.

Froufe, M., & Schwartz, C. (2001). Subliminal messages for increasing self-esteem: Placebo effect. *Spanish Journal of Psychology, 4*(1), 19–25.

Frydman, M. (1999). Television, aggressiveness and violence. *International Journal of Adolescent Medicine & Health, 11*(3–4), 335–344.

Fukuda, K., & Ishihara, K. (2001). Age-related changes of sleeping pattern during adolescence. *Psychiatry & Clinical Neurosciences, 55*(3), 231–232.

Fuligni, A. J. (1998). Authority, autonomy, and parent–adolescent conflict and cohesion: A study of adolescents from Mexican, Chinese, Filipino, and European Backgrounds. *Developmental Psychology, 34*(4), 782–792.

Fuller, T. D., Edwards, J. N., Vorakitphokatorn, S., & Sermsri, S. (1996). Chronic stress and psychological well-being: Evidence from Thailand on household crowding. *Social Science & Medicine, 42*(2), 265–280.

Funder, D. C. (2004). *The personality puzzle* (3rd ed.). New York: Norton.

Funk, J. B. (2005). Children's exposure to violent video games and desensitization to violence. *Child and Adolescent Psychiatric Clinics of North America, 14*(3), 387–404.

Fuqua, D. R., & Newman, J. L. (2002). Creating caring organizations. *Consulting Psychology Journal: Practice & Research, 54*(2), 131–140.

Furumoto, L., & Scarborough, E. (1986). Placing women in the history of psychology. *American Psychologist, 41,* 35–42.

Gable, S. L., Reis, H. T., Impett, E. A., & Asher, E. R. (2004). What do you do when things go right? *Journal of Personality & Social Psychology, 87*(2), 228–245.

Gabrieli, J. D. E. (1998). Cognitive neuroscience of human memory. *Annual Review of Psychology, 49,* 87–115.

Gadzella, B. M. (1995). Differences in processing information among psychology course grade groups. *Psychological Reports, 77,* 1312–1314.

Gaertner, S. L., Dovidio, J. F., Banker, B. S., Houlette, M., et al. (2000). Reducing intergroup conflict: From superordinate goals to decategorization, recategorization, and mutual differentiation. *Group Dynamics, 4*(1), 98–114.

Gagnon, J. H. (1977). *Human sexualities.* Glenview, IL: Scott, Foresman.

Galambos, N. L., Barker, E. T., & Tilton-Weaver, L. C. (2003). Who gets caught at maturity gap? A study of pseudomature, immature and mature adolescents. *International Journal of Behavioral Development, 27*(3), 253–263.

Galanter, E. (1962). Contemporary psychophysics. In *New directions in psychology* (Vol. 1), 87–156. New York: Holt, Rinehart & Winston.

Galati, D., Scherer, K. R., & Ricci-Bitti, P. E. (1997). Voluntary facial expression of emotion: Comparing congenitally blind with normally sighted encoders. *Journal of Personality & Social Psychology, 73*(6), 1363–1379.

Galea, S., Ahern, J., Resnick, H., Kilpatrick, D., et al. (2002). Psychological sequelae of the September 11 terrorist attacks in New York City. *New England Journal of Medicine, 346*(13), 982–987.

Galea, S., & Resnick, H. (2005). Posttraumatic stress disorder in the general population after mass terrorist incidents: Considerations about the nature of exposure. *CNS Spectrums, 10*(2), 107–115.

Gallup, G. H., Jr., & Newport, F. (1991). Belief in paranormal phenomena among adult Americans. *Skeptical Inquirer, 15,* 137–146.

Gamache, G. (2004). *Essentials in human factors.* San Mateo, CA: Usernomics.

Ganellen, R. J. (1996). Comparing the diagnostic efficiency of the MMPI, MCMI-II, and Rorschach. *Journal of Personality Assessment, 67*(2), 219–243.

Ganis, G., Thompson, W. L., & Kosslyn, S. M. (2004). Brain areas underlying visual mental imagery and visual perception: An fMRI study. *Cognitive Brain Research, 20*(2), 226–241.

Gannon, L. (1993). Menopausal symptoms as consequences of dysrhythmia. *Journal of Behavioral Medicine, 16*(4), 387–402.

García-Junco-Clemente, P., Linares-Clemente, P., & Fernández-Chacón, R. (2005). Active zones for presynaptic plasticity in the brain. *Molecular Psychiatry, 10*(2), 185–200.

Gardner, H. (1993). *Frames of mind.* New York: Basic Books.

Gardner, H. (1999). *Intelligence reframed: Multiple intelligences for the 21st century.* New York: Basic Books.

Gardner, H. (2002). The pursuit of excellence through education. In M. Ferrari (Ed.), *Learning from extraordinary minds*. Mahwah, NJ: Erlbaum.

Gardner, H. (2003). *Multiple intelligences after twenty years*. Invited Address, American Educational Research Association, April. Retrieved December 6, 2005, from http://www.pz.harvard.edu/PIs/HG_MI_after_20_years.pdf

Gardner, R. A., & Gardner, B. T. (1989). *Teaching sign language to chimpanzees*. Albany, NY: State University of New York Press.

Gardner, R. M., & Bokenkamp, E. D. (1996). The role of sensory and nonsensory factors in body size estimations of eating disorders subjects. *Journal of Clinical Psychology, 52*(1), 3–15.

Garland, A. F., & Zigler, E. (1993). Adolescent suicide prevention. *American Psychologist, 48*(2), 169–182.

Garland, A. F., & Zigler, E. (1999). Emotional and behavioral problems among highly intellectually gifted youth. *Roeper Review, 22*(1), 41–44.

Garnets, L. D. (2002). Sexual orientation in perspective. *Cultural Diversity and Ethnic Minority Psychology, 8*(2), 115–129.

Garnets, L. D., & Kimmel, D. (1991). Lesbian and gay male dimensions in the psychological study of human diversity. In *Psychological perspectives on human diversity in America*. Washington, DC: American Psychological Association.

Gates, A. I. (1958). Recitation as a factor in memorizing. In J. Deese (Ed.), *The psychology of learning*. New York: McGraw-Hill.

Gatz, M., & Pearson, C. G. (1988). Ageism revised and the provision of psychological services. *American Psychologist, 43*(3), 184–188.

Gauthier, J., Cote, G., & French, D. (1994). The role of home practice in the thermal biofeedback treatment of migraine headache. *Journal of Consulting & Clinical Psychology, 62*(1), 180–184.

Gayle, H. (2000). An overview of the global HIV/AIDS epidemic, with a focus on the United States. *AIDS, 14*(Suppl. 2), S8–S17.

Gazzaniga, M. S. (1970). *The bisected brain*. New York: Plenum.

Gazzaniga, M. S. (1995). On neural circuits and cognition. *Neural Computation, 7*(1), 1–12.

Gazzaniga, M. S., Ivry, R. B., & Mangun, G. R. (2002). *Cognitive neuroscience: The biology of the mind* (2nd ed.). New York: Norton.

Geary, N. (2004). Endocrine controls of eating: CCK, leptin, and ghrelin. *Physiology & Behavior, 81*(5), 719–733.

Gedo, J. E. (2002). The enduring scientific contributions of Sigmund Freud. *Perspectives in Biology and Medicine, 45*, 200–211.

Geehr, J. L., Burke, M. J., & Sulzer, J. L. (1995). Quality circles: The effects of varying degrees of voluntary participation on employee attitudes and program efficacy. *Educational & Psychological Measurement, 55*(1), 124–134.

Gegenfurtner, K. R., & Kiper, D. C. (2003). Color vision. *Annual Review of Neuroscience, 26*, 181–206.

Geiger, M. A. (1991) Changing multiple-choice answers: Do students accurately perceive their performance? *Journal of Experimental Education, 59*(3), 250–257.

Geiselman, R. E., Fisher, R. P., MacKinnon, D. P., & Holland, H. L. (1986). Eyewitness memory enhancement with the cognitive interview. *American Journal of Psychology, 99*, 385–401.

Genesee, F. (1994). Bilingualism. In V. S. Ramachandram (Ed.), *Encyclopedia of human behavior* (Vol. 1). San Diego, CA: Academic Press.

Georgiades, A., Serwood, A., Gullette, E. C., Babyak, M. A., et al. (2000). Effects of exercise and weight loss on mental stress-induced cardiovascular responses in individuals with high blood pressure. *Hypertension, 36*, 171–176.

Gepner, B., & Mestre, D. R. (2002). Brief report: Postural reactivity to fast visual motion differentiates autistic from children with Asperger syndrome. *Journal of Autism & Developmental Disorders, 32*(3), 231–238.

German, T. P., & Barrett, H. C. (2005). Functional fixedness in a technologically sparse culture. *Psychological Science, 16*(1), 1–5.

German, T. P., & Defeyter, M. A. (2000). Immunity to functional fixedness in young children. *Psychonomic Bulletin & Review, 7*(4), 707–712.

Gersh, R. D. (1982). Learning when not to shoot. *Santa Barbara News Press*, June 20.

Gershoff, E. T. (2002). Corporal punishment by parents and associated child behaviors and experiences: A meta-analytic and theoretical review. *Psychological Bulletin, 128*(4), 539–579.

Gershon, E. S., Badner, J. A., Goldin, L. R., Sanders, A. R., et al. (1998). Closing in on genes for manic-depressive illness and schizophrenia. *Neuropsychopharmacology, 18*(4), 233–242.

Gerstein, E. R. (2002). Manatees, bioacoustics, and boats. *American Scientist, 90*(March–April), 154–163.

Gerwood, J. B. (1998). The legacy of Viktor Frankl. *Psychological Reports, 82*(2), 673–674.

Geschwind, N. (1979). Specializations of the human brain. *Scientific American, 241*, 180–199.

Gewirtz, J. C., & Davis, M. (1998). Application of Pavlovian higher-order conditioning to the analysis of the neural substrates of fear conditioning. *Neuropharmacology, 37*(4–5), 453–459.

Ghadirian, A-M., Gregoire, P., & Kosmidis, H. (2001). Creativity and the evolution of psychopathologies. *Creativity Research Journal, 13*(2), 145–148.

Gibson, B., & Werner, C. M. (1994). The airport as a behavior setting: The role of legibility in communicating the setting program. *Journal of Personality and Social Psychology, 66*, 1049–1060.

Gibson, E. J., & Walk, R. D. (1960). The "visual cliff." *Scientific American, 202*(4), 67–71.

Gibson, K. R. (2002). Evolution of human intelligence: The roles of brain size and mental construction. *Brain, Behavior & Evolution, 59*(1–2), 10–20.

Gierl, M. J., & Rogers, W. T. (1996). A confirmatory factor analysis of the Test Anxiety Inventory using Canadian high school students. *Educational & Psychological Measurement, 56*(2), 315–324.

Gifford, R. (2002). *Environmental psychology: Principles and practice* (3rd ed.). Colville, WA: Optimal Books.

Gila, A., Castro, J., Cesena, J., & Toro, J. (2005). Anorexia nervosa in male adolescents: Body image, eating attitudes and psychological traits. *Journal of Adolescent Health, 36*(3), 221–226.

Gilbert, A. N., & Wysocki, C. J. (1987). The smell survey results. *National Geographic*, Oct., 514–524.

Gilbert, D. G., Stunkard, M. E., Jensen, R. A., & Detwiler, F. R. J. (1996). Effects of exam stress on mood, cortisol, and immune functioning. *Personality & Individual Differences, 21*(2), 235–246.

Gilbert, P. (2001). *Overcoming depression*. New York: Oxford.

Giliovich, T., Keltner, D., & Nisbett, R. (2005). *Social psychology*. New York: Norton.

Gill, S. T. (1991). Carrying the war into the never-never land of psi. *Skeptical Inquirer, 15*(1), 269–273.

Gillberg, M., & Akerstedt, T. (1998). Sleep loss performance: No "safe" duration of a monotonous task. *Physiology & Behavior, 64*(5), 599–604.

Gilligan, C. (1982). *In a different voice*. Cambridge, MA: Harvard University Press.

Gilligan, C., & Attanucci, J. (1988). Two moral orientations: Gender differences and similarities. *Merrill-Palmer Quarterly, 34*(3), 223–237.

Gilman, S. E., Cochran, S. D., Mays, V. M., Hughes, M., et al. (2001). Risk of psychiatric disorders among individuals reporting same-sex sexual partners in the National Comorbidity Survey. *American Journal of Public Health, 91*(6), 933–939.

Ginet, M., & Py, J. (2001). A technique for enhancing memory in eyewitness testimonies for use by police officers and judicial officials: The cognitive interview. *Travail Humain, 64*(2), 173–191.

Giniger, S., Dispenzieri, A., & Eisenberg, J. (1983). Age, experience, and performance on speed and skill jobs in an applied setting. *Journal of Applied Psychology, 68*, 469–475.

Ginott, H. G. (1965). *Between parent and child: New solutions to old problems*. New York: Macmillan.

Girodo, M. (1978). *Shy? (You don't have to be!)*. New York: Pocket Books.

Giuseppe, R. (2005). Virtual reality in psychotherapy: Review. *CyberPsychology & Behavior. Special Use of Virtual Environments in Training and Rehabilitation: International Perspectives, 8*(3), 220–230.

Gladstone, G. L., & Parker, G. B. (2002). When you're smiling, does the whole world smile for you? *Australasian Psychiatry, 10*(2), 144–146.

Gladwell, M. (2005). *Blink: The power of thinking without thinking*. New York: Little, Brown.

Glaser, R. (1986). The integration of instruction and testing. In E. Freeman (Ed.), *The redesign of testing in the twenty-first century: Proceedings of the 1985 ETS Invitational Conference*. Princeton, NJ: Educational Testing Service.

Gleason, J. B. (2005). *The development of language* (6th ed.). Boston: Allyn & Bacon.

Glik, D. C., Kronenfeld, J. J., & Jackson, K. (1996). Predictors of well role performance behaviors. *American Journal of Health Behavior, 20*(4), 218–228.

Glisky, M. L., Williams, J. M., & Kihlstrom, J. F. (1996). Internal and external mental imagery perspectives and performance on two tasks. *Journal of Sport Behavior, 19*(1), 3–18.

Gloaguen, V., Cottraux, J., Cucherat, M., Blackburnet, I. M., et al. (1998). A meta-analysis of the effects of cognitive therapy in depressed patients. *Journal of Affective Disorders, 49*(1) 59–72.

Globus, G. (1987). *Dream life, wake life: The human condition through dreams*. Albany: State University of New York Press.

Glomb, T. M. (2002). Workplace anger and aggression. *Journal of Occupational Health Psychology, 7*(1), 20–36.

Glover, R. J. (2001). Discriminators of moral orientation: Gender role or personality? *Journal of Adult Development, 8*(1), 1–7.

Glueck, J., Ernst, R., & Unger, F. (2002). How creatives define creativity. *Creativity Research Journal, 14*(1), 55–67.

Gluhoski, V. L. (1995). A cognitive perspective on bereavement: Mechanism and treatment. *Journal of Cognitive Psychotherapy, 9*(2), 75–84.

Gobet, F., & Simon, H. A. (1996). Recall of random and distorted chess positions: Implications for the theory of expertise. *Memory & Cognition, 24*(4), 493–503.

Goel, V., & Grafman, J. (1995). Are the frontal lobes implicated in "planning" functions? Interpreting data from the Tower of Hanoi. *Neuropsychologia, 33*(5), 623–642.

Goin, R. P. (1998). Nocturnal enuresis in children. *Child: Care, Health, & Development, 24*(4), 277–278.

Gold, P. E. (1987). Sweet memories. *American Scientist, 75*, (Mar.–Apr.), 151–155.

Goldberg, C. (2001). Of prophets, true believers, and terrorists. *The Dana Forum on Brain Science, 3*(3), 21–24.

Goldberg, R. (2003). *Clashing views on controversial issues in drugs and society* (5th ed.). New York: McGraw-Hill.

Golden, J. (2005). *Message in a bottle: The making of fetal alcohol syndrome*. Cambridge, MA: Harvard University Press.

Goldfried, M. R. (2001). Integrating gay, lesbian, and bisexual issues into mainstream psychology. *American Psychologist*, (Nov.), 977–987.

Goldfried, M. R., Greenberg, L. S., & Marmar, C. (1990). Individual psychotherapy: Process and outcome. *Annual Review of Psychology, 41,* 659–688.

Goldiamond, I. (1971). Self-control procedures in personal behavior problems. In M. S. Gazzaniga & E. P. Lovejoy (Eds.), *Good reading in psychology.* Englewood Cliffs, NJ: Prentice Hall.

Goldman, H. H. (1998). Deinstitutionalization and community care. *Harvard Review of Psychiatry, 6*(4), 219–222.

Goldstein, E. B. (2004). *Sensation and perception* (7th ed.). Belmont, CA: Wadsworth.

Goldstein, E. B. (2005). *Cognitive psychology.* Belmont, CA: Wadsworth.

Goldstein, I. L., & Gilliam, P. (1990). Training system issues in the year 2000. *American Psychologist, 45*(2), 134–143.

Goldstein, M. J. (1985). *The UCLA family project.* Presented at NIMH High-Risk Consortium, San Francisco. Cited by Mirsky & Duncan, 1986.

Goldstein, S. R., & Young, C. A. (1996). "Evolutionary" stable strategy of handedness in major league baseball. *Journal of Comparative Psychology, 110*(2), 164–169.

Goldstone, R. L. (1998). Perceptual learning. *Annual Review of Psychology, 49,* 585–612.

Goleman, D. (1995). *Emotional intelligence.* New York: Bantam.

Gondola, J. C., & Tuckman, B. W. (1982). Psychological mood state in "average" marathon runners. *Perceptual and Motor Skills, 55,* 1295–1300.

Good, M. (1995). A comparison of the effects of jaw relaxation and music on postoperative pain. *Nursing Research, 44*(1), 52–57.

Goodale, M. A., Milner, A. D., Jakobson, L. S., & Carey, D. P. (1991). A neurological dissociation between perceiving objects and grasping them. *Nature, 349,* 154–156.

Goodall, J. (1990). *Through a window: My thirty years with the chimpanzees of the Gombe.* Boston: Houghton Mifflin.

Goode, E. (1996). Gender and courtship entitlement: Responses to personal ads. *Sex Roles, 34*(3–4), 141–169.

Goodman, G. (1984). SASHA tapes: Expanding options for help-intended communication. In D. Larson (Ed.), *Teaching psychological skills.* Monterey, CA: Brooks/Cole.

Goodman-Delahunty, J. Greene, E., & Hsiao, W. (1998). Construing motive in videotaped killings: The role of jurors' attitudes toward the death penalty. *Law & Human Behavior, 22*(3), 257–271.

Goodwin, S. A., & Fiske, S. T. (2001). Power and gender. In R. K. Unger (Ed.), *Handbook of the psychology of women and gender.* New York: Wiley.

Gopnik, A., Meltzoff, A. N., & Kuhl, P. K. (1999). *The scientist in the crib.* New York: William Morrow.

Gordon, T. (1970). *P.E.T. parent effectiveness training: A tested new way to raise children.* New York: Peter H. Wyden.

Gorman, J. M. (1996). *The essential guide to mental health.* New York: St. Martin's Griffin.

Gosling, S. D., Vazire, S., Srivastave, S., & John, O. P. (2004). Should we trust Web-based studies? *American Psychologist, 59*(2), 93–104.

Gottfried, A. W., & Gottfried, A. E. (1994). *Gifted IQ.* New York: Plenum.

Gottlieb, G. (1998). Normally occurring environmental and behavioral influences on gene activity: From central dogma to probabilistic epigenesis. *Psychological Review, 105*(4), 792–802.

Gottman, J. M. (1994). *Why marriages succeed or fail.* New York: Simon & Schuster.

Gottman, J. M., & Krokoff, L. J. (1989). Marital interaction and satisfaction: A longitudinal view. *Journal of Consulting & Clinical Psychology, 57*(1), 47–52.

Gottselig, J. M., Bassetti, C. L., & Achermann, P. (2002). Power and coherence of sleep spindle frequency activity following hemispheric stroke. *Brain, 125,* 373–383.

Gould, D., & Udry, E. (1994). Psychological skills for enhancing performance: Arousal regulation strategies. *Medicine & Science in Sports & Exercise, 26*(4), 478–485.

Gould, R. (1975). Growth toward self-tolerance. *Psychology Today,* Feb., 74–78.

Grack, C., & Richman, C. L. (1996). Reducing general and specific heterosexism through cooperative contact. *Journal of Psychology & Human Sexuality, 8*(4), 59–68.

Grande, T., Rudolf, G., Oberbracht, C., & Pauli-Magnus, C. (2003). Progressive changes in patients' lives after psychotherapy. *Psychotherapy Research, 13*(1), 43–58.

Grant, B. F., & Dawson, D. A. (1997). Age at onset of alcohol use and its association with DSM-IV alcohol abuse and dependence. *Journal of Substance Abuse, 9,* 103.

Grant, I., Gonzalez, R., Carey, C., & Natarajan, L. (2001). Long-term neurocognitive fconsequences of marijuana. In *National Institute on Drug Abuse Workshop on Clinical Consequences of Marijuana,* August 13, Rockville, MD.

Graves, J. L. (2001). *The emperor's new clothes.* Piscataway, NJ: Rutgers University Press.

Graziottin, A. (1998). The biological basis of female sexuality. *International Clinical Psychopharmacology, 13*(Suppl. 6), S15–S22.

Green, K. C. (1989). A profile of undergraduates in the sciences. *American Scientist, 77,* 475–478.

Greene, D., & Lepper, M. R. (1974). How to turn play into work. *Psychology Today,* Sept., 49.

Greenfield, P. M. (1997). You can't take it with you: Why abilities assessments don't cross cultures. *American Psychologist, 52,* 1115–1124.

Greenfield, P. M., & Savage-Rumbaugh, E. S. (1993). Comparing communicative competence in child and chimp: The pragmatics of repetition. *Journal of Child Language, 20*(1), 1–26.

Greenglass, E. R., Burke, R. J., & Konarski, R. (1998). Components of burnout, resources, and gender-related differences. *Journal of Applied Social Psychology, 28*(12), 1088–1106.

Greenglass, E. R., Burke, R. J., & Moore, K. A. (2003). Reactions to increased workload: Effects on professional efficacy of nurses. *Applied Psychology: An International Review, 52*(4), 580–597.

Gregory, R. L. (1990). *Eye and brain: The psychology of seeing.* Princeton, NJ: Princeton University Press.

Gregory, R. L. (2000). Visual illusions. In A. Kazdin (Ed.), *Encyclopedia of psychology.* Washington, DC: American Psychological Association.

Grenier, G., & Byers, E. S. (1995). Rapid ejaculation: A review of conceptual, etiological, and treatment issues. *Archives of Sexual Behavior, 24*(4), 447–472.

Griffin, W. A. (2002). Family therapy. In M. Hersen & W. H. Sledge (Eds.), *Encyclopedia of psychotherapy.* San Diego: Academic Press.

Grigorenko, E. L. (2005). The inherent complexities of gene-environment interactions. *Journals of Gerontology: Series B: Psychological Sciences & Social Sciences. Special Research on Environmental Effects in Genetic Studies of Aging, 60B*(1, Spec. Issue), 53–64.

Gross, J. J. (2001). Emotion regulation in adulthood: Timing is everything. *Current Directions in Psychological Science, 10*(6), 214–219.

Grossenbacher, P. G. (2001). *Finding consciousness in the brain: A neurocognitive approach.* Amsterdam: John Benjamins.

Grubin, D., & Madsen, L. (2005). Lie detection and the polygraph: A historical review. *Journal of Forensic Psychiatry & Psychology, 16*(2), 357–369.

Grudnik, J. L., & Kranzler, J. (2001). Meta-analysis of the relationship between intelligence and inspection time. *Intelligence, 29*(6), 523–535.

Gruner, C. R., & Tighe, M. R. (1995). Semantic differential measurements of connotations of verbal terms and their doublespeak facsimiles in sentence contexts. *Psychological Reports, 77*(3, Pt. 1), 778.

Guastello, D. D., & Guastello, S. J. (2003). Androgyny, gender role behavior, and emotional intelligence among college students and their parents. *Sex Roles, 49*(11–12), 663–673.

Guéguen, N. (2002). Status, apparel and touch: Their joint effects on compliance to a request. *North American Journal of Psychology, 4*(2), 279–286.

Gullette, D. L., & Lyons, M. A. (2005). Sexual sensation seeking, compulsivity, and HIV risk behaviors in college students. *Journal of Community Health Nursing, 22*(1), 47–60.

Gump, B. B., & Kulik, J. A. (1997). Stress, affiliation, and emotional contagion. *Journal of Personality & Social Psychology, 72*(2), 305–319.

Gur, R. E., Cowell, P., Turetsky, B. I., Gallacher, F., et al. (1998). A follow-up magnetic resonance imaging study of schizophrenia. *Archives of General Psychiatry, 55*(2), 145–152.

Gustavson, C. R., & Garcia, J. (1974). Pulling a gag on the wily coyote. *Psychology Today,* May, 68–72.

Gustavsson, J. P., Weinryb, R. M., Göransson, S., Pedersen, N. L., et al. (1997). Stability and predictive ability of personality traits across 9 years. *Personality & Individual Differences, 22*(6), 783–791.

Guthrie, R. V. (2004). *Even the rat was white: A historical view of psychology* (2nd ed.). Boston: Allyn & Bacon.

Haas, L. J., Benedict, J. G., & Kobos, J. C. (1996). Psychotherapy by telephone: Risks and benefits for psychologists and consumers. *Professional Psychology: Research & Practice, 27*(2), 154–160.

Haber, R. N. (1969). Eidetic images; with biographical sketches. *Scientific American, 220*(12), 36–44.

Haber, R. N. (1970). How we remember what we see. *Scientific American, 222*(5), 104–112.

Haddy, R. I., & Clover, R. D. (2001). The biological processes in psychological stress. *Families, Systems & Health, 19*(3), 291–302.

Hadwin, A. F., Kirby, J. R., & Woodhouse, R. A. (1999). Individual differences in notetaking, summarization and learning from lectures. *Alberta Journal of Educational Research, 45*(1), 1–17.

Hafer, C. L., & Bègue, L. (2005). Experimental research on just-world theory: Problems, developments, and future challenges. *Psychological Bulletin, 131*(1), 128–167.

Haier, R. J., Jung, R. E., Yeo, R. A., Head, K., et al. (2004). Structural brain variation and general intelligence. *NeuroImage, 23,* 425–433.

Haier, R. J., Siegel, B. V., Nuechterlein, K. H., Hazlett, E., et al. (1988). Cortical glucose metabolic rate correlates of abstract reasoning and attention studied with positron emission tomography. *Intelligence, 12,* 199–217.

Haines, M. M., Stansfeld, S. A., Job, R. F. S., Berglund, B., et al. (2001). Chronic aircraft noise exposure, stress responses, mental health and cognitive performance in school children. *Psychological Medicine, 31*(2), 265–277.

Hakuta, K., Bialystok, E., & Wiley, E. (2003). Critical evidence: A test of the critical-period hypothesis for second-language acquisition. *Psychological Science, 14*(1), 31–38.

Halbert, J., Crotty, M., & Cameron, I. D. (2002). Evidence for the optimal management of acute and chronic phantom pain. *Clinical Journal of Pain, 18*(2), 84–92.

Hall, C. (1966a). *The meaning of dreams.* New York: McGraw-Hill.

Hall, C. (1974a). What people dream about. In R. L. Woods & H. B. Greenhouse (Eds.), *The new world of dreams: An anthology.* New York: Macmillan.

Hall, C., Domhoff, G. W., Blick, K. A., & Weesner, K. E. (1982). The dreams of college men and women in 1950 and 1980: A comparison of dream contents and sex differences. *Sleep, 5*(2), 188–194.

Hall, E. T. (1966b). *The hidden dimension.* Garden City, NY: Doubleday.

Hall, E. T. (1974b). *Handbook for proxemic research.* Washington, DC: Social Anthropology and Visual Communication.

Hall, J. A. (1996). Touch, status, and gender at professional meetings.

Journal of Nonverbal Behavior, 20(1), 23–44.

Hall, J. A., Coats, E. J., & LeBeau, L. S. (2005). Nonverbal behavior and the vertical dimension of social relations: A meta-analysis. *Psychological Bulletin, 131*(6), 898–924.

Hall, R. C. W., Platt, D. E., & Hall, R. C. W. (1999). Suicide risk assessment. *Psychosomatics, 40*(1), 18–27.

Hallahan, D. P., & Kauffman, J. M. (2006). *Exceptional learners* (10th ed.). Boston: Allyn & Bacon.

Halpern, D. F. (2000). Critical thinking. In N. J. Smelser & P. B. Baltes (Eds.), *International encyclopedia of the social and behavioral sciences*. Amsterdam: Pergamon.

Halpern, D. F. (2001). Sex difference research: Cognitive abilities. In J. Worell (Ed.), *Encyclopedia of women and gender*. New York: Oxford.

Halpern, D. F. (2003). *Thought and knowledge: An introduction to critical thinking* (4th ed.). Mahwah, NJ: Erlbaum.

Hamer D. H., Hu, S., Magnuson, V. L., Hu, N., et al. (1993). A linkage between DNA markers on the X chromosome and male sexual orientation. *Science, 16:261*(5119), 291–292.

Hamilton, V. L., & Sanders, J. (1995). Crimes of obedience and conformity in the workplace. *Journal of Social Issues, 51*(3), 67–88.

Hammer, J. C., Fisher, J. D., Fitzgerald, P., & Fisher, W. A. (1996). When two heads aren't better than one: AIDS risk behavior in college-age couples. *Journal of Applied Social Psychology, 26*(5), 375–397.

Hammer, L. B., Grigsby, T. D., & Woods, S. (1998). The conflicting demands of work, family, and school among students at an urban university. *Journal of Psychology, 132*(2), 220–226.

Hancock, P. A., & Ganey, H. C. N. (2003). From the inverted-U to the extended-U: The evolution of a law of psychology. *Journal of Human Performance in Extreme Environments, 7*(1), 5–14.

Handsfield, H. H. (2001). Resurgent sexually transmitted diseases among men who have sex with men. *Medscape Infectious Disease*, Medscape.com, http://www.medscape.com/viewarticle/446212 (accessed April 13, 2006).

Haney, C., Hurtado, A., & Vega, L. (1994). "Modern" death qualification: New data on its biasing effects. *Law & Human Behavior, 18*(6), 619–633.

Haney, M., Ward, A. S., Comer, S. D., Foltin, R. W., et al. (1999). Abstinence symptoms following oral THC administration to humans. *Psychopharmacology, 141*(4), 385–394.

Hannigan, S. L., & Reinitz, M. T. (2001). A demonstration and comparison of two types of inference-based memory errors. *Journal of Experimental Psychology: Learning, Memory, and Cognition, 27*(4), 931–940.

Hansel, C. E. M. (1980). *ESP and parapsychology: A critical reevaluation.* Buffalo, NY: Prometheus.

Hansell, J. H., & Damour, L. (2004). *Abnormal psychology*. San Francisco: Jossey-Bass.

Hansen, C. J., Stevens, L. C., & Coast, J. R. (2001). Exercise duration and mood state. *Health Psychology, 20*(4), 267–275.

Harding, D. J., Fox, C., & Mehta, J. D. (2002). Studying rare events through qualitative case studies. *Sociological Methods & Research, 31*(2), 174–217.

Harding, R. W., Morgan, F. H., Indermaur, D., Ferrante, A. M., et al. (1998). Road rage and the epidemiology of violence. *Studies on Crime & Crime Prevention, 7*(2), 221–238.

Hare, R. D. (1996). Psychopathy: A clinical construct whose time has come. *Criminal Justice and Behavior, 23*, 25–54.

Hare, R. D. (2002). Psychopathy and risk for recidivism and violence. In N. Gray, J. Laing, et al. (Eds.), *Criminal justice, mental health, and the politics of risk*. London: Cavendish.

Hare-Mustin, R. T., & Marecek, J. (1988). The meaning of difference. *American Psychologist, 43*(6), 455–464.

Harker, L., & Keltner, D. (2001). Expressions of positive emotion in women's college yearbook pictures and their relationship to personality and life outcomes across adulthood. *Journal of Personality & Social Psychology, 80*(1), 112–124.

Harlow, H. F., & Harlow, M. K. (1962). Social deprivation in monkeys. *Scientific American, 207*, 136–146.

Harlow, J. M. (1868). Recovery from the passage of an iron bar through the head. *Publications of the Massachusetts Medical Society, 2*, 327–347.

Harm, D. L. (2002). Motion sickness neurophysiology, physiological correlates, and treatment. In K. M. Stanney (Ed.), *Handbook of virtual environments: Design, implementation, and applications*. Hillsdale, NJ: Erlbaum.

Harris, B. (1996). Hormonal aspects of postnatal depression. *International Review of Psychiatry, 8*(1), 27–36.

Harris, C. (2004). The evolution of jealousy. *American Scientist, 92*, 62–71.

Harris, D. A. (1999). *Driving while black*. American Civil Liberties Union Special Report, June.

Harris, J. A., Rushton, J. P., Hampson, E., & Jackson, D. N. (1996). Salivary testosterone and self-report aggressive and pro-social personality characteristics in men and women. *Aggressive Behavior, 22*(5), 321–331.

Harris, J. R., & Liebert, R. M. (1991). *The child*. Englewood Cliffs, NJ: Prentice Hall.

Harrison, L. F., & Williams, T. M. (1986). Television and cognitive development. In T. M. Williams (Ed.), *The impact of television: A natural experiment in three communities*. Orlando, FL: Academic.

Harsch, N., & Neisser, U. (1989). *Substantial and irreversible errors in flashbulb memories of the Challenger explosion*. Poster presented at the meeting of the Psychonomic Society, November, Atlanta, GA.

Hart, B., & Risley, T. R. (1999). *The social world of children learning to talk*. Baltimore, MD: Paul H. Brookes.

Hartgens, F., & Kuipers, H. (2004). Effects of androgenic–anabolic steroids in athletes. *Sports Medicine, 34*(8), 513–554.

Hartlep, K. L., & Forsyth, G. A. (2000). The effect of self-reference on learning and retention. *Teaching of Psychology, 27*(4), 269–271.

Harvey, C. A., Curson, D. A., Pantelis, C., & Taylor, J. (1996). Four behavioural syndromes of schizophrenia. *British Journal of Psychiatry, 168*(5), 562–570.

Harvil, L. M., & Davis, G. (1997). Medical students' reasons for changing answers on multiple-choice tests. *Academic Medicine, 72*(10, Suppl. 1), S97–S99.

Harway, M. (Ed.). (2004). *Handbook of couples therapy*. San Francisco, CA: Jossey-Bass.

Hashimoto, I., Suzuki, A., Kimura, T., Iguchi Y., et al. (2004). Is there training-dependent reorganization of digit representations in area 3b of string players? *Clinical Neurophysiology, 115*(2), 435–447.

Hathaway, S. R., & McKinley, J. C. (1989). *MMPI-2: Manual for administration and scoring*. Minneapolis: University of Minnesota Press.

Hauck, F. R., Moore, C. M., Herman, S. M., Donovan, M., et al. (2002). The contribution of prone sleeping position to the racial disparity in sudden infant death syndrome. *Pediatrics, 110*, 772–780.

Hauri, P., & Linde, S. (1990). *No more sleepless nights*. New York: Wiley.

Havighurst, R. J. (1961). Successful aging. *Gerontologist, 1*, 8–13.

Hawkins, D. B., & Gruber, J. J. (1982). Little league baseball and players' self-esteem. *Perceptual and Motor Skills, 55*, 1335–1340.

Hay, I., Ashman, A. F., & Van Kraayenoord, C. E. (1998). Educational characteristics of students with high or low self-concept. *Psychology in the Schools, 35*(4), 391–400.

Hayes, C. (1951). *The ape in our house*. New York: Harper & Row.

Hayne, H., & Rovee-Collier, C. (1995). The organization of reactivated memory in infancy. *Child Development, 66*(3), 893–906.

Hays, W. S. T. (2003). Human pheromones: Have they been demonstrated? *Behavioral Ecology & Sociobiology, 54*(2), 89–97.

Hearold, S. L. (1987). Meta-analysis of the effects of television on social behavior. In G. Comstock (Ed.), *Public communication and behavior* (Vol. 1). New York: Academic.

Heath, D. B. (2001). Culture and substance abuse. *Psychiatric Clinics of North America, 24*(3), 479–496.

Heath, L., & Gilbert, K. (1996). Mass media and fear of crime. *American Behavioral Scientist, 39*(4), 379–386.

Hebb, D. O. (1966). *A textbook of psychology*. Philadelphia: Saunders.

Heckhausen, J. (1987). Balancing for weaknesses and challenging developmental potential. *Developmental Psychology, 23*(6), 762–770.

Heermann, J. A., Jones, L. C., & Wikoff, R. L. (1994). Measurement of parent behavior during interactions with their infants. *Infant Behavior & Development, 17*(3), 311–321.

Heiby, E. M. (1983). Assessment of frequency of self-reinforcement. *Journal of Personality & Social Psychology, 44*, 1304–1307.

Heilman, M. E., Wallen, A. S., Fuchs, D., & Tamkins, M. M. (2004). Penalties for success: Reactions to women who succeed at male gender-typed tasks. *Journal of Applied Psychology, 89*(3), 416–427.

Heiman, J. R. (2002). Sexual dysfunction: Overview of prevalence, etiological factors, and treatments. *Journal of Sex Research. Special Promoting Sexual Health and Responsible Sexual Behavior, 39*(1), 73–78.

Heimann, M., & Meltzoff, A. N. (1996). Deferred imitation in 9- and 14-month-old infants. *British Journal of Developmental Psychology, 14*(Mar.), 55–64.

Heine, S. J., & Lehman, D. R. (1999). Culture, self-discrepancies, and self-satisfaction. *Personality & Social Psychology Bulletin, 25*(8), 915–925.

Heinrichs, R. W. (2001). *In search of madness: Schizophrenia and neuroscience*. New York: Oxford University Press.

Heinze, H. J., Hinrichs, H., Scholz, M., Burchert, W., et al. (1998). Neural mechanisms of global and local processing. *Journal of Cognitive Neuroscience, 10*(4), 485–498.

Held, R. (1971). Plasticity in sensory-motor systems. In *Contemporary psychology*. San Francisco: Freeman.

Helgeson, V. S. (2005). *The psychology of gender* (2nd ed.). Englewood Cliffs, NJ: Prentice Hall.

Hellerstein, D. J., Rosenthal, R. N., Pinsker, H., Samstag, L. W., et al. (1998). A randomized prospective study comparing supportive and dynamic therapies. *Journal of Psychotherapy Practice & Research, 7*(4), 261–271.

Hellige, J. B. (1993). *Hemispheric asymmetry*. Cambridge, MA: Harvard University Press.

Helms, J. E. (1992). Why is there no study of cultural equivalence in standardized ability testing? *American Psychologist, 47*(9), 1083–1101.

Helson, H. (1964). *Adaptation-level theory*. New York: Harper & Row.

Helson, R., & Srivastava, S. (2002). Creative and wise people. *Personality & Social Psychology Bulletin, 28*(10), 1430–1440.

Helwig, A. A. (1998). Gender-role stereotyping: Testing theory with a longitudinal sample. *Sex Roles, 38*(5–6), 403–423.

Henderson, L. (1997). Mean MMPI profile of referrals to a shyness clinic. *Psychological Reports, 80*(2), 695–702.

Henderson, N. D. (1982). Human behavior genetics. *Annual Review of Psychology, 33*, 403–440.

Hendrick, S. S., & Hendrick, C. (1993). Lovers as friends. *Journal of Social & Personal Relationships, 10*(3), 459–466.

Henman, L. D. (2001). Humor as a coping mechanism. *Humor: International Journal of Humor Research, 14*(1), 83–94.

Hepper, P.G., McCartney, G. R., & Shannon, E. A. (1998). Lateralised behaviour in first trimester human foetuses. *Neuropsychologia, 36*(6), 531–534.

Herbert, T. B., & Cohen, S. (1993). Depression and immunity. *Psychological Bulletin, 113*(3), 472–486.

Herrnstein, R., & Murray, C. (1994). *The bell curve*. New York: Free Press.

Hersen, M. (2002). Rationale for clinical case studies. *Clinical Case Studies, 1*(1), 3–5.

Herxheimer, A., & Waterhouse, J. (2003). The prevention and treatment of jet lag. *British Medical Journal, 326*(7384), 296–297.

Herz, R. S. (2001). Ah sweet skunk! *Cerebrum, 3*(4), 31–47.

Herzog, A. R., Franks, M. M., Markus, H. R., & Holmberg, D. (1998). Activities and well-being in older age. *Psychology & Aging, 13*(2), 179–185.

Hess, E. H. (1959). Imprinting. *Science, 130,* 133–141.

Hetherington, E. M., & Kelly, S. (2002). *For better or for worse: Divorce reconsidered.* New York: Norton.

Hettich, P. I. (1998). *Learning skills for college and career.* Belmont, CA: Wadsworth.

Higbee, K. L. (1997). Novices, apprentices, and mnemonists: Acquiring expertise with the phonetic mnemonic. *Applied Cognitive Psychology, 11*(2), 147–161.

Higbee, K. L., Clawson, C., DeLano, L., & Campbell, S. (1990). Using the link mnemonic to remember errands. *Psychological Record, 40*(3), 429–436.

Hilgard, E. R. (1968). *The experience of hypnosis.* New York: Harcourt Brace Jovanovich.

Hilgard, E. R. (1977). *Divided consciousness.* New York: Wiley.

Hilgard, E. R. (1978). Hypnosis and pain. In R. A. Sternbach (Ed.), *The psychology of pain.* New York: Raven.

Hill, P. (1993). Recent advances in selected aspects of adolescent development. *Journal of Child Psychology & Psychiatry & Allied Disciplines, 34*(1), 69–99.

Hilsenroth, M. J. (2000). Rorschach test. In A. Kazdin (Ed.), *Encyclopedia of psychology.* Washington, DC: American Psychological Association.

Hinkel, E. (Ed.). (2005). *Handbook of research in second language teaching and learning.* Mahwah, NJ: Erlbaum.

Hinshaw, S. P. (2002). Preadolescent girls with attention-deficit/hyperactivity disorder. *Journal of Consulting & Clinical Psychology, 70*(5), 1086–1098.

Hirshberg, L. M., & Svejda, M. (1990). When infants look to their parents. *Child Development, 61*(4), 1175–1186.

Hiscock, M., Perachio, N., & Inch, R. (2001). Is there a sex difference in human laterality? *Journal of Clinical & Experimental Neuropsychology, 23*(2), 137–148.

Hite, S. (1976). *The Hite report.* New York: Macmillan.

"HIV/AIDS." (2004). UNAIDS 2004 Report on the global AIDS epidemic. New York: United Nations

Hixon, M. D. (1998). Ape language research: A review and behavioral perspective. *Analysis of Verbal Behavior, 15,* 17–39.

Hobson, J. A. (2000). Dreams: Physiology. In A. Kazdin (Ed.), *Encyclopedia of psychology.* Washington, DC: American Psychological Association.

Hobson, J. A. (2001). *Consciousness.* New York: Freeman.

Hobson, J. A., Pace-Schott, E. F., & Stickgold, R. (2000). Dream science 2000. *Behavioral & Brain Sciences, 23*(6), 1019–1035, 1083–1121.

Hobson, J. A., Pace-Schott, E. F., Stickgold, R., & Kahn, D. (1998). *Current Opinion in Neurobiology, 8*(2), 239–244.

Hodgson, R., & Miller, P. (1982). *Selfwatching.* New York: Facts on File.

Hofer, B. K., & Yu, S. L. (2003). Teaching self-regulated learning through a "Learning to Learn" course. *Teaching of Psychology, 30*(1), 30–33.

Hoff, K. E., & DuPaul, G. J. (1998). Reducing disruptive behavior in general education classrooms: The use of self-management strategies. *School Psychology Review, 27*(2), 290–303.

Hoffer, A., & Youngren, V. R. (2004). Is free association still at the core of psychoanalysis? *International Journal of Psychoanalysis, 85*(6), 1489–1492.

Hoffman, D. D. (1999). *Visual intelligence.* New York: Norton.

Hoffman, H. G., Garcia-Palacios, A., Carlin, A., Furness, T. A., et al. (2003). Interfaces that heal: Coupling real and virtual objects to treat spider phobia. *International Journal of Human–Computer Interaction, 16*(2), 283–300.

Hoffman, H. G., Patterson, D. R., Carrougher, G. J., & Sharar, S. (2001). The effectiveness of virtual reality pain control with multiple treatments. *Clinical Journal of Pain, 17*(3), 229–235.

Hofmann, W., Gawronski, B., Gschwendner, T., Le, H., et al. (2005). A meta-analysis on the correlation between the implicit association test and explicit self-report measures. *Personality & Social Psychology Bulletin, 31*(10), 1369–1385.

Hogan, E. H., Hornick, B. A., & Bouchoux, A. (2002). Focus on communications: Communicating the message: Clarifying the controversies about caffeine. *Nutrition Today, 37,* 28–35.

Hogben, D., & Lawson, M. J. (1992). Superiority of the keyword method for backward recall in vocabulary acquisition. *Psychological Reports, 71*(3, Pt. 1), 880–882.

Hoge, C. W., Castro, C. A., Messer, S. C., McGurk, D., et al. (2004). Combat duty in Iraq and Afghanistan, mental health problems, and barriers to care. *New England Journal of Medicine, 351*(1), 13–22.

Hohwy, J., & Rosenberg, R. (2005). Unusual experiences, reality testing and delusions of alien control. *Mind & Language, 20*(2), 141–162.

Holden, C. (1980). Twins reunited. *Science 80,* Nov., 55–59.

Holden, G. W., Coleman, S. M., & Schmidt, K. L. (1995). Why 3-year-old children get spanked. *Merrill–Palmer Quarterly, 41*(4), 431–452.

Holland, J. L. (1997). *Making vocational choices.* Odessa, FL: Psychological Assessment Resources.

Holmes, M. (2002). Rethinking the meaning and management of intersexuality. *Sexualities, 5*(2), 159–180,

Holmes, T., & Masuda, M. (1972). Psychosomatic syndrome. *Psychology Today,* Apr., 71.

Holstein, M. (1997). Reflections on death and dying. *Academic Medicine, 72*(10), 848–855.

Holtzworth-Munroe, A., & Hutchinson, G. (1993). Attributing negative intent to wife behavior. *Journal of Abnormal Psychology, 102*(2), 206–211.

Honzik, M. P. (1984). Life-span development. *Annual Review of Psychology, 35,* 309–331.

Hooks, G., & Mosher, C. (2005). Outrages against personal dignity: Rationalizing abuse and torture in the war on terror. *Social Forces, 83*(4), 1627–1646.

Horn, J., Nelson, C. E., & Brannick, M. T. (2004). Integrity, conscientiousness, and honesty. *Psychological Reports, 95*(1), 27–38.

Horne, J. A., & Reyner, L. A. (1996). Counteracting driver sleepiness: Effects of napping, caffeine, and placebo. *Psychophysiology, 33*(3), 306–309.

Horne, R. S. C., Andrew, S., Mitchell, K., Sly, D. J., et al. (2001). Apnoea of prematurity and arousal from sleep. *Early Human Development, 61*(2), 119–133.

Hortman, G. (2003). What do facial expressions convey? *Emotion, 3*(2), 150–166.

Horvath, A. O., & Goheen, M. D. (1990). Factors mediating the success of defiance- and compliance-based interventions. *Journal of Counseling Psychology, 37*(4), 363–371.

Horvath, L. S., Milich, R., Lynam, D., Leukefeld, C., et al. (2004). Sensation seeking and substance use: A cross-lagged panel design. *Individual Differences Research, 2*(3), 175–183.

Horwitz, W. A., Kestenbaum, C., Person, E., & Jarvik, L. (1965). Identical twin "Idiot savants" calendar calculators. *American Journal of Psychiatry, 121,* 1075–1079.

Hosch, H. M., & Cooper, D. S. (1982). Victimization as a determinant of eyewitness accuracy. *Journal of Applied Psychology, 67,* 649–652.

Hough, L. M., & Oswald, F. L. (2000). Personnel selection. *Annual Review of Psychology, 51,* 631–664.

Howard, A., Pion, G. M., Gottfredson, G. D., Flattau, P. E., et al. (1986a). The changing face of American psychology. *American Psychologist, 41,* 1311–1327.

Howard, I. P., & Rogers, B. J. (2001a). *Seeing in depth (Vol I): Basic mechanisms.* Toronto: Porteous.

Howard, I. P., & Rogers, B. J. (2001b). *Seeing in depth (Vol II): Depth perception.* Toronto: Porteous.

Howard, J. L., & Ferris, G. R. (1996). The employment interview context. *Journal of Applied Social Psychology, 26*(2), 112–136.

Howard, K. I., Kopta, S. M., Krause, M. S., & Orlinsky, D. E. (1986b). The dose–effect relationship in psychotherapy. *American Psychologist, 41,* 159–164.

Howes, C. (1997). Children's experiences in center-based child care as a function of teacher background and adult:child ratio. *Merrill–Palmer Quarterly, 43*(3), 404–425.

Howitt, D., Craven, G., Iveson, C., Kremer, J., et al. (1977). The misdirected letter. *British Journal of Social and Clinical Psychology, 16,* 285–286.

Hsia, Y., & Graham, C. H. (1997). Color blindness. In A. Byrne, D. R. Hilbert, et al., (Eds.), *Readings on color (Vol. 2): The science of color.* Cambridge, MA: MIT Press.

Hsiung, P. (1990). Expansion of field of view via wide angle imaging. Unpublished document.

Hu, S., Pattatucci, A. M., Patterson, C., Li. L., et al. (1995). Linkage between sexual orientation and chromosome Xq28 in males but not in females. *Nature Genetics, 11*(3), 248–256.

Hubble, M.A., Duncan, B. L., & Miller, S. D. (Eds.). (1999). *The heart and soul of change: What works in therapy.* Washington, DC: American Psychological Association.

Hubel, D. H. (1979). The visual cortex of normal and deprived monkeys. *American Scientist, 67,* 532–543.

Hubel, D. H., & Wiesel, T. N. (1979). Brain mechanisms of vision. *Scientific American, 241,* 150–162.

Huebner, R. (1998). Hemispheric differences in global/local processing revealed by same–different judgements. *Visual Cognition, 5*(4), 457–478.

Huesmann, L. R., Eron, L., Klein, L., Brice, P., et al. (1983). Mitigating the imitation of aggressive behaviors by changing children's attitudes about media violence. *Journal of Personality & Social Psychology, 44,* 899–910.

Huesmann, L. R., Moise, J. F., & Podolski, C. (1997). The effects of media violence on the development of antisocial behavior. In D. M. Stoff, J. Breilin, et al. (Ed.), *Handbook of antisocial behavior.* New York: Wiley.

Huesmann, L. R., Moise-Titus, J., Podolski, C., & Eron, L. D. (2003). Longitudinal relations between children's exposure to TV violence and their aggressive and violent behavior in young adulthood: 1977–1992. *Developmental Psychology, 39*(2), 201–221.

Hughes, J. N., & Hasbrouck, J. E. (1996). Television violence: Implications for violence prevention. *School Psychology Review, 25*(2), 134–151.

Hughes, J. R., Oliveto, A. H., Liguori, A., Carpenter, J., et al. (1998). Endorsement of DSM-IV dependence criteria among caffeine users. *Drug & Alcohol Dependence, 52*(2), 99–107.

Human Rights Watch. (2003). *Ill-equipped: U.S. prisons and offenders with mental illness.* New York: HRW.

Humphries, S. A., Johnson, M. H., & Long, N. R. (1996). An investigation of the gate control theory of pain using the experimental pain stimulus of potassium iontophoresis. *Perception & Psychophysics, 58*(5), 693–703.

Hunt E. (1995). The role of intelligence in modern society. *American Scientist, 83*(July–August), 356–368.

Hunter, E. (1998). Adolescent attraction to cults. *Adolescence, 33*(131), 709–714.

Hunter, J. P., Katz, J., & Davis, K. D. (2003). The effect of tactile and visual sensory inputs on phantom limb awareness. *Brain, 126*(3), 579–589.

Hurlbert, D. F., & Apt, C. (1995). The coital alignment technique and directed masturbation: A comparative study on female orgasm. *Journal of Sex & Marital Therapy, 21*(1), 21–29.

Hutchinson, S., Lee, L. H. L., Gaab, N., & Schlaug, G. (2003). Cerebellar volume of musicians. *Cerebral Cortex, 13*(9), 943–949.

Hutchison, K. E., McGeary, J., Smolen, A., Bryan, A., et al. (2002). The DRD4 VNTR polymorphism moderates craving after alcohol consumption. *Health Psychology, 21*(2), 139–146.

Hyde, J. S. (2004). *Half the human experience: The psychology of women* (6th ed.). Boston: Houghton Mifflin.

Hyde, J. S., & DeLamater, J. D. (2000). *Understanding human sexuality.* New York: McGraw-Hill.

Hyman, R. (1989). *The elusive quarry: A scientific appraisal of psychical research.* Buffalo, NY: Prometheus.

Hyman, R. (1996a). Evaluation of the military's twenty-year program on psychic spying. *Skeptical Inquirer, 20*(2), 21–23.

Hyman, R. (1996b). The evidence for psychic functioning: Claims vs. reality. *Skeptical Inquirer, 20*(2), 24–26.

Hyman, S. (1999). Susceptibility and "second hits." In R. Conlan (Ed.), *States of mind.* New York: Wiley.

Hyson, M. G., Hirsh-Pasek, K., Rescorla, L., Cone, J. et al. (1991). Ingredients of parental "pressure" in early childhood. *Journal of Applied Developmental Psychology, 12*(3), 347–365.

Ickes, W. (1993). Traditional gender roles: Do they make, then break, our relationships? *Journal of Social Issues, 49*(3), 71–86.

Ingram, V. (2003). Alzheimer's disease. *American Scientist, 91,* 312–321.

Institute of Medicine. (1990). *Broadening the base of treatment for alcohol problems.* Washington, DC: National Academy Press.

Ironson, G., Freud, B., Strauss, J. L., & Williams, J. (2002). Comparison for two treatments for traumatic stress: A community-based study of EMDR and prolonged exposure. *Journal of Clinical Psychology, 58*(1), 113–128.

Isaak, M. I., & Just, A. (1995). Constraints on thinking in insight and invention. In R. J. Sternberg & J. E. Davidson (Eds.) *The nature of insight.* Cambridge, MA: MIT Press.

Ito, T. A., Miller, N., & Pollock, V. E. (1996). Alcohol and aggression. *Psychological Bulletin, 120*(1), 60–82.

Ivanco, T. L., & Racine, R. J. (2000). Long-term potentiation in the pathways between the hippocampus and neocortex in the chronically implanted, freely moving, rat. *Hippocampus, 10,* 143–152.

Izard, C. E. (1977). *Human emotions.* New York: Plenum.

Izard, C. E. (1990). Facial expressions and the regulation of emotions. *Journal of Personality & Social Psychology, 58*(3), 487–498.

Izard, C. E., & Abe, J. A. (2004). Developmental changes in facial expressions of emotions in the strange situation during the second year of life. *Emotion, 4*(3), 251–265.

Izard, C. E., Fantauzzo, C. A., Castle, J. M., Haynes, O. M., et al. (1995). The ontogeny and significance of infants' facial expressions in the first 9 months of life. *Developmental Psychology, 31*(6), 997–1013.

Jablonski, N.G., & Chaplin, G. (2000). The evolution of human skin coloration. *Journal of Human Evolution, 39*(1), 57–106.

Jackson, R. J. (1994). A multimodal method for assessing and treating airsickness. *International Journal of Aviation Psychology, 4*(1), 85–96.

Jackson, T., Fritch, A., Nagasaka, T., & Gunderson, J. (2002). Towards explaining the association between shyness and loneliness. *Social Behavior & Personality, 30*(3), 263–270.

Jackson, T., Towson, S., & Narduzzi, K. (1997). Predictors of shyness. *Social Behavior & Personality, 25*(2), 149–154.

Jacob, A., Prasad, S., Boggild, M., & Chandratre, S. (2004). Charles Bonnet syndrome: Elderly people and visual hallucinations. *British Medical Journal, 328*(7455), 1552–1554.

Jacob, S., Hayreh, D. J. S., & McClintock, M. K. (2001). Context-dependent effects of steroid chemosignals on human physiology and mood. *Physiology & Behavior, 74*(1–2), 15–27.

Jacobs, M. (2003). *Sigmund Freud.* Thousand Oaks, CA: Sage.

Jacobs, M. K., Christensen, A., Snibbe, J. R., Dolezal-Wood, S., et al. (2001). A comparison of computer-based versus traditional individual psychotherapy. *Professional Psychology: Research & Practice, 32*(1), 92–96.

Jacobsen, P. B., Bovbjerg, D. H., Schwartz, M. D., Andrykowski, M. A., et al. (1993). Formation of food aversions in cancer patients receiving repeated infusions of chemotherapy. *Behavior Research & Therapy, 31*(8), 739–748.

Jaffe, J., Beatrice, B., Feldstein, S., Crown, C. L., et al. (2001). Rhythms of dialogue in infancy. *Monographs of the Society for Research in Child Development, 66*(2), vi–131.

Jahn, R. G. (1982). The persistent paradox of psychic phenomena. *Proceedings of the IEEE, 70*(2), 136–166.

James, T. W., Culham, J., Humphrey, G. K., Milner, A. D., et al. (2003). Ventral occipital lesions impair object recognition but not object-directed grasping: An fMRI study. *Brain, 126*(11), 2463–2475.

Jamison, K. R. (1999). A magical orange grove in a nightmare: Creativity and mood disorders. In R. Cohen (Ed.), *States of mind.* New York: Wiley.

Jamison, K. R. (2001). Suicide in the young: An essay. *Cerebrum, 3*(3), 39–42.

Jang, K. L., & Livesley, W. J. (1998). Support for a hierarchical model of personality. *Journal of Personality and Social Psychology, 74*(6), 1556–1565.

Janis, I. L. (1989). *Crucial decisions.* New York: Free Press.

Janis, I. L., & Mann, L. (1965). Effectiveness of emotional role-playing in modifying smoking habits and attitudes. *Journal of Experimental Research in Personality, 1,* 84–90.

Janis, I. L., & Wheeler, D. (1978). Thinking clearly about career choices. *Psychology Today, 11,* 66–78.

Janssen, S. A., & Arntz, A. (2001). Real-life stress and opioid-mediated analgesia in novice parachute jumpers. *Journal of Psychophysiology, 15*(2), 106–113.

Janus, S. S., & Janus, C. L. (1993). *The Janus report.* New York: Wiley.

Jarvik, M. E. (1995). "The scientific case that nicotine is addictive": Comment. *Psychopharmacology, 117*(1), 18–20.

Jarvin, L., & Sternberg, R. J. (2003). Alfred Binet's contributions to educational psychology. In B. J. Zimmerman & D. H. Schunk (Eds.), *Educational psychology: A century of contributions.* Mahwah, NJ: Erlbaum.

Jay, T. B. (2003). *Psychology of language.* Upper Saddle River, NJ: Prentice Hall.

Jeffery, R. W., & Wing R. R. (2001). The effects of an enhanced exercise program on long-term weight loss. *Obesity Research, 9*(3), O193.

Jellinek, E. M. (1960). *The disease concept of alcoholism.* New Haven: Hill House.

Jenkins, J. G., & Dallenbach, K. M. (1924). Oblivescence during sleep and waking. *American Journal of Psychology, 35,* 605–612.

Jennings, L., & Skovholt, T. M. (1999). The cognitive, emotional, and relational characteristics of master therapists. *Journal of Counseling Psychology, 46*(1), 3–11.

Jensvold, M. L. A., & Gardner, R. A. (2000). Interactive use of sign language by cross-fostered chimpanzees (Pan troglodytes). *Journal of Comparative Psychology, 114*(4), 335–346.

Jerabek, I., & Standing, L. (1992). Imagined test situations produce contextual memory enhancement. *Perceptual & Motor Skills, 75*(2), 400.

Jerome, L. W., DeLeon, P. H., James, L. C., Folen, R., et al. (2000). The coming of age of telecommunications in psychological research and practice. *American Psychologist, 55*(4), 407–421.

Jewell, L. N. (1998). *Contemporary industrial/organizational psychology.* Pacific Grove, CA: Brooks/Cole.

Johnson, B. T. (1991). Insights about attitudes: Meta-analytic perspectives. *Personality & Social Psychology Bulletin, 17*(3), 289–299.

Johnson, J. G., Cohen, P., Smailes, E. M., Kasen, S., et al. (2002). Television viewing and aggressive behavior during adolescence and adulthood. *Science, 295*(5564), 2468–2471.

Johnson, K. E., & Mervis, C. B. (1997). Effects of varying levels of expertise on the basic level of categorization. *Journal of Experimental Psychology: General, 126*(3), 248–277.

Johnson, M. H., Breakwell, G., Douglas, W., & Humphries, S. (1998). The effects of imagery and sensory detection distractors on different measures of pain. *British Journal of Psychology, 37*(2), 141–154.

Johnson, N. G., & Roberts, M. C. (1999). Passage on the wild river of adolescence. In N. G. Johnson, M. C. Roberts, et al. (Eds.), *Beyond appearance.* Washington, DC: American Psychological Association.

Johnson, S. (2005). *Everything bad is good for you: How today's popular culture is actually making us smarter.* New York: Riverhead.

Johnson, S. M., & White, G. (1971). Self-observation as an agent of behavioral change. *Behavior Therapy, 2,* 488–497.

Johnson, S. P., & Nanez, J. E. (1995). Young infants' perception of object unity in two-dimensional displays. *Infant Behavior & Development, 18*(2), 133–143.

Johnson, T. J. (2002). College students' self-reported reasons for why drinking games end. *Addictive Behaviors, 27*(1), 145–153.

Johnsrude, I. S, Owen, A. M., Zhao, W. V., & White, N. M. (1999). Conditioned preference in humans. *Learning & Motivation, 30*(3), 250–264.

Jokerst, M. D., Gatto, M., Fazio, R., Stern, R. M., et al. (1999). Slow deep breathing prevents the development of tachygastria and symptoms of motion sickness. *Aviation, Space, & Environmental Medicine, 70*(12), 1189–1192.

Jones, E. E., & Nisbett, R. E. (1971). The actor and observer: Divergent perceptions of the causes of behavior. In E. E. Jones, D. E. Kanouse, et al. (Eds.), *Attribution: Perceiving the causes of behavior.* Morristown, NJ: General Learning Press.

Jones, G. V., & Martin, M. (2001). Confirming the X–linked handedness gene as recessive, not additive. *Psychological Review, 108*(4), 811–813.

Jones, L., Hughes, M., & Unterstaller, U. (2001). Post-traumatic stress disorder (PTSD) in victims of domestic violence. *Trauma Violence & Abuse, 2*(2), 99–119.

Jones, L., & Petruzzi, D. C. (1995). Test anxiety: A review of theory and current treatment. *Journal of College Student Psychotherapy, 10*(1), 3–15.

Jones, M. E., Russell, R. L., & Bryant, F. B. (1998). The structure of rape attitudes for men and woman. *Journal of Research in Personality, 32*(3), 331–350.

Jones, M. K., & Menzies, R. G. (1998). Danger ideation reduction therapy (DIRT) for obsessive-compulsive washers. *Behaviour Research & Therapy, 36*(10), 959–970.

Jones, R. N. (2003). Racial bias in the assessment of cognitive functioning of older adults. *Aging & Mental Health, 7*(2), 83–102.

Jorm, A. F., Korten, A. E., Rodgers, B., Jacomb, P. A., et al. (2002). Sexual orientation and mental health. *British Journal of Psychiatry, 180*(5), 423–427.

Jourard, S. M. (1966). An exploratory study of body-accessibility. *British Journal of Social and Clinical Psychology, 5,* 221–231.

Jourard, S. M. (1974). *Healthy personality.* New York: Macmillan.

Jouvet, M. (1999). *The paradox of sleep*. Cambridge, MA: MIT Press.

Joy, L. A., Kimball, M. M., & Zabrack, M. L. (1986). Television and aggressive behavior. In T. M. Williams (Ed.), *The impact of television: A natural experiment involving three towns*. New York: Academic Press.

Julesz, B. (1971). *Foundations of cyclopean perception*. Chicago: University of Chicago Press.

Julien, R. M. (2004). *A primer of drug action: A comprehensive guide to the actions, uses, and side effects* (10th ed.). New York: Worth.

Jung, C. (1961). *Memories, dreams, reflections*. London: Collins, Fount Paperbacks.

Jurma, W. E., & Powell, M. L. (1994). Perceived gender roles of managers and effective conflict management. *Psychological Reports, 74*(1), 104–106.

Juster, H. R., Heimberg, R. G., Frost, R. O., & Holt, C. S. (1996). Social phobia and perfectionism. *Personality & Individual Differences, 21*(3), 403–410.

Kagan, J. (1971). *Change and continuity in infancy*. New York: Wiley.

Kagan, J. (1991). The theoretical utility of constructs for self. *Developmental Review, 11*(3), 244–250.

Kagan, J. (1999). Born to be shy? In R. Conlan (Ed.), *States of mind*. New York: Wiley.

Kagan, J. (2000). Temperament. In A. Kazdin (Ed.), *Encyclopedia of psychology*. Washington, DC: American Psychological Association.

Kagan, J. (2004). New insights into temperament. *Cerebrum, 6*(1), 51–66.

Kahneman, D. (2003). A perspective on judgment and choice. *American Psychologist, 58*(9), 697–720.

Kahneman, D., & Tversky, A. (1972). Subjective probability: A judgment of representativeness. *Cognitive Psychology, 3*, 430–454.

Kahneman, D., & Tversky, A. (1973). On the psychology of prediction. *Psychological Review, 80*, 237–251.

Kaitz, M., Zvi, H., Levy, M., Berger, A., et al. (1995). The uniqueness of mother-own-infant interactions. *Infant Behavior & Development, 18*(2), 247–252.

Kakigi, R., Matsuda, Y., & Kuroda, Y. (1993). Effects of movement-related cortical activities on pain-related somatosensory evoked potentials. *Acta Neurologica Scandinavica, 88*(5), 376–380.

Kalal, D. M. (1999). Critical thinking in clinical practice: Pseudoscience, fad psychology, and the behavioral therapist. *The Behavior Therapist, 22*(4), 81–84.

Kalat, J. W. (2004). *Biological psychology* (8th ed.). Belmont, CA: Wadsworth.

Kallio, S., & Revonsuo, A. (2003). Hypnotic phenomena and altered states of consciousness: A multilevel framework of description and explanation. *Contemporary Hypnosis, 20*(3), 111–164.

Kamin, L. J. (1981). *The intelligence controversy*. New York: Wiley.

Kandel, E. (1999). Of learning, memory, and genetic switches. In R. Conlan (Ed.), *States of mind*. New York: Wiley.

Kaplan, H. S. (1974). *The new sex therapy*. New York: Brunner/Mazel.

Kaplan, P. S. (1998). *The human odyssey*. Pacific Grove, CA: Brooks/Cole.

Kaplan, P. S., Goldstein, M. H., Huckeby, E. R., & Cooper, R. P. (1995). Habituation, sensitization, and infants' responses to motherese speech. *Developmental Psychobiology, 28*(1), 45–57.

Kapleau, P. (1966). *The three pillars of Zen*. New York: Harper & Row.

Kapur, S., & Lecrubier, Y. (Eds.). (2003). *Dopamine in the pathophysiology and treatment of schizophrenia: New findings*. Washington, DC: Taylor & Francis.

Karlberg, L., Krakau, I., & Unden, A. (1998). Type A behavior intervention in primary health care reduces hostility and time pressure. *Social Science & Medicine, 46*(3), 397–402.

Karon, B. P., & Widener, A. J. (1997). Repressed memories and World War II: Lest we forget! *Professional Psychology: Research & Practice, 28*(4), 338–340.

Karon, B. P., & Widener, A. J. (1998). Repressed memories: The real story. *Professional Psychology: Research & Practice, 29*(5), 482–487.

Karow, C. M., Marquardt, T. P., & Marshall, R. C. (2001). Affective processing in left and right hemisphere brain-damaged subjects with and without subcortical involvement. *Aphasiology, 15*(8), 715–729.

Karylowski, J. J., Motes, M. A., Curry, D., & Van Liempd, D. (2002). In what font color is Bill Cosby's name written? *North American Journal of Psychology, 4*(1), 1–12.

Kasper, M. E., Rogers, R., & Adams, P. A. (1996). Dangerousness and command hallucinations. *Bulletin of the American Academy of Psychiatry & the Law, 24*(2), 219–224.

Kasser, T., & Ryan, R. M. (1993). A dark side of the American dream: Correlates of financial success as a central life aspiration. *Journal of Personality & Social Psychology, 65*(2), 410–422.

Kasser, T., & Ryan, R. M. (1996). Further examining the American dream: Differential correlates of intrinsic and extrinsic goals. *Personality & Social Psychology Bulletin, 22*(3), 280–287.

Kassin, S. M., Tubb, V. A., Hosch, H. M., & Memon, A. (2001). On the "general acceptance" of eyewitness testimony research. *American Psychologist, 56*(5), 405–416.

Kataria, S. (2004). A clinical guide to pediatric sleep: Diagnosis and management of sleep problems. *Journal of Developmental & Behavioral Pediatrics, 25*(2), 132–133.

Katz, P. A. (2003). Racists or tolerant multiculturalists? *American Psychologist, 58*(11), 897–909.

Kaufman, A. S. (2000). Intelligence tests and school psychology: Predicting the future by studying the past. *Psychology in the Schools, 37*(1), 7–16.

Kaufman, J. C. (2001). The Sylvia Plath effect: Mental illness in eminent creative writers. *Journal of Creative Behavior, 35*(1), 37–50.

Kaufman, J. C., & Baer, J. (2002). Could Steven Spielberg manage the Yankees? Creative thinking in different domains. *Korean Journal of Thinking & Problem Solving, 12*(2), 5–14.

Kaufman, L., & Kaufman, J. H. (2000). Explaning the moon illusion. *Proceedings of the National Academy of Sciences, 97*(1), 500–505.

Kawai, K., Sugimoto, K., Nakashima, K., Miura, H., et al. (2000). Leptin as a modulator of sweet taste sensitivities in mice. *Proceedings: National Academy of Sciences, 97*(20), 11044–11049.

Kazdin, A. E. (1975). *Behavior modification in applied settings*. Homewood, IL: Dorsey Press.

Kearney, C. A., Sims, K. E., Pursell, C. R., & Tillotson, C. A. (2003). Separation anxiety disorder in young children: A longitudinal and family analysis. *Journal of Clinical Child & Adolescent Psychology, 32*(4), 593–598.

Kebbell, M. R., & Milne, R. (1998). Police officers' perceptions of eyewitness performance in forensic investigations. *Journal of Social Psychology, 138*(3), 323–330.

Kebbell, M. R., & Wagstaff, G. F. (1998). Hypnotic interviewing: The best way to interview eyewitnesses? *Behavioral Sciences & the Law, 16*(1), 115–129.

Keefe, F. J., Abernethy, A. P., & Campbell, L. C. (2005). Psychological approaches to understanding and treating disease-related pain. *Annual Review of Psychology, 56*, 601–630.

Keel, P. K., & Klump, K. L. (2003). Are eating disorders culture-bound syndromes? Implications for conceptualizing their etiology. *Psychological Bulletin, 129*(5), 747–769.

Keller, J. (2002). Blatant stereotype threat and women's math performance. *Sex Roles, 47*(3–4), 193–198.

Keller, M. C., & Young, R. K. (1996). Mate assortment in dating and married couples. *Personality & Individual Differences, 21*(2), 217–221.

Kellermann, A. L., Rivara, F. P., Rushforth, N. B., Banton, J. G., et al. (1993). Gun ownership as a risk factor for homicide in the home. *New England Journal of Medicine, 329*(15), 1084–1091.

Kelley, H. H. (1950). The warm–cold variable in first impressions of persons. *Journal of Personality, 18*, 431–439.

Kelley, H. H. (1967). Attribution in social psychology. *Nebraska Symposium on Motivation, 15*, 192–238.

Kelly, I. W. (1998). Why astrology doesn't work. *Psychological Reports, 82*, 527–546.

Kelly, I. W. (1999). "Debunking the debunkers": A response to an astrologer's debunking of skeptics. *Skeptical Inquirer*, Nov.–Dec., 37–43.

Kelly, I. W., & Saklofske, D. H. (1994). Psychology and pseudoscience. *Encyclopedia of human behavior, 3*, 611–618.

Kelly, J. B., & Emery, R. E. (2003). Children's adjustment following divorce: Risk and resilience perspectives. *Family Relations: Interdisciplinary Journal of Applied Family Studies, 52*(4), 352–362.

Kelly, T. H., Foltin, R. W., Emurian, C. S., & Fischman, M. W. (1990). Multidimensional behavioral effects of marijuana. *Progress in Neuro-Psychopharmacology & Biological Psychiatry, 14*(6), 885–902.

Kendler, K. S., Thornton, L. M., & Prescott, C. A. (2001). Gender differences in the rates of exposure to stressful life events and sensitivity to their depressogenic effects. *American Journal of Psychiatry, 158*(4), 587–593.

Kennaway, D. J., & Wright, H. (2002). Melatonin and circadian rhythms. *Current Topics in Medicinal Chemistry, 2*, 199–209.

Kennedy, J. M. (1983). What can we learn about pictures from the blind? *American Scientist, 71*, 19–26.

Kenneth, M., Carpenter, K. M., & Hasin, D. S. (1998). Reasons for drinking alcohol. *Psychology of Addictive Behaviors, 12*(3), 168–184.

Kenrick, D. T., & MacFarlane, S. W. (1986). Ambient temperature and horn honking: A field study of the heat/aggression relationship. *Environment and Behavior, 18*(2), 179–191.

Kessen, W., & Cahan, E. D. (1986). A century of psychology: From subject to object to agent. *American Scientist, 74*, 640–649.

Kessler, R. C. (1997). The effects of stressful life events on depression. *Annual Review of Psychology, 48*, 191–214.

Kessler, R. C., Sonnega, A., & Nelson, C. B. (1995). Posttraumatic stress disorder in the National Comorbidity Survey. *Archives of General Psychiatry, 52*(12), 1048.

Kety, S. S. (1979). Disorders of the human brain. *Scientific American, 241*, 202–214.

Key, W. B. (1973). *Subliminal seduction: Ad media's manipulation of a not so innocent America*. Englewood Cliffs, NJ: Prentice Hall.

Keyes, C. L. M., & Haidt, J. (2003). Introduction: Human flourishing. In C. L. M. Keyes & J. Haidt (Eds.), *Flourishing*. Washington, DC: American Psychological Association.

Kiecolt-Glaser, J. K., & Glaser, R. (1992). Psychoneuroimmunology: Can psychological interventions modulate immunity? *Journal of Consulting & Clinical Psychology, 60*(4), 569–575.

Kiecolt-Glaser, J. K., McGuire, L., Robles, T. F., & Glaser, R. (2002). Emotions, morbidity, and mortality. *Annual Review of Psychology, 53*, 83–107.

Kiewra, K. A., DuBois, N. F., Christian, D., McShane, A., et al. (1991). Note-taking functions and techniques. *Journal of Educational Psychology, 83*(2), 240–245.

Killen, J. D., & Fortmann, S. P. (1997). Craving is associated with smoking relapse. *Experimental and Clinical Psychopharmacology, 5*(2), 137–142.

Kim, J., Singer, R. N., & Radlo, S. J. (1996). Degree of cognitive demands in psychomotor tasks and the effects of the five-step strategy on achievement. *Human Performance, 9*(2), 155–169.

Kim, S. (2000). Bogglers. *Discover*, Dec., 98.

Kim, S. (2002). Participative management and job satisfaction: Lessons for management leadership. *Public Administration Review, 62*(2), 231–241.

Kim-Cohen, J., Moffitt, T. E., Caspi, A., & Taylor, A. (2004). Genetic and environmental processes in young children's resilience and vulnerability to socioeconomic deprivation. *Child Development, 75*(3), 651–668.

Kimble, C. E., & Hirt, E. R. (2005). Self-focus, gender, and habitual self-handicapping: Do they make a difference in behavioral self-handicapping? *Social Behavior & Personality, 33*(1), 43–56.

Kimball, M. M. (1986). Television and sex-role attitudes. In T. M. Williams (Ed.), *The impact of television: A natural experiment in three communities*. Orlando, FL: Academic Press.

Kimmel, D. C. (1988). Ageism, psychology, and public policy. *American Psychologist, 43*(3), 175–178.

King, A. (1992). Comparison of self-questioning, summarizing, and notetaking-review as strategies for learning from lectures. *American Educational Research Journal, 29*(2), 303–323.

King, A. (1995). Cognitive strategies for learning from direct teaching. In E. Wood, V. Woloshyn, et al. (Eds.), *Cognitive strategy instruction for middle and high schools*. Cambridge, MA: Brookline.

King, B. E. (2005). *Human sexuality today* (5th ed.). Englewood Cliffs, NJ: Prentice Hall.

King, H. E. (1961). Psychological effects of excitation in the limbic system. In D. E. Sheer (Ed.), *Electrical stimulation of the brain*. Austin: University of Texas Press.

King, L., & Napa, C. (1998). What makes a life good? *Journal of Personality & Social Psychology, 75*(1) 156–165.

King, L. A., Richards, J. H., & Stemmerich, E. (1998). Daily goals, life goals, and worst fears. *Journal of Personality, 66*(5), 713–744.

Kinnier, R. T., Tribbensee, N. E.. Rose, C. A., & Vaughan, S. M. (2001). In the final analysis: More wisdom from people who have faced death. *Journal of Counseling & Development, 79*(2), 171–177.

Kinnunen, L. H., Moltz, H., Metz, J., & Cooper, M. (2004). Differential brain activation in exclusively homosexual and heterosexual men produced by the selective serotonin reuptake inhibitor, fluoxetine. *Brain Research, 1024*(1–2), 251–254.

Kinsey, A., Pomeroy, W., & Martin, C. (1948). *Sexual behavior in the human male*. Philadelphia: Saunders.

Kinsey, A., Pomeroy, W., & Martin, C. (1953). *Sexual behavior in the human female*. Philadelphia: Saunders.

Kipper, D. A. (1992). The effect of two kinds of role playing on self-evaluation of improved assertiveness. *Journal of Clinical Psychology, 48*(2), 246–250.

Kirsch, I., & Lynn, S. J. (1995). The altered state of hypnosis. *American Psychologist, 50*(10), 846–858.

Kirsch, I., & Lynn, S. J. (1999). Automaticity in clinical psychology. *American Psychologist, 54*(7), 504–515.

Kirsch, I., Montgomery, G., & Sapirstein, G. (1995). Hypnosis as an adjunct to cognitive behavioral psychotherapy: A meta-analysis. *Journal of Consulting and Clinical Psychology, 63*, 214–220.

Kirsch, I., & Sapirstein, G. (1998). Listening to Prozac but hearing placebo: A meta-analysis of antidepressant medication. *Prevention & Treatment, 1*, www.journals.apa.org/treatment (accessed April 13, 2006).

Kisilevsky, B. S., Hains, S. M. J., Jacquet, A.-Y., Granier-Deferre, C., et al. (2004). Maturation of fetal responses to music. *Developmental Science, 7*(5), 550–559.

Kitayama, S., Markus, H. R., & Kurokawa, M. (2000). Culture, emotion, and well-being: Good feelings in Japan and the United States. *Cognition and emotion, 14*, 93–124.

Kitayama, S., Markus, H. R., Matsumoto, H., & Norasakkunkit, V. (1997). Individual and collective processes in the construction of the self. *Journal of Personality & Social Psychology, 72*(6), 1245–1267.

Kite, M. (2001). Gender stereotypes. In J. Worell (Ed.), *Encyclopedia of women and gender*. San Diego: Academic Press.

Kite, M. E., Russo, N. F., Brehm, S. S., Fouad, N. A., et al. (2001). Women psychologists in academe. *American Psychologist, 56*(12), 1080–1098.

Kite, M. E., Stockdale, G. D., Whitley, B. E., Jr., & Johnson, B. T. (2005). Attitudes toward younger and older adults: An updated meta-analytic review. *Journal of Social Issues, 61*(2), 241–266.

Kjellgren, A., Sundequist, U., Norlander, T., & Archer, T. (2001). Effects of flotation-REST on muscle tension pain. *Pain Research & Management, 6*(4), 181–189.

Klaus, M. H., Kennell, J. H., & Klaus, P. H. (1995). *Bonding*. Reading, MA: Addison-Wesley.

Klebanoff, M. A., Levine, R. J., DerSimonian, R., Clemens, J. D., et al. (1999). Maternal serum paraxanthine, a caffeine metabolite, and the risk of spontaneous abortion. *New England Journal of Medicine, 341*(22), 1639–1644.

Kleespies, P. K. (2004). *Life and death decisions: Psychological and ethical considerations in end-of-life care*. Washington, DC: American Psychological Association.

Klein, D. W., & Kihlstrom, J. F. (1986). Elaboration, organization, and the self-reference effect in memory. *Journal of Experimental Psychology: General, 115*, 26–38.

Klein, G., Wolf, S., Militello, L., & Zsambok, C. (1995). Characteristics of skilled option generation in chess. *Organizational Behavior & Human Decision Processes, 62*(1), 63–69.

Klein, K., & Boals, A. (2001a). Expressive writing can increase working memory capacity. *Journal of Experimental Psychology: General, 130*(3), 520–533.

Klein, K., & Boals, A. (2001b). The relationship of life event stress and working memory capacity. *Applied Cognitive Psychology, 15*(5), 565–579.

Klein, R. M. (2004). On the control of visual orienting. In M. I. Posner (Ed.), *Cognitive neuroscience of attention*. New York: Guilford.

Kleinke, C. L. (1986). *Meeting and understanding people*. New York: Freeman.

Kleinke, C. L., Peterson, T. R., & Rutledge, T. R. (1998). Effects of self-generated facial expressions on mood. *Journal of Personality and Social Psychology, 74*(1), 272–279.

Kleinplatz, P. J. (1996). The erotic encounter. *Journal of Humanistic Psychology, 36*(3), 105–123.

Klinger, E. (1990). *Daydreaming*. Los Angeles: J. P. Tarcher.

Klinger, E. (2000). Daydreams. In A. Kazdin (Ed.), *Encyclopedia of psychology*. Washington, DC: American Psychological Association.

Klintsova, A. Y., & Greenough, W. T. (1999). Synaptic plasticity in cortical systems. *Current Opinion in Neurobiology, 9*(2), 203–208.

Klohnen, E. C., & Luo, S. (2003). Interpersonal attraction and personality: What is attractive—self-similarity, ideal similarity, complementarity or attachment security? *Journal of Personality & Social Psychology, 85*(4), 709–722.

Klug, W. S., & Cummings, M. R. (2003). *Genetics: A molecular perspective*. Mahwah, NJ: Prentice Hall.

Knight, J. (2004). The truth about lying. *Nature, 428*(6984), 692–694.

Knoblauch, H., Schmied, I., & Schnettler, B. (2001). Different kinds of near-death experience. *Journal of Near-Death Studies, 20*(1), 15–29.

Knoops, K. T. B., de Groot, L. C., Kromhout, D., Perrin, A., et al. (2004). Mediterranean diet, lifestyle factors, and 10-year mortality in elderly european men and women. *Journal of the American Medical Association, 292*(12), 1433–1439.

Knox, D. (1984). *Human sexuality*. St. Paul, MN: West.

Knutson, J. (1995). Psychological characteristics of maltreated children. *Annual Review of Psychology, 46*, 401–431.

Koch, C. (2004). *The quest for consciousness: A neurobiological approach*. Englewood, CO: Roberts.

Koenig, S. M. (1996). Central sleep apnea. *Virginia Medical Quarterly, 123*(4), 247–250.

Koepke, J. E., & Bigelow, A. E. (1997). Observations of newborn suckling behavior. *Infant Behavior & Development, 20*(1), 93–98.

Kohlberg, L. (1969). The cognitive-developmental approach to socialization. In A. Goslin (Ed.), *Handbook of socialization theory and research*. Chicago: Rand McNally.

Kohlberg, L. (1981a). *Essays on moral development (Vol. I): The philosophy of moral development*. San Francisco: Harper.

Kohlberg, L. (1981b). *The meaning and measurement of moral development*. Worcester, MA: Clark University Press.

Kohler, I. (1962). Experiments with goggles. *Scientific American*, Offprint no. 465, 62–72.

Kolb, B. (1990). Recovery from occipital stroke: A self-report and an inquiry into visual processes. *Canadian Journal of Psychology, 44*(2), 130–147.

Kolb, B., & Whishaw, I.Q. (2005). *Introduction to brain and behavior* (2nd ed.). New York: Freeman-Worth.

Kolbe, L. J., Collins, J., & Cortese, P. (1997). Building the capacity of schools to improve the health of the nation. *American Psychologist, 52*(3), 256–265.

Kopta, M. S., Lueger, R. J., Saunders, S. M., & Howard, K. I. (1999). Individual psychotherapy outcome and process research. *Annual Review of Psychology, 50*, 441–469.

Korol, C., Craig, K. D., & Firestone, P. (2003). Dissociative and somatoform disorders. In P. Firestone & W. L. Marshall (Eds.), *Abnormal psychology: Perspectives* (2nd ed.). Toronto: Prentice Hall.

Korte, C., & Milgram, S. (1970). Acquaintance networks between racial groups. *Journal of Personality & Social Psychology, 15*, 101–108.

Koss, M. P. (1993). Rape. *American Psychologist, 48*(10), 1062–1069.

Koss, M. P. (2000). Blame, shame, and community: Justice responses to violence against women. *American Psychologist*, Nov., 1332–1343.

Kosslyn, S. M. (1983). *Ghosts in the mind's machine*. New York: Norton.

Kosslyn, S. M. (1985). Stalking the mental image. *Psychology Today*, May, 23–28.

Kosslyn, S. M., Ball, T. M., & Reiser, B. J. (1978). Visual images preserve metric spatial information: Evidence from studies of image scanning. *Journal of Experimental Psychology: Human Perception and Performance, 4*, 47–60.

Kosslyn, S. M., Thompson, W. L., & Alpert, N. N. (1995). Topographical representation of mental images in primary visual cortex. *Nature, 378*(6556), 496.

Kosslyn, S. M., Thompson, W. L., Costantini-Ferrando, M. F., Alpert, N. M., et al. (2000). Hypnotic visual illusion alters color processing in the brain. *American Journal of Psychiatry, 157*(8), 1279–1284.

Kosson, D. S., Suchy, Y., Mayer, A. R., & Libby, J. (2002). Facial affect recognition in criminal psychopaths. *Emotion, 2*(4), 398–411.

Kotkin, M., Daviet, C., & Gurin, J. (1996). The Consumer Reports mental health survey. *American Psychologist, 51*(10), 1080–1082.

Kottler, J. A. (2004). *Introduction to therapeutic counseling*. Belmont, CA: Wadsworth.

Kowert, P. A. (2002). *Groupthink or deadlock: When do leaders learn from their advisors? SUNY series on the presidency*. Albany: State University of New York Press.

Kozart, M. F. (2002). Understanding efficacy in psychotherapy. *American Journal of Orthopsychiatry, 72*(2), 217–231.

Krakow, B., Kellner, R., Pathak, D., & Lambert, L. (1996). Long-term reduction of nightmares with imagery rehearsal treatment. *Behavioural & Cognitive Psychotherapy, 24*(2), 135–148.

Krakow, B., & Neidhardt, J. (1992). *Conquering bad dreams and nightmares*. New York: Berkley Books.

Krantz, D. S., & McCeney, M. K. (2002). Effects of psychological and social factors on organic disease. *Annual Review of Psychology, 53*, 341–369.

Krantz, L. (1995). *Jobs rated almanac.* New York: Wiley.

Kratofil, P. H., Baberg, H. T., & Dimsdale, J. E. (1996). Self-mutilation and severe self-injurious behavior associated with amphetamine psychosis. *General Hospital Psychiatry, 18*(2), 117–120.

Kristof-Brown, A. L., Barrick, M. R., & Franke, M. (2002). Applicant impression management: Dispositional influences and consequences for recruiter perceptions of fit and similarity. *Journal of Management, 28,* 27–46.

Kropp, P., Gerber W. D., Keinath-Specht, A., Kopal, T., et al. (1997) Behavioral treatment in migraine. *Functional Neurology, 12*(1), 17–24.

Krosnick, J. A. (1999). Survey research. *Annual Review of Psychology, 50,* 537–567.

Krosnick, J. A., Betz, A. L., Jussim, L. J., & Lynn, A. R. (1992). Subliminal conditioning of attitudes. *Personality & Social Psychology Bulletin, 18*(2), 152–162.

Krueger, J., Ham, J. J., & Linford, K. M. (1996). Perceptions of behavioral consistency: Are people aware of the actor–observer effect? *Psychological Science, 7*(5), 259–264.

Kruger, J., & Dunning, D. (1999). Unskilled and unaware of it: How difficulties in recognizing one's own incompetence lead to inflated self-assessments. *Journal of Personality & Social Psychology, 77*(6), 1121–1134.

Kübler-Ross, E. (1975). *Death: The final stage of growth.* Englewood Cliffs, NJ: Prentice Hall.

Kubovy, M., & Holcombe, A. O. (1998). On the lawfulness of grouping by proximity. *Cognitive Psychology, 35*(1), 71–98.

Kuczka, K. K., & Treasure, D. C. (2005). Self-handicapping in competitive sport: Influence of the motivational climate, self-efficacy, and perceived importance. *Psychology of Sport and Exercise, 6*(5), 539–550.

Kuehner, C. (2003). Gender differences in unipolar depression: An update of epidemiological findings and possible explanations. *Acta Psychiatrica Scandinavica, 108*(3), 163–174.

Kuhl, P. K. (2004). Early language acquisition: Cracking the speech code. *Nature Reviews Neuroscience, 5*(11), 831–841.

Kuhn, C. M., & Wilson, W. A. (2001). Our dangerous love affair with Ecstasy. *Cerebrum, 3*(2), 22–33.

Kunkel, M. A. (1993). A teaching demonstration involving perceived lunar size. *Teaching of Psychology, 20*(3), 178–180.

Kunzendorf, R. G. (1989). After-images of eidetic images: A developmental study. *Journal of Mental Imagery, 13*(1), 55–62.

Kusseling, F. S., Shapiro, M. F., Greenberg, J. M., & Wenger, N. S. (1996). Understanding why heterosexual adults do not practice safer sex: A comparison of two samples. *AIDS Education & Prevention, 8*(3), 247–257.

Laan, E., Everaerd, W., van Bellen, G., & Hanewald, G. J. F. P. (1994). Women's sexual and emotional responses to male- and female-produced erotica. *Archives of Sexual Behavior, 23*(2), 153–169.

Laan, E., Everaerd, W., van der Velde, J., & Geer, J. H. (1995). Determinants of subjective experience of sexual arousal in women. *Psychophysiology, 32*(5), 444–451.

LaBar, K. S., & LeDoux, J. E. (2002). Emotional learning circuits in animals and man. In R. J. Davidson, K. R. Scherer, et al. (Eds.), *Handbook of affective sciences.* New York: Oxford University Press.

Laberge, L., Petit, D., Simard, C., Vitaro, F., et al. (2001). Development of sleep patterns in early adolescence. *Journal of Sleep Research, 10*(1), 59–67.

LaBerge, S. P. (1981). Lucid dreaming: Directing the action as it happens. *Psychology Today,* Jan., 48–57.

LaBerge, S. P. (1985). *Lucid dreaming.* Los Angeles: Tarcher.

Labov, W. (1973). The boundaries of words and their meanings. In C. J. N. Bailey & R. W. Shuy (Eds.) *New ways of analyzing variation in English.* Washington, DC: Georgetown University Press.

Lac, G., & Chamoux, A. (2004). Biological and psychological responses to two rapid shiftwork schedules. *Ergonomics, 47*(12), 1339–1349.

Lacayo, A. (1995). Neurologic and psychiatric complications of cocaine abuse. *Neuropsychiatry, Neuropsychology, & Behavioral Neurology, 8*(1), 53–60.

Lachman, M. E. (2004). Development in midlife. *Annual Review of Psychology, 55,* 305–331.

Lackner, J. R., & DiZio, P. (2005). Vestibular, proprioceptive, and haptic contributions to spatial orientation. *Annual Review of Psychology, 56,* 115–147.

Lacks, P., & Morin, C. M. (1992). Recent advances in the assessment and treatment of insomnia. *Journal of Clinical and Consulting Psychology, 60*(4), 586–594.

Lal, S. K. L., Henderson R. J., Carter, N., Bath A., et al. (1998). Effect of feedback signal and psychological characteristics on blood pressure self-manipulation capability. *Psychophysiology, 35*(4), 405–412.

Lamb, M. R., & Yund, E. W. (1996). Spatial frequency and attention. *Perception & Psychophysics, 58*(3), 363–373.

Lambert, M. J. (1999). Are differential treatment effects inflated by researcher therapy allegiance? *Clinical Psychology: Science & Practice, 6*(1), 127–130.

Lambert, M. J., & Cattani-Thompson, K. (1996). Current findings regarding the effectiveness of counseling. *Journal of Counseling & Development, 74*(6), 601–608.

Lambert, M. J., & Ogles, B. M. (2002). The efficacy and effectiveness of psychotherapy. In M. J. Lambert (Ed.), *Handbook of psychotherapy and behavior change* (5th ed.). New York: Wiley.

Lambert, W. E. (1987). The effects of bilingual and bicultural experiences on children's attitudes and social perspectives. In P. Homel, M. Palij, & D. Aaronson (Eds.), *Childhood bilingualism.* Hillsdale, NJ: Erlbaum.

Lance, C. E., LaPointe, J. A., & Stewart, A. M. (1994). A test of the context dependency of three causal models of halo rater error. *Journal of Applied Psychology, 79*(3), 332–340.

Landau, J. D., & Bavaria A. J. (2003). Does deliberate source monitoring reduce students's misconceptions about psychology? *Teaching of Psychology, 30,* 311–314.

Landy, F. J., & Conte, J. M. (2003). *Work in the 21st century: An introduction to industrial and organizational psychology.* Boston: McGraw-Hill.

Landy, F. J., Shankster, L. J., & Kohler, S. S. (1994). Personnel selection and placement. *Annual Review of Psychology, 45,* 261–296.

Lange, A., van de Ven, J.-P., Schrieken, B., & Emmelkamp, P. M. G. (2001). Interapy. Treatment of posttraumatic stress through the Internet: A controlled trial. *Journal of Behavior Therapy & Experimental Psychiatry, 32*(2), 73–90.

Langens, T. A., & Schmalt, H.-D. (2002). Emotional consequences of positive daydreaming: The moderating role of fear of failure. *Personality & Social Psychology Bulletin, 28*(12), 1725–1735.

Langer, E. J. (2000). Mindful learning. *Current Directions in Psychological Science, 9*(6), 220–223.

Langer, E. J., & Abelson, R. P. (1974). A patient by any other name: Clinician group difference in labeling bias. *Journal of Consulting and Clinical Psychology, 42*(1), 4–9.

Langleben, D. D., Schroeder, L, Maldjian, J. A., Gur, R. C., et al. (2002). Brain activity during simulated deception: An event-related functional magnetic resonance study. *NeuroImage, 15,* 727–732.

Langone, M. D. (2002). Cults, conversion, science, and harm. *Cultic Studies Review, 1*(2), 178–186.

Lantz, J. (1998). Dream reflection in logotherapy. *Journal of Contemporary Psychotherapy, 28*(1) 81–89.

Lanzetta, J. T., & Englis, B. G. (1989). Expectations of cooperation and competition and their effects on observers' vicarious emotional responses. *Journal of Personality & Social Psychology, 56*(4), 543–554.

Larner, A. J., Moss, J., Rossi, M. L., & Anderson, M. (1994). Congenital insensitivity to pain. *Journal of Neurology, Neurosurgery & Psychiatry, 57*(8), 973–974.

Larsen, R. J., & Buss, D. M. (2005). *Personality psychology* (2nd ed.). New York: McGraw-Hill.

Larsen, R. J., & Kasimatis, M. (1990). Individual differences in entrainment of mood to the weekly calendar. *Journal of Personality & Social Psychology, 58*(1), 164–171.

Larson, M. E., Houlihan, D., & Goernert, P. N. (1995). Effects of informational feedback on aluminum can recycling. *Behavioral Interventions, 10*(2), 111–117.

Latané, B., Nida, S. A., & Wilson, D. W. (1981). The effects of group size on helping behavior. In J. P. Rushton & R. M. Sorrentino (Eds.), *Altruism and helping behavior: Social, personality and developmental perspectives.* Hillsdale, NJ: Erlbaum.

Lattal, K. A., Reilly, M. P., & Kohn, J. P. (1998). Response persistence under ratio and interval reinforcement schedules. *Journal of the Experimental Analysis of Behavior, 70*(2), 165–183.

Latty-Mann, H., & Davis, K. E. (1996). Attachment theory and partner choice. *Journal of Social & Personal Relationships, 13*(1), 5–23.

Laumann, E., Michael, R., Michaels, S., & Gagnon, J. (1994). *The social organization of sexuality.* Chicago: University of Chicago Press.

Laurent, G., Stopfer, M., Friedrich, R. W., Rabinovich, M. I., et al. (2001). Odor encoding as an active, dynamical process. *Annual Review of Neuroscience, 24,* 263–297.

Laursen, B., Coy, K. C., & Collins, W. A. (1998). Resonsidering changes in parent–child conflict across adolescence. *Child Development, 69,* 817–832.

Lavallee, A. C. (1999). Capuchin (Cebus apella) tool use in a captive naturalistic environment. *International Journal of Primatology, 20*(3), 399–414.

Lavie, P. (2001). Sleep–wake as a biological rhythm. *Annual Review of Psychology, 52,* 277–303.

Lawrence, B., Myerson, J., & Hale, S. (1998). Differential decline of verbal and visuospatial processing speed across the adult life span. *Aging, Neuropsychology, & Cognition, 5*(2), 129–146.

Lay, C., & Verkuyten, M. (1999). Ethnic identity and its relation to personal self-esteem. *Journal of Social Psychology, 139*(3), 288–299.

Lazarus, R. S. (1981). Little hassles can be hazardous to health. *Psychology Today,* July, 12–14.

Lazarus, R. S. (1991b). Cognition and motivation in emotion. *American Psychologist, 46*(4), 352–367.

Lazarus, R. S. (1991a). Progress on a cognitive–motivational–relational theory of emotion. *American Psychologist, 46*(8), 819–834.

Lazarus, R. S. (1993). From psychological stress to the emotions: A history of changing outlooks. *Annual Review of Psychology, 44,* 1–21.

Lazev, A. B., Herzog, T. A., & Brandon, T. H. (1999). Classical conditioning of environmental cues to cigarette smoking. *Experimental and Clinical Psychopharmacology, 7*(1), 56–63.

Leal, M. C., Shin, Y. J., Laborde, M.-L., Calmels, M.-N., et al. (2003). Music perception in adult cochlear implant recipients. *Acta Oto-Laryngologica, 123*(7), 826–835.

Leary, M. R. (2004). *Introduction to behavioral research methods* (4th ed.). Boston: Allyn and Bacon.

Leavens, D. A., & Hopkins, W. D. (1998). Intentional communication by chimpanzees. *Developmental Psychology, 34*(5), 813–822.

LeBlanc, G., & Bearison, D. J. (2004). Teaching and learning as a bi-directional activity: Investigating dyadic interactions between child teachers and child learners. *Cognitive Development, 19*(4), 499–515.

Lecomte, D., & Fornes, P. (1998). Suicide among youth and young adults, 15 through 24 years of age. *Journal of Forensic Sciences, 43*(5), 964–968.

Lederman, S. J., & Klatzky, R. L. (2004). Haptic identification of common objects: Effects of constraining the manual exploration process. *Perception & Psychophysics, 66*(4), 618–628.

Lederman, S. J., Howe, R. D., Klatzky, R. L., & Hamilton, C. (2004). Force variability during surface contact with bare finger or rigid probe. In *12th International Symposium on Haptic Interfaces for Virtual Environment and Teleoperator Systems,* 154–160.

LeDoux, J. (1996). *The emotional brain: The mysterious underpinnings of emotional life.* New York: Simon & Schuster.

LeDoux, J. E. (2000). Emotion circuits in the brain. *Annual Review of Neuroscience, 23,* 155–184.

LeDoux, J. E., & Gorman, J. M. (2001). A call to action: Overcoming anxiety through active coping. *American Journal of Psychiatry, 158*(12), 1953–1955.

Lee, J. M., Ku, J. H., Jang, D. P., Kim, D., et al. (2002). Virtual reality system for treatment of the fear of public speaking using image-based rendering and moving pictures. *CyberPsychology & Behavior, 5*(3), 191–195.

Lee, M., Zimbardo, P. G., & Bertholf, M. (1977). Shy murderers. *Psychology Today,* Nov, 69.

Lee, T. D., & Carnahan, H. (1990). When to provide knowledge of results during motor learning: Scheduling effects. *Human Performance, 3*(2), 87–105.

Leeming, F. C. (1997). Commitment to study as a technique to improve exam performance. *Journal of College Student Development, 38*(5), 499–507.

Leenaars, A. A., Brown, C., Taparti, L., Anowak, J., et al. (1999). Genocide and suicide among indigenous people: The North meets the South. *Canadian Journal of Native Studies, 19*(2), 337–363.

Leenaars, A. A., Lester, D., & Wenckstern, S. (2005). Coping with suicide: The art and the research. In R. I. Yufit & D. Lester (Eds.), *Assessment, treatment, and prevention of suicidal behavior.* New York: Wiley.

Leeper, R. W. (1935). A study of a neglected portion of the field of learning: The development of sensory organization. *Pedagogical Seminary and Journal of Genetic Psychology, 46,* 41–75.

Lefcourt, H. M., & Thomas, S. (1998). Humor and stress revisited. In W. Ruch (Ed.), *The sense of humor.* Berlin: Walter De Gruyter.

Lehman, D. R., Chiu, C., & Schaller, M. (2004). Psychology and culture. *Annual Review of Psychology, 55,* 689–714.

Lejuez, C. W., Eifert, G. H., Zvolensky, M. J., & Richards, J. B. (2000). Preference between onset predictable and unpredictable administrations of 20% carbon-dioxide-enriched air. *Journal of Experimental Psychology: Applied, 6*(4), 349–358.

Lench, H. C. (2004). Anger management: Diagnostic differences and treatment implications. *Journal of Social & Clinical Psychology, 23*(4), 512–531.

Lenzenweger, M. F., & Gottesman, I. I. (1994). Schizophrenia. In V. S. Ramachandran (Ed.), *Encyclopedia of human behavior.* San Diego: Academic Press.

Leonard, C. M. (1997). Language and the prefrontal cortex. In N. A. Krasnegor, G. R. Lyon, et al. (Eds.), *Development of the prefrontal cortex: Evolution, neurobiology, and behavior.* Baltimore: Paul H. Brookes.

Leor, J., Poole, W. K., & Kloner, R. A. (1996). Sudden cardiac death triggered by earthquake. *New England Journal of Medicine, 334*(7), 413.

Lepore, F. E. (2002). When seeing is not believing. *Cerebrum, 4*(2), 23–38.

Lepper, M. R., Keavney, M., & Drake, M. (1996). Intrinsic motivation and extrinsic rewards. *Review of Educational Research, 66*(1), 5–32.

Leslie, K., & Ogilvie, R. (1996). Vestibular dreams: The effect of rocking on dream mentation. *Dreaming: Journal of the Association for the Study of Dreams, 6*(1), 1–16.

Lessow-Hurley, J. (2005). *Foundations of dual language instruction* (4th ed.). Boston: Allyn & Bacon.

Lester, D. (2000). Major dimensions of near-death experiences. *Psychological Reports, 87*(3, Pt. 1), 835–836.

Lettvin, J. Y. (1961). Two remarks on the visual system of the frog. In W. Rosenblith (Ed.), *Sensory communication.* Cambridge, MA: MIT Press.

Levant, R. F. (1996). The new psychology of men. *Professional Psychology: Research & Practice, 27*(3), 259–265.

Levant, R. F. (2001). Men and masculinity. In J. Worell (Ed.), *Encyclopedia of women and gender.* San Diego: Academic Press.

LeVay, S. (1993). *The sexual brain.* Cambridge, MA: MIT Press.

LeVay, S., & Valente, S. M. (2005). *Human sexuality* (2nd ed.). Sunderland, MA: Sinauer Associates.

Levenston, G. K., Patrick, C. J., Bradley, M. M., & Lange, P. J. (2000). The psychopathic observer. *Journal of Abnormal Psychology, 109,* 373–385.

Leventhal, E. A., Leventhal, H., Shacham, S., & Easterling, D. V. (1989). Active coping reduces reports of pain from childbirth. *Journal of Consulting & Clinical Psychology, 57*(3), 365–371.

Levesque, M. F., & Neuman, T. (1999). Human trials to begin. *Spinal Cord Society Newsletter, 246,* 3–4.

Levesque, M. J., Steciuk, M., & Ledley, C. (2002). Self-disclosure patterns among well-acquainted individuals. *Social Behavior & Personality, 30*(6), 579–592.

Levi, A. M. (1998). Are defendants guilty if they were chosen in a lineup? *Law & Human Behavior, 22*(4), 389–407.

Levine, M., Toro, P. A., & Perkins, D. V. (1993). Social and community interventions. *Annual Review of Psychology, 44,* 525–558.

Levine, R. V. (1998). *A geography of time.* New York: Basic Books.

Levine, R. V. (2003). The kindness of strangers. *American Scientist, 91*(May–June), 226–233.

Levinson, A. (1999). Memory champ an absent-minded lady. *Tucson Daily Star,* Feb.

Levinson, D. J. (1986). A conception of adult development. *American Psychologist, 41*(1), 3–13.

Levinson, D. J., & Levinson, J. D. (1996). *The seasons of a woman's life.* New York: Knopf.

Levis, D. J. (1989). The case for a return to a two-factor theory of avoidance: The failure of non-fear interpretations. In S. B. Klein & R. R. Mower (Eds.), *Contemporary learning theories.* Hillsdale, NJ: Erlbaum.

Levitsky, D. A., Nussbaum, M., Halbmaier, C.A., & Mrdjenovic, G. (2003). The Freshman 15: A model for the study of techniques to curb the "epidemic" of obesity. *Society for the Study of Ingestive Behavior: Annual Meeting,* July 15–19, University of Groningen, Haren, The Netherlands.

Levy, B. R., Slade, M. D., Kunkel, S. R., & Kasl, S. V. (2002). Longevity increased by positive self-perceptions of aging. *Journal of Personality & Social Psychology, 83*(2), 261–270.

Levy, J., & Reid, M. (1976). Cerebral organization. *Science, 194,* 337–339.

Lewchanin, S., & Zubrod, L. A. (2001). Choices in life: A clinical tool for facilitating midlife review. *Journal of Adult Development, 8*(3), 193–196.

Lewis, M. (1992). *Shame: The exposed self.* New York: Free Press.

Lewis, M. (1995). Self-conscious emotions. *American Scientist, 83*(Jan.–Feb.), 68–78.

Lewis, M., & Brooks-Gunn, J. (1979). *Social cognition and the acquisition of self.* New York: Plenum.

Lewis, P. S., Goodman, S. H., & Fandt, P. M. (1995). *Management.* St Paul, MN: West.

Lewy, A. J., Bauer V. K., Cutler, N. L., Sack, R. L., et al. (1998). Morning vs. evening light treatment of patients with winter depression. *Archives of General Psychiatry, 55*(10), 890–896.

Liddell, S. K. (2003). *Grammar, gesture and meaning in American Sign Language.* Cambridge: Cambridge University Press.

Lieberman, D. A. (1979). Behaviorism and the mind: A (limited) call for a return to introspection. *American Psychologist, 34,* 319–333.

Lieberman, D. A. (2004). *Learning and memory: An integrative approach.* Belmont, CA: Wadsworth.

Light, P. (1997). Computers for learning. *Journal of Child Psychology & Psychiatry & Allied Disciplines, 38*(5), 497–504.

Lilienfeld, S. O. (1999). Projective measures of personality and psychopathology. *Skeptical Inquirer,* Sept.–Oct., 32–39.

Lilienfeld, S. O. (2005). Pseudoscience, nonscience, and nonsense in clinical psychology: Dangers and remedies. In K. A. Fowler, J. M. Lohr, et al. (Eds.), *Destructive trends in mental health: The well-intentioned path to harm.* New York: Routledge.

Lindemann, B. (2000). A taste for umami. *Nature Neuroscience, 3,* 99–100.

Lindemann, B. (2001). Receptors and transduction in taste. *Nature, 413,* 219–225.

Linden, W. (2005). *Stress management: From basic science to better practice.* Thousand Oaks, CA: Sage.

Lindsay, E. W., Mize, J., & Pettit, G. S. (1997). Differential pay patterns of mothers and fathers of sons and daughters. *Sex Roles, 37*(9–10), 643–661.

Lindstrom, T. C. (1995). Anxiety and adaptation in bereavement. *Anxiety, Stress & Coping: An International Journal, 8*(3), 251–261.

Lindstrom, T. C. (2002). "It ain't necessarily so . . ." Challenging mainstream thinking about bereavement. *Family & Community Health, 25*(1), 11–21.

Linton, M. (1979). I remember it well. *Psychology Today,* July, 81–86.

Lipschitz, D. S., Kaplan, M. L., Sorkenn, J., & Chorney, P. (1996). Childhood abuse, adult assault, and dissociation. *Comprehensive Psychiatry, 37*(4), 261–266.

Lipsey, M. W., & Wilson, D. B. (1993). The efficacy of psychological, educational, and behavioral treatment: Confirmation from meta-analysis. *American Psychologist, 48,* 1181–1209.

Liu, X., Matochik, J. A., Cadet, J., & London, E. D. (1998). Smaller volume of prefrontal lobe in polysubstance abusers. *Neuropsychopharmacology, 18*(4), 243–252.

Liu, Y., Gao, J., Liu, H., & Fox, P. T. (2000). The temporal response of the brain after eating revealed by functional MRI. *Nature, 405,* 1058–1062.

Lobo, L. L., & Tufik, S. (1997). Effects of alcohol on sleep parameters of sleep-deprived healthy volunteers. *Sleep, 20*(1), 52–59.

Locke, B. D., & Mahalik, J. R. (2005). Examining masculinity norms, problem drinking, and athletic involvement as predictors of sexual aggression in college men. *Journal of Counseling Psychology, 52*(3), 279–283.

Loeber, R., & Hay, D. (1997). Key issues in the development of aggression and violence from childhood to early adulthood. *Annual Review of Psychology, 48,* 371–410.

Loehlin, J. C., McCrae, R. R., Costa, P. T., & John, O. (1998). Heritabilities of common and measure-specific components of the Big Five personality factors. *Journal of Research in Personality, 32*(4), 431–453.

Loftus, E. F. (1979). Words that could save your life. *Psychology Today,* Nov., 102, 105–106.

Loftus, E. F. (1980). *Memory.* Reading, MA: Addison-Wesley.

Loftus, E. F. (2003). Make-believe memories. *American Psychologist, 58*(11), 867–873.

Loftus, E. F., & Bernstein, D. M. (2005). Rich false memories: The royal road to success. In A. F. Healy (Ed.), *Experimental cognitive psychology and its applications.* Washington, DC: American Psychological Association.

Loftus, E. F., & Ketcham, K. (1994). *The myth of repressed memory: False memories and allegations of abuse.* New York: St. Martin's Press.

Loftus, E. F., & Palmer, J. C. (1974). Reconstruction of automobile destruction: An example of interaction between language and memory. *Journal of Verbal Learning and Verbal Behavior, 13,* 585–589.

Loftus, G. R., & Mackworth, N. H. (1978). Cognitive determinants of fixation location during picture viewing. *Journal of Experimental Psychology: Human Perception and Performance, 4,* 565–572.

LoLordo, V. M. (2001). Learned helplessness and depression. In M. E. Carroll & J. B. Overmier, (Eds.), *Animal research and human health: Advancing human welfare through behavioral science*. Washington, DC: American Psychological Association.

Long, E. C., & Andrews, D. W. (1990). Perspective taking as a predictor of marital adjustment. *Journal of Personality & Social Psychology, 59*(1), 126–131.

Long, V. O. (1989). Relation of masculinity to self-esteem and self-acceptance in male professionals, college students, and clients. *Journal of Counseling Psychology, 36*(1), 84–87.

López, S. R., & Guarnaccia, P. J. J. (2000). Cultural psychopathology. *Annual Review of Psychology, 51,* 571–598.

Lorenz, K. (1937). Imprinting. *The Auk, 54,* 245–273.

Lorenz, K. (1962). *King Solomon's ring.* New York: Time.

Lorenz, K. (1966). *On aggression.* Translated by M. Kerr-Wilson. New York: Harcourt Brace Jovanovich.

Lorenz, K. (1974). *The eight deadly sins of civilized man.* Translated by M. Kerr-Wilson. New York: Harcourt Brace Jovanovich.

Lovaas, O., & Simmons, J. (1969). Manipulation of self-destruction in three retarded children. *Journal of Applied Behavior Analysis, 2,* 143–157.

Low, K. G., & Feissner, J. M. (1998). Seasonal affective disorder in college students: Prevalence and latitude. *Journal of American College Health, 47*(3), 135–137.

Lubinski, D. (2000). Scientific and social significance of assessing individual differences. *Annual Review of Psychology, 51,* 405–444.

Lucas, F., & Sclafani, A. (1990). Hyperphagia in rats produced by a mixture of fat and sugar. *Physiology & Behavior, 47*(1), 51–55.

Lucas, J. L., & Heady, R. B. (2002). Flextime commuters and their driver stress, feelings of time urgency, and commute satisfaction. *Journal of Business & Psychology, 16*(4), 565–572.

Lucas, R. E., Clark, A. E., Georgellis, Y., & Diener, E. (2003). Reexamining adaptation and the set point model of happiness: Reactions to changes in marital status. *Journal of Personality & Social Psychology, 84*(3), 527–539.

Luce, G. G. (1965). *Current research on sleep and dreams.* Health Service Publication no. 1389. U.S. Department of Health, Education, and Welfare.

Luckie, W. R., & Smethurst, W. (1998). *Study power.* Cambridge, MA: Brookline.

Ludwig, T. D., Gray, T. W., & Rowell, A. (1998). Increasing recycling in academic buildings. *Journal of Applied Behavior Analysis, 31*(4), 683–686.

Lumley, M. A. (2004). Alexithymia, emotional disclosure, and health: A program of research. *Journal of Personality. Special Emotions, Personality, and Health, 72*(6), 1271–1300.

Lundh, L., Berg, B., Johansson, H., Nilsson, L., et al. (2002). Social anxiety is associated with a negatively distorted perception of one's own voice. *Cognitive Behaviour Therapy, 31*(1), 25–30.

Luria, A. R. (1968). *The mind of a mnemonist.* New York: Basic Books.

Luster, T., & Dubow, E. (1992). Home environment and maternal intelligence as predictors of verbal intelligence. *Merrill–Palmer Quarterly, 38*(2), 151–175.

Lustig, C., May, C. P., Hasher, L. (2001). Working memory span and the role of proactive interference. *Journal of Experimental Psychology: General, 130*(2), 199–207.

Luxem, M., & Christophersen, E. (1994). Behavioral toilet training in early childhood: Research, practice, and implications. *Journal of Developmental & Behavioral Pediatrics, 15*(5), 370–378.

Lykken, D. T. (1998). *A tremor in the blood: Uses and abuses of the lie detector.* New York, NY: Plenum.

Lykken, D. T. (2001). Lie detection. In W. E. Craighead & C. B. Nemeroff (Eds.), *The Corsini encyclopedia of psychology and behavioral science* (3rd ed.). New York: Wiley.

Lynch, K. B., Geller, S. R., & Schmidt, M. G. (2004). Multi-year evaluation of the effectiveness of a resilience-based prevention program for young children. *Journal of Primary Prevention, 24*(3), 335–353.

Lynch, T. R., Robins, C. J., Morse, J. Q., & MorKrause, E. D. (2001). A mediational model relating affect intensity, emotion inhibition, and psychological distress. *Behavior Therapy, 32*(3), 519–536.

Lyubomirsky, S., & Tucker, K. L. (1998). Implications of individual differences in subjective happiness for perceiving, interpreting, and thinking about life events. *Motivation & Emotion, 22*(2), 155–186.

Lyznicki, J. M., Doege, T. C., Davis, R. M., & Williams, M. A. (1998). Sleepiness, driving, and motor vehicle crashes. *Journal of the American Medical Association, 279*(23), 1908–1913.

Maas, J. (1999). *Power Sleep.* New York: HarperCollins.

Mabry, J. H. (1998). Something for the future. *Analysis of Verbal Behavior, 15,* 129–130.

Maccoby, E. E. (1990). Gender and relationships: A developmental account. *American Psychologist, 45*(4), 513–520.

Maccoby, E. E., & Jacklin, C. N. (1974). *The psychology of sex differences.* Stanford, CA: Stanford University Press.

Mack, A. (2002). Is the visual world a grand illusion? *Journal of Consciousness Studies, 9*(5–6), 102–110.

Mack, A., & Rock, I. (1998). *Inattentional blindness.* Cambridge, MA: MIT Press.

Mackey, M. C. (1995). Women's evaluation of their childbirth performance. *Maternal-Child Nursing Journal, 23*(2), 57–72.

Macklis, J. D. (2001). New memories from new neurons. *Nature, 410*(6826), 314–315.

Macmillan, R. (2001). Violence and the life course. *Annual Review of Sociology, 27,* 1–22.

Maddi, S. R., Kahn, S., & Maddi, K. L. (1998). The effectiveness of hardiness training. *Consulting Psychology Journal: Practice & Research, 50*(2), 78–86.

Maddox, K. B. (2004). Perspectives on racial phenotypicality bias. *Personality & Social Psychology Review, 8*(4), 383–401.

Madigan, S., & O'Hara, R. (1992). Short-term memory at the turn of the century. *American Psychologist, 47*(2), 170–174.

Madon, S., Jussim, L., & Eccles, J. (1997). In search of the powerful self-fulfilling prophecy. *Journal of Personality and Social Psychology, 72,* 791–809.

Madon, S., Smith, A., Jussim, L., Russell, D. W., et al. (2001). Am I as you see me or do you see me as I am? *Personality & Social Psychology Bulletin, 27*(9), 1214–1224.

Magee, W. J., Eaton, W. W., & Wittchen, H. (1996). Agoraphobia, simple phobia, and social phobia in the national comorbidity survey. *Archives of General Psychiatry, 53*(2), 159–168.

Maguire, E. A., Frackowiak, R. S. J., & Frith, C. D. (1997). Recalling routes around London: Activation of the hippocampus in taxi drivers. *Journal of Neuroscience, 17*(8), 7103.

Mah, K., & Binik, Y. M. (2001). The nature of human orgasm: A critical review of major trends. *Clinical Psychology Review, 21*(6), 823–856.

Mahay, J., & Laumann, E. O. (2004). Meeting and mating over the life course. In E. O. Laumann & R. Michael (Eds.), *The sexual organization of the city.* Chicago: University of Chicago Press.

Maheu, M. M., Pulier, M. L., Wilhelm, F. H., McMenamin, J. P., et al. (2004). *The mental health professional and the new technologies: A handbook for practice today.* Mahwah, NJ: Lawrence Erlbaum.

Maier, N. R. F. (1949). *Frustration.* New York: McGraw-Hill.

Major, B., Schmidlin, A. M., & Williams, L. (1990). Gender patterns in social touch: The impact of setting and age. *Journal of Personality & Social Psychology, 58*(4), 634–643.

Malamuth, N. M., Addison, T., & Koss, M. (2000). Pornography and sexual aggression: Are there reliable effects and can we understand them? *Annual Review of Sex Research, 11,* 26–91.

Malamuth, N. M., & Donnerstein, E. (1982). The effects of aggressive-pornographic of mass media stimuli. In L. Berkowitz (Ed.), *Advances in experimental social psychology* (Vol. 15). New York: Academic Press.

Malaspina, D., Harlap, S., Fennig, S., Heiman, D., et al. (2001). Advancing paternal age and the risk of schizophrenia. *Archives of General Psychiatry, 58*(4), 361–367.

Malaspina, D., Reichenberg, A., Weiser, M., Fennig, S., et al. (2005). Paternal age and intelligence: Implications for age-related genomic changes in male germ cells. *Psychiatric Genetics, 15*(2), 117–125.

Malinosky-Rummell, R., & Hansen, D. R. (1993). Long-term consequences of childhood physical abuse. *Psychological Bulletin, 114*(1), 68–79.

Malnic, B., Hirono, J., & Buck, L. B. (1999). Combinatorial receptor codes for odors. *Cell, 96*(5), 713.

Maloney, A. (1999). Preference ratings of images representing archetypal themes. *Journal of Analytical Psychology, 44*(1) 101–116.

Mamen, M. (2004). *Pampered child syndrome: How to recognize it, how to manage it and how to avoid it.* Carp, ON: Creative Bound.

Mandler, J. M., & McDonough, L. (1998). On developing a knowledge base in infancy. *Developmental Psychology, 34*(6), 1274–1288.

Mangels, J. A., Picton, T. W., & Craik, F. I. M. (2001). Attention and successful episodic encoding: An event-related potential study. *Brain Research, 11,* 77–95.

Manschreck, T. C. (1996). Delusional disorder: The recognition and management of paranoia. *Journal of Clinical Psychiatry, 57*(3, Suppl.), 32–38.

Mansouri, A., & Adityanjee. (1995). Delusion of pregnancy in males: A case report and literature review. *Psychopathology, 28*(6), 307–311.

Mantyla, T. (1986). Optimizing cue effectiveness: Recall of 600 incidentally learned words. *Journal of Experimental Psychology: Learning, Memory, and Cognition, 12*(1), 66–71.

Marcus, E. (2002). Psychoanalytic psychotherapy and psychoanalysis: An overview. In M. Hersen & W. H. Sledge (Eds.), *Encyclopedia of psychotherapy.* San Diego: Academic Press.

Margolin, G., & Gordis, E. B. (2000). The effects of family and community violence on children. *Annual Review of Psychology, 51,* 445–479.

Marion, S. L., Shayka, J. J., & Marcus, S. C. (1996). A short computer interview for obtaining psychiatric diagnoses. *Psychiatric Services, 47*(3), 293–297.

Markovits, H., & Nantel, G. (1989). The belief-bias effect in the production and evaluation of logical conclusions. *Memory and Cognition, 17,* 11–17.

Marks, D. F. (2000). *The psychology of the psychic.* Buffalo, NY: Prometheus.

Markus, H., Kitayama, S., & VandenBos, G. R. (1996). The mutual interactions of culture and emotion. *Psychiatric Services, 47*(3), 225–226.

Markus, H., & Nurius, P. (1986). Possible selves. *American Psychologist, 41,* 954–969.

Marriott, L. K., & Wenk, G. L. (2004). Neurobiological consequences of long-term estrogen therapy. *Current Directions in Psychological Science, 13*(5), 173–176.

Marsella, A. J. (1998). Urbanization, mental health, and social deviancy. *American Psychologist, 53*(6), 624–634.

Martens, R., & Trachet, T. (1998). *Making sense of astrology.* Amherst, MA: Prometheus.

Martin, A. J., & Marsh, H. W. (2003). Fear of failure: Friend or foe? *Australian Psychologist, 38*(1), 31–38.

Martin, C. L., & Fabes, R. A. (2001). The stability and consequences of young children's same-sex peer interactions. *Developmental Psychology, 37*(3), 431–446.

Martin, D. J., Garske, J. P., & Davis, M. K. (2000). Relation of the therapeutic alliance with outcome and other variables: A meta-analytic review. *Journal of Consulting & Clinical Psychology, 68*(3), 438–450.

Martin, D. W. (2004). *Doing psychology experiments* (6th ed.). Belmont, CA: Wadsworth.

Martin, G., & Pear, J. (2003). *Behavior modification* (7th ed.). Upper Saddle River, NJ: Prentice Hall.

Martin, K. A., Moritz, S. E., & Hall, C. R. (1999). Imagery use in sport. *Sport Psychologist, 13*(3), 245–268.

Martin, P. Y., & Benton, D. (1999). The influence of a glucose drink on a demanding working memory task. *Physiology & Behavior, 67*(1), 69–74.

Martin, S. (1995). Field's status unaltered by the influx of women. *APA Monitor,* Jan., 9.

Martin, W. L. B., & Freitas, M. B. (2002). Mean mortality among Brazilian left- and right-handers: Modification or selective elimination. *Laterality, 7*(1), 31–44.

Martinez-Gonzalez, M. A., Gual, P., Lahortiga, F., Alonso, Y., et al. (2003). Parental factors, mass media influences, and the onset of eating disorders in a prospective population-based cohort. *Pediatrics, 111,* 315–320.

Martino, G., & Marks, L. E. (2001). Synesthesia: Strong and weak. *Current Directions in Psychological Science, 10*(2), 61–65

Marx, B. P., Gross, A. M., & Adams, H. E. (1999). The effect of alcohol on the responses of sexually coercive and noncoercive men to an experimental rape analogue. *Sexual Abuse: Journal of Research & Treatment, 11*(2), 131–145.

Mashour, G. A., Walker, E. E., & Martuza, R. L. (2005). Psychosurgery: Past, present, and future. *Brain Research Reviews, 48*(3), 409–419.

Masi, G., Mucci, M., & Millepiedi, S. (2001). Separation anxiety disorder in children and adolescents. *CNS Drugs, 15*(2), 93–104.

Maslach, C., Schaufeli, W. B., & Leiter, M. P. (2001). Job burnout. *Annual Review of Psychology, 52,* 397–422.

Maslow, A. H. (1954). *Motivation and personality.* New York: Harper.

Maslow, A. H. (1967). Self-actualization and beyond. In J. F. T. Bugental (Ed.), *Challenges of humanistic psychology.* New York: McGraw-Hill.

Maslow, A. H. (1968). *Toward a psychology of being.* New York: Van Nostrand.

Maslow, A. H. (1969). *The psychology of science.* Chicago: Henry Regnery.

Maslow, A. H. (1970). *Motivation and personality.* New York: Harper & Row.

Maslow, A. H. (1971). *The farther reaches of human nature.* New York: Viking.

Masten, A. S. (2001). Ordinary magic: Resilience processes in development. *American Psychologist, 56*(3), 227–238.

Masters, W. H., & Johnson, V. E. (1966). *Human sexual response.* Boston: Little, Brown.

Masters, W. H., & Johnson, V. E. (1970). *The pleasure bond: A new look at sexuality and commitment.* Boston: Little, Brown.

Mateu-Gelabert, P., & Lune, H. (2003). School violence: The bidirectional conflict flow between neighborhood and school. *City & Community, 2*(4), 353–368.

Matheny, K. B., Brack, G. L., McCarthy, C. J., & Penick, J. M. (1996). The effectiveness of cognitively-based approaches in treating stress-related symptoms. *Psychotherapy, 33*(2), 305–320.

Matias, R., & Cohn, J. F. (1993). Are MAX-specified infant facial expressions during face-to-face interaction consistent with differential emotions theory? *Developmental Psychology, 29*(3), 524–531.

Matossian, M. K. (1982). Ergot and the Salem witchcraft affair. *American Scientist, 70,* 355–357.

Matson, J. L., Sevin, J. A., Fridley D., & Love, S. R. (1990). Increasing spontaneous language in three autistic children. *Journal of Applied Behavior Analysis, 23*(2), 223–227.

Matsuda, L. A., Lolait, S. J., Brownstein, M. J., Young, A. C., et al. (1990). Structure of a cannabinoid receptor and functional expression of the cloned cDNA. *Nature, 346*(6284), 561–564.

Matthews, P. H., & Matthews, M. S. (2004). Heritage language instruction and giftedness in language minority students: Pathways toward success. *Journal of Secondary Gifted Education, 15*(2), 50–55.

Mattson, S. N., Riley, E. P., Gramling, L., Delis, D. C., et al. (1998). Neuropsychological comparison of alcohol-exposed children with or without physical features of fetal alcohol syndrome. *Neuropsychology, 12*(1), 146–153.

May, M. (1996). Resistance: Friend or foe? *American Journal of Psychotherapy, 50*(1), 32–44.

Mayer, E. L. (2002). Freud and Jung: the boundaried mind and the radically connected mind. *Journal of Analytical Psychology, 47,* 91–99.

Mayer, J. D., & Hanson, E. (1995). Mood-congruent judgment over time. *Personality & Social Psychology Bulletin, 21*(3) 237–244.

Mayer, J. D., Salovey, P., Caruso, D. R., & Sitarenios, G. (2001). Emotional intelligence as standard intelligence. *Emotion, 1*(3), 232–242.

Mayer, R. E. (1995). *Thinking, problem solving, and cognition.* New York: Freeman.

Mayer, R. E. (2004). Should there be a three-strikes rule against pure discovery learning? *American Psychologist, 59*(1), 14–19.

Mays, V. M., & Cochran, S. D. (2001). Mental health correlates of perceived discrimination among lesbian, gay, and bisexual adults in the United States. *American Journal of Public Health, 91*(11), 1869–1876.

McAlister, A. L., Ama, E., Barroso, C., Peters, R. J., et al. (2000). Promoting tolerance and moral engagement through peer modeling. *Cultural Diversity and Ethnic Minority Psychology, 6*(4), 363–373.

McBride, W. J., Murphy, J. M., & Ikemoto, S. (1999). Localization of brain reinforcement mechanisms. *Behavioural Brain Research, 101*(2), 129–152.

McCabe, M. P. (1992). A program for the treatment of inhibited sexual desire in males. *Psychotherapy, 29*(2), 288–296.

McCann, S. L., & Stewin, L. L. (1988). Worry, anxiety, and preferred length of sleep. *Journal of Genetic Psychology, 149*(3), 413–418.

McCarley, R. W. (1998). Dreams: Disguise of forbidden wishes or transparent reflections of a distinct brain state? In R. M. Bilder, F. F. LeFever, et al. (Eds.), *Neuroscience of the mind on the centennial of Freud's Project for a Scientific Psychology.* New York: New York Academy of Sciences.

McCarthy, B. W. (1995). Bridges to sexual desire. *Journal of Sex Education & Therapy, 21*(2), 132–141.

McCarthy, B. W., & Fucito, L. M. (2005). Integrating medication, realistic expectations, and therapeutic interventions in the treatment of male sexual dysfunction. *Journal of Sex & Marital Therapy, 31*(4), 319–328.

McCartney, K., Bernieri, F., & Harris, M. J. (1990). Growing up and growing apart: A developmental meta-analysis of twin studies. *Psychological Bulletin, 107*(2), 226–237.

McCarty, R. (1998). Making the case for animal research. *APA Monitor,* Nov., 18.

McCaul, K. D., & Malott, J. M. (1984). Distraction and coping with pain. *Psychological Bulletin, 95,* 516–533.

McCleary, R., Chew, K. S., Hellsten, J. J., & Flynn-Bransford, M. (1991). Age- and sex-specific cycles in United States suicides, 1973 to 1985. *American Journal of Public Health, 81*(11), 1494–1497.

McClelland, D. C. (1961). *The achieving society.* New York: Van Nostrand.

McClelland, D. C. (1965). Achievement and entrepreneurship. *Journal of Personality & Social Psychology, 1,* 389–393.

McClelland, D. C. (1975). *Power: The inner experience.* New York: Irvington.

McClelland, D. C. (1994). The knowledge-testing–educational complex strikes back. *American Psychologist, 49*(1), 66–69.

McClelland, D. C., & Cheriff, A. D. (1997). The immunoenhancing effects of humor on secretory IgA and resistance to respiratory infections. *Psychology & Health, 12*(3), 329–344.

McClelland, D. C., & Pilon, D. A. (1983). Sources of adult motives in patterns of parent behavior in early childhood. *Journal of Personality & Social Psychology, 44,* 564–574.

McClelland, L., & Cook, S. W. (1980). Promoting energy conservation in master-metered apartments through group financial incentives. *Journal of Applied and Social Psychology, 10,* 20–31.

McClenon, J. (2005). Content analysis of a predominately African-American near-death experience collection: Evaluating the ritual healing theory. *Journal of Near-Death Studies, 23*(3), 159–181.

McCluskey, U. (2002). The dynamics of attachment and systems-centered group psychotherapy. *Group Dynamics, 6*(2), 131–142.

McCoy, N. L., & Pitino, L. (2002). Pheromonal influences on sociosexual behavior in young women. *Physiology & Behavior, 75*(3), 367–375.

McCrae, R. R. (1987). Creativity, divergent thinking, and openness to experience. *Journal of Personality & Social Psychology, 52*(6), 1258–1265.

McCrae, R. R., & Costa, P. T. (1990). *Personality in adulthood.* New York: Guilford.

McCrae, R. R., & Costa, P. T. (1997). Personality trait structure as a human universal. *American Psychologist, 52*(5), 509–516.

McCrae, R. R., & Costa, P. T. (2001). A five-factor theory of personality. In L. A. Pervin & O. P. John (Eds.), *Handbook of personality.* New York: Guilford.

McCrae, R. R., & Terracciano, A. (2005). Universal features of personality traits from the observer's perspective: Data from 50 cultures. *Journal of Personality & Social Psychology, 88*(3), 547–561.

McCrory, C., & Cooper, C. (2005). The relationship between three auditory inspection time tasks and general intelligence. *Personality & Individual Differences, 38*(8), 1835–1845.

McDaniel, M. A., & Schlager, M. S. (1990). Discovery learning and transfer of problem-solving skills. *Cognition & Instruction, 7*(2), 129–159.

McDermott, J. F. (2001). Emily Dickinson revisited: A study of periodicity in her work. *American Journal of Psychiatry, 158*(5), 686–690.

McEachin, J. J., Smith, T., & Lovaas, O. I. (1993). Long-term outcome for children with autism who received early intensive behavioral treatment. *American Journal of Mental Retardation, 97*(4), 359–372.

McGinnies, E. (1949). Emotionality and perceptual defense. *Psychological Review, 56,* 244–251.

McGinnis, J. M., & Foege, W. H. (1993). Actual causes of death in the United States. *Journal of the American Medical Association, 270*(18), 2207–2212.

McGinnis, J. M., & Foege, W. H. (2002). *Health, United States 2002.* Rockville, MD: Centers for Disease Control and Prevention.

McGregor, D. (1960). *The human side of enterprise.* New York: McGraw-Hill.

McGregor, I., & Little, B. R. (1998). Personal projects, happiness, and meaning. *Journal of Personality & Social Psychology, 74*(2), 494–512.

McGuire, J., & Scott, S. (2002). Universal Design for Instruction: A promising new paradigm for higher education. *Perspectives, 28,* 27–29.

McIntosh, W. D., Harlow, T. F., & Martin, L. L. (1995). Linkers and nonlinkers: Goal beliefs as a moderator of the effects of everyday hassles on rumination, depression, and physical complaints. *Journal of Applied Social Psychology, 25*(14), 1231–1244.

McKean, K. J. (1994). Using multiple risk factors to assess the behavioral, cognitive, and affective effects of learned helplessness. *Journal of Psychology, 128*(2), 177–183.

McKeever, W. F. (2000). A new family handedness sample with findings consistent with X-linked transmis-

sion. *British Journal of Psychology, 91*(1), 21–39.
McKeever, W. F., Cerone, L. J., Suter, P. J., & Wu, S. M. (2000). Family size, miscarriage-proneness, and handedness. *Laterality, 5*(2), 111–120.
McKenna, K. Y. A., & Bargh, J. A. (1998). Coming out in the age of the Internet: Identity "demarginalization" through virtual group participation. *Journal of Personality & Social Psychology, 75*(3), 681–694.
McKenna, M. W., & Ossoff, E. P. (1998). Age differences in children's comprehension of a popular television program. *Child Study Journal, 28*(1), 52–68.
McKim, W. A. (1997). *Drugs and behavior.* Upper Saddle River, NJ: Prentice Hall.
McLennan, J. (1992). "University blues": Depression among tertiary students during an academic year. *British Journal of Guidance & Counselling, 20*(2), 186–192.
McLoyd, V. (1998). Socioeconomic disadvantage and child development. *American Psychologist, 53*(2), 185–204.
McLoyd, V. C., & Smith, J. (2002). Physical discipline and behavior problems in African American, European American, and Hispanic children: Emotional support as a moderator. *Journal of Marriage & Family, 64*(1), 40–53.
McMahon, S., & Koltzenburg, M. (2005). *Wall & Melzacks textbook of pain* (5th ed.). London: Churchill Livingstone.
McManus, I. C., Sik, G., Cole, D. R., Muellon, A. F., et al. (1988). The development of handedness in children. *British Journal of Developmental Psychology, 6*(3), 257–273.
McMurdo, M. E., & Gaskell, A. (1991). Dark adaptation and falls in the elderly. *Gerontology, 37*(4), 221–224.
McNally, R. J., & Clancy, S. A. (2005). Sleep paralysis, sexual abuse, and space alien abduction. *Transcultural Psychiatry, 42*(1), 113–122.
McNamara, D. S., & Scott, J. L. (2001). Working memory capacity and strategy use. *Memory & Cognition, 29*(1), 10–17.
Mead, M. (1935). *Sex and temperament in three primitive societies.* New York: Morrow.
Meagher, M. W., Arnau, R. C., & Rhudy, J. L. (2001). Pain and emotion. *Psychosomatic Medicine, 63*(1), 79–90.
Mehrabian, A. (2000). Beyond IQ. *Genetic Social, and General Psychology Monographs, 126,* 133–239.
Mehrabian, A., & Blum, J. S. (2003). Physical appearance, attractiveness, and the mediating role of emotions. In N. J. Pallone (Ed.), *Love, romance, sexual interaction: Research perspectives from current psychology.* New Brunswick, NJ: Transaction.
Mehren, E. (1994). Study finds most child care lacking. *Los Angeles Times,* April 8, E-5.
Meichenbaum, D., Henshaw, D., & Himel, N. (1982). Coping with stress as a problem-solving process. In H. W. Krohne & L. Laux (Eds.), *Achievement, stress, and anxiety.* New York: Hemisphere.
Meier, R. P. (1991). Language acquisition by deaf children. *American Scientist, 79*(1), 60–70.
Meltzoff, A. N., & Moore, M. K. (1983). Newborn infants imitate adult facial gestures. *Child Development, 54,* 702–709.
Melzack, R. (1993). Pain: Past, present and future. *Canadian Journal of Experimental Psychology, 47*(4), 615–629.
Melzack, R. (1999). From the gate to the neuromatrix. *Pain. Special: A tribute to Patrick D. Wall, Suppl. 6,* S121–S126.
Melzack, R., & Wall, P. D. (1996). *The challenge of pain.* Harmondworth, UK: Penguin.
Mendolia, M. (2002). An index of self-regulation of emotion and the study of repression in social contexts that threaten or do not threaten self-concept. *Emotion, 2*(3), 215–232.
Mendolia, M., Moore, J., & Tesser, A. (1996). Dispositional and situational determinants of repression. *Journal of Personality & Social Psychology, 70*(4), 856–867.
Meneses, G. D., & Asunción, B. (2005). Recycling behavior: A multidimensional approach. *Environment and Behavior, 37*(6), 837–860.
"Mental health: Does therapy help?" (1995). *Consumer Reports,* Nov., 734–739.
Menzel, P., Eisert, S., Mann, C. C., & Kennedy, P. (1994). *Material world : A global family portrait.* San Francisco: Sierra Club Books
Mercer, J. G., Beck, B., Burlet, A., Moar, K. M., et al. (1998). Leptin (ob) mRNA and hypothalamic NPY in food-deprived/refed Syrian hamsters. *Physiology & Behavior, 64*(2), 191–195.
Merckelbach, H., & Muris, P. (1997). The etiology of childhood spider phobia. *Behaviour Research & Therapy, 35*(11), 1031–1034.
Merenda, P. F. (1996). BASC: Behavior Assessment System for Children. *Measurement & Evaluation in Counseling & Development, 28*(4), 229–232.
Merritt, J. M., Stickgold, R., Pace-Schott, E., Williams, J., et al. (1994). Emotion profiles in the dreams of men and women. *Consciousness & Cognition, 3*(1), 46–60.
Mesquita, B., & Frijda, N. H. (1992). Cultural variations in emotions. *Psychological Bulletin, 112*(2), 179–204.
Messer, S. B., & Kaplan, A. H. (2004). Outcomes and factors related to efficacy of brief psychodynamic therapy. In D. P. Charman (Ed.), *Core processes in brief psychodynamic psychotherapy: Advancing effective practice.* Mahwah, NJ: Lawrence Erlbaum.
Messick, D. M., & Mackie, D. M. (1989). Intergroup relations. *Annual Review of Psychology, 40,* 45–81.
Metcalfe, J. (1986). Premonitions of insight predict impending error. *Journal of Experimental Psychology: Learning, Memory, and Cognition, 12,* 623–634.
Meyer, G. J., Finn, S. E., Eyde, L. D., Kay, G. G., et al. (2001). Psychological testing and psychological assessment. *American Psychologist, 56*(2) 128–165.
Meyer, I. H. (1995). Minority stress and mental health in gay men. *Journal of Health & Social Behavior, 36*(1), 38–56.
Meyer, R. G., & Youngjohn, J. R. (1991). Effects of feedback and validity expectancy on responses in a lie detector interview. *Forensic Reports, 4*(3), 235–244.
Meyer-Bisch, C. (1996). Epidemiological evaluation of hearing damage related to strongly amplified music (Personal cassette players, discotheques, rock concerts). *Audiology, 35*(3), 121–142.
Michalko, M. (1998). *Cracking creativity.* Berkeley, CA: Ten Speed Press.
Michel, D. E., & Chesky, K. S. (1995). A survey of music therapists using music for pain relief. *Arts in Psychotherapy, 22*(1), 49–51.
Michotte, A. (1963). *The perception of causality.* New York: Methuen/Basic.
Mickelson, K. D., Kessler, R. C., & Shaver, P. R. (1997). Adult attachment in a nationally representative sample. *Journal of Personality & Social Psychology, 73*(5), 1092–1106.
Middaugh, S. J., & Pawlick, K. (2002). Biofeedback and behavioral treatment of persistent pain in the older adult: A review and a study. *Applied Psychophysiology and Biofeedback, 27*(3), 185–202.
Mielke, H. W. (1999). Lead in the inner cities. *American Scientist, 87*(Jan.–Feb.), 62–73.
Mignot, E. (2001). A hundred years of narcolepsy research. *Archives of Italian Biology, 139,* 207–220.
Mikulincer, M., & Nachshon, O. (1991). Attachment styles and patterns of self-disclosure. *Journal of Personality & Social Psychology, 61*(2), 321–331.
Milgram, S. (1963). Behavioral study of obedience. *Journal of Abnormal and Social Psychology, 67,* 371–378.
Milgram, S. (1965). Some conditions of obedience and disobedience to authority. *Human Relations, 18,* 57–76.
Milgram, S. (1967). The small-world problem. *Psychology Today,* May, 61–67.
Milgram, S. (1970). The experience of living in the cities: A psychological analysis. *Science, 167,* 1461–1468.
Milgram, S., Bickman, L., & Berkowitz, L. (1969). Note on the drawing power of crowds of different size. *Journal of Personality & Social Psychology, 13,* 79–82.
Miller, D. T. (2006). *An invitation to social psychology.* Belmont, CA: Wadsworth.
Miller, D. T., Turnbull, W., & McFarland, C. (1988). Particularistic and universalistic evaluation in the social comparison process. *Journal of Personality & Social Psychology, 55*(6), 908–917.
Miller, G. A. (1956). The magical number seven, plus or minus two: Some limits on our capacity for processing information. *Psychological Review, 63,* 81–87.
Miller, G. A. (1999). On knowing a word. *Annual Review of Psychology, 50,* 1–19.
Miller, G. E., & Cohen, S. (2001). Psychological interventions and the immune system. *Health Psychology, 20*(1), 47–63.
Miller, G. E., Cohen, S., & Ritchey, A. K. (2002). Chronic psychological stress and the regulation of pro-inflammatory cytokines. *Health Psychology, 21*(6), 531–541.
Miller, L. K. (1999). The Savant Syndrome: Intellectual impairment and exceptional skill. *Psychological Bulletin, 125*(1), 31–46.
Miller, M. A., & Rahe, R. H. (1997). Life changes scaling for the 1990s. *Journal of Psychosomatic Research, 43*(3), 279–292.
Miller, N., Pedersen, W. C., Earleywine, M., & Pollock, V. E. (2003). A theoretical model of triggered displaced aggression. *Personality & Social Psychology Review, 7*(1), 75–97.
Miller, N. E. (1944). Experimental studies of conflict. In J. McV. Hunt (Ed.), *Personality and the behavior disorders* (Vol. I). New York: Ronald Press.
Miller, N. E., & Bugelski. R. (1970). The influence of frustration imposed by the in-group on attitudes expressed toward out-groups. In R. I. Evans & R. M. Rozelle (Eds.), *Social psychology in life.* Boston: Allyn & Bacon.
Miller, S. J., & Binder, J. L. (2002). The effects of manual-based training on treatment fidelity and outcome. *Psychotherapy: Theory, Research, Practice, Training, 39*(2), 184–198.
Miller, W. C. (1999). Fitness and fatness in relation to health. *Journal of Social Issues, 55*(2), 207–219.
Miller-Jones, D. (1989). Culture and testing. *American Psychologist, 44*(2), 360–366.
Millon, T. (1981) *Disorders of personality: DSM-III: Axis II.* New York: Wiley.
Milner, B. (1965). Memory disturbance after bilateral hippocampal lesions. In P. Milner & S. Glickman (Eds.), *Cognitive processes and the brain.* Princeton, NJ: Van Nostrand.
Miltenberger, R. G. (2004). *Behavior modification* (3rd ed.). Belmont, CA: Wadsworth.
Miltner, W. H. R., Krieschel, S., Hecht, H., Trippe, R., et al. (2004). Eye movements and behavioral responses to threatening and non-threatening stimuli during visual search in phobic and nonphobic subjects. *Emotion, 4*(4), 323–339.
Milton, J., & Wiseman, R. (1997). *Guidelines for extrasensory perception research.* Hertfordshire, UK: University of Hertfordshire Press.
Milton, J., & Wiseman, R. (1999). A meta-analysis of mass-media tests of extrasensory perception. *British Journal of Psychology, 90*(2), 235–240.
Minda, J. P., & Smith, J. D. (2001). Prototypes in category learning. *Journal of Experimental Psychology: Learning, Memory, & Cognition, 27*(3), 775–799.
Mineka, S., & Hamida, S. B. (1998). Observational and nonconscious learning. In W. T. O'Donohue (Ed.), *Learning and behavior therapy.* Boston: Allyn & Bacon
Minton, H. L. (2000). Psychology and gender at the turn of the century. *American Psychologist, 55*(6), 613–615.
Miotto, K., Darakjian, J., Basch, J., Murray, S., et al. (2001). Gamma-

hydroxybutyric acid: Patterns of use, effects and withdrawal. *American Journal on Addictions, 10*(3), 232–241.

Miranda, J. (1992). Dysfunctional thinking is activated by stressful life events. *Cognitive Therapy & Research, 16*(4), 473–483.

Mirsky, A. F., Bieliauskas, L. M., Van Kammen, D. P., Jonsson, E., et al. (2000). A 39-year followup of the Genain quadruplets. *Schizophrenia Bulletin, 3,* 5–18.

Mischel, W. (2004). Toward an integrative science of the person. *Annual Review of Psychology, 55,* 1–22.

Mischel, W., & Shoda, Y. (1998). Reconciling processing dynamics and personality dispositions. *Annual Review of Psychology, 49,* 229–258.

Mitchell, D. (1987). Firewalking cults: Nothing but hot air. *Laser,* Feb., 7–8.

Mitchell, D. B. (1989). How many memory systems? Evidence from aging. *Journal of Experimental Psychology: Learning, Memory, and Cognition, 15*(1), 31–49.

Mitru, G., Millrood, D.L., & Mateika, J. H. (2002). The impact of sleep on learning and behavior in adolescents. *Teachers College Record, 104*(4), 704–726.

Miyake, A. (2001). Individual differences in working memory. *Journal of Experimental Psychology: General, 130*(2), 163–168.

Moerman, D. E. (2002). The meaning response and the ethics of avoiding placebos. *Evaluation & the Health Professions. Special Recent Advances in Placebo Research, 25*(4), 399–409.

Mogg, K., Bradley, B. P., Hyare, H., & Lee, S. (1998). Selective attention to food-related stimuli in hunger. *Behaviour Research & Therapy, 36*(2), 227–237.

Moghaddam, B. (2002). Stress activation of glutamate neurotransmission in the prefrontal cortex. *Biological Psychiatry, 51*(10), 775–787.

Mohanty, S., Pati, N. C., & Kumar, R. (1998). Effects of token economy on the rate of envelope making in the persons with mental retardation. *Social Science International, 14*(1–2), 84–97.

Mokdad, A. H., Marks, J. S., Stroup, D. F., & Gerberding, J. L. (2004). Actual causes of death in the United States, 2000. *Journal of the American Medical Association, 291*(March 10), 1238–1245.

Monahan, J., Steadman, H. J., Silver, E., Appelbaum, P. S., et al. (2001). *Rethinking risk assessment: The MacArthur Study of Mental Disorder and Violence.* New York, Oxford University Press.

Money, J. (1987). Sin, sickness, or status? *American Psychologist, 42*(4), 384–399.

Money, J., & Mathews, D. (1982). Prenatal exposure to virilizing progestins: An adult follow-up study of twelve women. *Archives of Sexual Behavior, 11,* 73–83.

Montgomery, G. (1989). The mind in motion. *Discover,* March, 58–68.

Moor, J. H. (2001). The status and future of the Turing test. *Minds & Machines, 11*(1), 77–93.

Moore, T. O. (2001). Testosterone and male behavior: Empirical research with hamsters does not support the use of castration to deter human sexual aggression. *North American Journal of Psychology, 3*(3), 503–520.

Moore-Ede, M. C., Sulzman, F. M., & Fuller, C. A. (1982). *The clocks that time us.* Cambridge, MA: Harvard University Press.

Moras, K. (2002). Research on psychotherapy. In M. Hersen & W. H. Sledge (Eds.), *Encyclopedia of psychotherapy.* San Diego: Academic Press.

Morelli, G. A., Rogoff, B., Oppenheim, D., & Goldsmith, D. (1992). Cultural variation in infants' sleeping arrangements. *Developmental Psychology, 28*(4), 604–613.

Moreno, J. L. (1953). *Who shall survive?* New York: Beacon.

Morgan, J. D. (1995). Living our dying and our grieving: Historical and cultural attitudes. In H. Wass & R. A. Neimeyer (Eds.), *Dying: Facing the facts.* Washington, DC: Taylor & Francis.

Morgan, J. P. (Ed.). (2005). *Psychology of aggression.* Hauppauge, NY: Nova Science.

Morgan, M. J. (2000). Ecstasy (MDMA): A review of its possible persistent psychological effects. *Psychopharmacology, 152,* 230–248.

Morgan, M. J., Hole, G. J., & Glennerster, A. (1990). Biases and sensitivities in geometrical illusions. Special Issue: Optics, physiology and vision. *Vision Research, 30*(11), 1793–1810.

Morgenstern, J., Labouvie, E., McCrady, B. S., Kahler, C. W. et al. (1997). Affiliation with Alcoholics Anonymous after treatment. *Journal of Consulting & Clinical Psychology, 65*(5), 768–777.

Morisse, D., Batra, L., Hess, L., & Silverman, R. (1996). A demonstration of a token economy for the real world. *Applied & Preventive Psychology, 5*(1), 41–46.

Moritz, A. P., & Zamchech, N. (1946). Sudden and unexpected deaths of young soldiers. *American Medical Association Archives of Pathology, 42,* 459–494.

Moriarty, T. (1975). A nation of willing victims. *Psychology Today,* April, 43–50.

Morris, L. L., & Knafl, K. (2003). The nature and meaning of the near-death experience for patients and critical care nurses, *Journal of Near-Death Studies, 21*(3), 139–167.

Morrison, R. G., & Wallace, B. (2001). Imagery vividness, creativity and the visual arts. *Journal of Mental Imagery, 25*(3–4), 135–152.

Morsella, E., & Krauss, R. M. (2004). The role of gestures in spatial working memory and speech. *American Journal of Psychology, 117*(3), 411–424.

Mortensen, E. L., Michaelsen, K. F., Sanders, S. A., & Reinisch, J. M. (2002). The association between duration of breastfeeding and adult intelligence. *Journal of the American Medical Association, 287*(18), 2365–2371.

Moser, D. (1965). The nightmare of life with Billy. *Life,* May 7.

Moss, K. (1989). Performing the light-switch task in lucid dreams: A case study. *Journal of Mental Imagery, 13*(2), 135–137.

Most, S. B., Scholl, B. J., Clifford, E. R., & Simons, D. J. (2005). What you see is what you set: Sustained inattentional blindness and the capture of awareness. *Psychological Review, 112*(1), 217–242.

Mshelia, A. Y., & Lapidus, L. B. (1990). Depth picture perception in relation to cognitive style and training in non-Western children. *Journal of Cross-Cultural Psychology, 21*(4), 414–433.

Muchinsky, P. M. (2006). *Psychology applied to work* (8th ed.). Belmont, CA: Wadsworth.

Mullen, P. E., Martin, J. L., Anderson, J. C., & Romans, S. E. (1996). The long-term impact of the physical, emotional, and sexual abuse of children: A community study. *Child Abuse & Neglect, 20*(1), 7–21.

Mullington, J., & Broughton, R. (1993). Scheduled naps in the management of daytime sleepiness in narcolepsy-cataplexy. *Sleep, 16*(5), 444–456.

Murray, B. (2001a). "A daunting unbelievable experience." *Monitor on Psychology,* Nov., 18.

Murray, B. (2001b). Fast-food culture serves up super-size Americans. *Monitor on Psychology,* Dec., 56.

Murray, C. B., & Warden, M. R. (1992). Implications of self-handicapping strategies for academic achievement. *Journal of Social Psychology, 132*(1), 23–37.

Murray, J. B. (1995). Evidence for acupuncture's analgesic effectiveness and proposals for the physiological mechanisms involved. *Journal of Psychology, 129*(4), 443–461.

Murray, J. B. (2002). Phencyclidine (PCP): A dangerous drug, but useful in schizophrenia research. *Journal of Psychology, 136*(3), 319–327.

Murray, S. H., Touyz, S. W., Beumont, P. J. V. (1996). Awareness and perceived influence of body ideals in the media: A comparison of eating disorder patients and the general community. *Eating Disorders: The Journal of Treatment & Prevention, 4*(1), 33–46.

Murray, S. L., & Holmes, J. G. (1993). Seeing virtues in faults. *Journal of Personality & Social Psychology, 65*(4), 707–722.

Murray, S. L., Holmes, J. G., & Griffin, D. W. (1996). The self-fulfilling nature of positive illusions in romantic relationships. *Journal of Personality & Social Psychology, 71*(6), 1155–1180.

Mussen, P. H., Conger, J. J., Kagan, J., & Geiwitz, J. (1979). *Psychological development: A life span approach.* New York: Harper & Row.

Musso, M., Weiller, C., Kiebel, S., Muller, S. P., et al. (1999). Training-induced brain plasticity in aphasia. *Brain, 122,* 1781–1790.

Mustanski, B. S., Chivers, M. L., & Bailey, J. M. (2002). A critical review of recent biological research on human sexual orientation. *Annual Review of Sex Research, 13,* 89–140.

Myers, H. F., Lesser, I., Rodriguez, N., Mira, C. B., et al. (2002). Ethnic differences in clinical presentation of depression in adult women. *Cultural Diversity & Ethnic Minority Psychology, 8*(2), 138–156.

Nagel, T. (1974). What is it like to be a bat? *The Philosophical Review, 83,* 435–450.

Nairne, J. S. (2002). Remembering over the short-term. *Annual Review of Psychology, 53,* 53–81.

Naitoh, P., Kelly, T. L., & Englund, C. E. (1989). *Health effects of sleep deprivation.* U.S. Naval Health Research Center Report no. 89-46.

Nakamura, J., & Csikszentmihalyi, M. (2003). The motivational sources of creativity as viewed from the paradigm of positive psychology. In L. G. Aspinwall & U. M. Staudinger (Eds.), *A psychology of human strengths: Fundamental questions and future directions for a positive psychology.* Washington, DC: American Psychological Association.

Nakashima, M., & Canda, E. R. (2005). Positive dying and resiliency in later life: A qualitative study. *Journal of Aging Studies, 19*(1), 109–125.

Naranjo, C. (1970). Present-centeredness: Technique, prescription, and ideal. In J. Fagan & I. L. Shepherd (Eds.), *What is Gestalt therapy?* New York: Harper & Row.

Natale, V., & Cicogna, P. (1996). Circadian regulation of subjective alertness in morning and evening types. *EDRA: Environmental Design Research Association, 20*(4), 491–497.

Nathan, P. E., & Langenbucher, J. W. (1999). Psychopathology. *Annual Review of Psychology, 50,* 79–107.

Nathan, P. E., Stuart, S. P., & Dolan, S. L. (2000). Research on psychotherapy efficacy and effectiveness: Between Scylla and Charybdis? *Psychological Bulletin, 126*(6), 964–981.

National Academy of Sciences. (2002). *The polygraph and lie detection.* Washington, DC: National Academies Press.

National Institute of Child Health and Human Development. (1999). The NICHD Study of Early Child Care.

National Television Violence Study. (1995–1996). Studio City, CA: Mediascope, Inc.

Navarro, M. (1995). Drug sold abroad by prescription becomes widely abused in U.S. *New York Times,* Dec. 9, 1, 9.

Naveh-Benjamin, M. (1990). The acquisition and retention of knowledge: Exploring mutual benefits to memory research and the educational setting. *Applied Cognitive Psychology, 4*(4), 295–320.

Neath, I. (2002). *Human memory.* Belmont, CA: Wadsworth.

Neave, N., & Wolfson, S. (2003). Testosterone, territoriality, and the "home advantage." *Physiology & Behavior, 78*(2), 269–275.

Needles, D. J., & Abramson, L. Y. (1990). Positive life events, attributional style, and hopefulness: Testing a model of recovery from depression. *Journal of Abnormal Psychology, 99*(2), 156–165.

Neff, F. (1990). Delivering sport psychology services to a professional sport organization. *Sport Psychologist, 4*(4), 378–385.

Nehlig, A. (Ed.). (2004). *Coffee, tea, chocolate, and the brain.* Boca Raton, FL: CRC Press.

Neisser, U. (1997). Rising scores on intelligence tests. *American Scientist, 85,* 440–447.

Neisser, U., Boodoo, G., Bouchard, T. J., Boykin, A. W., et al. (1996). Intelligence: Knowns and unknowns. *American Psychologist, 51*(2), 77–101.

Nelson, C. A. (1999). How important are the first 3 years of life? *Applied Developmental Science, 3*(4), 235–238.

Nelson, G., & and Prilleltensky, I. (Eds.). (2005). *Community psychology: In pursuit of liberation and well-being*. New York: Palgrave MacMillan.

Nelson, J. R., Smith, D. J., & Dodd, J. (1990). The moral reasoning of juvenile delinquents. *Journal of Abnormal Child Psychology, 18*(3), 231–239.

Nelson, T. D. (2002). *Psychology of prejudice*. Boston: Allyn & Bacon.

Nelson, T. O. (1987). Predictive accuracy of the feeling of knowing across different tasks and across different subject populations and individuals. In M. M. Grunegerg, P. E. Morris, et al. (Eds.), *Practical aspects of memory: Current research and issues*. Chinchester, U.K.: Wiley.

Nesca, M., & Koulack, D. (1994). Recognition memory, sleep and circadian rhythms. *Canadian Journal of Experimental Psychology, 48*(3) 359–379.

Neter, E., & Ben-Shakhar, G. (1989). The predictive validity of graphological inferences: A meta-analytic approach. *Personality and Individual Differences, 10*(7), 737–745.

Neubert, M. J. (1998). The value of feedback and goal setting over goal setting alone and potential moderators of this effect: A meta-analysis. *Human Performance, 11*(4), 321–335.

Neufeld, R. W. (1970). The effect of experimentally altered cognitive appraisal on pain tolerance. *Psychonomic Science, 20*(2), 106–107.

Neufeld, R. W. J., Carter, J. R., Nicholson, I. R., & Vollick, D. N. (2003). Schizophrenia. In P. Firestone & W. L. Marshall (Eds.), *Abnormal psychology: Perspectives* (2nd ed.). Toronto: Prentice Hall.

Neugarten, B. (1971). Grow old along with me! The best is yet to be. *Psychology Today*, Dec., 45.

Neuman, G. A., & Baydoun, R. (1998). An empirical examination of overt and covert integrity tests. *Journal of Business & Psychology, 13*(1), 65–79.

Neumeister, A. (2004). Neurotransmitter depletion and seasonal affective disorder: Relevance for the biologic effects of light therapy. *Primary Psychiatry. Special Neurotransmitter Depletion, 11*(6), 44–48.

Nevid, J. S., & Greene, B. (2005). *Abnormal psychology in a changing world, media and research update* (5th ed.). Upper Saddle River, NJ: Prentice Hall.

Newell, A., & Simon, H. A. (1972). *Human problem solving*. Englewood Cliffs, NJ: Prentice Hall.

Newman, A. W., & Thompson, J. W. (2001). The rise and fall of forensic hypnosis in criminal investigation. *Journal of the American Academy of Psychiatry & the Law, 29*(1), 75–84.

Newman, B. M., & Newman, P. R. (1987). The impact of high school on social development. *Adolescence, 22*(87), 525–534.

Newman, R. (1994). Electronic therapy raises issues, risks. *APA Monitor*, Aug., 25.

Niaura, R., Todaro, J. F., Stroud, L., Spiro, A., et al. (2002). Hostility, the metabolic syndrome, and incident coronary heart disease. *Health Psychology, 21*(6), 588–593.

Nickell, J. (2001). John Edward: Hustling the bereaved. *Skeptical Inquirer*, Nov.–Dec., 19–22.

Nickerson, R. S., & Adams, M. J. (1979). Long-term memory for a common object. *Cognitive Psychology, 11*, 287–307.

Niedzwienska, A. (2004). Metamemory knowledge and the accuracy of flashbulb memories. *Memory, 12*(5), 603–613.

Niehaus, D. J. H., Stein, D. J., Koen, L., Lochner, C., et al. (2005). A case of "Ifufunyane": A Xhosa culture-bound syndrome. *Journal of Psychiatric Practice, 11*(6), 411–413.

Niehoff, B. P., Moorman, R. H., Blakely, G., & Fuller, J. (2001). The influence of empowerment and job enrichment on employee loyalty in a downsizing environment. *Group & Organization Management, 26*(1), 93–113.

Nielsen, D. M., & Metha, A. (1994). Parental behavior and adolescent self-esteem in clinical and nonclinical samples. *Adolescence, 29*(115), 525–542.

Nijstad, B. A., Stroebe, W., & Lodewijkx, H. F. M. (1999). Persistence of brainstorming groups: How do people know when to stop? *Journal of Experimental Social Psychology, 35*(2), 165–185.

Nikles, C. D., Brecht, D. L., Klinger, E., & Bursell, A. L. (1998). The effects of current-concern- and non-concern-related waking suggestions on nocturnal dream content. *Journal of Personality & Social Psychology, 75*(1), 242–255.

Nisbett, R. E. (2005). Heredity, environment, and race differences in IQ: A commentary on Rushton and Jensen (2005). *Psychology, Public Policy, and Law, 11*(2), 302–310.

Nisbett, R. E., & Miyamoto, Y. (2005). The influence of culture: Holistic versus analytic perception. *Trends in Cognitive Sciences, 9*(10), 467–473.

Nist, S. L., Sharman, S. J., & Holschuh, J. L. (1996). The effects of rereading, self-selected strategy use, and rehearsal on the immediate and delayed understanding of text. *Reading Psychology, 17*(2), 137–157.

Njeri, I. (1991). Beyond the melting pot. *Los Angeles Times*, Jan. 13, E–1, E–8.

Noble, K. D., Subotnik, R. F., & Arnold, K. D. (1996). A new model for adult female talent development. In K. D. Arnold, K. D. Noble, et al. (Eds.), *Remarkable women*. Cresskill, NJ: Hampton Press.

Noble, P. (1997). Violence in psychiatric in-patients. *International Review of Psychiatry, 9*(2–3), 207–216.

Noice, H., & Noice, T. (1999). Long-term retention of theatrical roles. *Memory, 7*(3), 357–382.

Nolen-Hoeksema, S. (2004). *Abnormal psychology* (3rd ed.). New York: McGraw-Hill.

Noller, P., & Ruzzene, M. (1991). Communication in marriage. In G. J. O. Fletcher & F. D. Fincham (Eds.), *Cognition and close relationships*. Hillsdale, NJ: Erlbaum.

Norcross, J. C. (Ed.). (2002). *Psychotherapy relationships that work*. New York: Oxford.

Norcross, J. C. (2005). A primer on psychotherapy integration. In J. C. Norcross & M. R. Goldfried (Eds.), *Handbook of psychotherapy integration* (2nd ed.). London: Oxford.

Norcross, J. C., Hedges, M., & Prochaska, J. O. (2002). The face of 2010: A Delphi poll on the future of psychotherapy. *Professional Psychology: Research & Practice, 33*(3), 316–322.

Norenzayan, A., & Nisbett, R.E. (2000). Culture and causal cognition. *Current Directions in Psychological Science, 9*, 132–135.

Norenzayan, A., Smith, E. E., Kim, B. J., & Nisbett, R. E. (2002). Cultural preferences for formal versus intuitive reasoning. *Cognitive Science, 26*(5), 653–684.

Nori, G. (1998). Glucagon and the control of meal size. In G. P. Smith (Ed.), *Satiation: From gut to brain*. New York: Oxford University Press.

Norlander, T., Bergman, H., & Archer, T. (1998). Effects of flotation rest on creative problem solving and originality. *Journal of Environmental Psychology, 18*(4), 399–408.

Norlander, T., Bergman, H., & Archer, T. (1999). Primary process in competitive archery performance: Effects of flotation REST. *Journal of Applied Sport Psychology, 11*(2), 194–209.

Norman, A. D., Ramsay, S. G., Martray, C. R., & Roberts, J. L. (1999). Relationship between levels of giftedness and psychosocial adjustment. *Roeper Review, 22*(1), 5–9.

Norman, D. A. (1994) *Things that make us smart*. Menlo Park, CA: Addison-Wesley.

Normann, R. A., Maynard, E. M., Rousche, P. J., & Warren, D. J. (1999). A neural interface for a cortical vision prosthesis. *Vision Research, 39*(15), 2577–2587.

Norris, R. M., & Weinman, J. A. (1996). Psychological change following a long sail training voyage. *Personality & Individual Differences, 21*(2), 189–194.

North, C. S. (1987). *Welcome silence*. New York: Simon & Schuster.

Northcutt, R. G. (2004). Taste buds: Development and evolution. *Brain, Behavior & Evolution, 64*(3), 198–206.

Nosek, B. A., Greenwald, A. G., & Banaji, M. R. (2005). Understanding and using the implicit association test: II. Method variables and construct validity. *Personality and Social Psychology Bulletin, 31*(2), 166–180.

Nurmi, J. (1992). Age differences in adult life goals, and their temporal extension. *International Journal of Behavioral Development, 80*(4), 487–508.

Nurnberger, J. I., & Zimmerman, J. (1970). Applied analysis of human behaviors: An alternative to conventional motivational inferences and unconscious determination in therapeutic programming. *Behavior Therapy, 1*, 59–69.

Oakley, D. A., Whitman, L. G., & Halligan, P. W. (2002). Hypnotic imagery as a treatment for phantom limb pain. *Clinical Rehabilitation, 16*(4), 368–377.

Oakley R. (2004). *How the mind hurts and heals the body. American Psychologist, 59*(1), 29–40.

Oatley, K., & Jenkins, J. M. (1992). Human emotions: Function and dysfunction. *Annual Review of Psychology, 45*, 55–85.

Obernier, J. A., White, A. M., Swartzwelder, H. S., & Crews, F. T. (2002). Cognitive deficts and CNS damage after a 4-day binge ethanol exposure in rats. *Pharmacology, Biochemistry & Behavior, 72*(3), 521–532.

Obhi, S. S., & Haggard, P. (2004). Free will and free won't. *American Scientist, 92*(July–Aug.), 358–365.

O'Brien, R. M., Figlerski, R. W., Howard, S. R., & Caggiano, J. (1981). The effects of multi-year, guaranteed contracts on the performance of pitchers in major league baseball. Paper presented at the annual meeting of the American Psychological Association, Los Angeles, Aug.

O'Connor, M. G., Sieggreen, M. A., Bachna, K., Kaplan, B., et al. (2000). Long-term retention of transient news events. *Journal of the International Neuropsychological Society, 6*(1), 44–51.

O'Conner, T. G., Marvin, R. S., Rutter, M., Olrick, J. T., et al. (2003). Child–parent attachment following early institutional deprivation. *Development & Psychopathology, 15*(1), 19–38.

O'Craven, K. M., & Kanwisher, N. (2000). Mental imagery of faces and places activates corresponding stimulus-specific brain regions. *Journal of Cognitive Neuroscience, 12*(6), 1013–1023.

Oehman, A. (2002). Automaticity and the amygdala: Nonconscious responses to emotional faces. *Current Directions in Psychological Science, 11*(2), 62–66.

Oest, L. (1996). One-session group treatment of spider phobia. *Behaviour Research & Therapy, 34*(9), 707–715.

Oest, L., Svensson, L., Hellstroem, K., & Lindwall, R. (2001). One-session treatment of specific phobias in youths. *Journal of Consulting & Clinical Psychology, 69*(5), 814–824.

Ofosu, H. B., Lafreniere, K. D., & Senn, C. Y. (1998). Body image perception among women of African descent: A normative context? *Feminism & Psychology, 8*(3), 303–323.

Ogloff, J. R. P., & Chopra, S. R. (2004). Stuck in the dark ages: Supreme Court decision making and legal developments. *Psychology, Public Policy, and Law, 10*(4), 379–416.

Ohayon, M. M., Guilleminault, C., & Priest, R. G. (1999). Night terrors, sleepwalking, and confusional arousals in the general population. *Journal of Clinical Psychiatry, 60*(4), 268–276.

Olds, M. E., & Fobes, J. L. (1981). The central basis of motivation: Intracranial self-stimulation studies. *Annual Review of Psychology, 32*, 523–574.

Olio, K. A. (2004). The truth about "false memory syndrome." In P. J. Caplan & L. Cosgrove (Eds.), *Bias in psychiatric diagnosis. A project of the association for women in psychology*. Northvale, NJ: Jason Aronson.

Oliver, J. E. (1993). Intergenerational transmission of child abuse. *American Journal of Psychiatry, 150*(9), 1315–1324.

Oliver, M. B., & Hyde, J. S. (1993). Gender differences in sexuality. *Psychological Bulletin, 114*(1), 29–51.

Oliwenstein, L. (1993). The gene with two faces. *Discover*, May, 26.

Ollendick, T. H., & King, N. J. (1991). Origins of childhood fears. *Behaviour Research & Therapy, 29*(2), 117–123.

Olson, J. M., & Zanna, M. P. (1993). Attitudes and attitude change. *Annual Review of Psychology, 44*, 117–154.

Olson, R. L., & Roberts, M. W. (1987). Alternative treatments for sibling aggression. *Behavior Therapy, 18*(3), 243–250.

Olson, S. L., Bates, J. E., & Kaskie, B. (1992). Caregiver–infant interaction antecedents of children's school-age cognitive ability. *Merrill-Palmer Quarterly, 38*(3), 309–330.

O'Neil, K. M., Patry, M. W., & Penrod, S. D. (2004). Exploring the effects of attitudes toward the death penalty on capital sentencing verdicts. *Psychology, Public Policy, and Law, 10*(4), 443–470.

O'Neill, B. (2003). *Don't believe everything you read online.* BBC News. Retrieved 2006 from http://newswww.bbc.net.uk/1/hi/magazine/3151595.stm.

O'Neill, P. (2005) The ethics of problem definition. *Canadian Psychology, 46*, 13–20.

Ones, D. S., & Viswesvaran, C. (2001). Integrity tests and other criterion-focused occupational personality scales (COPS) used in personnel selection. *International Journal of Selection & Assessment, 9*(1–2), 31–39.

Ones, D. S.,Viswesvaran, C., & Schmidt, F. L. (2003). Personality and absenteeism: A meta-analysis of integrity tests. *European Journal of Personality. Special Issue: Personality and Industrial, Work and Organizational Applications, 17*(Suppl. 1), S19–S38.

Onwuegbuzie, A. J. (2000). Academic procrastinators and perfectionistic tendencies among graduate students. *Journal of Social Behavior & Personality, 15*(5), 103–109.

Orleans, C. T. (2000). Promiting the maintenance of health behavior change. *Health Psychology, 19*(Suppl. 1), 76–83.

Orleans, C. T., Gruman, J., & Hollendonner, J. K. (1999). Rating our progress in population health promotion: Report card on six behaviors. *American Journal of Health Promotion, 14*(2), 75–82.

Orlick, T. D. (1975). The sports environment: A capacity to enhance—a capacity to destroy. In B. S. Rushall (Ed.), *The status of psychomotor learning and sport psychology research*. Dartmouth, Nova Scotia: Sport Science Associates.

Ornstein, R. (1997). *The right mind.* San Diego, CA: Harcourt Brace.

Ornstein, R., & Ehrlich, P. (1989). *New world new mind.* New York: Simon & Schuster.

Ornstein, S., & Isabella, L. (1990). Age vs. stage models of career attitudes of women: A partial replication and extension. *Journal of Vocational Behavior, 36*, 1–19.

O'Roark, A. M. (2001). Personality assessment, projective methods and a triptych perspective. *Journal of Projective Psychology & Mental Health, 8*(2), 116–126.

Osgood, C. E. (1952). The nature and measurement of meaning. *Psychological Bulletin, 49*, 197–237.

Oskamp, S. (1995). Resource conservation and recycling: Behavior and policy. *Journal of Social Issues, 51*(4), 157–177.

Oskamp, S. (2000). A sustainable future for humanity? *American Psychologist, 55*(5), 496–508.

Oskamp, S. (2002). Summarizing sustainability issues and research approaches. In P. Schmuck & W. P. Schultz (Eds.), *Psychology of sustainable development*. Dordrecht, Netherlands: Kluwer.

Oskamp, S., & Schultz, P. W. (2005). *Attitudes and opinions* (3rd ed.). Mahwah, NJ: Erlbaum.

Osmon, D. C., & Jackson, R. (2002). Inspection time and IQ: Fluid or perceptual aspects of intelligence? *Intelligence, 30*(2), 119–128.

Osofsky, M. J., Bandura, A., & Zimbardo, P. G. (2005). The role of moral disengagement in the execution process. *Law and Human Behavior, 29*(4), 371–393.

"Outline for cultural formulation and glossary of culture-bound syndromes." (2000). In *DSM-IV-TR: Diagnostic and statistical manual of mental disorders* (5th ed.). Washington, DC: American Psychiatric Association.

Overmier, J. B., & LoLordo, V. M. (1998). Learned helplessness. In W. T. O'Donohue (Ed.), *Learning and behavior therapy.* Boston: Allyn & Bacon.

Owen, J. D. (1976). Flextime: Some problems and solutions. *Industrial and Labor Relations Review, 29*, 152–160.

Oyama, T., & Ichikawa, S. (1990). Some experimental studies on imagery in Japan. *Journal of Mental Imagery, 14*(3–4), 185–195.

Oyserman, D., Bybee, D., Terry, K., & Hart-Johnson, T. (2004). Possible selves as roadmaps. *Journal of Research in Personality, 38*(2), 130–149.

Page, K. (1999). The graduate. *Washington Post Magazine, 152*(May 16), 18–20.

Pagnin, D., de Queiroz, V., Pini, S., & Cassano, G. B. (2004). Efficacy of ECT in depression: A meta-analytic review. *Journal of ECT, 20*(1), 13–20.

Palfai, T., & Jankiewicz, H. (1991). *Drugs and human behavior.* Dubuque, IA: Wm. C. Brown.

Palm, K., & Gibson, P. (1998). Recovered memories of childhood sexual abuse: Clinicians' practices and beliefs. *Professional Psychology: Research & Practice, 29*(3), 257–261.

Palmer, S. E. (1992). Common region: A new principle of perceptual grouping. *Cognitive Psychology, 24*(3), 436–447.

Pandey, S. (1999). Role of perceived control in coping with crowding. *Psychological Studies, 44*(3), 86–91.

Papa, F. J., Aldrich, D., & Schumacker, R. E. (1999). The effects of immediate online feedback upon diagnostic performance. *Academic Medicine, 74*(Suppl. 10), S16–S18.

Papps, F., Walker, M., Trimboli, A., & Trimboli, C. (1995). Parental discipline in Anglo, Greek, Lebanese, and Vietnamese cultures. *Journal of Cross-Cultural Psychology, 26*(1), 49–64.

Paquette, V., Lévesque, J., Mensour, B., Leroux, J.-M., et al. (2003). "Change the mind and you change the brain": Effects of cognitive-behavioral therapy on the neural correlates of spider phobia. *NeuroImage, 18*, 401–409.

Paradis, C. M., Solomon, L. Z., Florer, F., & Thompson, T. (2004). Flashbulb memories of personal events of 9/11 and the day after for a sample of New York City residents. *Psychological Reports, 95*(1), 304–310.

Park, D. C., Smith, A. D., & Cavanaugh, J. C. (1990). Metamemories of memory researchers. *Memory & Cognition, 18*(3), 321–327.

Park, N., Peterson, C., & Seligman, M.E. P. (2004). Strengths of character and well-being. *Journal of Social & Clinical Psychology, 23*(5), 603–619.

Parke, R. D. (1995). Fathers and families. In M. H. Bornstein (Ed.), *Handbook of parenting* (Vol. 3). Mahwah, NJ: Erlbaum.

Parke, R. D. (2004). Development in the family. *Annual Review of Psychology, 55*, 365–399.

Parker, A., Ngu, H., & Cassaday, H. J. (2001). Odour and Proustian memory. *Applied Cognitive Psychology, 15*(2), 159–171.

Parker, J. D. A., Summerfeldt, L. J., Hogan, M. J., & Majeski, S. A. (2004). Emotional intelligence and academic success: Examining the transition from high school to university. *Personality & Individual Differences, 36*(1), 163–172.

Parkes, C. M. (1979). *Grief: The painful reaction to the loss of a loved one.* Monograph, University of California, San Diego.

Parsons, L. M., Fox, P. T., Downs, J. H., Glass, T., et al. (1995). Use of implicit motor imagery for visual shape discrimination as revealed by PET. *Nature, 375*(6526), 54–58.

Passman, R. H. (1987). Attachments to inanimate objects: Are children who have security blankets insecure? *Journal of Consulting & Clinical Psychology, 55*(6), 825–830.

Pasupathi, M., & Staudinger, U. M. (2001). Do advanced moral reasoners also show wisdom? *International Journal of Behavioral Development, 25*(5), 401–415.

Patrick, C. J., & Iacono, W. G. (1989). Psychopathy, threat, and polygraph test accuracy. *Journal of Applied Psychology, 74*(2), 347–355.

Patten, B. M. (1990). The history of memory arts. *Neurology, 40*(2), 346–352.

Patterson, C. J. (1995). Sexual orientation and human development: An overview. *Developmental Psychology, 31*(1), 3–11.

Patterson, C. J. (2002). Lesbian and gay parenthood. In M. Bornstein (Ed.*), Handbook of Parenting, 3, 4, 5.* Mahwah, NJ: Erlbaum.

Patterson, G. R. (1982). *Coercive family process.* Eugene, OR: Castilia Press.

Paulhus, D. L. (1998). Interpersonal and intrapsychic adaptiveness of trait self-enhancement. *Journal of Personality and Social Psychology, 74*(5), 1197–1208.

Pavlidis, I., Eberhardt, N. L., & Levine, J. A. (2002). Seeing through the face of deception. *Nature, 415*(6867), 35.

Pavlov, I. P. (1927). *Conditioned reflexes.* Translated by G. V. Anrep. New York: Dover.

Pavot, W., & Diener, E. (1993). Review of the Satisfaction with Life scale. *Psychological Assessments, 5*(2), 164–172.

Peeters, M. C. W., Buunk, B. P., & Schaufeli, W. B. (1995). A microanalysis exploration of the cognitive appraisal of daily stressful events at work. *Anxiety, Stress & Coping: An International Journal, 8*(2), 127–139.

Pelton, T. (1983). The shootists. *Science 83, 4*(4), 84–86.

Penfield, W. (1957). Brain's record of past a continuous movie film. *Science News Letter*, April 27, 265.

Penfield, W. (1958). *The excitable cortex in conscious man.* Springfield, IL: Charles C Thomas.

Pennebaker, J. W. (2004). *Writing to heal: A guided journal for recovering from trauma and emotional upheaval.* Oakland, CA: New Harbinger Press.

Pennebaker, J. W., & Francis, M. E. (1996). Cognitive, emotional, and language processes in disclosure. *Cognition & Emotion, 10*(6), 601–626.

Penner, L. A., Dovidio, J. F., Piliavin, J. A., & Schroeder, D. A. (2005). Prosocial behavior: Multilevel perspectives. *Annual Review of Psychology, 56*, 365–392.

Pennisi, E. (1992). Valentine bind. *Science News, 141* (Feb. 15), 110–111.

Pepler, D. J., & Craig, W. M. (1995). A peek behind the fence: Naturalistic observations of aggressive children with remote audiovisual recording. *Developmental Psychology, 31*(4), 548–553.

Pepler, D. J., Craig, W. M., & Roberts, W. L. (1998). Observations of aggressive and nonaggressive children on the school playground. *Merrill-Palmer Quarterly, 44*(1), 55–76.

Perin, C. T. (1943). A quantitative investigation of the delay of reinforcement gradient. *Journal of Experimental Psychology, 32*, 37–51.

Perkins, D. N. (1995). *Outsmarting IQ: The emerging science of learnable intelligence.* New York: Free Press.

Perkins, D. N., & Grotzer, T. A. (1997). Teaching intelligence. *American Psychologist, 52*(10), 1125–1133.

Perkins, K. A. (1995). Individual variability in responses to nicotine. *Behavior Genetics, 25*(2), 119–132.

Perlman, D., & Cozby, P. C. (1983). *Social psychology.* New York: Holt, Rinehart & Winston.

Perls, F. (1969). *Gestalt therapy verbatim.* Lafayette, CA: Real People.

Perreault, S., & Bourhis, R. Y. (1999). Ethnocentrism, social identification, and discrimination. *Personality & Social Psychology Bulletin, 25*(1), 92–103.

Perry, R. P. (2003). Perceived (academic) control and causal thinking in achievement settings. *Canadian Psychology, 44*(4), 312–331.

Perry, R. P., Hladkyj, S., Pekrun, R. H., & Pelletier, S. T. (2001). Academic control and action control in the achievement of college students: A longitudinal field study. *Journal of Educational Psychology, 93*(4), 776–789.

Perugini, E. M., Kirsch, I., Allen, S. T., Coldwell, E., et al. (1998). Surreptitious observation of responses to hypnotically suggested hallucinations. *International Journal of Clinical & Experimental Hypnosis, 46*(2), 191–203.

Pervin, L. A., Cervone, D., & John, O. P. (2005). *Personality: Theory and research* (9th ed.). New York: Wiley.

Pescatello, L. S. (2001). Exercising for health. *Western Journal of Medicine, 174*(2), 114–118.

Peters, L., Clark, D., & Carroll, F. (1998). Are computerized interviews equivalent to human interviewers? *Psychological Medicine, 28*(4), 893–901.

Peters, W. A. (1971). *A class divided.* Garden City, NY: Doubleday.

Petersen, A. C., Kennedy, R. E., & Sullivan, P. (1991). Coping with adolescence. In M. E. Colten & S. Gore (Eds.), *Adolescent stress.* New York: Aldine de Gruyter.

Peterson, B. E., & Klohnen, E. C. (1995). Realization of generativity in two samples of women at midlife. *Psychology & Aging, 10*(1), 20–29.

Petersen, S. E., Fox, P. T., Posner, M. I., Mintun, M., et al. (1988). Positron emission tomographic studies of the cortical anatomy of single-word processing. *Nature, 331*(6157), 585–589.

Peterson, C., & Chang, E. C. (2003). Optimism and flourishing. In C. L. M. Keyes & J. Haidt (Eds.), *Flourishing.* Washington, DC: American Psychological Association.

Peterson, C., & Seligman, M. E. P. (2004). *Character strengths and virtues.* Washington, DC: American Psychological Association.

Peterson, D. R. (2001). Choosing the PsyD. In S. Walfish & A. K. Hess (Eds.), *Succeeding in graduate school: The career guide for psychology students.* Mahwah, NJ: Erlbaum.

Peterson, J. (1995). How are psychologists perceived by the public? *APA Monitor,* March, 31.

Peterson, L. R., & Peterson, M. J. (1959). Short-term retention of individual verbal items. *Journal of Experimental Psychology, 58,* 193–198.

Peterson, P. L. (1979). Direct instruction: Effective for what and for whom? *Educational Leadership, 37,* 46–48.

Peterson, S. E. (1992). The cognitive functions of underlining as a study technique. *Reading Research & Instruction, 31*(2), 49–56.

Petri, H. (2003). *Motivation.* Belmont, CA: Wadsworth.

Petrie, T. A., & Diehl, N. S. (1995). Sport psychology in the profession of psychology. *Professional Psychology: Research & Practice, 26*(3), 288–291.

Petrill, S. A., Luo, D., Thompson, L. A., & Detterman, D. K. (2001). Inspection time and the relationship among elementary cognitive tasks, general intelligence and specific cognitive abilities. *Intelligence, 29*(6), 487–496.

Pettigrew, T. F. (1998). Intergroup contact theory. *Annual Review of Psychology, 49,* 65–85.

Pettit, G. S., Brown, E. G., Mize, J., & Lindsey, E. (1998). Mothers' and fathers' socializing behaviors in three contexts. *Merrill-Palmer Quarterly, 44*(2), 173–193.

Peverly, S. T., Brobst, K. E., Graham, M., & Shaw, R. (2003). College adults are not good at self-regulation. *Journal of Educational Psychology, 95*(2), 335–346.

Phillips, D. P., Liu, G. C., Kwok, K., Jarvinen, J., et al. (2001). The Hound of the Baskervilles effect: Natural experiment on the influence of psychological stress on timing of death. *British Medical Journal, 323*(7327), 1443–1446

Phillips, D. P., & Wills, J. S. (1987). A drop in suicides around major national holidays. *Suicide & Life-Threatening Behavior, 17,* 1–12.

Phillips, J. L. (1969). *Origins of intellect: Piaget's theory.* San Francisco: Freeman.

Piaget, J. (1951, original French, 1945). *The psychology of intelligence.* New York: Norton.

Piaget, J. (1952). *The origins of intelligence in children.* New York: International University Press.

Pierce, J. P. (1991). Progress and problems in international public health efforts to reduce tobacco usage. *Annual Review of Public Health, 12,* 383–400.

Pierce, W. D., & Cheney, C. D. (2004). *Behavior analysis and learning* (3rd ed.). Mahwah, NJ: Erlbaum.

Pierrehumbert, B., Ramstein, T., Karmaniola, A., Miljkovitch, R., et al. (2002). Quality of child care in the preschool years. *International Journal of Behavioral Development, 26*(5), 385–396.

Pierrel, R., & Sherman, J. G. (1963). Train your pet the Barnabus way. *Brown Alumni Monthly,* Feb., 8–14.

Piliavin, I. M., Rodin, J., & Piliavin, J. A. (1969). Good samaritanism: An underground phenomenon? *Journal of Personality & Social Psychology, 13,* 289–299.

Piliavin, J. A. (2003). Doing well by doing good: Benefits to the benefactor. In C. L. M. Keyes & J. Haidt (Eds.), *Flourishing.* Washington, DC: American Psychological Association.

Pillow, D. R., Zautra, A. J., & Sandler, I. (1996). Major life events and minor stressors: Identifying mediational links in the stress process. *Journal of Personality & Social Psychology, 70*(2), 381–394.

Pinel, J. P. J., Assanand, S., & Lehman, D. R. (2000). Hunger, eating, and ill health. *American Psychologist, 55*(10), 1105–1116.

Pines, A. M., Ben-Ari, A., Utasi, A., & Larson, D. (2002). A cross-cultural investigation of social support and burnout. *European Psychologist, 7*(4), 256–264.

Pinker, S., & Jackendoff, R. (2005). The faculty of language: What's special about it? *Cognition, 95*(2), 201–236.

Pinsof, W. M., Wynne, L. C., & Hambright, A. B. (1996). The outcomes of couple and family therapy. *Psychotherapy, 33*(2), 321–331.

Pisacreta, R. (1998). Superstitious behavior and response stereotypy prevent the emergence of efficient rule-governed behavior in humans. *Psychological Record, 48*(2), 251–274.

Piven, J., Arndt, S., & Palmer, P. (1995). An MRI study of brain size in autism. *American Journal of Psychiatry, 152*(8), 1145.

Pizam, A., Jeong, G.-H., Reichel, A., Van Boemmel, H., et al. (2004). The relationship between risk-taking, sensation-seeking, and the tourist behavior of young adults: A cross-cultural study. *Journal of Travel Research, 42,* 251–260.

Pliner, P., & Haddock, G. (1996). Perfectionism in weight-concerned and -unconcerned women. *International Journal of Eating Disorders, 19*(4), 381–389.

Plomin, R., & Rende, R. (1991). Human behavioral genetics. *Annual Review of Psychology, 42,* 161–190.

Plutchik, R. (2003). *Emotions and life.* Washington, DC: American Psychological Assocation.

Pogatchnik, S. (1990). Kids' TV gets more violent, study finds. *Los Angeles Times,* Jan. 26, F1, F27.

Poland, J., & Caplan, P. J. (2004). The deep structure of bias in psychiatric diagnosis. In P. J. Caplan & L. Cosgrove (Eds.), *Bias in psychiatric diagnosis. A project of the association for women in psychology.* Lanham, MD: Jason Aronson.

Polemikos, N., & Papaeliou, C. (2000). Sidedness preference as an index of organization of laterality. *Perceptual & Motor Skills, 91*(3, Pt. 2), 1083–1090.

Polivy, J., & Herman, C. P. (2002). Causes of eating disorders. *Annual Review of Psychology, 53,* 187–213.

Pollack, W. S. (2001). Preventing violence through family connection. *Brown University Child and Adolescent Behavior Letter, 17*(12), 1, 3–4.

Pollak, S. D., & Kistler, D. J. (2002). Early experience is associated with the development of categorical representations for facial expressions of emotion. *Proceedings of the National Academy of Sciences, 99*(June 25), 9072–9076.

Pollak, S. D., & Tolley-Schell, S. A. (2003). Selective attention to facial emotion in physically abused children. *Journal of Abnormal Psychology, 112*(3), 323–338.

Pollak, S. D., Vardi, S., Bechner, A. M. P., & Curtin, J. J. (2005). Physically abused children's regulation of attention in response to hostility, *Child Development, 76*(5), 968–977.

Pollner, M. (1998). The effects of interviewer gender in mental health interviews. *Journal of Nervous & Mental Disease, 186*(6), 369–373.

Pollock, V. E., Briere, J., Schneider, L., Knop, J., et al. (1990). Childhood antecedents of antisocial behavior. *American Journal of Psychiatry, 147*(10), 1290–1293.

Pope, H. G., Gruber, A. J., & Yurgelun-Todd, D. (1995). The residual neuropsychological effects of cannabis. *Drug & Alcohol Dependence, 38*(1), 25–34.

Porac, C., Friesen, I. C., Barnes, M. P., & Gruppuso, V. (1998). Illness and accidental injury in young and older adult left- and right-handers: Implications for genetic theories of hand preference. *Developmental Neuropsychology, 14*(1), 157–172.

Port, R. L., & Seybold, K. S. (1995). Hippocampal synaptic plasticity as a biological substrate underlying episodic psychosis. *Biological Psychiatry, 37*(5), 318–324.

Porter, S., Campbell, M. A., Birt, A. R., & Woodworth, M. T. (2003). "He said, she said": A psychological perspective on historical memory evidence in the courtroom. *Canadian Psychology, 44*(3), 190–206.

Posada, G., Jacobs, A., Richmond, M. K., Carbonell, O. A., et al. (2002). Maternal caregiving and infant security in two cultures. *Developmental Psychology, 38*(1), 67–78.

Potter, S. M., Wagenaar, D. A., & DeMaarse. T. B. (2006). Closing the loop: Stimulation feedback systems for embodied MEA cultures. In M. Taketani & M. Baudry (Eds.), *Advances in network electrophysiology: Using multi-electrode arrays.* New York: Springer.

Poulton, R. G., & Andrews, G. (1996). Change in danger cognitions in agoraphobia and social phobia during treatment. *Behaviour Research & Therapy, 34*(5–6), 413–421.

Powell, A. L., & Thelen, M. H. (1996). Emotions and cognitions associated with bingeing and weight control behavior in bulimia. *Journal of Psychosomatic Research, 40*(3), 317–328.

Powell, R. A., Symbaluk, D. G., & Macdonald, S. E. (2005). *Introduction to learning and behavior.* Belmont, CA: Wadsworth.

Pratkanis, A. R. (1992). The cargo-cult science of subliminal persuasion. *Skeptical Inquirer, 16*(Spring), 260–272.

Premack, A. J., & Premack, D. (1972). Teaching language to an ape. *Scientific American,* Oct., 92–99.

Premack, D. (1983). Animal cognition. *Annual Review of Psychology, 34,* 351–362.

Premack, D., & Premack, A. J. (1983). *The mind of an ape.* New York: Norton.

Prentice, D. A., & Miller, D. T. (1993). Pluralistic ignorance of alcohol use on campus. *Journal of Personality and Social Psychology, 64*(2), 243–256.

Pressley, M. (1987). Are key-word method effects limited to slow presentation rates? An empirically based reply to Hall and Fuson (1986). *Journal of Educational Psychology, 79*(3), 333–335.

Pressley, M., Symons, S., McDaniel, M., A., Snyder, B., et al. (1988). Elaborative interrogation facilitates acquisition of confusing facts. *Jour-*

nal of Educational Psychology, 80(3), 268–278.

Pressman, J. D. (1998). *Last resort: Psychosurgery and the limits of medicine.* New York: Cambridge University Press.

Priluck, R., & Till, B. D. (2004). The role of contingency awareness, involvement, and need for cognition in attitude formation. *Journal of the Academy of Marketing Science, 32*(3), 329–344.

Pritchard, R. M. (1961). A collimator stabilizing system. *Quarterly Journal of Experimental Psychology, 13,* 181–183.

Proite, R., Dannells, M., & Benton, S. L. (1993). Gender, sex-role stereotypes, and the attribution of responsibility for date and acquaintance rape. *Journal of College Student Development, 34*(6), 411–417.

Provencher, M. D., Dugas, M. J., & Ladouceur, R. (2004). Efficacy of problem-solving training and cognitive exposure in the treatment of generalized anxiety disorder: A case replication series. *Cognitive & Behavioral Practice, 11*(4), 404–414.

Provins, K. A. (1997). Handedness and speech. *Psychological Review, 104*(3), 554–571.

Puca, R. M., & Schmalt, H. (1999). Task enjoyment: A mediator between achievement motives and performance. *Motivation & Emotion, 23*(1), 15–29.

Pulkkinen, L., Nurmi J., & Kokke, K. (2002). Individual differences in personal goals in mid-thirties. In L. Pulkkinen & A. Caspi, (Eds.), *Paths to successful development.* New York: Cambridge University Press.

Pursch, J. A. (1983). Cocaine can give you the business. *Los Angeles Times,* June 12, VII–12.

Pychyl, T. A., Lee, J. M., Thibodeau, R., & Blunt, A. (2000). Five days of emotion: An experience sampling study of undergraduate student procrastination. *Journal of Social Behavior & Personality, 15*(5), 239–254.

Quinn, P. C., & Bhatt, R. S. (1998). Visual pop-out in young infants. *Infant Behavior & Development, 21*(2), 273–288.

Raag, T., & Rackliff, C. L. (1998). Preschoolers' awareness of social expectations of gender: Relationships to toy choices. *Sex Roles, 38*(9–10), 685–700.

Rabius, V., McAlister, A. L., Geiger, A., Huang, P., et al. (2004). Telephone counseling increases cessation rates among young adult smokers. *Health Psychology, 23*(5), 539–541.

Rachman, S. (2004). *Anxiety* (2nd. ed.). New York: Routledge.

Rader, P. E., & Hicks, R. A. (1987). Jet lag desynchronization and self-assessment of business related performance. Paper presented at the Western Psychological Association meeting in Long Beach, CA, April.

Rafaeli, A., & Klimoski, R. J. (1983). Predicting sales success through handwriting analysis: An evaluation of the effects of training and handwriting sample content. *Journal of Applied Psychology, 68,* 212–217.

Rahman, Q., & Wilson, G. D. (2003). Born gay? The psychobiology of human sexual orientation. *Personality & Individual Differences, 34*(8), 1337–1382.

Raison, C. L., Klein, H. M., & Steckler, M. (1999). The moon and madness reconsidered. *Journal of Affective Disorders, 53*(1), 96–106.

Ramachandran, V. S. (1992). Blind spots. *Scientific American,* May, 86–91.

Ramachandran, V. S. (1995). 2-D or not 2-D—that is the question. In R. Gregory, J. Harris, et al. (Eds.), *The artful eye.* Oxford: Oxford University Press.

Ramanaiah, N. V., Detwiler, F. R. J., & Byravan, A. (1995). Sex-role orientation and satisfaction with life. *Psychological Reports, 77*(3, Pt. 2), 1260–1262.

Ramey, C. T., Ramey, S. L., & Lanzi, R. G. (2001). Intelligence and experience. In R. J. Sternberg & E. L. Grigorenko (Eds.), *Environmental effects on cognitive abilities.* Mahwah, NJ: Erlbaum.

Ramirez-Valles, J., Zimmerman, M. A., & Newcomb, M. D. (1998). Sexual risk behavior among youth. *Journal of Health & Social Behavior, 39*(3), 237–253.

Randi, J. (1983). Science and the chimera. In G. O. Abell & B. Singer (Eds.), *Science and the paranormal.* New York: Scribner's.

Randi, J. (1997). *An encyclopedia of claims, frauds, and hoaxes of the occult and supernatural.* New York: St. Martin's Press.

Rando, T. A. (1995). Grief and mourning: Accommodating to loss. In H. Wass & R. A. Neimeyer (Eds.), *Dying: Facing the facts.* Washington, DC: Taylor & Francis.

Rangell, L. (2002). Mind, body, and psychoanalysis. *Psychoanalytic Psychology, 19*(4), 634–650.

Rathus, R., Nevid, J., & Fichner-Rathus, L. (2005). *Human sexuality in a world of diversity* (6th ed.). Boston: Allyn & Bacon.

Rau, H., Bührer, M., & Weitkunat, R. (2003). Biofeedback of R-wave-to-pulse interval normalizes blood pressure. *Applied Psychophysiology and Biofeedback, 28*(1), 37–46.

Raven, B. H. (1974). The analysis of power and power preference. In J. T. Tebeschi (Ed.), *Prospectus on social power.* Chicago: Aldine.

Read, J. (1995). Female sexual dysfunction. *International Review of Psychiatry, 7*(2), 175–182.

Reed, J. D., & Bruce, D. (1982). Longitudinal tracking of difficult memory retrievals. *Cognitive Psychology, 14,* 280–300.

Reed, S. K. (1996). *Cognition: Theory and applications* (3rd ed). Pacific Grove, CA: Brooks/Cole.

Reed, T. E., Vernon, P. A., & Johnson, A. M. (2004). Confirmation of correlation between brain nerve conduction velocity and intelligence level in normal adults. *Intelligence, 32*(6), 563–572.

Reevy, G. M., & Maslach, C. (2001). Use of social support: Gender and personality differences. *Sex Roles, 44*(7–8), 437–459.

Regan, P. C., Levin, L., Sprecher, S., Christopher, F. S., et al. (2000). Partner preferences: What characteristics do men and women desire in their short-term sexual and long-term romantic partners? *Journal of Psychology & Human Sexuality, 12*(3), 1–21.

Reid, M. R., Mackinnon, L. T., & Drummond, P. D. (2001). The effects of stress management on symptoms of upper respiratory tract infection, secretory immunoglobulin A, and mood in young adults. *Journal of Psychosomatic Research, 51*(6), 721–728.

Reid, P. T. (2002). Multicultural psychology. *Cultural Diversity and Ethnic Minority Psychology, 8*(2), 103–114.

Reiff, S., Katkin, E. S., & Friedman, R. (1999). Classical conditioning of the human blood pressure response. *International Journal of Psychophysiology, 34*(2), 135–145.

Reifman, A. S., Larrick, R. P., & Fein, S. (1991). Temper and temperature on the diamond: The heat-aggression relationship in major league baseball. *Personality & Social Psychology Bulletin, 17*(5), 580–585.

Reis, H. T., Sheldon, K. M., Gable, S. L., Roscoe, J., et al. (2000). Daily well-being. *Personality & Social Psychology Bulletin, 26,* 419–435.

Reiss, M., Tymnik, G., Koegler, P., Koegler, W., et al. (1999). Laterality of hand, foot, eye, and ear in twins. *Laterality, 4*(3), 287–297.

Reiss, S., & Havercamp, S. M. (2005). Motivation in developmental context: A new method for studying self-actualization. *Journal of Humanistic Psychology, 45*(1), 41–53.

Reiterman, T. (1993). Parallel roads led to Jonestown, Waco. *Los Angeles Times,* Apr. 23, A-24.

Reitman, D., Murphy, M. A., Hupp, S. D. A., & O'Callaghan, P. M. (2004). Behavior change and perceptions of change: Evaluating the effectiveness of a token economy. *Child & Family Behavior Therapy, 26*(2), 17–36.

Remland, M. S., Jones, T. S., & Brinkman, H. (1991). Proxemic and haptic behavior in three European countries. *Journal of Nonverbal Behavior, 15*(4), 215–232.

Renner, M. J., & Mackin, R. S. (1998). A life stress instrument for classroom use. *Teaching of Psychology, 25*(1), 46–48.

Rentfrow, P. J. & Gosling, S. D. (2003). The do re mi's of everyday life: The structure and personality correlates of music preferences. *Journal of Personality & Social Psychology, 84*(6), 1236–1256.

Reppucci, N. D., Woolard, J. L., & Fried, C. S. (1999). Social, community, and preventive interventions. *Annual Review of Psychology, 50,* 387–418.

Rescorla, R. A. (1987). A Pavlovian analysis of goal-directed behavior. *American Psychologist, 42,* 119–126.

Restak, R. M. (2001). *The secret life of the brain.* New York: Dana Press.

Reznick, J. S., & Goldfield, B. A. (1992). Rapid change in lexical development in comprehension and production. *Developmental Psychology, 28*(3), 406–413.

Rhine, J. B. (1953). *New world of the mind.* New York: Sloane.

Rhodewalt, F. (1994). Conceptions of ability, achievement goals, and individual differences in self-handicapping behavior. *Journal of Personality, 62*(1), 67–85.

Rice, M. E. (1997). Violent offender research and implications for the criminal justice system. *American Psychologist, 52*(4), 414–423.

Richards, J. M., & Gross, J. J. (2000). Emotion regulation and memory: The cognitive costs of keeping one's cool. *Journal of Personality & Social Psychology, 79*(3), 410–424.

Richards, L., Rollerson, B., & Phillips, J. (1991). Perceptions of submissiveness: Implications for victimization. *Journal of Psychology, 125*(4), 407–411.

Richelle, M. N. (1995). *B. F. Skinner: A reappraisal.* Hillsdale, NJ: Erlbaum.

Richter, W., Somorjai, R., Summers, R., Jarmasz, M., et al. (2000). Motor area activity during mental rotation studied by time-resolved single-trial fMRI. *Journal of Cognitive Neuroscience, 12*(2), 310–320.

Ricketts, M. S., & Galloway, R. E. (1984). Effects of three different one-hour single-session treatments for test anxiety. *Psychological Reports, 54,* 113–119.

Riefer, D. M., Keveri, M. K., & Kramer, D. L. (1995). Name that tune: Eliciting the tip-of-the-tongue experience using auditory stimuli. *Psychological Reports, 77*(3, Pt. 2), 1379–1390.

Rieke, M. L., & Guastello, S. J. (1995). Unresolved issues in honesty and integrity testing. *American Psychologist,* June, 458–459.

Riquelme, H. (2002). Can people creative in imagery interpret ambiguous figures faster than people less creative in imagery? *Journal of Creative Behavior, 36*(2), 105–116.

Ritchie, R. J., & Moses, J. L. (1983). Assessment center correlates of women's advancement into middle management: A 7-year longitudinal analysis. *Journal of Applied Psychology, 68,* 227–231.

Ritter, J. (1998). Uniforms changing the culture of the nation's classrooms. *USA Today,* Oct. 15, 1A, 2A.

Roberti, J. W. (2004). A review of behavioral and biological correlates of sensation seeking. *Journal of Research in Personality, 38,* 256–279.

Roberts, B. W., Caspi, A., & Moffitt, T. E. (2001). The kids are alright: Growth and stability in personality development from adolescence to adulthood. *Journal of Personality & Social Psychology, 81*(4), 670–683.

Roberts, R. E., Phinney, J. S., Masse, L. C., Chen, Y. R., et al. (1999). The structure of ethnic identity of young adolescents from diverse ethnocultural groups. *Journal of Early Adolescence, 19*(3), 301–322.

Robertson, L. C., & Sagiv, N. (2005). *Synesthesia: Perspectives from cognitive neuroscience.* New York: Oxford.

Robins, R. W., Gosling, S. D., & Craik, K. H. (1998). Psychological science at the crossroads. *American Scientist, 86*(July–Aug.), 310–313.

Robinson, A., & Clinkenbeard, P. R. (1998). Giftedness. *Annual Review of Psychology, 49,* 117–139.

Robinson, B., Frye, E. M., & Bradley, L. J. (1997). Cult affiliation and disaffiliation. *Counseling & Values, 41*(2), 166–173.

Robinson, D. L. (1999). The "IQ" factor: Implications for intelligence theory and measurement. *Personality & Individual Differences, 27*(4), 715–735.

Robinson, T. N., Wilde, M. L., Navracruz, L. C., Haydel, K. F., et al. (2001). Effects of reducing children's television and video game use on aggressive behavior. *Archives of Pediatrics and Adolescent Medicine, 155*(1), 17–23.

Robinson-Riegler, B., & McDaniel, M. (1994). Further constraints on the bizarreness effect: Elaboration at encoding. *Memory & Cognition, 22*(6), 702–712.

Robson, P. (1984). Prewalking locomotor movements and their use in predicting standing and walking. *Child Care, Health & Development, 10,* 317–330.

Roeckelein, J. E. (2004). *Imagery in psychology: A reference guide.* Westport, CT: Praeger.

Roediger, H. L. (1990). Implicit memory. *American Psychologist, 45*(9), 1043–1056.

Roediger, H. L., & McDermott, K. B. (1995). Creating false memories: Remembering words not presented on lists. *Journal of Experimental Psychology: Learning, Memory, and Cognition, 21*(4), 803–814.

Rogers, C. R. (1959). A theory of therapy, personality, and interpersonal relationships, as developed in the client-centered framework. In S. Koch (Ed.), *Psychology: A study of a science* (Vol. 3). New York: McGraw-Hill.

Rogers, C. R. (1961). *On becoming a person: A therapist's view of psychotherapy.* Boston: Houghton Mifflin.

Rogers, C. R. (1980). *A way of being.* Boston: Houghton Mifflin.

Rogers, S., & Silver, S. M. (2002). Is EMDR an exposure therapy? A review of trauma protocols. *Journal of Clinical Psychology, 58*(1), 43–59.

Rogerson, J. (1997). Canine fears and phobias: A regime for treatment without recourse to drugs. *Applied Animal Behaviour Science, 52*(3–4), 291–297.

Rohsenow, D. J., & Smith R. E. (1982). Irrational beliefs as predictors of negative affective states. *Motivation and Emotion, 6,* 299–301.

Roid, G. (2003). *Technical manual: Stanford-Binet Intelligence Scales* (5th ed.). Itasca, IL: Riverside.

Roizen, M. F. (1999). *Real age.* New York: HarperCollins

Rolling, B. L., & Belsky, J. (1992). The contribution of mother–child and father–child relationships to the quality of sibling interaction: A longitudinal study. *Child Development, 63*(5), 1209–1222.

Ronen, T., & Wozner, Y. (1995). A self-control intervention package for the treatment of primary nocturnal enuresis. *Child & Family Behavior Therapy, 17*(1), 1–20.

Roney, J. R. (2003). Effects of visual exposure to the opposite sex: Cognitive aspects of mate attraction in human males. *Personality & Social Psychology Bulletin, 29,* 393–404.

Roos, P. E., & Cohen, L. H. (1987). Sex roles and social support as moderators of life stress adjustment. *Journal of Personality & Social Psychology, 52,* 576–585.

Rosch, E. (1977). Classification of real-world objects: Origins and representations in cognition. In P. N. Johnson-Laird & P. C. Wason (Eds.), *Thinking: Reading in cognitive science.* Cambridge: Cambridge University Press.

Rose, R. J. (1995). Genes and human behavior. *Annual Review of Psychology, 46,* 625–654.

Rosen, G., Hugdahl, K., Ersland, L., Lundervold, A., et al. (2001). Different brain areas activated during imagery of painful and non-painful "finger movements" in a subject with an amputated arm. *Neurocase, 7*(3), 255–260.

Rosen, L. A., Booth, S. R., Bender, M. E., McGrath, M. L., et al. (1988). Effects of sugar (sucrose) on children's behavior. *Journal of Consulting & Clinical Psychology, 56*(4), 583–589.

Rosenberg, L. B. (1994). The effect of interocular distance upon depth perception when using stereoscopic displays to perform work within virtual and telepresent environments. *USAF AMRL Technical Report (Wright-Patterson),* July, AL/CF-TR-1994-0052.

Rosenberg, S. S., & Lynch, J. E. (2002). Fritz Perls revisited: A microassessment of a live clinical session. *Gestalt Review, 6*(3), 184–202.

Rosenfeld, P., Giacalone, R. A., & Tedeschi, J. T. (1983). Cognitive dissonance vs. impression management. *Journal of Social Psychology, 120,* 203–211.

Rosenhan, D. L. (1973). On being sane in insane places. *Science, 179,* 250–258.

Rosenman, R. H., Brand, R. J., Jenkins, C. D., Friedman, M., et al. (1975). Coronary heart disease in the Western Collaborative Group Study: Final follow-up experience of 8 1/2 years. *Journal of the American Medical Association, 233,* 872–877.

Rosenkranz, M.A., Jackson, D. C., Dalton, K. M., Dolski, I., et al. (2003). Affective style and in vivo immune response: Neurobehavioral mechanisms. *Proceedings of the National Academy of Sciences, 100,* 11148–11152.

Rosenthal, D., & Quinn, O. W. (1977). Quadruplet hallucinations: Phenotypic variations of a schizophrenic genotype. *Archives of General Psychiatry, 34*(7), 817–827.

Rosenthal, R. (1965). *Clever Hans: A case study of scientific method.* Introduction to *Clever Hans: (The horse of Mr. Von Osten),* by O. Pfungst. New York: Holt, Rinehart & Winston.

Rosenthal, R. (1973). The Pygmalion effect lives. *Psychology Today,* Sept., 56–63.

Rosenthal, R. (1994). Science and ethics in conducting, analyzing, and reporting psychological research. *Psychological Science, 5,* 127–134

Rosenthal, R., & DiMatteo, M. R. (2001). Meta-analysis: Recent developments in quantitative methods for literature reviews. *Annual Review of Psychology, 52,* 59–62.

Rosenthal, S. L., Von Ranson, K. M., Cotton, S., Biro, F. M., et al. (2001). Sexual initiation: Predictors and developmental trends. *Sexually Transmitted Diseases, 28*(9), 527–532.

Rosenthal, T. L. (1993). To soothe the savage breast. *Behavior Research & Therapy, 31*(5), 439–462.

Rosenthal, T. L., & Rosenthal, R. (1980). *The vicious cycle of stress reaction.* Memphis: Stress Management Clinic, Department of Psychiatry, University of Tennessee College of Medicine.

Rosenthal, T. L., & Steffek, B. D. (1991). Modeling methods. In F. H. Kanfer & A. P. Goldstein (Eds.), *Helping people change.* Elmsford, NY: Pergamon.

Rosnow, R. L., & Rosnow, M. (2002). *Writing papers in psychology: A student guide.* Belmont, CA: Wadsworth.

Ross, D. C., Jaffe, J., Collins, R. L., Page, W., & Robinette, D. (1999). Handedness in the NAS/NRC Twin Study. *Laterality, 4*(3), 257–264.

Ross, H. E., & Plug. C. (2002). *The mystery of the moon illusion.* Oxford: Oxford University Press.

Ross, M., Heine, S. J., Wilson, A. E., & Sugimori, S. (2005). Cross-cultural discrepancies in self-appraisals. *Personality and Social Psychology Bulletin, 31*(9), 1175–1188.

Rossi, A. S. (2004). The menopausal transition and aging processes. In O. G. Brim, C. D. Ryff, et al. (Eds.), *How healthy are we: A national study of wellbeing in midlife.* Chicago: University of Chicago Press.

Roth, W. T., Breivik, G., Jorgensen, P. E., & Hofmann, S. (1996). Activation in novice and expert parachutists while jumping. *Psychophysiology, 33*(1), 63–72.

Rourke, B. P., Ahmad, S. A., Collins, D. W., Hayman-Abello, B. A., et al. (2002). Early hydrocephalus. *Annual Review of Psychology, 53,* 309–339.

Rowe, B. (1998). *College survival guide: Hints and references to aid college students.* Belmont, CA: Wadsworth.

Rowe, D. C., Chassin, L., Presson, C., & Sherman, S. J. (1996). Parental smoking and the "epidemic" spread of cigarette smoking. *Journal of Applied Social Psychology, 26*(5), 437–454.

Rowe, J. W., & Kahn, R. L. (1998). *Successful aging.* New York: Dell.

Rozin, P., Kabnick, K., Pete, E., Fischler, C., et al. (2003). The ecology of eating: Smaller portion sizes in France than in the United States help explain the French paradox. *Psychological Science, 14*(5), 450–454.

Rubenstein, C. (1983). The modern art of courtly love. *Psychology Today, 17*(7), 43–49.

Rubenstein, C. (2002). What turns you on? *My Generation,* July–Aug., 55–58.

Rubenstein, C., & Tavris, C. (1987). Special survey results: 2600 women reveal the secrets of intimacy. *Redbook, 159,* 147–149.

Rubin, D. C. (1985). The subtle deceiver: Recalling our past. *Psychology Today,* Sept., 38–46.

Rubin, K. H. (1998). Social and emotional development from a cultural perspective. *Developmental Psychology, 34*(4), 611–615.

Rubin, V., & Comitas, L. (Eds.). (1975). *Ganja in Jamaica.* The Hague: Mouton.

Rubin, Z. (1970). Measurement of romantic love. *Journal of Personality & Social Psychology, 16,* 265–273.

Rubin, Z. (1973). *Liking and loving: An invitation to social psychology.* New York: Holt.

Rudd, M. D., Joiner, T. E., Jr., & Rajab, M. H. (2001). *Treating suicidal behavior.* New York: Guilford.

Rueckl, J. G., & Galantucci, B. (2005). The locus and time course of long-term morphological priming. *Language & Cognitive Processes, 20*(1), 115–138.

Rummens, J., Beiser, M., & Noh, S. (Eds.). (2003). *Immigration, ethnicity and health.* Toronto: University of Toronto Press.

Runco, M. A. (2003). *Critical creative processes.* Cresskill, NJ: Hampton Press.

Runco, M. A. (2004). Creativity. *Annual Review of Psychology, 55,* 657–687.

Ruscio, J., Whitney, D. M., & Amabile, T. M. (1998). Looking inside the fishbowl of creativity. *Creativity Research Journal, 11*(3), 243–263.

Russell, S., & Norvig, P. (2003). *Artificial intelligence: A modern approach* (2nd ed.). Englewood Cliffs, NJ: Prentice Hall.

Russell, T. G., Rowe, W., & Smouse, A. D. (1991). Subliminal self-help tapes and academic achievement: An evaluation. *Journal of Counseling & Development, 69*(Mar.–Apr.), 359–362.

Russo, M. B., Brooks, F. R., Fontenot, J., Dopler, D. M., et al. (1998). Conversion disorder presenting as multiple sclerosis. *Military Medicine, 163*(10), 709–710.

Russo, N. F. (1990). Forging research priorities for women's mental health. *American Psychologist, 45*(3), 368–373.

Rutledge, T., & Linden, W. (1998). To eat or not to eat: Affective and physiological mechanisms in the stress–eating relationship. *Journal of Behavioral Medicine, 21*(3), 221–240.

Rutter, M. (1995). Maternal deprivation. In M. H. Bornstein (Ed.), *Handbook of parenting* (Vol. 4). Mahwah, NJ: Erlbaum.

Ryan, M. P. (2001). Conceptual models of lecture learning. *Reading Psychology, 22*(4), 289–312.

Ryan, R. M., & Deci, E. L. (2000). Self-determination theory and the facilitation of intrinsic motivation, social development, and well-being. *American Psychologist, 55*(1), 68–78.

Ryff, C. D. (1995). Psychological well-being in adult life. *Current Directions in Psychological Science, 4*(4), 99–104.

Ryff, C. D., & Keyes, C. L. (1995). The structure of psychological well-being revisited. *Journal of Personality & Social Psychology, 69*(4), 719–727.

Ryff, C. D., & Singer, B. (2000). Interpersonal flourishing. *Personality & Social Psychology Review, 4,* 30–44.

Saadeh, W., Rizzo, C. P., & Roberts, D. G. (2002). Spanking. *Clinical Pediatrics, 41*(2), 87–88.

Saariluoma, P. (1994). Location coding in chess. *Quarterly Journal of Experimental Psychology: Human Experimental Psychology, 47A*(3), 607–630.

Sackett, P. R., Schmitt, N., Ellingson, J. E., & Kabin, M. B. (2001). High-stakes testing in employment, credentialing, and higher education. *American Psychologist, 56*(4), 302–318.

Sadker, M., & Sadker, D. (1994). *Failing at fairness: How America's schools cheat girls*. New York: Scribner's.

Saegert, S., Swap, W., & Zajonc, R. B. (1973). Exposure, context, and interpersonal attraction. *Journal of Personality & Social Psychology, 25,* 234–242.

Sagvolden, T., & Sergeant, J. A. (1998). Attention deficit/hyperactivity disorder: From brain dysfunctions to behaviour. *Behavioural Brain Research, 94*(1), 1–10.

Sahelian, R. (1998). *5-HTP.* Wakefield, RI: Moyer Bell.

Sales, B. D., & Hafemeister, T. L. (1985). Law and psychology. In E. M. Altmeir & M. E. Meyer (Eds.), *Applied specialties in psychology.* New York: Random House.

Salmela, J. H. (1974). An information processing approach to volleyball. *C.V.A. Technical Journal, 1,* 49–62.

Salmela, J. H. (1975). Psycho-motor task demands of artistic gymnastics. In J. H. Salmela (Ed.), *The advanced study of gymnastics: A textbook*. Springfield, IL: Charles C Thomas.

Salmon, P. (2001). Effects of physical exercise on anxiety, depression, and sensitivity to stress: A unifying theory. *Clinical Psychology Review, 21*(1), 33–61.

Salovey, P., & Mayer, J. (1997). *Emotional development and emotional intelligence*. New York: Basic Books.

Salovey, P., & Singer, J. A. (1989). Mood congruency effects in recall of childhood versus recent memories. *Journal of Social Behavior & Personality, 4*(2), 99–120.

Salthouse, T. A. (2004). What and when of cognitive aging. *Current Directions in Psychological Science, 13*(4), 140–144.

Sansone, R. A., Sansone, L. A., & Righter, E. L. (1998). Panic disorder. *Journal of Women's Health, 7*(8), 983–989.

Sarason, I. G., & Sarason, B. R. (2005). *Abnormal psychology* (11th ed.). Mahwah, NJ: Prentice Hall.

Sateia, M. J., & Nowell, P. D. (2004). Insomnia. *Lancet, 364*(9449), 1959–1973.

Saudino, K. J., Pedersen, N. L., Lichtenstein, P., McClearn, G. E., et al. (1997). Can personality explain genetic influences on life events? *Journal of Personality & Social Psychology, 72*(1), 196–206.

Saunders, T., Driskell, J. E., Johnston, J. H., Salas, E. (1996). The effect of stress inoculation training on anxiety and performance. *Journal of Occupational Health Psychology, 1*(2), 170–186.

Savage, A. R., Petersen, M. B., Pettay, D., Taft, L., et al. (1998). Elucidating the mechanisms of paternal non-disjunction of chromosome 21 in humans. *Human Molecular Genetics, 7,* 1221–1227.

Savage-Rumbaugh, S., & Lewin, R. (1996). *Kanzi*. New York: Wiley.

Savage-Rumbaugh, S., Murphy, J., Sevcik, R. A., Brakke, K. E., et al. (1993). Language comprehension in ape and child. *Monographs of the Society for Research in Child Development, 58*(3–4), v–221.

Savage-Rumbaugh, S., Sevcik, R. A., Brakke, K. E., Rumbaugh, D. M., et al. (1990). Symbols: Their communicative use, comprehension, and combination by bonobos (Pan paniscus). *Advances in Infancy Research, 6,* 221–278.

Savage-Rumbaugh, S., Shanker, S., & Taylor, T. (1998). *Apes, language, and mind.* New York: Oxford.

Sawa, A., & Snyder, S. H. (2002). Schizophrenia: Diverse approaches to a complex disease. *Science, 296*(5568), 692–695.

Sawyer, R. G., & Smith, N. G. (1996). A survey of situational factors at first intercourse among college students. *American Journal of Health Behavior, 20*(4), 208–217.

Saxe, L., Dougherty, D., & Cross, T. (1985). The validity of polygraph testing. *American Psychologist, 40,* 355–366.

Saywitz, K. J., Mannarino, A. P., Berliner, L., & Cohen, J. A. (2000). Treatment for sexually abused children and adolescents. *American Psychologist, 55*(9), 1040–1049.

Scarr, S. (1998). American child care today. *American Psychologist, 53*(2), 95–108.

Schachter, S. (1959). *Psychology of affiliation.* Stanford, CA: Stanford University Press.

Schachter, S., & Wheeler, L. (1962). Epinephrine, chlorpromazine and amusement. *Journal of Abnormal and Social Psychology, 65,* 121–128.

Schacter, D. L. (2000). Memory: Memory systems. In A. Kazdin (Ed.), *Encyclopedia of psychology.* Washington, DC: American Psychological Association.

Schacter, D. L. (2001). *The seven sins of memory.* Boston: Houghton Mifflin.

Schacter, D. L., Norman, K. A., & Koutstaal, W. (1998). The cognitive neuroscience of constructive memory. *Annual Review of Psychology, 49,* 289–318.

Schafer, M., & Crichlow, S. (1996). Antecedents of groupthink: A quantitative study. *Journal of Conflict Resolution, 40*(3), 415–435.

Schaie, K. W. (1988). Ageism in psychological research. *American Psychologist, 43*(3), 179–183.

Schaie, K. W. (1994). The course of adult intellectual development. *American Psychologist, 49*(4), 304–313.

Schaie, K. W. (2005). *Developmental influences on adult intelligence: The Seattle longitudinal study*. London: Oxford University Press.

Schall, J. D. (2004). On building a bridge between brain and behavior. *Annual Review of Psychology, 55,* 23–50.

Schaller, S. (1991). *A man without words.* New York: Summit.

Scheck, B., Neufeld, P., & Dwyer, J. (2000). *Actual innocence*. New York: Doubleday.

Scheck, M. M., Schaeffer, J. A., & Gillette, C. (1998). Brief psychological intervention with traumatized young women. *Journal of Traumatic Stress, 11*(1), 25–44

Schick, T., & Vaughn, L. (2001). *How to think about weird things: Critical thinking for a new age.* New York: McGraw-Hill.

Schilling, M. A. (2005). A "Small-World" network model of cognitive insight. *Creativity Research Journal, 17*(2–3), 131–154.

Schiraldi, G. R., & Brown, S. L. (2001). Primary prevention for mental health: Results of an exploratory cognitive-behavioral college course. *Journal of Primary Prevention, 22*(1), 55–67.

Schleicher, S. S., & Gilbert, L. A. (2005). Heterosexual dating discourses among college students: Is there still a double standard? *Journal of College Student Psychotherapy, 19*(3), 7–23.

Schlosberg, H. (1954). Three dimensions of emotion. *Psychological Review, 61,* 81–88.

Schmidt, F. L., & Hunter, J. E. (1998). The validity and utility of selection methods in personnel psychology. *Psychological Bulletin, 124*(2), 262–274.

Schmidt, F. L., Ones, D. S., & Hunter, J. E. (1992). Personnel selection. *Annual Review of Psychology, 43,* 627–670.

Schmitt, D. P., & Allik, J. (2005). Simultaneous administration of the Rosenberg Self-Esteem Scale in 53 nations: Exploring the universal and culture-specific features of global self-esteem. *Journal of Personality and Social Psychology, 89*(4), 623–642.

Schmitt, D. P., & Buss, D. M. (1996). Strategic self-promotion and competitor derogation. *Journal of Personality & Social Psychology, 70*(6), 1185–1204.

Schmitt, E. (2001). U.S. now more diverse, ethnically and racially. *New York Times*, Apr. 1, A–18.

Schmolck, H., Buffalo, E. A., & Squire, L. R. (2000). Memory distortions develop over time. *Psychological Science, 11*(1), 39–45.

Schneider, H. G., & Shugar, G. J. (1990). Audience and feedback effects in computer learning. *Computers in Human Behavior, 6*(4), 315–321.

Schneider, K. J. (2002). Humanistic psychotherapy. In M. Hersen & W. H. Sledge (Eds.), *Encyclopedia of psychotherapy*. San Diego: Academic Press.

Schneider, K. J., Bugental, J. F. T., & Pierson, J. F. (2001). Introduction. In *The Handbook of Humanistic Psychology.* Thousand Oaks, CA: Sage.

Schneiderman, N., Antoni, M. H., Saab, P. G., & Ironson, G. (2001). Health psychology. *Annual Review of Psychology, 52,* 555–580.

Schooler, C. (1998). Environmental complexity and the Flynn effect. In U. Neisser (Ed.), *The rising curve: Long-term gains in IQ and related measures*. Washington, DC: American Psychological Association.

Schotte, D. E., Cools, J., & McNally, R. J. (1990). Film-induced negative affect triggers overeating in restrained eaters. *Journal of Abnormal Psychology, 99*(3), 317–320.

Schouten, S. A. (1994). An overview of quantitatively evaluated studies with mediums and psychics. *Journal of the American Society for Psychical Research, 88*(3), 221–254.

Schredl, M. (1995). Creativity and dream recall. *Journal of Creative Behavior, 29*(1), 16–24.

Schreiber, E. H., & Schreiber, D. E. (1999). Use of hypnosis with witnesses of vehicular homicide. *Contemporary Hypnosis, 16*(1), 40–44.

Schreiber, F. R. (1973). *Sybil*. Chicago: Regency.

Schroeder, J. E. (1995). Self-concept, social anxiety, and interpersonal perception skills. *Personality & Individual Differences, 19*(6), 955–958.

Schroots, J. J. F. (1996). Theoretical developments in the psychology of aging. *Gerontologist, 36*(6), 742–748.

Schuel, H., Chang, M. C., Burkman, L. J., Picone, R. P., et al. (1999). Cannabinoid receptors in sperm. In G. Nahas, K. M. Sutin, et al. (Eds.), *Marihuana and medicine*. Totowa, NJ: Humana Press.

Schuerger, J. M., & Witt, A. C. (1989). The temporal stability of individually tested intelligence. *Journal of Clinical Psychology, 45*(2), 294–302.

Schuiling, G. A. (2004). Death in Venice: The homosexuality enigma. *Journal of Psychosomatic Obstetrics & Gynecology, 25*(1), 67–76.

Schultheiss, O. C., Wirth, M. M., & Stanton, S. J. (2004). Effects of affiliation and power motivation arousal on salivary progesterone and testosterone. *Hormones and Behavior, 46*(5), 592–599.

Schultz, H. T. (2004). Good and bad movie therapy with good and bad outcomes. *The Amplifier: Official Newsletter of APA Division 46, Media Psychology*, Fall/Winter. Retrieved October 25, 2005 from http://www.apa.org/divisions/div46/Amp%20Winter%2005/for%20Website/ampwinter05.html#therapy.

Schultz, P. W. (1999). Changing behavior with normative feedback interventions. *Basic & Applied Social Psychology, 21*(1), 25–36.

Schulz, R., & Heckhausen, J. (1996). A life span model of successful aging. *American Psychologist, 51*(7), 702–714.

Schulz, R. (1978). *The psychology of death, dying and bereavement.* Reading, MA: Addison-Wesley.

Schum, T. R., McAuliffe, T. L., Simms, M. D., Walter, J. A., et al. (2001). Factors associated with toilet training in the 1990s. *Ambulatory Pediatrics, 1*(2), 79–86.

Schunk, D. H. (1990). Goal setting and self-efficacy during self-regulated learning. Special issue: Self-regulated learning and academic achievement. *Educational Psychologist, 25*(1), 71–86.

Schuster, M. A., Stein, B. D., Jaycox, L. H., Collins, R. L., et al. (2001). A national survey of stress reactions after the September 11, 2001, terrorist attacks. *New England Journal of Medicine, 345*(20), 1507–1512.

Schwartz, M. S., & Andrasik, F. (Eds.). (2003). *Biofeedback: A practitioner's guide* (3rd ed.). New York: Guilford.

Schweickert, R. (1993). A multinomial processing tree model for degradation and redintegration in immediate recall. *Memory & Cognition, 21*(2), 168–175.

Schwinghammer, S. A., Stapel, D. A., & Blanton, H. (2006). Different

selves have different effects: Self-activation and defensive social comparison. *Personality and Social Psychology Bulletin, 32*(1), 27–39.
Sclafani, A., & Springer, D. (1976). Dietary obesity in adult rats: Similarities to hypothalamic and human obesity syndromes. *Psychology and Behavior, 17*, 461–471.
Scoboria, A., Mazzoni, G., Kirsch, I., & Milling, L. S. (2002). Immediate and persisting effects of misleading questions and hypnosis on memory reports. *Journal of Experimental Psychology: Applied, 8*(1), 26–32.
Scott, J. P., & Ginsburg, B. E. (1994). The Seville statement on violence revisited. *American Psychologist, 49*(10), 849–850.
Scott, L., & O'Hara, M. W. (1993). Self-discrepancies in clinically anxious and depressed university students. *Journal of Abnormal Psychology, 102*(2), 282–287.
Scott, S. S., McGuire, J. M., & Shaw, S. F. (2003). Universal design for instruction: A new paradigm for adult instruction in postsecondary education. *Remedial and Special Education.* Special Issue: *Adults with Learning Disabilities, 24*(6), 369–379.
Scroppo, J. C., Drob, S. L., Weinberger, J. L., & Eagle, P. (1998). Identifying dissociative identity disorder: A self-report and projective study. *Journal of Abnormal Psychology, 107*(2), 272–284.
Scurfield, R. M. (2002). Commentary about the terrorist acts of September 11, 2001: Posttraumatic reactions and related social and policy issues. *Trauma Violence & Abuse, 3*(1), 3–14.
Seal, D. W., & Palmer-Seal, D. A. (1996). Barriers to condom use and safer sex talk among college dating couples. *Journal of Community & Applied Social Psychology, 6*(1), 15–33.
Sears, R. R., Maccoby, E. E., & Levin, H. (1957). *Patterns of child rearing.* Evanston, IL: Row, Peterson.
Seckel, A. (2000). *The art of optical illusions.* London: Carlton Books.
Segraves, R. T., & Segraves, K. B. (1995). Human sexuality and aging. *Journal of Sex Education & Therapy, 21*(2), 88–102.
Segraves, T., & Althof, S. (2002). Psychotherapy and pharmacotherapy for sexual dysfunctions. In P. E. Nathan & J. M. Gorman (Eds.), *A guide to treatments that work* (2nd ed.). London: Oxford.
Seidman, B. F. (2001). Medicine wars. *Skeptical Inquirer,* Jan.–Feb., 28–35.
Sekuler, R., & Blake, R. (2006). *Perception* (5th ed.). New York: McGraw-Hill.
Seligman, M. E. P. (1972). For helplessness: Can we immunize the weak? In *Readings in psychology today* (2nd ed.). Del Mar, CA: CRM.
Seligman, M. E. P. (1989). *Helplessness.* New York: Freeman.
Seligman, M. E. P. (1994). *What you can change and what you can't.* New York: Knopf.
Seligman, M. E. P. (1995). The effectiveness of psychotherapy. *American Psychologist, 50*(12), 965–974.
Seligman, M. E. P. (1998). Why therapy works. *APA Monitor, 29*(12), 2.
Seligman, M. E. P. (2002). *Authentic happiness.* New York: Free Press.
Seligman, M. E. P. (2003). Positive psychology: Fundamental assumptions. *Source Psychologist, 16*(3), 126–127.
Seligman, M. E. P., & Csikszentmihaly, M. (2000). Positive psychology: An introduction. *American Psychologist, 55*, 5–14.
Selye, H. (1978). *The stress of life.* New York: McGraw-Hill.
Senden, M. V. (1960). *Space and sight.* Translated by P. Heath. Glencoe, IL: Free Press.
Senécal, C., Julien, E., & Guay, F. (2003). Role conflict and academic procrastination: A self-determination perspective. *European Journal of Social Psychology, 33*(1), 135–145.
Serbin, L. A., & O'Leary, K. D. (1975). How nursery schools teach girls to shut up. *Psychology Today,* Dec., 57–58, 102–103.
Service, R. F. (1994). Will a new type of drug make memory-making easier? *Science, 266*, 218–219.
Sessa, V. I., & London, M. (2006). *Continuous learning in organizations: Individual, group, and organizational perspectives.* Hillsdale, NJ: Erlbaum.
Seybolt, D. C., & Wagner, M. K. (1997). Self-reinforcement, gender-role, and sex of participant in prediction of life satisfaction. *Psychological Reports, 81*(2), 519–522.
Shaffer, D. R. (2002). *Developmental psychology.* Belmont, CA: Wadsworth.
Shaffer, J. B., & Galinsky, M. D. (1989). *Models of group therapy.* Englewood Cliffs, NJ: Prentice Hall.
Shafir, E. (1993). Choosing versus rejecting: Why some options are both better and worse than others. *Memory and Cognition, 21*, 546–556.
Shafton, A. (1995). *Dream reader.* Albany: State University of New York Press.
Shakesby, A. C., Anwyl, R., & Rowan, M. J. (2002). Overcoming the effects of stress on synaptic plasticity in the intact hippocampus: Rapid actions of serotonergic and antidepressant agents. *Journal of Neuroscience, 22*, 3638–3644.
Shalev, A.Y. (2001). What is posttraumatic stress disorder? *Journal of Clinical Psychiatry, 62*(Suppl. 17), 4–10.
Shanahan, T. L., Kronauer, R. E., Duffy, J. F., Williams, G. H., et al. (1999). Melatonin rhythm observed throughout a three-cycle bright-light stimulus designed to reset the human circadian pacemaker. *Journal of Biological Rhythms, 14*(3), 237–253.
Shapiro, F. (2001). *Eye movement desensitization and reprocessing: Basic principles, protocols and procedures* (2nd ed.). New York: Guilford Press.
Shapiro, F., & Forrest, M. S. (2004). *EMDR: The breakthrough therapy for overcoming anxiety, stress, and trauma.* New York: Basic Books.
Sharkey, K. M., & Eastman, C. I. (2002). Melatonin phase shifts human circadian rhythms in a placebo-controlled simulated night-work study. *American Journal of Physiology: Regulatory, Integrative, and Comparative Physiology, 282*, R454–R463.
Sharma, T., Lancaster, E., Lee, D., Lewis, S., et al. (1998). Brain changes in schizophrenia: Volumetric MRI study of families multiply affected with schizophrenia—the Maudsley Family Study 5. *British Journal of Psychiatry, 173*(Aug.), 132–138.
Shaw, J. S. (1996). Increases in eyewitness confidence resulting from postevent questioning. *Journal of Experimental Psychology: Applied, 2*(2), 126–146.
Shaywitz, B. A, Shaywitz, S. E., Pugh, K. R., Constable, R. T., et al. (1995). Sex differences in the functional organization of the brain for language. *Nature, 373*(6515), 607–609.
Shaywitz, S. E., & Gore, J. C. (1995). Sex differences in functional organization of the brain for language. *Nature, 373*(6515), 607.
Sheehy, M., & Cournos, F. (1992). What is mental illness? In F. I. Kass, J. M. Oldham, & H. Pardes (Eds.), *The Columbia University College of Physicians and Surgeons complete home guide to mental health.* New York: Sharpe Communications/ Henry Holt.
Sheldon, K. M., & Elliot, A. J. (1999). Goal striving, need satisfaction, and longitudinal well-being. *Journal of Personality & Social Psychology, 76*(3), 482–497.
Sheldon, K. M., Ryan, R. M., Rawsthorne, L. J., & Ilardi, B. (1997). Trait self and true self: Cross-role variation in the Big-Five personality traits and its relations with psychological authenticity and subjective well-being. *Journal of Personality & Social Psychology, 73*(6), 1380–1393.
Shepard, R. N. (1975). Form, formation, and transformation of internal representations. In R. L. Solso (Ed.), *Information processing and cognition: The Loyola Symposium.* Hillsdale, NJ: Erlbaum.
Sherif, M., Harvey, O. J., White, B. J., Hood, W. R., et al. (1961). *Intergroup conflict and cooperation: The Robbers Cave experiment.* University of Oklahoma, Institute of Group Relations.
Shires, A., & Miller, D. (1998). A preliminary study comparing psychological factors associated with erectile dysfunction in heterosexual and homosexual men. *Sexual & Marital Therapy, 13*(1), 37–49.
Shneidman, E. S. (1987a). At the point of no return. *Psychology Today,* Mar., 54–58.
Shneidman, E. S. (1987b). Psychological approaches to suicide. In G. R. VandenBos & B. K. Bryant (Eds.), *Cataclysms, crises, and catastrophes: Psychology in action.* Washington, DC: American Psychological Association.
Shore, H. (2003). Personal communication.
Shore, L. A. (1990). Skepticism in light of scientific literacy. *Skeptical Inquirer, 15* (Fall), 3–4.
Shrum, L. J. (2004). *The psychology of entertainment media: Blurring the lines between entertainment and persuasion.* Mahwah, NJ: Erlbaum.
Shulman, B. H. (2004). Cognitive therapy and the individual psychology of Alfred Adler. In A. Freeman, M. J. Mahoney, et al. (Eds.), *Cognition and psychotherapy* (2nd ed.). New York: Springer.
Shurkin, J. N. (1992). *Terman's kids.* Boston: Little, Brown.
Siau, Keng L. (1996). Group creativity and technology. *Journal of Creative Behavior, 29*(3), 201–216.
Sieber, J. E., & Saks, M. J. (1989). A census of subject pool characteristics and policies. *American Psychologist, 44*(7), 1053–1061.
Siegler, R. S. (1989). Mechanisms of cognitive development. *Annual Review of Psychology, 40*, 353–379.
Siegler, R. S. (2004). *Children's thinking* (4th ed.). Mahwah, NJ: Erlbaum.
Siever, L. J., & Koenigsberg, H. W. (2000). The frustrating no-man's-land of borderline personality disorder. *Cerebrum, 2*(4), 85–99.
Sigman, M. (1995). Current research findings on childhood autism. *Canadian Journal of Psychiatry, 40*(6), 289–294.
Silva, C. E., & Kirsch, I. (1992). Interpretive sets, expectancy, fantasy proneness, and dissociation as predictors of hypnotic response. *Journal of Personality & Social Psychology, 63*(5), 847–856.
Silver, S. M., Rogers, S., Knipe, J., & Colelli, G. (2005). EMDR therapy following the 9/11 terrorist attacks: A community-based intervention project in New York City. *International Journal of Stress Management, 12*(1), 29–42.
Silverman, K., Evans, S. M., Strain, E. C., & Griffiths, R. R. (1992). Withdrawal syndrome after the double-blind cessation of caffeine consumption. *New England Journal of Medicine, 327*(16), 1109–1114.
Silverman, L. K. (1998). Through the lens of giftedness. *Roeper Review, 20*(3), 204–210.
Silverstein, B. (1989). Enemy images. *American Psychologist, 44*(6), 903–913.
Simeon, D., Guralnik, O., Knutelska, M., & Schmeidler, J. (2002). Personality factors associated with dissociation: Temperament, defenses, and cognitive schemata. *American Journal of Psychiatry, 159*, 489–491.
Simeonova, D., Chang, K. D., Strong, C., & Ketter, T. A. (2005). Creativity in familial bipolar disorder. *Journal of Psychiatric Research, 39*(6), 623–631.
Simner, M. L., & Goffin, R. D. (2003). A position statement by the international graphonomics society on the use of graphology in personnel selection testing. *International Journal of Testing, 3*(4), 353–364.
Simon, A. (1998). Aggression in a prison setting as a function of lunar phases. *Psychological Reports, 82*(3, Pt. 1), 747–752.
Simon, G. E, Ludman, E. J., Tutty, S., Operskalski, B., et al. (2004). Telephone psychotherapy and telephone care management for primary care patients starting antidepressant treatment. *Journal of the American Medical Association, 292*, 935–942.
Simons, D. J., & Chabris, C. F. (1999). Gorillas in our midst: Sustained inattentional blindness for dynamic events. *Perception, 28*, 1059–1074.
Simons, D. J., & Levin, D. T. (1998). Failure to detect changes to people during a real-world interaction. *Psychonomic Bulletin & Review, 5*(4), 644–649.

Simonton, D. K. (1988). Age and outstanding achievement: What do we know after a century of research? *Psychological Bulletin, 104*(2), 251–267.

Simonton, D. K., & Baumeister, R. F. (2005). Positive psychology at the summit. *Review of General Psychology. Special Positive Psychology, 9*(2), 99–102.

Simpson, D. D., Joe, G. W., Fletcher, B. W., Hubbard, R. L, et al. (1999). A national evaluation of treatment outcomes for cocaine dependence. *Archives of General Psychiatry, 57*(6), 507–514.

Simpson, J. A. (1990). Influence of attachment styles on romantic relationships. *Journal of Personality & Social Psychology, 59*(5), 971–980.

Simpson, K. J. (2002). Anorexia nervosa and culture. *Journal of Psychiatric & Mental Health Nursing, 9,* 65–71.

Singer, J. D. (2005). Explaining foreign policy: U.S. decision-making and the Persian Gulf War. *Political Psychology, 26*(5), 831–834.

Singer, M. T. (2003). *Cults in our midst: The continuing fight against their hidden menace* (Rev. ed.). San Francisco: Jossey-Bass.

Singer, M. T., & Addis, M. E. (1992). Cults, coercion, and contumely. *Cultic Studies Journal, 9*(2), 163–189.

Singleton, J. L., & Newport, E. L. (2004). When learners surpass their models: The acquisition of American Sign Language from inconsistent input. *Cognitive Psychology, 49*(4), 370–407.

Sipos, A., Rasmussen, F., Harrison, G., Tynelius, P., et al. (2004). Paternal age and schizophrenia: A population based cohort study. *British Medical Journal, 329*(7474), 1070.

Sirkin, M. I. (1990). Cult involvement: A systems approach to assessment and treatment. *Psychotherapy, 27*(1), 116–123.

Sison, C. E., Alpert, M., Fudge, R., & Stern, R. M. (1996). Constricted expressiveness and psychophysiological reactivity in schizophrenia. *Journal of Nervous & Mental Disease, 184*(10), 589–597.

Skeels, H. M. (1966). Adult status of children with contrasting early life experiences. *Monograph of the Society for Research in Child Development, 31*(3), 105.

Skinner, B. F. (1938). *The behavior of organisms.* Englewood Cliffs, NJ: Prentice Hall.

Skinner, B. F. (1971). *Beyond freedom and dignity.* New York: Bantam.

Skipton, L. H. (1997). The many faces of character. *Consulting Psychology Journal: Practice & Research, 49*(4), 235–245

Skoog, I. (1996). Sex and Swedish 85-year-olds. *British Journal of Clinical Psychology, 334*(17), 1140–1141.

Skuy, M., Gewer, A., Osrin, Y., Khunou, D., et al. (2002). Effects of mediated learning experience on Raven's matrices scores of African and non-African university students in South Africa. *Intelligence, 30*(3), 221–232.

Slaby, A. E., Garfinkel, B. D., & Garfinkel, L. F. (1994). *No one say my pain.* New York: Norton.

Slater, A., Mattock, A., & Brown, E. (1990). Size constancy at birth: Newborn infants' responses to retinal and real size. *Journal of Experimental Child Psychology, 49*(2), 314–322.

Sledge, W. H., Tebes, J., Rakfeldt, J., Davidson, L. (1996). Day hospital/crisis respite care versus inpatient care: I. Clinical outcomes. *American Journal of Psychiatry, 153*(8), 1065–1073.

Sleek, S. (1998). How are psychologists portrayed on screen? *APA Monitor,* Nov., 11.

Slijper, F. M. E., Drop, S. L. S., Molenaar, J. C., de Muinck, K., et al. (2000). "Long-term psychological evaluation of intersex children": Reply. *Archives of Sexual Behavior, 29*(1), 119–121.

Slot, L. A. B., & Colpaert, F. C. (1999). Recall rendered dependent on an opiate state. *Behavioral Neuroscience, 113*(2), 337–344.

Slotkin, T. A. (1998). Fetal nicotine or cocaine exposure: Which one is worse? *Journal of Pharmacology and Experimental Therapeutics, 285*(3), 931–945.

Smedley, A., & Smedley, B. D. (2005). Race as biology is fiction, racism as a social problem is real. *American Psychologist, 60*(1), 16–26.

Smith, A. P., Clark, R., & Gallagher, J. (1999). Breakfast cereal and caffeinated coffee: Effects on working memory, attention, mood and cardiovascular function. *Physiology & Behavior, 67*(1), 9–17.

Smith, A. P., Sturgess, W., & Gallagher, J. (1999). Effects of a low dose of caffeine given in different drinks on mood and performance. *Human Psychopharmacology Clinical & Experimental, 14*(7), 473–482.

Smith, C., Carey, S., & Wiser, M. (1985). On differentiation: A case study of the development of the concepts of size, weight, and density. *Cognition, 21*(3), 177–237.

Smith, J. L., & Cahusac, P. M. B. (2001). Right-sided asymmetry in sensitivity to tickle. *Laterality, 6*(3), 233–238.

Smith, K. E., Landry, S. H., & Swank, P. R. (2000). Does the content of mothers' verbal stimulation explain differences in children's development of verbal and nonverbal cognitive skills? *Journal of School Psychology, 38*(1), 27–49.

Smith, K. H., & Rogers, M. (1994). Effectiveness of subliminal messages in television commercials: Two experiments. *Journal of Applied Psychology, 79*(6), 866–874.

Smith, L. F. (2002). The effects of confidence and perception of test-taking skills on performance. *North American Journal of Psychology, 4*(1), 37–50.

Smith, R. W., & Kounios, J. (1996). Sudden insight: All-or-none processing revealed by speed-accuracy decomposition. *Journal of Experimental Psychology: Learning, Memory, & Cognition, 22*(6), 1443–1462.

Smith, S. M, McIntosh, W. D., & Bazzini, D. G. (1999). Are the beautiful good in Hollywood? *Basic & Applied Social Psychology, 21*(1), 69–80.

Smith, T. W. (1990). *Adult sexual behavior in 1989: Number of partners, frequency, and risk.* Paper presented to the American Association for the Advancement of Science, February, New Orleans.

Smith, T. W., Glazer, K., Ruiz, J. M., & Gallo, L. C. (2004). Hostility, anger, aggressiveness, and coronary heart disease: An interpersonal perspective on personality, emotion, and health. *Journal of Personality. Special Emotions, Personality, and Health, 72*(6), 1217–1270.

Smith, T. W., Ruiz, J. M., & Uchino, B. N. (2004). Mental activation of supportive ties, hostility, and cardiovascular reactivity to laboratory stress in young men and women. *Health Psychology, 23*(5), 476–485.

Smyth, M. M., & Waller, A. (1998). Movement imagery in rock climbing. *Applied Cognitive Psychology, 12*(2), 145–157.

Snow, C. P. (1961). Either-or. *Progressive,* Feb., 24.

Snowden, P. L., & Christian, L. G. (1999). Parenting the young gifted child: Supportive behaviors. *Roeper Review, 21*(3), 215–221.

Sobel, E., Shine, D., DiPietro, D., & Rabinowitz, M. (1996). Condom use among HIV/infected patients in South Bronx, New York. *AIDS, 10*(2), 235–236.

Sobolewski, J. M., & Amato, P. R. (2005). Economic hardship in the family of origin and children's psychological well-being in adulthood. *Journal of Marriage and Family, 67*(1), 141–156.

Solomon, R. C., & Wynne, L. C. (1953). Traumatic avoidance learning: Acquisition in normal dogs. *Psychological Monographs, 67*(4, Whole no. 354).

Solomon, R. L. (1980). The opponent-process theory of acquired motivation. *American Psychologist,* Aug., 691–721.

Solowij, N., Stephens, R. S., Roffman, R. A., & the Marijuana Treatment Project Research Group. (2002). Cognitive functioning of long-term heavy cannabis users seeking treatment. *Journal of the American Medical Association, 287,* 1123–1131.

Solso, R. L., MacLin, M. K., & MacLin, O. H. (2005). *Cognitive psychology* (7th ed). Boston: Allyn and Bacon.

Somberg, D. R., Stone, G., & Claiborn, C. D. (1993). Informed consent: Therapist's beliefs and practices. *Professional Psychology: Research & Practice, 24*(2), 153–159.

Sorce, J. F., Emde, R. N., Campos, J. J., & Klinnert, M. D. (1985). Maternal emotional signaling: Its effect on the visual cliff behavior of 1-year-olds. *Developmental Psychology, 21,* 195–200.

Soussignan, R. (2002). Duchenne smile, emotional experience, and autonomic reactivity. *Emotion, 2*(1), 52–74.

Spackman, M. P., Belcher, J. C., Calapp, J. W., & Taylor, A. (2002). An analysis of the effects of subjective and objective instruction forms on mock-juries' murder/manslaughter distinctions. *Law and Human Behavior, 26*(6), 605–623.

Spangenberg, J. J., & Lategan, T. P. (1993). Coping, androgyny, and attributional style. *South African Journal of Psychology, 23*(4), 195–203.

Spector, P. E. (2005). *Industrial and organizational psychology: Research and practice* (4th ed.). New York: Wiley.

Spence, S., & David, A. (Eds.). (2004). *Voices in the brain: The cognitive neuropsychiatry of auditory verbal hallucinations.* London: Psychology Press.

Sperry, R. W. (1968). Hemisphere deconnection and unity in conscious awareness. *American Psychologist, 23,* 723–733.

Sperry, R. W. (1995). The riddle of consciousness and the changing scientific worldview. *Journal of Humanistic Psychology, 35*(2), 7–33.

Spiegel, D. (1986). Dissociation, double binds, and posttraumatic stress in multiple personality disorder. In B. G. Braun (Ed.), *Treatment of multiple personality disorder.* Washington, DC: American Psychiatric Press.

Spiegler, M. D., & Guevremont, D. C. (2003). *Contemporary behavior therapy.* Belmont, CA: Wadsworth

Spinella, M. (2005). Compulsive behavior in tobacco users. *Addictive Behaviors, 30*(1), 183–186.

Sporer, S. L. (2001). Recognizing faces of other ethnic groups. *Psychology, Public Policy, and Law, 7*(1), 36–97.

Sprecher, S. (1998). Insiders' perspectives on reasons for attraction to a close other. *Social Psychology Quarterly, 61*(4), 287–300.

Sprecher, S., & Hatfield, E. (1996). Premarital sexual standards among U.S. college students. *Archives of Sexual Behavior, 25*(3), 261–288.

Springer, S. P., & Deutsch, G. (1998). *Left brain, right brain.* New York: Freeman.

Squire, L. R. (2004). Memory systems of the brain: A brief history and current perspective. *Neurobiology of Learning & Memory, 82,* 171–177.

Squire, L. R., & Kandel, E. R. (2000). *Memory: From mind to molecule.* New York: Worth.

Squire, L. R., Knowlton, B., & Musen, G. (1993). The structure and organization of memory. *Annual Review of Psychology, 44,* 453–495.

Squire, L. R., & Zola-Morgan, S. (1988). Memory: Brain systems and behavior. *Trends in Neurosciences, 11*(4), 170–175.

Srivastava, S., John, O. P., Gosling, S. D., & Potter, J. (2003). Development of personality in early and middle adulthood: Set like plaster or persistent change? *Journal of Personality & Social Psychology, 84*(5), 1041–1053.

Sroufe, L. A., Egeland, B., Carlson, E., & Collins, W. A. (2005). Placing early attachment experiences in developmental context: The Minnesota Longitudinal Study. In K. E. Grossmann, K. Grossmann, et al. (Eds.), *Attachment from infancy to adulthood: The major longitudinal studies.* New York: Guilford.

Staats, P., Hekmat, H., & Staats, A. (1998). Suggestion/Placebo effects on pain: Negative as well as positive. *Journal of Pain & Symptom Management, 15*(4), 235–243.

Stanovich, K. E. (2004). *How to think straight about psychology* (7th ed.). Boston: Allyn & Bacon.

Staples, S. L. (1996). Human response to environmental noise. *American Psychologist, 51*(2), 143–150.

Staw, B. M., Sutton, R. I., & Pelled, L. H. (1994). Employee positive emotion and favorable outcomes at the workplace. *Organization Science, 5*(1), 51–71.

Steblay, N. M. (1987). Helping behavior in rural and urban environments: A meta-analysis. *Psychological Bulletin, 102*(3), 346–356.

Steblay, N. M. (1992). A meta-analytic review of the weapon focus effect. *Law and Human Behavior, 16,* 413–424.

Steele, C. M. (1997). A threat in the air. *American Psychologist, 52*(6), 613–629.

Steele, C. M., & Aronson, J. (1995). Stereotype threat and the intellectual test performance of African Americans. *Journal of Personality & Social Psychology, 69*(5), 797–811.

Stefanis, C., Dornbush, R. L., & Fink, M. (1977). *Hashish: A study of long-term use.* New York: Raven.

Stein, M. I. (1974). *Stimulating creativity* (Vol. 1). New York: Academic.

Stein, M. T., & Ferber, R. (2001). Recent onset of sleepwalking in early adolescence. *Journal of Development, Behavior, and Pediatrics, 22,* S33–S35.

Steinberg, L. (2000). We know some things: Parent–adolescent relations in retrospect and prospect. *Journal of Research on Adolescence, 11*(1), 1–19.

Steinberg, L. (2001). Adolescent development. *Annual Review of Psychology, 52,* 83–110.

Steinberg, L. D., Catalano, R., & Dooley, P. (1981). Economic antecedents of child abuse and neglect. *Child Development, 52,* 975–985.

Stenberg, G., & Hagekull, B. (1997). Social referencing and mood modification in 1-year-olds. *Infant Behavior and Development, 20*(2), 209–217.

Stephan, W., Berscheid, E., & Walster, E. (1971). Sexual arousal and heterosexual perception. *Journal of Personality & Social Psychology, 20*(1), 93–101.

Stephens, K., Kiger, L., Karnes, F. A., & Whorton, J. E. (1999). Use of nonverbal measures of intelligence in identification of culturally diverse gifted students in rural areas. *Perceptual & Motor Skills, 88*(3, Pt. 1), 793–796.

Steriade, M., & McCarley, R. W. (1990). *Brainstem control of wakefulness and sleep.* New York: Plenum.

Sterman, M. B. (1996). Physiological origins and functional correlates of EEG rhythmic activities: Implications for self-regulation. *Biofeedback & Self Regulation, 21*(1), 3–33.

Stern, D. (1982). Some interactive functions of rhythm changes between mother and infant. In M. Davis (Ed.), *Interaction rhythms, periodicity in communicative behavior.* New York: Human Sciences Press.

Sternbach, H. (1998). Age-associated testosterone decline in men: Clinical issues for psychiatry. *American Journal of Psychiatry, 155,* 1310–1318.

Sternberg, E. M. (2000). *The balance within: The science of connecting health with emotions.* New York: Freeman.

Sternberg, R. J. (1996). *Successful intelligence.* New York: Simon & Schuster.

Sternberg, R. J. (2001). What is the common thread of creativity? *American Psychologist, 56*(4), 360–362.

Sternberg, R. J. (2004). Culture and intelligence. *American Psychologist, 59*(5), 325–338.

Sternberg, R. J., & Davidson, J. D. (1982). The mind of the puzzler. *Psychology Today,* June, 37–44.

Sternberg, R. J., & Grigorenko, E. L. (2005). Cultural explorations of the nature of intelligence. In A. F. Healy (Ed.), *Experimental cognitive psychology and its applications.* Washington, DC: American Psychological Association.

Sternberg, R. J., Grigorenko, E. L., & Kidd, K. K. (2005). Intelligence, race, and genetics. *American Psychologist, 60*(1), 46–59.

Sternberg, R. J., & Lubart, T. I. (1995). *Defying the crowd.* New York: Free Press.

Sternberg, W. F., Bailin, D., Grant, M., & Gracely, R. H. (1998). Competition alters the perception of noxious stimuli in male and female athletes. *Pain, 76*(1–2), 231–238.

Steuer, F. B., & Hustedt, J. T. (2002). *TV or no TV? A primer on the psychology of television.* Lanham, MD: University Press of America.

Stewart, A. J., & Ostrove, J. M. (1998). Women's personality in middle age. *American Psychologist, 53*(11), 1185–1194.

Stewart, A. J., & Vandewater, E. A. (1999). "If I had it to do over again . . .": Midlife review, midcourse corrections, and women's well-being in midlife. *Journal of Personality & Social Psychology, 76*(2), 270–283.

Stewart, J. V. (1996). *Astrology: What's really in the stars.* Amherst, NY: Prometheus.

Stewart-Williams, S. (2004). The placebo puzzle: Putting together the pieces. *Health Psychology, 23*(2), 198–206.

Stickgold, R., Hobson, J. A., Fosse, R., & Fosse, M. (2001). Sleep, learning, and dreams: Off-line memory reprocessing. *Science, 294*(5544), 1052–1057.

Stiles, W. B., Agnew-Davies, R., Hardy, G. E., Barkham, M.E., et al. (1998). Relations of the alliance with psychotherapy outcome. *Journal of Consulting & Clinical Psychology, 66*(5), 791–802.

Stöber, J. (2004). Dimensions of test anxiety: Relations to ways of coping with pre-exam anxiety and uncertainty. *Anxiety, Stress & Coping: An International Journal, 17*(3), 213–226.

Stockhorst, U., Klosterhalfen, S., & Steingrueber, H. (1998). Conditioned nausea and further side-effects in cancer chemotherapy. *Journal of Psychophysiology, 12*(Supp. 1), 14–33.

Stokes, D. M. (2001). The shrinking filedrawer. *Skeptical Inquirer,* May–June, 22–25.

Stokoe, W. C. (2001). *Language in hand: Why sign came before speech.* Washington, DC: Gallaudet University Press.

Stolerman, I. P., & Jarvis, M. J. (1995). The scientific case that nicotine is addictive. *Psychopharmacology, 117*(1), 2–10.

Stone, J., Perry, Z. W., & Darley, J. M. (1997). "White men can't jump." *Basic and Applied Social Psychology, 19*(3), 291–306.

Stoney, S., & Wild, M. (1998). Motivation and interface design: Maximising learning opportunities. *Journal of Computer Assisted Learning, 14*(1), 40–50.

Stoppard, J. M., & McMullen, L. M. (Eds.). (2003). *Situating sadness: Women and depression in social context.* New York: New York University Press.

Storms, G., De Boeck, P., & Ruts, W. (2001). Categorization of novel stimuli in well-known natural concepts: A case study. *Psychonomic Bulletin & Review, 8*(2), 377–384.

Strack, F., Martin, L. L., & Stepper, S. (1988). Inhibiting and facilitating conditions of facial expressions: A non-obtrusive test of the facial feedback hypothesis. *Journal of Personality & Social Psychology, 54,* 768–777.

Straneva, P. A., Maixner, W., Light, K. C., Pedersen, C. A., et al. (2002). Menstrual cycle, beta-endorphins, and pain sensitivity in premenstrual dysphoric disorder. *Health Psychology, 21*(4), 358–367.

Strange, J. R. (1965). *Abnormal psychology.* New York: McGraw-Hill.

Straus, M. A., & Mouradian, V. E. (1998). Impulsive corporal punishment by mothers and antisocial behavior and impulsiveness of children. *Behavioral Sciences & the Law, 16*(3), 353–374.

Strayer, D. L., Drews, F. A., & Johnston, W. A. (2003). Cell phone–induced failures of visual attention during simulated driving. *Journal of Experimental Psychology: Applied, 9*(1), 23–32.

Strickler, E. M., & Verbalis, J. G. (1988). Hormones and behavior: The biology of thirst and sodium appetite. *American Scientist,* May–June, 261–267.

Strier, F. (1999). Whither trial consulting? Issues and projections. *Law & Human Behavior, 23*(1), 93–115.

Stroebe, M., Stroebe, W., Schut, H., Zech, E., et al. (2002). Does disclosure of emotions facilitate recovery from bereavement? *Journal of Consulting & Clinical Psychology, 70*(1), 169–178.

Stroeher, S. K. (1994). Sixteen kindergartners' gender-related views of careers. *Elementary School Journal, 95*(1), 95–103.

Strong, B., & DeVault, C. (1994). *Understanding our sexuality.* St. Paul, MN: West.

Strongman, K. T. (1996). *The psychology of emotion.* New York: Wiley.

Strote, J., Lee, J. E., & Wechsler, H. (2002). Increasing MDMA use among college students: Results of a national survey. *Journal of Adolescent Health, 30*(1), 64–72.

Sturges, J. W., & Sturges, L. V. (1998). In vivo *systematic desensitization* in a single-session treatment of an 11-year-old girl's elevator phobia. *Child & Family Behavior Therapy, 20*(4), 55–62.

Stuss, D. T., & Alexander, M. P. (2000). The anatomical basis of affective behavior, emotion and self-awareness: A specific role of the right frontal lobe. In G. Hatano, N. Okada, & H. Tanabe (Eds.), *Affective minds. The 13th Toyota conference.* Amsterdam: Elsevier.

Stuss, D. T., & Levine, B. (2002). Adult clinical neuropsychology. *Annual Review of Psychology, 53,* 401–433.

Sue, D., Sue, D. W., & Sue, S. (1996). *Understanding abnormal behavior.* Boston: Houghton Mifflin.

Suedfeld, P. (1990). Restricted environmental stimulation and smoking cessation. *International Journal of Addictions, 25*(8), 861–888.

Suedfeld, P., & Borrie, R. A. (1999). Health and therapeutic applications of chamber and flotation restricted environmental stimulation therapy (REST). *Psychology & Health, 14*(3), 545–566.

Suedfeld, P., & Piedrahita, L. E. (1984). Intimations of mortality: Integrative simplification as a precursor of death. *Journal of Personality and Social Psychology, 47,* 848–852.

Sugihara, Y., & Warner, J. A. (1999). Endorsements by Mexican-Americans of the Bem Sex-Role Inventory: Cross-ethnic comparison. *Psychological Reports, 85*(1), 201–211.

Suinn, R. M. (1975). *Fundamentals of behavior pathology* (2nd ed.). New York: Wiley.

Suinn, R. M. (1999). Scaling the summit: Valuing ethnicity. *APA Monitor,* March, 2.

Suinn, R. M. (2001). The terrible twos—Anger and anxiety. *American Psychologist, 56*(1), 27–36.

Sullivan, M. J., Johnson, P. I., Kjelberg, B. J., Williams, J., et al. (1998). Community leadership opportunities for psychologists. *Professional Psychology: Research and Practice, 29*(4), 328–331.

Suls, J. (1989). Self-awareness and self-identity in adolescence. In J. Worell & F. Danner (Eds.), *The adolescent as decision-maker.* New York: Academic Press.

Sumathipala, A., Siribaddana, S. H., & Bhugra, D. (2004). Culture-bound syndromes: The story of dhat syndrome. *British Journal of Psychiatry, 184*(3), 200–209.

Sumerlin, J. R. (1997). Self-actualization and hope. *Journal of Social Behavior & Personality, 12*(4), 1101–1110.

Sumerlin, J. R., & Bundrick, C. M. (1996). Brief Index of Self-Actualization: A measure of Maslow's model. *Journal of Social Behavior & Personality, 11*(2), 253–271.

Sumi, K., & Kanda, K. (2002). Relationship between neurotic perfectionism, depression, anxiety, and psychosomatic symptoms. *Personality & Individual Differences, 32*(5), 817–826.

Sunnafrank, M., Ramirez, A., & Metts, S. (2004). At first sight: Persistent relational effects of get-acquainted conversations. *Journal of Social & Personal Relationships, 21*(3), 361–379.

Swanson, J. (Ed.). (1999). *Sleep disorders sourcebook.* New York: Omnigraphics.

Swanson, M. W., Streissguth, A. P., Sampson, P.D., & Carmichael-Olson, H. (1999). Prenatal cocaine and neuromotor outcome at four months: Effect of duration of exposure. *Journal of Developmental & Behavioral Pediatrics, 20*(5), 325–334.

Swim, J. K., & Sanna, L. J. (1996). He's skilled, she's lucky: A meta-analysis of observers' attributions for women's and men's successes and failures. *Personality & Social Psychology Bulletin, 22*(5), 507–519.

Taeuber, C. M. (1993). *Sixty-five plus in America*. Washington, DC: United States Bureau of Census.

Takooshian, H., Haber, S., & Lucido, D. J. (1977). Who wouldn't help a lost child? You, maybe. *Psychology Today*, Feb., 67.

Talbott, J. A. (2004). Deinstitutionalization: Avoiding the disasters of the past. *Psychiatric Services. Special Issue: A Tribute to John A. Talbott, M.D., 55*(10), 1112–1115.

Talley, P. F., Strupp, H. H., & Morey, L. C. (1990). Matchmaking in psychotherapy: Patient–therapist dimensions and their impact on outcome. *Journal of Consulting & Clinical Psychology, 58*(2), 182–188.

Tallis, F. (1996). Compulsive washing in the absence of phobic and illness anxiety. *Behaviour Research & Therapy, 34*(4), 361–362.

Tang, S., & Hall, V. C. (1995). The overjustification effect: A meta-analysis. *Applied Cognitive Psychology, 9*(5), 365–404.

Tanner, J. M. (1973). Growing up. *Scientific American*, Sept., 34–43.

Taraban, R., Rynearson, K., & Kerr, M. (2000). College students' academic performance and self-reports of comprehension strategy use. *Reading Psychology, 21*(4), 283–308.

Tardif, T. Z., & Sternberg, R. J. (1988). What do we know about creativity? In R. J. Sternberg (Ed.), *The nature of creativity*. New York: Cambridge University Press.

Tart, C. T. (1986). Consciousness, altered states, and worlds of experience. *Journal of Transpersonal Psychology, 18*(2), 159–170.

Taylor, K. (2004). *Brainwashing: The science of thought control*. New York: Oxford University Press.

Taylor, S. E. (2002). Classical conditioning. In M. Hersen & W. H. Sledge (Eds.), *Encyclopedia of psychotherapy*. San Diego: Academic Press.

Taylor, S. E. (2006). *Health psychology* (6th ed.). New York: McGraw-Hill.

Taylor, S. E., Kemeny, M. E., Reed, G. M., Bower, J. E., et al. (2000). Psychological resources, positive illusions, and health. *American Psychologist, 55*(1), 99–109.

Taylor, S. E., Lerner, J. S., Sherman, D. K., Sage, R. M., et al. (2003). Are self-enhancing cognitions associated with healthy or unhealthy biological profiles? *Journal of Personality & Social Psychology, 85*(4), 605–615.

Taylor, T. E. (1983). *Learning studies of higher cognitive levels in short-term sensory isolation environment*. Paper delivered at First International Conference on REST and Self-Regulation, Denver, Colorado, March 17.

Taylor-Seehafer, M., & Rew, L. (2000). Risky sexual behavior among adolescent women. *Journal of Social Pediatric Nursing, 5*(1), 15–25.

Tedeschi, J. T., Lindskold, S., & Rosenfeld, P. (1985). *Introduction to social psychology*. St. Paul: West.

"Teen sex: Not for love." (1989). *Psychology Today*, May, 10.

Tenenbaum, G., Bar-Eli, M., & Eyal, N. (1996). Imagery orientation and vividness: Their effect on a motor skill performance. *Journal of Sport Behavior, 19*(1), 32–49.

Teng, E., & Squire, L. R. (1999). Memory for places learned long ago is intact after hippocampal damage. *Nature, 400*(6745), 675–677.

Terman, L. M., & Merrill, M. A. (1937, revised 1960). *Stanford–Binet Intelligence Scale*. Boston: Houghton Mifflin.

Terman, L. M., & Oden, M. (1959). *The gifted group in mid-life: Vol. 5. Genetic studies of genius*. Stanford, CA: Stanford University Press.

Terry, D. J., & Hogg, M. A. (1996). Group norms and the attitude–behavior relationship. *Personality & Social Psychology Bulletin, 22*(8), 776–793.

Teti, D. M. (1996). And baby makes four: Predictors of attachment security among preschool-age firstborns during the transition to siblinghood. *Child Development, 67*(2), 579–596.

Thase, M. E., & Kupfer, D. L. (1996). Recent developments in the pharmacotherapy of mood disorders. *Journal of Consulting & Clinical Psychology, 64*(4), 646–659.

Thelen, E. (2000). Infancy: Perception and motor development. In A. Kazdin (Ed.), *Encyclopedia of psychology*. Washington, DC: American Psychological Association.

"They'd kill for $1 million." (1991). *Los Angeles Times*, July 1, A-8.

Thompson, C. P., Cowan, T. M., & Frieman, J. (1993). *Memory search by a menorist*. Hillsdale, NJ: Lawrence Erlbaum.

Thompson, R. A., & Nelson, C. A. (2001). Developmental science and the media. *American Psychologist, 56*(1), 5–15.

Thornburg, H. D. (1984). *Introduction to educational psychology*. St. Paul: West.

Thorson, J. A., & Powell, F. C. (1990). Meanings of death and intrinsic religiosity. *Journal of Clinical Psychology, 46*(4), 379–391.

Thyen, U., Richter-Appelt, H., Wiesemann, C., Holterhus, P. M., et al. (2005). Deciding on gender in children with intersex conditions: Considerations and controversies. *Treatments in Endocrinology, 4*(1), 1–8.

Tice, D. M., & Baumeister, R. F. (1997). Longitudinal study of procrastination, performance, stress, and health: The costs and benefits of dawdling. *Psychological Science, 8*(6), 454–458.

Tidwell, M. O., Reis, H. T., & Shaver, P. R. (1996). Attachment, attractiveness, and social interaction. *Journal of Personality & Social Psychology, 71*(4), 729–745.

Tierny, J. (1987). Stitches: Good news; Better health linked to sin, sloth. *Hippocrates*, Sept.–Oct., 30–35.

Tiffany, S. T., Martin, E. M., & Baker, T. B. (1986). Treatments for cigarette smoking: An evaluation of the contributions of aversion and counseling procedures. *Behavior Research & Therapy, 24*(4), 437–452.

Tijerino, R. (1998). Civil spaces: A critical perspective of defensible space. *Journal of Architectural & Planning Research, 15*(4), 321–337.

Till, B. D., & Priluck, R. L. (2000). Stimulus generalization in classical conditioning: An initial investigation and extension. *Psychology & Marketing, 17*(1), 55–72.

Timmerman, I. G. H., Emmelkamp, P. M. G., & Sanderman, R. (1998). The effects of a stress-management training program in individuals at risk in the community at large. *Behaviour Research & Therapy, 36*(9), 863–875.

Tipples, J., Atkinson, A. P., & Young, A. W. (2002). The eyebrow frown: A salient social signal. *Emotion, 2*(3), 288–296.

Tittle, C. R., & Rotolo, T. (2000). IQ and stratification. *Social Forces, 79*(1), 1–28.

Tobler, N. S., Roona, M. R., Ocshorn, P., Marshall, D. G., et al. (2000). School-based adolescent drug prevention programs: 1998 meta-analysis. *Journal of Primary Prevention, 20*, 275–337.

Tolman, E. C., & Honzik, C. H. (1930). Introduction and removal of reward and maze performance in rats. *University of California Publications in Psychology, 4*, 257–275.

Tolman, E. C., Ritchie, B. F., & Kalish, D. (1946). Studies in spatial learning: II. Place learning versus response learning. *Journal of Experimental Psychology, 36*, 221–229.

Tomasello, M. (2003). *Constructing a language: A usage-based theory of language acquisition*. Cambridge, MA: Harvard University Press.

Torrance, M., Thomas, G. V., & Robinson, E. J. (1991). Strategies for answering examination essay questions: Is it helpful to write a plan? *British Journal of Educational Psychology, 61*(1), 46–54.

Torrey, E. F. (1988). *Surviving schizophrenia: A family manual*. New York: Harper & Row.

Torrey, E. F. (1996). *Out of the shadows*. New York: John Wiley & Sons.

Tourangeau, R. (2004). Survey research and societal change. *Annual Review of Psychology, 55*, 775–801.

Trappey, C. (1996). A meta-analysis of consumer choice and subliminal advertising. *Psychology & Marketing, 13*(5), 517–530.

Treffert, D. A. (2000). Savant syndrome. In A. E. Kazdin (Ed.), *Encyclopedia of psychology*. Washington, DC: American Psychological Association.

Treffert, D. A., & Christensen, C. D. (2005). Inside the mind of a savant. *Scientific American, 293*(6), 108–113.

Treharne, G. J., Lyons, A. C., & Tupling, R. E. (2001). The effects of optimism, pessimism, social support, and mood on the lagged relationship between daily stress and symptoms. *Current Research in Social Psychology, 7*(5), 60–81.

Trehub, S. E., Unyk, A. M., & Trainor, L. J. (1993a). Adults identify infant-directed music across cultures. *Infant Behavior & Development, 16*(2), 193–211.

Trehub, S. E., Unyk, A. M., & Trainor, L. J. (1993b). Maternal singing in cross-cultural perspective. *Infant Behavior & Development, 16*(3), 285–295.

Trepel, C., & Racine, R. J. (1998). Long-term potentiation in the neocortex of the adult, freely moving rat. *Cerebral Cortex, 8*, 719–729.

Triandis, H. C., & Suh, E. M. (2002). Cultural influences on personality. *Annual Review of Psychology, 53*, 133–160.

Troll, L. E., & Skaff, M. M. (1997). Perceived continuity of self in very old age. *Psychology & Aging, 12*(1), 162–169.

Truax, S. R. (1983). Active search, mediation, and the manipulation of cue dimensions: Emotion attribution in the false feedback paradigm. *Motivation and Emotion, 7*, 41–60.

Tryon, R. C. (1929). The genetics of learning ability in rats. *University of California Publications in Psychology, 4*, 71–89.

Tsai, C., Hoerr, S. L., & Song, W. O. (1998). Dieting behavior of Asian college women attending a US university. *Journal of American College Health, 46*(4), 163–168.

Tsai, G., & Coyle, J. T. (2002). Glutamatergic mechanisms in schizophrenia. *Annual Review of Pharmacology & Toxicology, 42*, 165–179.

Tsai, W.-C., Chen, C.-C., & Chiu, S.-F. (2005). Exploring boundaries of the effects of applicant impression management tactics in job interviews. *Journal of Management, 31*(1), 108–125.

Tse, L. (1999). Finding a place to be: Ethnic identity exploration of Asian Americans. *Adolescence, 34*(133), 121–138.

Tugade, M. M., Fredrickson, B. L., & Barrett, L. F. (2004). Psychological resilience and positive emotional granularity: Examining the benefits of positive emotions on coping and health. *Journal of Personality. Special Emotions, Personality, & Health, 72*(6), 1161–1190.

Tuholski, S. W., Engle, R. W., & Baylis, G. C. (2001). Individual differences in working memory capacity and enumeration. *Memory & Cognition, 29*(3), 484–492.

Tulley, M., & Chiu, L. H. (1995). Student teachers and classroom discipline. *Journal of Educational Research, 88*(3), 164–171.

Tulving, E. (1989). Remembering and knowing the past. *American Scientist, 77*(4), 361–367.

Tulving, E. (2000). *Concepts of memory*. In E. Tulving & F. I. M. Craik (Eds.), *The Oxford handbook of memory*. New York: Oxford.

Tulving, E. (2002). Episodic memory. *Annual Review of Psychology, 53*, 1–25.

Turk, D. C., & Melzack, R. (2001). *Handbook of pain assessment*. New York: Guilford.

Turkheimer, E. (1998). Heritability and biological explanation. *Psychological Review, 105*(4), 782–791.

Turner, S. J. M. (1997). The use of the reflective team in a psychodrama therapy group. *International Journal of Action Methods, 50*(1) 17–26.

Turton, M. D., O'Shea, D., Gunn, I., Beak, S. A., et al. (1996). A role for glucagons-like peptide-1 in the central regulation of feeding. *Nature, 379*(6560), 69–74.

Turvey, M. T. (1996). Dynamic touch. *American Psychologist, 51*(11), 1134–1152.

Tversky, A., & Kahneman, D. (1981). The framing of decisions and the psychology of choice. *Science, 211,* 453–458.

Tversky, A., & Kahneman, D. (1982). Judgments of and by representativeness. In D. Kahneman, P. Slovic, et al. (Eds.), *Judgment under uncertainty: Heuristics and biases.* Cambridge: Cambridge University Press.

Twenge, J. M. (1999). Mapping gender: The multifactorial approach and the organization of gender-related attributes. *Psychology of Women Quarterly, 23*(3), 485–502.

Twenge, J. M., & Campbell, W. K. (2001). Age and birth cohort differences in self-esteem. *Personality & Social Psychology Review, 5*(4), 321–344.

Tye-Murray, N., Spencer, L., & Woodworth, G. G. (1995). Acquisition of speech by children who have prolonged cochlear implant experience. *Journal of Speech & Hearing Research, 38*(2), 327–337.

Tyler, J. M., & Feldman, R. S. (2006). Deflecting threat to one's image: Dissembling personal information as a self-presentation strategy. *Basic and Applied Social Psychology, 27*(4), 371–378.

Tzeng, M. (1992). The effects of socioeconomic heterogamy and changes on marital dissolution for first marriages. *Journal of Marriage and Family, 54,* 609–619.

Tzuriel, D., & Shamir, A. (2002). The effects of mediation in computer assisted dynamic assessment. *Journal of Computer Assisted Learning, 18*(1), 21–32.

Udvari-Solner, A., Villa, R. A., & Thousand, J. S. (2002). Access to the general education curriculum for all: The universal design process. In J. S. Thousand, R. A. Villa, et al. (Eds.), *Creativity and collaborative learning: The practical guide to empowering students, teachers, and families* (2nd ed.). Baltimore: Paul H. Brookes.

Ulrich, R. E., Stachnik, T. J., & Stainton, N. R. (1963). Student acceptance of generalized personality interpretations. *Psychological Reports, 131,* 831–834.

Underwood, B. J. (1957). Interference and forgetting. *Psychological Review, 64,* 49–60.

UNESCO. (1990). The Seville statement on violence. *American Psychologist, 45*(10), 1167–1168.

Unsworth, G., & Ward, T. (2001). Video games and aggressive behaviour. *Australian Psychologist, 36*(3), 184–192.

Urdan, T., & Midgley, C. (2001). Academic self-handicapping. *Educational Psychology Review, 13*(2), 115–138.

Vaillant, G. E. (2002). *Aging well.* Boston: Little, Brown.

Vaillant, G. E., & Mukamal, K. (2001). Successful aging. *American Journal of Psychiatry, 158*(6), 839–847.

Valery, J. H., O'Connor, P., & Jennings, S. (1997). The nature and amount of support college-age adolescents request and receive from parents. *Adolescence, 32*(126), 323–338.

Valian, V. (1998). Running in place. *The Sciences,* Jan.–Feb., 18–23.

Valins, S. (1966). Cognitive effects of false heart-rate feedback. *Journal of Personality & Social Psychology, 4,* 400–408.

Valins, S. (1967). Emotionality and information concerning internal reactions. *Journal of Personality & Social Psychology, 6,* 458–463.

Vandell, D. L. (2004). Early child care: The known and the unknown. *Merrill–Palmer Quarterly. Special: The maturing of the human developmental sciences: Appraising past, present, and prospective agendas, 50*(3), 387–414.

van der Hart, O., Lierens, R., & Goodwin, J. (1996). Jeanne Fery: A sixteenth-century case of dissociative identity disorder. *Journal of Psychohistory, 24*(1), 18–35.

van Dierendonck, D., & Te Nijenhuis, J. (2005). Flotation restricted environmental stimulation therapy (REST) as a stress-management tool: A meta-analysis. *Psychology & Health, 20*(3), 405–412.

Vane, J. R., & Guarnaccia, V. J. (1989). Personality theory and personality assessment measures: How helpful to the clinician? *Journal of Clinical Psychology, 45*(1), 5–19.

Van Goozen, S. H. M., Cohen-Kettenis, P. T., Gooren, L. J. G., & Frijda, N. H. (1995). Gender differences in behaviour: Activating effects of cross-sex hormones. *Psychoneuroendocrinology, 20*(4), 343–363.

van Lawick-Goodall, J. (1971). *In the shadow of man.* New York: Houghton Mifflin.

van Rooij, J. J. F. (1994). Introversion–extraversion: Astrology versus psychology. *Personality & Individual Differences, 16*(6), 985–988.

Van Wyk, P. H., & Geist, C. S. (1995). Biology of bisexuality: Critique and observations. *Journal of Homosexuality, 28*(3–4), 357–373.

Vasquez, M. J. T., & de las Fuentes, C. (1999). American-born Asian, African, Latina, and American Indian adolescent girls: Challenges and strengths. In N. G. Johnson, M. C. Roberts, et al. (Eds.), *Beyond appearance.* Washington, DC: American Psychological Association.

Vecera, S. P., Vogel, E. K., & Woodman, G. F. (2002). Lower region: A new cue for figure-ground assignment. *Journal of Experimental Psychology: General, 131*(2), 194–205.

Velakoulis, D., & Pantelis, C. (1996). What have we learned from functional imaging studies in schizophrenia? *Australian & New Zealand Journal of Psychiatry, 30*(2), 195–209.

Venkatagiri, H. S. (2005). Recent advances in the treatment of stuttering: A theoretical perspective. *Journal of Communication Disorders, 38*(5), 375–393.

Verkuyten, M., & Lay, C. (1998). Ethnic minority identity and psychological well-being: The mediating role of collective self-esteem. *Journal of Applied Social Psychology, 28*(21), 1969–1986.

Vernoy, M. W. (1989). Simultaneous adaptation to size, distance, and curvature underwater. *Human Factors, 31*(1), 77–85.

Videon, T. M. (2005). Parent–child relations and children's psychological well-being: Do dads matter? *Journal of Family Issues, 26*(1), 55–78.

Viegener, B. J., Perri, M. G., Nezu, A. M., Renjilian, D. A., et al. (1990). Effects of an intermittent, low-fat, low-calorie diet in the behavioral treatment of obesity. *Behavior Therapy, 21*(4), 499–509.

Vogler, R. E., & Bartz, W. R. (1982). *The better way to drink.* New York: Simon and Schuster.

Vogler, R. E., & Bartz, W. R. (1992). *Teenagers and alcohol.* Philadelphia: Charles Press.

Vogler, R. E., Weissbach, T. A., Compton, J. V., & Martin, G. T. (1977). Integrated behavior change techniques for problem drinkers in the community. *Journal of Consulting and Clinical Psychology, 45,* 267–279.

Volkmann, J., Schnitzler, A., Witte, O. W., & Freund, H. J. (1998). Handedness and asymmetry of hand representation in human motor cortex. *Journal of Neurophysiology, 79*(4), 2149–2154.

Volkow, N. D., Gillespie, H., Mullani, N., & Tancredi, L. (1996). Brain glucose metabolism in chronic marijuana users at baseline and during marijuana intoxication. *Psychiatry Research: Neuroimaging, 67*(1), 29–38.

Volpicelli, J. R., Ulm, R. R., Altenor, A., & Seligman, M. E. P. (1983). Learned mastery in the rat. *Learning and Motivation, 14,* 204–222.

Von Baumgarten, R., Benson, A., Berthoz, A., Brandt, T., et al. (1984). Spatial orientation in weightlessness and readaptation to earth's gravity. *Science, 225,* 205–225.

Vygotsky, L. S. (1962). *Thought and language.* Cambridge, MA: MIT Press.

Vygotsky, L. S. (1978). *Mind in society.* Cambridge, MA: Harvard University Press.

Wager, T. D., Rilling, J. K., Smith, E. E., Sokolik, A., et al. (2004). Placebo-induced changes in fMRI in the anticipation and experience of pain. *Science, 303*(Feb. 20), 1162–1166.

Wagstaff, G., Brunas-Wagstaff, J., Cole, J., & Wheatcroft, J. (2004). New directions in forensic hypnosis: Facilitating memory with a focused meditation technique. *Contemporary Hypnosis, 21*(1), 14–27.

Waid, W. M., & Orne, M. T. (1982). The physiological detection of deception. *American Scientist, 70*(July–Aug.), 402–409.

Wainright, J. L., Russell, S. T., & Patterson, C. J. (2004). Psychosocial adjustment, school outcomes, and romantic relationships of adolescents with same-sex parents. *Child Development, 75*(6), 1886–1898.

Wakefield, J. C. (1992). The concept of mental disorder. *American Psychologist, 47*(3), 373–388.

Wald, J., & Taylor, S. (2000). Efficacy of virtual reality exposure therapy to treat driving phobia. *Journal of Behavior Therapy & Experimental Psychiatry, 31*(3–4), 249–257.

Waldvogel, J. A. (1990). The bird's eye view. *American Scientist, 78*(4), 342–353.

Walker, E., Kestler, L. Bollini, A., & Hochman, K. M. (2004). Schizophrenia: Etiology and course. *Annual Review of Psychology, 55,* 401–430.

Walker, I., & Crogan, M. (1998). Academic performance, prejudice, and the jigsaw classroom. *Journal of Community & Applied Social Psychology, 8*(6), 381–393

Wallach, M. A. (1985). Creativity testing and giftedness. In F. D. Horowitz & M. O'Brien (Eds.), *The gifted and talented: Developmental perspectives.* Washington, DC: American Psychological Association.

Wallach, M. A., & Kogan, N. (1965). *Modes of thinking in young children.* New York: Holt.

Wallerstein, J. S., Lewis, J. M., & Blakeslee, S. (2000). *The unexpected legacy of divorce: A 25 year landmark study.* New York: Hyperion.

Walsh, J. K., & Scweitzer, P. K. (1999). Ten-year trends in the pharmacological treatment of insomnia. *Sleep, 22*(3), 371–375.

Walster, E. (1971). Passionate love. In B. I. Murstein (Ed.), *Theories of attraction and love.* New York: Springer.

Walton, C. E., Bower, M. L., & Bower, T. G. (1992). Recognition of familiar faces by newborns. *Infant Behavior & Development, 15*(2), 265–269.

Wampold, B. E., Mondin, G. W., Moody, M., Stich, E., et al. (1997). A meta-analysis of outcome studies comparing bona fide psychotherapies. *Psychological Bulletin, 122*(3), 203–215.

Wandersman, A., & Florin, P. (2003). Community interventions and effective prevention. *American Psychologist, 58*(6–7), 441–448.

Wang, Q., & Conway, M. A. (2004). The stories we keep: Autobiographical memory in American and Chinese middle-aged adults. *Journal of Personality, 72*(5), 911–938.

Wang, S. S., & Brownell, K. D. (2005). Public policy and obesity: The need to marry science with advocacy. *Psychiatric Clinics of North America, 28*(1), 235–252.

Ward, C., & Rana-Deuba, A. (1999). Acculturation and adaptation revisited. *Journal of Cross-Cultural Psychology, 30*(4), 422–442.

Ward, E., & Ogden, J. (1994). Experiencing vaginismus: Sufferers' beliefs about causes and effects. *Sexual & Marital Therapy, 9*(1), 33–45.

Wark, G. R., & Krebs, D. L. (1996). Gender and dilemma differences in real-life moral judgment. *Developmental Psychology, 32*(2), 220–230.

"Warning signs." (2000). Washington, DC: American Psychological Association.

Warrington, E. K., & McCarthy, R. A. (1995). Multiple meaning systems in the brain: A case for visual semantics. *Neuropsychologia, 32*(12), 1465–1473.

Warwick-Evans, L. A., Symons, N., Fitch, T., & Burrows, L. (1998). Evaluating sensory conflict and postural instability: Theories of motion sickness. *Brain Research Bulletin, 47*(5), 465–469.

Watson, D. L., & Tharp, R. G. (2002). *Self-directed behavior: Self-modification for personal adjustment* (8th ed.). Belmont, CA: Wadsworth.

Watson, D. L., deBortali-Tregerthan, G., & Frank, J. (1984). *Social psychology: Science and application.* Glenview, IL: Scott, Foresman.

Watson, J. B. (1913/1994). Psychology as the behaviorist views it. *Psychological Review. Special Issue: The Centennial Issue of the Psychological Review, 101*(2), 248–253.

Weaver, C. N., & Matthews, M. D. (1987). What white males want from their jobs: Ten years later. *Personnel, 4*(9), 62–65.

Wechsler, H., & Wuethrich, B. (2002). *Dying to drink.* Emmaus, PA: Rodale Books.

Wechsler, H., Lee, J. E., Kuo, M., Seibring, M., et al. (2002). Trends in college binge drinking during a period of increased prevention efforts. *Journal of American College Health, 50*(5), 203–217.

Weekley, J. A., & Jones, C. (1997). Video-based situational testing. *Personnel Psychology, 50*(1), 25–49.

Weems, C. F. (1998). The evaluation of heart rate biofeedback using a multi-element design. *Journal of Behavior Therapy & Experimental Psychiatry, 29*(2), 157–162.

Wehr, T. A., Duncan, W. C., Sher, L., Aeschbach, D., et al. (2001). A circadian signal of change of season in patients with seasonal affective disorder. *Archives of General Psychiatry, 58*(12), 1108–1114.

Weinberg, R. A. (1989). Intelligence and IQ. *American Psychologist, 44*(2), 98–104.

Weiner, I. B. (1997). Current status of the Rorschach Inkblot Method. *Journal of Personality Assessment, 68*(1), 5–19.

Weinstein, R. S., Gregory, A., & Strambler, M. J. (2004). Intractable self-fulfilling prophesies. *American Psychologist, 59*(6), 511–520.

Weintraub, M. I. (1983). *Hysterical conversion reactions.* New York: SP Medical & Scientific Books.

Weintraub, S. (2003). Cognitive aging. In G. Adelman & B. Smith (Eds.), *Encyclopedia of Neuroscience.* New York: Elsevier Science.

Weisburd, D. E. (1990). Planning a community-based mental health system: Perspective of a family member. *American Psychologist, 45*(11), 1245–1248.

Weisenberg, R. W. (1986). *Creativity.* New York: W. H. Freeman.

Weisfeld, G. E., & Beresford, J. M. (1982). Erectness of posture as an indicator of dominance or success in humans. *Motivation and Emotion, 6,* 113–131.

Weiss, J. (1990). Unconscious mental functioning. *Scientific American,* Mar., 103–109.

Weiss, S. J., Wilson, P., Seed, M., & Paul, S. M. (2001). Early tactile experience of low birth weight children: Links to later mental health and social adaptation. *Infant & Child Development, 10*(3), 93–115.

Weiten, W. (1998). Pressure, major life events, and psychological symptoms. *Journal of Social Behavior & Personality, 13*(1), 51–68.

Wells, B. E., & Twenge, J. M. (2005). Changes in young people's sexual behavior and attitudes, 1943–1999: A cross-temporal meta-analysis. *Review of General Psychology, 9*(3), 249–261.

Wells, G. L. (1993). What do we know about eyewitness identification? *American Psychologist, 48*(5), 553–571.

Wells, G. L. (2001). Police lineups: Data, theory, and policy. *Psychology, Public Policy, & Law, 7*(4), 791–801.

Wells, G. L., & Olsen, E. A. (2003). Eyewitness testimony. *Annual Review of Psychology, 54,* 277–295.

Wells, G. L., Small, M., Penrod, S., Malpass, R. S., et al. (1999). Eyewitness identification procedures: Recommendations for lineups and photospreads. *Law & Human Behavior, 22*(6), 603–647.

Wells, N. (1994). Perceived control over pain: Relation to distress and disability. *Research in Nursing & Health, 17*(4), 295–302.

Werner, C. M., & Makela, E. (1998). Motivations and behaviors that support recycling. *Journal of Environmental Psychology, 18*(4), 373–386.

Wertheimer, M. (1959). *Productive thinking.* New York: Harper & Row.

Wespes, E., & Schulman, C. C. (2002). Male andropause: Myth, reality, and treatment. *International Journal of Impotence Research,* Feb. 14, Suppl. 1, S93–S98.

Wessel, I., & Wright, D. B. (Eds.). (2004). *Emotional memory failures.* Hove, UK: Psychology Press.

West, L. J. (1993). A psychiatric overview of cult-related phenomena. *Journal of the American Academy of Psychoanalysis, 21*(1), 1–19.

West, T. G. (1991). *In the mind's eye.* Buffalo, NY: Prometheus.

Westen, D. (1998). The scientific legacy of Sigmund Freud: Toward a psychodynamically informed psychological science. *Psychological Bulletin, 124*(3), 333–371.

Wethington, E. (2003). Turning points as opportunities for psychological growth. In C. L. M. Keyes & J. Haidt (Eds.), *Flourishing.* Washington, DC: American Psychological Association.

Wettach, G. E. (2000). The near death experience as a product of isolated subcortical brain function. *Journal of Near-Death Studies, 19*(2), 71–90.

Wexler, M., Kosslyn, S. M., & Berthoz, A. (1998). Motor processes in mental rotation. *Cognition, 68*(1), 77–94.

Wexler, M. N. (1995). Expanding the groupthink explanation to the study of contemporary cults. *Cultic Studies Journal, 12*(1), 49–71.

Whatley, M. A., Webster, J. M., Smith, R. H., & Rhodes, A. (1999). The effect of a favor on public and private compliance. *Basic & Applied Social Psychology, 21*(3), 251–259.

Whipple, B. (2000). Beyond the G spot. *Scandinavian Journal of Sexology, 3*(2), 35–42.

White, B. L., & Watts, J. C. (1973). *Experience and environment* (Vol. 1). Englewood Cliffs, NJ: Prentice Hall.

White, G. L., & Taytroe, L. (2003). Personal problem-solving using dream incubation: Dreaming, relaxation, or waking cognition? *Dreaming, 13*(4), 193–209.

White, S. D., & DeBlassie, R. R. (1992). Adolescent sexual behavior. *Adolescence, 27*(105), 183–191.

Whitley, B. E. (1999). Right-wing authoritarianism, social dominance orientation, and prejudice. *Journal of Personality & Social Psychology, 77*(l), 126–134.

Whyte, G. (2000). Groupthink. In A. E. Kazdin (Ed.), *Encyclopedia of psychology* (Vol. 4). Washington, DC: American Psychological Association.

Wickett, J. C., Vernon, P. A., & Lee, D. H. (2000). Relationships between factors of intelligence and brain volume. *Personality & Individual Differences, 29*(6), 1095–1122.

Widiger, T. A. (2005). Classification and diagnosis: Historical development and contemporary issues. In J. E. Maddux & B. A. Winstead (Eds.), *Psychopathology: Foundations for a contemporary understanding.* Mahwah, NJ: Erlbaum.

Wiederhold, B. K., & Wiederhold, M. D. (2004). *Virtual reality therapy for anxiety disorders.* Washington, DC: American Psychological Association.

Wiederman, M. W. (1999). Volunteer bias in sexuality research using college student participants. *Journal of Sex Research, 36*(1), 59–66.

Wiederman, M. W. (2001). Gender differences in sexuality: Perceptions, myths, and realities. *Family Journal-Counseling & Therapy for Couples & Families, 9*(4), 468–471.

Wilder, D. A., Simon, A. F., & Faith, M. (1996). Enhancing the impact of counterstereotypic information. *Journal of Personality & Social Psychology, 71*(2), 276–287.

Wilding, J., & Valentine, E. (1994a). Memory champions. *British Journal of Psychology, 85*(2), 231–244.

Wilding, J., & Valentine, E. (1994b). Mnemonic wizardry with the telephone directory: But stories are another story. *British Journal of Psychology, 85*(4), 501–509.

Wilhelm, J. L. (1976). *The search for superman.* New York: Simon & Schuster.

Wilkinson, G., Piccinelli, M., Roberts, S., Micciolo, R., et al. (1997). Lunar cycle and consultations for anxiety and depression in general practice. *International Journal of Social Psychiatry, 43*(1), 29–34.

Wilkinson, R. B. (1997). Interactions between self and external reinforcement in predicting depressive symptoms. *Behaviour Research & Therapy, 35*(4), 281–289.

Williams, D. G., & Morris, G. (1996). Crying, weeping or tearfulness in British and Israeli adults. *British Journal of Psychology, 87*(3), 479–505.

Williams, G., Cai, X. J., Elliott, J. C., & Harrold, J. A. (2004). Anabolic neuropeptides. *Physiology & Behavior. Special Reviews on Ingestive Science, 81*(2), 211–222.

Williams, J. M. (1995). Applied sport psychology: Goals, issues, and challenges. *Journal of Applied Sport Psychology, 7*(1), 81–91.

Williams, J. M. (2006). *Applied sport psychology: Personal growth to peak performance* (5th ed.). New York: McGraw-Hill.

Williams, L. J. (1995). Peripheral target recognition and visual field narrowing in aviators and nonaviators. *International Journal of Aviation Psychology, 5*(2), 215–232.

Williams, L. M., Senior, C., David, A. S., Loughland, C. M., et al. (2001). In search of the "Duchenne Smile": Evidence from eye movements. *Journal of Psychophysiology, 15*(2), 122–127.

Williams, N. (2002). The imposition of gender: Psychoanalytic encounters with genital atypicality. *Psychoanalytic Psychology, 19*(3), 455–474.

Williams, R. (1989). *The trusting heart: Great news about Type A behavior.* New York: Random House.

Williams, R., & Vinson, D. C. (2001). Validation of a single screening question for problem drinking. *Journal of Family Practice, 50*(4), 307–312.

Williams, R. L. (1975). The Bitch-100: A culture-specific test. *Journal of Afro-American Issues, 3,* 103–116.

Williams, R. L., Agnew, H. W., & Webb, W. B. (1964). Sleep patterns in young adults: An EEG study. *Electroencephalography & Clinical Neurophysiology, 17,* 376–381.

Williams, R. L., & Eggert, A. (2002). Notetaking predictors of test performance. *Teaching of Psychology, 29*(3), 234–236.

Williams, R. L., & Long, J. D. (1991). *Toward a self-managed life style.* Boston: Houghton Mifflin.

Williams, W. M., & Ceci, S. J. (1997). Are Americans becoming more or less alike? *American Psychologist, 52*(11), 1226–1235.

Willoughby, T., Wood, E., Desmarais, S., Sims, S., et al. (1997). Mechanisms that facilitate the effectiveness of elaboration strategies. *Journal of Educational Psychology, 89*(4), 682–685.

Wilson, F. L. (1995). The effects of age, gender, and ethnic/cultural background on moral reasoning. *Journal of Social Behavior & Personality, 10*(1), 67–78.

Wilson, G. T. (1987). Chemical aversion conditioning as a treatment for alcoholism: A re-analysis. *Behaviour Research and Therapy, 25*(6), 503–516.

Wilson, T. D. (2002). *Strangers to ourselves: Discovering the adaptive unconscious.* Cambridge, MA: Harvard University Press.

Winner, E. (2003). Creativity and talent. In M. H. Bornstein, L. Davidson, et al. (Eds.), *Well-being: Positive development across the life course.* Mahwah, NJ: Erlbaum.

Winningham, R. G., Hyman, I. E., & Dinnel, D. L. (2000). Flashbulb memories? The effects of when the initial memory report was obtained. *Memory, 8*(4), 209–216.

Wise, J. (1982). A gentle deterrent to vandalism. *Psychology Today,* Sept., 31–38.

Wise, R. A., & Rompre, P. P. (1989). Brain dopamine and reward. *An-*

nual Review of Psychology, 40, 191–225.

Witelson, S. F. (1991). Neural sexual mosaicism: Sexual differentiation of the human temporo-parietal region for functional asymmetry. *Psychoneuroendocrinology, 16*(1–3), 131–153.

Withers, N. W., Pulvirenti, L., Koob, G. F., & Gillin, J. C. (1995). Cocaine abuse and dependence. *Journal of Clinical Psychopharmacology, 15*(1), 63–78.

Witt, S. D. (1997). Parental influences on children's socialization to gender roles. *Adolescence, 32*(126), 253–259.

Wolfe, J. B. (1936). Effectiveness of token rewards for chimpanzees. *Comparative Psychology Monographs, 12*(5), Whole no. 60.

Wolpe, J. (1974). *The practice of behavior therapy* (2nd ed.). New York: Pergamon.

Wolpe, J., & Plaud, J. J. (1997). Pavlov's contributions to behavior therapy. *American Psychologist, 52*(9), 966–972.

Wolpin, M., Marston, A., Randolph, C., & Clothier, A. (1992). Individual difference correlates of reported lucid dreaming frequency and control. *Journal of Mental Imagery, 16*(3–4), 231–236.

Wolraich, M. L., Wilson, D. B., & White, J. W. (1995). The effect of sugar on behavior or cognition in children. *Journal of the American Medical Association, 274*(20), 1617–1621.

Wong, C. Y., Sommer, R., & Cook, E. J. (1992). The soft classroom 17 years later. *Journal of Environmental Psychology, 12*(4), 337–343.

Wong, J. L., & Whitaker, D. J. (1993). Depressive mood states and their cognitive and personality correlates in college students. *Journal of Clinical Psychology, 49*(5), 615–621.

Wood, E., & Willoughby, T. (1995). Cognitive strategies for test-taking. In E. Wood, V. Woloshyn, et al. (Eds.), *Cognitive strategy instruction for middle and high schools.* Cambridge, MA: Brookline.

Wood, J. M., & Bootzin, R. R. (1990). The prevalence of nightmares and their independence from anxiety. *Journal of Abnormal Psychology, 99*(1), 64–68.

Wood, J. M., Bootzin, R. R., Kihlstrom, J. F., & Schacter, D. L. (1992). Implicit and explicit memory for verbal information presented during sleep. *Psychological Science, 3*(4), 236–239.

Wood, W. & Eagly, A. H. (2002). A cross-cultural analysis of the behavior of women and men. *Psychological Bulletin, 128,* 699–727.

Woodruff-Pak, D. S. (2001). Eyeblink classical conditioning differentiates normal aging from Alzheimer's disease. *Integrative Physiological & Behavioral Science, 36*(2), 87–108.

Woods, D. W., Miltenberger, R. G., & Lumley, V. A. (1996). A simplified habit reversal treatment for pica-related chewing. *Journal of Behavior Therapy & Experimental Psychiatry, 27*(3), 257–262.

Woods, S. C., Schwartz, M. W, Baskin, D. G., & Seeley, R J. (2000). Food intake and the regulation of body weight. *Annual Review of Psychology, 51,* 255–277.

Woods, S. C., Seeley, R. J., & Porte, D. (1998). Signals that regulate food intake and energy homeostasis. *Science, 280*(5368), 1378–1383.

Woodward, J., & Goodstein, D. (1996). Conduct, misconduct and the structure of science. *American Scientist, 84*(5), 479–490.

Woody, S. R. (1996). Effects of focus of attention on anxiety levels and social performance of individuals with social phobia. *Journal of Abnormal Psychology, 105*(1), 61–69.

Work in America. (1973). Special Task Force, Department of Health, Education and Welfare. Cambridge, MA: MIT Press.

Worthen, J. B., & Marshall, P. H. (1996). Intralist and extralist sources of distinctiveness and the bizarreness effect. *American Journal of Psychology, 109*(2), 239–263.

Worthen, J. B., & Wade, C. E. (1999). Direction of travel and visiting team athletic performance: Support for a circadian dysrhythmia hypothesis. *Journal of Sport Behavior, 22*(2), 279–287.

Wright, D. B. (1993). Recall of the Hillsborough disaster over time: Systematic biases of "flashbulb" memories. *Applied Cognitive Psychology, 7*(2), 129–138.

Wright, T. A., & Cropanzano, R. (2000). Psychological well-being and job satisfaction as predictors of job performance. *Journal of Occupational Health Psychology, 5*(1), 84–94.

Wu, C. W. H., & Kaas, J. H. (2002). The effects of long-standing limb loss on anatomical reorganization of the somatosensory afferents in the brainstem and spinal cord. *Somatosensory & Motor Research, 19*(2), 153–163.

Wulf, G., Shea, C. H., & Matschiner, S. (1998). Frequent feedback enhances complex motor skill learning. *Journal of Motor Behavior, 30*(2), 180–192.

Wyatt, J. W., Posey, A., Welker, W., & Seamonds, C. (1984). Natural levels of similarities between identical twins and between unrelated people. *Skeptical Inquirer, 9,* 62–66.

Yagmurlu, B., Berument, S. K., & Celimli, S. (2005). The role of institution and home contexts in theory of mind development. *Journal of Applied Developmental Psychology, 26*(5), 521–537.

Yalom, I. D. (1980). *Existential psychotherapy.* New York: Basic.

Yardley, L. (1992). Motion sickness and perception. *British Journal of Psychology, 83*(4), 449–471.

Yarmey, A. D. (2003). Eyewitness identification: Guidelines and recommendations for identification procedures in the United States and in Canada. *Canadian Psychology, 44*(3), 181–189.

Yedidia, M. J., & MacGregor, B. (2001). Confronting the prospect of dying. *Journal of Pain & Symptom Management, 22*(4), 807–819.

Yeh, C. J. (2003). Age, acculturation, cultural adjustment, and mental health symptoms of Chinese, Korean, and Japanese immigrant youths. *Cultural Diversity and Ethnic Minority Psychology, 9*(1), 34–48.

Yehuda, R. (2002). Post-traumatic stress disorder. *New England Journal of Medicine, 346*(2), 108–114.

Yokota, F., & Thompson, K. M. (2000). Violence in G-rated animated films. *Journal of the American Medical Association, 283*(20), 2716.

Yontef, G. M. (1995). Gestalt therapy. In A. S. Gurman & S. B. Messer (Eds.), *Essential psychotherapies.* New York: Guilford.

Yoshida, M. (1993). Three-dimensional electrophysiological atlas created by computer mapping of clinical responses elicited on stimulation of human subcortical structures. *Stereotactic & Functional Neurosurgery, 60*(1–3), 127–134.

Yost, W. (2000). *Fundamentals of hearing: An introduction.* San Diego: Academic Press.

Yuille, J. C., & Daylen, J. (1998). The impact of traumatic events on eyewitness memory. In C. Thompson, D. Herrmann, et al. (Eds.), *Eyewitness memory: Theoretical and applied perspectives.* Mahwah, NJ: Erlbaum.

Zakzanis, K. K., & Young, D. A. (2001). Memory impairment in abstinent MDMA ("Ecstasy") users: A longitudinal investigation. *Neurology, 56*(7), 966–969.

Zametkin, A. J. (1995). Attention-deficit disorder: born to be hyperactive? *Journal of the American Medical Association, 273*(23), 1871–1874.

Zeidner, M. (1995). Adaptive coping with test situations: A review of the literature. *Educational Psychologist, 30*(3), 123–133.

Zeki, S. (1991). Cerebral akinetopsia (Visual motion blindness): A review. *Brain, 114,* 811–824.

Zelezny, L. C. (1999). Educational interventions that improve environmental behaviors: A meta-analysis. *Journal of Environmental Education, 31*(1), 5–14.

Zellner, D. A., Harner, D. E., & Adler, R. L. (1989). Effects of eating abnormalities and gender on perceptions of desirable body shape. *Journal of Abnormal Psychology, 98*(1), 93–96.

Zemishlany, Z., Aizenberg, D., & Weizman, A. (2001). Subjective effects of MDMA ("Ecstasy") on human sexual function. *European Psychiatry, 16*(2), 127–130.

Zetlin, A., & Murtaugh, M. (1990). Whatever happened to those with borderline IQs? *American Journal on Mental Retardation, 94*(5), 463–469.

Zhang, A. Y., & Snowden, L. R. (1999). Ethnic characteristics of mental disorders in five U.S. communities. *Cultural Diversity and Ethnic Minority Psychology, 5*(2), 134–146.

Zimbardo, P. G., Haney, C., & Banks, W. C. (1973). A Pirandellian prison. *New York Times Magazine,* April 8.

Zimbardo, P. G., Pilkonis, P. A., & Norwood, R. M. (1978). The social disease called shyness. In *Annual editions, personality and adjustment 78/79.* Guilford, CT: Dushkin.

Zimmerman, B. J. (1996a). Enhancing student academic and health functioning: A self-regulatory perspective. *School Psychology Quarterly, 11*(1), 47–66.

Zimmerman, J. D. (1996b). A prosocial media strategy. *American Journal of Orthopsychiatry, 66*(3), 354–362.

Zohar, D. (1998). An additive model of test anxiety: Role of exam-specific expectations. *Journal of Educational Psychology, 90,* 330–340.

Zola, S. M., & Squire, L. R. (2001). Relationship between magnitude of damage to the hippocampus and impaired recognition in monkeys. *Hippocampus, 11,* 92–98.

Zucker, A. (1995). Rights and the dying. In H. Wass & R. A. Neimeyer (Eds.), *Dying: Facing the facts.* Washington, DC: Taylor & Francis.

Zuckerman, M. (1990). The psychophysiology of sensation seeking. *Journal of Personality, 58*(1), 313–345.

Zuckerman, M. (1996). Item revisions in the Sensation Seeking Scale Form V (SSS-V). *EDRA: Environmental Design Research Association, 20*(4), 515.

Zuckerman, M. (2000). Sensation seeking. In A. Kazdin (Ed.), *Encyclopedia of psychology.* Washington, DC: American Psychological Association.

Zuckerman, M. (2002). Genetics of sensation seeking. In J. Benjamin, R. P. Ebstein, et al. (Eds.), *Molecular genetics and the human personality.* Washington, DC: American Psychiatric Publishing.

Zuckerman, M., Kieffer, S. C., & Knee, C. R. (1998). Consequences of self-handicapping. *Journal of Personality & Social Psychology, 74*(6), 1619–1628.

Zuckerman, M., & Tsai, F.-R. (2005). Costs of self-handicapping. *Journal of Personality, 73*(2), 411–442.

Zuwerink, J. R., Devine, P. G., Monteith, M. J., & Cook, D. A. (1996). Prejudice toward blacks: With and without compunction? *Basic & Applied Social Psychology, 18*(2), 131–150.

Photo Credits

This page constitutes an extension of the copyright page. We have made every effort to trace the ownership of all copyrighted material and to secure permission from copyright holders. In the event of any question arising as to the use of any material, we will be pleased to make the necessary corrections in future printings. Thanks are due to the following authors, publishers, and agents for permission to use the material indicated.

Introduction. 1: Eric Audras/PhotoAlto/Jupiterimages

Chapter 1. 11: Corbis Images/Jupiterimages; **12:** Jeff Greenberg/PhotoEdit; **15:** bottom left, Anne-Marie Weber/Getty Images; top left, Mireille Vauier/Woodfin Camp/PictureQuest; top right, Eric A. Wessman/Stock, Boston Inc./PictureQuest; bottom right, Greg Johnston/Lonely Planet Images; **16:** Anna Clopet/Corbis; **17:** Archives of the History of American Psychology, University of Akron; **18:** left, Archives of the History of American Psychology, University of Akron; right, Archives of the History of American Psychology, University of Akron; **19:** Neena Leen/Life Magazine/Timepix/Getty Images; **20:** all, Archives of the History of American Psychology, University of Akron; **21:** left, Archives of the History of American Psychology, University of Akron; right, Bettmann/Corbis; **24:** Joseph Sohm/Stock, Boston; **25:** Universal Studios/The Kobal Collection; **29:** Dan McCoy/Rainbow; **31:** Baron Hugo van Lawick/National Geographic Society; **38:** Esbin-Anderson/The Image Works; **43:** Bettmann/Corbis; **44:** Dennis Coon; **47:** John Nordell/The Image Works

Chapter 2. 51: Arthur Toga, UCLA/Photo Researchers, Inc.; **56:** Spencer Grant/PhotoEdit; **59:** Phanie/Photo Researchers, Inc.; **61:** AJPhoto/Photo Researchers, Inc.; **62:** left, Huntington Magnetic Resonance Center, Pasadena, CA; right, Washington University School of Medicine, St. Louis; **63:** Washington University School of Medicine, St. Louis; **64:** Courtesy of Richard Haier, University of California, Irvine; **67:** Ronald C. James; **70:** Shaywitz et al., 1995 NMR Research/Yale Medical School; **75:** left, Getty Images; right, Amanda Edwards/Getty Images; **76:** Getty Images; **78:** Bob Daemmrich/The Image Works; **80:** Custom Medical Stock Photo

Chapter 3. 83: FogStock/Index Stock Imagery; **84:** Biophoto Associates/Photo Researchers, Inc.; **86:** Myrleen Ferguson Cate/PhotoEdit; **87:** Petit Format/Photo Researchers, Inc.; **88:** left, Ted Wood; right, Michael Newman/PhotoEdit; **89:** Anna Kaufman Moon/Stock, Boston; **91:** Margaret Miller/Photo Researchers, Inc.; **92:** top, From A.N. Meltzoff & M.K. Moore, "Imitation of facial and manual gestures by human neonates," Science, 1977,198, 75–78; bottom left, Courtesy of David Linton; Rubberball Productions/Getty Images; **93:** Michael Newman/PhotoEdit; **95:** Chris Lowe/Index Stock Imagery; **96:** left, Nina Leen/TimePix; right, Michael Newman/PhotoEdit; **97:** Ryan McVay/Getty Images; **99:** left, Courtesy of Harry Harlow, U. of WI Primate Laboratory; right, Brownie Harris/Corbis; **102:** D. L. Baldwin/Photo Network; **104:** Jeff Greenberg/PhotoEdit; **108:** Gary Conner/Index Stock Imagery; **109:** Tony Freeman/PhotoEdit; **110:** left, Yves De Braine/stockphoto.com; right, FogStock LLC/Index Stock Imagery; **116:** SW Production/Index Stock Imagery

Chapter 4. 121: Michael Newman/PhotoEdit; **123:** Sarah Putnum/Index Stock Imagery; **124:** Jeff Greenberg; **125:** Jonathan Nourok/PhotoEdit; **128:** David Young-Wolff/PhotoEdit; **131:** Los Angeles County Department of Children's Services; **133:** left, Bettmann/Corbis; right, David Young-Wolff/PhotoEdit; **135:** Michael Siluk/The Image Works; **137:** Bananastock/Jupiterimages; **143:** Royalty-Free/Corbis; **144:** Tony Ranze/AFP/Getty Images; **145:** left, Lori Adamski Peek/Getty Images; right, Jeff Greenberg/Index Stock Imagery; **147:** Michael Newman/PhotoEdit; **148:** Blackmore 1993; **149:** Craig Aurness/Corbis; **150:** Esbin/Anderson/The Image Works

Chapter 5. 155: Douglas Kirkland/Corbis; **158:** © Robert Rattner; **163:** Omnikron/Photo Researchers, Inc.; **165:** Tom McCarthy/PhotoEdit; **167:** Michael Newman/PhotoEdit; **169:** Jon L. Barken/Index Stock Imagery; **173:** Dr. G. Oran Bredberg/SPL/Photo Researchers, Inc.; **174:** Richard Costana, *Discover Magazine*, 1993; **175:** Tim Davis/Getty Images; **179:** JSC/NASA; **180:** Roger Ressmeyer/Corbis; **182:** Herve Donnezan/Photo Researchers, Inc.; **184:** Esbin-Anderson/Photo Network/PictureQuest

Chapter 6. 188: © 2006 "Pintos" by Bev Doolittle®, courtesy of The Greenwich Workshop, Inc. www.greenwichworkshop.com; **190:** left, "Marilyn Numerisee #420" © Yvaral 1990, Courtesy Circle Gallery; left, Mark Richards/PhotoEdit; **194:** E.R. Degginger/Animals Animals; **195:** Mark Richards/PhotoEdit; **196:** Bob Western; **197:** © 2003 Magic Eye Inc.; **199:** Dennis Coon; **200:** M. C. Escher's "Convex and Concave" © 2002 Cordon Art B. V. Baarn—Holland. All rights reserved; **202:** Dennis Coon; **203:** Bettmann/Corbis; **204:** left, Mark McKenna; right, David Young-Wolff/PhotoEdit; **205:** Andrew G. Wood/Photo Researchers, Inc.; **207:** Dennis Coon; **209:** Bob Daemmrich/The Image Works; **211:** Randy Ury/Corbis; **212:** The Museum of Modern Art, New York; **214:** Susan Van Etten/PhotoEdit; **215:** Dennis Coon; **217:** AP/Wide World Photo

Chapter 7. 223: Image Source/SuperStock; **225:** Joel Gordon, 1991; **226:** Timothy Ross/The Image Works; **228:** Yale Joel/TimePix/Getty Images; **229:** Martin M. Potker, Taurus; **231:** Detroit Institute of the Arts/SuperStock; **235:** Michael Newman/PhotoEdit; **238:** Dennis Coon; **239:** Dennis Coon; **240:** Dennis Coon; **240:** Dennis Coon; **245:** National Library of Medicine; **248:** top, The Everett Collection; bottom, Mark C. Burnett/Stock, Boston; **251:** Creasource/Series/PictureQuest; **254:** left, "Marijuana and the Brain," *Science News*, Vol. 143; right, Courtesy of Dr. Lester Grinspoon/Harvard Medical School; **256:** Courtesy of Maryanne Mott

Chapter 8. 261: Jeff Greenberg/PhotoEdit; **267:** Dennis Coon; **273:** Yale Joel/Life Magazine/TimePix/Getty Images; **275:** Chimp-O-Mat, Yukes Regional Primate Resesarch Center, Emory University; **279:** Christoph Wilhelm/Getty Images; **281:** Carleton Ray/Photo Researchers, Inc.; **283:** Tony Freeman/PhotoEdit; **288:** top, Mark Andersen/Rubberball/Jupiterimages; bottom, Courtesy of Albert Bandura/Stanford University; **289:** Tony Freeman/PhotoEdit; **291:** Rubberball/SuperStock

Chapter 9. 296: Richard Heinzen/SuperStock; **299:** Malcolm Linton/Liaison/Getty Images; **301:** Wilder Penfield, *The Excitable Cortex in Conscious Man*, 1958. Courtesy of the author and Charles C. Thomas Publisher, Springfield, Illinois; **302:** bottom, Tom Carter/Index Stock Imagery; top, Dennis Coon; **303:** A. Ramey/PhotoEdit; **307:** SW Production/Index Stock Imagery; **314:** Paul Conklin/PhotoEdit; **315:** Andy Reynolds/Getty Images; **316:** Rick Martin/San Jose Mercury News; **318:** AP/Wide World Photo; **319:** © Tulving, E. (1989). Remembering and knowing the past. *American Scientist*, 77(4), 361–367; **320:** Jeffrey L. Rotman/Corbis; **322:** Robbie Jack/Corbis; **324:** Ulrike Welsch

Chapter 10. 329: Dave Umberger/AP/Wide World Photo; **330:** AP/Wide World Photo; **331:** B. Busco/Getty Images; **332:** Dennis Coon; **333:** Brian Bailey/Getty Images; **334:** Robert Bowman/Austin MacRae Photography; **336:** Javier Plerin/Latin Stock/Corbis; **338:** top, Guy Edwardes/Getty Images; bottom, Myrleen Ferguson Cate/PhotoEdit; **340:** Robin Nelson/PhotoEdit; **345:** left, Archiv/Photo Researchers, Inc.; right, Courtesy of Cray Computer; **348:** left, Popperfoto/Retrofile; **351:** top, Roger Viollet/Getty Images; center, T. J. Floian/Rainbow; bottom, John Barr/Getty Images

Chapter 11. 362: Kaluzny-Thatcher/Getty Images; **364:** David Young-Wolff/Photo Edit, Inc.; **367:** AP/Wide World Photo; **369:** Hulton-Deusch Collection/Corbis; **372:** bottom left, Dan McCoy/Rainbow; bottom right, Christiana Dittmann/Rainbow; top, Mobile Press Register/Getty Images; **373:** Richard Green; **374:** Stan Godlweski/Getty Images; **380:** Getty Images

Chapter 12. 387: Mike Brinson/Getty Images; **389:** David Austen/Woodfin Camp & Associates; **392:** left, Courtesy of Neal E. Miller**,** Rockefeller University; right, John Sholtis, Rockefeller University; **393:** Royalty-Free/Corbis; **396:** left, Janet Hass/Rainbow; right, AP/Wide World Photo; **397:** Evan Agostini/Getty Images; **398:** Alain Evrard/Photo Researchers, Inc.; **400:** Courtesy of Harry F. Harlow; **401:** Jeffrey L. Rotman; **404:** left, David Frazier/The Image Works; right, Alex Bartel/SPL/Photo Researchers, Inc.; **405:** AP/Wide World Photo; **407:** Reuters/Corbis; **408:** left, Rick Friedman/Corbis; right, Gregory A. Beaumont/® The Great Arcata to Ferndale World Championship Cross Country Kinetic Sculpture Race; **412:** Bob Daemmrich/The Image Works; **415:** Dennis Coon; **416:** top, Gary Conner/PhotoEdit; center, Sergei Karpukhgin/

Reuters/Corbis; bottom, Amy Etra/PhotoEdit; **418:** Michael Grecco/Stock, Boston/PictureQuest; **419:** Dennis Coon

Chapter 13. 426: David Lo Tai Wai/Getty Images; **433:** left, Robert Caputo/Stock, Boston; right, Steve Dunwell Photography, Inc./Index Stock Imagery/PictureQuest; **434:** left, Kevin Fitzgerald/Getty Images; right, Vario Press/Imapress/The Image Works; **444:** ABC-TV/The Kobal Collection/Brakha, Moshe; **448:** Leonard Lessin/Photo Researchers, Inc.

Chapter 14. 458: Andre Forget/AP/Wide World Photo; **460:** left, Matthew Mendelsohn/Corbis; right, Michael Newman/PhotoEdit; **461:** O'Brien Productions/Corbis; **466:** Eleanor Bentall/Corbis; **467:** Alris Upitis/stockphoto.com; **470:** "All is Vanity" by Allen Gilbert; **471:** Bettmann/Corbis; **474:** Alison Wright/Stock, Boston; **475:** fotostock/SuperStock; **476:** David Young-Wolff/PhotoEdit; **478:** Laura Dwight/PhotoEdit; **481:** photolibrary/PictureQuest; **484:** Zia Soleil/Getty Images; **486:** David McNew/Newsmakers/Getty Images; **491:** Digital Vision/Getty Images

Chapter 15. 496: Royalty-Free/Corbis; **498:** left, Darren Robb/Getty Images; right, Jeffery Allan Salter/Corbis; **502:** left, Daniel G. Lavoie/Corbis; right, Bob Daemmrich/The Image Works; **504:** Ken Cedeno/Corbis; **506:** Tony Anderson/Getty Images; **507:** Royalty-Free/Corbis; **512:** Scott Cunningham/Getty Images; **513:** Stephen Rose/Rainbow; **514:** Barbara Stitzer/PhotoEdit; **517:** Purestock/SuperStock; **518:** Morton Beebe/Corbis; **519:** Dan McCoy/Rainbow; **520:** Hisham Ibrahim/Getty Images; **522:** Tim Pannell/Corbis; **524:** Tom Stewart/Corbis

Chapter 16. 531: Tim Pannell/Corbis; **533:** Rick Friedman/Corbis; **536:** left, American Psychiatric Association; right, Scott Camazine/Photo Researchers, Inc.; **537:** Courtesy of Ulrike Kantor Gallery; **541:** Cary Wolinsky/Stock, Boston; **542:** Courtesy of Robert Hare; **544:** Brent Stirton/Getty Images; **545:** bottom left, Bettmann/Corbis; bottom right, Dennis Coon; right, Paula Bronstein/Getty Images; **546:** Bruce Ayres/Getty Images; **550:** top, Benelux Press/Getty Images; bottom, Bettmann/Corbis; **551:** top, Joe Sohm/The Image Works; bottom, Alan Oddie/PhotoEdit, Inc.; **553:** left, Peter Granser/Laif/Aurora Photos; right, Grunnitis/Photo Researchers, Inc.; **554:** bottom, Bruce Ely; top, Curt Borgwardt/Corbis Sygma; **556:** Derik Bayes/Courtesy Guttman-Maclay Life Picture Service; **557:** left, Dennis Brack/stockphoto.com; right, The Brookhaven National Laboratory; **560:** Darren Robb/Getty Images; **561:** Dan McCoy/Rainbow; **563:** Tony Freeman/PhotoEdit

Chapter 17. 569: Zigy Kalunv/Getty Images; **571:** Danielle Pellegrini/Photo Researchers, Inc.; **572:** left, Mary Evans Picture Library/Photo Researchers, Inc.; center, Bettmann/Corbis; right, Archive/Photo Researchers, Inc.; **574:** Courtesy of Dr. Natalie Rogers; **576:** Getty Images; **579:** Christopher A. Record/AP/Wide World Photo; **580:** Courtesy of Albert Bandura; **581:** left, Courtesy of Larry Hodges, Thomas and Rob Kooper; right, Georgia Tech Telephoto; **587:** Jon Bradley/Getty Images; **591:** Gilles Mingasson/Getty Images; **593:** left, Courtesy of Rodger Casier; right, Will & Deni McIntyre/Photo Researchers, Inc.; **594:** Peter Southwick/Stock, Boston; **595:** Ed Kashi/Corbis; **597:** Sheila Terry/Photo Researchers, Inc.

Chapter 18. 604: Paul Chesley/Getty Images; **606:** Bonnie Kamin/PhotoEdit; **608:** Spencer Grant/PhotoEdit; **609:** AFP/Getty Images; **610:** Altrendo Images/Getty Images; **612:** Mark Richards/Photo Edit; **613:** Jeff Greenberg/Rainbow; **614:** John W. Gertz/zefa/Corbis; **615:** Ralf-Finn Hestoft/Corbis; **618:** Anthony B. Woods/Stock, Boston; **619:** Roy Morsch/Corbis; **622:** Scenes from the film "Obedience," by Stanley Milgram, The Pennsylvania State University Audio Visual Services. Used by permission; **623:** Rubberball/Jupiterimages; **626:** Michael Newman/PhotoEdit

Chapter 19. 631: Nick Clements/Getty Images; **633:** Pralash Singh/AFP/Getty Images; **634:** Bob Llewellen/Pictor International Ltd./PictureQuest; **635:** Joel Gordon; **637:** Greg Smith/Corbis; **638:** Bettmann/Corbis; **642:** NBAE/Getty Images; **643:** David Young-Wolff/ PhotoEdit; **644:** AP/Wide World Photo; **645:** Mary Kate Denny/PhotoEdit; **646:** Jonathan Nourok/PhotoEdit; **647:** Getty Images; **648:** Jon Love/Getty Images; **651:** The Photo Works/Photo Researchers, Inc.; **653:** Robert Brenner/PhotoEdit, Inc.

Chapter 20. 661: Jose L. Pelaez/Corbis; **663:** Courtesy of the General Electric Company; **665:** Bill Aron/PhotoEdit, Inc.; **667:** Yellow Dog Productions/Getty Images; **670:** F. Pedrick/The Image Works; **671:** Joel Gordon; **673:** Laura Dwight/Corbis; **674:** top left, Daniel Barry/Getty Images; left, Jeff Greenberg/PhotoEdit; right, UNEP/Photog/The Image Works; **676:** top and bottom, Peter Ginter/Material World; **677:** Cleo/PhotoEdit; **679:** Bill Aron/PhotoEdit, Inc.; **681:** Getty Images; **682:** Tony Savion/The Image Works; **683:** top, Oliver Maire/Corbis; bottom, Richard Pasley/Stock, Boston

Appendix. 690: Dennis Coon

Name Index

Abe, J. A., 94
Abel, T, 277, 320
Abelson, R. P., 213
Abernethy, A.P, 239
Abi-Dargham, 98, 556
Abraham, J., 108
Abraham, M., 499
Abrahamson, D. J., 451
Abrahamson, L. S., 451
Abrams, D. B, 248
Abramson, L. Y., 512, 515
Abuhamdeh, S., 684
Accordino, D. B., 467
Accordino, M. P., 467
Acebo, C, 227
Achermann, P., 229
Adams, B., 403
Adams, G., 538
Adams, H. B., 241
Adams, H. E., 446
Adams, J., 241, 344, 357
Adams, M., 312, 313
Adams, P. A., 550
Adams-Curtis, L. E., 446, 650
Addis, M E., 306
Addis, M. E., 637
Addison, T., 650
Adelman, P. K., 419, 420
Adityanjee, 549
Adler, A., 21, 397, 472, 473
Adorno, T., 641
Aeschbach, D., 561
Ahissar, M., 202
Ahmad, S. A., 375
Ainsworth, M., 97
Aizenberg, D., 246
Ajzen, I., 632, 634
Akerstedt, T., 226, 228, 403
Akert, R. M., 623
al'Absi, M., 520
Alarcon, R. D., 23
Alberti, R., 628
Alberto, P. A., 285
Albonetti, S, 555
Alcock, J. E., 214, 216
Alexander, M. P., 67
Alfeld-Liro, C., 481
Alicke, M. D., 614
Allan, J. S., 403
Allen, J. J. B., 129, 159
Allen, J. L., 654
Allen, K., 523, 527
Allen, M., 682
Allgower, A., 498
Allhusen, V., 89
Allik, J., 462
Allin, J. D., 365
Alloy, L. B., 512
Allport, G., 464, 640
Alonso, Y., 396
Alpert, M., 550
Alpert, N. N., 332
Alsaker, F. D., 133
Altemeyer, B., 641
Althof, S. E., 451, 452
Altman, L. K., 449
Alvarado, N., 488
Alvino, J., 111, 372
Alvir, J. M. J., 592
Ama, E., 657
Amabile, T., 357, 408
Amato, P. R., 89
Ambady, N., 353
American Psychological Association, 23
Ancis, J. R., 538
Anderegg, D., 352
Anderson, 03, 650
Anderson, C. A., 289, 505, 644, 648
Anderson, J. R., 346
Anderson, K. B., 648
Anderson, M. C., 316, 317
Anderson, N. B., 644
Anderson, S, 513
Andrasik, F., 518
Andrews, D. W., 454
Andrews, G., 548
Andrykowski, M. A., 395
Annett, M., 80
Anowak, J., 590
Anshel, H. M., 685
Anthony, W. A., 596
Antle, M. C., 402
Antoni, M. H., 524
Anwyl, R., 320
Appelbaum, A. G., 211
Appelbaum, P. S., 554
Apt, C., 452
Arauz, R. M., 365
Arbona, C. B., 580
Areily, D., 6
Armeli, S., 521
Arnau, R. C., 184
Arndt, J., 129, 159
Arnett, J., 132, 134, 135
Arnold, K. D., 406
Arntz, A., 56, 182
Aron, A. P., 419
Aronoff, J., 416
Aronson, E., 614, 623, 635, 646
Aronson, J., 643
Arthur, W., 465
Ary, D, 500
Asch, S. E., 619, 622
Ash, D. W., 322
Ashanasy, N. M., 422
Ashby, F. G., 333
Asher, E. R., 522
Ashman, A. E., 104, 105
Ashner, E. R, 422
Aslin, R. N., 195
Assanand, S., 394, 395
Aston-Jones, G., 246
Asunción, B., 277
Athenasiou, R., 444
Atkinson, A. P., 414
Attanucci, J., 137
Aussprung, J., 515
Austen, D., 389
Ayers, L., 351
Ayllon, T., 275, 582
Azrin, N. H., 275, 285

Baard, P. P., 407
Baberg, H. T., 245
Babulas, V., 555
Babyak, M. A., 499
Bachan, K., 311
Bachman, J. G., 123
Backs-Dermott, G. J., 584
Badner, J. A., 561
Baer, D., 579
Baer, J. M., 347, 348, 351, 352
Bagley, C., 440
Bahrick H. P., 312
Bahrke, M. S., 76
Bailey, J. M., 439
Baillargeon, R., 111, 113
Bain, S. K., 365
Bajracharaya, S. M., 445
Baker, T. B., 578
Bakich, I., 451
Bakker, F. C., 333
Baldo, O., 451
Balk, D. E., 488
Balkin, T. J., 230
Ball, B., 593
Ball, T., 308
Ballinger, K. M., 527
Baltes, 99, 668
Balts, P., 142, 144, 145
Banaji, M. R., 613, 640
Bandura, A., 268, 285, 288, 476, 478, 503–504, 644, 648, 649
Bank, B. J., 126, 615
Banker, B. S., 645
Banks, A., 439
Banks, T., 648
Banks, W. C., 606
Banton, J. G., 648
Bar-Eli, M., 684
Bar-Hillel, M., 43
Bar-Tal, D., 641
Barabasz, A., 237
Baranek, G. T., 129
Barber, T. X., 239
Barclay, A. M., 416
Bard, P., 418
Bargh, J. A., 417, 620
Barker, E. A., 44
Barker, E. T., 132
Barlow, D. H., 451, 543, 545, 547, 588
Barnet, A. B., 89, 129, 377
Barnet, R. J., 89, 129, 377
Barnett, R. C., 140
Baron, R. A., 605, 664
Baron, R. S., 619, 620, 657
Barowsky, E. L., 519
Barrett, D., 258, 343
Barrett, L. F., 500
Barrick, M. R., 465, 664
Barroso, C., 657
Barsalou, L. W., 300
Barsky, S. H., 254
Barth, A., 519
Bartholow, B. D., 290
Bartlett, J. C., 203
Bartol, A. M., 680
Bartol, C. R., 680
Bartoshuk, L., 176
Bartoshuk, L. M., 176
Bartz, W. R., 14, 45, 252
Basadur, M., 358
Basch, J., 248
Baskin, D. G., 390–391, 392
Bassetti, C. L., 229
Basson, R., 436
Baston, C. D., 654
Batejat, D. M., 228
Bates, J. E., 101
Bates, T. C., 379
Bath, H., 117
Batra, L., 583
Batterham, R. L., 391
Bauer, V. K., 561
Baum, A., 674, 675, 677
Baumeister, R. F., 5, 22, 462
Baumrind, D., 105
Baur, K., 398, 427, 438, 444
Bavaria, A. J., 13
Baydoun, R., 488
Baylis, G. C., 298
Bazzini, D. G., 246, 614
Beach, F. A., 441
Beak, S. A., 391
Bear, J., 416
Bearison, D. J., 114, 115
Bearman, P. S., 447
Beaton, S., 351
Beauchamp P.H., 685
Beaulieu, C. M. J., 608, 609
Beck, A. T., 514, 564, 584, 585
Beck, B., 392
Beck, B. L., 5
Beck, R. C, 236
Beck, R. C., 388, 406
Becker, S. W., 655
Beebe, B., 107
Beeman, M. J., 67
Bégue, L., 656
Behl, L. E., 129
Beiser, M., 518
Belcher, J. C., 680
Bell, T., 316
Bellebaum, C, 268
Bellezza, F. S., 310
Bellisle, F., 175
Belohlav, J. A., 666
Belsham, B., 556
Belsky, J., 89, 98, 126
Bem, S., 434
Ben-Abba, E., 43
Ben-Ari, A., 520
Ben-Shakhar, G., 43, 413
Benbow, C. P., 80
Benedetti, F., 38
Benedict, J. G., 576
Benet, A., 363
Benjafield, J. G., 18
Benloucif, S., 89
Bennet, E. L., 89
Bennett, A. K., 597, 598
Bennett, E. A., 681
Bennett, S., 212
Bensley, L., 290
Benson, E., 175, 340
Bentley, D. L., 671
Benton, A. L., 323
Berchick, R. J., 564
Beresford, J. M., 417
Berg, B., 491
Berglund, B., 674
Berko, E. H., 415
Berkowitz, L., 619
Berliner, L., 443
Berman, S., 108
Bernat, J. A, 446
Berne, E., 591
Bernieri, F., 86
Bernstein, H. J., 317
Berry, J. W., 518, 614
Berschied, E., 613, 616
Bertholf, M., 490
Berthoz, A., 331
Bertsch, G. J., 283
Berument, S. K., 111
Betancur, C., 80
Bhatt, R. S., 157
Bialystock, E., 337
Bickman, L., 606, 619
Bieliauskas, L. M., 40
Bigelow, A. E., 90
Biggers, J., 402
Biglan, A., 500
Bigler, E. D., 73, 319
Bilu, Y., 43
Binder, J. L., 590
Binet, A., 365
Binik, Y. M., 441
Binks, P. G., 226
Biondi, M., 497, 524
Birch, H. G., 126
Birch, J., 168

Biro, F. M., 445
Birren, J. E., 141, 145
Bjork, R. A., 48, 226, 238, 239, 241, 406
Blackmore, C., 148
Blackmore, S., 14, 258
Blackwell, D. L., 485, 614
Blair, I. V., 640
Blake, D. M., 156, 181
Blakely, G., 669
Blakemore, C., 204
Blakeslee, S., 126
Blanke, D. M., 148
Blanton, H., 613
Blascovich, J., 523, 527
Block, J., 433
Blok, S. V., 334
Blood, A. J., 73
Bloom, J. W., 577
Bloom, R., 405
Blum, J. S., 422, 614
Blumberg, M. S., 32
Blunt, A., 6
Boals, A., 527
Bockting, W. O., 438
Boergers, J., 564
Bohannon, J. N., 107
Bohart, A. C., 574
Bokenkamp, E. D., 396
Boland, J. E., 205
Bollini, A., 555, 556–558, 593
Bonanno, G. A., 422
Bond, R., 620
Bongard, S., 520
Bonham, V., 383, 644, 657
Bonifazi, D. Z., 516
Boodoo, G., 368
Book, H. E., 573
Booker, J. M., 561
Booth-LaForce, C., 89
Bootzin, R. R., 48, 232–233
Borman, W. C., 663, 664, 665
Bornstein, M. H., 86, 87, 104
Bornstein, R. F., 534
Borod, J. C., 66, 67
Borrie, R. A., 241
Boschker, M. S. J., 333
Bouchard, T. J., Jr., 368, 467
Bouchoux, A., 246
Bourhis, R. Y., 641, 663
Boutros, N. N., 52, 61, 67
Bovbjerg, D. H., 265, 395
Bowe, F., 680
Bower, G., 300, 312, 314, 317, 324
Bower, J. E., 498, 501, 505, 522
Bower, M. L., 91
Bower, T. G., 91
Bowers, K. S., 239, 303
Boykin, A. W., 368
Brack, G. L., 528
Bradley, L. J., 637
Bradley, L. P., 87, 89
Bradley, M. M., 542
Bradley, R., 588
Bradley, R. H., 89, 90
Braffman, W., 237
Braid, J., 237
Bramsen, I., 546
Brandon, T. H., 291
Brannick, M. T., 488
Brannon, L., 143, 144, 497
Bransford, J. D., 111, 334, 342
Bratko, D., 401
Braun, A. R., 230, 246
Brawman-Mintzer, O., 543
Bray, S. R., 685
Breakwell, G., 184
Breedlove, S. M., 431
Brehm, S. S., 432, 608, 614, 619
Breier, A., 593
Breivik, G., 403
Brenner, V., 285
Breslau, N., 247, 546
Bressi, C., 555
Brewer, J. S., 442
Brewer, K. R., 288
Brice, P., 650
Bridges, L. J., 94
Bridwell, A. M., 103, 683
Brief, A. P., 667, 668
Briere, J., 542
Brim, O. G., 139
Bringham, J. C., 682
Brinkman, H., 608
Britton, B. K., 6
Brock, T. C., 634
Brody, N., 369, 371, 377, 381
Brooks, F. R., 547
Brooks-Gunn, J., 95, 133
Brothen, T., 4
Brotto, L. A., 436
Broughton, R, 334
Brower, A. M., 249
Brower, K. J., 76
Brown, A. M., 91
Brown, A. S., 555
Brown, B. B., 671
Brown, C., 564, 590
Brown, E., 189
Brown, P., 534
Brown, R., 248
Brown, R. L., 244
Brown, R. T., 6
Brown, S. A., 251
Brown, S. L., 528
Brown, T. D., 358, 644
Browne, K., 443
Brownell, K. D., 394, 395
Bruce, D., 323
Bruch, M. A., 415, 491
Brunner, J., 91
Bryan, A., 251
Bryan, J. H., 289
Bryant, D. M., 374
Bucci, W., 573
Buchanan, R. W., 593
Bucholz, K. K., 97
Buchwald, A., 486
Buck, L. A., 174, 571
Buckelew, S. P., 519
Buckhout, R., 218
Budak, F., 379
Budney, A. J., 254
Buffalo, E. A., 318
Bugelski, R., 640
Bugental, J. F. T., 21
Bührer, M., 519
Bundrick, C.M., 480
Bunting, M. F., 181
Burchinal, M. R., 100
Burgess, C. A., 238
Burgess, P., 545
Burgner, D., 611
Burka, J. B., 5
Burke, M. J., 667
Burke, R. J., 502
Burkman, L. J., 254
Burlet, A., 392
Burlingame, G. M., 586, 600
Burnett, R. C., 334
Burns, D. D., 584, 596
Burns, J., 214, 216
Burrows, L., 180
Burton, C. M., 527
Burtt, 307
Bushman, B. J., 289, 290, 505, 644, 648, 650
Buss, A., 491, 492
Buss, D., 617
Buss, D. M., 409, 460, 461, 613, 618
Butcher, J. N., 487, 532
Butkovic, A., 401
Butler, J. C., 641
Butler, R., 399
Buunk, B. P., 505
Buyer, L. S., 358
Bybee, D., 482
Byers, E. S., 453
Byravan, A., 435
Byrne, S. M., 397, 605, 619, 657
Byrnes, J. P., 37
Cabanieu, G., 89
Cadinur, M., 643
Caggiano, J., 271
Cahan, E. D., 369
Cahill, S. P., 581
Cahusac, P. M. B., 410
Calapp, J. W., 680
Caldwell, B. M., 90
Calhoun, J., 672
Calhoun, J. B., 528
Calhoun, K. S., 446
Calhoun, L. G., 528
Calkins, M., 20
Callaghan, T., 111
Calmels, M.-N., 172
Calment, J., 142
Camara, W. J., 448
Cameron, L. D., 183, 527
Cammann, C., 606, 667
Campbell, B., 381
Campbell, F. A., 377
Campbell, J. B., 463
Campbell, J. D., 462
Campbell, L., 239, 381
Campbell, M. A., 317
Campbell, S., 325
Campbell, W. K., 419, 462
Campfield, L. A., 390
Campion, M. A., 408, 669
Campos, A., 4, 324
Campos, J. J., 195
Camras, L. A., 94
Canda, E. R., 147
Canivez, G. L., 368
Canli, T., 410
Cann, A., 528
Cannon, W., 390, 418
Cao, Y, 58
Caplan, P. J., 534
Capron, C., 377
Capuzzi, D., 587
Carbonell, O. A., 98
Cardoso, S. H., 72
Carducci, B. J., 491
Carey, C., 254
Carey, D. P., 164
Carey, J. C., 402
Carlin, A., 580
Carlsmith, J. M., 636
Carlson, C. L., 128
Carlson, J. G., 581
Carlson, M., 648
Carlson, N. R., 53, 68, 72, 75, 169, 177, 178
Carmichael-Olsen, H., 87
Carnahan, H., 276
Carnegie Corporation, 89
Carney, R., 325
Carpenter, J., 247
Carpenter, K. M., 588
Carpenter, S., 251
Carrigan, M. H., 581
Carroll, F., 484
Carroll, J. M., 414
Carroll, L., 309, 550
Carrougher, G. J., 184
Carskadon, M. A., 227
Carter, N., 519
Carter, W. E., 254
Cartwright, R., 236, 256, 257, 258
Caruso, D. R., 422
Carver, L., 128
Casey, P., 546
Caspi, A., 105, 460
Cassaday, H. J., 314
Cassano, G. B., 594
Castro, C. A., 246, 546
Castro, J. R., 127, 467
Castro, S. D., 376
Catalano, L. D., 506
Catalano, R., 506
Cattani-Thompson, K., 588
Cattell, R. B., 464
Cautela, J. R., 578, 597, 598
Ceci, S, 377, 384
Cecil, H, 248
Celimli, S., 111
Centers for Disease Control (CDC), 392
Cervone, D., 476, 483
Cesena, J., 127
Chabas, C, 334
Chabris, C., 210
Chakos, M. H., 592
Chamberlin, J., 594, 598
Chambers, R. A., 244
Chambless, D. L., 584
Chamorro-Premuzic, T., 465
Chamoux, A., 403
Chan, G. C-K., 255
Chance, P., 265, 280, 282, 285
Chandler,M J., 590
Chang, E. C., 522
Chang, K. D., 352
Chang, M. C., 254
Chansler, P. A., 606, 667
Chapanis, A., 193
Chaplin, G., 657
Charness, N., 356, 406
Chartrand, T., 417
Chassin, L., 500
Chastain, G., 2
Chasteen, 05, 643
Chaves, J. F., 238, 239
Check, J., 446
Cheek, J., 491
Chemtob, C. M., 581
Chen, C.-C., 664
Chen, E.Y. H., 66
Chen, Y., 538
Chen, Z., 344, 620
Cheney, C. D., 271
Cheng, H., 58
Cheriff, A. D., 528
Chesky, K. S., 184
Chess, S., 86, 101, 126
Chesson, A. L., 232
Chiarello, C., 67
Chimpsky, N., 340
Chiu, L. H., 23, 285
Chiu, S.-F., 664
Chivers, M. L., 439
Chomsky, N., 107, 337–328
Chopra, S. R., 682
Chorney, P., 546
Christensen, A., 600
Christensen, C. D., 373
Christian, A. G., 248
Christian, C., 573
Christopher, F. S., 617, 618
Christophersen, E., 94
Chua, H. F., 205
Chua, P., 205, 435
Chung, T., 333
Cialdini, R., 624, 625, 634
Cialdini, R. B., 408, 607
Ciarrochi, J., 513
Cicogna, P., 402
Cinciripini, P. M., 248
Clack. R. J., 677
Claiborn, C. D., 600
Clair, J. M., 144
Clancy, S. A., 231, 392
Clapham, M. M., 358
Clara, I. P., 467
Clark, D., 52, 61, 67, 484
Clark, K., 646
Clark, M. C., 4
Clark, R., 323, 644
Clark, V. R., 644
Claux, M. L., 111
Clawson, C., 325
Clayton, L. D., 681
Click, P., 656
Clifford, E. R., 192
Cline, V. B., 650
Clinkenbeard, P.R., 372
Clore, G., 645
Clothier, A., 258
Clover, R. D., 522
Coast, J. R., 130, 527
Coats, E.J., 608

Cochran, S. D., 440
Coffman, T. L., 642
Cohen, D. J., 212
Cohen, G., 312
Cohen, J. A., 443
Cohen, J. E., 672, 675
Cohen, L. H., 521
Cohen, L.H., 435
Cohen, M., 596
Cohen, M. A., 391
Cohen, N. L., 516
Cohen, P., 289, 555
Cohen, R. J., 364
Cohen, S., 523, 524, 674
Cohen-Kettenis, P., 398
Colapinto, J., 430
Cole, J., 177
Cole, P. H., 576
Coleman, E., 438
Coleman, S. M., 131
Colin, A. K., 210, 219
Collins, A. M., 304
Collins, D. W., 375
Collins, Deutch, 645
Collins, F. S., 383, 644, 657
Collins, J., 499
Collins, K. A., 613
Collins, R. L., 79, 254, 504
Collins, W. A., 98
Colpaert, F. C., 314
Comer, R. J., 533
Comer, S. D., 254
Comitas, L., 254
Comperatore, C. A., 403
Compton, W. C., 22, 410, 571
Condon, W., 106
Conoley, C. W., 652
Conte, J. M., 662, 667
Conway, A. R.A., 181
Conway, M. A., 312
Conway, R., 519
Conyne, R. K, 677
Cook, D. A., 656
Cook, E. J., 672
Cook, S. W., 676
Cooke, B.M., 431
Cooley, T., 321
Cools, J., 392
Cooper, C., 379
Cooper, D. S., 218
Cooper, G., 204
Cooper, G. D., 241
Cooper, J., 316, 635, 636, 681
Cooper, M., 439
Cooper, M. J., 396
Cooper, P. J., 560
Cooper, R. P., 108
Coopersmith, S., 104
Corballis, M. C., 328
Corbin, W. R., 449
Cordova, D. L., 277
Coren, S., 78, 80, 168, 192, 199, 207, 226
Corkin, S., 319
Cornell, D. G., 652
Correa-Chávez, M., 365
Corrigan, P. W., 554, 562, 583
Corteen, P. W., 289
Cortese, P., 499
Corwyn, R. F., 89
Costa, P. T., 460, 465, 466, 467
Cote, G., 518
Cote, S., 666
Cotton, S., 445
Coulton, C. J., 677
Couresy, R. D., 596
Courrier, S., 650
Court, J. H., 317
Court, P. C., 317
Cover, J. D., 634
Cowan, N., 114, 181, 300
Cowan, T. M., 310
Cowell, P., 557
Cowles, J. T., 275
Cox, B. J., 467
Cox, W. E., 214
Coye, R. W, 666
Coyle, J. T., 556
Cozby, P. C., 681
Craig, K. D., 546
Craig, W. M., 32
Craik, F. I. M., 312
Craik, K. H., 22
Crandall, C. S., 515
Crano, W. D, 619, 620
Cravatt, B. F., 228
Crawford, C. B., 133
Crawley, S. B., 101
Creamer, M., 545
Cregler, L. L., 245
Crencavage, L. M., 589
Crews, F. T., 291
Crichlow, S., 620
Crocker, J., 105
Croft, R. G., 650
Crogan, M., 646
Cromdal, J., 337
Cronbach, L., 487
Cronk, N. J., 97
Crooks, R., 398, 427, 438, 444
Cropanzano, R., 318, 666
Crosby, R. A., 449
Cross, T., 413
Crotty, M., 183
Crouch, J. L., 129
Crowe, L. C., 438
Crowther, J. H., 516
Csikszentmihalyi, M., 22, 408, 684
Cuddy, A. J. C., 641–642
Cull, M., 430
Cullen, F. T., 445
Cumming, B. G., 197
Cumming, E., 143
Cumming, M. R., 85
Cumming, S., 594
Cummins, D. D., 654
Curry, D., 335
Cushner, K., 23
Cutler, N. L., 561
Czeisler, C. A., 227, 402, 403

Dabbs, J. M., Jr., 648
Daigle, L. E., 445
Dallenbach, K. M., 314
Dalton, K. M., 524
Damour, L., 536
Dane, F. C., 217, 358, 644
Daniels, M., 377
Darakjian, J., 248
Darley, J., 653
Darley, J. M., 16, 642
Darling, C. A., 442
Darou, W. S., 366
Darwin, C., 18, 414
Das, J. P., 374
DasGupta, B., 503
Daum, I., 268
Daumrind, D., 102–103
Davanloo, H., 573
David, A. S., 415
David, H., 159, 206
Davidson, J., 342–343
Davidson, J. K., 442
Davidson, L., 594
Davies, M., 446
Daviet, C., 588
Davis, A. J., 101
Davis, D., 354
Davis, E. B., 290
Davis, G., 7
Davis, G. E., 600, 678
Davis, J. R., 179
Davis, K. D., 183
Davis, K. E., 617
Davis, M., 268
Davis, M. F., 641
Davis, M. K., 589
Davis, M. R., 303
Daw, J., 26
Dawson, G., 128
Daylen, J., 218
Dayton, T., 342
De Boeck, P., 334
de Bono, E., 357
de Groot, G., 651
de Groot, L. C., 499
De Haan, E. H. F., 69
de Jong, T., 268
de las Fuentes, C., 133, 134
de Luccie, M. F., 101
de Muinck, K., 430
de Queiroz, V., 594
de Rios, M. D., 225
Dean, F. P., 513
Dean-Church, L., 435
DeAngelis, G. C., 197
Deary, I. J., 379
Deaux, K., 611
DeBlassie, R. R., 132
deBortali-Tregerthan, G., 680
Deci, E. L., 407, 408
Deckers,L., 390
Deckro, G. R., 527
Deco, G., 164
Deeb, S. S., 167
Deese, J., 321
Deffenbacher, J. L., 580
DeFries, J. C., 376
Degirmencioglu, S. M., 134
DeGood, D. E., 501
DeKlyen, M., 285
DeLamater, J. D., 443
DeLano, L., 325
DeLeon, P. H., 577
Delgado, B. M., 103, 134
Delis, D. C., 251
Dement, W., 235, 236
Denmark, F. L., 23, 41
Denollet, J., 521
Deregowski, J. B., 201
Derleg, V. J., 484
Dermer, A., 100
Deshon, R. P., 664
Desimone, R., 209
Desmarais, S., 301
Desmond, J. E., 410
Detterman, D., 373
Detterman, D. K., 379
Detwiler, F. R. J., 435
Deuser, W. E., 519, 648
Deutch, M., 645
Deutsch, G., 65, 67, 79, 80
Deutsch, M., 646
DeVault, C., 444, 455
Devine, D. J, 681
Devine, P. G., 656
Devlin, B., 377
Di Marzo, V., 391
Diamond, L., 440
Dickens, W. T., 377
Dickerson, F. B., 583
Dickinson, D., 381
Dickinson, D. J., 321
Diehl, N. S., 685
Diekstra, R. F., 564
Diener, E., 150, 151
Dieter, J. N., 90, 100
Dignon, A. M, 484
Diller, L. H., 128
DiMatteo, M. R., 36
Dimsdale, J. E., 245
Dinges, D. F., 226
Dinkmeyer, D. Jr., 116
Dinkmeyer, D., Sr., 118
Dinnel, D. L., 318
Dion, K. L., 656
DiPietro, D., 449
Dirkzwager, A. J. E., 546
Dixon, R., 128
DiZio, P., 179
Dobelle, W. H., 157
Dobson, K. S., 560, 584
Doctor, J. N., 501
Doctor, R. M., 501
Dodd, J., 136
Dodds, J. B., 93
Doidge, N., 573
Dolan, S. L., 590
Dolev, K., 413
Dollard, 475, 476
Dolski, I., 524
Domingo, R. A., 107
Donaldson, D., 564
Donne, J., 605
Donnerstein, E., 650
Dooley, P., 506
Dooling, D. J., 298
Dopler, D. M., 547
Doran, S. M., 226
Dorfman, J., 357
Dornbush, R. L., 254
Dosher, B. A., 313
Doty, R. M., 641
Dougherty, D., 413
Douglas, W., 184
Douvan, E., 123, 133
Dove, A., 382
Doverspike, D., 465
Dovidio, J. F., 639, 643, 645, 651, 654, 656
Dowdall, G., 499
Dozois, D. J. A., 584
Draguns, J. G., 589, 590
Drake, M., 407
Dretzke, B. J., 324
Drews, F. A., 210
Drigotas, S. M., 482
Driskell, J. E., 528
Drob, S. L., 546
Drolet, G., 57
Drop, S. L. S., 430
Drucker, P., 573
Druckman, D., 48, 226, 238, 239, 241, 406
Druhan, J., 246
Drummond, P. D., 524
DSM-IV-TR, 97, 128, 233, 234, 373–374, 534, 535, 536, 541, 542, 544, 549, 551, 552, 553, 559
Dubow, E. F., 90
Duclos, S. E., 419, 420
Duffy, J. F., 402, 403
Duffy, V. B., 176
Dugas, M. J., 548
Dulewicz, V., 422
Dumont, E. C., 57, 482
Duncan, B. L., 600
Duncan, J., 68, 209
Duncan, T. E., 500
Duncan, W. C., 561
Duncker, K., 341, 343
Dunford, B. B., 681
Dunning, D., 462
DuPaul, G. J., 128
Durham, M. D., 217, 644
Durham, M.D., 358
Durso, F. T., 342
Dusek, J. B., 132
Dutra, L., 588
Dutton, D. G., 419
Duymne, M., 377
Duyne, M., 377
Dwons, J. H., 333
Dwyer, J., 218
Dyer, K., 147
Dywan, J., 303
Dziub-Leatherman, J., 129
Dzokoto, V. A., 538

Eagle, P., 546
Eagly, A. H., 415, 430, 433, 655
Eardley, I., 451
Earleywine, M., 506
Eastman, C. I., 403
Eaton, W. W., 544
Ebbinghus, H., 311, 312
Eberhardt, N. L., 413
Ebster, C., 175
Eccles, J. S., 38, 134
Eckerman, D. A., 280
Eckman, P., 415
Eddy, K. T., 588
Edwards, D. J. A., 40
Edwards, J. N., 673

Egeland, B., 130
Eggert, A., 3
Ehrlich, P., 211
Eich, E., 314
Eichorn, D. H., 368
Eidelson, J. I., 641
Eidelson, R. J., 641
Eifert, G. H., 501, 578, 580
Eimas, P. D., 114
Eimer, B. N., 239
Einstein, A., 647
Eisenberg, N., 105, 408
Eisert, S., 676
Ekman, P., 414, 416, 417, 419
Eliot, A. J., 87, 99, 109
Elkind, D., 133, 134
Elli, K. Ak., 320
Ellickson, P. L., 254
Ellingson, J. E., 384
Elliot, A. J., 151, 656
Elliott, M., 443, 600
Ellis, A., 585
Ellis, H. C., 341
Ellis, P. J., 664
Ellis, S. M., 391
Elovainio, M., 668
Emery, R. E., 126
Emmelkamp, P. M. G., 558
Emmelkamp, P.M. G., 577
Emmons, K., 248
Emmons, K. M., 499
Emmons, M., 628
Emmons, R. A., 151
Emory, E. K., 90
Emswiller, T., 611
Emurian, C. S., 253
Engle, R. W., 298
Englis, B. G., 657
Enns, J. T., 168, 192, 199, 207
Enns, M. W., 467
Epstein, D. R., 232–233
Erasmus, 321
Erdelyi, M. H., 211
Ericsson, K. A., 145, 310, 356, 406
Erikson, E., 21, 122–125, 138, 472
Ernst, E., 182, 356
Eron, L., 650, 651
Eronen, S., 150
Escher, M. C., 200
Espie, C. A., 232, 233
Espy, K. A., 87
Esser, J. K., 620
Ethier, K. A., 447
Evans, G. W., 674, 678
Evans, R. J., 248
Evans, S., 130
Evans, S. M., 372
Evens, G. W., 674
Everaerd, W., 436
Everard, K. M., 144
Everly, G. S., 596
Everson, C. A., 226
Eyal, N., 684
Eyde, L. D., 487
Eyer, D. E., 97
Eyesenck, M. W., 298
Eysenck, H. J., 462, 573

Fabes, R. A., 105, 136, 433
Fabrega, H., Jr., 534
Fairclough, S. H., 226
Faith, M. S., 588, 640, 643
Falkowski, C., 248
Famularo, R., 129
Fandt, P. M., 667, 669
Fantz, R. L., 91
Farrimond, T., 190
Farroni, T., 92
Farvolden, P., 317
Fazio, R. H., 180, 636
FDA Consumer, 562
Fein, S., 608, 619
Feingold, A., 614, 618
Feissner, J. M., 561
Feist, J., 143, 144, 497
Feldhusen, J. F., 349
Feldman, R. S., 244, 613
Fellous, J. M., 73, 411
Felsenfeld, S., 127
Fennig, S., 555
Fenton, G. W., 594
Fernald, A., 108
Fernandez, E., 184
Fernández-Chacón, R., 320
Fernlad, A., 108
Ferrante, A. M., 505
Ferrari, J. R., 6
Ferris, G. R., 664
Ferster, C. B., 291
Festinger, L., 612, 635, 636
Fetsch, R. J., 130
Feuerstein, R., 377
Fichner-Rathus, L., 430, 439
Fields, R. M., 504
Figlerski, R. W., 271
Filiz, T. M., 379
Fink, M., 254, 593
Finke, R., 351
Finkelhor, D., 129
Finn, S. E., 487
Firestone, P., 546
First, M. B, 535
Firth, U., 129
Fischer, A. H., 415
Fischler, C., 394
Fischman, M. W., 253
Fish, J. M., 589, 590
Fisher, B. S., 445
Fisher, C. D., 422
Fisher, J. D., 449
Fisher, L. M., 141, 145
Fisher, R. P., 236, 303, 323
Fisher, S. G., 516
Fisher, W. A., 449
Fiske, S. T., 641–642, 643
Fitch, T., 180
Fitzgerald, P., 449
Fitzgibbon, M., 397
Fitzsimmons, G. M., 615
Flashman, L. A., 64
Flattau, P. E., 20
Flavell, J. H., 109
Fleming I., 674, 675
Fleming, J., 339
Fletcher, B. W., 246
Florin, P., 500
Flynn, J.R., 377
Flynn, K. J., 397
Fobair, P., 600
Fobes, J. L., 274
Fochtmann, L. J., 546
Foege, W. H., 497
Folen, R., 577
Folkman, S., 503, 504, 505
Follett, K., 610
Follette, W. C., 354
Foltin, R. W., 253, 254
Fones, C. S. L., 544
Fontaine, K. R., 498
Fontenelle, D.H., 116, 118
Fontenot, J., 547
Foos, P., 4
Forbes, G. B., 446, 650
Ford, G. G., 103, 683
Foreyt, J. P., 248
Fornes, P., 564
Forrest, M. S., 581
Forsyth, J. P., 578
Fortmann, S. P., 247
Foss, R. D., 654
Fosse, R., 236
Foster, C. A., 419
Foster, G., 32
Fouad, N. A., 432
Fournier, J. F., 685
Fouts, D., 340
Fouts, R., 339, 340
Fowers, B. J., 656
Fowles, D. C., 555
Fox, C., 39
Fox, P. T., 333, 392
Fox, R. A., 285
Foxhall, K., 218
Fraley, R. C., 616, 617
Franche, R., 560
Frank, J., 589, 680
Frank, J. D., 589
Frank, M. G., 415
Franke, M., 664
Frankenburg, W. K., 93
Frankl, V., 575
Franks, M. M., 144
Fraser, C., 183
Fraser, S. C., 624
Fredrickson, B. L., 397, 422, 500, 522
Freedman, J. L., 624
Freeman, A, 214, 216
Freeman, D., 553
Freeman, J., 372
Freeman, W. J., 174
Freitas, M. B., 80
Freize, 443
French, C. C., 44
French, D., 518
Freud, A., 21
Freud, B., 581
Freud, S., 20, 236, 256, 469–472, 510, 572, 574, 662
Fridley, D., 271
Fried, C. S., 446
Fried, P. A., 130, 254, 255
Friedman, M., 520
Friedman, R., 267
Friedman, R. C., 573
Friedrich, R. W., 174
Frieman, J., 310
Friesen, W. V., 416, 419
Frijda, N. H., 398, 411
Fritch, A., 491
Froh, J. J., 22
Fromme, K., 449
Frone, M. R., 668
Frost, R. O., 548
Froufe, M., 159
Frueh, B. C., 581
Frydman, M., 651
Frye, E. M., 637
Fuchs, D., 432
Fucito, L. M., 454
Fudge, R., 550
Fuhriman, A., 586
Fujino, D. C., 435
Fukuda, K., 227
Fuligni, A. J., 134
Fulker, D. W., 376
Fuller, J., 669
Fuller, T. D, 673
Funder, D., 459, 467
Funk, J. B., 290
Fuqua, D. R., 669
Furness, T. A., 580
Furnham, A., 465
Furumoto, L., 20

Gable, S. L., 422, 522
Gabrieli, J. D. E., 304, 319, 320
Gaertner, S. L., 639, 643, 645, 656
Gagnon, J., 436, 438
Galambos, N. L., 132, 135
Galantucci, B., 308
Galati, D., 414
Galea, S., 504
Galinsky, M. D., 587
Gallacher, F., 557
Gallagher, J., 323
Gallagher, S. H., 103, 683
Gallo, L. C., 521
Galloway, R. E., 402
Gallup Poll, 444
Gamache, G., 193
Ganellen, R. J., 488
Ganey, H. C. N., 400
Ganis, G., 331
Gannon, L., 140
Gao, J., 392
Garcia, J., 395
Garcia-Junco-Clemente, P., 320
Garcia-Palacios, A., 580
Gardner, A., 339
Gardner, H., 380, 384, 396
Gardner, R., 226
Garety, P. A., 553
Garfinkel, B. D., 564
Garfinkel, L. F., 564
Garland, A. F., 564, 565
Garnefski, N., 564
Garnets, L. D., 438, 439, 441
Garske, J. P., 589
Gartner, G., 352
Gartrell, N. K., 439
Gaskell, H., 169
Gates, A. I., 321
Gatto, M., 180
Gatz, M., 145
Gauthier, J., 518
Gawronski, B., 640
Gayle, H., 448
Gazzaniga, M. S., 64, 66, 67
Geary, N., 392
Gedo, J. E., 20
Geehr, J. L., 667
Geer, J. H., 436
Gegenfurtner, K. R., 166
Geiger, A., 577
Geiger, M. A., 7
Geiselman, R. E., 303, 323
Genessee, F., 337
George, W. H., 438
Georgiades, A., 499
Gepner, B., 66
Gerber, W. D., 518
Gerberding, J. L., 497, 499
German, T.P., 337
Gershoff, E. T., 131, 284, 285
Gershon, E. S., 561
Gerstein, E. R., 158
Geschwind, N., 68, 80
Gewer, A., 377
Gewirtz, J. C., 268
Ghadirian, A-M., 352
Giacalone, R. A., 636, 648
Gibson, E. J., 195
Gibson, P., 317
Gielen, U. P., 589, 590
Gierl, M. J., 402
Gifford, R., 671, 678
Gila, A., 127
Gilbert, K., 633
Gilbert, L. A., 436
Gilbert, P., 524, 584
Giliovich, T., 656
Gill, S. T., 14
Gillberg, M., 226
Gillette, C, 581
Gilliam, P., 686
Gilligan, C., 41, 136–137
Gillin, J. C., 246
Gilman, S. E., 440
Gilroy, F. D., 435
Ginet, M., 303
Giniger, S., 145
Ginott, H., 117
Ginsburg, B. E., 648
Girodo, M., 492
Giuseppe, R., 580
Gladstone, G. L., 415
Gladwell, M., 353
Glaser, R., 384, 523
Glass, T., 333
Glazer, K., 521
Gleason, J. B., 106
Glennerster, A., 208
Glick, P., 639, 641–642
Glik, D. C., 499
Glisky, M. L., 87, 333
Globus, G., 257
Glomb, T. M., 669
Glover, G., 410
Glover, R. J., 137
Glueck, J., 356

Gluhoski,V. L., 148
Gobet, F., 346
Goel, V., 68
Goernert, P. N., 677
Goffin, R. D., 43
Goh, B. E., 349
Goheen, M. D., 233
Goin, R. P., 127
Gold, P. E., 319
Goldberg, C., 638
Goldberg, R., 242
Golden, J., 87
Goldfield, B. A., 106
Goldfried, M. R., 440, 587
Goldiamond, L., 291
Goldin, L. R., 561
Goldman, H. H., 596
Goldstein, A. P., 652
Goldstein, E. B., 167, 301
Goldstein, I. L., 686
Goldstein, M., 555
Goldstein, N. J., 624, 625
Goldstein, S. R., 78
Goldstein-Alpren, N., 107
Goldstone, R. L., 203
Goleman, H. H., 411
Gondola, J. C., 683
Gonzales, R., 254
Good, M., 184
Goodale, M. A., 164
Goodall, J., 31
Goode, E., 618
Goodman, G., 592
Goodman, S. H., 667, 669
Goodman-Delahunty, J., 682
Goodstein, D., 43
Goodwin, J., 572
Gooren, L. J. G, 398
Goparaju, S. K., 391
Gopnik, A., 90, 91, 92, 106, 111, 115
Gordis, E. B., 650
Gordon, J., 225
Gordon, L. R., 620
Gore, J. C., 70
Gorman, J. M., 504, 540, 559, 594
Gosling, S., 463
Gosling, S. D., 22, 460
Gosselin, I., 57, 482
Gottesman, I. I., 555
Gottfredson, G. D., 20
Gottman, J. M., 453, 454, 615
Gottselig, J. M., 229
Gould, D., 685
Gould, R., 138–139
Grack, C., 645
Grafman, J., 68
Graham, C. H., 167
Graham, R., 226
Grande, T., 589
Granholm, E., 251
Grant, I., 254
Graves, J. L., 657
Gray, R., 254, 255
Gray, T. W., 676
Graziottin, A., 398, 438
Greemberg, L. S., 587
Green, B. L., 408
Green, C., 317
Green, J. D., 419
Green, M. C., 634
Green, R. G., 650
Green-Paden, L. D., 583
Greenberg, J., 129, 159
Greenberg, R. L., 514
Greenberg, R. P., 236
Greene, B., 558
Greene, D., 408
Greene, E., 682
Greene, J., 588
Greenfield, P, M, 382, 383
Greenfield, P., 366
Greenglass, E. R., 502
Greenough, W. T., 320
Greenwald, A. G., 640
Greenwood, K. M., 303
Greenwood, M. R. C., 395
Gregoire, P., 352
Gregory, A., 38
Gregory, R., 189, 207, 208
Grenier, G., 453
Griffin, W. A., 587
Griffiths, R. R., 372
Grigorenko, E. L., 363, 376, 379, 383, 657
Grigsby, T. D., 606
Grob, C. S., 225
Gross, 02, 421
Gross, A. M., 446
Grossenbacher, P. G., 225
Grotzer, T. A., 378
Gruber, A. J., 317
Gruber, C.L., 254
Gruber, J. J., 683
Grubin, D., 413
Grudnik, J. L., 379
Gruman, J., 498
Gruner, C. R., 334
Gschwendner, T., 640
Gual, P., 396
Guarnaccia, P. J. J., 538, 540
Guarnaccia, V. J., 487, 488
Guary, F., 606
Guastello, D. D., 435
Guastello, S. J., 435, 488
Guéguen, 02, 608
Guevremont, D. C., 275, 578, 579, 583
Gullette, D. L., 401
Gullette, E. C., 499
Gump, B. B., 612
Gunderson, J., 491
Gunn, I., 391
Gunnar, M. R., 98
Gunthert, K. C., 521
Gur, R. E., 557
Guralnik, O., 546
Gurin, J., 588
Gustavson, C. R., 395
Guthrie, R. V., 23, 41
Gwiazda, J., 195

Haas, L. J., 576
Haase, R. F., 415
Haber, R. N., 307, 309
Haber, S., 674
Haddock, G., 397
Haddy, R. I., 522
Hadley, C. N., 357, 408
Hadwin, A. F., 322
Hafemeister, T. L., 681, 682
Hafer, C. L., 656
Hagekull, B., 96
Haggard, P., 56
Haidt, J., 480
Haier, R. J., 64, 70, 182
Haines, M. M., 674
Hakuta, K., 337
Halbert, J., 183
Halbmaier, C. A., 392
Hale, S., 369
Hall, C., 235, 256, 564, 608
Hall, C. R., 684
Hall, E. T., 564, 608
Hall, J. A., 608
Hallahan, D. P., 371, 373, 375
Hallett, D., 590
Halligan, P. W., 239
Halliwell, W. R., 685
Halpern, D. F., 12, 14, 30, 32, 431
Ham, J. J., 610
Hambright, A. B., 587
Hamer, D. H., 439
Hamida, S. B., 269
Hamlton, V. L., 623
Hammer, J. C., 449
Hammer, L. B., 606
Hancock, P. A., 400
Handsfield, H. H., 449
Haney, C., 606, 682
Haney, M., 254
Hannigan, S. L., 302
Hansel, C. E. M., 214
Hansell, J. H., 536
Hansen, C. J., 130, 527
Hansford, S. L., 615
Hanson, E., 18
Hanson, M. A., 663, 664, 665
Harding, R. W., 39, 505
Hare, R. D., 542
Hare-Mustin, R. T., 431
Hargrove, M. F., 648
Harkavy-Friedman, J., 555
Harker, L., 460
Harlap, S., 555
Harlow, H., 99
Harlow, H. E., 286
Harlow, J. M., 39
Harlow, M. K., 286
Harlow, T. F, 514
Harm, D. L., 180
Harner, D. E., 397
Harris, B., 561
Harris, C., 618
Harris, J. R., 93
Harris, M. F., 86
Harrision, L. F., 289
Harrison, G., 555
Harsch, N., 318
Hart, B., 108
Hart-Johnson, T., 482
Hartgens, F., 76
Harvey, O. J., 645
Harvil, L. M., 7
Hasbrouck, J. E., 289
Hasbrouck, J. N., 650
Hasher, L., 314
Hashimoto, I., 68
Hasin, D. S., 251
Hathaway, S. R., 487
Hauck, F. R., 235
Hauri, P., 402
Havercamp, S. M., 406, 479
Havighurst, R. J., 144
Hawkins, D. B., 683
Hawley, C. W., 463
Hay, I., 104, 105
Hay, P., 594
Hayes, C., 339
Hayman-Abello, B. A., 375
Hayne, H., 93
Hayreh, D. J. S., 175, 590
Heady, R. B., 668
Hearold, S. L., 652
Heath, D. B., 225
Heath, L., 633
Hebb, O. O., 240
Heckhausen, J., 141, 144
Hecth, H., 544
Hedge, J. W., 663, 664, 665
Hedlund, N. L., 581
Heiby, E. M., 477
Heilman, M. E., 432
Heiman, D., 555
Heiman, J. R., 451
Heimann, M., 91
Heimberg, R. G., 548
Heine, S. J., 462
Heinrichs, R. W., 552
Heinze, S. J., 67
Hekmat, H., 184
Held, R., 205
Helgeson, V. S., 431, 434
Hellekson, C. J., 561
Hellerstein, D. J., 571
Hellige, J. B., 67, 79
Hellstroem, K., 579
Helms, J. E., 383
Helson, L. H., 206
Henderson, C., 195
Henderson, L., 491
Henderson, R. J., 519
Hendrick, C., 616
Hendrick, S. S., 616
Henman, L. D., 528
Henry, W. E., 143
Henshaw, D., 652
Hepper, P. G., 79, 80
Herbert, T. B., 524
Herman, C. P., 396
Herrnstein, R., 383
Herscovitch, P., 230
Hersen, M., 39
Herxheimer, A., 403
Herz, R. S., 174
Herzog, A. R., 144
Herzog, T. A., 291
Hess, E., 96
Hess, L., 583
Hess, T. M., 610
Hetherington, E. M., 126
Heusel, C., 648
Hewstone, M., 611
Hiatt, S., 195
Hicks, R. A., 402
Higbee, K. L., 325
Higgs, M., 422
Hilgard, E., 238
Hill, P., 134
Hilsenroth, M. J., 488
Himel, N., 652
Hinds, T. R., 255
Hinkle, E., 337
Hinshaw, S. P., 128
Hiripi, E., 247, 546
Hironon, 174
Hirsch, J., 390
Hirshberg, L. M., 96
Hirt, E. R., 611
Hiscock, M., 431
Hite, S., 442
Hladkyj, S., 4
Hobosn, A., 236
Hobson, A., 258
Hobson, J. A., 224, 225, 230, 236
Hochman, K. M., 555, 556–558, 593
Hodges, L., 581
Hodson, G., 639, 643
Hoerr, S. L., 397
Hofer, B. K., 1
Hoff, K. E., 128
Hoffer, A., 572
Hoffman, H. G., 184, 580
Hoffman, M., 377
Hofmann, S., 403
Hofmann, W., 640
Hogan, C. W., 246
Hogan, M. J., 422
Hogben, D., 325
Hoge, C. W., 546
Hogg, M. A., 634
Hohwy, J., 206
Holcome, A. O., 191
Holden, C., 468
Holden, G. W., 131
Holding, D. H., 322
Hole, G. J., 208
Holland, J., 664
Hollendonner, J. K., 498
Holmberg, D., 144
Holmes, J. G., 616, 636
Holmes, M., 430
Holmes, T., 515
Holschuh, J. L., 321
Holstein, M., 147
Holt, C. S., 548
Holt, K., 528
Holterhus, P. M., 430
Holtzworth-Munroe, A., 610
Honomichi, R., 344
Honzik, C., 286
Honzik, M. P., 368, 369
Hood, W. R., 645
Hooks, G., 644
Hooley, J., 487, 532
Horn, J., 488
Horne, J. A., 226, 234
Horney, K., 21, 473
Hornick, B. A., 246
Horowitz, B., 164
Hortman, G., 409

Horvath, A. O., 233
Horvath, L. S., 401
Horwitz, W. A., 363
Hosch, H. M., 218, 313
Hough, L. M., 663, 664
Houlette, M., 645
Houlihan, D., 677
Howard, A., 20
Howard, I. P., 197
Howard, J. L., 664
Howard, K. I., 588
Howard, S. R., 271
Howes, C, 100
Hoyt, M., 527
Hsia, Y., 167
Hsiao, W., 682
Hsiung, P. K., 198
Hu, N., 439
Hu, S., 439
Huang, P., 577
Hubbard, R. L., 246
Hubble, M. A., 600
Hubel, D., 156, 162
Hudson, W., 201
Huebner, R., 67
Huesmann, L. R., 650
Hughes, J. N., 289
Hughes, J. R., 247, 650
Hughes, M., 440, 545
Hulse, S. J., 321
Human Rights Watch, 596
Humphries, S. A., 181, 184
Hunt, E., 374, 378, 380, 384
Hunt, H., 351
Hunt, J. V., 368
Hunt, M., 444
Hunt, R. R., 341
Hunter, E., 637, 638
Hunter, J. E., 663
Hunter, J. P., 183
Hupp, S. D. A., 583
Hurlbert, D. F., 452
Hurry, M., 226
Hurtado, A., 682
Hustedt, J. T., 633
Hutchinson, G., 610
Hutchinson, K. E., 71
Hutchison, K. E., 251
Hyde, J. S., 41, 140, 370, 438, 443
Hyman, I. E., 318
Hyman, R., 52, 215, 216
Hyson, M. G., 111

Iacono, W. G., 413
Ichikawa, S., 333
Ickes, W., 435
Iguchi, Y., 68
Ikemoto, S., 274
Ilardi, B., 481
Impett, E. A., 422, 522
Impey, S., 255
Inch, R., 431
Indermaur, D., 505
Institute of Medicine, 253
Ironson, G., 524, 581
Isaak, M. I., 343
Isabella, L., 140
Isberner, F. R., 445
Ishihara, K., 227
Ising, H., 674
Ito, T. A., 648
Ivanco, T. L., 320
Ivry, A. E., 67
Izard, C. E., 94, 419

Jablonski, N. G., 657
Jackendoff, R., 339
Jacklin, C. N., 433
Jackson, D. C., 524
Jackson, K., 499
Jackson, R., 379
Jackson, R. J., 180
Jackson, T., 491, 492
Jacob, S., 206
Jacobs, A., 98
Jacobs, M., 469
Jacobs, S., 590
Jacobsen, P. B., 265, 395
Jacobson, N. S., 600
Jacobvitz, D., 130
Jaffe, J., 79, 108
Jahn, R. G., 214
Jakobson, L. S., 164
James, D., 254, 255
James, L. C., 577
James, W., 18, 164, 417
Jamison, K. R., 564
Jang, D. P., 580
Jang, K. L., 467
Janis, I. L., 620, 635, 668
Jankiewicz, H., 253
Janssen, 182
Janssen, S. A., 56
Janus, C. L., 42, 438, 440, 442, 444, 445
Janus, S. S., 42, 438, 440, 442, 444, 445
Jarmasz, M., 331
Jarvik, L., 363
Jarvin, L., 363
Jarvinen, J., 412
Jarvis, M. J., 247
Jaycox, L. H., 504
Jeffery, R. W., 394
Jellinek, E. M., 251
Jenkins, J. G., 314
Jenkins, J. M., 409
Jenni, O. C., 227
Jennings, L., 134, 600
Jennings, R. T., 183
Jennings, S., 134
Jensen, M. R., 377
Jeong, G. H., 401
Jerabek, I., 314
Jerome, L. W., 577
Jewell, 98, 667
Job, R. F. S., 674
Joe, G. W., 246
Johansson, H., 491
John, O., 467
John, O. P., 460, 476, 483
Johnson, A. M., 141, 322
Johnson, B. T., 614, 640
Johnson, E., 451, 454
Johnson, E. O., 247, 546
Johnson, J. G., 289
Johnson, K. E., 333
Johnson, L. D., 123
Johnson, M., 184
Johnson, M. H., 92, 181
Johnson, N. G., 111, 132
Johnson, P. I., 27
Johnson, S., 377, 378
Johnson, T. E., 379
Johnson, T. J., 252
Johnson, V., 440–441
Johnson, W. A., 210
Johnsonn, J. H., 528
Johnsrude, I. S., 266
Joiner, T. E., Jr., 564
Jokerst, M. D., 180
Jones, C., 486
Jones, E. E., 610
Jones, G. V., 79, 545
Jones, L., 402
Jones, M. K., 584
Jones, R. N., 382
Jones, T. S., 608
Jones, W. H., 484
Jordan, C. L., 431
Jorgensen, P. E., 403
Jourard, S., 219
Jouvet, M., 226, 230
Joy, L. A., 289
Judge, T. A., 465
Julesz, B., 196
Julien, E., 606
Julien, R. M., 242, 244, 246, 247, 253, 592
Jung, C., 21, 460, 473–474
Jussim, L., 38
Just, A., 343
Juster, H. R., 548

Kaas, J. H., 183
Kabin, M. B., 384
Kabnick, K., 394
Kagan, J., 85, 86, 91, 459
Kah, S., 521
Kahana, M. J., 306
Kahler, C. W., 253
Kahn, R. L., 142
Kahn, S., 126
Kahneman, D., 353–354
Kaismatis, R. J., 410
Kaitz, M., 97
Kakigi, R., 185
Kalat, J. W., 411
Kalish, D., 286
Kallgren, C. A., 608
Kallio, S., 237
Kalliomaeki-Levanto, T., 668
Kamin, L., 383
Kamin, L. J., 377
Kaplan, A. H., 573
Kaplan, B., 311
Kaplan, M. L., 546
Kaplan, P. S., 103, 106, 122
Kapleau, P., 220
Kapur, S., 556
Karlins, M., 642
Karnes, F. A., 383
Karon, B. P., 316
Karow, C. M., 66
Karp, D. A., 144
Karylowski, J. J., 335
Kasen, S., 289
Kasimatis, M., 410
Kaskie, B., 101
Kasl, S. V., 145
Kasper, M. E., 550
Kasser, T., 405, 407
Kassin, S., 218
Kassin, S. B., 313
Kassin, S. M., 608, 619
Kataria, S., 233
Katkin, E. S., 267
Katz, B., 596
Katz, J., 183
Katz, P. A., 640
Kauffman, J. M., 371, 373, 375
Kaufman, A. S., 363
Kaufman, J. C., 351, 352
Kaufman, J. H., 201, 202
Kaufman, L., 201, 202
Kaufmann, P. M., 87
Kawai, K, 395
Kawakami, K., 639, 643
Kay, G. G., 487
Keane, M. T., 298
Kearney, A. J., 578, 597, 598
Kearney, C. A., 97
Keavney, M., 407
Kebbell, M. R., 217
Keefe, F. J., 239
Keel, P., 538
Keinath-Specht, A., 518
Keller, J., 643
Keller, M. C., 614
Kellerman, A. L., 648
Kelley, H., 610
Kelley, H. M., 212
Kelly, I. W., 44
Kelly, J. B., 126
Kelly, J. W., 44
Kelly, S., 126
Kelly, T. H., 253
Kelter, D., 460
Keltner, D., 656
Kemeny, M. E., 498, 501, 505, 522
Kennard, W., 596
Kennaway, D. J., 75
Kennedy, J. M., 194
Kennedy, P., 676
Kennedy, R. E., 132
Kennell, J. H., 97
Kenneth, M., 251
Kenrick, D., 13
Kerr, M., 2
Kershaw, T., 447
Kessen, W., 369
Kessler, R., 247, 546
Kessler, R. C., 560
Kessler, R. S., 617
Kesteler, L., 593
Kestenbaum, C., 363
Kestler, L., 555, 556–558
Ketcham, K., 302, 317
Ketter, T. A., 352
Kety, S. S., 550
Keveri, M. K., 306
Keyes, C. L. M., 141, 480
Khunou, D., 377
Kidd, K. K., 657
Kiebel, S., 74
Kiecolt-Glaser, J. K., 522, 523, 524
Kieffer, S. C., 611
Kiesner, J., 643
Kiewra, K. A., 3
Kiger, L., 383
Kihlstrom, J. F., 48, 226, 333, 357
Kilcoyne, J., 443
Killen, J. D., 247
Kim, D., 580
Kim, J., 685
Kim, K., 500
Kim, S., 347, 666
Kim-Cohen, J., 105
Kimball, M. M., 289
Kimble, C. E., 611
Kimmel, D., 441
Kimmel, D. C., 145
Kimura, T., 68
King, A., 3
King, B. E., 446, 451, 452, 453
King, H. E., 72
King, L., 150, 151
King, L. A., 527
King, N. J., 269
Kinkead, R., 57, 482
Kinnier, R. T., 148
Kinnunen, L. H., 439
Kinsey, A., 436, 444
Kiper, D.C., 166
Kirby, A. W., 403
Kirby, J. R., 322
Kirk-Smith, M., 175
Kirkpatrick, B., 593
Kirsch, I., 37, 38, 237, 238, 239, 303
Kisilevsky, B. S., 87
Kistler, D. J., 130
Kitayama, S., 414, 415, 462
Kite, M. E., 432, 640
Kivimaeki, M., 668
Kjelberg, B. J., 27
Kjellgren, A., 241
Klatsky, R. L., 193
Klaus, M. H., 97
Klebanoff, M. A., 246
Kleerup, E. C., 254
Kleespies, P. K., 147
Klein, G., 346
Klein, K., 527
Klein, L., 650
Klein, R. M., 209
Kleinke, C. L., 420, 687
Kleinplatz, P. J., 454
Klimoski, R. J., 43
Klinger, E., 349
Klintsova, A. Y., 320
Klohnen, E. C., 123, 618
Kloner, R. A., 412
Klosterhalfen, S., 395
Klug, W. S., 85
Klump, K., 538
Knafl, K., 148
Knee, C. R., 611
Knight, J., 413
Knoops, K. T. B., 499
Knop, J., 542

Knowlton, B., 305
Knox, D., 454
Knutelaska, M., 546
Knutson, J., 130
Kobos, J. C., 576
Koch, C., 224, 225
Koegler, P., 79
Koegler, W., 79
Koen, L., 590
Koenigsberg, H. W., 540
Koening, S. M., 234
Koepke, J. E., 90
Koestner, R., 685
Kofler, W. W., 674
Kogan, N., 350
Kohlberg, L., 41, 136–137
Kohler, I., 204
Kohler, S. S., 664, 665, 666
Kohn, J. P., 291
Kokke, K., 101
Kolb, B., 66, 73
Kolbe, L. J., 499
Koltzenburg, M., 184, 398
Konarski, R., 502
Koob, G. F., 246
Koons, S. R., 5
Kopal, T., 518
Kopta, S. M., 588
Korbin, J. E., 677
Koreen, A., 592
Korol, C., 546
Korte, C., 605
Kosmidis, H., 352
Koss, M. P., 445, 650
Kosslyn, S., 237, 308, 331, 332
Kosson, D. S., 542
Kotkin, M., 558
Kottler, J. A., 585, 586, 591
Koulack, D., 319
Kounios, J., 342
Koutstaal, W., 302
Kowert, P. A., 620
Kozart, M. F., 589
Krakow, B., 233, 334
Kramer, S. J., 357
Kramer, S. l, 306
Kramer,S. J., 408
Krantz, D. S, 520, 521
Krantz, D. S., 674
Krantz, L., 521
Kranzier, J., 379
Kratofil, P. H., 245
Krause, M. S., 588
Krebs, D. L., 137
Krieschel, S., 544
Kristof-Brown, A. L., 664
Krokoff, L. J., 454
Kromhout, D., 499
Kronauer, R. E., 403
Kronenfeld, J. J., 499
Kropp, P., 518
Krosnick, J. A., 40, 42, 159
Krueger, J. I., 462, 610
Ku, J. H., 580
Kübler-Ross, E., 146–147
Kubovy, M., 191
Kuczka, K. K., 611
Kuhl, P. K., 90, 91, 92, 106, 111, 316
Kuipers, H., 76
Kulik, J. A., 612
Kumar, R., 583
Kunkel, S. R., 145
Kunzendorf, R. G., 308
Kupfer, D. L., 593
Kurokawa, M., 415
Kwok, K., 412

L'odewijkx, H. F. M., 358
Laan, E., 436
LaBar, K. S., 73
LaBerge, L., 227
LaBerge, S., 258
Labin, D., 641
Laborde, M.-L., 172
Labouvie, E., 253
Labov, W., 334
Lac, G., 403
Lacayo, A., 245
Lachman, M. E., 140
Lachman, R., 298
Lackner, J. R., 179
Lacks, P., 233
Lacy, B. A., 103, 683
Ladd-Franklin, C., 20
Ladouceur, R., 548
Lafreniere, K. D., 397
Lagarde, D. P., 228
Lahortiga, F., 396
Laird, J. D., 419, 420
Lal, S. K. L., 519
Lalande, K., 422
Lalonde, C. E., 590
Lamberg, L., 236, 256, 257
Lambert, M. J., 32
Lambert, W. E., 656
Lamert, M. J., 588
Lampe, S., 488
Lampinen, J. M., 297
Lancaster, E., 557
Lance, C. E., 485
Landau, J. D., 13
Landry, S. H., 114
Landy, F. J., 662, 664, 665, 666, 667
Lange, A., 577
Lange, C., 417
Lange, P. J., 542
Langenbucher, J. W., 534
Langens, T. A., 349
Langer, E. J., 213, 343
Langone, M. D., 638
Lantz, J., 575
Lanzetta, J. T., 657
Lanzi, R. G., 377
Lapidus, L. B., 201
LaPointe, J. A., 485
Larner, A. J., 178
Larsen, R. J., 410, 460, 461
Larson, D., 520
Larson, M. E., 677
Lashley, K., 319
Latané, B., 16, 653
Lategan, T. P., 435
Lattal, K. A., 280, 320
Latty-Mann, H., 617
Lauman, E., 444
Laumann, E., 438
Laumann, O. E., 445
Laurent, G., 174
Laursen, B., 134
Lavie, P., 226, 227, 228
Lawrence, B., 369
Lawson, M. J., 325
Lawson, R. B., 620
Lay, C., 134, 462
Lazarus, R., 503, 516
Lazarus, R. S., 510
Lazev, A. B., 291
Le Moal, M., 89
Le Roux, C. E., 391
Le Vay, S., 439
Le, H., 640
Leal, M. C., 172
Leary, T., 12, 29, 30
LeBeau, L. S., 608
LeBlanc, G., 114, 115
Lecomte, D., 564
Lecrubier, Y., 556
Lederman, S. J., 193
Ledley, C., 58, 614
LeDoux, J., 73, 410, 411, 471, 504
Lee, D., 557
Lee, D. H., 64
Lee, J. E., 246
Lee, J. M., 6, 580
Lee, M., 490
Lee, T., 594
Lee, T. D., 276
Leeming, 6
Leenaars, A., 564, 565, 590
Lefcout, M. M., 528
Lehman, D. R., 23, 394, 395, 462
Leikind, B., 47
Leirens, R., 572
Leiter, M. P., 502
Lejuez, C. W., 501, 578, 580
Lench, H. C., 652
Lenzenweger, M. F., 555
Leonard, C. M., 68
Leonard, T., 244
Leor, J., 412
Lepore, F. E., 206
Lepore, S. J., 678
Lepper, F. E., 277
Lepper, M. R., 407, 408
Lercher, P., 674
Lerner, J. S., 514
Leroux, J.-M., 74
Leslie, K., 258
Lesser, I., 560
Lessow-Hurley, J., 337
Lester, D., 148, 564, 565
Lettvin, J. Y., 156
Leukefeld, C., 401
Levant, R. F, 434
Levant, R. F., 433
LeVay, S., 429, 430, 431
Leven, J. R., 325
Levenson, R. W., 419
Levenston, G. K., 542
Leventhal, E. A., 185
Lévesque, J., 74
Levesque, M. J., 58, 614
Levin, D. T., 313
Levin, H., 476
Levin, J. R., 324, 325
Levin, L., 617, 618
Levine, J. A., 413
Levine, M., 596
Levine, R. V., 66, 670, 674
Levinson, A, 321
Levinson, A., 139–140
Levinson, D., 139–140
Levis, D. J., 284
Levitsky, D. A., 392
Levitt, E. B., 291
Levy, B. R., 145
Levy, J., 79
Lewchanin, S., 140
Lewin, R., 340
Lewis, J. B., 447
Lewis, J. M., 126
Lewis, M., 95
Lewis, P. S., 667, 669
Lewis, S., 557
Lewy, A. J., 561
LIbby, J., 542
Lichtenstein, P., 467
Lichter, D. T., 485, 614
Liddell, S. K., 328
Lieberman, D. A., 17, 297, 303, 319, 324
Lieberman, H. R., 403
Liebert, R. M., 93
Lierens, R., 572
Light, K. C., 57
Light, P., 276
Liguori, A., 247
Lilienfeld, S., 47
Lillard, A., 111
Linares-Clemente, P., 320
Linde, S., 402
Linden, W., 392, 526
Lindenbaum, L. E., 193
Lindenberger, V., 142, 144, 145
Lindermann, B., 175
Lindsay, E. W., 102
Lindskold, S., 681
Lindstrom, T. C., 149
Lindwall, R., 579
Linford, K. M., 610
Linton, M., 316
Linz, D., 650
Lipschitz, D. S., 546
Lipsey, M. W., 588
Little, B. R., 151
Liu, G. C., 412
Liu, H., 392
Liu, X., 68
Liu, Y., 392
Livesley, W. J., 467
Lobo, L. L., 232, 235
Lochner, C., 590
Locke, B. D., 446
Loehlin, J. C., 467
Loewi, O., 257
Loftus, E. F., 662
Loftus, E., 297, 302, 317
Loftus, G., 209
LoLordo, V. M., 512, 560
London, M., 669
Long, E. C., 454
Long, J. D., 293, 578, 598
Long, N. R., 181
Long, V. O., 435
López, S. R., 538, 540
Lopiano, L., 38
Lorenz, K., 96, 647
Loughland, C. M., 415
Lovaas, I., 129
Lovaas, O., 583
Lovallo W. R., 520
Love, S. R., 271
Low, K. G., 561
Lubart, T., 351, 357, 358, 408
Luborsky, L., 573
Lucas, F., 151
Lucas, J. L., 668
Lucchina, L., 176
Luce, G. G., 226
Lucido, D. J., 674
Luckie, W. R., 3, 4, 6, 7
Ludman, E. J., 577
Ludwig, T.D., 676
Lui, J., 391
Lumley, V. A., 127
Lundh, L., 491
Lune, H., 652
Luo, D., 379
Luo, S., 618
Luria, A., 309
Luster, T., 90
Lustig, C., 314
Luxem, M., 94
Lydiard, R. B., 543
Lykken, D., 412, 413
Lykken, D. T., 467
Lynch, J. E., 576
Lynch, T. R, 105
Lynn, S. J., 37, 237, 238
Lynnam, D., 401
Lyons, A. J., 516
Lyons, M. A., 401
Lyubomirsky, S., 522
Lyznicki, J. M., 225

Ma, J., 313
Maas, J., 226, 233
Maass, A., 643
Mabry, E., 682
Mabry, J. H., 276
Maccoby, E. E., 433, 476
Macdonald, S. E., 281
MacFarlane, S., 13
MacGregor, B., 147
Mack, A., 209–210
Mackey, M. C., 88
Mackie, D. M., 657
Mackin, R. S., 525
Mackinnon, L. T., 524
Macklis, J. D., 319
MacLin, M. K., 330, 342
MacLin, O. H., 330, 342
MacLin, R. L., 342
Macmillian, R., 649
Macworth, N., 209
Madden, P. A. F., 97
Maddi, K. L., 521
Maddi, S. R., 521
Maddox, K. B., 642
Maddox, W. T., 333

Madigan, S., 20
Madon, S., 38
Madsen, L., 413
Magee, W. J., 544
Maggi, G., 38
Magnuson, V. L., 439
Maguire, E. A., 73
Mah, K., 441
Mahalik J. R., 446
Mahay, J., 445
Maheu, M. M., 576
Maier, N. R. F., 507
Maixner, W., 57
Majeski, S. A., 422
Major, B., 608
Makela, E., 277, 677
Malamuth, N. M., 446, 650
Malaspina, D., 555
Malinosky-Rummell, R., 130
Malnic, B., 174
Maloney, 473
Malott, J. M., 185
Malpass, R. S., 307
Mamen, M., 105
Mandler, J. M., 91
Manfro, G. G., 544
Mangels, J. A., 312
Mangun, G. R., 67
Mann, C., 676
Mann, L., 635
Mannarino, A. P., 443
Manne, S. L., 265
Manning, M., 80
Manschreck, T. C., 551
Mansouri, A., 549
Manstead, A. S. R., 415
Mantyla, T., 322
Marcus, E., 572, 573
Marcus, H. R., 484
Marcus, S. C, 484
Marcus-Hewhall, A., 648
Marecek, J., 431
Margolin, G., 650
Margolin, J., 504
Marion, S. L., 484
Mark, H., 245
Markovits, H., 353
Marks, D. F., 214, 216, 331
Marks, J. S., 497, 499
Markus, H., 482
Markus, H. R., 144, 414, 415
Marmar, C., 587
Marriott, L. K., 140
Marsella, A. J., 672
Marsh, H. W., 514
Marshall, A., 379
Marshall, I., 379
Marshall, P. H., 325
Marston, A., 258
Marston, W., 412–413
Martens, R., 44
Martin, A, J., 514
Martin, C., 436
Martin, C. L., 433
Martin, D. J., 589
Martin, E. M., 578
Martin, G., 291
Martin, K. A., 684
Martin, L. L., 420
Martin, M., 79, 80
Martin, P. Y., 323
Martin, S., 12, 20
Martinez-Gonzales, M. A., 396
Martino, G., 254, 331
Martuza, R. L., 594
Marvin, R. S., 98
Marx, B. P., 446
Mashour, G.A., 594
Masi, G., 97
Maslach, C., 502
Maslow, A., 21, 22, 219, 406, 407, 479, 480, 483
Massaccesi, S., 92
Masten, A. S., 105
Masters, W., 440–441, 451, 454
Mateika, J. H., 227
Mateu-Gelabert, P., 652
Matheny, K. B., 528
Mathews, D., 431
Matossian, K. M., 572
Matschiner, S., 276
Matson, J. L., 271
Matsuda, L. A., 253
Matthews, M. D., 667
Mattock, A., 189
Mattson, J. L., 87
Maxwell, K. L., 374
May, C. P., 314
May, M., 573
Mayer, 02, 473
Mayer, A. R., 542
Mayer, J. D., 18, 422
Mayer, R. E., 335
Mays, V. M., 440
Mazzie, C., 108
Mazzoni, G., 303
McAlister, A., 657
McAlister, A. L., 577
McBride, W. J., 274
McCabe, M. P., 452
McCann, S. L., 227
McCarley, R. L., 228, 236
McCarrell, N. S., 334
McCarthy, B. W., 454
McCarthy, C. J., 528
McCarthy, R. A., 69
McCartney, K., 79, 86
McCartney, S., 446
McCarty, R., 16
McCaul, K. D., 185
McCeney, M. K., 520, 521
McClearn, G. E., 467
McClelland, C. L., 669
McClelland, D. C., 371, 384, 405, 408, 476, 528
McClelland, L., 676
McClintock, M. K., 175
McClure, J. B., 248
McCluskey, U., 586
McConnell, R., 506
McCoy, N. L., 175
McCrady, B. S., 253
McCrae, R. R., 351, 460, 465, 466, 467
McCrory, C., 379
McDaniel, M. A., 287, 322, 325
McDermott, J. F., 302
McDonald, J. L., 248
McDonnough, L., 108
McEachin, J. J., 129
McFarland, C., 613
McFarlane, A. C., 545
McGeary, J., 251
McGinnies, J. M., 159
McGinnis, J. M., 497
McGregor, D., 666
McGregor, I., 151
McGue, M., 467
McGuire, J. M., 680
McGuire, L, 523
McGurk, D., 546
McIntoch, W. D., 514
McIntosh, B., 620
McIntosh, W. D., 246, 614
McKay, G., 116
McKean, K. J., 512
McKeever, W. F., 79, 168
McKelton, D., 682
McKenna, K. Y. A., 620
McKenna, M. W., 615
McKim, W. A., 248, 525
McKinley, J. C., 487
McLean, N. J., 397, 605, 619, 657
McLennan, J., 514
McLoyd, V., 89, 284
McMahon, K., 184
McMahon, M., 303
McMahon, S., 398
McManus, I. C., 80
McMenamin, J. P., 576
McMullen, L. M., 560
McMurdo, M. E., 169
McNally, R., 231
McNally, R. J., 392
McNamara, D. S., 325
Mead, M., 432
Meagher, M. W., 184
Medin, D. L., 334
Mehrabian, A., 422, 614
Mehren, E., 100
Mehta, J. D., 39
Meichenbaum, D., 528, 652
Meier, R. P., 328
Meis, M., 674
Meltzoff, A. N., 90, 91, 92, 106, 111, 115, 128
Melzack, R., 181, 182, 183, 184, 185
Memon, A., 313
Mendes, W. B., 523, 527
Mendez, M., 52, 61, 67
Mendolia, M., 316, 510
Menese, G. D., 277
Mensour, B., 74
Menzel, P., 676
Menzies, R. G., 584
Mercer, J. G., 392
Merchelbach, H., 268
Merenda, P. F., 485
Merritt, M. A., 236
Mervis, C. B., 333
Mesmer, F., 237
Mesquita, B., 411
Messer, S. B., 573
Messer, S. C., 546
Messick, D. M., 657
Mestre, D. R., 66
Metcalfe, J, 342
Metha, A., 105
Metts, S., 613
Metz, J., 439
Meyer, G. J., 487
Meyer, I. H., 439, 440
Meyer, J., 244
Meyer, R. G., 414
Meyer-Bisch, C., 173
Micciolo, R., 477
Michael, G., 94
Michael, R., 438
Michaels, S., 438
Michaelsen, K. F., 100
Michalko, M., 348, 357, 358, 371
Michel, D. E., 184
Michel, G., 184
Michotte, A., 191
Mickelson, K. D., 617
Middahugh, S. J., 519
Midgley, C., 611
Mielke, H. W., 550, 551
Mignot, E, 334
Mikulincer, M., 616
Milgram, S., 605, 622, 623, 626, 673
Milgrim, S., 5
Milich, R., 128, 401
Militello, L., 346
Millepiedi, S., 97
Miller, D., 451
Miller, D. C., 37
Miller, D. T., 608, 612, 613, 653
Miller, G., 300
Miller, G. E., 523, 524
Miller, I. J., 176
Miller, K. M., 614
Miller, L. K., 335, 363, 373
Miller, M., 515
Miller, N., 475, 476, 506, 648
Miller, N. E., 508, 640
Miller, S. D., 600
Miller, S. J., 590
Miller-Jones, D., 383
Millgram, S., 619
Milling, L. S., 303
Millorood, D. L, 227
Milnder, B., 319
Milne, R., 217
Milner, A. D., 164
Miltenberger, R. G., 127, 578, 583
Miltner, W. H., 544
Milton, J., 214, 215
Minda, J. P., 334
Mineka, S., 269, 487, 532
Miotto, K., 248
Mira, C. B, 560
Mirabile, R., 635
Miranda, J., 560
Mirsky, A. F., 40
Mischel, W., 459, 466, 474, 476
Mistlberger, R. E., 402
Mitchell, D. B., 305
Mitru, G., 227
Miura, H., 395
Miyake, A., 298
Miyamoto, Y., 205
Mize, J., 102
Mo, L., 344
Moar, K. M., 392
Moerman, D. E., 37, 38
Moffitt, T. E., 105, 460
Mogg, K., 159, 210
Moghaddam, B., 556
Mohanty, S., 583
Mokdad, A. H., 497, 499
Molenaar, J. C., 430
Moltz, H., 439
Monahan, J., 554
Money, J., 431
Monteith, M. J., 656
Montgomery, G., 63, 239
Moody, J., 447
Moody, M., 600
Moor, J. H., 346
Moore, J., 210, 219
Moore, J. H., 648
Moore, K., 91, 613
Moore, K. A., 502
Moore, T. E., 91
Moorman, R. H., 669
Moras, K., 588
Morelli, G. A., 96
Moreno, J. L., 586
Morey, L. C., 600
Morgan, F. H., 505
Morgan, J. P., 648
Morgan, M. J., 146, 149, 208
Morgan, M.J., 246
Morgenstern, J., 253
Moriarty, T., 625
Morin, C. M., 233
Morisse, D., 583
Moritz, A. P., 411
Moritz, S. E., 684
Morris, G., 416
Morris, R. G., 148
Morsella, E., 328
Mortensen, E. L., 100
Moser, D., 127
Moses, J. L., 666
Mosher, C., 644
Mosier, J., 586
Moskowitz, J., 503, 504, 505, 519
Moss, K., 258
Most, S. B., 192
Motes, M. A., 335
Moudin, G. W., 600
Moun, M. K., 465
Mouradian, V. E., 285
Mrdjenovic, G., 392
Mshelia, A. Y., 201
Mucci, M., 97
Muchinsky, P. M., 662, 665, 670
Mukamal, K., 498
Mullen, P. E., 130
Muller, S. P., 74
Mullington, J., 334
Muris, P., 268
Murphy, J. M., 274
Murphy, M. A., 583
Murray, B., 394, 577
Murray, C., 383
Murray, C. B., 611
Murray, J. B., 182, 556
Murray, L., 560

Murray, S., 248
Murray, S. L., 616
Murry, S. L., 636
Murtaugh, M., 374
Musen, G., 305
Musen, P. H, 305, 318
Mussen, P. H., 107
Musso, M., 74
Mustanski, B. S., 439
Myers, H. F., 560
Myerson, J., 369

Nachshon, O., 616
Nagasaka, T., 491
Nagel, T., 225
Nairne, J. S., 300, 314
Naitoh, P., 226
Nakamura, J., 408, 684
Nakashima, K., 395
Nakashima, M., 147
Nanez, J. E., 111
Nantel, G., 353
Napa, C., 150
Naranjo, C., 576
Narduzzi, K., 491, 492
Natale, V., 402
Natarajan, L., 254
Nathan, P. E., 320, 534, 590
National Academy of Sciences, 412, 414
National Institute of Child Health and Human Development, 100
Navarro, M., 248
Naveh-Behjamin, M., 4
Neath, I., 298, 300, 308, 309, 314, 315, 322, 325
Neave, N., 671
Needles, D. J., 515
Neff, F., 682
Nehlig, A., 246
Neidhardt, J., 233
Neisser, U., 318, 368, 371, 376, 377, 381, 383
Nelson, C., 656
Nelson, C. A., 87, 88, 89
Nelson, C. E., 488
Nelson, G., 211
Nelson, J. R., 136
Nelson, T. D., 639
Nesca, M., 319
Neter, E., 43
Neubert, M. J., 666
Neufeld, P., 218
Neufeld, R. W., 184, 552
Neugarten, B., 145–146
Neuman, G. A., 58, 488
Neurmeister, A., 562
Nevid, J., 430, 439
Nevid, J. S., 558
Newcomb, M. D., 449
Newcomb, T., 634
Newell, A., 346
Newman, A. W., 303
Newman, B. M., 108, 134
Newman, J. L., 669
Newman, P. R., 108, 134
Newman, R., 577
Newport, E. L., 338
Nezu, A. M., 394
Ngu, H., 314
Niaura, R., 520
Niaura, R. S., 248
Niccolai, L., 447
Nicholls, G., 527
Nickell, J., 44, 47
Nickerson, R., 312, 313
Nida, S. A., 653
Niedzwienska, A., 318
Niehaus, D. J. H., 590
Niehoff, B. P., 669
Nielsen, D. M., 105
Nijstad, B. A., 358
Nikles, C. D., 236
Nilsson, L., 491
Nisbett, R. E., 205, 377, 383, 610, 656
Nist, S. L., 321
Njeri, I., 23, 657
Nobel, K. D., 406
Noble, P., 554
Noh, S., 518
Noice, H., 322
Noice, T., 322
Nolen-Hoeksema, 536
Nolen-Hoeksema, S., 534
Noller, P., 610
Norcross, J. C., 589, 600
Norenzayan, A., 205, 383
Nori, G., 391
Norlander, T., 241
Norman, D., 193
Norman, K. A., 302
Normann, A. D., 157
Norris, R. M., 513
Norsek, B. A., 640
North, C., 532, 550
Northcutt, R. G., 175
Norvig, P., 345
Norwood, R. M., 492
Novaco, R., 506
Nowell, P. D., 232
Nurius, P., 482
Nurmi, J., 101, 150
Nurnberger, J. I., 291, 293
Nussbaum, M., 392

O'Brien, R. M., 271
O'Callaghan, P. M., 583
O'Connell, D. Q., 321
O'Conner, P., 134
O'Conner, T. G., 98
O'Connor, M. G., 311
O'Hara, M. W., 20, 481, 514
O'Leary, K. D., 478
O'Neil, K. M., 682
O'Neill, B., 45
O'Neill, P., 16, 211
O'Roark, A. M., 488
O'Shea, D., 391
O'Sullivan, M., 417
Oakley, D. A., 239
Oakley, R., 519
Oatley, K., 409
Oberbracht, C., 589
Obernier, J. A., 251
Obhi, S. S., 56
Ochsner, K. N., 316
Oest, L., 579
Ofosu, H. B., 397
Ogden, J., 453
Ogilvie, R., 258
Ogles, B. M., 588
Ogloff, J. R. P., 682
Ohayon, M. M., 233
Olds, 274
Oliver, J. E., 130
Oliver, M. B., 438
Oliveto, A. H., 247
Oliwenstein, L., 226
Ollendick, T. H., 269, 584
Olrick, J. T., 98
Olsen, E. A., 307
Olsen, J. M., 645
Olson, J. M., 633
Olson, L., 58
Olson, R. L., 582
Olson, S. L., 101
Ones, D. S., 488, 663
Onwuegbuzie, A. J., 5
Operskalski, B., 577
Orleans, C. T., 498, 500
Orlick, T. D., 683
Orlinsky, D. E., 588
Orne, M. T., 413
Ornstein, R., 67, 211
Ornstein, S., 140
Osgood, C. E., 335
Oskamp, S., 632, 634, 635, 672, 675, 676, 678
Osma, J., 580
Osmon, D. C., 379
Osofsky, M. J., 644
Osrin,Y., 377
Ossoff, E. P., 615
Ostrove, J. M., 138, 140
Oswald, F. L., 663, 664
Overmier, J. B., 512
Owen, J. D., 668
Oyama T., 333
Oyserman, D., 482

Pace-Schott, E. F, 230
Page, W., 79
Pagnin, D, 594
Palfai, T., 253
Palm, K., 317
Palmer, J., 302
Palmer, S. E., 129, 191
Palmer-Seal, D. A., 448
Panagiotides, H., 128
Pandey, S., 673
Panelis, C., 557
Papa, A., 422
Papa, F. J., 276
Papaeliou, C., 80
Papasouiotis, O., 244
Papps, F., 104
Paquette, V., 74
Park, D. C., 312
Park, L. E., 105
Park, N., 480
Parke, R. D., 90, 103, 104
Parker, G. B., 415
Parker, J., 519
Parker, J. D. A., 422
Parkes, C. M., 148
Parsons, L. M., 333
Passarello, L. C., 442
Passman, R. H., 99
Pasupathi, M., 137
Pati, N. C., 583
Patrick, C. J., 413, 542
Patry, M. W., 682
Patten, B. M., 324
Patteron, C. J., 440
Patterson, C. J., 439
Patterson, D. R., 184
Patterson, G. R., 104
Paul, S. M., 99
Pauli-Magnus, C., 589
Pavlidis, I., 413
Pavlov, I., 18, 263
Pavot, W., 150
Pawlick, K., 519
Pear, J., 291
Pearson, C. G., 145
Pedersen, C. A., 57
Pedersen, N. L., 467
Pedersen, W. C., 506
Peeters, M. C. W., 505
Pekrun, R. H., 4
Pelhan, W. E., 128
Pelled, L. H., 668
Pelletier, S. T., 4
Pelton, T., 683
Penfield, W., 301
Penick, J. M., 528
Penn, D. L., 562
Penner, L. A., 651, 654
Pennisi, E., 175
Penrod, S., 307
Penrod, S. D., 682
Pepler, D. J., 32
Perachio, N., 431
Perez, M. J., 4, 324
Perin, C. T., 272
Perkins, D. N., 378, 380
Perkins, D. V., 596
Perlman, D., 681
Perls, F., 257, 576
Perreault, S., 641
Perri, M. G., 394
Perrin, A., 499
Perry, R. P., 4, 512
Perry, Z. W., 642
Person, E., 363
Persons, J., 584
Perugini, E. M., 237
Pervin, L. A., 476, 483
Pescatello, L. S., 499
Pete, E., 394
Peters, R. J., 657
Peters, W. A., 484, 644
Petersen, A. C., 62, 132
Petersen, M. B., 375
Peterson, B. E., 641
Peterson, C, 522
Peterson, C., 480, 512
Peterson, J., 25
Peterson, L. R., 301
Peterson, M. J., 301
Peterson, P. L., 680
Peterson, S. E., 321
Peterson, T. R., 420
Petit, D., 227
Petri, H., 398
Petrie, T. A., 685
Petrill, S. A, 379
Petruzzi, D. C., 402
Pettay, D., 375
Pettigrew, T. F., 646
Pettit, G. S., 102
Philips, J. L., 112
Phillips, D. P, 412
Phillips, D. S., 310
Phillips, J., 626
Piaget, J., 109–114
Piccinelli, M., 477
Picone, R. P., 254
Piction, T. W., 312
Picton, T. W., 312
Piedrahita, L. E., 369
Pierce, J. P., 248, 271
Pierrehumbert, B., 100
Pierrel, R., 272
Pierson, J. F., 21
Piliavin, I. M., 654
Piliavin, J. A., 651, 654, 655
Pilkonis, P. A., 492
Pillow, D. R., 516
Pilon, D. A., 476
Pincus, H. A., 535
Pinel, J. P. J., 394, 395
Pines, A. M., 502
Pini, S., 594
Pinker, S., 339
Pinof, W. M., 587
Pinsker, H., 571
Pion, G. M., 20
Pisacreta, R., 272
Pitino, L., 175
Piven,J., 129
Pividori, D., 92
Pizam, A., 401
Platt, D. E., 564
Plaud, J. J., 579
Pliner, P., 397
Plomin, R., 555
Plug, C., 201, 202
Plutchik, R., 409, 422
Pogatchnik, S., 289
Poland, J., 534
Polemikos, N., 80
Polivey, J., 396
Pollack, M. H., 544
Pollack, W. S., 652
Pollak, S. D., 130
Pollner, M., 484
Pollock, V. E., 506, 542
Pomeroy, W., 436
Poole, W. K., 412
Pope, H. G., 254
Porac, C., 80
Port, R. L., 556
Porte, D., 392
Porter, S., 317
Posada, G., 98
Posey, A., 468
Potenza, M. N., 244
Potter, J., 460

Poulton, R. G., 548
Powell, A. A., 654
Powell, A. L., 281, 397
Powell, F. C., 146
Pratkanis, A. R., 159
Preisler, J. J., 515
Premack, A. J., 339
Premack, D., 328–339
Prentice, D. A., 608, 613
Pressley, M., 322, 325
Presson, C. C., 500
Prilleltensky, I., 211
Priluck, R. L., 266
Pritchard, R. M., 181
Provencher, M. D., 548
Provins, K. A., 79
Puca, R. M., 405
Pulier, M. L., 576
Pulkkinen, L., 101
Pulvirenti, L., 246
Pursch, J. A., 246
Pursell, C. R., 97
Py, J., 303
Pychyl, T. A., 6

Quero, S., 580
Quillian, M. R., 304
Quinn, P. C., 39, 114, 157

Raag, T., 433
Rabinowitz, M., 449
Rabinowitz, V. C., 23, 41
Rabionovich, M. I., 174
Rabius, V., 577
Rachman, S., 542, 547
Racine R. J., 320
Rackliff, C. L., 433
Rader, P. E., 402
Radio, S. J., 685
Rafaeli, A., 43
Rahe, R., 515
Rahman, Q., 439
Rajab, M. H., 564
Rakfeldt, J., 594
Ramachandran, V. S., 156
Ramanaiah, N. V., 435
Ramey, C. T., 90, 377
Ramirez, A., 613
Ramirez-Valles, J., 449
Ramsay, D., 195
Rana-Deuba, A., 518
Rand, Y., 377
Randi, J., 213, 216
Rando, T. A., 149
Randolph, C., 258
Rangell, L., 573
Rank, O., 21
Rasmussen, F., 555
Rathus, R., 430, 439
Rau, H., 519
Raven, B.H, 621
Rawsthorne, L. J., 481
Razzoli, E., 555
Rea, C. B., 342
Read, J., 451
Read, S. K., 452
Redd, W. H., 265
Redden, D. T., 498
Redmond, G., 436
Reed, G. M., 498, 501, 505, 522
Reed, T. E., 322, 323, 379
Regan, P., 613, 616
Regan, P. C., 617, 618
Reichel, A., 401
Reichenberg, A., 555
Reid, M., 79
Reid, M. R., 524
Reid, P. T., 23, 41
Reilly, M. P., 320
Reinisch, J. M., 100
Reinitz, M. T., 302
Reis, H. T., 98, 141, 422, 522, 617
Reiser, B., 308
Reiss, M., 79
Reiss, S., 406, 479
Reiterman, T., 637
Reitman, D., 583
Remland, M. S., 608
Rende, R., 555
Renjilian, D. A., 394
Renner, M. J., 525
Reno, R. R., 608
Rentflow, P., 463
Reppucci, N. D., 130, 446
Rescorla, R. A., 266
Resnick, H., 504
Restak, R. M., 244
Restak, R. M., 111
Revonsuo, A., 237
Rew, L., 448
Reyner, L. A., 226
Reznick, J. S., 106
Rhine, J. B., 214
Rhoads, K., 408
Rhodes, A., 624
Rhodewalt, F., 611
Rhudy, J. L., 184
Ricci-Bitti, P. E., 414
Rice, K. G., 467
Rice, M. E., 541, 554
Richards, J. B., 501
Richards, J. H., 151
Richards, L., 626
Richardson, F. C., 656
Richelle, M. N., 18
Richman, C. L., 645
Richmond, M. K., 98
Richter, W., 331
Richter-Appelt, H., 430
Ricketts, M. S., 402
Riefer, D. M., 306
Rieff, S., 267
Rieke, M. L., 488
Rieser, J., 342
Righter, E. L., 543
Rilling, J. K., 37
Rimmer, D. W., 402, 403
Riquelme, H., 351
Risley, T. R., 108
Ritchey, A. K., 523
Ritchie, B. F., 286
Ritchie, R. J., 666
Ritter, J., 645
Rivara, F. P., 648
Rizzo, C. P., 284
Robels, T. F., 523
Robert, S., 477
Roberti, J. W., 401
Roberts, B. W., 460
Roberts, D. G., 284
Roberts, M. C., 132, 134
Roberts, M. W., 582
Roberts, W. L., 32
Robertson, L. C., 331
Robinette, D., 79
Robins, R. W., 22
Robinson, A., 372
Robinson, B., 637
Robinson, D. L., 381
Robinson, E. J., 7
Robinson-Riegler, B., 325
Robson, P., 93
Rochat, P., 111
Rock, I., 209–210
Rock, S. L., 90
Rodin, J., 654
Rodriguez, N., 560
Rodriquez Mosquera, P. M., 415
Roeckelein, J. E., 308
Roeder, K., 377
Roediger, H. L., 302, 308
Rogers, B. J., 197
Rogers, C., 21, 479, 480, 481, 482
Rogers, C. R., 548, 574, 575
Rogers, J. A., 594
Rogers, M., 159
Rogers, R., 550
Rogers, S., 581
Rogers, W. T., 402
Rogerson, J., 268
Rogoff, B., 365
Rohsenow, D. J., 585
Roid, G., 365
Roizen, M. F., 144
Rokeach, M., 641
Rollerson, B., 626
Rolling, B. L., 126
Rolls, E. T., 164
Rompre, P. P., 73
Ronen, T., 127
Roney, J. R., 438
Roos, P. E., 435
Rosabinanca, A., 643
Rosch, E., 334
Rose, R. J., 375, 379, 467
Rosen, G., 183
Rosenbaum, M., 390
Rosenberg, E., 414
Rosenberg, R., 198, 206
Rosenberg, S. S., 576
Rosenfeld, P., 636, 681
Rosenhan, D., 562
Rosenkranz, M. A., 524
Rosenman, R. H., 520
Rosenthal, R., 29, 36, 38, 39, 353
Rosenthal, R. N., 571
Rosenthal, S. L., 445
Rosenthal, T. L., 268, 288, 527, 561, 598
Rosenzweig, M. R., 89
Ross, D., 288
Ross, D. C., 79
Ross, H. E., 201, 202
Ross, M., 462
Ross, N. O., 334
Ross, S. A., 288
Rossi, A. S., 140
Roth, M. D., 254
Roth, W. T., 403
Rothbaum, B., 581
Rotolo, T., 371
Rourke, B. P., 375
Rovee-Collier, C., 93
Rowan, M. J., 320
Rowe, J. W., 142
Rowe, W., 159
Rowell, A., 676
Rozin, P., 394
Rubenstein, C., 138, 444
Rubin, D. C., 318
Rubin, K. H., 103
Rubin, V., 254
Rudd, M. D., 564
Rudman, L. A., 639
Rudolf, G., 589
Rueckl, J. G., 308
Ruiz, J. M., 521, 523, 527
Rumbaugh, D., 340
Rummens, J., 518
Runco, M. A., 347, 348, 349, 358, 371
Ruscio, J., 408
Rushforth, N. B., 648
Rusnak, K., 581
Russ, E., 588
Russell, D. W., 38
Russell, J. A., 414
Russell, S., 345
Russell, S. T., 439
Russell, T. G., 159
Russo, M. B., 547
Russo, N. F., 432, 560
Ruthsatz, J., 373
Rutledge, T., 392, 420
Ruts, W., 334
Rutter, M., 86, 98
Ruzzene, M., 610
Ryan, A. M., 664
Ryan, M. P., 3
Ryan, R. M., 405, 407, 408, 481
Ryff, C. D., 140, 141, 151
Rynearson, K., 2

Saab, P. G., 524
Saadeh, W., 284
Sachdev, P., 594
Sack, R. L., 561
Sackett, P. R., 384
Sadker, D., 478
Sadker,M., 478
Saegrt, S., 613
Sage, R. M., 514
Sagiv, N., 331
Sagvolden, T., 128
Sahelian, R., 233
Saklofske, D. H., 43
Saks, M. J., 40
Salas, E., 528
Sales, B. D., 681, 682
Salmela, J. H., 683
Salmon, P., 526
Salovey, P., 314, 422
Salthouse, T. A., 142
Sampson, P. D., 87
Samstag, L. W., 571
Sander, L., 106
Sanderman, R., 558
Sanders, A. R., 561
Sanders, J., 623
Sanders, S. A., 100
Sandler, I., 516
Sanftner, J., 516
Sanna, L. J., 611
Sansone, L. A., 543
Sansone, R. A., 543
Santy, P. A., 183
Sapirstein, G., 38, 239
Sarvela, P. D., 445
Sateia, M. J., 232
Saudino, K. J., 467
Saunders, L. A., 244
Saunders, T., 528
Savage, A. R., 375
Savage-Rumbaugh, S., 340
Savsevitz, J., 578
Sawa, A., 556
Sawyer, R. G., 445
Saxe, L., 413
Saywitz, K. J., 443
Scarborough, E., 20
Schachter, S., 418, 419
Schacter, D. L., 48, 226, 302, 312, 320, 322
Schacter, S, 612
Schaeffer, J. A., 581
Schafer, M., 620
Schafer, W. D., 37
Schaie, W. D., 142, 145
Schaller, S., 22, 23, 328
Schaufeli, W. B., 502
Scheck, M. M., 581
Scher, S. J., 6, 635
Scherer, K. R., 414
Schick, B., 215, 216
Schick, T., 483
Schilling, M. A., 342
Schiraldi, G. R., 528
Schlager, M. S., 287
Schleicher, S. S., 436
Schlosberg, H., 416
Schmalt, H., 405
Schmalt, H.-D., 349
Schmeidler, J., 546
Schmidlin, A. M., 608
Schmidt, F. L., 663
Schmidt, K. L., 131
Schmitt, D. P., 462, 618
Schmitt, E., 23
Schmitt, F. L., 488
Schmitt, N., 384
Schmolck, H., 318
Schneider, D. L., 448
Schneider, H. G., 276
Schneider, K. J., 21, 574
Schneider, L., 542
Schneiderman, K. J., 524
Schoenfield, D., 340
Scholl, B. J., 192
Schoote, D. E., 392
SchredL, M., 257
Schreiber, F. R., 546

Schrieken, B., 577
Schroeder, A., 678
Schroeder, D. A., 651, 654
Schroeder, J. E., 492
Schroots, J. J. F., 144
Schuel, H., 254
Schulman, C. C., 140
Schultheiss, O. C., 74
Schultz, C. J., 130
Schultz, D., 538
Schultz, H. T., 25
Schultz, P. W., 632, 634, 635, 677
Schulz, R., 141, 144, 148
Schuman, C. C., 94
Schunk, D. H., 6
Schuster, M. A., 504
Schwartz, C., 159
Schwartz, M. D., 395
Schwartz, M. S., 518
Schwartz, M. W., 390–391, 392
Schwinghammer, S. A., 613
Schwinn, S., 488
Sclafani, A., 392
Scoboria, A., 303
Scott, J. P., 241, 648
Scott, L., 481, 514
Scott, S. S., 680
Scroppo, J. C., 546
Scweitzer, P. K., 232
Seal, D. W., 448
Seamonds, C., 468
Searcy, J., 203
Sears, R. R., 476
Sechzer, J. A., 23, 41
Seed, M., 99
Seeley, R. J., 392
Seftel, A. D., 451
Segal, N. L., 467
Segraves, K. B., 437–438, 451
Segraves, R. T., 437–438, 451
Segraves, T., 452
Seidman, B. F., 38
Sekuler, A., 156, 181
Seligman, M. E. P., 22, 411, 422, 480, 512–513, 560, 589, 599
Selye, H., 501, 522
Senécal C., 606
Senior, C., 415
Senn, C. Y., 397
Serbin, L. A., 478
Sergeant, J. A., 128
Sermsri, S., 673
Service, R. F., 320
Serwood, A., 499
Sessa, V. I., 669
Sevin, J. A., 271
Seybold, K. S., 556
Seybolt, D. C., 477
Seying, R., 681
Shaffer, D., 114
Shaffer, J. B., 587
Shafir, E., 354
Shafton, A., 230, 235, 236
Shakesby, A. C., 320
Shakespeare, W., 249
Shames, J., 357
Shamir, A., 377
Shananhan, T. L., 403
Shanker, S., 340
Shankster, L. J., 664, 665, 666
Shannon, E. A., 79
Shapiro, F., 581
Sharar, S., 184
Sharkey, K. M., 403
Sharma, T., 557
Sharman, S. J., 321
Shaughnessy, J. J., 323
Shaver, P. R., 98, 444, 616, 617
Shaw, G. L., 218
Shaw, S. F., 680
Shayka, J. J., 484
Shaywitz, S. E., 70
Shea, C. H., 276
Sheldon, K. M., 151, 481
Shepard, R. N., 331
Shepherd, K. L., 516
Sher, L., 561
Sherif, M., 608, 645
Sherman, D. K., 514
Sherman, M. F., 272
Sherman, S. J., 500
Sherrod, K. B., 101
Sherwood, R., 342
Shin, Y. J., 172
Shine, D., 449
Shires, A., 451
Shneidman, E., 564
Shoda, Y., 466, 474, 476
Shore, H., 577
Shore, L. A., 14
Shrager, E. E., 395
Shrum, L. J., 159
Shugar, G. J., 276
Shurkin, J., 371
Siau, K. L., 358
Sieber, J. E., 40
Sieggreen, M. A., 311
Siever, L. J., 540
Sigelman, C. K., 481
Sigman, M., 128
Silva, C. E., 237
Silver, E., 554
Silver, S. M., 581
Silverman, K., 247
Silverman, L. K., 372
Silverman, R., 583
Simard, C., 227
Simeon, D., 546
Simeonova, D., 352
Simmons, J., 583
Simner, M. L., 43
Simon, A., 47
Simon, A. F., 640, 643
Simon, G. E., 577
Simon, H. A., 346
Simonotto, E., 379
Simons, D, 210
Simons, D. J., 192, 313
Simonton, D. K., 22
Simpson, D. D., 246
Simpson, J. A., 617
Simpson, K. J., 127, 397
Sims, K. E., 97
Sims, S., 301
Singer, D., 651
Singer, J., 651
Singer, J. D., 620
Singer, M. T., 637, 638
Singer, R. N., 685
Singleton, J. L., 338
Sipos, A., 555
Sirkin, M. I., 638
Sison, C. E., 550
Sitarenios, G, 422
Six, L. S., 310
Skaff, M. M., 461
Skeels, H. M., 377
Skinner, B. F., 18–19, 270, 271, 278–279
Skipton, L. H., 459
Skovholt, T. M., 134, 600
Skuy, M., 377
Slaby, A. E., 564
Slade, M. D., 145
Slaney, R. B., 467
Slater, A., 189
Sledge, W. H., 594
Sleek, S., 25
Slijper, F. M. E., 430
Slot, L. A. B., 314
Slotkin, T. A., 87
Slutske, W. S., 97
Smailes, E. M., 289
Small, M., 307
Smedley, A., 657
Smedley, B. C, 657
Smethuyrst, W., 3, 4, 6, 7
Smith, A. P., 323
Smith, C. L., 105
Smith, D. J., 136
Smith, E. E., 37
Smith, F. J., 390
Smith, J. D., 334
Smith, J. L., 410
Smith, K. E., 114
Smith, K. H., 159
Smith, L. B., 195
Smith, L. F., 402
Smith, N. G., 445
Smith, P. B., 620
Smith, R. E., 585
Smith, R. H., 624
Smith, R. W., 342
Smith, S. M., 246, 614
Smith, T., 129
Smith, T. W., 438, 444, 521, 523, 527
Smolen, A., 251
Smouse, A. D., 159
Snow, C. P., 624
Snowden, L. R., 538
Snyder, B., 322
Snyder, S. H., 556
Sobel, E., 449
Sobolewski, J. M., 89
Sokol, B. W., 590
Sokolik, A., 37
Solomon, R. C., 284
Solomon, R. L., 403
Solowij, R. L., 254
Solso, R. L., 342
Somberg, D. R., 600
Sommer, C., 486
Sommer, R., 672
Somorjai, R., 331
Song, W. O., 397
Sorce, J. F., 96
Sorkenn, J., 546
Soussignan, R., 415, 419
Spackmann, M. P., 680
Spanenberg, J. J., 435
Spector, P. E., 488, 669
Spence, J. T., 206
Spencer, L., 172
Sperry, R. W., 19, 65, 66
Spiegel, D., 546
Spiegler, M. D, 578, 579, 583
Spiegler, M. D., 275
Spinella, M., 247
Spirito, A., 564
Spiro, A., 520
Sporer, S. L., 204
Sprecher, S., 617, 618
Springer, D., 392
Springer, S. P., 65, 67, 79, 80
Springston, F., 300
Squire, L. R., 304, 305, 318, 319, 320
Srivastava, S., 460
Sroufe, L. A., 130
Staats, A., 184
Staats, P., 184
Stackhouse, T. L., 325
Stafanis, C., 254
Standing, L., 314
Stanhope, N., 312
Stanley, D. A., 402
Stanley, M. A., 248
Stanovich, K. E., 13, 14, 28, 30, 48, 107
Stansfeld, S. A., 674
Stantion, S. J., 74
Stanton, A. L., 74
Stapel, D. A., 613
Staska, M., 108
Staudinger, U. M., 137, 142, 144, 145
Staw, B. M., 668
Steadman, H. J., 554
Steblay, N. M., 218, 674
Steciuk, M., 58, 614
Steele, C. M., 643
Steen, N., 668
Steffek, B. D., 288
Stein, B. D., 504
Stein, D. J., 590
Stein, M. T., 342, 357
Stein, N. D., 491
Steinberg, L. D., 506
Steinberg, R.J., 132, 133, 134
Steingrueber, H., 395
Stellar, E., 395
Stemmerich, E., 151
Stenberg, G., 96
Stephan, W, 211
Stephan, W., 277
Stephens, K., 383
Stepper, S., 420
Steptoe, A., 498
Steriade, M., 228
Stern, R. M., 107, 180, 550
Sternbach, H., 140
Sternberg, E. M., 501, 515
Sternberg, R. J., 342–343, 351, 352, 357, 358, 363, 364, 365, 383, 408, 657
Sternberg, R., 380
Steurer, F. B., 633
Stevens, L. C., 130, 527
Stevenson, L. A., 416
Stewart, A. J., 138, 140
Stewart, A. M., 485
Stewart, B. L., 564
Stewart, J. V., 44
Stewart-Williams, S., 37
Stewin, L. L., 227
Stich, E., 600
Stickgold, R., 230, 235, 236
Stöber, J., 402
Stockdale, G. D., 640
Stockhorst, U., 395
Stokes, D. M., 214, 216
Stokoe, W. C., 328
Stokols, D., 674
Stolerman, I. P., 247
Stolp, S., 446
Stone, G., 600
Stone, J., 642
Stoney, S., 277
Stopfer, M., 174
Stoppard, J. M., 560
Storm, D. R., 255
Storms, G., 334
Stough, C., 379
Stovel, K., 447
Strack, F., 420
Strain, E. C., 372
Strambler, M. J., 38
Straneva, P. A., 57
Strange, J. R., 76
Strauss, J. L., 581
Strayer, D. L., 210
Streissguth, A. P., 87
Strickler, E. M., 398
Strier, F., 682
Stroebe, W., 149, 358
Stroeher, S. K., 433
Strong, B., 444, 455
Strong, C., 352
Strongman, K. T., 420, 421
Strote, J., 246
Stroud, L., 520
Stroup, D. F., 497, 499
Strupp, H. H., 600
Stuart, S. P., 590
Sturges, J. W., 579
Sturges, L. V., 579
Stuss, D. T., 66, 67
Su, M., 677
Subotnik, R. F., 406
Suchy, Y., 542
Sue, D, 443
Sue, D. W., 443
Sue, S., 443
Suedfeld, P., 241, 369
Sugihara, Y., 435
Sugimori, S., 462
Sugimoto, K., 395
Suh, E. M., 478
Suinn, R. M., 500, 543, 553, 580, 657
Sukel, H. L., 681
Sullivan, J., 94
Sullivan, M. J., 27

Sullivan, P., 132
Suls, J., 133
Sulzer, J. L., 667
Sumerlin, J. R., 479, 480
Summerfeldt, L. J., 422
Summers, R., 331
Sunnafrank, M., 613
Sutton, R. I., 668
Suzuki, A., 68
Svejda, M., 96
Svensson, L., 579
Swamidass, P. M., 606, 667
Swank, P. R., 114
Swanson, J., 232
Swanson, M. W., 87
Swap, W., 613
Swartzwelder, H. S., 291
Swerdlik, M. E., 364
Swim, J. K., 611
Symbaluk, D. G., 281
Symons, N., 180
Symons, S., 322

Taft, L., 375
Takooshian, H., 674
Talbott, J. A., 596
Talley, P. F., 600
Tallis, F., 545
Tallman, K., 574
Tamis-LaMonda, C. S., 86
Tamkins, M. M., 432
Tan, Ü, 379
Taparti, L., 590
Tapert, S. F., 251
Taraban, R., 2
Tardif, T. Z., 351
Tart, C. T., 224
Tavris, C., 444
Taylor, A., 105, 680
Taylor, F., 666
Taylor, J. R., 244
Taylor, K., 637
Taylor, S., 580
Taylor, S. E., 265, 498, 501, 505, 514, 517, 522
Taylor, T., 340
Taylor, T. E., 240
Taylor-Seehafer, M., 448
Taytroe, L., 236
Te Nijenhuis, J., 241
Tebes, J., 594
Tedeschi, J. T., 636, 648, 681
Tenenbaum, G., 684
Teng, E., 320
Tenhula, W. N., 583
Terman, L., 365, 371
Terry, D. J., 634
Terry, K., 482
Tesser, A., 6
Tharp, R. G., 271, 291, 402
Thase, M. E., 593
Thelen, E., 93
Thelen, M. H., 397
Thibodeau, R., 6
Thomas, A., 86, 101, 126
Thomas, G. V., 7
Thomas, S., 528
Thompson, C. P., 310
Thompson, J. W., 303
Thompson, K. M., 289
Thompson, L. A., 379
Thompson, R. A., 87
Thompson, W. L., 331
Thomson, W. L., 332
Thornberg, H. D., 680
Thorndike, E. L., 269
Thorson, J. A., 146
Thousand, J. S., 680
Thurber, S., 2
Thyen, U., 430
Tice, D. M., 5
Tidwell, M. O., 98, 617
Tiffany, S. T., 578
Tighe, M. R., 334
Tijerino, R., 671
Till, B. D., 266
Tillotson, C. A., 97
Tilton-Weaver, L. C., 132
Timmerman, I. G. H., 558
Tipples, J., 414
Titchener, E. B., 17
Tittle C. R., 371
Todaro, J. F., 520
Tolley-Schell, S. A., 130
Tolman, E. C., 41, 46, 286
Tomasello, M., 107, 108
Topsever, P., 379
Toro, J., 127
Toro, P. A., 596
Torrance, M., 7
Torry, E. F., 549, 596
Tourangeau, R., 40, 42
Towson, S., 491, 492
Trachet, T., 44
Trappey, C., 159
Traux, S. R., 419
Treasure, D. C., 611
Treffert, D. A., 363, 373
Treharne, G. J., 516
Trehub, S. E., 108
Tremblay, P., 440
Triandis, H. C., 478
Tripp, P., 226
Trippe, R., 544
Troll, L. E., 461
Troutman, A. C., 285
Tryon, R. C., 376
Tsai, C., 397
Tsai, F.-R., 611
Tsai, G., 556
Tsai, W.-C., 664
Tse, L., 134
Tubb, V. A., 313
Tucker, K. L., 522
Tuckman, B. W., 683
Tufik, S., 232, 235
Tugade, M. M., 500
Tuholski, S. W., 298
Tulley, M., 285
Tulving, E., 304, 305, 319, 320
Tupling, R. E., 516
Turetsky, B. I., 557
Turk, D. C., 184
Turkheimer, E., 379
Turnbull, W., 613
Turner, S. J. M., 587
Turton, M. D., 391
Turvey, M. T., 179
Tutty, S., 577
Tversky, A., 353–354
Twenge, J. M., 434, 444, 462
Tye-Murray, N., 172
Tyler, J. M., 613
Tymnik, G., 79
Tynelius, P., 555
Tzeng, M., 614
Tzuriel, D., 377

Uchino, B. N., 523, 527
Udari-Solner, A., 680
Udry, E., 685
Underwood, B. J., 315
UNESCO, 648
Unger, F., 356
Unsworth, G., 290
Unterstaller, U., 545
Urdan, T., 611
Utasi, A., 520

Vaillant, G. E., 498
Valente, S. M., 429, 430, 431
Valentine, E., 310–311, 324
Valery, J. H., 134
Valian, V., 432
Valiente, C., 105
Valins, S., 677
Van Boemmel, H., 401
van de Ven, J-P., 577
van der Hart, O., 572
Van Der Ploeg, H. M., 546
Van der Veld, J., 436
van Dierendonck, D., 241
Van Dongen, H. P., 226
Van Eenwyk, J., 290
Van Goozen, S. H. M., 398
Van Heck, G. L., 521
Van Kammen, D. P., 40
Van Kraayenoord, C. E., 104, 105
Van Lawick-Goodall, 31
Van Liempd, D., 335
van Vianen, A. E. M., 415
Vandell, D. L., 100
VandenBos, G. R., 414
Vanderploeg, J. M., 183
Vandewater, E. A., 140
Vane, J. R., 487, 488
Vasquez, M. J. T., 133, 134
Vaughn, L., 215, 216, 483
Vecera, S., 203
Vega, L. A., 358, 682
Velakoulis, D., 557
Velez, A., 89
Venkagagiri, H. S., 127
Verbalis, J. G., 398
Verkuyten, M., 134, 462
Vernon, P. A., 64, 141, 322, 379
Vernoy, P. A., 205
Videon, T. M., 101
Viegener, B. J., 394
Villa, R. A., 680
Viswesvaran, C., 488
Vitaro, F., 227
Vogel, E., 203
Vogler, R., 252, 578
Vohs, K. D., 462
Volkmann, N. D., 78
Volkow, N. D., 255
Von Baumgarten, R., 180
Von Ranson, K. M., 445
Vorakitphokatorn, S., 673
Vredenburg, D. S., 614
Vye, N., 342
Vygotsky, L., 114–115

Wade, C. E., 683
Wager, M. K., 37
Wagner, M. K., 477
Wagstaff, G. F., 238
Wahler, J. J., 130
Waid, W. M., 413
Wainright, J. L., 439
Wakefield, J. C., 532, 534
Walbek, N. H., 289
Wald, J., 580
Waldvogel, J. A., 198
Walk, R. D., 195
Walker, E. E., 555, 556–558, 593, 594
Walker, I., 646
Wall, P., 181, 182, 184
Wallach, M. A., 349, 350
Wallen, A. S., 432
Wallerstein, J. S., 126
Walsh, J. K., 232
Walster, E., 419
Walters, G., 642
Walters, R., 285, 288
Walton, C. E., 91
Waltzman, S. B., 516
Wambach, C., 4
Wampoid, B. E., 600
Wandersman, A., 500
Wang, C., 498
Wang, L., 391
Wang, Q., 298
Wann, D. L., 288
Ward, A. S., 254
Ward, C., 518
Ward, E., 453
Ward, L. M., 168, 192
Ward, T., 290
Ward-Alexander, L., 596
Warden, M. R., 611
Wardle, J., 498
Wark, G. R., 137
Warner, J. A., 435
Warren, M. P., 133
Warrington, E. K., 69
Warshauer-Baker, E., 383, 644, 657
Warwick-Evens, L. A., 180
Washburn, A. L., 390
Washburn, M., 20
Wasserman, A. W., 682
Wasserman, E. A., 32
Waterhouse, J., 403
Waters, W. F., 226
Watkins, W. L., 368
Watkinson, B., 254, 255
Watson, A. C., 554
Watson, D. L., 271, 291, 402, 680
Watson, J. B., 18
Watts, J. C., 101
Weaver, C. N., 667
Webster, J. M., 624
Wechsler, H., 246
Wecshler, H., 251, 499
Weekley, J. A., 486
Weems, C. F., 519
Wehr, T. A., 561
Weiller, C., 74
Weinberg, R. A., 377
Weinberger, J. L., 546
Weiner, I. B., 488
Weinman, J. A., 513
Weinstein, R. S., 38
Weintraub, S., 369
Weisburd, D. E., 535
Weiser, M., 555
Weisfeld, G. E., 417
Weiss, H. M., 667, 668
Weiss, J., 589
Weiss, S. J., 99
Weitkunt, R., 519
Weizman, A., 246
Welker, W., 468
Wells, B. E., 444
Wells, G. L., 184, 217, 307
Wenckstern, S., 564, 565
Wenk, G. L., 140
Werner, C. M., 277, 677
Wertenbroch, K., 6
Wertheimer, M., 19–20, 287
Wespes, E., 140
West, A. N., 210, 219, 613
West, B. J., 664
West, L. J., 638
West, T. G., 332
Westen, D., 21, 588
Westfall, A. O., 498
Westphal, M., 422
Wethington, E., 140
Wettach, G. E., 148
Wetter, D. W., 248
Wexler, M. N., 331, 638
Whatley, M. A., 624
Wheeler, D, 668
Wheeler, L., 418
Whipple, B., 441
Whishaw, I. Q., 73
Whitaker, D. J., 514
White A. M., 291
White, B. J., 645
White, B. L., 101
White, G. L., 236
White, J. W., 128
White, K. B., 446
White, S. D., 43, 132
Whitely, B. E., 641
Whitley, B. E., Jr., 640
Whitman, L. G., 239
Whitney, D. M., 408
Whorton, J. E., 383
Whyte, G., 620
Wickett, J. C., 64
Widener, A. J., 316
Widiger,T. A., 534
Widmeyer, W. N., 685
Wiederhold, B. K., 580
Wiederhold, M. D., 580
Wiederman, M. W., 41, 438

Wiesel, T. N., 156, 162
Wiesemann, C., 430
Wilcher, M., 527
Wild, M., 277
Wilder, D. A., 640, 643
Wilding, J., 310–311, 324
Wiley, E., 337
Wilhelm, F. H., 576
Wilkinson, R. B., 47
Wilkinson,G., 477
Williams, D., 600
Williams, D. G., 416
Williams, D. R., 644
Williams, G., 392
Williams, G. H., 403
Williams, J., 27, 581
Williams, J. M., 165, 333, 684
Williams, L., 608
Williams, L. J., 683
Williams, L. M., 415
Williams, N., 430
Williams, R., 521
Williams, R. L., 3, 228, 289, 383, 578, 598
Williams, T., 289
Willoughby, T., 6, 301, 325
Wilson, A. E., 462
Wilson, D. B., 128, 588
Wilson, D. W., 653
Wilson, F. L., 43, 137
Wilson, G. D., 439
Wilson, P., 99
Wilson, T. D., 353, 623
Wing, R. R., 394
Winner, E., 351, 372
Winningham, R. G., 318
Winstead, B. A., 484
Winter, D. G., 641
Wirth, M. M., 74
Wise, J., 672
Wise, R. A., 73
Wiseman, R., 214, 215
Witcher, B. S., 419
Witelson, S. F., 430
Withers, N. W., 246
Witt, S. D., 430
Wittchen, H., 544
Woerner, M., 592
Wolf, S., 346
Wolfe, J. B., 275
Wolfson, S., 671
Wolpe, J., 579, 598
Wolpin, M., 258
Wolraich, M., 43
Wolraich, M. L., 128
Wong, C. Y., 672
Wong, F. Y., 588
Wong, J. L., 514
Wood, E., 301
Wood, E. T., 6
Wood, J. M., 48, 226, 233
Wood, W., 415
Woodhouse, R. A., 322
Woodman, G., 203
Woodruff-Pak, D., 268
Woods, D. W., 127
Woods, S., 606
Woods, S. E, 390–391, 392
Woodward, J., 43
Woodworth, G. G., 172
Woodworth, M. T., 317
Woody, E. Z., 239
Woody, S. R., 548
Woolard, J. L., 130, 446
Worthen, J. B., 325, 683
Wozner, Y., 127
Wright, D. B., 75
Wright, H., 75
Wright, T. A., 318, 666
Wu, C., 183
Wuethrich, B., 251
Wulf, G., 276
Wundt, W., 17
Wyatt, J. W., 468
Wynne, L. C., 284, 587

Xu, J., 641–642

Yagmurlu, B., 111
Yalom, 575
Yarber, W. L., 449
Yardley, J. K., 668
Yardley, L., 180
Yarmey, A. D., 218
Yedidia,M. J., 147
Yeh, C. J., 518
Yesalis, C. E., 76
Yoels, W. C., 144
Yokota, F., 289
Yontef, G. M., 575
Yoshida, M., 61
Yost, W., 170
Young, A. W., 414
Young, D. A., 246
Young, R. K., 614
Young, R. L., 78
Youngjohn, J. R., 487
Youngren, V. R., 572
Ysseldyke, G., 32
Yu, S. L., 1, 572
Yudelson, H., 500
Yuen, L. M., 5
Yuille, J. C., 218
Yurak, T.J., 614
Yurgelun-Todd, D., 254, 317
Zajonc, R. B., 419, 420, 613
Zakzanis, K. K., 246
Zamchech, N., 411
Zametkin, A. J., 128
Zanna, M. P., 633, 645
Zannino, M., 497, 524
Zatorre, R. J., 73
Zaurtra, A. J., 516
Zechmeister, E. B., 323
Zeidner, M., 402
Zeki, S, 164
Zelezny, L. C., 676
Zellner, D. A., 397
Zemishlany, Z., 246
Zetlin, A., 374
Zhang, Y. A., 538
Zhao, Z., 410
Zigler, E., 564, 565
Zimbardo, P. G., 490, 492, 606, 644
Zimmerman, B. J., 5, 652
Zimmerman, J., 293
Zimmerman, M. A., 449
Zion, C., 656
Zohar, D., 402
Zola, S. M., 320
Zola-Morgan, S., 304
Zsambok, C., 346
Zubrod, L. A., 140
Zuckerman, M., 400, 401, 611
Zuerink, J. R., 656
Zuwerink, J. R., 656
Zvolensky, M. J., 501
Zweig, J. B., 519

Subject Index

AA. *See* Alcoholics Anonymous
Ablation, 60
Abnormalities. *See also* Mental disorders
  core features of, 534–535
  cultural relativity, 534
  defining, 532–534
  politics of, 534
  situational context, 534
  statistical, 532
  statistical definitions, 533
Absolute threshold, 158
Accommodation
  light, 160
  mental, 110
  as muscular cue, 196
Acculturative stress, 518
Acetylcholine, 55
Achieved roles, 605–606
Achievement
  giftedness and, 371–372
  IQs and, 370–371
  need for, 405
  self-confidence and, 406
Acquisition, 265
Acromegaly, 75
Action potential, 53
Activation-synthesis hypothesis, 236–237
Active listening, 3, 591
Activity theory, 144
Actor-observer bias, 610
Acupuncture, 182
Adaptability, 434–435
Adaptation
  habituation and, 210
  perceptual learning, 205–206
  sensory, 180–181
Addams, Jane, 479
Additive bilingualism, 337
ADHD. *See* Attention-deficit/hyperactivity disorder (ADHD)
Adjustment disorders, 542
Adjustments, sexual, 453–454
Adler, Alfred, 21, 473
Adolescents
  adult transition and, 135
  characterization, 123
  defined, 132
  eating disorders and, 397
  identity formation and, 133–134
  imaginary audiences in, 134
  maturation timing in, 132–133
  parents and, 134
  peers, 134
  puberty *vs.*, 132
  social markers, 133
Adorno, Theodore, 641
Adrenal cortex, 76
Adrenal glands, 76
Adrenal medulla, 76
Adulthood
  depth perception in, 195
  midlife crisis, 139–141
  stages of, 124
  transition to, 135
Advice avoidance, 591
Aerial perspective, 200
Affiliations, 612–613
African Americans
  dieting and, 397
  IQ testing and, 382–384
  parenting styles, 103
  racial profiling, 639
Afterimages, 165
Age
  chronological, 366
  cognitive development and, 109
  happiness and, 151
  mental, 366
  regression, 239
  suicide and, 564
Ageism, 145, 639
Aggression. *See also* Violence
  anger control and, 652
  biological aspects, 648
  characterization, 627
  cues, 648
  defined, 647
  displacing, 506, 639–640
  frustration and, 505–506, 648
  instincts and, 647
  models, 649
  pornography and, 650
  preventing, 650–652
  punishment and, 285
  television and, 289–290, 649–652
Aging
  activity theory, 144
  attitude and, 144–145
  biological, 141
  compensation and, 144
  course of, 141–142
  disengagement theory, 143
  mental abilities and, 141–142
  milestones, 141
  myths, 145–146
  sleep patterns and, 227–228
  successful, 143–145
Agnosia, 68–69, 164
Agoraphobia, 543–544
AI. *See* Artificial intelligence (AI)
Alarm reaction, 522
Albert, Robert, 628
Alcohol
  abuse, 251–253
  characterization, 250
  effects of, 250
  health risk of, 499
Alcoholics Anonymous, 253
Alcoholism, 578–579
Alda, Alan, 317
Alice's Adventures in Wonderland (Carroll), 309, 550
All-or-nothing thinking, 335
All-or-nothing events, 53
Allen, Woody, 146
Allport, Gordon, 640
Alternative responses, 292
Alzheimer's disease, 551
Ambiguous stimuli, 192
Ambivalence, 508
Ambivalent attachment, 617
American Psychological Association (APA)
  first women president, 20
  media award, 25
  specialty divisions, 27–28
  website, 8–9
American Sign Language (ASL), 338
Amnesia
  dissociative, 546
  hypnosis and, 238–239
  skill memory and, 304
Amok, 538
Amos, Tori, 52
Amphetamines, 244–245
Amygdala, 72, 410–411
Amytal, 317
Anagrams test, 349
Analyze This (film), 25
Androgens, 398, 428
Androgyny, 434–435
Andropause, 141
Anesthesia, glove, 547
Angelou, Maya, 122
Anger, 130, 652
Anger Management (film), 25
Anhedonia, 246
Anima, 474
Animal language, 338–339
Animal models
  depth perception, 198
  function of, 15–16
  imprinting, 96
  motherless monkeys, 99
  naturalistic observation, 31–32
Animus, 474
Anorexia nervosa, 127, 396
Anosmia, 174
ANS. *See* Autonomic nervous system
Antecedents, 262, 292
Anthropomorphic error, 32
Antidepressants, 592
Antipsychotics, 592
Antisocial personality, 541–542
Anxiety
  basic, 473
  as defense mechanism, 510
  drugs for, 592
  moral, 470
  neurotic, 470
  pain and, 184
  separation, 97
  test, 402
Anxiety disorders
  adjustment, 542–543
  defined, 537
  dissociative, 546
  generalized, 543
  OCD, 544–545
  panic, 543–544
  phobias, 544
  somatoform, 546–547
  stress, 545–546
  treatment approaches, 548
Anxiolytics, 592
APA. *See* American Psychological Association (APA)
Aphasia, 68, 74
Apparent-distance hypothesis, 201–202
Approach-approach conflicts, 507
Approach-avoidance conflicts, 508
Approximations, 272
Aptitude tests, 664–665
Aptitudes, 364
Arab-Americans, 104
Archetypes, 473–474
Architectural psychology, 677
Archives, 8
Army Alpha, 369
Aronson, Elliot, 646
Arousal
  ANS, 420
  circadian rhythms and, 402–403
  defined, 400
  disorder, 451
  emotions and, 411–414
  empathic, 654
  labeling, 418
  levels of, 400–401
  peak performance and, 684
  sexual, 436–437, 451
  theory, 400
  Yerkes-Dodson law, 401
Artificial intelligence (AI)
  cognition and, 345–346
  defined, 345
  future of, 346–347
  working with, 346
As Nature Made Him (Colapinto), 430
Asch experiment, 619–620
Asians
  dieting and, 397
  emotional expression, 414–415
  parenting styles, 103–104
  self-esteem and, 462
ASL. *See* American Sign Language (ASL)
Aspartame, 374
Assertiveness training, 627–628
Assessments, behavioral, 485
Assessments, environmental, 677
Assimilation, 110, 518
Association cortex, 68
Astigmatism, 160
Astrology, 44
Ataque de nervois, 538
Attachment
  animal studies, 99
  breast-feeding and, 99–100
  day care and, 100
  importance of, 97
  love and, 616–617
  mate selection and, 617–618
  quality, 97–98
  secure, 98–99
  styles of, 98
  types of, 617
Attention
  divided, 209
  motives, 210–211
  pain, 184
  perception and, 209–210
  selective, 181, 209
  value of, 219–220
Attention-deficit/hyperactivity disorder (ADHD), 128
Attentional overload, 673–674
Attitudes
  aging and, 144–145
  behavior and, 634
  brainwashing, 636–637
  changing, 634–636
  cognitive dissonance theory, 635–636
  cults and, 637–638
  defined, 632
  formation, 632–634
  measurement, 634
  persuasion and, 634–635
  prejudicial, 639–641
  role playing and, 635
  sexual behavior, 444–445
Attraction. *See* Interpersonal attraction
Attractiveness, 614
Attribution theory
  actor and observers, 610–611
  characterization, 609
  concepts of, 610–611
Attributions
  arousal and, 419
  demonstrating, 418–419
  double standards, 611
  making, 610
  process of, 608
Authentic smiles, 415
Authenticity, 574
Authoritarian parents, 102
Authoritarian personality, 641, 681

Autism, 128–129
Autocide, 505–506
Autokinetic effect, 607–608
Autonomic nervous system (ANS)
  arousal, 76
  branches, 411
  function of, 58–59
  hormones, 76
Autonomy, 123
Autosuggestion, 239
Aversion therapy, 578–579, 597
Aversive stimuli, 648
Avoidance-avoidance conflicts, 507–508
Avoidant attachment, 617
Awareness
  in Gestalt, 575
  improving, 220
  levels of, 471–472
  perceptual, 219
Axon terminals, 52

Babbling, 107
Bait shyness, 395
Barbiturates, 249
Bard, Phillip, 418
Barney and Friends, 651
Barnum effect, 44–45
Barnum, P. T., 44–45
Barriers, 507
Base rate, 354
Basic anxiety, 473
Basic suggestion effect, 238
Beautiful Mind, A (film), 206
Behavior
  assertive, 627–628
  assessments, 485
  attitudes and, 634
  attributions and, 610
  atypical sexual, 442–444
  compliance, 624–626
  conformity, 619–620
  critical thinking and, 14
  endocrine system and, 74
  gender differences, 433–434
  health risk, 497–498
  health-promoting, 499
  ineffective, 527–528
  instrumental, 433
  jury, 680–681
  maladaptive, 534
  modern views of, 21–22
  modification, 128
  nonverbal, 681
  obedience, 621–624
  personality and, 463, 475–476
  prosocial, 651–655
  self-managed, 291–292
  sexual, 398–399, 436–437
  space effect on, 608
  STDs and, 448–449
  territorial, 671
  views of, 23
Behavior, gateways to, 2–3
Behavioral contracts, 292–293
Behavioralism. *See also* Classical conditioning; Operant conditioning
  anxiety explanation, 548
  aversion, 578–579, 597
  characterization, 578
  cognitive, 19
  desensitization, 579–583
  diets and, 394–395
  emphasis of, 23
  genetics, 466–467
  history of, 18–19
  medicine, 497
  radical, 18–19
  rational-emotive, 585
  setting, 671
  thought stopping, 597–598
Beliefs
  authoritarian, 641
  common-sense, 13
  component, 632
  irrational, 585–586
  just-world, 656
  shy, 492
Bell Curve, The (Herrnstein, Murray), 383
Bereavement, 148. *See also* Death; Grief
Bern Sex Role Inventory (BSRI), 434
Beta-endorphin, 182
Bias
  actor-observer, 610
  gender, 41
  observer, 32
  samples, 40
Bilingualism, 337
Binge drinking, 251
Biodata, 663
Biofeedback, 517, 519
Biological aging, 141
Biological predisposition, 107
Biological rhythm, 226
Biopsychological theory, 23
Biopsychologists, 15
Biopsychology, 60
Biopsychosocial model, 519
Bipolar disorders, 559–560
Bisexuality, 438
Blind spots, 162, 163
Blindness
  color, 166–169
  inattentional, 210
  night, 169
Bloom, Benjamin, 405
BMI. *See* Body mass index (BMI)
Body language, 416–417
Body mass index (BMI), 393
Boiled frog syndrome, 211
Borderline personality disorder, 540
Bottom-up processing, 211
Brains
  central biasing system, 182
  cerebral cortex, 63–70
  color messages, 166
  dendrites, 88
  drugs effect on, 243–244
  electrical stimulation, 61
  emotions and, 410–411
  functions of, 73
  gender differences, 70
  handedness and, 77–80
  hemispheric specialization, 65–67
  hunger control function, 391–392
  imaging, 61–62
  information processing, 380
  memory loci, 319–320
  schizophrenic, 555–557
  smell receptors, 174
  structure functions, 60–61
  subcortex, 71–73
  vision receptors, 162
Brainstem, 71
Brainstorming, 358–359
Brainwashing, 636–637
Branch Davidians, 637
Breast-feeding, 99–100
Brief psychodynamic therapy, 573
Brightness, 160
Brightness constancy, 190
Broca's area, 68
Broken record, 627
Brothers, Joyce, 48
Browser, 9
Bryant, Kobe, 682
BSRI. *See* Bern Sex Role Inventory (BSRI)
Buchwald, Art, 486
Bulimia nervosa, 396
Burnout, 502
Bush, George W., 158
Buss, David, 617
Bystander apathy, 653
Bystander intervention
  arousal and, 654
  emergency defining, 654
  individual characteristics, 654–655
  noticing, 653
Caffeine, 246–247
CAI. *See* Computer-assisted instruction (CAI)
Calhoun, John, 672
Calkins, Mary, 20
Cannon, Walter, 418
Cannon-Bard theory, 418
Carcinogens, 247–248
Cardiac personality, 520–521
Career decisions, 668
Careers. *See* Work
Caregiving styles, 101–102
Caring, morality of, 136–137
Carroll, Lewis, 309, 550
Cartwright, Rosalind, 256–257
Carver, George Washington, 680
Case studies
  critical thinking, 42–43
  defined, 39
  function of, 39–40
Castration, 437–428
Catatonic schizophrenia, 553
Cattell, Raymond B., 464
Causation, 32–33, 699
Cause and effect, 36
CD-ROMs, 9
Central nervous system (CNS), 57
Central tendency, measures of, 692–694
Central traits, 464
Cerebellum, 71
Cerebral cortex
  association areas, 68–70
  characterization, 63
  description, 64
  function, 63–64
  hemispheres, 64–67
  lobes of, 67–68
Cerebrum, 63
Character, 459
Charles Bonnet syndrome, 206
Charles, Ray, 512
Child abuse
  cycle of, 130
  parent profile, 129
  preventing, 130–131
  sexual, 443–444
Child's Guide to Life on Earth, A (Vygotsky), 114
Childbirth, 88, 185
Childhood
  disorders, 128–129
  early experiences, 86
  normal problems of, 125–126
  serious problems of, 126–129
  stages, 123–124
Childhood and Society (Erikson), 122
Children. *See also* Infants
  cognitive development, 109–114
  divorce and, 126
  early experiences, 86
  egocentricity of, 111
  gifted, 371–372
  growth sequence, 85–86
  immunization, 500
  intersexual, 430
  moral development, 135–137
  pampered, 105
  parental relationships, 116–117
  play and, 407–408
  in poverty, 89–90
  rearing attitudes, 633
  resilience in, 105
  self-esteem, 104–105
  sensitive periods, 87
  styles, 101–104
  temperament, 85–86
Chromosomes, 84
Chronological age, 366
Churchill, Winston, 555
Cigarette smoking, 87, 247–249
Circadian rhythms, 402–403
Citizenship, organizational, 670
Clairvoyance, 213
Classical conditioning
  aversion therapy, 578–579
  defined, 262–263
  desensitization, 579–581
  emotional responses, 267–268
  in humans, 267–269
  principles of, 265–267
  vicarious, 269
Clever Hans, 29
Client-centered therapy, 574–575
Climacteric age, 141
Clinging, 126
Clinical method, 30, 39–40
Clinical psychologists, 25
Clinical studies, 60
Clinton, Hillary, 122, 432
Cliques, 134
Clore, Gerald, 645
Clozaril, 593
CNS. *See* Central nervous system (CNS)
Cocaine, 245–246
Cochlea, 170, 172
Coefficient of correlation, 33
Coercive power, 621
Cognition
  AI and, 345–346
  anxiety explanation, 548
  defined, 330
Cognitive behaviorism, 19
Cognitive development
  age-associated stages, 109
  concrete operational stage, 111
  formal operations stage, 112
  infants, 112–114
  mental adaptations, 110
  parenting and, 112
  Piaget's theory of, 110–114
  preoperational stage, 110–111
  sensorimotor stage, 110
  Vygotsky's theory, 114–115
Cognitive dissonance theory, 635–636
Cognitive learning, 286–288
Cognitive therapy
  application, 584
  on behavior, 23
  description, 15
  emotion theory of, 418–419
  interviews, 303
  maps, 286
  REBT, 585
Cohesiveness, 606–607
Collective unconscious, 473
College Life Stress Inventory, 525
Color
  blindness, 166–168
  brightness, 165
  constructing, 166
  detection of, 162
  theories, 165–166
  weakness, 167
Colostrum, 99
Columbine, 652
Common region, principle of, 191
Common traits, 464
Common-sense beliefs, 13
Communication. *See also* Language
  childhood disturbances, 127
  early, 107–109
  effective, 117–118, 686–687
  listening and, 687
  in sexual interactions, 454–455
Community health, 500
Community mental health centers, 596
Community surveys, 681
Comparative psychologists, 15
Comparison levels, 615
Comparison, social, 612–613
Compensation, 144, 511–512
Competence, 614
Competition, 657
Complacent style, 668

Compliance
defined, 624
determining factors, 624
gaining, 624–625
passive, 625–626
Computed tomography (CT), 62
Computer simulations, 345–346
Computer-assisted instruction (CAI), 276–278
Computerized interviews, 484
Concepts
defined, 331, 333
faulty, 335
forming, 333–334
types of, 334–335
Conceptual rule, 334
Concrete operational stage, 111
Conditioned responses, 18, 264
Conditioned stimulus, 264
Conditioning. *See also* Classical conditioning; Operant conditioning
Pavlov's studies, 263–265
reinforcement, 274–280
secondhand, 268–269
stimulus control, 280–282
vicarious, 268–269
Conditioning chamber, 271
Conduct disorder, 128
Conduction deafness, 172
Cones, 161–162, 164
Confidentiality, 592
Conflicts
diagrams, 508
managing, 509
multiple, 508–509
occurrence, 507
role, 606
types of, 507–509
Conformity
Asch experiment, 619–620
defined, 619
group factors, 620
norms, 619
Congenital problems, 87
Connector neurons, 60
Connotative meaning, 334–335
Conscience, 470
Conscientiousness, 465
Consciousness
altered state of, 224
culture and, 225
drug-altered, 242–244
hypnosis and, 237–240
sensory deprivation, 240–241
walking, 224
Consequences, 262
Conservation, 111, 676–677
Consistency, 116
Consolidation, 318–319
Constructive processing, 302
Contact comfort, 99
Context, 205–206
Contiguity, principle of, 191
Continuation, principle of, 191
Continuity. *See* Continuation
Continuous reinforcement, 278
Contracting behavior, 292–293
Control
defined, 16
groups, 35, 47
pain, 184
questions, 413
Conventional moral reasoning, 136
Convergent thinking, 348
Conversation, 492
Conversion, 638
Conversion disorder, 547
Convictions, 634
Cooing, 107
Coolidge effect, 399
Coolidge, Calvin, 399
Cooper, Gordon, 164
Coping
with depression, 514–515
with frustration, 507
statements, 528
stress, 504–505
Corpus callosum, 64
Correlational method, 30
Correlational studies
causation, 32–33
coefficients, 32
defined, 32
Correlations
causation, 699
coefficients, 698
predictions, 698–699
relationships, 697–698
visualizing, 697
Corticalization, 64
Corticoids, 76
Cosby, Bill, 336
Counseling psychologists, 25
Counterirritation, 185
Covert reinforcement, 598
Covert sensitization, 597
Cowan, Fred, 490
Cranial nerves, 60
Creativity
characteristics of, 347–348
daydreams and, 349
dreams and, 257–258
enhancing, 356–359
impact of, 347
lifestyles and, 359
mental illness and, 352
motivation and, 408
personality and, 351–352
stages of, 350–351
tests of, 349
Cretinism, 375
Crisis hotlines, 599
Crisis intervention, 596
Critical incidents, 663
Critical situations, 477
Critical thinking
behavior and, 14
case study, 42–43
importance of, 14
Crowding, 672–673, 677
Crystal, Billy, 25
Crystallized abilities, 142
CT. *See* Computed tomography (CT)
Cue-dependent forgetting, 313–314
Cues
aggression, 648
bad habits and, 292
memory and, 313–314, 322
personality, 476
Cults
characterization, 637
conversion, 638
implications, 638
recruitment, 637–638
Cultural awareness, 657–658
Cultural psychologists, 15
Cultural relativity, 23
Culture
abnormal behavior and, 534
consciousness and, 225
creativity and, 350
defined, 605
diet and, 395
dieting and, 397
diversity and, 22–23
emotions and, 414–415
gender roles and, 432–433
impact of, 23
IQ and, 382–384
memory and, 299
organizational, 669–670
parenting and, 103–104
perception and, 205
personality and, 462
problem solving, 344
psychopathology and, 538
spatial norms and, 608–609
teen identity and, 133–134
Culture shock, 518
Curvilinear relationships, 34
Cybertherapy, 577
Dahmer, Jeffrey, 554
Dark adaptation, 167, 169
Darwin, Charles, 18
Data reduction system, 156
Day care, 100
Daydreams, 349
Deafness, 172–173
Death. *See also* Bereavement; Grief
emotional reactions to, 147–148
hospice movement, 147
impending, 146–147
instinct, 469
statistics on, 146
sudden, 411–412
Death-qualified juries, 681
Declarative memory, 304
Deductive thought, 347
Deep lesioning, 60
Defense mechanisms
anxiety, 510
compensation, 511–512
denial, 510
failure of, 512
projection, 511
rationalization, 511
reaction formation, 511
repression, 510
sublimation, 512
Defensive-avoidant style, 668
Deinstitutionalization, 594–595
Delayed speech, 127
Delusional disorders, 551–552
Dementia, 551
Demographic information, 681
Demonology, 571–572
Dendrites, 52, 88
Denial, 510
Dependent variables, 35
Depressants, 242
Depression
biology and, 561
cognitive therapy for, 584
coping with, 514–515
drugs for, 592
learned helplessness and, 512–513
postpartum, 560–561
recognizing, 514
social impact of, 514
Deprivation, 88–89
Depth cues, 196–197, 199–202
Depth perception
apparent-distance hypothesis, 201–202
defined, 195
moon illusion, 201–202
muscular cues, 196–197
pictorial cues, 199–202
stereoscopic vision and, 197–198
testing for, 195–196
Desensitization
aggression and, 650
characterization, 579
performing, 579
relaxation and, 580
self-directed, 598
as trauma therapy, 581
vicarious, 580
virtual reality exposure, 580
Desirability, 41–42
Desire disorders, 450–451
Desk rage, 669
Despair, integrity *vs.*, 124
Detoxification, 253
Development. *See also* Life stages
cognitive, 109–114
emotional, 94
influences on, 90
language, 106–109
milestones, 122
moral, 135–137
motor, 93–94
personality (*See* Personality development)
prejudices, 639–640
sexual, 427–435
social, 95–100
theory, 30
Developmental psychology, 84
Developmentally disabled. *See* Mental retardation
Devi, Shakuntala, 330
Deviation IQs, 368
Deviation, sexual, 442–444
Dhat, 538
Diagnostic interviews, 484
Dictionary of Afro-American Slang (Williams), 383
Dieting
behavioral, 394–395
cultural factors, 397
yo-yo, 394
Diets. *See also* Eating disorders
behavior and, 394–395
content, 393–394
defined, 393
evolution and, 394
Difference thresholds, 158
Differences, significant, 696–697
Dilemmas, 122
Direct contact, 632–633
Direct instruction, 679
Direct observations, 485–486
Discipline. *See also* Punishment
child abuse and, 131
constructive, 116
self-esteem and, 104
types of, 104
Discrimination
conditioning, 266–267
impact of, 639
stimulus control, 281–282
Discriminative stimuli, 281
Discussion Forum, 8
Disease-prone personality, 499
Disengagement theory, 143
Dishabituation, 219
Disinhibition, 650
Disordered behavior. *See* Abnormality
Disorganized schizophrenia, 552–553
Displaced aggression, 506, 639–640
Displacement, 256
Dissatisfaction, 126
Dissociation, 238
Dissociative disorders, 537, 546
Distinctiveness, 610
Distraction, 185
Distribution frequency, 692
Disturbances, childhood, 127
Divergent thinking, 348
Diversity
culture and, 22–23
prejudice and, 656–658
social norms and, 23
Divided attention, 209
Divorce, 126
Dixon, Jeanne, 47
DNA, 84
DNA testing, 218
Dogmatism, 641
Dominant genes, 84–85
Donne, John, 605
Door-in-the-face effect, 624
Dopamine, 245
Double approach-avoidance conflicts, 509
Double-blind experiments, 37–38
Double standards, 611
Dove counterbalance intelligence test, 382
Down syndrome, 375
Dreams
analyzing, 235–236, 572–573
creativity and, 257–258
lucid, 258
processes, 256
sleep and, 230–231, 235
symbols, 236, 573
theories, 236–237
theorists, 256
work, 257
Drive, 388, 476

Drug abuse
  alcohol, 250–253
  amphetamines, 244–249
  caffeine, 246–247
  cocaine, 245–246
  GHB, 249
  MDMA, 246
  nicotine, 247–249
  patterns, 244
  tranquilizers, 249–250
Drug-dependency insomnia, 232
Drugs
  abuse patterns, 244
  dependency, 244
  depressants, 249–253
  hallucinogens, 253–254
  interactions, 249
  marijuana, 253–254
  psychedelic, 556
  psychoactive, 242–244
  stimulants, 244–249
  therapeutic, 592–593
  truth, 317
Dual memory, 299
Duchenne smiles, 415
Dwarfism, 75

Eardrum. *See* Tympanic membrane
Ears. *See also* Hearing
  anatomy of, 171
  ringing in, 173
  structures of, 170
Eating disorders, 396–397
Ebbinghaus curve, 312
Eclectic, defined, 21
ECS. *See* Electroconvulsive shock (ECS)
Ecstasy. *See* Methylenedioxymethamphetamine
ECT. *See* Electroconvulsive therapy (ECT)
Edison, Thomas, 646
Education
  bilingual, 337
  classroom violence, 652
  early childhood, 377
  GATE programs, 372
  goals, 150
  psychology in, 679–680
EEG. *See* Electroencephalograph (EEG)
Effector cells, 60
Ego, 470
Ego ideal, 471
Eidetic imagery, 308–309
Einstein, Albert, 479, 647
Ejaculation, 442
Elaborative rehearsal, 301
Electrical stimulation, 274
Electrical stimulation brains (ESB), 61
Electroconvulsive shock (ECS), 318–319
Electroconvulsive therapy (ECT), 593–594
Electrodes, 60
Electroencephalograph (EEG), 61
Electromagnetic spectrum, 156
Electronic media, 7–9
Elliot, Jane, 643–644
EMDR. *See* Eye movement desensitization and reprocessing
Emergency defining, 654
Emmons, Michael, 628
Emotion-focused coping, 504
Emotional appraisal, 420
Emotional consequence, 585
Emotional expressions, 409
Emotional feelings, 409
Emotional intelligence, 422–423
Emotions. *See also* Arousal; Facial expressions
  accepting, 117
  arousal and, 411–414
  body language, 416–417
  brain and, 410–411
  classical conditioning and, 267–268
  contemporary model of, 420
  cultural differences, 414–415
  death-associate, 147
  early development of, 94
  expressing, 414–417
  focus on, 591
  forms of, 410
  Freud's views, 20
  function of, 408
  gender differences, 415
  happiness and, 150
  judgment and, 354
  overreaction to, 411–412
  physiological aspects, 409
  positive, 422–423
  primary, 409–410
  problem solving and, 345
  restating, 591–592
  suppressing, 420
  theories of, 417–421
  universal, 415–416
Empathic arousal, 654
Empathy, 574
Empathy-helping relationships, 654
Empiricism
  defined, 12
  examples of, 13
  types, 13
Empty nest syndrome, 140
Encoded memory, 297
Encoding failure, 312–313
Encopresis, 127
Encounter groups, 587
Encouragement, 117
Endocrine system, 74–76
Endorphins, 55
Engram, 319
Enkephalins, 55
Enrichment, 88–89, 668–669
Enuresis, 127
Environments
  assessing, 677
  defined, 86
  deprived, 88–89
  early experiences, 86–87
  enriched, 88–89
  heredity interactions, 90
  influence of, 672
  IQ and, 377–378
  learning and, 4
  motives and, 404–406
  physical, 671
  prenatal, 87–88
  schizophrenia and, 555
  social, 671
  stressful, 672–674
  toxic, 675–678
  urban, 670–678
Epinephrine, 76
Episodic drive, 398
Episodic memory, 305
Equal-status contact, 645, 646
Erectile disorder, 451–452
Ergot, 572
Erikson, Erik, 122–124
Erogenous zones, 436, 471
Eron, Leonard, 650
ESB. *See* Electrical stimulation brains (ESB)
Escape, 284, 506
Escher, M. C., 200
ESP. *See* Extrasensory perception (ESP)
Essay tests, 6–7
Estrogen, 398, 428
Estrus, 398
Ethics, 27
Ethnicity, 538, 540
Ethnocentrism, 641
Eugenics, 376
Evolutionary psychologists, 15
Evolutionary psychology, 617–618
Exercise, 233, 526–527
Exhaustion, stage of, 522–523
Exhibitionism, 443
Existential therapy, 575
Expectancies, 211–213, 266
Expectancy, 476
Experimenter effect, 38
Experiments
  cause and effects, 36
  controls, 36
  double-blind, 37–38
  evaluating, 36–37
  groups, 35–36
  groups for, 35
  methods, 30
  performing, 35
  placebo effects, 37–38
  self-observation, 17
  variables, 35–36
Expert power, 621
Expert witness, 540
Explicit memory, 308
Expressions, 414–415
External causes, 609
External frustration, 505
Extinction
  bad habits, 292
  conditioning, 266
  nonreinforcement and, 582–583
  operant, 272–273
Extracellular thirst, 398
Extraneous variables, 35, 36
Extrasensory perception (ESP)
  appraisals of, 214–215
  basic forms, 213
  chance and, 214–215
  fraud and, 214
  implications of, 216
  skepticism and, 214
  stage, 215–216
  statistics and, 214–215
  study of, 213
Extrinsic motivation, 407–408
Extroverts, 460, 465
Eye movement desensitization and reprocessing, 581
Eyes. *See also* Vision
  blind spots, 162, 163
  focus, 160
  light control by, 161
  movements, 181
  receptor cells, 156–157, 161–162
  structure, 160
  visual acuity, 164
Eysenck, Hans, 462
Eyewitness testimony, 217–218

Facial agnosia, 69
Facial expressions
  beauty and, 415
  cultural aspects, 414
  feedback hypothesis, 419–420
  universal, 415–416
Facial feedback hypothesis, 419–420
Fact memory, 304–306
Fallacy of positive instances, 44
Familial retardation, 374
Family theory, 587
FAS. *See* Fetal alcohol syndrome (FAS)
Fears. *See also* Phobias
  childhood, 126
  learned, 268
  overcoming, 598
  urban, 677
Features, perceptual, 204
Feedback, 276
Feeding disturbances, 127
Feeling of knowing, 306
Feelings. *See* Emotions
Fetal alcohol syndrome (FAS), 87
Fetal vulnerability, 87
Fight-or-flight syndrome, 267, 411
Figure-ground organization, 191
Fixations, 343–344
Fixed interval, 280
Fixed ratio, 279
Flashbulb memory, 317–318
Flat affect, 550
Flexibility, 347, 422
Flextime, 668
Fluency, 347
Fluid abilities, 142
Fluid reasoning, 365–366
Flynn effect, 378
fMRI. *See* Functional magnetic resonance imaging (fMRI)
Food intake, 233
Food values, 395
Foot-in-the door effect, 624
Forced teaching, 112
Forcible rape, 446–447
Forebrain, 72–73
Foreclosed identity, 134
Forensic memory, 303
Forgetting. *See also* Memory
  causes, 310
  cue-dependent, 313–314
  curve of, 310
  disuse factors, 313
  encoding and, 312–313
  interference and, 314–315
  memory decay and, 313
  order effects and, 315
  state-dependent learning and, 314
  time factors, 310–311
Formal operations stage, 112
Fragile-X syndrome, 375
Frames
  acceptance, 591
  mind, 380–381
  reference, 21, 206
Framing, 354
Frankl, Victor, 575
Franklin, Eileen, 316
Fraternal twins, 376
Fraud, 214
Free association, 572
Free will, 21
Frequency distribution, 692
Frequency theory, 170
Freud, Anna, 21
Freud, Sigmund, 236, 256
  on defense mechanisms, 510
  legacy of, 21
  personality development, 471–472
  personality dynamics, 470–471
  personality structure, 469–470
  theories, 20
  therapy developed by, 572
Friendship, 523, 615
Frontal lobes, 68
Frustration
  aggression and, 648
  aversive stimuli, 648
  coping with, 507
  defined, 505
  reactions to, 505–506
  stress and, 516–517
Fugue, dissociative, 546
Functional fixedness, 343
Functional magnetic resonance imaging (fMRI), 62, 74
Functional solutions, 341
Functionalism, 18
Functioning, levels of, 535
Fundamental attributional error, 610

G-factor, 381
G.A.S. *See* General adaptation syndrome (G.A.S.)
Gall, Franz, 43
Galvanic skin response (GSR), 412
Ganzfeld, 215
Gate control theory, 181, 185
GATE programs, 372
Gates, Bill, 122, 351
Gateways, 2–3
Geller, Uri, 213, 215–216
Genain sisters, 39–40
Gender
  bias, in research, 41
  defined, 427

identity, 429–431
identity disorders, 537
prejudice, 640
psychologists, 15
Gender differences. *See also* Men; Women
behavior, 433–434
brain specialization, 70
emotions and, 415
IQs, 370
mood disorders and, 560
origins of, 431–434
sexual development, 427–428
success acknowledgment, 611
suicide and, 563–564
Gender roles
culture and, 432–433
influence of, 431
rape and, 446
socialization, 433–435
stereotypes, 431–432
General adaptation syndrome (G.A.S.), 522–523
General solution, 341
Generalizations, 266, 281
Generalized anxiety disorder, 543
Generativity, 124
Genes. *See also* Heredity
associated disorders, 87
defined, 84
patterns, 85
types, 84–85
Genetic sex, 429
Genital sex, 429
Genovese, Kitty, 653
Gerontologists, 142
Gestalt therapy
bases, 575–576
defined, 19
perception principles, 191–194
Gestural languages, 338
GHB, 249
Ghost sickness, 538
Giftedness, 371–372
Gilligan, Carol, 41, 136–137
Glenn, John, 122, 144
Glove anesthesia, 547
GLP-1. *See* Glucagon-like peptide 1 (GLP-1)
Glucagon-like peptide 1 (GLP-1), 392
Goals
happiness and, 151
motivation for, 404–405
psychology's, 16
setting, 6
superordinate, 645–646
Godfather, The (film), 74
Golden Psi Media Award, 25
Gonadal sex, 429
Gonads, 428
Goodall, Jane, 31
Google, 7–8
Gore, Al, 158
Grammar, 337
Graphical data, 33–34
Graphical statistics, 691–692
Graphologists, 43–44
Grasping reflex, 91
Gray matter, 64
Grief. *See also* Bereavement; Death
coping with, 149
defined, 148
pattern of, 148
reactions to, 148–149
Group therapy
awareness training, 587–588
defined, 586
family, 587–588
psychodrama, 587–588
Groups
affiliation needs, 612–613
cohesiveness, 606–607
conformity, 619–620
cults, 637–638
in, 606
norms, 607–608
out, 606
prejudice, 640
sanctions, 620
status, 606–607
structures, 606
Groupthink, 620
Growth hormone, 75
Growth needs, 406
Growth spurt, 132
GSR. *See* Galvanic skin response (GSR)
Guided imagery, 527
Guilt, 123–124
Gustation. *See* Taste

Habits
changing, 241
defined, 475
learning, 292–293
perceptual, 203–205
prejudice and, 656
Habituation, 210, 219
Hair cells, 170
Hall, Calvin, 256
Hallucinations, 206, 231, 550
Halo effect, 614
Handedness
advantages, 78–80
causes, 77
defined, 77
determining, 78
hemisphere dominance and, 78–79
impact of, 77–78
Happiness
authentic, 423
goals, 151
life events and, 150
life satisfaction and, 150
personal factors, 150–151
Hardy personality, 521–522
Hassles, 516
Hawking, Stephen W., 330
Health
behavioral risk factors, 497–499
biopsychosocial, 519
medical model, 519
nicotine impact on, 247–248
personality and, 520–523
prevention, 499–500
social support and, 522
stress and, 515–517
Health psychology
aims of, 497
community education, 499–500
wellness programs, 500
Hearing. *See also* Ears
artificial, 172
deafness, 172–173
mechanisms, 170, 173
stimulus for, 170
Hemispheres
connections, 64
handedness and, 77–79
specialization, 64–65
Heredity. *See also* Genes
defined, 84
environments interactions, 90
homosexuality and, 469
influence of, 85–86
IQ and, 376–377
personality and, 466–468
processes of, 84–85
schizophrenia and, 555
temperament and, 85–86
Herrnstein, Richard, 383
Heterosexuality, 438
Heuristics, 341–342
Hidden observer, 239
Hierarchy
constructing, 598
function, 579
human needs, 406
Higher order conditioning, 265
Hindbrain, 71–72
Hinkley, John, Jr., 556
Hippocampus, 73, 319
Hispanic-Americans, 103
Histogram, 692
HIV/AIDS, 448
Hoffman, Dustin, 373
Homeostasis, 390, 400
Homogamy, 614
Homosexuality
defined, 438
heredity and, 439
hostility toward, 439–440
national percents, 440
Hopelessness, 512
Hormones. *See also* specific hormones
defined, 74
sex drive and, 398
sexual development and, 428–429
sleep, 228
Horney, Karen, 21, 473
Hospices, 147
Hospitalization, 594–595
Hostility, 521
Hot topics, 8
Hothousing, 112
Hotlines, 599
Huberty, James, 554
Hudson test picture, 201
Hue, 160
Human factors engineers, 193
Human growth sequence, 85
Humanism
anxiety explanation, 548
on behavior, 23
characterization, 479
evaluation, 483
history, 21
positive traits, 480
self theory, 480–481
self-actualization and, 479–480
therapies, 574–575
Humans. *See also* Groups; Men; Women
affiliation needs, 612–613
conditioning and, 267–269
interpersonal attraction, 613–615
mate selection, 617–618
space needs, 608–609
in social context, 605–606
Hunger. *See also* Diet
brain's role in, 391–392
causes of, 390
cultural factors, 395
memory and, 323
set point, 392
taste factors, 395–396
Hydrocephaly, 374–375
Hyperopia, 160
Hypersomnia, 227
Hyperthyroidism, 76
Hypervigilant style, 668
Hypnagogic images, 240
Hypnosis
defined, 237
effects of, 238–239
false memory and, 303
stage, 239–240
susceptibility, 237–238
Hypoactive sexual desire, 450
Hypochondriacs, 517
Hypochondriasis, 546
Hypoglycemia, 648
Hypopituitary, 75
Hypothalamus, 72, 391
Hypothesis, 29
Hypothyroidism, 76

I-messages, 117–118
Id, 469–470
Ideal self, 481
Identical twins, 376
Identity
in adolescence, 123, 133–134
foreclosed, 134
sexual, 438–439, 478
Illogical thought, 347
Illumination, creative, 350
Illusions, 206–208
Imagery. *See also* Mental images
guided, 527
rehearsal, 233–234
Images
hypnagogic, 240
internal, 308
mental, 331–333
Imaginary audiences, 134
Imitation, 478
Immune system, 523–524
Immunization, 500
Implicit memory, 308
Imprinting, 96–97
In the Shadow of Man (Goodall), 31
In-groups, 606
Inattentional blindness, 210
Incentives, value of, 389
Income, 564
Incongruent person, 481
Independent variables, 35
Individual traits, 464
Individuating information, 656
Inductive thought, 347
Industrial-organizational psychologists, 662
Industry, 123
Infants. *See also* Children
birth injuries, 374
breast-feeding, 99–100
cognition, 112–114
congenital problems, 87
contact comfort, 99
depth perception, 195
emotional development, 94
engagement scale, 107
insecure-avoidant, 97–98
language development, 106–109
maturation, 93
motor development, 93–94
neonates, 90–92
readiness, 94
social development, 95–100
Inferential statistics, 696–697
Inferiority, 123
InfoTrac, 8
Information
bits, 300
chunks, 300
demographic, 681
individuating, 656
processing, 380
recalling, 306
rehearsing, 300–301
Initiative, 123
Inkblot test, 488
Insanity, 540
Insecure-avoidant infants, 97–98
Insight, 342–343
Insomnia, 232–233
Instincts
aggression and, 647
death, 469
life, 469
Instrumental behavior, 433
Instrumental learning. *See* Operant conditioning
Integration, 518
Integrity, 124, 151
Intelligence. *See also* Giftedness; Mental retardation
aspects of, 365–366
defining, 364–365
emotional, 422–423
index of, 384
information processing and, 380
inspecting, 379
neural bases for, 379–380
types of, 380–381
working memory and, 366
Intelligence quotients (IQ)
determining, 366–367
development of, 365

deviation, 366–367
environment and, 377–378
hereditary and, 376–377
retardation and, 373–374
scores, 370–371
stability of, 368–369
variations in, 370–371
Intelligence tests
bell curve, 383–384
criticism of, 382–384
cultural issues, 382–384
reliability, 364–365
standardization, 365
standardized, 384
types, 369–371, 382
validity, 364–365
Intention, paradoxical, 233
Interactive Activities, 8
Interference, 314–315
Internal causes, 609
Internal images, 308
Internet
resource center, 8
rumors on, 48
search engines, 7–8
surveys, 41
therapy, 577
websites, 8–9
Interpersonal attraction
competence and, 614
defined, 613
gendered friendships, 615
love and, 616–617
physical attractiveness, 614
physical proximity and, 613
self-disclosure and, 614–615
similarity and, 614
Interposition. *See* Overlap
Interpretation, 184
Interpretation of Dreams, The (Freud), 236
Intersexual person, 430
Intervention
bystander, 653–654
crisis, 596
suicide, 565
Interviews
cognitive, 303
computerized, 484
limitations, 484–485
personal, 664
personality assessments by, 484–486
Intimacy, 124, 454–455
Intimate distance, 608
Intracellular thirst, 398
Intrinsic motivation, 407–408
Introspection, 17–18
Introverts, 460
Intuition, 353–355
Intuitive thought, 110
Inverted U function, 400
Inverted vision, 204–205
Ions
channels, 53
defined, 52
potassium, 54
sodium, 53
IQ. *See* Intelligence quotients (IQ)
Iris, 161
Irrational beliefs, 585–586
Ishihara test, 168
Isolation, 124
Izard, Carrol, 419

Jackson, Michael, 412, 682
James, Henry, Sr., 18
James, William, 18, 417, 479
James-Lange theory, 417
Janis, Irving, 668
Jet lag, 402–403
Jigsaw classrooms, 646
JNDs. *See* Just noticeable differences
Jobs. *See* Work
Johnson, Virginia, 440–441
Jones, Jim, 637, 638
Jonestown, 637, 638
Judgment errors, 353–354
Jung, Carl, 460, 473–474
Juries
behavior, 680–681
death-qualified, 681
selecting, 681–682
Just noticeable differences, 158
Just-world beliefs, 656
Justice, 136–137
Justification, 636

Kaczynski, Theodore, 554
Kaman, Dean, 408
Kanzi, 340
Kasparov, Garry, 345
Keating, Jack, 662
Keller, Helen, 511–512
Kelley, Harold, 610
Kennedy, John F., 318
Kinesics, 416
Kinesthetic images, 333
Kinesthetic senses, 177
King, B. B., 58
King, Martin Luther, 318
Knowledge, 276, 366
Kohlberg, Laurence, 41, 136
Kolb, Bryan, 66
Koresh, David, 637
Koro, 538
Kübler-Ross, Elisabeth, 146–147

LaBerge, Stephen, 258
Ladd-Franklin, Christine, 20
LaLanne, Jack, 511
Lamaze method, 88
Lange, Carl, 417
Language. *See also* Communication
acquisition, 106
animal, 338–339
body, 416–417
defined, 331
early communication, 107–109
gestural, 338
parentese, 108–109
roots of, 106–107
structure of, 337–338
study of, 336–337
terrible twos and, 106
Large group awareness training, 587–588
Lashley, Karl, 319
Latent content, 572–573
Latent learning, 286
Lateralization, 81
Law and Order: Special Victims Unit (television), 25
LCUs. *See* Life change units
Leaderless group discussion, 665
Learned helplessness
characterization, 512
depression and, 512–513
hope and, 513–514
Learning. *See also* Relearning
aids, 276–278
antecedents, 262
capacity for, 364
classical conditioning, 262–269
cognitive, 286–288
consequences, 262
defined, 262
discovery, 286–287
disorders, 128
escape, 284
fears, 268
habits, 292–293
instrumental, 267–277
latent, 286
observational (*See* Modeling)
over, 5
part, 322
perceptual, 202–208
punishment and, 282–283
readiness for, 94
self-regulated, 5
serial position, 322
social, 649–650
state-dependent, 314
teaching styles and, 679–680
video games and, 290
whole, 322
Learning theories of personality
approaches to, 474–475
behavior, 475–476
development, 477
evaluation, 483
social, 476–477
Leaving-the-field reaction, 508
Legitimate power, 621
Levine, Robert, 670
Levinson, Daniel, 139–140
Lexigrams, 340
Libido, 469
Life
events, 150, 515–516
expectancy, 143
instincts, 469
satisfaction, 150
Life change units, 515–516
Life stages
adolescence, 132–134
adulthood, 138–141
childhood, 123–129
dying, 146–149
middle age, 140, 143
moral development, 135–137
old age, 141–146
transitions, 139
Life-span perspective, 122, 124
Lifestyles
diseases, 497–498
risky, 497–498
sustainable, 675
Light and shadow, 200
Light sleep, 229
Limbic system, 72–73
Lincoln, Abraham, 479
Linear perspective, 199
Linear relationships, 34
LISAN, 3–4
Listening, 591, 687
Lithium carbonate, 560
Lobes, 67–68
Lock and key theory, 174
Locura, 538
Loewi, Otto, 257–258
Loftus, Elizabeth, 317, 662
Logic, 352–353
Logical consequences, 118
Long sleepers, 227
Long-term memory
constructing, 301–302
encoding, 298–299
organizing, 303–304
permanence of, 301
Looking chambers, 91–92
Lopez, Jennifer, 122
Lorenz, Konrad, 647
Love, 616–617
Low-ball technique, 624
LSD, 253
Lying, 412–414, 417

Ma, Yo Yo, 52, 55, 62, 67
Magnetic resonance imaging (MRI), 62, 557
Mahadevan, Rajan, 310
Maintenance rehearsal, 300–301
Maladaptive behavior, 534
Management, 666–667
Manic-depression. *See* Bipolar disorders
Manifest content, 573
Marginalization, 518
Marijuana, 253, 254–255
Marriage, 150–151
Marston, William, 412
Maslow, Abraham, 21, 22, 479
Massed practice, 4, 5, 322
Masters, William, 440–441
Mastery training, 513–514
Masturbation, 438
Maternal influences, 101
Maternity blues, 560
Matrix (film), 183
Maturation, 93, 132–133
McClelland, David, 405
McGwire, Mark, 76
MDMA. *See* Methylenedioxymethamphetamine
Mead, Margaret, 432
Mean, 693
Mean worldview, 633
Means-ends analysis, 346
Measures of central tendency, 692–694
Measures of variability, 694
Mechanical solutions, 341
Media
aggression and, 649–652, 651
APA award, 25
electronic, 7–9
modeling and, 289–290
psychological reports in, 46–48
psychologists, 48, 576
Median, 693
Medical model, 519
Medical therapy
drugs, 592–593
ECT, 593–594
hospitalization, 594–595
surgery, 594
Medicated childbirth, 88
Medication, 497
Meditation, 527
Medulla, 71
Meet the Author, 8
Melatonin, 75, 403
Melnick, Michael, 39
Memory. *See also* Forgetting
champions, 310–311
consolidation, 318–319
cues, 313–314
culture and, 299
decay, 313
dual, 299
exceptional, 308–311
explicit, 308
fact, 304–306
flashbulb, 317–318
forensic, 303
formation, 318–323
hunger and, 323
hypnosis and, 238
implicit, 308
improving, 320–323
long-term, 298–300, 301–304
mnemonics and, 324–326
partial, 306–307
pill, 320
recovered, 316–317
redintegrative, 304
sensory, 297
short-term, 297, 300–301
skill, 304–306
sleep and, 322
strategies, 321
structure, 303–304
suppression of, 316–317
system of, 297
updating, 302
working, 297, 366
Men. *See also* Gender differences
becoming, 478
friendships, 615
orgasm disorders, 452–453
sexual disorders, 451–454
sexual response, 442
Menarche, 427
Menopause, 140, 427–428

Mental abilities, 141–142
Mental age, 366
Mental disorders. *See also* Abnormality
  anxiety-based, 542–546
  classification, 535, 536
  creativity and, 352
  dissociative, 546
  DSM-IV categories, 539
  ethnicity and, 538, 540
  labeling, 562
  mood, 536–537, 558–562
  organic, 536
  overview of, 535–538
  psychosis, 550–558
  risk factors, 538, 540
  social stigma, 562
  somatoform, 546–547
  suicide and, 563–565
  violence and, 554
Mental images
  defined, 331
  forms of, 331
  kinesthetic, 333
  nature of, 331
  reversed, 332
  using, 332–333
Mental practice, 684
Mental retardation
  causes of, 374
  defined, 373
  levels of, 373–374
  organic sources of, 374–375
  in perspective, 375
Meta-analysis, 36–37
Meta-needs, 407
Methylenedioxymethamphetamine, 246
Micro-electrodes, 61
Microcephaly, 374
Microsleep, 225
Microstressors, 516
Midlife crisis, 139–141
Milgram, Stanley, 622–623
Mind of a Mnemonist, The (Luria), 309
Mindblindness. *See* Agnosia
Minnesota Multiphasic Personality Inventory-2 (MMPI-2), 486–487
Mirror technique, 587
Miss Cleo, 214
Mistrust, 123
Mitchell, Edgar, 215
MMPI-2. *See* Minnesota Multiphasic Personality Inventory-2
Mnemonics, 4, 5, 324–326
Mock juries, 680
Mode, 693–694
Modeling
  causing, 288
  defined, 288
  imitation and, 288–289
  television and, 289–290
Molestation, 443–444
Mood disorders. *See also* Depression
  causes, 560–562
  creativity and, 352
  definition, 536
  general types, 558–559
  major, 559–560
  types, 536–537
Moods, 410
Moon illusion, 201–202
Moral anxiety, 470
Moral development
  Gilligan's theories, 136–137
  Kohlberg's theories, 136
  onset of, 136
Moreno, Jacob L., 586–587
Moriarty, Thomas, 625
Moro reflex, 91
Motherless monkeys, 99
Motion parallax, 200
Motivation
  achievement and, 405
  blocked, 505
  creativity and, 408
  defined, 388
  extrinsic, 407–408
  hierarchy of, 406–407
  hunger as, 390–395
  incentives, 389
  intrinsic, 407–408
  origins of, 388
  stimulus drives, 399–409
  success and, 405–406
Motives. *See also* Primary motives
  attention and, 210–211
  homeostasis and, 390
  learned, 404–406
  social, 404–405
  types of, 389–390
Motor development, 93–94
Motor program, 684
Motor skills, 684
Mozart, Wolfgang Amadeus, 348
MRI. *See* Magnetic resonance imaging (MRI)
Muir, John, 479
Müller-Lyer illusion, 207, 208
Multiculturalism, 656–658
Multimedia computerized tests, 665
Multiple intelligences, 380–381
Murray, Charles, 383
Muscular cues, 196–197
Mutism, 553
Myelin, 57
Myopia, 160

NakaMats, Yoshiro, 351
Narcolepsy, 234
Nash, John, 206
Nason, Susan, 316
National Enquirer, 46
Natural clinical tests, 39
Natural consequences, 118
Naturalistic observations
  described, 31
  limitations, 31–32
  recording observations, 32
Nature. *See* Heredity
NDE. *See* Near-death experience
Near-death experience, 148
Nearness, principle of, 191
Needs
  affiliation, 612
  growth, 406
  motivation and, 388
Negative after potential, 54
Negative correlation, 32
Negative reinforcement, 273–274
Negative transfer, 316
Negativism, 126
Neo-Freudians, 20–21
Neonates, 90–92
Nerve cells. *See* Neurons
Nerves
  characterization, 165
  cranial, 60
  deafness, 172
  pain, 178
  spinal, 60
  vision pathways, 65
Nervous system
  central, 57–58
  dendrites, 88
  intelligent, 379–380
  neural networks, 57–58
  neurons in, 57
  peripheral, 58–59
  spinal cord, 59–60
Neugarten, Bernice, 145–146
Neural networks, 57–58
Neurilemma, 57
Neurological soft signs, 65, 66
Neurons
  communication, 55–57
  connector, 60
  defined, 52
  function, 57
  impulses, 52–54
  parts, 52
  regulators, 55, 57
  sensory, 60
Neuropeptide Y (NYP), 391–392
Neuropeptides, 55
Neurotic anxiety, 470
Neuroticism, 465
Neurotransmitters
  defined, 55
  function, 55, 57
Neutral stimulus, 264
Nicholson, Jack, 25
Nicotine. *See also* Cigarette smoking
  abuse, 247
  characterization, 247
  health impact of, 247–248
Night blindness, 169
Night terrors, 233–234
Nightmares, 233–234
Noise pollution, 674
Nonreinforcement, 582–583
Nonverbal behavior, 681
Noradrenaline, 245–246
Norepinephrine, 76
Normal acuity, 164
Normal curve, 695–696
Norms
  conformity and, 619
  defined, 23, 607
  group, 607–608
  spatial, 608–609
North, Carol, 532, 534, 550
Note-taking, 3–4
Nurture. *See* Environments
NYP. *See* Neuropeptide Y (NYP)

Obedience
  defined, 621
  limits of, 621–622
  studies, 622–624
Obesity, 393–394
Object permanence, 110
Objective tests, 6–7, 365
Observational record, 32
Observer bias, 32
Observer effect, 31–32
Obsessive-compulsive disorder (OCD), 544–545
Occipital lobes, 67–68
OCD. *See* Obsessive-compulsive disorder (OCD)
Odor receptors, 174
Olfaction, 173–174
One-step-ahead strategy, 112
Online counseling. *See* Cybertherapy
Online flash cards, 8
Online quizzes, 8
Open teaching, 679–680
Operant conditioning
  acquiring, 271–272
  bases of, 263
  defined, 269
  extinction, 272–273
  information, 270
  negative reinforcement, 273–274
  partial reinforcers, 278–280
  positive reinforcement, 269
  primary reinforcers, 274
  principles, 582–583
  reinforcement, 271–272
  secondary reinforcers, 274–276
  shaping, 272
  social reinforcers, 276–278
  superstitions and, 272
  theory development, 269–270
  timing of, 271–272
  token reinforcers, 276
Operational definitions, 29
Opponent-process theory, 165–166, 404
Order effects, 315
Organ of Corti, 170
Organic mental disorders, 536
Organic psychosis, 550–551
Organization, 321–322
Organizational citizenship, 670
Orgasmic disorders, 452–453
Orientation response, 210
Orientation, creative, 350
Originality, 347
Osama bin Laden, 638
Osbourne, Ozzy, 352
Ossicles, 170
Other-race effect, 204
Otolith organs, 179–180
Out-groups, 606
Overdisclosure, 614–615
Overgeneralization, 584
Overlap, 200
Overlearning
  in assertiveness training, 627
  memory and, 322
  reasons for, 4
Overload, 673

Pain
  avoidance, 398
  controlling, 184
  coping with, 185
  disorder, 547
  gates, 181–182
  receptors, 178
  relief, hypnosis and, 239
  sexual, 453
Palmistry, 43
Pampered Child Syndrome (Mamen), 105
Panic disorder, 543–544
Paradoxical intention, 233
Paranoid psychosis, 552
Paranoid schizophrenia, 553–554
Paraphilias, 443
Paraprofessionals, 596
Parapsychology, 213
Parasympathetic branch, 59, 411–412
Parasympathetic rebound, 411
Parentese, 108–109
Parents
  abusive, 129
  adolescents and, 134
  authoritarian, 102
  caregiving styles, 101–103
  -child relationships, 116–117
  cultural differences, 103
  effective, 115–118
  influence of, 101
  life stages, 123–124
  one-step-ahead strategy, 112
  permissive, 102
  TV guidance by, 651
Parietal lobes, 68
Partial hospitalization, 594
Partial reinforcement, 278–280
Participative management, 666
Passive compliance, 625–626
Pavlov, Ivan, 263–265
Peak performance, 684–685
Peek, Kim, 373
Peer counselors, 599–600
Peer groups, 134
Penn, Sean, 609
Perception
  attention, 209–213
  awareness, 219
  brightness constancy, 190
  defined, 157, 189
  depth, 195–202
  expectations and, 211–213
  extrasensory, 213–216
  eyewitness and, 217–218
  Gestalt principles, 191–194
  habituation and, 210
  problem solving and, 345
  shape constancy, 189–190
Perceptual defense, 158–159
Perceptual features, 156–157
Perceptual learning
  adaptation level, 205–206
  defined, 202
  examples, 202–203

Perceptual learning *(continued)*
features, 204
frames of reference, 206
habits of, 203–205
illusions, 206–208
inverted vision, 204–205
Perceptual organization, 191
Perceptual reconstruction, 217
Peripheral nervous system, 58–59
Peripheral vision, 165
Perls, Fritz, 596
Persona, 473
Personal distance, 608
Personal growth, 575
Personal interviews, 664
Personal prejudice, 640
Personal space, 608–609
Personal unconscious, 473
Personality
anxiety and, 475
archetypes, 473–474
aspects of, 459–460
authoritarian, 641, 681
behavior and, 463
cardiac, 520–521
classification, 464–465
creativity and, 351–352
culture and, 462
defined, 459
development, 471–472, 477
dimensions, 465–466
disease-prone, 499
dynamics of, 470–471, 481–482
happiness and, 151
hardy, 521–522
heredity and, 466–468
humanistic theory of, 479–482
learning theories of, 474–479
positive traits, 480
prejudice, 641
projective tests of, 487–488
psychoanalytic theories of, 468–472
psychodynamic theories of, 472–474
self-concept of, 461–462
self-esteem and, 461–462
shyness, 491–494
structure of, 469–470, 481–482
superiority and, 473
theories, comparison, 482–483
traits, 460, 463–468
twin studies, 467–468
types, 460–461
Personality assessments
direct observations, 485–486
inkblot test, 488
interviews, 484–485
murders, case study, 490
projective testing, 488–489
questionnaires, 486–487
rating scales, 485–486
situational testing, 485–486
TAT, 488–489
Personality development
behaviorist view, 477–478
Freudian view, 471–472
humanist view, 482–483
Personality disorders
antisocial, 541–542
anxiety-based, 541–547
defined, 537
example, 540
maladaptive patterns, 541
Personnel psychology
characterization, 662
job analysis and, 663
selection procedures and, 663–666
Persuasion, 634–635
PET. *See* Positron emission tomography (PET)
Peterson, Scott, 412
Phantom limbs, 183
Phenomena, 213
Phenylketonuria (PKU), 374
Phenylthiocarbamine, 175
Pheromones, 175
Phobias, 544
Phonemes, 337
Phosphenes, 156–157
Photographic memory. *See* Eidetic imagery
Photons, 158
Photothrapy, 561–562
Phrenology, 43
Physical attractiveness, 614
Physical environments, 671
Physical proximity, 613
Piaget, Jean, 110–114
Pica, 127
Picasso, Pablo, 348
Pictorial depth cues, 199–202
Pineal gland, 75
Pinel, Phillipe, 572
Pinna, 170
Pituitary gland, 75
PKU. *See* Phenylketonuria (PKU)
Place theory, 172
Placebo effects
controlling, 37–38
defined, 37
impact of, 37
Plaster set, 460
Play, 407–408
Play skills, 100
Pleasure principle, 469
Polygenic genes, 84
Polygraphs, 412–414
Pons, 71
Populations, 40–41, 696
Pornography, 650
Positive correlation, 32
Positive instances, fallacy of, 44
Positive psychology, 22
Positive reinforcement, 269, 582
Positive relationships, 697–698
Positive transfer, 316
Positron emission tomography (PET), 62, 64, 557
Postconventional moral reasoning, 136
Postpartum depression, 560–561
Posttraumatic stress disorder (PTSD), 545
Potassium ions, 54
Poverty, 89–90
Power. *See* Social power
Practice, 322
Precognition, 213
Preconventional moral reasoning, 136
Prediction, 16
Pregnancy, 87–88
Prejudices
combating, 644–645
defined, 639
development of, 639–640
diversity and, 656–658
experiments, 643–646
forms of, 639
gender, 640
group, 640
personal, 640
personality and, 641
roots of, 641–643
social competition and, 657
stereotypes and, 641–643
symbolic, 642
Premack principle, 292
Premature ejaculation, 452–453
Premature puberty, 76
Prenatal environment, 87–88
Preoperational stage, 110–111
Preparation, creative, 350
Prepared childbirth, 88
Presbyopia, 161
Pressure, 501
Prevention
aggressive behavior, 650–652
early, 499–500
suicide, 564–565
Primary motives
defined, 389, 397–399
homeostasis, 390
mechanism, 397
pain, 398
sex, 398–399
thirst, 398
Primary reinforcers, 274
Primary sexual characteristics, 427
Priming, 308
Principles of Psychology (James), 18
Private self-consciousness, 491–492
Proactive interference, 315
Problem finding, 349
Problem solving
barriers to, 344–345
creative, 351
culture and, 344
fixations and, 343–344
heuristics in, 341–342
ideal, 342
insightful, 342–344
mechanical solutions, 341
random search strategy, 341
understanding in, 341
Problem-focused coping, 504
Procedural memory, 304
Processing, 211
Procrastination, 5–6
Programmed instruction, 276–278
Progressive relaxation, 527
Projection, 511
Projective tests, 487–488
Prosocial behavior
bystander apathy, 653
bystander intervention, 653–654
defined, 651
encouraging, 654
Prototypes, 334
Proust, Marcel, 575
Proxemics, 608
Pseudo-psychology
Barnum effect, 44–45
positive instances, 44
types of, 43–44
uncritical acceptance of, 44
PsycDIRECT, 8
Psyche, 469
Psychedelic drugs, 556
Psychiatric social workers, 26
Psychiatrists, 26
Psychoactive drugs, 242–244
Psychoanalysis
anxiety explanation, 548
elements of, 572–573
history, 20–21
modern developments, 573
practitioners, 26
theories of, 20–21
Psychoanalytic theory of personality
basic beliefs, 468–469
dynamics, 470–471
evaluation, 483
personality structure, 469–470
Psychodrama, 586–587
Psychodynamic theory, 21, 23
Psychodynamic theory of personality, 472–474, 483
Psychokinesis, 213
Psychological situations, 476
Psychological testing, 664–666
Psychological trauma, 555
Psychologists
activities, 26
basic skills, 590–592
defined, 25
engineering, 193
ethics, 27
evaluating, 600
industrial, 662
key qualities, 590
legal requirements, 27
locating, 599–600
media, 48, 576
paraprofessionals, 596
public impressions of, 25
qualifications, 600
scientific method and, 29
specialties, 27–28
telephone, 576–577
training of, 25
types of, 24, 25
women, 19–20
Psychology. *See also* Social psychology
defined, 12
education and, 679–680
empiricism and, 12–13
goals of, 16
history of, 17–22
law and, 680–682
in media, 46–48
schools of, 17–21
sports, 682–685
Psychoneuroimmunology, 523
Psychophysics, 158
Psychosexual stages, 471–472
Psychosis
delusional disorders, 551–552
major features, 549–550
organic, 550–551
paranoid, 552
schizophrenia, 552–558
sleep-deprivation, 226
Psychosocial dilemmas, 122
Psychosomatic disorders and, 517
Psychosurgery, 594
Psychotherapy
assessing need for, 596–597, 598
basic skills, 590–592
behavioralism, 578–582
client-centered, 574–575
cognitive, 584–586
core features, 589
defined, 570
dimensions of, 570–571
effectiveness, 588–589
existential, 575
family, 587
future of, 590
Gestalt, 575–576
group, 586–588
humanist, 574–576
Internet, 577
master therapists, 590
media, 576
meta-analysis, 588
myths, 571
origins, 571–572
telephone, 576–577
PsycINFO, 8, 9
PsycLIT, 8
PsycNOW, 9
PsycPORT, 9
PTC. *See* Phenylthiocarbamine
PTSD. *See* Posttraumatic stress disorder (PTSD)
Puberty, 76, 132–133
Public distance, 608
Public self-consciousness, 491–492
Publications, 30–31
Punishment. *See also* Discipline
defined, 273
in operant therapy, 582
side effects, 284–285
use considerations, 285
variables affecting, 282–283
wise use of, 283–284
Pupil, 161

Quality circles, 667
Quantitative reasoning, 366
Questionnaires, 486–487
Questions, 413, 592
Quinlan, Karen Ann, 249–250

Racial profiling, 639
Racism, 639
Rain Man (film), 373
Ramona, Gary, 317
Randi, James, 216

Random assignment, 36
Random search strategy, 341
Range, the, 694
Rank, Otto, 21
Rape
crime of, 445–446
defined, 445
forcible, 446–447
gender roles and, 446
myths, 446
Rapid eye movement, 230, 235
RAS. *See* Reticular activating system (RAS)
Rating scales, 485–486
Rational concepts, 334
Rational Recovery and Secular Organizations for Sobriety (SOS), 253
Rational-emotive behavior therapy, 585
Rationalization, 511
Reaction formation, 511
Readiness, 94
Reagan, Ronald, 556
Reality principle, 470
Reality testing, 218–219
Reasoning, 365–366
Rebellion, 126
Recall, 306, 310
Receptor sites, 55
Recessive genes, 84–85
Reciprocal inhibition, 579
Recitation, 321
Recognition, 306–307
Reconstruction, 217
Recovered memory, 316–317
Recovery, spontaneous, 266
Redintegrative memories, 304
Reeves, Keanu, 183
Reference, frames of, 206
Referent power, 621
Referred pain, 178
Reflexes, 91, 262
Refractory period, 442
Rehearsal
elaborative, 301
imagery, 233–234
maintenance, 300–301
memory improvement and, 321
Reinforcement
contingent, 271
covert, 598
defined, 262
partial, 278–280
positive, 582
primary, 274
schedules of, 278–279
secondary, 274–276
social, 276–278
token, 276
token economies, 583
value, 476
Reinterpretation, 185
Relationships
curvilinear, 34
empathy-helping, 654
graphical data, 33–34
linear, 34
parent-child, 116–117
statistical, 697–698
Relative motion, 200
Relative size, 199
Relativity, 23
Relaxation
desensitization and, 580
hypnosis and, 241
insomnia and, 233
progressive, 527
Relearning, 307–308
Reliability, 364–365
Religion, 151
REM. *See* Rapid eye movement
Reminding system, 178, 181–182
Repetitious stimuli, 209
Representative samples, 40
Representativeness, 353–354
Repression
defined, 20
Freud's views, 510
memory suppression and, 316–317
Research
animal, 15–16
clinical method, 39–40
correlational studies, 32–33
experiments, 35–38
function of, 13–14
gender bias, 41
method comparison, 42
methods, 14, 31
publishing, 30
scientific method, 29–30
specialties, 14–15
survey method, 40–42
Research and Teaching Showcase, 8
Resilience, 105
Resistance, 522, 573
Resources, wasted, 675
Response
alternative, 292
chaining, 272
chains, 292
conditioned, 18, 264
conditioned emotional, 267–268
defined, 388
personality, 476
sexual, 440–442
unconditioned, 264
Resting potential, 53
Results, knowledge of, 321
Retardation. *See* Mental retardation
Reticular activating system (RAS), 71
Reticular formation (RF), 71
Retina, 161, 163
Retinene, 169
Retrieved memory, 297
Reward power, 621
Rewards, 583
RF. *See* Reticular formation (RF)
Rice, Condolezza, 432
Risk takers, 405
Risperdal, 593
Rivalries, 126
Rods
color sensitivity of, 165
function of, 161–162
visual acuity and, 164
Rogers, Carl, 21, 479–481, 574–575
Role modeling, 651–652
Role playing
assertiveness, 627
attitudes and, 635
cognitive dissonance theory, 635–636
Roles
conflicts, 606
confusion in, 123
reversals, 587
types of, 605–606
Roosevelt, Eleanor, 479
Rorschach, Hermann, 488
Rowling, J. K., 122
Rubinstein, Arthur, 144
Rules
conceptual, 334
transformation, 338
verbal, 684
Run of luck, 214–215

SAD. *See* Seasonal affective disorder (SAD)
Samples, 40, 696
Sanctions, 620
Santana, Carlos, 52
SATs. *See* Scholastic aptitude tests
Savant syndrome, 363, 373
Scaffolding, 114
Scapegoating, 506
Scatter diagram, 697
Schachter, Stanley, 418
Schedules, 6
Schedules of reinforcement, 278–279
Schizophrenia
brain chemistry and, 555
catatonic, 553
causes, 555–557
characterization, 552
disorganized, 552–553
drugs for, 592–593
environmental factors, 555
paranoid, 553–554
stress-vulnerability model, 558
undifferentiated, 554–555
Scholastic aptitude tests (SAT), 370
Schumann, Robert, 352
Scientific jury election, 681
Scientific management, 666
Scientific method
application, 29
observations, 13
theory development, 30
Scripts, 436–437
SD. *See* Sensory deprivation
Seasonal affective disorder (SAD), 561–562
Secondary elaboration, 256
Secondary motives, 389
Secondary reinforcers, 274–276
Secondary sexual characteristics, 427
Secondary traits, 464
Secondhand conditioning, 268–269
Secure attachment, 617
Sedatives, 249–253
Selection, 321
Selective attention, 181, 209
Selective perception, 584
Self
assertion, 627
confidence in, 406
evaluation of, 21
ideal, 481
theory of, 480–481
Self-actualization
characteristics of, 479–480
confidence and, 406
defined, 21, 479
feelings of, 480
Self-consciousness, 491–492
Self-directed desensitization, 598
Self-disclosure, 614–615
Self-efficacy, 476
Self-esteem
defined, 461
discipline and, 104–105
personality and, 461–462
Self-fulfilling prophecy, 38, 656–657
Self-handicapping, 611
Self-image, 21, 481
Self-managed teams, 666–667
Self-management, 291–292
Self-observation, experimental, 17
Self-recording, 292
Self-regulated learning, 5
Self-reinforcement, 476–477
Self-testing, 4
Semantic memory, 304
Semantics, 336
Semicircular canals, 180
Sensate focus, 451–452
Sensation seekers, 400
Sensation-seeking scale, 401
Sensitive periods, 87
Sensitivity groups, 587
Sensitization, 597
Sensorimotor stage, 110
Sensory conflict theory, 180
Sensory deprivation (SD), 240–241
Sensory systems
adaptation, 180–181
analysis, 156–157
aural, 160–173
changes, 239
coding, 156–157
enhancement, 240–241
gating, 181–182
general properties, 156
gustation, 173
localization, 157
memory, 297
neurons, 60
olfaction, 173–175
perceptual defense and, 158–159
selective attention, 181
somesthetic, 177–182
subliminal perception and, 158–159
thresholds, 158–160
vestibular, 179–180
visual, 160–170
Separation, 518
Separation anxiety disorder, 97
Serial position effect, 306
Set points, 392
Sex
defined, 427
dimensions of, 429
drive, 437–428
happiness and, 151
Sex drive, 398–399
Sexism, 639
Sexual arousal, 436–437
Sexual aversion, 450
Sexual development
gender aspects, 427–428
hormones and, 428–429
orientation, 438–439
prenatal, 429–430
psychosexual stages, 471–472
Sexual disorders, 537
Sexual identity, 427
Sexual interactions
atypical, 442–444
changing attitudes, 444
changing behavior, 444–445
communications, 454–455
disease risks, 447–449
double standards, 445
dysfunctional, 450–455
female response, 441–442
intimacy and, 454–455
male response, 442
relationships and, 453–454
responsibility and, 449
safety concerns, 447–449
studies, 440–441
Sexual orientation. *See also* Heterosexuality; Homosexuality
defined, 438
genetics and, 439
heredity and, 439
personal identity and, 438–439
Sexual scripts, 436–437
Sexually transmitted diseases (STDs)
common, 447
defined, 447
risky behaviors, 448–449
transmission of, 447–448
Shakespeare, William, 250, 348
Shame, 123
Shape constancy, 189–190
Shaping, 272, 582
Shapiro, Francine, 581
Shift work, 402–403
Short answer tests, 7
Short sleepers, 227
Short-term memory
duration of, 300–301
function of, 297
use of, 300
Shyness
beliefs and, 492
conversation and, 492
defined, 491
dynamics of, 491–492
elements of, 491
situational causes, 491
social skills, 492
Sibling rivalry, 126
SIDS. *See* Sudden infant death syndrome

Signals, 107
Significance, statistical, 697
Significant differences, 696–697
Significant numbers, 696–697
Silence, 592
Similarity, 191, 614
Simpson, O. J., 682
Simultaneous color contrast, 166
Singer, Margaret, 637
Situational demands, 610
Situational judgment tests, 665
Situational testing, 485–486
Situations, 476, 477
Sixteen Personality Factor Questionnaire, 464
Size-distance invariance, 207
Skepticism, 214
Skill memory, 304–306
Skin receptors, 177–179
Skinner's box
 invention of, 19
 punishment and, 283
 reinforcement and, 271–272
Skinner, B. F., 18–19, 271–272
Sleep
 apnea, 234–235
 consciousness and, 224, 226–228
 deprivation, 226
 disturbances, 126, 232–235
 dreaming and, 230–231
 hormone, 228
 memory and, 322
 need for, 225–226
 NREM, 230
 patterns, 227–228
 REM, 230
 restriction, 233
 spindles, 229
 stages of, 229–231
Sleeptalking, 233
Sleepwalking, 233
Smell. *See* Olfaction
Smiles, 415
Social comparison theory, 612–613
Social development
 attachment, 97–99
 early, 95
 referencing, 95–96
Social distance, 608
Social environments, 671
Social exchange theory, 615
Social learning theory, 476–477, 649–650
Social markers, 133
Social motives. *See* Goals
Social nonconformity, 533
Social norms. *See* Norms
Social phobia, 544
Social power
 compliance with, 624–626
 obedience and, 621–624
 types of, 621
Social psychologists, 15
Social psychology
 attribution theory, 609–612
 comparison theory, 612–613
 defined, 605
 exchange theory, 615
 group norms, 605–607
 interpersonal attraction, 613–615
 spatial norms, 608–609
Social Readjustment Rating Scale (SRRS), 515–516
Social referencing, 95–96
Social reinforcers, 276–278
Social roles, 605–606
Social skills, 100, 492
Social smiles, 94, 415
Social stigma, 562
Social support, 522
Social workers. *See* Psychiatric social workers
Socialization, 430–431, 433–435
Sociocultural theory, 114–115
Sociopaths, 541–542
Sodium ions, 53
Solutions, 341, 342
Soma, 52
Somatic pain, 178
Somatization disorders, 546
Somatoform disorders, 537
Somesthetic senses, 177–179
Sommer, Carol, 486
SOS. *See* Rational Recovery and Secular Organizations for Sobriety
Sounds, 170, 173
Source traits, 464
Space
 attraction and, 613
 personal, 608–609
 territorial markers, 671
Spaced practice, 4, 5, 322
Spatial grammar, 338
Spatial norms, 608–609
Specific phobias, 544
Speech disturbances, 127
Speed of processing, 379
Spinal cord, 59–60
Spinocerebellar degeneration, 71
Split-brain operation, 65–66
Spontaneous recovery, 266
Sports psychology
 advantages, 683
 application, 682–683
 defined, 682
 motor skills, 684
 peak performance and, 684–685
SQ4R method, 1–2
SRRS. *See* Social Readjustment Rating Scale (SRRS)
Stage ESP, 215–216
Stagnation, 124
Standard deviation, 694
Standard scores, 694
Standardization, 365
Stanford Hypnotic Susceptibility Scale, 237
Stanford-Binet Intelligence Scale, 363, 367
Star Trek (television), 46
State-dependent learning, 314
Statistical significance, 36, 697
Statistics
 correlations, 697–699
 descriptive, 691–692
 graphical, 691–692
 inferential, 696–697
 measures of central tendency, 692–694
 measures of variability, 694
 normal curve, 695–696
 standard scores, 694
Status, 606–607
STDs. *See* Sexually transmitted diseases
Steele, Claude, 643
Stereocilia, 170
Stereoscopic vision, 197–198
Stereotypes
 avoiding, 656
 defined, 641
 gender roles, 431–432
 irrationality of, 643
 racial, 642
 self-fulfilling prophecies and, 656–657
 victims, 643
 war and, 644
Sterilization, 437–428
Stimulants
 defined, 242
 insomnia and, 233
 types, 244–249
Stimulation deafness, 173
Stimulation, electrical, 274
Stimulus
 conditioned, 264
 control, 232–233, 280–282, 582
 defined, 17, 18
 generalization, 266
 motives, 389
 neutral, 264
Stimulus drives
 anxiety and, 402
 arousal theory, 400–401
 function of, 399–400
Stored memory, 297
Stress
 acculturative, 518
 adjustment disorders and, 542–543
 burnout and, 501–502
 childhood, 126
 disorders, 545–546
 evaluating, 516
 friendship and, 523
 frustration and, 516–517
 G.A.S., 522–523
 immune system and, 523–524
 impact of, 500
 job, 501
 life events and, 515–516
 psychosomatic disorders and, 517
 traumatic, 504
Stress management
 bodily reactions and, 526–527
 coping statement and, 528
 function of, 525
 ineffective behavior and, 527–528
 upsetting thoughts and, 527–528
Stress-vulnerability model, 558
Stressors
 appraising, 503–505
 biofeedback and, 517, 519
 conflicts, 507–510
 coping with, 504–505
 defenses, 510–512
 defined, 501
 frustration, 505–507
 learned helplessness and, 512–515
 micro-, 516
 nature of, 503–504
 preparing for, 528
 urban, 672–674
Striving for superiority, 473
Stroboscopic movement, 206
Strokes, 66
Stroop interference task, 336
Structuralism, 17–18
Study strategies
 environment and, 4
 goal setting, 6
 mnemonics, 4
 overlearning, 4
 self-testing, 4
 spaced sessions, 4
 taking test, 6–7
 time management, 5–6
Stuttering, 127
Subjective well-being, 150
Subjects, 35, 40–41
Sublimation, 512
Subliminal perception, 158–159
Subliminal Seduction (Key), 158
Substance-related disorders, 537
Success, motivation and, 405–406
Successive approximations, 272
Sucking reflex, 91
Sudden death, 411–412
Sudden infant death syndrome, 234–235
Suggestibility, 240
Suggestion, 212
Suicide
 age and, 564
 crisis intervention, 565
 gender and, 563–564
 immediate causes, 564
 income and, 564
 preventing, 564–565
 season and, 563
Superego, 470
Superiority, striving for, 473
Superordinate goals, 645–646
Superstitions, 272
Surface traits, 464
Surveys
 description, 40
 Internet, 41
 method, 30
 populations, 40–41
 samples, 40
 social desirability, 41–42
Susceptibility, hypnotic, 237
Syllogisms, 352
Symbolic prejudice, 642
Symbols, dream, 236
Synapses
 defined, 55
 function, 57
 newborns', 88
Synesthesia, 331
Syntax, 337, 340

Taste
 aversion, 395
 basic sensations, 175
 buds, 175
 function of, 173
 sensitivity, 176–177
 spicy, 176
 sweet, 176
TAT. *See* Thematic apperception tests (TAT)
Tchambuli, 432–433
Teaching strategies, 679–680
Telehealth, 577
Telepathy, 213
Television. *See* Media
Temperament, 85–86, 459
Temporal lobes, 68
Tension-release method, 580
Teratogens, 87
Term schedules, 6, 7
Territorial behavior, 671
Territorial markers, 671
Terrorism, 413
Tested by relearning, 307
Testosterone, 429
Tests
 anagram, 349
 anxiety, 402
 aptitude, 664–665
 creativity, 349
 depth perception, 195–196
 DNA, 218
 essay, 6–7
 hypothesis, 29
 inkblot, 488
 intelligence, 364–365, 382–384
 Ishihara, 168
 for lying, 412–414
 natural clinical, 39
 objective, 6–7, 365
 personality, 487–488
 projective, 487–488
 psychological, 664–666
 reality, 218–219
 relearning and, 307
 short answer, 7
 situational, 485–486
 standardized, 365
 taking skills, 6–7
 vocational, 664–665
Texture gradients, 200
Thalamus, 72
Thanatologist, 146
Thanatos, 469
Thematic apperception tests (TAT), 488–489
Theory of mind, 111
Theory X, 666–667
Theory Y, 666–667
Therapeutic alliance, 589
Therapists. *See* Psychologists
Therapy. *See* Medical therapy; Psychotherapy
Thermostats, 390
Thirst, 398
Thorndike, Edward L., 269–270

Thoughts
- all-or-nothing, 335
- basic units, 330–331
- concepts, 333–335
- creative, 347–352, 349–359
- forms of, 348
- Freud's views, 20
- imagery in, 331
- intuition, 352–355
- logic forms, 347, 352–355
- mental images, 331–333
- problem solving, 341–345
- reflecting, 591–592
- stopping, 597–598
- upsetting, 527–528

Threats. *See* Stressors
Throw-away society, 277
Thyroid gland, 76
Time management, 5–6
Time out, 582
Tinnitus, 173
Tip-of-the-tongue state, 306
Titchener, Edward B., 17
Toilet-training disturbances, 127
Token economies, 583
Token reinforcers, 276
Tolerance, 657–658
Top-down processing, 211
TOT state. *See* Tip-of-the-tongue state
Touch
- dynamic, 179
- norms, 607
- receptors, 177

Toxic environments, 675–678
Training
- assertiveness, 627–628
- group awareness, 587–588
- mastery, 513–514
- transfer of, 316

Trait theories of personality
- approaches to, 463
- behavior prediction, 463
- evaluation of, 466–468
- genetics, 466–468
- key dimensions, 465–466
- trait-situation interactions, 466
- type classification, 464–465

Trait-situation interactions, 466
Tranquilizers, 249–250
Transducer, 156
Transfer, 316
Transference, 573
Transformation rules, 338
Transformations, 109
Transition periods, 139
Trauma
- psychological, 555
- stress and, 504
- therapy for, 581

Trepanning, 571
Trichromatic theory, 165
Trust, 123
Tryptophan, 233
Tunnel vision, 165
Twin studies
- IQ, 376–377
- personality, 467

Tympanic membrane, 170
Type A personality
- characterization, 460–461
- health and, 520–521
- urban life and, 670

Umami, 175
Unconditional positive regard, 574
Unconditioned response, 264
Unconscious
- collective, 473
- personal, 473
- thoughts, 20

Understanding, 16, 341
Undifferentiated schizophrenia, 554–555
Unusual uses test, 349
Urban environments
- influence of, 672
- rating, 670
- stressors, 672–674

Validity, 364–365
Values, 476
Variability, measures of, 694
Variables
- defined, 35
- intervals, 280
- ratios, 280
- types, 35–36

Verbal rules, 684
Verification, creative, 350
Vestibular systems, 179–180
Vicarious classical conditioning, 269
Vicarious conditioning, 268–269
Video games, 290
Vigilant style, 668
Violence. *See also* Aggression
- mental disorders and, 554
- school, 652
- at work, 669

Virilism, 76
Virtual reality exposure, 580
Visceral pain, 178
Visible spectrum, 160
Vision. *See also* Eyes
- color, 165–167
- dark adaptation, 167, 169
- inverted, 204–205
- nerve pathways, 65
- peripheral, 165
- problems with, 160–161
- stereoscopic, 197–198
- tunnel, 165

Vistibular senses, 177
Visual acuity, 164
Visual agnosia, 164
Visual pigments, 165–166
Visual-spatial processing, 366
VNO. *See* Vomeronasal organ
Vocational interest tests, 664–666
Vomeronasal organ, 175
vos Savant, Marilyn, 367
Vygotsky, Leo, 114–115

Wain, Louis, 556
Waking suggestibility, 240
Walking consciousness, 224
Warning systems, 178
Washburn, Margaret, 20
Watson, Doc, 512
Watson, John B., 18
Wealth, 150
Weapons effect, 648
Weber's law, 158
Wechsler tests, 369
Weekly time schedules, 6, 7
Well-being, 150–151
Wellness programs, 500
Wernicke's area, 68
Wertheimer, Max, 19–20
Wheeler, Dan, 668
White matter, 59–60
Whitman, Walt, 479
Wilf, Andy, 537
Winfrey, Oprah, 122
Wisdom, 354–355
Wish fulfillment, 235
Wolpe, Joseph, 627
Women. *See also* Gender differences
- aggression against, 650
- appropriate sexuality, 445
- becoming, 478
- friendships, 615
- menopause, 140
- mood disorders and, 560–561
- orgasm disorders, 452
- prejudices against, 640
- psychologists, 19–20
- research bias and, 41
- sexual disorders, 452–453
- sexual response, 441–442

Wonder Women, 412
Wonder, Stevie, 512
Woods, Tiger, 122
Work
- career decisions, 668
- coping styles, 668
- creativity and, 408
- culture, 669–670
- enriching, 668–669
- flextime, 668
- gender roles and, 432
- happiness and, 151
- I-O psychologist at, 662
- job analysis and, 663
- management theories, 666–668
- personnel psychology, 662–666
- psychological testing, 664–666
- satisfaction in, 667–668
- selection procedures, 663–666
- shift, 402–403
- stress-associated, 501–502

Working memory, 297
World Wide Web. *See* Internet
Worldview, 633
Wundt, Wilhelm, 17

X chromosomes, 429

Y chromosomes, 429
Yerkes-Dodson law, 401

Zar, 538
Zener cards, 214
Zone of proximal development, 114

TO THE OWNER OF THIS BOOK:

I hope that you have found *Introduction to Psychology: Gateways to Mind and Behavior*, 11th edition, useful. So that this book can be improved in a future edition, would you take the time to complete this sheet and return it? Thank you.

School and address: ____

____

Department: ____

Instructor's name: ____

1. What I like most about this book is: ____

____

____

2. What I like least about this book is: ____

____

____

3. My general reaction to this book is: ____

____

____

4. The name of the course in which I used this book is: ______________________________

____

5. Were all of the chapters of the book assigned for you to read? ______________________

   If not, which ones weren't? ____

6. In the space below, or on a separate sheet of paper, please write specific suggestions for improving this book and anything else you'd care to share about your experience in using this book.

____

____

____

____

____

____

____

DO NOT STAPLE. TAPE HERE.

DO NOT STAPLE. TAPE HERE.

FOLD HERE

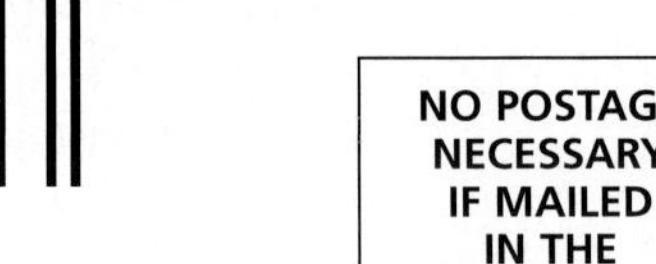

BUSINESS REPLY MAIL

FIRST-CLASS MAIL PERMIT NO. 34 BELMONT CA

POSTAGE WILL BE PAID BY ADDRESSEE

Attn: Marianne Taflinger, Psychology Editor

Wadsworth/Thomson Learning
10 Davis Dr
Belmont CA 94002-9801

FOLD HERE

OPTIONAL:

Your name: ______________________________ Date: ________________

May we quote you, either in promotion for *Introduction to Psychology: Gateways to Mind and Behavior*, 11th edition, or in future publishing ventures?

Yes: __________ No: __________

Sincerely yours,

Dennis Coon and John Mitterer